ART NOW

Edward Lucie-Smith

ART NOW

FROM ABSTRACT EXPRESSIONISM TO SUPERREALISM

WILLIAM MORROW AND COMPANY, INC.
New York 1977

Text
EDWARD LUCIE-SMITH

Brief Biographies
LARA VINCA MASINI

Introduction
GILLO DORFLES

Editors
MARIELLA DE BATTISTI
MARISA MELIS

Graphic Production
ENRICO SEGRÉ

Library of Congress Catalog Card Number 77-76724
ISBN 0–688–03201–X

Printed and bound in Italy by Arnoldo Mondadori Editore—Verona

The Birth of Modernism

Modern art was born into a world very different from the one we know today. If we date the birth of Modernism from the first public appearance of the Fauves, in the Paris Salon d'Automne of 1905, we are looking back to a society which was in many respects very different from our own. In the first decade of the twentieth century, technology, it is true, was making very rapid advances, but these advances had not yet had anything like their full impact upon the daily lives of the majority of Europeans. The internal combustion engine, to cite one example, had already established itself as something a great deal more than a toy. In Paris one-third of the wheeled traffic in the streets in the year 1905 was propelled by that engine rather than by horses. Yet the full possibilities of the invention were far from being realized, and the new motor car still bore a strong resemblance to the horse-drawn conveyances which it was starting to replace. In most minor details the manner in which people lived was far closer to the mode of existence that had prevailed during the nineteenth century than to anything that exists now. The Franco-Prussian War of 1870–71 was a relatively recent memory; the American Civil War still had many living eyewitnesses. The terrible social conditions that had shocked leading nineteenth-century writers such as Dickens and Zola were still largely unremedied, and the gulf between the different classes of society remained very wide in all the European nations. In the United States, with the rise of a new plutocracy—Astors, Vanderbilts, Guggenheims, Goulds—it even seemed to be growing wider still as the immense wealth of America increasingly made its way into the hands of a privileged few.

It was universally assumed that art was, and would remain, the business of a group which, in comparison to the rest of the social mass, was indeed very small: it consisted of the aristocracy, the plutocracy, and (its largest component) the prosperous and cultivated middle class. Such attempts as there were to bring art to a larger public—the Victoria and Albert Museum and the Whitechapel Art Gallery, though both in London, are well-contrasted examples—owed their existence to philanthropic impulses as characteristic of the nineteenth century in one way as its social injustices were in another. Typically, the management of these enterprises remained in middle-class hands. If the Fauves of 1905 were truly "wild beasts", as the critics of the day jokingly dubbed them, then they threatened the tranquillity of a few people only.

The intimate, even cloistered nature of their rebellion can be judged from the subject matter of some of the paintings they produced. Henri Matisse's *Dessert, Harmony in Red* (Plate 1), which dates from 1908, makes use of visual materials which were commonplaces for the artists of the time, whatever aesthetic persuasion they followed, and which had indeed been part of the European stock-in-trade since the Dutch genre painters of the seventeenth century. A maid with a starched collar and cuffs, and wearing a white apron, is seen arranging fruit on a tazza. Another tazza stands ready upon the table, accompanied by two decanters of wine. What gives this domestic scene its originality is the treatment of colour and form. The colour is, as the title claims, harmonious, but it is also unnaturally powerful. This and the drastic simplification of the drawing alike pay little attention to the way in which the eye perceives things in real life.

The use of colour in this way was not something entirely unheard of in painting, though Matisse was pushing his experiments to new extremes. James McNeill Whistler had already put forward the idea that colour could be treated in musical terms, and used for its own sake, though the hues

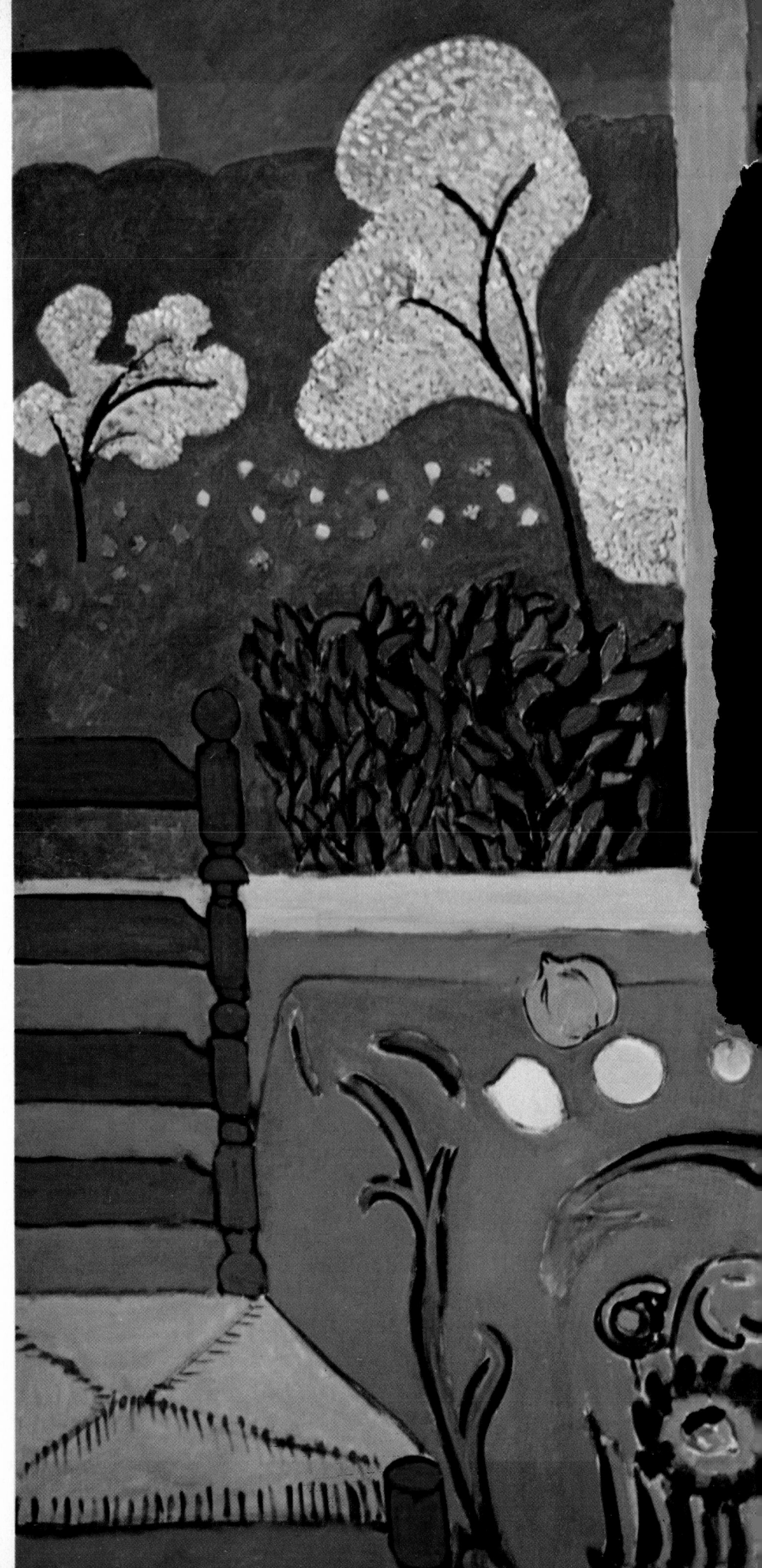

1.
Henri Matisse
La Desserte, harmonie en rouge
1908; 180 × 220 cm. (70 × 86 in.)
Leningrad, The Hermitage

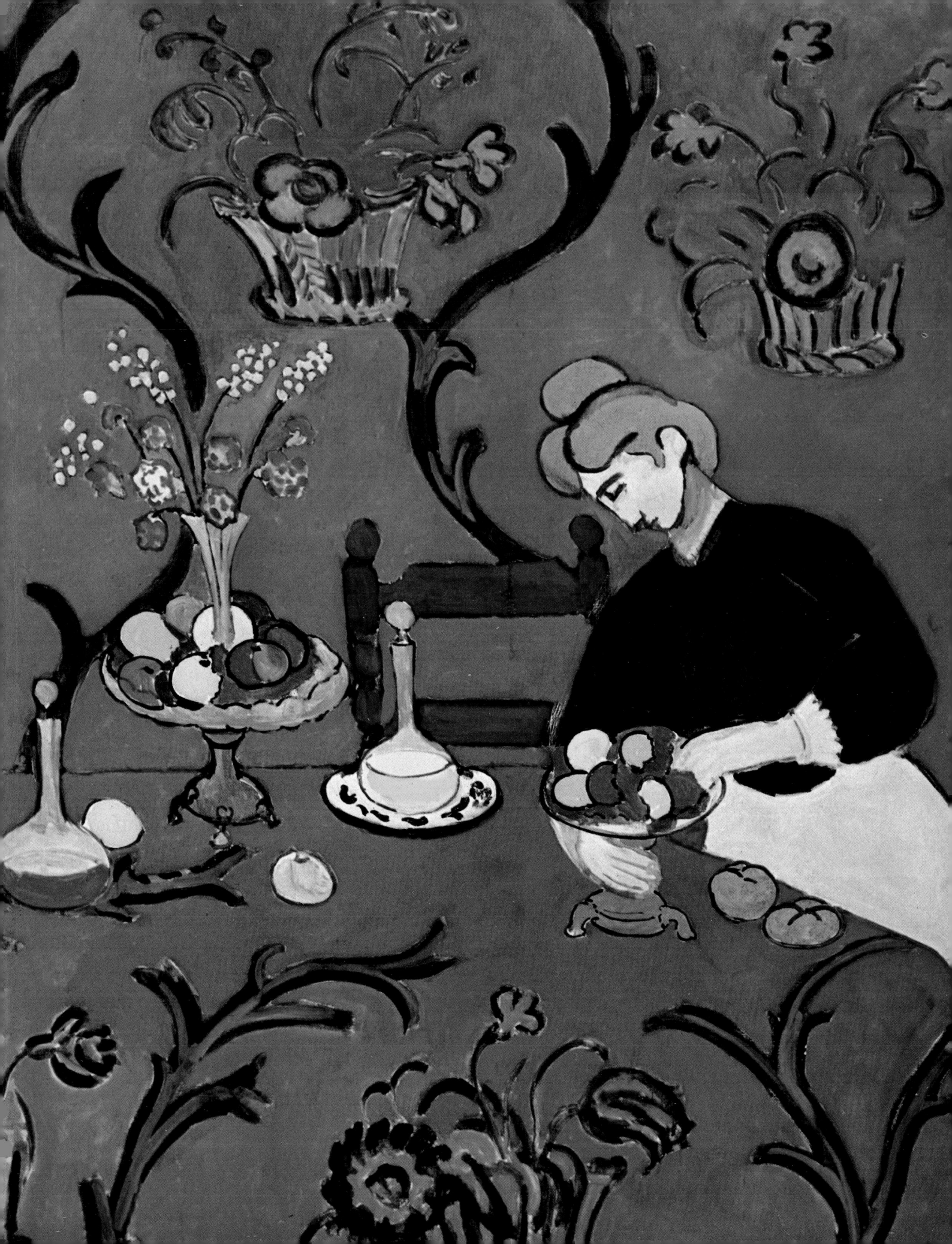

2.
Henri Matisse
La Danse (The Dance)
1910; 260 × 391 cm. (101 × 152 in.)
Leningrad, The Hermitage

3. Opposite
Ernst Ludwig Kirchner
Funf Frauen auf der Strasse (Five Women in the Street)
1913; 120 × 91 cm. (47 × 35 in.)
Cologne, Wallraf-Richartz Museum

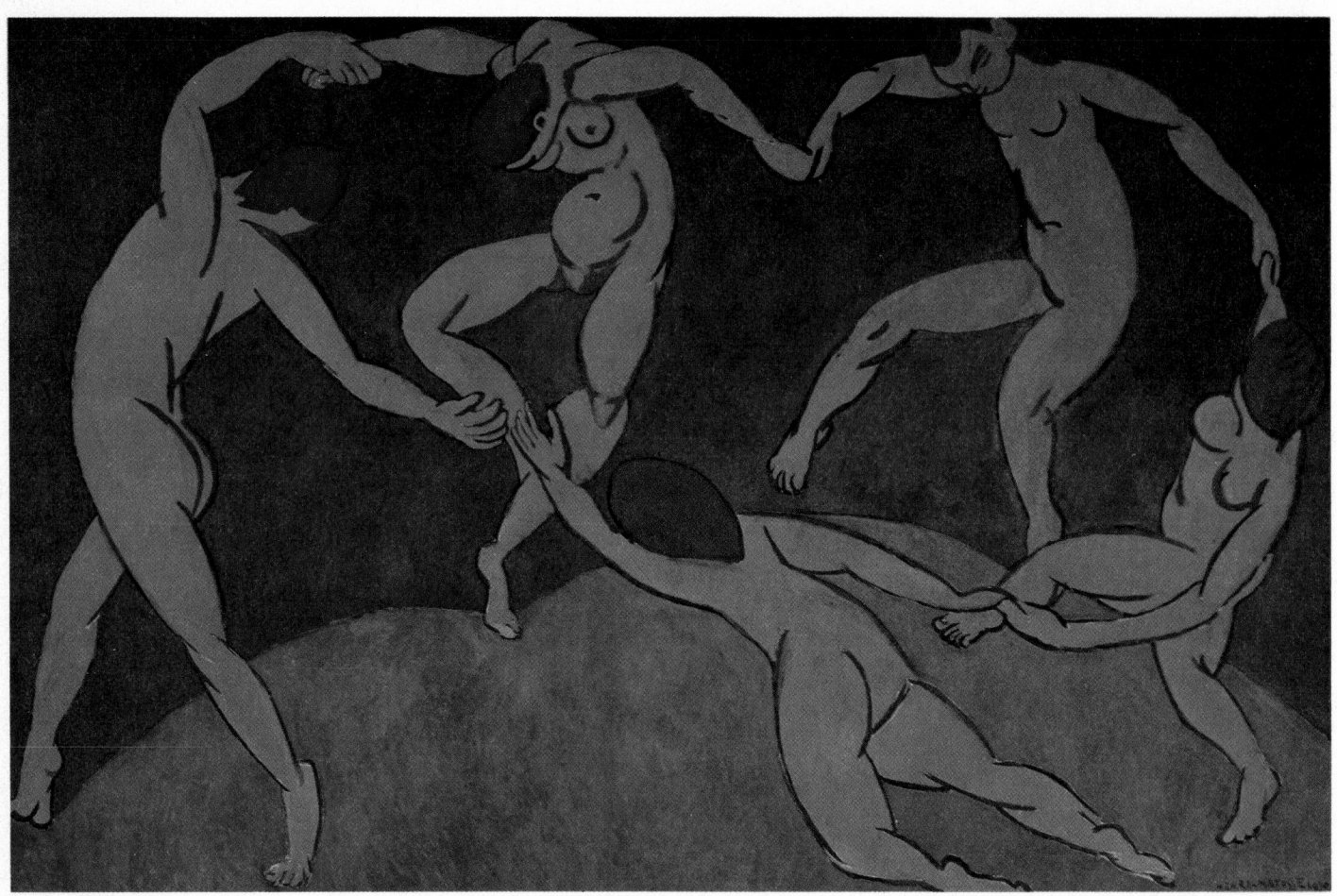

he favoured were subdued. The Symbolist painters in France, pursuing a slightly different line, had begun to accept that colour was something that could be used to express not the look of things as the physical eye perceived it, but the subjective mood they evoked.

Matisse's predecessors in the use of bold and violent hues had been the two great Post-Impressionist masters, Paul Gauguin and Vincent van Gogh. Van Gogh's use of colour was liberating because its violence was so obviously connected to the violence of the painter's own emotions, and for the first time artists were presented with a new kind of rhetoric—a rhetoric of anguish and suffering which went a long way beyond anything the Romantic movement had achieved. The Expressionist strain in European art, which began in the late nineteenth century but

has prolonged itself into the twentieth, is in many respects the main link between Romantic and Modernist painting, and therefore the most conspicuously "traditional" element within Modernism itself.

In Germany, in the years just preceding the First World War, Expressionism achieved the status of a school, and German Expressionism of this type is typified by Ernst Ludwig Kirchner's *Five Women in the Street* (1913), which is illustrated here (Plate 3). But there are many important modern painters who can be classified as Expressionists even though they are independent of any school or movement. One of the most typical of these is the Russian-born Jewish artist Chaim Soutine, who later emigrated from Russia and came to live in Paris. Soutine always worked in isolation, and what he produced was entirely personal to himself

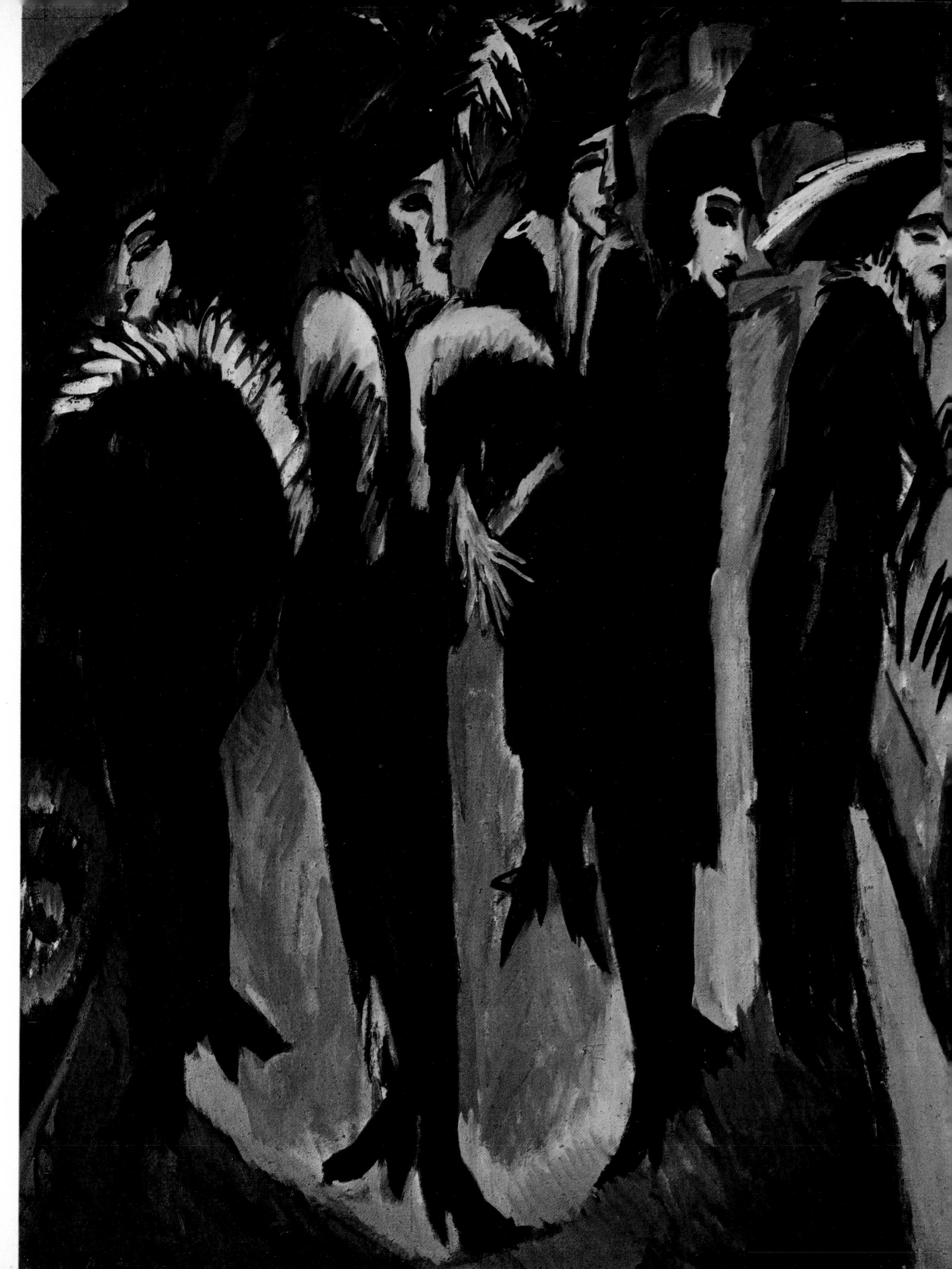

(Plate 4). His chosen images are obsessively repeated; he frequently painted the same motif again and again. But the precise significance of his choice often remains obscure, just as it does here in the artist's portrait of a young page boy. What we are chiefly aware of when we look at the painting is not the boy's character, but the artist's use of paint as a vehicle for his own anguish. We have here a revival of the Romantic assertion that the movements of the individual soul are of paramount interest, and that furthermore the artist unjustly limits himself, and tends to destroy his own potentiality, if he sets any bounds to his own ego. The claim of the artist to be an exceptional man in an increasingly egalitarian environment was to have, as we shall see, important consequences for the visual arts in the post-1945 period.

If we compare Soutine's *Page Boy* to the interior by Matisse, we note a significant difference. This is that, though both are apparently violent in colour, the Matisse lacks the feeling of emotional stress which emanates so powerfully from the work by Soutine. Though he was dubbed the leader of the "wild beasts" by the critics, Matisse was in fact essentially calm and luxurious in temperament. This mood is evoked very powerfully in what is nevertheless one of the most radical of his early works, *The Dance* (Plate 2), painted in 1910. This is one of the decorative compositions in which Matisse most obviously paid homage to Gauguin.

Gauguin may not have been a greater painter than Van Gogh, but he was an artist whose work had perhaps a wider import for the subsequent development of the visual arts. Unlike Van Gogh, Gauguin was regarded as a leader in his own day, even though this leadership was accorded to him by a very restricted coterie of other artists and writers. Not only did he seem to them to find new ways of developing ideas that were already implicit in Symbolism, but his decision to leave France altogether and to go and live and work in the South Seas had an enormous moral impact. What Gauguin celebrated was the primacy of instinct. "Our modern intelligence," he remarked, "lost as it is in the details of analysis, cannot perceive what is too simple or too visible." In this he

too paid tribute to Romanticism, which had always made a cult of the simple life. But Gauguin was prepared to go further. He looked among a primitive people, still with the vestiges of their pre-Christian tribal culture, for the qualities that he thought were missing from contemporary European society. And in this sense he was one of the founders of the cult of barbarism which swept through advanced circles on the eve of the First World War.

The Dance is affected both by Gauguin's own vision and, in a more general sense, by the feeling that Matisse shared with many of his contemporaries that the society they lived in was stiflingly elaborate as well as stiflingly conventional, that it was necessary to destroy much before art could be rebuilt from its foundations. The war itself, which was to destroy so much and to transform the structure of its society, seemed to many people in its first moments the great ecstatic release of destructive energy which so many artists had longed for.

A painting which reflects this negative and destructive spirit far more obviously than anything produced by Matisse is Pablo Picasso's early masterpiece, *Les Demoiselles d'Avignon* (Plates 5 and 6). Painted three years before *The Dance*, this is a much more radical statement of disaffection. Indeed, everything leads us to suppose that it was a large part of Picasso's intention to produce a picture which any middle-class spectator would find unacceptably hideous. This suspicion is confirmed by the title, originally given to the work by the poet André Salmon. "Young ladies of Avignon" is an ironic description indeed—these are the whores who plied their trade in the Calle d'Avignon of Picasso's native Barcelona.

Academic historians of Modernism have often claimed that the most significant thing about *Les Demoiselles d'Avignon* is not this element of hostility towards the public, but the fact that the painting ushers in Picasso's so-called Negro Period, which leads in turn to the birth of Cubism. If we look at the five female figures, we note a distinct progression from left to right. The head of the nude on the extreme left is a tribute to the Polynesian faces characteristic of Gauguin's late

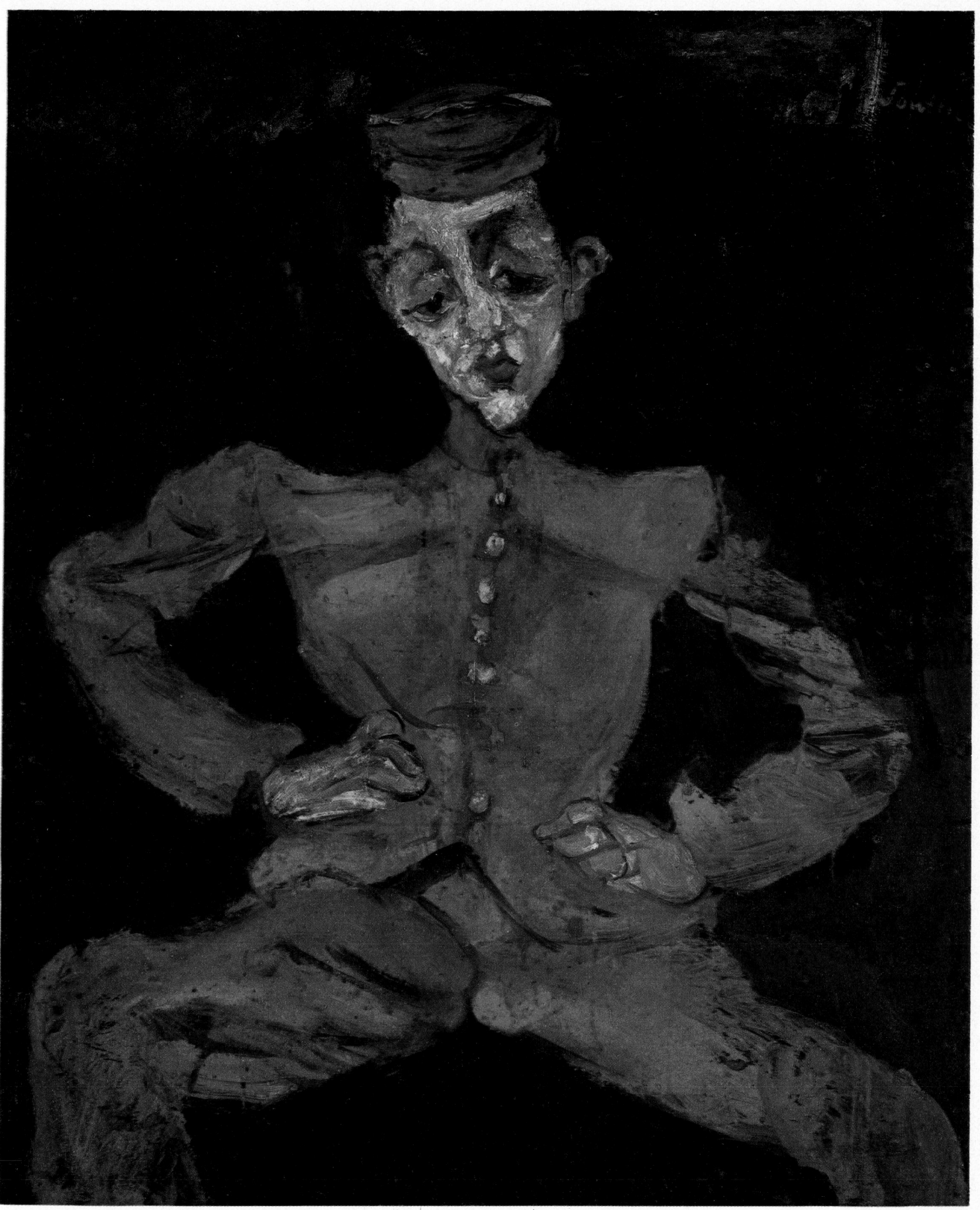

5 and 6.
Pablo Picasso
Les Demoiselles d' Avignon
1907; 243 × 234 cm. (95 × 91 in.)
New York, Museum of Modern Art
Opposite, detail

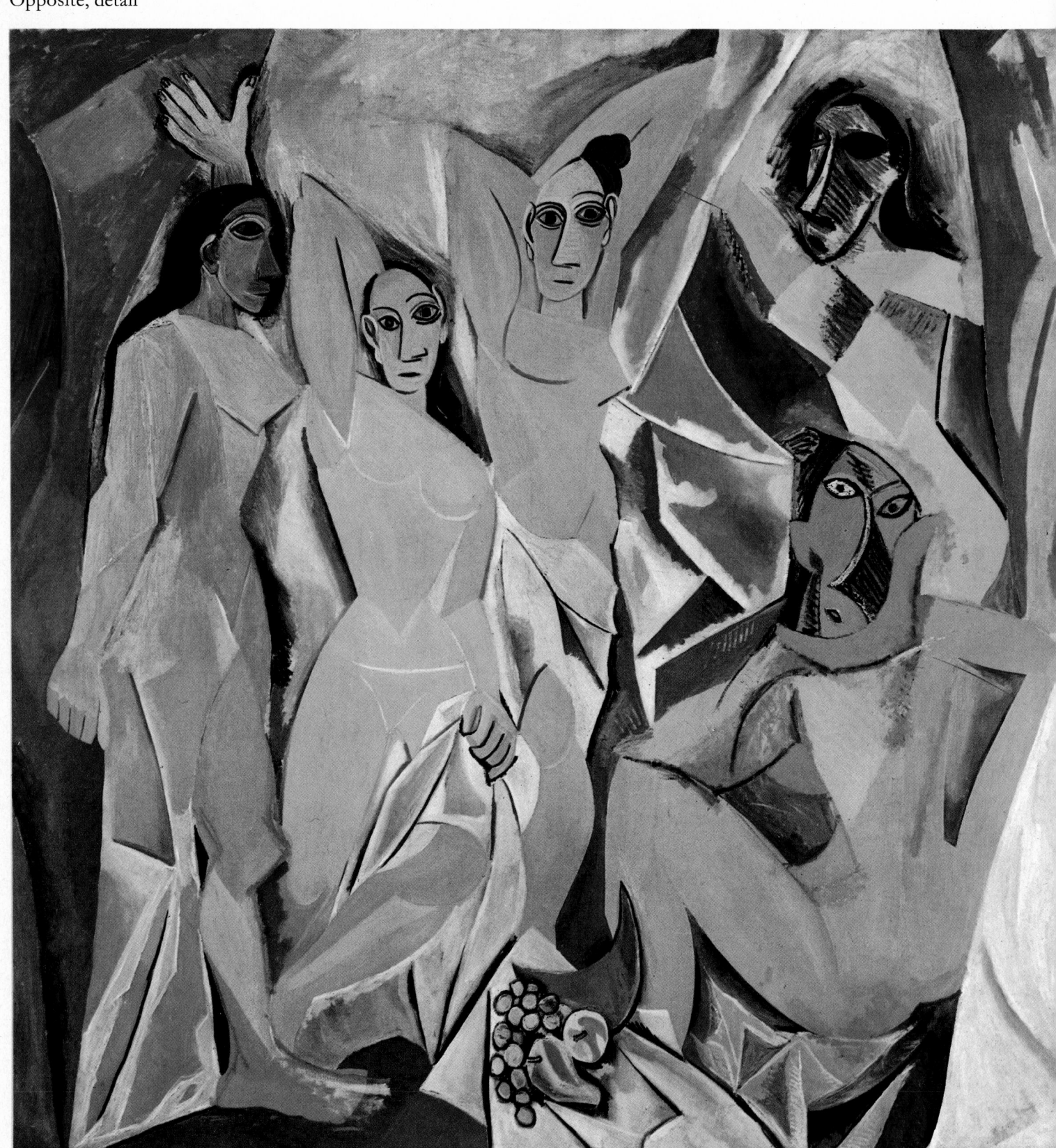

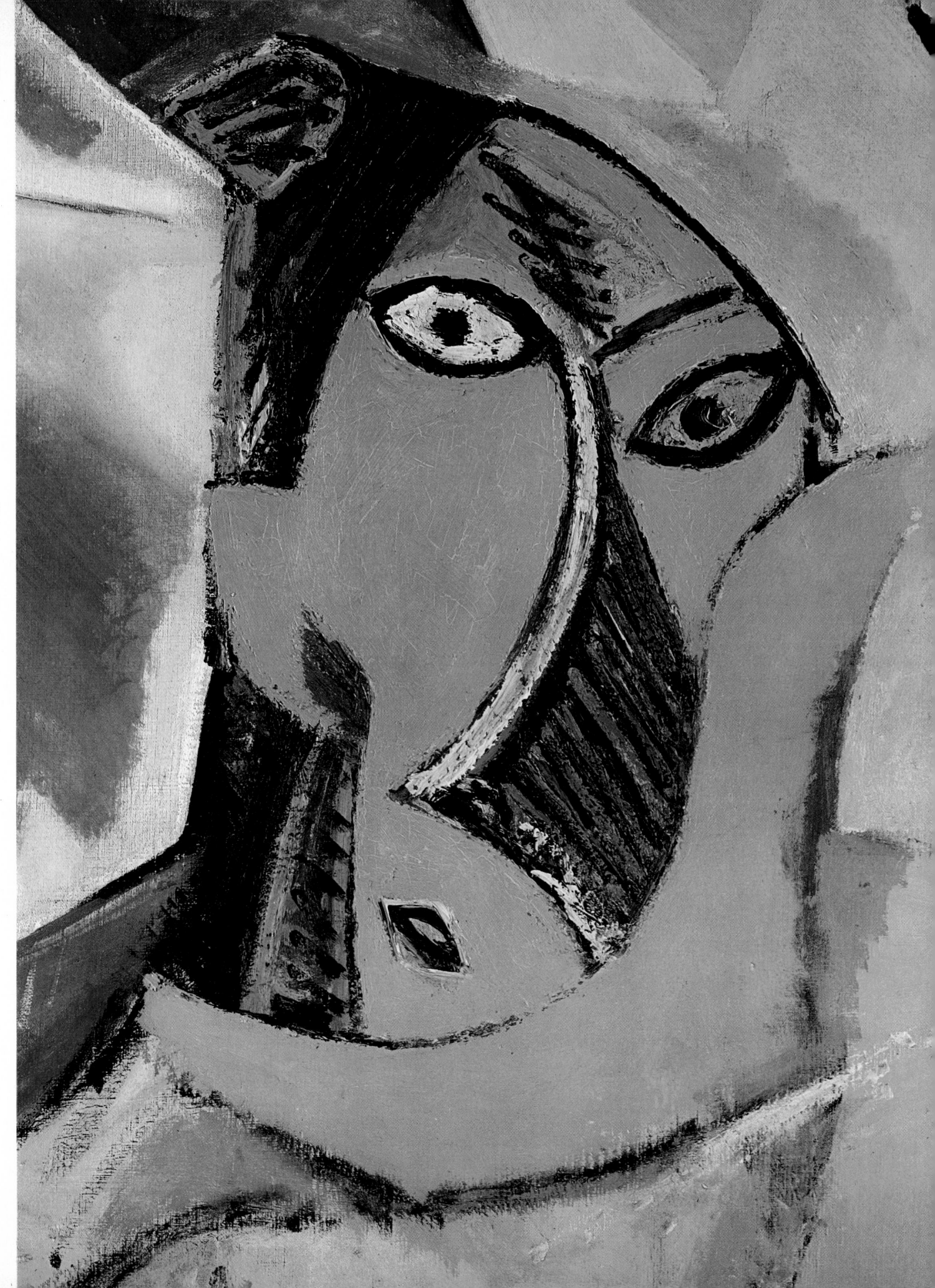

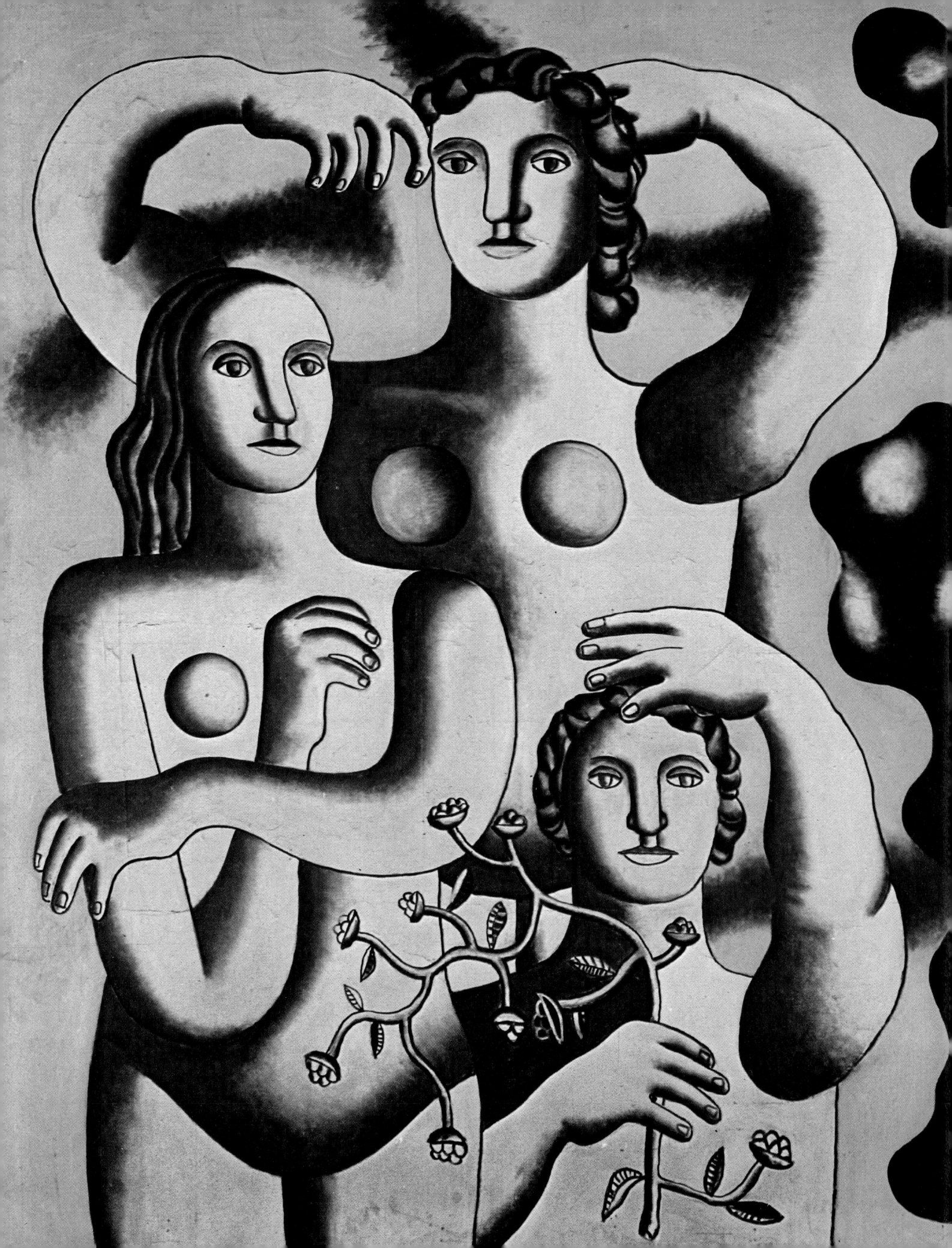

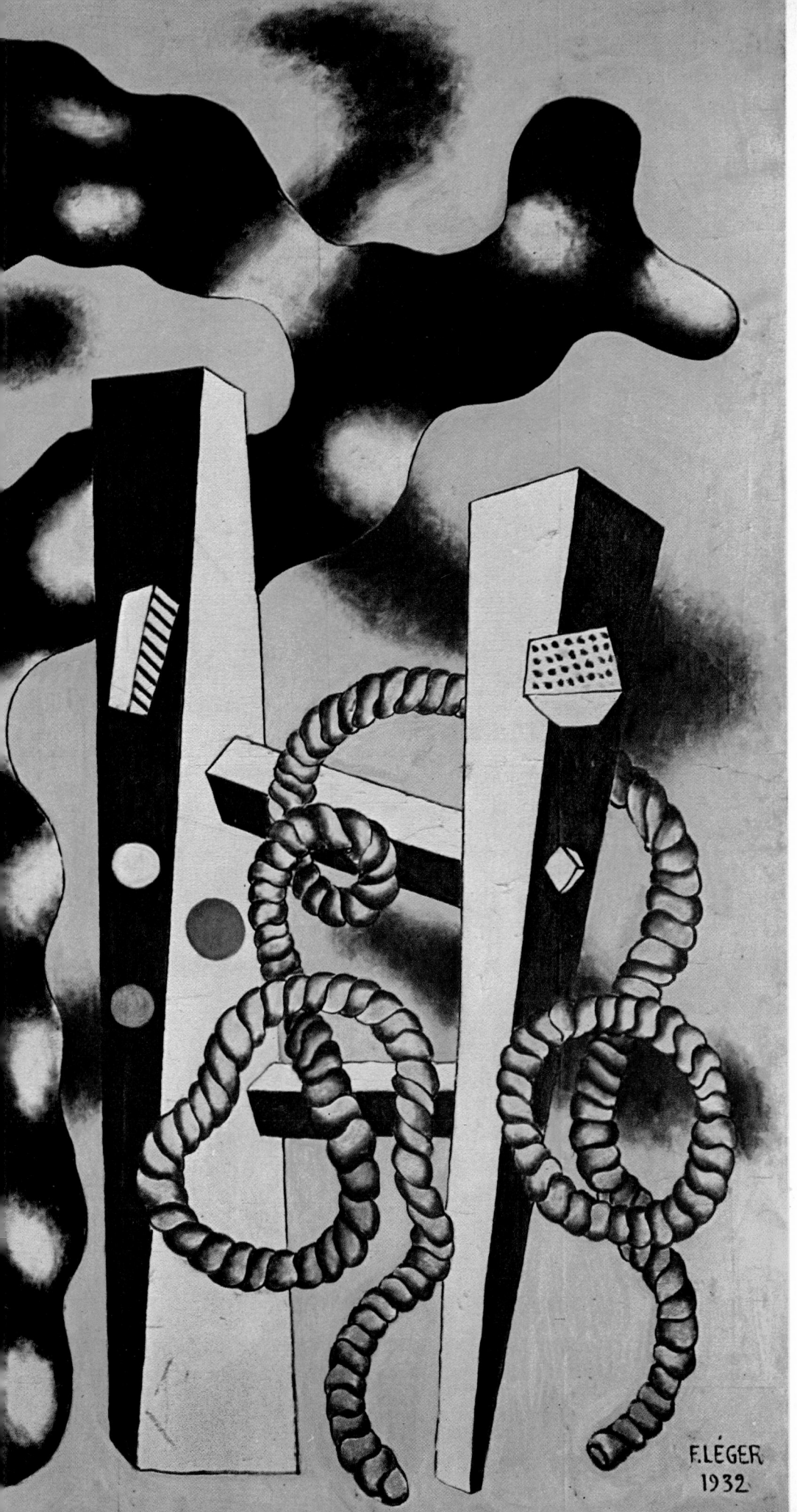

7.
Fernand Léger
Composition aux trois figures
(Three Women)
1932; 182 × 282 cm. (72 × 111 in.)
Paris, Musée National
d'Art Moderne

8.
Georges Braque
La femme à la guitare (Woman with Guitar)
1912; 130 × 74 cm. (51 × 29 in.)
Paris, Museé National d'Art Moderne

9. Opposite
Pablo Picasso
Portrait of Ambroise Vollard
1909–10; 92 × 66 cm. (36 × 26 in.)
Moscow, Pushkin Museum

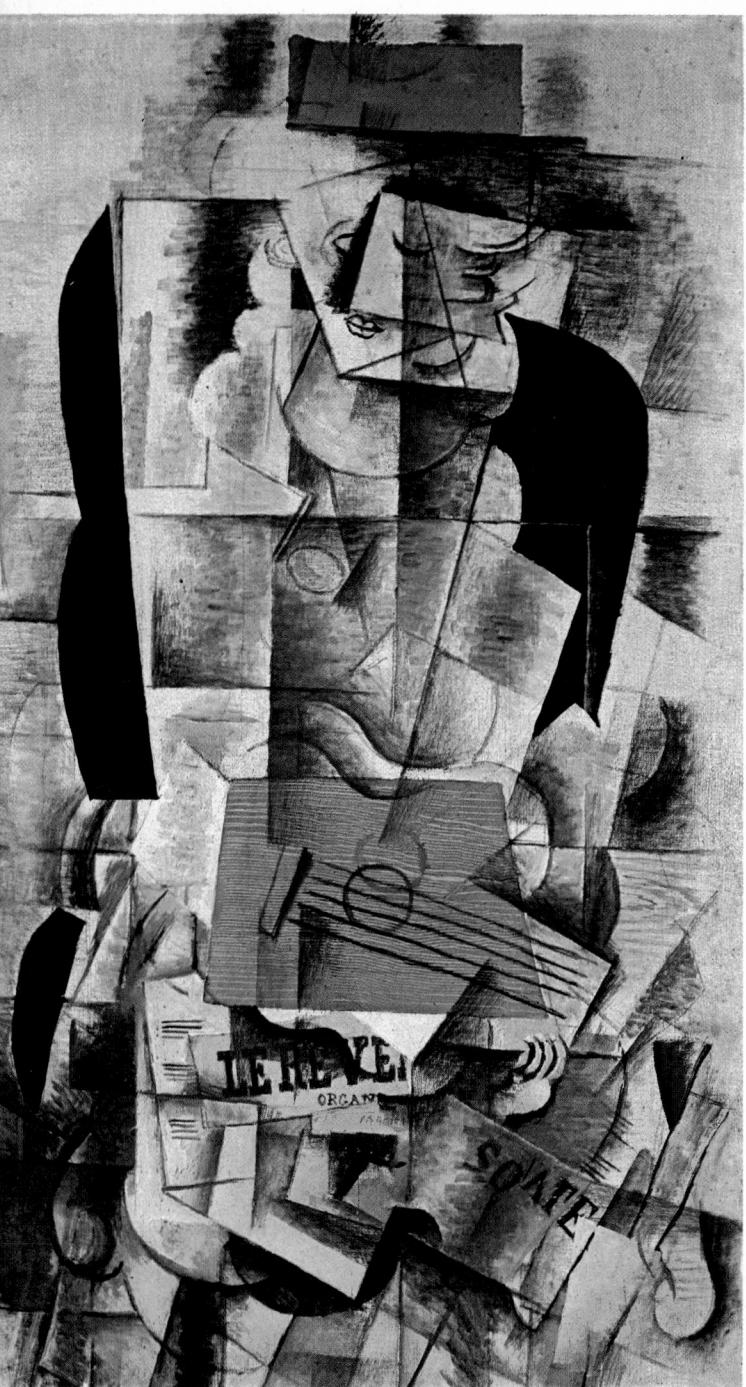

work. The two heads on the extreme right are very different. They are evidently based on the African masks which were just starting to attract the interest and enthusiasm of avant-garde artists. The intention to be "barbarous" in this sense is therefore unequivocally stated.

It is one of the curiosities of the early history of Modernism that this harsh and uncomfortable painting should lead directly to the most sophisticated of early Modernist styles—Analytic Cubism. Georges Braque's *Woman with Guitar* of 1912 (Plate 8) is in all respects typical of the work that both he and Picasso were producing at this time.

Until recently the claim that Cubism was the fountainhead of all subsequent Modernist art passed almost unchallenged. Yet there is a good case for claiming that it is a by-way, or perhaps even a cul-de-sac. Negro art was part of Analytic Cubism's parentage because the primitive artists of Africa had the habit of using faceted forms, in which the planes of the carving are distinguished from one another by a firm and visible boundary. A more important ancestor was Paul Cézanne. Cézanne, too, developed the habit of breaking up the forms he was using into facets, but in his case these were displayed on a flat surface.

During their Analytic Cubist period—it was very brief—Picasso and Braque were determined to see how far Cézanne's researches could be taken. They were fascinated by the problem of representing three-dimensional objects in two dimensions, without betraying their three-dimensionality, yet at the same time without allowing the spectator to forget for a moment that the surface itself was flat. What they did was to discard conventional perspective—and therefore any pretense at illusion—and show what they were painting from multiple points of view. Cubist paintings have often loosely been described as "abstract", whereas in fact they are the very opposite. They strive for the uttermost concreteness, the most precise and refined description of form.

Though contemporary artists have continued to be interested in a notion which Cubism introduced—that painting is in fact a kind of language, which can be used to translate one

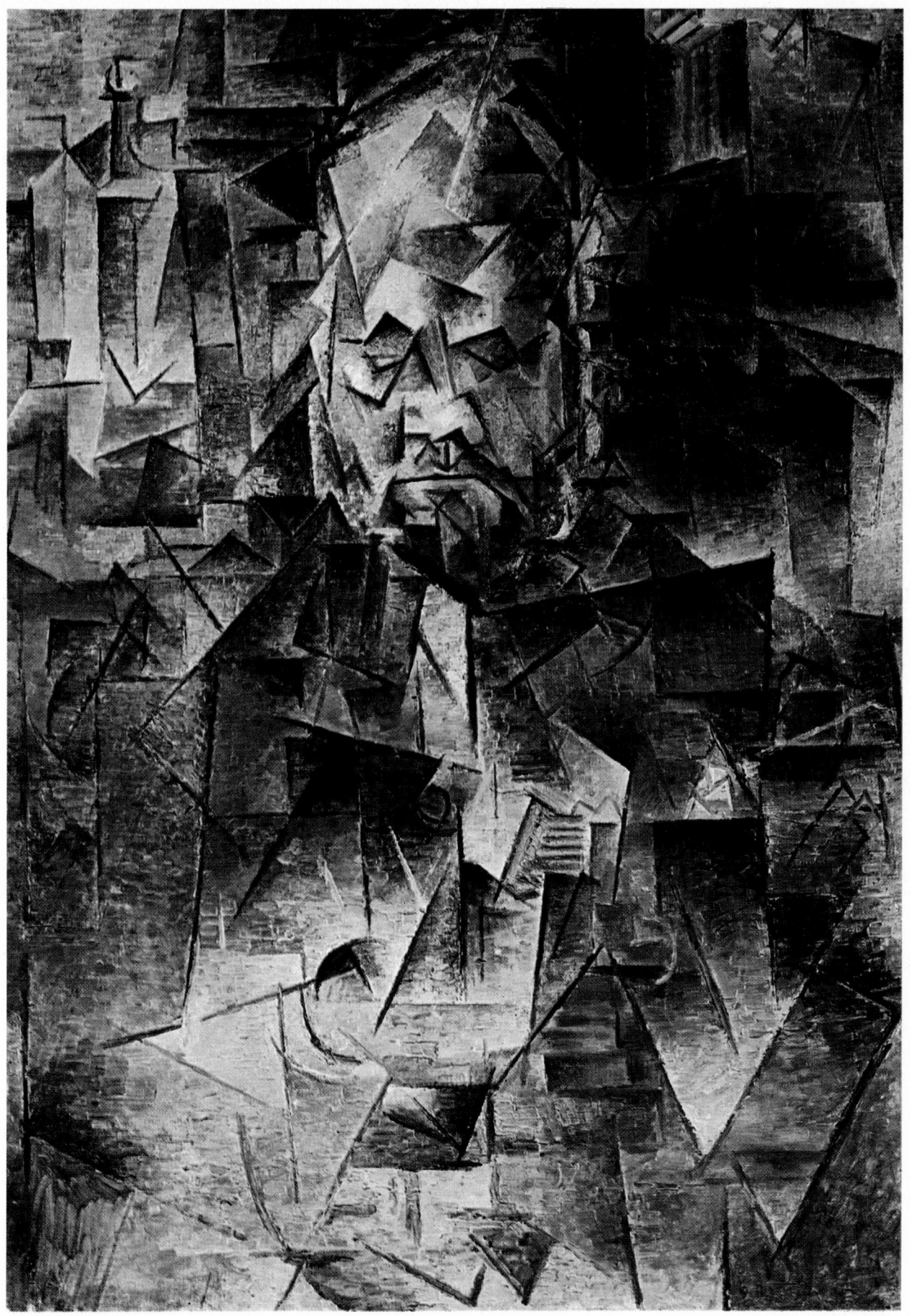

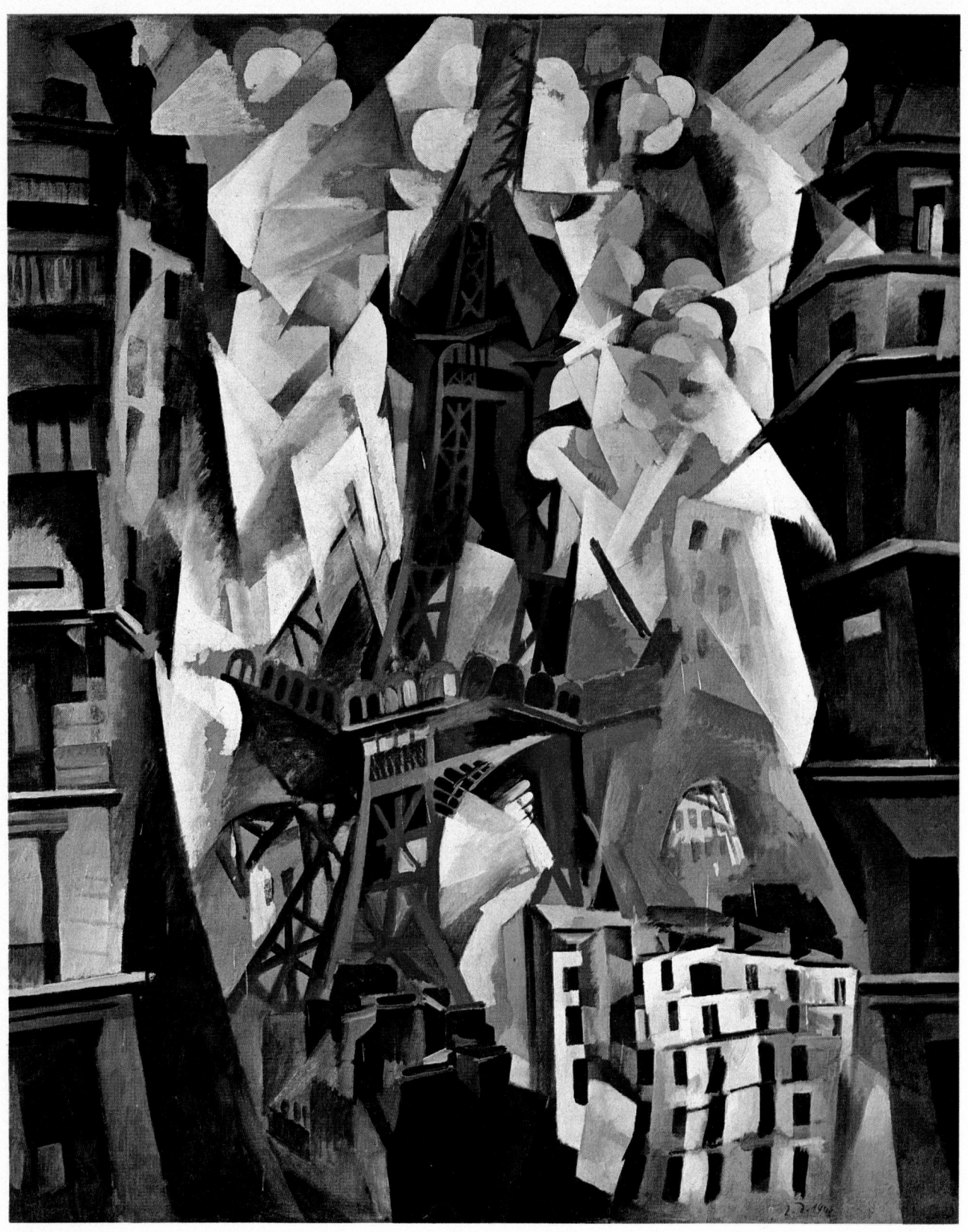

10.
Robert Delaunay
Champs de Mars, La Tour Rouge
1911; 162.6 × 130.9 cm. (63 × 51 in.)
Chicago, Art Institute of Chicago

11. Opposite
Gino Severini
Geroglifico dinamico del Bal Tabarin
1912; 161 × 156 cm. (63 × 61 in.)
New York, by courtesy of the Museum of Modern Art

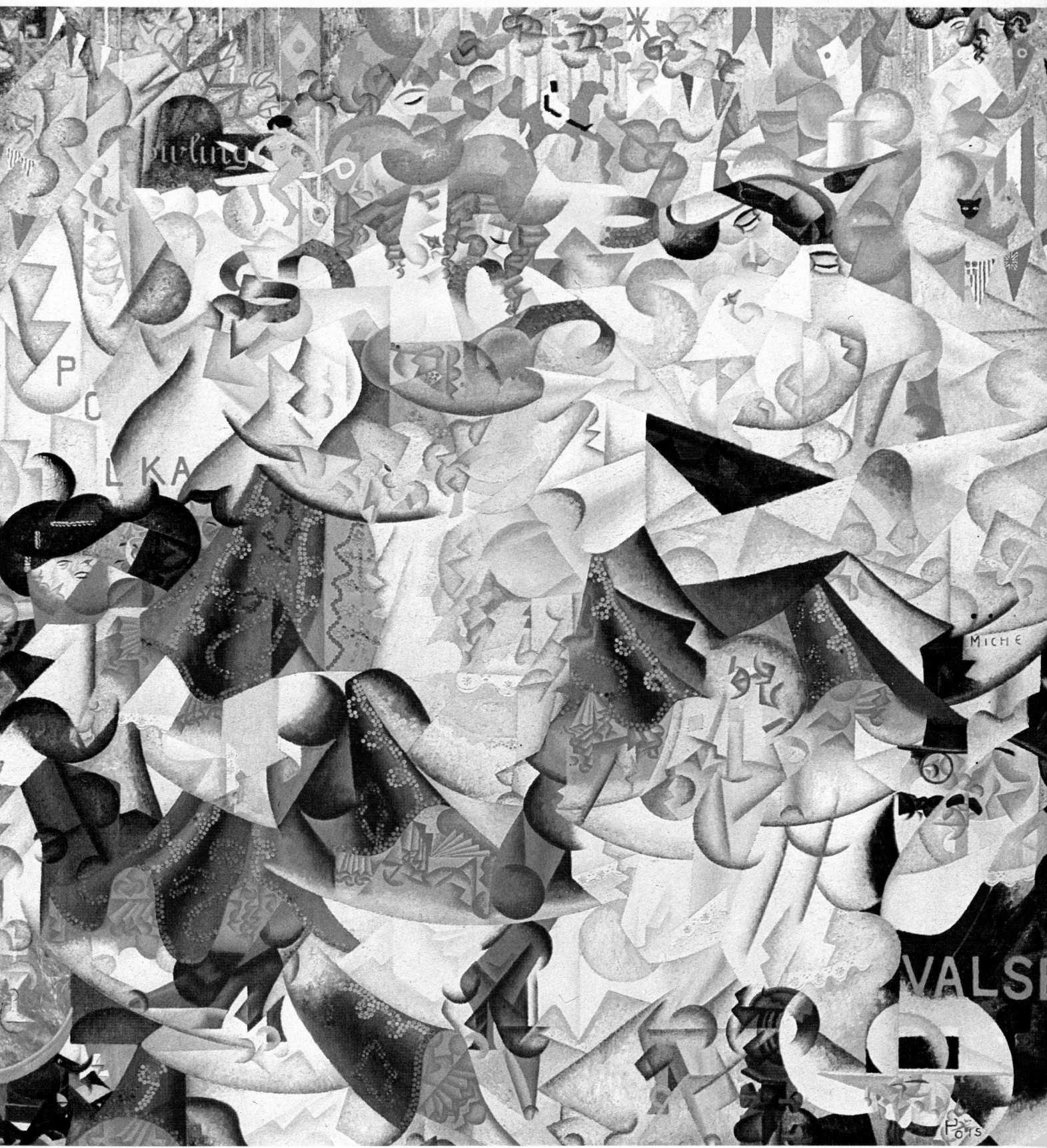

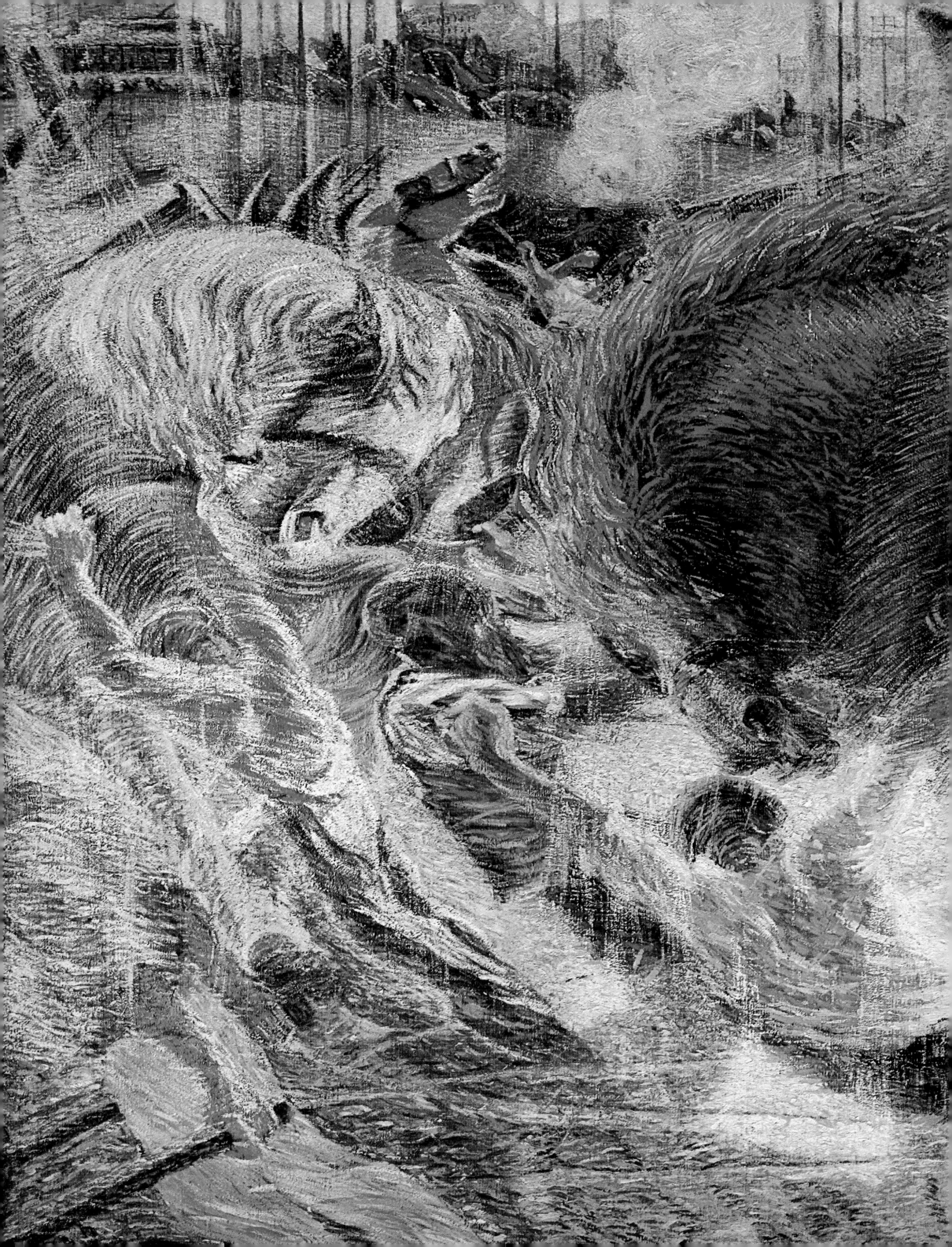

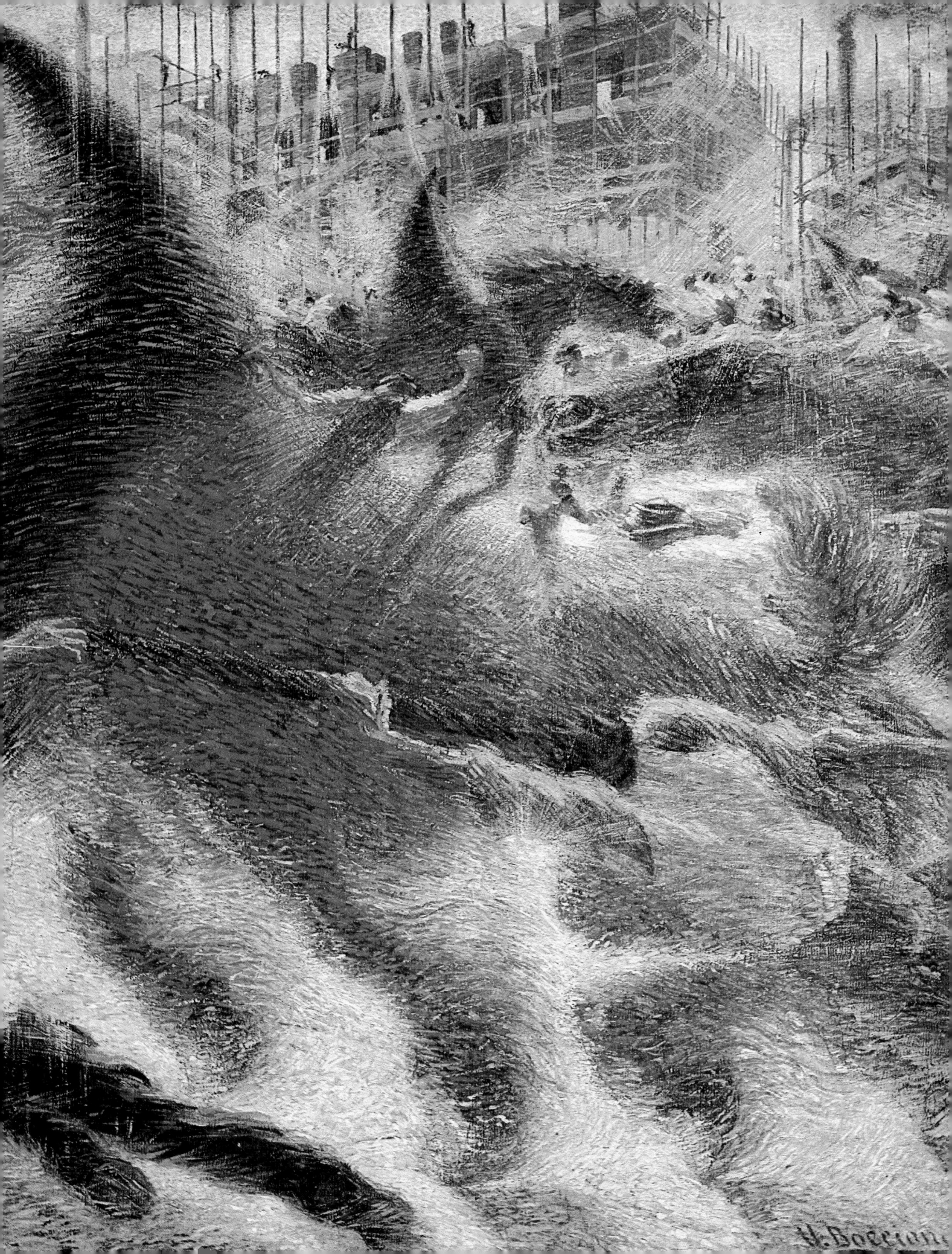

reality into the very different terms of another—they have ceased to regard appearances themselves as paramount. Analytic Cubism can be thought of, paradoxically, as the last manifestation of the Naturalist spirit which affected so much of the art of the late nineteenth century, and even as the logical culmination of academic Salon painting.

After the traumatic shock of the First World War, painters and sculptors in France were half-inclined to abandon the experimental attitudes they had favoured a decade earlier. Cubism had already moved from a stringent analysis of what was seen to a laxer synthesis of decorative elements. The overlapping planes which had once been used to render the three-dimensionality of the object were now employed in a purely conventional way.

In the period between the two wars there was even an inclination, among those who had been associated with Cubism, to revert to the long-established French classical tradition—that of Nicolas Poussin in the seventeenth century and Jean-Auguste-Dominique Ingres in the nineteenth. The influence of Poussin, for example, is visible in Fernand Léger's monumental *Three Women* (Plate 7), painted in 1932. We see in this a tendency, which can also be found in Poussin, to turn details such as eyes, hands, and breasts into purely conventional symbols, with no element of first-hand observation. There seem to be two reasons for this. One is that Léger, as a kind of classicist, believed that a blandly generalized artistic language was likely to be more effective in conveying general ideas—about order and tranquillity, for example. But we also get the feeling that the artist (who was a Communist) was haunted by the suspicion that Modernism had already gone too far, and had put itself out of touch with the masses whom it was destined to serve. The difficulty in reconciling political and artistic radicalism is something that has bedeviled Modernism throughout its career.

Without attempting to deny the quality of the best Cubist work, it must nevertheless be said that the main line of development seems to run in another direction. Cubism did have an offshoot, in the form of the Orphism of Robert Delaunay, which was enthusiastically supported by the poet and publicist Guillaume Apollinaire, but Delaunay failed to persist in his more radical explorations. He began with a derivation of Cubism which stressed the value of colour and movement (Plate 10), in place of the rather static composition favoured by Braque and Picasso at this point, and progressed from this to one of the earliest varieties of pure abstraction, with paintings showing areas of pure colour that seemed to interpenetrate and revolve around one another. In these, too, as in his figurative work, a sense of dynamic movement was paramount.

Delaunay's interest in rendering movement had already been anticipated by the work of the Italian Futurists. The importance of this group to the early history of Modernism is still somewhat underestimated, though the justice has to some extent been rectified by retrospective exhibitions in Turin and elsewhere. One of the peculiarities of Futurism was the fact that the leader of the movement was not himself a painter. F. T. Marinetti, who published the first Futurist Manifesto in a Paris newspaper in February, 1909, was an Italian poet long resident in France. His manifesto, however, dealt entirely with the Italian situation—it was a blast directed at the cultural apathy into which Italy had fallen and the deadweight of the past. Its most famous sentences run as follows: "We maintain that the splendours of the world have been enriched by a new beauty: the beauty of speed. A racing automobile is more beautiful than the *Victory of Samothrace*." The manifesto also declared that "Beauty exists only in struggle. A work that is not aggressive cannot be a masterpiece. Art must be conceived as a violent assault against the forces of the unknown, designed to subject them to man."

Futurism is of great interest to the student of Modernism for at least three reasons. The first is that it perfectly sums up the aggressive spirit that typified the international avant-garde in the years immediately preceding the First World War. Marinetti was a nationalist, a super-patriot, and he glorified the idea of armed conflict. He looked forward eagerly to war, as something which would let a great gust of fresh air into the musty

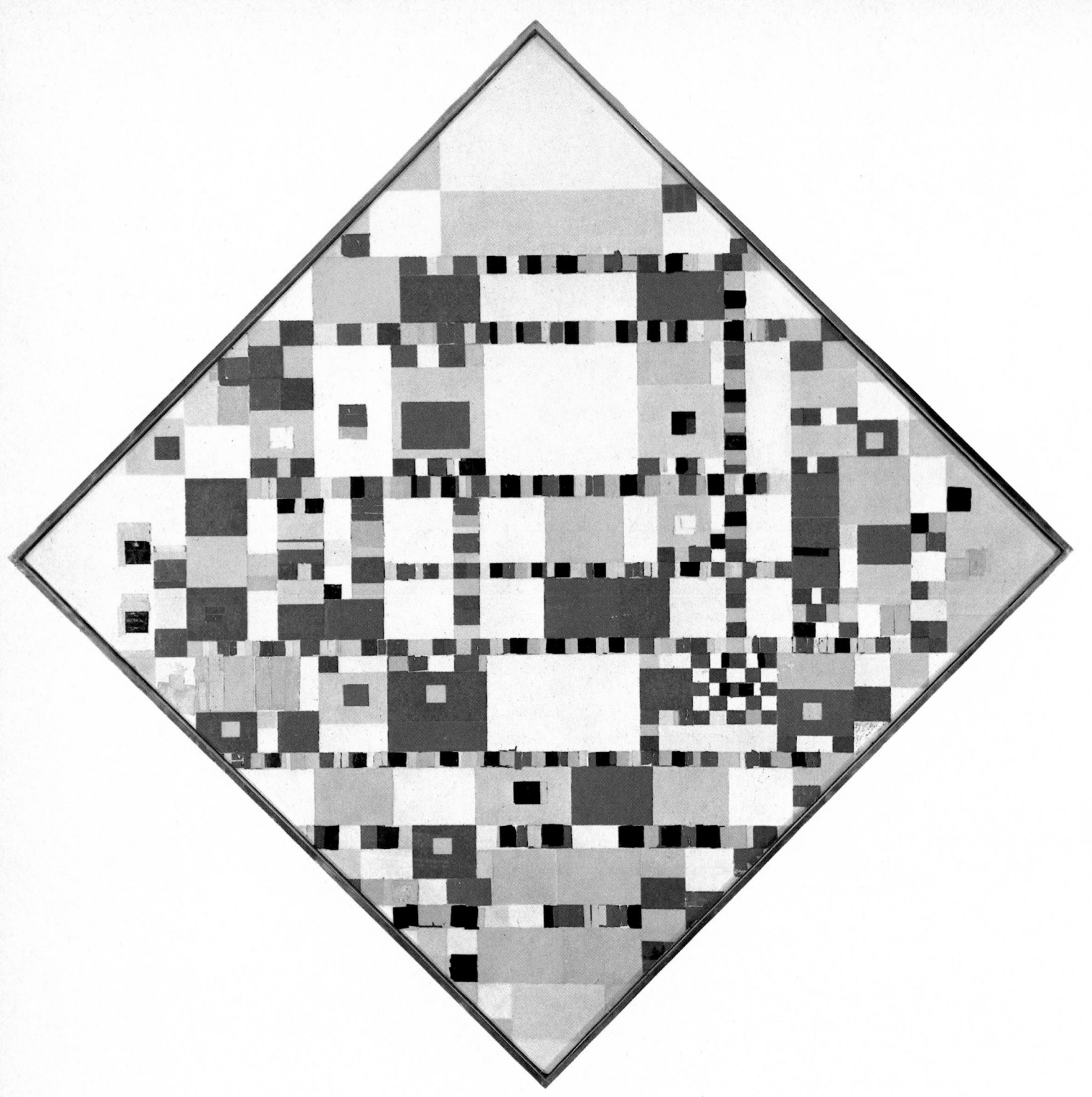

attics of the past. This love of violence was shared by poets and artists elsewhere. We find it loudly expressed by the English Vorticists and by some of the Russian Futurists. The more extreme members of the avant-garde were at this moment only too eager to bring the whole social structure of Europe down upon their own heads. Marinetti himself, however, was not a man of the left but of the radical right. After a brief period during which he treated Mussolini as a political rival rather than as an ally, he ended his life as a faithful Fascist.

The second important aspect of Futurism is that it was the earliest of the organized, self-conscious avant-garde movements, eager to invent and publicize an identity, rather than leave this task to the critics. Publicity, indeed, was Marinetti's strong suit. He held Futurist demonstrations throughout Italy; and, from 1912 onwards, throughout Europe. The success of these gatherings was measured in the manuals of the

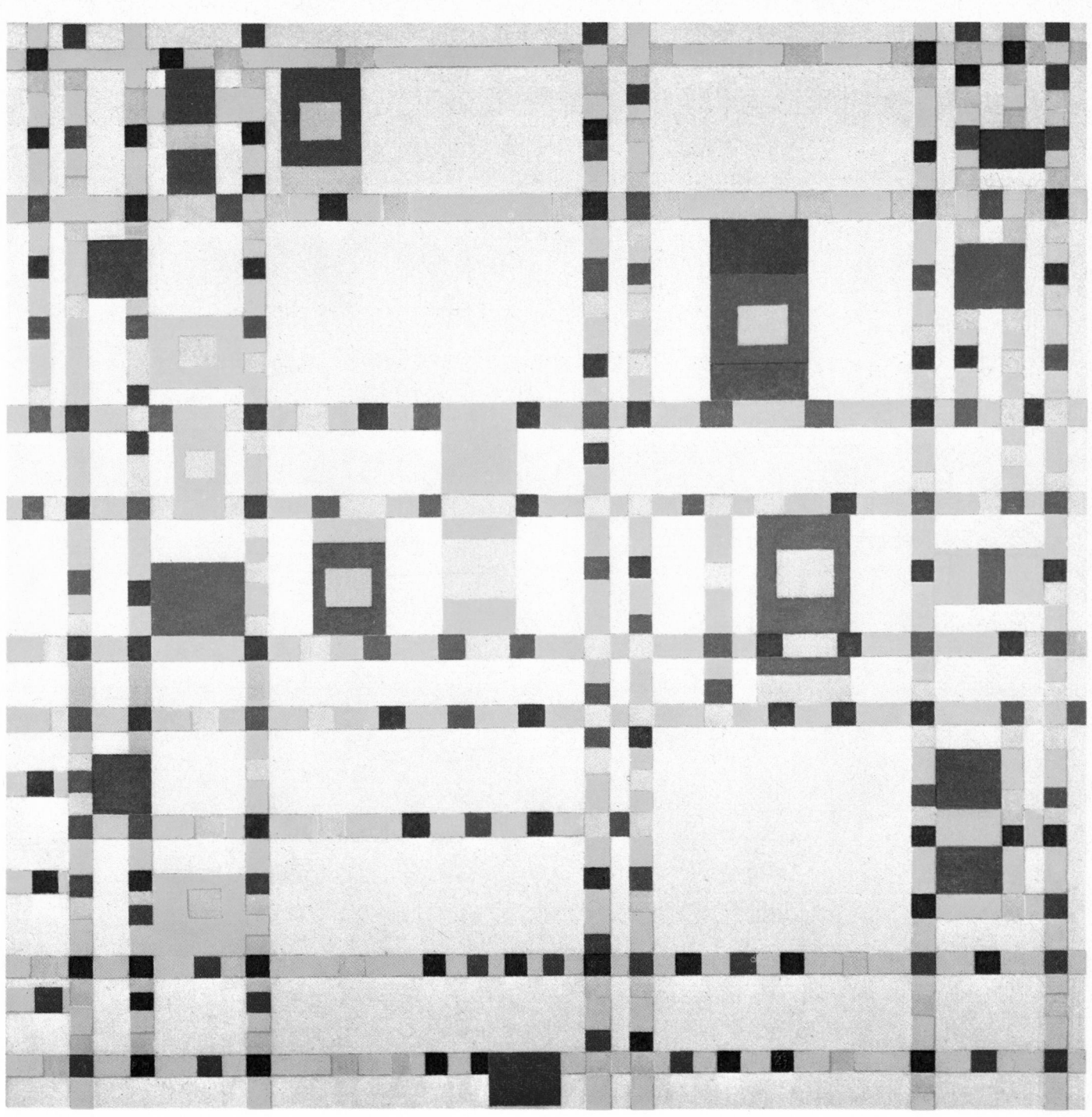

14. Opposite
Piet Mondrian
Victory Boogie-Woogie
1943–44; 127 × 127 cm. (50 × 50 in.)
Connecticut, coll. Mr. and Mrs. Burton Tremaine

15.
Piet Mondrian
Broadway Boogie-Woogie
1942–43; 127 × 127 cm. (50 × 50 in.)
New York, Museum of Modern Art

organizers, by the riots they provoked.

But Futurism is also interesting for a third reason; the talent of the artists whom Marinetti succeeded in attracting to his banner, and the direction their work took under his influence. The most prominent of the Futurists—Giacomo Balla, Umberto Boccioni, Gino Severini (all of them signatories of the Technical Manifesto of Futurist Painting, which was issued in 1910)—plunged themselves into the task of representing and

16. Below
László Moholy-Nagy
Composition A-XX
1924; 135 × 115 cm. (53 × 45 in.)
Paris, Musée National d'Art Moderne

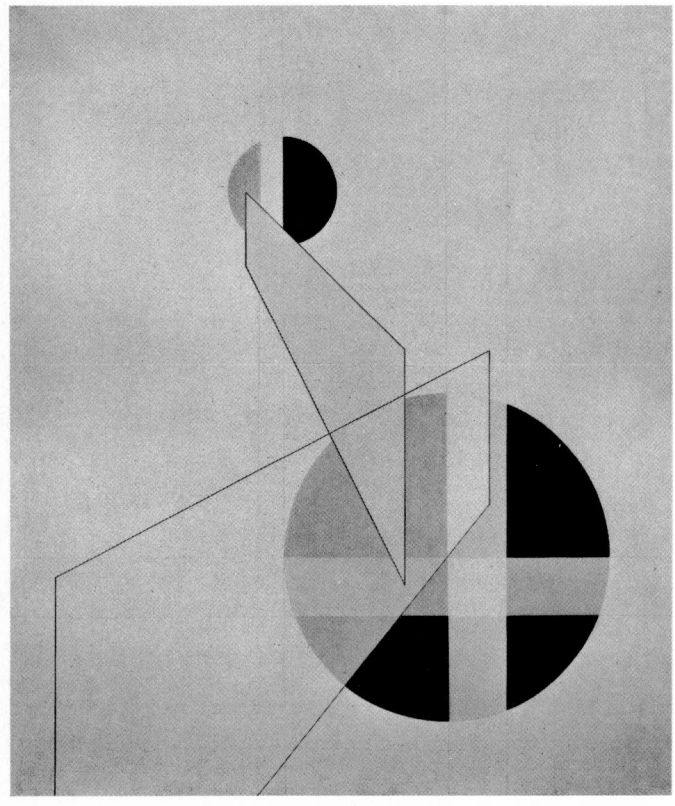

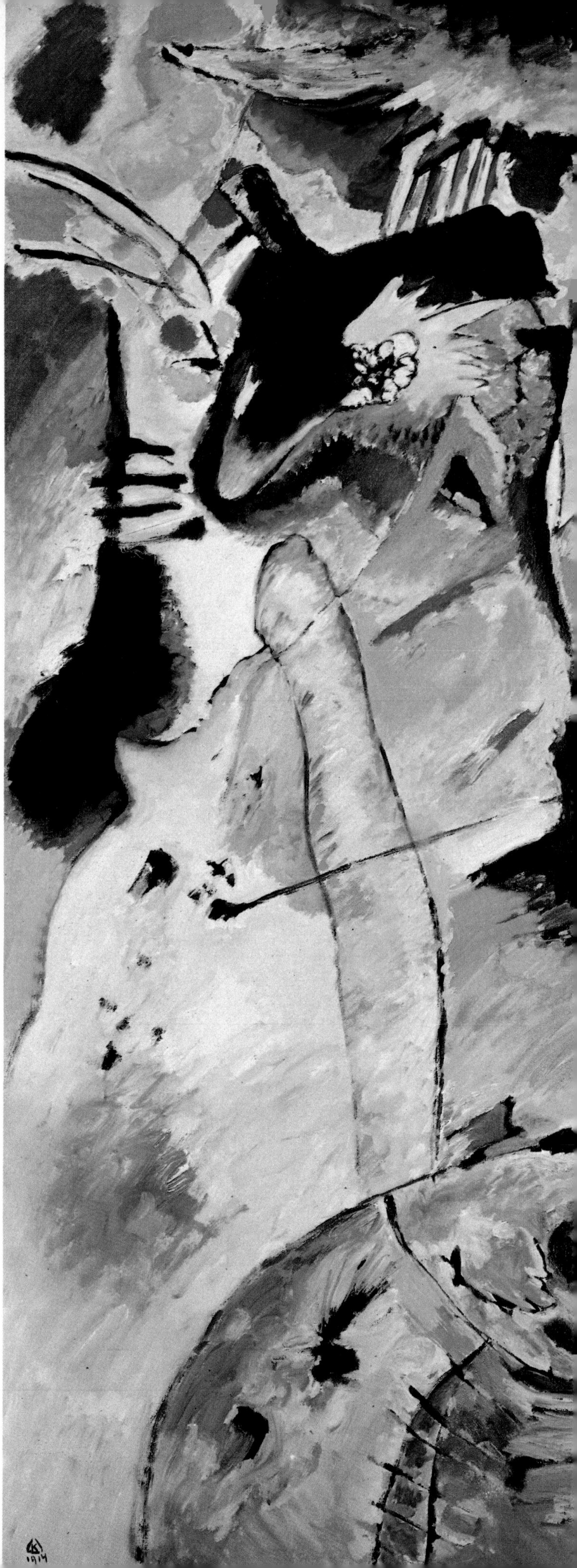

17. Right
Wassily Kandinsky
Panel (3)
1914; 162 × 94 cm. (63 × 37 in.)
New York, Museum of Modern Art

18. Opposite
Wassily Kandinsky
Panel (4)
1914; 162 × 80 cm. (63 × 31 in.)
New York, Museum of Modern Art

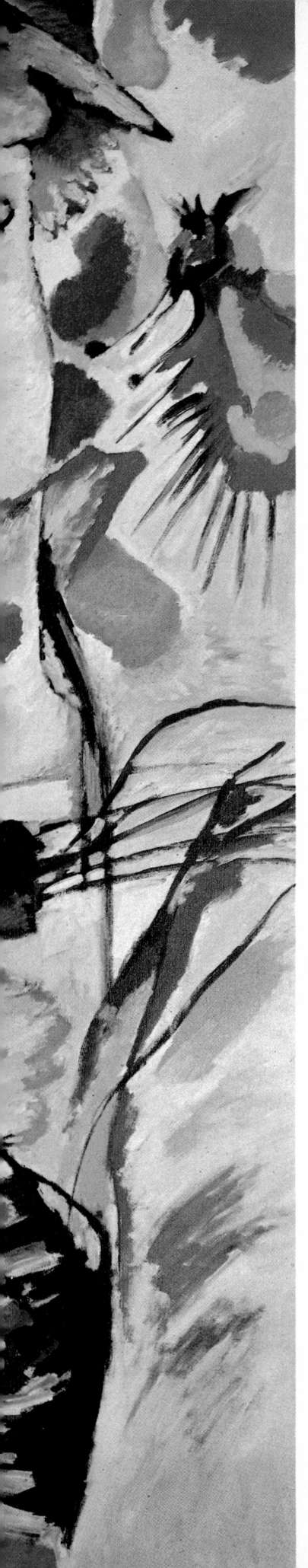

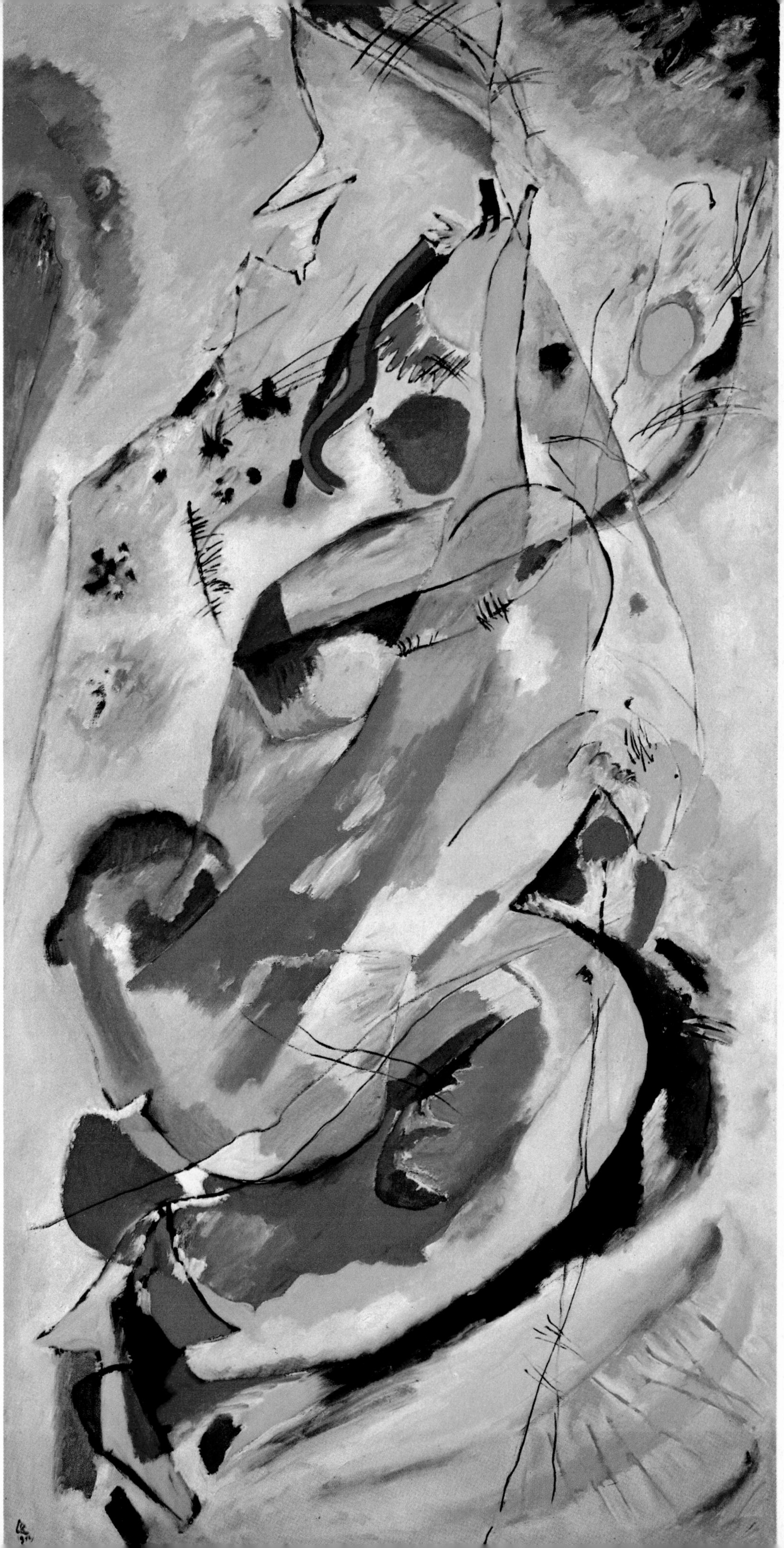

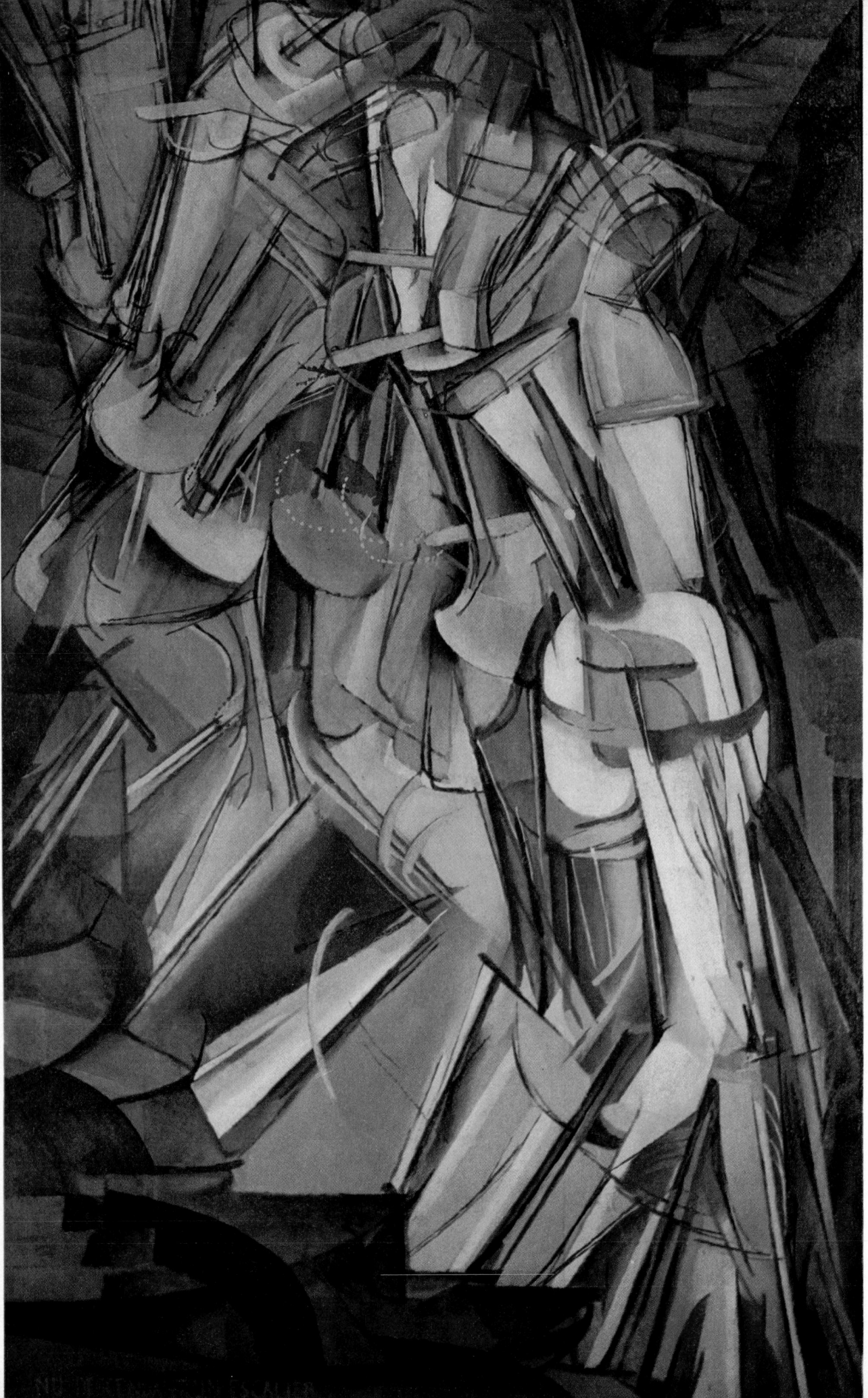

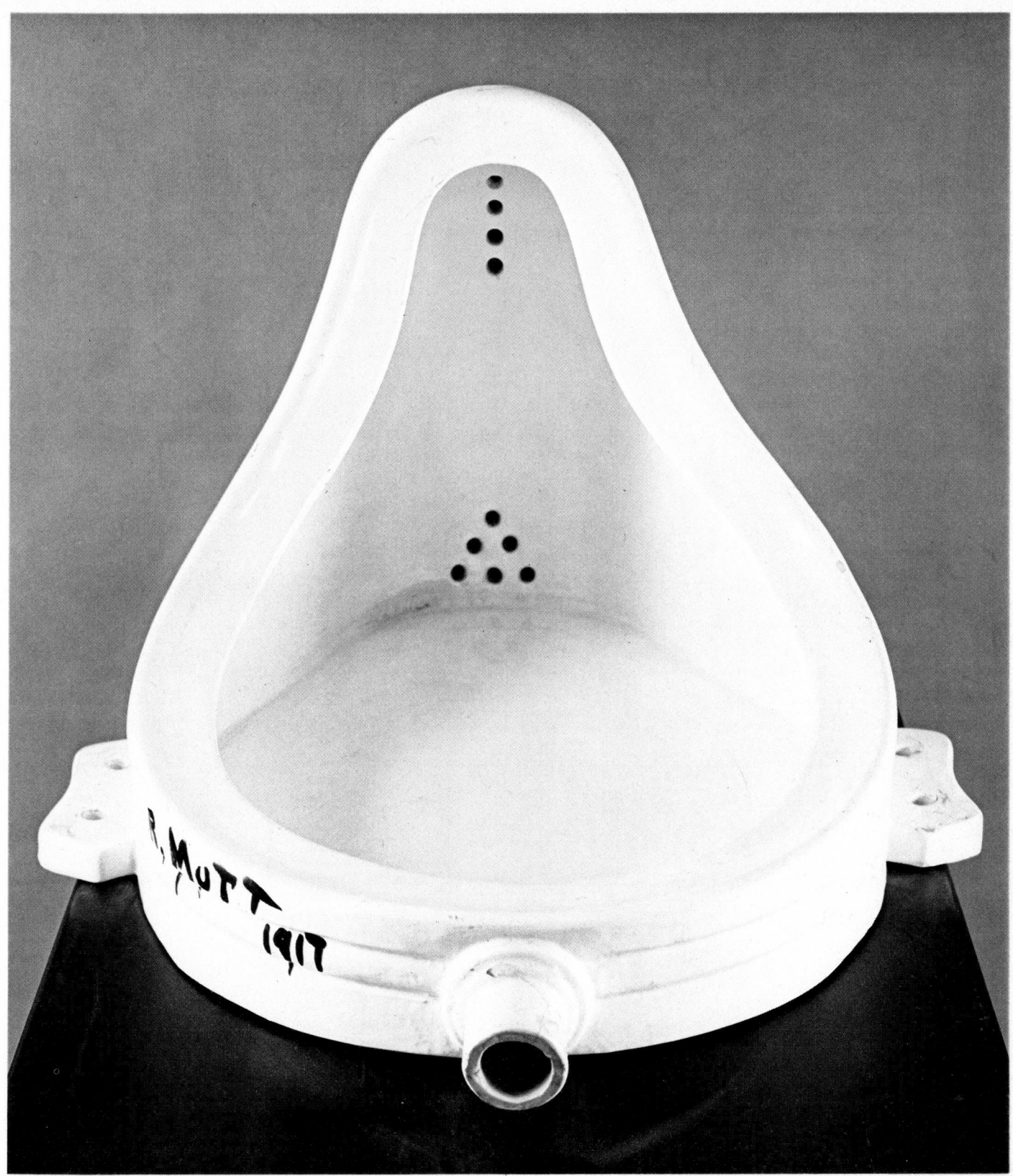

19. Opposite
Marcel Duchamp
Nu descendant un escalier No. 2 (Nude Descending a Staircase No. 2)
1912; 147 × 89 cm. (57 × 35 in.)
Philadelphia, Philadelphia Museum of Art

20.
Marcel Duchamp
Fountain
1964 (replica of 1917 original); 63 × 46 × 36 cm.
(25 × 18 × 14 in.)
Milan, Galleria Schwarz

21. Below left
Marcel Duchamp
Roue de bicyclette
1964 (replica of 1913 original); 126 cm. (49 in.)
Milan, Galleria Schwarz

22. Below right
Marcel Duchamp
Porte-bouteille
1964 (replica of 1914 original); 66 cm. (26 in.)
Milan, Galleria Schwarz

reflecting modern life, which they saw as being characterized by frantic speed and dynamism. Boccioni's *The City Rises*, 1910 (Plate 12), is in these respects typical of their work. Interest in movement led the Futurist painters to consider the problem of simultaneity: several phases of movement were represented on the same canvas, in a manner which was probably suggested by the experiments with chronophotography made some decades earlier by E. J. Marey. The Cubist concern to represent a given object in successively unfolding views was taken a stage further, since a temporal element was now introduced. For the first time since the birth of perspective Western art comprehended the ideas of a temporal lapse within the boundaries of the canvas, and the artist no

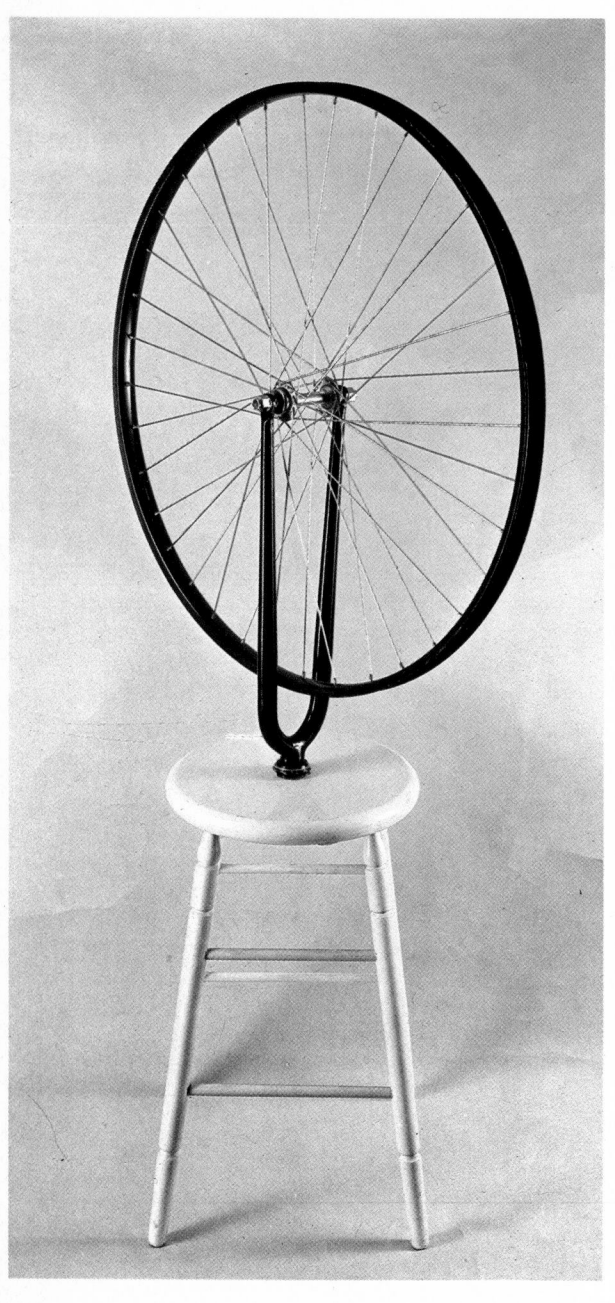

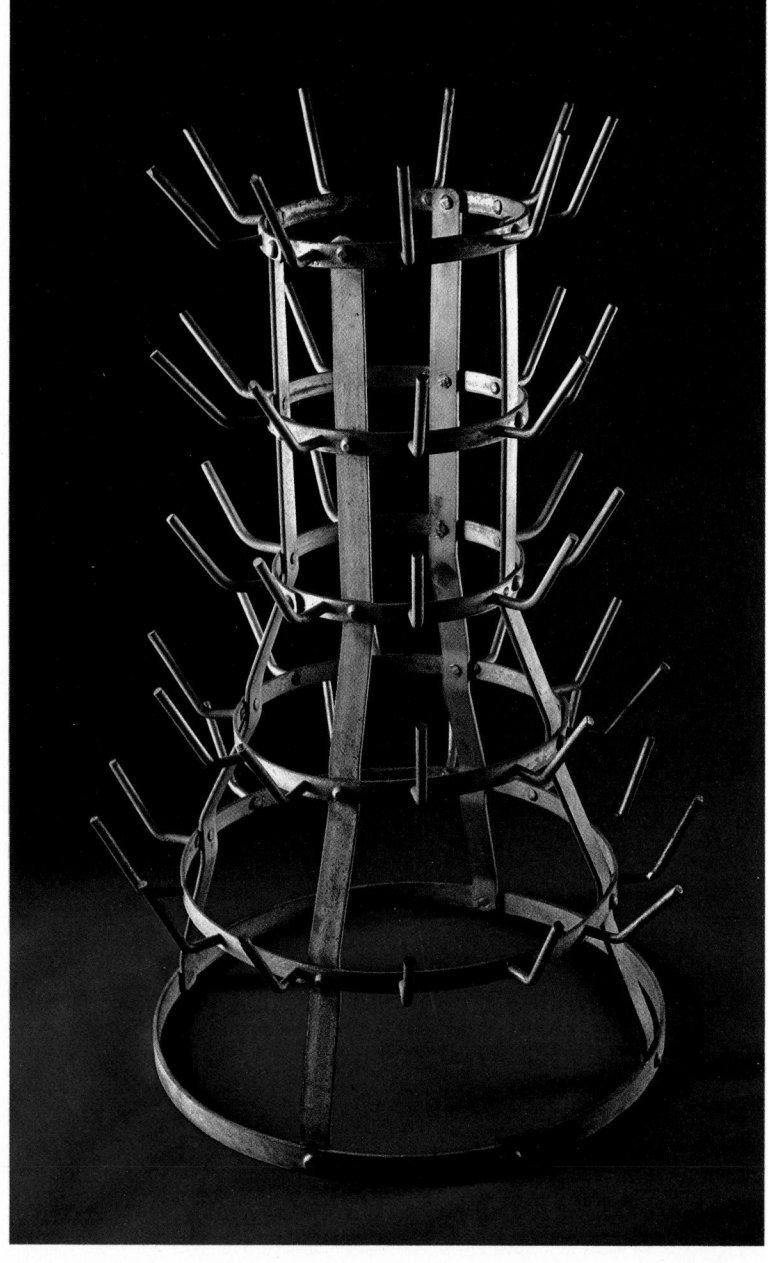

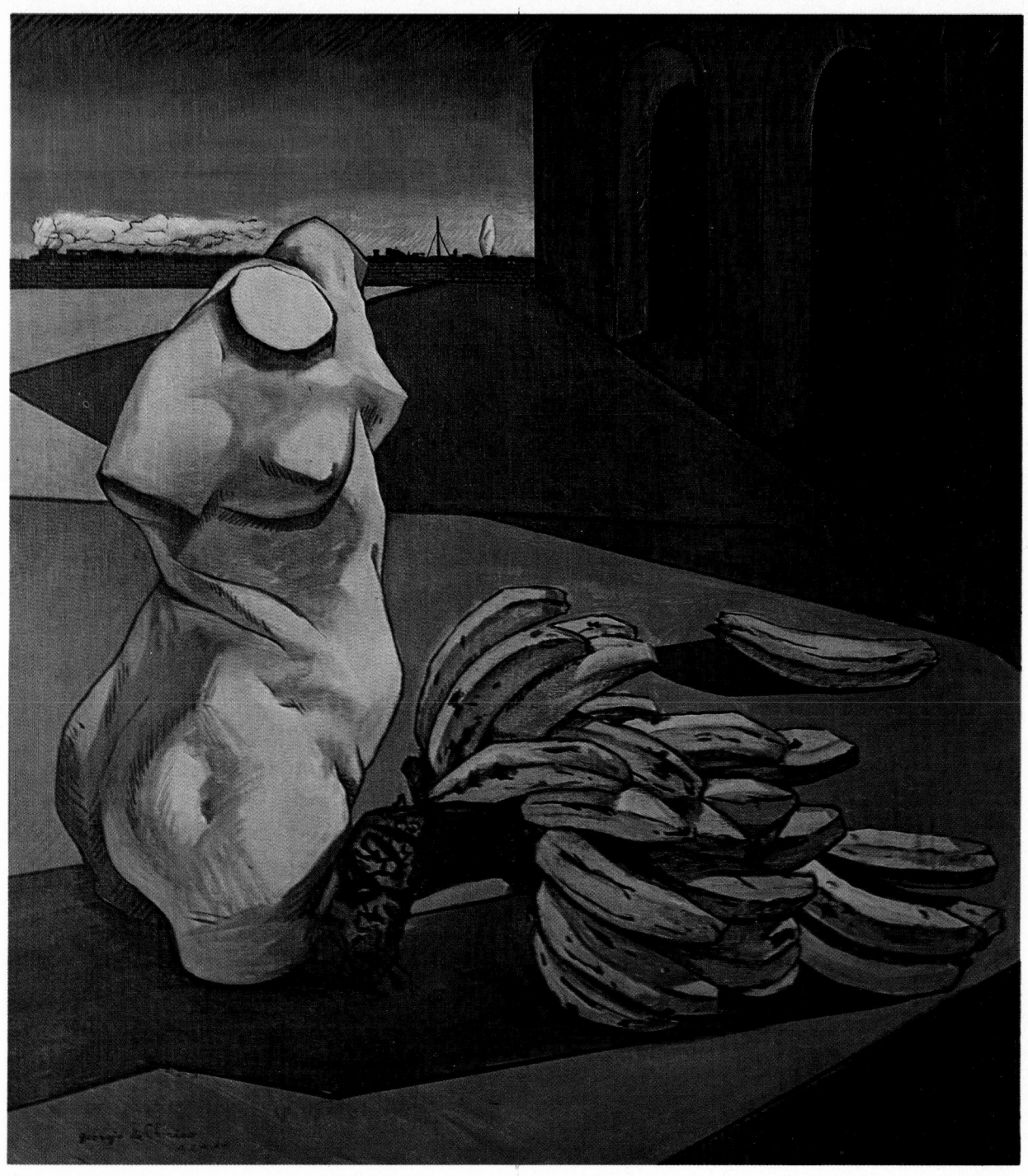

23.
Giorgio de Chirico
L'incertezza del poeta
1913; 106 × 94 cm. (41 × 37 in.)
London, coll. Sir Roland Penrose

longer confined himself to the representation of a single, frozen moment. This was to be full of consequences for the future.

The avant-garde movement elsewhere which most closely resembled Italian Futurism and which was most closely allied to it in ideas and methods was the Futurism that soon afterwards appeared in Russia, basing itself chiefly in Moscow. The Russian avant-garde differed from its Italian equivalent in being far more eclectic, and in undergoing a more complex development. The leading Russian artists, for example, often went through a phase of neo-primitivism which related their work to that of the Fauves. This development is visible in the work of Kasimir Malevich as well as in that of Mikhail Larionov and Natalia Goncharova. They also felt the attraction of Cubism. One of the most striking things about Russian Futurism, however, was the early appearance of pure abstraction, and the extreme lengths to which it was taken. Malevich's *Suprematist Compositions* (Plate 13), painted early in the war, were at least as extreme as anything produced by any member of the avant-garde during the next thirty years.

Many of the problems that have continued to preoccupy modern artists were first formulated in Russia during the years just before and just after the Revolution of 1917. In the immediately post-Revolutionary period, the Russian avant-garde, led by Malevich's great rival Vladimir Tatlin, moved towards a total abolition of art under the banner of a new movement, Constructivism. They insisted that the artist must become a technician in a technological society, using the tools and materials of modern production for the benefit of all. "Our Constructivism," declared Alexei Gan, in an important text written in 1920, "has declared unconditional war on art, for the means and qualities of art are not able to systematize the feelings of a revolutionary environment."

Constructivism was one of the direct ancestors of the hard-edge geometric abstraction which is still practised by many contemporary artists. But the roots of this are also to be found in Holland and in Germany. In Holland, Constructivism had its counterpart in the group which dubbed itself De Stijl, founded at the height of the war in 1917. The greatest artist connected with this group was Piet Mondrian. After Symbolist beginnings, Mondrian was influenced by Analytical Cubism during a stay in Paris from 1910–14. Cut off in Holland by the outbreak of hostilities, he started to evolve a purely geometrical style, stripped of all references to the figure or to landscape. At last he reached the point where the formal elements in his paintings had been simplified to the uttermost.

Narrow black bands divided the surface into compartments of black, white, grey, and the three primary colours. Towards the end of his life, exiled in America, Mondrian was to demonstrate that this minimal style had an unexpected capacity for development in the work which he produced in the United States. The late masterpiece *Broadway Boogie-Woogie* (Plate 15) anticipates some of the inventions of post-war kinetic art.

The artists associated with the Bauhaus, founded in Weimar in 1919, had close connections with those who belonged to the De Stijl group in Holland. Their aim, like that of the Constructivists, was to produce a rational art, in harmony with the modern technological environment. And like the Constructivists, they increasingly came to think of the fine arts as little more than experimental forms of industrial design. This tendency is clearly discernible in the work produced in the early Twenties by one of the most typical of the Bauhaus masters, László Moholy-Nagy (Plate 16).

Even in the Bauhaus, however, not all abstract art tended towards functionalism. This is particularly true of the work of Wassily Kandinsky, who was at one period closely associated with the school. Kandinsky is a key figure because he, if

24. Opposite
Max Ernst
Deux enfants sont menacé par un rossignol (Two Children Are Menaced by a Nightingale)
1924; 46 × 33 cm. (18 × 13 in.)
New York, Museum of Modern Art

25. Overleaf left
Kurt Schwitters
Merzbild 25 A. Das Sternenbild
1920; 104 × 79 cm. (41 × 31 in.)
Düsseldorf, Kunstsammlung Nordrhein-Westfalen

26. Overleaf right
Kurt Schwitters
Bild mit Heller Mitte
1919; 84 × 65.7 cm. (33 × 26 in.)
New York, Museum of Modern Art

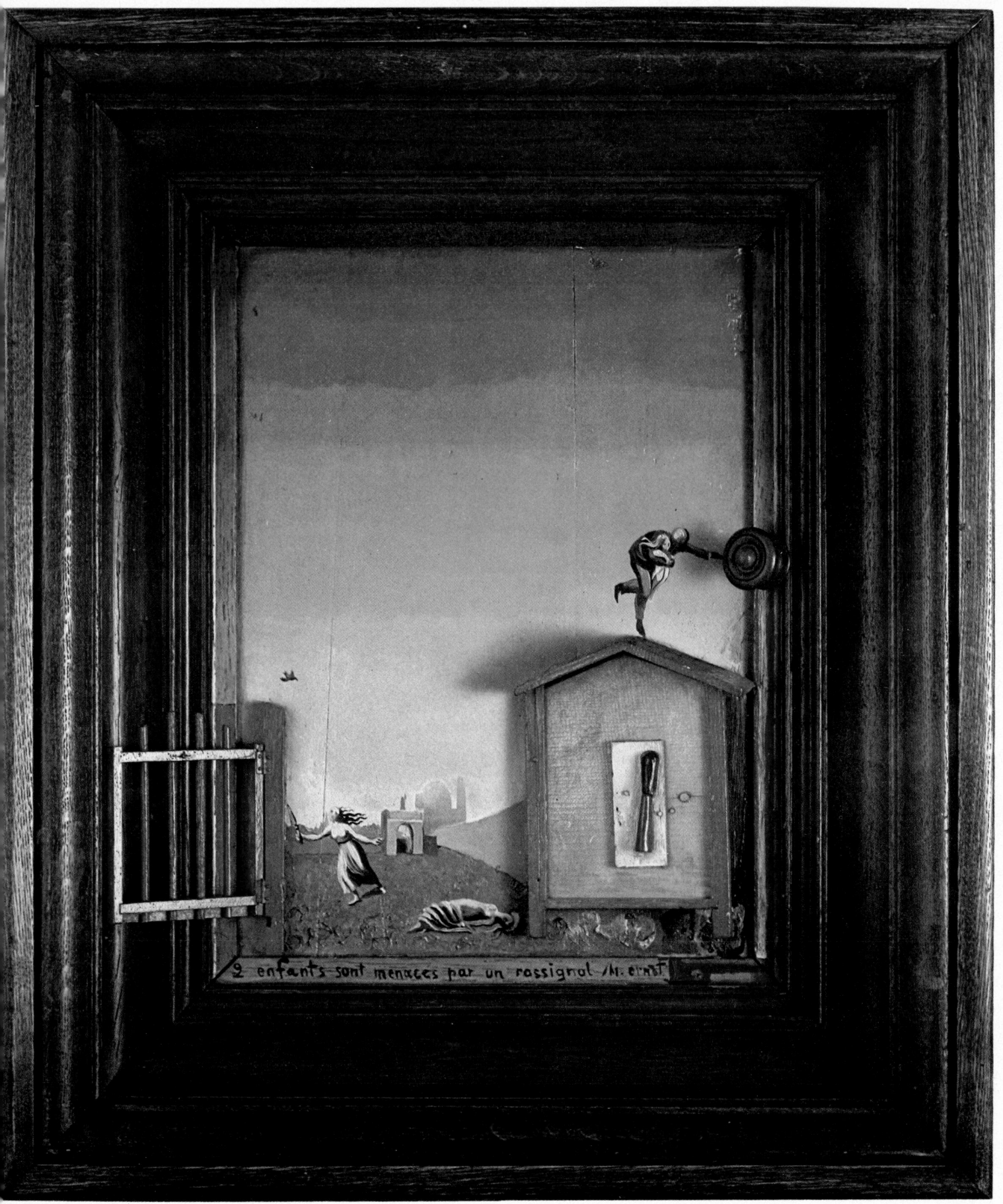

2 enfants sont menacés par un rossignol /M. ernst

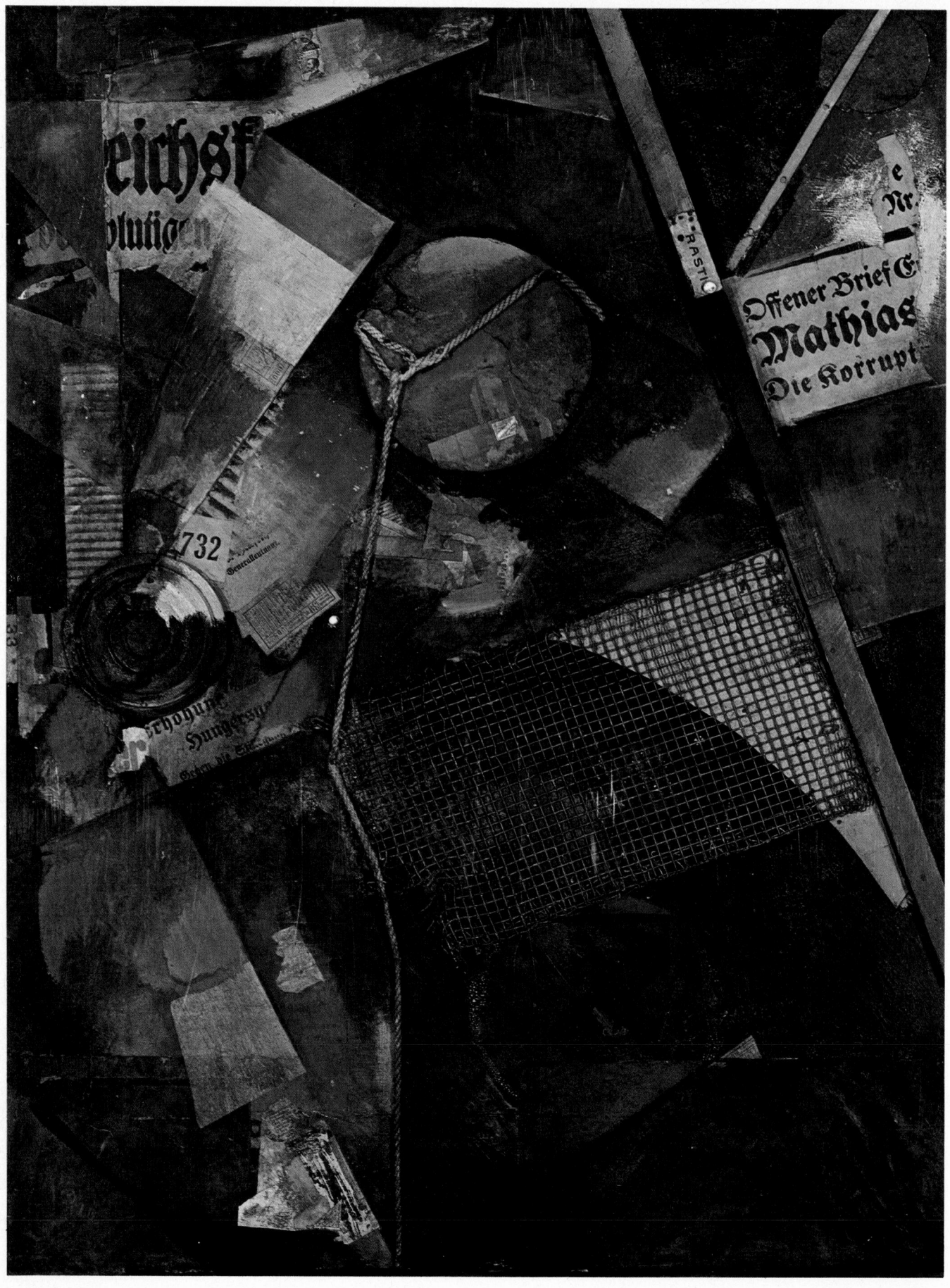

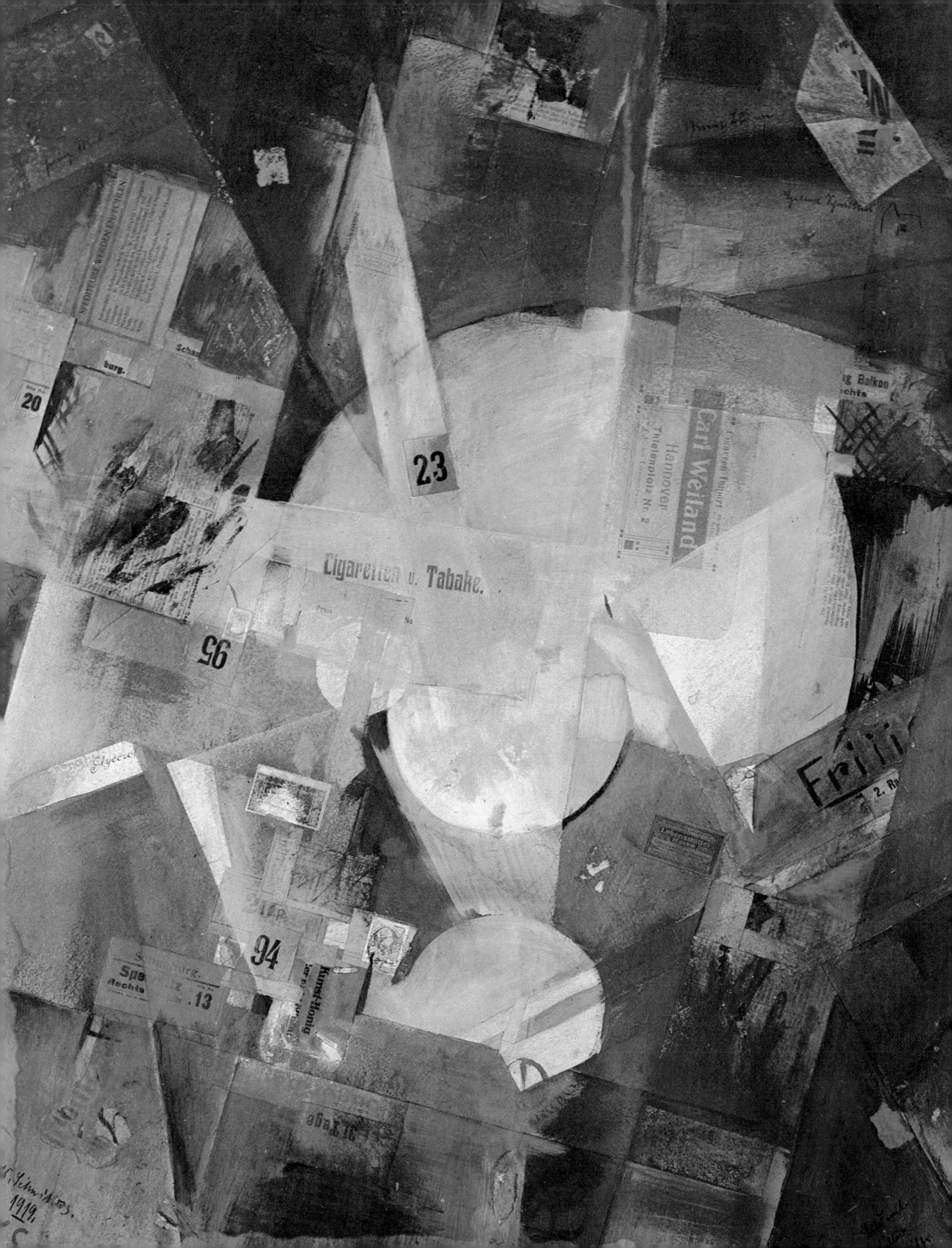

anyone, has the best claim to be regarded as the inventor of a purely abstract art. Yet for him abstraction had a very different significance from what some of his colleagues intended. For them it was a means of demystifying art, making it mundane; for Kandinsky, on the contrary, it was a way of heightening its spiritual and mystical content. Painting, for him, was as much a matter of explaining his own identity as it was for Soutine.

Kandinsky was born in Moscow in 1866, but did not take up painting until he was thirty. He moved from Russia to Germany, studying in Munich under the leading Symbolist Franz von Stuck, and soon making a name for himself as a leader of the avant-garde. To the influence of the German Jugendstil upon his own work, he added that of Fauvism. He also studied the colour theories of the French Pont-Aven group. His studies led him to the conclusion that the only law for the artist must be his own "inner necessity": "The harmony of colours and forms can be based on only one thing: a purposive contact with the human soul." Gradually Kandinsky began to loosen his own ties with the images he saw around him in nature, and in 1910 he painted his first wholly abstract picture. These early improvisations (Plate 18) are joyous outbursts of mystical feeling. They find their justification not in any duty the artist may feel he owes to society, but in his duty to himself, his need to make visible the inner core of his own being.

Even before Kandinsky joined the staff of the Bauhaus—an event which took place in 1922—his style had become more disciplined and less lyrical under the impact of Constructivism. But he could never submit to a purely utilitarian aesthetic. The little book he published in 1912, *Concerning the Spiritual in Art*, was to be a textbook for artists of a later generation, particularly in the United States.

The radicalism of the first Modernist generation did not express itself through abstract art alone. The First World War brought with it a revulsion against what the artists now saw as the meaningless and terrifying violence of their time—even though this violence was something which they, or at any rate their colleagues, had been anxious to instigate. The optimistic energy of Futurism was

succeeded by the frivolous or despairing nihilism of the various Dada movements which sprang up during the war. The most active Dadaist centres were Zurich and New York, both of them places on the fringe of the conflict. Those who participated in this new outburst of activity were poets as well as painters, and were wide-ranging in nationality—Dada was even more cosmopolitan than the various art movements that had preceded it. In essence, the most destructive aspect of Dada was the way in which it questioned the nature of art itself.

The most intellectual of the Dadaists, and the one whose importance seems greatest today, was Marcel Duchamp. Duchamp came from a family of artists. His elder brothers were the painter Jacques Villon and the sculptor Raymond Duchamp-Villon. In 1913 his painting *Nude Descending a Staircase* was the sensation of the already sensational Armory Show in New York. One newspaper described this rather derivative Cubo-Futurist work as "an explosion in a shingle factory", and, with the phrase, the painter's reputation was made.

But Duchamp never seems to have had a high opinion of his own talents as an artist. Instead, he set out to be the smiling philosopher of Modernism. The most devastating of his inventions was the "ready-made". In one sense, the ready-made is best described by reference to the inventor himself. "Duchamp's attitude," said an old friend in later years, "is that life is a melancholy joke, not worth the trouble of investigating. To his superior intelligence the total absurdity of life, the contingent nature of a world denuded of all values, are logical consequences of Descartes' *Cogito ergo sum*."

By asserting that any object could be turned into a work of art merely by labelling it as such, Duchamp gave free rein to a vein of distinctive irony. How amusing, for example, to submit a porcelain urinal (Plate 20) to an avant-garde art exhibition, under the signature "R. Mutt", and then wait for his fellow jurors to betray their own libertarian principles!

Yet the ready-mades do pose a very important question: How do we recognize a work of art *as a*

27.
Salvador Dali
Presage of Civil War; Construction with Boiled Beans
1936; 100 × 100 cm. (39 × 39 in.)
Philadelphia, Philadelphia Museum of Art

28. Overleaf
Salvador Dali
Persistence of Memory
1931; 24 × 33 cm. (9 × 13 in.)
New York, Museum of Modern Art

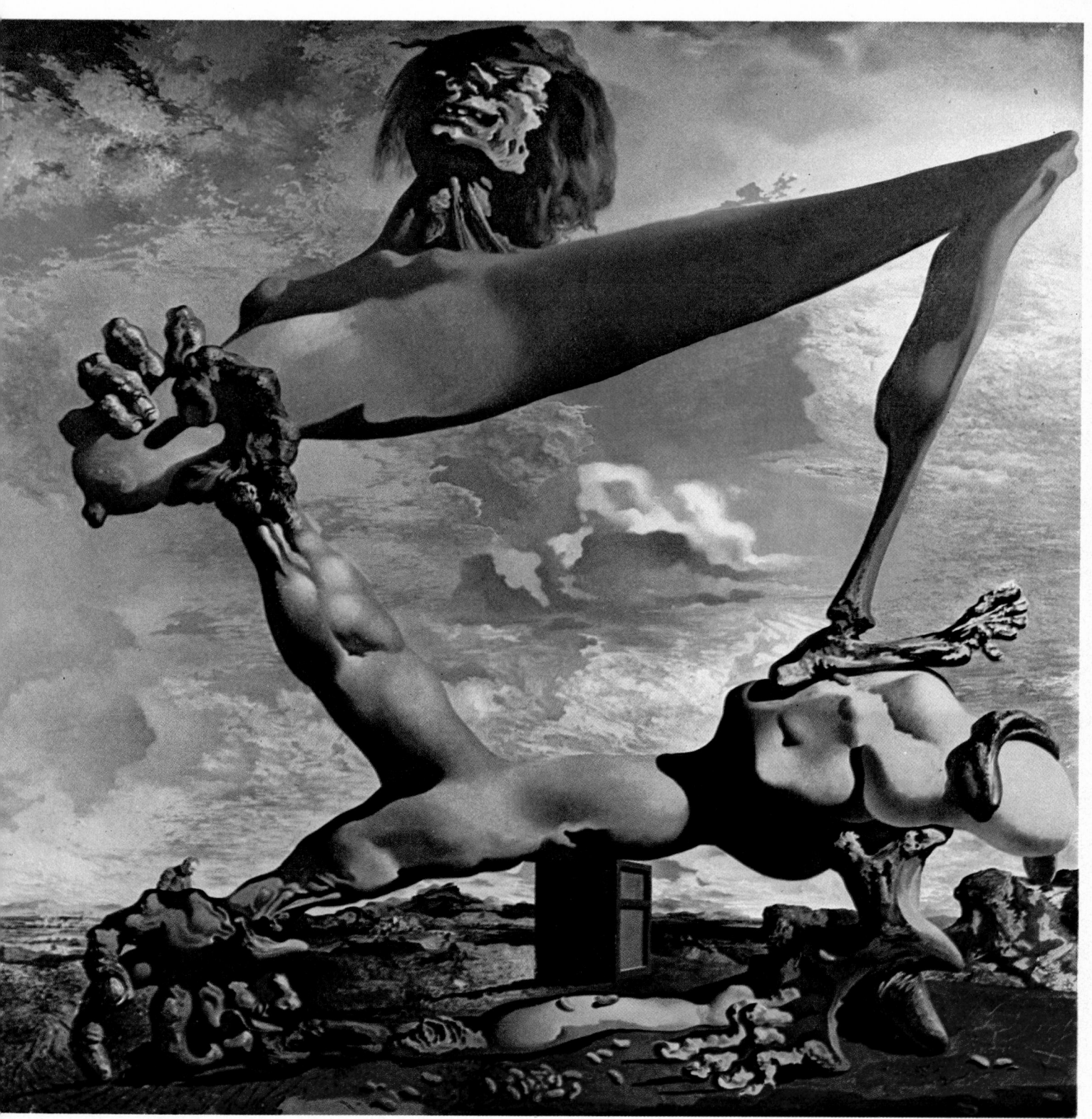

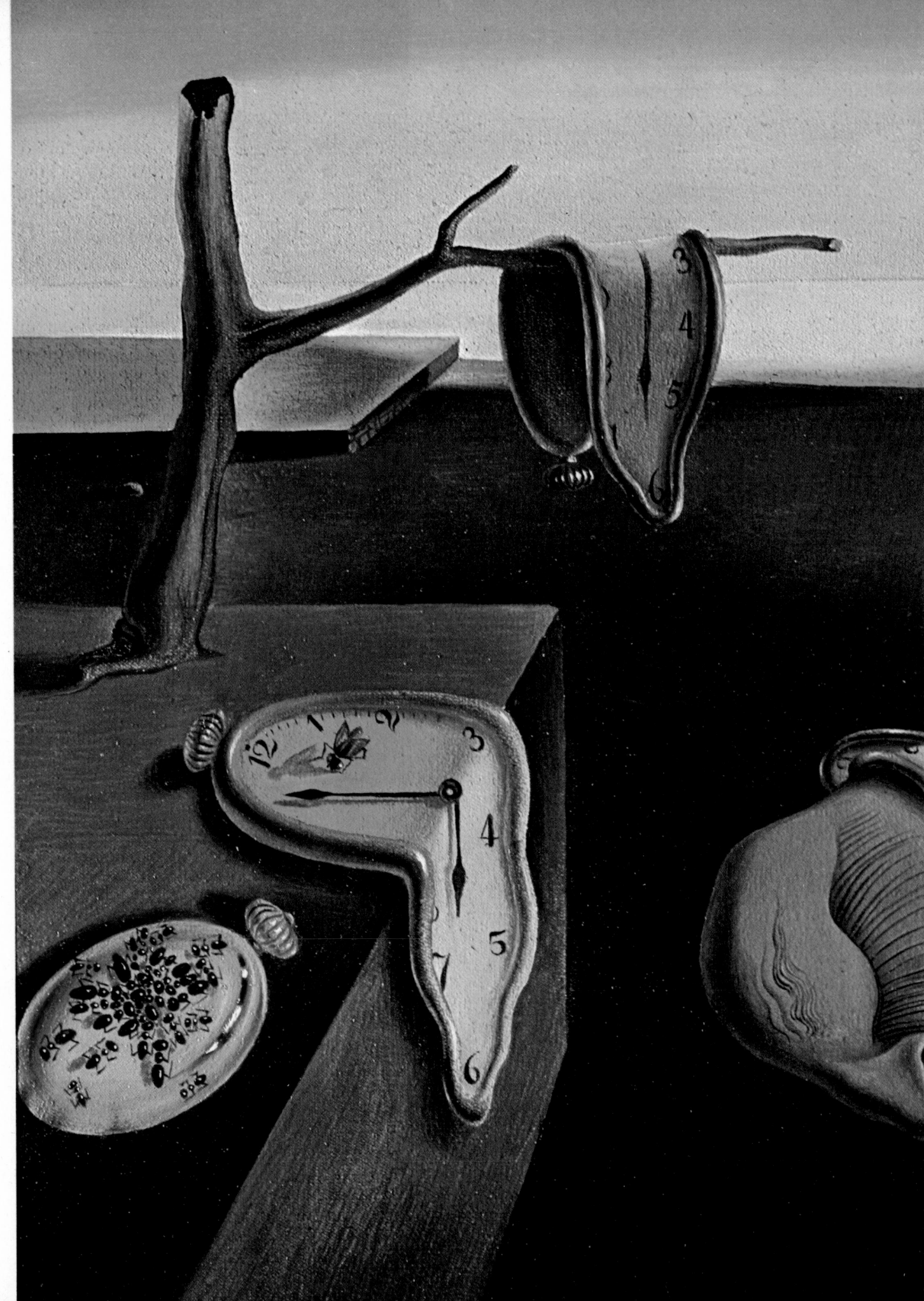

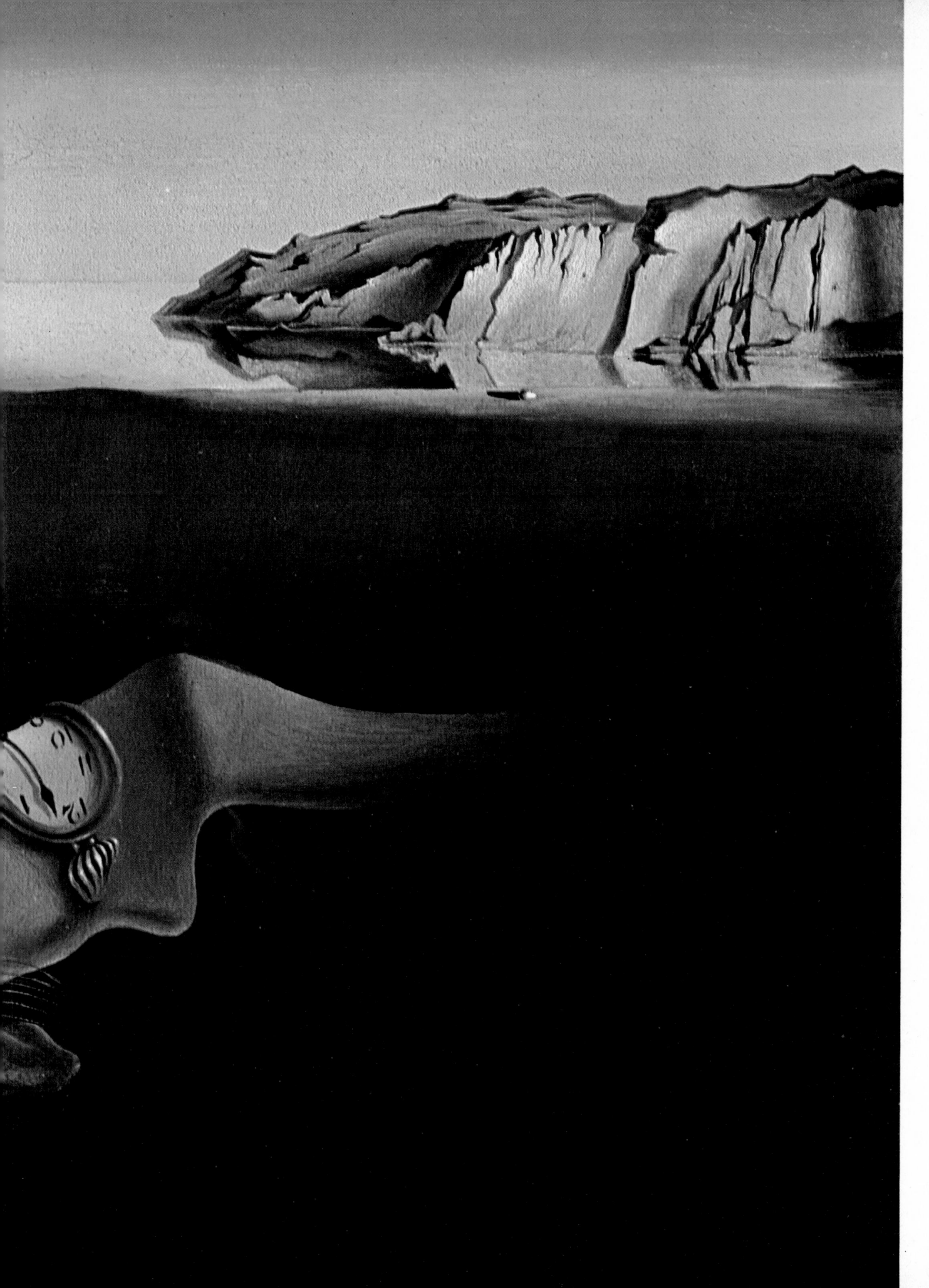

29.
René Magritte
The Voice of Blood
1959; 114 × 87.5 cm. (44 × 34 in.)
Vienna, Museum des 20. Jahrhundert

work of art? Duchamp offers a disconcerting answer: only because we are already prepared in advance to do so, to accept that the thing presented to us belongs to a special category. He was insistent that his choice of ready-mades "was never dictated by aesthetic delectation. The choice was based on a reaction of *visual indifference* with a total absence of good or bad taste . . . in fact a complete anesthesia." What Duchamp did was to cut the ground from under traditionally established criteria of aesthetic judgment. It has never been possible to stabilize the situation since.

Dada was too nihilistic to survive for long. Elsewhere there were already signs of the direction art might take. One of the most important of these signposts was supplied by Pittura Metafisica, which began as the personal expression of the young Italian painter Giorgio de Chirico around 1911 or 1912, and, during the war years, burgeoned into an art movement when De Chirico won the allegiance of the Futurist Carlo Carrà. De Chirico and Carrà wanted to revive the serenity of classic Italian painting—one of the qualities the Futurists had sought to destroy. At the same time they were aware of a profound change in consciousness. "We use painting," De Chirico said, "to create a new metaphysical psychology of things" (Plate 23). The visual world invented by the metaphysical painters often had an anguished, nightmarish quality underlying its apparent serenity, because it revealed, whether the artist desired it or not, hidden aspects of his own nature.

It was left to the post-war Surrealist movement to codify this discovery and to erect it into a principle. Surrealism was fascinated by the discoveries of Freud, and wanted to use art as a means of revealing the hidden world of the unconscious.

Max Ernst, who had formed a Dada group in Cologne in 1919, moved to Paris in 1922 and became perhaps the first recognizably Surrealist painter. *Two Children Are Menaced by a Nightingale* (Plate 24) is one of the best-known of his early Surrealist works. Technically it harks back to Analytic Cubism through the employment of collage, and one can also make a comparison to the work of another German Dadaist, Kurt Schwitters (Plates 25 and 26). But Ernst's aim is different from either of these. Cubism seeks to stress the dichotomy between painted reality and "real" reality, by the sudden intrusion of the latter into the former. Schwitters tried to redeem what has been discarded as rubbish—old bus tickets and scraps of wrapping paper—by organizing it as art. What Ernst wanted to do was to bring us face to face with a universe full of fruitful but unexpected combinations. The objects he employed were chosen for their value as images.

Since Surrealism lays such stress on spontaneity and the intuitions of the subconscious, it is perhaps surprising to find that some of its best-known exponents are academic in technique—to the point where they seem to reject many of the discoveries of an earlier epoch. But artists such as Salvador Dali and René Magritte are so intent on showing us their vision as clearly as possible that they choose the mode of presentation they hope we will find most accessible (Plates 27, 28, and 29). It is one reason why an artist such as Magritte managed to remain stylistically static almost throughout his career. Paint was never an end in itself but merely a convenient method of communication.

A number of leading Surrealists thought this was a sacrifice of qualities that painting still ought to possess. One of these was Joan Miró, whose *Dutch Interior* of 1928 (Plate 30) shows a treatment of spatial problems which owes much to Cubism. In this painting we see the beginning of a style which Miró was to develop much further—a way of painting which is more like writing, where emblematic forms are deployed on the canvas as if they were a series of hieroglyphs. As we shall see in the next chapter this development was pregnant with consequences for art after 1945.

But what is worth considering at this juncture is not the development of individual Surrealists, however eminent, but the nature of the Surrealist movement itself. Its history, which embraces poetry and politics as well as the visual arts, is well documented, even if the interpretation of the facts is often a matter of controversy. The Surrealist movement was officially founded in 1924, with the

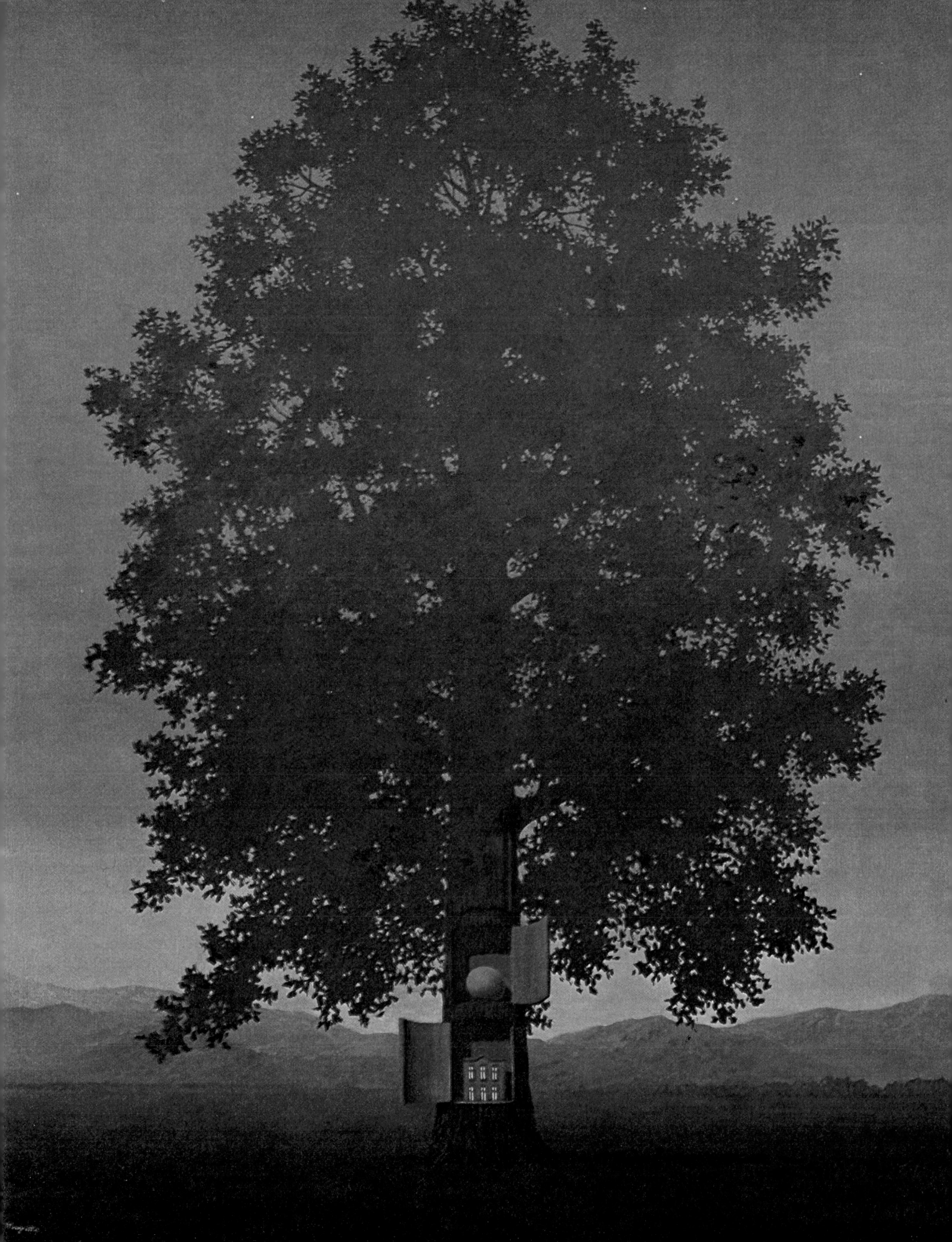

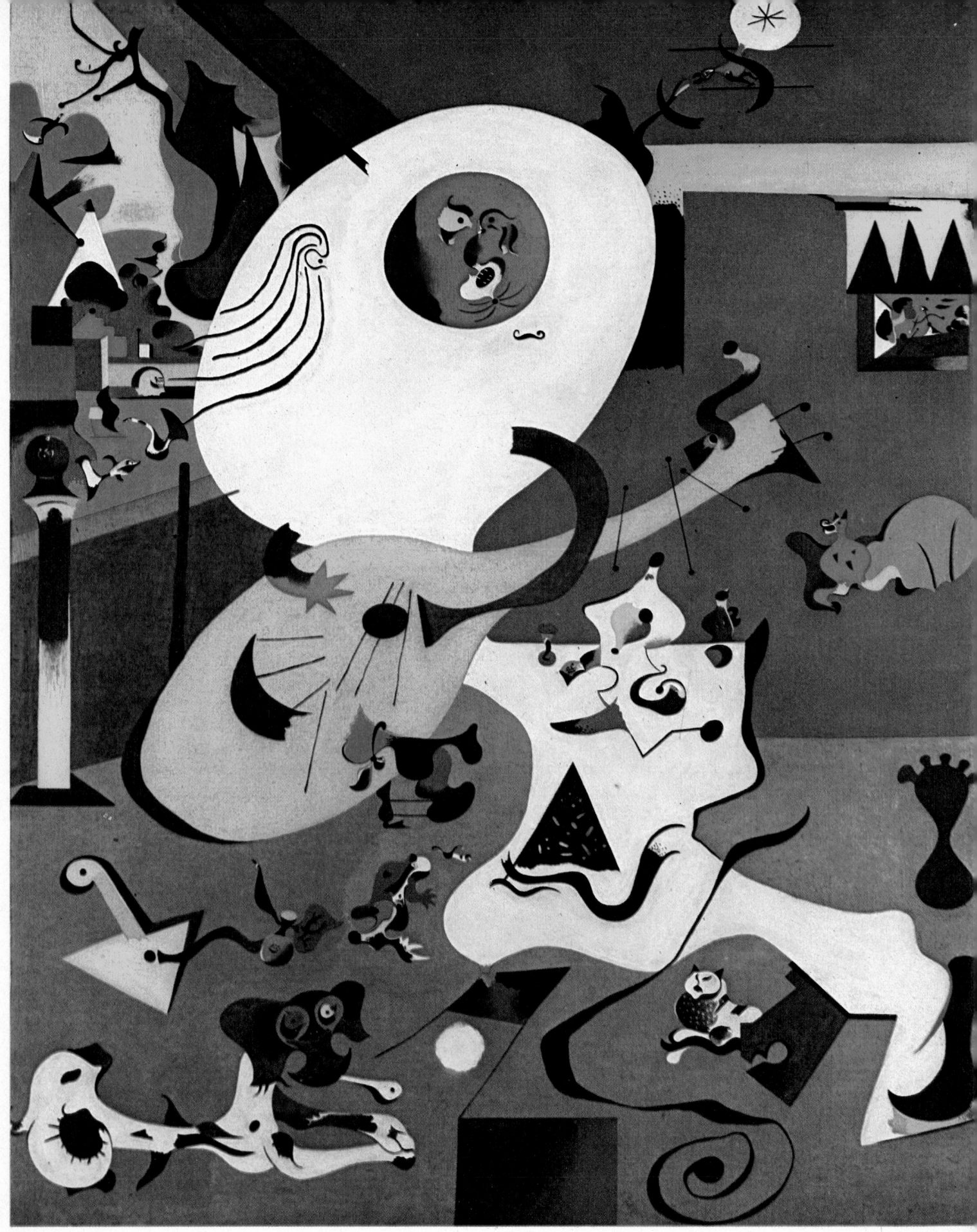

Joan Miró
Dutch interior
1928; 91.8 × 73 cm. (36 × 28 in.)
New York, by kind permission of the
Museum of Modern Art

publication of the First Surrealist Manifesto, a document of comparable importance to the Futurist Manifesto of 1909. In it the word *surrealism* is defined thus: "Pure psychic automatism, by which an attempt is made to express, either verbally, in writing, or in any other manner, the true functioning of thought. The dictation of thought, in the absence of all control by the reason, excluding any aesthetic or moral preoccupation." But soon enough this definition was to be stretched, and some might think distorted, by the effort to bring the movement into line with political events, and more especially with what was happening in Russia. When the poet Louis Aragon broke with his fellow Surrealists in 1930, to go over wholly to the cause of communism, this marked a turning point in the history of the movement as a whole. André Breton, the acknowledged "pope" of the Surrealists, continued to try to find a brand of left-wing politics in accord with his own aesthetic and philosophical principles, but never quite succeeded in doing so. Meanwhile, the Surrealists remained dependent, as the Fauves and Cubists had before them, on the financial support of a rich and fashionable elite.

In their different ways, Surrealism and Constructivism provide the first instances of the apparent incompatibility between radical art and radical politics, which was to continue to haunt committed Modernists in the period after 1945. In this connection, it is worth recalling what the Spanish philosopher Ortega y Gasset had to say on the subject fifty years ago—that is to say, at a moment when the evidence available to him was mainly that supplied by Cubism and its derivatives. "In my opinion," he remarked, in his famous essay "The Dehumanization of Art," "the characteristic of contemporary art 'from the sociological point of view' is that it divides the public into these two classes of men: those who understand it and those who do not. . . . Modern art, evidently, is not for everybody, as was Romantic art, but from the outset is aimed at a special, gifted minority. . . . Accustomed to dominate in everything, the masses feel that their 'rights' are threatened by modern art, which is an art of privilege, of an aristocracy of instinct." Increasingly, this is an unpopular, even a heretical, point of view. It is also one we shall have reason to consider carefully as this study proceeds.

Abstract Expressionism

In the repertoire of art styles after the Second World War, Abstract Expressionism enjoys a unique eminence. It is not only that it was the first in a long procession of stylistic experiments, but it also seems to mark a definite watershed, a handing over of power. Just as the United States emerged from the conflict as the most powerful nation on earth, so, too, the emergence of Abstract Expressionism seemed to mark the coming of age of American art, and the replacement of Paris by New York as the centre of the artistic universe.

Though this view does contain an element of truth, it must be qualified. Abstract Expressionism, though it was later to become a vehicle for the chauvinism of certain American critics, was in essence a reaction against narrowly nationalist sentiment. During the Great Depression of the Thirties, American art had been in an introverted phase. This introversion took different forms. There was the political conservatism of the regionalists, led by Thomas Hart Benton. Their work showed a nostalgic concern with rural America and the American past. In contrast to this there was the Marxism of many of the artists who participated in the Federal Art Project, beneath the umbrella of the Work Projects Administration set up to alleviate some of the worst miseries of the slump. The Federal Art Project produced little that was memorable, but did alter the relationship between artists and society by giving people a new consciousness of contemporary art. In addition, it fostered an esprit de corps among the artists themselves.

The regionalists were of course figurative, and so were most of the artists connected with WPA enterprises. Nevertheless, the authorities responsible for the scheme made no formal distinction between abstract and representational art, and this essentially democratic decision was full of consequences for the future.

Abstract art did survive during the American Thirties, though it had a hard time. In 1936 the Museum of Modern Art in New York organized an influential exhibition entitled "Cubism and Abstract Art", and in the same year the younger abstract artists banded themselves together in an association known simply as American Abstract Artists. Unlike most of their fellows, these painters did have a vision of modern art as an international community, but their own work remained derivative and dependent upon foreign, principally French, exemplars. A number of the members of AAA also belonged to the French critic Michel Seuphor's Abstraction-Creation group. The style that nearly all of these American painters favoured was strictly geometric. It derived ultimately from De Stijl and from Constructivism.

Even during the Thirties the American art scene began to be leavened by the arrival of talented refugees, among them Josef Albers, who had taught at the Bauhaus, and Hans Hofmann, who had taught in Munich from 1915 until 1932, the year he settled in the United States. Hofmann opened a new school, the Eighth Street School, in New York in 1934, and this became one of the principal channels whereby young Americans were introduced to advanced European concepts.

The decisive event, however, was the outbreak of war. This brought almost the entire Surrealist movement to New York, in flight from the conflict. Matta arrived as early as 1939. In the early Forties he was followed by Ernst, Dali, and André Masson among the painters, and also by André Breton, the "pope" of the movement. Breton still formed a focal point around whom most of the others revolved. Peggy Guggenheim, at that time married to Max Ernst, provided a home for the activities of the group by opening a gallery, Art of This Century, in 1942. This was to exhibit the

31.
André Masson
Sketch for the ceiling of the national theatre of the Odéon
1965 ; 220 × 200 cm. (86 × 78 in.)
Paris, Centre National d'Art Contemporain

32. Opposite
André Masson
Le Peintre et le temps
1938 ; 116 × 73 cm. (45 × 28 in.)
Milan, Galleria Schwarz

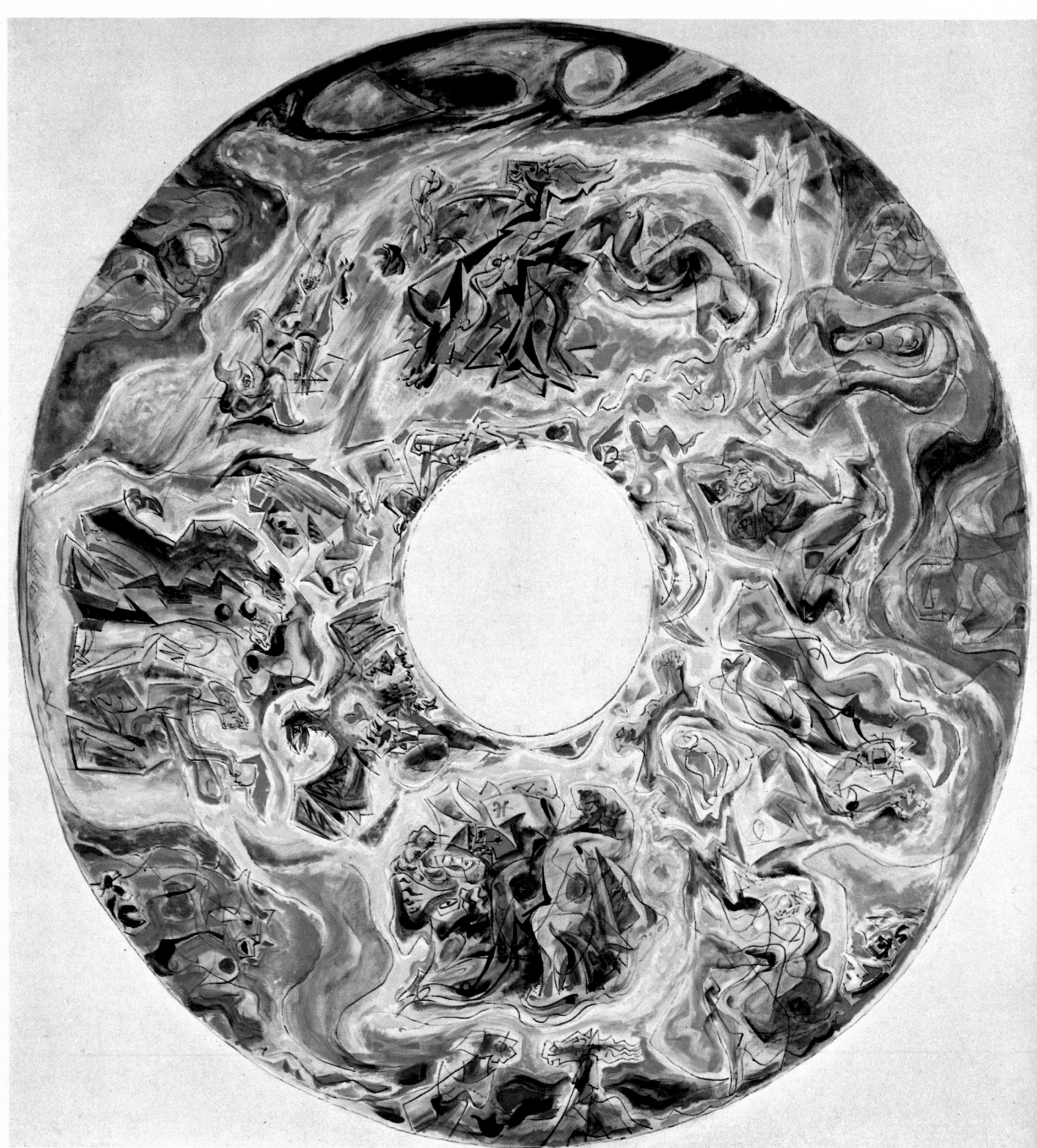

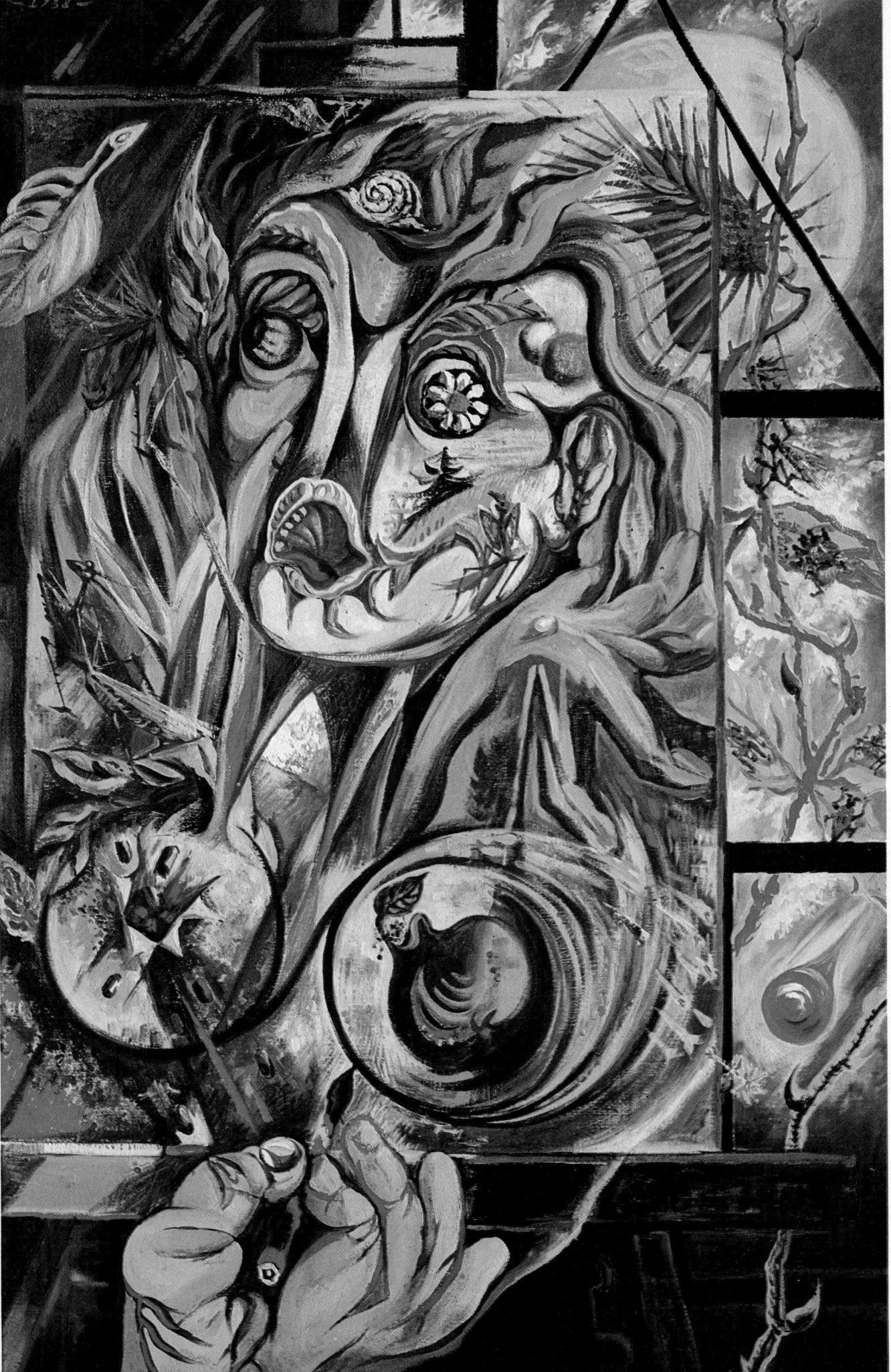

work of young American painters as well as that of the Surrealist exiles.

Contacts, however, were at first not easy. The Surrealists remained fiercely cliquish, and ill at ease with their surroundings. A number of them, notably Breton, refused even to learn English. One of the few American painters to build up a relationship with them was the Armenian immigrant Arshile Gorky, and it is Gorky's painting which forms the bridge between European Surrealism and what a new generation of Americans was to make of it, following the original Surrealist principle of transformation.

Before taking Gorky's work into consideration, it is necessary to say a word about the art of Masson and Matta, two Surrealists whose work differs in important respects from that of painters such as Dali and Magritte, whom I have already considered. Masson, born in 1896, had been an early adherent of the Surrealist movement, which he joined in 1924, at the time of his first exhibition. He was never happy with Breton's authoritarian rule, and by 1933 had broken with the group. His complaint, both then and later, was that official Surrealist doctrine paid too little attention to the painter's special needs: "The Surrealist Movement

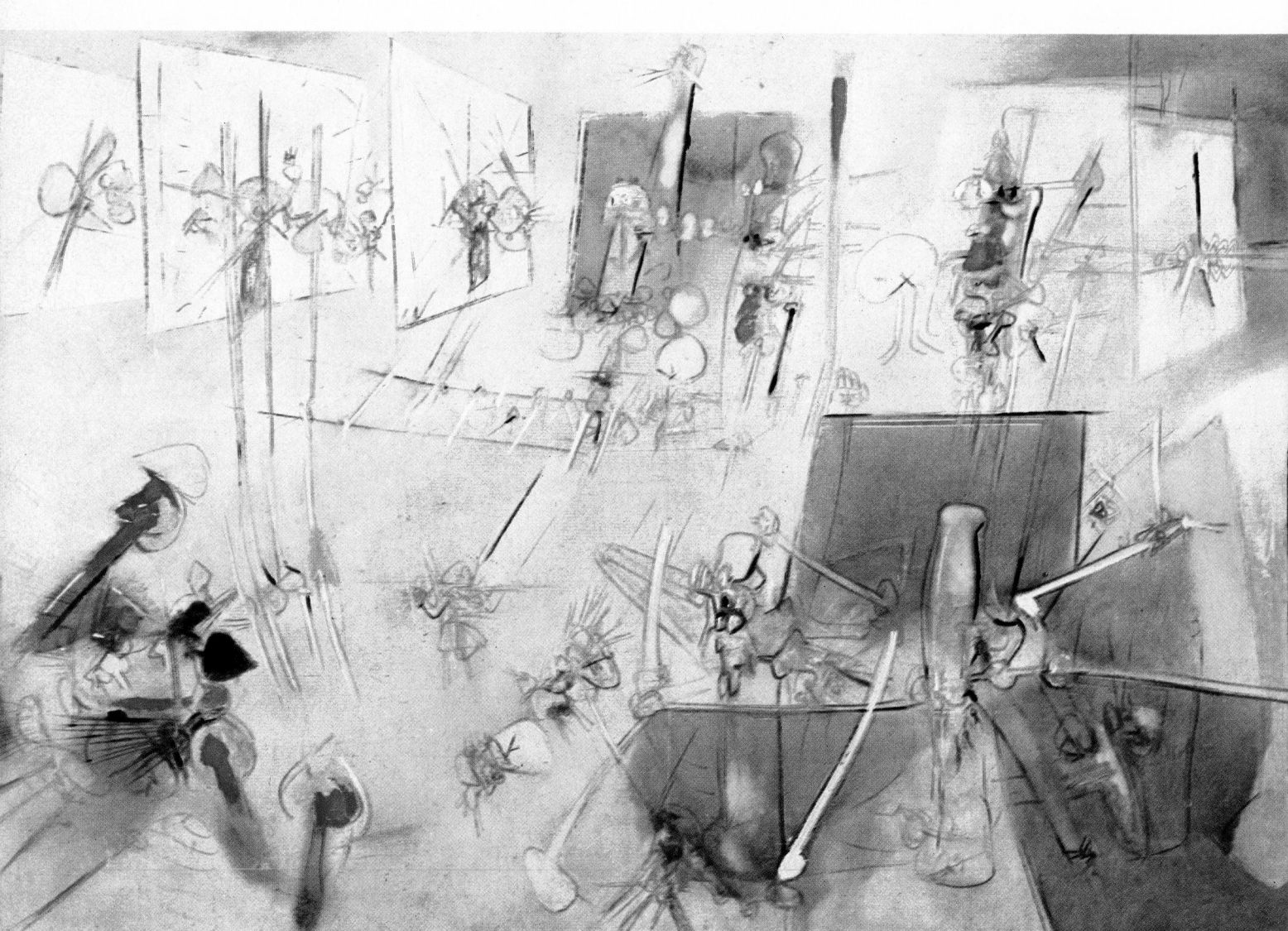

34.
Matta (Roberto Matta Echaurren)
However
1947; 218 × 365 cm. (85 × 142 in.)
Amsterdam, Stedelijk Museum

is essentially a literary movement. . . . In literature the surrealists are as insistent on the exact word as Boileau; but when it comes to painting they are very liberal in matters of structure. The spiritual directors of surrealist painting are not of the profession" (André Masson, "Eleven Europeans in America," *Museum of Modern Art Bulletin,* Vol. XIII, Nos. 4–5 [1946], p. 4).

As can be seen from the typical example reproduced here (Plate 32), Masson's work is not veristic, in the manner of Dali and Magritte, but calligraphic. One critic has described his most typical compositions as "delirious germinations complicated to the point of becoming nothing more than labyrinthine tangles of vegetable, organic, or mental circuits." One is reminded, too, of the general comment made by the Greek-American writer Nicolas Calas: "In surrealist art, the artist *viewed as dreamer* becomes the subject of art."

One thing which is conspicuous in Masson's work is its close relationship to the Surrealist doctrine of automatism. For Surrealist writers, the technique called "automatic writing" had long been one of the principal means whereby the artist put himself in touch with his own unconscious.

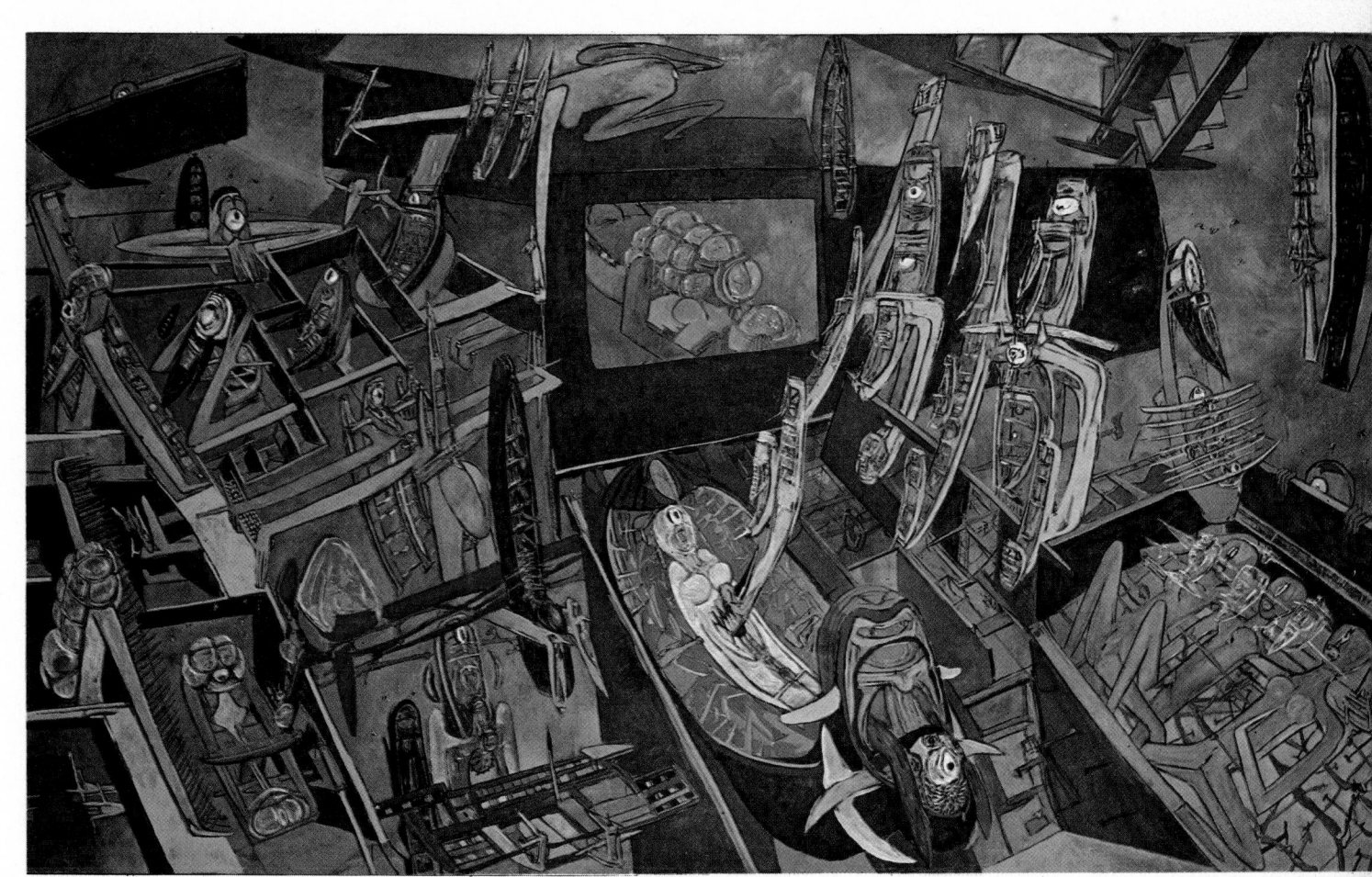

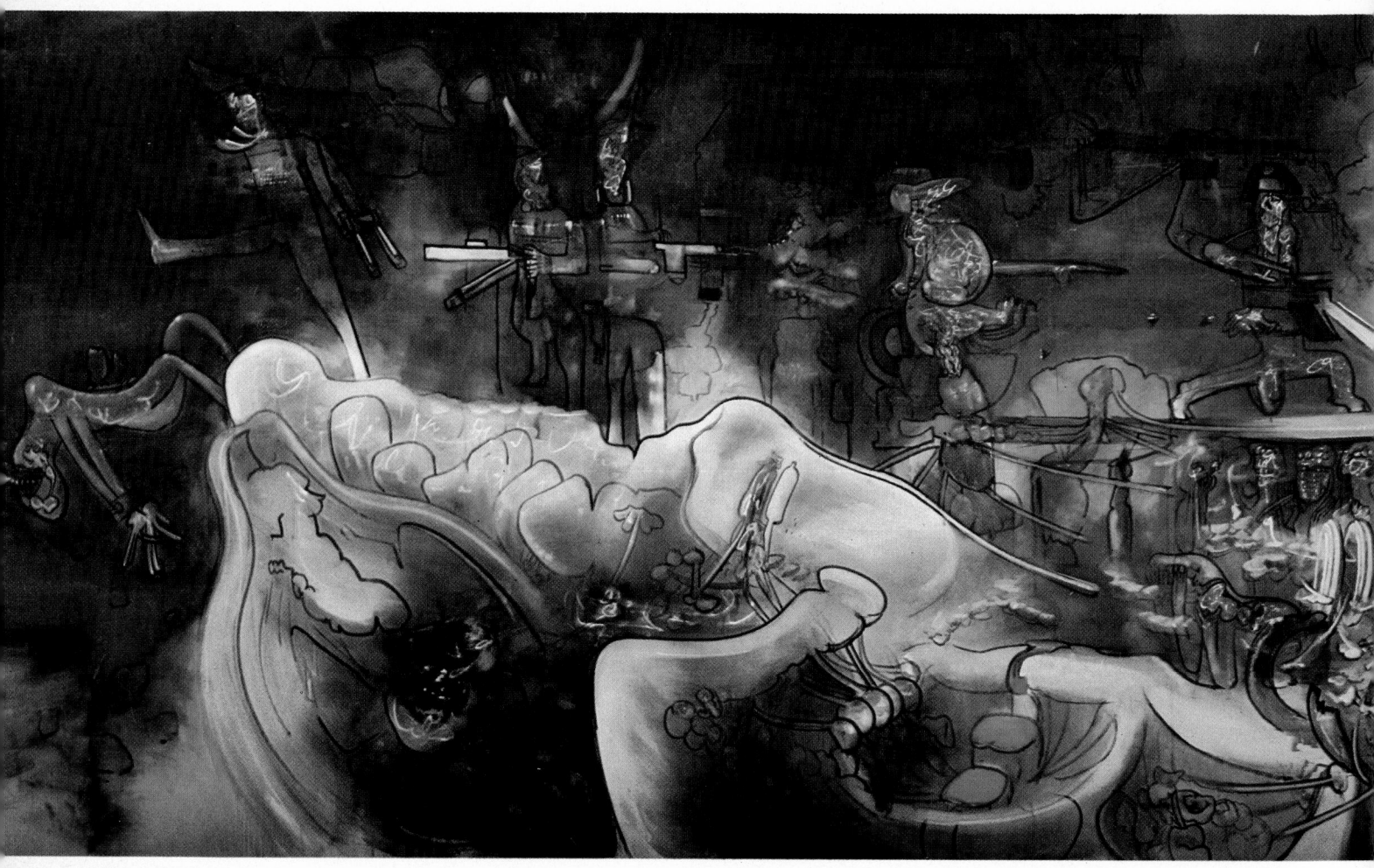

Sitting before a piece of blank paper, a pen or pencil in his hand, the writer allowed his thoughts and associations to flow without impediment onto the paper. Similarly, Masson, despite his distrust of literature, allowed his calligraphic brushstrokes to conjure up the presence of images that were unknown to, or at least unsuspected by, their creator until the very moment of their appearance.

Matta was a much younger man than Masson, a Chilean who did not come into contact with the Surrealist group in America until the middle Thirties. Extremely intelligent as well as extremely ambitious, he was quick to realize that he must try to extend the scope of accepted Surrealist techniques if he was to make a worthwhile personal contribution to Modernism. As Calas

somewhat portentously put it, Matta "replaced the repressed microcosm with the unobtainable macrocosm". What he meant by that was that Matta's paintings often seem to suggest a parallel universe, of the kind we find in popular science fiction (Plate 33). Yet the imagery of Matta's paintings has an elusiveness which suggests, correctly, that much of it has been generated by the use of automatic gestures. What the artist did was to spread transparent washes of colour on the canvas, usually with a rag; he then developed forms from these beginnings which became more particularized and more illustrative as the work proceeded.

In this respect Matta's work forms a striking contrast to that of Arshile Gorky, whom Breton

35.
Matta (Roberto Matta Echaurren)
Watchman What of the Night
1968; 300 × 1000 cm. (117 × 390 in.)
Archives Alexandre Iolas, New York, Paris, Geneva,
Milan, Rome

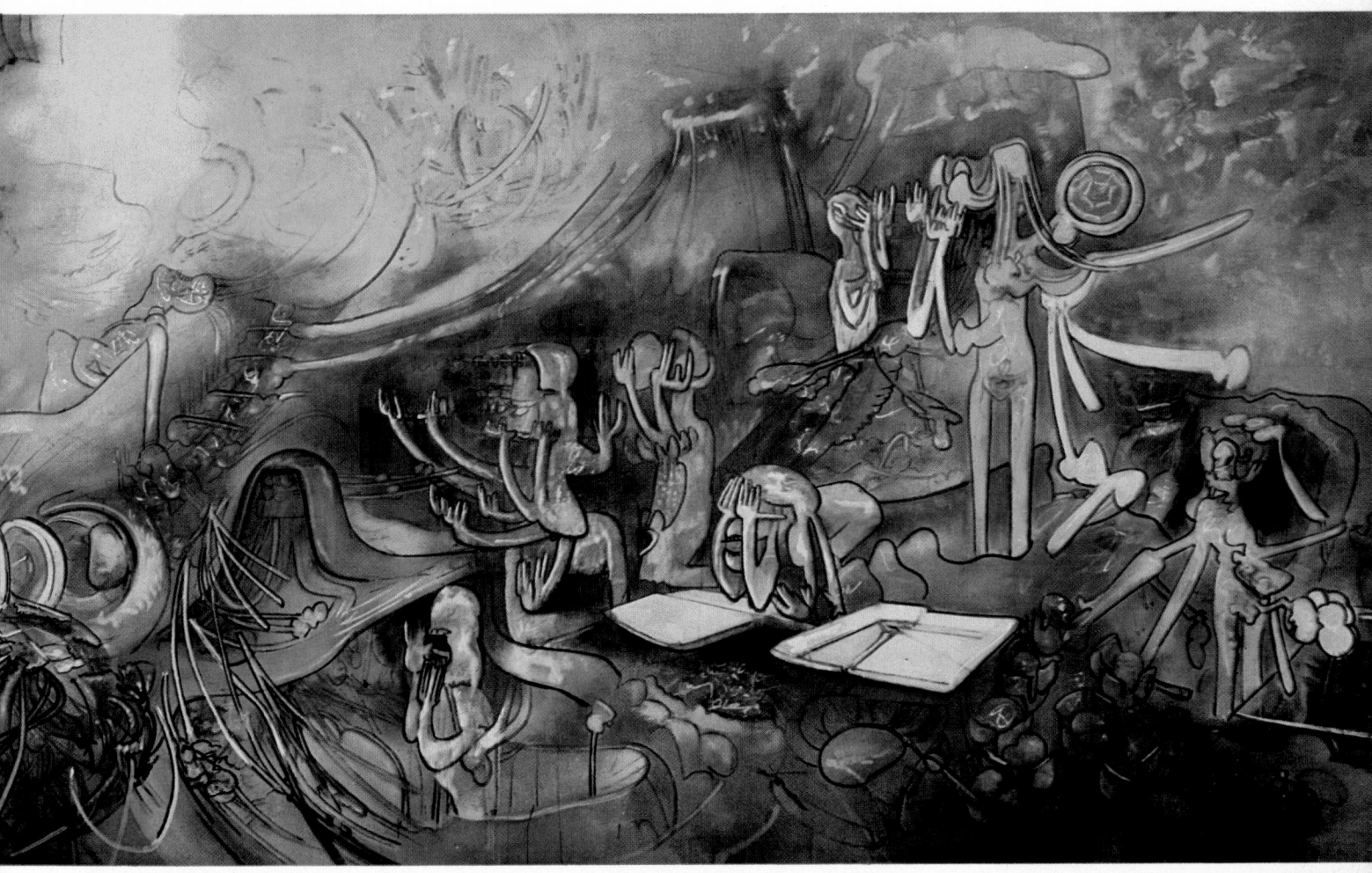

himself regarded as the most important American recruit to Surrealism. Gorky's late pictures make use of automatism, but they often take their starting point from drawings which are more specific than the paintings which derive from them. Gorky also differs from Matta (who was for a while not only an important influence but a close friend) in the fact that his characteristic imagery derives from the natural world—it alludes to ripeness, tumescence, flowering, and fruiting—while Matta's is mechanistic.

Before he became a Surrealist, Gorky underwent a long apprenticeship—chiefly to Cubism, although it also seemed that he discovered within himself the urge to recapitulate every accepted style of modern art. His subservience to Picasso

was the subject of ill-natured jesting in the New York art community. But when he finally reached artistic maturity these studies paid a considerable dividend. In particular, he was equipped to understand the Cubist use of shallow space which Miró, in particular, employed in many of his canvases. William Rubin, in one of the best studies of Gorky's work, puts the matter thus: "That it was possible for Gorky to synthesize Miró and Masson into his Cubism, whereas to do the same with surrealists like Dali and Tanguy would have been unthinkable, makes sense if we recall that Miró and Masson alone among the surrealists had earlier been convinced Cubists. While their organic forms strayed far from the morphology of Cubism, they rarely sacrificed the taste for shallow (as opposed to deep) space and for disposing the composition comfortably inside the frame, which they had learned during their Cubist apprenticeship" (William Rubin, "Arshile Gorky", *Art International*, Vol. VII, No. 2 [February 25, 1963]).

Yet it is Gorky's sensibility as well as his technique which makes him such a pivotal figure in the history of twentieth-century American painting. When we look at a late Gorky, such as *The Betrothal* of 1947 (Plate 38), we are immediately aware that the canvas which confronts us is almost nakedly autobiographical. These apparently unspecific forms nevertheless speak with great precision about what the painter feels and is. We sense the painter's own masochism from the way in which the forms seem to attack one another.

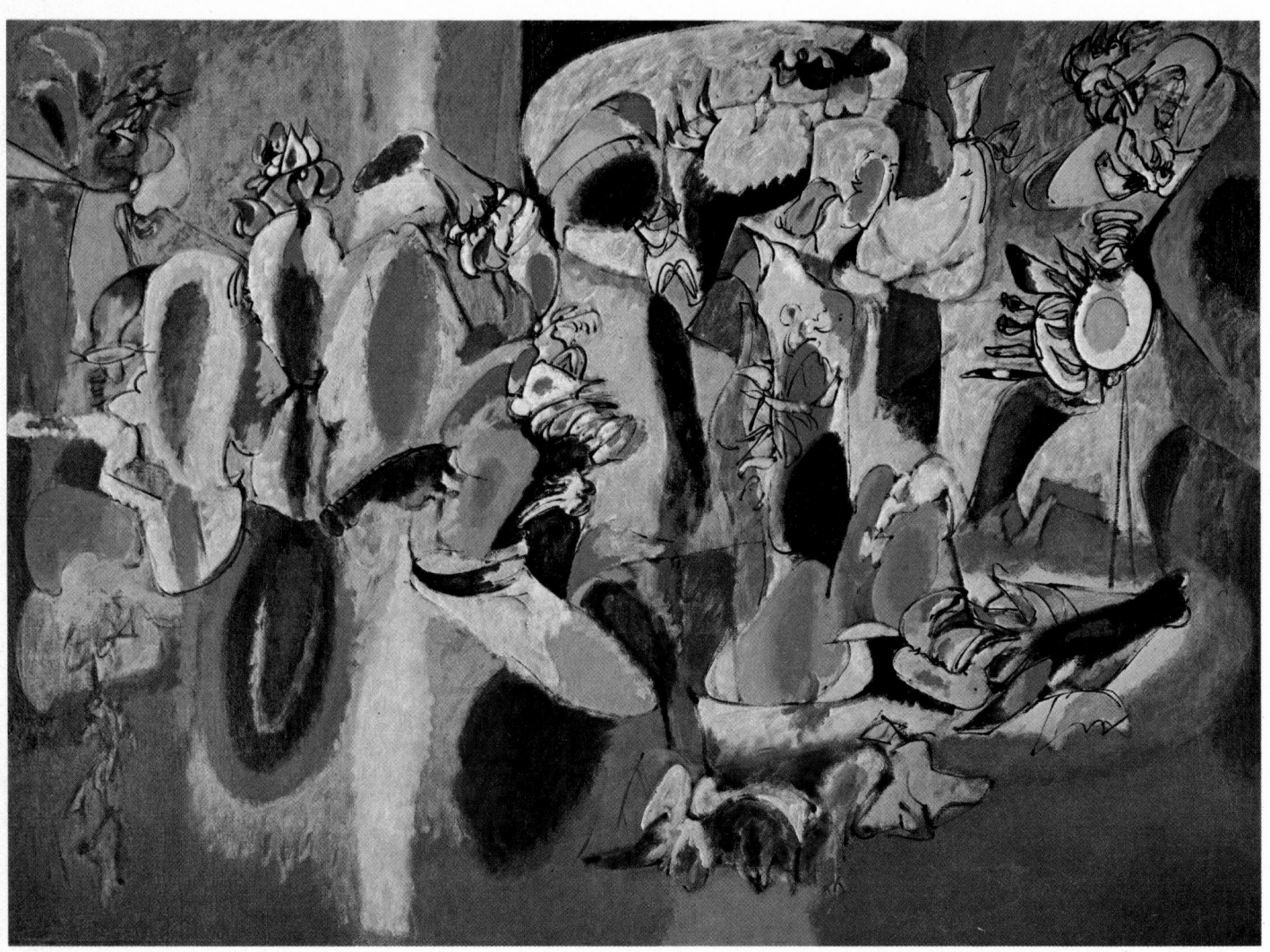

36.
Arshile Gorky
The Liver Is the Cock's Comb
1944; 72 × 98 cm. (28 × 38 in.)
California, Pasadena Art Museum

37. Opposite
Arshile Gorky
Water of the Flowery Mill, detail
1944; 107.3 × 123.8 cm. (42 × 48 in.)
New York, Metropolitan Museum of Art

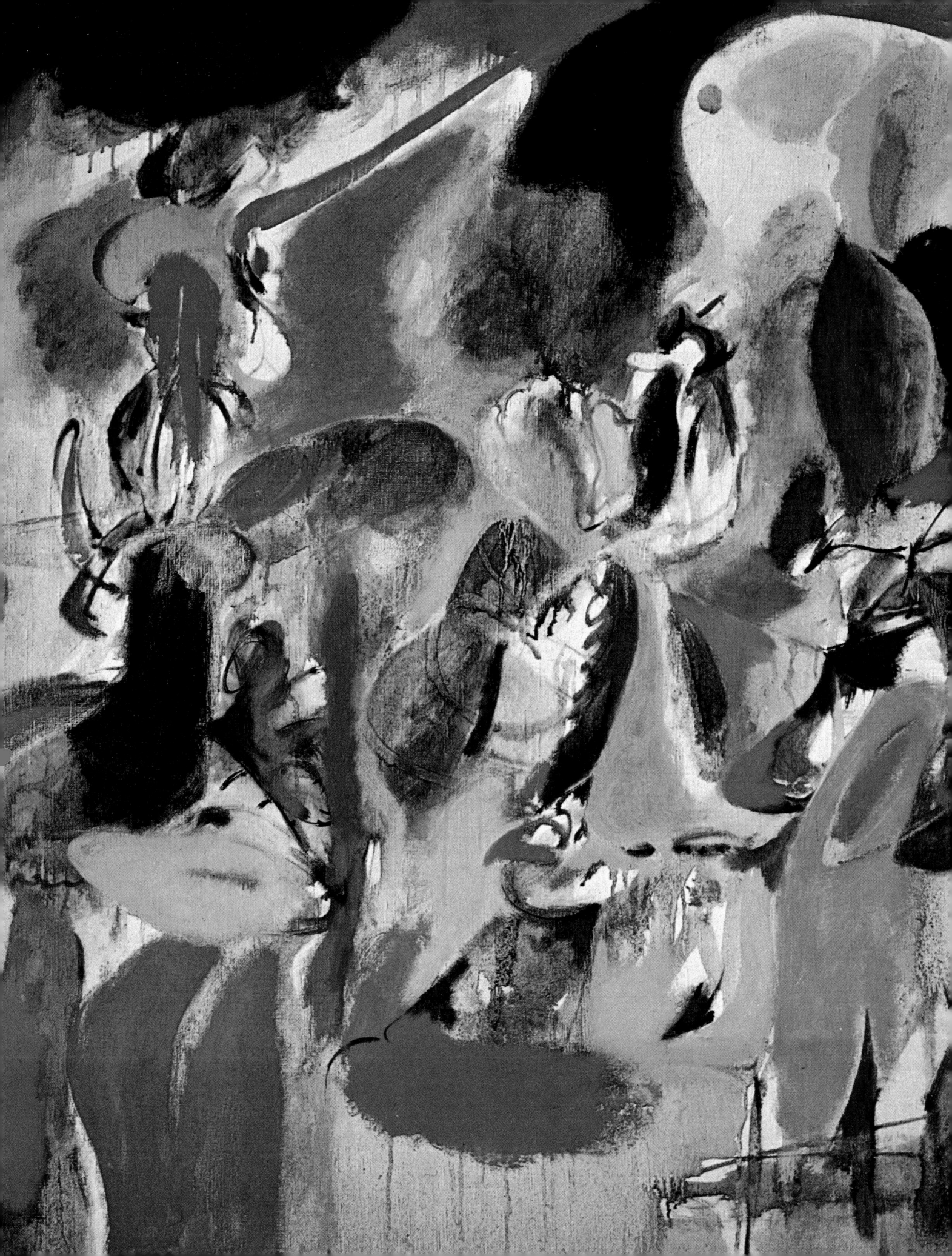

38.
Arshile Gorky
The Betrothal II
1947; 126.9 × 95 cm. (49 × 37 in.)
New York, Whitney Museum of American Art

Claws and tendrils sprout from what is apparently soft and harmless. Rubin has spoken of the painter's "emotional fragility", a phrase perhaps justified by Gorky's suicide, after a long series of personal misfortunes, in 1948. One is, however, aware that this fragility is also a form of aggression. Gorky exalts the "I" more openly than any European painter had yet dared to do.

If Gorky remained upon one side of the divide that separates Surrealism from Abstract Expressionism, then Pollock was the man who made the decisive step across the gap. Jackson Pollock began his career in the camp of the regionalists. In the years 1929–31 he studied with Thomas Hart Benton. Later, like many other American painters, he was supported by the WPA. In 1939 he worked in the studio of the Mexican social realist David Siqueiros, and he was also in contact with other leading Mexican painters of the same school.

By 1943 Pollock was in contact with the circle of Surrealist exiles and in particular with the Art of This Century gallery. In November of that year Peggy Guggenheim gave him a one-man show. His work in the early and middle Forties was based on automatic techniques, but could not be described as abstract (Plates 40 and 41). Pollock was at this stage making use of pictographs and ideograms which were in part suggested by his study of Jung and of Red Indian mythology, and in part prompted by the influence of Miró and Masson. But these works had a quality of American rawness which was immediately recognized as something new, even by critics who disliked Pollock's work and thought it uncouth. The rawness was a matter of choice. Later Pollock, describing his own technique, was to say: "I don't work from drawings or color sketches. My painting is direct. The method of painting is the natural growth out of a need. I want to express my feelings rather than to illustrate them. Technique is just a means of arriving at a statement. When I am painting I have a general notion as to what I am about. I can control the flow of the paint; there is no accident just as there is no beginning and no end" (commentary by Jackson Pollock for the film *Jackson Pollock*, made in 1951 by Hans Nemuth and Paul Falkenberg).

By 1947 Pollock had made the breakthrough to the series of drip paintings which are now considered not only his own most characteristic products, but perhaps the most characteristic products of the Abstract Expressionist movement taken as a whole. The artist once provided a description of the way in which a canvas such as *Autumn Rhythm* (Plate 43) was painted. Even though it is so very well-known, it is worth quoting again here: "On the floor [Pollock now worked with the canvas spread on the floor of the studio rather than placed on an easel] I am more at ease. I feel nearer, more a part of the painting, since this way I can walk round it, work from the four sides and literally be in the painting. This is akin to the method of the Indian sand painting of the West. When I am in my painting, I am not aware of what I am doing. It is only after a sort of 'get acquainted' period that I can see what I have been about. I have no fears about making changes, destroying the image, etc. because the painting has a life of its own. I try to let it come through. It is only when I lose contact with the painting that the result is a mess. Otherwise there is pure harmony, an easy give and take, and the painting comes out well" (Jackson Pollock, "My Painting", *Possibilities I*, New York, Winter 1947–48).

The sense of harmony which Pollock claims to have felt is reflected in the paintings themselves, which are astonishingly serene and decorative compared to the artist's earlier work.

Admiring as they are of Pollock's art, leading contemporary critics have often seemed at a loss as to how to interpret it. Bryan Robertson, author of the most important monograph on the artist, declares that "Pollock was never concerned with communicating in the sense of description." Irving Sandler, author of the standard history of Abstract Expressionism, speaks of "an expansive web of forces, suspended in front of the passive canvas plane". In a study which tries to link American painting of this kind to the tradition of northern Romantic art, Robert Rosenblum has this to add: "The classic Pollock of the late 1940s and early 1950s almost becomes a spectacle of nature, a whirlwind vortex of sheer energy that may take us to the cosmological extremes of

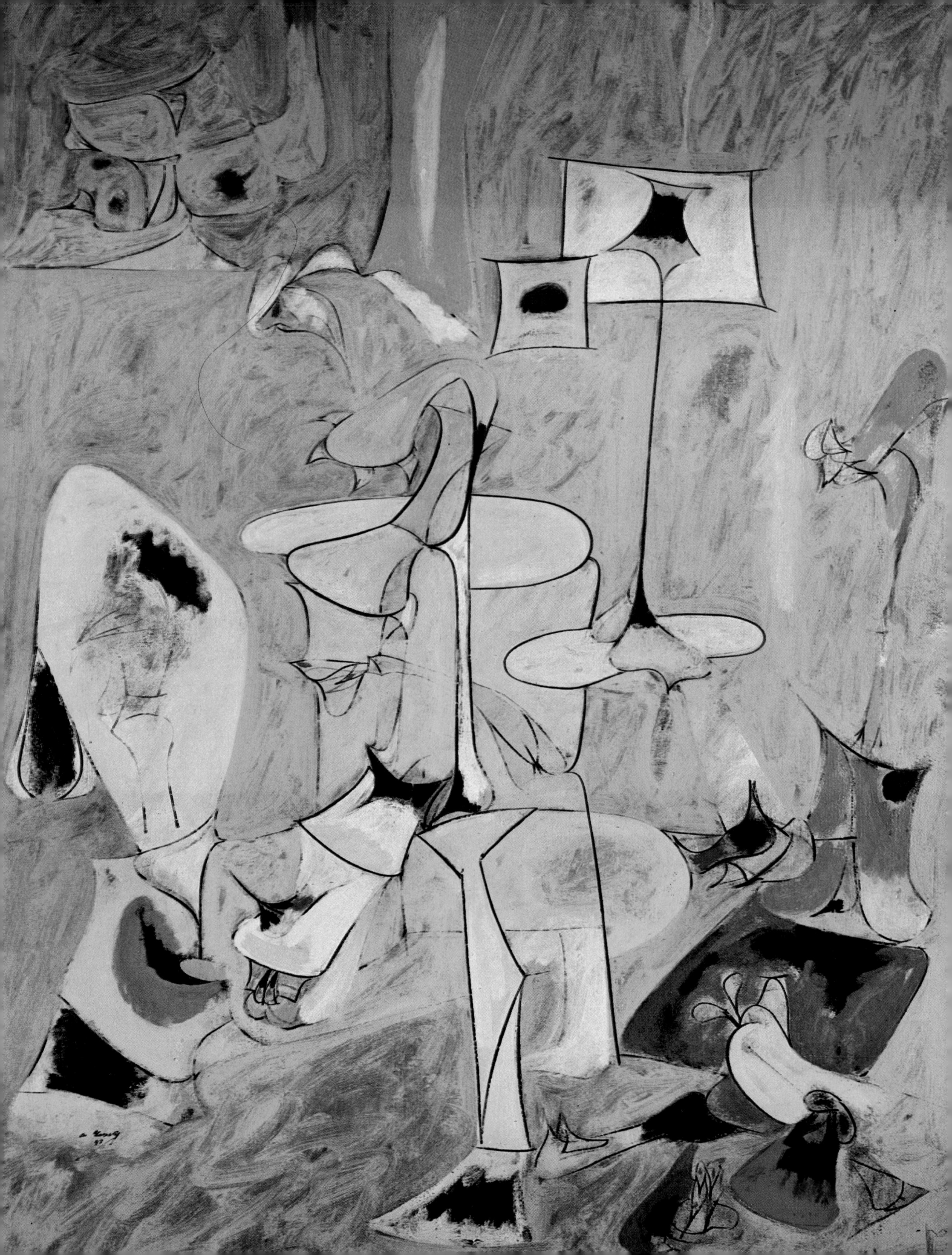

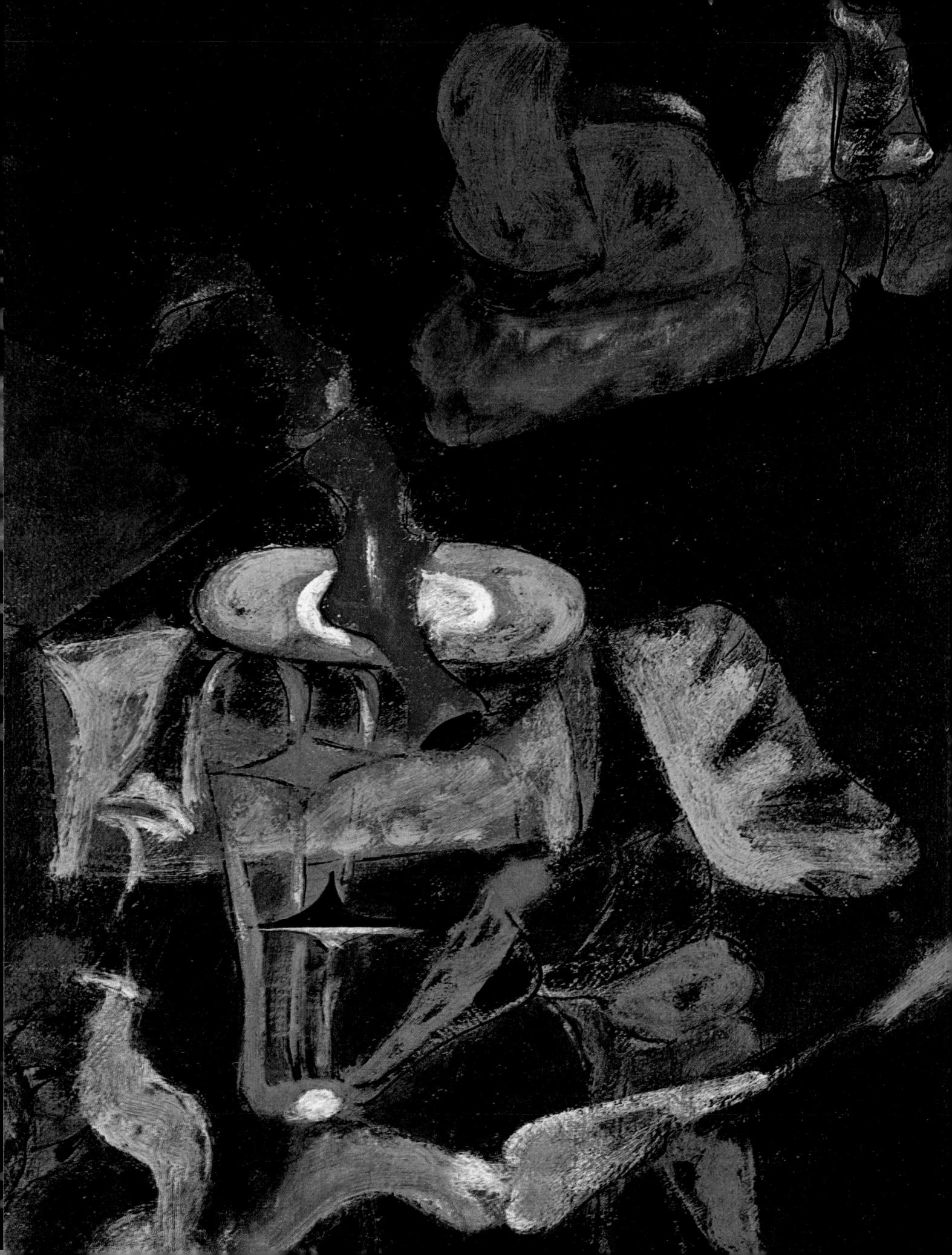

microscopic and telescopic vision—glimpses of some galactic or atomic explosion, or in more terrestrial terms, the overpowering forces of nature's most impalpable elements, air, fire and water" (Robert Rosenblum, *Modern Painting and the Northern Romantic Tradition*, London, 1975, p. 203).

There is a certain justice in this last interpretation, but it does not seem to account for the somewhat enclosed feeling one gets from Pollock's paintings, despite their physical expansiveness. What Pollock has to communicate is a sense of selfhood so all-pervasive that the outside world makes little impact upon the artist.

This theme can be examined from another angle by looking at the work of two other painters of decidedly lesser stature. One of these is Franz Kline, an Abstract Expressionist of a slightly later generation than that of the true founders of the school. Kline was always and primarily a draftsman, and his typical black-and-white canvases look at first glance like Chinese ideograms on an enormous scale (Plate 44). This comparison, however, gives a false impression of the painter's real sources, which were to be found in the techniques of graphic illustration, and in the scaffolding, girders, railways, and bridges of urban New York. The impact of these paintings is very powerful when one first encounters them, and there are those who continue to find them powerful still. The critic Robert Goldwater speaks of the way in which they seem "the spontaneous unretouched record of an impulsive mood, noted in broad, confident strokes". But he goes on to note an inherent contradiction in the way the paintings were created: "Only a few pictures were executed at one sitting. Many broad directional strokes, whose force seems the product of a single inspirational gesture, were actually painted with small brushes; many an entire outsize work had its model in one of Kline's innumerable small sketches" (Robert Goldwater, "Franz Kline: Darkness Visible", *Art News*, Vol. 66, No 1 [March, 1967], pp. 38 ff.).

The other painter who prompts a comparison with Pollock comes from a very different milieu. He is the West Coast artist Mark Tobey, who devoted a period of intense study to Japanese

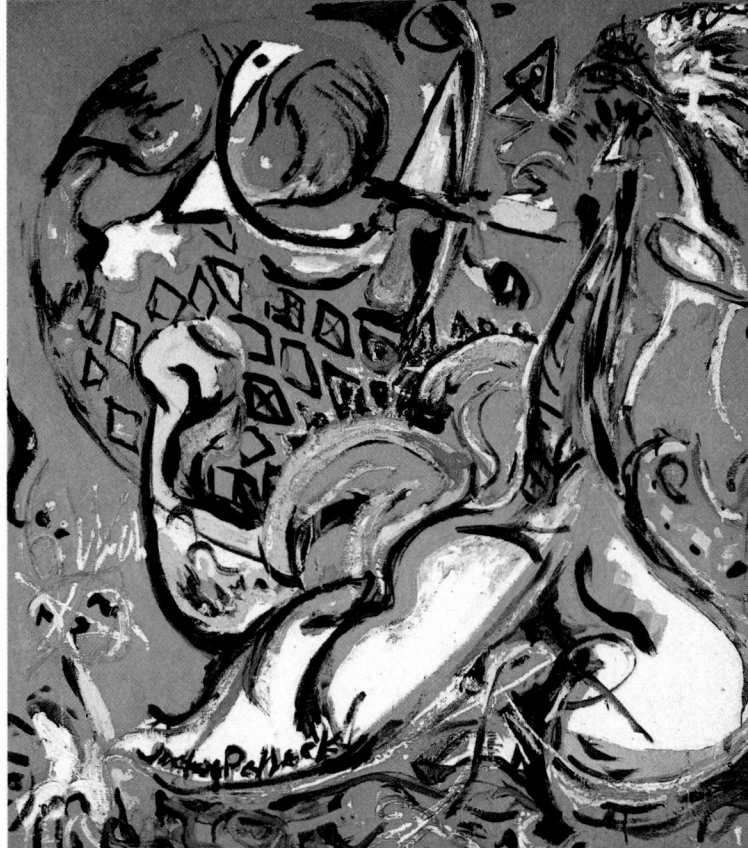

39. Opposite
Arshile Gorky
Dark Green Painting, detail
c. 1948; 11.1 × 142.2 cm. (4 × 55 in.)
Pennsylvania, coll. Mrs. H. Gates Lloyd

40. Above
Jackson Pollock
Male and Female
1942; 186 × 124.4 cm. (73 × 49 in.)
Pennsylvania, coll. Mrs. H. Gates Lloyd

41.
Overleaf left
Jackson Pollock
Night Ceremony
1944; 182.9 × 109.5 cm. (71 × 43 in.)
New York, coll. Mrs. Barbara Reis Poe

42.
Overleaf right
Jackson Pollock
Lucifer, detail
1947; 104.1 × 268 cm. (41 × 105 in.)
New York, coll. Joseph H. Hazen

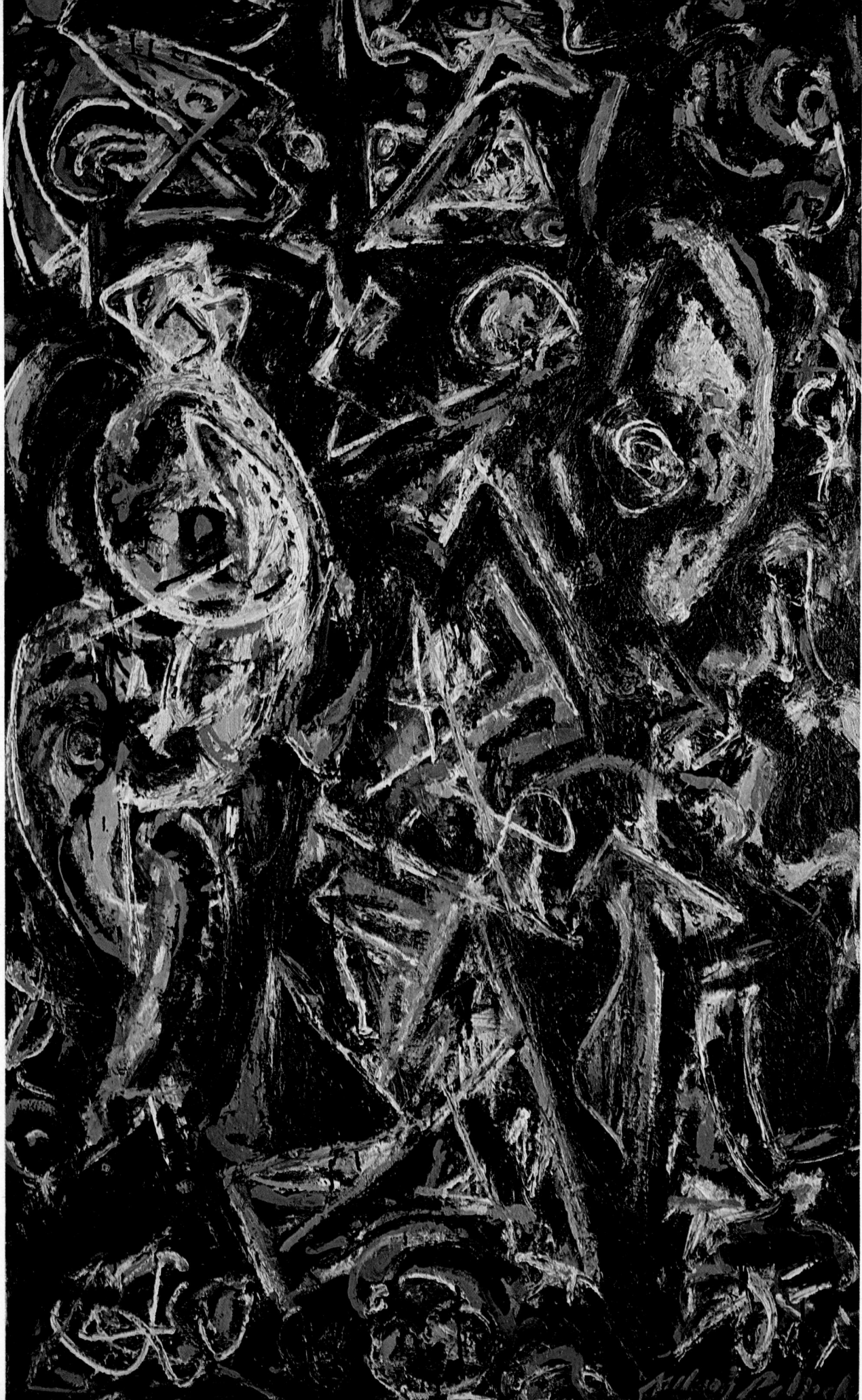

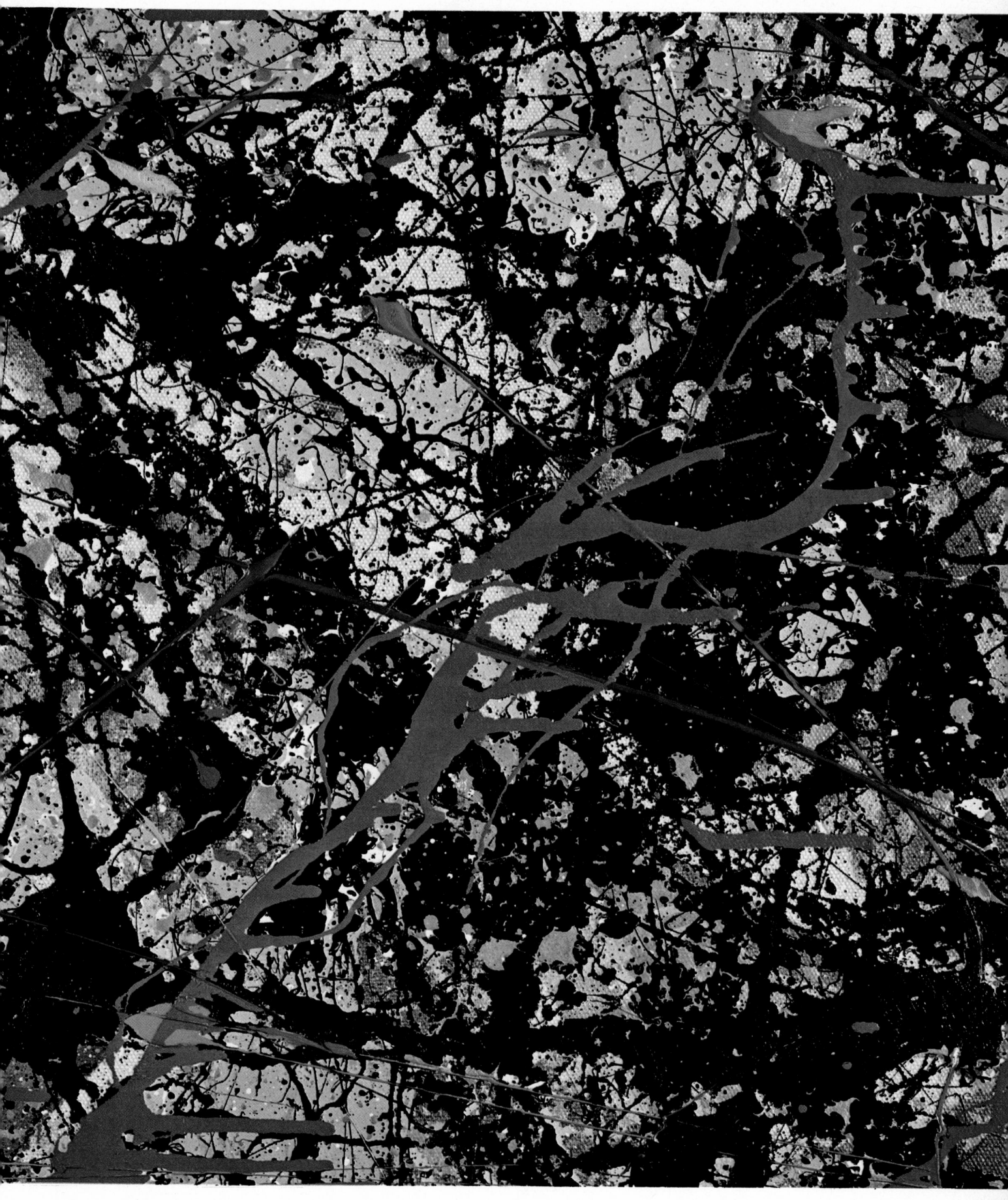

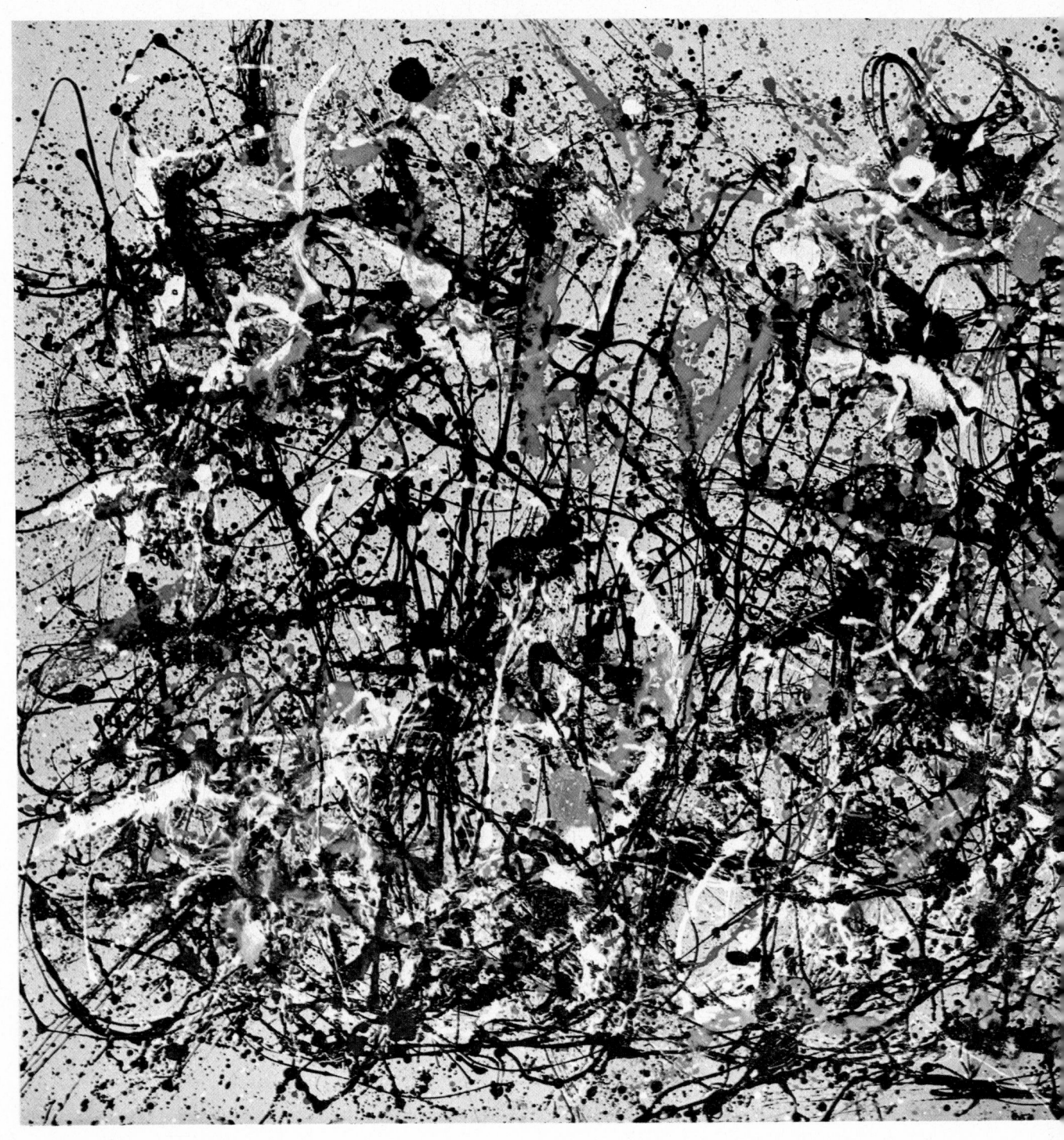

calligraphy (Plate 46). With Oriental source
material as his direct inspiration, he developed the
method he dubbed "white writing". But he had
more weapons in his armoury than this. As he tells
us himself, in the catalogue introduction to his
retrospective exhibition at the Stedelijk Museum,
Amsterdam, which was held in 1966: "Over the
past fifteen years, my approach to painting has
varied, sometimes being dependent on brushwork, sometimes on lines, dynamic white strokes,

43.
Jackson Pollock
Autumn Rhythm
1950; 266.7 × 525.8 cm. (88 × 205 in.)
New York, Metropolitan Museum of Art, property of
Jackson Pollock, George A. Hearn Fund

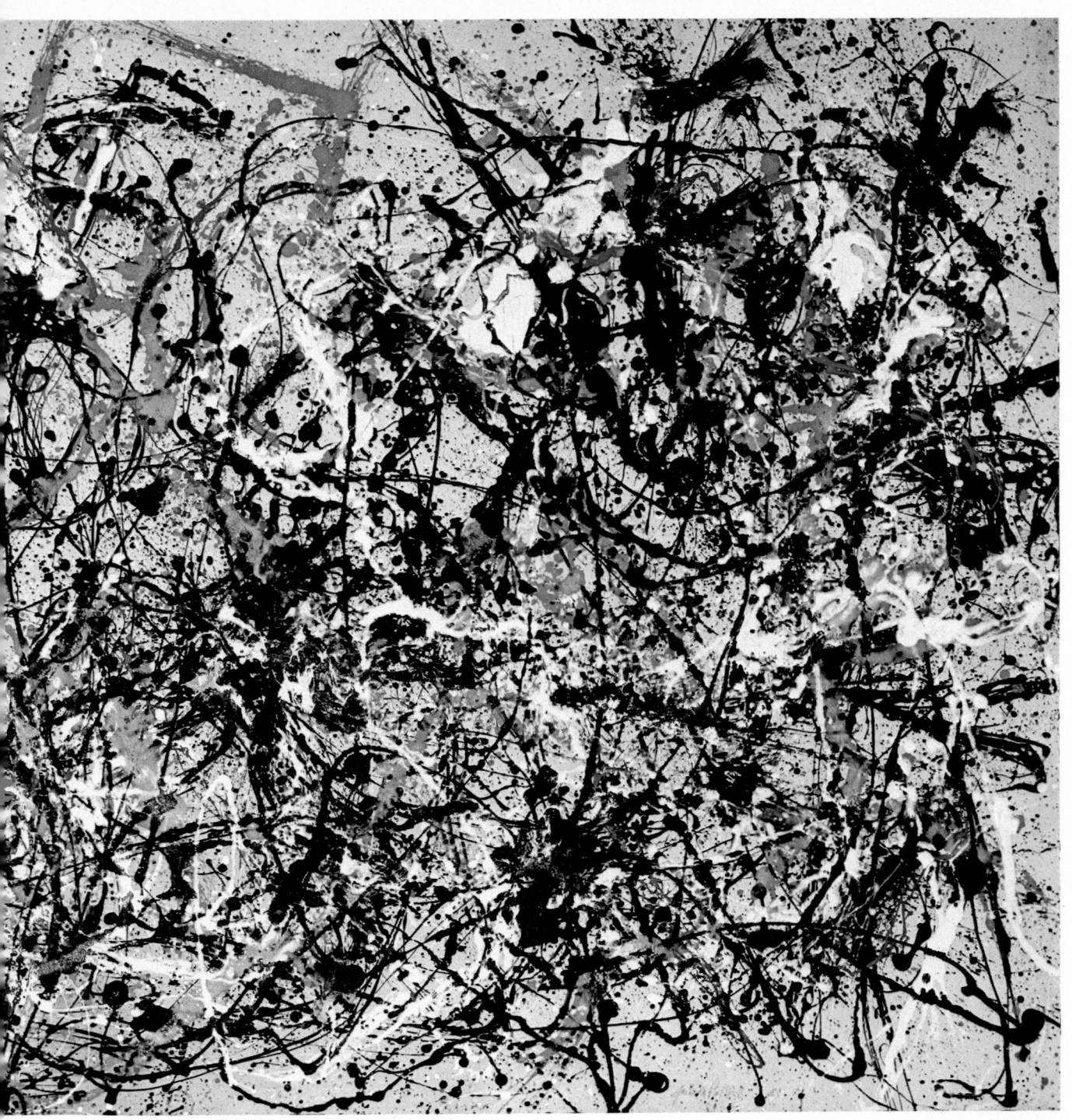

geometric space. I have nevertheless tried to pursue a particular style in my work. For me, the road has been a zig-zag into and out of old civilizations, seeking new horizons through meditation and contemplation. . . . I have sought to make my painting 'whole', but to attain this I have used a whirling mass."

Tobey differs from Pollock and Kline in two important respects—in his very different sense of scale and in his nostalgic feeling for what is ancient (something Pollock avoided even when he made use of primitive pictographs). But when we look at his paintings we get a feeling which we also sometimes get from theirs: that the supposedly "direct" language of gestural abstraction is in fact more special and hermetic, more thoroughly cut off from the society that produced it, than the historians of modern art have found it comfortable to admit. In fact, it is often as ambiguous as its own technical procedures.

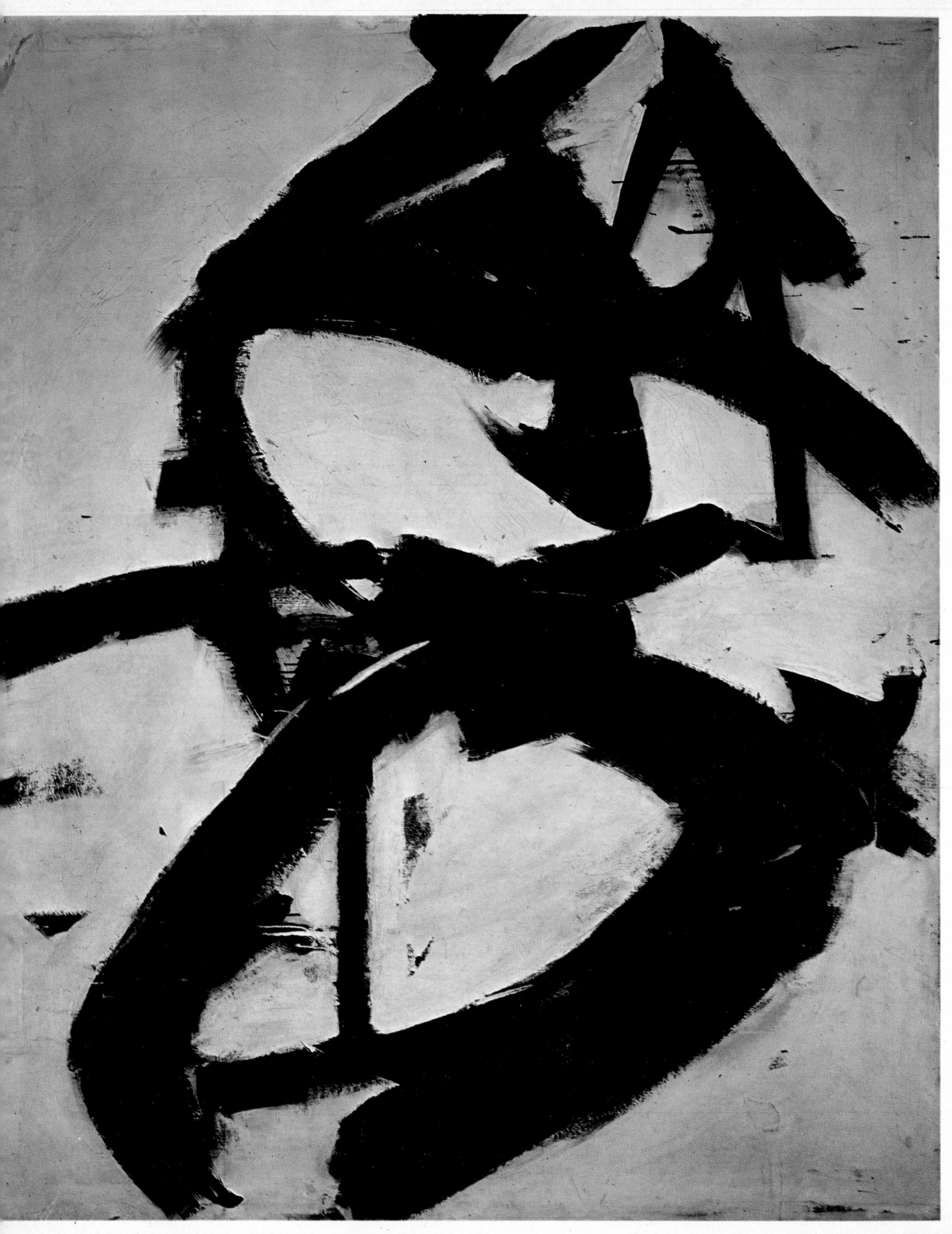

The Abstract Expressionists themselves, often well read in Marx as much as in Freud and Jung, were of course aware of the dangers they ran, and it is interesting to see some of the solutions which were proposed to the dilemma of the isolated artist. The most forthright and in a sense the most brutal was that proposed by Clyfford Still (Plate 48).

Still's *oeuvre* is somewhat monotonous. He was one of the earliest of the Abstract Expressionists to arrive at a personal and characteristic image, and he stuck to it doggedly thereafter. The monotony is implicit in Still's conception of the artist as an American pioneer: "It was a journey that one must make, walking straight and alone . . . until one had crossed the darkened and wasted valleys and come at last into clear air and could stand on a high and limitless plain. Imagination, no longer fettered by the laws of fear, became as one with vision. And the Act, intrinsic and absolute, was its meaning, and the bearer of its passion" (letter to Gordon M. Smith, dated January 1, 1959; published in the

44. Opposite
Franz Kline
Figure Eight
1952; 204.5 × 161.3 cm. (80 × 63 in.)
New York, coll. William S. Rubin

45. Above
Franz Kline
Orange and Black Wall
1959; 168.9 × 365.8 cm. (66 × 143 in.)
New York, coll. Mr. and Mrs. Robert C. Scull

46. Overleaf left
Mark Tobey
Festival
1953; 100.5 × 75 cm. (39 × 29 in.)
Washington, coll. Mr. and Mrs. Bagley Wright

47. Overleaf right
Mark Tobey
Edge of August
1953; 121.9 × 71.1 cm. (48 × 28 in.)
New York, Museum of Modern Art

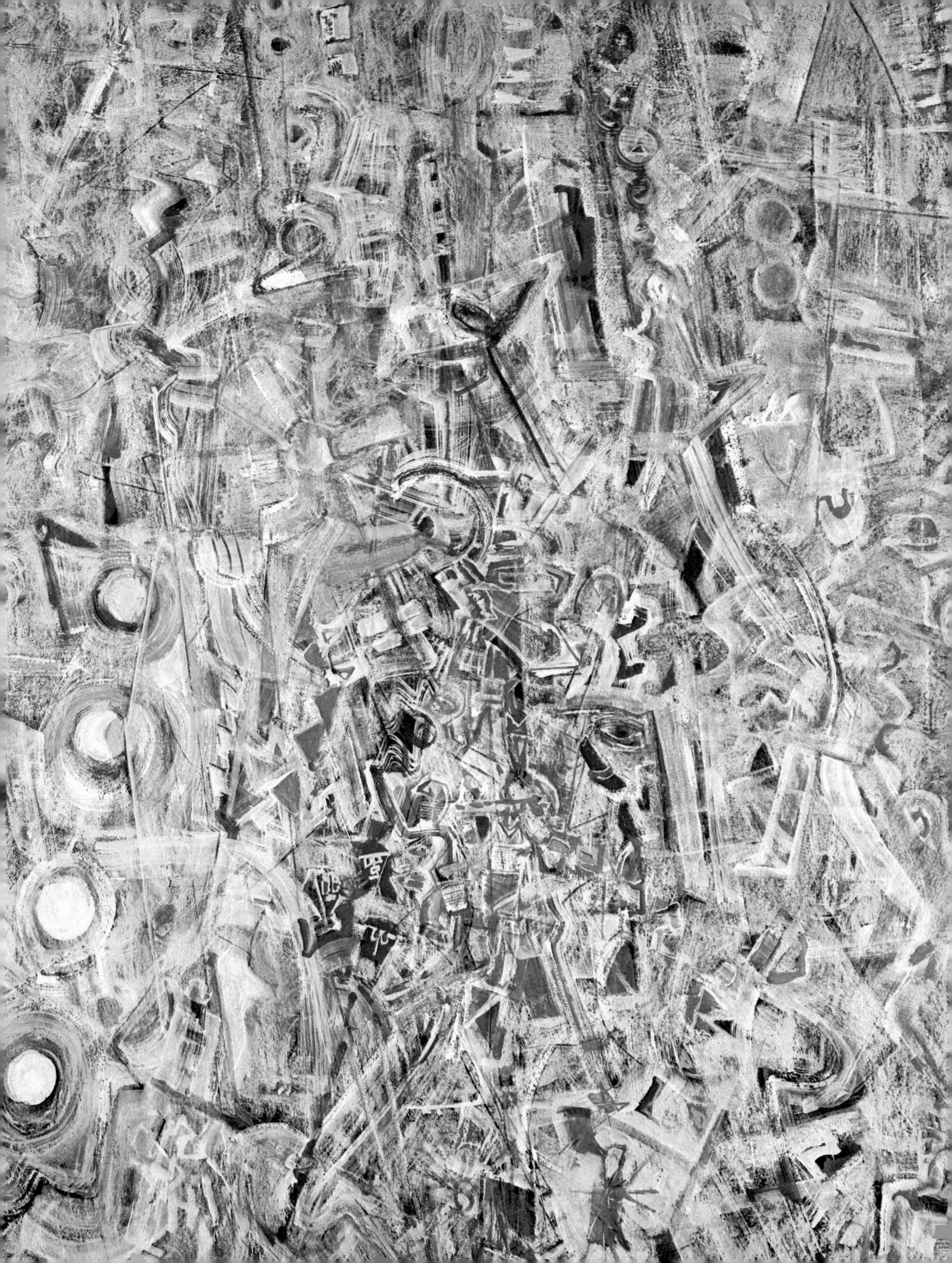

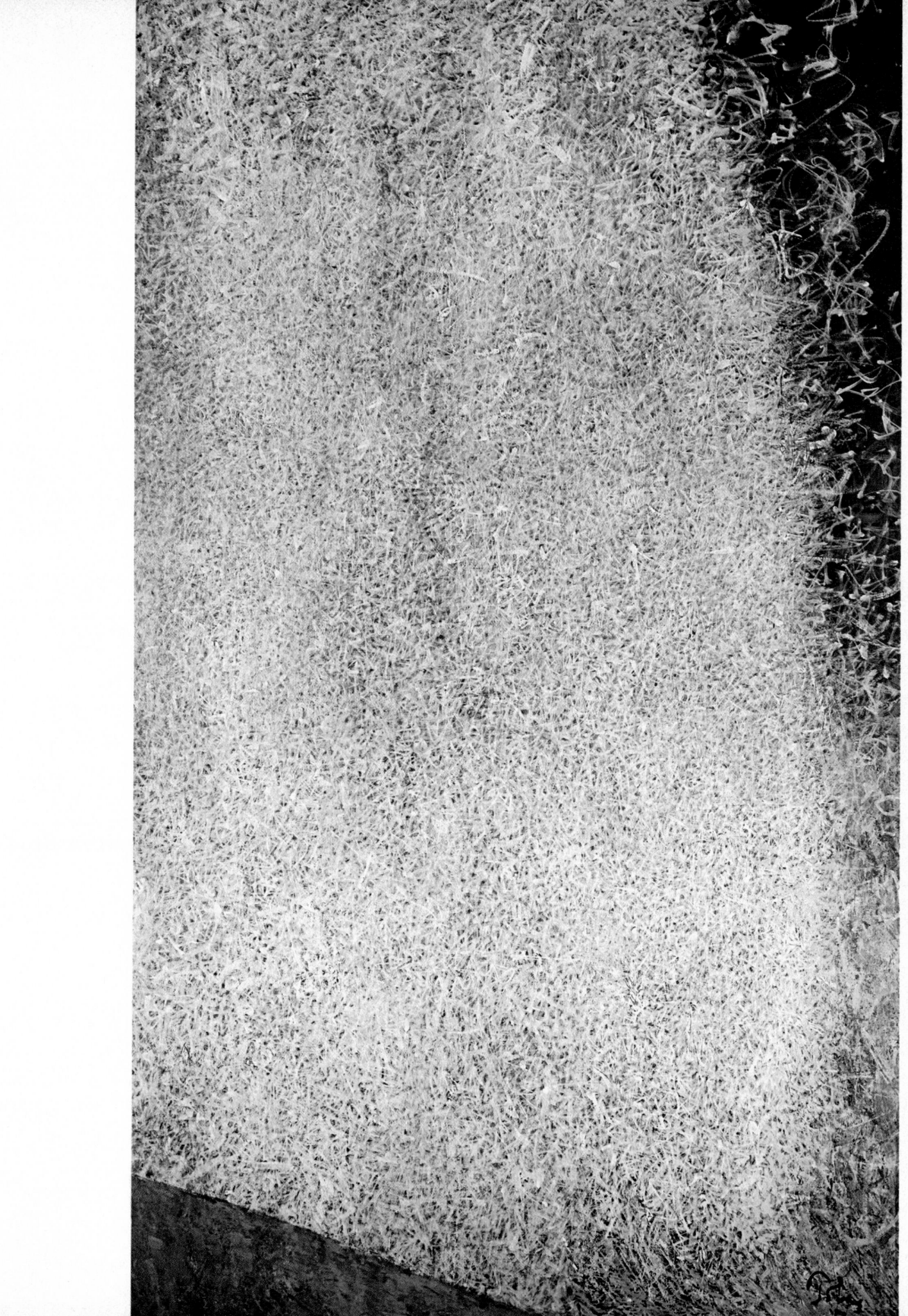

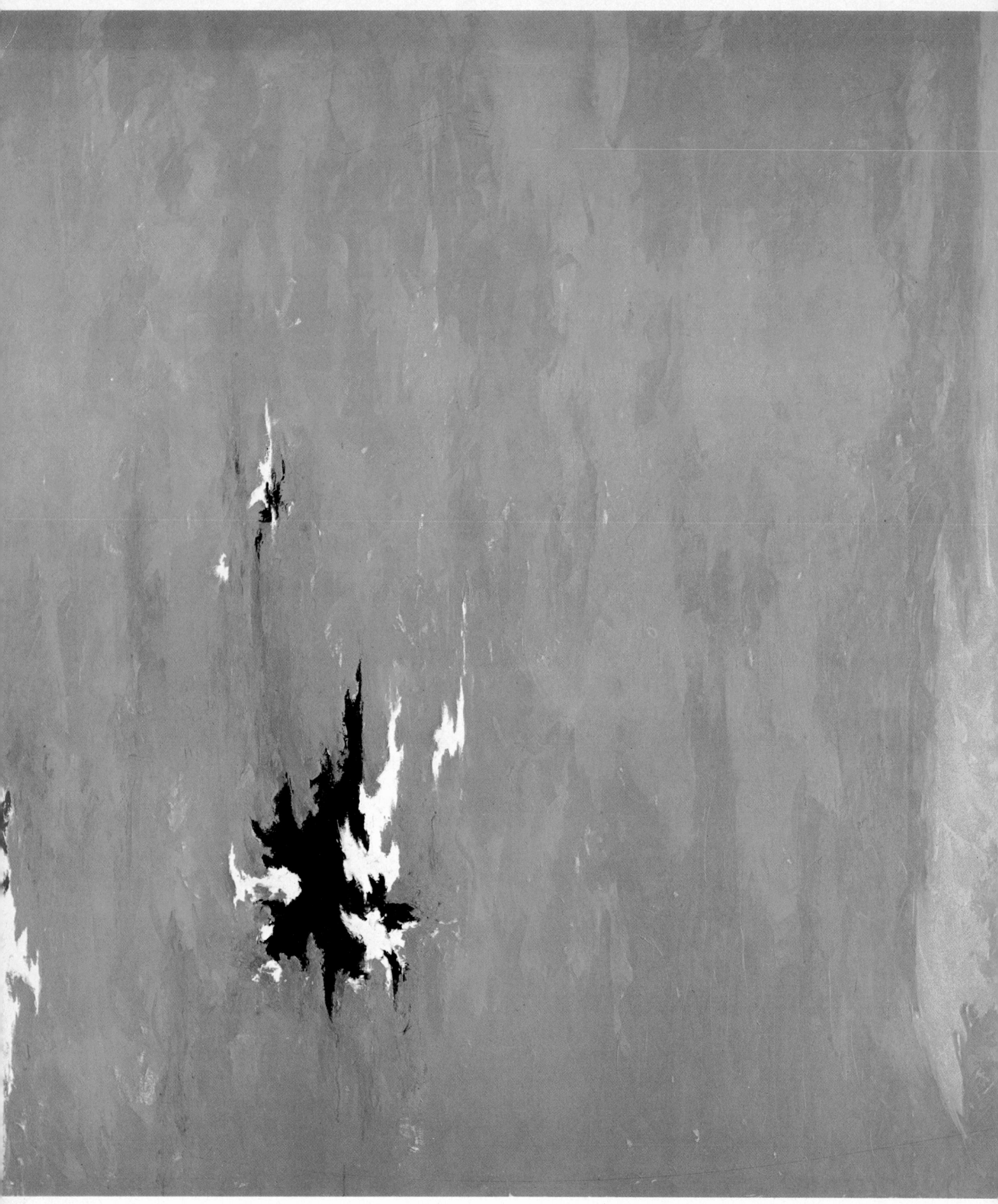

48. Opposite
Clyfford Still
Painting 1948-D
1948; 236.5 × 202.2 cm. (92 × 79 in.)
New York, coll. William S. Rubin

49.
Robert Motherwell
Work
1968; 28.4 × 36.1 cm. (11 × 14 in.)
California, coll. Mr. and Mrs. Frederick R. Weisman

catalogue to the Clyfford Still retrospective at the Albright-Knox Art Gallery, Buffalo, New York, 1959).

Robert Rosenblum has shrewdly compared Still's painting, with its shapes like flames or clouds or stalactites, to that of a slightly senior and much less celebrated contemporary, Augustus Vincent Tack, whose large, late Symbolist canvases are to be seen in the Phillips Gallery in Washington. Rosenblum demonstrates that Tack is the link between Still on the one hand and

American Romantics such as Albert Pinkham Ryder and even Albert Bierstadt upon the other. It must be said that this comparison does not really increase our respect for Still's achievement, which seems in this context both cranky and provincial.

At the opposite end of the spectrum from Still, both temperamentally and intellectually, is Robert Motherwell. Motherwell played a conspicuous role in the early history of Abstract Expressionism, and in particular was responsible for bringing a number of his colleagues into contact with the Surrealist exiles from Europe. He was more keenly aware of the historical development of the

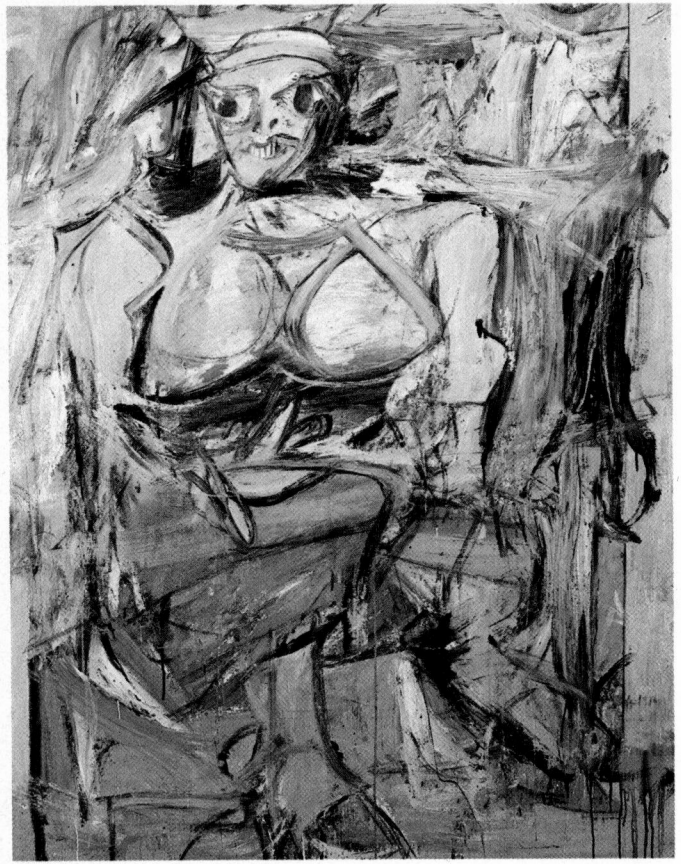

50 and 51
Willem de Kooning
Woman I
1950–52; 192.7 × 147.3 cm. (75 × 57 in.)
New York, Museum of Modern Art
Opposite, detail

Modernist aesthetic than any other American artist. An advocate of automatist techniques, he nevertheless was aware of their disadvantages, "To give oneself over completely to the unconscious is to become a slave." But he defended automatism by means of a paradox: "Plastic automatism though perhaps not verbal automatism . . . is actually very little a question of the unconscious. It is more a plastic weapon with which to invent new forms. As such it is one of the twentieth century's greatest formal inventions."

He tried to incorporate the moral force that some of the Abstract Expressionists claimed for their work into a more traditional aesthetic, declaring rather uneasily to the critic Dore Ashton: "Sometimes I have a painting which is aesthetically beautiful, and I pause. But then I go on because it doesn't really correspond to my judgment of the world." The slow rhythm of Motherwell's most typical compositions (Plate 49) runs the constant risk of seeming devitalized—and an Abstract Expressionist work which lacks vitality is by definition a failure.

No one could level the same accusation against the powerfully various work of Willem de Kooning. De Kooning's *oeuvre* is one of the places where the "expressionist" component of Abstract Expressionism becomes most clearly visible. One reason for this is that De Kooning is the most European of all the leading Abstract Expressionists, with the possible exception of Hofmann, having arrived in the United States in 1926, when he was already an adult. His best-known paintings are perhaps the various series of *Women* (Plates 50 and 51). These begin as a statement of raw sexuality, but later examples have a sugary prettiness which has suggested a comparison to Jean Honoré Fragonard. But within the apparent inconsistency can be discovered a certain steadiness of aim: "For De Kooning, the urge is to include everything, to leave nothing out, even if it means working in a turmoil of contradictions and, as has been suggested, a turmoil of contradictions is his favourite medium" (Thomas B. Hess, *De Kooning's Recent Paintings*, 1967).

De Kooning's perpetual restlessness has led him

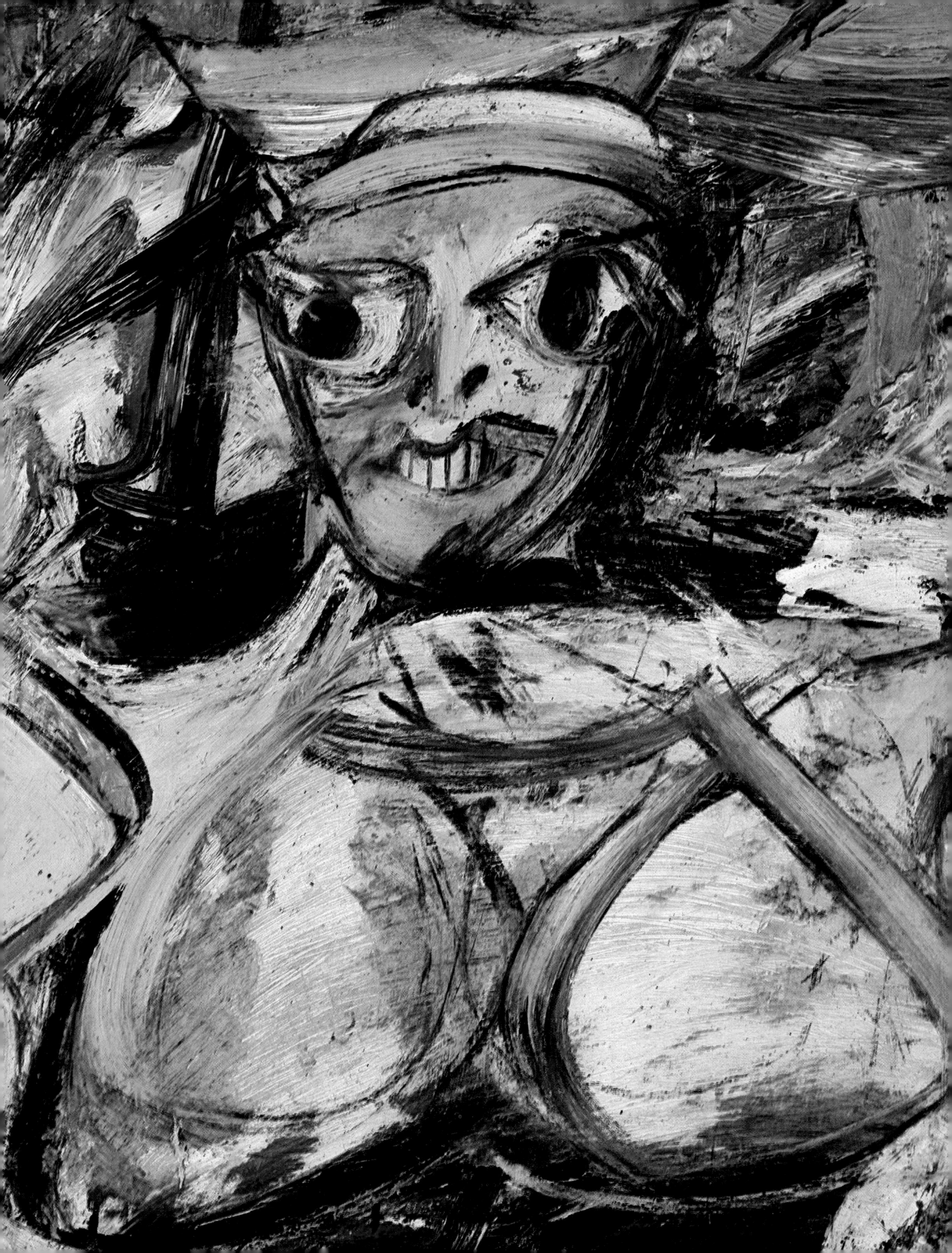

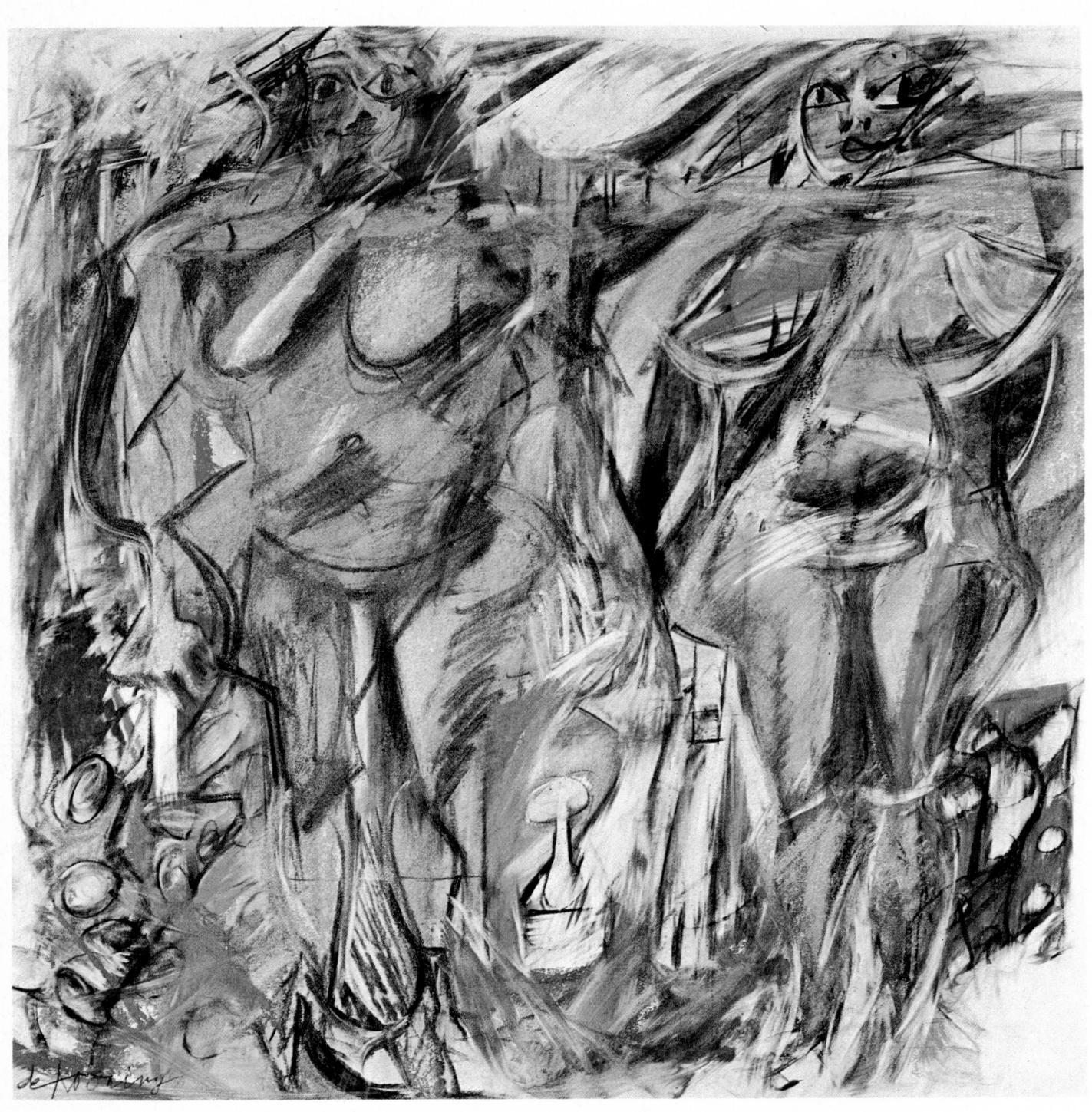

52.
Willem de Kooning
Two Women with Still Life
1952; 59.7 × 56.5 cm. (23 × 22 in.)
Los Angeles, coll. Weisman

53. Opposite
Willem de Kooning
Police Gazette
1954–55; 109.9 × 127.6 cm. (43 × 50 in.)
New York, coll. Mr. and Mrs. Robert C. Scull

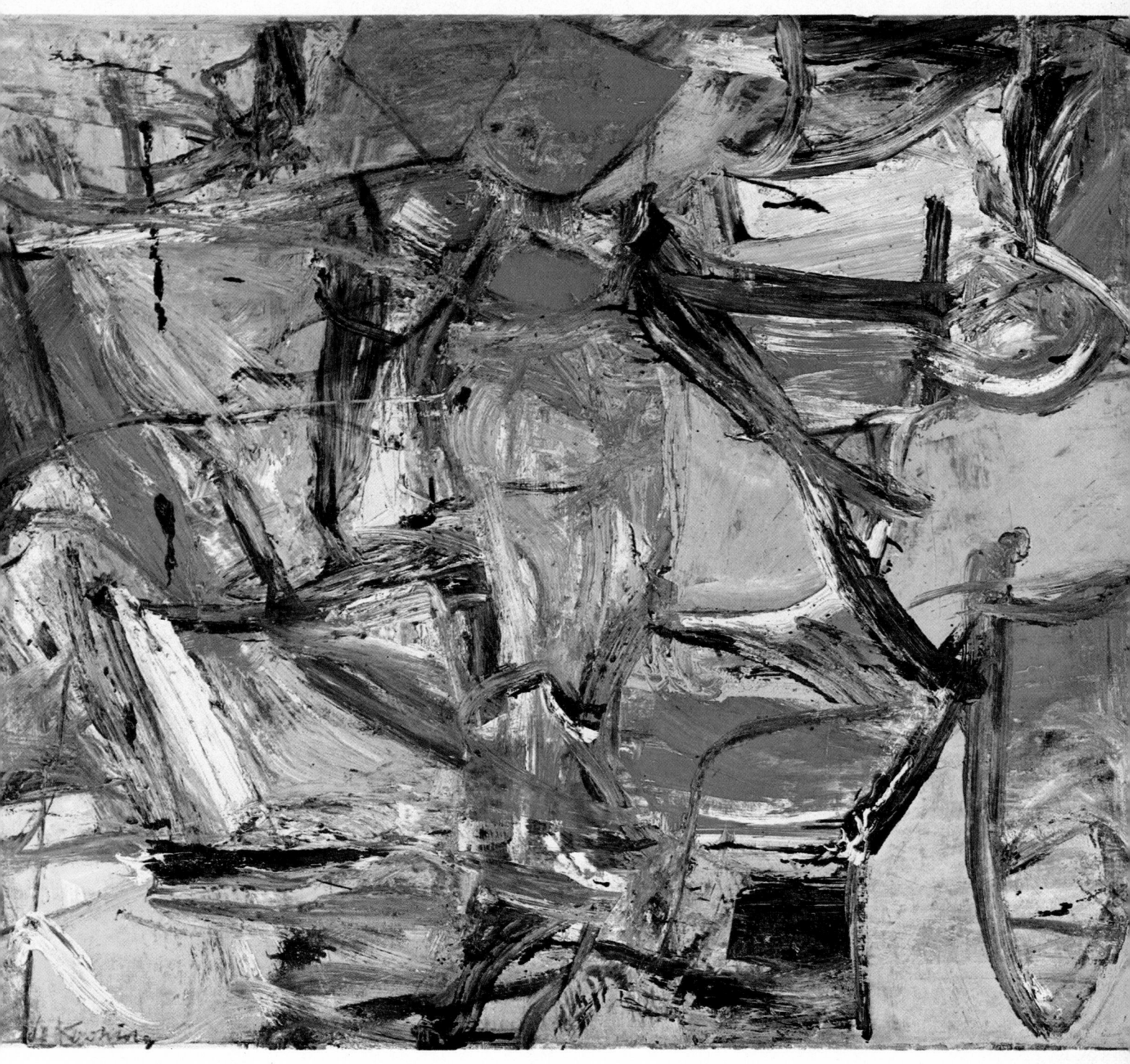

to explore a number of traditional genres. In addition to the series of female nudes, for example, there is a series of impressive landscapes which hover just on the border of total abstraction (Plate 54). A comparison of the artist's *Door to the River* with the landscape-derived paintings of minor Abstract Expressionists such as Grace Hartigan (Plate 55) or Helen Frankenthaler (Plate 56) reveals how brilliantly the balancing act is sustained. De Kooning contrives to convey the *genius loci* without ever lapsing into specifics, and the canvas thus retains its power to play upon the spectator's imagination. Yet his landscapes suffer from the defect we also discover in the landscape sketches of a romantic painter such as John Constable. They are unresolved; they propose no solution. In this sense they are just a fragment of experience wrenched out of context, and existing in a moral void.

The question of a morality for painting was undoubtedly important to the Abstract Expressionists, as we find when we move on to examine the work of a group of artists who were somewhat different from those who have already been discussed. The gesture painters, such as Pollock and Kline, hoped to induce a kind of leap of communication which was somewhat akin to the spiritual leap of late medieval mystics. But they had colleagues who were somewhat less sanguine about the possibility of such a movement of the mind or soul. Among them were to be numbered men such as Adolph Gottlieb, William Baziotes, Mark Rothko, and Barnett Newman.

One of the things that drove them towards a new and radical art in the America of the 1940's was despair, within which paradoxically there was also a kind of hope. Barnett Newman was later to declare: "In 1940, some of us woke up to find ourselves without hope—to find that painting did not really exist. Or to coin a modern phrase, painting, a quarter of a century before it happened to God, was dead. The awakening had the exaltation of a revolution. It was that awakening that inspired the aspiration—the high purpose— quite a different thing from ambition—to start from scratch, to paint as if painting had never existed before. It was that naked revolutionary moment that made painters out of painters" (Barnett Newman, in "Pollock: An Artist" Symposium, Part 1. *Art News*, Vol. 57, No. 16 [October, 1958]).

Adolph Gottlieb said: "The situation was so bad that I know I felt free to try anything, no matter how absurd it seemed. What was there to lose? Neither Cubism nor Surrealism could absorb someone like myself—we felt like derelicts" (ibid.).

The "enormous vacuum" which Gottlieb described was to be filled, in the first instance, by an effort to re-create the force of primitive myth and symbol, things which would have contemporary value and yet be both "tragic and timeless", as Rothko and Gottlieb were to say in a famous joint letter to the *New York Times*, published in June 1943.

The concern with the pictograph was to be most thoroughly stable and constant in the work of William Baziotes. We find it expressed even in a late work, such as the handsome *Pompeii* of 1955 (Plate 57). Lawrence Alloway, in the catalogue preface for the exhibition of Baziotes's work staged at the Guggenheim Museum in 1965, gives a good survey of the artist's affinities, influences and sources: "The conversion of surrealist techniques in the direction of organically unified imagery and, in Baziotes' case, in the direction of 'beautiful painting', is characteristic of American art in the 40's. What Baziotes did in fact, with biomorphism, is indicative of the situation. He went around the movement, behind it to the original traditions of fantastic art. His slow automatism, prudent and sensitive, is closer to Paul Klee than it is to André Masson. . . Baziotes's anxious musing is more like the mysteries of Odilon Redon than the Surrealist's drama of revelation or exhortation."

As Alloway recognizes, in another passage in the same essay, Baziotes tended to remain somewhat apart from the other American artists of the same group, because "he retained an essentially scenic conception of the picture space, within which a cast of distinct forms is displayed". In this respect, he retains affinities to Gorky in particular.

Gottlieb and Rothko, starting from much the same point, continued in a different and more dramatic way. Gottlieb developed his pictographs until their large simplified forms were centralized, and came to dominate the canvas (Plate 58). But the sense of imagery remains, even when the glyphs have grown sufficiently large and dominant to shed their original function and identity: "The radical change of scale accomplished by the elimination of his pictographic vocabulary and the isolation of a few large forms on a field creates an imagery which, in its directness, has an immediate and total impact on the viewer. There are, however, secondary impulses. A body of minutiae in the play of textures, the brushstrokes, the delicate nuances of colour in them, complicate the way one sees the painting" (Diane Waldman, "Gottlieb: Signs and Suns", *Art News*, Vol. 66, No. 10 [February, 1968], p. 68).

Perhaps the most radical aspect of Gottlieb's

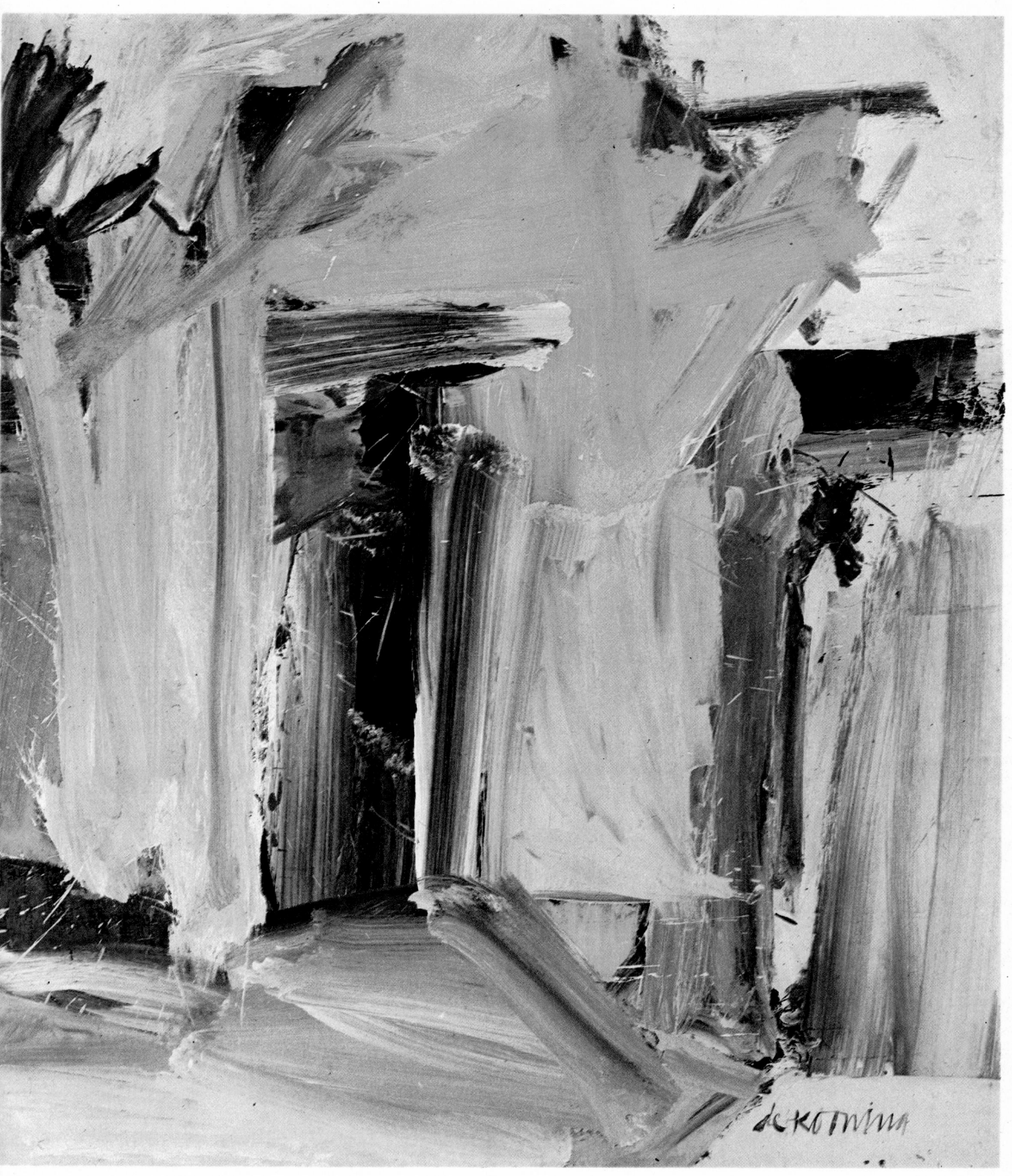

painting is, however, the abandonment of any pretence at traditional composition. The use of centralized, heraldic imagery is as fundamental to his mature painting as the freely calligraphic line is to Pollock's. Even Gottlieb did not press this development as far as Rothko and Newman, and it is for this reason, I suspect, that the two latter now seem the more commanding artists.

Rothko has more and more come to seem absolutely pivotal to any assessment of the achievement of Abstract Expressionism. His earlier works in the Abstract Expressionist idiom, such as *Entombment I* of 1946 (Plate 59), are pictographic, but more painterly than Baziotes, for example, was ever to be. But even before this picture was painted, Rothko had the yearning for

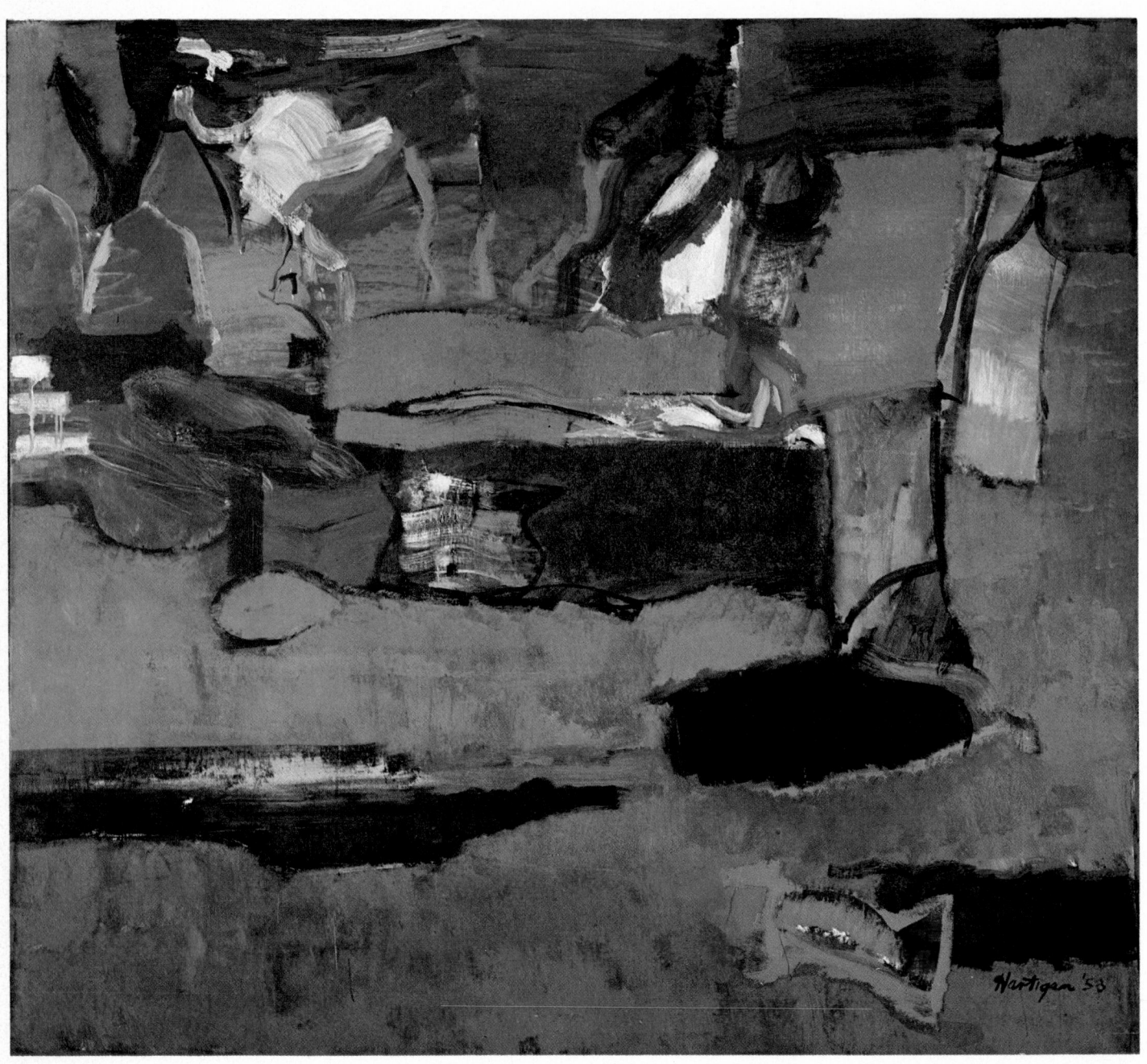

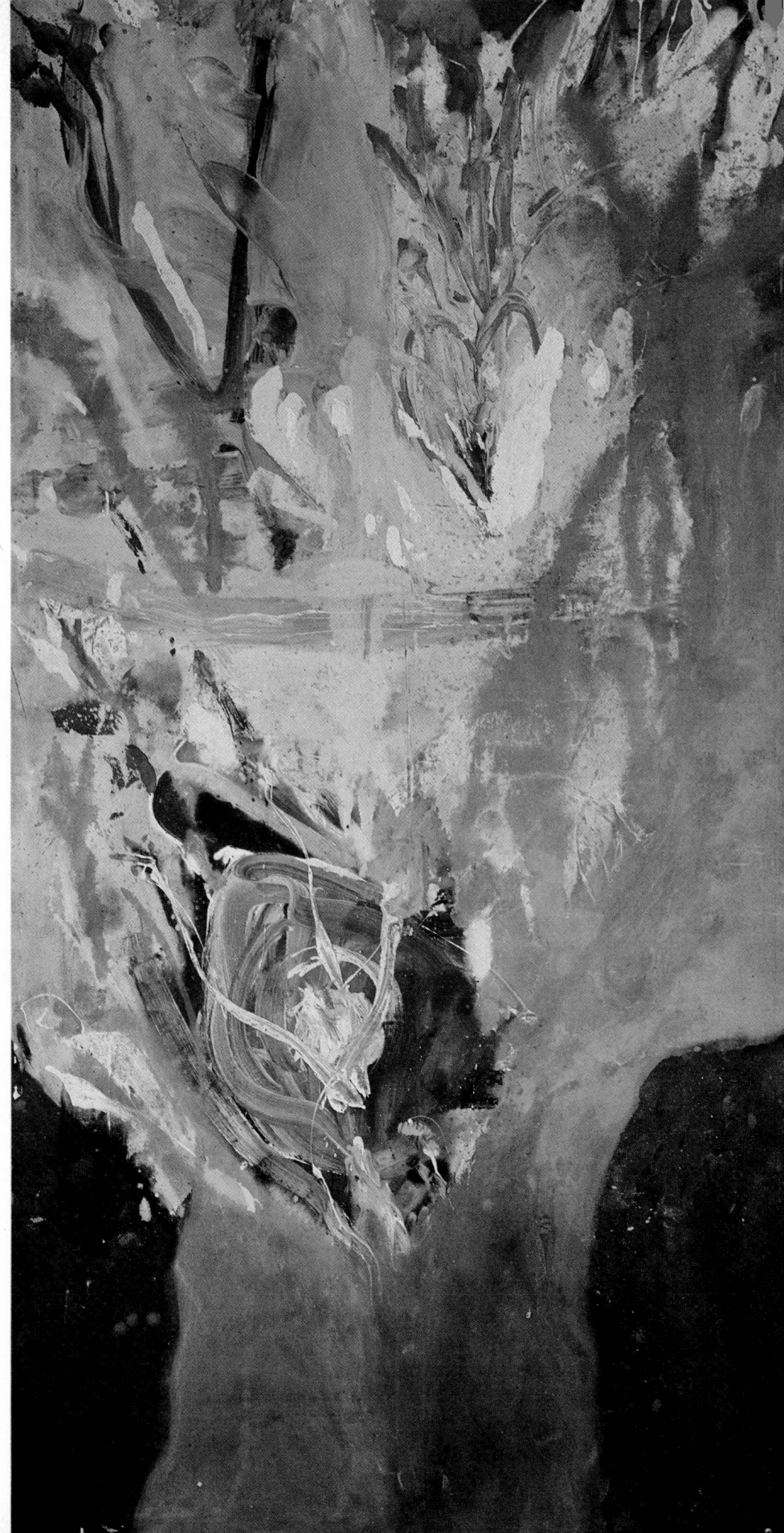

55. Opposite
Grace Hartigan
Frederickstead
1958; 207.3 × 225.7 cm.
(81 × 88 in.)
Brandeis University,
Massachusetts, Rose Art Museum

56.
Helen Frankenthaler
Blue Territory
1955; 287 × 147.3 cm.
(112 × 57 in.)
New York,
Whitney Museum of American Art

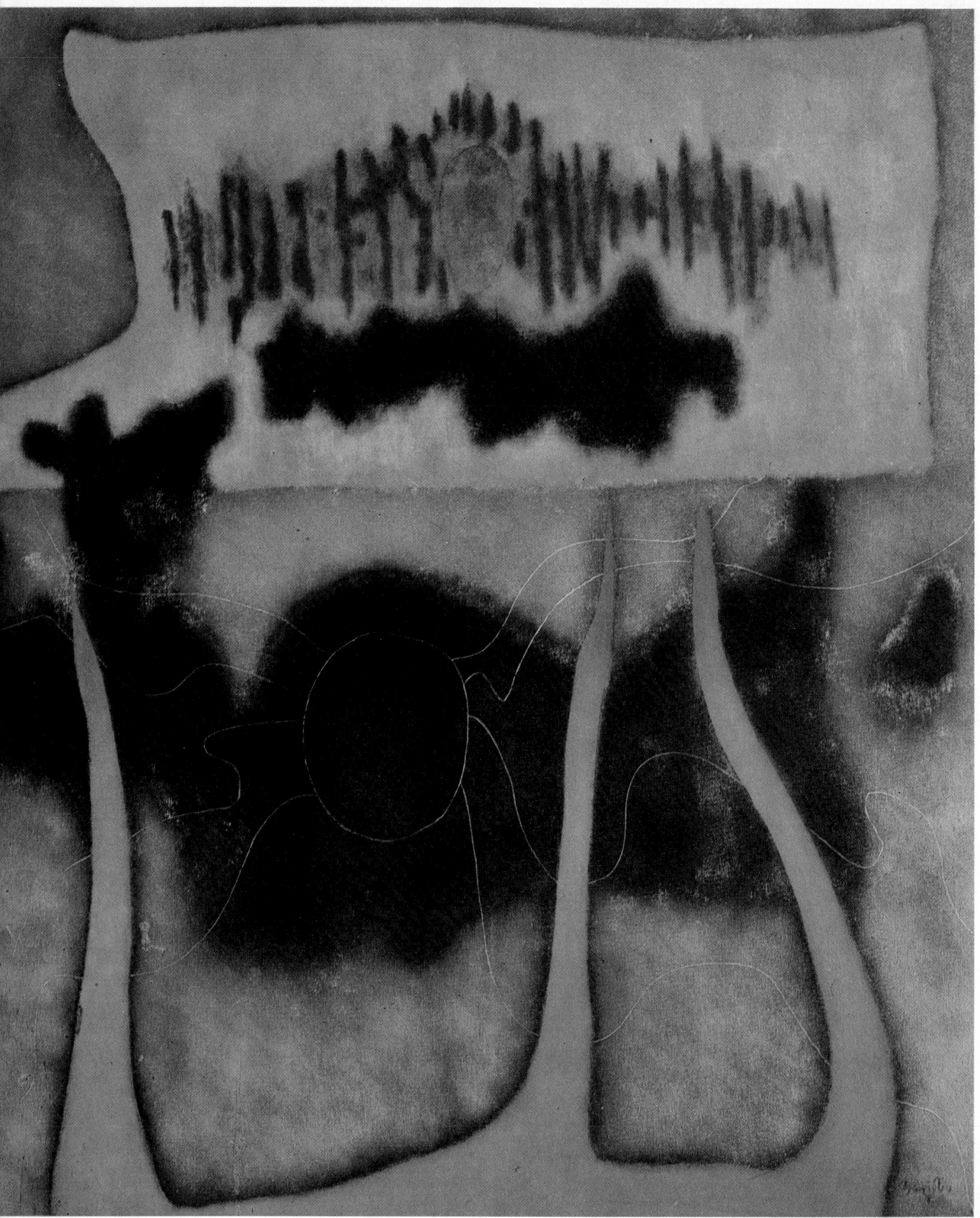

57. Opposite
William Baziotes
Pompeii
1955; 152.4 × 121.9 cm. (59 × 48 in.)
New York, Museum of Modern Art

58.
Adolph Gottlieb
Sign
1962; 228.6 × 213.4 cm. (89 × 83 in.)
New York, collection of the artist

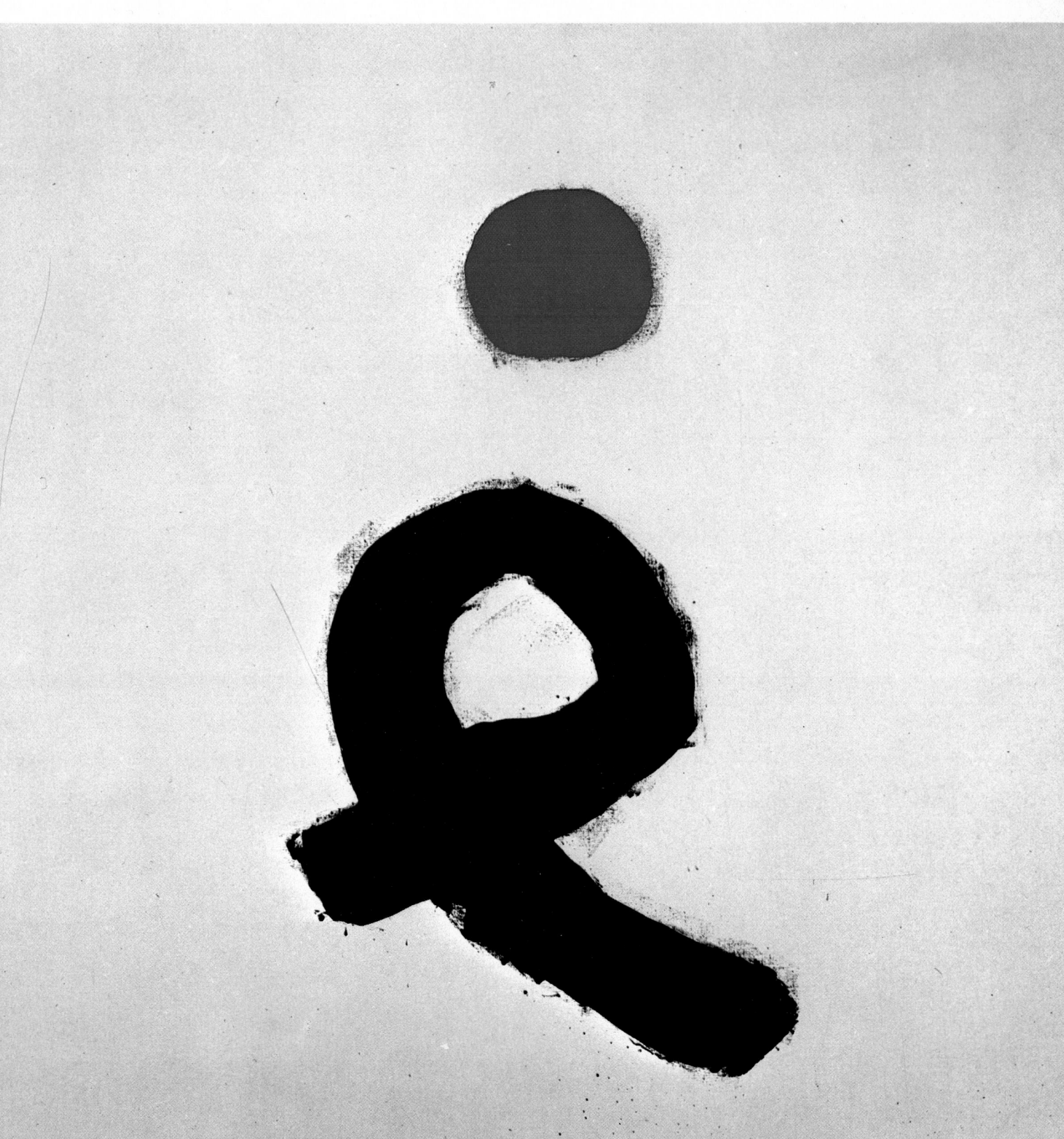

something which would be less specific and more unitary. By 1948 he was ready to assert that he wanted a mode which would have "no direct association with any particular visual experience", and the next year he called for "the elimination of all obstacles between the idea and the observer". His solution, in the search for what would be communicative yet unspecific, was to evolve the centred compositions of softly brushed rectangles of paint floating against a more thinly painted ground which are now associated with his name (Plate 60). Rothko had a clear idea of what kind of effect he wanted to achieve: "The progress of the painter's work, as it travels in time from point to point, will be towards clarity; towards the elimination of all obstacles between the painter and the idea, and between the idea and the observer. As examples of such obstacles, I give

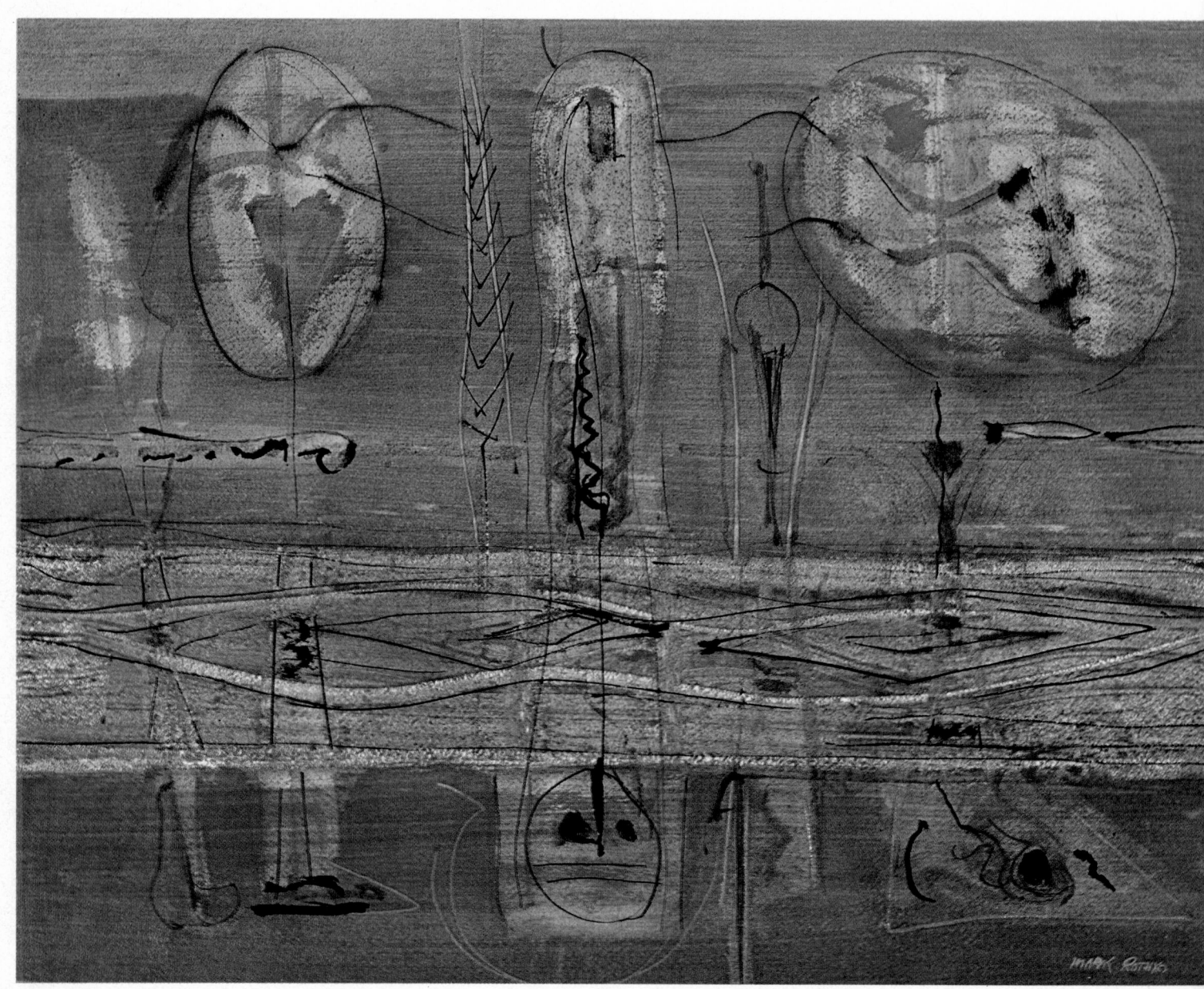

59. Opposite
Mark Rothko
Entombment I
1946; 51.8 × 65.4 cm. (20 × 26 in.)
New York, Whitney Museum of American Art

60.
Mark Rothko
Black, Pink, and Yellow over Orange
1951–52; 295 × 235 cm. (115 × 92 in.)
New York, coll. William S. Rubin

(among others) memory, history or geometry" (Mark Rothko, in "Artists' Statements", catalogue of the exhibition "New American Painting", Museum of Modern Art, 1958–59; the statement first appeared in *The Tiger's Eye*, October, 1949).

His success in reaching his declared aim can be judged, not only from the absolute recognizability of his art, but also from the sense of almost religious communion which many people have found in it. Yet there is, too, a certain justice in

61.
Barnett Newman
Vir Heroicus Sublimis
1950–51; 242 × 543 cm. (94 × 212 in.)
New York, Museum of Modern Art,
gift of Mr. and Mrs. Heller

Harold Rosenberg's comment that it remained escapist "in the deepest traditional sense—rich in the romance of self-estrangement".

This romance is apparently absent from the painting of Barnett Newman, one of the most articulate and most radical of the Abstract Expressionists, yet for this reason one of the slowest to achieve recognition. With Newman we see the beginning of a return to the idea of the painting as object, rather than that of the painting as the portrait of an individual soul. His huge canvases are even more uncompromising than Rothko's in their refusal to have anything to do with traditional ways of composing a picture (Plates 61 and 62), though the titles still tend to suggest a degree of aspiration. "Newman's art", comments one American critic, "is about color in relation to size and shape; it amounts to a strategy of scale. Where he differs from Rothko and Still, who are up to something similar, is in his absolute distaste for any atmospheric illusion and textural painting" (E. C. Goosens, "The Philosophic Line

of Barnett Newman", *Art News*, Vol. 57, No. 4 [Summer 1968], p. 63). Harold Rosenberg comments, with a certain asperity, that "In pushing painting as near as possible to extinction, Newman showed it to survive as an act of faith rather than as a normal attribute of modern culture" (*The Re-Definition of Art*, p. 97).

Rothko and Newman present the problem in a different form from the way in which it confronts us in Pollock, but they still bring us back to the question of how art is to function in a modern society. They also draw our attention to an aspect of the New York School of painting in the 1940's and 1950's which has perhaps received insufficient attention, which is its connection with traditional Jewish culture. Rothko was in fact, like De Kooning and Gorky, an immigrant. He was born at Dvinsk, within the Russian Pale of Settlement.

The more one studies the products of the nongestural wing of the Abstract Expressionist movement (and the majority of the artists who belonged to this group were indeed Jews), the more one perceives that it is in a way an extension of the Russian-Jewish Hassidic tradition, and the strangely transplanted expression of a culture

62.
Barnett Newman
Day One
1951–52; 335 × 133 cm. (131 × 52 in.)
New York, Whitney Museum of American Art

63. Opposite
Hans Hofmann
Fantasia in Blue
1954; 152.4 × 132.1 cm. (59 × 52 in.)
New York, Whitney Museum of American Art

64. Overleaf
Sam Francis
Moby Dick
1958; 236.2 × 370.8 cm. (92 × 145 in.)
New York, coll. Mr. and Mrs. Armand Bartos

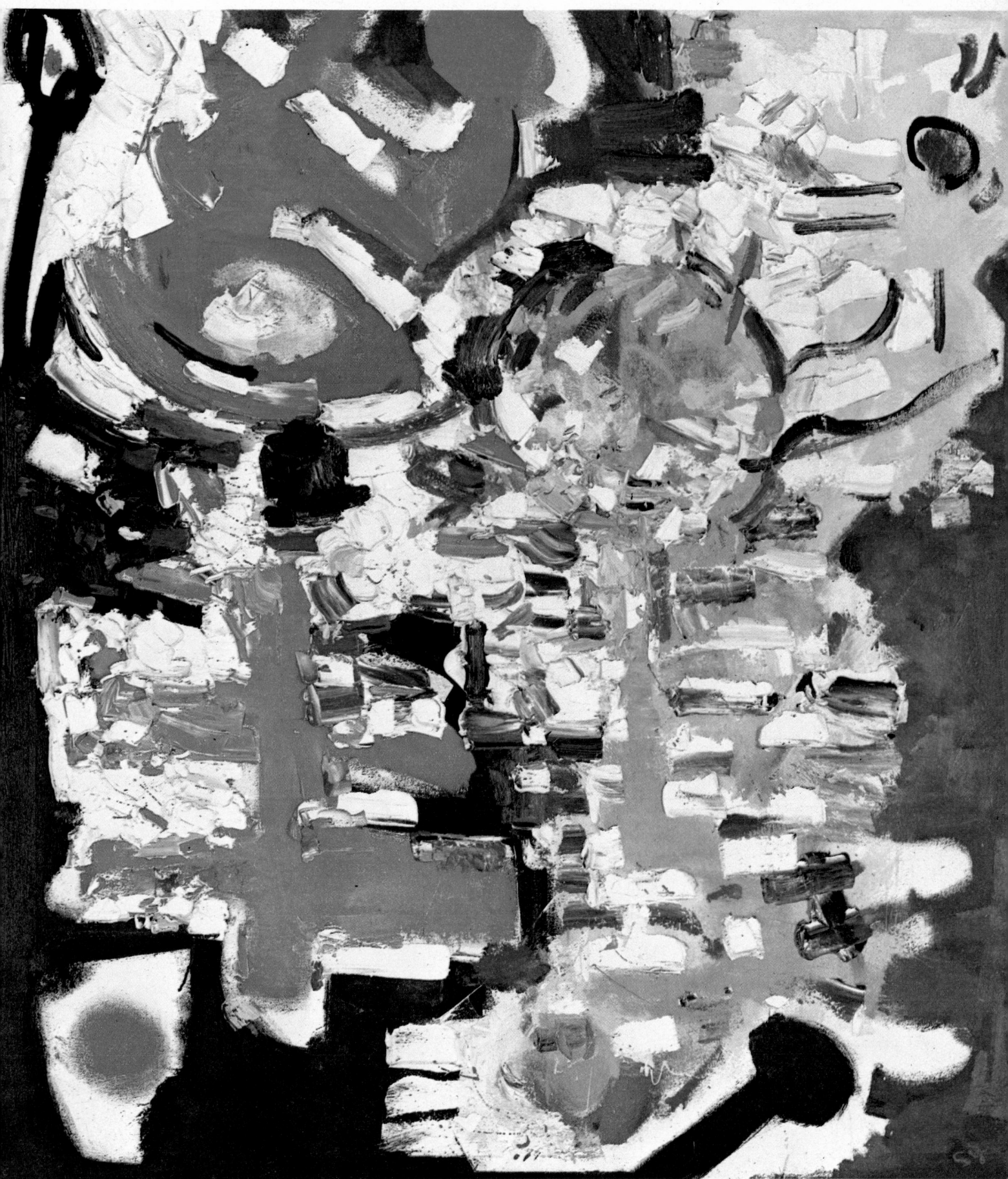

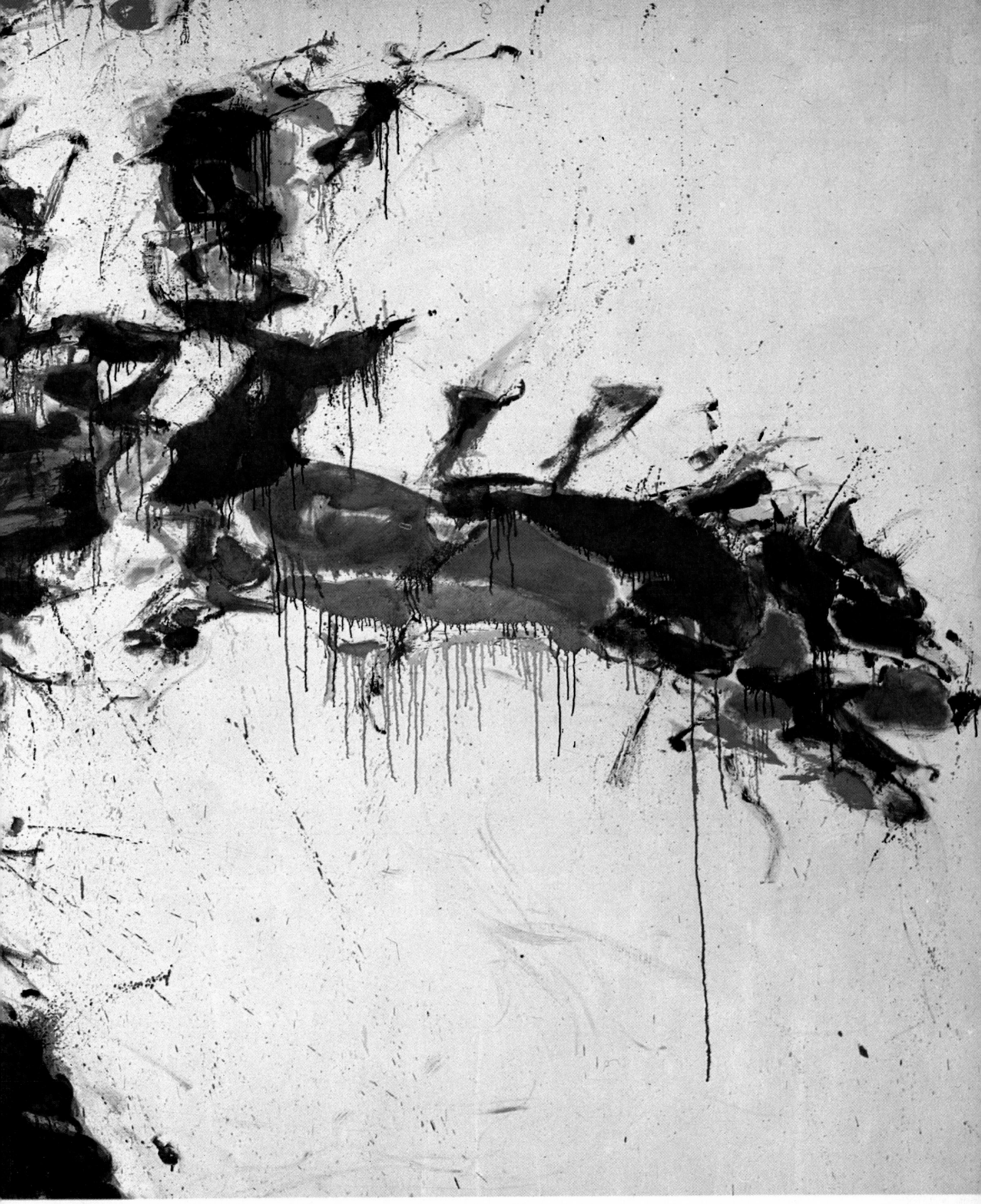

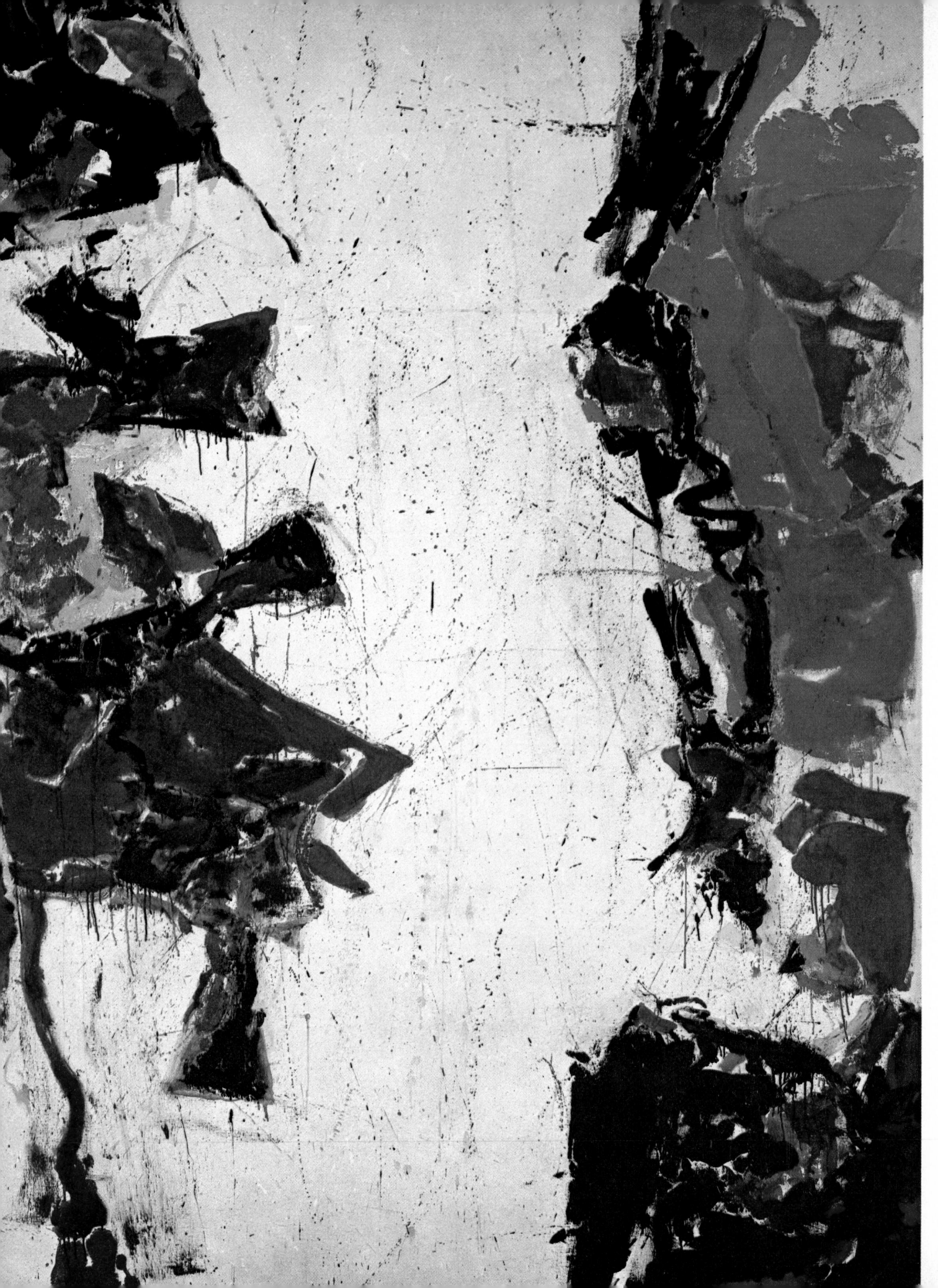

65. Opposite
Sam Francis
Untitled
1958; 274.3 × 191.7 cm. (107 × 75 in.)
California, Pasadena Art Museum

66. Overleaf
Ad Reinhardt
Red Painting
1952; 198 × 366 cm. (77 × 143 in.)
New York, Metropolitan Museum of Art,
Arthur H. Hearn Fund

which had already been destroyed in its native place. This seems to me as important as the connection that Robert Rosenblum has traced between the cosmic aspirations of a Romantic landscapist such as Caspar David Friedrich and similar sentiments as expressed by Rothko.

Once we recognize the connection, certain consequences follow. We note that the distaste for specific imagery is traditional in a Jewish sense, as well as radical in terms of the development of Western painting. We note, too, that the search for some kind of "ultimate" is linked to the Hassidic teachings which were so typical of the Pale. And, finally, one notes that the social impotence, the ability to make connections only within the art community, can be read as a curious and significant transmogrification of the ghetto mentality. With Abstract Expressionism, the artist takes up the position that art can only make an efficient contribution to society by becoming a substitute religion. More ordinary types of communication will not do.

Abstract Expressionism was in one sense an extremely powerful and fruitful artistic explosion.

One of the best proofs of its fertilizing power is what it did to Hans Hofmann's work towards the end of his career. Hofmann, who had been a commanding teacher rather than a commanding creative artist, became towards the end of his life "his pupils' best pupil", as Nicolas Calas has said, and produced canvases at least as powerful as those painted by other Abstract Expressionist leaders (Plate 63). On the other hand, the idiom could easily slip into being a pleasant decorative convention (Sam Francis, Plates 64 and 65).

The most powerful expression of the eventual bankruptcy of Abstract Expressionist ideas was provided by Ad Reinhardt, a painter who was the eternal gadfly of the movement without being able, in his own work, to make the final surrender of certain Abstract Expressionist aspirations (Plate 66). Reinhardt declared that his aim was "To paint and repaint the same thing over and over again, to repeat and refine the one uniform form again and again. Intensity, consciousness, perfection in art come only after long routine, preparation and intention" (Ad Reinhardt, "Art-as-Art", *Environments I*, No. 1 [Autumn 1962], p. 81).

Post-war Europe

In Europe, in the years that immediately followed the Second World War, the situation for modern art was paradoxical. On the one hand, the hostility of Nazism and fascism to the Modernist movement gave the latter a new respectability now that the dictatorships were defeated. Not unreasonably, people identified contemporary painting with the liberal spirit which the armies of the Allies had been fighting to preserve. The senior Modernist painters such as Picasso, Braque, and Matisse found themselves elevated, finally, to the status of Old Masters, and the public thronged to showings of their work. There was also a tendency to turn the artist himself into a revered cultural object, with an existence quite separate from that of his work, and young American GI's paid pilgrimages to Picasso's studio in much the same spirit as they would previously have gone to visit the *Venus de Milo* or the *Mona Lisa*.

The initial euphoria nevertheless did little to conceal the real difficulties that confronted a new generation of modern artists. The mass emigration of Surrealists to the United States (even if most of them returned to Europe shortly after the war was over) had meant a break in the continuity of modern painting. Young painters felt themselves overshadowed by the achievement of the Modernist pioneers, yet curiously without relationship to them. If on the one hand people recognized the birth of a new era, on the other hand the weariness and depression left behind by the war made them feel disinclined to strenuous activity.

The despair, indeed, struck deep, and some of the most characteristic post-war painting was an expression of it. One of the mushroom reputations of the late Forties was made by the young Frenchman Bernard Buffet. Significantly, he belonged to a group called L'homme témoin. Among its other members were French romantic realists such as Paul Rebeyrolle, Minaux, and Venard. Buffet's *Pietà* (Plate 67), painted when the artist was only eighteen, is representative of the mood which then prevailed. At the time when he first made his reputation, the public and many of the critics ignored Buffet's essential superficiality because he so exactly fulfilled their expectations.

In England another, and very different, artist made a striking success. This was Francis Bacon, whose *Three Studies for a Crucifixion* caused a sensation in London when it was first shown there in 1945. Bacon was a much older man than Buffet, and he had been a long time in discovering his true vocation as a painter, though he actually started to paint as early as 1929, when he was twenty. In 1936, he was refused a place in the large Surrealist exhibition then being organized in London, on the grounds that his work was insufficiently Surrealist. Bacon has since disowned the paintings produced during this period of search, and nearly all of them have been destroyed. When he began work on the *Three Studies* in 1944, he was making a completely new beginning as an artist.

Bacon's work excited people from the first because it seemed to reflect some of the more horrifying aspects of contemporary experience—war, starvation, the mass slaughter of the concentration camps. His early paintings, such as the untitled canvas of 1946 illustrated here (Plate 68), suggested a complex web of references—in the first place to Old Masters such as Velásquez and Rembrandt (here powerfully suggested by the flayed carcass hanging behind the figure), in the second place to Expressionists such as Soutine, and thirdly and more superficially to Surrealism. Yet Bacon was then, and was to remain, stylistically isolated.

Throughout his career he has continued to portray the themes of horror and suffering which announced themselves in his first mature canvases. The *Three Studies for a Crucifixion* of 1962 (Plate 70)

67.
Bernard Buffet
Pietà
1946; 172 × 255 cm. (67 × 99 in.)
Paris, Musée National d'Art Moderne

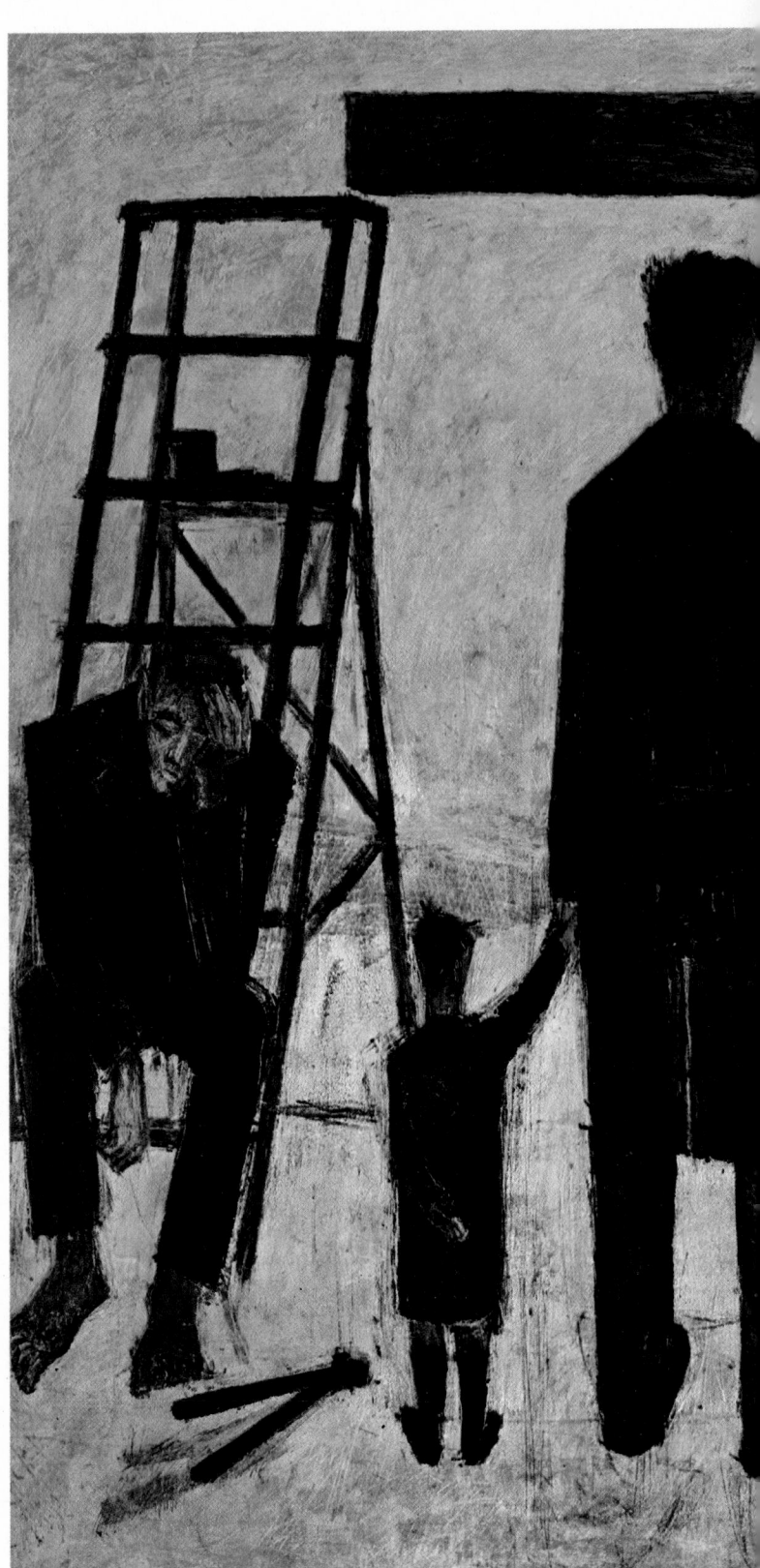

is an even more ferocious restatement of the material in the original triptych of seventeen years earlier. As Bacon once remarked to an interviewer: "One always loves the story and the sensation to be cut down to its most elemental state. That's how one longs for one's friends to be, isn't it? One can do so much without the padding" (quoted by Lawrence Gowing, in *The Irrefutable Image*, Marlborough Fine Art, London, 1968).

Yet, despite the professed search for essentials, the unprejudiced spectator will also detect in many of Bacon's works an element of rhetoric—a rhetoric of suffering, instantly recognizable, and not always, it seems, completely justified by the subject-matter. Bacon's paintings, when they first stunned the public, seemed to speak with a universal accent, and to find a form for what many people felt about the devastated world which surrounded them. As his career has progressed, he has come to seem more and more isolated, and his images are now almost claustrophobically special and personal. Great artist as he undoubtedly is, the main line of development in post-war European art does not run through him.

We are closer to the roots when we look at the work of two Paris-based painters of considerably lesser stature: Fautrier and Wols. In 1945, Jean Fautrier, who was already an established painter, exhibited his series of *Otages* at the René Drouin Gallery (Plate 72). These were inspired by the faces of the hostages whom the artist had seen being taken out to be shot during the war. Fautrier was by inclination an abstractionist—he had painted his first abstracts as early as 1928—and, in order to cope with his chosen subject matter, he had devised a technique which would be simultaneously abstract and figurative. It partook of the "psychic improvisation" pioneered by the Surrealists but contained other elements as well. Among these was an interest in child art, and a sophisticated appreciation of archaeology—a taste later to be popularized by André Malraux's propaganda for the concept of the *musée imaginaire*, or imaginary museum. The perhaps surprising thing about Fautrier's work was its consistently luxurious texture, which seemed to contradict its tragic subject-matter. Fautrier was one of the

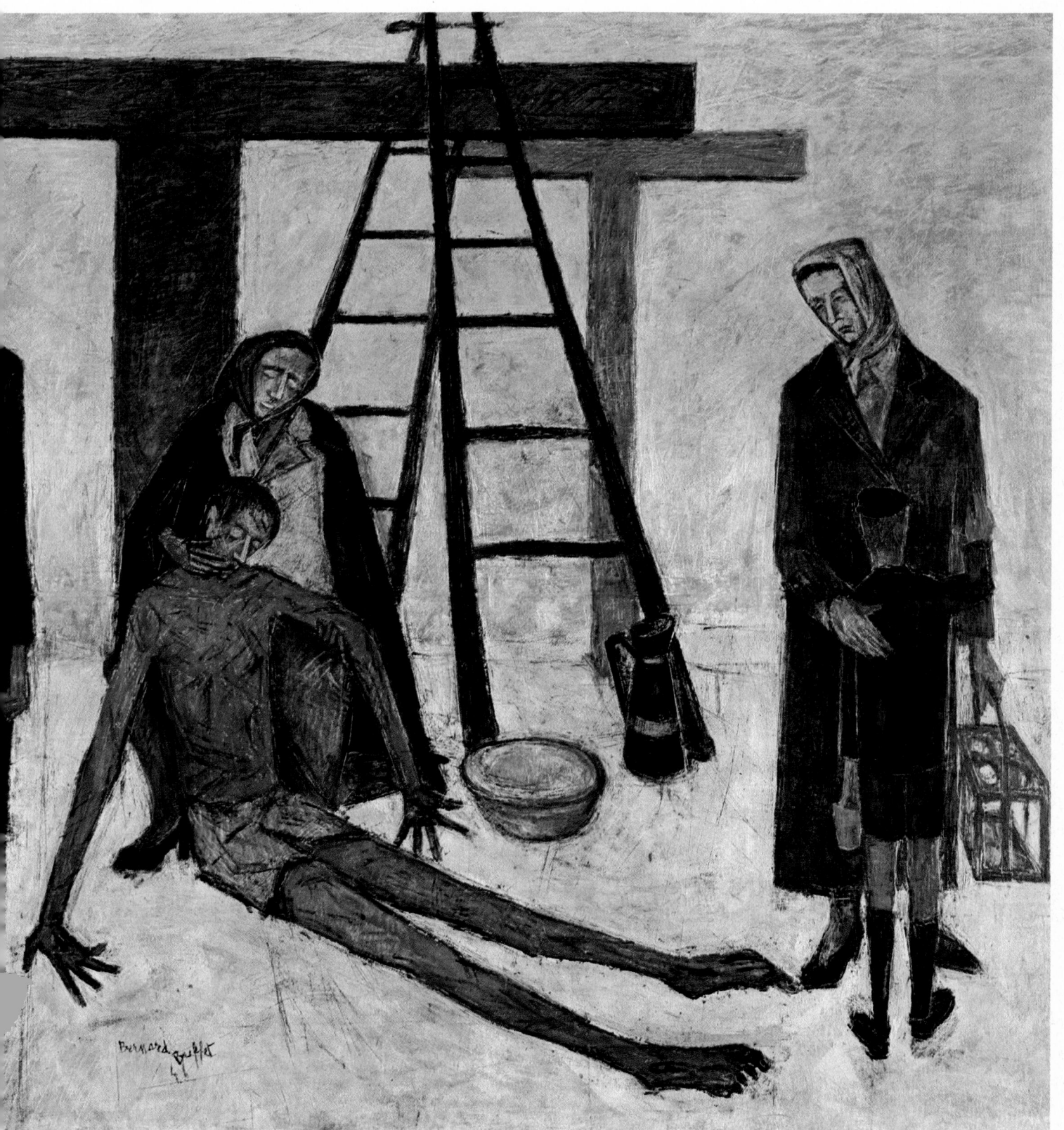

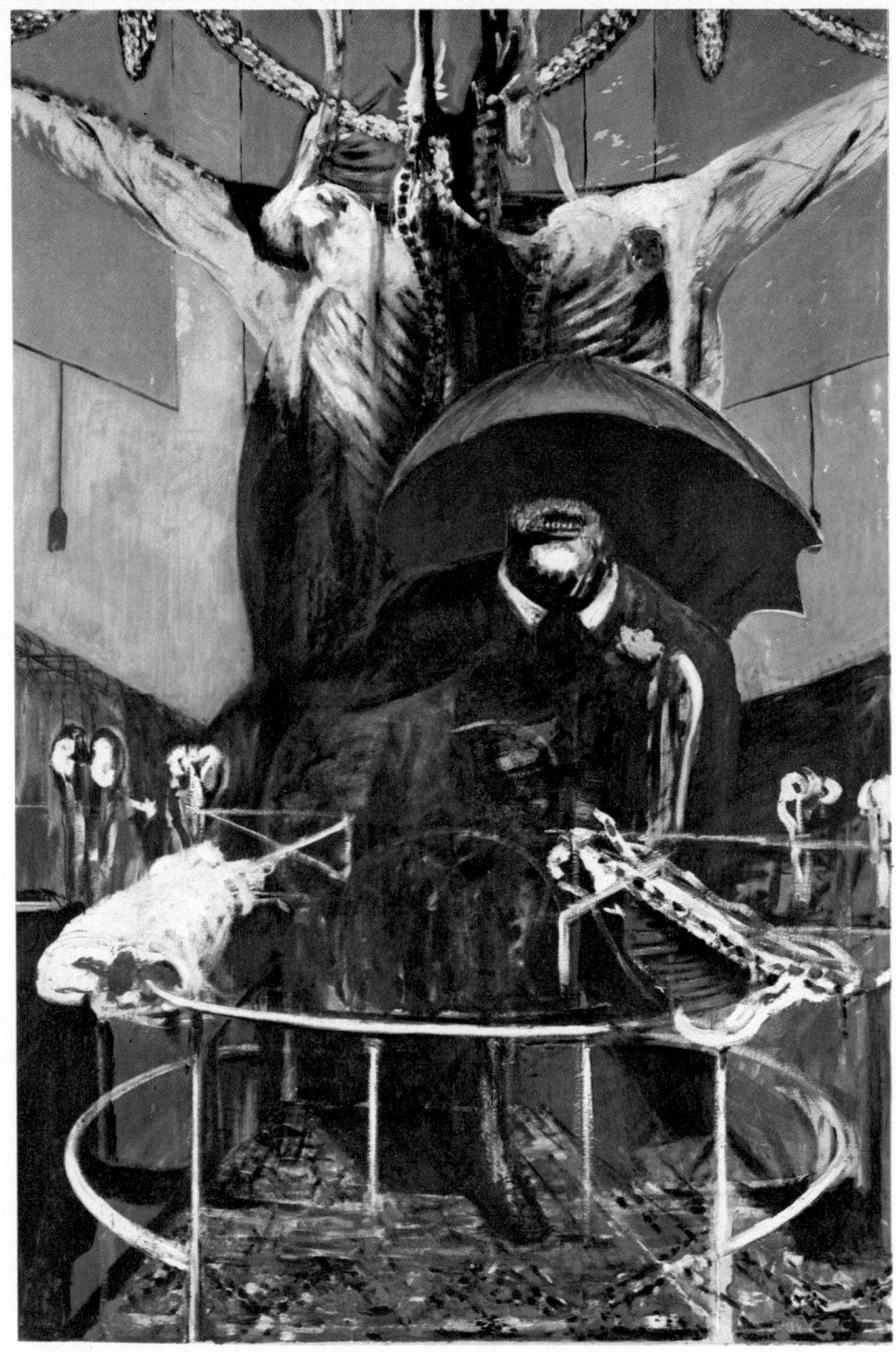

pioneers of the so-called *haute pâte* technique, which was to attract so many European abstractionists during the decade which followed. *Haute pâte* became a logical extension of the long-established French predilection for a sensual, painterly surface.

"Wols" was the pseudonym of a German artist, Wolfgang Schultze. He had studied briefly at the Bauhaus under Mies van der Rohe, in the early Thirties, and had moved to Paris in 1932, when the

68.
Francis Bacon
Painting
1946; 196.8 × 132.1 cm. (77 × 52 in.)
New York, Museum of Modern Art

69. Opposite
Francis Bacon
Lying Figure No. 3
1959; 198.5 × 142 cm. (77 × 55 in.)
Düsseldorf, Kunstammlung Nordrhein-Westfalen

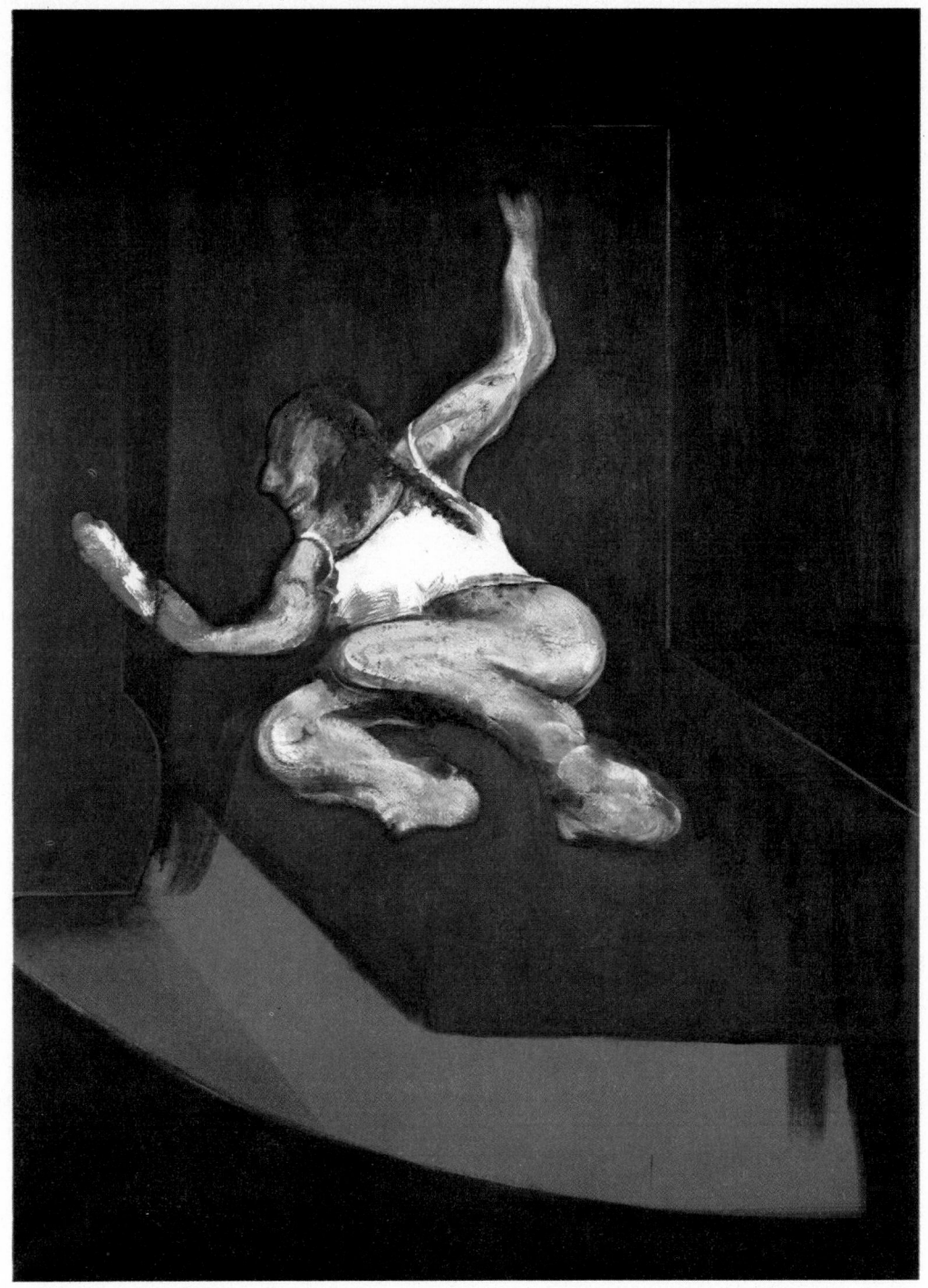

situation began to deteriorate in Germany. There he became an associate of the Surrealists, but worked as a photographer. It took a spell of internment during the war to turn him first into a draftsman, then into a painter. He then became linked to the new group of Existentialist philosophers and writers, led by Jean-Paul Sartre; and he, too, had a successful show at the Drouin Gallery in 1945.

The striking thing about Wols's work is its spontaneous, scribbled calligraphy. He was working on lines parallel to those of the American Abstract Expressionists at a time when their work was still unknown in Europe (1949). But Wols's influence was more than a merely technical one. In his own life he revived the Romantic idea of the artist as a doomed soul, condemned to being devoured by his art. He died in 1951.

Fautrier and Wols heralded the birth of European *tachisme*, a style which was to enjoy a

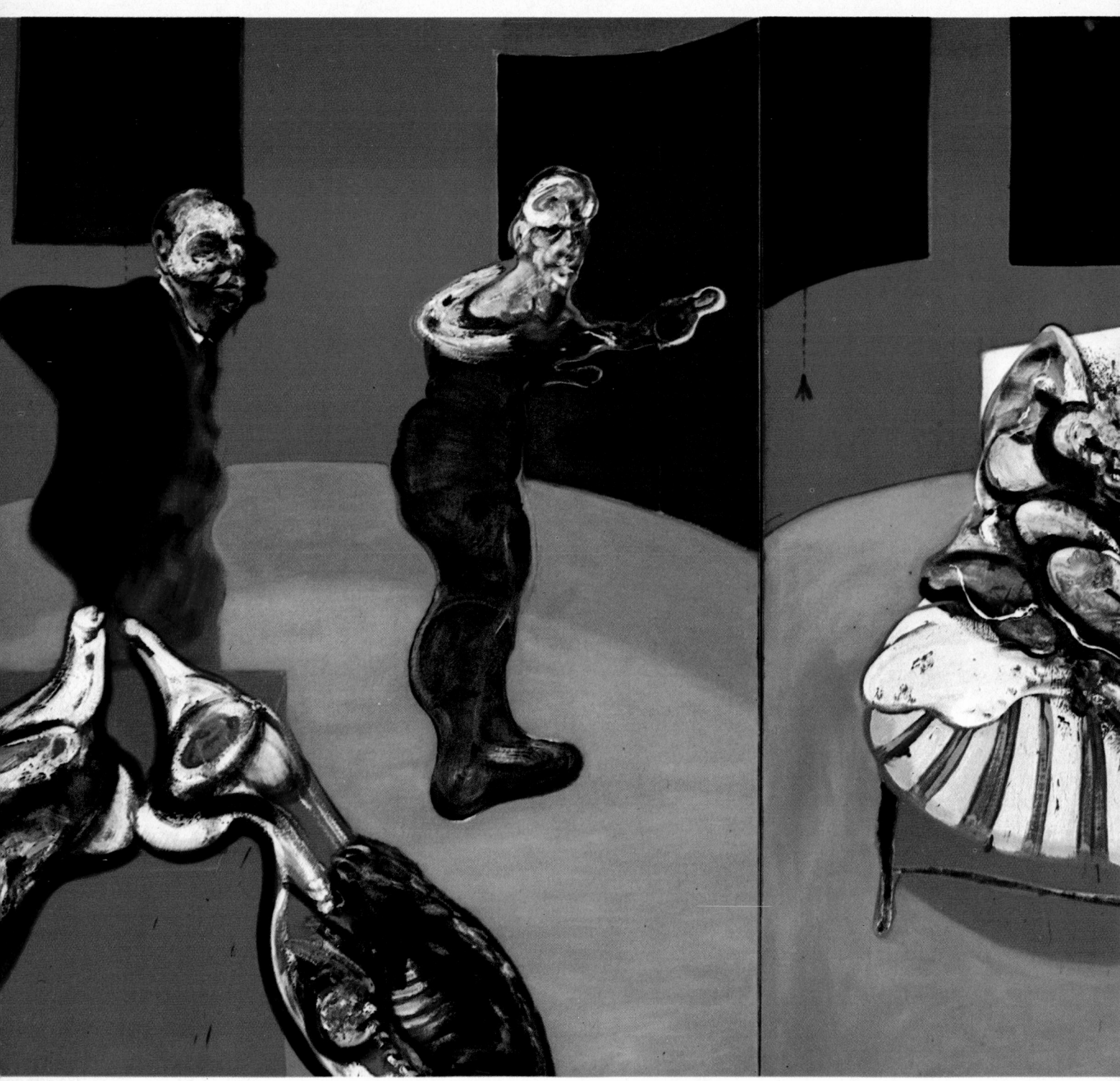

huge critical and financial success before it was eclipsed by the rise of Pop Art. The painters associated with this phase of Modernism are currently very difficult to assess, so completely has much recent critical opinion rejected them. Their downfall has also been intimately connected with the decline in prestige of Paris as an international art centre.

70.
Francis Bacon
Three Studies for a Crucifixion
1962; 198.1 × 434.3 cm. (77 × 169 in.)
New York, Solomon R. Guggenheim Museum

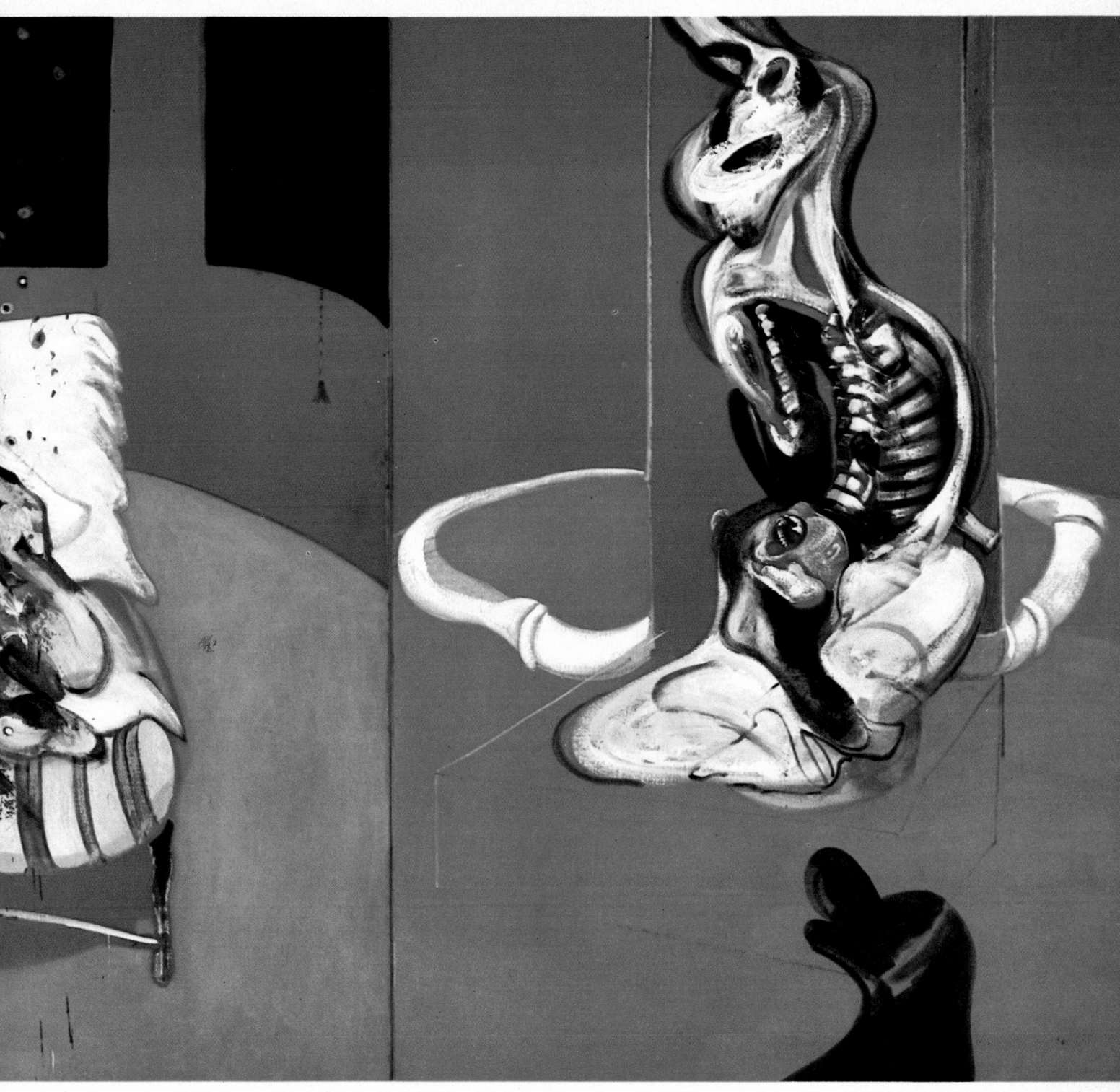

One of the most typical of European *tachistes* is Georges Mathieu. High claims have been made for Mathieu, even comparatively recently. Werner Haftmann, one of the most respected of the historians of Modernism, wrote of him as follows: "There are three concepts which return regularly and give a certain continuity to his work: *le jeu, la fête, le sacré*. It is round this triad of the playful, the festive and the sacred that his imagination plays. . . . [F]aced with the liberating emptiness of the canvas, he covered it with fleeting arabesques like personal signatures which, if the paintings succeeded, left behind a splendid and audacious pattern which represented his liberation from *angst*. It is this aspect of his painting which makes it like some grand decorative scheme, but it

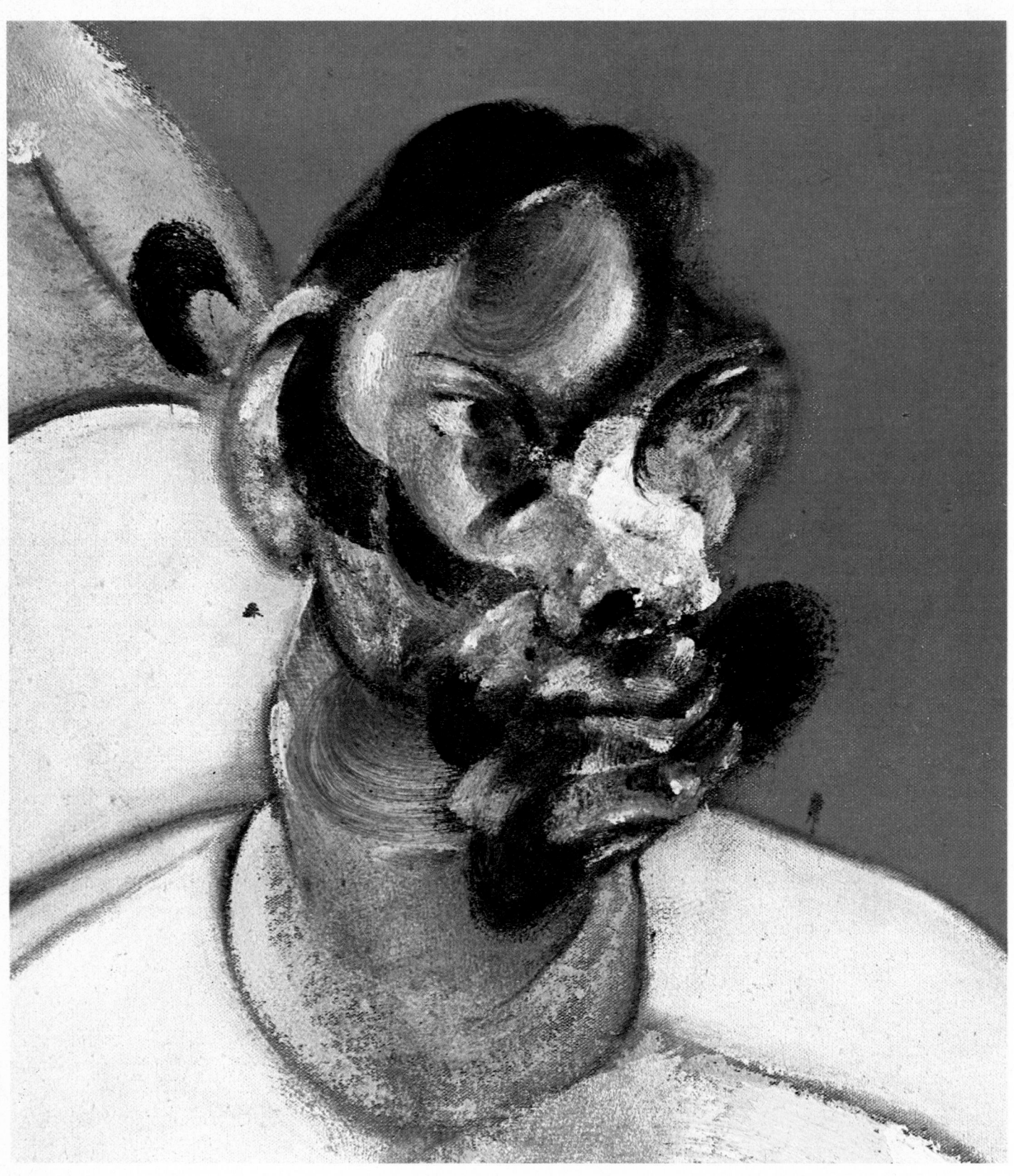

71.
Francis Bacon
Double Portrait of Lucien Freud and Frank Auerbach, detail
1964; 165 × 287 cm. (64 × 112 in.)
Stockholm, Moderna Museet

72. Opposite
Jean Fautrier
Tête d'Otage No. 1
1943; 35 × 27 cm. (14 × 11 in.)
Varese, coll. Giuseppe Panza di Biumo

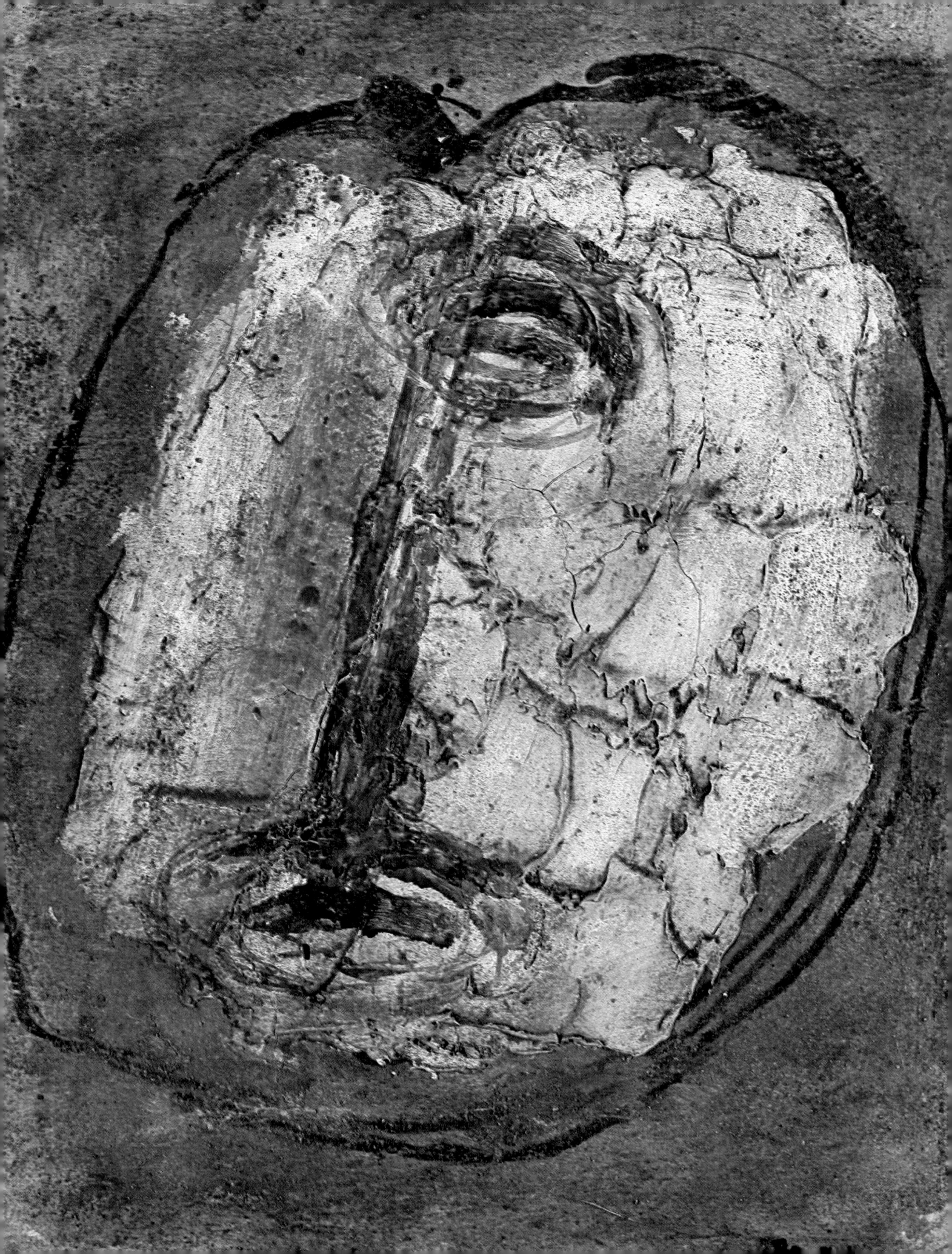

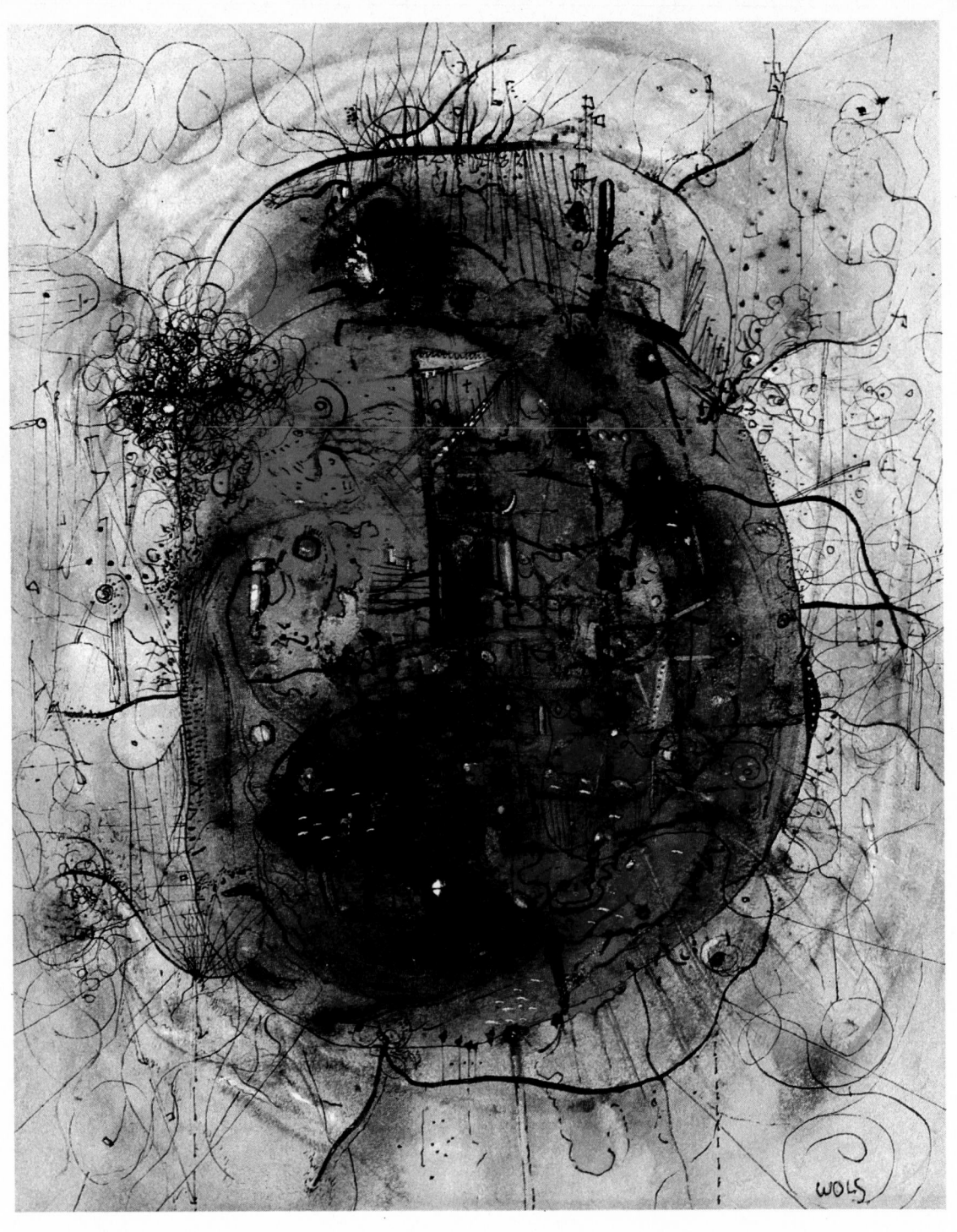

73.
Wols (Alfred Otto Wolfgang Schulze)
Composition V
1946; 15.9 × 12.3 cm. (6 × 5 in.)
Paris, Musée National d'Art Moderne

74. Opposite
Wols (Alfred Otto Wolfgang Schulze)
Painting
1944–45; 79.7 × 80 cm. (31 × 31 in.)
New York, Museum of Modern Art,
gift of Dominique and John de Menil

75. Overleaf
Georges Mathieu
Composition in Red on Brown
1952; 129.5 × 195.6 cm. (51 × 76 in.)
Connecticut, coll. Mr. and Mrs. Burton Tremaine

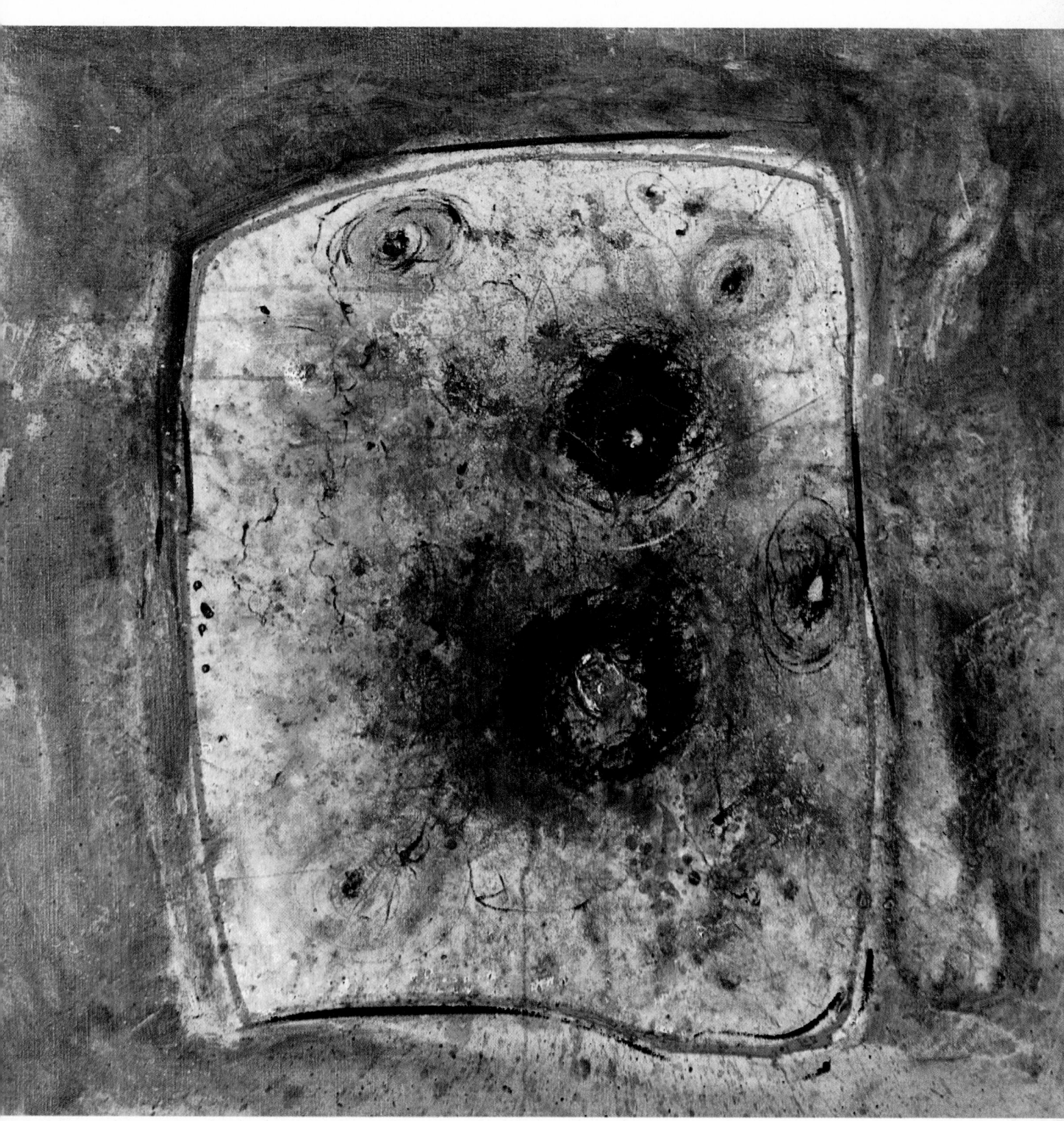

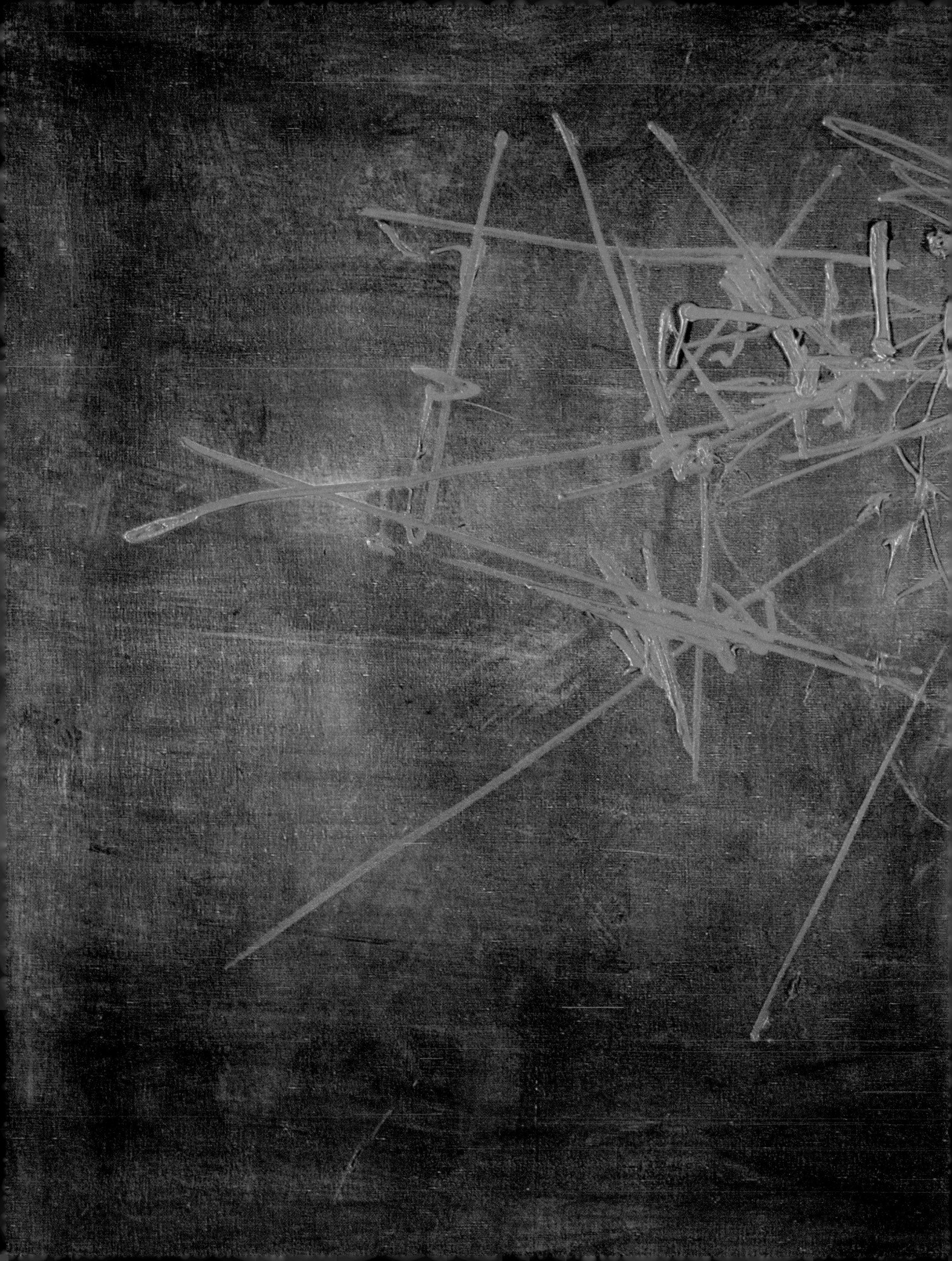

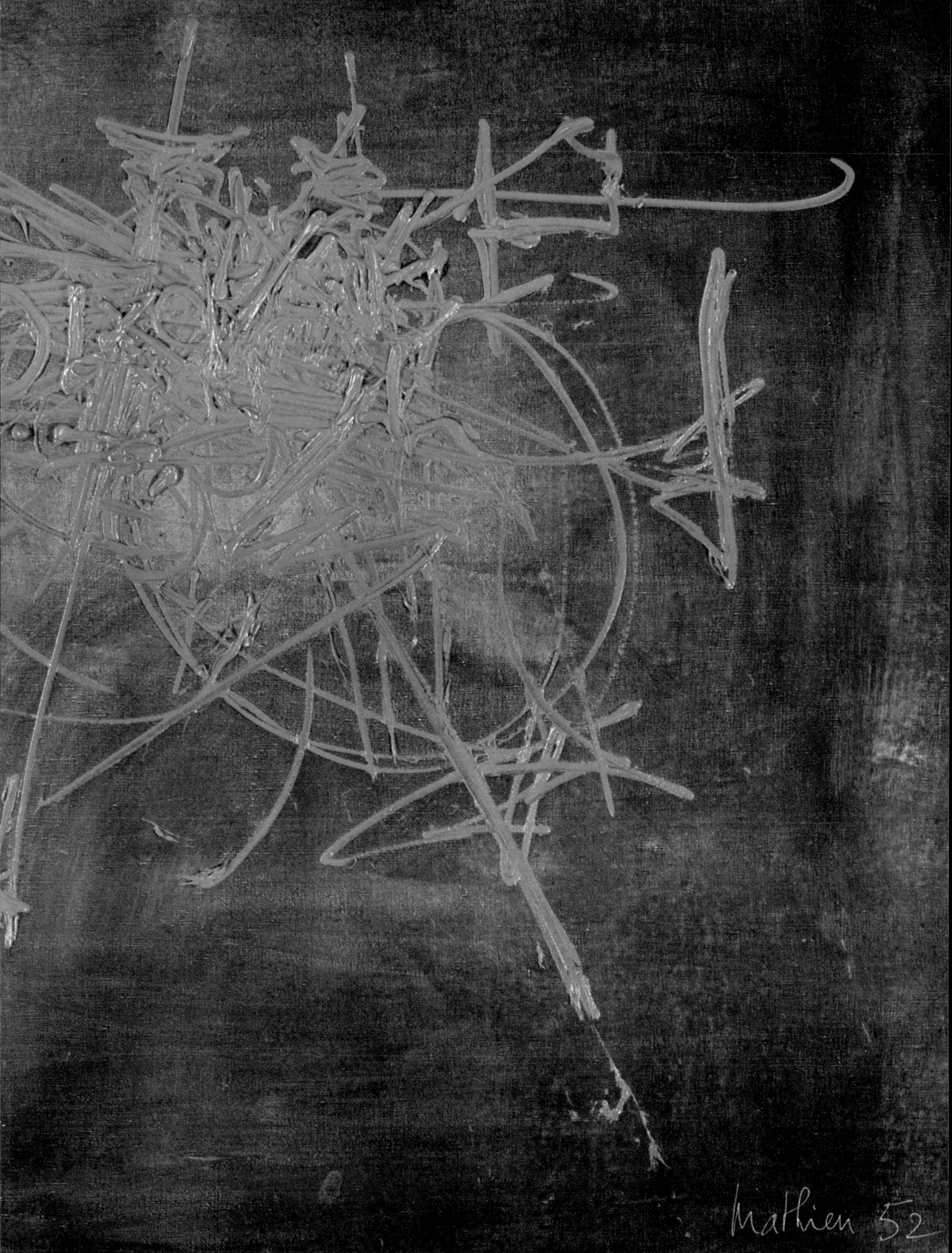

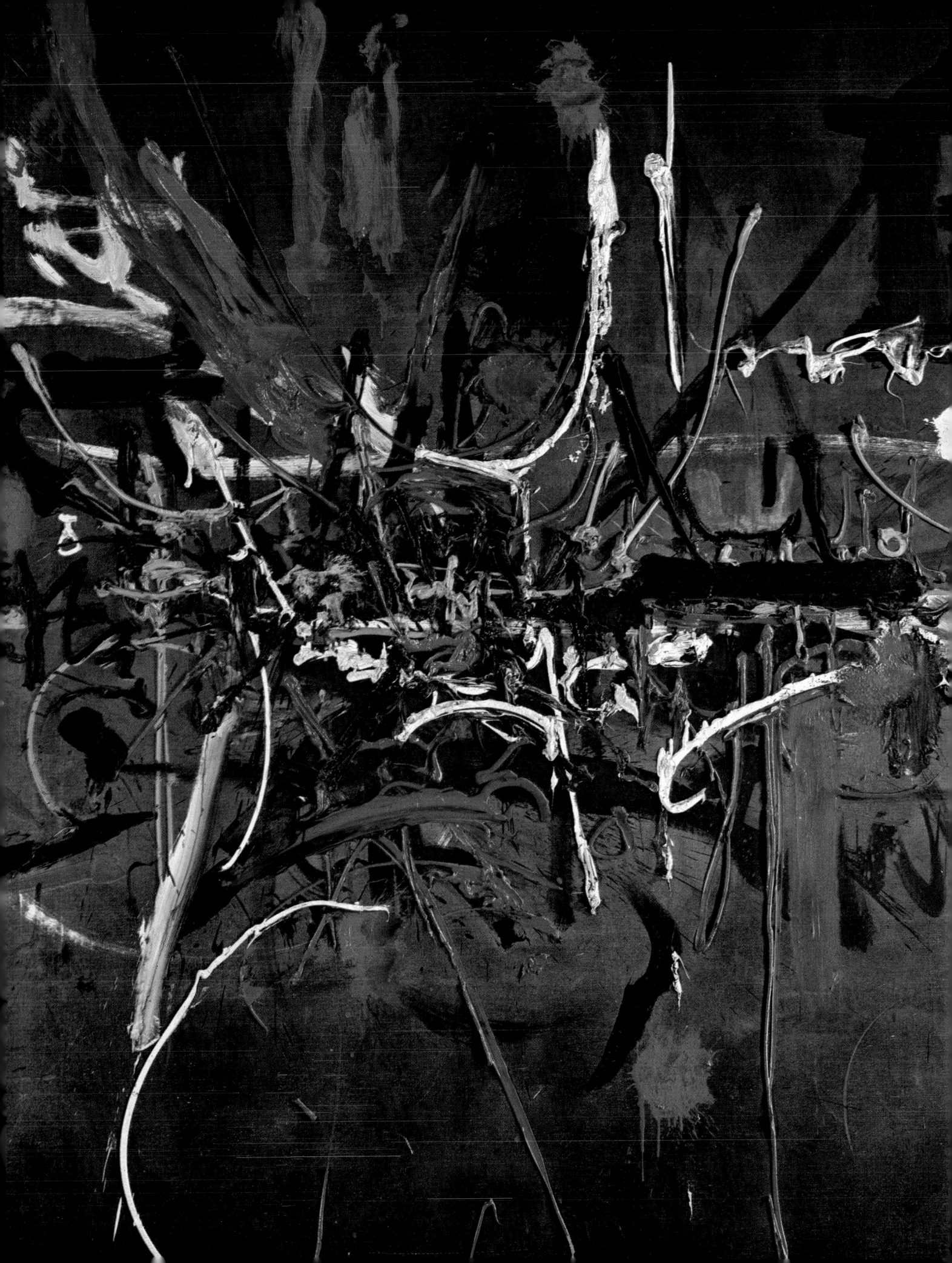

nevertheless retains its own peculiar meditative quality. It is rather like the painting of the age of Louis XIV which Mathieu so much admired" (Werner Haftmann, "Master of Gestural Abstraction", *Abstract Art Since 1945*, London, 1971, p. 48).

This summary does at least have the merit not only of telling us a good deal about the appearance of Mathieu's most typical paintings, but also of suggesting, if only between the lines, why severe criticism has been levelled at his work. Mathieu's art is in fact decorative, but in a perjorative sense. When we compare a large Mathieu (Plate 75) to a Pollock on the same scale, the former seems both superficial and inflated. Mathieu has spoken of an "intrinsic autonomy" as being "the only quiddity possible for the work of art in its relation with its own existence." But in his own work this autonomy all too often seems like mere egotism.

Mathieu's real importance lies not in his personal achievement as a painter, but in his function as an *animateur*. He was one of the first Europeans to realize the importance of the new American art, when actual specimens of this began to make their appearance in Europe in 1947—the year in which the Galerie Maeght in Paris showed work by Gottlieb and Baziotes. He was also eager to explore the resources of Oriental calligraphy and led other European painters to share his interest in this. Finally, he was an effective showman, capable of painting a huge painting on stage in a theatre, before an invited audience, as an attempted justification of his "aesthetic of speed".

Nineteen forty-seven was an important year for the growth of what came to be called Lyrical Abstraction. Jean Atlan exhibited with Maeght, and Hans Hartung at the Lydia Conti Gallery. Pierre Soulages made an impact with a canvas in typical style at the Salon des Surindépendants in the same year. There seemed to be some reason for critics to hail the rebirth of the prewar Ecole de Paris as a dominant force on the international art scene.

Of the three painters I have just mentioned, Soulages (Plate 77) is perhaps the one who currently seems the most impressive. The pattern of heavy black calligraphy is more than a little reminiscent of Kline, but one senses in Soulages' work a more profound respect for traditional methods of composing a picture, as well as a more succulent approach to the actual paint.

Hartung (Plate 78) is a desperately monotonous artist, with his seldom-varied formula of bundled sheaves of lines. Atlan (Plate 79) is eclectic rather than monotonous, striving to bring together Surrealist elements and Expressionist ones, morphological transformations with a lingering attachment to landscape.

Whatever one may think of it now, Lyrical Abstraction was certainly dominant in European painting during the late Forties and throughout the Fifties, and many versions of its basic attitudes were evolved. An artist such as Jean Bazaine (Plate 80) retained elements derived from Cubism in order to try and keep his links with the past. One is aware, too, of the concealed play of natural forms. Nature, lightly disguised, similarly plays her part in typical compositions by Alfred Manessier (Plates 81 and 82), while Manessier's near-namesake Jean Messagier (Plate 83) sometimes produces paintings which look like less successful versions of some of De Kooning's landscapes.

76. Opposite
Georges Mathieu
Les Capétiens Partout, detail
1954; 295 × 600 cm. (115 × 234 in.)
Paris, Musée National d'Art Moderne

77. Overleaf left
Pierre Soulages
Painting
1956; 194 × 129.9 cm. (76 × 51 in.)
New York, Solomon R. Guggenheim Museum

78. Overleaf right
Hans Hartung
Painting 54-16
1954; 130 × 97 cm. (51 × 38 in.)
Paris, Musée National d'Art Moderne

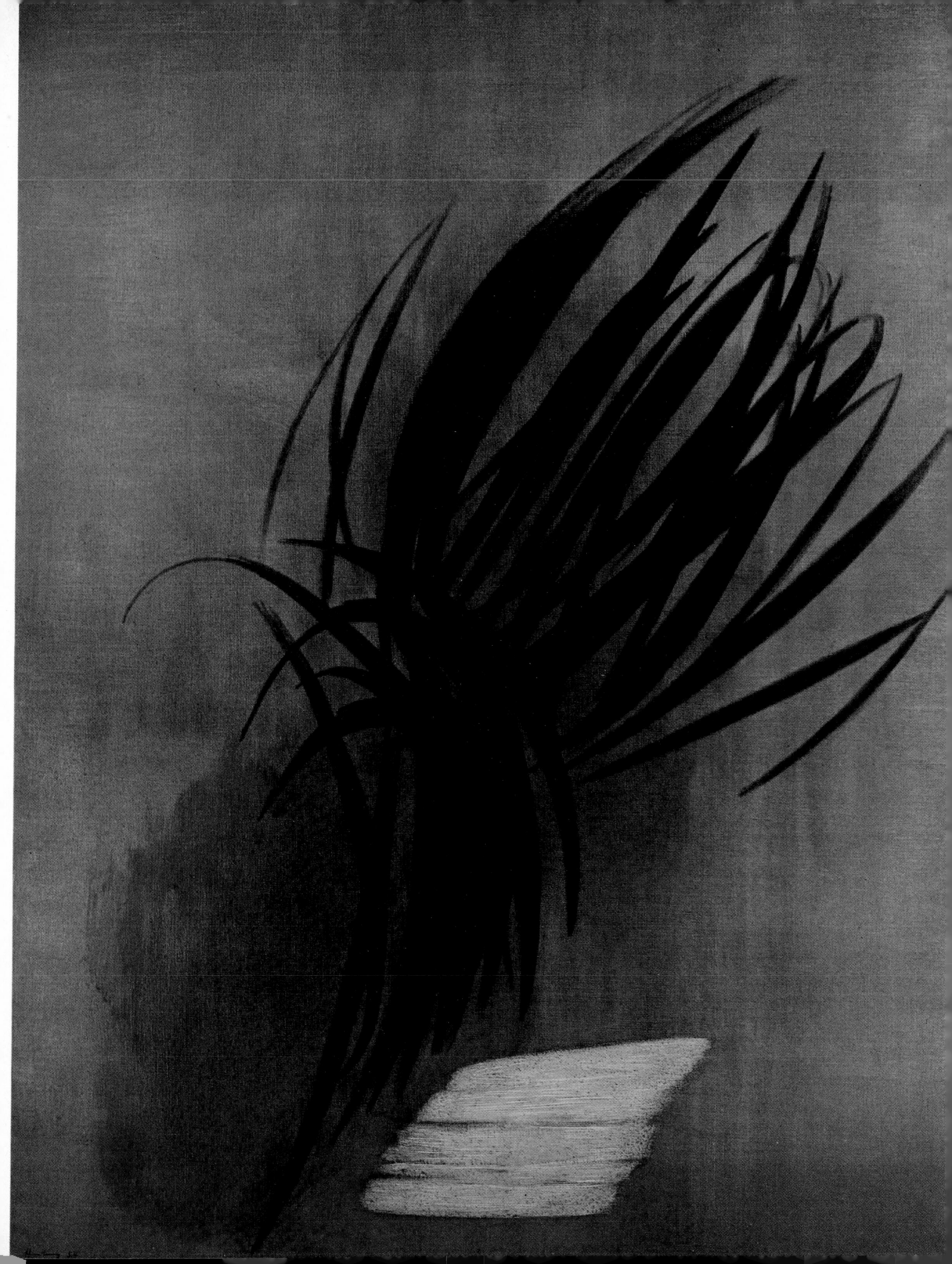

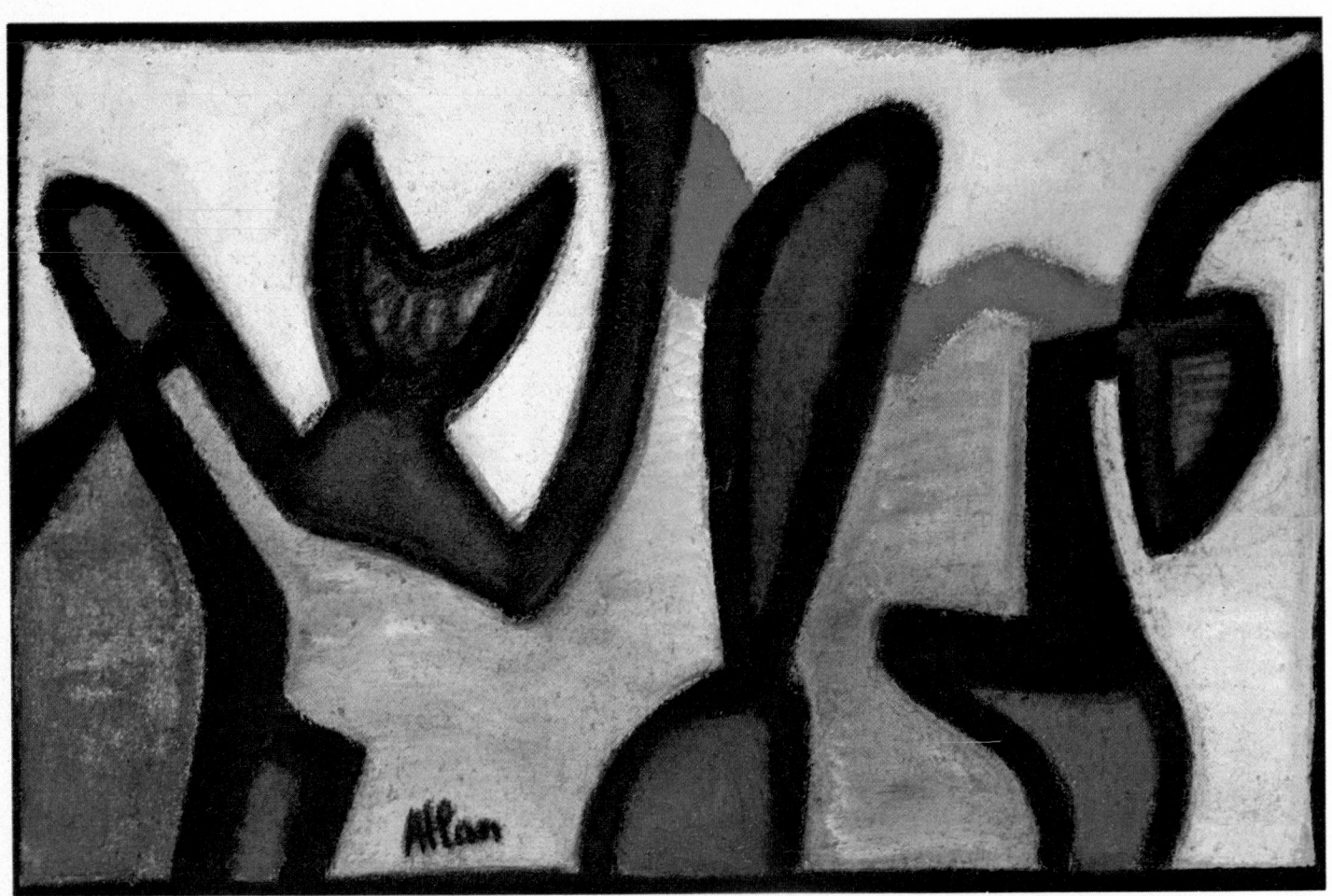

One striking thing about the new school was its internationalism. We find versions of it among artists from all the principal European countries. For Germans such as Willi Baumeister (Plate 84) and E. W. Nay (Plate 85), free abstraction became a statement of liberation from the nightmare of the immediate past. Nay's work is interesting not only as an abstract version of things which had been attempted in figurative painting by the original German Expressionists, but also thanks to the artist's attempt to make freedom systematic through the use of colour disks "with each colour group of disks constituting an unobjective figuration".

We recognize a different kind of national sensibility at work in the paintings of the Franco-Russian painter Serge Poliakoff (Plate 86), where the characteristic colour gamut has affinities with the colour schemes we find in Russian ikons.

Among Italian artists, some felt the traditional pull of Paris. One of these was Emilio Vedova (Plate 87), whose paintings certainly owe a great deal to Wols. Others, among them Giuseppe Capogrossi, were on the very fringes of Lyrical Abstraction, and produced work which was more personal (Plate 88). The appearance of Capogrossi's work has been well described by Roland Penrose: "The individual marks resemble, especially when arranged in series, alphabets in languages that we cannot read, yet the appearance of sequence and order is so strong as to imply the presence of meaning. . . . Capogrossi's pictures are like the bills and accounts of long-dead places . . . the clean, simple finish of his paintings is

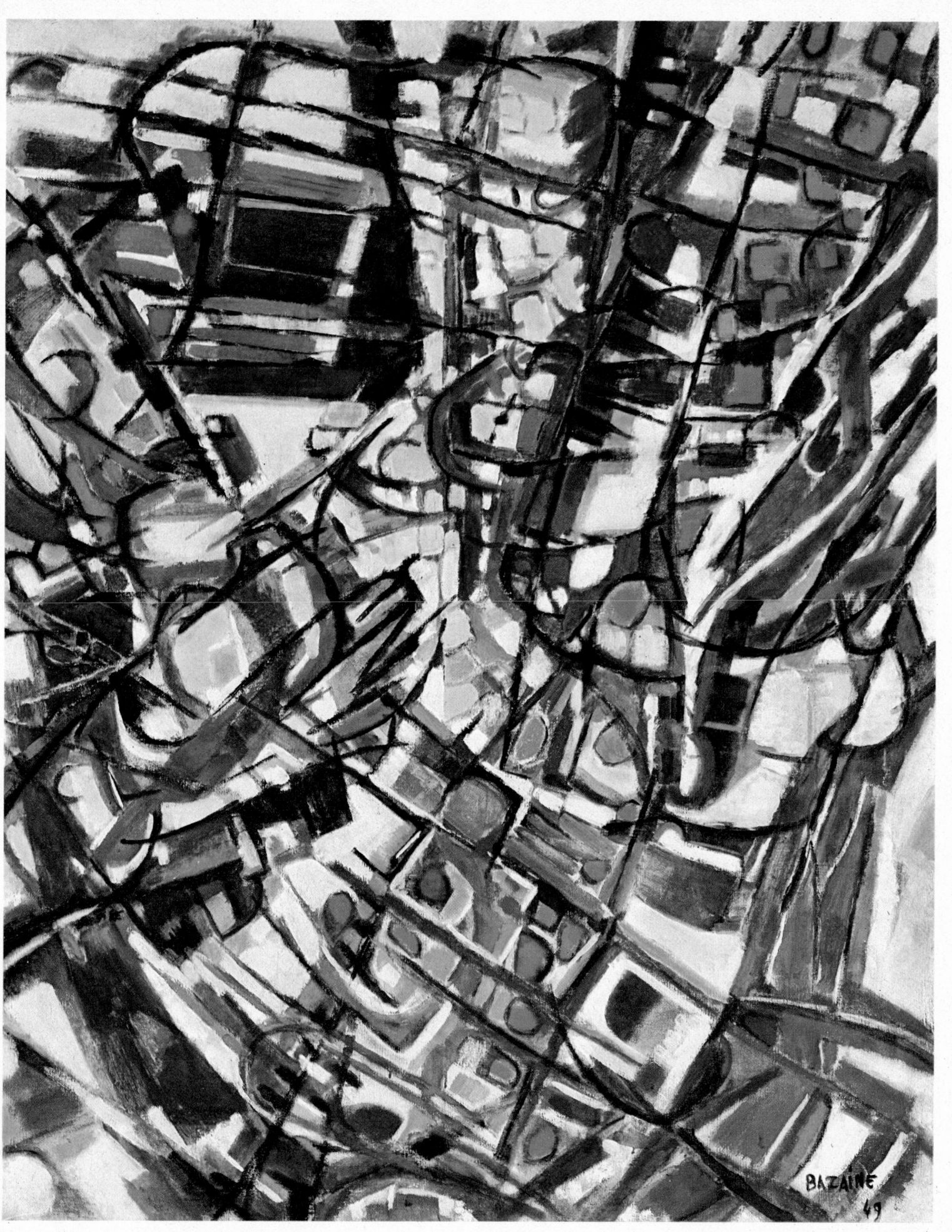

81. Opposite
Alfred Manessier
Nuit de Gethsémani
1952; 198 × 148 cm. (77 × 58 in.)
Düsseldorf, Kunstsammlung Nordrhein-Westfalen

82.
Alfred Manessier
Fire
1957; 80 × 98.5 cm. (31 × 38 in.)
Cologne, Wallraf-Richartz Museum

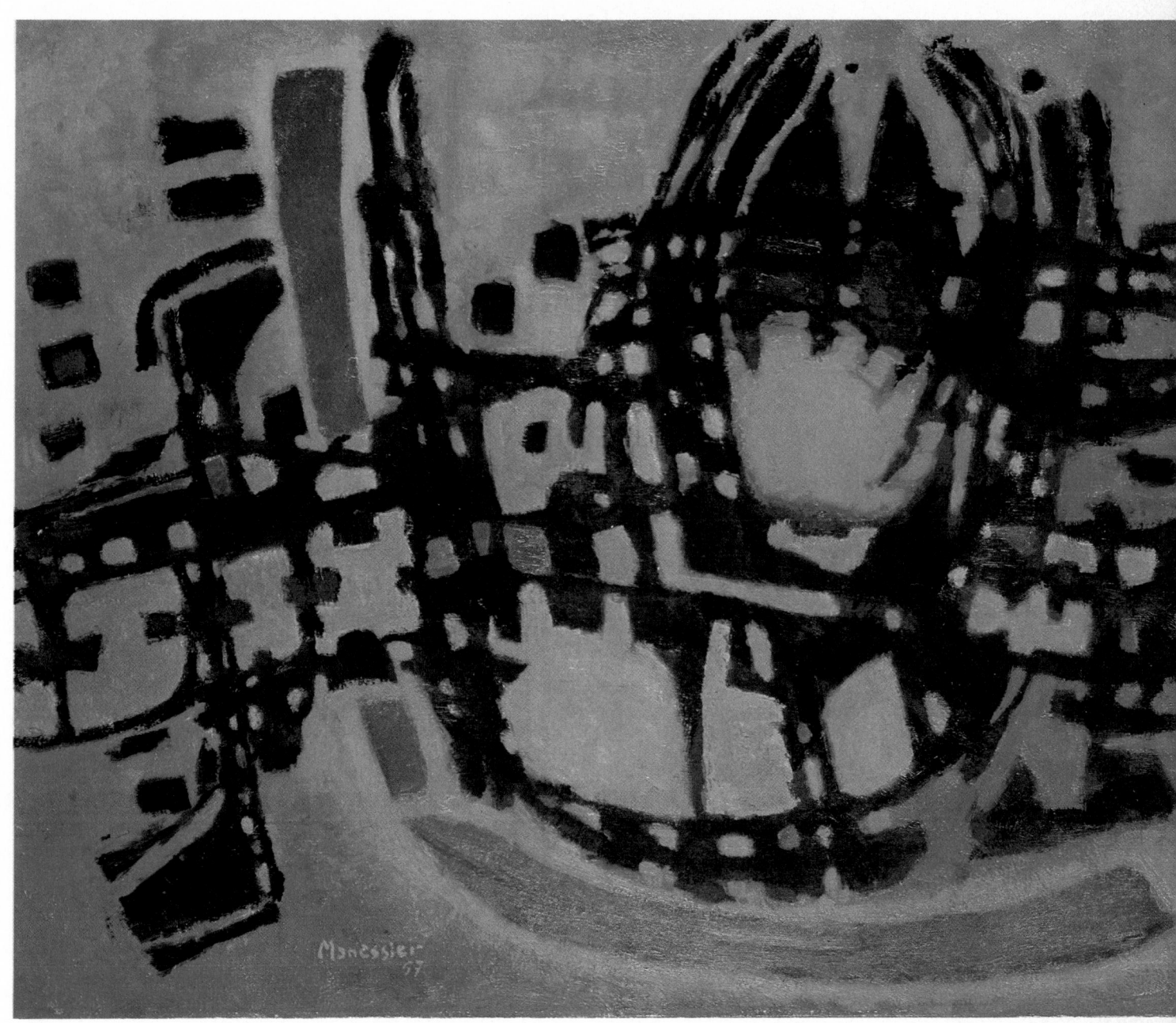

impersonal and contemporary. It is of the same family as a piece of competent packaging, such as we might find in any city" (Roland Penrose, "Giuseppe Capogrossi", introduction to the catalogue of an exhibition at the Institute of Contemporary Arts, London, 1957).

The impersonal look of Capogrossi's work, which Penrose draws to our notice, is in fact one of the things that most sharply marks him off from his contemporaries.

Impersonality was never the aim of the Spanish painters who also began to attract attention during the Fifties, somewhat to the surprise of those who had expected little of interest to emerge from Franco's Spain, the last survivor of the Fascist dictatorships. Some of these painters, such as

115

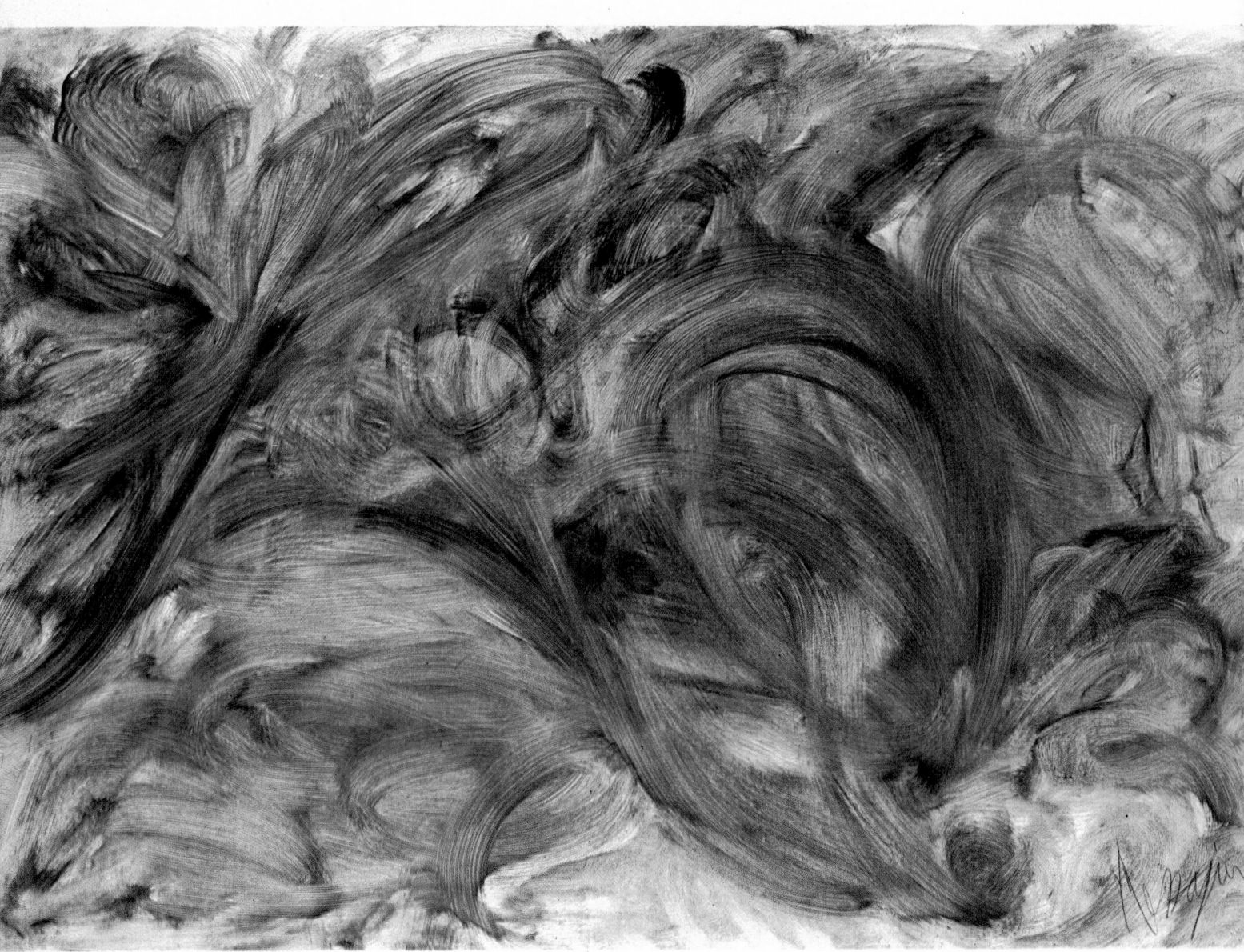

Antonio Saura (Plate 89), soon transferred their activity to Paris, and their work shows the inherent weaknesses which affected their Parisian colleagues, the inflated formlessness to which Lyrical Abstraction could all too easily lead.

One Spanish artist stands head and shoulders above the rest. This is the Catalan painter Antoni Tàpies. Where Lyrical Abstraction for the most part failed, Tàpies was able to show that many of its ideas, if badly executed by others, were not in fact worthless. Comparing a painting by Tàpies to one by a leading American Abstract Expressionist—for example, to the work of Motherwell (doubly relevant because the latter feels a fascination for Spain and things Spanish)—we note the extreme slowness of the rhythms, the patient way in which the work has been evolved: "The corroded surfaces, fissures, and peeled areas convey a sense of stratification, of one level below another, which is rich in evoked antiquity. The

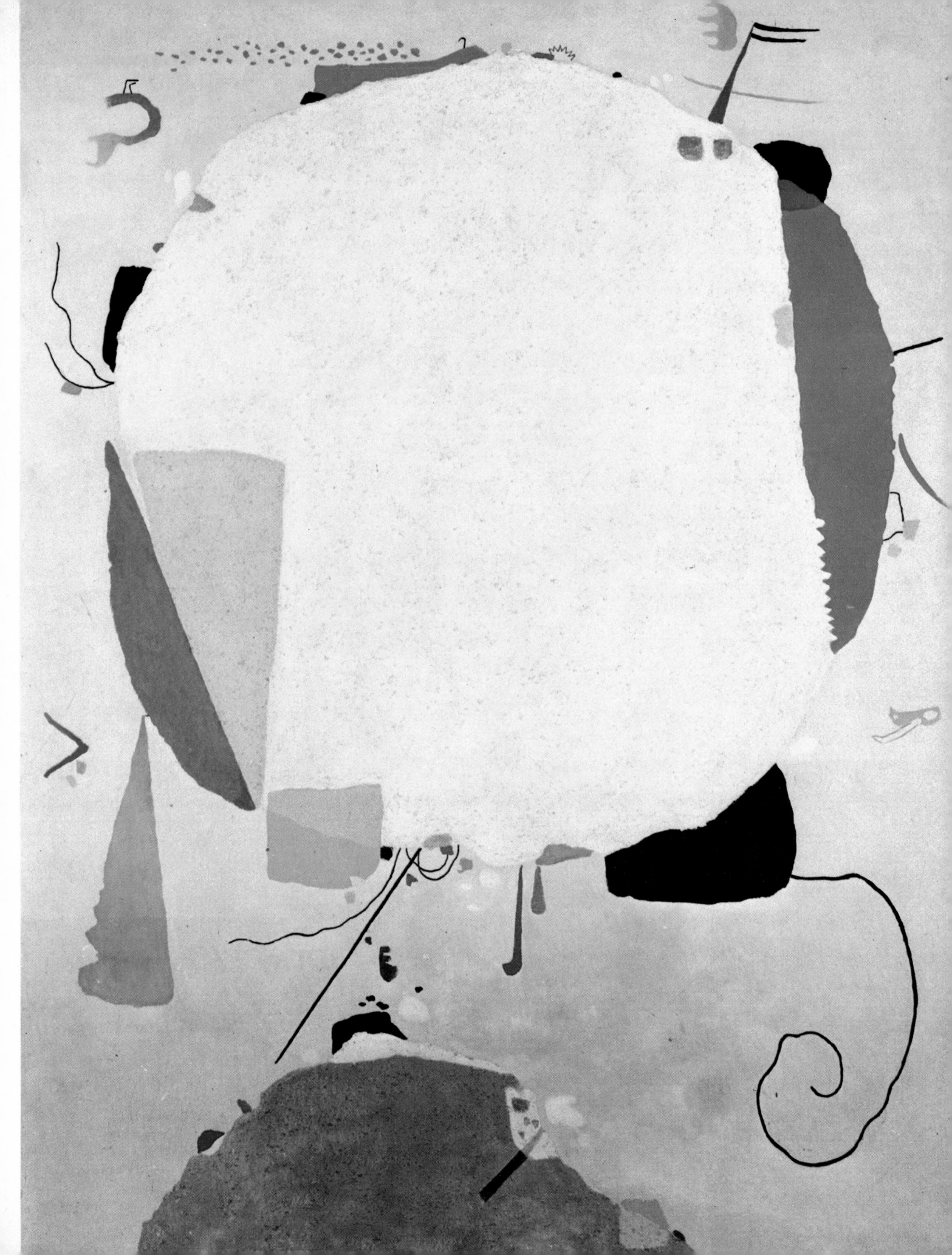

85.
Ernst Wilhelm Nay
Gelbe Scheiben
1954; 60 × 80 cm. (23 × 31 in.)
Cologne, coll. Alfred Otto Müller

86. Opposite
Serge Poliakoff
Composition
1950; 130.5 × 97.2 cm. (51 × 38 in.)
New York, Solomon R. Guggenheim Museum

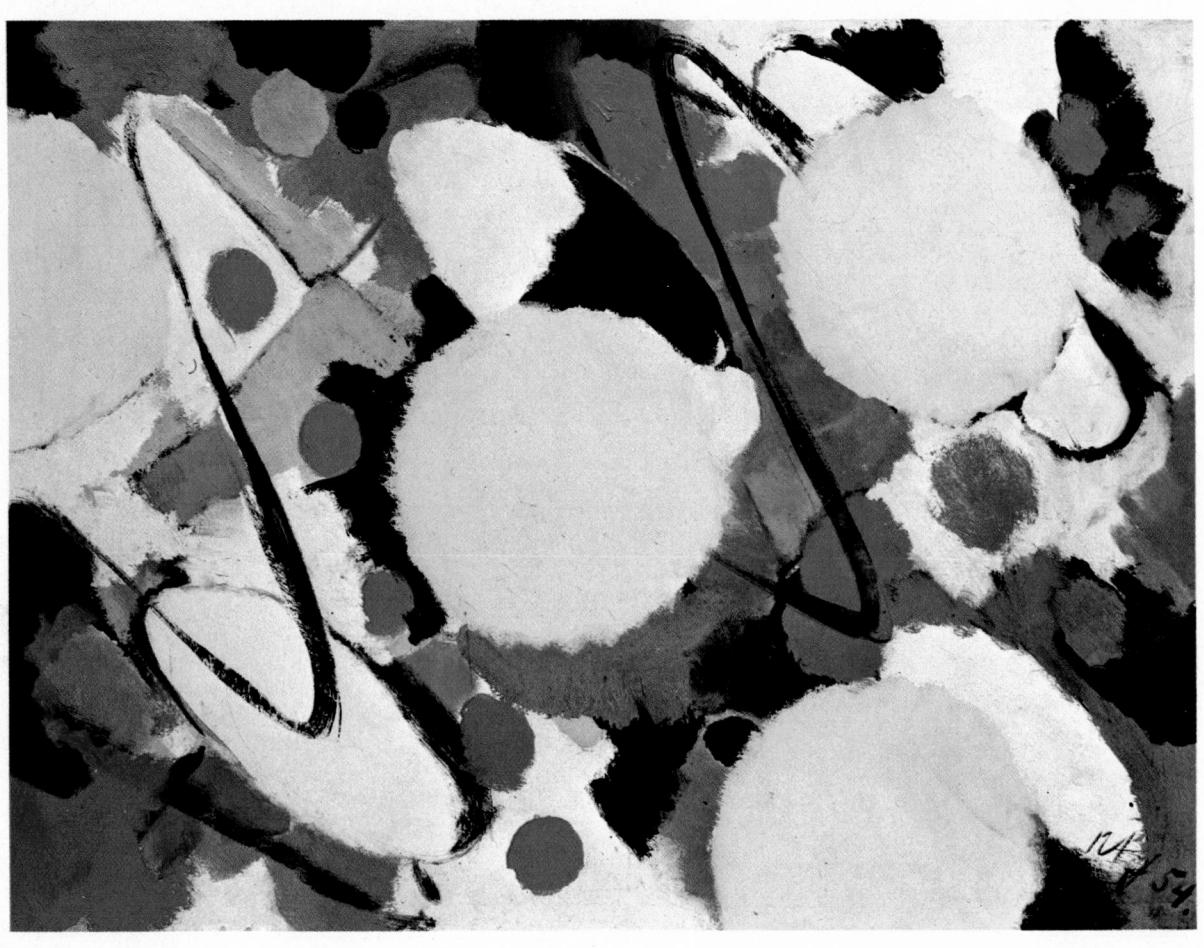

paint surfaces seem worn by a duration greater than that of an individual artist. . . . The processes of the hand as an analogy of time's shaping make elegance a natural result of partial destruction" (Lawrence Alloway, catalogue foreword for the exhibition "Antoni Tàpies", at the Solomon R. Guggenheim Museum, New York, 1962).

The sense of elapsed time in Tàpies' work is indeed very strong, and it is one element that gives his painting its continued power. It is worth comparing his sensitivity in the use of thick paint with the insensitivity of surface which one finds in the work of the French-Canadian artist Jean-Paul Riopelle (Plate 91).

An aspect that today tends to make us mistrust the talent of Riopelle—or of artists such as Mathieu or Hartung for that matter—is their monotony. There seems no reason to prefer one work by the same hand to another, when all are essentially the same. Yet this standardization of the product has certainly contributed to the success of Lyrical Abstraction with collectors. The Fifties witnessed a massive growth in the market for modern art, and for the first time it was abstract art which was favoured. One reason for this was that many artists had evolved a way of painting which was so instantly recognizable that the artist himself became the subject of his picture. One collector, visiting another, would have no trouble in recognizing a work by Hartung, and would feel no need to know its title. A number of collections were formed on the "one of each" principle—by buying a specimen of the work of a whole list of "approved" artists. Another reason was that the style that had evolved from the anguish of the post-war period became, in the hands of the

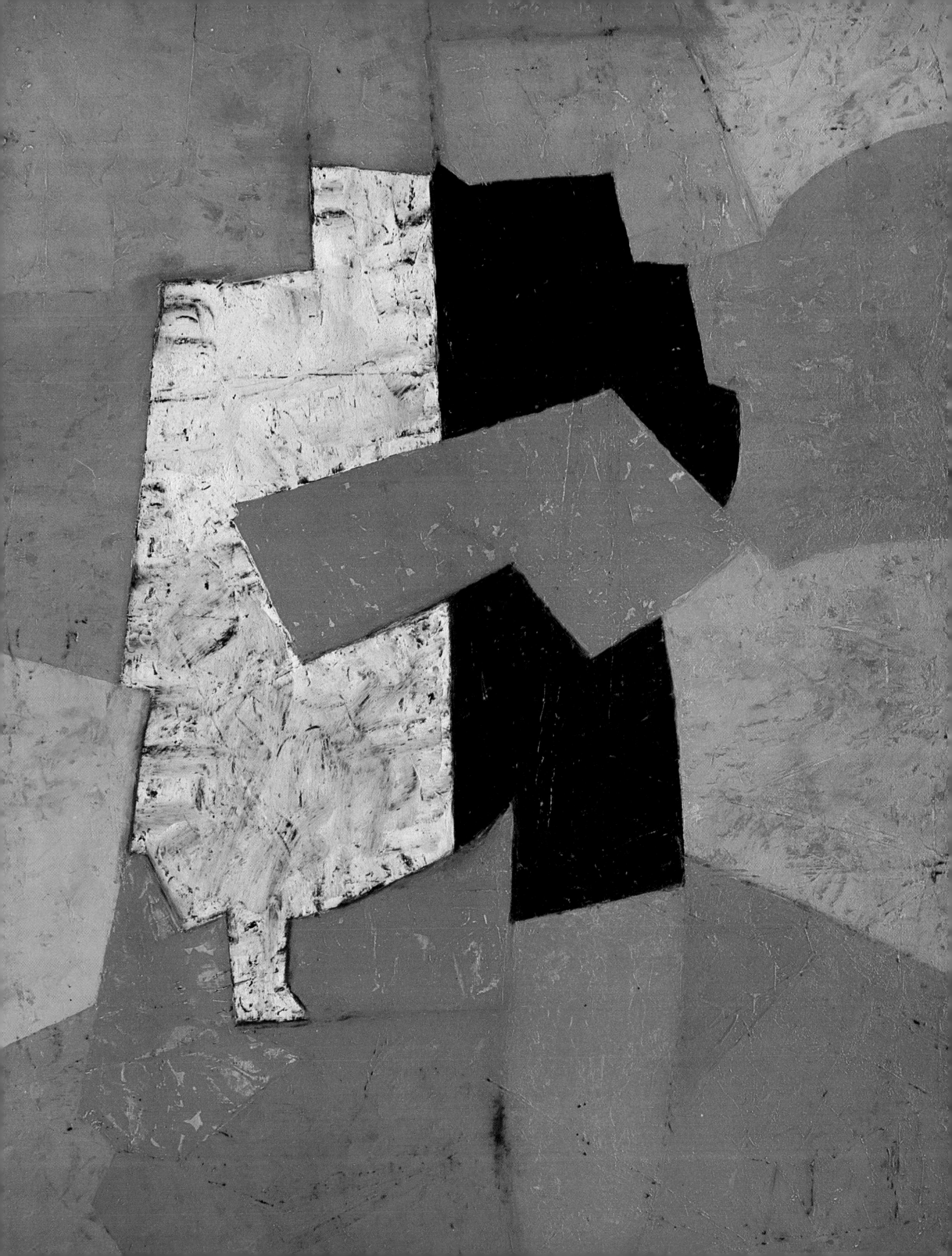

87.
Emilio Vedova
Documenta No. 2
1952; 144.8 × 189.2 cm. (56 × 74 in.)
Wadsworth Atheneum, Connecticut,
gift of Peggy Guggenheim

88. Opposite
Giuseppe Capogrossi
Superficie No. 305
1959; 74 × 61 cm. (29 × 24 in.)
Cologne, coll. Alfred Otto Müller

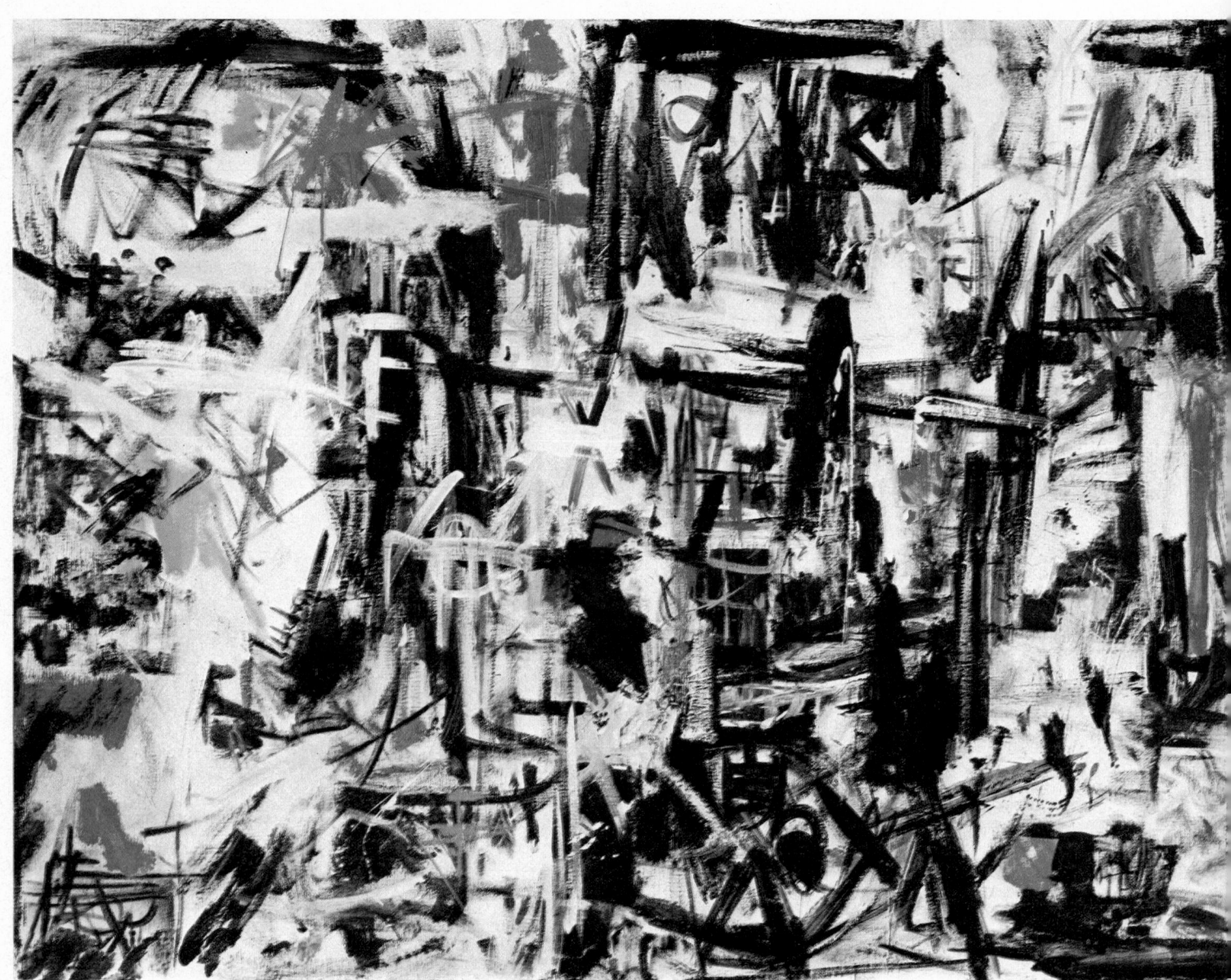

Lyrical Abstractionists, so purely decorative that it caused no discomfort to a clientele grown prosperous in the sudden boom. The opulent paint surface matched the opulence of the context.

Despite the post-war triumph of abstract art, a number of artists were uneasy. They were attracted by the new freedom the painter had received, but were unwilling to surrender the specific entirely. One of these was the Portuguese-born woman artist Vieira da Silva, who had once been a pupil of Léger. Her delicate paintings (Plates 92 and 93) suggest landscapes or townscapes without ever quite being specific about what is being shown. They bear a fascinating resemblance to the kind of work Mondrian produced in the period when he was moving towards total abstraction.

The most important of these painterly but figurative artists is, however, Nicolas De Staël, whom some critics have sought to see as one of the

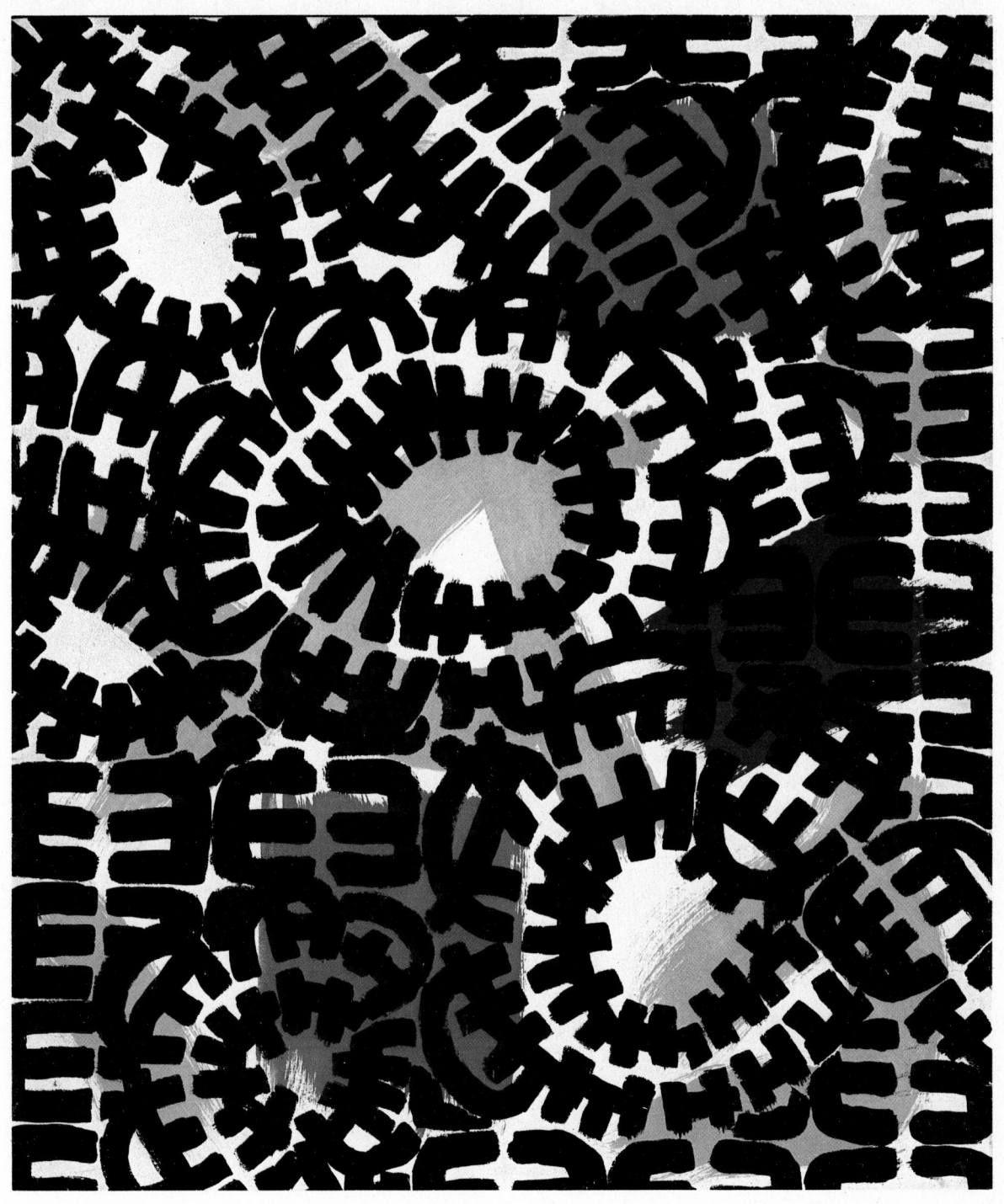

half-dozen most important painters to have made a reputation since the war. De Staël deliberately moved against the prevalent current of his time. A Franco-Russian like Poliakoff, he began his career as an abstractionist, painting first in a geometrical style derived from Synthetic Cubism. Gradually, following the spirit of the time, he began to paint more freely, now making use of coloured blocks and cubes arranged in rhythmic patterns. Even at this stage De Staël's designs often seemed to have hidden figurative connotations, and in 1952 the figuration became specific. De Staël's method was now to paint pictures which had the simplicity and discipline of his abstract work, but which nevertheless resolved themselves, on a second glance, into something recognizable—a figure or a landscape (Plate 94). His great gift was as a colourist. Perhaps no painter of the time showed a greater control of powerful hues. At the end of his life, he wrote to the critic and collector Douglas

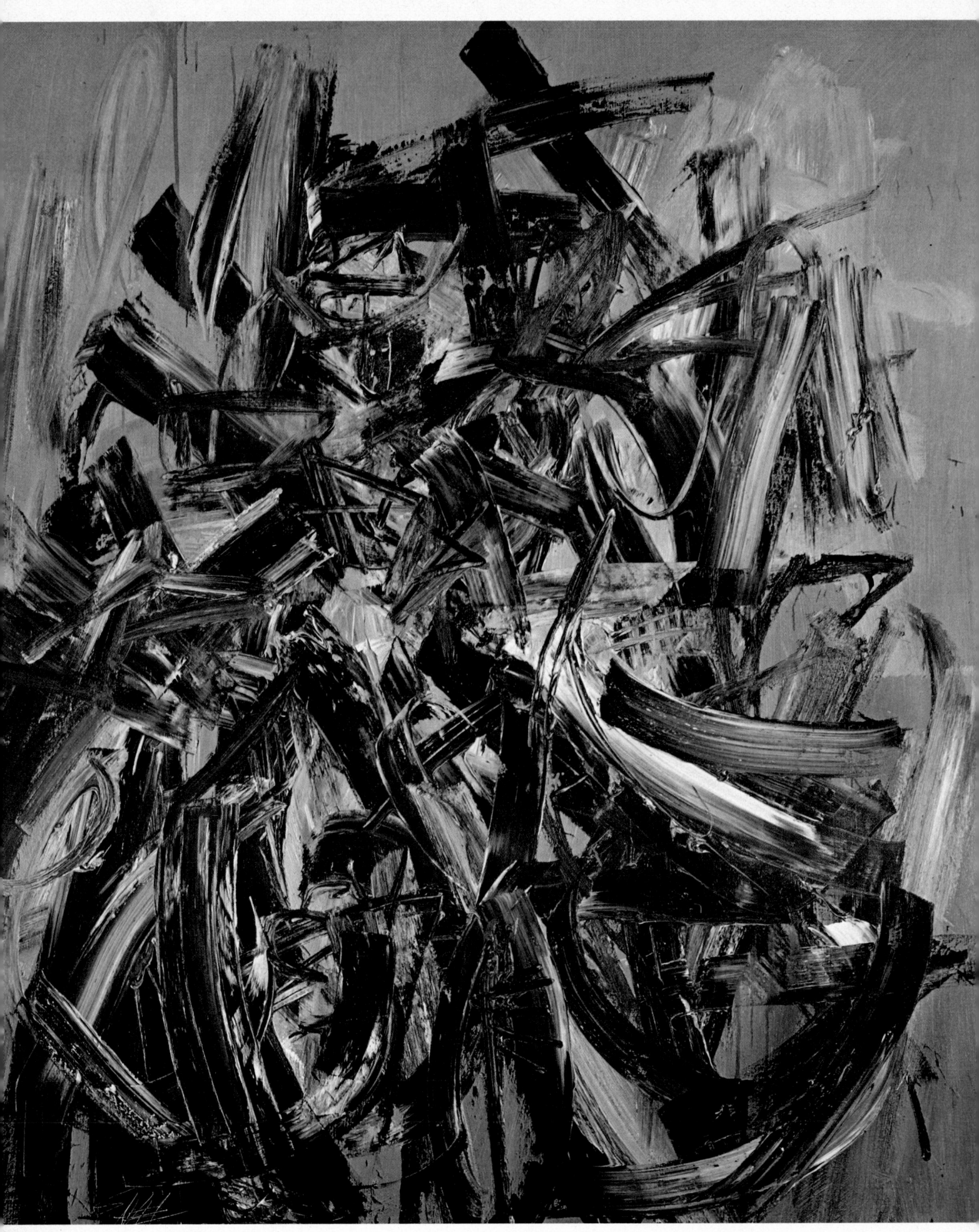

89. Opposite
Antonio Saura
Ingegerd
1958; 412.1 × 130.2 cm. (161 × 51 in.)
Brandeis University, Massachusetts, Rose Art Museum

90.
Antoni Tàpies
Large Painting
1958; 200.7 × 260.7 cm. (78 × 102 in.)
New York, Solomon R. Guggenheim Museum

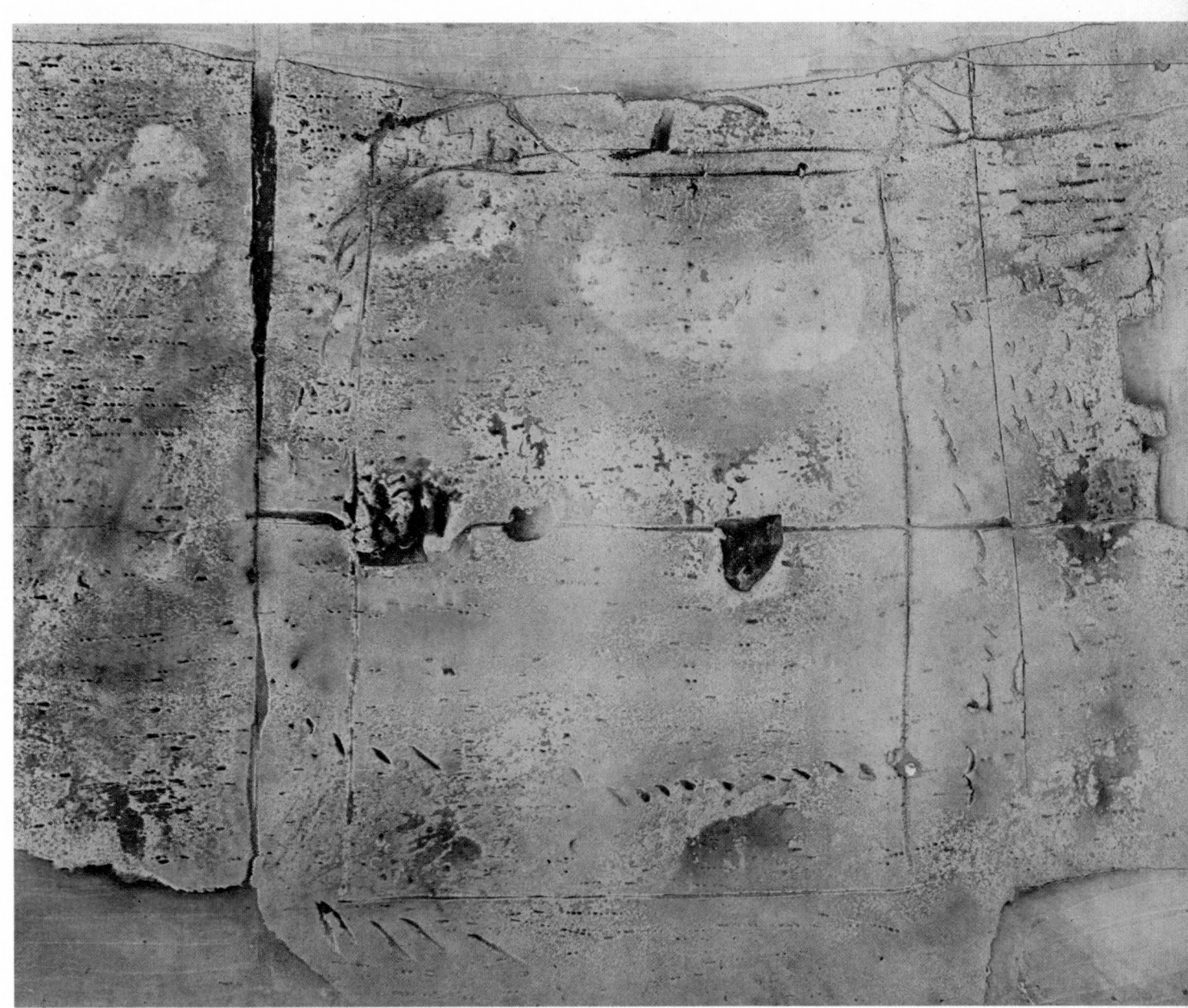

Cooper: "The harmonies have to be strong, subtle, very subtle, the values direct, indirect, or even inverse values. What matters is that they should be true. That always. But the more the approach to this differs from one picture to another, the more absurd the way of achieving it seems, the more interested I am in pursuing it!"

It is possible to detect in this declaration, so apparently confident on the surface, a note of uncertainty. De Staël was pursuing not a synthesis of abstraction and figuration, but an impossible compromise—a method of painting which would give the finished canvas the acceptability of the figurative, and the new respectability which belonged to abstraction. His suicide, though ultimately attributable to personal tragedies, was also a response to an impasse in his work.

Of all the painters of the French school who

123

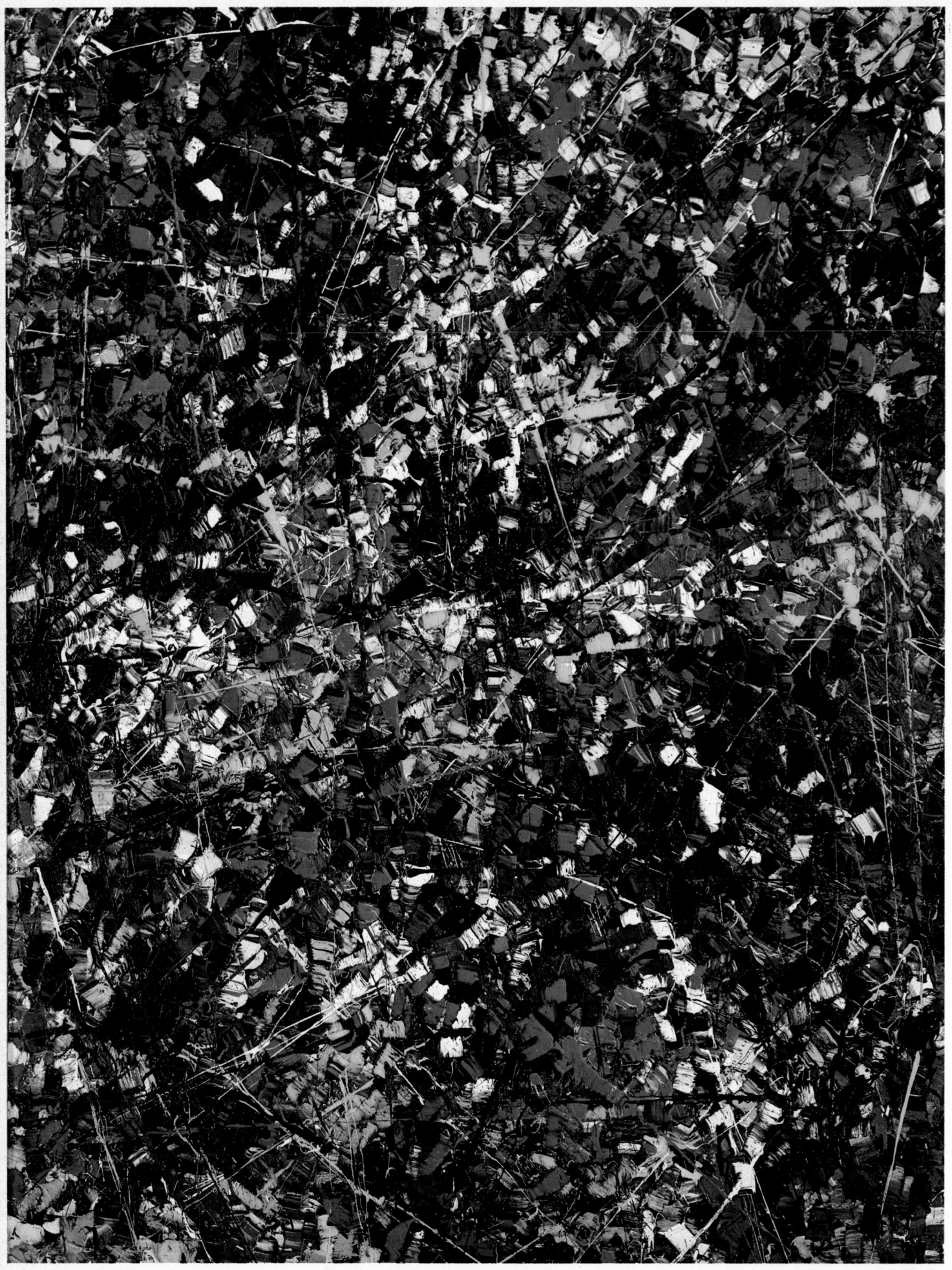

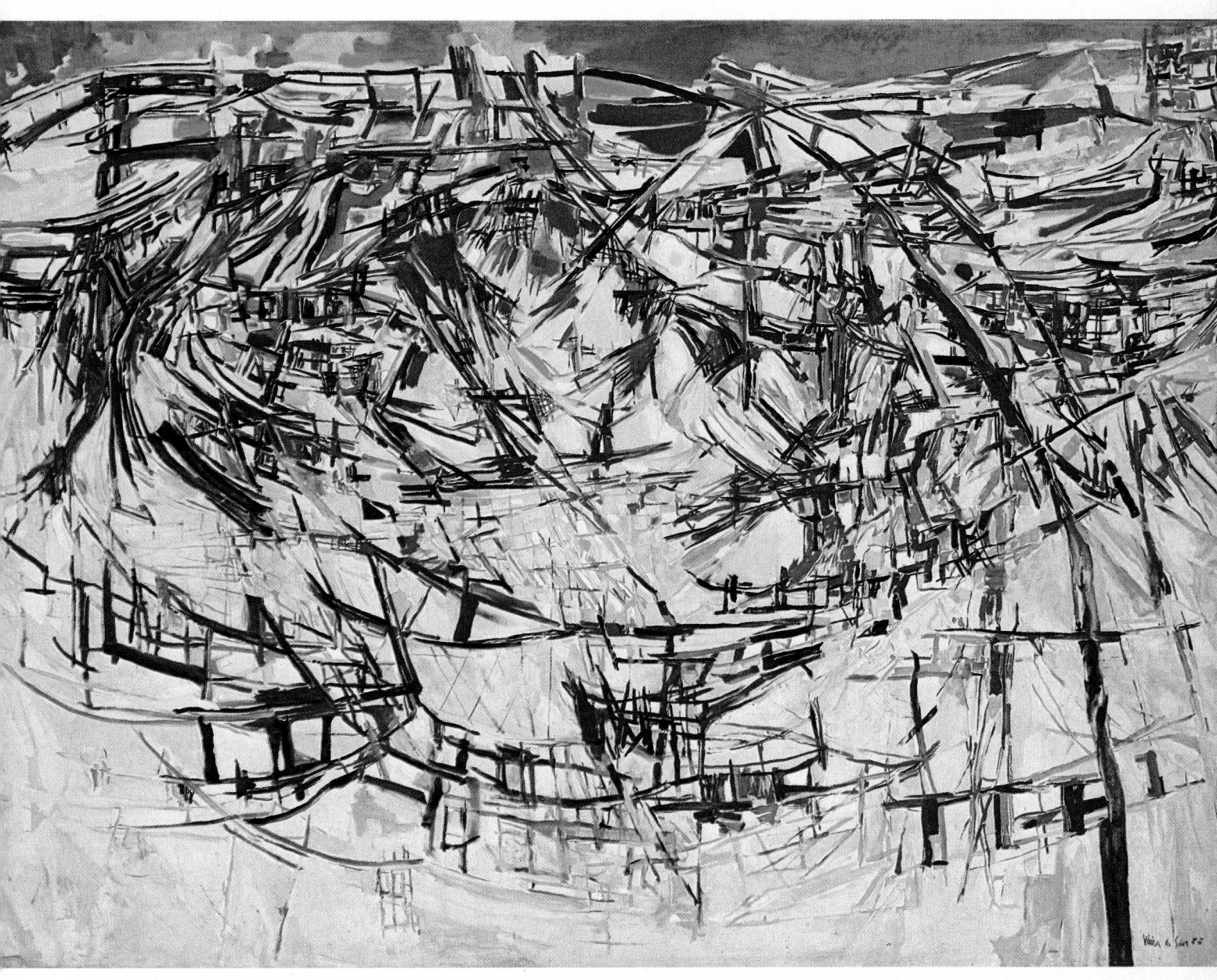

91. Opposite
Jean-Paul Riopelle
Suit of Stars
1952; 200 × 150 cm. (78 × 59 in.)
Cologne, Wallraf-Richartz Museum

92.
Vieira da Silva
Le Métroaérien
1955; 160 × 220 cm. (62 × 86 in.)
Düsseldorf, Kunstsammlung Nordrhein-Westfalen

93. Overleaft left
Vieira da Silva
Suspended garden
1955; 165 × 113 cm. (64 × 44 in.)
Paris, Musée National d'Art Moderne

94. Overleaf right
Nicolas de Staël
Figures au bord de la mer
1952; 161.5 × 129.5 cm. (63 × 51 in.)
Düsseldorf, Kunstsammlung Nordrhein-Westfalen

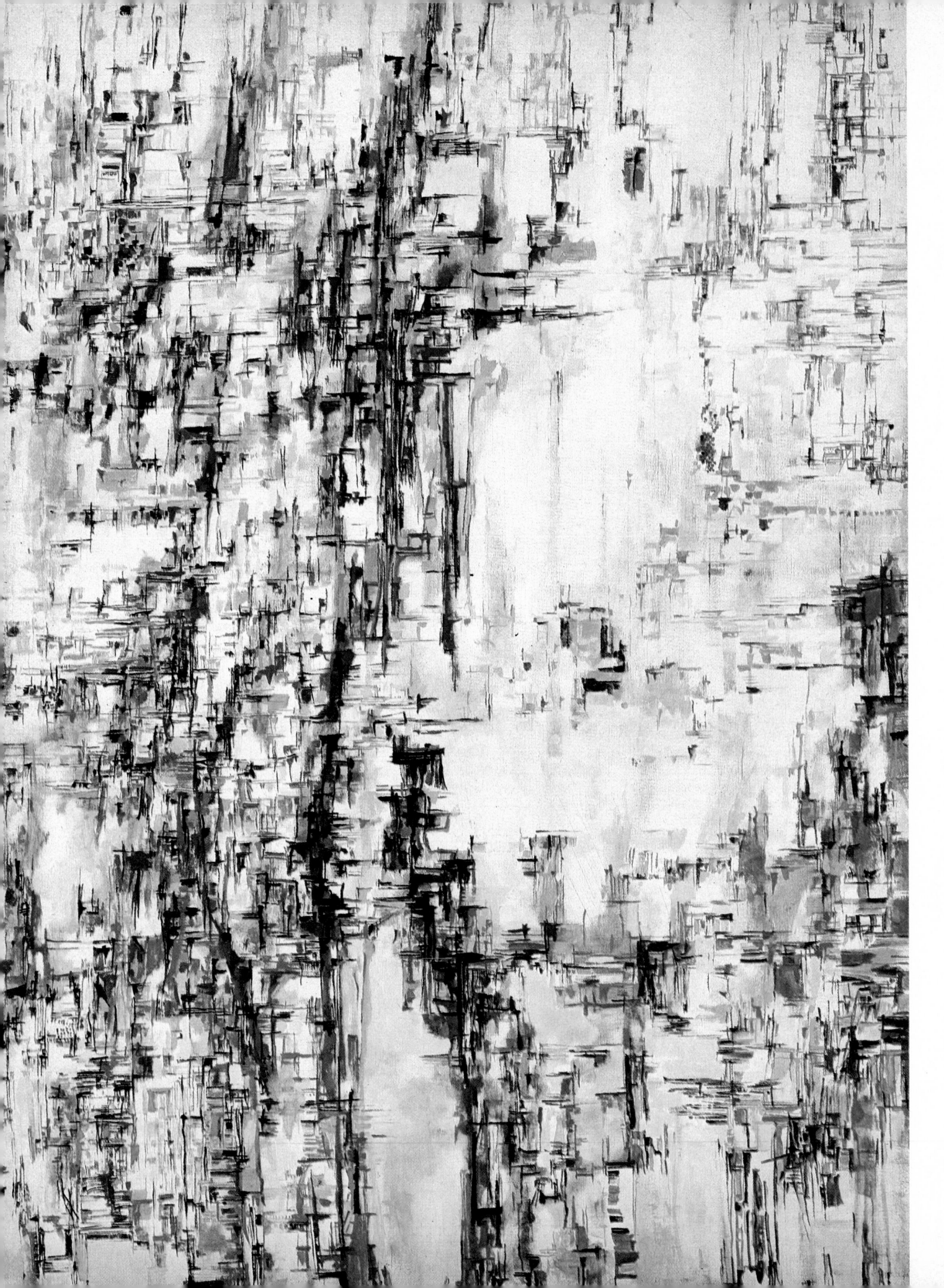

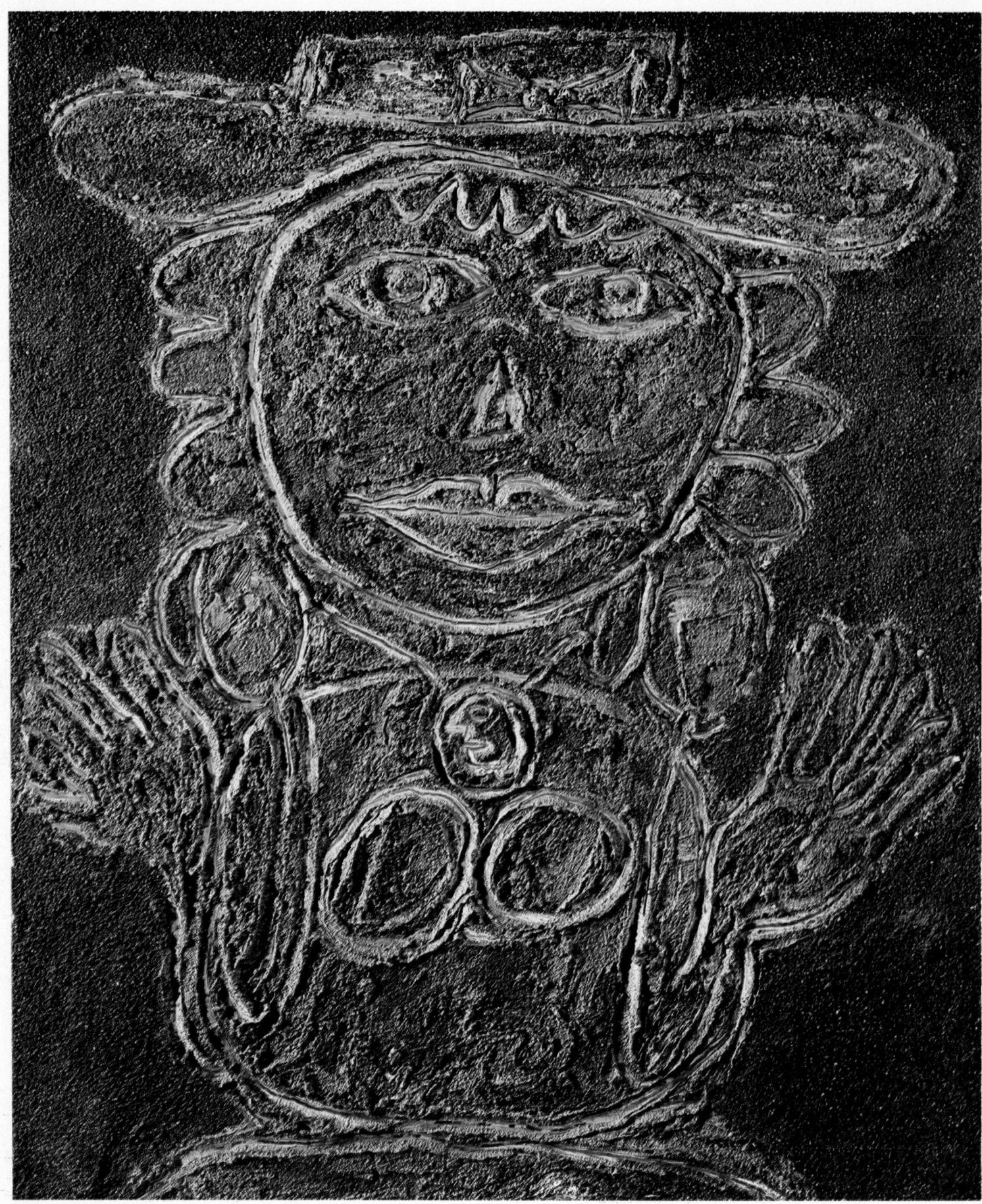

95. Opposite
Jean Dubuffet
Noeud au Chapeau
1946; 81 × 65 cm. (32 × 25 in.)
Stockholm, Moderna Museet

96.
Jean Dubuffet
Vie inquiète
1953; 130 × 195 cm. (51 × 76 in.)
London, Tate Gallery

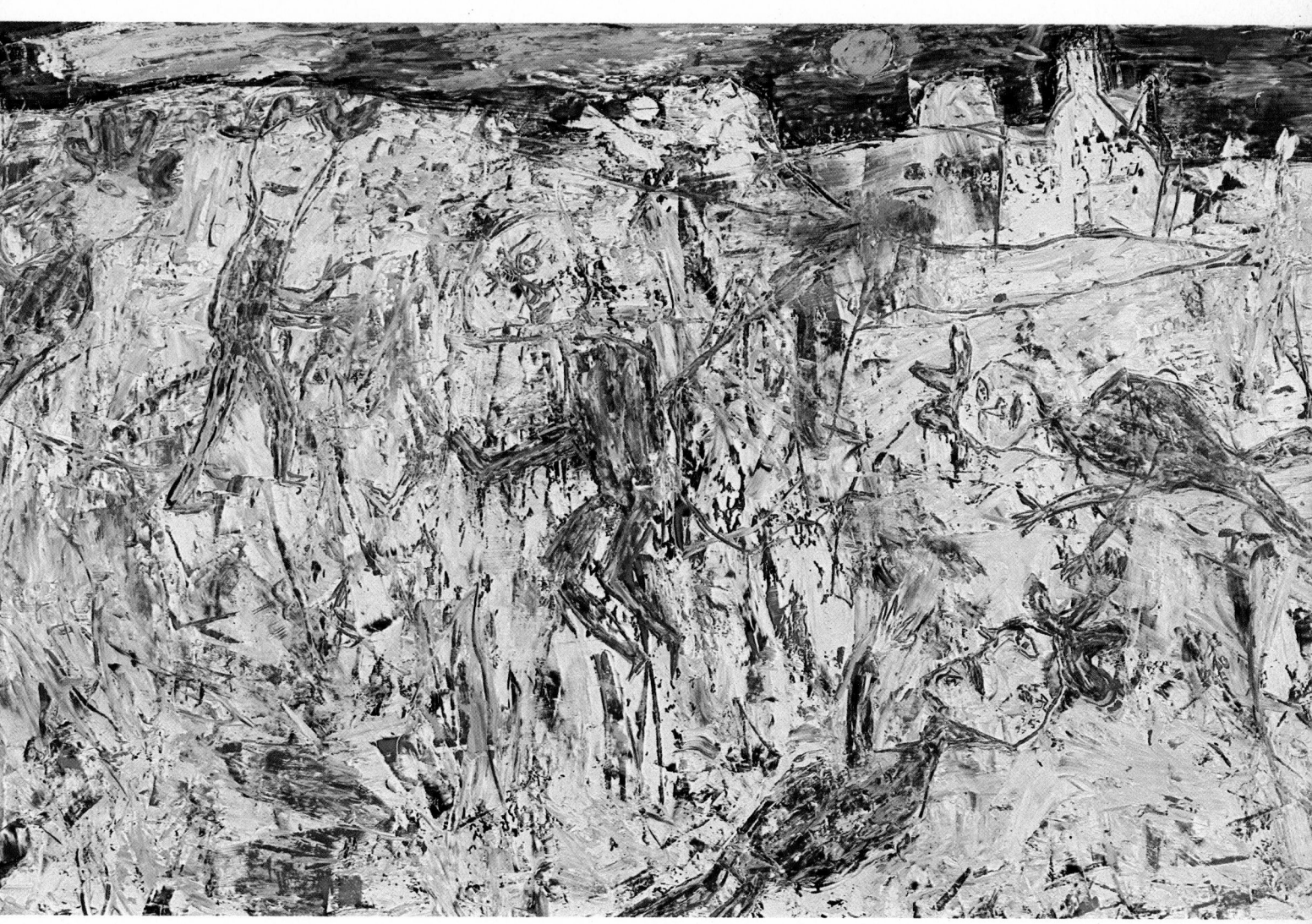

have made a reputation after the war, the hardest to absorb, but ultimately the most significant, is Jean Dubuffet. Immensely prolific, Dubuffet is quite unlike any other post-war artist, though one may detect fleeting resemblances to a large number of different contemporaries. Born in 1901, he painted intermittently during the Twenties and Thirties. He did not turn to art full-time until 1942.

In the immediately post-war period, Dubuffet was influenced by the *haute pâte* technique of Fautrier and in a more general sense by the aesthetic of Paul Klee. A typical work of this period, like the *Noeud au Chapeau* of 1946 (Plate 95), shows the charm, the naïveté, the apparent lightness of what he was doing then. But beneath the frivolity lay a serious purpose. Dubuffet believed, for example, that there was more truth in child art and naïf art than in much so-called serious painting. From the Dadaists he had inherited a love of perversity, of "mistakes" and awkwardnesses which may or may not be deliberate. He preserves "The accidental blotches, clumsy blunders, forms clearly wrong, anti-real, colours that don't work and are inappropriate—all sorts of things that must be unbearable to some people and

129

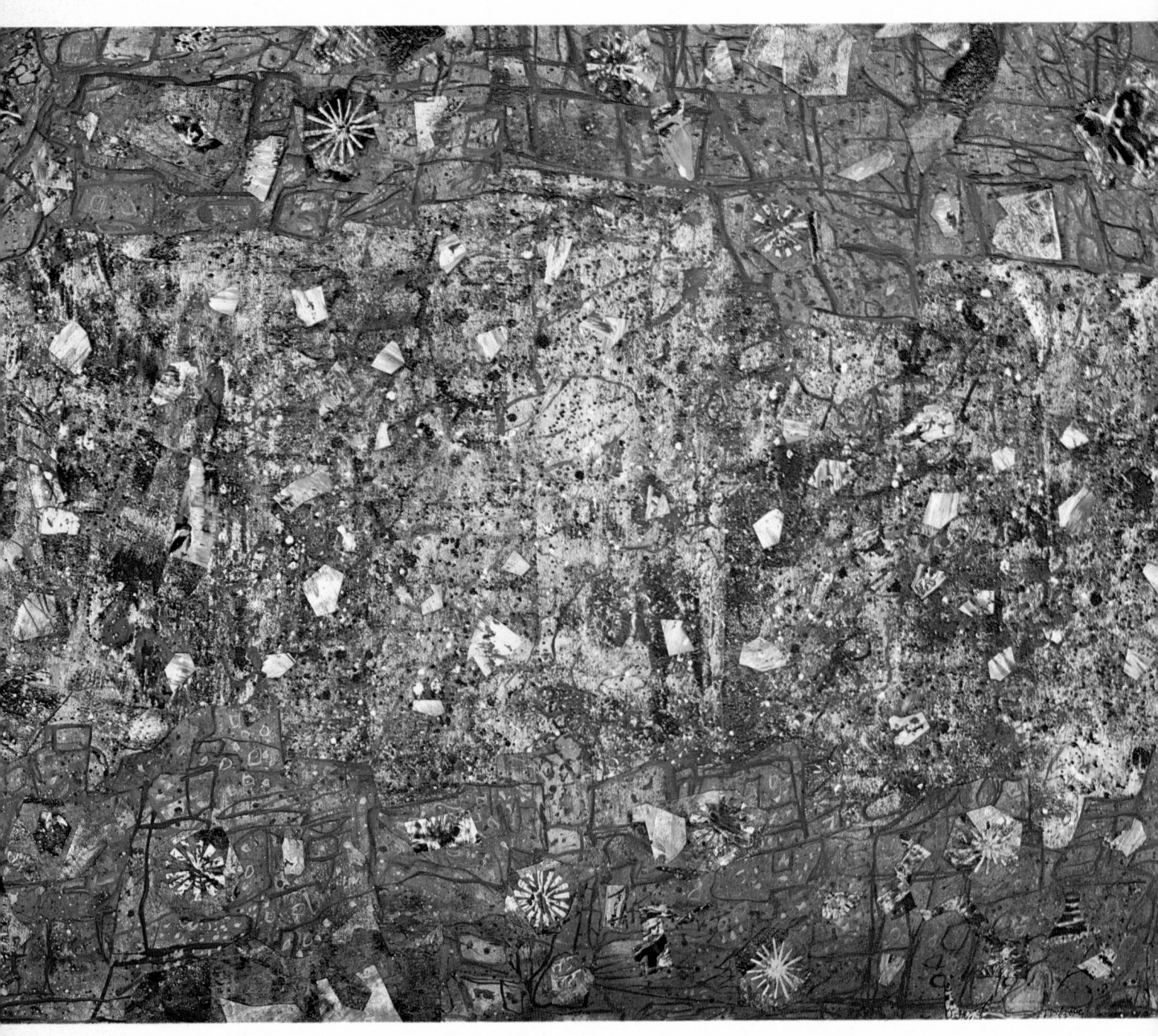

97.
Jean Dubuffet
Menues pierres éparsés sur le chemin (Small Stones Scattered upon the Road)
1957; 120 × 148 cm. (47 × 58 in.)
Private collection

98.
Opposite
Jean Dubuffet
Topografia increspata
1959; 79 × 89 cm. (31 × 35 in.)
Vienna, Museum des 20. Jahrhundert

130

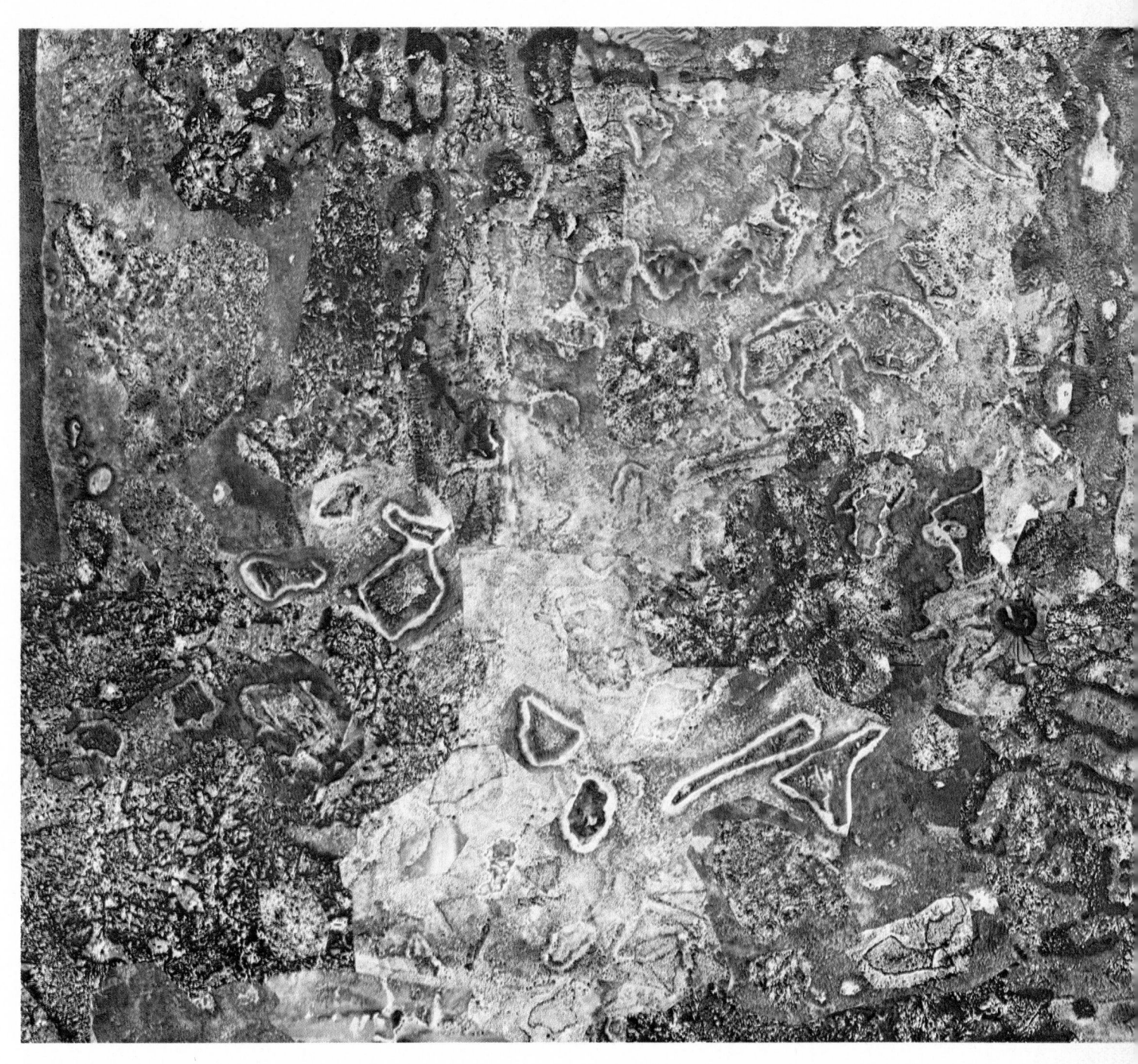

99. Overleaf left
Karel Appel
La Hollandaise
1969; 130 × 97 cm. (51 × 38 in.)
Paris, Galerie Ariel

100. Overleaf right
Karel Appel
Tête 2 (Femme cubiste)
1968; 166.5 × 126 cm. (65 × 49 in.)
London, Gimpel Fils

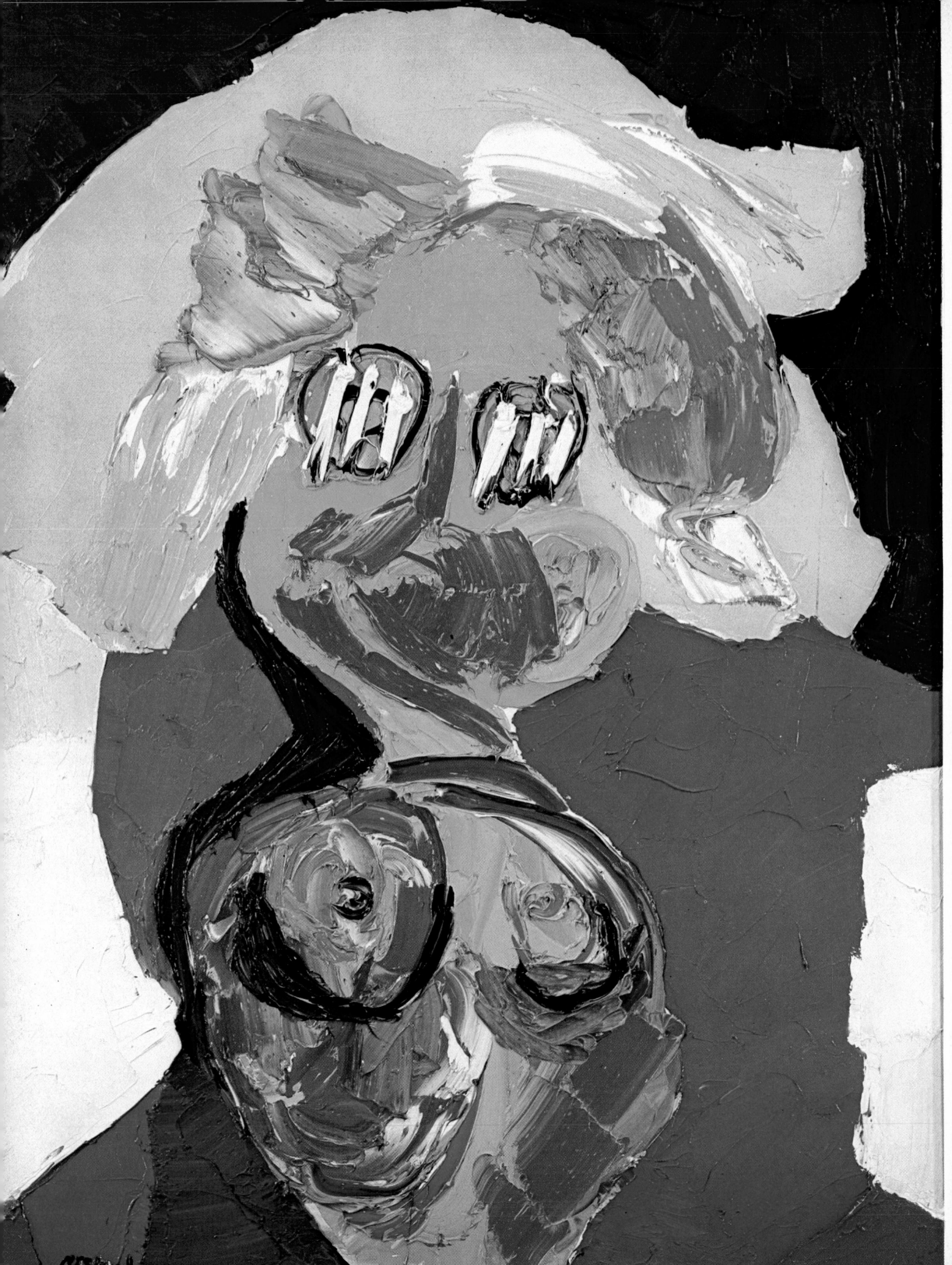

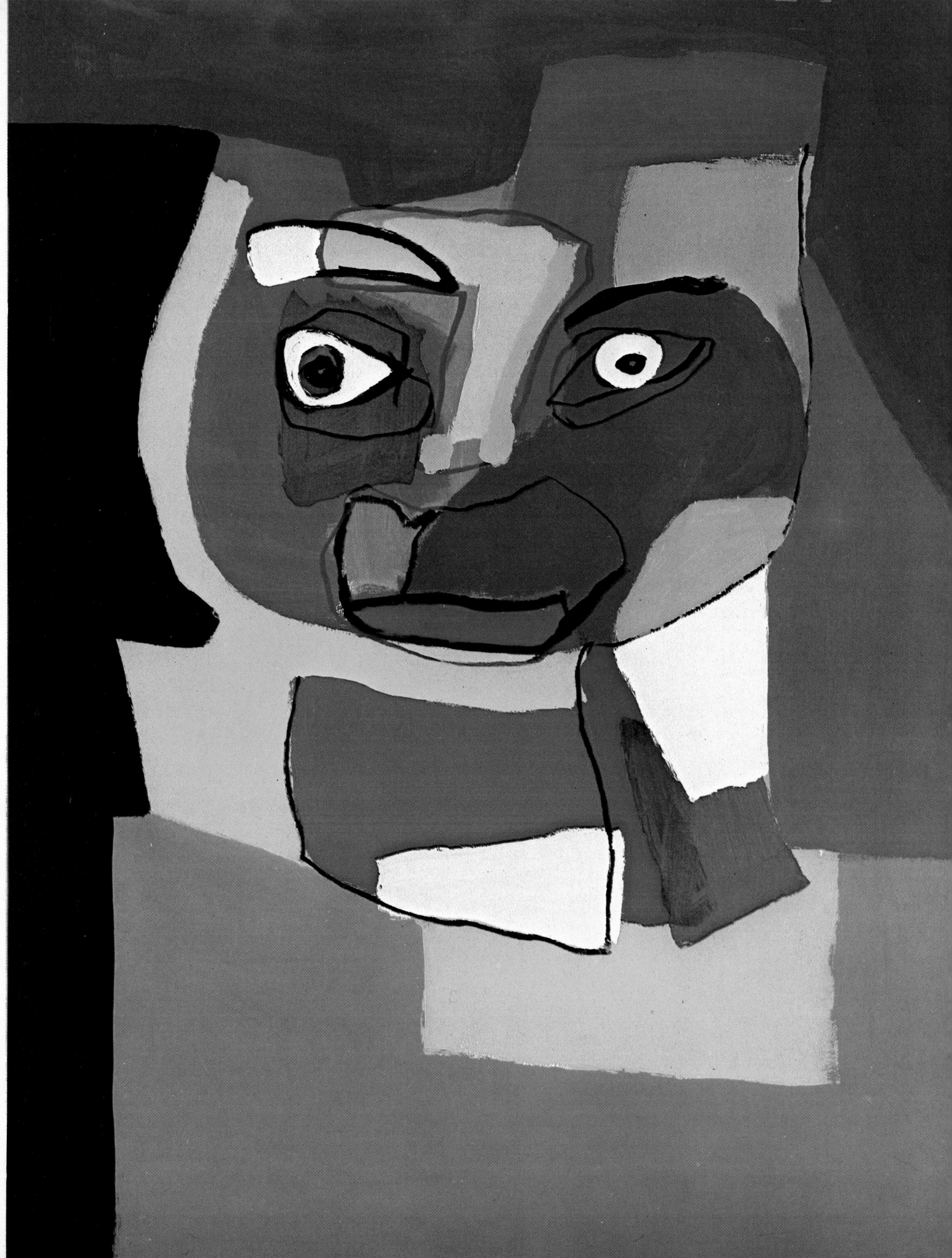

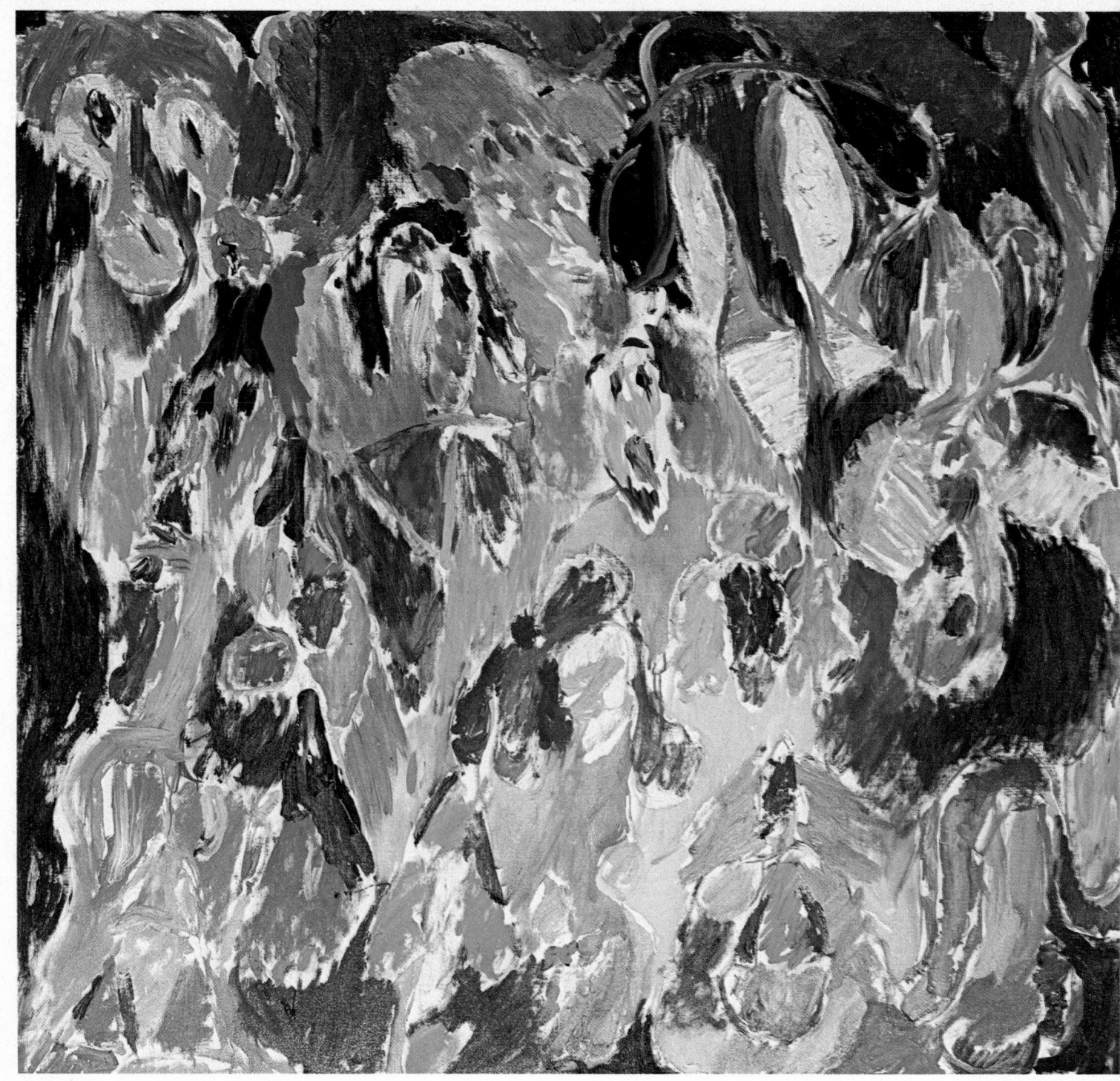

even make me a bit uneasy because they often destroy the effect. But I accept them, because in fact it keeps one aware of the painter's hand in the picture, and prevents the object from dominating and stops things taking shape too clearly" (artist's statement, catalogue of the Dubuffet exhibition, Tate Gallery, 1966).

In spite of this, Dubuffet is a master of his materials—one of the great "cooks" of contemporary art. He has the disconcerting habit of

101.
Pierre Alechinsky
Loin d'Ixelles
1965; 138 × 143 cm. (54 × 56 in.)
New York, private collection

102. Opposite
Lucebert (Lucebertus J. Swaanswijk)
The Golden Boy
1959; 64.5 × 52 cm. (25 × 20 in.)
Copenhagen, coll. Henny and Aby Besjakov

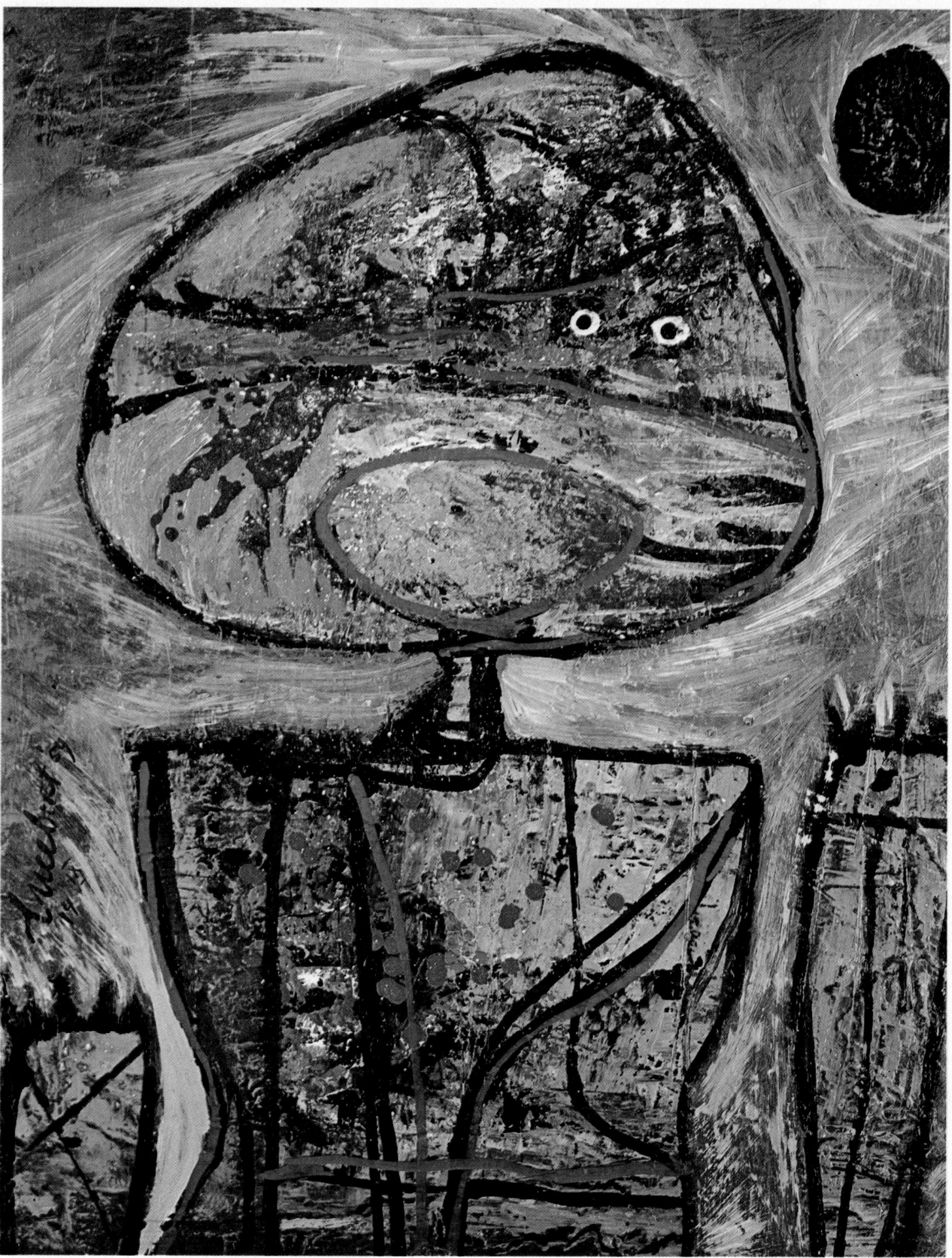

arriving at an effect or a surface for quite different reasons from what one might suppose. A painting such as *Small Stones Scattered upon the Road* of 1957 (Plate 97) looks at first glance like one of the all-over abstract compositions which both Americans and Europeans were then producing. But it has no ambitious programme behind it. Its intentions—quite literally—are down to earth.

Lacking pretentiousness, Dubuffet also lacks weight. His prolific output seems to stand to one side of the tradition of Modernist painting, just as the prose texts of his contemporary Francis Ponge stand aside from the main course of development of modern poetry. Ponge says that his ambition is to bestow upon any object he may happen to encounter "the good fortune to be born into words". Dubuffet offers the same chance-selected subject-matter the luck to be born into paint. Like Ponge, he recognizes "the object's basic rights, its inalienable rights in opposition to poetic objectives". Compared to Klee, however, Dubuffet seems to lack stringency. The rules of the games he plays, with himself and with the spectator, lack stringency.

There is sometimes a certain resemblance between Dubuffet's work with its reliance upon ideas taken from children's drawings, and the work of some members of the CoBrA Group. But there is also a fundamental difference of attitudes and sympathies. CoBrA represents a kind of Nordic protest against the attempt to renew the dominance of Paris, and we find in it more than a trace of the Expressionism of early Modernist masters such as Edvard Munch and Kirchner.

Despite this, CoBrA itself was formed at a meeting in a Paris café—by a group of painters from Denmark, Belgium, and Holland who named it by combining the first letters of the names of their respective native cities—Copenhagen, Brussels, Amsterdam. Prominent among them were Karel Appel, from Holland; the Belgians Pierre Alechinsky and Corneille; and the Dane Asger Jorn. Atlan, although of French Algerian origin, was also a member, but his work was never typical. The first CoBrA exhibition was held in 1949 in Amsterdam. This year also saw the publication of a magazine; it contained articles about children's art, folk art, and the art of schizophrenics.

The aim of the typical CoBrA painter was always the directest possible expression of personal fantasy: "My paint tube [said Karel Appel in 1956] is like a rocket which describes its own space. I try to make the impossible possible. What is happening I cannot foresee; it is a surprise. Painting, like passion, is an emotion full of truth and rings with a living sound, like the roar coming from the lion's breast" (quoted by Hugo Claus, *Karel Appel*, New York, 1962).

The bright colours of Appel's work (Plates 99 and 100) in fact convey an emotion very different from the one we find in the paintings of the pioneer Expressionists—something far less introverted and anguished. It is as if the artist now has such ready access to his own subconscious that he has little reason to fear what it contains. The same comment could be made about Alechinsky (Plate 101), whose work seems to invite a comparison with James Ensor's which it cannot sustain. Lucebert, another Dutch member of the group, repeats Appel's formulae in a more sombre key (Plate 102).

Corneille (Plate 103) is attracted to landscape rather than to the figure. His compositions are often distilled from experiences gathered during his extensive travels. Here one seems to feel the impact of the late Van Gogh—but can Van Gogh function as a mere tourist? Asger Jorn (Plate 104) was, though over-prolific and uneven, probably the most impressive of all the CoBrA artists. His paintings reflect his own wide-ranging curiosity and intellectual energy. We find in them allusions to magic, hermetic knowledge, alchemical secrets—the signposts are half-hidden beneath the turbulent paint surfaces. Jorn's lack of discipline is compensated for, in his best work, by the tremendous energy and commitment he displays.

Nevertheless, if we compare the work of any of the CoBrA group to their Expressionist predecessors of the period before the First World War, we are instantly aware that this is a lesser kind of art, one which has sacrificed complexity of allusion in return for apparent freedom. The anti-intellectual stance of the CoBrA painters now

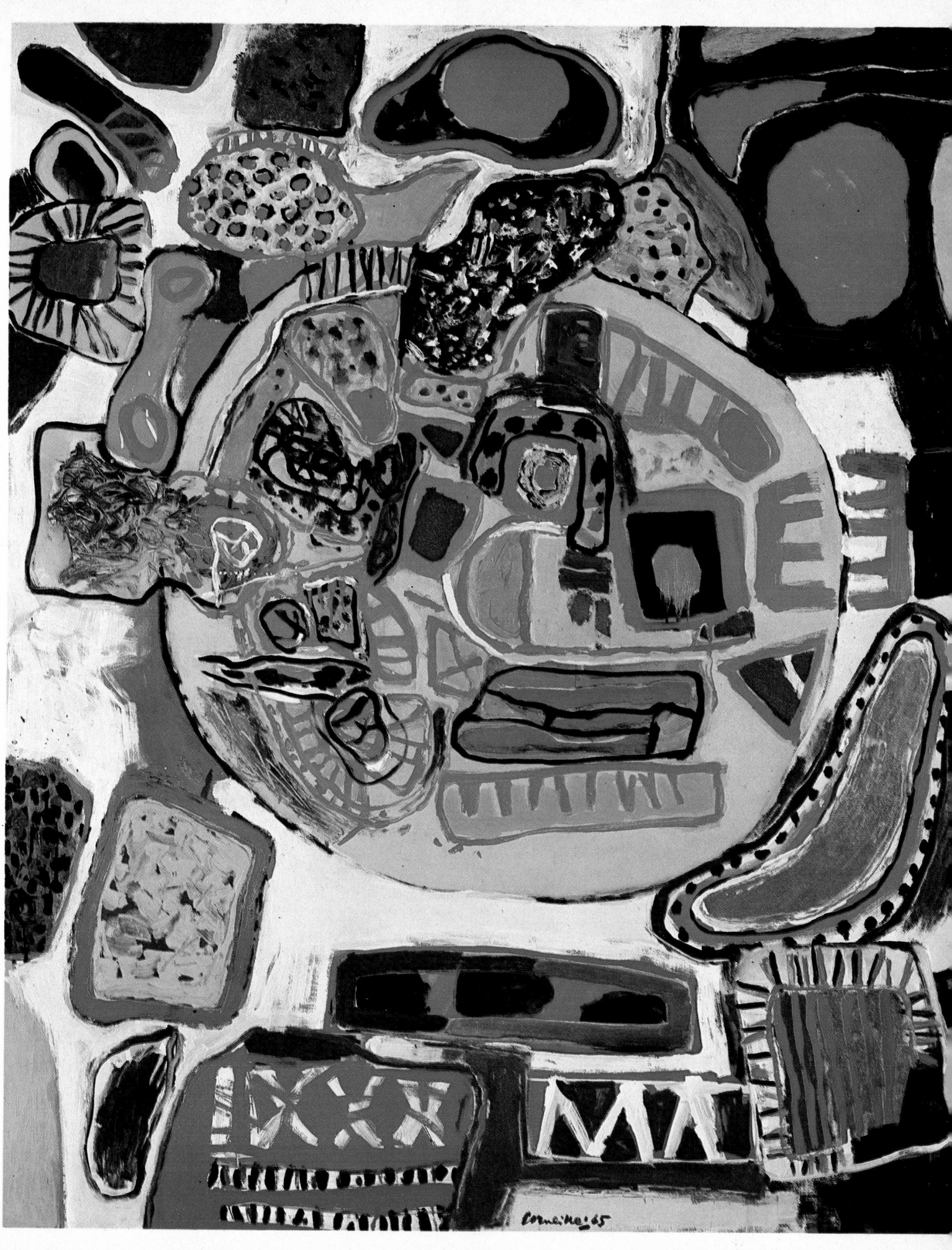

Corneille '65

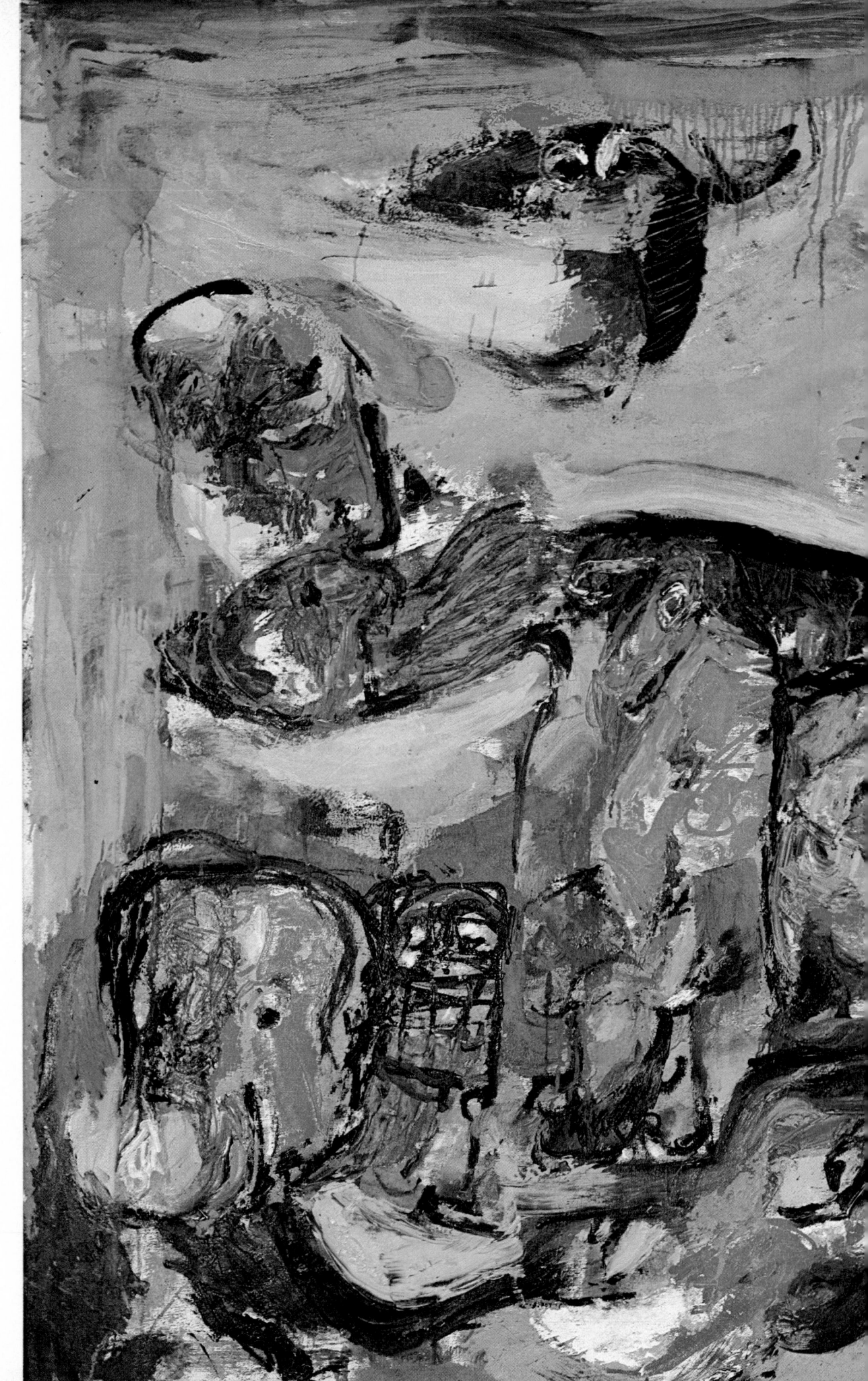

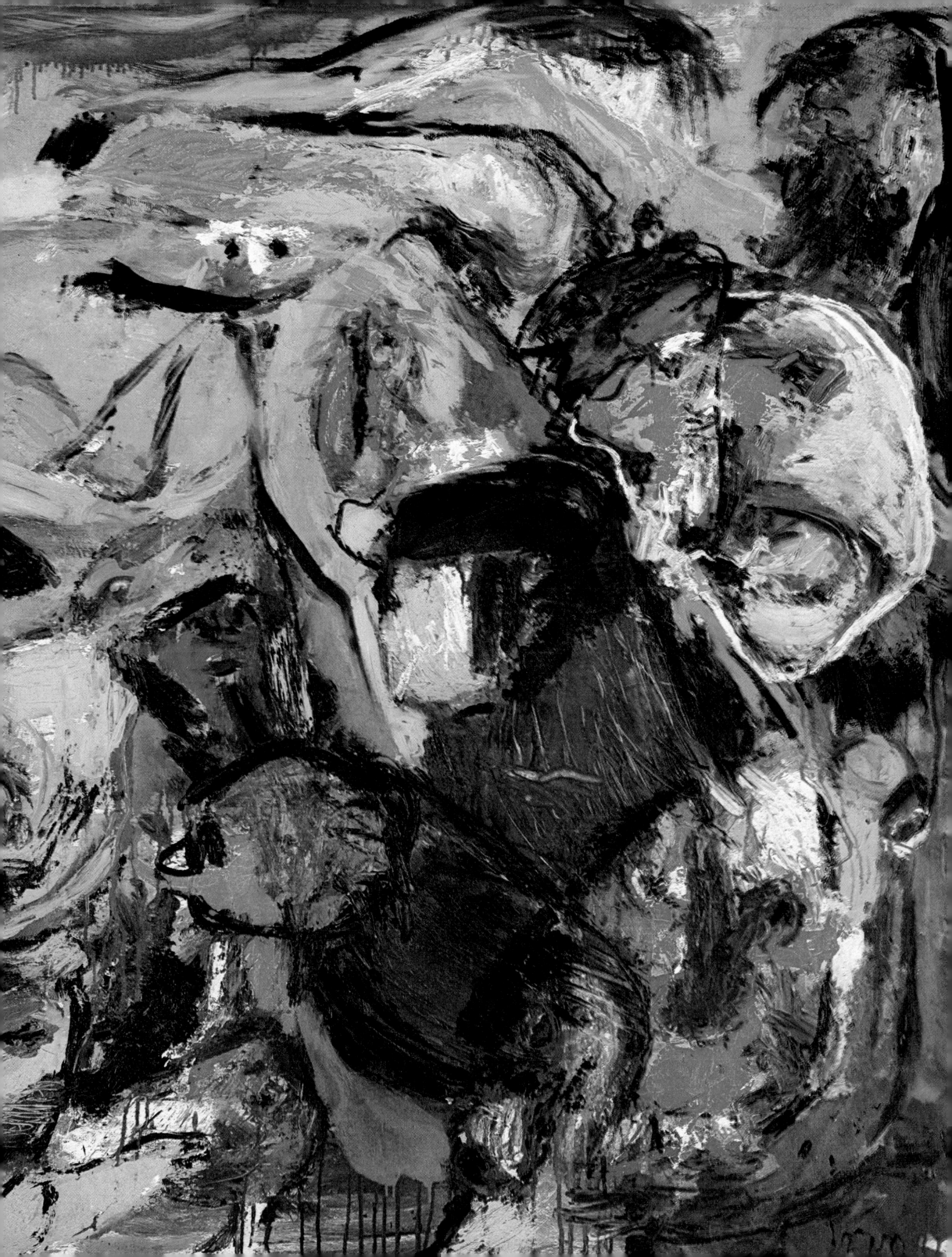

makes their work seem simplistic, for all its restlessness of design.

The classic Surrealist movement, though it had lost much of its energy in the new conditions that prevailed after 1945, continued to put forth fresh shoots. A marginal but sympathetic role was played by the writer-painter Henri Michaux, whose calligraphic doodlings are an extension of his activity as a writer. He is one of the clearest examples of the direct link between the technique of automatic writing and automatism in painting (Plate 105). Michaux has said in this connection: "Instead of the one vision which excludes others, I would have liked to draw the moments that, placed side by side, go to make up a life. To expose the interior phrase for people to see, the phrase that has no words, a rope which uncoils sinuously, and intimately accompanies everything that impinges from the outside or the inside. I wanted to draw the consciousness of existence and the flow of time. As you would take your pulse" (quoted by John Ashbery, "Henri Michaux: Painter Inside Poet", *Art News*, Vol. 60, No. 1 [March, 1961], p. 65).

Even veristic Surrealism survived, and it attracted new recruits. One of the most powerful

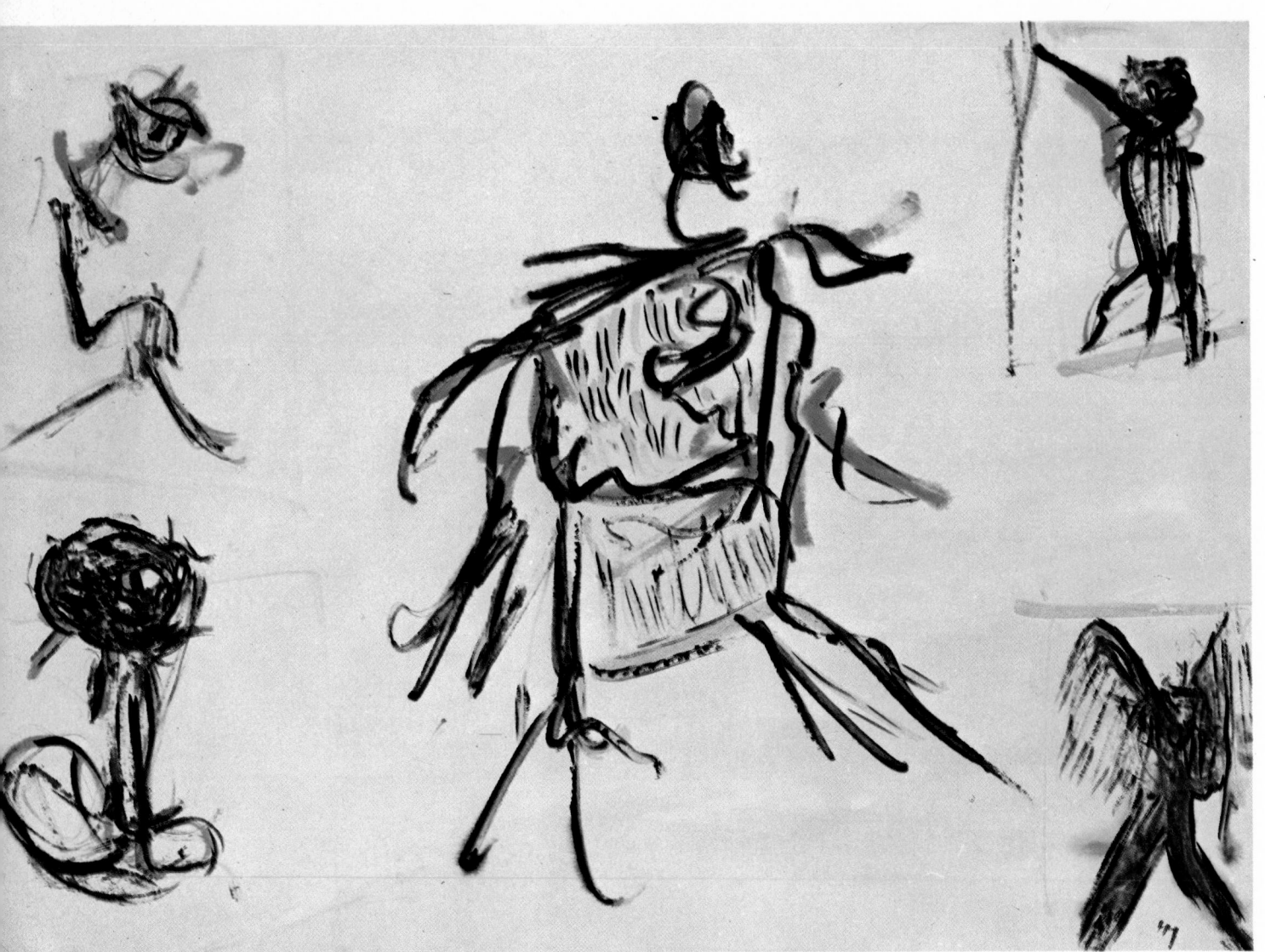

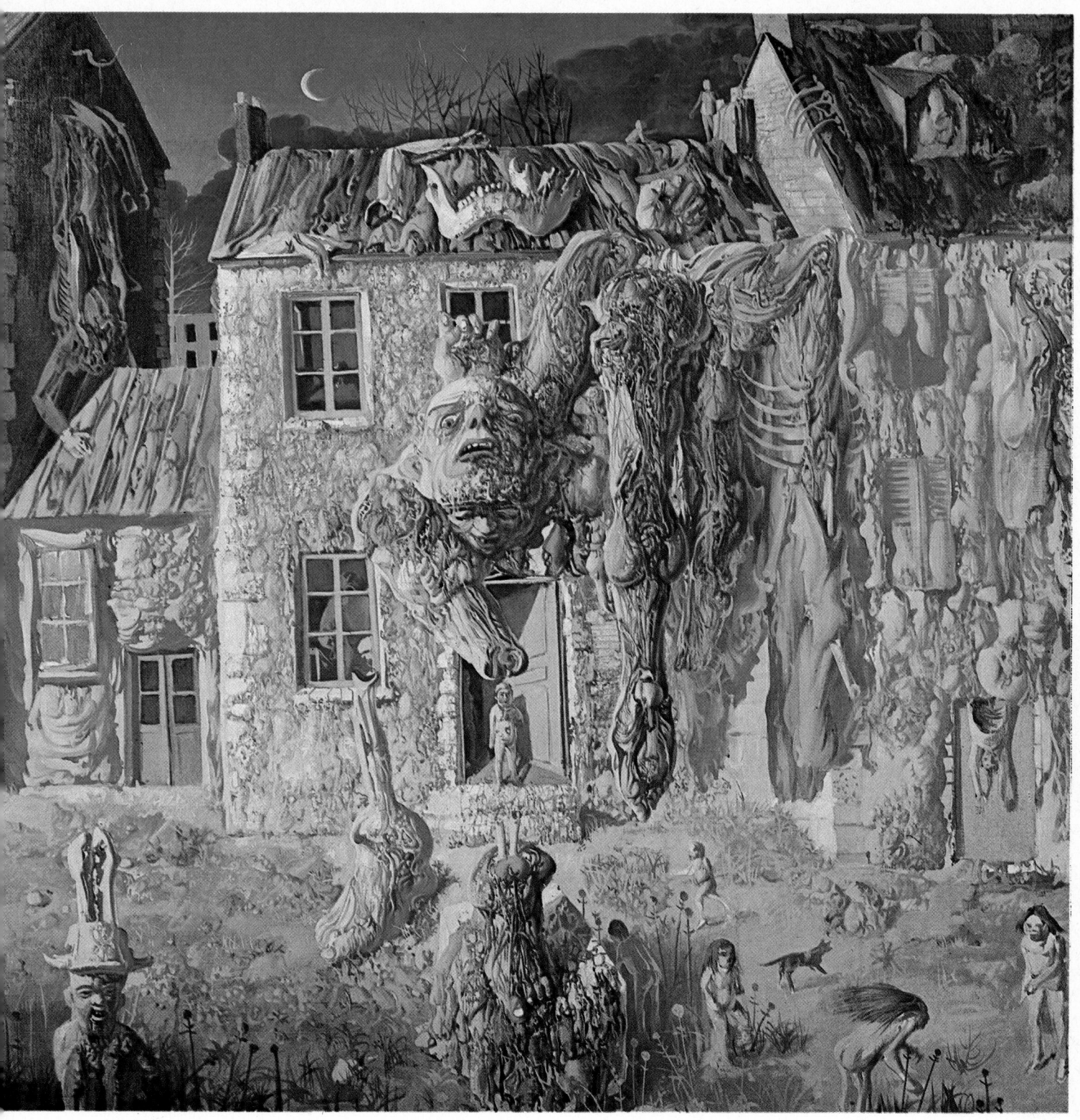

105. Opposite
Henri Michaux
Untitled
N.d. 49 × 64.5 cm. (19 × 25 in.)
Copenhagen, coll. Henny and Aby Besjakov

106.
Dado (Miodrag Djuric)
La Guerre civile
1967; 120 × 120 cm. (49 × 49 in.)
Paris, Galerie André François Petit

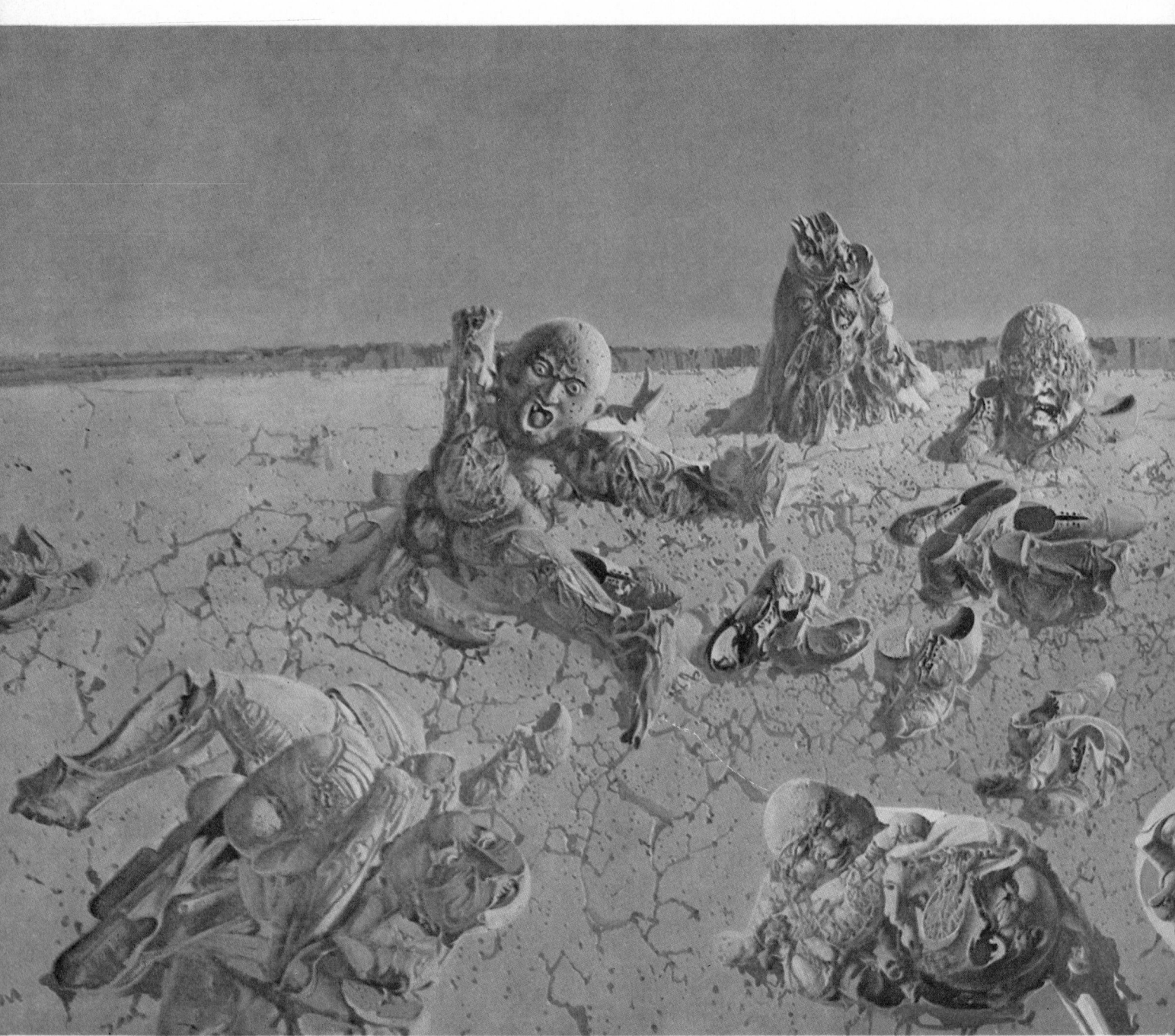

of these was the Yugoslavian artist Dado (Miodrag Djuric), who made his way to Paris in the middle Fifties and made contact with Dubuffet. Compared to Dubuffet's wit and lightness, Dado's work (Plates 106 and 107) is curiously solemn. One finds in it, though strangely transformed, the ambition to create those large-scale academic machines which obsessed the painters of the nineteenth century.

It is perhaps significant in this connection that

107.
Dado (Miodrag Djuric)
Grande plage bleue
1969; 162 × 403 cm. (63 × 157 in.)
Paris, Musée National d'Art Moderne, loan of the Centre
National d'Art Contemporain

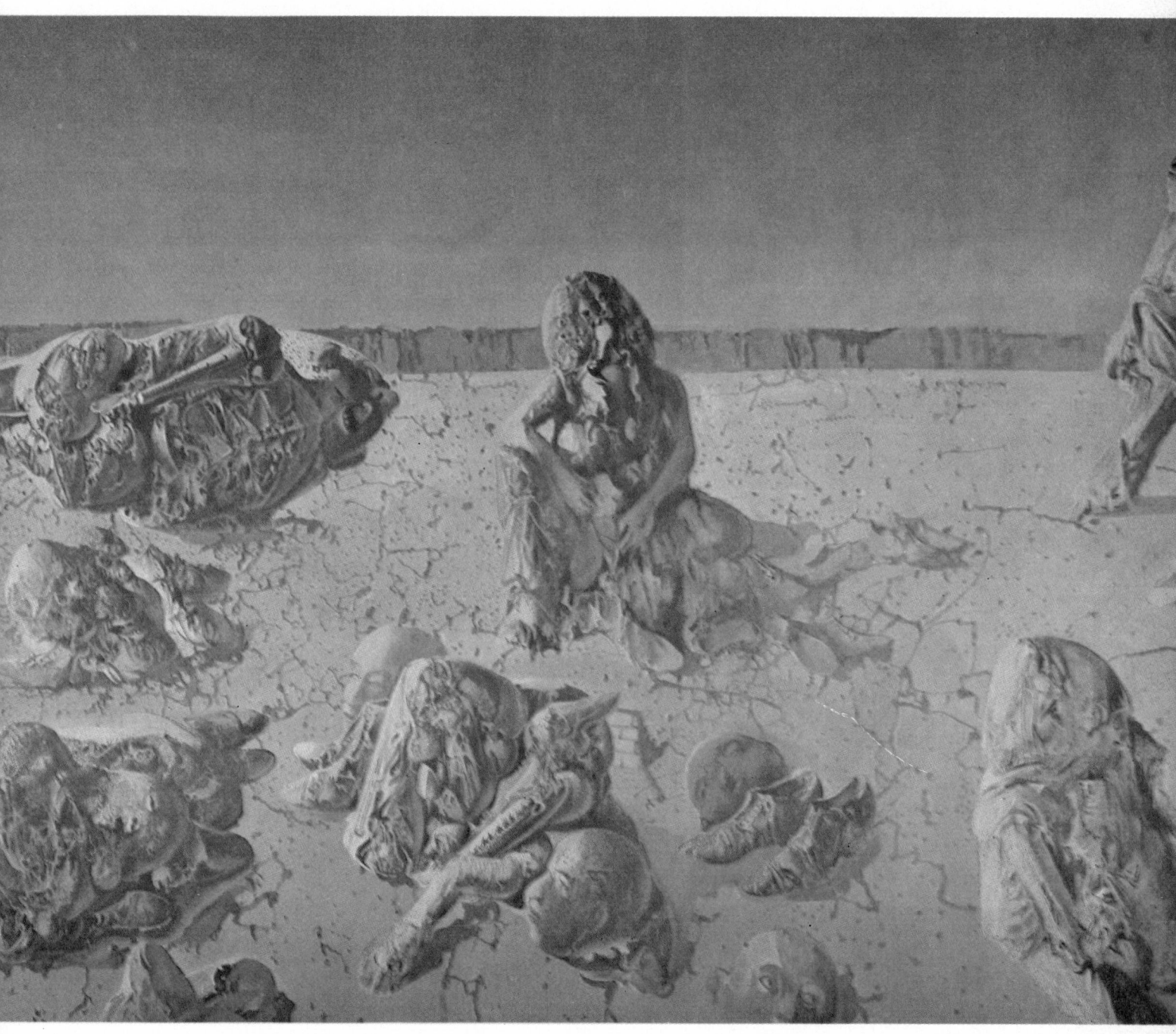

Dado comes from a country on the margin of the modern art scene. The place where veristic Surrealism has flourished most notably in the years since the Second World War is undoubtedly Austria. The work of Ernst Fuchs (Plate 108) is characteristic of what came to be dubbed the Vienna School: "His dreams and nightmares [one critic has written of Fuchs], as transmitted in his paintings, are autobiographical to the point where his own visage frequently emerges in his repre-

143

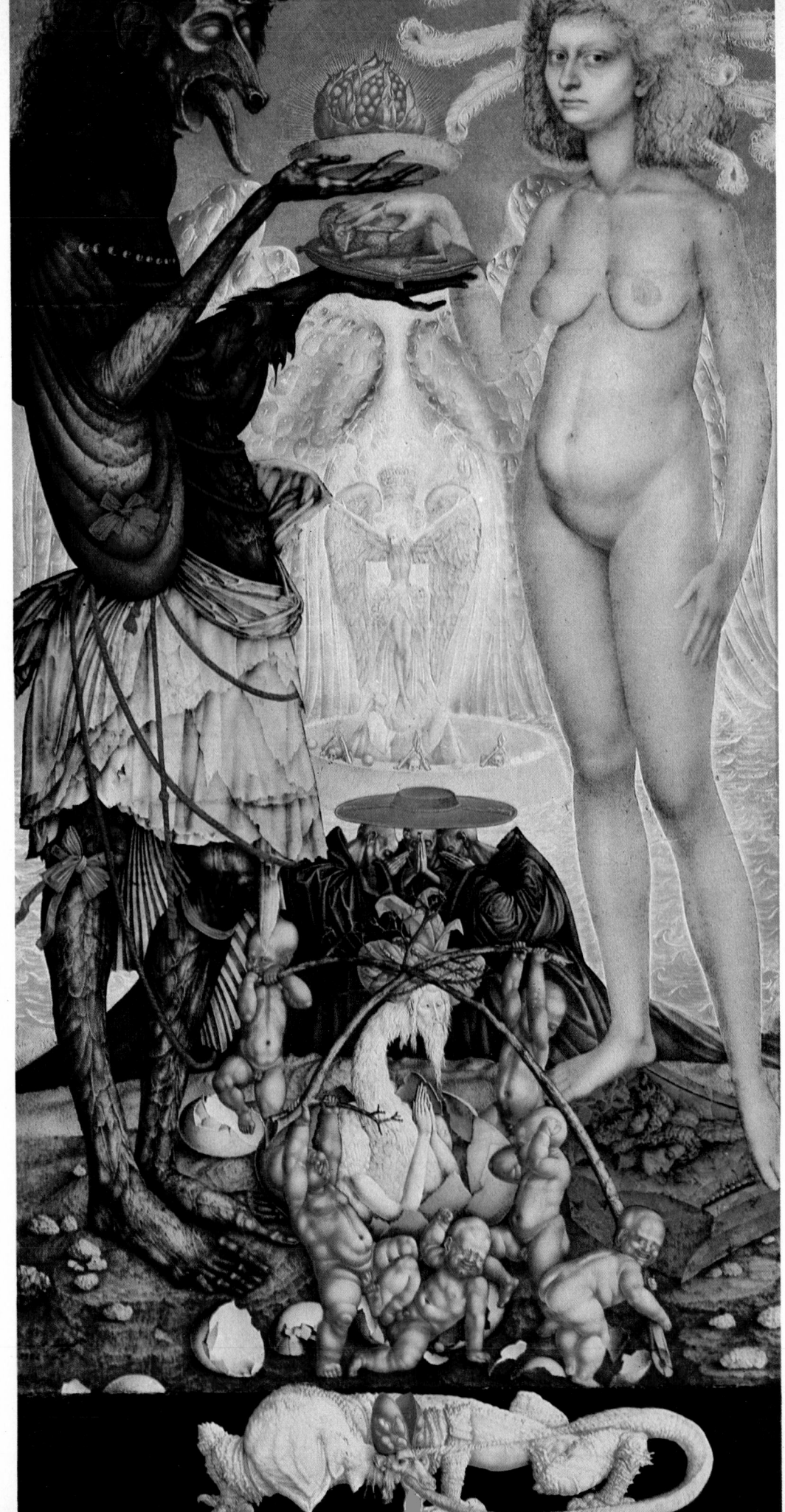

144

108.
Ernst Fuchs
Die Hochzeit von Unicorn
1952–60; 71 × 36 cm. (28 × 14 in.)
Vienna, collection of the artist

sentations of saints and deities. With biblical symbols and century-old techniques Fuchs creates complex ikons that speak of death and transfiguration and reflect his belief in redemption" (H. Seldis, "The Vienna School", *Art International,* Vol. X, No. 4 [April, 1966], p. 47).

What one notes in the work of Fuchs and his Viennese colleagues—among them Erich Brauer, Wolfgang Hutter, and Anton Lehmden—is the reversion to medieval modes. Hieronymus Bosch is as conspicuous an influence on their work as Yves Tanguy or Dali, and they have turned back to conservative values that André Breton would have condemned. Their art seems an appropriate expression of the provincialism of the Austrian cultural situation.

The emergence of "national" schools of this kind was, however, the exception rather than the rule in the conditions that prevailed after 1945. In the European democracies modern painting made an enormous upsurge. It matched in quantity, if not in quality, what was happening in the United States in the same epoch, and it established for itself a more or less international language. Any stylistic innovation was rapidly transmitted from country to country. The main organs of dissemination were exhibitions, art books and magazines, and the so-called dealer-critic network.

Major exhibitions of modern art were now a regular feature of the cultural scene in most capital cities. Museums were in the process of democratiz-ing themselves and were making strenuous efforts to reach a new mass public. And this public was itself in the throes of making art into a kind of secular religion. The artist was increasingly admired as the ideal towards which everyone aspired—the truly liberated man. Technical progress in printing and publishing, and especially improved methods of colour reproduction, soon made the publication of art books one of the most flourishing activities of the whole European publishing industry, a situation which benefited modern art even more than it did the visual arts in general, as it was now worth a publisher's while to take the risk of producing books about it, given the seemingly inexhaustible thirst for new titles. The leading art magazines had a particularly strong impact on young students of painting and kept them keenly aware of new developments.

The dealer-critic network—the world of the private dealers and the critics who promoted their wares—was at its most powerful in the Fifties and early Sixties, because modern art itself had not as yet rebelled against the commercialism of the market. The Fifties witnessed a boom in contemporary art which matched the boom generated by the new industrial money of the nineteenth century. Abstract paintings sold almost as easily as the works of Ernest Meissonier had done eighty years previously. The fifteen years after 1945 saw modern art in perhaps the least self-questioning phase of its existence.

Assemblage and Neo-Dadaism

The renewed interest in collage and *assemblage* techniques, signalled by an important exhibition entitled "The Art of Assemblage", held at the Museum of Modern Art in New York in 1961, was visible evidence not so much of a change in attitude towards materials and the way they were used as of a change in the artist's attitude towards the society he lived in.

There had been no break in continuity from the days of Cubism and early Surrealism so far as technique itself was concerned. Throughout the Thirties and Forties artists had continued to explore the freedom which collage gave them. The American artist Joseph Cornell, for instance, had been making small-scale poetic *assemblages* in boxes since the early Thirties. His first one-man show, held at the Surrealist-oriented Julien Levy Gallery in New York in 1932, was entitled "Minutiae, Glass Bells, Shadow Boxes, Coups d'oeil, Jouets surréalistes". Cornell's work (Plates 109–110) perfectly exemplifies the point made by William C. Seitz in a book issued in connection with the "Art of Assemblage" show: "Figuratively, the practice of assemblage raises materials from the level of formal relations to that of associational poetry, just as words and numbers, on the contrary, tend to be formalized. Transmutation tends also to move in the opposite direction in Abstract Expressionist painting, in which the subject is absorbed into the medium" (William C. Seitz, *The Art of Assemblage*, New York, 1961, p. 84).

One must not, however, conclude that *assemblage* techniques were entirely hostile to the Abstract Expressionist sensibility. Alfonso Ossorio, a Philippine artist closely associated with the New York School, started to develop an elaborate collage technique during the late Fifties and employed it to increasing effect during the following decade (Plates 111, 112, and 113). In his work the frenzied accumulation of heterogenous forms and materials provides an equivalent for the complicated calligraphy one discovers in a Pollock, and serves the same purpose, to reveal the personal sensibility of the artist.

In fact, one of the striking things about *assemblage* is that the method itself tends to preclude the idea of a style. It can be used to great effect for humorous purposes, for example. The imaginary portraits created by the Italian artist Enrico Baj teeter just on the verge of caricature (Plates 114 and 115); they are first cousins to the kind of Saul Steinberg cartoon that would be printed in *The New Yorker*. Baj creates a dialogue between the materials used and what is being portrayed. The oddments of military finery which appear in Baj's collage *The General* are not there simply because they happen to be appropriate to the subject (though indeed they are). They are also present because the artist can use them to create exactly the form he wants. Comment and structure are fused, and a quality of visual punning gives the work its special flavour.

Compared to many of the artists who began to employ *assemblage* in the late Fifties and early Sixties, Baj is, however, unadventurous and retrograde. Having discovered a pleasing formula, he is quite content to stick to it. His work has none of the disturbing quality which fills that produced by the two Americans who are now most commonly thought of as the link between Abstract Expressionism and the Pop Art which was to follow. Jasper Johns and Robert Rauschenberg do indeed provide this link, but their work has other connections and characteristics which are perhaps even more important in the development of art after 1945. For one thing, they were the twin standard-bearers of the Dada revival which was to have such a tremendous influence over the thinking of all young artists during the 1960's and early 1970's. The revival itself had started as early

109.
Joseph Cornell
Bird in a Box
1943; 32 × 29 × 7 cm. (12 × 11 × 3 in.)
Krefeld, Kaiser Wilhelm Museum, coll. Lauffs

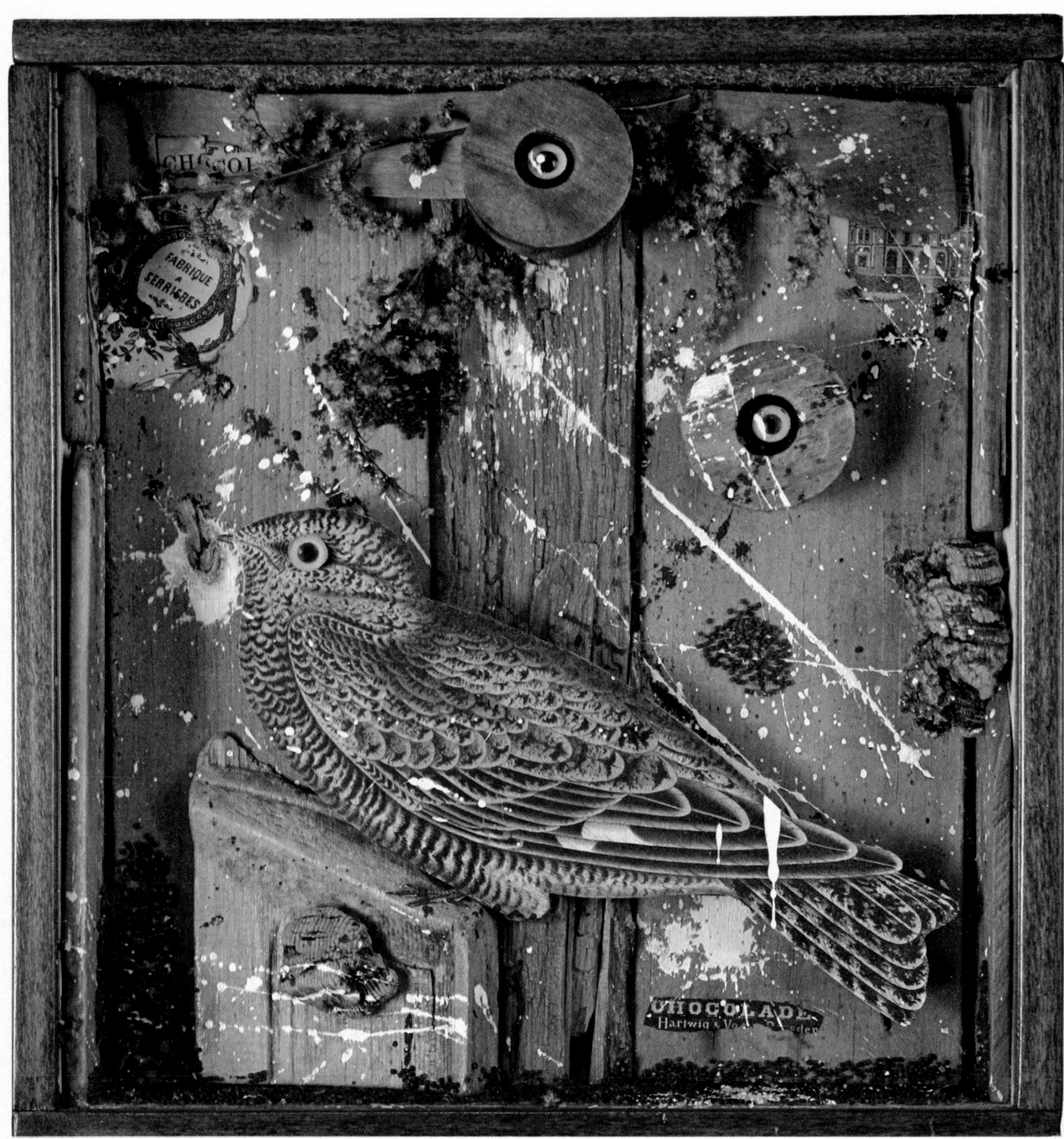

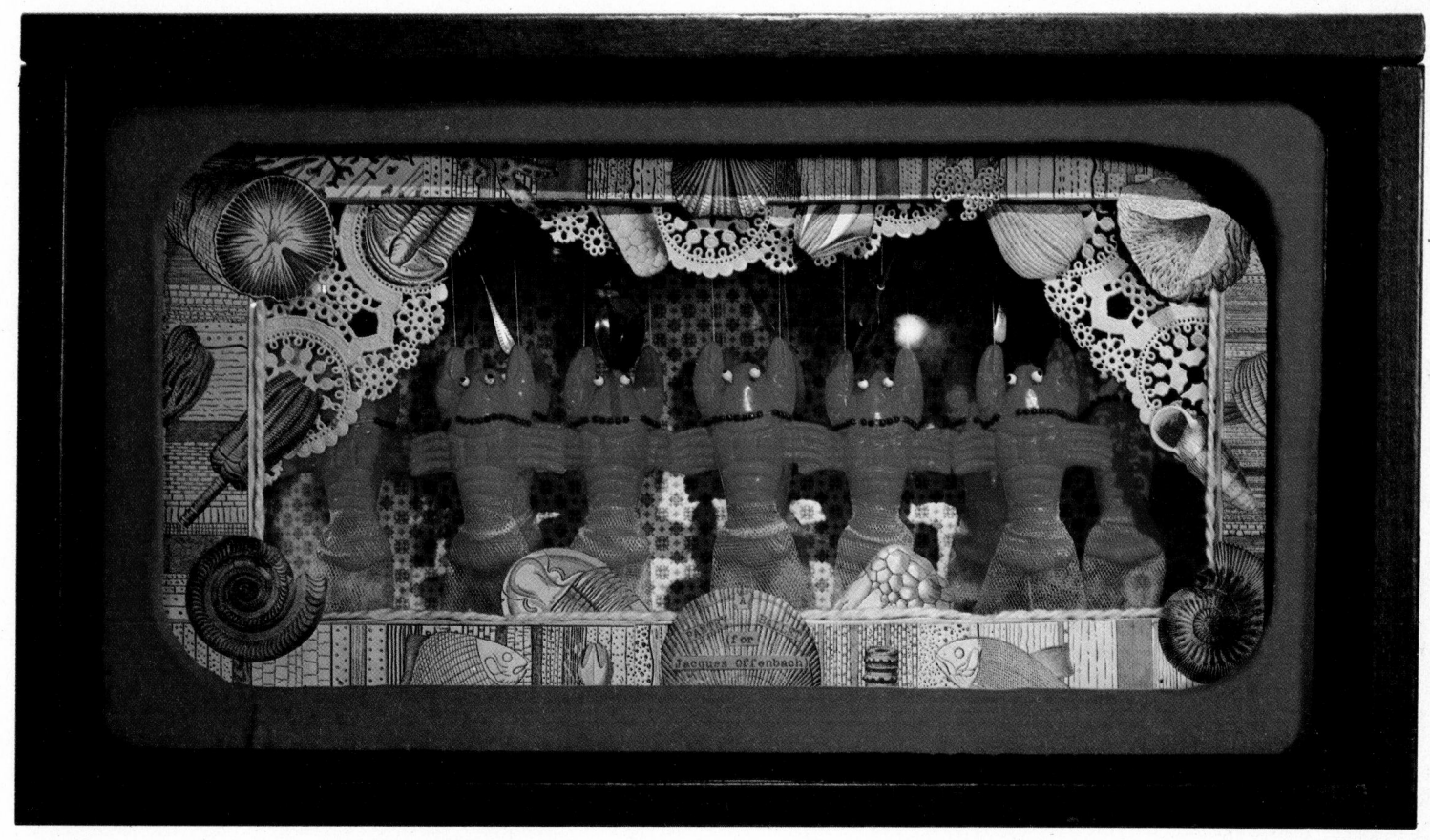

as 1951, when the leading Abstract Expressionist painter Robert Motherwell published an important anthology devoted to the work of the Dada painters and poets. But it was Johns and Rauschenberg who changed Dada from being a historical phenomenon, something safely encapsulated and neutralized, into something which was once again vivifying and controversial. In his introduction to the catalogue of the Jasper Johns retrospective exhibition held at the Whitechapel Art Gallery, London, in 1964, the American critic Alan R. Solomon wrote: "The plain fact remains that the issues of sensibility raised by Dada (apart from whatever significance it may or may not otherwise have), and subsequently raised again by the new generation of American artists, together with a broad re-examination of the meaning of objective reality stimulated by exploration of these issues, challenge all of our basic premises defining the aesthetic experience." A statement of this kind would have been unthinkable even a decade before. The rapidity as well as the magnitude of the change wrought in modern art during the late Fifties is a tribute to the influence exercised by these two American artists.

Of the two, it is Rauschenberg who at first seems the more accessible. Lawrence Alloway remarks: "Johns's imagery is characteristically monolithic—with a massive central object—or serial, as in the parades of alphabets or numbers. Rauschenberg's work is characteristically scenic, with a cluster of points of equivalent interest distributed like islands. Where Rauschenberg accepts the abundance which jumps fully formed from society's head, Johns is elegiac or memorial. . . . Rauschenberg's art samples a plenty that reflects both the sensory input of the city dweller and the industrial output of material goods and waste. Johns's art is concerned with subtle minimums, laconic in style and sceptical in timing.

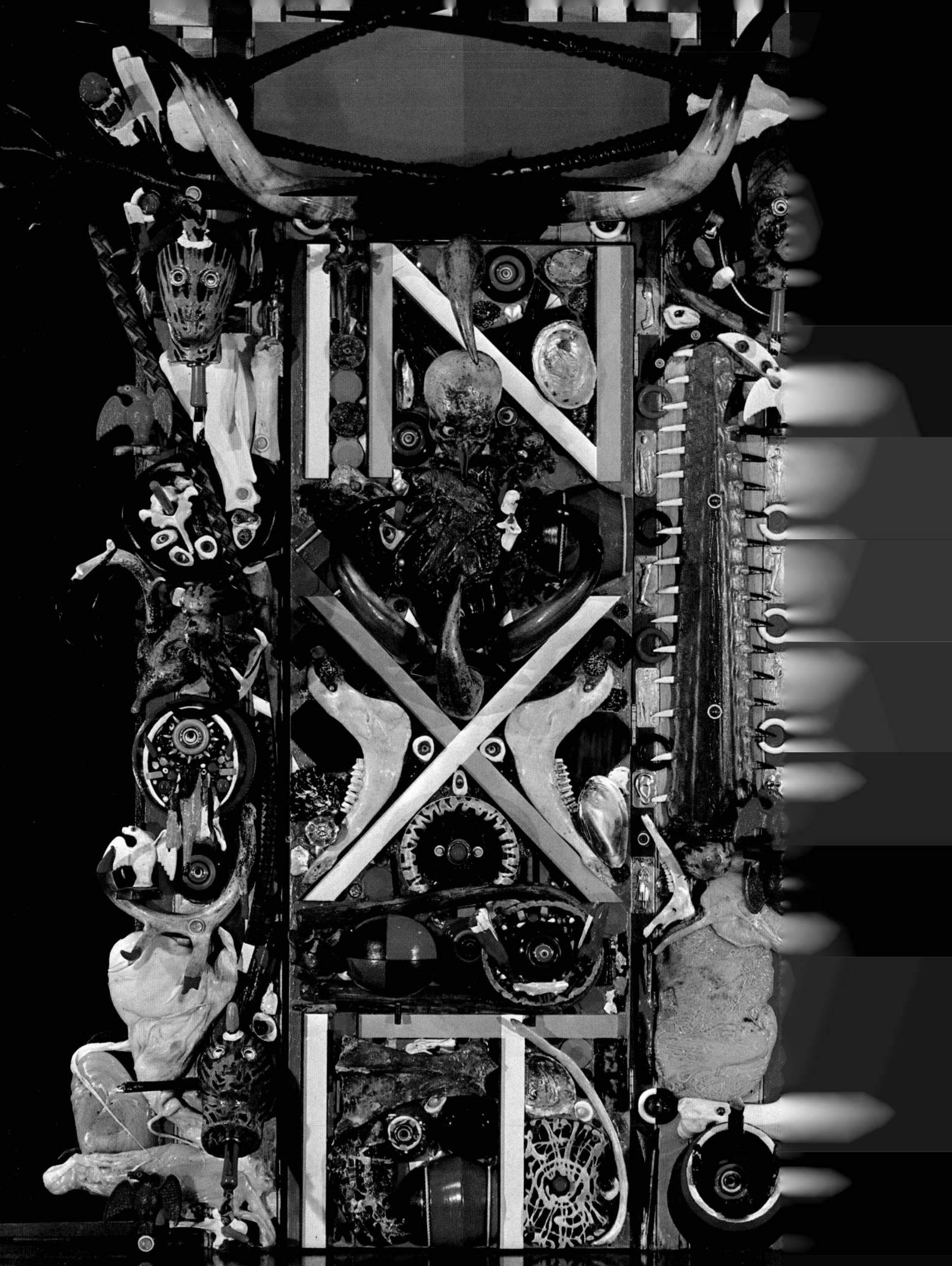

111. Opposite
Alfonso Ossorio
INXIT
1968; 244 × 183 cm. (95 × 71 in.)
New York, coll. Edward F. Dragon

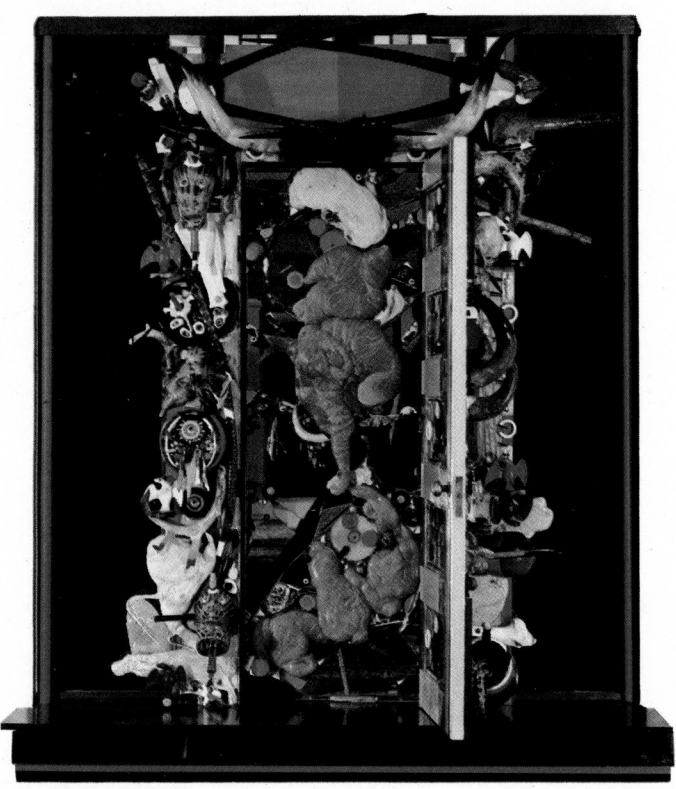

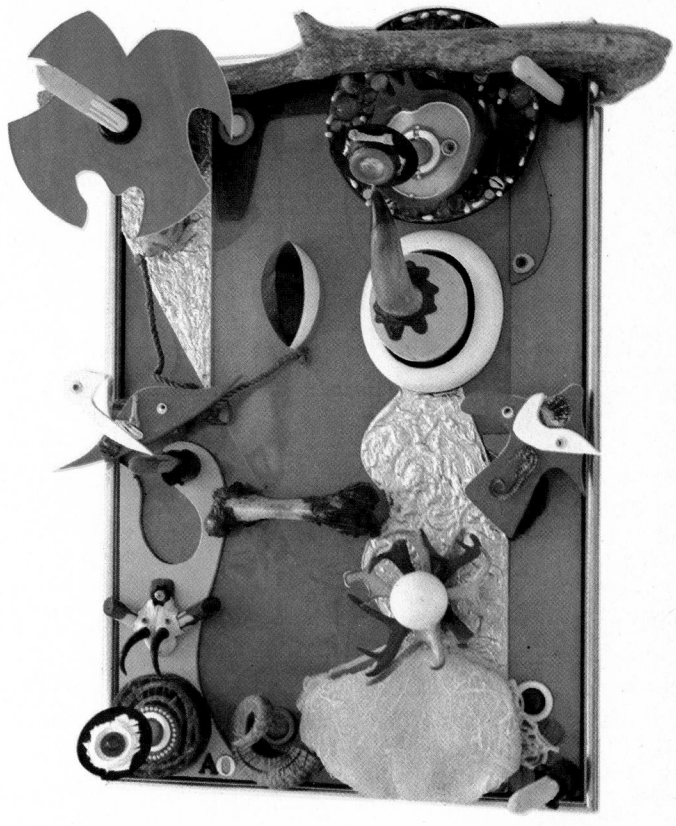

He opposes a malicious monumentality to Rau-schenberg's documentary sense" (Lawrence Alloway in *Figurative Art since 1945*, London, 1971, p. 202).

This description admirably establishes the parameters within which the two artists seem to operate. The most formative part of Rau-schenberg's early career was undoubtedly the years 1948–49, which he spent at the experimental Black Mountain College in North Carolina. This institution was briefly the focus of a number of important talents. Albers taught there, and so did the poet Charles Olson. Rauschenberg's most important contact was not with these but with the avant-garde composer John Cage. It was Cage who implanted in Rauschenberg's mind the notion of "acting in the gap between art and life" which was to result in the creation of the combine-paintings and combine-objects which are his most typical productions.

Works such as *Interview* (Plate 117) or *Retroactive I* (Plate 116) undoubtedly contain elements that

112. Left
Alfonso Ossorio
INXIT
Back

113. Above and right
Alfonso Ossorio
Multiflora
1969; 132 × 89 cm. (51 × 35 in.)
Brandeis University, Massachusetts, Rose Art Museum

114. Overleaf left
Enrico Baj
Busto di donna con cappello
1969; 146 × 114 cm. (57 × 44 in.)
Milan, Galleria Studio Marconi

115. Overleaf right
Enrico Baj
Il Generale (The General)
1962; 146 × 114 cm. (57 × 44 in.)
Milan, Galleria Studio Marconi

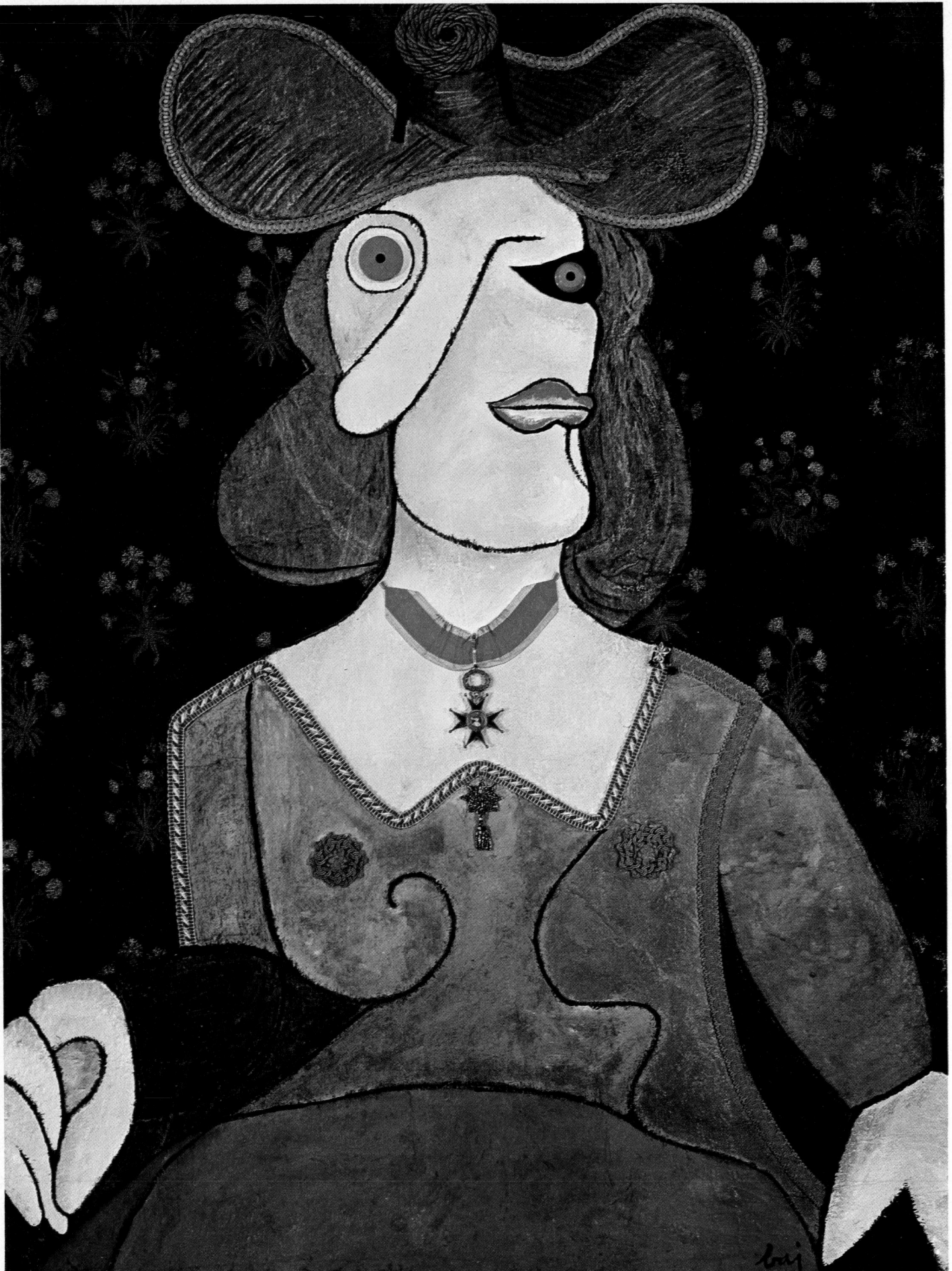

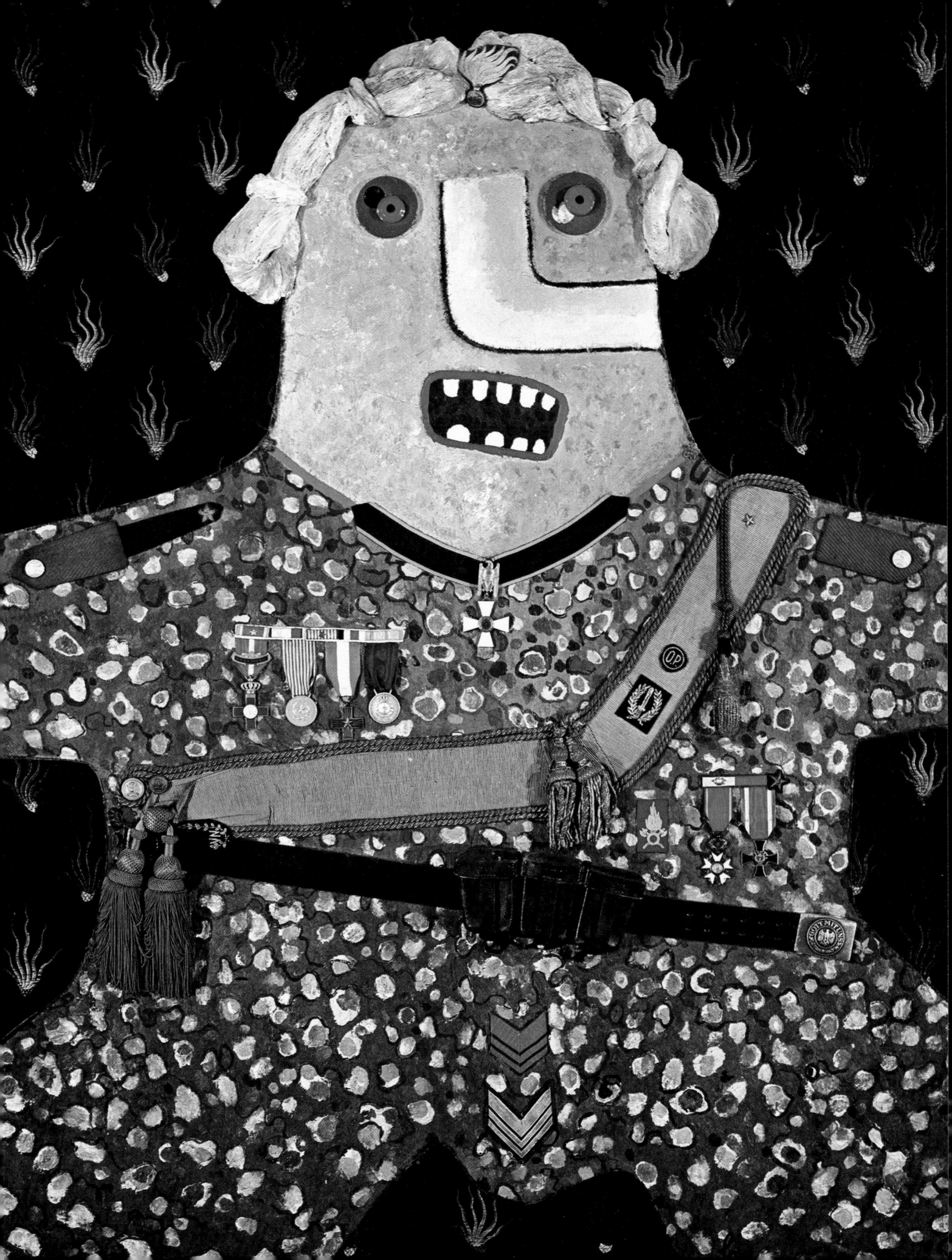

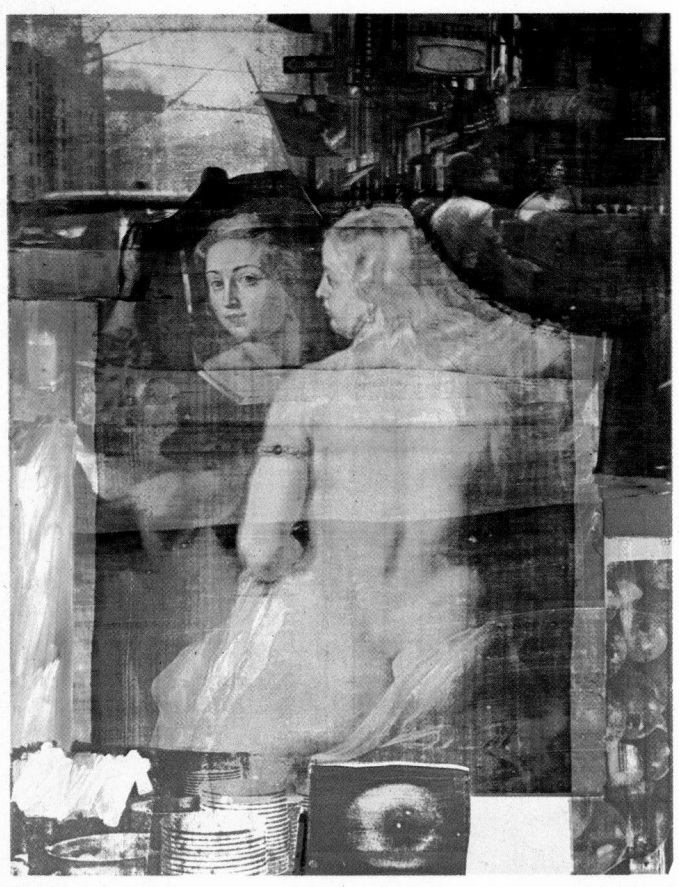

(G. S. Whittet, *Studio International* [April, 1964], p. 158). To which another critic has subsequently replied: "Life has penetrated his work through and through, and each work, rather than impose a definition of art, springs from a questioning of all the possible contexts in which art can happen" (Andrew Forge, *Rauschenberg*, New York, 1970, p. 15).

In fact, these comments probably set the boundaries too wide. Rauschenberg is undoubtedly experimental not merely because that is what a modern artist ought to be, but because he himself is possessed by the spirit of exploration. The famous combine-object *Monogram* (Plate 120) of 1955–59, whose principal component is a stuffed goat, proposes to the spectator a dizzying leap of sensibility. How and why should this be considered a work of art? It is only a work of art if the conjunction of elements provides a certain kind of *frisson*, and that *frisson* can no more be explained than the psychic shock that the reader gets from certain images in modern poetry.

But much of Rauschenberg's work does not impose such strenuous tests. One of the logical elements in his creative career has been his relationship to the urban and technological society which surrounds him. The conjunctions of imagery which we discover in what he does are not juxtapositions peculiar to himself, but ones which assail us at every moment of urban existence. Rauschenberg was the direct pioneer of many of the innovations afterwards attributed to Pop Art. In 1955, he made a series of paintings using comic strips. He has also interested himself in the distortions imposed on the art of the past by modern techniques of mass reproduction. We frequently find in the combines the notion of re-using and recycling urban detritus, of "redeeming" it, as Schwitters did before him.

But Rauschenberg does not confine his associative leaps (the ones he makes himself and the ones he imposes on the spectator) to purely contemporary and popular material. He has a habit of using his work to reflect aspects of the art and culture of the past. A striking example of this is the series of drawings made as illustrations to Dante's *Inferno*. In creating these Rauschenberg was

derive from Abstract Expressionism. As late as 1964 Max Kozloff was afraid that the artist would "continue to be dismissed as a belated Abstract Expressionist, one whose dribbles and splatters of paint have merely thinned and shrunk to give way to objects or reproduced images of daily life". But in fact his originality was quickly recognized. To the fluidity which was a leading characteristic of the painting of the Pollock-Kline group of Abstract Expressionists, he opposed images which remained discrete and themselves, which insisted on maintaining a value and identity which had nothing to do with their own presence in the picture. This put traditional criticism in a dilemma. As one reviewer remarked, concerning the retrospective at the Whitechapel Art Gallery which made Rauschenberg's European reputation: "Art by being absent does nothing to assist our reaction to life; Rauschenberg offers *neat* life; it is for us to find the art in it for ourselves"

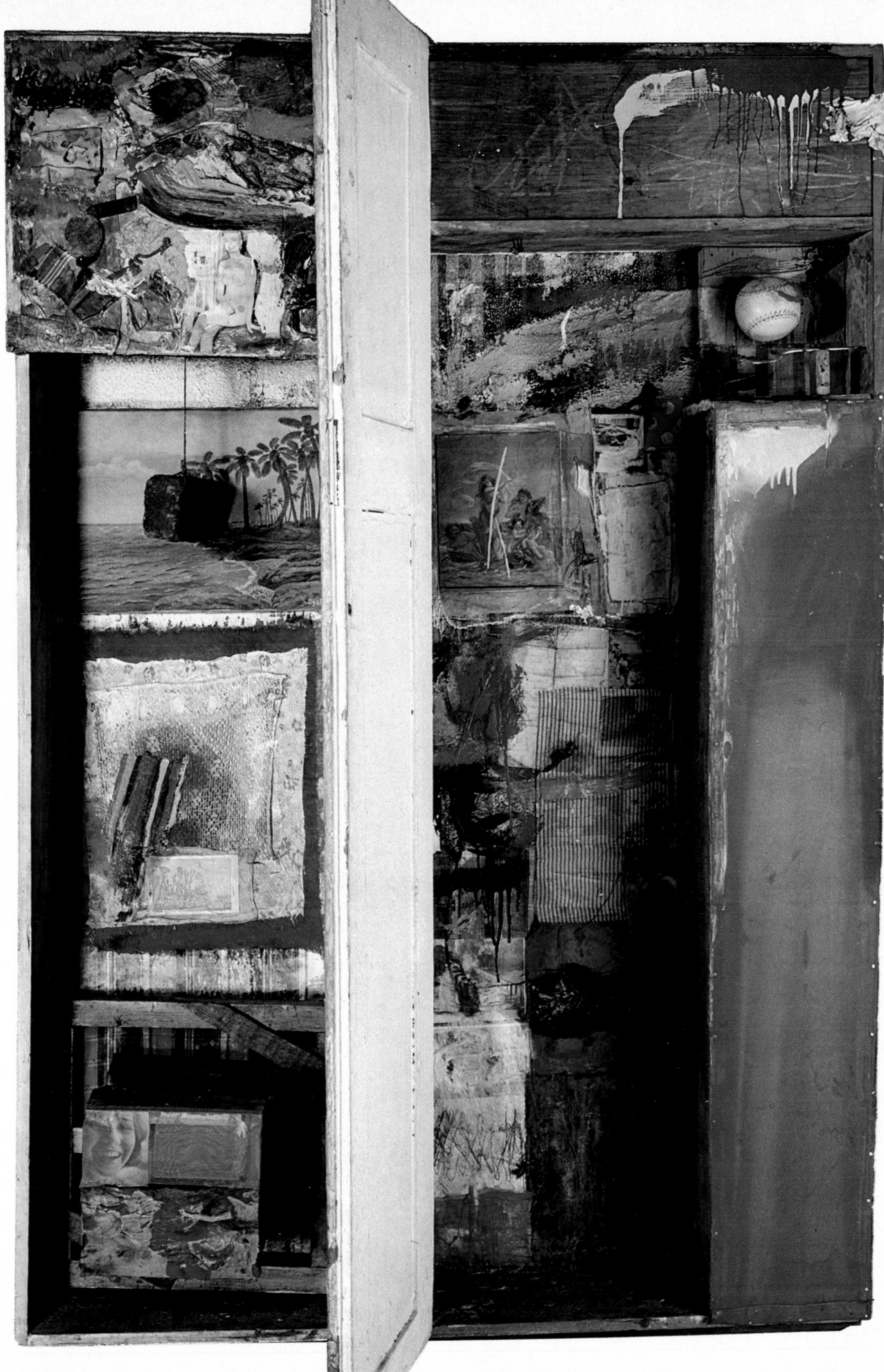

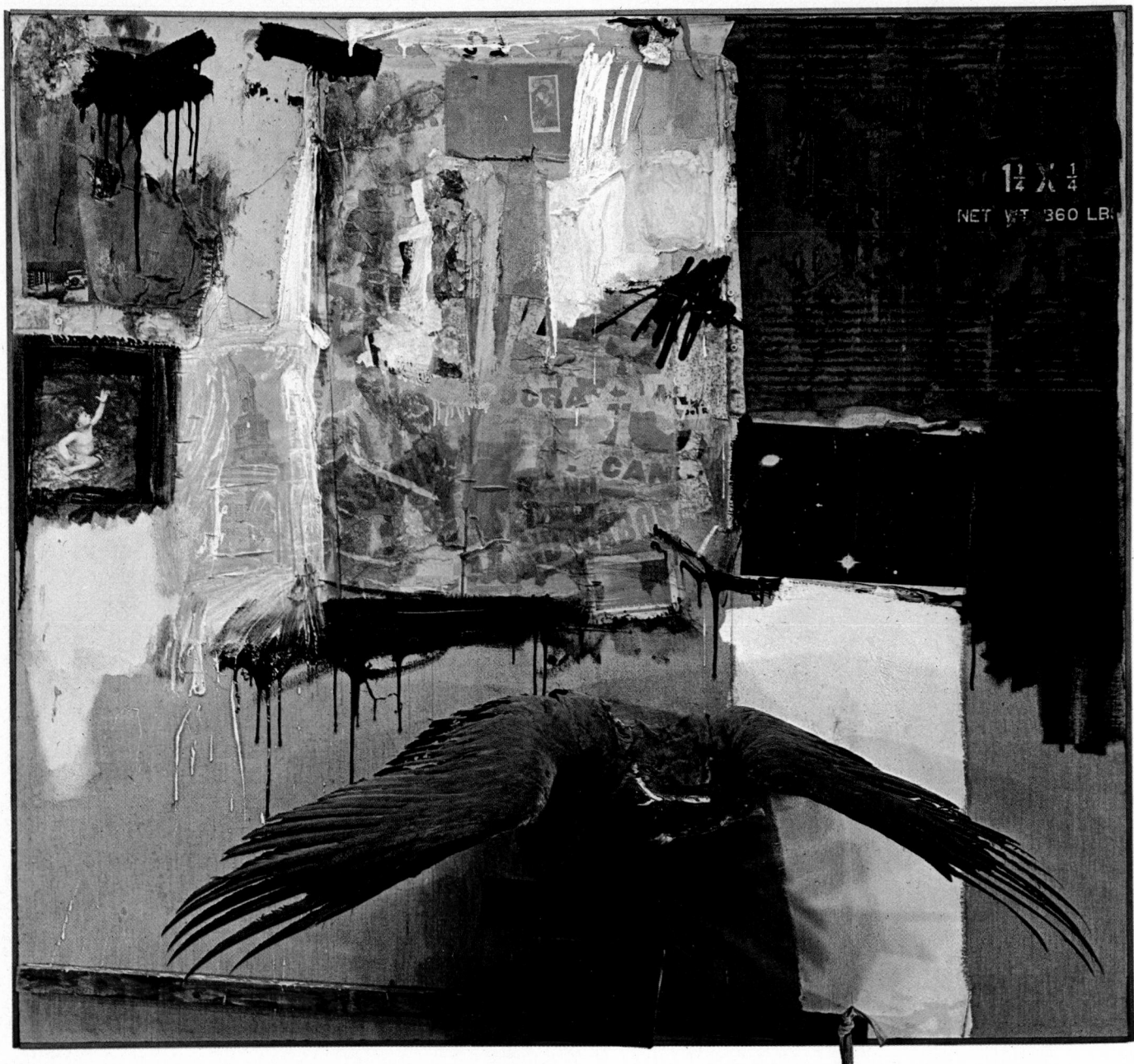

following in the footsteps of many other illustrators of Dante, among them William Blake and Sandro Botticelli. His achievement is to show the continuing relevance of the great poet, by relating his poem directly to the things we see about us. The city, he reminds us, may be a mechanism for alienation, but on the other hand it offers the key to many varieties of human achievement. The great museums are as typically urban as slums and decaying rubbish dumps.

Jasper Johns's career offers many parallels with Robert Rauschenberg's, and, at a crucial point in their joint development, the two artists shared a New York studio. Johns, too, has concerned

118.
Robert Rauschenberg
Canyon
1959; 216 × 176 × 58 cm. (84 × 69 × 23 in.)
California, Pasadena Art Museum

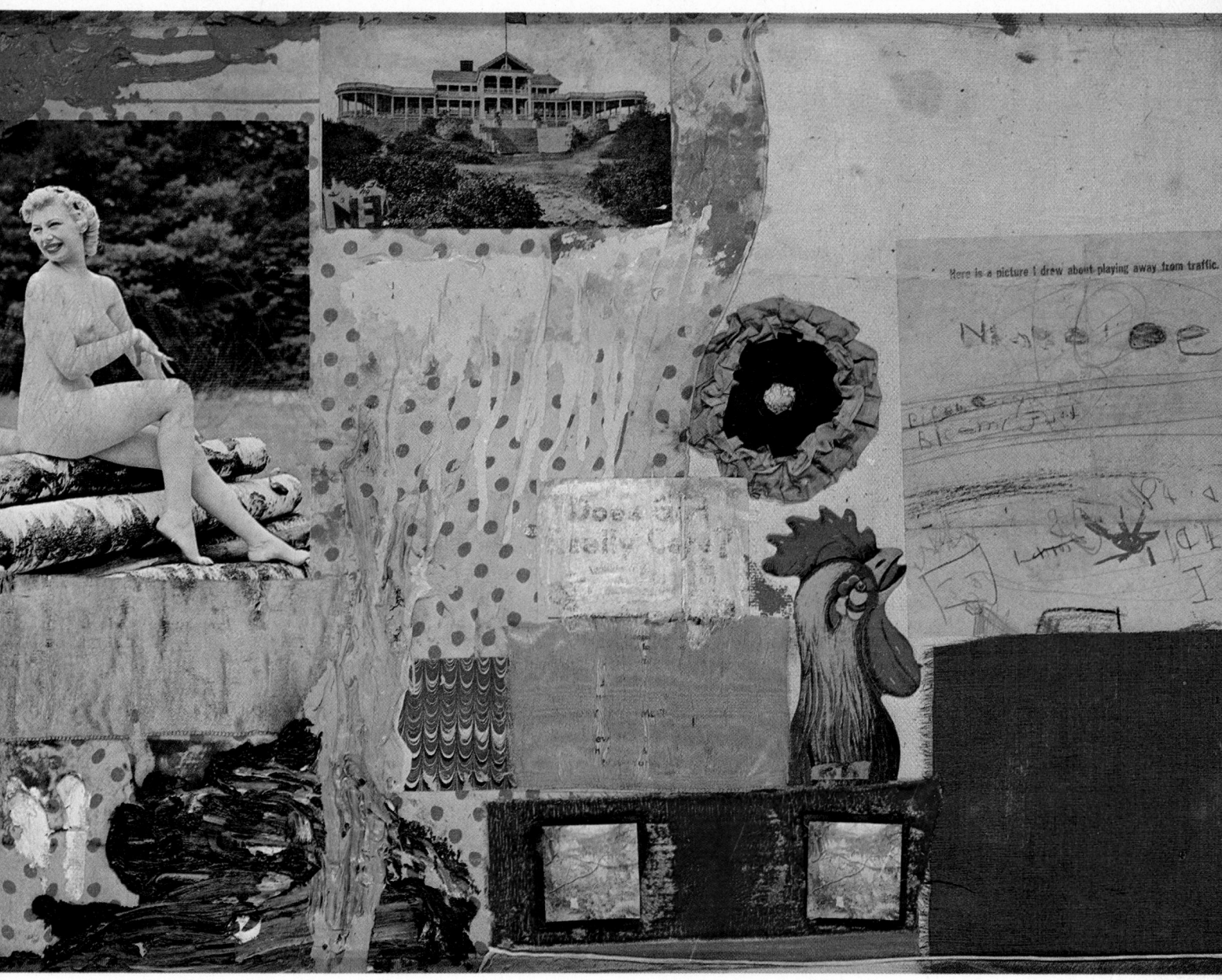

119.
Robert Rauschenberg
Untitled
1955; 39.4 × 52.7 cm. (15 × 21 in.)
New York, coll. Jasper Johns

120. Overleaf
Robert Rauschenberg
Monogram
1955–59; 163 × 160.5 × 95 cm. (64 × 63 × 37 in.)
Stockholm, Moderna Museet

himself with the different layers of reality: "I am concerned with a thing's not being what it was, with its becoming other than what it is, with any moment in which one identifies a thing precisely and with the slipping away of this moment, with any moment seeing or saying and letting it go at that" (quoted by G. R. Swenson, "What is Pop Art? Part II, Jasper Johns", *Art News*, Vol. 62, No. 10 [February, 1964], p. 43).

Assemblage is very much part of Johns's technical armoury, and there is, too, a popular, urban component in his work. But unlike Rauschenberg he is not tremendously interested in recording the way that urban experience impinges

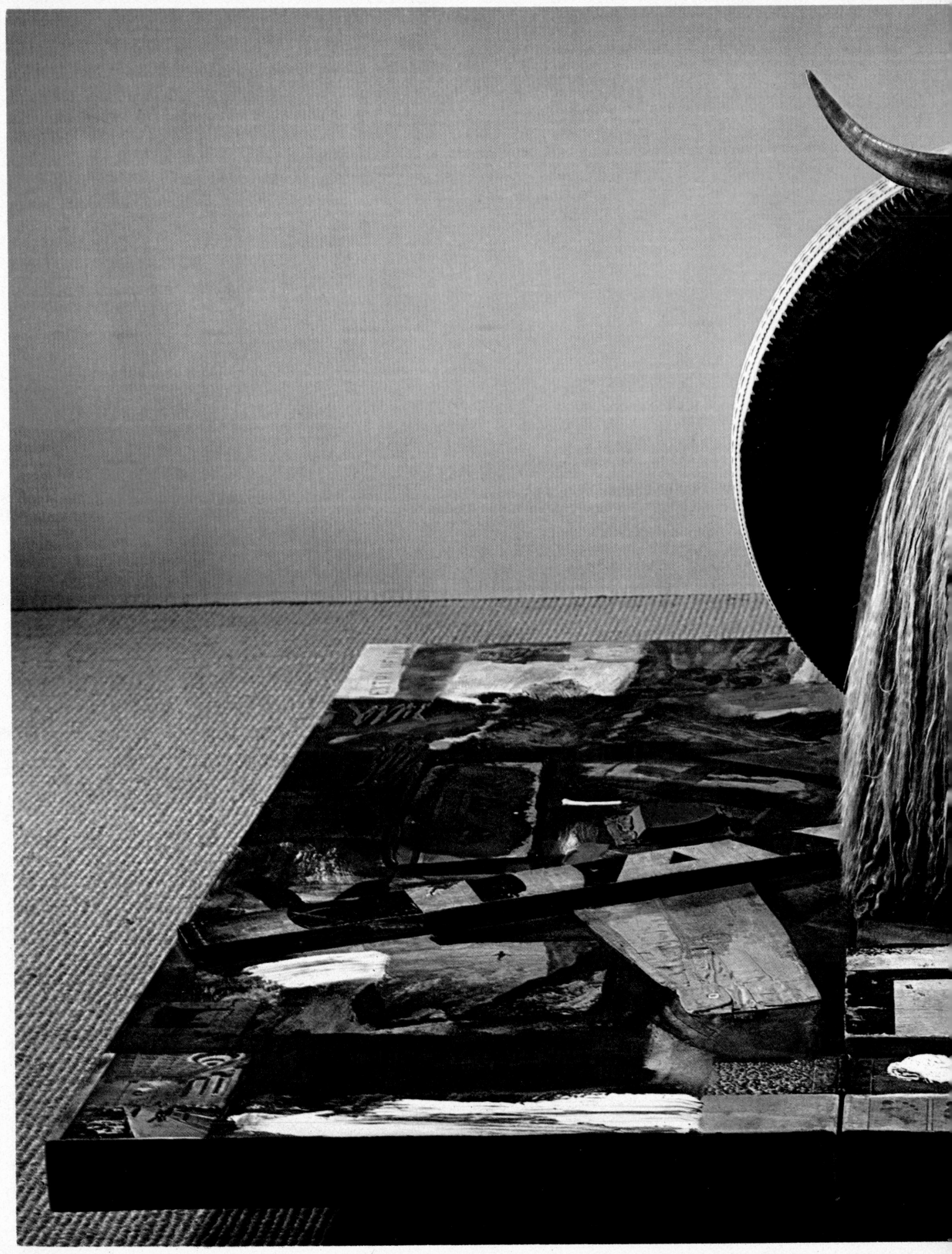

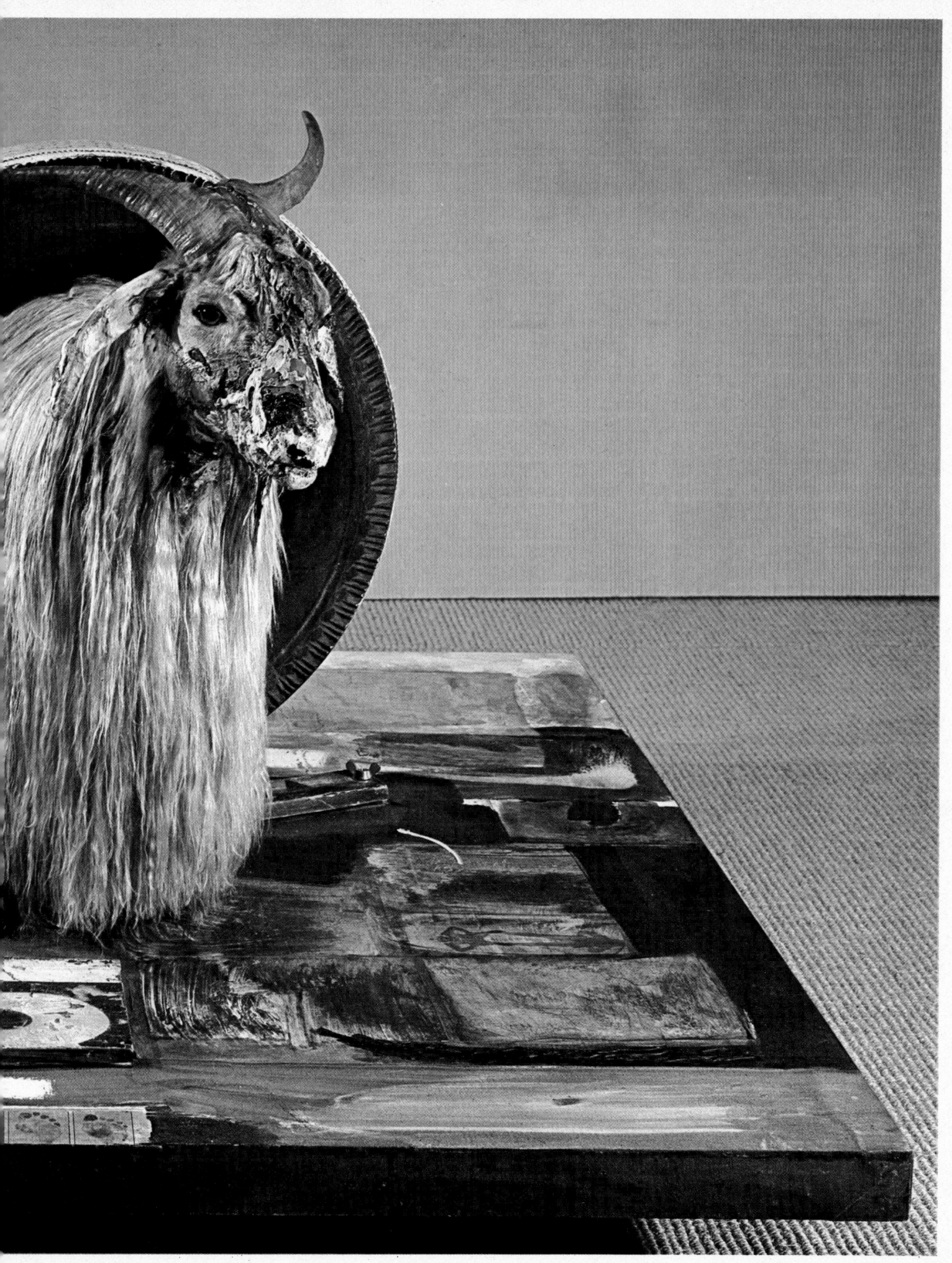

121.
Jasper Johns
Three Flags
1958; 78.4 × 115.6 cm. (31 × 45 in.)
Connecticut, coll. Mr. and Mrs. Burton Tremaine

122. Opposite
Jasper Johns
Target with Four Faces
1958; 75.6 × 66 cm. (29 × 26 in.)
New York, Museum of Modern Art,
gift of Mr. and Mrs. Robert C. Scull

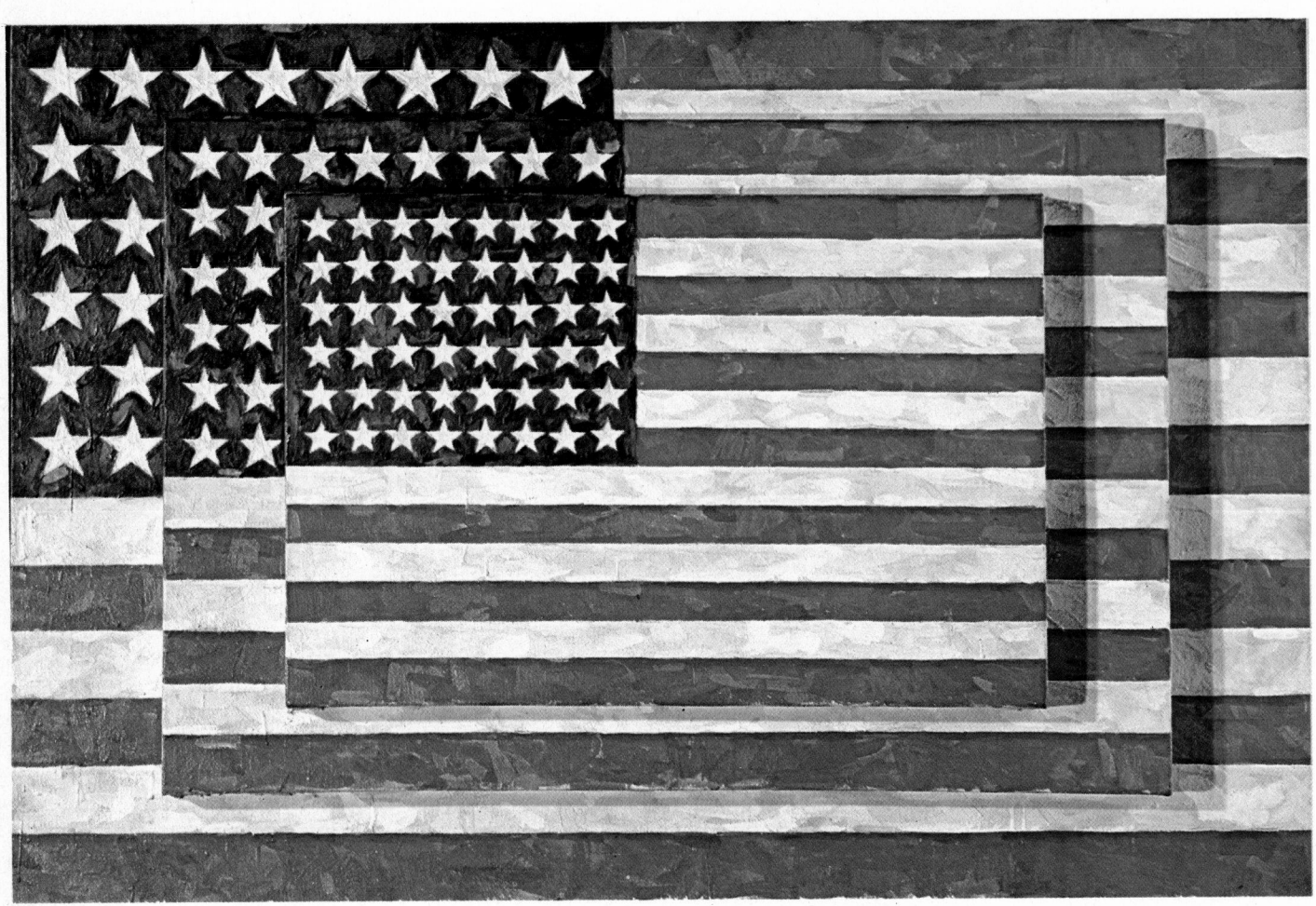

upon his own sensibility. His work has ikon-like characteristics which link it directly to that of a man like Rothko upon the one hand and to Pop artists such as Roy Lichtenstein and Andy Warhol upon the other. In a series of works painted during the middle Fifties he used the American flag as his chosen image (Plate 121). The familiar pattern is presented completely frontally, so that the spectator is forced to ask himself what difference exists between a real flag and this simulacrum of one which is presented as "art". Johns himself said that he chose for his iconography "things the mind already knows. That gave me room to work on other levels." His view is that "Meaning is determined by the use of a thing, the way an audience uses a painting once it is put in public."

An examination of Johns's flag paintings does

nevertheless reveal an "art" component of a perfectly traditional kind. This is to be found in the way they are painted. For these works Johns made use of encaustic, a medium he handles with the utmost refinement, and the marks that go to make the image, though in no sense rhetorical or even gestural, are instantly recognizable as the artist's personal handwriting.

Another inert sign which Johns made use of at this period was the target. Subsequently targets were to have a long career in American art and were to be used for a number of different reasons. Johns's reason does seem to be connected with the function of a target as a mark to be aimed at. One of the best-known works from this particular series is the *Target with Four Faces* of 1958 (Plate 122). The faces are life masks of a nose and mouth

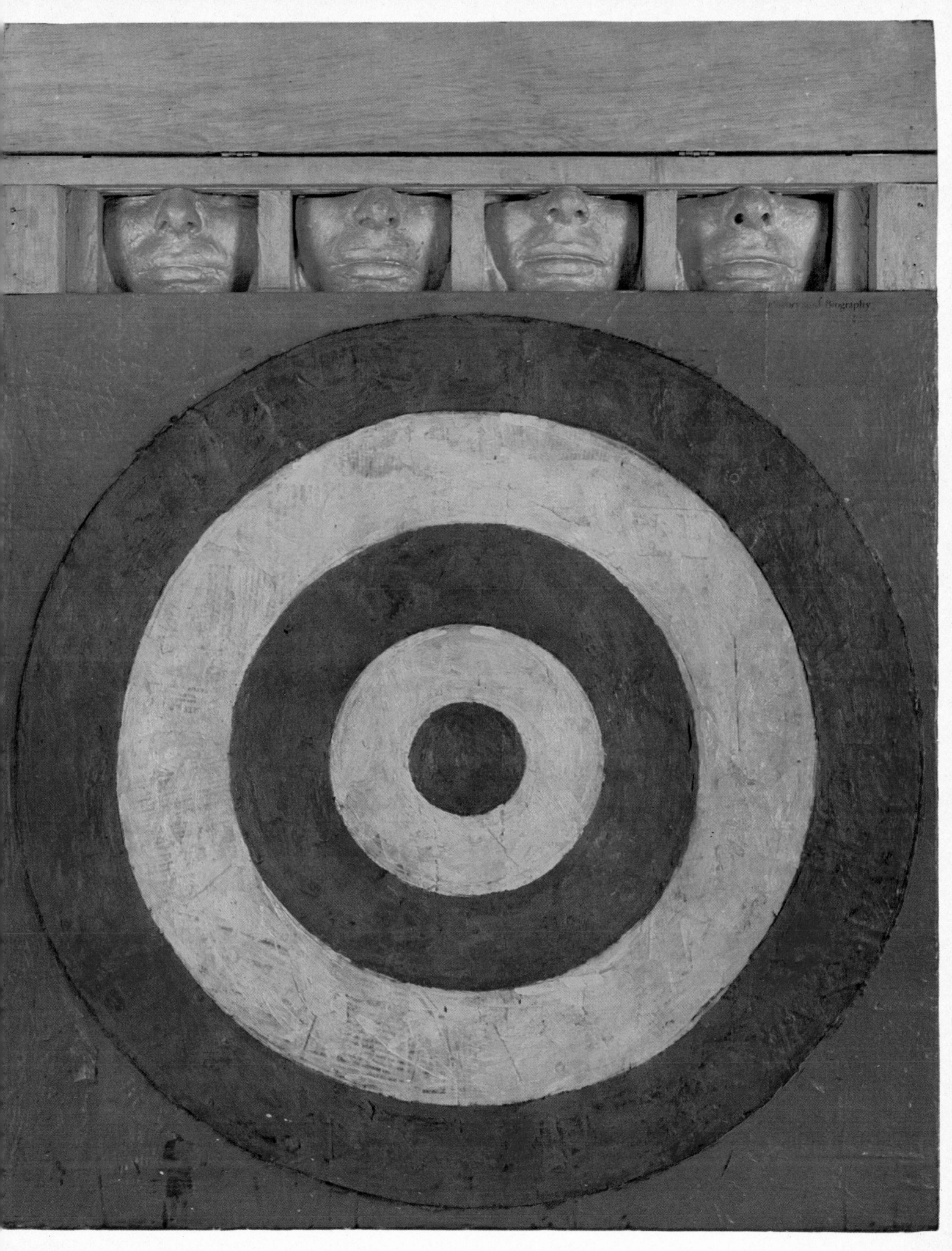

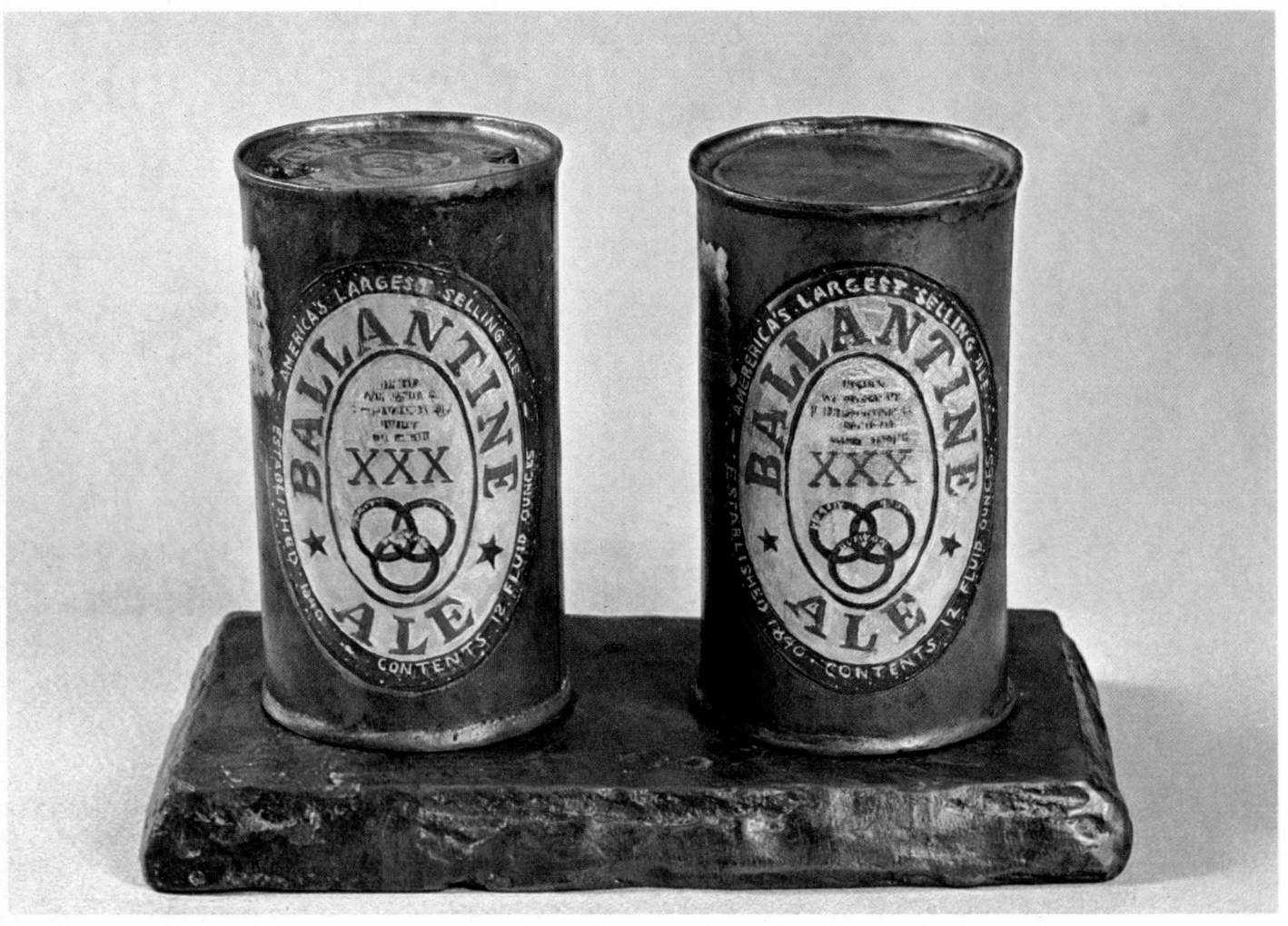

only. They are identical and are placed in a row above the target itself. Situated thus, they have an air of vulnerability which is disturbing. But, as if to protect the spectator from any discomfort he might feel, the faces are provided with a hinged cover which can be used to conceal them.

This, however, is only one possible interpretation of a profoundly ambiguous work. Lawrence Alloway, discussing it, sees the principal function of the faces as being to reinforce the symmetry of the target itself, thanks to the repetition of identical forms. This repetition, he believes, cancels out any sense of mutilation we might have because the mask is incomplete. "The whole form of the target . . ." he adds, "is echoed by the all-or-nothing cover."

123.
Jasper Johns
Painted Bronze II: Ale Cans
1964; 137 × 20 × 11.2 cm. (53 × 9 × 4 in.)
New York, collection of the artist

124. Opposite above
Jasper Johns
The Critic Smiles
1959; 4 × 18.1 × 3.8 cm. (2 × 7 × 1 in.)
New York, collection of the artist

125. Opposite below
Jasper Johns
High School Days
1964; 30 cm. (12 in.)
New York, collection of the artist

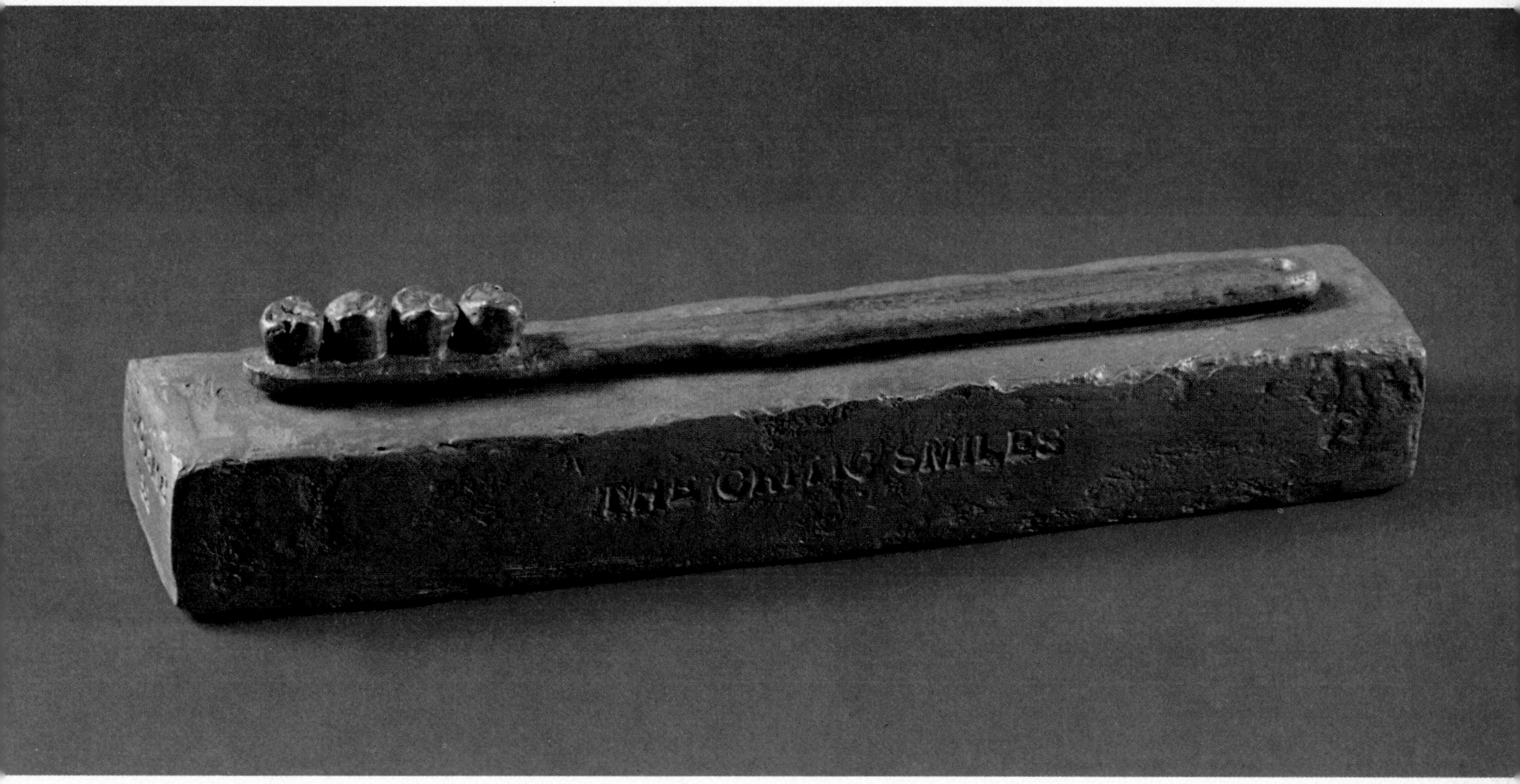
THE CRITIC SMILES

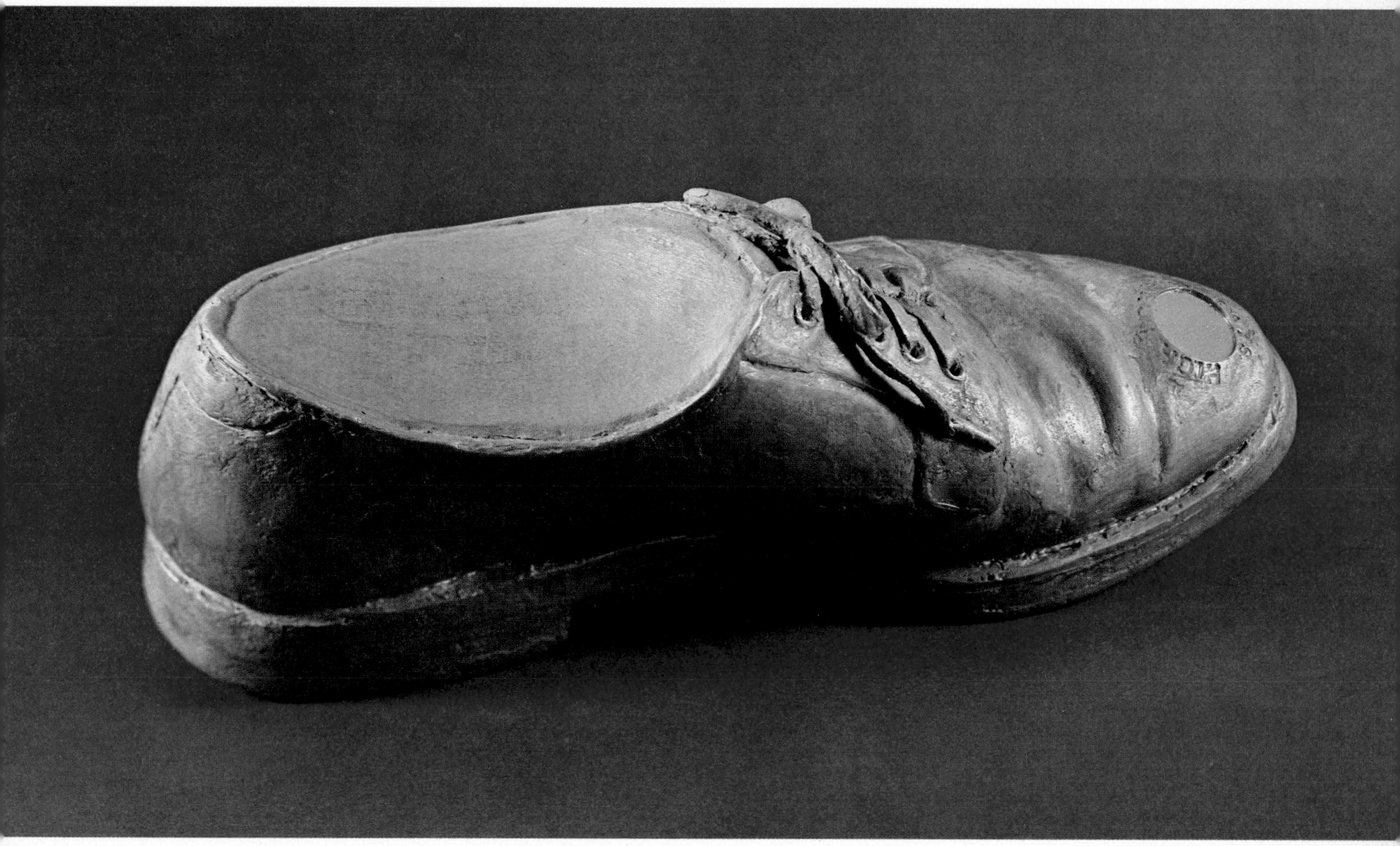

126.
Yves Klein
Suaire ANT-SU 2
1962; 128 × 66 cm. (50 × 26 in.)
Stockholm, Moderna Museet

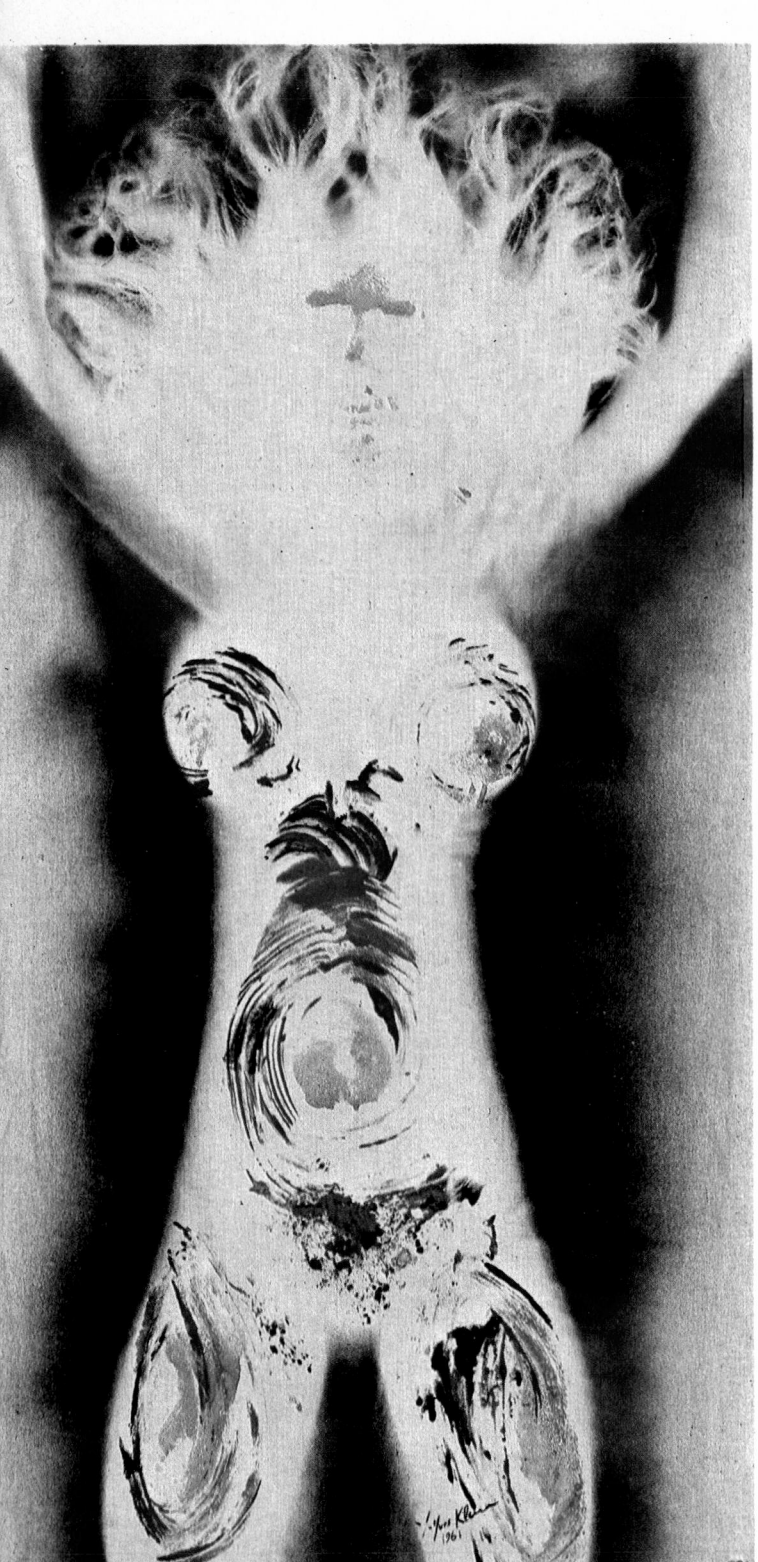

Johns's irony and ambiguity link him very closely indeed to Duchamp, and the link is stressed by a small series of Sculpmetal objects, which are the American artist's equivalent of the Duchamp ready-mades. One, a pair of beer cans on a plinth, is said to have been made as a retort to the remark that Johns's dealer, Leo Castelli, "could sell anything, even a can of beer". Another, *The Critic Smiles*, features a toothbrush and is a directer-than-usual assault on the state of criticism.

The most endearing of these objects is probably the one the artist has entitled *High School Days* (Plate 125). This is a Sculpmetal cast of a teenager's shoe. Johns means it to be emblematic, not only of aspects of the American growing-up process, but also of his own nostalgia for that period in his own life. At the same time we are conscious of a deliberate attempt—also discernible in the paintings of flags and of the maps of the United States—to acclimatize the avant-garde in terms which would be purely American. In this sense Johns continued the effort already begun by the Abstract Expressionists.

That which most closely corresponded to what Johns and Rauschenberg were doing, so far as Europe was concerned, was the work of the New Realism group, organized by the French critic Pierre Restany. New Realism did not officially come into being until 1960, though a number of the artists who participated in the group had already made reputations for themselves during the late Fifties. Among the founding members were Yves Klein, Fernandez A. Arman, Martial Raysse, Daniel Spoerri, and Jean Tingueley. The sculptor César gave his adherence soon afterwards, and a later recruit was the Bulgarian artist Christo. Some of these members, such as Raysse and Tingueley, no longer seem particularly relevant to the aims of New Realism. Raysse is better considered in the context of European Pop Art and Tingueley in that of Kineticism.

The striking personality was Yves Klein. Restany relates how Klein, on the beach at Nice in 1946, when he was eighteen, received a revelation of the "energetic infinity" of the sky. Because birds in their passage disturbed the purity of the blue he saw above him, he wanted to kill them.

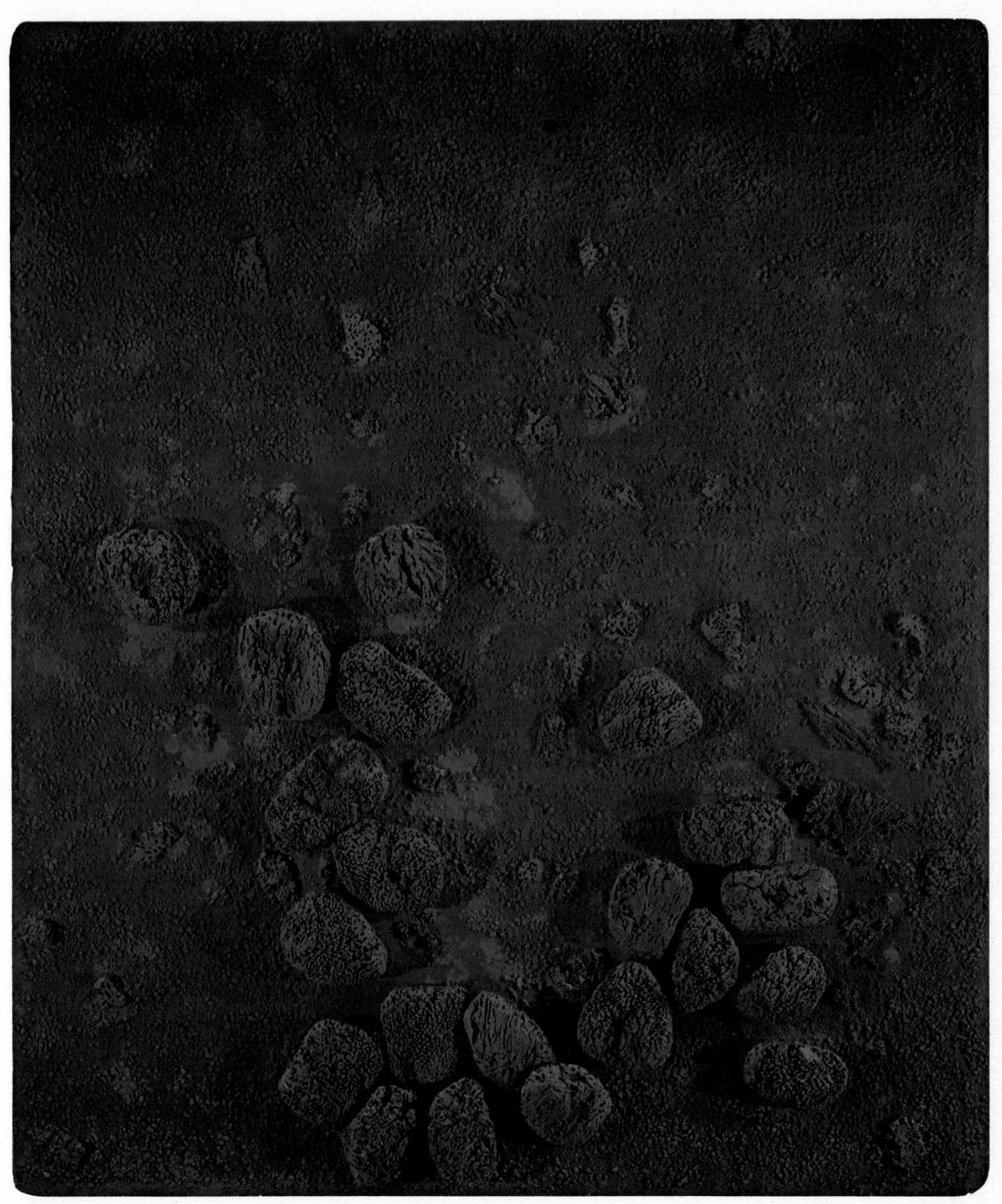

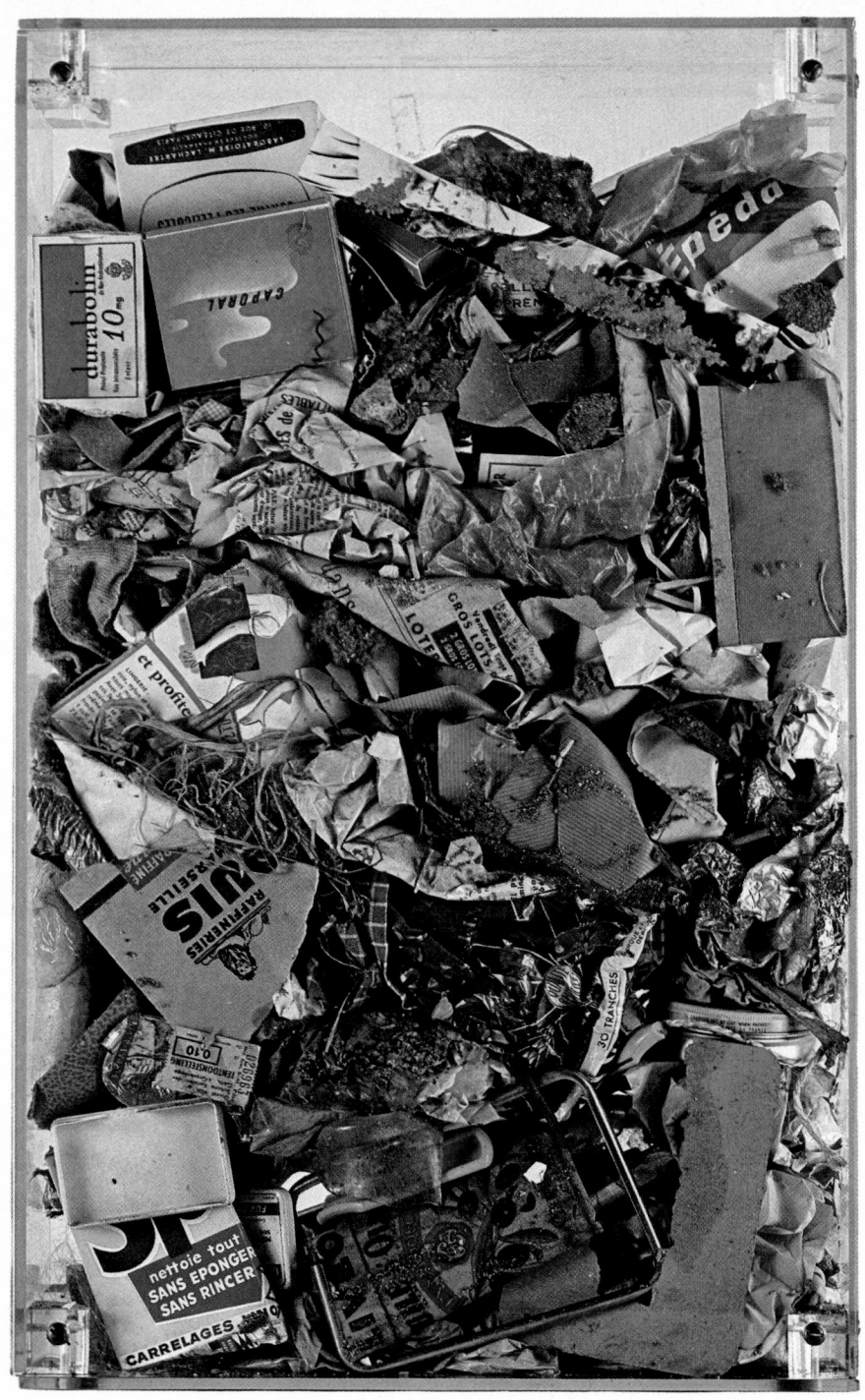

128. Opposite
Yves Klein
Monogold: MG 18
1961; 78.5 × 55.5 cm. (31 × 22 in.)
Cologne, Wallraf-Richartz Museum

129.
Fernandez Arman
Poubelle I (Dustbin I)
1960; 65 × 40 × 10 cm. (25 × 16 × 4 in.)
Krefeld, Kaiser Wilhelm Museum

130. Overleaf left
Fernandez Arman
Nucléide
1964; 123 × 92 cm. (48 × 36 in.)
Amsterdam, Stedelijk Museum

131. Overleaf right
Fernandez Arman
Soyeux Temps modernes: accumulation d'engranages
1965; 79.5 × 60 cm. (31 × 23 in.)
Paris, Galerie Mathias Fels

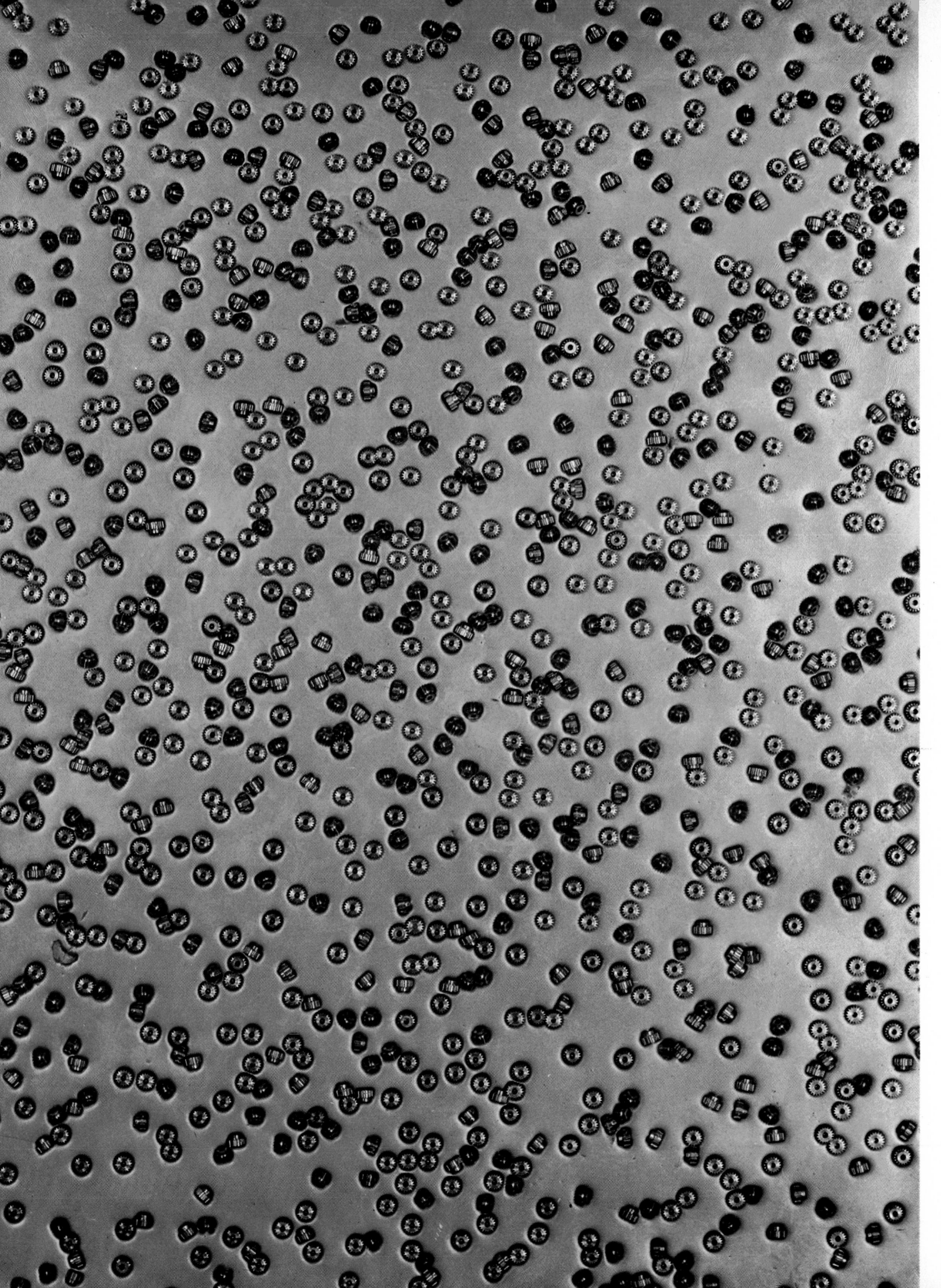

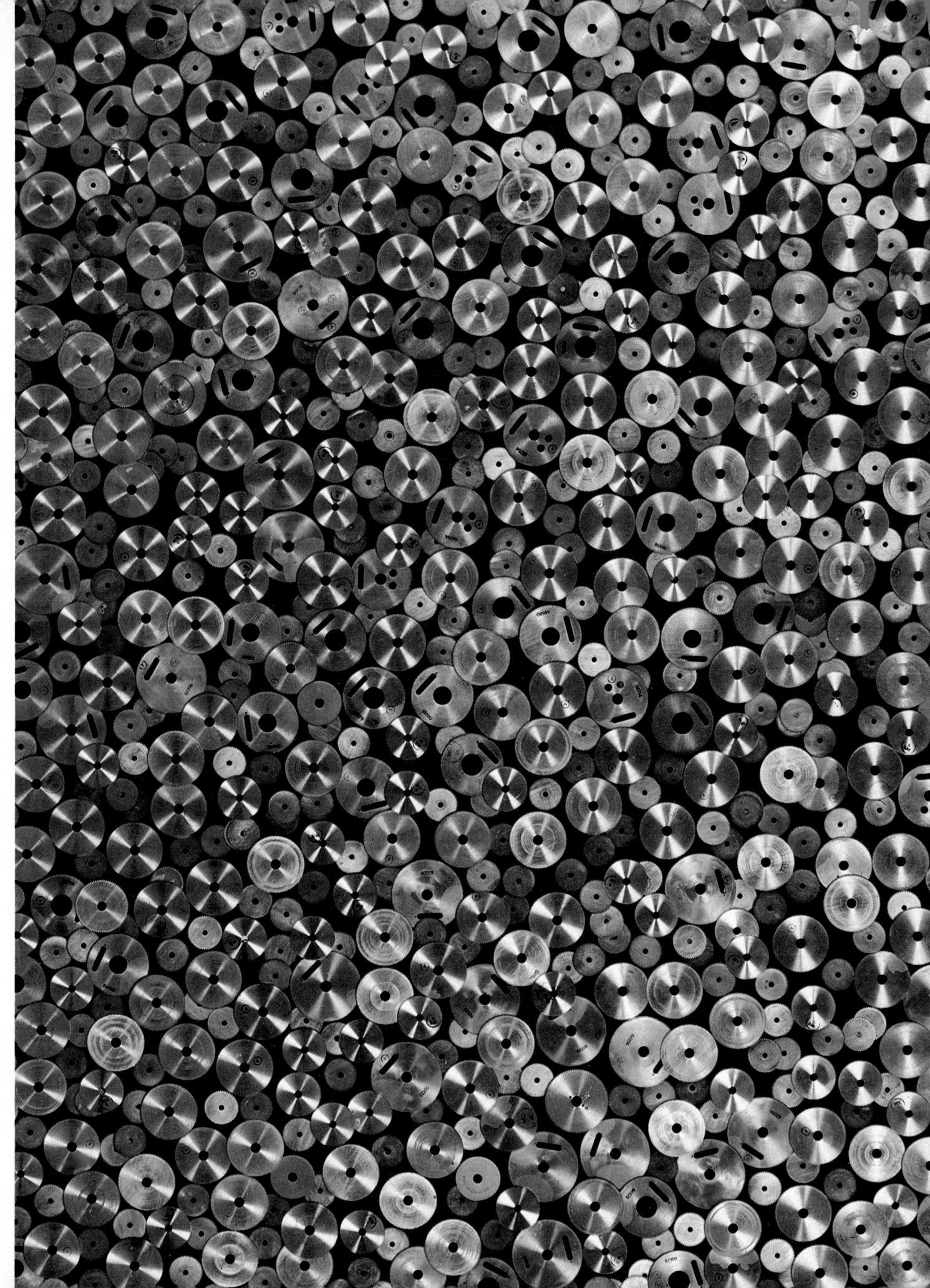

132.
Vic Gentils
Untitled
1955–64; 62.1 × 49.2 cm. (24 × 19 in.)
Cologne, coll. Mr. and Mrs. Müller

What Restany calls the "tendency towards a visionary monopoly" was early implanted in the artist.

In practical terms, the results were unpredictable. Klein was one of the most gifted creators of artistic scandals of his time and, until his premature death in 1962, managed to keep the European art world in a ferment. Klein's drive was always towards the boundless, the immaterial. This was the real point of the exhibition he staged at the Iris Clert Gallery in Paris in April, 1958. This was entitled "*Le Vide*"—"The Void"—and at the preview the invited guests discovered that the artist meant precisely what he said. The gallery walls were entirely bare, and the space was "sensitized" only by the artist's presence.

Later Klein was to say: "To sum up, mine is a dual proposal: first of all to record the imprint of man's affectivity in present-day civilization, and then to record the trace of precisely that which has engendered the same civilization, which is to say, that of fire. And all this because my essential preoccupation has always been with the void, and I hold it as assured that, in the heart of the void as in the heart of man, there are fires that burn" (written in New York in 1961; from the catalogue of the exhibition "Yves Klein", Iolas Gallery, Paris, 1965).

These words were written in connection with the group of paintings in which Klein used "natural" forces to achieve his effects: a flame-thrower, rain falling on a canvas which was first tied to the roof of a car, then driven through the wet. But Klein experimented with a number of other methods as well. For example, he made use of human paintbrushes. Girls were asked to strip and then to dip their bodies in paint. After this they impressed their outlines upon the canvas, or allowed themselves to be dragged across it (Plate 126). Klein often turned these painting sessions into public ceremonies—some people count them among the earliest happenings. His genius for publicity certainly at least equalled that of Mathieu.

Today his most typical works seem to be his monochromes. Many of these were painted in a special shade of blue which the artist patented under the name of International Klein Blue (Plate 127). The sponges attached to the surface of some examples were another favourite material of Klein's, presumably because the substance was both formless and absorbent. Perhaps the most beautiful of all the monochrome works are the *Monogolds*. These are usually dented as if the artist had struck them with a padded hammer, as if to draw attention to the parallel between resonance of sound and the visual resonance of the surface (Plate 128).

There is a strong resemblance between these *Monogolds* and the plain gold screens sometimes produced by the Japanese. This draws attention to the link between Klein's cosmic transcendentalism and Zen philosophy. This connection is not an accidental one. Klein, in addition to his activities as an artist, was an expert in judo, and wrote a handbook on the subject. The strong element of Dada provocation in his activities must therefore be balanced against a strain of quietism which also appears in the work of Johns and Rauschenberg. Rauschenberg, for instance, produced a series of all-white paintings during his sojourn at Black Mountain College, in which the only "figuration" was produced by the cast shadows of those who moved in front of them. Zen, of course, exercised a profound influence over the musical activities of John Cage.

Klein's closest associate—they were friends from the time of their youth in the South of France—was Arman. But the latter did not develop rapidly as an artist. From 1946, when he first met Klein, until 1956, he was no more than a Sunday painter, recapitulating the historical progression of Modernist styles from Fauvism to abstract post-Cubism. After this he progressively abandoned the practice of painting, in favour of a method of accumulation—what he came to call "the language of quantity". Objects would be presented in random accumulations, as in the *Dustbin I* of 1960 (Plate 129). To show the chance-selected contents of a dustbin as a work of art is surely an idea to delight any Dadaist. Another gambit of Arman's was to embed a mass of objects of the same type in a matrix of liquid polyester, which imparted to them a spurious preciousness

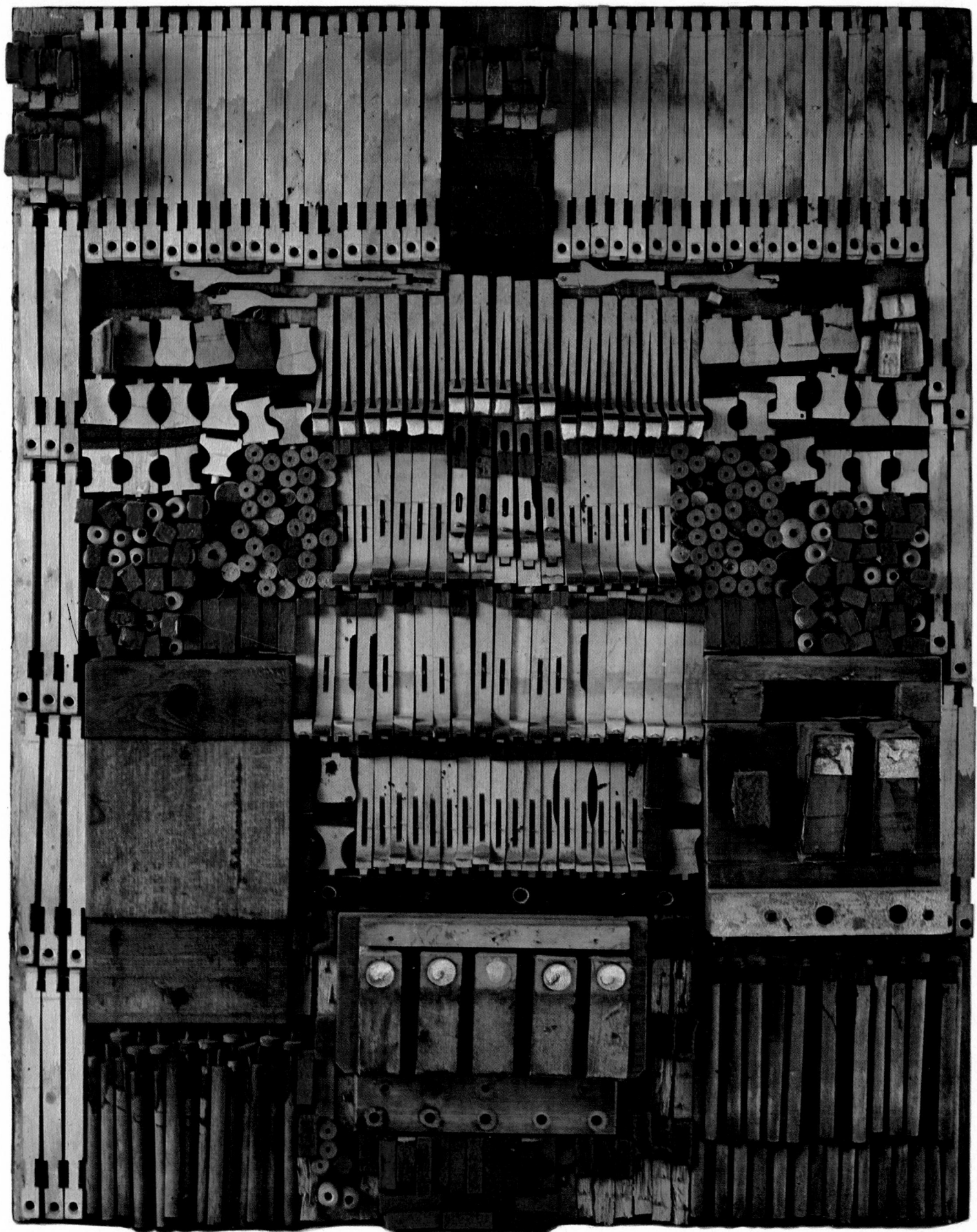

133.
John Latham
Film Star
1961; 160 × 200 × 25.4 cm. (62 × 78 × 10 in.)
London, Tate Gallery

134. Opposite
Fernandez Arman
Torse aux gants (Glove Torso)
1967; 85 cm. (33 in.)
Cologne, Wallraf-Richartz Museum, coll. Ludwig

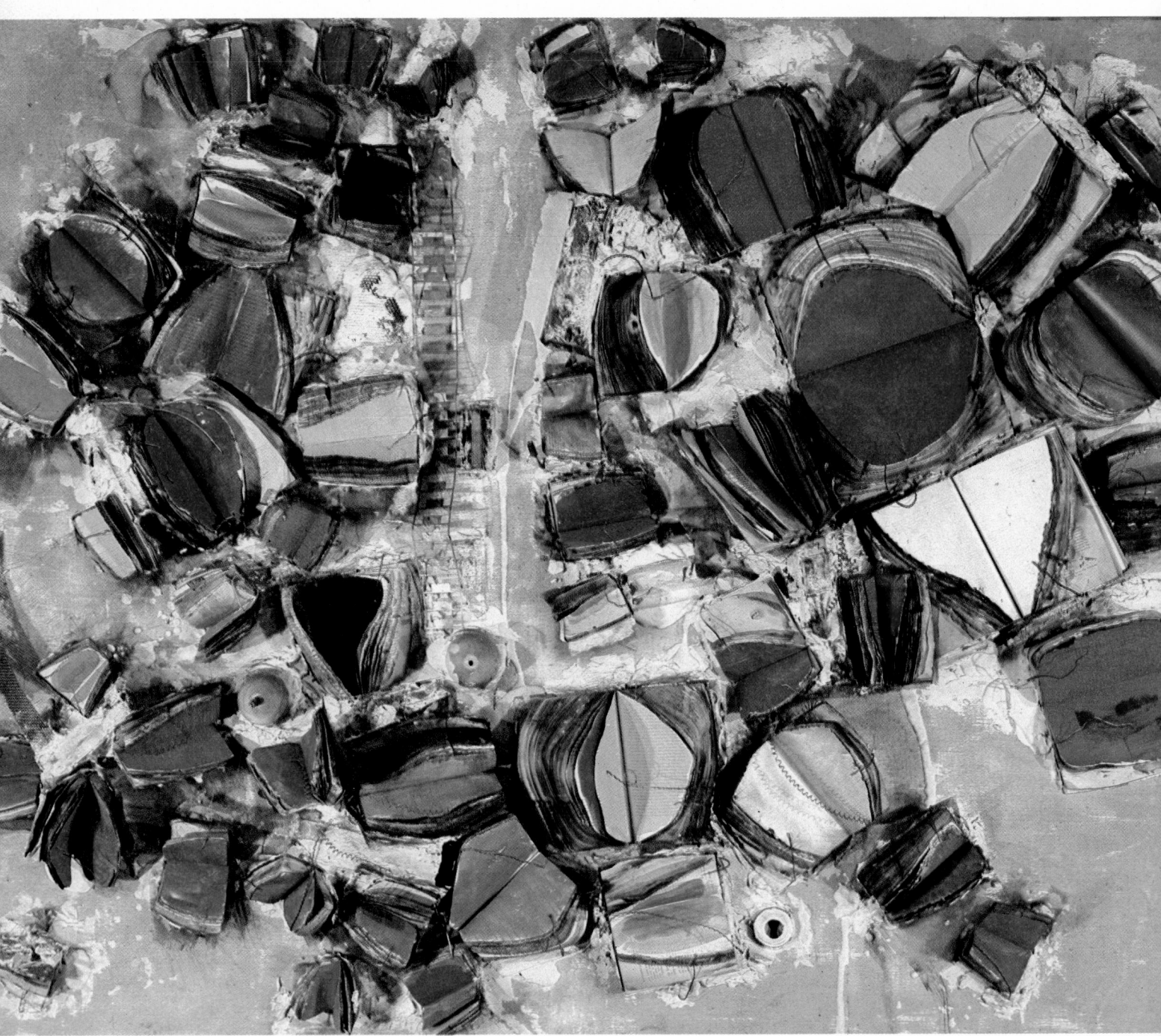

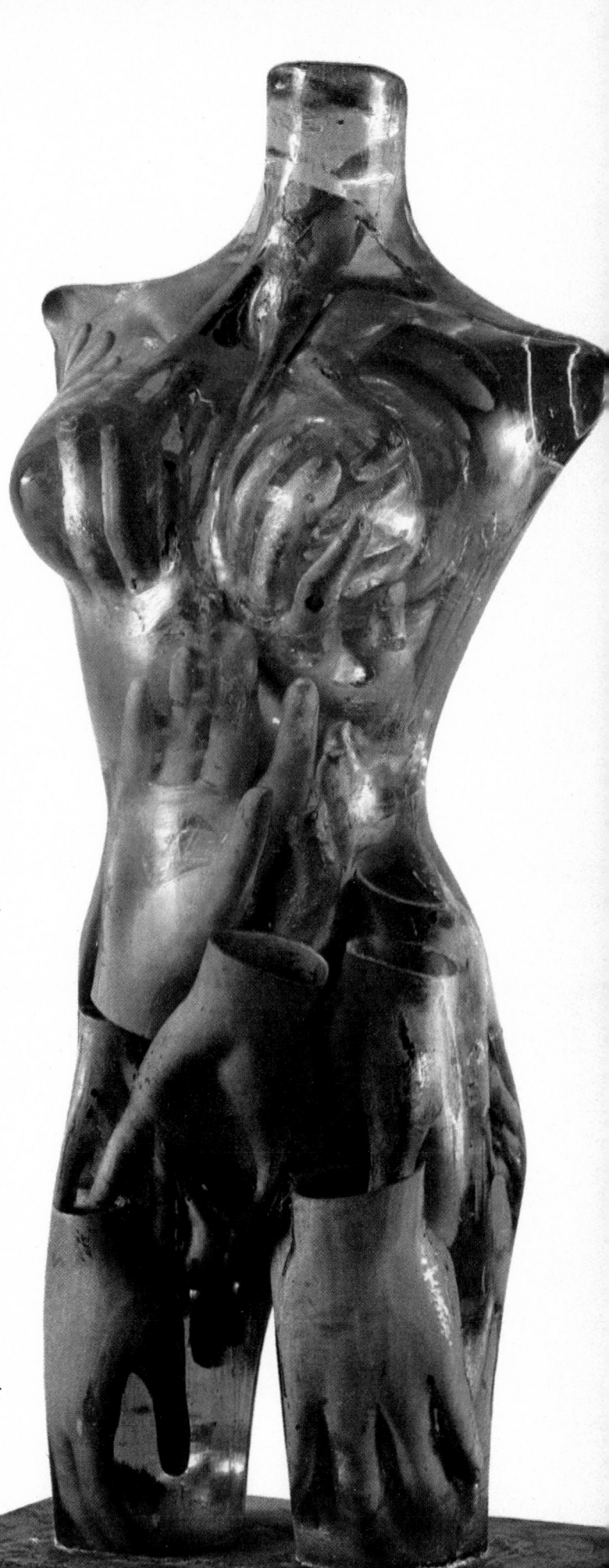

135. Overleaf
Daniel Spoerri
Tableau Piège
1966; 109 × 185 × 30 cm. (43 × 72 × 12 in.)
Paris, Galerie Mathias Fels

and glamour, as if the cogwheels in *Nucléide* (Plate 130) were diamonds in a jeweler's shop-window Arman said, in the catalogue-preface to a retrospective exhibition of his work held at the Stedelijk Museum, Amsterdam, in 1969: "My technique of accumulation consisted in allowing [the objects I used] to compose themselves. In the long run there is nothing more controllable than chance. Since chance depends on laws, on quantity, for instance, it is no longer chance. Chance is my basic material, my blank page." The last sentence of this quotation might certainly have been attributed to Duchamp rather than to Arman.

The effect of these random accumulations is nevertheless not particularly Duchampian. They have a quality of "all overness" which immediately reminds one of the compositional formulae of a drip painter, such as Pollock. As with Pollock's work the eye is given no place to settle. One's glance continually zigzags across the surface of the composition, without being able to decide what the most important segment of it is.

Arman was not the only artist using *assemblage* as a primary method to employ random accumulation as a method of composition which superseded more traditional ones. The wooden relief composed of piano parts by Vic Gentils illustrated here (Plate 132) is close to Arman's *assemblages* that use destroyed violins as their basic material. The same can be said of *Film Star* (Plate 133), which is the work of another English artist, John Latham. *Film Star* was produced at a time when Latham's basic concern was with mutilated books, and it is interesting to recall the moral shock which these works caused when they were first shown in England—something perhaps out of proportion to their real originality. Arman's dismembered musical instruments have a similar effect. We feel, rightly or wrongly, that the artist has in fact made a significant choice, in choosing to assault an object emblematic of traditional cultural values.

Arman is certainly capable of the kind of black humour which has always been associated with Dada and Surrealism. Perhaps the best known of all his works is the *Glove Torso* of 1967 (Plate 134). This uses the familiar method of embedding a

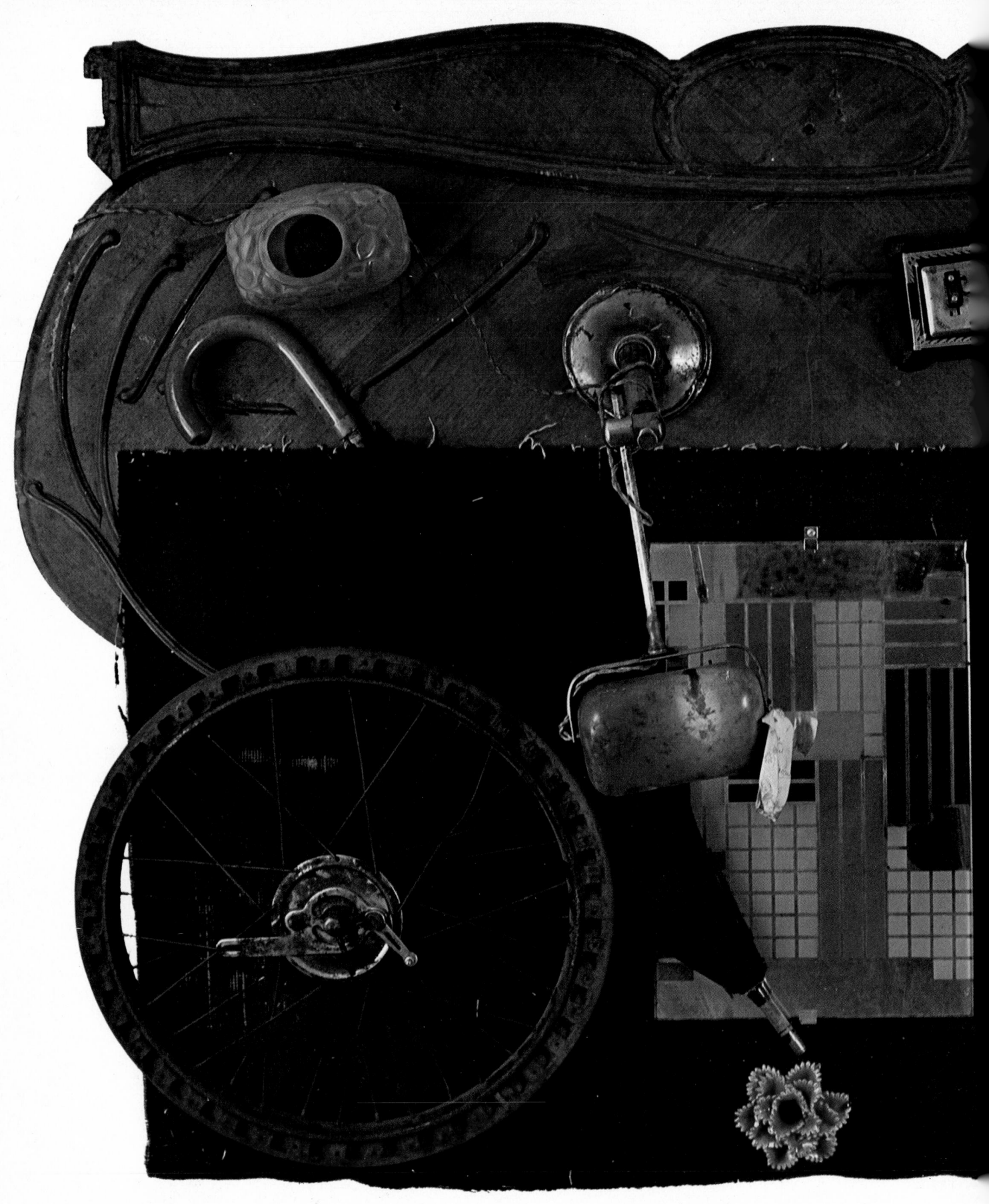

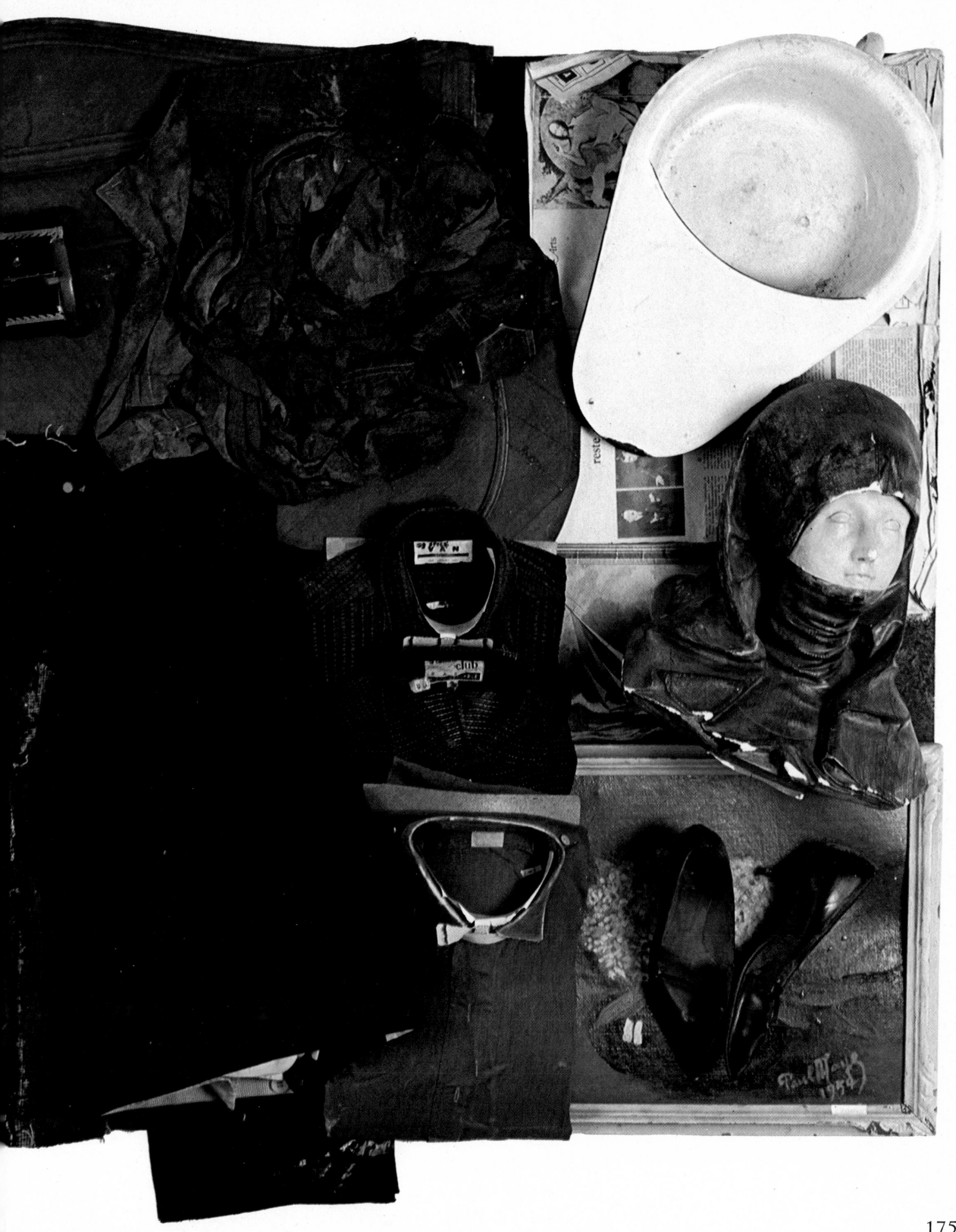

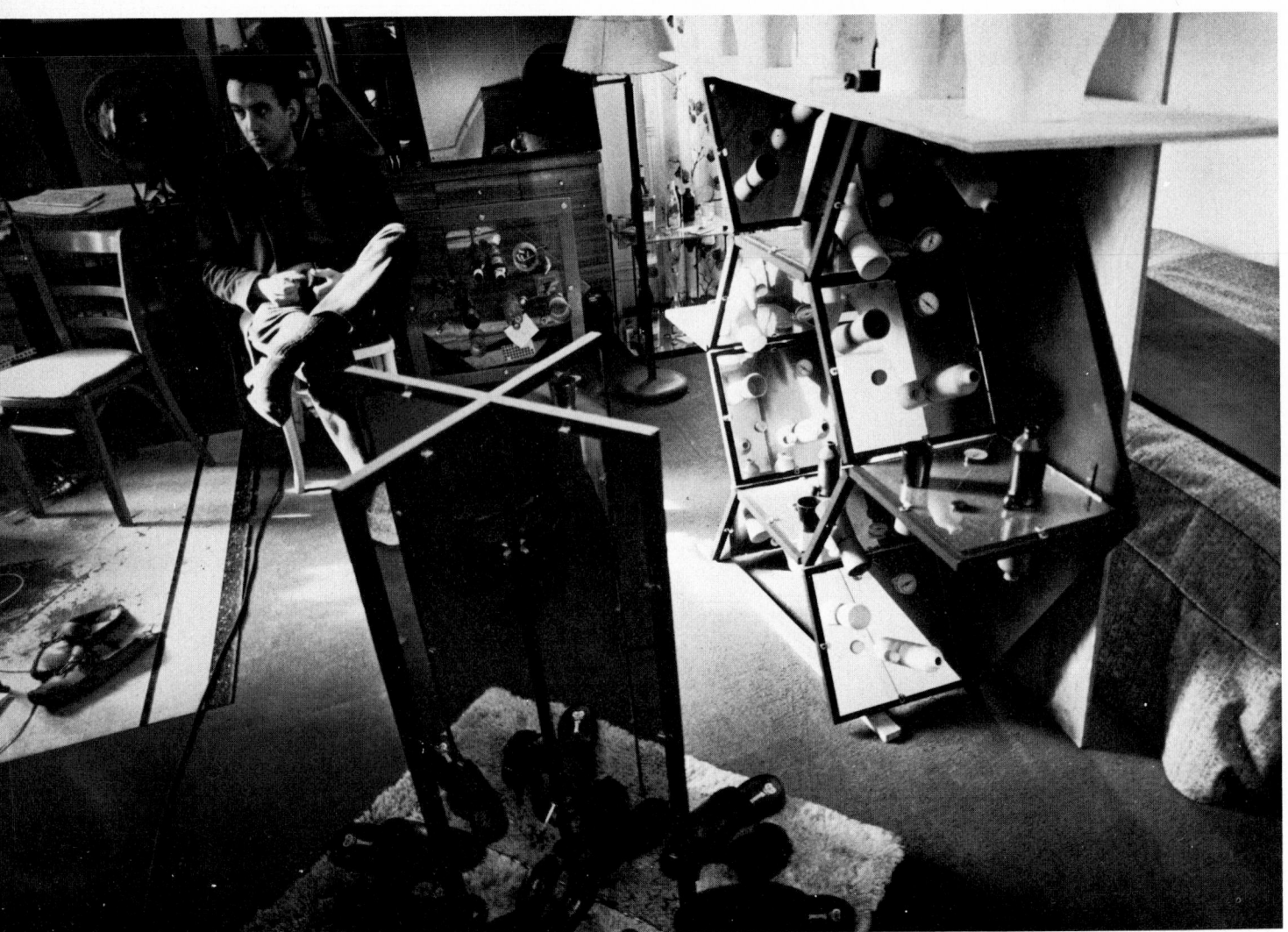

large number of objects, all of them belonging to a single category, in transparent polyester. On this occasion the objects are a multitude of rubber gloves, and the polyester has been shaped to form a female torso. The effect is not neutral but powerfully erotic. It is as if the gloves are hands, feeling this resilient flesh. They may be a doctor's hands, conducting some kind of intimate and slightly humiliating medical examination. Or else they may be the hands of someone who is making a sexual assault on the woman.

Other members of the New Realist movement who call for a comment here are Daniel Spoerri and Christo. Spoerri is of Roumanian birth and

began his career as a dancer. He has been a pioneer in several fields, for example in that of multiple art, but is best-known for his "trap-pictures" (Plate 135). This particular example shows a selection of objects from the artist's room. The aim is not to produce a work of art in any conventional sense, but to take possession of a particular moment. Spoerri himself describes the method employed as follows: "Situations discovered by chance in order or disorder are fixed (trapped) just as they are upon their support of the moment (chair, table, box, etc.), only the orientation with respect to the spectator is altered. The result is declared to be a work of art (attention—work of art). What was

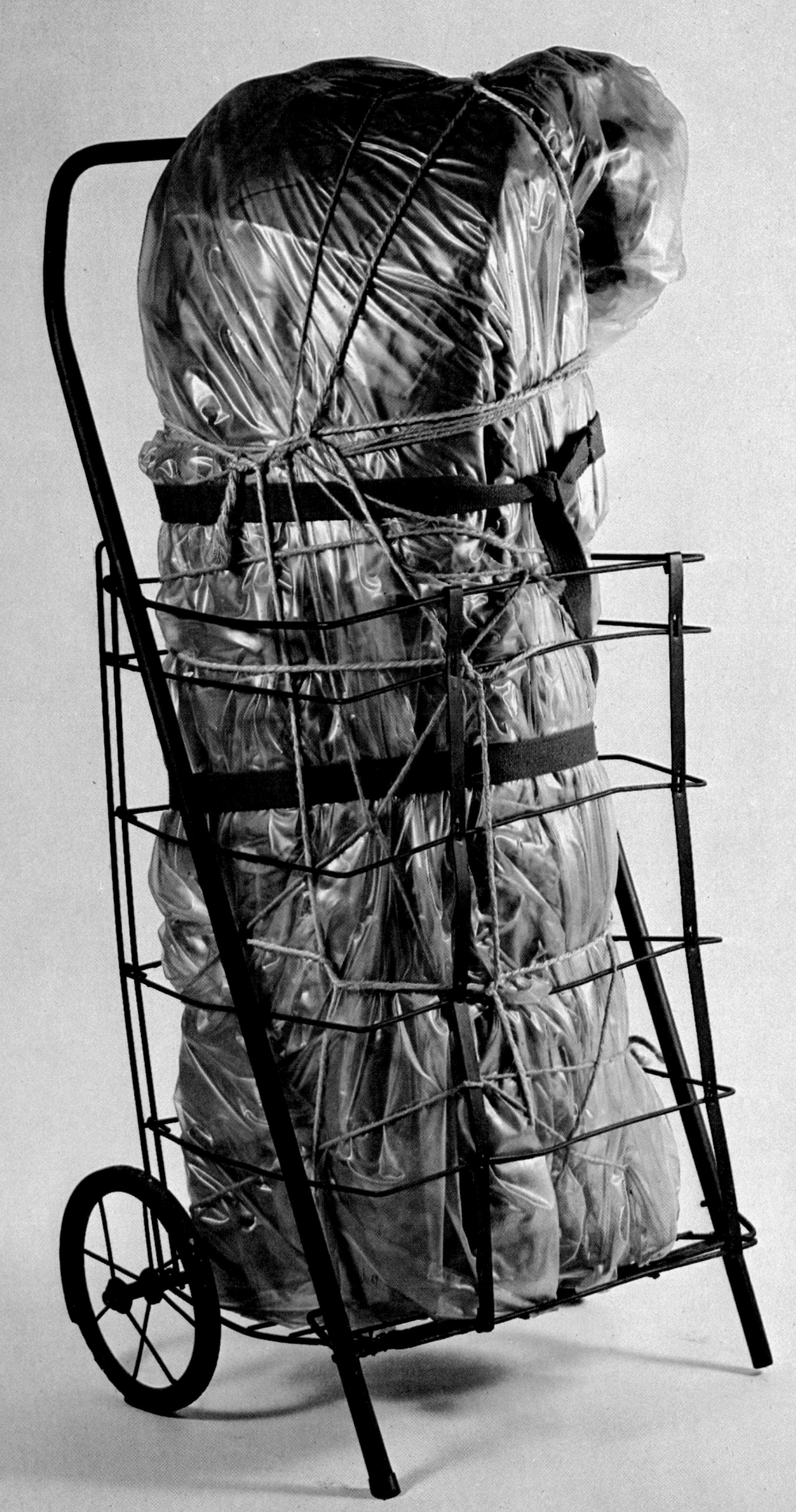

138.
Christo (Christo Jaracheff)
Wrapped Bottle
1958; 45 × 7.5 cm. (18 × 3 in.)
Colorado, coll. Kimiko and John Powers

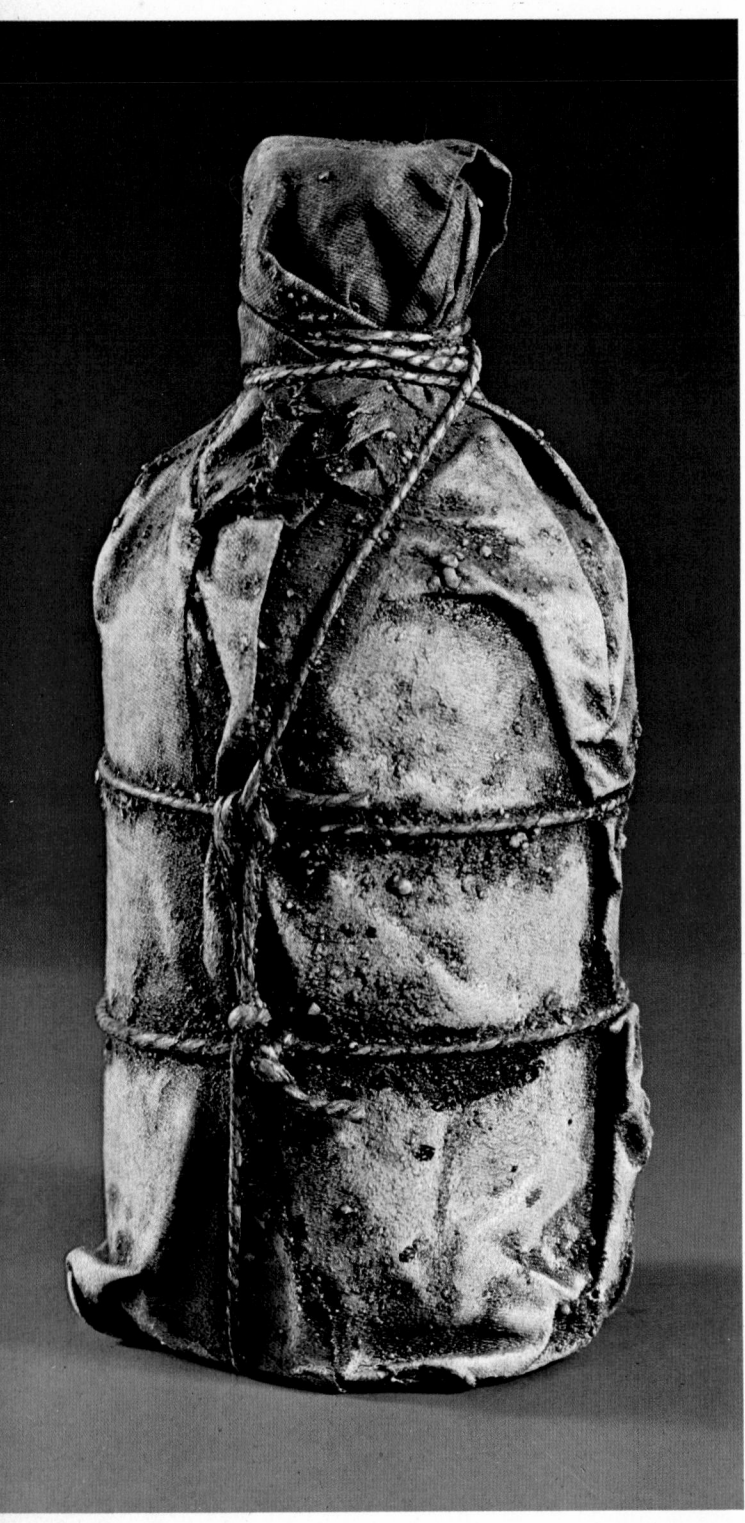

horizontal becomes vertical—for instance, the remains of breakfast, put on a board resting on a chair, are fixed in their positions, and the whole thing hung on the wall" (statement from the catalogue of Spoerri's exhibition at CNAC, Paris, 1972).

The trap-pictures often have a somewhat sinister air, and Spoerri's work has in fact grown increasingly black in mood. One series called *The Dangers of Multiplication* consisted of a number of boxes with the bones of rats, a child's shoes, and other debris. In the early Seventies, Spoerri made a group of works with death as their announced subject matter. In these he employed the cadavers of animals and the weapons used to kill the victims. Yet, at the same time, he is one of the artists who have tried to break down the museum situation, and who have wanted to marry avant-gardism to populism. In 1965, for instance, Spoerri opened his hotel room at the Hotel Chelsea, New York, as a public exhibition.

Christo is famous for his obsession with the mysteriously wrapped object (Plates 137 and 138). It seems that there is nothing he will not attempt to turn into a package, from an adding machine to a mile-long stretch of coastline in Australia. The direct ancestor of these *empaquetages* is the wrapped sewing machine by the American Dadaist and photographer Man Ray, which its author has entitled *The Enigma of Isidore Ducasse*. Christo's intention is identical: to evoke disquiet by alienating the everyday.

An artist who did not participate in the New Realist movement, but who seems in some respects closely related to both Spoerri and Christo, is the Greek-American Lucas Samaras. Samaras, like Joseph Cornell, puts much of his work into boxes. But the boxes are not chosen merely for convenience of format. Samaras from early childhood has been fascinated by the idea of erotic, forbidden objects. His boxes have strongly sadomasochistic overtones (Plate 139). Samaras seems to regard art chiefly as a means of "declassifying hush-hush feelings", whatever these may happen to be. This was certainly the motivation for a long series of Polaroid self-portraits which he exhibited at the Kassel

139.
Lucas Samaras
Untitled
1966; 21.6 × 27.9 × 20.3 cm. (8 × 11 × 8 in.)
California, coll. Robert Halff and Carl W. Johnson

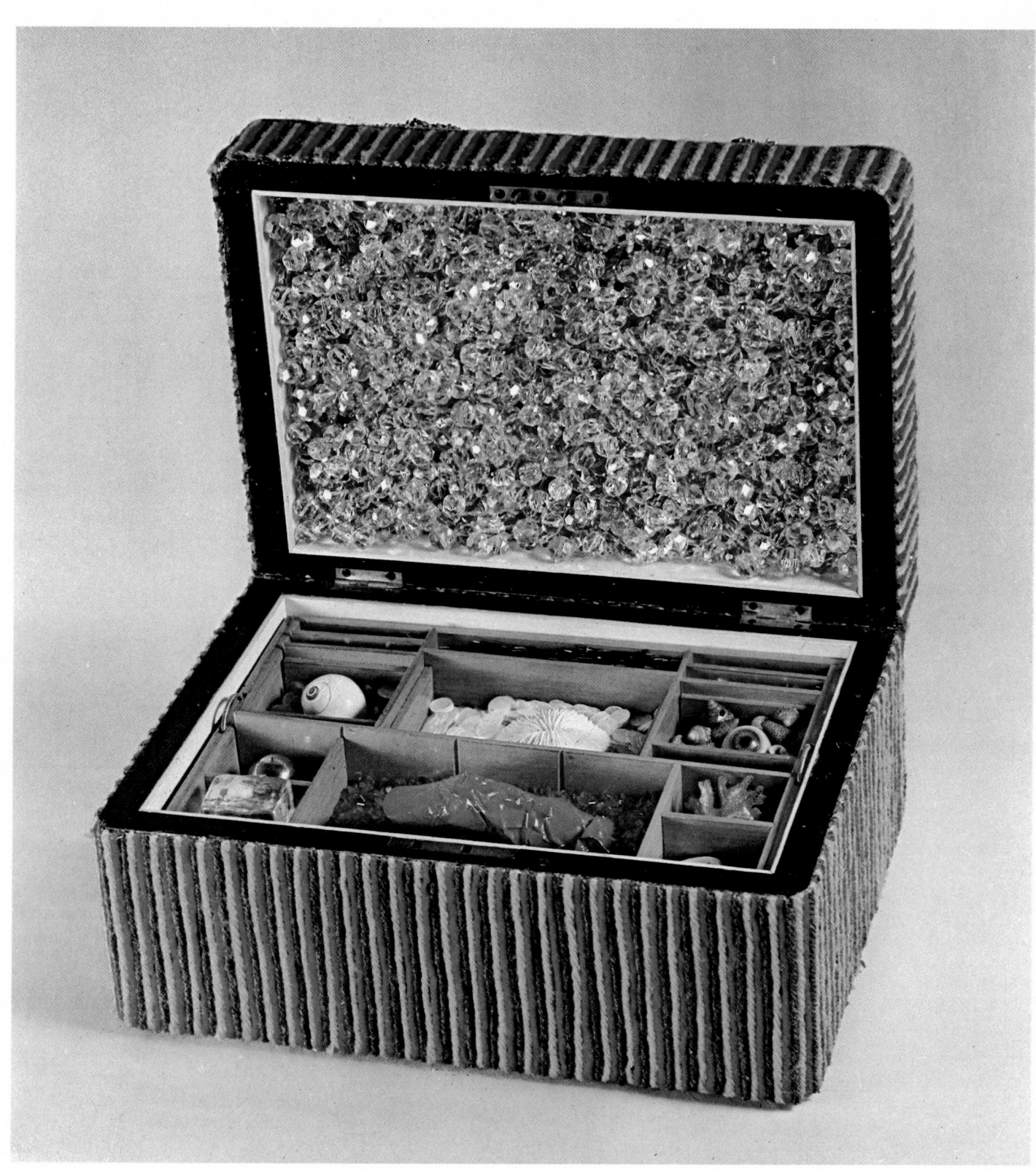

140.
Edward Kienholz
Gossip
1963; 60 × 35 × 45 cm. (23 × 14 × 18 in.)
Los Angeles, coll. Mr. and Mrs. Melvin Hirsh

141. Opposite
Edward Kienholz
Odious to Rauschenberg
1960
Los Angeles, coll. Mr. and Mrs. Melvin Hirsh

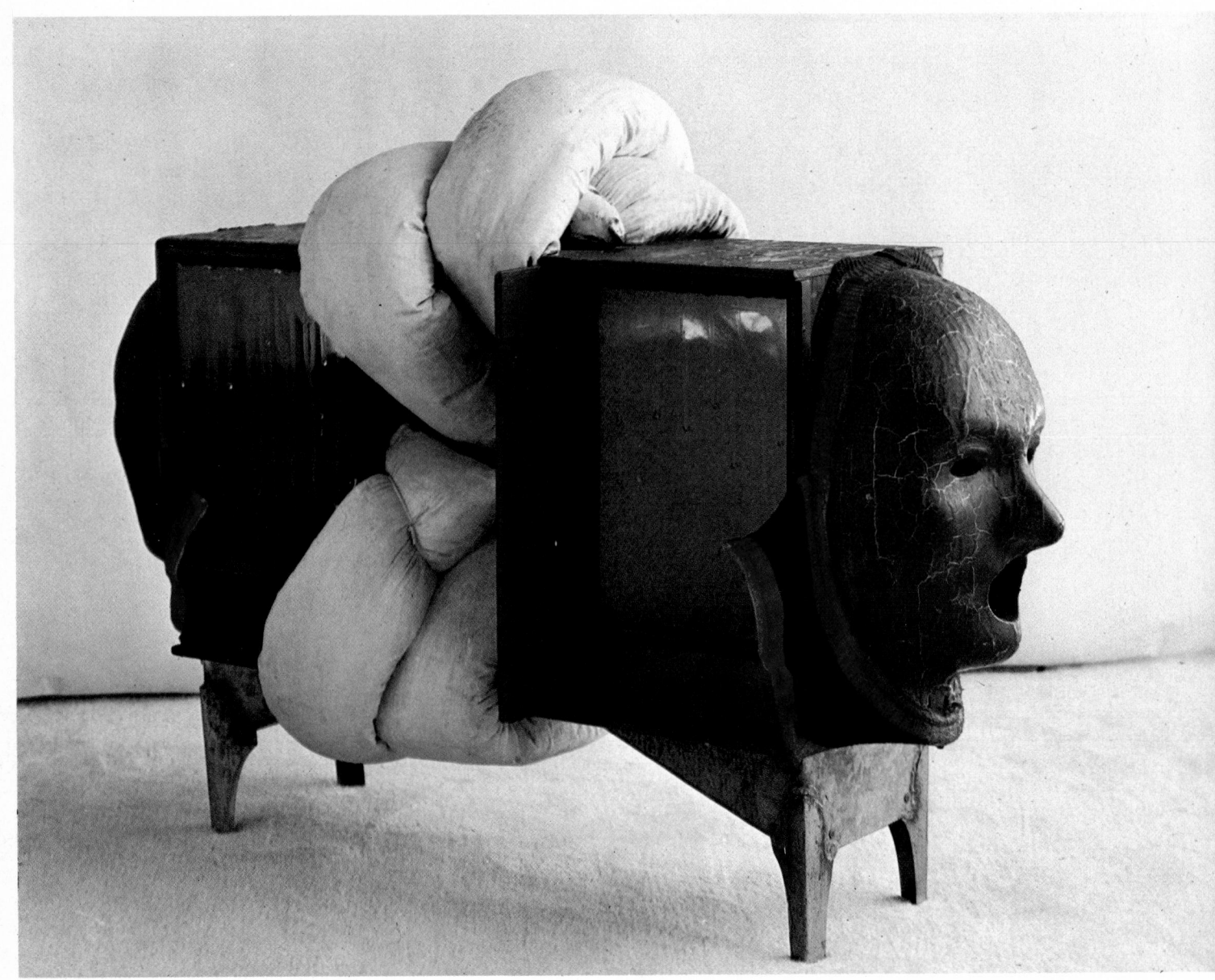

Documenta of 1972. These made an extraordinarily candid record of both physical and spiritual self-obsession.

The wide range open to the assemblagist is neatly illustrated by the contrast between Samaras's boxes and the vast environments often constructed by another American, Edward Keinholz, whose enormous political tableau, *Five Car Stud*, was shown in the same Kassel Documenta. This represented the castration of a Negro by five southerners, who have caught him drinking at night in his pick-up truck with a white woman. A tableau of this type is a precise contemporary equivalent of the large-scale historical scenes (Paul Delaroche's *The Execution of Lady Jane Grey* is a well-known example) which it was customary to exhibit in the large Salons of the nineteenth century.

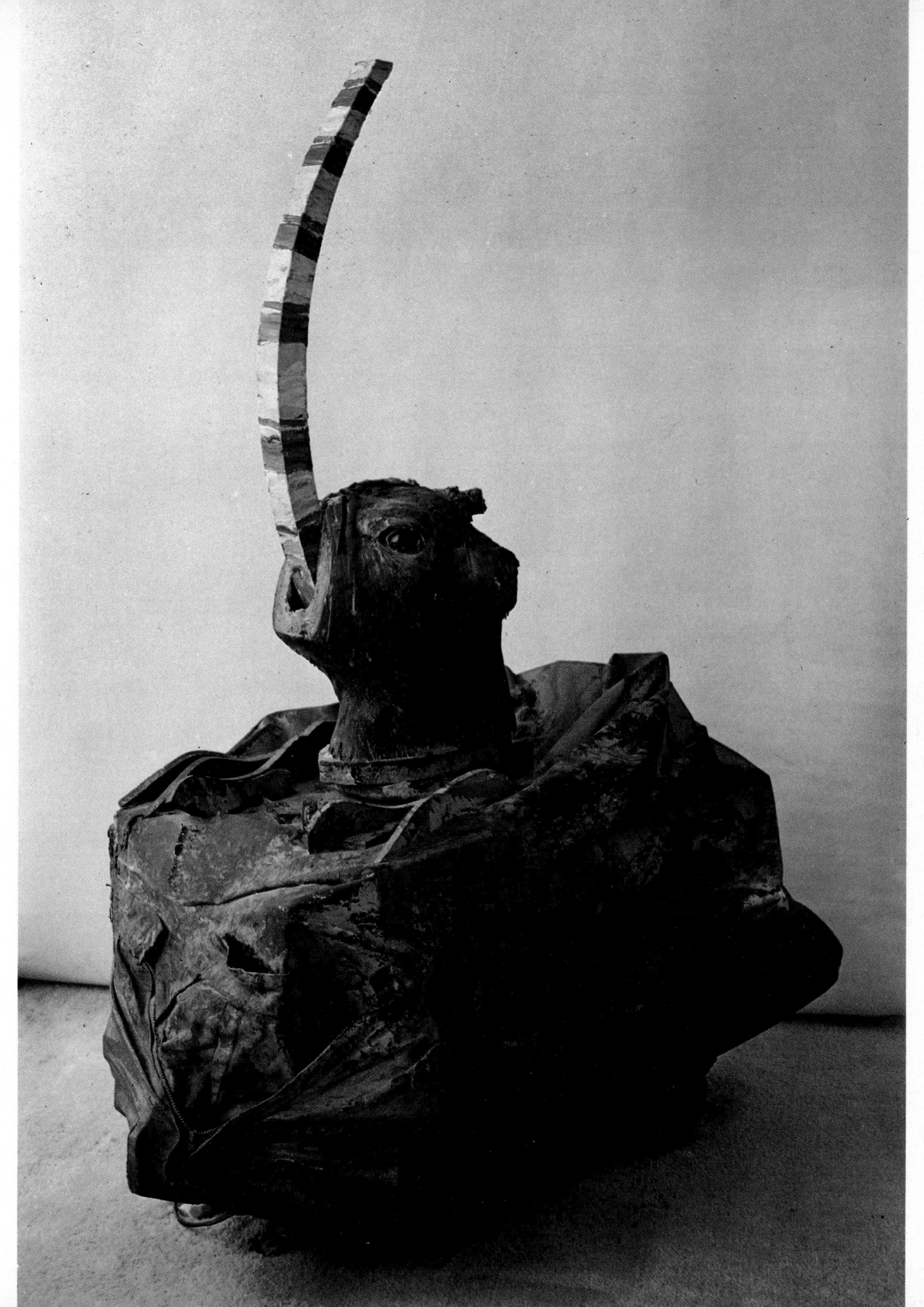

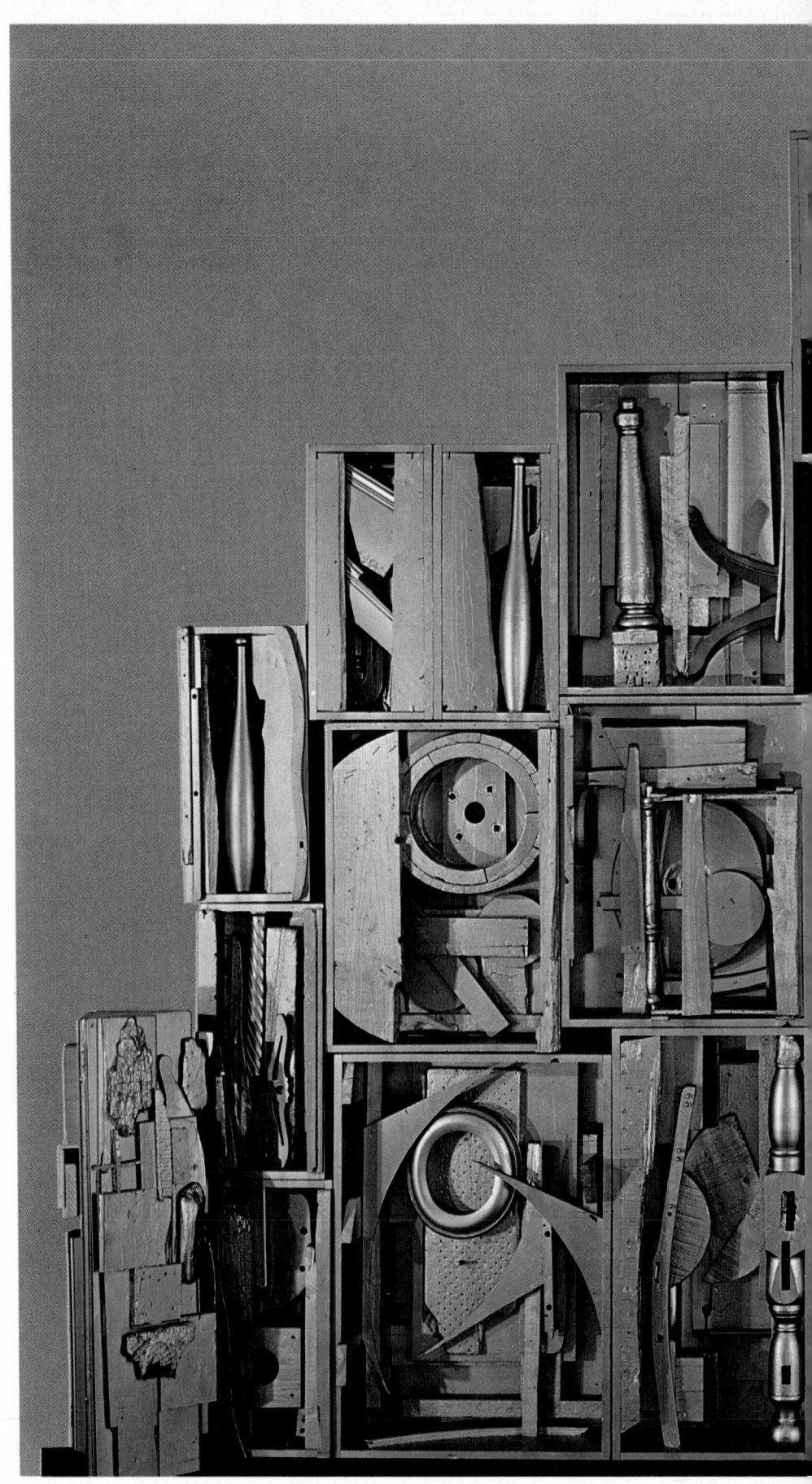

142.
Louise Nevelson
Royal Tide IV
1960; 335.3 × 426.7 cm. (131 × 166 in.)
Cologne, Wallraf-Richartz Museum

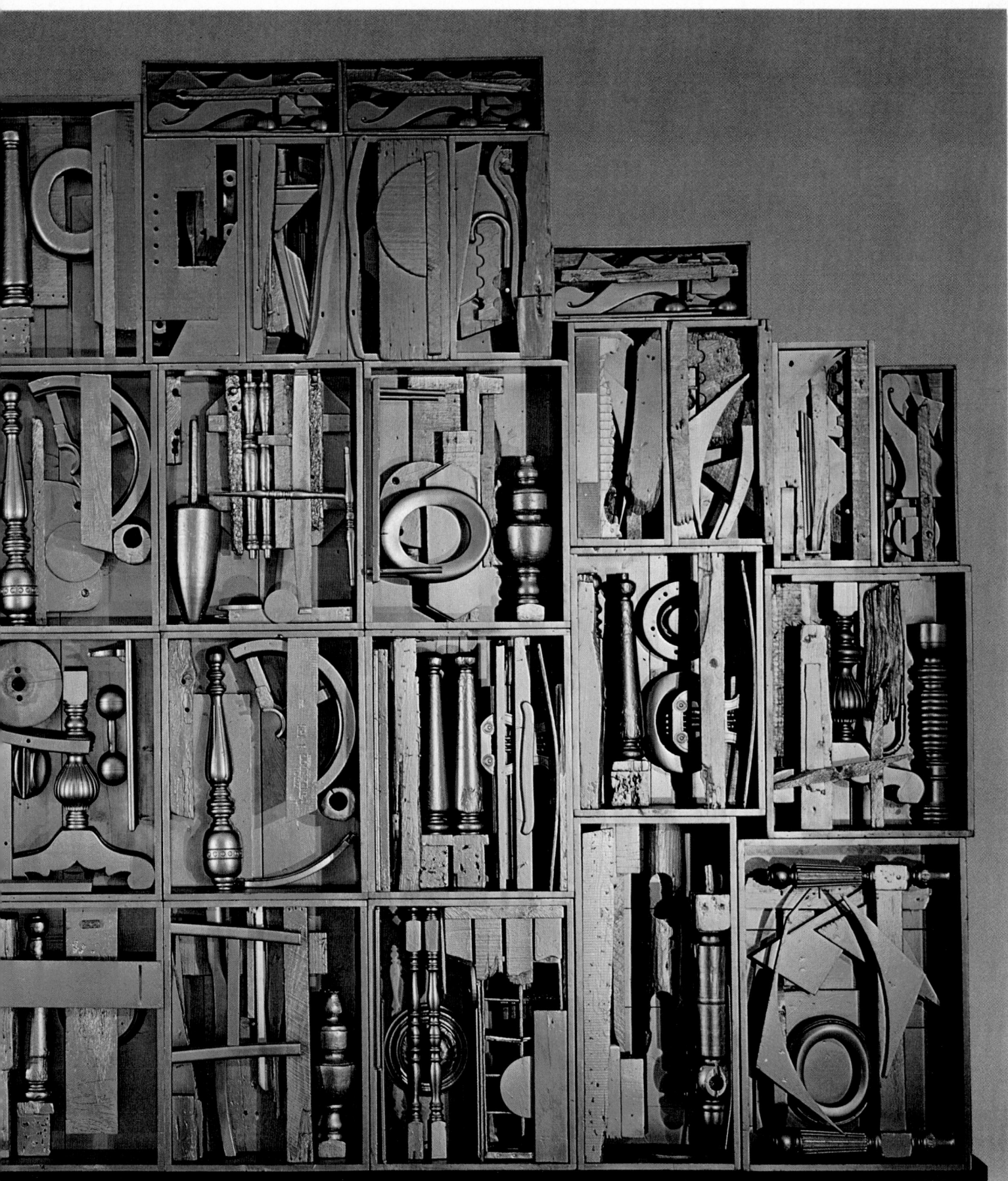

143.
John Chamberlain
Dolores James
1962; 190 × 243 × 97.5 cm. (74 × 95 × 38 in.)
New York, Leo Castelli Gallery

144. Opposite
César (César Baldaccini)
The Yellow Buick
1961; 149 × 79 × 62 cm. (58 × 31 × 24 in.)
New York, Museum of Modern Art

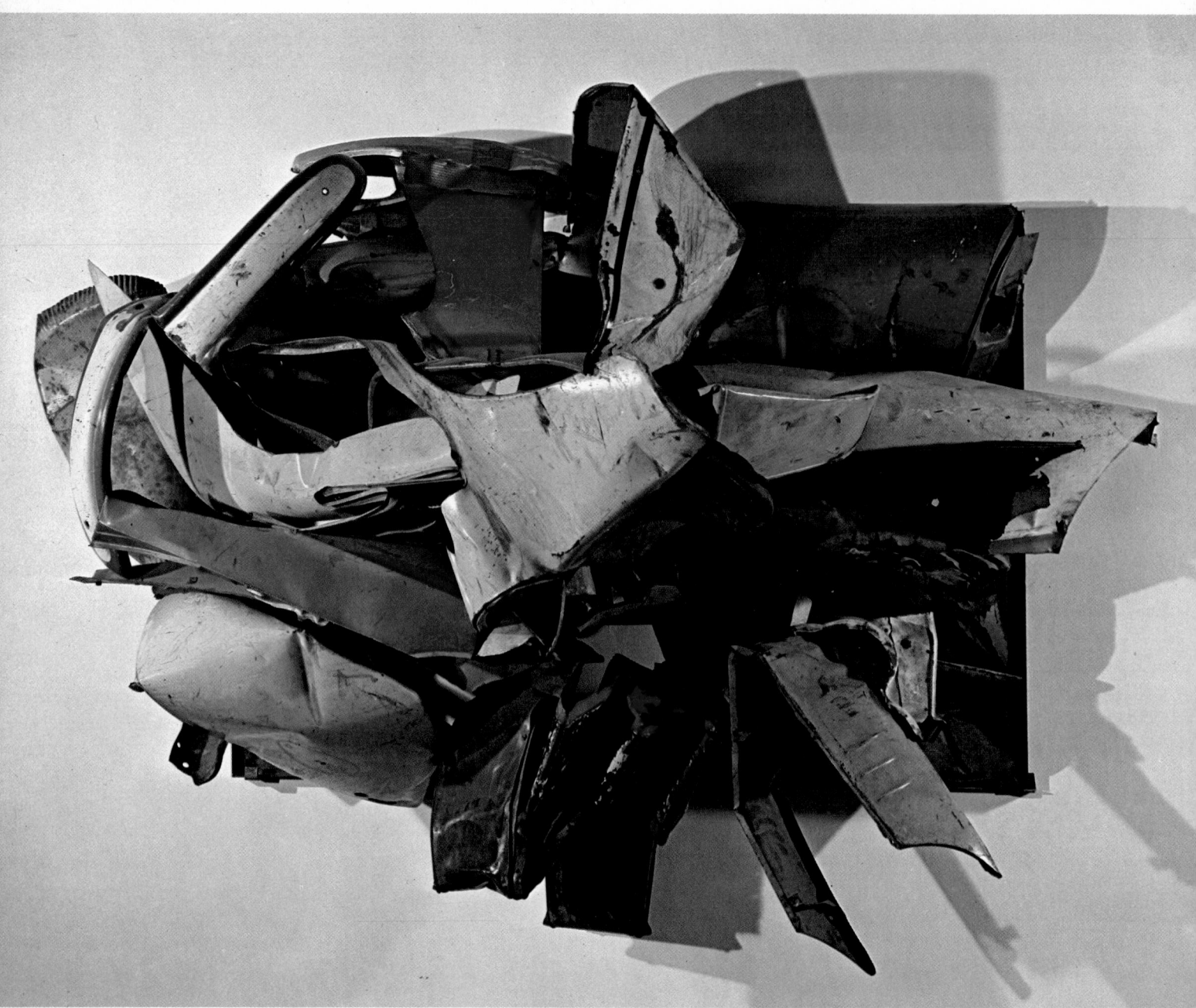

Keinholz's work was not always so specific or so academic. The earlier piece entitled *Gossip* (Plate 140), which is illustrated here, shows a freer and more Surrealist combination of elements, and a more suggestive and less literary end result.

On the whole, it is the American *assemblage* artists who have been the more concerned with urban context, if not with the need (as Keinholz has) to convey a social message. One of the most respected American sculptors of the post-war years, Louise Nevelson, is a perhaps unexpected example. Nevelson works in wood, for the most part, though more recently she has also experimented with metal. Her wooden sculptures are constructed on the box principle which seems to attract so many assemblagists, perhaps simply because of its convenience. The boxes are then themselves combined to make massive reliefs, wall-like and wall-sized (Plate 142). The vocabulary of forms Nevelson uses is not for the most part invented by herself, but is selected from the surrounding environment. She uses offcuts and fragments of natural wood, but also found objects, such as parts of chairs, other fragments of furniture, door panels and stair balusters.

Wood is a material with its own connotations—connotations of natural growth and decay—and this has perhaps tended to conceal the fact that Nevelson's is essentially an art of the New York environment, feeding off the city's detritus, its demolitions, its continual process of change. Nevelson has said: "My total conscious search in life has been for a new seeing, a new image, a new insight. The search not only includes the object, but the in-between place. The dawns and the dusk" (quoted in *Time* magazine, "One Woman's World", [February 3, 1958], p. 58). But these dawns and these dusks are those Hart Crane celebrated in *The Bridge*. They belong emphatically to a particular place. It is not for nothing that a big Nevelson *assemblage* tends to have a haunting resemblance to typical New York architecture.

But there is another point which is worth noticing about Nevelson, in addition to her close connection to the spirit of place. And this is the way in which she straddles the gap between "the art of *assemblage*" and true sculpture. It is generally agreed that there is a gap between "objects" and true sculptures, and that most *assemblages* fall into the former category. As we have noted, the object works by means of suggestion and association; the sculpture through the impact of form. Nevelson was one of the first to pioneer the use of ready-made parts to make what are recognizably sculptures, and in this she stands on the same footing as David Smith, who is generally considered the most important of American post-war sculptors. Her custom of painting her wooden sculptures one colour, black or gold, emphasizes the formal relationships of the parts.

It is an easy move, in one sense, from

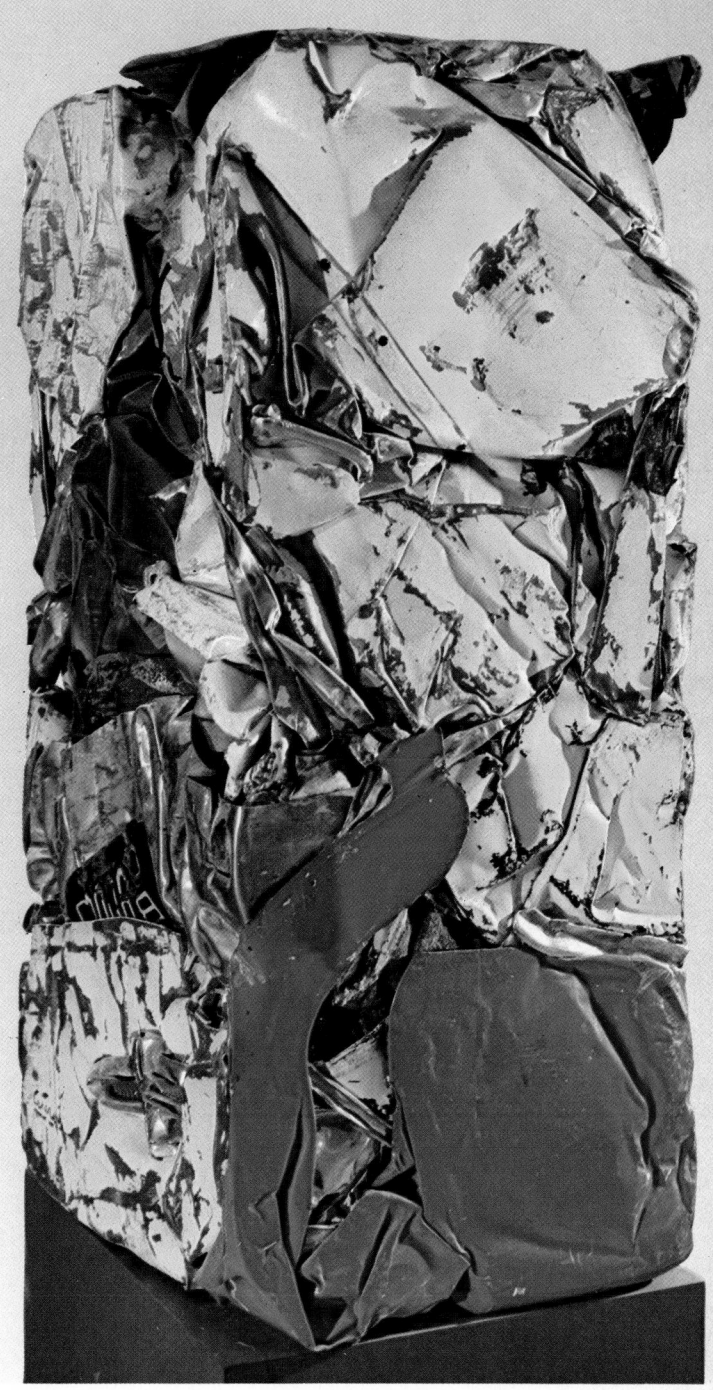

Nevelson's work to that of her compatriot John Chamberlain, and thence to that of yet another New Realist, the French sculptor César.

Chamberlain's characteristic material is fragments of wrecked automobiles; César, too, has made use of this modern and urban form of detritus, often producing effects which at first

145.
Ernst Trova
Power Kit
1965; 35.6 × 44.5 × 108 cm. (14 × 17 × 42 in.)
Colorado, coll. Kimiko and John Powers

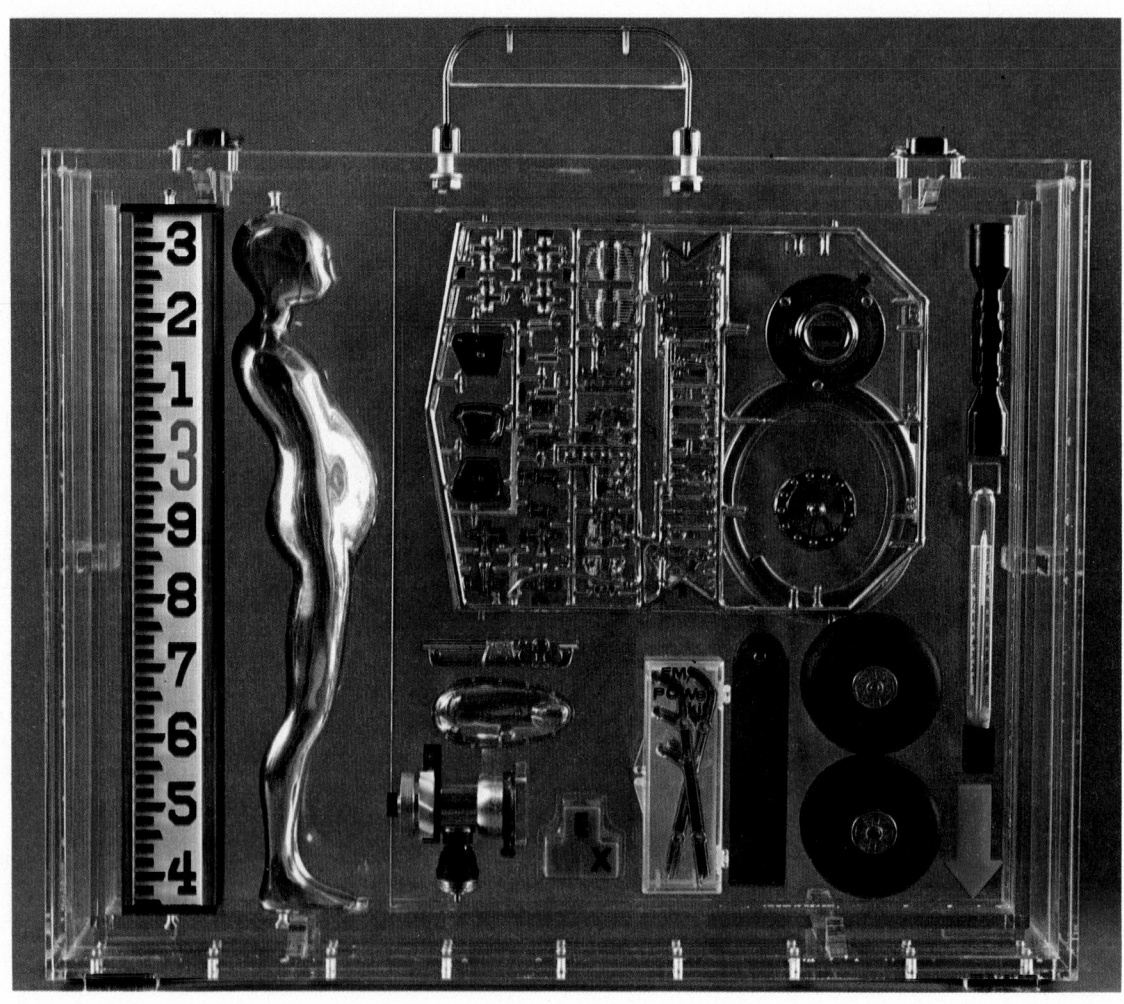

sight seem almost indistinguishable from those obtained by his American colleague (Plates 143 and 144). Chamberlain, however, is interested in the result, while César seems to be fascinated chiefly by the process that leads to that result. For Chamberlain the chosen material has several attractions—its connotations, because by using it the artist is recycling waste and redeeming squalor much as Schwitters did with his collages of discarded labels and bus tickets; and the further possibility of using colour without sentimentality. Unlike Nevelson, he welcomes polychromy. César, who began his career as a "traditional modernist", in the group of post-war romantics which included Germaine Richier, used the automobile sculptures as the most startling means

he could discover of announcing his adherence to a new philosophy. They were made with the help of the baling machines employed in scrapyards, and for this reason the artist dubbed them his "controlled compressions". Unlike Chamberlain, he had no intention of imposing a style upon the material, and quickly moved on to something else.

The battle of style versus theory or process was often, it seems, the battle of American versus European art in the years after 1950. The work of Ernst Trova, for example, has qualities which make it seem characteristically American. Trova makes *assemblages*, but of a very different sort from those we have encountered hitherto. Since the early Sixties, nearly every piece he has produced has included the manikin-like image of the

146.
Ernst Trova
Falling Man Series: Six Figures
1964; 40.6 × 48.3 × 48.3 cm. (16 × 19 × 19 in.)
New York, Whitney Museum of American Art, Larry
Aldrich Foundation Fund

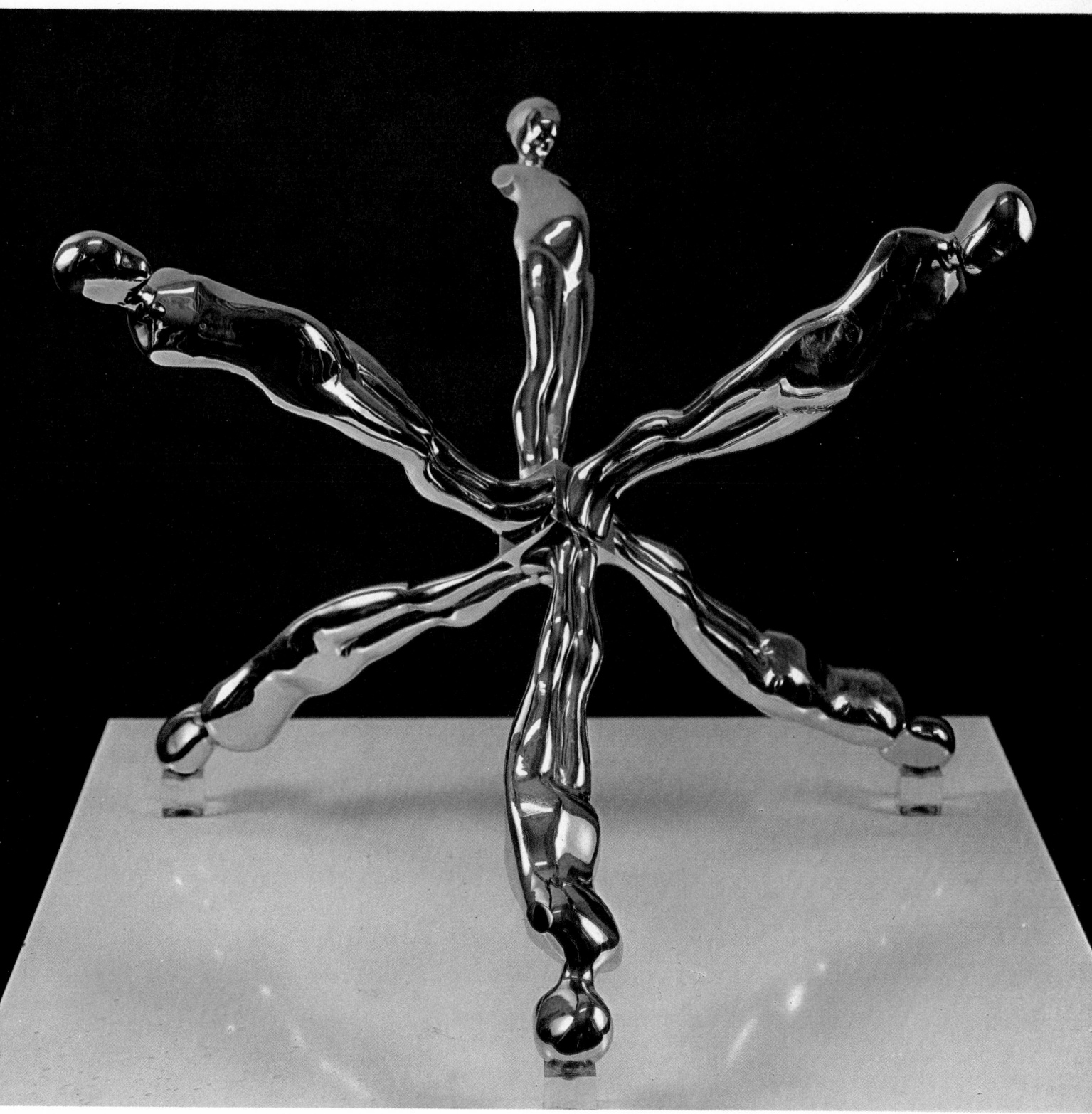

147.
Lucio Fontana
Tela tagliata
c. 1960
Private collection
(Photo: Ugo Mulas)

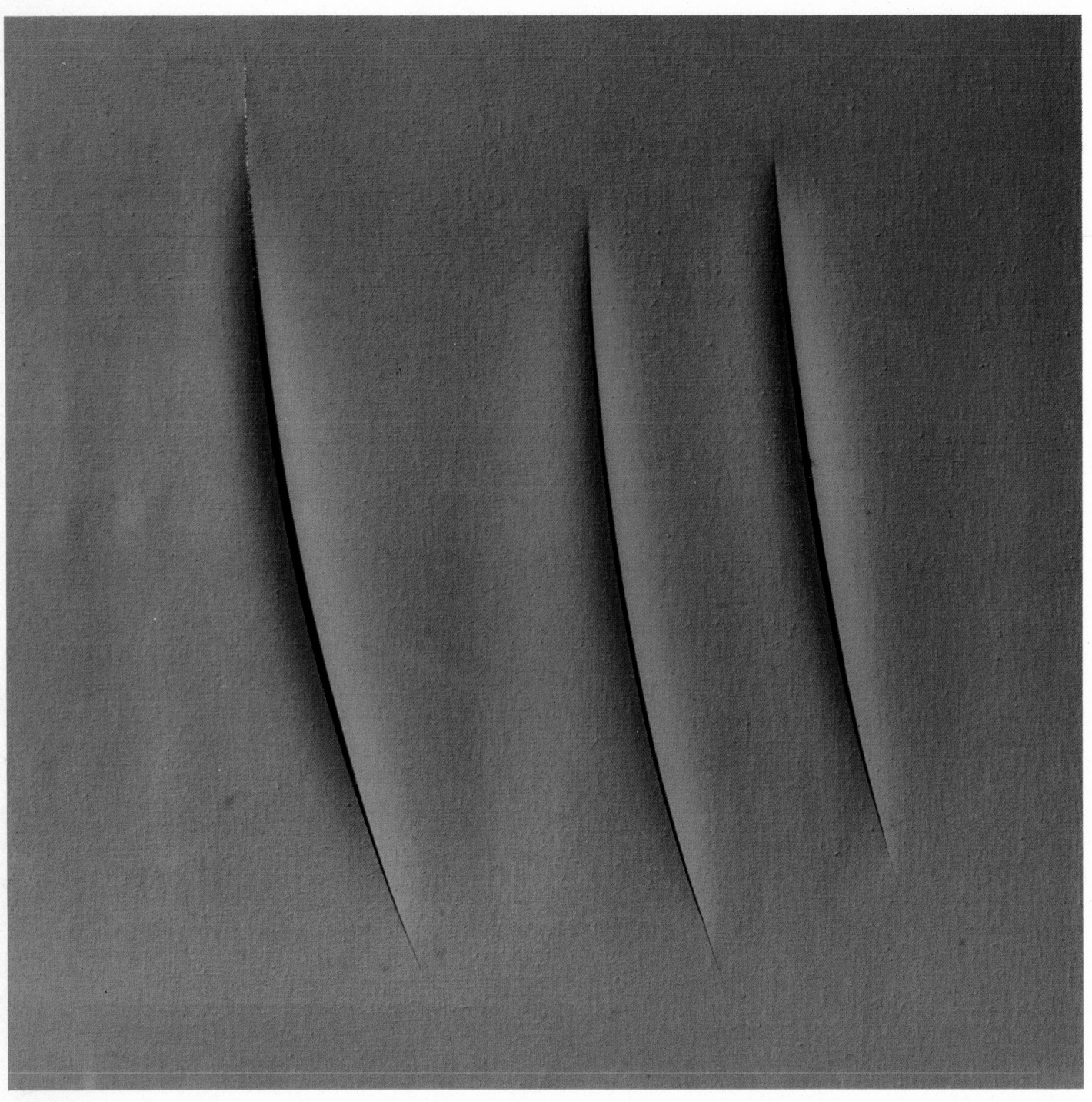

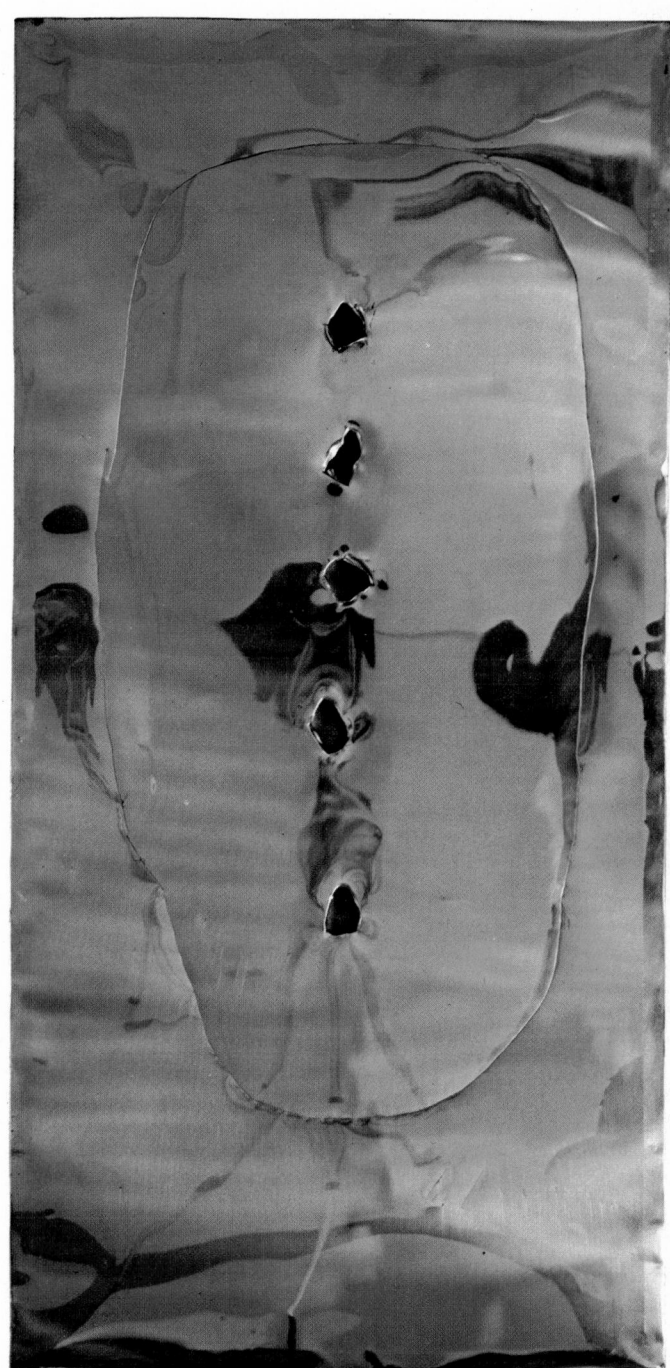

"Falling Man" (Plate 146) which Trova first invented as a symbol of purification from the expressive, romantic art which he had produced formerly (Plate 145). The manikin rapidly became a recognizable trademark, the sign that the product was an authentic Trova. The commercial quality of Trova's work links him to Pop Art— like Warhol's paintings, his *assemblages* are ironic, though we are never certain whether the irony is directed at the artist himself or at the audience that solemnly receives them as art. Yet the irony cannot destroy their status as glossy, expensive toys, tributes to the spending power of the collector who buys them.

At first sight the work of a typically European artist such as Lucio Fontana has an equivalent glossy elegance (Plates 147, 148 and 149). Fontana did indeed produce commercial decorative works for a large part of his career, but he was also one of the first to become impatient with the limits of easel painting, and to think about how these might be overcome. The "black spatial environment" which he created in 1947 anticipated the obsession with environmental works which was to obsess the avant-garde by considerably more than a decade. But it is the "holed" and "slit" canvases by which Fontana is best remembered today. Those with holes were produced as early as 1948, those with slits a decade later. These had a shock effect at the time, and they continue to be cited as examples of the nihilism of modern art.

Fontana's own attitude towards them was different. He said: "As a painter, while working on one of my perforated canvases, I do not want to make a painting; I want to open up space, create a new dimension for art, tie in at the cosmos as it endlessly expands beyond the confining plane of the picture. With my innovation of the hole pierced through the canvas in repetitive formations, I have not attempted to decorate a surface, but, on the contrary, I have tried to break its dimensional limitations. Beyond the perforations a newly gained freedom of interpretation awaits us, but also, and just as inevitably, the end of art" (quoted by Jan Van der Marck in the catalogue introduction to the Lucio Fontana exhibition, Walker Art Center, Minneapolis, 1966).

149.
Lucio Fontana
Concetto spaziale-Teatrino
1968; 110 × 110 cm. (43 × 43 in.)
Cologne, coll. Alfred Otto Müller

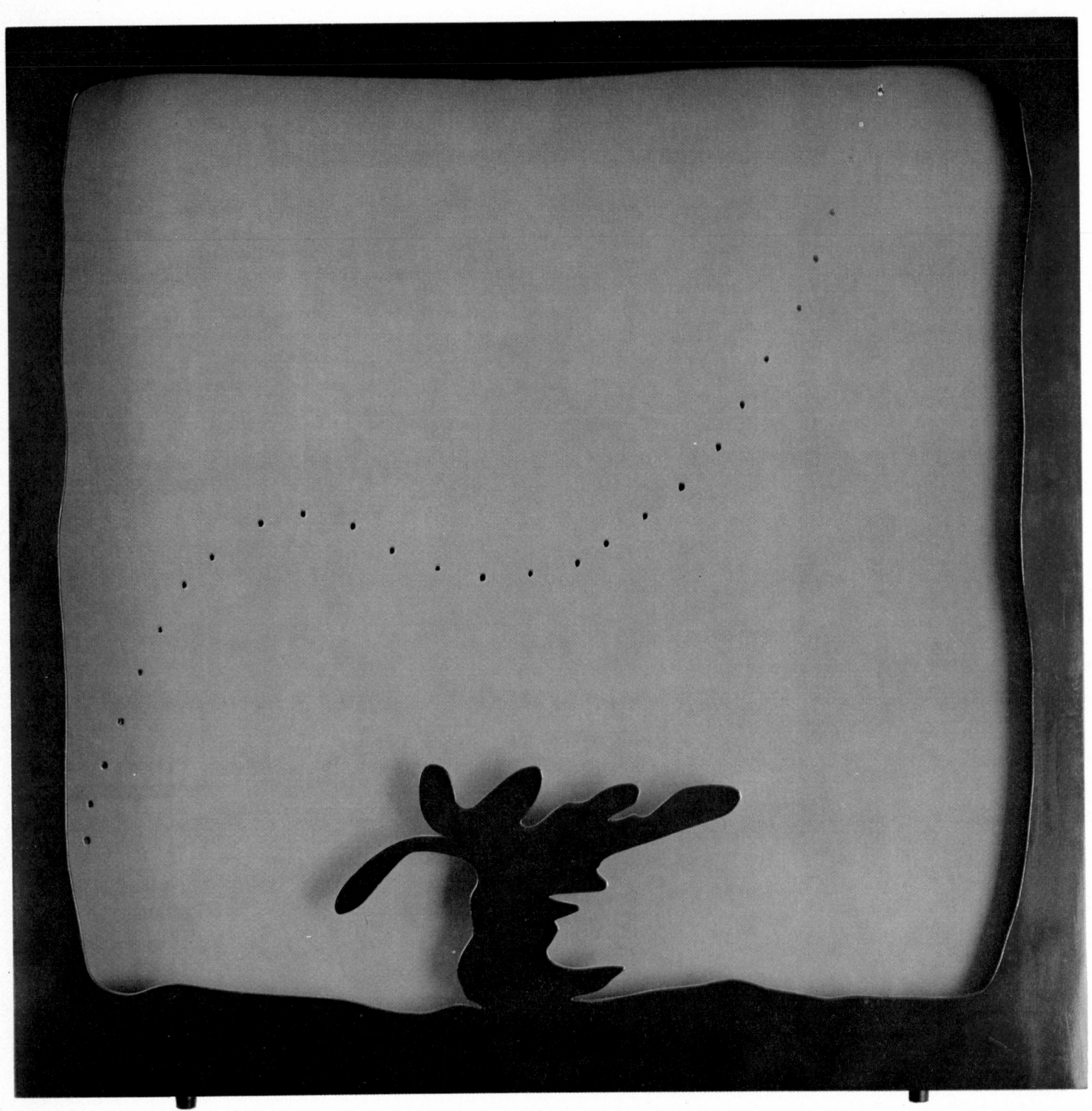

There is an obvious relationship to be discovered between this statement and some of the attitudes expressed by Yves Klein. Klein's feeling for the "energetic infinity" of the sky parallels Fontana's desire to open up spatial possibilities to the utmost. In addition, both artists seem to see the true purpose of art as being its own abolition. One is also reminded of Ad Reinhardt's declaration that he was "just making the last painting that anyone can make", though Reinhardt does not seem nearly so typical of the aesthetic situation of the American artist.

It has been possible to combine the extremes in this chapter—works of rigorous purity and works which refuse to edit the artist's experience at all—because, however different they are in superficial appearance, they were responses to the same situation. If Abstract Expressionism and *tachisme* had been, in their various ways and with whatever private hesitations, symptoms of faith in the continuing possibilities of art, then the revival of Dada was a clear signal of doubt. Either the artist, through the development and extension of *assemblage*, plunged himself into the "real" and submitted his inspiration to the pre-existing facts represented by his materials, or else he retreated into a transcendental ivory tower. Pop Art was to be an attempt to find a way out of this impasse.

Pop Art in America

Pop is generally considered to be the typical art style of the 1960's—as characteristic of the decade as Abstract Expressionism had been of the late Forties and early Fifties. Because it is thought of as something fully developed and coherent, it has already attracted a lot of attention from the historians of modern art.

In fact, Pop, like all art movements, had roots deep in the past. The deepest of these, as I have already suggested in the preceding chapter, were in Dada. But it had other sources as well. In America, for instance, the language of Cubism had developed an accent of its own, particularly in the work of Stuart Davis. Born in 1894, Davis was already using commonplace domestic objects—an electric fan, a rubber glove, and an egg-beater—as material for the still lifes he painted in the late Twenties. By the late Forties he was making extensive use of lettering as the basis for his compositions. At this period he spoke of the "need to neutralize certain emotional irrelevancies". An ambitious late painting, such as *Switchsky's Syntax* (Plate 150), can therefore contain many of the elements we now recognize as typically Pop, while not being in any sense an attempt made by an older artist to ape his juniors.

For art historians Pop Art has shown a geographical as well as a purely temporal divide. They have made a distinction between American and British Pop Art, and between British Pop Art and what happened in the rest of Europe. Many of them have pointed out that the Pop phenomenon was recognizable earlier in Britain than it was in the United States. They cite the exhibitions "Collages and Objects" (1954) and "Man, Machine & Motion" (1956) at the Institute of Contemporary Arts in London; and in particular they point to Richard Hamilton's contribution to the "This Is Tomorrow" show at the Whitechapel Art Gallery in 1955. Nevertheless, it seems to make

better sense to look first at what happened in the United States, because America and the quality of American life were the basic inspiration of most Pop artists, wherever they happened to hail from.

The quality of this involvement varied according to the individual's own temperament. There is a tremendous difference for example, in attitude as well as in method, between the work of Andy Warhol and that of Jim Dine. Both, however, are leading American exponents of the Pop style.

In his technique Dine represents a direct development from the Neo-Dadaism of Johns and (especially) Robert Rauschenberg. He makes extensive use of collage, and it is even possible to speak of the painterly quality which is inherent in his work (*Three Panel Study for Child's Room*, Plate 151). Dine himself has declared that he cannot see any sharp break between his own attitudes and those of the Abstract Expressionists: "Pop Art is only one facet of my work. More than popular images I'm interested in personal images, in making paintings about my studio, my experience as a painter, about painting itself, about color charts, the palette, about elements of realistic landscape—but used differently" (interview with G. R. Swenson, *Art News*, November, 1963, reprinted in *Pop Art Redefined*, by John Russell and Suzi Gablik, London, 1969, p. 61).

For Dine, as for Pollock, what counts is the problem he sets himself, rather than the eventual solution: "I paint about problems of how to make a picture work, the problems of seeing, of making people aware without handing it to them on a silver platter" (ibid., pp. 62–63). Yet there are elements in Dine's painting which make him recognizably part of the Pop pantheon. One of these is his sly eroticism (Plate 153), which is an ironic commentary on the degree of commercial eroticism in our society. Another is his passionate interest in the banal—his collage elements, almost

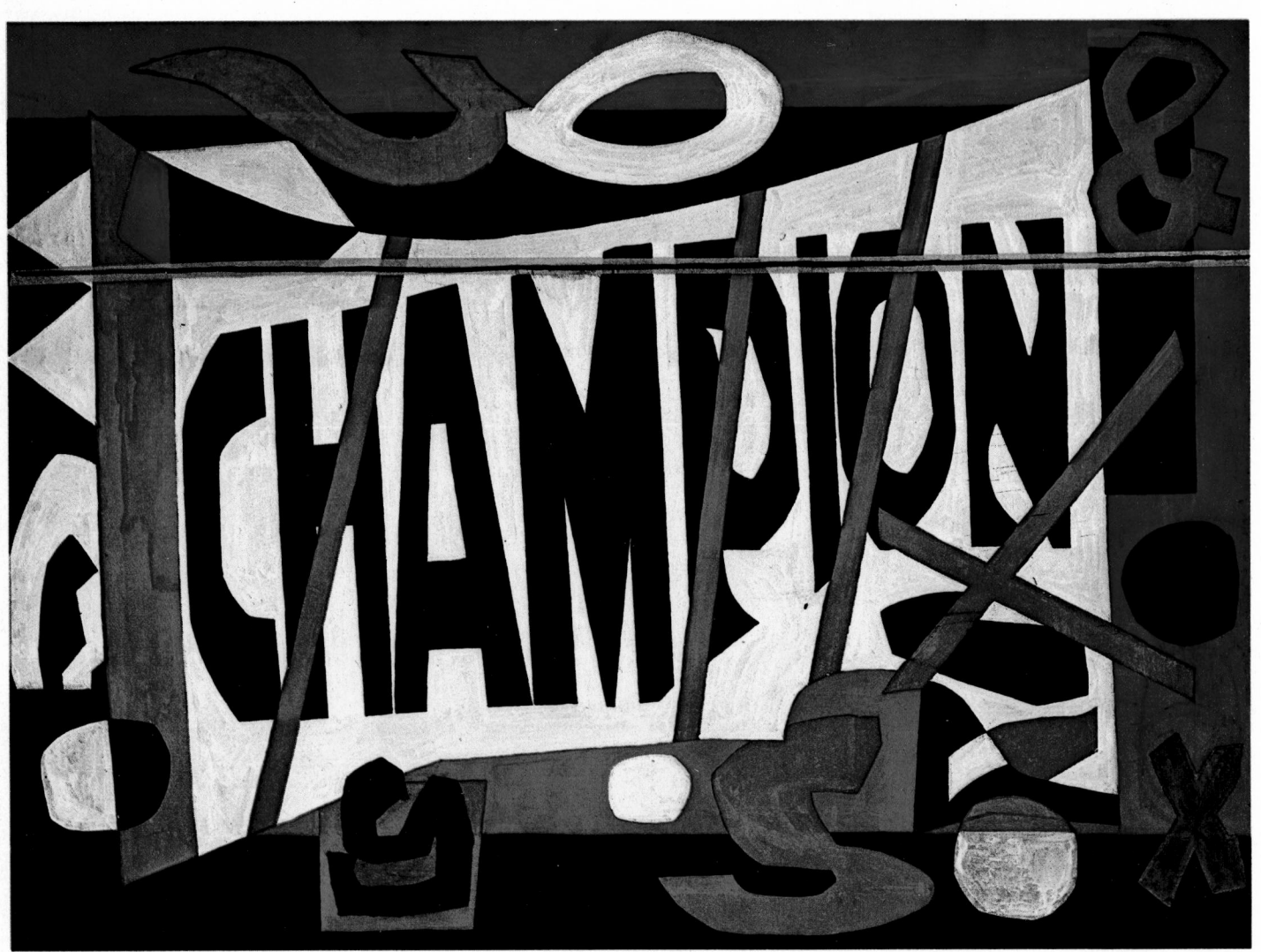

exclusively, are thoroughly commonplace objects, ties, coats, shoes, a washbasin and its fittings. A third, though many would claim that this is what makes him inferior to the best of Pop, is his sentimental attachment to the everyday; his desire to make "ordinary life", as everyone experiences it in the urban and industrial societies of the West, into something which has the dignity of art.

Warhol is a far more enigmatic personality than Dine, and, many would claim, a more important innovator. His background was not a conventional fine-arts one, but commercial illus-

tration. He did window displays and made drawings for shoe illustrations and greetings cards. He recalled later, when answering an interviewer's questions, his own absolute submission to what the client wanted; and the amount of emotion—not his own but the client's—which nevertheless went into the work. These years of commercial experience seem to have given him a desire for art that would be absolutely blank, without "style" or emotion of any kind.

Warhol's transition from commercial art to "high art" was perfectly logical. He achieved it via

194

151.
Jim Dine
Three Panel Study for Child's Room
1962; 210 × 180 cm. (82 × 70 in.)
Colorado, coll. Kimiko and John Powers

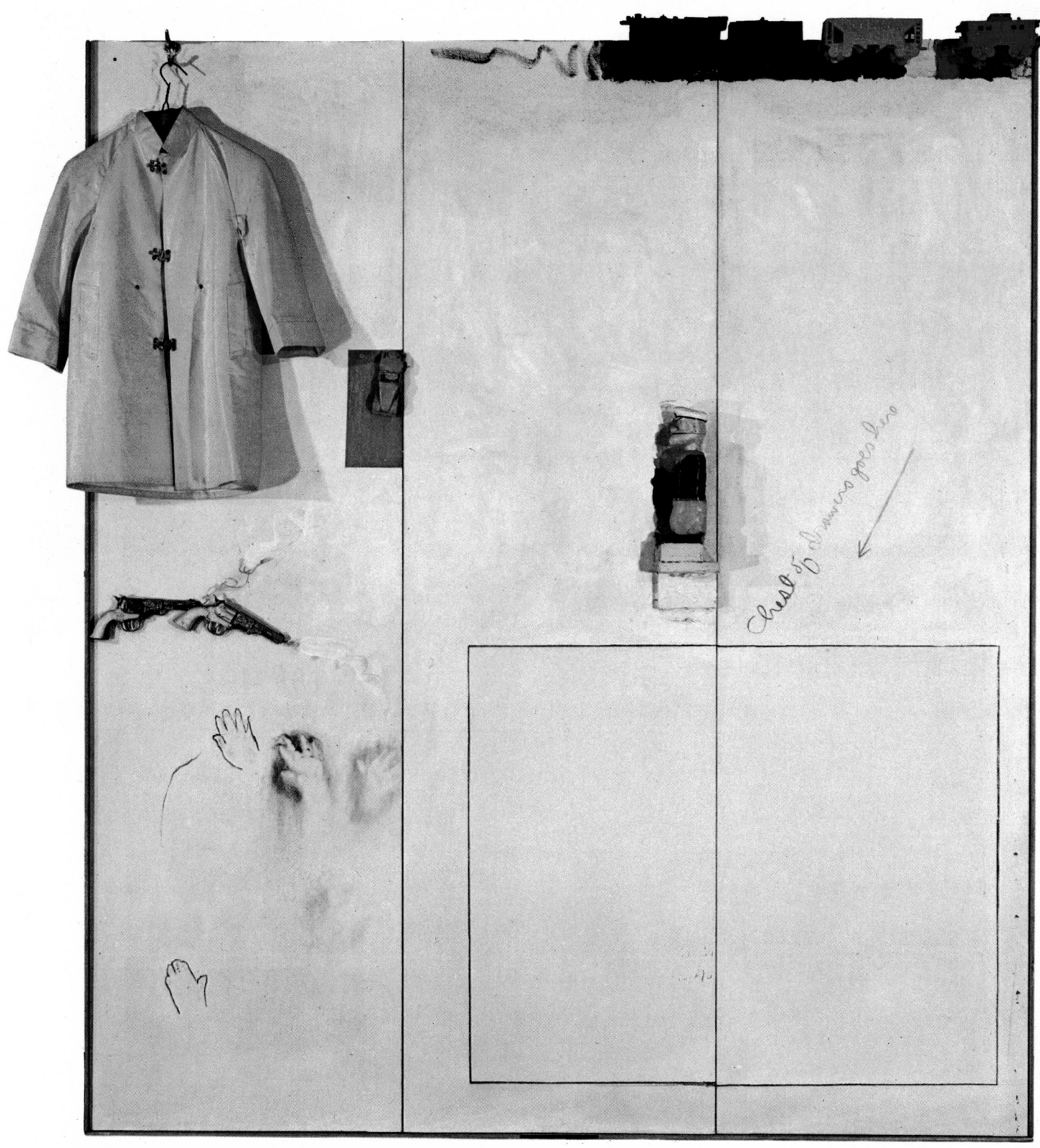

152.
Jim Dine
The White Suit
1964; 183 × 92 × 7.5 cm. (71 × 36 × 3 in.)
Amsterdam, Stedelijk Museum

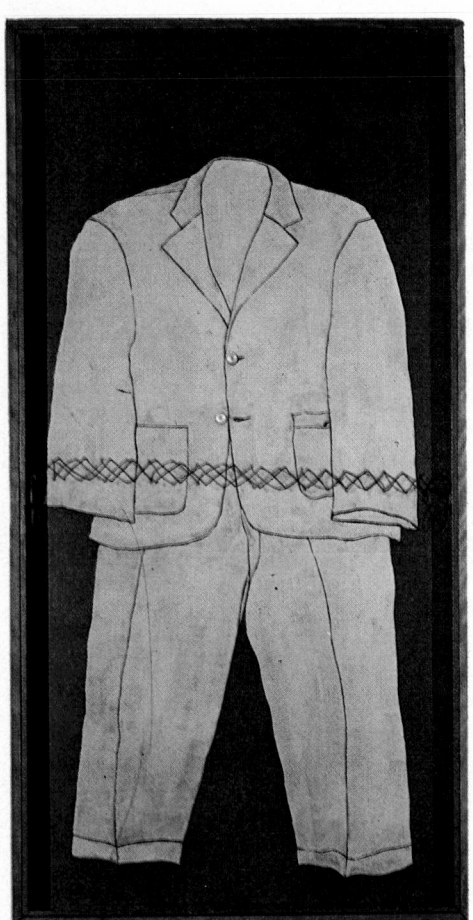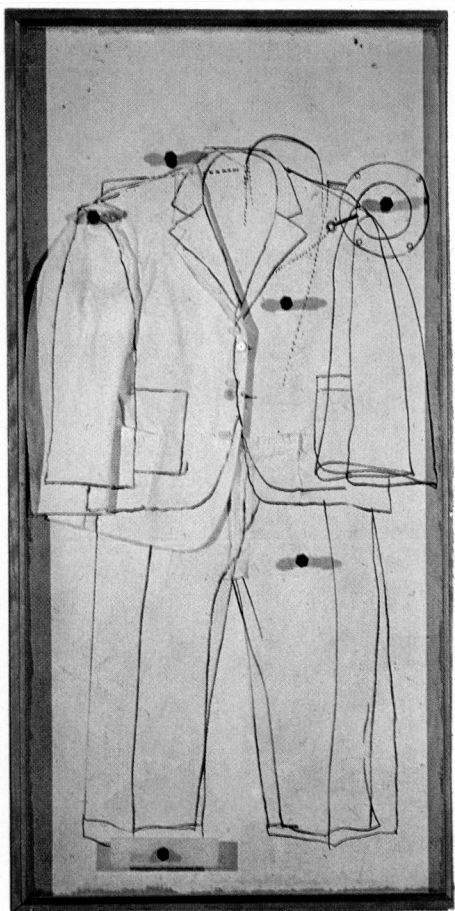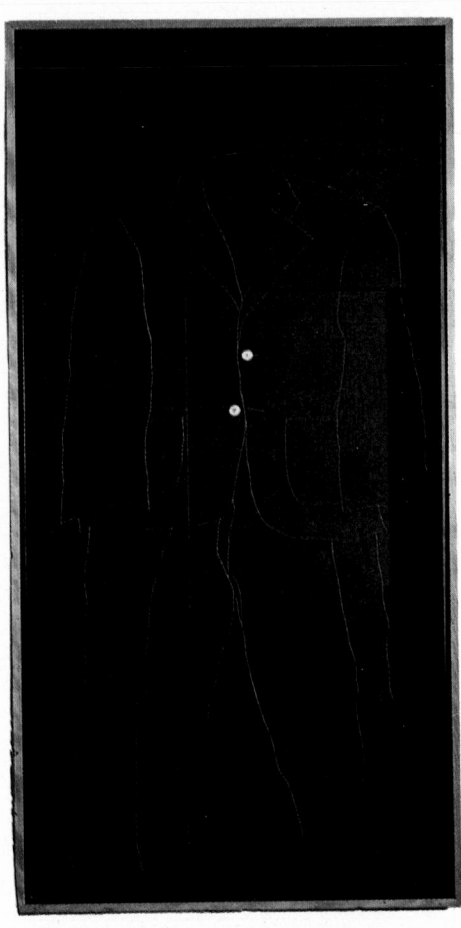

the comic strip. The earliest Warhols were blown-up versions of the Dick Tracy comic strip which were used as part of a window display for the New York department store Lord and Taylor's (Plate 154). Just before these he had made some drawings, also based on comic strips, which were shown at the novelty shop Serendipity and also at an art gallery. One of the interesting things about the Dick Tracy paintings is undoubtedly the uncertainty of their technique. Warhol has never been a "natural" artist like Dine, and this may account for his subsequent development towards a kind of art in which all emphasis on handling, on the painter's personal thumbprint, has been abolished.

The next phase in Warhol's career is the one which established him as being among the most prominent of the new Pop artists. It was also the one in which he adopted—"invented" would perhaps be too strong a word—the most famous of his images, the Campbell's soup can (Plate 155). When an interviewer asked him why he started painting these cans, Warhol gave a typical but not very enlightening reply: "Because I used to drink it. I used to have the same lunch every day, for twenty years I guess, the same thing over and over again. Someone said my life has dominated me; I liked that idea. I used to want to live at the Waldorf Towers and have soup and a sandwich, like that scene in the restaurant in *Naked Lunch* ..." (interview with G. R. Swenson, *Art News*, November, 1963, reprinted in *Pop Art Redefined*, by John Russell and Suzi Gablik, London, 1969, p. 117).

From single representations of soup cans Warhol soon progressed to multiple ones, where

153.
Jim Dine
All in One Lycra Plus Attachments
1965; 120 × 150 cm. (47 × 59 in.)
Eindhoven, Van Abbe Museum

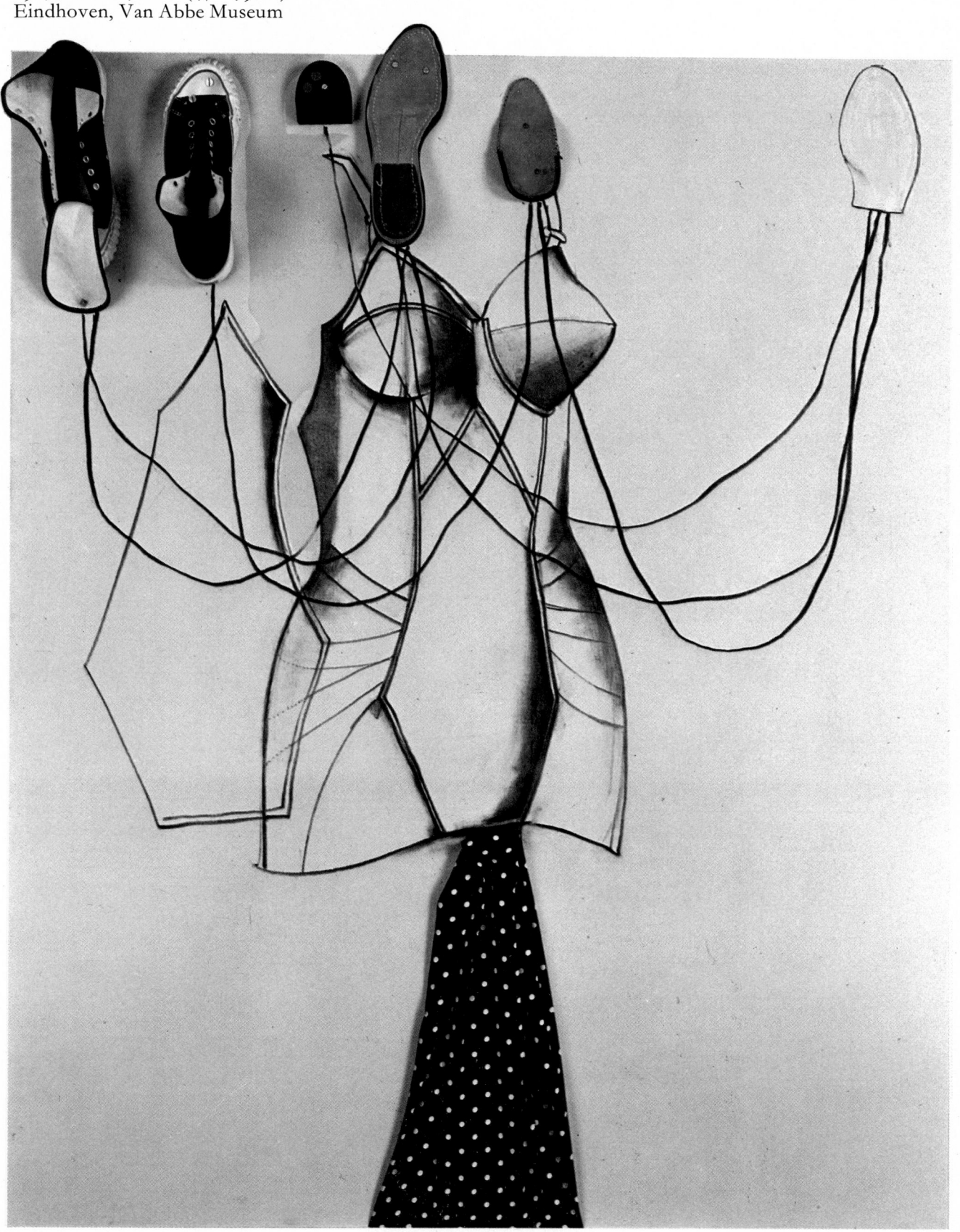

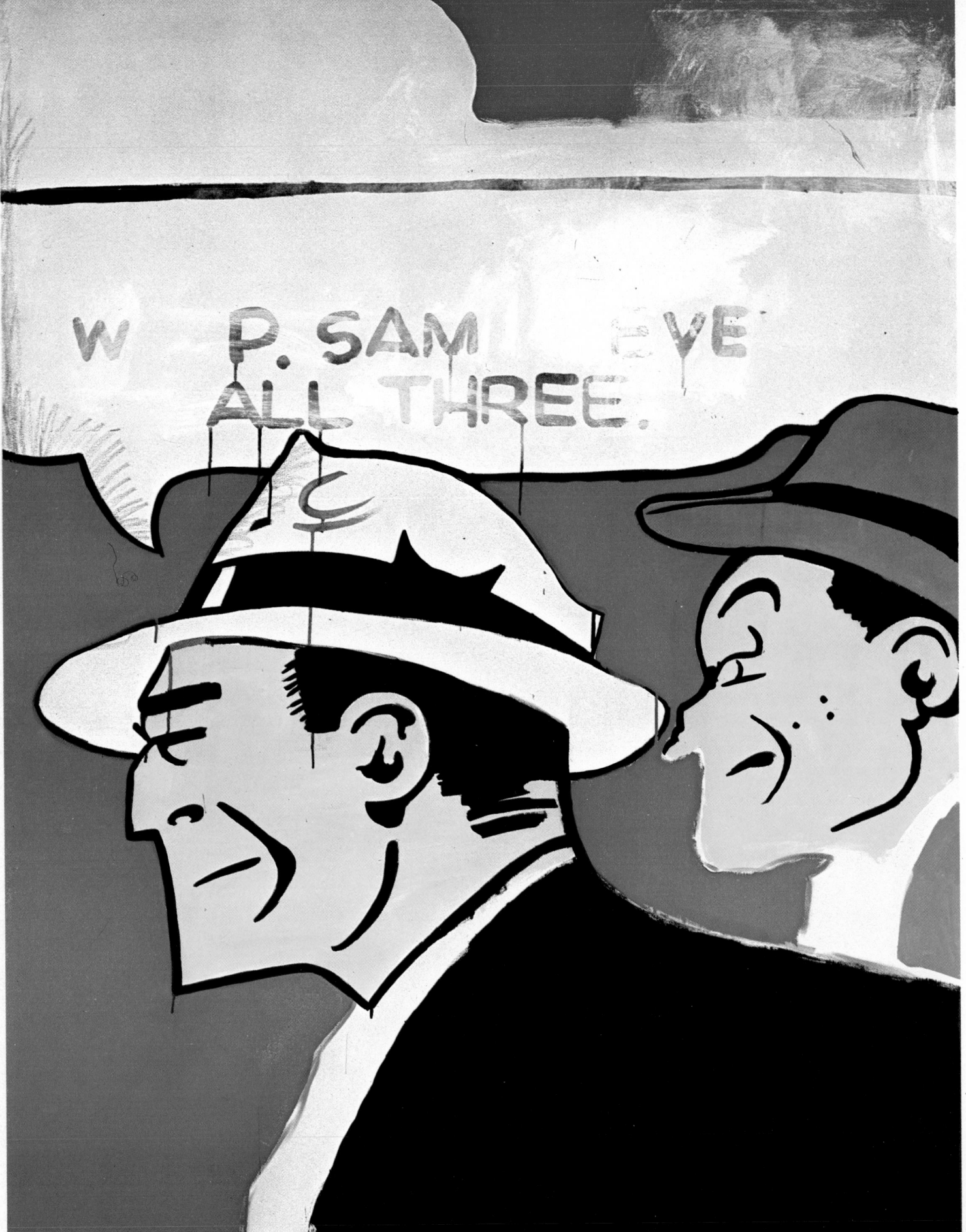

the same image is repeated over and over again, as if to remove any air of significance it might have possessed when viewed on its own, in isolation. From this in turn it was an easy step to the abandonment of handwork in favour of a mechanical process, in this case silk-screen. Warhol produced a series of ikons of well-known personalities—Marilyn Monroe, Elizabeth Taylor, Jacqueline Kennedy, Elvis Presley. Silk-screen in the Marilyns (Plate 158), and indeed in all the others, is used with deliberate crudity, and it is not even certain that Warhol has himself intervened personally in the production of the images that now bear his name. This is because he believes that art should have the egalitarian anonymity of the life he observes around him. "Everybody looks alike and acts alike," he avers, "and we're getting more and more that way." It is this feeling which prompted his famous statement, often quoted and often misunderstood: "The reason I'm painting this way is that I want to be a machine, and I feel that whatever I do and do machine-like is what I want to do" (ibid., p. 117).

Warhol's nihilism, however, goes even deeper than this. Another characteristic series of paintings are those he has dubbed the *Disasters*. These are silk-screened images of ghastly car crashes, of race riots, and of the electric chair (Plates 159 and 160). The shocking image is often slicked over and partly obscured by a wash of Day-Glo colour, orange or mauve or pink. These pictures are at one and the same time an acknowledgment of a deep streak of negative emotion, and a deliberate cauterization of that emotion: "When you see a gruesome picture over and over again, it doesn't really have any effect."

It comes as no surprise that Warhol's development eventually took him away from painting altogether. First he began to concentrate increasingly on films, then, as the films themselves became commercial rather than avant-garde, he became celebrated merely for being Warhol, and scarcely intervened in the activity which still went on around him, and which continued to bear his name.

Yet it took far more than the activities of Dine and Warhol to exhaust the possibilities of Pop. A

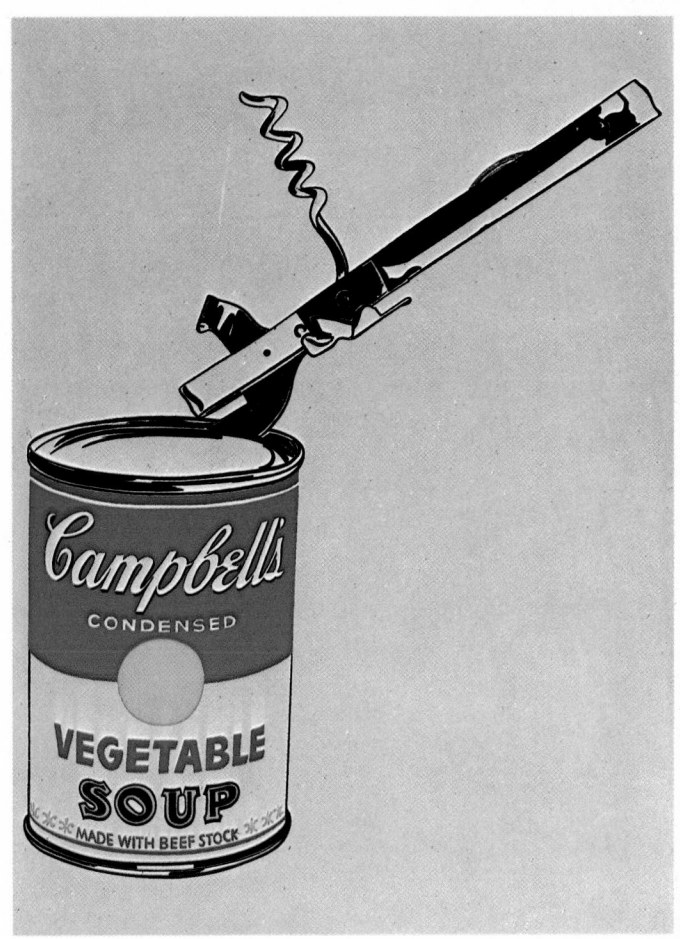

very different aspect of the American movement is revealed by the work of Roy Lichtenstein. Lichtenstein was early fascinated with Americana. Paintings done in the early Fifties deal with subjects like cowboys and bathing beauties, though not yet in the style that was to become associated with the artist's name. His approach to Pop Art, when an abrupt stylistic change came over his work in 1961, was largely negative—"anti-contemplative, anti-nuance, anti-getting-away from the tyranny of the rectangle, anti-movement-and-light, anti-mystery, anti-paint-quality, anti-Zen, and anti all of those brilliant ideas of preceding movements which everyone understands so thoroughly" (from an interview with Lichtenstein in "Picasso to Lichtenstein" exhibition catalogue, Tate Gallery, 1974). But the

156. Opposite
Andy Warhol
Campbell's Soup Cans 200, detail
1962; 183 × 254 cm. (71 × 99 in.)
Colorado, coll. Kimiko and John Powers

157.
Andy Warhol
Elvis I and II
1964; 208.3 × 208.3 cm. (81 × 81 in.)
Toronto, Art Gallery of Ontario, donated in 1966 by the Women's Committee Fund

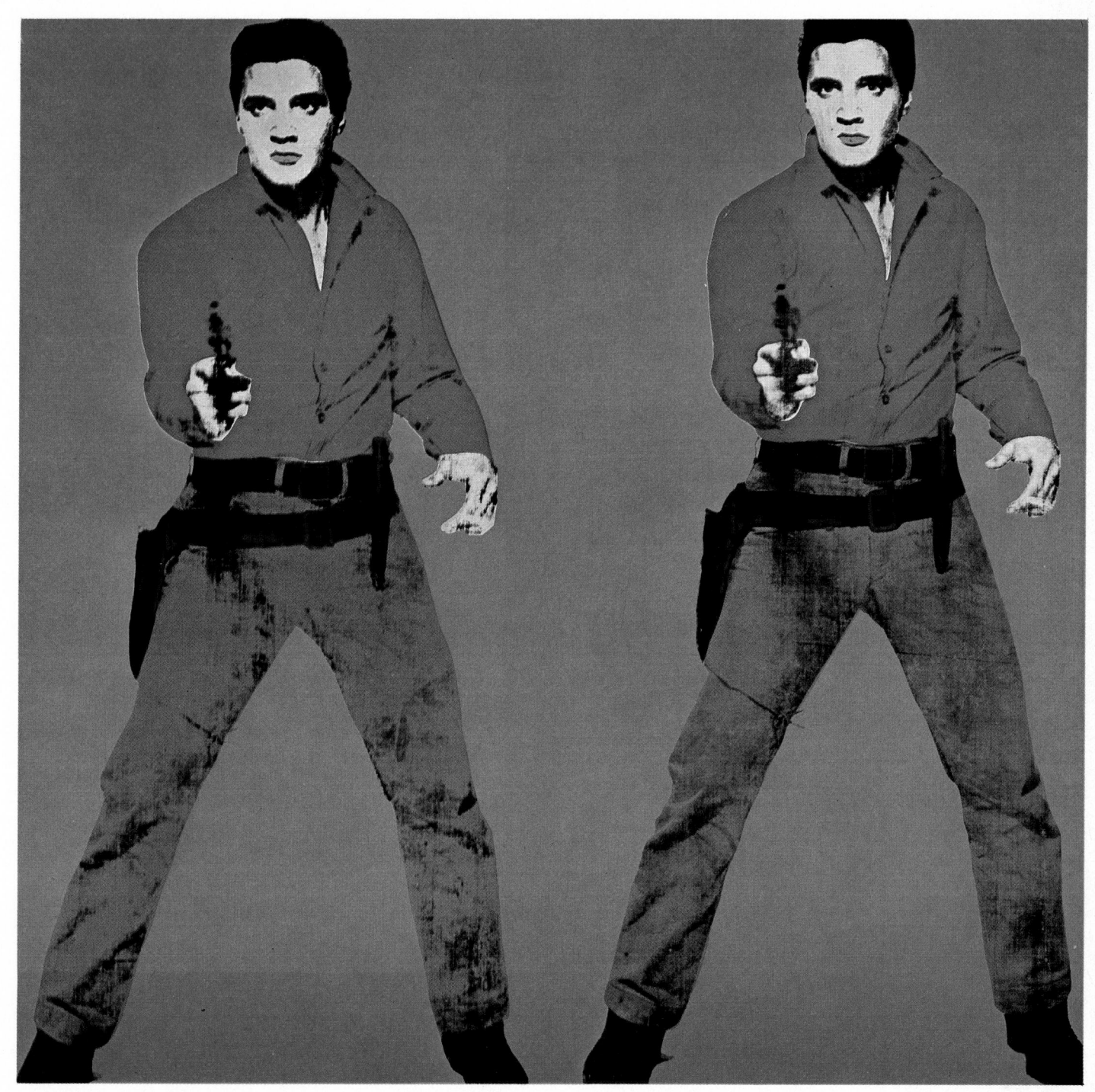

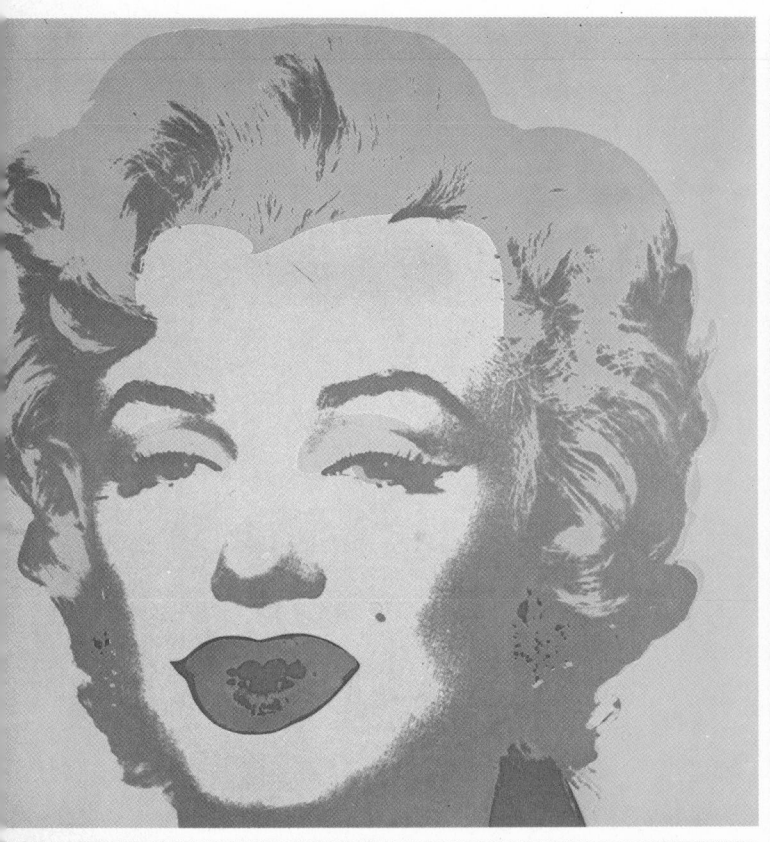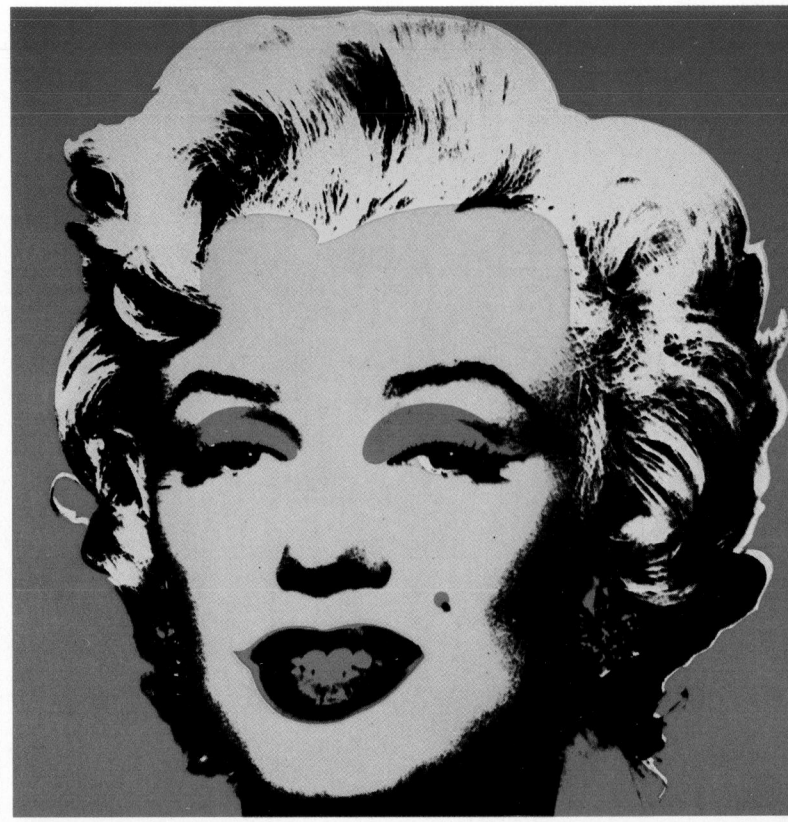
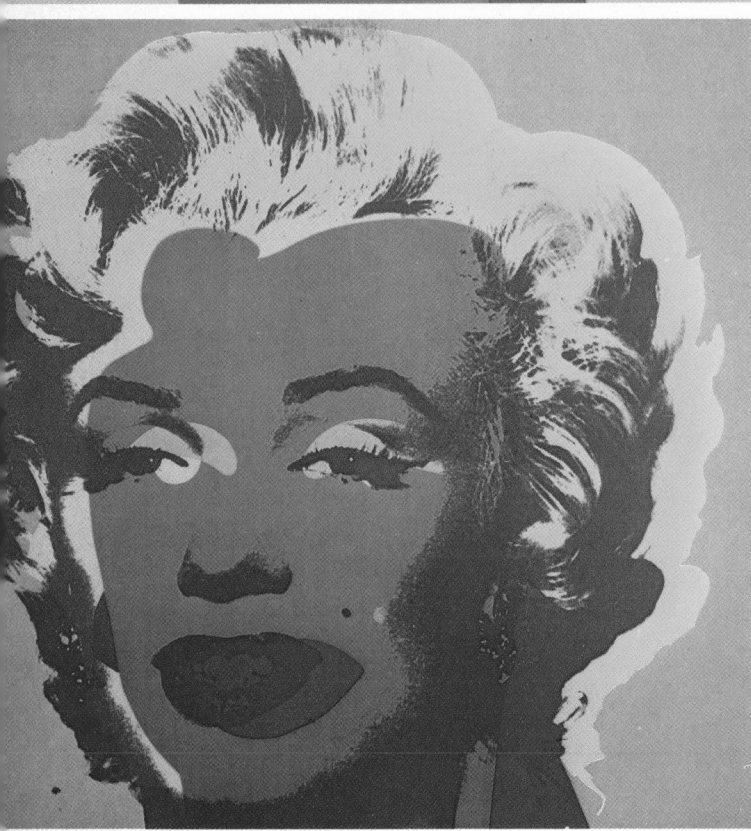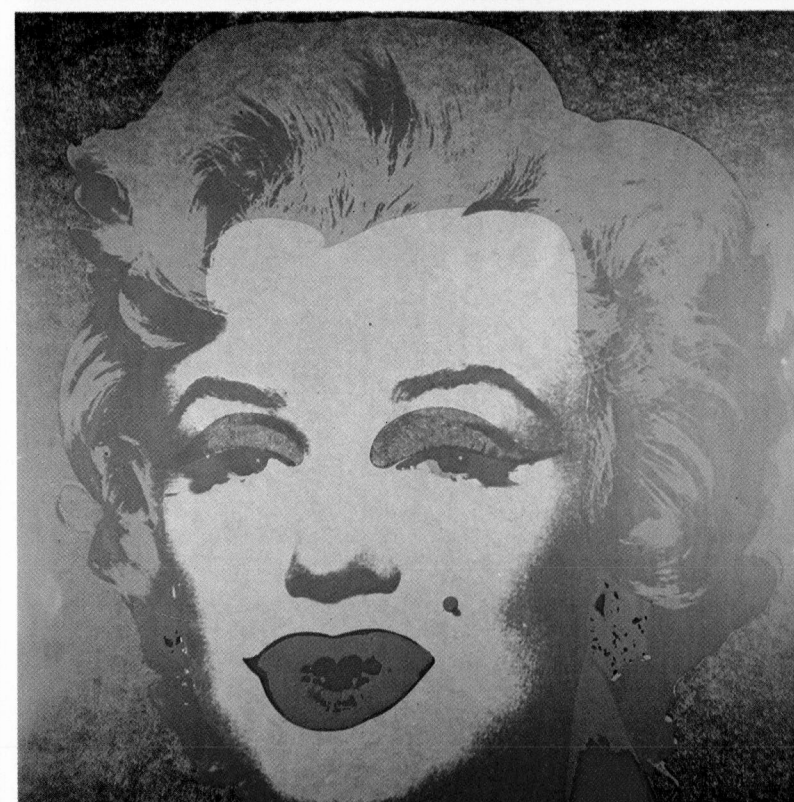

202

158.
Andy Warhol
Marilyn Monroe
1967; 92 × 92 cm. (36 × 36 in.)
Colorado, coll. Kimiko and John Powers

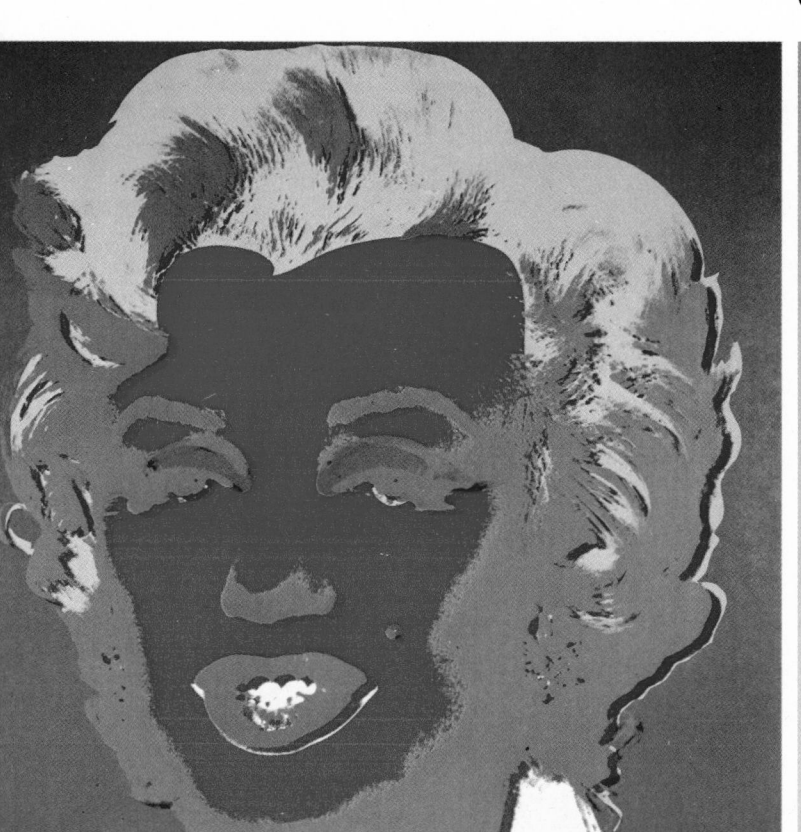
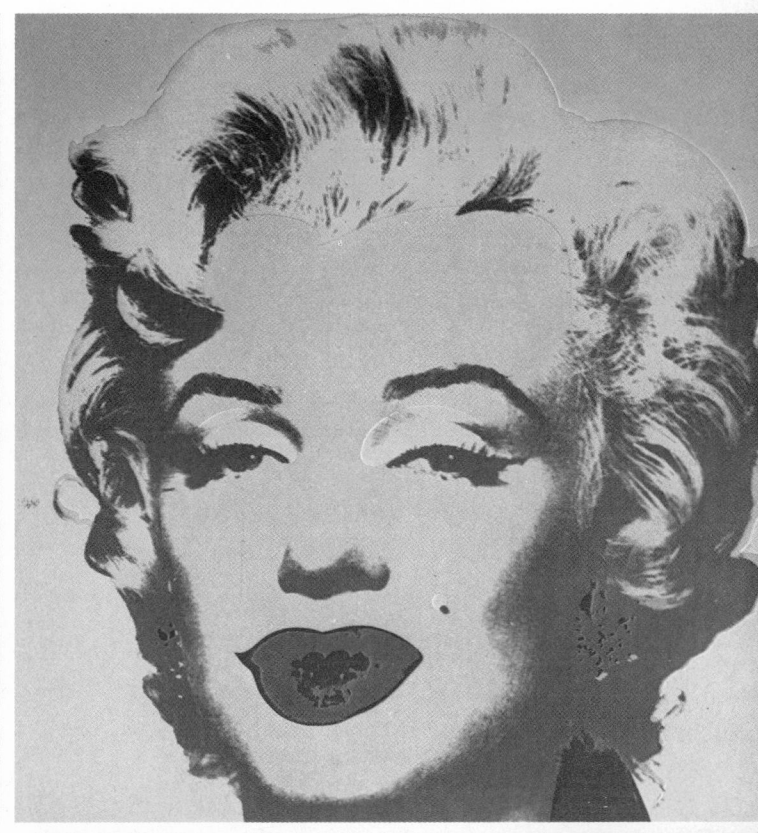
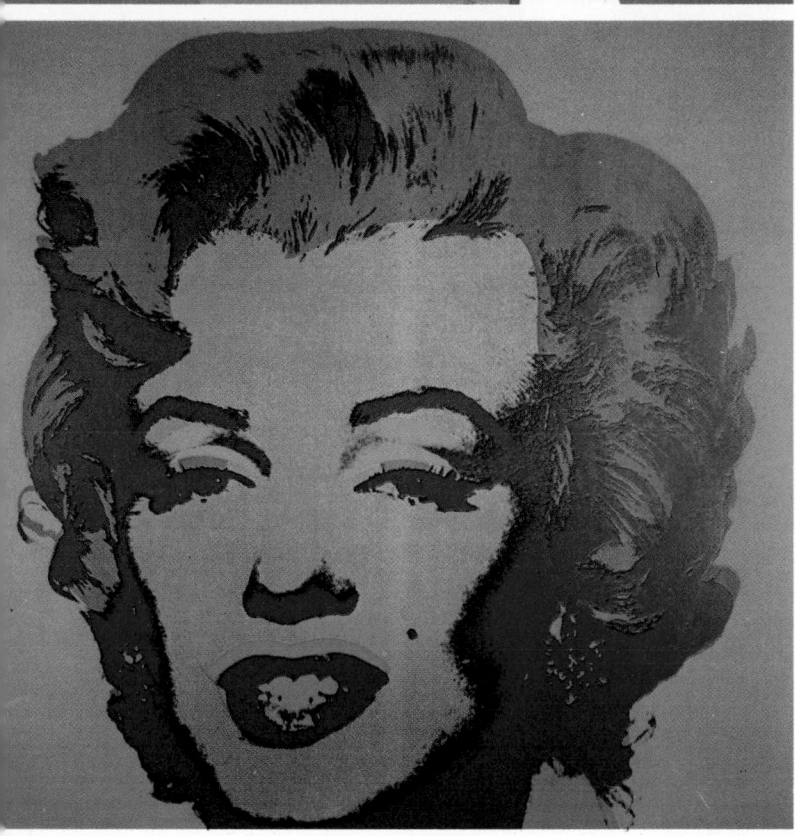
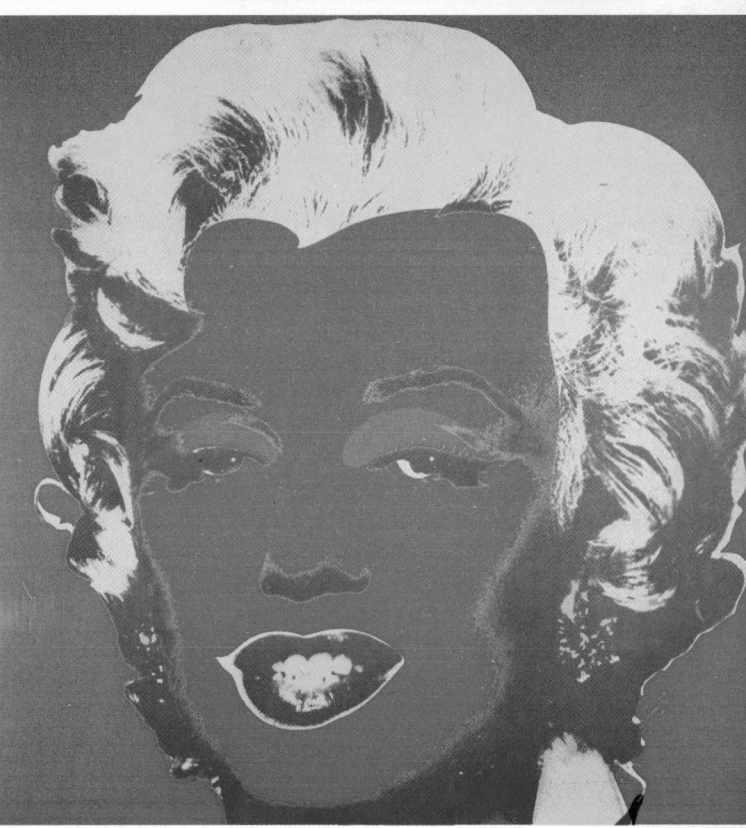

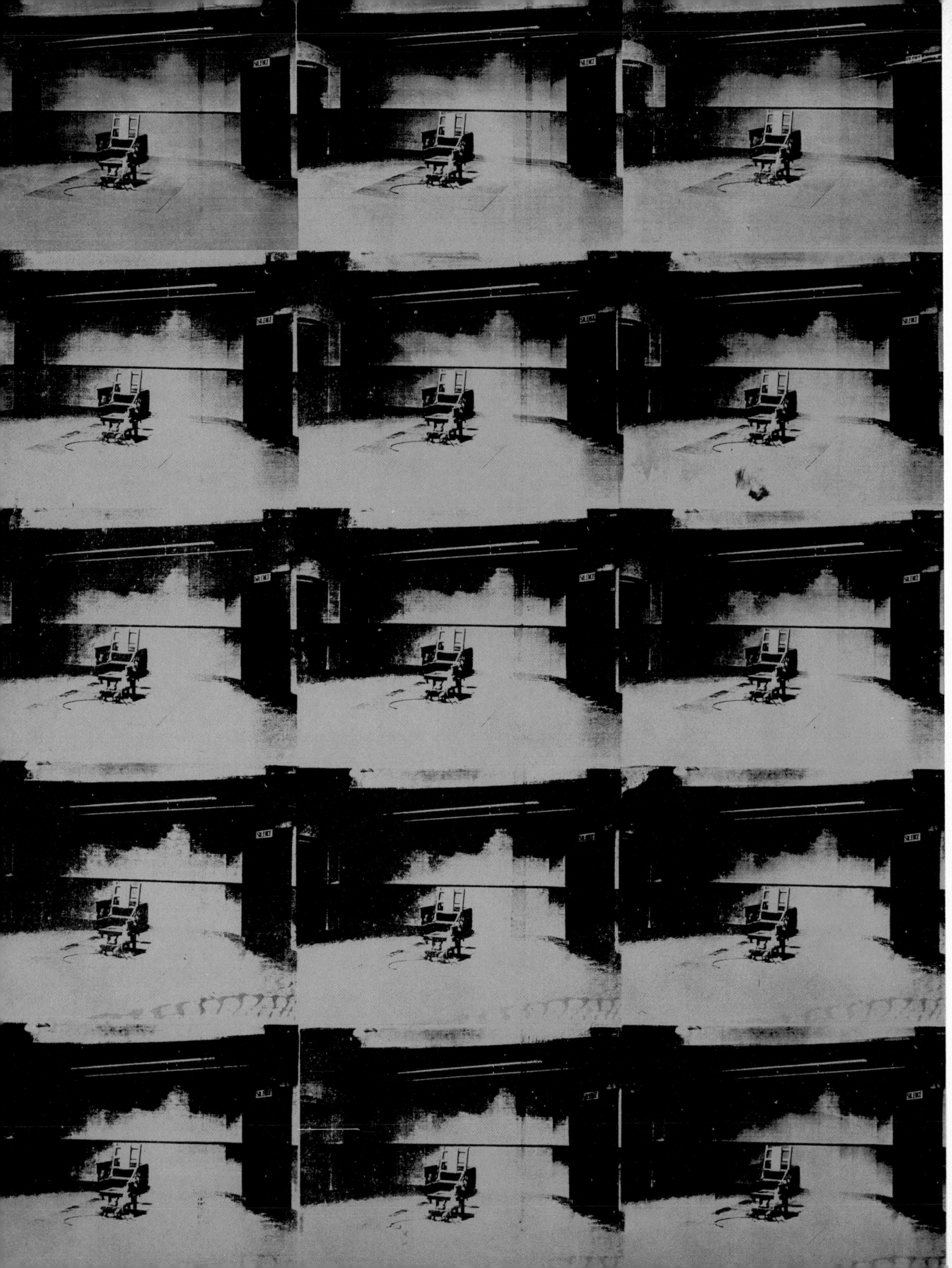

159. Opposite
Andy Warhol
Orange Disaster
1963; 269.2 × 208.3 cm. (105 × 81 in.)
New York, coll. Harry N. Abrams family

160.
Andy Warhol
Race Riot
1964; 76.5 × 84.1 cm. (30 × 33 in.)
Detroit, Detroit Institute of Arts

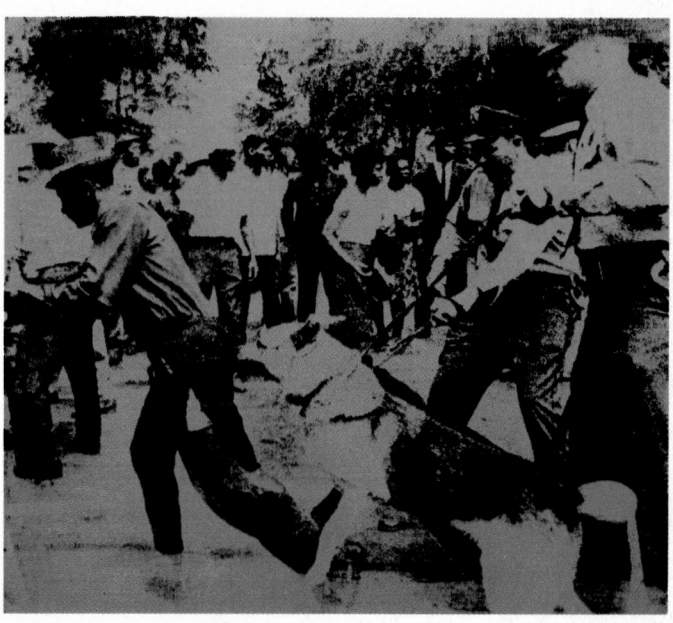

impulse to say no sprang from very different motivations from those which had directed Andy Warhol.

Lichtenstein, unlike Warhol, is deeply interested in questions of style, though the interest is often expressed in an extremely paradoxical and ironic way. To say, as Lichtenstein did, that the idea was "to get a painting that was despicable enough so that no one would hang it" nevertheless implies a keen interest in the paintings that people do in fact put on the wall, in art galleries, and in their own homes.

Lichtenstein's first material, like Warhol's, was the comic strip, but the material extracted from this source was treated in a particularly refined and subtle kind of way. The artist might reproduce all the conventions he found in his material—the black outlines, the coarse screen of dots characteristic of cheap colour-printing (*M-Maybe*, Plate 161)—but in fact the material is substantially revised. Lichtenstein declares: "What I do is form, whereas the comic strip is not formed in the sense I'm using the word: the comics have shapes but there has been no attempt to make them intensely unified.... And my work is actually different from comic strips in that every mark is really in a different place, however slight the difference seems to some. The difference is often not great, but it is crucial. ... One of the things a cartoon does is to express violent emotion and passion in a completely mechanical and removed style. To express this thing in a painterly style would dilute it; the techniques I use are not commercial, they only appear to be commercial—and the ways of seeing and composing and unifying are different and have different ends" (interview with G.R.Swenson, "What is Pop Art?", *Art News*, Vol. 62, No. 7 [November, 1963], p. 24–27).

This approach soon led the artist to apply the same techniques to totally different subject matter, not initially connected with comic strips at all, though translated into comic-strip terms. Thus Lichtenstein painted a series of large *Brushstrokes*, which were intended as a satire on Abstract Expressionist pretensions to total artistic freedom. He also made revised versions of works by the greatest Modernist innovators—Cézanne, Mon-

drian, and Picasso. In these one finds a dual strategy. On the one hand, Lichtenstein seems to be trying to distance the paintings he chooses to copy, so that a rational assessment can be made of them. On the other, he seems to ask us to consider how our reaction to a representation changes when the convention used for that representation is altered.

At his best Lichtenstein has some of the traditional monumentality of Georges Seurat or even of Poussin. Strangely enough, this happens most often with the paintings that derive from comic strips. None of his transpositions of Picasso has anything like the authority possessed by a painting such as *Whaam!* (Plate 163), in the Tate Gallery. At his weakest, on the other hand, Lichtenstein seems the very opposite of a truly popular artist. He is claustrophically obsessed with art itself and ideas about art. This may be one reason why he has been one of the most successful of the American Pop artists with European audiences.

Dine, Lichtenstein, and Warhol have all made reputations for activities on the margin of what they have achieved as painters. Warhol's film making has already been mentioned. His earlier and more personal films used a fixed camera and

205

161.
Roy Lichtenstein
M-Maybe
1965; 152.4 × 152.4 cm. (59 × 59 in.)
Cologne, Wallraf-Richartz Museum, coll. Ludwig

162.
Roy Lichtenstein
Pow!
N.d.; 96 × 71 cm. (37 × 28 in.)
Aachen, Neue Galerie, coll. Ludwig

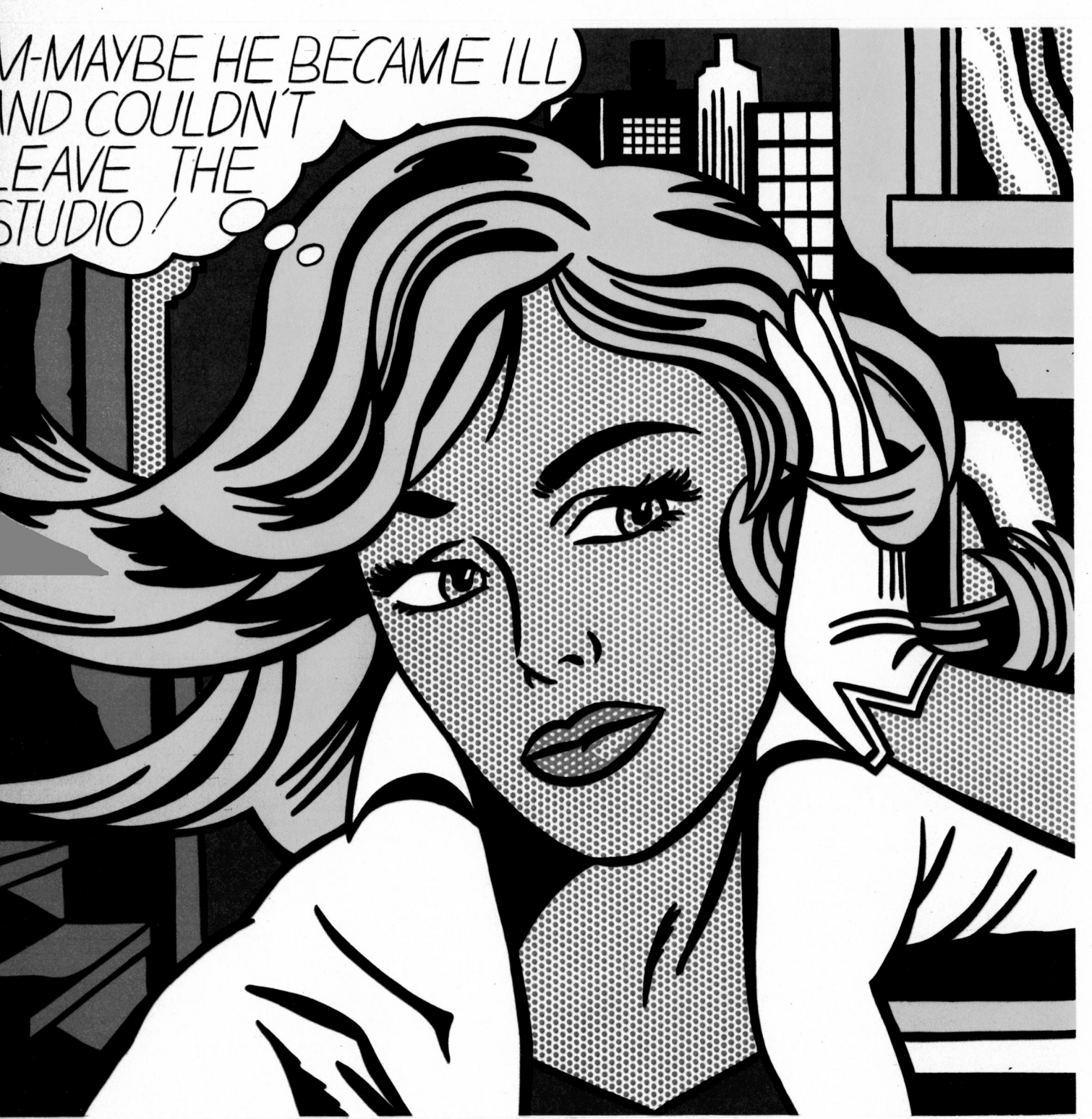

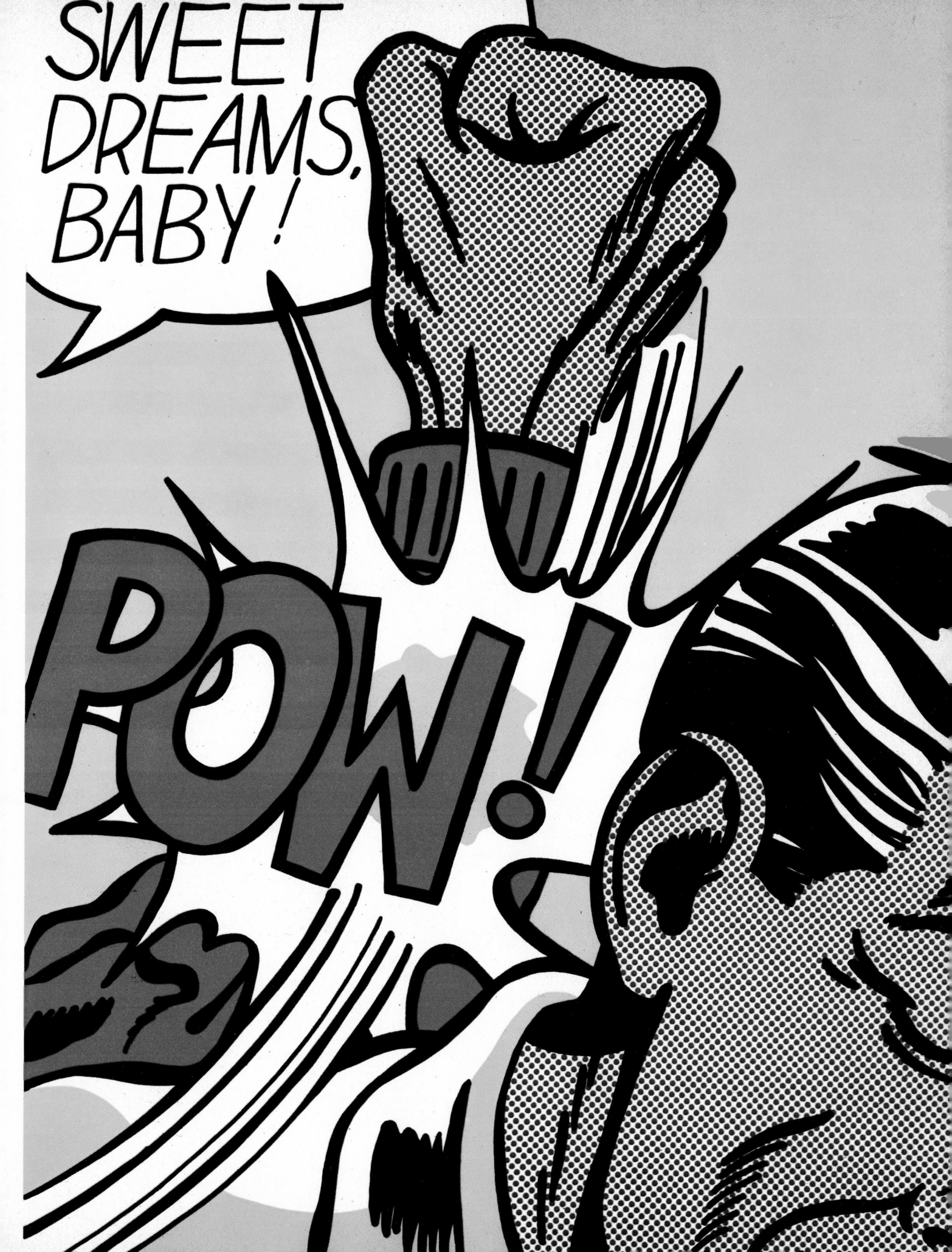

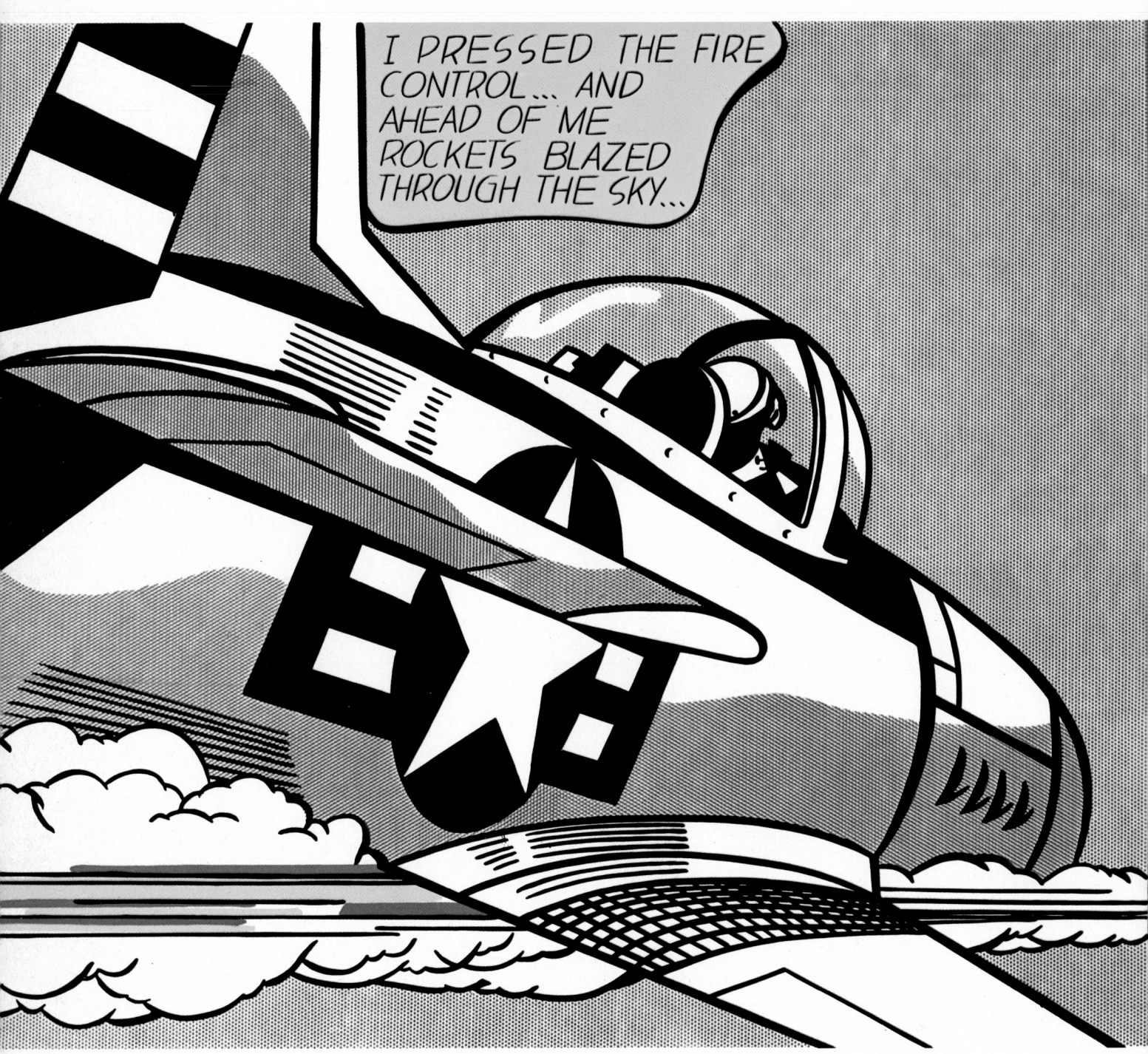

163.
Roy Lichtenstein
Whaam!
1963; 173 × 406.5 cm. (67 × 159 in.)
London, Tate Gallery

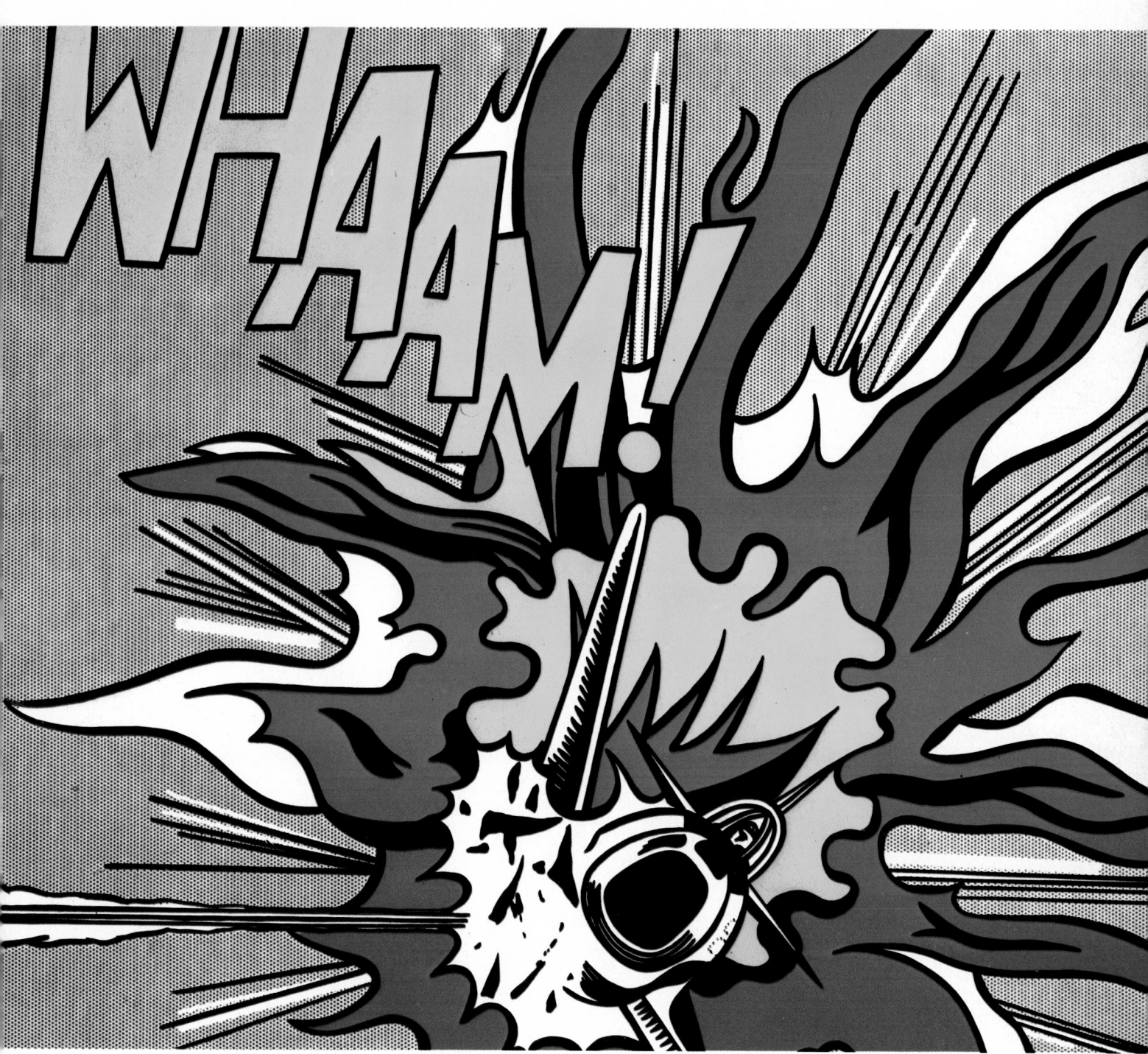

164.
Roy Lichtenstein
Ceramic Head with Blue Shadow
1966; 38.11 cm. (15 in.)
Connecticut, coll. Mr. and Mrs. Burton Tremaine

165. Opposite
Roy Lichtenstein
Wall Explosion No. 1
1964; 251 × 160 cm. (98 × 62 in.)
Cologne, Wallraf-Richartz Museum, coll. Ludwig

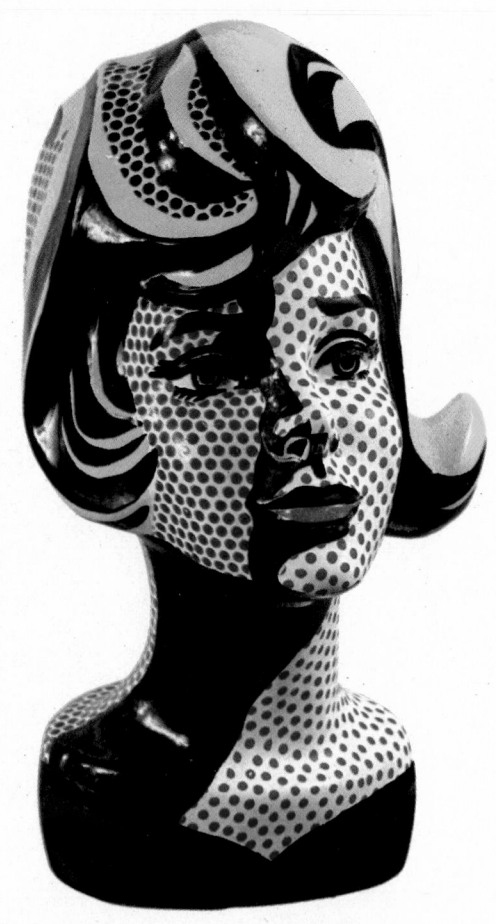

the transition being noticeable. It was a case of the scenery creating the theatrical event, rather than vice versa.

Lichtenstein extended his work in a very different direction still. From being a painter, he also became a sculptor (Plates 164 and 165). His sculptures are in general much weaker and less interesting than his work in two dimensions. They make more clearly evident the degree of mannerism which is also found in his painting.

Pop Art has indeed included, within its stylistic boundaries, work in three dimensions. Perhaps the most important of the Pop object makers is Claes Oldenburg. Oldenburg was born in Sweden and educated in the United States and in Scandinavia. He thus has a dual perspective on American urbanism and industrialism, and this perspective reveals itself not in a horrified rejection, but in a curiously joyous acceptance of the American scene. Like the other important Pop artists, Oldenburg had been practising as an artist for some time before he suddenly reached the point of breakthrough into a new style. In 1959, he began work on a project he called *The Street*, a collection of graffiti-like sketches and objects made from discarded material. At this time he became friendly with Dine and with Allan Kaprow. Kaprow, like Dine, was one of the progenitors of the Happening. A second version of *The Street*, which was exhibited in 1960, was accompanied by a number of group performances. It was followed by a second project called *The Store*.

The Store launched Oldenburg into a career as a maker of objects. Sometimes these objects, like *Salmon Mayonnaise* of 1964 (Plate 166), were merely reproductions, or more often over-scaled versions, of things that existed in real life. The subjects were not, however, items that would traditionally have been considered worthy of a sculptor's attention. In reproducing the mummified, artifically coloured food he saw in delicatessens, Oldenburg was following the example of the commercial artists and sign makers. His sources were window displays and the strange objects that loom up by the side of American

Gradually Oldenburg came to understand the

were essentially explorations of our power to endure boredom. There was also the idea that the fixed, unblinking scrutiny of the camera lens would eventually force the subject, whether animate or inanimate, to yield up secrets which might otherwise remain unrevealed. Dine's extra-curricular work was in total contrast to this. He was responsible for staging some of the earliest "Happenings". The Happening was a theatrical event in revolt against then prevalent theatrical conventions. Instead of a plot it offered a collage of sensations, and was essentially an extension of the interest in collage, especially collage which had grown to monumental size, and which surrounded the spectator after the manner of the *Merzbaus* or environmental constructions made of found material created by Kurt Schwitters. If sounds and moving bodies were added, the static environment became the dynamic Happening, almost without

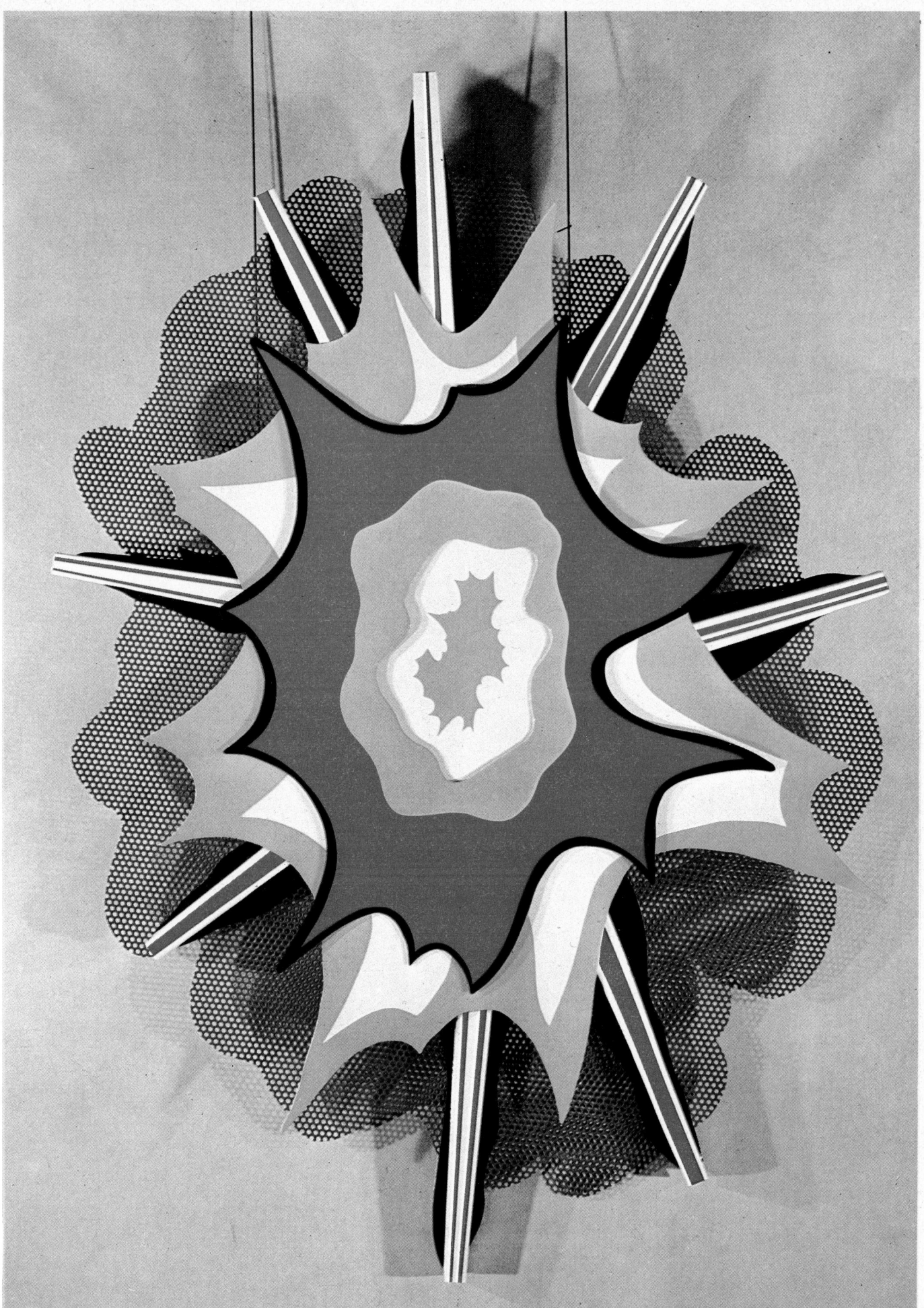

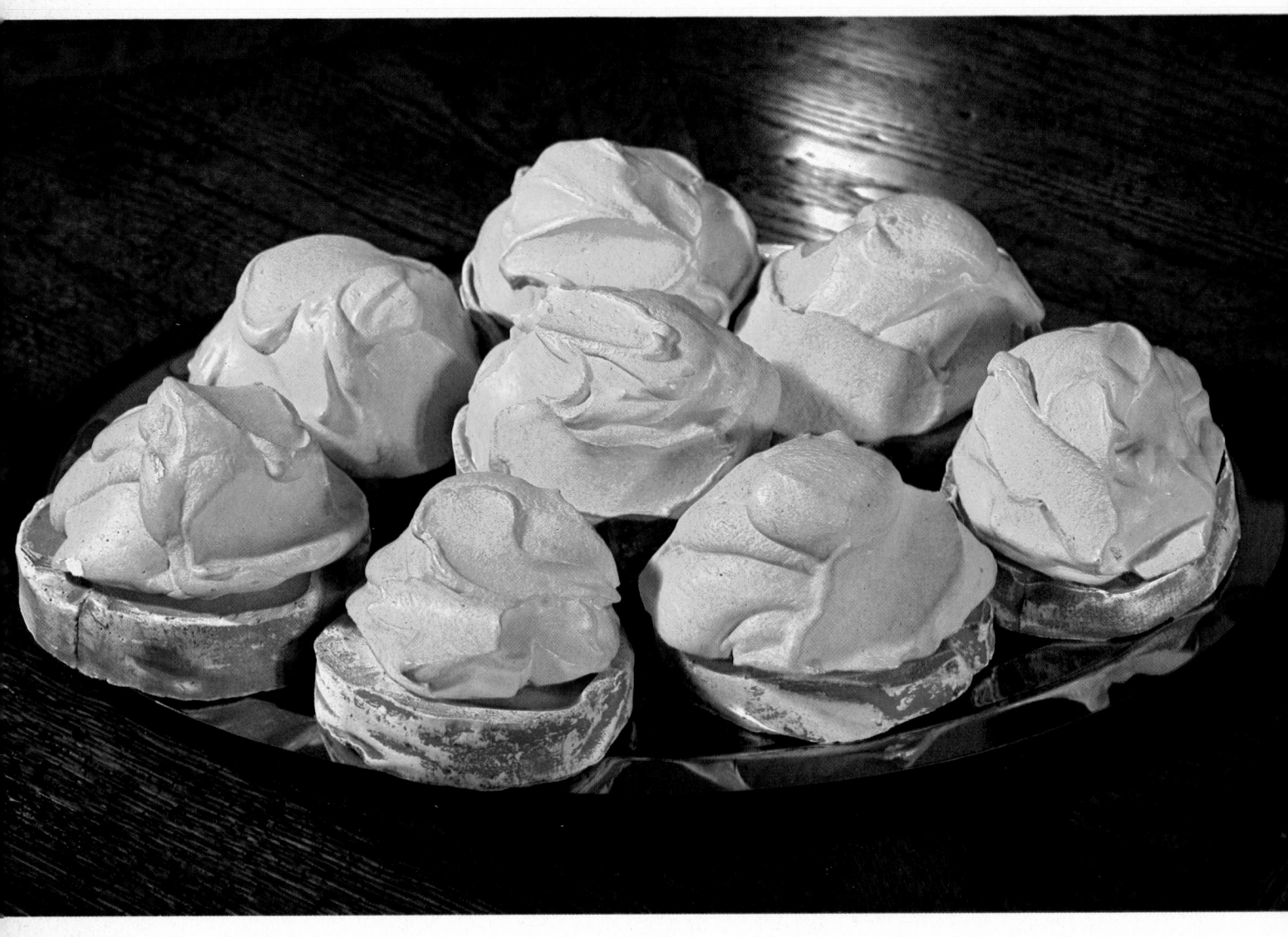

166.
Claes Oldenburg
Salmon Mayonnaise
1964; 12.7 × 44.5 cm. (5 × 17 in.)
New York, coll. Mr. and Mrs. Robert C. Scull

167. Opposite
Claes Oldenburg
Trowel, Scale B
1971; 12.2 m. (40 ft.)
New York, collection of the artist

168. Overleaf left
Claes Oldenburg
Giant Soft Swedish Light Switch
1966; 130 cm. (51 in.)
Cologne, Wallraf-Richartz Museum, coll. Ludwig

169. Overleaf right
Claes Oldenburg
Giant Fireplug Sited in the Civic Center, Chicago
1968; 26.3 × 20.6 cm. (10 × 8 in.)
Colorado, coll. Kimiko and John Powers

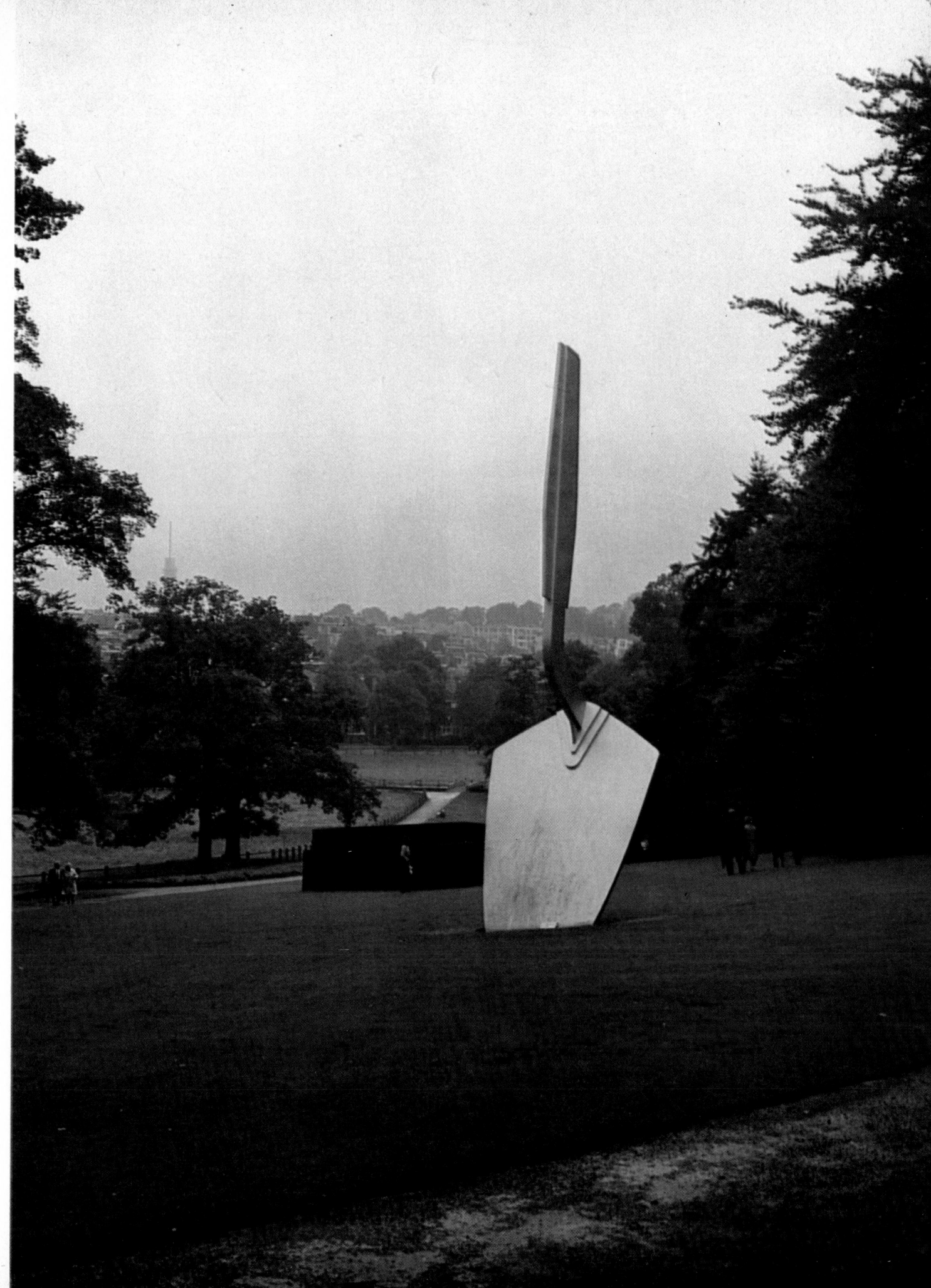

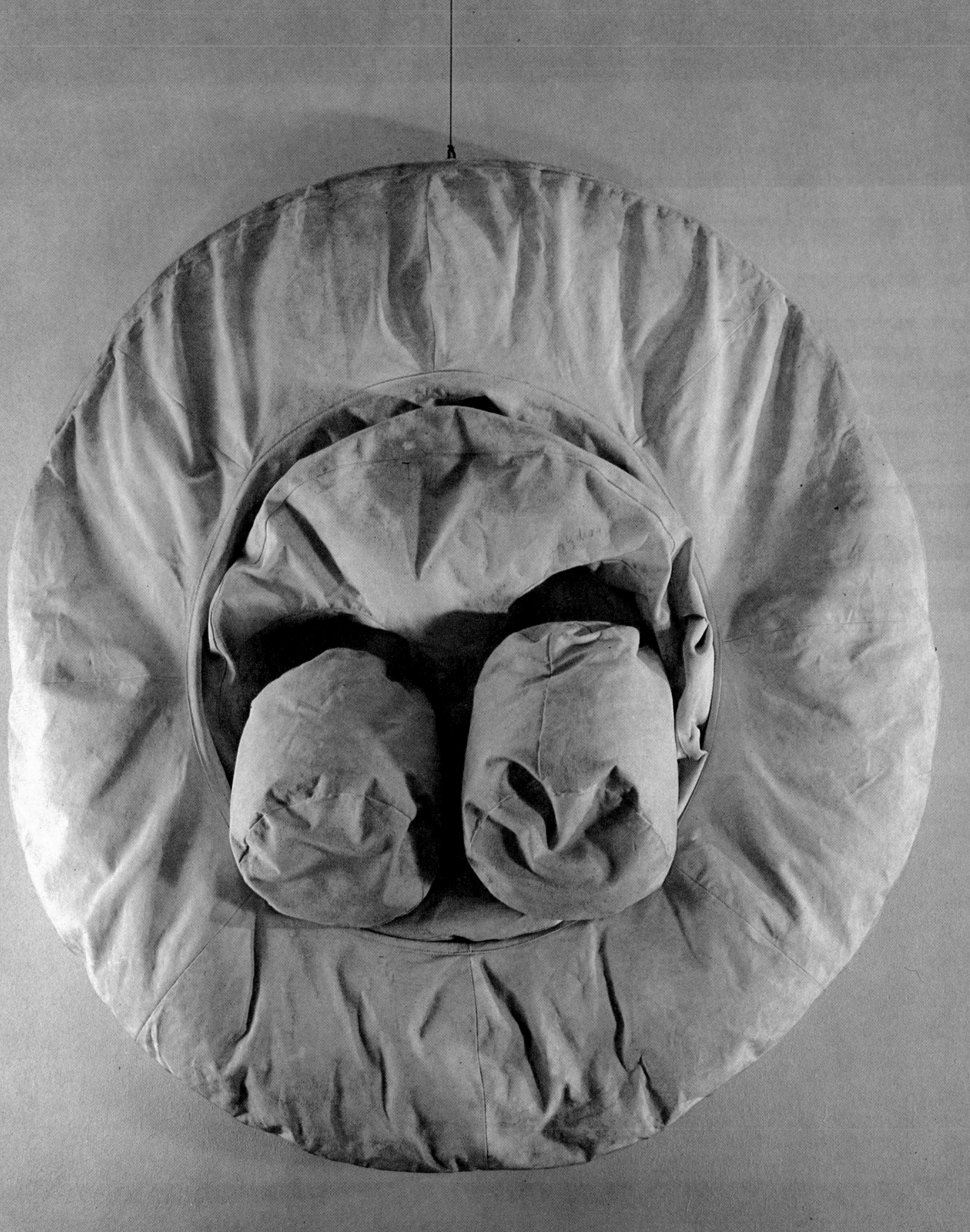

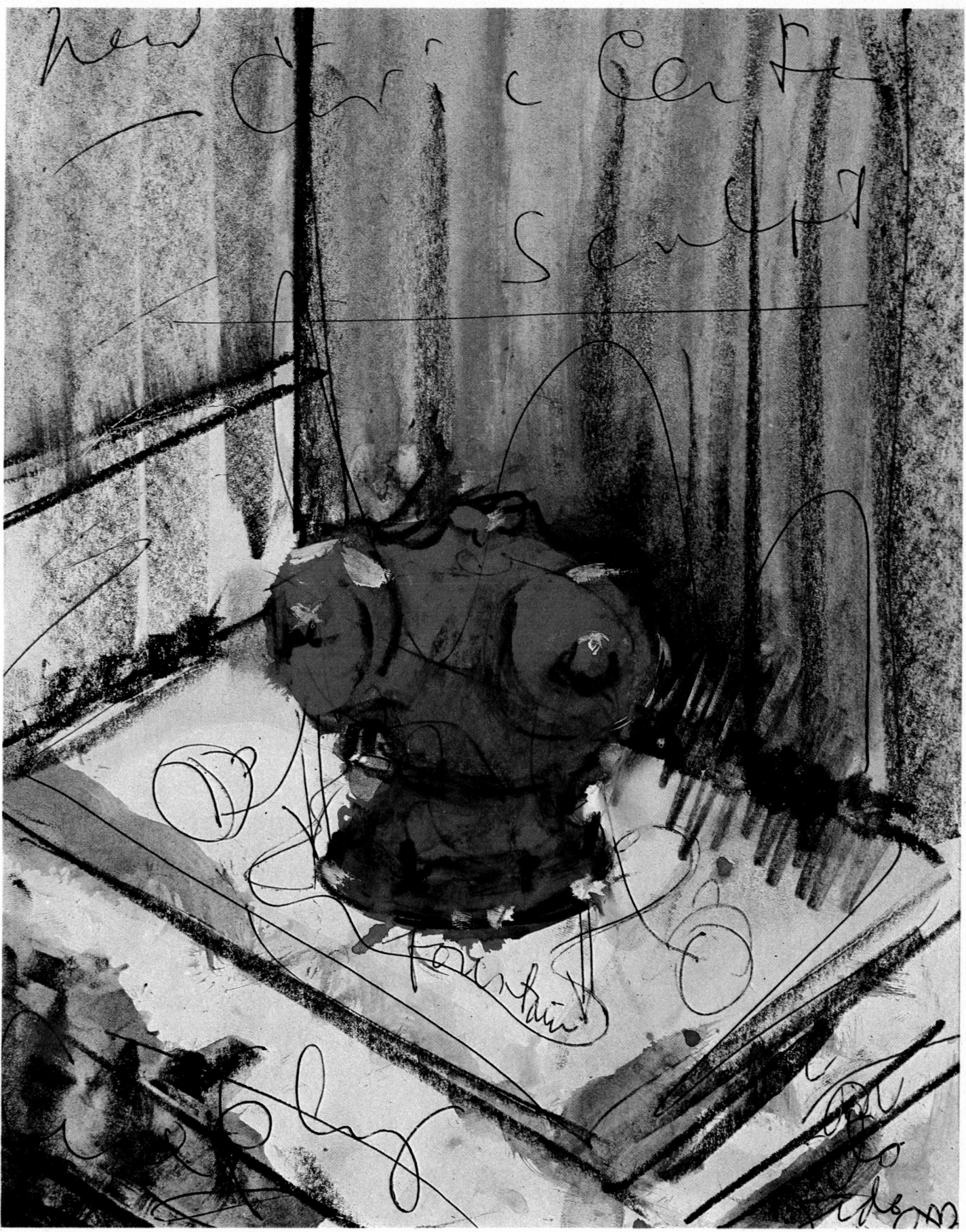

215

effects that could be derived not merely from making his objects over-scale, but also from using inappropriate materials, and even from allowing the original form to assume an inappropriate shape. This is what has happened to *Giant Soft Swedish Light Switch* (Plate 168), which is representative of a whole series of soft sculptures made of vinyl or other material and loosely stuffed with kapok. The forms, often extremely erotic, assumed by these transformations of ordinary objects are part of the artist's campaign to make us re-examine the world that surrounds us. He has expressed this desire in another way in his projects for open-air monuments. The *Giant Fireplug Sited in the Civic Center, Chicago* (Plate 169) is only one of a very considerable number of these. "I am for an art", Oldenburg once said, "that is political-erotical, mystical, that does something other than sit on its ass in a museum."

There are no other Pop sculptors or object makers who achieve anything like Oldenburg's vitality and impact. The work of the Venezuelan sculptor Marisol, however, does have personality and charm. Her slightly Surrealist wooden sculptures (Plates 170 and 171) have been classified as Pop Art for a number of not entirely convincing reasons. The first of these is that she has clearly been influenced by some aspects of the work of Johns and Rauschenberg, notably their use of plaster casts of parts of the human body as ingredients in some of their *assemblages*. Secondly, Marisol made her reputation in New York in the early Sixties, just at the time when Pop became the "boss" style, and when any figurative artist who happened to be attracting attention was immediately assimilated into it.

Her true source is nevertheless thoroughly American. She often seems to be a less gifted reincarnation of Elie Nadelman. Nadelman's late work shows a brilliant assimilation of American folk art, and there is more than a trace of this in Marisol. Her inclusion here is a reminder of the sentimentally populist side of Pop Art, which so many artists and critics have attempted to deny.

More central, and certainly far more important in historical terms, is the sculpture of George Segal. Segal, after working under Hans Hofmann,

and painting figurative work in the manner of Matisse, of Pierre Bonnard, and of the Abstract Expressionists—a range of styles which revealed his own stylistic uncertainty—began experimenting with life-size figures made of plaster and wire in 1958. By late 1960 he had stopped painting altogether and had started making casts of identifiable models which were then placed in architectural settings.

The point of Segal's work is very simple. It consists in the contrast between his ghostlike plasters and what surrounds them (Plates 172 and 173). Segal has said: "I use the premise of walking into a real space, intensifying it by working very carefully with the space between the figures and the objects surrounding them" (from the introduction by Martin Friedman to the catalogue of the exhibition "Figure/Environments" at the Walker Art Center, Minneapolis, 1970).

The plasters themselves remain surprisingly academic in style despite the far-from-academic technical method by which they have been produced. It was possible to go in two different, indeed opposite, directions from the position at which Segal found himself when Pop was at its height in the middle and late Sixties. One is that chosen by the various Super Realist sculptors, among them Duane Hanson and John de Andrea. Their effort has been to make the figure as lifelike as possible, by giving it glass eyes and real hair, colouring it naturalistically, etc. Segal has gone the other way, and has more and more edited his figures to look like the traditional *beaux-arts* work of the end of the nineteenth century. Recent

170. Opposite
Escobar Marisol
Ruth
1962; 167.6 cm. (65 in.)
Brandeis University, Massachusetts, Rose Art Museum

171. Overleaf
Escobar Marisol
Party
1965–66
New York, by kind permission of Sidney Janis Gallery

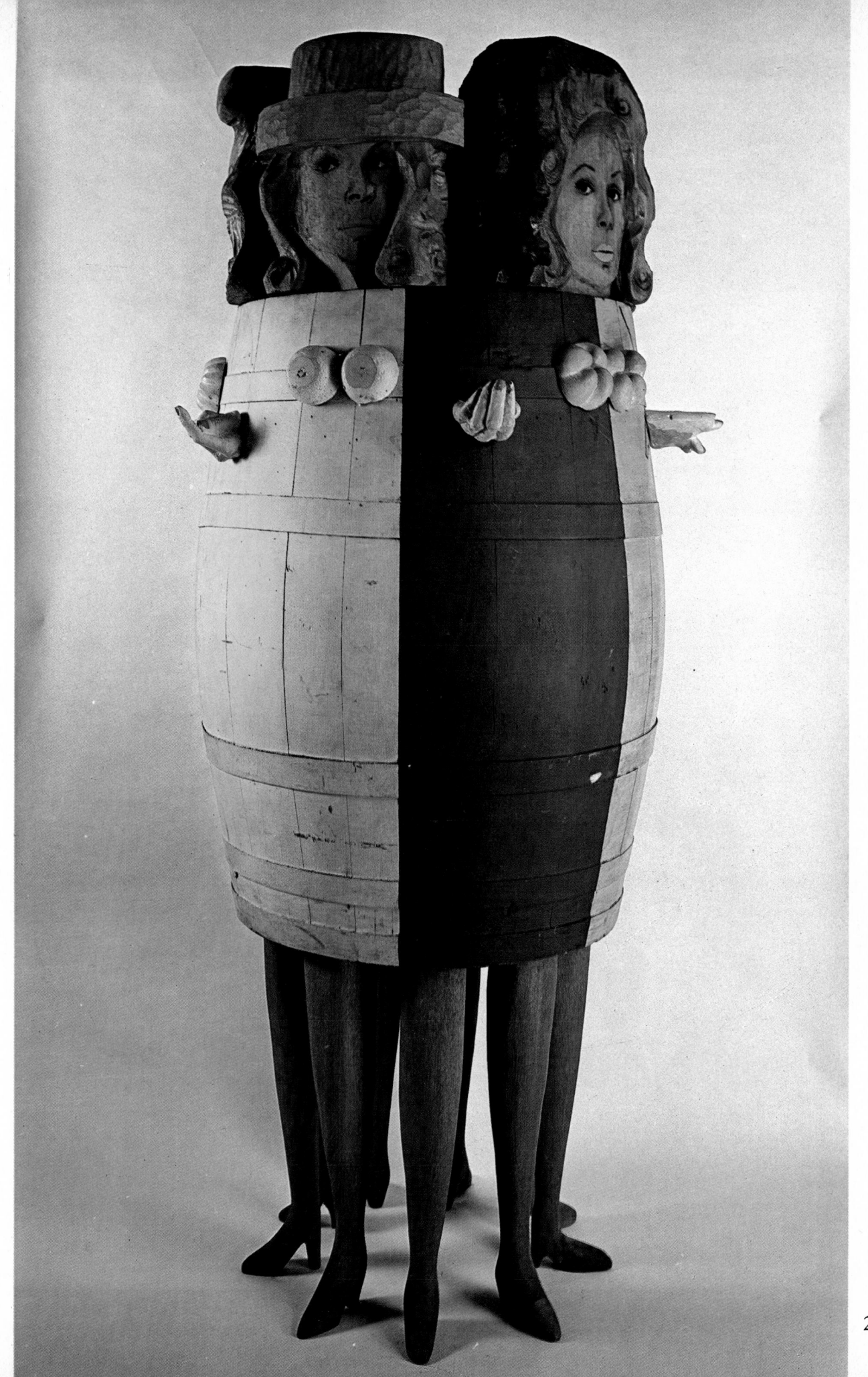

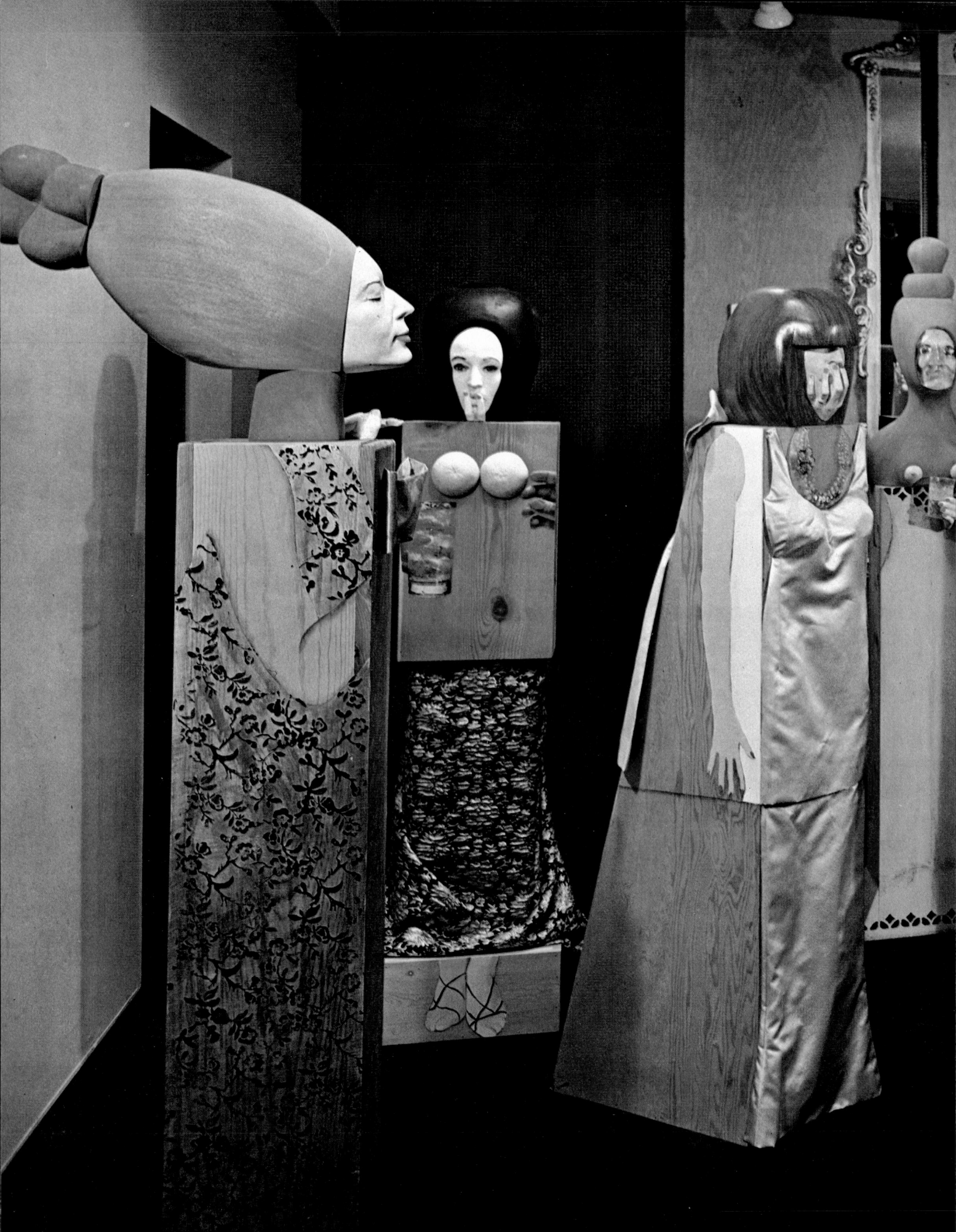

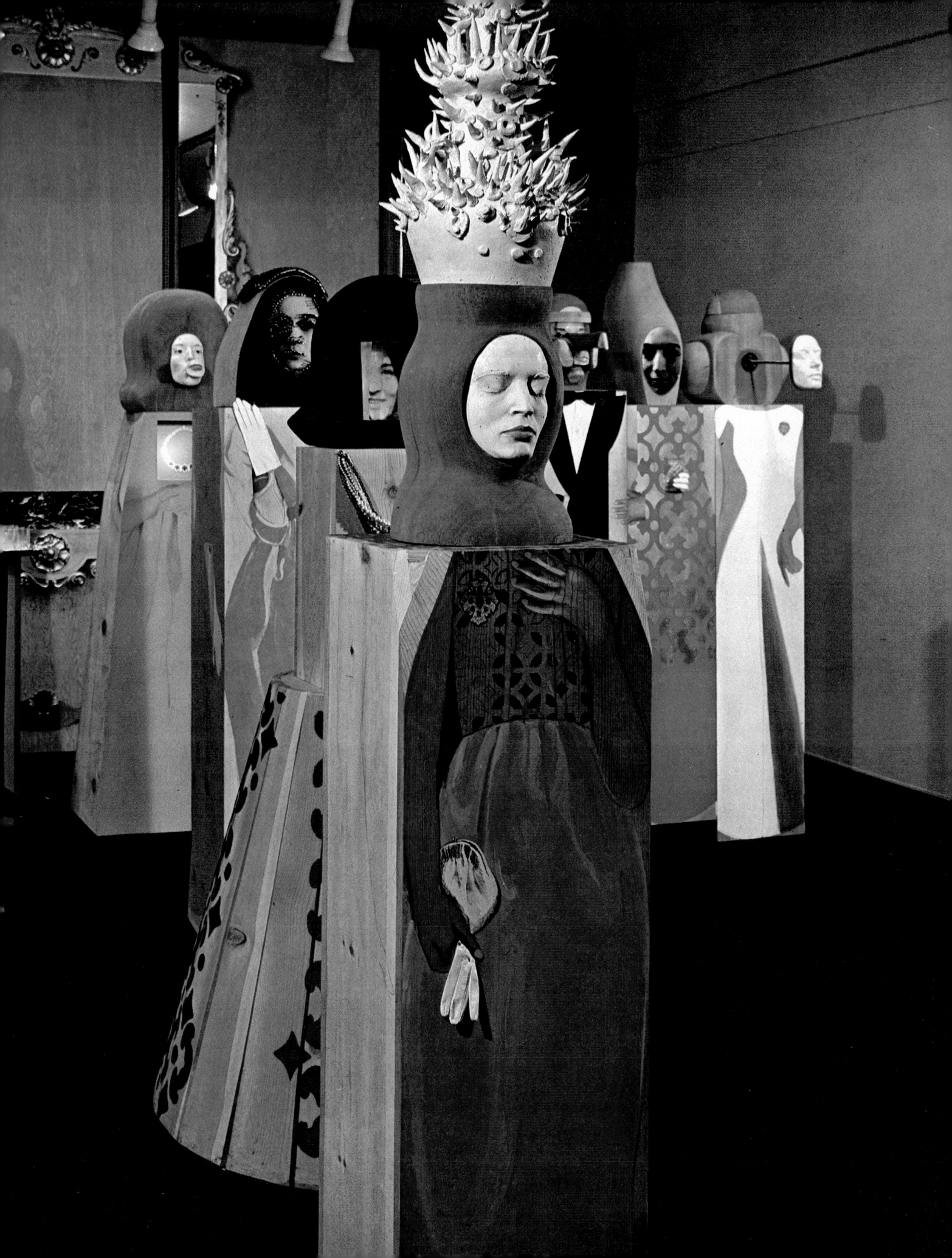

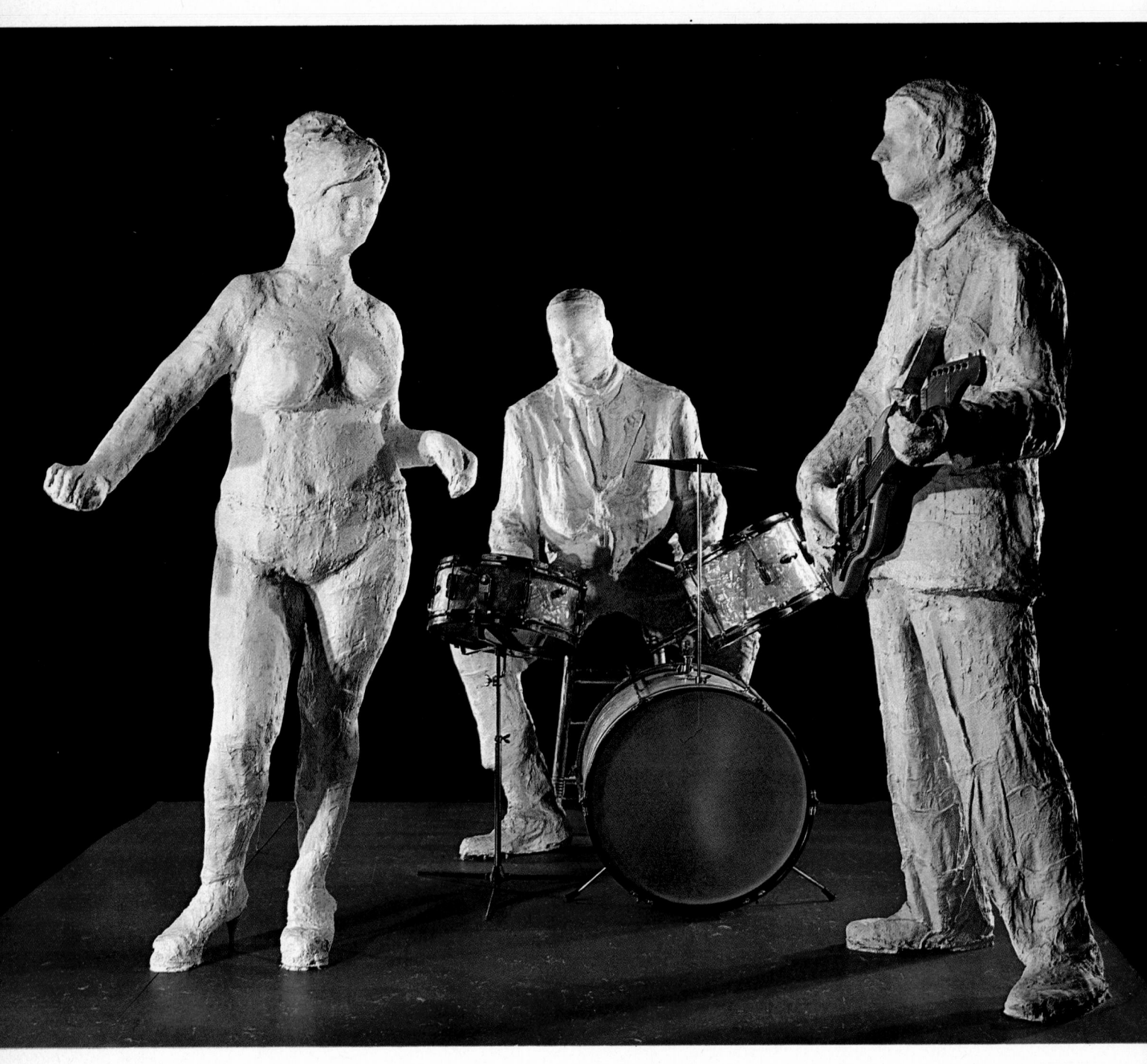

172.
George Segal
Rock 'n Roll Combo
1964; 186 × 190 × 145 cm. (73 × 74 × 57 in.)
Darmstadt, Hessisches Landesmuseum, coll. Karl Strobel

173. Opposite
George Segal
Film Poster
1967; 188 × 71.1 cm. (73 × 28 in.)
Colorado, coll. Kimiko and John Powers

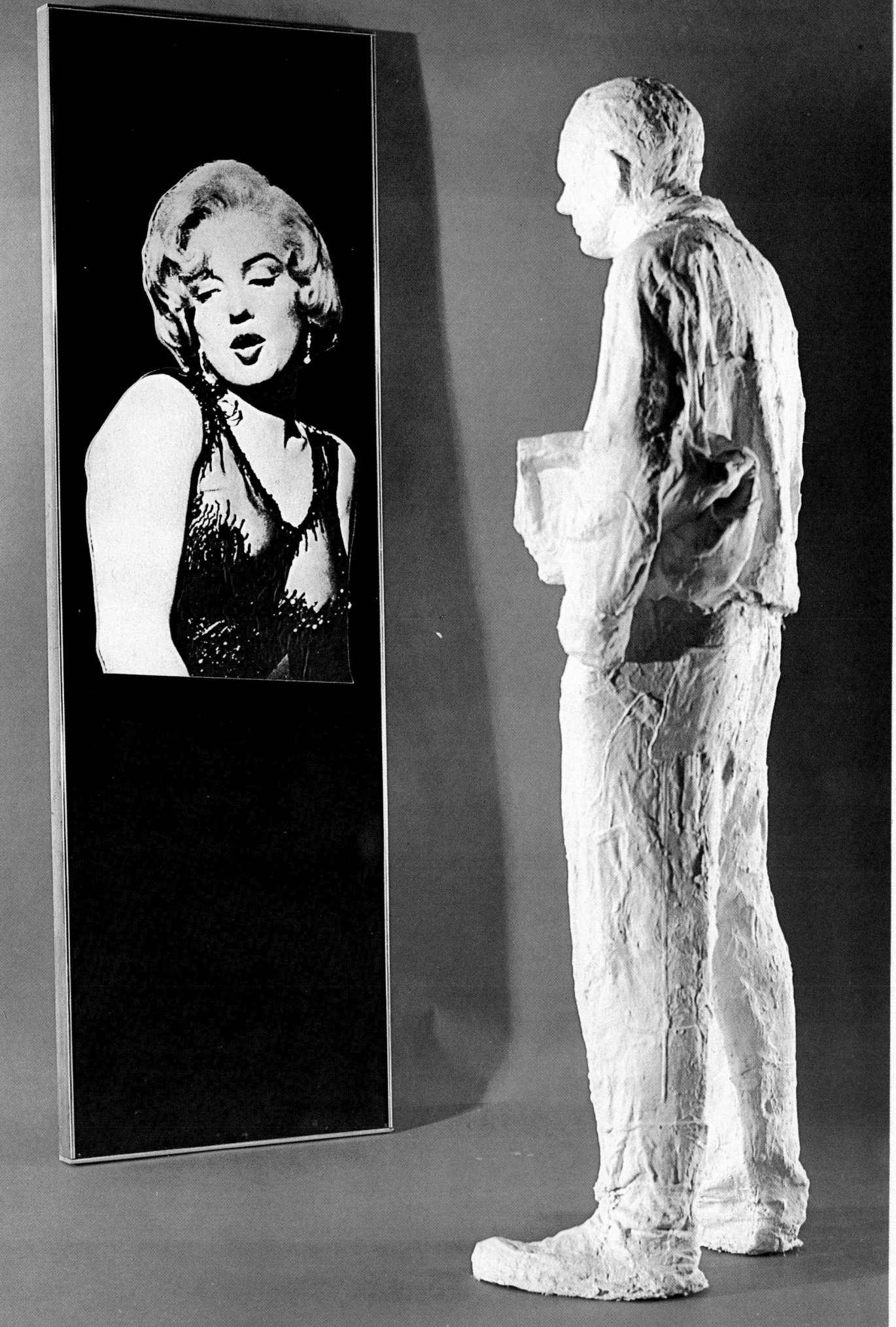

174.
Tom Wesselman
Great American Nude No. 8
1961; 119.7 cm. (47 in.)
Connecticut, coll. Mr. and Mrs. Burton Tremaine

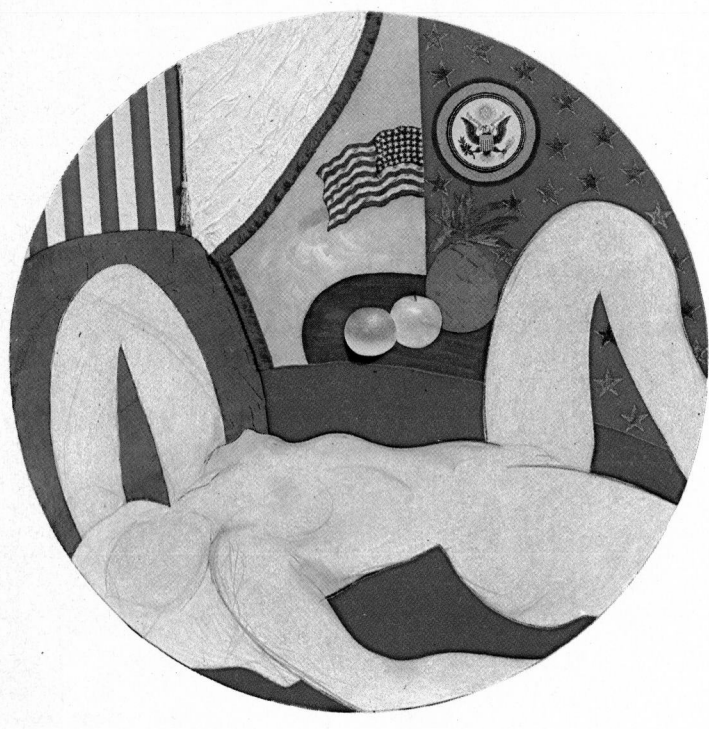

175 and 176.
Tom Wesselman
Bathtub Collage No. 3
1963; 213 × 270 × 45 cm. (83 × 105 × 18 in.)
Cologne, Wallraf-Richartz Museum, coll. Ludwig
Opposite, detail

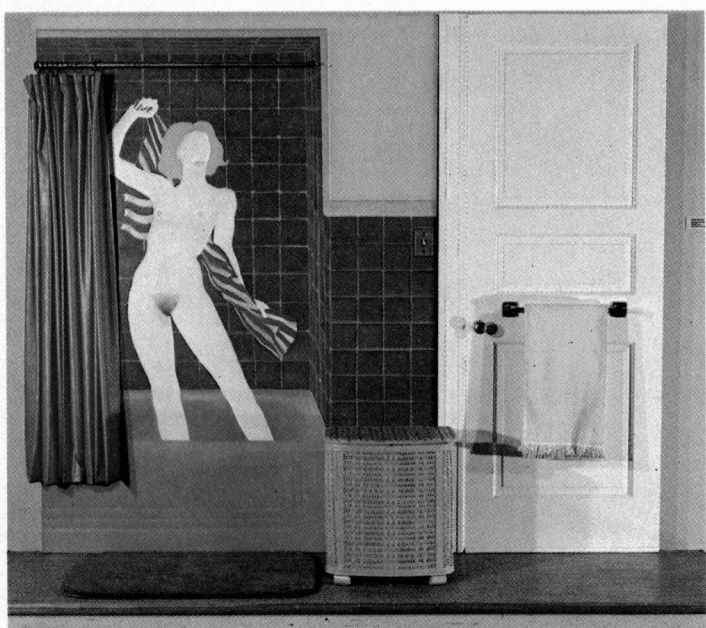

reliefs, showing figures and parts of figures emerging from a rough plaster surface, have been feeble tributes to Michelangelo and Rodin.

Of the American Pop artists who have not so far been mentioned, the most interesting is probably Tom Wesselman. Wesselman claims that his first important influence was the work of De Kooning. "That," he declares, "was what I wanted to be, with all its self-dramatization." But though he liked De Kooning's subject-matter, especially the nudes, the sloppiness of Abstract Expressionism distressed him. He found that what he wanted to do was to establish an absolutely concrete situation which was nevertheless full of jarring yet stimulating contrasts: "throughout the picture all the elements compete with one another."

Most of Wesselman's work can be divided into two major series, the nudes (Plates 174, 175, 176, and 177) and the still lifes (Plate 178). Often these have included collage elements, in order to get the contrasts the artist desires, but he is capable of producing much the same shocks without these added elements. What impresses about Wesselman's work is a rather brash energy. The nudes in particular demonstrate the male chauvinism of a great deal of Pop to perfection. The girls themselves are reduced to what is most erogenous—to eyes, nipples, patches of pubic hair. But there is no evidence that this depersonalization is as deliberately engineered as it is in Warhol's work. It is just something that happens to be there.

In addition to the major creative figures in the movement, Pop inevitably produced a swarm of less important but still interesting artists. Some people might feel that James Rosenquist deserves better than to be put in this category. Certainly, if scale is anything to go by, Rosenquist is important. Some of his canvases are among the biggest ever painted by a Pop artist. This interest in large scale may have been due to Rosenquist's experience, in the late Fifties, as a painter of billboards. While he was doing this to earn a living, he was also attending a drawing class organized by Claes Oldenburg and Robert Indiana, whose work will also be discussed in this chapter.

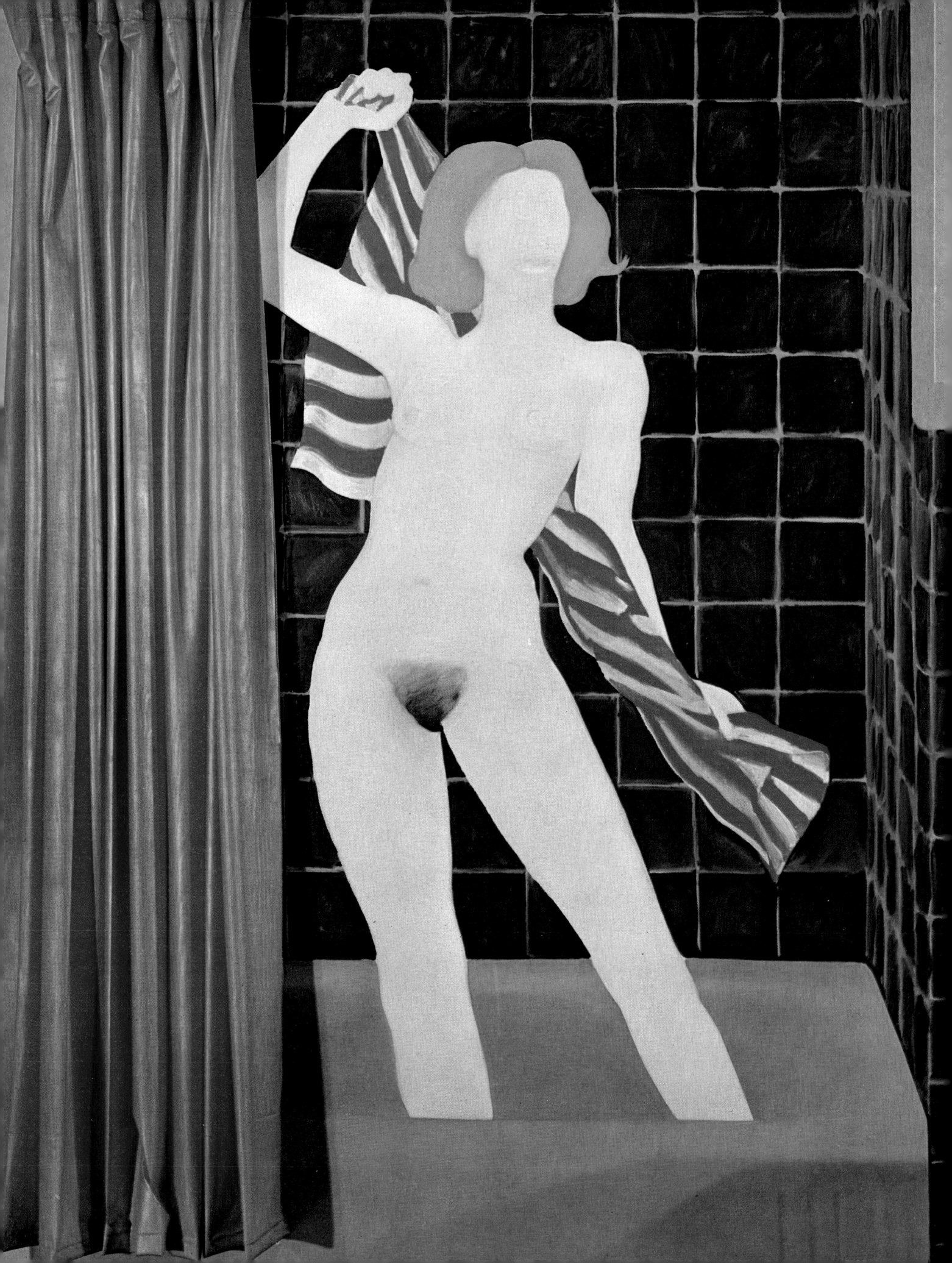

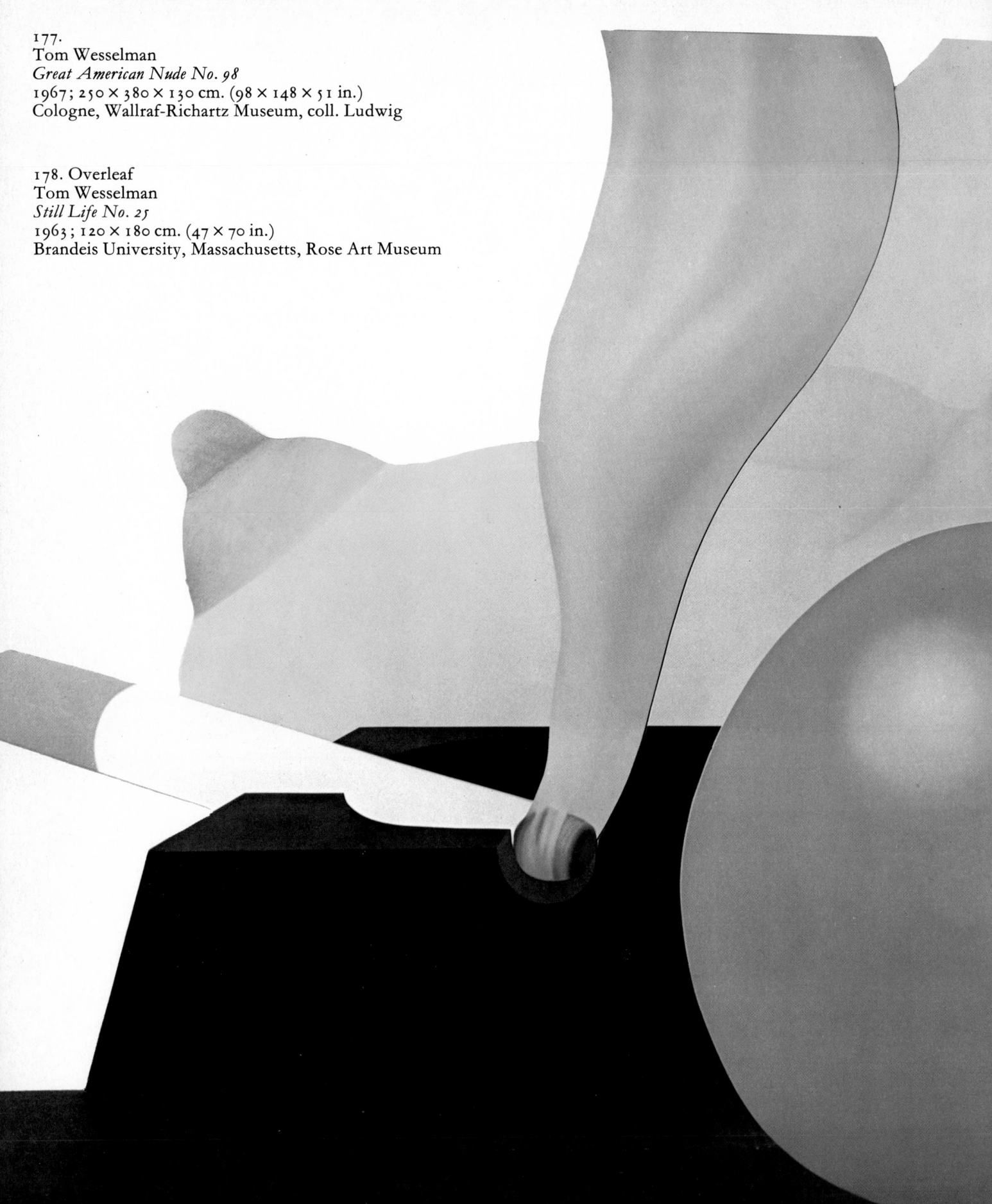

177.
Tom Wesselman
Great American Nude No. 98
1967; 250 × 380 × 130 cm. (98 × 148 × 51 in.)
Cologne, Wallraf-Richartz Museum, coll. Ludwig

178. Overleaf
Tom Wesselman
Still Life No. 25
1963; 120 × 180 cm. (47 × 70 in.)
Brandeis University, Massachusetts, Rose Art Museum

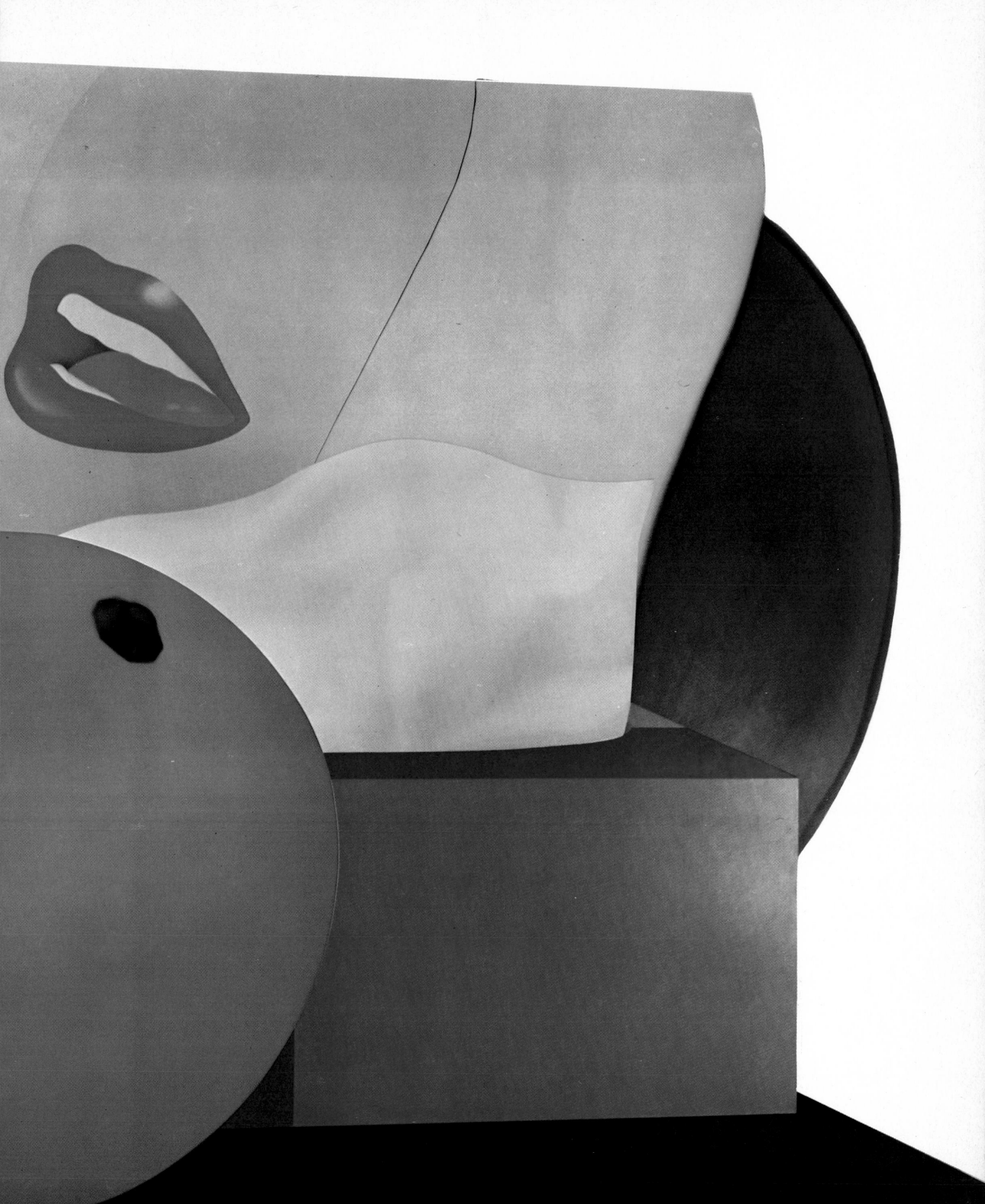

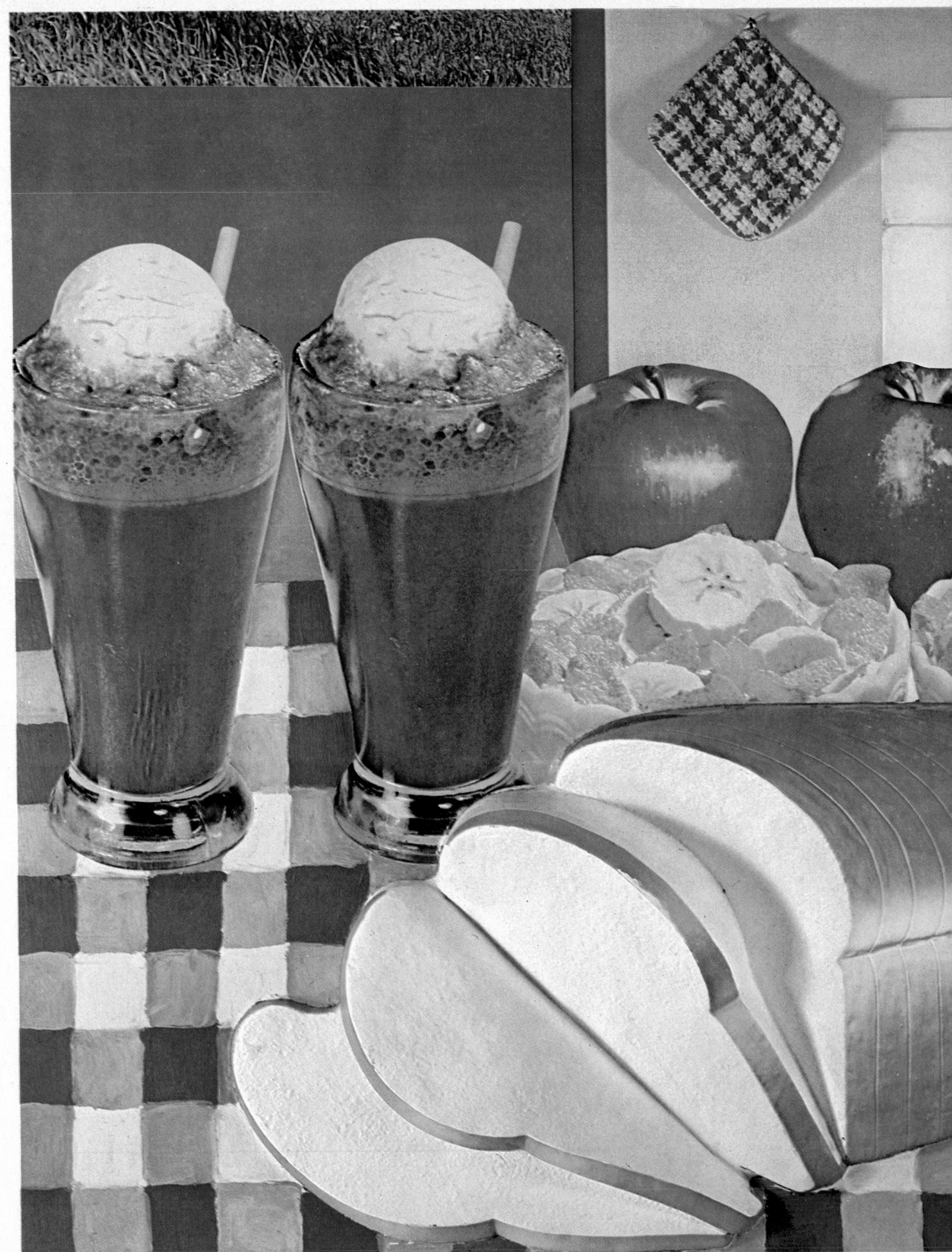

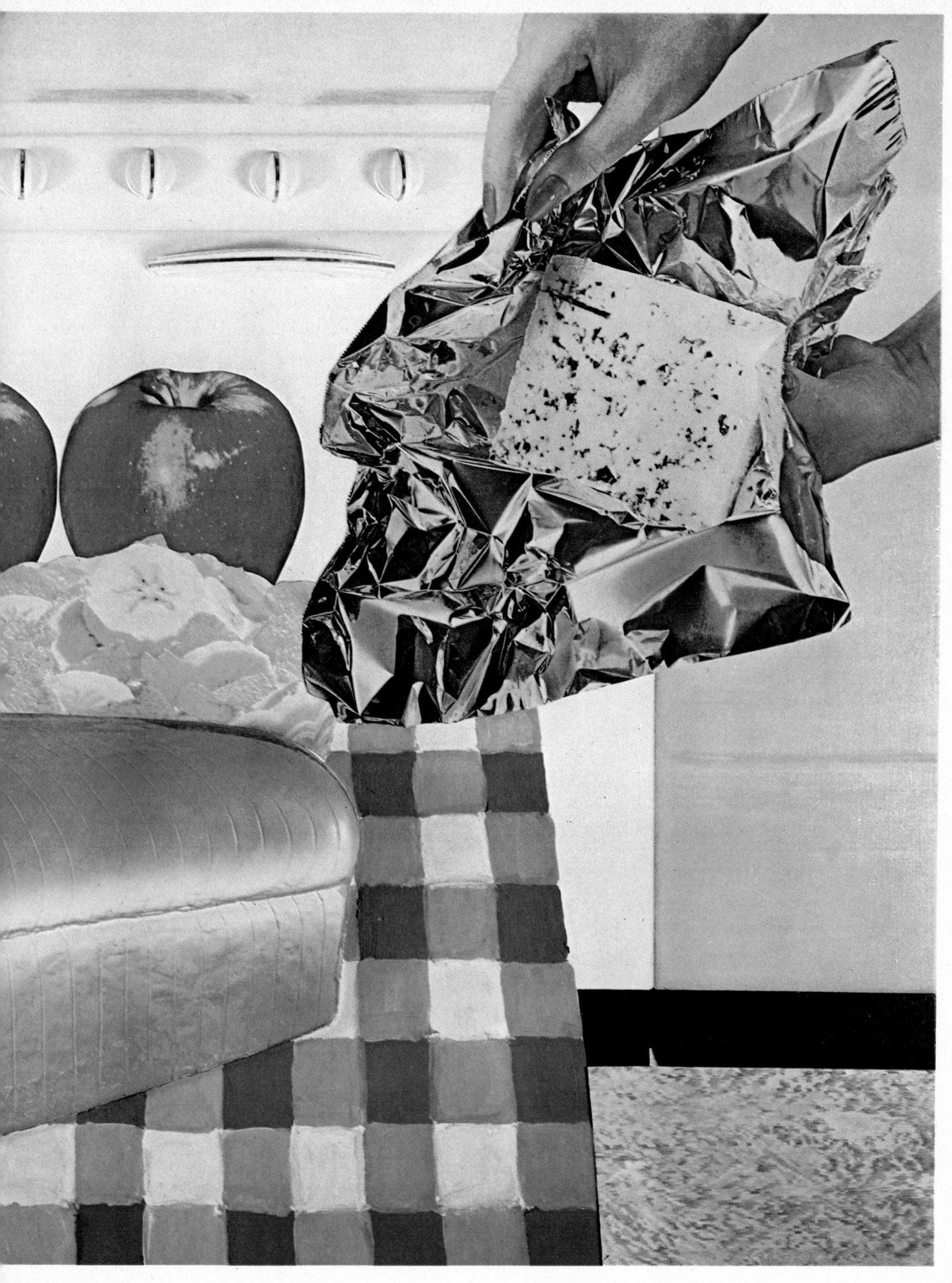

179.
James Rosenquist
I Love You with My Ford
1961; 210 × 237.5 cm. (82 × 93 in.)
Stockholm, Moderna Museet

180. Opposite
Robert Indiana
The American Dream
1961; 180.3 × 150.3 cm. (70 × 59 in.)
New York, Museum of Modern Art, Larry Aldrich
Foundation Fund

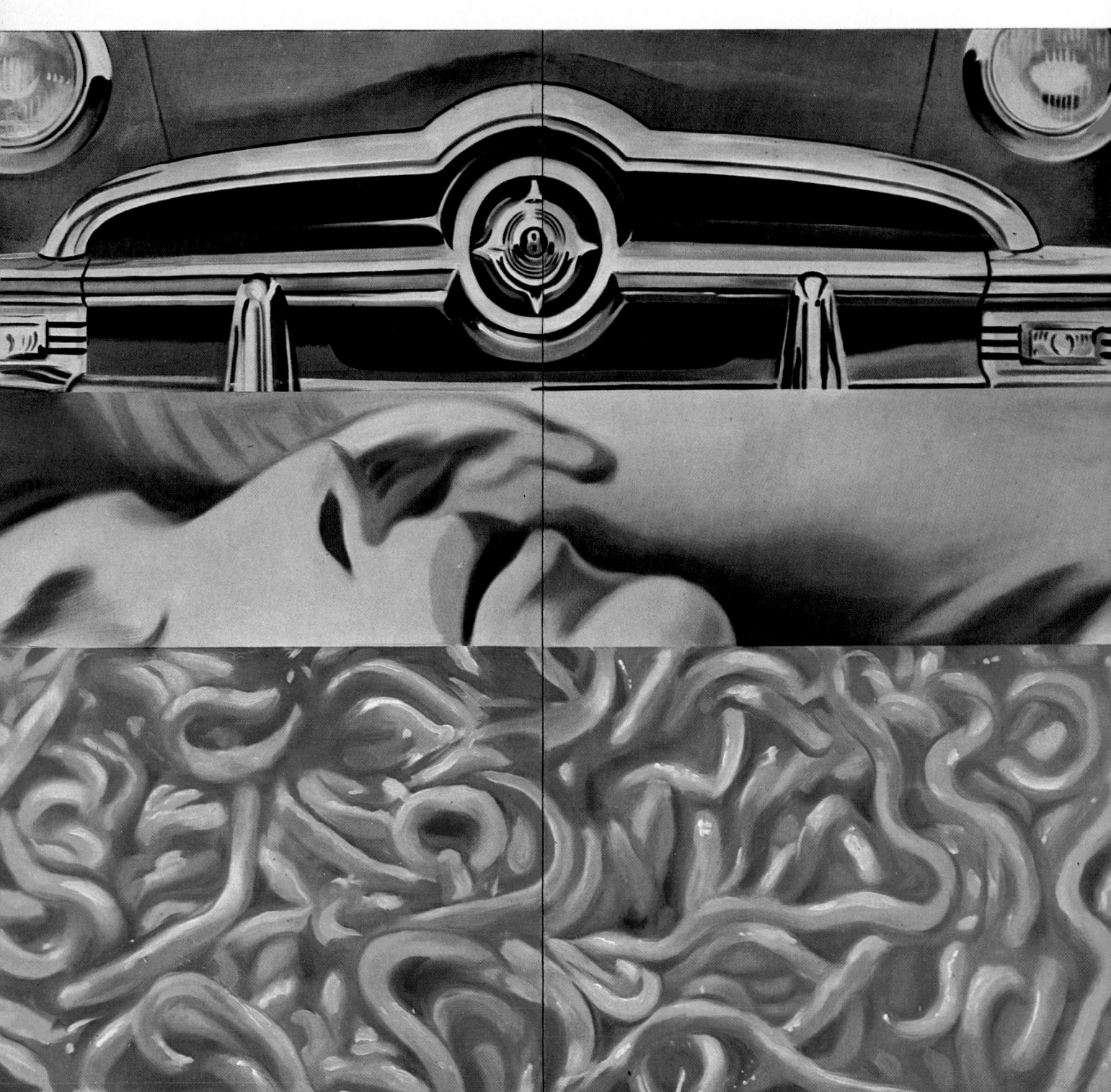

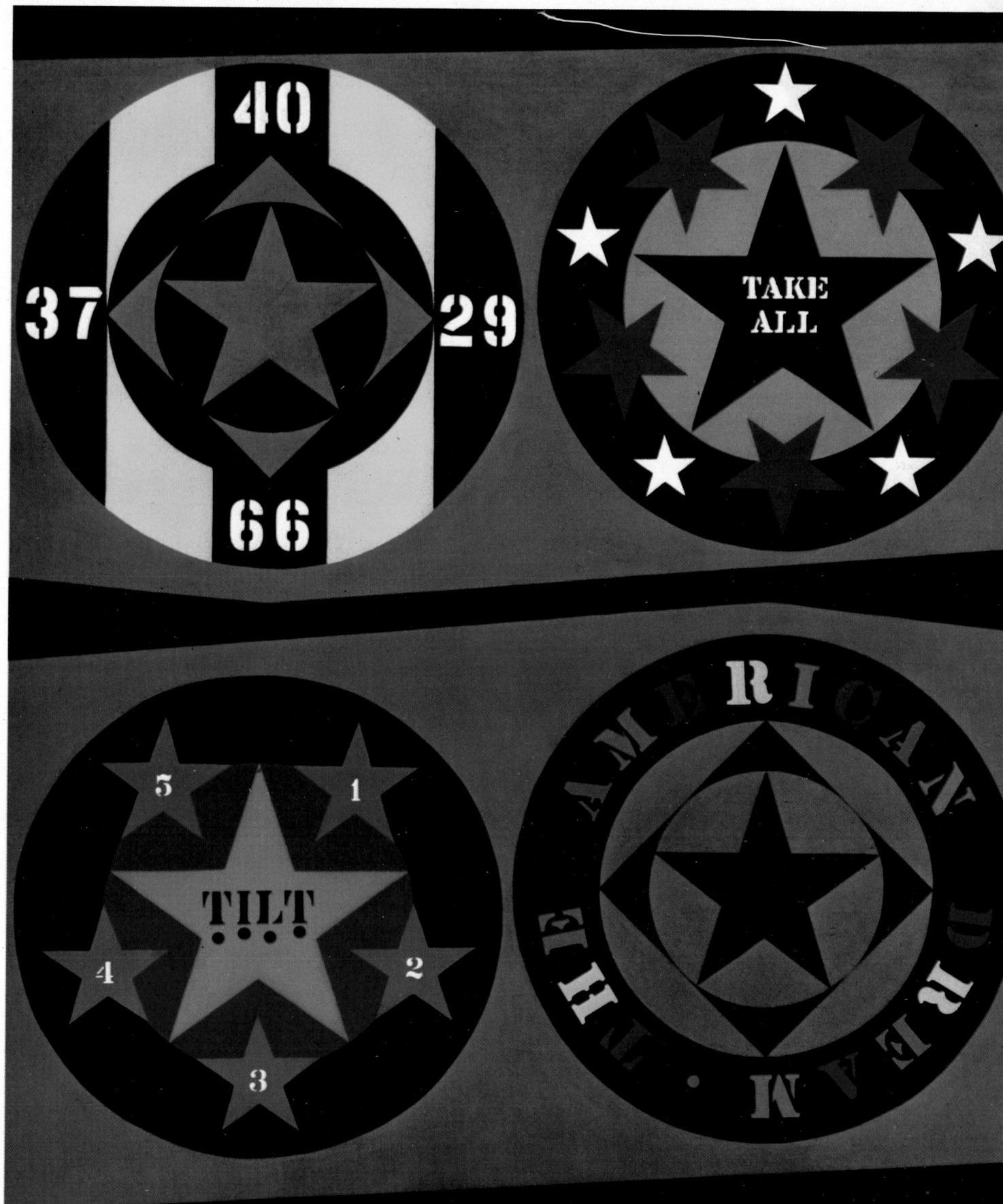

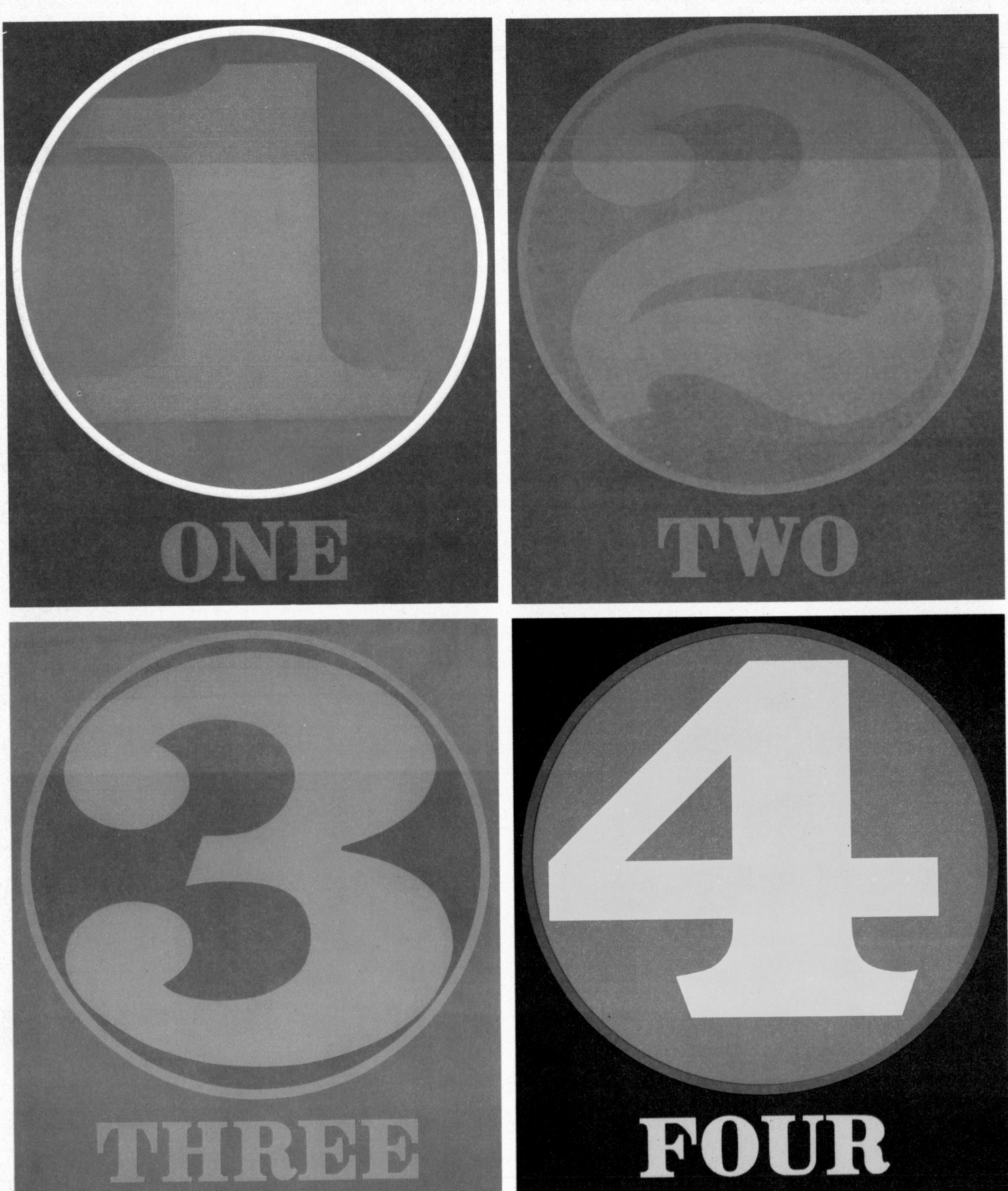

181. Opposite
Robert Indiana
Numbers (from 0–9)
1968; 63.6 × 49 cm. (25 × 19 in.)
Colorado, coll. Kimiko and John Powers

182.
Allan d'Arcangelo
Full Moon
1963; 162.6 × 155 cm. (63 × 60 in.)
Colorado, coll. Kimiko and John Powers

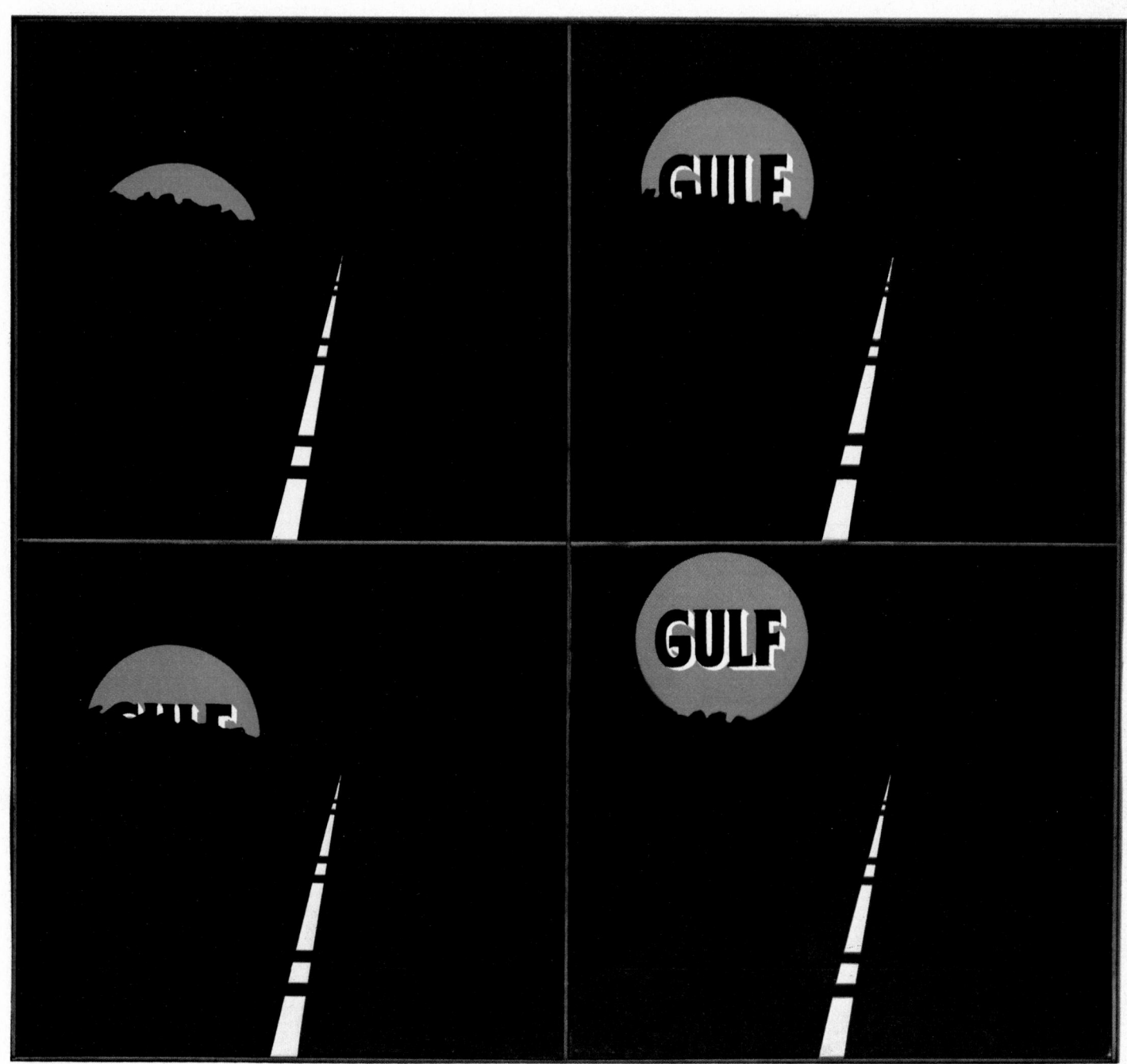

What Rosenquist does (Plate 179) is to put together in collage various images painted in billboard style, in the hope that something significant will emerge from the conjunction. He sees himself as a willing collaborator with the commercial society he lives in: "I geared myself, like an advertiser or a large company, to this visual inflation—in commercial advertising which is one of the foundations of our society. I'm living in it, and it has such impact and excitement in its means of imagery. Painting is probably more exciting than advertising—so why shouldn't it be done

231

with that power and gusto, with that impact? ...
My metaphor, if that is what you can call it, is my
relations to the power of commercial advertising
which is in turn related to our free society, the
visual inflation which accompanies the money that
produces box tops and space cadets. . . ." (from an
interview with G. R. Swenson, *Art News* [February, 1964], reprinted in *Pop Art Redefined*, by
John Russell and Suzi Gablik, London, 1969, p.
111).

The difficulty is that this uncritical acceptance of
his surroundings makes Rosenquist into a rather
insensitive painter as compared with, say, Roy
Lichtenstein. There is no real subtlety of visual
arrangement in his work, which eventually

becomes as monotonous to look at as the billboard
art from which it derives.

Robert Indiana (born Robert Clark) is another
Pop artist who has committed himself to the
American dream, in much the same way that
Rosenquist has. In fact, one of his most typical
canvases is actually entitled *The American Dream*
(Plate 180). It derives its basic imagery from
pinball machines, and it might seem possible at
first glance to read its message as ironic. But this
would not appear to be in line with the painter's
own interpretation. In his view the American
dream, using the words in a general rather than a
specific sense, is "optimistic, generous, and
naïve".

183.
Ed Ruscha
Hollywood
1968; 31.7 × 103.5 cm. (12 × 40 in.)
Düsseldorf, coll. Heinz Beck

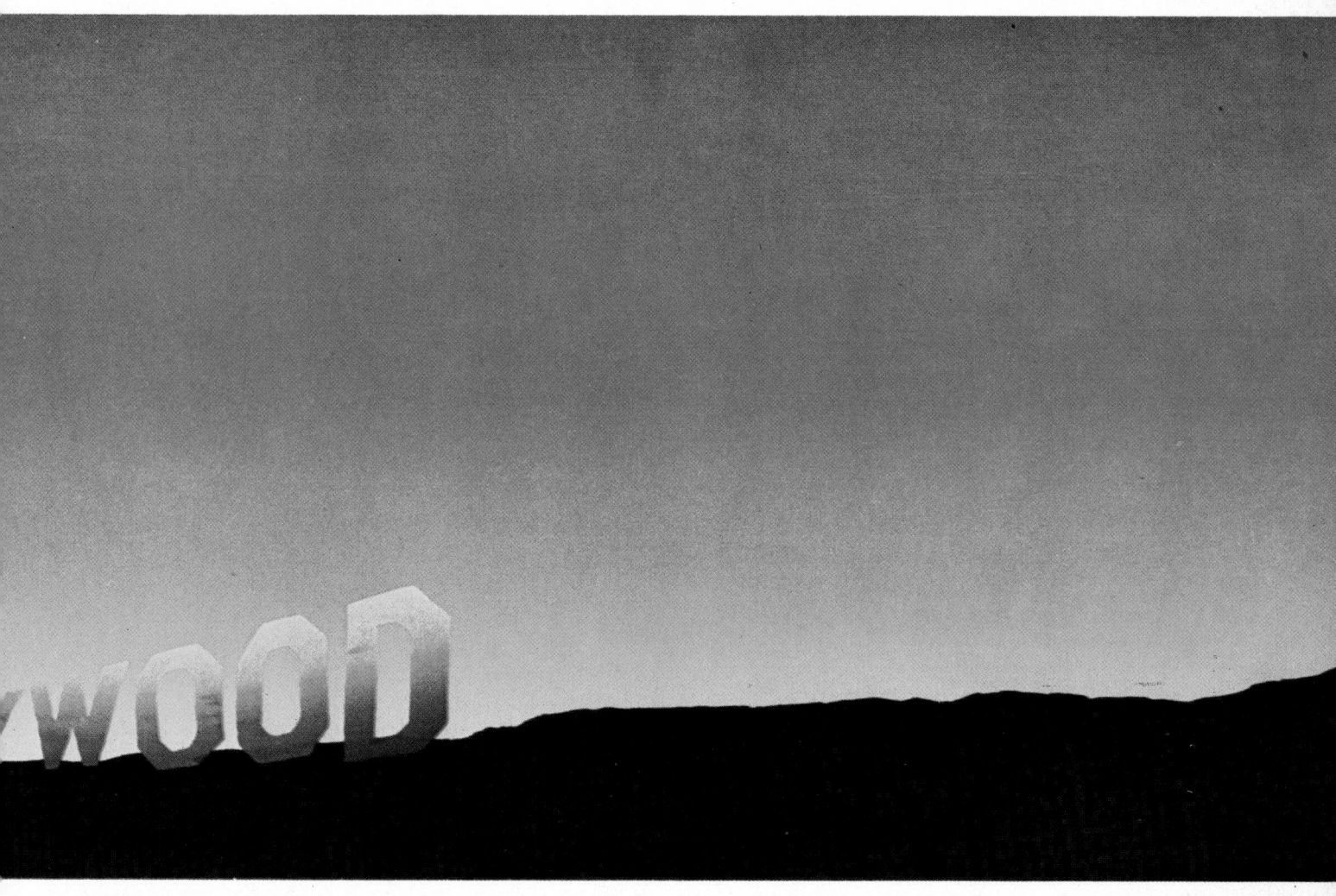

Indiana's strength is his hostility to closed systems and to art for art's sake. Pop, he says, "is death to smuggery and the Preconceived-Notion-of-What-Art-Is diehards". He opposes himself utterly to the idea that great art must be difficult art. In a mass society these are undoubtedly sympathetic doctrines. But there is something disconcertingly bare and bleak about the work that Indiana proposes to substitute for the things he attacks.

A painter who in some ways resembles Indiana is Allan D'Arcangelo. In his painting, too, we find an emphasis on lettering, a crisp, no-nonsense way of presenting the image. But where images are juxtaposed, they tend to be similar rather than contrasted (Plate 182). D'Arcangelo can thus at moments resemble an optimistic Warhol. The most important aspect of his work, however, is not so much the way he presents his imagery as the imagery itself. D'Arcangelo, among Pop artists, is the poet of the highway, the celebrator of American distances.

The artist who shares this particular pre-occupation is Ed Ruscha, who is a somewhat isolated figure in the American Pop school taken as a whole. What tends to set Ruscha apart is his commitment to the West rather than the East of the United States, to Los Angeles rather than New York. Some of Ruscha's work (Plate 183) is a refined and elegant version of Pop, with a sleekness that seems typically Californian. But much of the rest has nothing to do with Pop Art at all, but belongs to the category which is labelled "process art" by some critics. This is true, for instance, of the long series of books and booklets which Ruscha has issued. One of these is called "Stains", and each page contains a stain made by some common substance. Ruscha is an example of the fact that one can produce Pop Art without being a full-time Pop artist.

There are also several painters who lie on the margins of the Pop school because some aspect of their work seems consistently untypical. Two who come to mind are Wayne Thiebaud and Larry Rivers, and in each case what makes them seem exceptional is their handling of paint, which has an individuality which is uncommon in Pop Art, at least in America. Wayne Thiebaud's technique (Plate 184) can make him seem a descendant of the American realists of the Thirties, particularly Edward Hopper. There is the same blunt but extremely personal touch. Thiebaud's chosen subject-matter is remarkably narrow. He devotes himself to food, and in particular to pies (Plate 184). In this connection he once remarked: "A pie has all kinds of marvellous complex associations. The whiteness of meringue becomes for me of great poetic preoccupation: it's like snow, like frost, like the concept of purity, and, from a painter's standpoint, white both absorbs light and reflects light—it's composed of all colours, like Chardin's tablecloths" (from an interview conducted by Le Grace G. Benson and David Shoarer in *Leonardo*, Vol. 2, No. 1, Oxford, 1969).

The implied comparison to Chardin is a reasonably shrewd piece of self-assessment, but also implies the deliberate self-restriction which has prevented Thiebaud from becoming a major figure.

Far more difficult to assess than Thiebaud, and certainly much more uneven, is Larry Rivers. Rivers has a most seductive fluency with the brush (Plate 186). He seems to aim at re-creating the effects caught by Edouard Manet, using opalescent colour and loose, virtuoso handling. But the subject-matter he chooses is often Pop-oriented, though the most important reason for choosing it often appears to be a rather childish desire to shock. In the early Fifties, before Pop itself arrived on the scene, Rivers painted a series of brilliant female nudes, which owed a technical debt to the male nudes of Théodore Géricault. For most of these the subject was his ageing mother-in-law, Berdie. This was also the period at which he defiantly painted a large historical picture, *Washington Crossing the Delaware*, which was quite specifically intended as a revival of nineteenth-century academic art. It caused a satisfactory uproar among the New York avant-garde of the period.

Later in the decade Rivers was using commonplace objects as his subject-matter, though by now employing a less solid and more vaporous technique which was related to Abstract Expressionism. But when the Pop movement began, the artist, with pliant flexibility, began to explore the kind of material that was in vogue with the new group. He painted paraphrases of commercial packaging, such as the Camel cigarette pack, and employed collage techniques. One of his most successful series resulted from the absorption of Pop influence. Called *Parts of the Body*, it explored the possibilities offered by the conjunction of crude, stencilled lettering, and of figures and heads painted in Rivers's usual virtuoso style.

Rivers is such a gifted artist that it may seem surprising that he has had so little influence on the development of American painting. This failure must be attributed to his constant changes of direction, and to the apparent lack of conviction which seems to motivate them. He often seems little more than a highly talented ventriloquist.

A movement as successful as American Pop Art naturally attracted foreign adherents. Those who found it easiest to assimilate themselves to the New York scene were usually young Englishmen. Many English artists spent long periods in the city, which they found a far more sympathetic environment for modern art than the London they had left. One or two came to identify themselves with America almost entirely. The most gifted of these was Gerald Laing. He seems to have felt the impact of the highly competitive New York art world chiefly as a stimulus to ambition, rather than

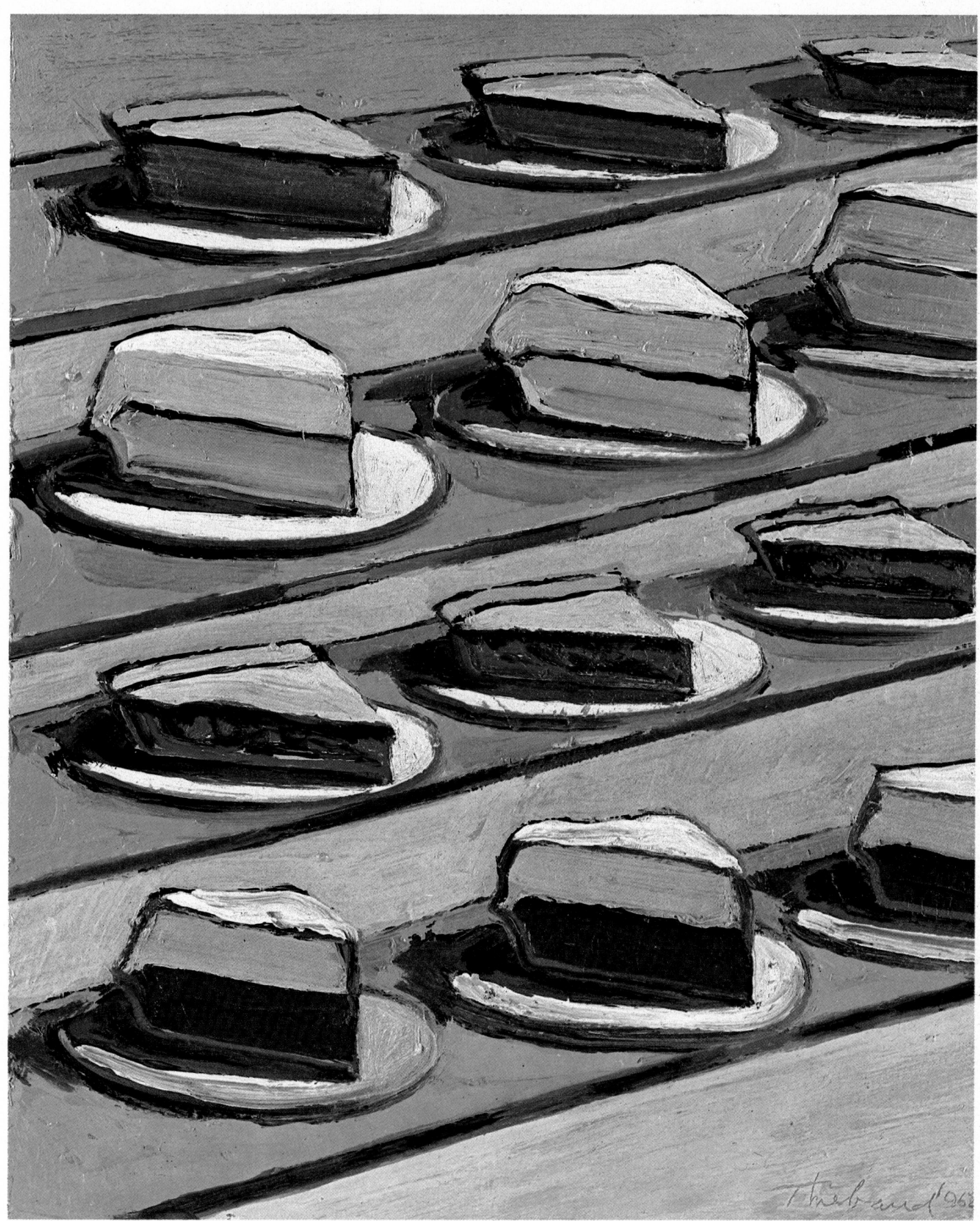

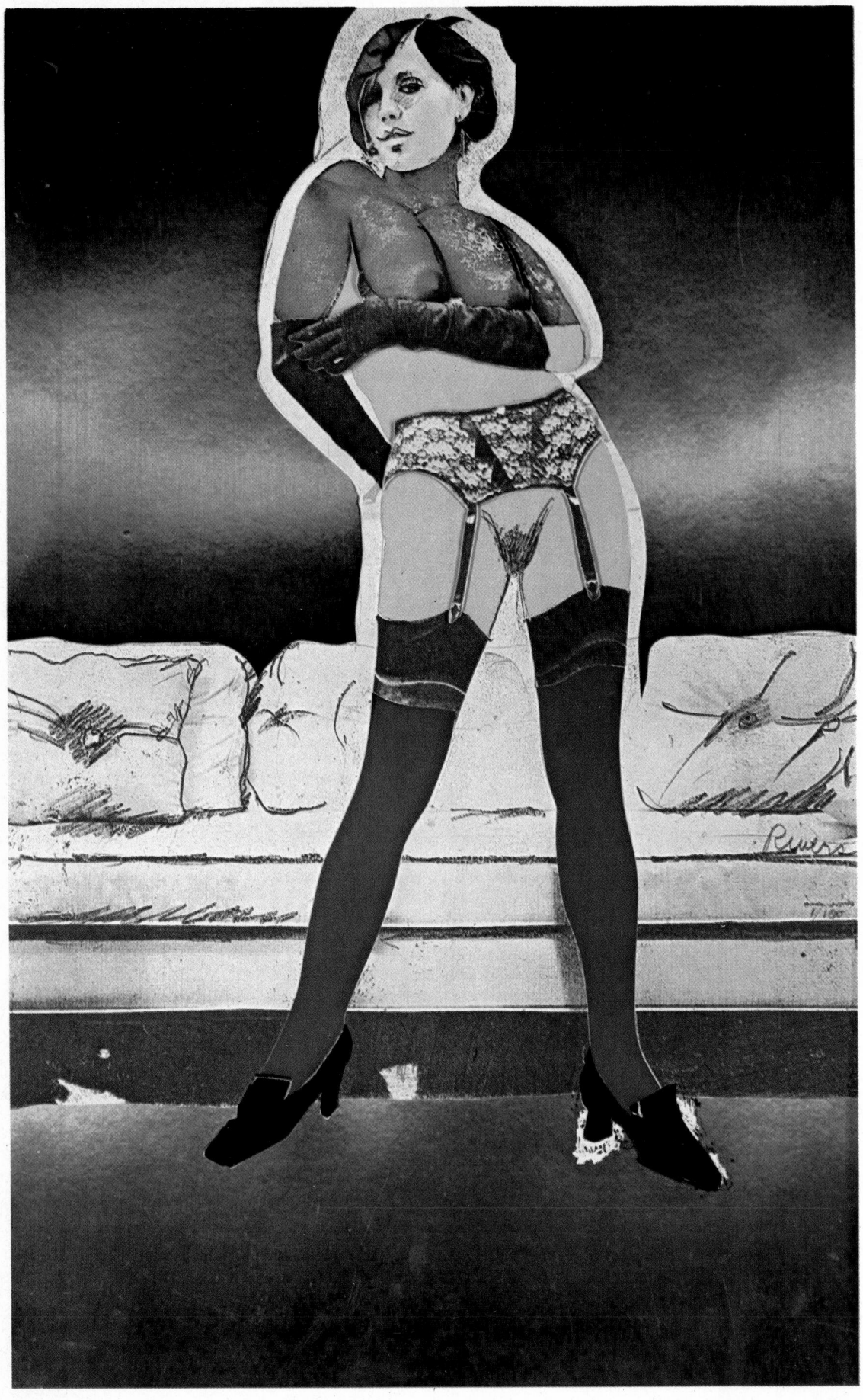

185.
Larry Rivers
Girlie
1970; 76 × 46 cm.
(30 × 18 in.)
New York,
Marlborough Graphics

186. Opposite
Larry Rivers
*Parts of the Body:
French (cut out)*
1964; 33 × 21.6 cm
(13 × 8 in.)
New York, by kind
permission of the
Dwan Gallery

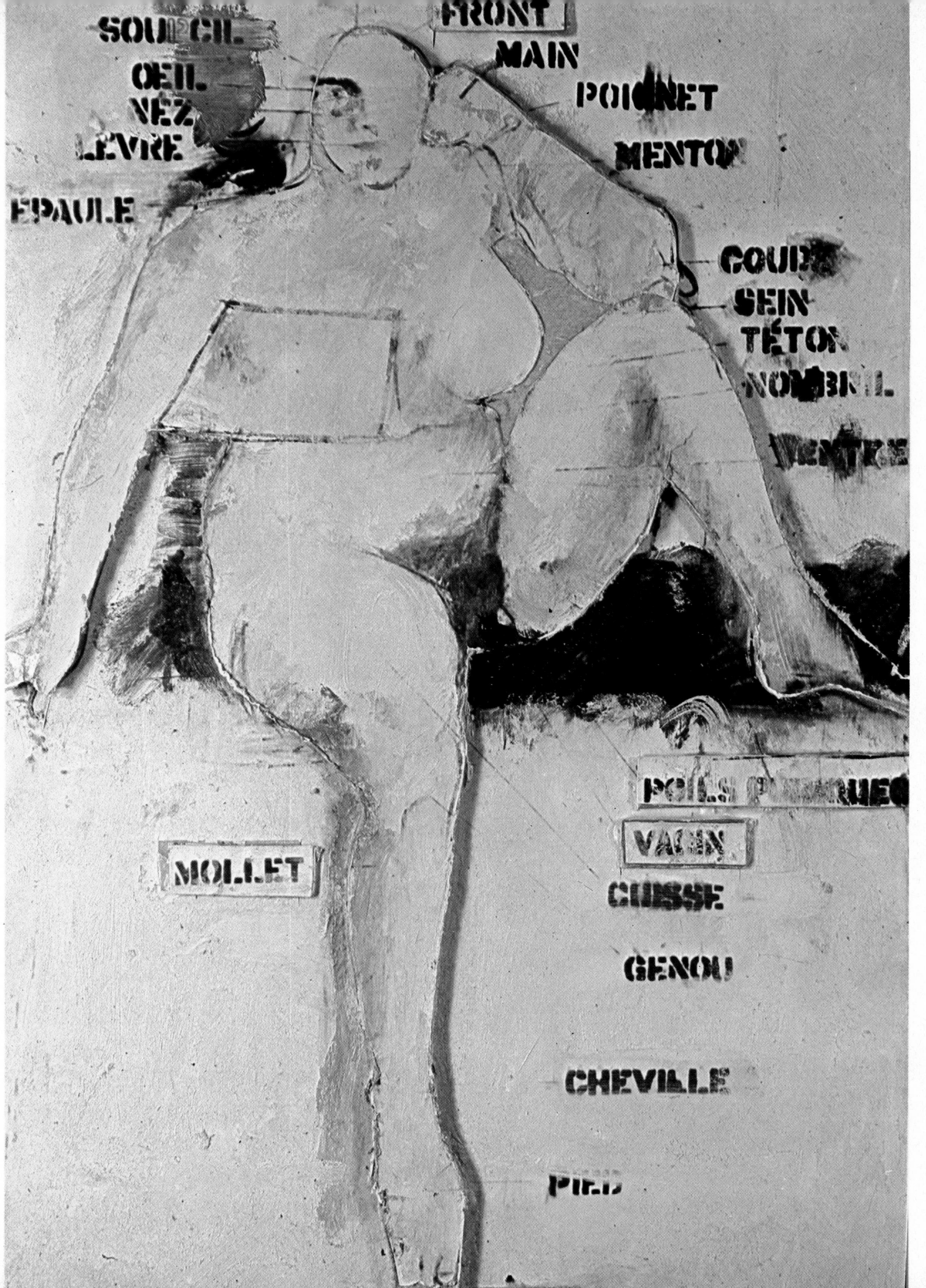

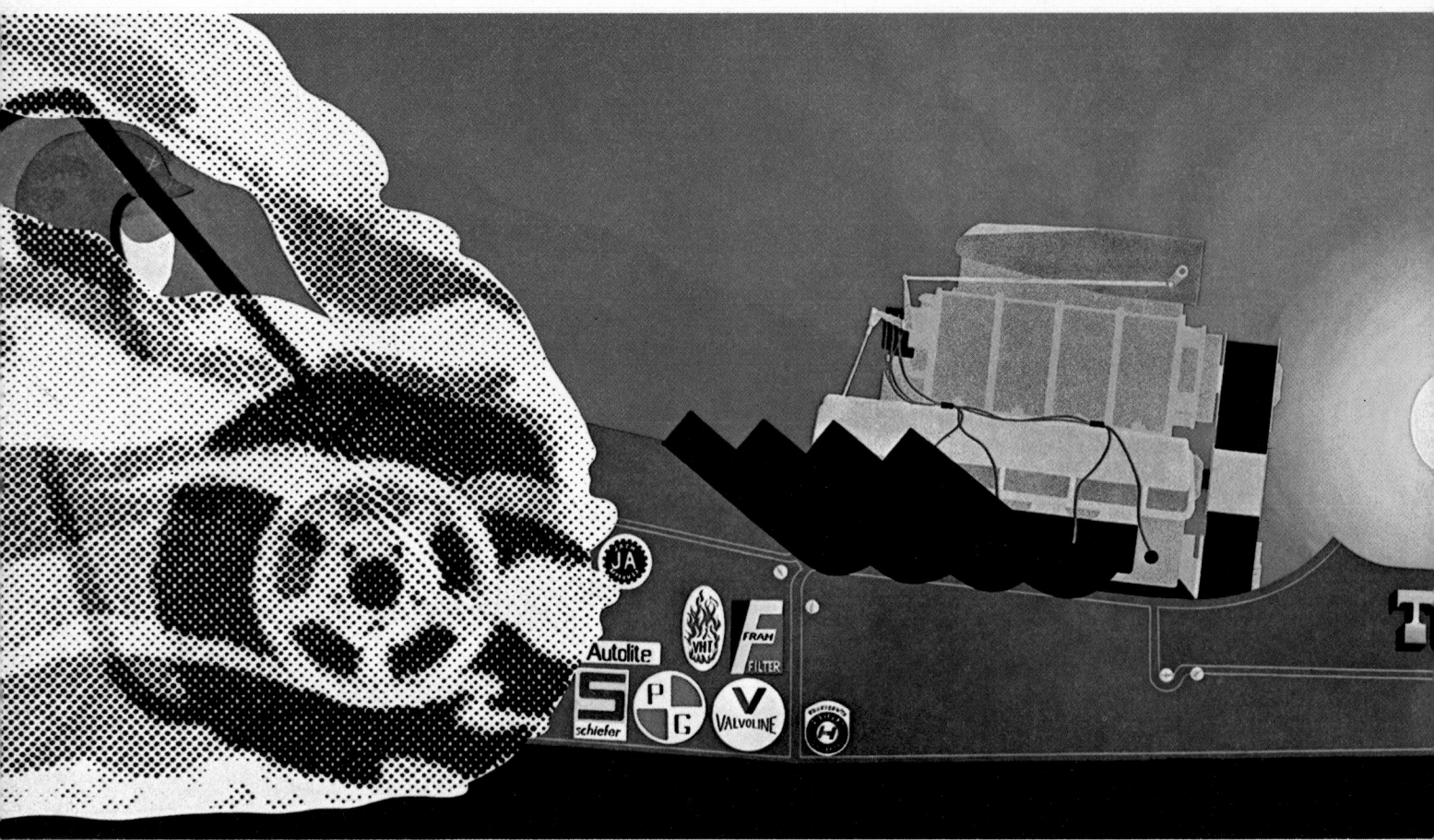

as something which prompted any radical process of rethinking or change of style. In 1964, when he participated at a group show at the Institute of Contemporary Arts in London, his catalogue statement read in part: "My work is developed from the idea of the hero-image as presented by mass-media. In the first instance I began painting newspaper photographs of people, rather than the people themselves. Since then I have been trying to create images using mass-media techniques— half-tone areas and flat areas of colour as used in printing." This statement would have been just as applicable to the work he was doing some five years later, after his departure from London (Plate 187), except that it was now more elaborate and much larger in scale. One feels that Laing was already so committed to America even before he got there that the country had little to tell him.

A more interesting case is that of the much older German artist, Richard Lindner. Lindner was born in Hamburg in 1901. He fled from Germany in 1933, subsequently living and working in France. After he came to America in 1941, at first he worked as an illustrator; and only in the early Fifties did he give up illustration for painting. By 1953 he had established a basic visual vocabulary, including the corseted woman, "Lulu", who frequently appears in his paintings (Plate 188). Though Lindner's work seems to owe much to the artists of the Weimar Republic, such as George Grosz, and to memories of the pre-war German theatre, it also owes a good deal, especially from about 1961 onwards, to the New York environment. A "typical" Lindner certainly has a distinctly Pop look to it, and it is difficult to decide how much of this was already inherent in

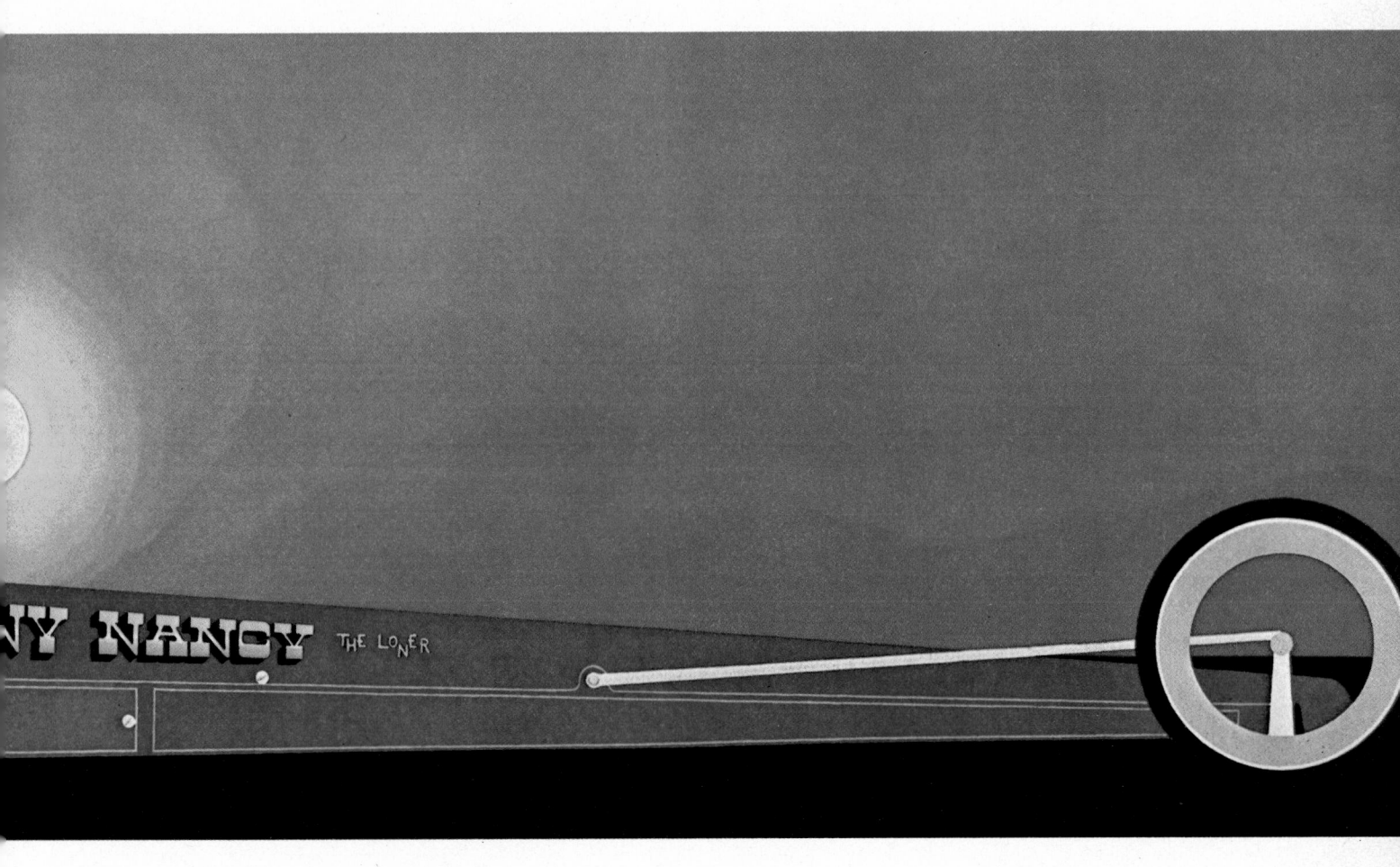

187.
Gerald Laing
The Loner
1969; 152.4 × 648.6 cm. (59 × 253 in.)
Richard Feigen Gallery, New York, Chicago

188. Overleaf left
Richard Lindner
Ice
1966; 177.8 × 152.4 cm. (69 × 59 in.)
New York, Whitney Museum of American Art

189. Overleaf right
Richard Lindner
Cushion
1966; 177.8 × 152.4 cm. (69 × 59 in.)
Cologne, Wallraf-Richartz Museum, coll. Ludwig

Lindner's style, formed as it was in isolation from the main currents of modern painting, and how much was due to a fresh current of inspiration. One thing, however, is indisputable, and that is Lindner's power to create erotic images of obsessional force, and of far greater psychological complexity than most of those which appear in the Pop Art created by men who are considerably junior to him.

Pop was basically a one-generation phenomenon. Few of those who did not belong to the first wave succeeded in making any contribution to the movement. In America the exception to this has been Mel Ramos. Ramos' aims as an artist are essentially straightforward. He says: "I try to celebrate folk heroes and sex queens in a straightforward manner. While their likeness is not faithful, their character is obvious" (from the

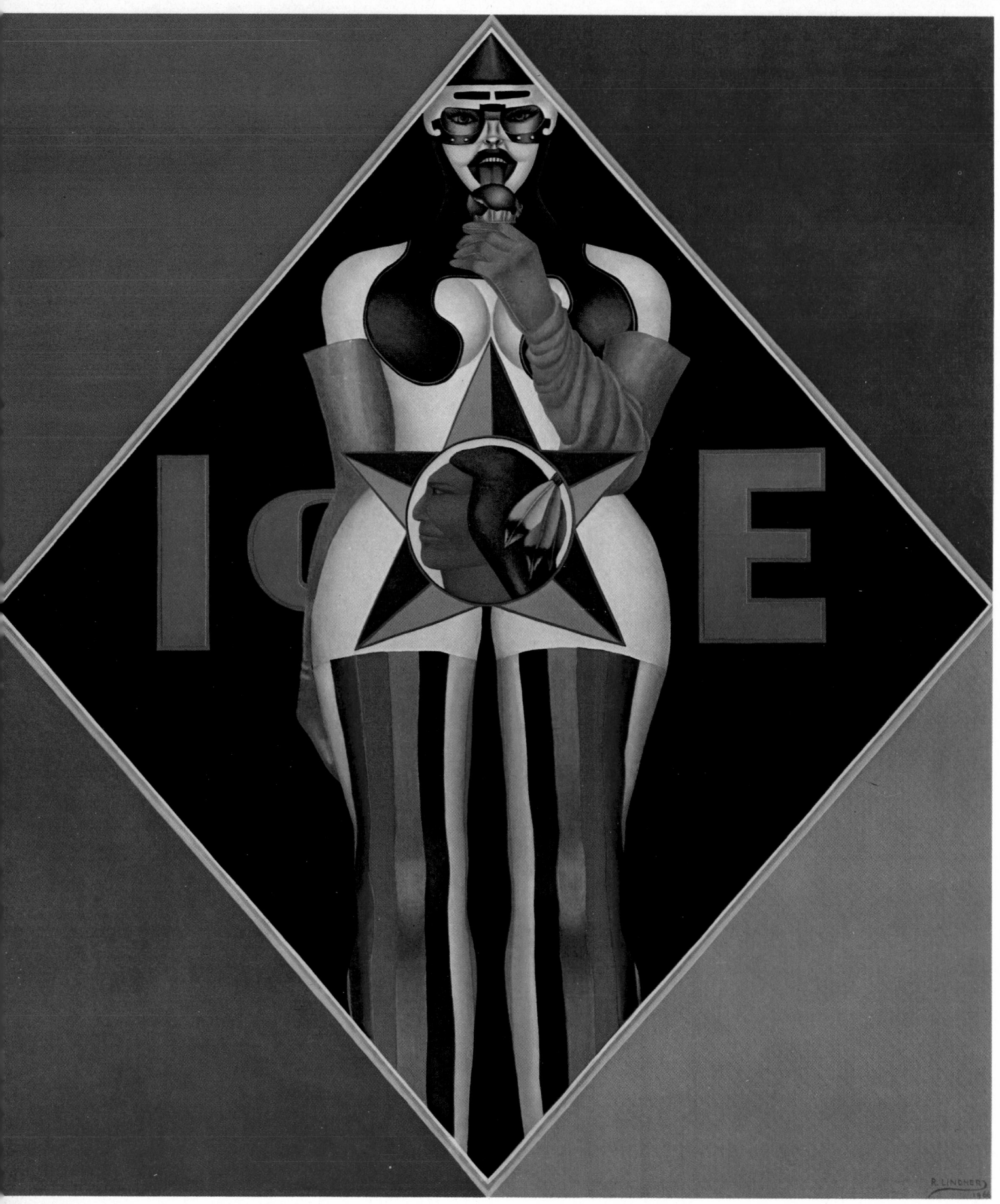

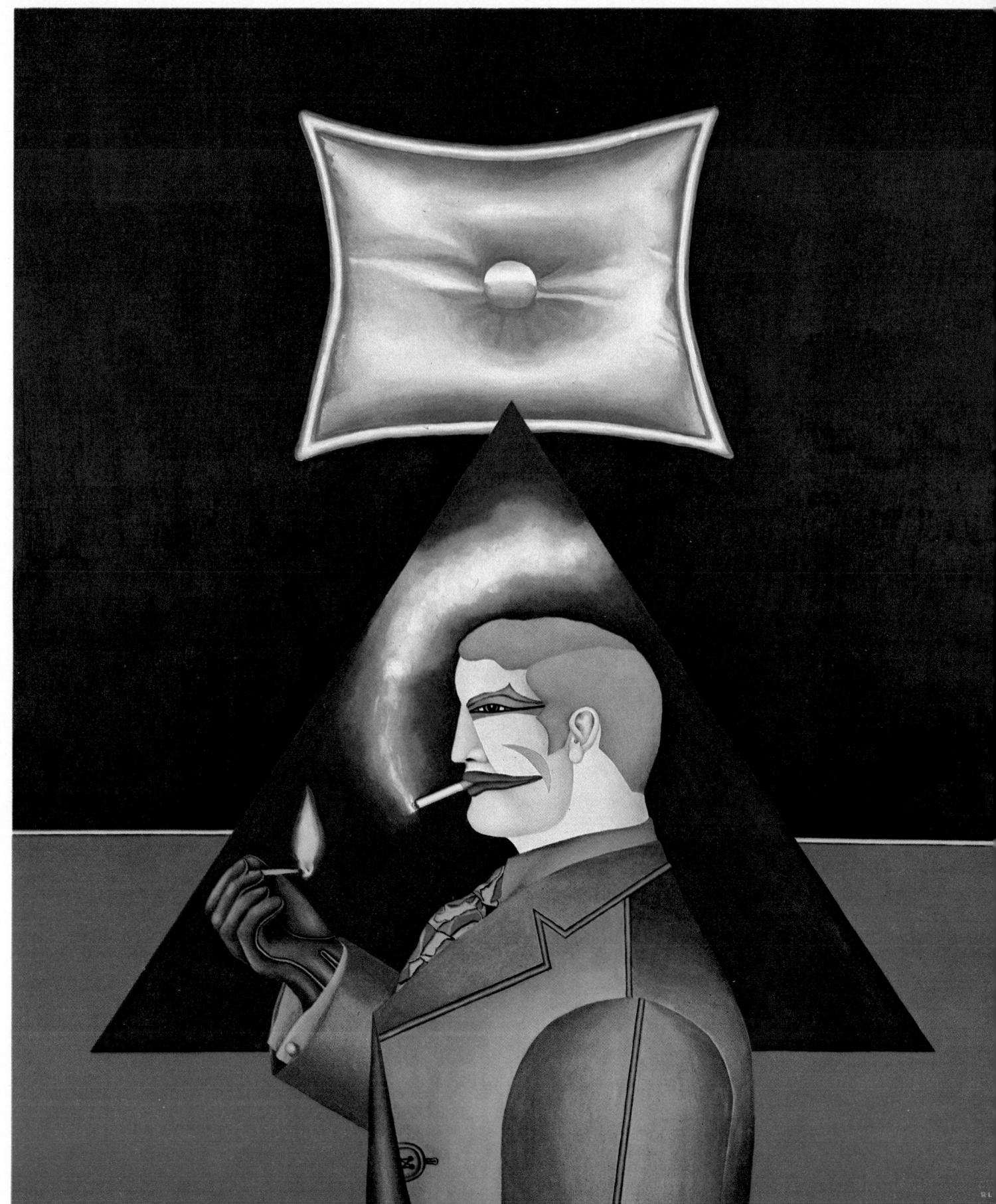

190.
Mel Ramos
Hippopotamus
1967; 180 × 247 cm. (70 × 96 in.)
Aachen, Neue Galerie, coll. Ludwig

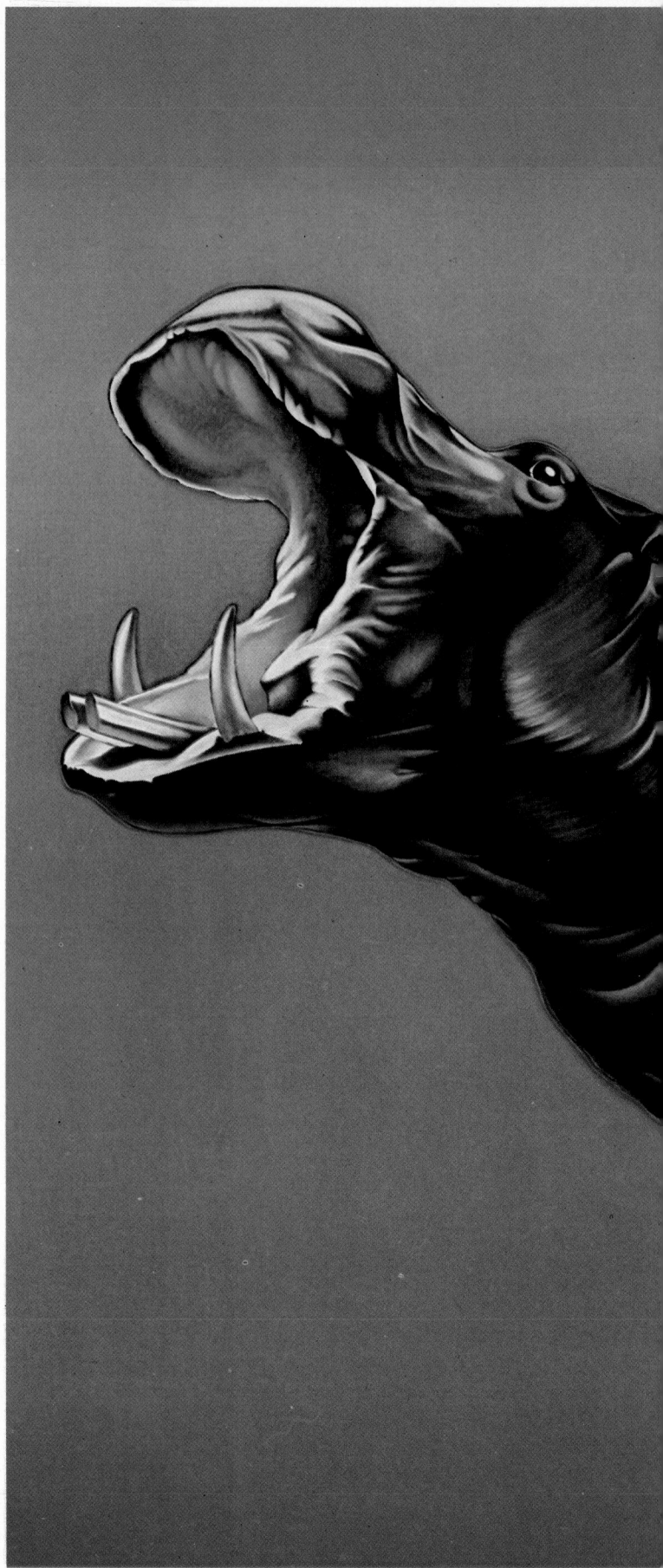

introduction to the "Six More" exhibition at the Los Angeles County Museum of Art, 1963).

What makes Ramos's work attractive, in addition to its straightforwardness, is its technical confidence (Plate 190). If one compares a painting of his to those using similar subject-matter done by artists who made their reputations slightly earlier, one notes that Ramos approaches the material with utter confidence, and also with a total lack of self-consciousness. Lawrence Alloway, always a shrewd judge, has noted the way in which the "painterly handling ripples through the heraldic scheme".

Of all the art styles that have arisen since the war, Pop Art, and especially American Pop, was the one which seemed to mesh most successfully with the society that produced it. In this connection it is important to note that its success was made by dealers and collectors, rather than by critics. When the first Pop works made their appearance in the New York galleries, they were eagerly welcomed by buyers, but the reaction from established writers on modern art was almost universally unfavourable. Just as Pop Art was making its first impact, Harold Rosenberg, who had been one of the chief supporters of Abstract Expressionism, issued the following denunciation: "The new American illusionist contrivances have a deeper identification with commercial art than the plagiarism or adaptation of its images. They share the impersonality of advertising-agency art-department productions. They are entirely cerebral and mechanical; the hand of the artist has no part in the evolution of the work but is the mere executor of the idea-man's command, though in this case the artist himself is usually the idea-man (sometimes the idea for a work comes from friends or sponsors). Nor is the self of the artist involved in the process of creation" (Harold Rosenberg, *The Anxious Object*, London, 1965, p. 75). This was fairly typical of what the most-respected critics had to say on the subject.

It was only towards the mid-Sixties that some art theorists became more tolerant. In an article published in 1964, Robert Rosenblum pointed out that the Pop label had already been used to cover a whole diversity of styles. He was ready to declare,

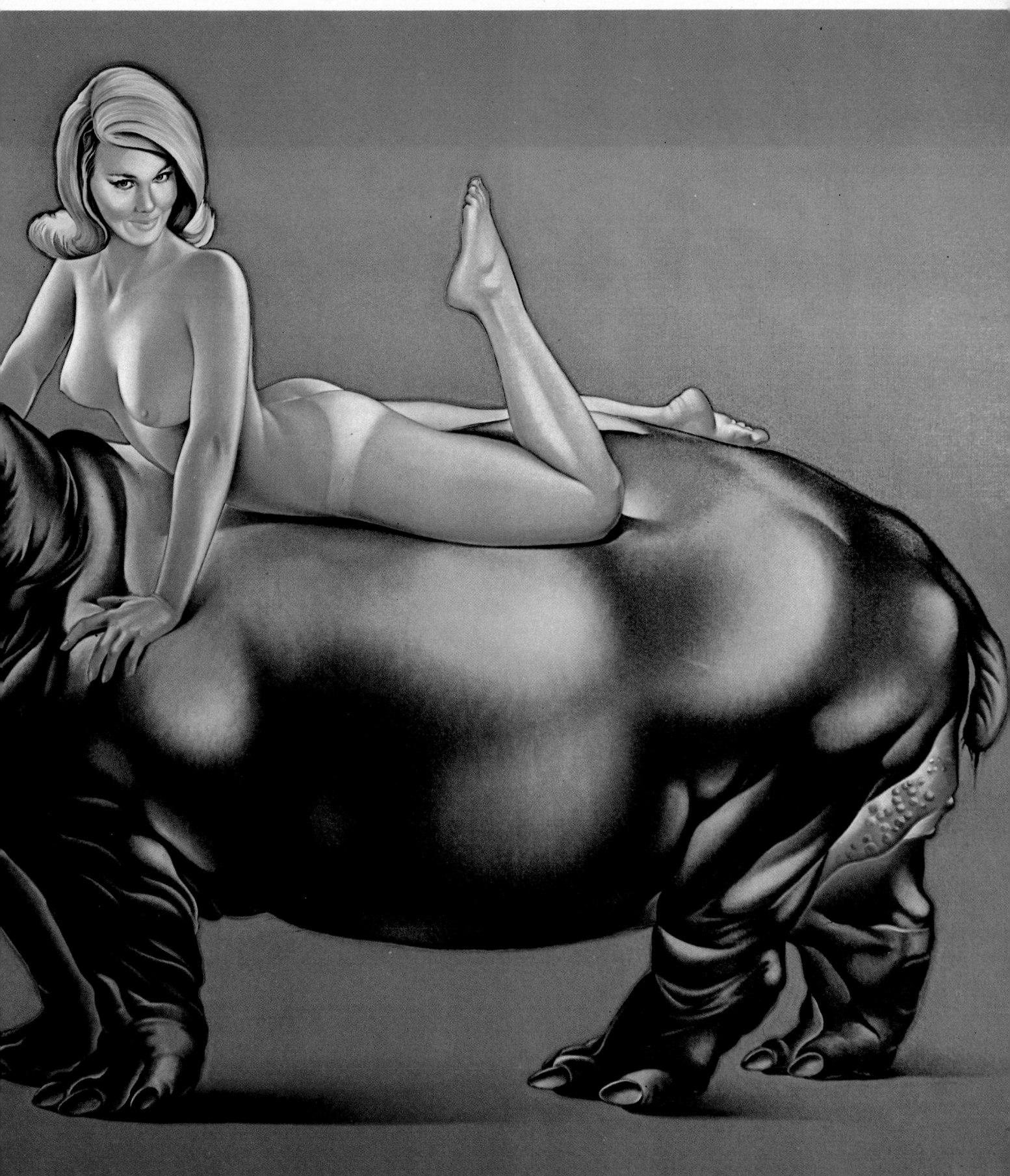

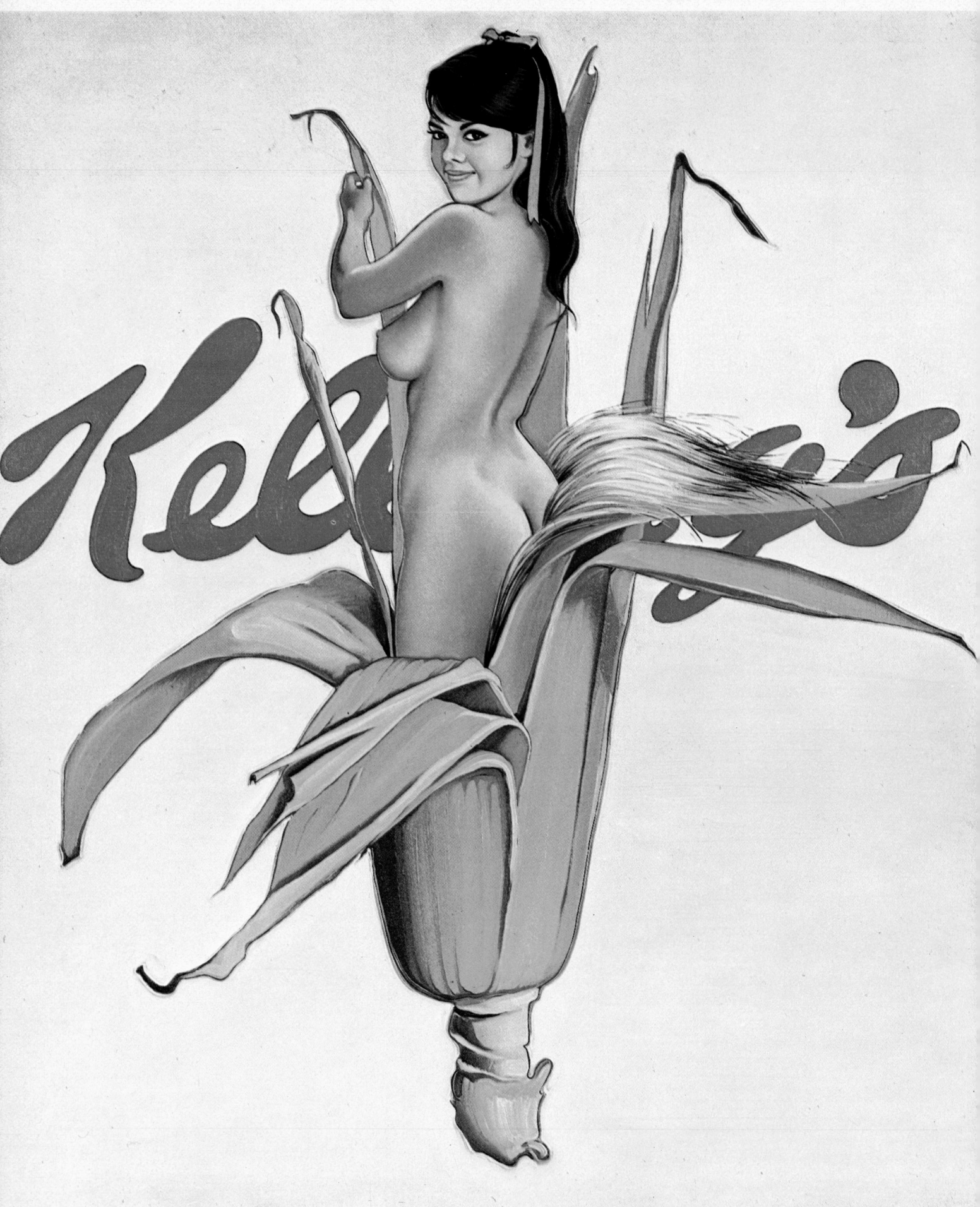

191.
Mel Ramos
Miss Corn Flakes
1964; 183 × 152.5 cm. (71 × 59 in.)
Colorado, coll. Kimiko and John Powers

indeed, that the boundary between Pop and abstract art was an illusory one. This article, for all the good sense which it displayed in detail, was nevertheless a sign that Pop was being painlessly absorbed, that it was becoming part of the art consensus. For there are several ways of approaching Pop Art. One is to regard it as a cultural conspiracy, a plot by both ends against the middle. In this case the respective ends are the mass and the avant-garde. The avant-garde takes up and uses the characteristic images and artifacts of mass culture as a way of disconcerting the bourgeois centre, whose members regard themselves as the custodians of culture. In this interpretation, the most important aspect of Pop is its irony.

But, as has appeared from a number of the artists' statements that I have quoted in this chapter, Pop was also celebratory. The artists actually liked the source material they drew upon—it gave them pleasure to contemplate it. They liked it for its own sake, and because it was emblematic of aspects of the culture around them which they enjoyed: its speed, energy, eroticism, enthusiasm for novelty. Because of the dissident position traditionally occupied by members of the avant-garde, it took some courage for artists to make the declaration that they were not in fact disaffected, that on balance they enjoyed the context that surrounded them. They had to overcome deep-seated blockages within themselves in order to paint Pop pictures and create Pop objects, and it was this which gave the images they made a certain emotional force.

Enjoyment of Pop culture was also linked to a certain nihilism. This nihilism was different from the same emotion as it manifested itself in Dada because society had undergone so many transitions in the interval. The Pop artist admired the "cool" of the jazz musician and the street hipster; he wanted to demonstrate that he, too, belonged to the same breed. Acceptance of modern industrial society, with all its crudity and ugliness, was a way of preserving oneself from emotional damage. If the label Pop covered a wide variety of artistic styles, it nevertheless designated quite accurately a concern for "stylishness" which had its roots in a willed emotional distance.

The relationship between Pop Art and its audience was a good deal more complex than it appeared on the surface because the public tended to be impervious to irony and did not share the artists' concern with the nuances of a vocabulary of representation. Nevertheless, Pop was the nearest that avant-garde art had got, during its more than fifty years of activity, to achieving a broad-based popular acceptance.

Pop Art as an International Style

As has already been noted, artists in Britain were quick to discover the possibilities offered by Pop imagery—even quicker, in fact, than artists in the United States. The man who, where British Pop was concerned, occupied a position analogous to that of Rauschenberg and Johns in America was Richard Hamilton. The similarity is increased by the fact that Hamilton has taken a lifelong interest in Dada. He became a personal friend of Marcel Duchamp towards the end of the latter's life, and was responsible for the reconstruction of the *Large Glass* shown in the Duchamp restrospective exhibition at the Tate Gallery.

Hamilton has always been an artist with a strong element of social consciousness, and it is this perhaps which prevents him from being a pure Dadaist in the Duchamp mould. Another thing which has influenced his work is the fact that he is virtually an autodidact. He left elementary school at the age of fourteen, and worked in advertising while attending evening classes at various art schools. He thus, like Warhol, had personal experience of the kind of source material he was afterwards to use. A third powerful influence on Hamilton's painting is his own experience as a teacher—he taught for a long time, not fine art, but courses in design. This led him to place great stress on the idea of problem solving. It also turned him into an habitual pragmatist. The English critic Richard Morphet has commented on his "aversion from predetermination of the character of the work by fidelity to style as such".

Despite the extensive use he makes of American material, Hamilton could never be mistaken for an American artist, not least because whatever he does has a consistently dandified quality which is the signal that he is happy to use what the Pop milieu offers him, but by no means to identify himself with it. He is always very willing to supply explanations, often elaborate ones, of his own work, and these explanations give many clues to his attitudes. The painting *She* (Plate 192), for instance, is the subject of a long exposition, some excerpts from which are worth quoting here. "Art's Woman in the fifties [Hamilton remarks] was anachronistic—as close to us as a smell in the drain; bloated, pink-crutched, pin-headed and lecherous; remote from the cool woman image outside fine art. There she is truly sensual but she acts her sexuality and the performance is full of wit. Although the most precious of adornments, she is often treated as just a styling accessory. The worst thing that can happen to a girl, according to the ads, is that she should fail to be exquisitely at ease in her appliance setting—the setting that now does much to establish our attitude to woman in the way that her clothes alone used to. Sex is everywhere, symbolized in the glamour of mass-produced luxury—the interplay of fleshy plastic, and smooth, fleshier metal" (*Architectural Design*, October, 1962).

She is a compilation from various advertising sources—a picture of a "cornucopic" refrigerator, advertisements for vacuum cleaners and other electrical appliances, an *Esquire* pin-up photograph.

A somewhat later painting, *I'm Dreaming of a White Christmas* (Plate 193), subjects a clip from a movie to an elaborate series of transformations. In particular, the artist has substituted colour-negative for colour-positive, so that the singer is transformed into a Negro, as an ironic allusion to the title of his song. The element of irony does not, however, rule out nostalgia. Hamilton's work, in common with that of other British Pop artists, has a sentimental tinge which makes it seem more charming and less deliberately aggressive than the work produced by his American colleagues.

An interesting, though only partial, exception to this rule is the work of the American artist

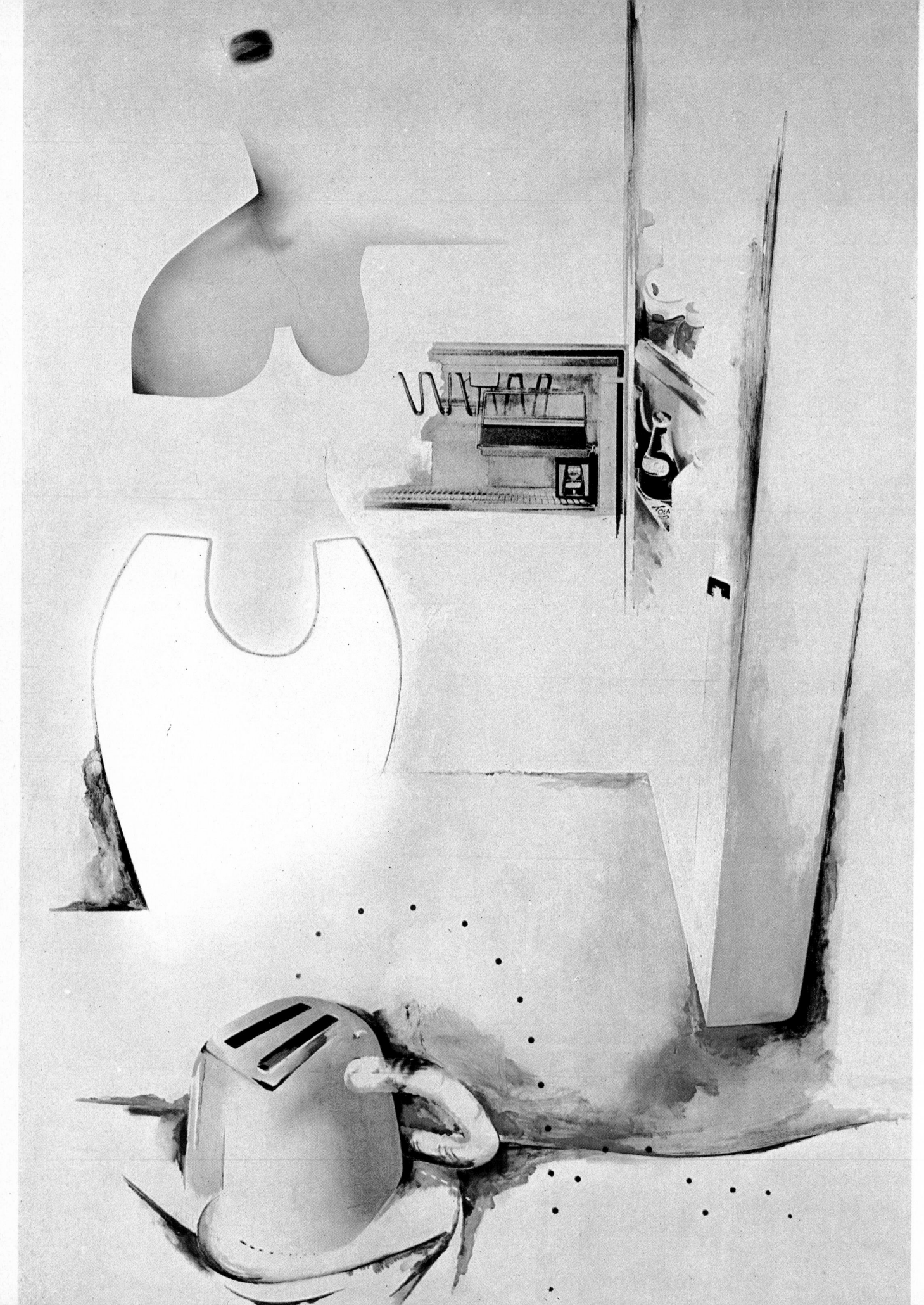

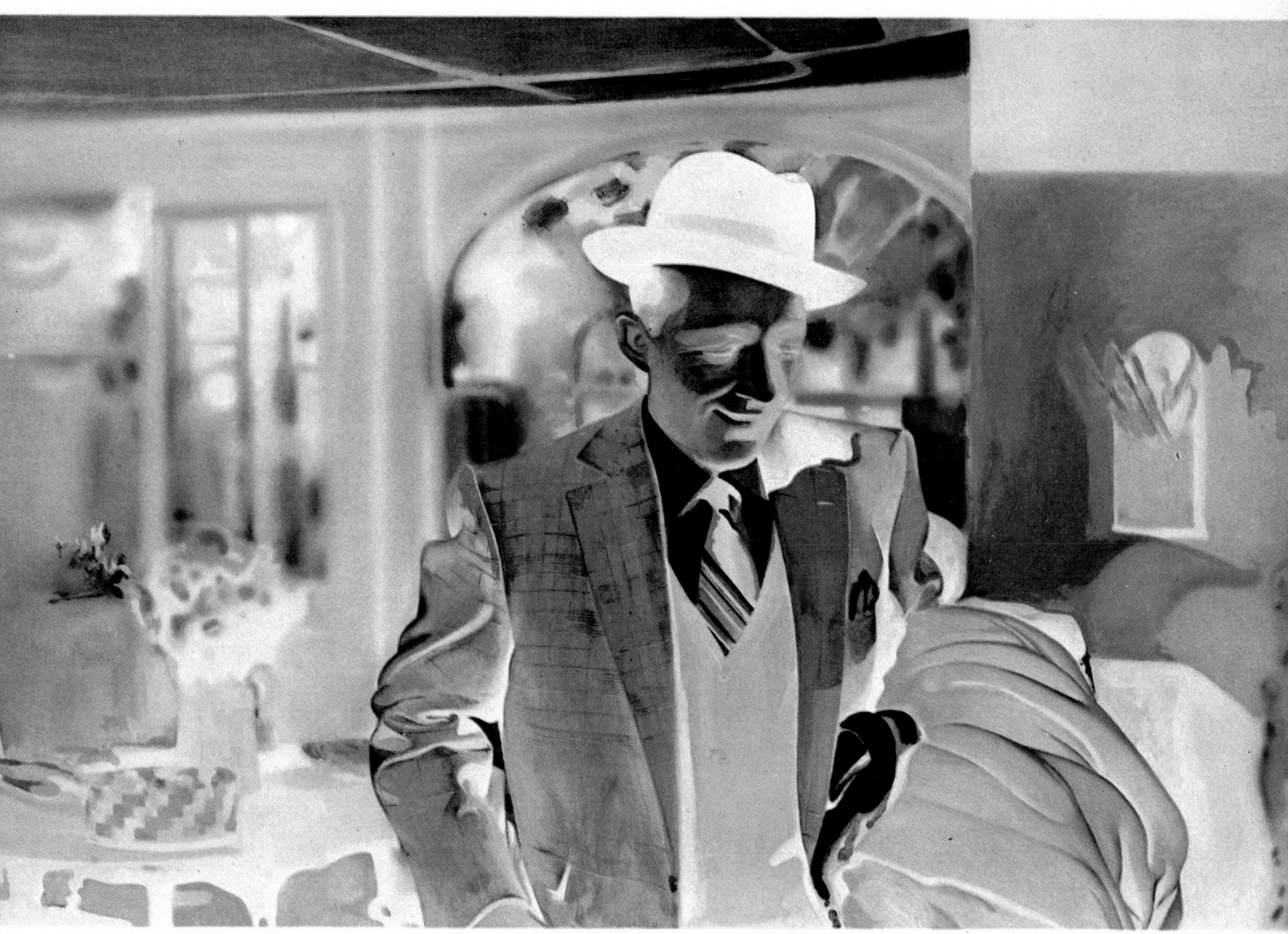

R. B. Kitaj. Kitaj is an émigré who has spent the most important part of his career in England, first arriving in 1958 to study at the Royal College of Art. What Kitaj has in common with Hamilton is that his painting, like Hamilton's, is filled with complex ideas which often require verbal as well as visual expression to make themselves fully apparent. Kitaj is a great admirer of the American expatriate poet Ezra Pound, and his paintings (Plate 194) seem meant to contain, and to sustain, a whole complex of allusions, many of them deliberately hermetic, as if the artist were trying to produce a painted equivalent of one of the more involuted segments of Pound's *Cantos*. Kitaj is an intensely literary painter, probably the most literary which the post-war period has so far produced. But he is also a humanist. As Wieland Schmied remarked in the catalogue preface to the Kitaj exhibition at the Kestner Gesellschaft, Hanover, in 1970, the canvases are meant "to bear the possibility or occasion of delivering something like human character into picture making". The honesty and the defects of Kitaj's humanism are well suggested by the qualifications which fill out this description. His work is indeed full of possibilities—it seems meant to keep the artist's

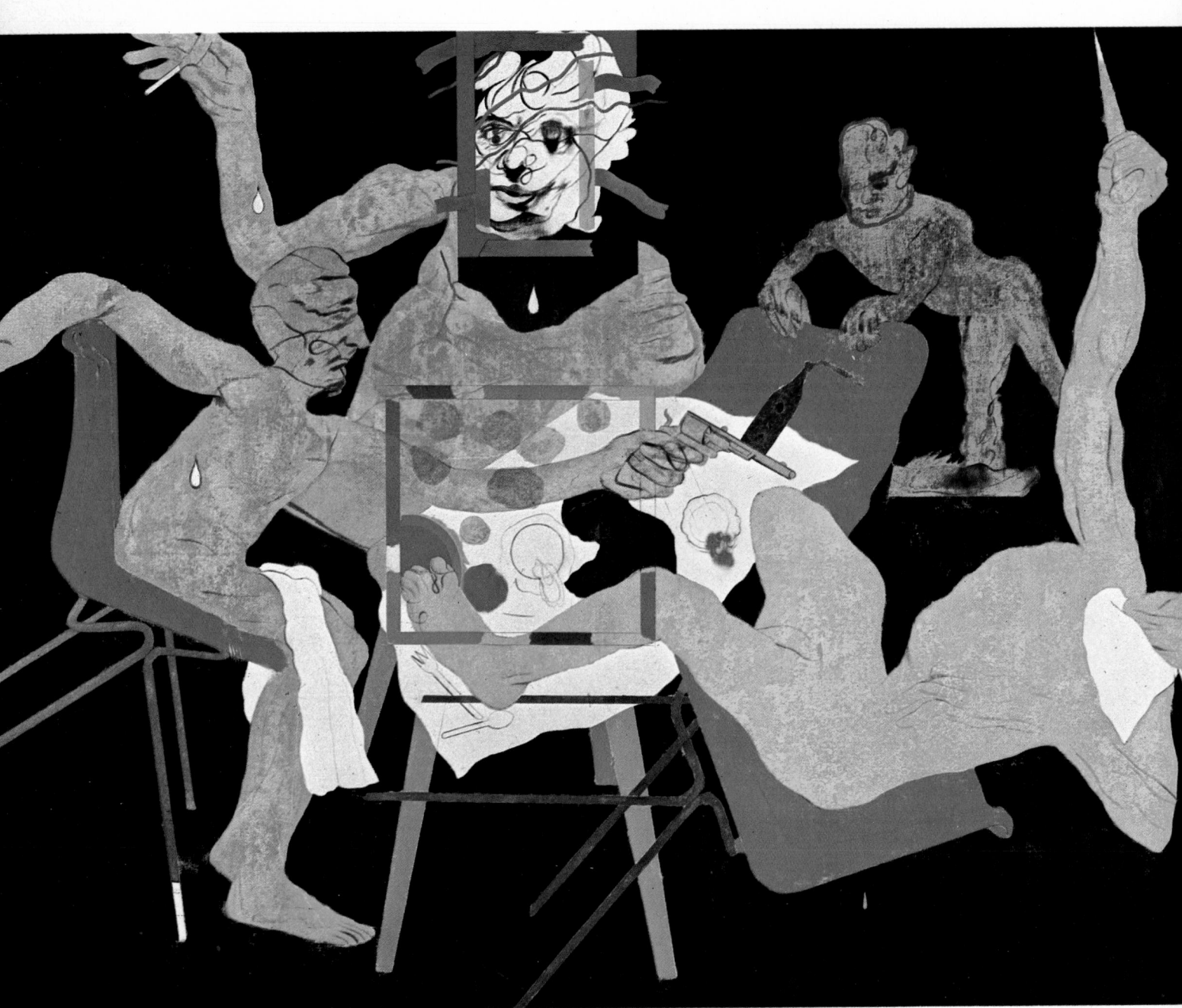

choices, as well as the spectator's, completely open. In this respect it is unlike most of the rest of Pop Art because it so entirely lacks the brash directness associated with the style.

Kitaj exercised a significant influence over the English artists with whom he came in contact at the Royal College of Art, and the college itself played an important role in the formation of an English Pop style. There was, however, room for artists of very different persuasions within the walls of the institution, room even for those interested by the same kind of source material. Peter Blake, for instance, remained the most resolutely English of artists, despite his enduring affection for popular

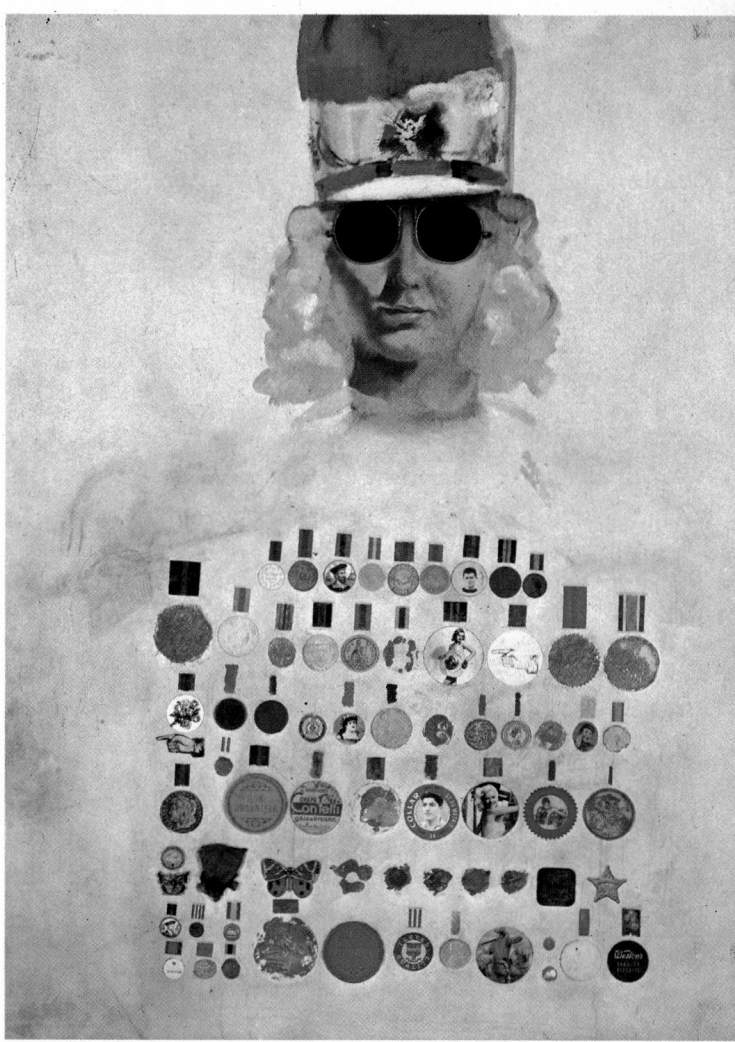

artifacts of all kinds (Plate 196). What Blake valued about Pop was simply the sense of freedom which it gave him: "Pop Art changed a lot of things in the way people look at pictures—so now I don't have to step from one to the other—one day I can do a drawing for a magazine and the next day a drawing for an exhibition, and they will be identical. I don't have a graphic style: it is exactly the same sort of drawing as I would be doing as fine art" (artist's statement from the catalogue *Three Painters: Blake, Dine, Hamilton*, Midlands Art Centre, Birmingham, 1967).

The nostalgic element in his work is even stronger than it is in Hamilton's, so much so that Blake can seem a Victorian artist born out of his time, never more so than in a beautiful series of illustrations for Lewis Carroll's *Alice's Adventures in Wonderland*. When Blake makes use of a specifically twentieth-century technique, such as collage, he immediately manages to remind us that the method was in fact taken to heights of considerable elaboration by Victorian amateurs pasting scraps onto screens. Even the basic materials of Blake's collages are often reminders of his roots in an earlier sensibility. He makes extensive use of Victorian and Edwardian post-cards, as well as of modern pin-ups.

The boy wonder of the British Pop scene of the 1960's was not Peter Blake but David Hockney. From the sociological (though not from the artistic) point of view, Hockney provides a British equivalent for the meteoric career of Andy Warhol, and in their different fashions they both of them illustrate the way in which the successful artist suddenly became the culture hero of the period, in London as well as in New York.

One of Hockney's characteristics is the marked lack of an American accent in his work, despite the importance of the American experience to his personal development. When he was a student, his work showed distinct signs of the influence of Dubuffet, and this influence is still traceable in the paintings produced during the early Sixties, when Hockney first made his reputation (Plate 198). It was apparently Dubuffet who first aroused Hockney's interest in child art. He has always been an artist with a tremendous gift for draftsmanship,

and these early pictures rely heavily upon the sensitivity of his line, to the point where they can seem to be enlarged drawings, rather than works which necessitated the elaboration of oil paint. But one should not overlook the sophistication of his approach to the problems of visual representation. Discussing the picture in Plate 198, he once said: "I placed [the two figures] in the painting in a rather ambiguous setting. It looks as though they are standing on a desert island with white sand and a palm tree. But the white at the bottom is only a base for them to stand on, and the rest of their setting is intended to be slightly out of focus, apart from the ecclesiastical shape in the bottom left-hand corner (an association with marriage). I called

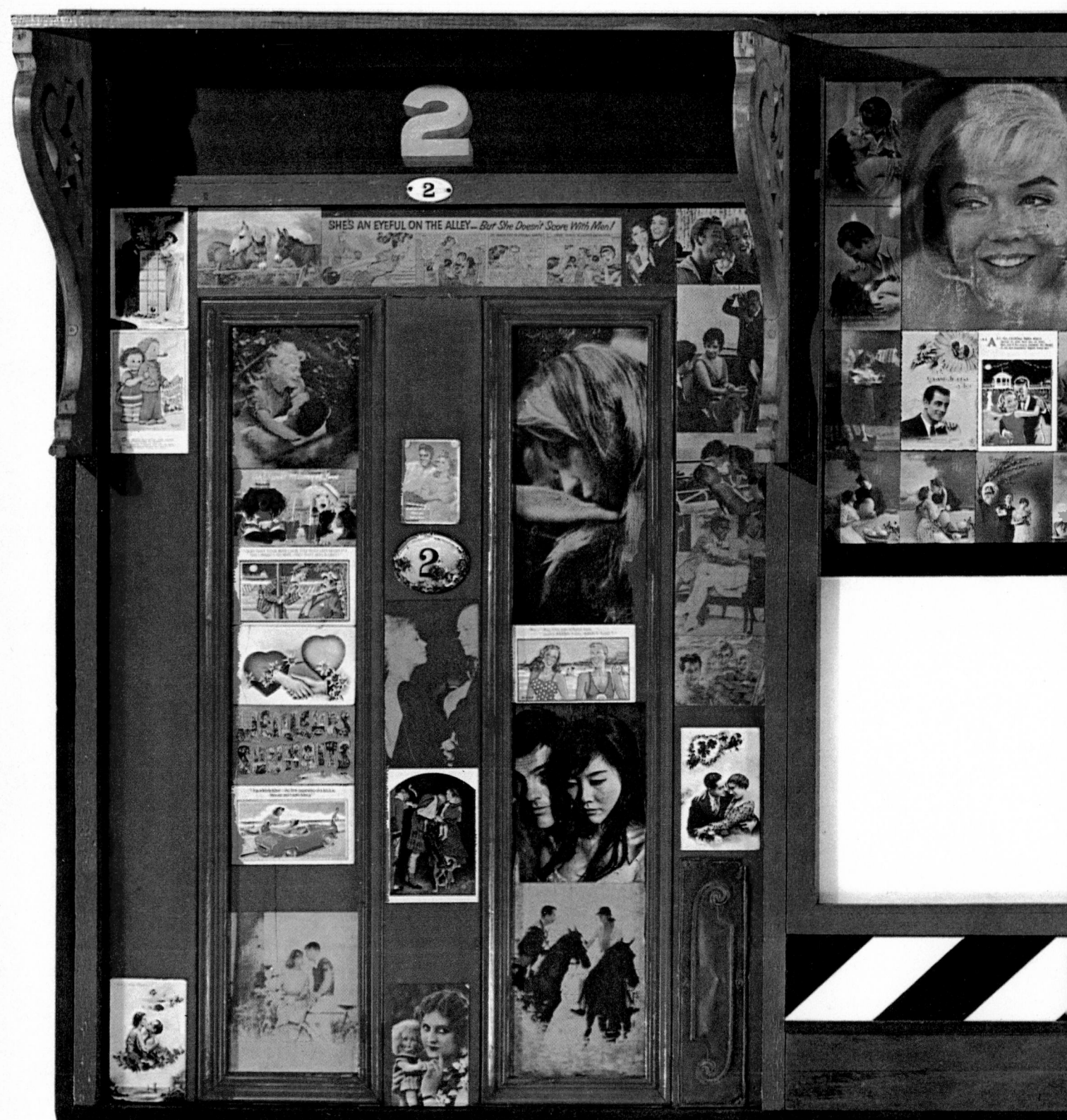

196.
Peter Blake
The Love Wall
1961; 124.5 × 236.2 × 23 cm. (49 × 92 × 9 in.)
London, The Calouste Gulbenkian Foundation

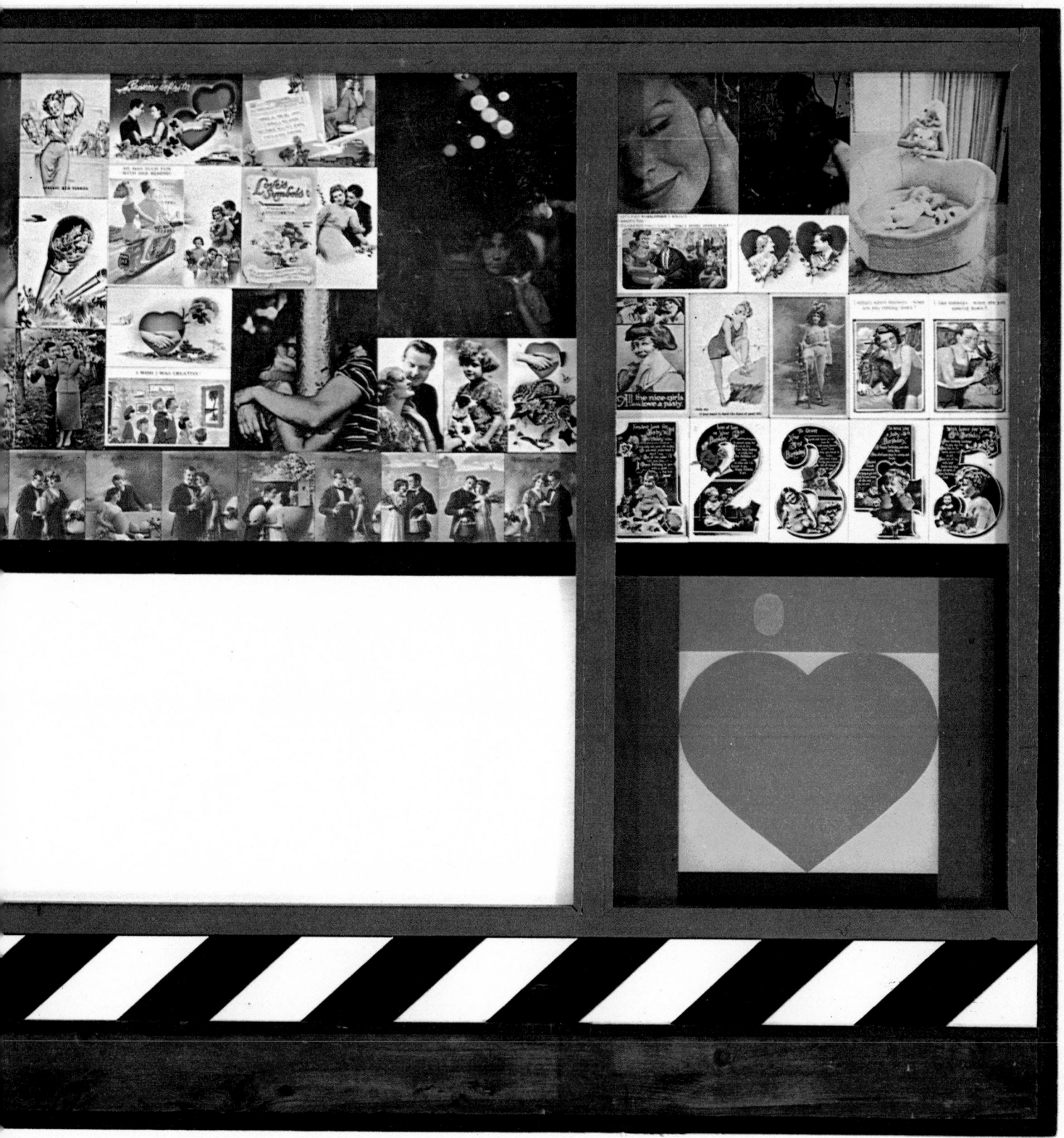

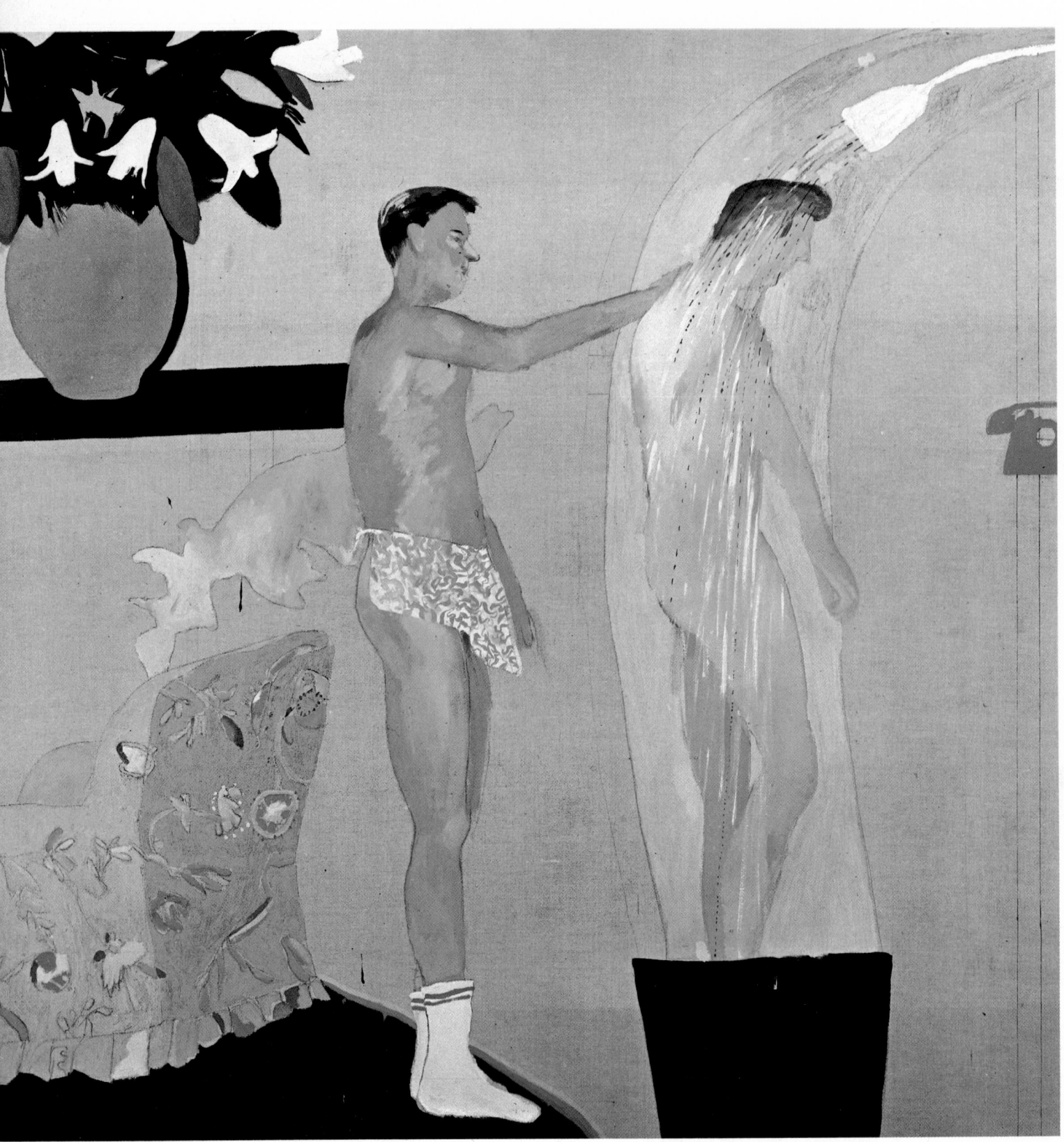

198.
David Hockney
The First Marriage
1962; 183 × 214.5 cm. (71 × 84 in.)
London, Tate Gallery

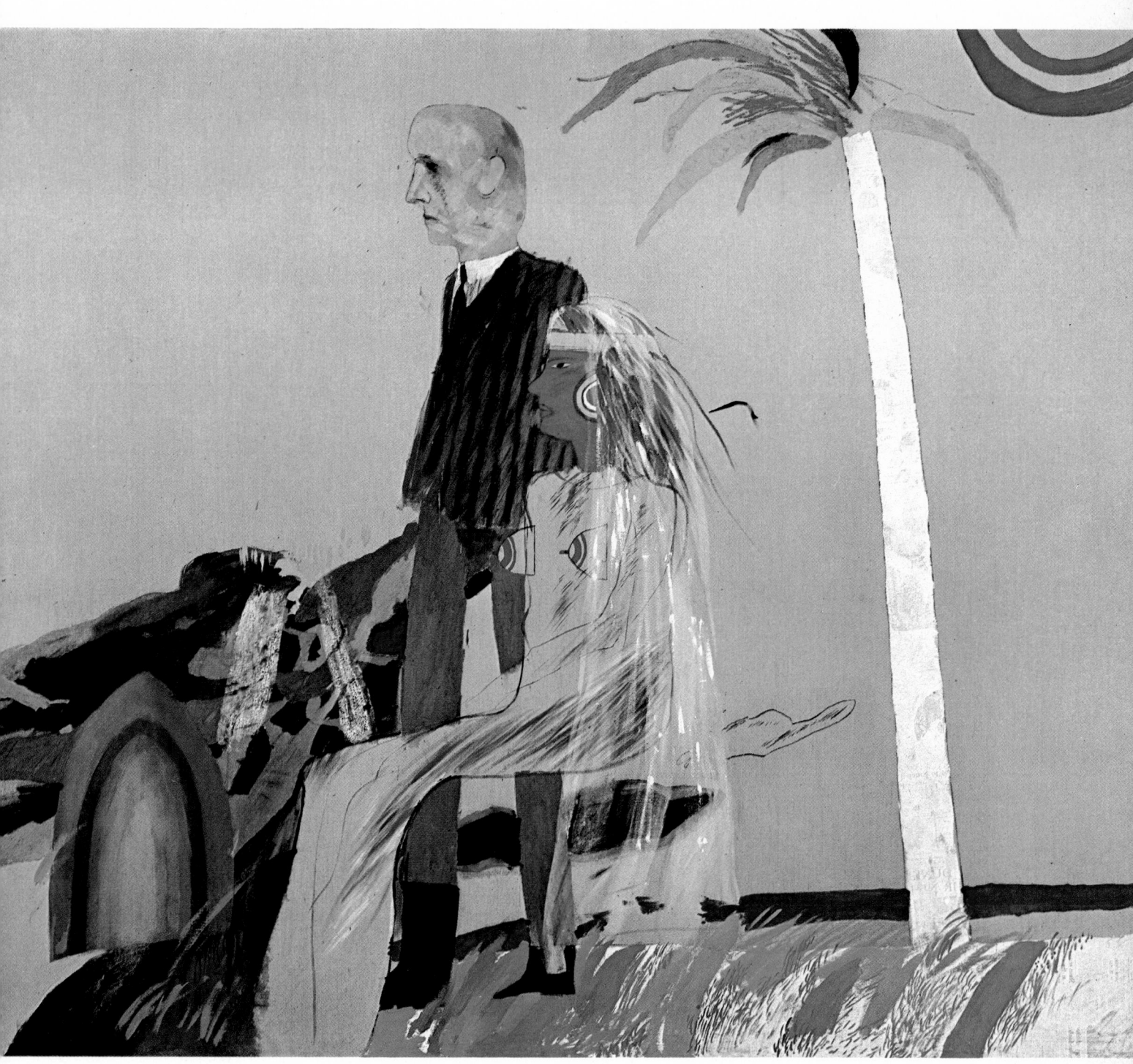

199.
Peter Phillips
Futuristic Revamp
1968; 59.5 × 94 cm. (23 × 37 in.)
Düsseldorf, coll. Heinz Beck

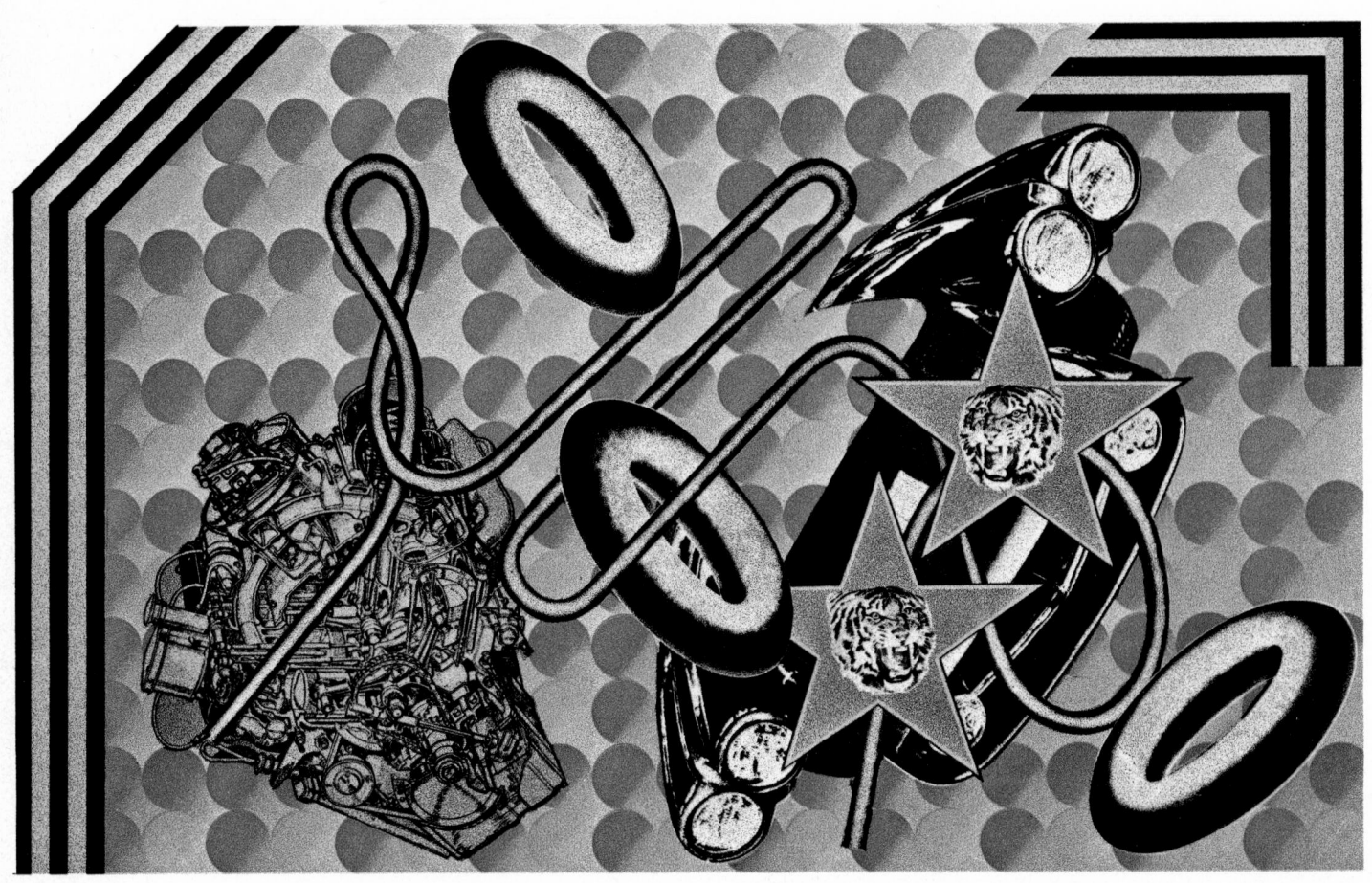

it *First Marriage* because I regarded it as a sort of marriage of style. The heavily stylized female figure with the not so stylized 'bridegroom'" (from an article in *Cambridge Opinion*, 37, 1963, reprinted in the catalogue of the David Hockney exhibition at the Whitechapel Art Gallery, London, 1970).

What Hockney was able to do, in this early phase of his work, was to combine two very different approaches. On the one hand he was interested in exploring the workings of accepted visual convention, and on the other he created paintings which seemed uniquely accessible because of the mixture of confessional autobiography and genial wit.

America was important to Hockney because he found it personally liberating. Though his famous suite of etchings *The Rake's Progress*, which records his first visit to New York, is full of criticisms of the American scene, what comes across most strongly is a sense of euphoria. New York and later Los Angeles were for the artist the legendary Land of Cockaigne, where any kind of experience was possible, and where all feelings of guilt and constraint could be shed. Hockney came to stand for an opposition to English provincialism. He himself was a provincial boy from the industrial town of Bradford—the pictures he painted represented a process of self-transformation. Their unique quality was their detachment, their ability to record the artist's follies and foibles without indulging them.

Most of the other artists connected with the English Pop movement were distinctly more conventional in their approach. The most typical of them, in many respects, were Peter Phillips and Allen Jones. Phillips (Plates 199 and 200) represents the nearest approach by an Englishman to the Pop ikons produced in America—his

200.
Peter Phillips
Tribal 1 × 4
1962; 107 × 99 cm. (42 × 39 in.)
Paris, Galerie Mathias Fels

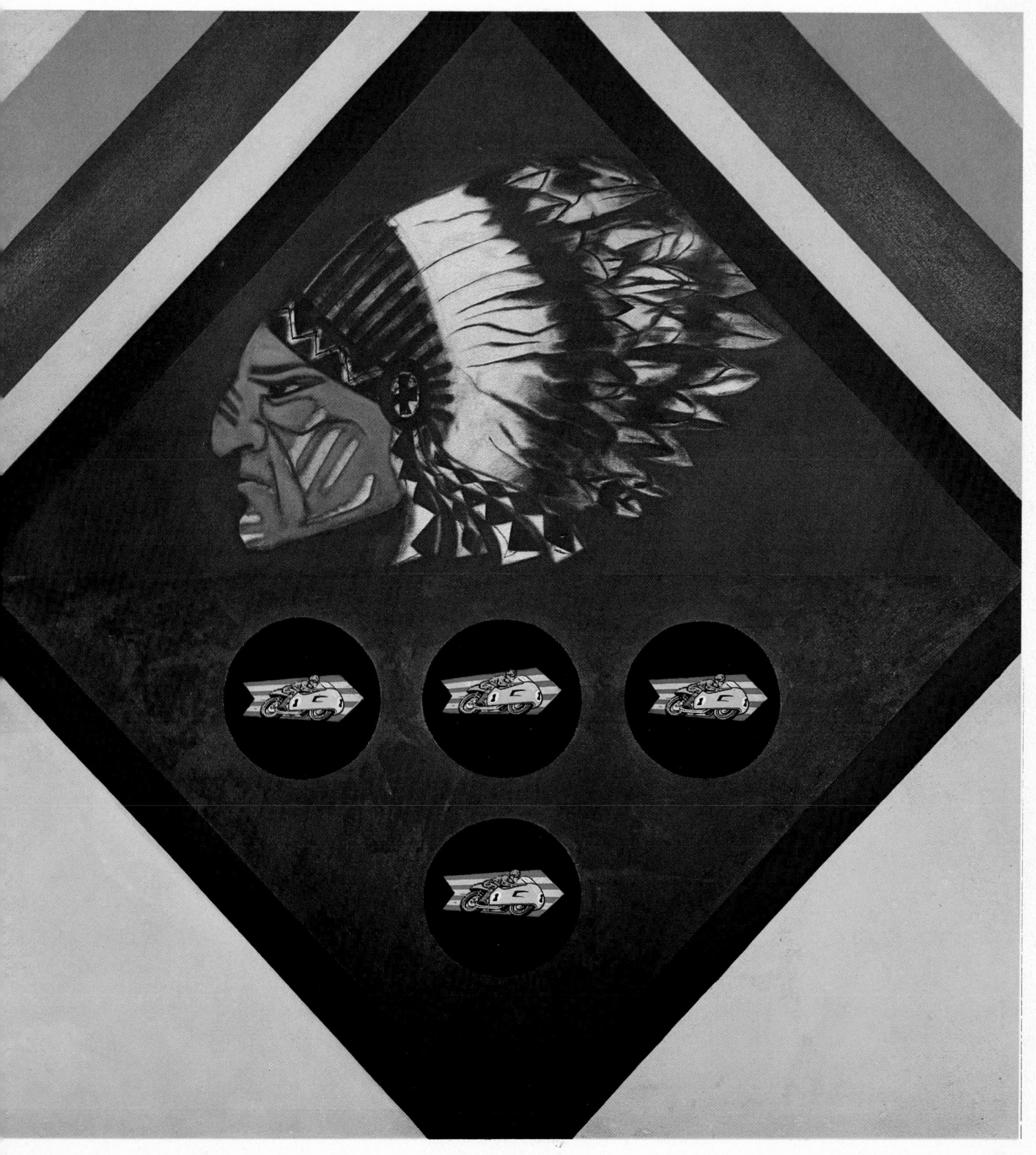

201.
Allen Jones
Curious Woman
1964–65; 121.9 × 101.6 × 10.2 cm. (48 × 40 × 4 in.)
Colorado, coll. Kimiko and John Powers

202. Opposite
Allen Jones
Perfect Match
1966–67; 280 × 93 cm. (109 × 36 in.)
Cologne, Wallraf-Richartz Museum, coll. Ludwig

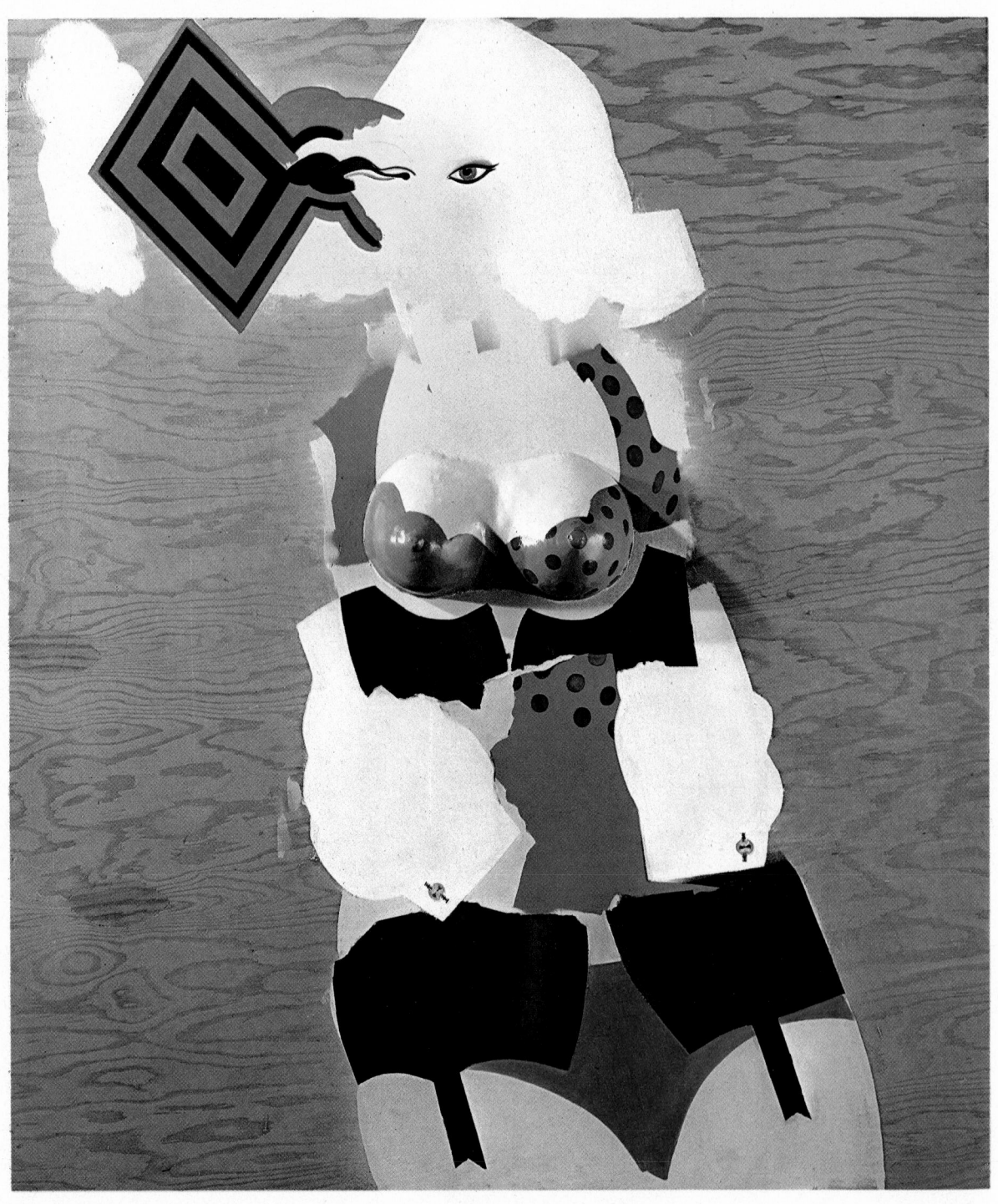

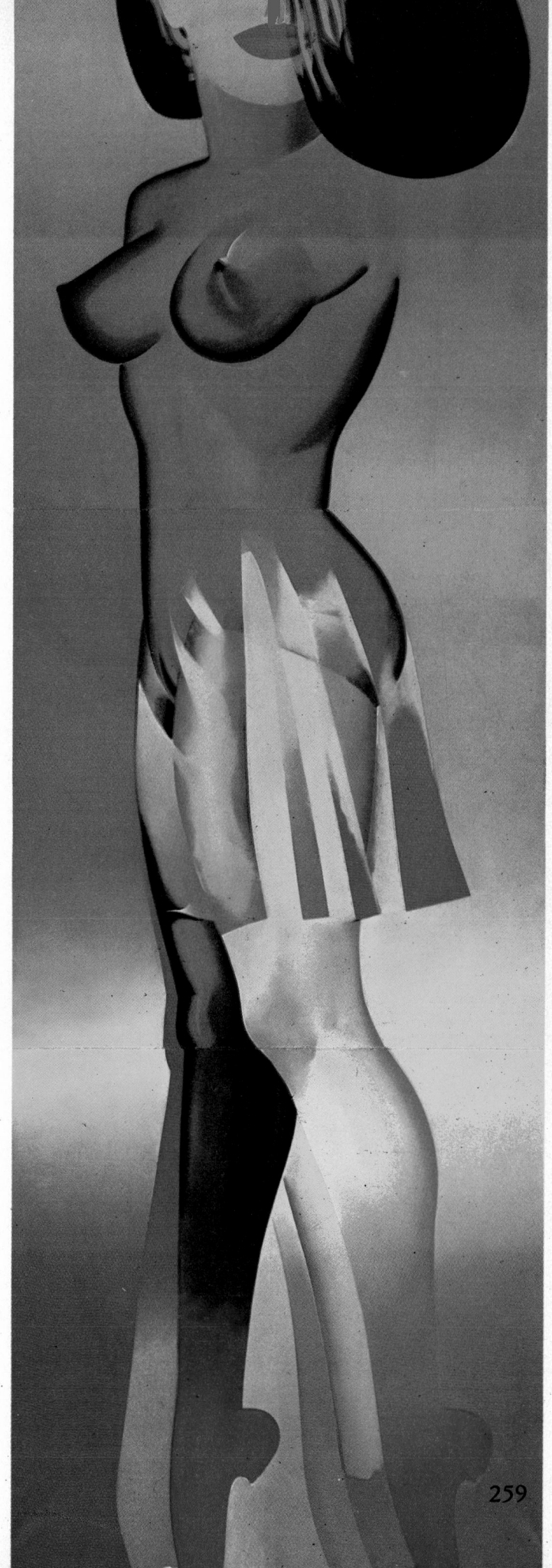

203. Overleaf
Allen Jones
Hatstand, Table, Chair
1969; 184 × 76 × 62 cm. (72 × 30 × 24 in.)
Aachen, Neue Galerie, coll. Ludwig

versions differ from the native product only because of their romanticism. Many of Phillips' favourite images have a fetishistic tinge, but he has consistently denied that this is an important part of their meaning: "My crash-helmets and motor-cycles are not 'kinky'; I use them for different ends than just fetishism. The imagery is not important or significant for itself; it is the way it is painted and used that matters" (quoted by Mario Amaya, *Pop as Art*, London, 1965, p. 132).

Despite this specific denial, the spectator remains aware of a sexual overtone. But it is carefully distanced by the technique, especially in those canvases from the mid-Sixties onwards in which the artist makes use of the impersonal finish which can be got with an airbrush. This was adopted as part of a search for mechanical perfection. "I don't want to be a machine like Warhol," Phillips said, "but I love the idea of using one." Yet it also seems to be a device for holding violent and perhaps threatening emotions at a safe distance.

The eroticism in Allen Jones's work is more openly acknowledged, though he also said in 1965, at about the time when *Curious Woman* (Plate 201) was produced: "I have no special regard for figuration; it is simply a means of commencing, and any recurrence of an image could be said to reflect the inability to solve a pictorial problem" (quoted by Michael Compton, *Pop Art*, New York, 1970, p. 69). Much of the basic material of his earlier painting came from the kinkier kind of girlie magazine, but translated into terms of Matisse's brushwork and colour-schemes. Jones is a gifted painter. He has outstanding inventiveness with both imagery and colour, combining and recombining stringently patterned and freely painterly elements, breaking up human anatomy to re-arrange it in new ways. In the early Sixties, at a time when he was working in New York, he was deeply interested in the theme of hermaphro-ditism, and played a series of inventive variations upon it. Americans were fascinated by the way in which he managed to combine the traditional preoccupations of European painting with the new, and on the surface very different, concerns of Pop. Jones at that stage seemed to work with

259

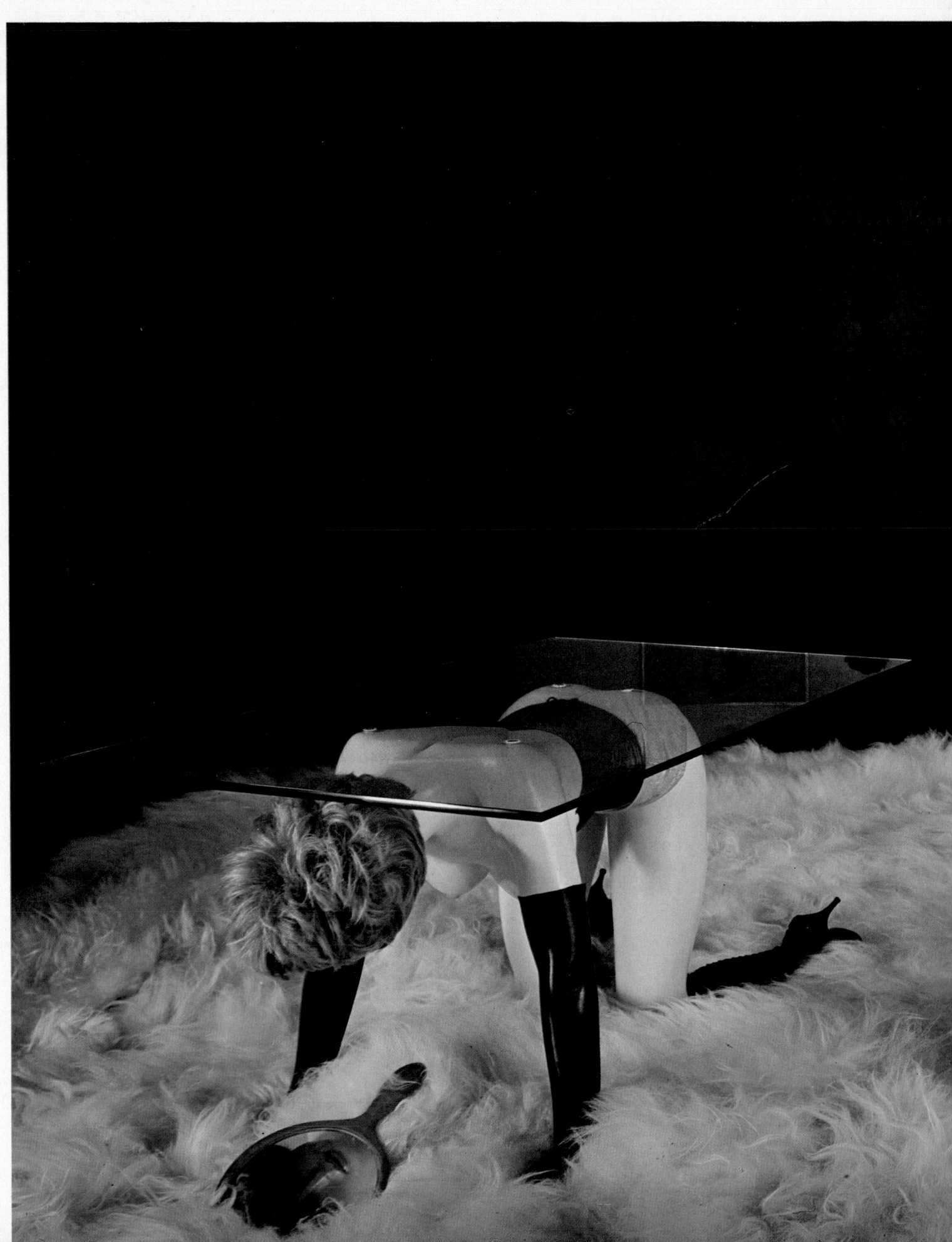

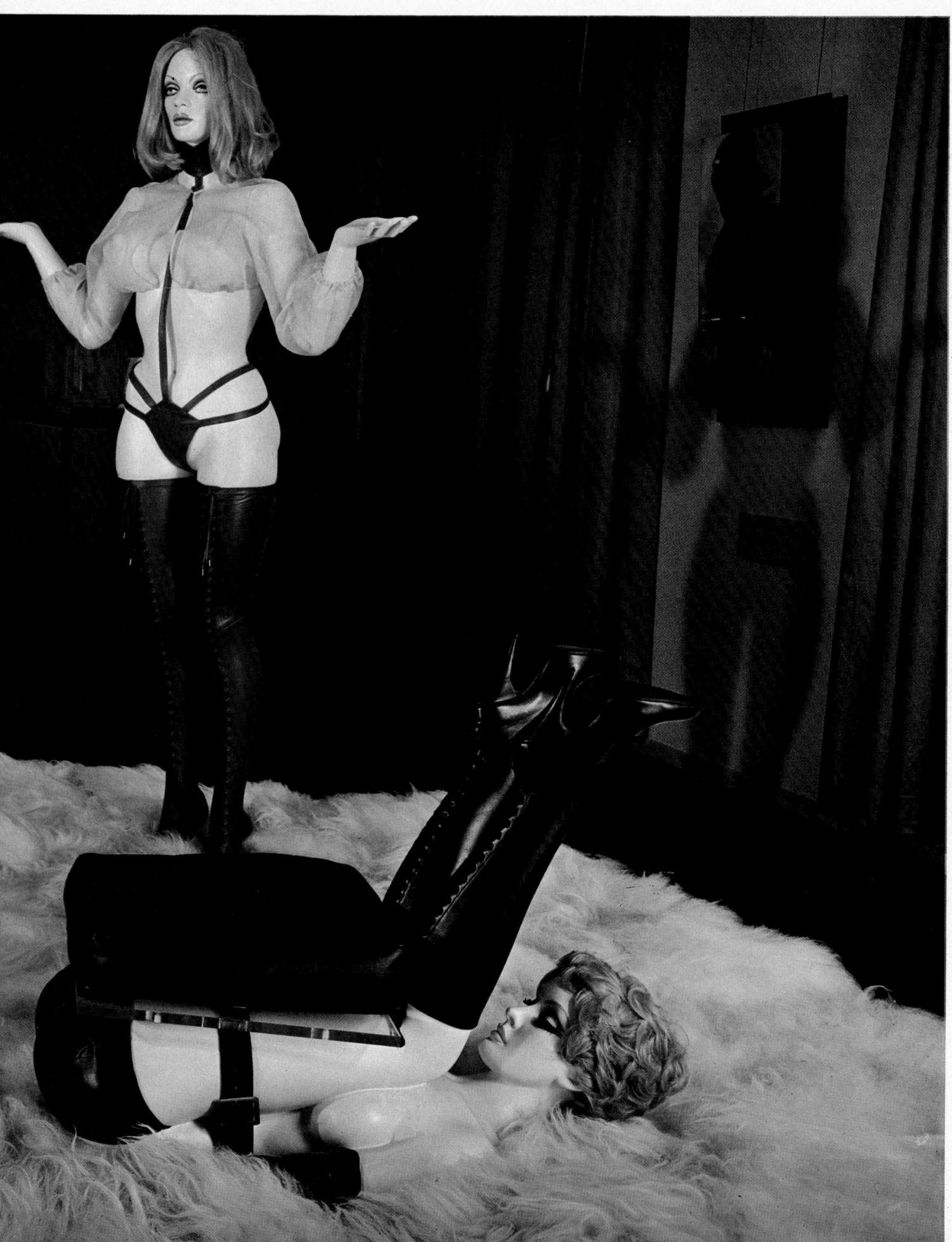

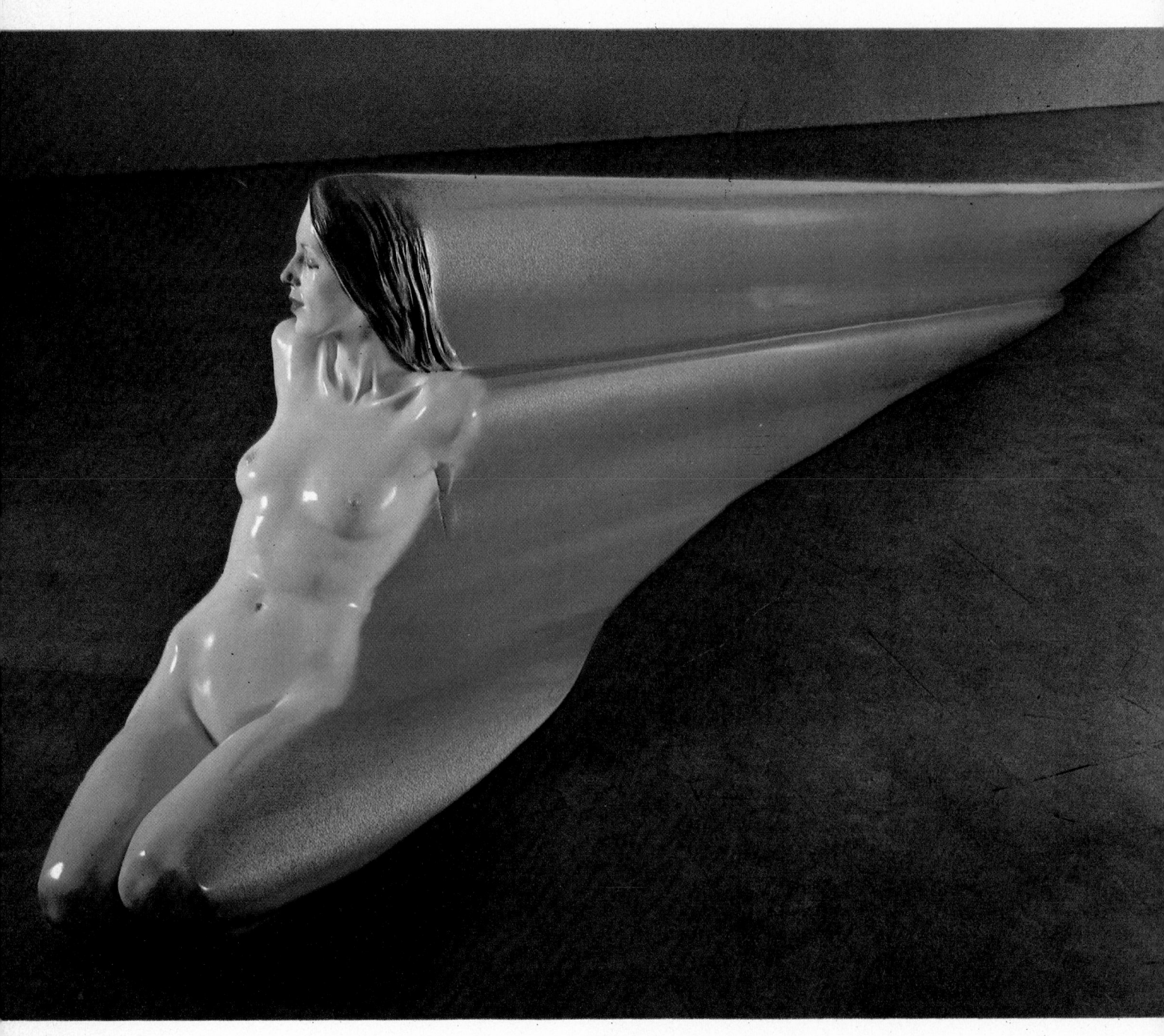

204.
Anthony Donaldson
Girl Sculpture "Red 'n Gold"
1970; 75 × 448 cm. (29 × 175 in.)
London, Rowan Gallery

205. Opposite
Anthony Green
The Red Chair
1970; 216 × 211 cm. (84 × 82 in.)
London, Rowan Gallery

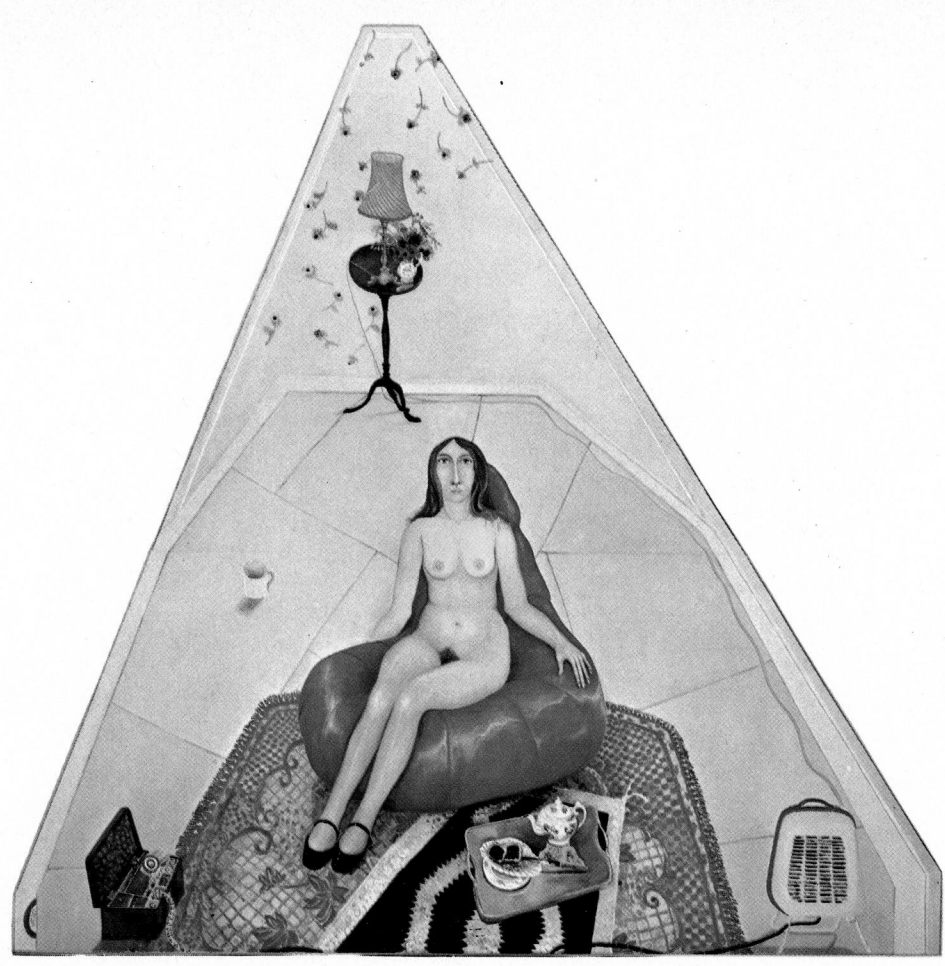

greater technical freedom than either Tom Wesselman or Richard Lindner, both of whom had something in common with him so far as subject-matter was concerned.

More recently, Jones's fetishistic obsessions have often seemed to get the better of his artistic judgment. He has made a series of sculptures (Plate 203) which are expressions of sadistic sexual fantasy, and the Super Realist style in which these pieces are executed makes it difficult to decide in what way the spectator is intended to react to them. Are they an ironic commentary on the limited nature of contemporary eroticism? Or does the artist present these images with complete confidence in their intrinsic interest?

Obsessional eroticism is one of the leading characteristics of British Pop Art, far more so than with American Pop. Few of the leading British artists of this group are free from it—we encounter it not only in Phillips and Jones but also in the art of Hockney and Peter Blake. Yet another example is the work of Anthony Donaldson, who has a visual repertoire based on variations of the pin-up.

Donaldson's paintings can look rather tame when put beside those of some of his rivals, but he is one of the few Pop artists to have become more inventive as he grew older, and his recent streamlined sculptures (Plate 204), combining the architectural features of Los Angeles with typical girlie-magazine images, are a witty new variation on a rather worn theme.

One British artist, connected to Pop Art but not in the mainstream, who shows a rather different kind of eroticism in his work is Anthony Green. Green employs some of the conventions of naïve painting without being in any sense a naïf. He has described his own paintings as follows: "They tell stories about my immediate surroundings, about people who are close to me—my wife, relatives, children. I want them to reach a wide section of the community, the expert as well as the 'man on the street' because I feel the appreciation of paintings exists on many levels" ("Anthony Green at Rowan Gallery", *Studio International*, Vol. 184, London [November, 1972]). But the artist's candour makes no concessions. He paints his wife,

206.
Joe Tilson
Is This Che Guevara?
1969; 101.6 × 68.6 cm. (40 × 27 in.)
London, Tate Gallery

calm and naked (rather than nude) in the surroundings of their apartment (Plate 205), and he has even painted a group of canvases which are candid, and also touching, depictions of the act of love.

In seeking for an explanation of this powerful erotic streak in the British art of the Sixties, one is tempted to point to the difference in social context between Britain and America. In many ways, the sexual sense not least among them, the Sixties were a more thoroughly liberating decade in London than they were in New York. The reason is simple: prosperity came more suddenly, and the British had greater freedoms to win. The sexuality in American Pop Art tends to be of two kinds—either it is a tribute to a revered cultural object, in this case the pin-up; or else (as in Warhol's movies) it is a covert expression of American violence. That is to say, it is sexual only at some secondary level. In Britain things are different. There is a feeling of confessional release and self-discovery in the images used by British Pop artists.

On a different plane, it is also interesting to note differences of technique. American Pop artists created ikons or fully developed three-dimensional objects. Their flirtations with the shaped canvas were comparatively mild. In Britain experiments of this type assumed a great deal more importance. At an early stage in his career, Hockney employed shaped canvases, but one associates them chiefly with the work of Peter Phillips, Allen Jones, and Richard Smith—the third named is one of the few artists to have made the move from Pop figuration to complete abstraction. The shaped paintings produced in Britain invite a comparison with a quite different school in the United States, that of the Post-Painterly Abstractionists (see Chapter VIII), and particularly with the work of Frank Stella. The resemblance indicates the more eclectic and more prolix nature of British art.

Unlike American Pop, but like some of that produced in Europe, British Pop had a political component. Richard Hamilton was again one of the leaders in this field, with the series of canvases *Swingeing London*, inspired by the arrest on drugs charges of the Rolling Stones, and with the large-edition print inspired by the shootings at Kent State. Another artist who produced a good deal of politically oriented work was Joe Tilson, whose print *Is This Che Guevara?* (Plate 206) became one of the best-known "radical" images of the decade. Tilson has always been an intellectual—interested in language games (which form the subject of the series of painted reliefs entitled *Geometry*), and interested in the way the visual and verbal language of the mass media affects the way in which we apprehend the world. He said to an interviewer: "I am interested in the environment of the mind, what goes on inside rather than outside. . . . By celebrating the ephemeral you change people's attitudes towards it, make them more aware of non-permanence and the inevitability of change" (Richard Cork, "Talking with Tilson", *Art and Artists*, Vol. IV, No. 12, London [March, 1970], p. 27).

As it happens, Tilson's own work has a certain air of transience, based on the triviality of his approach to the subject-matter, which seems circumscribed by Pop conventions. *Is This Che Guevara?*, though it dates from the very end of the decade, now seems even more of a period piece than most examples of Sixties Pop Art. Looking at it, one recalls that a fashion boutique called Che Guevara was founded in London at almost the same moment, in inappropriate tribute to the Cuban guerrilla leader's death.

There is one British painter usually classified as Pop who stands in striking contrast to the rest of those who find themselves placed in that category. This is Patrick Caulfield. Caulfield's work has much in common with that of Roy Lichtenstein (Plate 208). His source material is not comic strips, but the cheapest kind of department-store art reproduction. From these he has deduced a set of conventions which he applies to a wide range of subject-matter. Like Lichtenstein, Caulfield uses what seems on first sight to be a harsh and cruel technique with surprising subtlety and classicism, using a heavy black line to divide the canvas into colour areas, and pitching the colours themselves against one another with such skill that one never notices the total absence of modelling. Caulfield has stuck even more firmly than Lichtenstein to

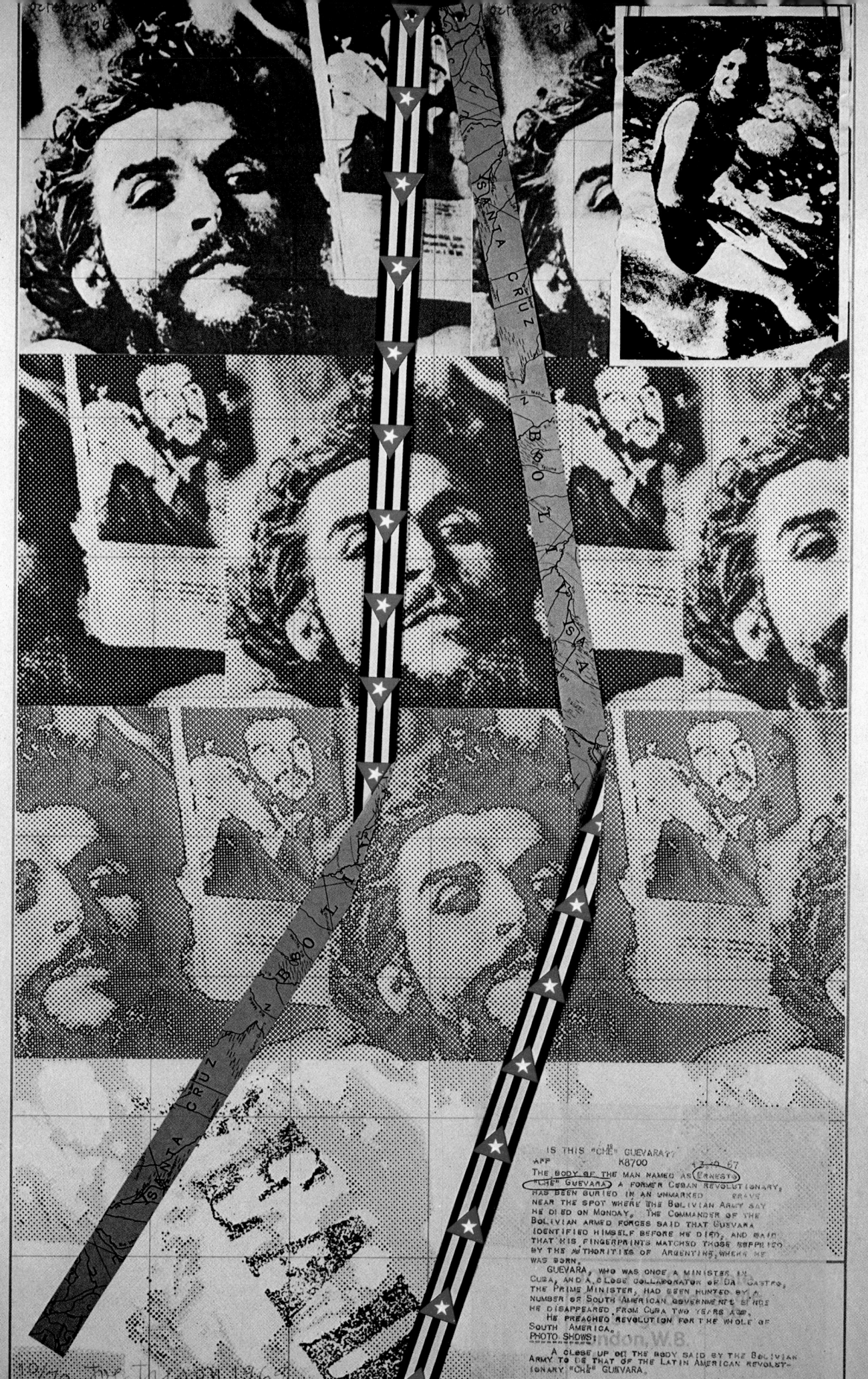

IS THIS "CHE" GUEVARA?
AFP   K8700   13.10.67
THE BODY OF THE MAN NAMED AS Ernesto
"CHE" GUEVARA, A FORMER CUBAN REVOLUTIONARY,
HAS BEEN BURIED IN AN UNMARKED GRAVE
NEAR THE SPOT WHERE THE BOLIVIAN ARMY SAY
HE DIED ON MONDAY. THE COMMANDER OF THE
BOLIVIAN ARMED FORCES SAID THAT GUEVARA
IDENTIFIED HIMSELF BEFORE HE DIED, AND SAID
THAT HIS FINGERPRINTS MATCHED THOSE SUPPLIED
BY THE AUTHORITIES OF ARGENTINE, WHERE HE
WAS BORN.
   GUEVARA, WHO WAS ONCE A MINISTER IN
CUBA, AND A CLOSE COLLABORATOR OF DR. CASTRO,
THE PRIME MINISTER, HAD BEEN HUNTED BY A
NUMBER OF SOUTH AMERICAN GOVERNMENTS SINCE
HE DISAPPEARED FROM CUBA TWO YEARS AGO.
   HE PREACHED REVOLUTION FOR THE WHOLE OF
SOUTH AMERICA.
PHOTO SHOWS: London, W.8.
   A CLOSE UP OF THE BODY SAID BY THE BOLIVIAN
ARMY TO BE THAT OF THE LATIN AMERICAN REVOLUT-
IONARY "CHE" GUEVARA

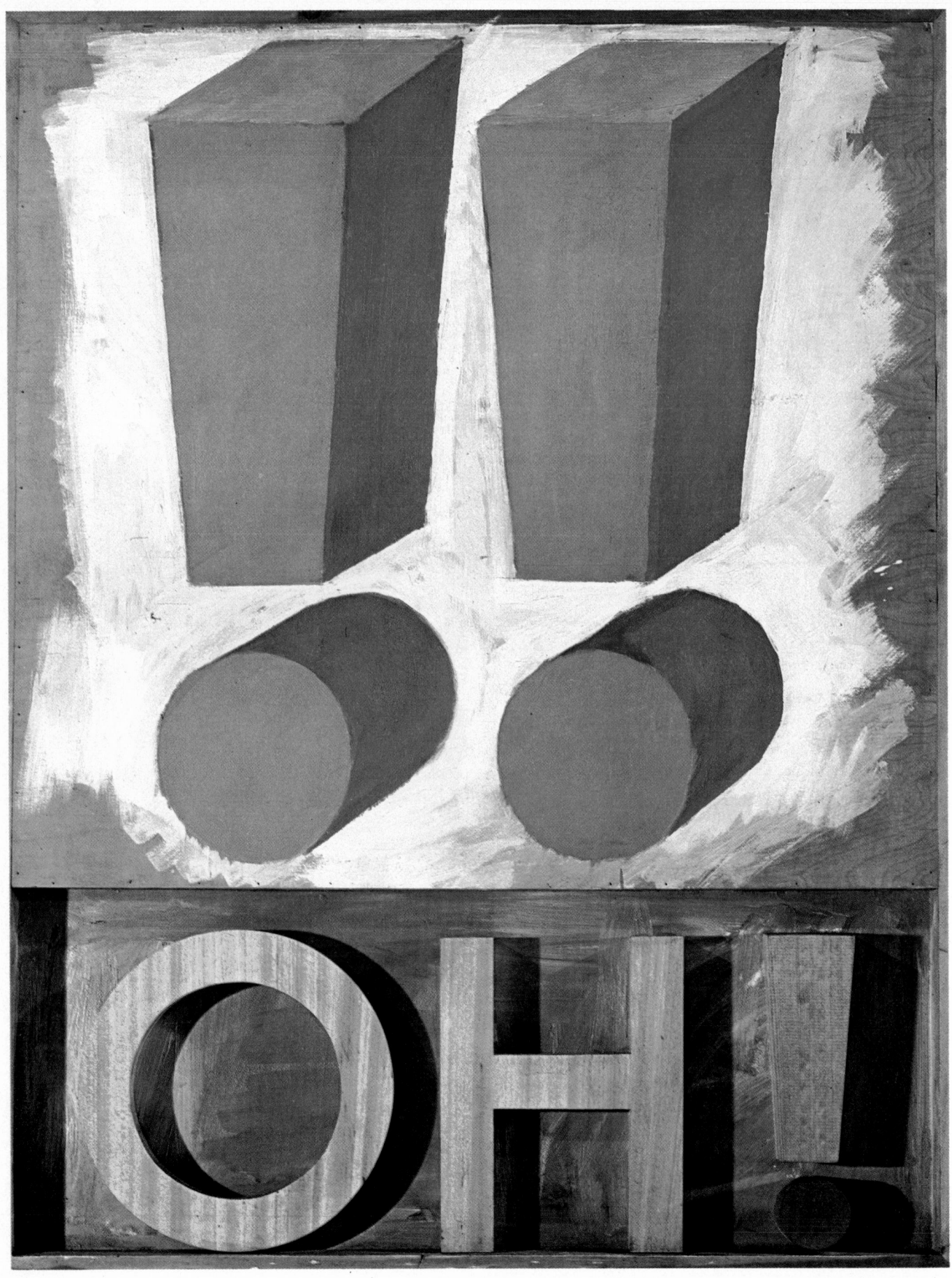

207. Opposite
Joe Tilson
OH!
1963; 124.5 × 94 cm. (49 × 37 in.)
Boston, The 180 Beacon Collection

208.
Patrick Caulfield
Pottery
London, Tate Gallery

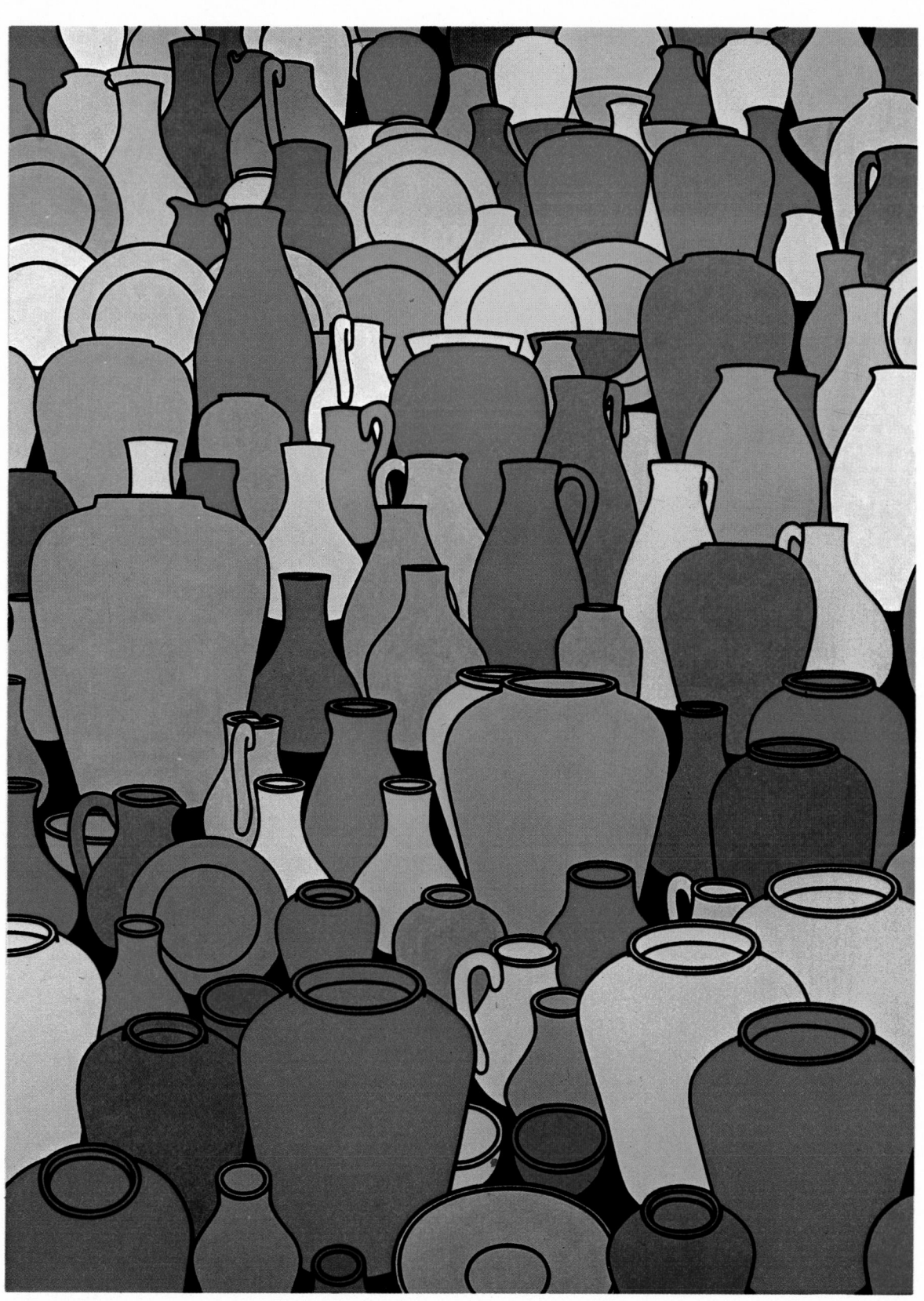

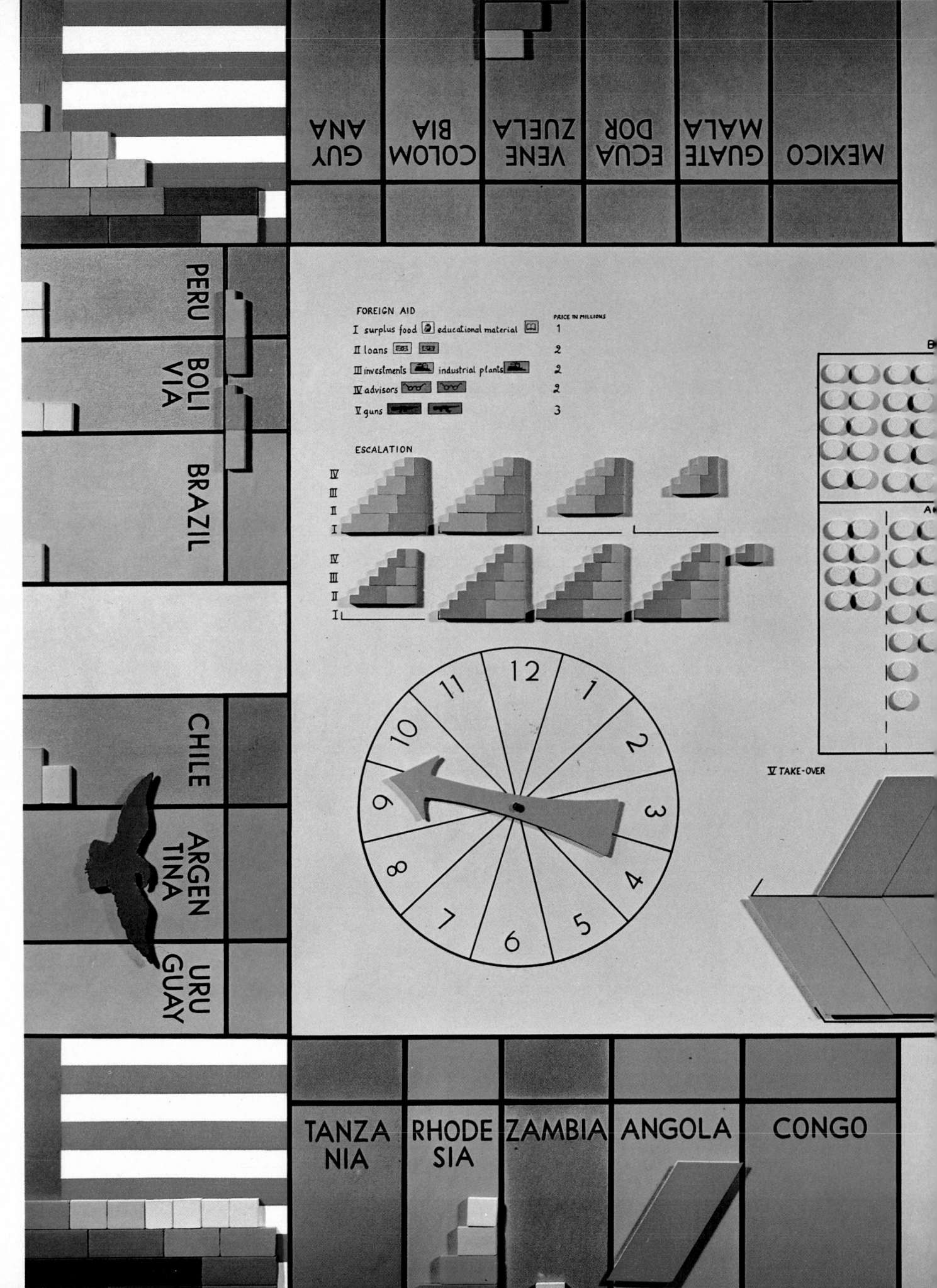

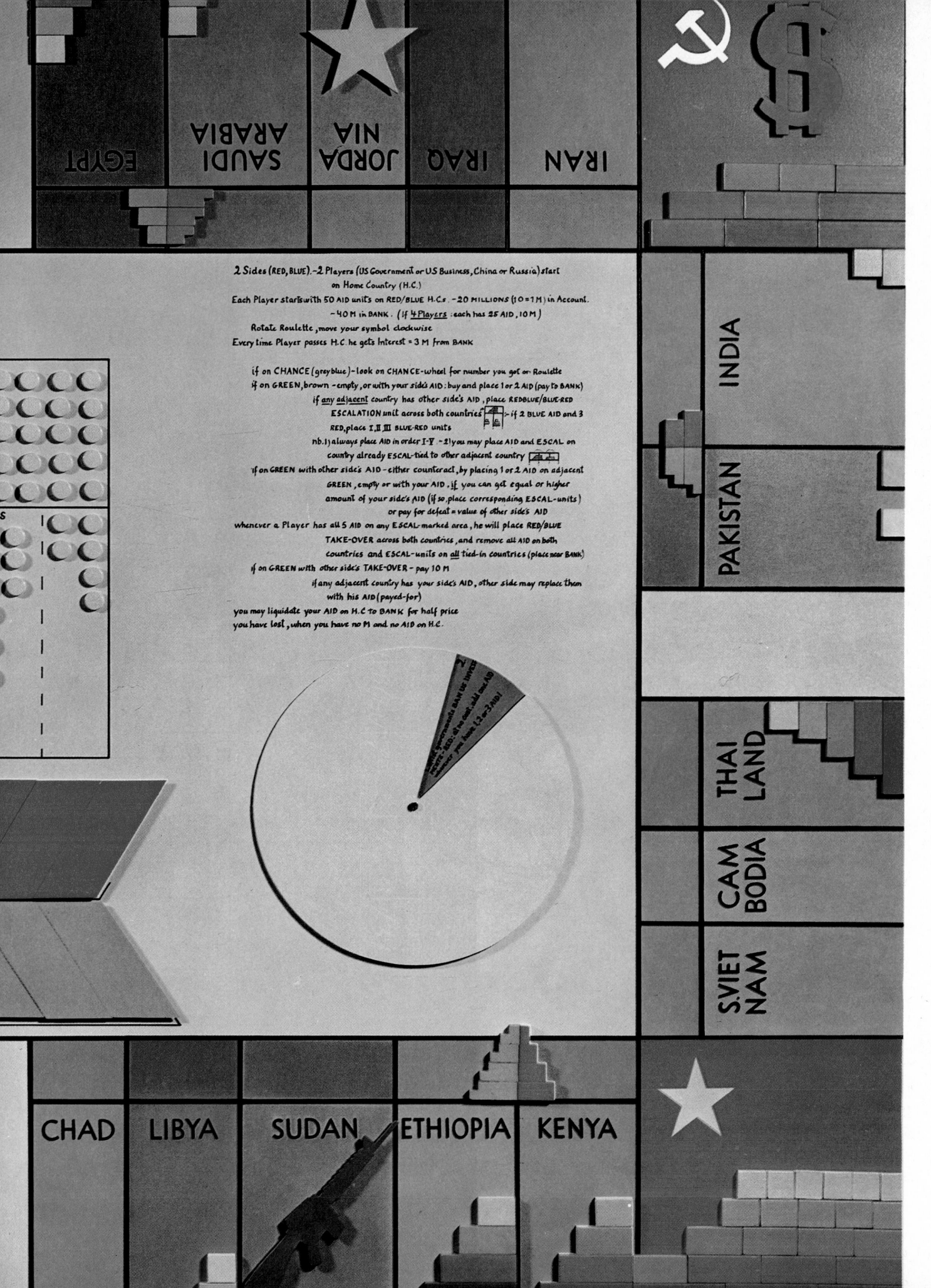

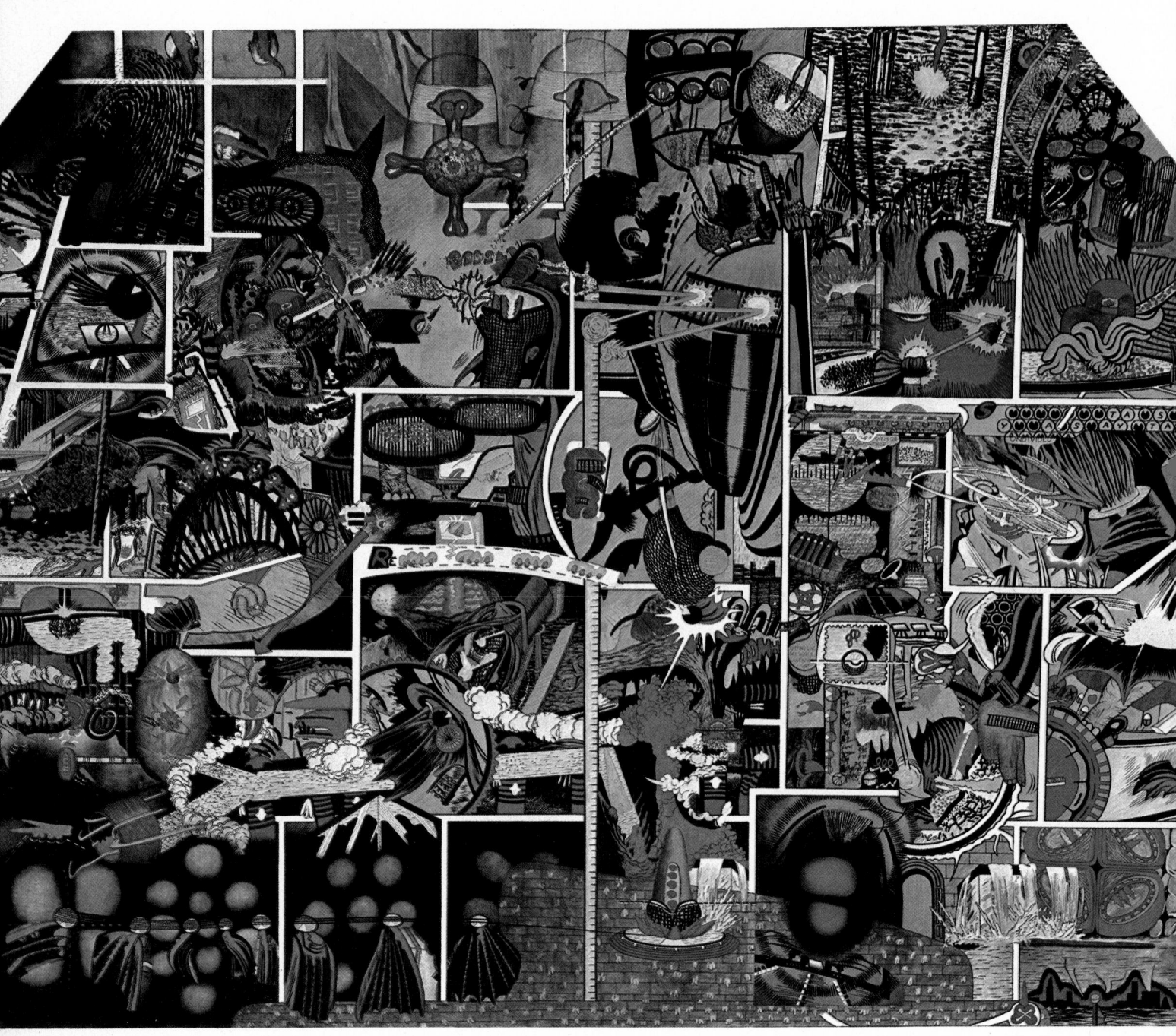

209. Overleaf
Öyvind Fahlström
World Trade Monopoly
1970; 63.5 × 98 cm. (25 × 38 in.)
New York, by kind permission of the Sidney Janis Gallery

210.
Öyvind Fahlström
Eddie in the Desert
1966; 77.5 × 128 cm. (30 × 50 in.)
Stockholm, Moderna Museet

270

211. Overleaf
Erró (Gudmundur Gudmundson)
Foodscape
1964; 201 × 303 cm. (78 × 118 in.)
Stockholm, Moderna Museet

his métier as a painter, and has produced an increasingly impressive body of work.

Pop has often been thought of, in the English-speaking countries, as an exclusively Anglo-American phenomenon. The large survey exhibition, "Pop Art Redefined", organized by John Russell and Suzi Gablik in London in 1969 contained only one artist not usually domiciled either in Britain or in the United States. This was the Swede Öyvind Fahlström, who in any case keeps in close touch with what is going on in New York. But his work, nevertheless, has traits which mark it off from the British or American product. The chief of these is its didacticism. Fahlström tells himself to "Consider art as a way of experiencing a fusion of 'pleasure' and 'insight'. Reach this by impurity, or multiplicity of levels, rather than by reduction. . . . The importance of bisociation (Koestler). In painting, factual images of erotic or political character, for example, bisociated, within a game-framework, with each other and/or with 'abstract' elements (character-forms), will not exclude but may incite to 'meditational' experiences. These, in turn, do not exclude probing on everyday moral, social levels" (statement from *Pop Art Redefined*, by John Russell and Suzi Gablik, London, 1969, p. 68). What he means by this may perhaps be deduced by looking at a work such as his *World Trade Monopoly* (Plate 209), where the political situation of 1970 is interpreted in terms of a well-known board game.

The humour in Fahlström's work is, despite his close links with the American art world, recognizably European in character, with an irony which resembles that of Bertolt Brecht rather than that of Andy Warhol because it is directed towards making an absolutely specific moral point.

The Pop Art produced by Scandinavian or German artists does in fact have a rigorous, uncompromising quality which seems to mark it off from that created elsewhere. The Icelandic painter Erró has been associated with the Paris avant-garde, but his teeming *Foodscape* (Plate 211) has an Expressionist quality which gives Pop subject-matter a completely new twist and which seems recognizably northern in its satire upon an oppressive abundance. By contrast, there is a northern bleakness about the highway image in Peter Brüning's *Autobahndenkmal* (Plate 212) which makes the image seem different from those created by Ruscha and D'Arcangelo, though these have clearly exercised an influence.

For northerners, Pop might seem a contemporary extension of the long-standing realist tradition. For Frenchmen, on the other hand, its status was more controversial. By the time Pop Art arose, the Paris art world was already worried by the threat to its hegemony represented by New York. Pop, with its American accent, was not sure of a welcome, and French artists who adopted Pop techniques and attitudes ran the risk of arousing the chauvinism of their own countrymen. In addition to this, Pop culture was less deeply rooted in France than it was in either Britain or America, and what was commonplace in the English-speaking countries (the excesses of consumer advertising, for example) still seemed exotic in France.

Despite this, the attraction of the Pop movement was so powerful that a number of French artists were drawn into its ranks. The one who achieved the most widespread international reputation was Martial Raysse, partly through his association with the New Realism group formed by Pierre Restany. Among Raysse's most typical works are his new versions of classic paintings—for instance, the paraphrase of an Ingres *Baigneuse* illustrated here (Plate 213). The artist has always denied that there is any sarcastic intention in these works, and the claim has been repeated by his admirers: "Martial Raysse has taken the colors and textures of this attractive world of the supermarket and made a poem of them. The colors are the lurid pastel and fluorescent ones of useful articles: the textures are those of new aluminum, plastic and nylon . . . unlike some of his colleagues he is not trying to put across an ironic message. Things are left as they are. 'I want everything in my work to be good-looking and brand-new,' he once said wistfully" (John Ashbery, from the catalogue introduction to the "Raysse Beach" exhibition at the Dwan Gallery, Los Angeles, 1965). Otto Hahn has spoken of Raysse's desire to artificially penetrate life, to beautify, to reach

271

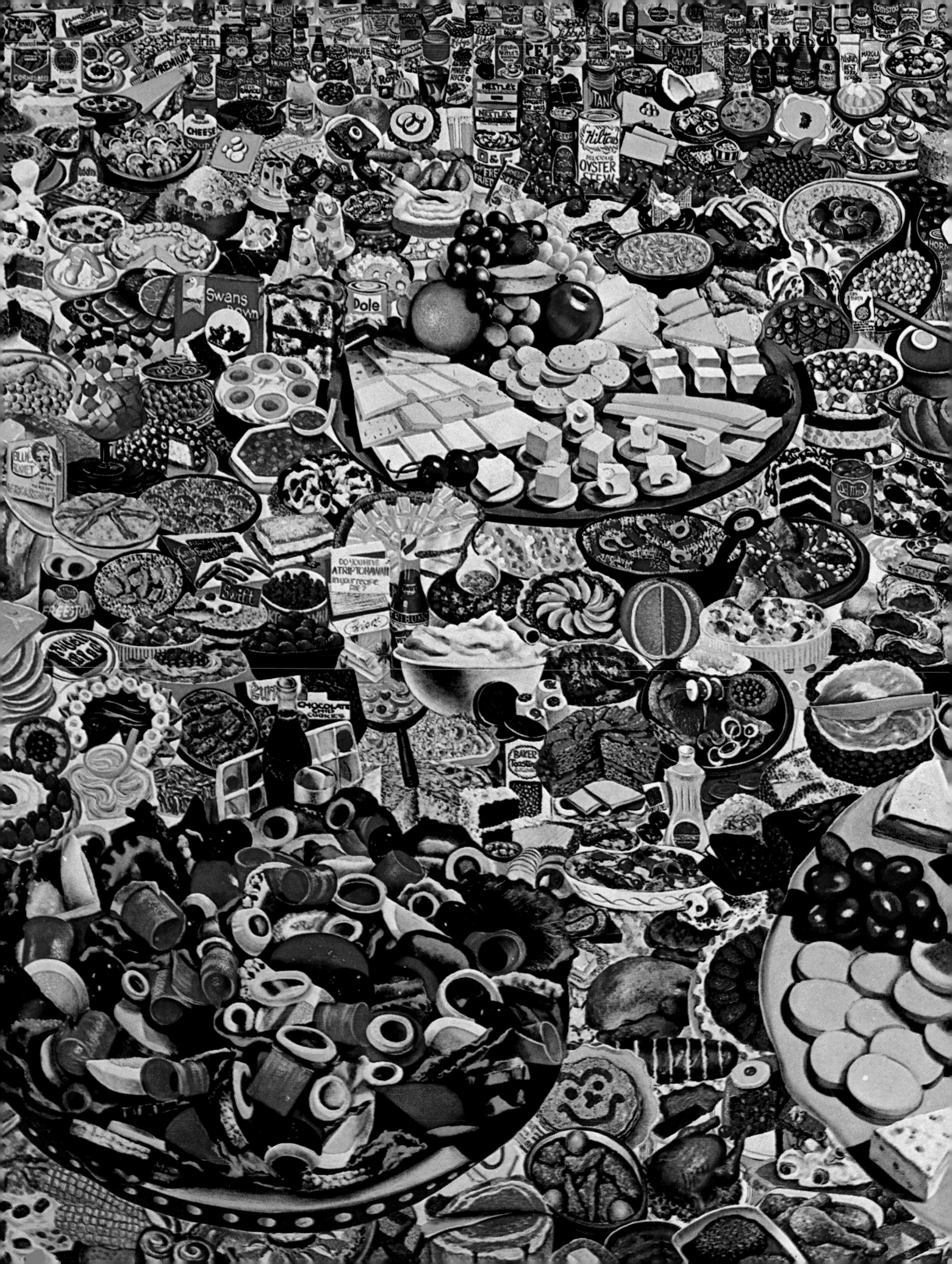

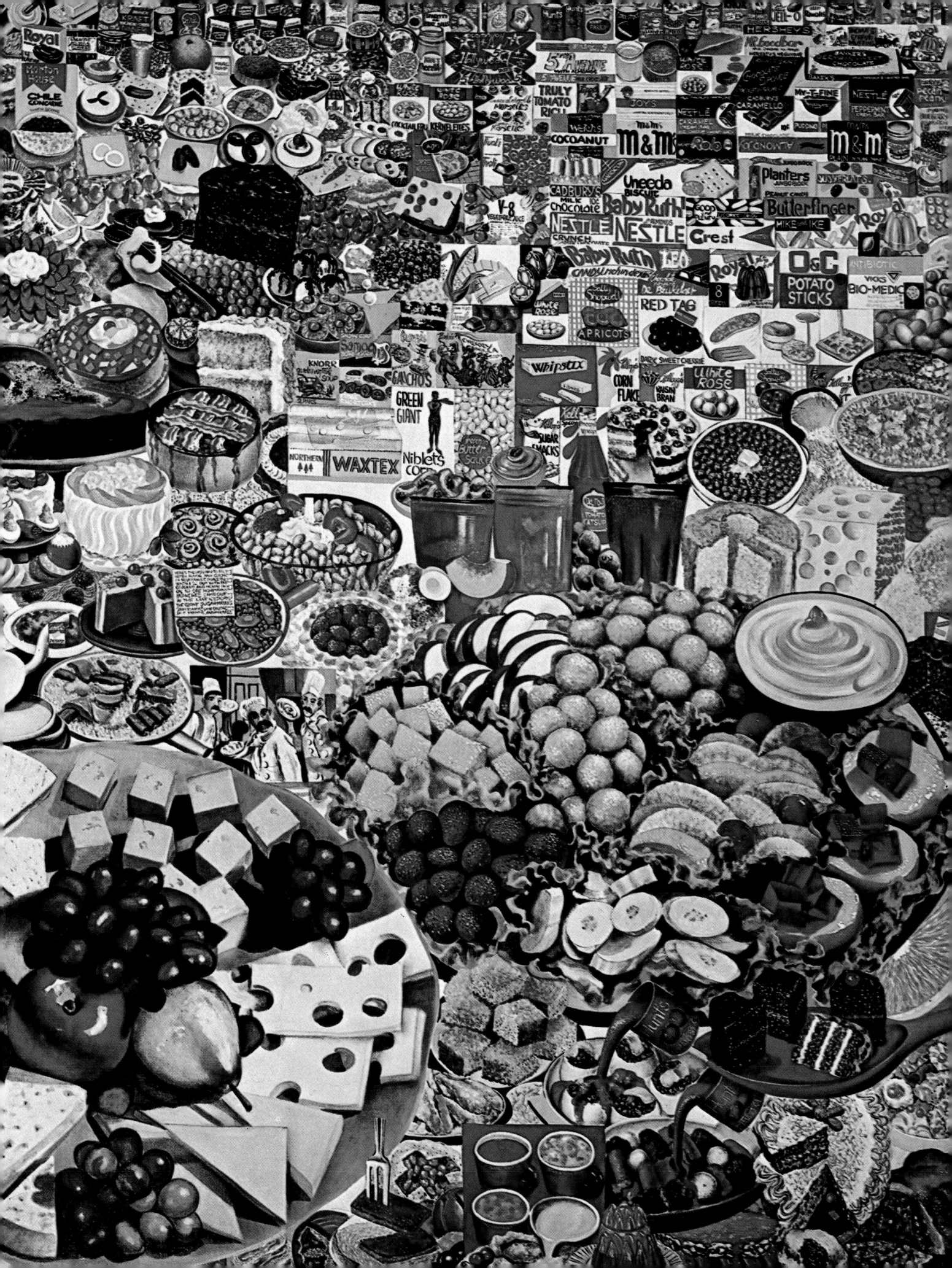

212.
Peter Brüning
Autobahndenkmal
1968; 42 × 75.5 cm. (16 × 29 in.)
Düsseldorf, coll. Heinz Beck

213. Opposite
Martial Raysse
Made in Japan in Martialcolor
1964; 116 × 89 cm. (45 × 35 in.)
Archives Galerie Alexandre Iolas, New York, Paris,
Geneva, Milan, Rome

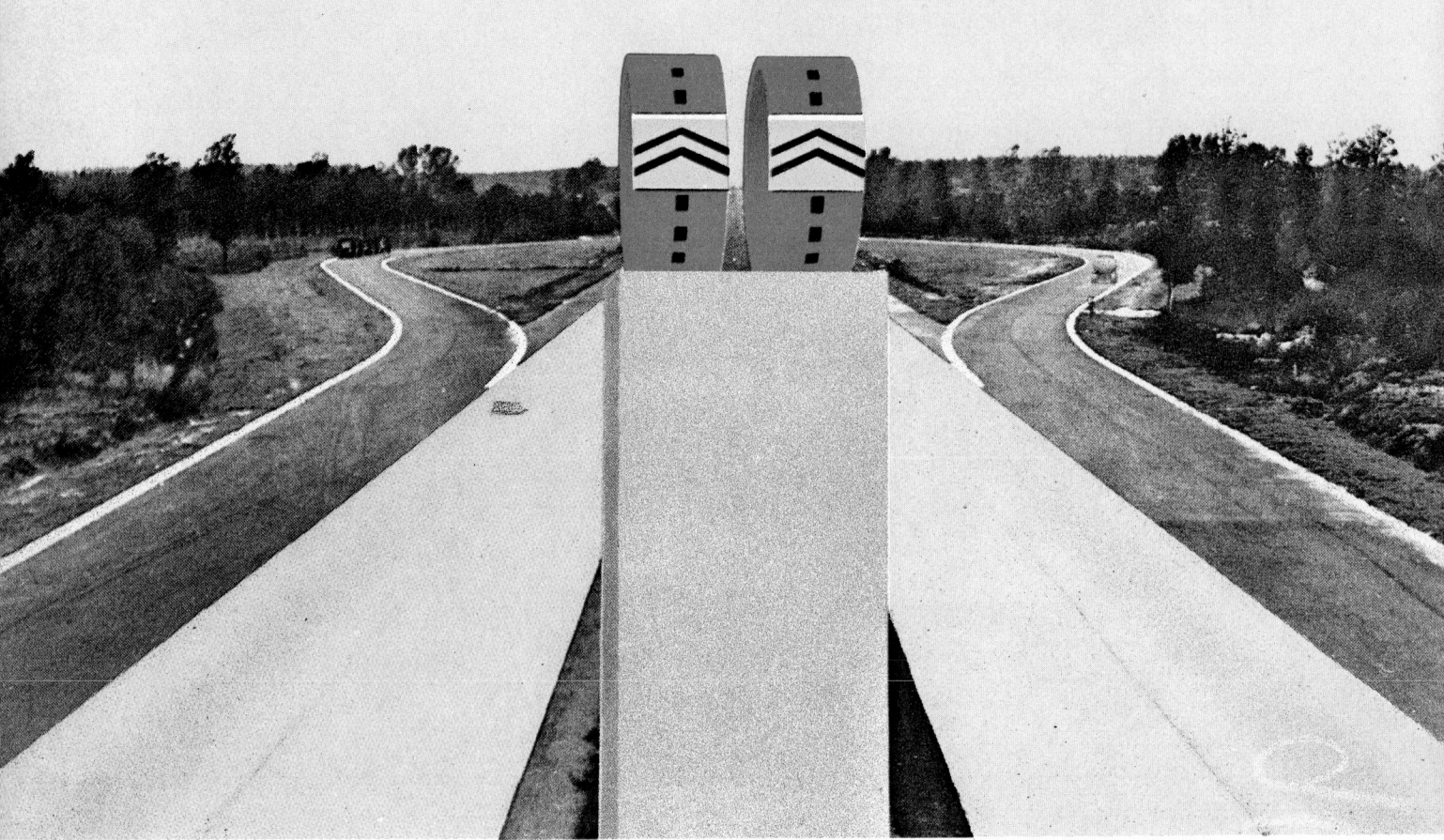

by any means the highest degree of intensity".

What this means in practice is the extensive application of "bad taste"—neon tubes in garish colours, surfaces flocked with plastic fibres in vivid colours—to images which are usually considered the height of "good taste". It is as if Raysse feels that these images have lost all intensity, and need to be rescued by the means that lie closest to hand, however drastic the process may seem.

Other French Pop artists such as Alain Jacquet and Jacques Monory give the same impression of being burdened to the point of rebellion by the artistic tradition which they have inherited. Jacquet (Plates 215 and 216) has made extensive use of photomechanical processes as a way of alienating familiar material, and of making the

spectator look at it with a fresh eye. Monory (Plate 217) also relies heavily on the transforming power of the camera, and on the emotional distance imposed by his monochrome colour schemes: "What Monory does is to bring us back to this prison of familiar gestures whose significance eludes us like certain faces in the blue and rose mist of his canvases. A certain lassitude seems to be the price of this effort to achieve lucidity without illusions, where woman plays the role of sovereign palliative and omnipresent idol" (Gérald Gassiot-Talabot, catalogue introduction to "Jacques Monory—Velvet Jungle/NY", Amsterdam, Stedelijk Museum, 1972).

Much of Monory's work has the same fugitive quality and the same emotional ambiguity as the films of French New Wave moviemakers.

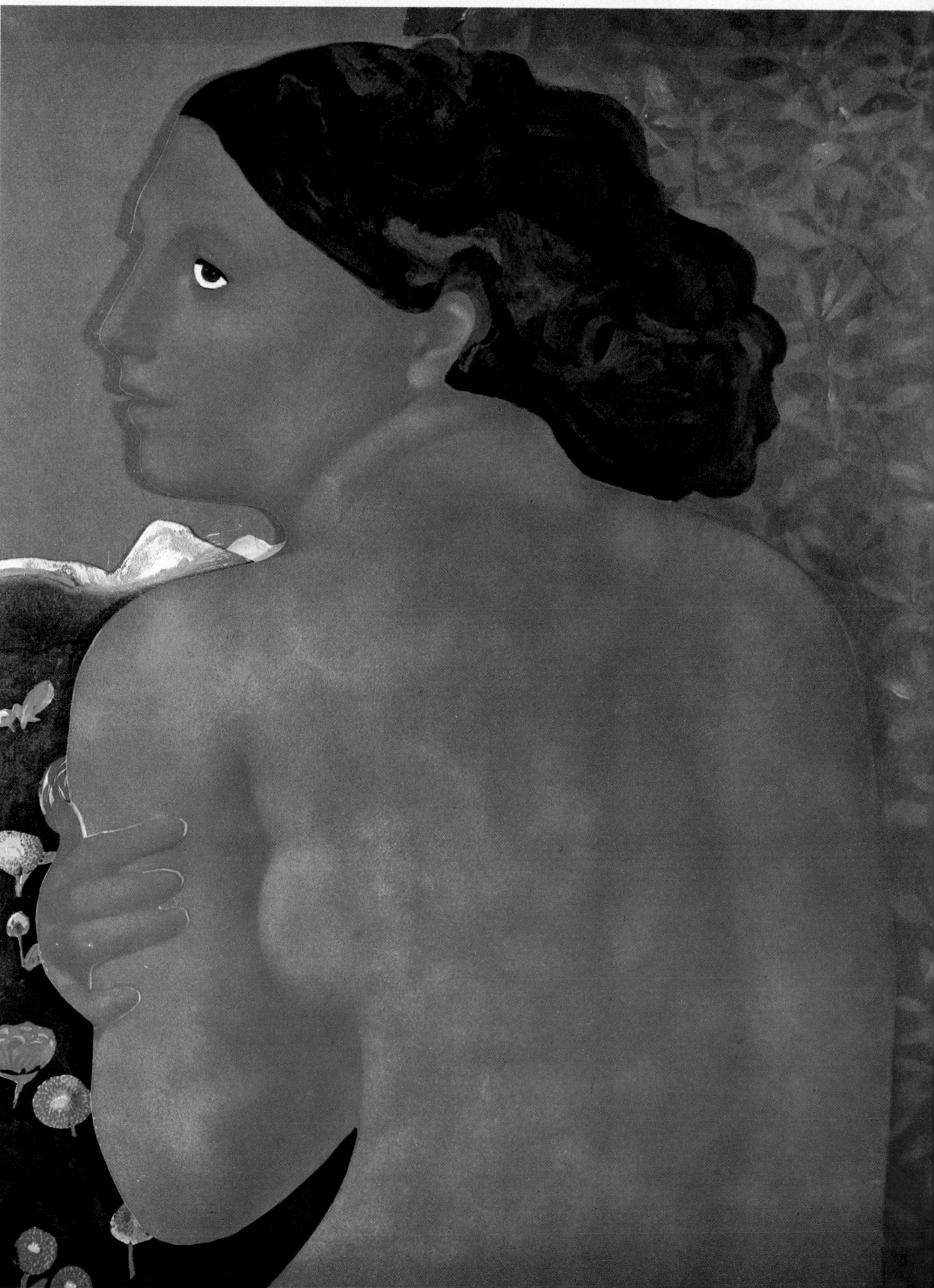

214.
Martial Raysse
Simple and Tranquil Painting
1965; 129.5 × 175.6 × 16.5 cm. (51 × 68 × 6 in.)
Cologne, Wallraf-Richartz Museum, coll. Ludwig

215. Opposite
Alain Jacquet
The Rape of Europa
1965; 76 × 53.5 cm. (30 × 21 in.)
Düsseldorf, coll. Heinz Beck

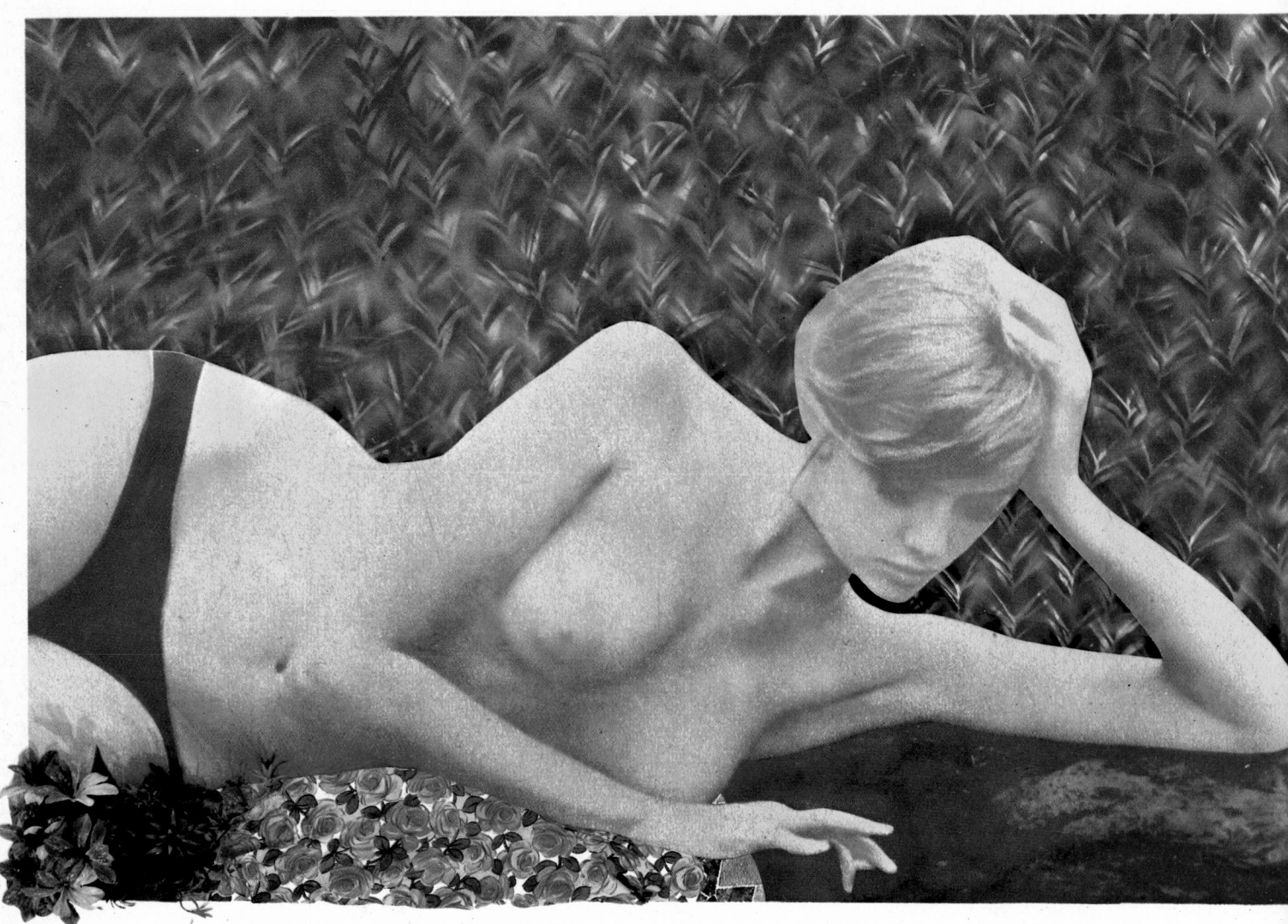

The extreme degree of contrast between the women who appear in Monory's work and the cheerful "Nanas" created by Niki de Saint-Phalle (Plate 218) prompts one to reflect on what now, in the mid-Seventies, seems the least acceptable aspect of the Pop Art movement in general, which was its conspicuous streak of male chauvinism. Almost everywhere they appeared in Pop painting or in Pop sculpture, women were represented as mere objects. They were allowed no independent existence outside the confines of male fantasy. Saint-Phalle's figurines offer a striking contrast to Allen Jones's fetishistic sculptures. Bulging and brightly decorated, they seem to echo female,

rather than male, fantasies about the female body and female existence. As "sculpture" they are essentially and endearingly unpretentious.

Another French artist who produced sculpture in a recognizably Pop idiom was the chameleon-like César, whose giant versions of his own thumb (Plate 219) fall into this category, and seem to offer a Parisian equivalent to Oldenburg. But it is difficult to find these mammoth examples of self-glorification original or significant, especially as they seem, though unconsciously, to echo so many Renaissance notions concerning the artist as divine creator.

Pop also had its impact upon the art scene in

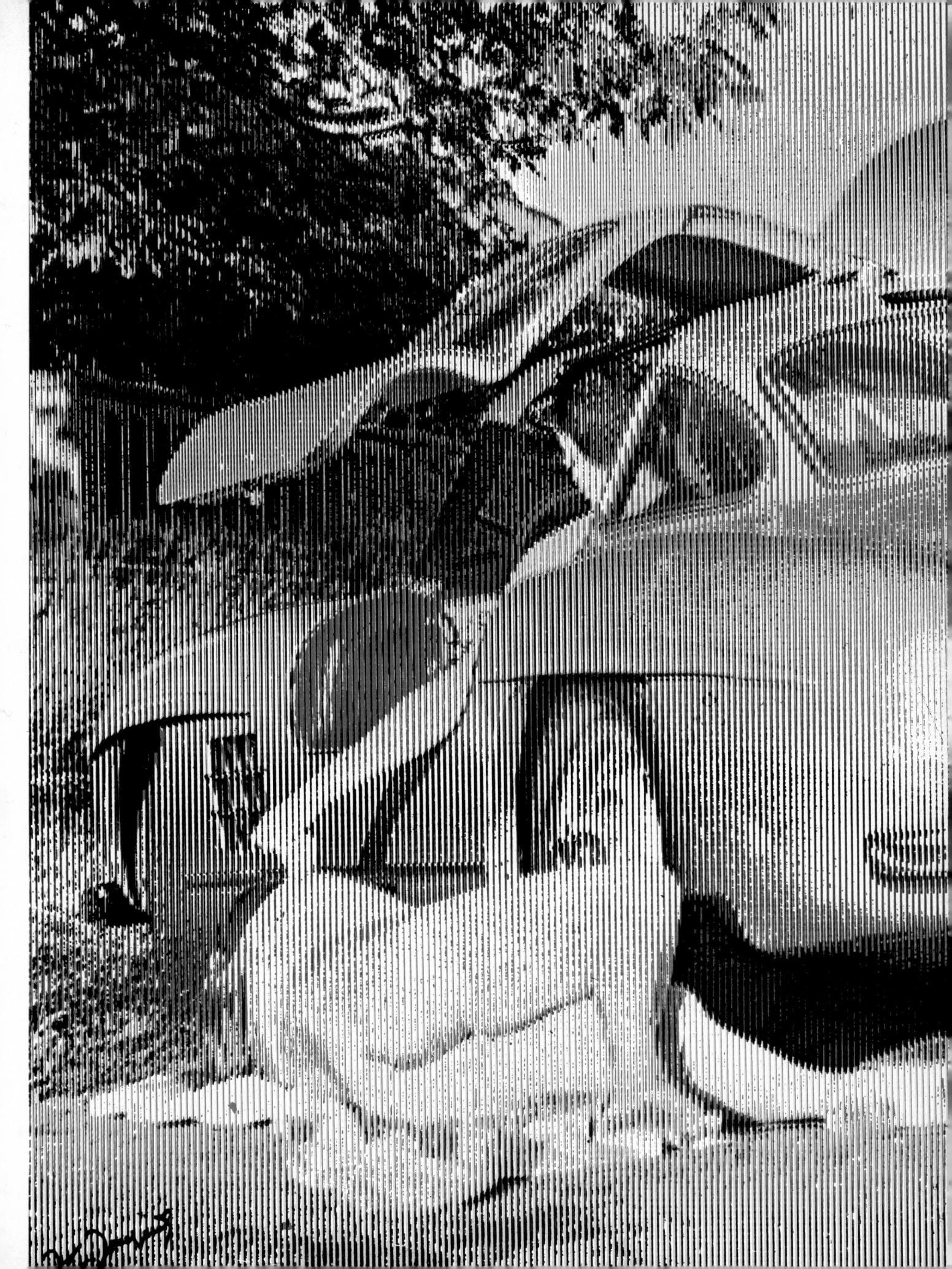

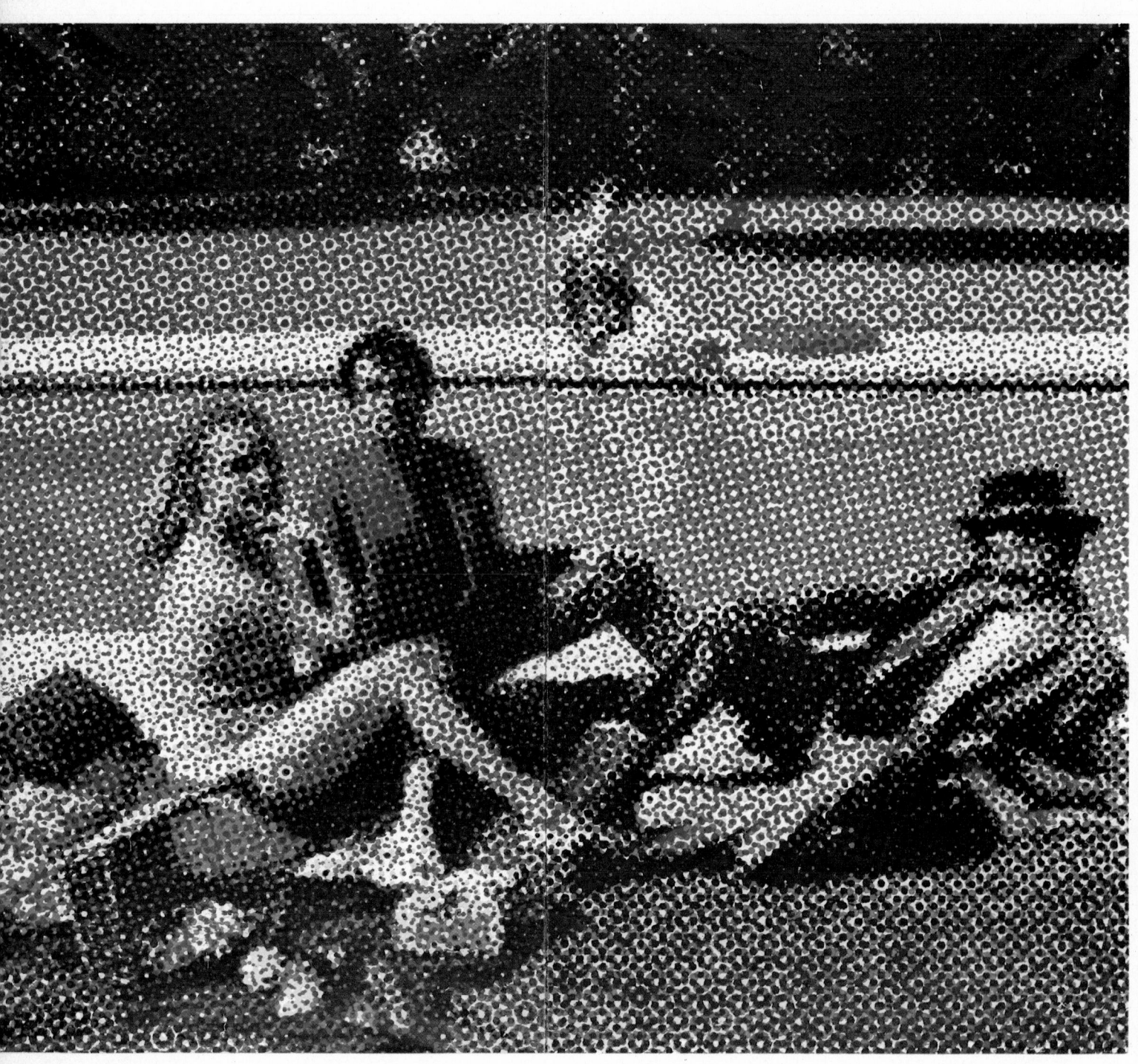

216.
Alain Jacquet
Déjeuner sur l'herbe
1964; 175 × 197 cm. (68 × 77 in.)
Rome, Galleria Nazionale d'Arte Moderna

217. Opposite
Jacques Monory
Hypersensitive
1970; 201 × 150 cm. (78 × 59 in.)
Aachen, Neue Galerie, coll. Ludwig

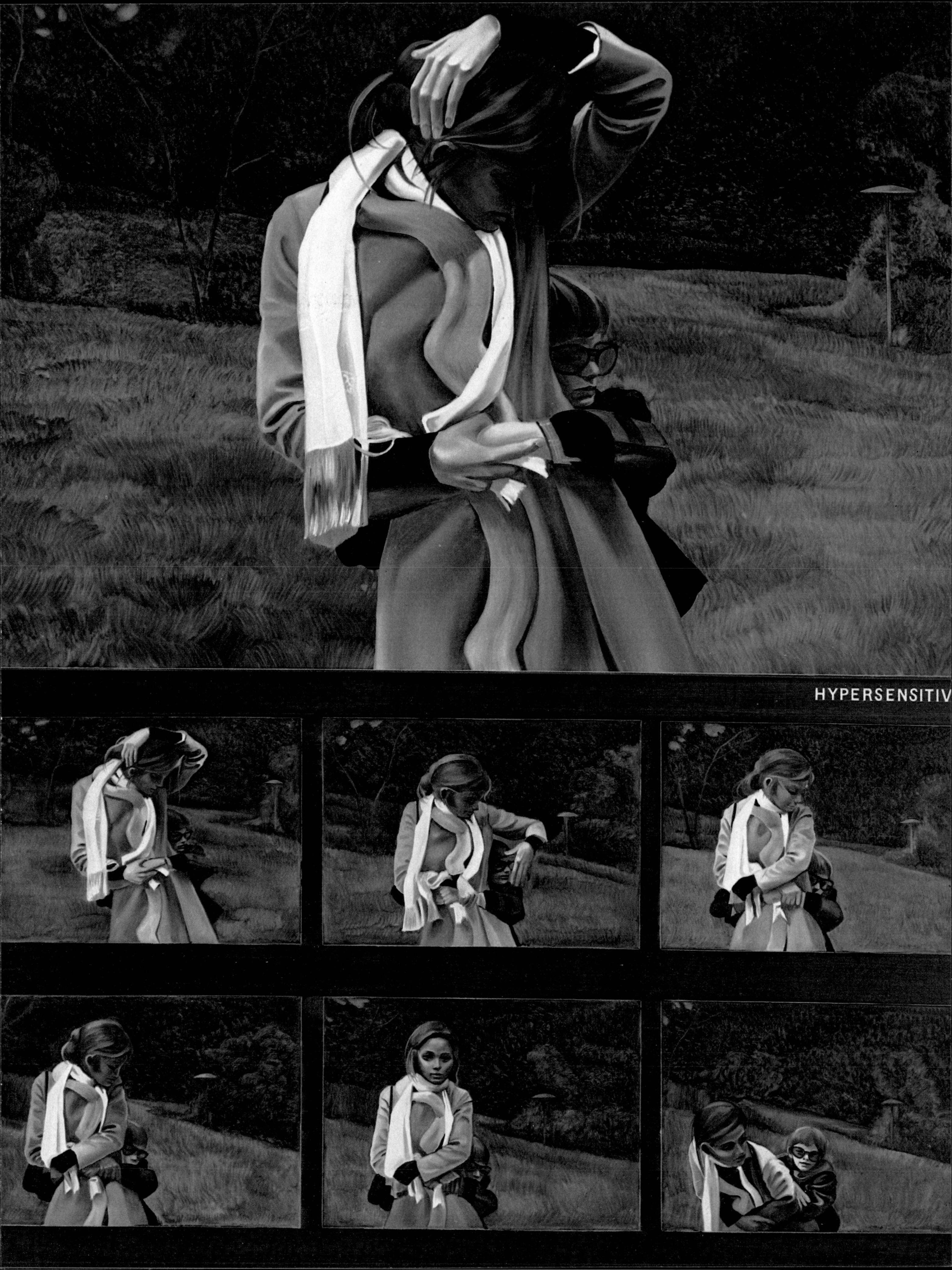

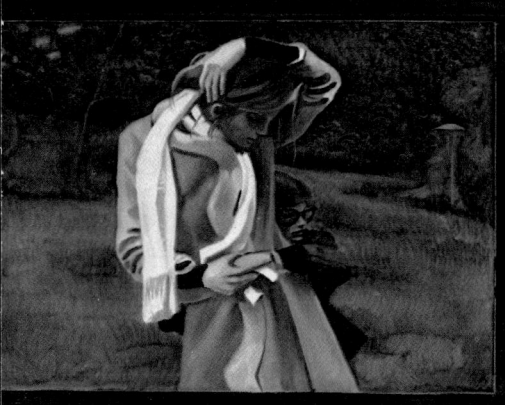

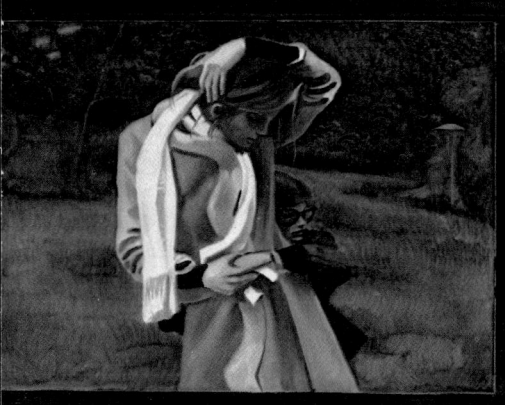
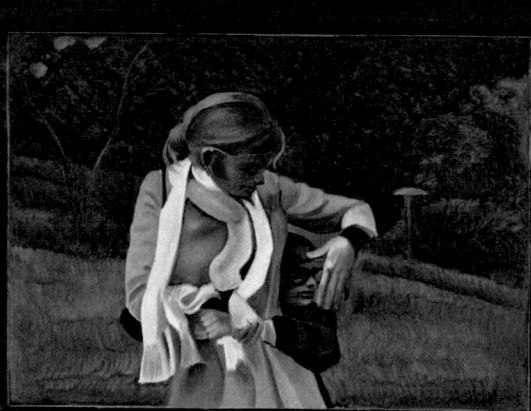
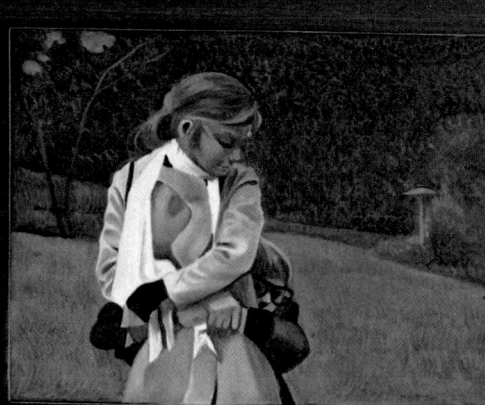
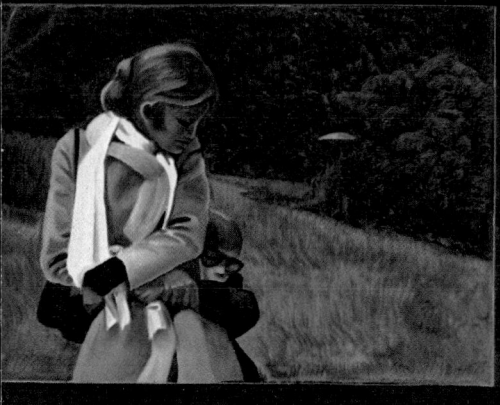
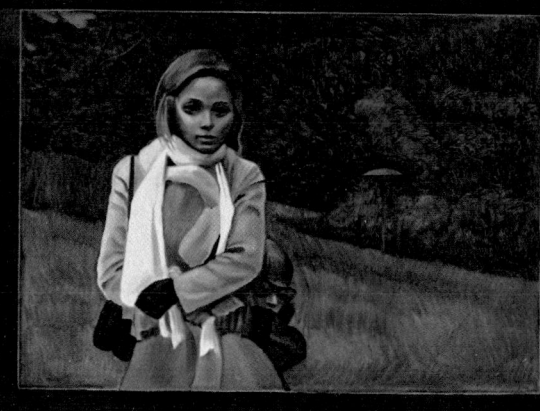
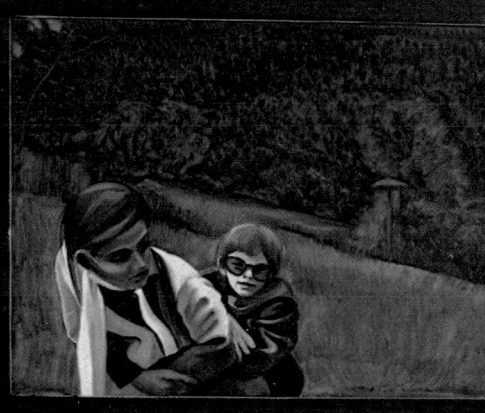

218.
Niki de Saint-Phalle
Un Ensemble de "Les Nanas"
1965;
Archives Galerie Alexandre Iolas, New York, Paris,
Geneva, Milan, Rome

219. Opposite
César (César Baldaccini)
Le Pouce
1976; 90 × 50 × 42 cm. (35 × 20 × 16 in.)
Paris, Galerie Claude Bernard

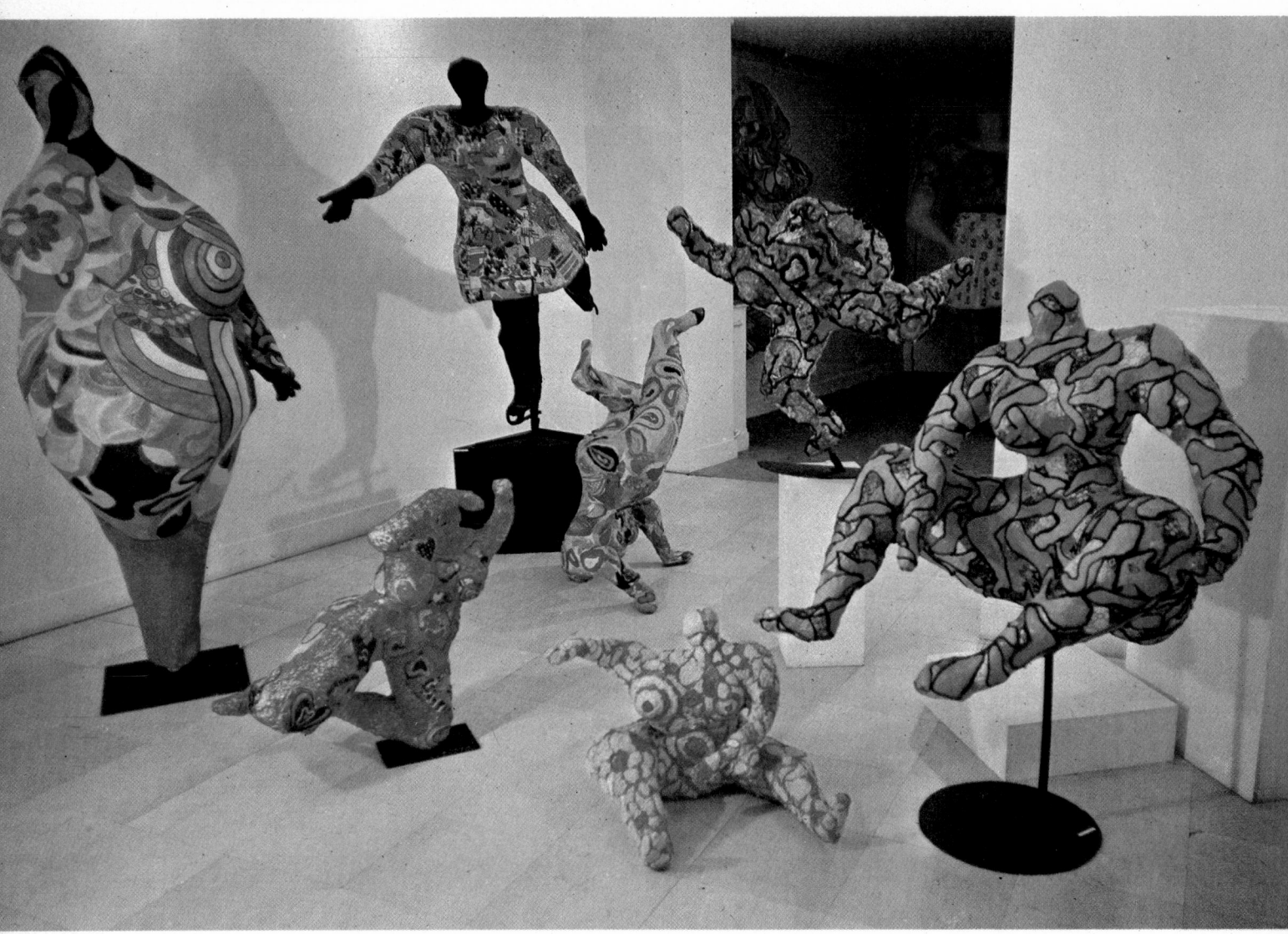

Italy, and here the results were perhaps more interesting than they were in France. Some Italian artists had close connections with those in Paris. One of these was Mimmo Rotella (rather older than most Pop artists, since he was born in 1918), who, like Raysse and César, formed part of Restany's band of New Realists. Rotella's place in the Pop pantheon was earned by a series of collages made of torn posters and newspapers mounted on canvas (Plate 220). These were a translation into "gallery" terms of the accidental conjunctions which the artist saw in the streets.

Another Italian artist who won widespread acceptance in Paris was Valerio Adami, who in 1970 was the subject of a large-scale retrospective at the Musée de l'Art Moderne de la Ville de Paris. From the point of view of technique, the nearest equivalent to Adami's work is that of Patrick Caulfield. We meet again there the hard black outlines, with the intervening areas filled with flat colour (Plate 221). But Adami does not depict his subject-matter with Caulfield's literalism. He declares: "I think the spectator should relive, in his own way, the formative process which the image

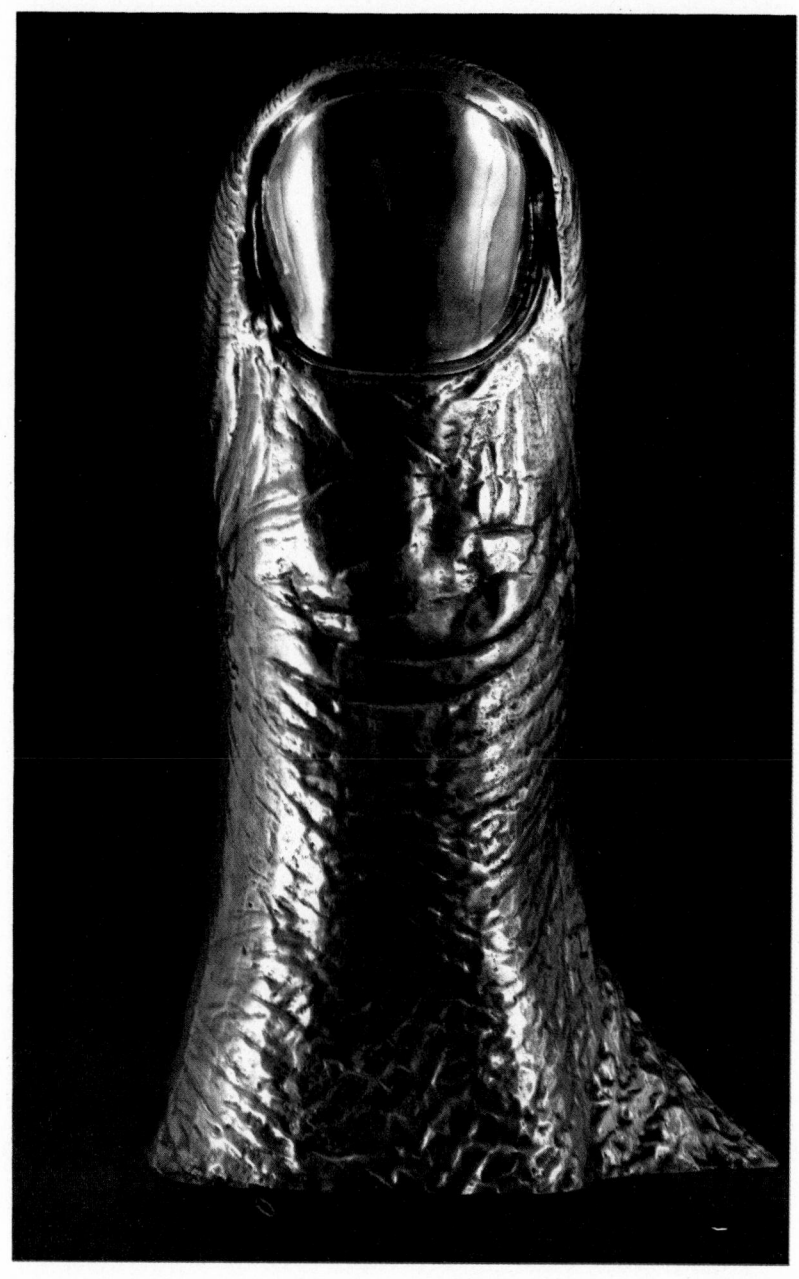

has followed. He should not find himself faced with a closed, immobile object. He should find himself implicated in something which is still in the process of happening. The picture is a complex proposition in which anterior visual experiences form unpredictable combinations; the imagination creating incessantly new associations—one image expands into another and its original form is in continual transformation" (from the catalogue of the exhibition "Adami Privacy Galerie", by B. Mommaton, Paris, 1968).

In practice this means a compromise between Surrealism and Pop. The metamorphoses familiar from Surrealist paintings present themselves, in Adami's work, not with the three-dimensional actuality familiar from the painting of Dali and Tanguy, or with the melting painterliness which we find in the mature works of Arshile Gorky, but with heraldic flatness and toughness of outline.

Other Italians connected with the Pop movement show a fascination with observed reality which takes us back to the great tradition of Italian art, and especially to Caravaggio. The most literal interpretation of "realism" is that provided by

220.
Mimmo Rotella
Omaggio al Presidente
1963; 82 × 175 cm. (32 × 68 in.)
Paris, Galerie Mathias Fels

221. Opposite
Valerio Adami
Interno coloniale
1976; 198 × 147 cm. (77 × 57 in.)
Paris, Musée National d'Art Moderne, loaned by the
Centre National d'Art Contemporain

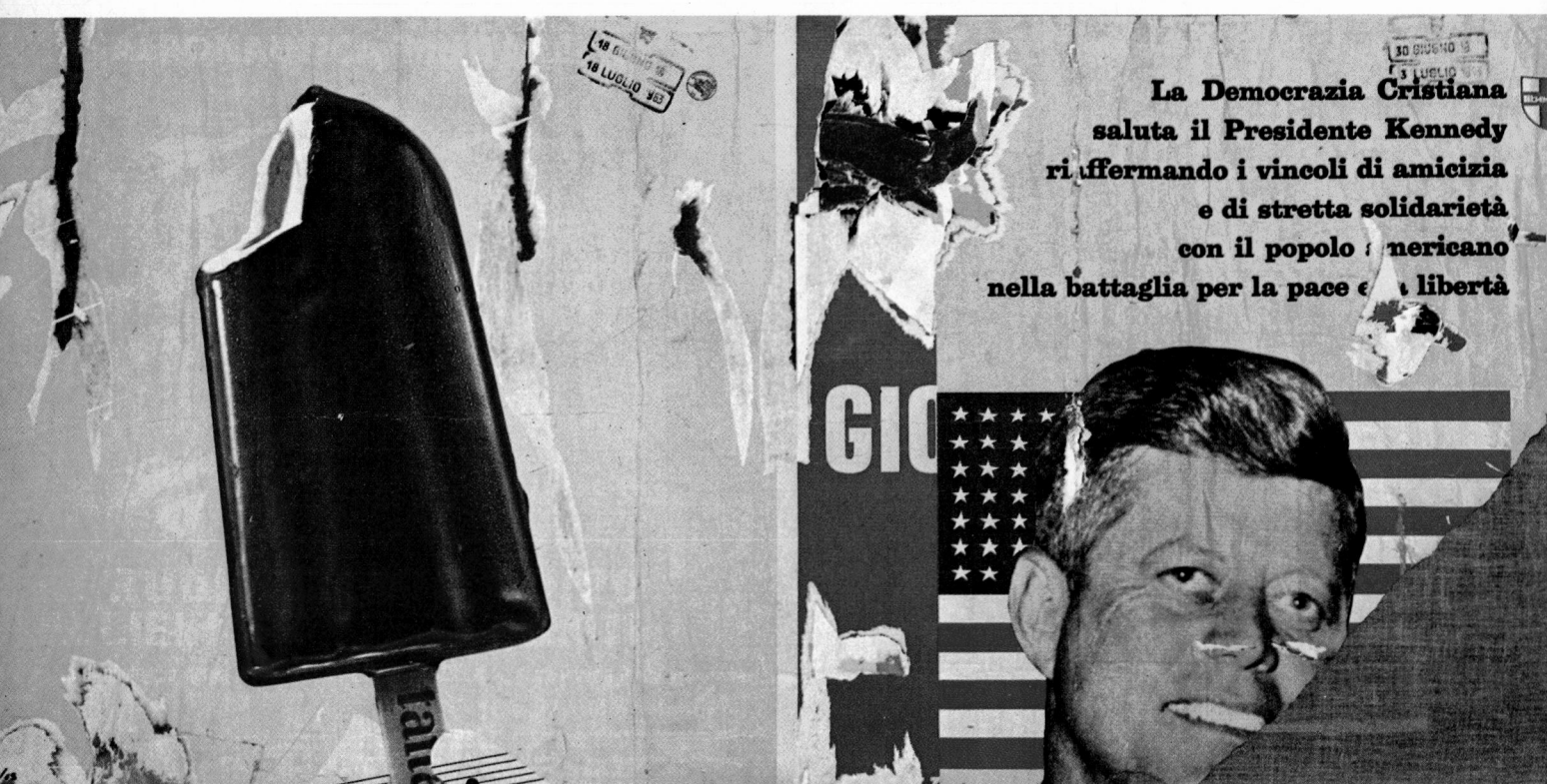

Michelangelo Pistoletto. He made a series of "mirror paintings" by reproducing photographs of people and everyday objects on sheets of polished steel. To these the spectator becomes a random addition, as he stands in front of the work (Plate 223). This has led the critic Henry Martin to deny that Pistoletto is a Pop artist in any recognizable sense: "His paintings are the meeting place of several different kinds of vision, and the meaning of the paintings lies in the way that these kinds of vision interact and manage to transform themselves into a single new and different and perhaps 'visionary' vision. Whereas Pop, along with its equivalents and predecessors, is a search for metaphor within reality and with respect to objects abstracted from their representation of reality. Pistoletto is at one step removed—he plays a game with the various orders of reality and does not fall in love with the photographic reality he reproduces. The absolute staticness of the photographs became the absolute immobility of the represented figure. The 'instant death' quality of

the photograph became translated into the figure's absolute expressionlessness" (Henry Martin, introduction to the catalogue of the Pistoletto exhibition, Museum Boymans-van Beuningen, Rotterdam, 1969).

Piero Gilardi has a more romantic, even sentimental, approach, with his painstaking three-dimensional reproductions of natural things (Plate 222). He says: "I have faith in our technological civilization, because it can reproduce the facts of nature while triumphing over death." Fragments of existence, separated from the context in which we usually find them, and brought to our attention without apparent editing, take on a strangely touching and vulnerable quality.

Another Italian artist with an interest in the apparently insignificant fragment was the late Domenico Gnoli. Gnoli's speciality was extreme close-up views of perfectly ordinary things, but particularly of clothing (Plate 224). These, in his hands, acquired hallucinatory intensity, thanks chiefly to an accomplished but never showy

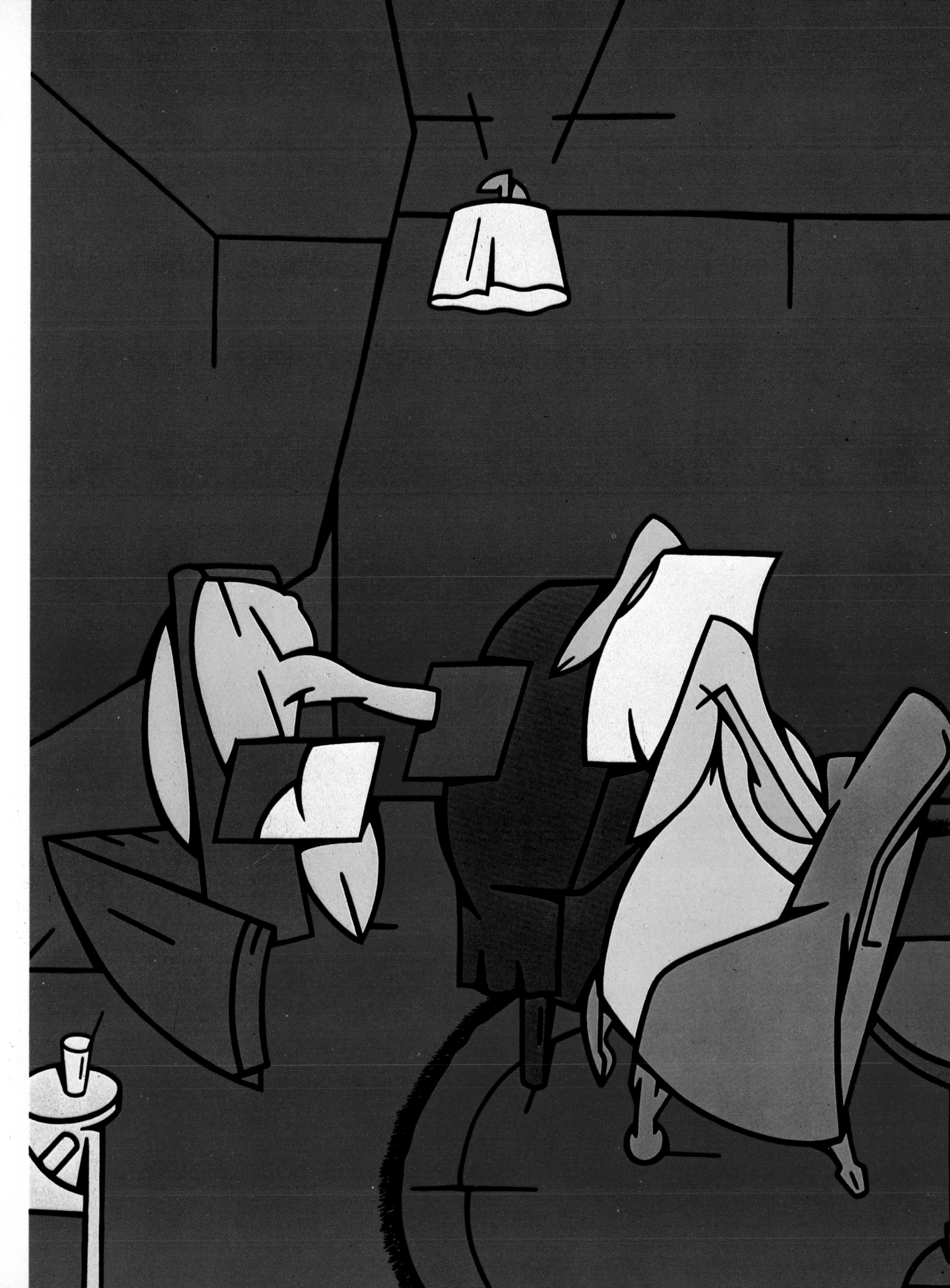

222.
Piero Gilardi
Orto
1967; 160 × 160 cm. (62 × 62 in.)
Boston, The 180 Beacon Collection

223. Opposite
Michelangelo Pistoletto
Uomo che legge
1968; 228 × 120 cm. (89 × 47 in.)
New York, Kornblee Gallery

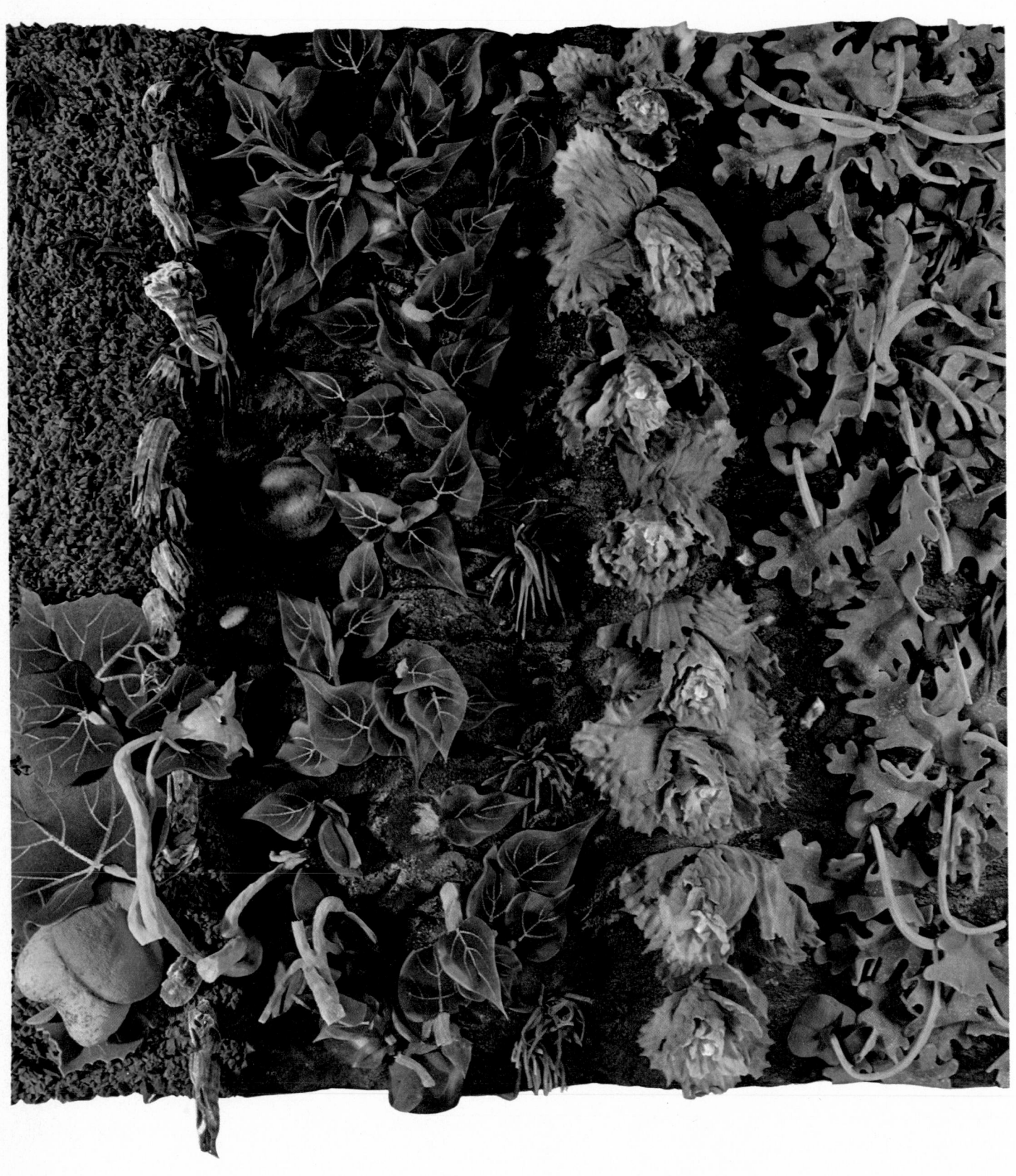

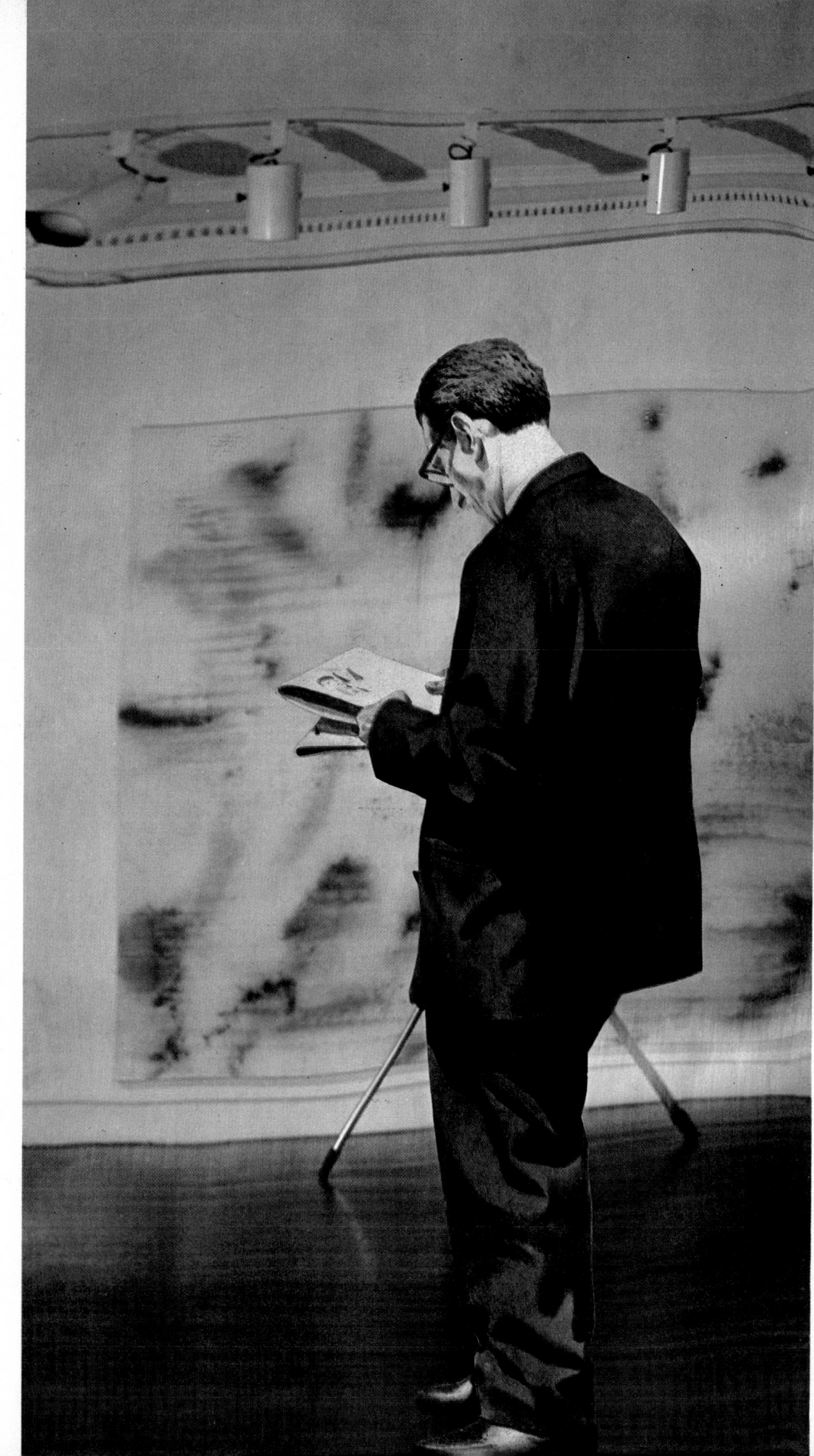

224.
Domenico Gnoli
Uomo double-face
1964; 149 × 72 cm. (58 × 28 in.)
Cologne, Wallraf-Richartz Museum, coll. Ludwig

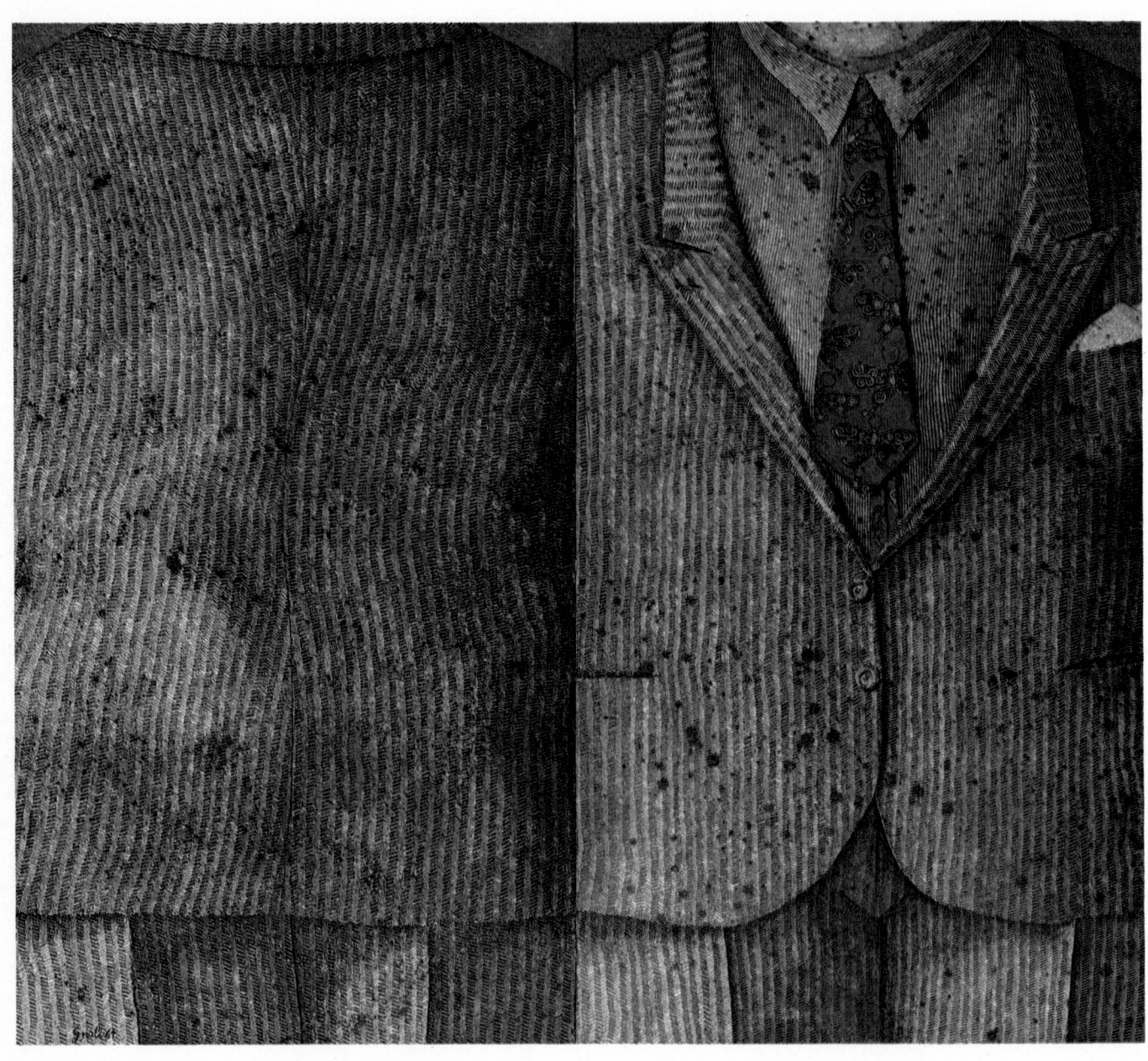

technique. Gnoli's paintings communicate the value and the strangeness of quotidian existence, and in this sense they are outside the Pop tradition and in direct line of descent from the still-life painting of Giorgio Morandi. Gnoli's wonderful control of tone and texture was in marked contrast to the deliberate cheapness of much of the fashionable painting produced during the 1960's.

In Spain, hardly any art appeared which deserved the Pop label, chiefly, and quite logically, because Spain was still to a large extent a preindustrial society. The nearest approach to convincingly popular imagery was to be found in the ominous paintings of Juan Genovés (Plate 225), which looked like excerpts taken at random from news reels showing riots, executions, civil

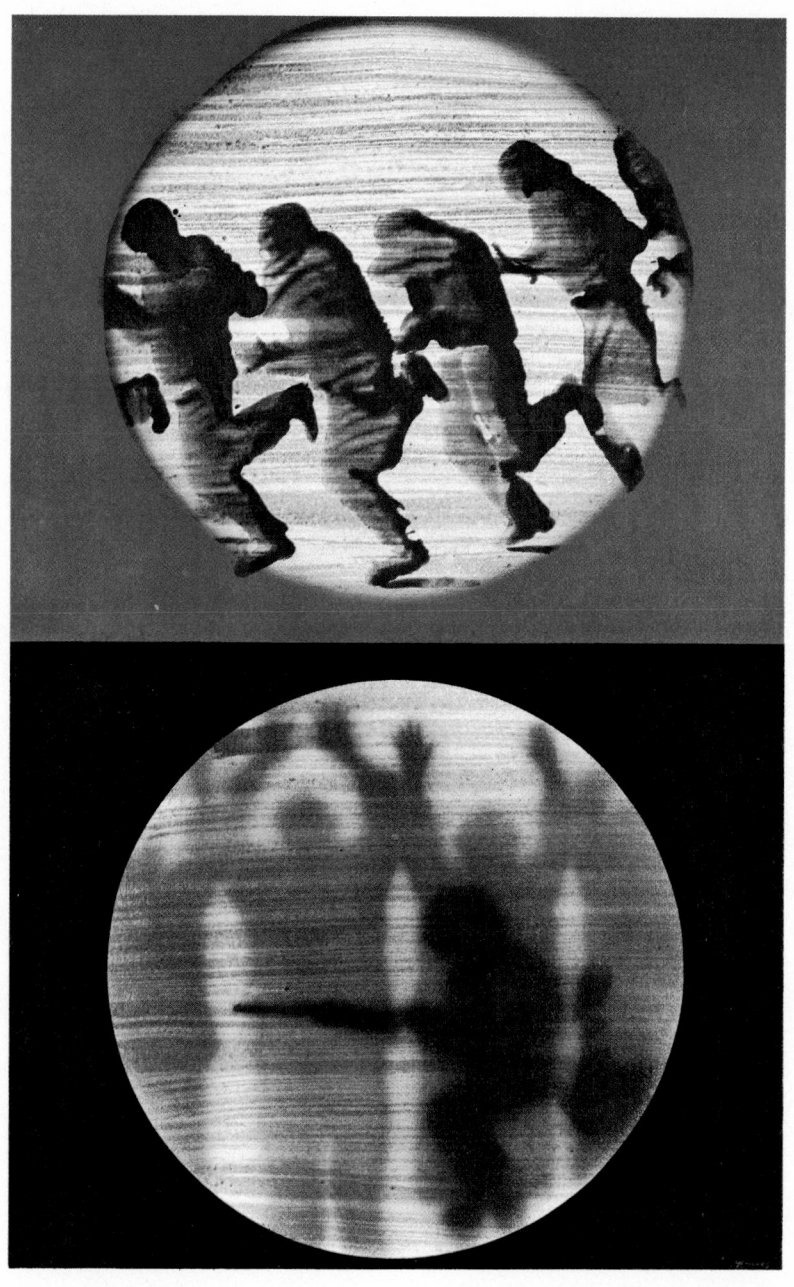

war, and revolution. It was a strange kind of art to make its emergence under the still repressive regime of General Franco. In fact, Genovés seems to intend his paintings not so much as a report on the condition of the world as it is now, but as a kind of prophetic dream of an apocalyse to come. They thus, like Adami's work, contain a strong Surrealist element. What does relate them to Pop Art, however, is the decision to rely on the way the camera sees, as recorded on film, rather than on the way the eye sees (or upon the mind's interpretation of what is brought to it by the eye).

Finally, something must be said about the progress of Pop Art in the only fully industrialized nation in Asia. The style enjoyed an enormous success in Japan, far greater than that of other

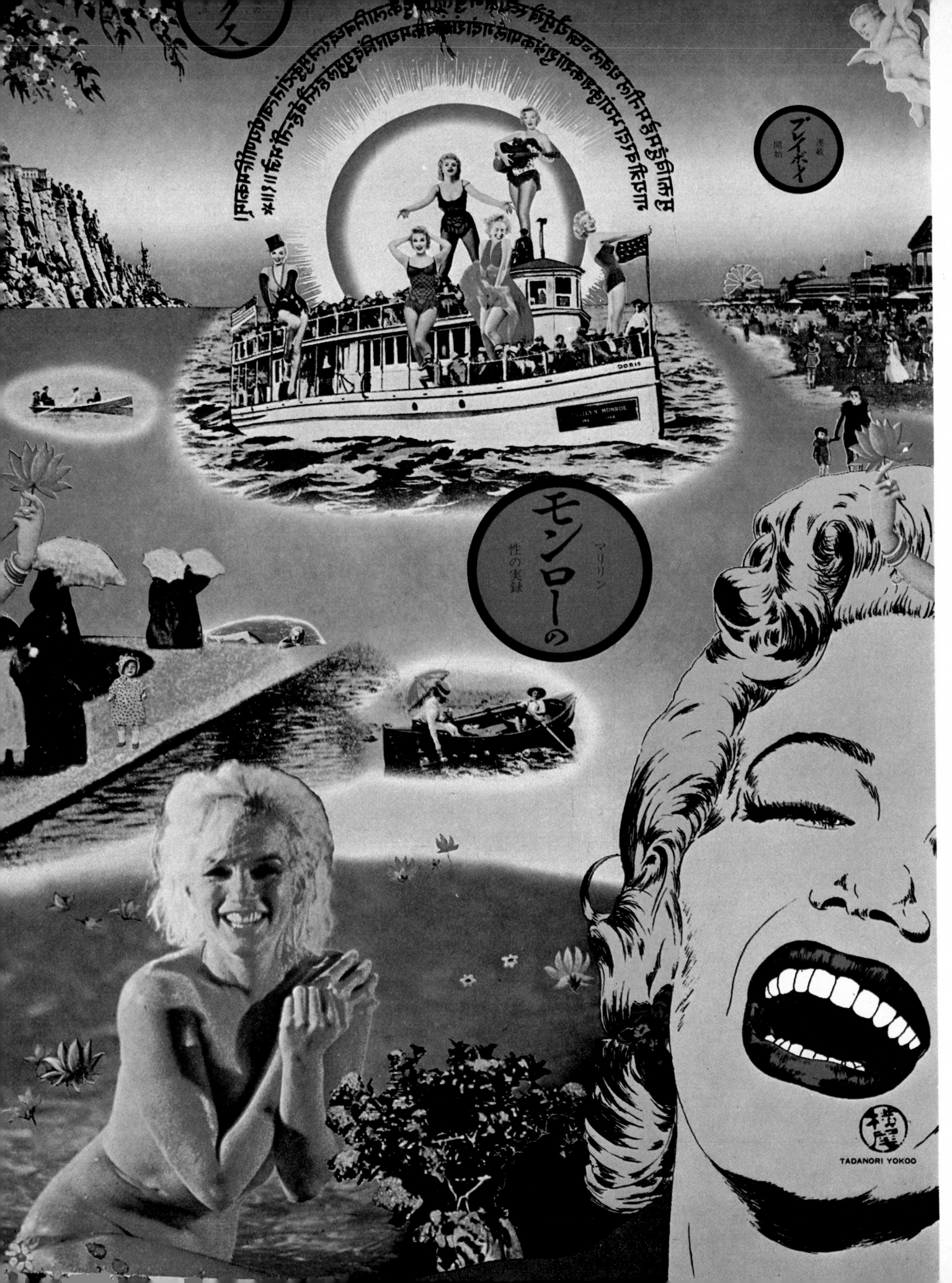

TADANORI YOKOO

226. Opposite
Tadanori Yoko-o
A Document of Marilyn Monroe's Sex Life
1970; 85 × 60.2 cm. (33 × 23 in.)

227.
Tomio Miki
Ear Pink 12
1967; 270 × 144 × 98 cm. (105 × 56 × 38 in.)

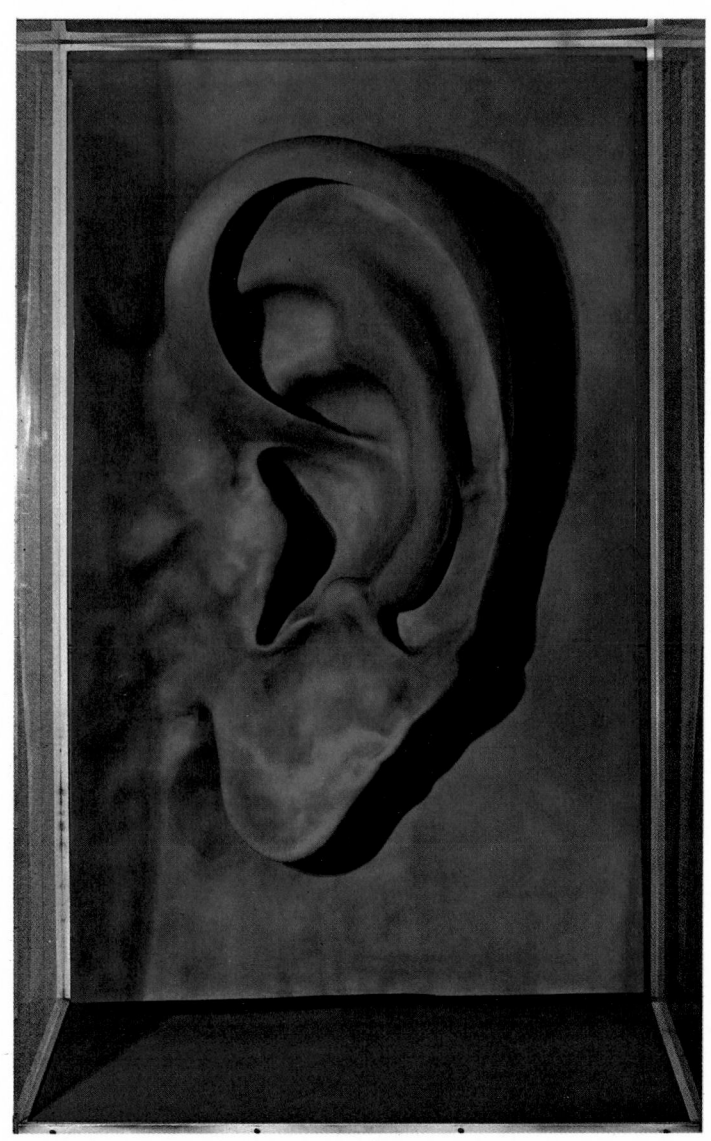

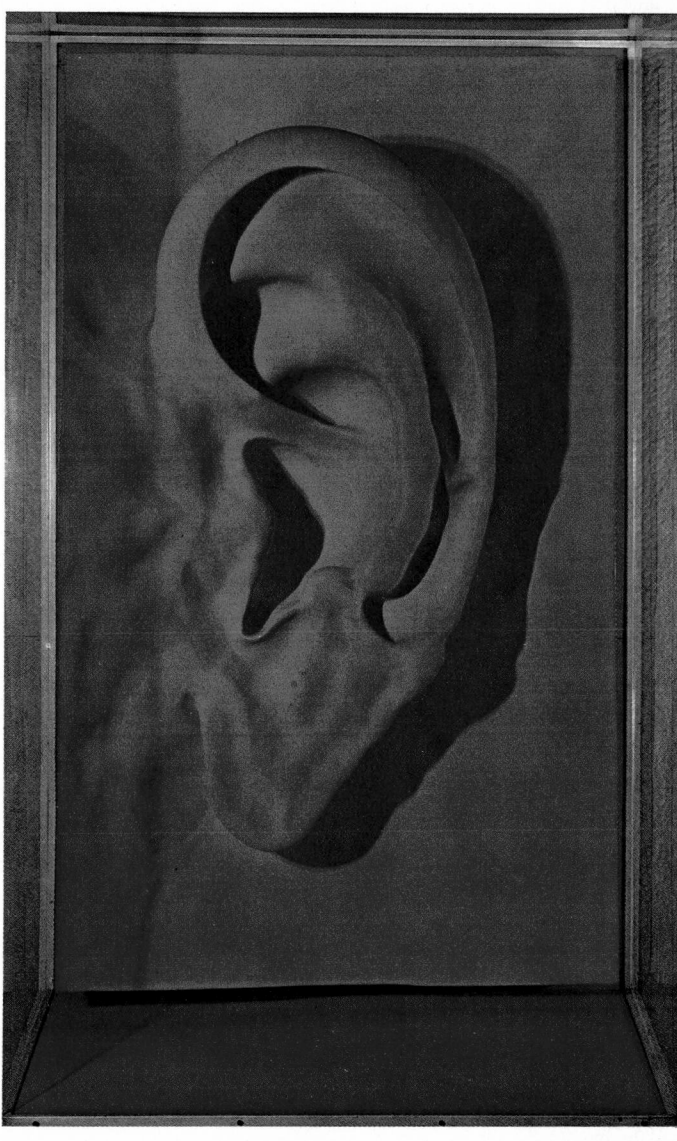

kinds of avant-garde painting which might actually be said to owe something to Oriental calligraphy or the quietism of Zen philosophy. A work such as Tadanori Yoko-o's *A Document of Marilyn Monroe's Sex Life* (Plate 226) strangely combines Japanese and European elements, making use of material borrowed from Japanese prints at the tail end of the *ukiyoe* tradition as well as of photographic images such as an American or a European would have used. But perhaps it is significant that the choice of Marilyn herself seems to have been *de rigueur*.

Often Japanese Pop is indistinguishable from what was being produced elsewhere. Tomio Miki's giant ears (Plate 227) exhibit no essential point of difference from César's giant thumbs.

Pop's universal success was a tribute to its appositeness to the time which produced it, and to its ability to communicate to a broad spectrum of people. But it also deserves examination as an instance of unconscious cultural imperialism—a visual language imposed by technologically advanced societies upon those which were less thoroughly developed.

Op Art and Kinetic Art

At the height of their vogue, optical (nicknamed Op) and kinetic art were often presented as the destined successors of Pop—the logical response in a dialogue of styles. There was some truth in this idea, but as a theory it was too superficial. In many respects, these developments were the reassertion of a long-established tradition within Modernism, a reaction not to Pop as such, but to the attitude towards society which formed the background to the activities of Pop artists and to their success with the public. If Pop had its roots in Dada, then Op and kinetic art had theirs in the rich soil of Futurism and Constructivism. Pop was simultaneously celebratory and ironic, while those who gave their allegiance elsewhere tended to think of themselves as being opposed to the present in the cause of the future. At the same time, however, they often retained a romantic love of the machine which Pop had outgrown. Pop artists liked not the machine, but its consequences.

Op and kinetic art grew up simultaneously with Pop in the Sixties, but were somewhat slower in attracting the attention of the mass public. Indeed, experiments of this type were already being made by many artists during the middle Fifties, as they moved towards a new attitude to abstract art in general. Almost from the beginning, these experiments attracted the attention of informed and intelligent critics. As a result, this phase of post-war Modernism has been the subject of a considerable amount of intelligent analysis. Perhaps the most useful book on the subject is Frank Popper's *Origins and Developments of Kinetic Art* (London, 1968; first published in French in 1967), and it is Popper's system of categories that I shall make use of here.

He divides art of this kind into six classifications. The first of these he calls "Abstract Visual Inducements". By this he means work which induces a psycho-physiological reaction in the spectator, by the use of dazzle patterns or moiré effects. Works of this kind are, strictly speaking, the only ones that can be described as purely optical. Next there are works that in some way require the intervention of the spectator. He must himself move in order to activate them. Thirdly, there are actual machines. Then there are "mobiles"—things which have real movement of their own, but are not machine-powered. Popper's two final categories are works that incorporate both light and movement; and those, more elaborate still, which are best thought of as spectacle and environment rather than as independent objects.

None of these categories was completely new in the 1960's, and artists had made experiments with many of them almost from the beginning of Modernism itself. Both the Russian Futurist Alexander Rodchenko and the Dadaist Man Ray had made suspended mobiles as early as 1920. Naum Gabo, the great Constructivist sculptor, produced a simple kinetic piece powered by a motor in the same year, but did not follow up the experiment. In the early Twenties, Marcel Duchamp was experimenting with optical illusions produced by means of rotating discs.

Perhaps the first artist to establish himself almost entirely through works which incorporated movement as an essential part of their effect was the American Alexander Calder. Born in 1898, Calder graduated as a mechanical engineer from the Stevens Institute of Technology in 1919. He continued to work as an engineer while studying at the Art Students League of New York during the middle Twenties. And in 1926 he made the then (for American artists) mandatory pilgrimage to Paris. It was at this period that he made the miniature circus with personages of wire and wood which has come to be recognized as the precursor of the mobiles which made him famous.

228 and 229.
Alexander Calder
Two mobiles: opposite
Little Spider; c. 1940; 140 × 127 cm. (55 × 50 in.)
New York, Perls Galleries

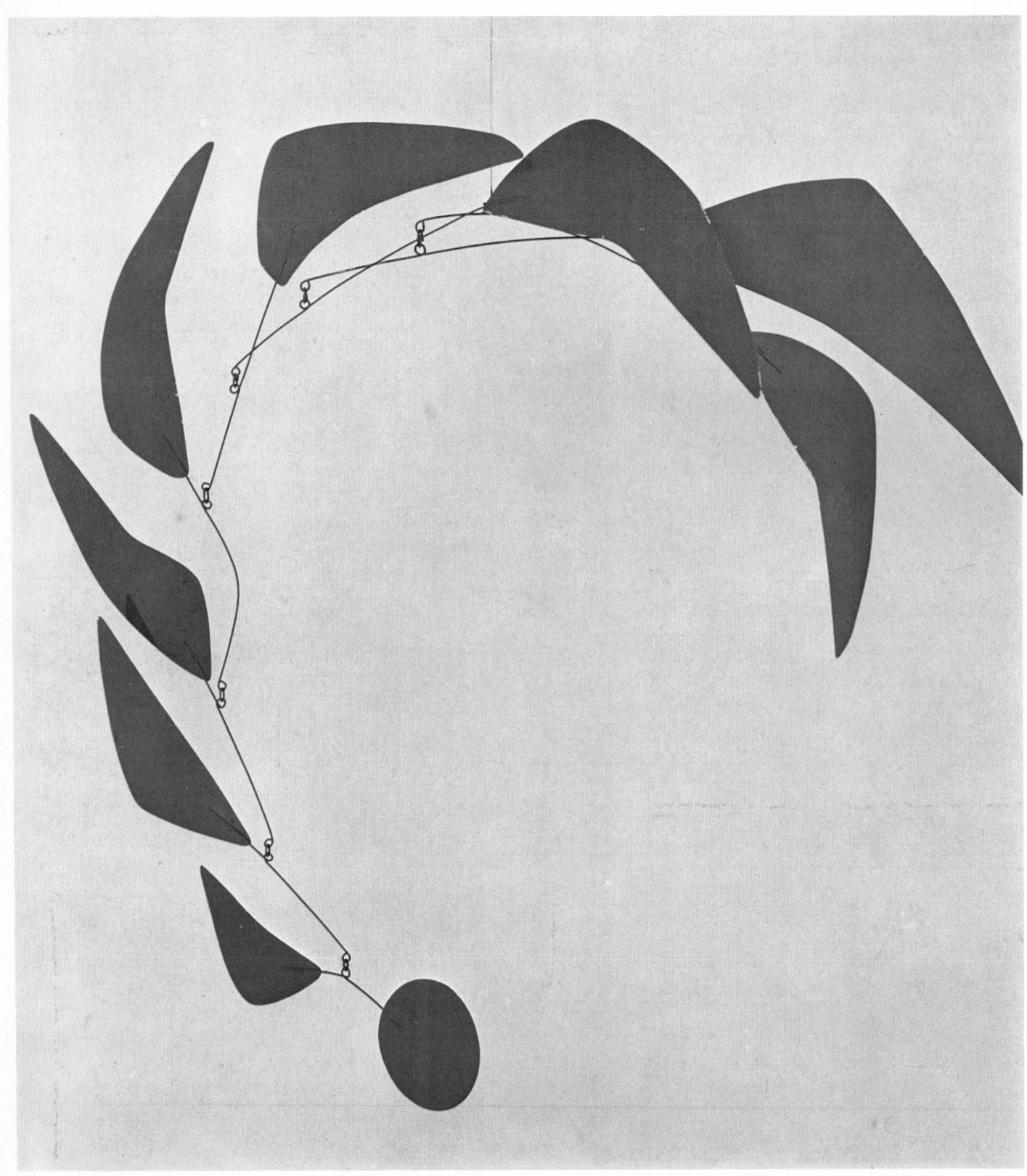

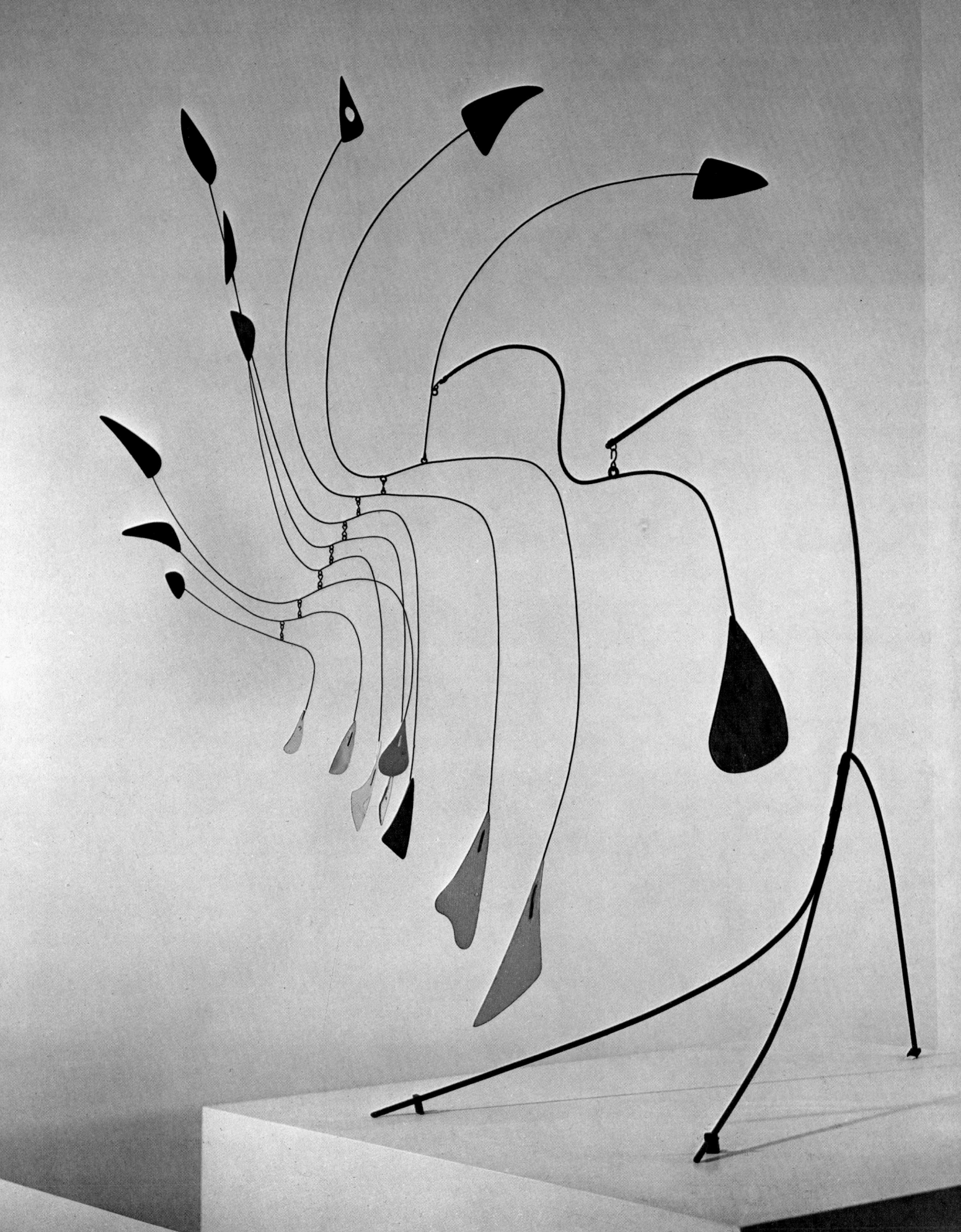

230.
George Rickey
Six Lines Horizontal
1964; 61 cm. (24 in.)
Colorado, coll. Kimiko and John Powers

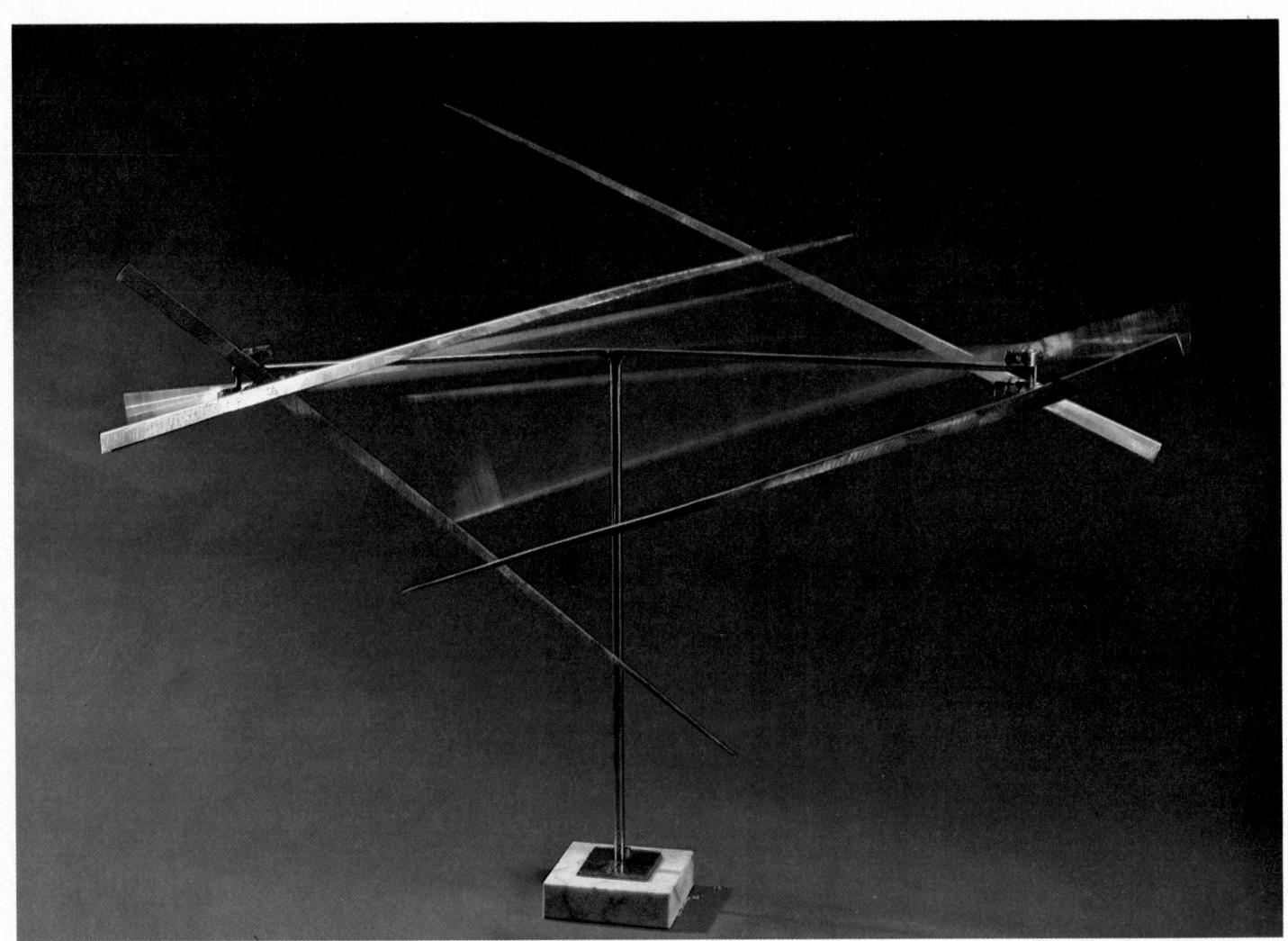

The first of these were exhibited in 1932.

Calder's mobiles, even at this time (Plates 228 and 229), were fully developed works of kinetic art, dependent for the effect they made on the movement of forms, rather than upon the forms themselves. The essential difference between the mobile and the powered object is that the mobile is random, and dependent upon chance for its juxtapositions; though it is true, of course, that the experienced maker of these objects can calculate with some precision what kind of effects he is likely get. Indeed, it has sometimes been

complained that the apparent freedom given by random movement conceals within itself such stringent limitations that the mobile, however skilfully made, soon begins to pall, and does not have the presence of true sculpture. This complaint, however, applies to unsuccessful examples. In successful ones, as another American maker of mobiles, George Rickey, remarks, the "movement is as intrinsic as that of a Gramophone record or an airplane in flight; without it the object would be something else."

Rickey's own mobiles are more solidly con-

231.
Günter Haese
Oase
1964; 28 cm. (11 in.)
Cologne, Wallraf-Richartz Museum, coll. Ludwig

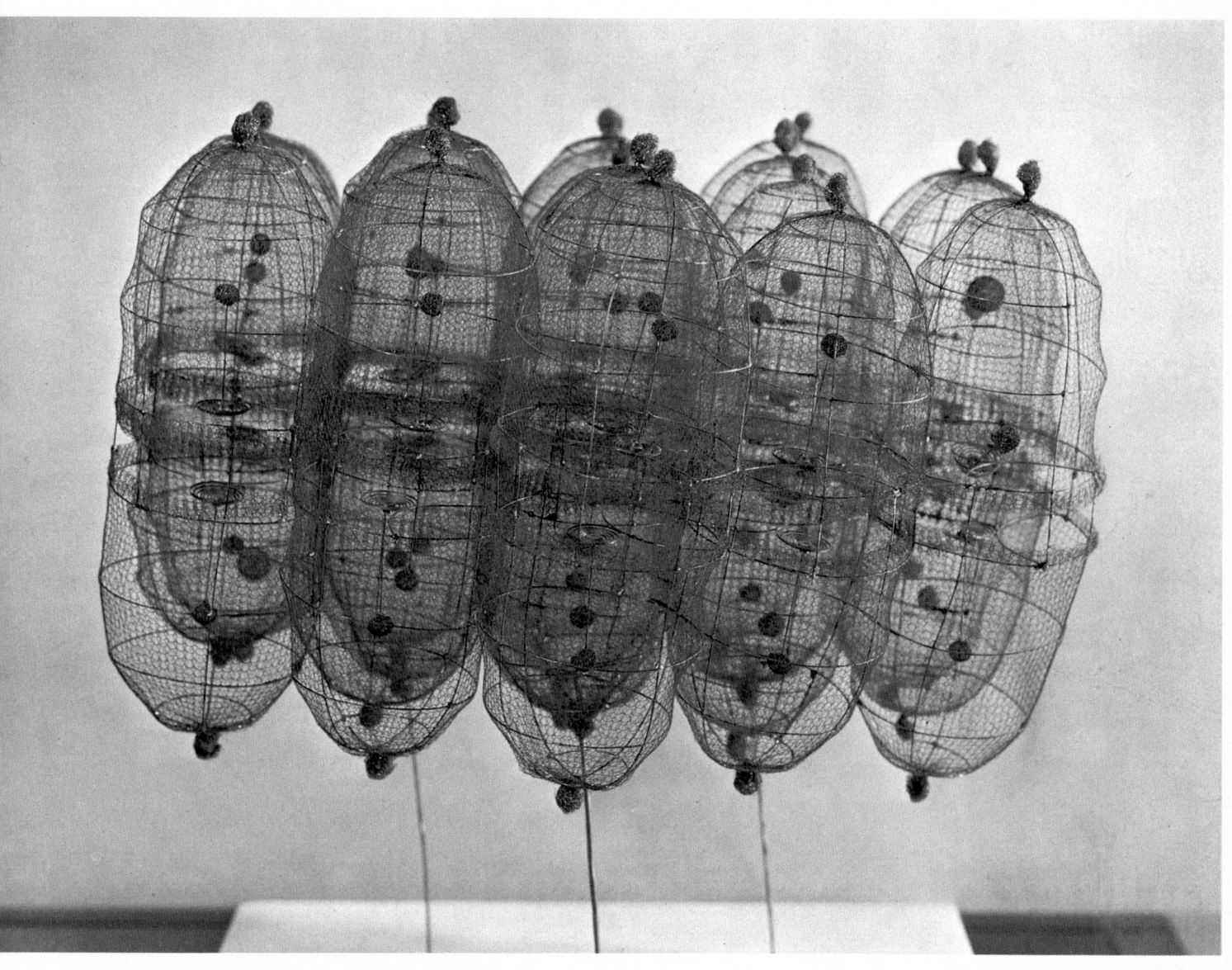

structed than Calder's (Plate 230), and the possible range of movement is apparently more restricted. He believes that one can establish a theoretical classification of, at most, six or eight types of motion, and is himself content to use only two or three of these types—yet he feels, with justification, that the effect produced is always a surprise. "When you construct an object in movement," he remarks, "you are always surprised by the movement itself: however well worked out the design may be, the movement seems to come from somewhere else." One thing which Rickey and Calder have in common, in addition to American nationality and their interest in mobiles as opposed to kinetic machines, is their tendency to stand firmly outside the groupings that abound in kinetic art. These have served to reinforce the "scientific" and deliberately experimental, rather than purely aesthetic, character of the movement. Also entirely opposed to this tendency is the poetic work of the German sculptor Günter Haese. Haese makes small-scale constructions out of wire. Typically, a framework which is itself delicate and flexible will contain numerous vibrating elements (Plate 231). A German critic has spoken of them as being "a kind of graphic art in space", and the resemblance in spirit, if not in form, to the drawings of Paul Klee is indeed striking. Haese seems to recapture in three dimensions much of Klee's wit, and there is, too, a similar vein of ambiguity and melancholy. Nor is Haese an abstract artist in the true sense of the word, any more than Klee was, and in this also his sculpture differs from the more typical

232.
Victor Vasarely
Zett-Kek
1966; 140 × 140 cm. (55 × 55 in.)
New York, by kind permission of the Sidney Janis Gallery

233. Opposite
Victor Vasarely
Aran
1964; 81 × 81 cm. (32 × 32 in.)
Colorado, coll. Kimiko and John Powers

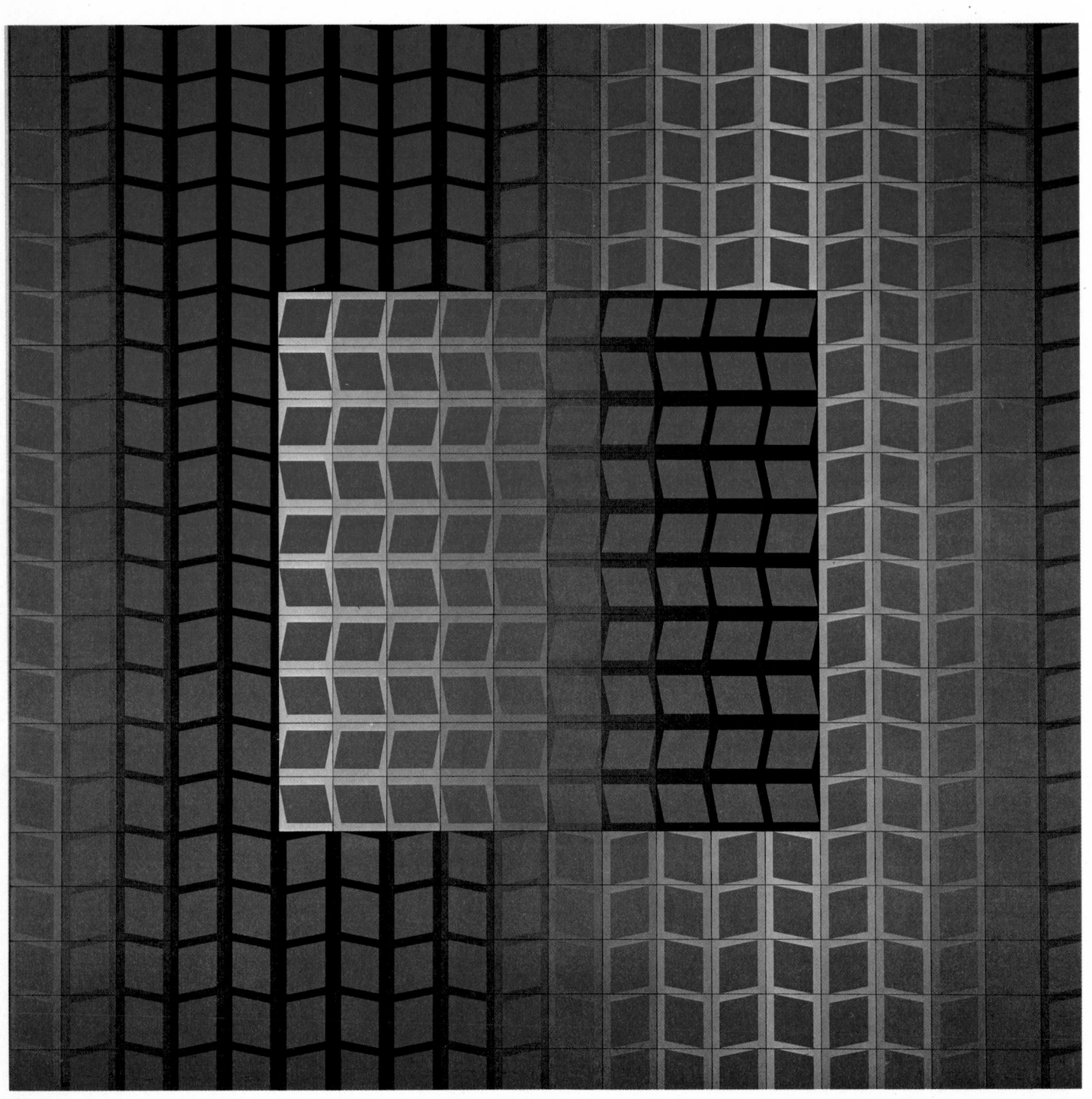

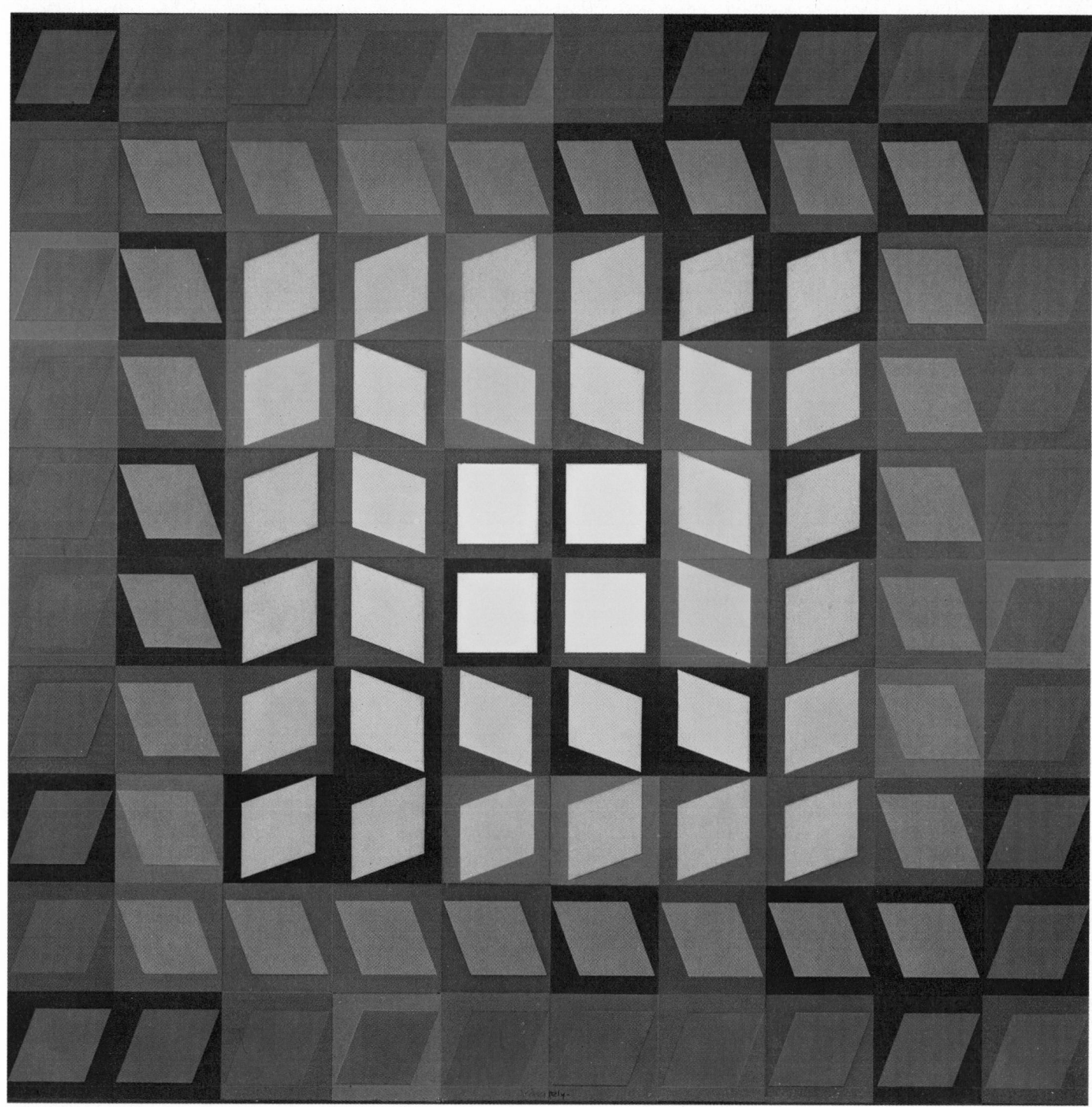

manifestations of kinetic and optical art.

In Europe, which has been the stronghold of the movement, the dominating influence has undoubtedly been the Hungarian-born painter Victor Vasarely, and it is of great importance that Vasarely made his early studies at the Mühely, the Budapest Bauhaus. The spirit of the Bauhaus has always pervaded his own work, and he has passed on essential elements of the Bauhaus tradition to the younger artists who have entered his orbit.

Though Vasarely's name is now connected with pure abstraction, he moved towards this through the study of nature, a fact which he himself has been perfectly willing to recognize. But he feels that it was essential to his own art, and will be essential to others, to leave behind the last traces of figuration, in pursuit of a vision of the "new city— geometrical, sunny and full of colours," in which art will be "kinetic, multi-dimensional and communal. Abstract, of course, and closer to the

234.
Pietro Dorazio
Murale
1965; 170 × 110 cm. (66 × 43 in.)
Berlin, Galerie Springer

finally, thanks to, and through, the machine" (Vasarely in Aldo Pellegrini, *New Tendencies in Art*, London, 1966, pp. 166–7).

The element of movement in Vasarely's work can therefore be regarded as a substitute for things which the hand-made object possesses, and which the machine-made one can no longer have. It supplies the animation which formerly came from the evidence of the artist's touch.

One of Vasarely's most typical devices is that of opposing systems of perspective (Plate 232, *Zett-Kek*). These call attention, as much as his writings do, to the strongly architectural character of his work. He also makes use of another of the typical tools of Op art—the opposition of colour areas which are violently contrasted in hue, but the same in tonal value. A black-and-white photograph of *Aran* (Plate 233), for instance, would consist of almost identical tones of grey.

But Vasarely has not been content to work on pictures and prints alone. He has experimented with designs painted on layers of cellophane or acrylic sheets, which were then superimposed and placed at some distance from one another, so that the effect altered as the spectator changed position. He has also been concerned with large-scale decorative projects which involved the animation, by optical means, of outside walls and facades. One such project was carried out at the University of Caracas.

Nevertheless, it is true to say that his followers have been more intimately concerned than he has been himself with the three-dimensional object. In contrast to this, the optical painters who have flourished since the war have pursued interests somewhat different from Vasarely's. One reason for this is that the most prominent of them have been English or American, and have therefore inherited a very different tradition. One of the few to share some of Vasarely's preoccupations has been the Italian Piero Dorazio (Plate 234), who also, though in less complex form, reproduces some of the former's effects. Interestingly enough, Dorazio began his career, in the immediately post-war epoch, as a painter of social realist themes.

In the United States, where Op art enjoyed a brief period of violent popularity in the middle

sciences." Vasarely goes well beyond Kineticism as such, and envisages a new function for the artist and his work in a society changed by the hoped-for social revolution. In this he echoes not only the ideas of the Bauhaus, but also those put forward by the Russian Constructivists during their most extreme phase: "If the art of yesterday signified 'to feel and to do', today it signifies 'to conceive and to order to do'. If yesterday the durability of the work resided in the excellence of the materials, in the technical perfection and in the mastery of the hand, today it rests in the knowledge of a possibility for *re-creation*, *multiplication* and *expansion*. Thus the artifact disappears with the myth of uniqueness and the diffusible work triumphs

235.
Richard Anuskiewicz
Luminous
1965; 61 × 61 cm. (24 × 24 in.)
Los Angeles, coll. Mr. and Mrs. Melvin Hirsch

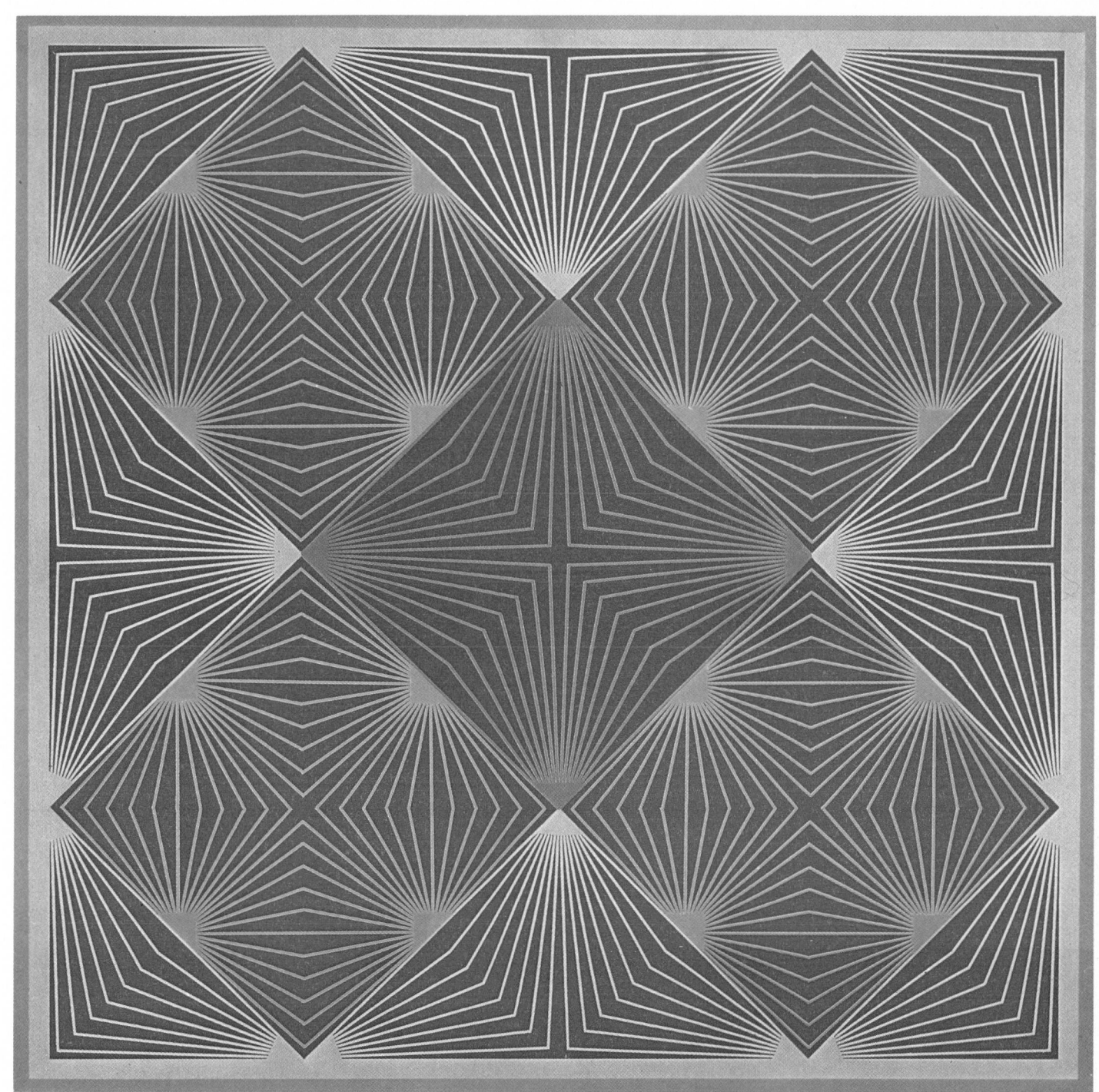

Sixties, the most skilful exponent of purely optical effects was Richard Anuskiewicz (Plate 235). Anuskiewicz was an inheritor of the Bauhaus tradition, but only in the limited sense that he studied for a period with Josef Albers at Yale. A brilliant technician, he devised some of the most striking dazzle patterns to appear on canvas, and imbued them with a typically American elegance. But there is something limited and even monotonous about his talent. His tendency to organize his patterns in squares and diamonds suggests, of course, an affinity with Albers, who was his master. It also suggests an informative comparison with the work of Ad Reinhardt, whose glimmering rectangular patterns produce surprisingly powerful optical effects if one gazes at them for long enough.

Reinhardt is often thought of, not as a true Abstract Expressionist, but as the link between Abstract Expressionism and Post-Painterly Abstraction (the art movement which will be dealt with in the next chapter). He is thus equivalent to Arshile Gorky, whose career provides the bridge between Surrealism and Abstract Expressionism. Another American painter who occupies a similarly indeterminate position is Larry Poons. As Kermit S. Champa pointed out in an article in the influential magazine *Artforum*, Poons and Pollock have much in common: "Like Pollock's great works of 1949–50, Poons's have accepted responsibility for more of the available surface area, and they have worked that area in a way which stresses continuity rather than focus. The image which is characteristic of both painters continually restates the whole of the painted surface through the cadenced repetition of similar pictorial units. Pollock's units were primarily linear, Poons's primarily coloristic, but the function is identical" (Kermit S. Champa, "New Paintings by Larry Poons", *Artforum*, Vol. VI, No. 10 [Summer, 1968], pp. 39–42).

Yet it is interesting to note that Poons, even more than Reinhardt, can properly be described as an Op painter during an important phase of his career. *Double Speed* (Plate 236), which dates from 1962–63, is representative of this aspect of his work. The design consists of not one but two superimposed patterns of colour dots, though the dots in each system are identical in colour. The eye, trying to distinguish one pattern from another, soon becomes unable to focus properly, thanks to the brilliance of the colour contrast; and because of this the dots themselves seem continually to change position. The effect is reinforced by the fact that the design is carried right up to the edges of the canvas. There is even a hint that it continues beyond the edges of the area provided.

Poons was not to persist with these strongly optical effects. The colour, instead of being clear and forcefully contrasted, became muddy, while the dots were enlarged and took on the shapes of the slipper bacilli which can be seen with the help of a microscope in a drop of muddy pond-water. Though these paintings are less attractive than the earlier ones, they retain a sense of movement and energy which differentiates them from the inertia of a more "central" Post-Painterly Abstractionist such as Kenneth Noland.

Energy is one of the most striking qualities of the painting of the English artist Bridget Riley, who has claims to be thought of as the most successful of all the painters who have experimented with optical effects during the period since 1945. In his introduction to the catalogue of Riley's exhibition at the Venice Biennale of 1968, David Thompson said: "One of the most distinctive characteristics of Bridget Riley's art is that it 'insists' with such concentration that it changes sensory response into something else. The sensation which Riley offers is closely related to the creation of visual analogues expressive of emotion, or, more exactly, to the creation of visual analogues for sharply particularised states of mind. The very intensity of the assault which her painting makes on the eye drives it, as it were, past the point at which it is merely a matter of optical effect to the point at which it becomes acute physical sensation, apprehended kinesthetically as mental tension or mental release, anxiety or exhilaration, heightened self-awareness of heightened awareness of unfamiliar or even alien states of being" (David Thompson, "Bridget Riley", catalogue to the British Pavilion exhibit, Venice Biennale, 1968).

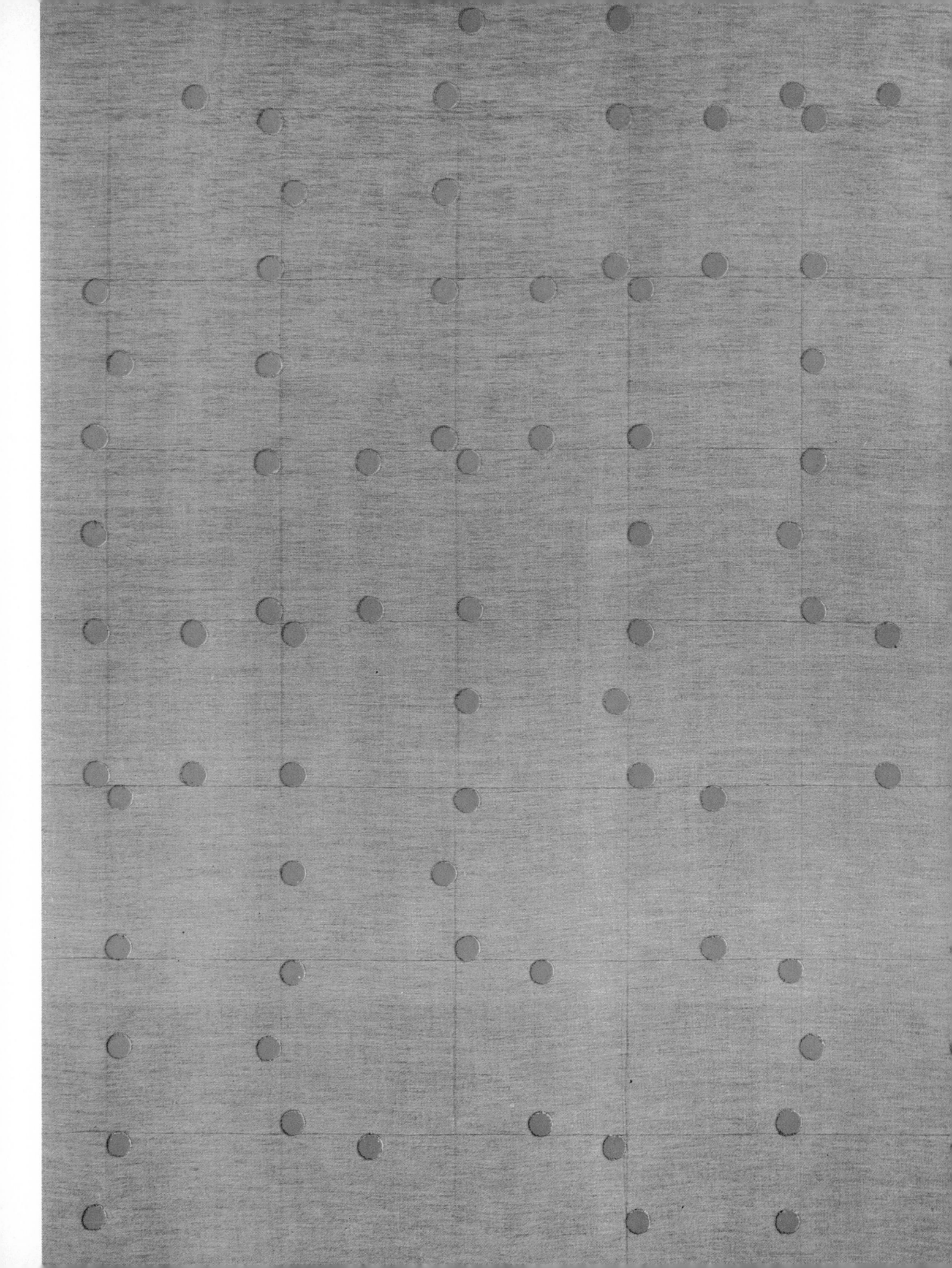

237.
Bridget Riley
Current
1964; 135 × 150 cm. (53 × 59 in.)
New York, Museum of Modern Art, Philip Johnson Fund

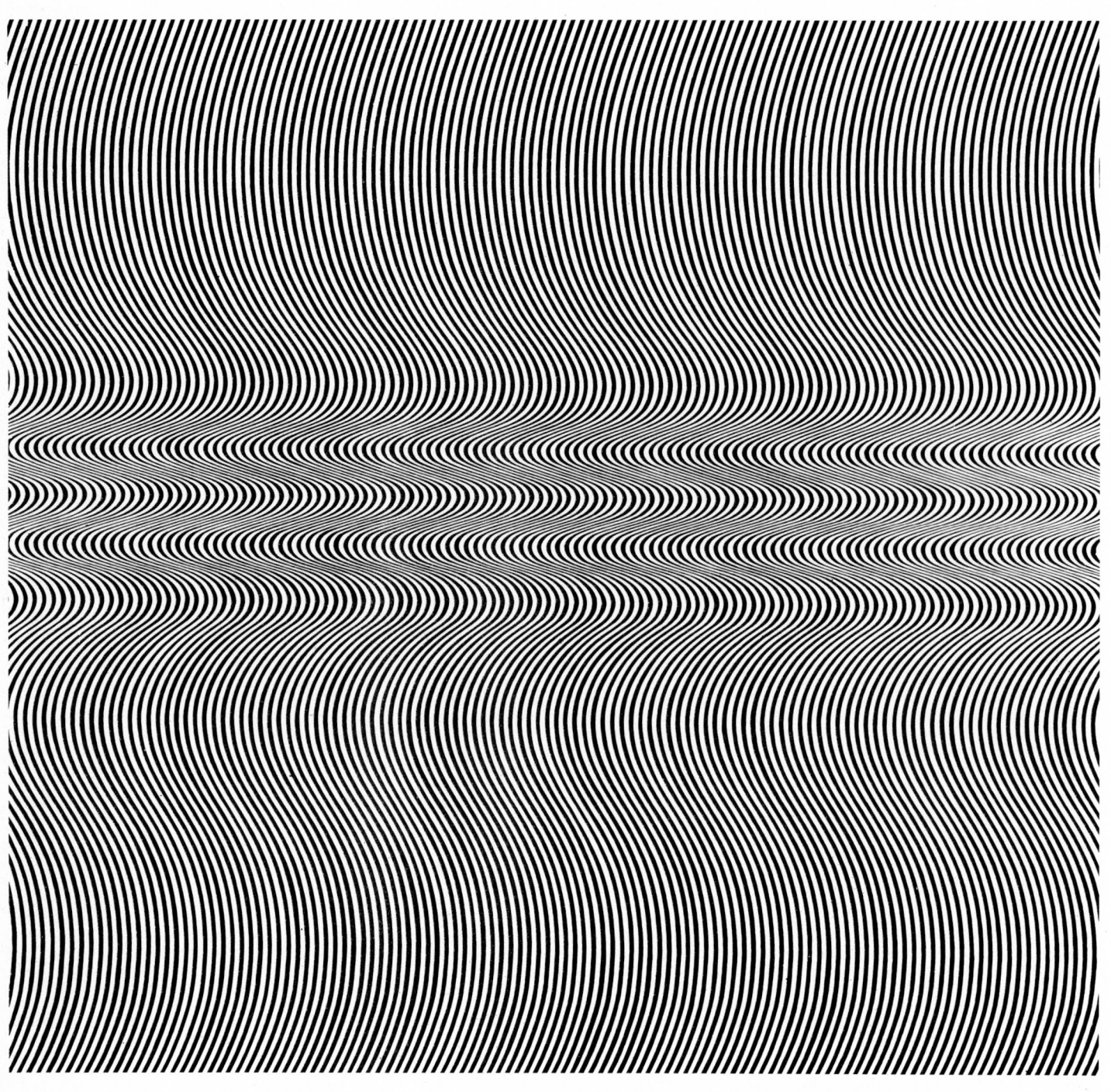

238.
Bridget Riley
Cataract III
1967; London, coll. British Council, by kind permission of
the Rowan Gallery

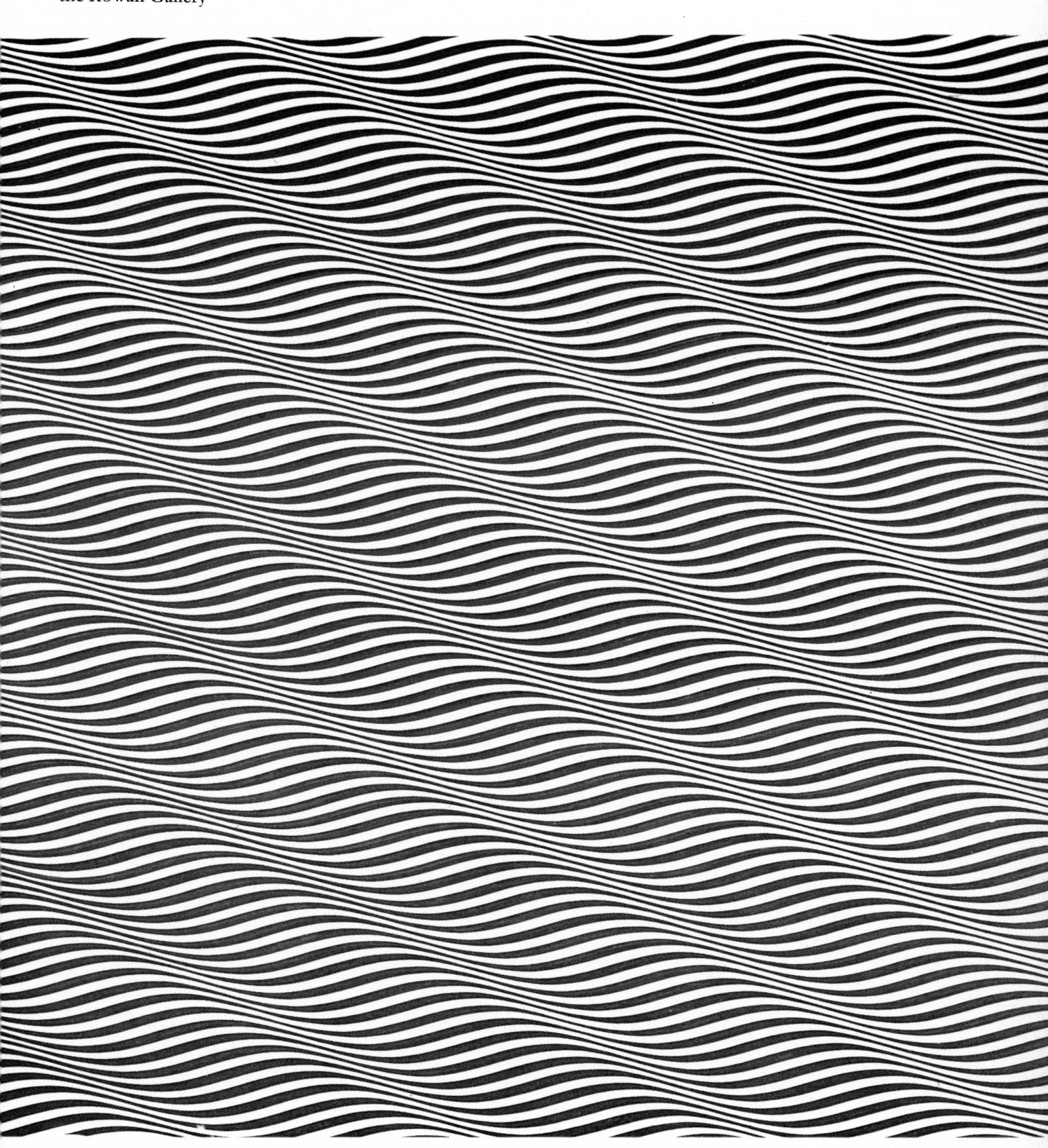

What Thompson acutely seizes upon in this passage is the fact that Riley's work, though intensely energetic, is not expressive of energy alone. Unlike many of the kinetic artists who are her contemporaries, she is not satisfied with quasi-scientific investigation of optical properties, but wants to use the effects she discovers for personal ends, to express some element in her own personality. In this she differs from the detached and impersonal spirit of communal art, as advocated by Vasarely and his followers.

Riley's early influences included the work of Georges Seurat (she made some beautiful Neo-Impressionist paraphrases during her student years) and the Italian Futurists, though she did not discover the latter until she made a journey to Italy in 1960. Her first optical paintings date from the same year.

During the early 1960's, and indeed until 1967, Bridget Riley worked entirely in black and white. *Current* (Plate 237), which dates from 1964, is typical of what she was producing at this time. Riley's paintings are very much dependent on the precise scale chosen by the artist (one reason why she dislikes nearly all reproductions of her work), but the optical effect here is so powerful that the design has a powerful impact even when it has been greatly reduced in size. As the title suggests, the work, though abstract, has accepted a suggestion from what the artist has observed in nature. The pattern seems to be a formalization of the pattern of ripples observed upon the surface of a stream.

The landscape element, so astonishingly persistent in British art, reappears in Riley's *Cataract III* of 1967 (Plate 238). Here the ripple pattern of the earlier picture has been smoothed out and regularized. The artist has been able to do this because she has now begun to introduce colour, and it is colour which supplies the place of the disturbance in the pattern which served to animate the earlier picture. For the first time, although the hues are not pure, we encounter the phenomenon of "optical bleed", which was to fascinate the artist henceforth. Optical bleed is the mechanism whereby the eye can be induced to see a colour which is not in fact present, projecting complementary after-images onto areas which lie beside those where the colour itself is strongest.

By 1970, when *Apprehend* (Plate 239) was painted, Riley felt sure enough of her command over colour to abandon the use of all but the simplest patterns—stripes, and sometimes elongated chevrons. It is the relationship of the various hues which now provides the picture with its drama. Since simple stripes form so important a part of the repertoire of recent American painting, it is instructive to compare the use which Riley

240.
Peter Sedgley
Yellow Attenuation
1965 ; 122 × 122 cm. (48 × 48 in.)
London, Tate Gallery

241 and 242.
Yaacov Agam
Double Metamorphosis
1968–69; 127 × 188 cm. (50 × 73 in.)
Paris, Centre National d'Art Contemporain

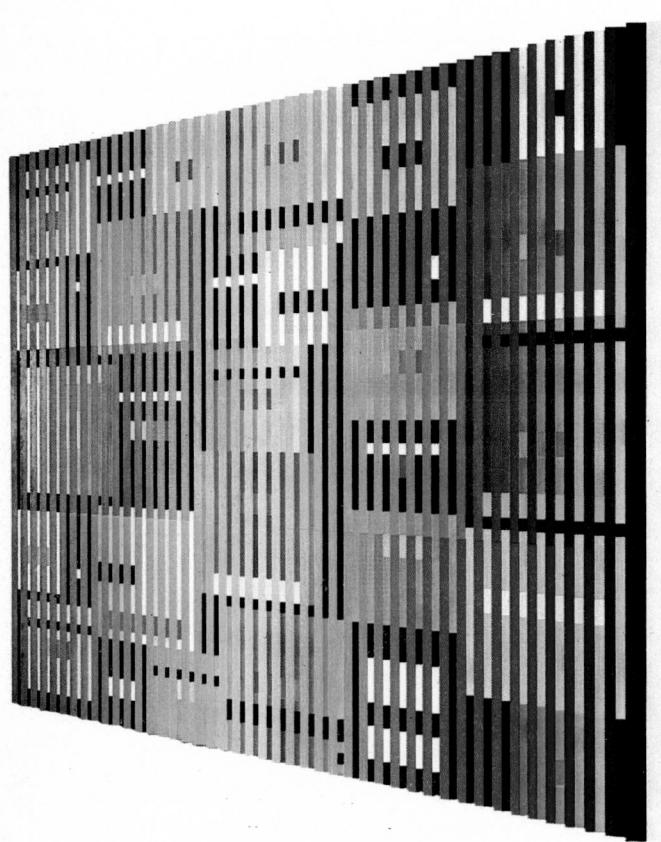

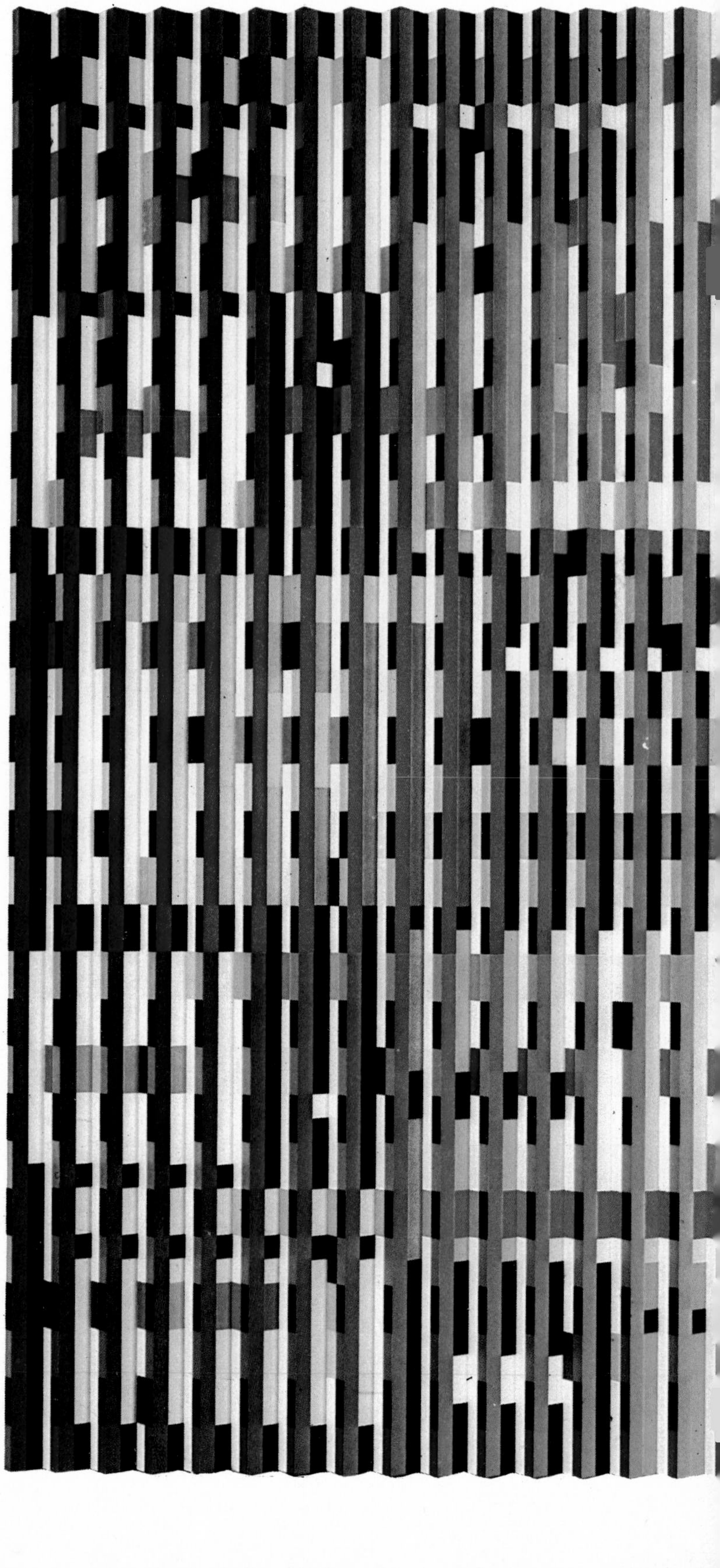

makes of the device with that way in which it is employed by Kenneth Noland or Frank Stella. She still maintains the tremendous energy which was associated with her earlier work, even in a format which critics have tended to associate with a willed passivity.

Riley was anticipated in this particular method of using colour stripes by another British artist, Peter Sedgley, whose *Yellow Attenuation* (Plate 240) dates from 1965. Sedgley and Riley have been closely associated, and their work shows signs of mutual influence. Sedgley has, however, essayed a format which never seems to have tempted Bridget Riley: the circular target pattern which has played so conspicuous a role in recent American art. Here, too, there is a difference of effect which seems to sum up some of the differences between American and European abstract painting. Where Noland's targets remain static, or at most suggest a slow rotation through the use of actual colour bleed at the edges of the design, Sedgley's show powerful illusory pro-

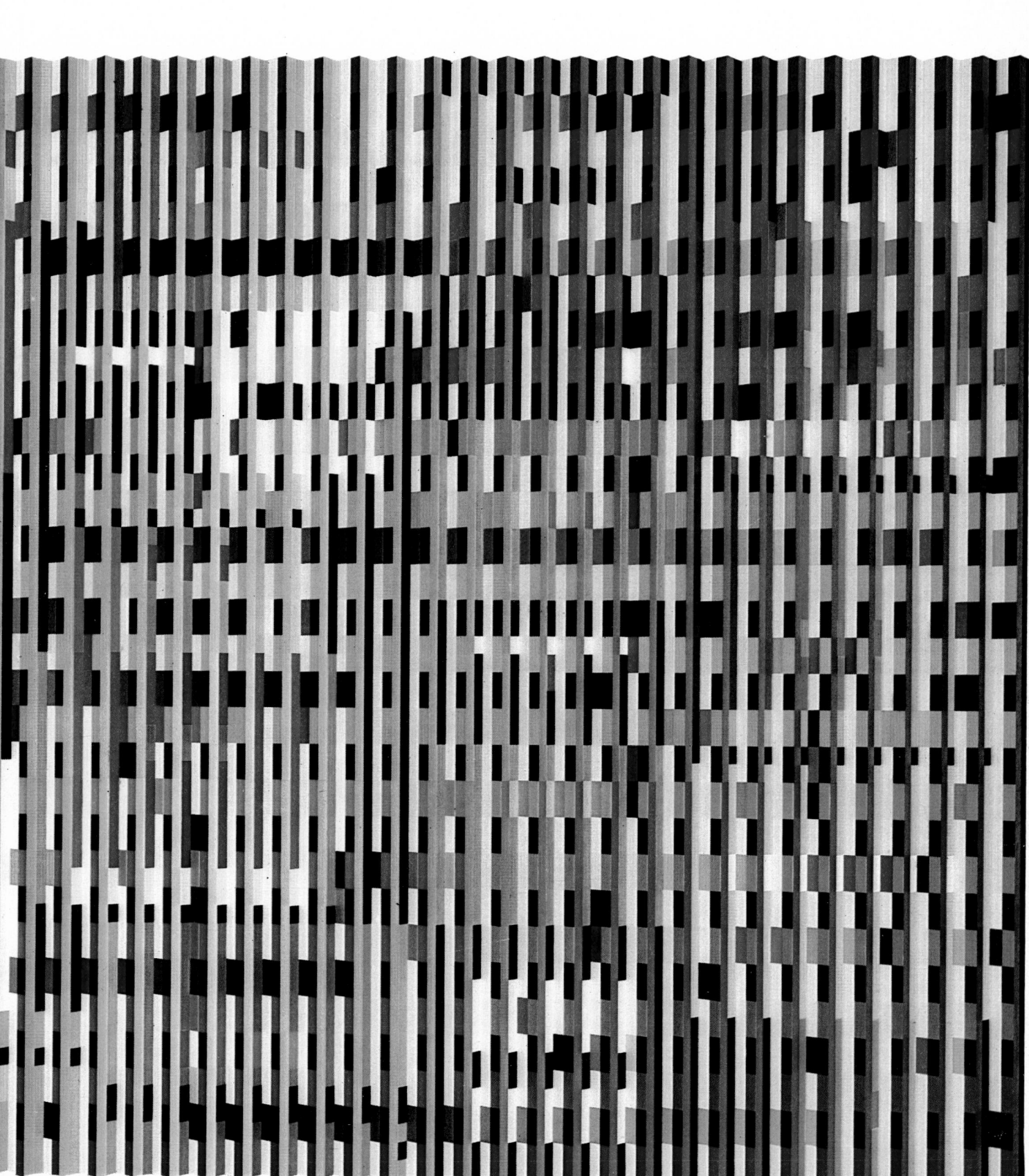

jection and recession, so that the whole surface of the picture becomes unstable.

Sedgley has used these target paintings as a basis for further experiments. He has illuminated them with colour filters and has set them in actual physical motion with the use of rotors. In 1969, these experiments culminated in an ambitious kinetic environment, making use of a light programme inside a dome.

British artists have been less active in exploring true kinetic effects, as opposed to purely optical ones, and in this sense have stood a little aside from the international kinetic movement, which has had its home base in Paris, but which has included artists from all over the world. The essential impersonality of this kind of art—something we have already encountered in the work of Vasarely—has perhaps made it easier for artists from very different backgrounds to discover a common language.

The Israeli artist Yaacov Agam and the Venezuelan Carlos Cruz-Diez supply a case in point, since they work along lines which are very similar. Both have chiefly concerned themselves with work which, to revert to Frank Popper's system of classification, "requires the intervention of the spectator". More specifically, what they make only has its intended effect when the spectator moves his position in relation to it.

Agam's work spans a wider gamut than this description might suggest. Jasia Reichardt, in her study of the artist, has this to say about his creative attitudes: "To Agam, a static picture approximates an idol. As such, it cannot be acceptable to him, since it is contrary to the very essence of what he believes. Precariousness and change are the only permanent concepts recognized by the Hebrew religion, and Agam's involvement with them as exemplified by movement and change, appearance and disappearance, is as strongly related to them as the basic formal aspects of creating a work of art" (Jasia Reichardt, *Yaacov Agam*, London, 1966).

The pursuit of movement and change has involved Agam in a great variety of experiments since he first began to create transformable works in 1951. The first series could be changed either by the use of a pivoting element, or by means of elements whose relationship to one another the spectator himself could modify. These led, in turn, to works which unfolded either "contrapuntally" or "polyphonically" as the spectator passed in front of them (Plates 241 and 242). Agam has said about the paintings which he has labelled polyphonic: "The surfaces of these paintings are composed of parallel triangles in relief, which set up a rhythmic measure over which the different themes are painted. I can paint up to eight distinct themes in one work: these appear to be integrated with one another if one stands straight in front of the picture, but they separate and recompose in turns when one moves to the right or the left" (quoted by Frank Popper, *Origins and Development of Kinetic Art*, London, 1968, p. 111).

Agam has also ventured into a field related to the mobile by making paintings with elements attached by means of springs, which vibrate at the slightest contact, and in turn give rise to various optical illusions.

Cruz-Diez adopted a slightly different system from that used by Agam in his polyphonies. Instead of painting the design on parallel triangles with their points turned towards the spectator, he uses narrow slats placed at right angles to the picture plane. It is these which carry the actual colour, which is reflected onto the surface of the picture plane (Plate 243). Once again, the effect varies as the spectator changes position.

There is a relationship between Cruz-Diez's work and that of his fellow Venezuelan J. R. Soto, because both make use of the moiré effect which also plays such a prominent part in the early works of Bridget Riley. In Soto's case, however, there is an even clearer link to the tradition of hard-edge abstraction founded by Mondrian. Though his later work has moved a long way from what would conventionally be thought of as "painting", the artist nevertheless sees himself as searching for an art which would be its own master, wholly independent of the natural world, in much the same way that Mondrian did.

Soto's earliest notable works, produced soon after his arrival in Paris at the beginning of the Fifties, consisted of works which made use of

243.
Carlos Cruz-Diez
Physichromie No. 326
1967; 120 × 180 cm. (47 × 70 in.)
Cologne, Wallraf-Richartz Museum, coll. Ludwig

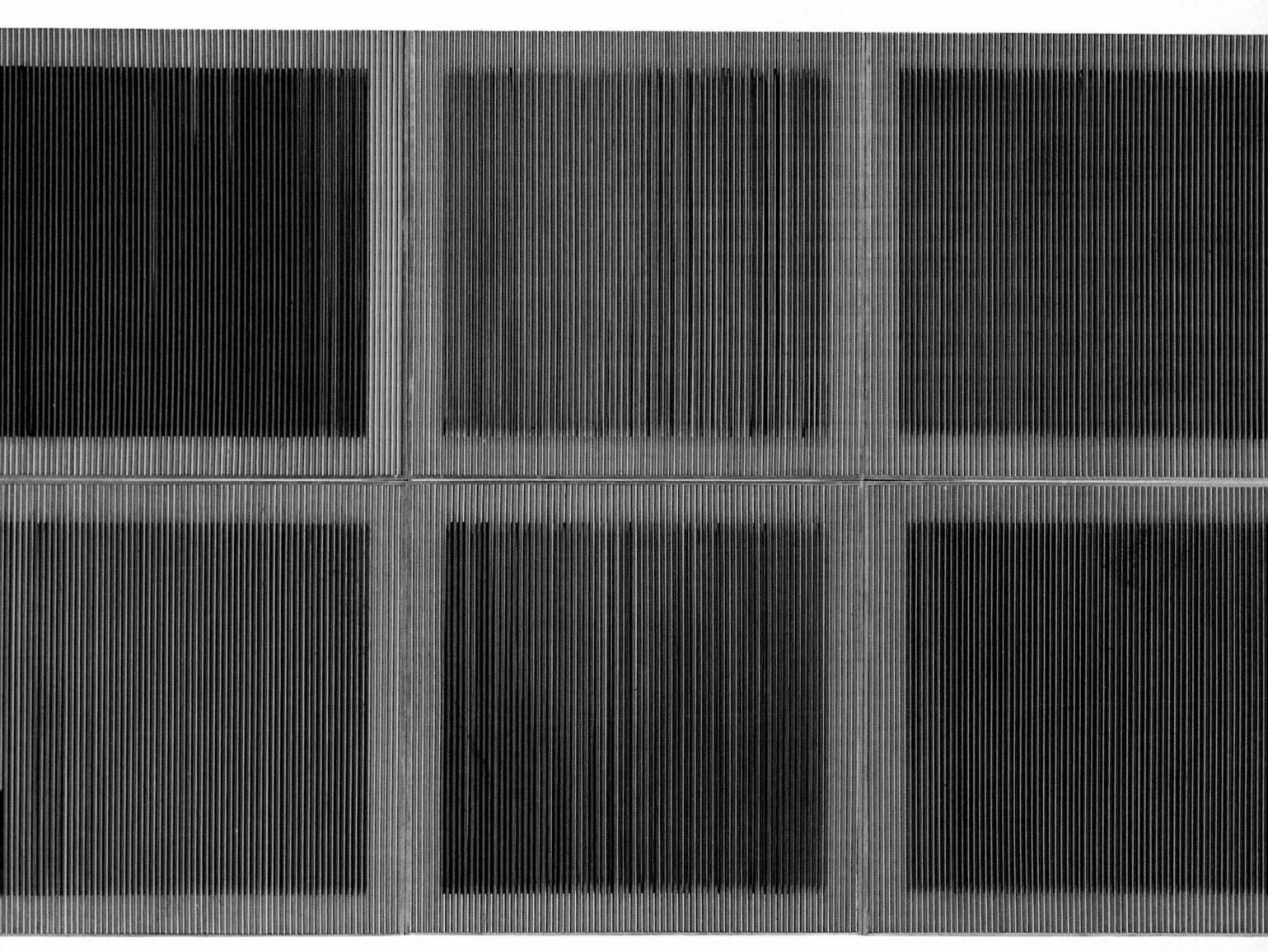

identical and multipliable elements. The aim, said the artist, was to reduce the sign to total anonymity, in the effort to get away from subjective art. He then began to use interchangeable colours which were arranged by chance. The transition to kinetic art came in 1955, when Soto began making Plexiglas superimpositions. Spirals traced upon Perspex were superimposed in depth. The optical movement that resulted was in direct relationship to the interval between the surfaces.

It was from these superimpositions in Perspex that Soto moved to a different kind of superimposition. Now he began to place suspended wires and other metallic elements in front of a striped background (*Vibration*, Plate 244). The effect of the striped background is strange—it seems to attack, and partly to dissolve, the forms which are placed in front of it. The effect is enhanced by any movement of the spectator's body or head. The English critic Guy Brett has spoken of the lack of "mystification" in Soto's work. "It establishes a concrete relationship with our perceptions," he asserts, "however diffuse the experience may be." It is certainly true to say that the artist makes use of optical illusion in a curiously anti-illusionistic way. This is true even

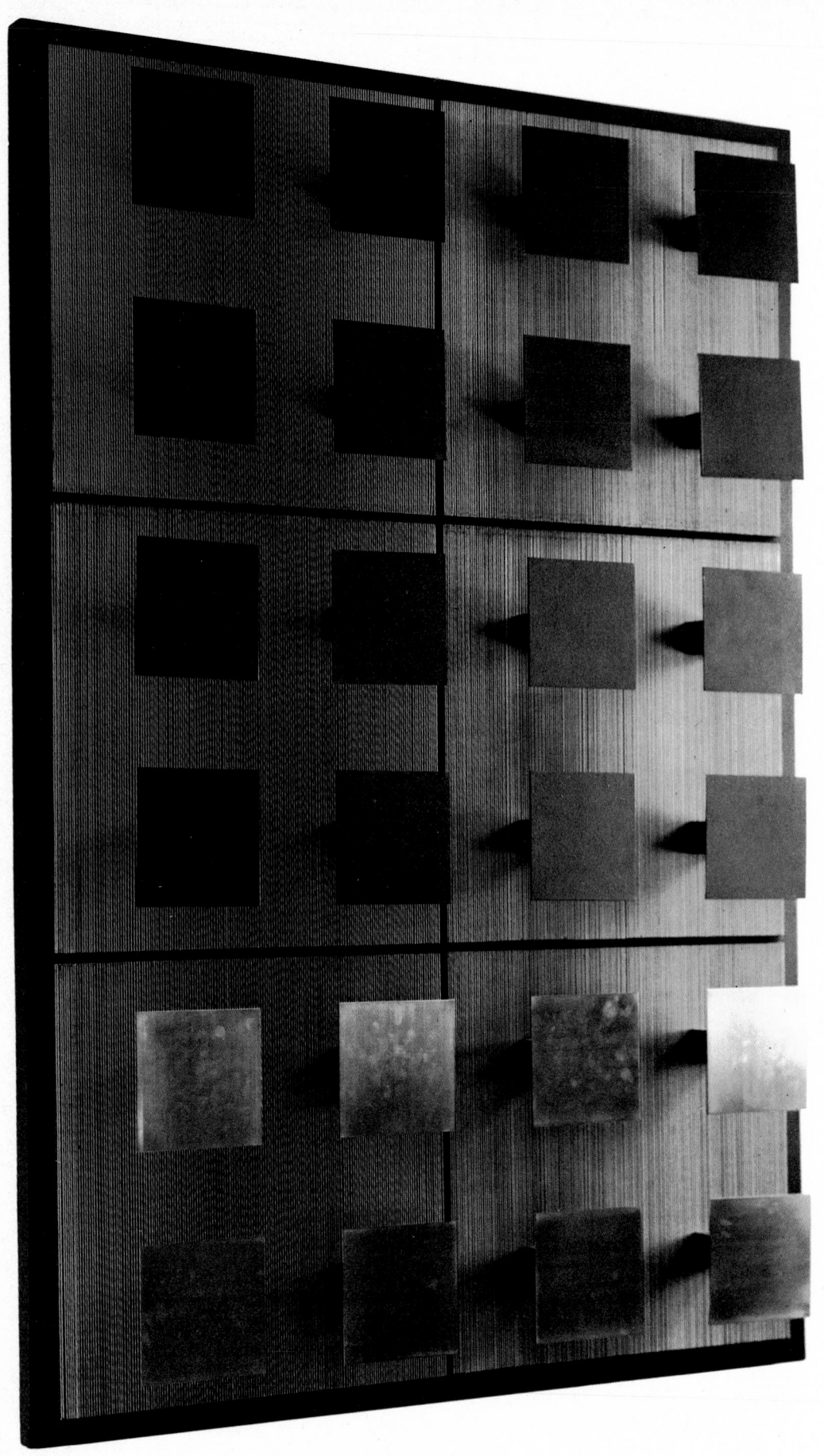

244.
Jesus Rafael Soto
Vibration
1965; 158 × 107 × 15 cm.
(62 × 42 × 6 in.)
New York, Solomon R.
Guggenheim Museum

245. Opposite
Jesus Rafael Soto
*Gran muro panoramico
vibrante*, detail
1966; 273 cm. (106 in.)
Rome, Galleria Nazionale
di Arte Moderna

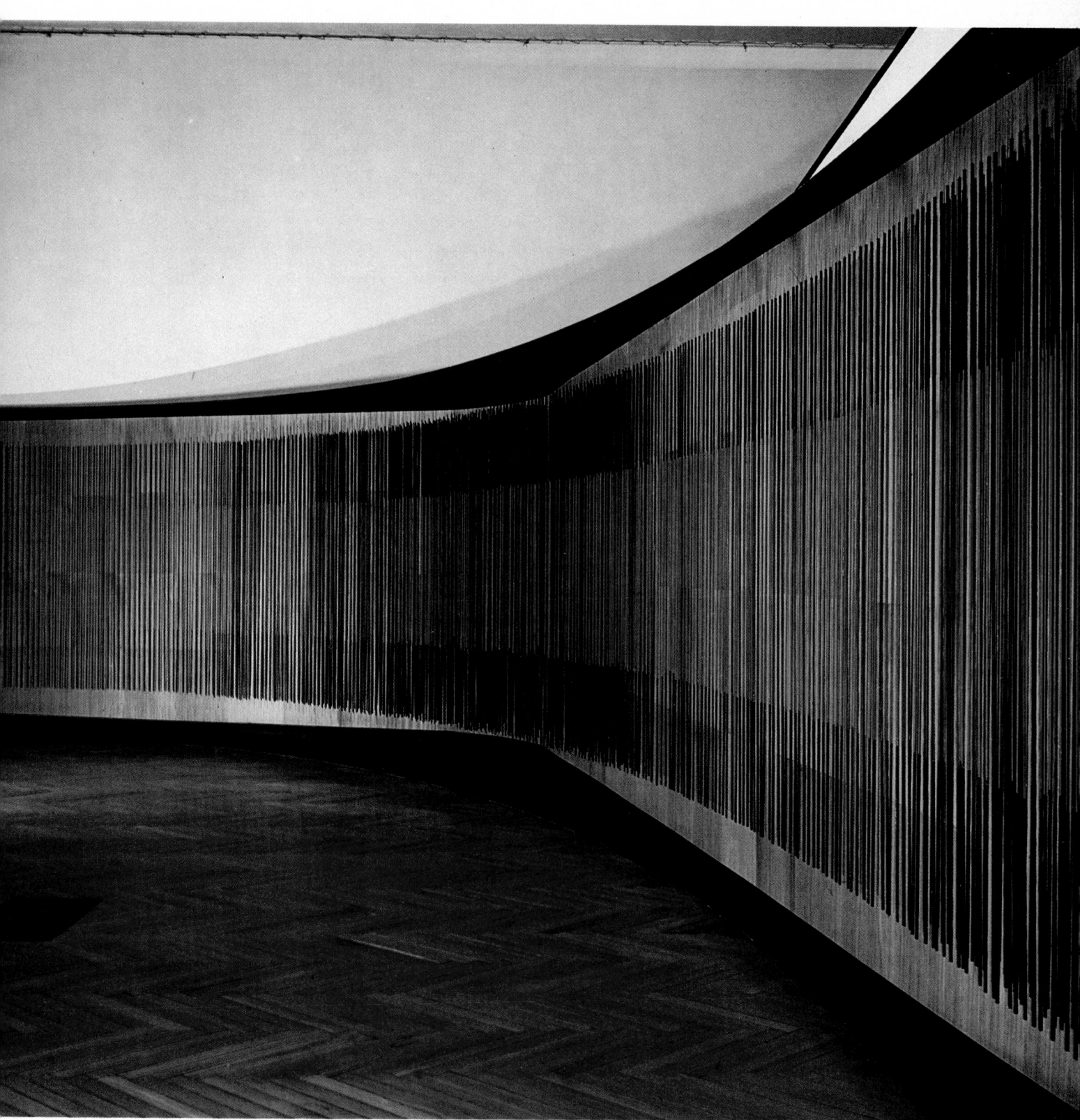

246.
Günther Uecker
Nagelrelief
1969; 149 × 150 cm. (58 × 59 in.)
Aachen, Neue Galerie, coll. Ludwig

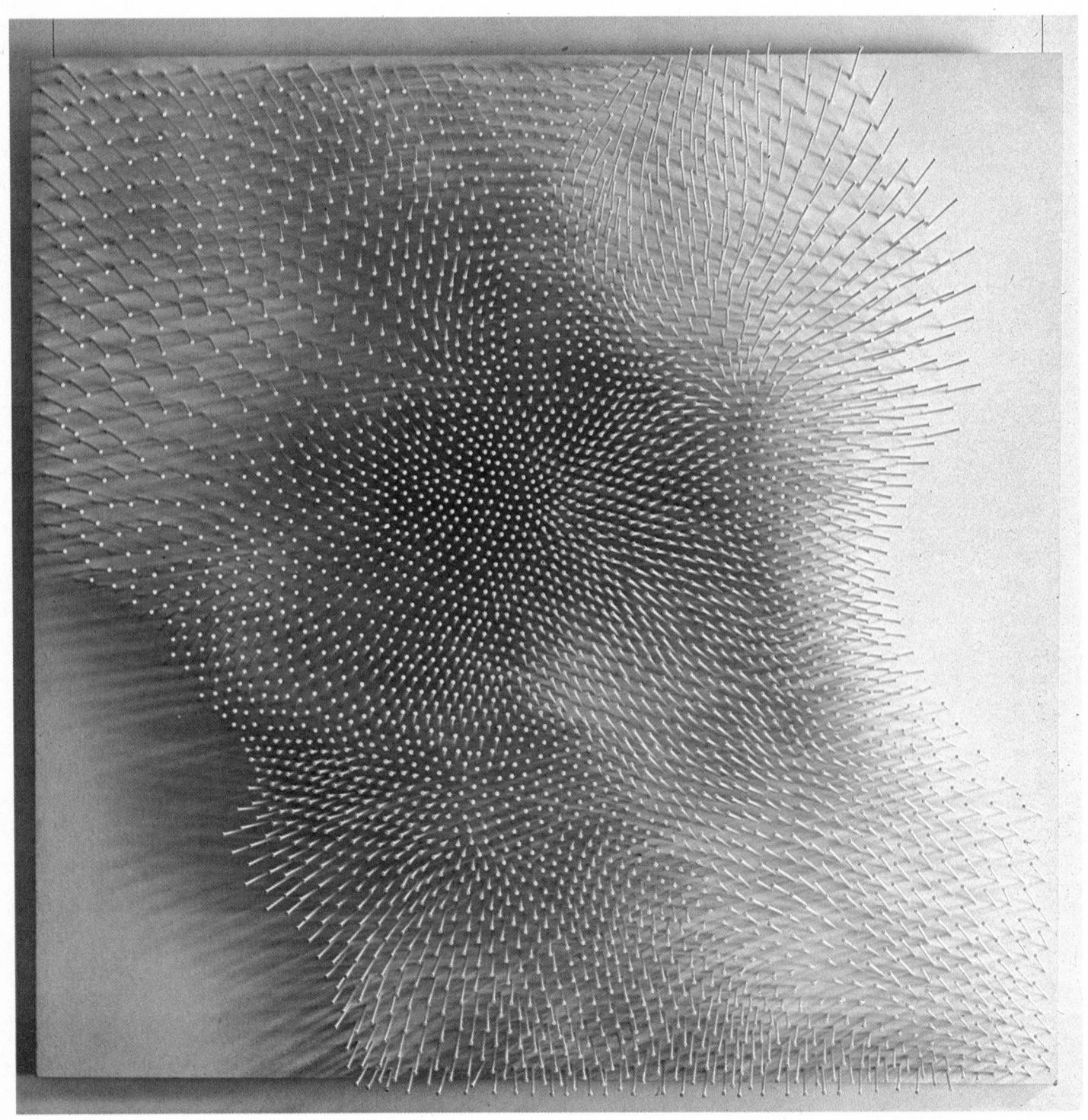

247.
Sergio de Camargo
Rilievo No. 267
1970; 100 × 100 cm. (39 × 39 in.)
London, Gimpel Fils

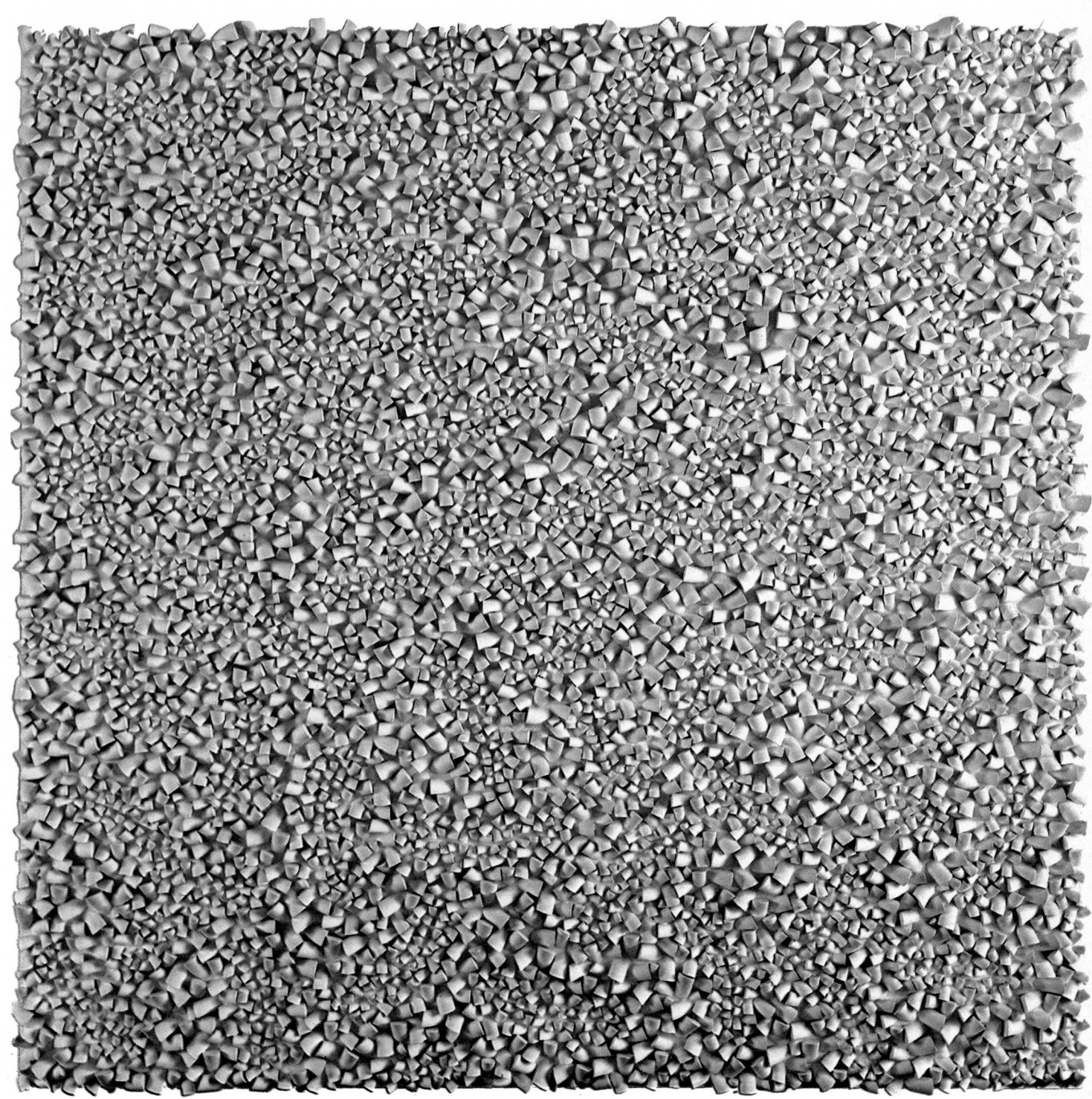

of his occasional ventures into environmental art. Some of the most impressive of his works consist simply of metal rods or nylon threads hung from the ceiling, so as to envelop the space. The spectator's perception of the architecture that surrounds him is thereby completely dissolved. A sense of complete disorientation results (Plate 245).

The *Nailreliefs* of the German artist Günther Uecker (Plate 246) produce a somewhat similar effect on a smaller scale. The white-painted nails driven into an equally white surface have the effect of partly dissolving the physical identity of the work, as the eye no longer has a stable plane surface to rest upon. A somewhat similar device animates the white-painted wooden reliefs of the Brazilian artist Sergio de Camargo (Plate 247). Here the surface is covered with segments cut from a small-diameter rod. Each segment is sliced at a different angle, and, while the curved sides of each volume attract shadow, the sliced ends catch and distribute the light in a multitude of different directions. Yet another variant of this play of light over a white surface is encountered in the canvases of Enrico Castellani, where nails and cuts are used to produce an irregular grid pattern in low relief (Plate 248). It can be no accident that both Uecker and Castellani were influenced by Yves Klein, since each of them seems to use a moderate degree of optical illusion (perhaps not enough for their work to be classified as fully kinetic) in the effort to make the work of art less solidly and soberly material. Castellani has spoken of "the myopia of subjectivism" and of "the necessity of the absolute"—both strikingly Kleinian concepts.

For the large audiences who flocked to the major kinetic art exhibitions of the Sixties, none of the art which has so far been discussed in this chapter would seem particularly relevant to their own concerns in visiting these shows. What the public was excited by, and looked for, was art which had made a successful alliance with the machine, and which could therefore be thought of as having attuned itself to modern technological civilization.

In a sense, this alliance was a polite fiction. Modern artists have very seldom had access to the most advanced technology our society can offer,

and on those few occasions when the two have come together, the results have been disappointing. The "Evenings in Art and Technology" staged in New York in 1966, as an attempted collaboration between artists and engineers, were generally thought disappointing; and during the succeeding decade no attempt has been made to repeat them. It is significant in this connection that the United States, though technologically the most advanced society in the world, has not been in the forefront where kinetic art is concerned. It is better to think of machine-powered art as an expression of feelings about the machine, rather than as an attempt to discover what the machine can in fact do for the artist. This is the case whether the artist describes himself as "experimentally" oriented or not.

In some cases, indeed, the artist has been anxious to preserve the mystery of the mechanical means he employs to get his effects. This is the case with the Belgian artist Pol Bury. For him, movement should be "anonymous, silent, and supernatural", and his pieces can be regarded as a contemporary equivalent of the automata produced by eighteenth-century craftsmen. Bury's roots are in the Surrealist movement, not in Futurism or Constructivism, and in the late Forties he became a member of the CoBrA group. He has shown great ingenuity in the use of simple mechanisms, with a particular penchant for slow movement, often so slow as to be almost imperceptible. The temptation is, as Frank Popper suggests, to see the slowly waving metal or nylon stalks of some of Bury's works as metaphors suggested by marine life—the movements of sea-urchins and sea-anenomes—and to perceive in others ideas taken from planetary movements. The artist himself does not approve of romantic interpretations of this kind, and wishes only to present movement for movement's sake—an idea which emerges clearly from the example illustrated here, with its ranged balls and cubes (Plate 249).

Bury's attitudes towards the machine may be contrasted with those of Jean Tingueley. Tingueley is fascinated by the machine for its own sake. He celebrates it and satirizes it at one and the same time, and uses it, too, to satirize aspects of

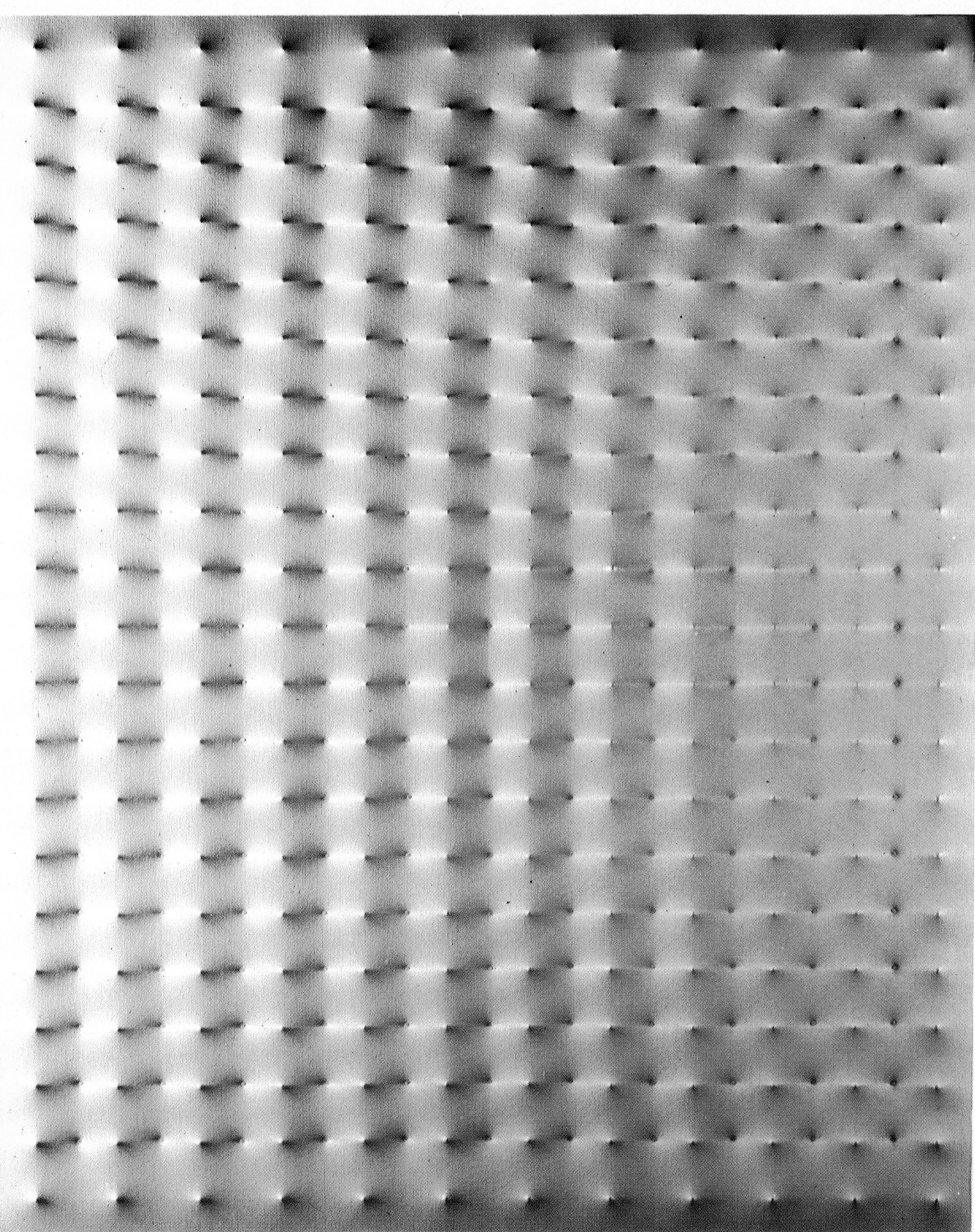

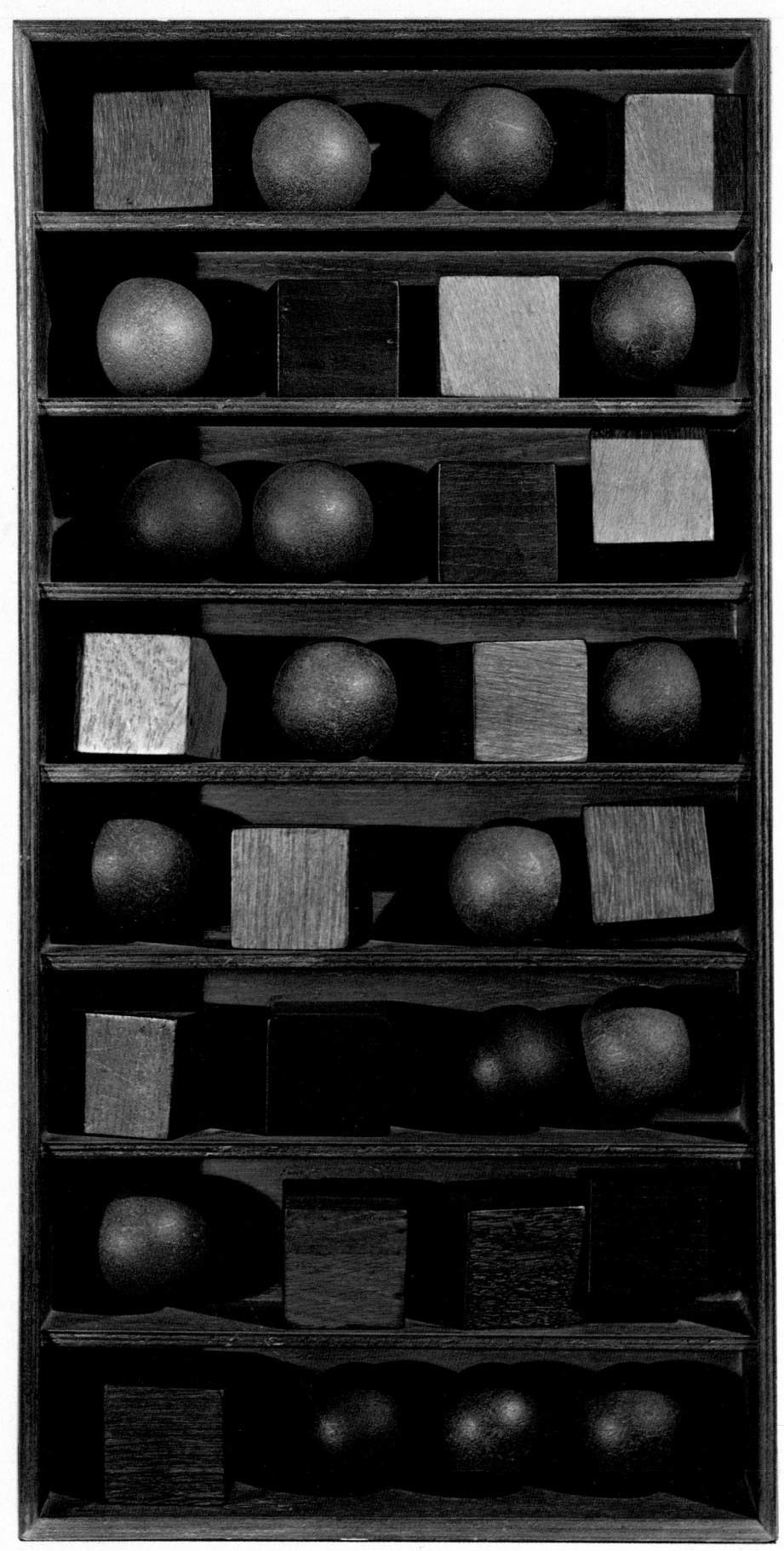

249.
Pol Bury
16 Balls and 16 Cubes on 7 Shelves
1966; 80 × 40 × 20 cm.
(31 × 16 × 8 in.)
London, Tate Gallery

250. Opposite
Jean Tingueley
Baluba No. 3
1959; 144 cm. (56 in.)
Cologne, Wallraf-Richartz Museum,
coll. Ludwig

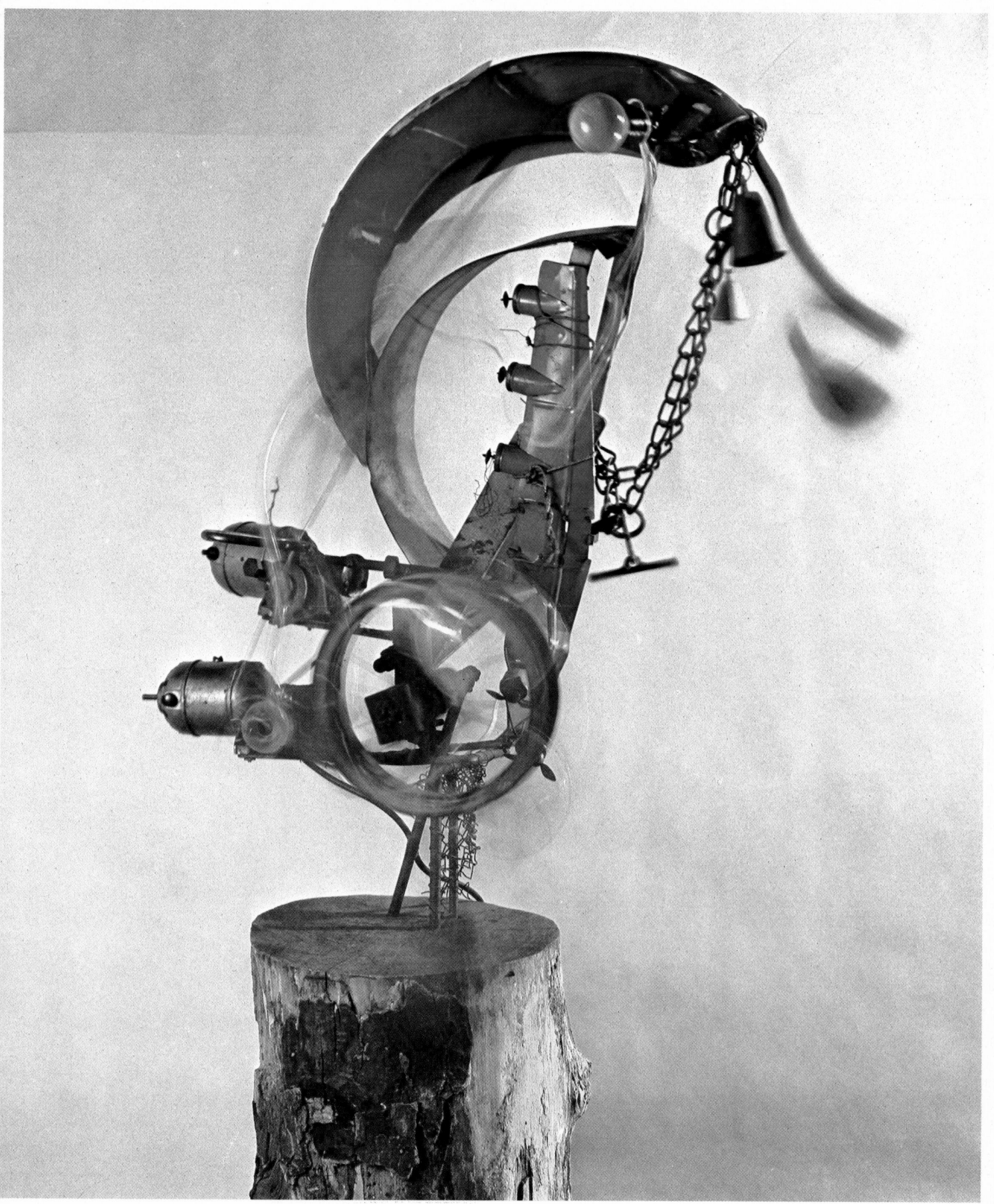

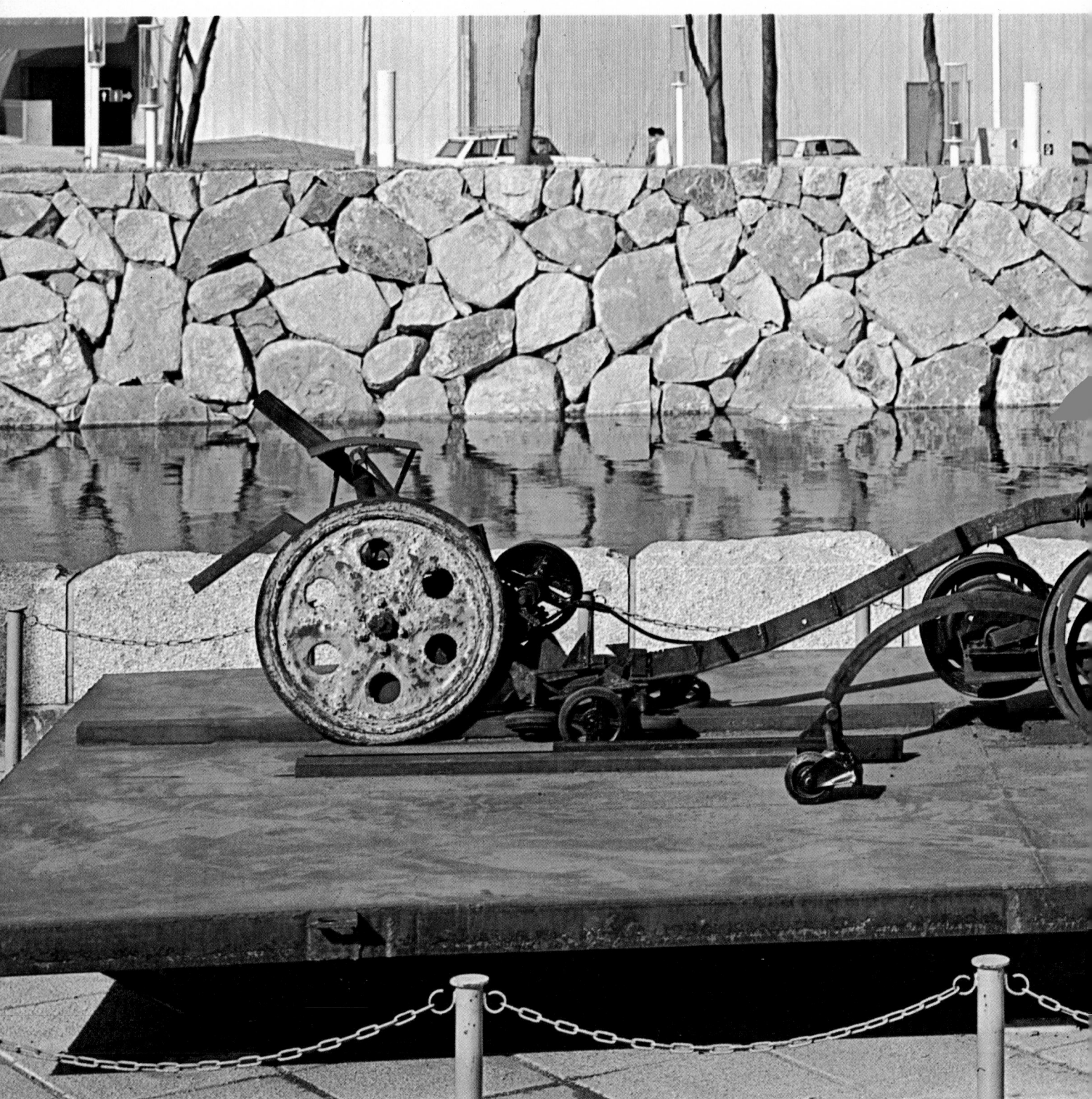

251.
Jean Tingueley
Kamikaze Monument 1962–1969
1969; 500 × 300 × 200 cm. (195 × 117 × 78 in.)
Kanagawa, open-air museum of Hakone

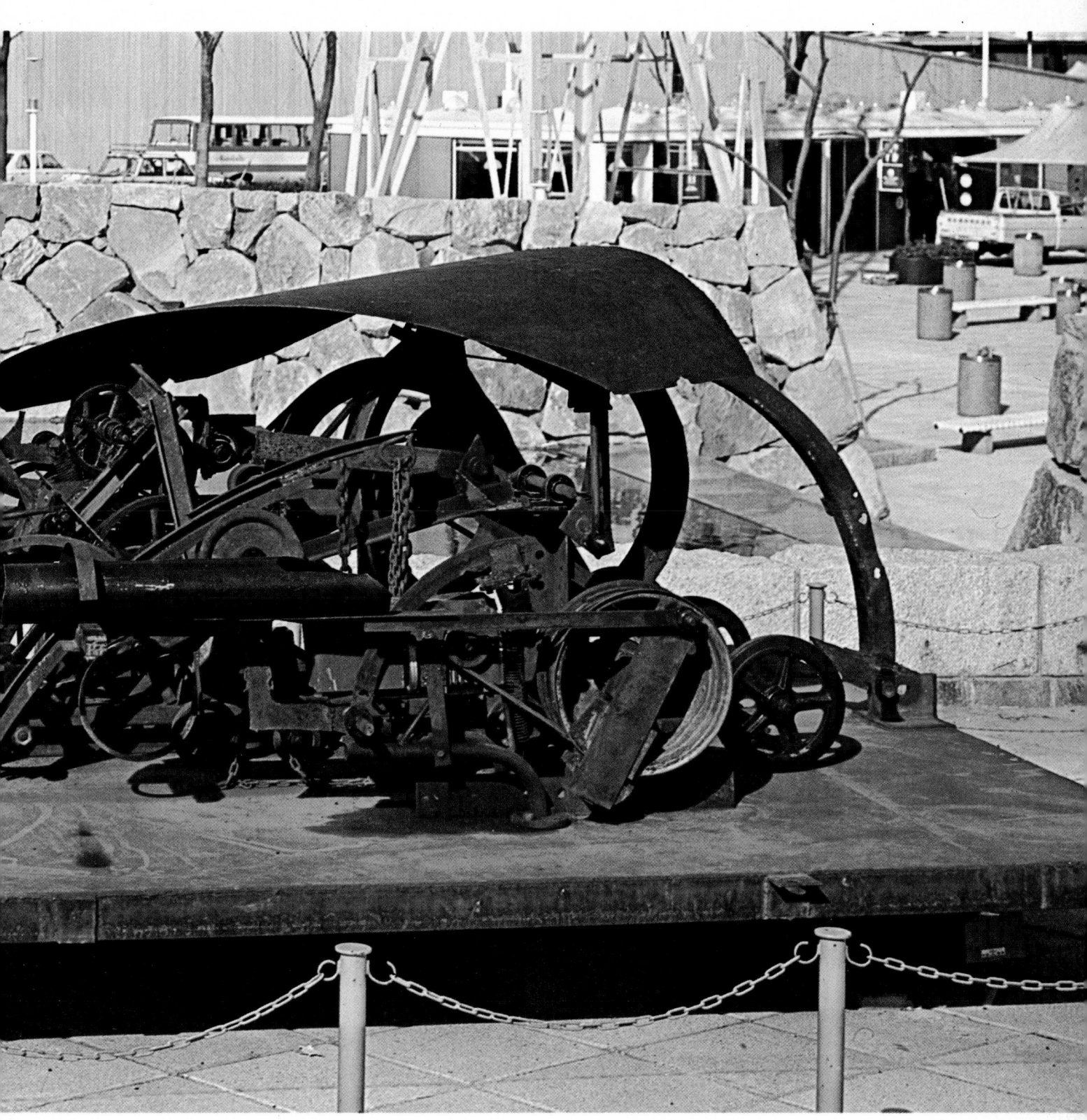

contemporary art. He has, for example, devised mechanisms capable of making "Abstract Expressionist" paintings or drawings. But the satire is never wholly disrespectful to the machine itself. "From Tingueley's point of view," Frank Popper remarks, "the machines which he devises are living creatures which inspire him at one stage with fear, and at another with astonishment or admiration." Instead of the neatness of Bury, Tingueley's pieces have an endearing raffishness (Plate 250, *Baluba No. 3*). Some, indeed, are programmed chiefly to destroy themselves, as with the chief actor in the "Machine Happening" which the artist devised for the Museum of Modern Art in 1960. Others place great emphasis on the capacity of the machine to undergo a rapid process of deterioration (Plate 251, *Kamikaze Monument*). Almost always his constructions have an unmechanical waywardness: "With their unpredictable and unique movements and sequences, Tingueley's machines exist in an enviable freedom. Their vitality, spontaneity and lyricism bring us ecstatic moments of life divorced entirely from moral precept or inhibition, from work and evil right and wrong, beautiful or ugly . . . they subvert the established order and convey a sense of anarchy and individual liberation which would otherwise not exist" (K. G. Hulten, in the introduction to the catalogue of the exhibition "Two Kinetic Sculptors: Nicolas Schöffer and Jean Tingueley", at the Jewish Museum, New York, 1966).

Tingueley himself paradoxically affirms that "Movement is the only static, final, permanent and certain things. . . . Today we can no longer believe in permanent laws, defined religions, durable architecture or eternal kingdoms. Immobility does not exist. All is movement. All is static" (From *Zero 3*, Dusseldorf, 1961, p. 44).

If Pol Bury demonstrates that kinetic art, though its origins for the most part lie elsewhere, is not necessarily irreconcilable with Surrealism, Tingueley's prolific *oeuvre* is a reminder of the link between kinetics and Dada. In particular, he is a direct descendant of Marcel Duchamp.

Yet another approach to this kind of art can be found in the work of Takis. With Takis, it is not the machine as such which is the focus of his activity; it is what the machine makes visible. It is for this reason that he makes widespread use of magnets in his work: "At one blow the magnet provided him with an entirely new language of space. . . . the magnet freed Takis from the architects' and engineers' methods of construction which, for example, Gabo had used. The construction system in a Takis sculpture is a flexible network of electro-magnetic energy, not unlike a planetary system" (Guy Brett, *Kinetic Art: The Language of Movement*, London, 1968, p. 28).

In a typical Takis work (Plate 252), an electromagnet supplies a pole of energy which is switched on and off in a regular rhythm. When the magnet is on, it attracts positive magnets in its surroundings and repels negative ones. When it is off, the positive and negative magnets are drawn towards one another. Whenever the machine is active, all its components are therefore engaged in a perpetual dance. In other magnetic sculptures, the artist makes use of needles which apparently defy gravity as they float in a magnetic stream.

Since Takis's sculptures are concerned with energy rather than matter, they have no formal qualities as such. If the machine is switched off, it has no hint of the presence it possesses when activated, unlike a work by Bury or Tingueley. On the other hand, at those times when they are working, the sounds Takis's sculptures emit are often nearly as important as the spectacle they present.

Light and sound are quite commonly important additional elements in kinetic sculpture. The *Silberroter* of Heinz Mack (Plate 253) provides a simple example of the importance of light. As the disk within the piece revolves, so reflected light begins to ripple off its surfaces.

The most ambitious works in this category are, however, those which have been produced by Nicolas Schöffer. Like Vasarely, Schöffer was born in Hungary, and he has since settled in France. Since 1959 he has been developing what he has dubbed "spatiodynamics" and "luminodynamics" (Plate 254). Moving metal constructions are used in combination with lights which are reflected from their surfaces, and transmitted

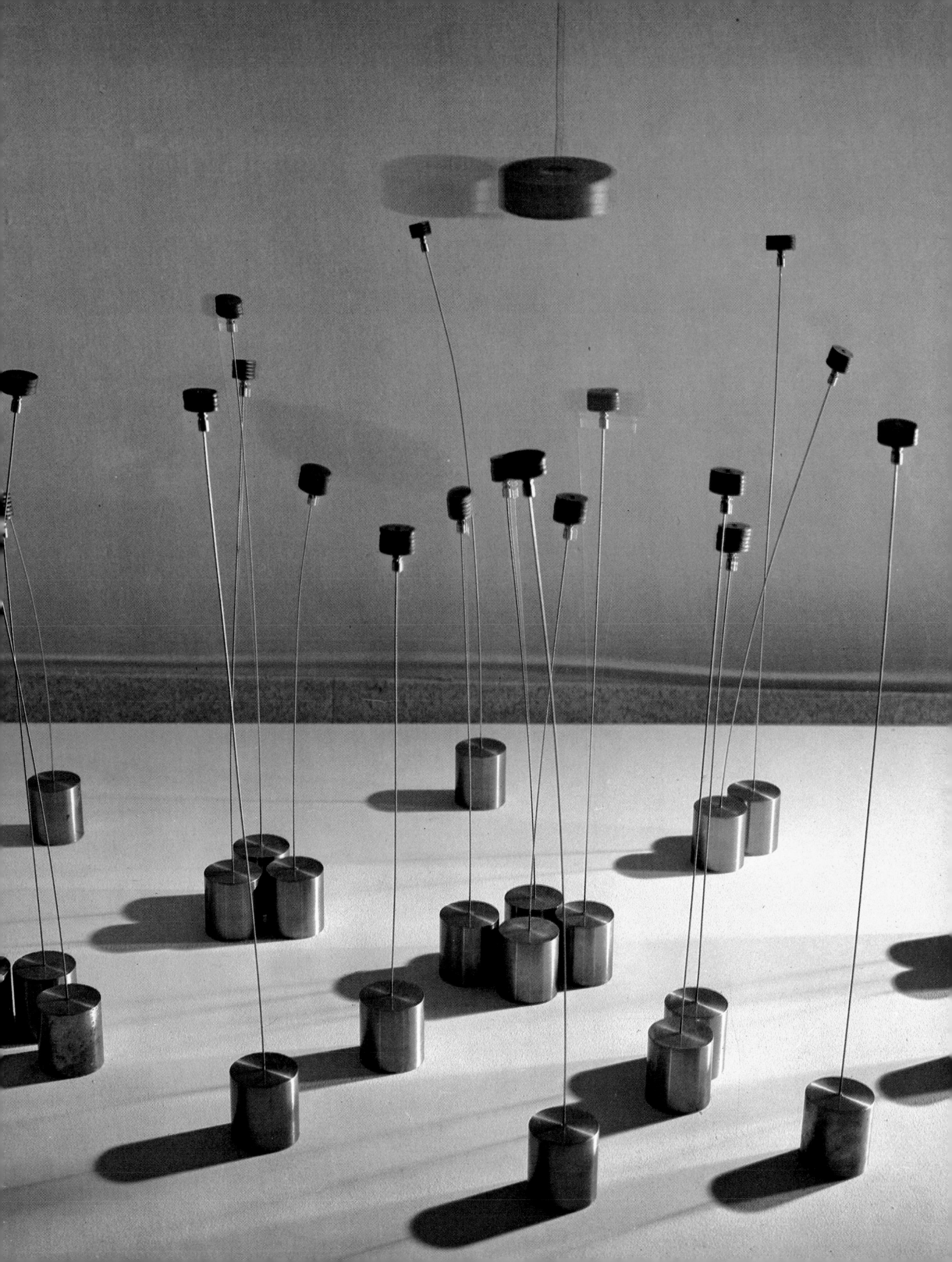

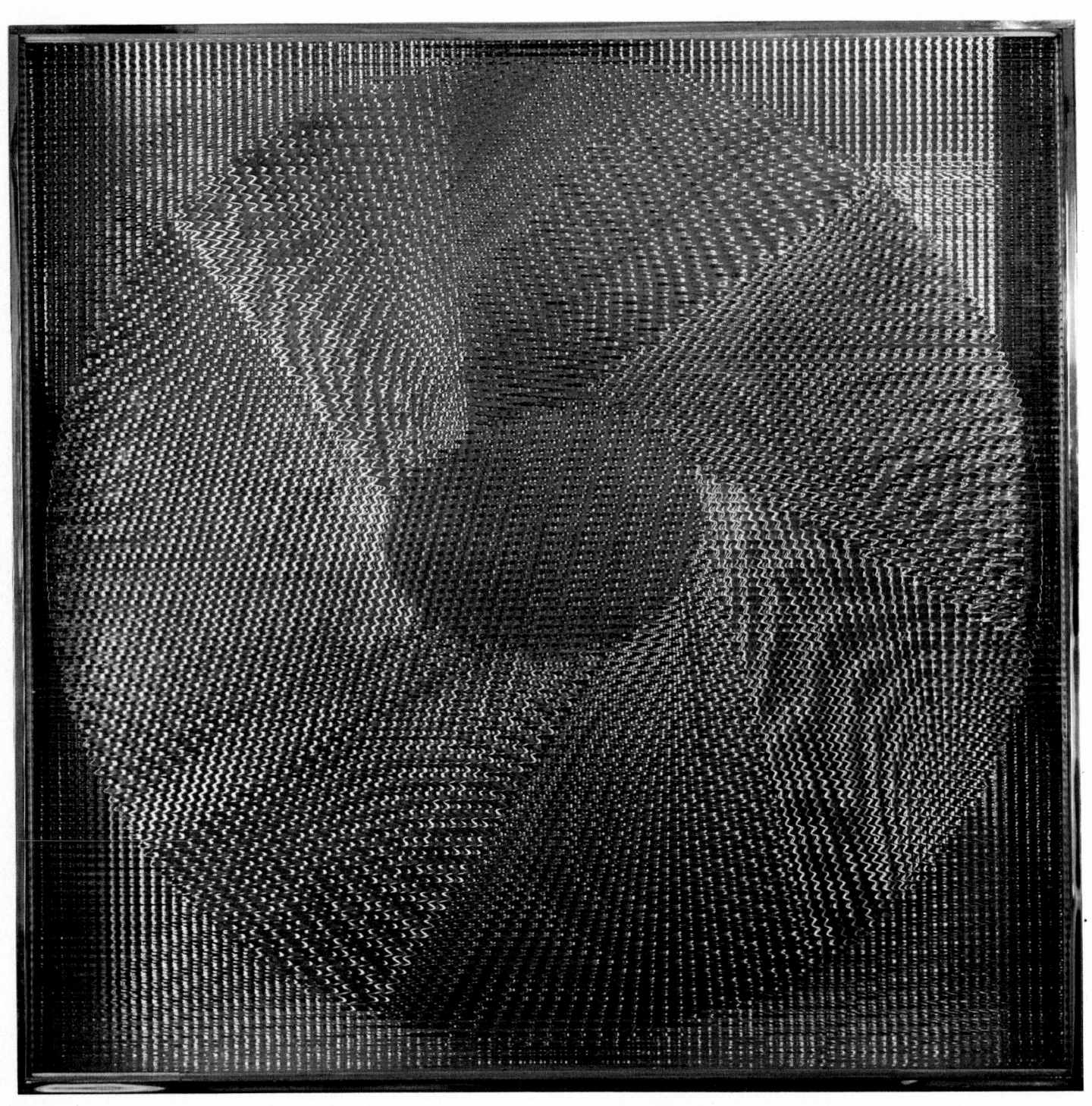

through sheets of coloured plastic Sometimes a musical accompaniment is added. Schöffer often works on a very ambitious scale—his sound-equipped luminodynamic tower made for the Bouverie Park, Liège, in 1961 is 52 metres (171 feet) in height. The theatrical nature of what Schöffer does is accentuated by his own attitudes towards it. He regards the necessary dynamism

254.
Nicolas Schöffer
Sculptures Spatio-Dynamiques
N.d.; 107 × 90 × 75 cm. (42 × 35 × 29 in.)
Paris, Musée National d'Art Moderne

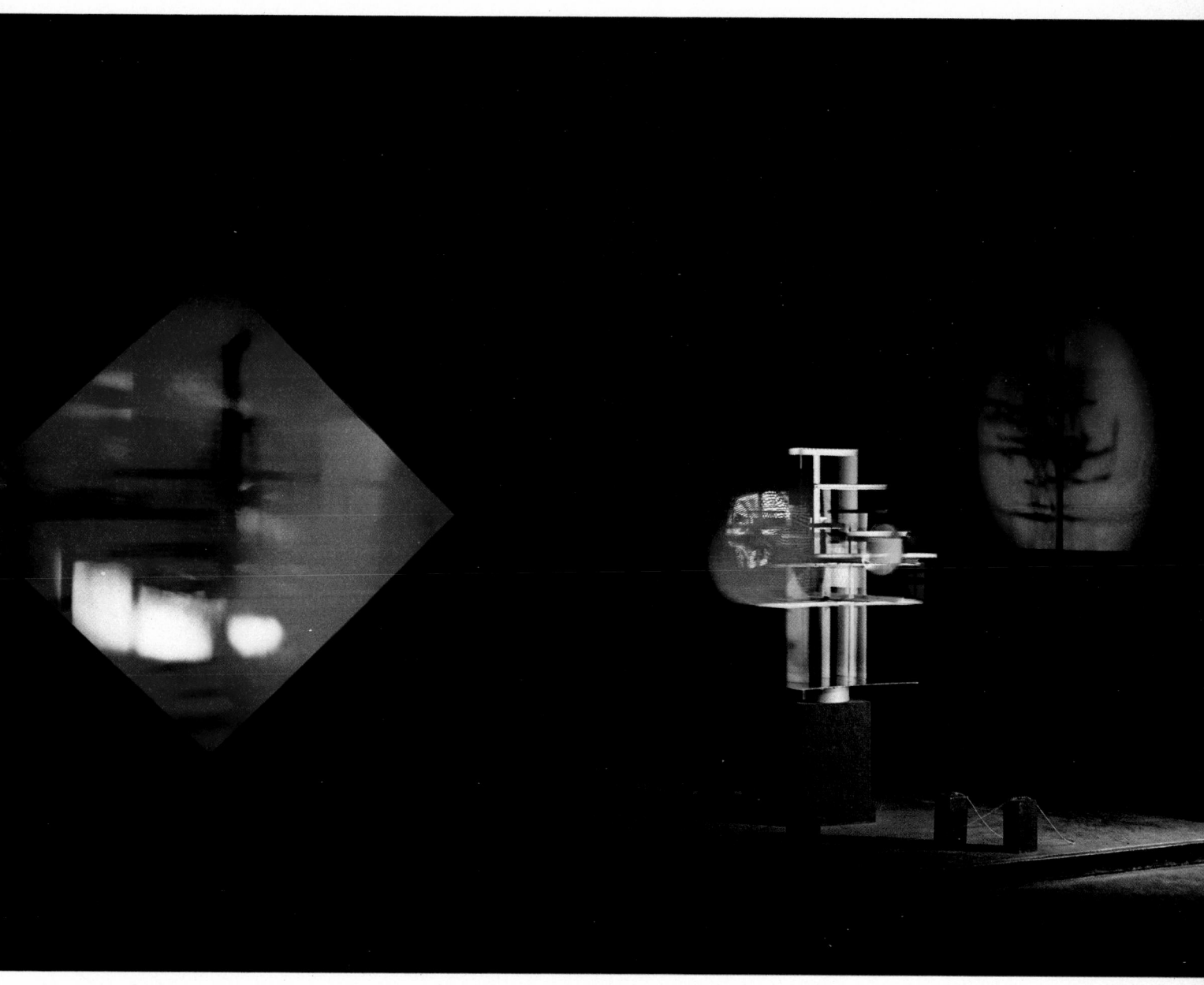

within the work as being very much the product of the chaos of emotion and intuition from which it arises in the first place, and the elaborate engineering of his constructions by no means rules out the idea of random motion, and therefore includes the kind of unpredictable relations which are part of the excitement of true theatre.

Schöffer's kinetic constructions take us to the very borders of both environmental art and of the Happening, and therefore demonstrate another of the ways in which the apparently closed and specialized world of kinetic and optical art stretches out to make contact with what is being done elsewhere on the contemporary scene.

Post-Painterly Abstraction

The art movement commonly dubbed Post-Painterly Abstraction presents the critic writing in the 1970's with some of his most ticklish problems of judgment. The reason for this is the considerable literature which has already accumulated about a kind of art which, viewed superficially, might not seem to lend itself to verbal elaboration.

The tone of the criticism devoted to work by leading members of the group is best represented by quotation from Michael Fried's essay *Three American Painters*, published in 1965. The three painters concerned were Kenneth Noland, Jules Olitski, and Frank Stella, but the remarks cited here were intended by Fried as a general comment upon the situation of both the painter and the critic: "While modernist painting has increasingly divorced itself from the concerns of the society in which it precariously flourishes, the actual dialectic by which it is made has taken on more and more of the denseness, structure and complexity of moral experience—that is, of life itself, but of life lived as few are inclined to live it: in a state of continuous intellectual and moral alertness.

"The formal critic of modernist painting, then, is also a moral critic: not because all art is at bottom a criticism of life, but because modernist painting is at least a criticism of itself. And because this is so, criticism that shares the basic premises of modernist painting finds itself compelled to play a role in its development closely akin to, and only somewhat less important than, the paintings themselves" (Michael Fried, *Three American Painters*, Cambridge, Massachusetts, 1965, pp. 9–10).

It will be seen that Fried not only claims a moral as well as a physical autonomy for certain kinds of modern art, but that he ranks the critic as a kind of collaborator of the painter, though at the same time conceding that this may be "an intolerably arrogant conception" of his task.

In fact, it seems to me that criticism has tended to obfuscate, rather than to elucidate, important aspects of Post-Painterly Abstraction. One of these is the question of its precise ancestry. The more enthusiastic of the supporters of artists such as Morris Louis, Noland, and Stella have wanted to see them as the direct descendants and true heirs of Abstract Expressionism, forming the second and perhaps more important phase of an American art which outclasses its European rivals, and which in fact owes nothing to anything which has happened in Europe since 1940, though an ultimate debt to the "shallow space" of Cubism is more or less proudly admitted. While there is, indeed, some truth in the contention that Post-Painterly Abstraction is a natively American style, its origins are more complex and the actual quality of the painting is more questionable than its supporters have been prepared to admit.

Fried's essay, which is the most important, and also the most closely argued, manifesto issued on behalf of the painters of this group, seeks to derive their work in the first place from the all-over drip paintings produced by Jackson Pollock in the years 1947 to 1950, and in the second place, though in a more muted way, from Barnett Newman. He also admits—and it is, after all, a well-established historical fact—the impact made by Helen Frankenthaler's work on Morris Louis and on Noland when they visited her studio in 1953.

Nowhere, however, does one find a discussion of two subjects which seem to be closely related to his argument. The first of these is the relationship between figurative and abstract art in the America of the 1960's, and the second is the relevance of certain hard-edge abstract painters, notably Josef Albers and Ellsworth Kelly, to what the Post-Painterly Abstractionists were trying to do.

Figurative art in these circumstances can only mean Pop Art, and if Fried ignores this, it is

255.
Josef Albers
Homage to the Square Series : Assertive
1958; 81 × 81 cm. (32 × 32 in.)
New York, by kind permission of the Sidney Janis Gallery

256.
Josef Albers
Homage to the Square Series: Fall Fragrance
1964; 102 × 102 cm. (40 × 40 in.)
New York, by kind permission of the Sidney Janis Gallery

257. Overleaf
Ellsworth Kelly
Red, Blue, Green
1962; 213 × 396 cm. (83 × 154 in.)
California, Pasadena Art Museum

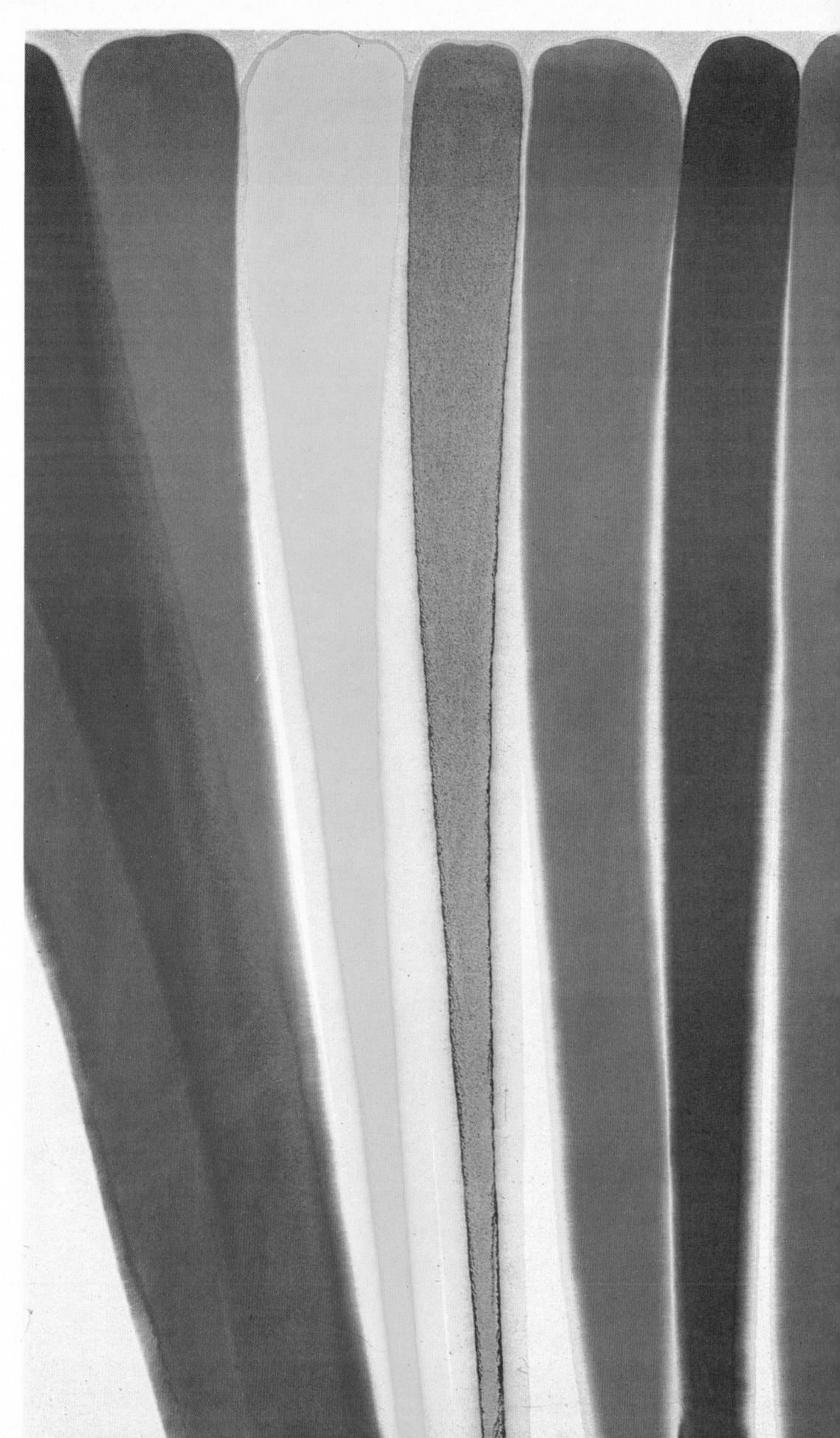

258.
Morris Louis
While
1959; 245 × 347 cm.
(96 × 135 in.)
New York, coll. of the
Harry N. Abrams family

manifestly because he thinks that Pop Art is not only worthless, but in his terms immoral—a deliberate debasement of what art ought to be. This opinion was fairly generally shared by major American art critics, who had great difficulty in coming to terms not only with Pop Art itself, but with its success with the public. In particular, those who had supported Abstract Expressionism tended to see the Pop reaction against it as a cynical betrayal of everything American art had achieved during the Forties and Fifties.

In this respect Post-Painterly Abstraction is a conservative rather than a radical style But this must not lead us into asserting that it grew up in direct opposition to Pop Art. On the contrary, this new version of American abstraction had already started to evolve in the mid-Fifties, and chronologically reached a recognizable maturity somewhat before Pop did.

The precise terms that art critics and theorists elected to use, when discussing artists such as Louis, Noland, and Stella in the years after 1960, were, however, strongly influenced by distaste for the alternative, which was Pop figuration.

The relevance of Albers, and to a lesser extent of Kelly, springs to the eye when one looks at the paintings themselves. Josef Albers, after teaching at the Bauhaus, emigrated to America in the early Thirties and found himself at Black Mountain College. His work, after an early Expressionist phase, which can be studied in surviving woodcuts, became imbued with the logically experimental Bauhaus spirit, which can also be detected in the work of Moholy-Nagy. The study of colour became a particular preoccupation with Albers during his American years. In 1949 he wrote: "A painter works to formulate with or in color. Some painters regard color as a concomitant of form, and hence as subordinate. For others, and in ever-increasing proportion, color is the chief medium of their pictorial language. Here color attains autonomy. My painting represents the second trend. I am particularly interested in the psychic effect, an aesthetic experience that is evoked by the interaction of juxtaposed colors" (quoted by Eugen Gomringer, *Josef Albers*, New York, 1968, p. 104).

This statement, so relevant not only to Albers' own art but to the colour stripes of Louis and Noland, was written before Albers embarked on the *Homage to the Square* series by which he is best known. These paintings, apparently so simple in their format, are a fascinating fusion of European and American themes. They are European because the artist sums up in them the best of his Bauhaus experience. The squares, for example, are proportioned according to a strict mathematical formula—the pictures are composed according to a horizontal and vertical division consisting of ten units in each case. The optical quality of the colour, deliberately sought, has its roots in Bauhaus investigations of illusion, and thus has a direct relationship to the Op art produced in postwar Europe. Albers arranges his hues so as to persuade the planes to separate from the ground on which they are painted, and float free in space (Plates 255 and 256).

What is un-European about these works is their symmetry—the refusal to compromise the search for fully activated colour by resorting to traditional compositional devices. There is a relevant comparison here between Albers and Rothko. Rothko's centred rectangles of colour float free of the ground in just the same way that Albers' do, though the technical means used to achieve the effect is different in each case.

If Ellsworth Kelly's work conveys a slight sense of isolation from the rest of the New York scene, this may be due to the pattern of his training and development. He studied painting in Paris under the G. I. Bill and did not return to America until the middle Fifties, when he had already absorbed the lessons of European Constructivism. Impressed by the scale and power of Abstract Expressionism, he adjusted the scale of the clear, flat images he had inherited from the Constructivists so as to conform to the new mode (Plate 257). But this adjustment meant an increased concentration upon colour. As Lawrence Alloway remarks: "The center of his work is a painterly command of color. Not color in terms of glazes, or variations, or light and shade, but solid color. His hues are controlled not by gradation but by exact adjustments of their internal density and

259.
Morris Louis
Alpha-Pi
1961; 260 × 450 cm. (101 × 176 in.)
New York, Metropolitan Museum of Art, Arthur H.
Hearn Fund

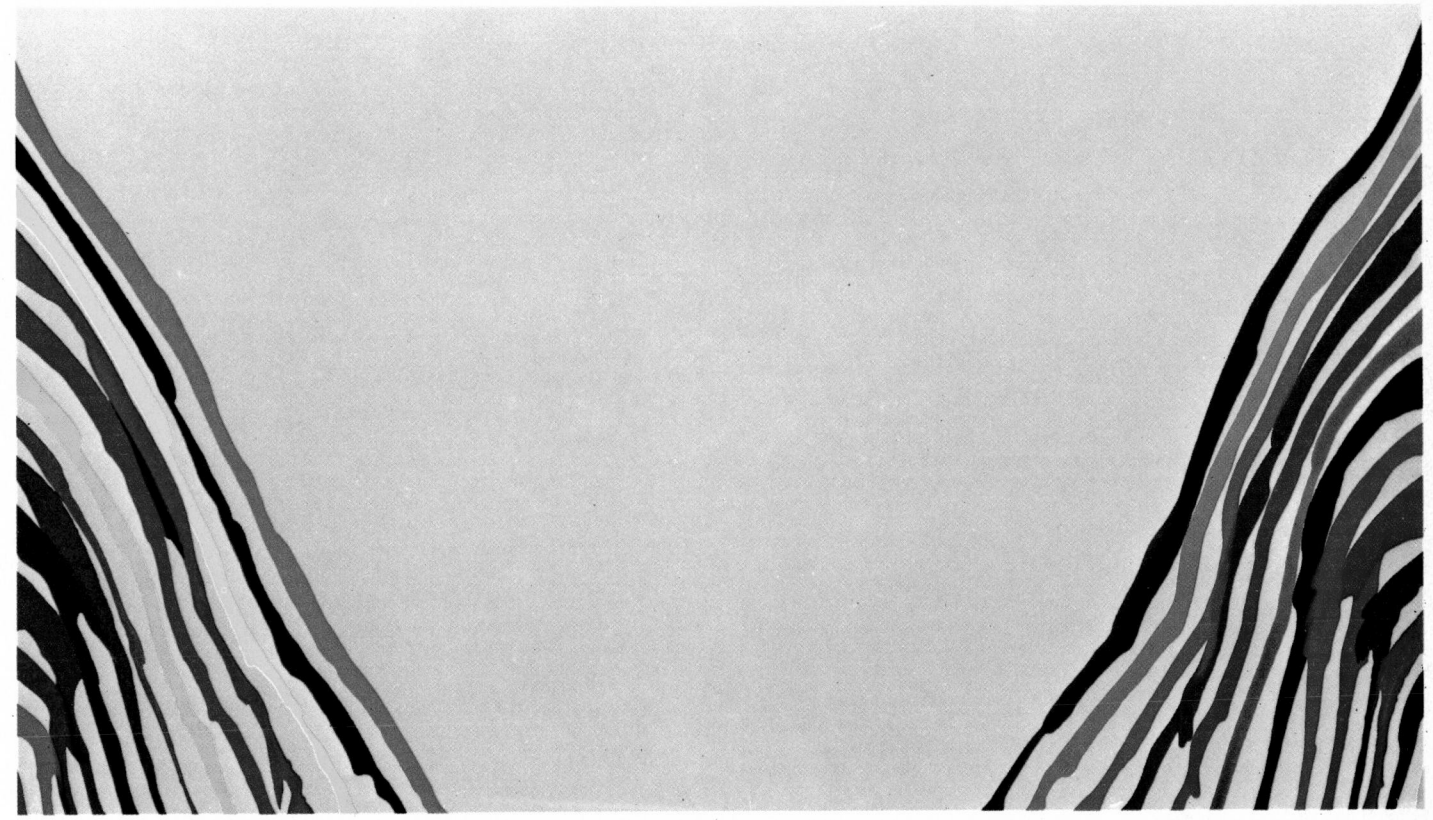

their outer contours" (Lawrence Alloway, catalogue to the American Pavilion, Venice, Esposizione d'Arte, 1966).

If one compares Kelly's works to Albers's, one notes that the former does not resort to effects which are definably "optical", at least as that adjective is commonly used in connection with painting. But it is nevertheless the colour which forces adjustments on the eye. The conception one forms of the various areas into which the canvas is divided depends as much on one's reaction to the hues they are painted as on one's estimate of their size and shape.

Curiously enough, the resemblance between Albers and Kelly and Morris Louis is far less than the resemblance between the same two artists and the later work of Noland and Stella. It is in Louis's painting that one is most conscious of the genuine and intimate connection between Post-Painterly Abstraction and Abstract Expressionism. Louis supplies us with an outstanding example of what

has been called the break-through phenomenon in contemporary American art. Before 1954, Louis, though a dedicated artist, had made only a minor contribution. After 1954, he gradually came to be seen as a painter of major importance. The key event was a visit which Louis, who lived and worked in Washington, paid to New York in 1953. He was accompanied by Kenneth Noland, already a friend of his, and one of the people whom they saw was the critic Clement Greenberg, and it was Greenberg who took them to Helen Frankenthaler's studio.

For Louis, Frankenthaler's work had the force of a revelation, but it was a revelation of a very special kind. What impressed him was not so much the content of her work as some aspects of her technique, in particular the habit of using thinned acrylic paint and of letting this stain the canvas as if it was watercolour used upon absorbent paper. Greenberg tells us: "The crucial revelation he got from Pollock and Frankenthaler had to do with

333

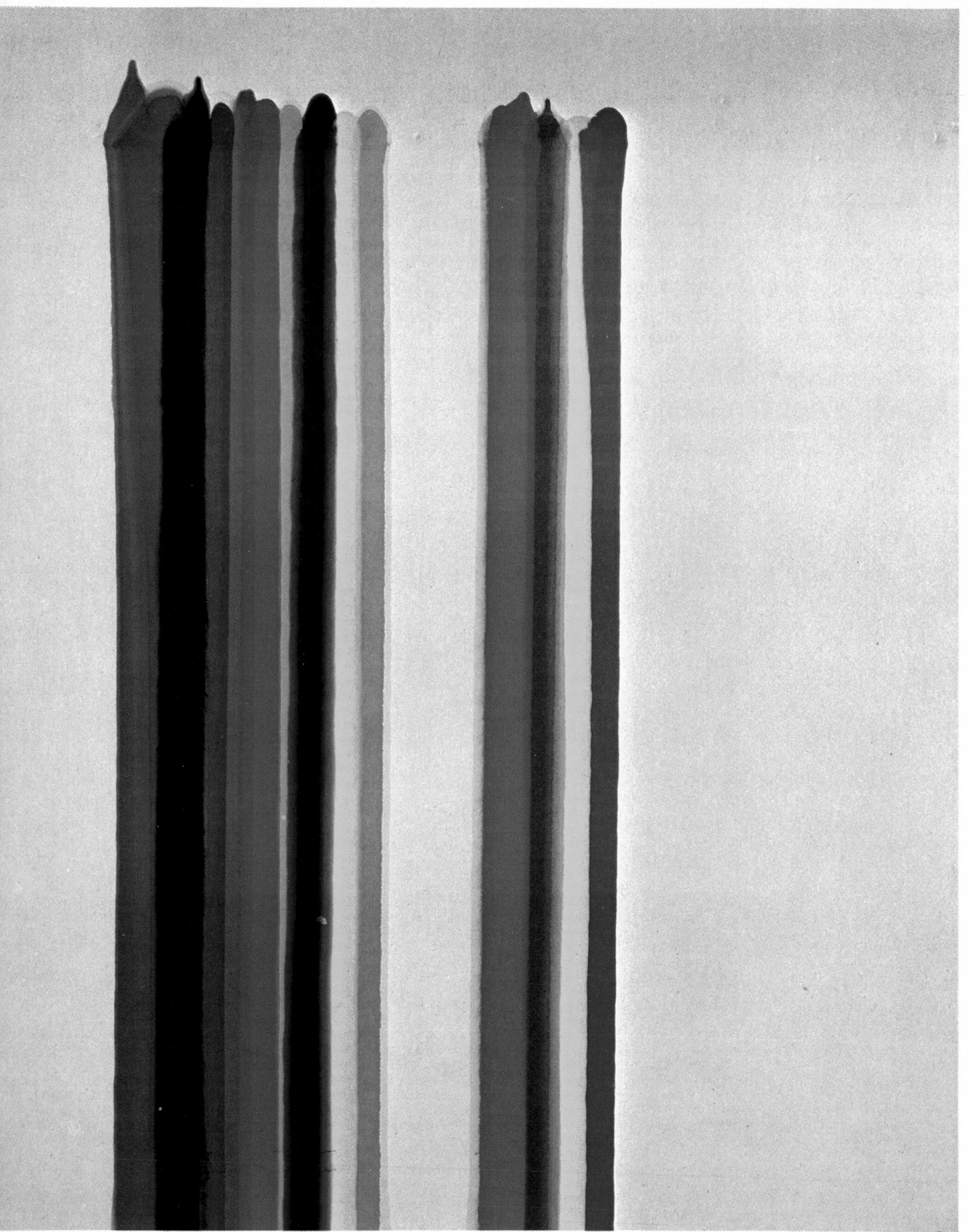

260. Opposite
Morris Louis
No. 180
1961; 226 × 186 cm. (88 × 73 in.)
California, Pasadena Art Museum

261.
Morris Louis
Hot Half
1962; 161 × 161 cm. (63 × 63 in.)
Washington, D.C., coll. Mrs. Abner Brenner

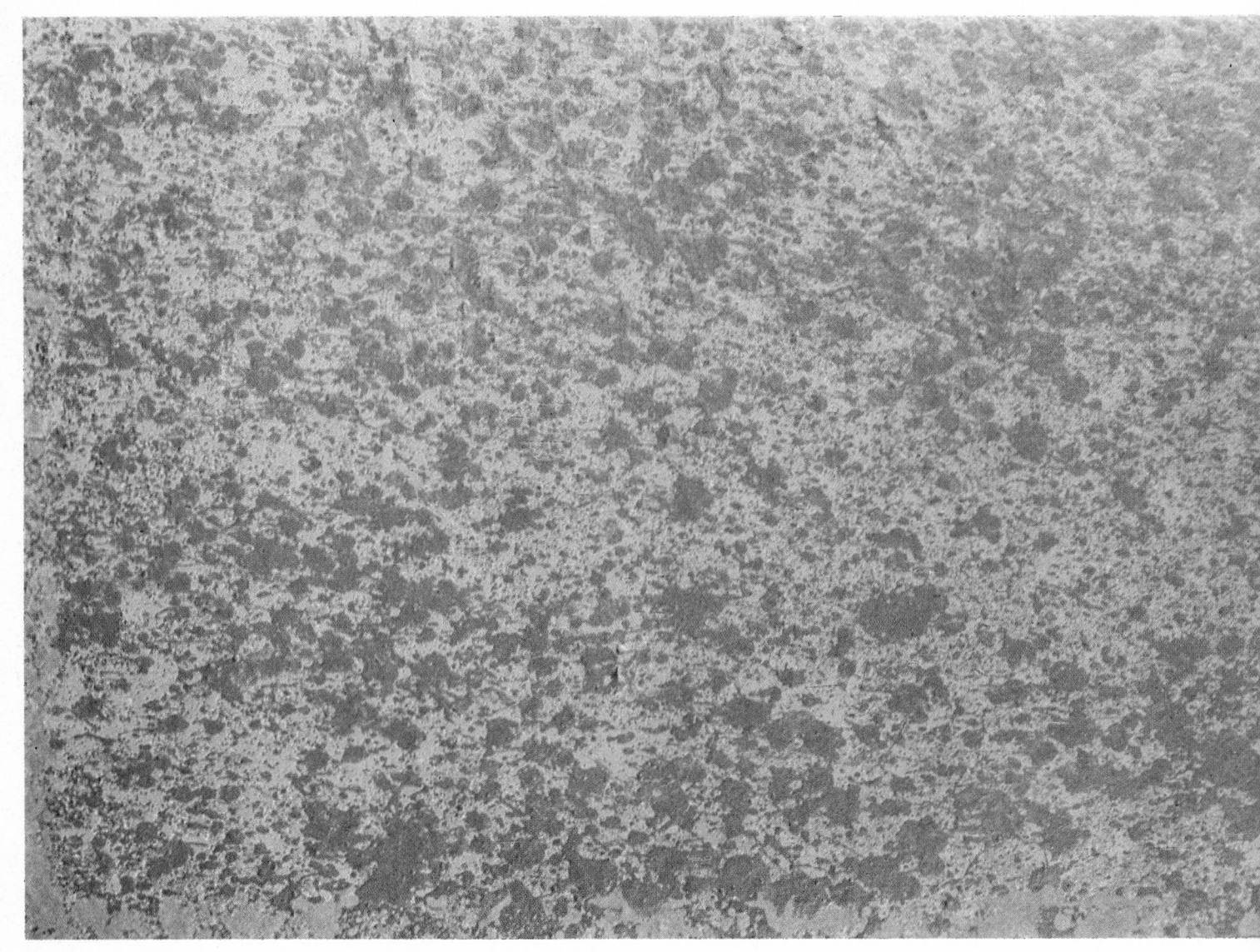

facture as much as anything else. The more closely color could be identified with its ground, the freer it would be from the interference of tactile associations" (Clement Greenberg, *Art International*, Vol.IV, No. 5 [May, 1960], pp. 26–9).

When Louis adopted a new range of techniques, these involved important consequences for his art. For one thing, the paintings became more impersonal, though they remained painterly. The colour was either poured onto the horizontal canvas, or applied to it with commercial rollers, and there was no place for the bravura touch of an Abstract Expressionist such as De Kooning. While the staining might produce the illusion of painterliness, it was only an illusion.

At the same time, the colour was no longer on but actually *in* the weave of the canvas, and this was particularly true after Louis abandoned the use of sized canvas for unsized cotton duck. This caused the painter, and later the spectator, to think of the work itself in new terms, as a homogenous object, an independent addition to a world of objects.

Thirdly, and this applied chiefly to Louis's

262.
Jules Olitski
11th Move
1969
London, Kasmin Gallery Ltd.

earlier and freer experiments, the staining produced a contour which was not drawn; and repeated streams of paint would actually produce a contour *within* a contour, if that was what the artist wanted (*While*, 1959, Plate 258).

Once the initial breakthrough was made, Louis, like many contemporary artists, tended to work in connected series or groups. The *Veils* were followed by the *Unfurleds* (*Alpha-Pi*, 1961, Plate 259), and these in turn by a series in which the colour was arranged in simple stripes (*No. 180*, 1961, Plate 260). In some final canvases, executed just before Louis's final illness and death, the stripes were arranged diagonally (*Hot Half*, 1962, Plate 261). The development of his work is always towards the more stringent, the more rigorous, the more fully controlled. It is possible to imbue the *Veils* and the *Unfurleds* with some kind of transcendental or mystical meaning, or at any rate to see them as "objects for meditation" on more or less the same footing as Rothko's later painting, but the stripes reject interpretations of this kind.

The work of Kenneth Noland is generally discussed in close association with that of Morris

337

263.
Kenneth Noland
Reverberation
1961 ; 244 × 244 cm. (95 × 95 in.)
Colorado, coll. Kimiko and John Powers

264. Opposite
Kenneth Noland
17th Stage
1964 ; 244 × 213 cm. (95 × 83 in.)
New York, coll. Mr. and Mrs. Eugene Schwartz

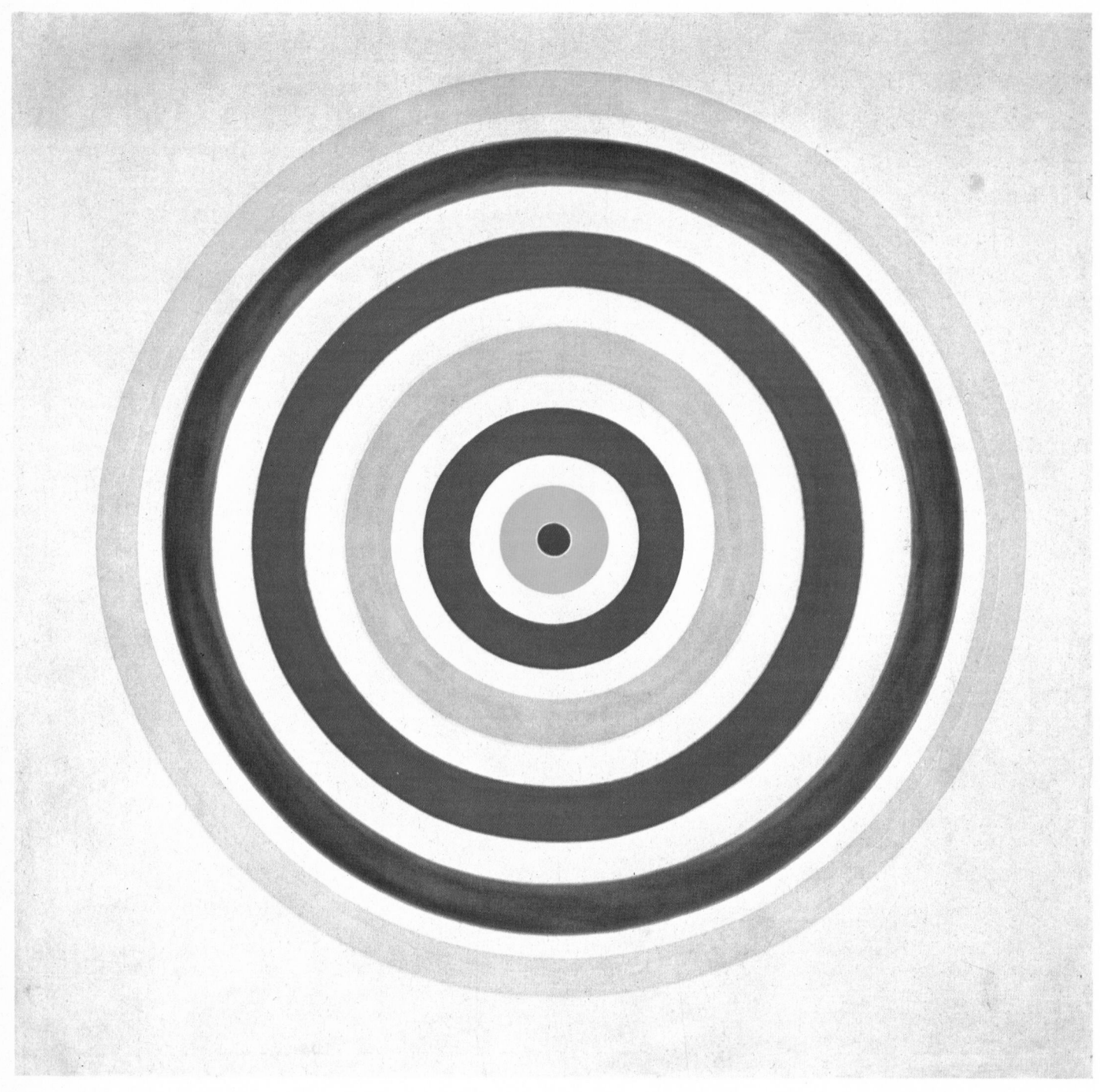

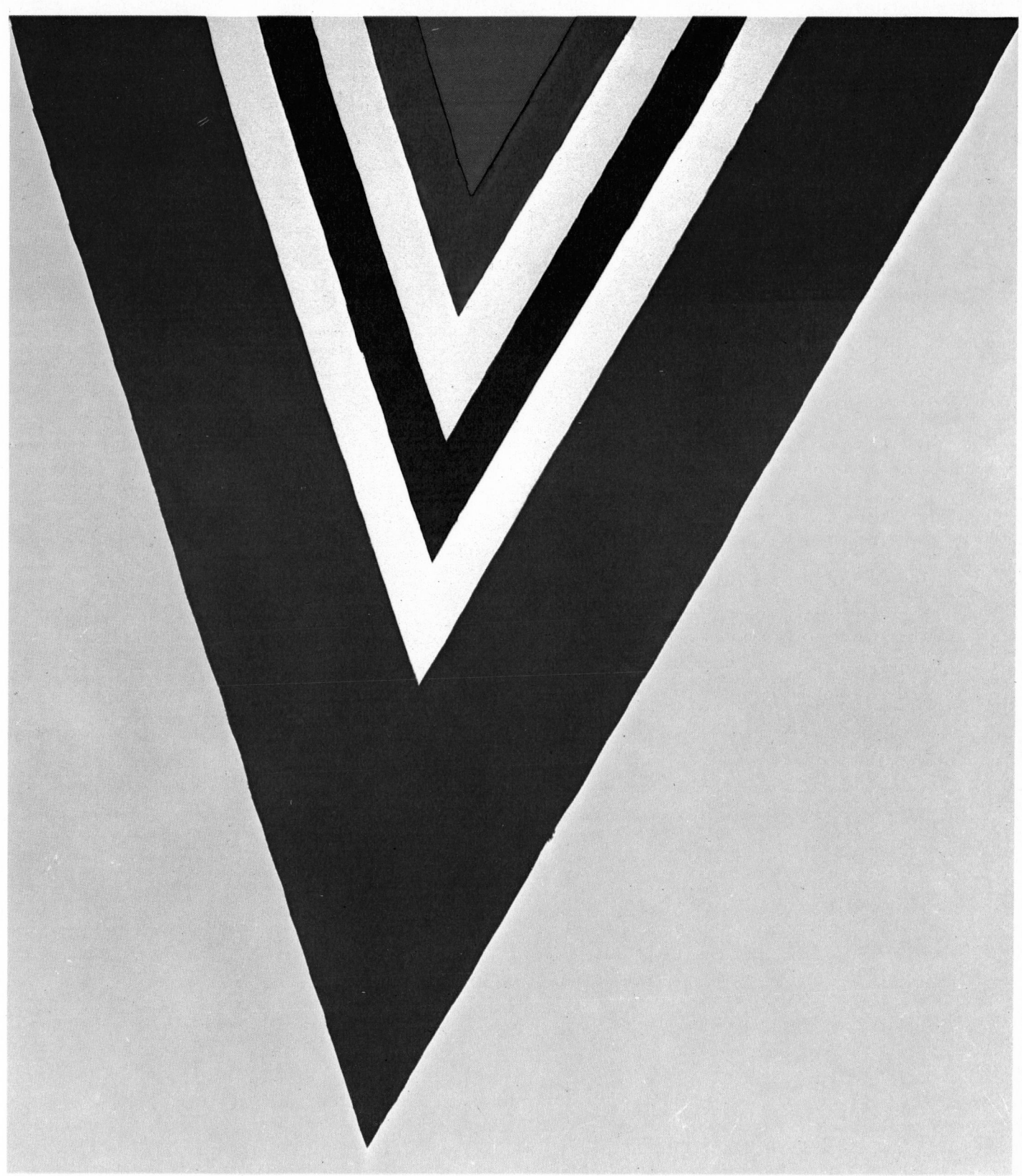

Louis, simply because the two artists were not only personal friends but shared important phases of artistic development. But before passing to Noland's work, we have good reason to consider that of Jules Olitski. Olitski's fascination with veils of tender colour has a relevance to Noland's earlier work, just as Noland's stripes can be referred to what Louis did later.

Olitski's paintings have provoked some extravagant comparisons. Fried, for example, has compared him to Van Eyck: "Putting aside for a moment their obvious differences, what the paintings of Van Eyck and Olitski have in common is a mode of pictorial organization that does not present the beholder with an instantaneously apprehensible unity." This sounds like a critic desperate to justify a preference, and in fact one of the striking things about Olitski is the difference of sensibility to be found between his art and that of the painters with whom he is usually grouped. The difference can be summed up by saying that he has a different area of failure: he seems sentimental (Plate 262) on occasions where they would seem numb. Olitski's background—liky Ellsworth Kelly, he spent some of his formative years in Paris—may help to explain this. The gap between his work and Louis's is similar to the gap that exists between that of Franz Kline and Soulages.

What deserves respect in Olitski's work, despite its fundamental uncertainty and lack of poise, is its respect for feeling. This emotionalism stands firmly opposed to the cynicism of a great deal of Pop Art, and to the schooled indifference of so much that has followed it.

Kenneth Noland, though he was a friend of Louis's from 1952 onwards, and though he accompanied Louis on the latter's all-important visit to New York in the following year, was slower to find his own identity as an artist. His first wholly individual paintings date from 1958–59. Since he had, during the middle years of the decade, been deeply under Louis's spell, it is worth enumerating some of the differences between them. There was, for instance, Noland's tendency to leave more of the canvas unpainted, and his preference at that time for a precisely centred

image—often the target pattern that Jasper Johns used in such a different sense (*Reverberation*, Plate 263). The large areas of raw canvas to be found in Louis's *Unfurleds* derive from Noland, rather than vice versa.

By 1962 Noland had come to feel that the centred image was too confining, and this year saw the appearance of the first chevron paintings (*17th Stage*, 1964, Plate 264). Later still, he began to fill the entire canvas with stripes of colour, at first using a lozenge-shaped support, so as to keep some of the visual dynamism of the chevrons, and later relying on horizontal stripes on immense canvases, where the sheer size of the picture kept the eye moving by preventing it from settling on any one area, or indeed from apprehending the work as shape rather than colour.

One of the main impressions made by Noland's painting (and in this he is quite the contrary of Olitski) is its single-mindedness. Barbara Rose remarks: "To create the most powerful impact he was willing to jettison anything that interfered with the instantaneous communication of the image. This included the elimination of any kind of detail or internal inflection within the work, even such minor surface variations as those created through transparency" (Barbara Rose, "Retrospective Notes on the Washington Color School", in the catalogue of the Vincent Melzac Collection, Corcoran Gallery of Art, Washington, 1971, p. 31). A corollary of this is that it is easier to define what Noland does in negative rather than positive terms. It has no reverberation, either physical or emotional, beyond itself. It exists simply as visual information, and reaches out into no other field of activity or experience.

Rigorous as it is, Noland's art is less rigorous than the early work of Frank Stella, who is both the youngest of the leading Post-Painterly Abstractionists and the member of the group who seems to mark a transition to another and rather different way of thinking about the visual arts, though it is a transition he himself has been unable to accomplish fully.

Stella first made his reputation with a series of monochrome paintings, based, once again, on the theme of the stripe. Now it was monochrome

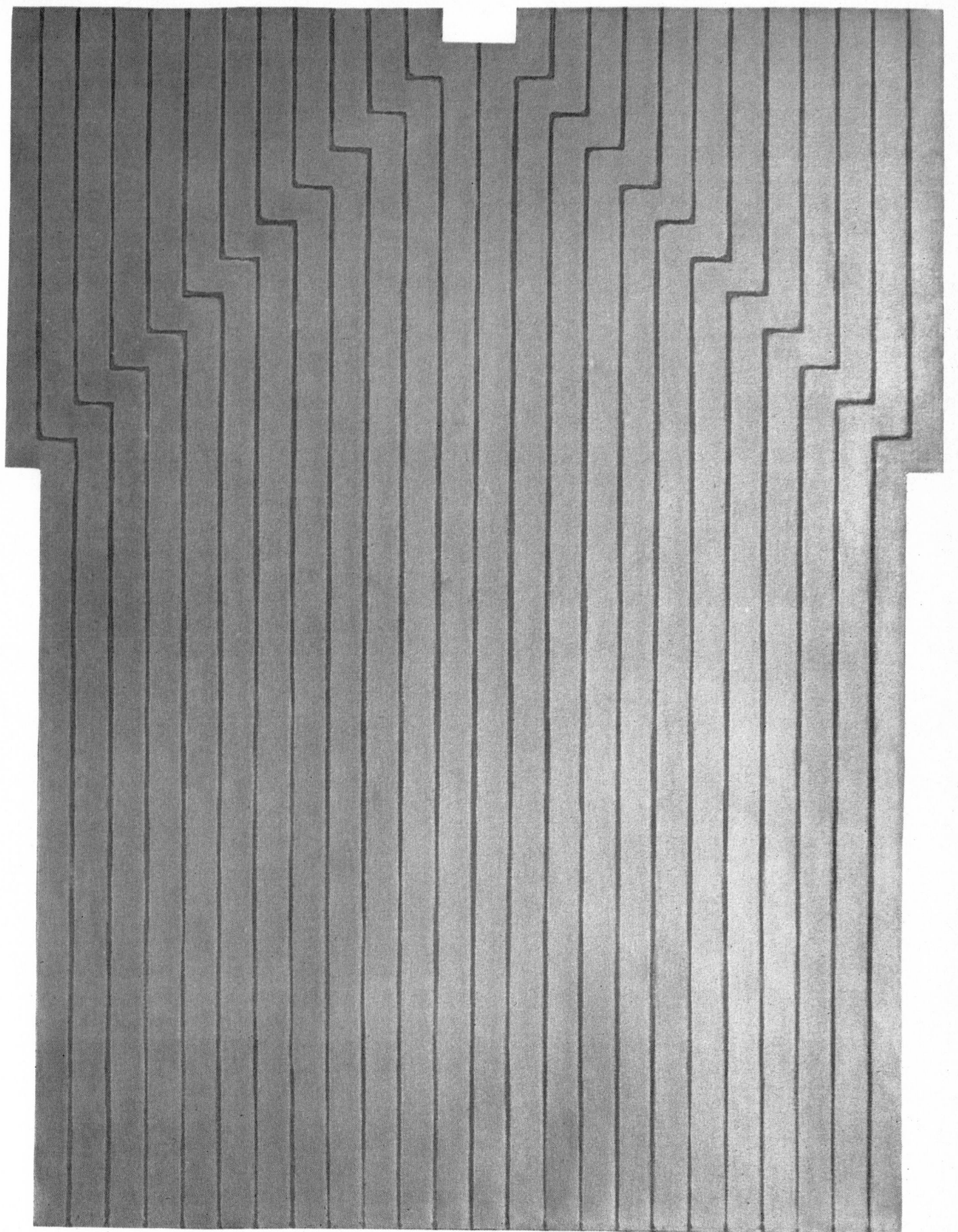

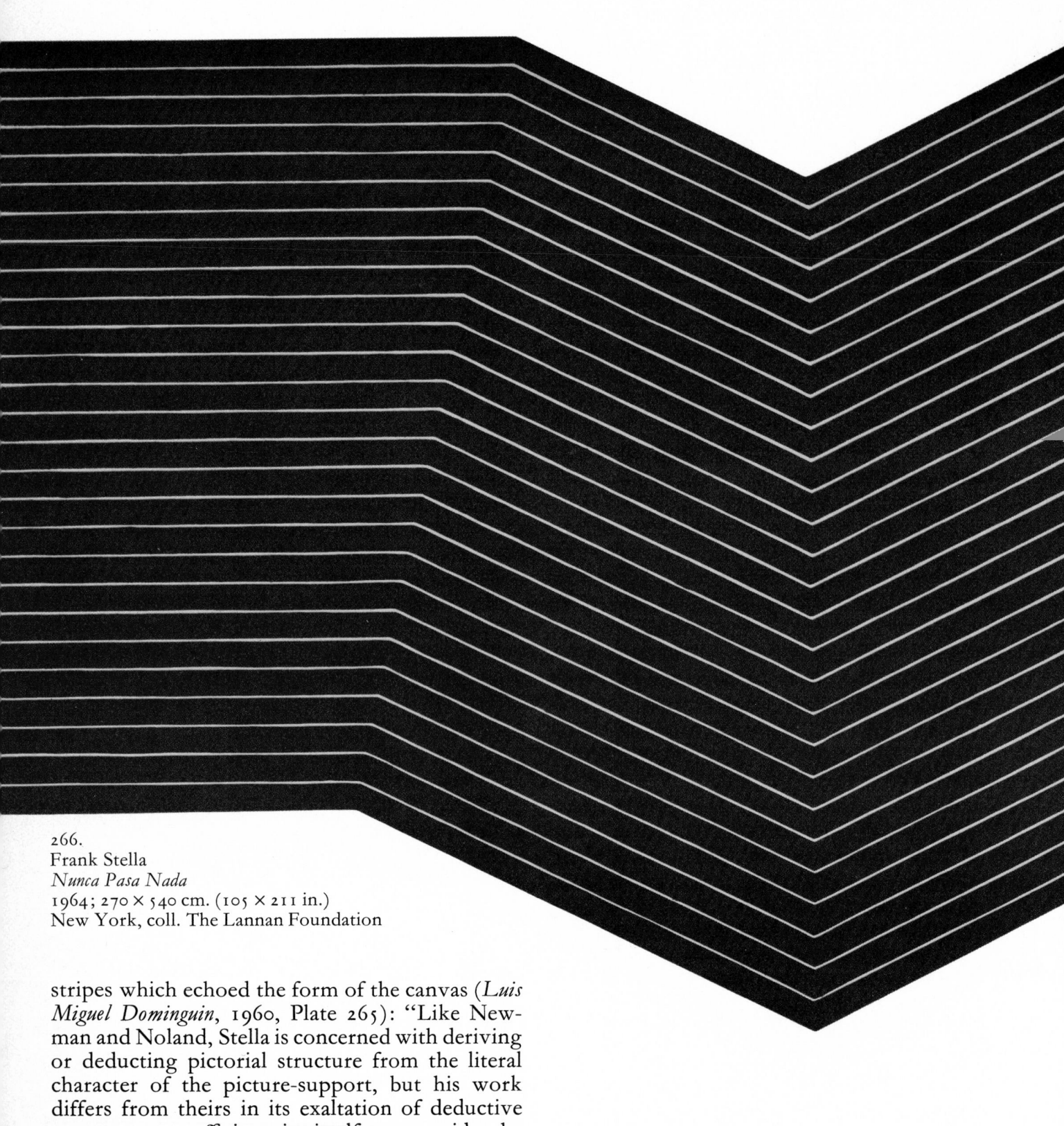

266.
Frank Stella
Nunca Pasa Nada
1964; 270 × 540 cm. (105 × 211 in.)
New York, coll. The Lannan Foundation

stripes which echoed the form of the canvas (*Luis Miguel Dominguin*, 1960, Plate 265): "Like Newman and Noland, Stella is concerned with deriving or deducting pictorial structure from the literal character of the picture-support, but his work differs from theirs in its exaltation of deductive structure as sufficient in itself to provide the substance, and not just the scaffolding or syntax, of major art" (Michael Fried, *op. cit.*, p. 40).

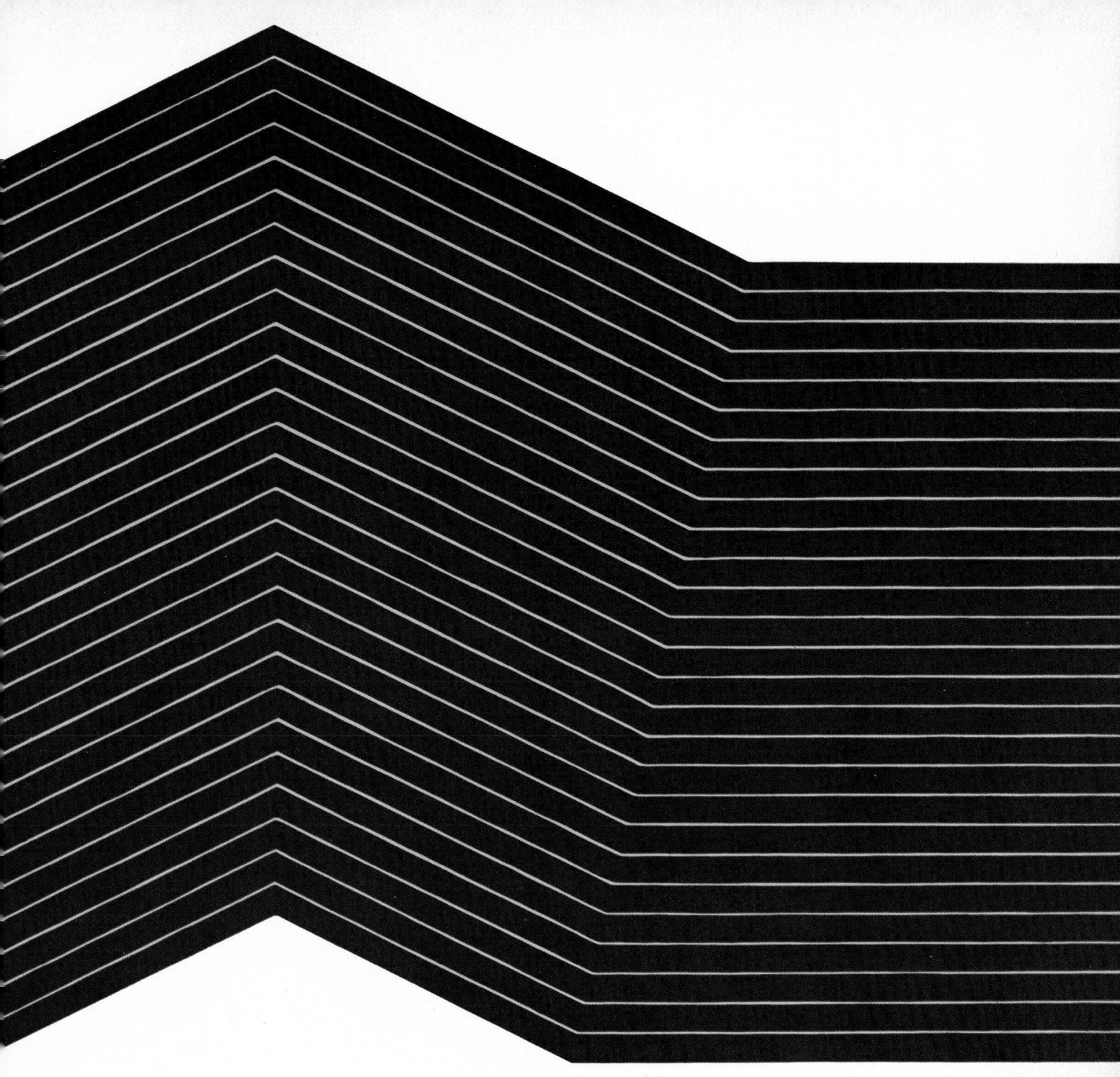

One characteristic of these stripe paintings was that they proceeded from the edge inwards (some of Stella's striped canvases had an actual void in the centre) rather than from the centre outwards, as for example with Rothko or Pollock. This seemed to lay additional emphasis on their quality as objects rather than as painted surfaces. Stella said in an interview given in 1966: "My painting is based on the fact that only what can be seen there is there. It really is an object. All I want anyone to get out of my paintings, and all I ever get out of them, is the fact that you can see the whole idea without any confusion. What you see is what you see" (Frank Stella in "Questions to Stella and Judd", by Bruce Glaser, edited by Lucy Lippard, *Art News*, Vol. 65, No. 5 [September, 1966], p. 58).

By the time this interview was given, he had already begun to develop the sculptural impli-

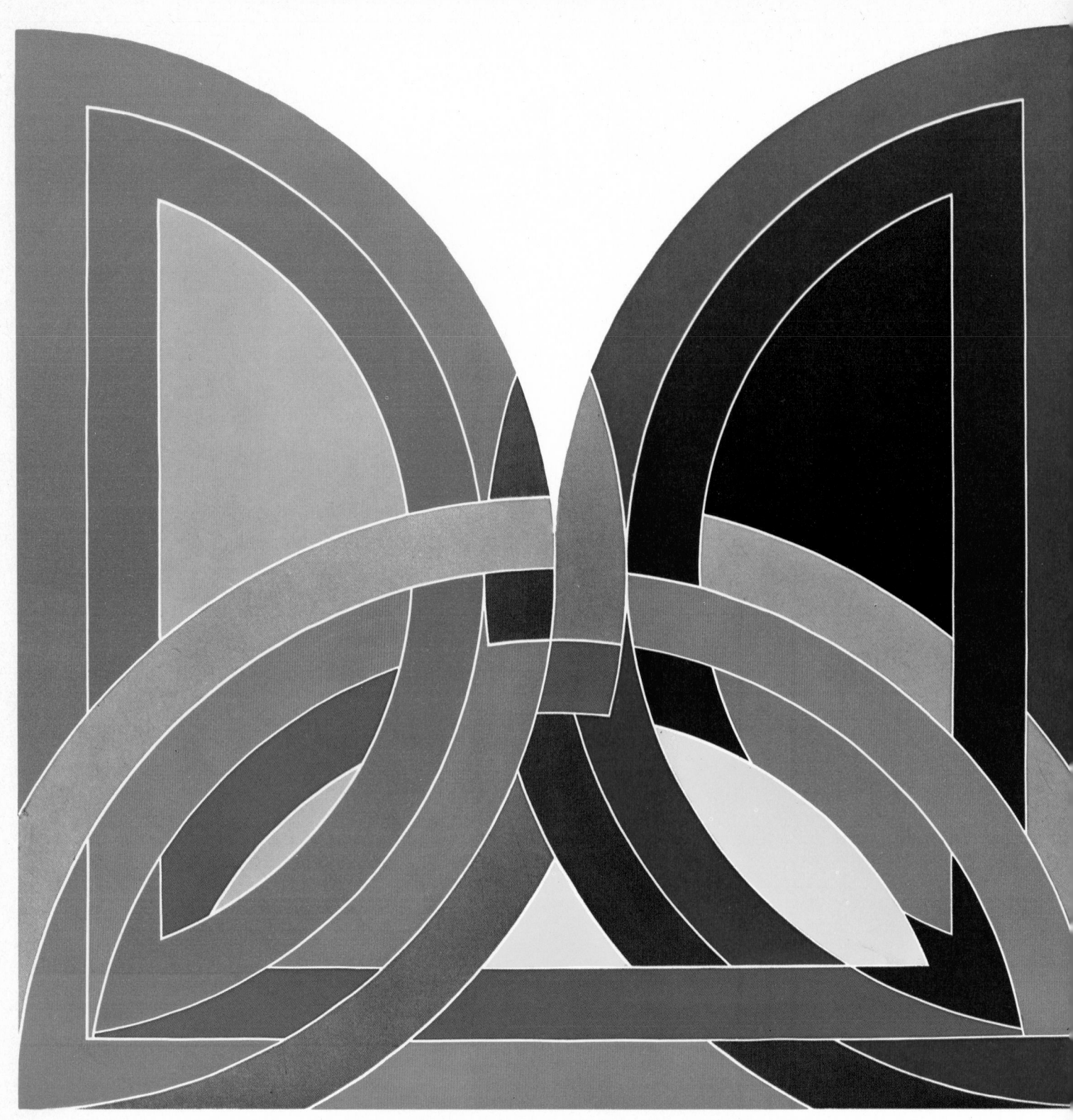

cations implicit in what he was doing in a series of paintings where the actual shape of the canvas was really much more important than anything that might be happening on its surface (*Nunca Pasa Nada*, 1964, Plate 266). He was in any case wholly opposed to any notion of inflection: "One could

267.
Frank Stella
Tahkt I-Sulayman I
1967; 305 × 610 cm. (119 × 238 in.)
California, Pasadena Art Museum

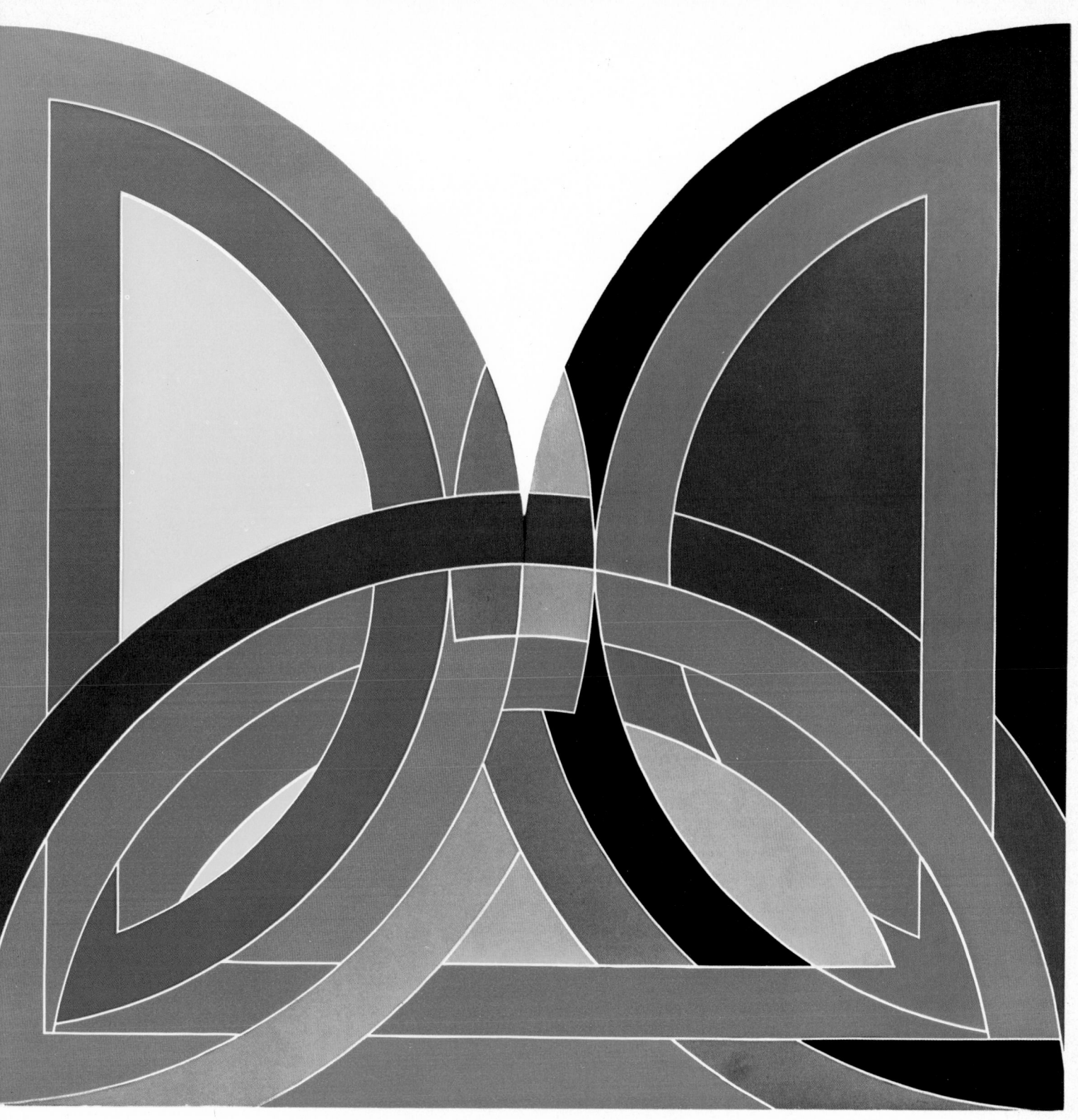

stand in front of any Abstract Expressionist's work for a long time, and walk back and forth, and inspect the depths of the pigment and the inflection and all the painterly brushwork for hours. . . . I feel that you should know after a while that you're just sort of mutilating the paint. . . . If you have some feeling about either color or direction of line or something, I think you can state it. You don't have to knead the material and grind it up. That seems destructive to me; it makes me very nervous" (Frank Stella, *op. cit.*, p. 59).

It is not too much to say that there is implicit, in

268.
Frank Stella
Ossippee I
1966; 242 × 350 cm. (94 × 137 in.)
New York, coll. Mr. and Mrs. Ernest Kafka

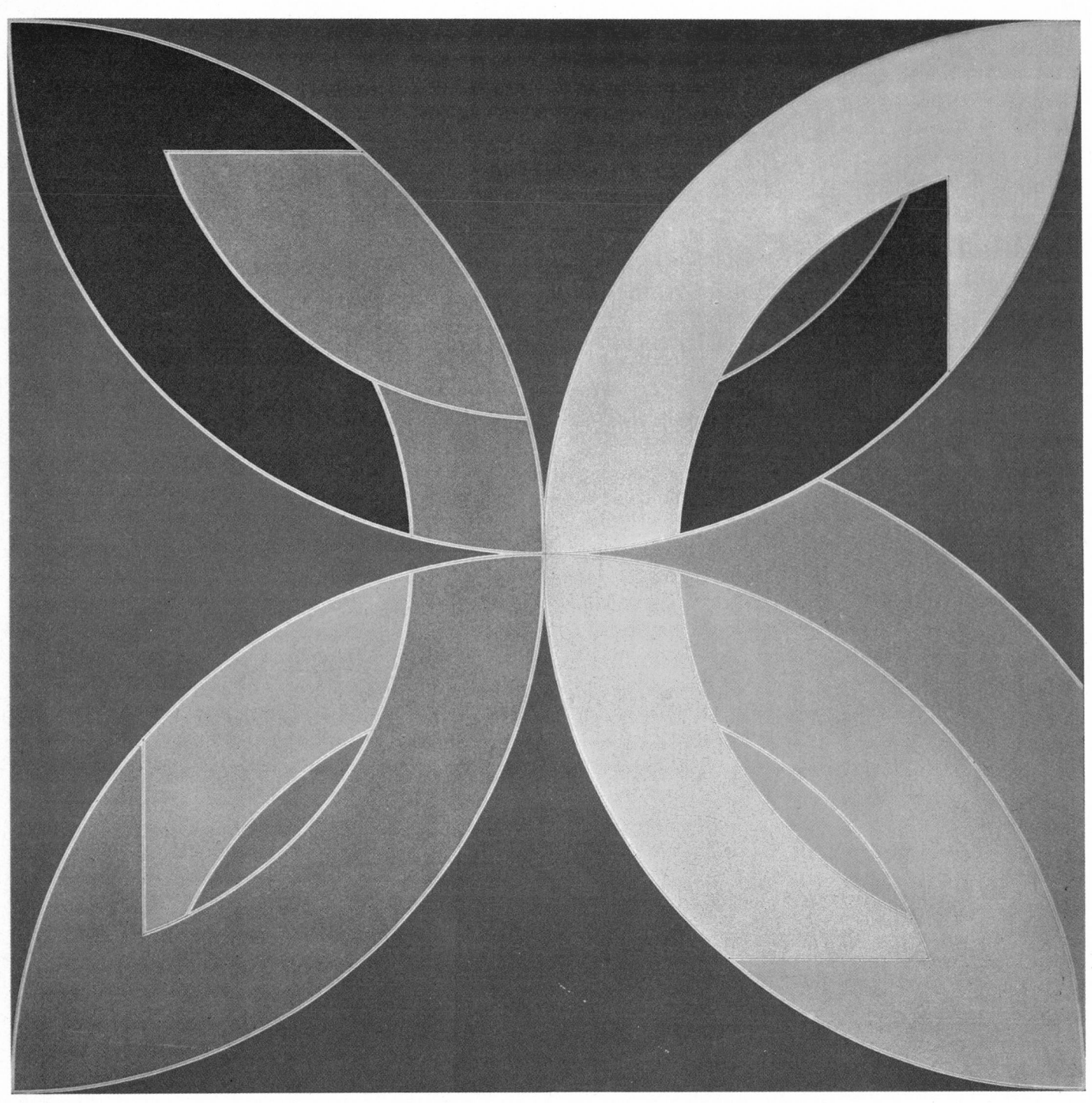

Stella's work during the earlier part of his career, a philosophy closely related to, though not precisely the same as, that of the group of sculptors who became known as the Minimalists.

Stella's change of direction, during the later part of the Sixties, was a shock to those who had hitherto supported his work, not so much because of its violence (violent changes of this type have, since Picasso, come to be expected of leading modern artists) but because of what it implied. Like Bridget Riley, who had also been devoted to monochrome, Stella took the plunge into colour, but with far more disconcerting results (*Tahkt I-Sulayman I*, 1976, Plate 267). It is worth recording the comment of a leading American reviewer when the series to which the illustrated work belongs was first shown: "The interdependence between literal and depicted shape fails to materialize. In its place I simply see circular armatures behind the arcs ... rays of color recede in vertiginous traditional illusionism ... it feels very strange to see a painting by Frank Stella in the light of Cubism ..." (Rosalind R. Krauss, "On Frontality", *Artforum*, Vol. VI, No. 9, [May, 1968], pp. 40–5).

In fact, the move to colour brought the informed spectator face to face with the decorative element which had always lurked within the apparent austerity of Stella's work. Worse still, it was now decoration of a recognizable kind. Like Lichtenstein in some of his weaker paintings, and certainly with some of his sculptures, Stella had aligned himself not so much with Cubism in its pure form as with the Art Deco revival which was sweeping through fashionable circles in New York, Paris, and London. The new works, even when they *were* new, had all the false seduction of the period piece, and their weaknesses even imported this slightly tainted flavour into much of what Stella had produced before.

Even more than with most art movements, Post-Painterly Abstraction loses coherence when it is examined closely. There is a great difference between the works Morris Louis produced immediately following his breakthrough and the *Protractor* series of Frank Stella—a difference of intention as well as of quality. There is, and this is more important, a visible difference between the *Veils* and *Unfurleds* of Louis, and the works with which Stella made his reputation. Louis immediately after 1954, and indeed until the advent of the striped paintings, remains within the current of Abstract Expressionism. His is a more refined, more rarefied, less vital version of what had already been accomplished by artists such as Pollock and Rothko, and no amount of talk about the unity between colour and ground can alter that fact. It would be unjust not to concede that Louis was, for a brief period, a painter who made an original contribution to the development of abstract art in America. At the same time, it is necessary to admit that this contribution was of a special kind—he took an established tradition to the point where it could progress no further, rather as G. B. Tiepolo did with the baroque in Italy.

With Stella we see, as early as 1960, a groping towards the Minimal Art which was to exercise so powerful an influence a little later, but we also find, encapsulated in his earlier paintings, the nihilism which was to paralyze so many artists in the Sixties and Seventies. Michael Fried's assertion that a painter such as Stella is forced to live "in a state of continuous intellectual and moral alertness" now seems to state not the truth of the situation, but what is diametrically opposite to the truth. These are nerveless works, which suppress intellect, morality, and above all, alertness, as much as they are able. When Stella finds the dehumanized situation in which he has placed himself intolerable, and attempts to break out, the only escape he can find is to the kitsch which had already been exploited, with more intelligence and poise, by the adherents of Pop Art.

Like Warhol, Stella is an important figure, not because one can in conscience assert that his painting is good, but because one can locate in it the crisis which was to overtake Modernism as the Sixties progressed—a crisis which is still with us, in a yet acuter form, during the 1970's.

Sculpture in the Post-war Period: Towards Minimal Art

Concern with the status of the painted canvas as an object in a world of objects gradually brought painting and sculpture closer together during the 1960's, to the point where what had seemed to be very different realms of artistic activity became, at least in the minds of many artists and critics, almost interchangeable. The term "sculpture" acquired a prestige, and also a breadth of meaning, which it had not possessed during the earlier part of the twentieth century, when the modern movement first came into being.

The dominance of painting over sculpture was something that early Modernism inherited from the nineteenth century. Painting was the less expensive and therefore more independent medium. The artist who was prepared to starve, or at least to exist with the help of only a few private patrons, could still hope to produce important works of art. No such opportunity was open to the sculptor out of tune with his time.

The result of this situation was that Modernism itself developed through painters and through painting. When sculptural experiments were made, it was men who thought of themselves as being primarily painters who made them, with a few important exceptions. Thus we may list Matisse, Picasso, Modigliani, and Boccioni as being among the most important pioneers of modern sculpture.

It is true that, as the modern movement progressed, certain men emerged whose main activity was making sculpture. Among them were Julio Gonzalez, Raymond Duchamp-Villon, Alexander Archipenko, the Constructivists Gabo and Antoine Pevsner, and Constantin Brancusi. But the painters rather than the sculptors continued to be the experimental vanguard. The new styles that arose—Cubism and Surrealism—found their first and most convincing embodiment in two dimensions rather than in three. In fact, there were certain aspects of both these styles which tended to inhibit the sculptor rather than to inspire him.

In the case of Cubism, the overriding concern with the representation of what was three-dimensional upon a flat surface tended to make sculpture itself seem irrelevant. Attempts were indeed made to adapt the ideas of the Synthetic Cubists to sculpture in stone—the early work of Henri Laurens is a good example. But Laurens found himself in a curiously contradictory situation. For example, when he made stone reliefs in a Cubist style inspired by Braque, he found himself impelled to colour them. "I wanted", he later said, "to do away with the effects of variations of light on statues." Cubist sculpture tends to look both decorative and decorous when set beside the paintings that inspired it. Worse still, it tends to look illogical. Why, we ask ourselves, should the planes be flattened in this way, when a sculptor is fully at liberty to develop them in real space?

A more powerful and more important artist, Julio Gonzalez, also showed the mark of the struggle to escape from Cubist influences, and from that of Picasso in particular. But in Gonzalez's case the struggle was in the end beneficial, as he was forced to find new techniques in order to express himself. In particular, he experimented with the process of oxy-acetylene welding, which he had learned when he worked at the Renault car factory during the First World War. This led him to think of sculpture not so much as the creation of three-dimensional forms as of executing a drawing in space. It also led him to see that a sculpture need not be unitary, but could be an accumulation of parts, with a corresponding emphasis on the way in which these parts were joined together. "To project into space and draw with it", Gonzalez declared, "with the help of new mediums; to use this space and build with it, as if it were a newly discovered material—that is my whole endeavour."

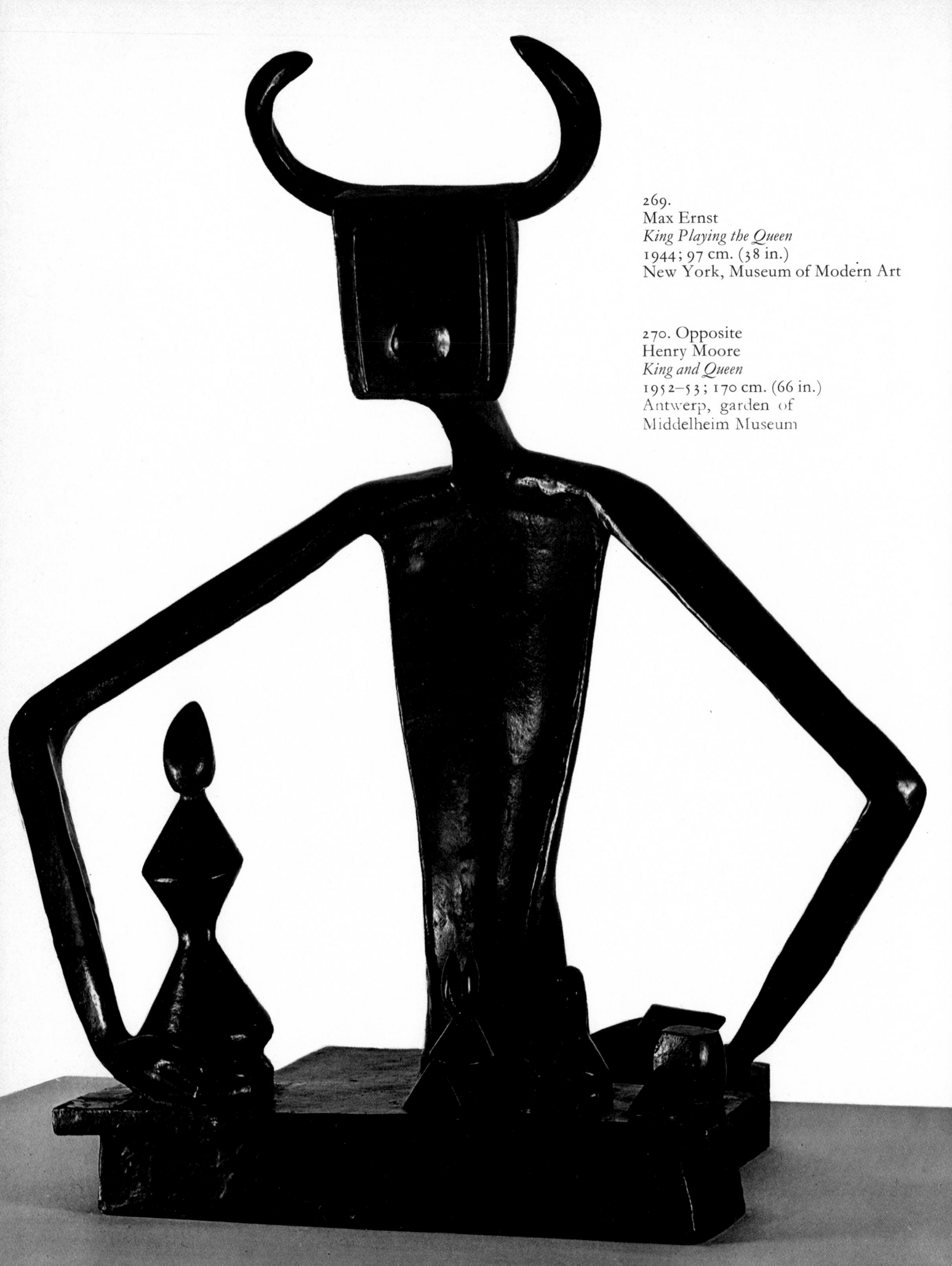

269.
Max Ernst
King Playing the Queen
1944; 97 cm. (38 in.)
New York, Museum of Modern Art

270. Opposite
Henry Moore
King and Queen
1952–53; 170 cm. (66 in.)
Antwerp, garden of
Middelheim Museum

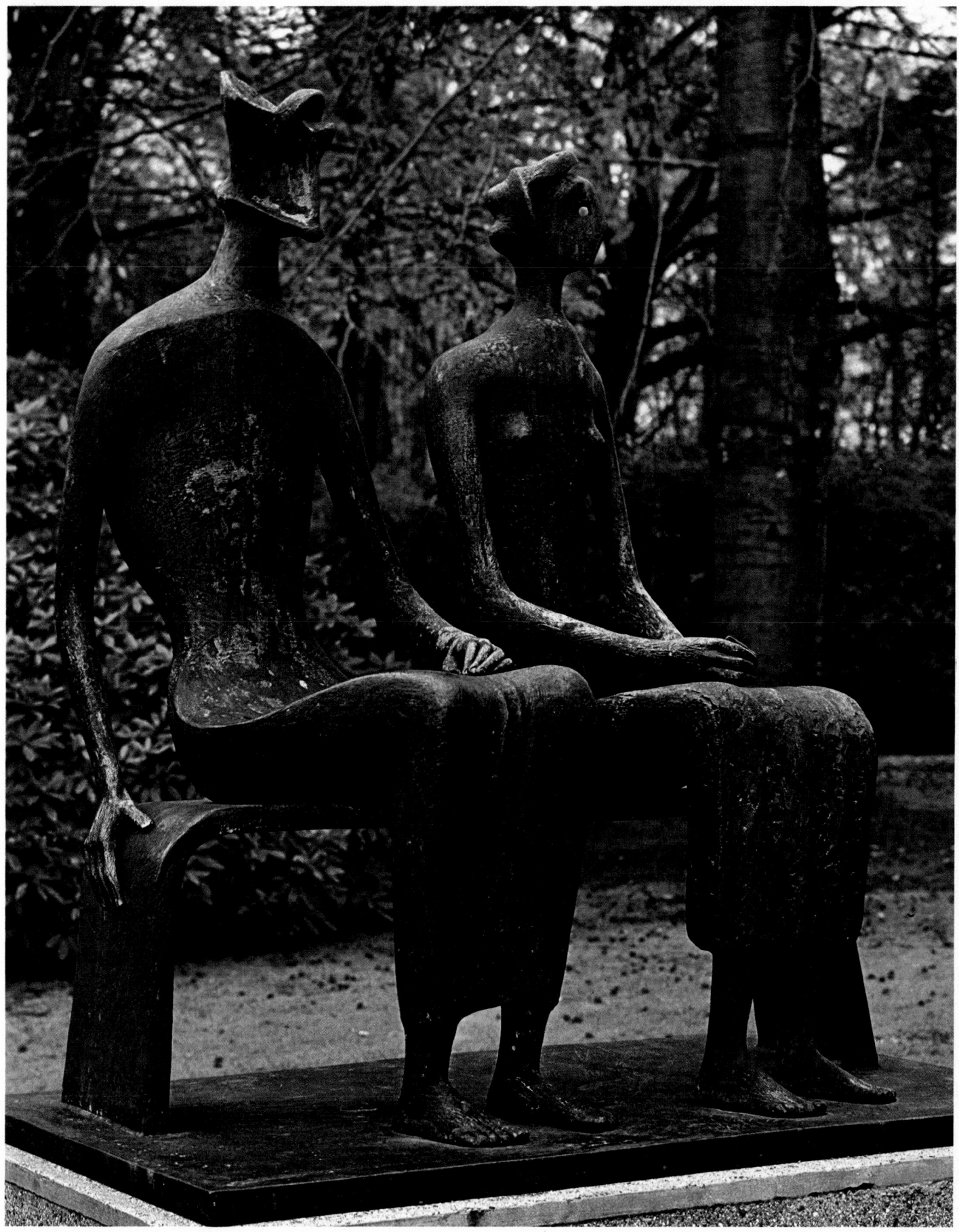

Surrealism hampered the development of modern sculpture in a subtler way than Cubism. Where Cubist painters seemed to question the necessity for sculpture, since painting itself could now be made to express what was previously the province of the three-dimensional work, the Surrealists gave sculpture a rival, in the form of the Surrealist object. The object, so typical of the production of many Surrealist artists, is something which exists in three dimensions, but which makes no claim to be thought of as sculpture, that is, as a statement concerning form and formal relationships. Where the object is concerned, all relationships are those of association, of memory, fantasy, and dream. As has appeared in some of the earlier chapters of this book, the object has known a long and prosperous career under Modernism, and has survived quite comfortably into the post-war world, as we can see from the work of artists such as Oldenburg and Rauschenberg.

The various disadvantages under which the sculptor laboured, during the period from 1905 to 1945, meant that three-dimensional work never acquired the coherence of aim which we discover in early Modernist painting. The sculptor tended to exist rather on the fringes of group activity, and the isolation in which he worked made it more difficult for him to exercise a real influence over the course of events.

The most distinguished sculptor of the early Modernist epoch was Constantin Brancusi, and in many ways Brancusi's career seems to sum up the essential isolation of the art he practised. Brancusi belonged to no movement, though the leading members of the Cubist and Surrealist fraternities knew and respected him. What he sought, almost throughout his life, was an alternative road to that taken by Auguste Rodin, who had exercised a powerful influence over Brancusi's early work. Where Rodin was theatrical, dramatic, full of sentiment, Brancusi sought impersonality and restraint. The search led him back to objects produced by archaic civilizations, though he never fell into the trap of archaistic imitation. His search for archetypes was to exercise an enormous influence over sculptors junior to himself.

Despite all the difficulties I have just outlined, modern sculpture did, during the Thirties in particular, begin to establish a place for itself in the hierarchy of Modernism. In England, Henry Moore, after difficult beginnings, earned a reputation among those who were interested in modern art (a tiny band) for work which was influenced by Surrealism, but which also seemed to respond to Brancusi's search for archetypes. Barbara Hepworth also attracted attention, for work which went in much the same direction as Moore's, but which seemed, too, to owe a debt to Constructivism. In France, Alberto Giacometti emerged as a leading Surrealist. His work also demonstrated the irresistible attraction of the archaic—in this case, to the Cycladic artifacts which were just beginning to attract attention among collectors and archaeologists. In Italy, Marino Marini had begun to look for ways of reviving the Italian sculptural tradition through the study of Far Eastern art as well as that of Egyptian, Etruscan, and Roman Republican work.

Perhaps because they had already had so much to contend with, these sculptors survived the hiatus of the war years more successfully than some of the painters who were their contemporaries. We are conscious of a definite break in the development of painting during the 1940's, and of a transfer of power from Paris to New York. No such gap is visible in the history of modern sculpture. The break had yet to occur, and did not in fact happen until much later. Nor was there any sudden shift from Europe to America, perhaps because the development of the new American painting was not matched by any corresponding upsurge in sculpture, despite the activity of artists such as Ibram Lassaw and Reuben Nakian.

If we look at the condition of sculpture in the years immediately following 1945, we observe first of all the continuation of tendencies which had already established themselves before the war, though sometimes with a different emphasis to suit changed circumstances. Max Ernst, for example, though still primarily a painter, had been seriously interested in sculpture from the middle Thirties onwards. During his period of exile in

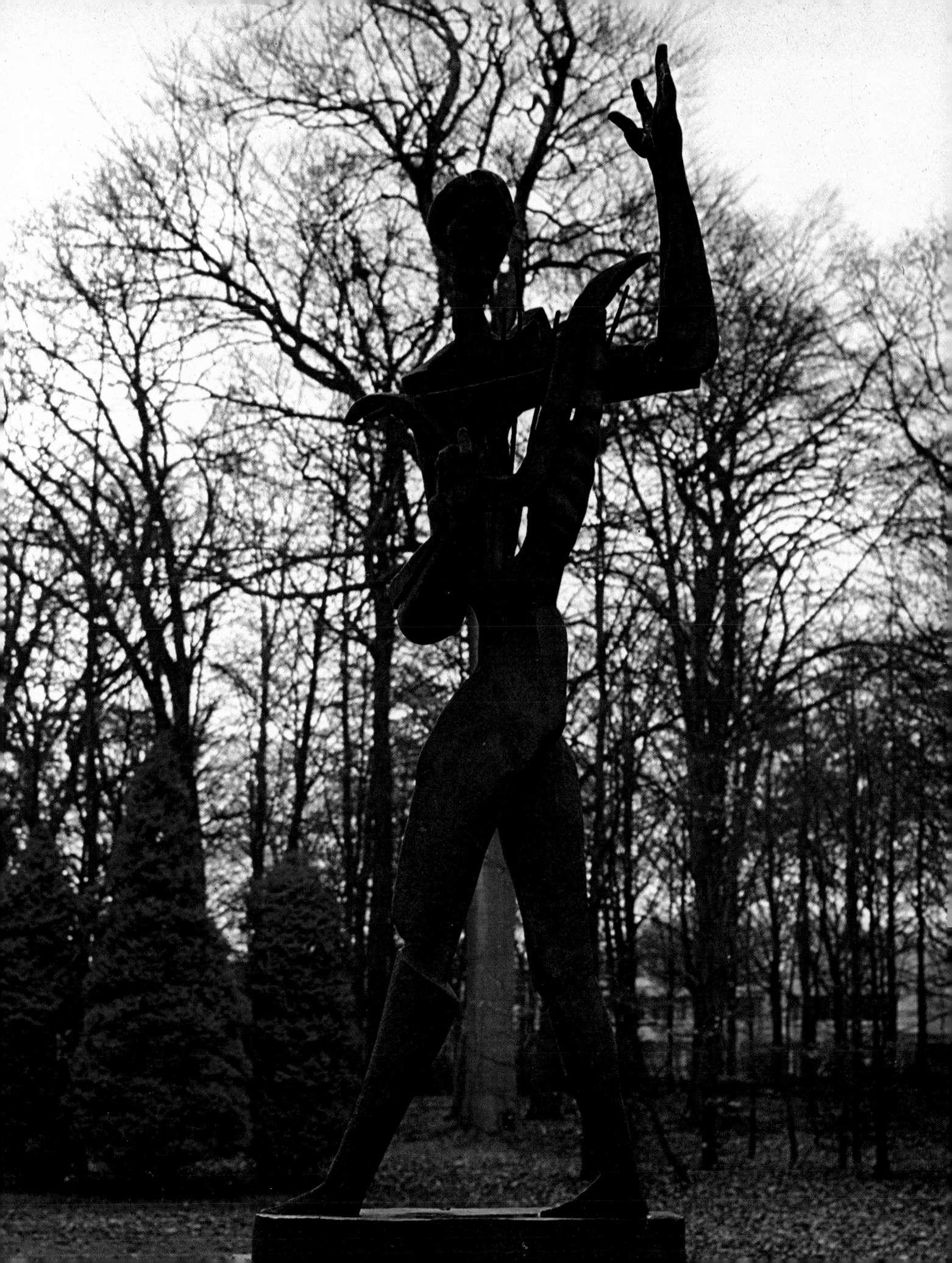

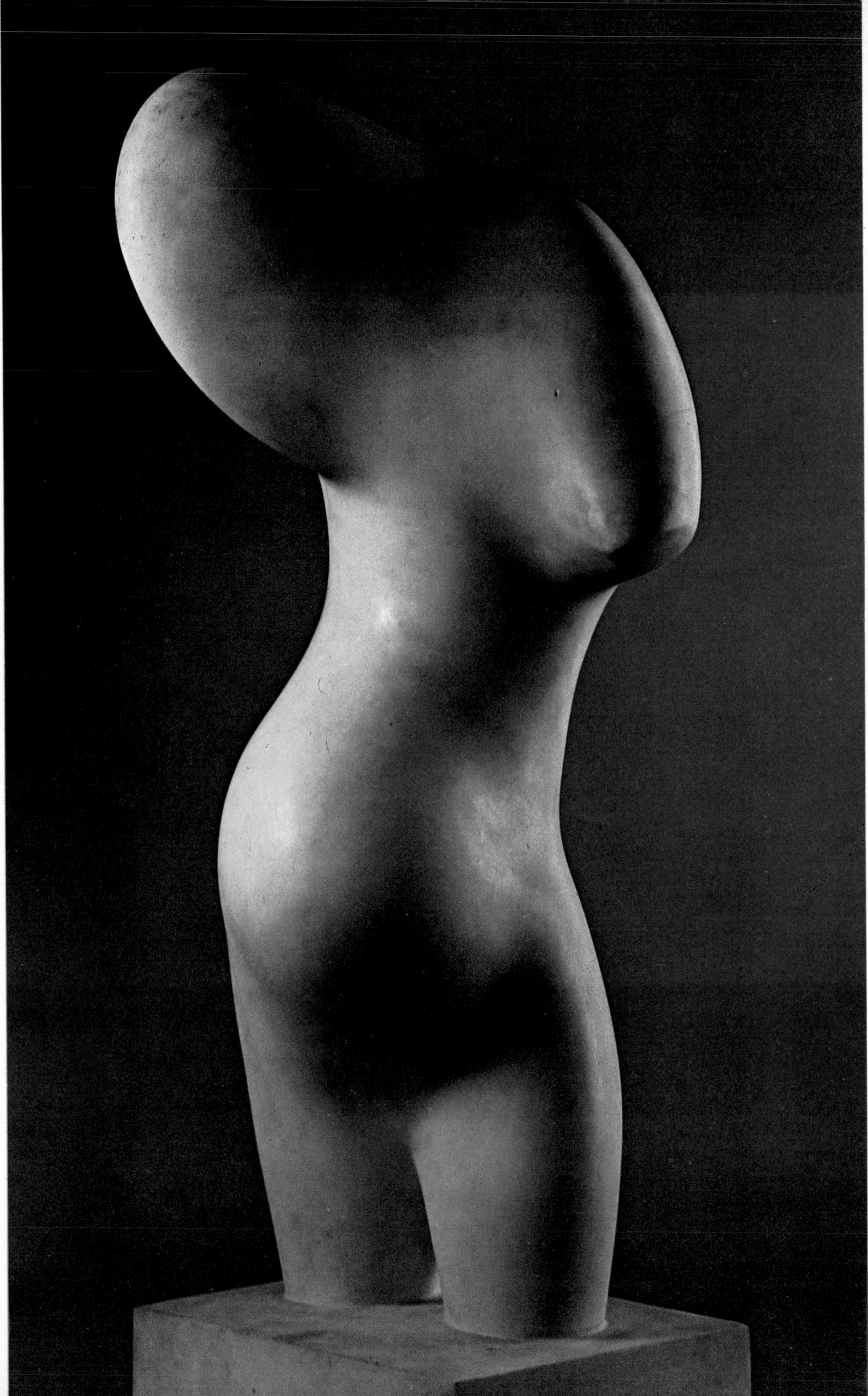

272. Opposite
Jean Arp
Torse de Femme
1953; 80 cm. (31 in.)
Cologne, Wallraf-
Richartz Museum

273.
Alberto Giacometti
Uomo che indica
1947; 178 cm. (69 in.)
New York, Museum
of Modern Art,
gift of Mrs. John D.
Rockefeller III

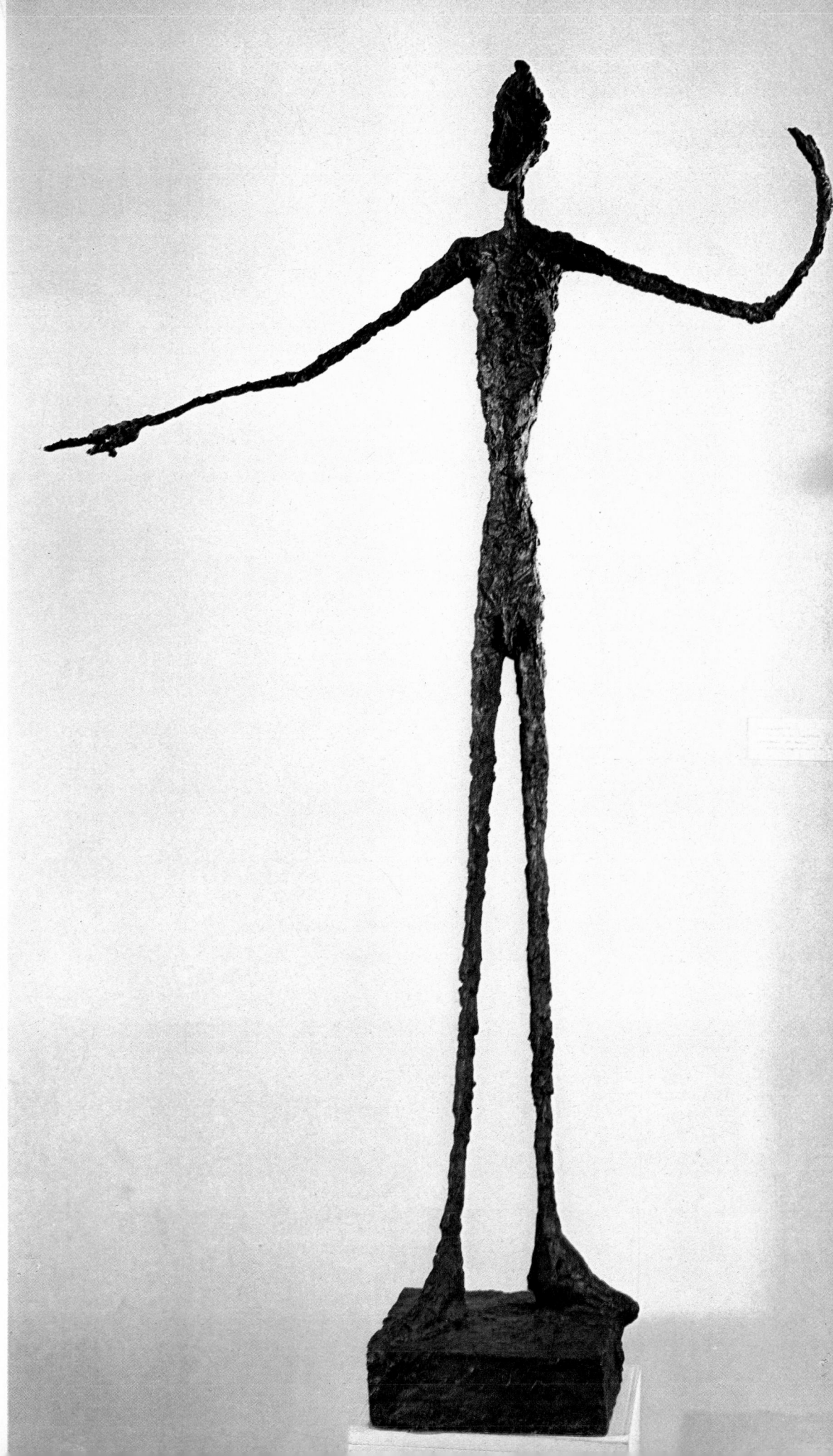

274.
Barbara Hepworth
Three Obliques (Walk-in)
1968–69; 290 cm. (113 in.)
London, Gimpel Fils

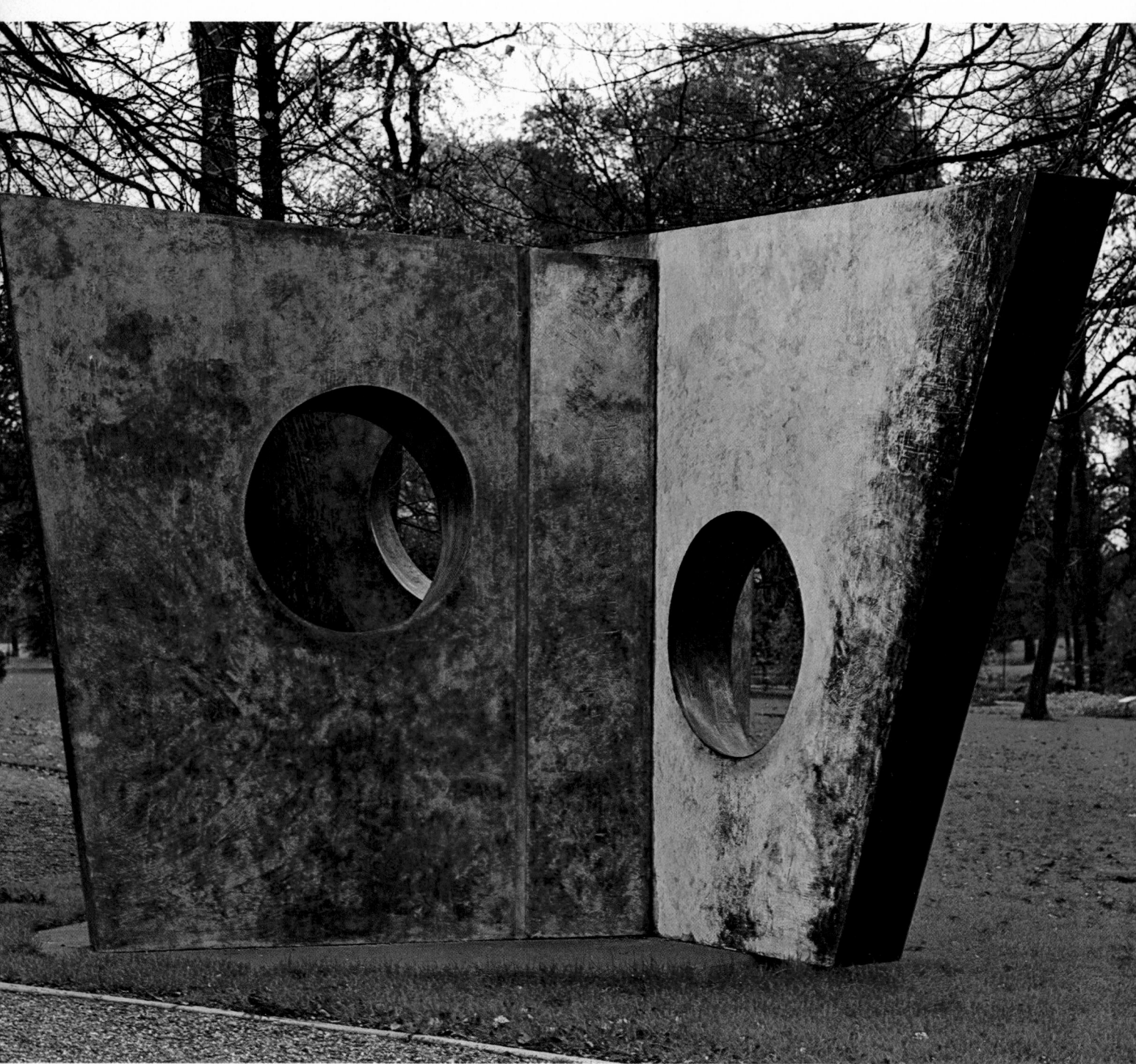

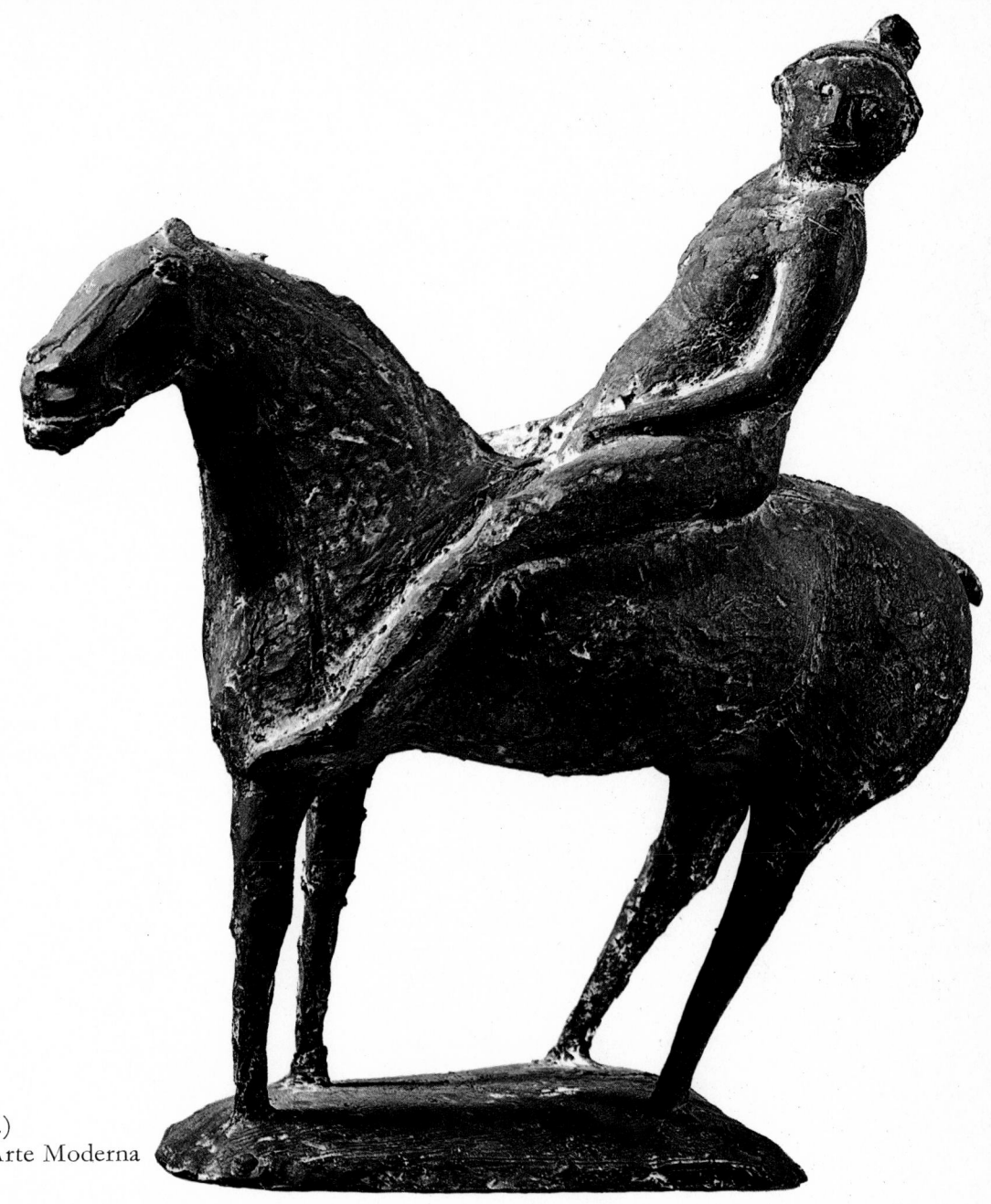

275.
Marino Marini
Cavaliere
Bronze
1946; 50 × 45 cm. (20 × 18 in.)
Rome, Galleria Nazionale d'Arte Moderna

America this interest continued, and indeed some of his most important sculptures, such as the *King Playing the Queen* (Plate 269) of 1944, were produced during his sojourn in the United States. Ernst's *King Playing the Queen* makes an instructive comparison with one of the best known of Henry Moore's post-war bronzes, the *King and Queen* of 1952–53 (Plate 270). Moore's sculpture has been accused of being in some respects formally incoherent. Commentators have pointed to the inconsistency of style between the stylized heads and the naturalistic hands and feet of the figures. Despite this, one notices that Moore's work has a density and fullness which is denied to the Ernst

piece. The longer one looks at the latter, the more it comes to seem a capricious *assemblage* of bits and pieces which in fact have very little relationship to one another.

The figure by Ossip Zadkine (Plate 271) is at any rate the work of an artist whose main activity is sculpture. It has a swaggering confidence and professionalism which reminds the spectator, not unjustly, of the work of the sculptors who showed in the various French Salons towards the end of the nineteenth century. Indeed, Zadkine's work does show a strange trajectory, from close association with the avant-garde to disguised academicism. Zadkine, a Russian Jew, was born in

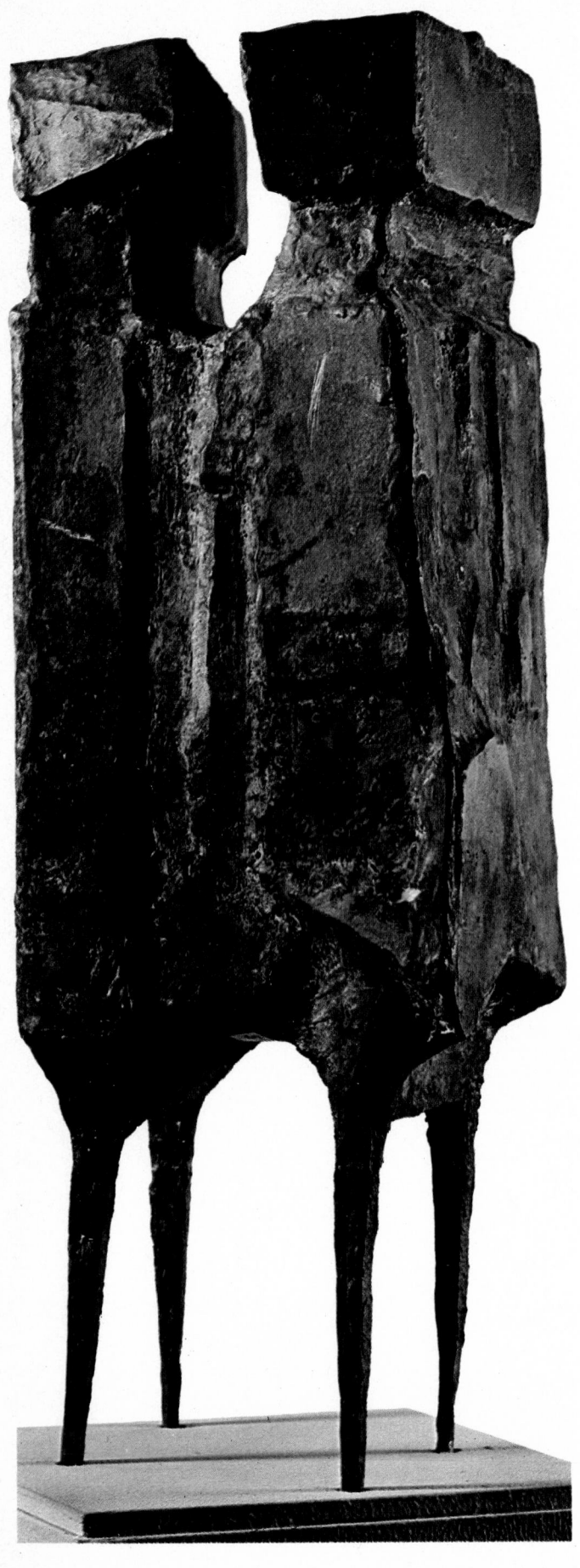

276.
Lynn Chadwick
Two Guardians V
1960; 57.5 cm. (22 in.)
Cologne, Wallraf-Richartz Museum,
gift of Wilhelm Grosshenning

Smolensk, but by 1909 he had made his way to Paris, where he, like his colleague Jacques Lipchitz, was drawn into the circle of the Cubists. Between the wars he more or less abandoned Cubism, and by 1930 a baroque element had started to reveal itself in his work, closely allied to the decorative fashions of the time. Eventually, after emigrating to America in 1937, Zadkine began to experiment with ways of opening up the massive forms of his sculptures so as to give them greater lightness and energy. The idea of penetrating the form in this way had already occurred to Moore and Hepworth, who used it in a far more daring and inventive fashion. In itself the device can be regarded as a Cubist legacy, and as being something which sprang from the desire to show different aspects—front and back, inner and outer—from the same point of view and simultaneously.

The use of this device in a piece such as *Orphée* is, however, of much less importance than the bland classicism of the outline. Fluently and rather emptily decorative, Zadkine's late work seems to tell us that nothing has changed in sculpture since the late nineteenth century. The influence of genuine innovators, such as Gonzalez, is painlessly absorbed. The post-war Zadkine was at his most effective when faced with the kind of commission which any nineteenth-century academic sculptor would have found familiar. The efficiently rhetorical *Commemorative Monument to the Destruction of Rotterdam*, a shouting figure raising anguished arms to the sky, is in direct line of descent from works like the reliefs by François Rude which ornament the Arc de Triomphe in Paris.

Jean Arp came from a different background and developed in a different way. Arp, born in Alsace, was bilingual as well as multi-talented. He was first associated with the world of avant-garde art in Germany, exhibiting at the second show of the Blaue Reiter group in Munich in 1912. During the war years he was one of the originators of Dada in Zurich. At this period he wrote burlesque poems, made collages, and illustrated the poems of his friends, as well as producing the reliefs in painted wood by which his activity during those years is

277.
Germaine Richier
Chess Piece: Queen
1959
Hamburg, Kunsthalle

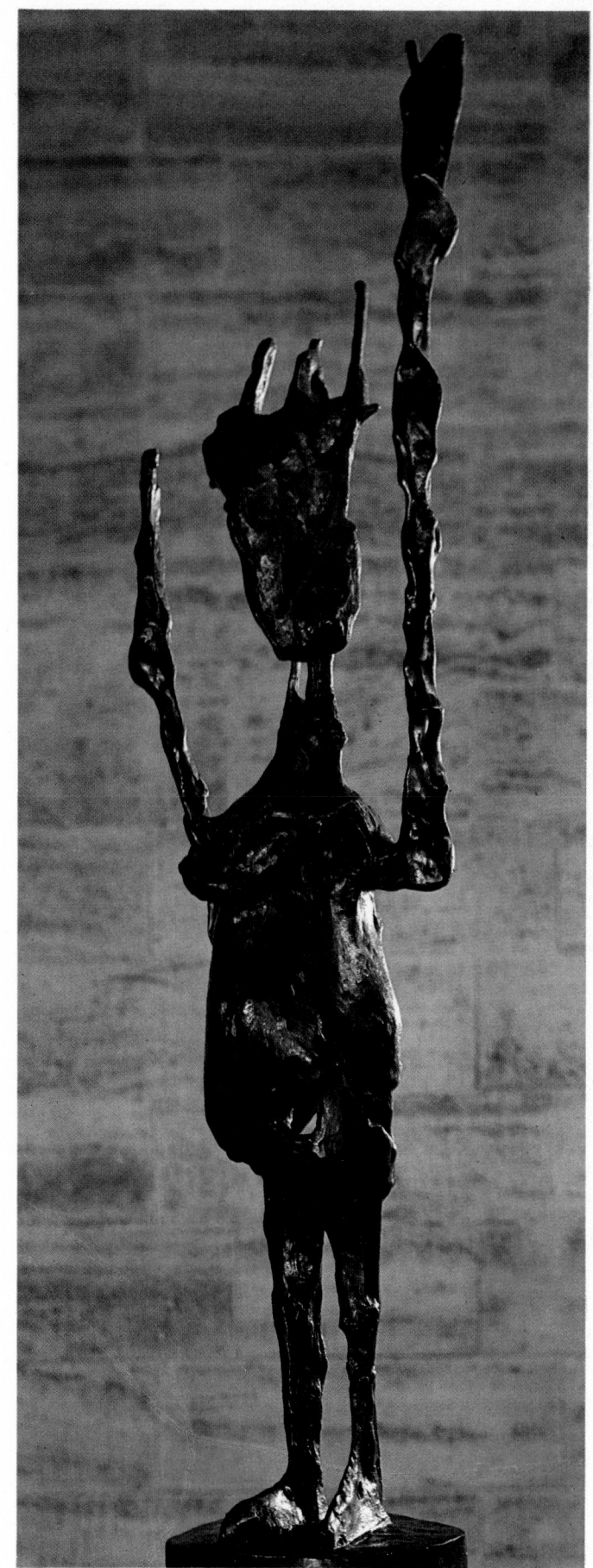

now best remembered. He did not return to sculpture in the round (he had had a brief flirtation with it before the war) until 1930, when he was living near Paris. Gradually his work moved into a more solemn and romantic phase, related on the one hand to the simplicity of Brancusi and on the other to the biomorphic forms that populate the compositions of Tanguy. A French critic asserts that it was Arp who "demonstrated that a sculptor could find the equivalent of the automatic writing of the poets" (Sarane Alexandrian, *Connaissance des Arts*, July, 1972, p. 55).

Having discovered what seemed to be a viable sculptural style, Arp stuck to it firmly, and the works produced after the war (Plate 272) are very little different from those created in the late Thirties. The American critic Harold Rosenberg has justly commented with reference to the later phases of Arp's career: "For the non-militant avant-gardist, maturity consists in passing from games in the garden of the imagination to the inventions of a professional in a world of institutionalized values" (Harold Rosenberg, *The Re-Definition of Art*, London, 1972, p. 80).

Artists like Arp and Zadkine seemed an integral part of the immediately post-war sculptural scene chiefly because the scene was so stagnant. Nevertheless, there were artists who seemed to be trying to bring new life to the Modernist tradition. These can be divided into those who had already made reputations before 1945 and those who were newcomers.

Giacometti possessed one of the most important of the established names, and the direction taken by his art was extremely important for sculpture in general. He had joined the Surrealist movement in 1929, and his return to working from the model in 1935, which led to his being denounced by his Surrealist colleagues, was in every way a significant decision. The years 1935–45 were those which Giacometti spent in forging the new style which was to have such an impact upon the post-war public. The most striking characteristic of this second phase of the sculptor's work was the extreme attenuation of the figures (Plate 273). Usually these very thin sculptures were provided with relatively massive

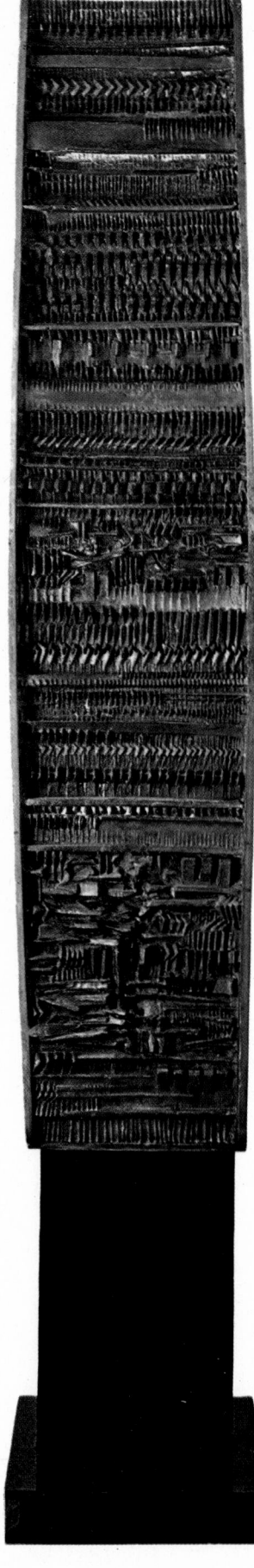

bases, which served to increase the impression of distance and alienation from the viewer.

In immediately post-war Paris the "ungraspability" of Giacometti's personages was immediately equated with the essential ungraspability of human experience, as preached by the newly prominent existentialist philosophers, such as Jean-Paul Sartre. If this was legitimate (Giacometti formed important friendships within the existentialist group), it was perhaps less legitimate to equate these skeletal figures with the general misery and depression of post-war existence, and in particular with the appearance of those who had survived imprisonment in German concentration camps. Nevertheless the comparison was made. Giacometti, who was the most private of artists, found that he had become the symbol of a new humanist concern among modern artists—a humanism which focused its attention upon social problems and evils.

The post-war Henry Moore did not seem as radically different from his former self as the post-war Giacometti. For Moore, unlike most other modern artists, the war years had been to some extent at least a period of opportunity. Working in the shelters during the Blitz, Moore produced a remarkable documentation of a nation's ordeal. Later, when he was able to resume work as a sculptor, Moore, like many of the artists working at that time in Britain, showed a move towards work with a broad popular appeal—the famous *Madonna* for St. Matthew's, Northampton, is perhaps the best-known case in point. And when the conflict at last came to an end, the sculptor had established himself as a figure whose importance was admitted by a broad spectrum of people. His international stature was meanwhile confirmed by an exhibition which the British Council sent to New York.

Presented with opportunities such as no modern sculptor had had before him, Moore was able to take advantage of them to the full, thanks to his outstanding creative energy. A technical change took place in his work, in that, from being primarily a carver of stone and wood, he now made bronze his chief medium of expression. Some critics saw in this a tendency on the part of

278. Opposite
Arnaldo Pomodoro
La colonna del viaggiatore
1961; 134 × 29 × 8.5 cm. (52 × 11 × 3 in.)
Cologne, coll. of Mr. and Mrs. Alfred Otto Müller

279.
Arnaldo Pomodoro
Cubo
1965–75; 130 × 130 × 130 cm. (51 × 51 × 51 in.)
Gedola (Saudi Arabia), sculpture Park

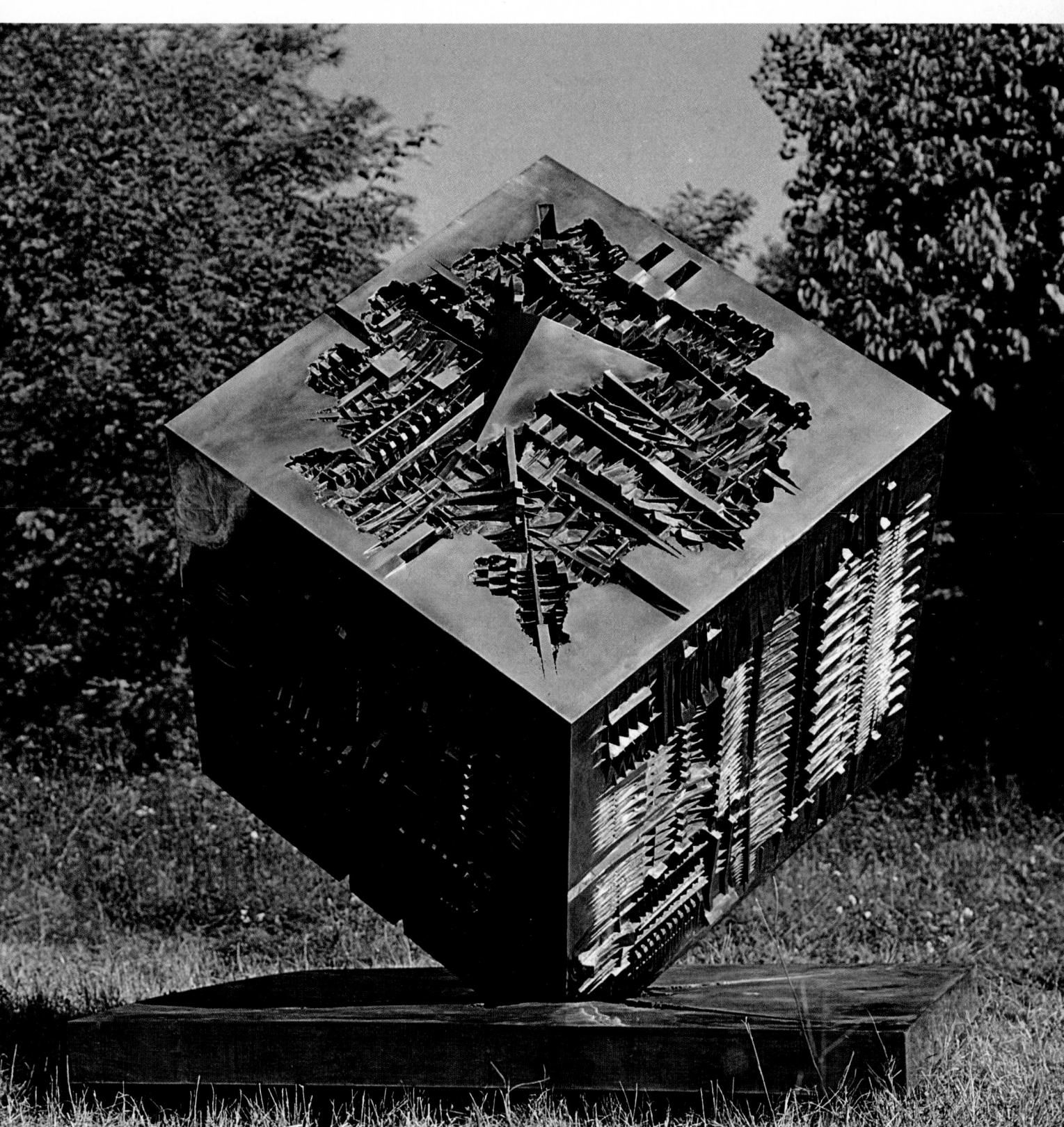

the artist to compromise the standards he had hitherto maintained. But there was no denying Moore's ability to create memorable images. This was accompanied by an astonishing flexibility of style. Moore never seemed to abandon an idea or a theme, but moved from works which were almost Rodinesque, such as the *Hand Relief No. 2* of 1952, to others as grandly abstract as the *Locking Piece* of ten years later.

The reputation of British sculpture was also sustained by the career of Barbara Hepworth. The direction taken by her work in the late Forties was influenced by the friendship which she and her then husband, the painter Ben Nicholson, formed with the veteran Russian Constructivist Naum Gabo during the preceding decade. Gabo arrived in England in 1935, and he was in close contact with Hepworth and her husband for the next ten years. Her work, however, could never be described as fully Constructivist, since it had a strongly surviving element of poetic irrationality, reinforced by the landscapes and seascapes which the artist saw about her in Cornwall, where she lived and worked from 1939 onwards. "From the sculptor's point of view," she later remarked, "one can either be the spectator of the object or the object itself. For a few years I became the object."

The intensity Hepworth achieved during the late Forties was not entirely sustained during the decade that followed, which brought, only a little behind Moore, a great expansion of her reputation and therefore of the opportunities open to her as an artist. Carving had been even more central to her original aesthetic than it had been to Moore, but now she too was tempted into using bronze, a material in which it was so much easier and quicker to attain monumental scale. These late monumental works (Plate 274) are not likely to enhance her reputation when a final assessment is made.

In Italy, Marino Marini's reputation grew in a way analogous to what happened to Moore and Hepworth after 1945. His equestrian groups (a theme he had attempted as early as the mid-Thirties) became one of the type-images of modern art (Plate 275), and many people cited his work as proof that contemporary sculpture could keep its integrity and yet convey a message to a broad public. Marini and his near-contemporary Giacomo Manzù became the standard-bearers in Italy of a new figurative and humanist sculpture, just as Giacometti had done in France.

The energy of artists such as Giacometti, Moore, and Marini, and the attention which naturally focused on their activities, made it hard for new sculptors to find a footing in the immediately post-war years. The group that emerged most prominently did so, surprisingly enough, in England. It included Lynn Chadwick (Plate 276) and Reg Butler, both of them major prize-winners in the Unknown Political Prisoner competition of 1953. This, with its emotionally charged subject matter, did much to attract attention to a new generation of artists. Butler and Chadwick, together with Kenneth Armitage and Bernard Meadows, were shown by the British Council at the Venice Biennale of 1952, and this exhibition, in a rather narrower sense, also seemed significant in showing what sculpture might become in the future. All the four artists I have mentioned were exponents of a romantic figurative style which owed something to Surrealism without being fully Surrealist. The human figure, in their hands, was transformed and distorted so that it became a metaphor for the emotions felt by the artist.

This strictly subjective realism appeared, though in more developed fashion, in the work of the French sculptor Germaine Richier, who spent four years as a private pupil of Émile-Antoine Bourdelle. Richier's sculptures are caught in the very midst of a process of transformation (Plate 277)—the figure here is always in the midst of turning into something not human at all, be it an insect or a hurricane, in a way that resembles the transformations of imagery we find in modern poetry, for example in the work of Richier's husband, the French poet René de Solier. In this rather specialized sense Richier was a literary artist. She is at any rate literary enough to seem incredibly remote from much of the sculpture that followed her death in 1959.

Humanistic sculpture of this type was not, however, the only option open to artists during

280.
Max Bill
Endless Surface
1953–56; 125 × 125 × 80 cm. (49 × 49 × 31 in.)
Antwerp, garden of Middelheim Museum

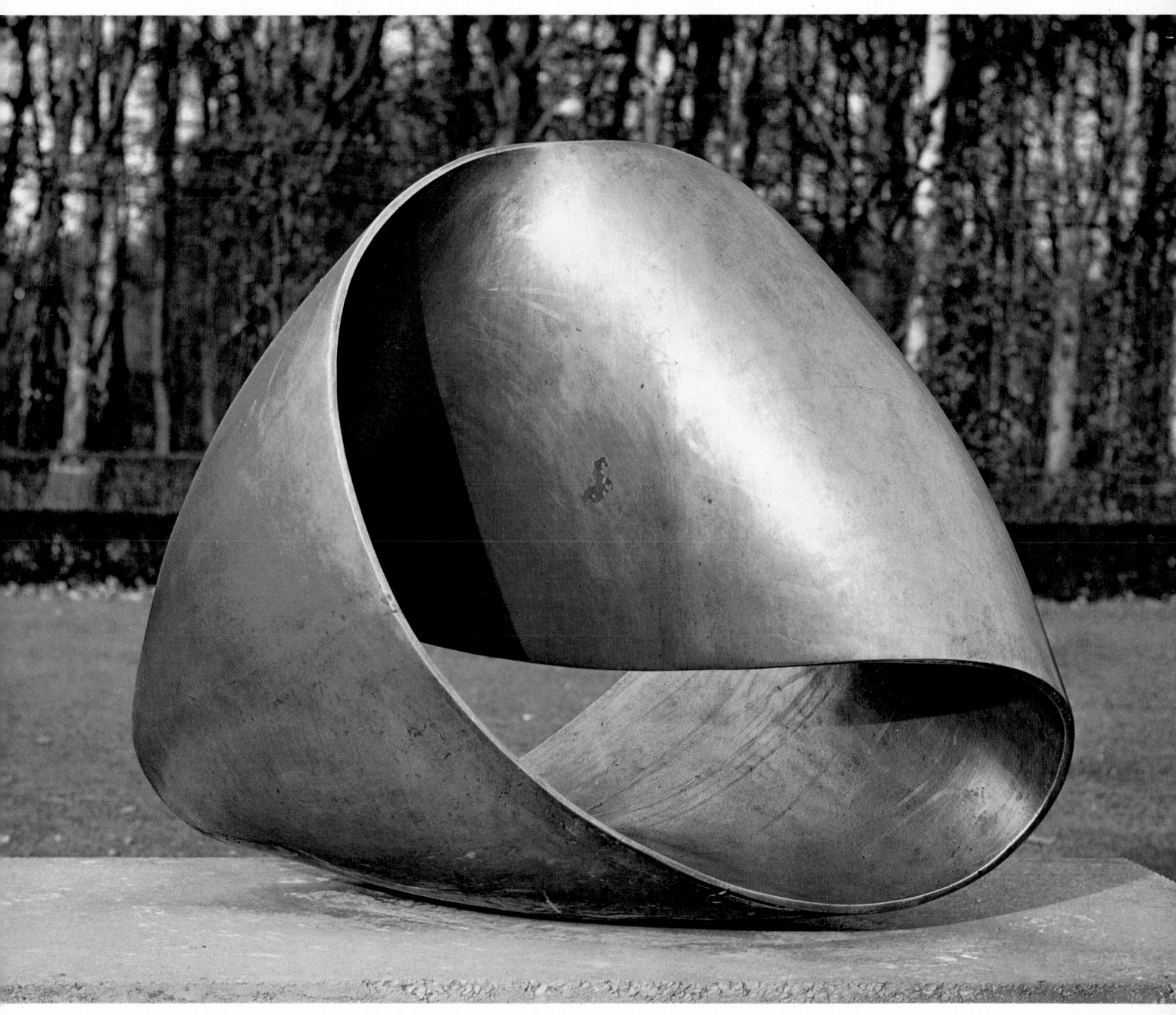

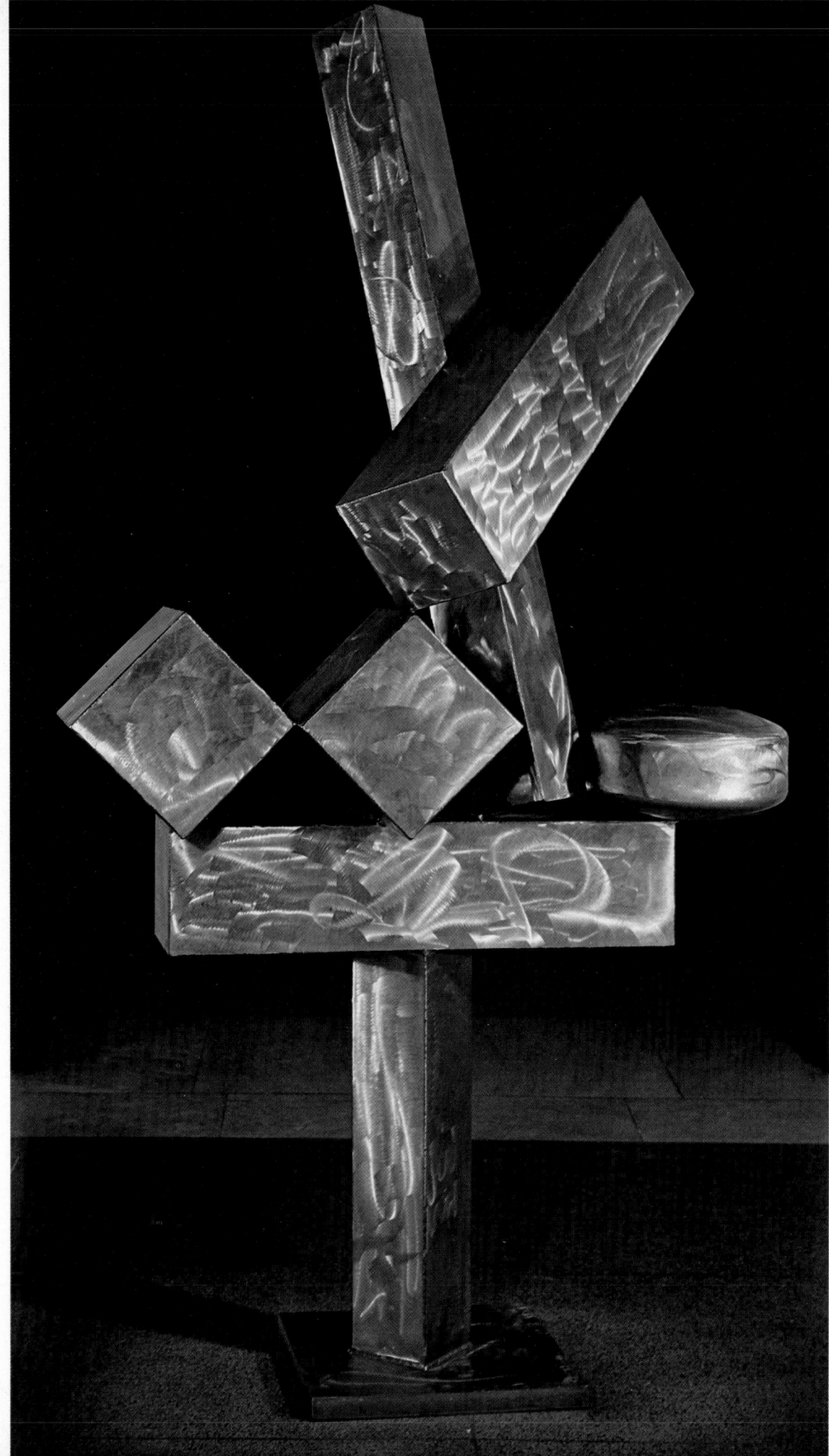

281. Opposite
David Smith
Cubi XIX
1964; 287 × 156 × 105 cm. (112 × 61 × 41 in.)
London, Tate Gallery

282.
David Smith
Primo Piano III
1962; 315 × 368 × 46 cm. (123 × 144 × 18 in.)
New York, Marlborough-Gerson Gallery

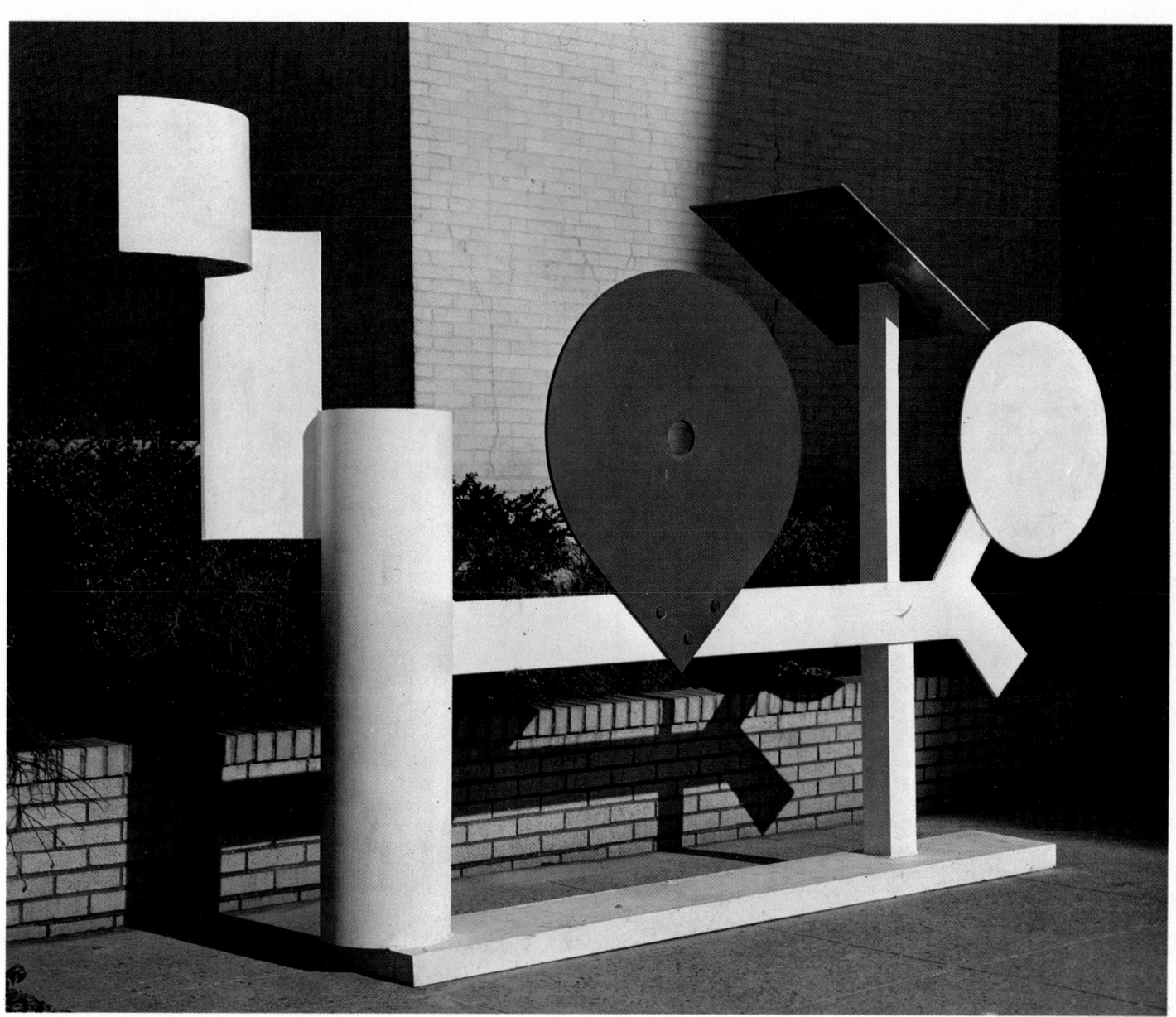

the 1950's. Some, for example, tried to evolve an idiom which would supply an equivalent for the abstract painting of the time. This is probably the best way of approaching the work of Arnaldo Pomodoro, who held his first exhibition in Venice in 1955. Like his brother, Giò Pomodoro, Arnaldo Pomodoro began as a designer, decorator, and metalsmith—that is, he began with the material, and with a keen awareness of its sensuous qualities. It was through manipulation of metal that he became a sculptor, and his subtle contrasts of smoothly polished and apparently corroded surfaces (Plates 278 and 279) are an equivalent of what an artist such as Tàpies does with paint.

Another approach, different again, was through the impersonal logic of the old Constructivist tradition. Perhaps the most interesting exponent of this in the post-war world has been the Swiss

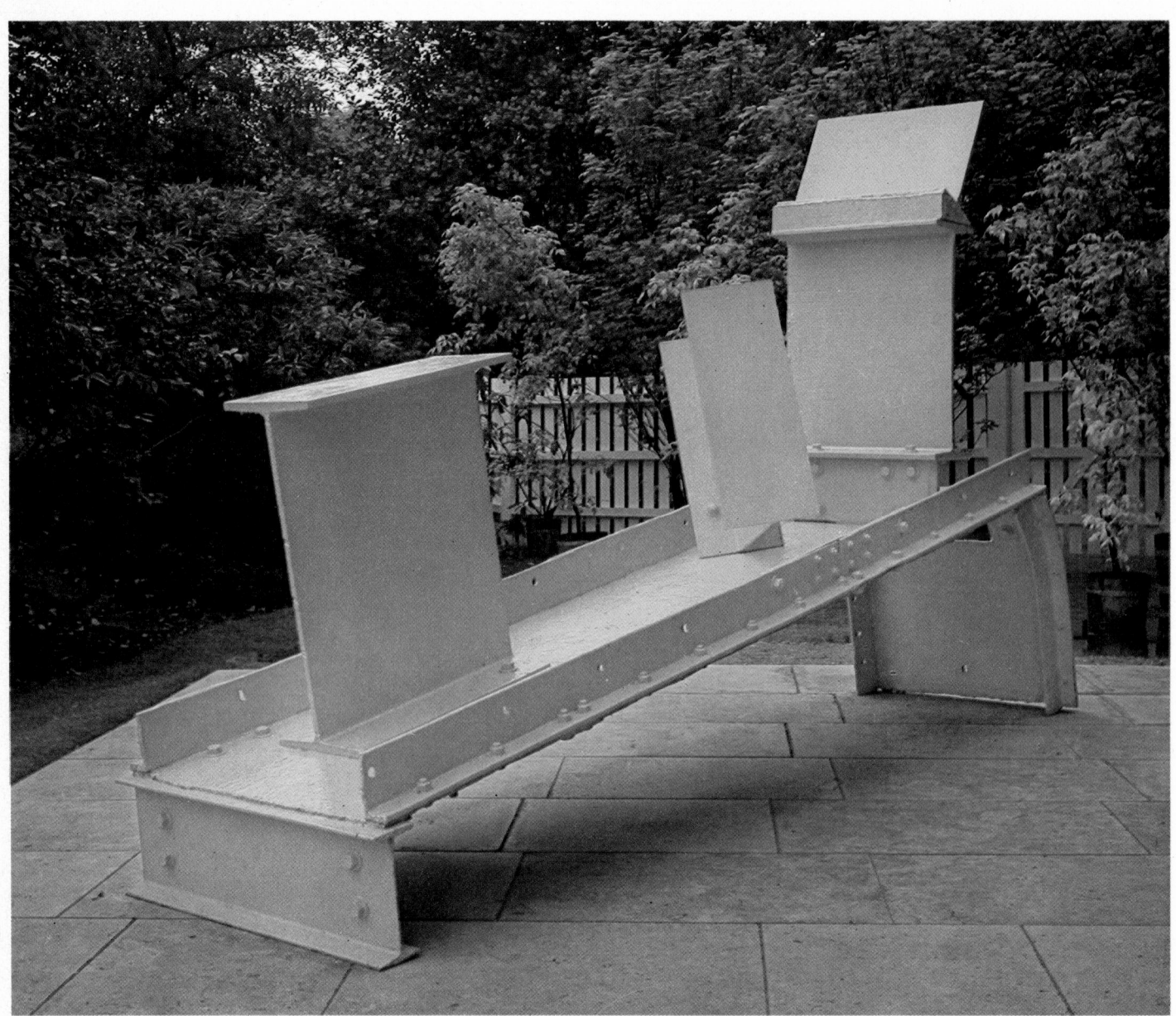

sculptor-architect Max Bill (Plate 280). Bill was a pupil of the Dessau Bauhaus in 1927–29, and the rest of his career has been devoted to an elaboration of Bauhaus ideas. His sculptures approach the problems of three-dimensionality in a spirit of detached curiosity. How, for instance, can a frontal, static quality be avoided, so that the piece has no main aspect, but only an unfolding series of aspects, each of which seems "right" at the moment when it is looked at, but each of which nevertheless urges the spectator onward to a new and different viewpoint, until the circuit is completed? Sculpture, for Bill, is a question of experiments with form. Emotion is irrelevant. In this he has much in common with younger men, yet it is difficult to trace any specific connection between his *oeuvre* and what was to succeed it.

The revolution in sculpture, when it came, took place in several stages. The first and most important stage is represented by the work of two

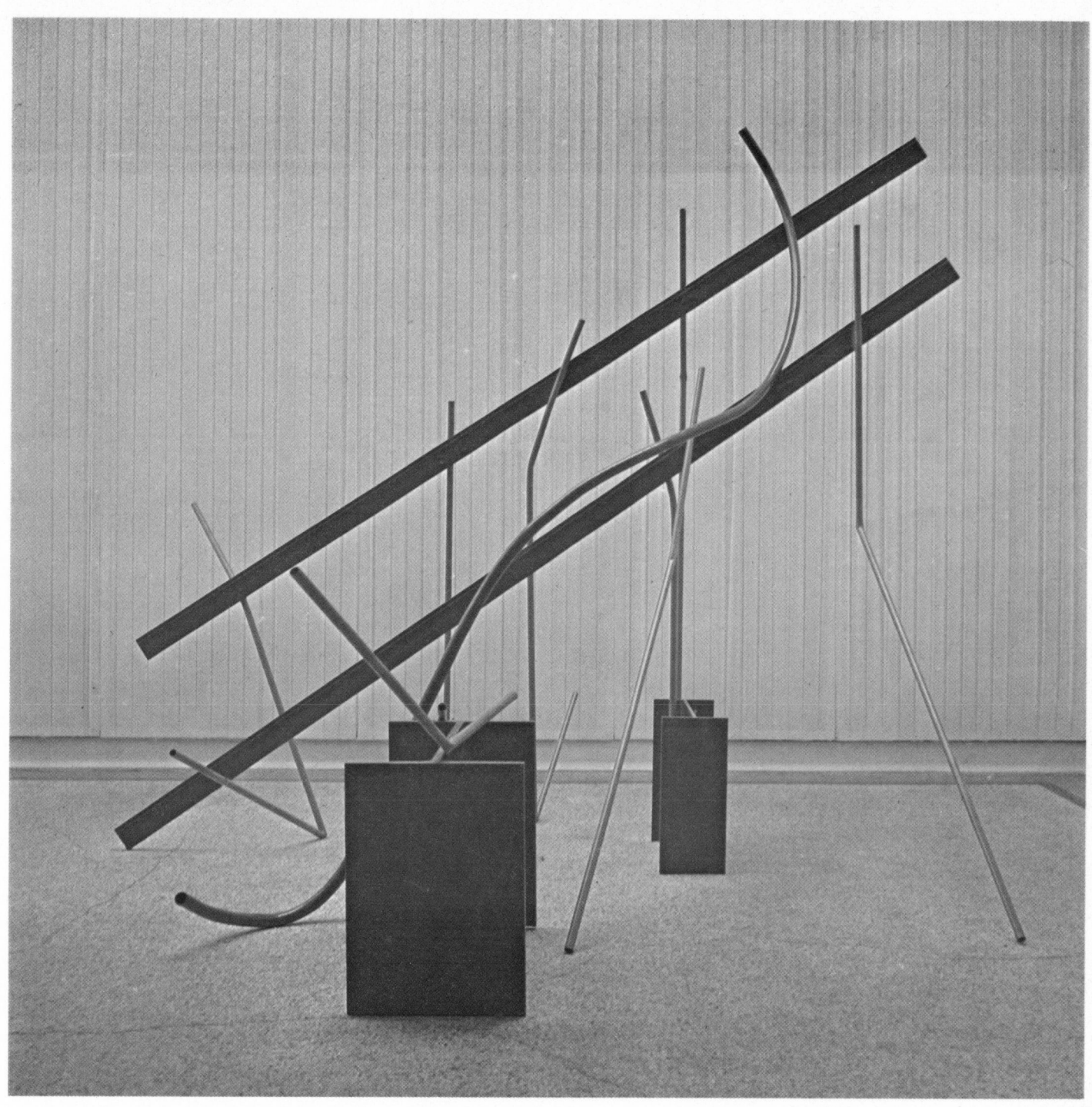

artists, an American and an Englishman: David Smith and Anthony Caro. Smith was a contemporary of the leading Abstract Expressionist painters, and his evolution has some resemblance to theirs. Born in 1906, he was attracted to art from his high school years, but did not actually succeed in making any reputation as an artist until the mid-Thirties, at which time he was associated with the Federal Art Project. This reputation was consolidated during the war, when Smith caught the attention of the influential critic Clement Greenberg; but it was not until the 1950's that his artistic identity was fully visible.

The technique that assumed great importance for David Smith was direct welding. He moved towards this from two different directions—from his experience on the assembly line of the Studebaker plant at South Bend, Indiana, in the middle Twenties, and from his admiration for the welded sculpture of Picasso and Julio Gonzalez.

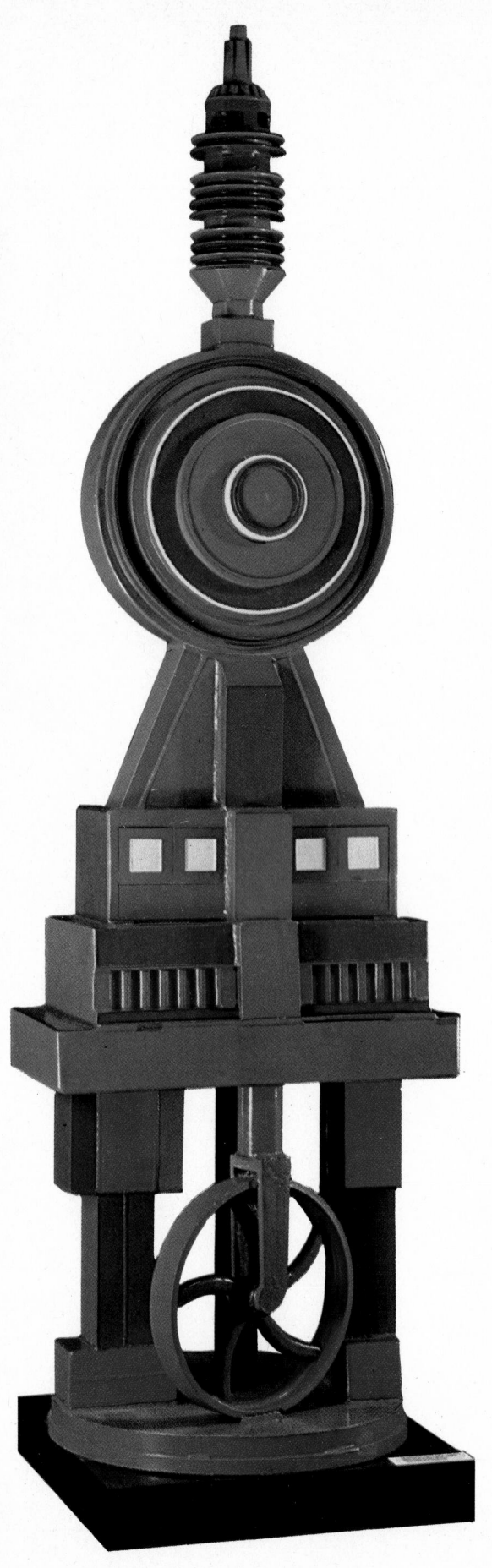

285.
Eduardo Paolozzi
Last of the Idols
1963; 244 × 61 × 11 cm. (95 × 24 × 4 in.)
Cologne, Wallraf-Richartz Museum, coll. Ludwig

286. Opposite
Philip King
Through
1965; 213 × 335 × 274 cm. (83 × 131 × 107 in.)
Bedfordshire, collection of the artist

He first became aware of their work from reproductions of it in a copy of *Cahiers d' Art* which he saw in 1931. Later, during the Second World War, Smith again had a welding job at the American Locomotive Company plant in Schenectady.

Smith began his career as an artist uncertain of whether he wanted to be a painter or a sculptor, and long after he opted definitely for sculpture his work relied upon a kind of draftsmanship in metal. The effect is particularly pronounced in some beautiful sculptures of around 1950, which look like an attempt to rival Abstract Expressionist calligraphy in painted steel.

Soon after this, Smith's work became increasingly industrial in style and handling. In the *Agricola* and *Tanktotem* series of 1952 and 1953, he started to make use of ready-made industrial parts. This was not an entirely new venture. As early as 1933 Smith had made use of found objects. But now, in the early Fifties, Smith began to break away from the Surrealist attitude towards the found object. What it might evoke counted more for this than its inherent formal qualities: "I find many things [he said to an interviewer], but I only choose certain ones that fit a niche in my mind, fit into a relationship I need, and that relationship is somewhat of a geometric nature" (interview with Thomas B. Hess, 1964, reprinted in *David Smith*, edited by Garnett McCoy, London, 1973).

Smith found that by using industrial parts, some of them ordered from manufacturers' catalogues, he was able to make sculptures of substantial size both easily and rapidly. His tendency to work in series, from the 1950's onwards, was prompted by this. It led, in turn, to a rather different attitude towards sculpture itself than that taken up by his predecessors. The late sculptures of the *Cubi* series (Plate 281) have an improvised, almost provisional

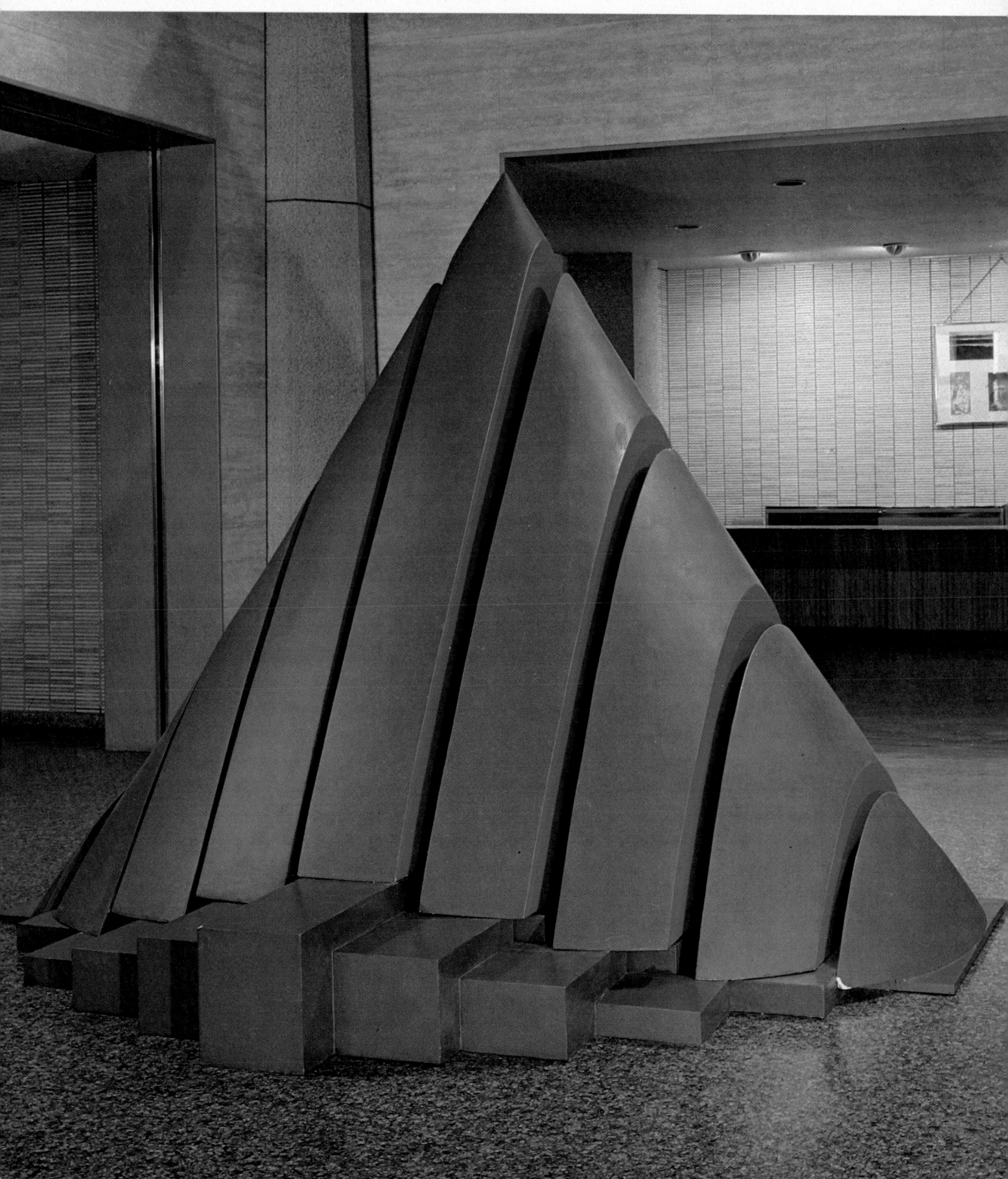

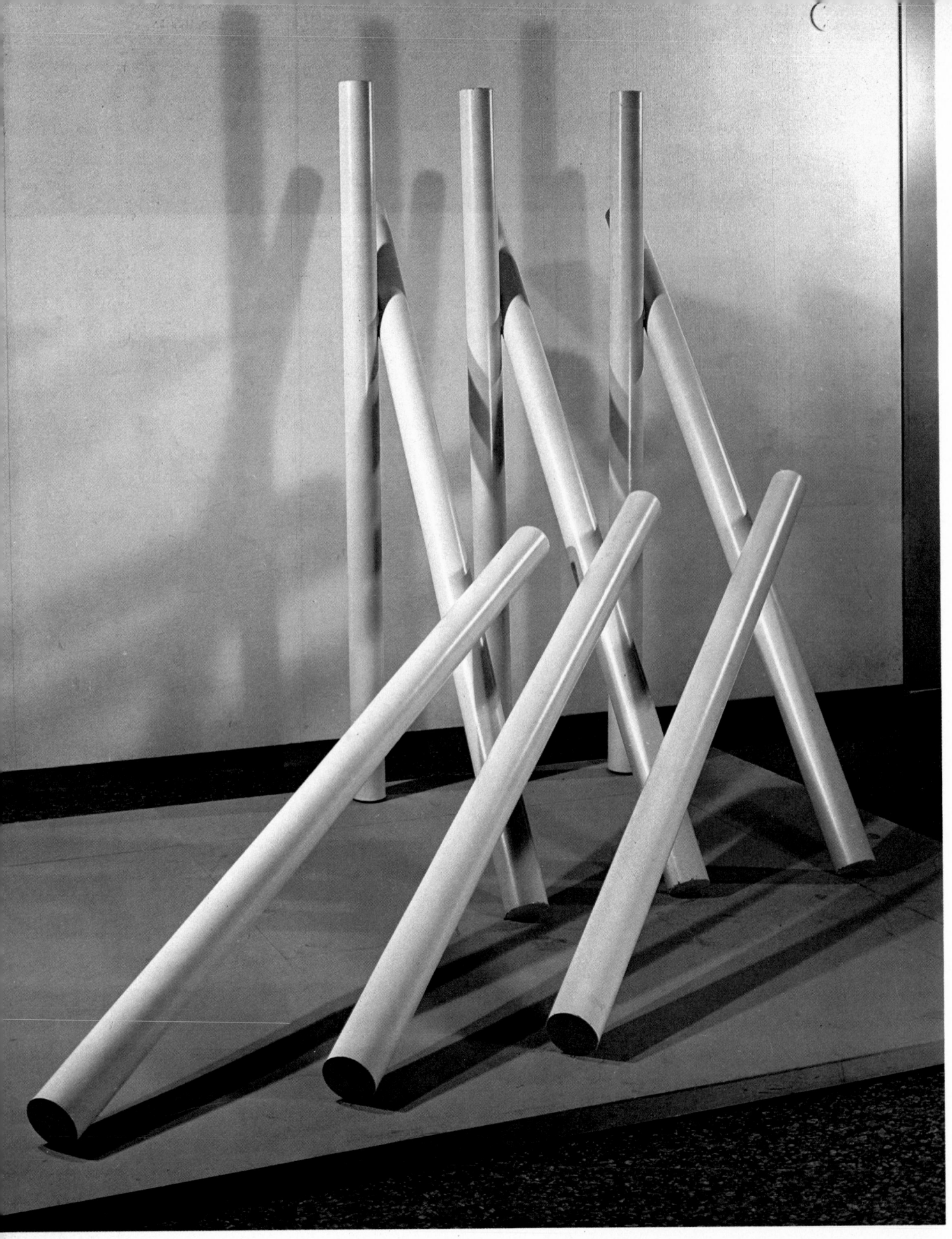

287. Opposite
William Tucker
Nine Poles
1967; 224 × 91 cm. (87 × 35 in.)
London, Kasmin Ltd.

288.
Kenneth Snelson
Audrey I
1965
Colorado, coll. Kimiko and John Powers

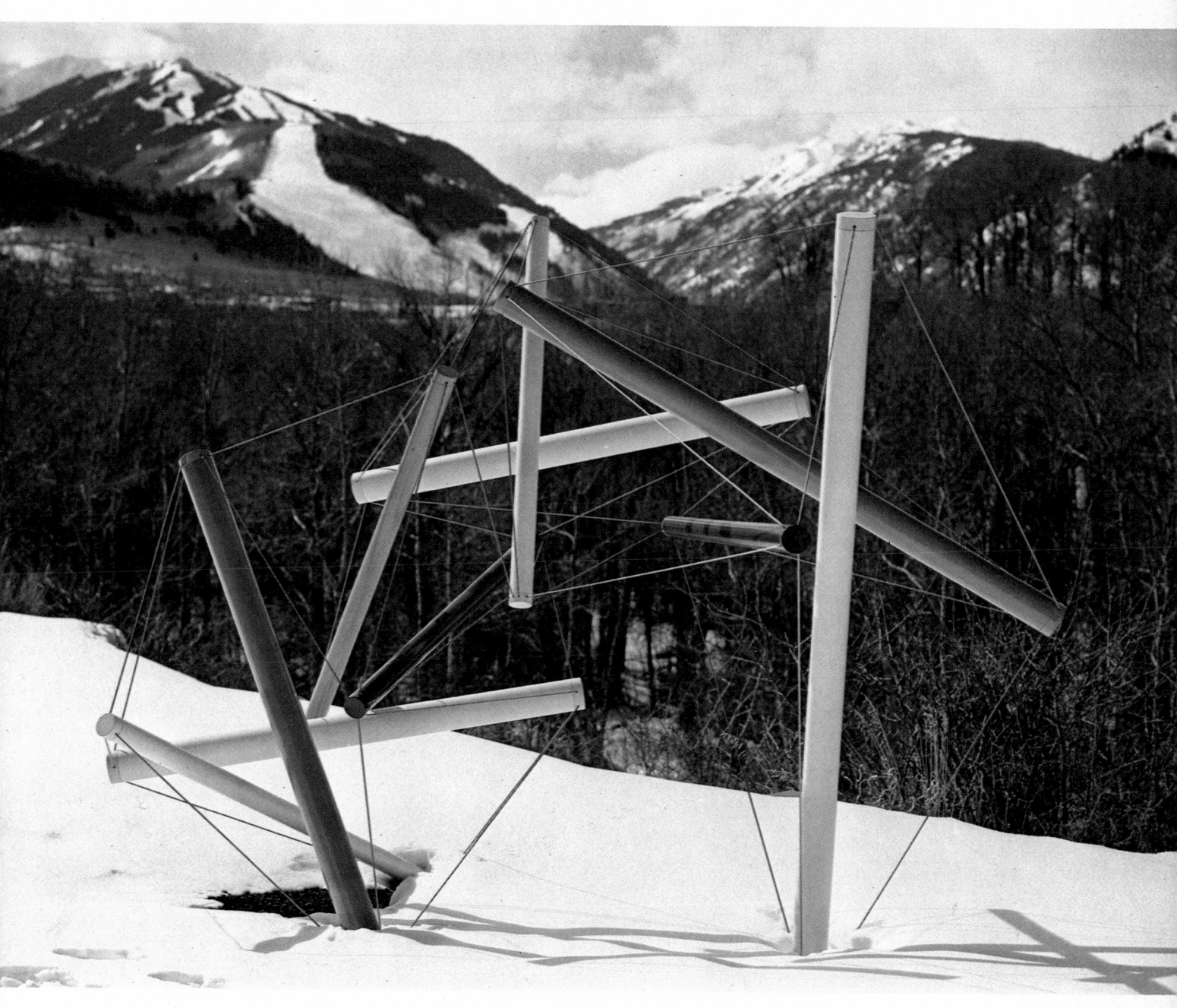

quality. The gain in dynamism is balanced by a corresponding loss of the authority that sculpture is traditionally supposed to possess.

The majority of the *Cubi* series do, however, retain some vestiges of tradition. With most the sculpture starts from a base; and many can be interpreted as paraphrases, though distant ones, of the human figure. In other work of the Sixties Smith was even further from the conventional notion of sculpture (*Primo Piano III*, Plate 282), though it must be noted that sculptures of this type have a strong resemblance to some of the more ambitious "stabiles"—as opposed to mobiles—produced by Alexander Calder.

371

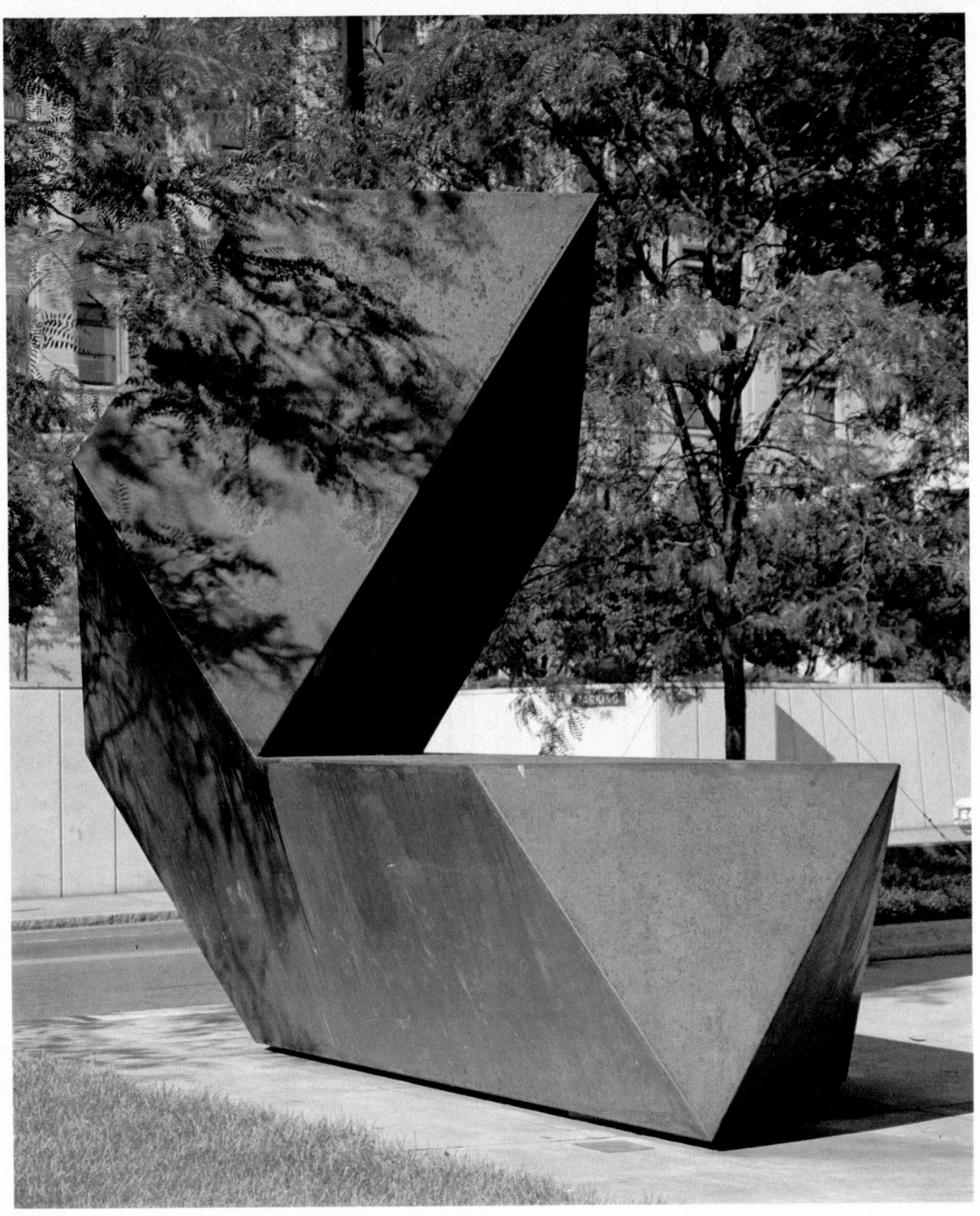

Smith's work, coupled with advice and encouragement from Clement Greenberg, was destined to have a decisive impact upon the work of the British sculptor Anthony Caro, who in 1959 paid a first visit to the United States. In the course of this he saw work by Noland and Louis, as well as sculpture by Smith. Before this, Caro had worked for a time as an assistant to Henry Moore, enlarging Moore's small-scale models to final sculptures. He had also produced a number of figurative sculptures of his own in a boldly Expressionist style. Now, like Smith, Caro started making sculptures out of scrap steel, girders, and sheet metal.

The earliest of these, for example, *Midday*, which dates from 1960 (Plate 283), are more closed in form, and more massive, than subsequent work. But already there are marked differences between

289. Opposite
Tony Smith
Amaryllis
1965; 350 × 129 × 350 cm. (137 × 50 × 137 in.)
Connecticut, Wadsworth Atheneum

290.
Larry Bell
Ellipse
1965; 136 × 35.6 × 35.6 cm. (53 × 14 × 14 in.)
New York, Whitney Museum of American Art,
gift of Howard and Jean Lipman

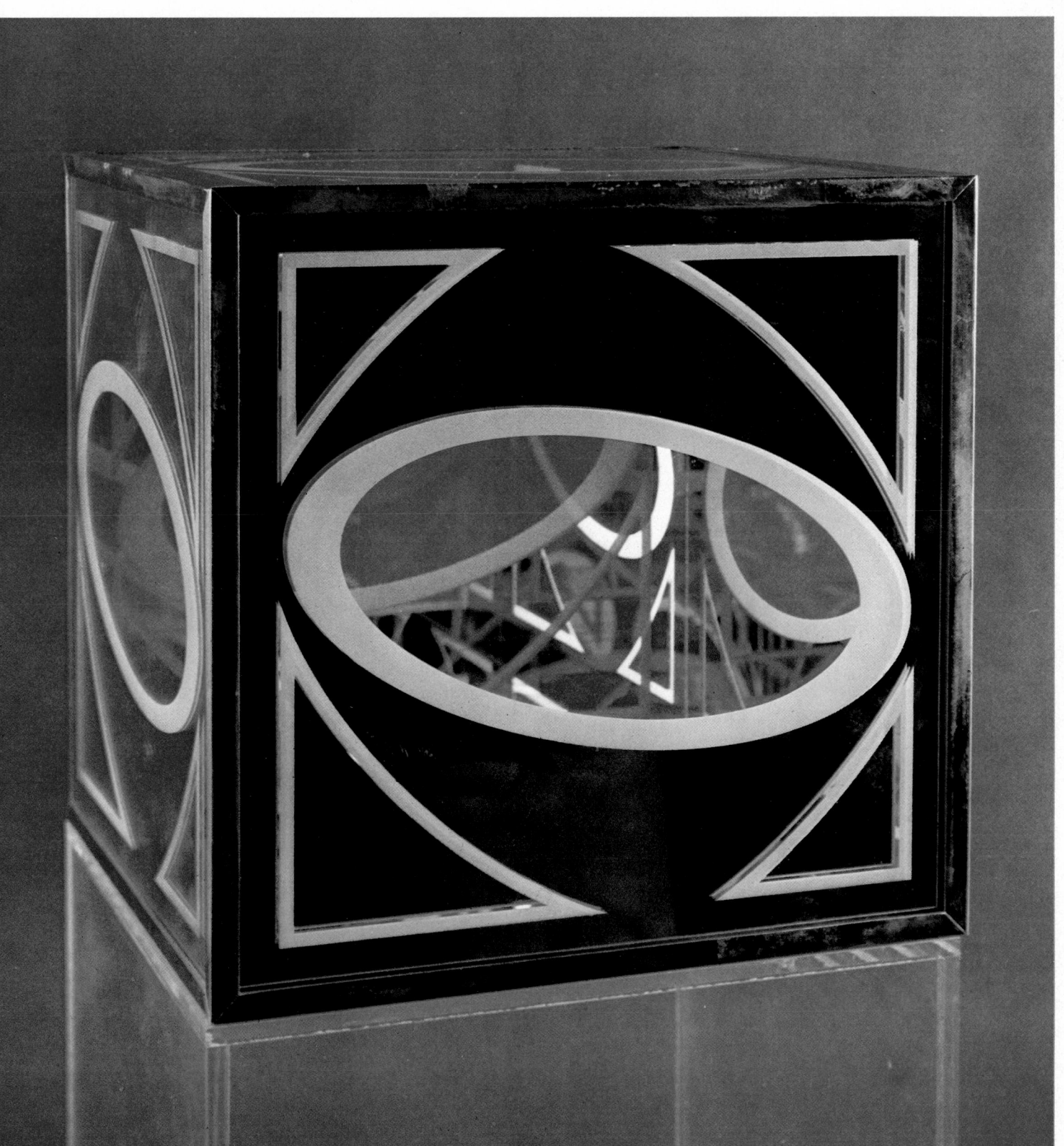

291.
Donald Judd
Untitled
1966; 122 × 305 × 305 cm. (48 × 119 × 119 in.)
Connecticut, coll. Mr. and Mrs. Howard Lipman

292. Opposite
Donald Judd
Untitled, detail
1968; 23 × 102 × 79 cm. (9 × 40 × 31 in.)
Los Angeles, County Museum of Art

Caro and Smith. Caro abolishes the base altogether, and his sculptures tend to be horizontal in orientation. Many are entirely below eye level. The rambling quality of much of Caro's work (*Month of May*, Plate 284) prevents the spectator from anthropomorphizing it. But the free interplay of parts has a strong effect upon the whole of the surrounding space. A sculpture like *Month of May* is not environmental in the exact sense of the term. It does not surround the viewer, nor can he walk through it as well as around it. But its chief function is, nevertheless, to alter spatial perception.

An interesting comparison can be drawn between Caro's work of the early Sixties and that being done at the same moment by another British sculptor, Eduardo Paolozzi (Plate 285). Paolozzi, during the previous decade, had been closely involved with the beginnings of the Pop Art movement in Britain, but his own work had remained a compromise between nascent Pop

ideas and Surrealism. The two allegiances were neatly epitomized in Paolozzi's most characteristic technical device, which was to create an intricate surface pattern upon sheets of wax, using small cogwheels, wheels from toy motor cars and similar small objects, and then to form these sheets into slightly monstrous creatures which were afterwards cast in bronze, the traditional material of the sculptor. But now Paolozzi, too, started using ready-made industrial parts, which were welded together and brightly painted. The forms he made with them, however, were recognizably humanoid—witty fantasies based upon the robots and Martians in comic strips.

Caro exerted an important influence on younger British sculptors through his work as a teacher at the St. Martin's School of Art. This influence announced itself in an exhibition called "The New Generation: 1965", which was held at the Whitechapel Art Gallery in London. The majority of the exhibitors had studied at St. Martin's under

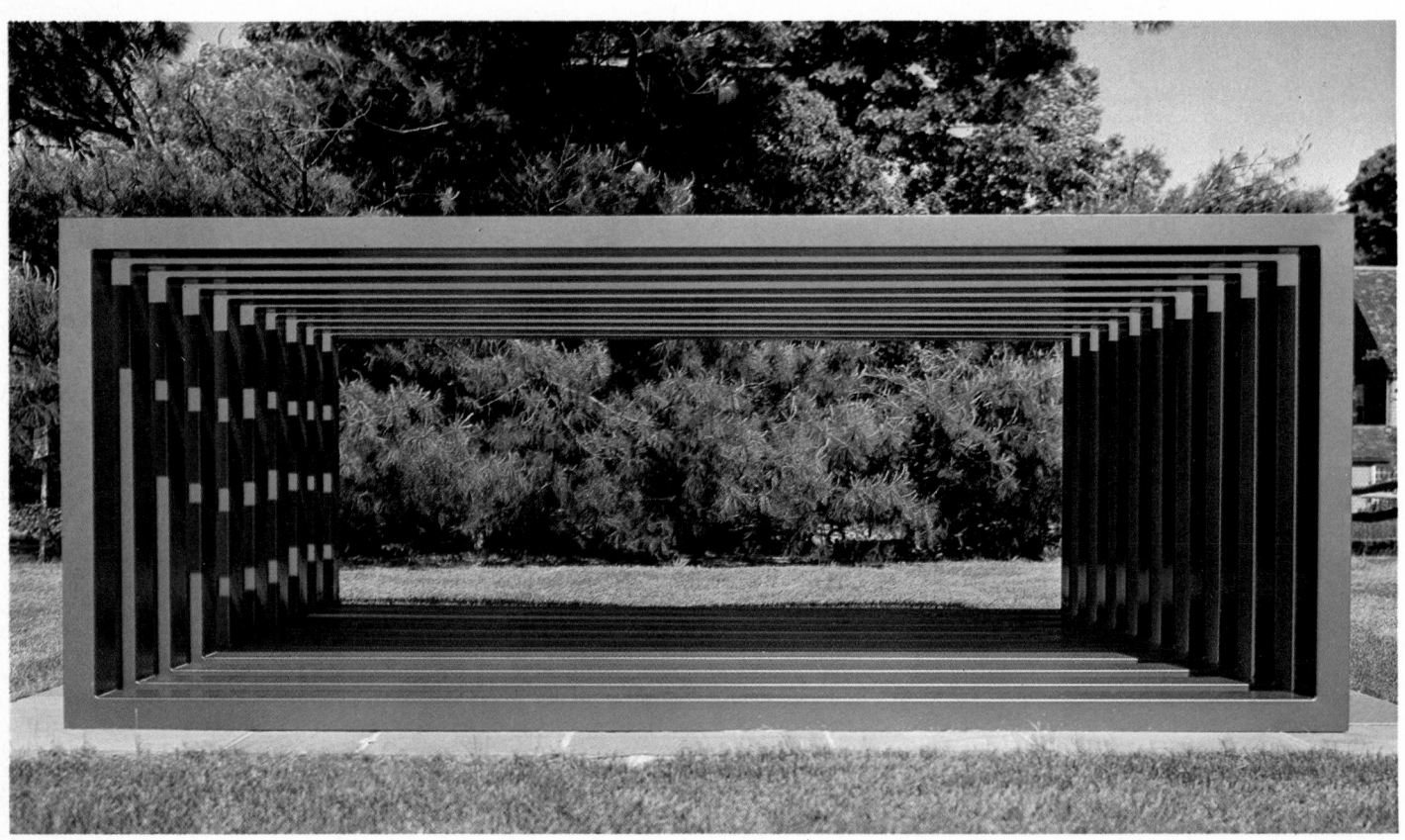

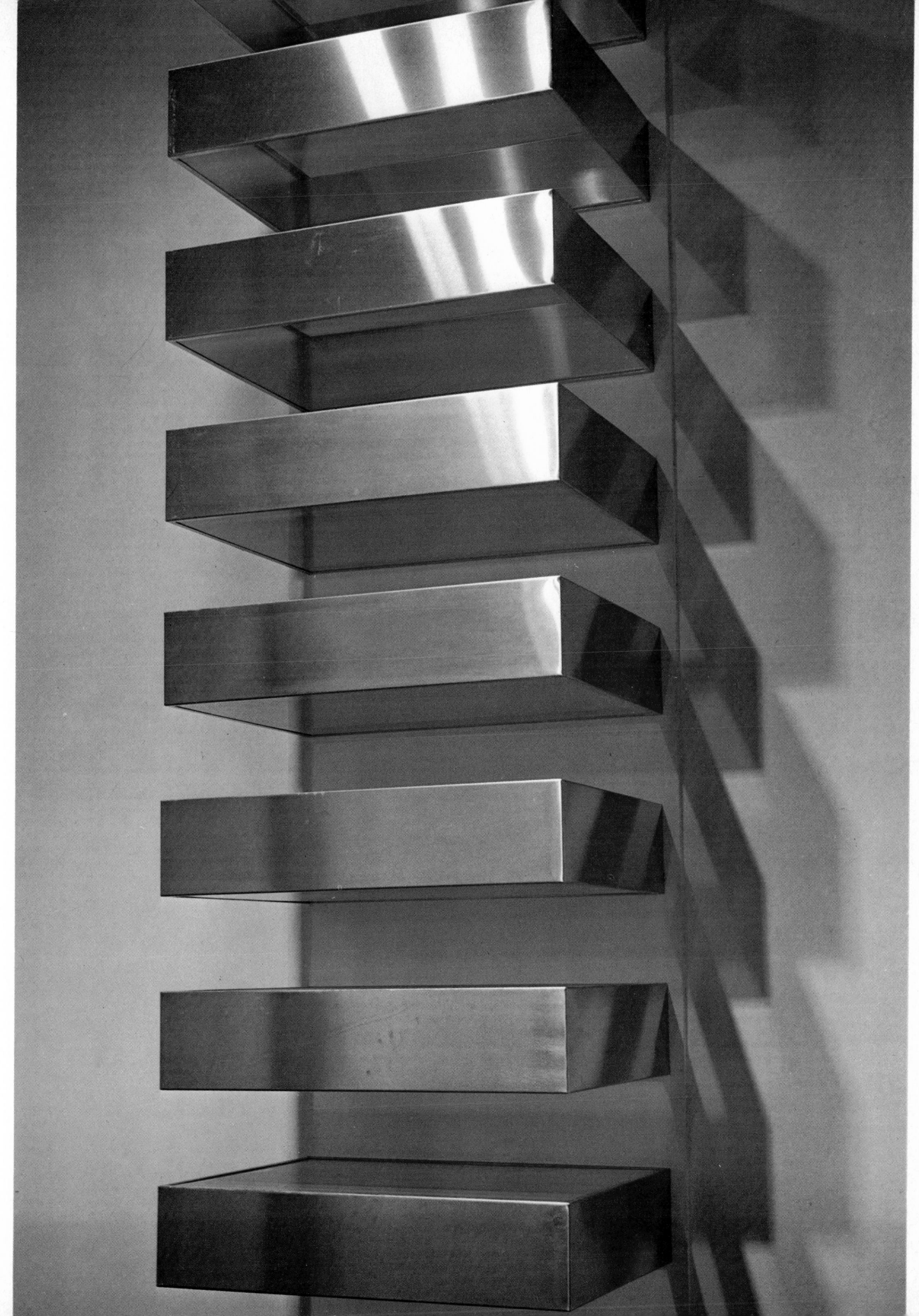

293.
Carl Andre
64 Pieces of Copper
1969; 20 × 20 × 1 cm. (9 × 9 × ½ in.)
New York, private collection

294. Opposite
Sol LeWitt
3 Part Set 789 (B)
1968; 80 × 208 × 50 cm. (31 × 81 × 20 in.)
Cologne, Wallraf-Richartz Museum, coll. Ludwig

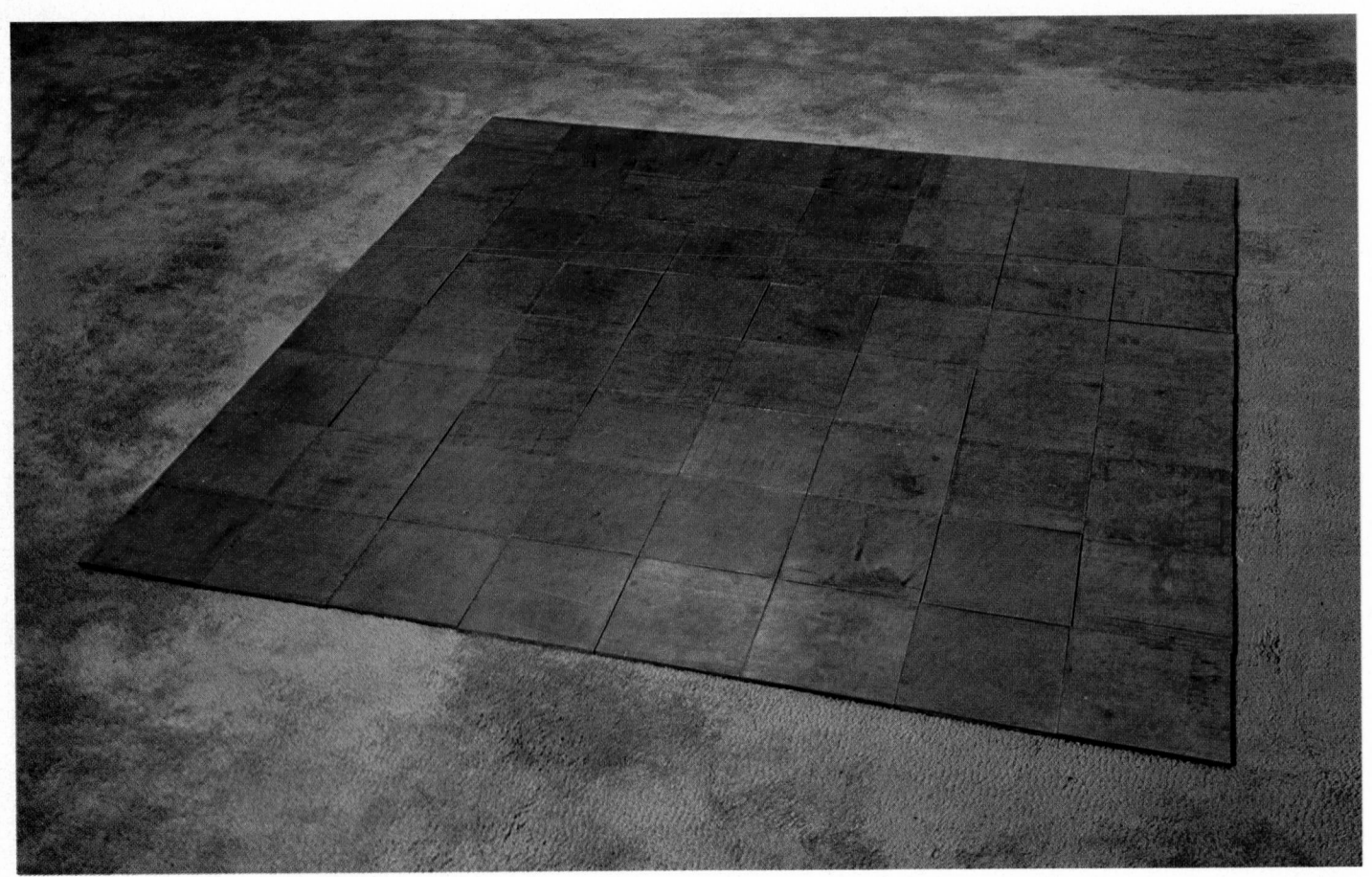

Caro. Among them were Philip King and William Tucker. King's *Through* (Plate 286) dates from the same year as the Whitechapel exhibition and exemplifies many of the qualities to be found in this new group of artists—a feeling for formal ambiguity, which is nevertheless closely controlled, combined with a determination to get away from any kind of external or nostalgic association, even the associations conjured up by Caro's girders. A neutral material—fibreglass—is given life with deliberately synthetic colour, and it is the play of colour, as much as the interaction of form, that gives life to the piece.

William Tucker (Plate 287) sticks much closer to Caro's example, but a comparison between *Month of May* and *Nine Poles* reveals that a tidying-up process has taken place. Tucker's sculpture has a rather arid logic which is quite different from

Caro's use of similar elements.

The feeling for logic and regularity which showed itself in King and Tucker was to reappear in far more drastic guise in the American sculpture of the same period. There were, of course, certain resemblances to what was being produced in Britain at the same time. One can see, for instance, a distinct kinship between *Nine Poles* and Kenneth Snelson's *Audrey I* (Plate 288). Both make logical use of linear units. But the more closely one examines the two pieces, the less alike they seem. Snelson takes up and exaggerates one aspect of David Smith's work: the feeling of instability. An American critic, discussing the sculpture illustrated, remarks: "*Audrey I* is a dynamic structure which achieves only a very tenuous and threatened balance. Poised lightly upon the apexes of triangular units, its insubstantiality is emphasized

376

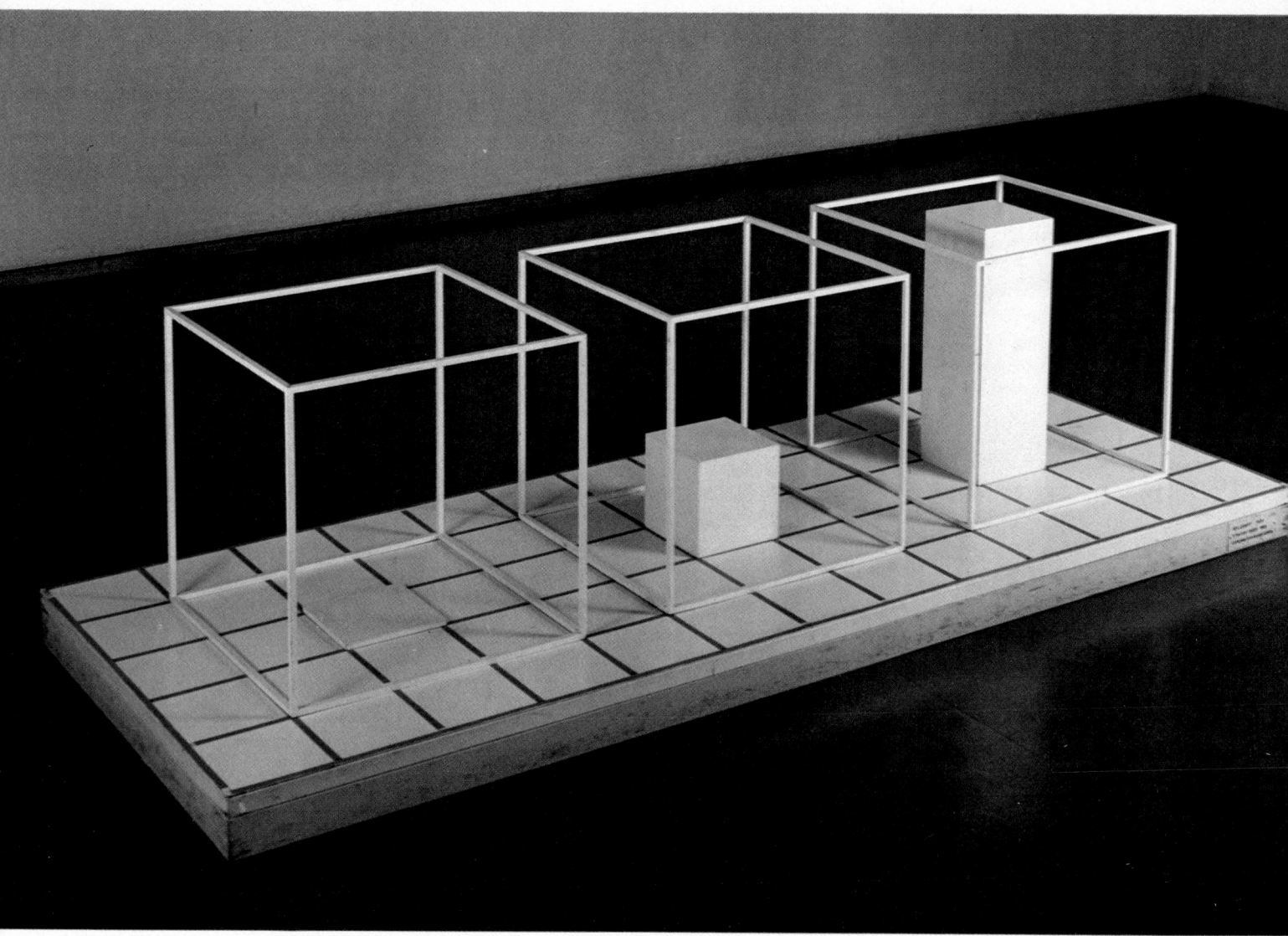

as well as its dependence upon the strength of the cable system" (Stephen A. Kurtz, "Kenneth Snelson: The Elegant Solution", *Arts Magazine*, New York, 1968).

Snelson takes the provisional quality of David Smith's work a stage further by introducing a means of construction which is genuinely precarious, instead of just seeming so.

Snelson's work is outside the mainstream of American sculpture of the Sixties because, despite the simplicity of the parts, they are used to create a complex structure. Even he, as it happened, was to simplify his work and make it more regular and stable in appearance in the course of the decade.

The term "Minimal Art" was coined by the British philosopher Richard Wollheim in 1965. He used it to describe the kind of contemporary art object that seems to rely, for its aesthetic impact, on a paradoxical absence of art content. The readymades of Marcel Duchamp would be a case in point. Almost immediately, this term came to be used by art critics as a convenient label for a particular kind of extremely simplified sculpture then being produced in America. Such works were also dubbed "Primary Structures"—the title of an exhibition held at the Jewish Museum in New York in 1966—and the movement which gave birth to them was dubbed "Structuralism". Among the artists whose work was included in the show at the Jewish Museum were Larry Bell, Dan Flavin, Donald Judd, Sol LeWitt, John McCracken, and Robert Morris.

The artist who most clearly demonstrates the derivation of Structuralism from the late sculptures of David Smith is the latter's namesake Tony Smith. The way that Tony Smith's sculptures look

295.
Robert Morris
Untitled
1966; 61 × 244 cm. (24 × 95 in.)
Colorado, coll. Kimiko and John Powers

296. Opposite
Robert Morris
Untitled
1970; 183 × 244 cm. (71 × 95 in.)
New York, Leo Castelli Gallery

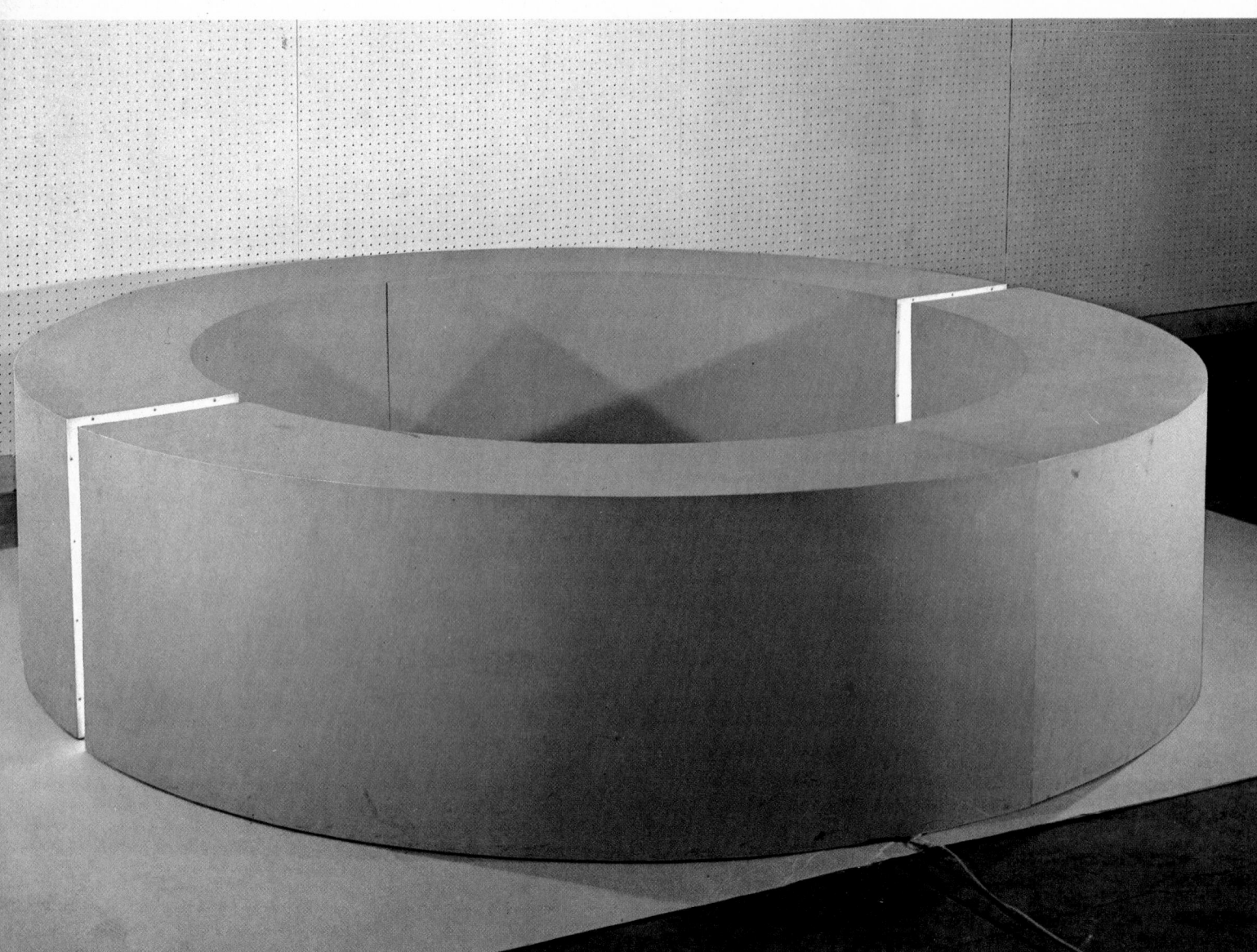

is in part at least the product of the circuitous route by which he came to making sculpture. Born in 1912, he had made a career in architecture, working as an assistant to Frank Lloyd Wright in the late Thirties, then during two decades independently designing numerous buildings. It was not until 1960 that he started his career as a sculptor, and the decision was in large part due to his impatience with the impurity of architecture— to the fact that the architect's intentions were always compromised and distorted by the pressures of human use and human need.

But there is also to be found in Tony Smith's work a version of the cult of inexpressiveness which we have already encountered in the paintings of Andy Warhol. Describing the genesis of his piece *Amaryllis* (Plate 289), the artist said: "I set out to make something like a cave. I wanted to make the space and light as tangible as possible and in other ways it was to be the architecture of an

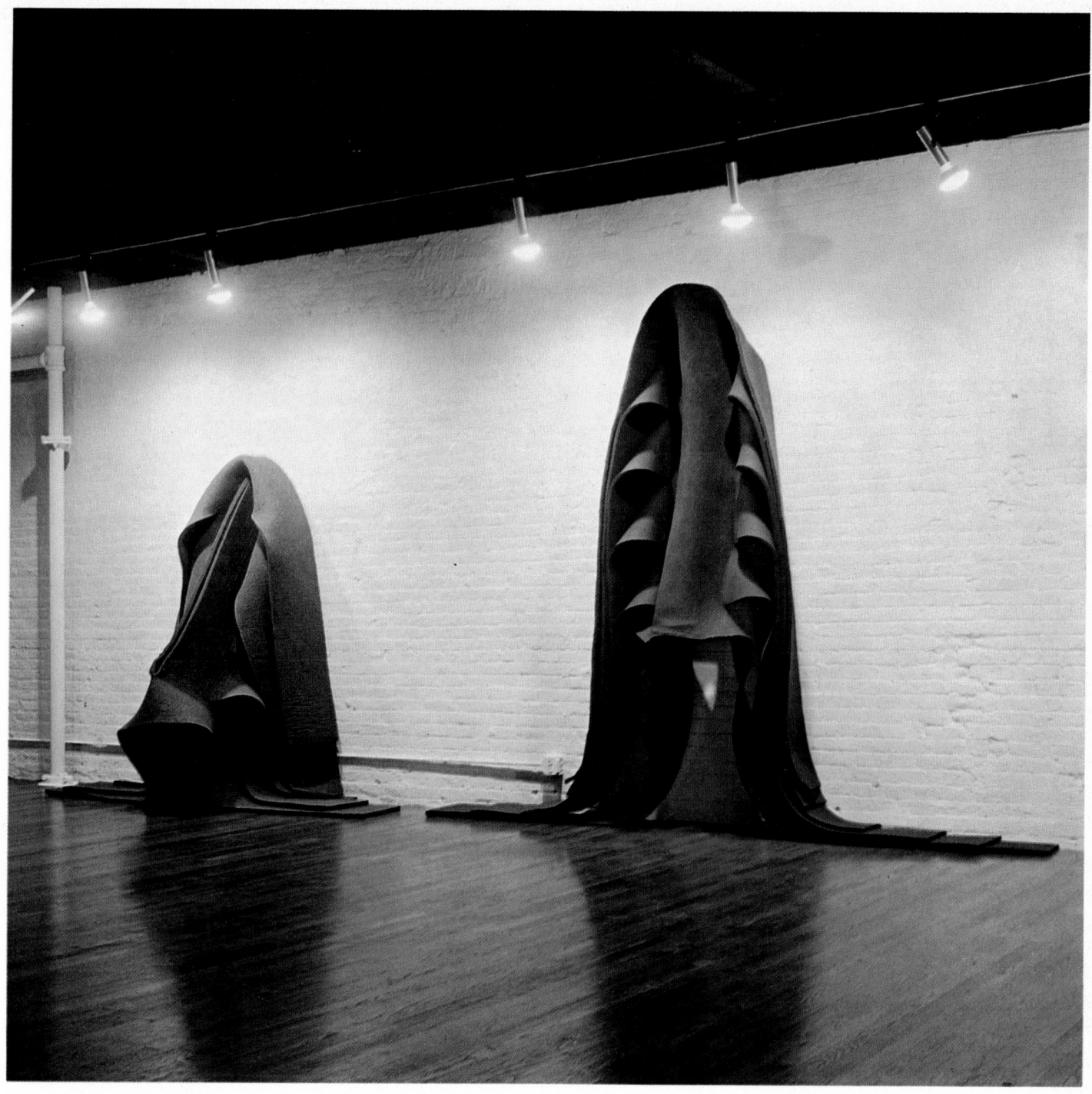

idiot" (Tony Smith in the catalogue of "Tony Smith—Two Exhibitions of Sculpture", shown at the Wadsworth Atheneum, Hartford, Connecticut, 1966, and at the ICA, Philadelphia, 1966–67).

This piece makes the connection with David Smith very clear. *Amaryllis* is a large box structure made of sheet metal, which looks like a flowing-together and enlargement of certain parts of the *Cubi* series. Its large scale seems to reflect Tony Smith's long experience as an architect. But this characteristic is not confined to his work alone. Very many Minimal sculptures are of monumental size, and this fact, like the bland banality of their forms, has been linked by commentators to the ideas of Gestalt psychology. The "good Gestalt" the spectator is unconsciously in search of resides, according to this theory, in the soothing uniformity of these vast shapes, and in the fact that they are big enough to block all other objects from our view.

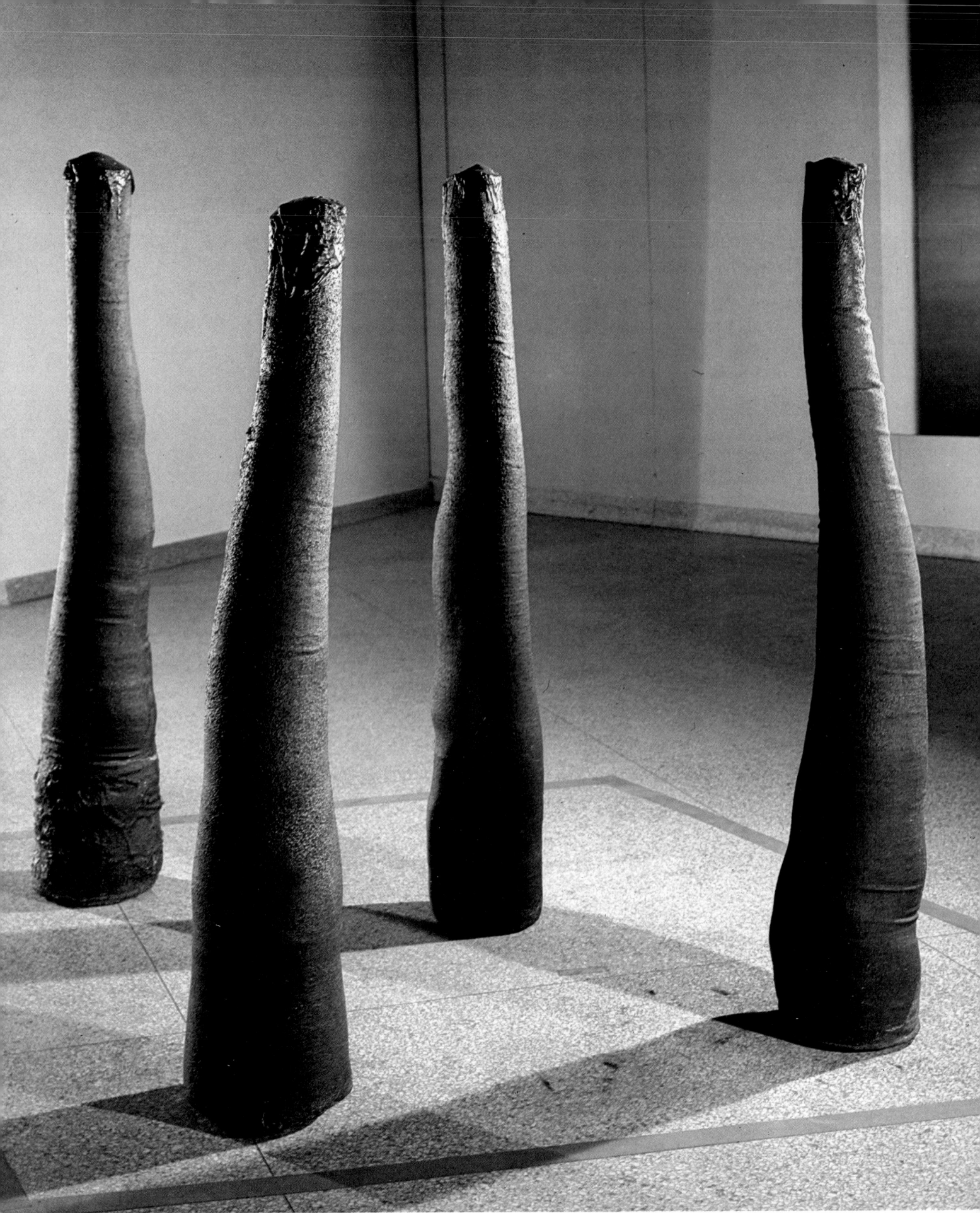

380

297. Opposite
Barry Flannagan
Four Rahsbs 4, 1967
1967, 127 × 152.4 × 152.4 cm. (50 × 59 × 59 in.)
New York, Solomon R. Guggenheim Museum

298.
Richard Serra
Untitled 1969
1969; 268 × 272 × 47.5 cm. (105 × 106 × 19 in.)
New York, coll. Jasper Johns

Not everything placed under the heading of Minimal Art was as inherently simple as the phrase itself suggested. There was a complex play of reflection in the coated glass cubes made by Larry Bell (Plate 290), even in those made when he had ceased to inscribe designs upon the surface. And when he stopped making cubes, and instead simply placed sheets of coated glass at right angles to one another, the play of imagery continued to be the main subject of the work.

At the heart of Minimal Art lay an austere puritanism which makes an artist like Bell seem slightly divorced from its real purposes. This puritanism is especially conspicuous in the work of a sculptor such as Donald Judd, with its passion for total visibility and the absence of any ambiguity (Plates 291 and 292). Judd asserts: "A shape, a volume, a color, a surface is something itself. It shouldn't be concealed as part of a fairly different whole. The shapes and materials should not be altered by the context. One or four boxes in a row, any single thing or such a series, is local

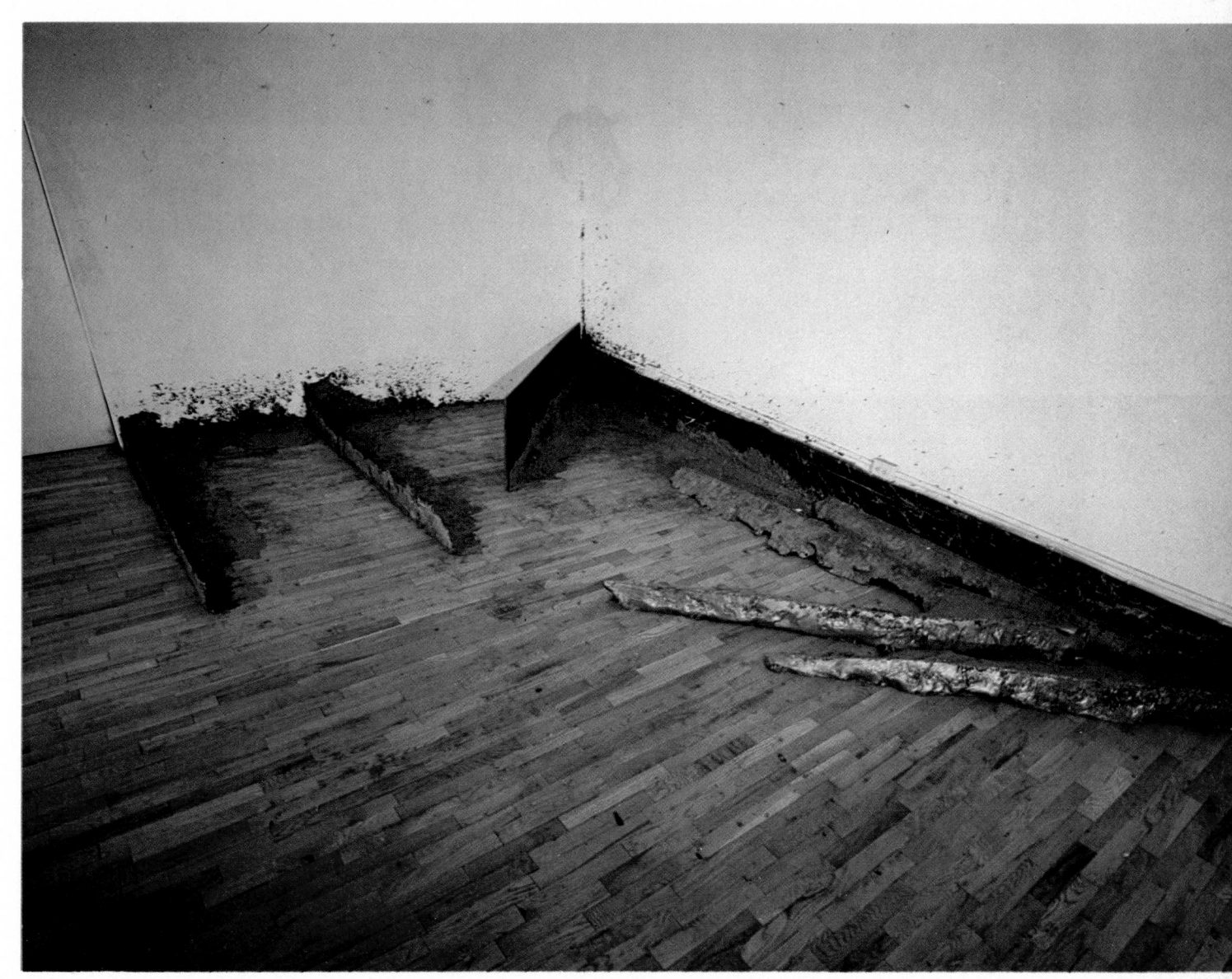

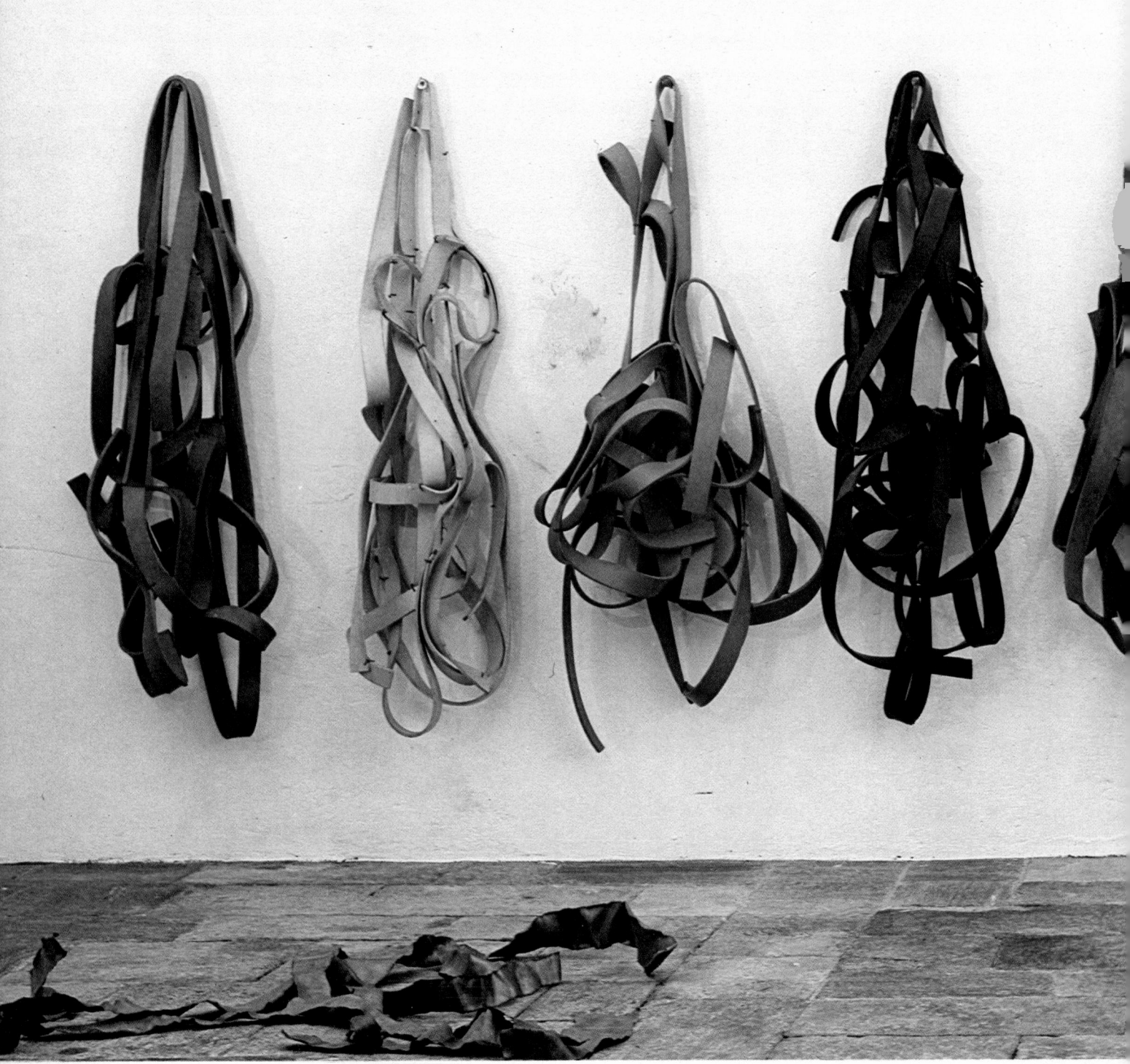

299.
Richard Serra
9 Rubber Belts and Neon
1968; 190 × 553 × 44 cm. (74 × 216 × 17 in.)
Varese, coll. Giuseppe Panza di Biumo

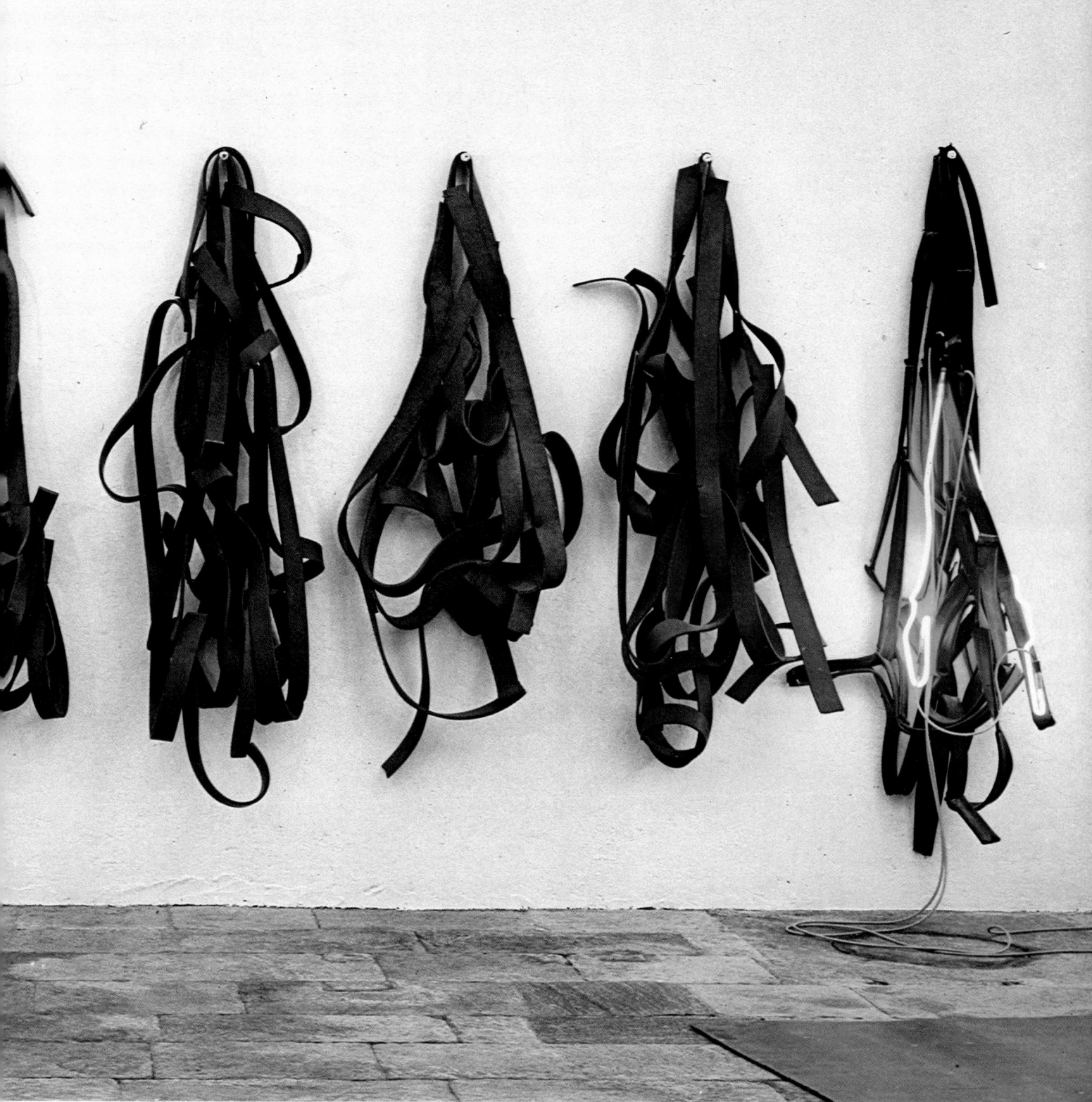

order, just an arrangement, barely order at all. The series is mine, someone's, and clearly not some larger order. It has nothing to do with either order or disorder in general. Both are matters of fact. The series of four or six doesn't change the galvanized iron or steel or whatever the boxes are made of" (Donald Judd, "Perspecta II, 1967", *Portfolio: 4 Sculptors*, New York, 1967).

The one concession Judd makes to ambiguity of any kind lies in the fact that his sculptures, like Kenneth Noland's stripe paintings or, before that, the *Endless Column* of Brancusi, give the impression that the sequence of identical shapes could be indefinitely prolonged.

We find another version of this idea in the floor pieces of Carl Andre (Plate 293), where the units (in this case copper plaques) have even less formal interest than Judd's boxes. Andre's work also demonstrates a number of other characteristics that tend to appear frequently in Minimal Art—the emphasis upon the plane of the floor, and the fact that the sculpture is what has come to be called an "installation piece", made to fit a particular physical situation, and without fixed identity, since all the components are movable.

There is an affinity between Andre's work and that of Sol LeWitt, but also a difference. LeWitt's structures, such as *3 Part Set 789 (B)* (Plate 294) are demonstrations of the conflict between "conceptual order and visual disorder". What LeWitt exploits is the contradiction between what we know to be there and what we actually see. The work *3 Part Set* presents a mathematical series in visual form, but our apprehension of this series is confused by matters extraneous to the real content of the work—perspective effects, the fact that one part may stand in front of another, cast shadows, and so forth. The conceptual content of LeWitt's sculptures links them directly to his wall drawings and prints. Here the marks are made according to rigid sets of rules, which are designed to eliminate the effects of either taste or accident.

One of the chief theoreticians of the Structuralist movement has been Robert Morris, and his personal evolution has, correspondingly, been among the most interesting. Earlier works, such as *Untitled* of 1966 (Plate 295), show the rigidity of post-David Smith sculpture. In this particular case the artist has even chosen to emphasize the nature of the structure by putting a light inside it, and by providing two slits at opposite sides through which the light can be seen. That is, he demonstrates to us that a ring-like form which we might in fact accept as solid and unitary is in fact hollow. Later works (Plate 296) are the opposite of rigid, and seem to owe a good deal to the soft sculptures of Claes Oldenburg. Morris explained his change of orientation thus, in an article in the influential art magazine *Artforum*: "In object-type art, process is not visible. Materials often are. When they are, their reasonableness is usually apparent. Rigid industrial materials go together at right angles with great ease. But it is the *a priori* evaluation of the well-built that dictates the materials. The well-built form of objects preceded any consideration of means."

The solution, according to Morris, is to follow the lead given by the material itself: "Sometimes a direct manipulation of a given material without the use of any tool is made. In these cases considerations of a given material begun as means result in forms which were not projected in advance. Considerations of ordering are necessarily casual and imprecise and unemphasized. Random piling, loose stacking, hanging, give passing form to the material. Chance is accepted and indeterminacy is implied since replacing will result in another configuration, since disengagement with preconceived enduring forms and orders for things is a positive assertion" (Robert Morris, "Anti-Form", *Artforum*, New York, April, 1968).

Morris's argument, which is, in effect, that to be truly Minimal sculpture must abandon fixed form altogether, has found an echo among quite a number of avant-garde artists. The English sculptor Barry Flannagan, with his *Four Rahsbs 4, 1967* (Plate 297), seems to be making at least a tentative protest against the kind of work that was simultaneously being turned out by members of the "New Generation", a group of sculptors who took their name from an exhibition at the Whitechapel Art Gallery, London, in 1965. The forms can be read as a kind of parody of what other

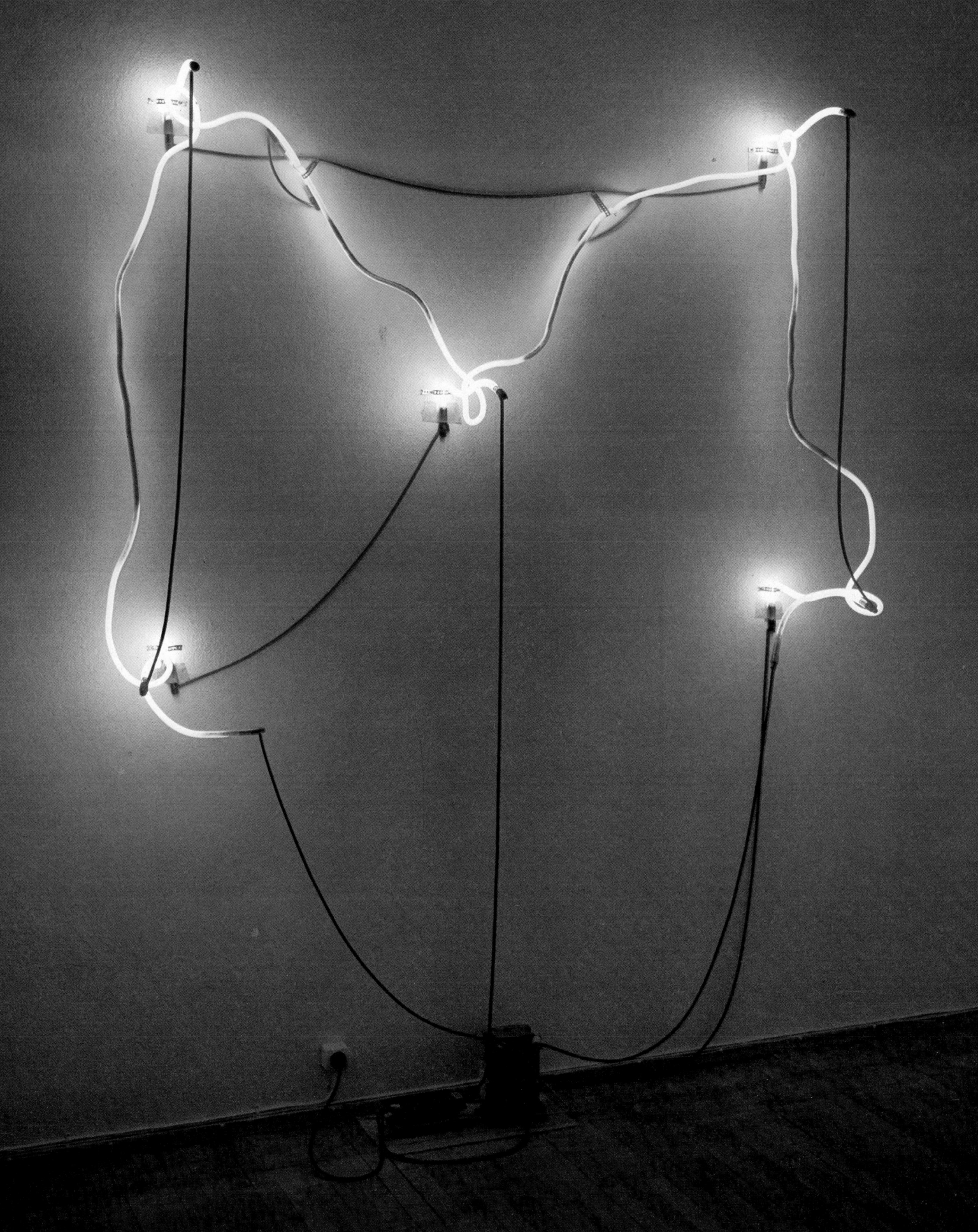

301.
Reiner Ruthenbeck
Paper Heap
1970; 250 cm. (98 in.)

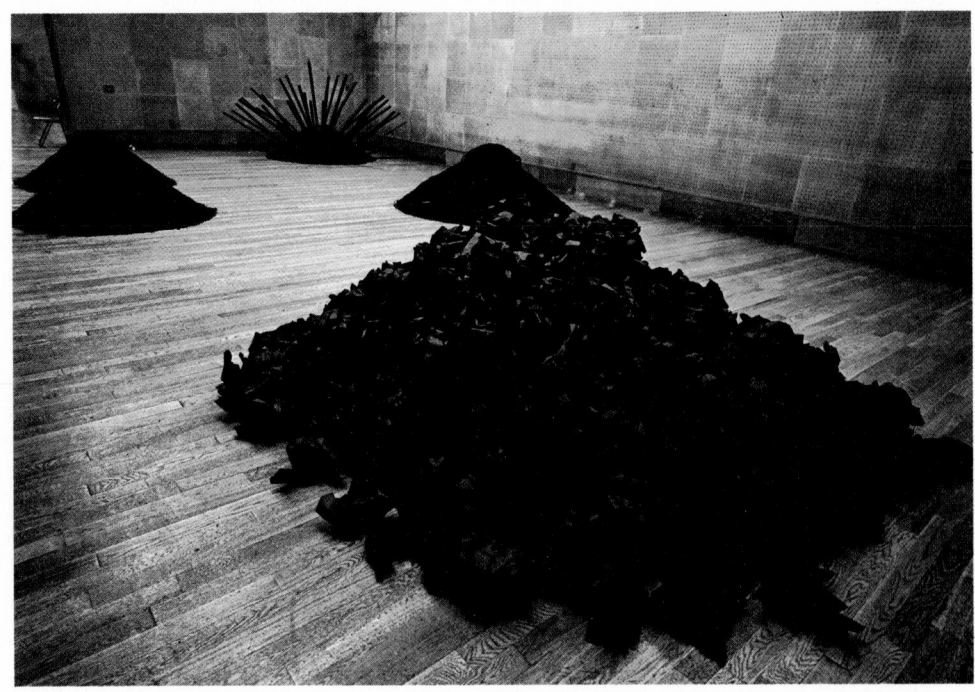

English artists were doing at the same moment. Flannagan's piece, for instance, dates from the same year as William Tucker's *Nine Poles*.

Richard Serra's *Untitled 1969* (Plate 298) looks like an attempt to achieve the same kind of "anti-form" as Morris's work, using more intractable materials; and, like Morris's felt pieces, it has a simple but hidden principle of order, since the metal shapes have been formed by pouring molten lead into the corners of the room where they are shown, and the results of what happened have been accepted as something "given". Serra's *9 Rubber Belts and Neon* (Plate 299) of 1968 is directly comparable to Judd's hanging felt pieces of the same year. The bent neon tube which forms part of one of the tangles of rubber belting could be read, indeed, as an ironic commentary on the claim made by Morris that the chosen material will dictate its own form. In Keith Sonnier's *Wrapped Neon Piece* (Plate 300) the calligraphy of the tubes seems to stand in the same relationship to some of Morris's work as Lichtenstein's *Brushstrokes* do to the techniques of Abstract Expressionism.

The extreme of Minimal anti-form is reached with the *Paper Heap* of the German artist Reiner Ruthenbeck (Plate 301). This, though done six years ago, seems to mark the extreme limit of post-war sculpture's trajectory. It is hard to think of anything at a further extreme from the immediately post-1945 work of Henry Moore.

The impulse towards the minimal was sufficiently strong to draw along with it a number of artists whose sensibility remained slightly at odds with the doctrines that men such as Judd and Morris were attempting to propagate. Dan Flavin's sculptures are formed out of ready-made fluorescent light fixtures. A piece like *Monument for V. Tatlin* (Plate 302) leads the spectator's mind in several different directions. The title and indeed the form suggest a parody or paraphrase of Tatlin's project for a *Monument to the Third International*. In this sense there is a dual connection—to Constructivism on the one hand and to Pop Art on the other. The chosen material, neon tubing, in any case has Pop associations because of its employment in advertising signs and shop fascias. On the other hand the putting together of ready-made industrial parts indicates that, in terms of his technical approach, Flavin can be considered yet another descendant of David

386

302.
Dan Flavin
Monument for V. Tatlin
1964–69
New York, Leo Castelli Gallery

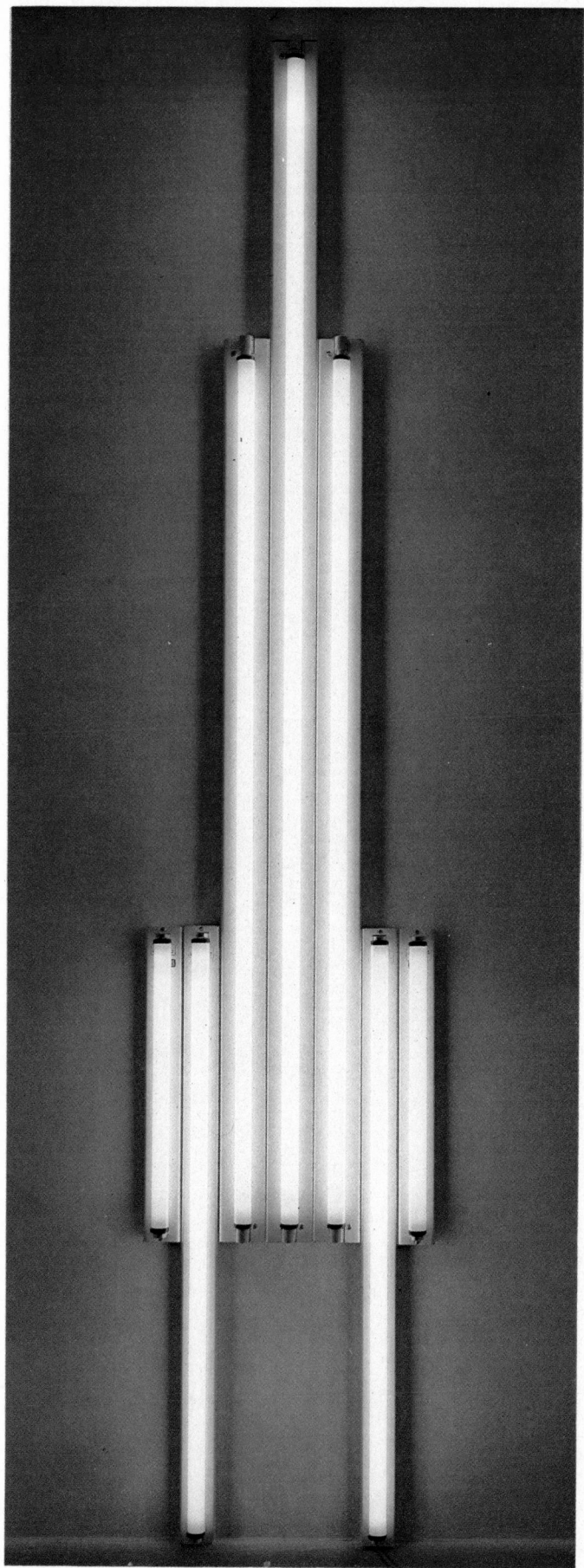

Smith. His work therefore, despite its apparent simplicity, brings together a whole complex of associations, at least for the informed spectator. Nevertheless, Flavin would not want any symbols we may find in his work to take precedence over what is actually seen: "As I have said for years, I believe that art is shedding its vaunted mystery for a common sense of keenly realized decoration. Symbolizing is dwindling—becoming slight. We are pressing downward toward no art—a mutual sense of psychologically indifferent decoration—a neutral pleasure of seeing known to everyone" (Dan Flavin, from the catalogue of the exhibition "A New Aesthetic", Washington Gallery of Modern Art, 1967, p. 35).

John McCracken and Craig Kauffman differ from the Structuralists with whom they are sometimes grouped because they both have a sense of the seductive and the decorative which relates them to other kinds of art produced during the Sixties in California (where they both come from), and especially to the ultra-refined Pop of Ed Ruscha. Kauffman began his career as an artist in the late Fifties, at which time he was a painter working in the standard Painterly Abstract style then prevalent in San Francisco. By 1963 he had made his first factory-produced plastic pictures based on organic forms, and in 1967 he made a series of vacuum-formed rectangles with rounded corners (Plate 303). These are still his best-known works. Though they are three-dimensional, it is an open question whether they should be classified as sculpture or painting, in view of the artist's own comments: "I began working in plastic with an idea of form, it is true, but my principal impetus was a passion for a kind of color, a kind of light, a sensual response to material . . ." (Craig Kauffman, ibid., p. 51).

McCracken's reputation rests on a series of brightly coloured slabs which lean against the wall (*Red Plant*, Plate 304). The artist himself seems to think of these as being definably sculptural: "I'm concerned with making things that exist and operate in real space in an integrated and non-static way. I want a sculpture to have a definite presence and individuality of its own, but at the same time to function interactively with things

303.
Craig Kauffman
Untitled, Wall Relief
1967; 128 × 196 cm. (50 × 76 in.)
Los Angeles, County Museum of Art, loaned by the
Kleiner Foundation, Beverly Hills

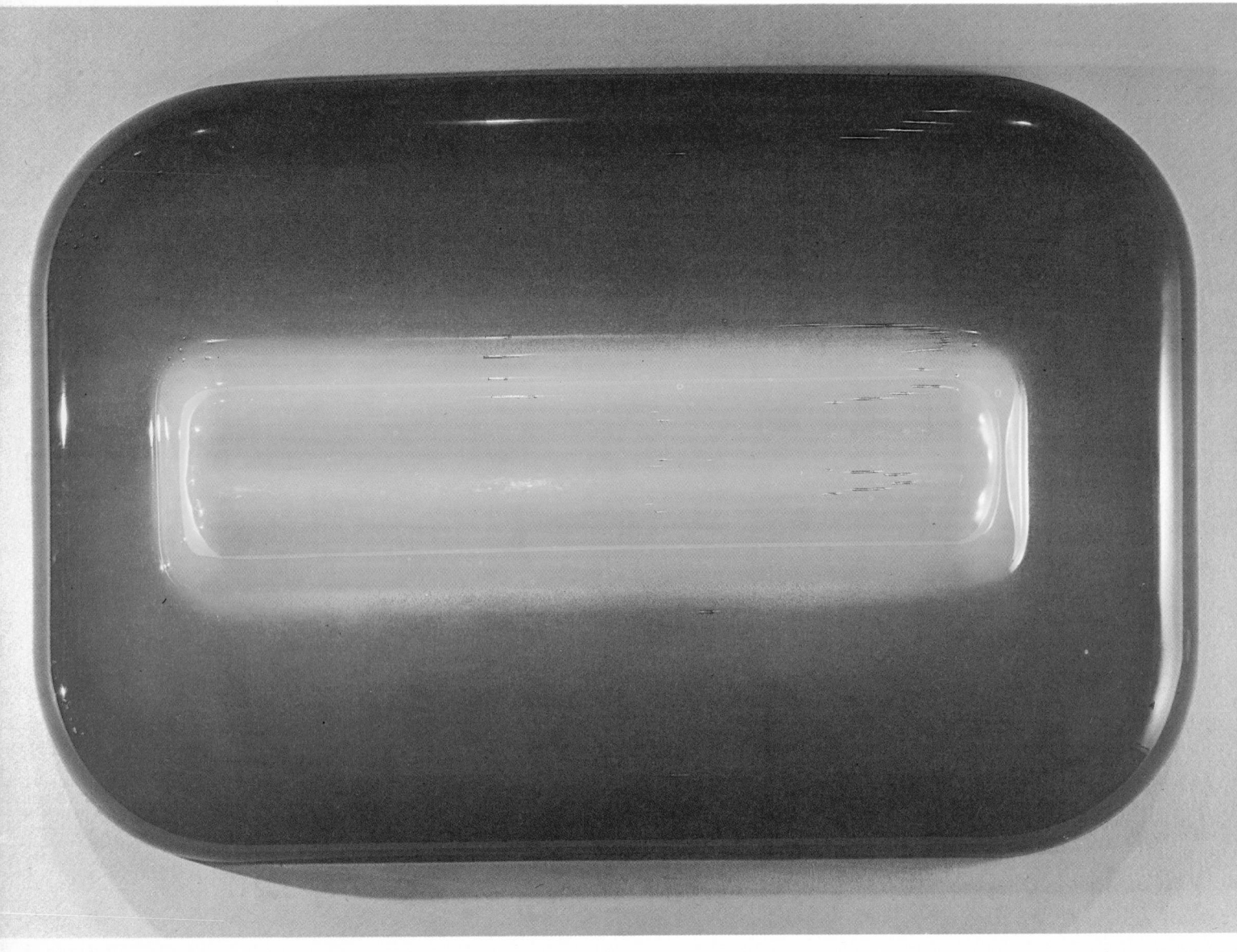

around it" (John McCracken, ibid., p. 37).

On the other hand, he does not deny the importance of colour itself: "I think of color as being the structural material I use to build the forms I am interested in. The fact that in another sense I use plywood, fiberglass and lacquer as structural materials is of less importance. I have found that a certain combination of color intensity and transparency and surface finish provide me with the expressive means I want, at least for the present" (John McCracken, from "New Talent USA", *Art in America*, Vol. 54, New York [July, 1966]).

McCracken's work, more perhaps than that of any other artist, makes one aware of the degree to which the distinction between painting and sculpture has broken down.

The erection of Minimal Art into a successful, indeed a momentarily dominant, style, is a phenomenon which may require a good deal of explanation from the art historians of the future. Even at this distance of time it is possible to see

304.
John McCracken
Red Plant
1967; 259 × 45 × 7.5 cm. (101 × 18 × 3 in.)
Los Angeles, coll. L. M. Asher family

that the art of the late Sixties represented a serious
crisis in the relationship of modern art and its
public. Clement Greenberg, the major promotor,
or perhaps the inventor, of Post-Painterly Abstraction, and the convinced admirer of David
Smith and Anthony Caro, denounced the Minimalists as men who had turned what he called
"the far out" into an end in itself. That is, he
believed that a dynamic of extremism had
developed, and that young artists were now
competing with one another for the leadership of
an avant-garde which had become institutionalized.

There are indeed indications that Minimalist
developments were due in part to a struggle for
dominance within a closed society of artists. If one
reads the writings of a theoretician-artist like
Robert Morris, one notes that the concepts which
he puts forward are elaborated in direct proportion to the simplicity of the work. One also
notes that not Morris only but nearly all Minimal
artists presume that the spectator will bring to
their work not only a high degree of aesthetic
sophistication, but also a self-conscious awareness
of his own sensibility and the pitfalls into which it
may lead him. An art which eschews taste
nevertheless demands, from those who come to
look at it, a keen awareness of what taste is and
how it operates. This amounts to saying that
Minimal Art is a conspicuously mandarin style.

How does a mandarin style—rarefied and
elitist—operate in a democratic society? The
answer seems to be that Minimal Art owed a great
deal to the increasing institutionalization of
Modernism. The point at which it arose, in the
mid-Sixties, was certainly also the point at which
one began to notice, not indeed for the first time
but more acutely, the fact that avant-garde art
activity had become almost entirely dependent
upon official or semi-official patronage. The more
avant-garde he was (granted that stable criteria for
vanguard activity could be found), the more
confidently the artist looked to the public sector
for support.

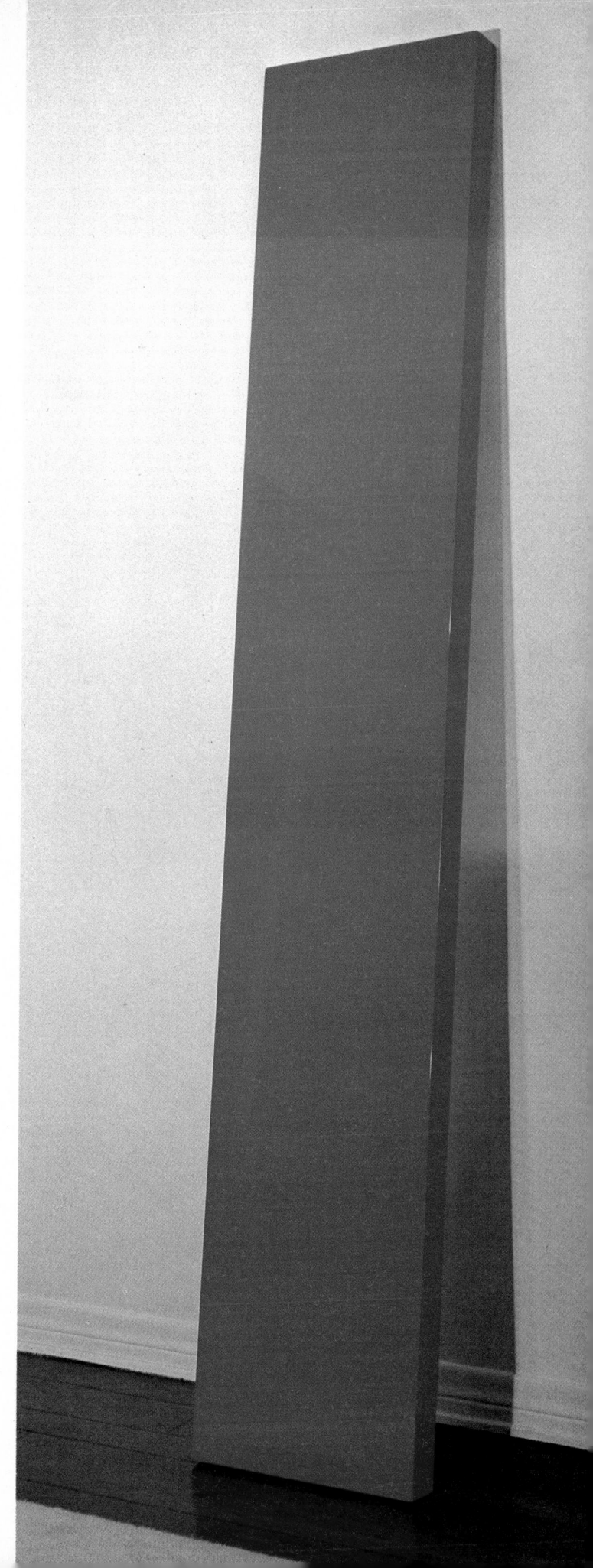

Happenings and Environments

If Minimal Art seems to represent post-war Modernism at its most elitist—or very nearly so (as we shall see, Conceptual Art has claims to be considered more elitist still)—then the Happenings and other events staged by avant-garde artists can be thought of as an attempt at populism.

One must be careful not to present the cult of the Happening as a movement or style, the equivalent of Pop or Op. Rather, it was a phenomenon connected with a number of art movements. A further and perhaps more serious error is to regard the Happening as the product of the artistic climate that grew up after 1945. Instead, it was a revival of some aspects of the earliest Modernism. Before the First World War, both the Italian and Russian Futurists had staged performances of various kinds. During the war, the Dadaist Cabaret Voltaire in Zurich had been one of the most important manifestations of the spirit of Dada. Later still, the Surrealists had been responsible for various collective demonstrations, which brought what they were trying to do to the attention of the public.

Italian Futurism was the first Modernist movement to abandon the studio and the art gallery for the lecture hall, the theatre, and the street. F. T. Marinetti, the founder of the movement, was a publicist of genius. As early as 1908, he had realized that "articles, poems and polemics were no longer adequate. It was necessary to change methods completely, to go out into the streets, to launch assaults from theatres and to introduce the fisticuff into the artistic battle."

Some amusing accounts survive of the "Futurist evenings" organized by Marinetti and his colleagues. Here, for example, is a glimpse of one such performance in Naples, as described by Marinetti's friend and collaborator Francesco Cangiullo: "Suddenly a storm broke in the orchestra seats, the room was beginning to divide in two: friends and enemies. The latter inveighing against the Futurists in gusts of insult and profanity, fists shaking, faces twisted into masks. The others clapped insanely. 'Viva Marinetti!... Abbasso!... Viva!... Abbasso!... Idiots! Cretins! Sons of whores!' The whole was crowned by a rain of vegetables: potatoes, tomatoes, chestnuts ... an homage to Ceres. Finally, in a moment of calm (very relatively speaking), the chief of Futurism began..." (quoted by R. W. Flint, in his introduction to *Marinetti: Selected Writings*, London, 1969, p. 24).

The Russian Futurists, who almost from the beginning kept in close touch with what Marinetti was doing, followed his example by staging performances of their own. The poet V. V. Mayakovsky strolled through the streets of Moscow in a yellow shirt with a wooden spoon stuck in his buttonhole. Other members of the Futurist group had strange signs painted on their faces—one had a urinating dog on his cheek "to show that he had a sense of smell". In the years 1913–14, Mayakovsky, together with his friends the Burliuk brothers and Vassily Kamensky, made a tour of seventeen Russian cities to publicize their ideas. David Burliuk had the words "I—Burliuk" written on his forehead, in the hope of provoking the proper kind of stir.

Yet despite their determination to outrage their audience—one Russian Futurist manifesto, issued in 1912, is actually called "A Slap in the Face of Public Taste"—the Moscow avant-garde found their antics were disconcertingly popular with the local bourgeoisie who were also becoming collectors of their work.

The Zurich Dadaists were equally anxious to provoke and puzzle the public. Hugo Ball, the leader of the group, describes one performance in some detail in his diary. His legs, he tells us, were encased in a tight-fitting cylinder of blue cardboard which reached as high as his hips. Above this was a cardboard garment, at once collar and coat, scarlet outside and gold inside, which the performer could flap with his elbows. Ball also wore a tall, cylindrical witch-doctor's hat. Thus attired, he proceeded to recite an "abstract poem" made up of meaningless sounds. After a few moments of puzzlement the audience exploded: "In the midst of the storm Ball stood his ground (in his cardboard costume he could not move anyway) and faced the laughing, applauding crowd of pretty girls and solemn bourgeois, like Savonarola, motionless, fanatical and unmoved" (Hans Richter, *Dada*, London, 1965, p. 42).

When, in the years that immediately followed the war, Dada moved its headquarters to Paris and was eventually transformed into Surrealism, the tradition of performances and events continued. A hostile journalist described an early Max Ernst exhibition as follows: "With characteristic bad taste, the Dadas have now resorted to terrorism. The stage was in the cellar, and all the lights in the shop were out; groans rose from a trap-door. Another joker hidden behind a wardrobe insulted the persons present . . . the Dadas, without ties and wearing white gloves, passed back and forth . . . . André Breton chewed up matches, Ribemont-Dessaignes kept screaming 'It's raining on a skull,' Aragon caterwauled. Philippe Soupault played hide-and-seek with Tzara, while Bejamin Péret and Charchoune shook hands every other minute. On the doorstep, Jacques Rigaut counted the automobiles and the pearls of the lady visitors . . ." (Maurice Nadeau, *The History of Surrealism*, New York, 1967, pp. 62–3).

If one looks for common factors in all these early avant-garde manifestations, one finds, sure enough, the qualities that the Italian critic Renato Poggioli declares to be the true indices of avant-gardism—he summarizes them as "activism, antagonism, nihilism, and agonism". But one also finds something else which is perhaps more unexpected. From the very beginning, avant-garde demonstrations owed a great deal to the popular theatre.

To understand why this was so we must again look to Italian Futurism, and, in particular, to the manifesto on "The Variety Theatre" which appeared in 1913. This is one of the most significant of all the Futurist manifestoes. Among the reasons it gives for exalting the variety theatre we find the following: "The authors, actors and technicians of the Variety Theatre have only one reason for existing and triumphing: incessantly to invent new elements of astonishment. Hence the absolute impossibility of arresting or repeating oneself, hence an excited competition of brains and muscles to conquer the various records of agility, speed, force, complication, and elegance."

And we also find: "Today the Variety Theatre is the crucible in which the elements of an emergent new sensibility are seething. Here you find an ironic decomposition of all the worn-out prototypes of the Beautiful, the Grand, the Solemn, the Religious, the Ferocious, the Seductive, and the Terrifying, and also the abstract elaboration of the new prototypes that will succeed these" (*Marinetti: Selected Writings*, edited by F. W. Flint, London, 1969, pp. 116–7).

It is scarcely possible to give, even today, a better description of the aims of the Happening at its most ambitious. The obvious connection between the avant-garde performances of the Sixties and Seventies and the popular entertainments of the time when Modernism began is one of the paradoxes of the history of the avant-garde.

In the period that immediately followed the Second World War, there was, as we have seen, a mood of introversion in the arts that was scarcely propitious to the large-scale "performance" as the Futurists had understood it. Futurism itself, in any case, was in almost total eclipse because of Marinetti's worship of war and violence, and his close association with fascism during the later years of his career.

Nevertheless, the Modernist thirst for self-publicity and the need for direct confrontation with the public remained. In 1950, Georges Mathieu presented a "Night of Poetry" at the Théâtre Sarah Bernhardt in Paris, in the course of which he painted an enormous picture on stage. It took him twenty minutes. The next year the same artist organized a series of "Ceremonies to Commemorate the Second Condemnation of Siger

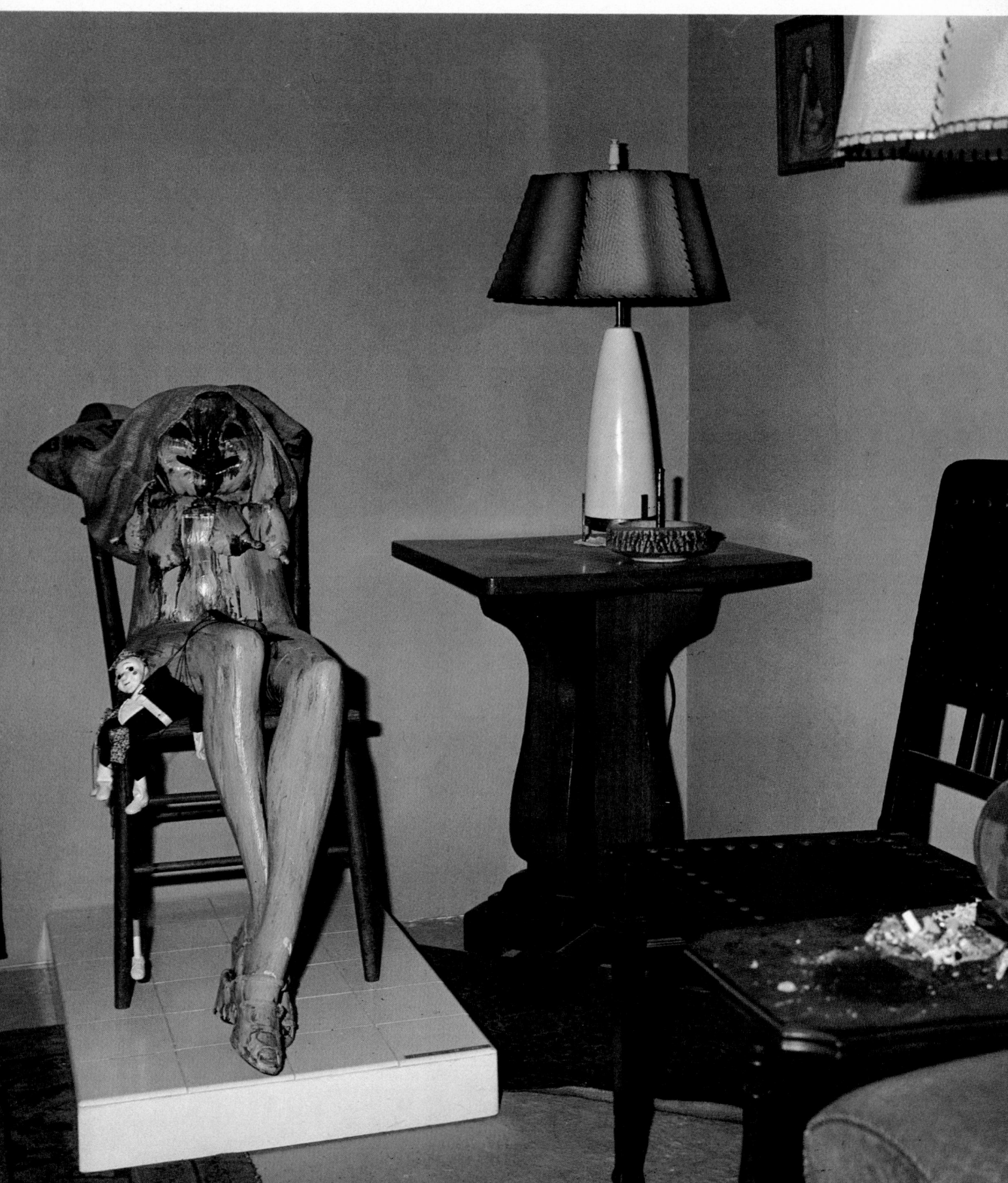

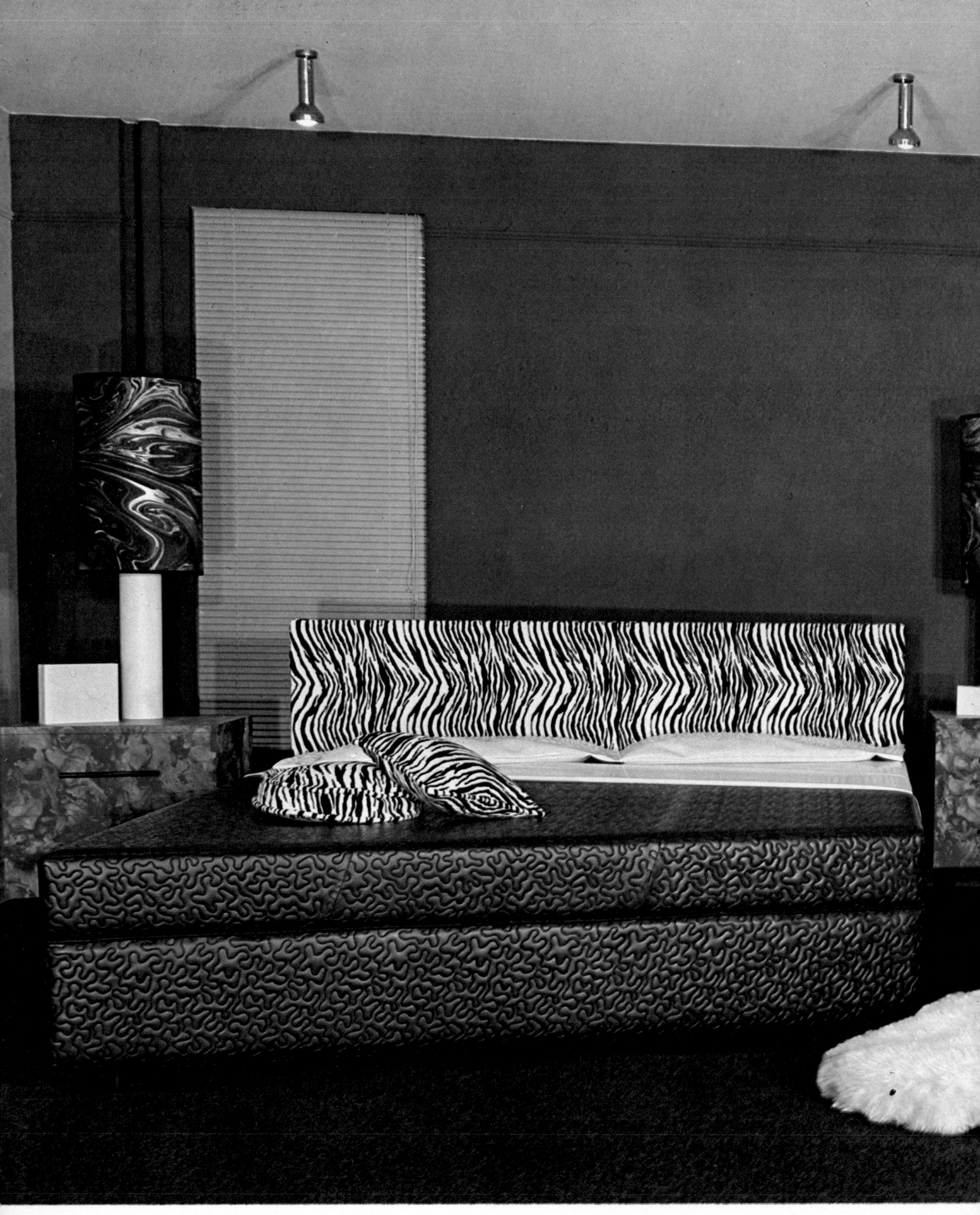

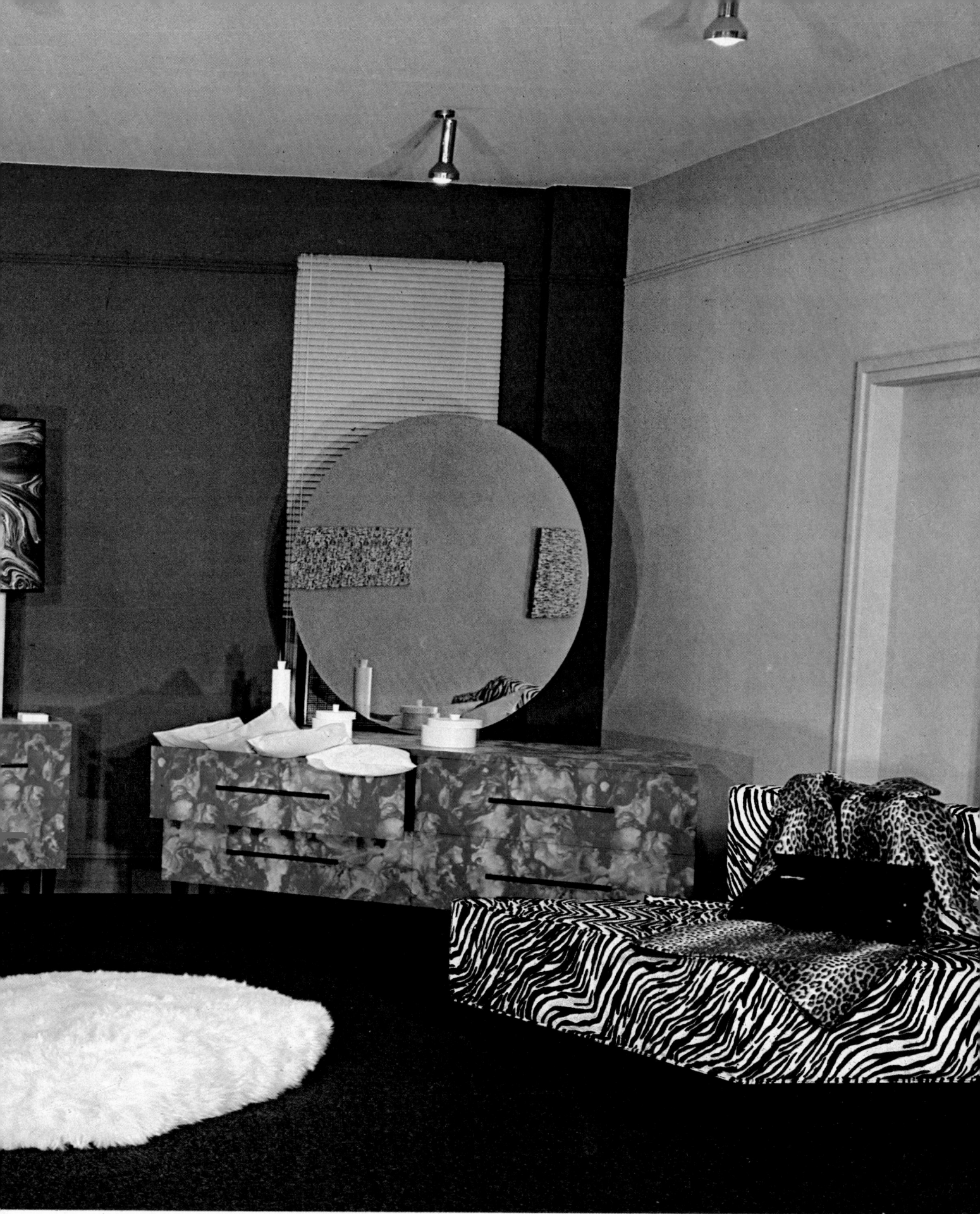

de Brabant". There were four cycles of change—*Cycle sacredotal, Cycle royal, Cycle bourgeois,* with Voltaire, Diderot, and others represented as hanged men, and a portrait of Descartes to walk on, and finally a contemporary cycle featuring Frigidaires and juke-boxes.

Some of the more interesting events of the period took place in relatively remote locations, and were symptoms less of the need to attract attention than of impatience with the condition of things within the art world itself. In 1952 the musician John Cage organized an evening at Black Mountain College, where he then taught. The audience, seated in four triangular, inward-facing blocks, was treated to a lecture by Cage himself, delivered from the top of a ladder, to poems by Charles Olson, delivered from another ladder, and to various kinds of music (Robert Rauschenberg played a wind-up Gramophone). Meanwhile, dancers moved through the seating spaces.

From the mid-Fifties onwards, the Gutai Group was active in Japan. Many of the things done by its members anticipated things which were only to be done considerably later in Europe. As early as 1955, for example, Kazuo Shiraga was creating outdoor performance pieces in which his own body became the medium of expression. In the Gutai Group we seem to see a fusion of the age-old Japanese taste for elaborate rituals with the new tenets of Modernism.

The real rise of the Happening, however, is connected with the birth of the Pop Art movement in America. Most of the major Pop Art names created or took part in Happenings during the early Sixties, and there were some specialists, such as Allan Kaprow, who made reputations for this kind of activity alone.

As has already been noted, there is a connection between the Pop Happening and the Pop Environment. Keinholz's elaborate *Roxy's* (Plate 305), a Surrealist re-creation of a 1940's brothel, seems the kind of setting in which a Happening might take place. The same is true of Oldenburg's massive *Bedroom Ensemble I* (Plate 306). Environments did not precede Happenings—the two developed hand in hand.

Oldenburg's "thematic" show, *The Store,* of

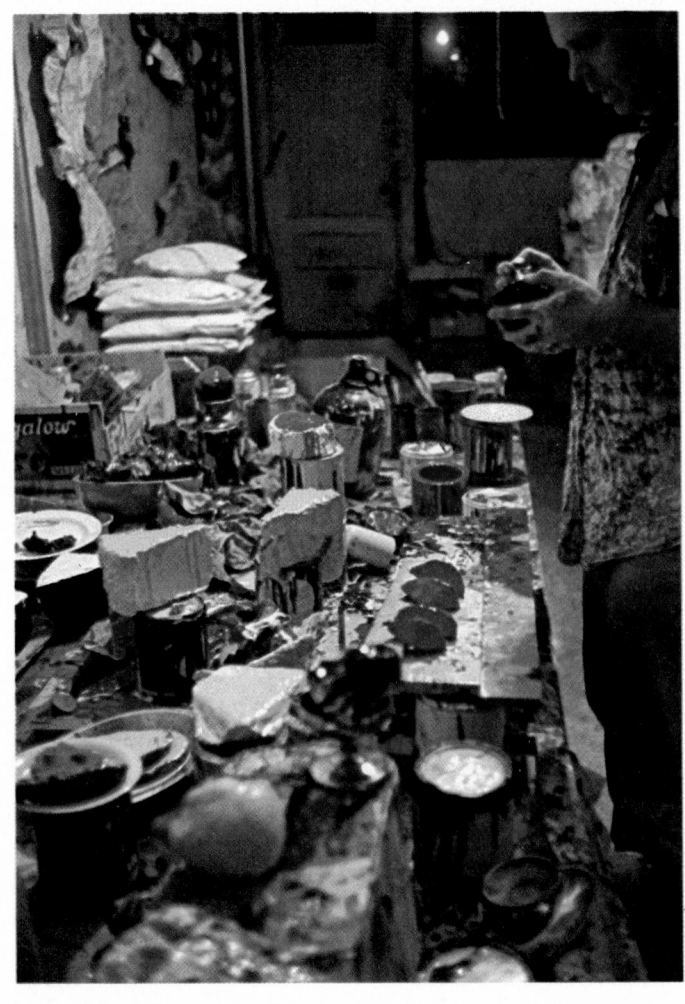

307.
Claes Oldenburg
Claes paints the work on which he was working on in that period in the Store
1962, New York
© 1962 by Robert R. McElroy

308. Opposite above
Jim Dine
Vaudeville Act
1960, New York
© 1960 by Robert R. McElroy

309. Opposite below
Jim Dine
The Smiling Workman
1960, New York
© 1960 by Robert R. McElroy

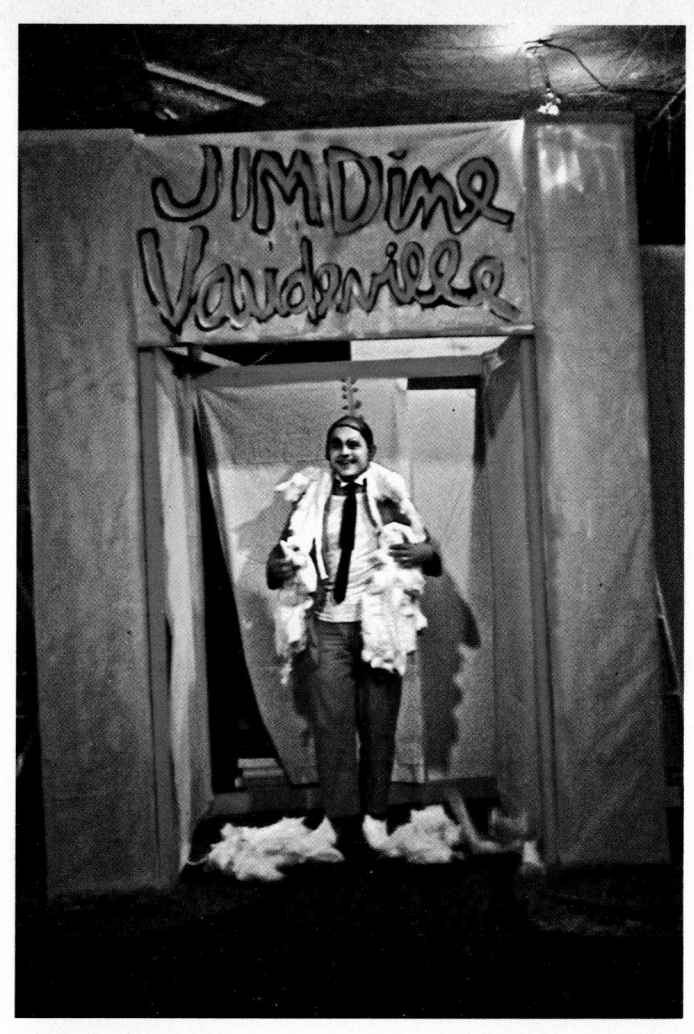

1961 (Plate 307), provided the artist with a setting which could be used for further activity. The Happening itself, for Oldenburg, is simply a direct extension of the kind of work involved in the creation of *The Store*. It is, he says, "one or another method of using *objects in motion*, and this I take to include people, both in themselves and as agents of object motion". *The Store* therefore led to the creation of *Store Days I*. This took place in three adjacent rooms: *The Bedroom—Jail*; *The Living Room—Funeral Parlor—Whorehouse*; *The Kitchen—Butcher Shop*. There were also three "periods" of action: *A Customer Enters*, *A Bargain*, and *How the Founders Struggled*. Each room had several "stations" related to the various phases of what was taking place. These elaborate subdivisions of place and time were contrasted to the simplicity of the actions themselves.

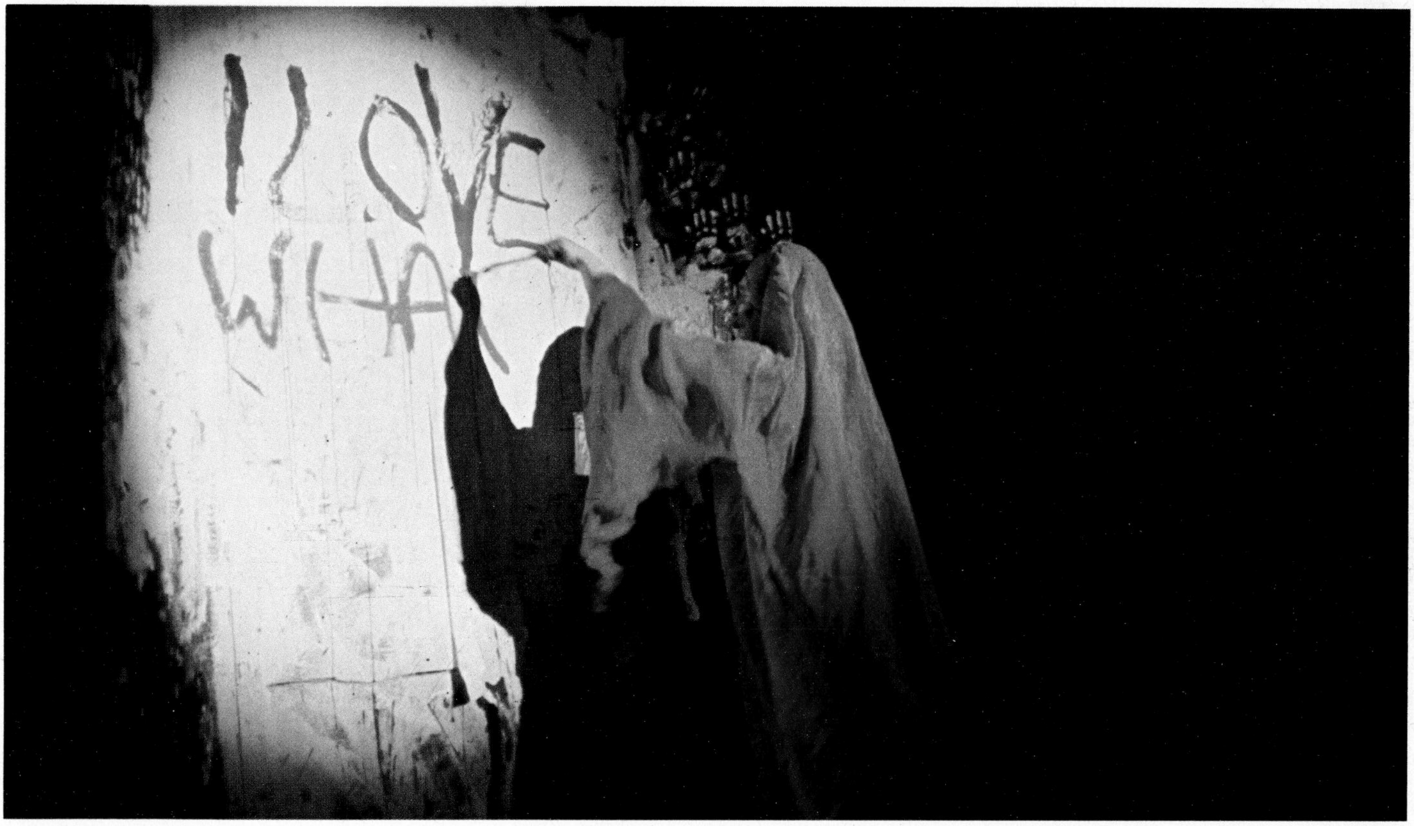

Jim Dine, too, thought of the visual side of the Happenings he staged as an "extension" of his paintings, but added that "there were other things involved—since I think on two levels". The point was made again, and more graphically, in *The Smiling Workman*, a brief event staged at the Judson Church in New York in 1960 (Plate 309). Dine himself has described what took place: "I had a flat built. It was a three-panel flat with two sides and one flat. There was a table with three jars of paint and two brushes on it, and the canvas was painted white. I came around it with one light on me. I was all in red with a big, black mouth: all my head and face were red, and I had a red smock on, down to the floor. I painted 'I love what I'm doing' in orange and blue. When I got to 'what I'm doing', it was going very fast, and I picked up one of the jars and drank the paint, and then I poured the other two jars of paint over my head, quickly, and dove, physically, through the canvas. The light went off" (Jim Dine in *Happenings*, by Michael Kirby, New York, 1965, p. 185).

Vaudeville Act (Plate 308), which was the successor to *The Smiling Workman*, has also been described by Dine: "It was all kinds of crazy things: organ music, me talking—it was a collage on tape. I came out with a red suit on and cotton all over me, my face painted yellow. To the music that was going on, I pulled the cotton off and just let it fall to the floor until there was no cotton on me. Then I walked out" (ibid., p. 186). The performance did not conclude with the artist's disappearance. After he had gone, there was a dance of strung cabbages, carrots, lettuces, and celery. Red paint was poured down the flats, and then Dine himself reappeared in a red suit and a straw hat, carrying a cardboard puppet of a nude girl on each

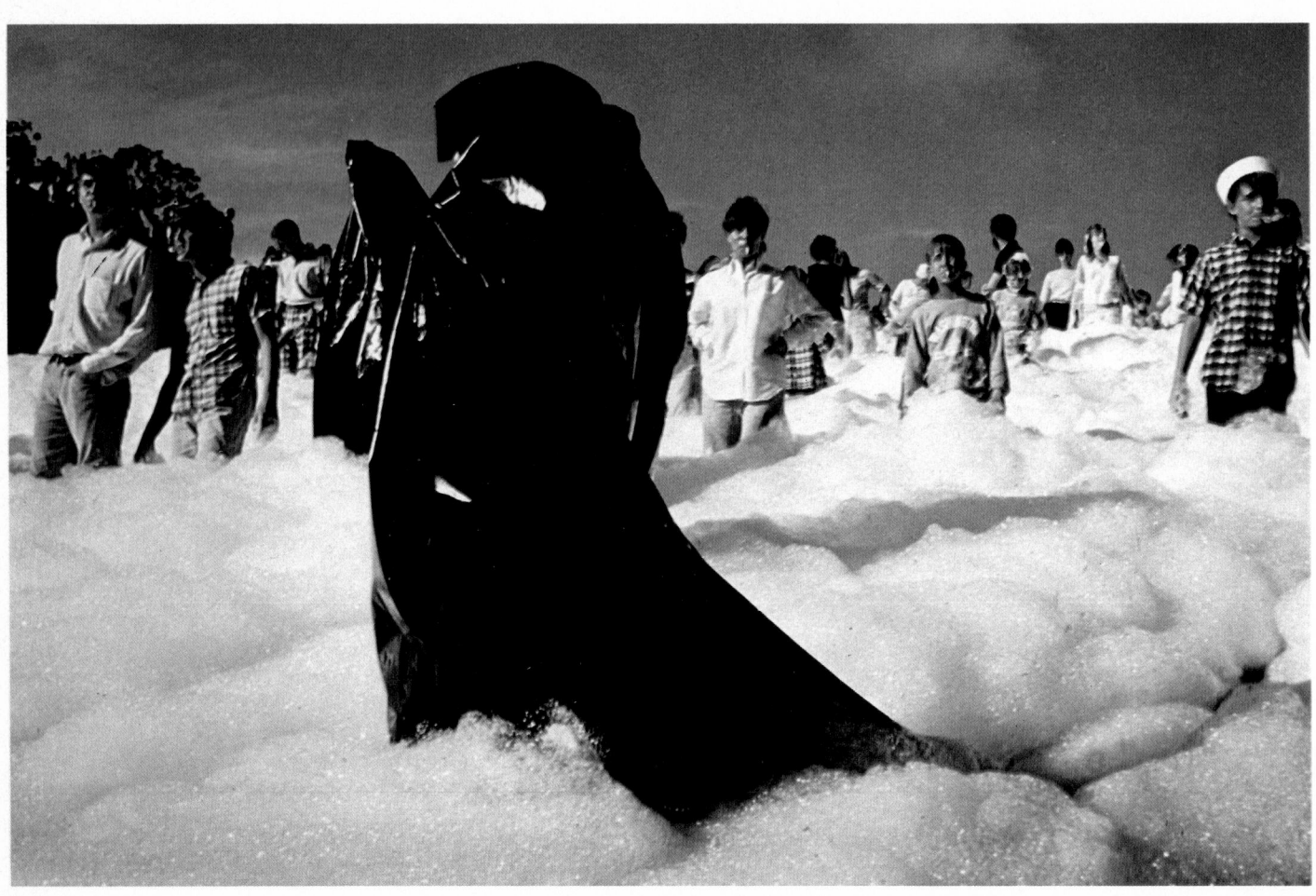

arm, made in such a way that each of his arms became the inner arm of one of the puppets. With these puppets he then did a dance.

Anyone reading this description of *Vaudeville Act* may well be reminded, not only of the Futurist manifesto concerning the variety theatre, which has already been quoted above, but also of accounts of the two Eric Satie ballets *Parade* and *Relâche*. A recent London revival of *Parade*—an apparently faithful reconstitution of the original—showed it to be a startling anticipation of the Happenings of the 1960's, with its roots in the same soil of popular entertainment.

Among the other prominent makers of Happenings in the United States during the 1960's were Red Grooms, Robert Whitman, Allan Kaprow, and Carolee Schneeman. Grooms, whose

Burning Building dates from 1959, and was one of the earliest manifestations of the new interest in performance art in America, has spoken of the influence exercised over his childhood imagination by the big circuses—Ringling Brothers, Barnum & Bailey—which still flourished in those days. He has also declared that "the structure of my performances came from the idea of building a set like an acrobat's apparatus." Here yet again we meet the ideas and images we have encountered elsewhere.

Where Oldenburg, Dine, and Grooms have moved away from the creation of events, Robert Whitman and Allan Kaprow have continued their involvement with this form of visual activity. Whitman offers a contrast to Dine and Oldenburg because his work is a great deal more abstract than

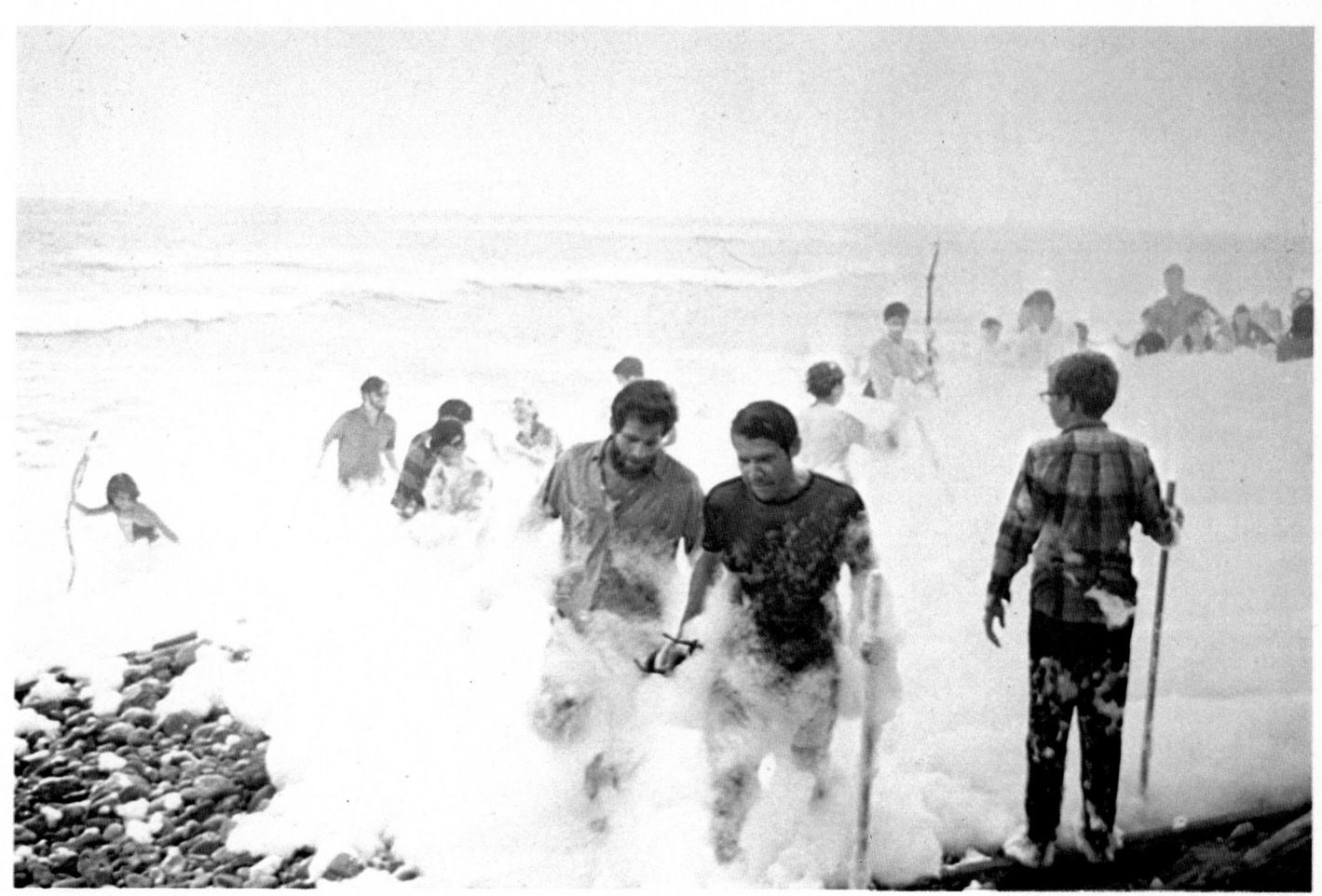

theirs. The thing that interests him is not so much the manipulation of objects as the manipulation of time: "The thing about the theatre that most interests me is that it takes time. Time for me is something material. I like to use it that way. It can be used in the same way as paint or plaster or any other natural material. It can describe other natural events" (Robert Whitman, ibid., p. 134).

Though his Happenings seem more abstract than those of Dine and Oldenburg, they are still intended as "stories of physical experience and realistic, naturalistic descriptions of the physical world". Whitman has made extensive use of film in many of his performance pieces, exploiting the contrast between the action recorded on the celluloid (already one degree removed from the spectator) and the action taking place in his presence. *Cinema Piece* of 1968 makes a direct confrontation between what is real and what is a recording of reality. Here there is a shower with a film of a girl taking a shower projected on to the curtain.

Allan Kaprow has been described, by Adrian Henri in his authoritative book *Environments and Happenings*, as "the central figure in the rise of the happening, and the main authority on the way in which it evolved out of the environment". Kaprow has always had two aspects to his career: on one side an academic one, as a professor of art history; and on the other side involvement as a creative artist, beginning first as an Abstract Expressionist, then becoming, in the mid-Fifties, a maker of *assemblages*. The *assemblages* became increasingly environmental, and from this, in turn, there came a perception that "every visitor to the Environment was part of it".

Though his Happenings arose in such an informal way, they were at first elaborately scripted and conscientiously rehearsed. But Kaprow soon found that he was encountering various difficulties. Actors were useless because they wanted stellar roles, and were in any case self-conscious and awkward. Friends were unreliable. Kaprow decided that on each occasion he would have to make deliberate use of whatever was available, the people as well as the environment. But even this decision brought its own difficulties,

chiefly the lack of rehearsal time when doing a Happening outside New York, with a completely fresh group of amateur performers: "So the next thing was to find a method to do a performance without a rehearsal—to make use of the available people on the spot as quickly as possible. ... So I thought of the simplest situations, the simplest images—the ones having the least complicated mechanics or implications on the surface. Written down on a sheet of paper sent in advance, these actions could be learned by anyone. Those who wished to participate could decide for themselves. Then, when I arrived shortly before the scheduled event, I already had a committed group, and I could then discuss the deeper implications of the Happening with them as well as the details of the performance" (Allan Kaprow, ibid., p. 49).

It was thus purely practical considerations that led Kaprow to shift the emphasis in his performance pieces away from the value derived from them by the spectator, and towards those got from them by the actual participant. What we see in his work is a move towards the concept of the Happening as a therapeutic ritual. This is particularly visible in a piece like *Gas* (1966, Plates 310, 311, and 312), which was carried out at a number of different locations and which therefore, by its very nature, was fully apprensible only to those who took part in it.

Kaprow's work prompts a consideration of the true nature of the Happening, at least as it developed in America. Michael Kirby, author of one of the first textbooks on the subject, proposes the following definition. Happenings, he says, are "a form of theatre in which diverse elements, including non-matrixed performing, are organised in a compartmented structure". By "compartmented structure" he means that the Happening is made up of self-contained units of action, which may or may not take place simultaneously. He suggests a comparison here to the activities in a three-ring circus. "Non-matrixed performing", according to Kirby, means the absence of the matrix of time, place, and character which we get in almost any kind of play.

This definition was proposed in 1965 and seems to fit the work of the artists whom Kirby chooses

312.
Allan Kaprow
Southampton Parade (part of the collective Happening *Gas*)
1966, Southampton, Long Island, New York
© 1966 by Peter Moore

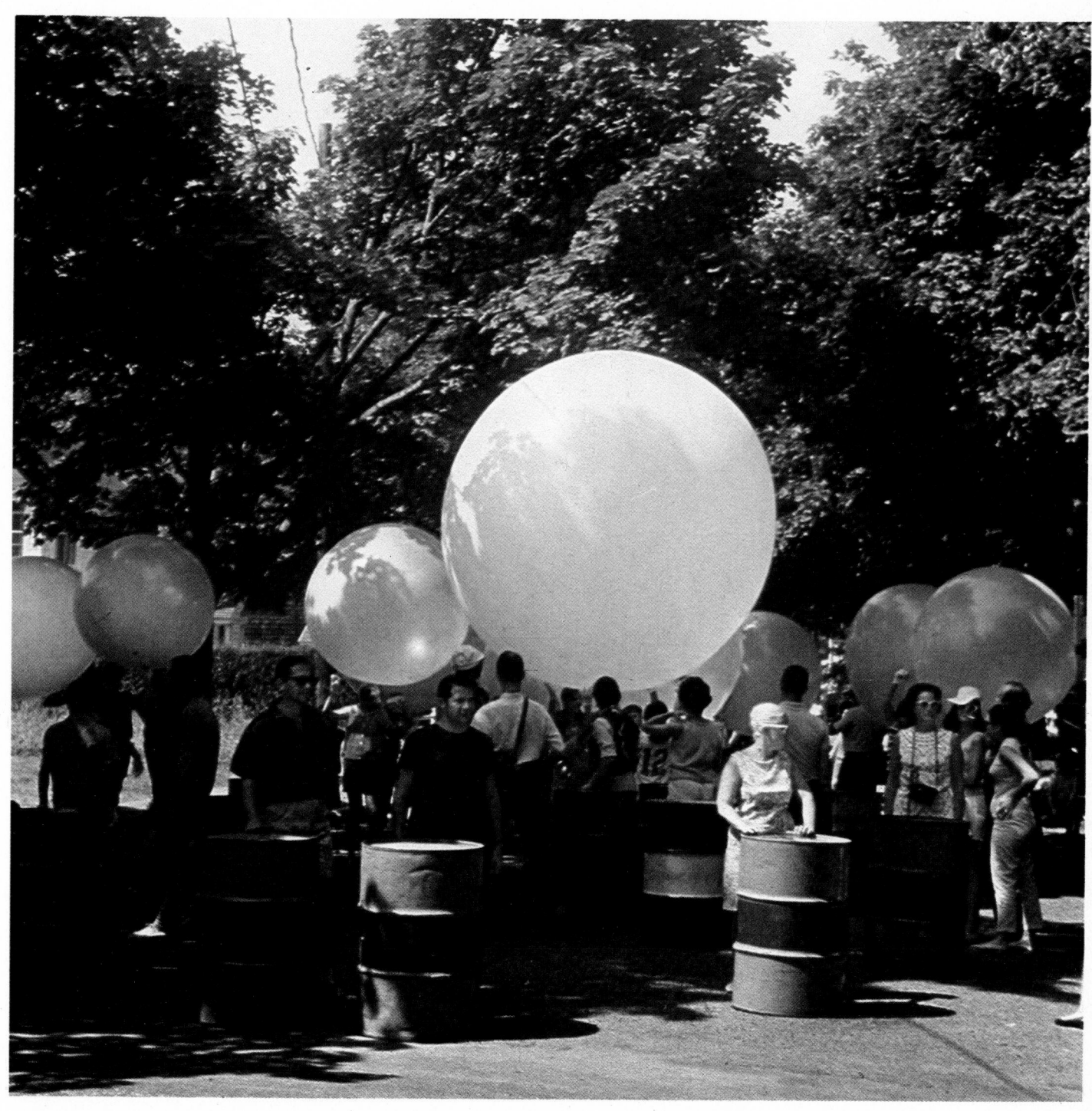

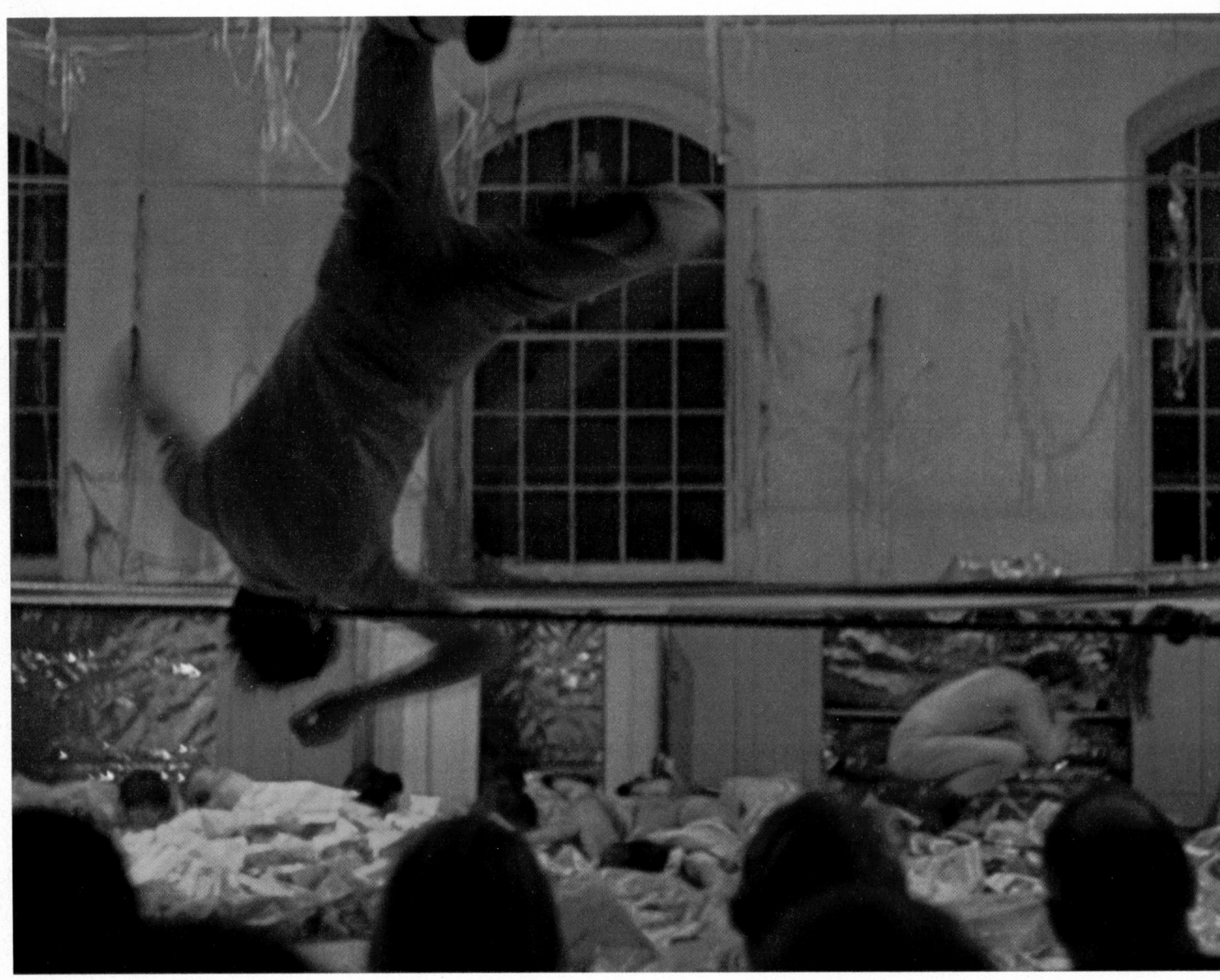

313.
Carolee Schneeman
Happening
1966, New York, St. Mark's Church

to discuss—Dine, Oldenburg, Kaprow, Grooms, and Whitman—more than adequately. The interesting thing is that it seems a good deal less adequate to performers whom Kirby has left outside his scope. Even in the work of Carolee Schneeman (Plate 313) there is an element of deliberate bravura, an acceptance and simultaneous defiance of moral as well as theatrical convention which supplies a very definite matrix for what is taking place.

Once Happenings had established themselves as a recognized part of the New York art scene (they rapidly attracted the attention of fashionable and would-be fashionable people, just as the Futurist cabarets had done in pre-Revolutionary Moscow), the performance medium began to develop in different directions. Many of these were inimical to the survival of the Happening itself as a definable art form. The legitimate theatre, against which the artists had staged this effective but anarchic revolt,

314.
Robert Rauschenberg
Dance Event
1966, New York, Judson Church

315. Below
Yvonne Rainer
Performance
1971, New York
© 1971 by Peter Moore

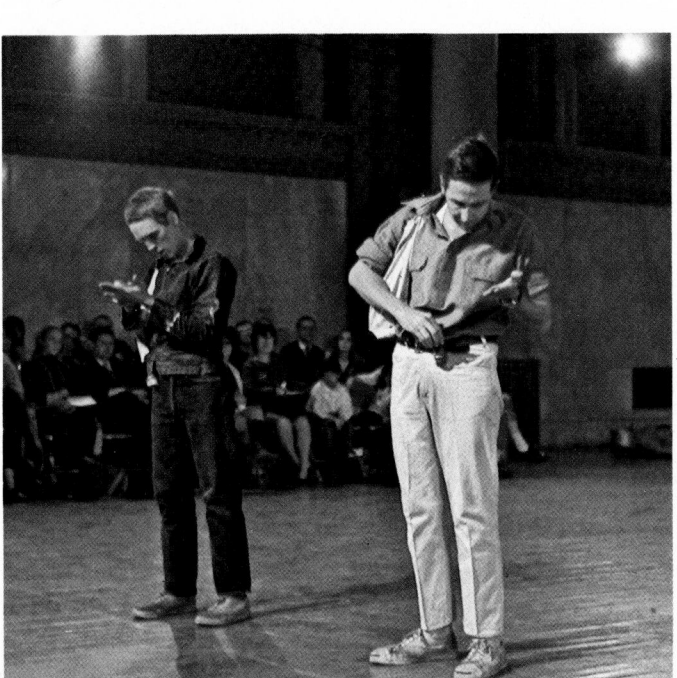

was quick to borrow from its critics. The Off-Broadway and especially the Off-Off-Broadway theatre owes an immense amount to the Happening. The stranglehold of narrative was broken, and it became possible for dramatists to communicate with their audiences by means of visual and verbal images which would have seemed impossibly irrational and outré only a few years previously. At the same time there was a renewal of interest in improvisation, and the actors learned to shed the self-consciousness which Allan Kaprow had once found so frustrating.

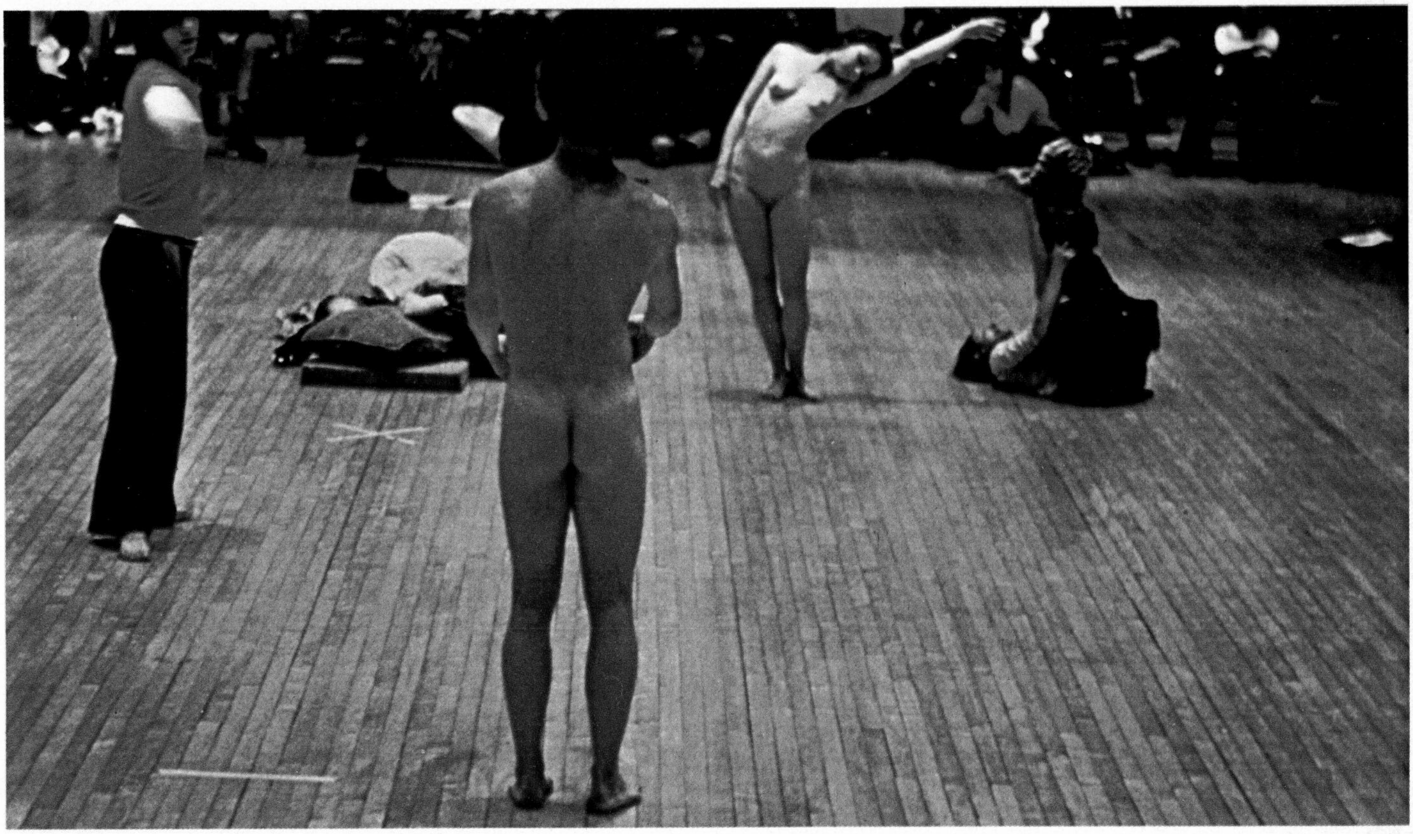

The Happening also had a marked impact on the dance in America. Avant-garde dance companies, that of Merce Cunningham, for example, had been involved with the movement from the very beginning, but the way of thinking initiated by men like Whitman and Kaprow set them free for bold experimentation. The barrier between the professional and the amateur dancer—far more

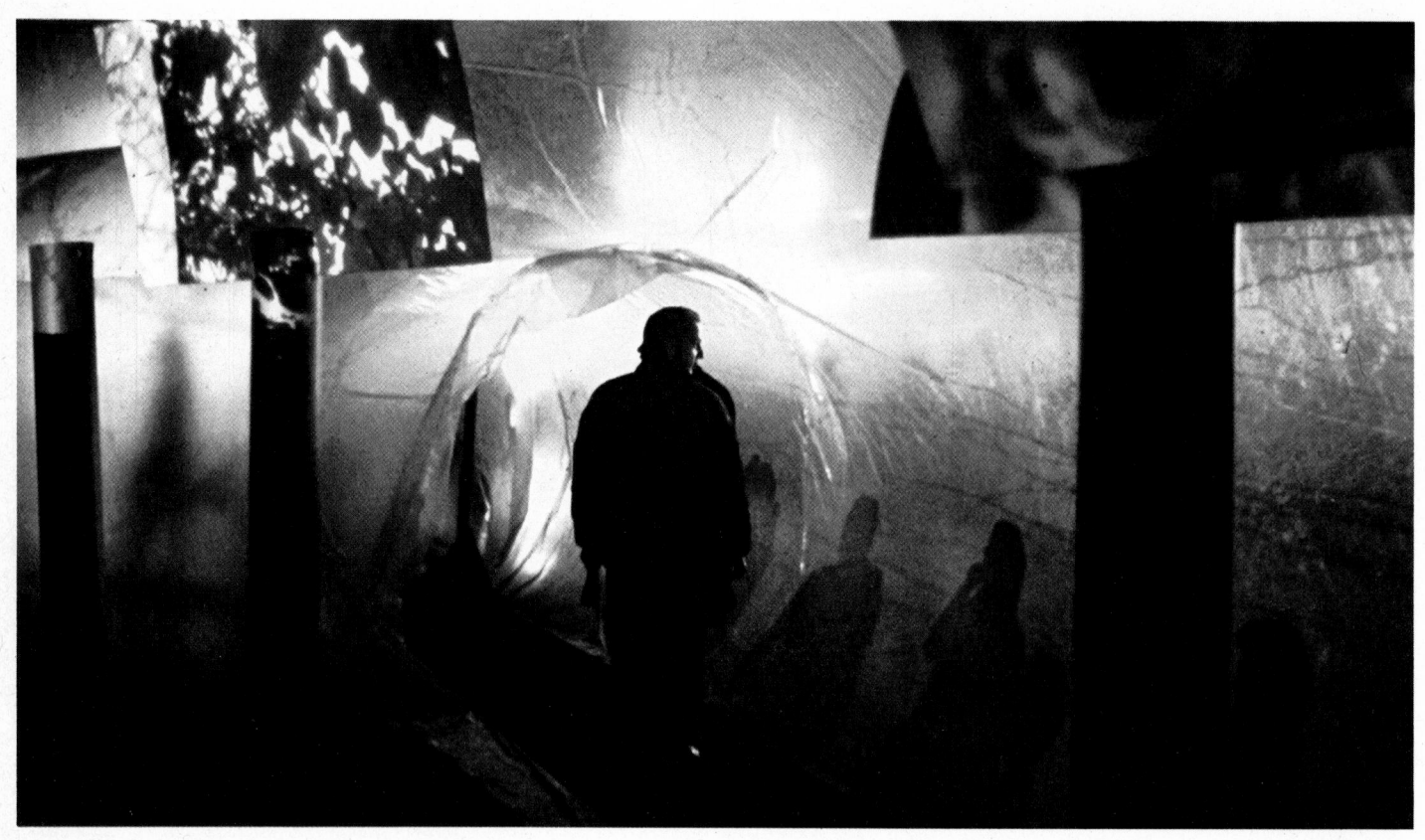

rigid than that between the professional and amateur actor—was to some extent at least broken down. Artists, notably Rauschenberg, who in any case had had a long association with Cunningham, could now appear in a dance context without seeming ridiculous (Plate 314). At the same time professional dancers, such as Yvonne Rainer, found themselves freed to do things onstage which they might not otherwise have dared to attempt (Plate 315).

The "Evenings in Art and Technology" which have already been mentioned (Chapter VII) represented a somewhat less reassuring development (Plate 316—Steve Paxton, *Physical Things*). Big business was now willing to put its resources, those of advanced technology and money, at the service of something that had originally represented a revolt against everything that big

business might be supposed to stand for. The main beneficiary was once again the protean Rauschenberg, who was able to absorb the technological experience and use it in works such as *Soundings* (Plate 318). Projects like Stan van der Beek's environmental *Movie Drome* (Plate 319) were also distantly related to the Happening, as indeed were the spectacular light shows favoured by leading rock groups such as the Pink Floyd in the late Sixties.

Missing from the American-bred Happening was the element of confrontation, which had played so large a role in the original Futurist and Dadaist events. When European artists such as Wolf Vostell, or even Japanese ones such as Ay-O, worked in America, their events and performances seemed to be distinguished from the native product by the undercurrent of political and social

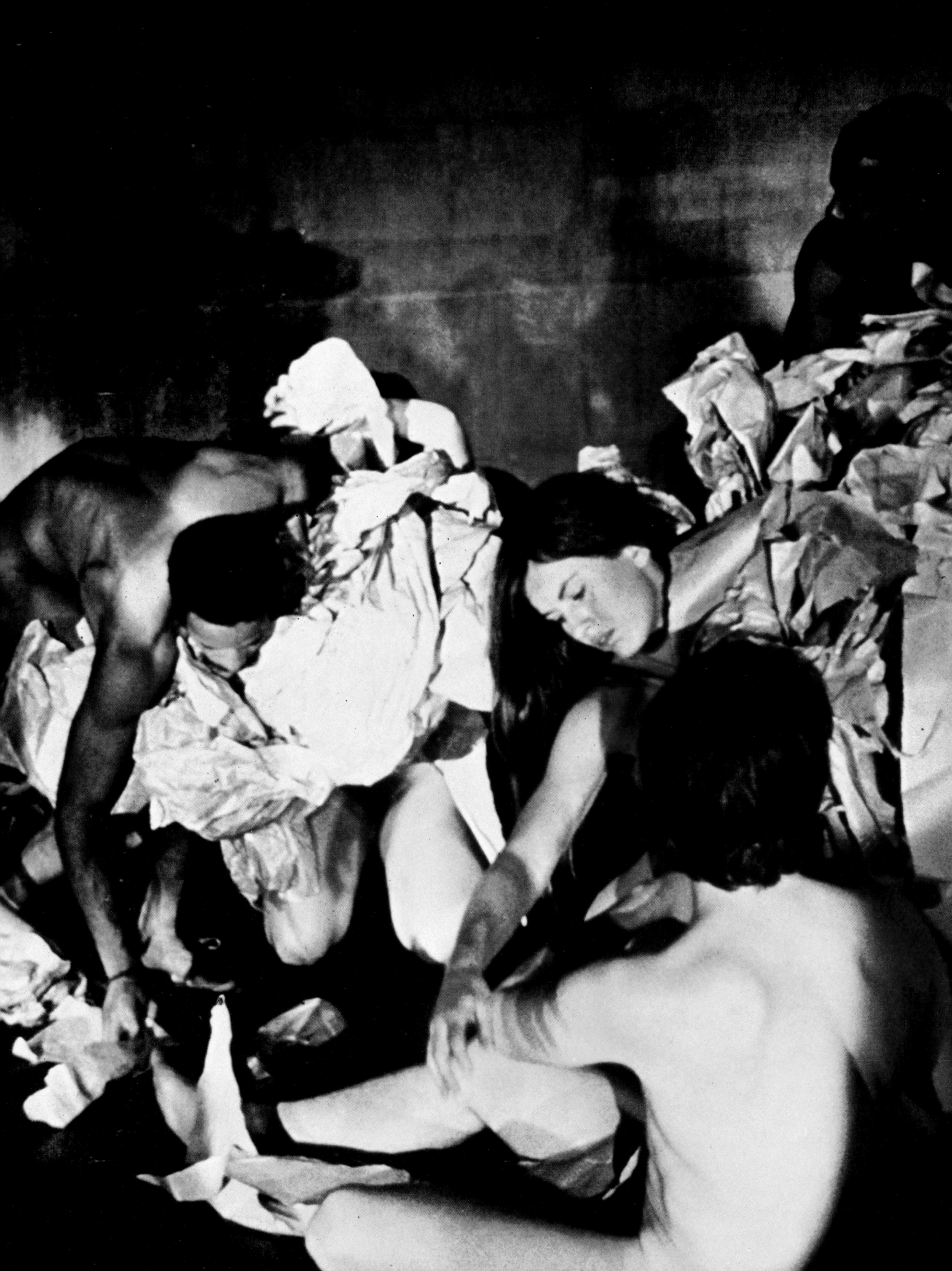

318.
Robert Rauschenberg
Soundings
1968; 240 × 1100 cm. (94 × 429 in.)
Cologne, Wallraf-Richartz Museum, coll. Ludwig

commentary. This made itself felt, for example, in Ay-O's *Kill Paper, Not People*, presented at the Fluxus Paper Concert in New York in 1967 (Plate 320). Vostell's use of what he called "decollage" as a creative principle (Plate 321) was also a symptom of this rather different orientation, though in a more general sense. Vostell has informally defined his way of thinking thus: "What fascinated me was the symptoms and the emanations of a constant metamorphosis in the environment and in artistic expression, in which destruction in general, together with dissolution and juxtaposition, is the strongest element. Dé-coll/age is a production principle which makes use of destruction and

autodestruction, in contradistinction to collage, in which mostly undestroyed, although heterogenous, objects are assembled" (Wolf Vostell, from *vor der collage zur assemblage*, Institut für moderne Kunst, Nuremberg, 1968).

A natively American idea of confrontation in the arts had to await the bitter period of the Vietnam War. There was a certain amount of activity of this kind on the West Coast, in San Francisco and Los Angeles. The Los Angeles Provos (whose name was borrowed from a Dutch organization) on one occasion had the idea of collecting unwanted possessions from the Watts ghetto and then distributing them to the pros-

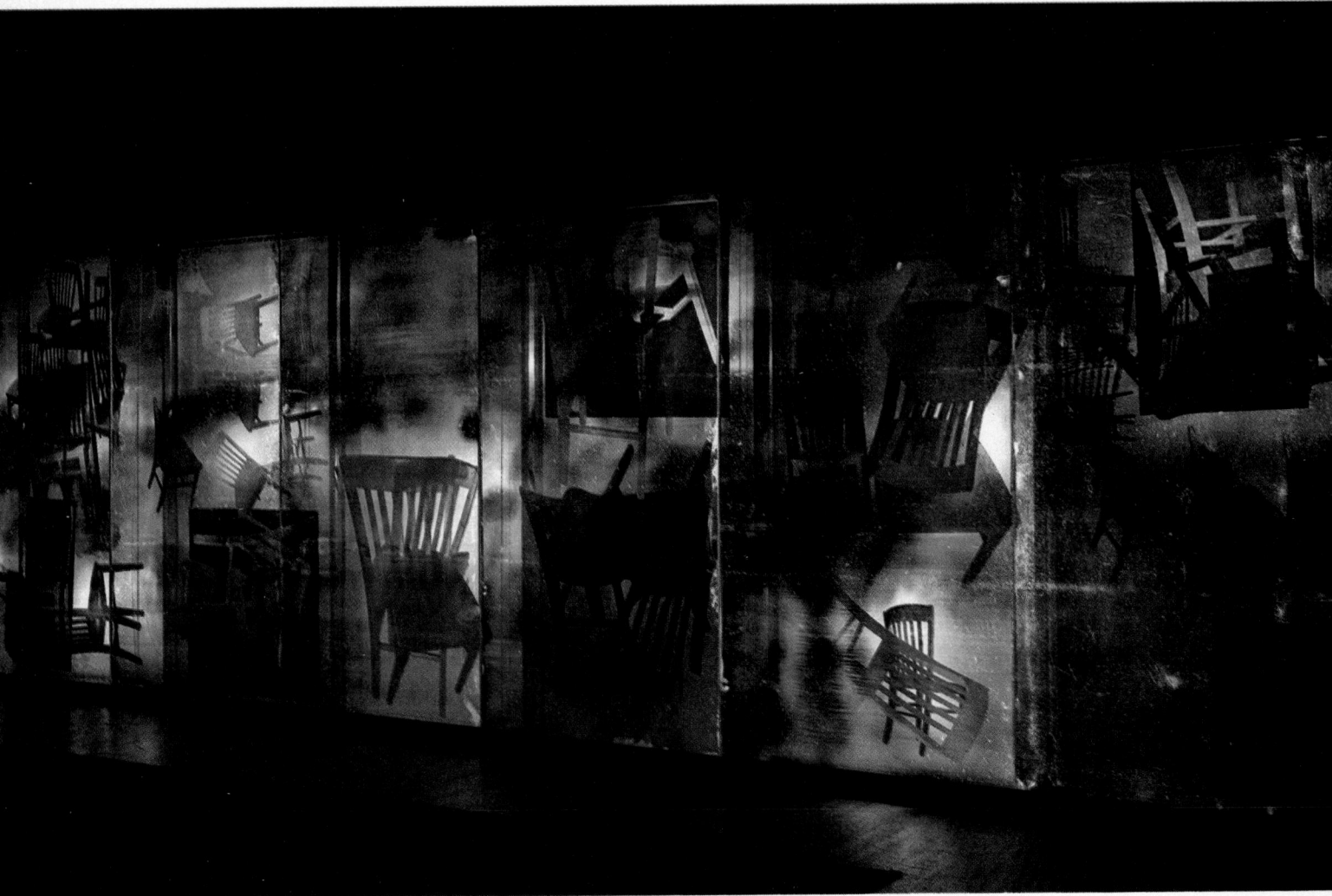

perous suburbs from a decorated truck. In New York, the Art Workers' Coalition was established at a meeting in April, 1969. The militant wing of this formed the Guerrilla Art Action Group. This was involved in a demonstration mounted in front of Picasso's *Guernica* to protest against the Song My massacre. In the course of the demonstration there were readings from the Bible and from reports of the massacre which had been printed in *Life* magazine. Members of GAAG also took part in mounting an exhibition called "The People's Flag Show", in which various artists showed works with the American flag as a common basis. Since the design of the flag is protected by American law, the exhibition was closed by the police, and some of the artists (no doubt to their secret delight) were prosecuted as a result of it.

Events such as this in America were tame compared to the activities of members of the Institute of Direct Art in Vienna. Post-war Austrian society was markedly more conservative than any other free society in Europe. In this sense it provided an equivalent to Marinetti's pre-1914 Italy, and it is fascinating to note how soon Neo-Dada activity made its appearance there. By the mid-Sixties a whole school of artists were making themselves notorious for their acting out of sadistic fantasies. Hermann Nitsch, announcing

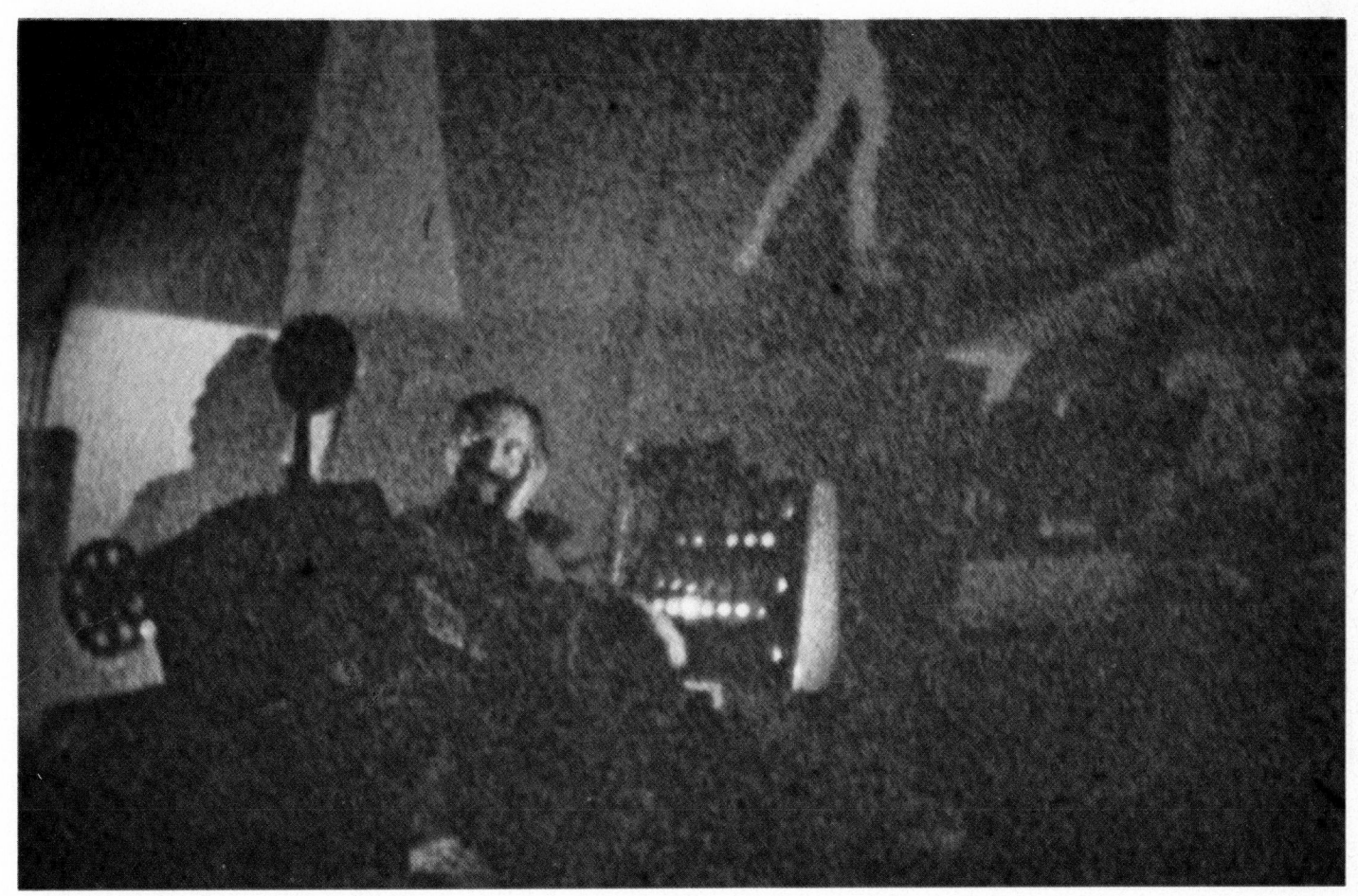

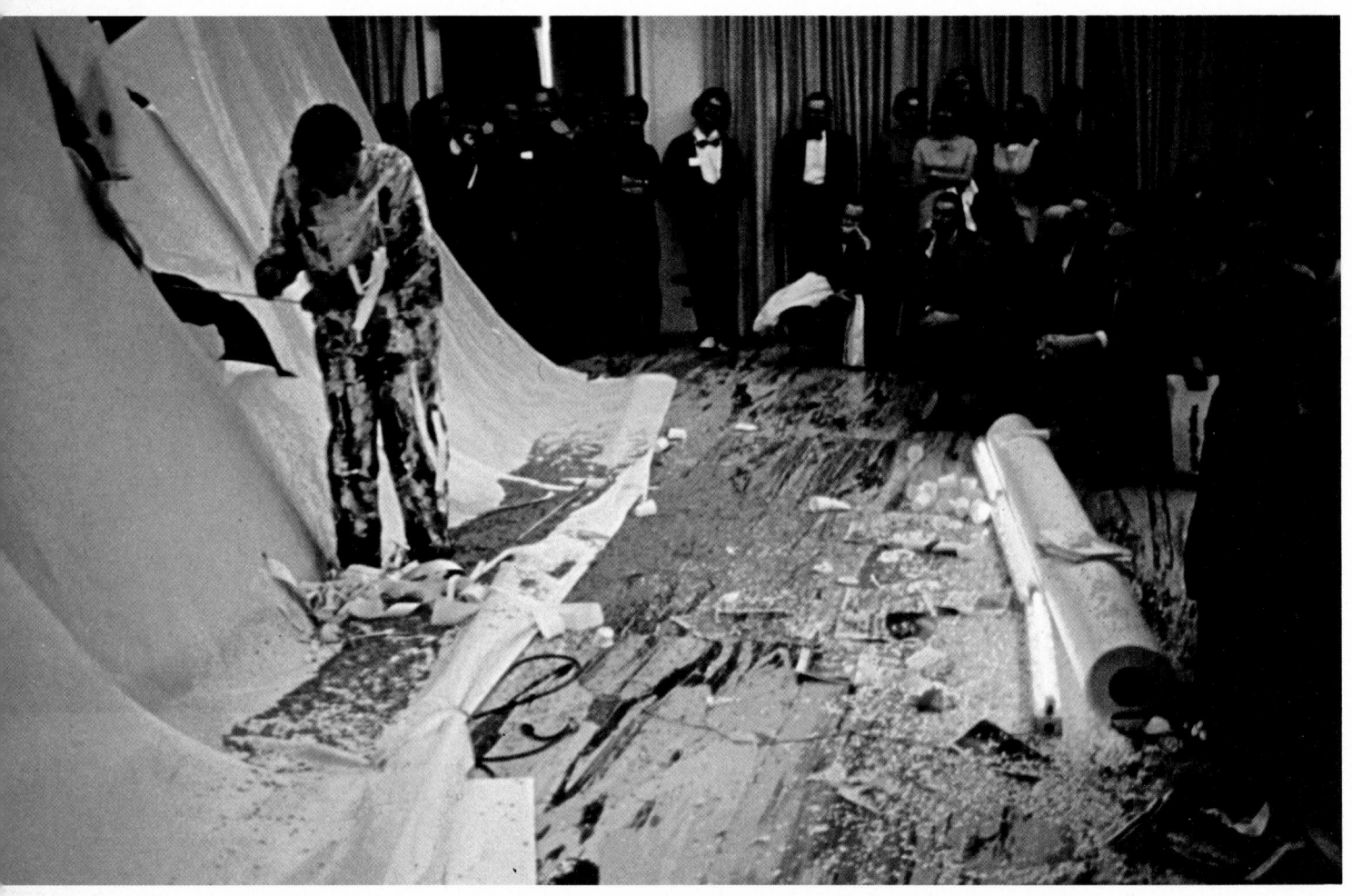

his intention (in June, 1962) to "disembowel, tear, and pull to pieces a dead lamb", continued with the claim: "Through my artistic production (a form of the mysticism of being), I take upon myself the apparent negative, unsavoury, perverse, obscene, the passion and the hysteria of the act of sacrifice so that YOU are spared the sullying, shaming descent into the extreme" (Hermann Nitsch, *Orgien Mysterien Theater*, Frankfurt, 1969).

Another artist, Günter Brus, performed what he dubbed a *Scheiss-Aktion* in 1967—this involved an act of ritual public defecation and was filmed. In 1969, a third member of the Viennese group, Otto Mühl, was the principal performer in an event called *Libi*. In the course of this an egg was broken into the vagina of a menstruating girl, who then positioned herself so as to allow the egg to drip into the artist's mouth.

Actions such as these seem designed as a protest, not against any specific form of social evil, but against the humiliation of the human condition. They are the products of Poggioli's nihilism and agonism, rather than of his activism and antagonism.

The extremism of the Viennese group might seem to exclude it permanently from any kind of artistic establishment, but even here the social organism showed an astonishing capacity to absorb just those elements which had been designed to be totally unacceptable to it. The Kassel Documenta of 1972, the premier exhibition of modern art in Europe, contained a section devoted to the work of Günter Brus and another which documented that of Hermann Nitsch. Both

321.
Wolf Vostell
Decollage Happening-You
1964, Great Neck, New York
© 1964 by Peter Moore

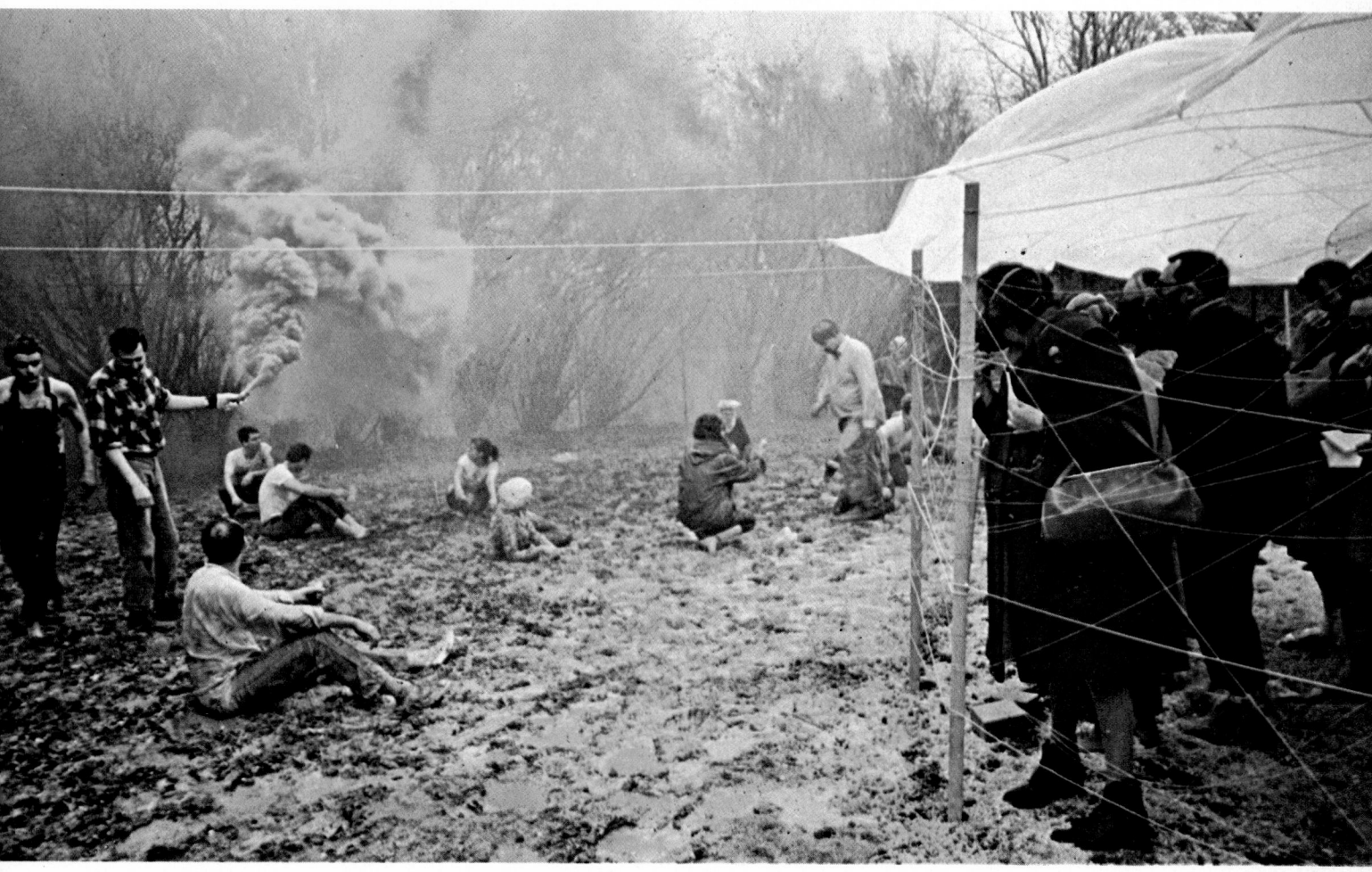

found themselves categorized under the anodyne heading "Individual Mythologies" and seemed to rouse no particular sense of excitement or wonder among the throngs of visitors who came to see the show.

Though the Happening attracted so much attention in America, the roots of the art "event" or "performance" were perhaps deeper in Europe, and one reason why the Viennese artists whom I have just mentioned won a certain degree of acceptance was that their work was perceived as only part of a wide spectrum. The buried moralism of Brus or Nitsch appeared quite openly in events staged by other, chiefly German artists, among them Klaus Rinke (*Masculine, Feminine*, Plates 322 and 323). In Holland, as might have been expected, this mode of expression formed a close

link with the "ecological" art of a man like Ger van Elk (Plate 324).

But it was in England during the late Sixties and early Seventies that performance art seemed to enter into a new phase of expression. There were a number of reasons for this. The most important was lack of competition from media like experimental video and experimental film which increasingly occupied the attention of the American avant-garde. The British theatre, too, proved to be far more flexible than its American counterpart; and this meant that in Britain there was not the sharp contrast between Broadway and Off-Broadway which for a long time polarized theatrical energies in New York. By an ironic paradox, this meant that those individuals in Britain who saw themselves as truly "avant-garde" or experimental

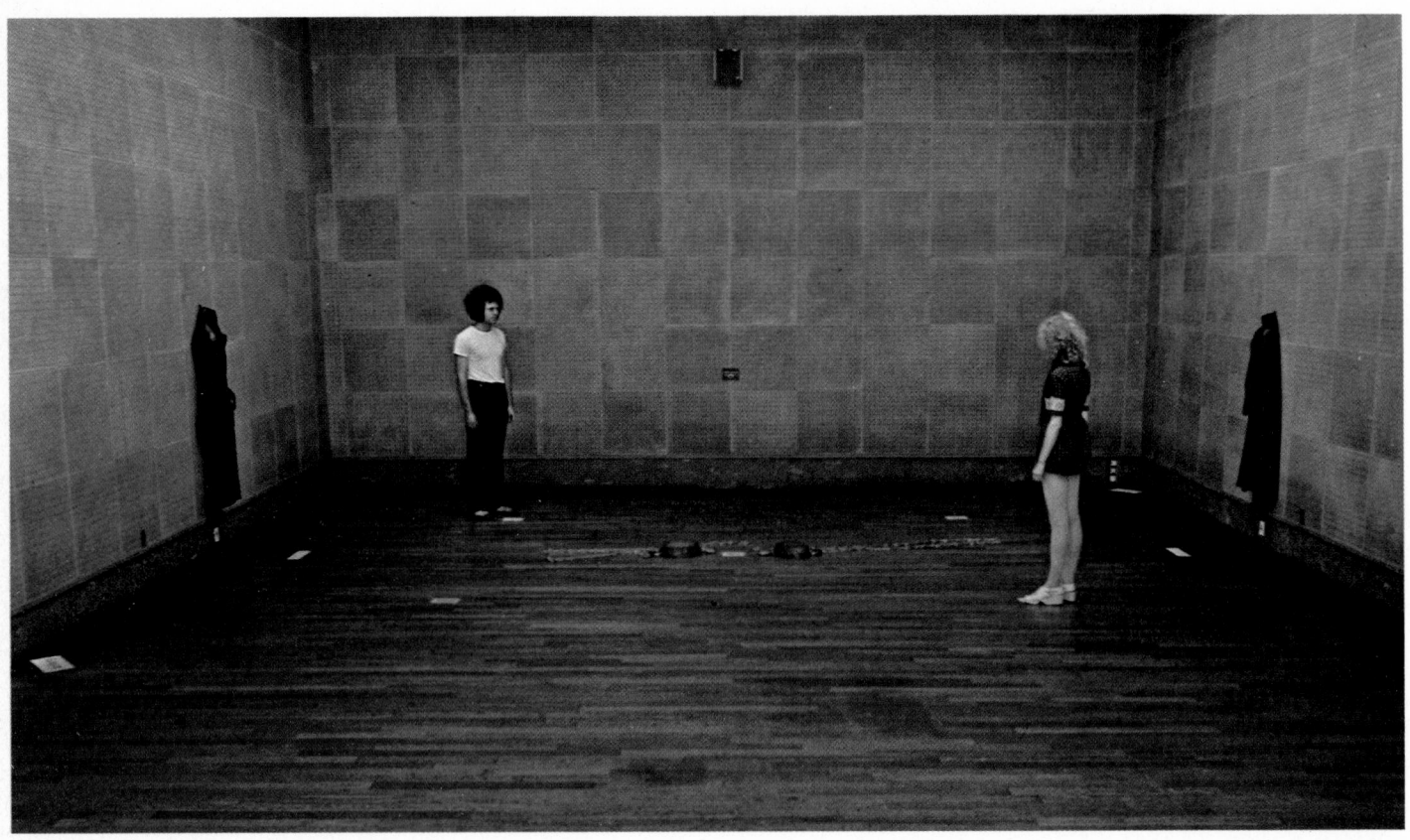

tended to turn their backs on any kind of recognizably theatrical format—at least for a time. I say "at least for a time" because it is clear that the British "event" or "performance" was usually essentially more theatrical than its American counterpart.

Another characteristic of British performance art was its tendency to be at its most flourishing and effective outside London, while the American Happening was, by contrast, a New York phenomenon which subsequently spread elsewhere, chiefly to places like universities and colleges where New York exercised its greatest influence.

The earliest performance events to be put on in England—or at any rate the earliest in the postwar period—were those staged in Liverpool as part of a Merseyside Arts Festival in 1962. The moving spirit was the poet-painter Adrian Henri, who describes them as being "a mixture of poetry,

rock'n'roll, and assemblage" (*Environments and Happenings* by Adrian Henri, New York, 1974). Liverpool is still a regular venue for environmental and mixed-media events, most of them based on the Great Georges Project, a large converted neo-classical church in a socially deprived area of central Liverpool.

Yorkshire, particularly the cities of Leeds and Bradford, was another place where performance art made rapid headway in the 1960's. In Bradford, the focus of energy was provided by Albert Hunt, and by the Complementary Studies Department run by Hunt at the Bradford College of Art. In 1967, for instance, Bradford became the stage for a Hunt-inspired re-creation of the October Revolution in Petrograd, whose fiftieth anniversary fell that year.

The most notable product of Yorkshire, however, was the Welfare State, the largest, most ambitious, and most successful of all British

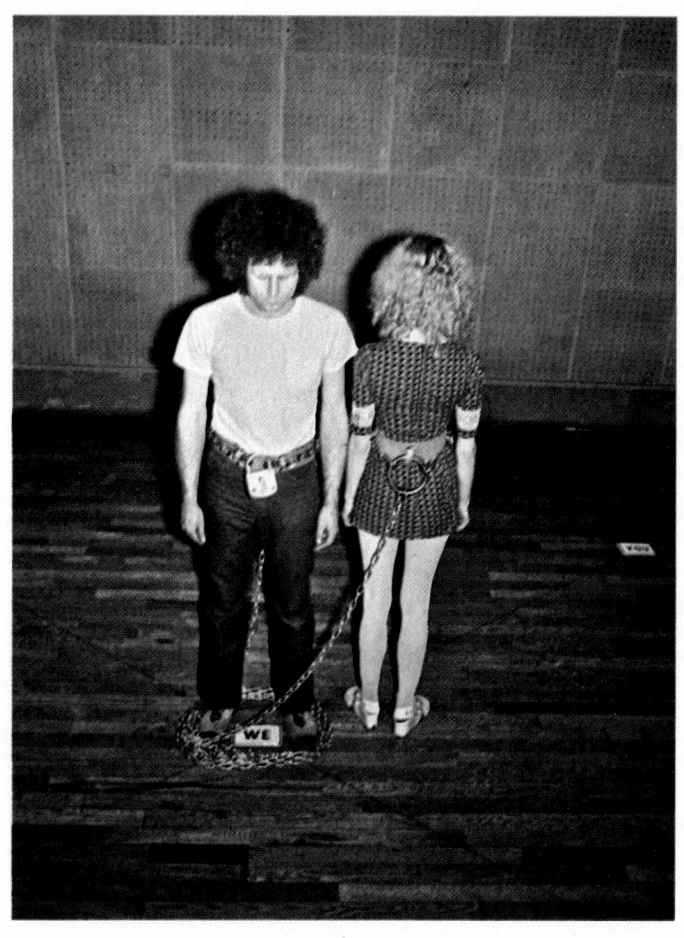

performance groups. This was founded and led by John Fox. There is some argument as to whether the Welfare State's activities can be described as performance art or not. Certainly, group members till recently insisted on describing themselves as "artists" rather than actors, though the Welfare State as an entity is now usually described as an experimental theatre company. Fox and those he gathered around him had a great gift for generating unexpected and memorable poetic images, through techniques which mingled ideas borrowed from traditional music hall with others taken from primitive ritual. A manifesto issued by the group reads in part: "We make art using the traditions of popular theatre such as mummers, circus, fairground, puppets, music-hall, so that as well as being entertaining and funny and apparently familiar in style to the popular audience our work also has a more profound implication. We will react to new stimulus and situations spontaneously and dramatically and continue to fake unbelievable art as a necessary way of offsetting cultural and organic death" (quoted by Adrian Henri, *op. cit.*, p. 119).

Still more in the "popular" or music-hall vein is the work done by the group variously called (according to caprice and circumstances) John Bull's Puncture Repair Kit and the Yorkshire Gnomes. Its activities also owe more than a little to anarchic British radio comedy of the Forties and Fifties, and especially "The Goon Show".

Not all British performance work was in this knockabout vein. Stuart Brisley turns the Happening into an endurance test for performance and audience alike—immersing himself, for example, in a bath in which float animal entrails, or enduring long periods of isolation in a room where nevertheless his every action could be observed. In fact, one of the most interesting aspects to the events done in Britain is their sheer variety, and

324.
Ger van Elk
Confounding the Word OK
1971 ; Marken, Holland
Courtesy Art & Project

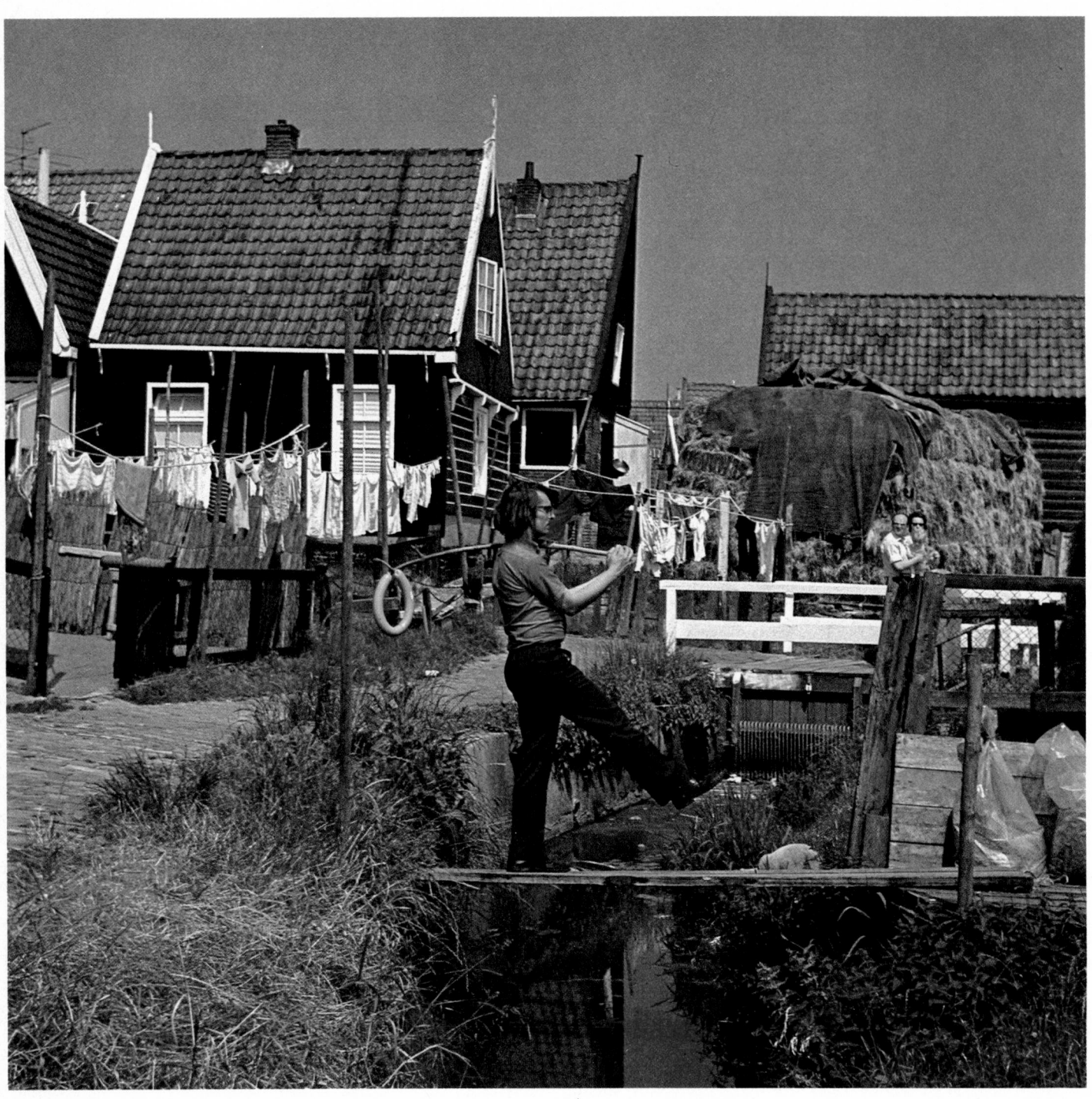

325.
Peter Kuttner
Coloured Food Event "Edible Rainbow"
1971; London, Chessington Zoo
By kind permission of the artist

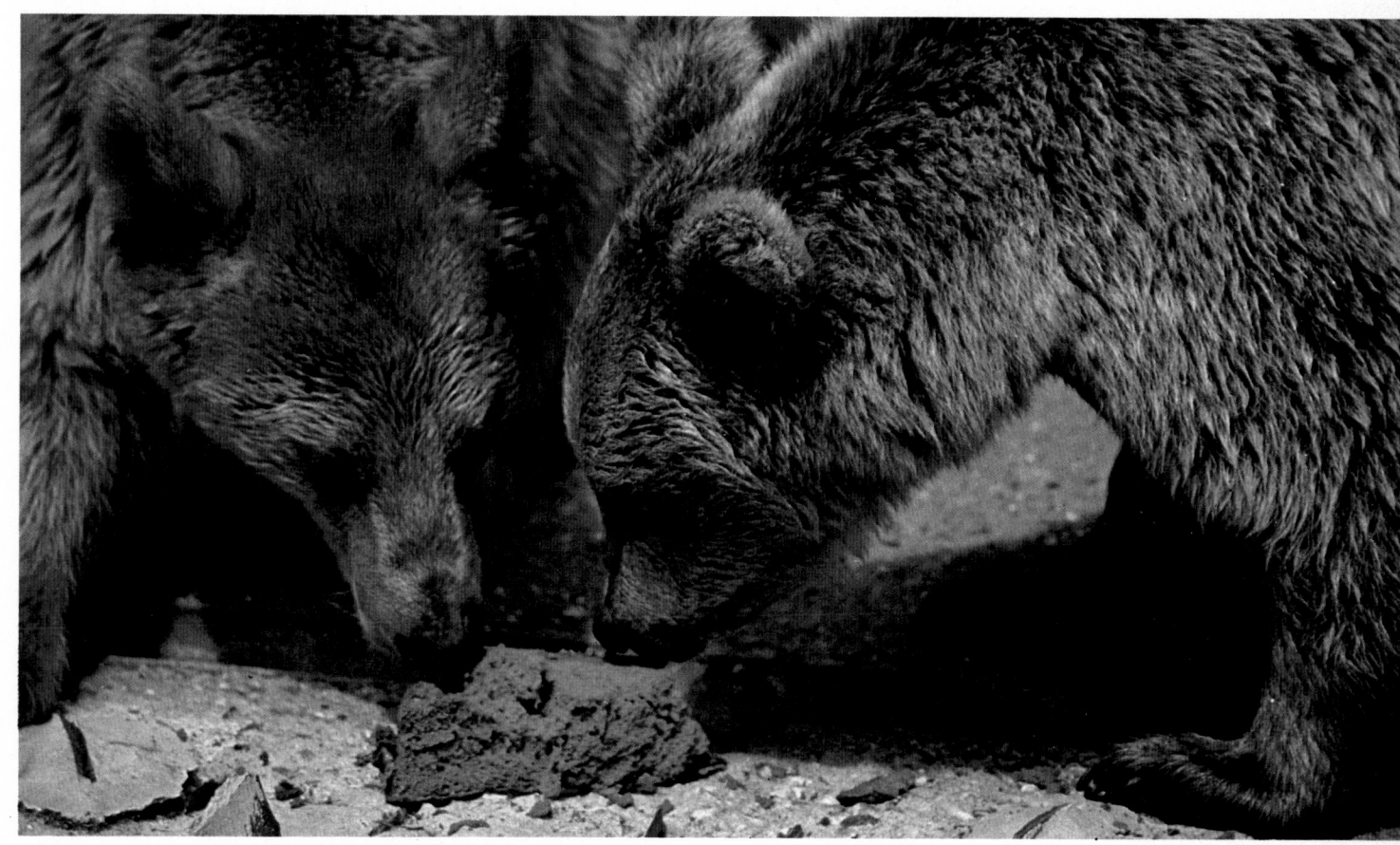

the number of different techniques they have involved. Peter Kuttner (Plate 325) has made a specialty of food, tinted in garishly improbable colours but nevertheless perfectly edible; while Peter Dockley (Plate 326) makes use of wax figures, as well as, in the instance illustrated here, reverting to the science-fiction imagery which has proved so popular with all types of Pop artist.

The effort to disentangle the chief themes and purposes of performance art during the post-war period cannot be an easy one. There is no single simple explanation for the tremendous amount of energy that has been put into this medium of expression since the early Sixties. For some commentators, the art event is primarily a response to an oppressive political climate. It is the confrontation with the established order which is valuable. By this interpretation, the Paris "events" of 1968 were simply a Happening writ large. But one only has to examine the argument to see how specious it is. As a form of political communication, Happenings, like most other manifestations of Modernism, are almost uniquely inefficient, since formal considerations invariably get in the way of the message to be delivered. The most ambitious Happening delivers less, in terms of effective political propaganda, than a moderately well-attended political rally.

Other commentators see art events and performances as being chiefly valuable as an attempt to democratize the avant-garde, and to make its ideas accessible to a broader spectrum of people, more especially to those who would never dream of setting foot in a museum. The participatory nature of many art events responds, according to this argument, to the desire that people themselves have to take a more active part in culture. An offshoot of the interest in Happenings has been, in

413

326.
Peter Dockley
Spaced
1970, London, Round House
By kind permission of the artist

327. Opposite
Yukihisa Isobe
Hot Air Balloon
1969; at the Seventh annual New York Avant-Garde
Festival, Wards Island, by kind permission of the artist

a number of European countries, the so-called community-art movement, which aims to bring the making of art, as well as its appreciation, down to local grass-roots level. It is sad to have to point out first that what makes the street performance popular is generally its most traditional and nostalgic elements—knockabout physical comedy, clowns, and circus tricks; and secondly that the community-art movement has involved, for better or worse, a concerted attack on the notion of artistic standards, on the grounds that they are both obstructive and undemocratic. Modernism has consistently sought not to abolish standards of judgment, but to change them, and if the community-art movement succeeded on a large scale, the avant-garde as we now recognize it would certainly be the first victim.

A third way of looking at Happenings is to see them as rituals—as having a therapeutic function for the performers and also, to a lesser extent, for the spectators. There is certainly a powerful argument for regarding much modern art as a

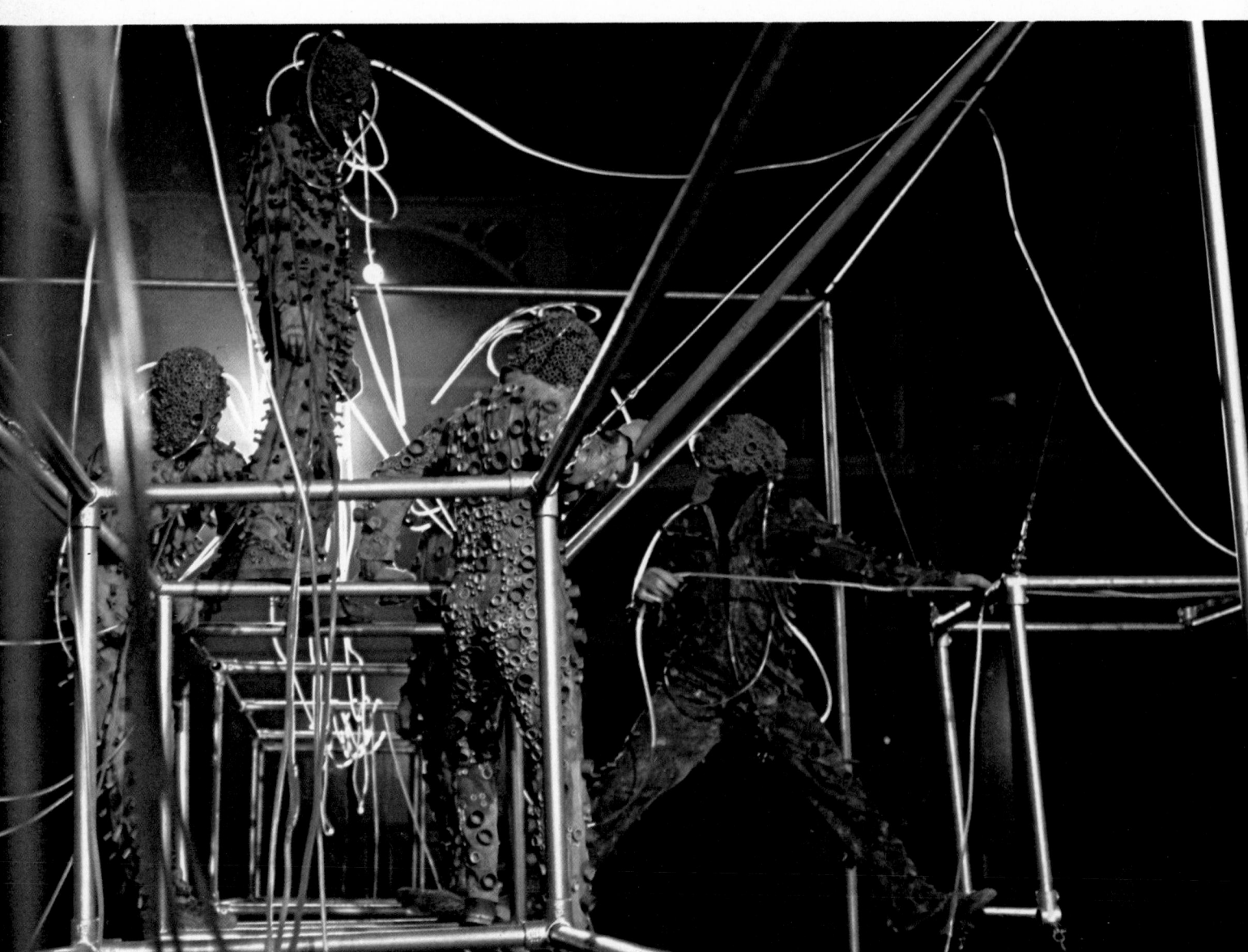

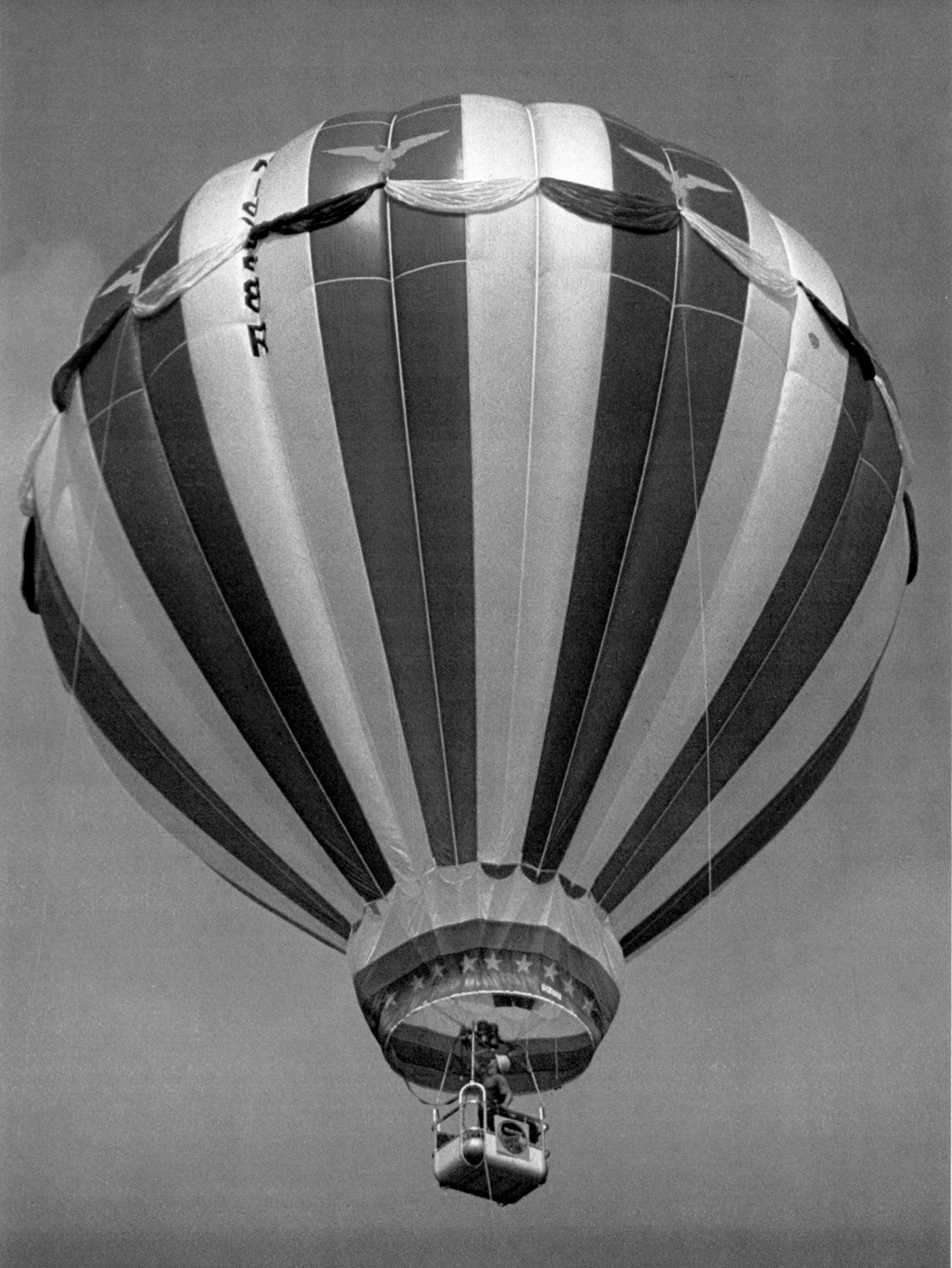

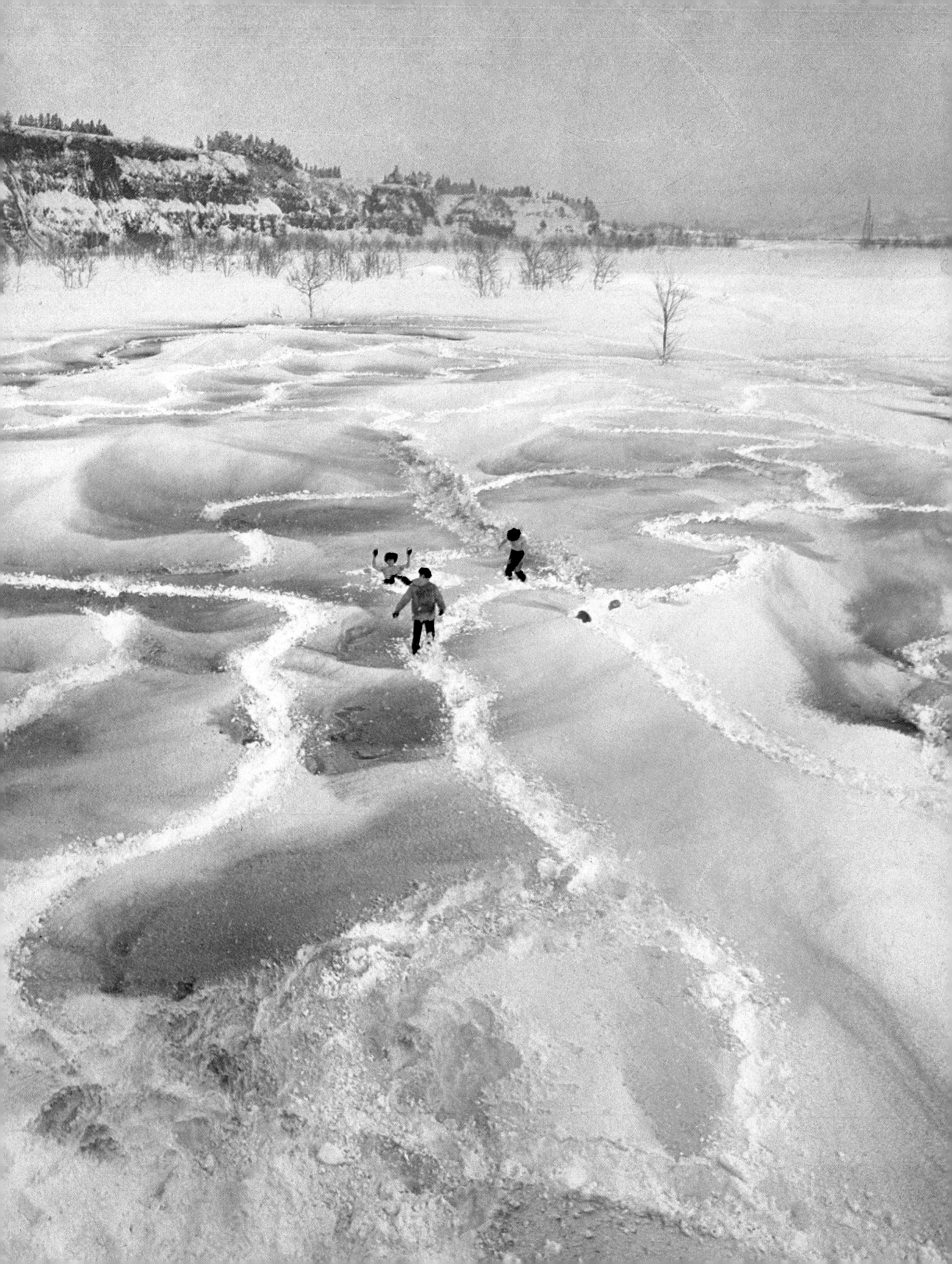

328. Opposite
GUN
Event for the Image-Change of Snow
1970; 1 sq. km. (39 sq. mi.)

substitute for religion in a now-secularized society. Freud foresaw that art would have to fulfil this function, and discusses his insight in *Civilization and Its Discontents*.

But is the therapy as effective as the supporters of the avant-garde would like to assume? Udo Kultermann, in his recent book *Art-Events and Happenings*, compares the makers of events to the traditional shaman: "The shaman does not produce objects, although he is usually an artist in primitive communities, and he acts like an artist by renouncing the self and by bringing a sacrifice for society. In that he is himself engaged, he activates healing forms of behaviour in others. Seen in this light, the Happening is the consequence and expression of modern shamanism" (Udo Kultermann, *Art-Events and Happenings*, London, 1971, p. 12).

The objection to this is that it takes the will for the deed. There is no evidence that the rituals devised by modern artists have elicited any deep sense of commitment from the mass. Indeed, when mass audiences occasionally come in contact with activities of this sort, they greet them with the detached, mildly ironic curiosity evoked by the more trivial kind of news event.

The Happening is at its most effective when it fulfils the traditional function of the Renaissance "triumph" or the baroque pageant. Not surprisingly, it is Japanese groups and artists who have shown the acutest sense of this, often in works which show the traditional Oriental impulse towards unity with nature. Yukihisa Isobe's hot-air balloon (Plate 327), shown at the seventh annual New York Avant-Garde Festival, was no more avant-garde than the brothers Montgolfier—indeed, a good deal less so, given the strides made by technology in the course of two hundred years. But it still had the power to delight. The *Event for the Image-Change of Snow* (Plate 328), put on by the GUN group in Japan, provided a pictorial image worthy of a Hiroshige or a Hokusai.

Earth Art and Concept Art

Since the rise of Minimal Art there has been no absolutely dominant art style or movement—nothing which, as Pop Art did, seemed to bring everything into relationship with itself, whether through the influence that it exercised or by the opposition it aroused. On the other hand, it is possible to trace a line of development, with the attitudes embodied in Minimalism as its source. Art manifestations which seem superficially very different from one another turn out to have hidden intellectual links.

In the case of what came to be called Earth Art, the connections with Minimal sculpture are not hidden but obvious, and often the same artists were involved with both forms of expression. The cult of anti-form, initiated by Robert Morris, led to experimentation with all kinds of materials. Rafael Ferrer's *Hay, Grease, Steel* (Plate 330), shown at the Whitney Museum in 1969, is only a brief step away from Morris's soft sculptures on the one hand, and one or two of Christo's more ambitious environmental pieces upon the other (*Wrapped Floor*, 1970, Plate 329). But even anti-form, for some artists, was not enough. They wanted a direct confrontation with "outside" reality. One way of achieving this was to bring the outside, as literal earth and stones, into the art gallery. This was what Robert Smithson did with his *Sandstone with Mirror* (1969, Plate 331).

It was more logical, however, to remove the art work from the gallery altogether, and to create it through intervention in the natural environment. Smithson's *Spiral Jetty*, in Great Salt Lake, Utah (Plate 332), has become, in the handful of years since its creation, perhaps the best-known single example of Earth Art.

Like many apparently simplistic recent art works, *Spiral Jetty* has been the focus for complex explanations: "The very form of the work, a spiral, is an open one, which, in terms of Gestalt, is impossible to grasp without accepting the notion of the infinite. Contrary to all the Minimal artists who have been preoccupied with cubic volumes, which have a 'closed' Gestalt, Smithson has always preferred volumes that imply a geometric progression" (Grégoire Müller, *The New Avant-Garde*, London, 1972, p. 17).

But an approach through Gestalt psychology was not the only possible one, according to Smithson's commentators and critics. For example, there were the physical properties of the Great Salt Lake itself—the high density of salt which gives the water a reddish colour and which promotes crystallization on the edges of the work. There were also legendary associations—one legend claims that the lake was once connected with the ocean, another that it contained a dangerous whirlpool (of which the *Spiral Jetty* became the symbol). Created at a time when "underground" culture was taking a passionate interest in the possible esoteric meanings of prehistoric monuments, most notably barrows, earthworks, and turf figures, Smithson's piece could also be regarded as an effort to re-create and rival prehistory.

One of the most important things about *Spiral Jetty*, however, was its inaccessibility. Sited in a sparsely inhabited tract of country, it could only be fully apprehended from the air. For most of the people who theorized about it, it could only be known through photographic and other documentation. The "reality" of the piece thus, by a paradox, existed chiefly at one remove from the spectator.

Michael Heizer, who at one stage collaborated with Smithson, takes the process of abstraction even further. His *Displaced, Replaced Mass* at Silver Springs, Nevada (Plates 334 and 333), is in fact one of the more conventional of his works, because it seems at least to propose a formal equation. *Double*

Negative, another example, is notable not so much for its form as for the enormous mass of material that had to be removed in order to make it—no less than 240,000 tons of earth and rock. Its form was determined by the nature and conformation of the ground, at least as much as it was by the artist's intentions. *Double Negative* was nevertheless the subject of a massive documentary effort on the part of its creator. He took over a thousand photographs of the piece, at right angles and from an equal distance, in order to overcome the effects of perspective distortion. These images, when brought together, preserved the "true" form of the piece.

Neither Smithson nor Heizer is as indifferent to the final embodiment of their ideas as Douglas Huebler (Plate 335). A catalogue statement issued by this artist reads as follows: "The existence of each sculpture is documented by its documentation.

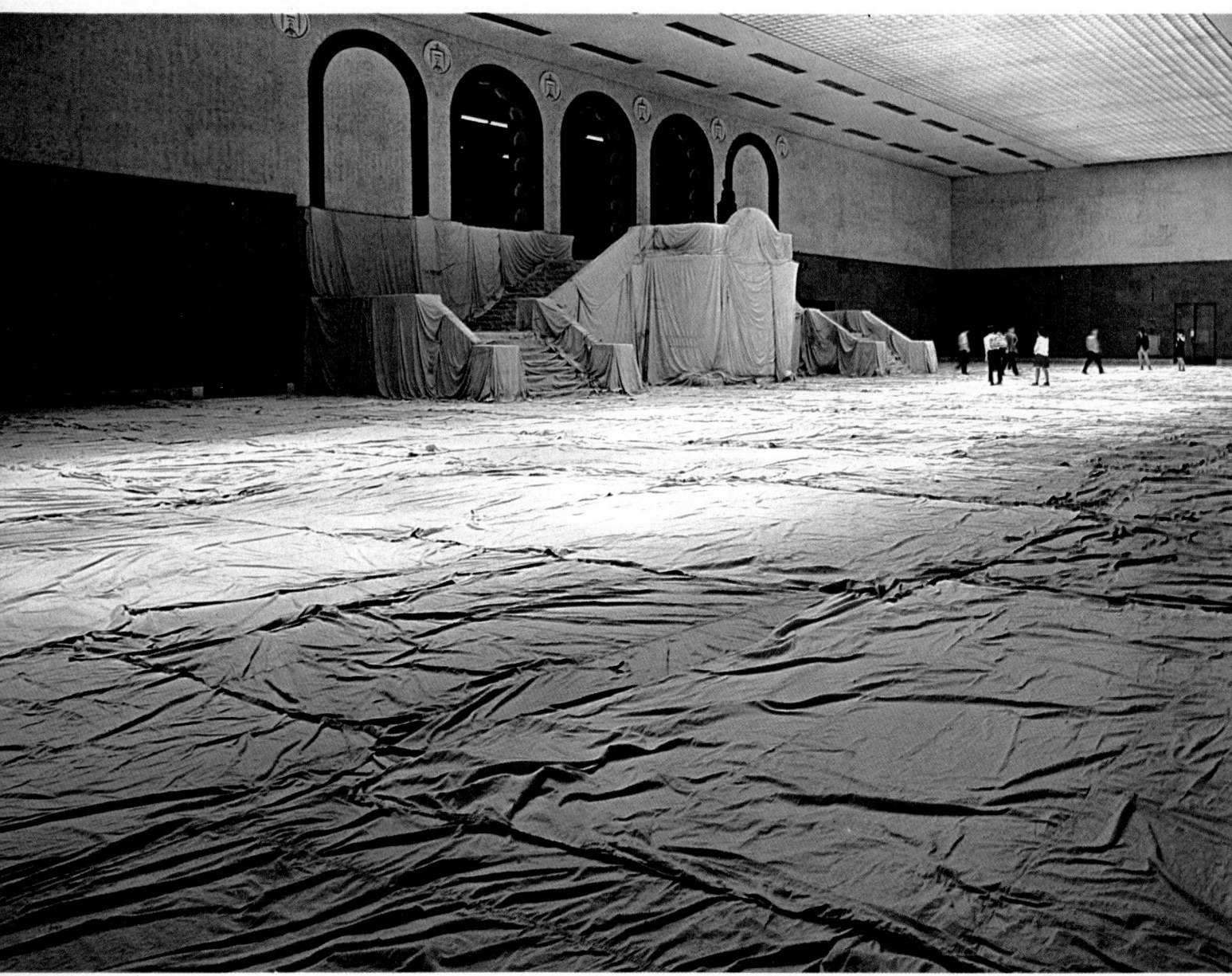

420

329. Below
Christo (Christo Jaracheff)
Wrapped Floor
1970; 1240 sq. m. (1476 sq. yd.)

330. Right
Rafael Ferrer
Hay, Grease, Steel
1969
New York, Whitney Museum of American Art

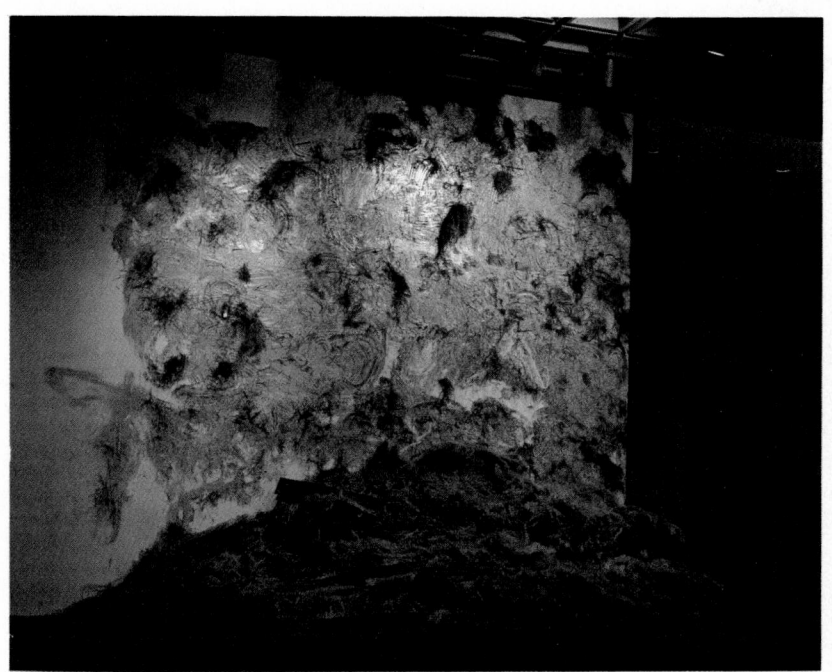

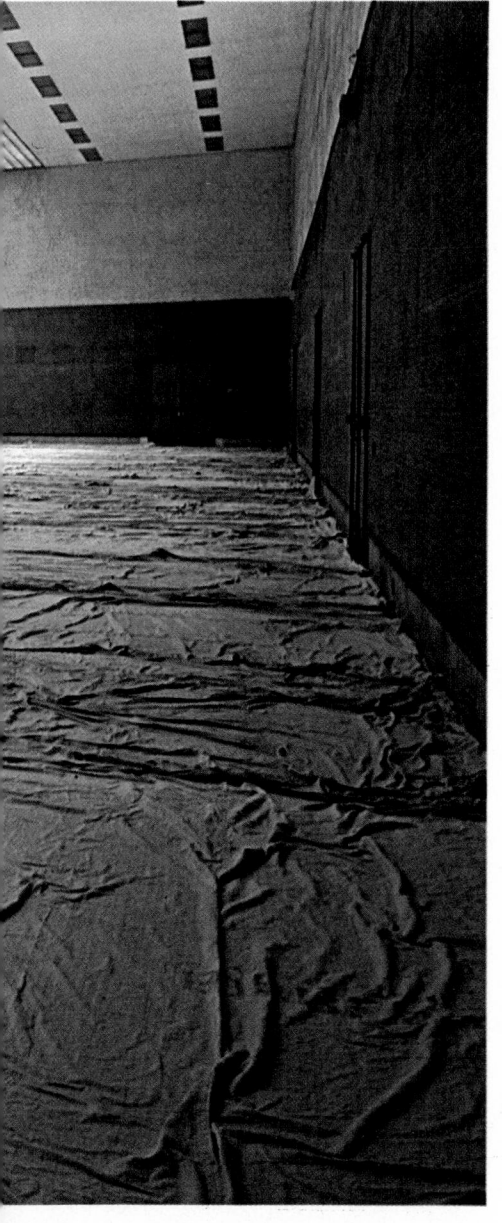

"The documentation takes the form of photographs, maps, drawings and descriptive language.

"The marker 'material' and the shape described by the location of the markers have no special significance, other than to demark the limits of the piece.

"The permanence and destiny of the markers have no special significance.

"The duration pieces exist only in the documentation of the marker's destiny within a selected period of time.

"The proposed projects do not differ from the other pieces as idea, but do differ to the extent of their material substance" (catalogue of the exhibition "Douglas Huebler", at the Seth Siegelaub Gallery, New York, November, 1968).

Here the importance of the original concept, as well as that of the documentation in support of the concept, seems to be far more important than the actual physical embodiment of the work. Huebler says that none of his works can be experienced as physical presence, and that he attaches no significance to the sites of his pieces: "When I go to the site to document it—to 'mark' it—I think 'here it is' and that's all. As a matter of fact I

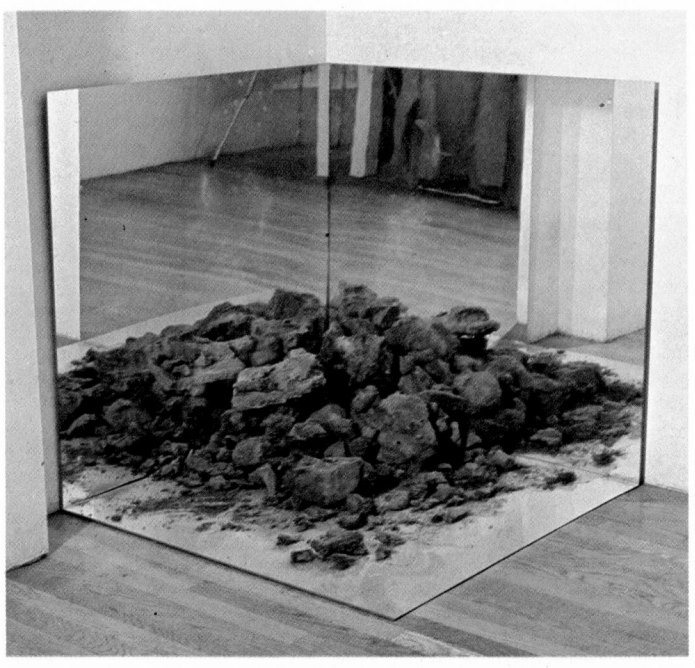

331.
Robert Smithson
Sandstone with Mirror
1969; 91.4 × 91.4 cm. (36 × 36 in.)
New York, John Weber Gallery

consider it important that it is no different from the next ten feet or next block or whatever. Both the sites selected and the shape that they describe are 'neutral' and only function to form 'that' work" (Douglas Huebler, interviewed by Arthur Rose, in *Idea Art*, a critical anthology edited by Gregory Battcock, New York, 1973, pp. 143–4).

Huebler's work is a reminder of the fact that Earth Art does not necessarily involve the transportation from one place to another of many tons of earth and rock. To mark the site in one way or another may be enough to create the piece.

Other artists working with variants of Huebler's ideas tend to be more romantic than he is. In fact, it is surprising to discover in them what looks like a survival of early nineteenth-century attitudes towards nature. Walter de Maria's *Las Vegas Piece* (Plate 337) is a mile-long line drawn in the Nevada desert. De Maria's original idea with pieces of this kind was that any photographic reproduction of them would be forbidden, so that the spectator, in order to experience them, would actually have to go out into the wastelands where they were situated. Dennis Oppenheim's *Branded Mountain* (Plate 338) evokes the world of cattle kings and cattle rustlers, in fact the whole of the American cowboy myth—since the brand is an enlargement of the kind of brand used to indicate the ownership of cattle. Oppenheim has also created examples of Earth Art by interfering with the pattern of growth in crops (Plate 339) and by cutting curving channels in the ice of a frozen lake.

Earth Art occasionally made its appearance in an urban context, for instance with Serra's *To Encircle: Base Plate (Hexagram)* (Plate 340), with its fashionable reference to the *I Ching*, but here the idea is not so much to identify with the context as to contrast simple elements of order or disorder— the circle is an "area of order", the *I Ching*'s symbols are arrived at by the random tossing of yarrow stalks or coins.

Essentially, however, Earth artists seem to have intended a reaffirmation of oneness with nature and natural forces. This impulse makes itself especially conspicuous in the work of two English practitioners of the genre, Richard Long and Hamish Fulton. Richard Long has clearly been

influenced by Bronze Age earthworks, such as the impressive mound of unknown origin and purpose at Silbury Hill in Wiltshire, and both he and Fulton document their work with conspicuously romantic photographs. On the other hand there is also an element (which we also recognize in men like J. M. W. Turner and Lord Byron) of the desire to pit oneself against one's surroundings. The artist, for example, sets himself to accomplish a trek of a given distance in a given number of days or hours. Earth Art thus becomes linked to performance art, and to the widespread notion that ritualized behaviour, rather than the actual production of objects, now forms the most important part of the avant-garde artist's activity.

Earth Art can involve co-operation with natural processes as well as the wilful alteration or even contradiction of nature. One sees this contradiction in simple guise in Wolf Kahlen's *Baum-Raumsegment* (Plate 341), where a tree is partially sprayed with paint. Earth Art seems to move into another category, however, when the emphasis shifts to documentation and process. At this point we seem to cross a frontier and to be exploring a different category: the phenomenon that critics have called Conceptual or Concept Art.

332.
Robert Smithson
Spiral Jetty
1970, Great Salt Lake, Utah
By kind permission of the artist

One artist who often seems to exist on the borderline between the two is the Dutchman Jan Dibbets (Plate 342). He uses a wide range of different media—maps, the mail, photography, tape recordings, and videotape—but is perhaps best known for his "perspective corrections". These are photographs of landscape in which the camera has been manipulated to produce an alternative image to the true one. For example, Dibbets uses the camera to build mountains out of the flat lands of his native Holland.

Dibbets clearly regards the way of thinking, the method of approach, as being far more important than the actual subject-matter: "I really believe [he says] in having projects which in fact can't be carried out, or which are so simple that anyone could work them out. I once made four spots on the map of Holland, without knowing where they were. Then I found out how to get there and went to the place and took a snapshot. Quite stupid. Anyone can do that" (quoted in Ursula Meyer, *Conceptual Art*, New York, 1972, p. 121).

One of the paradoxes of Concept Art is that it can embody itself in almost any form the artist chooses to adopt. Thus there is a strongly conceptual element in the work of Tom Phillips,

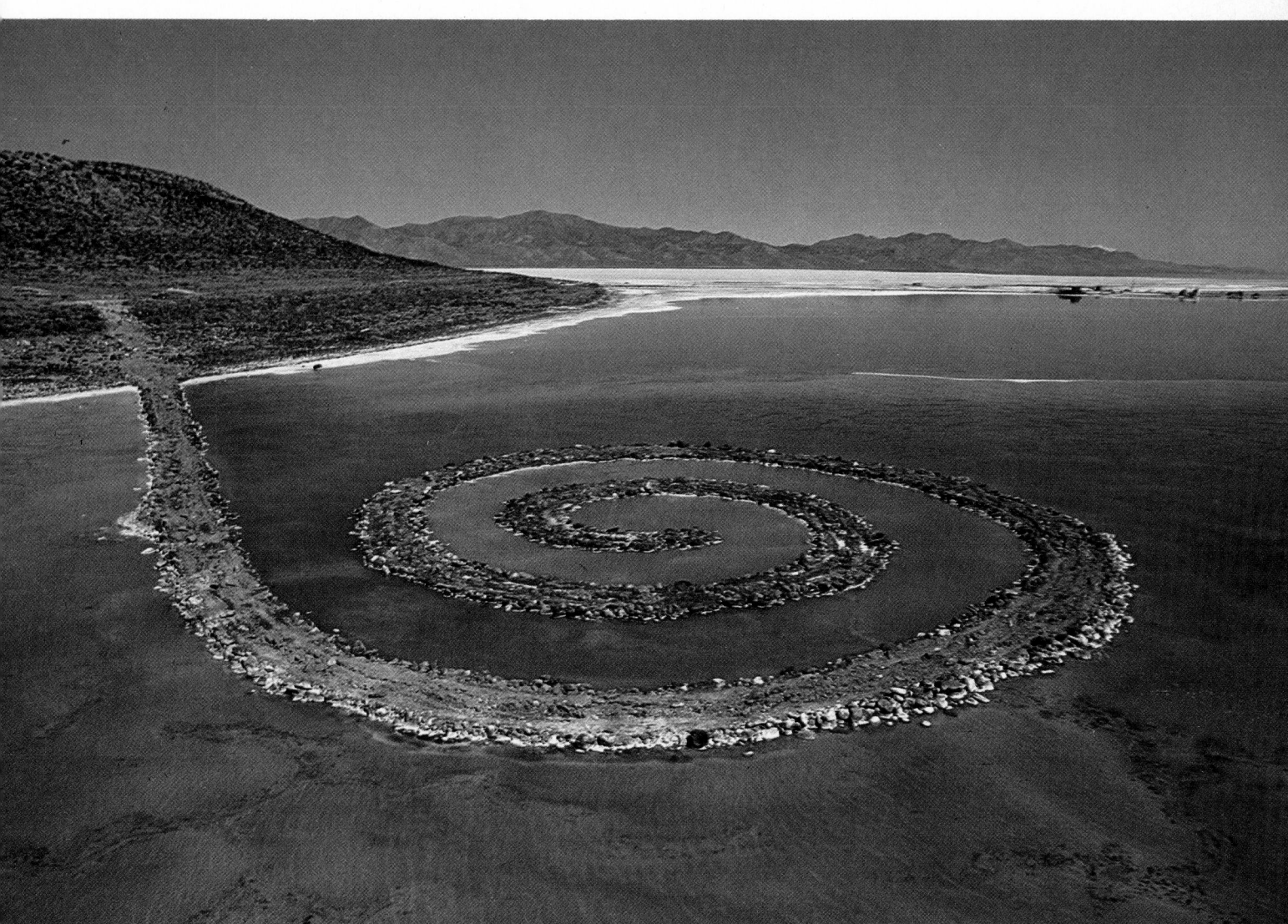

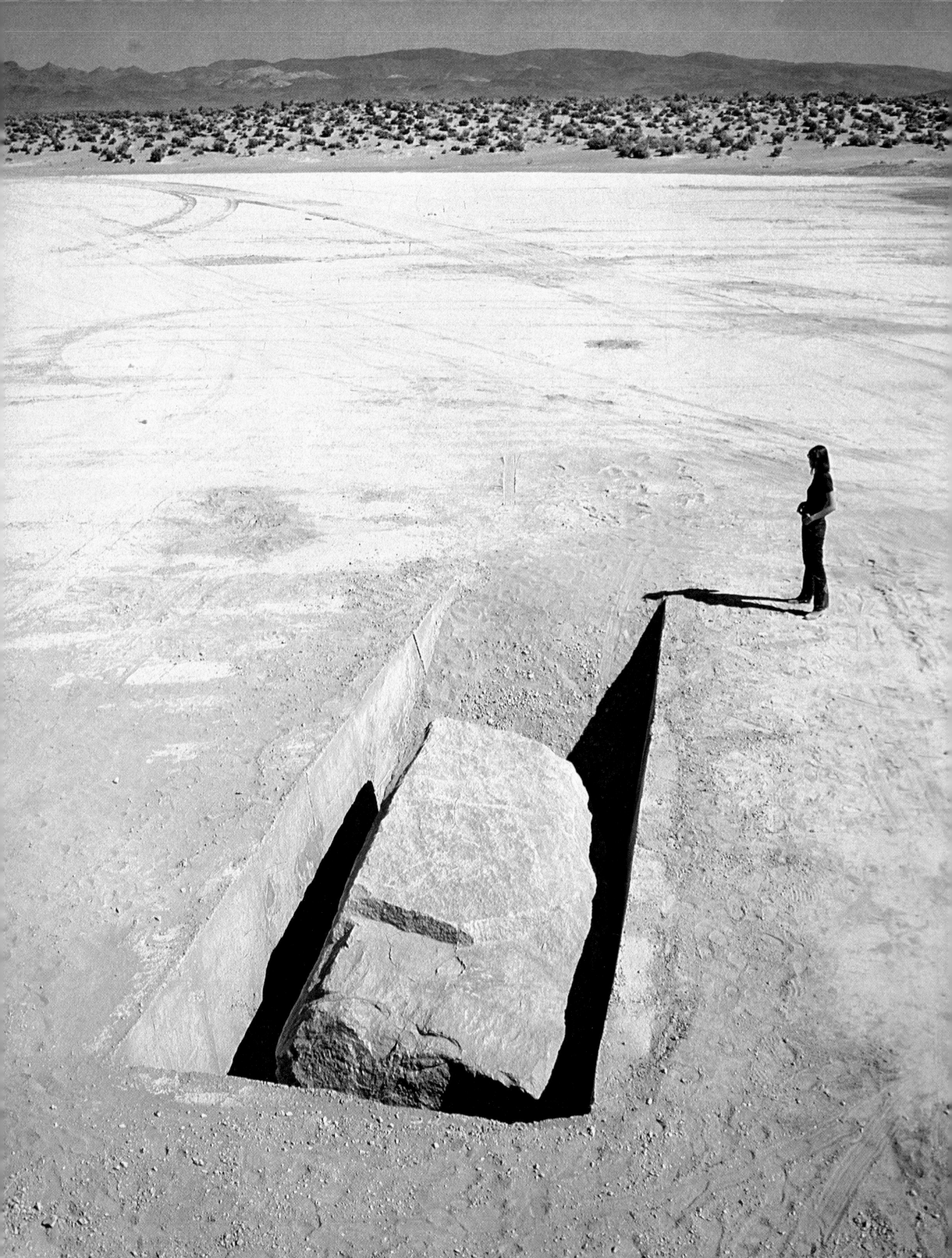

even though it is embodied in a relatively conventional format, in paint on canvas. The painting *Benches* (Plate 344) is a good example of his method of work.

It began with the chance purchase of a postcard at a railway station. The image, which showed people sitting on a bench, had a strong connection with mortality in the artist's mind because of a childhood recollection. This connection gave the main "subject" of the work. There are also connections with T. S. Eliot's *The Waste Land*, Dante's *Inferno*, and the Brahms *Requiem*—the artist and his wife sang in the choir when a recording of this work was made by Otto Klemperer. In addition to this, the vertical intervals in the work were determined by means of random coin-tossing procedures, and the conspicuous striped areas form a "colour-catalogue"

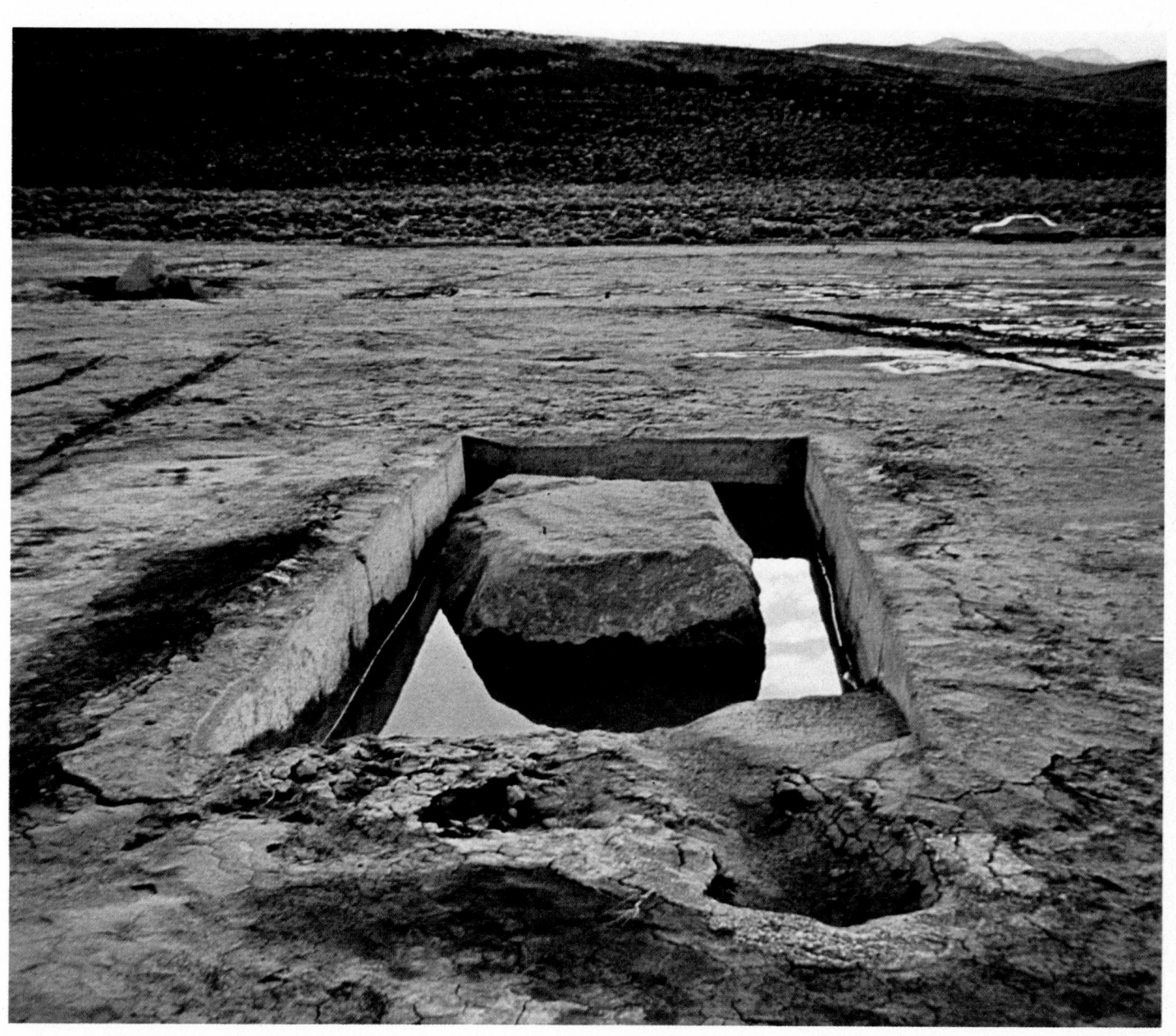

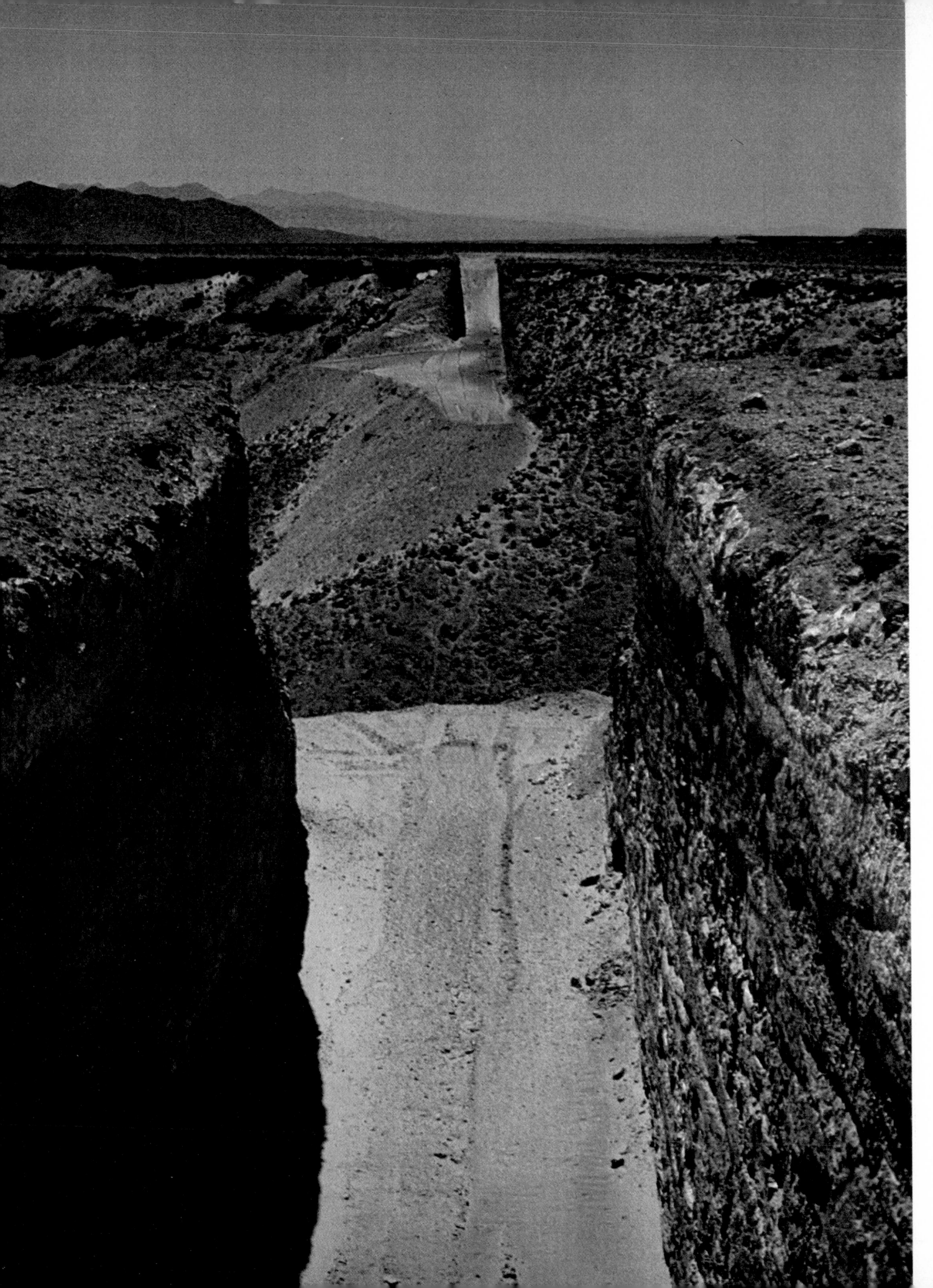

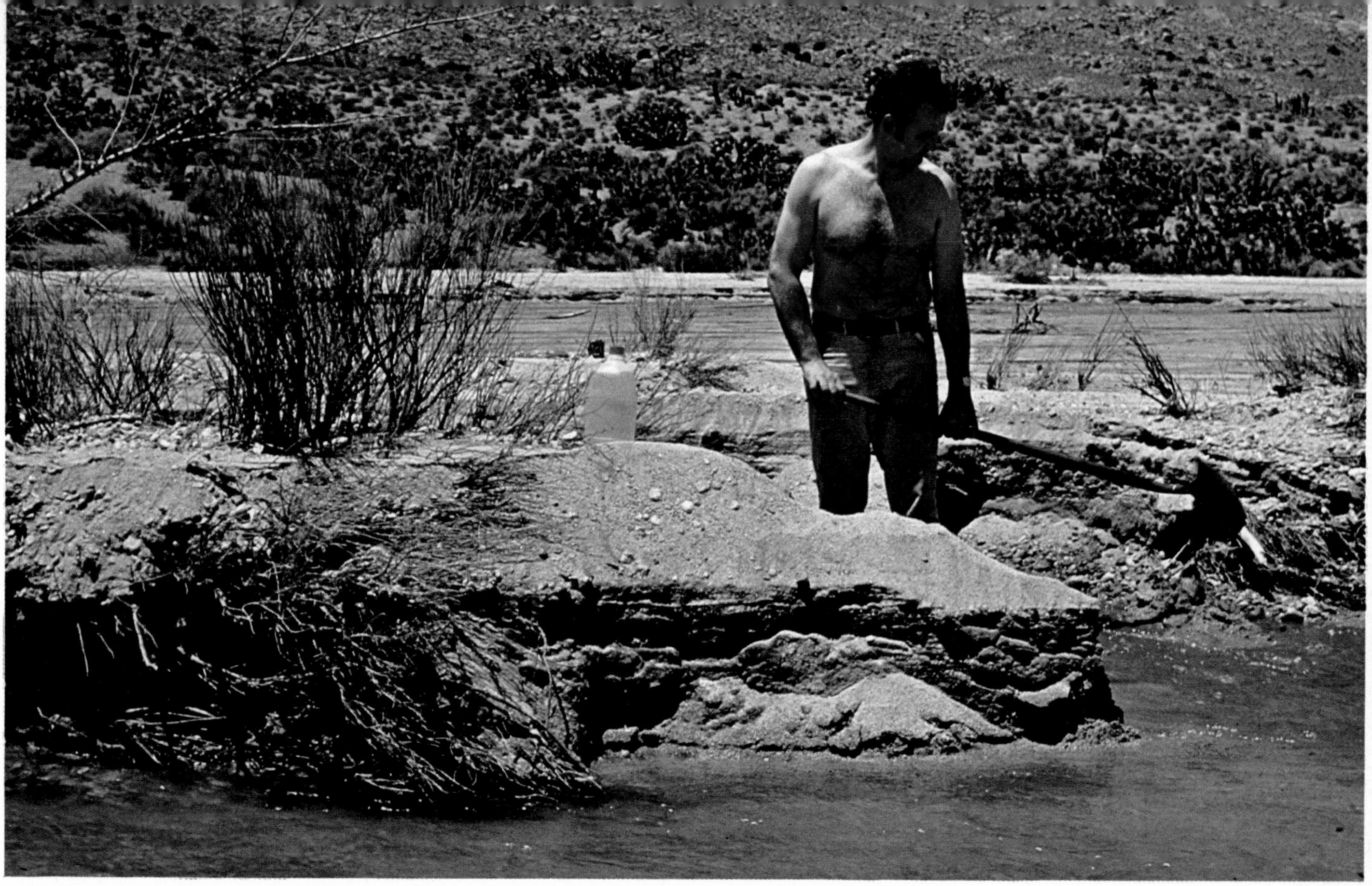

336. Above
Douglas Huebler
Location Piece No. 13
1969, in the desert twenty miles from Mojave, California
(Photo: Frederic Tuten)

337. Below
Walter de Maria
Las Vegas Piece
1969, in the desert of southern Nevada
By kind permission of the artist

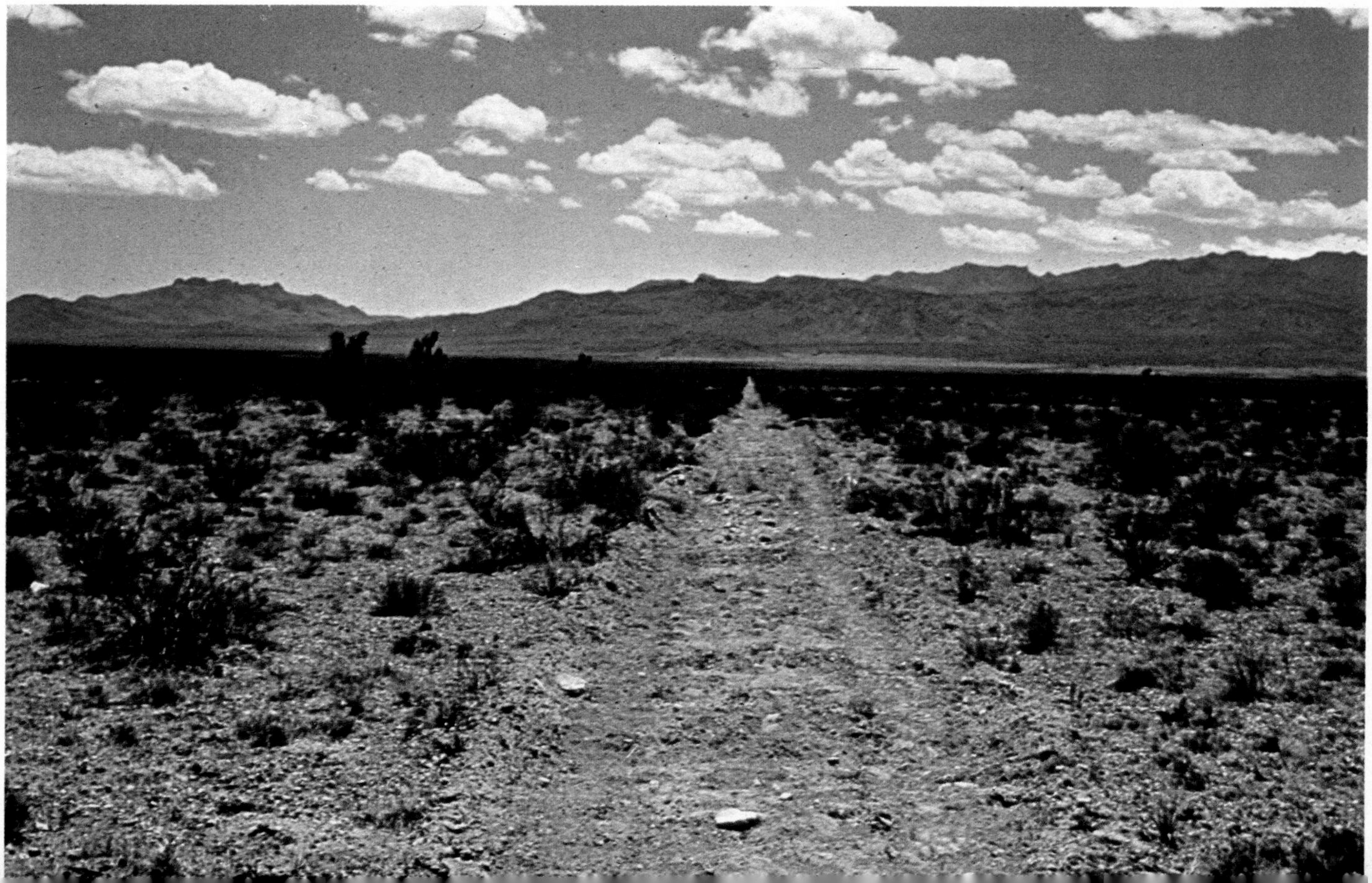

338.
Dennis Oppenheim
Branded Mountain
1969; 9.2 m. (30 ft.); San Pablo, California
By kind permission of the Sonnabend Gallery,
New York, Paris

of all the hues employed. The artist remarks: "A curious chicken/egg state of affairs subsisted in this picture and others with regard to the relation of stripes to image. The image generates the colours to fill the stripes; the stripes condition the procedure of painting the image" (Tom Phillips, *Works. Texts. To 1974*, Stuttgart, London, Reykjavik, 1975, p. 145).

Phillips perhaps differs from other artists in the conceptual field not so much because he sticks to a traditional means of expression—paint on canvas—but because he still clings to a humanist view of the artist's function: "What I most want the picture to do is what art has always done, to help people see the world; art continues as its main function (perhaps even more emphatically in the 20th century or with justified urgency) to lead people to see more of the world, more in the world; the natural and the man made; the spaces even that lie between things in the world, 'the

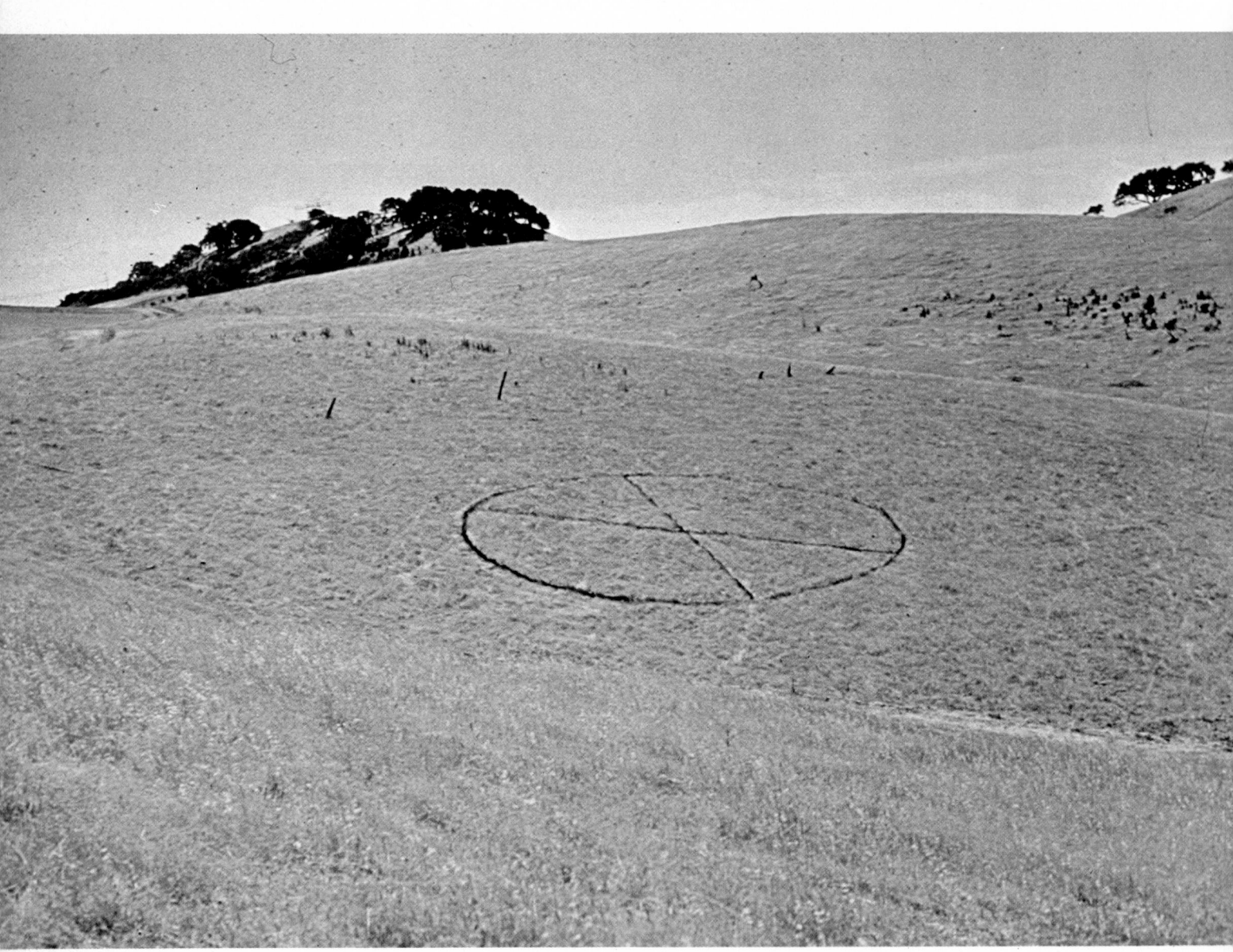

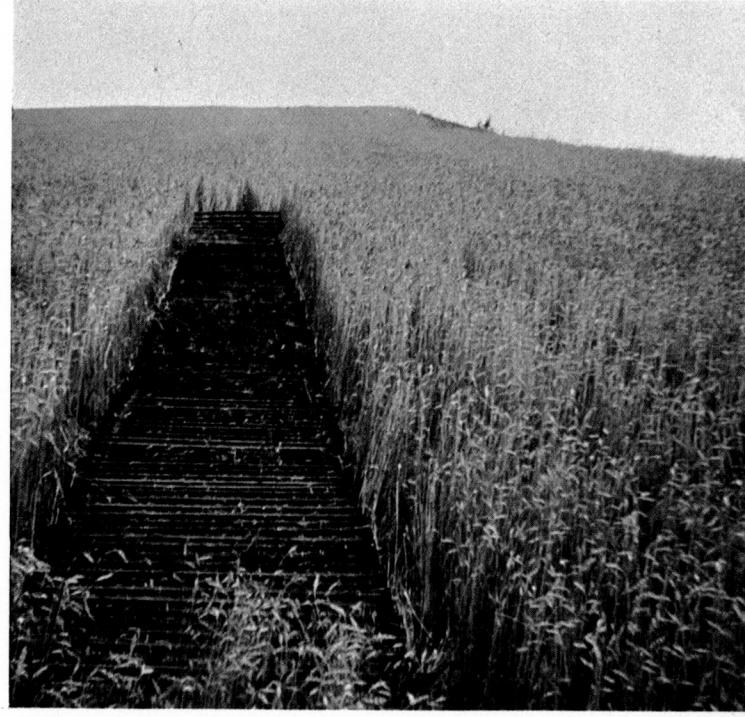

339.
Dennis Oppenheim
Surface Indentation
1968; 15.3 m. (50 ft.); Hamburg
By kind permission of the Sonnabend Gallery,
New York, Paris

atomic facts' (Wittgenstein) one by one.

"From this picture people may look at post-cards (and back to things), may look at benches, may examine the actions they perform and the ritual places of these actions and come to view them as metaphors" (ibid.).

One thing, nevertheless, that makes it appropriate to include *Benches* in a discussion of Concept Art is the heavy reliance upon inscriptions in addition to the images.

Though Concept Art stems very largely, as we have seen, from ideas that first took shape with the rise of Minimal sculpture, it also has an important link with Pop, since Pop was the first art movement to give such prominence to the inscription or incorporated caption. This habit derived in part from the advertisements and comic strips which Pop artists used as their raw material, and in part from the employment of letters and numerals by Jasper Johns.

With Pop Art, however, the word was still relatively subordinate—at any rate, it was not the whole of the work. With Shusaku Arakawa's *Look at It* (Plate 345) we reach a rather different situation. Here the verbal content of the painted diagram dominates the rest. Moreover, the work itself is about the correspondence, or lack of it, between what we see, how we see it, and how we verbalize our experience of what we have seen. The point is more brutally and less ambiguously put in Mel Bochner's *Language Is Not Transparent* (Plate 346), though here the hand-drawn lettering and the dripping of the background paint still keep us within touching distance of the physical world inhabited by Abstract Expressionist painting.

When we arrive at a work such as Joseph Kosuth's *Neon Electrical Light English Glass Letters* (Plate 347), it is reasonable to say that we have come to a point where the intellectual input is more important than any message the senses may happen to receive. Kosuth's piece is a tautology: it announces what it is, it is what it announces. The same is just as true, and perhaps truer, of Pier Paolo Calzolari's *Zero* (Plate 348), Stephen Kaltenbach's *Art Works* (Plate 268) and Alighiero Boetti's *Oro Longchamp 2 234 2288* (Plate 350). In varying degrees, and with a variable tone of irony,

they are all three of them statements of the self-evident.

Kosuth is one of the best informed, philosophically, of the artists working in his field, and his views may be regarded as authoritative. For him Conceptual Art is "An enquiry by artists that understand that artistic activity is not solely limited to the framing of art propositions, but further, the investigation of the function, meaning and use of any, and all (art) propositions, and their consideration within the concept of the general term 'art', and as well, that an artist's dependence on the critic or writer on art to cultivate the conceptual implications of his art propositions and argue their explication, is either intellectual irresponsibility or the naivest kind of mysticism" (Joseph Kosuth, in the catalogue of the "Information" exhibition, Museum of Modern Art, New York, 1970).

This amounts to saying that the critic, even in the role of auxiliary moralist (which is that claimed for him by Michael Fried), is now entirely superfluous. In another context, Kosuth has claimed that "The validity of artistic propositions

340.
Richard Serra
To Encircle: Base Plate (Hexagram)
1970; 7.9 m. (26 ft.)
Bronx, Webster Avenue and 183rd Street, New York

is not dependent on any empirical, much less any aesthetic, presupposition about the nature of things. For the artist, as an analyst, is not directly concerned with the physical properties of things. He is concerned only with the way (1) in which art is capable of conceptual growth and (2) how his propositions are capable of logically following that growth. In other words, the propositions of art are not factual, but linguistic in *character*—that is, they do not describe the behaviour of physical, or even mental objects; they express definitions of art, or the formal consequences of definitions of art" (Joseph Kosuth, "Art After Philosophy", in Ursula Meyer, *Conceptual Art*, p. 165).

A comment made by the veteran critic Harold Rosenberg arguably provides an appropriate marginal note to this particular declaration: "To qualify as a member of the art public, an individual must be tuned to the appropriate verbal reverberation of objects in art galleries, and his

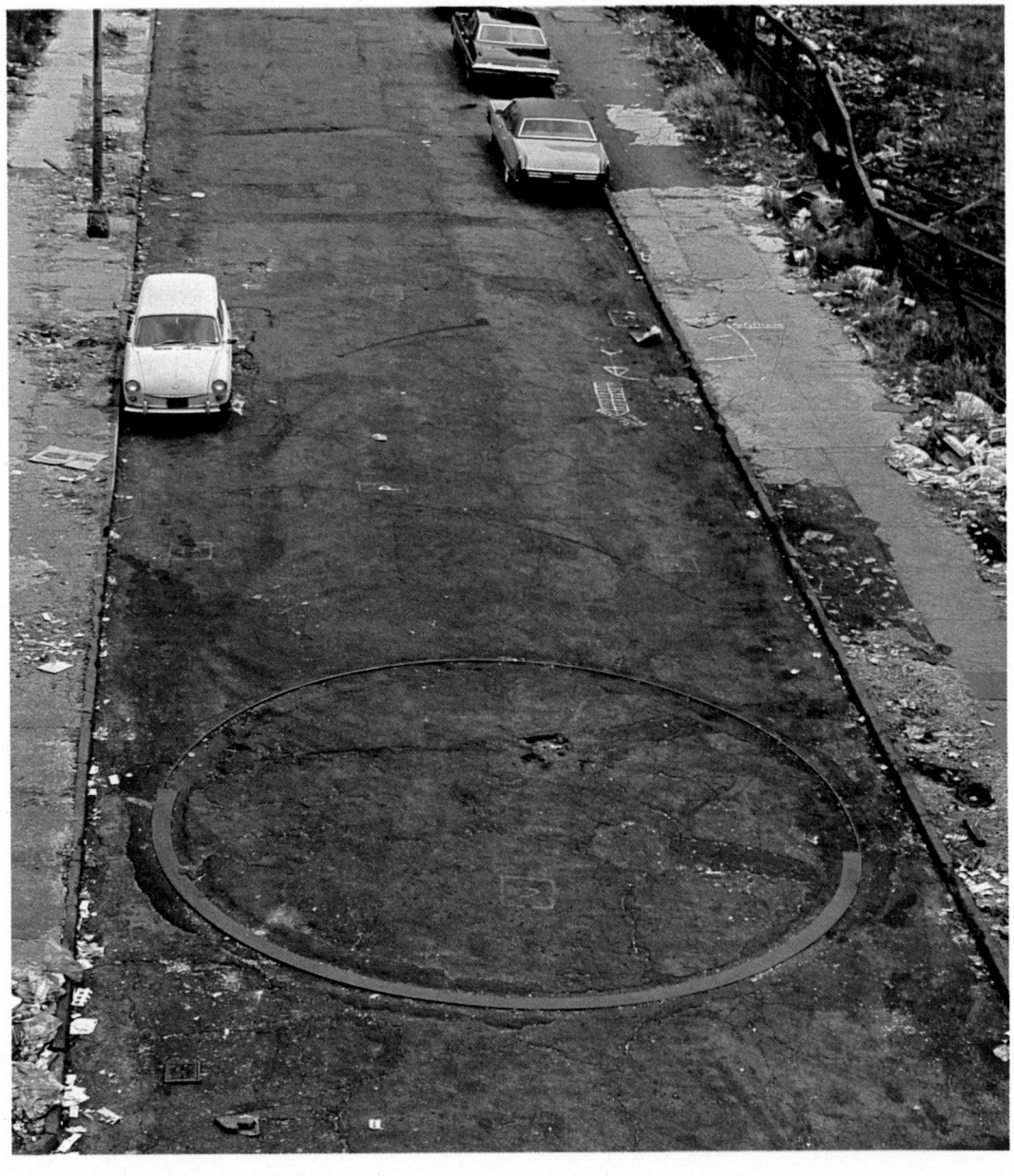

341.
Wolf Kahlen
Baum-Raumsegment
1970, Monschau
By kind permission of the artist

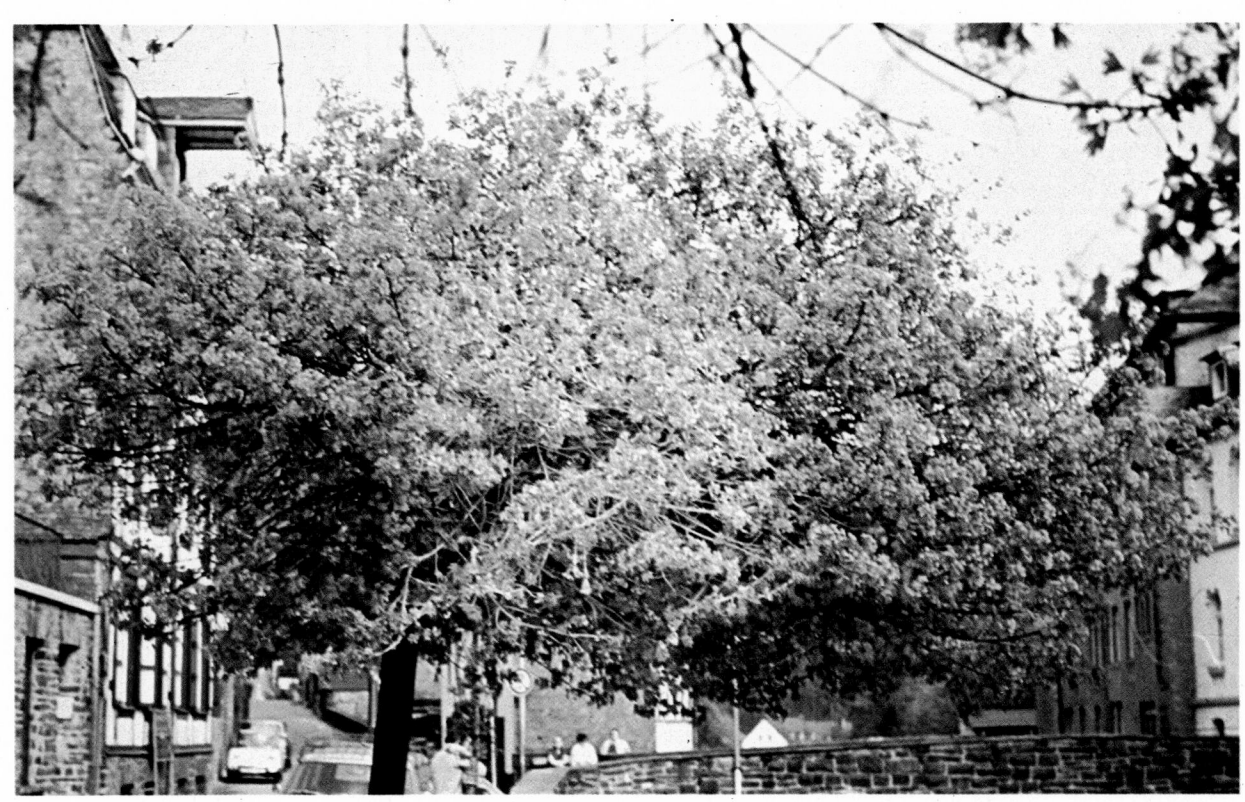

receptive mechanism must be constantly adjusted to oscillate to new vocabularies" (Harold Rosenberg, "Art and Words", in *Idea Art*, edited by Gregory Battcock, New York, 1973, pp. 153–4).

As it happens, the examples of Concept Art that have already been mentioned are by no means the "purest" available. For Mario Merz, various mathematical demonstrations and propositions can be art—for example, *610 Functions of 15* (Plate 351). Merz has spent a number of years exploring the possibilities of the Fibonacci series, discovered by a monk of the same name during the Middle Ages. This series is a progression obtained by adding 1 to 2, 2 to 3, 3 to 5, 5 to 8, and so on. Reduced to geometrical terms, the series defines a perfect spiral—precisely defined and yet open.

Hans Haacke, a German artist who lives in the United States, has interested himself in systems both inorganic and organic (Plate 352, *Chickens Hatching*), and he has also interested himself in social and political phenomena. In 1970, he conducted a poll of visitors to the Museum of Modern Art in New York, concerning the attitude taken by the then governor of New York, Nelson Rockefeller, towards the war in Vietnam (Plate 353).

More neutral presentations of research as art are the projects undertaken by the husband-and-wife team Bernhard and Hilde Becher, who make photographic documentations of items of anonymous industrial architecture, such as watertowers (Plates 354 and 355).

Finally, there are Concept Art "pieces" which consist of statements only, in which the movements of the mind alone constitute the "art" experience. The following, by Donald Burgy, may serve as an example:

"*Name Idea No. 1*

"Observe something as it changes in time. Record its names.

"Observe something as it changes in scale. Record its names.

"Observe something as it changes in hierarchy. Record its names.

431

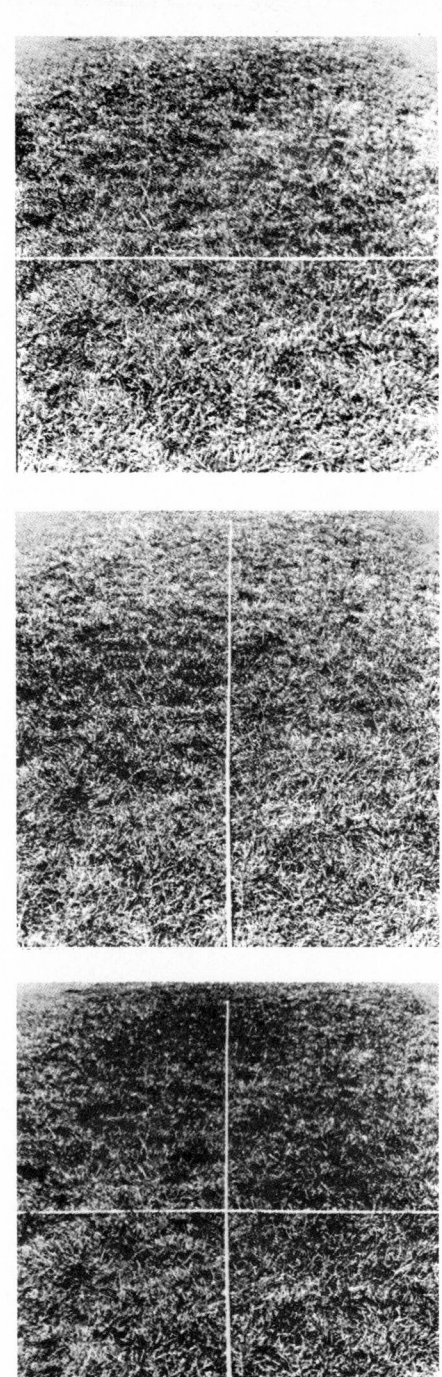

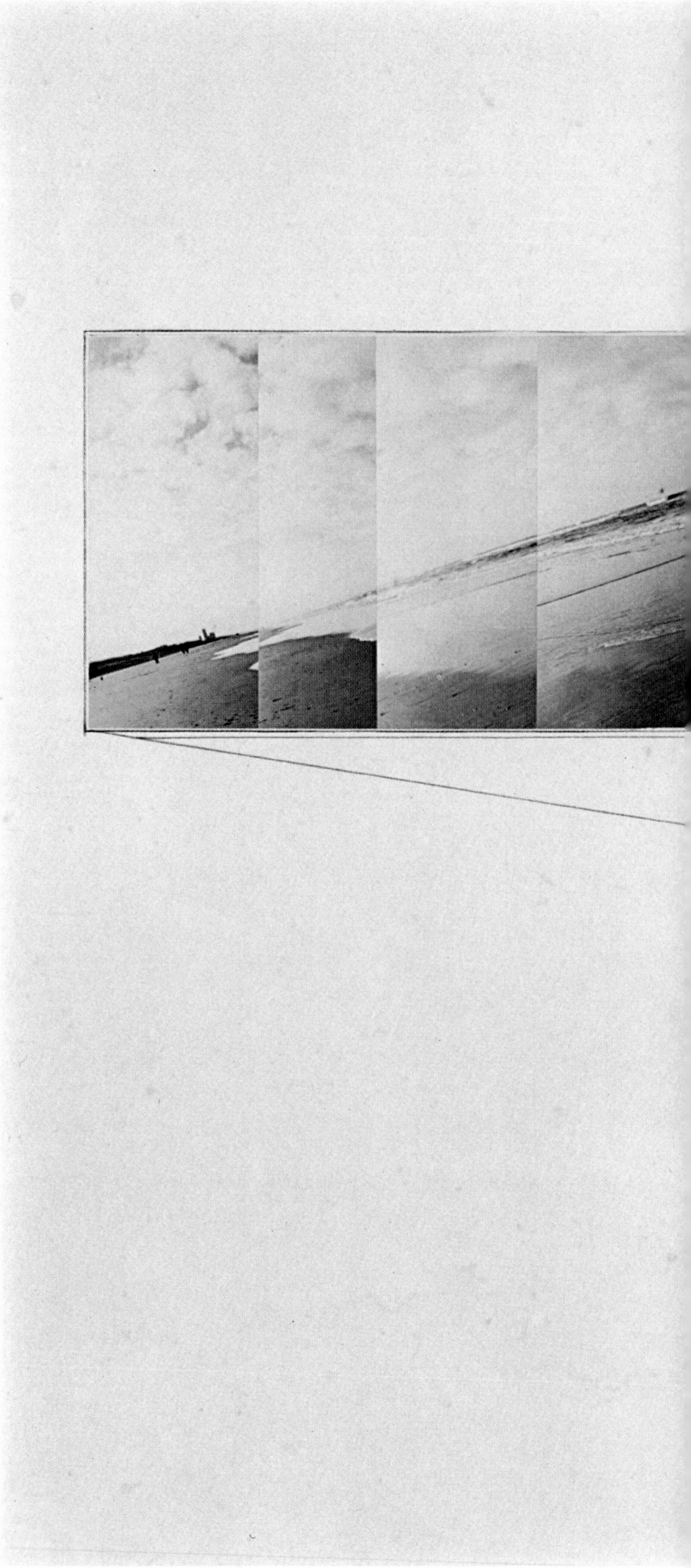

342.
Jan Dibbets
The Perspective Correction: Horizontal, Vertical, Cross
1968; 120 × 120 cm. (47 × 47 in.)

343. Opposite
Jan Dibbets
Panorama with Mountain, Sea II A
London, Tate Gallery

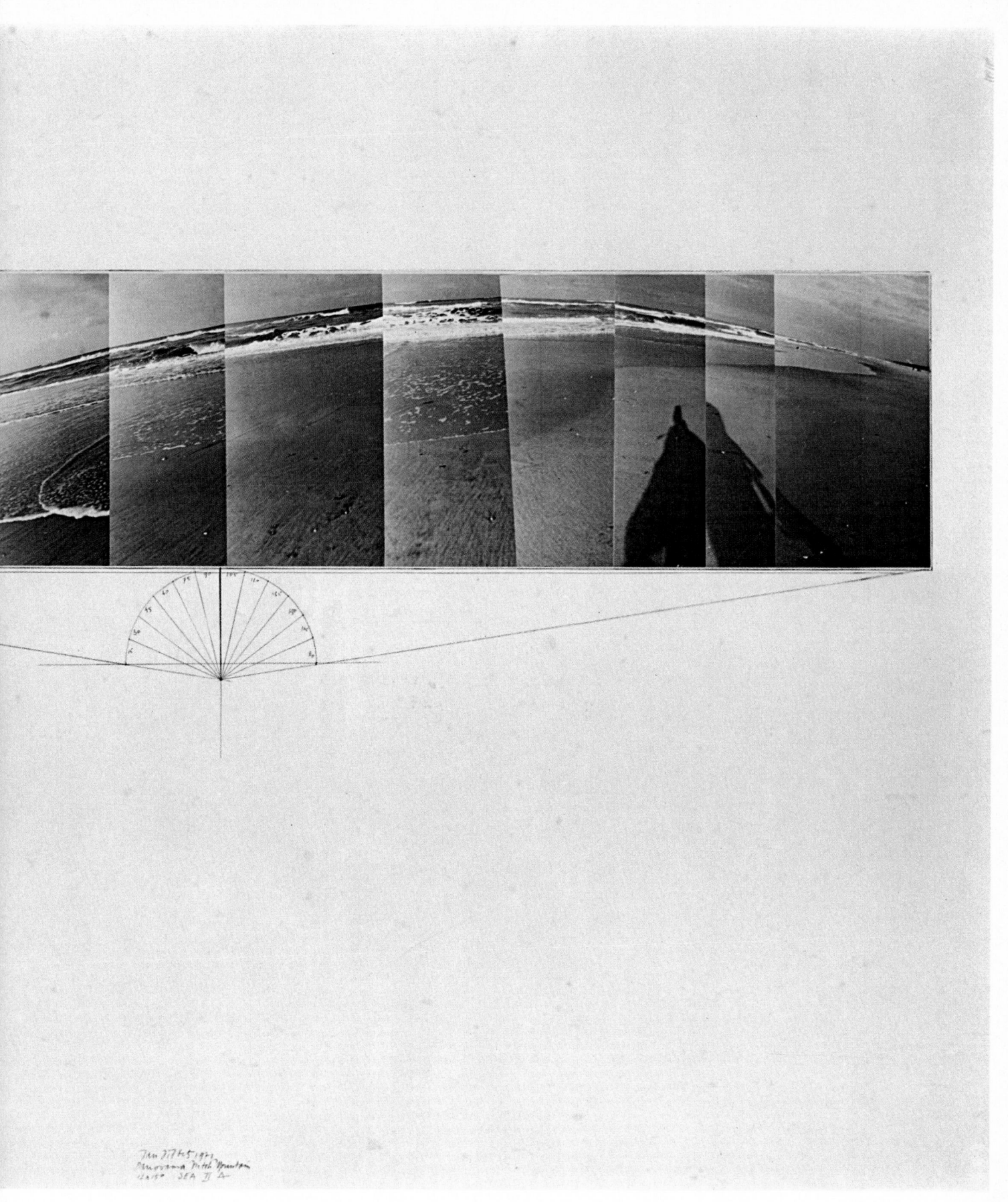

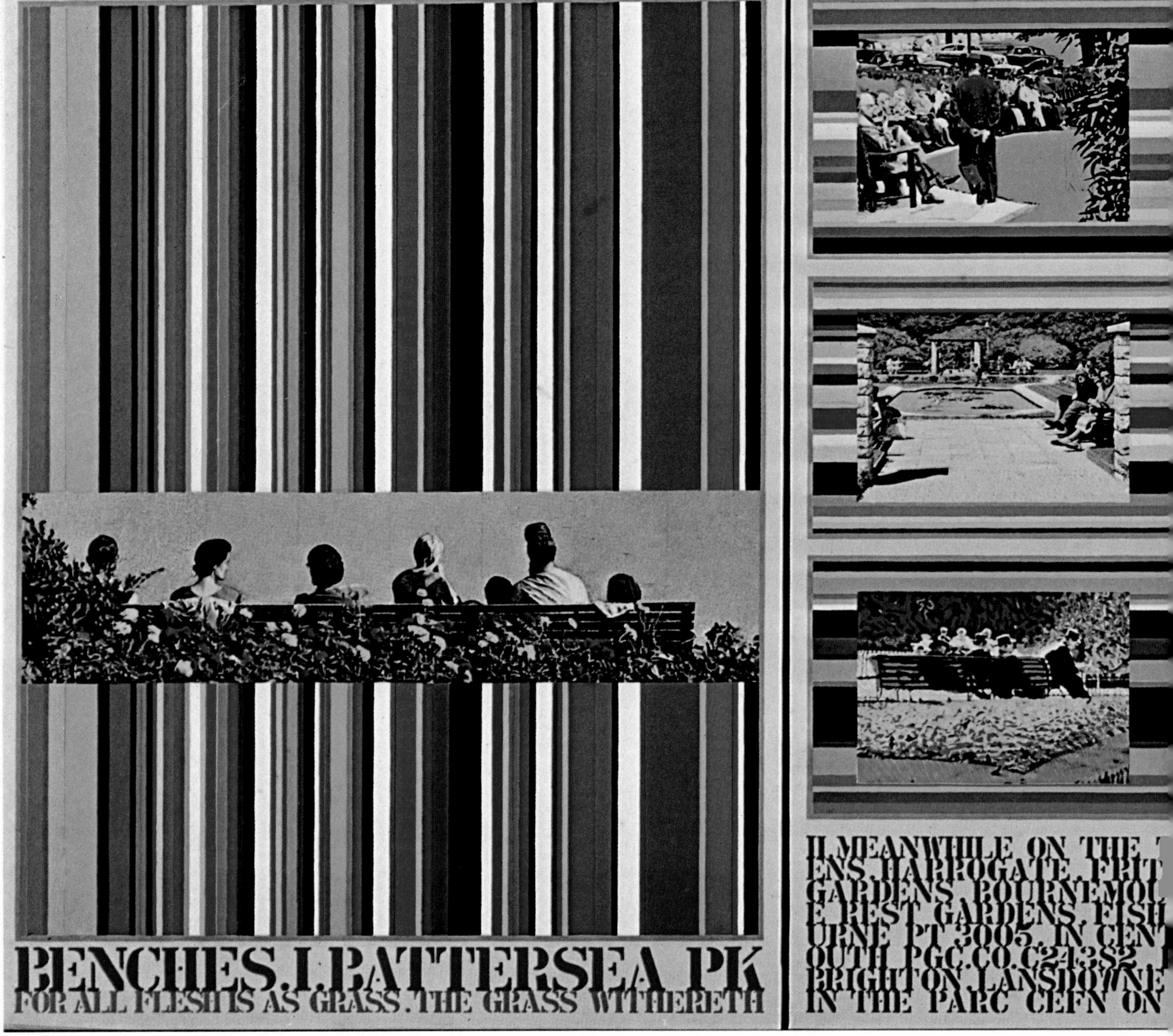

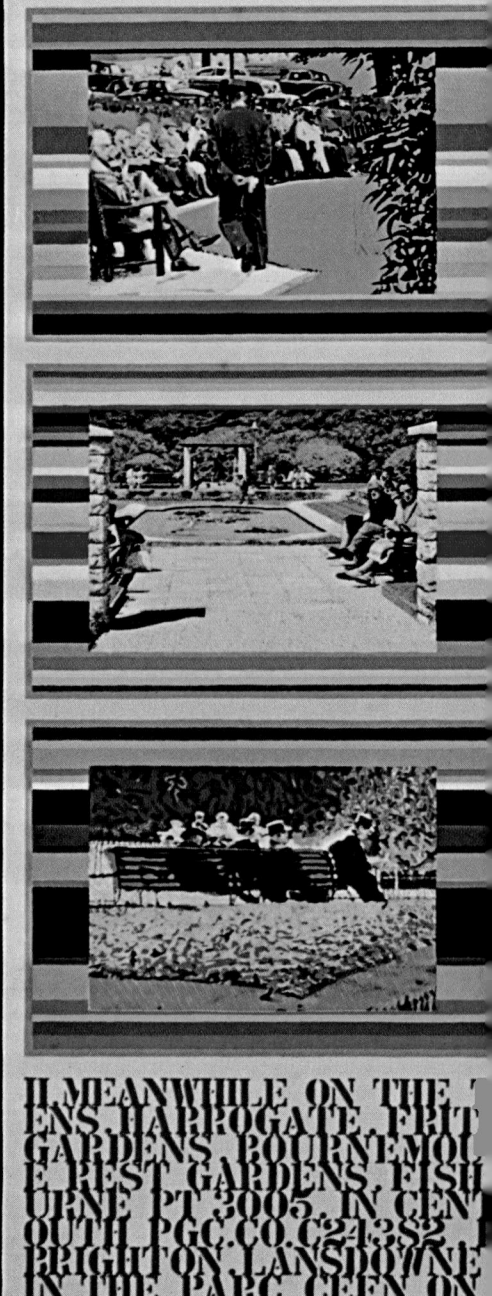

BENCHES. I. BATTERSEA PK
FOR ALL FLESH IS AS GRASS. THE GRASS WITHERETH

II MEANWHILE ON THE I
ENS HARROGATE FH T
GARDENS BOURNEMOU
E REST GARDENS FISH
URNE PT 8005 IN CEN
OUTH PGC CO C 2438 2
BRIGHTON LANSDOWNE
IN THE PARC CEFN ON

Tom Phillips
Benches
London, Tate Gallery (Photo: John Webb)

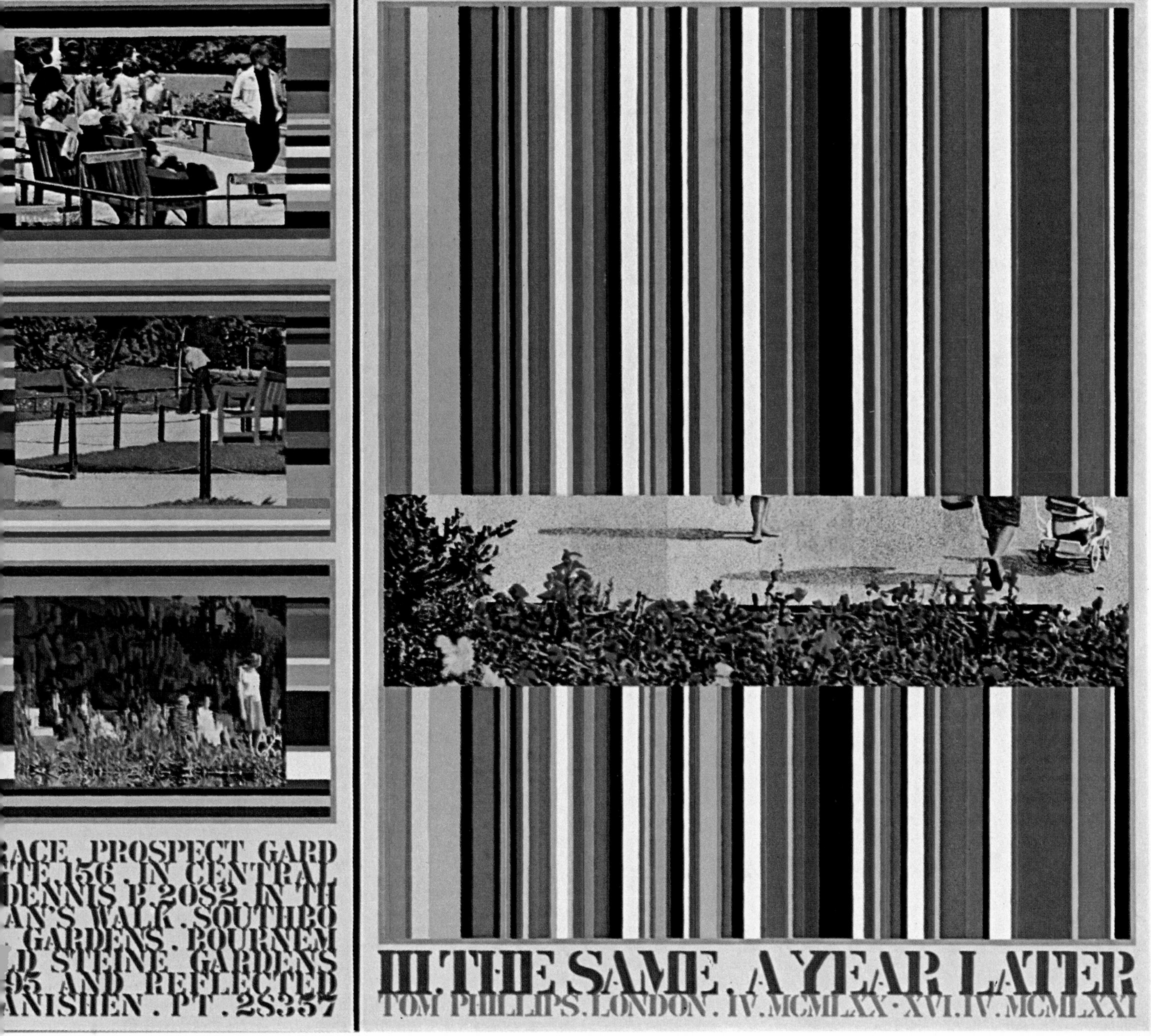

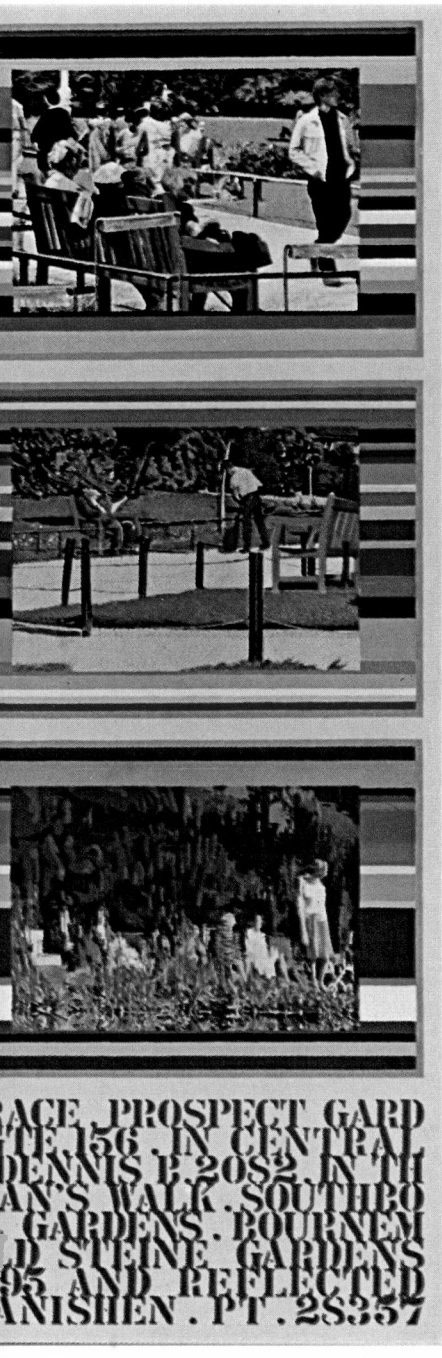

345.
Shusaku Arakawa
Look at It
1968; 91 × 122 cm. (35 × 48 in.)
Tokyo, Minami Gallery

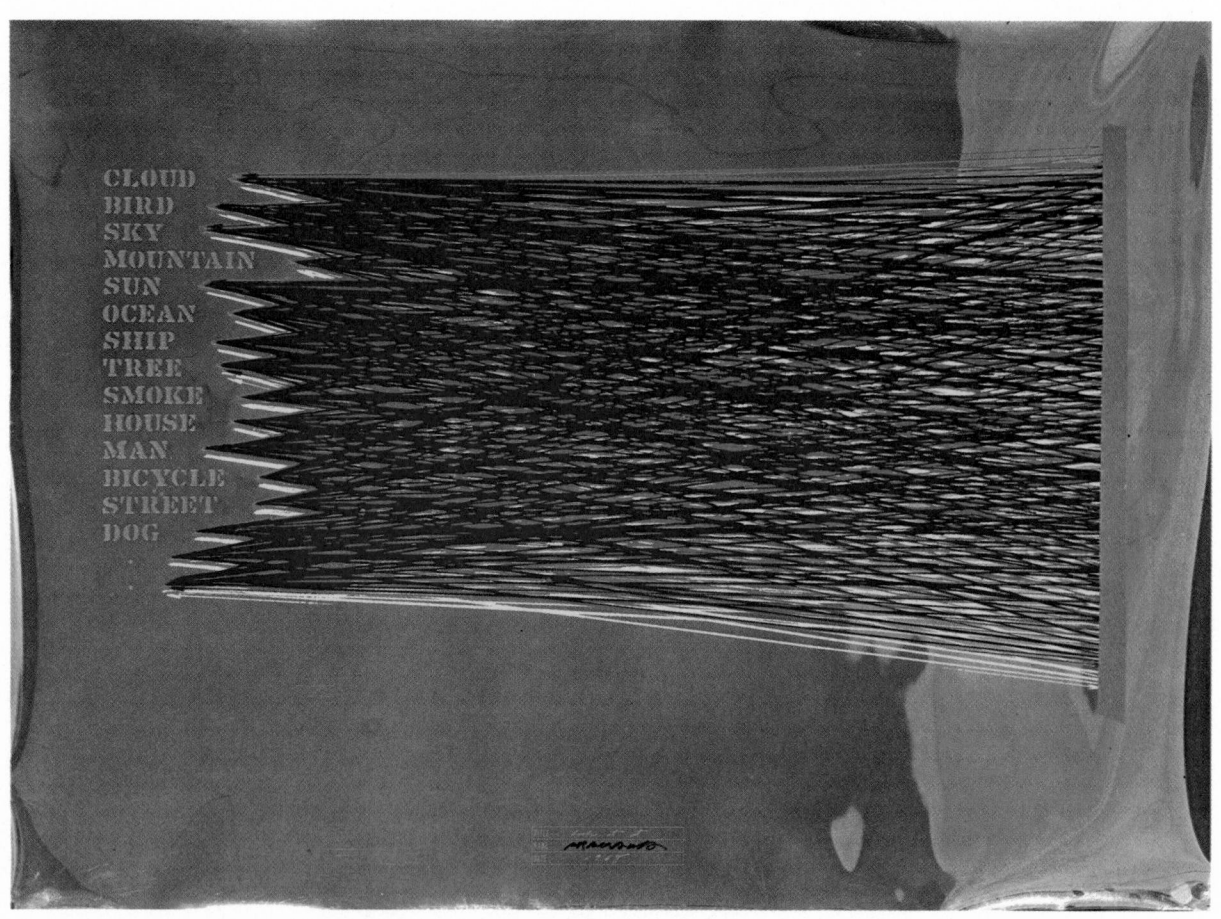

"Observe something as it changes in differentiation. Record its names.

"Observe something as it changes under different emotions. Record its names.

"Observe something as it changes in different languages. Record its names.

"Observe something which never changes. Record its names.

"September, 1969" (from Ursula Meyer, *Conceptual Art*, New York, 1972, p. 90).

The apparent impersonality of Concept Art does, nevertheless, conceal a paradox which is not as apparent as it might be from the instances which have so far been given. This paradox is related to the way in which Concept focuses upon the person and personality of the artist. If the art work as such is abolished, then attention turns to the person who, despite this, claims to possess or embody the notion of art.

In one way this is an intensification of something that has already been going on for a long time. Abstract Expressionism asked the spectator to focus his intention upon the psyche of the artist, which was reflected in the turbulent swirls of paint. The act of painting the picture—the processes whereby it came about—was thus of equal interest to the finished result, or perhaps even more interesting. Increasingly, during the years that followed, art came to be thought of as being essentially a record of its own making. The work of Tom Phillips, discussed in this chapter, is an excellent example of so-called process art, in which one of the main aims of the artist is to supply, actually within what has been done, a full history of the work from its inception to its completion.

When the artist enacts rituals rather than creating objects, logically the process of making

436

346.
Mel Bochner
Language Is Not Transparent
1970; 195.6 × 127 cm. (76 × 50 in.)
New York, by kind permission of the Dwan Gallery

347. Below
Joseph Kosuth
Neon Electrical Light English Glass Letters
1966
Varese, coll. G. Panza di Biumo

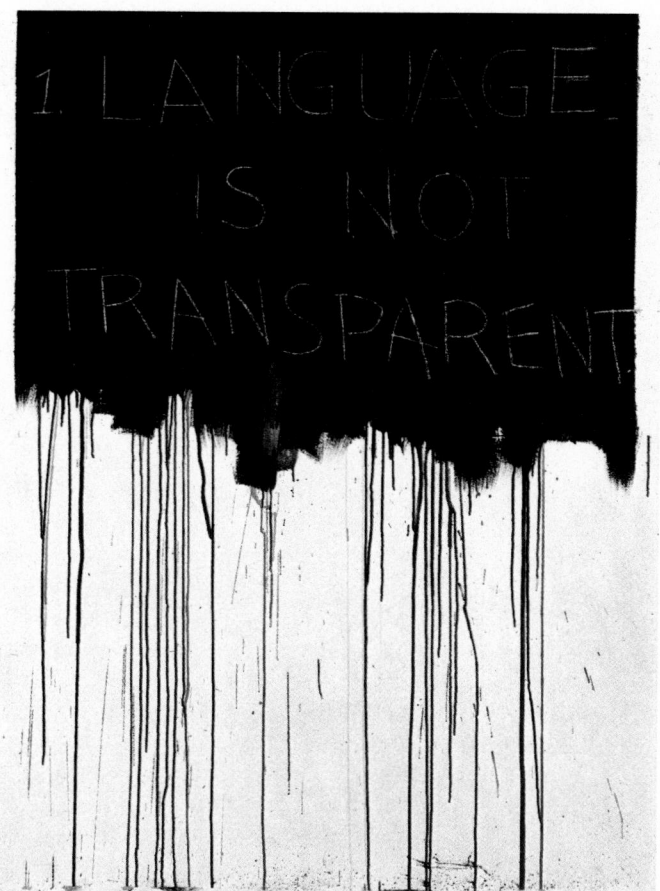

art manifests itself directly in, as well as through, him. An almost ludicrously simple example of what I mean can be found in some of the activities of Dennis Oppenheim. Oppenheim's *Reading Position for a Second Degree Burn* demonstrates how the artist deliberately inflicted a bad sunburn upon himself (Plate 356). The open book used to protect the unburnt area of skin is significantly entitled *Tactics*. Oppenheim says that, for him, what is now labelled Body Art arose directly from his involvement with Earth Art: "My concern for the Body came from constant physical contact with large bodies of land. This demands an echo from the artist's body. Now I'm doing microscopic slides of skin tissue: the focus is becoming more and more intimate. It fascinates me how the body changes under different stimuli and pressures" (Dennis Oppenheim, quoted by Douglas Davis in *Newsweek*, May 25, 1970).

Another artist associated with Body Art is Bruce Nauman. His *Bound To Fail* (Plate 357) is an exemplification of a statement of intent made in a leading art magazine: "Examination of physical or psychological response to simple or even over-simplified situations which can yield clearly experienceable phenomena" (Bruce Nauman,

348.
Pier Paolo Calzolari
Zero
1970
Paris, by kind permission of the Sonnabend Gallery
New York, Paris

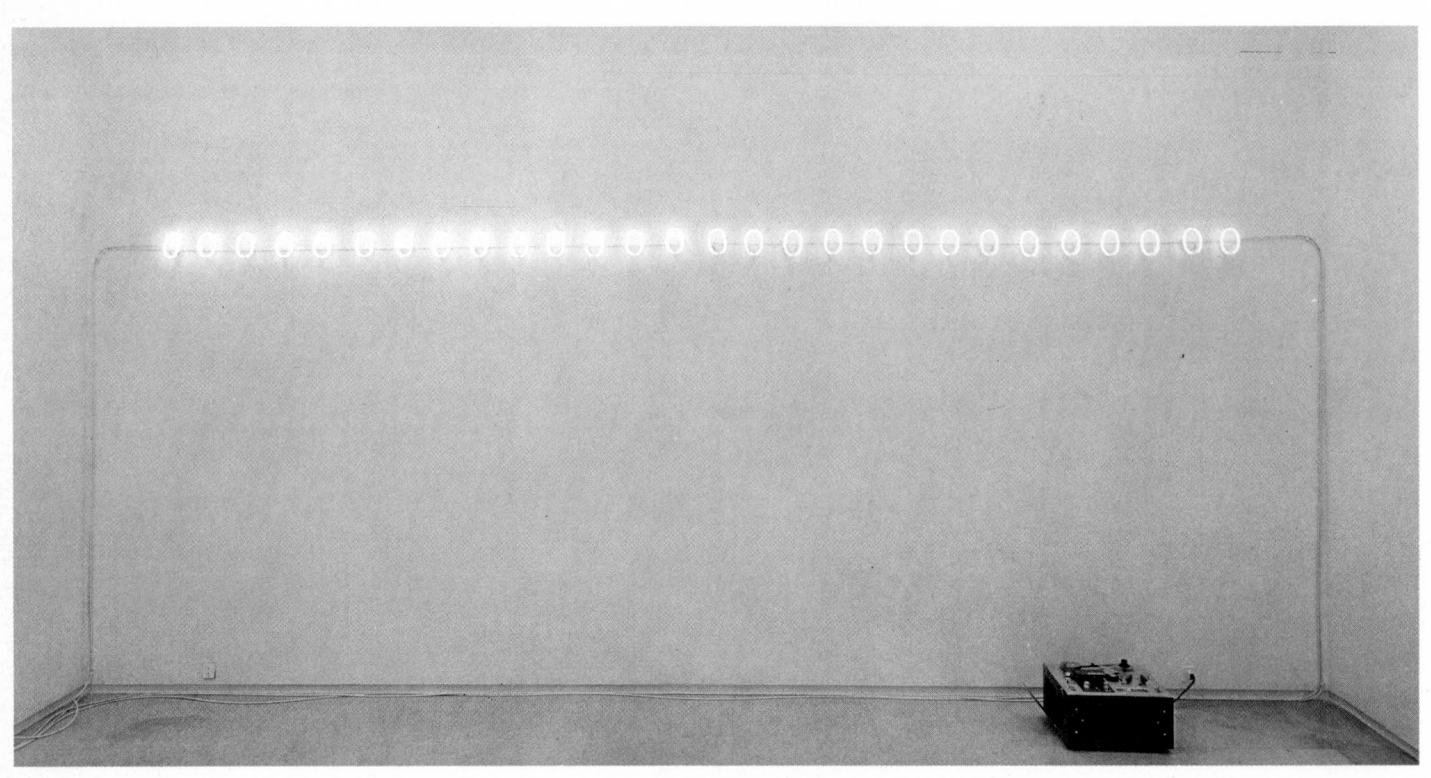

349. Below left
Stephen James Kaltenbach
Art Works
1968; by kind permission of the artist

350. Right
Alighiero Boetti
Oro Longchamp 2 234 2288
1967–70; 72 × 72 cm. (28 × 28 in.)
Rome, by kind permission of the Galleria Sperone

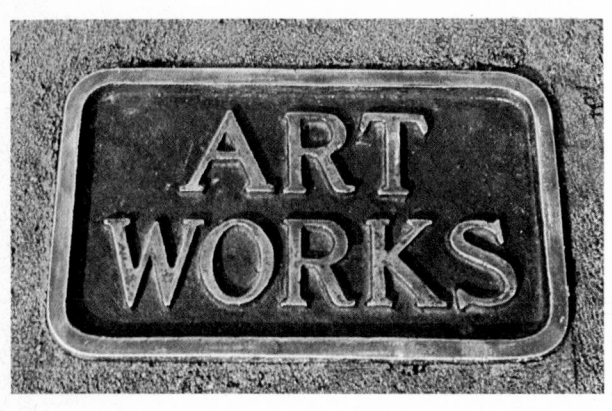

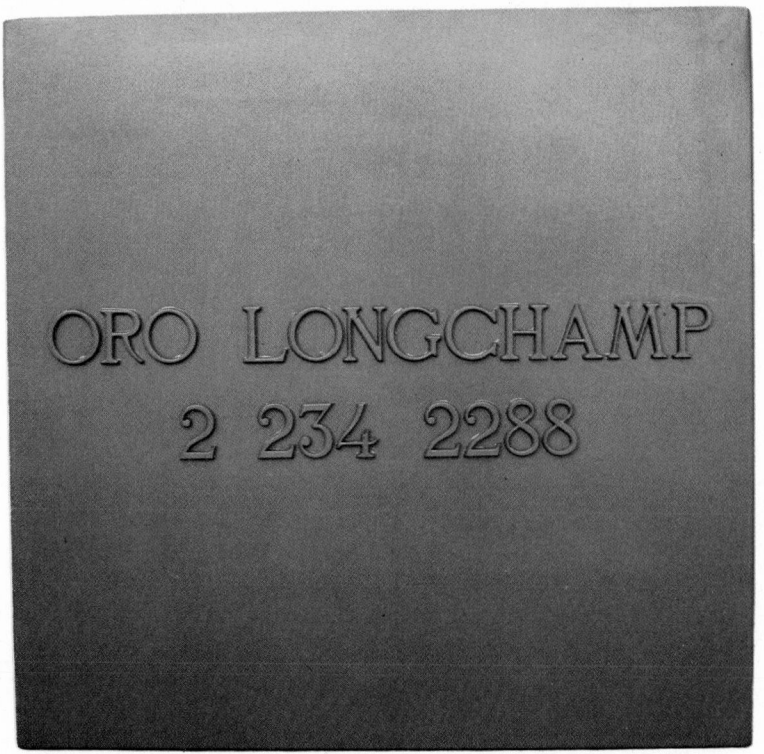

351.
Mario Merz
610 functions of 15
1971; 345 × 157 × 57 cm. (135 × 61 × 22 in.)
New York, John Weber Gallery

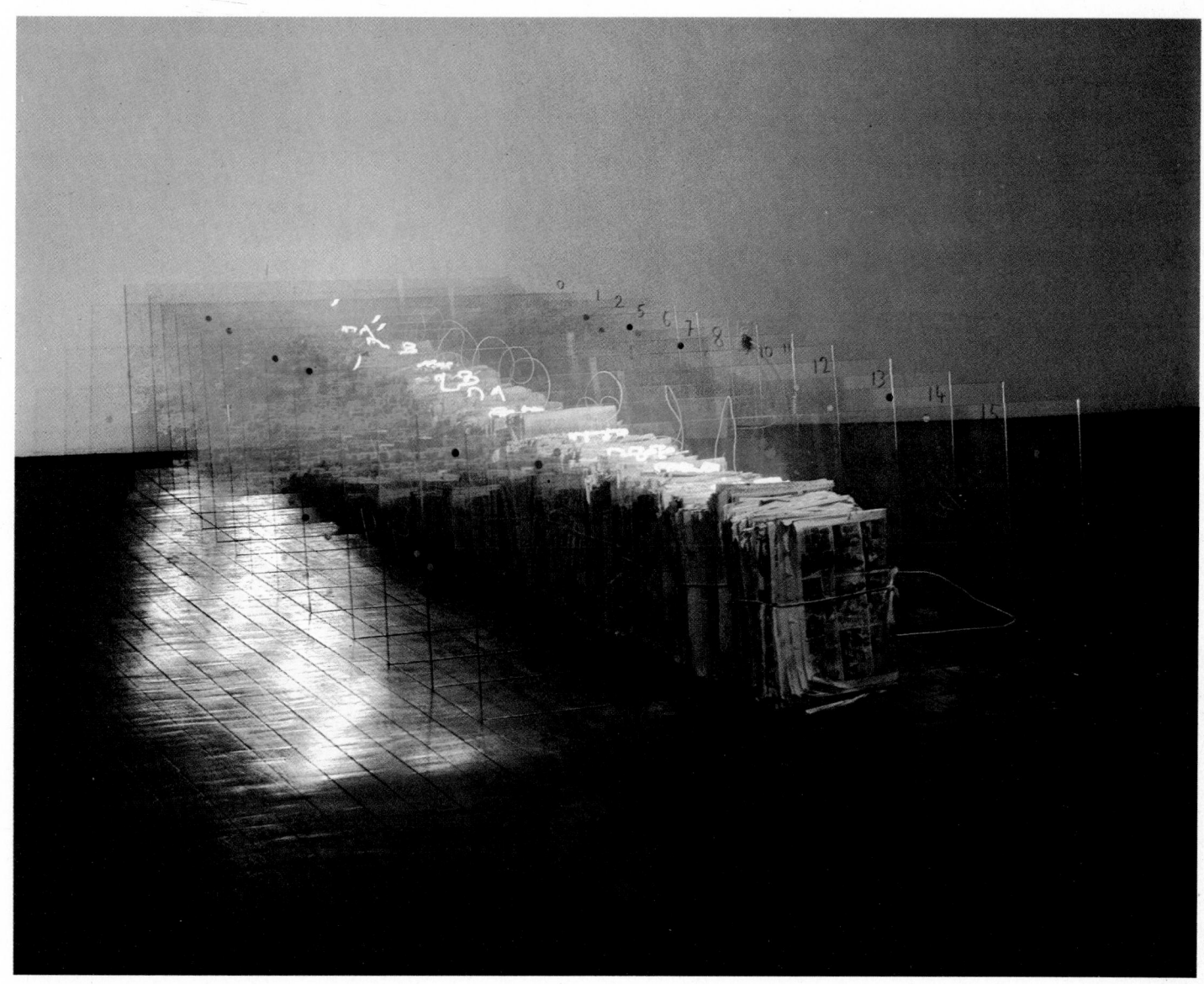

"Notes and Projects", *Artforum*, December, 1970).

It has been said of Nauman that his true originality lies not in the invention of one language but of various languages, that he is interested in all the different and overlapping ways in which a given thing can be expressed: "Being 'invented', these forms of language are the result of an 'unconscious choice'. They are exclusive of other forms of language and might be adequate only in one kind of environment. By slightly altering this environment, Nauman makes evident the inadequacies of our forms of language and forces us to find new systems of relationships with a changing reality" (Grégoire Müller, *The New Avant-Garde*, London, 1972, p. 22).

In the light of this interpretation, *Bound to Fail* might be said to be "about" the gap between the three words which form the title and what is shown in the picture.

There is obviously a close connection between Body Art and the Happening. Some of Stuart Brisley's "actions" might be interpreted as belonging simultaneously to both categories. But

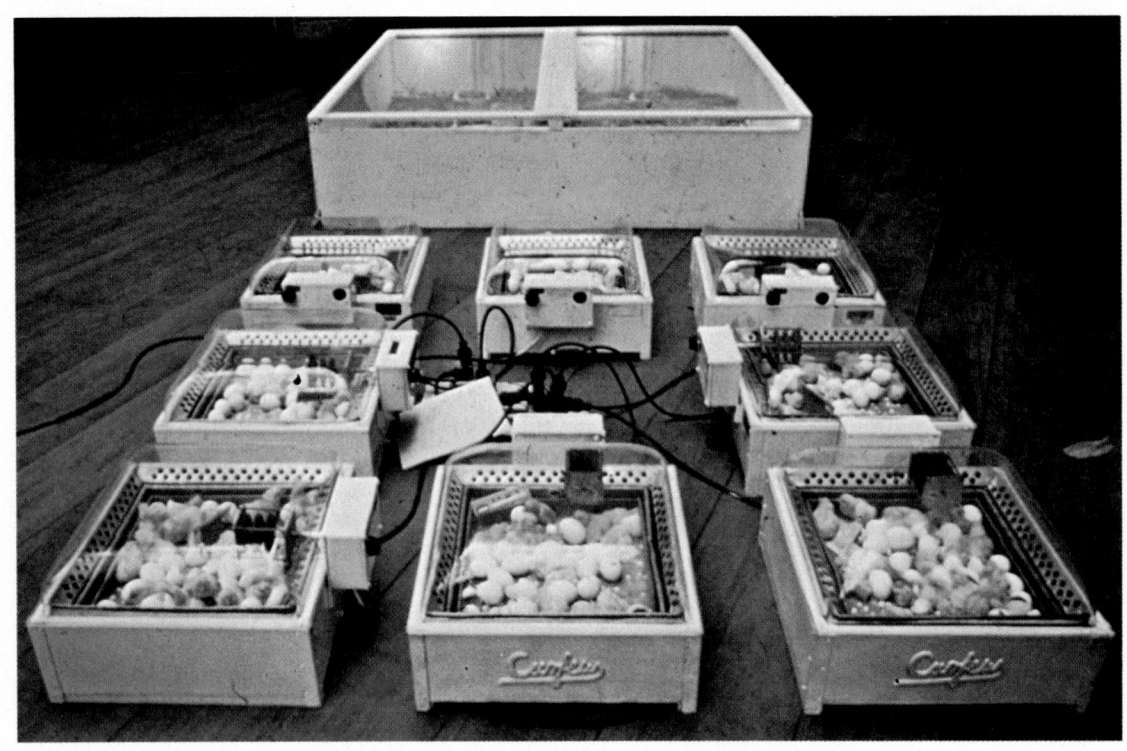

other questions also arise. One of the most interesting of these is "What happens when the artist insists on being continuously not only an artist, but actually art?" Some members of the avant-garde wish us to think of every detail of their existence as being part of a continuously evolving work. Perhaps the best instances of this are the two Englishmen Gilbert & George.

Gilbert & George operate through an organization called Art for All. Much of their material goes out through the mail. A typical specimen of one of their cards is *A Sculpture Sample Entitled Sculptors' Samples* (Plate 358). The artists send physical mementos of themselves—hair, clothing, food—and give us to understand that this is "sculpture" and also a series of excerpts from a larger and more complex work: Gilbert & George themselves, continuing their quotidian existence. The boundary between art and life has been summarily abolished.

For this reason one cannot speak of Gilbert & George as artists who fit into any particular category—all categories have been rendered

nonexistent by their basic aesthetic premise. At one moment they are performers, miming to a record of the music-hall song "Underneath the Arches". At another they are painters in the most thoroughly conventional and Victorian way, with a series of self-portraits of themselves in sylvan settings, entitled *Ourselves in the Nature*. At yet another they are making videotapes, or are happy to allow some aspect of their daily existence to be recorded by a camera. As far as the artists are concerned, all of these, however diverse they may seem, are still "sculpture" (Plates 359 and 360). It shows how far the meaning of the word has now been stretched.

If Gilbert & George have attained not only considerable reputations within the avant-garde but even a certain celebrity outside it, it is probably because they inject an element of sly humour into almost everything they do. This makes them acceptable as the successors of the Pop artists who flourished in the Sixties. In particular, they seem to have inherited Hockney's mantle of glamour, his ability to associate with the fashionable world

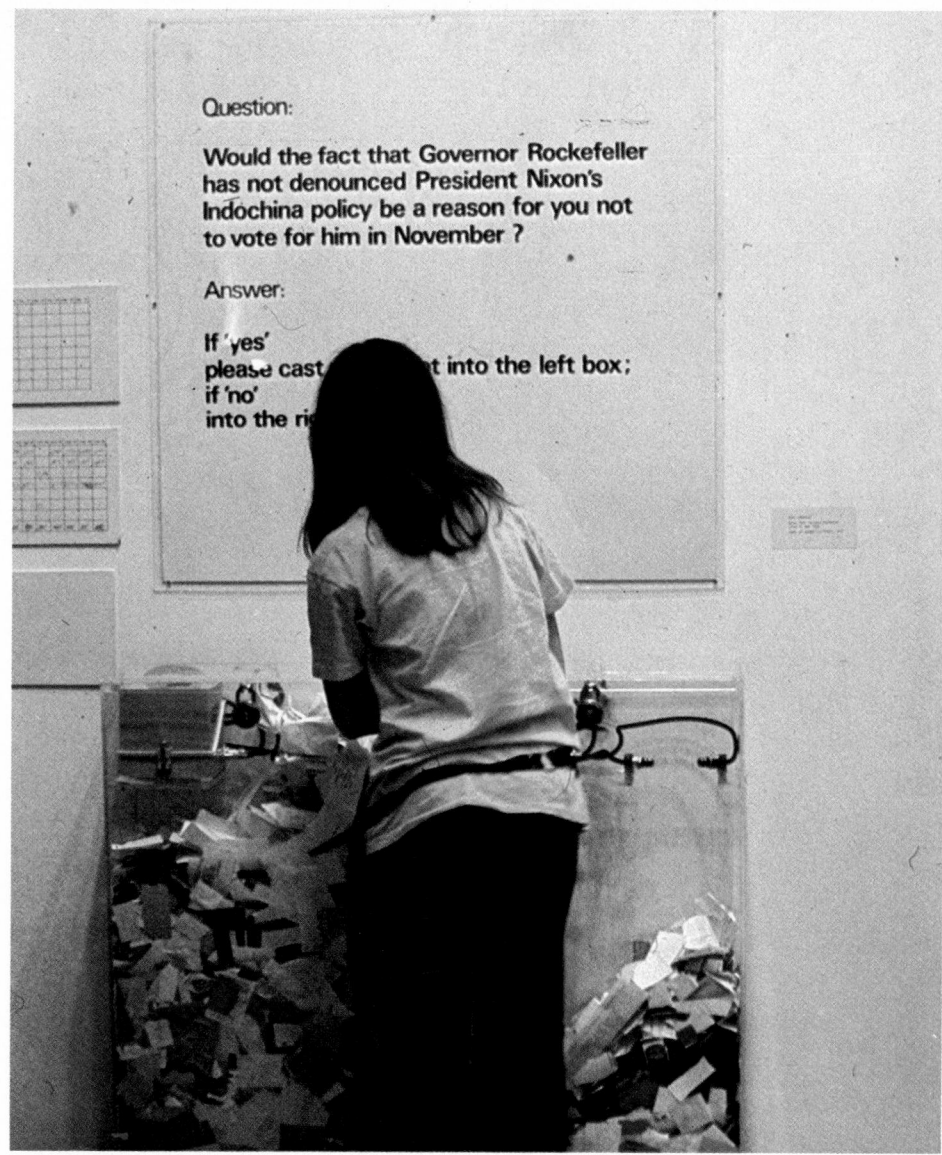

without being contaminated by it.

Joseph Beuys, who has built up an even more powerful legend than that of Gilbert & George, is an artist in deadly earnest. Beuys has been around for a considerable time. His first exhibition was held in 1953 in Wuppertal, Germany, at the Museum von der Heydt. But it was not until the middle Sixties that he began to excite widespread curiosity. At this time he was making *assemblages* (Plate 361, *Chair with Fat*, 1964) and creating environments (Plates 362 and 363, *Room Sculpture*, 1968), which seemed more "radical" than anything being done by other artists. One element which fascinated spectators was the use of apparently inappropriate materials for symbolic purposes. *Chair with Fat* belongs to a series which Beuys dubbed *Fat Corners*, which combined, in his own interpretation, the energy of fat with the regularity and order of the right-angled corner.

Beuys's reputation was really cemented, however, by the effect he made in performance pieces. One of the most celebrated of these was his *How To Explain Paintings to a Dead Hare* (Düsseldorf, 1965). Another "action", which exists on film, was *Eurasienstab*. In this we see Beuys apparently alone in a room, in which there are a number of boards covered with felt, a metal pole, and some margarine. The artist dons a pair of metal shoes, which seem to anchor him to the ground, and which make his subsequent tasks more difficult, then proceeds to take one board after another and build with them a kind of enclosure. Within this "sacred" space Beuys performs a kind of foundation rite, transforming chaos into cosmos, which he completes by pointing the curved end of the metal pole—the *Eurasienstab* itself—from left

354.
Bernhard and Hilde Becher
Pitheads
1971
Property of the artists

355. Opposite
Bernhard and Hilde Becher
Pitheads
1972–73
London, Nigel Greenwood Inc.

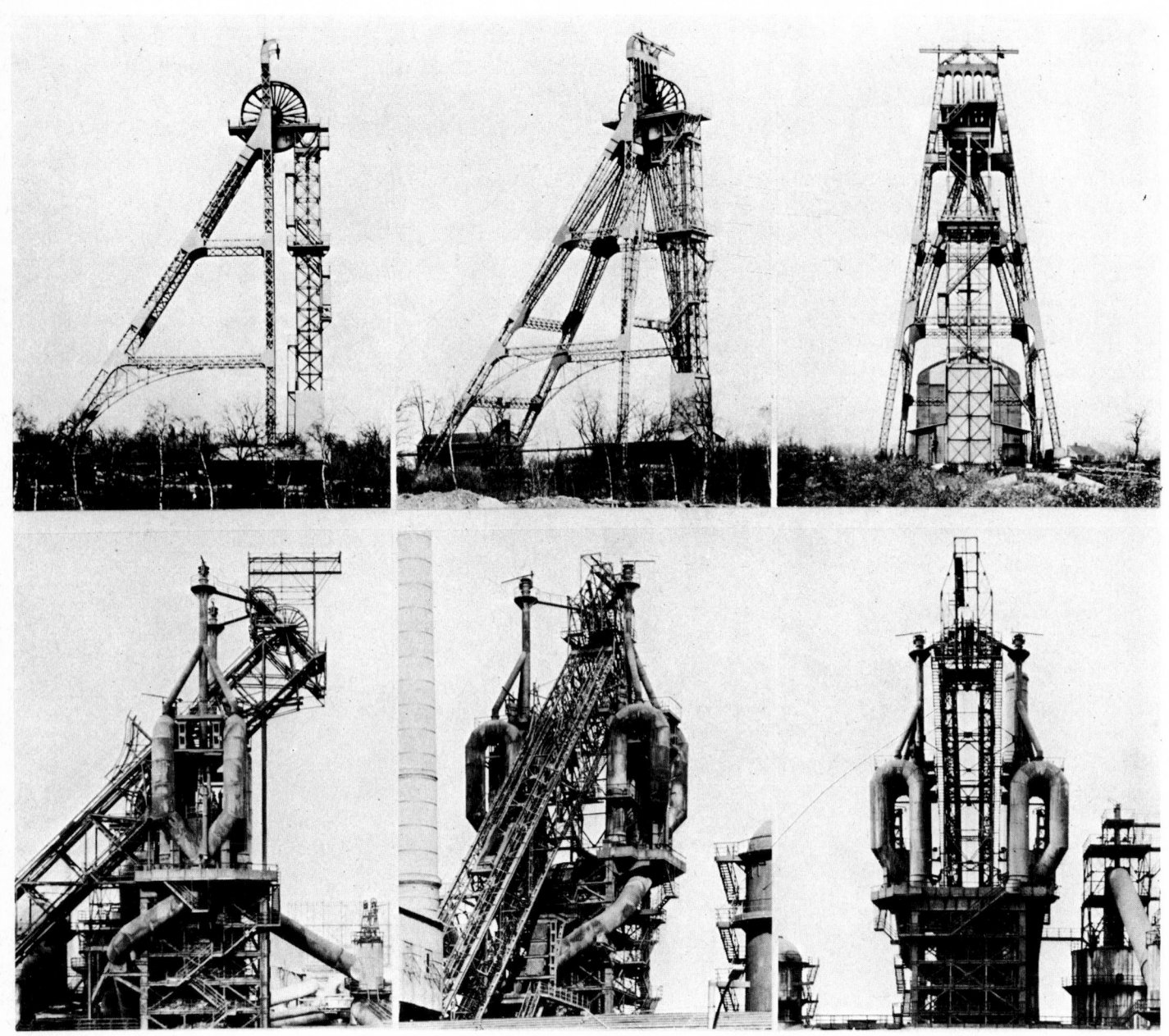

to right, west to east, that is, towards the direction from which the experience of initiation comes. Meanwhile, the margarine, which first appears in an unformed state, gradually becomes a triangular block.

Beuys has a powerful personality and has impressed nearly all those with whom he has come in contact. It has been said of him that he is "an actor with a mask which reminds us of the faces of certain actors in the silent movies, above all the impassioned, secretly pathetic mask of Buster Keaton". But it was not until he began to close the distance between the performer and the everyday persona that he achieved a fame which no other post-war German artist had enjoyed. What happened was that he became a teacher and a politician who asserted that teaching and politics were now to be considered his means of artistic expression.

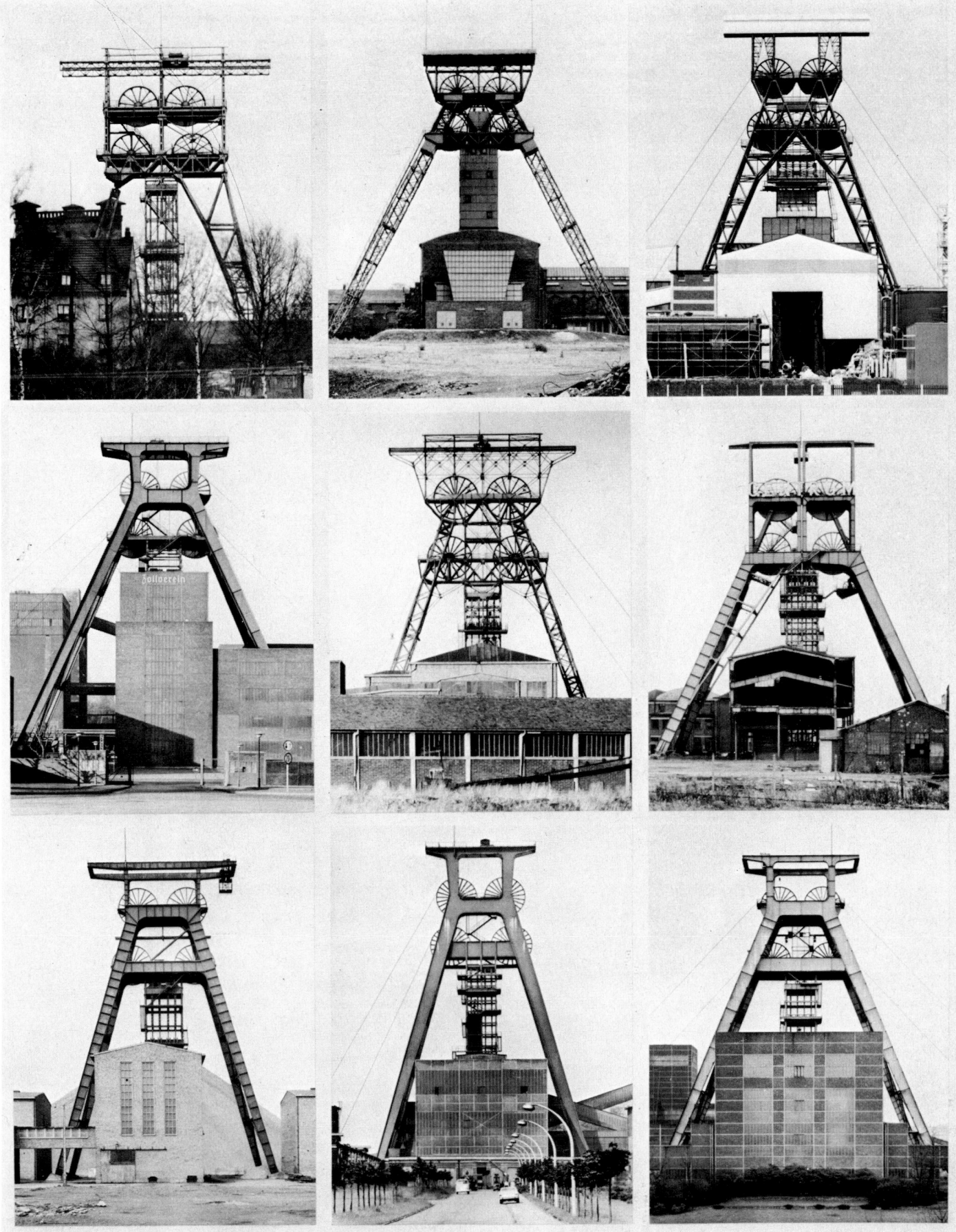

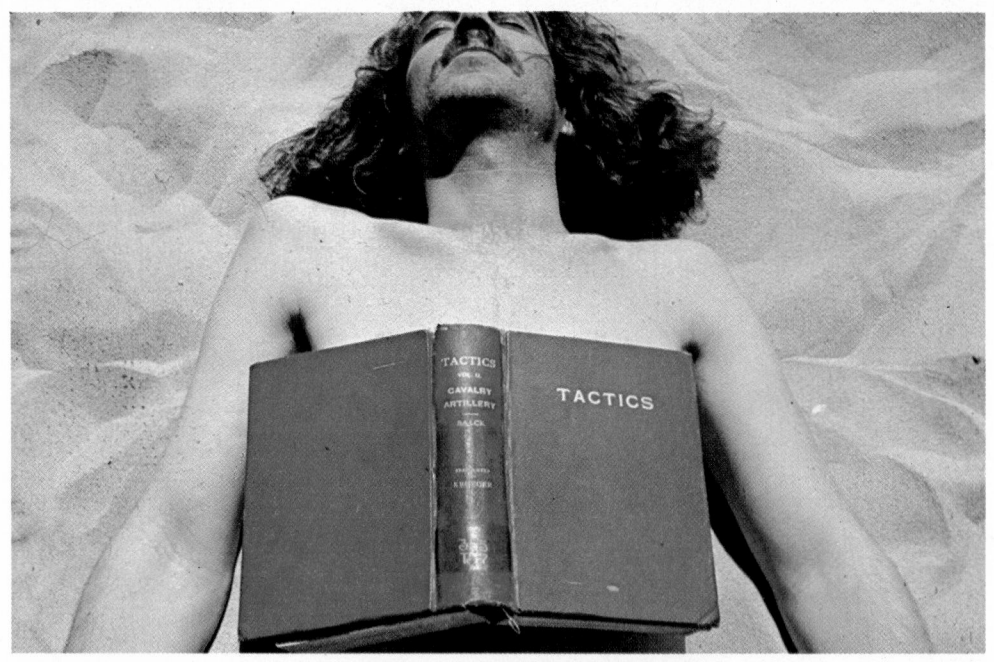

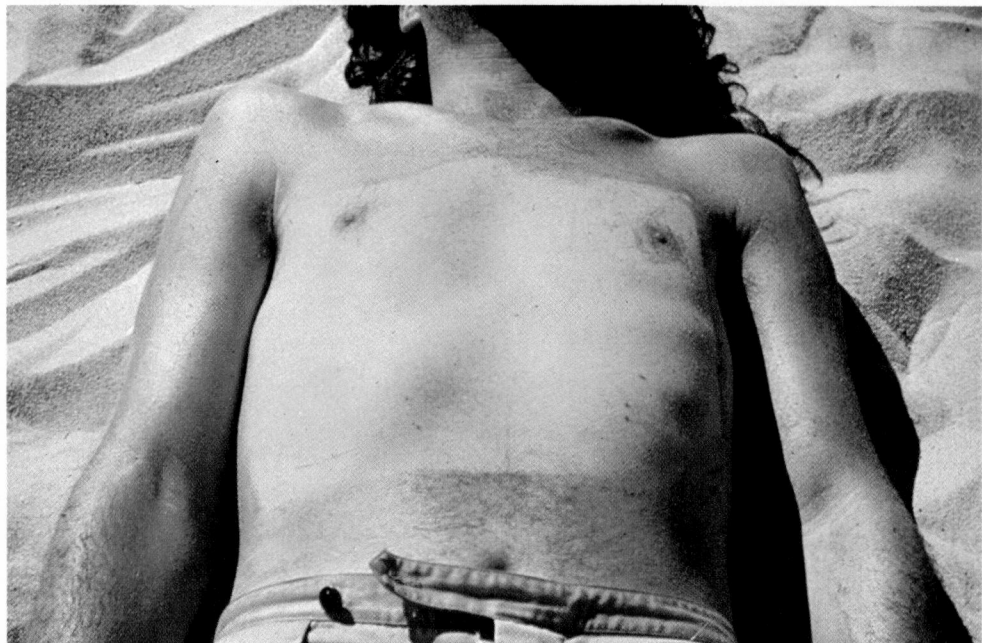

Gradually he abandoned the idea of performing at all, in favour of appearances in which he explained his ideas directly to the public and answered any questions that those who were present might care to put to him. The connection with art was usually that these confrontations took place in art galleries—Beuys conducted a daylong seminar at the Tate, and was given an office at the Kassel Documenta. However, he also opened a shop-front office in Düsseldorf, the city where he was employed as a professor at the Düsseldorf Kunstakademie, in an effort to reach the kind of public that would not normally visit an art exhibition or a museum.

The message that Beuys preaches on these occasions can be summed up in the following quotation from an interview: "Even though sociology is a science of man, even though it cannot come into existence without the help of what is schematically called science, nonetheless, because of a series of positivistic hestitations, it assumes a polemical attitude with respect to art: art has no value, has no social purpose, is useless, is in no way a means of revolution, only science can

444

356. Opposite
Dennis Oppenheim
Reading Position for a Second Degree Burn
1970; by kind permission of the Sonnabend Gallery,
New York, Paris

357.
Bruce Nauman
Bound To Fail
1967–70
New York, Leo Castelli Gallery

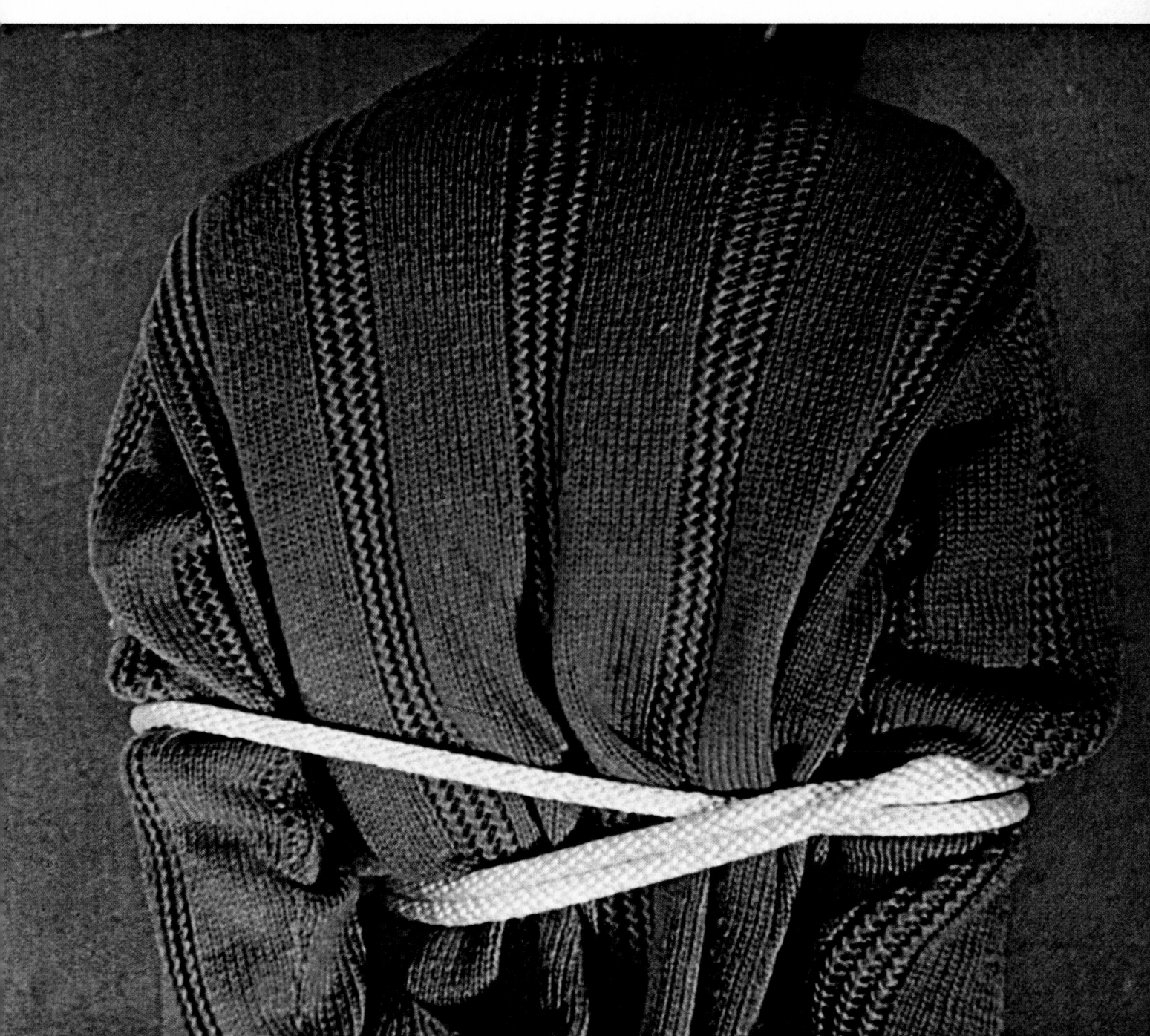

358.
Gilbert & George
A Sculpture Sample entitled Sculptors' Samples
1971

359. Opposite
Gilbert & George
Bad Thoughts
1975
London, Nigel Greenwood Inc.

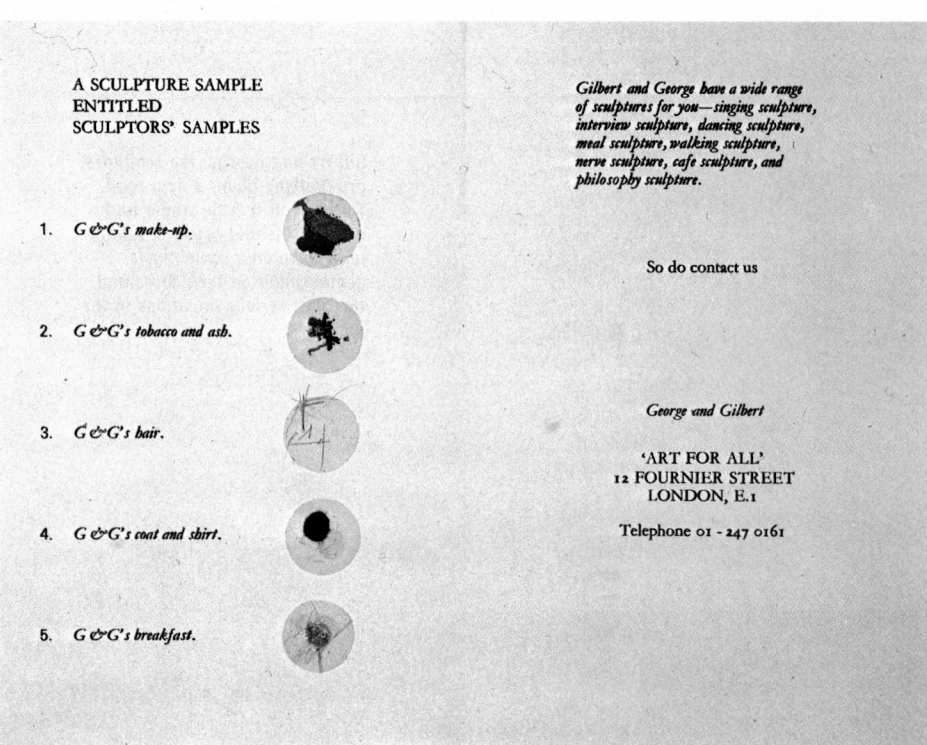

A SCULPTURE SAMPLE
ENTITLED
SCULPTORS' SAMPLES

1. *G & G's make-up.*

2. *G & G's tobacco and ash.*

3. *G & G's hair.*

4. *G & G's coat and shirt.*

5. *G & G's breakfast.*

Gilbert and George have a wide range of sculptures for you—singing sculpture, interview sculpture, dancing sculpture, meal sculpture, walking sculpture, nerve sculpture, cafe sculpture, and philosophy sculpture.

So do contact us

George and Gilbert

'ART FOR ALL'
12 FOURNIER STREET
LONDON, E.1

Telephone 01 - 247 0161

be revolutionary. But from where I stand, I affirm that only art can be revolutionary, and especially so when one manages to liberate the concept of art from its traditional technical meanings by passing from the zone of art to anti-art, to the gesture and to the action, in order to put it at man's complete disposition. Which is to say ART = LIFE, ART = MAN. The only revolutionary means is a global concept of art that also gives birth to a new concept of science" (*A Score by Joseph Beuys: We Are the Revolution*, Naples, 1971).

It can be seen from this that Beuys makes very large claims for art—provided that we are prepared to accept his definition of what art is. In fact, the extra dimension added to Beuys's utterances by his own extraordinary personality makes it difficult to decide if his remarks have any general validity.

Beuys is especially interesting because he seems to symbolize, and to sum up in his own person, the role of the artist in the society of the 1970's. Or, rather, he gives us a vivid sense of what artists would like their role to be. To a somewhat lesser extent, we see the same thing in the *modus operandi* adopted by Gilbert & George, and by a Body artist such as Dennis Oppenheim. The artist sees himself as a shaman, and he also sees himself as a "chosen" being, whose claims to be recognized as an artist are dependent not upon anything he has produced or may produce, but upon some inherent quality which the rest of us, audience rather than artists, are bound to recognize and equally bound to acknowledge with enthusiasm. Art having become sufficient unto itself, like the Deity, artists themselves are sacred beings who can claim special consideration without violating our sense of democracy. One point that supports this contention is the way in which art—Richard Long's and Hamish Fulton's timed walks, Oppenheim's sunburn, the self-amputations of the Viennese artist Rudolf Schwarzkogler—has taken on the character of a test or ordeal. One is reminded of the way in which the shaman discovers his vocation through suffering; and, still more, of the way in which the Indian fakir achieves merit by staring fixedly at the sun or lying on a bed of nails.

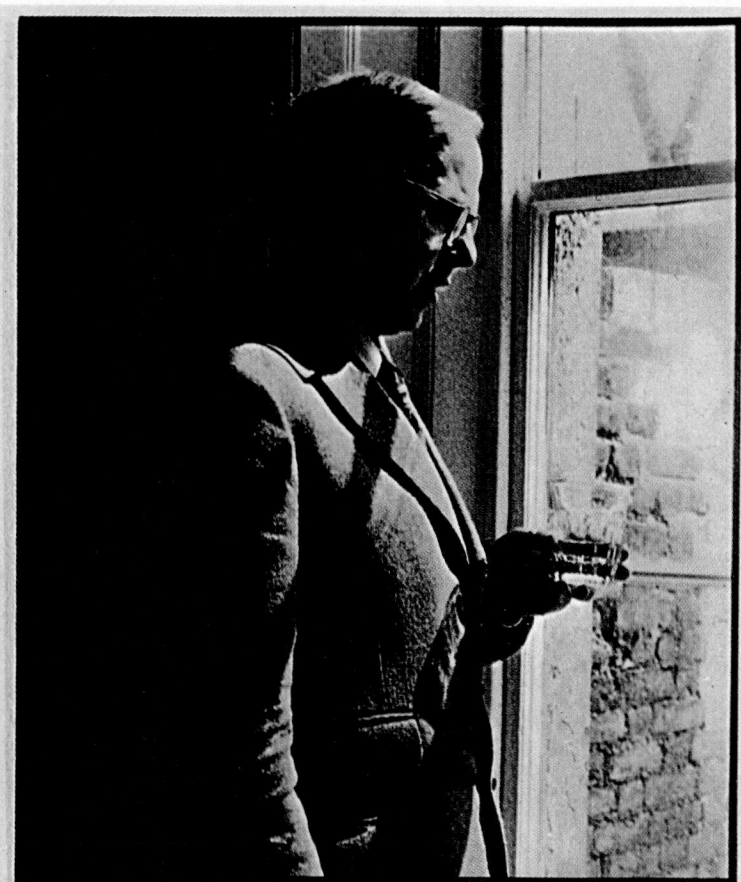
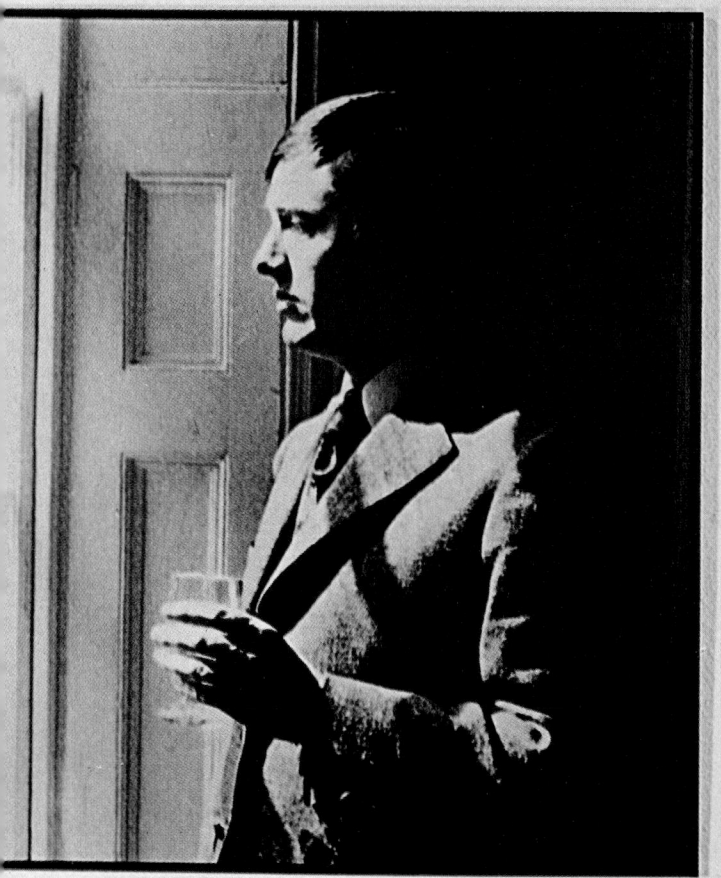
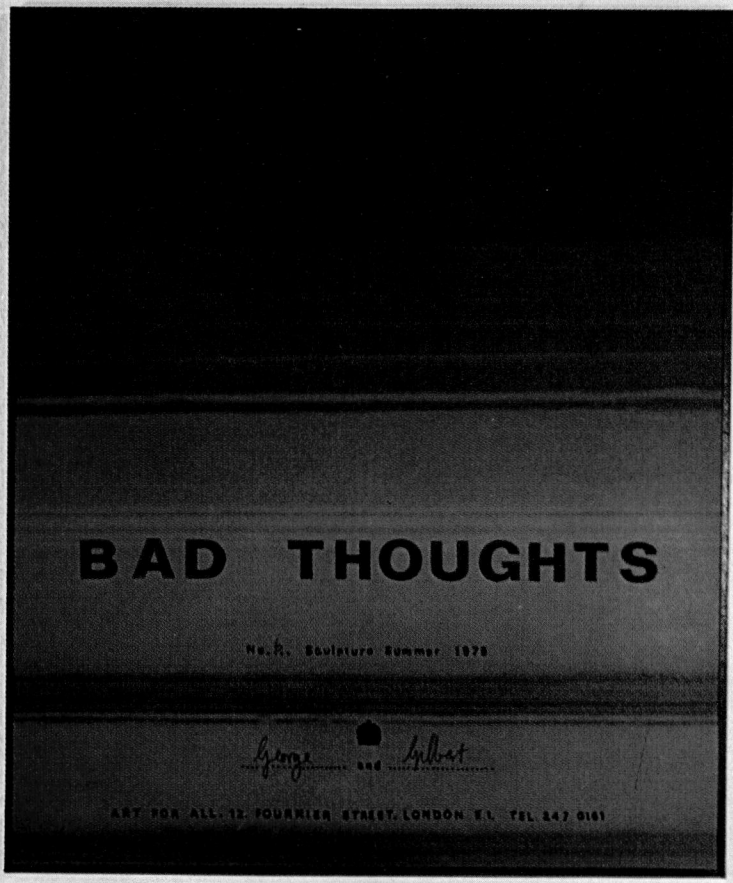

360.
Gilbert & George
Singing Sculpture
1971
New York, Sonnabend Gallery (Photo: Thomas Haar)

The question we have to ask ourselves is whether conduct of this kind has any validity in the context of the industrial and technological society we know. It can be argued that the *faux naïf* behaviour and apparent frivolity of the Zen philosopher have age-old roots in the culture of China and Japan. Zen is at once a refinement and an exaggeration of something which has always existed. But the modern artist cannot make his gestures meaningful simply by claiming that they are so. What he does has to mesh with the world around him.

Some artists have tried to achieve this through a passionate engagement with the things which seem to them to typify the times. In the Seventies one of the most active fields of avant-garde experimentation has been video. Video Art, as it has come to be called, already covers a very broad spectrum. The best definition of what artists have tried to do with the medium is supplied by Ernest Gusella's list of negatives. In reply to a questionnaire from the magazine *Art-Rite* he said: "My video is not:

"—Accompanied by a 'pink sludge' rock and roll soundtrack.

"—Documentation of a conceptual perfor-

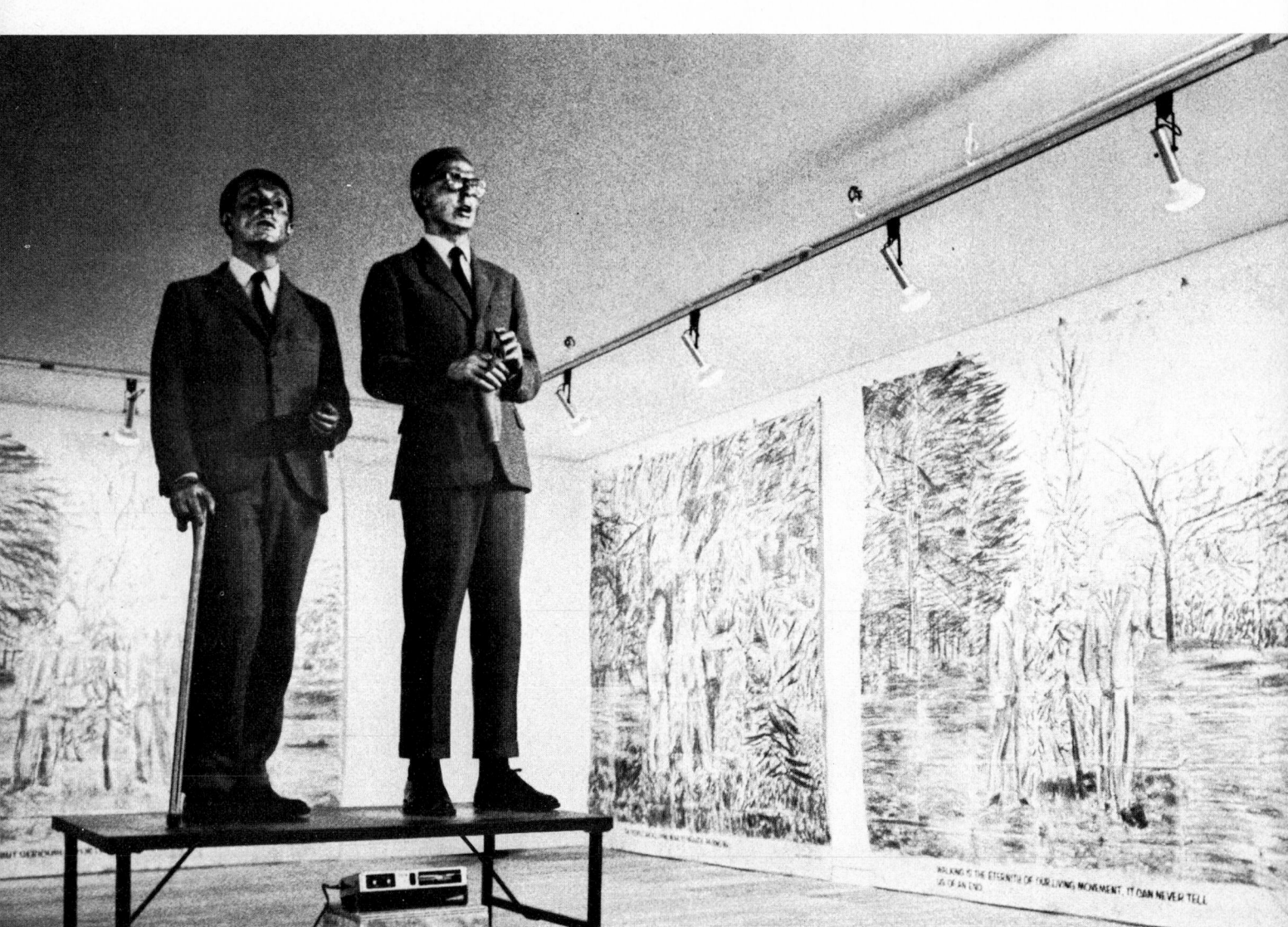

361.
Joseph Beuys
Stuhl mit Fett (Chair with Fat)
1964; 47 × 42 × 100 cm. (18 × 16 × 39 in.)
Darmstadt, Hessisches Landesmuseum, coll. Karl Ströher

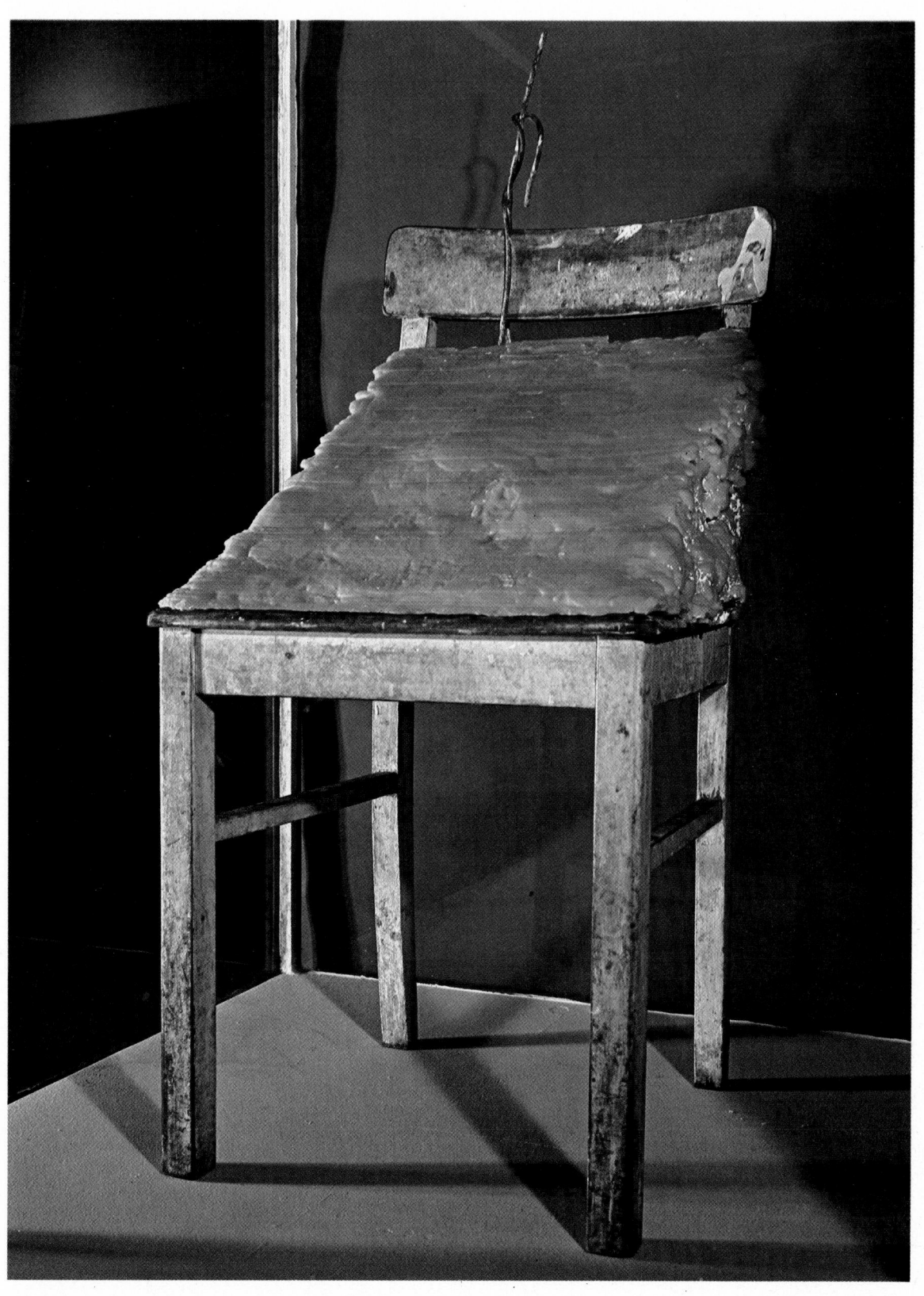

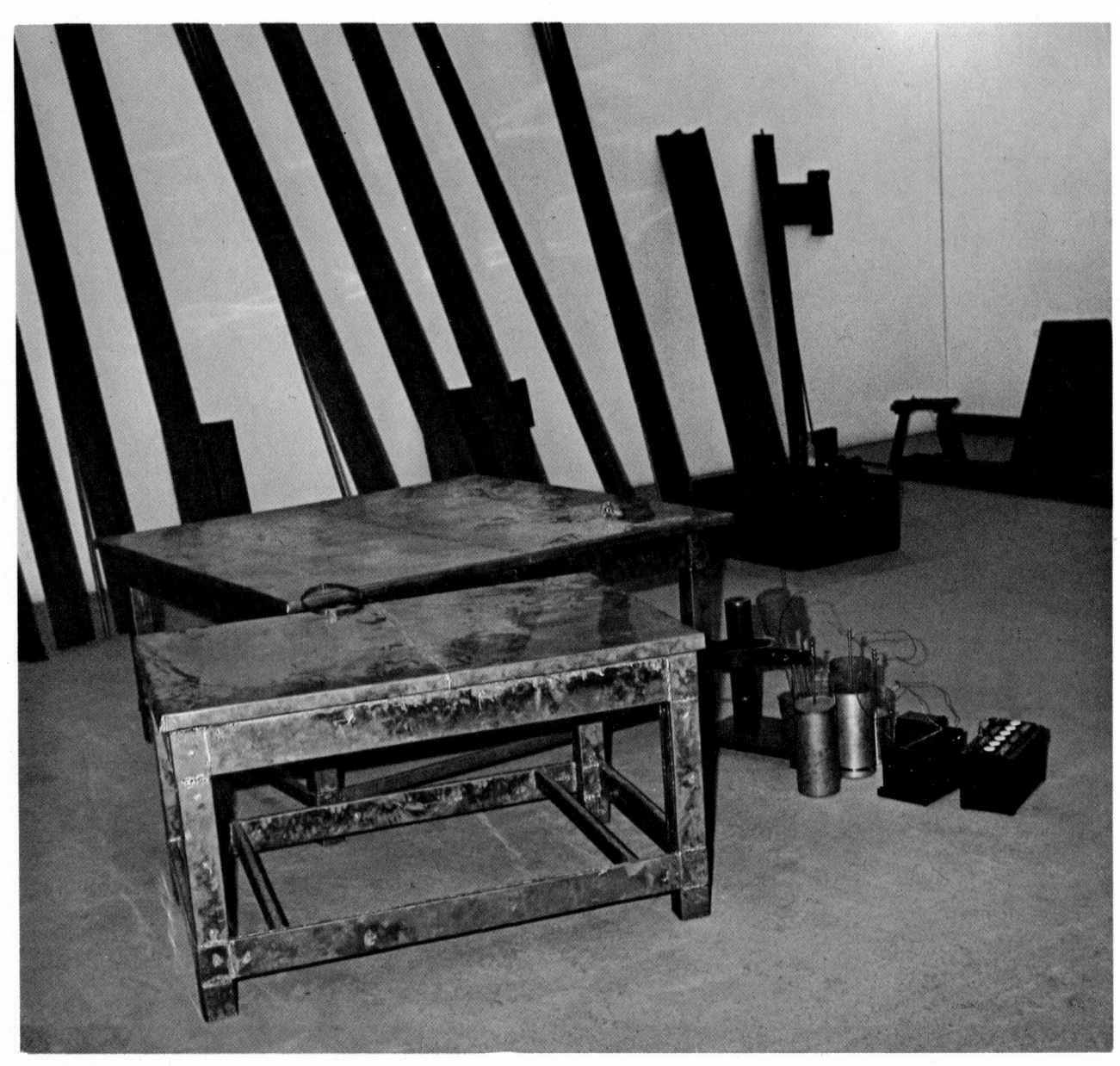

mance in which I jump out of a 13th story window to test the laws of chance.

"—Synthetic images created with rebuilt surplus World War I airplane parts.

"—Shot with two cameras attached under each armpit and one between my legs.

"—A group therapy encounter between the Neo-Nazi Anarchists and the Bowery Satanists.

"—An underground sex-opera starring all my beautiful friends.

"—A presentation about the 3rd coming of the Punjab of Mysore to bless his freebies in America.

"—Product with future marketing potential" (*Art-Rite*, No. 7, p. 11).

This baleful catalogue at least gives a good notion of all the things video has tried to be. They range from "alternative" politics masquerading as art to a prettier and more complex version of the old-fashioned kaleidoscope. The perils and pleasures of technically experimental video can best be

362 and 363. Below and opposite
Joseph Beuys
Raumplastik (Room Sculpture)
1968; 10 × 12 m. (33 × 39 ft.)
Darmstadt, Hessisches Landesmuseum, coll. Karl Ströher

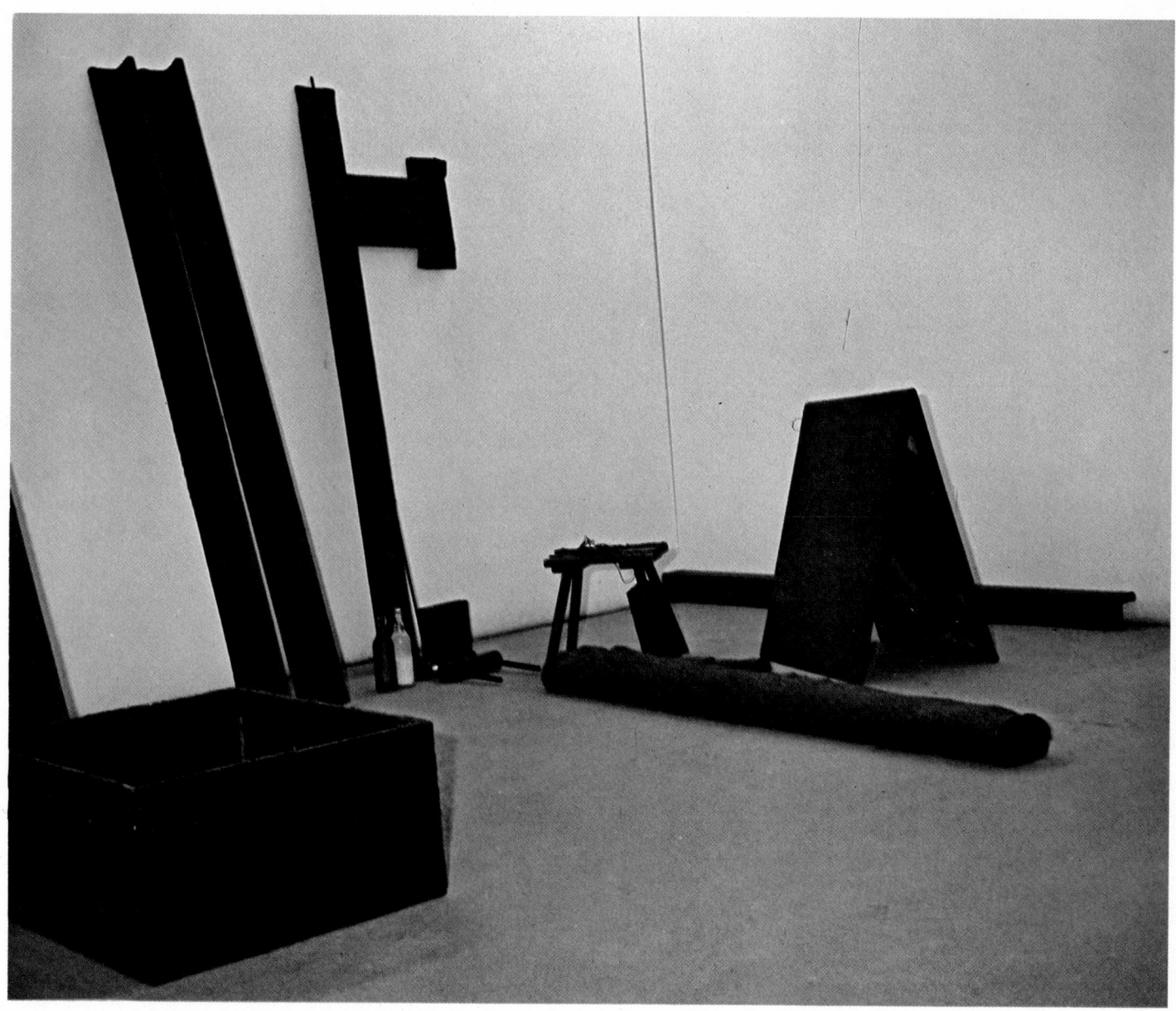

sampled in the work of the Korean artist Nam June Paik. The *Paik-Abe Synthesizer* (Plate 364) delivers a flood of astonishing images which eventually become boring because they have no stability and therefore no point of rest for eye or mind. Further adventures, such as Paik's collaboration with the cellist Charlotte Moorman, who sometimes plays her adapted instrument bare-breasted (Plate 365), suggest a desperate search for novelty at any price.

But even technological top-dressing of the kind supplied by video cannot disguise the fact that the artist, or one kind of contemporary artist, has come very close to the total abolition of art. On the one hand, as Kosuth does, he calls for an activity which is totally self-sufficient and immune from criticism and even description (since the only true account of the work is given by itself). On the other hand, as Beuys does, he claims that art is a totality so vast, so powerful, and so all-embracing

451

364.
Nam June Paik
Paik-Abe Synthesizer
1971
© 1971 by Peter Moore

365. Opposite
Nam June Paik
T.V. Cello (with cellist Charlotte Moorman)
1971, New York

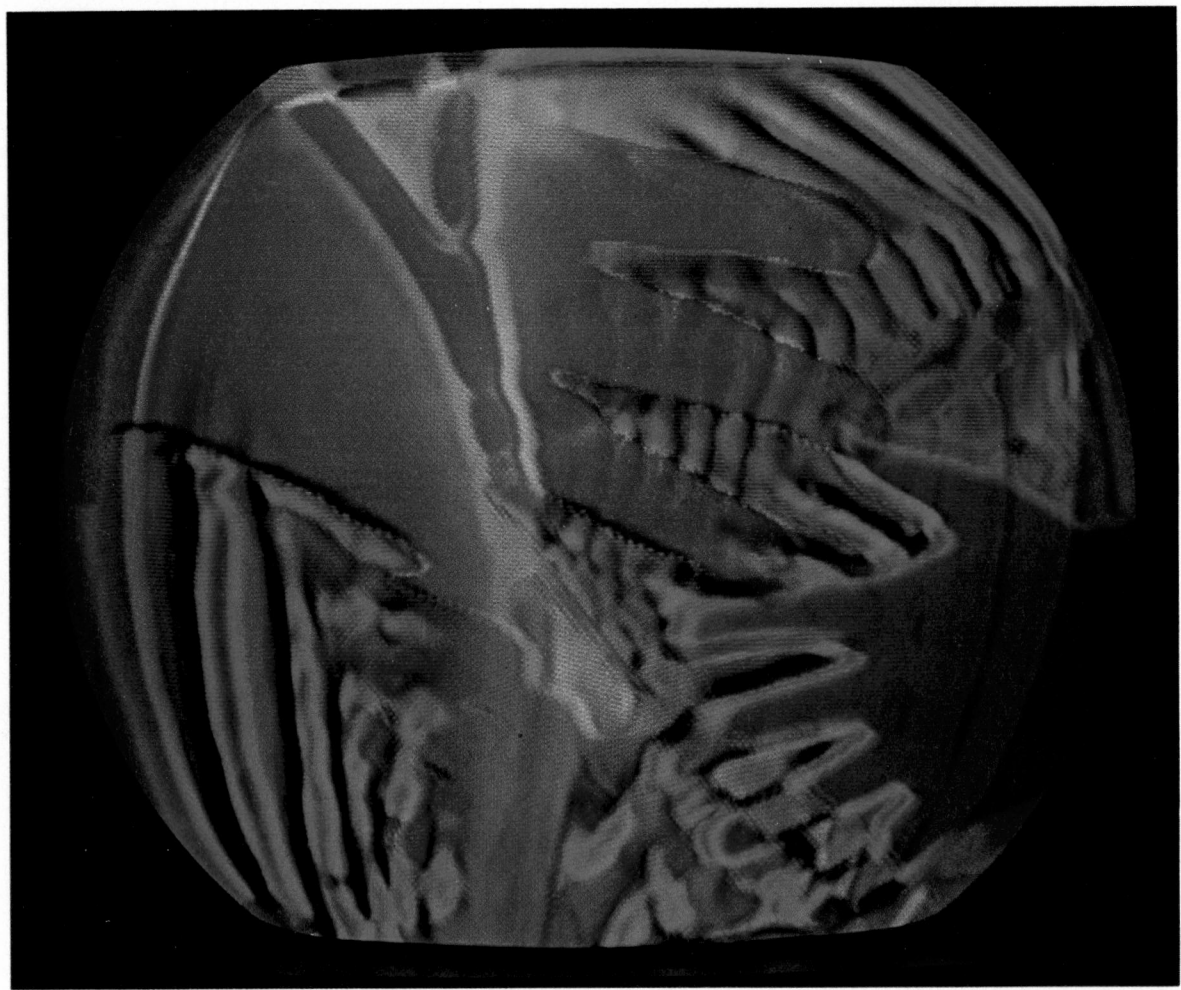

that it needs no embodiment other than the person of the artist.

Art's struggle to escape from itself presents a far from reassuring spectacle—that is, if one continues to believe in the shibboleths of the avant-garde. If the Seventies seem a significant decade in the history of Modernism, it is because they supply an increasing quantity of evidence that the accepted theory of the avant-garde is breaking down. Since 1905, the development of art has been interpreted in terms of a frontier which was always being pushed forward, and the assumption was that this process could be continued indefinitely. A secondary theme, apparently contradictory but in fact very closely related to the first, was the development of nihilism, so that the progress of art was measured by its tendency to turn itself into some new variety of anti-art. The one thing which was never invoked was the law of diminishing returns.

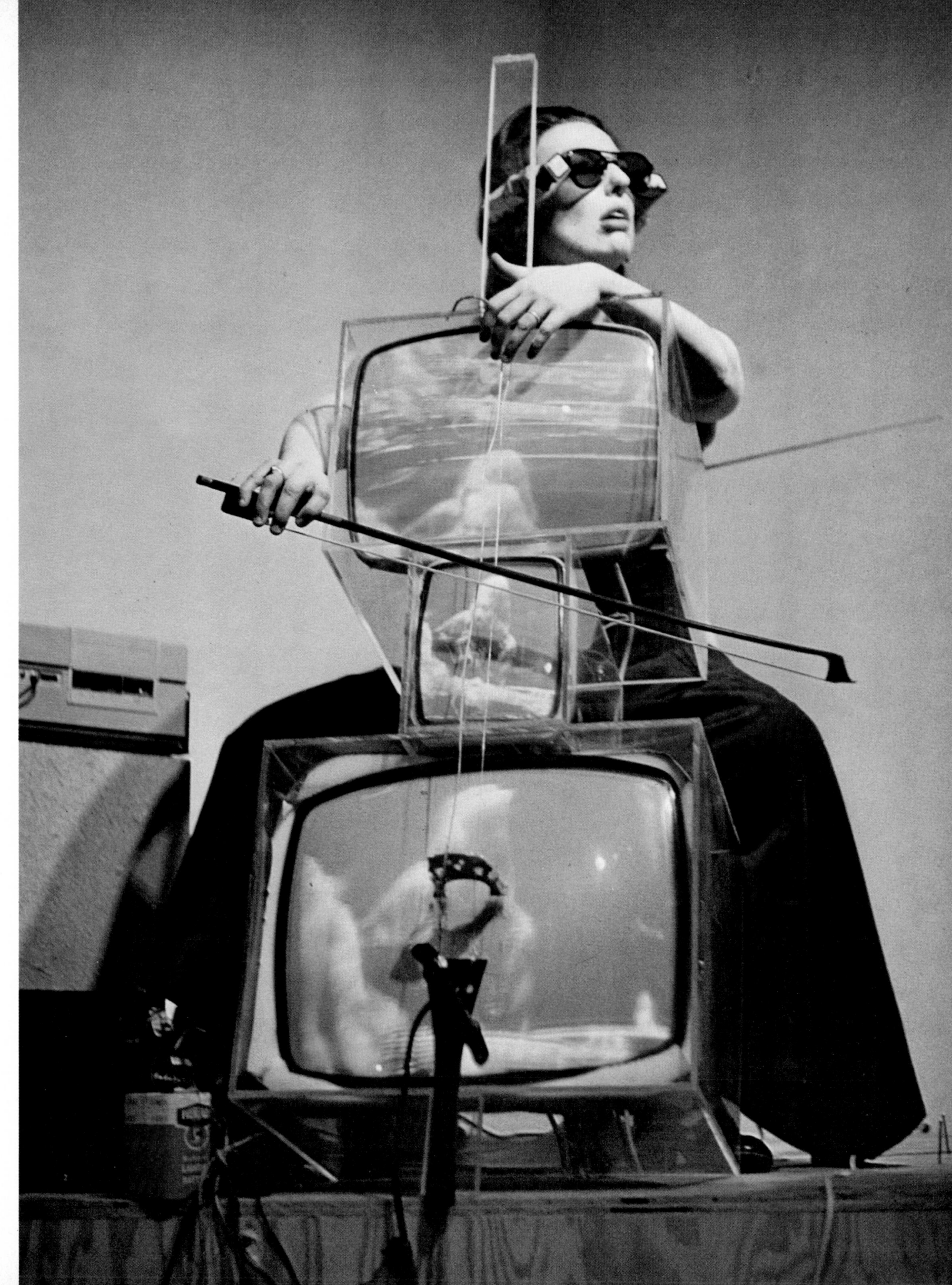

Superrealism

However great their success with critics and museum curators, the various Minimal and Conceptual styles did not completely sweep the field. They faced serious competition from a way of painting pictures and making sculpture which seemed the polar opposite of such abstract and cerebral modes. The name given to this artistic phenomenon was Hyper Realism or Superrealism. Superrealism, like its predecessor Pop Art, enjoyed a tremendous success with collectors and dealers, but attracted less than unanimous critical support. Indeed, even those critics who had finally accepted Pop tended to feel dubious about this new manifestation. This was understandable—on the face of it, Superrealist artists were trying to return art to the condition which it had been in not only before Modernism, but before the triumph of Impressionism. It seemed as if, by a final cynical paradox, the advocates of Superrealism were trying to assert that the only style worthy of a truly avant-garde artist was the academic Salon painting of the late nineteenth century. The wheel had come full circle.

In fact, in the years since 1945, realism had never quite ceased to assert itself. There was even a handful of artists who escaped the label "academic" while practising what was recognizably a kind of realism. In Italy, for example, there was the intensely prolific Renato Guttuso, whose realist works, tinged with Expressionism, were the product of his Marxist political convictions. In France there was Balthus, whose strangely erotic paintings of pubescent girls distilled a Surrealist atmosphere without being overtly Surrealist in any detail. In England there was Lucien Freud, who, beginning as a neo-romantic, proceeded to evolve a plain, direct style which owed something to Walter Sickert and a great deal to the camera. British Pop Art always remained close to straightforward realism, particularly in the work of Peter Blake. Blake himself refused to accept the Pop label and always insisted that he was most accurately described as being simply a "realistic" painter. As his work matured, it seemed as if Blake's deepest ambition was to be recognized as a belated colleague of the Pre-Raphaelites (who in the 1960's and 1970's continued to enjoy an immense popularity with the gallery-going public).

Another British painter with increasingly close links to traditional realism was the boy wonder of Pop Art, David Hockney. Hockney has often asserted that one of the things which fascinates him about painting is the contrast between the different conventions of representation an artist can use. Now the conventions he chose were those which the masters of the Renaissance would have recognized as familiar. Hockney's *Double Portrait of Ossie and Celia* (Plate 366) is, from the point of view of the committed Modernist, a brilliant but disturbing work. It is undoubtedly intensely contemporary, in that it distills the essence of the fashionable London world of the late Sixties. In this respect it resembles works such as John Singer Sargent's portrait of the Wertheimer sisters, which performs the same service for the Edwardian age. But the contemporaneity of Hockney's painting goes further than this. We find in it a way of arranging the forms, a response to certain colours, even to a certain kind of light, which makes it intensely evocative of the moment at which it was created. Now that the Sixties are already fading one can see that it evokes the spirit of the time as no other work could do. Yet it is exactly this quality—and the painter's keen eye for social nuances—which makes it seem anachronistic compared to the art since the Second World War.

There is, however, a difference between Hockney's painting, even in this phase, and the kind of painting that was being done by the American artist Philip Pearlstein (Plate 367).

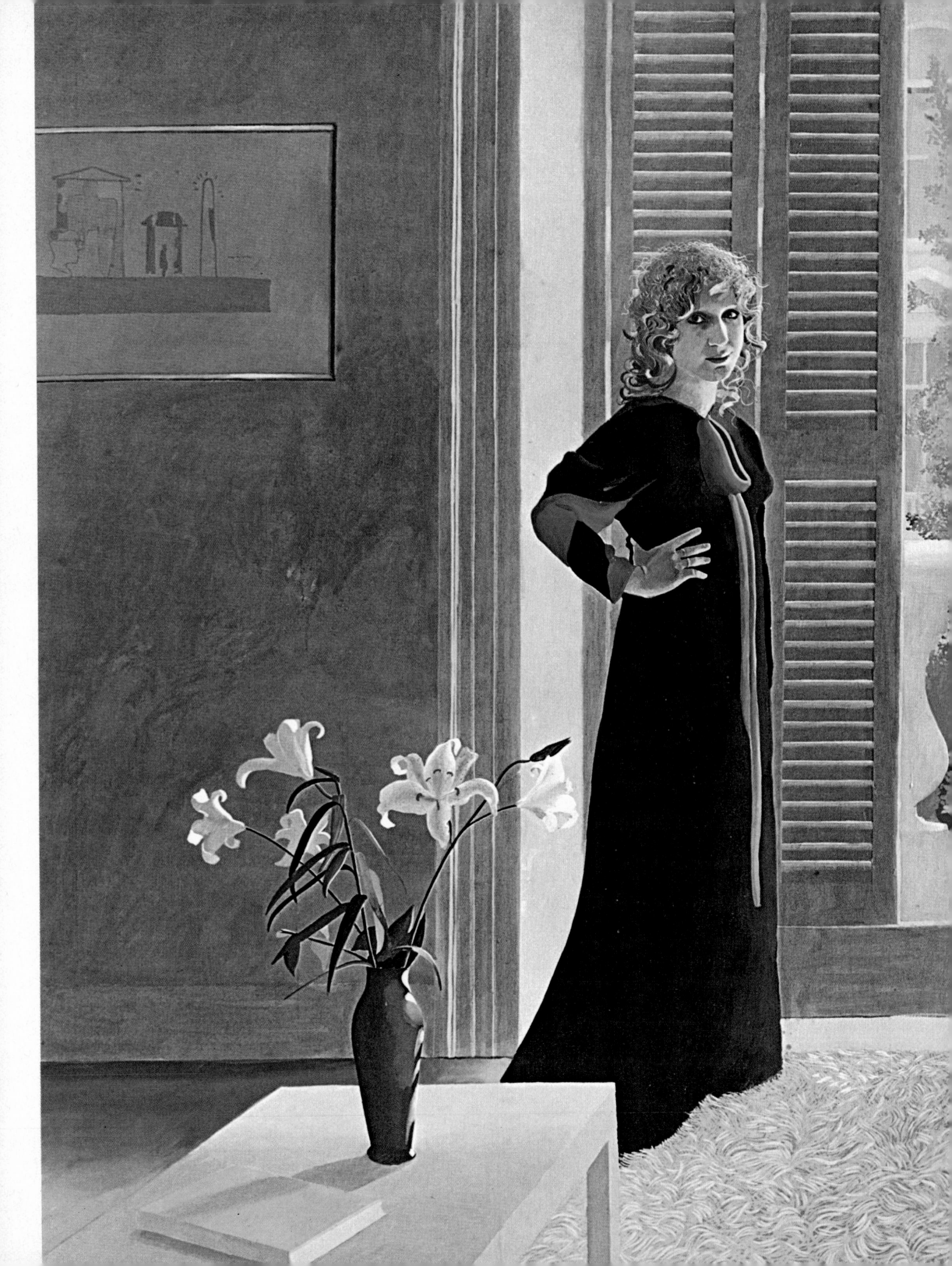

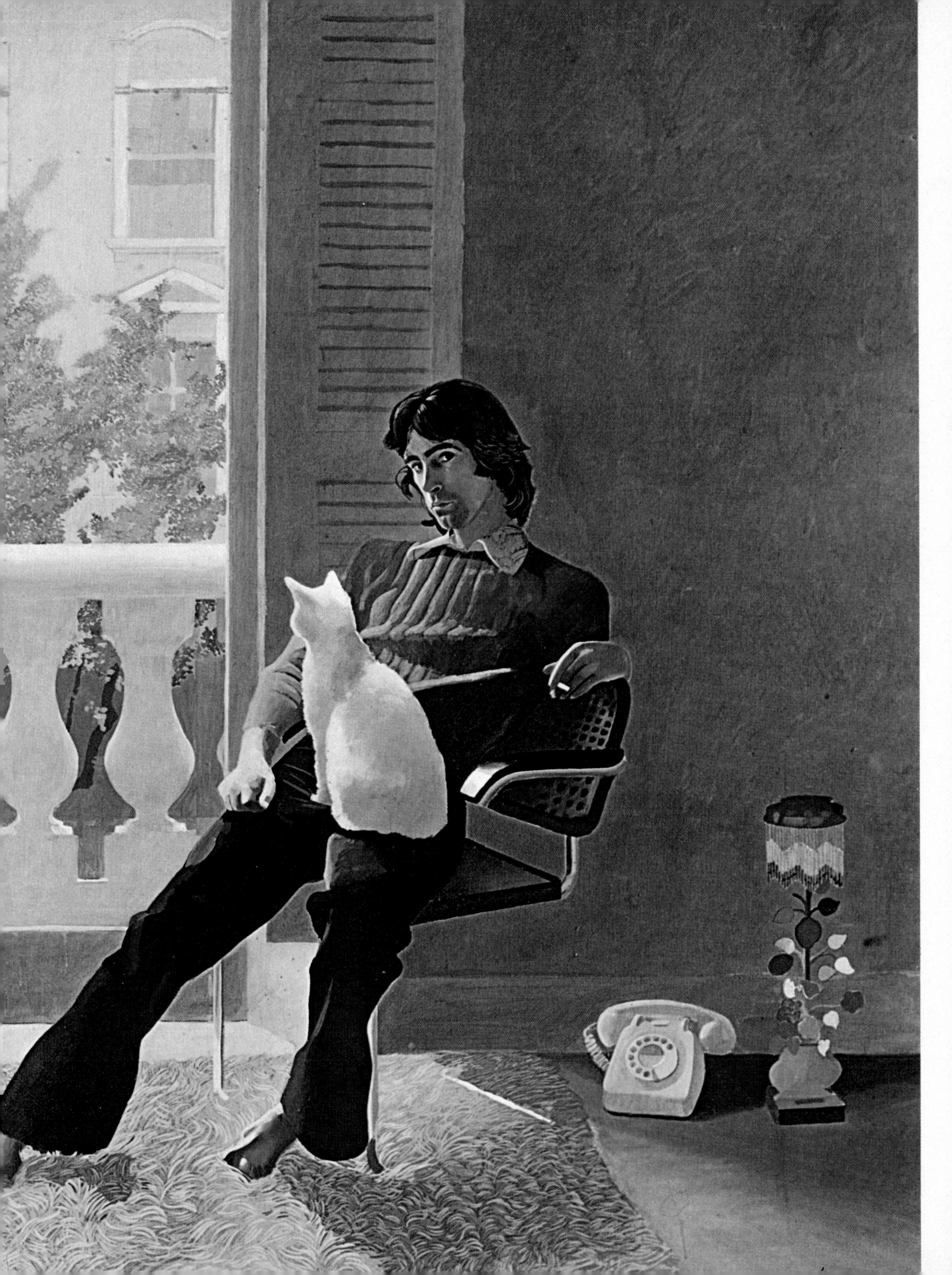

Pearlstein's obsessive concentration upon the nude—usually but not always the female nude—has been thought to make him one of the sources of Superrealism. This is not true, except in the general sense that Pearlstein preserved, and made available to other American artists, the tradition of American realism which had had a strong revival during the 1930's, and which is well represented in the work of Edward Hopper.

Pearlstein differs from the painters of the Superrealist group and from Hockney, too, because he will have nothing to do with the camera. His nudes are painted from life, usually by artificial light. One quality which might lead us to think that they are not life studies is the arbitrary way in which they are cropped, just as an unskilled amateur photographer will often succeed in framing his subject in a way that he doesn't intend. In Pearlstein's case the cropping seems rooted in the method of work. The artist does not deliberately "compose" the picture, but starts with a single detail and moves outward from that, stopping when he reaches the edge of the canvas. This, in turn, makes him seem very different from those who painted the figure during the nineteenth century or, for that matter, earlier. Pearlstein's method announces to us that it is the whole process of perceiving something and then of rendering it into paint that counts. The arbitary cropping of the image does not matter so long as the process itself is fully demonstrated.

The idea of process also enters very strongly into the work of Malcolm Morley, an English artist now domiciled in America, who may be regarded as the true founder of Superrealism. Morley invented a variation of the Pop Art approach to the "given" image. What Lichtenstein does, in his paintings derived from comic strips, is first to take something which seems to have been irremediably coarsened by the processes of cheap colour reproduction, and then to refine and formalize this before using it as the basis for a picture. The fact that the painting shows a series of mannerisms and conventions that derive from the original printed source serves in a way to distance it from that source. We know, from the scale alone, but also from other aspects as well, that this is not simply a frame from a comic strip, but the transformation of such a frame.

Morley, following the dialectical pattern of so much art after 1945, set out to criticize Lichtenstein's method. In the middle Sixties he produced a series of paintings which, instead of being based upon crude comic-strip images, derived from high-quality four-colour reproductions of photographs, pictures of the kind one finds used to decorate the offices of shipping lines and to illustrate the brochures of travel agents (Plate 368). Morley has since said that he did not find the pictures themselves particularly interesting. What did interest him was the process of making a painted equivalent—of doing by hand what the machine already did so efficiently. For this reason he adopted an arbitrary method of copying. The printed original was divided into a number of squares, and all but one of these squares was covered while the artist was working on his copy. He only saw how near he had managed to come to what he was trying to imitate when the whole job was finished. To add to the arbitrariness of the procedure, the original was often copied upside down.

One finds similar attitudes at work in the painting of John Clem Clarke, another painter who can be regarded as forming part of the transition between Pop and Superrealism. Clarke is an extremely prolific and uneven artist, whose work shows many changes of direction. Among his most significant pictures are his versions of the Old Masters. He does not seem to undertake these in quite the same spirit as that which animates Martial Raysse, in the latter's versions of Ingres and Pierre Paul Prud'hon. Clarke has no quality of sarcasm. As far as he is concerned, these "translations" are simply a method of making the works he chooses available to his own time. If the translation also involves a degree of cheapening, the artist is prepared to accept this, as a comment on the society which he himself inhabits.

Clarke's *Three Graces* series has unusual complexity, because here he is parodying not an "established" kind of art, but one which in 1970, when the pictures were painted, was still in some disfavour. The obvious source is A.

367.
Philip Pearlstein
Female Model Reclining on Bentwood Love Seat
1974; 120 × 150 cm. (47 × 59 in.)
New York, Allan Frumkin Gallery

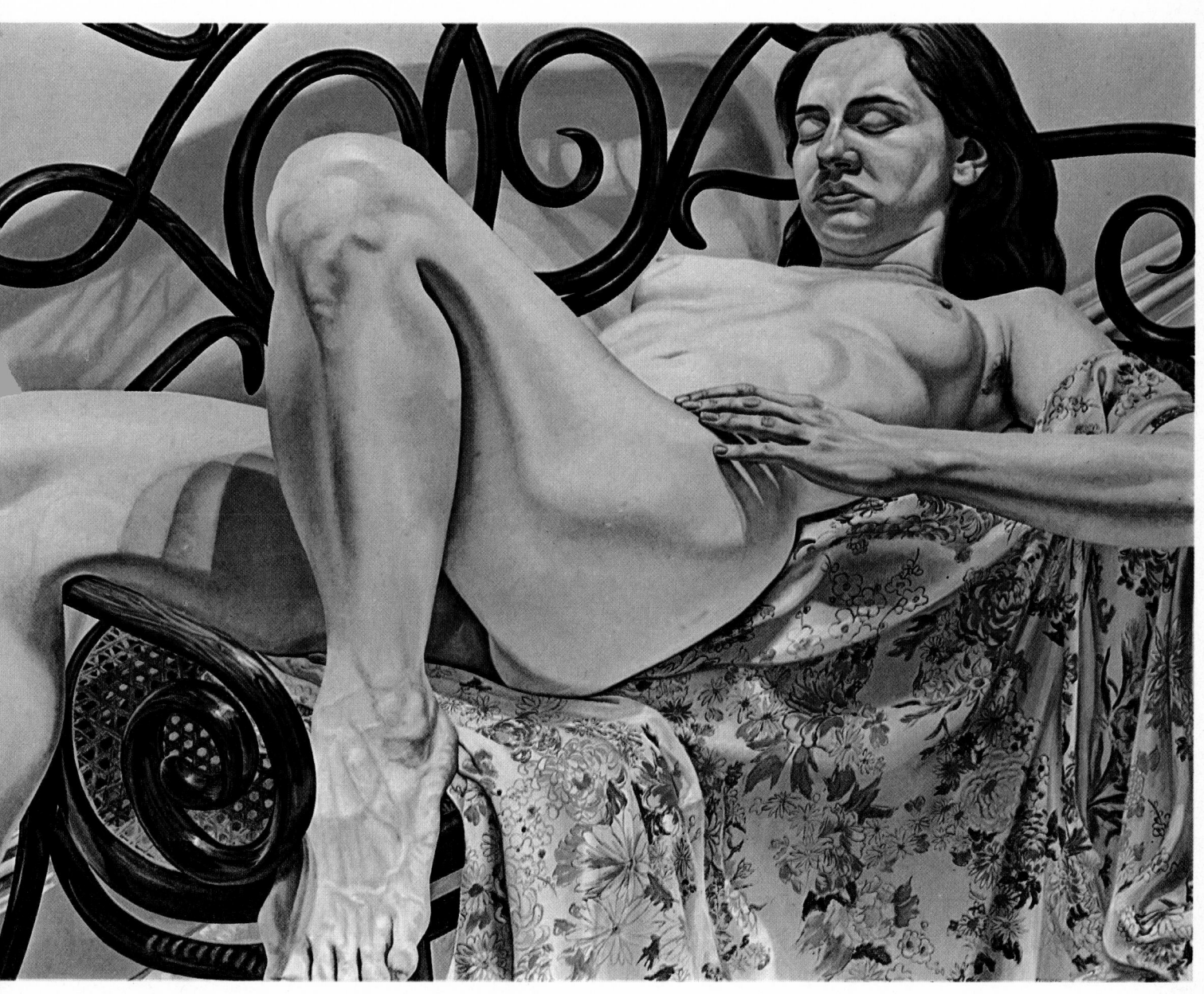

W. Bouguereau, whose paintings of nudes were star items in the Paris Salons of the late nineteenth century, and who was admired particularly by the rich American collectors of that time. Even in 1970, Bouguereau was beinning to attract renewed interest, but there was certainly still something perverse or anti-art about professing an admiration for him. Clarke does not make a direct transcription of his work. Instead, he suggests a contemporary equivalent. These are Bouguereau's nudes seen through the eyes of the camera. But it is important to make the point that they are not pin-ups. None of these girls would ever make the centrefold of *Playboy*. The artist therefore manages to pack quite a lot of comment into a single canvas—about changes in erotic tastes, changes in artistic style, about the difference between the camera's true vision and the apparently "photographic" vision of popular Salon painting.

Indeed, Clarke seems to be divided from the

368.
Malcolm Morley
SS "Amsterdam" in Front of Rotterdam
1966
Courtesy of the artist

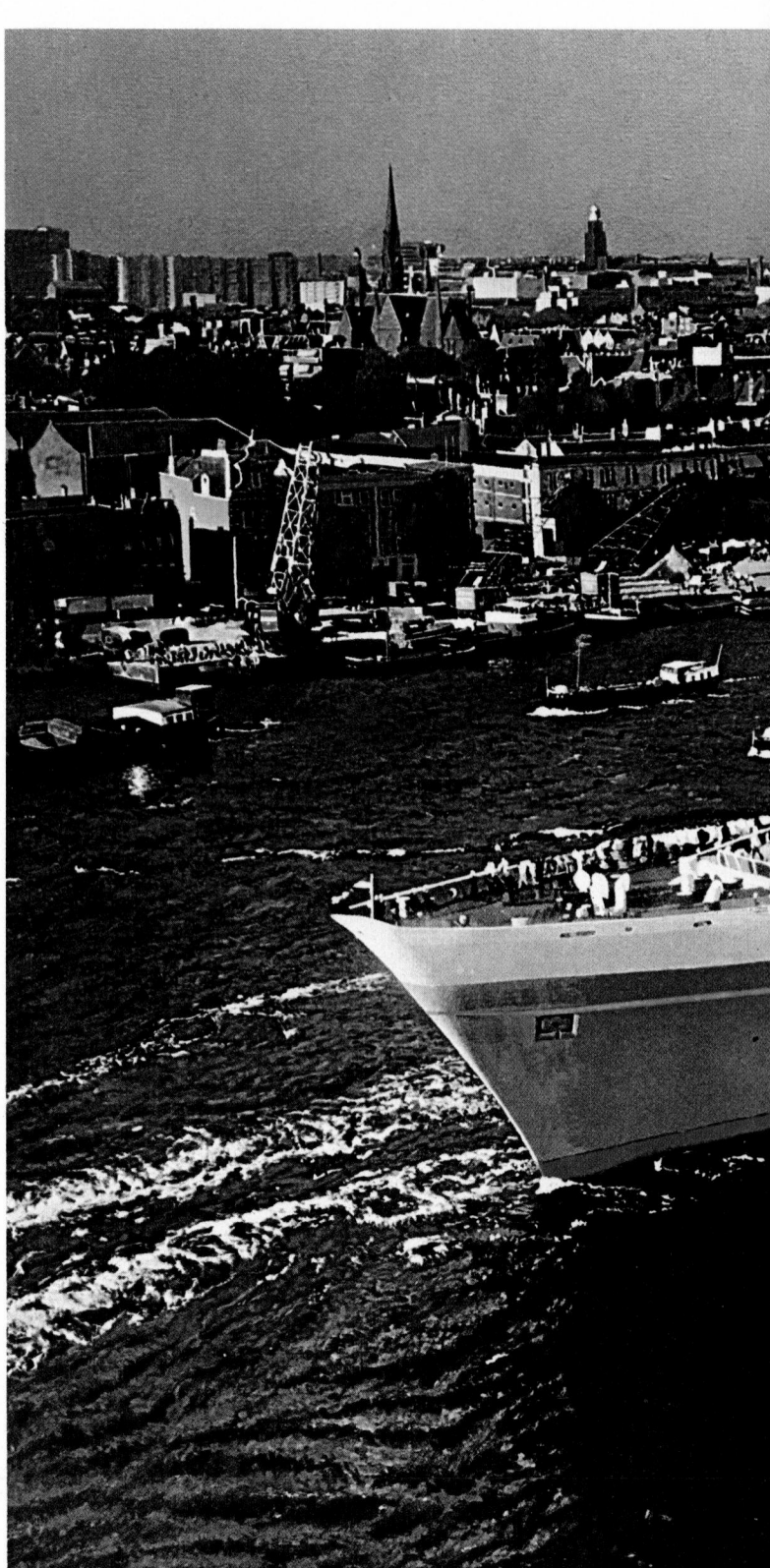

mainstream of Superrealist painting by the amount of comment embodied in his activity. The true Superrealist aspires to be strictly neutral. This at least is the theoretical defence put up for it by the handful of critics who have bothered to investigate it. They see these canvases, with their deliberate lack of an imposed style and their apparently slavish dependence upon the camera, as a new variation upon the theme of the found object. They find in Superrealism a nihilistic streak which goes even beyond Minimalism.

Of course the painters now classified as Superrealists are as keenly aware of the Modernist heritage as artists who work in other styles. Gerhard Richter, a German artist who is an occasional adherent of the movement, has even produced a parody version of Duchamp's *Nude Descending a Staircase* (Plate 370). He bases it upon the fact that Duchamp's nude takes as its own original source the experiments with simultaneous photography made by men such as Marey, and retranslates the action of the figure into present-day photographic terms.

Another item that preoccupies Superrealist painters is the modern reflex camera—both its powers and its limitations. The artist in whose work we can most easily examine its influence is Charles Close, who specializes in large-scale paintings of heads (Plates 371 and 372). These paintings, which are often of fantastic technical refinement, raise a number of important questions. The first of these is that of scale. The effect of enormously enlarging the heads is to make them seem, not less real in a general sense, but less, rather than more, like the person they are supposed to represent. At the same time this enlargement serves as a reminder that the camera, too, has no inbuilt sense of scale. This lack manifests itself in several ways. In the first place, it is possible to enlarge the image on a modern negative to almost any dimension—the tiniest object can be blown up to monumental size. The dynamic range of enlargement is increased by the fact that the camera is a sophisticated optical instrument, which can be fitted with lenses that make it possible to record aspects that the naked eye cannot perceive. Secondly, when we look at

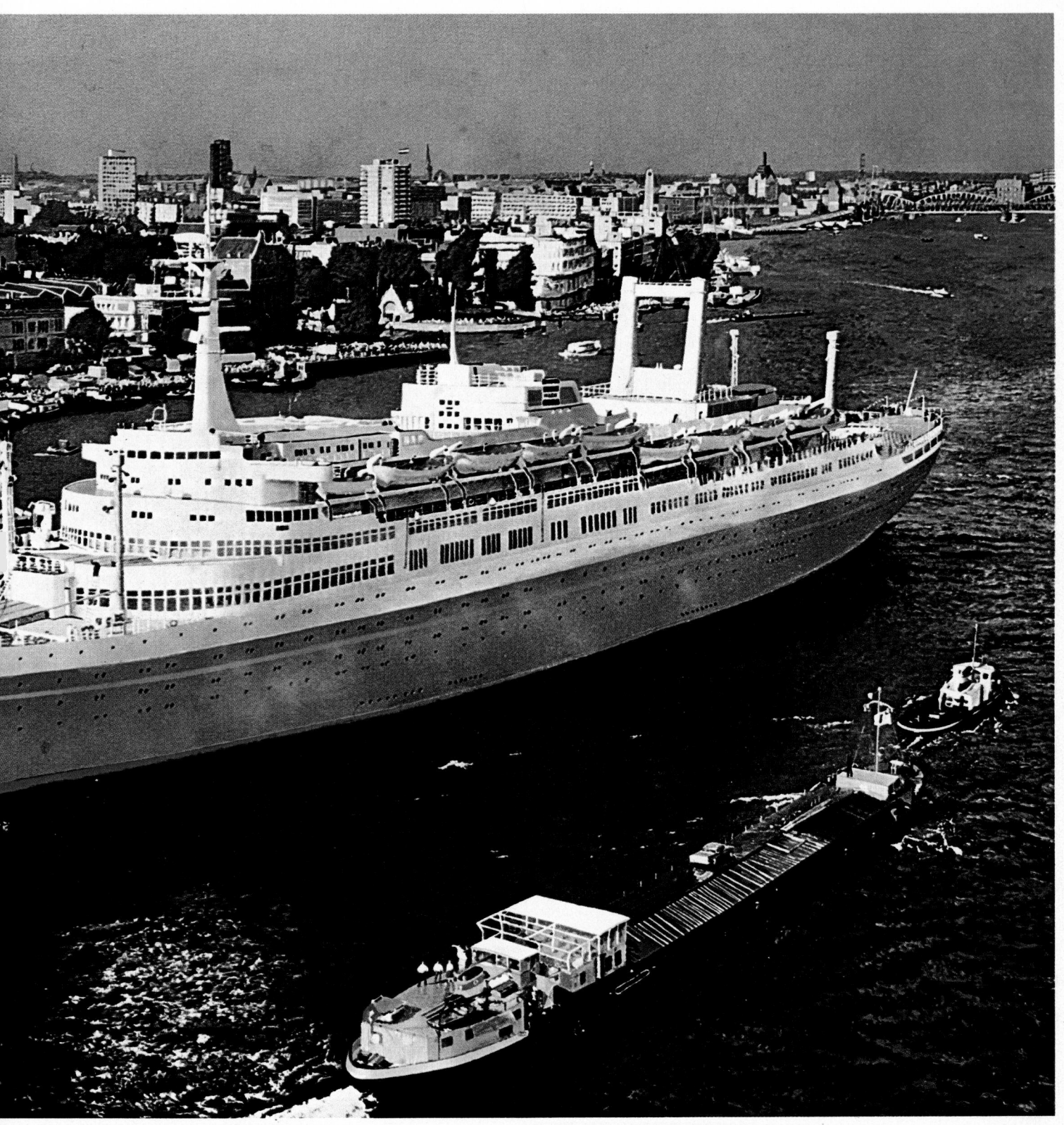

369.
John Clem Clarke
Small Bacchanal
1970
New York, O. K. Harris Gallery

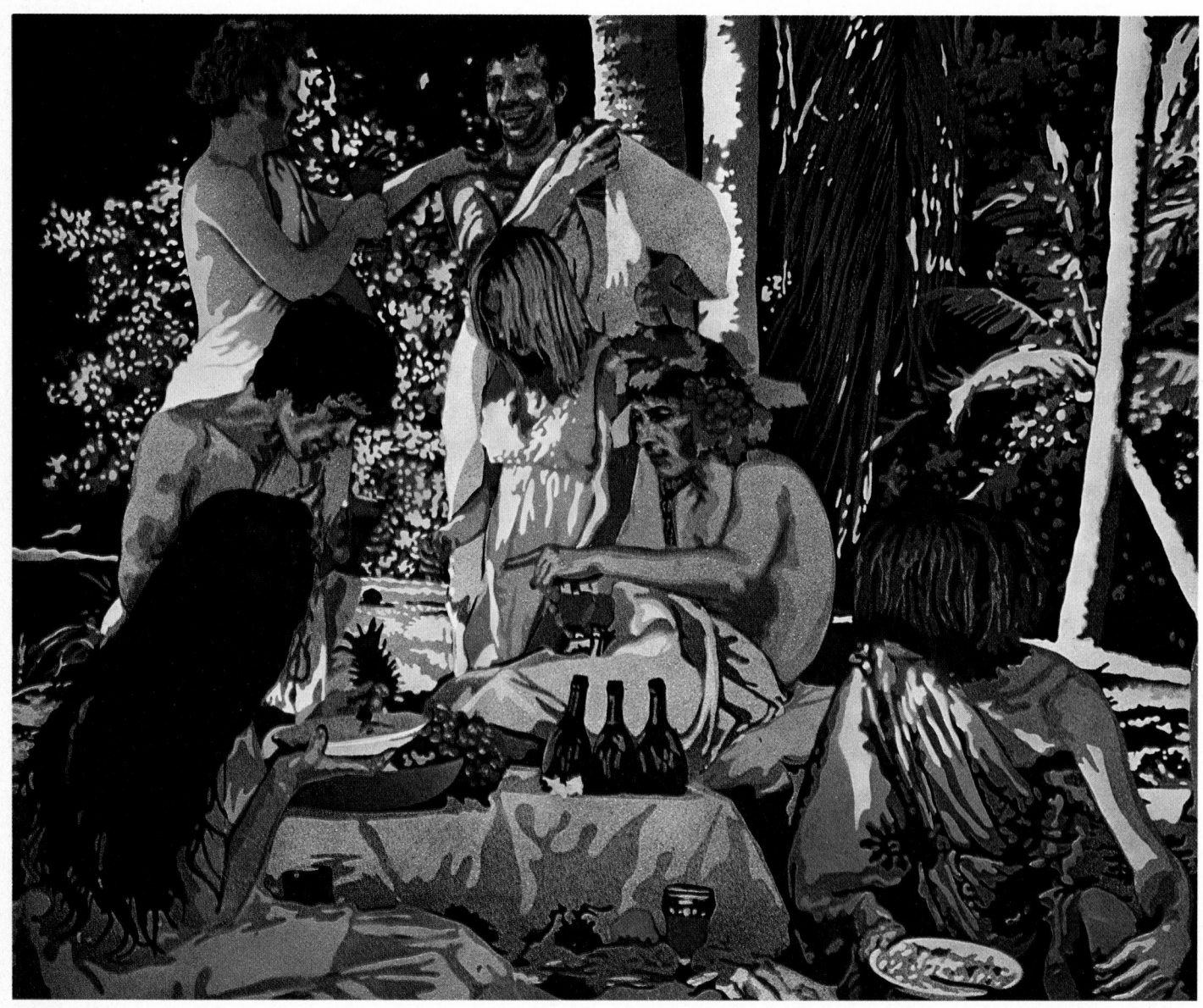

photographs, we are often uncertain of the relative proportions of the objects *within the frame*, especially if the picture has been unskilfully composed. We are often able to judge the height of a building, or the size of a statue, only because the photographer has been careful to include a human figure. Close's portraits destroy scale, and are in this sense disorienting.

Another problem in photography is that of the "all over" quality of the camera's vision. When photography was born, in the nineteenth century, the men of that time were astonished by the sheer quantity of details which the lens recorded on the sensitized plate or paper. There were far more of these details, they realized, than even the most industrious artist could hope to include in his painting or drawing. (This made them feel, naively, that photography was inherently superior to painting. Superrealism often seems to concede this superiority, which other art disputes.) Close grapples with this problem in two ways. The first is by reducing the content of the work—a single

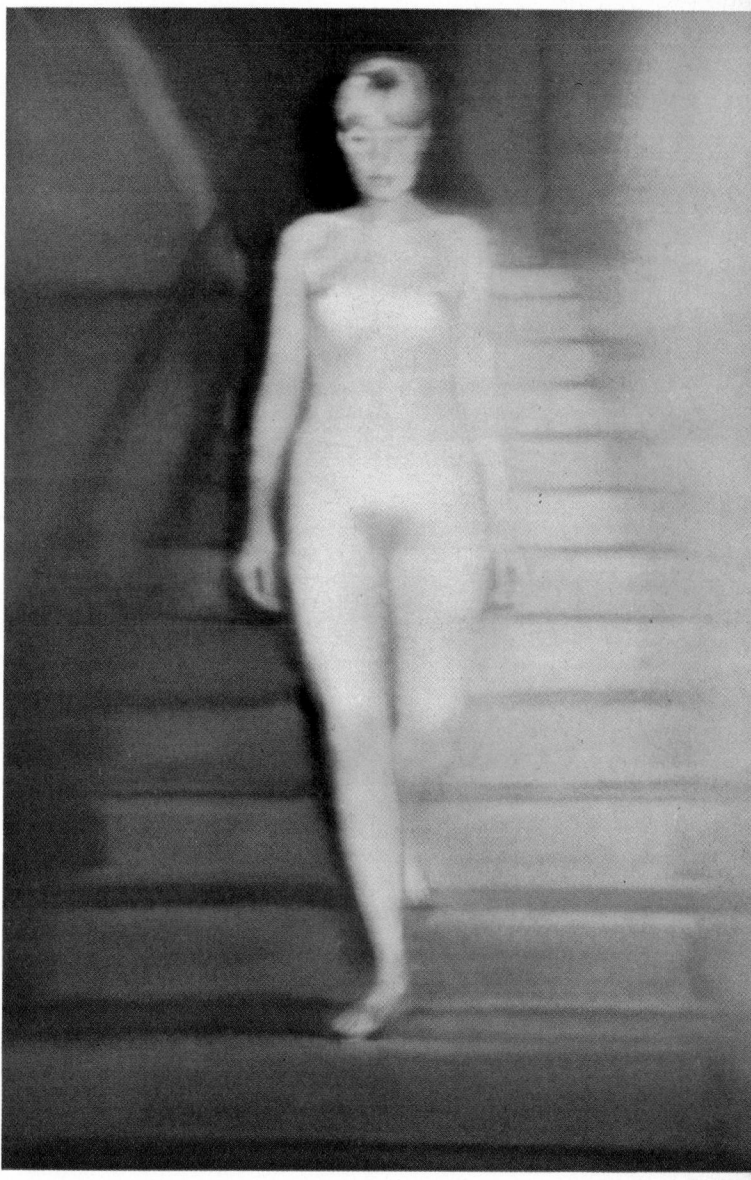

head is all he is willing to paint. The second is by a laborious effort to reproduce precisely what the camera has seen. He can at any rate examine this vision minutely and at leisure on the print, which permits a scrutiny closer and more intimate than that which could be given to the living sitter.

In many of his paintings, especially the more recent ones, Close also tries to echo the camera's faults as well as its virtues. He seems anxious to reproduce the aberrations of vision that are peculiar to the camera lens. Sophisticated as lenses may now have become, they are in most respects less sensitive and flexible than the human eye. The principle of the variable aperture, which allows the photographer to adjust his instrument to different lighting conditions, brings with it certain penalties. In particular, the wider the aperture the photographer uses, the shallower the zone in which the image is in sharp focus. This can create difficulties in close-up work. In taking a picture of a head, the photographer may find that if he gets the tip of the nose in focus, the eyes, in a directly frontal view, are already not quite sharp. He juggles with the problem as best he can, usually choosing to have the plane of focus resting on the eyes and cheekbones, rather than on the tip of the nose. Close reproduces these defects without editing them. In some of his portraits the tip of the nose is slightly blurred, and the blurring begins again behind the focal zone—with the ears, for instance, and the hair as it springs away from the forehead.

Another characteristic of his paintings is that, like photographs, they are the product of monocular rather than binocular vision. This gives the portraits an intensity, as does the rigidity imposed by a mechanical way of seeing. The eye collates impressions through a scanning process, focusing on different areas in turn in a way that we are usually unaware of. The camera has no such facility of adjustment.

Close's work also directs our attention towards another characteristic of Superrealist painting as a whole, which is that it is impossible to reproduce it satisfactorily. The image borrowed from a photograph, when reduced in size and turned into another photograph, re-assumes the qualities it had at first, before the artist began work on the image.

It may perhaps be asked why these looming heads should be of any more interest to the spectator than the photographic originals upon which they are based. The easiest answer to this question is to say that they exercise the fascination that has always been attributed to *trompe l'oeil*—the kind of painting which reproduces reality in such a way that we mistake what is painted for the real thing. Since Close bases his work so closely upon a photographic original, it might even be said that he is not in fact a portraitist, but a still-life painter

371.
Chuck Close
Susan
1972; 252 × 226.5 cm. (98 × 88 in.)

372. Opposite
Chuck Close
Richard
1969
Aachen, Neue Galerie, coll. Ludwig
(Photo: Ann Munchow)

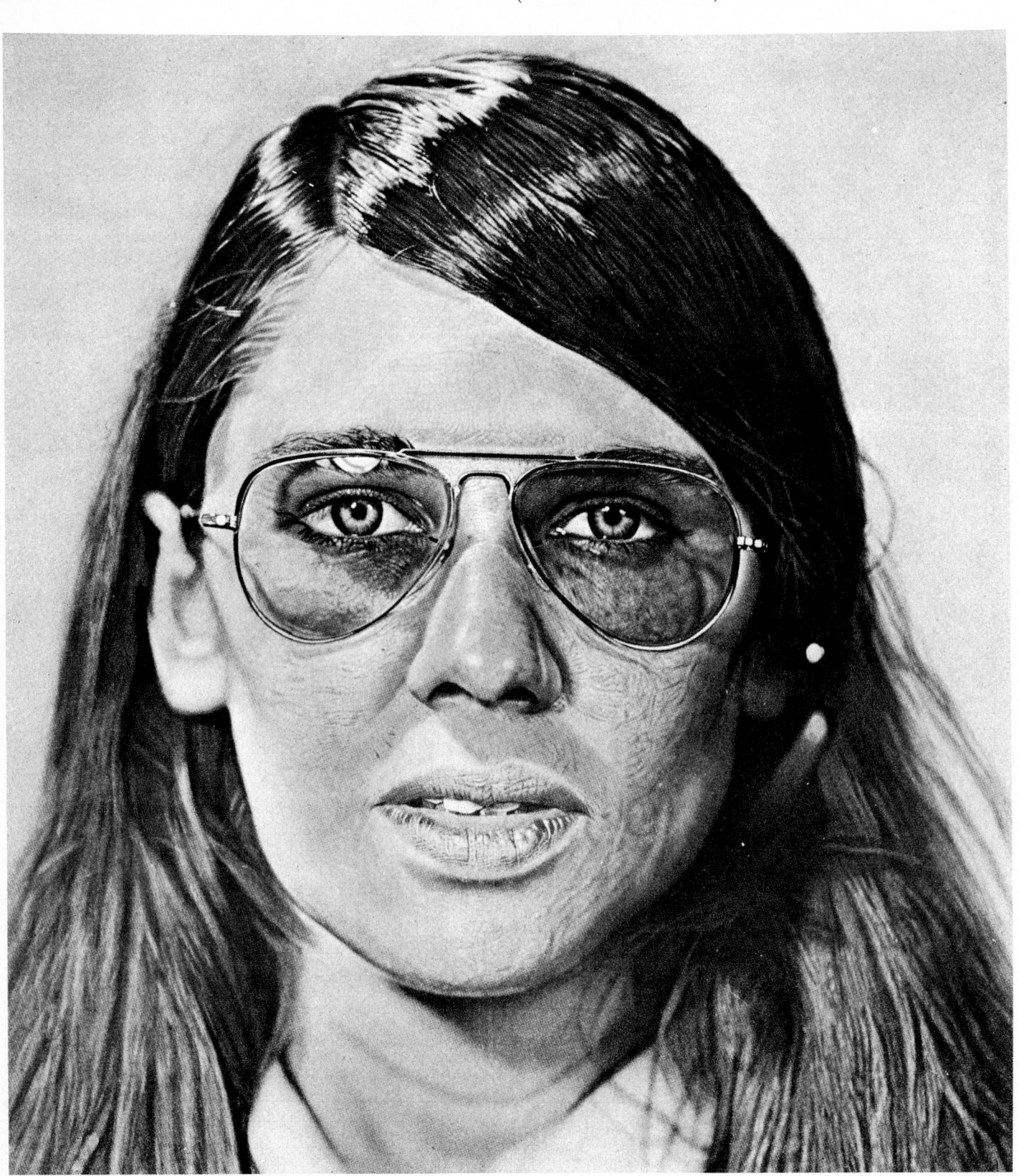

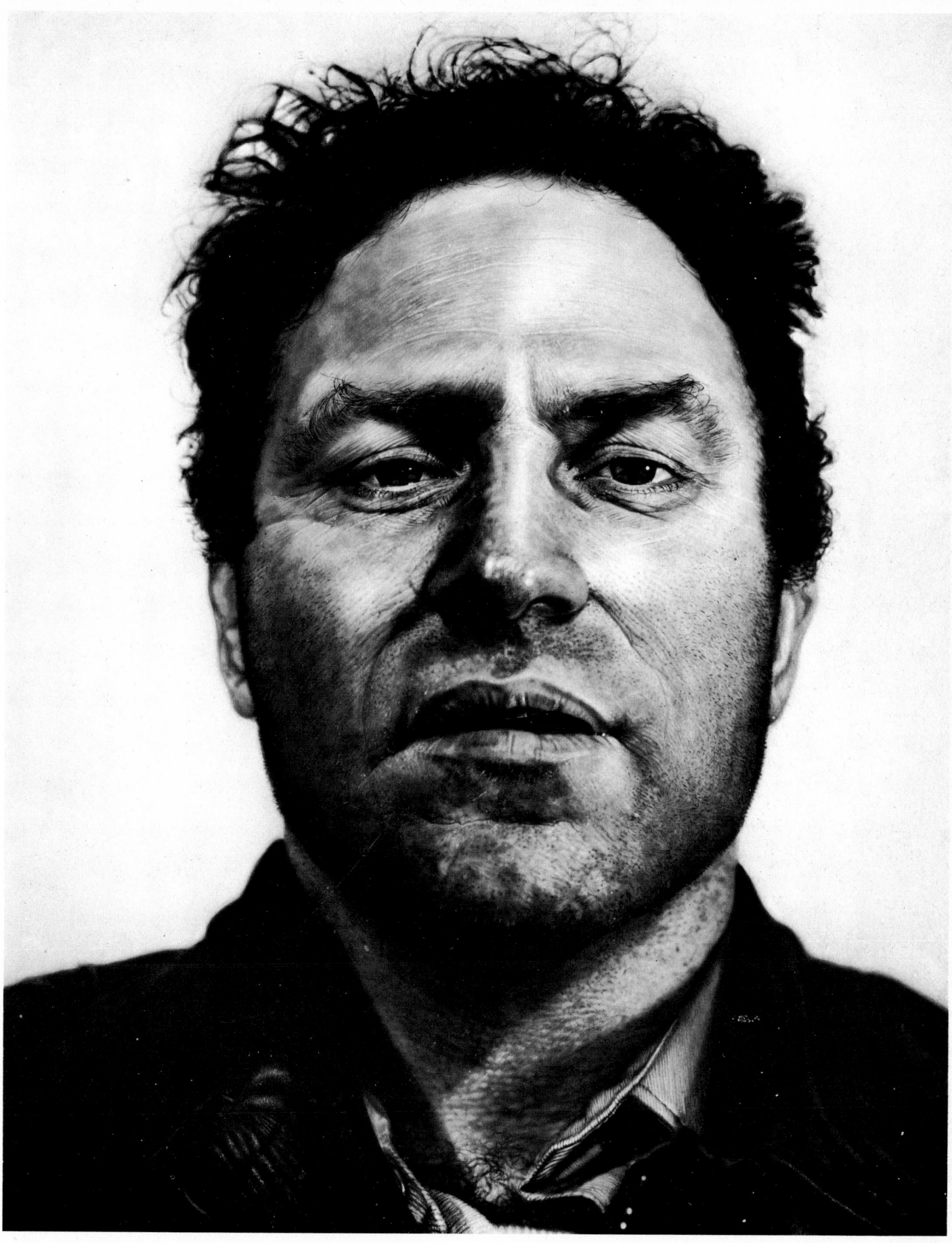

whose chosen subject happens to be the photographic print. It is really only the change in scale which militates against this argument, and even that is not conclusive, since, as I have already noted, the photographic print itself can be made upon almost any scale.

In fact, it is not merely the technical skill of the performance which makes Close interesting as an artist, but the inevitable gap between the simulacrum and the reality—even if this "reality" is itself a simulacrum. Close, unlike Roy Lichtenstein, does not admit that he makes adjustments in the original image. Rather he asserts the opposite—that he wants to reproduce the original as closely as he can. But, nevertheless, in making this statement he is forced to admit that there will be an area of difference, however slight, between what he sets out to do and what he actually accomplishes. This tiny discrepancy is enough to animate his paintings, to give them life as works of art.

Another artist who works in this severely restricted yet interesting area is Richard McClean. As nearly all the Superrealist painters do, he confines himself to a very narrow range of subject-matter. In his case, he limits himself almost entirely to paintings of horses and riders. Usually these are based either on publicity photographs or on the kind of picture that is taken of a winning racehorse, with its jockey up and its owner or trainer proudly holding the bridle (Plate 373). In fact, McClean has turned himself into a kind of contemporary George Stubbs, but with this proviso—he does not seem to work for the owners of the prize-winning beasts but rather to examine this equine world with an ironic fascination, a tendency to stress its philistinism and bad taste. Yet to say this is probably to read something into the paintings which is not present in the artist's mind. What probably interests him most is the exercise of making a "hand-made" version of a mechanical original.

If one is inclined to deny McClean's work any significant sociological content, this is not the case with other leading Superrealist artists. Four men who in various ways seem to typify the style, and to explain the very direct reaction it arouses, are Robert Cottingham, Richard Estes, John Salt, and Ralph Goings. In each of these we find an unmistakable, and obviously intentional, reflection of salient features of contemporary American life.

Cottingham is a painter whose work once again underlines the close connection between Superrealism and Pop Art. His specialty is the sign. He portrays the words and letters which adorn the movie-house marquees and department-store facades of his native New York. He thus presents us with a version of Pop's fascination with the written word and with advertising. The signs that Cottingham choose to paint (Plate 374) are inevitably viewed through the lens of the camera, and it is the camera which is used to impose the arbitrary croppings which sometimes rob the letters of meaning, and at other times supply meanings different from those they possess in reality—as, for instance, when the word MART is transformed, by a piece of symbolic legerdemain, into ART. Cottingham's clean style of painting gives his work a slightly simplified look, which also tends to suggest a relationship to the somewhat more drastic simplifications typical of Pop.

A striking thing about Cottingham's work is that it is so thoroughly urban. The same is true of the work of Richard Estes. Of all the Superrealist painters whose work is illustrated here, Estes is formally the most complex, and this fact alone brings him closest to painting of a traditional kind. As his colleagues do, Estes uses colour transparencies as his prime materials. These transparencies, however, are not only rigorously winnowed but most selectively employed. Estes is the poet of the modern city and, in particular, the poet of New York. The glittering glass facades of New York buildings, with their multiple reflections, and reflections within reflections, exercise an obsessional fascination over him, only rivalled by the equivalent effects to be discovered in the glittering metallic maze of the subway system. If the figure makes an appearance in his paintings, it generally does so in a completely subordinate role—dimly seen within a store or cafeteria, or reflected, ghostlike, in a shop-window. Estes's subject is architecture, not people (Plate 375).

373.
Richard McLean
Still Life with Black Jockey
1969; 150 × 150 cm. (59 × 59 in.)
New York, Whitney Museum

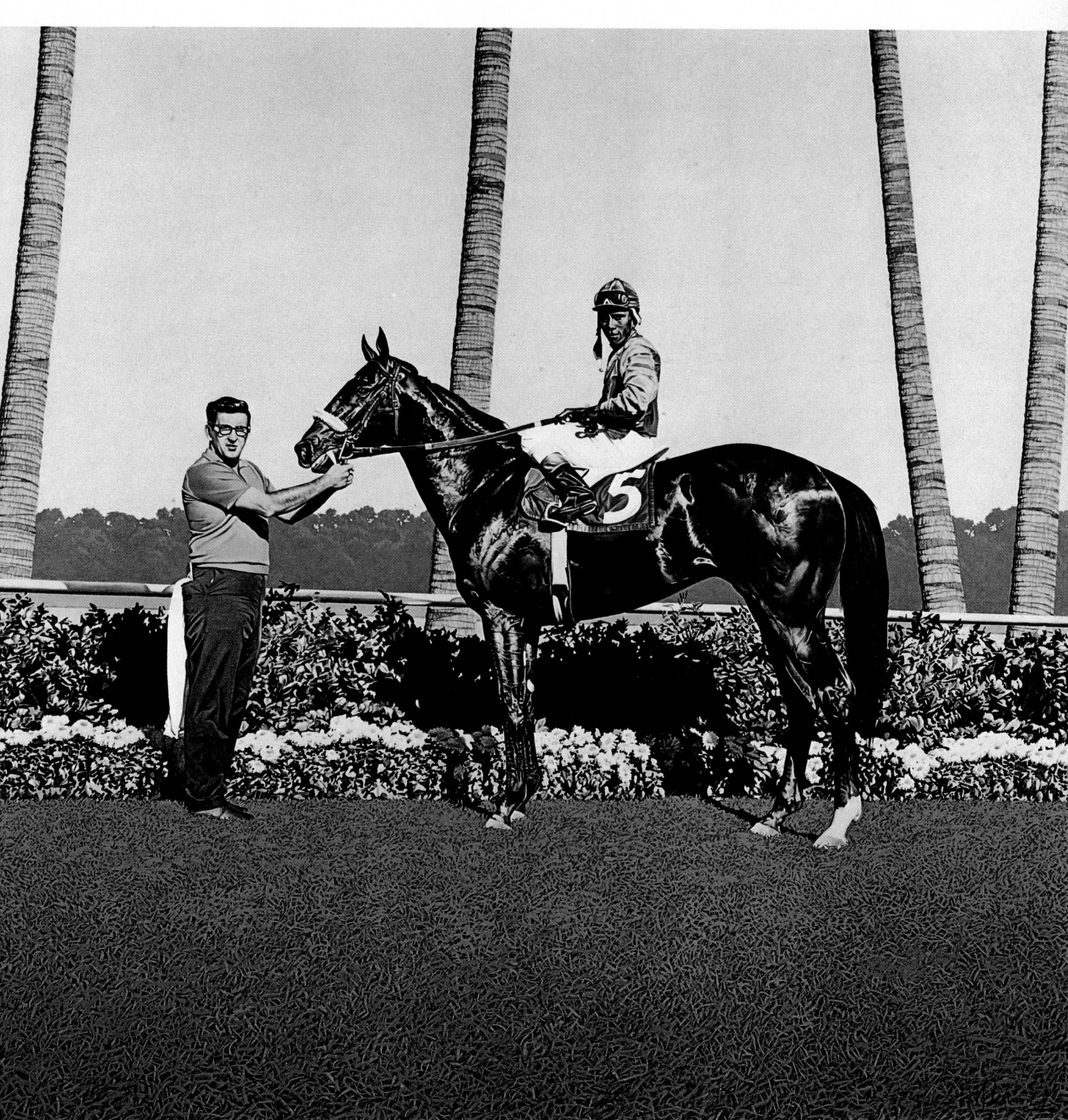

374.
Robert Cottingham
F.W.
1975 ; 200 × 200 cm. (78 × 78 in.)
Collection of the artist

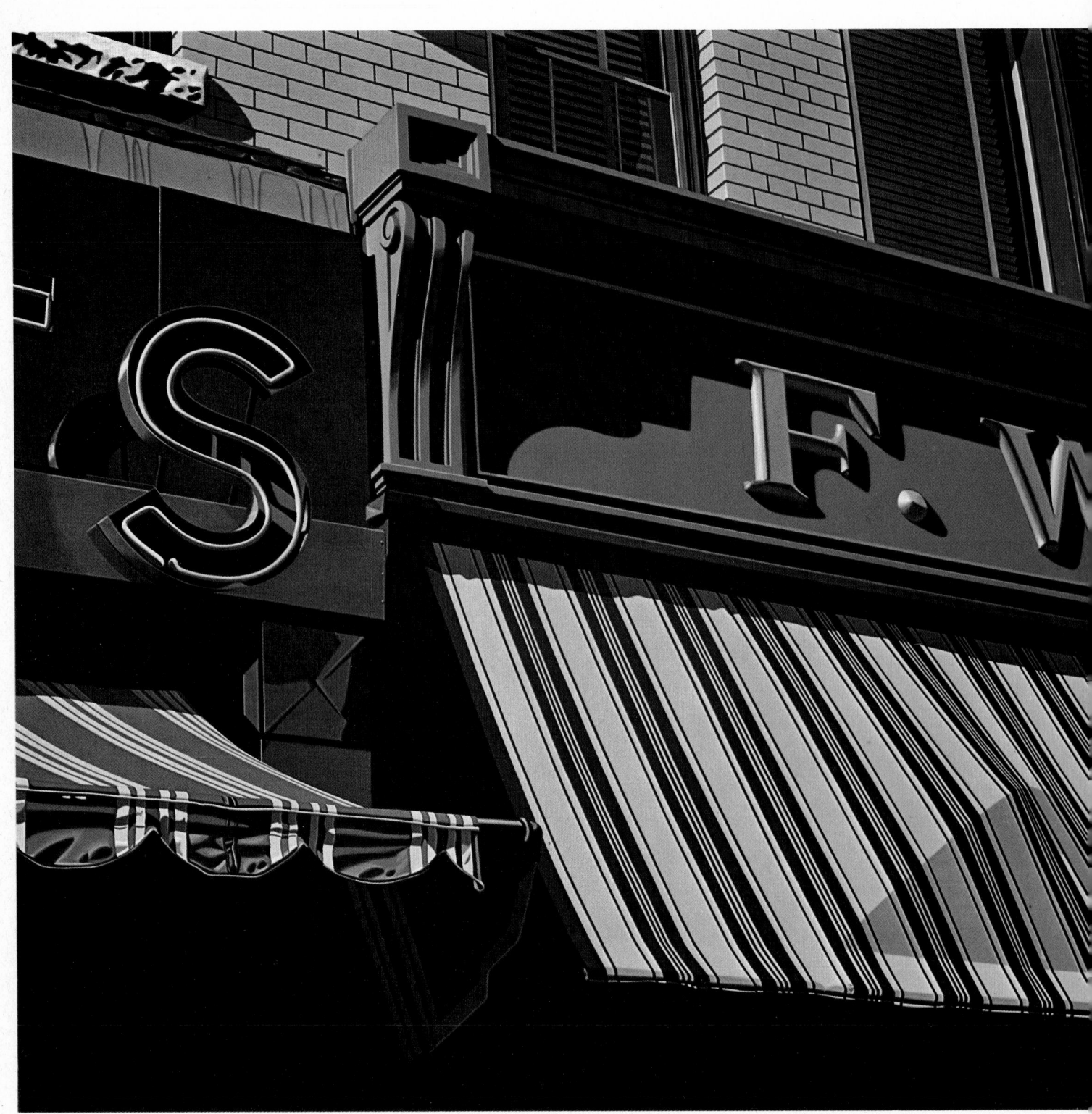

Richard Estes
Façade
1974
Courtesy, Allan Stone Gallery

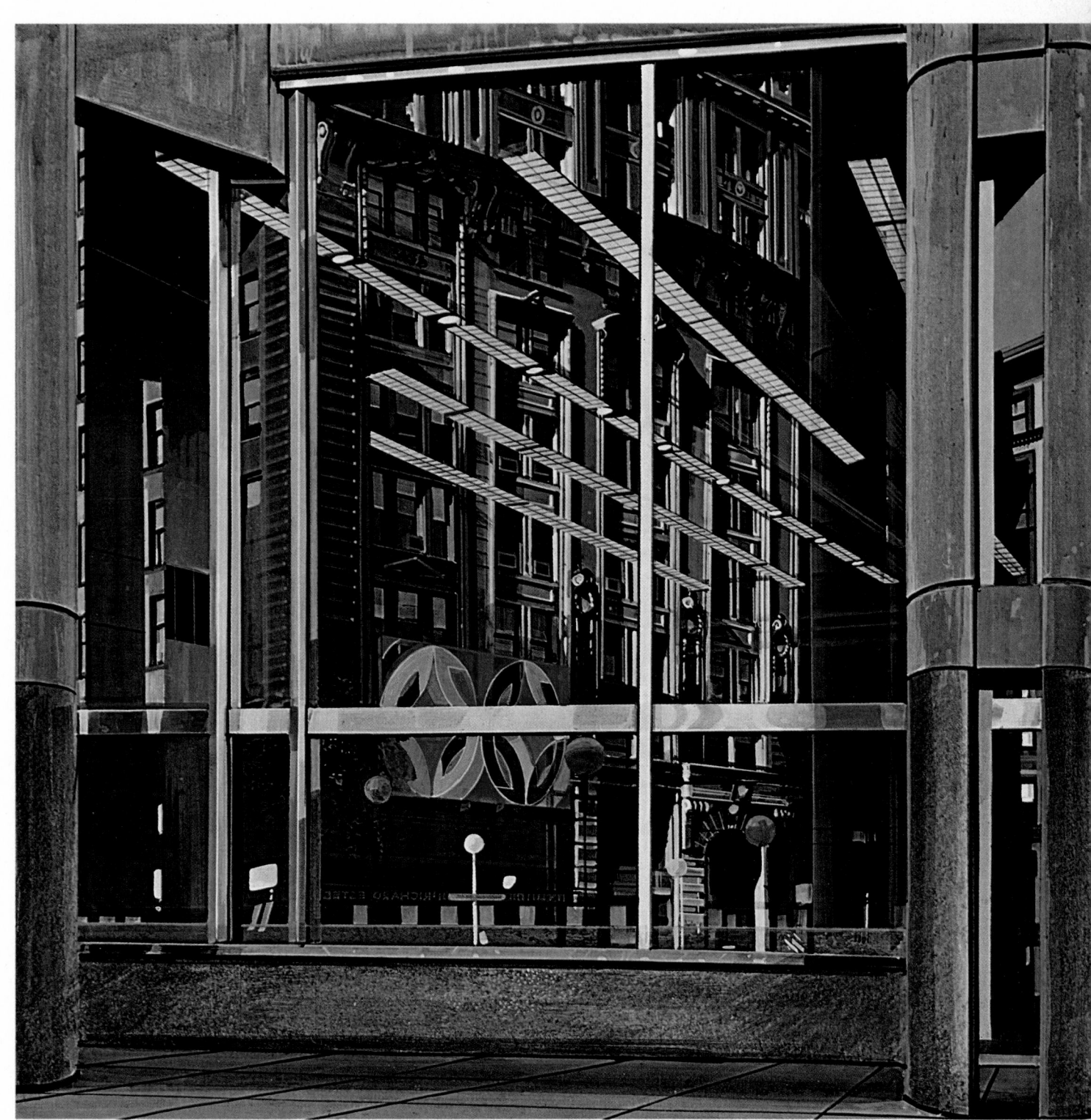

376.
Ralph Goings
Paul's Corner
1970; 120 × 189.4 cm. (47 × 74 in.)
New York, O. K. Harris Gallery

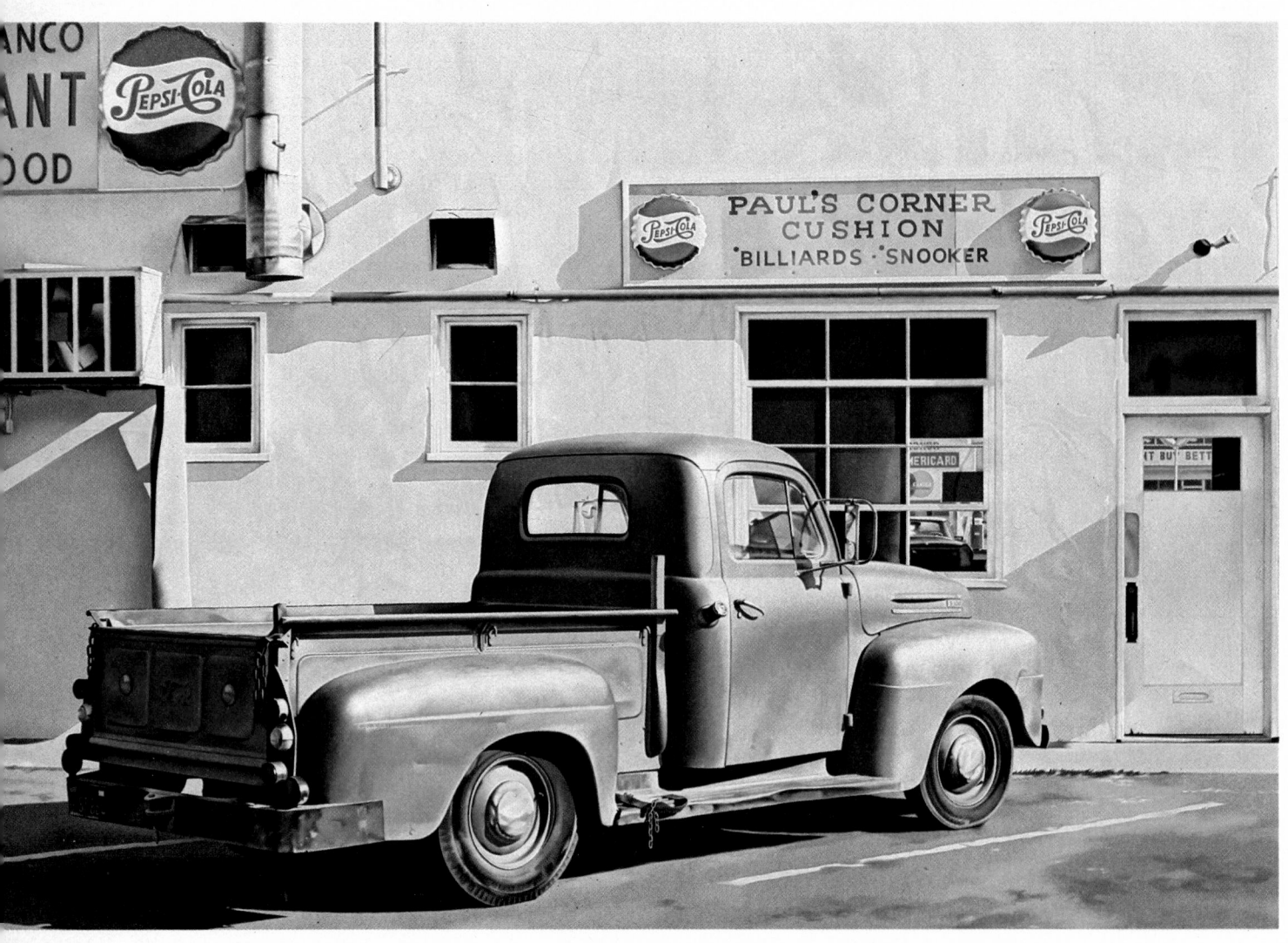

It soon becomes apparent, if one examines Estes's work at all closely, that he, as Roy Lichtenstein does, makes innumerable small adjustments in the selected image. These adjustments, as are those made by Lichtenstein, are aimed at imposing order upon chaos. Estes makes virtuosic use of a complex geometry of planes and angles. Within each of his compositions is concealed an abstract organization almost as complex as that to be discovered in a Kandinsky. In fact, there is a close resemblance in method to the work of some of the leading architectural painters of the past, in particular to the best of all the Dutch seventeenth-century painters of church architecture, Pieter Saenredam. The latter, like Estes, is an artist who

extracted a very wide variety of effects from apparently limited subject-matter.

Ralph Goings is a Californian, and his paintings do for the urban landscape of California what those of Estes do for New York (Plate 376). Automobiles occupy the forefront of his paintings; and the flimsy drive-in stores and eateries lining the great Californian superhighways usually form the background. To some extent, Goings therefore tends to parallel the work of the Californian Pop artist Ed Ruscha, who has been attracted by the architecture of American filling stations. Goings, with the majority of Superrealist artists, makes use of the airbrush, a technique which originated in advertising design studios,

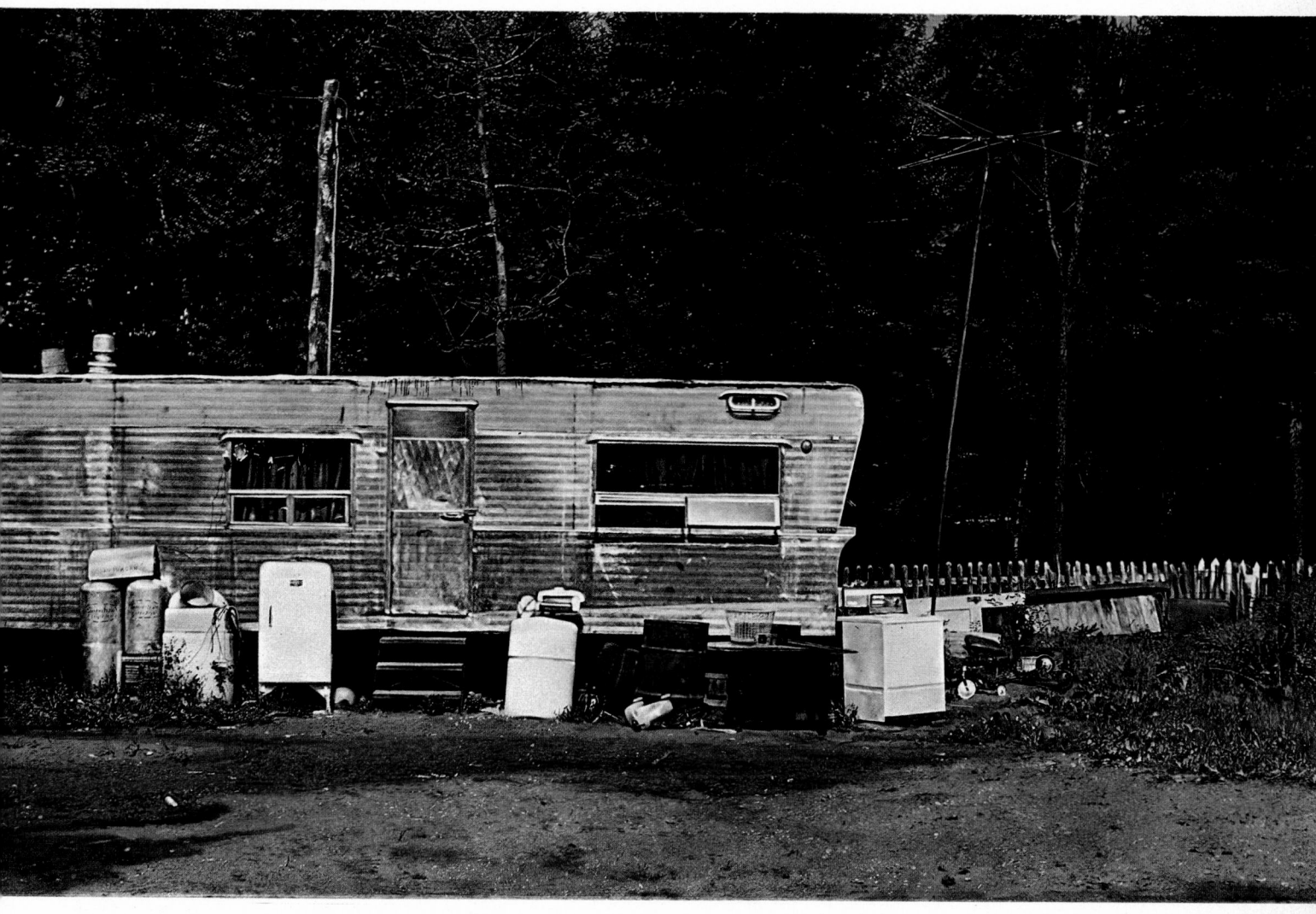

and which gives a smooth, meticulously impersonal finish to the work. He is perhaps the best known of a whole group of artists now resident in California who treat similar subject-matter in a more or less identical way.

The fact that Goings, even more than Estes, chooses to paint a landscape with no apparent redeeming features has been used to support the argument that he, too, is a nihilist, in search, like so many avant-garde artists before him, of acceptably "unacceptable" subjects. This seems to me to beg the question. It was not until the time of the Romantic movement that people began to think that the painter, and the landscape painter in particular, must make beauty only from what was

already agreed to be beautiful. And even during the Romantic period the rule was as much honoured in the breach as in the observance. Philippe de Loutherbourg painted *Coalbrookdale by Night* in 1801, thus making art out of the worst horrors of the Industrial Revolution. Turner performed much the same feat a little later with his *Keelmen Hauling Coals by Moonlight*, that hymn to the beauty of industrial Tyneside. The fact is that artists traditionally tend to look for subjects that are "original"—that is, unsullied by the attempts of previous artists. They do this at least as often as they choose a subject that is already guaranteed to be "artistic". At the same time there is an understandable tendency on the part of the more

378.
Stephen Posen
Portrait of a Space
1975
New York, O. K. Harris Gallery
(Photo: Eric Pollitzer)

original and adventurous painters to seek out subjects that seem to them to be typical of their own time, as a means of saying something about the society they live in. Goings and the other Californian Superrealists have been able to prove, in however unambitious a fashion, that art is still capable of fulfilling some of the functions which used to be attributed to it—if this is the direction in which the artist himself chooses to go.

One Superrealist whose pictures seem to have a marked symbolic content is the émigré Englishman John Salt. His chosen subject-matter is automobiles, and in this he resembles not only Ralph Goings but also numerous other artists of the same school, among them Robert Bechtle and Don Eddy. But Salt's cars are not roadworthy—they are the battered wrecks on American automobile dumps. Even when he chooses to paint one of the great trailers which so aptly symbolize American mobility and American leisure, he shows it apparently abandoned and surrounded by debris—old refrigerators and non-functional washing machines (Plate 377). It is hard not to see his paintings as deliberate reflections of affluence and waste, and indeed I can think of no reason why the spectator should resist this interpretation.

Not all the art classified under the rubric Superrealist is interpretable in this way. As we have already seen, the explanation would not apply to Charles Close. Nor would it serve as a means of approaching the curious work of Stephen Posen (Plate 378). Posen takes banal objects, in this case some streamers and an elaborate birdcage, and subjects them to an unwavering scrutiny. This scrutiny seems designed to bring out the sense of alienation the artist feels. Another device favoured by Posen is a kind of still-life painting based on a group of cardboard boxes covered with a cloth. Here, too, but more obviously, we are informed of the way the mysterious and the ordinary intermingle with one another. Posen shows virtuoso power in depicting his chosen subject-matter, but the world he inhabits is peculiarly narrow and claustrophobic.

Another, and a much more various and engaging, virtuoso is Howard Kanovitz. Kan-ovitz, indeed, is too various to be easily classifiable. Some of his paintings, like the deadpan *The Opening* (Plate 379), are best thought of as offshoots of Pop. Others, such as *The Painting Wall, The Water-bucket Stool* (Plate 380), have a metaphysical quality which seems to owe a good deal to Magritte. This direction—a movement towards the surprising and the magical—is that taken by his more recent work. Kanovitz demonstrates that irrational elements can survive successfully within an idiom that is apparently totally realistic. Indeed, the sudden leap into irrationality which occurs in many of Kanovitz's most successful paintings is fuelled by the virtuosity of his technique, which includes a marked ability to manipulate *trompe l'oeil* effects without allowing *trompe l'oeil* (as it so often does) to dominate the composition into which it has been introduced.

One of the curious things about the fully developed Superrealist style is that it is so firmly rooted in the United States. Those Englishmen, such as Malcolm Morley and John Salt, who have made a name for themselves by practising this kind of realism have actually been domiciled in America. There seem to be two reasons for this. One is the tradition of American realism, deep-rooted and stubborn even in the early twentieth century, at a time when realist styles were in retreat almost everywhere else except in Soviet Russia. The second reason is not historical but economic. Superrealism is a style which has depended for its support, unlike other recent Modernist styles, upon the enthusiasm of private patrons. The United States was the place where the greatest remaining reservoir of private patronage was to be found.

But there is a possible third reason as well. It has been said that the curiously "closed" quality of Superrealist art is a reflection of the numb conservatism of Nixon's America. Art responds to the stagnation of politics by developing a kind of carapace, an insulating brilliance of technique. In support of this argument there is the fact that the only other place where a considerable realist group has made its mark in recent years is Spain. The best known of the Spanish realists (actually a Chilean

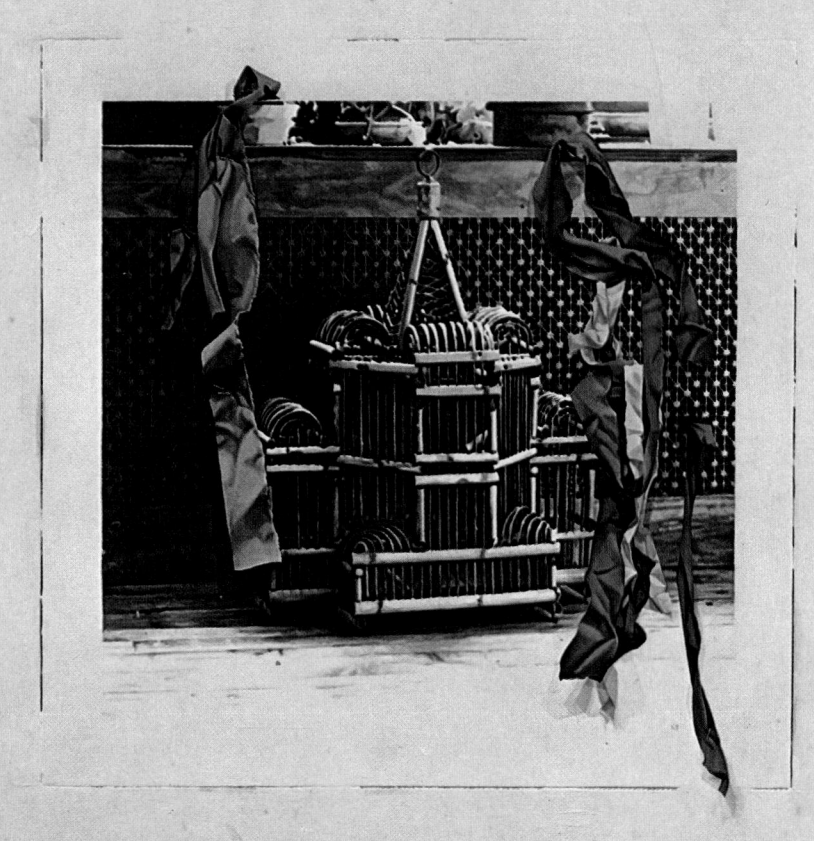

379.
Howard Kanovitz
The Opening
1967; 49 × 69.5 cm. (19 × 27 in.)
Cologne, Wallraf-Richartz Museum, coll. Ludwig

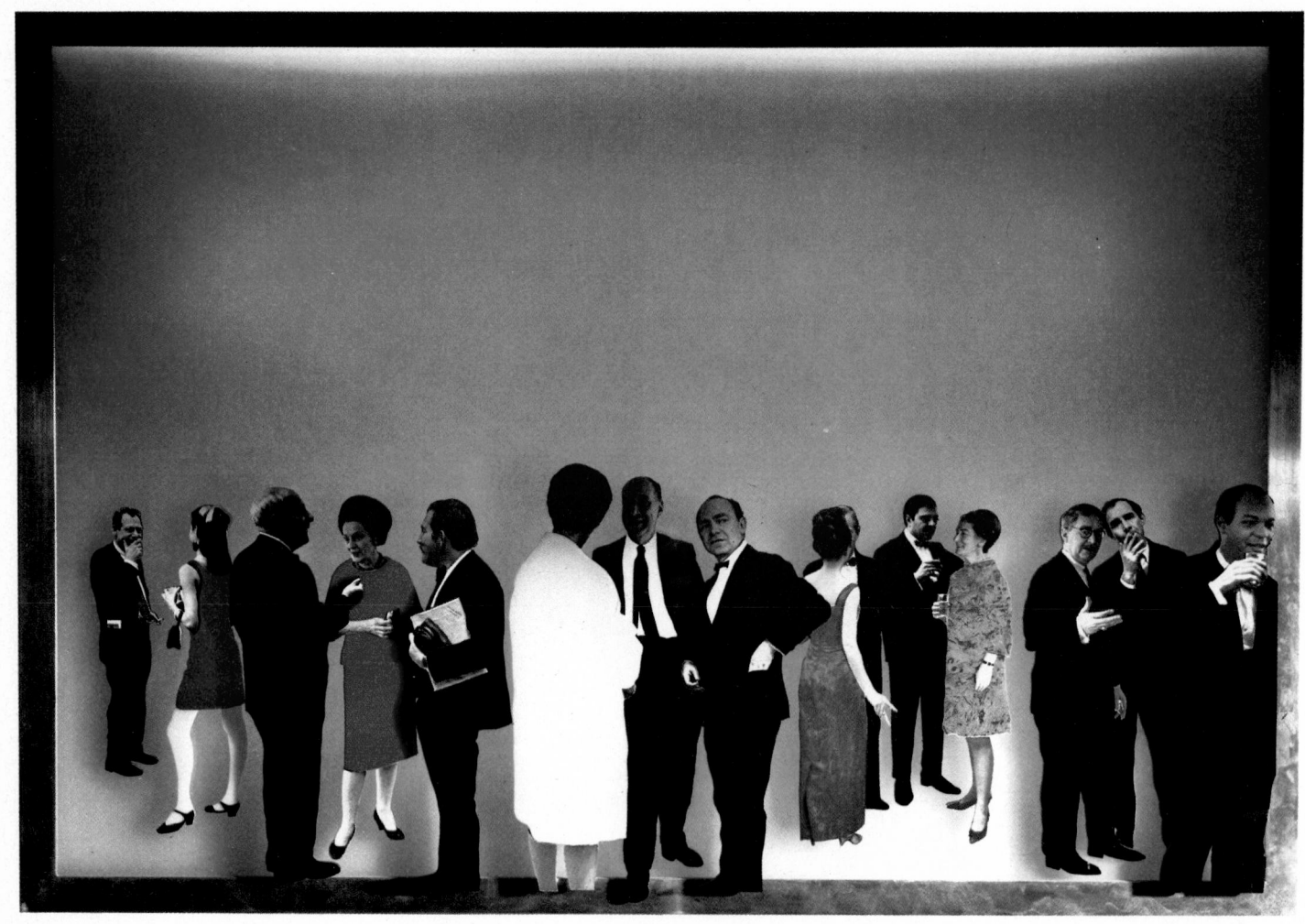

domiciled in Spain) is Claudio Bravo, whose work can look very like that of his American contemporaries (Plate 381).

Up to this point I have said nothing about Superrealist sculptors. Indeed, even though it exists, Superrealist sculpture may still seem uncomfortably paradoxical, especially if we consider the fact that Superrealist painting is so largely concerned with the illusionistic rendering of three-dimensional objects upon a flat surface. Even at those times in the past when European art was most concerned with realism—the seventeenth century, for example—sculpture tended to maintain a distance between itself and the moving flux of life. However illusionistic Gianlorenzo Bernini's sculptures became, the spectator was in

no danger of mistaking them for living people. One of the few exceptions to this rule is supplied by Spanish art. Here, indeed, some seventeenth-century religious images, with their painted faces, glass eyes, jewels, and real clothes made of silk and satin, have an astonishing resemblance to living beings. To those who came to worship, they were in fact as close to living people as made no difference.

American Superrealist sculpture, as exemplified by the work of John de Andrea and Duane Hanson, does indeed tend to strike the spectator as disturbing, almost indecorous. The same spectator would be most unlikely to have a reaction of an identical kind to the work of Superrealist painters, however pronounced the *trompe l'oeil* element.

380. Opposite
Howard Kanovitz
The Painting Wall, The Water-bucket Stool
1968; 240 × 295 cm.; 97 × 45 cm. (94 × 115 in.; 39 × 18 in.)
Aachen, Neue Galerie, coll. Ludwig

381. Overleaf
Claudio Bravo
Il pacchetto blu
1971; 111 × 140 cm. (43 × 55 in.)
London, Marlborough Fine Art

Speaking of realist art in the 1920's, when it was everywhere in retreat, the Spanish philosopher-critic Ortega y Gasset touched upon the subject of the waxwork. Waxworks, he said, had a peculiar effect upon us because they were neither one thing nor the other, neither art nor life.

Are Superrealist sculptures no more than waxworks brought up to date and promoted to the art galleries? It is tempting to say that they are. In many ways, they are more realistic, less illusionistic, than the wax figures in Mme. Tussaud's. Contrary to popular belief, for example, waxworks are not cast from the living body, whereas Superrealist sculpture is often put together from

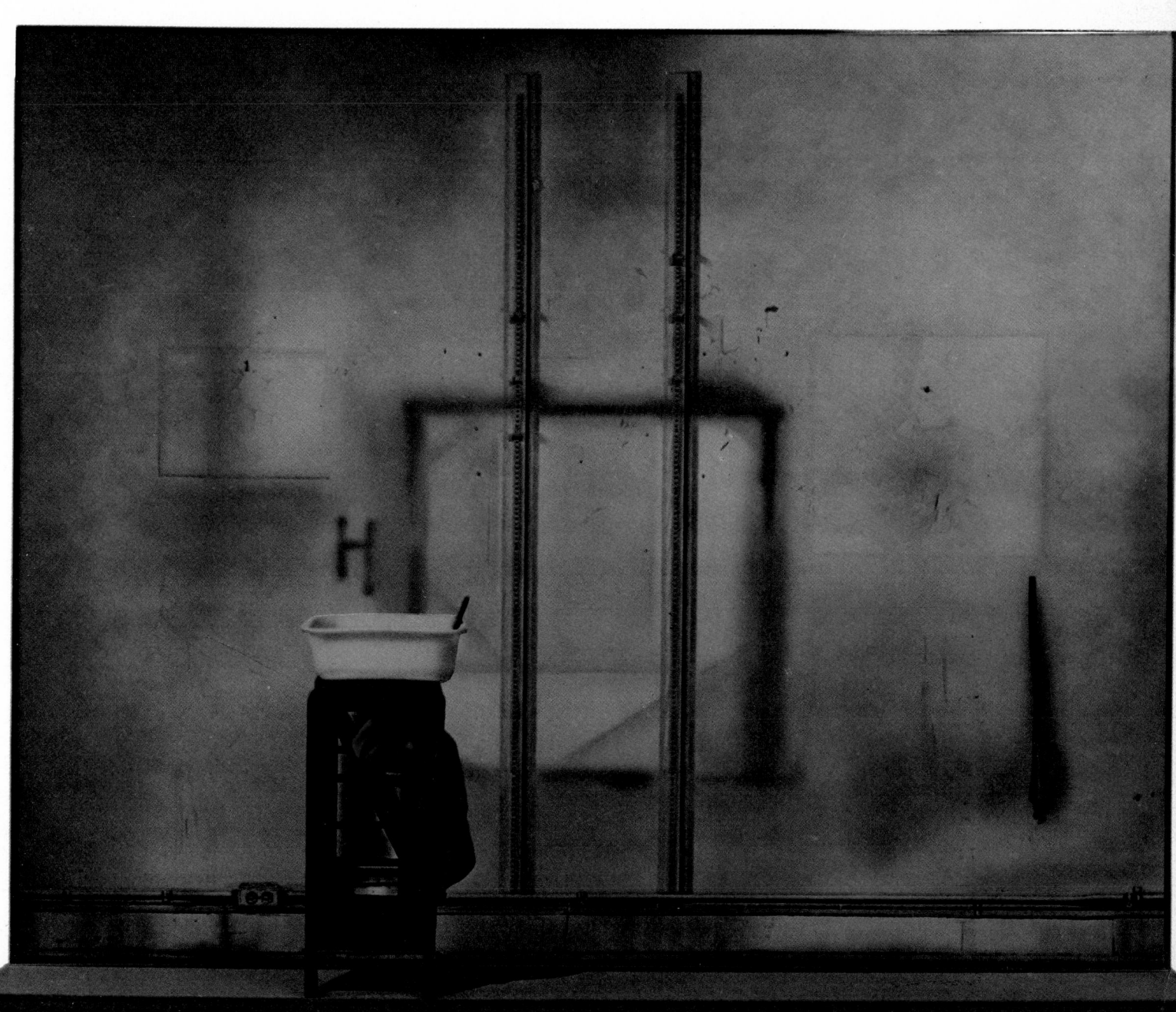

475

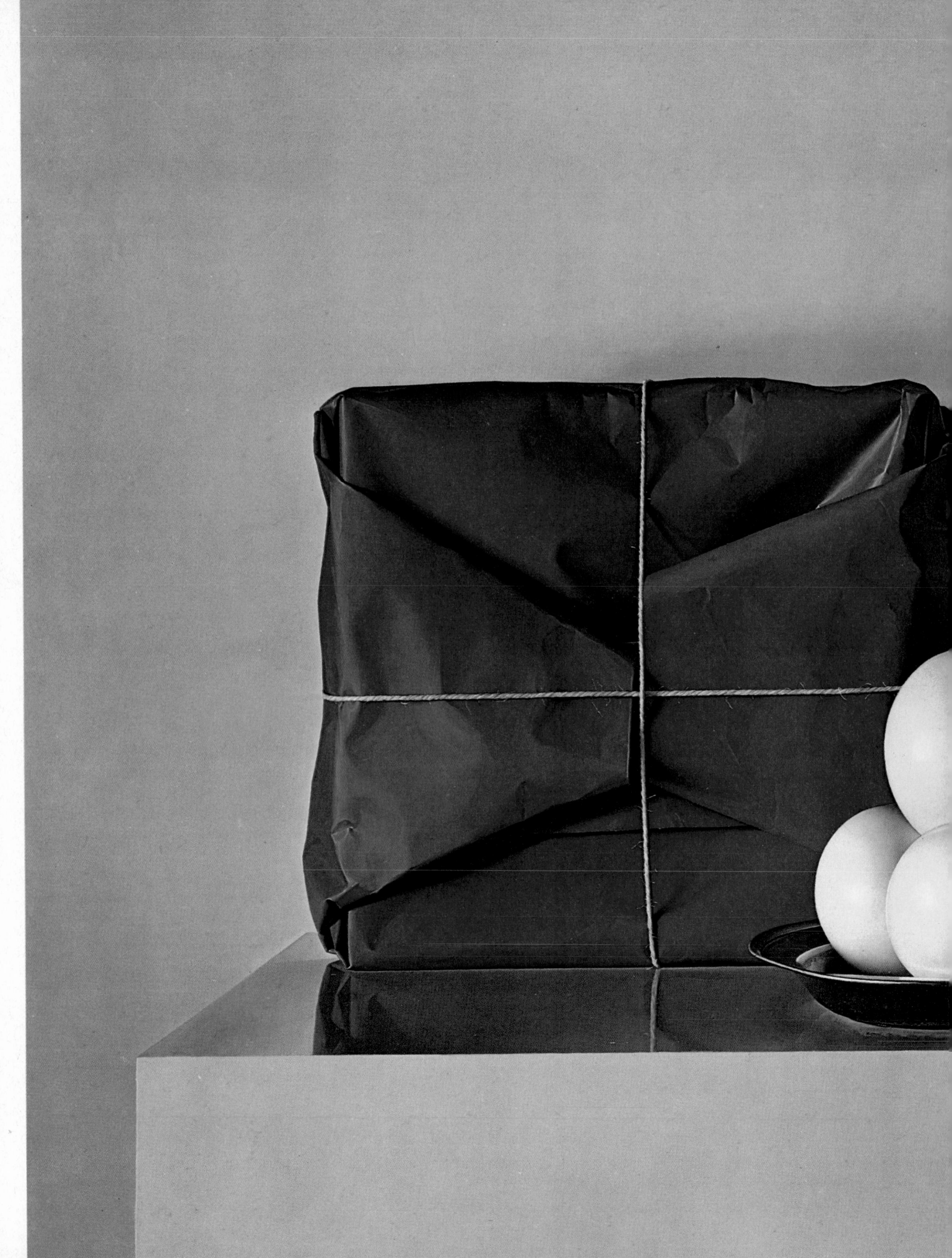

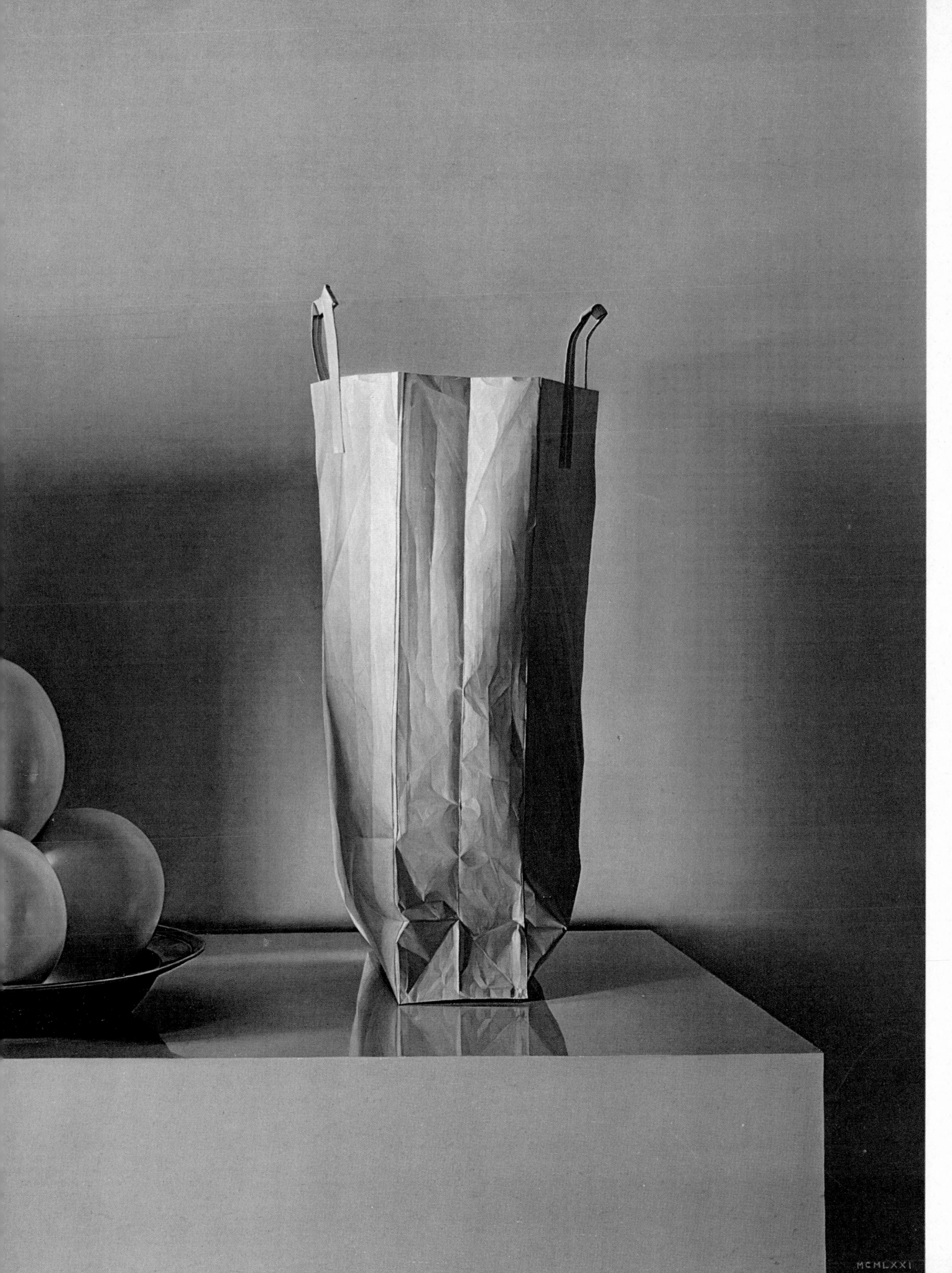

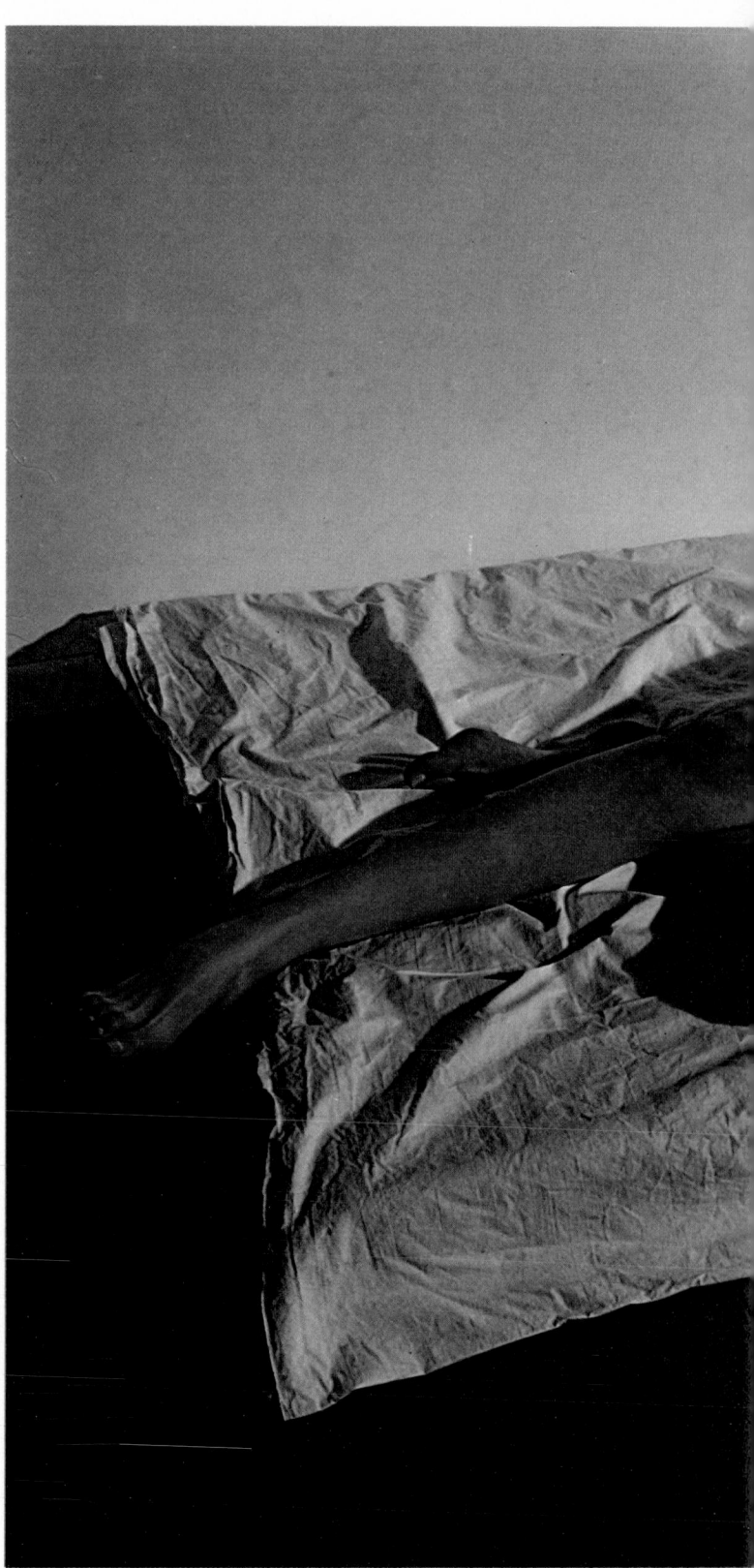

casts made in this way. Technically, the work of De Andrea and Hanson derives directly from that of George Segal. What these two artists have done is to take Segal's method of casting from life and perfect it. Now the figure emerges, not as a white and slightly clumsy version of the original model, but as a simulacrum which is exact in every detail—smoothed over, coloured to resemble life, provided with real hair and eyelashes and a pair of glass eyes; with clothing, too, where this in appropriate.

De Andrea does not clothe his figures. His nudes (Plate 382) are bland duplications of the American middle-class kids who are their originals—handsome and well built for the most part, but not hardened by any real effort of endurance. They somehow give away both their class and their national origin through details of hair style, posture, and expression. The fact that one can feel a mild dislike for De Andrea's sculptures, thought of simply as people, says something for their quality of lifelikeness, but it is still difficult to argue that they in any way transcend the waxworks which they so closely resemble. It has been argued that one of the things which makes modern art "modern" is its desire to break down the barrier that separates art from life. Thus Duchamp's bicycle wheel is simultaneously a work of art *and* a bicycle wheel, Warhol's Brillo box remains a Brillo box, and so forth. De Andrea's work lends continuing support to this theory, which is perhaps the best that can be said for it.

Duane Hanson is a different matter. What he does for the most part is to present us with a gallery of American types, brilliantly if somewhat cruelly observed. Occasionally he attempts a more elaborate tableau—there is one of a race riot—but these are usually less successful. Hanson's claim to be an artist is founded upon the exercise of traditional talents for observation and synthesis. No American housewife could ever be as representative of the whole race of American housewives as his bulging *Woman with a Shopping Cart* (Plate 383). Hanson is, in fact, that extreme rarity, an artist who uses sculpture, rather than painting or drawing, as a vehicle for social criticism.

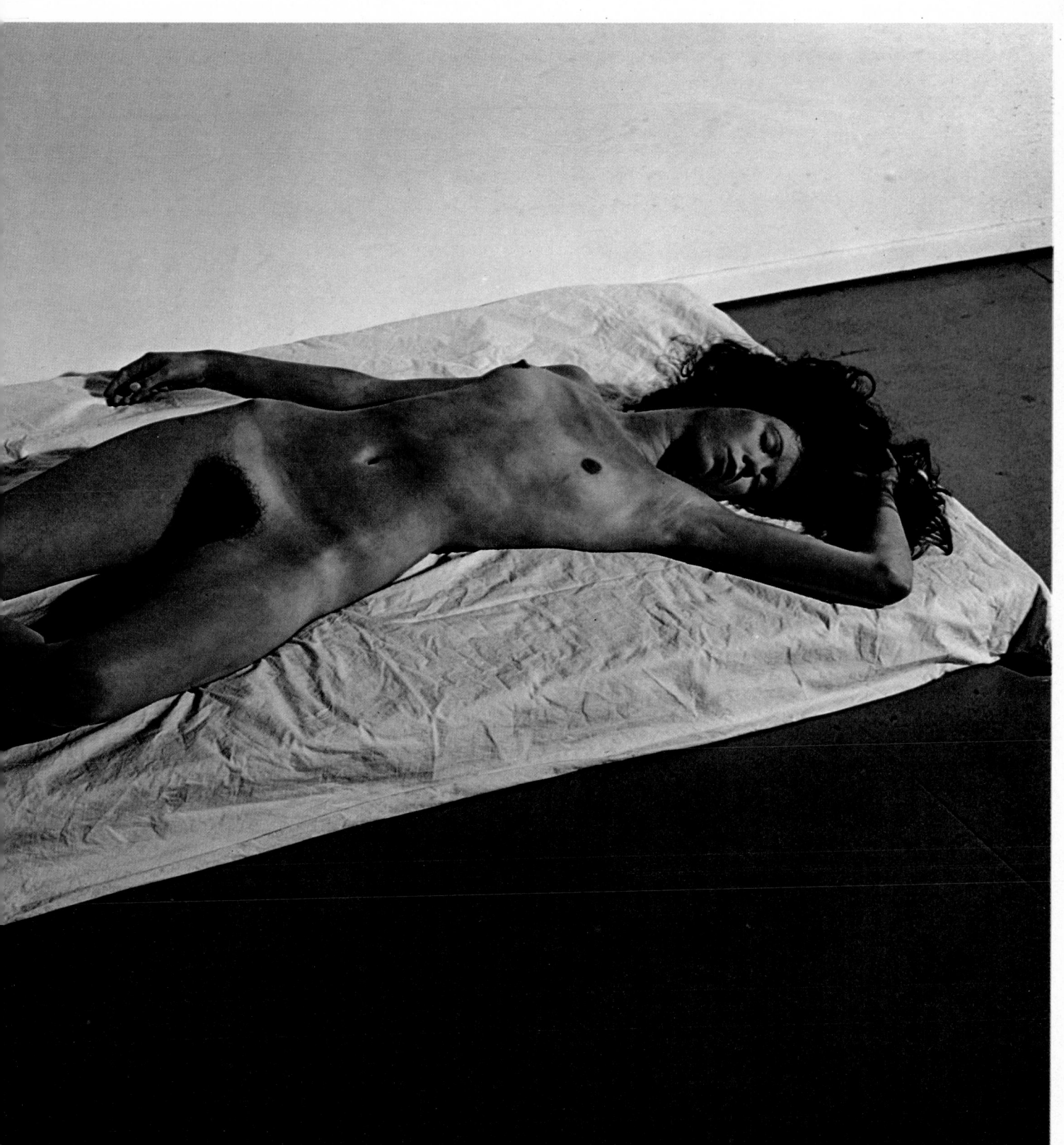

European artists have made even less impact upon the progress of Superrealist sculpture than they have upon that of Superrealist painting. Almost the only exception to this is the young British sculptor John Davies (Plate 384). Like De Andrea and Hanson, Davies sometimes makes use of the technique of casting from life. He also uses real cloth to make garments for his figures, though he now stiffens the material to make it more firmly plastic and sculptural. But his figures are not coloured to resemble life. Instead they are a greyed echo of life. Also they are often provided with strange additions—false noses, contraptions of board and wire. These give Davies an obvious affinity to the Surrealists—the labels Surrealist and Superrealist have an obvious linguistic connection. But his figures still have an extraordinary veracity which is far from typical of classic Surrealism. This is not the world of dream or fantasy but an alternative universe. He has a power to touch on emotions directly which is often denied to the modern artist.

As I have already half suggested at the beginning of this chapter, Superrealism seems to represent a point of rest in the development of modern art. The Seventies, insofar as one can judge a decade at its midway point, seem likely to be characterized by a profound reconsideration of the role of the modern movement.

Irving Howe, in his *The Idea of the Modern in Literature and the Arts*, published in 1967, remarked that "Modernism must always struggle and never quite triumph, and then, after a time, must struggle in order not to triumph." To this perception Daniel Bell has more recently added the following comment: "Modernism, seen as a whole, exhibits a striking parallel to the social science of the late nineteenth century. For Marx, Freud and Pareto, the surface rationality of appearances belied the irrationality of the substructures of reality. For Marx, beneath the exchange process was the anarchy of the market; for Freud, beneath the tight reins of the ego was the limitless unconscious, driven by instinct; for Pareto, under the forms of logic were the residues of irrational sentiment and emotion. Modernism, too, insists on the meaninglessness of appearance and seeks to uncover the substructure of the imagination. This expresses itself in two ways. One, stylistically, is an attempt to eclipse 'distance'—psychic distance, social distance and aesthetic distance—and insist on the absolute presentness, the simultaneity and immediacy, of experience. The other, thematically, is the insistence on the absolute imperiousness of the self, of man as the 'self-infinitizing' creature who is impelled to search for the beyond" (Daniel Bell, *The Cultural Contradictions of Capitalism*, London, 1976, p. 47).

Modernism, as Professor Bell points out, is basically a response to major social changes which took place during the nineteenth century. Its extraordinary power of endurance, in the very midst of its own insistence on change, is not the least extraordinary thing about it.

There are, however, signs—and the Minimalism of the Sixties was one of the most striking of them—that Modernism has become institutionalized to a point where it has begun to contradict its own nature. The insistence of the Modernist (or at least of the majority of Modernists) that revolution in the arts was to be equated with revolution in politics has long since been disproved, though it is interesting to see that the artists themselves feel compelled to keep on reviving this untruth, because to them it is a necessary myth. Much nearer to the mark is Thomas Mann's notion that Modernism cultivates "a sympathy for the abyss": "Whatever the political stripe, the modern movement has been united by rage against the social order as the first cause, and a belief in the apocalypse as the final cause. It is this trajectory which provides the permanent appeal and the permanent radicalism of that movement" (Daniel Bell, ibid., p. 51).

When rage against the social order itself begins to depend upon the very institutions it condemns for the most basic and necessary support, its credibility is seriously undermined. Nor has the long postponement of the feared and longed-for apocalypse made the apocalyptic vision of the artist any easier to believe in.

This does not mean that the basic achievements of modern art must be discarded, because the

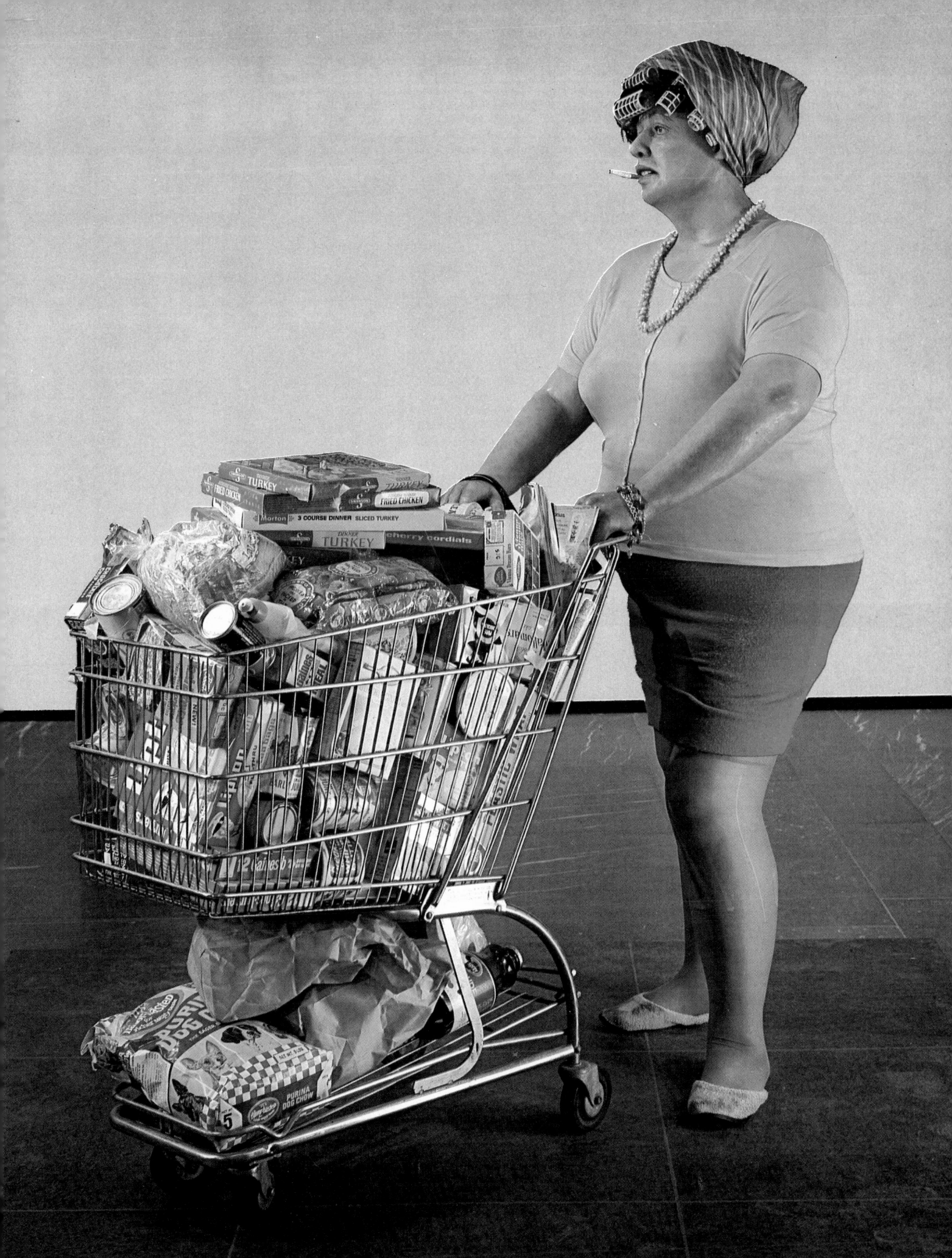

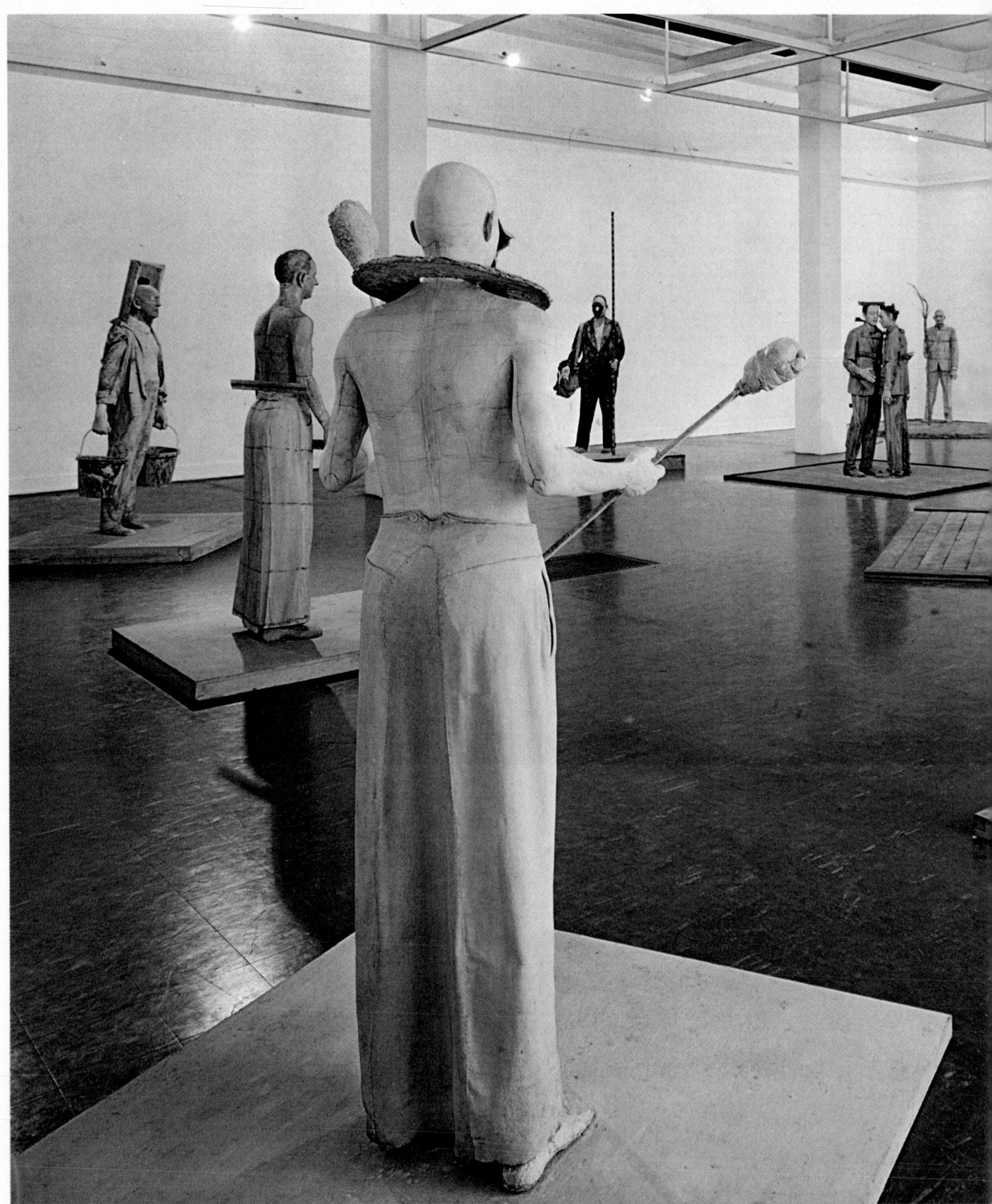

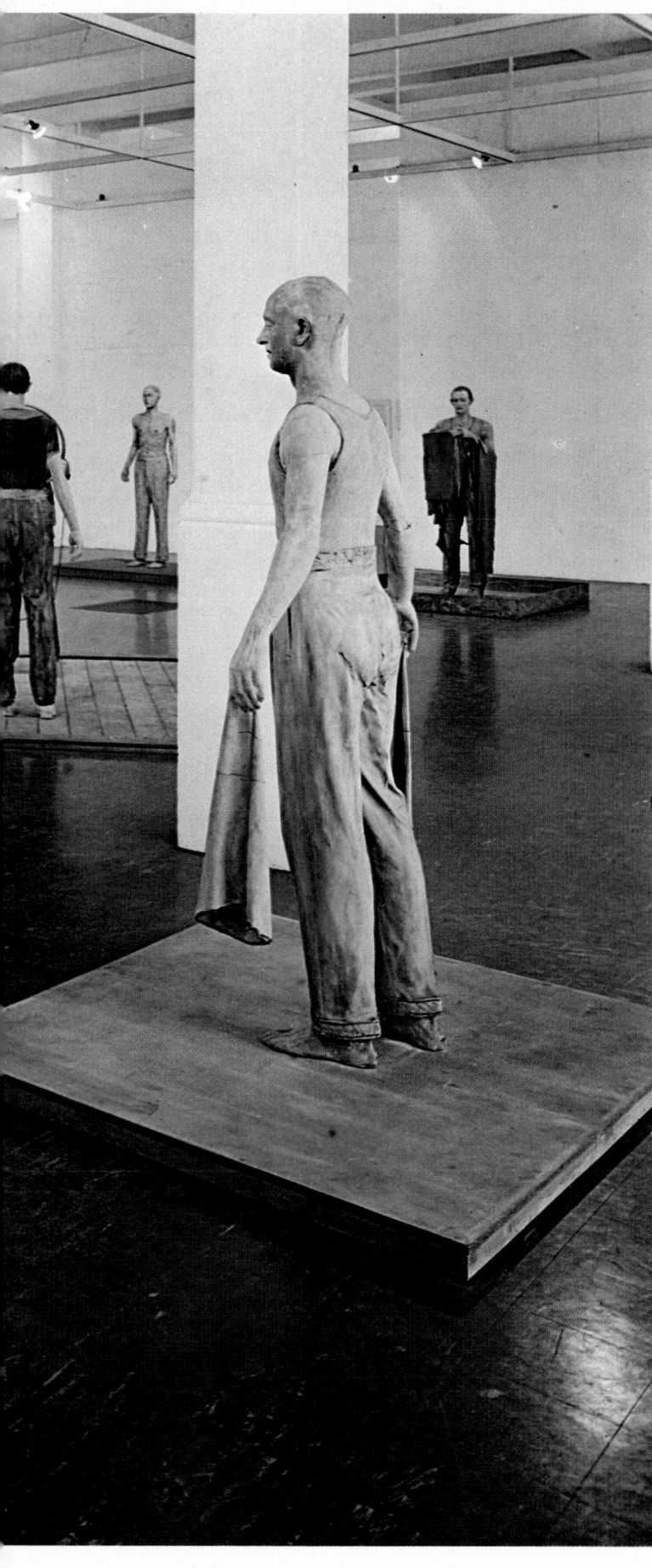

384.
John Davies
View of the Show
1975
London, Whitechapel Art Gallery
(Photo: Annely Judah Fine Art)

premises upon which they were based seem likely to be proved false. The Renaissance and the baroque both triumphantly survive the destruction of the framework of ideas which was their scaffolding. What it does mean, on the other hand, is that Modernism itself must now be seen not as something present and immediate, but as something which, to be fully understood, must be set in a historical context which is no longer the one which we ourselves inhabit.

Perhaps the most important point to make at the present moment is that the promised "destruction of art"—the apparent motivating force of each new Modernist style—is never in fact the destruction of art, though it may indeed involve the supersession of whatever artistic idiom happens to be dominant at the moment. The impulse to make art is so deep-rooted that it seems likely to continue as long as human society exists. The only way to destroy art is to destroy society, and this is one reason why avant-garde artists have so often seemed to campaign not merely against the existing social order, but also against the continuing existence of the social organism.

Yet despite this, it is society which teaches us to interpret art—this is at least as true as the contrary proposition, which is that art teaches us to interpret and understand society. The gallery of illustrations in this book supply us with a mirror image of the fears and contradictions which existed in European society during the period which it covers. The aesthetic truth we may find in them is at least rivalled by the social truth.

It is impossible to predict what the art of the next quarter of a century will be like, and even more impossible to prophesy what artists will be doing in the first decades of the new millennium. It will surely be quite unlike the work that is illustrated here, which will then have taken its proper place as historical and sociological as well as aesthetic evidence of the strengths and weaknesses of the mid-twentieth century. The one prediction which I will venture, with whatever becoming degree of hesitation, is that the concept of Modernism will by that time have been replaced by something else, whose essential nature we are not as yet able to perceive.

Brief Biographies

Adami, Valerio
(Bologna, 1935). Italian painter. Studied in Milan at the Brera Academy from '53 to '57; worked in London from '61 to '62 and in Paris from '62 to '64. Lives in Milan. Makes use of the images of consumer design, of mass communications, using also their flat tonal colour, breaking it down apparently according to a methodology originally Cubist, actually in a dynamic disordering of the habitual context of the image as it is offered by the mass media.

Agam, Yaacov
(Richon Lezion, Israel, 1928). French painter and sculptor. Interested in literature, music, theatre, and photography. Studied in Jerusalem up to '48. In Zurich from '50–'51; living since '51 in Paris. Began as a painter with "polymorphic" works, creating surfaces on corrugated steel panels arranged so as to change shape with the spectator's change of viewpoint; he has also produced "transformable" and tactile paintings, and mobiles. In '67 he developed a series of transformable sculptures made up of free modular elements, which allow the composition to be varied.

Albers, Josef
(Bottrop, 1888). Naturalized American painter, born in Germany. At Weimar between '20 and '23, student at the Bauhaus; stayed on at Weimar from '24–'33 as a teacher. In '33, when the Bauhaus school was closed by the Nazi government, he emigrated to America and taught at Black Mountain College, in North Carolina ('33 and '49). Later taught at Harvard University, in the Graduate School of Design, and in many other American universities up to '60 (Princeton University). A member of the international Abstraction-Creation group. Albers is a representative of one of the main European artistic tendencies transported to America. With Mondrian he is alone in the United States in remaining faithful to the geometric-concrete vision in an organized way. He uses colour-light in geometrical relationships as a means of plastic organization. His predominant theme, "the square within the square", offers him inexhaustible opportunities for luminous-chromatic variations, within a closed formula, absolutely dependent on internal relationships.

Alechinsky, Pierre
(Brussels, 1927). Belgian painter. Studied up to '47 at the College of Architecture and Decorative Arts in Brussels, then made a number of study trips (Morocco, Yugoslavia). In '48 he joined the group *Jeune Peinture Belge*. Made a first stay in Paris and in '49, once again in Brussels, with Appel, Corneille, Jorn, Pedersen, and the writer Christian Dotremont, he was among the founders of the CoBrA group, and remained a member until its break-up in '51, after which he moved to Paris. In '53 he became technical director of the first number of the magazine *Phases* and also became a member of the "October Committee". In '55 he visited the Far East, afterwards making the film *Calligraphies Japonaises* (which won the '57 Bergamo Festival prize and a certificate of honour at the Tokyo Festival, '61).

Andre, Carl
(Quincy, Massachusetts, 1935). American art worker. Studied at the Phillips Academy in Andover (Massachusetts) from '51 to '53. From '53 he worked in Patrick Morgan's studio and from '58 with Frank Stella. From '60 to '64 was stoker and ticket collector on the Pennsylvania Railway. Lives in New York. Works in the field of Minimal Art (primary structures), using elementary geometrical constituents, also of "poor" materials, as a means of spatial denotation.

Anuszkiewicz, Richard
(Erie, Pennsylvania, 1930). American artist. His works are strictly in the field of optical art, of a perceptual and optical-dynamic type. He was one of the participants in "The Responsive Eye" review begun by the Museum of Modern Art in New York in '65.

Appel, Karel
(Amsterdam, 1921). Dutch painter. Studied in Amsterdam from '40 to '43. In '48 was one of the founders of the Reflex Group, which in '49 combined with the international CoBrA group. Has lived in Paris since '50. Won the UNESCO prize in the Venice Biennale of '54. Trained as an Expressionist, he has made a long study of the modern tradition in painting, from the Impressionists to Picasso. He has also followed the development of the School of Paris. Later devoted himself to the study of primitives and naïfs. His gestural, abstract interpretation of colour as an emotive, vitalistic fact expresses itself in a vivid, violent rendering of the image, interpreted in an Expressionist manner, with a personal vision of great feeling and irrational violence.

Arakawa, Shusaku
(Nagoya, 1936). Japanese painter. In '63 initiated a schematic type of pictorial technique in which the images, reduced to graphic silhouettes, relate to design objects in the field of technology. Slowly images gave way to a calligraphy composed of different texts in a sort of pregnant vacuum, out of which are created new possibilities for organizing images as if to illustrate the workings of the imagination through the systematic analysis of language. He is also the author of extremely interesting art films.

Archipenko, Alexander
(Kiev, 1887–New York, 1944). Russian sculptor, naturalized French and then American. In Paris in 1908 he studied ancient Egyptian and Central American sculpture. In '10 he made contact with the Analytic Cubism group. In '12 he experimented in his sculpture with holes and cavities which bring out the relationship with space. A member of the Sturm group from '13. In '14 he developed his sculpto-paintings, which were syntheses of painting and sculpture. In '21 he moved to Berlin and in '23 to the United States. With his "Archipentura" he later attempted a synthesis between painting, space, and time, introducing movement into his works. In his later years arrived at a type of sculpture ever more involved with spatial dynamics, including light and movement within the work by means of a Plexiglas filter. As Moholy-Nagy did, he calls these "light modulators".

Arman, Fernandez A.
(Nice, 1928). French art worker. Studied at the National School of Decorative Arts in Nice and at the Louvre School in Paris. From '67 to '68 he taught at UCLA. In '60 was one of the founders of the New Realism group, whose theorist was Pierre Restany. From informal poetics he moved to New Dada, by an accumulative process which he applied both to the *assemblage* of objects of the same kind, as well as parallel sections of the same object (mandolins, commemorative statuettes), and to a kind of frozen immersion in Perspex of coloured paint from different tubes, to show, as Restany wrote, "the pure and simple taking possession (accumulation) or pure and simple destruction (anger … conservation, the discharge of hostility) in relation to the world's impenetrability".

Armitage, Kenneth
(Leeds, Yorkshire, 1916). English sculptor. Studied at Leeds Art College and became head of the Department of Sculpture at Bath Academy of Art. Figurative. Bases his dynamic-vitalistic research on a highly suggestive, geometrically structured framework, in a dialectical opposition that makes a lively visual impact.

Arp, Jean
(Strasbourg, 1887–Basel, 1960). German painter and sculptor, naturalized French. Began his artistic studies in Strasbourg and later went to the city's Art School until 1907. First went to Paris in 1904 (the year in which he published his first poems in *Das Neue Magazin*). In 1908 he went to the Académie Julian in Paris. In 1909, at Weggis in Switzerland, he first made contact with many artists with whom later, in '11, he founded the *Moderne Bund*. In '11 he also made the acquaintance of Klee and Wiggs, and in '12, in Munich, of Kandinsky and Delaunay, taking part in the second exhibition of the Blaue Reiter. In '13 in Cologne he met Max Ernst; in '14, in Paris, Picasso, Jacob, and Apollinaire; and in '15 Sophie Tauber, whom he later married. After this he withdrew to Zurich, where he took part in the Dadaist meetings at

the Cabaret Voltaire in '16. In '19, with Janco, he founded the *Association des Artistes Revolutionnaires* and took part in various Dadaist initiatives in Cologne, with Max Ernst, and in Berlin; in '23 he contributed to Schwitters' Dadaist review *Merz*. From '20 to '30 he was a member of the Surrealist group and took part in their first exhibition ('25). After '30 he joined the *Cercle et Carré* group and in '31 joined the group called Abstraction-Creation. He was one of the most vital and interesting figures of the contemporary artistic movement and was in the forefront of the principal avant-garde movements, constantly maintaining within each his own unmistakable personal expression, always aiming at an extreme formal purity within the freedom of an organic structure inspired by the spontaneous growth of nature.

Atlan, Jean
(Constantine, Algeria, 1913–Paris, 1960). French painter. Orthodox Jew. Moved to Paris in '30 and devoted himself to the study of philosophy and the formulation of a type of experimental poetry. From '41 he devoted himself to painting. Was interned in a psychiatric hospital during the German occupation. In '44 he published his first volume of poetry (*Le Sang profond*). Was a member of the group of artists from the School of Paris. His painting develops themes of signs, of a symbolic and almost totemistic character, vividly reminiscent of pre-Columbian and Negro art.

Ay-O
Japanese art worker. Was a member of the international Fluxus group. Works in the field of environments and happenings in an interdisciplinary form of expression, integrating music as well in his funk and "poor art" works in which he actively involves the onlooker.

Bacon, Francis
(Dublin, 1910). Irish painter of English origin. In '26 he began to make study trips to London, Berlin, and Paris. Having moved to London, he established contact with Sutherland, with whom he worked for a time. His works show a pitiless analysis of the atrocity of the existential condition of modern man, shown through the monstrous deformation of his image. For this purpose he has often chosen to rework famous portraits (Velásquez's *Innocent III*), which he transforms, with a violently expressive energy, into figures fixed in distraught expressions emerging from a gelatinous, organic, oppressive background, so as to symbolize the destruction of man. Bacon, with Giacometti, is considered the leader of the "New Figuration", existentialist in character.

Baj, Enrico
(Milan, 1924). Italian painter. After studying law in Italy and making a number of study trips to Paris and Brussels, he founded the *Movimento Nucleare* ('51) with Crippa, Dova, and others, and he published its manifesto in Brussels. In '53, with Asger Jorn, he promoted the *Mouvement International pour un Bauhaus imaginiste* against the New Bauhaus at Ulm, founded by Max Bill. He developed his own ironic and demystifying language of a Neo-Dadaist type. He used collages of different materials (medals, broken mirrors, trimmings, etc.) with which he created his robot figures (the *Generals*, the *Ubu*), symbolizing the degeneration of the middle-class world. He branded this with his acute, satirical style, also denouncing the "appropriation" of all kinds of contemporary artistic expression (from the informal to Picasso) and the deforming manipulation that the self-interested consumerism of mass communication exerts on artistic activity.

Balla, Giacomo
(Turin, 1874–Rome, 1958). Italian painter. Lived in Rome from 1895; in 1900 he made a study trip to Paris, where he met Pissarro and joined the Pointillist movement. Later met Marinetti and in '10 joined the Futurists and signed the first Futurist Manifesto with Boccioni, Carrà, Luigi Russolo, and Severini. His experience of Divisionism helped in his explorations of Futurist dynamics, interpreted as a rapid fanlike shifting of the image, as in the photodynamics of Bragaglia and as in Duchamp's *Nu descendant l'escalier* (his *Cagnolino al guinzaglio* [*Dog on a Leash*] belongs, like Duchamp's work, to '12). He searched for the same dynamics in colours in his *Compenetrazioni iridescenti* (*Iridescent Interpenetrations*), which remain, almost prophetically, among the first outstanding examples of optical-dynamic research and of the interaction of colours as light. In '14 he published, with Despero, the manifesto entitled *Ricostruzione futurista dell'universo* (*Futurist Reconstruction of the Universe*).

Baumeister, Willi
(Stuttgart, 1889–1955). German painter. First visited Paris in '12; in '14 he again went to Paris, with Oskar Schlemmer, and their association is reflected in his first non-figurative works, which were highly disciplined in composition. He later met Kokoschka and Loos. Following this, he came closer to the purism of Le Corbusier and Ozenfant. In '33 he left the School of Fine Arts in Frankfurt because of Nazi persecution of what was defined as "degenerate art". In '37 he began to insert biomorphic motifs into his paintings, transforming them into great symbolic ideograms, and in his later years accentuated their ties with matter by making reliefs in sand. He had contact with Miró, Ernst, and Klee.

Bazaine, Jean
(Paris, 1904). French painter. Among the main representatives of the School of Paris, in '41 he organized, in Paris, the exhibition of the group called *Jeunes Peintres de Tradition Française*; he was also the group's theorist. Reasserting the chromatic values expressed first in Cubism and by the Fauves, he sought the essence of form expressed through colour and elementary structuring. After the war he moved from a figuration developed on these theories to an essential abstractionism developed from the dynamic structure of the sign. He is also the author of *Notes sur la peinture d'aujourd'hui* (*Notes on Contemporary Painting*).

Baziotes, William
(Pittsburgh, 1912–1963). American painter. Studied at the National Academy of Design in New York. During the war he remained in contact with American artists. In '48, with Motherwell, Newman, and Rothko, he was one of the founders of the "Subject of the Artist" school, forerunner of what was later termed the Pacific School. He interpreted the language of Abstract Expressionism in emblematic terms, with references to Oriental theories, and this gives life at times to symbolic and mysterious images.

Becher, Bernhard and Hilde
(Bernhard, Siegen, 1931; Hilde, Berlin). German art workers. Live in Düsseldorf. Work in the field of conceptual research, with anthropo-sociological implications. They use photographic means to document a fast disappearing industrial typology, with the intention of offering documentary material for archaeology in the future.

Bell, Larry
(Chicago, 1939). American art worker and sculptor. Lives at Ranchos de Taos New Mexico. Develops his plastic works in a form of Minimal Art, using neon light as a structural element and Plexiglas as a dynamic element, to enliven the structure of the image.

Beuys, Joseph
(Kleve, 1921). German art worker. Lives in Düsseldorf. Uses all kinds of media from photographs to felt, margarine, copper, even his own body, in an attempt to free the individual from the restrictions of an authoritarian society, anticipating certain themes of "behavioural" and Body Art, to show the present exploitation of man's capabilities.

Bill, Max
(Winterthur, 1908). Swiss architect, painter, sculptor, and designer. Studied in Zurich until '29; from '29 to '32 was a student at the Bauhaus in Dessau. From '31 he was a member of the Abstraction-Creation group. From '44 to '45 he taught in Zurich and from '51 to '56 he was director of the Hochschule fur Gestaltung (the New Bauhaus) at Ulm, which he had founded on the model of Gropius' Bauhaus. He has developed a pictorial and plastic language based on a rigorous structuring of form. His didactic interests developed according to a lucidly rational projectuality.

Blake, Peter
(Dartford, 1932). English painter. Studied at the Royal College of Art in London. One of the exponents of English Pop Art, he analyzes the world of advertising and television images, those of a depersonalized society, using photographic material which combines with his pictorial technique.

Boccioni, Umberto
(Reggio Calabria, 1882–Sorte, Verona, 1916). Italian painter and sculptor. Moved to Rome in 1901, and with Severini, Sironi, and Cambellotti he frequented Balla's studio. He began with Divisionism, which after 1907, in Milan, he interpreted, together with Previati, according to a psychological interest of the image, from which he later developed his theory of "states of mind". Meanwhile, he had stayed for long periods in Paris, Russia, Padua, and Venice. He was interested in the symbolist culture of the Secession, in Munch, and in German culture, and after a careful reading of Bergson's philosophical works he came to define his concepts of "dynamism" and "simultaneity", which later formed the basis of Futurist poetics, as a synthesis of plastic and chromatic elements. On February 11, 1910,

after a series of meetings with Carrà, Russolo, and Marinetti, Boccioni signed the Manifesto of Futurist Painters and shortly afterwards, with Carrà, Russolo, Severini, and Balla, he also signed the Technical Manifesto of Futurist Painting, in which he put forward the theories of plastic dynamism and of states of mind. In '13 he wrote the essay *Pittura e Scultura futurista* (*Futurist Painting and Sculpture*). In '13 he also wrote the *Manifesto tecnico della scultura futurista*. In the same period he painted *La città che sale* (*The City Rises*), 1910; *Visioni simultanee* (*Simultaneous Visions*), 1911; *Gli addii* (*The Farewells*), 1911. In the meantime he was an active proselytizer, making frequent trips abroad. In '15, gradually detaching himself from Futurist poetics, Boccioni became increasingly interested in plastic images through Cézanne's influence. However, having volunteered, he was killed in the war.

Bochner, Mel
(Pittsburgh, 1940). American painter and art worker. Lives in New York. In the field of conceptual art he uses mathematical and geometric "measurements" as instruments for the analysis of space.

Boetti, Alighiero
(Turin, 1940). Studied in Turin and later moved to Rome. He analyzed the creative process by which completed experiences of different kinds are transposed into art. From this he also developed the analysis of the creative process of the image.

Brancusi, Constantin
(Pestisani Gory, Roumania, 1876–Paris, 1957). Roumanian sculptor, naturalized French. Lived in Paris from 1904 and worked for Rodin from 1906–07. From 1908, after a post-Cubist and neo-Cézanne period, he turned to a search for a closer adherence to the essence of his materials (*The Kiss*, 1908), also maintaining his concentration on the motifs of Negro art. But his purist structural vision soon brought him to elaborate an individual language in defining a compact ovoid shape of a rare and extraordinary formal, as well as symbolic, intensity.

Braque, Georges
(Argenteuil, 1882–Paris, 1963). French painter. Lived in Le Havre from 1890 until his move to Paris in 1900 and there, through Othon Friesz's influence, he joined the Fauves. In 1907 he was at L'Estaque; there, through the study of Cézanne and inspired by a visit to Picasso at the Bateau Lavoir in Paris, where he saw *Les Demoiselles d'Avignon*, he developed the principles of Cubism, which linked him to Picasso in a union that lasted until '14. His initial themes, during the first (Analytic) and the second (Synthetic) Cubist periods, are still lifes. In these he introduced the use of techniques different from those of traditional painting, to assert the artist's freedom in the use of means of expression (the inclusion in his paintings of letters and numbers, *papier collé* and collage). The breaking up of the plastic form in space, reproduced on the surface, and the reduction of temporal "duration" in a space-time synthesis are dominant themes of the Cubism which Braque developed with Picasso. The First World War separated the two artists, and afterwards Braque's work proceeded entirely independently. After '40 the themes of interiors and the flight of birds predominate in a new, dynamic conception of form in space, developing an extraordinarily coherent vision, even through the variations of themes and formulas which make Braque's language among the most effective.

Bravo, Claudio
(Valparaiso, Chile, 1936). Chilean painter. Lives in Madrid. He belongs to the Hyper Realist movement and is known for his nudes, such as his *Adam and Eve*, of which he has produced two versions with the images seen alternatively from the front and from behind, and for his portraits, characterized by a cold, analytic realism.

Brüning, Peter
(Düsseldorf, 1929). German painter and sculptor. Studied at the Stuttgart Academy of Art under the guidance of Baumeister from '50 to '52. In his early days as a painter he came under the gestural influence of Twombly. Since '64 he has elaborated his own kind of pictorial language in which the sign becomes a symbol, based on cartographic elements, with a clear reference to the modern urban and industrial environment.

Buffet, Bernard
(Paris, 1928). French painter. Began painting in '43. With Rebeyrolle, Minaux, Mottet, Venard, and other young members of the group called *L'homme témoin*, which he joined in '49, he rejected abstract tendencies for a spare and concise figuration, which resolves itself in the use of black in clean lines, in a sectional development according to the contours of the images, reduced to outlines in cold and livid tones.

Burri, Alberto
(Città di Castello, 1915). Italian painter. He began to paint in '44, when he was a prisoner of war in Texas. Has lived in Rome since '45. He was a member of the *Origine* group from '50 to '52, with Ballocco, Capogrossi, and Colla. Already non-figurative in '47, he concentrated from '48 to '49 on studies of materials. His first *Sacks* belong to '52 and the first *Cinders* to '56; they are followed by *Plastic*, *Wood*, *Paper*, in a crescendo of denunciation of the waste and the spoilt, burnt, shattered, filthy remains that man leaves behind, evidence of his condition in the modern world. Between '57 and '60 he worked on the *Iron* series; later came the backgrounds of burnt cellophane and the *Cellotex*.

Bury, Pol
(Haine-Saint-Pierre, Belgium, 1922). Belgian art worker. Studied at the Mons Academy of Art until '38; in '39 he met Chavet and Laurent, two poets of the *Rupture* group; in '48, influenced by Magritte and Tanguy, he took part in the international Surrealist exhibition at Brussels. In '47 he was one of the group *Jeune Peinture Belge*; after '49 he took part in the activity of the international CoBrA group with Alechinsky. In '54 he gave up painting to present his "mobile planes" for the first time. Since then he has been occupied with kinetic art.

Calder, Alexander
(Philadelphia, 1898–New York, 1976). American sculptor. After graduating in engineering he studied design at evening classes. In '26 he moved to Paris, where in '27 he exhibited his first sculptures in steel wire, in which he had already tackled the possibilities of movement. In '28 he held his first personal exhibition in New York and, on his return to Paris, became the friend of Arp, Miró, Mondrian, and Léger. In '31 he joined the Abstraction-Creation group and created the first abstract sculptures, which Arp called "stabiles". He followed them with his first sculptures driven by a working motor, and from these moved on to "mobiles", structures whose movement depends on that of the air.

Calzolari, Pier Paolo
(Bologna, 1943). Italian art worker. Lives in Bologna and works in the area of "Process" art, with connections in "poor art" and Conceptual Art, according to a fairy-tale vision of the world and of existence which permits him to capture the poetic quality of everyday things transposed into a strange setting.

Camargo, Sergio de
(Rio de Janeiro, 1930). Brazilian sculptor. Worked first at Buenos Aires with Emilio Pettoruti and Lucio Fontana. In '48 he went to Paris for the first time and concentrated on the study of Brancusi and Arp. He was again in Paris from '51 to '53, and in '54 he visited China. Since '61 he has lived in Paris. He has developed an optical-dynamic language, creating monochromatic surfaces made up of modular cylindrical sections arranged in a close series at different angles, producing an interesting and lively chiaroscuro effect.

Capogrossi, Giuseppe
(Rome, 1900–1972). Italian painter. After attending the Carena studio he was in Paris until '32, producing works in a Post-Cubist style. In Rome after '32, with Cagli, Cavalli, Mafai, and Pirandello, he formed the group later known as the Roman School. After a series of journeys to Austria and Sardinia he moved in '49 to abstract art, becoming with Burri a member of the *Origine* group. In '53 he signed the Sixth Spatialist Manifesto with Fontana, Crippa, and Dova. Since '46 he has developed an emblematic synthesis of form, consisting in the identification of a kind of elementary graphic lettering, echoing the archaic symbols of remote civilizations and characterized by a lively emotive force and great formal dignity.

Caro, Anthony
(London, 1924). British sculptor. From '51 to '53 he was Henry Moore's assistant. In '59 he made his first visit to America, where he taught from '63 to '64. In this period he met Albers, Noland, and David Smith. From his American experience he derived a new idea of sculptural language, in which the plastic element, reduced to its essence in accumulations of material in direct relation to the surrounding space, rejects any implications of formalism.

Carrà, Carlo
(Quargnento, 1881–Milan, 1966). Italian painter. Trained at the Brera, after a visit to Paris in 1900, and in London, with Tallone. He was active in anarchist circles in Milan and London; as a painter he moved from Divisionism to Futurism, signing in '10 the Painters' Manifesto with Balla, Boccioni, Russolo, and

Severini. In '13 he contributed to *Lacerba*, and in '15 he published *War Painting*. His love for the Old Masters and his meeting with De Chirico and Savinio in the Ferrara military hospital in '16 impelled him towards a metaphysical vision of reality and thence to the "magical realism" which was the basis of the Italian *Novecento* movement. Carrà was among the founders of this movement and was one of the advocates of a new conception of sculptural representation, of fifteenth-century inspiration.

Castellani, Enrico
(Castellamare, Rovigo, 1930). Italian painter. After moving to Brussels at the age of twenty-two, he studied painting and sculpture at the Academy there. In '53 he graduated in architecture. In '59 he founded the magazine *Azimut* with Piero Manzoni and Vincenzo Agnetti. He developed a rigorous and precious formal language from an optical-plastic source created by the incidence of light on the canvas, using negative and positive reliefs obtained by fixing the canvas in the frame or raising it out.

Caulfield, Patrick
(London, 1936). British painter. From '57 to '60 he studied at the Chelsea School of Art and from '60 to '63 at the Royal College of Art. He teaches at the Chelsea School of Art. He works in the manner of Lichtenstein, basing his own paintings on the images of the mass media, using them for their visual implications rather than for their literary significance.

César (César Baldaccini)
(Marseille, 1921). French sculptor. After studying at the School of Fine Arts in Marseille and having worked in the studio of the sculptor Cornu, he was in Paris in '43, attending Gaumont's studio. In the field of New Realism, he works violently on industrial waste material from which, by "compression", he draws disturbing images that symbolize the destructive stress man suffers daily in the consumer society. He is well known for his "compressions" of car bodies.

Cézanne, Paul
(Aix-en-Provence, 1839–1906). French painter. In Paris from 1861 he identified himself with Camille Pissarro and the future Impressionists. During the Franco-Prussian War in 1870 he withdrew to L'Estaque. He later returned to Paris, and in '73–'74 he stayed with the well-known Dr. Gachet. Through his contact with Pissarro he came closer to the Impressionists and exhibited with them at Nadar's studio in '74. In '78 he settled permanently in Provence, except for a brief stay in Paris in '88, when he discovered Gauguin, Van Gogh, and Bernard. In '95 he held his great Paris exhibition, organized by Vollard, but it was his great retrospective in 1907 that revealed the innovatory force of Cézanne's painting, the significance of his "modelling through colour", of his *"refaire Poussin sur nature"*. His well-known decision "to treat nature by means of the cylinder, the sphere, and the cone" later came to be an article of faith for the Cubists, who took from him the structural and plastic significance of volume in space.

Chadwick, Lynn
(London, 1914). British sculptor. Studied architecture and turned to sculpture in '45,

under the influence of Calder. Later developed a sculptural representation of a symbolic kind (insects, monstrous animals), in a dynamic and rigorous synthesis which the critic Herbert Read called the "geometry of fear".

Chamberlain, John
(Rochester, Indiana, 1927). American sculptor. From '41 to '44 he served in the American Navy; from '50 to '54 he attended classes at the professional school of the Art Institute of Chicago. He taught from '55 to '56 at Black Mountain College in North Carolina with Charles Olson. He lives in New York and Los Angeles. Worked in Abstract Expressionism and later developed a Neo-Dadaist type of plastic expression, based on the *assemblage* of technological materials rendered visually aggressive by the use of vivid industrial colour.

Christo (Jaracheff)
(Gabrovo, 1935). Bulgarian sculptor. Lives in New York. Works in the area of New Realism and of performance art. His *empaquetages* of objects began about '58 and suggest the increasing anonymity to which consumer culture is leading us. Carried onto an environmental scale, they relate to the poetic of land art, resulting in visual effectiveness.

Clarke, John Clem
American art worker. Works along the lines of American Hyper Realism in the new objective manner, creating pictures from photographic materials, where the reality of the image is crystallized and frozen by the technique.

Close, Charles
(Monroe, Washington, 1910). American painter. Lives in New York. Works in Post-Pop pictorial activity, intent on re-creating the realistic image as it is given us by means of actual reproduction (from photography to rotogravure); in this the image takes on a stereotyped character, "more real than real", crystallized by a vision which is not that of realistic optics. He belongs to the Hyper Realist group.

Corneille (Cornelis van Beverloo)
(Liège, 1922). Belgian painter. Studied in Amsterdam from '40 to '43. In '48, with Appel and Constant, he was one of the founders of the "Experimental Group" of the magazine *Reflex* and later, with Appel, Alechinsky, and Jorn, of the CoBrA group. He has lived permanently in Paris since '49 but makes frequent trips to Denmark, Sweden, Tunisia ('48), South America, the Antilles, and New York ('58).

Cornell, Joseph
(Nyack, New York, 1903). American sculptor. After beginning in painting he soon abandoned it to develop *assemblages* of heterogeneous objects, which he arranged in a painted case, with symbolic suggestions of a kind of memory-objects. His repertory later grew more complex with the inclusion of constantly different elements (glass, mirrors, photographs, stuffed birds), to increase the sense of narrative profundity and multiplicity.

Cottingham, Robert
(Brooklyn, New York, 1935). American painter, living in Los Angeles. Studied at the Pratt Institute in New York and belongs to the Hyper Realist movement.

Cruz-Diez, Carlos
(Caracas, 1923). Venezuelan painter and sculptor, living in Paris. Works in the optical-perceptual area and belongs to the international group *Nouvelles Tendances*. He draws on perceptions based on effects of anamorphosis and of false perspective.

Dado (Miodrag Djuric)
(Cettigne, Montenegro, 1923). Yugoslavian painter. After studying in Montenegro he moved in '56 to Paris, where he worked as a lithographer until he was discovered by Dubuffet and began to exhibit ('58). Dado's language, stimulated by a Surrealistic symbolism and expressed in almost naïve forms, reveals itself in a proliferation of images which all appear as if drawn from excrescences of nature, vegetable or mineral.

Dali, Salvador
(Figueras, 1904). Catalan painter. Trained in Madrid, friend of Federico Garcia Lorca and Luis Buñuel. After a first period of varying experiences, Futurist, metaphysical, and Cubist, he met Picasso, Miró, Breton, and Éluard in Paris in '27 and became a Surrealist; he developed, however, his own haunted and extravagant vision, which he described as his "paranoiac-critical method", based on psychoanalysis and automatism. He has written various books (*La Femme visible*, '30; *The Secret Life of Salvador Dali*, '42), contributed to *Minotaure* and *Cahiers d'art*, and worked, with Buñuel, on the screenplay of the Surrealist films *Le Chien andalou* ('29) and *L'Age d'or* ('20). He abandoned Surrealism in '34 after being repudiated by Breton. His language thereafter became one of almost academic realism, increasingly elaborate and artificial. In '39 he settled in the United States. The extravagance of his behaviour has always echoed his eccentric and exhibitionistic pictorial vision.

D'Arcangelo, Allan
(Buffalo, 1930). American painter. Lives in New York. In Pop Art, D'Arcangelo analyzes the new visual reality of the landscape expressed in the road, whose linguistic dimension is reflected in the sharp partition of lines and stripes, and in the incidence of traffic signs or of the "signs" and "traces" of events (such as the assassination of John Kennedy seen in the car's broken driving mirror), all of which replace direct contact with a nature unconditioned by urban man, with a new technological nature.

Davies, John
(Cheshire, 1946). British sculptor. Studied painting at the Manchester College of Art and sculpture at the Slade School in London. In '70 he won the Sainsbury Prize. He has exhibited in various European cities and recently at Edinburgh in an exhibition organized by Annely Juda Fine Art. His sculptures, similar to those of the Surrealists, are created by casting from life and aim at mirroring the greyness of daily life.

Davis, Stuart
(Philadelphia, 1894–New York, 1964). American painter. Studied in New York from '10 to '13 and was present at the famous Armory Show ('13). On that occasion he abandoned the academic education of Robert Henri and became a follower of Synthetic Cubism in large

works, imitating collages and pasted papers ('17–'21). He then moved on to Constructivism and later, after journeys to New Mexico ('23) and Paris ('28–'29), he developed his brilliant vision of the modern city.

De Andrea, John
(Denver, Colorado, 1941). American art worker, living in Denver. Studied at the University of Colorado. A Hyper Realist, he creates sculptures in coloured polyester that seem perfect casts of the persons he represents, caught in the actions of ordinary life; as in the example of the couple (*Arden Anderson and Nora Murphy*, '72) exhibited at Kassel in '72.

De Chirico, Giorgio
(Volos, 1888). Italian painter, born in Greece. He studied in Athens and in Munich from 1906. At the height of the Secession he came under the Symbolist influence of Boecklin and became interested in the philosophical theories of Nietzsche, Schopenhauer, and Weiniger; Weiniger's ideas were later essential to the formation of his own metaphysical aesthetic. In 1908 he was in Milan and in '11, after a short stay in Turin, a city that for him evoked magical images, he was in Paris, where he stayed until '15, together with Apollinaire and Picasso. In '15, while in Ferrara for his military service, he met Carrà and from this friendship and his acquaintance with Morandi, De Chirico developed the "metaphysical painting" which he pursued until '18. During this period he produced *Le Piazze d'Italia* (*Italian Piazzas*), *Le Muse Inquietanti* (*The Disquieting Muses*), *Ettore e Andromaca* (*Hector and Andromache*). At the same time, with Carrà, Savinio, Morandi, and Broglio, he contributed to the magazine *Valori plastici* (*Plastic Values*), which aimed to lead Italian painting back to its original values. He was in Paris once again in '24 and the next year he took part in the first Surrealist exhibition, his pictures having aroused great interest in those circles. But already since '18 he had begun a period of cultural revision of the past, which after '24 led him to return to a monumental classicism in the general Italian climate of "a return to order". In Paris, in dispute with André Breton, De Chirico produced, together with his classical-realist works, a number of fantastic paintings in which he rendered his own individual Surrealist vision. In the meantime he attempted new techniques elaborating a kind of painting with a thick impasto, giving a bright, enamelled, pearly surface. This is the period of the *Mannequins*, the *Gladiators*, and the *Horses*. About '40, after a series of visits to America and Europe, De Chirico settled permanently in Rome.

De Kooning, Willem
(Rotterdam, 1904). Dutch painter, naturalized American. After studying in Holland, in '26 he was in New York. In '34 he was already painting abstract as well as figurative works. In '46 his language defined itself in the automatic use of the gesture, Surrealist in origin but in its psycho-dynamic function foreshadowing action painting.

Delaunay, Robert
(Paris, 1885–Montpellier, 1941). French painter. After a Fauvist period he turned through the study of Cézanne to Cubism and initiated its third phase, that of "Orphic" Cubism (according to Apollinaire's definition). This was seen as a study of colour-light, of the interpenetration, the simultaneity, and the dynamism of the planes of colour (the series of *The City of Paris* and *Windows* and, later, *Circular Rhythms* and *Simultaneous Discs*), in which the planes of light are broken down into facets, creating dynamic whirling syntheses, along the lines of Seurat's and Chevreuil's theories of colour. After returning, around '25, to figurative painting, he redeveloped the abstract style in about '30, seeking, with his wife, an architectonic integration of his work in murals.

De Maria, Walter
(Albany, California, 1935). American art worker. Works in the field of land art and "actions", with Conceptual implications.

Dibbets, Jan
(Veert, 1941). Dutch art worker. In his Conceptual works he uses photography as an instrument for the analysis of visual perception in its temporal aspect. In this he uses images in sequence to form a kind of diagram of the temporal and spatial development of the event being perceptually investigated.

Dine, Jim
(Cincinnati, 1935). American painter. After training in Boston he moved to New York in '58 and, with Chamberlain, Oldenburg, and Stella, joined the Pop Art movement. This, however, he elaborated in an expressive development of action painting in a Neo-Dadaist manner, following a special technique of *assemblage* of objects positioned in the painting in a kind of collection which does not aim to assume a plastic or symbolic significance but to present the object as a real, contingent presence.

Dockley, Peter
American art worker. He has been one of the exponents of the tendency which, following Allan Kaprow, has produced spectacular Happenings and "Action-Environments", representing man's life in present-day society.

Donaldson, Anthony
(Godalming, Surrey, 1939). British painter. Studied at the Slade School and from '58 took part in the Young Contemporaries exhibitions. A representative of Pop Art in England, he uses a figuration developed through backgrounds of flat colour by rotogravure, combining painted images with photographs.

Dorazio, Piero
(Rome, 1927). Italian painter. Studied architecture in Rome, exhibiting while very young with the Roman group *Arte sociale*. After the war he worked with Perilli, Guerrini, and Buratti; and in '47, with Accardi, Attardi, Consagra, Guerrini, Perilli, Sanfilippo, and Turcato, he signed the *Forma Uno* manifesto, the expression of Italian abstract painting at that period. His work, constantly renewing itself, focuses on values of "sign-colour-light", realized through textures of fine colour signs with intense effects of light or in intersecting bands of colour, or expanses of colour in which variously arranged blotches spread over the canvas.

Dubuffet, Jean
(Le Havre, 1901). French painter. After classical studies he devoted himself to music, literature, and commerce. From '33 he concentrated on painting, only to abandon it in '37 for a business career and take it up once again for good in '47. Starting from the use of the informal technique in the manner of Fautrier, Dubuffet elaborated a style derived from the noncultural manifestations of figurative art (drawings by children, the insane, or primitives) which he calls *art brut*. In varied, complex works aimed at investigating the possibilities of the materials and of spontaneous expression can be recognized the dreamlike element and the automatism typical of Surrealist themes. His three trips to the Sahara ('49) greatly influenced his work. His painting developed in great cycles: the series *Peinture de la vie moderne* (*Paintings of Modern Life*), '39–'43; the series of *Grotesque Landscapes*, of the *Corps des dames* and *Sols et terrains* ('46–'52), developing his studies of materials; *Assemblages* and *Texturologies* ('53–'59), using collages of different materials; *Phénomènes* ('58–'62); *Matériologies* ('59–'60), *L'Hourloupe* ('61–'62), with Neo-Dadaist and Expressionistic echoes; *Cabinet Logologique* ('67); *Découpés peints* ('71). Particularly interesting is his relationship with Jorn, with whom he composed music in '60.

Duchamp, Marcel
(Blainville, 1887–Neuilly, 1968). French painter. After beginning as a caricaturist he went through phases of Fauvism and Cubism. In '11 he joined the *Section d'or*. In '12 he painted his first *Nu descendant l'escalier*, which created a great scandal when exhibited in '13 at the Armory Show. With this work Duchamp related the demands of Cubism to those of Futurist photodynamics. In '14 Duchamp invented the ready-made, the common object, taken from its usual context and re-employed as the artist's "work", with the purpose of demystifying and profaning the traditional concept of art. On his first trip to New York, Duchamp met Man Ray, the photographer Stieglitz, and Picabia, and with them he initiated the Dadaist movement in America; as in Europe this proposed the nihilistic and ironic overthrow of all established academic institutions in the world of art and consequently in society as well. His great work on glass, *La Mariée mise à nu par ses célibataires, même* (the *Large Glass*), on which he worked incessantly from '15 to '23 and which he left unfinished, is the synthesis of all his alchemic-magic theories and of his idea of art as a "mental" fact. During the 1920's he worked on kinetic objects and produced the Dadaist-Surrealist film *Anémic Cinéma*. He stopped painting in '23, although he continued his busy activity of demystifying art and liberating it from outmoded, traditional dogma. In his last years he produced a series of multiples from his most famous ready-mades and a work for the Philadelphia Art Museum, *Etant donnés* (a sculptural-erotic environment), which was closed to the public, except for a peephole, according to his wishes.

Duchamp-Villon, Raymond
(Danville, 1876–Cannes, 1918). French sculptor, brother of Jacques Villon, Marcel, and Suzanne Duchamp. Abandoned medicine for sculpture. Studied in Paris. Applied to sculpture the Cubist principles of shifting planes and simultaneity.

Ensor, James
(Ostend, 1860–1949). Belgian painter and engraver. Was one of the major contributors to

the Symbolist movement between 1880 and '90, and one of the most important exponents of Surrealism, which he interpreted with an inexhaustible vein of invention and magical, fantastic imagination. He lived for most of his life in Ostend except for a brief period in Brussels. After an unhappy childhood under the influence of a dominating mother and a sensitive and weak father who died an alcoholic in '87, Ensor studied at the Brussels Academy. In '83 he joined the group called *Les XX* and later joined *La Libre Esthétique* ('94). After a naturalistic-realist period he passed to a so-called dark period ('79–'83), during which he used a special chiaroscuro technique. He later achieved the fantastic vision of a symbolic-grotesque kind which became typical of his work and which anticipated many later tendencies such as Expressionism and Fauvism.

Ernst, Max

(Brühl, 1891–Paris, 1976). German painter and sculptor. Studied philosophy at Bonn (1909–11); later met Macke and became associated with the Blaue Reiter movement ('13). He moved from the climate of Abstract Expressionism to that of Dadaism and took part, with Arp and Baargeld, in the formation of the Cologne Dadaist group ('19). In Paris in '21 he was among the founders of Surrealism. In '25 he discovered the technique of *frottage*, obtained by rubbing with black lead on a sheet of paper placed over rough surfaces (wood, bark, cloth). In contrast to the automatist theory of Breton he developed a conception of Surrealism based on the symbolic significance of the image, about which he wrote his *Traité de la peinture surréaliste*. From '25 to '39 he worked on several series of well-known works from *Histoire naturelle* ('25), to *Une semaine de bonté*, a series of graphic works with a marked fantastic emphasis, to the organic series of *Forests* ('27) and *Cities* ('35–'36). After '39 he moved to the United States, where he greatly influenced young artists. Since the war he accentuated the narrative element in his works, while an historical-anthropological dimension enriched his vein of lyrical fantasy. He also invented the technique of "dripping" (the dripping of colour directly onto the canvas), which became characteristic of Pollock's action painting.

Errò, Gudmundur Gudmundson

(Olafsvik, Iceland, 1932). Icelandic painter, naturalized French. Studied in Reykjavik and Oslo; has lived in Paris since '58. In the field of realistic representation Errò has developed a kind of narrative *assemblage* of images drawn from every period of history in a proliferation at once naïve and also linked partly to the realist vision of Mexican murals.

Estes, Richard

(Evanston, 1936). American painter. A member of the Hyper Realist movement, which aims to reproduce the raw objectivity of the image, mixed and stereotyped by the methods of actual reproduction, from photography to rotogravure, which crystallize and finally denature an immobilized moment of reality.

Fahlström, Öyvind

(São Paulo, 1928). Brazilian painter, naturalized Swede. Lived in Sweden from '39 to '61, when he settled in New York. He began by studying archaeology and the history of art, writing poetry and dramatic pieces and working in journalism. In '52, while working with the Fries Opera, he began to paint, with narrative and dynamic intentions. In '62 he produced the first examples of variable paintings, composed of two or three basic elements which have a dominant colour. His work presupposes the presence of the spectator who actively participates in the artistic process, arranging the parts of the composition according to his own idea of form. Often the individual parts of a Fahlström work are magnetized, for ease of movement. His subjects relate to the political, social, and scientific events of today.

Fautrier, Jean

(Paris, 1898–1964). French painter. Studied in London and moved back to Paris at the outbreak of the First World War. From '20 to '30 he produced works of a realistic type. In '34 he ran a hotel in the mountains of Upper Savoy and worked as a ski instructor. He was back in Paris in '40 and in '43, with his *Otages*, he initiated European informal art, creating material-gestural systems of great expressive force.

Ferrer, Rafael

(San Juan, Puerto Rico, 1933). Puerto Rican art worker. Lives in Philadelphia. Studied at the University in Puerto Rico and at Syracuse University; he has taught at the Philadelphia College of Art. He works in "poor art" with connections in land art.

Flannagan, John Bernard

(Fargo, North Dakota, 1895–New York, 1942). American sculptor. After studying painting from '14 to '17 at the Minnesota Institute of Arts and with Arthur Davies, he turned to sculpture. He preferred to use stone, revealing its rough, natural surface. His favourite subjects were animals, which he rendered in his own formal synthesis, and birth, the origin of life and of form, with results that were always very much his own and vitalized by his personal touch.

Flavin, Dan

(New York, 1933). American art worker. His works seek a perceptible realization of space, against which he sets elementary structures (in the manner of the exponents of Minimal Art), employing neon tubes as instruments of his expressive technique.

Fontana, Lucio

(Rosario de Santa Fé, Argentina, 1899–Milan, 1964). Italian painter and sculptor. From childhood he lived in Milan, and he studied at the Brera with Wildt. In '34 he was a member of the Parisian Abstraction-Creation group and in '35 exhibited in Turin and Milan with the first Italian abstract artists. Meanwhile, he worked in ceramics. From '39 to '46 he was in Argentina, where he published the *Manifesto Blanco* with his pupils; back in Milan in '47, he founded Spatialism and, at the Naviglio Gallery, created the first "spatial environment" with black light. In '49 came the first "holes" in his *Spatial Concepts* and in '58 the first "slashes". In '61 his *Spatial Concepts* were dedicated to the American city. Fontana's importance in contemporary Italian art has been fundamental because of his revolutionary role, the clarity with which he established his language, the richness of his creative fantasy, and the human feeling conveyed in his work. He was the first to identify in Secessionist art the possibility of its transformation into the language of the avant-garde. The school of Wildt and the influence of baroque culture (which remained the indispensable principles of his expression) provided the range and the richness of content of his spatial abstraction, permitting him, in cases such as the sketches for the doors of Saint Peter's, to achieve a very vital and articulate figurative language. The focal point of his work is in the *Spatial Concepts* (the "holes" and later the "slashes") where the artistic process is revealed in the dynamic gesture, the onslaught on the material that dominates and at the same time liberates it, which some ten years later developed into the violent "slashes" of the canvas.

Francis, Sam

(San Mateo, California, 1923). American painter. He was the pupil of Clyfford Still at San Francisco after the war, during which he was wounded while serving in the Air Force. In '50 he was in Paris, where he joined the group of American painters, with Riopelle. Later he journeyed to the Far East. He belongs with Abstract Expressionism and action painting but has developed within them his own symbolic-gestural style.

Frankenthaler, Helen

(New York, 1928). American painter. Studied with Rufino Tamayo at the Dalton School in New York. After a period of redeveloping the language of Cubism she moved to Abstract Expressionism through the study of Gorky and Kandinsky. In '50 she was working with Hans Hofmann and knew the work of Pollock and De Kooning. In '58 she married Robert Motherwell. Her style shows itself in a sensitive and lyrical treatment of colour, which she uses in broad thick strokes, strictly controlled even with the freedom of the movement. She uses predominantly acrylic colours.

Fuchs, Ernst

(Vienna, 1930). Austrian painter. Studied at the Vienna Academy with Gütersloh from '46 to '50. He lives in Vienna and Paris. He is one of the members of the new Viennese school which develops figurative themes, "Fantastic Realism". Inspired by mystical symbolism and by German graphics of the sixteenth century, their works are distinguished by their special magical, Surrealist character, with many psychological implications.

Gabo, Naum (Naum Neemia Pevsner)

(Bryanks, Russia, 1890). Russian-American sculptor. The brother of Antoine Pevsner, he began by studying medicine and natural sciences at the University of Munich, where he also followed Wölfflin's seminars on the history of art. He visited Italy in '12 and '13, and in '14 visited his brother, who was living in Paris; the latter introduced him to Cubism and Orphism. At the outbreak of the First World War he went to Oslo, where his brother joined him. In '17, after returning to Russia, the two brothers published the "Realist Manifesto", in which they put forward the Constructivist programme ('20). In '22, when it was clear that Russia was not supporting the avant-garde, Gabo moved to Berlin and stayed there for ten years, maintaining contact with the Bauhaus and the Dutch De Stijl group. In '30 he held his first personal exhibition, entitled *Konstruktive Plastik*, in Hanover. Two years later he moved to Paris, where he became one of the organizers of the Abstraction-Creation group. In '35 he was in London, where with other contributors he directed the magazine *Circle*. In '38 he made his first visit to the United States, where he has lived since '46.

Gauguin, Paul
(Paris, 1848–Marquesas, 1903). French painter. As a child (1851) he lived in Lima with his family. On returning to France he studied in Orléans, and after a spell as a trainee pilot in the merchant navy he worked as a stockbroker in Paris and began a comfortable, middle-class existence. His friendship with the painter Schuffenecker encouraged him to take up painting. He later met Pissarro, who introduced him to the Impressionist group ('80). In '83 he gave up his job and followed his wife to Copenhagen. In '85 he was back in Paris and in '86 was at Pont-Aven, in Brittany, leaving immediately afterwards for Martinique, with his friend Laval. In '88 he was once again at Pont-Aven, and with Emile Bernard he initiated the Pont-Aven School, based on "Synthetist" theories and the antinaturalist technique of *cloisonnisme*, which was related to the technique used in medieval stained-glass windows in which the colours are enclosed within a metal framework. The idea of a new spirituality inspired all the new painting, giving its character to the image, colour, composition, and subject of the painting. At Pont-Aven, Gauguin met Sérusier, who was to transmit the Symbolist inspiration to Paris through the *Talisman* painting. Meanwhile, Gauguin met Van Gogh at Arles, but their relationship was broken up tragically by Van Gogh's aggression and the flight of Gauguin. In '91 he went to Tahiti for the first time, returning in '93 and again in '95 (the second Tahiti period). In 1901 he moved to the Marquesas Islands, no longer able to separate himself from the subjects essential to his painting, which sought in the savage or primitive world the origins of the symbolic spirituality that the civilized world had forgotten.

Genovés, Juan
(Valencia, Spain, 1930). Spanish painter. Studied at the Valencia Academy until '50. Lives in Madrid. His subjects relate to the progressive standardization of the human being, which he represents in dense groupings seen from the air, that form almost solid conglomerations, with collective expressions of fear or of obsessive and irrational will.

Gentils, Vic
(Ilfracombe, England, 1919). British sculptor, living at Antwerp. He interprets the New Realist style in an individual manner, creating *assemblages* of objects from ordinary life with a nineteenth-century flavour, in a sort of memory-totem of a gently familiar, poetic, and intimate world.

Giacometti, Alberto
(Stampa, Grigioni, 1901–Paris, 1966). Swiss painter and sculptor. After studying at Geneva he was in Italy from '20 to '21 and he settled in Paris in '22, studying with Bourdelle at the Académie de la Grande Chaumière. He developed from plastic work of a Cubist type to Surrealism ('29–'35) and after the Second World War achieved a definition of his own figurative language, emphasizing an existential relation between the image and space, as a symbol of the extreme impoverishment and alienation man suffers in society.

Gilardi, Piero
(Turin, 1942). Italian art worker, living in Turin. Working in the artistic activities that have developed from Pop Art, Gilardi has elaborated an artificial re-creation of nature, demonstrating with an acute and cold irony the ever-more-obvious impossibility for urban man of being able to establish a direct contact with nature.

Gilbert & George
(Gilbert, Italy, 1943; George, Orven, England, 1942). British art workers, working in London. They work in performance art, offering their own bodies as "living sculpture". In this they appear together, often with their faces painted silver, stick in hand, and making banal, minimal gestures.

Gnoli, Domenico
(Rome, 1933–New York, 1970). Italian painter. After receiving a classical education from his father, which led him to a traditional style of painting, he concentrated from about '50 on set designing. Moving to the United States, he developed his own interpretation of the expanded image characteristic of Pop Art, examining details of commonly used objects on a distortingly exaggerated scale and representing the object with a pictorial technique close to fresco.

Goings, Ralph
(Corning, California, 1928). American painter. Studied at the California College of Arts and Crafts up to '53 and at Sacramento State College ('66). Belongs to the Hyper Realist group of painters, also known as the Sharp-Focus Realism group.

Gonzales, Julio
(Barcelona, 1876–Paris, 1942). Spanish sculptor and painter. Born into a family of goldsmiths, he exhibited at the International Exhibition of Barcelona in 1892, at the height of the Art Nouveau period. He was in Paris in 1900, in Picasso's circle. After '27 he concentrated on metal sculpture, being the first to use the techniques of relief and of welding which Picasso later used, techniques Gonzales had experimented with during the war in the Renault car-welding section. After '27 he also took part in *Cercle et Carré*, formed in Paris by Torres Garcia.

Gorky, Arshile
(Tiflis, Armenia, 1904–Sherman, Texas, 1948). Armenian painter and naturalized American. He emigrated with his family to Transcaucasia during the First World War and worked as a typographer at Erivan. In '20 he moved to the United States. From '26 he attended the Central School of Art in New York, where he later taught, and became the friend of De Kooning, Stuart Davis, and later Max Ernst and Tanguy, through whom he came permanently under Surrealist influence. He later joined the group of American Abstract Artists ('30–'40). From '36 he worked for the WPA (Federal Art Project), creating frescoes, now destroyed, for the Newark Airport in '36 and for the aviation building at the New York World's Fair ('38). After meeting Matta and Breton ('44) he turned towards lucidly tense and dramatic painting, reflecting visionary influences, in which the Surrealist elements combine with a violent and dynamic gesturality of great expressive force. In '46 a fire in his studio destroyed forty-seven works. In '47 he became gravely ill; and in June, '48, in an accident he was seriously disabled. That July he took his own life.

Gottlieb, Adolph
(New York, 1903). American painter. A student of Jung's psychology, he developed a version of Abstract Expressionism which began from the meditative and contemplative assumptions of the Pacific School and resulted in a kind of action painting.

Guttuso, Renato
(Bagheria, 1912). Italian painter. After studying at Palermo he came to Rome as a young man and established contact with the artists of the Roman School. In '32 he formed the "Corrente" group in Milan and there developed the political-social beliefs that later led him to fight in the Resistance. After the war he belonged to the "New Front for the Arts". He is the most authoritative representative of Italian social realism, which takes its starting point from Picasso's post-Cubism and from the realist Expressionism of Mexican painting.

Haacke, Hans
(Cologne, 1936). German art worker, living in New York. He develops his work in Conceptual Art in an ideological fashion, in an analysis by means of photographs relating to urban life and the economy.

Haese, Günter
(Kiel, 1924). German sculptor. Studied with Bruno Goller at the Düsseldorf Academy and later worked as an assistant to Ewald Mataré until '48. His fragile, vibrant constructions in thin metal wire, combined with pieces of watch mechanism and mobile elements, achieve a delicate poetic lyricism recalling the lightness and lucid freshness of some of Klee's images.

Hamilton, Richard
(London, 1922). British painter. He is one of the major representatives of Pop Art and one of the first, even including the Americans. His first Pop collage (*Interior I*), of '56, shows a caustic intelligence in its use of photography as one of the means of expression closest to the iconography of the mass media.

Hanson, Duane
(Alexandria, Minnesota, 1945). American painter, living in New York. His work in Hyper Realism uses outlines of plastic and reproduces figures from different social levels in banal attitudes, ironically attacking the standardization of contemporary life.

Hartigan, Grace
(Newark, New Jersey, 1922). American painter. After graduating from Millburn High School in '40 she worked at first in New York. In '49 she was in San Miguel de Allende, in

Mexico. Back in New York she became a member of the Abstract Expressionist group but abandoned it for a time to return to a figuration in which her Mexican experiences were reflected.

Hartung, Hans
(Leipzig, 1904). French painter of German origin. From his German education he absorbed the cultural influences which developed after '21–'22 in studies of the expressive value of the sign that were already abstract in intention. To escape Nazi persecution he left Dresden in '35 for Paris. During the Second World War he enrolled in the Foreign Legion. Wounded in Alsace, he had a leg amputated. He returned to painting in '45, resuming his studies of the sign.

Heizer, Michael
(Berkeley, California, 1944). American art worker. With the need felt by the artist after the objectualization of Pop and Op Art, Heizer attempts a recovery of the natural. His land art works make a visible impression on the natural environment, using rollers and various other instruments to score, for instance, a frozen river and preserving the results by photography, which provides their only record. His work, like all land art or Earth Art, has many Conceptual elements.

Hepworth, Barbara
(Wakefield, 1903–1975). British sculptor. From a type of traditional sculpture, belonging to Post-Impressionist figurativism, she moved to the development of forms in dialectic interpenetration with space. In '33, with Moore, Nash, and Nicholson, she became a member of the Unit One group, the basis of which was the organic nature of form. The vitality Hepworth infused into geometric form reveals itself in the dynamic relation between the external and the internal and between space and light. She often used linear elements (wires, string) which link different parts of the sculpture in a rhythmical scansion. She died in a fire at her studio.

Hockney, David
(Bradford, 1937). British painter. A representative of English Pop Art. He attacks with vivid irony, in works of an emblematic type, the false and hypocritical complacency expressed in the images of well-being projected by advertising onto bourgeois society.

Hofmann, Hans
(Weissenburg, 1880–New York, 1966). American painter of German origin. From music and scientific research he moved on to painting. He was in Paris from 1903 until the outbreak of the First World War. He worked at the Académie de la Grande Chaumière with Matisse and later became the friend of Delaunay, meeting Picasso and Braque. After the war he opened an art school in Munich. In '30 he was invited to lecture in California at Los Angeles and Berkeley. In '52 he settled in the United States, where he continued his work, directed on one side towards geometric abstraction and on the other to a freer, organic gesturalism.

Hopper, Edward
(Nyack, New York, 1882–1967). American painter. From 1900 to 1906 he studied in New York and from 1906 to '10 travelled in Europe.

In Paris he got to know Cézanne, the Fauves, and Cubism. He returned to America in '25 and pursued a kind of painting later described as "American realism", full of volumetric solidity but pervaded by a set, almost metaphysical approach which was to have echoes in recent American Hyper Realism.

Huebler, Douglas
(Ann Arbor, Michigan, 1924). American art worker, living in Truro, Mass. He uses photography in a Conceptual manner to examine the temporal variations in everyday actions caused by voluntarily provoked rejections which in some way upset the temporal development.

Indiana, Robert (Robert Clark)
(New Castle, Indiana, 1928). American painter. He studied in Indianapolis, New York, and Chicago and, from '53 to '54, at the Edinburgh College of Art. He settled in New York in '56. Rather than on Abstract Expressionism, he has concentrated on the visual panorama represented by marks and sign systems, which he interprets with disturbing symbolic allusiveness in a kind of "poptical" art (Amaya), close to what in the 1920's and 1930's in North America was called Precisionism.

Isobe, Yukihisa
(Japan, 1932). Japanese painter and art worker, living in Japan. He produces Environments made with inflatable materials, using air pressure to define structure.

Jacquet, Alain George Frank
(Neuilly-sur-Seine, 1939). French painter. He studied architecture at Grenoble and Paris and was an actor for a time before turning to painting. Lives in Paris and is a representative of the movement associated with Pop Art.

Johns, Jasper
(Augusta, Georgia, 1930). American painter. Studied at Columbia and since '52 has lived in New York. He belongs to the American Neo-Dadaist movement. If Duchamp introduced the real object into art, transforming it into an "art object" by the disorientating change of context (the ready-made), Johns brought the object back to the painting, invading the area of painting with the object itself and trying to express the representational quality of everyday objects (the American flag, targets), an idea which Johns has since transferred to Pop Art.

Jones, Allen
(Southampton, 1937). British painter and graphic artist; belongs to the English Pop Art movement. His themes, developed with extremely free association of images, are those of erotic mass advertising.

Jorn, Asger
(Veirun, Denmark, 1914). Danish painter. Studied with Léger and Ozenfant in Paris from '36 but soon went beyond Purism to achieve a fluid and automatic calligraphy of Surrealist origin. In '48 with Appel, Constant, Corneille, Bille and Mortensen, he founded the CoBrA group, which reasserted the freedom of imagination and gesture against rational procedures. Later, with other artists, he also founded a movement for a *Bauhaus imaginiste*, in opposition to the New Bauhaus at Ulm, founded and directed at that time by Max Bill. In '53 Jorn published a plan for a *Methodology of the Arts*.

Judd, Donald
(Excelsior Springs, Missouri, 1928). American sculptor. In seeking to reduce artistic phenomenon to its essentials, he has worked in Minimal sculpture, reducing his works to essentials of a basic geometry, though worked out on a large scale.

Kahrlen, Wolf
German art worker. He works in the area of land art, creating architectural luminous structures arranged in the open, such as the *Baum Raumsegment* exhibited at Monschau in '70.

Kaltenbach, Stephen
Belongs to a new generation of American artists who try to overcome the distance between art and life, working in an ideological and socially conscious manner in opposition to the deforming influences of the system. He puts forward an identification of art and daily life.

Kandinsky, Wassily
(Moscow, 1866–Neuilly-sur-Seine, 1944). Russian painter. He studied law in Moscow but in 1896 he was already working as a painter in Munich at the height of the Secessionist period. In 1902 he initiated the *Die Phalanx* group; in 1909, with Jawlensky and Izdebsky, he founded the *Neue Kunstlervereinigung* (the New Artists' Association) in Munich. In '12, with Klee and Marc, he founded the Blaue Reiter (Blue Rider, a name taken from one of his paintings of 1903); in the same year he published *Concerning the Spiritual in Art*. Again in Moscow during the First World War and the October Revolution, he became director there of the Museum of Pictorial Culture ('19) and was one of the founders of the Academy of Arts and Sciences ('21). He returned to Germany in '22. He taught at the Bauhaus and was its president ('22–'23). In '26 he published his second essay, *Point and Line to Plane*, and with Klee, Feininger, and Jawlensky founded the group of the "Blue Four". Condemned by the Nazis as a degenerate artist, he emigrated to Paris. His pictorial development reflects that of a part of modern painting: from a naturalistic Impressionism he moved through work of a Jugendstil type, through Pointillism, Fauvism, and Expressionism, always moving further away from objective experience to adopt the manner and forms of an expressive gesturalism, close to musical expression, which increasingly resulted in abstraction. His first *Abstract Watercolour* dates from '10. The development of his later work is usually divided into the "dramatic" period ('10–'14), the "architectural" ('20–'24), the period "of circles" ('26–'28), the "concrete" or "romantic" ('28–'35), and the period of "the great synthesis" (last period). He is usually considered to be the originator of Abstract Expressionism, based on the lyricism and spirituality of artistic expression, against (German) Expressionism, based on immediate sensation.

Kanovitz, Howard
(Fall River, Massachusetts). American painter, living in New York. A forerunner of Hyper Realism, in the 1960's he represented the female body in a strongly realistic manner, very similar to photographic reproduction, setting it against elements with classical associations and so providing a contrast between the ideal formal transformation and reality.

Kaprow, Allan

(Atlantic City, 1927). American art worker of Russian origin. From '57 he began an artistic activity which excluded the use of traditional techniques and involved the physical presence of man and his environment. His Happenings and Environments, developed within Neo-Dadaist poetics, deal with men's relationships with each other and with the social reality in which they live.

Kauffman, Craig

(Los Angeles, 1932). American painter, living at Venice, California. He uses intense colours in such a way as to obtain volumetric depth in curved forms in relief, to be interpreted in a spatial-temporal manner.

Kelly, Ellsworth

(Philadelphia, 1913). American painter. He works in the area of reductive "radical painting", reductive, that is, in tending to reduce the painting to its primary essential elements (the pictorial means, colour, the surface of the canvas), without seeking any other thematic reference. He creates structural spreads of colour that are seen as two-dimensional space.

Kienholz, Edward

(Fairfield, Washington, 1927). American art worker, living in Los Angeles. He has developed from a type of post-Pop activity, producing *assemblages* of objects drawn from everyday life, to the creation of sculptures and Environments which tend to be presented as a mirror of the violence of present-day society. As a critical activity his work approaches in this aspect that of the New Realism.

King, Philip

(Tunisia, 1934). British sculptor. Living in Britain since '45, he studied languages at Cambridge University. From '57 to '58 he studied sculpture with Anthony Caro at St. Martin's School of Art in London and from '58 to '59 he was also Henry Moore's assistant. Since '59 he has lived in London, and he teaches at St. Martin's School. He was the first British sculptor to use polyester and glass fibre. His works are produced according to a system of "addition" by which they can be arranged repeatedly in varying ways.

Kirchner, Ernst Ludwig

(Aschafenburg, 1880–Davos, 1938). German painter. Studied at Dresden and came to painting through the study of Dürer and the German engravers. He was also interested in Japanese painting and in Negro sculpture. He was an admirer of Van Gogh, Munch, Toulouse-Lautrec, and Vallotton. In 1905 with Heckel, Bleyl, and Schmidt Rottluff, he formed the group called *Die Brücke* (The Bridge) in Dresden, the first organized manifestation of German Expressionism. Later the group was joined by Emil Nolde and Pechstein. After he moved to Berlin together with the group ('11), his subjects changed from portrait and landscape to images of the city. Even with the break-up of *Die Brücke* ('13) Kirchner continued his work in Expressionist art, practising sculpture as well as painting and graphics, at which he worked from 1902. During the war in '14 he fell ill and went into a sanatorium, first in Germany and later in Switzerland. After his paintings had been included in the exhibition of "degenerate art" ordered by the Nazis in Berlin in '37, Kirchner committed suicide.

Kitaj, R. B.

(Cleveland, 1932). American painter, naturalized British. He has interpreted the Pop Art movement with sensitivity and with frequent references to literature and visual culture. In his paintings, rendered in a free and rapid style or with flat images, he refers especially to the themes of rotogravure advertising.

Klee, Paul

(Münchenbuchsee, Bern, 1879–Muralto, Locarno, 1940). Swiss painter and designer. Studied at Munich with Von Stuck. He was in Italy from 1901–02, in Paris in 1906, and in Munich from 1906 to 1920. The friend of Macke, Kandinsky, Marc, and Jawlensky, he was in '12 among the founders, with Marc and Kandinsky, of the Blaue Reiter (Blue Rider), an avant-garde group which anticipated Abstract Expressionism, and he took part in the group's second exhibition. In Paris in '12 he met and studied Delaunay and in '14 made a study trip to Tunisia. He taught at the Bauhaus in Weimar ('21–'24) and in Dessau ('26–'31). The results of his teaching are preserved in his *Theory of Form and Figuration*, published in '52, and his ideas on art in *The Artist's Confession*, written in '17–'18. Later he taught at the Düsseldorf Academy ('31–'33). In '25 he took part in the first Surrealist exhibition in Paris. Labelled by the Nazis as a "degenerate artist", he returned to Bern, Switzerland. Klee's style developed independently of contemporary artistic work, according to a vision which is among the most representative and "projective" of the period and among the most revolutionary; in it he reduces into vibrations of lines and colours the latent structural geometry of nature, which he investigated in complete freedom from conventional schemes in the inexhaustible and continual rhythm of growth and organic formation.

Klein, Yves

(Nice, 1928–Paris, 1962). French painter and sculptor. His discoveries of the symbolic value of monochrome belong to '46, when he painted a completely blue sky. In this period he also studied Oriental theories and the cosmogonal theories of the Rosicrucians. In '47 he created his *Monotone Symphony* (a continuous note followed by a prolonged silence). Later came his *Monochrome* developments. Between '48 and '53 he travelled in Europe and Asia and in '54 became technical director of the Spanish Judo Federation. In '55 he exhibited his *Monochromes* in Paris. He then became leader of the Nice School, which in '60 gave way to the New Realism. Other members of the group were Arman, Raysse, Tingueley, and Hain as well as the theorist and critic Pierre Restany. Meanwhile, in '58, continuing his search for a kind of immaterial energy, he had organized the "Exhibition of the Void" in Paris and in collaboration with Walter Runhan, the "architect of the air", he worked on the project for the acclimatization of the atmosphere and the control of natural phenomena which was presented at the Sorbonne in '59 in two lectures on *The Evolution of Art and Architecture towards Immateriality*. In '59 he exhibited *Bas-reliefs in a Forest of Sponges* and, developing cosmogonal theories with the trilogy of fire, water, and rose-gold, he created other works using "living brushes" (the bodies of models covered with blue paint and made to move over paper, which constitute the *Anthropométries*), which were followed by *Cosmogonies*, painted with a rain of powdered paint. In '61 he produced his *Tableaux-feu*, exhibited at Krefeld, for which Klein used the gas jets from a blast furnace to create sculpture with sheets of asbestos. His last works were *Relief-portraits*, cast from life.

Kline, Franz

(Wilkes-Barre, 1910–New York, 1962). American painter. Studied in Philadelphia and in Boston until '35. From '37 to '38 he was in London and in '39 in New York. He developed from a post-Cubist figurativism to a violent orientalized gesturalism; this fills the canvas with large gestures, giving it its structure, in an expanded, macroscopic interpretation of action painting, and so expresses the sensation of vast spaces and of the violent tensions provoked by the dynamic structures of great cities.

Kosuth, Joseph

(Toledo, Ohio, 1945). American art worker. He is one of the principal figures of Conceptual Art, which he presents as a linguistic analysis of the concept of art from the inside.

Kuttner, Peter

German art worker, belonging to the Düsseldorf group. His works belong with performance art and are intended to explore current myths.

Laing, Gerald

(Newcastle-on-Tyne, 1936). American painter and sculptor, living in New York and London. He is one of the artists who have worked in the area of Pop Art.

Latham, John

(Africa, 1921). African, naturalized British, sculptor. Studied at the Chelsea School of Art. Since '58 he has begun to use books as the materials for *assemblage*, creating works and panels of great force and symbolic significance.

Laurens, Henri

(Paris, 1885–1954). French sculptor. Studied in Paris, concentrating first on painting and then on sculpture, beginning by following the development of Post-Impressionism. In '11 he met Braque in Paris, who introduced him to other Cubist artists and to Apollinaire. He then joined the group and within it applied Cubist theories about the breaking up of planes to his own sculpture.

Léger, Fernand

(Argentan, Orne, 1881–Paris, 1955). French painter. He studied architecture in an architect's office in Caen and then moved to Paris, to the Académie Julien and to Gérôme's studio. In '10 he was already pursuing Cubist pictorial theories, reflecting their purist, mechanistic element. In '11 he exhibited in the Salon des Indépendants in Paris with Metzinger, Gleizes, and Delaunay. His *Still Lifes* of this period are already distinguished by a new structural vitality which Léger expresses through rounded forms with smooth spreading and through the use of primary, tonal colour. Later he became more interested in the symbols of industrial and mechanical civilization. He also discussed this subject in essays (*The Aesthetics of the Machine*, '23; *The New Realism Continues*, '36; *Colour in Architecture*, '46). In '24, with Ozenfant, he had founded a free school in which he gave one of the most advanced examples of collaboration between the arts. The period from '25 to '30 is described as "architectonic" because of the monumental character of the works he produced; the next period is called "dynamic" because of the new interests in the realization of Cubist themes. He produced murals, stage sets, tapestries, and mosaics, large ceramic pieces, and animated films (the *Ballet Mécanique*). From '39 to '45 he taught in America, at Yale and at Mills College.

LeWitt, Sol
(Hartford, 1928). American art worker, living in New York. He uses the surface or the third dimension as the scope for Conceptual work. On the surface he creates a network that unites points in different possible spatial dimensions; he produces geometrical, three-dimensional structures of a Minimal type as the means of a graduated and modular definition of the surrounding space.

Lichtenstein, Roy
(New York, 1923). American painter, living in New York. One of the most interesting innovators in American painting among the representatives of Pop Art. He uses enlarged comic-strips and blown-up images to express, through the same means as advertising images, the trivializing of everything real by the mass media, even of the artistic achievements of the past, which he often uses as the subjects of his works, enlarging them by means of a projector and reproducing them with the almost Pointillist technique of the printing screen.

Licini, Osvaldo
(Montevidoncorrado, 1894–1958). Italian painter. Studied in Bologna, where he met Morandi. He served in the First World War and from '20 to '30 developed his own line of tonal figurative work, one quite close to that of Morandi. In '31 he turned to abstract art as one of the group of Italian abstract artists formed around the Milione Gallery in Milan (Bogliardi, Ghiringhelli, Magnelli, Reggiani, Soldati, and Fontana, as well as Meloni and the Como group, Radice, Rho, and Badiali).

Lindner, Richard
(Hamburg, 1901). German painter, naturalized American. He studied music in Bavaria and began a career as a concert performer. From '22 he devoted himself to painting. He studied painting at the Kunstegewerbeschule in Nuremberg and at the Munich Academy of Art. In '33, during the Nazi period, he left Germany for Paris, where he met Picasso and Gertrude Stein. He fought in the French and British armies during the war. In '41 he was in the United States, where he worked as an illustrator for magazines such as *Fortune*, *Vogue*, and *Harper's Bazaar* and for books (*Madame Bovary*, '44; *Tales of Hoffman*, '46). Since '51 he has concentrated entirely on painting and on teaching at the Pratt Institute in New York.

Lipchitz, Jacques
(Druskinikinkai, Lithuania, 1891–Paris, 1973). Lithuanian sculptor, naturalized French and later American. From 1909 he studied in Paris. He became involved with Cubism in '13, developing its themes of simultaneity and "space-time" in sculpture. After '25 in his plastic works the volumetric relations were brought out with greater clarity in the contrasts of substance and void, to the point of producing a kind of plastic arabesque, culminating in the "transparent sculptures" of '26–'28. He later returned to forms connected with figuration. From '41 he lived in the United States.

Louis, Morris
(Baltimore, 1912–Washington, 1962). American painter. He studied in Baltimore and later taught in Washington. In '39 he worked on the WPA (Federal Art Project). He lived in Washington. After a period of figurative work under the influence of Mexican murals, he developed a style which almost combines the New York gestural school with the Pacific School.

Lucebert (Lucebertus J. Swaanswijk)
(Amsterdam, 1924). Dutch painter, graphic artist, and poet. Studied at the Amsterdam School of Arts and Crafts from '38. In '48 he joined the international CoBrA group and showed a series of *Poèmes-Peintures* at the group's first exhibition. In '52 he visited Berlin at Bertolt Brecht's invitation. He now lives at Bergen, in Holland. Within the Expressionist gestural language of the CoBrA group he has developed an informal style in which emerge suggestions of phantom images, expressing terror or menace.

Mack, Heinz
(Lollar, Rhineland, 1931). German sculptor. Studied at the Düsseldorf Academy of Art from '50 to '53 and graduated in philosophy from Cologne University in '56. He creates luminous reliefs in mirror-like metal. In '58 he founded the Zero group with Otto Piene, and with the other members edited the three publications of the group. He then began to develop luminous vibrant columns and in '61–'62 created his "dynamic-luminous" objects, consisting of metallic surfaces which move irregularly by means of plates of curved glass and electric motors.

Magritte, René
(Lessines, 1898-Brussels, 1967). Belgian painter. Studied at the Brussels Academy. After early work of a Cubist type he came to know the painting of De Chirico about '23 and, also through a personal acquaintance with Breton (during his stay in Paris between '27 and '30), he moved towards Surrealism, joining that movement and in fact becoming one of its most distinguished representatives.

Malevich, Kasimir
(Kiev, 1878–Leningrad, 1935). Russian painter. From a Post-Impressionist style he moved to "Rayonism" (1908–10) and in '15 together with Larionov and avant-garde Russian poets he drew up the Suprematist Manifesto, becoming the leader of the Russian Cubo-Futurist movement. In '12 he took part in the second exhibition of the Blaue Reiter with all the Russian avant-garde. In '13 he produced his famous *Black Square on a White Ground*, the first example of Suprematist art. In '12 he organized the "Donkey's Tail" exhibition and did some stage sets. In '17 he produced his famous *White Square on a White Ground*. In '19, after actively participating in the Russian revolutionary struggle, promoting a new advanced cultural policy, he was nominated professor at the Moscow National School. Later he lost favour with the government and was transferred to Leningrad. In '15 he had published *The World of Representation*, which was brought out in '17 as a Bauhaus edition. He visited the Bauhaus in '26 and met Kandinsky.

Manessier, Alfred
(St. Ouen, 1911). French painter. Studied at Amiens. In '31 he moved to Paris, where he attended the École des Beaux Arts and the Académie Ranson, under the direction of Bissière, whom he met in '35. In '41, at the height of the war, with Bertholl, Marchand, Bazaine, Estève, Lapicque, Singier, and Le Moal, he organized an exhibition in Paris of the group *Jeunes Peintres de Tradition Française*, which aimed to combine Cubism with a new realist vision. In '44 his pictorial form became more geometrical without renouncing its emotional intensity and its character of offering a record of experience and a profoundly religious inspiration. In '58 Manessier made a journey to the South of France, which proved a revelation to him. His style became more flexible and more relaxed, his colour more vibrant. He also worked in the decoration of glass windows.

Manzù, Giacomo
(Bergamo, 1908). Italian sculptor. Studied at the Accademia Cicognini in Verona and moved to Milan in '30. He was in Paris in '33 and in '36. In '41 he joined the Albertina Academy group in Turin and from '43 to '54 taught at the Brera in Milan. After a period of redeveloping the styles of Renaissance sculpture, making a special study of Donatello, he came under the influence of the Post-Impressionists and in particular Rodin and Medardo Rosso. About '40 he returned to the classical style and developed a type of figurative sculpture related to the canons of classical beauty.

Marini, Marino
(Pistoia, 1901). Italian sculptor, graphic artist, and painter. Studied at Florence as the pupil of Trentacoste. From '29 to '40 he taught at the Scuola d'Arte di Villa Reale in Monza, succeeding Arturo Martini. In '40 he was professor at the Accademia di Brera. He has spent long periods in other countries. Lives in Milan. He has close relations with major European artists and his reputation quickly became international. Having begun in sculpture and in design, developed with a sensitive naturalism inspired by Medardo Rosso, he later achieved an individual symbolism characterized by a sophisticated historical-cultural synthesis (in which an historical awareness of the Etruscans and the Egyptians is fused with twentieth-century culture) and culminating in the recurring themes of his work (the *Pomone*, the *Horses*, the *Riders*). In his *Portraits*, which are of particular importance, he transcribes in a careful psychological analysis a refined historical perception that is informed by a profound sense of personal experience and of artistic vitality, and ranges from a mannered archaism to nineteenth-century realism, from Rodin to the historic avant-garde movements. After '43

493

his sculpture moved away from the use of the rounded block, with its firmly architectonic foundation, and towards developments in which form was stripped down, in a concern with existential problems. Besides his sculpture Marini has produced many graphic works and a considerable pictorial achievement, which has been nourished by an historically informed artifice and enriched by a limpid chromatic density.

Marisol (Marisol Escobar)
(Paris, 1930). French sculptor, living since '50 in New York. In her *assemblages* she has developed a series of outline images which she colours according to a vision that has links with folklore, and in which she includes real objects, producing a wittily ambiguous and ironic but also often haunted activity of the memory.

Masson, André
(Balagny, 1896). French painter and engraver. Studied in Brussels and Paris. At first influenced by the Cubism of Juan Gris ('22–'24), he turned later to work of a visionary and irrational character. His work was noticed by Breton, and as one of the Surrealists he developed automatic and almost gestural techniques, still, however, maintaining direct contact with the natural world. From '34 to '36 he lived in Catalonia. Returning to Paris in '37, he took part in the '38 Surrealist international exhibition. At the outbreak of war he took refuge in the United States ('41–'45), where he had a marked influence on the American painters later associated with action painting and where he found stimulus in Indian and primitive art. He returned to Paris in '46 and later settled in Aix-en-Provence.

Mathieu, Georges
(Boulogne-sur-Mer, 1921). French painter. After studying law and philosophy he devoted himself to painting from '42. In Paris he exhibited from '47 at the Salon des Réalités Nouvelles and with the poet and painter Camille Bryen founded "Psychic Nonfiguration", which was oriented towards a kind of automatic *tachisme*. Meanwhile, with Bryen, he organized the exhibition called "The Imaginary". In '48 he organized another exhibition of all those painters who were to be the masters of informal art in Europe and America (from De Kooning to Gorky, Pollock, Rothko, Tobey, Hartung, and Wols). In '56, on the occasion of the International Festival of Dramatic Art, he painted a work in oils, of 39 × 13 feet, on the stage of the Sarah Bernhardt Theatre in Paris. In Tokyo he produced twenty-one paintings in three days, among them one 26 feet and another 49 feet long. In New York he painted fifteen canvases in a day.

Matisse, Henri
(Le Cateau, 1869–Cimiez, Nice, 1954). French painter. Studied law in Paris and turned to painting in 1890 after reading a treatise on art. He joined Moreau's studio, where he met Marquet, Manguin, and Camoin. He also attended the Académie Julien, the École des Beaux Arts, and finally the Académie Carrière and the École de la Rue Étienne Marcel. He moved from a naturalistic style developed through chiaroscuro and relationships of colour and light to an almost tonal use of pure colour. In '98 in Carrière's studio he met Derain and quickly became one of the creators of Fauvism. After a visit to Brittany ('95–'97) his colour became clearer and continued to develop with the image, becoming a direct means of creation. In *Luxe, Calme, et Volupté* and in *Joie de Vivre*, both of 1905, his idea of art is defined in an entirely autonomous fashion, as an intimate vocation, a spiritualized contemplation, in contrast with the rationalism expressed, for example, by Cubism. Oriental art, Negro sculpture, and Persian ceramics contributed something to Matisse's style. After a journey to Africa, returning with some Negro statuettes that he showed to Picasso, he visited Russia, Spain, and Morocco. He took part in the exhibition of the Secession in Berlin and the Armory Show in New York ('13). He also engaged in stage designs and in graphics. In his last years, while living between Cimiez and Vence, he designed and frescoed the chapel at Vence. Towards the Fifties he discovered the use of *découpage* in graphics, by which he cut out the images in paper painted in pure watercolours.

Matta, Echaurren Sebastian
(Santiago, Chile, 1912). Chilean painter. Studied at the College of the Sacred Heart in Santiago and at the Catholic University, where he graduated in architecture in '31. In Europe from '36, he worked as a draftsman ('36–'37) in Paris with Le Corbusier. In Spain in '36 he met Garcia Lorca, Neruda, and Rafael Alberti, and in '38 he joined the Surrealist group. At the outbreak of war he moved to New York. In '48 he was again in Europe and from '50 to '54 in Rome, then again in Paris. He has tended to enlarge Surrealist themes from the individual to the collective subconscious. He uses mechanistic and symbolic techniques to create a kind of allegorical representation of the alienating evils of our time.

McCracken, John
(Berkeley, California, 1934). American painter, living at Costa Mesa, California. He has been an exponent of Pop Art and has developed a pictorial language connected with Hyper Realism.

McLean, Richard
(Hoquiam, Washington, 1934). American painter. He studied in various institutions and universities, such as New Meadows High School, Idaho, '53, Boise Junior College, Idaho, '53–'55, California College of Arts and Crafts, '55–'58 and Mills College, Oakland, '60–'62. He lives in Oakland, California, and has been a member of San Francisco State College since '63. He belongs to the Hyper Realist movement, which is also known as New Realism, Cool Realism, Radical Realism, and Sharp-Focus Realism.

Merz, Mario
(Milan, 1925). Italian art worker, living in Turin. Works in Conceptual Art, applying Fibonacci's theory of progressive numerical series to artistic activity and demonstrating how the progressive growth of those things closest to nature (such as the igloo) happens by natural rather than strictly mathematical laws.

Messagier, Jean
(Paris, 1920). French painter. Studied in Paris. Since '46 he has made a number of study trips to Algeria and Italy, where he has studied and copied Piero della Francesca and Fra Angelico. In '61, with the architect Jean Louis Veret, he designed the new mill at Colombier Fontaine, where he had settled. He has developed a gestural style which is, however, contained within an almost symmetrical organization of signs. At times he has used *assemblages* and collages of various objects, and he has also produced designs for tapestries.

Michaux, Henri
(Namur, 1899). Belgian poet and painter, naturalized French. He was in Paris in '23 and immediately afterwards made long journeys to India, China, Japan, Egypt, Uruguay, and Argentina. He began to paint about '25, translating his Surrealist poetic language into painting. Since '48 his pictorial and graphic output has constituted an independent activity, parallel to his literary output. He has developed the poetics of Surrealist automatic writing informally, giving it the mystical-symbolic significance of Oriental calligraphy, and has arrived at an analysis of the subconscious and the irrational, also by means of drugs.

Miki, Tomio
Japanese painter. He belongs to the international movement that has developed the language of American Pop Art, which he interprets with lucid and detached irony.

Miró, Joan
(Montroig, 1893). Spanish painter. Studied at Barcelona. In Paris in '19 he came under the influence of Cubism, but after '23 he turned to Dadaism and Surrealism ('24). He interpreted Surrealism, whose manifesto he signed, in emblematic and fabulous terms, in a concentration of cultural experiences that are filtered through a transcription suggesting a kind of "rediscovered childhood". In '28 Miró was in Holland, and in '40 he returned to Spain, to Palma de Mallorca. He also worked in graphics, ceramics and sculpture, maintaining in these too his fairy-tale language and his delight in the fantastic.

Modigliani, Amedeo
(Leghorn, 1884–Paris, 1920). Italian painter and sculptor. He studied with Micheli, the pupil of Fattori, at Leghorn. His first journey, to Capri for the sake of his health, took him to Florence, Rome, and Naples. On his return (1902) he enrolled at the Academy in Florence and later moved to Venice, where he came to know the work of Klimt and the Viennese Secession. He was in Paris in 1906, installed at the Bateau Lavoir. The discovery of Negro sculpture and his familiarity with Brancusi and Picasso led him to that volumetric and linear synthesis which characterized his sculpture and his painting, the latter being sustained by an individual and profound chromatic density. In '14 he met the British poetess Beatrice Hastings, Paul Guillaume, and Leopold Zhorowsky, great friends and collectors of his work. His health was undermined by tuberculosis, and he died in the Charité Hospital in Paris.

Moholy-Nagy, László
(Bàcs-Borsod, 1895–Chicago, 1946). Hungarian painter, sculptor, and designer. Between '19 and '21 he was inspired by the theories of Suprematism and of Russian Constructivism, sharing the conception of the social function of art. From '23 to '28 he taught at the Bauhaus,

where he developed a type of teaching based especially on experiment. As well as his kinetic and luminous works his experiments led him to the use of photography (in which at the same time as Man Ray he explored new techniques and methods, such as the "rayograph") and of abstract film. He was also responsible for the publication of fourteen *Bauhausbücher*. After leaving the Bauhaus he went to Paris, where he took part in the Abstraction-Creation exhibitions ('32–'36) and to Chicago, where he was among the founders of the New Bauhaus. His transparent sculptures in Perspex and his *Space Modulators* belong to this period. In '47 his *Vision in Motion* was published posthumously, in which he set out his theories and teaching.

Mondrian, Piet

(Amersfoort, 1872–New York, 1944). Dutch painter. Studied at the Amsterdam Academy from 1892 to 1897. He reflects the influence of his Calvinist upbringing and his theosophical initiation. Until 1907 he worked according to the principles of Post-Impressionist figurativism; from 1907 to 1910 he went through a Fauve period, with Expressionist features. He moved to Paris in '11 and remained there until '14. In this period, under Cubist influence, he pursued an abstract synthesis of form (on the theme of *The Tree*). On returning to Holland because of his father's illness, he was overtaken by the war and could not return to Paris until '19. However, in Holland in '17, with Theo van Doesburg he founded the neoplastic De Stijl movement and the review of the same title, the organ of the movement, which proposed "a common need for clarity and order" against subjective individualism, according to a structural language of organic spatiality. In '20 Mondrian published in French, in Paris, his essay on De Stijl, which was later issued in '25 as one of the Bauhausbücher with the title *Neue Gestaltung*. He was in London in '38, and when the Second World War broke out he took refuge in New York, where he further developed in a rhythmic-dynamic direction his themes of the breaking up of the surface of the painting (*New York City*, '42, *Broadway Boogie-Woogie*, '43).

Monory, Jacques

(Paris, 1934). French painter. His painting can be seen as belonging to narrative realism; he deals with subjects ideological in intention. He combines photographic techniques with painting.

Moore, Henry

(Castleford, 1898). British sculptor. He studied in Leeds and London until '25. He then travelled in France and Italy with a study grant. In '36 he took part in the International Surrealist Exhibition in London. He took up the themes of the avant-garde revival in sculpture, accentuating the process of formal abstraction and developing the relation between the work and space, in terms of architectural structure and integration. After a short phase of post-Picasso Surrealism ('22–'23), he reached his period of greatest abstraction about '38 (*String Figures*). After '40 he returned to an essential figuration in sculpture. During the war he produced the celebrated drawings of life in the air-raid shelters (*Shelter Book*). Since the war his sculpture has been characterized by mythical images, set in landscape or framed by a building, in monumental, hollowed-out forms which also recall inorganic shapes.

Morandi, Giorgio

(Bologna, 1890–1964). Italian painter and engraver. Studied at Bologna, which during the rest of his life he left only for brief journeys. He was able, however, to grasp the significance of the modern movement and, although isolated and very reserved, succeeded in forming his critical judgment. Starting from the study of Cézanne, his ideal guide, he progressed through a revised Cubism from which he turned to a scholarly rediscovery of Renaissance structure, from Giotto to Piero della Francesca and Paolo Uccello. Between '18 and '20 he belonged to the metaphysical movement with Carrà and De Chirico. After '20, in a total revision of formal purism and of tonal values in painting, from Corot to Chardin, he turned to a style of painting in which objects (still lifes, bottles) are immersed in colour-light, achieving an essential completeness which, not formally but for the rigour of technique and ascetic aspiration, brings him close to Mondrian.

Morley, Malcolm

(London, 1931). British painter, living in New York. He uses the photographic image as the starting point for his painting, on themes relating to mass tourism (often representing life on board ship) and to the traditional American sagas, such as the cowboy rodeos, which have now become a commercialized tourist spectacle.

Morris, Robert

(Kansas City, 1931). American sculptor and art worker. The author of essays on art published in *Art News*, *Art in America*, and *Aujourd'hui*, he moved from a Minimal phase (producing great Primary Structures with elementary geometric form and works in scraps of felt to be hung on the wall or spread on the floor) to a performance art, with Happenings of various kinds. Later he progressed to land-art activities, worked out in the open ('70–'71).

Motherwell, Robert

(Aberdeen, Washington, 1915). American painter. He graduated from Stanford and studied engraving with Seligman and Hayter before concentrating on painting. He took part in the activities of the New York School, tempering the symbolic gestural violence of action painting with a rigorous, rational organization of the pictorial work. With Baziotes, Newman, and Rothko, he founded the "Subject of the Artist" school in '48 which then became The Club, almost a forerunner of the Pacific School.

Nauman, Bruce

(Fort Wayne, Indiana, 1941). American art worker. Works in performance art, substituting operations of a Conceptual type for the artistic object and using the neon tube in a kind of gestural writing, with an environmental setting.

Nay, Ernst Wilhelm

(Berlin, 1902). German painter. He studied in Berlin with Karl Hofer, who helped him to an understanding of Expressionism. He was in Norway from '36 to '37, and he also visited Italy. In '44 he served in the army in France but succeeded in working at Le Mans, in the studio of a French friend. After a post-Cubist phase of an Orphist tendency, he developed towards a formal synthetism.

Nevelson, Louise

(Kiev, 1900). Russian sculptor, naturalized American. She has lived in America from early childhood and studied in New York. In '31 she was in Europe and painted under the guidance of Hans Hofmann. In '32 she collaborated with Diego Rivera on murals of New York. A journey to Mexico encouraged her interest in archaeology. Her *assemblages* of *objets trouvés* (waste, fragments of wood, and, later, serial elements), organized as the structures of the memory, appear totem-like symbols, archaeological discoveries of the present-day world.

Newman, Barnett

(New York, 1905). American painter. From '22 to '26 he studied in New York. In '48, with Baziotes, Motherwell, and Rothko, he formed the school which was later called the Pacific and which is distinguished from action painting by its orientalizing and contemplative interests, expressed in great expanses of pure colour. He took part in the exhibition of "The New American Painting" ('58–'59) and in the 1960 Lewerkusen exhibition "Monochrome Malerei", together with the Italians Manzoni, Fontana, and Castellani.

Noland, Kenneth

(Asheville, North Carolina, 1924). American painter. He studied at Black Mountain College with Albers and in Paris with Zadkine. He lived in Washington until '63 and then moved to South Shaftsbury, Vermont. He belongs to the movement called New Abstraction. He works on large surfaces with uniform spreading and pure tonal colours, developing powerfully emotive structures of basic geometry or of large concentric circles (the *Targets*), which almost magically capture the onlooker's imagination.

Oldenburg, Claes

(Stockholm, 1929). Swedish sculptor, naturalized American. He studied in Chicago and at Yale University. In '53–'54 he attended the Art Institute of Chicago. In '56 he was in New York, and in '60 he organized the first Happenings. As one of the exponents of American Pop Art, he represents the objects of everyday life in a grotesque form, as soft and unnatural, new horrors of contemporary life (the soft typewriter, the soft handbasin), and a repertory of foods and objects of the consumer society blown up in an aggressively monstrous fashion.

Olitski, Jules

(Gomel, Russia, 1922). Russian painter, naturalized American. He studied at the Academy of Design in New York, then at the Académie de la Grande Chaumière in Paris until '50 and later at Ossip Zadkine's school. He has taught at C. W. Post College, New York University, and Bennington College. From '52 to '59 he worked on informal themes but later abandoned them for a wider vision of the pictorial surface. Since '63 he has treated the canvas as a lyrical mental space, with a direct vision in which contrasts of differently painted zones appear to develop, while a greater thickness of colour marks the borders of the picture.

Oppenheim, Dennis

(Mason City, Iowa, 1938). American art worker, living in New York. Works in land art, using macroscopic signs (tracks, furrows, and gigantic lines on snowy ground), visible also from above, to symbolize the repossession of nature by man and the modification of the environment. He also works in the area of performance art.

Ossorio, Alfonso
(Manila, Philippines, 1916). American painter, living in the United States since '29. He studied at Harvard University and afterwards, for a year, at the Rhode Island School of Design. From '43 to '46 he served in the Army. He belongs to the Abstract Expressionist movement; he made use of the dripping technique up to '55 and afterwards developed fantastic images in the informal medium of his painting. After '60 with the spreading of colour he combined a collage of various objects—shells, beads, and twine—which embellish and enrich the surface of his works.

Paik, Nam June
(Seoul, 1932). American art worker. He uses various techniques in his Body Art works, including the body (often of a naked woman with a violoncello), which he records on videotape, manipulating the image from a distance with the monitor, to repossess the technological means for creative purposes.

Paolozzi, Eduardo
(Edinburgh, 1924). English sculptor of Italian origin. He studied in Edinburgh and London. From '47 to '50 he worked in Paris, where he exhibited with the group *Les Mains Éblouies* in the Maeght Gallery. He taught fabric design in Paris from '49 to '55, and sculpture from '55 to '58. He has also worked on architectural projects. After a period influenced by Dadaism and by Dubuffet's Primitivism he moved to the creation of *assemblages* (which he had already used in '47). His *assemblages* are developed in a "brutalist" fashion, creating totemistic images of the machine society and anticipating some of the characteristic devices of Pop Art.

Paxton, Steve
In Conceptual Art he has produced films intended to contrast anonymity (to which city life daily submits the individual) with the recovery of personality and of individual attitudes outside the urban environment.

Pearlstein, Philip
(United States, 1924). American painter, belonging to the Hyper Realist movement. He often uses photography to make clear the reference to a reality fixed by a mechanical technique.

Pevsner, Antoine
(Orel, 1886–Paris, 1962). French painter and sculptor of Russian origin, brother of Naum Gabo. From 1902 to 1909 he studied at the Kiev School of Art, later entering the St. Petersburg Academy of Art, which he had to leave after a few months of training. At that time he was interested in medieval Russian ikons and in the modern French painting he saw in Moscow collections. In '11 he was in Paris, where he saw the Cubists. Again in Paris in '13, he entered Cubist circles, introduced by Archipenko and Modigliani. He added to this an awareness of Italian Futurism. In '14 he joined his brother, Naum Gabo, in Oslo and with him pursued Constructivist work in painting. In '17 the two brothers, returning to Russia, published the Realist Manifesto, in which they put forward

the bases of Constructivist theories. In '23 Pevsner abandoned painting for sculpture and, leaving Russia, stayed for a short time in Berlin before moving to Paris ('24), where he met Marcel Duchamp and Katherine Dreier. In '30 he became a French citizen and in '31 joined the Abstraction-Creation group with Gabo, Herbin, Kupka, and Mondrian. The characteristic of his sculpture is the development of a dynamic surface through linear elements.

Phillips, Tom
(London, 1937). British painter, musician, and art worker, living in London. From '56 to '59 he was a student at Oxford and in '61 at the Camberwell School of Art, becoming afterwards a teacher at the Wolverhampton College of Art and at the Bath Academy in Corham ('62–'70). He presented his musical works in '68, and his opera *Irma* was performed for the first time in '73. He works on the photographic medium, transcribing the photographic image distorted by the screen, by being out of context, by fabricated colours, so as to re-create mentally the real image.

Picasso, Pablo
(Malaga, 1881–Mougins, 1973). Spanish painter, sculptor, engraver, and ceramist. He trained in Barcelona, where in 1901 he founded the magazine *Arte Joven*. He was in Paris for the first time in 1900, and he settled after 1904 in the famous Bateau Lavoir, inhabited by artists whose leader he soon became. From the naturalistic figuration that he had concentrated on from his youth, he moved to a vivid and intense version of French Fauvism, which was also reminiscent of medieval Catalan sculpture and had connections with Post-Impressionist and Symbolist painting up to the point of treating the realistic social subject matter of the time (the Blue Period, 1901–04), which brought him close in some respects to the sharp impact of Expressionism. Afterwards he developed a more direct formal structure (the Pink Period, 1905–06) and then, following Cézanne and the new discovery of Negro sculpture and of primitive arts, he achieved a new pictorial form, Cubism (1907). This was anticipated in the painting *Les Demoiselles d'Avignon*, which Georges Braque saw in his studio, and developed by Picasso with Braque and Juan Gris. The bases of Cubism consist in the breaking down of the image into its various facets and in its treatment of volumes, all brought into the same plane, in a dynamic which introduces the temporal dimension into the painting, bringing it back to the simultaneity of vision. From Analytical Cubism (resulting in the breaking down of plastic form in the surface, 1907–11), Picasso moved to a Synthetic Cubism ('12–'14), in which the form is recomposed in a volumetric synthesis. Later, in the general atmosphere of the "return to order", came the Neo-Classical Period ('17–'24) and a phase of revised Neo-Cubism ('24–'26). In '25 Picasso approached Surrealist poetics (the Neo-Romantic Period, '25–'32), acquiring impulses of lively social commitment, of a fascinating expressive force, which culminated in the famous *Guernica* of '37, dedicated to the Spanish Civil War. This phase of Picasso's work was to have an extraordinary influence, and it had consequences for the entire neorealist tradition, from the Mexican murals up to post-Cubist developments, with their strong Expressionist

elements, in the post-war period. Picasso's later work continued in this area of critical classical-Expressionist revision. The originator of many techniques and styles, Picasso used collage and *assemblage*, created sculptures of heterogeneous materials, and inaugurated the reconsideration of the nineteenth-century tradition, becoming through the force of his temperament the model and guide of generations of artists.

Pistoletto, Michelangelo
(Biella, 1933). Italian painter and art worker. He began with figurative painting and moved in '62 to the use of mirror glass as a "different" response to nature and as an ironic reflection of the current image of life and its socially accepted organization. The image in the mirror obtained by photographic means and by transfer becomes involved with the environment in which it is set, and the mirror involves both the onlooker and the setting in an ambiguous play of fiction and reality. From work of this type Pistoletto progressed to collective and spectacular "actions" and to environment operations of a Conceptual kind, still playing on interpretative ambiguity.

Poliakoff, Serge
(Moscow, 1906). Russian painter, naturalized French. After a luxurious youth (his father owned large stud farms) he fled from Russia at the outbreak of the Revolution and joined an aunt in Constantinople. She was a well-known variety singer, and Poliakoff accompanied her for a time on the guitar. He wandered through Europe, playing the guitar, until he settled in Paris in '23 and concentrated on painting. He was in London from '35 to '37, attending the Slade School, and on his return to Paris associated with the Delaunays and Kandinsky. This led to his development towards geometric abstraction, which he interpreted in a personal fashion, creating a suggestive field of chromatic and luminous relations out of elementary forms and pure tonal scansions. These relations suggest meditative contemplation and an evocation of space reminiscent of ikon tradition. He belongs to the *Réalité Nouvelle* group.

Pollock, Jackson
(Cody, Wyoming, 1912–Springs, Long Island, 1956). American painter. He studied in Los Angeles and from '29 to '31 in New York with Thomas Benton, one of the representatives of the American scene. At first he also felt the influence of Albert Pinkham Ryder, the Mexican muralists, and Indian folklore. Then followed the post-Cubist example of Picasso and that of the Surrealist automatism of Masson, Matta, and Miró. He later resolved Expressionist and Surrealist influences in an identification of his own self with the painting, reflected in action painting and in the technique of "dripping" (that is, making the colour drip directly from the tube onto the canvas). Pollock arranged the painting on the ground and violently attacked it in a kind of excited ballet, almost becoming himself the immediate and direct gesture of the painting. Around '51 he painted in black and white. From '53 to '56 his paintings present images disguised in the tangle of the sign and the expanded dimensions of the painting, which is no longer an "object" but the expression of action. In this Pollock is the first contemporary painter to work on a large scale, abandoning easel painting.

Pomodoro, Arnaldo
(Marciano di Romagna, 1926). Italian sculptor. He came to sculpture after doing sophisticated work as a goldsmith and designer of modern jewelry in Florence with his brother Giò and Giorgio Perfetti in the "3 P" group, with whom he also worked on stage and interior designs. In '61-'62 he organized the exhibitions of the *Continuità* group, with Perilli, Novelli, Dorazio, Bemporad, and Fontana. In '56 he visited Paris for the first time, in '57 Brussels, and the United States in '59, where he organized the review *New York from Italy*. In '61 he was again in the United States and in Mexico, and in '63 he visited Brazil. He applies the poetics of the informal and of the sign to sculpture welded in metal, a poetics which he puts in continual dialectic with the lucid, mirror-like surface of the metal (often brass or gilded bronze). This contrast with the gestural tensions of the sculpture reveals an organic microstructural design, suggestive at times of an archaic script from the tables of some primeval law.

Poons, Larry
(Tokyo, 1937). American painter. He studied first at the New England Conservatory of Music and later at the Boston Museum School of Fine Arts ('55-'57). His relationship with the avant-garde musician John Cage has had a great influence on his work, introducing him to the methods of casual composition, which he has applied to painting. His first work was based on rhythmic progressions of musical origin and on graduated relations of broken geometric forms, as in the last American works of Mondrian. His later acquaintance with Pollock's work and the colour-field painting of Barnett Newman encouraged him to include in his paintings a visually effective combination of colours in dynamic relation.

Posen, Stephen
(St. Louis, 1939). Studied at Washington University, St. Louis ('58-'62) and at the Yale University School of Music and Art in '61. From '62 to '64 he went to Yale University and now lives in New York. He has also visited Italy, where he exhibited in '65 and '66. He is a member of the Hyper Realist group and interprets the realistic image in a provocatory and iconoclastic manner.

Rainer, Yvonne
She worked in the area of post-Pop Environments before coming to express herself through performance and action art.

Ramos, Mel
(Sacramento, 1935). American painter, living in Sacramento. He is one of the exponents of American Pop Art; his themes are drawn from erotic, sensual mass communications.

Ray, Man
(Philadelphia, 1890–1976). American painter, photographer, and film artist. He studied architecture, engineering, and painting in New York from 1897 to 1908. He then worked in advertising design. His meeting with Joseph Stella in '14 and his friendship with Duchamp and Picabia in New York from '15 were crucial for the development of American Dadaism. From '18 he painted with the air-brush, which until then had only been used in advertising.

From '20 he began the use of the ready-made, that is, the transformation into works of art objects from everyday life, which the artist modified very little or not at all; their definition as "works of art" was due exclusively to their being used by an artist and put into a different context. The aim was an ironic debunking of the sacred concept of art and, as in the case of Duchamp, there was the shifting of the "artistic" from the work to the artist. In the same period he produced the "rayographs" (photographic images obtained without the use of a camera with the imprinting of objects on sensitive paper) and the solarizations (obtained by exposing the photographic plate to light while it was being developed). In '22 he produced his "writings with light". In '21, after having published *New York Dada* with Duchamp, he moved to Paris, where he also worked in the cinema, applying to it the iconoclastic techniques of Dadaism. He was in the United States from '40 to '51 and then returned to Paris, continuing to work in a Dadaist way.

Raysse, Martial
(Nice, 1936). French painter. He started painting in Nice in '57. He worked in the field of Neo-Dadaism and later in New Realism, using the techniques of the new technological panorama which has now replaced the natural panorama (fluorescent colours, neon, photography), aiming to liberate his works from the myths developed and imposed by advertising in a mechanized society.

Rauschenberg, Robert
(Port Arthur, Texas, 1925). American painter. In '50 he studied in Paris, and in '55 he worked for the Merce Cunningham Dance Company, producing stage designs and costumes. He is a representative of the Neo-Dadaist movement, emerging from the various strands of informal art, and has produced "combine paintings", using collage technique and the *assemblage* of non-art objects, which reflect a satiric intention in an ironic celebration of the consumer myths and figures of our time.

Reinhardt, Ad
(Buffalo, 1913–New York, 1967). American painter. He was the initiator of the "reductive" tendency in painting, directed towards analysis of the activity itself, without other content. With this radical intention he developed uniform black spreads of colour containing geometrical shapes, also in black, to create a kind of "event" which reflects in itself a concept of art defined by the artist, "art as art".

Richier, Germaine
(Grans, Provence, 1904–Montpellier, 1959). French sculptor. She studied at Montpellier under Guignes, the pupil of Rodin. From '25 she lived in Paris, first as a pupil of Bourdelle and after '29 in her own studio. She developed from a renewed classicism to an existential interpretation of the human figure, withered by the instruments of destruction in contemporary civilization (atomic wars, institutionalized genocide). From the period of the *Insect Women* ('45) she went on to the *Orages*, in which the luminous sensitivity of Rodin was transformed into a violent, almost animalistic portrayal of terror. Germaine Richier later produced *La Feuille*, *L'Ouragane*, and the *Tauromachia*, in which she attempted a more direct abstraction while retaining an animal vitality in her forms.

Richter, Gerhard
(Waltersdorf, 1932). German painter. He started with the alienating photographic record, adding in a "different" medium a progressive blurring by means of superimposed brushstrokes, in a rediscovery of informal gesturality, and arrived at the complete obliteration of the image in almost uniform strokes of colour.

Rickey, George
(South Bend, Indiana, 1907). American sculptor and painter. He has studied at New York, Paris, and Oxford. He began as a painter, working on numerous murals. In '65 he completed his first mobile, and he continued in kinetic plastic work, using stainless steel and various other metals in an abstract style characterized by lightness and clarity of form.

Riley, Bridget
(London, 1931). English painter. Studied in London. She is among those whose experiments in perceptual and optical-kinetic art have given the initiative to Op art. She has contributed to international exhibitions and to the review "The Responsive Eye", organized by the Museum of Modern Art in New York.

Rinke, Klaus
(Wattenskied, 1939). German art worker, living in Düsseldorf. He is an exponent of Body Art and uses the body as a system of elementary signs, excluding any subjective and intentional implications.

Riopelle, Jean-Paul
(Montreal, 1923). Canadian painter. He was a pupil, at the Montreal Ecole du Meuble, of Paul Emile Borduas ('43-'44), through whom Canadian artistic culture achieved international recognition. He moved at once to abstract art and belonged, with Borduas, Mousseau, Leduc, and Gauvreau, to the *Automatisme* group, whose aim was the renewal of spontaneity in creative activity. In '48 he signed Borduas' *Refus Global* manifesto. Since '48 he has lived in Paris. Since then his language has developed towards a lyrical and dramatic Abstract Expressionism based on a striking fragmented calligraphy.

Rivers, Larry
(New York, 1923). American painter and sculptor. He at first studied music and also wrote poetry. He began painting with Hans Hofmann in a dynamic abstract style. In Europe in '50 he moved to a figurative style, which he has developed, however, with methods of combination and montage characteristic of Abstract Expressionism.

Rosenquist, James
(North Dakota, 1933). American painter, living in New York since '58. He works in advertising. He progressed from Abstract Expressionism to Pop Art, whose language is drawn from advertising graphics, taking from them the dilated scale of the image, the wall-poster style of design, and the typographical technique, which Rosenquist applies to large panels in flat, commercial colours, as in printing, so as to overturn by a change of context the contemporary world conditioned by the destructive machinery of consumerism. His best-known work is *F-111*, a panel 85 feet long.

Rotella, Mimmo
(Catanzaro, 1918). Italian painter. Studied in Naples and immediately afterwards moved to Rome. In '52 he went to the University of Kansas City in the United States. His work was already tending towards the use of photographic material, to decollage, photomontage, and phonetic poetry. Since '57 he has used "double decollage": he glues posters torn from city walls onto the canvas only to tear them off again.

Rothko, Mark
(Dvinsk, 1903–New York, 1970). Russian painter, naturalized American. He emigrated to Oregon in '13 and studied there until '21, when he went to Yale University. From '25 he attended Max Webern's courses at the Art Students League in New York. In '35, with Adolph Gottlieb, he was one of the founders of the Expressionist group The Ten. In '36–'37 he worked on the WPA (Federal Art Project). In '45 he became a Surrealist. But from '46 his work tended towards the definition of an individual language based on the elaboration of vast expanses of luminous colour. In '48 he founded the "Subject of the Artist" school with Gottlieb, Motherwell, and Newman. In '58, after a period of travel in Europe, he began the series of large murals for the Seagram Building in New York, designed by Mies van der Rohe (he later decided not to place them there). He committed suicide in '70 at the height of his fame. He is considered one of the principal figures of the abstract-concrete Pacific School. His murals establish themselves as real space, as space-quantity, light-quantity, and colour-quantity; the space of the image is interpreted as a concrete plane of perception, in terms of perspective and light. At the same time as Pollock was identifying space with life, as a convulsive restless drama in its development, Rothko through light interpreted the space of man, perceived space, as an achieved equilibrium, as contemplation. He arranged colour in successive and parallel planes, according to an architectural vision of relative space, determined in a regular, articulated manner in a simple, extremely pure structure; in this every superfluous movement is replaced by an emotive concentration, expressed in a luminous uniformity reminiscent of the contemplative theories of Oriental philosophy.

Ruscha, Ed
(Omaha, 1937). American art worker, living in Los Angeles. He has developed from his own, almost naturalistic, version of Pop Art to work of a Conceptual type which makes deliberately modest use of photography and is collected in series of a typological character with qualities of ironic and at times macabre banality.

Ruthenbeck, Reiner
(Velbert, 1937). German painter, living in Düsseldorf. He uses "poor" techniques and materials to demonstrate the need for a new "naturalness" in seeking a different image of the world.

Saint-Phalle, Niki de
(Paris, 1930). French sculptor. After living in New York as a child she returned to Paris in '51 and began to paint in '52. She lives at Soisy-sur-École (Essonne) and belongs to the international New Realist group. Since her "surprise pictures" of '61 (plaster panels of uneven surface from which tubes of liquid colour emerged as if out of sacks; the spectator was invited to shoot at the painting, which disgorged colour, so colouring the surface in different ways) she has developed to the creation of abnormally inflated three-dimensional images, a kind of monstrous, enormous caricatures of explosive, erupting vitality. In these works, some monumental in scale, with a variety of "events" inside, she approached Pop Art and anticipated the Environment but from a Neo-Dadaist angle.

Salt, John
(Birmingham, 1937). British painter. Studied at the Birmingham College and at the Slade School of Fine Arts in London. He lives and teaches in New York. He has followed the American Hyper Realists, working on enlarged, coldly objective, photographic representations of the detail of technological objects.

Samaras, Lucas
(Kastoria, Greece, 1936). Greek art worker, living in New York. His works analyze the environment and objects in common use (bed, chair), which are seen in a manner that shatters the myth of comfort. He creates disorienting settings, playing on ambiguities of perspective through the use of light.

Saura, Antonio
(Huesca, 1930). Spanish painter. A representative of European "informal" art, he makes use of an impetuous gesturalism, attacking the rich material of his paintings. He reflects the influence of De Kooning.

Schneeman, Carolee
German art worker. She works in the area of event art, in "actions" and "performances", using her body as instrument, as in the performance she staged in Berlin in '70 in which she presented herself in a series of transformations, clothed in different materials and objects.

Schöffer, Nicolas
(Calocsa, Hungary, 1912). Hungarian architect, sculptor, and painter, naturalized French. He studied in Budapest and later settled in Paris. In '50 he turned to abstract spatial sculpture characterized by a dynamic illusion, founding "spatiodynamism" in '48 and "luminodynamism" in '57. More recently he has realized his spatio-dynamic intentions through the use of electronic instruments that produce moving coloured images.

Schwitters, Kurt
(Hanover, 1887–Ambleside, 1948). German painter, sculptor, poet, and writer. He studied at Dresden and was in Hanover from '17 until he left Germany in '37. He began with post-Cubist and Expressionist work and from '19 took part in the European Dadaist movement. About '23 he was in contact with the Constructivists Moholy-Nagy and El Lissitzky, and with Van Doesburg, who was his guide on a visit to Holland. Hence his temporary adherence to the Concrete art movement and to the Cercle et Carré and the Abstraction-Creation groups ('23–'26). In the Neo-Dadaist movement Schwitters collected all his pictorial and literary work under the name *Merz* (from *Commerz*). In '19 he published a volume of poetry, *Anna Blume*, and produced the first *Merz* by the *assemblage* technique. Between '23 and '32 he published twenty numbers of the *Merz* review. Meanwhile, in his house in Hanover, he constructed the *Merzbau*, an architectural *assemblage* made up of the most disparate objects, which soon rose so high as to force him to demolish two floors of his house (it was destroyed by a bomb in the Second World War). In '40 Schwitters, in Norway, withdrew to England. While almost all the Dadaists turned to Surrealism, Schwitters chose a line of his own, anticipating a kind of New Realism.

Sedgley, Peter
(Britain, 1930). British painter. Began with optical perceptual work associated with Pop Art to create new possibilities in optical dynamics.

Segal, George
(New York, 1924). American sculptor. Associated with Pop Art, he created human figures from life, using plaster casts, capturing them in familiar activities and settings, and accentuating the anonymity of the actions imposed by society. His first environmental sculptures date from '61. In '64 the Sidney Janis Gallery in New York held an exhibition of works by Dine, Oldenburg, Rosenquist, and Segal entitled "Environments by 4 New Realists".

Serra, Richard
(San Francisco, 1939). American art worker, living in New York. He works in a variety of basic materials with the intention of demonstrating in a conceptual way their ability to express energy, developing latent tensions and autonomous structural relations.

Severini, Gino
(Cortona, 1883–Paris, 1966). Italian painter. In 1899 Severini left Tuscany for Rome, where he met Boccioni in Balla's studio. Devoting himself to painting, from 1904–05 he studied and copied the Old Masters and the Florentine Renaissance. In 1906 he was in Paris, where he met Modigliani, Max Jacob, Suzanne Valadon, Utrillo, Dufy, and the artists of Picasso and Braque's circle. In '10 with Balla, Boccioni, and Carrà he signed the manifestoes of Futurism, which he introduced in that year to Paris. He contributed to *Lacerba* and in '30 became the friend of Juan Gris, who introduced him to Léonce Rosenberg. In '21 he published *Du Cubisme au Classicisme* and in the meantime, after a very advanced abstract phase, he returned to a classicist figuration with metaphysical overtones. Through different phases and different technical and formal experiments Severini developed his own abstract-geometric language, enriched by a classical, traditional basis.

Smith, Anthony
(South Orange, New Jersey, 1912). American architect and sculptor, closely associated with the New York School artists. He has worked with Frank Lloyd Wright. As a sculptor he has developed a lucid reduction of plastic language into basic geometric forms, in the manner of Minimal Art (Primary Structures).

Smith, David
(Decatur, Indiana, 1906–Bennington, 1965). American sculptor. He studied in Ohio and came to New York at the age of twenty, earning

his living as a metal-worker while studying painting. In '30, influenced by Picasso and Gonzales, he began to include a variety of materials in his paintings, creating *assemblages*. In '32 he devoted himself to sculpture in wood and in '33 was the first in America to use welding in iron. He travelled in Europe in 1935, visiting Greece. Meanwhile, his sculpture was developing in Surrealist directions. In '40 he settled at Bolton Landing, near New York. From '48 to '50 he taught at Sarah Lawrence College and at the universities of Arkansas and Mississippi. In the 1950's his sculpture developed under Constructivist influences in unadorned monumental structures of spatial organization.

Smithson, Robert
(Passaic, 1938–Texas, 1973). American art worker. He worked along the lines of land art, using mechanical devices (rollers, carts) in various spaces and territorial zones with the object of modifying the landscape in accordance with geometric laws. His *Spirals* are to be understood in this way, being made of materials drawn from the same ground that they are created on.

Snelson, Kenneth
(Pendleton, Oregon, 1927). American sculptor. He works in Environmental art and the development of Minimal structures.

Sonnier, Keith
American art worker, living in New York. He works in activities which go beyond the specifically artistic, carrying the artistic "dimension" into life itself.

Soto, Jesus Rafael
(Ciudad Bolivar, Venezuela, 1923). Venezuelan aesthetic-visual worker. He has lived in Paris since '50, after being director of the Maracaibo Academy. Beginning from a neo-Concrete art, he has developed a study of optical dynamics on an enlarged scale with light filtered by means of thin linear diaphragms that move with the movement of the air or if touched by the spectator.

Soulages, Pierre
(Rodez, 1909). French painter. From an early interest in Celtic and Roman prehistory and archaeology, he moved to modern art in '39 in Paris. He was then in the war and on his return worked near Montpellier until '46. He returned to Paris in '46 and devoted himself to painting and scene painting. He is a representative of European Abstract Expressionism, which he expresses in large, symbolic movements structured in broad zones of colour (black, blue, brown), creating a plastic structuring of great expressive force.

Soutine, Chaim
(Smilivic, 1894–Paris, 1943). Russian painter, naturalized French. At thirteen he fled to Minsk, where he began to study design. In '10 he was at the Vilna Academy. In '13 he succeeded in reaching Paris, where he met Chagall, Léger, Delaunay, and Cendrars and was the friend of Modigliani. In '19, with the assistance of the merchant Zhorowsky, he was able to withdraw to Céret, in the Pyrenees. In '41, at the time of the German occupation, he took refuge at Champigny-sur-Vende. A visionary Expressionist, constantly engrossed in his private vision, he explored the extremes of colour as the means of representing a crude and painful psychic realism.

Spoerri, Daniel
(Galati, Roumania, 1930). Roumanian painter and art worker, belonging to the New Realism group. He creates *assemblages* of objects of daily use, preserved in the deteriorating squalor caused by use which turns them into the wreckage and revealing refuse of modern life.

Staël, Nicolas de
(St. Petersburg, 1914–Antibes, 1955). Russian painter, naturalized French. His family left Russia during the Revolution and settled in Belgium until '38. From '38 De Staël was in Paris. Coming to painting only after '40, he developed an intense, personal, and dramatically expressive style.

Stella, Frank
(Malden, Massachusetts, 1936). American painter. He creates basic geometric images, reducing the significance of the painting to objective expression without references of any kind. His "radical" pictorial work develops the same process which in sculpture is represented in the activities of Minimal Art (Primary Structures). His works, developed in terms of two-dimensional space, are composed of rhythmic bands and cruciform sections in moulded compositions on projecting canvases, along the lines of "shaped canvases".

Still, Clyfford
(Grandin, North Dakota, 1904). American painter. He studied at Spokane and in '41 moved to San Francisco, where he met Rothko and took part in the activity of what was to be called the Pacific School. An Abstract Expressionist from '40 to '50 (in '48 with Rothko, Motherwell, Baziotes, Hare, and others he belonged to the founding group of the "Subject of the Artist" school, and in '50 he worked in New York with Pollock and De Kooning). He later turned to structural work of a neo-Concrete type.

Takis (Vassilakis)
(Athens, 1925). Greek sculptor, naturalized French. His first sculptures date from '46, his "signal sculptures" from '54–'58, and his first "telemagnetic sculptures" from '58. In '57 he caused some spherical bronze sculptures to explode on a hill in Athens, and in the streets of Paris he presented "firework sculptures". Rather than the formal result, Takis has always sought to demonstrate in his sculptures the force of latent energy that nature expresses in its vital manifestations of explosive violence.

Tàpies, Antoni
(Barcelona, 1923). Spanish painter. He devoted himself to drawing from early childhood, having ample means of study in the extensive family library, and while still a boy he found himself in the midst of the Civil War ('36), which left indelible marks on him. In '43 he began to study law, as his father wished, but soon abandoned it for painting. He moved from a variety of preliminary phases, the study of the Expressionists and of Picasso, towards a type of Surrealism inspired by Klee, Miró, and Ernst. In '46 he founded the *Dan al Set* group. Already at that time, in linguistically inspired works with Expressionist figuration, there appear the themes later dominant, the interest in matter-colour, the monochrome, and the subjects of "matter-mud". In Paris in '52 he met the critic Tapié, who became interested in his work. Later he approached a type of informal art which rejected painting as gesture, since existentially he rejects action, taking up a position of not acting, not being.

Tatlin, Vladimir (Avgrafovic)
(Karlow, Russia, 1885–Moscow, 1953). Russian sculptor, architect, and painter. He ran away from home at eighteen and became a sailor. In 1904 he studied at Pensa and in '10 at Moscow, where he became the friend of Vesnin and took part in the exhibitions of the "Donkey's Tail" ('12). In '13 he visited Berlin and Paris, where the work of Picasso made a strong impression on him. Returning to Moscow, he began the *Reliefs* that led the way to Russian Constructivism, which in contrast with Malevich's Suprematism favoured contact between art and technology and later brought about the birth of industrial design. His *Project for the Monument to the Third International*, one of the first examples of contemporary kinetic art, dates from '19–'20. In '22 he was summoned to teach at St. Petersburg. In '27 he returned to Moscow, where he taught at the advanced technical art institute.

Thiebaud, Wayne
(Mesa, Arizona, 1920). American painter, director, and graphic artist. He worked in New York as cartoonist, designer, and publicity artist. He occupies a special place among the representatives of Pop Art for his violently distorted rendering of images (especially convenience food) which a bright, advertising use of colour makes still more emphatically false and synthetic.

Tilson, Joe
(London, 1928). British painter and sculptor. He studied at the Royal College of Art in London and also in Italy. With Phillips, Kitaj, Blake, Jones, and Caulfield, he is one of the representatives of British Pop Art, which is more allusive and ambitious than American Pop Art. He produces compositions in relief in painted wood, using collage and presenting in a rigorous, emblematic manner what he himself calls "the ambiguous images of the great city".

Tingueley, Jean
(Fribourg, 1925). Swiss painter and sculptor. He studied at the Fribourg Academy of Fine Arts from '41 to '45, and he has constructed watermills supplied with sound tracks in a forest. Between '45 and '52 he developed his own interpretation of Dadaism, making abstract constructions in iron, other metals, wood, and paper. In Paris in '52 he developed "metal mechanism", creating *Speaking Metal Robots* and *Painting Machines*. Constantly poised between kinetic and New Realist work, he creates self-propelling, edible, and musical machines (John Cage often supplies sound tracks).

Tobey, Mark
(Centerville, Wisconsin, 1890). American painter. He studied at the Chicago Art Institute and in '11 moved to New York. In '22 he moved to Seattle, where he taught painting. From his

youth he has been interested in Oriental mystical and cosmogonal theories (especially in Bahai beliefs, which are based on the spiritual unity and equality of man and which spread in America after the First World War). About '23 he was initiated by the Chinese painter Teng Kwei into the technical processes of Oriental painting and calligraphy. He then travelled in Europe and in the East. He studied Chinese calligraphy at Shanghai and Zen painting at Kyoto. From '31 to '38 he lived in England. In '38, again in Seattle, he worked for the WPA (Federal Art Project). After '35 he introduced the sign element into his painting with a dynamic-luminous function (this is the period of the "white writing"). Developing his work on light as a "unifying idea", he later came to abandon any reference to a realistic image and to create dense, continuous surfaces, swarming with minute signs, through which he attempts to convey the sense of the frenetic rhythm of life and of the city.

Trova, Ernst
(St. Louis, 1927). American sculptor, living in St. Louis. Working in the area of Pop Art, he has developed a stereotyped image of man, reduced to a depersonalized metallic marionette, worked out in volumetric terms and often enclosed in containers, which accentuate the sense of any human object, and even its representation, as being "merchandise".

Tucker, William
(Cairo, 1935). British sculptor, living in Britain since '37. After studying languages at college he pursued sculpture at the St. Martin's School of Art with Anthony Caro and at the Central School of Art in London from '58 to '60. He teaches at the St. Martin's School and lives in London. His sculptures are abstract constructions in fibre glass, put together in painted modular parts produced industrially and capable of being assembled in different ways.

Uecker, Günther
(Wendorf, Mecklenburg, 1930). German sculptor. Studied in Berlin and Düsseldorf. He produces works with nails sticking out of the wood, almost like organic growths, which he elaborates by adding sources of light. In '61, with Piene and Mack, he joined the Zero group in Düsseldorf.

Van der Beek, Stan
(United States, 1928). American art worker. He has worked at the Massachusetts Institute of Technology in Boston, experimenting with electronic computers. He is well-known for his films, in which he uses a computer to subdivide the sections of microfilm in different planes, to create abstract, isolated, animated images.

Van Elk, Ger
(Amsterdam, 1941). Dutch art worker, living in Amsterdam and Los Angeles. Working in "poor" art, he has created some interesting films, one of a box projected onto the box and one of a pennant projected on itself. He also uses photographs to which he adds pictorial devices.

Van Gogh, Vincent
(Groot-Zundert, 1853–Auvers-sur-Oise, 1890). Dutch painter. After an initial period of exalted mysticism which led him, at about the age of twenty, to teach in a mining village in England and in '78 to be a preacher in Borinage, about '80 he turned to painting. In '86 in Paris, where he had gone at the invitation of his brother Theo, he developed from realism in Millet's manner to Neo-Impressionism, which he had discovered through Pissarro, Seurat, Toulouse-Lautrec, and Gauguin. In '88 he moved to Arles, where his frenetic pictorial activity began. Abandoning Neo-Impressionism, he turned to a tonal enkindling of colour, enhanced by the vibrant incisiveness of the sign. Gauguin joined him at Arles and there occurred his tragic attack on Gauguin and his self-punishing mutilation of his own ear. This led to the crises which in '89 caused him to enter the mental hospital in Saint-Rémy. In '90 Van Gogh moved to Auvers, near Dr. Gachet, the collector and friend of artists. In the same year he committed suicide.

Vasarely, Victor
(Pecs, 1908). Hungarian painter, naturalized French. At first he studied medicine in Budapest. He then went on to study art at the Mühely Academy of Alexander Bortnyik, the Budapest Bauhaus, where he was a pupil of Moholy-Nagy. In Paris in '30 he joined the Abstraction-Creation group, and in '44 he founded the Denise Réné Gallery. In '55 he published the *Jaune* manifesto and began the period of optical kinetic experiment which made him one of the pioneers of optical art. His studies of perception in its possibilities of creating virtual and ambiguous images, permutable "binary structures", still using exact geometric principles, represent one of the most extensive and fascinating investigations in the optical-perceptual field.

Vedova, Emilio
(Venice, 1919). Italian painter. Basically self-taught, in '37 he studied in Rome, and in '38 he was again in Venice. He was in the Resistance between '43 and '45 and was wounded during an ambush. In '46 he joined the New Secession and New Front for the Arts in Venice. In '52 he was in Venturi's "Group of Eight". From a kind of post-Cubism, filtered through a personal Expressionistic violence and through a fine revision of eighteenth-century Venetian graphics, he arrived at a dynamic, abstract-gestural language with political and existential content. Later, with the *Plurimi*, he moved to the acquisition of real space in his gesturality.

Vieira da Silva, Maria Elena
(Lisbon, 1908). French-Portuguese painter. She studied sculpture in Paris with Bourdelle and Despiau and later with Dufresne, Friesz, and Léger. She then turned to painting, elaborating linear surfaces in neutral tones. Later she accentuated the perspective relations of the surface structures, giving an ideal reference to urban structures with a dynamic perspective effect. She uses clear colours and a soft light which give the composition sensitivity and a mysterious emotiveness.

Vostell, Wolf
(Leverkusen, 1932). German art worker, living in Berlin. One of the international Fluxus group, he produces Happenings of various kinds, with the purpose of demonstrating means of organized violence against the social system. He involves the public in his "actions" in order to identify them ideologically.

Warhol, Andy
(Philadelphia, 1930). American painter. He began as a commercial artist and studied at the Carnegie Institute. He became one of the leading figures of Pop Art and of the new Super Realism. He reproduces the objects of mass industrial consumerism in their obsessive multiplicability and uniformity, developing an inexorable and bitterly ironic criticism of mass society in which nevertheless he sees himself as an "integrated" consumer. In his pictures Warhol uses photographic materials and the industrial colours of offset printing with their crude violence. He has also made films which develop the same unrelenting themes.

Wesselman, Tom
(Cincinnati, Ohio, 1931). American painter. An exponent of Pop Art, he treats themes of mass communication in emphatic enlargement, rendering them with aggressive irony in clear, direct colours and with explosive visual force.

Wols (Alfred Otto Wolfgang Schulze)
(Berlin, 1913–Paris, 1951). German painter and graphic artist. The son of a musician, he was a respected violinist from his youth. He studied in Dresden and Frankfurt, where he followed Frobenius' course at the Institute of African Studies. For a short time he then attended the Berlin Bauhaus, studying architecture with Mies van der Rohe and Moholy-Nagy. In '32 he was in Paris and was in contact with the Surrealists, working meanwhile as a photographer. At the beginning of the war, being German, he was interned in a concentration camp, where he began to make designs. In '45 he held his first personal exhibition. In '47 he began the series of illustrations for Sarte, Kafka, Artaud, and Paulhan. He belonged, with Fautrier and Dubuffet, to the founding triad of informal art in Europe (*tachisme*). The psychic impulse is transformed in Wols's works into a sign without the filters of memory. To see is to discover in oneself the complex reality of the spirit; this is interpreted in the delicate intricacy of signs and machines which makes up his painting, in a subterranean search for the process of organic growth in nature.

Yoko-o, Tadanori
Japanese art worker and painter. In the wake of the international diffusion of Pop Art he analyzes the erotic element in much of the mass media, from advertising to the commercial cinema, in an ironic and iconoclastic way.

Zadkine, Ossip
(Smolensk, 1890–Paris, 1967). Russian sculptor, naturalized French. He studied in Scotland and London; in 1909 he was in Paris, where after briefly attending the courses at the École des Beaux Arts he opened his own studio. The friend of Archipenko and Lipchitz and in close contact with Léger, Chagall, and Soutine, he was in the thick of avant-garde experiments. During the First World War he fought in the French army; and suffering from gas poisoning in '18, he returned to Paris, where, penniless and ill, he doggedly took up his work again. From a Cubist starting point he elaborated during the 1920's a plastic representation that united metaphysical elements reminiscent of De Chirico to Expressionist motifs, which often led him to a monumental heightening of the plastic image.

Bibliography

Abstract Art since 1945 (essays by various authors), London, 1971

Amaya, Mario, *Pop as Art*, London, 1965

Ashton, Dore, *The Life and Times of the New York School*, Bath, 1972

Bann, Stephen, with Reg Gadney, Frank Popper, and Philip Steadman, *Four Essays in Kinetic Art*, London, 1966

Barrett, Cyril, *Op Art*, London, 1970

Battcock, Gregory (ed.), *Minimal Art—a Critical Anthology*, London, 1968

———— (ed.), *Idea Art*, New York, 1973

Berger, John, *Selected Essays and Articles—The Look of Things*, London, 1972

Brett, Guy, *Kinetic Art*, London, 1968

British Painting and Sculpture 1960–1970, catalogue of the exhibition at the National Gallery of Art, Washington, D.C., November 12, 1970–January 3, 1971

Calas, Nicolas, *Art in the Age of Risk*, New York, 1968

Cobra 1948–51, catalogue of an exhibition at the Boymans-van Beuningen Museum, Rotterdam

Coutts-Smith, Kenneth, *The Dream of Icarus*, London, 1970

Creedy, Jean (ed.), *The Social Context of Art*, London, 1970

Davis, Douglas, *Art and the Future*, London, 1973

54–64, Painting and Sculpture of a Decade, catalogue of an exhibition organized by the Calouste Gulbenkian Foundation at the Tate Gallery, London, April 22–June 28, 1964

Figurative Art since 1945 (essays by various authors), London, 1971

Finch, Christopher, *Pop Art—Object and Image*, London and New York, 1968

Fried, Michael, *Three American Artists*, catalogue of an exhibition at the Fogg Art Museum, Harvard University, 1965

Geldzahler, Henry, *New York Painting and Sculpture 1940–1970*, catalogue of an exhibition at the Metropolitan Museum of Art, New York—London, 1969

Greenberg, Clement, *Art and Culture*, Boston, 1961

———— *Recentness of Sculpture*, "American Sculpture of the Sixties", catalogue of an exhibition at the Los Angeles County Museum of Art, April 28–June 25, 1967, and at the Philadelphia Museum of Art, September 19–October 29, 1967

Haftmann, Werner, *Painting in the Twentieth Century*, 2nd edition, London, 1965

Henri, Adrian, *Environments and Happenings*, London, 1974; published in the United States with the title *Total Art*, New York, 1974.

Kepes, Gyorgy (ed.), *The Nature and Art of Motion*, London and New York, 1965

Kirby, Michael, *Happenings*, New York, 1965

Kostelanetz, Richard (ed.), *The New American Arts*, New York, 1967

Kozloff, Max, *Renderings*, London, 1968

Kultermann, Udo, *The New Sculpture*, London and New York, 1968

———— *Art-Events and Happenings*. London, 1971

———— *New Realism*, New York, 1972

Lippard, Lucy R., *Pop Art*, London and New York, 1966

Lucie-Smith, Edward, *Movements in Art since 1945*, 2nd edition, London, 1976; published in the United States with the title *Late Modern*, 2nd edition, New York, 1976

———— *Thinking about Art*, London, 1968

Mailland, Robert (ed.), *A Dictionary of Modern Sculpture*, Paris, 1960; London, 1962

McMullen, Roy, *Art, Affluence and Alienation*, London, 1968

Meyer, Ursula, *Conceptual Art*, New York, 1972

Mueller, Robert E., *The Science of Art*, New York, 1967, London, 1968

Müller, Grégoire, *The New Avant-Garde*, Venice and London, 1972

O'Doherty, Brian, *Object and Idea*, New York, 1967

Pellegrini, Aldo, *New Tendencies in Art*, New York, 1966, London, 1967

Popper, Frank, *Naissance des arts cinétiques*, Paris, 1967

Reichardt, Jasia, *The Computer in Art*, London and New York, 1971

Restany, Pierre, catalogue of the "Superlund" exhibition, Lund (Sweden), 1967

Richardson, Tony, and Nikos Stangos (eds.), *Concepts of Modern Art*, London, 1974

Rodman, Selden, *Conversations with Artists*, New York, 1961

Rose, Barbara, *American Art since 1900*, London and New York, 1967

Rosenberg, Harold, *The Tradition of the New*, London and New York, 1962

———— *The Anxious Object*, London and New York, 1964

———— *The Re-Definition of Art*, London and New York, 1972

———— *Art on the Edge*, New York, 1975; London, 1976

Russell, John, and Suzi Gablik, *Pop Art Redefined*, London and New York, 1969

Sandler, Irving, *Abstract Expressionism: The Triumph of American Painting*, London and New York, 1970

Seitz, William C., *The Art of Assemblage*, catalogue of an exhibition at the Museum of Modern Art, New York, 1961

———— *The Responsive Eye*, catalogue of an exhibition at the Museum of Modern Art, New York, 1965

Tomkins, Calvin, *Ahead of the Game*, London, 1968

Tuchman, Maurice (ed.), *The New York School: Abstract Expressionism in the 40's and 50's*, London, 1970

Vergine, Lea, *Il Corpo come Linguaggio*, Milan, 1974

Walker, John A., *Art since Pop*, London, 1975

Weber, J., *Pop-Art: Happenings und neue Realisten*, Munich, 1970

Index of Illustrations

502

504

HSP Math

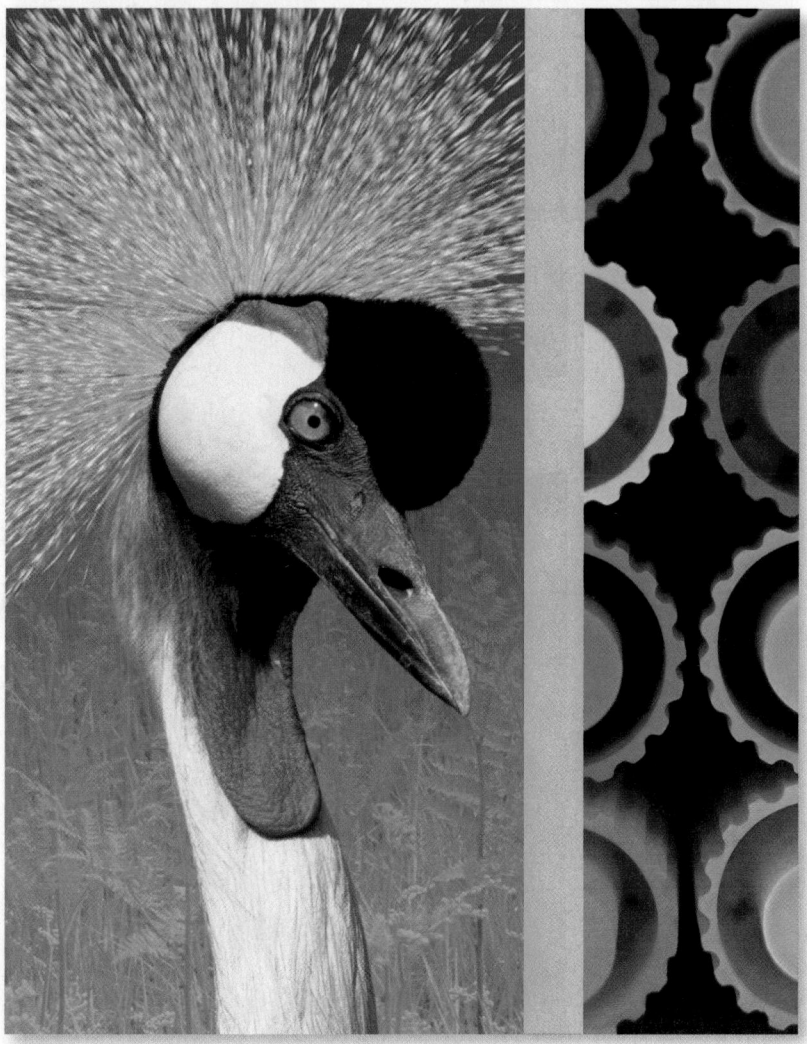

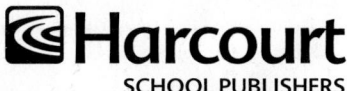

Harcourt
SCHOOL PUBLISHERS

Visit *The Learning Site!*
www.harcourtschool.com

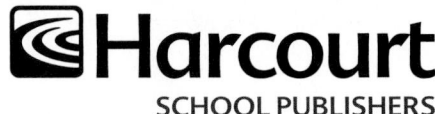

SCHOOL PUBLISHERS

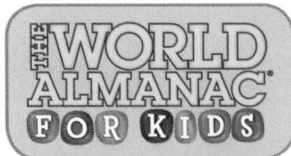

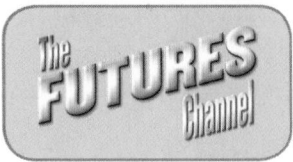

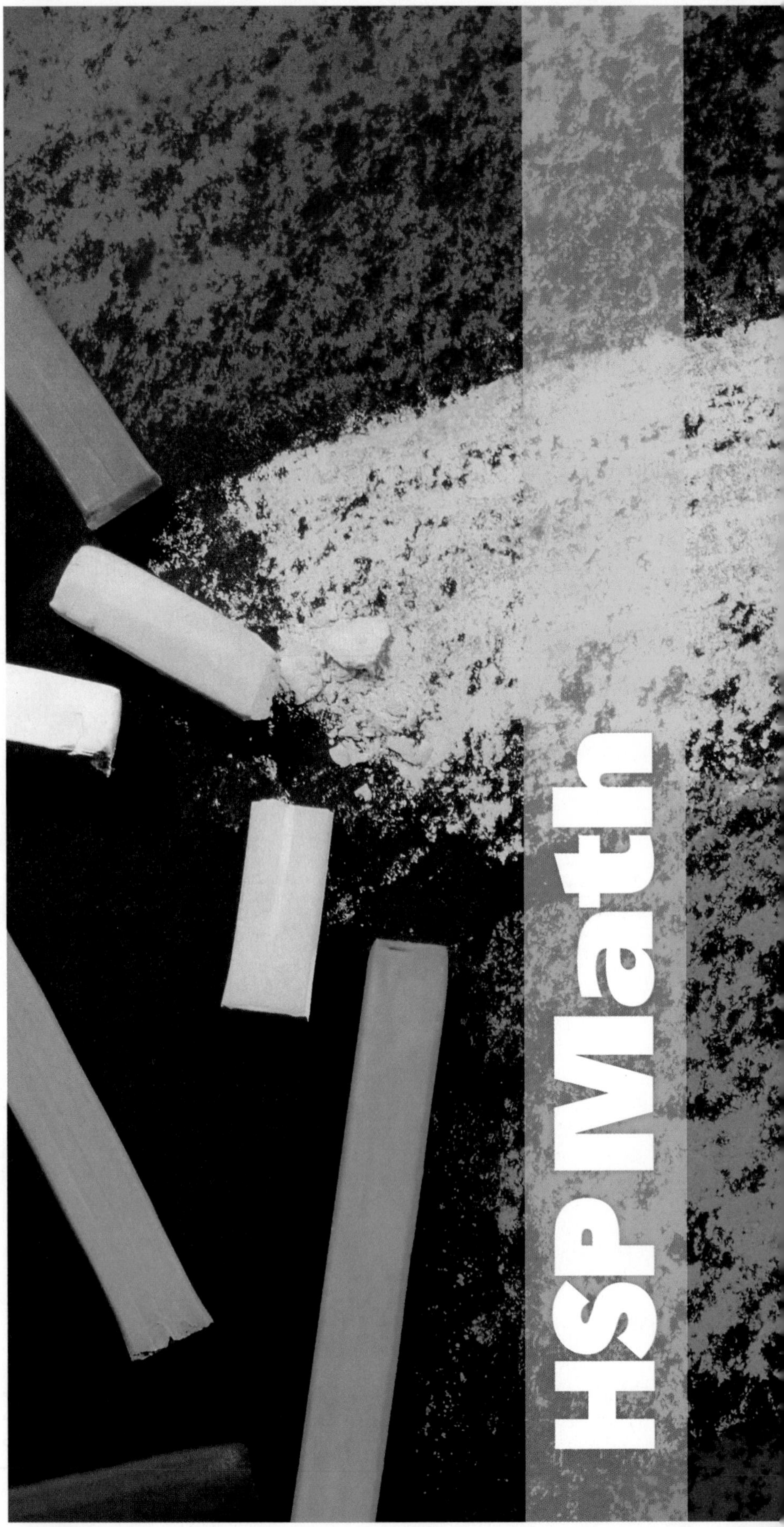

ISBN 13: 978-0-15-341261-5
ISBN 10: 0-15-341261-5

2 3 4 5 6 7 8 9 10 032 16 15 14 13 12 11 10 09 08

HSP Math

Mathematics Advisors

James A. Mendoza Epperson
Associate Professor
Department of Mathematics
The University of Texas
    at Arlington
Arlington, Texas

David G. Wright
Professor
Department of Mathematics
Brigham Young University
Provo, Utah

Senior Authors

Evan M. Maletsky
Professor Emeritus
Montclair State University
Upper Montclair, New Jersey

Joyce McLeod
Visiting Professor, Retired
Rollins College
Winter Park, Florida

Authors

Angela G. Andrews
Assistant Professor of
    Math Education
National Louis University
Lisle, Illinois

Lynda Luckie
Director, K-12 Mathematics
Gwinnett County Public Schools
Suwanee, Georgia

Janet K. Scheer
Executive Director
Create-A-Vision
Foster City, California

Juli K. Dixon
Associate Professor of
    Mathematics Education
University of Central Florida
Orlando, Florida

David G. Wright
Professor
Department of Mathematics
Brigham Young University
Provo, Utah

Vicki Newman
Classroom Teacher
McGaugh Elementary School
Los Alamitos Unified
    School District
Seal Beach, California

Karen S. Norwood
Associate Professor of
    Mathematics Education
North Carolina State University
Raleigh, North Carolina

Jennie M. Bennett
Mathematics Teacher
Houston Independent
    School District
Houston, Texas

David D. Molina
Program Director, Retired
The Charles A. Dana Center
The University of Texas
    at Austin

James A. Mendoza Epperson
Associate Professor
Department of Mathematics
The University of Texas
    at Arlington
Arlington, Texas

Tom Roby
Associate Professor of
    Mathematics
Director, Quantitative
    Learning Center
University of Connecticut
Storrs, Connecticut

Minerva Cordero-Epperson
Associate Professor of
    Mathematics and
Associate Dean of the
    Honors College
The University of Texas
    at Arlington
Arlington, Texas

Barbara Montalto
Mathematics Consultant
Assistant Director
    of Mathematics, Retired
Texas Education Agency
Austin, Texas

Program Consultants and Specialists

Michael DiSpezio
Writer and On-Air Host,
    JASON Project
North Falmouth,
    Massachusetts

Valerie Johse
Elementary Math Specialist
Office of Curriculum
    & Instruction
Pearland I.S.D.
Pearland, Texas

Concepion Molina
Southwest Educational
    Development Lab
Austin, Texas

Lydia Song
Program Specialist–Mathematics
Orange County Department
    of Education
Costa Mesa, California

Rebecca Valbuena
Language Development
    Specialist
Stanton Elementary School
Glendora, California

Robin C. Scarcella
Professor and Director
Program of Academic English
    and ESL
University of California,
    Irvine
Irvine, California

Tyrone Howard
Assistant Professor
UCLA Graduate School
    of Education
Information Studies
University of California
    at Los Angeles
Los Angeles, California

Russell Gersten
Director, Instructional
    Research Group
Long Beach, California
Professor Emeritus of
    Special Education
University of Oregon
Eugene, Oregon

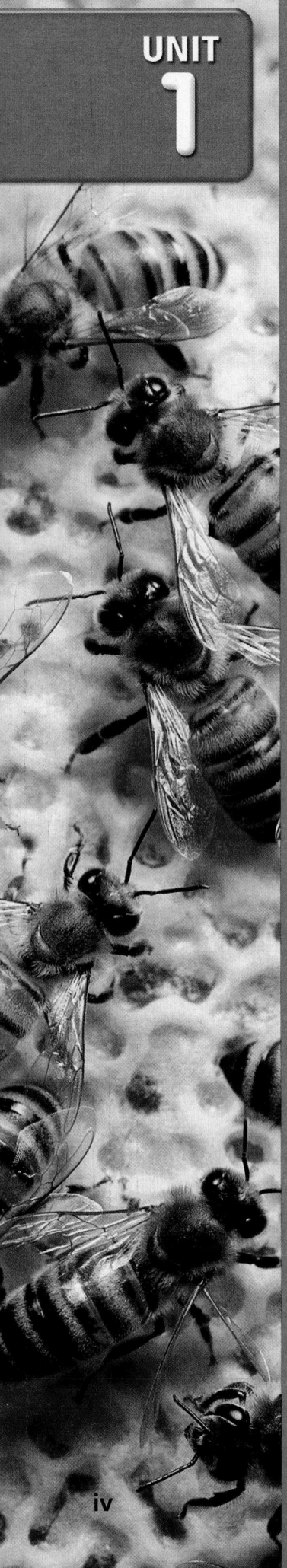

Place Value, Addition, and Subtraction

1 Understand Place Value   2

2 Compare, Order, and Round Numbers   26

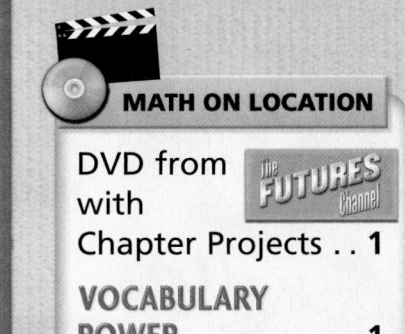

MATH ON LOCATION

DVD from with The FUTURES Channel
Chapter Projects . . 1

VOCABULARY
POWER 1

GO ONLINE Technology

Harcourt Mega Math: Chapter 1, p. 12; Chapter 2, p. 30; Chapter 3, p. 57; Chapter 4, p. 83; Extra Practice, pp. 20, 40, 68, 98
The Harcourt Learning Site: www.harcourtschool.com
Multimedia Math Glossary: www.harcourtschool.com/hspmath

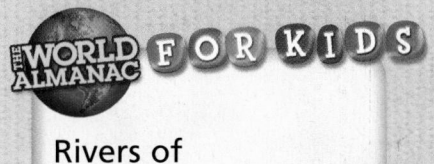

THE WORLD ALMANAC FOR KIDS

Rivers of the World 104

v

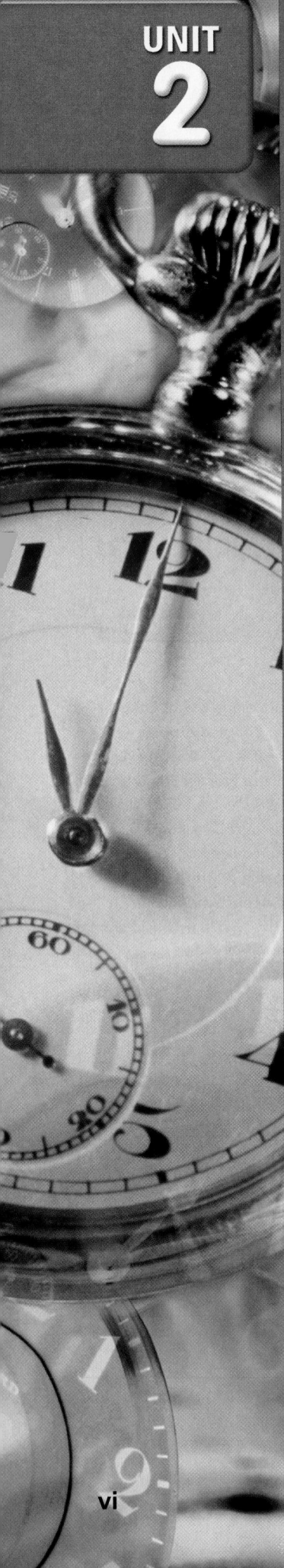

Money and Time, Data, and Probability

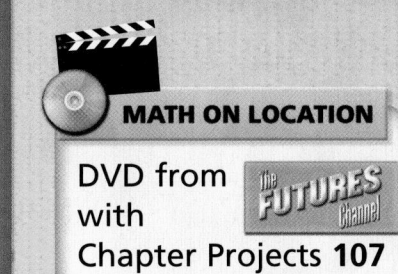
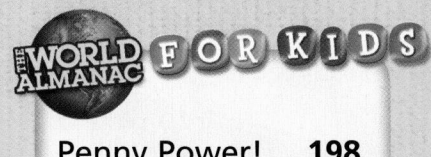

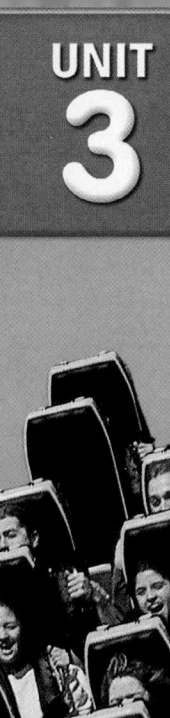

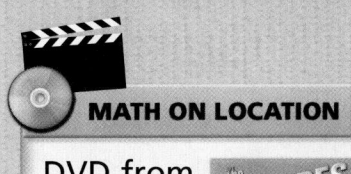

MATH ON LOCATION

DVD from The FUTURES Channel with Chapter Projects 201

VOCABULARY POWER 201

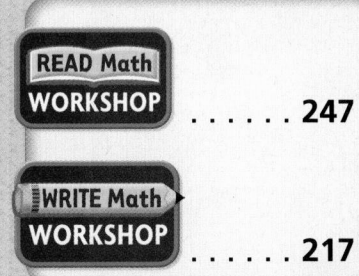

READ Math **WORKSHOP** 247

WRITE Math **WORKSHOP** 217

GO ONLINE **Technology**

Harcourt Mega Math: Chapter 8, p. 208; Chapter 9, p. 239; Chapter 10, p. 259; Extra Practice, pp. 224–225, 248, 266
The Harcourt Learning Site: www.harcourtschool.com
Multimedia Math Glossary: www.harcourtschool.com/hspmath

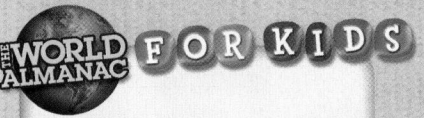

All About Animals 272

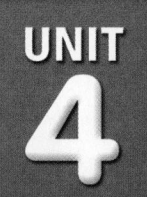

UNIT 4

Division Concepts and Facts

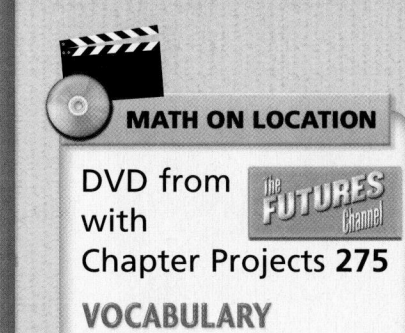

MATH ON LOCATION

DVD from 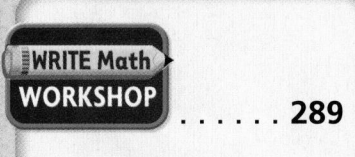 with
Chapter Projects **275**

**VOCABULARY
POWER** **275**

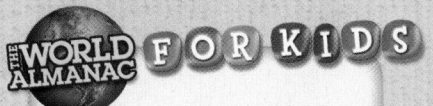

Technology

Harcourt Mega Math: Chapter
11, p. 285; Chapter 12, p. 310;
Chapter 13, p. 334; Extra
Practice, pp. 294, 314, 338
The Harcourt Learning Site:
www.harcourtschool.com
Multimedia Math Glossary:
www.harcourtschool.com/
hspmath

THE WORLD ALMANAC FOR KIDS

The Wheel Is
a Big Deal **344**

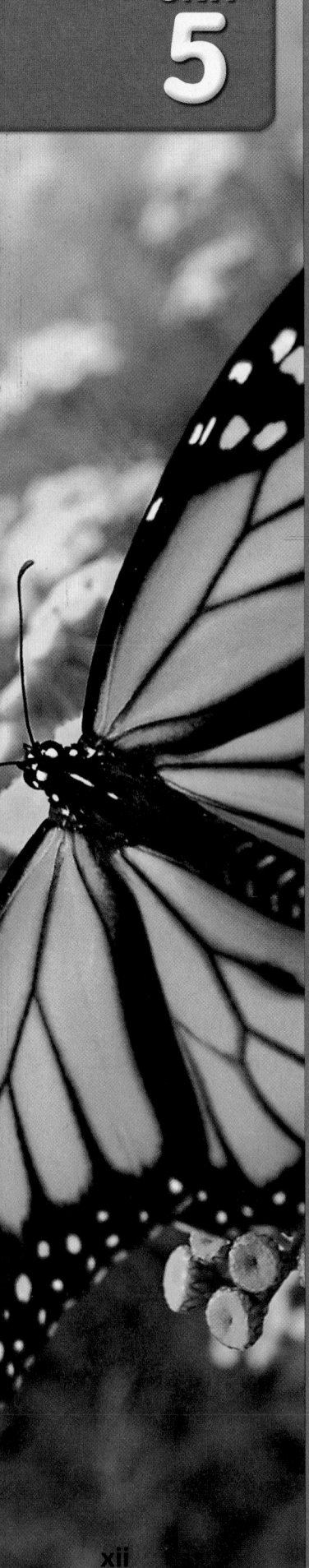

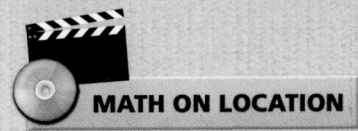

MATH ON LOCATION

DVD from with FUTURES Channel
Chapter Projects **347**

VOCABULARY
POWER **347**

READ Math
WORKSHOP **407**

WRITE Math
WORKSHOP **353**

GO ONLINE   Technology

Harcourt Mega Math: Chapter 14, p. 362; Chapter 15, pp. 385, 387; Chapter 16, p. 402; Chapter 17, p. 423; Extra Practice, pp. 370–371, 392, 414, 434
The Harcourt Learning Site:
www.harcourtschool.com
Multimedia Math Glossary:
www.harcourtschool.com/hspmath

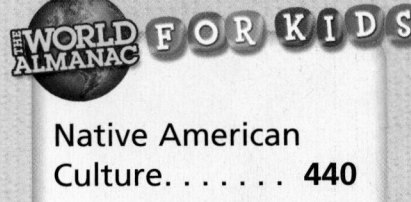

THE WORLD ALMANAC FOR KIDS

Native American Culture. **440**

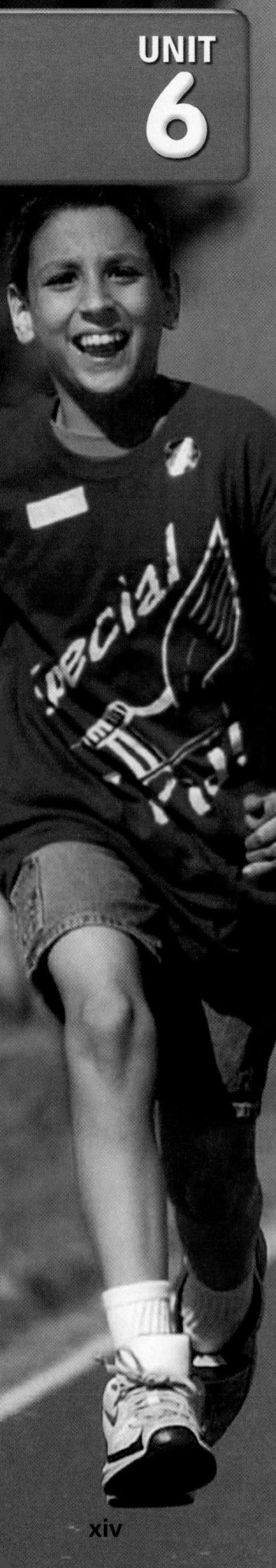

Fractions and Decimals

18 Understand Fractions 444

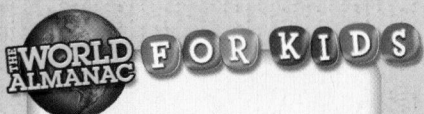

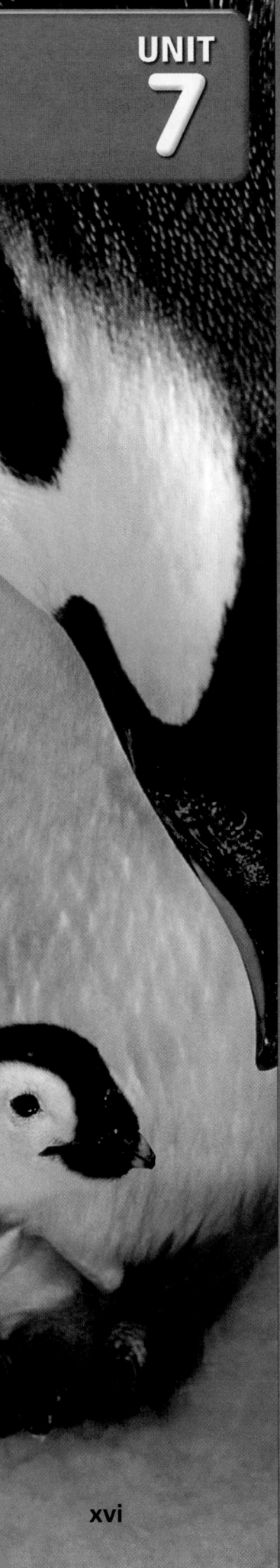

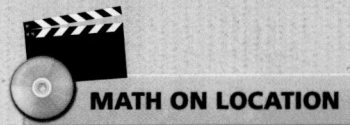

MATH ON LOCATION

DVD from 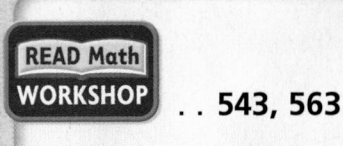 with Chapter Projects **509**

VOCABULARY POWER **509**

READ Math WORKSHOP . . **543, 563**

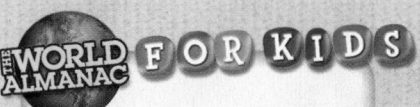

GO ONLINE   **Technology**

Harcourt Mega Math: Chapter 20, p. 516; Chapter 21, p. 545; Chapter 22, pp. 562, 566; Extra Practice, pp. 530, 552, 574
The Harcourt Learning Site:
www.harcourtschool.com
Multimedia Math Glossary:
www.harcourtschool.com/hspmath

THE WORLD ALMANAC FOR KIDS

Fish Stories **580**

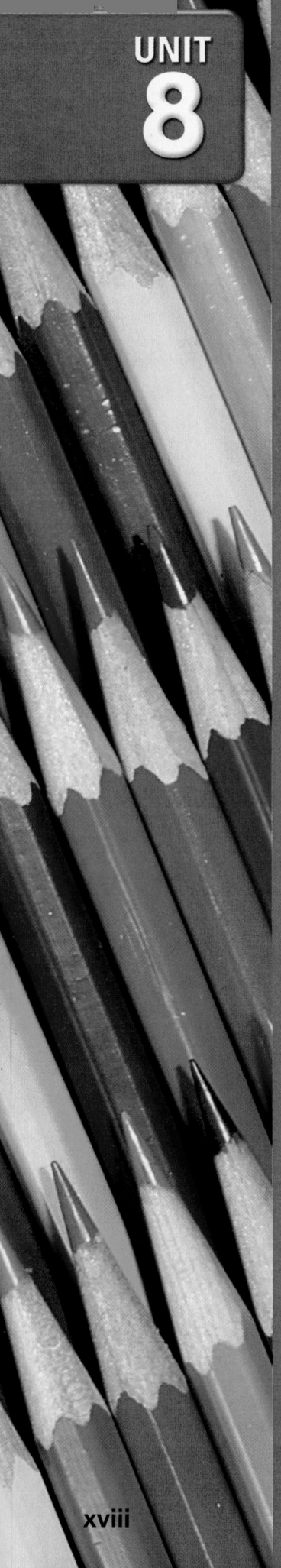

Multiply and Divide by 1 Digit

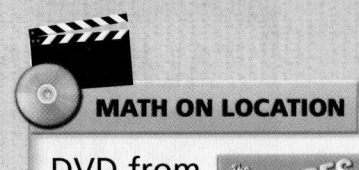

MATH ON LOCATION

DVD from with **The FUTURES Channel** Chapter Projects **583**

VOCABULARY POWER **583**

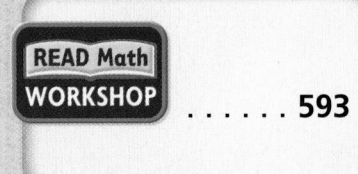

READ Math WORKSHOP **593**

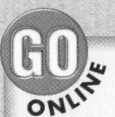

GO ONLINE — Technology

Harcourt Mega Math: Chapter 23, p. 597; Chapter 24, p. 621; Extra Practice, pp. 604, 624
The Harcourt Learning Site:
www.harcourtschool.com
Multimedia Math Glossary:
www.harcourtschool.com/hspmath

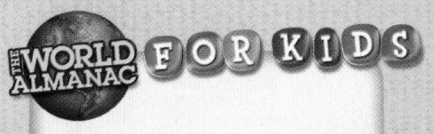

THE WORLD ALMANAC FOR KIDS

Model Trains. **630**

Mathematics is a language of numbers, words, and symbols.

This year, you will learn ways to communicate about math as you **talk**, **read**, and **write** about what you are learning.

The tally table and the bar graph show the number of long-legged wading birds seen along the bay shore of South Padre Island. Marta and her family counted the birds they saw.

Long-Legged Wading Birds

Name	Tallies
Glossy Ibis	卌
Great Blue Heron	卌 I
Roseate Spoonbill	卌 IIII
Snowy Egret	IIII

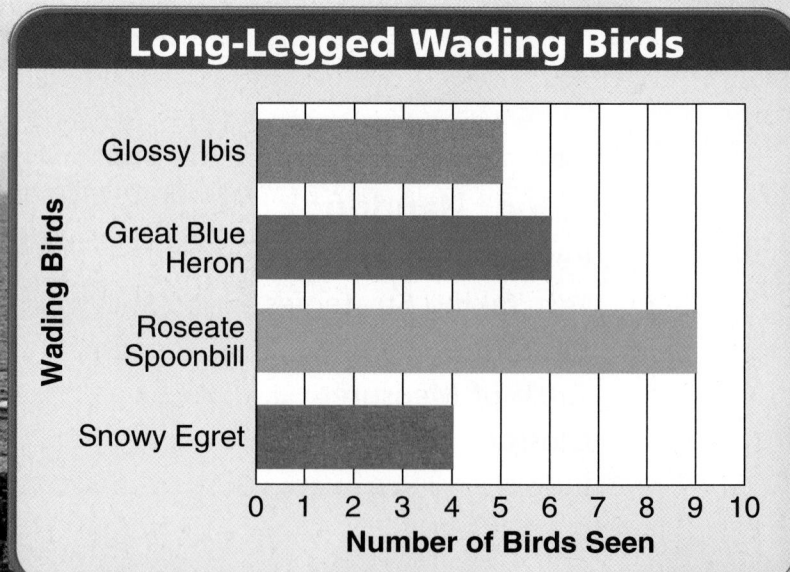

Long-Legged Wading Birds

TALK Math

Talk about the tally table and the bar graph.

1. Why are the titles of the tally table and the bar graph the same?

2. How is the information on the tally table and the bar graph alike? How it is different?

3. How do you use the numbers along the bottom of the bar graph?

Read the data on the bar graph.

4. How many Snowy Egrets were seen?

5. Were more Glossy Ibises or Snowy Egrets seen?

6. How many more Roseate Spoonbills than Great Blue Herons were seen?

7. How many birds were counted in all?

WRITE Math ▸

Write a problem about the graph.

This year, you will write many problems. When you see **Pose a Problem**, you look at a problem on the page and use it to write your own problem.

> In your problem, you can
> - change the numbers or some of the information.
> - exchange the known and unknown information.
> - write an open-ended problem that can have more than one correct answer.

These problems are examples of ways you can pose your own problem. Solve each problem.

Problem How many more Roseate Spoonbills than Snowy Egrets were seen?

- **Change the Numbers or Information.**
  Marta saw 2 more Great Blue Herons, but she forgot to put tally marks on the tally table. How many more Great Blue Herons than Snowy Egrets did she see?

- **Exchange the Known and Unknown Information.**
  Marta tallied a total of 13 Roseate Spoonbills and Snowy Egrets. If she tallied 4 Snowy Egrets, how many Roseate Spoonbills did she tally?

- **Open-Ended**
  Marta visited the seashore again and counted the same birds. She counted a total of 14 birds. She saw 3 Snowy Egrets. How many Glossy Ibises, Great Blue Herons, and Roseate Spoonbills might she have seen?

Pose a Problem Choose one of the three ways to write a new problem. Use the information on the tally table and the bar graph.

Place Value, Addition, and Subtraction

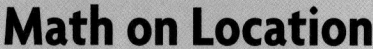

A DVD FROM
The Futures Channel

with
Chapter Projects

1

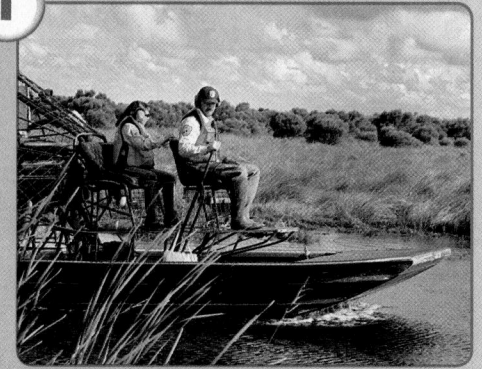

The biologist visits thousands of acres of refuges by airboat to keep track of birds and other animals.

2

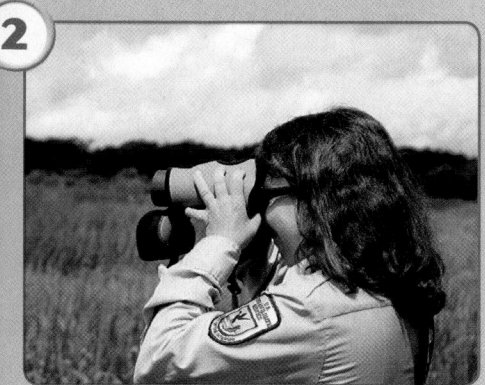

The biologist counts and records the number of egrets to tell if the number is increasing or decreasing.

3

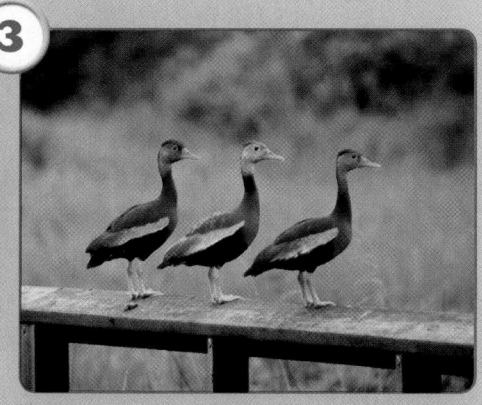

Great numbers of birds and ducks arrive daily so totals are estimated.

VOCABULARY POWER

TALK Math

What math do you see in the **Math on Location** photographs? How can you tell if the number of egrets is increasing or decreasing?

READ Math

REVIEW VOCABULARY You learned the words below when you learned about place value last year. How do these words relate to **Math on Location**?

compare to describe whether numbers are equal to, less than, or greater than each other

estimate to find about how many or how much

place value the value of each digit in a number, based on the location of the digit

WRITE Math

Copy and complete a Word Association Tree Diagram like the one below. Use what you know about place value to fill in the blanks.

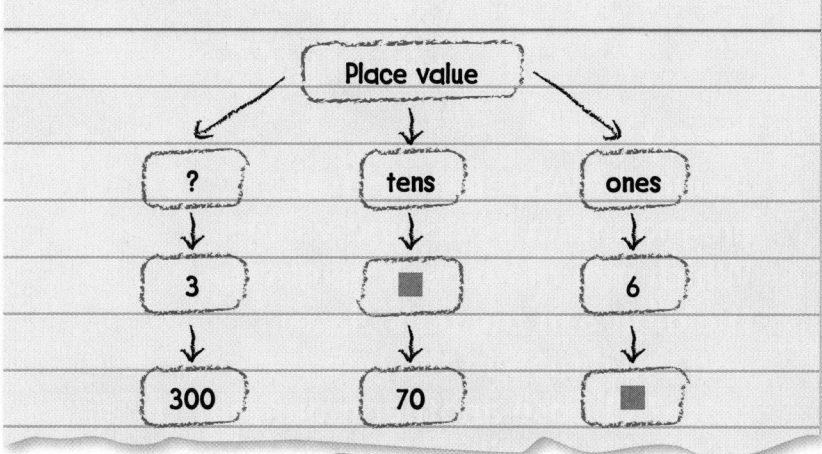

GO ONLINE
Technology
Multimedia Math Glossary link at
www.harcourtschool.com/hspmath

Unit 1 • Chapters 1–4   1

1 Understand Place Value

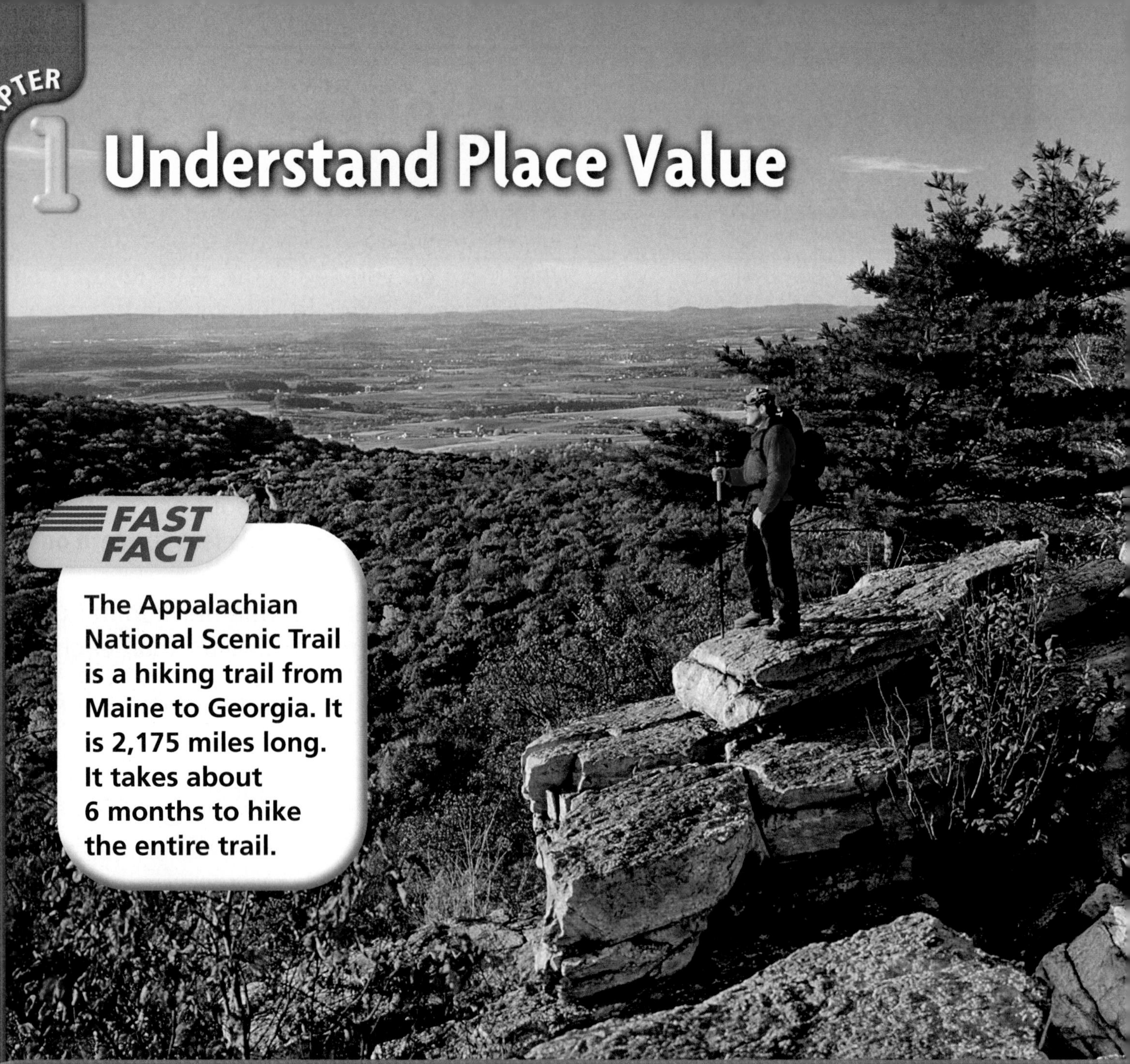

≡FAST FACT

The Appalachian National Scenic Trail is a hiking trail from Maine to Georgia. It is 2,175 miles long. It takes about 6 months to hike the entire trail.

Investigate

Along the Appalachian Trail are mountain peaks and valleys. Which mountain peak height has the digit 8 in the tens place and the digit 6 in the hundreds place? Choose another mountain peak and describe its height by using place value.

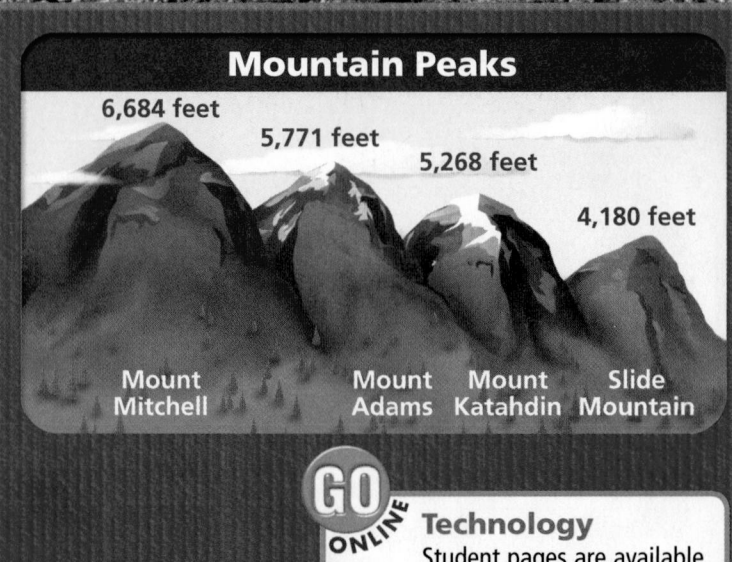

Mountain Peaks

6,684 feet

5,771 feet

5,268 feet

4,180 feet

Mount Mitchell

Mount Adams

Mount Katahdin

Slide Mountain

GO ONLINE

Technology
Student pages are available in the Student eBook.

Show What You Know

Check your understanding of important skills needed for success in Chapter 1.

▶ **Place Value: Tens and Ones to 100**

Write the value of the blue digit.

1. 37   **2.** 81   **3.** 53   **4.** 29   **5.** 14

▶ **Understand Place Value**

Write the number shown.

6. 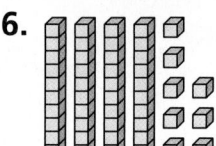   **7.** 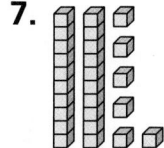   **8.**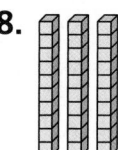

9. 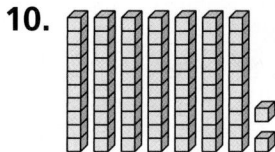   **10.**   **11.**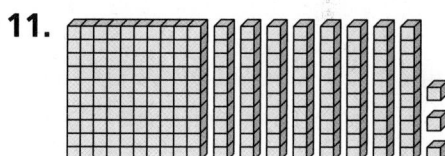

▶ **Tens and Ones**

Write each number.

12. 90 + 3   **13.** 20 + 6

14. seventeen   **15.** thirty-one

VOCABULARY POWER

CHAPTER VOCABULARY	WARM-UP WORDS
digits	**digits** The symbols 0, 1, 2, 3, 4, 5, 6, 7, 8, and 9
even	
expanded form	**even** A whole number that has a 0, 2, 4, 6, or 8 in the ones place
odd	
standard form	**odd** A whole number that has a 1, 3, 5, 7, or 9 in the ones place
word form	

1 Algebra: Patterns on a Hundred Chart

OBJECTIVE: Find number patterns on a hundred chart.

Quick Review

Find the sum.

1. $5 + 5$ 2. $10 + 5$
3. $15 + 5$ 4. $20 + 5$
5. $25 + 5$

Vocabulary

even   **odd**

Investigate

Materials ■ hundred chart

You can use a hundred chart to find number patterns.

Ⓐ Choose a number from 2 through 5.

Ⓑ Shade that box on the hundred chart.

Ⓒ Skip-count by your number and shade each box you land on.

Draw Conclusions

1. Describe the pattern you see on your hundred chart.

2. Compare your hundred chart with those of other classmates. What do you notice about the patterns?
How are they alike?
How are they different?

3. **Analysis** Look at a hundred chart. What pattern will you get if you start at 10 and skip-count by tens?

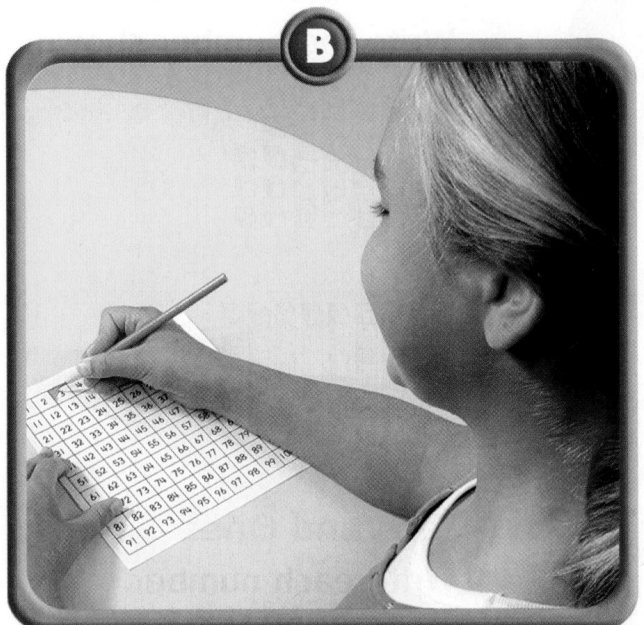

Connect

You can use a hundred chart to identify even and odd numbers.

Step 1

Start at 2. Shade the box on the hundred chart.

1	2	3	4	5	6	7	8	9	10
11	12	13	14	15	16	17	18	19	20
21	22	23	24	25	26	27	28	29	30
31	32	33	34	35	36	37	38	39	40
41	42	43	44	45	46	47	48	49	50
51	52	53	54	55	56	57	58	59	60
61	62	63	64	65	66	67	68	69	70
71	72	73	74	75	76	77	78	79	80
81	82	83	84	85	86	87	88	89	90
91	92	93	94	95	96	97	98	99	100

Step 2

Skip-count by twos. Shade each box you land on. What pattern do you see?

1	2	3	4	5	6	7	8	9	10
11	12	13	14	15	16	17	18	19	20
21	22	23	24	25	26	27	28	29	30
31	32	33	34	35	36	37	38	39	40
41	42	43	44	45	46	47	48	49	50
51	52	53	54	55	56	57	58	59	60
61	62	63	64	65	66	67	68	69	70
71	72	73	74	75	76	77	78	79	80
81	82	83	84	85	86	87	88	89	90
91	92	93	94	95	96	97	98	99	100

The numbers that are shaded are **even** numbers.
Even numbers end in 2, 4, 6, 8, or 0.

The numbers that are not shaded are **odd** numbers.
Odd numbers end in 1, 3, 5, 7, or 9.

- How does a hundred chart help you identify even and odd numbers?

TALK Math

How can you tell whether a number is odd or even?

Practice

Use the hundred chart. Find the next number in the pattern.

1. 10, 20, 30, 40, ■

2. 5, 10, 15, 20, ■

3. 77, 75, 73, 71, ■

✓4. 3, 6, 9, 12, ■

Use the hundred chart. Tell whether each number is *odd* or *even*.

5. 16

6. 25

7. 34

✓8. 23

9. 81

10. 92

11. 47

12. 78

13. **WRITE Math** ▸ If you start at 3 and skip-count by twos, will the pattern include even numbers, odd numbers, or both? **Explain.**

Locate Points on a Number Line

OBJECTIVE: Locate and name points on a number line.

Quick Review

Write the next number in the pattern.

1. 2, 4, 6, 8, ■
2. 5, 10, 15, 20, ■
3. 1, 3, 5, 7, ■
4. 10, 20, 30, 40, ■
5. 4, 8, 12, 16, ■

Learn

PROBLEM Ryan is playing a game that uses a number line. His game piece is on the point labeled X. What number does point X represent?

A number line shows numbers in order from least to greatest.

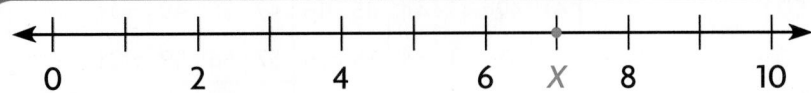

0   2   4   6 X 8   10

This number line shows marks for numbers from 0 through 10. The numbers shown count by twos from left to right. Point X is between 6 and 8.

So, point X represents 7.

Examples Find the number represented by the letter.

A
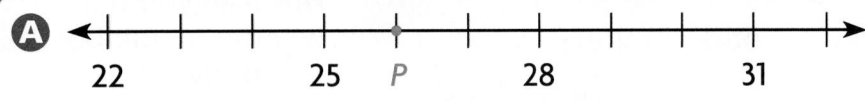

22   25 P 28   31

Point P is between 25 and 28.

Think: There are two marks between 25 and 28. Those marks represent 26 and 27. Point P is the first mark.

So, point P represents 26.

B
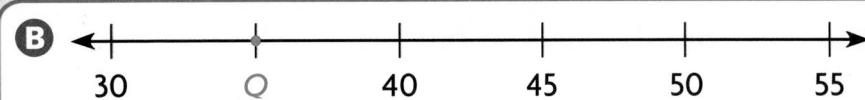

30   Q 40   45   50   55

Point Q is between 30 and 40.

Think: The number line shows counting by fives. Count on to find the number that Q represents.

So, point Q represents 35.

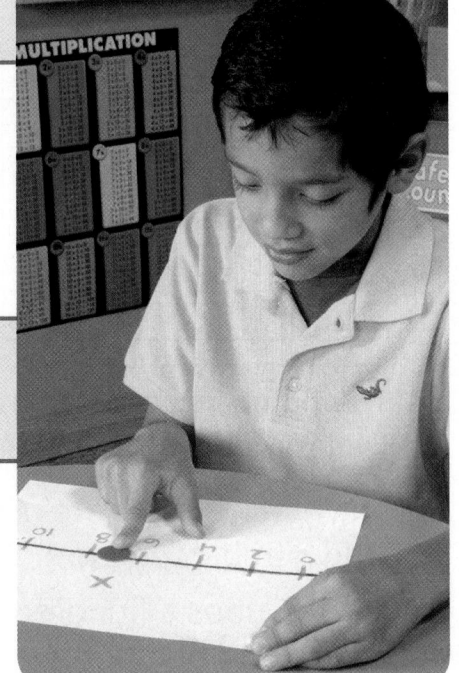

Guided Practice

1. Skip-count by threes to find the number that point Z represents on the number line.

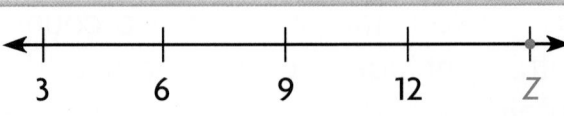

3   6   9   12 Z

Find the number that point X represents on the number line.

2.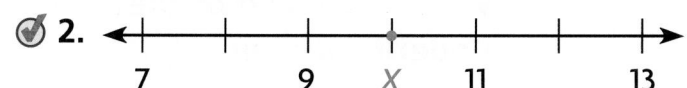

3.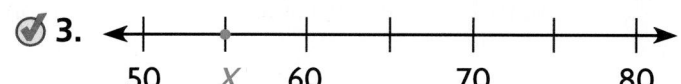

4. **TALK Math** **Explain** how you can use the numbers and marks that are on a number line to find the missing numbers.

Independent Practice and Problem Solving

Find the number that point X represents on the number line.

5.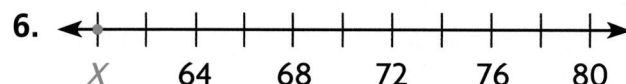

6.

For 7–8, use the number line.

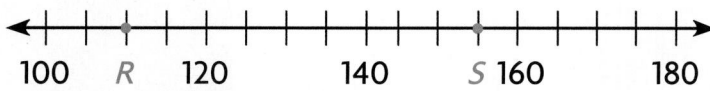

7. Robin's score is shown by point R on the number line above. What is her score?

8. Reasoning Steve's score is shown by point S. What will Steve's next score be if he gets 10 more points? 5 fewer points?

9. What's the Error? On the number line below, Laura says that the difference between point X and point Y is 10. What error did Laura make?

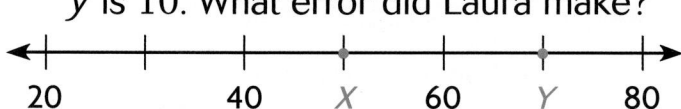

10. **WRITE Math** **Sense or Nonsense** Brian says every other whole number on every number line is an even number. Does Brian's statement make sense?

Mixed Review and Test Prep

11. What is the next number in this pattern? (p. 5)

12, 15, 18, 21, ■

12. Each pen costs $4. What is the total cost of 5 pens? (Grade 2)

13. Test Prep What number does point X represent?

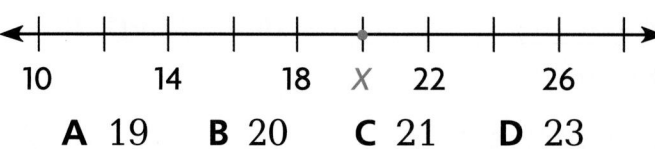

A 19   **B** 20   **C** 21   **D** 23

Extra Practice on page 20, Set A

Place Value: 3 Digits

OBJECTIVE: Use place value to read, write, and represent 3-digit numbers.

Quick Review

Write the value of the underlined digit.

1. 1**8**
2. **2**5
3. **1**0
4. 6**1**
5. 4**2**

Vocabulary

digits   expanded form
standard form   word form

Learn

The symbols 0, 1, 2, 3, 4, 5, 6, 7, 8, and 9 are **digits**. Numbers are made up of digits.

PROBLEM The Otto family visited the world's longest cave at Mammoth Cave National Park. The cave is 367 miles long. What is the value of the digit 6 in 367?

Show 367 with base-ten blocks and a place-value chart.

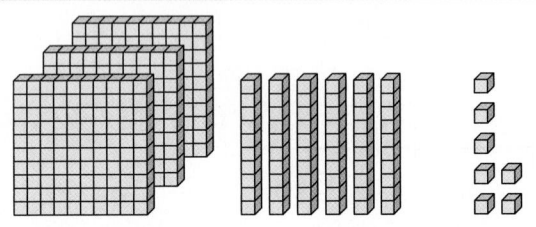

HUNDREDS	TENS	ONES
3	6	7

3 hundreds   6 tens   7 ones
    300   60   7

So, the value of the digit 6 in 367 is 6 tens, or 60.

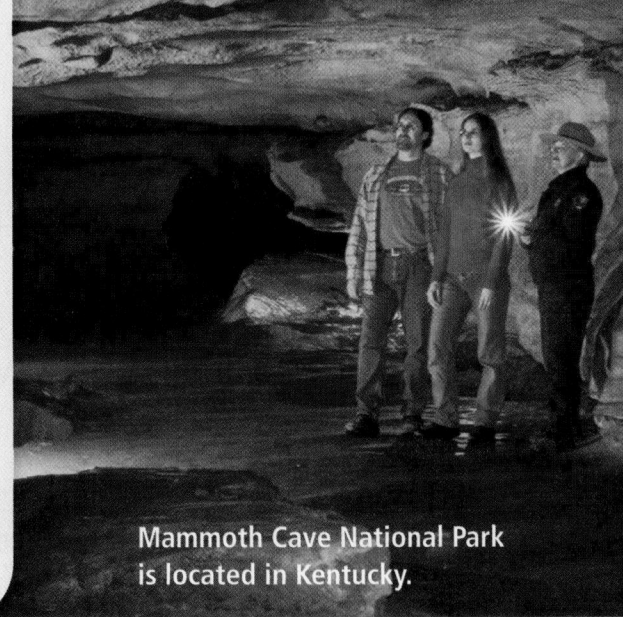

Mammoth Cave National Park is located in Kentucky.

You can write a number in different ways.
Standard form: 367
Expanded form: 300 + 60 + 7
Word form: three hundred sixty-seven

READ Math

When you read whole numbers, do not say "and." The number 367 is read "three hundred sixty-seven."

Guided Practice

1. Write the value of each digit in the chart.

HUNDREDS	TENS	ONES
4	9	5

Write the value of the underlined digit.

2. 9**2**1   3. 53**7**   ✓4. **6**24   ✓5. 75**0**

6. **TALK Math** The campground has 109 campsites. **Explain** what the zero in 109 means.

Write the value of the underlined digit.

7. 58<u>1</u>   **8.** 6<u>7</u>2   **9.** <u>1</u>20   **10.** <u>2</u>08

11. 91<u>4</u>   **12.** <u>8</u>45   **13.** 7<u>1</u>3   **14.** 6<u>9</u>3

Write each number in standard form.

15. 700 + 80 + 1   **16.** 200 + 10 + 9   **17.** 600 + 40 + 3

18. three hundred eighty-five   **19.** 5 hundreds 4 ones   **20.** eight hundred nine

Write each number in expanded form.

21. 842   **22.** 329   **23.** four hundred fifty-four

USE DATA For 24–25, use the table.

24. What is the length of Fisher Ridge Cave written in expanded form?

25. Which cave's length has a 1 in the tens place?

United States Caves	
Cave	**Length in Miles**
Jewel Cave	129
Wind Cave	116
Fisher Ridge Cave	107

26. **≡FAST FACT** Jewel Cave in South Dakota has a depth of 632 feet. What is the value of the digit 3 in 632?

27. ▮WRITE Math▸ **What's the Error?** Tanya wrote four hundred seven as 470. Explain her error. Write the number in standard form.

28. **Reasoning** Write as many 3-digit numbers as you can with the digits 1, 2, and 3 in each number. Write the greatest number in expanded form.

29. I am an odd number between 21 and 40. The sum of my digits is 8. What number am I?

Mixed Review and Test Prep

30. Cory read 43 pages. Blake read 28 pages. How many more pages did Cory read than Blake? (Grade 2)

31. Jordan has three dollar bills and one quarter. How much money does he have? (Grade 2)

32. **Test Prep** Which shows 806 written in expanded form?

A 800 + 60

B 800 + 6

C 80 + 60

D 80 + 6

Extra Practice on page 20, Set B

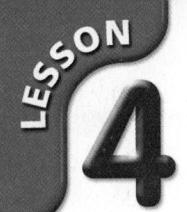

Place Value: 4 Digits

OBJECTIVE: Use place value to read, write, and represent 4-digit numbers.

Quick Review

Write the value of the underlined digit.

1. 8<u>2</u>5
2. <u>4</u>17
3. <u>2</u>51
4. 19<u>8</u>
5. 6<u>3</u>4

Learn

PROBLEM Most peanuts grown in the United States are used to make peanut butter. It takes about 1,000 peanuts to make a jar of peanut butter! What does 1,000 of an object look like?

Activity

Materials ■ paper clips

Model 1,000 using paper clips.

Step 1

Make a chain of 10 linked paper clips. Then make 9 more chains of 10 paper clips.

Step 2

Skip-count by tens.
How many paper clips have you used?

Step 3

Now link your 10 chains to make one long chain of 100 paper clips.

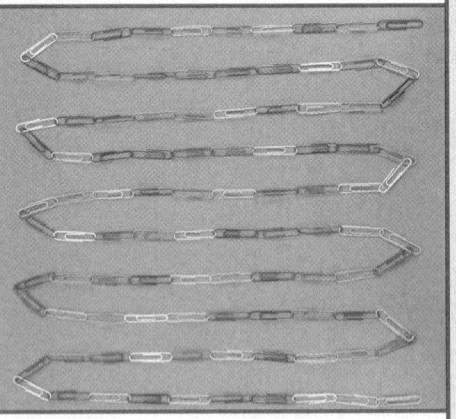

Step 4

Combine your chain of 100 paper clips with the chains from 9 other groups.

• How many chains of 100 paper clips did it take to make 1,000?

So, now you know what 1,000 looks like.

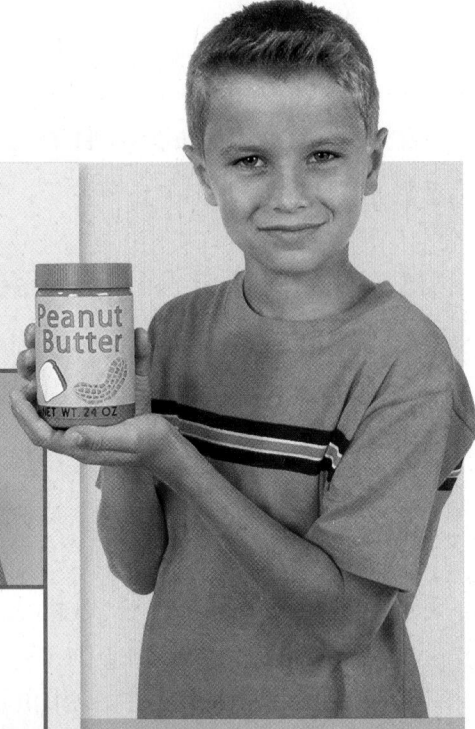

▲ Did you know that the peanut is not a nut? The peanut is actually a vegetable.

Understand Thousands

Base-ten blocks can help you understand thousands.

There are 10 ones in 10.   There are 10 tens in 100.

There are 10 hundreds in 1,000.

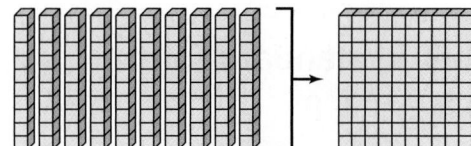

- How many hundreds are in 3,000?

Mr. Jackson sold 2,186 jars of homemade peanut butter. What is the value of the digit 2 in 2,186?

Model the number with base-ten blocks.

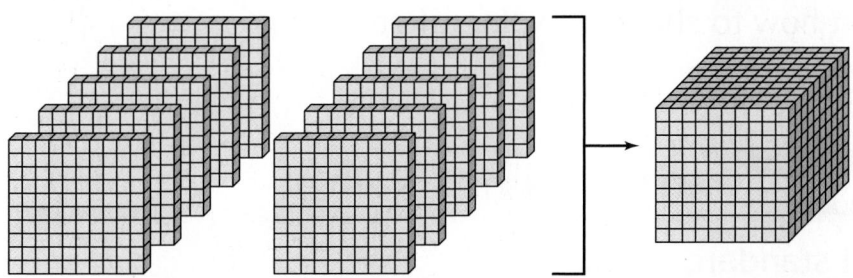

Write the number in a place-value chart.

THOUSANDS	HUNDREDS	TENS	ONES
2,	1	8	6

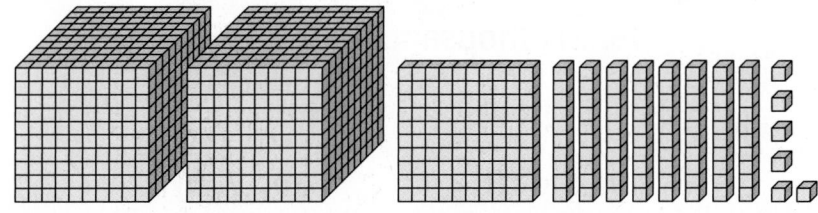

2 thousands	1 hundred	8 tens	6 ones
2,000	100	80	6

So, the value of the digit 2 in 2,186 is 2 thousands, or 2,000.

Here are three ways to write this number.

Standard form: 2,186
Expanded form: 2,000 + 100 + 80 + 6
Word form: two thousand, one hundred eighty-six

> **Math Idea**
> A comma is used to separate the thousands and the hundreds.

Guided Practice

1. Write this number in standard form and in expanded form.

THOUSANDS	HUNDREDS	TENS	ONES
1,	3	4	7

Write each number in standard form.

2. $8,000 + 200 + 50 + 8$

3. three thousand, one hundred fourteen

✓ 4. $1,000 + 300 + 8$

✓ 5. two thousand, thirty-four

6. **TALK Math** Explain how to show the value of each digit in the number 9,248.

Independent Practice and Problem Solving

Write each number in standard form.

7. $9,000 + 700 + 30 + 1$

8. $1,000 + 20 + 4$

9. eight thousand, five hundred two

10. seven thousand, three hundred ninety-one

Write each number in expanded form.

11. 2,389

12. 7,241

13. 6,170

14. 4,502

15. one thousand, eighteen

16. six thousand, four

Write the value of the underlined digit.

17. <u>6</u>,452

18. 3,<u>8</u>01

19. <u>5</u>,018

20. 7,3<u>14</u>

Algebra **Find the missing number.**

21. $1,000 + \blacksquare + 40 + 8 = 1,748$

22. $3,000 + 200 + \blacksquare + 6 = 3,296$

23. $4,000 + 600 + \blacksquare = 4,620$

24. $\blacksquare + 50 + 4 = 8,054$

25. Write a 4-digit number that has a 7 in the hundreds place.

26. Write a number that is 1,000 more than 6,243.

27. How many hundreds are in 6,000? How many tens?

28. **WRITE Math** ▸ **Sense or Nonsense** Brett says that the greatest possible 4-digit number is 9,000. Does Brett's statement make sense? **Explain.**

Technology
Use Harcourt Mega Math, The Number Games, *Tiny's Think Tank*, Level A; Country Countdown, *Block Busters*, Level T.

Extra Practice on page 20, Set C

Learn About | Names For Numbers

You can name numbers in many different ways. Here are some of the different names for 78, 152, and 2,046.

78	152	2,046
70 + 8	100 + 50 + 2	2,000 + 40 + 6
25 + 25 + 25 + 3	50 + 50 + 52	2,000 + 46
80 − 2	155 − 3	2,100 − 54
100 − 22	200 − 48	1,000 + 1,000 + 20 + 20 + 6

Try It

Write two other names for each number.

29. 45   **30.** 215   **31.** 698   **32.** 1,523   **33.** 4,267

34. 61   **35.** 992   **36.** 457   **37.** 29   **38.** 3,514

39. 2,199   **40.** 53   **41.** 95   **42.** 722   **43.** 816

44. 375   **45.** 6,358   **46.** 186   **47.** 74   **48.** 163

Mixed Review and Test Prep

49. Maggie wants to buy a kite that costs 63¢ and a tablet that costs 24¢. She has 85¢. How much more money does she need? (Grade 2)

50. Test Prep Which number shows eight thousand ninety?

  A 890

  B 8,009

  C 8,090

  D 8,900

51. In a class survey of favorite pets, 6 students chose dogs, 7 students chose cats, and 3 students chose fish. How many students in all voted? (Grade 2)

52. Test Prep What is the value of the underlined digit in 6,4$\underline{7}$2?

  A 7

  B 70

  C 700

  D 7,000

Place Value: 5 and 6 Digits

OBJECTIVE: Use place value to read and write 5- and 6-digit numbers.

Learn

PROBLEM The highest peak in California is Mount Whitney. It has a height of 14,494 feet. What is the value of the digit 1 in 14,494?

Use a place-value chart. The place to the left of the thousands place is the ten-thousands place.

TEN THOUSANDS	THOUSANDS	HUNDREDS	TENS	ONES
1	4,	4	9	4

So, the value of the digit 1 in 14,494 is 10,000.

You can write this number in different ways.
Standard form: 14,494
Expanded form: 10,000 + 4,000 + 400 + 90 + 4
Word form: fourteen thousand, four hundred ninety-four

Mount Whitney is in Sequoia National Park, which is next to Kings Canyon National Park. These parks have a total area of 865,952 acres.

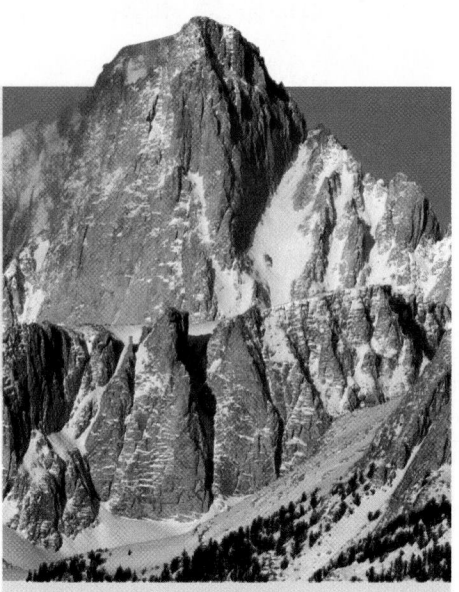

▲ Mount Whitney is part of the mountain range called the Sierra Nevada.

Look at this number in a place-value chart. The place to the left of the ten-thousands place is the hundred-thousands place.

HUNDRED THOUSANDS	TEN THOUSANDS	THOUSANDS	HUNDREDS	TENS	ONES
8	6	5,	9	5	2

You can write this number in different ways.
Standard form: 865,952
Expanded form: 800,000 + 60,000 + 5,000 + 900 + 50 + 2
Word form: eight hundred sixty-five thousand, nine hundred fifty-two

Remember
Put a comma between the thousands place and the hundreds place.
865,952
↑
comma

Guided Practice

1. Complete the expanded form for 17,598.   10,000 + ■ + 500 + 90 + ■

Write the value of the underlined digit.

2. 1<u>4</u>0,278   **3.** 5<u>2</u>,167   ✓**4.** <u>2</u>3,890   ✓**5.** <u>5</u>74,302

6. [TALK Math] Explain how to show the value of each digit in the number 623,714.

Independent Practice (and Problem Solving)

Write the value of the underlined digit.

7. 7<u>2</u>,180   **8.** <u>8</u>26,351   **9.** 2<u>6</u>5,817   **10.** 19,<u>3</u>42

Write each number in standard form.

11. 200,000 + 500 + 90 + 4   **12.** 60,000 + 8,000 + 700 + 40 + 3

13. nine hundred twelve thousand, two hundred six

USE DATA For 14–15, use the graph.

14. Write the height of Mount Rainier in expanded form.

15. Find the height of Mount Hood. What is the value of the digit in the hundreds place?

16. Reasoning Tammy baked 21 cookies. She ate 2 cookies and put the rest in bags with 3 cookies in each bag. How many cookies are not in a bag?

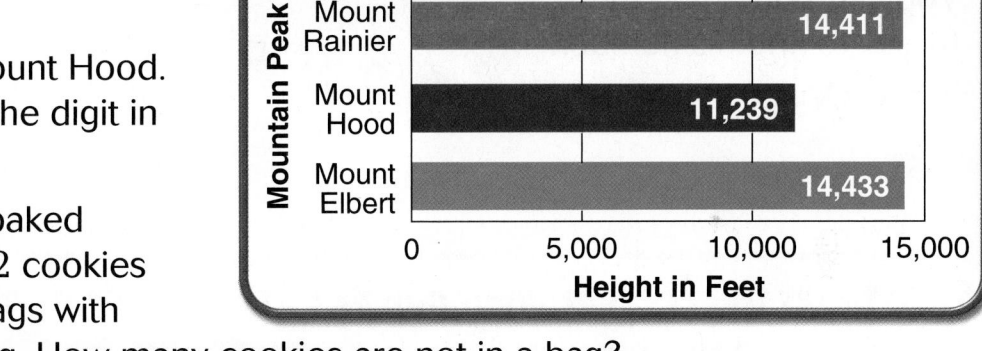

Mountain Heights

Mount Rainier — 14,411
Mount Hood — 11,239
Mount Elbert — 14,433

Mountain Peak / Height in Feet: 0, 5,000, 10,000, 15,000

17. [WRITE Math] Write a 6-digit number that has a zero in the thousands place. **Explain** how to write your number in expanded form.

Mixed Review and Test Prep

18. Derek walks home from school in 15 minutes. School gets out at 3:30. At what time does Derek get home? (Grade 2)

19. Beth's dog weighs 18 pounds more than her cat. Her cat weighs 9 pounds. How much does Beth's dog weigh? (Grade 2)

20. Test Prep How is 43,867 written in expanded form?

A 4,000 + 800 + 60 + 7

B 40,000 + 800 + 60 + 7

C 40,000 + 3,000 + 60 + 7

D 40,000 + 3,000 + 800 + 60 + 7

Extra Practice on page 20, Set D

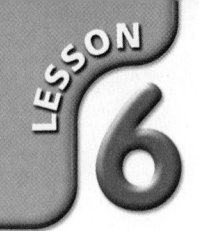

Problem Solving Workshop
Strategy: Use Logical Reasoning

OBJECTIVE: Solve problems by using the strategy *use logical reasoning*.

Learn the Strategy

Logical reasoning can help you solve problems. When you use logical reasoning, you compare facts and think about clues.

Sometimes the facts or clues can be organized in a list.

Vince plays soccer. The players on his team have the numbers 1 to 11 on their uniforms.

Vince's uniform has an odd number.

His number is greater than 6.

You can skip-count by threes to find his number.

What is Vince's number?

1 2 3 4 5 6 7 8 ⑨ 10 11

Sometimes the facts or clues can be put in a table or chart.

Sue, Rick, and Heather were in a race.

Sue finished first.

Rick did not finish second.

In what position did Heather finish?

	1st	2nd	3rd
Sue	yes	no	no
Rick	no	no	yes
Heather	no	yes	no

TALK Math

Explain why there is a *yes* for Heather in the second column.

Use the Strategy

PROBLEM Anna used a riddle for the invitations to her birthday party. Her friends had to use the clues at the right to find her address on Pine Street.

My address is a 2-digit number. The number is greater than 80. The sum of the digits is 15. The ones digit is 1 less than the tens digit.

What is my address?

Read to Understand

 **Reading Skill**
- Use a graphic aid to understand the clues.
- What information is given?

Plan

- **What strategy can you use to solve the problem?**
  You can use logical reasoning.

Solve

- **How can you use the strategy to solve the problem?**
  Look at one clue at a time. Use a hundred chart.

  The number has two digits, so cross out 1 through 9 and 100. The number is greater than 80, so cross out 80 and all the numbers less than 80.

1	2	3	4	5	6	7	8	9	10
11	12	13	14	15	16	17	18	19	20
21	22	23	24	25	26	27	28	29	30
31	32	33	34	35	36	37	38	39	40
41	42	43	44	45	46	47	48	49	50
51	52	53	54	55	56	57	58	59	60
61	62	63	64	65	66	67	68	69	70
71	72	73	74	75	76	77	78	79	80
81	82	83	84	85	86	87	88	89	90
91	92	93	94	95	96	97	98	99	100

  Add the digits of each number that is not crossed out. Circle the numbers with digits whose sum is 15.

| 81 | 82 | 83 | 84 | 85 | 86 | 87 | 88 | 89 | 90 |
| 91 | 92 | 93 | 94 | 95 | 96 | 97 | 98 | 99 | 100 |

  Find the circled number with a ones digit that is 1 less than its tens digit.

$$96 \rightarrow 9 - 6 = 3 \ X$$
$$87 \rightarrow 8 - 7 = 1 \ \checkmark$$

  So, Anna's address is 87 Pine Street.

Check

- **How do you know your answer is correct?**

1. Anna wants to mail an invitation to Steve. He gave her his address on Oak Road in the riddle below.

   • My address is a 2-digit number between 46 and 64.
   • The sum of the digits is 12.
   • The ones digit is 2 more than the tens digit.

   What is Steve's address?

   First, use a copy of a hundred chart and read the first clue. Cross out numbers less than 46 and greater than 64.

   Then, add the digits of each number not crossed out. Circle the numbers whose sum is 12.

   Finally, use the last clue to find Steve's address.

1	2	3	4	5	6	7	8	9	10
11	12	13	14	15	16	17	18	19	20
21	22	23	24	25	26	27	28	29	30
31	32	33	34	35	36	37	38	39	40
41	42	43	44	45	46	47	48	49	50
51	52	53	54	55	56	57	58	59	60
61	62	63	64	65	66	67	68	69	70
71	72	73	74	75	76	77	78	79	80
81	82	83	84	85	86	87	88	89	90
91	92	93	94	95	96	97	98	99	100

2. **What if** the sum of the digits is 10? What is Steve's address?

3. Julie is thinking of an even number between 12 and 29. The sum of the digits is the same as the digit in the tens place. What is Julie's number?

Problem Solving Strategy Practice

Use logical reasoning to solve.

4. Use the hundred chart and the clues. Cary is thinking of an odd number between 32 and 48. The sum of the digits is 5. What is Cary's number?

5. Copy the chart and use the clues. Andy, Beth, Mary, and Rod brought Anna gifts.

   Rod's gift had to be put together. Beth's gift was not the teddy bear or the soccer ball. Andy's gift was not the skates. Mary's gift was the soccer ball.

	Skates	Puzzle	Teddy Bear	Soccer Ball
Andy	?	no	?	?
Beth	?	no	?	?
Mary	?	no	?	?
Rod	no	yes	no	no

   What was Andy's gift?

Mixed Strategy Practice

USE DATA For 6–11, use the calendars.

6. Jami's birthday is on a Saturday in July. It is not July 7. It is not an even number. What date is Jami's birthday?

7. Carl's birthday invitations have a riddle theme. He wants his friends to find the date of his party. He gave them the following clues.

> My party is on a Friday in July.
>
> The date of my party is a two-digit
>
> even number.

What date is Carl's party?

8. Michelle's birthday is June 22. Kim's birthday is 9 days before Michelle's birthday. What date is Kim's birthday?

9. Jon's birthday is June 30. Rachel's birthday is 12 days after Jon's. What date is Rachel's birthday?

10. **Open-Ended** Shawn's birthday is June 16. Mark's birthday is two weeks later. Tell two ways you could find the date of Mark's birthday.

11. **Pose a Problem** Look back at Problem 9. Write a similar problem by changing the date of Rachel's birthday.

Choose a STRATEGY

Draw a Diagram or Picture

Make a Model or Act It Out

Make an Organized List

Find a Pattern

Make a Table or Graph

Predict and Test

Work Backward

Solve a Simpler Problem

Write a Number Sentence

Use Logical Reasoning

June

Sun	Mon	Tue	Wed	Thu	Fri	Sat
					1	2
3	4	5	6	7	8	9
10	11	12	13	14	15	16
17	18	19	20	21	22	23
24	25	26	27	28	29	30

July

Sun	Mon	Tue	Wed	Thu	Fri	Sat
1	2	3	4	5	6	7
8	9	10	11	12	13	14
15	16	17	18	19	20	21
22	23	24	25	26	27	28
29	30	31				

CHALLENGE YOURSELF

Thirteen children in Kim's class have a birthday in either June, July, or August.

12. Two more children have a birthday in July than in June. In July and August there are the same number of birthdays. How many children have a birthday in August?

13. Michael's birthday falls on a Thursday in August. The sum of the digits of his birthday is 5. **Explain** how you know when Michael's birthday is.

Extra Practice

Set A Find the number that point *X* represents on the number line. (pp. 6–7)

1.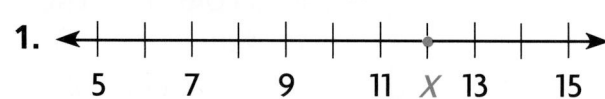

2.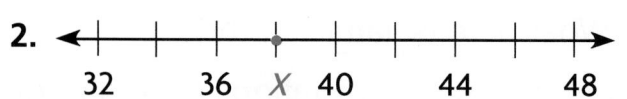

Set B Write the value of the underlined digit. (pp. 8–9)

1. 67<u>2</u>

2. 1<u>5</u>8

3. 8<u>9</u>0

4. <u>4</u>35

5. There are 253 students in Talia's school. How do you write the number in expanded form?

6. There are 922 seats in the theater. What is the value of the digit 9 in 922?

Set C Write each number in standard form. (pp. 10–13)

1. 4,000 + 800 + 10 + 3

2. 9,000 + 600 + 50 + 2

3. 7,000 + 20 + 2

4. Mr. Price drove 2,947 miles in one week. What is the value of the digit 2 in 2,947?

5. The library has 7,163 children's books. How do you write 7,163 in expanded form?

Write each number in expanded form.

6. 2,064

7. 5,839

8. 6,127

9. 3,905

Set D Write the value of the underlined digit. (pp. 14–15)

1. 1<u>3</u>,781

2. 8<u>4</u>0,526

3. <u>5</u>71,903

4. 7<u>1</u>4,200

Write each number in standard form.

5. eighty thousand, seven hundred ninety-six

6. two hundred fifteen thousand, thirty

7. 10,000 + 6,000 + 400 + 90 + 7

8. 400,000 + 5,000 + 800 + 2

iTools: Base-Ten Blocks

Use Base-Ten Blocks to Show Numbers.

Bob has 6 hundreds, 8 tens, and 16 ones.
What number does this show?

Step 1	Click on *Base-Ten Blocks*. Then click on the third tab at the bottom. Click on *Hide*.
Step 2	Click on the hundreds block at the left. Click 6 times in the hundreds column. Do the same thing with 8 tens and 16 ones. If you make a mistake, click on the eraser.
Step 3	Click on *Line Up* at the bottom. Then click on the *Regroup* arrow in the **ones** column. Ten **ones** blocks will group together and move to the tens column.
Step 4	Count the hundreds, tens, and ones blocks. Write the 3-digit number. Click on *Show* to check your answer.

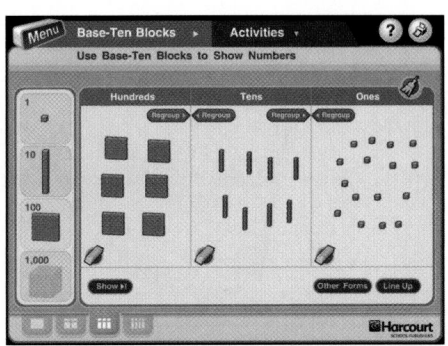

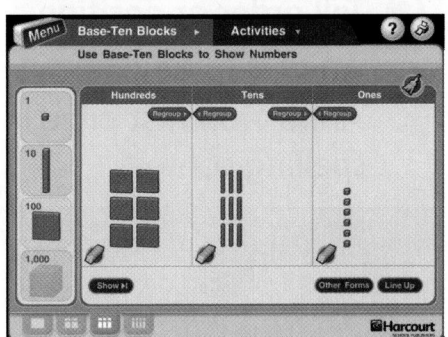

So, Bob's number is 696.
Click on the broom to clear the workspace.

Try It

Follow the steps above to make each 3-digit number.

1. 7 hundreds, 12 tens, 6 ones   **2.** 3 hundreds, 5 tens, 14 ones

Use Base-Ten Blocks to show each number.

3. 825   **4.** 917   **5.** 256   **6.** 379   **7.** 568

8. Explore More Karen has 4 hundreds, 9 tens, and 11 ones. Benson has 3 hundreds, 19 tens, and 12 ones. Use Base-Ten Blocks to show the numbers. Who has the greater number? **Explain.**

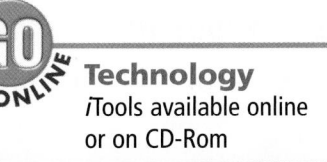

Technology
iTools available online
or on CD-Rom

Numbers are used in many ways.

Examples

A Count or tell how many.

Mark has 2 boxes of crayons.

There are 10 crayons in each box.

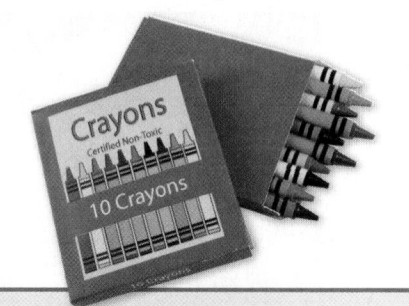

B Measure.

Sarah's book is 8 inches wide.

The book weighs 5 pounds.

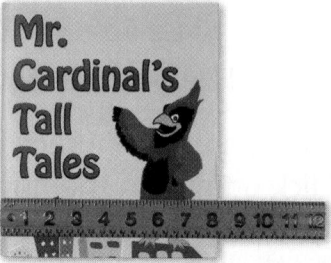

C Tell order or position.

Anita is third in line.

Anita won first prize in the spelling contest.

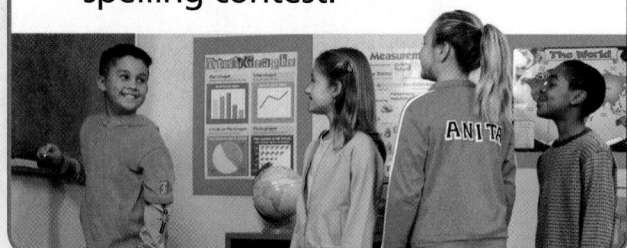

D Name or label.

Mr. Sanchez teaches in Room 27.

The school's address is 400 Main Street.

Tom's phone number is 555-2610.

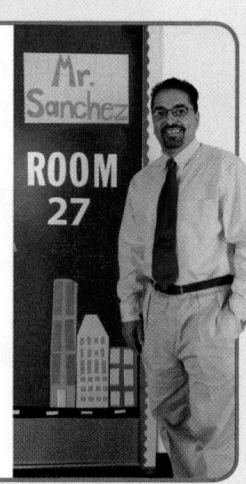

Try It

Tell how each number is used. Write *count, measure, position,* **or** *label.*

1.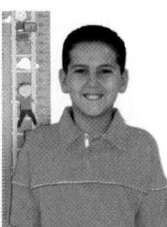

2.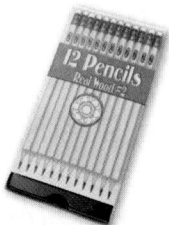

3.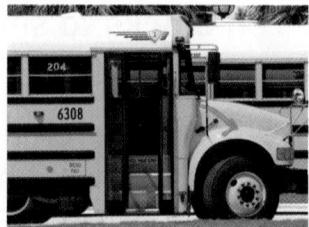

4. **WRITE Math** ▶ Write a list of things you did to get ready for school this morning. In your list, use numbers that tell order.

Chapter 1 Review/Test

Check Vocabulary and Concepts

Choose the best term from the box.

VOCABULARY
digits   even   odd
standard form
expanded form

1. Numbers ending with 2, 4, 6, 8, or 0 are <u>?</u> numbers.
   (p. 5)

2. There are six <u>?</u> in the number 457,390. (p. 14)

3. <u>?</u> is a way to write numbers by showing the value of each digit. (p. 8)

4. The <u>?</u> of three hundred seventeen is 317. (p. 8)

Check Skills

Use a hundred chart. Find the next number in the pattern. (pp. 4–5)

5. 3, 6, 9, 12, ■

6. 65, 70, 75, 80, ■

Find the number that point X represents on each number line. (pp. 6–7)

7.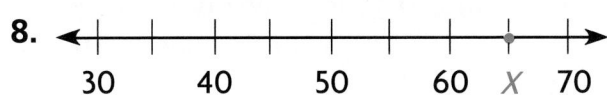

| 11 | | 13 | X | 15 | | 17 | | 19 |

8.

| 30 | | 40 | | 50 | | 60 | X | 70 |

Write the value of the underlined digit. (pp. 10–13, 14–15)

9. 4<u>7</u>6,521

10. 1,<u>9</u>64

11. <u>8</u>30,795

12. 63,4<u>2</u>8

Write each number in standard form. (pp. 8–9, 10–13, 14–15)

13. five hundred thirty-two

14. seven thousand, three hundred five

15. 5,000 + 100 + 40 + 8

16. 60,000 + 2,000 + 10 + 7

17. eighty-four thousand, sixteen

18. 200,000 + 3,000 + 900 + 20 + 6

Check Problem Solving

For 19, use the table. Solve. (pp. 16–19)

19. Jack's score is a 4-digit number. The hundreds digit is an even number. The tens digit is odd. What is his score?

20. **⊫WRITE Math** ▸ Beth, Sasha, Jake, and Tyrone ran in a race. Tyrone finished first. Sasha did not finish second. Beth finished last. **Explain** how you can tell in which place Jake finished.

Game Scores	
Players	**Scores**
Player A	4,602
Player B	897
Player C	3,415

Standardized Test Prep
Chapter 1

Number and Operations

1. Lily put 43 marbles in a jar. Joe put 28 marbles in the jar. How many marbles did Lily and Joe put in the jar all together? (Grade 2)

   A 15

   B 25

   C 61

   D 71

Test Tip **Choose the answer.**

See item 2. If your answer doesn't match one of the choices, check your computation.

2. $53 - 26 = \blacksquare$ (Grade 2)

   A 23   **C** 33

   B 27   **D** 77

3. Which fraction of this shape is shaded? (Grade 2)

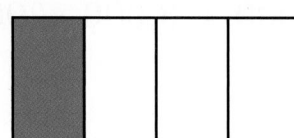

   A $\frac{1}{4}$ **C** $\frac{1}{2}$

   B $\frac{1}{3}$ **D** $\frac{3}{4}$

4. **WRITE Math** ▶ **Explain** how you can find the value of the digit 6 in the number 16,782. (p. 14)

Algebraic Reasoning

5. Which addition fact helps you find the difference? (Grade 2)

$$17 - 9 = \blacksquare$$

   A $10 + 10 = 20$

   B $8 + 9 = 17$

   C $4 + 4 = 8$

   D $1 + 7 = 8$

6. What is the next number in the pattern? (p. 4)

$$20, 24, 28, 32, \blacksquare$$

   A 30   **C** 36

   B 34   **D** 37

7. What number makes this number sentence true? (Grade 2)

$$9 + \blacksquare = 14$$

   A 7   **C** 5

   B 6   **D** 4

8. **WRITE Math** ▶ Find the difference.

$$70¢ - 24¢$$

Explain how you can check your answer by using addition. (Grade 2)

Measurement

9. What is the area of the figure? (Grade 2)

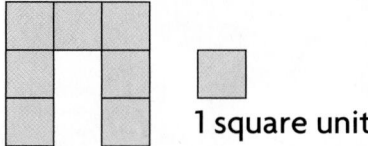

1 square unit

- **A** 6 square units
- **B** 7 square units
- **C** 8 square units
- **D** 9 square units

10. Use the inch ruler. About how long is the nail? (Grade 2)

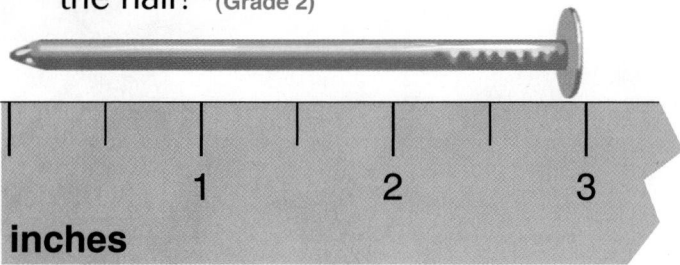

- **A** 1 inch
- **B** 2 inches
- **C** 3 inches
- **D** 4 inches

11. **WRITE Math** Does this bag of apples weigh about 5 ounces or about 5 pounds? **Explain** how you know.

(Grade 2)

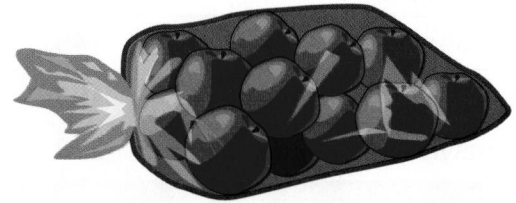

Data Analysis and Probability

12. How many more boxes of cookies were sold in Week 2 than Week 3?

(Grade 2)

Cookie Sales	
Week	**Number of Boxes Sold**
1	15
2	25
3	20
4	10

- **A** 5
- **C** 15
- **B** 10
- **D** 20

13. How many students in all voted for their favorite fruit? (Grade 2)

Favorite Fruit	
Place	**Votes**
Banana	ⵑⵑ ⵑⵑ I
Grapes	ⵑⵑ ⵑⵑ ⵑⵑ
Apple	ⵑⵑ ⵑⵑ III

- **A** 21
- **C** 28
- **B** 26
- **D** 39

14. **WRITE Math** From which bag is it more likely to pull a red tile than a blue tile? **Explain.** (Grade 2)

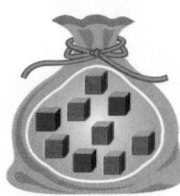
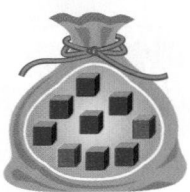

Bag A   **Bag B**

Compare, Order, and Round Numbers

The Ohio State Capitol building, in Columbus, Ohio, is 158 feet tall and is about 150 years old. The floor in one of its rooms is covered with about 5,000 pieces of marble.

Investigate

How does the height of each capitol building compare to the height of the Ohio State Capitol? Round the height of each building to the nearest hundred, and then compare. Explain why you may not want to compare rounded heights.

Heights of State Capitol Buildings

State	Height in Feet
Michigan	267
Mississippi	180
New Jersey	145
New York	108
Pennsylvania	272

GO ONLINE

Technology
Student pages are available in the Student eBook.

Check your understanding of important skills
needed for success in Chapter 2.

▶ **Order on a Number Line to 100**

Write the numbers in order from least to greatest.

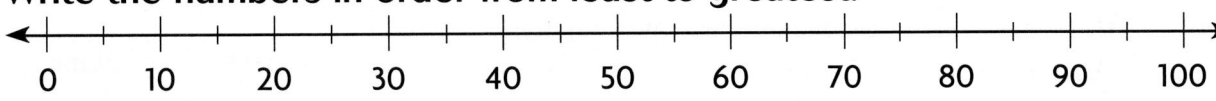

0   10   20   30   40   50   60   70   80   90   100

1. 27, 34, 22   **2.** 41, 38, 50

3. 80, 90, 60   **4.** 83, 86, 72

5. 20, 14, 19   **6.** 61, 52, 68

▶ **Compare 2-Digit Numbers Using Place Value**

Write <, >, or = for each ●.

7. 15 ● 23   **8.** 77 ● 58   **9.** 31 ● 34

10. 82 ● 82   **11.** 91 ● 19   **12.** 46 ● 61

13. 27 ● 28   **14.** 45 ● 40   **15.** 53 ● 63

VOCABULARY POWER

CHAPTER VOCABULARY

compare
equal to =
greater than >
less than <
order
round

WARM-UP WORDS

greater than > A symbol used to compare two
numbers, with the greater number given first

less than < A symbol used to compare two
numbers, with the lesser number given first

round To replace a number with another
number that tells about how many or how much

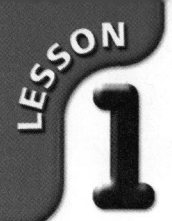

LESSON

1 Compare Numbers

OBJECTIVE: Use models, place value, and number lines to compare 3-, 4-, and 5-digit numbers.

Quick Review

Write the greater number.

1. 9 or 12   **2.** 8 or 3

3. 22 or 25   **4.** 29 or 39

5. 68 or 91

Vocabulary

compare   equal to =

less than <   greater than >

Learn

PROBLEM The State Capitol Building in Springfield, Illinois, is 361 feet tall. The United States Capitol Building in Washington, D.C., is 288 feet tall. Which building is taller?

You can **compare** numbers in different ways to find which number is greater.

    greater than >   **less than <**   **equal to =**

ONE WAY   **Use base-ten blocks.**

Compare from left to right.

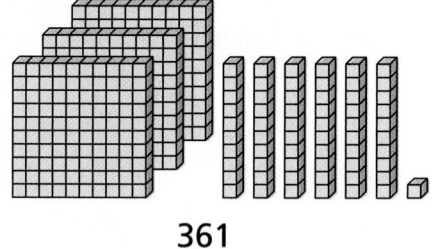

361   288

3 hundreds is greater than 2 hundreds. 361 > 288

So, the Illinois State Capitol Building is taller.

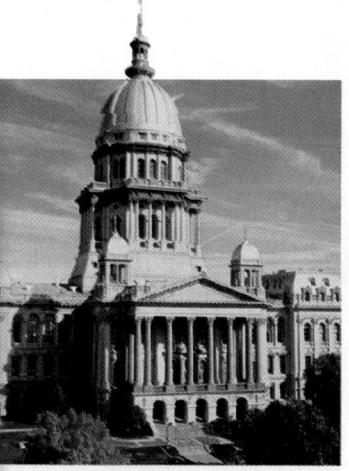

▲ **The Illinois State Capitol Building**

OTHER WAYS

Ⓐ Use a number line.

The numbers are in order from least to greatest.

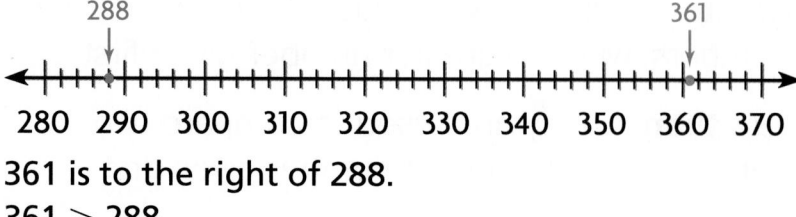

      288   361

280   290   300   310   320   330   340   350   360   370

361 is to the right of 288.
361 > 288

Ⓑ Use a place-value chart.
Compare digits in the same place-value position from left to right.

HUNDREDS	TENS	ONES
3	6	1
2	8	8

↑

3 hundreds is greater than 2 hundreds. 361 > 288.

28

Compare 4- and 5-Digit Numbers

Example

Compare 1,324 and 1,249.

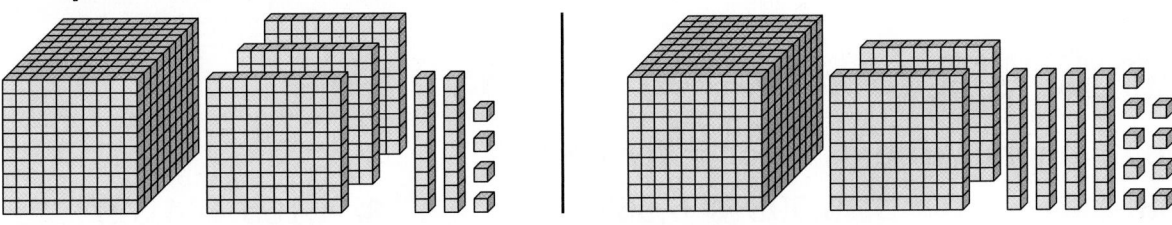

The thousands are the same, so compare the hundreds.
3 hundreds is greater than 2 hundreds. So, 1,324 > 1,249.

More Examples

A Compare 3,158 and 3,372.

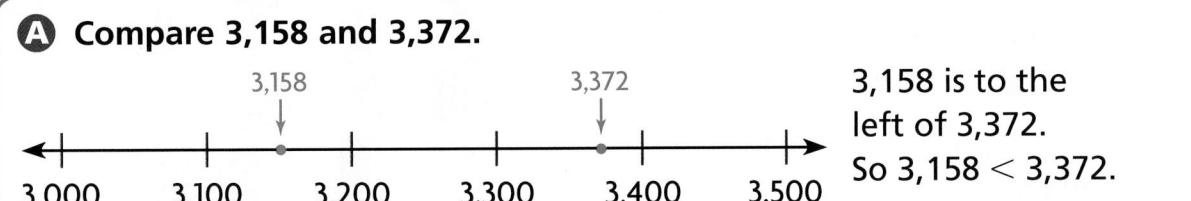

3,158 is to the left of 3,372. So 3,158 < 3,372.

B Compare 27,468 and 27,513.

TEN THOUSANDS	THOUSANDS	HUNDREDS	TENS	ONES
2	7,	4	6	8
2	7,	5	1	3

↑ Ten thousands are the same.   ↑ Thousands are the same.   ↑ 5 > 4

So, 27,468 < 27,513.

- In Example B, what if you were comparing 27,468 and 9,563? Explain why you do not need to compare the thousands, the hundreds, the tens, and the ones.

Guided Practice

1. Which number has more hundreds? Which number is greater?

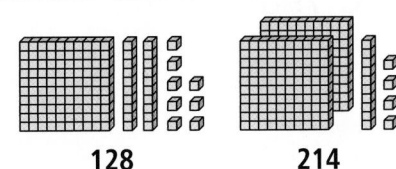

128   214

Compare the numbers. Write <, >, or = for each ⬤.

2. 567 ⬤ 567   ✓**3.** 5,228 ⬤ 5,628   ✓**4.** 1,004 ⬤ 789

5. [TALK Math] **Explain** two ways to compare 368 and 386.

Independent Practice and Problem Solving

Compare the numbers. Write <, >, or = for each ⬤.

6. 485 ⬤ 98

7. 6,598 ⬤ 6,587

8. 4,165 ⬤ 4,327

9. 2,000 ⬤ 487

10. 521 ⬤ 521

11. 75,362 ⬤ 73,659

12. 3,446 ⬤ 3,446

13. 38,047 ⬤ 39,102

14. 8,389 ⬤ 8,398

USE DATA For 15–17, use the table.

15. Compare the heights of the tallest buildings in Texas and California.

16. Compare the heights of the Key Tower and One Liberty Place.

17. [WRITE Math] ▸ **What's the Error?** Dana compared 947 and 1,002. She says 947 is greater than 1,002 because 9 is greater than 1. What was Dana's error?

18. ≡**FAST FACT** • The tallest building in Indiana, the Chase Tower, is 830 feet tall. The tallest building in New Jersey, the Goldman Sachs Tower, is 781 feet tall. Compare the heights.

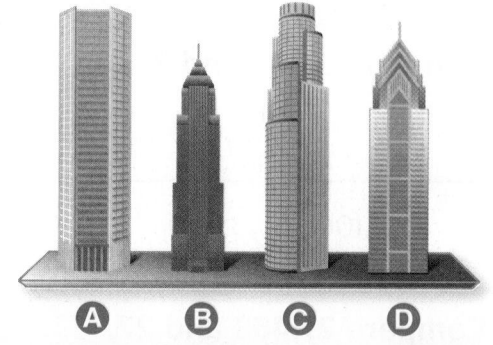

Tallest Buildings in 4 States		
State	**Building**	**Height in Feet**
Texas	Ⓐ JPMorgan Chase Tower	1,002
Ohio	Ⓑ Key Tower	947
California	Ⓒ U.S. Bank Tower	1,018
Pennsylvania	Ⓓ One Liberty Place	945

Mixed Review and Test Prep

19. Sarah said that it is 278 days until her birthday. What is 278 written in expanded form? (p. 8)

20. **Test Prep** Which number is greater than 822?

   A 637   **B** 743   **C** 798   **D** 826

21. Karen read a book that had 1,028 pages. Is 1,028 an even number or an odd number? What is the value of the 2 in 1,028? (pp. 5, 11)

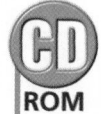

Technology
Use Harcourt Mega Math, Country Countdown, *Harrison's Comparisons,* Levels L and M; Fraction Action, *Number Line Mine,* Level B.

(Extra Practice)on page 40, Set A

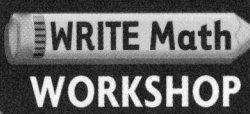

Write to Explain

Justin is using data from the table to compare the heights of the Chrysler Building and the John Hancock Center. He wants to find out which building is taller.

This is how Justin explained how he compared the heights of the buildings.

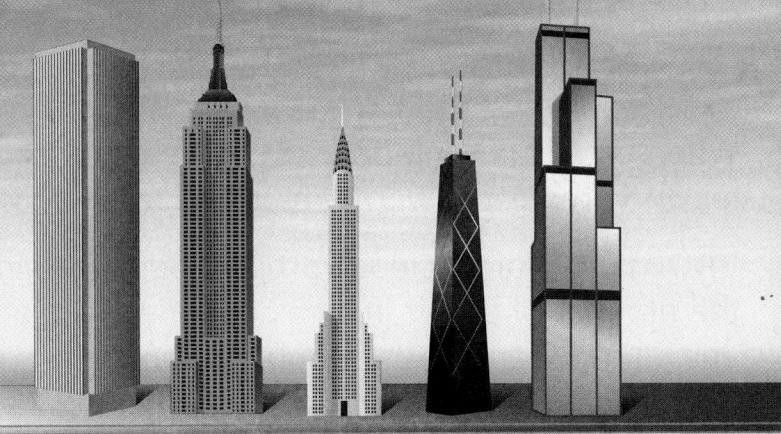

Aon Center   Empire State Building   Chrysler Building   John Hancock   Sears Tower

First, I looked at the table to find the heights of the Chrysler Building and John Hancock Center.

Next, I recorded the heights of the buildings.

Chrysler Building   1,046 feet
John Hancock Center   1,127 feet

Tall Buildings in the United States		
Building	**City**	**Height in feet**
Aon Center	Chicago	1,136
Chrysler Building	New York	1,046
Empire State Building	New York	1,250
John Hancock Center	Chicago	1,127
Sears Tower	Chicago	1,450

Then, I compared the heights. Since both numbers have a 1 in the thousands place, I compared the hundreds digits. The John Hancock Center has a 1 and the Chrysler Building has a 0 in the hundreds place. Since 1 > 0, I know that the John Hancock Center is taller than the Chrysler Building.

Tips

To write an explanation:
- Write the steps you took to solve the problem.
- Use words such as *first*, *next*, and *then*.
- State your answer in the last sentence of your explanation.

Problem Solving Use the data in the table. Explain how to solve each problem.

1. Is the Aon Center or the John Hancock Center taller?

2. Is the Sears Tower or the Empire State Building taller?

Order Numbers

LESSON 2

OBJECTIVE: Use a number line and place value to order 3-, 4-, and 5-digit numbers.

Learn

When you **order** numbers, you write them from least to greatest or from greatest to least.

PROBLEM For a science project, Ben listed in a table the number of bones in a cat, a human, and a dog. Which animal has the greatest number of bones?

ONE WAY Use a number line.

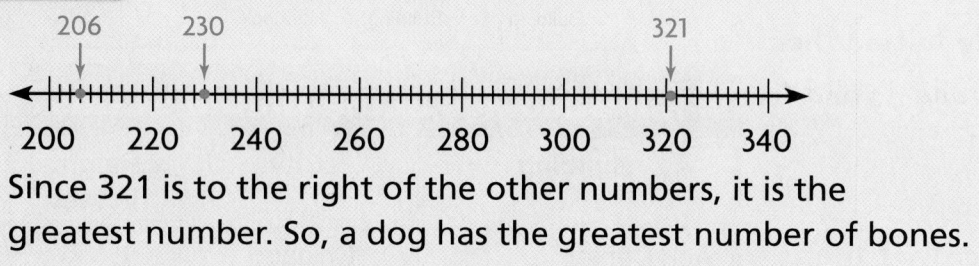

206   230   321

200   220   240   260   280   300   320   340

Since 321 is to the right of the other numbers, it is the greatest number. So, a dog has the greatest number of bones.

Bones

Animal	Number
Cat	230
Human	206
Dog	321

ANOTHER WAY Use place value.

Example 1 Order 2,387; 2,475; and 2,190 from least to greatest.

Step 1	Step 2
2,387 2,475 2,190 Compare the thousands. $2 = 2 = 2$	2,387 2,475 2,190 Compare the hundreds. $1 < 3 < 4$

So, the order is 2,190; 2,387; 2,475.

Example 2 Order 54,926; 56,718; and 55,302 from greatest to least.

Step 1	Step 2
54,926 56,718 55,302 Compare the ten thousands. $5 = 5 = 5$	54,926 56,718 55,302 Compare the thousands. $6 > 5 > 4$

So, the order is 56,718; 55,302; 54,926.

ERROR ALERT

Compare the digits with the greatest place value first.

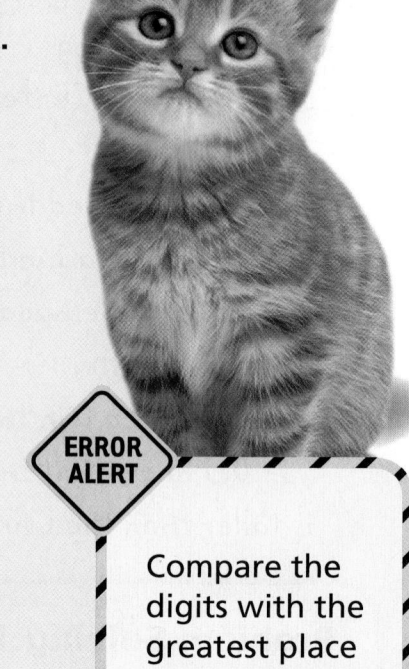

Guided Practice

1. Use the number line to order 851, 912, and 796 from least to greatest.

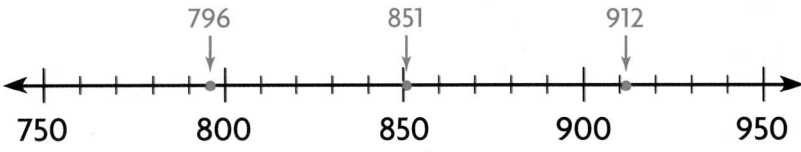

750　　800　　850　　900　　950

Write the numbers in order from greatest to least.

2. 540, 527, 536

✓ 3. 2,079; 2,178; 2,122

✓ 4. 20,794; 21,786; 21,157

5. **TALK Math** **Explain** how you know that 458, 572, and 613 are in order from least to greatest.

Independent Practice and Problem Solving

Write the numbers in order from greatest to least.

6. 310, 440, 390

7. 914, 896, 910

8. 993; 1,399; 949

9. 5,091; 5,136; 5,109

10. 3,403; 3,430; 3,034

11. 79,880; 79,188; 78,899

Write the numbers in order from least to greatest.

12. 645, 456, 654

13. 372, 452, 289

14. 898; 3,786; 3,981

15. 4,570; 4,550; 4,660

16. 9,223; 9,280; 9,275

17. 63,215; 63,149; 62,768

For 18–19, use the pictures.

18. Order the weights of the tiger, lion, and giant panda from greatest to least.

19. **WRITE Math** ▶ **What's the Error?** Alex ordered the three animal weights from least to greatest. He wrote 220, 330, 250. What is Alex's error? Write the weights in the correct order.

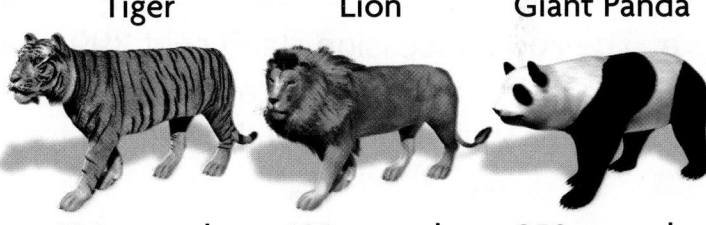

Tiger　　　Lion　　　Giant Panda

220 pounds　　330 pounds　　250 pounds

Mixed Review and Test Prep

20. Sixty thousand, seventy-eight people attended a football game. Write this number in standard form. (p. 14)

21. Casey, Ben, and Ted ran a race. Casey did not finish last. Ted finished before Casey. Who finished first? (p. 16)

22. **Test Prep** Which number is less than 408 but greater than 390?

　A 400　　　　**C** 410

　B 408　　　　**D** 480

Extra Practice on page 40, Set B

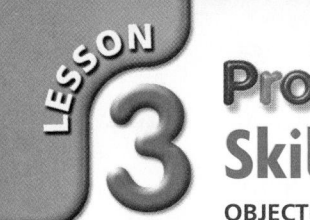

Problem Solving Workshop
Skill: Use a Model

OBJECTIVE: Solve problems by using the skill *use a model.*

Use the Skill

PROBLEM A zoo has a rhinoceros that weighs 2,812 pounds, a camel that weighs 1,520 pounds, a giraffe that weighs 2,233 pounds, and a polar bear that weighs 1,450 pounds. Which animal has the second-greatest weight?

The animal weights are shown on the number line.

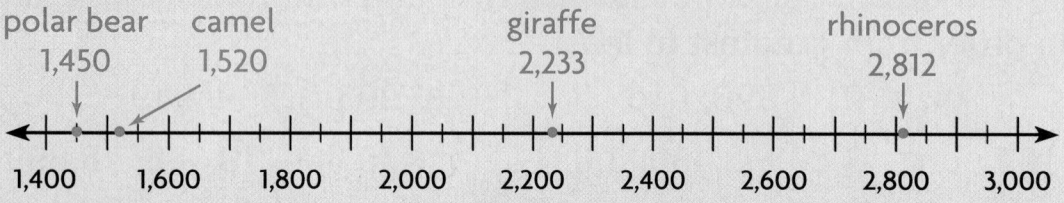

The animal with the greatest weight is on the right.

The rhinoceros has the greatest weight.
So, the giraffe has the second-greatest weight.

Think and Discuss

Use the number line to solve the problem.

a. The zoo concession stand sold 399 sodas, 438 bags of popcorn, 384 candy apples, and 420 ice-cream cones. Which item had the second-least sales?

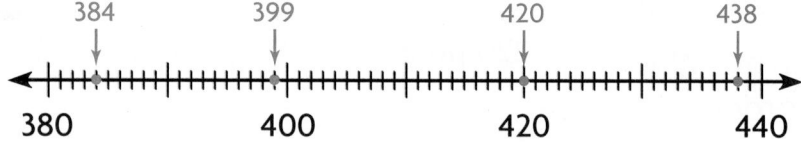

b. The petting zoo had 1,038 visitors in May, 1,240 in June, 1,287 in July, and 952 in August. List the number of petting zoo visitors in order from greatest to least.

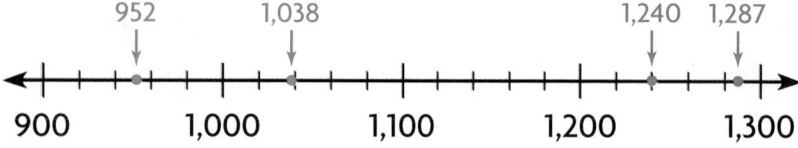

Use the number line to solve the problem.

1. The zoo had 2,918 visitors in May, 3,976 in June, 3,298 in July, and 2,287 in August. Which month had the least number of visitors?

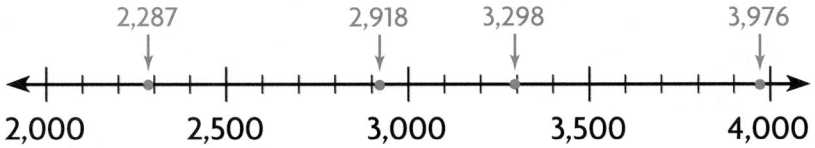

Use the number line.

Think: Where would the least number be on the number line?

2. **What if** there were 2,283 visitors in September? Which month would have had the least number of visitors?

3. The bird show had 2,498 visitors in June, 2,675 visitors in July, and 2,189 visitors in August. Write the number of visitors at the bird show in order from greatest to least.

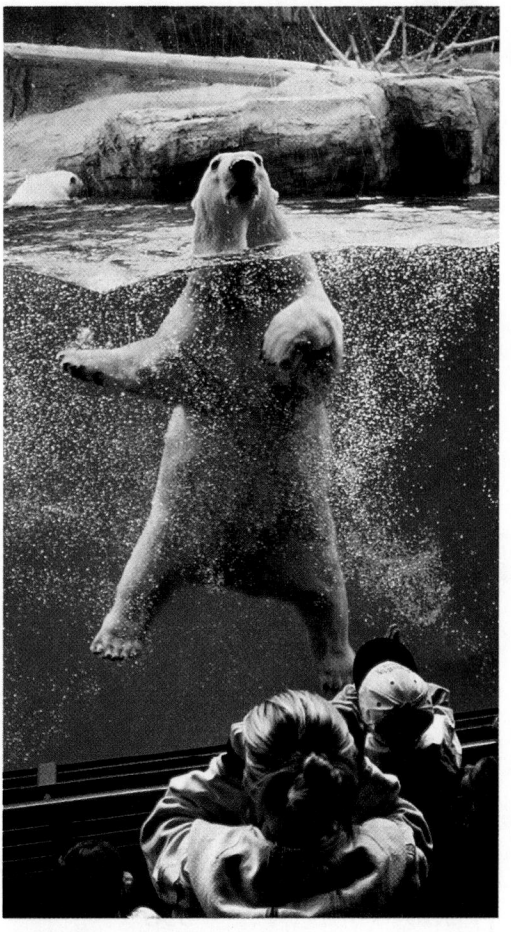

Mixed Applications

USE DATA For 4–5, use the table.

4. Write the names of the animals in order from least to greatest number of minutes of sleep each day.

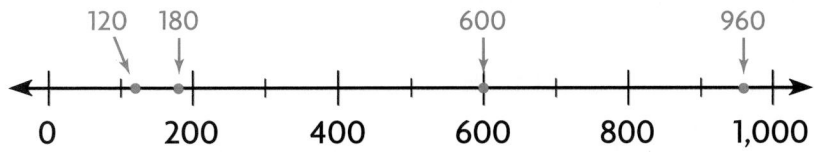

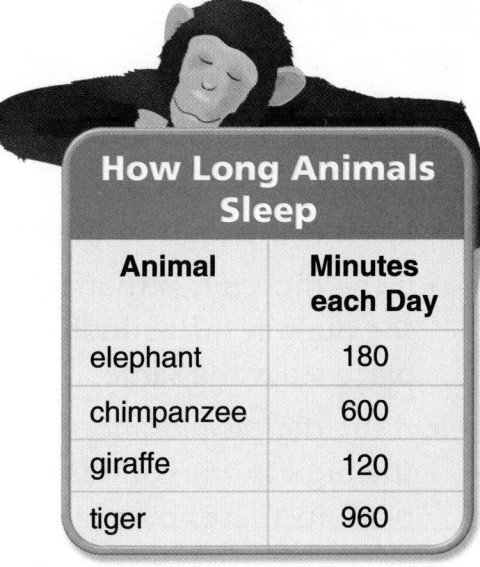

How Long Animals Sleep	
Animal	**Minutes each Day**
elephant	180
chimpanzee	600
giraffe	120
tiger	960

5. How many more minutes each day does a tiger sleep than a chimpanzee?

6. Kelly bought 2 pencils for 25¢ each and an eraser for 50¢ in the zoo gift shop. How much did Kelly spend in all?

7. Hector's family lives 46 miles from the zoo. They have driven 28 miles. How many more miles do they have to drive to reach the zoo?

Round to the Nearest Ten and Hundred

OBJECTIVE: Use the number line and rounding rules to round numbers to the nearest ten and nearest hundred.

Learn

When you **round** a number, you find a number that tells you *about* how much or *about* how many.

PROBLEM Carlos has collected 317 baseball cards. To the nearest ten and to the nearest hundred, about how many baseball cards does Carlos have?

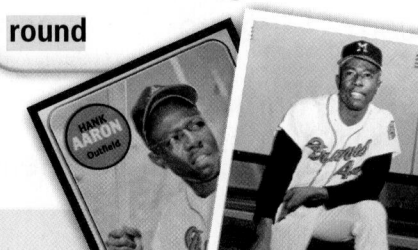

ONE WAY Use a number line.

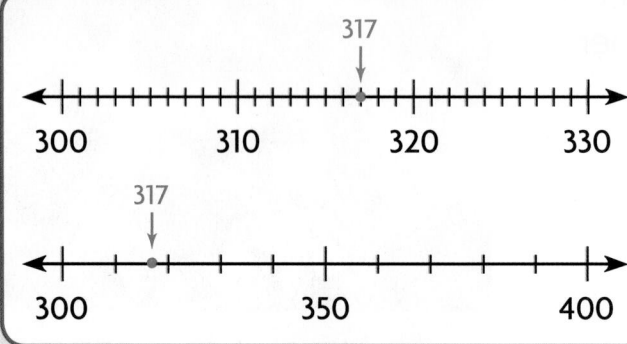

317 is closer to 320 than to 310.
So, to the nearest ten, 317 rounds to 320.

317 is closer to 300 than to 400.
So, to the nearest hundred, 317 rounds to 300.

ANOTHER WAY

Use rounding rules.

- Find the place to which you want to round.
- Look at the digit to the right.
- If the digit is less than 5, the digit in the rounding place stays the same.
- If the digit is 5 or more, the digit in the rounding place increases by one.
- Write a zero for the digit to the right.

Examples

Round 672 to the nearest ten.

672
↑

Look at the ones digit.

Since the ones digit is less than 5, the tens digit stays the same. Write a zero for the digit to the right.

So, 672 rounds to 670.

Round 672 to the nearest hundred.

672
↑

Look at the tens digit.

Since the tens digit is greater than 5, the hundreds digit increases by 1. Write a zero for each digit to the right.

So, 672 rounds to 700.

1. Use the number line. Is 458 closer to 450 or to 460?

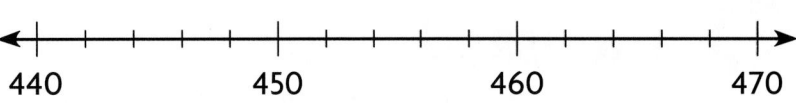

440   450   460   470

Round the number to the nearest ten and to the nearest hundred.

2. 128   3. 361   4. 835   5. 657   ✔6. 232   ✔7. 944

8. **TALK Math** Explain how you would round 726 to the nearest ten and to the nearest hundred.

Independent Practice and Problem Solving

Round the number to the nearest ten and to the nearest hundred.

9. 152   10. 576   11. 298   12. 663   13. 791   14. 499

15. 283   16. 364   17. 519   18. 455   19. 844   20. 172

USE DATA For 21–22 and 26, use the table.

21. What is the number of dog stickers rounded to the nearest ten?

22. Round the number of horse stickers to the nearest ten and to the nearest hundred.

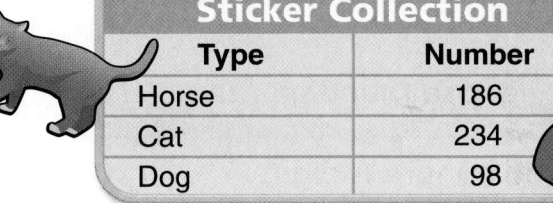

Hannah's Animal Sticker Collection	
Type	**Number**
Horse	186
Cat	234
Dog	98

23. **WRITE Math** Explain how rounding 296 to the nearest ten and to the nearest hundred are alike.

24. **Reasoning** A 3-digit number has the digits 3, 7, and 9. To the nearest hundred, it rounds to 1,000. What is the number?

Mixed Review and Test Prep

25. Order the numbers 6,598; 6,782; and 6,516 from least to greatest.
(p. 32)

26. Compare the number of horse stickers and cat stickers in Hannah's collection. (p. 28)

27. **Test Prep** The number of seashells in Stella's collection, rounded to the nearest ten, is 520. How many seashells could Stella have?

A 552   C 527

B 531   D 522

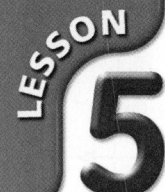

LESSON 5

Round to the Nearest Thousand

OBJECTIVE: Use the number line and rounding rules to round numbers to the nearest thousand.

Quick Review

Round to the nearest hundred.

1. 514
2. 459
3. 4,387
4. 7,428
5. 3,982

Learn

PROBLEM There were 2,773 people in the world's largest pillow fight in 2004. To the nearest thousand, about how many people were in the pillow fight?

Round 2,773 to the nearest thousand.

ONE WAY Use a number line.

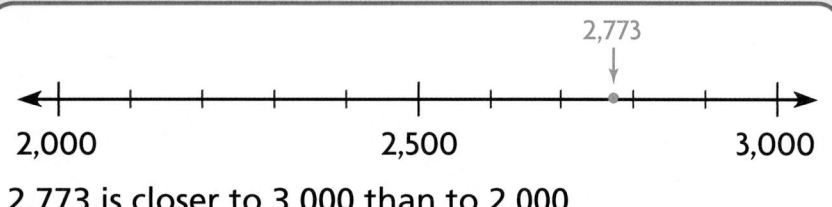

2,773 is closer to 3,000 than to 2,000.
2,773 rounds to 3,000.

So, there were about 3,000 people in the pillow fight.

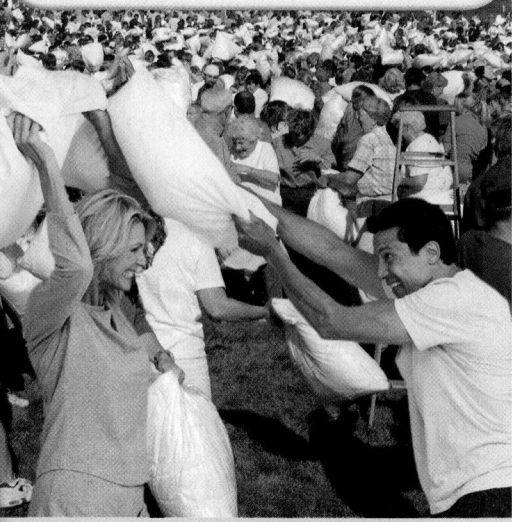

▲ World's largest pillow fight in 2004 in Dodgeville, Wisconsin

ANOTHER WAY Use rounding rules.

Look at the hundreds digit.

2,773
↑

Since 7 > 5, the thousands digit increases by 1. Write a zero for each digit to the right.

So, 2,773 rounds to 3,000.

Math Idea
Always look at the digit to the right of the rounding digit.

Examples

A Round 6,429 to the nearest thousand.

Look at the hundreds digit.

6,429
↑

Since 4 < 5, the thousands digit stays the same.

So, 6,429 rounds to 6,000.

B Round 4,591 to the nearest ten, hundred, and thousand.

Look at the ones digit. 1 < 5, so 4,591 rounds to 4,590.

Look at the tens digit. 9 > 5, so 4,591 rounds to 4,600.

Look at the hundreds digit. 5 = 5, so 4,591 rounds to 5,000.

Guided Practice

1. Between which two thousands is 8,714? To which thousand is it closer?

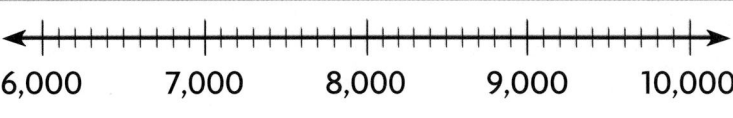

6,000 7,000 8,000 9,000 10,000

Round to the nearest thousand.

2. 1,403   3. 5,148   4. 8,747   ☑5. 2,501   ☑6. 3,274

7. [TALK Math] **Explain** how to round 4,681 to the nearest thousand.

Independent Practice and Problem Solving

Round to the nearest thousand.

8. 5,484   9. 8,273   10. 4,593   11. 1,935   12. 2,222

Round to the nearest thousand, to the nearest hundred, and to the nearest ten.

13. 1,376   14. 2,632   15. 6,648   16. 7,051   17. 8,475

USE DATA For 18–19, use the table.

18. To the nearest thousand, about how many people played musical chairs?

19. To the nearest thousand, about how many people had a snowball fight?

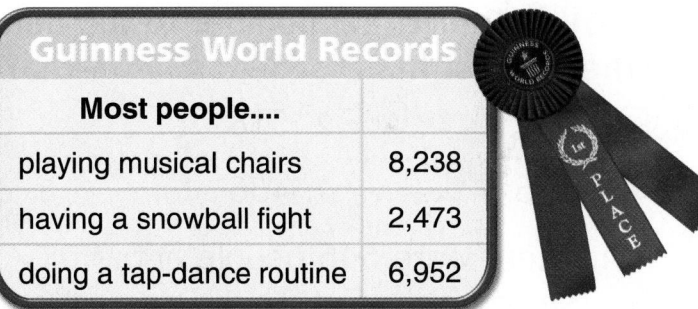

Guinness World Records	
Most people....	
playing musical chairs	8,238
having a snowball fight	2,473
doing a tap-dance routine	6,952

20. [WRITE Math] ▸ **What's the Question?** A total of 1,927 people performed sign language at the same time to the same song. The answer is 2,000.

21. **Reasoning** When rounding to the nearest thousand, what is the greatest number that rounds to 6,000? What is the least number?

Mixed Review and Test Prep

22. What is six thousand, two hundred eight written in standard form? (p. 10)

23. What tool would Kevin use to measure how much juice his glass holds? (Grade 2)

24. **Test Prep** What is 6,871 rounded to the nearest thousand?

   A 6,000   C 6,900

   B 6,870   D 7,000

Extra Practice on page 40, Set D

Extra Practice

Set A Compare the numbers. Write <, >, or = for each ⬤. (pp. 28–31) ————

1. 867 ⬤ 904   **2.** 3,281 ⬤ 3,281   **3.** 43,208 ⬤ 39,756

4. 1,882 ⬤ 1,828   **5.** 71,023 ⬤ 70,968   **6.** 5,618 ⬤ 6,158

7. 65,358 ⬤ 59,970   **8.** 8,945 ⬤ 9,217   **9.** 14,306 ⬤ 41,306

Set B Write the numbers in order from least to greatest. (pp. 32–33) ————

1. 526; 589; 564   **2.** 1,728; 1,717; 1,731   **3.** 8,015; 9,317; 6,273

4. 3,956; 1,516; 3,870   **5.** 27,990; 38,185; 19,654   **6.** 8,102; 5,973; 7,318

7. A farm produced 1,099 pounds of cherries in June. It produced 998 pounds of cherries in July, and another 901 pounds in August. During which month did the farm produce the most cherries?

8. Ryan saved 359 pennies. His brother Allen saved 368 pennies, and his sister Marla saved 360 pennies. Order the numbers from least to greatest.

Set C Round the number to the nearest ten and to the nearest hundred. (pp. 36–37) ————

1. 657   **2.** 518   **3.** 642   **4.** 109   **5.** 756

6. 235   **7.** 456   **8.** 313   **9.** 711   **10.** 544

11. There were 546 people at the summer concert. To the nearest hundred, about how many people attended the concert?

12. Sarah rounded 495 to the nearest hundred. Lee rounded it to another place and got the same answer. To what place did Lee round 495?

Set D Round to the nearest thousand. (pp. 38–39) ————

1. 3,333   **2.** 2,590   **3.** 4,938   **4.** 1,296   **5.** 7,557

6. 8,432   **7.** 5,356   **8.** 4,209   **9.** 6,750   **10.** 9,917

11. 1,848   **12.** 6,172   **13.** 2,691   **14.** 7,415   **15.** 8,763

CD ROM Technology — Use Harcourt Mega Math, Fraction Action, *Number Line Mine*, Levels B, C.

Building Numbers

Prepare!

3 players

Plan!
- Number cube numbered 1–6
- 1 gameboard for each player

A

THOUSANDS   HUNDREDS   TENS   ONES

B

THOUSANDS   HUNDREDS   TENS   ONES

C

THOUSANDS   HUNDREDS   TENS   ONES

Build!

- Players take turns rolling the number cube.

- Player 1 writes the rolled number in the ones, tens, hundreds, or thousands place in one of the place-value charts.

- Once a number is placed in a chart, it cannot be moved to another place-value position.

- Play continues until each player has built a 4-digit number.

- Players compare their 4-digit numbers. The player with the greater number earns 1 point.

- The game continues until each player has built a 4-digit number in each place-value chart.

- The player with more points wins.

MATH POWER — Benchmark Numbers

Numbers that help you estimate a number of objects without counting them are called **benchmark numbers**. Any useful number, such as 10, 25, 50, or 100, can be a benchmark.

About how many jellybeans are in Jar B?

You can use the 25 jellybeans in Jar A as a benchmark.

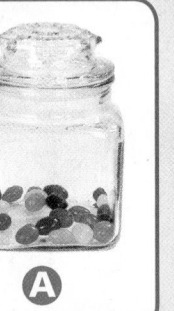

A

There are about ■ jellybeans in Jar B.

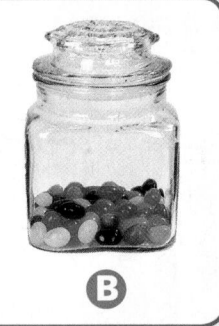

B

There are about twice as many jellybeans in Jar B.
So, there are about 50 jellybeans in Jar B.

Try It

**Estimate the number of jellybeans in each jar.
Use Jars C and D as benchmarks.**

Jar C has 10 jellybeans.

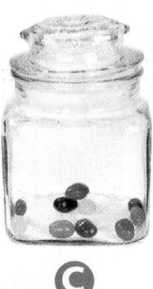

C

Jar D has about 100 jellybeans.

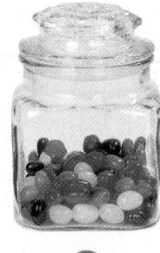

D

1.

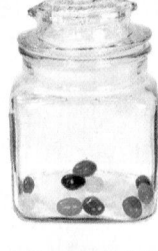

10 or 50?

2.

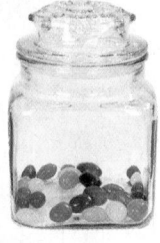

25 or 50?

3.

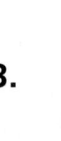

100 or 200?

4. **WRITE Math** ▶ **Explain** how you might use a benchmark of 25 jellybeans to fill a jar that will hold about 100 jellybeans.

Chapter 2 Review/Test

Check Vocabulary and Concepts

Choose the best term from the box.

1. One way to __?__ numbers is to use <, >, or =. (p. 28)

2. You __?__ a number to find *about* how much or how many. (p. 36)

3. The symbol < means __?__. (p. 28)

Check Skills

Compare the numbers. Write <, >, or = for each ●. (pp. 28–31)

4. 5,329 ● 5,498   **5.** 879 ● 1,001   **6.** 3,867 ● 3,867

7. 980 ● 890   **8.** 1,226 ● 1,490   **9.** 29,694 ● 26,949

Write the numbers in order from greatest to least. (pp. 32–33)

10. 498, 569, 389   **11.** 1,267; 1,098; 1,330 **12.** 24,013; 22,798; 32,564

13. 8,780; 8,870; 8,078   **14.** 843, 627, 762   **15.** 6,636; 6,950; 5,910

Round to the nearest thousand, to the nearest hundred, and to the nearest ten. (pp. 36–39)

16. 8,687   **17.** 2,341   **18.** 7,924   **19.** 4,567   **20.** 1,212

21. 6,478   **22.** 3,633   **23.** 5,295   **24.** 9,526   **25.** 2,877

Check Problem Solving

Solve. Use a number line. (pp. 34–35)

26. The zoo sold 378 tickets on Monday, 389 tickets on Tuesday, 403 tickets on Wednesday, and 369 tickets on Thursday. On which day was the least number of tickets sold?

27. The zoo concession stand sold 1,483 juice drinks, 1,347 fruit smoothies, and 1,429 sandwiches. Order the numbers from least to greatest.

28. **WRITE Math** Jenny, Todd, and Gene collect stamps. Jenny has 220 stamps, Todd has 216 stamps, and Gene has 261 stamps. **Explain** how you can find who has the second-greatest number of stamps.

Standardized Test Prep
Chapters 1–2

Number and Operations

1. How is twenty thousand, five hundred four written in standard form? (p. 14)

   A 20,054

   B 20,504

   C 20,540

   D 25,004

2. Use the number line to order these numbers from greatest to least: 3,350; 3,240; 3,150; 3,260 (p. 32)

   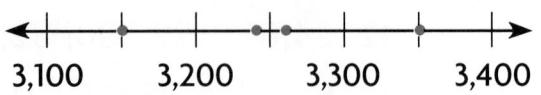

   A 3,150; 3,230; 3,260; 3,350

   B 3,350; 3,230; 3,260; 3,150

   C 3,350; 3,260; 3,240; 3,150

   D 3,260; 3,240; 3,350; 3,150

3. **WRITE Math** Cara has 187 photos and Molly has 178 photos. Who has more photos? Write a number sentence that compares the number of photos. **Explain** how place value can help you solve the problem.

   (p. 28)

Algebraic Reasoning

4. What is the next number in the pattern? (p. 4)

   $$33, 36, 39, 42, \blacksquare$$

   A 40

   B 43

   C 45

   D 55

5. Which addition fact helps you find the difference? (Grade 2)

   $$13 - 6 = \blacksquare$$

   A $7 + 6 = 13$

   B $3 + 3 = 6$

   C $4 + 2 = 6$

   D $13 + 6 = 19$

> **Test Tip** Check your work.
>
> See item 6. Use subtraction to check your answer.

6. **WRITE Math** Which number makes the number sentence true? **Explain** your answer. (Grade 2)

   $$8 + \blacksquare = 14$$

Geometry

7. Mary has these three triangles. Which figure can be made from the three triangles? (Grade 2)

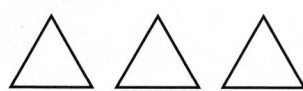

A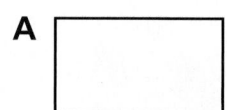

B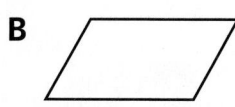

C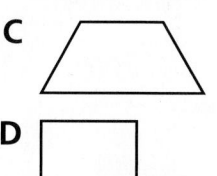

D

8. How many faces does a rectangular prism have? (Grade 2)

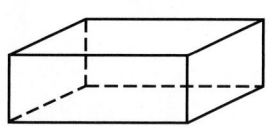

A 4

B 6

C 7

D 8

9. **WRITE Math** ▸ Which solid figure has more faces, a square pyramid or a cube? **Explain** how you know.

(Grade 2)

Data Analysis and Probability

For 10–12, use the Favorite Juice graph.

10. Ms. Parker's class made a bar graph to show the results of their class survey. Which juice did the most students choose? (Grade 2)

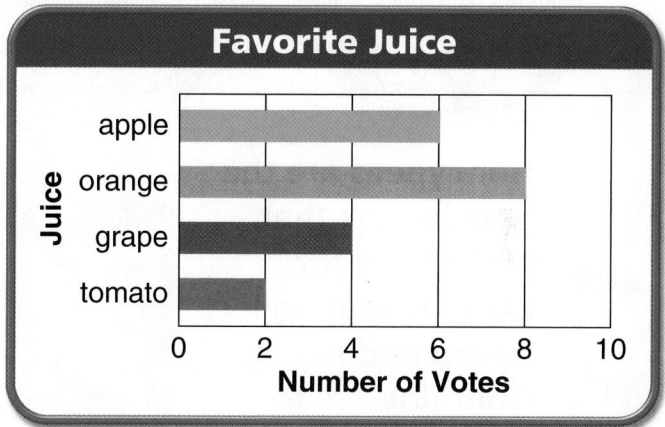

A apple   **C** grape

B orange   **D** tomato

11. How many more students chose apple than grape juice? (Grade 2)

A 8

B 6

C 4

D 2

12. **WRITE Math** ▸ What is the difference between the greatest number of votes and the least number of votes? **Explain** how you found your answer.

3 Addition

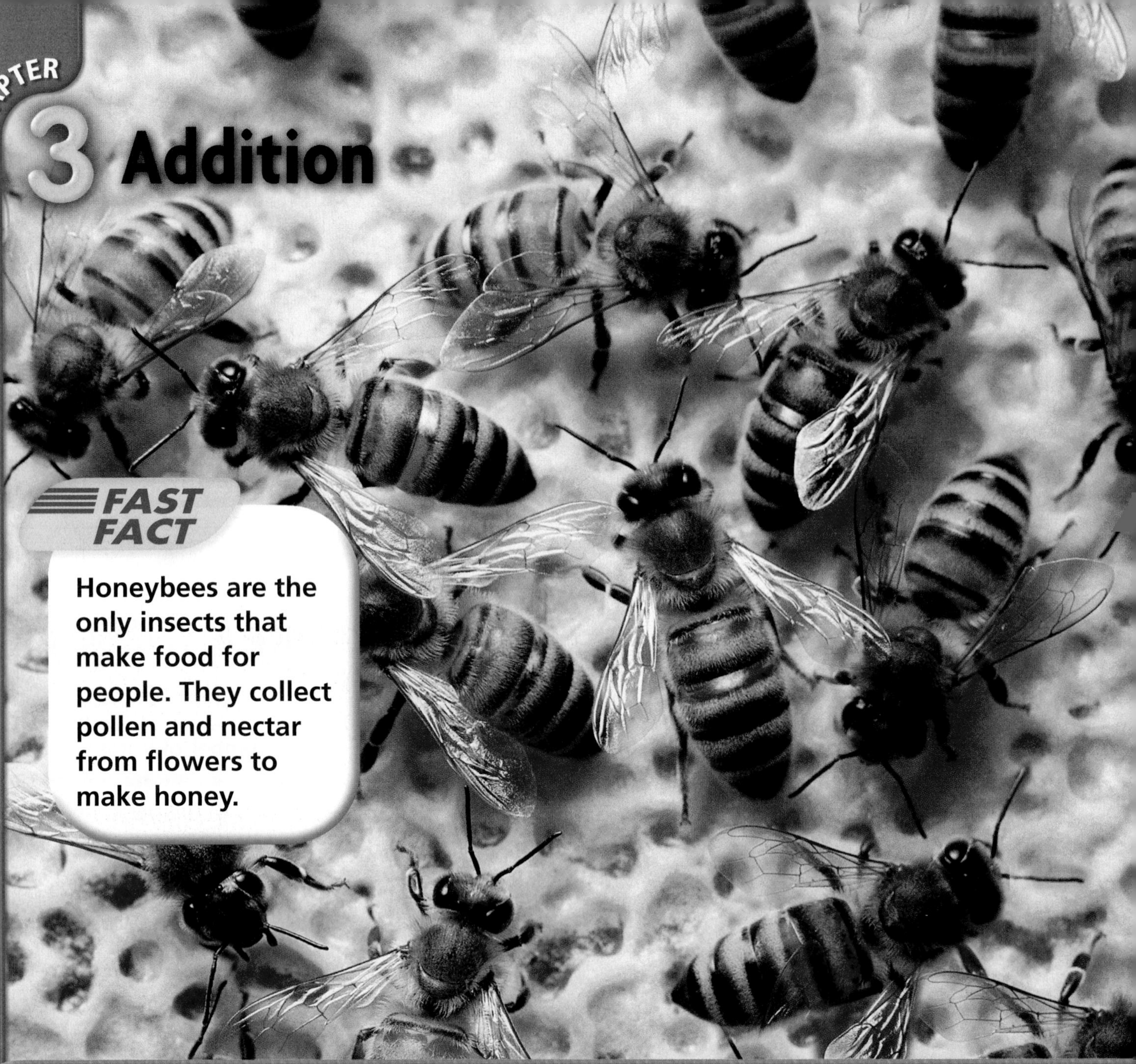

≡ FAST FACT

Honeybees are the only insects that make food for people. They collect pollen and nectar from flowers to make honey.

Investigate

Honey is used in a variety of recipes. The pictograph shows the amount of honey used in five different recipes. Choose three of the recipes. Tell how much honey you would need to make all three of those recipes.

Honey Recipes

Honey muffins	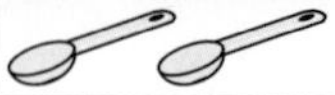 🥄🥄
Honey BBQ chicken	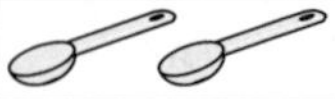 🥄🥄
Honey baked apples	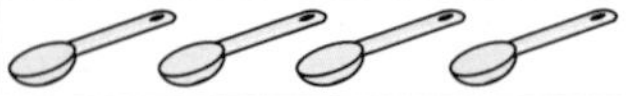 🥄🥄🥄🥄
Honey mustard dressing	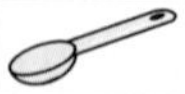 🥄
Honey banana pops	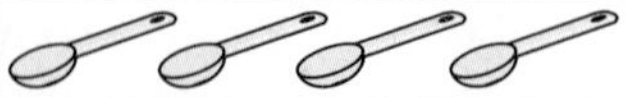 🥄🥄🥄🥄🥄

Key: Each 🥄 = 2 tablespoons.

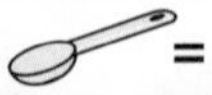

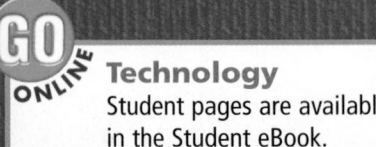

Technology
Student pages are available in the Student eBook.

Check your understanding of important skills needed for success in Chapter 3.

▶ **Add 1-Digit Numbers**

Add.

1. 5 +2	**2.** 3 +7	**3.** 8 +6	**4.** 9 +4	**5.** 1 +8

▶ **Model 2-Digit Addition**

Use the models. Find each sum.

6. $15 + 18 =$ ■ 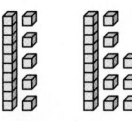   **7.** $27 + 31 =$ ■ 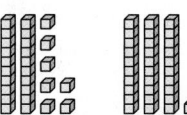

8. $45 + 19 =$ ■ 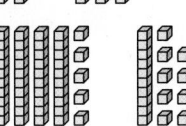   **9.** $50 + 24 =$ ■ 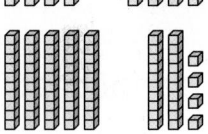

▶ **2-Digit Addition Without Regrouping**

Add.

10. 14 +11	**11.** 32 +24	**12.** 27 +62	**13.** 48 +30	**14.** 34 +15

VOCABULARY POWER

CHAPTER VOCABULARY

Associative Property of
   Addition
Commutative Property of
   Addition
compatible numbers
estimate
Identity Property of
   Addition
missing addend
number sentence

WARM-UP WORDS

Associative Property of Addition The property that states that you can group addends in different ways and still get the same sum

Commutative Property of Addition The property that states that you can add two or more numbers in any order and get the same sum

Identity Property of Addition The property that states that when you add zero to a number, the result is that number

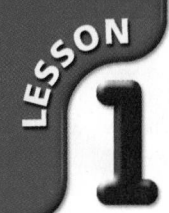

ALGEBRA
Addition Properties

OBJECTIVE: Use properties of addition to solve problems.

Quick Review

1. $5 + 8$ 2. $6 + 6$

3. $7 + 3$ 4. $8 + 7$

5. $9 + 6$

Vocabulary

Commutative Property of Addition

Identity Property of Addition

Associative Property of Addition

Learn

PROBLEM Ana saw 9 seagulls on Monday and 5 seagulls on Tuesday. How many seagulls did she see in all?

Commutative Property of Addition

You can add numbers in any order and get the same sum.

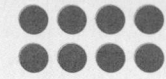

$$9 + 5 = 14$$
↑   ↑   ↑

addend + addend = sum

$$5 + 9 = 14$$
↑   ↑   ↑

addend + addend = sum

So, $9 + 5 = 5 + 9$. Ana saw 14 birds.

Identity Property of Addition

Ana saw 8 fish. Beth did not see any. How many fish did the girls see in all?

If you add zero to any number, the sum is that number.
$8 + 0 = 8$

So, the girls saw 8 fish in all.

Associative Property of Addition

Ana collected 7 brown shells, 4 white shells, and 6 gray shells. How many shells did she collect in all?

You can group addends in different ways, and the sum will be the same.

$$(7 + 4) + 6 = 7 + (4 + 6)$$
$$11 + 6 = 7 + 10$$
$$17 = 17$$

So, Ana collected 17 shells in all.

Math Idea
Parentheses ( ) show which numbers to add first.

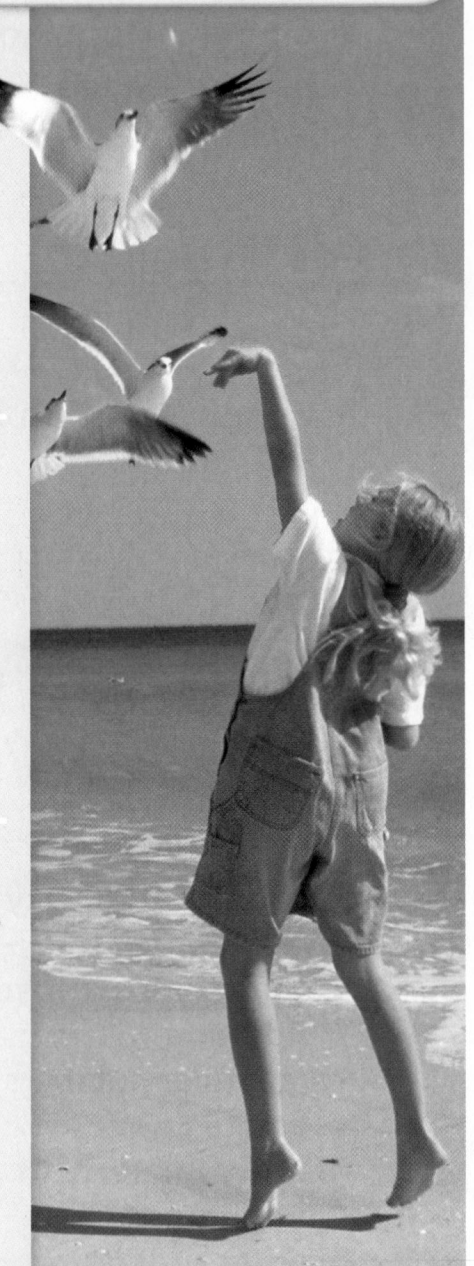

Guided Practice

1. What is the sum when you add 0 to 6?
   6 turtles + 0 turtles = ■ turtles

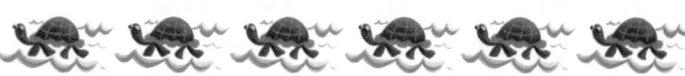

Find each sum. Name the property used.

2. 8 + 4 = ■
   4 + 8 = ■

3. 0 + 23 = ■
   23 + 0 = ■

✓4. 6 + 3 = ■
   3 + 6 = ■

✓5. (2 + 7) + 1 = ■
   2 + (7 + 1) = ■

6. **TALK Math** **Explain** how you can use the Associative Property of Addition to find 15 + 7 + 3.

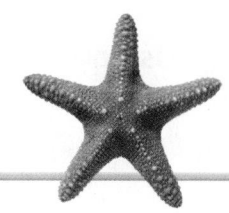

Independent Practice and Problem Solving

Find each sum. Name the property used.

7. 10 + 2 = ■
   2 + 10 = ■

8. 1 + (16 + 4) = ■
   (1 + 16) + 4 = ■

9. 6 + 0 = ■
   0 + 6 = ■

10. 3 + (5 + 9) = ■
    (3 + 5) + 9 = ■

Find each sum two different ways. Use parentheses to show which numbers you added first.

11. 8 + 9 + 1 = ■

12. 25 + 25 + 15 = ■

13. 30 + 70 + 15 = ■

14. A saltwater fishtank has 2 starfish, 3 sea horses, and 5 clown fish. How many animals are in the tank in all? Draw a picture and write a number sentence.

15. **What if** 4 of each animal are added to the tank? How many animals are there in all now?

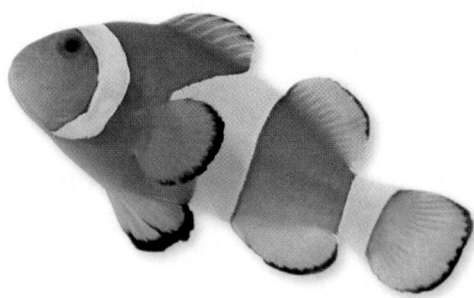

16. **WRITE Math** Do you think there is a Commutative Property of Subtraction? **Explain** why or why not.

Mixed Review and Test Prep

17. What is 759 rounded to the nearest hundred? (p. 36)

18. There are 2 red marbles and 5 green marbles in a bag. Which color marble are you more likely to choose? (Grade 2)

19. **Test Prep** Which is the sum?
    $$(6 + 6) + 7 = ■$$

    A 12   **C** 19

    B 13   **D** 20

Extra Practice on page 68, Set A

ALGEBRA
Missing Addends

OBJECTIVE: Identify missing addends in addition sentences.

Quick Review

1. $4 + 7$
2. $5 + 9$
3. $8 + 4$
4. $9 + 3$
5. $7 + 6$

Learn

PROBLEM Nick's family spent the day at an amusement park. They rode roller coasters a total of 12 times. They rode roller coasters 7 times before lunch. How many times did they ride roller coasters after lunch?

ONE WAY Use an addition fact.

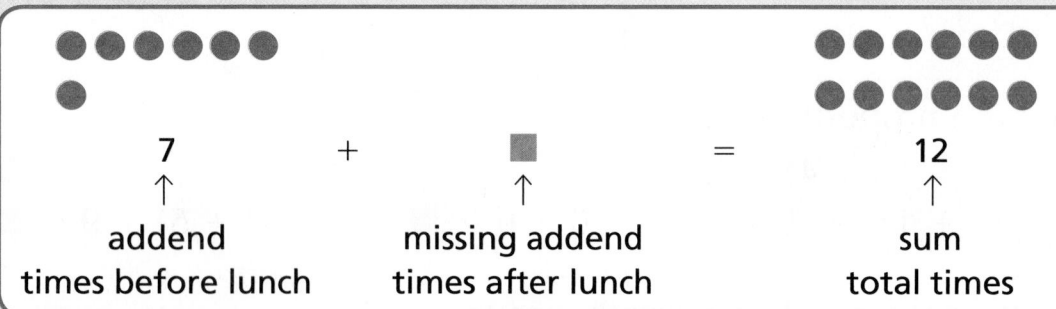

7	+	■	=	12
↑		↑		↑
addend		missing addend		sum
times before lunch		times after lunch		total times

$7 + 5 = 12$

ANOTHER WAY Use a related subtraction fact.

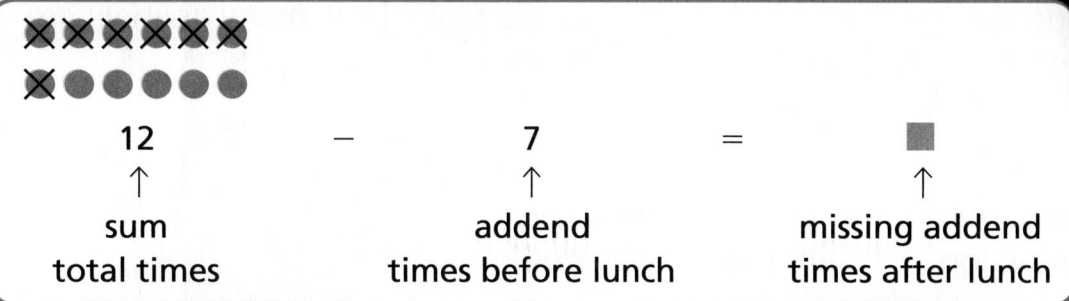

12	−	7	=	■
↑		↑		↑
sum		addend		missing addend
total times		times before lunch		times after lunch

$12 - 7 = 5$

So, Nick's family rode roller coasters 5 times after lunch.

• **What if** Nick's family had ridden roller coasters 3 times before lunch? How many times would they have ridden roller coasters after lunch?

Guided Practice

1. What addition fact can help you find $3 + ■ = 10$? What related subtraction fact can help you?

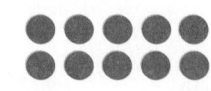

Find the missing addend. You may want to use counters.

2. $4 + \blacksquare = 12$ **3.** $\blacksquare + 6 = 6$ ✓**4.** $8 + \blacksquare = 10$ ✓**5.** $\blacksquare + 5 = 11$

6. [TALK Math] **Explain** how to use a related subtraction fact to find $8 + \blacksquare = 13$.

Independent Practice and Problem Solving

Find the missing addend. You may want to use counters.

7. $6 + \blacksquare = 16$ **8.** $\blacksquare + 5 = 12$ **9.** $\blacksquare + 9 = 9$ **10.** $\blacksquare + 17 = 17 + 6$

11. $6 + \blacksquare = 20$ **12.** $5 + \blacksquare = 13$ **13.** $\blacksquare + 3 = 18$ **14.** $19 + 12 = 12 + \blacksquare$

Find the missing number.

15. $7 + 8 = \blacksquare$ **16.** $9 + \blacksquare = 18$ **17.** $\blacksquare + 8 = 14$ **18.** $10 + 0 = \blacksquare$

USE DATA For 19–21, use the table.

19. The table shows the amount of food sold at an amusement park on Friday. How many more hot dogs and nachos were sold than hamburgers?

Food Sold	
Food	**Number Sold**
Hamburgers	41
Hot dogs	29
Nachos	35

20. Pose a Problem Look back at Problem 19. Write a similar problem by changing the number of items sold to numbers less than 20 and by changing the question.

21. [WRITE Math] If Sue's family bought 8 hot dogs, how many hot dogs were bought by other people? **Explain** how you know.

Mixed Review and Test Prep

22. Leah wrote eight thousand, three hundred four. What is Leah's number in standard form? (p. 10)

23. Dan caught 12 baseballs. Jim didn't catch any. Which addition property is shown by this example? $12 + 0 = 12$

(p. 48)

24. Test Prep Which is the missing addend for $12 + \blacksquare = 17$?

A 3

B 4

C 5

D 6

Estimate Sums

OBJECTIVE: Estimate sums of 2- and 3-digit numbers by using rounding and compatible numbers.

Learn

PROBLEM There are many types of birds at Lake Whitney, in Texas. One day Jacob counted 128 birds. Paul counted 73 birds. About how many birds did Jacob and Paul count in all?

To find *about* how many, you can **estimate**.

Vocabulary

estimate
compatible numbers

Example Estimate. 128 + 73

ONE WAY Use rounding.

Round each number to the nearest ten. Then add.

$$
\begin{array}{r}
128 \rightarrow 130 \\
+ \ 73 \rightarrow + \ 70 \\
\hline
200
\end{array}
$$

ANOTHER WAY Use compatible numbers.

Compatible numbers are close numbers that are easy to compute mentally.

$$
\begin{array}{r}
128 \rightarrow 125 \\
+ \ 73 \rightarrow + \ 75 \\
\hline
200
\end{array}
$$

So, 200 is a reasonable estimate of how many birds were counted.

• What other compatible numbers could be used to estimate the sum?

More Examples

A Use rounding.

$$
\begin{array}{r}
19 \rightarrow 20 \\
+ 66 \rightarrow + 70 \\
\hline
90
\end{array}
$$

B Use rounding.

$$
\begin{array}{r}
492 \rightarrow 500 \\
+ 219 \rightarrow + 200 \\
\hline
700
\end{array}
$$

C Use compatible numbers.

$$
\begin{array}{r}
306 \rightarrow 300 \\
+ 286 \rightarrow + 285 \\
\hline
585
\end{array}
$$

Guided Practice

1. Copy the problem at the right. Round both 324 and 48 to the nearest ten. Then estimate their sum.

$$
\begin{array}{r}
324 \\
+ \ 48 \\
\hline
\end{array}
$$

Use rounding or compatible numbers to estimate each sum.

2. 37
   + 51

3. 307
   + 181

4. 476
   + 239

✓ 5. 29
   + 44

✓ 6. 148
   + 151

7. **TALK Math** Use rounding and then use compatible numbers to estimate 128 + 381. Which way do you think gives an answer closer to the exact sum for this problem? **Explain.**

Independent Practice and Problem Solving

Use rounding to estimate each sum.

8. 42
   + 35

9. 61
   + 95

10. 319
   + 54

11. 289
   + 407

12. 526
   + 361

Use compatible numbers to estimate each sum.

13. 42
   + 37

14. 51
   + 48

15. 172
   + 27

16. 326
   + 176

17. 248
   + 121

USE DATA For 18–20, use the table.

18. **Reasoning** If you went along the shoreline of Lake Conroe two times, would that distance be about the same as going one time along Lake Fork? **Explain** using compatible numbers.

Shorelines of Texas Lakes	
Lake	Distance in Miles
Lake Fork	315
Lake Conroe	157
Lake Buchanan	124

19. **WRITE Math** Some lakes in Texas have shorelines along which people hike and fish. **Explain** how you would estimate the sum of Lake Fork's and Lake Conroe's shorelines.

20. **≡FAST FACT** Lake Livingston is the second-largest lake in Texas. It has 450 miles of shoreline. Estimate the sum of Lake Livingston's and Lake Buchanan's shorelines.

Mixed Review and Test Prep

21. Write the numbers in order from least to greatest. (p. 32)

    2,219; 2,178; 2,198

22. What is the missing addend? (p. 50)

    9 + ■ = 18

23. **Test Prep** A plane flew 732 miles and then flew 476 miles. About how many miles did the plane fly in all?

    A 200 miles

    B 1,000 miles

    C 1,200 miles

    D 2,000 miles

Extra Practice on page 68, Set C

Add 2-Digit Numbers

OBJECTIVE: Add 2-digit numbers with and without regrouping.

Quick Review

1. $6 + 8$
2. $8 + 9$
3. $7 + 7$
4. $8 + 4$
5. $6 + 4 + 5$

Learn

PROBLEM Shannon picked 29 red apples at the orchard. Katrina picked 57 green apples. How many apples did Shannon and Katrina pick in all?

Example 1 **Add.** $29 + 57$

Estimate. $30 + 60 = 90$

ONE WAY Use place value.

Step 1

Add the ones.
$9 + 7 = 16$ ones
Regroup 16 ones
as 1 ten 6 ones.

$$\begin{array}{r} \overset{1}{2}9 \\ + 57 \\ \hline 6 \end{array}$$

Step 2

Add the tens.
$1 + 2 + 5 = 8$ tens

$$\begin{array}{r} \overset{1}{2}9 \\ + 57 \\ \hline 86 \end{array}$$

ANOTHER WAY Use mental math.

	Add the tens.	Add the ones.	Add the sums.
$\begin{array}{r}29\\+57\\\hline\end{array}$	$\begin{array}{r}20\\+50\\\hline 70\end{array}$	$\begin{array}{r}9\\+7\\\hline 16\end{array}$	$\begin{array}{r}70\\+16\\\hline 86\end{array}$

So, Shannon and Katrina picked 86 apples in all. Since 86 is close to the estimate of 90, the answer is reasonable.

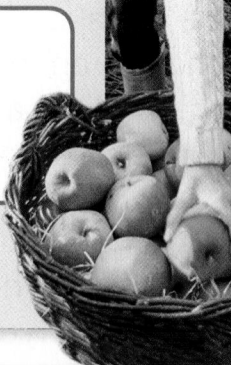

Sometimes when you add 3 addends, you can make a ten.

Example 2 **Add.** $35 + 26 + 54$

Step 1

Add the ones.
$5 + 6 + 4 = 15$ ones
Regroup 15 ones
as 1 ten 5 ones.

$$\begin{array}{r} \overset{1}{3}5 \\ 26 \\ + 54 \\ \hline 5 \end{array}$$ Make a ten.

Step 2

Add the tens.
$1 + 3 + 2 + 5 = 11$ tens
Regroup 11 tens
as 1 hundred 1 ten.

$$\begin{array}{r} \overset{1}{3}5 \\ 26 \\ + 54 \\ \hline 115 \end{array}$$

ERROR ALERT

Remember to add the regrouped ten.

• How can you use mental math to find $43 + 22 + 18$?

1. Find 45 + 68 using mental math.
   Complete the number sentences.

   $\begin{array}{r} 45 \\ +68 \\ \hline \end{array}$ $40 + 60 = \blacksquare$
   $5 + 8 = \blacksquare$

Estimate. Then find each sum using place value or mental math.

2. $\begin{array}{r} 17 \\ +54 \\ \hline \end{array}$

3. $\begin{array}{r} 22 \\ 48 \\ +13 \\ \hline \end{array}$

4. $\begin{array}{r} 84 \\ +35 \\ \hline \end{array}$

✓5. $\begin{array}{r} 24 \\ +39 \\ \hline \end{array}$

✓6. $\begin{array}{r} 47 \\ 23 \\ +28 \\ \hline \end{array}$

7. **TALK Math** **Explain** how you would use place value to find 56 + 19 + 31.

Independent Practice and Problem Solving

Estimate. Then find each sum using place value or mental math.

8. $\begin{array}{r} 98 \\ +36 \\ \hline \end{array}$

9. $\begin{array}{r} 19 \\ +42 \\ \hline \end{array}$

10. $\begin{array}{r} 53 \\ +29 \\ \hline \end{array}$

11. $\begin{array}{r} 16 \\ 12 \\ +28 \\ \hline \end{array}$

12. $\begin{array}{r} 33 \\ 10 \\ +85 \\ \hline \end{array}$

13. $66 + 35 = \blacksquare$ 14. $21 + 46 = \blacksquare$ 15. $18 + 18 = \blacksquare$ 16. $21 + 37 + 19 = \blacksquare$

USE DATA For 17–19, use the picture.

17. For the class party, Carlos brought 2 gallons of apple juice. How many cups can he pour?

18. Kate brought 2 dozen apples for the class party. Only 22 apples were eaten. How many apples were left?

19. **WRITE Math** Sarah bought 3 dozen apples to make applesauce. How many apples did Sarah buy? **Explain** how you know.

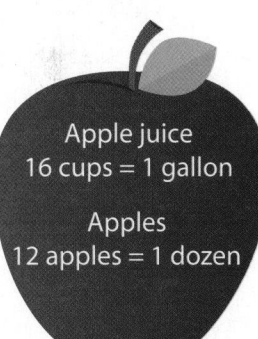

Apple juice
16 cups = 1 gallon

Apples
12 apples = 1 dozen

Mixed Review and Test Prep

20. What is 576 rounded to the nearest hundred? (p. 36)

21. Kyle cut apart a square. What figures did he make? (Grade 2)

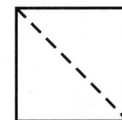

22. **Test Prep** Which is the sum?

    $56 + 41 + 73 = \blacksquare$

    A 160   **C** 170

    B 161   **D** 171

5 Model 3-Digit Addition

OBJECTIVE: Explore adding 3-digit numbers with and without regrouping.

Quick Review

Regroup.

1. 10 ones = ■ ten 0 ones
2. 17 ones = 1 ten ■ ones
3. ■ ones = 1 ten 4 ones
4. 12 tens = ■ hundred 2 tens
5. 19 tens = 1 hundred ■ tens

Investigate

Materials ■ base-ten blocks

You can use base-ten blocks to help add numbers.

A Model the numbers 246 and 175.

Use your model to find the sum of 246 and 175.
Add the ones, tens, and hundreds.
Regroup the blocks when needed.

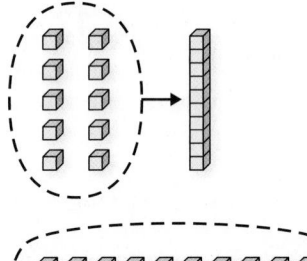

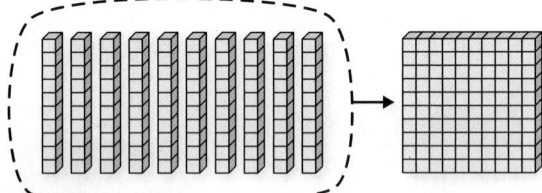

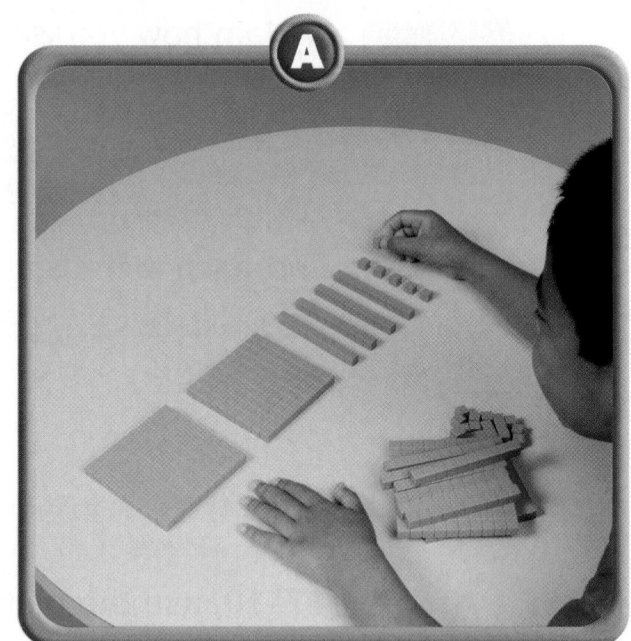

B Draw a picture to show the sum.
Record your answer.

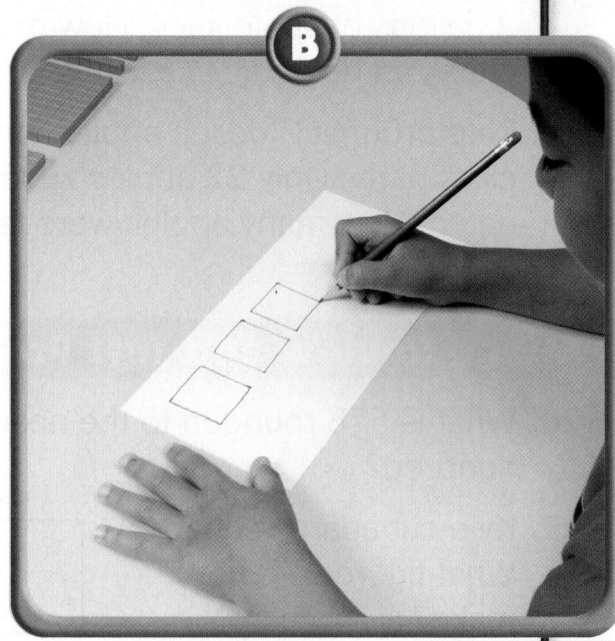

Draw Conclusions

1. Explain how your model helped you find the sum.

2. When do you need to regroup?

3. **Analysis** Can the sum of two 3-digit numbers equal a 4-digit number? Explain. Give an example.

Connect

Here is a way to record addition.

To add 138 and 267, first line up the hundreds, tens, and ones.

```
 H T O
   1 3 8
 + 2 6 7
```

Step 1	Step 2	Step 3
Add the ones. 8 + 7 = 15 ones	Add the tens. 1 + 3 + 6 = 10 tens	Add the hundreds. 1 + 1 + 2 = 4 hundreds
Regroup. 15 ones = 1 ten 5 ones	Regroup. 10 tens = 1 hundred 0 tens	

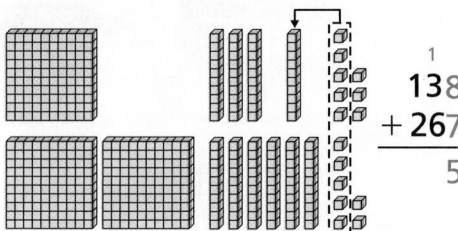

$$\begin{array}{r} 1\\ 138 \\ +267 \\ \hline 5 \end{array}$$

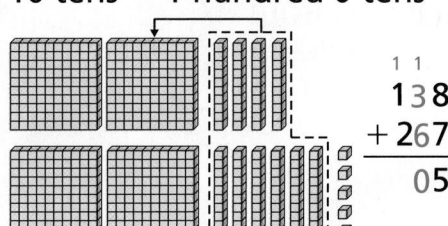

$$\begin{array}{r} 1\ 1\\ 138 \\ +267 \\ \hline 05 \end{array}$$

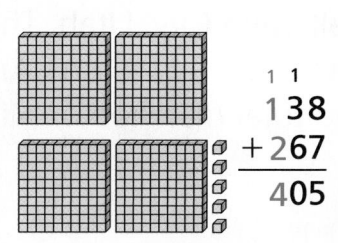

$$\begin{array}{r} 1\ 1\\ 138 \\ +267 \\ \hline 405 \end{array}$$

So, 138 + 267 = 405.

TALK Math

Explain how to find the sum of 485 and 429. Tell if you need to regroup.

Practice

Use base-ten blocks to find each sum.

1. 511 + 253 = ■
2. 183 + 214 = ■
3. 455 + 346 = ■
4. 268 + 258 = ■
5. 123 + 155 = ■
✓6. 352 + 191 = ■

Find each sum.

7. 434
   + 517

8. 185
   + 309

9. 594
   + 156

10. 233
    + 128

✓11. 457
    + 465

12. 193
    + 796

13. 216
    + 261

14. 377
    + 140

15. 615
    + 284

16. 545
    + 389

17. **Reasoning** Will the sum of 625 and 718 be greater than or less than 1,000? How do you know?

18. **WRITE Math** **Explain** how to use base-ten blocks to model 182 + 376. What is the sum?

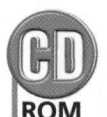

Technology
Use Harcourt Mega Math, Country Countdown, *Block Busters,* Levels U, V.

6 Add Greater Numbers

OBJECTIVE: Add 3- and 4-digit numbers with and without regrouping.

Learn

PROBLEM Mia is planning a trip to Los Angeles, California. Her airplane leaves from New York City and stops in Salt Lake City, Utah. Then it flies from Salt Lake City to Los Angeles. What is the total distance of Mia's flight?

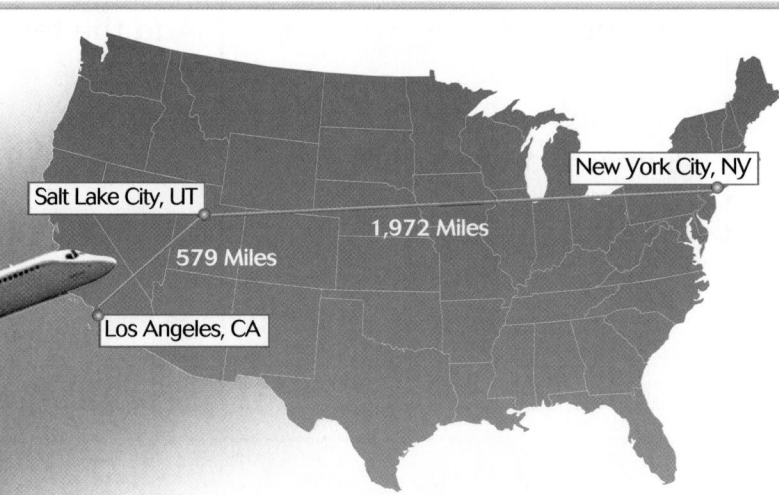

Salt Lake City, UT

New York City, NY

1,972 Miles

579 Miles

Los Angeles, CA

Example Add. 1,972 + 579   **Estimate.** 2,000 + 600 = 2,600

Step 1	Step 2	Step 3	Step 4
Add the ones. Regroup.	Add the tens. Regroup.	Add the hundreds. Regroup.	Add the thousands.
11 ones = 1 ten 1 one	15 tens = 1 hundred 5 tens	15 hundreds = 1 thousand 5 hundreds	
$\begin{array}{r} {\scriptstyle 1} \\ 1,972 \\ +\ \ 579 \\ \hline 1 \end{array}$	$\begin{array}{r} {\scriptstyle 1\ 1} \\ 1,972 \\ +\ \ 579 \\ \hline 51 \end{array}$	$\begin{array}{r} {\scriptstyle 1\ 1\ 1} \\ 1,972 \\ +\ \ 579 \\ \hline 551 \end{array}$	$\begin{array}{r} {\scriptstyle 1\ 1\ 1} \\ 1,972 \\ +\ \ 579 \\ \hline 2,551 \end{array}$

So, the total distance of Mia's flight is 2,551 miles. Since 2,551 is close to the estimate of 2,600, the answer is reasonable.

More Examples

A Regrouping

$\begin{array}{r} {\scriptstyle 1} \\ 436 \\ +182 \\ \hline 618 \end{array}$

B No regrouping

$\begin{array}{r} 5,242 \\ +\ \ 654 \\ \hline 5,896 \end{array}$

C Regrouping

$\begin{array}{r} {\scriptstyle 1\ 1\ 1} \\ 2,764 \\ +6,648 \\ \hline 9,412 \end{array}$

1. Copy the problem at the right. Do you need to regroup? Find the sum.

$$534 \\ +319$$

Estimate. Then find each sum.

2. $$604 \\ +263$$
3. $$532 \\ +419$$
4. $$3,163 \\ +3,644$$
✓5. $$2,833 \\ +\ 175$$
✓6. $$1,825 \\ +4,617$$

7. **TALK Math** Explain how to use place value to add 1,258 and 1,376.

Independent Practice and Problem Solving

Estimate. Then find each sum.

8. $$479 \\ +352$$
9. $$241 \\ +325$$
10. $$5,963 \\ +\ 778$$
11. $$2,071 \\ +1,985$$
12. $$3,729 \\ +4,541$$

13. $643 + 167 = \blacksquare$

14. $469 + 860 = \blacksquare$

15. $9,514 + 2,858 = \blacksquare$

USE DATA For 16–17, use the table.

16. Ms. Sloan flies from Boston to Washington, D.C. Then she flies from Washington, D.C., to Atlanta. She flies the same distance to return home. What is the total distance she flies?

17. **WRITE Math** **What's the Error?**
A plane flies from Philadelphia to Chicago and then to Las Vegas. Keith says the total flight distance is 1,191 miles. Describe his error. Find the correct distance.

Flight Distances Between Cities	
Cities	**Distance in Miles**
Boston to Washington, D.C.	394
Washington, D.C. to Atlanta	541
Philadelphia to Chicago	665
Chicago to Las Vegas	1,526

Mixed Review and Test Prep

18. What is the mode? (Grade 2)

$$4, 3, 9, 6, 3, 2, 8$$

19. Write $<$, $>$, or $=$ to compare. (p. 28)

$$2,178 \ \bullet \ 2,187$$

20. **Test Prep** Which is the sum of 3,579 and 453?

A 4,032   **C** 3,922

B 3,932   **D** 3,126

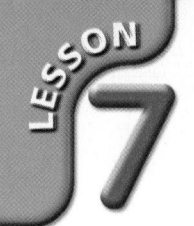
Problem Solving Workshop
Strategy: Predict and Test

OBJECTIVE: Solve problems by using the strategy *predict and test*.

Learn the Strategy

Sometimes, the best way to solve a problem is to predict and test. After reading the problem, you predict, or guess, what the answer might be. Then you use information in the problem to test, or check, if your answer is too low, too high, or just right.

Predict and test to find numbers whose sum is 39.

Three numbers in a row have a sum of 39. What are the numbers?

Predict	Test	Notes
9, 10, 11	$9+10+11 = 30$	too low
13, 14, 15	$13+14+15 = 42$	too high
12, 13, 14	$12+13+14 = 39$	just right

Predict and test to find the number of books each boy has.

Mark has 3 more books than Chad. Together, they have 25 books. How many books does each boy have?

Predict: 12 and 9	Predict: 16 and 13	Predict: 14 and 11
Test: $12+9 = 21$	Test: $16+13 = 29$	Test: $14+11 = 25$
too low	too high	just right

Predict and test to find the amount of time spent on each activity.

Melanie spends 60 minutes reading and exercising. She exercises 10 minutes more than she reads. How much time does Melanie spend doing each activity?

Predict		Test	
Read	Exercise	Total	Notes
30	$30+10 = 40$	$30+40=70$	too high
20	$20+10 = 30$	$20+30=50$	too low
25	$25+10 = 35$	$25+35=60$	just right

TALK Math

Explain how you can use the results from one guess to make another guess.

Use the Strategy

PROBLEM Jacob and Gabe play on different football teams. Jacob's team scored 7 more points than Gabe's team. There were 35 points total scored in the game. How many points did each team score?

Read to Understand

Reading Skill

- **Use graphic aids to organize your predictions and test the results.**
- **What information is given?**
- **Is there information you will not use? If so, what?**

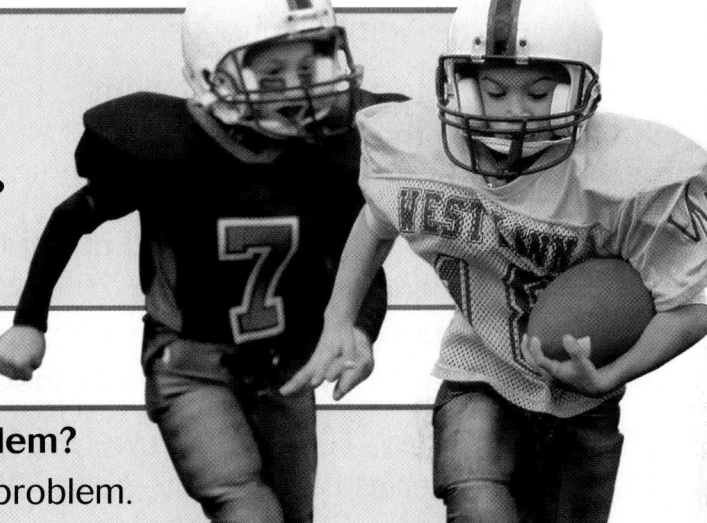

Plan

- **What strategy can you use to solve the problem?**
  You can predict and test to help you solve the problem.

Solve

- **How can you use the strategy to solve the problem?**
  Make a table to organize your predictions and test the results.

  Predict the number of points scored by Gabe's team. Add 7 to that number to find the points scored by Jacob's team. Then test to see if the sum of the numbers is 35.

  So, Gabe's team scored 14 points, and Jacob's team scored 21 points.

Predict		Test	
Gabe's Team	Jacob's Team	Total	Notes
11	11 + 7 = 18	11 + 18 = 29	too low
16	16 + 7 = 23	16 + 23 = 39	too high
14	14 + 7 = 21	14 + 21 = 35	just right

Check

- **How do you know your answer is correct?**

Guided Problem Solving

Read to
Understand
Plan
Solve
Check

1. Fifty children signed up for the youth basketball league. There were 20 more boys than girls. How many girls and how many boys signed up for the basketball league?

   First, predict the number of girls.

   Then, add 20 to that number to find the number of boys.

   Finally, test to see if the sum is 50. If the sum is not 50, try other numbers.

Predict		Test	
Girls	Boys	Total	Notes
20	20+20=40	20+40=60	too high
10	10+20=		

2. **What if** 72 children signed up for the league and there were still 20 more boys than girls? How many girls and how many boys would have signed up?

3. In a survey, 100 students were asked to choose swimming or soccer as their favorite sport. Of those, 14 more chose soccer than swimming. How many students chose soccer?

Problem Solving Strategy Practice

Predict and test to solve.

4. For a volleyball game, 200 tickets were sold. There were 70 more student tickets sold than adult tickets. How many of each type of ticket were sold?

5. The snack bar at the football field has 500 cups. There are 80 more small cups than large cups. How many small cups are there?

6. The youth softball league ordered 48 T-shirts in two colors. There were 10 fewer red shirts ordered than blue shirts. How many of each color were ordered?

7. **WRITE Math** During basketball practice, Jacob attempted 40 free-throw shots. He made 6 more than he missed. How many free-throw shots did Jacob make? **Explain** how you know.

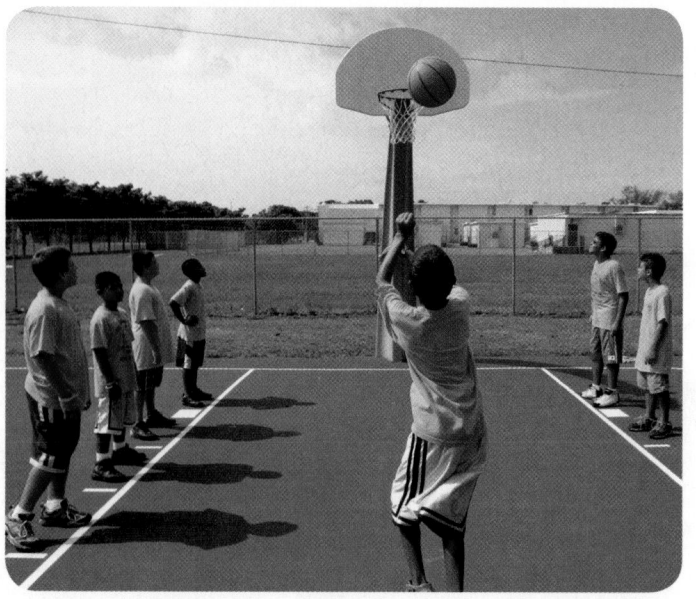

Mixed Strategy Practice

USE DATA For 8–10, use the graph.

8. For Game 1, the number of fans for the home team was 200 more than the number of fans for the visiting team. How many visiting fans were at Game 1?

9. The coach said that the number of fans at Game 2 was 235 fewer than he expected. How many fans did the coach expect at Game 2?

10. **Pose a Problem** Look back at Problem 9. Write a similar problem by changing the number of fans the coach expected to a number greater than 300.

11. **Open-Ended** At Game 3, each fan was given a 3-digit number for a prize drawing. Justin's number had three even digits. The digit in the tens place was greater than the digit in the ones place. The digit in the hundreds place was greater than the digit in the tens place. What could Justin's number have been?

CHALLENGE YOURSELF

In the first three games of the season, Sam scored 23, 18, and 26 points.

12. In Game 4, Sam scored 5 more points than he did in one of the first three games. He scored fewer than 94 points in all for the first four games. How many points did he score in Game 4?

13. Sam scored more than 100 points over the first 5 games. He scored the same number of points in Games 4 and 5. What is the least number of points he could have scored in Game 5?

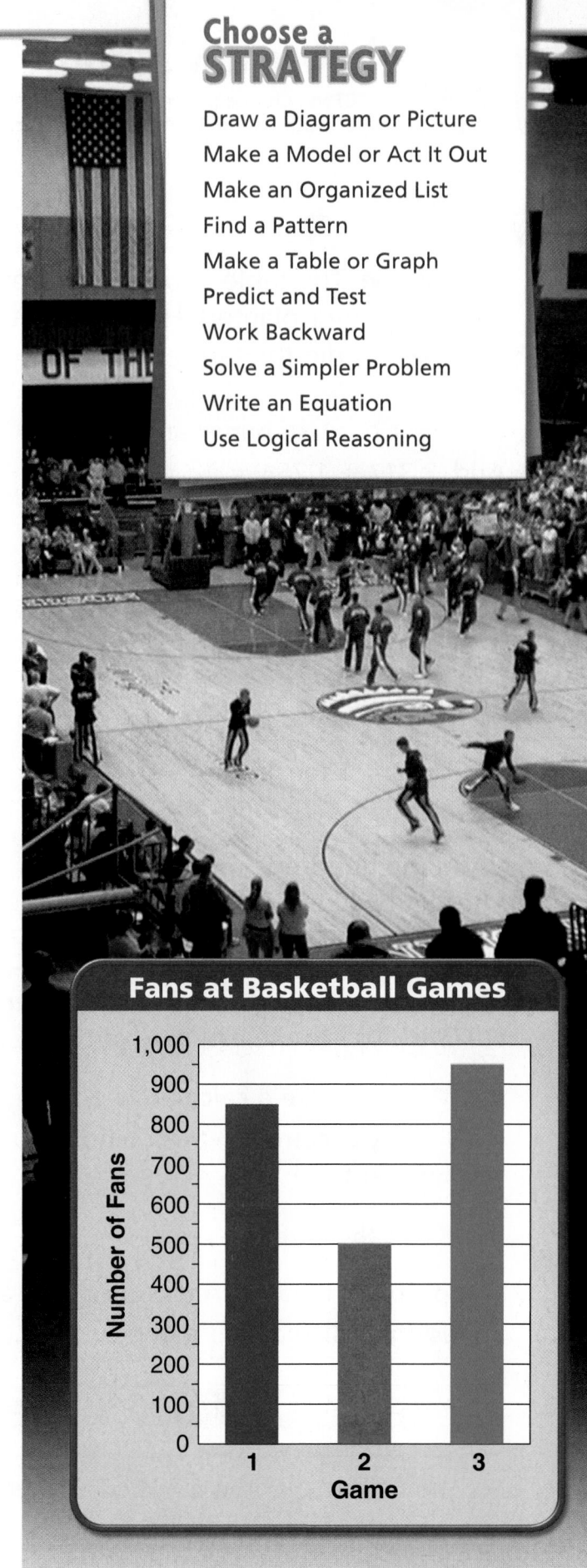

Choose a
STRATEGY

Draw a Diagram or Picture
Make a Model or Act It Out
Make an Organized List
Find a Pattern
Make a Table or Graph
Predict and Test
Work Backward
Solve a Simpler Problem
Write an Equation
Use Logical Reasoning

Fans at Basketball Games

Choose a Method

OBJECTIVE: Choose paper and pencil, a calculator, or mental math to add 3- and 4-digit numbers.

There are 130 students at Prairie School. There are 275 students at Lincoln School. What is the total number of students at both schools?

Learn

PROBLEM The table shows the number of vegetable seeds a farmer planted. How many cucumber and bean seeds did the farmer plant?

Seeds Planted

Seed	Number Planted
Cucumber	3,317
Carrot	875
Bean	1,754
Lettuce	2,612

Example 1 Use paper and pencil.

Add. $3,317 + 1,754 = \blacksquare$

Estimate. $3,000 + 2,000 = 5,000$

The problem involves regrouping and adding two numbers. So, using paper and pencil is a good choice.

Step 1

Add the ones.
Regroup.
11 ones = 1 ten 1 one

$$\begin{array}{r} \overset{1}{}\\ 3,317 \\ + 1,754 \\ \hline 1 \end{array}$$

Step 2

Add the tens.

$$\begin{array}{r} \overset{1}{}\\ 3,317 \\ + 1,754 \\ \hline 71 \end{array}$$

Step 3

Add the hundreds.
Regroup. 10 hundreds =
1 thousand 0 hundreds

$$\begin{array}{r} \overset{1}{}\overset{1}{}\\ 3,317 \\ + 1,754 \\ \hline 071 \end{array}$$

Step 4

Add the thousands.

$$\begin{array}{r} \overset{1}{}\overset{1}{}\\ 3,317 \\ + 1,754 \\ \hline 5,071 \end{array}$$

So, the farmer planted 5,071 cucumber and bean seeds. Since 5,071 is close to the estimate of 5,000, the answer is reasonable.

Example 2 Use a calculator.

How many cucumber, carrot, and lettuce seeds did the farmer plant?

$3,317 + 875 + 2,612 = \blacksquare$

The problem involves regrouping and adding three large numbers. So, using a calculator is a good choice.

Math Idea

Since you may enter a wrong number when using a calculator, it is important to check your answer.

3 3 1 7 **+** 8 7 5 **+** 2 6 1 2 **=** 6804.

So, the farmer planted 6,804 cucumber, carrot, and lettuce seeds.

Example 3 Use mental math.

Pete and Michael bought vegetable plants for their farm. They bought 120 radish plants and 438 broccoli plants. How many plants did they buy?

$$120 + 438 = \blacksquare$$

No regrouping is needed. So, using mental math is a good choice.

Think: Add the hundreds. $100 + 400 = 500$
Add the tens. $20 + 30 = 50$
Add the ones. $0 + 8 = 8$
Find the sum. $500 + 50 + 8 = 558$

So, Pete and Michael bought 558 plants.

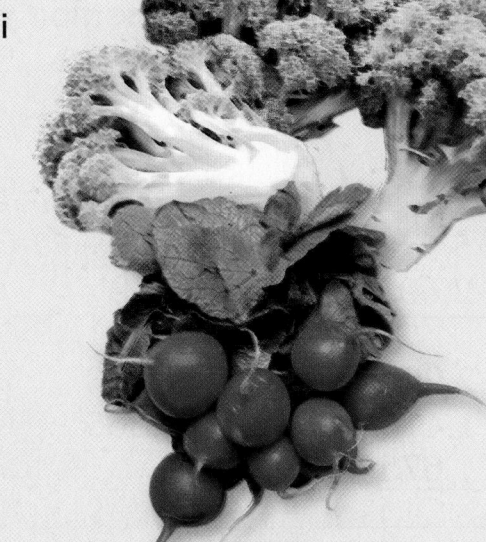

More Examples

A Use paper and pencil.

$$\begin{array}{r} {}^{1} \\ 581 \\ + \ 495 \\ \hline 1,076 \end{array}$$

B Use a calculator.

$$\begin{array}{r} 4,835 \\ 2,462 \\ + \ 1,684 \\ \hline 8,981 \end{array}$$

C Use mental math.

$$\begin{array}{r} 503 \\ + 324 \\ \hline 827 \end{array}$$

• What is another method you could use to find the sum in Example B?

Guided Practice

1. Find $247 + 230$ using mental math. Use the number sentences to help you.

$$\begin{array}{r} 247 \\ + 230 \\ \hline \end{array}$$

$200 + 200 = \blacksquare$
$40 + 30 = \blacksquare$
$7 + 0 = \blacksquare$

Find the sum. Tell which method you used.

2. $\begin{array}{r} 898 \\ + 365 \\ \hline \end{array}$

3. $\begin{array}{r} 1,650 \\ + 4,103 \\ \hline \end{array}$

4. $\begin{array}{r} 5,784 \\ 2,257 \\ + \ \ 836 \\ \hline \end{array}$

5. $\begin{array}{r} 135 \\ + 610 \\ \hline \end{array}$

✓6. $\begin{array}{r} 3,862 \\ + 2,839 \\ \hline \end{array}$

7. $611 + 156 = \blacksquare$

8. $2,754 + 4,526 = \blacksquare$

✓9. $3,722 + 4,180 + 1,359 = \blacksquare$

10. **TALK Math** **Explain** which strategy would be a good choice to use to add 457 and 963. Then find the sum.

Find the sum. Tell which method you used.

11. 608
    + 241

12. 1,895
    + 1,542

13. 456
    + 372

14. 1,211
     3,849
    + 1,970

15. 968
    + 453

16. 5,570
    + 2,695

17. 786
    + 274

18. 1,054
    + 622

19. 110
    + 373

20. 4,545
    + 3,687

21. 2,904
     1,418
    + 675

22. 4,103
    + 2,865

23. 324
     510
    + 143

24. 3,908
    + 2,712

25. 293
    + 862

26. $942 + 528 + 896 = $ ■   27. $859 + 364 = $ ■   28. $463 + 216 = $ ■

29. $309 + 185 = $ ■   30. $6,214 + 1,305 = $ ■   31. $5,285 + 3,789 = $ ■

USE DATA For 32–35, use the table.

32. Sarah's family owns a farm that is 2,852 acres. How many acres planted with corn, broccoli, and lettuce does the family have?

33. Eric's family plants 878 more acres of lettuce than Sarah's family does. How many acres of lettuce does Eric's family plant?

34. **Reasoning** Is the total number of acres planted with corn and peas greater than or less than the number of acres planted with broccoli? **Explain** your answer.

35. **WRITE Math** ▸ **What's the Question?** Jessica used the data in the table. The answer is 507.

36. On Friday, Dan and his father picked some tomatoes. On Saturday, they picked 36 more tomatoes. Now they have 89 tomatoes. How many tomatoes did they pick on Friday?

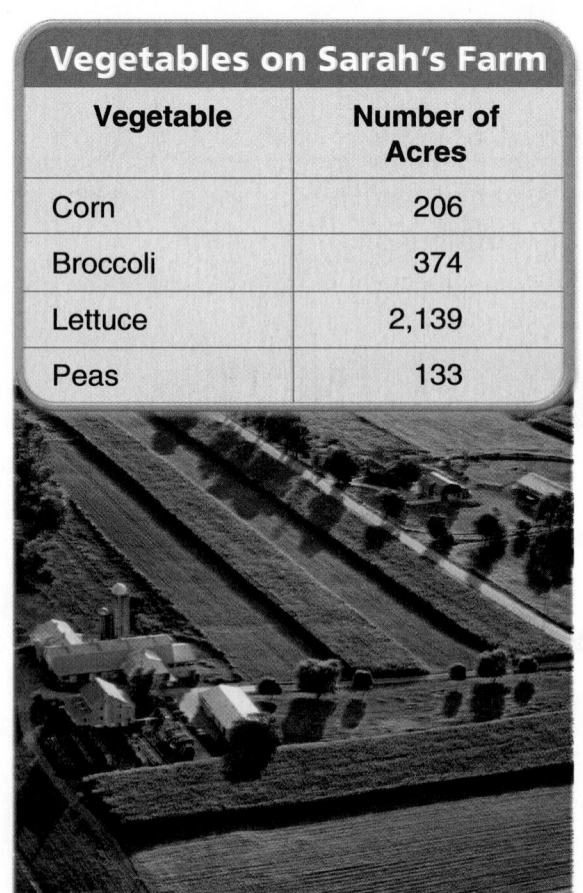

Vegetables on Sarah's Farm	
Vegetable	**Number of Acres**
Corn	206
Broccoli	374
Lettuce	2,139
Peas	133

▲ An acre of land is about the size of a football field.

Learn About) Addition Riddle

Copy and find each sum. Use mental math.

S 216 +153	B 352 +617	O 750 +248	A 332 +504	I 425 +250
E 793 +206	T 526 +361	R 319 +320	G 182 +607	C 453 +116
H 853 +134	N 630 +230	K 445 +424	y 223 +513	

To answer the riddle, match the letters from the sums above to the numbers below.

What food likes to listen to music? Why?

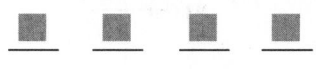 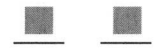 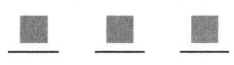 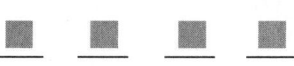

569 998 639 860   675 887   987 836 369   999 836 639 369

Mixed Review and Test Prep

37. Write the numbers in order from least to greatest. (p. 32)

245, 278, 236

38. Test Prep Drew's family drove 512 miles to his uncle's farm. Then they drove 173 miles to Drew's grandmother's house. How many miles did Drew's family drive in all?

A 339 miles

B 456 miles

C 572 miles

D 685 miles

39. What is the greatest whole number you can make by using the digits 4, 7, 3, and 5? Use each digit only once. (p. 10)

40. Test Prep Junie's father runs a shipping business. He shipped 870 boxes on Tuesday. He shipped 765 boxes on Wednesday. How many boxes did he ship on both days? **Explain** what method you used.

Extra Practice

Set A Find each sum. Name the property used. (pp. 48–49)

1. $8 + 3 = \blacksquare$
   $3 + 8 = \blacksquare$

2. $0 + 14 = \blacksquare$
   $14 + 0 = \blacksquare$

3. $13 + 5 = \blacksquare$
   $5 + 13 = \blacksquare$

4. $(4 + 2) + 3 = \blacksquare$
   $4 + (2 + 3) = \blacksquare$

Set B Find the missing addend. You may want to use counters. (pp. 50–51)

1. $\blacksquare + 2 = 8$
2. $9 + \blacksquare = 17$
3. $\blacksquare + 5 = 22$
4. $15 + \blacksquare = 2 + 15$

Set C Use rounding to estimate each sum. (pp. 52–53)

1.	2.	3.	4.	5.
51	89	22	678	487
+ 47	+ 56	+ 72	+ 113	+ 391

Use compatible numbers to estimate each sum.

6.	7.	8.	9.	10.
49	63	354	477	761
+ 52	+ 21	+ 126	+ 226	+ 131

Set D Estimate. Then find each sum
using place value or mental math. (pp. 54–55)

1.	2.	3.	4.	5.
43	38	86	27	53
31	+ 93	64	+ 18	+ 67
+ 22		+ 54		

Set E Estimate. Then find each sum. (pp. 58–59)

1.	2.	3.	4.	5.
367	5,742	890	502	2,670
+ 243	+ 2,961	+ 539	+ 319	+ 6,529

6. Andy's family drove 214 miles on Friday and 329 miles on Saturday. How many miles did they drive in all?

7. Becky sold 1,587 shirts one month and 1,703 shirts the next month. How many shirts did she sell in all?

Set F Find the sum. Tell which method you used. (pp. 64–67)

1.	2.	3.	4.	5.
329	258	965	1,404	4,433
+ 693	+ 640	711	+ 7,294	+ 5,376
		+ 179		

CD ROM **Technology**
Use Harcourt Mega Math, Country Countdown,
Block Busters, Levels M, U, V.

Auto Addition

Get in the Car!
2 players

Start Your Engines!
- 2 two-color counters

START

32 + 14

1

59 + 82

4

28 + 67

3

43 + 91

2

67 + 64

5

48 + 33

6

99 + 87

7

64 + 63

8

85 + 72

29 + 75

9

15 + 18

10

77 + 62

6

94 + 29

5

81 + 90

FINISH

11 + 48

10

7

9

50 + 48

83 + 74

START

54 + 28

1

35 + 71

2

29 + 43

4

46 + 54

3

ROUTE 62

73 + 19

8

Drive to the Picnic!

- Each player selects a different color counter and places it on the matching START color.

- Players follow the highway color that matches the color of their counter.

- Players complete the addition problem to get to the first Stop Sign. Use paper and pencil to solve. Players will check each other's answers.

- If the player's answer to a problem is wrong, the player does not move forward. The player must wait until his or her next turn to try to solve the problem again.

- Players take turns solving addition problems in order to move to the next Stop Sign.

- The first player to reach the picnic wins the game.

iMagic SQUARES

Magic Squares are a fun way to practice finding sums. In a Magic Square, the sums of each column, row, and diagonal are the same.

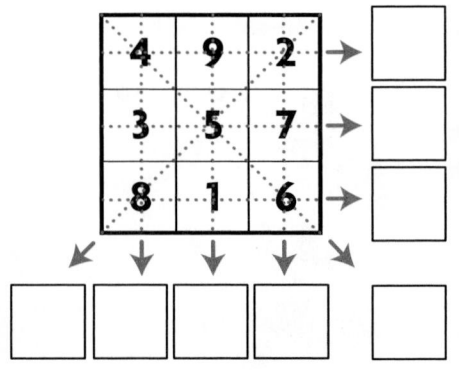

Example

The Magic Square to the right is called the *Lo Shu* Magic Square. To find the answer to this Magic Square, follow these steps.

Step 1 Find the sums of the horizontal rows.

$4 + 9 + 2 = \blacksquare$, $3 + 5 + 7 = \blacksquare$, $8 + 1 + 6 = \blacksquare$

Step 2 Find the sums of the vertical columns.

$4 + 3 + 8 = \blacksquare$, $9 + 5 + 1 = \blacksquare$, $2 + 7 + 6 = \blacksquare$

Step 3 Find the sums of the diagonals.

$4 + 5 + 6 = \blacksquare$, $2 + 5 + 8 = \blacksquare$

So, the answer to the Magic Square is 15.

Try It

1. Copy and complete the Magic Square by using the numbers below. The answer is 18.

| 2 | 3 | 5 | 6 | 9 | 10 |

		7
4		8

2. **WRITE Math** ▶ Work with a partner to find the sum of one row in Benjamin Franklin's Magic Square. **Explain** how you found your answer.

Benjamin Franklin's Magic Square

14	3	62	51	46	35	30	19
52	61	4	13	20	29	36	45
11	6	59	54	43	38	27	22
53	60	5	12	21	28	37	44
55	58	7	10	23	26	39	42
9	8	57	56	41	40	25	24
50	63	2	15	18	31	34	47
16	1	64	49	48	33	32	17

Chapter 3 Review/Test

Check Vocabulary and Concepts

Choose the best term from the box.

VOCABULARY

Associative Property of Addition

Commutative Property of Addition

Identity Property of Addition

1. The ? says that if you add zero to any number, the sum is that number. (p. 48)

2. The ? says that you can add numbers in any order and get the same sum. (p. 48)

Check Skills

Find each sum. Name the property used. (pp. 48–49)

3. $4 + 0 = \blacksquare$
   $0 + 4 = \blacksquare$

4. $8 + (2 + 4) = \blacksquare$
   $(8 + 2) + 4 = \blacksquare$

5. $7 + 6 = \blacksquare$
   $6 + 7 = \blacksquare$

Find the missing addend. (pp. 50–51)

6. $\blacksquare + 8 = 13$

7. $5 + \blacksquare = 9 + 5$

8. $6 + \blacksquare = 12$

9. $\blacksquare + 3 = 12$

Use rounding or compatible numbers to estimate each sum. (pp. 52–53)

10. 57
    $+ 24$

11. 782
    $+ 131$

12. 34
    $+ 59$

13. 542
    $+ 279$

Estimate. Then find each sum. (pp. 54–55, 58–59)

14. 57
    $+ 24$

15. 782
    $+ 119$

16. $4{,}213$
    $+ 1{,}732$

17. $2{,}394$
    $+ 6{,}278$

Check Problem Solving

Solve. (pp. 60–63)

18. There were 150 fans at a soccer game. There were 30 more children than parents. How many children were at the game?

19. Caleb and Mary scored a total of 14 points at the basketball game. Mary scored 6 more points than Caleb. How many points did each player score?

20. **WRITE Math** ▸ **Sense or Nonsense** Three numbers in a row have a sum of 45. Kathy says the numbers are 15, 16, and 17. Does her statement make sense? **Explain.**

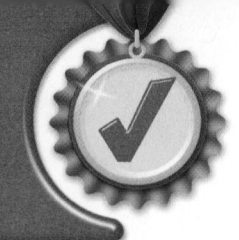

Standardized Test Prep
Chapters 1–3

Number and Operations

1. Which numeral means the same as
500 + 30 + 7? (p. 8)

   A 537

   B 573

   C 5,037

   D 5,307

Test Tip **Eliminate choices.**

See item 2. First, estimate the sum. Then, find the answer choices that are close to your estimate. Finally, add to find the correct answer choice.

2. The school library has 289 science books and 332 animal books. How many science and animal books does the library have altogether?
(p. 58)

   A 511

   B 521

   C 611

   D 621

3. **WRITE Math** ▶ On Sunday there were 643 visitors at the amusement park. Rounded to the nearest hundred, about how many people were at the park? **Explain** how to find the answer using the tens digit. (p. 36)

Algebraic Reasoning

4. Cars have 4 wheels. Greg wants to find out how many wheels are on 5 cars. Use the table below to find the answer. (Grade 2)

number of cars	1	2	3	4	5
number of wheels	4	8	12	16	■

   A 24   **C** 20

   B 22   **D** 18

5. Which are the next two figures in the pattern below? (Grade 2)

□△○□△○□△○ ? ?

   A □△

   B □○

   C ○□

   D △○

6. **WRITE Math** ▶ Brad had 4 toy cars and got 3 more. Pete had 3 toy cars and got 4 more. Who has more toy cars now? **Explain** which addition property helps you to solve the problem. (p. 48)

Measurement

7. Which time is shown on the clock?

(Grade 2)

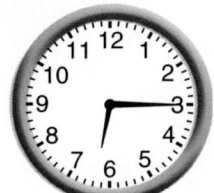

A 3:30

B 6:15

C 6:30

D 7:15

8. Which temperature does the thermometer show? (Grade 2)

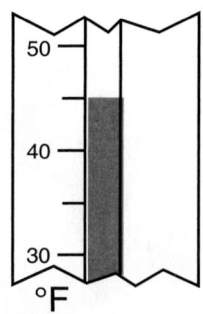

A 50°F

B 45°F

C 40°F

D 35°F

9. ⬛ WRITE Math ▸ Keith ate a snack at three forty. **Explain** where the hands of the clock point at three forty.

(Grade 2)

Data Analysis and Probability

10. Betty has 10 crayons in a bag. There are 1 green, 6 red, 1 yellow, and 2 blue crayons. Which color crayon is Betty more likely to choose? (Grade 2)

A Blue

B Red

C Yellow

D Green

11. Mrs. Totten's class made a tally table to show the number of books they read in each subject. How many science and social studies books did they read altogether? (Grade 2)

Books Read	
Subject	**Number of Books**
Social Studies	||||
Science	JHT |||
Music	||

A 4

B 6

C 11

D 12

12. ⬛ WRITE Math ▸ If Mrs. Totten's class wanted to make a picture graph using the data shown in Problem 11, how many pictures would they use? **Explain.** (Grade 2)

4 Subtraction

Investigate

The elephant is the largest land mammal, but not the fastest. Look at the animal facts listed in the table. Choose two animals and compare them to the elephant. Write about the differences in miles per hour.

Animal Facts

Animal	Height	Speed
Elephant	13 feet	25 mph
Cheetah	3 feet	70 mph
Antelope	6 feet	61 mph
Lion	4 feet	50 mph

GO ONLINE
Technology
Student pages are available in the Student eBook.

**Check your understanding of important skills
needed for success in Chapter 4.**

▶ **Subtract 1-Digit from 2-Digit Numbers**

Subtract.

1. 12 − 8	**2.** 17 − 7	**3.** 15 − 6	**4.** 11 − 0	**5.** 18 − 9

▶ **Model 2-Digit Subtraction**

Use the models. Find the difference.

6. 35 − 12 = ■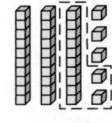

7. 48 − 26 = ■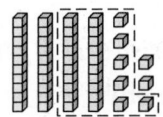

8. 53 − 43 = ■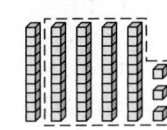

9. 69 − 23 = ■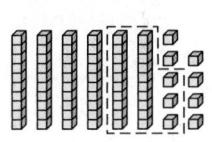

▶ **2-Digit Subtraction Without Regrouping**

Subtract.

10. 76 − 32	**11.** 29 − 13	**12.** 65 − 54	**13.** 92 − 50	**14.** 38 − 18

VOCABULARY POWER

CHAPTER VOCABULARY

fact family
inverse operations

WARM-UP WORDS

fact family A set of related addition and subtraction, or multiplication and division, number sentences

inverse operations Opposite operations, or operations that undo each other, such as addition and subtraction or multiplication and division

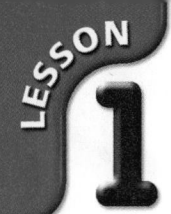

ALGEBRA
Fact Families

OBJECTIVE: Identify and write addition and subtraction fact families.

Quick Review

1. $4 + 5$
2. $12 - 4$
3. $3 + 8$
4. $5 + 6$
5. $13 - 7$

Learn

PROBLEM Rory is baking a cake. She has 12 eggs. She uses 3 eggs to make the cake. How many eggs does Rory have left?

Vocabulary

fact family

inverse operations

You can write a number sentence to solve the problem.

$12 - 3 = 9$ So, Rory has 9 eggs left.

The numbers 3, 9, and 12 can be used to make a fact family. A **fact family** is a group of related number sentences that use the same numbers.

Addition and subtraction are opposite, or **inverse operations**. Fact families are examples of inverse operations.

Fact Family for 3, 9, and 12

$3 + 9 = 12$ $9 + 3 = 12$

$12 - 9 = 3$ $12 - 3 = 9$

If both addends are the same, there are only two facts in the fact family.

Fact Family for 4, 4, and 8

$4 + 4 = 8$ $8 - 4 = 4$

Guided Practice

1. Copy and complete the fact family.

$8 + 5 = 13$ $5 + 8 = \blacksquare$ $13 - 5 = 8$ $13 - 8 = \blacksquare$

Complete.

2. $12 - 6 = 6$, so $6 + 6 = \blacksquare$.   ✓**3.** $4 + 3 = 7$, so $\blacksquare - 3 = 4$.

Write the fact family for each set of numbers.

4. 4, 5, 9   **5.** 5, 9, 14   **6.** 1, 6, 7   ✔**7.** 5, 7, 12

8. [TALK Math] **Explain** why some fact families have four facts and others have only two facts.

Independent Practice and Problem Solving

Complete.

9. $11 - 2 = 9$, so $2 + \blacksquare = 11$.   **10.** $4 + 8 = 12$, so $\blacksquare - 8 = 4$.

11. $6 + 9 = 15$, so $15 - 6 = \blacksquare$.   **12.** $10 - 5 = 5$, so $5 + \blacksquare = 10$.

13. $16 - 5 = 11$, so $\blacksquare + \blacksquare = 16$.   **14.** $7 + 6 = 13$, so $\blacksquare - 7 = \blacksquare$.

Write the fact family for each set of numbers.

15. 2, 8, 10   **16.** 4, 7, 11   **17.** 3, 6, 9   **18.** 7, 7, 14

USE DATA For 19–21, use the picture.

19. Write a number sentence that shows the total number of muffins sold. Then write the fact family for the number sentence.

20. On Tuesday, 3 blueberry muffins and 4 apple muffins were sold. How many more muffins were sold on Monday than on Tuesday?

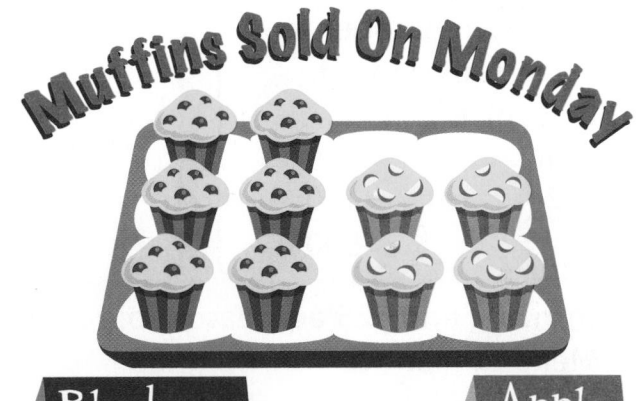

21. Pose a Problem Look back at Problem 20. Write a similar problem by changing the day and the numbers of muffins sold.

22. [WRITE Math] ▸ Draw and label four pictures to show the fact family for 2, 4, and 6. **Explain** how you used inverse operations to find the facts.

Mixed Review and Test Prep

23. The school store has 325 black pens and 115 blue pens. How many pens are there altogether? (p. 58)

24. What is the name of a figure with 6 sides? (Grade 2)

25. Test Prep Which number sentence is in the same fact family as $3 + 4 = 7$?

A $3 + 5 = 8$ **C** $4 + 7 = 11$

B $7 + 3 = 10$ **D** $4 + 3 = 7$

Extra Practice on page 98, Set A

Estimate Differences

OBJECTIVE: Estimate differences of 2- and 3-digit numbers by using rounding and compatible numbers.

Quick Review

Round each number to the greatest place value.

1. 24   **2.** 65
3. 391   **4.** 847
5. 588

Learn

PROBLEM The largest Mekong giant catfish caught by fishers weighed 646 pounds. The largest blue catfish caught weighed 124 pounds. About how much more did the Mekong giant catfish weigh than the blue catfish?

To find *about* how much more, you can estimate.

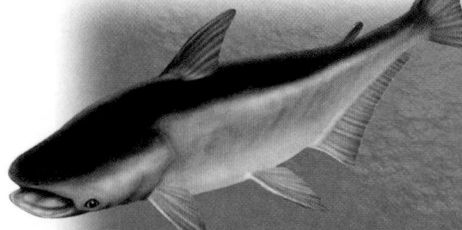

▲ The Mekong giant catfish is the largest known freshwater fish and is an endangered species.

Example Estimate. 646 − 124

ONE WAY Use rounding.

Round each number to the nearest hundred. Then subtract.

$$\begin{array}{rcr} 646 & \rightarrow & 600 \\ -124 & \rightarrow & -100 \\ \hline & & 500 \end{array}$$

ANOTHER WAY Use compatible numbers.

$$\begin{array}{rcr} 646 & \rightarrow & 650 \\ -124 & \rightarrow & -125 \\ \hline & & 525 \end{array}$$

Remember

Compatible numbers are numbers that are easy to compute mentally.

So, both 500 and 525 are reasonable estimates of how much more the Mekong giant catfish weighed.

• Why are 650 and 125 compatible numbers?

More Examples

A Use compatible numbers.

$$\begin{array}{rcr} 73 & \rightarrow & 75 \\ -22 & \rightarrow & -25 \\ \hline & & 50 \end{array}$$

B Use compatible numbers.

$$\begin{array}{rcr} 476 & \rightarrow & 475 \\ -248 & \rightarrow & -250 \\ \hline & & 225 \end{array}$$

C Use rounding.

$$\begin{array}{rcr} 87 & \rightarrow & 90 \\ -19 & \rightarrow & -20 \\ \hline & & 70 \end{array}$$

Guided Practice

1. Copy the problem at the right. Round both 319 and 133 to the nearest hundred. Then estimate their difference.

$$\begin{array}{r} 319 \\ -133 \end{array}$$

Use rounding or compatible numbers to estimate each difference.

2.	3.	4.	✓5.	✓6.
52	94	691	736	487
− 24	− 56	− 137	− 327	− 248

7. **TALK Math** **Explain** ways you could estimate 567 − 209.

Independent Practice and Problem Solving

Use rounding or compatible numbers to estimate each difference.

8.	9.	10.	11.	12.
88	65	98	378	42
− 41	− 19	− 67	− 312	− 19

13.	14.	15.	16.	17.
774	936	415	587	86
− 349	− 421	− 187	− 208	− 24

18.	19.	20.	21.	22.
694	94	798	561	63
− 593	− 42	− 726	− 349	− 37

Algebra Estimate to compare. Write <, >, or = for each ●.

23. 456 − 162 ● 200   24. 798 − 726 ● 10   25. 542 − 331 ● 300

USE DATA For 26–27, use the table.

26. About how much more is the total weight of the Pacific halibut and conger than the weight of the yellowfin tuna?

27. **WRITE Math** About how much more did the yellowfin tuna weigh than the conger? **Explain** how you know.

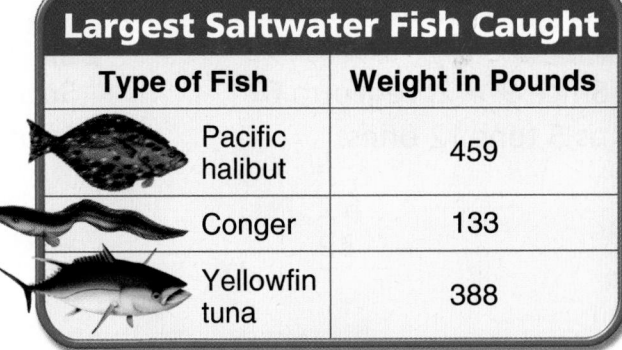

Largest Saltwater Fish Caught

Type of Fish	Weight in Pounds
Pacific halibut	459
Conger	133
Yellowfin tuna	388

Mixed Review and Test Prep

28. Use the Associative Property to complete the number sentence. (p. 48)

$$3 + (2 + 5) = (\blacksquare + \blacksquare) + 5$$

29. Which color marble is more likely to be pulled from the bag? (Grade 2)

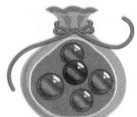

30. **Test Prep** Fred estimated 591 − 128. He rounded each number to the nearest hundred. Then he subtracted. What was Fred's estimate?

A 400   C 600

B 500   D 700

Extra Practice on page 98, Set B

Subtract 2-Digit Numbers

OBJECTIVE: Subtract 2-digit numbers with and without regrouping.

Learn

PROBLEM Ken saw a grizzly bear that was 39 inches tall. He saw a polar bear that was 62 inches tall. How much taller was the polar bear than the grizzly bear?

Example 1 Subtract. 62 − 39   **Estimate.** 60 − 40 = 20

ONE WAY Use mental math.

Step 1	Step 2	Step 3
Add to the lesser number to make a ten.	Add the same number to the greater number.	Subtract your answers.
62 − 39 → 40	62 → 63 − 39 → 40	62 → 63 − 39 → − 40 23
Think: 39 + 1 = 40	Think: 62 + 1 = 63	

▲ When standing on all four legs, a polar bear can be up to 64 inches tall.

ANOTHER WAY Use place value.

Step 1	Step 2
Since 9 > 2, regroup 62 as 5 tens 12 ones. 5 12 6 2 − 3 9	Subtract the ones. Subtract the tens. 5 12 6 2 23 Add to − 3 9 + 39 check. 2 3 62

Math Idea
Adding the same amount to both numbers does not change the difference.

So, the polar bear was 23 inches taller than the grizzly bear.

Since 23 is close to the estimate of 20, the answer is reasonable.

Example 2 Subtract. 43 − 16

Use mental math.	Use place value.

Think: 16 + 4 = 20
 43 + 4 = 47   43 → 47
             − 16 → − 20
                  27
	Regroup 43 as 3 13
	 3 tens 13 ones. 4 3
	 Subtract the ones. − 1 6
	 Subtract the tens. 2 7

1. To find 31 − 17 by using mental math, what number should you add to both 17 and 31?

Estimate. Then find each difference.

2. 94	3. 58	4. 87	✓5. 72	✓6. 79
− 15	− 29	− 54	− 24	− 36

7. **TALK Math** Explain how to use place value to find 93 − 68.

Independent Practice and Problem Solving

Estimate. Then find each difference.

8. 61	9. 46	10. 77	11. 51	12. 45
− 48	− 23	− 19	− 34	− 27

Find each difference. Use addition to check.

13. 55 − 31 = ■   **14.** 86 − 28 = ■   **15.** 68 − 14 = ■   **16.** 93 − 76 = ■

USE DATA For 17–18, use the graph.

17. A brown bear grew 6 inches more than the average height. An American black bear grew 3 inches more than the average height. What is the difference between their heights?

18. **WRITE Math** Explain how you can use mental math to find how much taller the polar bear is than the brown bear.

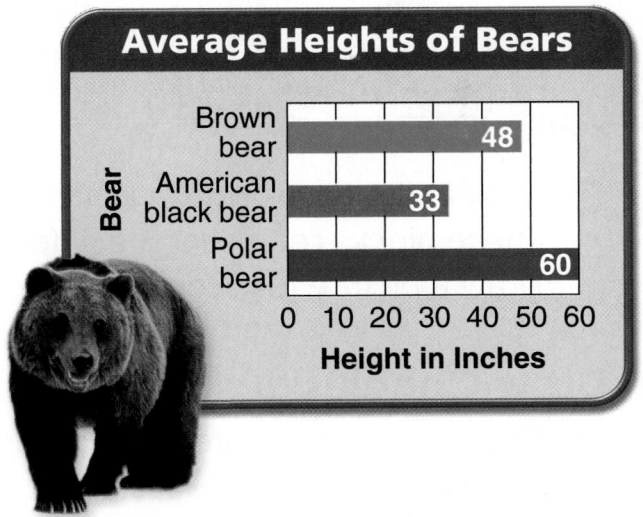

Average Heights of Bears

Mixed Review and Test Prep

19. What is 5,399 rounded to the nearest thousand? (p. 38)

20. There are 324 girls and 271 boys at school. About how many students are at school? (p. 52)

21. **Test Prep** Craig sold 54 shirts to raise money for the swim team. He has delivered 17 of them. How many shirts does he have left to deliver?

   A 17   **B** 37   **C** 47   **D** 71

Extra Practice on page 98, Set C

4 Model 3-Digit Subtraction

OBJECTIVE: Explore subtracting 3-digit numbers with and without regrouping.

Quick Review

Write the numbers in expanded form.

1. 656 2. 703
3. 182 4. 599
5. 250

Investigate

Materials ■ base-ten blocks

You can use base-ten blocks to subtract numbers.

A Model the number 345.

B Use your model to find 345 − 158. Subtract the ones, tens, and hundreds. Regroup the blocks when needed.

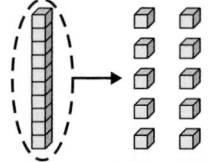

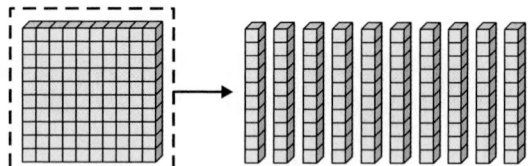

C Look at the base-ten blocks that are left. These blocks represent the difference. Draw a picture to record your answer.

Draw Conclusions

1. **Explain** why there are 3 hundreds, 3 tens, and 15 ones in Picture B.

2. How did you know you had to regroup one of the hundreds?

3. **Synthesis** How could you use base-ten blocks and addition to check your answer?

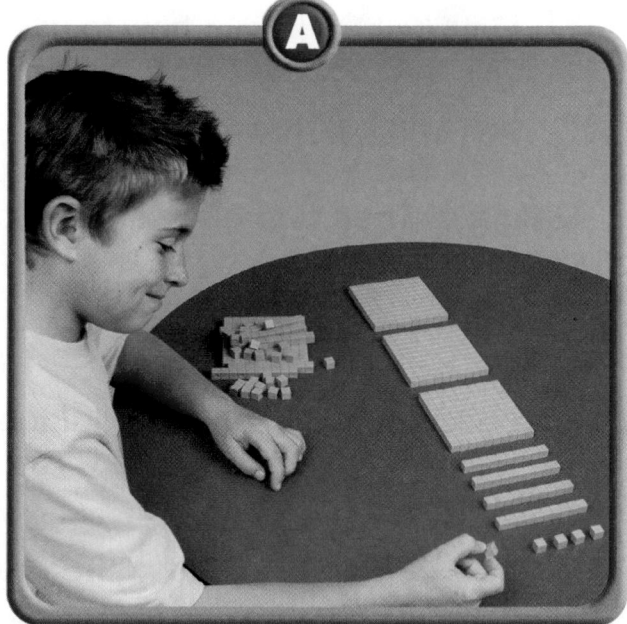

A

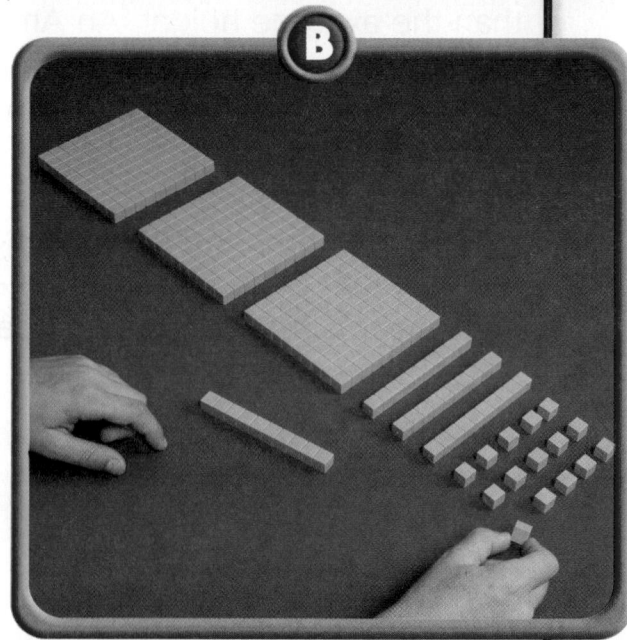

B

You can record your steps with paper and pencil.

Example Subtract. 221 − 146

Step 1	Step 2	Step 3
Subtract the ones. Since 6 > 1, regroup. 2 tens 1 one = 1 ten 11 ones	Subtract the tens. Since 4 > 1, regroup. 2 hundreds 1 ten = 1 hundred 11 tens	Subtract the hundreds.

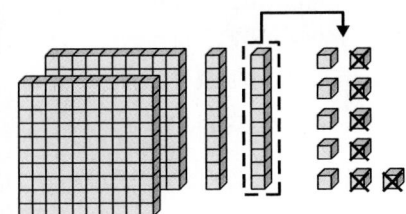

$$\begin{array}{r} {\scriptstyle 1\ \ 11} \\ 2\ 2\ \cancel{1} \\ -1\ 4\ 6 \\ \hline 5 \end{array}$$

$$\begin{array}{r} {\scriptstyle 11} \\ {\scriptstyle 1\ \cancel{2}\ 11} \\ 2\ \cancel{2}\ \cancel{1} \\ -1\ 4\ 6 \\ \hline 7\ 5 \end{array}$$

$$\begin{array}{r} {\scriptstyle 11} \\ {\scriptstyle 1\ \cancel{2}\ 11} \\ \cancel{2}\ \cancel{2}\ \cancel{1} \\ -1\ 4\ 6 \\ \hline 7\ 5 \end{array}$$

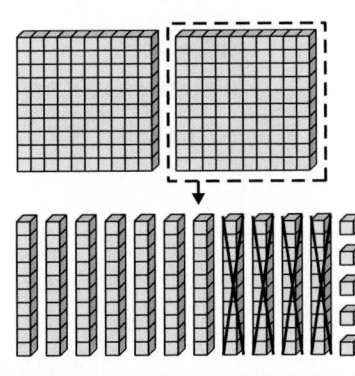

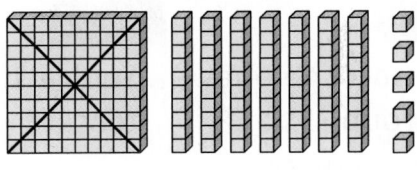

TALK Math

Explain how to find 462 − 299.

So, 221 − 146 = 75.

Practice

Use base-ten blocks to find each difference.

1. 299 − 186 = ■   **2.** 309 − 281 = ■   ✓**3.** 443 − 267 = ■

Find each difference.

4. 435
− 319

5. 585
− 124

6. 458
− 283

7. 796
− 435

✓**8.** 851
− 615

9. 909
− 350

10. 374
− 126

11. 614
− 327

12. 451
− 286

13. 640
− 337

14. **WRITE Math** **Explain** how modeling with base-ten blocks helps you see when you need to regroup for subtraction.

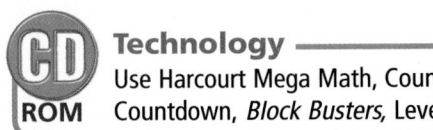

Technology
Use Harcourt Mega Math, Country Countdown, *Block Busters*, Levels X, Y.

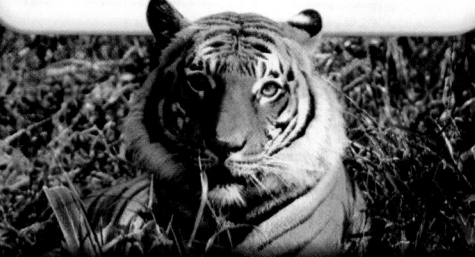
▲ Indo-Chinese tigers live in the tropical forests of seven different countries.

LESSON 5

Subtract Greater Numbers

OBJECTIVE: Subtract 3- and 4-digit numbers with and without regrouping.

Learn

PROBLEM Lena is researching endangered tigers. There are 1,785 Indo-Chinese tigers and 426 Siberian tigers in the wild. How many more Indo-Chinese tigers are in the wild than Siberian tigers?

Example Subtract. 1,785 − 426

Estimate. 1,800 − 400 = 1,400

Step 1	Step 2	Step 3	Step 4
Subtract the ones. Regroup. 8 tens 5 ones = 7 tens 15 ones	Subtract the tens.	Subtract the hundreds.	Subtract the thousands.
7 15 1,785 − 426 ——— 9	7 15 1,785 − 426 ——— 59	7 15 1,785 − 426 ——— 359	7 15 1,785 − 426 ——— 1,359

So, there are 1,359 more Indo-Chinese tigers in the wild than Siberian tigers. Since 1,359 is close to the estimate of 1,400, the answer is reasonable.

More Examples

A Regrouping

```
  4 14
  5̶4̶8
−383
————
 165
```

B No Regrouping

```
 6,896
−1,524
——————
 5,372
```

C Regrouping

```
      12
    8 2̶ 15
 4,9̶3̶5̶
−2,277
——————
 2,658
```

Guided Practice

1. Copy the problem at the right. Do you have to regroup? Find the difference.

```
  562
−295
```

Estimate. Then find each difference.

| 2. | 654
− 544 | 3. | 425
− 248 | 4. | 5,867
− 2,998 | ✓ 5. | 7,404
− 781 | ✓ 6. | 8,153
− 4,322 |

7. ⬛TALK Math⬛ **Explain** how to find the difference between 3,695 and 1,486.

Independent Practice and Problem Solving

Estimate. Then find each difference.

| 8. | 518
− 305 | 9. | 304
− 124 | 10. | 671
− 268 | 11. | 948
− 659 | 12. | 1,632
− 546 |

| 13. | 2,519
− 1,400 | 14. | 6,187
− 2,275 | 15. | 4,710
− 2,547 | 16. | 9,346
− 4,419 | 17. | 659
− 424 |

⭐**Algebra** Compare. Write <, >, or = for each ●.

18. $732 − 284$ ● $824 − 392$ 19. $5,476 − 2,132$ ● $8,288 − 4,502$

20. $481 − 256$ ● $629 − 404$ 21. $9,109 − 8,387$ ● $3,637 − 2,543$

USE DATA For 22–24, use the table.

22. What is the difference between the number of Bengal tigers and the number of Indo-Chinese tigers?

23. What if the number of each type of tiger increased by 150? How many tigers would there be in all?

24. ⬛WRITE Math⬛ **Explain** how you would find how many more Bengal tigers there are than Siberian tigers.

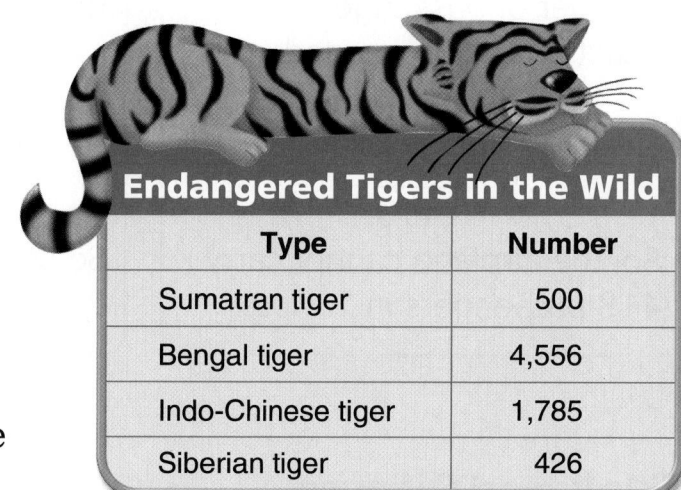

Endangered Tigers in the Wild

Type	Number
Sumatran tiger	500
Bengal tiger	4,556
Indo-Chinese tiger	1,785
Siberian tiger	426

Mixed Review and Test Prep

25. Find the missing addend. (p. 50)

$$23 + ■ = 41$$

26. A bookmobile has 327 books. Amy ordered 156 more books. How many books will there be in all? (p. 58)

27. **Test Prep** What is the difference between 2,345 and 1,695?

   A 1,650   **C** 750

   B 1,350   **D** 650

⬛Extra Practice⬛ on page 98, Set D

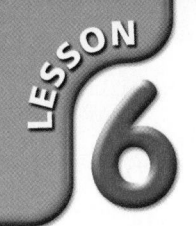
Problem Solving Workshop
Skill: Estimate or Exact Answer

OBJECTIVE: Solve problems by using the skill *estimate or exact answer.*

Use the Skill

PROBLEM A Boeing 757 airplane that can carry 208 passengers flies from Dallas to St. Louis several times each day. The 547-mile trip takes 95 minutes.

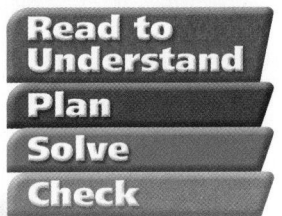

Sometimes, you need an exact answer to solve a problem. Sometimes, an estimate is all you need.

Examples

A Can the airplane carry 418 passengers in 2 trips?

Since the question asks if the airplane can carry an exact number of passengers, an exact answer is needed.

$$
\begin{array}{r}
208 \\
+\,208 \\
\hline
416
\end{array}
$$

So, the airplane cannot carry 418 passengers in 2 trips.

B About how many minutes will 2 trips take?

Since the question asks *about* how many, you can estimate to solve.

$$
\begin{array}{rcl}
95 & \rightarrow & 100 \\
+\,95 & \rightarrow & +\,100 \\
\hline
& & 200
\end{array}
$$

So, 2 trips will take about 200 minutes.

Think and Discuss

Tell whether you need an exact answer or an estimate. Then solve.

a. A Boeing 747 has 416 seats. A Boeing 767 has 245 seats. What is the greatest number of passengers the two airplanes can carry altogether?

b. Wendy and her family flew on a Boeing 727 last week. They flew 422 miles to Tulsa, Oklahoma, from Jackson, Mississippi. About how many miles is a round trip?

1. Woodfield Mall is the largest mall in Illinois. It has 294 stores. The nation's largest mall is the Mall of America in Minnesota. It has 520 stores. About how many more stores does the Mall of America have than Woodfield Mall?

   Do you need an estimate or an exact answer? To find out, see if the problem is asking for about how many or an exact answer.

2. **What if** the Mall of America had 568 stores? About how many more stores would the Mall of America have than Woodfield Mall?

3. A Boeing 777 that can carry 368 passengers is traveling from Dallas to Chicago. A one-way trip is 803 miles. Can the airplane carry 1,080 people in 3 one-way trips? Explain.

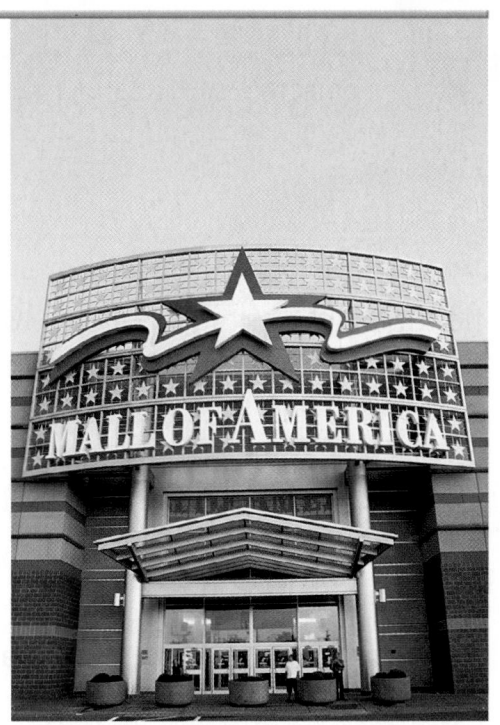

Mixed Applications

4. Randy wrote a 2-page story for a contest. His story must be 1,250 words or less. Randy's first page has 572 words. How many words can his second page have?

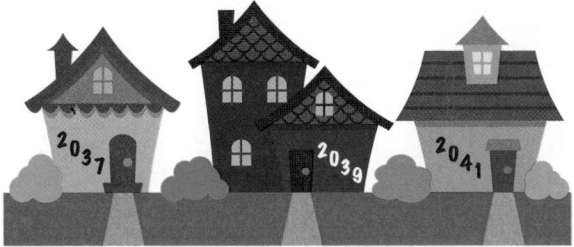

5. The Sunnyville Tree Nursery has 782 oak trees. The Lakeview Tree Nursery has 319 oak trees. About how many fewer oak trees does The Lakeview Tree Nursery have than The Sunnyville Tree Nursery?

6. **Reasoning** The picture shows three houses on Main Street. Hank, Derek, and Jill live in the houses. Derek does not live next to Jill. The sum of the digits in Jill's house number is 12. Who lives at 2041 Main Street? **Explain** your answer.

7. Joel read 10 pages of his book on Monday, 15 pages on Tuesday, and 20 pages on Wednesday. If the pattern continues, how many pages will he read on Friday?

8. **WRITE Math** For social studies, each student wrote about a year in history. Katie picked 1812. Josh's year was 96 years later. What year did Josh pick? **Explain** how you know.

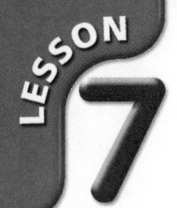

Subtract Across Zeros

OBJECTIVE: Subtract 3- and 4-digit numbers across zeros.

Quick Review
1. $700 - 200$
2. $516 - 300$
3. $324 - 102$
4. $479 - 281$
5. $815 - 347$

Learn

PROBLEM Colin is playing arcade games to win tickets. He wants to collect 300 tickets to exchange for a coloring book. He already has 184 tickets. How many more tickets does Colin need?

Example 1 **Subtract.** $300 - 184$ **Estimate.** $300 - 200 = 100$

MODEL	THINK	RECORD
Step 1	Look at the ones. Since $4 > 0$, regroup tens. There are 0 tens, so regroup hundreds. 3 hundreds 0 tens = 2 hundreds 10 tens	$\begin{array}{r} \overset{2\ 10}{\cancel{3}00} \\ -184 \end{array}$
Step 2	Now you can regroup tens. 10 tens 0 ones = 9 tens 10 ones	$\begin{array}{r} \overset{9}{\overset{2\ 10\ 10}{\cancel{3}\cancel{0}0}} \\ -184 \end{array}$
Step 3	Subtract the ones. Subtract the tens. Subtract the hundreds.	$\begin{array}{r} \overset{9}{\overset{2\ 10\ 10}{\cancel{3}\cancel{0}0}} \\ -184 \\ \hline 116 \end{array}$

So, Colin needs to collect 116 more tickets. Since 116 is close to the estimate of 100, the answer is reasonable.

• Explain why you need to regroup twice to find $300 - 184$.

Example 2

Anita and Jim need 2,000 tickets to get a board game.
They have 1,273 tickets. How many more tickets do they need?

Subtract. 2,000 − 1,273   **Estimate.** 2,000 − 1,300 = 700

Step 1	**Step 2**	**Step 3**	**Step 4**
Since 3 > 0, regroup tens. There are no tens or hundreds, so regroup thousands. 2 thousands 0 hundreds = 1 thousand 10 hundreds	Regroup hundreds. 10 hundreds 0 tens = 9 hundreds 10 tens	Regroup tens. 10 tens 0 ones = 9 tens 10 ones	Subtract the ones. Subtract the tens. Subtract the hundreds. Subtract the thousands.
1 10 2̸,0̸ 00 − 1,273	9 1 10 10 2̸,0̸ 0̸ 0 − 1,273	9 9 1 10 10 10 2̸,0̸ 0̸ 0̸ − 1,273	9 9 1 10 10 10 2̸,0̸ 0̸ 0̸ − 1,2 7 3 <u></u> 7 2 7

So, Anita and Jim need 727 more tickets. Since 727 is close to
the estimate of 700, the answer is reasonable.

More Examples

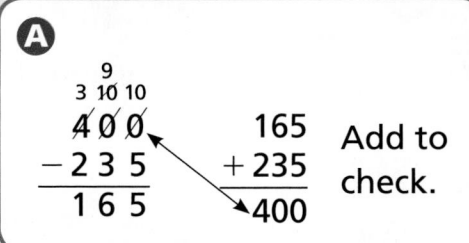

A
9
3 10 10
4̸ 0̸ 0̸
− 2 3 5
<u></u>
1 6 5

165
+ 235
<u></u>
400

Add to check.

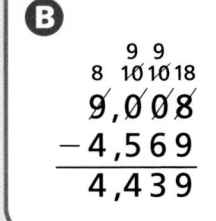

B
9 9
8 10 10 18
9,0̸ 0̸ 8̸
− 4,5 6 9
<u></u>
4,4 3 9

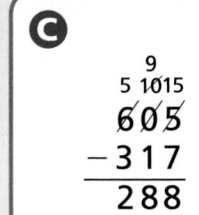

C
9
5 10 15
6̸ 0̸ 5̸
− 3 1 7
<u></u>
2 8 8

ERROR ALERT

Don't forget to regroup the tens after regrouping the hundreds.

Guided Practice

1. Look at the model for 203. What do you need to do to find 203 − 174?

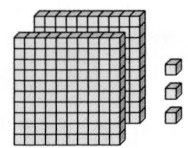

Estimate. Then find each difference.

2. 506 − 457	**3.** 700 − 374	**4.** 3,070 − 1,832	✓**5.** 5,004 − 1,286	✓**6.** 6,500 − 2,144

7. [TALK Math] **Explain** how to find 900 − 658.

Estimate. Then find each difference.

8.	9.	10.	11.	12.
402 − 165	758 − 442	600 − 227	4,400 − 3,215	8,000 − 2,480

13.	14.	15.	16.	17.
5,075 − 2,012	201 − 173	3,711 − 3,520	900 − 677	6,070 − 1,463

Find each difference. Use addition to check.

18. $805 − 346 = $ ■   **19.** $4,002 − 2,105 = $ ■   **20.** $7,000 − 2,259 = $ ■

⭐**Algebra** Copy and complete each table.

Subtract 436.	
21. 957	■
22. 708	■
23. 500	■

Subtract 3,045.	
24. 5,179	■
25. 4,000	■
26. 8,450	■

Subtract 1,823.	
27. 3,902	■
28. 6,456	■
29. 2,000	■

USE DATA For 30–31, use the picture.

30. How many more tickets are needed for a backpack than for a puzzle?

31. Sheila has 100 tickets. Tim gives her 54 tickets. How many more tickets does Sheila need to get a hat?

32. ▐WRITE Math▌ ▸ **What's the Error?** Oscar wrote this subtraction problem. **Explain** his error. Find the correct difference.

$$\begin{array}{r} \overset{9}{\cancel{8}}\overset{10}{\cancel{0}}\overset{10}{\cancel{0}} \\ -\ 5\ 7\ 9 \\ \hline 3\ 2\ 1 \end{array}$$

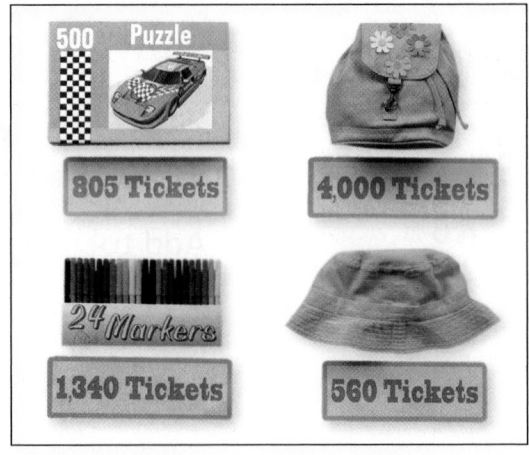

500 Puzzle

805 Tickets

4,000 Tickets

24 Markers

1,340 Tickets

560 Tickets

Mixed Review and Test Prep

33. Kelly had 435 trading cards. She gave away 118 cards. How many cards does she have left? (p. 84)

34. How many vertices does a hexagon have? (Grade 2)

35. **Test Prep** Which number will make the number sentence true?

$$5,002 − 3,416 = ■$$

A 2,696   **C** 1,696

B 2,414   **D** 1,586

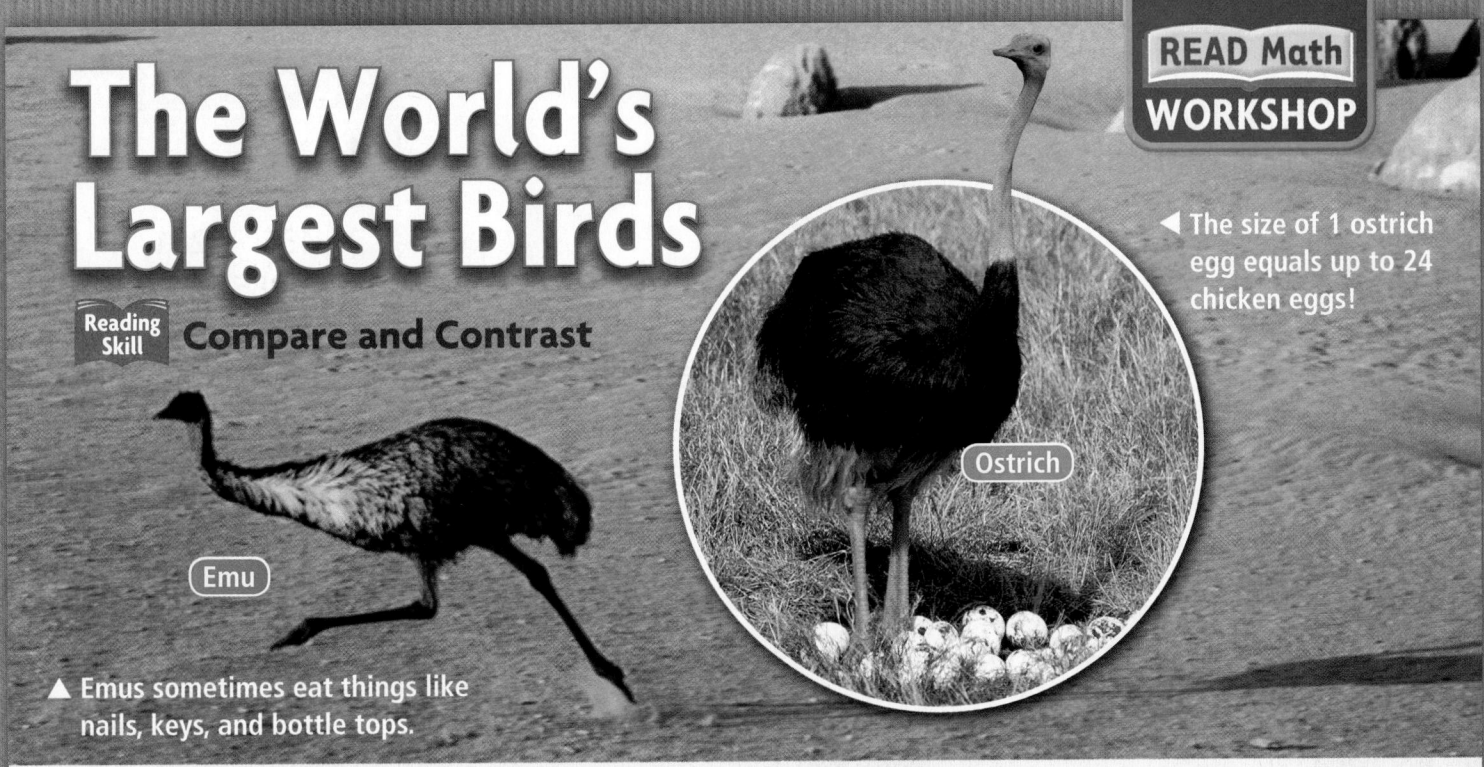

The World's Largest Birds

Reading Skill Compare and Contrast

◄ The size of 1 ostrich egg equals up to 24 chicken eggs!

Ostrich

Emu

▲ Emus sometimes eat things like nails, keys, and bottle tops.

Emus live in Australia and weigh about 120 pounds. They can grow to be about 6 feet tall and can run as fast as 40 miles per hour.

Ostriches live in Africa and weigh about 300 pounds. They can grow to be about 9 feet tall and can run as fast as 40 miles per hour.

When you compare things, you decide how they are alike. When you contrast things, you decide how they are different. Use the table to compare and contrast the birds. How are they different?

	Emus	Ostriches
Where do they live?	Australia	Africa
How much do they weigh?	120 pounds	300 pounds
How tall are they?	6 feet tall	9 feet tall
How fast can they run?	40 miles per hour	40 miles per hour

Problem Solving Compare and contrast to solve.

1. Solve the problem above by using the table to tell how the birds are different.

2. Ostriches have 2 toes on each foot. They protect themselves by kicking with their toes. Emus have 3 toes on each foot. They use them for protection. How are the birds alike?

8 Choose a Method

OBJECTIVE: Choose paper and pencil, a calculator, or mental math to subtract 3- and 4-digit numbers.

Learn

PROBLEM For her science project, Ella compared the weights of different animals that she saw at the zoo. How much more does the rhinoceros weigh than the walrus?

Example 1 Use paper and pencil.

Subtract. $4,750 - 2,840 = \blacksquare$ **Estimate.** $5,000 - 3,000 = 2,000$

The problem involves one regrouping. So, using paper and pencil is a good choice.

Step 1		Step 2	
Subtract the ones. $0 - 0 = 0$	$\begin{array}{r} 4,750 \\ -\,2,840 \\ \hline 0 \end{array}$	Subtract the tens. $5 - 4 = 1$	$\begin{array}{r} 4,750 \\ -\,2,840 \\ \hline 10 \end{array}$

Step 3		Step 4	
Subtract the hundreds. Since $8 > 7$, regroup. $17 - 8 = 9$	$\begin{array}{r} {\scriptstyle 3\ \ 17} \\ 4,\!\cancel{7}50 \\ -\,2,\!840 \\ \hline 9\,10 \end{array}$	Subtract the thousands. $3 - 2 = 1$	$\begin{array}{r} {\scriptstyle 3\ \ 17} \\ 4,\!\cancel{7}50 \\ -\,2,\!840 \\ \hline 1,\!9\,10 \end{array}$

So, the rhinoceros weighs 1,910 pounds more than the walrus. Since 1,910 is close to the estimate of 2,000, the answer is reasonable.

Example 2 Use a calculator.

How much more does the elephant weigh than the giraffe? $9,000 - 2,765 = \blacksquare$

The problem involves subtracting across zeros. So, using a calculator is a good choice.

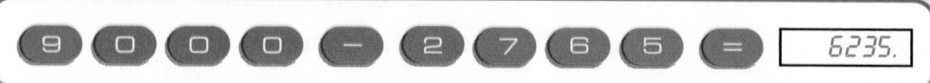

So, the elephant weighs 6,235 pounds more than the giraffe.

• How can you use addition to check your answer?

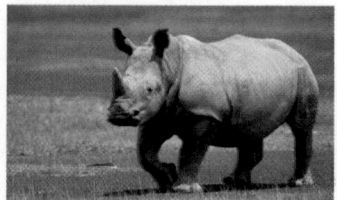

White rhinoceros weight: 4,750 pounds

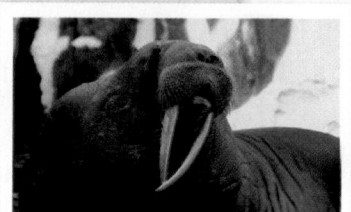

Walrus weight: 2,840 pounds

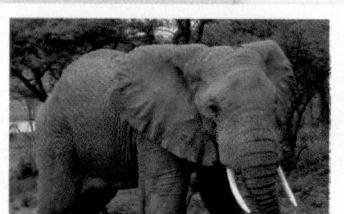

Elephant weight: 9,000 pounds

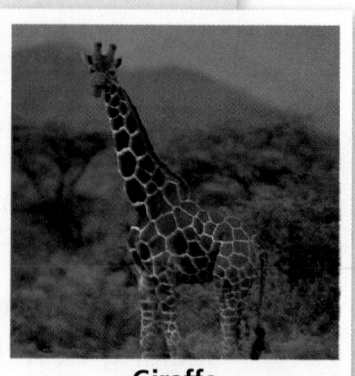

Giraffe weight: 2,765 pounds

Example 3 Use mental math.

A giraffe can be 218 inches tall.
An ostrich can be 108 inches tall.
How much taller is the giraffe than the ostrich?

$$218 - 108 = \blacksquare$$

There is no regrouping. So, using
mental math is a good choice.

Think:	Subtract the hundreds.	$200 - 100 = 100$
	Subtract the tens.	$10 - 0 = 10$
	Subtract the ones.	$8 - 8 = \underline{0}$
		110

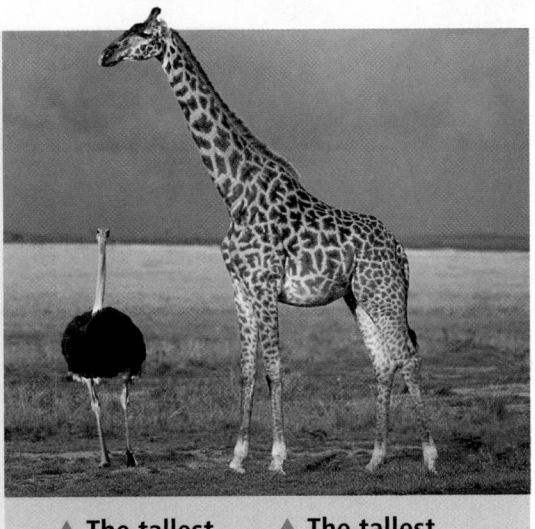

▲ The tallest bird is the ostrich. ▲ The tallest mammal is the giraffe.

So, the giraffe is 110 inches taller than the ostrich.

More Examples

A Use paper and pencil.

$$\begin{array}{r} \overset{7\ 12}{78\cancel{2}} \\ -457 \\ \hline 325 \end{array}$$

B Use mental math.

$$\begin{array}{r} 871 \\ -430 \\ \hline 441 \end{array}$$

C Use a calculator.

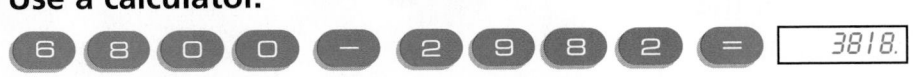

6 8 0 0 − 2 9 8 2 = | 3818. |

Guided Practice

1. Find $561 - 120$ by using mental math.
   Use the number sentences to help you.

   $$\begin{array}{r} 561 \\ -120 \end{array}$$

   $500 - 100 = \blacksquare$
   $60 - 20 = \blacksquare$
   $1 - 0 = \blacksquare$

Find the difference. Tell which method you used.

2. $\begin{array}{r} 748 \\ -205 \end{array}$

3. $\begin{array}{r} 8,165 \\ -4,823 \end{array}$

4. $\begin{array}{r} 9,120 \\ -3,576 \end{array}$

5. $\begin{array}{r} 400 \\ -267 \end{array}$

✓ 6. $\begin{array}{r} 1,790 \\ -1,218 \end{array}$

7. $357 - 189 = \blacksquare$

8. $6,051 - 4,370 = \blacksquare$

✓ 9. $895 - 722 = \blacksquare$

10. **TALK Math** Explain what method you would use to
    subtract 1,612 from 5,294. Then find the difference.

Find the difference. Tell which method you used.

| 11. | 6,000
− 2,781 | 12. | 428
− 311 | 13. | 7,194
− 3,720 | 14. | 317
− 105 | 15. | 520
− 419 |

| 16. | 570
− 269 | 17. | 8,952
− 4,743 | 18. | 9,543
− 6,221 | 19. | 650
− 376 | 20. | 4,737
− 3,259 |

| 21. | 904
− 418 | 22. | 3,983
− 1,720 | 23. | 1,324
− 193 | 24. | 6,241
− 5,719 | 25. | 875
− 233 |

26. $900 - 500 = \blacksquare$

27. $2,214 - 1,702 = \blacksquare$

28. $8,522 - 2,789 = \blacksquare$

29. $5,415 - 3,002 = \blacksquare$

30. $736 - 228 = \blacksquare$

31. $400 - 162 = \blacksquare$

Algebra Find the missing number.

32. $683 - \blacksquare = 331$

33. $\blacksquare - 165 = 164$

34. $397 - \blacksquare = 255$

35. $\blacksquare - 1,379 = 2,463$

36. $5,721 - \blacksquare = 3,575$

37. $\blacksquare - 4,784 = 1,601$

USE DATA For 38–40, use the table.

38. How many more animals live at the National Zoo than at the Miami Metrozoo?

39. Reasoning If 1,786 of the animals at the San Diego Zoo are male, how many of the animals are female?

40. How many fewer animals live at the Minnesota Zoo than at the Miami Metrozoo and the San Diego Zoo?

41. WRITE Math ▸ **What's the Question?** There are 359 fish in a large fish tank at a zoo. A zookeeper adds more fish to the tank for a total of 524 fish. The answer is 165 fish.

42. ☰**FAST FACT** The heaviest African lion in the wild weighed 690 pounds. The heaviest African lion at a zoo weighed 826 pounds. What is the difference in their weights?

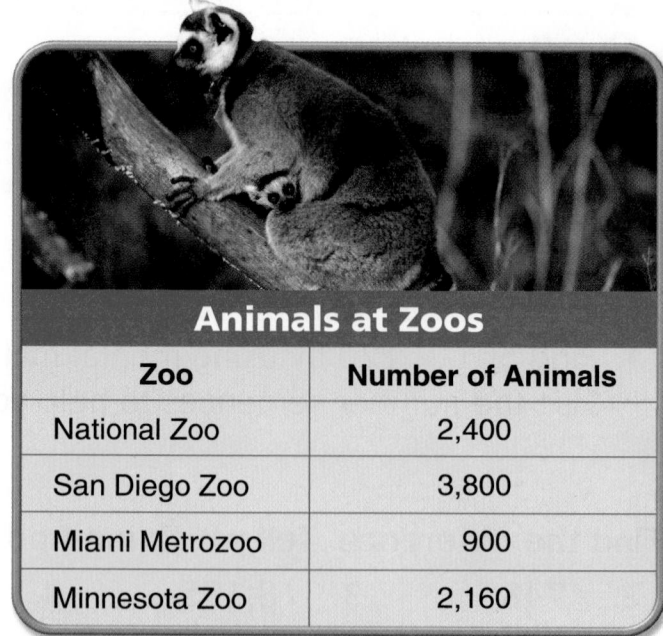

Animals at Zoos

Zoo	Number of Animals
National Zoo	2,400
San Diego Zoo	3,800
Miami Metrozoo	900
Minnesota Zoo	2,160

Learn About

MENTAL MATH
Subtract Across Zeros

Using mental math can make subtracting across zeros easy.

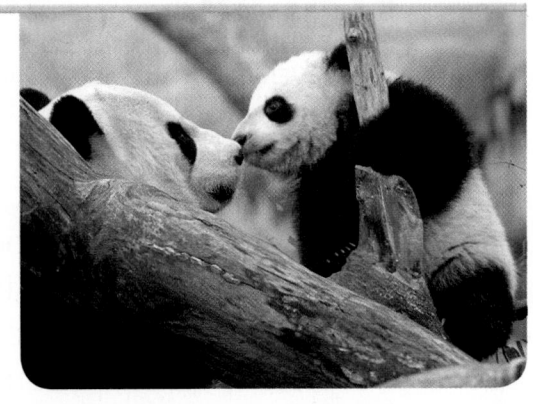

Example

Sharon went to 4 different zoos in June. She saw 300 animals in all. Of the animals, 138 were babies. How many animals were not babies?

Subtract. 300 − 138

You can use addition. To find 300 − 138 = ■, think: 138 + ■ = 300. Count on from 138 to make 300.

Step 1	Step 2	Step 3
Add to make a ten.	Add to make a hundred.	Add to make 300.
Think: 138 + 2 = 140	Think: 140 + 60 = 200	Think: 200 + 100 = 300

Now add the numbers to find 300 − 138. 2 + 60 + 100 = 162

So, 162 animals were not babies.

Try It

Use mental math to subtract.

43. 500 − 265   **44.** 800 − 311   **45.** 400 − 23   **46.** 700 − 541

47. 600 − 417   **48.** 800 − 348   **49.** 500 − 276   **50.** 300 − 79

Mixed Review and Test Prep

51. Kay spun the pointer. Which color is the pointer less likely to land on? (Grade 2)

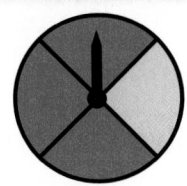

52. Test Prep An elephant is 136 inches tall. A giraffe is 212 inches tall. What is the difference in their heights?

  A 348 inches   **C** 124 inches

  B 176 inches   **D** 76 inches

53. On Friday, 1,689 adults and 2,784 children visited the zoo. How many people visited the zoo in all? (p. 58)

54. Test Prep A white rhinoceros weighs 4,505 pounds, and a giraffe weighs 2,680 pounds. How much more does the white rhinoceros weigh?

  A 1,825 pounds   **C** 2,185 pounds

  B 1,925 pounds   **D** 2,825 pounds

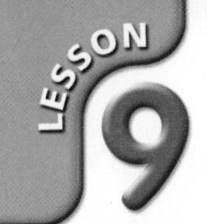

LESSON 9

Problem Solving Workshop
Skill: Choose the Operation

OBJECTIVE: Solve problems by using the skill *choose the operation.*

Read to Understand

Plan

Solve

Check

Use the Skill

PROBLEM Ms. Wells counted books in the school library. She counted 123 animal books in one section. She counted 305 sports books in another section. How many more sports books did Ms. Wells count than animal books?

This chart will help you decide which operation you can use to solve the problem.

Add	Join groups to find how many in all, or the total.
Subtract	Take away, or compare, to find how many more, how many fewer, or how many are left.

Since the question asks you to find how many more sports books Ms. Wells counted than animal books, you can subtract.

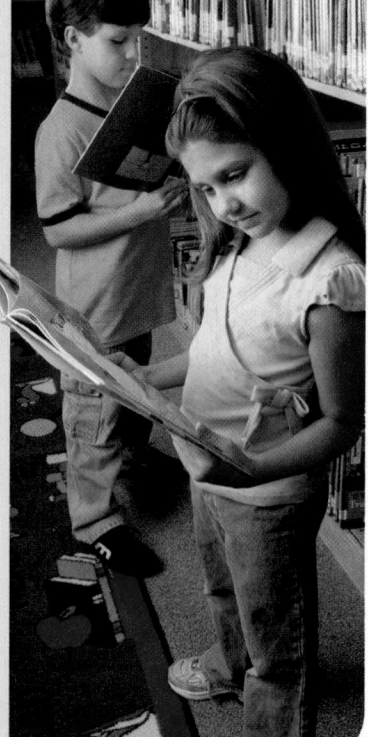

number of sports books		number of animal books		how many more sports books than animal books
↓		↓		↓
305	−	123	=	182

$$\begin{array}{r} {\overset{2\ 10}{\cancel{3}\cancel{0}5}} \\ -123 \\ \hline 182 \end{array}$$

So, Ms. Wells counted 182 more sports books than animal books.

Think and Discuss

Tell which operation you would use. Then solve the problem.

a. Gina's family has 165 books on shelves. They also have 277 books in the attic. How many books does Gina's family have in all?

b. Carlos likes word puzzles. He bought a puzzle book that has 275 word puzzles. He has 132 puzzles left to complete. How many puzzles has Carlos already completed?

96

Guided Problem Solving

1. Zack has 65 photos of his vacation and 48 photos of his family in his photo album. He has room for 137 more photos. How many photos can Zack's album hold in all?

   Copy and complete the table.

Clues	Meaning
has ■ photos of vacation and ■ photos of family	has a total of ■ photos
has room for ■ more photos	■ more photos can go in the album
How many photos can Zack's album hold in all?	What is the total number of ___?___ the album holds?

   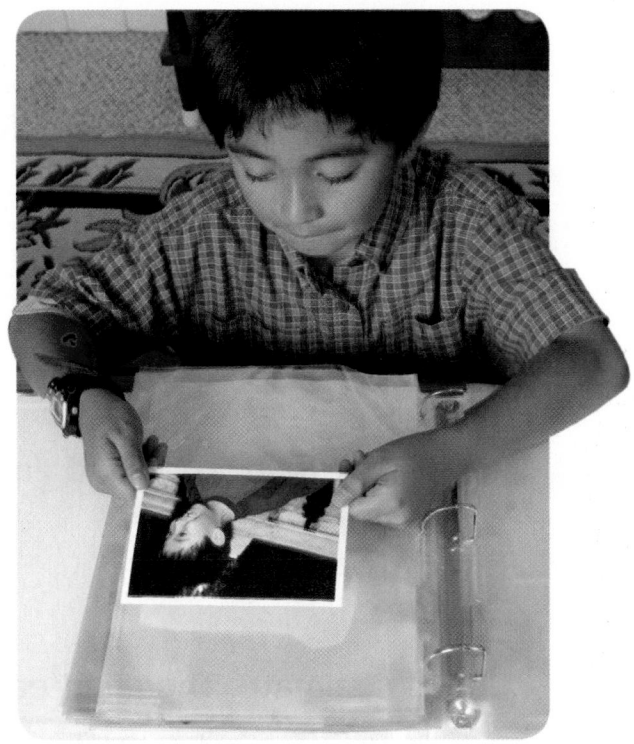

   Which operation can you use to find how many in all? Write a number sentence that shows the answer.

2. **What if** Zack had room for 175 more photos? How many photos would Zack's album hold in all?

3. Brad has room for 100 baseball cards in his binder. He has 64 cards already. How many more cards does he need to fill his binder?

Mixed Applications

4. Erin collects stamps. She has 279 stamps in an album. She gives away 47 stamps to her friends. How many stamps does Erin have left?

5. Kyle and Josh have a total of 64 CDs. Kyle has 12 more CDs than Josh. How many CDs does each boy have?

6. Joseph has 2 coins in his pocket. Their total is 30¢. What are the two coins?

7. Mrs. Gregory has 189 books in her office. Mrs. Moore has 168 books in her office. Who has more books? How many more?

8. **WRITE Math** Kim is reading a book that has 382 pages. She reads 28 pages each night. How many more pages will she have left to read after 3 nights? **Explain** how you know.

9. **Reasoning** Brad's album can hold 225 photos. He has 144 photos in the album. He wants to put 79 more photos in the album. **Explain** how to tell if he has enough space left for the photos.

Extra Practice

Set A Write the fact family for each set of numbers. (pp. 76–77)

1. 4, 9, 13   **2.** 2, 5, 7   **3.** 6, 8, 14   **4.** 3, 8, 11
5. 6, 6, 12   **6.** 1, 7, 8   **7.** 4, 6, 10   **8.** 7, 9, 16

Set B Use rounding or compatible numbers to estimate each difference. (pp. 78–79)

1. 76	**2.** 89	**3.** 506	**4.** 795	**5.** 448
− 24	− 12	− 354	− 133	− 227

6. Maggie read 87 pages of her book. Alan read 51 pages of his book. About how many more pages did Maggie read?

Set C Estimate. Then find each difference. (pp. 80–81)

1. 93	**2.** 78	**3.** 56	**4.** 85	**5.** 62
− 59	− 37	− 11	− 26	− 44

Set D Estimate. Then find each difference. (pp. 84–85)

1. 386	**2.** 519	**3.** 865	**4.** 4,786	**5.** 2,429
− 107	− 185	− 378	− 2,432	− 1,236

6. Sue is saving money to buy a bike for $220. So far she has saved $136. How much more money does Sue need to save?

Set E Estimate. Then find each difference. (pp. 88–91)

1. 600	**2.** 402	**3.** 330	**4.** 7,800	**5.** 5,906
− 328	− 238	− 119	− 4,183	− 2,557

Set F Find the difference. Tell which method you used. (pp. 92–95)

1. 580	**2.** 792	**3.** 1,843	**4.** 6,900	**5.** 9,478
− 461	− 521	− 376	− 1,263	− 4,105

CD ROM **Technology**
Use Harcourt Mega Math, Country Countdown, *Block Busters*, Levels R, X, Y.

Time to Subtract

On Your Mark!
2 players

Get Set!
• Timer

12 27 35 59 68 84

16 29 41 54 73 87

18 33 46 61 80 98

24 38 50 65 76 92

Play!

- Each player chooses a type of animal. Each player uses the 6 numbers on his or her animals to write and solve problems.

- Using their 6 numbers, players write and solve as many subtraction problems as they can in 2 minutes.

- When both players are ready, set the timer for 2 minutes and begin.

- After the 2 minutes are up, players trade papers and check each other's answers.

- The player with more correct answers receives a point.

- Each player chooses a different animal and continues to play.

- The first player to reach 3 points wins.

Odd or EVEN?

Every number is either **odd** or **even**.

Odd numbers end in 1, 3, 5, 7, or 9.

41, 197, and 1,433 are odd.

Even numbers end in 0, 2, 4, 6, or 8.

28, 374, and 4,562 are even.

You can look for clues to predict if the sum or difference of two numbers will be odd or even.

▲ Mancala is one of the oldest board games in the world. The game has 6 small holes on each side. Is the total number of small holes an odd or even number?

Examples

Addition Complete the table to find each answer.

NUMBERS	EXAMPLE	SUM	ODD OR EVEN?
even + even	2 + 6	8	even
odd + odd	73 + 7	■	■
odd + even	45 + 30	■	■
even + odd	2,116 + 517	■	■

Subtraction Complete the table to find each answer.

NUMBERS	EXAMPLE	DIFFERENCE	ODD OR EVEN?
even − even	8 − 4	4	even
odd − odd	87 − 49	■	■
odd − even	835 − 22	■	■
even − odd	474 − 367	■	■

Remember
The ones digit helps you see if a number is even or odd.

Try It
Find the sum or difference. Write *odd* or *even*.

1. 7 + 3 **2.** 1 + 12 **3.** 84 + 18 **4.** 734 + 15 **5.** 565 + 259

6. 10 − 5 **7.** 33 − 12 **8.** 196 − 80 **9.** 775 − 401 **10.** 9,827 − 6,378

11. 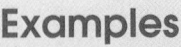 WRITE Math ▸ Choose two numbers to add. Is the sum of your numbers an odd or even number? **Explain** how you know.

Chapter 4 Review/Test

Check Vocabulary and Concepts

Choose the best term from the box.

VOCABULARY

fact family
inverse operations
regrouping

1. Addition and subtraction are opposite, or _?_ . (p. 76)

2. A group of related number sentences that use the same numbers is a _?_ . (p. 76)

Check Skills

Write the fact family for each set of numbers. (pp. 76–77)

3. 2, 8, 10   **4.** 6, 6, 12   **5.** 3, 4, 7   **6.** 7, 8, 15

Use rounding or compatible numbers to estimate each difference. (pp. 78–79)

7. $56 - 19$ **8.** $64 - 23$ **9.** $661 - 185$ **10.** $942 - 316$

Estimate. Then find each difference. (pp. 80–81, 84–85, 88–91)

11. $48 - 17$ **12.** $77 - 49$ **13.** $80 - 35$ **14.** $374 - 253$

15. $507 - 230$ **16.** $583 - 179$ **17.** $97 - 58$ **18.** $7{,}800 - 3{,}567$

19. $8{,}605 - 6{,}386$ **20.** $7{,}004 - 4{,}112$ **21.** $864 - 775$ **22.** $8{,}624 - 6{,}248$

Check Problem Solving

Solve. (pp. 86–87, 96–97)

23. Mr. Patrick read 216 pages of his book. Mrs. Wu read 197 pages of her book. How many pages have they read in all?

24. A car show had 559 visitors. Of the visitors, 165 were children and the rest were adults. About how many of the visitors were adults?

25. **WRITE Math** ▶ Did you need an estimate or an exact answer for Problem 24? **Explain** how you know.

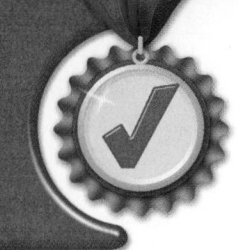

Unit Review/Test
Chapters 1–4

Multiple Choice

1. The Aon Center in California is 858 feet tall. The US Bank Plaza in Idaho is 267 feet tall. About how many feet taller is the Aon Center than the US Bank Plaza? (p. 78)

   A 400 feet

   B 500 feet

   C 600 feet

   D 700 feet

2. Gavin has a score of 300 on a computer game. Ben needs 188 more points to tie Gavin's score. What is Ben's score? (p. 88)

   A 112

   B 122

   C 212

   D 222

3. There are 8,537 people living in a town. What is this number rounded to the nearest thousand? (p. 38)

   A 8,000

   B 8,500

   C 8,540

   D 9,000

4. On Tuesday, 879 people visited the history museum. There were 452 visitors on Wednesday. How many visitors were there on Tuesday and Wednesday? (p. 58)

   A 427

   B 1,221

   C 1,231

   D 1,331

5. Which set of numbers is in order from greatest to least? (p. 32)

   A 475, 466, 584, 568

   B 568, 584, 466, 475

   C 584, 568, 475, 466

   D 466, 475, 568, 584

6. Which number is even? (p. 4)

   A 29   **C** 65

   B 32   **D** 81

7. Which digit is in the hundreds place in the number 6,794? (p. 10)

   A 9   **C** 6

   B 7   **D** 4

GO **Technology** Use *Online Assessment.*
ONLINE

8. Which number equals
4,000 + 80 + 6? (p. 10)

   A 486

   B 4,086

   C 4,806

   D 4,860

9. What is the sum of 5,209 and 3,881?
(p. 58)

   A 9,090

   B 9,080

   C 8,090

   D 8,080

10. Which number has a 5 in the tens
place and a 7 in the hundreds place?
(p. 10)

   A 1,575   **C** 8,752

   B 7,725   **D** 8,957

Short Response

11. The third-grade classes collected
3,694 pennies for the school
fundraiser. The fourth-grade classes
collected 3,496 pennies. Which
grade collected more pennies? (p. 28)

12. Write the number 15,102 in
expanded form. (p. 14)

13. There were 1,268 people at a
football game. Round this number
to the nearest hundred and to the
nearest thousand. (p. 38)

14. Juan's family is traveling 365 miles
to visit his grandmother. They have
already driven 179 miles. How much
farther do they need to drive? (p. 84)

Extended Response WRITE Math ▶

15. The table shows the weights of
fish that were caught in a fishing
tournament. Who caught fish that
were more than 500 grams heavier
than Paul's fish? **Explain** how you
found your answer. (p. 58)

Name	Weight in Grams
Paul	2,340
Andrew	3,080
Donna	2,790
Ted	2,930

16. Using each of the digits 2, 4, 6, and
8 once, what is the greatest possible
sum you can make from two 2-digit
numbers? **Explain** how you found
your answer. (p. 54)

THE WORLD ALMANAC FOR KIDS

Rivers of the World

Winding Water

There are rivers on every continent. Rivers can be used for transportation, to generate electricity, to water crops, for water to drink, and for fun. Over many thousands of years, rivers can even cut through rock. In the United States, the Colorado River carved out the Grand Canyon, which is about one mile deep.

Mediterranean Sea

The Nile River flows north through Africa from Lake Victoria to the Mediterranean Sea.

Africa

Nile River

Lake Victoria

FACT·ACTIVITY›

For 1–4, use the data in the table.

Longest Rivers on Six Continents		
Continent	River	Length
Africa	Nile	4,160 miles
Asia	Chang (Yangtze)	3,964 miles
Australia	Murray-Darling	2,310 miles
Europe	Volga	2,290 miles
North America	Mississippi	2,340 miles
South America	Amazon	4,000 miles

1 How many rivers are longer than the Mississippi River?

2 Which river is more than 1,800 miles longer than the Mississippi River?

3 Write the lengths of the rivers in order from the longest to the shortest.

4 Two different rivers have a combined length of exactly 4,600 miles. Which two rivers are they?

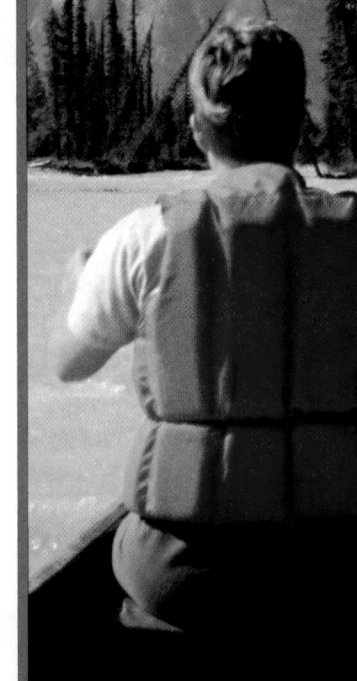

River Riddles

The Mississippi River is the longest in the United States. It touches 10 different states: Arkansas, Illinois, Iowa, Kentucky, Louisiana, Minnesota, Mississippi, Missouri, Tennessee, and Wisconsin. Many other rivers flow into the Mississippi River.

A river has a mouth. At its mouth, a river flows into another body of water. A river begins at its source, which may be an underground spring or a place high in the mountains where rain or melting snow collects to form a small stream.

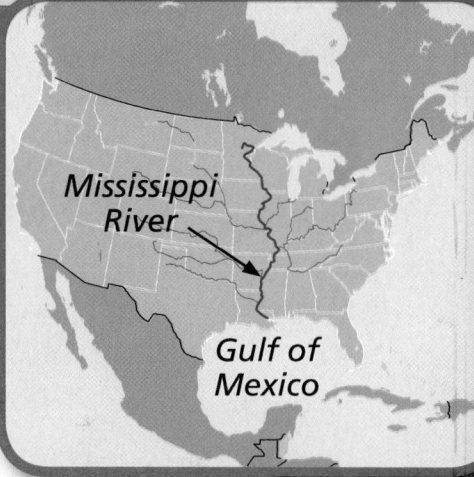

Mississippi River

Gulf of Mexico

Facts About Some U.S. Rivers

Name of River	Source State	Mouth	Length
Arkansas	Colorado	Mississippi River	1,459 miles
Colorado	Colorado	Gulf of California	1,450 miles
Delaware	New York	Delaware Bay	390 miles
Hudson	New York	Upper New York Bay	306 miles
Mississippi	Minnesota	Gulf of Mexico	2,340 miles
Missouri	Montana	Mississippi River	2,315 miles
Ohio	Pennsylvania	Mississippi River	981 miles
Potomac	Maryland	Chesapeake Bay	383 miles
Wabash	Ohio	Ohio River	512 miles

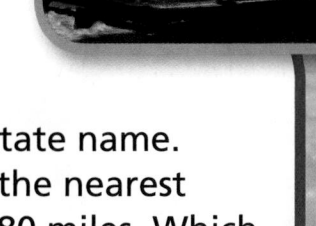

FACT·ACTIVITY

For 1–3, use the data in the table.

1 I have four i's, but I can't see. My length has a 0 in the ones place. Which river am I?

2 My name is not a state name. When rounded to the nearest ten, my length is 380 miles. Which river am I?

3 **Pose a Problem** Write three riddles using the river lengths. Have a classmate solve your riddles.

2 Money and Time, Data and Probability

Math on Location

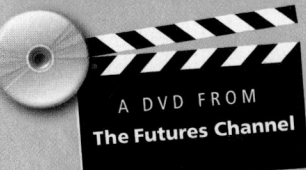

A DVD FROM
The Futures Channel

with
Chapter Projects

1

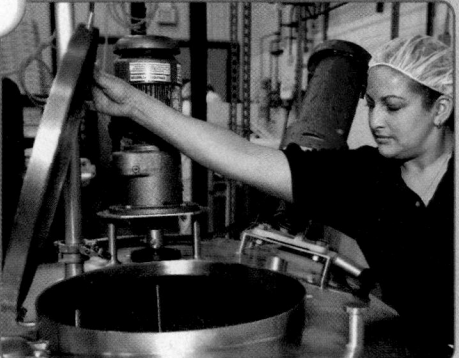

Maria checks that there will be enough gallons of each flavor to meet the needs for that day.

2

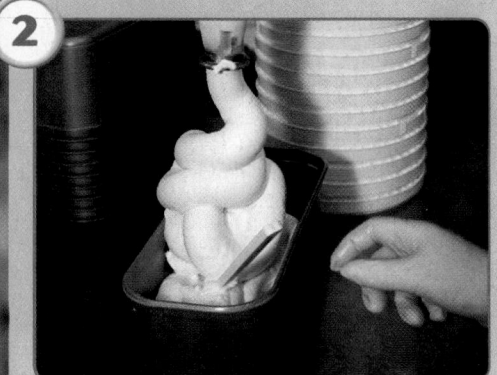

The elapsed time is recorded from cleaning the machine to filling the containers with the ice cream.

3

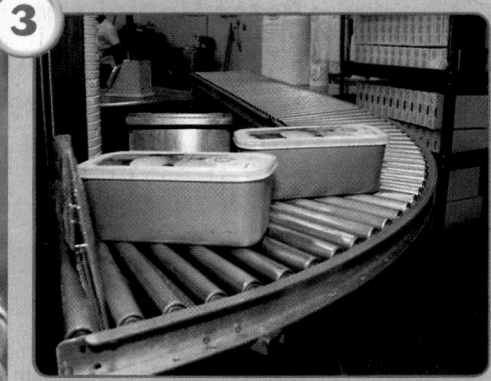

The cost of the ice cream is affected by the cost of the ingredients.

VOCABULARY POWER

TALK Math

What information is collected and talked about in the **Math on Location** photographs? How can you find the time between cleaning the machine and filling the containers?

READ Math

REVIEW VOCABULARY You learned the words below when you learned about time and data. How do these words relate to **Math on Location**?

graph a picture that represents a mathematical relationship

hour a unit used to measure time; in one hour, the hour hand on a clock moves from one number to the next

WRITE Math

Copy and complete a Freyer Model like the one below. Use what you know about data to add more words.

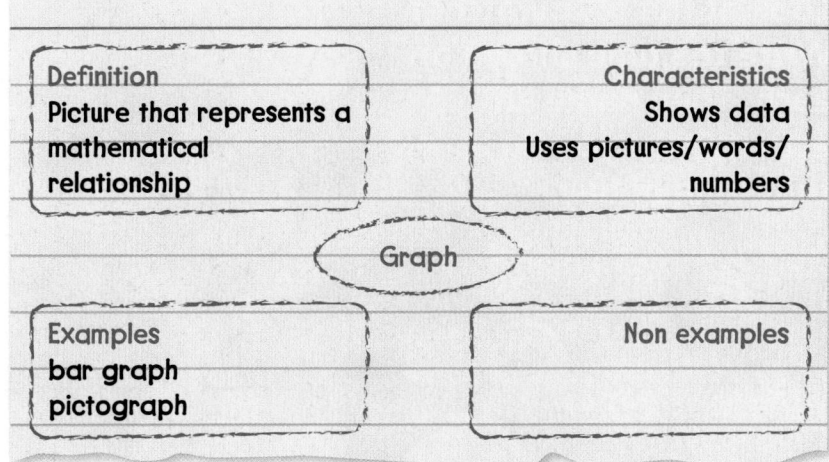

Definition	Characteristics
Picture that represents a mathematical relationship	Shows data. Uses pictures/words/numbers

Graph

Examples	Non examples
bar graph pictograph	

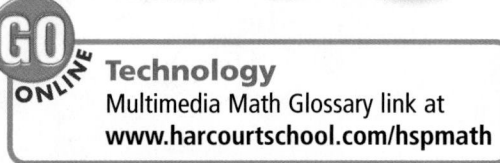

Technology
Multimedia Math Glossary link at
www.harcourtschool.com/hspmath

Unit 2 • Chapters 5–7   107

5 Money and Time

Investigate

Watches come in many different shapes and sizes. Look at the four watches. Write the time shown on each. Then name an activity that you do at that time of day.

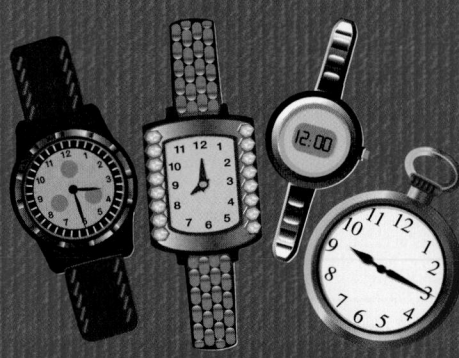

FAST FACT

The first pocket watch was invented in the 1500's by Peter Henlein. It only had an hour hand. The minute hand was added in the late 1600's.

GO ONLINE

Technology
Student pages are available in the Student eBook.

Show What You Know

Check your understanding of important skills needed for success in Chapter 5.

▶ **Count Coins**

Count and write the amount.

1. ⬤⬤⬤⬤

2. ⬤⬤⬤

3. ⬤⬤⬤⬤⬤⬤⬤

4. ⬤⬤⬤⬤⬤⬤

▶ **Quarters**

Count and write the amount.

5. ⬤⬤⬤⬤⬤⬤ ⬤ ⬤

6. ⬤⬤⬤⬤⬤ ⬤⬤⬤

7. ⬤⬤⬤⬤⬤⬤⬤⬤

8. ⬤⬤⬤⬤⬤⬤⬤⬤

9. ⬤⬤⬤⬤⬤⬤⬤ ⬤⬤⬤⬤

10. ⬤⬤⬤⬤⬤ ⬤⬤⬤⬤⬤⬤⬤

VOCABULARY POWER

CHAPTER VOCABULARY

change
decimal point
dollar
equivalent

WARM-UP WORDS

change The money you get back if you have paid for an item with coins or bills that have a value greater than the cost of the item

decimal point A symbol used to separate dollars from cents in money

equivalent Two or more sets that name the same amount

Count Bills and Coins

OBJECTIVE: Count, read, and write money amounts with groups of coins and bills.

Quick Review

Find the next number in the pattern.

1. 5, 10, 15, ■
2. 10, 20, 30, ■
3. 25, 30, 35, ■
4. 15, 25, 35, ■
5. 25, 50, 75, ■

Vocabulary

equivalent   dollar

decimal point

Learn

PROBLEM Brian has some coins in his piggy bank. How much money does he have?

Brian's Money

half dollar	quarter	dime	nickel	penny
50¢	25¢	10¢	5¢	1¢

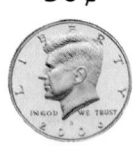 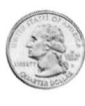   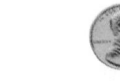

50¢ → 75¢ → 85¢ → 90¢ → 91¢

Start with the coin of greatest value. Count on to find the total.

So, Brian has 91¢ in his bank.

Example

25¢ → 50¢ → 60¢ → 70¢ → 80¢ → 85¢ → 86¢

Remember

Every coin has a "heads" side and a "tails" side.

heads   tails

Activity

Materials ■ play money coins

• Choose a handful of play money coins.

• Find the value of the coins. Start with the coins of greatest value.

• Record your count. Then find the value of the coins in a different order.

• Is the value of the set of coins different when you count in a different order? Explain.

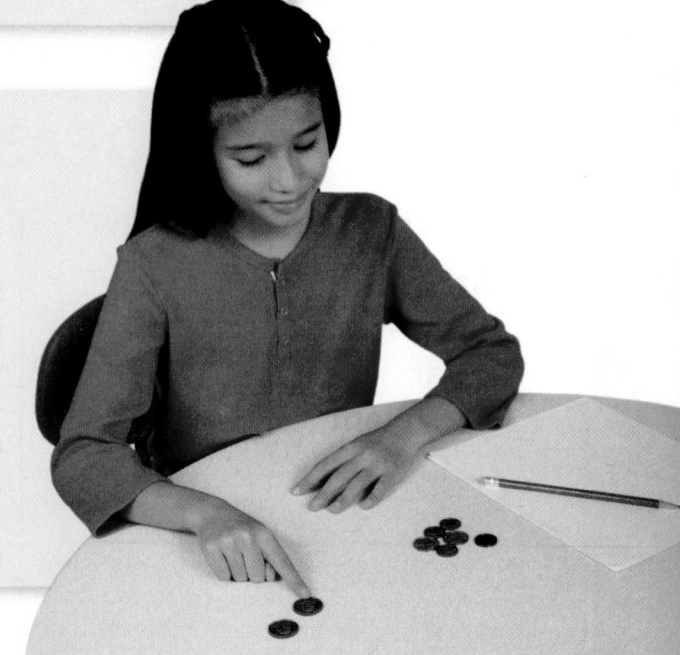

Equivalent Amounts

Sets of money that have the same value are **equivalent**.

Example 1 Show $1.06 two different ways.

ONE WAY	ANOTHER WAY
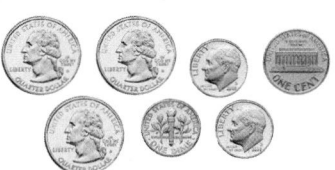	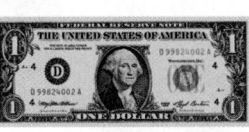 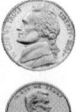
3 quarters = $0.75	one $1 bill = $1.00
3 dimes = $0.30	1 nickel = $0.05
+ 1 penny = $0.01	+ 1 penny = $0.01
total value = $1.06	total value = $1.06

Each set has a value of $1.06. The sets are equivalent.

Write	**Read**
dollar sign → $1.06	one **dollar** and six cents

↑
decimal point

• What does the 0 in $1.06 mean?

Example 2 Juanita and Tony have the money shown below.

Juanita's money	Tony's money
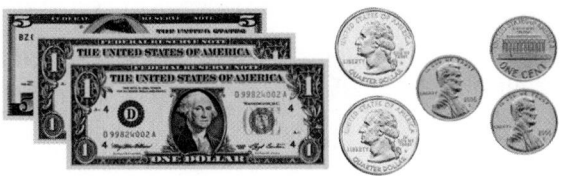	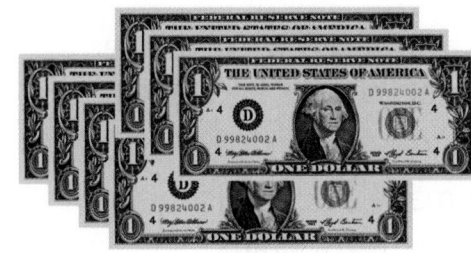 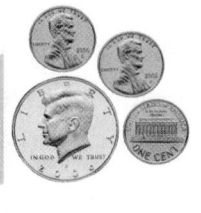
one $5 bill → $5.00	seven $1 bills → $7.00
two $1 bills → $2.00	1 half-dollar → $0.50
2 quarters → $0.50	3 pennies → $0.03
3 pennies → $0.03	$7.53
$7.53	

So, Juanita and Tony each have $7.53. The amounts are equivalent.

Guided Practice

1. What is the value of 5 nickels?

Write the amount.

2.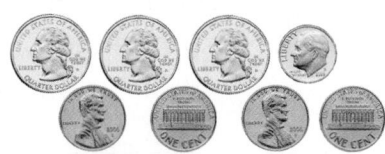

3.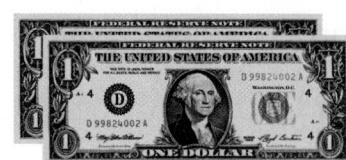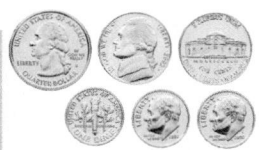

4. **TALK Math** Describe two ways to show $1.25.

Independent Practice and Problem Solving

Write the amount.

5.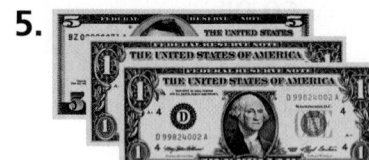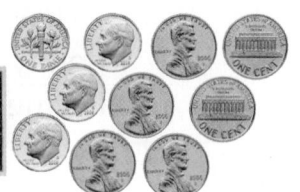

6.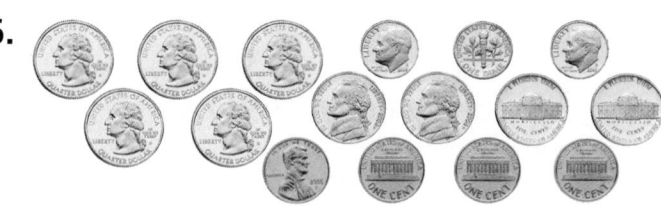

Find two equivalent sets for each. List the coins and bills.

7. 70¢

8. 38¢

9. $1.20

10. $6.74

Algebra Write the missing number.

11. 2 quarters + ■ dimes = 80¢

12. 2 nickels + ■ pennies = 23¢

USE DATA For 13–14, use the prices.

13. Tom wants to buy a smoothie. List the fewest bills and coins he can use.

14. **Reasoning** Kayla wants a fruit chiller. Describe two sets of bills and coins Kayla can use.

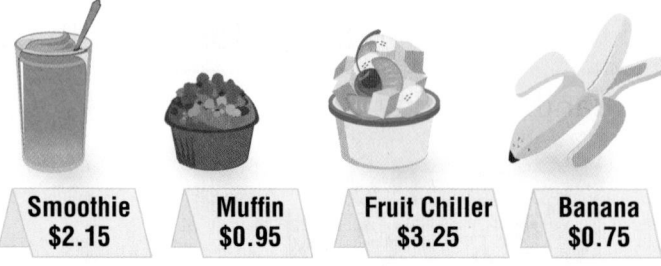

| Smoothie $2.15 | Muffin $0.95 | Fruit Chiller $3.25 | Banana $0.75 |

15. How can you make 87¢ by using the fewest coins? the most coins?

16. **WRITE Math** Alex has $1.48. **Explain** how you know he has at least six coins.

Mixed Review and Test Prep

17. Josh wants 200 postcards. He has 159 postcards. How many more does he need? (p. 88)

18. What number goes in the ■ to make the number sentence true?
      63 + ■ = 89 (p. 50)

19. **Test Prep** Jared has two $1 bills, 1 quarter, and 3 nickels. How much money does Jared have in all?

CD ROM **Technology** Use Harcourt Mega Math, The Number Games, *Buggy Bargains*, Levels A and B.

Write a Conclusion

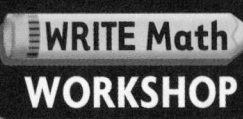

WRITE Math WORKSHOP

Writing a conclusion helps you use the information you are given and what you find out to make a decision.

Jessica and Alex are comparing the bills and coins they have. Do they have equivalent amounts of money?

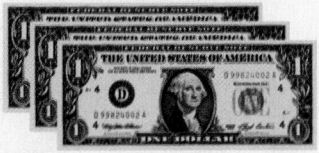

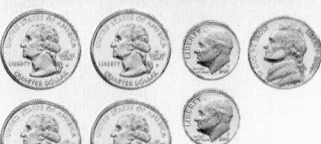

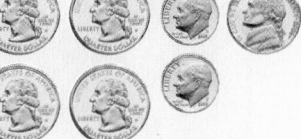

Jessica's Money

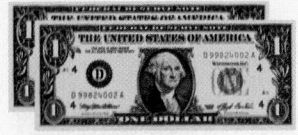

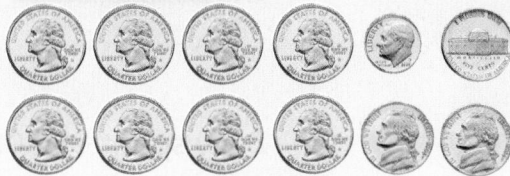

Alex's Money

Jessica wrote this paragraph to explain her answer.

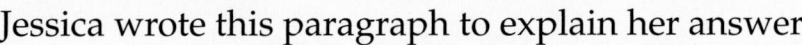

First, I counted my money. I have $3.00 + $1.00 + $0.20 + $0.05. I have $4.25.

Next, I counted Alex's money. He has $2.00 + $2.00 + $0.10 + $0.15. He has $4.25.

Then, I compared the two amounts of money. Alex and I have equivalent amounts.

Tips
- To write a conclusion, first, study the information you are given.
- Then, write the steps you took to help you make a decision.
- Use words such as first and next.
- Then state your conclusion in the last sentence.

Problem Solving Write a conclusion for each problem.

1. Tina has 2 quarters, 2 dimes, and 2 pennies. Jacob has 5 dimes, 5 nickels, and 2 pennies. Do they have equivalent amounts of money?

2. Ron has two $1 bills, 3 dimes, and 4 nickels. Lois has one $1 bill, 4 quarters, and 5 dimes. Do they have equivalent amounts of money?

2 Compare Money Amounts

OBJECTIVE: Compare money amounts with bills and coins.

Quick Review

Compare. Use <, >, or = for each.

1. 6 ⬤ 8
2. 11 ⬤ 13
3. 15 ⬤ 12
4. 134 ⬤ 145
5. 229 ⬤ 226

Learn

PROBLEM Sarah and Zoey each bought a pair of sunglasses. They paid the amounts shown below. Who spent more money?

Example 1 Count and compare the money amounts.

Sarah	Zoey
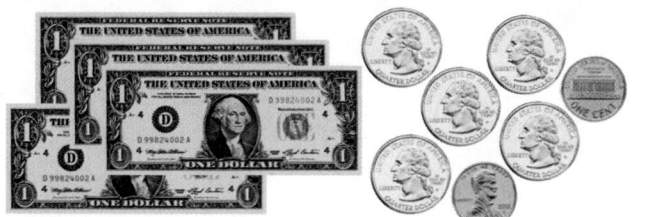	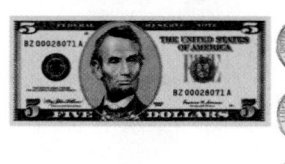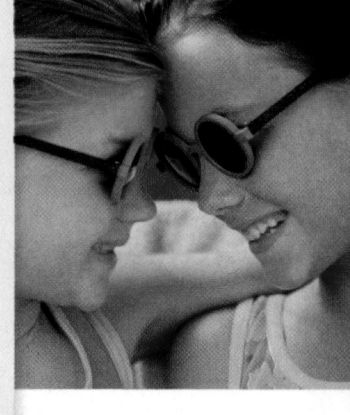
Sarah spent $5.27.	Zoey spent $5.30.

$5.27 < $5.30, or $5.30 > $5.27

So, Zoey spent more money.

- If you have a greater number of bills and coins than someone else, do you always have the greater amount of money? Explain.

Example 2 Use place value to compare $3.56 and $3.54.

DOLLARS	.	DIMES	PENNIES
$3	.	5	6
$3	.	5	4

The number of dollars and dimes are equal.
Compare the number of pennies.
6 > 4, so $3.56 > $3.54.

Remember

< means
is less than.

> means
is greater than.

Guided Practice

1. Which is the greater money amount, 2 quarters or 6 dimes?

Use <, >, or = to compare the amounts of money.

2.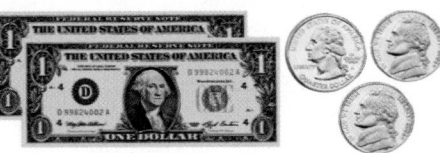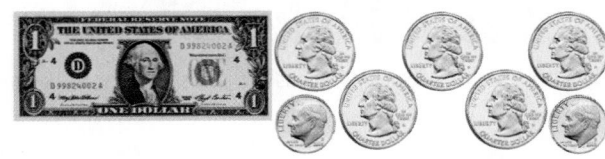

3.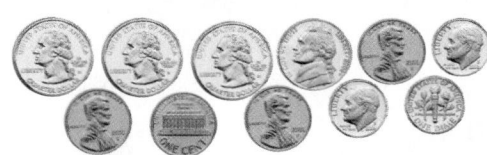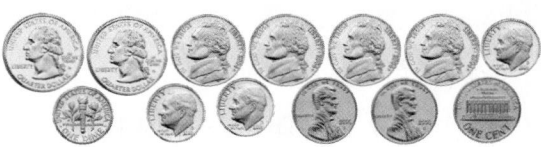

4. [TALK Math] **Explain** how to compare $5.28 and $5.41 by using place value.

Independent Practice and Problem Solving

Use <, >, or = to compare the amounts of money.

5.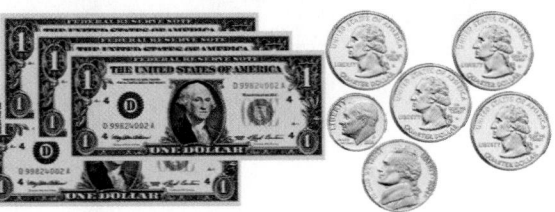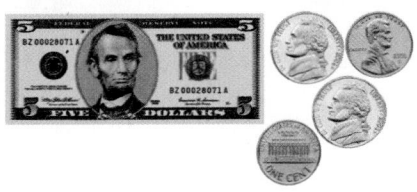

Which amount is greater?

6. $6.82 or $6.90   **7.** $1.10 or 5 quarters   **8.** $1.90 or 7 quarters

9. $3.26 or $2.63   **10.** 4 dimes or 4 quarters   **11.** 3 dimes 3 nickels, or 5 dimes

USE DATA For 12–13, use the table.

12. Write the prices in order from greatest to least. What is the difference between the greatest and the least amount?

13. [WRITE Math] Hayley has $5.00. Which item can she buy at the Beach Shop? **Explain** how you know.

Beach Shop	
Item	**Price**
Towel	$5.82
Water Bottle	$2.87
Sunscreen	$5.12

Mixed Review and Test Prep

14. Marcus poured milk into his glass. What tool should he use to measure how much milk he poured? (Grade 2)

15. Bianca estimated 688 − 432 by rounding each number to the nearest hundred. What was her estimate? (p. 78)

16. Test Prep Amber has only quarters. She has more than 75¢. Which amount could Amber have?

A $0.85   **C** $1.50

B $1.05   **D** $1.70

Extra Practice on page 138, Set B

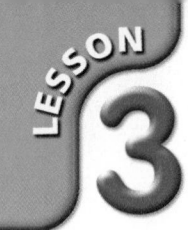
Problem Solving Workshop
Strategy: Make a Table

OBJECTIVE: Solve problems by using the strategy *make a table.*

Learn the Strategy

Using a table can help you understand the information in some problems.

A table can help you see how items in a problem are related. This table shows a number pattern.

Matt and his dad build wagons. Each wagon has 4 wheels.

Wagons	1	2	3
Wheels	4	8	12

A table can help you record choices. This table shows how students voted.

Mika asked his classmates to vote for their favorite meal.

Favorite Meal

Meal	Votes
Breakfast	⫿⫿⫿ ‖
Lunch	⫿⫿⫿ ‖‖
Dinner	⫿⫿⫿ ⫿⫿⫿

A table can help you find possible answers. This table shows equivalent sets of money.

Opal has a $1 bill, some dimes, and some nickels. She uses it all to buy a fruit drink for $1.50.

$ 1 bills	Dimes	Nickels	Total Value
1	2	6	$1.50
1	3	4	$1.50
1	4	2	$1.50

TALK Math

What questions can be answered by using each of the tables above?

116

Use the Strategy

PROBLEM Damon has the bills and coins pictured below. He wants to rent ice skates for $3.25. How many different ways can Damon make $3.25?

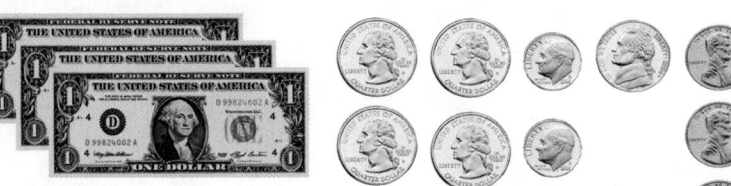

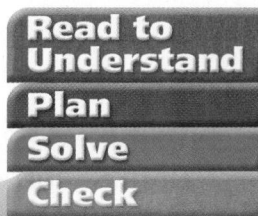

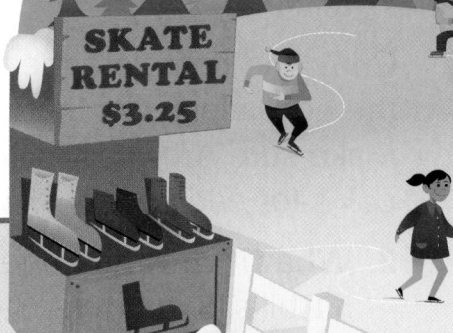

Read to Understand

Reading Skill

• **What information is given in the graphic aid?**
• **Is any information not needed?**

Plan

• **What strategy can you use to solve the problem?**
  You can make a table to help you solve the problem.

Solve

• **How can you use the strategy to solve the problem?**
  Make a table to show all the equivalent sets of bills and coins that equal $3.25.

$1 bills	Quarters	Dimes	Nickels	Pennies	Total Value
3	1	0	0	0	$3.25
3	0	2	1	0	$3.25
3	0	2	0	5	$3.25
2	4	2	1	0	$3.25
2	4	2	0	5	$3.25

So, there are 5 equivalent sets Damon can make to equal $3.25.

Check

• **How can you make sure each set of bills and coins equals $3.25?**
• **What other way could you solve the problem?**

Guided Problem Solving

1. Amy has six $1 bills, 4 quarters, 3 dimes, and 4 nickels. She needs to pay $6.85 to ice skate for an hour. How many different ways can Amy make $6.85?

Copy and complete the table. Find all the equivalent sets that equal $6.85. Make sure Amy has enough bills and coins for each set.

✓2. **What if** Amy had one $5 bill, two $1 bills, 3 quarters, 3 dimes, and 3 nickels? Name two ways Amy could make $6.85.

✓3. Tyler has 7 quarters, 4 dimes, and 6 nickels. He wants to buy a hot dog for $1.45. How many different ways can Tyler make $1.45?

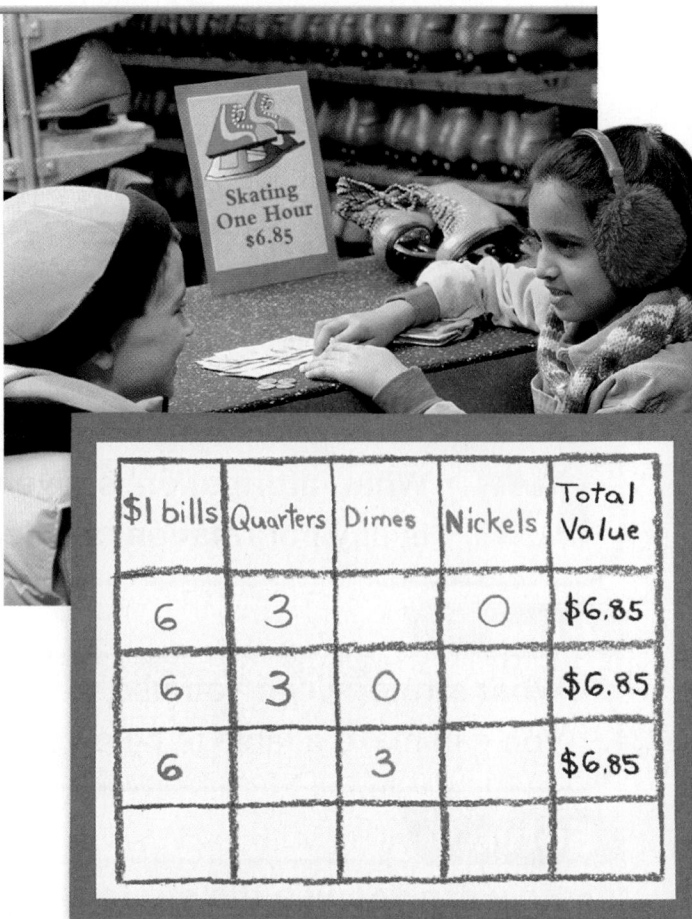

$1 bills	Quarters	Dimes	Nickels	Total Value
6	3		0	$6.85
6	3	0		$6.85
6		3		$6.85

Problem Solving Strategy Practice

USE DATA For 4–6, use the list.
Make a table to solve.

4. Kim had a class skating party for her birthday. Each student chose one juice flavor. How many students were at Kim's party? How many students chose each flavor?

5. How many more students chose grape juice than chose apple juice?

6. Kim's mother bought 2 juice boxes for each student at the party. How many juice boxes did she buy in all?

List your favorite juice.

grape apple   apple   berry
  grape berry apple   grape
berry   grape grape   berry
apple   apple   berry grape
berry berry   apple
grape   berry berry
apple grape   grape   grape

7. Eric has five $1 bills, 3 quarters, 5 dimes, 1 nickel, and 5 pennies. How many different equivalent sets of bills and coins can he use to pay for earmuffs that cost $5.75?

Mixed Strategy Practice

USE DATA For 8–10, use the table below.

8. Jen and Tina sold lemonade and cookies to raise money for an ice-skating class. On Friday, they counted 11 coins. List the coins they could have on Friday.

9. On Saturday, Taylor bought 4 cookies. He gave Jen and Tina 5 dimes and 8 pennies. How much more than that did the girls earn on Saturday?

10. After selling the lemonade and cookies on Sunday, the girls had 2 bills and 6 coins. What bills and coins did the girls have?

Choose a
STRATEGY

Draw a Diagram or Picture

Make a Model or Act It Out

Make an Organized List

Find a Pattern

Make a Table or Graph

Predict and Test

Work Backward

Solve a Simpler Problem

Write an Equation

Use Logical Reasoning

Friday	$2.75
Saturday	$5.58
Sunday	$6.30
Monday	$3.65

11. **WRITE Math** ▸ Duane scored 2 goals during ice hockey practice. Robbie scored 2 more goals than Duane. Jack scored 1 less goal than Robbie. **Explain** how you can find the number of goals each boy scored.

12. Casey bought ice hockey supplies. She spent $5 and bought 3 items. Which items did she buy?

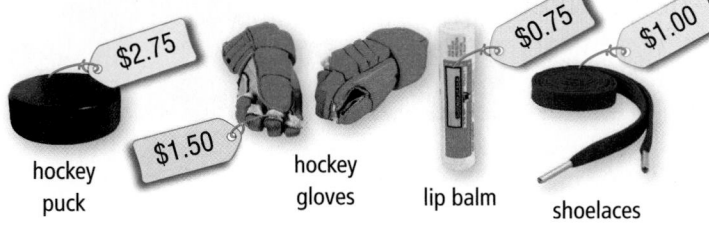

hockey puck — $2.75 $1.50   hockey gloves   lip balm — $0.75   shoelaces — $1.00

13. **Pose a Problem** Look back at Problem 9. Write a similar problem by changing the amount of money the girls had on Saturday.

14. **Open-Ended** Becca dropped her coins on the ice. The coins were four different sizes. There were more of the smallest coin than of any other coin. What coins could Becca have dropped? How much money would that be?

CHALLENGE YOURSELF

The Snow Cats are playing against the Polar Bears in ice hockey. Tickets for the game are $8.00 for adults and $5.00 for children.

15. Mr. Meyers buys 1 adult ticket. He pays with 3 bills and 6 coins. What bills and coins does he use?

16. Mr. Hall pays $31 for tickets. **Explain** how you can find the number of adult tickets and the number of children's tickets that he buys.

Model Making Change

OBJECTIVE: Make change by counting on.

Quick Review

Jody has a $1 bill, 3 pennies, and 1 quarter. How much money does Jody have in all?

Vocabulary

change

Learn

PROBLEM Marla buys a kitten toy for $3.68. She pays with a $5 bill. How much change should she get?

Change is the money you get back if you have paid for an item with coins or bills that have a value greater than the cost of the item.

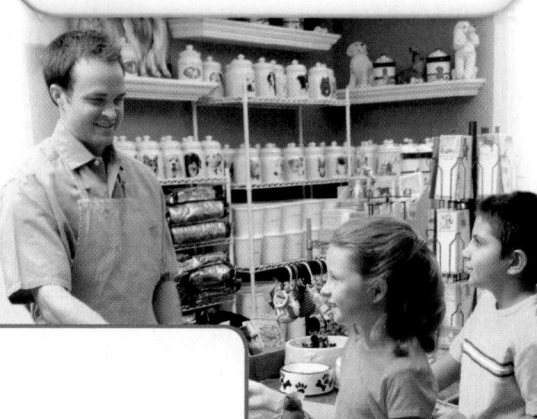

 **Activity 1 Make change from $5.00.**

Materials ■ play money

Start with the cost of the item.
Count up with coins and bills to the amount Marla paid.

cost of item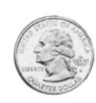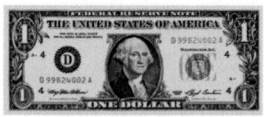

$\downarrow$

$3.68 \rightarrow$ $3.69 \rightarrow$ $3.70 \rightarrow$ $3.75 \rightarrow$ $4.00 \rightarrow$ $5.00 $\leftarrow$ amount paid

Then count the value of the bills and coins she received.

So, Marla should get $1.32 in change.

 **Activity 2 Make change from $10.00.**

Alex buys a leash for his dog for $7.70. He pays with a $10 bill. What change should Alex get?

cost of item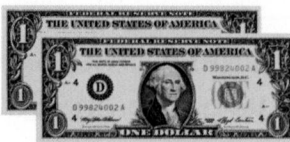

$\downarrow$

$7.70 \rightarrow$ $7.80 \rightarrow$ $7.90 \rightarrow$ $8.00 \rightarrow$ $9.00 \rightarrow$ $10.00 $\leftarrow$ amount paid

So, Alex should get $2.30 in change.

1. Count up from $5.18 to $6.00. Name the coins that are missing.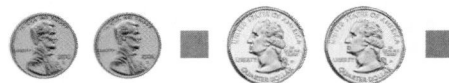

Find the amount of change. Use play money to help.

✓ 2. Brenda buys a comic book for $3.42. She pays with a $5 bill.

✓ 3. Ivy buys a sandwich for $5.25. She pays with a $10 bill.

4. **TALK Math** Explain how to count up from $2.09 to $5.00.

Independent Practice and Problem Solving

Find the amount of change. Use play money to help.

5. Pete buys a new dictionary for $4.59. He pays with a $5 bill.

6. Rose buys a carton of yogurt for $0.68. She pays with a $5 bill.

7. Omar buys a dog collar for $7.22. He pays with a $10 bill.

8. Morgan buys a stuffed animal for $3.85. She pays with a $10 bill.

USE DATA For 9–11, use the picture.

9. Ed buys a yo-yo. He pays with a $5 bill. How much change should he receive?

$5.99

$2.89

$8.65

10. **WRITE Math** Mena buys a stuffed bear. She pays with a $10 bill. How much is Mena's change? What bills and coins does she get? **Explain** how you know.

11. Valerie buys a jump rope. She pays with a $5 bill and 4 quarters. How much change should she receive?

12. **Reasoning** Jane bought a book. She paid with $3.00. She got 2 quarters, 2 dimes, and 3 pennies in change. What did her book cost?

Mixed Review and Test Prep

13. A year usually has 365 days. What is the value of the digit 3 in 365? (p. 8)

14. There are 328 boys and 182 girls at camp. Estimate the total number of campers. (p. 52)

15. **Test Prep** Kim buys lunch for $4.17. She pays with a $5 bill. How much change does she get?

   A $0.75   C $0.81

   B $0.78   D $0.83

Extra Practice on page 138, Set C

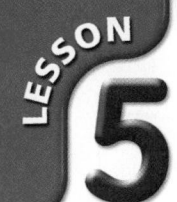

LESSON

5 Add and Subtract Money Amounts

OBJECTIVE: Add and subtract money amounts.

Quick Review

1. 31 + 57 = ■
2. 309 + 112 = ■
3. 450 − 200 = ■
4. 305 − 47 = ■
5. 1,251 + 3,070 = ■

Learn

PROBLEM Tony bought a robot for $12.42 and a book for $13.82. How much did Tony spend?

Example 1 **Add.** $12.42 + $13.82

Estimate to the nearest dollar. $12 + $14 = $26

Step 1	Step 2	Step 3
Line up the decimal points. $12.42 + $13.82	Add money like whole numbers. ₁ $12.42 + $13.82 26 24	Write the sum in dollars and cents. $12.42 + $13.82 $26.24

So, Tony needs $26.24. Since $26.24 is close to the estimate of $26, the answer is reasonable.

- How would you line up the decimal points to find $12.42 + $3.82?

Example 2 Megan bought a jacket for $28.19. She paid with $40.00. How much change did she get?

Estimate to the nearest ten dollars. $40 − $30 = $10

Step 1	Step 2	Step 3
Line up the decimal points. $40.00 − $28.19	Subtract money like whole numbers $40.00 − $28.19 11 81	Write the difference in dollars and cents. $40.00 − $28.19 $11.81

So, Megan got $11.81 in change. Since $11.81 is close to the estimate of $10, the answer is reasonable.

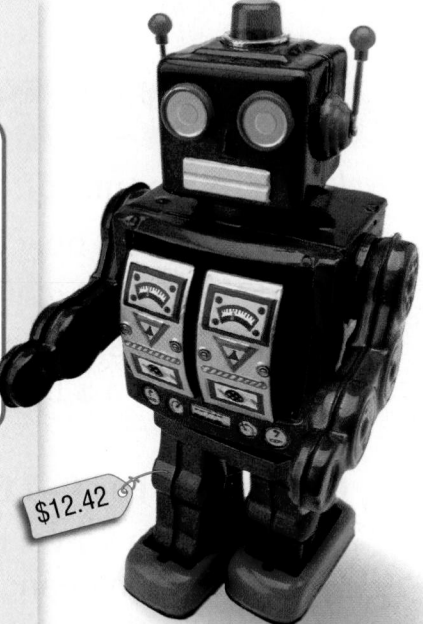

$12.42

$13.82

1. How would you line up the decimal points to find
   $8.64 + $7.22? Find the sum.

Estimate. Then find the sum or difference.

☑**2.** $45.76
          − $31.28

☑**3.** $16.25
          + $13.12

4. $3.81
         − $1.29

5. $20.51
         − $16.84

6. **TALK Math** **Explain** how you would find $2.43 − $1.25.

Independent Practice and Problem Solving

Estimate. Then find the sum or difference.

7. $2.57
         + $7.21

8. $52.94
         − $21.52

9. $4.00
         − $3.51

10. $32.50
          − $14.75

11. $0.62
          + $1.87

12. $22.15 + $18.39

13. $50.00 − $42.38

14. $1.23 + $6.50 + $4.27

15. $3.61 + $0.41

16. $46.87 − $29.19

17. $6.50 + $4.12 + $4.12

Algebra **Find the missing number.**

18. $6.50 − ■ = $2.50

19. $10.00 + ■ = $15.20

20. $10.70 + ■ = $50.00

USE DATA For 21–22, use the pictures.

21. Eric paid for glitter and glue with a
    $5 bill. How much change did he get?

22. **WRITE Math** **What's the Question?**
    Shelly bought construction paper and
    craft sticks. The answer is $2.06.

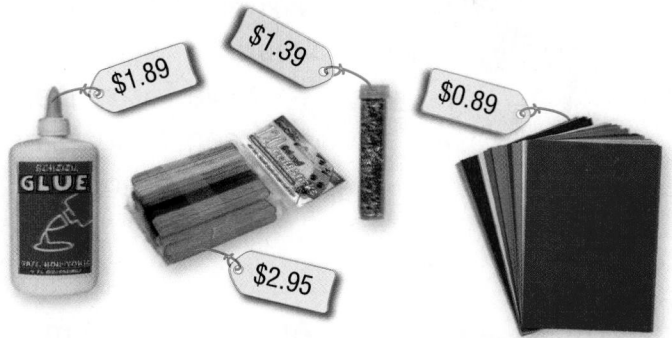

Mixed Review and Test Prep

23. A bag has 7 red cubes and 2 blue
    cubes. Which color cube are you
    more likely to choose? (Grade 2)

24. A cafeteria has 253 seats. One
    hundred sixteen seats are being
    used. How many seats are not
    being used? (p. 84)

25. **Test Prep** Ron buys a book for
    $6.12. He pays with a $10 bill. How
    much change does Ron get?

    A $3.58   **C** $3.88

    B $3.86   **D** $3.98

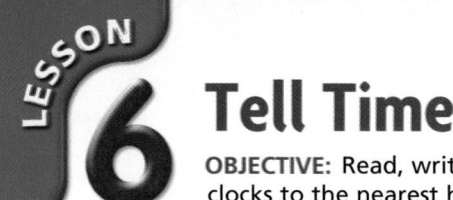

Tell Time

OBJECTIVE: Read, write, and tell time on analog and digital clocks to the nearest half hour, quarter hour, and minute.

Quick Review

Roberto skip-counted to 60 by fives. What numbers did Roberto count?

Vocabulary

half hour	quarter hour
hour minute	analog clock
digital clock	second

Learn

In one **hour**, the hour hand on a clock moves from one number to the next. In one **minute**, the minute hand on a clock moves from one mark to the next.

PROBLEM Carrie fed her puppy, Buster, at the 3 times shown below. At what times did she feed Buster?

Example In the morning

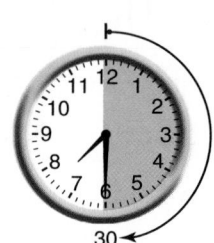

A **half hour** has 30 minutes.
Write: 7:30
Read:
• seven thirty
• thirty minutes after seven
• half past seven

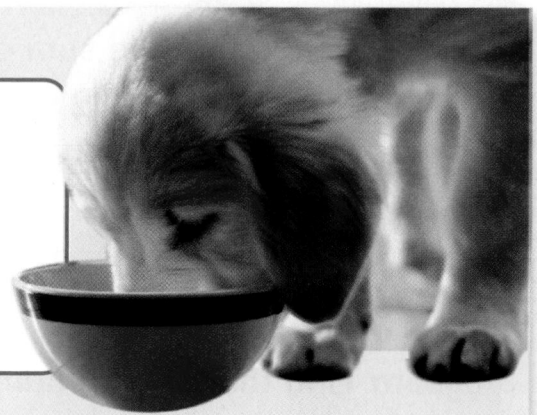

In the afternoon

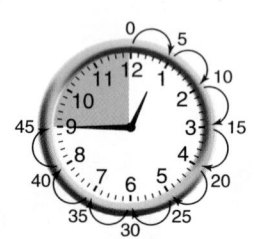

A **quarter hour** has 15 minutes.
Write: 12:45
Read:
• twelve forty-five
• fifteen minutes before one
• quarter to one

READ Math

An **analog clock** has a minute hand and an hour hand. Some clocks have second hands.

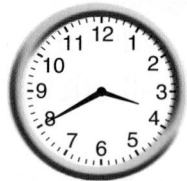

A **digital clock** shows the time by using numbers. The numbers to the left of the colon show the hour. The numbers to the right show the minutes after the hour.

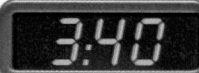

In the evening

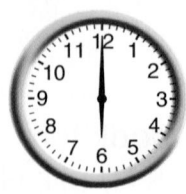

An **hour** has 60 minutes.
The hour hand is pointing to the 6.
The minute hand is pointing to the 12.
Write: 6:00
Read:
• six o'clock

So, Carrie fed Buster at 7:30, 12:45, and 6:00.

• Describe how the minute hand moves when the time goes from 8:00 to 9:00.

Time to the Minute

Example 1
Minutes after the hour

To find the number of minutes after the hour, count by fives and ones to where the minute hand is pointing.

Write: 11:23

Read:
- eleven twenty-three
- twenty-three minutes after eleven

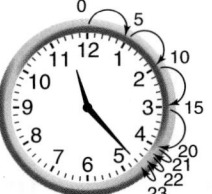

Example 2
Minutes before the hour

When a clock shows 31 or more minutes *after* the hour, you can read the time as a number of minutes *before* the next hour.

Write: 2:48

Read:
- twelve minutes before three
- two forty-eight

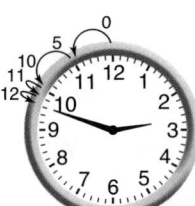

More Examples

A Minutes after the hour

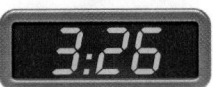

Write: 3:26

Read:
- three twenty-six
- twenty-six minutes after three

Think: 3:26 is almost half past 3.

B Minutes before the hour

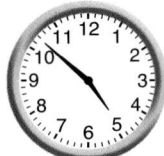

Write: 4:52

Read:
- four fifty-two
- eight minutes before five

Think: 52 minutes after an hour is 8 minutes before the next hour.

Guided Practice

1. How would you read the time shown on this clock two different ways?

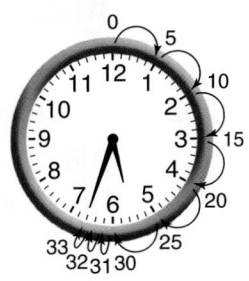

Write the time. Then write two ways you can read the time.

2.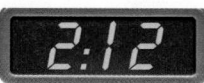

3.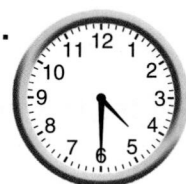

4.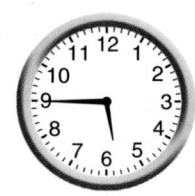

5.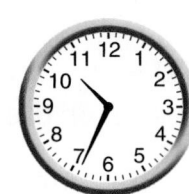

6. **TALK Math** **Explain** where the hour and minute hands are on a clock when it is 15 minutes after 9.

Independent Practice and Problem Solving

Write the time. Then write two ways you can read the time.

7.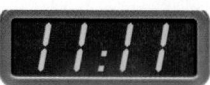

8.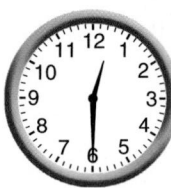

9.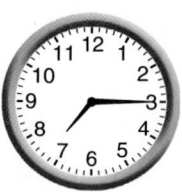

10.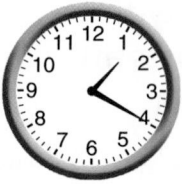

For 11–18, write the letter of the clock that shows the time.

a.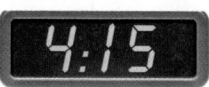

b.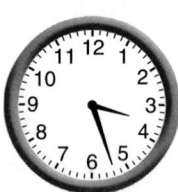

c.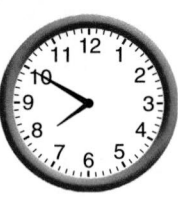

d.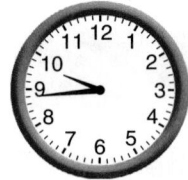

11. seven fifty

12. quarter past four

13. three twenty-seven

14. ten minutes before eight

15. sixteen minutes before ten

16. 3:27

17. 9:44

18. four fifteen

19. 50 minutes past 7

For 20–22, use the clocks.

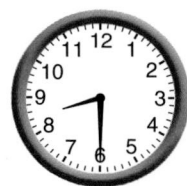

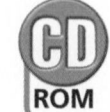

20. Bryan woke up at 8:30. Does this clock show that time? Explain how you know.

21. Tanya went home at a quarter after 10. Does this clock show that time? Explain how you know.

22. Art class ends at 5 minutes before 2. Does this clock show that time? Explain how you know.

Technology
Use Harcourt Mega Math, Country Countdown,
ROM *Clock-a-Doodle-Doo,* Levels I and J.

Extra Practice on page 139, Set E

USE DATA For 23–25, use the chart of Buster's Feeding Times.

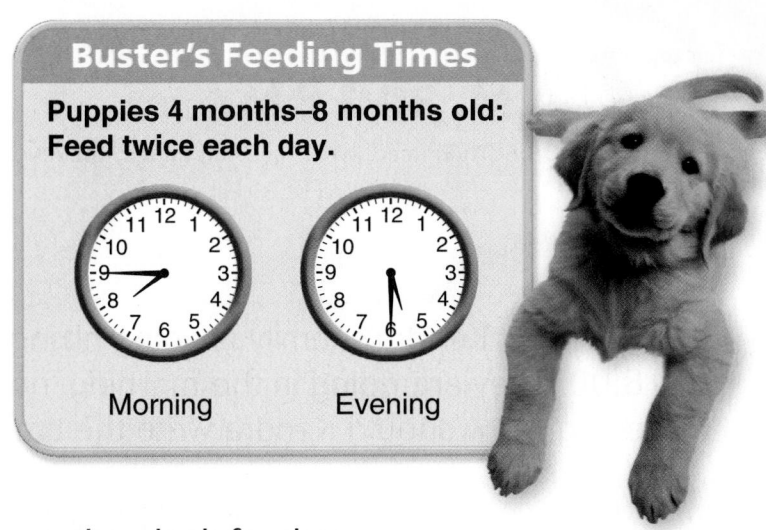

Buster's Feeding Times

Puppies 4 months–8 months old: Feed twice each day.

Morning   Evening

23. When Buster is 6 months old, Carrie will feed him twice each day at the times shown on the clocks. At what times will Carrie feed Buster?

24. Suppose Carrie fed Buster 5 minutes earlier than the evening time shown on the clock. At what time did she feed Buster?

25. **WRITE Math** ▸ **What's the Error?** Carrie says the clock for the morning feeding shows quarter past seven. **Explain** her error. Write the correct time.

Learn About Seconds

A **second** is a very short time. It takes about 1 second to take a step, clap your hands, or hop on one foot. Some clocks have second hands.

Math Idea
60 seconds = 1 minute
60 minutes = 1 hour
24 hours = 1 day

Try It

Write the time.

26.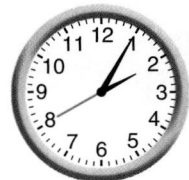

27.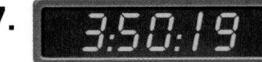

28.

29.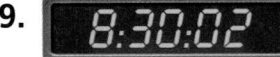

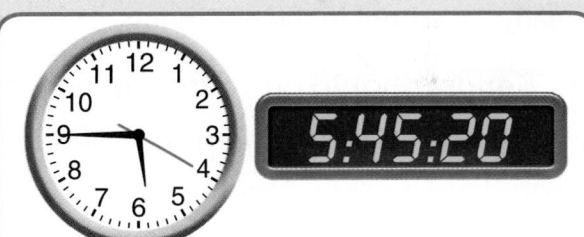

Write: 5:45:20
Read: 20 seconds after 5:45 **or** 5:45 and 20 seconds

Mixed Review and Test Prep

30. Bryan's mother bought a television set for $394. What is 394 rounded to the nearest hundred? (p. 36)

31. **Test Prep** Laura ate lunch at quarter to one. Which shows her lunch time?

    A 12:15   **B** 12:45   **C** 1:15   **D** 1:45

32. Three numbers are 46, 48, and 50. If the pattern continues, what is the next number? (p. 4)

33. **Test Prep** Write the time as it would look on Alex's digital watch at five minutes after six.

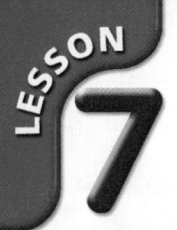

A.M. and P.M.

OBJECTIVE: Read, write, and tell time in the A.M. and P.M.

Learn

PROBLEM Kendra's family is going hiking tomorrow at 8:00. They are going in the morning, not in the evening. How should Kendra write the time?

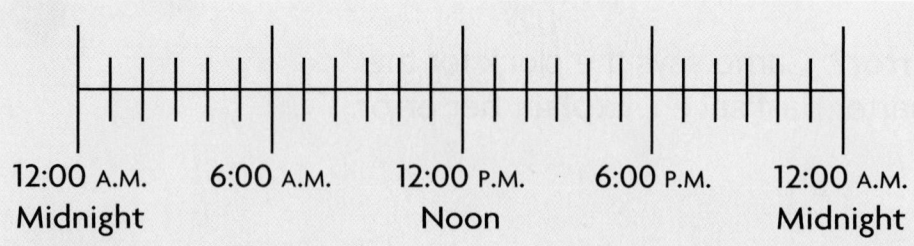

12:00 A.M.   6:00 A.M.   12:00 P.M.   6:00 P.M.   12:00 A.M.
Midnight   Noon   Midnight

A time line can help you understand the hours in a day.

Midnight is 12:00 at night.	**Noon** is 12:00 during the day.
For times from midnight to noon, write **A.M.** Midnight is 12:00 A.M.	For times from noon to midnight, write **P.M.** Noon is 12:00 P.M.
You wake up, eat breakfast, and get ready for school in the A.M. hours.	You come home from school, eat dinner, and go to bed in the P.M. hours.

So, Kendra should write the hiking time as 8:00 A.M.

• How do you write the time when it is one minute after noon?

Guided Practice

1. Name something you do in the A.M. hours. Name something you do in the P.M. hours.

Write the time for each activity. Use A.M. or P.M.

☑ **2.** play soccer

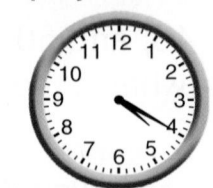

3. go shopping

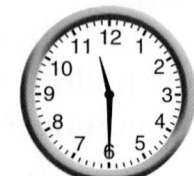

☑ **4.** look up at the stars

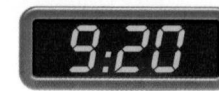

5. put on pajamas

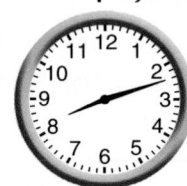

6. **TALK Math** Explain how you decide whether to use A.M. or P.M. when you write the time.

Write the time for each activity. Use A.M. or P.M.

7. eat breakfast

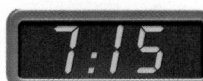

8. have math class

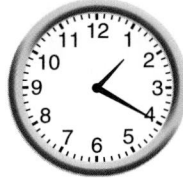

9. play outside

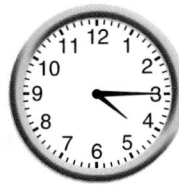

10. watch a sunset

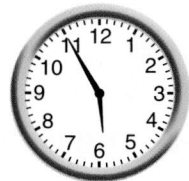

Write the time by using numbers. Use A.M. or P.M.

11. quarter after 8 in the morning

12. 5 minutes before 9 at night

13. one half hour past midnight

14. 20 minutes before noon

15. ≡**FAST FACT** Daylight Saving Time begins on the second Sunday in March at 2:00 in the morning. Write the time, and use A.M. or P.M.

USE DATA For 16–18, use the table.

16. Ken wants to go to the tile art class. Write the time for the class, using A.M. or P.M.

17. Brad took the earliest classes in the morning and afternoon. Which classes did he take?

18. [WRITE Math ▸] Mary eats lunch at noon. What classes are before Mary's lunch? **Explain** how you know.

Morning and Afternoon Craft Classes

Scrapbooking	8:50
Tile Art	10:30
Stamp a Card	1:00
Make Soap	2:45

Mixed Review and Test Prep

19. Use <, >, or = to make this number sentence true.

$$14 - 2 \ \blacksquare \ 10 + 2 \ \text{(p. 28)}$$

20. Carlos had 17 markers. He found 4 more. Then he gave Louis 9 markers. How many does Carlos have now?

(p. 80)

21. **Test Prep** At which of the times shown are most third graders asleep?

A 8 A.M.

B 12:00 P.M.

C 7:00 P.M.

D 12:00 A.M.

8 Model Elapsed Time

OBJECTIVE: Use a clock to measure elapsed time.

Learn

Elapsed time is the amount of time that passes from the start of an activity to the end of the activity.

PROBLEM The Library of Congress in Washington, D.C., is the largest library in the world. One of its buildings is the Thomas Jefferson building. It opens at 10:00 A.M. and closes at 5:30 P.M. For how long is the building open each day?

Hands On Activity

Materials ■ clock with moveable hands

Model 10:00 on your clock.

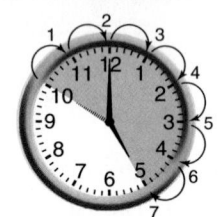

10:00 to 5:00 is 7 hours.
Move the hour hand.
Count the hours.

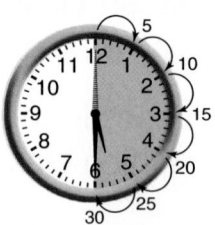

5:00 to 5:30 is 30 minutes.
Move the minute hand.
Count the minutes.

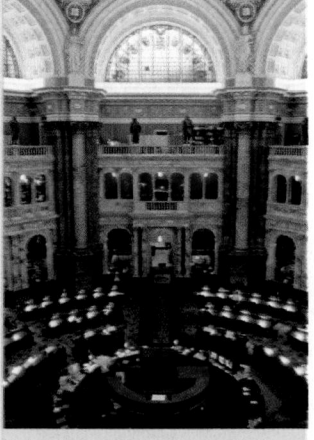

▲ The Library of Congress has more books than any library in the world.

So, the building is open for 7 hours 30 minutes.

More Examples

A Hours and Minutes

Start: 1:00
End: 3:30

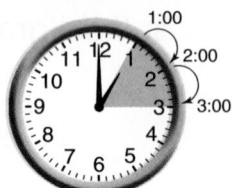

Move the hour hand.
Count the hours.

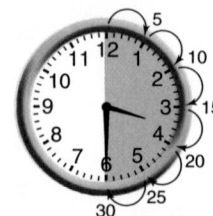

Move the minute hand.
Count the minutes.

Elapsed time: 2 hours 30 minutes

B Minutes

Start: 5:10
End: 5:38

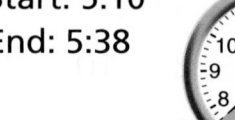

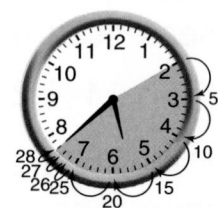

Move the minute hand.
Count the minutes.

Elapsed time: 28 minutes

1. How much time elapses from 4:15 P.M. until 7:15 P.M.?

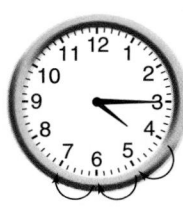

Use a clock to find the elapsed time.

2. Start: 8:30 A.M.
   End: 10:30 A.M.

3. Start: 4:20 A.M.
   End: 5:00 A.M.

4. Start: 11:50 A.M.
   End: 2:30 P.M.

5. **TALK Math** Explain how to use a clock to find the elapsed time from noon until 3:45 P.M.

Independent Practice and Problem Solving

Use a clock to find the elapsed time.

6. Start: 2:20 A.M.
   End: 5:30 A.M.

7. Start: 8:45 A.M.
   End: 2:00 P.M.

8. Start: 10:30 A.M.
   End: 6:15 P.M.

Tell what time it will be.

9. 15 minutes after 12:45 P.M.

10. 2 hours 30 minutes after 1:10 A.M.

11. 4 hours after 10:22 A.M.

12. 3 hours 10 minutes after 11:30 A.M.

13. Sam and his family arrived at the Library of Congress at 10:30 A.M. They took a sixty-minute tour. At what time was their tour over?

14. **WRITE Math** Sam's family toured the White House from 2:15 P.M. until 3:20 P.M. **Explain** how you know that the tour was less than 2 hours.

Mixed Review and Test Prep

15. Tim saw a very large sea turtle. About how much does it weigh?

    (Grade 2)

    779 pounds   779 ounces

16. Olivia has 12 nickels and 4 pennies. Toby has 5 dimes and 15 pennies. Who has more money? How much more? (p. 114)

17. **Test Prep** What time is 2 hours 30 minutes after 5:15 P.M.?

    A 7:15 P.M.   **C** 7:30 P.M.

    B 7:18 P.M.   **D** 7:45 P.M.

Use a Calendar

OBJECTIVE: Use a calendar to determine elapsed time.

Quick Review

Charles skip-counted by sevens from 0 to 35. What numbers did Charles count?

Vocabulary

calendar

Learn

A **calendar** shows the days, weeks, and months of a year. There are 12 months in one year. You can use a calendar to find elapsed time that is more than one day.

PROBLEM Sunrise Elementary School is having a school play. Tom's class begins practicing for the play on October 3. The play is in 3 weeks. On what date is the school play?

October						
Sun	Mon	Tue	Wed	Thu	Fri	Sat
			1	2	③	4
5	6	7	8	9	10	11
12	13	14	15	16	17	18
19	20	21	22	23	㉔	25
26	27	28	29	30	31	

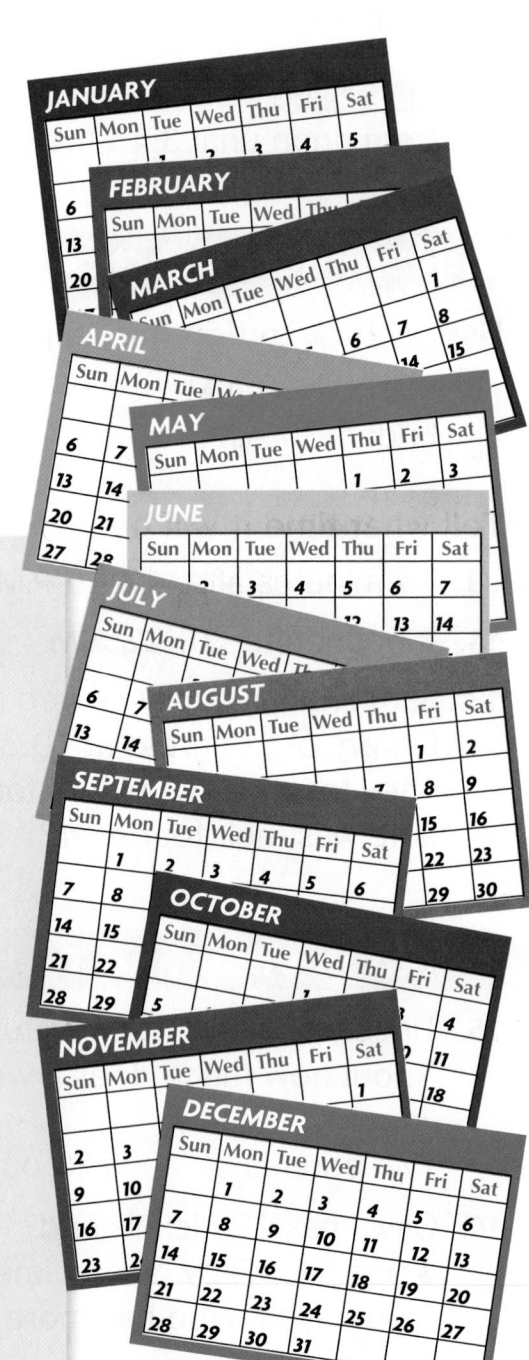

ONE WAY

Count by days.

Start on October 3, and count on one day to October 4, two days to October 5, and so on.

Count all the days that are shaded.
There are 21 days. 21 days = 3 weeks.

So, the school play is on October 24.

ANOTHER WAY

Count by weeks.

Start on October 3. Count down the Friday column one week to October 10, two weeks to October 17, and three weeks to October 24.

So, the school play is on October 24.

• How would you find the number of weeks from October 1 until October 29?

Units of Time

Time can be measured in small units, such as minutes and hours, by using a clock. Time can also be measured in larger units, such as days, weeks, and months, by using a calendar.

Units of Time
60 minutes = 1 hour
24 hours = 1 day
7 days = 1 week
12 months = 1 year
365 days = 1 year
52 weeks = 1 year

Example 1 Abby is visiting her cousin. The first day of her visit is June 18. The last day of her visit is July 10. How long is Abby's visit?

Count each day of her visit. The first day of the visit is June 18. The second day of the visit is June 19, and so on. Count all the days that are shaded. There are 23 days.

June

Sun	Mon	Tue	Wed	Thu	Fri	Sat
1	2	3	4	5	6	7
8	9	10	11	12	13	14
15	16	17	⑱	19	20	21
22	23	24	25	26	27	28
29	30					

July

Sun	Mon	Tue	Wed	Thu	Fri	Sat
		1	2	3	4	5
6	7	8	9	⑩	11	12
13	14	15	16	17	18	19
20	21	22	23	24	25	26
27	28	29	30	31		

So, the visit is 23 days, or 3 weeks and 2 days.

- How many days are in 3 weeks and 4 days?

Example 2 Eric loves baseball. Suppose it is Monday, August 4, at 3:00 P.M. Eric's next baseball game is on Tuesday, August 5, at 5:00 P.M. How long does Eric have to wait until his next baseball game?

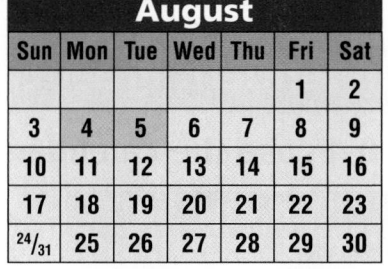

August

Sun	Mon	Tue	Wed	Thu	Fri	Sat
					1	2
3	4	5	6	7	8	9
10	11	12	13	14	15	16
17	18	19	20	21	22	23
24/31	25	26	27	28	29	30

Think:

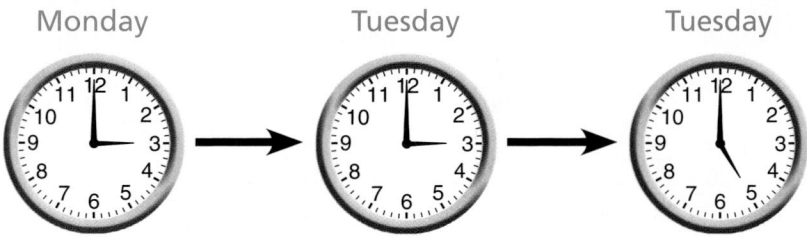

Monday   Tuesday   Tuesday

1 day = 24 hours   3:00 P.M. to 5:00 P.M. = 2 hours

24 hours + 2 hours = 26 hours

So, Eric has to wait 26 hours, or 1 day and 2 hours.

- How many hours are in 1 day and 6 hours?

1. The school's book fair runs for 5 days beginning on September 15. What is the last day of the book fair?

| September |||||||
Sun	Mon	Tue	Wed	Thu	Fri	Sat
	1	2	3	4	5	6
7	8	9	10	11	12	13
14	15	16	17	18	19	20
21	22	23	24	25	26	27
28	29	30				

For 2–5, use the calendars.

| January |||||||
Sun	Mon	Tue	Wed	Thu	Fri	Sat
		1	2	3	4	5
6	7	8	9	10	11	12
13	14	15	16	17	18	19
20	21	22	23	24	25	26
27	28	29	30	31		

| February |||||||
Sun	Mon	Tue	Wed	Thu	Fri	Sat
					1	2
3	4	5	6	7	8	9
10	11	12	13	14	15	16
17	18	19	20	21	22	23
24	25	26	27	28	29	

| March |||||||
Sun	Mon	Tue	Wed	Thu	Fri	Sat
						1
2	3	4	5	6	7	8
9	10	11	12	13	14	15
16	17	18	19	20	21	22
$^{23}/_{30}$	$^{24}/_{31}$	25	26	27	28	29

2. Today is January 3. Bob's birthday is January 12. How long is it until Bob's birthday? Write your answer two ways.

3. Today is February 11. Nikki began reading her book on January 30. She reads her book every day. Counting today, for how many days has Nikki been reading her book?

4. Suppose it is 8:00 A.M. on March 6. Julie is leaving on vacation at 11:00 A.M. on March 7. How long must Julie wait for her vacation to begin?

5. **TALK Math** **Explain** how to find the number of days from January 10 through January 25.

Independent Practice and Problem Solving

For 6–8, use the calendars.

| April |||||||
Sun	Mon	Tue	Wed	Thu	Fri	Sat
		1	2	3	4	5
6	7	8	9	10	11	12
13	14	15	16	17	18	19
20	21	22	23	24	25	26
27	28	29	30			

| May |||||||
Sun	Mon	Tue	Wed	Thu	Fri	Sat
				1	2	3
4	5	6	7	8	9	10
11	12	13	14	15	16	17
18	19	20	21	22	23	24
25	26	27	28	29	30	31

| June |||||||
Sun	Mon	Tue	Wed	Thu	Fri	Sat
1	2	3	4	5	6	7
8	9	10	11	12	13	14
15	16	17	18	19	20	21
22	23	24	25	26	27	28
29	30					

6. On April 11, Ms. Hines announced that there would be a class picnic in 2 weeks. On what date will the class have its picnic?

7. Manny began practicing the piano on May 26. He practiced for 1 hour every day through June 10. For how many days did Manny practice the piano?

8. **Reasoning** Jon and his family went camping at noon on May 20. They returned home at 5:00 P.M. on May 22. For how long did Jon's family camp? Write your answer in two ways.

Extra Practice on page 139, Set H

USE DATA For 9–10, use the calendar.

9. Suppose today is the second Monday in February. How many weeks is it until Presidents' Day?

10. **WRITE Math** ▶ **What's the Error?** Rob says that Valentine's Day is the third Thursday in February. Describe Rob's error. What correct statement could Rob make?

February						
Sun	**Mon**	**Tue**	**Wed**	**Thu**	**Fri**	**Sat**
					1	2
3	4	5	6	7	8	9
10	11	12	13	14 Valentine's Day	15	16
17	18 Presidents' Day	19	20	21	22	23
24	25	26	27	28	29	

Learn About) Visual Thinking

You can use the knuckles on your hands to help you remember the number of days in each month.

The months on the knuckles have 31 days. The months in between have 30 days, except February.

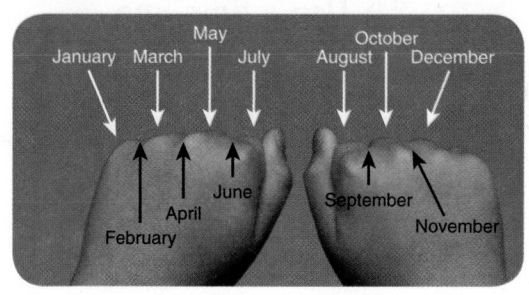

Try It

Write the number of days in each month.

11. September

12. August

13. November

Mixed Review and Test Prep

14. Beth is playing a game with a number line. Her game piece is on 505. If she moves 10 to the right, what number will she be on? (p. 34)

15. Della and Jasmine collected 98 shells at the beach. Della counted 46 shells and then found 4 more in her pocket. How many shells did Jasmine collect? (p. 80)

16. **Test Prep** Suppose it is 10:00 A.M. on Friday. Maggie's party will be at 1:00 P.M. on Saturday. How long is it until Maggie's party?

17. **Test Prep** Tim's birthday is February 13. Jena's birthday is February 20. How many days after Tim's birthday is Jena's birthday?

A 5 days   C 10 days

B 7 days   D 13 days

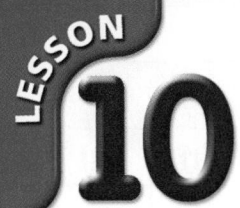
10 Sequence Events

OBJECTIVE: Use a clock, a calendar, and a time line to determine a sequence of events.

Learn

PROBLEM Ben drew a time line to show some events in the life of his kitten, Pogo. Did Pogo begin to walk before or after his weight doubled?

A time line shows the **sequence,** or order, of events. Read a time line from left to right. Events on the left happened before, or earlier than, events on the right.

Vocabulary

sequence

Example Use a time line.

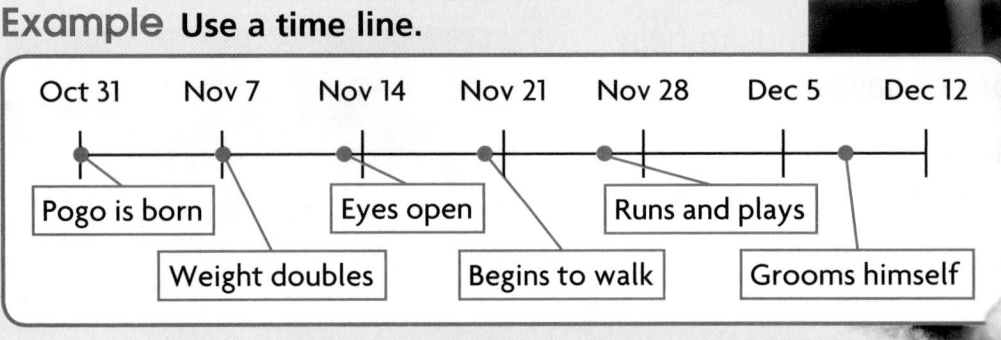

| Oct 31 | Nov 7 | Nov 14 | Nov 21 | Nov 28 | Dec 5 | Dec 12 |

Pogo is born | Eyes open | Runs and plays
Weight doubles | Begins to walk | Grooms himself

"Begins to walk" is to the right of "weight doubles." So, Pogo began to walk after his weight doubled.

- Pogo was 3 weeks old when he started getting his teeth. What other event on the time line happened about the same time?

More Examples

A Use a calendar.

April						
Sun	Mon	Tue	Wed	Thu	Fri	Sat
		1	2	3 Soccer	4	5 Party
6	7	8 Music	9	10	11	12
13	14 Zoo	15	16	17	18	19
20	21	22	23	24	25	26
27	28	29	30			

The order of Judy's activities: soccer game, birthday party, music lesson, and trip to the zoo.

B Use a clock.

4:20	6:15	7:00
Soccer practice	dinner	homework

Todd uses a clock to order his activities.

Which activity will Todd do first?

Guided Practice

For 1–4 use the time line.

1. *The Lion King* is to the right of the other movies on this time line. Was it first shown before or after the other movies?

Years in Which Movies Were First Shown

1940 1950 1960 1970 1980 1990 2000

Cinderella

101 Dalmatians

The Little Mermaid

The Lion King

Which movie was shown earlier?

☑ 2. *The Little Mermaid* or *Cinderella*   ☑ 3. *101 Dalmatians* or *The Lion King*

4. **TALK Math** Explain how to use the time line to tell which movie was shown before any of the others.

Independent Practice and Problem Solving

Use the calendar and the clocks. Which activity is earlier?

5. tennis or swimming

6. music or kickball

7. movie or book report

May						
Sun	**Mon**	**Tue**	**Wed**	**Thu**	**Fri**	**Sat**
				1 Book Report	2	3 Movie
4	5	6	7	8	9 Swim	10 Tennis

music	**1:00**
lunch	**11:30**
kickball	**10:15**

USE DATA For 8–9, use the table.

8. Sal's puppy was born on May 2. Which event was likely to happen on May 16?

9. **WRITE Math** Make a time line and explain how to show the events for Sal's puppy on it.

How a Puppy Grows

Event	Age
eyes open	2 weeks
walks	3 weeks
plays with puppies	4 weeks
eats puppy food	8 weeks

Mixed Review and Test Prep

10. Heath has 8 coins in his pocket. Six are pennies. Is he likely or unlikely to choose a penny? (Grade 2)

11. Jen left at 8 A.M. It took her 12 minutes to walk to the bus stop. The bus arrived at 8:20 A.M. For how many minutes did Jen wait for the bus? (p. 130)

12. **Test Prep** Use the calendar. Which event is Justin going to do last?

June						
Sun	**Mon**	**Tue**	**Wed**	**Thu**	**Fri**	**Sat**
1	2	3	4 Soccer	5	6	7
8 Swimming	9	10	11	12 Library	13	14 Camping

Extra Practice on page 139, Set I

Extra Practice

Set A Write the amount. (pp. 110–113)

1.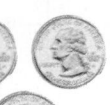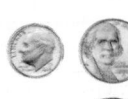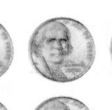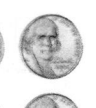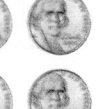

2.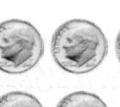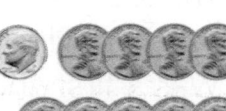

Find two equivalent sets for each. List the coins and bills.

3. 68¢   4. 80¢   5. $2.57   6. $1.14

Set B Use <, >, or = to compare the amounts of money. (pp. 114–115)

1.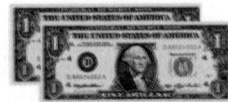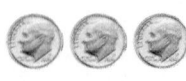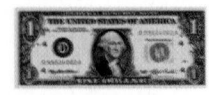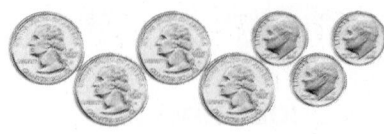

Which amount is greater?

2. $8.61 or $8.60   3. $3.25 or 3 one-dollar bills   4. $4.32 or $4.23

5. $1.10 or $1.01   6. $7.69 or $9.76   7. $5.15 or $5.51

Set C Find the amount of change. Use play money to help. (pp. 120–121)

1. Sofia buys a sandwich for $3.42. She pays with a $5 bill.

2. Kim buys a fruit salad for $4.74. She pays with a $5 bill.

3. Grace buys a calculator for $8.37. She pays with a $10 bill.

4. Brett buys a puzzle book for $7.99. He pays with a $10 bill.

5. Tony buys a model for $6.70. He pays with a $10 bill.

6. Matt buys a dog toy for $5.59. He pays with a $10 bill.

Set D Estimate. Then find the sum or difference. (pp. 122–123)

1. $6.21
   +$5.72

2. $3.65
   +$2.17

3. $27.18
   −$18.43

4. $70.00
   −$58.96

5. $48 + $39   6. $5.37 + $0.83   7. $21.76 − $14.19   8. $1.19 − $0.63

Technology
Use Harcourt Mega Math, The Number Games, *Buggy Bargains*, Levels D, G, I.

Set E Write the time. Then write two ways you can read the time. (pp. 124–127)

1.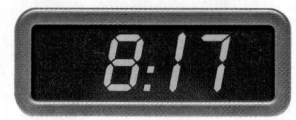

2.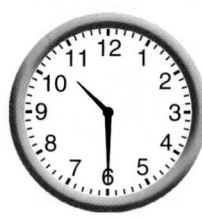

3.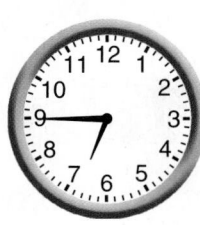

4.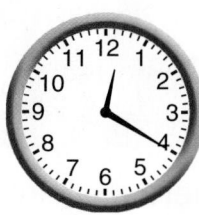

For 5–8, write the letter of the clock that shows the time.

a.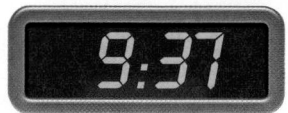

b.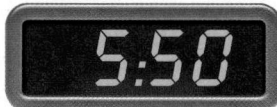

c.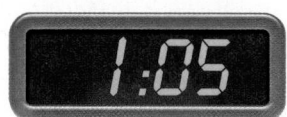

d.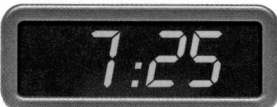

5. seven twenty-five

6. 1:05

7. nine thirty-seven

8. 5:50

Set F Write the time for each activity. Use A.M. or P.M. (pp. 128–129)

1.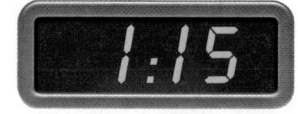
science class

2.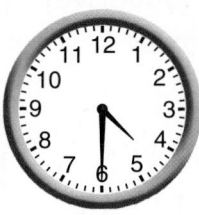
baseball game

3.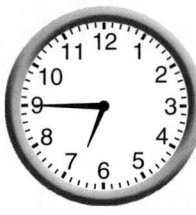
eat breakfast

4.
get ready for bed

Set G Use a clock to find the elapsed time. (pp. 130–131)

1. Start: 6:40 A.M.
End: 8:00 A.M.

2. Start: 2:45 P.M.
End: 4:15 P.M.

3. Start: 11:50 A.M.
End: 12:40 P.M.

Set H For 1–2, use the calendar. (pp. 132–135)

1. Marcie is going on vacation in 18 days from today. Today is June 3. On what date is Marcie going on vacation?

2. Rosa is visiting her aunt from June 16 through June 25. How many days is Rosa visiting her aunt?

June						
Sun	Mon	Tue	Wed	Thu	Fri	Sat
1	2	3	4	5	6	7 parade
8	9	10	11	12	13 visit cousin	14
15	16	17	18	19	20	21
22 beach	23	24	25 soccer	26	27	28
29	30					

Set I Use the calendar. Which activity is earlier? (pp. 136–137)

1. go to the beach or to the parade?

2. play soccer or go to the beach?

3. visit cousins or play soccer?

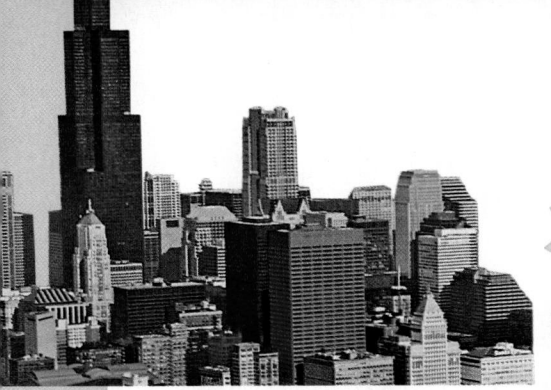
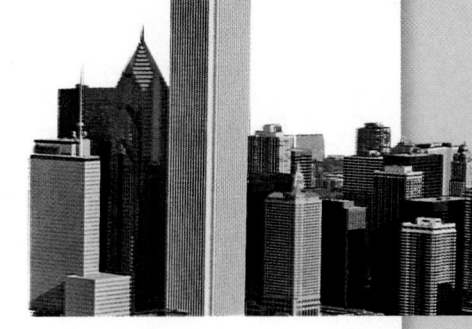

MATH POWER — Time Zones
Telephone Time

There are four time zones in the continental United States. There is a difference of one hour between each time zone.

Dial the Phone

Beth lives in San Francisco and her sister Shannon lives in Denver. If Beth calls Shannon when it is 9 A.M. in San Francisco, what time will it be in Denver?

Step 1

Find San Francisco on the map. San Francisco is in the Pacific time zone.

Step 2

Find Denver on the map. Denver is in the Mountain time zone.

Step 3

Find the difference in hours between the Pacific and Mountain time zones. It is one hour later in the Mountain time zone than in the Pacific time zone.

So, when it is 9 A.M. in San Francisco, it will be 10 A.M. in Denver.

UNITED STATES TIME ZONES

7 A.M.   8 A.M.   9 A.M.   10 A.M.

Seattle · MOUNTAIN
PACIFIC · Chicago · Boston
Denver · CENTRAL · EASTERN
San Francisco · Dallas · Miami

Try It

Use the map to solve.

1. Beth's cousin Randy lives in Dallas. If Beth calls him when it is 3:00 P.M. in San Francisco, what time will it be in Dallas?

2. Beth calls her grandmother at 8:00 A.M. each Sunday. Beth's grandmother lives in Miami. What time is it in Miami when Beth calls?

3. Beth calls her brother Mike when it is 4:00 P.M. in Chicago. What time is it in San Francisco when Beth calls her brother?

4. Beth's parents live in Seattle. If they call Beth at 7:00 P.M. once a week, what time is it in San Francisco?

5. **WRITE Math** ▸ Beth's brother Lewis lives in Boston. If Lewis calls Beth at 9:00 P.M. Eastern time, what time will it be in San Francisco? **Explain** how you know.

Chapter 5 Review/Test

Check Vocabulary and Concepts

Choose the best term from the box.

1. Times from noon to midnight are indicated by writing __?__ after the time. (p. 128)

2. A __?__ is thirty minutes. (p. 124)

3. The amount of time that passes is called __?__. (p. 130)

4. Sets of money that have the same value are __?__. (p. 110)

Check Skills

Find two equivalent sets for each. List the coins and bills. (pp. 110–113)

5. 72¢   6. 43¢   7. $3.35

Estimate. Then find the sum or difference. (pp. 122–123)

8. $8.37
  + $6.29

9. $53.25
  + $37.16

10. $65.71
   − $53.46

11. $28.00
   − $ 7.32

Write the time using numbers. Use A.M. or P.M. (pp. 128–129)

12. 25 minutes after two in the afternoon

13. one half hour past five in the evening

14. 40 minutes after nine in the morning

15. 50 minutes after one in the afternoon

16. 10 minutes after noon

17. 15 minutes before three in the afternoon

Check Problem Solving

Solve. (pp. 116–119)

18. Ryan wants to buy a snow globe for $2.17. What are two ways to use coins and bills to show $2.17?

19. Ava has 1 $5 bill, 4 $1 bills, 5 quarters, 6 dimes, and 2 nickels. She has to pay $5.95 for a new calculator. What are two ways Ava can make $5.95?

20. **WRITE Math** ▸ Yolanda bought a map for $1.50, sunblock for $4.75, and a bottle of water for $2.25. Write two ways Yolanda can pay for all three items. **Explain** how you found your answers.

Standardized Test Prep
Chapters 1–5

Number and Operations (p. 14)

1. The deepest part of the Gulf of Mexico is Sigsbee Deep. It is 12,714 feet deep. What is the value of the digit 2 in 12,714?

A 20

C 2,000

B 200

D 20,000

2. Lucy's book has 39 pages. Angela's book has 48 pages. How many more pages are in Angela's book? (p. 80)

A 6

C 8

B 7

D 9

Test Tip **Understand the problem.**

See item 3. What is the question? What information do you need to answer the question? Write down all of the numbers in the problem and solve.

3. **WRITE Math** Jaime and Kathy bought maps at a yard sale. Jaime's map cost $8.05. Kathy's map cost $7.95. Who spent the most money? **Explain** how you know. (p. 114)

Algebraic Reasoning

4. Which number completes the fact family? (Grade 2)

$6 + \blacksquare = 13$ $\blacksquare + 6 = 13$
$13 - 6 = \blacksquare$ $13 - \blacksquare = 6$

A 6

B 7

C 13

D 19

5. How many wheels are on 6 bicycles? (p. 4)

Bicycles	1	2	3	4	5	6
Wheels	2	4	6	8	10	$\blacksquare$

A 11

B 12

C 14

D 18

6. **WRITE Math** Describe the pattern unit and draw the next two shapes. **Explain** how to continue the pattern. (Grade 2)

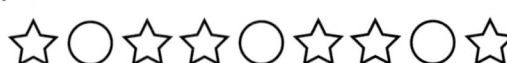

Measurement

7. What is the correct temperature? (Grade 2)

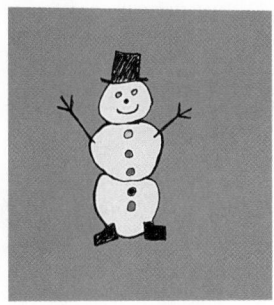 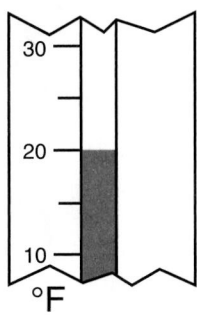

| **A** 20°F | **C** 30°F |
| **B** 25°F | **D** 35°F |

8. The clock shows the time Michael and his family eat dinner. At what time do they eat? (p. 124)

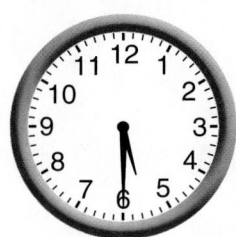

A 5:00

B 5:30

C 6:25

D 6:30

9. **WRITE Math** ▶ **Explain** where the hands on the clock will be when the time is 9:25. (p. 124)

Data Analysis and Probability

10. How many more students chose orange juice than apple juice? (Grade 2)

Juices We Like	
Apple	🍎🍎🍎
Orange	🍎🍎🍎🍎🍎
Grape	🍎🍎
Key: Each 🍎 = 1 student.	

A 1

B 2

C 3

D 4

11. Which pizza topping did the most students choose? (Grade 2)

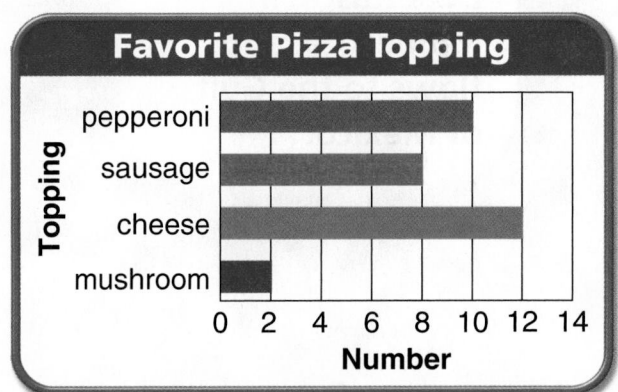

| **A** Pepperoni | **C** Cheese |
| **B** Sausage | **D** Mushroom |

12. **WRITE Math** ▶ A bag has 4 green tiles, 3 yellow tiles, and 7 red tiles. Which color are you most likely to pull? **Explain** how you know. (Grade 2)

6 Data

The Mississippi River is the longest river in the United States. It begins at Lake Itasca, in Minnesota, and flows to the Gulf of Mexico.

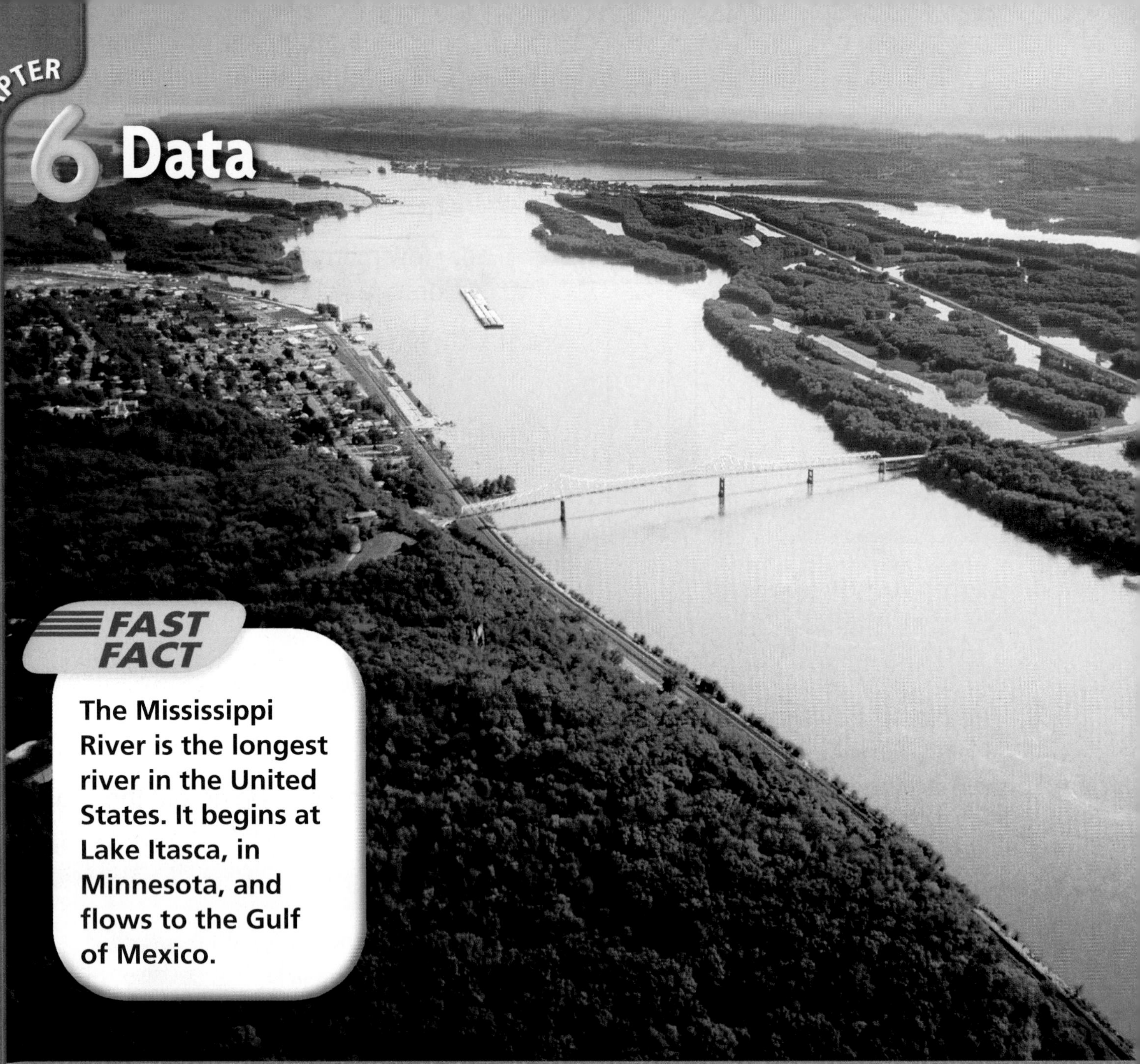

Investigate

Many rivers flow into the Mississippi River. Look at the map. Show another way you can display the data about the river lengths.

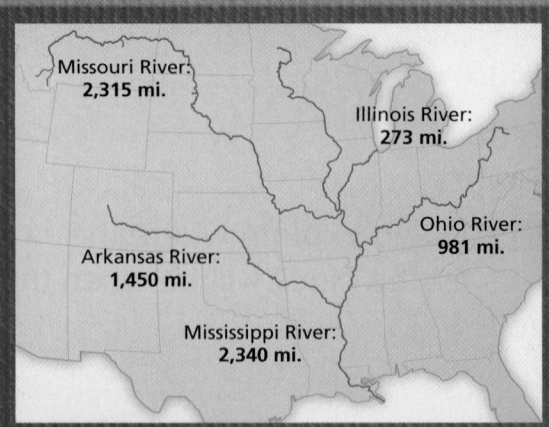

Missouri River: 2,315 mi.

Illinois River: 273 mi.

Ohio River: 981 mi.

Arkansas River: 1,450 mi.

Mississippi River: 2,340 mi.

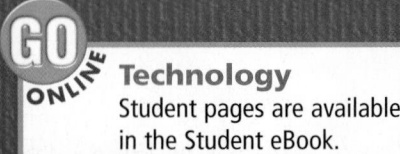

Technology
Student pages are available in the Student eBook.

Check your understanding of important skills needed for success in Chapter 6.

▶ **Read a Tally Table**

For 1–3, use the tally table.

Which pet do you have?	
Dog	卌 卌 IIII
Cat	卌 卌 II
Bird	IIII
Fish	卌 III

1. How many students have a dog?

2. How many students have fish?

3. How many students answered the question?

▶ **Column Addition**

Find the sum.

4. 3	5. 9	6. 6	7. 8	8. 7
2	3	2	1	9
5	1	8	4	2
+7	+4	+3	+6	+7

▶ **Read a Chart**

For 9–11, use the bar graph.

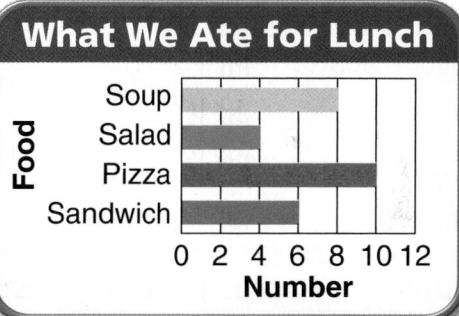

9. How many students ate a sandwich?

10. Which food did most students eat?

11. How many students ate lunch?

VOCABULARY POWER

CHAPTER VOCABULARY

bar graph
classify
data
frequency
  table
grid
horizontal bar
  graph

key
line graph
line plot
mode
ordered pair
pictograph
range
results

scale
survey
tally table
trends
vertical bar
  graph

WARM-UP WORDS

bar graph A graph that uses bars to show data

data Information that is collected about people or things

tally table A table that uses tally marks to record data

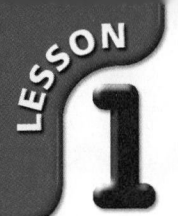

Collect Data

OBJECTIVE: Collect, organize, and record data in tally tables and frequency tables.

Learn

Data is information that is collected about people or things.

PROBLEM The students in Moira's class voted for their favorite ice cream flavors. Moira showed the results two ways. Which flavor got the greatest number of votes? Which flavor got the least number of votes?

You can record data in a **tally table** by making tally marks as you gather data.

Favorite Ice Cream

Flavor	Tally
Rocky Road	ⅢⅠ Ⅰ
Vanilla	ⅢⅠ ⅠⅠ
Chocolate	ⅢⅠ ⅠⅠⅠ
Strawberry	ⅠⅠⅠⅠ

You can show the number of tally marks in a **frequency table** to make the data easier to read.

Favorite Ice Cream

Flavor	Number
Rocky Road	6
Vanilla	7
Chocolate	8
Strawberry	4

The number of votes from greatest to least is 8, 7, 6, and 4.

So, chocolate got the greatest number of votes.
Strawberry got the least number of votes.

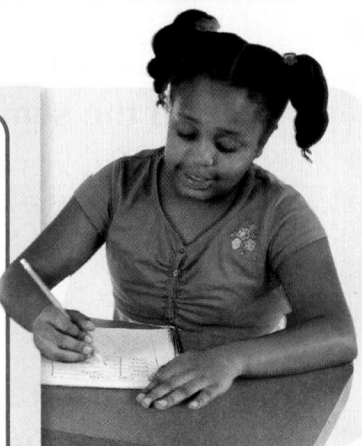

Activity   Materials ■ tally table

Collect data about your classmates' favorite ice cream. Organize the data in a tally table. Then make a frequency table.

Step 1	Step 2
Make a tally table. Write the title and headings. List the possible flavors. Make a tally mark for each vote.	Count the number of tally marks. Record the numbers in a frequency table.

Favorite Ice Cream

Flavor	Tally

Favorite Ice Cream

Flavor	Number

Guided Practice

1. What number would you write in a frequency table to show ⅢⅢ ⅢⅢ Ⅲ?

For 2–3, use the Favorite Sport table.

✓ 2. How many students in all voted for soccer and baseball?

✓ 3. How many students voted in all?

4. **TALK Math** **Explain** why a frequency table can be a good way to show data.

Favorite Sport	
Sport	**Tally**
Basketball	ⅢⅢ Ⅱ
Soccer	ⅢⅢ ⅢⅢ
Baseball	ⅢⅢ Ⅰ

Independent Practice and Problem Solving

For 5–6, use the Shirt Color list.

5. Kelly made this list of the shirt colors the students in her class were wearing. Make a tally table and a frequency table to organize her data.

6. How many more students are wearing white or blue shirts than red or green shirts?

Shirt Color			
Jen	white	Kim	blue
Patty	red	Lee	red
Matt	blue	Pam	white
Jared	white	Brad	red
Carl	green	Jake	blue

For 7–8, use the Favorite Juice table.

7. How many students voted for their favorite juice in this survey?

8. **What if** 13 more students voted for orange juice? How would the table change?

9. **WRITE Math** How are a tally table and a frequency table alike? How are they different?

Favorite Juice	
Flavor	**Number**
Grape	16
Orange	4
Berry	5
Apple	6

Mixed Review and Test Prep

10. Julie had 45 inches of ribbon. She cut 9 inches off each end. How many inches of ribbon are left? (p. 80)

11. A play began at 1:10 P.M. and ended at 3:20 P.M. How long did the play last? (p. 130)

12. **Test Prep** Jen made a tally table to record her friends' votes for their favorite pet. Her chart shows ⅢⅢ ⅢⅢ Ⅱ next to Dog. How many voted for dog?

   A 7　　　　　**C** 12

   B 10　　　　 **D** 15

Extra Practice on page 170, Set A

2 Read a Pictograph

OBJECTIVE: Read and interpret data in a pictograph.

Use the tally table.

Favorite Pet	
Pet	**Tally**
Dog	卌 卌 l
Cat	卌 llll
Bird	llll

How many people voted for cat?

Learn

A **pictograph** uses pictures to show information.

PROBLEM Areas that are part of the national park system are good places to vacation and to learn about plants and animals. The pictograph shows the number of those areas in some states. How many are there in Pennsylvania?

National Parks	
Massachusetts	🌲🌲🌲🌲🌲
Michigan	🌲🌿
New Jersey	🌲🌲🌿
New York	🌲🌲🌲🌲🌲🌲
Pennsylvania	🌲🌲🌲🌲🌲🌲
Key: Each 🌲 = 4 national parks.	

Math Idea
In this graph,
🌲 = 4 parks,
so 🌿 = 2 parks.

The title tells that the pictograph is about national parks.

Each row has a label that tells the name of a state.

The **key** tells that each picture stands for 4 national parks.

To find the number of national parks in Pennsylvania, count the number of 🌲 by fours.

$$4 + 4 + 4 + 4 + 4 + 4 = 24$$

So, there are 24 national parks in Pennsylvania.

• Which state in the pictograph has the most national parks? How many parks does it have?

• Explain how many national parks are in New Jersey.

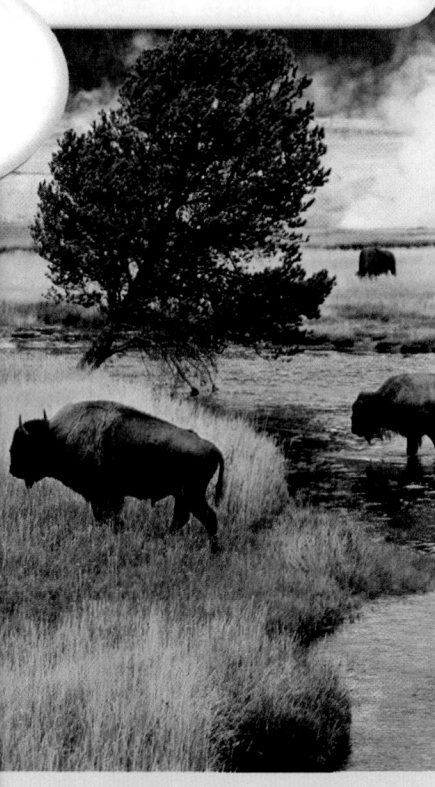

▲ Yellowstone National Park, in Wyoming, was the first named national park in the United States.

pictograph   key

Guided Practice

1. How many national parks are in Massachusetts?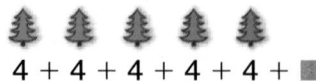

4 + 4 + 4 + 4 + 4 + ■

For 2–3, use the National Parks pictograph on page 148.

2. Which state in the pictograph has the fewest national parks?

3. How many more national parks are there in Pennsylvania than in Massachusetts?

4. **TALK Math** **Explain** why you need a key to read a pictograph.

Independent Practice and Problem Solving

For 5–7, use the National Parks pictograph at the right.

5. Kyle has visited every national park in Arizona. How many parks has he visited?

6. Which two states combined have the same number of national parks as Arizona?

7. **Pose a Problem** Look back at problem 5. Write a similar problem by changing the name of the state.

National Parks	
Arizona	🌲🌲🌲🌲🌲
Colorado	🌲🌲🌲
Kansas	🌲🌲
Oregon	🌲🌲
Key: Each 🌲 = 5 national parks.	

For 8–10, use the Favorite Park Activity pictograph.

8. How many people in all voted?

9. How many more people voted for hiking and fishing than for biking?

10. **WRITE Math** ▸ **What if** 25 people had voted for swimming? How would you show this in the pictograph?

Favorite Park Activity	
Biking	☺ ☺ ☺ ☺
Hiking	☺ ☺ ☺ ☺
Boating	☺ ☺ ☺
Fishing	☺ ☺
Key: Each ☺ = 10 votes.	

Mixed Review and Test Prep

11. Find the missing addend.
$$19 + \blacksquare = 32 \text{ (p. 50)}$$

12. Wendy bought a book for $7.59. She paid with a $10 bill. How much change did she receive? (p. 120)

13. **Test Prep** Lester made a pictograph to show how many books he has. This is his key.

Each 📕 = 10 books.

How many books does 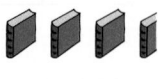 stand for?

A 7   **B** 8   **C** 35   **D** 40

Technology
Use Harcourt Mega Math, The Number
Games, *ArachnaGraph*, Level A.

Problem Solving Workshop
Strategy: Make a Graph

OBJECTIVE: Solve problems by using the strategy *make a graph*.

Learn the Strategy

There are many ways to show data. Some ways are lists, tables, and graphs.

You can show the data in this table in a pictograph.

Students' Pets

Type of Pet	Number
Cat	9
Dog	12
Fish	4
Hamster	3

Step 1

Write the title at the top of the graph. Write a label for each row.

Students' Pets

Cat	
Dog	
Fish	
Hamster	

Step 2

Look at the numbers. Choose a key that tells how many each picture represents.

Write the key at the bottom of the graph.

Students' Pets

Cat	
Dog	
Fish	
Hamster	

Key: Each 🐾 = 2 students.

Step 3

Draw the correct number of pictures for each type of pet.

Students' Pets

Cat	🐾 🐾 🐾 🐾 🐾
Dog	🐾 🐾 🐾 🐾 🐾 🐾
Fish	🐾 🐾
Hamster	🐾 🐾

Key: Each 🐾 = 2 students.

TALK Math

What do the pictures in the row for Dog in the pictograph tell you?

Remember

A half picture has half the value of a whole picture.
🐾 = 2 students
🐾 = 1 student

Use the Strategy

PROBLEM Mrs. Keller asked all the third grade students where they would like to go for a field trip. Eight students voted for the art museum, 26 students voted for the science center, 28 students voted for the aquarium, and 14 students voted for the zoo. What is one way the votes could be shown in a graph?

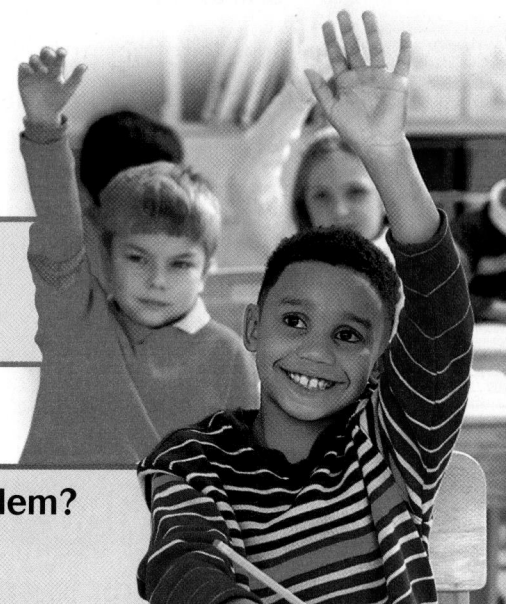

Read to Understand

- **Is there any information you will not use? If so, what?**

Plan

Reading Skill

- **What graphic aid could help you solve the problem?**
- **What strategy can you use?**

  You can make a pictograph.

Solve

- **How can you use the strategy to solve the problem?**

  Make a pictograph.

  Choose a title.
  Write a label for each row.
  Choose a key to tell how many votes each picture stands for.
  Decide how many pictures should be placed next to each field trip choice.
  Show the correct number of pictures beside each field trip choice.

Field Trip Choices	
Art museum	☺☺
Science center	☺☺☺☺☺☺☺
Aquarium	☺☺☺☺☺☺☺
Zoo	☺☺☺☺
Key: Each ☺ = 4 votes.	

Check

- **How do you know whether each row has the correct number of pictures? Give an example.**
- **Could you have used another number for the key? Explain.**

Guided Problem Solving

Read to Understand
Plan
Solve
Check

1. The science center gift shop sold 20 stuffed animals, 30 books, 15 stickers, and 10 T-shirts. How can you display the data?

   Copy the pictograph. Complete it by using the data. In your key, let each 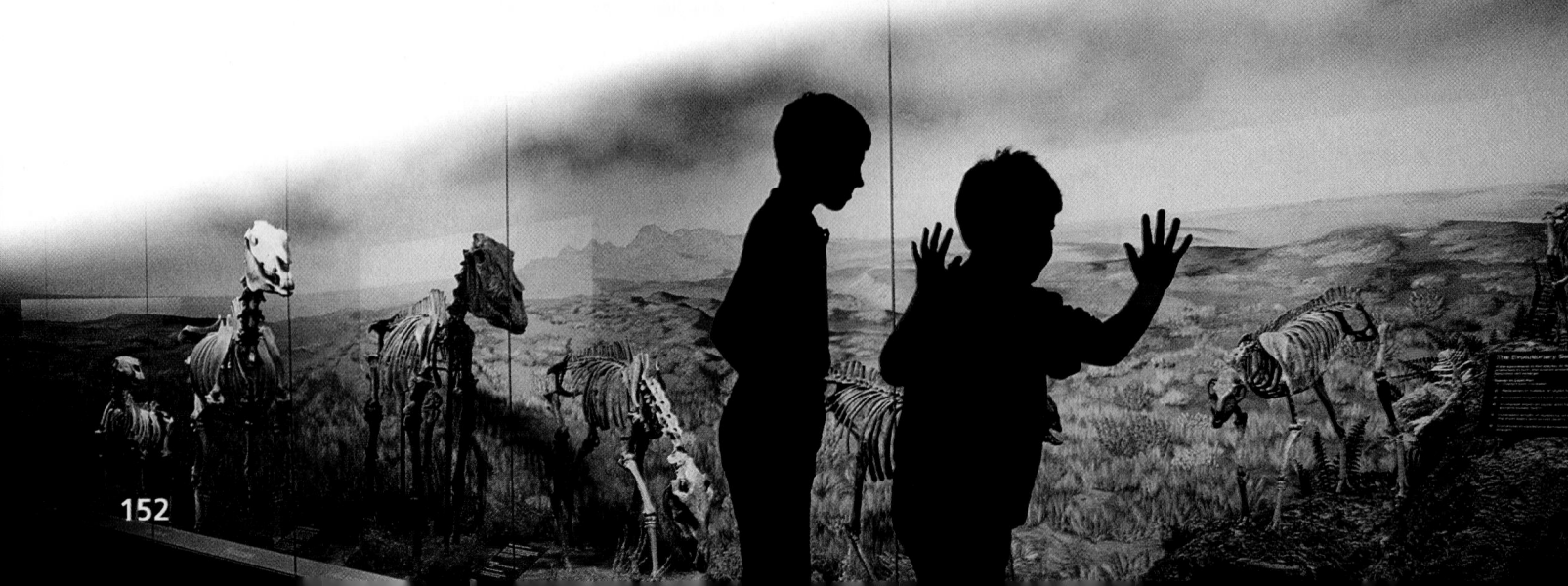 stand for 10 items.

2. **What if** the gift shop sold 25 posters? Explain how you would display that on the pictograph.

3. Which item at the gift shop was bought the most? The least?

Science Center Gift Shop

Stuffed Animals	🔋 🔋

Key: Each 🔋 = 10 items.

Problem Solving Strategy Practice

Make a pictograph to solve.

4. Some students voted for their favorite science center exhibit. The results are in the table at the right. Make a pictograph for the data. Let each picture stand for 3 students.

5. **WRITE Math** ▸ **Explain** how you knew how many pictures to draw for the light and sound exhibit.

6. **Reasoning** If the key is changed so that each picture stands for 6 students, how many pictures should be used for the number of students who voted for the nature exhibit?

Favorite Exhibit	
Nature	卌 IIII
Solar system	卌 I
Light and sound	卌 卌 卌
Human body	卌 卌 II

152

Mixed Strategy Practice

For 7–10, use the information about the constellations.

7. Make a pictograph to show the number of stars in each constellation. Which constellation has the fewest stars?

8. How many more stars are in Orion than in Ursa Minor? Write a number sentence that shows your answer.

9. **Pose a Problem** Look back at problem 8. Write a similar problem about Ursa Major and Ursa Minor.

10. **WRITE Math** ▸ **What's the Error?** Gina says that Ursa Minor has 2 fewer stars than Cassiopeia. What error did Gina make? **Explain.**

11. **Open-Ended** After the constellation show, Rick bought a poster for $1.45. He gave the clerk $2.00. What are three combinations of coins Rick could have received as change?

Choose a STRATEGY

Draw a Diagram or Picture
Make a Model or Act It Out
Make an Organized List
Find a Pattern
Make a Table or Graph
Predict and Test
Work Backward
Solve a Simpler Problem
Write a Number Sentence
Use Logical Reasoning

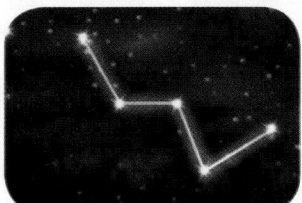
▲ Cassiopeia: 5 stars

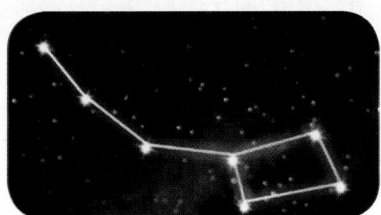
▲ Ursa Minor: 7 stars

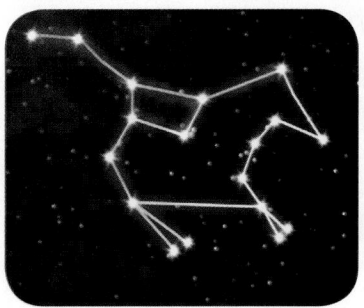
▲ Ursa Major: 18 stars

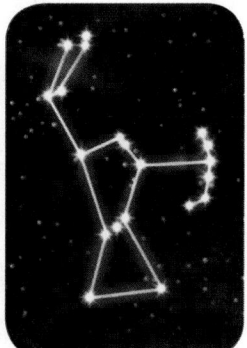
▲ Orion: 20 stars

CHALLENGE YOURSELF

The seats in the science center's planetarium are divided into 3 sections. Each section has 48 seats. The table shows the numbers of third grade students from Cypress Park School who are visiting the planetarium.

| Third Grade Students from Cypress Park School ||
Teacher	Number of Students
Mrs. Parker	31
Mr. Daniels	28
Ms. McCarthy	26

12. Mrs. Parker's students took their seats first, followed by Mr. Daniels's students. After the first section was filled, how many of Mr. Daniels's students sat in the second section of seats?

13. Ms. McCarthy's class was seated last. Explain how you can find the number of empty seats in the planetarium after everyone, including the teachers, took a seat.

Read a Bar Graph

OBJECTIVE: Read and interpret data in a bar graph.

Learn

PROBLEM Erin's family is planning to visit an amusement park. They want to ride as many roller coasters as possible. Which amusement park has the greatest number of roller coasters?

A **bar graph** uses bars to show data. A **scale** of numbers helps you read the number each bar shows. On the bar graphs below, the scale shows the numbers 0, 4, 8, 12, and 16. Each space between the numbers represents 4 roller coasters.

These bar graphs show the same data.

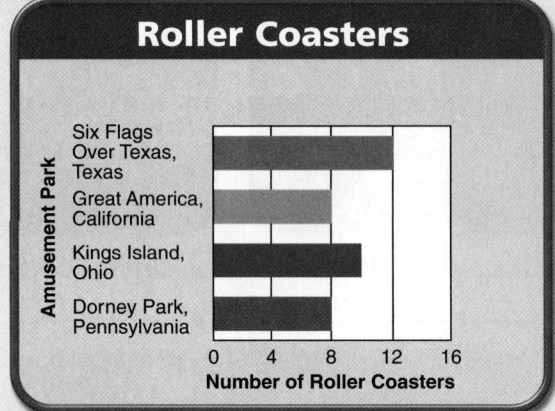

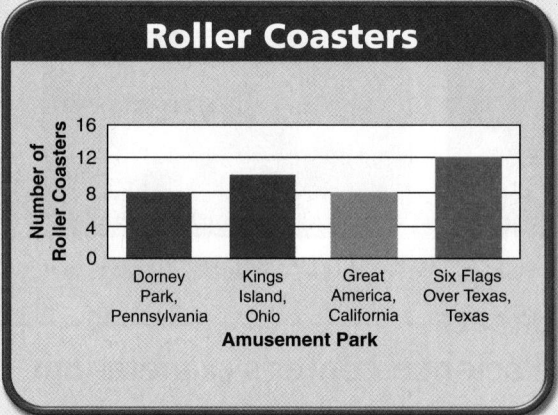

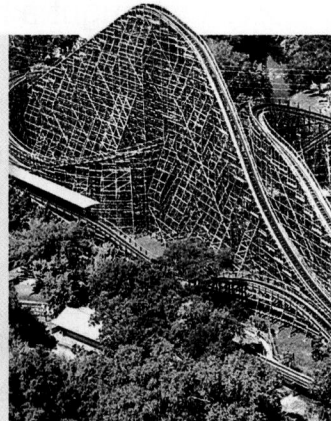

▲ The Texas Giant is a wooden roller coaster. It has 81,370 bolts holding it together!

In a **horizontal bar graph**, the bars go across from left to right.

In a **vertical bar graph**, the bars go up from the bottom.

The longest bar ends at 12. It is for Six Flags Over Texas.

So, Six Flags Over Texas has the greatest number of roller coasters.

Guided Practice

For 1–4, use the Roller Coasters graphs above.

1. Which amusement parks have the same number of roller coasters? **Think:** Which bars have the same length?

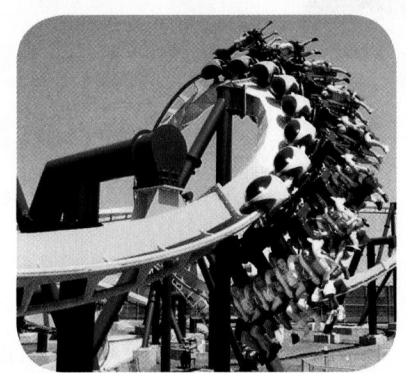

✓ **2.** How many roller coasters does Dorney Park have?

✓ **3.** How many more roller coasters does Six Flags Over Texas have than Great America?

4. [TALK Math] **Explain** how you would use the bar graph to tell how many roller coasters Kings Island has.

Independent Practice (and Problem Solving)

For 5–7, use the Favorite Ride graph.

5. How many students voted for roller coaster?

6. Did more students vote for ferris wheel and merry-go-round or for roller coaster and bumper cars? **Explain** your answer.

7. How many students voted in all?

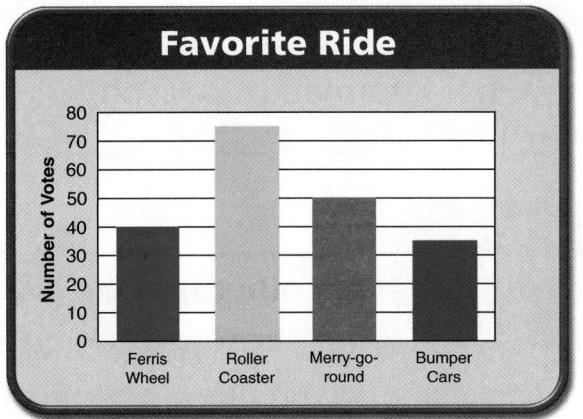

For 8–10, use the Roller Coaster Speed graph.

8. How much faster is Superman, The Escape than Nitro?

9. Which roller coaster has a bar that is twice as long as the bar for Gemini?

10. [WRITE Math] ▸ **Sense or Nonsense?** Jane says that Gemini is faster than Nitro. Does her statement make sense? **Explain.**

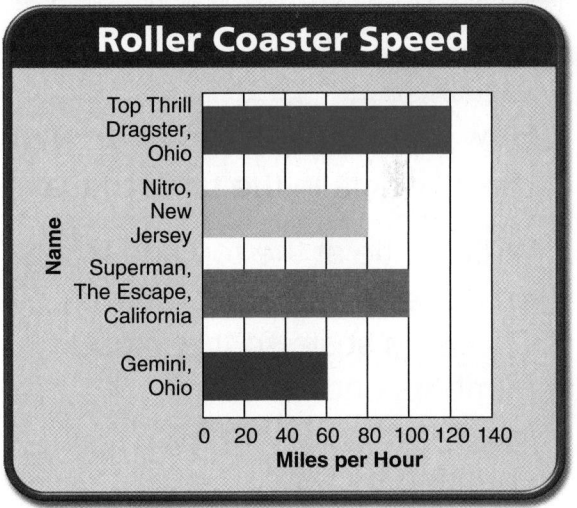

Mixed Review and Test Prep

11. Ty and his friends spent 7 hours at an amusement park. They arrived at 10:30 A.M. At what time did they leave? (p. 130)

12. Arthur placed two squares together side-by-side. What shape did Arthur make? (Grade 2)

13. Test Prep Melinda made a bar graph to show how many pets her friends have. Which pet has the shortest bar?

A 8 dogs   **C** 6 cats

B 4 hamsters   **D** 3 birds

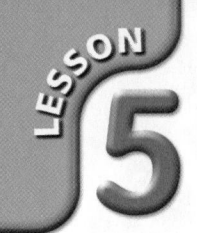
Problem Solving Workshop
Strategy: Make a Graph

OBJECTIVE: Solve problems by using the strategy *make a graph*.

PROBLEM Ella and Lou played a game with a spinner. Lou recorded the result of each spin in a tally table. What is another way he can show the results?

Spinner Results	
Color	Tally
Red	ⅣⅣ ⅣⅣ |||
Blue	ⅣⅣ ⅣⅣ
Yellow	ⅣⅣ |||
Green	ⅣⅣ ⅣⅣ ||

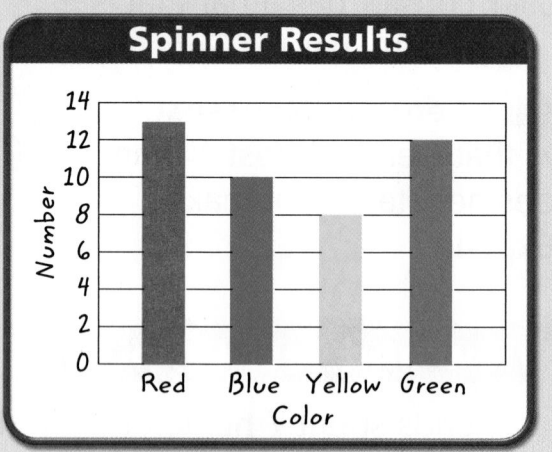

Read to Understand

• **What information is given?**

Plan

Reading Skill

• **What other graphic aid could you use?**
• **What strategy can you use to solve the problem?**
  You can make a bar graph.

Solve

• **How can you use the strategy to solve the problem?**
  Use the data in the table to make a bar graph.

Write a title at the top and labels on the side and at the bottom. Choose a scale so that most numbers end on a line. Make the scale 0 to 14, counting by twos. Red has 13 tally marks, so the bar for red ends halfway between 12 and 14.

Spinner Results

Check

• **How can you check your bar graph?**

1. Marta and Jordan took a survey of their classmates' favorite types of games. Jordan recorded the results in a table. Show the results in a bar graph.

Favorite Type of Game	
Type	Number
Board games	7
Card games	5
Puzzles	8
Playground games	10

First, write the title and labels. Write the types of games on the bottom and the number of votes on the side.

Then, choose a scale so that most bars end on a line.

Finally, draw the bars.

2. **What if** 3 students chose board games instead of playground games as their favorite type of game? How would the graph change?

3. Adrienne pulled her stuffed animals out of her toy box. She pulled out 5 bears, 8 frogs, and 4 rabbits. Make a bar graph to show Adrienne's results. Which bar is twice as long as the bar for rabbits?

Choose a STRATEGY

Draw a Diagram or Picture

Make a Model or Act It Out

Make an Organized List

Find a Pattern

Make a Table or Graph

Predict and Test

Work Backward

Solve a Simpler Problem

Write an Equation

Use Logical Reasoning

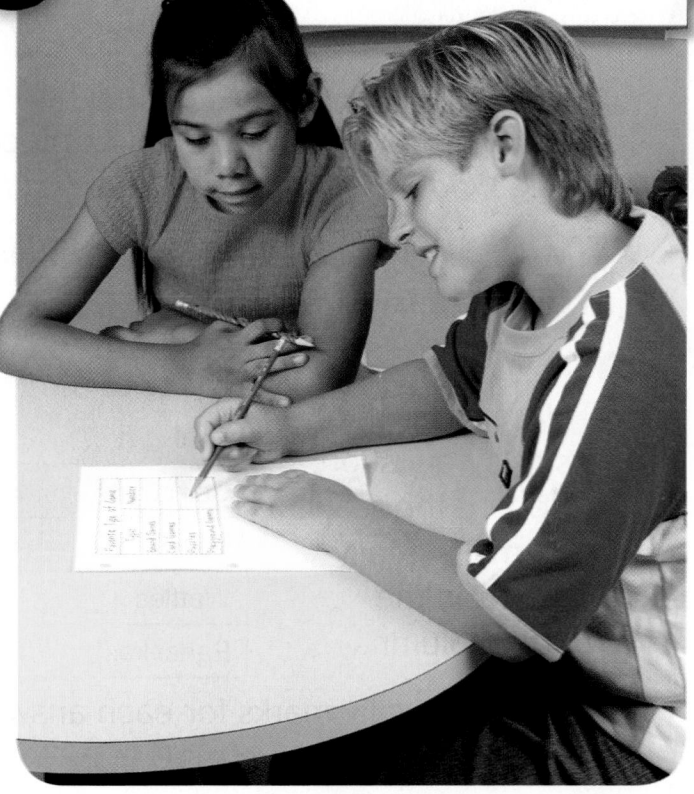

Mixed Strategy Practice

USE DATA For 4–5, use the Team Sports table.

4. Use the data in the table to make a bar graph. Which sport received the fewest votes?

5. Write a number sentence that shows how many more people chose soccer than baseball.

Favorite Team Sports	
Sport	Number
Soccer	12
Basketball	4
Baseball	9
Football	10

6. Ed scored more points than Amy but fewer points than Darren. Who scored the fewest points?

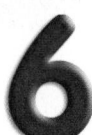
6 Hands On: Take a Survey

OBJECTIVE: Take a survey, and record the results in a tally table, pictograph, and bar graph.

Investigate

Materials ■ tally table

A **survey** is a way of collecting information or data. The answers collected are the **results** of the survey.

Take a survey in your classroom. Record the results in a tally table.

A Think of a survey question that has several answer choices. For example, you could ask, *What is your favorite breakfast food?*

B Make a tally table. Write a title and labels. List the answer choices.

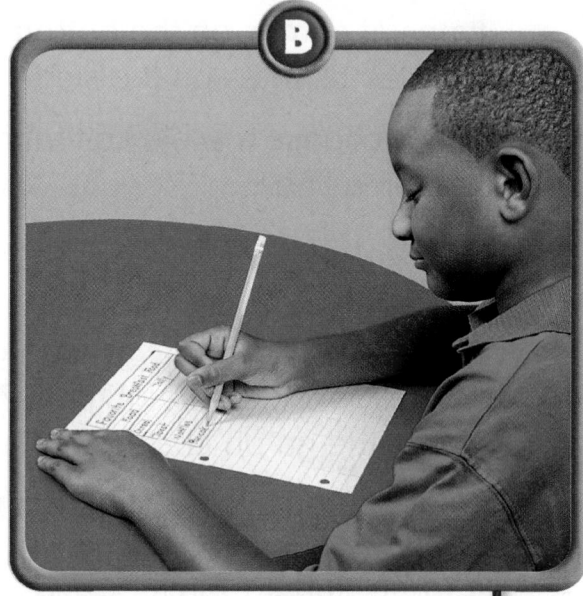

C Ask your classmates the survey question. Record the results by making tally marks in the *Tally* column.

Favorite Breakfast Food	
Food	**Tally**
Cereal	
Toast	
Waffles	
Pancakes	

D Count the tally marks for each answer. Share the results with the class.

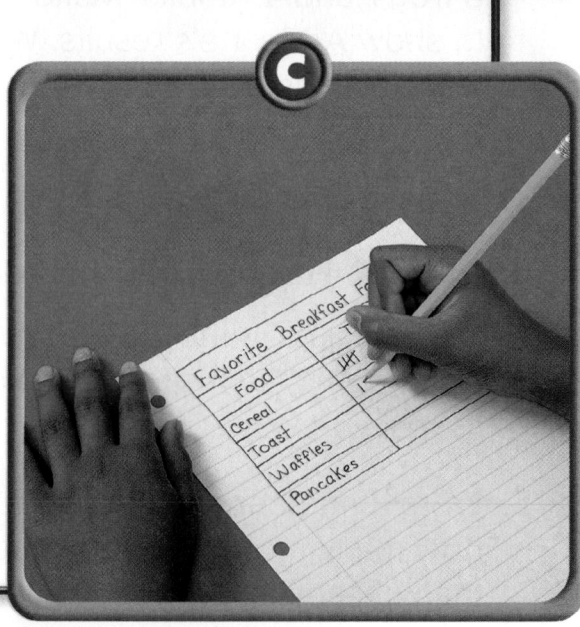

Draw Conclusions

1. What answer choices did you use for your survey?

2. Which answer choice for your survey has the most tally marks? Which has the fewest?

3. **Analysis** Do you think each classmate collected the same results in his or her survey? **Explain.**

You can show the data you collected by making a pictograph and a bar graph.

ONE WAY **Make a pictograph.**

Write a title and a label for each row.
Choose a key to tell how many each picture stands for.
Write the key at the bottom.
Copy and complete your pictograph.

Favorite Breakfast Food

Cereal	
Toast	
Waffles	
Pancakes	

Key: Each ■ = ■ students.

ANOTHER WAY **Make a bar graph.**

Write a title and labels.
Write the answer choices.
Choose a scale to show the number of answers.
Copy and complete your bar graph.

TALK Math

How do your graphs show the choice with the fewest tally marks? The most tally marks?

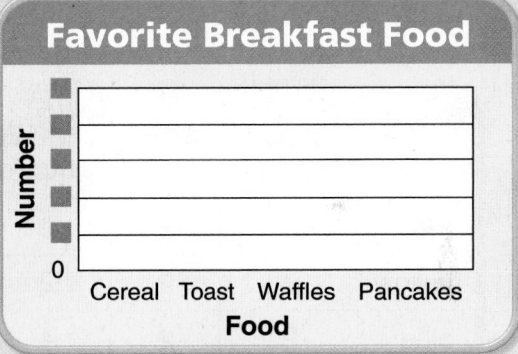

Favorite Breakfast Food

Number

0

Cereal Toast Waffles Pancakes

Food

Practice

For 1–2, use your tally table and graph.

1. What is the title of your tally table and your graph?

2. How many classmates in all answered your survey?

3. Think of another survey question. Write several possible answer choices. Ask your classmates your survey question. Show the results in a pictograph and in a bar graph.

4. **WRITE Math** ► How are the data in your pictograph and bar graph alike? How are they different?

7 Classify Data

OBJECTIVE: Use a table to organize data.

Quick Review

Find the sum.

1. 2 + 3 + 4

2. 4 + 6 + 3

3. 2 + 7 + 5

4. 3 + 5 + 8

5. 7 + 6 + 5

Vocabulary

classify

Learn

To **classify** is to group pieces of data according to how they are the same. You can classify by shape, color, or size.

PROBLEM Cathy and Tom are playing a game. Their game pieces are shown below. What are some ways Cathy and Tom can classify the game pieces?

Data can be organized into a table. A table can show two ways at a time to classify the data.

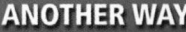 **By shape and color**

Game Pieces			
	triangle	circle	square
red	3	2	3
yellow	4	2	2
blue	2	2	4

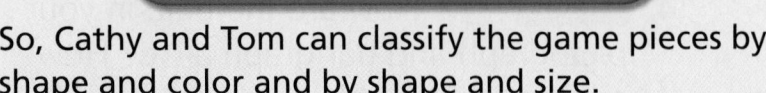 **By shape and size**

Game Pieces			
	triangle	circle	square
small	2	2	4
medium	3	2	3
large	4	2	2

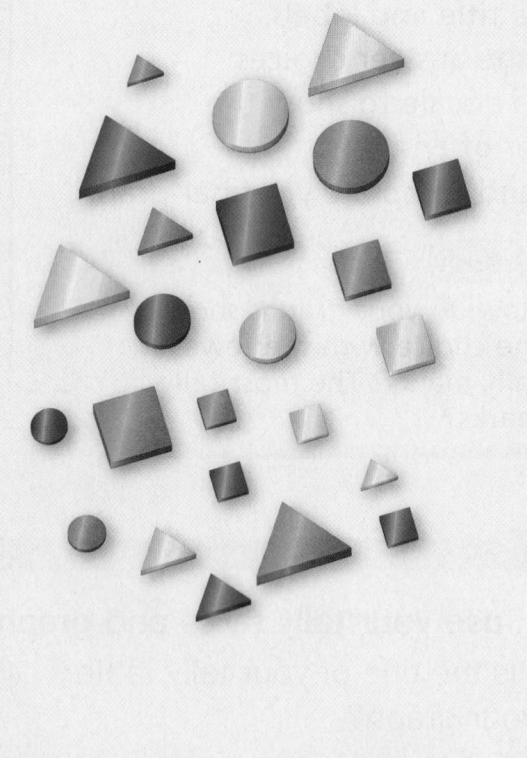

So, Cathy and Tom can classify the game pieces by shape and color and by shape and size.

• What other way can Cathy and Tom classify the game pieces?

Guided Practice

For 1–5, use the Juice Boxes table.

1. How are the juice boxes classified?

2. How many large apple juice boxes are there?

✓3. How many grape juice boxes are there?

✓4. How many more small juice boxes than large juice boxes are there?

5. **TALK Math** **Explain** how to find the total number of juice boxes.

Juice Boxes			
	orange	apple	grape
small	4	5	6
medium	5	4	4
large	5	5	4

Independent Practice and Problem Solving

For 6–9, use the Class Shoe Color table.

6. How many girls are wearing black shoes?

7. How many students are wearing blue shoes?

8. How many more boys than girls were surveyed?

9. How many students were surveyed in all?

Class Shoe Color		
	girls	boys
white	4	5
blue	3	2
black	2	3

10. Look at the stars at the right. Make a table to classify them two ways. **Explain** how you classified them.

11. **WRITE Math** ▸ **Explain** three ways you can classify the students in your class.

Mixed Review and Test Prep

12. Susan had $3.45. Then her sister gave her some money. Now Susan has $5.90. How much money did Susan's sister give her? (p. 122)

13. Alex is making a pictograph. His key is 📙 = 10 books. How many books are represented by 📙📙📙📙📗 (p. 150)

14. **Test Prep** Which shows two ways to classify a group of hats?

   A happy or sad

   B quiet or loud

   C size or color

   D sweet or salty

Extra Practice on page 170, Set D

Line Plots

OBJECTIVE: Read and make line plots, and find the range and mode.

Learn

A **line plot** shows each piece of data on a number line.

PROBLEM The students in Mrs. Young's class planted lima bean seeds for a science project. The line plot below shows the heights of the seedlings after 4 weeks. What height was recorded most often?

In this line plot, each **x** stands for 1 seedling. The numbers show the heights of the seedlings in inches.

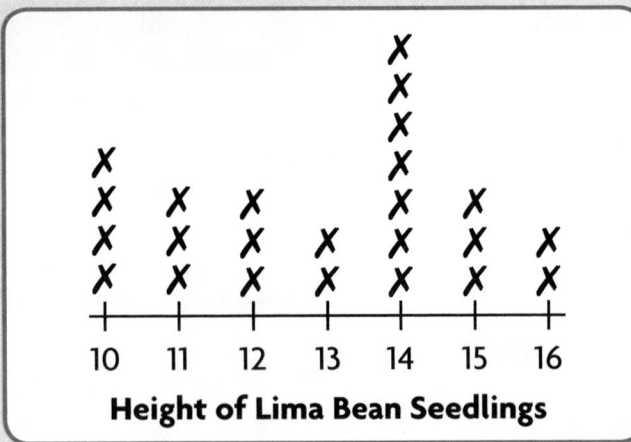

Height of Lima Bean Seedlings

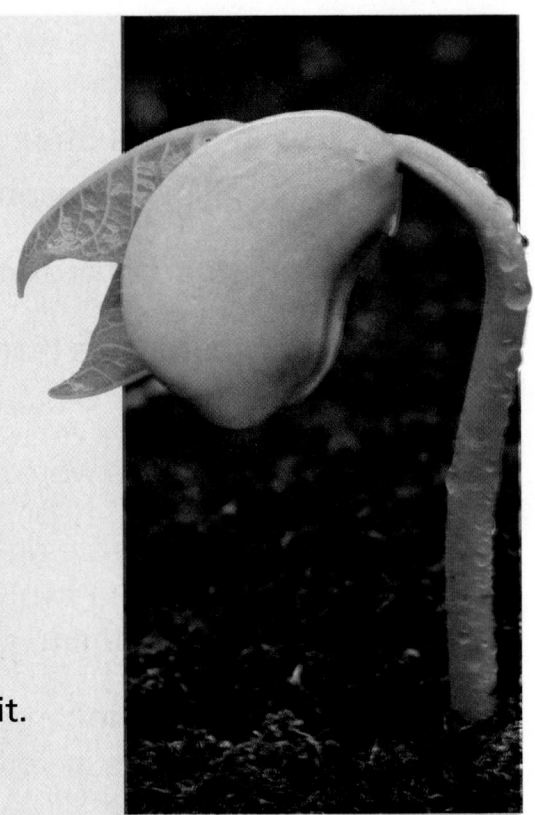

▲ Fordhook lima bean plants can reach about 20 inches in height.

The **mode** is the number or item found most often in a set of data.

Find the number on the line plot with the most **x**'s above it. There are 7 **x**'s above 14 inches.

So, the height recorded most often was 14 inches tall.

- How many seedlings were taller than 14 inches?

- **What if** 4 more lima bean seedlings were 10 inches tall? Would that change the mode? Explain.

The **range** is the difference between the greatest number and the least number in a set of data.

greatest number		least number		range
16	−	10	=	6

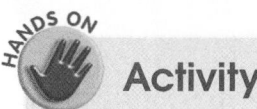

Activity

Materials ■ number line

Sarah rolled a number cube 20 times. She recorded the number rolled each time in a tally table.

You can also show these data in a line plot.

Sarah's Experiment

Number rolled	Tally
1	IIII
2	III
3	II
4	III
5	ЖI
6	III

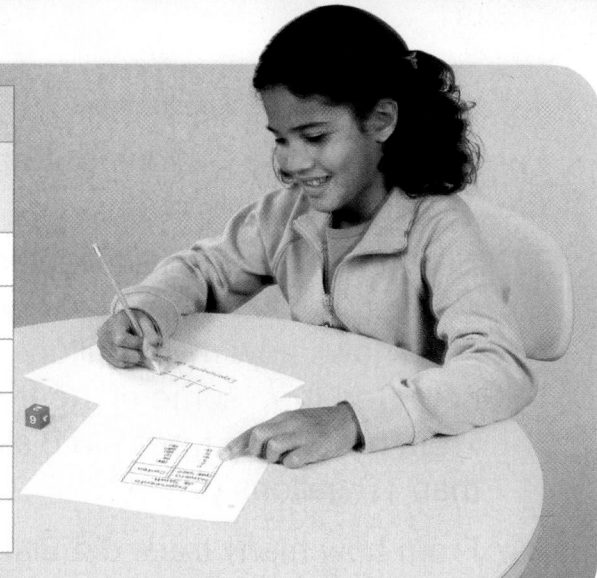

Step 1

Copy the line plot. Write a title. Label the numbers from 1 to 6 to show the numbers on the number cube.

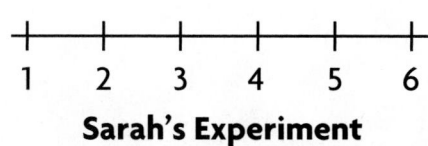

Sarah's Experiment

Step 2

Draw *x*'s above the number line to show how many times Sarah rolled each number.

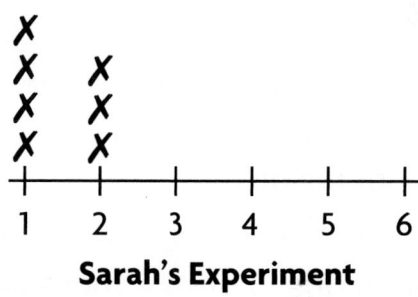

Sarah's Experiment

• How are the tally table and the line plot alike? How are they different?

Guided Practice

For 1–5, use your line plot.

1. How can you find the mode in Sarah's experiment?

   Think: Which number did Sarah roll most often?

2. How many times did Sarah roll a 1?

3. What is the range of Sarah's data?

4. Which number did Sarah roll the fewest times?

5. How many more times did Sarah roll a 5 than a 3?

6. **TALK Math** **Explain** why you would use a line plot to show data.

For 7–12, use the Gallons of Sap Collected line plot.

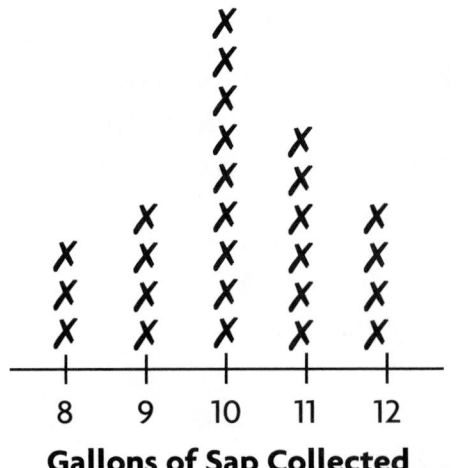

7. **≡FAST FACT** Sap is collected from sugar maple trees to make maple syrup. The line plot shows how many gallons of sap Blake collected from some of the trees on his farm. From how many trees did Blake collect fewer than 10 gallons of sap?

8. From how many trees did Blake collect more than 10 gallons of sap?

9. What is the range of the data?

10. **WRITE Math** ▸ **What's the Error?** Julie says the mode of the data is 9. Describe her error. What is the mode?

11. **Pose a Problem** Look back at problem 7. Write a similar problem by changing the number of gallons.

12. **Reasoning** Suppose Blake collected 11 gallons of sap from 4 more trees. Will the range of the data change? **Explain.**

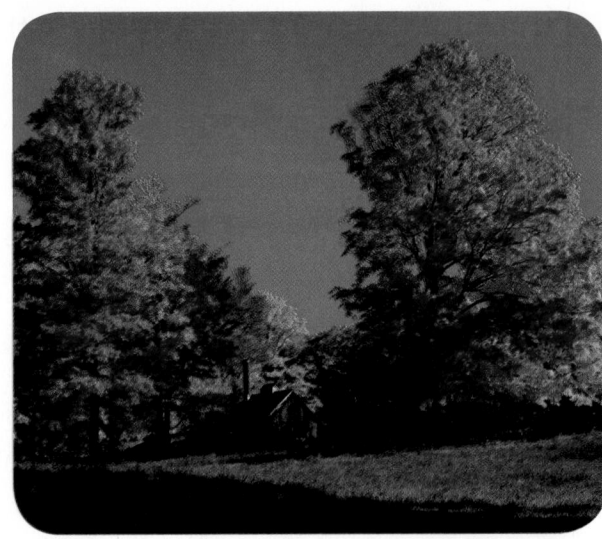

Mixed Review and Test Prep

13. The Missouri River is 2,315 miles long. The Mississippi River is 2,340 miles long. Which river is longer?

    (p. 28)

14. Matt has one $5 bill and 6 nickels. Peter has four $1 bills, 6 quarters, and 1 nickel. Compare the amounts of money. (p. 114)

15. **Test Prep** Madeline made the line plot below.

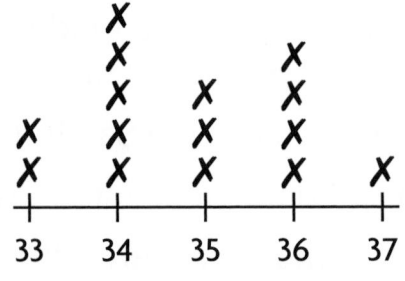

    Points Scored

    What is the mode of the data?

    A 4   **B** 5   **C** 34   **D** 36

CD
ROM

Technology —
Use Harcourt Mega Math, The Number Games, *ArachnaGraph*, Level F.

164

Extra Practice on page 171, Set E

The table shows the average life spans of different animals. Which graph shows the data in the table correctly?

Compare Graphs A and B to the data in the table.

Graph A

Graph B

Animal Life Spans

Animal	Years
chipmunk	6
mouse	3
opossum	1
squirrel	10

Animal Life Spans

chipmunk	🐾 🐾 🐾 🐾 🐾 🐾
mouse	🐾 🐾
opossum	🐾
squirrel	🐾 🐾 🐾 🐾 🐾

Key: Each 🐾 = 2 years.

Animal Life Spans

Graph A shows 1 picture, or 2 years, for the opossum and 6 pictures, or 12 years, for the chipmunk. This does not match the data in the table.

Each bar in Graph B correctly shows the data in the table. So, Graph B matches the data.

Try It

1. Which graph shows the data in the table correctly?

Graph C

Graph D

Animal Life Spans

Animal	Years
elephant	40
box turtle	100
bear	25
lion	15

Animal Life Spans

elephant	🐾 🐾 🐾 🐾
box turtle	🐾 🐾 🐾 🐾 🐾 🐾 🐾 🐾 🐾 🐾
bear	🐾 🐾 🐾
lion	🐾 🐾

Key: Each 🐾 = 10 years.

Animal Life Spans

2. **WRITE Math** ▸ **Explain** how you know which graph does NOT show the data in the table correctly.

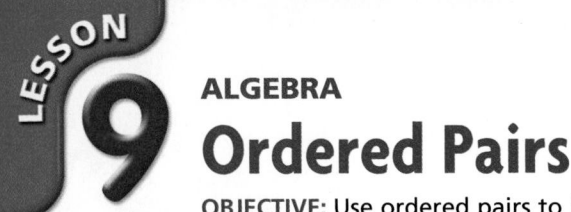

ALGEBRA
Ordered Pairs

OBJECTIVE: Use ordered pairs to locate points on a grid.

Quick Review

Identify the number named by each point.

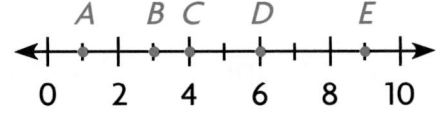

1. A   2. B   3. C
4. D   5. E

Vocabulary

grid   ordered pair

Learn

PROBLEM Myra and her family are visiting Washington, D.C. They are using the map below to find the places they want to visit. What ordered pair names the location of the Washington Monument?

The horizontal and vertical lines on the map make a **grid**.

An **ordered pair** of numbers within parentheses, like (2,3), names a point on a grid.

Find the Washington Monument on the grid.

Start at 0.
Move 4 spaces to the right.
Then move 3 spaces up.

So, the ordered pair (4,3) names the location for the Washington Monument.

The first number tells   → (4,3) ←   The second number
how many spaces to   tells how many
move from 0 to the right.   spaces to move up.

• How would you locate the Lincoln Memorial?

• What is located at (4,1)?

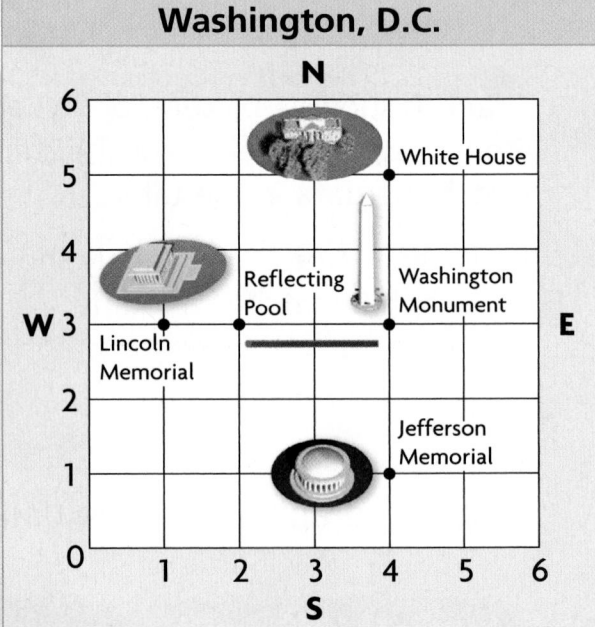

Washington, D.C.

Math Idea
Another way to write *up*, *down*, *left*, and *right* is *north*, *south*, *west*, and *east*.

Guided Practice

1. Use the Washington, D.C. map. What is located at (4,5)?
   Think: Start at 0. Move 4 spaces to the right. Then move 5 spaces up.

For 2–5, use the school grid at the right.

2. What ordered pair names the point between the music room and the art room?

✓3. What ordered pair names the location of the cafeteria?

✓4. What is located at $(6,1)$?

5. [TALK Math] Explain how to locate the computer lab.

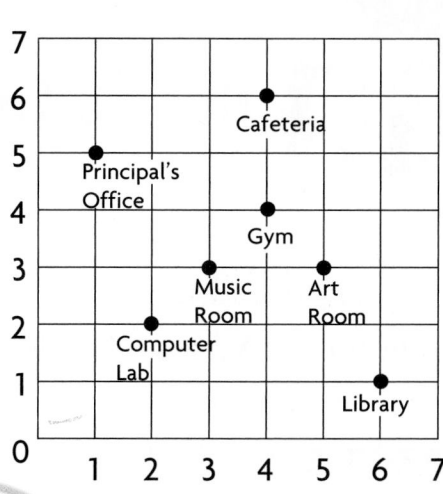

Independent Practice and Problem Solving

Write the ordered pair for each letter.

6. *J*   7. *B*   8. *G*   9. *K*   10. *C*

Write the letter that names the point for each ordered pair.

11. $(4,2)$ 12. $(1,1)$ 13. $(2,7)$ 14. $(6,3)$ 15. $(2,3)$

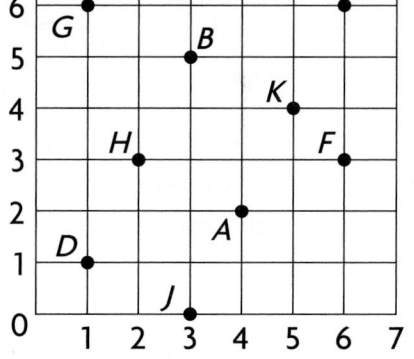

For 16–19 use the garden grid below.

16. What ordered pair names the location of the corn?

17. What is located at $(4,3)$?

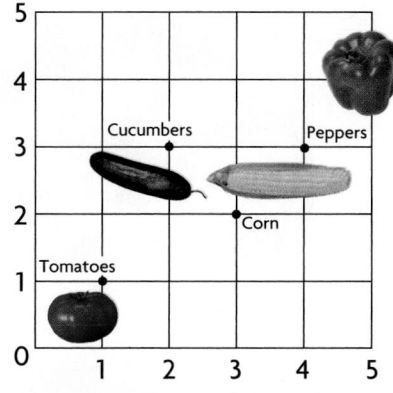

18. **Reasoning** What if Geoff planted lettuce at $(1,4)$ and Janna planted carrots at $(3,4)$? What ordered pair would name the point between the lettuce and the carrots?

19. [WRITE Math] **Explain** how a point located at $(2,3)$ is different than a point located at $(3,2)$.

Mixed Review and Test Prep

20. Sergio practiced soccer for 1 hour and 25 minutes. For how many minutes did he practice? (p. 124)

21. What number is missing in Jon's pattern? (p. 4)

    17, 27, 37, ■, 57

22. **Test Prep** Margie drew a grid. She started at 0, moved 4 spaces to the right and 6 spaces up. At what point did Margie end?

    A $(0,4)$ **C** $(4,6)$

    B $(6,4)$ **D** $(10,0)$

Extra Practice on page 171, Set F

Read a Line Graph

OBJECTIVE: Read and interpret data in a line graph.

Learn

A **line graph** uses a line to show how data change over time.

PROBLEM Isabella and her mother did an experiment to see how long it took water to boil. The line graph shows the data they collected. What was the water temperature at 2 minutes?

You can locate points on a line graph as you locate points on a grid.

> Find the vertical line for 2 minutes. Move up to the point. Follow the horizontal line left to the scale showing degrees.
>
> The point for 2 minutes is at 140 degrees.

So, the temperature of the water at 2 minutes was 140 degrees.

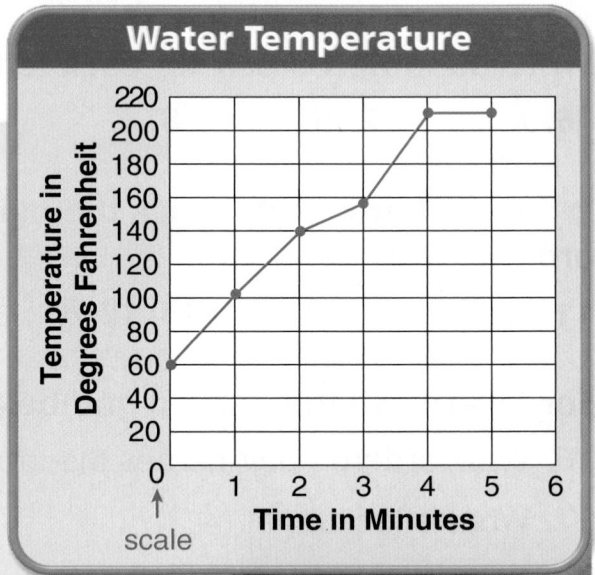

On a line graph, you can see **trends**, or areas where data increase, decrease, or stay the same over time.

• What does the blue line tell you?

• Between which two minutes did the temperature increase the most?

Guided Practice

For 1–4 use the Water Temperature graph.

1. What was the water temperature at 1 minute?
   Think: Find the vertical line for 1 minute. Move up to the point, and follow the horizontal line left to the scale.

✓2. What was the water temperature at 3 minutes?

✓3. By about how many degrees did the temperature increase between 2 minutes and 3 minutes?

4. **TALK Math** Explain a trend you see in the line graph.

For 5–7, use the Depth of Water graph.

Matthew measured the depth of the water in an outside bucket each day for 6 days.

5. How deep was the water on Friday?

6. Between which two days did the depth of the water increase 3 inches?

7. When the sun warms water, the water evaporates, or changes from a liquid to a gas. Suppose it did not rain and Matthew's bucket did not have a leak. How much water evaporated between Thursday and Saturday? **Explain** how you know.

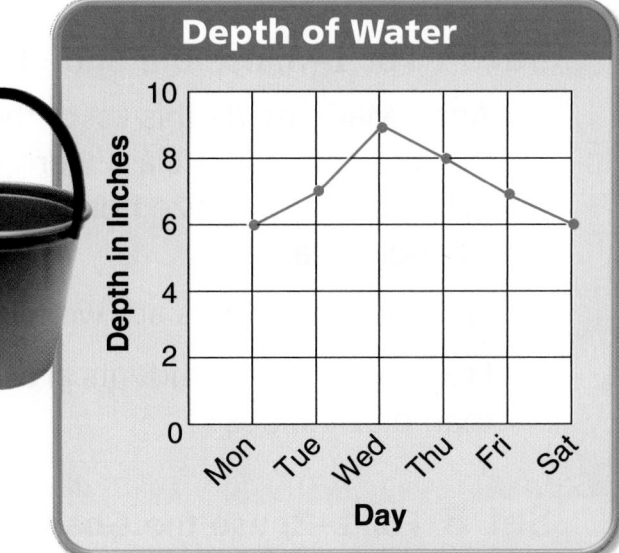

Depth of Water

For 8–10, use the Plant Growth graph.

8. How tall was the plant at 2 weeks?

9. How did the height of the plant change every week?

10. **WRITE Math** ▸ **Sense or Nonsense?** Sam thinks that the plant will be 7 inches tall at week 6. Does Sam's statement make sense? Explain.

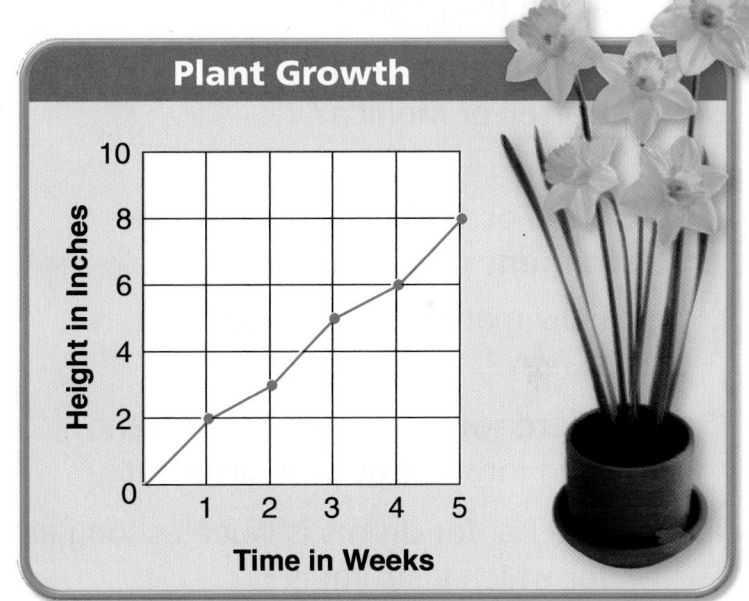

Plant Growth

Mixed Review and Test Prep

11. What is the name of this shape?
    (Grade 2)

12. The heights in inches of six students are: 36, 40, 38, 40, 39, and 40. What is the mode? (p. 162)

13. **Test Prep** How many books did Scott read in February?

    A 2 books

    B 3 books

    C 4 books

    D 6 books

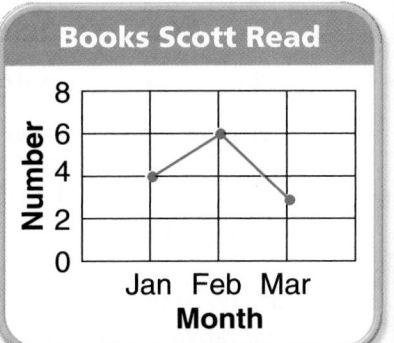

Books Scott Read

Extra Practice

Set A For 1–3, use the Shoe Color list. (pp. 146–147)

1. Anne Marie made this list of the shoe colors the students in her class were wearing. Make a tally table to organize her data. Then make a frequency table.

2. How many students are wearing brown shoes?

3. How many more students are wearing blue shoes than black shoes?

Shoe Color	
Jack	blue
Mike	brown
Trisha	black
Shelly	blue
Greta	white
Manuel	brown
Tyler	brown
Samantha	black
Hunter	blue
Morgan	brown

Set B For 1–2, use the Goals Scored pictograph. (pp. 148–149)

1. How many more goals did Monica score than Tony?

2. Who scored more goals—Tony and Darrell or Monica?

Goals Scored

Tony	⚽ ⚽ ⚽ ⚽
Darrell	⚽ ⚽
Monica	⚽ ⚽ ⚽ ⚽ ⚽

Key: Each ⚽ = 2 goals.

Set C For 1–4, use the Favorite Instrument graph. (pp. 154–155)

1. How many students voted in this survey?

2. There was 1 more vote for piano than for what other instrument?

3. The bar for drums is twice as long as for which instrument?

4. How many more students voted for drums than for piano?

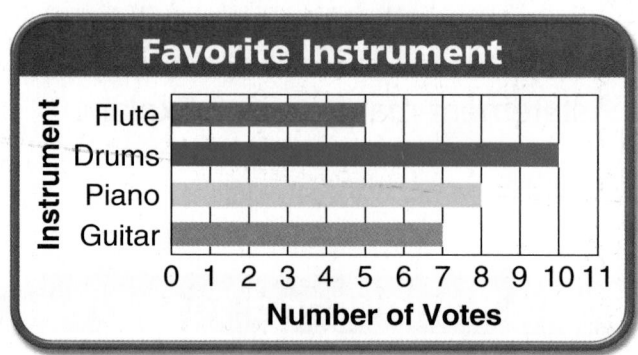

Set D For 1–3, use the Types of Books Read table. (pp. 160–161)

1. How many puzzle books have James and Maddie read?

2. Who has read the greater number of books?

3. How many more sports books has Maddie read than James?

Types of Books Read		
	James	**Maddie**
animal	4	1
puzzle	6	3
sports	6	9

Set E For 1–5, use the Baskets of Blueberries Picked line plot. (pp. 162–165)

1. How many people picked 9 baskets of blueberries?

2. What is the range of the data?

3. What is the mode of the data?

4. How many people picked fewer than 7 baskets of blueberries?

5. How many people picked more than 6 baskets of blueberries?

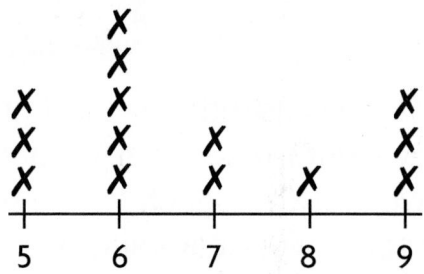

Baskets of Blueberries Picked

Set F For 1–4, use the classroom grid. (pp. 166–167)

1. What is located at (2,2)?

2. What is located at (1,1)?

3. What ordered pair names the location of the computer?

4. The teacher put a rug between the reading area and the bookshelf. What ordered pair names the point where the rug is?

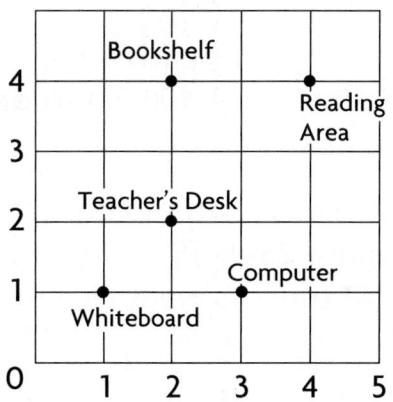

Set G For 1–3, use the Plants Sold graph. (pp. 168–169)

1. How many plants were sold on Monday?

2. How many more plants were sold on Saturday than on Sunday?

3. There were 5 more plants sold on Wednesday than on Tuesday. How many plants were sold on Wednesday?

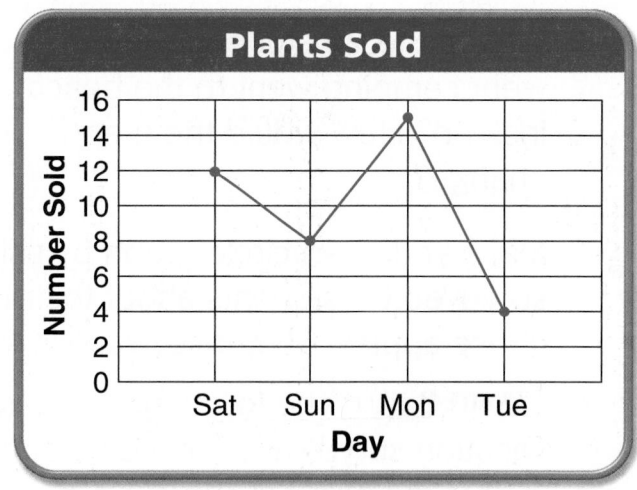

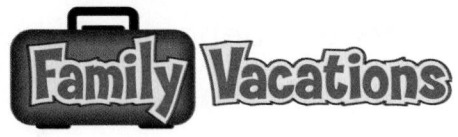

MATH POWER Circle Graphs

Family Vacations

Mr. Spear's class asked 100 third grade students where they went for summer vacation. Some students went to the beach, some went to a theme park, and some went camping. The class showed the data in a circle graph. A **circle graph** shows data as parts of a whole circle.

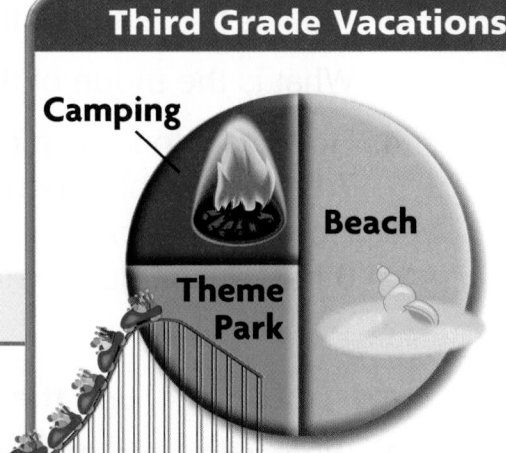

Third Grade Vacations

Camping

Beach

Theme Park

Example

- The whole circle represents all 100 students in the survey.

- The section for beach is half of the circle. Since 50 + 50 = 100, 50 students went to the beach.

- The sections for camping and theme park are the same size. Since 25 + 25 = 50, 25 students went camping, and 25 students went to a theme park.

Try It
For 1–2, use the Third Grade Vacations graph.

1. What if the 25 students who went camping went to the beach instead? How would the graph change?

2. What if 25 of the students who went to the beach went to a family reunion instead? How would the graph change?

3. Make your own circle graph by using these data: Robbie surveyed 60 students about their favorite fruit. Half chose apples, 10 chose oranges, and 20 chose grapes.

4. **WRITE Math** ▶ The fourth grade classes did their own vacation survey. Half of the students went camping. If 120 students were surveyed, how many went camping? Explain.

Chapter 6 Review/Test

Check Vocabulary and Concepts

Choose the best term from the box.

1. To __?__ is to group pieces of data according to how they are the same. (p. 160)

2. A way to record the number of tally marks is in a __?__. (p. 146)

3. A __?__ uses pictures to show information. (p. 148)

Check Skills

For 4–6, use the Miles Biked table. (pp. 160–161)

4. How many miles did Max bike on Saturday and Sunday?

5. Who biked the greater number of miles?

6. On which day did Laura bike more miles than Max?

Miles Biked		
	Max	**Laura**
Friday	4	3
Saturday	8	7
Sunday	9	10 ·

For 7–9, use the Number of Goals Scored line plot. (pp. 162–165)

7. How many soccer players scored 4 goals?

8. What is the mode of the data?

9. How many soccer players scored fewer than 2 goals?

Number of Goals Scored

Check Problem Solving

Make a pictograph to solve. (pp. 150–153)

10. The third grade classes voted on locations for their field trip. The results are shown in the frequency table. Make a pictograph for the data. Let each picture stand for 4 votes.

11. How many pictures did you draw for amusement park?

12. **WRITE Math** ▶ When Randy made his pictograph, he let each picture stand for 8 votes. **Explain** how the votes for the science center look different than on your pictograph.

Field Trip Locations	
Location	**Number of Votes**
Zoo	16
Amusement park	20
Nature museum	8
Science center	24

Standardized Test Prep
Chapters 1–6

Number and Operations

Test Tip Check the answer.

See Item 1. Subtract to find the answer. If the difference does not match one of the answer choices, check your subtraction.

1. The cafeteria at Ramon's school served 300 lunches on Tuesday. It served 257 lunches on Wednesday. How many more lunches were served on Tuesday? (p. 88)

   A 42   C 52

   B 43   D 53

2. Meredith lives 182 miles from her friend James. What is the value of the digit 8 in 182? (p. 8)

   A 8,000   C 80

   B 800   D 8

3. **WRITE Math** Cheryl has a collection of 413 stamps. Patty has a collection of 329 stamps. How many stamps do they have altogether? Did you use mental math or paper and pencil to solve the problem? **Explain.** (p. 64)

Algebraic Reasoning

4. Look at the pattern. What are the next two shapes? (Grade 2)

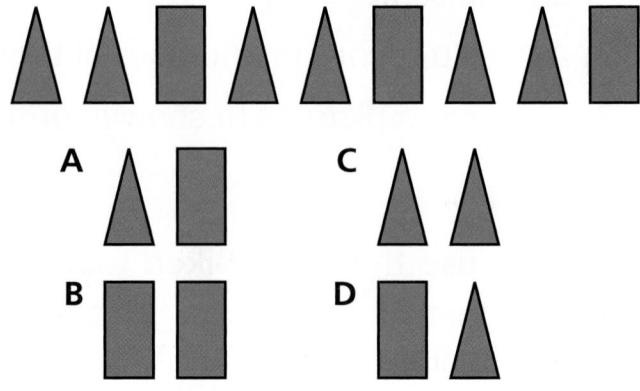

5. Look at the pattern. What comes next? (Grade 2)

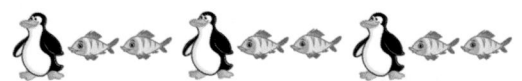

   A 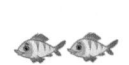   C

   B   D

   A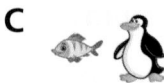

6. **WRITE Math** Sarah had 4 puzzle books. She got 9 more. Her sister Emily had 9 puzzle books. She got 4 more. Who has more puzzle books? **Explain.** (p. 48)

Geometry

7. What is the name of the shape?

(Grade 2)

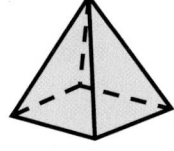

A Square

B Hexagon

C Rectangle

D Triangle

8. Look at the solid figure. Which plane figure is one face of the solid figure?

(Grade 2)

A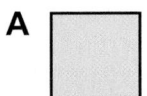

B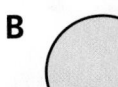

C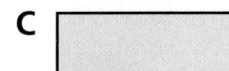

D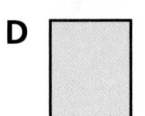

9. ⬛WRITE Math ▶ **Explain** how this cube and rectangular prism are alike.

(Grade 2)

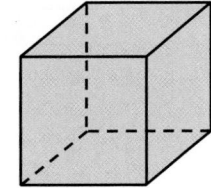 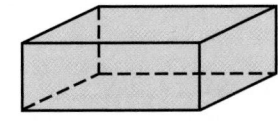

Data Analysis and Probability

10. Students voted for their favorite ice cream topping. How many students in all voted? (p. 154)

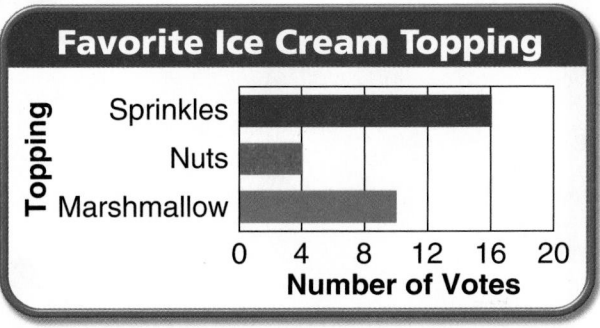

A 16   **C** 26

B 20   **D** 30

11. Which color marble is least likely to be pulled? (Grade 2)

A Yellow

B Blue

C Green

D Red

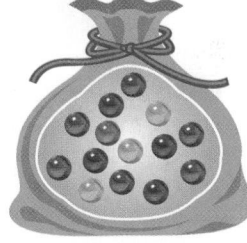

12. ⬛WRITE Math ▶ Sherri is making a pictograph to show the number of books the students in her class have read. Her key is Each 📕 = 5 books. There are 3 books next to Eric's name. How many books has he read? **Explain.** (p. 148)

Students, parents, and teachers in Ontario, Canada, set a world record by making 15,851 snow angels on February 2, 2004.

Investigate

Suppose you want to break the world record for the most snow angels. Use the line graph of normal monthly snowfall amounts to choose a month for your event. Explain your choice.

Normal Monthly Snowfall Amounts

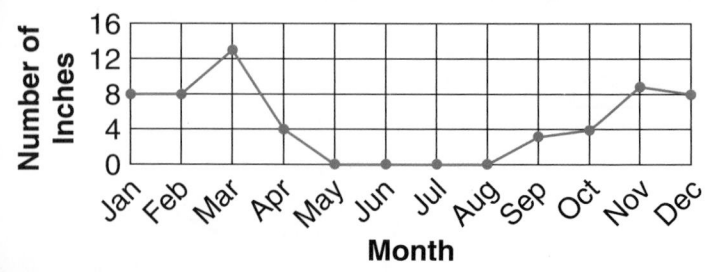

Number of Inches (y-axis: 0, 4, 8, 12, 16)
Month (x-axis: Jan, Feb, Mar, Apr, May, Jun, Jul, Aug, Sep, Oct, Nov, Dec)

GO ONLINE

Technology
Student pages are available in the Student eBook.

Check your understanding of important skills needed for success in Chapter 7.

▶ **Read a Tally Table**

For 1–4, use the tally table.

Which sport do you play?	
Baseball	卌 卌 l
Soccer	卌 卌 lll
Football	卌 lll
Basketball	卌 llll

1. How many students play baseball?

2. How many students play football?

3. How many students answered the question?

4. How many more students play soccer than basketball?

▶ **Compare Parts of a Whole**

For 5–8, write the color shown by the largest part of each spinner.

5. 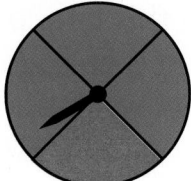   6. 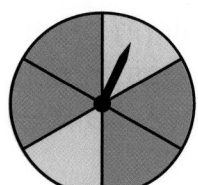   7. 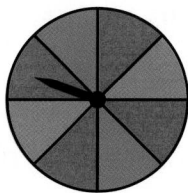   8.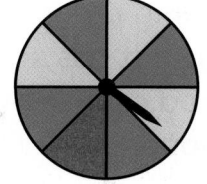

VOCABULARY POWER

CHAPTER VOCABULARY

certain
combination
equally likely
event
experiment
impossible

likely
outcome
predict
probability
tree diagram
unlikely

WARM-UP WORDS

event Something that might happen

outcome A possible result of an experiment

probability The chance that a given event will occur

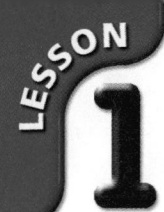

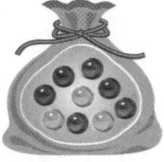

1 Probability: Likelihood of Events

OBJECTIVE: Decide if an event is likely, unlikely, certain, or impossible.

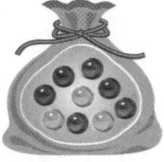
Learn

An **event** is something that might happen. **Probability** is the chance that an event will happen.

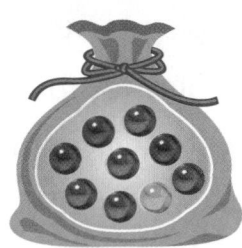

PROBLEM Ted is going to pull a marble out of this bag without looking. Is it likely, unlikely, certain, or impossible that Ted will pull a red marble?

Vocabulary

event	probability
likely	unlikely
impossible	certain

Use these examples.

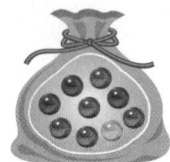 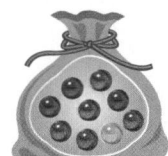 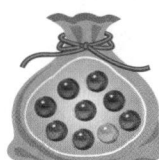 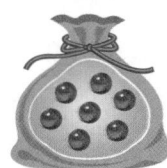

Pulling red is **likely**. It has a good chance of happening.

Pulling yellow is **unlikely**. It does not have a good chance of happening.

Pulling green is **impossible**. It will never happen.

In this bag, pulling red is **certain**. It will always happen.

Ted's bag has more red marbles than blue or yellow marbles.

So, it is likely that Ted will pull a red marble.

• Is Ted more likely to pull a blue marble or a yellow marble?

Guided Practice

1. Which color marble are you unlikely to pull?

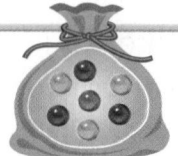

If you spin the pointer one time, tell whether each event is *likely, unlikely, certain,* or *impossible.*

2. The pointer will land on green.   **3.** The pointer will land on red.

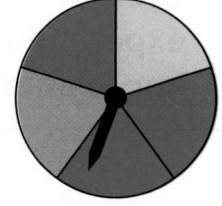

✓**4.** The pointer will land on blue.   ✓**5.** The pointer will land on blue, yellow, or green.

6. **TALK Math** **Explain** why landing on yellow is unlikely.

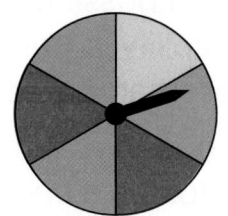

If you pull one marble, tell whether each event is *likely, unlikely, certain,* or *impossible*.

7. pulling a red marble

8. pulling a yellow marble

9. pulling a blue marble

10. pulling a yellow, green, or red marble

For 11–12, use the spinner.

11. Which color are you likely to spin?

12. Which color are you unlikely to spin?

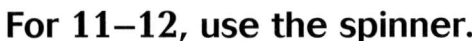

★ **Algebra** Find the missing addend.

13. $18 + \blacksquare = 24$

14. $\blacksquare + 79 = 92$

15. $205 + \blacksquare = 472$

USE DATA For 16–19, use the table. Tom pulls one sock from his drawer without looking.

16. Is it likely or unlikely that Tom will pull a white sock?

17. Is it certain or impossible that Tom will pull a blue sock?

18. **What if** Tom had 16 more black socks? How many more black socks than brown socks would he have?

Tom's Socks	
Color	**Number**
Black	14
Brown	12
White	2

19. **WRITE Math** **What if** Tom had 30 more white socks? **Explain** how your answer to Problem 16 would change.

20. Morgan took a survey of her friends' favorite kind of snack. She recorded the results in a tally table. Her table shows 卌 ‖ next to popcorn. How many friends chose popcorn? (p. 146)

21. Laura has 20 marbles in her collection. There are 5 green, 4 red, 9 white, and 2 blue marbles. She wants to make a bar graph to show her marble collection. Which color will have the shortest bar? (p. 156)

22. **Test Prep** Pulling a green marble from this bag is _?_.

A likely

B unlikely

C certain

D impossible

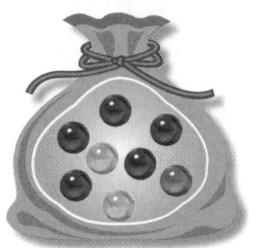

2 Possible Outcomes

OBJECTIVE: Find the possible outcomes for simple events.

When you toss a coin, there are two possible results. In probability, a possible result is called an **outcome**.

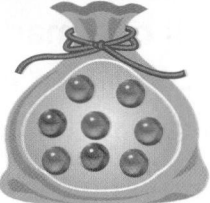

The possible outcomes in a coin toss are *heads up* and *tails up*.

The outcomes *heads up* and *tails up* are **equally likely** because each has the same chance of happening.

Quick Review

Without looking, Roz pulls one marble from the bag. Name a likely event and an impossible event.

Vocabulary

outcome   equally likely   predict

Investigate

Materials ■ coin, tally table

Record the outcomes of tossing a coin. Before the first toss, **predict** the results, or tell what you think they will be.

Ⓐ Predict the number of times the coin will land heads up.

Ⓑ Toss the coin. Record the outcome in a tally table.

Ⓒ Toss the coin 25 times. Record each outcome.

Draw Conclusions

1. How many times did the coin land heads up? tails up?

2. How did your prediction compare to the results?

3. **Synthesis** Would you predict the same number if you were going to toss the coin 25 more times? **Explain.**

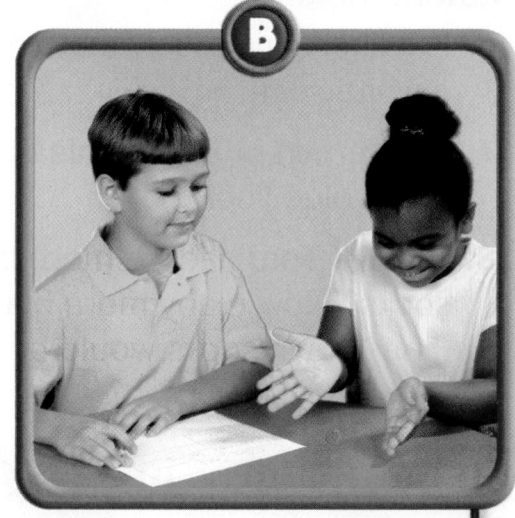

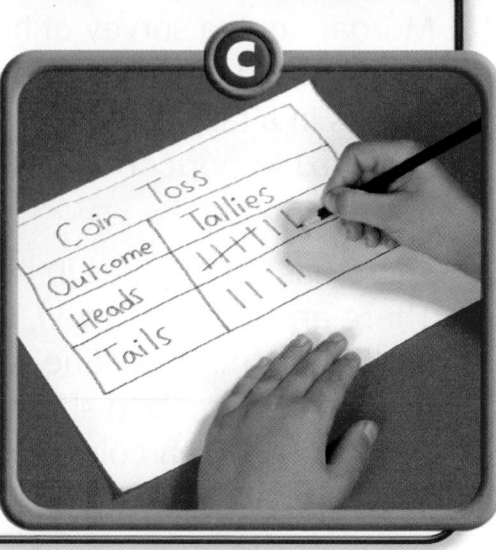

Connect

You can display the results of the coin toss in a bar graph.

Step 1

Jill tossed a coin 25 times. She recorded the results in a tally table.

Coin Toss Results

Heads	Tails
ѴИ ѴИ IIII	ѴИ ѴИ I

Step 2

Jill made a bar graph from the data in the tally table.

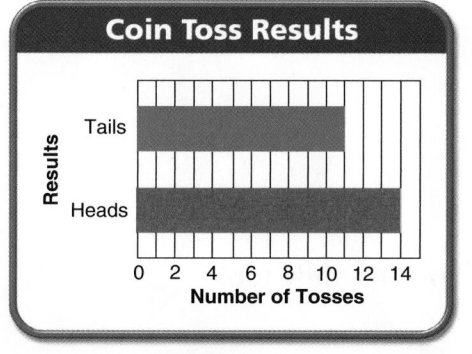

TALK Math

How does the bar graph help you compare Jill's results?

• Why are there 25 tally marks in the tally table?

Practice

For 1–2, list a possible outcome for each.

1. Henry will toss a quarter.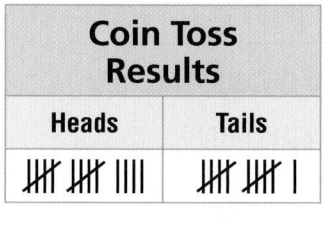

✓2. Marsha will use the spinner.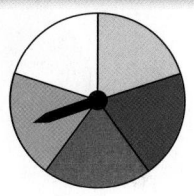

For 3–4, use the bag of marbles.

✓3. Billy is going to pull 1 marble from the bag. What are the possible outcomes for 1 pull?

4. **WRITE Math** ▸ **Sense or Nonsense** Billy says that pulling a red marble is equally likely as pulling a green marble. Does his statement make sense? **Explain.**

5. What are the possible outcomes for tossing a number cube? Which outcomes are equally likely?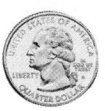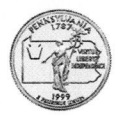

6. **Reasoning** Mario drew a spinner with 8 equal sections. Three sections are yellow. Landing on yellow and landing on red are equally likely. How many sections are red? **Explain.**

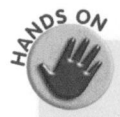

3 Experiments

OBJECTIVE: Conduct probability experiments, record the results, and describe the probability of outcomes.

Quick Review

Name a possible outcome for 1 spin of the pointer.

Vocabulary

experiment

Learn

An **experiment** is a test you can do to find out something. You can do probability experiments to explore how likely outcomes are.

HANDS ON

Activity

Materials ■ 5-part spinner pattern, crayons, tally table, bar graph pattern

Step 1

Make a spinner that has 5 equal parts. Color the parts yellow, red, green, purple, and blue.

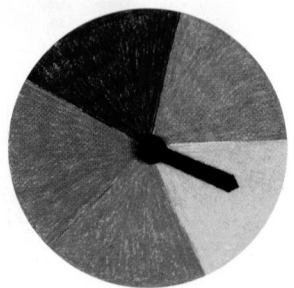

Step 2

Make a tally table. List all the possible outcomes. Spin 20 times. Record the results in the table.

Spinner Experiment	
Color	Tallies
Yellow	
Red	
Green	
Purple	
Blue	

Step 3

Make a bar graph of your data to show the results of your experiment.

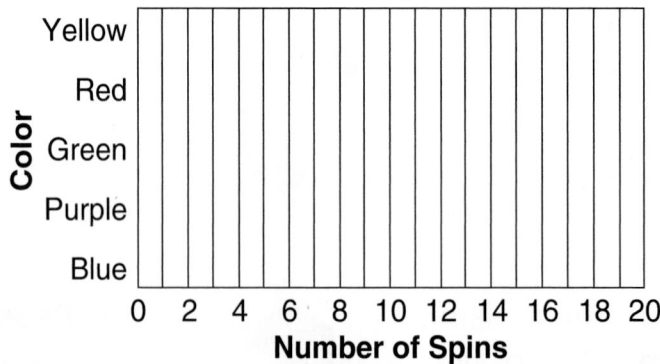

- Did the pointer land on each color about the same number of times?

- **What if** 2 sections of the spinner were blue? How would the results of your experiment change?

182

More About Experiments

Look at Spinner A.
There are 5 possible outcomes: green, red, blue, purple, or yellow. Each outcome is equally likely.

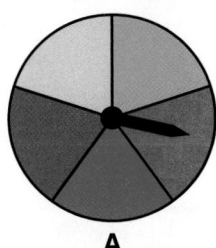

A

The probability of spinning blue is 1 out of 5.
You can write the probability as the fraction $\frac{1}{5}$.

Look at Spinner B.
There are 5 possible outcomes: yellow, yellow, blue, blue, or green.

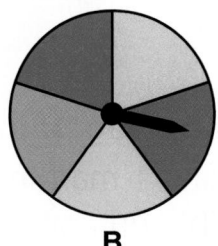

B

The probability of spinning blue is 2 out of 5.
You can write the probability as the fraction $\frac{2}{5}$.

- For Spinner B, what is the probability of spinning green?
- For Spinner B, which outcomes are equally likely?

If an event is certain, the probability that it will happen is 1.
If an event is impossible, the probability that it will happen is 0.

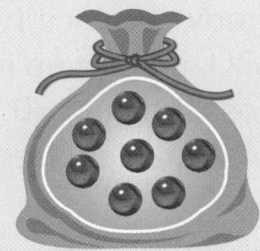

The probability that you will pull a red marble from this bag is 8 out of 8, the fraction $\frac{8}{8}$, or 1.

The probability that you will pull any other color is 0 out of 8, the fraction $\frac{0}{8}$, or 0.

Guided Practice

1. In spinner C, which outcome is most likely?
   Think: Which color is shown most often?

For 2–5, use the bags of tiles at the right.

2. For Bag D, which outcomes are equally likely?

3. What are the possible outcomes if you pull 1 tile from Bag E?

✓ 4. What is the probability of pulling a green tile from Bag D?

5. **TALK Math** Explain why the outcomes in Bag E are equally likely.

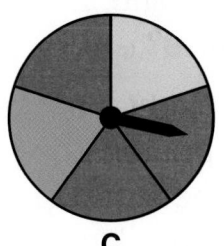

C

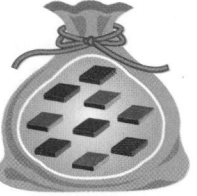

Bag D

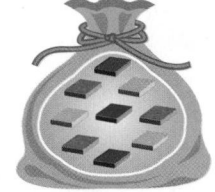

Bag E

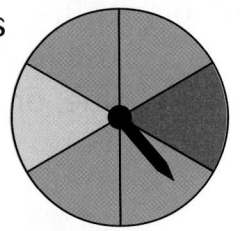

6. Which outcome is most likely?

7. What is the probability of spinning red?

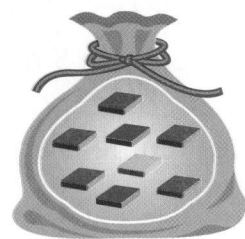

8. Which outcome is least likely?

9. What is the probability of pulling a green tile?

For 10–13, use the bag of marbles.

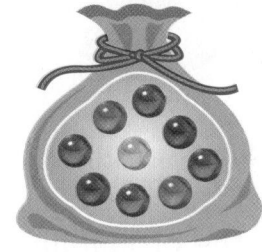

10. Cheryl is pulling 1 marble from this bag. What are the possible outcomes?

11. Which outcomes are equally likely?

12. What is the probability that Cheryl will pull a red marble?

13. **Pose a Problem** Look back at Problem 12. Write a similar problem by changing the color of the marble.

14. **WRITE Math** There are 6 red, 1 green, 2 blue, and 3 yellow tiles in a bag. **Explain** how to find the probability of pulling a yellow tile.

15. Predict the number of times a coin will land tails up in an experiment. Toss the coin 30 times. Then make a tally table to record the results.

16. **≡FAST FACT** The first machine-made glass marbles were produced in Akron, Ohio, in 1905. How many years ago was that?

Mixed Review and Test Prep

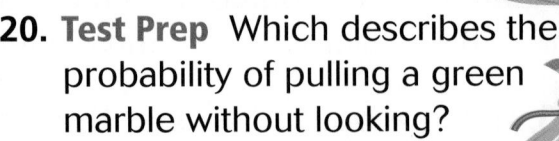

17. Is it likely, unlikely, certain, or impossible to pull a red tile from a bag of 1 blue, 2 green, 1 yellow, and 6 red tiles? (p. 178)

18. Dale bought a package of paper for his printer. The package had 500 sheets of paper. Dale used 112 sheets. How many sheets of paper are left? (p. 88)

19. **Test Prep** What is the probability of pulling a blue tile from this bag?

20. **Test Prep** Which describes the probability of pulling a green marble without looking?

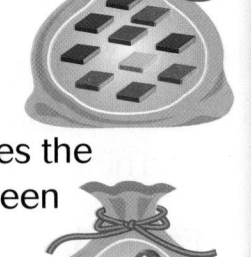

   A likely   **C** certain

   B unlikely   **D** impossible

Extra Practice on page 192, Set B

CD ROM **Technology** Use Harcourt Mega Math, Fraction Action, *Last Chance Canyon*, Level D.

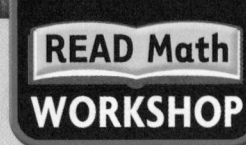
Spinning Around

 Reading Skill **Make an Inference**

The tables below show the results of 30 spins on each person's spinner. What inference can you make about the yellow section of Eve's spinner? When you make an inference, you develop ideas based on information given in a problem.

Julie's Results	
Color	**Times**
Orange	5
Yellow	4
Blue	6
Green	6
Red	5
Purple	4

Eve's Results	
Color	**Times**
Orange	5
Yellow	15
Blue	6
Green	0
Red	4
Purple	0

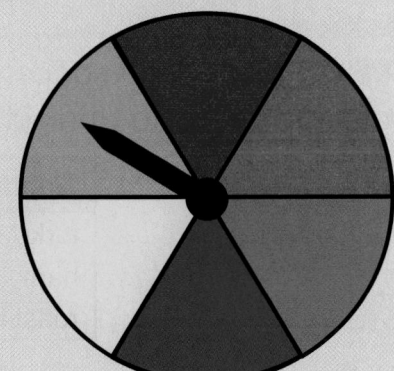

Julie's Spinner

Eve's Spinner

Use what you know about probability and the data in the tables to make an inference about the yellow section of Eve's spinner.

On Julie's spinner, the pointer landed on each color about an equal number of times. On Eve's spinner the pointer landed on yellow about 3 times more often than it landed on the other colors.

So, you can infer that the yellow section of Eve's spinner is larger than the other sections.

Problem Solving **Make an inference to solve the problems.**

1. How many times did the pointer on Eve's spinner land on purple or green? What inference can you make?

2. How many times did the pointer on Eve's spinner land on orange, blue, or red? What inference can you make? **Explain.**

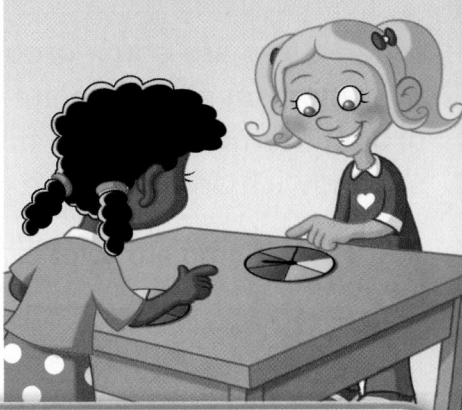

Combinations

OBJECTIVE: Use a tree diagram to find all the possible combinations.

Quick Review

Judy wants a piece of fruit for a snack. She has an apple, a banana, and an orange. How many snack choices does Judy have? What are they?

_____

Vocabulary

tree diagram   combination

Learn

PROBLEM Each soccer player will have the choices of sandwich and drink shown below for lunch.

Sandwich	Drink
turkey	juice
ham	milk
roast beef	

A **combination** is a result of joining two or more things. How many different combinations of 1 sandwich and 1 drink are possible?

You can use a **tree diagram** to find the possible combinations.

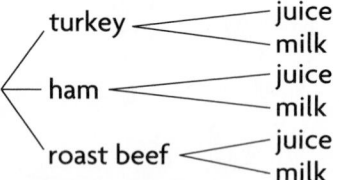

The first combination shown is a turkey sandwich and juice.

So, there are 6 possible combinations of 1 sandwich and 1 drink.

When there are equal groups, you can multiply to find how many in all. There are 3 groups with 2 in each group. Multiply 3 × 2 to find how many combinations of sandwich and drink are possible. 3 × 2 = 6

• **What if** cheese was added to the sandwich choices? How many combinations of 1 sandwich and 1 drink would be possible?

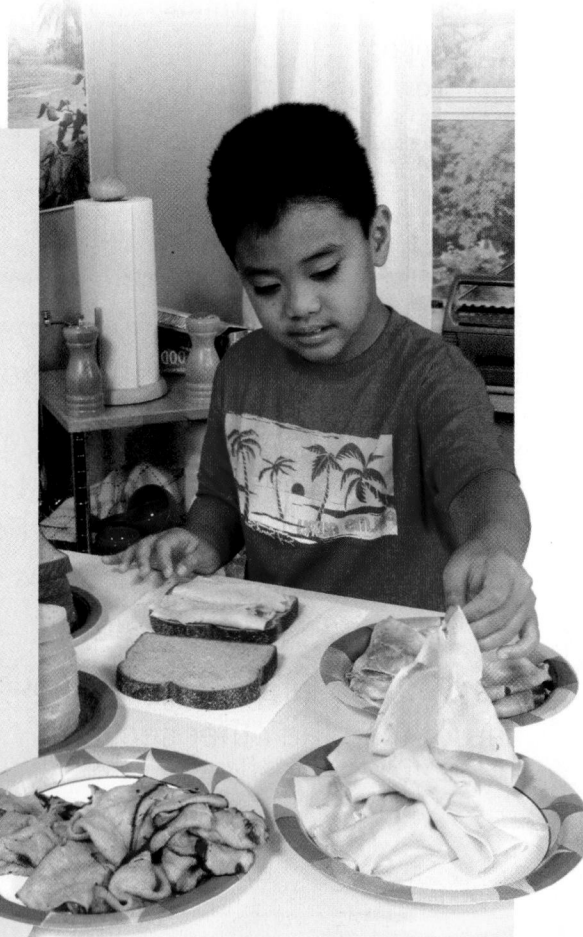

Guided Practice

1. What are the possible combinations of vanilla yogurt and 1 topping? Look at the tree diagram at the right.

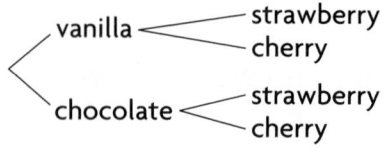

Make a tree diagram to show all the combinations.
Tell the number of combinations.

✓ **2.**

Soup	Fruit
tomato	banana
chicken noodle	apple
chili	

✓ **3.**

Shoes	Colors
sneakers	red
sandals	black
boots	white

4. **TALK Math** Eric has blue, yellow, and red shirts and black and brown shorts. **Explain** how he can use a tree diagram to find the number of possible shirt and shorts combinations.

Independent Practice and Problem Solving

Make a tree diagram to show all the combinations.
Tell the number of combinations.

5. side orders: grits, potatoes
meats: ham, bacon, sausage

6. shirts: yellow, green, striped, plaid
pants: jeans, shorts

USE DATA For 7–8, use the table.

7. John has the bills and coins shown in the table. How many combinations of 1 coin and 1 bill can he make?

8. **What if** John also had a $10 bill? How many combinations of 1 coin and 1 bill could he make?

9. **WRITE Math** **What's the Error?** Oliver has 2 hats and 4 jackets. He says he has 6 combinations of 1 hat and 1 jacket. Describe his error.

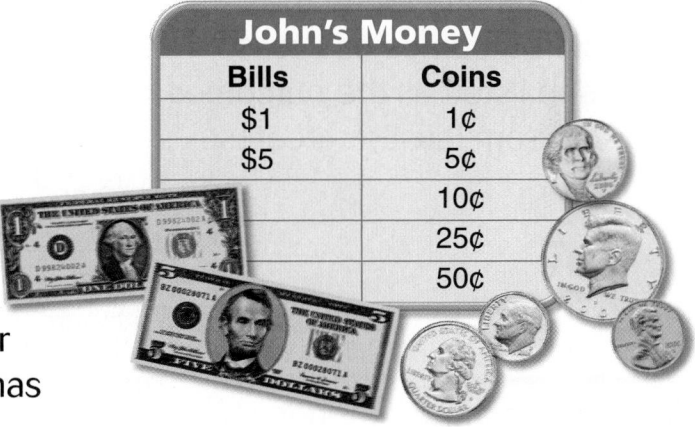

John's Money	
Bills	**Coins**
$1	1¢
$5	5¢
	10¢
	25¢
	50¢

Mixed Review and Test Prep

10. What shape is each face of a number cube? (Grade 2)

11. Jill is doing a coin toss experiment. How many possible outcomes are there? (p. 180)

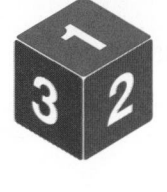

12. **Test Prep** Zach's printer has 3 colors of paper and 3 colors of ink. How many combinations of paper and ink color are possible?

A 1   **B** 5   **C** 6   **D** 9

Extra Practice on page 192, Set C

Problem Solving Workshop
Strategy: Make an Organized List

OBJECTIVE: Solve problems by using the strategy *make an organized list.*

Learn the Strategy

You can make an organized list to help solve problems.

Joy has 5 pennies, 5 nickels, and 5 dimes. She listed some of the different ways she can make 20¢.

Ways to make 20¢
20¢ 2 dimes
20¢ 1 dime, 2 nickels
20¢ 1 dime, 1 nickel, 5 pennies
20¢ 3 nickels, 5 pennies
20¢ 4 nickels

Allie is doing a number cube experiment. She found the possible outcomes of 1 toss. Then she listed all the outcomes in order from least to greatest.

Allie
1
2
3
4
5
6

Scott is serving his friends snacks and drinks after school. He listed the possible snack and drink combinations.

pretzels, juice
pretzels, water
popcorn, juice
popcorn, water
chips, juice
chips, water

TALK Math

Look at Scott's list. How many combinations of 1 snack and 1 drink are possible?

Use the Strategy

PROBLEM Sonya is having a birthday party. She is planning to serve chocolate cupcakes and yellow cupcakes at her party. Her guests can choose chocolate, vanilla, or strawberry frosting. How many combinations of a cupcake and frosting are there?

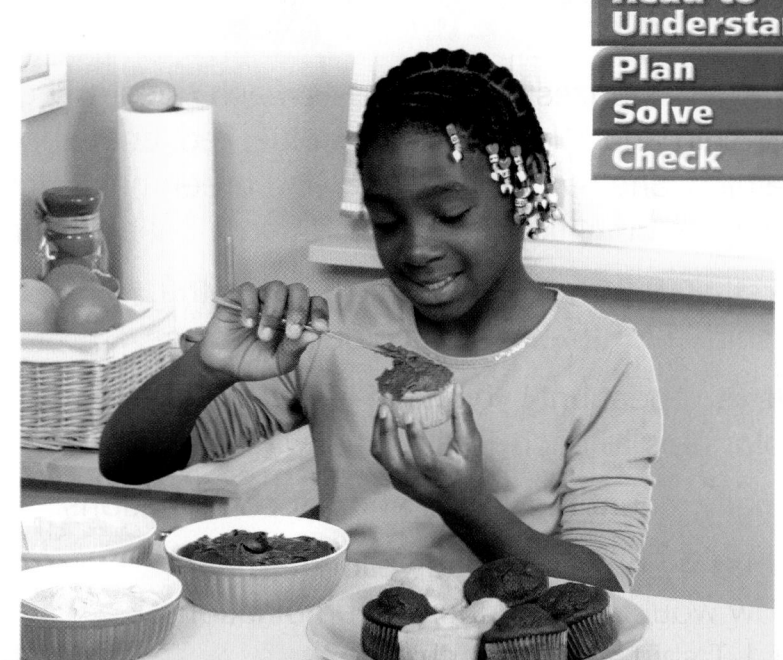

Read to Understand

Reading Skill

- **Identify the details of the problem.**
- **Is there any information you will not use? If so, what?**

Plan

- **What strategy can you use to solve the problem?** You can make an organized list of the combinations.

Solve

- **How can you use the strategy to solve the problem?**

  Make a list of the possible combinations. Start with one cupcake flavor. Match the cupcake flavor to each frosting flavor.

  Match the other cupcake to each frosting.

  Then, count the combinations.

  So, there are 6 combinations of a cupcake and frosting.

chocolate, chocolate
chocolate, vanilla
chocolate, strawberry
yellow, chocolate
yellow, vanilla
yellow, strawberry

Check

- **Is your answer reasonable? Explain.**

Guided Problem Solving

1. Sonya has prizes for her guests. Each guest will get 1 T-shirt and 1 hat. Sonya has blue, red, and white T-shirts. She has purple, blue, and green hats. How many combinations of 1 T-shirt and 1 hat are there?

   First, start with 1 T-shirt color. Match the T-shirt color to each hat color.

   Next, repeat until you have listed each hat color next to each T-shirt color.

   Finally, count the T-shirt and hat combinations.

2. **What if** Sonya also had yellow T-shirts? How would the number of combinations of 1 T-shirt and 1 hat change?

3. Lana's class is having a contest. Each student can choose 1 pencil and 1 notebook as a prize. There are smiley-face and animal pencils. The notebooks are blue and red. How many combinations of 1 pencil and 1 notebook are there?

○	blue, purple
	blue, blue
	blue, green
	red, purple
	red, blue
○	red, green
	white, purple
	white, blue
	white, green
○	

Problem Solving Strategy Practice

USE DATA For 4–6, use the table.

4. There are 3 bags of party prizes. Marty pulls out 1 prize from the balloon bag and 1 prize from the trading-card bag. How many combinations of 1 balloon and 1 trading card are there?

5. Rico pulls out 1 prize from the bookmark bag and 1 prize from the trading card bag. How many combinations of 1 bookmark and 1 trading card are there?

6. **WRITE Math** Sheree will pull 1 bookmark and 1 balloon. **Explain** how to find the number of bookmark and balloon combinations there are.

Party Prizes

Balloons	Bookmarks	Trading Cards
red	ribbon	baseball
white	paper	superhero
blue		

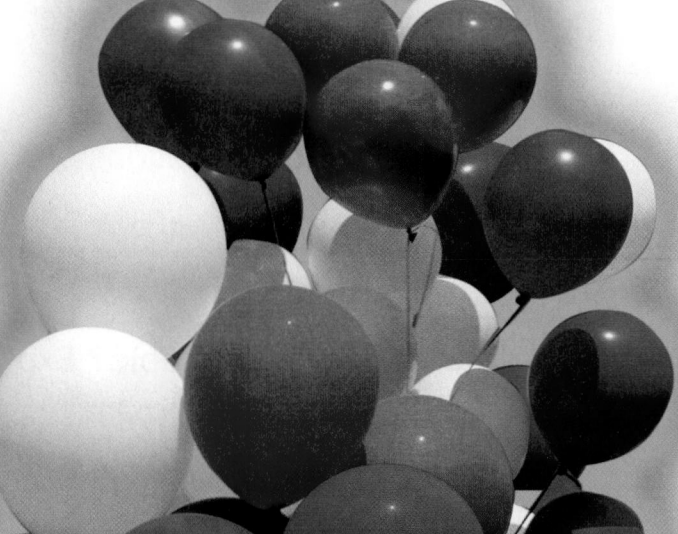

190

Mixed Strategy Practice

USE DATA For 8 and 10, use the pictures and prices.

7. Sonya is buying lollipops and yo-yos as party favors. She wants every guest to have one of each. She can buy orange or cherry lollipops and green or blue yo-yos. Make a list to show how many combinations of 1 lollipop and 1 yo-yo Sonya can buy.

8. **Pose a Problem** Look back at Problem 7. Write a similar problem by adding another color yo-yo.

9. **WRITE Math** ▸ **What's the Question?** Jared had $5.00 to spend at the store. He bought 1 item. The answer is $3.45.

10. **Open-Ended** Suppose you have $10.00 to spend on party favors. There will be 10 guests, and each guest will receive 2 favors. Choose the favors you would give, and find the total cost.

11. **Reasoning** A party store sold 86 packs of party hats in one day. There were 22 more packs sold in the afternoon than in the morning. How many packs were sold in the morning?

Choose a STRATEGY

Draw a Diagram or Picture
Make a Model or Act It Out
Make an Organized List
Find a Pattern
Make a Table or Graph
Predict and Test
Work Backward
Solve a Simpler Problem
Write an Equation
Use Logical Reasoning

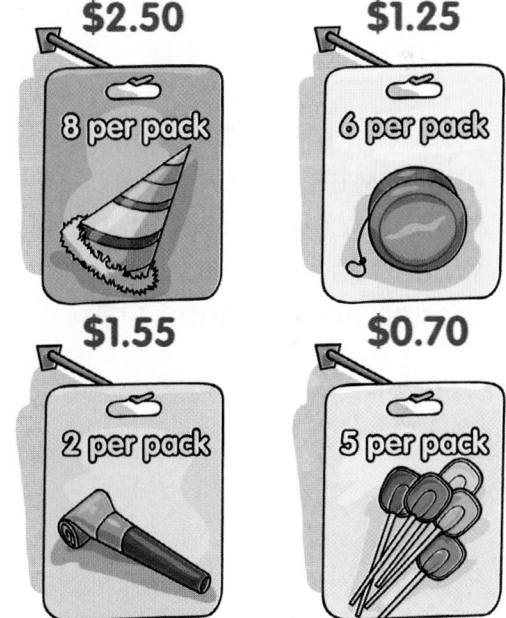

$2.50 — 8 per pack

$1.25 — 6 per pack

$1.55 — 2 per pack

$0.70 — 5 per pack

CHALLENGE YOURSELF

Ted invited 12 friends to his party. He bought whistles for party favors. Each friend will get 1 whistle. The whistles come in packs of 4 for $2 or packs of 10 for $3.

12. Ted wants to buy the whistles in a way that will cost the least amount of money. Explain how you can find which packs Ted should buy and how many of each pack.

13. Each friend brought Ted a stamp for his collection. Now he has 40 stamps. There are 12 more stamps in his second album than there are in his first album. How many stamps are in each album?

Extra Practice

Set A If you spin the pointer one time, tell whether each event is *likely, unlikely, certain,* or *impossible.* (pp. 178–179)

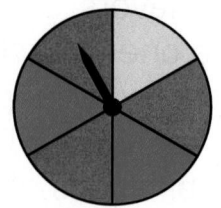

1. The pointer will land on yellow.

2. The pointer will land on green.

3. The pointer will land on red, blue, or yellow.

4. The pointer will land on red.

Set B For 1–2, use the spinner. For 3–4, use the bag of marbles. (pp. 182–185)

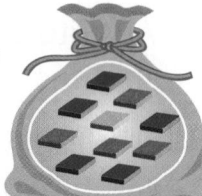

1. Which outcomes are equally likely?

2. What is the probability of spinning red?

3. What are the possible outcomes if you pull 1 tile?

4. What is the probability of pulling a red tile?

5. Rebecca made this tally table to show the results of a number cube experiment. What was the probability of tossing an odd number?

Experiment	
Number	**Tallies**
1	IIII
2	IIII
3	III
4	IIII I
5	IIII
6	III

Set C Make a tree diagram to show all the combinations. Tell the number of combinations. (pp. 186–187)

1. **ice cream:** vanilla, chocolate
   toppings: marshmallow, chocolate, caramel

2. **sandwich bread:** white, wheat, rye
   meats: turkey, ham, salami

3. **place to go:** school, store, park
   transportation: bike, walk

4. **what to read:** book, magazine
   where to read: bedroom, library, family room, school

5. Jeff has 4 sweaters and 2 pairs of jeans. Explain how many combinations of 1 sweater and 1 pair of jeans there are.

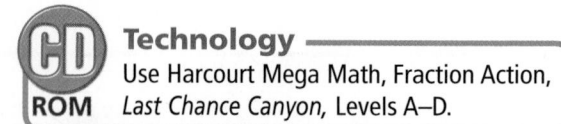

Technology
Use Harcourt Mega Math, Fraction Action, *Last Chance Canyon,* Levels A–D.

TECHNOLOGY ★ CONNECTION

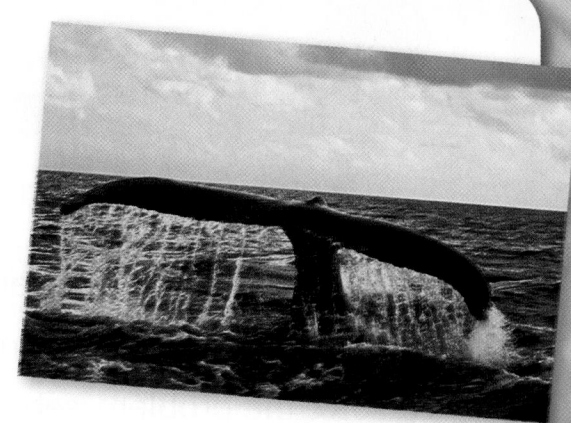

Computer: Spreadsheet

Use a Spreadsheet to Show Data

Carol studied humpback whales during June, July, and August. She looked for 3 humpback whales. Then she recorded how many times she saw each of the whales each month. Carol's findings are shown below.

BANDIT

June ⊪⊪
July ‖
August |

MIDNIGHT

June ‖‖
July ⊪⊪|
August ‖‖‖

OWEN

June ⊪⊪
July ⊪⊪‖‖
August ⊪⊪‖‖

Record Carol's data on a spreadsheet.

Step 1	Type labels in Row 1. Tab across the row, or use the mouse or arrow keys to move. Type *Name* in Column A, *June* in Column B, *July* in Column C, and *August* in Column D.
Step 2	Use the mouse or arrow keys to move to Row 2. Type *Bandit* in Column A. Then type the data for Bandit in Columns B, C, and D.
Step 3	Fill in the data for the other whales in the same way in Rows 3 and 4.

	A	B	C	D
1	Name	June	July	August
2				
3				

	A	B	C	D
1	Name	June	July	August
2	Bandit	5	2	1
3				

Try It

1. Ed kept track of how many food pellets his fish ate on 4 days. Fin ate 1, 0, 2, and 3 pellets. Flip ate 2, 1, 0, and 3. Stripe ate 0, 2, 2, and 2. Make a spreadsheet to show the amount of food eaten by each fish on the 4 days.

2. **Explore More** Record how many pages of homework you had on each day of one week. Ask four friends to do the same. Enter all the data on a spreadsheet. **Explain** what labels you need on the spreadsheet.

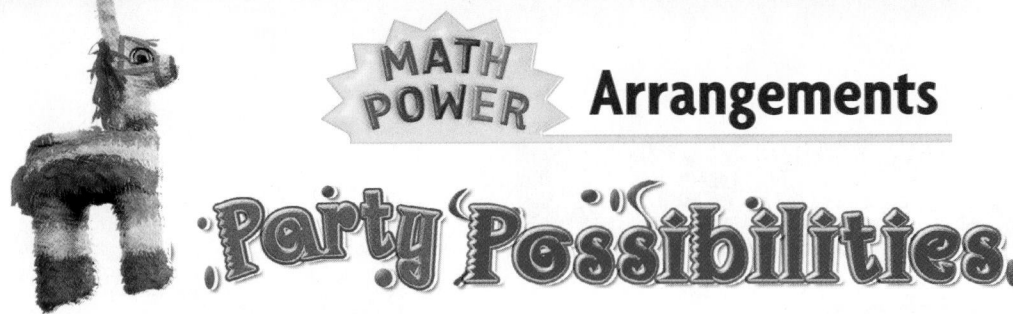

MATH POWER Arrangements

Party Possibilities

Rory is planning her birthday party. Her guests will play games, eat birthday cake, and break a piñata. In how many different ways can Rory plan the order of the 3 activities?

When the order is important, you need an **arrangement**.

To solve the problem, select each activity and then combine it with each of the other activities.

Examples

Step 1 Choose **games** to be first. Write down all the ways to do the 3 activities with games first.

Step 2 Next, choose **cake** to be first. Write down all the ways to do the 3 activities with cake first.

Step 3 Then, choose the **piñata** to be first. Write down all the ways to do the 3 activities with piñata first.

FIRST	SECOND	THIRD
games	cake	piñata
games	piñata	cake
cake	games	piñata
cake	piñata	games
piñata	cake	games
piñata	games	cake

Now count the ways. The order of the activities can be arranged 6 ways.

Try It
Make a chart or list to solve.

1. Paula is arranging her stuffed animals on a shelf. She has a tiger, a lion, and an elephant. In how many ways can Paula arrange her animals?

2. Choose 4 numbers from 1 through 9. Using each number once, in how many ways can you arrange the numbers in a 4-digit number?

3. **WRITE Math** Jillian and Molly are visiting New York City. They want to visit the places on the list at the right. In how many different ways can they visit the places? **Explain.**

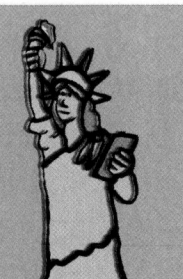

PLACES TO VISIT

Empire State Building
Times Square
Statue of Liberty
Central Park

Chapter 7 Review/Test

Check Vocabulary and Concepts

Choose the best term from the box.

1. An ___?___ is a possible result. (p. 180)

2. ___?___ is the chance that an event will happen. (p. 178)

3. An ___?___ is a test you can do to find out something. (p. 182)

Check Skills

For 4–6, if you pull one marker, tell whether each event is *likely, unlikely, certain,* **or** *impossible.* (pp. 178–179)

4. You will pull an orange marker.

5. You will pull a blue marker.

6. You will pull a red marker.

For 7–9, use the spinner. (pp. 182–185)

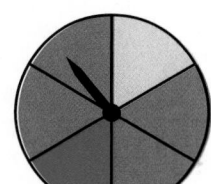

7. What are the possible outcomes of spinning the pointer one time?

8. What is the probability of spinning green?

9. Which outcomes are equally likely?

Make a tree diagram to show all the combinations. Tell the number of combinations. (pp. 186–187)

10. **bed cover:** quilt, comforter
    pattern: stripes, polka-dots, plaid

11. **container:** mug, glass, cup
    drink: milk, water, juice, lemonade

Check Problem Solving

For 12–13, use the table. (pp. 188–191)

12. Eva chooses 1 drink and 1 dessert. How many combinations of 1 drink and 1 dessert are there?

13. **WRITE Math** ▶ Dion chooses 1 drink and 1 fruit. **Explain** how to find the number of drink and fruit combinations there are.

Picnic Food		
Fruit	**Drink**	**Dessert**
watermelon	iced tea	brownie
orange	lemonade	cookie
banana		

Unit Review/Test
Chapters 5–7

Multiple Choice

1. Use the grid. Name the ordered pair for Mark's house. (p. 166)

   A (1,2)

   B (2,0)

   C (3,3)

   D (3,4)

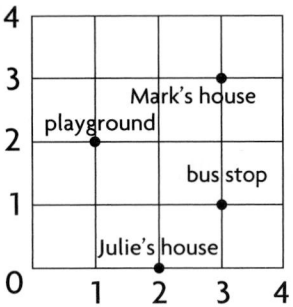

2. Which color tile is likely to be pulled? (p. 178)

   A blue

   B yellow

   C green

   D red

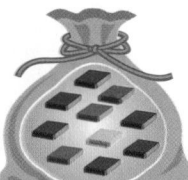

3. The tally table shows the results of pulling a marble 20 times. How many more times was red pulled than blue? (p. 146)

   A 3

   B 4

   C 5

   D 8

Marbles Pulled	
Color	**Number**
red	ЖЖ |||
orange	|||
purple	||||
blue	ЖЖ

4. Kaelynn's swimming lesson started at 1:30. It lasted 90 minutes. At what time did her lesson end? (p. 130)

   A 12:00

   B 1:00

   C 3:00

   D 4:00

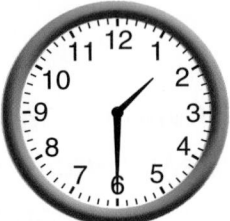

5. How many students are wearing jeans? (p. 146)

   A 2

   B 4

   C 6

   D 12

Clothes Worn Today	
Clothes	**Number of Votes**
shorts	4
skirt	2
jeans	12
pants	6

6. How much longer is the Meadow Trail than the Lakeside Trail? (p. 154)

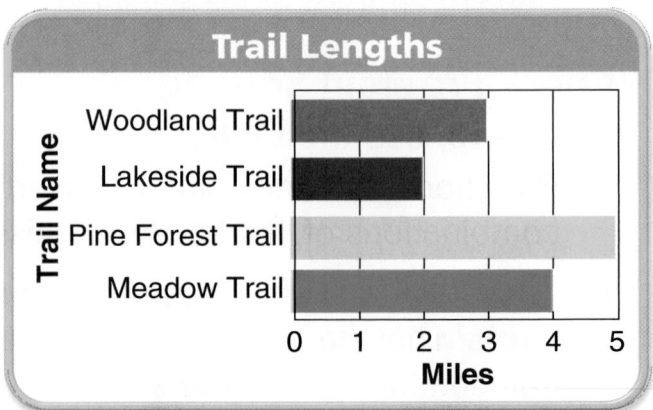

   A 1 mile   C 3 miles

   B 2 miles   D 4 miles

GO ONLINE Technology Use *Online Assessment.*

7. Julia bought 3 souvenirs. The T-shirt cost $7.20, the poster cost $4.50, and the magnet cost $2.10. How much did she spend in all? (p. 122)

A $12.70

C $13.90

B $13.80

D $14.80

8. What is the probability of spinning green? (p. 182)

A 1 out of 5, or $\frac{1}{5}$

B 2 out of 5, or $\frac{2}{5}$

C 3 out of 5, or $\frac{3}{5}$

D 4 out of 5, or $\frac{4}{5}$

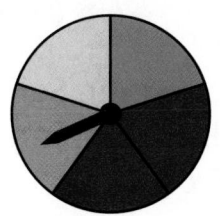

9. What is the range of the data? (p. 162)

A 2

B 3

C 4

D 5

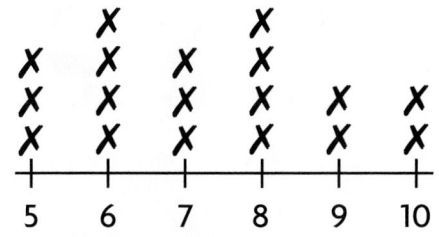

Number of Trees Planted

10. Find an equivalent set of coins. (p. 110)

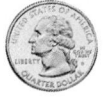

A 4 dimes, 1 nickel, 1 penny

B 6 nickels, 1 dime, 1 penny

C 1 quarter, 3 nickels, 1 penny

D 2 quarters, 1 dime, 2 pennies

Short Response

11. Which is better to show high temperatures over a 2-week period—a line graph or bar graph? (p. 168)

12. Ray has one $5 bill. He bought fruit snacks for $3.25. How much change should he get back? (p. 120)

13. Michelle pulls one cube from this bag. What are the possible outcomes? (p. 180)

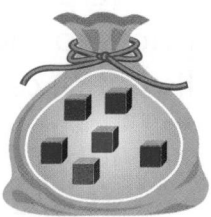

Extended Response 🖊 **WRITE Math** ▶

14. Ben has 2 jackets. The jackets are blue and black. He has 4 hats. The hats are white, red, green, and brown. How many combinations of 1 jacket and 1 hat are there? **Explain.** (p. 186)

15. Rebecca is at gymnastics class. What time is it? **Explain** how you know. (p. 124)

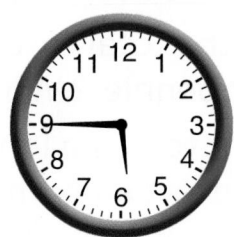

Penny Power!

Pennies Yesterday and Today

The penny is the oldest coin made by the United States Mint. The first copper penny was made in 1793.

What would life be like without pennies?

FACT·ACTIVITY

If we did not have pennies, prices might be higher. Sellers might raise prices to the next higher nickel. Something that now sells for 72 cents might sell for 75 cents.

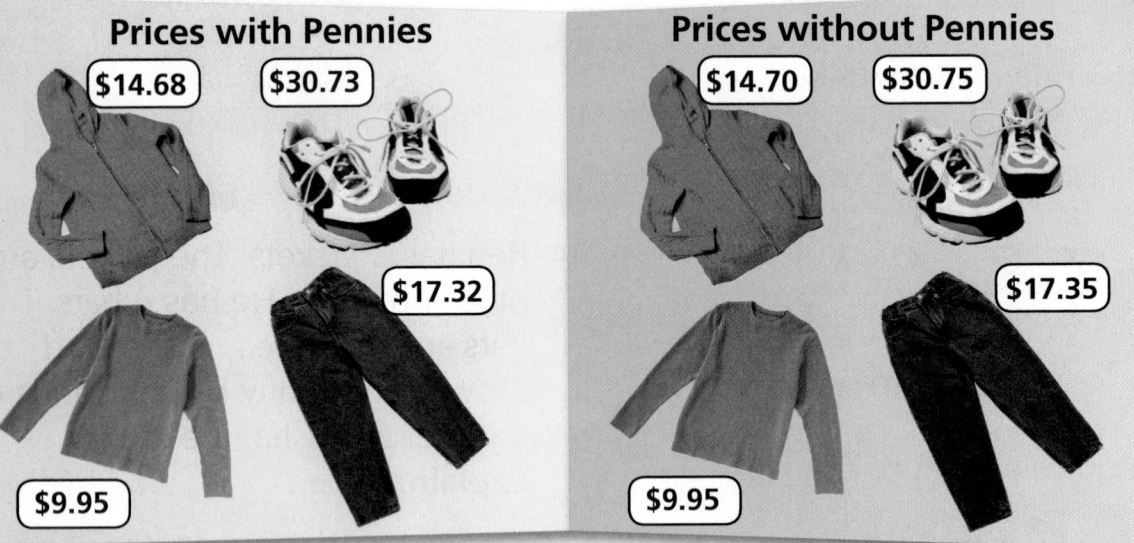

Prices with Pennies

$14.68 $30.73

$17.32

$9.95

Prices without Pennies

$14.70 $30.75

$17.35

$9.95

Use the information from the pictures.

1. Which items have higher prices when pennies are not used?

2. What is the total cost of the jacket and pants with pennies? Without pennies? Which total cost is greater? How much greater?

3. You want to buy a long-sleeved T-shirt for $9.95. How would you pay the exact amount for the shirt, using the fewest bills and coins?

Survey: Pennies

ALMANAC Fact

A coin usually lasts for about 30 years.

A one-dollar bill usually lasts about 2 years.

Some people think it is time to stop making and using pennies. The idea was talked about in Congress, but members voted to keep making and using pennies.

The table shows what some people think about getting rid of pennies.

Should We Stop Making and Using Pennies?

Yes	No
1. Vending machines don't take pennies.	1. Pennies keep prices down.
2. Pennies get lost in sofas and car seats.	2. Rolls of pennies can be exchanged for dollars.
3. Pennies are too heavy to carry around.	3. Pennies have been around for a long time.

FACT·ACTIVITY

Do you think it is time to stop making and using pennies? What do other students think? Survey 10 students.

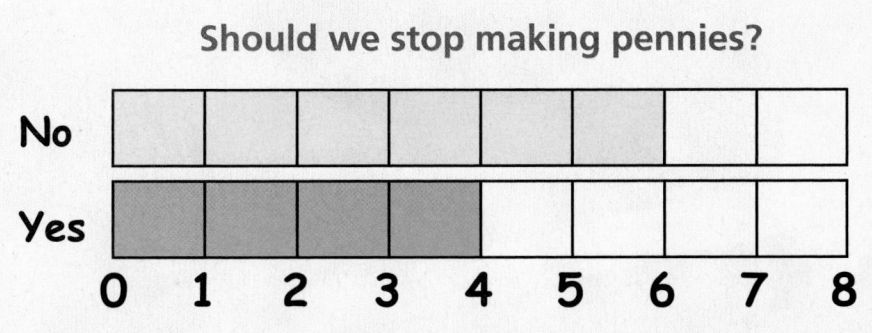

Should we stop making pennies?

No
Yes
0 1 2 3 4 5 6 7 8

❶ Make a list of 10 students to survey.

❷ Record their answers in a tally table.

❸ Make a bar graph like this one.

❹ Which answer did more students choose?

WRITE Math ▸ If we stop using pennies, what could be done with the ones we already have? Make a list of three or more ideas.

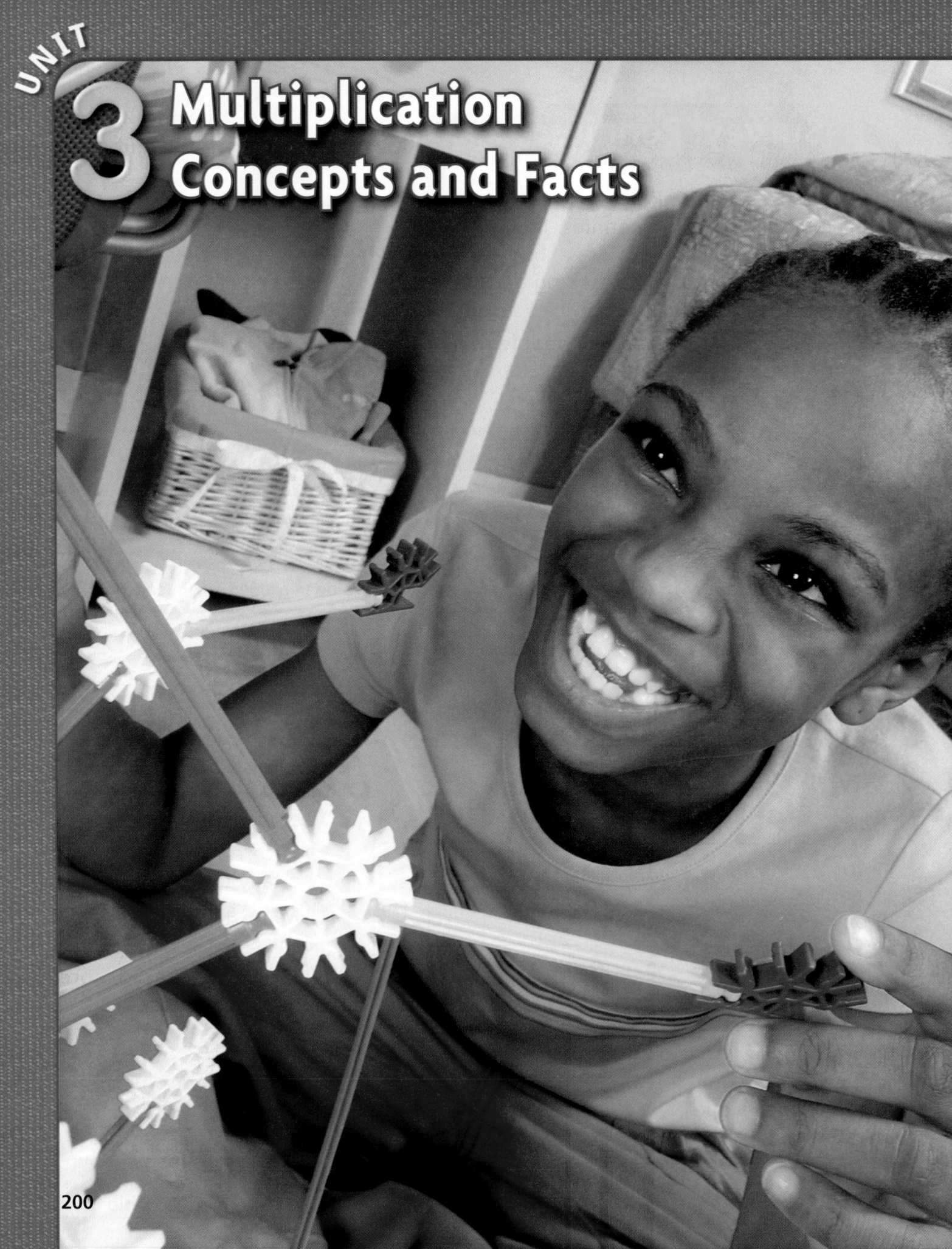

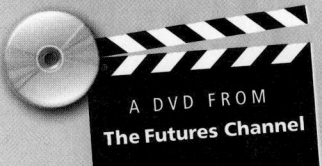

with
Chapter Projects

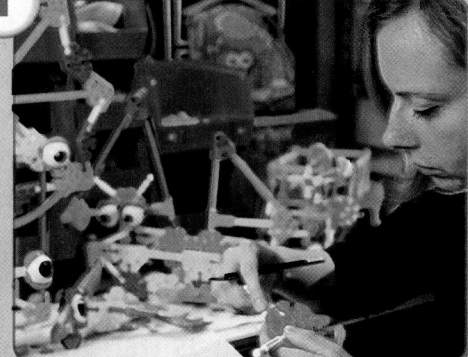

A new toy is invented by starting with an idea, making a drawing, and combining pieces for a kit.

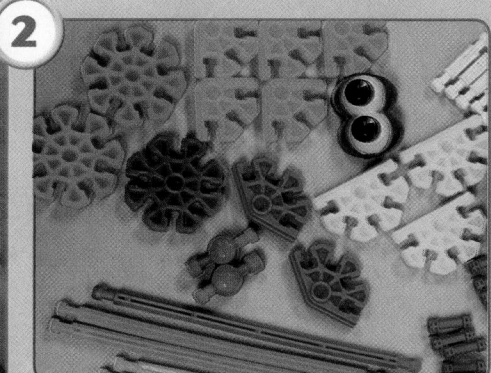

The unassembled kit shows multiple numbers of each different piece.

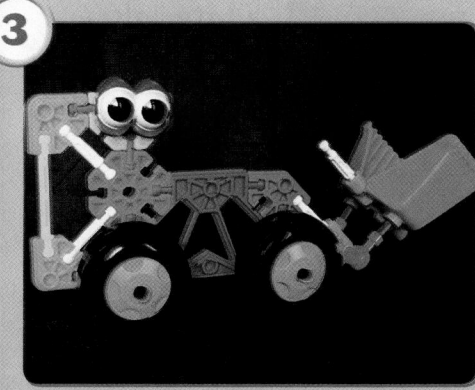

The designers use imagination and creativity when designing small toys or large, movable toys.

VOCABULARY POWER

TALK Math

What math is shown in the **Math on Location** photographs? How can you use multiplication to tell how many pieces there are?

READ Math

REVIEW VOCABULARY You learned the words below when you learned about multiplication last year. How do these words relate to **Math on Location**?

factor a number that is multiplied by another number to find a product

multiply to combine equal groups to find how many in all

product the answer in a multiplication problem

WRITE Math

Copy and complete a Word Definition Map like the one below. Use what you know about multiplication.

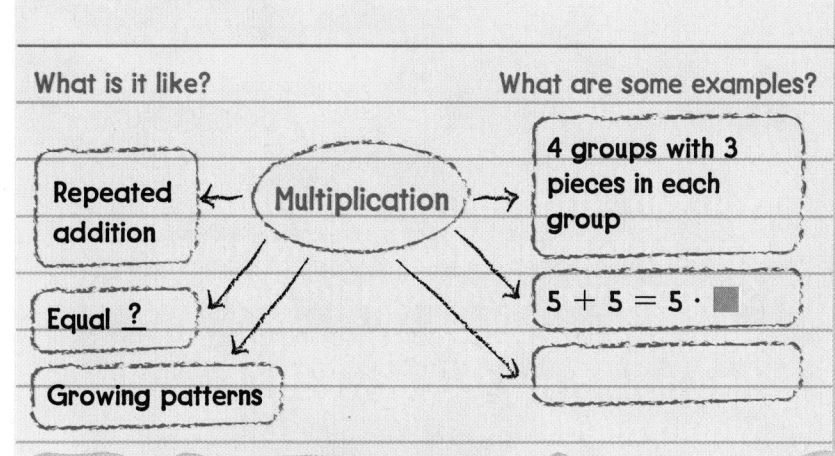

What is it like?

Repeated addition ← Multiplication →

What are some examples?

4 groups with 3 pieces in each group

Equal _?_

$5 + 5 = 5 \cdot \blacksquare$

Growing patterns

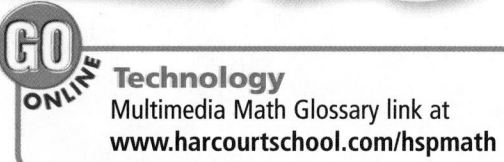

Technology
Multimedia Math Glossary link at
www.harcourtschool.com/hspmath

8 Understand Multiplication

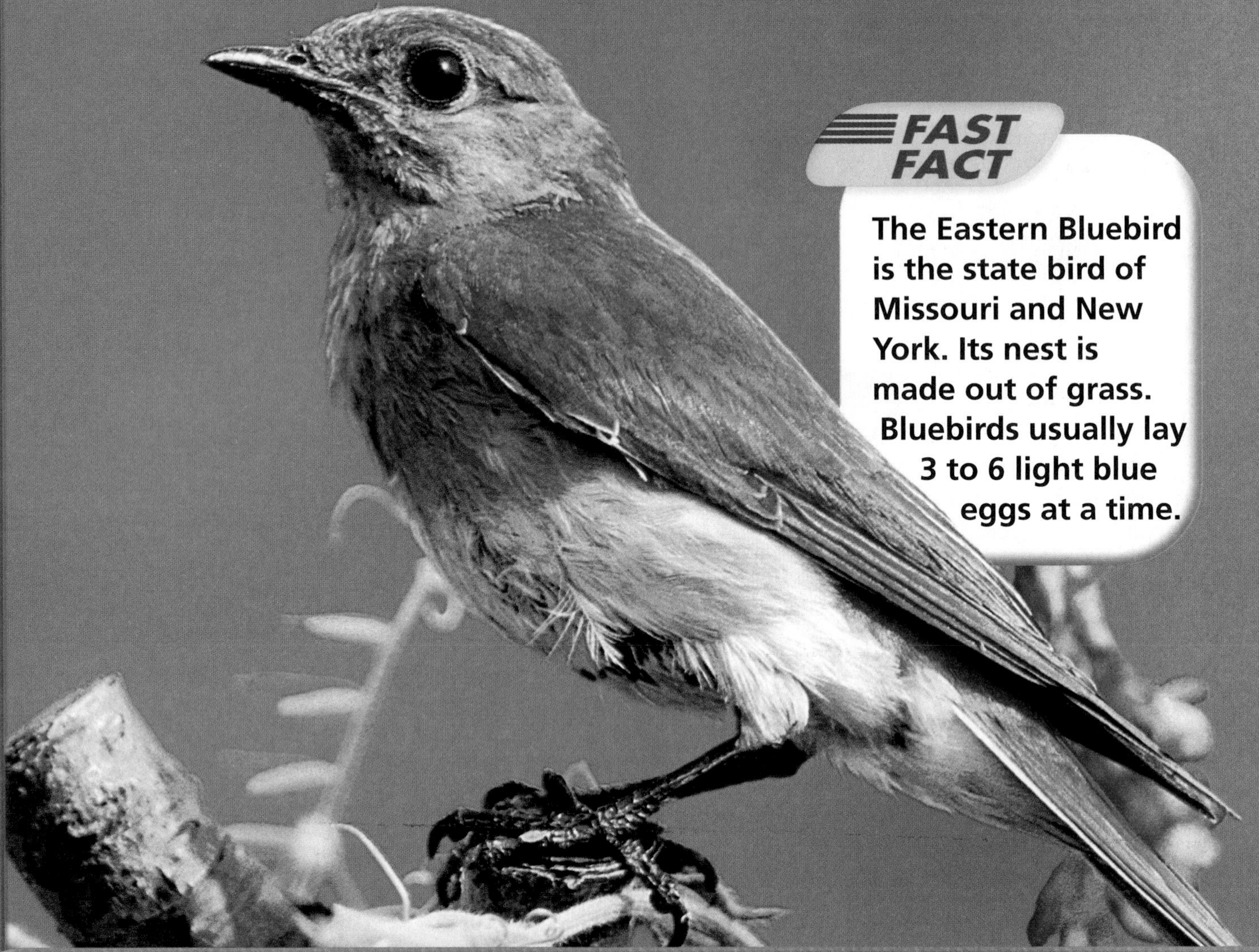

≡ FAST FACT

The Eastern Bluebird is the state bird of Missouri and New York. Its nest is made out of grass. Bluebirds usually lay 3 to 6 light blue eggs at a time.

Investigate

You can attract bluebirds to your yard by putting up a bluebird house. Suppose you want to make more than one birdhouse. How could you find how many feet of wood you would need?

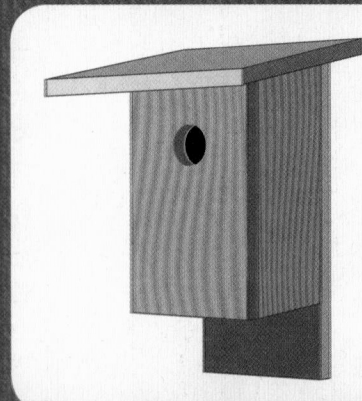

Materials:
6-foot piece of wood
nails
1 eye screw
wood screws

GO ONLINE

Technology
Student pages are available in the Student eBook.

Check your understanding of important skills needed for success in Chapter 8.

▶ **Skip-Count**

Skip-count to find the missing numbers.

1. 2, 4, 6, 8, ■, ■, ■

2. 3, 6, 9, ■, ■, ■

3. 5, 10, 15, ■, 25, ■, ■

4. 10, 20, ■, ■, 50, ■, ■

▶ **Equal Groups**

Write how many there are in all.

5.

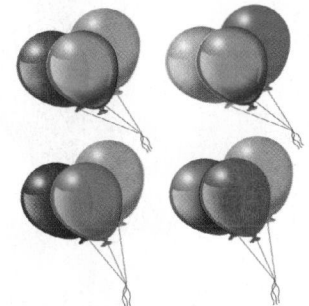

6.

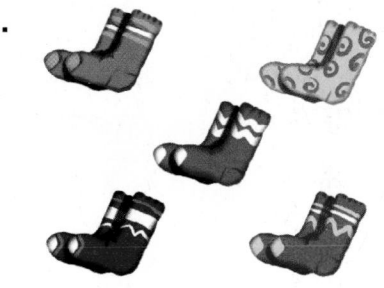

7.

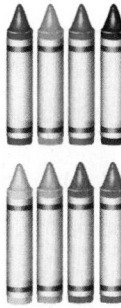

4 groups of 3 = ■   5 groups of 2 = ■   2 groups of 4 = ■

Find how many in all. You may wish to draw a picture.

8. 3 groups of 6   **9.** 2 groups of 2   **10.** 4 groups of 5

11. 2 groups of 4   **12.** 4 groups of 3   **13.** 5 groups of 6

VOCABULARY POWER

CHAPTER VOCABULARY

array
Commutative
   Property of
   Multiplication
factor
Identity Property of
   Multiplication

multiplication
multiply
product
Zero Property of
   Multiplication

WARM-UP WORDS

array An arrangement of objects in rows and columns

factor A number that is multiplied by another number to find a product

product The answer in a multiplication problem

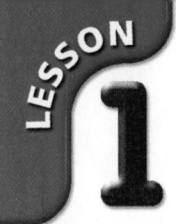

ALGEBRA
Relate Addition to Multiplication

OBJECTIVE: Relate addition and multiplication.

Quick Review

Add.

1. 4 + 4 + 4
2. 5 + 5 + 5 + 5
3. 7 + 7 + 7
4. 2 + 2 + 2
5. 3 + 3 + 3

Vocabulary

multiplication   multiply

Learn

PROBLEM Jasmine needs 3 bananas to make 1 loaf of banana bread. The same number of bananas are in each loaf. How many bananas does Jasmine need to make 4 loaves?

ONE WAY   **Use addition.**

Use counters to show the bananas. Show 3 counters for each loaf of bread. Make 4 groups to show the 4 loaves.

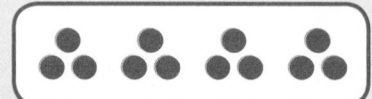

Find the total number of counters. Write the addition sentence.

$$3 + 3 + 3 + 3 = 12$$

So, Jasmine needs 12 bananas to make 4 loaves of bread.

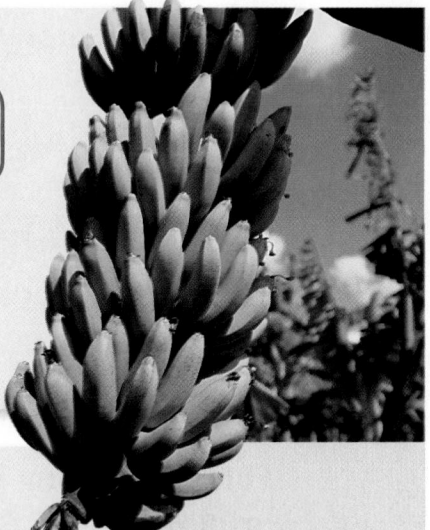

▲ There are about 200 bananas in some bunches.

ANOTHER WAY   **Use multiplication.**

When groups are equal, you can use **multiplication** to find the total. When you **multiply**, you combine equal groups to find how many in all.

Think: 4 groups of 3

Write: $4 \times 3 = 12$ **Read:** 4 times 3 equals 12.

A table can show the addition and multiplication.

Equal Groups	Think:	Addition Sentence	Multiplication Sentence
	4 groups of 3	3 + 3 + 3 + 3 = 12	4 × 3 = 12

• **What if** Jasmine makes 5 loaves of bread? How many bananas will she need? Use multiplication to show your answer.

1. Write a multiplication sentence that shows
   $2 + 2 + 2 + 2 + 2 = 10$.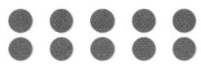

**Use counters to model. Then write an addition sentence
and a multiplication sentence for each.**

2. 2 groups of 4   3. 3 groups of 2   ✔4. 5 groups of 4   ✔5. 3 groups of 3

6. [TALK Math] **Explain** how you know that both $3 + 3$ and 2×3 equal 6.

Independent Practice (and Problem Solving)

**Use counters to model. Then write an addition sentence
and a multiplication sentence for each.**

7. 3 groups of 4   8. 2 groups of 5   9. 4 groups of 6   10. 3 groups of 7

Write a multiplication sentence for each.

11. 12. 13. 14.

15. $2 + 2 + 2 + 2 = 8$ 16. $4 + 4 + 4 + 4 = 16$ 17. $9 + 9 + 9 = 27$

USE DATA For 18–19, use the table.

18. John bought 3 oranges. How much do the
    oranges weigh in all?

19. Which weighs more, 3 apples or 4 bananas?
    How much more?

20. [WRITE Math] **Sense or Nonsense** Jared says
    that he can write a multiplication sentence and an addition sentence
    for $5 + 4 + 4$. Does Jared's statement make sense? **Explain.**

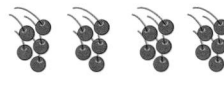

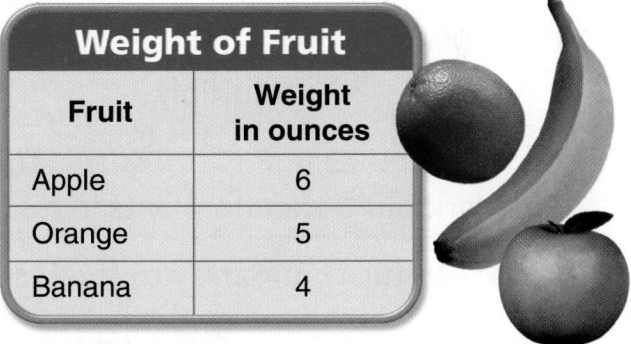

Weight of Fruit	
Fruit	Weight in ounces
Apple	6
Orange	5
Banana	4

Mixed Review and Test Prep

21. Tell whether the event is certain or
    impossible. Next year, May 2 will
    come before May 3. (p. 178)

22. Drew pulls 1 marble from
    the bag. List the possible
    outcomes. (p. 180)

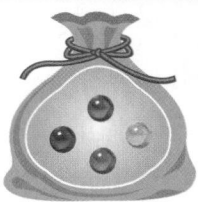

23. **Test Prep** What is another way to show $2 + 2 + 2 + 2$?

   A 2×2 **B** 6×2 **C** 4×2 **D** 2×8

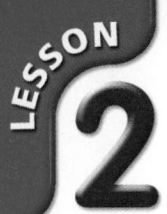

ALGEBRA
Model with Arrays

OBJECTIVE: Use arrays to understand multiplication and the Commutative Property of Multiplication.

Quick Review

Find how many in all.

1. 3 groups of 2
2. 2 groups of 6
3. 4 groups of 3
4. 3 groups of 5
5. 5 groups of 2

Learn

PROBLEM Mark has a garden. He planted 2 rows of tomato plants with 3 plants in each row. How many tomato plants did Mark put in his garden?

An **array** is a group of objects in rows and columns.

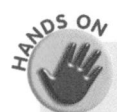

Activity

Materials ■ square tiles

Make an array with 2 rows and 3 columns to show Mark's tomato plants.

column
↓

row →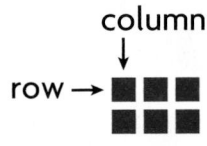

2 rows of 3 = ■

Now find the total number of tiles.

Add.   Multiply.

$3 + 3 = 6$ $2 \times 3 = 6$

So, Mark put 6 tomato plants in his garden.

You can turn your array to show 3 rows of 2.

3 rows of 2 = ■

Find the total number of tiles.

Add.   Multiply.

$2 + 2 + 2 = 6$ $3 \times 2 = 6$

• What happened to the number of tiles in the array when you turned it?

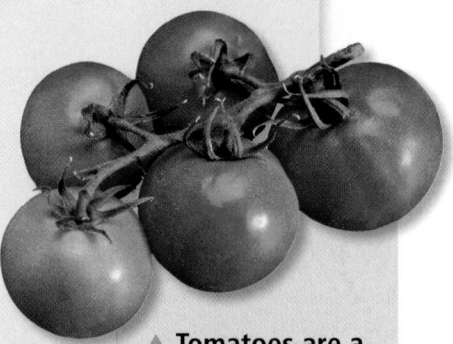

▲ Tomatoes are a good source of vitamins.

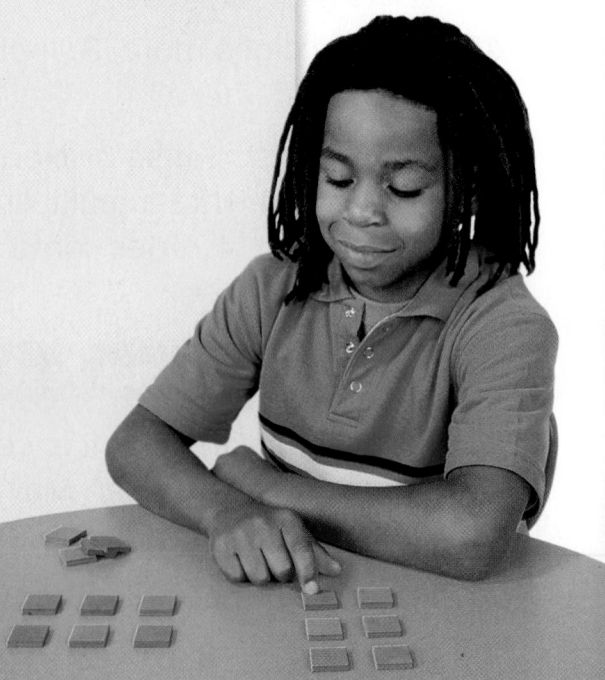

Commutative Property of Multiplication

In multiplication, the numbers you multiply are called **factors**. The answer is called the **product**.

The **Commutative Property of Multiplication**, or Order Property of Multiplication, states that factors can be multiplied in any order and their product is the same.

$$2 \quad \times \quad 3 \quad = \quad 6$$
$$\uparrow \qquad \uparrow \qquad \uparrow$$
factor   factor   product

You can use a table to see the Commutative Property.

Model	Draw	Write a Multiplication Sentence
2 rows of 3		$2 \times 3 = 6$
3 rows of 2		$3 \times 2 = 6$
2 rows of 5		$2 \times 5 = 10$
5 rows of 2		$5 \times 2 = 10$
3 rows of 4		$3 \times 4 = 12$
4 rows of 3		$4 \times 3 = 12$

Guided Practice

1. Write the multiplication sentences these arrays show.

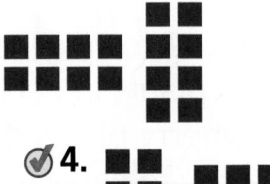

Write a multiplication sentence for each array.

2.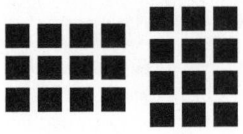

✓**3.**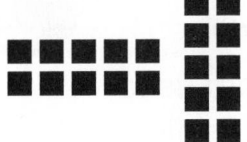

✓**4.**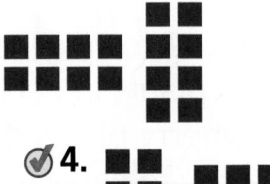

5. **TALK Math** Explain why the Commutative Property is also called the Order Property.

Write a multiplication sentence for each array.

6.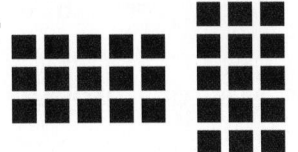

7.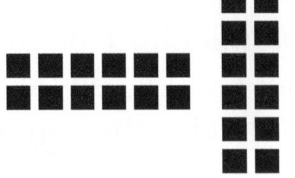

8.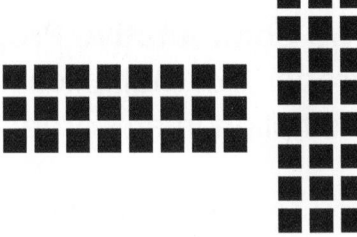

9.

10.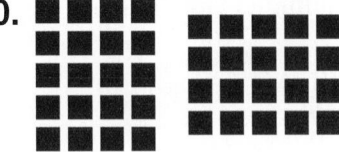

11.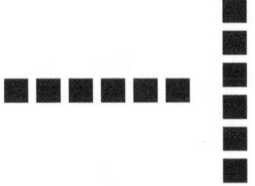

Write the multiplication sentence for each array.
Then draw the array that shows the Commutative Property.

12.

13.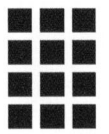

14.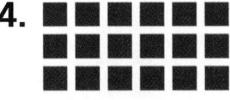

15. Mary placed 24 cans of tomato sauce in 6 rows. How many cans were in each row?

$$6 \text{ rows of } \blacksquare = 24$$

16. Mark picked 5 peppers from each of the 2 rows in his garden. He used 3 peppers to make a salad. How many peppers does he have left?

17. **Reasoning** Jenna and her mother baked apple pies. They picked 18 apples and put the same number of apples in each of 3 pies. Draw an array to show how many apples they put in each pie.

18. John planted 4 rows of strawberries. There are 8 plants in each row. How many strawberry plants did John grow? Draw an array to show your answer.

19. **WRITE Math** Eddie and Jackie both used 12 square tiles to make an array. Eddie's array had 4 rows. Jackie's array had 3 rows. Is this possible? **Explain.**

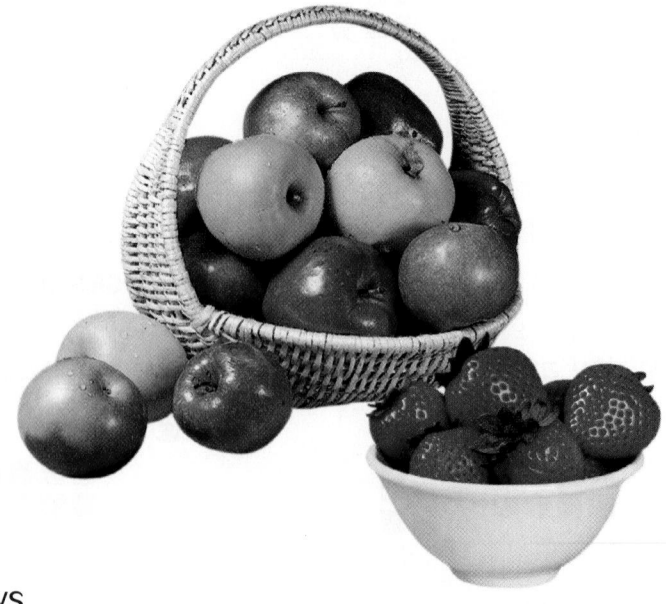

208 Extra Practice on page 224, Set B

Technology
Use Harcourt Mega Math, Country
Countdown, *Counting Critters,* Level W.
CD ROM

Learn About Square Numbers

If both factors are the same, the product is called a **square number**. When you use the factors to make an array, the array is a square.

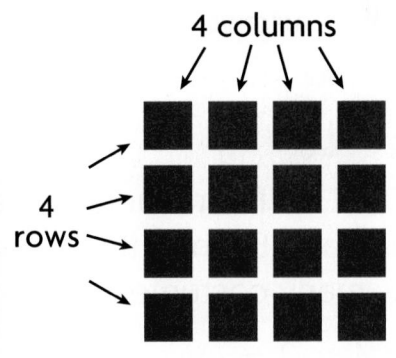

4 columns

4 rows

$4 \times 4 = 16$

16 is a square number.

Work with a partner to draw arrays that show square numbers.

Use tiles to make a square array with 3 rows and 3 columns.

Draw the array and write the multiplication sentence.

$3 \times 3 = 9$

So, 9 is a square number.

Try It

Draw each array. Write the multiplication sentence. Then circle the square number in each sentence.

20. 5×5 **21.** 7×7 **22.** 8×8

23. 6×6 **24.** 9×9

25. [WRITE Math] Is 10 a square number? **Explain** how you know.

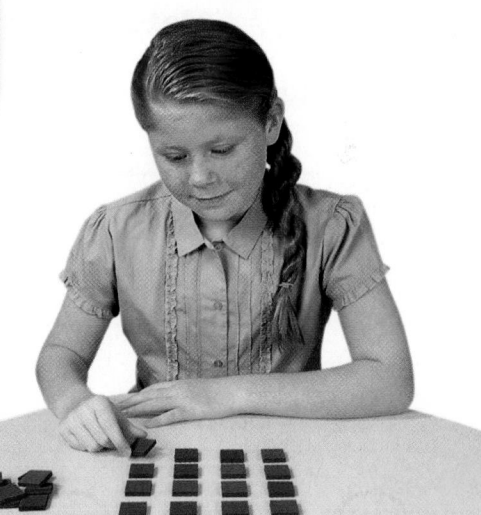

Mixed Review and Test Prep

26. ≡**FAST FACT** The world's largest Catsup Bottle is one hundred seventy feet tall. Write this number in standard form. (p. 8)

27. A notebook has 2 pockets for loose paper. Write an addition sentence and a multiplication sentence to show how many pockets 4 notebooks would have. (p. 204)

28. Test Prep Which is an example of the Commutative Property of Multiplication?

A $6 + 4 = 2 + 4$ **C** $4 \times 6 = 6 \times 4$

B $4 \times 6 = 4 + 6$ **D** $4 \times 6 = 3 \times 8$

29. Test Prep The art students hung up their paintings. There are 5 rows with 6 paintings in each row. How many paintings are there in all?

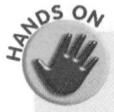

LESSON 3

Multiply with 2

OBJECTIVE: Multiply with the factor 2.

Learn

PROBLEM Four students are putting on a play for their class. Each of the 4 students has 2 costumes. How many costumes do the students have in all?

Find $4 \times 2 = \blacksquare$.

Activity Materials ■ counters

Use counters.

MODEL	THINK	RECORD
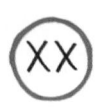 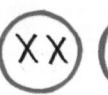 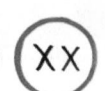	4 groups of 2 2 + 2 + 2 + 2	$4 \times 2 = 8$ $\begin{array}{r} 2 \\ \times 4 \\ \hline 8 \end{array}$

Draw a picture.

DRAW	THINK	RECORD
(XX) (XX) (XX) (XX)	4 groups of 2 2 + 2 + 2 + 2	$4 \times 2 = 8$ $\begin{array}{r} 2 \\ \times 4 \\ \hline 8 \end{array}$

So, the students have 8 costumes in all.

Example

You can also multiply by 2 by doubling the other factor.

$3 \times 2 = 2 \times 3 = 3 + 3 = 6$

$4 \times 2 = 2 \times 4 = 4 + 4 = 8$

$5 \times 2 = 2 \times 5 = 5 + 5 = 10$

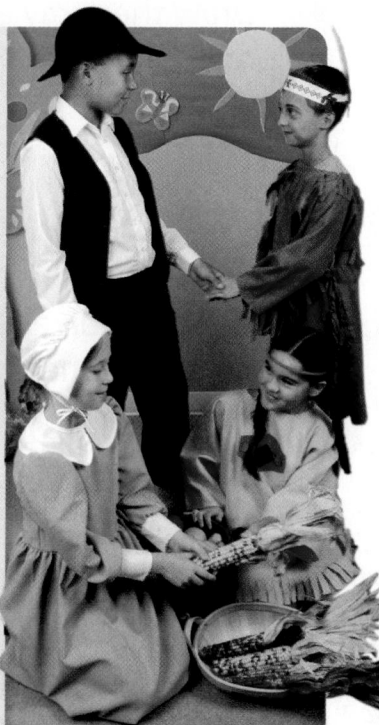

Guided Practice

1. Write the multiplication sentence the drawing shows.

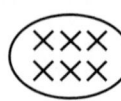 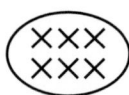

Write the multiplication sentence for each.

2. ✓3. ✓4.

5. **TALK Math** **Explain** how 6×2 can help you find the product for 2×6.

Independent Practice and Problem Solving

Write a multiplication sentence for each.

6. 7. 8.

Find the product.

9. $\begin{array}{r} 1 \\ \times 2 \\ \hline \end{array}$ 10. $\begin{array}{r} 2 \\ \times 2 \\ \hline \end{array}$ 11. $\begin{array}{r} 4 \\ \times 2 \\ \hline \end{array}$ 12. $\begin{array}{r} 2 \\ \times 9 \\ \hline \end{array}$ 13. $\begin{array}{r} 6 \\ \times 2 \\ \hline \end{array}$ 14. $\begin{array}{r} 2 \\ \times 7 \\ \hline \end{array}$

Copy and complete.

	×	1	2	3	4	5	6	7	8	9	10
15.	2	■	■	■	■	■	■	■	■	■	■

USE DATA For 16–17, use the graph.

16. How many tickets did Tyrone and Julia sell in all?

17. **WRITE Math** **Explain** how you find out how many tickets Lee sold for the school play.

Play Tickets

Name	Tickets Sold
Tyrone	🎟🎟🎟🎟
Julia	🎟🎟🎟🎟🎟🎟🎟
Lee	🎟🎟🎟🎟🎟🎟

Key: Each 🎟 = 2 tickets.

Mixed Review and Test Prep

18. What is the next number in Tom's pattern? (p. 4)

$$6, 12, 18, 24, \blacksquare$$

19. Write 2 multiplication sentences that use the factors 3 and 6. What property do the sentences show?

(p. 206)

20. **Test Prep** Jenna and Matt each wear 5 costumes in the play. Which number sentence shows their total number of costumes?

A $2 + 5 = 7$ **C** $2 \times 2 = 4$

B $5 + 2 = 7$ **D** $2 \times 5 = 10$

Extra Practice on page 224, Set C

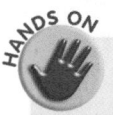

LESSON 4

Multiply with 4

OBJECTIVE: Multiply with the factor 4.

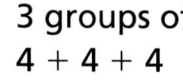

Quick Review

1. 2×3
2. 2×5
3. 8×2
4. 2×6
5. 10×2

Learn

PROBLEM Matchbox® cars were invented by Jack Odell in 1952. Caleb has 3 Matchbox cars. Each car has 4 wheels. What is the total number of wheels on Caleb's cars?

Find $3 \times 4 = \blacksquare$.

HANDS ON Activity   **Materials** ■ counters, number line

ONE WAY Use counters.

MODEL	THINK	RECORD
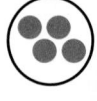	3 groups of 4 $4 + 4 + 4$	$3 \times 4 = 12$ $\begin{array}{r} 4 \\ \times 3 \\ \hline 12 \end{array}$

So, Caleb's cars have a total of 12 wheels.

OTHER WAYS Use a number line.

MODEL	THINK	RECORD
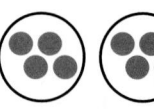 0 1 2 3 4 5 6 7 8 9 10 11 12	Skip-count by 4. 4, 8, 12	$3 \times 4 = 12$ $\begin{array}{r} 4 \\ \times 3 \\ \hline 12 \end{array}$

Use doubles.

Multiplying with 4 is the same as multiplying by 2 and doubling the product.

	Multiply by 2.	Double the product.
$3 \times 4 = \blacksquare$ Think: $2 + 2$	$3 \times 2 = 6$ ●● ●● ●●	$6 + 6 = 12$, so $3 \times 4 = 12$
$5 \times 4 = \blacksquare$ Think: $2 + 2$	$5 \times 2 = 10$ ●● ●● ●● ●● ●●	$10 + 10 = 20$, so $5 \times 4 = 20$

• How can you double a 2's fact to find 6×4?

212

1. How can you use this number line to find 4×4?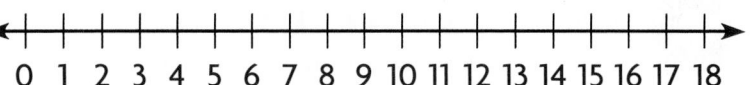

0 1 2 3 4 5 6 7 8 9 10 11 12 13 14 15 16 17 18

Find the product.

2. $6 \times 4 = \blacksquare$ 3. $3 \times 4 = \blacksquare$ ✅ 4. $5 \times 4 = \blacksquare$ ✅ 5. $8 \times 4 = \blacksquare$

6. **TALK Math** **Explain** how knowing the product of 2×8 helps you find the product of 4×8.

Independent Practice and Problem Solving

Find the product.

7. $4 \times 4 = \blacksquare$ 8. $7 \times 4 = \blacksquare$ 9. $6 \times 4 = \blacksquare$ 10. $4 \times 5 = \blacksquare$

Copy and complete.

	×	1	2	3	4	5	6	7	8	9	10
11.	2	■	■	■	■	■	■	■	■	■	■
12.	4	■	■	■	■	■	■	■	■	■	■

USE DATA For 13–14, use the graph.

13. Tina, Charlie, and Amber have Matchbox cars. How many wheels do their cars have altogether?

14. **WRITE Math** **What's the Error?** Charlie says that since $5 \times 2 = 10$, his cars have a total of 10 wheels. What is Charlie's error?

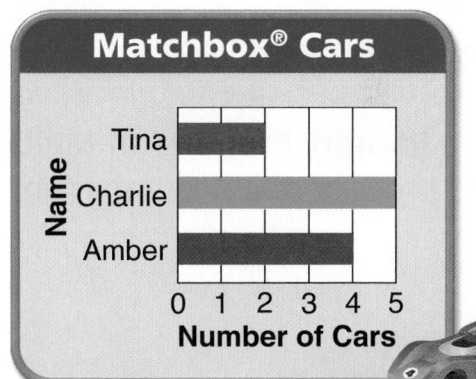

Matchbox® Cars

Mixed Review and Test Prep

15. In a pictograph, how would you show 9 votes using the key each ☺ = 3 votes? (p. 148)

16. What shape has 4 equal sides and 4 square corners? (Grade 2)

17. **Test Prep** There are 4 rows of 5 cars on the toy shelf. How many cars are there in all?

   A $4 + 5 = 9$ **C** $4 \times 5 = 20$

   B $4 \times 4 = 16$ **D** $5 \times 5 = 25$

ALGEBRA
Multiply with 1 and 0
OBJECTIVE: Multiply with the factors 1 and 0.

Quick Review
1. 6 + 1   2. 5 + 0
3. 1 + 4   4. 7 + 0
5. 9 + 1

Vocabulary
Identity Property of Multiplication

Zero Property of Multiplication

Learn

PROBLEM Luke saw 4 doghouses. Each doghouse had 1 dog in it. How many dogs were there in all?

ONE WAY Draw a picture.

Step 1

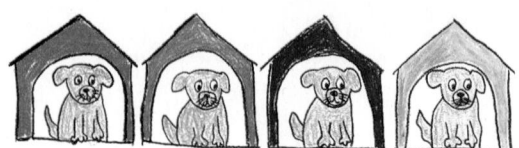

Step 2

Write the multiplication sentence.

$$4 \times 1 = 4$$

↑	↑	↑
number of groups	number in each group	number in all

So, there were 4 dogs in all.

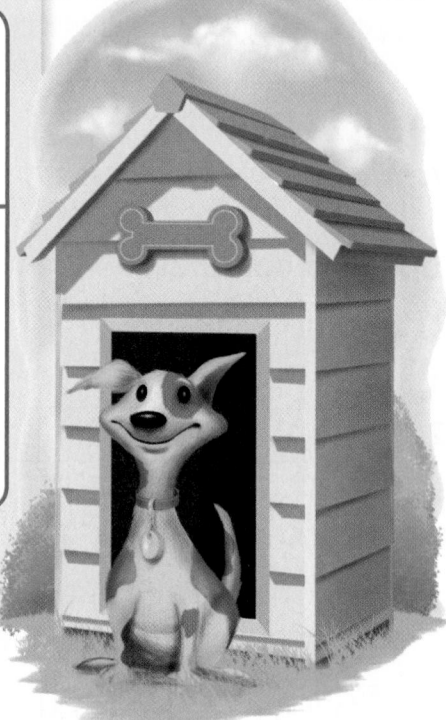

The **Identity Property of Multiplication** states that the product of any number and 1 is that number.

$$7 \times 1 = 7 \qquad 6 \times 1 = 6$$
$$1 \times 7 = 7 \qquad 1 \times 6 = 6$$

OTHER WAYS

Ⓐ Use counters.

4 groups
1 in each group
4 in all
$4 \times 1 = 4$

Ⓑ Use a number line.

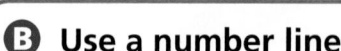

0   1   2   3   4

4 jumps of 1
4 in all
$4 \times 1 = 4$

ERROR ALERT

Be sure to look carefully at the operation signs.
$4 + 1 = 5$
$4 \times 1 = 4$
$1 + 5 = 6$
$1 \times 5 = 5$

Multiply with Zero

Lilly saw 4 doghouses. There were 0 dogs in each doghouse.
How many dogs were there in all?

ONE WAY Draw a picture.

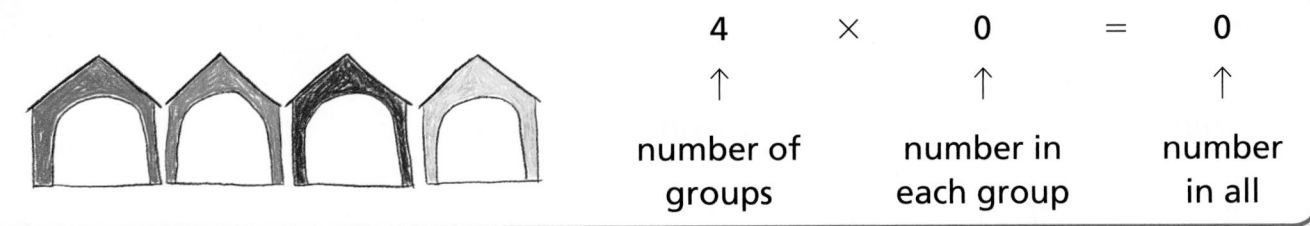

$$4 \quad \times \quad 0 \quad = \quad 0$$

number of groups · · · number in each group · · · number in all

So, there were 0 dogs in all.

The **Zero Property of Multiplication** states that
the product of zero and any number is zero.

$$0 \times 10 = 0 \qquad 5 \times 0 = 0$$

ANOTHER WAY Use a multiplication table.

Look at the row and column for 0.

- What do you notice about the products that have 0 as a factor?

Look at the row and column for 1.

- What do you notice about the products that have 1 as a factor?

×	0	1	2	3	4	5	6	7	8	9	10
0	0	0	0	0	0	0	0	0	0	0	0
1	0	1	2	3	4	5	6	7	8	9	10
2	0	2									
3	0	3									
4	0	4									
5	0	5									
6	0	6									
7	0	7									
8	0	8									
9	0	9									
10	0	10									

Guided Practice

1. What multiplication sentence is shown in this picture? Find the product.

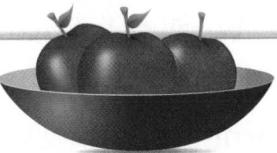

2. $3 \times 1 = \blacksquare$ 3. $0 \times 2 = \blacksquare$ ☑4. $4 \times 0 = \blacksquare$ ☑5. $1 \times 6 = \blacksquare$

6. **TALK Math** Explain how 3×1 and $3 + 1$ are different.
Draw a picture to show your answer.

Find the product.

7. $5 \times 1 = $ ■   **8.** $8 \times 0 = $ ■   **9.** $1 \times 9 = $ ■   **10.** $0 \times 7 = $ ■   **11.** $1 \times 1 = $ ■

12. $\begin{array}{r} 1 \\ \times 0 \\ \hline \end{array}$ **13.** $\begin{array}{r} 1 \\ \times 7 \\ \hline \end{array}$ **14.** $\begin{array}{r} 0 \\ \times 6 \\ \hline \end{array}$ **15.** $\begin{array}{r} 2 \\ \times 1 \\ \hline \end{array}$ **16.** $\begin{array}{r} 8 \\ \times 1 \\ \hline \end{array}$ **17.** $\begin{array}{r} 0 \\ \times 5 \\ \hline \end{array}$

Write a multiplication sentence shown on each number line.

18.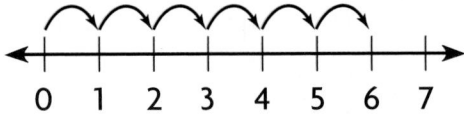

19.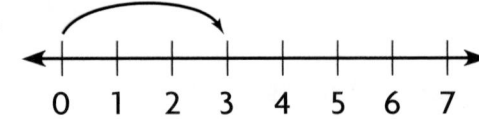

Find the missing number.

20. $3 \times$ ■ $= 0$ **21.** $5 \times 1 = $ ■ $\times 5$ **22.** ■ $\times 28 = 28$ **23.** $0 \times 46 = $ ■

USE DATA For 24–26, use the table.

24. At the circus Jon saw 5 unicycles. How many wheels are on the unicycles in all? Draw a picture and write a multiplication sentence.

25. Brian's family has 3 bicycles and 1 tricycle. How many wheels are there in all?

26. **WRITE Math** ▸ **What's the Question?** Josh used multiplication by 1 and the information in the table. The answer is 6.

Vehicle	Number of Wheels
Car	4
Tricycle	3
Bicycle	2
Unicycle	1

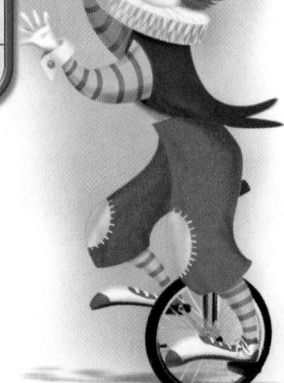

Mixed Review and Test Prep

27. There are 5 marbles in a bag. There are 4 orange marbles and 1 green marble. What color marble are you likely to choose? (p. 178)

28. Amy earned $9.75 raking leaves for a neighbor. Michelle earned $9.25 selling lemonade. How much more did Amy earn? (p. 122)

29. **Test Prep** Eric has 6 boxes. He has 1 pencil in each box. Which number sentence shows how many pencils Eric has?

A $6 + 1 = 7$ **C** $0 \times 6 = 0$

B $6 - 1 = 5$ **D** $6 \times 1 = 6$

Extra Practice on page 225, Set E

Pose a Problem

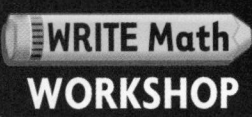

Writing a problem helps you become a better problem solver. Sarah is learning how to multiply with 1 and 0. Her teacher asked her to write a problem about multiplying with 1 and another problem about multiplying with 0. Sarah wrote the problems below.

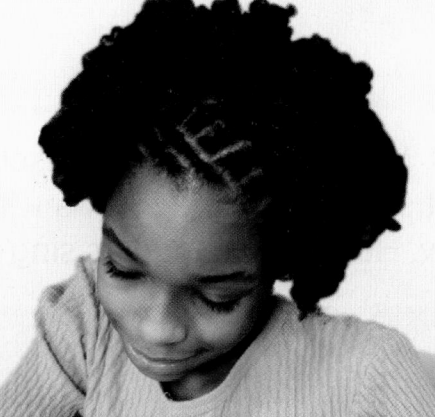

Marcos bought 1 box of crayons. There are 8 crayons in the box. How many crayons does Marcos have?

Each box of crayons has 8 crayons in it. James did not get a box. How many crayons does James have?

Tips

To pose a problem, think about these things:

- the information you will give
- the question you will ask
- the math idea your problem will be about
- the numbers you will use in your problem
- how to solve the problem

Problem Solving Write problems to show that you understand how to multiply with 1 and 0.

1. Multiply with 1.

2. Multiply with 0.

6 Multiply with 5 and 10

OBJECTIVE: Multiply with the factors 5 and 10.

Learn

PROBLEM Mandi is singing in the school chorus. For the first song, there are 3 rows with 5 students in each row. How many students sing the first song?

Multiply. $3 \times 5 = \blacksquare$

ONE WAY Make an array.

Use tiles to make an array with 3 rows of 5.

Count the tiles. $3 \times 5 = 15$

So, 15 students sing the first song.

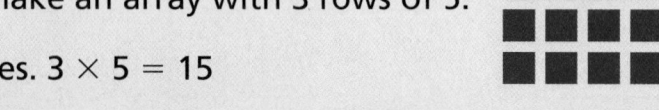

ANOTHER WAY Use a number line.

Start at 0. Make 3 jumps of 5 spaces each.

$$3 \times 5 = 15 \qquad \begin{array}{r} 5 \\ \times 3 \\ \hline 15 \end{array}$$

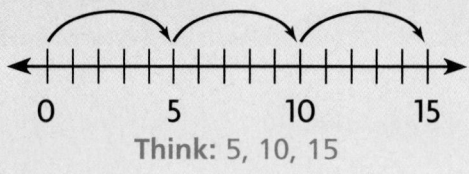

Think: 5, 10, 15

For the last song, there are 3 rows with 10 students in each row. How many students sing the last song?

Multiply. $3 \times 10 = \blacksquare$

ONE WAY Use zeros.

To find a 10's product, write a zero after the 1's product.

$1 \times 1 = 1$	$1 \times 10 = 10$
$2 \times 1 = 2$	$2 \times 10 = 20$
$3 \times 1 = 3$	$3 \times 10 = 30$

So, 30 students sing the last song.

ANOTHER WAY Use doubles.

Find the 5's product. $\qquad 3 \times 5 = 15$

Double that product. $\qquad 15 + 15 = 30$

So, $3 \times 10 = 30$.

> **Math Idea**
> The product of 10 and any factor always looks like the other factor followed by a zero.

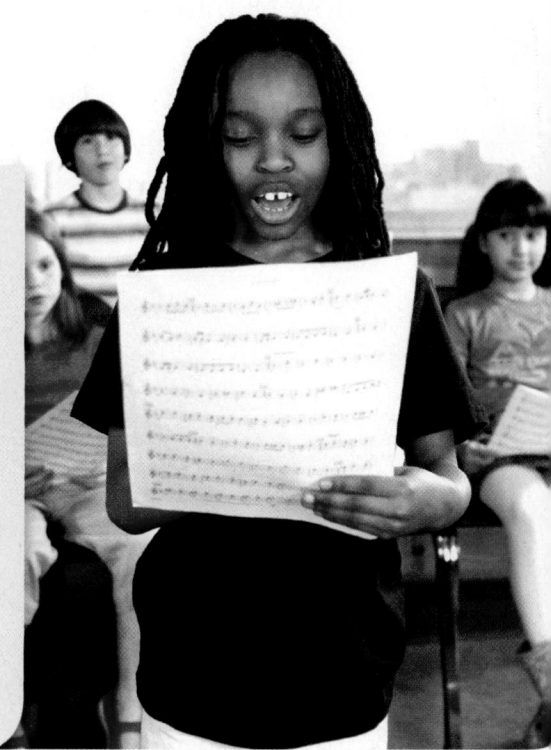

Guided Practice

1. How can you use this number line to find 4×10?

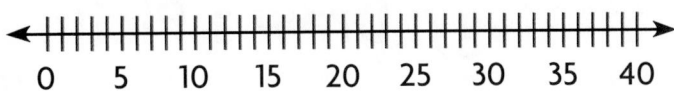

0   5   10   15   20   25   30   35   40

Find the product.

2. $2 \times 5 = $ ■

3. ■ $= 6 \times 10$

✓ 4. ■ $= 5 \times 5$

✓ 5. $10 \times 7 = $ ■

6. **TALK Math** Explain how 4×5 can help you find 4×10.

Independent Practice and Problem Solving

Find the product.

7. $10 \times 2 = $ ■

8. ■ $= 5 \times 3$

9. ■ $= 10 \times 10$

10. $6 \times 5 = $ ■

11. $10 \times 5 = $ ■

12. $9 \times 5 = $ ■

13. ■ $= 2 \times 10$

14. ■ $= 5 \times 9$

15. $\begin{array}{r} 10 \\ \times\ 0 \\ \hline \end{array}$

16. $\begin{array}{r} 7 \\ \times 5 \\ \hline \end{array}$

17. $\begin{array}{r} 5 \\ \times 8 \\ \hline \end{array}$

18. $\begin{array}{r} 10 \\ \times\ 9 \\ \hline \end{array}$

19. $\begin{array}{r} 5 \\ \times 6 \\ \hline \end{array}$

20. $\begin{array}{r} 10 \\ \times\ 8 \\ \hline \end{array}$

USE DATA For 21–22, use the table.

21. Draw a picture to show how many strings are on 4 banjos. Then write a multiplication sentence.

22. Mr. Case has 2 guitars, 4 banjos, and 1 mandolin. What is the total number of strings on Mr. Case's instruments?

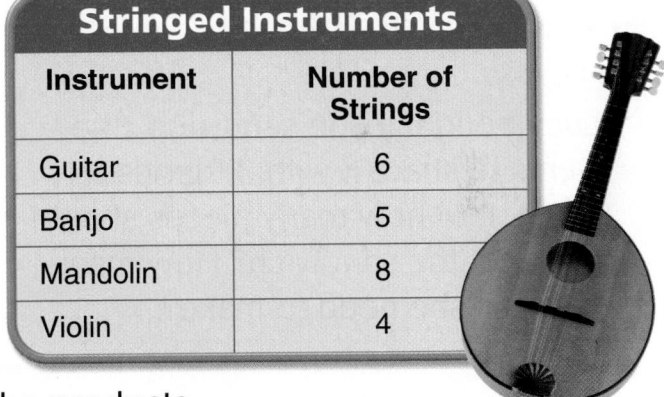

Stringed Instruments	
Instrument	**Number of Strings**
Guitar	6
Banjo	5
Mandolin	8
Violin	4

Mandolin

23. **WRITE Math** When you multiply by 5, are the products odd or even? **Explain** how you know.

Mixed Review and Test Prep

24. A music store sold 586 guitar books and 297 piano books. How many more guitar books were sold? (p. 84)

25. Which symbol makes this number sentence true?

$7 \bullet 4 = 28$ (p. 212)

26. **Test Prep** A music store has guitars displayed on 5 shelves. There are 5 guitars on each shelf. How many guitars are there in all?

A 10

C 20

B 15

D 25

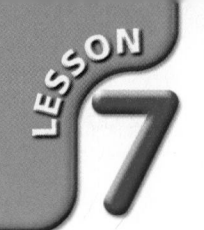

Problem Solving Workshop
Strategy: Draw a Picture

OBJECTIVE: Solve problems by using the strategy *draw a picture*.

Learn the Strategy

Drawing a picture can help you understand a problem and see how to solve it. You can draw pictures to solve different types of problems.

A picture can show how many in all.

There are 4 flower pots on the Langs' front porch. Mrs. Lang wants to plant 3 flowers in each pot. How many flowers will she plant in all?

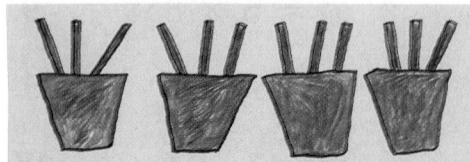

A picture can show how to divide a whole.

Lucy bought a sub sandwich. She wants to share it with 3 friends for lunch. Into how many pieces should Lucy cut the sandwich? How many cuts will she need to make?

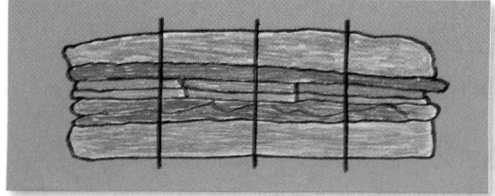

A picture can show order.

Morgan built a snowman. She put 5 buttons on it. The blue button was below the red button. The green button was above the red one. The black button was between the red and blue buttons. The yellow button was just above the green button. Which button was at the top?

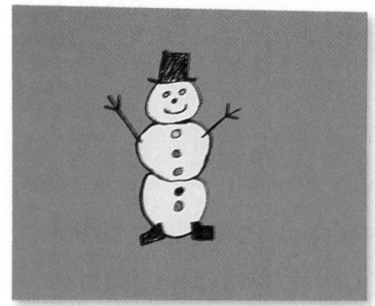

TALK Math

Choose one of the problems. Tell how the picture helps you solve it.

To draw a picture, carefully read the information in the problem. Keep your drawing simple.

Use the Strategy

PROBLEM There are 2 rows of drummers in the drum section of a marching band. There are 7 drummers in each row. How many drummers are there in all?

Read to Understand

Reading Skill

- **Summarize what you are asked to find.**
- **What information will you use?**

Plan

- **What strategy can you use to solve the problem?**
  You can draw a picture to help you solve the problem.

Solve

- **How can you use the strategy to solve the problem?**
  Draw a picture with stick people to show the drummers.

  Draw 2 rows.
  Show 7 stick people in each row.

  Add or multiply to find the total number of drummers in all.

  $$7 + 7 = 14$$
  $$2 \times 7 = 14$$

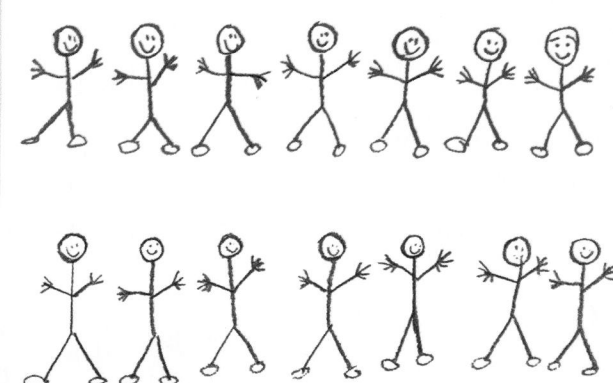

So, there are 14 drummers in all in the drum section.

Check

- **How can you check your answer?**
- **What other ways could you solve the problem?**

Guided Problem Solving

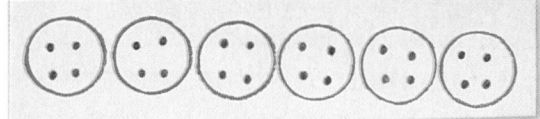

1. The marching band has 6 groups of 4 people who play the trumpet. How many people play the trumpet?

   First, draw a picture of the problem.
   Show 6 circles with 4 dots in each circle.

   Next, find the total number of dots.

   $6 \times 4 = \blacksquare$

2. **What if** there are 5 groups instead of 6 in Problem 1? How many people would play the trumpet?

3. There are 3 rows of flute players in the marching band. There are 7 people in each row. How many flute players are in the marching band?

Problem Solving Strategy Practice

For 4–6, draw a picture to solve.

4. Each drummer needs 2 drumsticks. How many drumsticks do 6 drummers need?

5. During band practice, 7 students each twirled 1 flag. How many total flags did the students twirl?

6. Twelve students in Mrs. Taylor's class want to start a band. Seven of the students made drums. The rest made 2 maracas each. How many maracas in all were made?

USE DATA For 7–8, use the table.

7. How many rubber bands will seven students need to make their drums?

8. **WRITE Math** ▶ Three students want to use maracas in the class band. How many water bottles do they need in all to make their maracas? Explain how you can draw a picture to find the answer.

9. **Reasoning** The class band has 12 students. Show two different ways the band members can stand in equal rows to march.

Materials Needed for Making Instruments	
Drum	**Maracas**
1 coffee can	2 plastic water bottles
1 large rubber band	1 roll of tape
1 trash bag	Dried beans

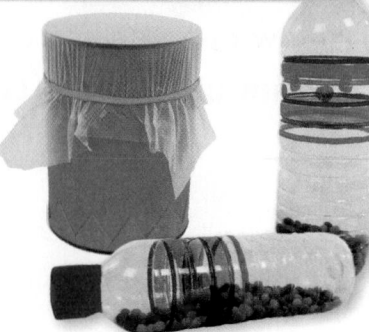

Mixed Strategy Practice

USE DATA For 10–12, use the Favorite Instrument Survey.

10. The table shows how students in Jillian's class voted. How many students voted for the guitar? Draw a picture to show your answer.

11. On the day of Jillian's survey, two students in the class were absent. The table shows the votes of all other students in the class, including Jillian. How many students in all are in Jillian's class?

12. Reasoning Jillian added the number of votes for two instruments and got a total of 12 students. Which two instruments did she add?

13. ≡FAST FACT The electric guitar was invented in 1931. How many years ago was that?

14. Open-Ended Tony and Mike surveyed 50 students about their favorite instrument: flute, trumpet, drum, or guitar. Choose a key and show a possible survey result in a table like the one at the right.

Choose a STRATEGY

Draw a Diagram or Picture
Make a Model or Act It Out
Make an Organized List
Find a Pattern
Make a Table or Graph
Predict and Test
Work Backward
Solve a Simpler Problem
Write an Equation
Use Logical Reasoning

Favorite Instrument Survey

Instrument	Number of Children
Flute	☺ ☺
Trumpet	☺ ☺ ☺
Drums	☺ ☺ ☺ ☺
Guitar	☺ ☺ ☺ ☺ ☺

Key: Each ☺ = 2 children.

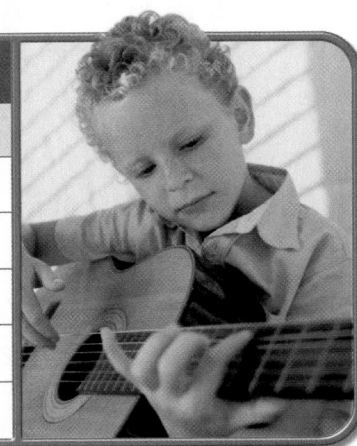

CHALLENGE YOURSELF

Ari, Beth, Corey, and Dan each play a different instrument. One plays the flute, one plays the trumpet, one plays the drum, and one plays the guitar. Read the clues to find out who plays which instrument.

15. Who plays the guitar? Who plays the trumpet?

16. Explain how you know which instrument Ari plays.

	Clues
a.	Ari's instrument does not have strings.
b.	Beth uses her mouth to play her instrument.
c.	Corey does not use sticks with his instrument.
d.	Dan's instrument is shaped like a cylinder.
e.	Ari's instrument is wider at one end than at the other.

Extra Practice

Set A Use counters to model. Then write an
addition sentence and a multiplication sentence for each. (pp. 204–205)

1. 3 groups of 4   **2.** 2 groups of 2   **3.** 2 groups of 3   **4.** 5 groups of 2

5. 6 groups of 1   **6.** 4 groups of 5   **7.** 3 groups of 6   **8.** 7 groups of 3

Write a multiplication sentence for each.

9. $3 + 3 + 3 = 9$ **10.** $2 + 2 + 2 + 2 = 8$ **11.** $4 + 4 = 8$

12. $7 + 7 + 7 + 7 = 28$ **13.** $1 + 1 + 1 = 3$ **14.** $6 + 6 + 6 + 6 = 24$

15. $5 + 5 + 5 = 15$ **16.** $3 + 3 = 6$ **17.** $8 + 8 + 8 = 24$

Set B Write a multiplication sentence for each array. (pp. 206–209)

1. 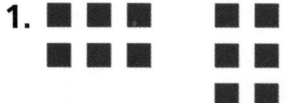   **2.** 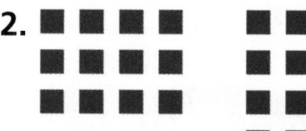   **3.**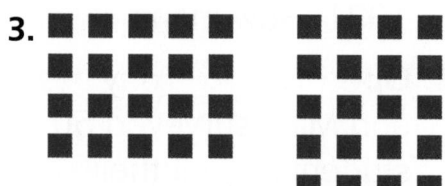

4. Jamal put 20 model cars in 5 rows. How many cars were in each row?
5 rows of ■ cars = 20 cars

5. Mary picked 6 tomatoes from each of the 3 rows in her garden. She used 4 tomatoes to make salsa. How many tomatoes does she have left?

Set C Find the product. (pp. 210–211)

Write a multiplication sentence for each.

1. 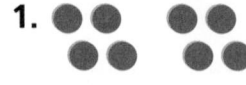   **2.** 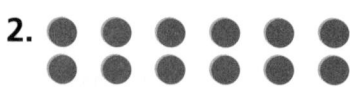   **3.**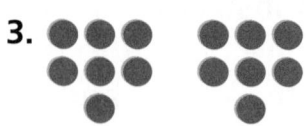

4. $2 \times 4 = $ ■   **5.** $9 \times 2 = $ ■   **6.** $2 \times 2 = $ ■   **7.** $2 \times 1 = $ ■

8. $2 \times 3 = $ ■   **9.** $5 \times 2 = $ ■   **10.** $2 \times 7 = $ ■   **11.** $8 \times 2 = $ ■

12. $\begin{array}{r} 2 \\ \times 7 \\ \hline \end{array}$ **13.** $\begin{array}{r} 5 \\ \times 2 \\ \hline \end{array}$ **14.** $\begin{array}{r} 2 \\ \times 2 \\ \hline \end{array}$ **15.** $\begin{array}{r} 6 \\ \times 2 \\ \hline \end{array}$ **16.** $\begin{array}{r} 2 \\ \times 8 \\ \hline \end{array}$ **17.** $\begin{array}{r} 3 \\ \times 2 \\ \hline \end{array}$

CD ROM Technology — Use Harcourt Mega Math, Country Countdown, *Counting Critters*, Levels V, Z.

Set D Find the product. (pp. 212–213)

1. $2 \times 4 = \blacksquare$ **2.** $9 \times 4 = \blacksquare$ **3.** $4 \times 4 = \blacksquare$ **4.** $4 \times 1 = \blacksquare$

5. $4 \times 3 = \blacksquare$ **6.** $5 \times 4 = \blacksquare$ **7.** $4 \times 7 = \blacksquare$ **8.** $8 \times 4 = \blacksquare$

9. $\begin{array}{r} 9 \\ \times 4 \\ \hline \end{array}$
10. $\begin{array}{r} 2 \\ \times 4 \\ \hline \end{array}$
11. $\begin{array}{r} 7 \\ \times 4 \\ \hline \end{array}$
12. $\begin{array}{r} 8 \\ \times 4 \\ \hline \end{array}$
13. $\begin{array}{r} 1 \\ \times 4 \\ \hline \end{array}$
14. $\begin{array}{r} 6 \\ \times 4 \\ \hline \end{array}$

Copy and complete.

×	1	2	3	4	5	6	7	8	9	10
15. 2	▪	▪	▪	▪	▪	▪	▪	▪	▪	▪
16. 4	▪	▪	▪	▪	▪	▪	▪	▪	▪	▪

Set E Find the product. (pp. 214–217)

1. $6 \times 0 = \blacksquare$ **2.** $4 \times 1 = \blacksquare$ **3.** $3 \times 0 = \blacksquare$ **4.** $0 \times 1 = \blacksquare$

5. $1 \times 5 = \blacksquare$ **6.** $0 \times 9 = \blacksquare$ **7.** $1 \times 1 = \blacksquare$ **8.** $4 \times 0 = \blacksquare$

9. $\begin{array}{r} 2 \\ \times 0 \\ \hline \end{array}$
10. $\begin{array}{r} 7 \\ \times 1 \\ \hline \end{array}$
11. $\begin{array}{r} 8 \\ \times 0 \\ \hline \end{array}$
12. $\begin{array}{r} 6 \\ \times 1 \\ \hline \end{array}$
13. $\begin{array}{r} 0 \\ \times 3 \\ \hline \end{array}$
14. $\begin{array}{r} 9 \\ \times 1 \\ \hline \end{array}$

Find the missing number.

15. $5 \times \blacksquare = 0$ **16.** $3 \times 1 = \blacksquare \times 3$ **17.** $\blacksquare \times 14 = 14$ **18.** $0 \times 89 = \blacksquare$

19. $\blacksquare \times 8 = 8$ **20.** $24 \times 0 = \blacksquare$ **21.** $11 \times \blacksquare = 11$ **22.** $1 \times 7 = \blacksquare \times 1$

23. Tom had 4 boxes. He put 1 car in each box. How many cars does he have in all?

24. Lucy has 2 fish bowls. There are no fish in the bowls. How many fish does she have in all?

Set F Find the product. (pp. 218–219)

1. $4 \times 5 = \blacksquare$ **2.** $\blacksquare = 3 \times 10$ **3.** $\blacksquare = 5 \times 2$ **4.** $\blacksquare = 6 \times 10$

5. $10 \times 7 = \blacksquare$ **6.** $\blacksquare = 2 \times 5$ **7.** $\blacksquare = 5 \times 10$ **8.** $5 \times 5 = \blacksquare$

9. $\begin{array}{r} 9 \\ \times 5 \\ \hline \end{array}$
10. $\begin{array}{r} 10 \\ \times 0 \\ \hline \end{array}$
11. $\begin{array}{r} 8 \\ \times 5 \\ \hline \end{array}$
12. $\begin{array}{r} 10 \\ \times 2 \\ \hline \end{array}$
13. $\begin{array}{r} 5 \\ \times 6 \\ \hline \end{array}$
14. $\begin{array}{r} 3 \\ \times 10 \\ \hline \end{array}$

15. A music store has CDs in 10 boxes. There are 8 CDs in each box. How many CDs are there in all?

16. A grocery store has boxes of cereal on 5 shelves. There are 6 boxes on each shelf. How many boxes of cereal are there in all?

Value of Shapes

Shape Solvers

Using shapes instead of numbers can help you practice addition, subtraction, and multiplication facts.

Find the value of the 💜 and ✳ by answering the questions.

$$💜 - ✳ = 3$$
$$✳ \times ✳ = 16$$

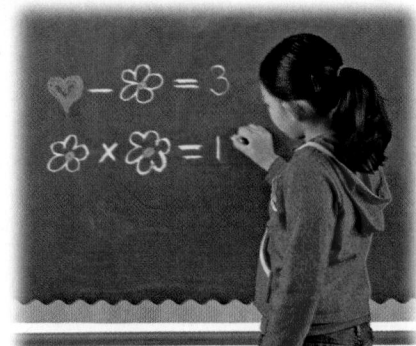

Step 1	Step 2
The ✳ is in both problems, so find the value of the ✳ first. **Think:** What number multiplied by itself equals 16? $4 \times 4 = 16$, so ✳ $= 4$.	Now you can find the value of the 💜. Using the value of the ✳, you know that 💜 $- 4 = 3$. Find the value of 💜 by adding. $4 + 3 = 7$. $7 - 4 = 3$, so 💜 $= 7$.

So, ✳ $= 4$ and 💜 $= 7$.

Try It
Find the value for each shape in the puzzles below.

1. ▲ + ⬡ $= 8$
   ⬡ × ▲ $= 12$

   ▲ $=$ ■
   ⬡ $=$ ■

2. ⬠ + ⬠ $= 6$
   ⬠ × ⬠ $= 9$

   ⬠ $=$ ■

3. 🍁 − 🌳 $= 5$
   🍁 × 🌳 $= 24$

   🍁 $=$ ■
   🌳 $=$ ■

4. **WRITE Math** ▸ How can knowing ★ $= 3$ help you to solve the puzzle below? **Explain.**

   ★ + ▽ $= 12$
   ★ × ★ $=$ ▽

Chapter 8 Review/Test

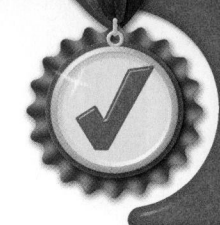

Check Vocabulary and Concepts

Choose the best term from the box.

1. When you __?__, you combine equal groups to find how many in all. (p. 204)

2. The __?__ states that the product of any number and 1 is that number. (p. 214)

> **VOCABULARY**
> array
> Identity Property
>   of Multiplication
> multiply
> Zero Property
>   of Multiplication

Check Skills

Use counters to model. Then write an addition sentence and a multiplication sentence for each. (pp. 204–205)

3. 7 groups of 3   **4.** 3 groups of 6   **5.** 4 groups of 5   **6.** 2 groups of 8

Write a multiplication sentence for each array. (pp. 206–209)

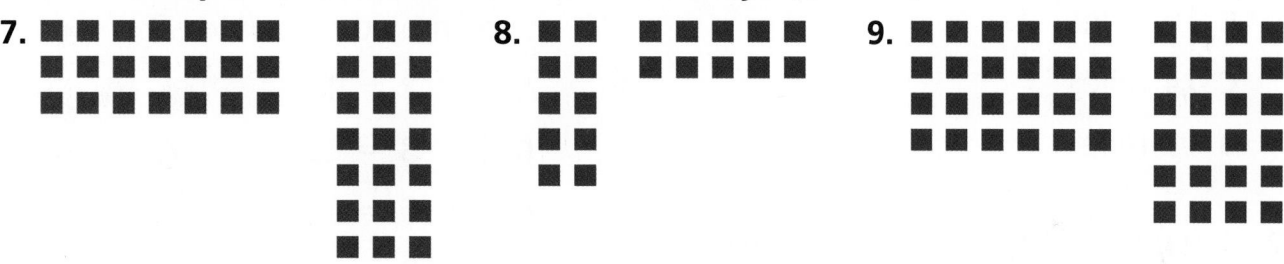

Find the product. (pp. 210–211, 212–213, 214–217, 218–219)

10. $5 \times 2 = \blacksquare$ **11.** $4 \times 1 = \blacksquare$ **12.** $0 \times 7 = \blacksquare$ **13.** $4 \times 4 = \blacksquare$

14. $2 \times 8 = \blacksquare$ **15.** $9 \times 0 = \blacksquare$ **16.** $1 \times 1 = \blacksquare$ **17.** $9 \times 5 = \blacksquare$

18. $\begin{array}{r} 2 \\ \times 2 \\ \hline \end{array}$ **19.** $\begin{array}{r} 10 \\ \times 6 \\ \hline \end{array}$ **20.** $\begin{array}{r} 7 \\ \times 1 \\ \hline \end{array}$ **21.** $\begin{array}{r} 6 \\ \times 2 \\ \hline \end{array}$ **22.** $\begin{array}{r} 10 \\ \times 4 \\ \hline \end{array}$ **23.** $\begin{array}{r} 8 \\ \times 4 \\ \hline \end{array}$

Check Problem Solving

Solve. (pp. 220–223)

24. Ten students are in the school play. Three students will play instuments and one student will sing a song. The rest of the students will make 2 props each. How many props will the students make in all?

25. **WRITE Math** Three students sold tickets for the play. They sold 10 tickets each. How many tickets did they sell in all? **Explain** how you know.

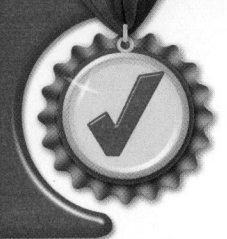

Standardized Test Prep
Chapters 1–8

Number and Operations

1. How many miles did Larry and Mike walk altogether? (p. 148)

School Walk-a-Thon

Sue	👟 👟 👟 👟 👟
Mike	👟 👟 👟
Jenny	👟
Larry	👟 👟 👟 👟

Key: Each 👟 = 2 miles.

A 18 miles

B 16 miles

C 14 miles

D 12 miles

2. Johanna's family drove 618 miles during their vacation. What is 618 rounded to the nearest ten? (p. 36)

A 600

B 610

C 620

D 630

3. **WRITE Math** ▸ **Explain** how knowing the product 9×2 can help you to find the product 9×4. (p. 212)

Algebraic Reasoning

4. Which array shows the product 6×3? (p. 206)

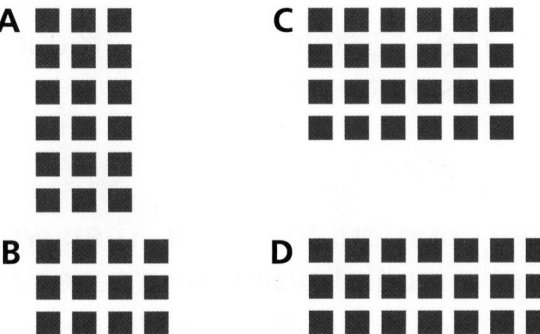

5. Which multiplication sentence is shown by the counters? (p. 204)

A $6 \times 3 = 18$

B $4 \times 3 = 12$

C $2 \times 6 = 12$

D $4 \times 2 = 8$

6. **WRITE Math** ▸ Write the addition sentence $5 + 5 + 5 + 5 = 20$ as a multiplication sentence. **Explain** how you know. (p. 204)

Measurement

Test Tip **Eliminate choices.**

See item 7. First find the time that names the correct hour shown on the clock. Then find the time that names the correct minutes.

7. Walter's swim practice ends at the time shown on the clock. What time does Walter's swim practice end?

(p. 124)

A 5:15

B 4:45

C 4:15

D 3:45

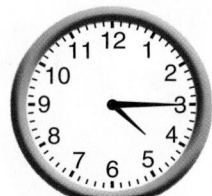

8. Jim is playing outside in the snow. Which temperature does the thermometer show? (Grade 2)

A 5° F

B 15° F

C 25° F

D 35° F

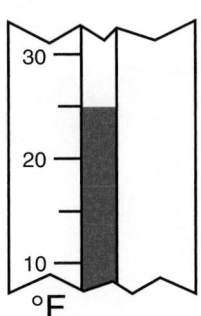

9. **WRITE Math** Would you use inches, feet, or yards to measure the length of the school playground? **Explain.**

(Grade 2)

Data Analysis and Probability

10. Randy recorded the results of a probability experiment. How many marbles did Randy pull in all? (p. 146)

A 12

B 13

C 14

D 15

Marbles Pulled	
Color	Number of Times Pulled
orange	|||
red	||
green	##t |||
blue	||

11. How many more red shirts than blue shirts does Matt have? (p. 154)

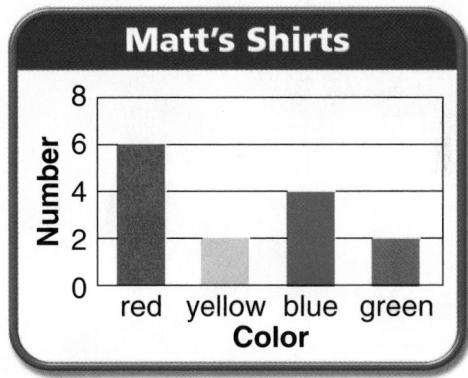

A 4

C 2

B 3

D 1

12. **WRITE Math** List the possible outcomes of spinning the pointer 1 time. **Explain** how you know. (p. 180)

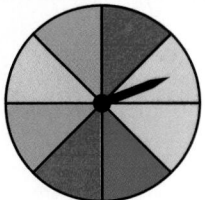

CHAPTER 9 Facts and Strategies

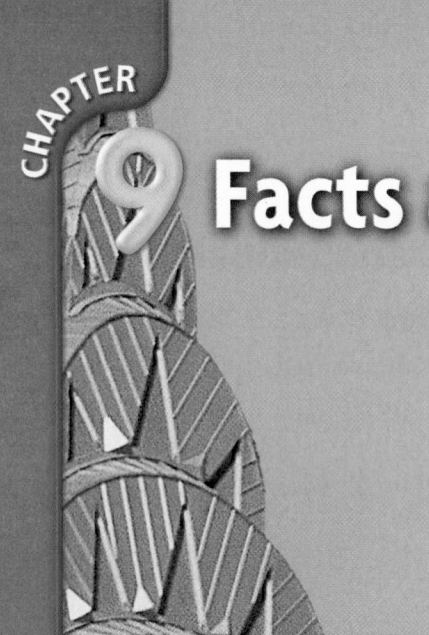

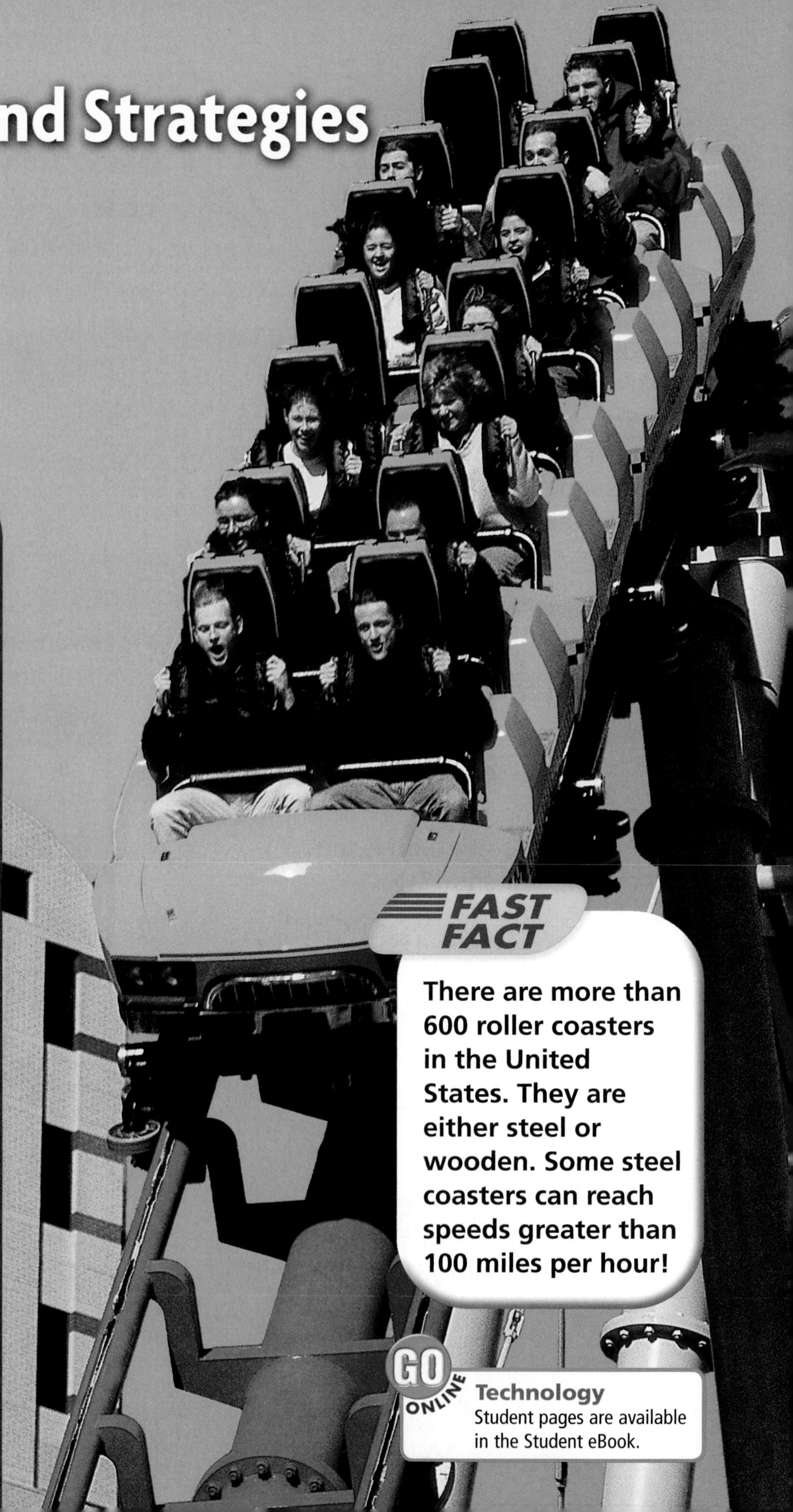

Investigate

Each train in the Manhattan Express roller coaster has 4 cars that hold 4 riders each for a total of 16 riders. Choose a roller coaster. How many cars and riders per car could the roller coaster have? Make a list of the possible combinations.

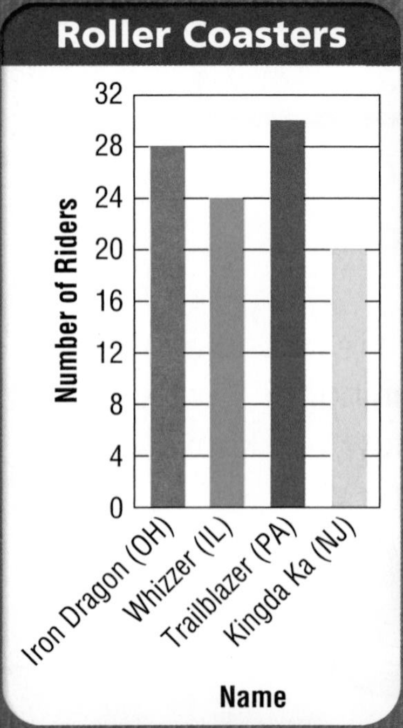

Roller Coasters
Number of Riders
0
4
8
12
16
20
24
28
32
Iron Dragon (OH)
Whizzer (IL)
Trailblazer (PA)
Kingda Ka (NJ)
Name

FAST FACT

There are more than 600 roller coasters in the United States. They are either steel or wooden. Some steel coasters can reach speeds greater than 100 miles per hour!

GO ONLINE **Technology** Student pages are available in the Student eBook.

Check your understanding of important skills needed for success in Chapter 9.

▶ **Equal Groups**

Write how many there are in all.

1.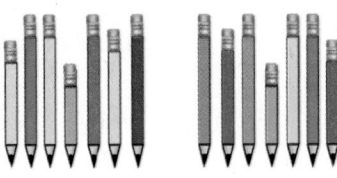

    2 groups of 7 = ■

2.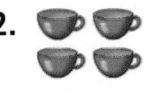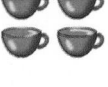

    3 groups of 4 = ■

3.

    6 groups of 2 = ■

▶ **Arrays**

Find the product.

4.

$3 \times 5 = ■$

5.

$2 \times 7 = ■$

6.

$3 \times 3 = ■$

7.

$4 \times 6 = ■$

▶ **Multiply with 2 and 4**

Multiply.

8. $4 \times 4 = ■$ 9. $3 \times 2 = ■$ 10. $5 \times 4 = ■$ 11. $2 \times 9 = ■$

VOCABULARY POWER

CHAPTER VOCABULARY

array
factor
multiple
multiplication
multiply
product

WARM-UP WORDS

multiple A number that is the product of a given number and a counting number

multiply When you combine equal groups, you can multiply to find how many in all.

product The answer in a multiplication problem

Multiply with 3

OBJECTIVE: Multiply with the factor 3.

Learn

PROBLEM Paula is making a design with 4 triangles. How many sides do 4 triangles have?

$$4 \times 3 = \blacksquare$$

A triangle has 3 sides. To find the number of sides in 4 triangles, find 4×3.

equilateral triangle

3 inches ⟋⟍ 3 inches

3 inches

ONE WAY Draw a picture.

Step 1 Draw 4 triangles.

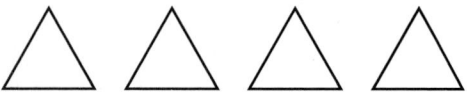

Step 2 Count the sides.

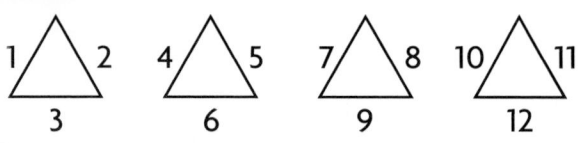

$$4 \times 3 = 12$$

So, 4 triangles have 12 sides.

OTHER WAYS

A Use counters.
Make 4 groups of 3.

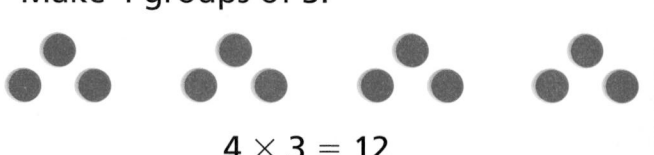

$$4 \times 3 = 12$$

B Look for a pattern.

Triangles	Sides	Total
1	3	3
2	3	6
3	3	9
4	3	12

$$4 \times 3 = 12$$

Guided Practice

1. Use the picture and tell how to find the number of sides in 6 triangles.

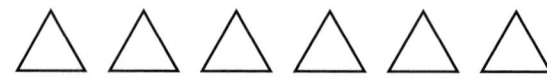

Find the product.

2. $3 \times 5 = \blacksquare$ **3.** $\blacksquare = 3 \times 6$ **✓4.** $\blacksquare = 7 \times 3$ **✓5.** $9 \times 3 = \blacksquare$

6. TALK Math Explain how you can use counters to find 5×3.

Independent Practice and Problem Solving

Find the product.

7. $6 \times 3 = \blacksquare$ **8.** $\blacksquare = 8 \times 3$ **9.** $\blacksquare = 3 \times 0$ **10.** $3 \times 3 = \blacksquare$

11. $2 \times 3 = \blacksquare$ **12.** $\blacksquare = 9 \times 3$ **13.** $\blacksquare = 3 \times 1$ **14.** $3 \times 7 = \blacksquare$

15. $\begin{array}{r} 3 \\ \times 6 \\ \hline \end{array}$ **16.** $\begin{array}{r} 8 \\ \times 3 \\ \hline \end{array}$ **17.** $\begin{array}{r} 5 \\ \times 3 \\ \hline \end{array}$ **18.** $\begin{array}{r} 3 \\ \times 2 \\ \hline \end{array}$ **19.** $\begin{array}{r} 7 \\ \times 3 \\ \hline \end{array}$ **20.** $\begin{array}{r} 3 \\ \times 9 \\ \hline \end{array}$

⭐**Algebra** Complete.

21. $2 \times 3 = \blacksquare \times 2$ **22.** $8 \times 1 = \blacksquare \times 8$ **23.** $5 \times 2 = \blacksquare \times 5$

24. $2 \times 3 = \blacksquare + 1$ **25.** $8 \times 1 = \blacksquare + 1$ **26.** $5 \times 2 = \blacksquare + 1$

27. A square has 4 sides. Which have more sides, 5 squares or 6 triangles? Show your work.

28. Reasoning Use the factors 3 and 4 to show the Commutative Property of Multiplication. Draw a picture.

USE DATA For 29–30, use the table.

29. How many squares are there in 3 pieces of the quilt pattern? Draw a picture to show your answer.

30. WRITE Math ▶ Explain how to find the total number of sides of all the shapes in the quilt pattern. Some sides will be counted more than once.

Quilt Pattern	
Shape	**Number in 1 pattern piece**
Square	6
Triangle	4
Rectangle	4

Amish pattern used ▶ in making quilts.

Mixed Review and Test Prep

31. Jon has 2 quarters, 2 dimes, and 3 nickels. Tom has 1 quarter, 5 nickels, and 27 pennies. Who has more money? How much more? (p. 114)

32. Ryan has 2 sheets of stickers. Each sheet has 8 stickers. How many stickers does Ryan have? (p. 210)

33. Test Prep There are 9 color pencils in each of 3 packages. How many color pencils are there in all?

A 6   **B** 12   **C** 24   **D** 27

Extra Practice on page 248, Set A

Multiply with 6

OBJECTIVE: Multiply with the factor 6.

Quick Review

1. 3×2
2. 9×3
3. 5×3
4. 3×4
5. 6×3

Vocabulary

multiple

Learn

PROBLEM A lightning bug has 6 legs. How many legs do 5 lightning bugs have?

$$5 \times 6 = \blacksquare$$

ONE WAY **Use an array.**

Make 5 rows with 6 tiles in each row.

Count the tiles.

$$5 \times 6 = 30 \qquad \begin{array}{r} 6 \\ \times\, 5 \\ \hline 30 \end{array}$$

So, 5 lightning bugs have 30 legs.

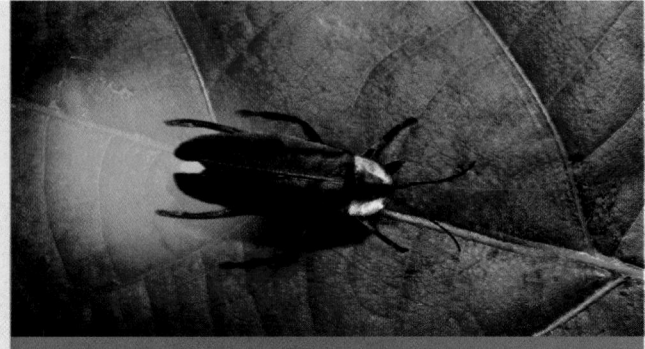

▲ Lightning bugs are also called fireflies.

OTHER WAYS

A **Use a number line.**
Make 5 jumps of 6 spaces each.
$$5 \times 6 = 30$$

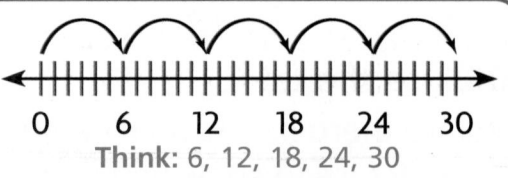

0   6   12   18   24   30

Think: 6, 12, 18, 24, 30

A **multiple** of 6 is any product that has a 6 as one of its factors.
Some multiples of 6 are 6, 12, 18, 24, and 30.

B **Use a multiplication table.**
Find the product for 5×6 where row 5 and column 6 meet. $5 \times 6 = 30$

C **Use doubles.**
First, find the 3s product. $\qquad 5 \times 3 = 15$
Then double that product. $\qquad 15 + 15 = 30$
$\qquad\qquad\qquad$ So, $5 \times 6 = 30$.

• Look at the columns for 3 and 6 in the table.
What do you notice about their products?

column ↓

×	0	1	2	3	4	5	6	7	8	9
0	0	0	0	0	0	0	0	0	0	0
1	0	1	2	3	4	5	6	7	8	9
2	0	2	4	6	8	10	12	14	16	18
3	0	3	6	9	12	15	18	21	24	27
4	0	4	8	12	16	20	24	28	32	36
5	0	5	10	15	20	25	30	35	40	45
6	0	6	12	18	24	30	36	42	48	54
7	0	7	14	21	28	35	42	49	56	63
8	0	8	16	24	32	40	48	56	64	72
9	0	9	18	27	36	45	54	63	72	81

row →

1. Use the array to find 3×6.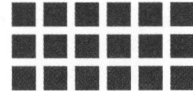

Find the product.

2. $6 \times 1 = \blacksquare$ 3. $\blacksquare = 3 \times 6$ ⓥ 4. $\blacksquare = 6 \times 4$ ⓥ 5. $6 \times 8 = \blacksquare$

6. **TALK Math** Name a product that is a multiple of 3 and 6. **Explain** how you know.

Independent Practice and Problem Solving

Find the product.

7. $6 \times 5 = \blacksquare$ 8. $\blacksquare = 8 \times 6$ 9. $\blacksquare = 6 \times 6$ 10. $0 \times 6 = \blacksquare$

11. $10 \times 6 = \blacksquare$ 12. $4 \times 5 = \blacksquare$ 13. $\blacksquare = 1 \times 6$ 14. $\blacksquare = 5 \times 5$

| 15. | 6 | 16. | 3 | 17. | 9 | 18. | 6 | 19. | 6 | 20. | 6 |
| | $\times 5$ | | $\times 5$ | | $\times 6$ | | $\times 7$ | | $\times 6$ | | $\times 3$ |

★ **Algebra** Copy and complete each table.

Multiply by 3.	
21.	6	$\blacksquare$
22.	$\blacksquare$	30

Multiply by 6.	
23.	3	$\blacksquare$
24.	7	$\blacksquare$

25.

Multiply by $\blacksquare$.	
6	30
5	25

USE DATA For 26–28, use the table.

26. How many wings do 6 honeybees have?

27. How many more wings do 6 beetles have than 6 flies?

28. **WRITE Math** Write a number sentence that shows how many wings 3 flies have. **Explain** how this fact can help you find the number of wings 6 flies have.

Winged Insects	
Insect	**Number of Wings**
Fly	2
Beetle	4
Honeybee	4

Mixed Review and Test Prep

29. Ten flies each had 2 wings. How many wings did they have in all? (p. 210)

30. Write the time shown on the clock. (p. 124)

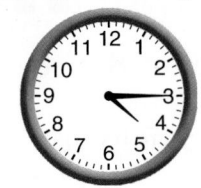

31. **Test Prep** Sean saw 8 ladybugs while he was camping. Each one had 6 legs. How many legs did the 8 ladybugs have in all?

   A 12   **B** 16   **C** 48   **D** 54

3 Multiply with 8

OBJECTIVE: Multiply with the factor 8.

Learn

PROBLEM A scorpion has 8 legs. How many legs do 4 scorpions have?

$$4 \times 8 = \blacksquare$$

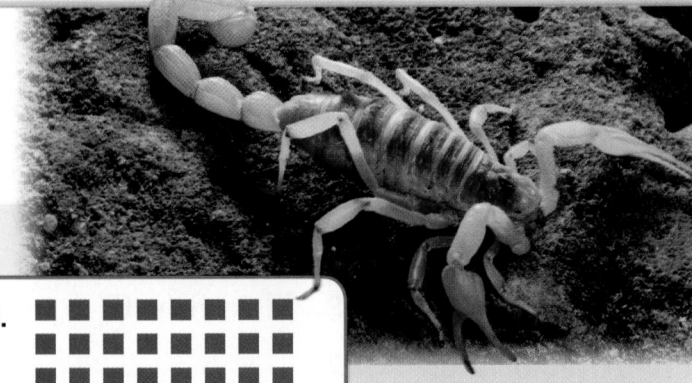

ONE WAY Make an array.

Use tiles to make an array with 4 rows of 8.

Count the tiles. $4 \times 8 = 32$

So, 4 scorpions have 32 legs.

▲ Scorpions are found in hot dry places, such as Arizona, Texas, and central Oklahoma.

OTHER WAYS

A Use the Commutative Property.

Use facts you know to find 4×8.

$8 \times 4 = 32$, so $4 \times 8 = 32$.

8 groups of 4   4 groups of 8

B Use doubles.

$4 \times 4 = 16$

$16 + 16 = 32$

So, $4 \times 8 = 32$.

Guided Practice

1. **Explain** how you would use this array to find 7×8.

Find the product.

2. $6 \times 8 = \blacksquare$ 3. $\blacksquare = 3 \times 8$ ⦿4. $\blacksquare = 8 \times 8$ ⦿5. $9 \times 8 = \blacksquare$

6. **TALK Math** **Explain** how you can use 5×4 to help you find 5×8.

Find the product.

7. $10 \times 8 = \blacksquare$ **8.** $2 \times 8 = \blacksquare$ **9.** $\blacksquare = 3 \times 8$ **10.** $\blacksquare = 8 \times 7$

11. $8 \times 4 = \blacksquare$ **12.** $\blacksquare = 6 \times 8$ **13.** $\blacksquare = 0 \times 8$ **14.** $5 \times 8 = \blacksquare$

15. $\begin{array}{r} 8 \\ \times 8 \\ \hline \end{array}$ **16.** $\begin{array}{r} 10 \\ \times 3 \\ \hline \end{array}$ **17.** $\begin{array}{r} 9 \\ \times 8 \\ \hline \end{array}$ **18.** $\begin{array}{r} 1 \\ \times 8 \\ \hline \end{array}$ **19.** $\begin{array}{r} 8 \\ \times 2 \\ \hline \end{array}$ **20.** $\begin{array}{r} 5 \\ \times 7 \\ \hline \end{array}$

21. $\begin{array}{r} 6 \\ \times 4 \\ \hline \end{array}$ **22.** $\begin{array}{r} 7 \\ \times 3 \\ \hline \end{array}$ **23.** $\begin{array}{r} 5 \\ \times 5 \\ \hline \end{array}$ **24.** $\begin{array}{r} 3 \\ \times 8 \\ \hline \end{array}$ **25.** $\begin{array}{r} 6 \\ \times 5 \\ \hline \end{array}$ **26.** $\begin{array}{r} 7 \\ \times 8 \\ \hline \end{array}$

⭐ **Algebra** Copy and complete each table.

Multiply by 4.	
27. 9	$\blacksquare$
28. 3	$\blacksquare$
29. 5	$\blacksquare$

Multiply by 8.	
30. 4	$\blacksquare$
31. $\blacksquare$	56
32. $\blacksquare$	24

33.

Multiply by $\blacksquare$.	
3	18
6	36
34. 9	$\blacksquare$

USE DATA For 35–37 use the table.

35. About how much rain falls in the Chihuahuan Desert in 4 years? **Explain** how you can use doubles to find the answer.

36. In 2 years, how many more inches of rainfall are there in the Sonoran Desert than in the Mojave Desert?

37. ✏️ **WRITE Math** ▸ **Explain** how you can find about how many inches of rain fall in the Chihuahuan Desert in 5 years.

Average Yearly Rainfall in North American Deserts

Desert	Inches
Chihuahuan	8
Great Basin	9
Mojave	4
Sonoran	9

Mixed Review and Test Prep

38. About 460 inches of rain falls on Mt. Waialeale, Hawaii, each year. What is the value of the 4 in 460? (p. 8)

39. Carrie has 3 bags of oranges. Each bag has 4 oranges. How many oranges is that? (p. 212)

40. **Test Prep** A black widow spider has 8 legs. How many legs do 7 black widow spiders have?

A 1   **C** 48

B 15   **D** 56

Extra Practice on page 248, Set C

4 ALGEBRA
Patterns with 9
OBJECTIVE: Multiply with the factor 9.

Learn

PROBLEM Melissa's class is studying the solar system. Students are making models of 9 planets that orbit, or revolve around, the sun. How many planets are in 5 solar system models?

$$5 \times 9 = \blacksquare$$

▲ Planets orbit the sun.

ONE WAY Use patterns of 9.

Look at the products in the table of 9s facts.

The tens digit is 1 less than the factor that is multiplied by 9.

$$5 \times 9 = 4\ \blacksquare$$
$$\downarrow \qquad \downarrow$$
$$5 - 1 = 4$$

The sum of the digits in the product equals 9.

$$4 + 5 = 9$$

So, $5 \times 9 = 45$

So, there are 45 planets in 5 solar system models.

• How can you use patterns of 9 to complete the table?

Table of 9s	
Factors	**Product**
$1 \times 9 =$	9
$2 \times 9 =$	18
$3 \times 9 =$	27
$4 \times 9 =$	36
$5 \times 9 =$	$\blacksquare$
$6 \times 9 =$	54
$7 \times 9 =$	63
$8 \times 9 =$	$\blacksquare$
$9 \times 9 =$	$\blacksquare$
$10 \times 9 =$	$\blacksquare$

ANOTHER WAY Use a related 10s fact.

To multiply by 9, first multiply by 10.

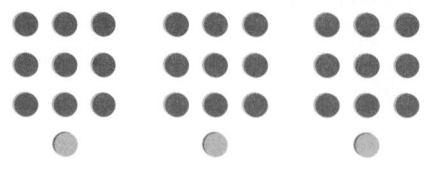

$$3 \times 10 = 30$$

Then subtract the first factor.

$$30 - 3 = 27$$
$$\text{So, } 3 \times 9 = 27$$

Guided Practice

1. How can you use a related 10s fact to find 4×9?

Find each product.

2. $9 \times 8 = \blacksquare$ **3.** $\blacksquare = 2 \times 9$ ✓**4.** $\blacksquare = 9 \times 6$ ✓**5.** $9 \times 1 = \blacksquare$

6. TALK Math **Explain** how to use the 9s pattern to find 7×9.

Independent Practice and Problem Solving

Find each product.

7. $\blacksquare = 9 \times 0$ **8.** $5 \times 9 = \blacksquare$ **9.** $\blacksquare = 6 \times 9$ **10.** $\blacksquare = 1 \times 9$

11. $9 \times 2 = \blacksquare$ **12.** $\blacksquare = 9 \times 9$ **13.** $9 \times 4 = \blacksquare$ **14.** $3 \times 9 = \blacksquare$

15. $\begin{array}{r} 9 \\ \times 8 \\ \hline \end{array}$ **16.** $\begin{array}{r} 9 \\ \times 7 \\ \hline \end{array}$ **17.** $\begin{array}{r} 10 \\ \times 5 \\ \hline \end{array}$ **18.** $\begin{array}{r} 4 \\ \times 6 \\ \hline \end{array}$ **19.** $\begin{array}{r} 8 \\ \times 4 \\ \hline \end{array}$ **20.** $\begin{array}{r} 9 \\ \times 5 \\ \hline \end{array}$

⭐**Algebra** Compare. Write <, >, or = for each ●.

21. $2 \times 9 ● 3 \times 6$ **22.** $5 \times 9 ● 6 \times 7$ **23.** $1 \times 9 ● 3 \times 3$

24. $9 \times 4 ● 7 \times 5$ **25.** $9 \times 0 ● 2 \times 3$ **26.** $5 \times 8 ● 3 \times 9$

USE DATA For 27–29, use the table.

27. The number of moons of one of the planets can be found by multiplying 7×9. Which planet is it?

28. Reasoning This planet has 9 times as many moons as Mars and Earth together have. Which planet is it? **Explain** your answer.

29. WRITE Math ▸ Nine groups of students made models of Mars and its moons. How many moons were made in all? **Explain** how to find the answer.

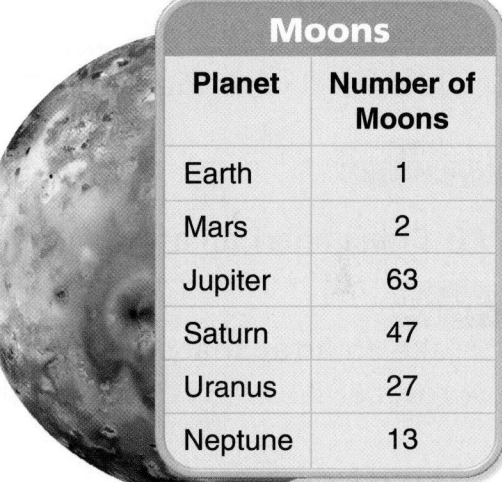

Moons	
Planet	**Number of Moons**
Earth	1
Mars	2
Jupiter	63
Saturn	47
Uranus	27
Neptune	13

Mixed Review and Test Prep

30. The school library has 87 books about space. John checked out 9 of them. How many books about space does the library have left? (p. 80)

31. Ten students each checked out 3 books from the library. How many books did the students check out?

(p. 232)

32. Test Prep Maddie has 5 sheets of star stickers. Each sheet has 9 stars on it. How many star stickers are there in all?

A 50   **C** 36

B 45   **D** 14

Extra Practice on page 248, Set D

CD ROM **Technology**
Use Harcourt Mega Math, The Number Games, *Up, Up, and Array*, Level B and C.

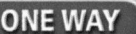
5 Multiply with 7

OBJECTIVE: Multiply with the factor 7.

Quick Review

1. 7×1 2. 7×4
3. 7×3 4. 7×2
5. 7×5

Learn

PROBLEM Jason's family has a new puppy. Jason walks the puppy once a day. How many times will Jason walk the puppy in 4 weeks?

$$4 \times 7 = \blacksquare$$

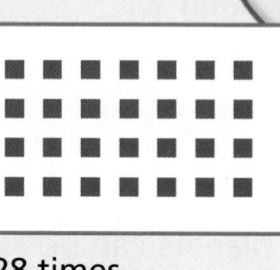

Remember
There are 7 days in 1 week.

ONE WAY Make an array.

Make 4 rows of 7 tiles.

$$\begin{array}{r} 7 \\ \times 4 \\ \hline 28 \end{array}$$

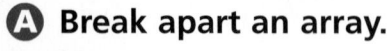

So, Jason will walk the puppy 28 times.

OTHER WAYS

A Break apart an array.

Step 1	Step 2	Step 3
Make an array that shows 4 rows of 7.	Break the array into two smaller arrays.	Add the products of the two arrays.
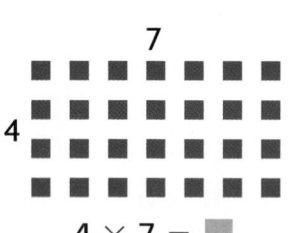	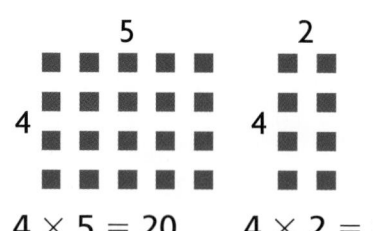	$\begin{array}{r} 20 \\ + 8 \\ \hline 28 \end{array}$
$4 \times 7 = \blacksquare$	$4 \times 5 = 20$ $4 \times 2 = 8$	So, $4 \times 7 = 28$.

• What is another way to break apart the 4×7 array?

B Use the Commutative Property.

If you know 7×4, use that fact to find 4×7.

$7 \times 4 = 28$, so $4 \times 7 = 28$.

1. **Explain** how you could break apart 8×7 into two arrays to help you find the product. Use tiles to help.

Find the product.

2. $9 \times 7 = \blacksquare$ 3. $\blacksquare = 6 \times 7$ ✓ 4. $\blacksquare = 3 \times 7$ ✓ 5. $7 \times 1 = \blacksquare$

6. [TALK Math] How could you use the Commutative Property to find 6×7?

Independent Practice and Problem Solving

Find the product.

7. $\blacksquare = 7 \times 7$ 8. $7 \times 6 = \blacksquare$ 9. $\blacksquare = 1 \times 8$ 10. $\blacksquare = 7 \times 2$

11. $\begin{array}{r} 7 \\ \times 3 \\ \hline \end{array}$
12. $\begin{array}{r} 10 \\ \times\ 6 \\ \hline \end{array}$
13. $\begin{array}{r} 9 \\ \times 7 \\ \hline \end{array}$
14. $\begin{array}{r} 5 \\ \times 7 \\ \hline \end{array}$
15. $\begin{array}{r} 6 \\ \times 8 \\ \hline \end{array}$
16. $\begin{array}{r} 7 \\ \times 6 \\ \hline \end{array}$

17. $\begin{array}{r} 8 \\ \times 9 \\ \hline \end{array}$
18. $\begin{array}{r} 0 \\ \times 7 \\ \hline \end{array}$
19. $\begin{array}{r} 8 \\ \times 8 \\ \hline \end{array}$
20. $\begin{array}{r} 7 \\ \times 4 \\ \hline \end{array}$
21. $\begin{array}{r} 3 \\ \times 6 \\ \hline \end{array}$
22. $\begin{array}{r} 8 \\ \times 7 \\ \hline \end{array}$

USE DATA For 23 and 25, use the table.

23. Lori has a dog named Midnight. How many baths will Midnight have in 7 months?

24. ☰**FAST FACT** A dog's heartbeat depends on its size. Some dogs' hearts beat 70 times a minute. What 7s fact equals 70?

25. [WRITE Math] Jose's dog, Sunny, eats 4 cups of food a day. In 7 days, does Sunny eat more or less than Midnight eats? **Explain.**

Midnight's Care	
Food	3 cups a day
Water	4 cups a day
Bath	2 times a month

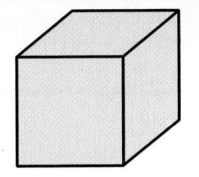

Mixed Review and Test Prep

26. How many faces does a cube have? (Gr. 2)

27. *Purr* cat food costs 9¢ per ounce. How much does a 5 ounce can of the food cost? (p. 238)

28. **Test Prep** Sam walks 3 miles a day. How many miles does he walk in one week?

  A 3 miles   **C** 21 miles

  B 10 miles   **D** 28 miles

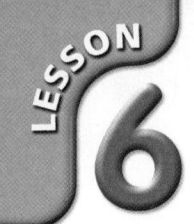

Problem Solving Workshop
Strategy: Compare Strategies

OBJECTIVE: Compare different strategies to solve problems.

PROBLEM The nine-banded armadillo usually has 9 bands across its back. How many bands would 4 armadillos have?

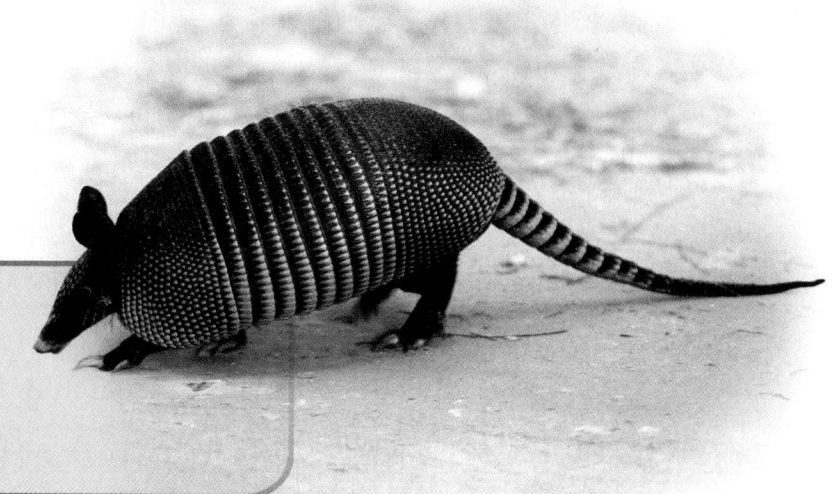

Read to Understand

Reading Skill

- Summarize what you are asked to find.
- What information is given?

Plan

- **What strategy can you use to solve the problem?**

Many times you can use more than one strategy to solve a problem. For example, you can *draw a picture* or *make a table* to solve this problem.

Solve

- **How can you use each strategy to solve the problem?**

Draw a picture of 4 armadillos with 9 bands on each one.

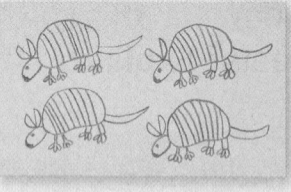

$4 \times 9 = 36$

So, 4 armadillos will have 36 bands.

Make a table to show the number of bands on four armadillos.

Armadillo Bands				
Number of armadillos	1	2	3	4
Number of bands	9	18	27	36

Check

- **How do you know your answer is correct?**

TALK Math
Which strategy would you use to solve the problem? Explain.

Choose a STRATEGY

Make a Model or Act It Out
Draw a Diagram or Picture
Make an Organized List
Find a Pattern
Make a Table or Graph
Predict and Test
Work Backward
Solve a Simpler Problem
Write an Equation
Use Logical Reasoning

1. Julie saw 6 robins each time she went bird-watching. How many robins did Julie see in 5 days?

   Draw a picture.

   First, draw a picture of 6 birds.

   Next, draw 4 more groups of 6 birds so there are 5 groups in all.

   Last, count to find the total number of birds.

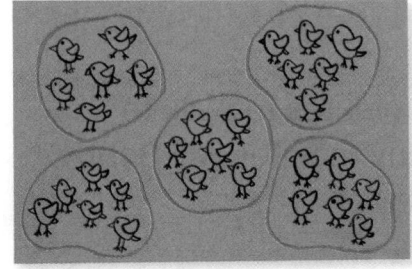

$$5 \times 6 = \blacksquare$$

   Make a table.

   First, decide what information should be in each row.

   Next, write the information from the problem in the table.

   Last, fill in the table through 5 days.

Bird-Watching					
Day	1	2	3	4	5
Number of birds	6	12	18	24	

2. **What if** Julie saw 6 robins every day for 6 days? How many would she have seen in all?

3. Mark hiked a trail every day for 5 days. Each day he saw 9 cactus plants. How many cactus plants did he see in all?

Mixed Strategy Practice

USE DATA For 4–6, use the recipe.

4. Jane doubles the cactus jelly recipe. How many lemons does she need?

5. Joan, Michelle, Samantha, and Gerri each use the recipe to make cactus fruit jelly. How many cups of sugar do they use in all?

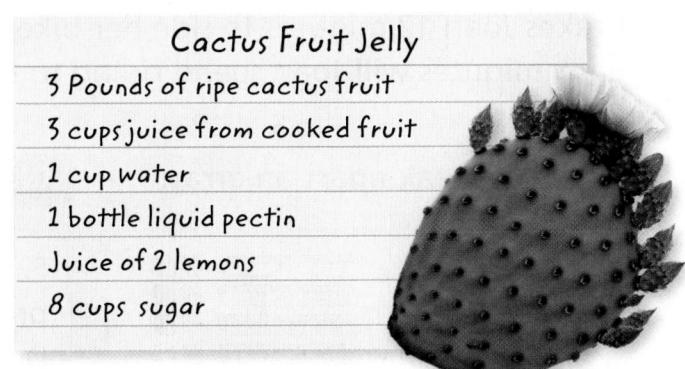

Cactus Fruit Jelly
3 Pounds of ripe cactus fruit
3 cups juice from cooked fruit
1 cup water
1 bottle liquid pectin
Juice of 2 lemons
8 cups sugar

6. **Reasoning** Joel has 7 pounds of ripe cactus fruit. How many pounds will he have left if he makes 2 batches of jelly? **Explain** your answer.

7. Lilly took a 4-mile walk every day for 9 days. How many miles in all did Lilly walk?

8. **WRITE Math** Louis planted a cactus garden. He bought 48 cactus. He planted 8 cactus each day. How many days did it take Louis to plant all of the cactus? **Explain** how you know.

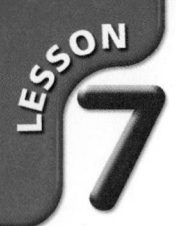

ALGEBRA
Multiplication Facts through 12

OBJECTIVE: Multiply with the factors 11 and 12 and practice multiplication facts by using various strategies.

Learn

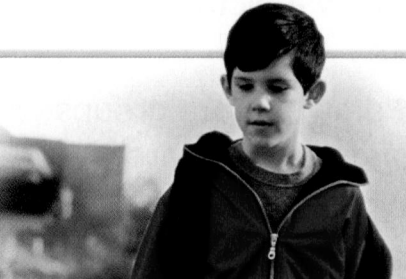

PROBLEM It takes Bobby 11 minutes to walk to school each morning. How many minutes will Bobby spend walking to school in 5 days?

$$5 \times 11 = \blacksquare$$

ONE WAY Break apart an array.

Make 5 rows of 11.

Use the 10s facts and the 1s facts to multiply by 11.

$5 \times 10 = 50$ $5 \times 1 = 5$
$5 \times 11 = 50 + 5 = 55$

5×10 5×1

So, Bobby will spend 55 minutes walking to school.

ANOTHER WAY

Look at the table of 11s facts.

To find 5×11, write the first factor twice.

$5 \times 11 = 55$

• What pattern do you see in the 11s facts through 9?

11s Facts

$1 \times 11 = 11$
$2 \times 11 = 22$
$3 \times 11 = 33$
$4 \times 11 = 44$
$5 \times 11 = \blacksquare$
$6 \times 11 = 66$
$7 \times 11 = 77$
$8 \times 11 = 88$
$9 \times 11 = 99$
$10 \times 11 = 110$

It takes Joan 12 minutes to ride her bike to school. How many minutes will Joan spend riding to school in 5 days?

$$5 \times 12 = \blacksquare$$

ONE WAY Break apart an array.

Make 5 rows of 12.

Use the 10s facts and the 2s facts to multiply by 12.

5×10 5×2

$5 \times 10 = 50$ $5 \times 2 = 10$
$5 \times 12 = 50 + 10 = 60$

So, Joan will spend 60 minutes riding to school.

ANOTHER WAY Double a 6s fact.

Find the 6s product.
Double that product.

$5 \times 6 = 30$
$30 + 30 = 60$
So, $5 \times 12 = 60$.

12s Facts

$0 \times 12 = 0$
$1 \times 12 = 12$
$2 \times 12 = 24$
$3 \times 12 = 36$
$4 \times 12 = 48$
$5 \times 12 = 60$
$6 \times 12 = 72$
$7 \times 12 = 84$
$8 \times 12 = 96$
$9 \times 12 = 108$
$10 \times 12 = 120$
$11 \times 12 = 132$
$12 \times 12 = 144$

Practice the Facts

You can multiply by using a variety of strategies.

OTHER WAYS

Ⓐ Use a number line.
Skip-count by 3s. $6 \times 3 = 18$

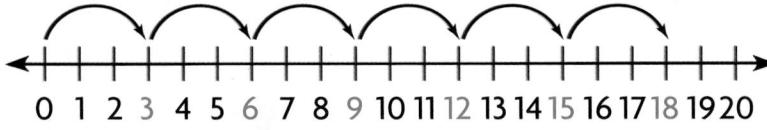

Think: 3, 6, 9, 12, 15, 18

Ⓑ Use counters.
Make 6 groups of 3.

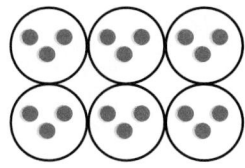

$6 \times 3 = 18$

Ⓒ Make an array.
Make 6 rows of 3 tiles.

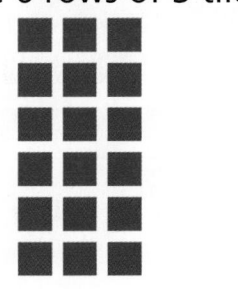

$6 \times 3 = 18$

Ⓓ Draw a picture.
Draw 6 groups of 3.

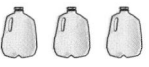 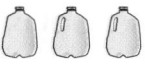 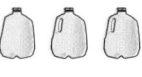

$$\begin{array}{r} 3 \\ \times\,6 \\ \hline 18 \end{array}$$

$6 \times 3 = 18$

Ⓔ Use doubles.
Find the 3s product. $3 \times 3 = 9$
Double that product. $9 + 9 = 18$
So, $6 \times 3 = 18$.

Ⓕ Use the Commutative Property.
Change the order of the factors.
$3 \times 6 = 18$, so $6 \times 3 = 18$.

- How would you find 3×6 by using a number line?

Guided Practice

1. How can you use the 10s facts and the 2s facts to find 4×12?

Find the product.

2. $9 \times 11 = \blacksquare$ 3. $\blacksquare = 12 \times 7$ ⊘4. $\blacksquare = 4 \times 11$ ⊘5. $12 \times 3 = \blacksquare$

6. **TALK Math** How does knowing $11 \times 6 = 66$ help you find 11×12?

Independent Practice and Problem Solving

Find the product.

7. $6 \times 8 = $ ■   **8.** ■ $= 5 \times 6$ **9.** ■ $= 4 \times 2$ **10.** $0 \times 9 = $ ■

11. $4 \times 7 = $ ■   **12.** $2 \times 6 = $ ■   **13.** ■ $= 5 \times 5$ **14.** ■ $= 6 \times 7$

15. ■ $= 10 \times 1$ **16.** $7 \times 2 = $ ■   **17.** $8 \times 3 = $ ■   **18.** $6 \times 9 = $ ■

19. ■ $= 11 \times 11$ **20.** $6 \times 12 = $ ■   **21.** ■ $= 10 \times 9$ **22.** ■ $= 0 \times 12$

23. $10 \times 11 = $ ■   **24.** ■ $= 11 \times 8$ **25.** $11 \times 3 = $ ■   **26.** $2 \times 12 = $ ■

27. $\begin{array}{r} 11 \\ \times\ 4 \\ \hline \end{array}$ **28.** $\begin{array}{r} 12 \\ \times\ 9 \\ \hline \end{array}$ **29.** $\begin{array}{r} 12 \\ \times\ 0 \\ \hline \end{array}$ **30.** $\begin{array}{r} 11 \\ \times\ 9 \\ \hline \end{array}$ **31.** $\begin{array}{r} 12 \\ \times\ 7 \\ \hline \end{array}$ **32.** $\begin{array}{r} 12 \\ \times\ 6 \\ \hline \end{array}$

USE DATA For 33–34, use the graph.

33. The graph shows the number of miles some students travel to school. How many miles will Carlos travel to school in 10 days?

34. Mandy takes 11 trips to school. Matt takes 12 trips to school. Who travels more miles? **Explain** your answer.

35. **WRITE Math** ▶ Mr. Lane is putting 6 cartons of eggs on the shelf. There are 12 eggs in each carton. How many eggs in all are there? **Explain** two ways to find the answer.

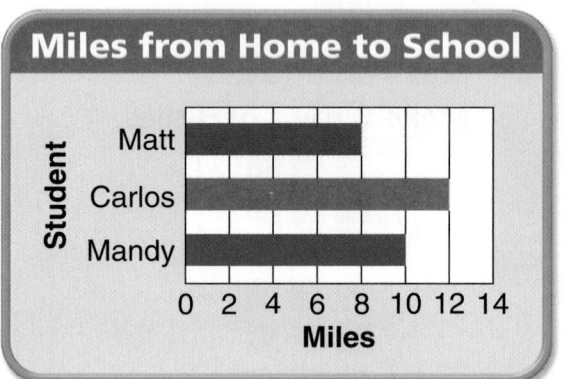

Mixed Review and Test Prep

36. Corey goes to soccer practice at 4:30 P.M. Two hours later, he eats dinner. At what time does Corey eat dinner? (p. 130)

37. There are 9 red marbles and 1 blue marble in a bag. Sam pulls a marble without looking. Is it certain, likely, unlikely, or impossible that Sam will pull a red marble from the bag? (p. 178)

38. **Test Prep** There are 12 desks in each of 3 rows. How many desks in all are there?

A 8   **B** 16   **C** 36   **D** 48

39. **Test Prep** Sharon has 4 necklaces. There are 12 beads on each necklace. **Explain** how you would find the total number of beads on all of Sharon's necklaces.

246   Extra Practice on page 248, Set F

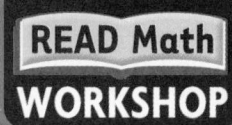

Healthy Foods for Good Health

 Reading Skill Use Graphic Aids

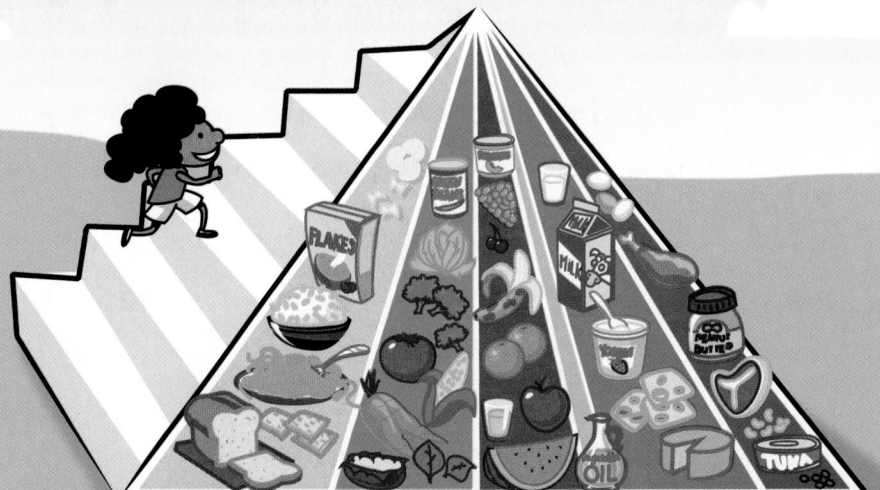

▶ The food pyramid shows amounts of different food groups people need for good health. The person climbing up the stairs reminds us that it is important to exercise as well as eat healthy foods.

To help you stay healthy, you should eat a balanced diet and exercise every day. The table shows the recommended daily servings for third graders. For good health, you should eat the right amounts of each food group. To stay healthy, you also need to limit the amount of foods you eat that have a lot of fat and sugar in them.

Recommended Daily Servings

Food Group	Servings
Whole grains (bread, cereal)	6 ounces
Vegetables (beans, corn)	2 cups
Fruits (apples, oranges)	1 cup
Dairy products (milk, cheese)	3 cups
Meat, beans, fish, eggs, nuts	5 ounces
8 ounces = 1 cup	

Problem Solving Look at the graphic aids. Use the information to solve the problems.

1. A slice of wheat bread weighs about 1 ounce. How many ounces of whole grains, such as bread and cereal, should a third grader eat in 1 week? Think: 1 week = 7 days

2. How many cups of vegetables and fruits should a third grader eat in 1 day? In 1 week?

3. How many cups of dairy products, such as milk and cheese, should a third grader have in 1 day? In 10 days?

4. **WRITE Math** ▶ What's the Question? Kendra ate the recommended number of vegetable servings each day for 7 days. The answer is 14 cups.

Extra Practice

Set A Find the product. (pp. 232–233)

1. $3 \times 5 = \blacksquare$ **2.** $\blacksquare = 4 \times 3$ **3.** $\blacksquare = 3 \times 10$ **4.** $7 \times 3 = \blacksquare$

5. $3 \times 9 = \blacksquare$ **6.** $\blacksquare = 3 \times 2$ **7.** $\blacksquare = 4 \times 6$ **8.** $3 \times 3 = \blacksquare$

Set B Find the product. (pp. 234–235)

1. $7 \times 6 = \blacksquare$ **2.** $\blacksquare = 3 \times 6$ **3.** $\blacksquare = 5 \times 6$ **4.** $6 \times 2 = \blacksquare$

5. $4 \times 6 = \blacksquare$ **6.** $1 \times 7 = \blacksquare$ **7.** $\blacksquare = 2 \times 5$ **8.** $\blacksquare = 1 \times 6$

9. $\begin{array}{r} 6 \\ \times 6 \\ \hline \end{array}$ **10.** $\begin{array}{r} 5 \\ \times 6 \\ \hline \end{array}$ **11.** $\begin{array}{r} 6 \\ \times 8 \\ \hline \end{array}$ **12.** $\begin{array}{r} 6 \\ \times 4 \\ \hline \end{array}$ **13.** $\begin{array}{r} 1 \\ \times 6 \\ \hline \end{array}$ **14.** $\begin{array}{r} 10 \\ \times 6 \\ \hline \end{array}$

Set C Find the product. (pp. 236–237)

1. $3 \times 8 = \blacksquare$ **2.** $1 \times 8 = \blacksquare$ **3.** $5 \times 8 = \blacksquare$ **4.** $8 \times 0 = \blacksquare$

5. $\begin{array}{r} 6 \\ \times 6 \\ \hline \end{array}$ **6.** $\begin{array}{r} 0 \\ \times 8 \\ \hline \end{array}$ **7.** $\begin{array}{r} 7 \\ \times 8 \\ \hline \end{array}$ **8.** $\begin{array}{r} 2 \\ \times 7 \\ \hline \end{array}$ **9.** $\begin{array}{r} 4 \\ \times 8 \\ \hline \end{array}$ **10.** $\begin{array}{r} 8 \\ \times 9 \\ \hline \end{array}$

Set D Find each product. (pp. 238–239)

1. $3 \times 9 = \blacksquare$ **2.** $9 \times 5 = \blacksquare$ **3.** $0 \times 9 = \blacksquare$ **4.** $9 \times 7 = \blacksquare$

Compare. Write $<$, $>$, or $=$ for each ●.

5. $9 \times 3 ● 7 \times 4$ **6.** $4 \times 3 ● 2 \times 6$ **7.** $9 \times 2 ● 6 \times 3$

Set E Find the product. (pp. 240–241)

1. $7 \times 10 = \blacksquare$ **2.** $3 \times 7 = \blacksquare$ **3.** $5 \times 7 = \blacksquare$ **4.** $7 \times 4 = \blacksquare$

5. A photo album has 7 pictures on 8 pages. How many photos are there in all?

6. Malik rides his bike 7 miles every day. How many miles does he ride in one week?

Set F Find the product. (pp. 244–247)

1. $11 \times 9 = \blacksquare$ **2.** $3 \times 11 = \blacksquare$ **3.** $12 \times 2 = \blacksquare$ **4.** $11 \times 8 = \blacksquare$

5. $7 \times 11 = \blacksquare$ **6.** $3 \times 12 = \blacksquare$ **7.** $6 \times 12 = \blacksquare$ **8.** $8 \times 12 = \blacksquare$

CD ROM Technology
Use Harcourt Mega Math, The Number Games, *Up, Up, and Array*, Levels B, C, and D.

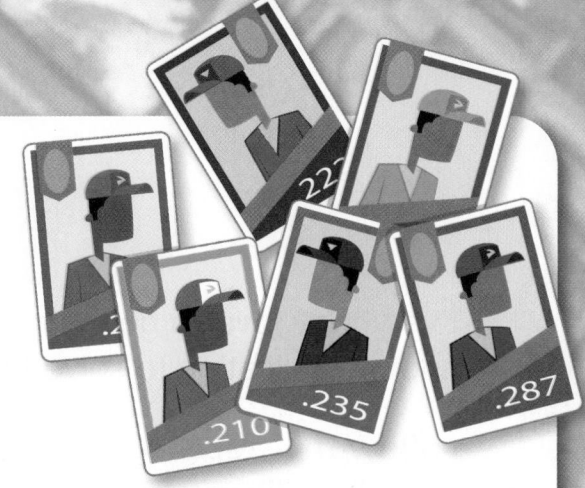

TECHNOLOGY ★ CONNECTION

iTools: Counters

Use Counters to Multiply

Trading cards come in packs of 6. If Seth has
8 packs, how many cards does he have in all?

Step 1 Click on *Counters.* Then click on
Multiply in the *Activities* menu.

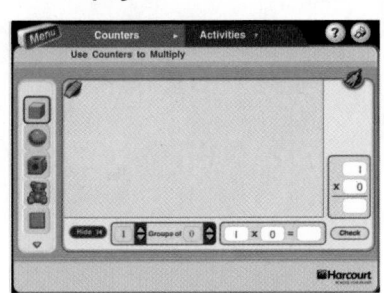

Step 2 Click on the workmat 6 times to
show 6 counters.

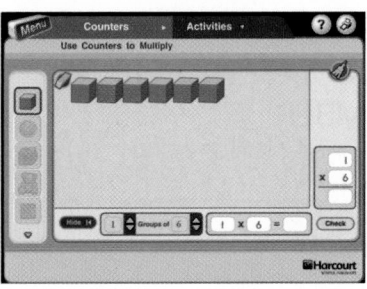

Step 3 Click on the up arrow before *Groups
of* to set the number of groups.
There should be 8 groups of 6.

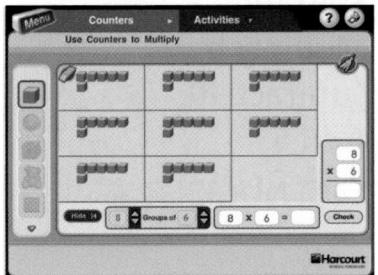

Step 4 Count or multiply the counters.
Type your answer in one of the
answer boxes. Click on *Check.*

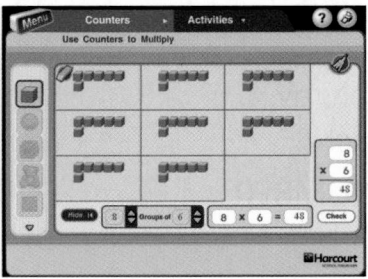

Try It

Follow the same steps to solve these problems.

1. $3 \times 9 = $ ■ **2.** $5 \times 6 = $ ■ **3.** $6 \times 4 = $ ■ **4.** $10 \times 8 = $ ■ **5.** $4 \times 7 = $ ■

6. $2 \times 8 = $ ■ **7.** $4 \times 9 = $ ■ **8.** $6 \times 7 = $ ■ **9.** $5 \times 8 = $ ■ **10.** $6 \times 3 = $ ■

11. Explore More Eighteen students went apple picking.
Half of them picked 6 apples each. The other half
picked 5 apples each. **Explain** how you can find out
how many apples were picked by the whole class.

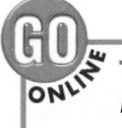

Technology
*i*Tools available online or
on CD-ROM

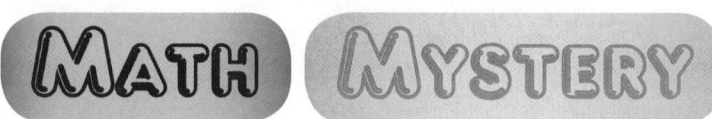

MATH POWER — Number Riddles

MATH MYSTERY

Everybody loves a good mystery! Use addition, subtraction, and multiplication to solve the riddle below.

Follow the steps to begin solving the riddle.

Start with 5.	5	**A**
Add 4.	5 + 4 = 9	
Multiply by 2.	9 × 2 = 18	
Subtract 3.	18 − 3 = 15	
END NUMBER: ■	15	
	So, **A** = 15.	

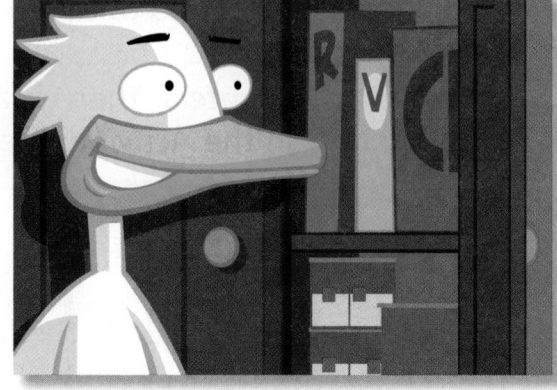

Try It

Copy the riddle below. Find the value of each letter.
Then write the letters in the correct spaces.

1. Start with 9.   **Q**
   Subtract 3.
   Multiply by 4.
   Subtract 4.
   END NUMBER: ■

2. Start with 4.   **C**
   Add 2.
   Subtract 3.
   Multiply by 6.
   END NUMBER: ■

3. Start with 8.   **K**
   Multiply by 3.
   Subtract 10.
   Add 5.
   END NUMBER: ■

4. Start with 7.   **U**
   Subtract 3.
   Multiply by 9.
   Add 4.
   END NUMBER: ■

5. Start with 10.   **E**
   Multiply by 5.
   Subtract 6.
   Add 11.
   END NUMBER: ■

6. Start with 6.   **R**
   Multiply by 8.
   Add 9.
   Subtract 22.
   END NUMBER: ■

7. What is a duck's favorite food?

A		?	?	?	?	?	?	?!
15		20	40	15	18	19	55	35

8. **WRITE Math** ▸ Create a riddle with at least 4 steps.
   Explain your riddle.

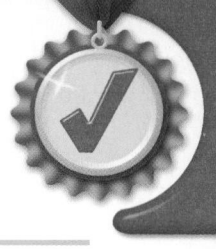

Chapter 9 Review/Test

Check Concepts

1. **Explain** how you can use the picture to find how many sides 4 triangles have. (pp. 232–233)

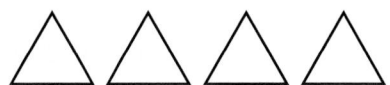

Make an array to solve. (pp. 236–237, 240–241)

2. Maria puts 8 ice cubes into each of 3 glasses for her friends. How many ice cubes has she used in all?

3. There are 7 days in a week. How many days are there in 4 weeks?

Check Skills

Find the product. (pp. 232–233, 234–235, 236–237, 238–239, 240–241, 244–247)

4. $2 \times 12 = \blacksquare$
5. $8 \times 4 = \blacksquare$
6. $3 \times 11 = \blacksquare$
7. $5 \times 7 = \blacksquare$

8. $7 \times 8 = \blacksquare$
9. $11 \times 7 = \blacksquare$
10. $9 \times 8 = \blacksquare$
11. $12 \times 4 = \blacksquare$

12. $9 \times 10 = \blacksquare$
13. $\blacksquare = 3 \times 4$
14. $6 \times 6 = \blacksquare$
15. $\blacksquare = 3 \times 7$

16. $\begin{array}{r} 5 \\ \times 4 \\ \hline \end{array}$
17. $\begin{array}{r} 3 \\ \times 8 \\ \hline \end{array}$
18. $\begin{array}{r} 5 \\ \times 6 \\ \hline \end{array}$
19. $\begin{array}{r} 11 \\ \times 9 \\ \hline \end{array}$
20. $\begin{array}{r} 12 \\ \times 3 \\ \hline \end{array}$
21. $\begin{array}{r} 8 \\ \times 4 \\ \hline \end{array}$

Compare. Write $<$, $>$, or $=$ for each ●. (pp. 238–239)

22. 4×3 ● 5×2
23. 6×5 ● 7×4
24. 4×5 ● 10×2

25. 8×2 ● 5×3
26. 8×3 ● 2×12
27. 7×5 ● 9×4

Check Problem Solving

Solve. (pp. 242–243)

28. Linda can paint 4 pictures in one day. How many pictures can she paint in 5 days?

Number of days	1	2	3	4	5
Pictures painted	4	8	■	■	■

29. Jerod buys 4 packages of markers and 5 packages of paper. Each package of markers costs $5, and each package of paper costs $3. How much does Jerod spend in all?

30. **WRITE Math** ▶ What if each package of paper costs $6? How much does Jerod spend in all for paper and markers then? **Explain** how you found your answer.

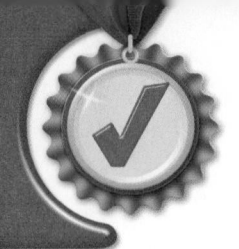

Standardized Test Prep
Chapters 1–9

Number and Operations

1. Jody's school is having a craft fair. There are 7 rows of tables with 5 tables in each row. How many tables are set up for the craft fair?
(p. 218)

  A 25

  B 30

  C 35

  D 40

 Test Tip — **Understand the problem.**

See item 2. What is the question asking you to find? Read the problem again to find the information you need to answer the question.

2. There was a talent show at Wanda's school on Friday and Saturday. On Friday, 495 people saw the talent show. In all, 867 people saw the talent show. How many people saw the talent show on Saturday? (p. 84)

  A 262   **C** 362

  B 272   **D** 372

3. **WRITE Math** ► How can this picture help you find 5×6? **Explain.** (p. 234)

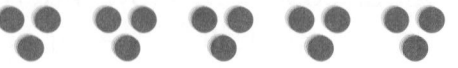

Algebraic Reasoning

4. What is the ordered pair for the post office? (p. 166)

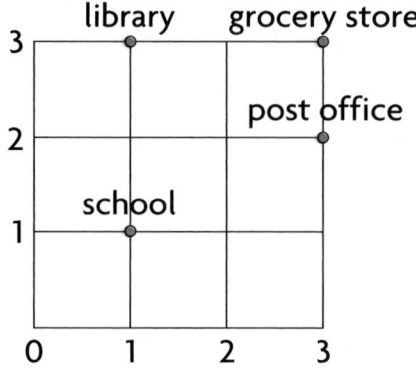

  A (3, 3)

  B (3, 2)

  C (1, 3)

  D (2, 3)

5. Which array shows 6×2? (p. 206)

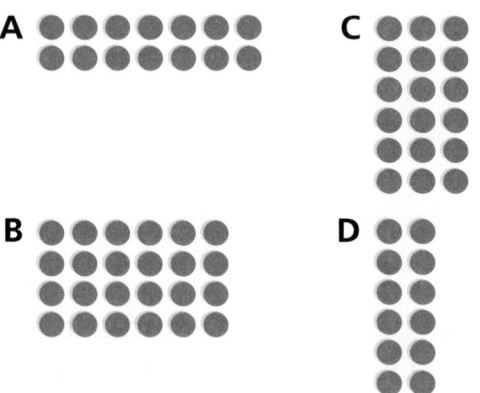

6. **WRITE Math** ► What is one way to find 8×4? **Explain.** (p. 212)

Geometry

7. These faces can be put together to make which solid figure? (Grade 2)

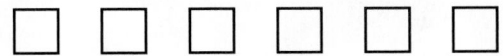

A Rectangular prism

B Cylinder

C Cube

D Square pyramid

8. Which solid figure has exactly 5 faces? (Grade 2)

A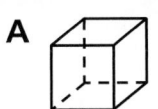

B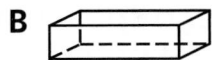

C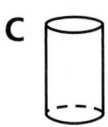

D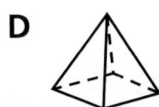

9. **WRITE Math** ▶ **Explain** how this square and this rectangle are alike. (Grade 2)

Data Analysis and Probability

10. How many more students chose blue than green as their favorite color? (p. 154)

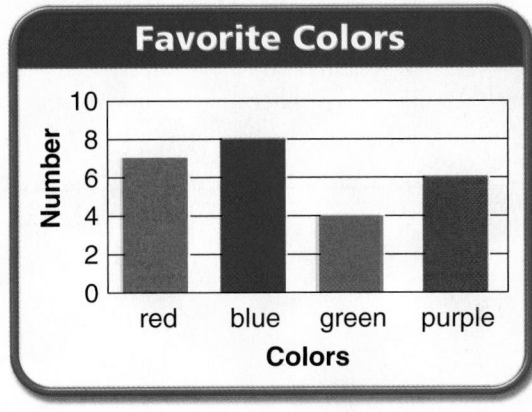

A 1   **C** 3

B 2   **D** 4

11. Which color block is Brian least likely to pull? (p. 178)

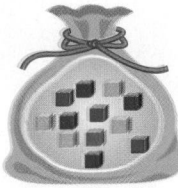

A Blue

B Green

C Red

D Yellow

12. **WRITE Math** ▶ What if Brian's bag had 10 yellow blocks and 2 green blocks. Which color would he be more likely to pull? **Explain** your answer. (p. 178)

10 Algebra: Facts and Properties

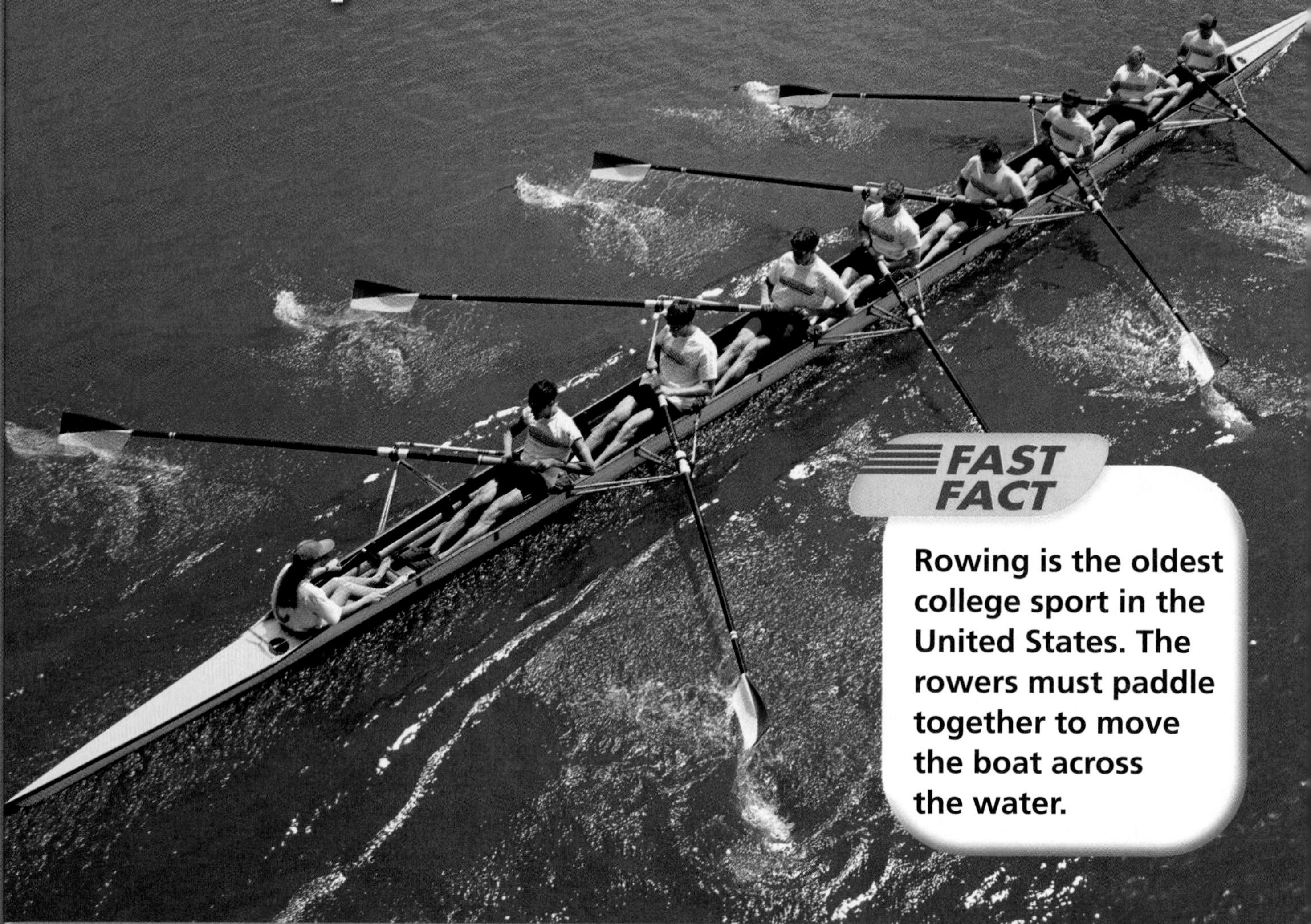

FAST FACT

Rowing is the oldest college sport in the United States. The rowers must paddle together to move the boat across the water.

Investigate

The boat used in sport rowing is called a shell. Other types of boats also use oars or paddles. Choose a boat from the graph. Explain how you can use multiplication to find how many boats you would need for your whole class to go boating.

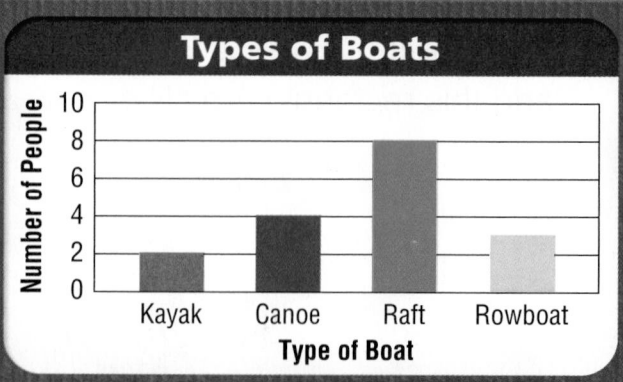

Types of Boats

Number of People (vertical axis): 0, 2, 4, 6, 8, 10

Type of Boat (horizontal axis): Kayak, Canoe, Raft, Rowboat

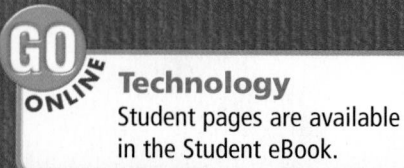

GO ONLINE

Technology
Student pages are available in the Student eBook.

Check your understanding of important skills needed for success in Chapter 10.

▶ **Arrays**

Complete.

1.

 2 rows of ■ = 16

 2 × 8 = ■

2.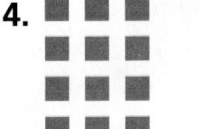

 4 rows of ■ = 20

 4 × 5 = ■

3.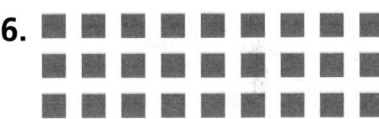

 3 rows of ■ = 21

 3 × 7 = ■

4.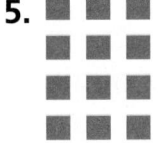

 4 rows of ■ = 12

 4 × 3 = ■

5.

 5 rows of ■ = 15

 5 × 3 = ■

6.

 3 rows of ■ = 27

 3 × 9 = ■

▶ **Multiplication Facts Through 10**

Find the product.

7. 4 × 4 = ■   **8.** 3 × 6 = ■   **9.** 7 × 9 = ■   **10.** 5 × 10 = ■

VOCABULARY POWER

CHAPTER VOCABULARY

Associative Property of Multiplication
Commutative Property of Multiplication
Identity Property of Multiplication
variable
Zero Property of Multiplication

WARM-UP WORDS

Associative Property of Multiplication The property that states that when the grouping of factors is changed, the product remains the same

variable A symbol or a letter that stands for an unknown number

Zero Property of Multiplication The property that states that the product of zero and any number is 0

1 Find a Rule

OBJECTIVE: Find a rule for a numerical pattern shown on a function table.

Learn

PROBLEM The camping club is planning a trip. Each camper will need a flashlight. One flashlight uses 3 batteries. How many batteries are needed for 7 flashlights?

Example Look for a pattern. Write a rule.

Flashlights	1	2	3	4	5	6	7
Batteries	3	6	9	12	15	18	■

Pattern: The number of batteries equals the number of flashlights times 3.

Rule: Multiply the number of flashlights by 3.

To find how many batteries are needed for 7 flashlights, multiply 7 times 3.

$$7 \times 3 = 21$$

So, 21 batteries are needed for 7 flashlights.

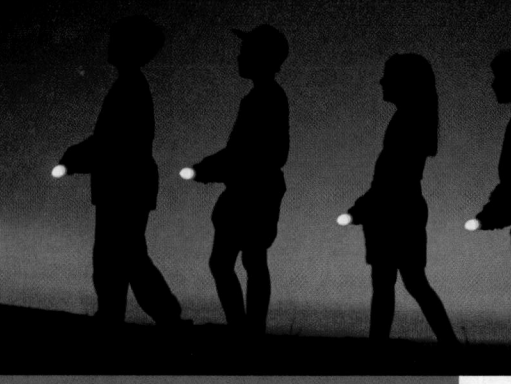
▲ The flashlight was invented in 1896.

More Examples Describe the pattern. Write a rule.

A

Packs of batteries	1	2	3	4	5
Number of batteries	4	8	■	16	■

Pattern: The number of batteries equals the number of packs times 4.

Rule: Multiply the number of packs of batteries by 4.

• How many batteries are in 3 packs? 5 packs?

B

Packs of batteries	1	2	3	4
Cost	$5	$10	$15	■

Pattern: The cost equals the number of packs times $5.

Rule: Multiply the number of packs of batteries by $5.

• How much do 4 packs cost? 7 packs?

• How does knowing the pattern rule help you find the next number in the pattern?

1. **Explain** how to use a rule to find how many batteries are needed for 9 flashlights.

Flashlights	1	2	3
Batteries	3	6	9

Write a rule for each table. Then copy and complete the table.

2.

Tents	2	3	4	5	6	7
Campers	4	6	8	10	■	■

3.

Campers	1	2	3	4	5
Flashlights	1	2	3	■	■

4. **TALK Math** **Explain** how you can make a table to find how many plates on 6 tables. Pattern: The number of plates equals the number of tables times 4.

Independent Practice and Problem Solving

Write a rule for each table. Then copy and complete the table.

5.

Hours	1	2	3	4	5
Miles Hiked	2	4	■	■	■

6.

Cabins	3	4	5	6	7
Campers	27	36	■	■	■

USE DATA For 7–10, use the table.

7. Write a rule for the table at the right. What pattern do you see?

Rafts	1	2	3	4
People	6	12	18	■

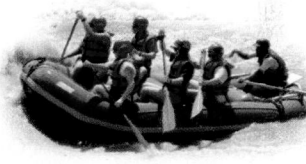

8. The camping club rents 4 rafts. How many people can 4 rafts hold?

9. The cost to rent a raft is $10 per person. There is a $2 launch fee per raft. What is the cost for a group of 6 people?

10. **WRITE Math** **What's the Question?** The answer is 30 people. What is the question?

Mixed Review and Test Prep

11. Are you more likely or less likely to spin blue on this spinner? (p. 178)

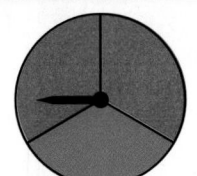

12. Tim bought 4 boxes of granola bars. There are 6 bars in each box. How many bars did Tim buy? (p. 234)

13. **Test Prep** At the store, two notebooks cost $4 and three notebooks cost $6. Jenny wants to buy 6 notebooks. How much will she spend?

A $6   **B** $10   **C** $12   **D** $24

Missing Factors

OBJECTIVE: Use an array and a multiplication table to find missing factors.

Learn

PROBLEM Brandy plans to invite 24 people to a picnic. The invitations come in packs of 8. How many packs of invitations does Brandy need to buy?

$$\blacksquare \times 8 = 24$$

A **variable** is a letter or symbol that stands for an unknown number.

ONE WAY Make an array.

Activity **Materials** ■ square tiles

Make an array with 24 tiles.
Use 8 tiles in each row.

Count the rows of 8 tiles.

column
↓

row →

$$\blacksquare \quad \times \quad 8 \quad = \quad 24$$
$$\uparrow \qquad \uparrow \qquad \uparrow$$
factor   factor   product
rows   columns   total number of tiles

There are 3 rows of 8 tiles. The missing factor is 3.
$$3 \times 8 = 24$$

So, Brandy needs 3 packs of invitations.

ANOTHER WAY Use a multiplication table.

Start at the column for 8.
Look down to the product, 24.
Look left across the row from 24.
The missing factor is 3.

$$a \times 8 = 24$$
$$3 \times 8 = 24$$

✕	0	1	2	3	4	5	6	7	8	9
0	0	0	0	0	0	0	0	0	0	0
1	0	1	2	3	4	5	6	7	8	9
2	0	2	4	6	8	10	12	14	16	18
3	0	3	6	9	12	15	18	21	24	27
4	0	4	8	12	16	20	24	28	32	36
5	0	5	10	15	20	25	30	35	40	45
6	0	6	12	18	24	30	36	42	48	54
7	0	7	14	21	28	35	42	49	56	63
8	0	8	16	24	32	40	48	56	64	72
9	0	9	18	27	36	45	54	63	72	81

Guided Practice

1. What is the missing factor shown by this array?

    $5 \times \blacksquare = 35$

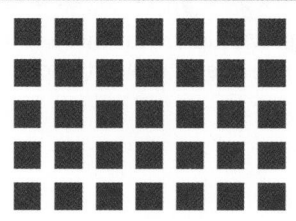

Find the missing factor.

2. $\blacksquare \times 3 = 27$ 3. $6 \times b = 30$ ☑ 4. $c \times 5 = 20$ ☑ 5. $\blacksquare \times 2 = 14$

6. **TALK Math** **Explain** how to use the multiplication table on page 258 to find the missing factor in $\blacksquare \times 6 = 42$.

Independent Practice and Problem Solving

Find the missing factor.

7. $\blacksquare \times 2 = 18$ 8. $4 \times \blacksquare = 28$ 9. $\blacksquare \times 3 = 9$ 10. $\blacksquare \times 7 = 63$

11. $5 \times \blacksquare = 40$ 12. $8 \times \blacksquare = 56$ 13. $\blacksquare \times 6 = 36$ 14. $9 \times \blacksquare = 72$

15. $a \times 4 = 24$ 16. $7 \times y = 7$ 17. $m \times 3 = 15$ 18. $b \times 8 = 48$

19. $3 \times 6 = n \times 9$ 20. $9 \times d = 70 + 2$ 21. $5 \times g = 35 - 5$

USE DATA For 22–24, use the table.

22. Brandy needs 48 bowls for the picnic. How many packs of bowls should she buy?

23. What is the total cost for 3 tablecloths and 2 packs of napkins?

24. **WRITE Math** **What's the Error?** Brandy needs 5 packs of cups. She gives the cashier $8. What is Brandy's error?

Picnic Supplies		
Item	Number per pack	Cost
Bowls	6	$4
Cups	8	$3
Tablecloth	1	$2
Napkins	36	$6
Forks	50	$3

Mixed Review and Test Prep

25. Eric bounced the ball 170 times. What is 170 in expanded notation?
    (p. 8)

26. The gym teacher divides the class into 4 teams. There are 9 students on each team. How many students are in the class? (p. 238)

27. **Test Prep** What is the missing factor?

    $\blacksquare \times 6 = 12$

    A 18 **C** 3

    B 6 **D** 2

CD ROM **Technology**
Use Harcourt Mega Math, Ice Station Exploration, *Arctic Algebra*, Level C.

Multiply 3 Factors

OBJECTIVE: Multiply with three factors using the Associative (Grouping) Property of Multiplication.

Learn

PROBLEM The Mr. Freeze Roller Coaster in Texas has 5 cars. Each car has 2 rows of seats. Each row has 2 seats. How many seats in all are on the ride?

ONE WAY Multiply $5 \times (2 \times 2) = \blacksquare$.

Make an array to show 5 groups of 2 times 2.

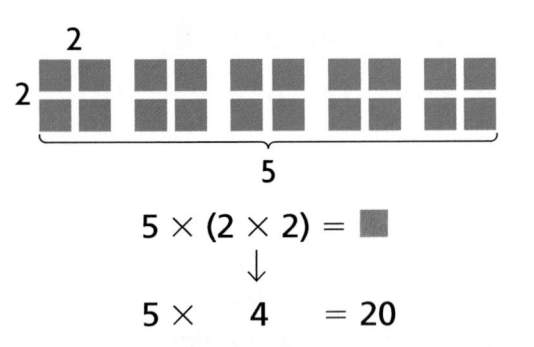

$$5 \times (2 \times 2) = \blacksquare$$
$$\downarrow$$
$$5 \times \quad 4 \quad = 20$$

Multiply the numbers in parentheses first.

ANOTHER WAY Multiply $(5 \times 2) \times 2 = \blacksquare$.

Make an array to show 2 groups of 5 times 2.

$$(5 \times 2) \times 2 = \blacksquare$$
$$\downarrow$$
$$10 \quad \times 2 = 20$$

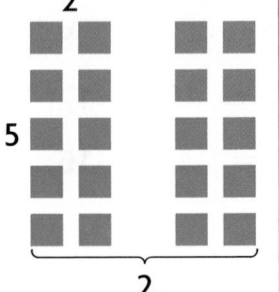

So, there are 20 seats in all on the roller coaster.

The **Associative Property of Multiplication**, or Grouping Property, states that when the grouping of factors is changed, the product remains the same.

• What if you change the order of the factors and multiply $(2 \times 5) \times 2$? What will the product be?

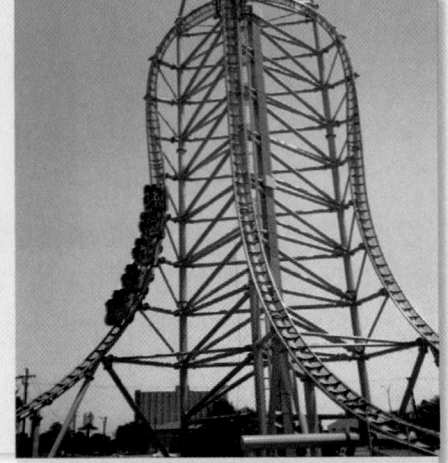

▲ Mr. Freeze Roller Coaster in Arlington, Texas, can go from 0 to 70 miles per hour in 4 seconds!

Guided Practice

1. What number sentence does this array represent? Use tiles. Write another way to group the factors.

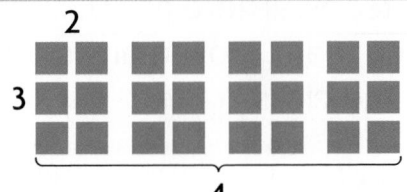

Find the product. Write another way to group the factors.

2. $(2 \times 1) \times 7$ **3.** $3 \times (5 \times 2)$ ✅**4.** $4 \times (3 \times 3)$ ✅**5.** $(3 \times 2) \times 6$

6. **TALK Math** Heidi multiplies $(3 \times 2) \times 5$, and Jesse multiplies $3 \times (2 \times 5)$. Will they get the same product? **Explain.**

Independent Practice and Problem Solving

Find the product. Write another way to group the factors.

7. $(5 \times 2) \times 2$ **8.** $8 \times (3 \times 2)$ **9.** $(1 \times 3) \times 2$ **10.** $(3 \times 2) \times 7$

11. $(6 \times 1) \times 4$ **12.** $(2 \times 2) \times 7$ **13.** $9 \times (3 \times 3)$ **14.** $5 \times (2 \times 4)$

Use parentheses. Find the product.

15. $3 \times 1 \times 9$ **16.** $1 \times 3 \times 5$ **17.** $4 \times 2 \times 6$ **18.** $2 \times 3 \times 6$

Find the missing factor.

19. $(2 \times \blacksquare) \times 7 = 28$ **20.** $6 \times (5 \times \blacksquare) = 30$ **21.** $\blacksquare \times (3 \times 2) = 54$

USE DATA For 22–23, use the graph.

22. Each car on Steel Force has 3 rows with 2 seats in each row. How many seats are on a train?

23. **Reasoning** A Kingda Ka train has 4 seats per car but the last car has only 2 seats. How many people can ride in one Kingda Ka train?

24. **WRITE Math** **Sense or Nonsense** Ken works 2 days for 4 hours each day and earns $5 an hour. Len works 5 days for 2 hours each day and earns $4 an hour. Ken says they both earn the same. Does his statement make sense? **Explain.**

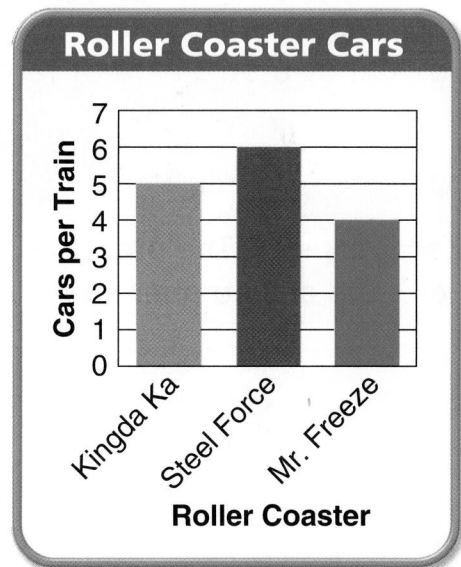

Mixed Review and Test Prep

25. Renee is 3 times as old as Jim. Jim is 5 years old. Write a number sentence to show Renee's age. (p. 218)

26. The product of two factors is 24. One factor is 4. What is the other factor?

(p. 258)

27. **Test Prep** Multiply. $3 \times 2 \times 5 = \blacksquare$

  A 11

  B 13

  C 16

  D 30

Extra Practice on page 266, Set C

Multiplication Properties

OBJECTIVE: Use the Identity, Zero, Commutative, and
Associative Properties of Multiplication to find products.

Vocabulary

Identity Property

Zero Property

Commutative Property

Associative Property

Learn

PROBLEM Mandy knit 3 scarves. She used 1 ball of
yarn for each scarf. How many balls of yarn did she
use in all?

You can use multiplication properties
to help you find products.

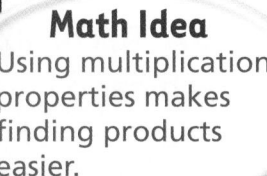

Example Multiply 3×1.

The **Identity Property** states that the
product of 1 and any number equals
that number.

$$3 \times 1 = 3 \quad \blacksquare \ \blacksquare \ \blacksquare$$

So, Mandy used 3 balls of yarn.

Math Idea
Using multiplication
properties makes
finding products
easier.

More Examples

Zero Property The product of
zero and any number equals 0.

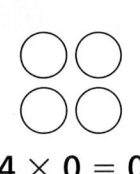

$$4 \times 0 = 0$$

Commutative Property When you multiply two
factors in any order the product is the same.

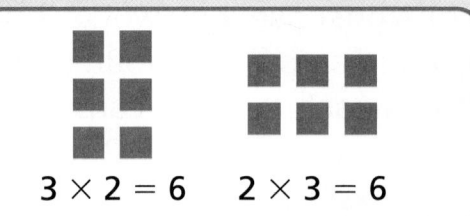

$$3 \times 2 = 6 \quad 2 \times 3 = 6$$

Associative Property
When you group factors in different ways the product is the same.

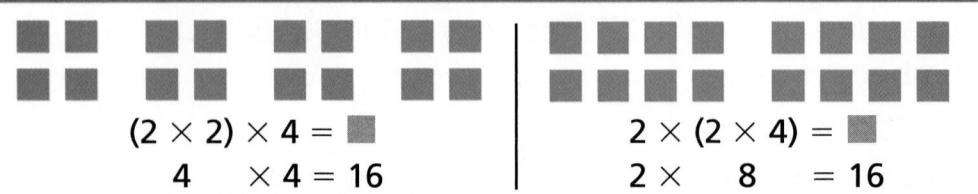

$$(2 \times 2) \times 4 = \blacksquare \qquad 2 \times (2 \times 4) = \blacksquare$$
$$4 \quad\ \times 4 = 16 \qquad\qquad 2 \times \quad 8 \quad\ = 16$$

• Which multiplication property can you use to find 85×0?

1. Which property is shown in this array?

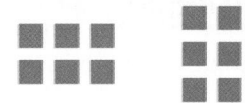

Find the product. Tell which property you could use.

2. 5×1 **3.** 8×4 ✓**4.** 0×9 ✓**5.** $3 \times (3 \times 7)$

6. [**TALK Math**] Which costs more—5 balls of yarn for $3 each or 3 balls of yarn for $5 each? **Explain** your answer.

Independent Practice and Problem Solving

Find the product. Tell which property you could use.

7. 0×7 **8.** 8×1 **9.** 9×2 **10.** 7×2

11. $(5 \times 2) \times 7$ **12.** 9×3 **13.** 6×0 **14.** $(3 \times 3) \times 8$

Algebra Find the missing factor.

15. $5 \times \blacksquare = 6 \times 5$ **16.** $3 \times (2 \times 4) = (\blacksquare \times 2) \times 4$ **17.** $\blacksquare \times 3 = 3 \times 9$

USE DATA For 18–19 and 21, use the pictograph.

18. Amy bought 3 balls of yarn. How much did she spend?

19. Katie bought one pack of needles, a knitting book, and 2 balls of yarn. What was the total cost?

Knitting Supplies		
Needles	🧶 🧶 🧶	
Book	🧶 🧶 🧶 🧶 🧶	
Yarn	🧶 🧶	
Key: Each 🧶 = $1.		

20. **Reasoning** What is the missing number? **Explain** your answer.

$$\blacksquare \times 0 = 0$$

21. [**WRITE Math**] ▸ Sandy bought 8 balls of yarn. **Explain** how you can use the Commutative Property to find the cost.

Mixed Review and Test Prep

22. Kevin has 3 packs of baseball cards. Each pack has 9 cards. How many baseball cards does he have? (p. 238)

23. A school's auditorium has 950 seats. There were 843 students who attended an assembly. How many seats were empty? (p. 84)

24. **Test Prep** Which is an example of the Identity Property?

A $5 \times 3 = 3 \times 5$

B $0 \times 6 = 0$

C $7 \times 1 = 7$

D $(8 \times 1) \times 4 = 8 \times (1 \times 4)$

Extra Practice on page 266, Set D

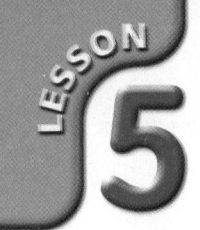

Problem Solving Workshop
Skill: Multistep Problems

OBJECTIVE: Solve problems by using the skill multistep problems.

Use the Skill

PROBLEM The circus is in town! Tickets cost $7 for adults and $5 for children. Mr. Kimble buys 5 tickets for his family. He buys 2 adult tickets and 3 child tickets. How much does it cost for the Kimble family to go to the circus?

Use the tickets to help you solve the problem.

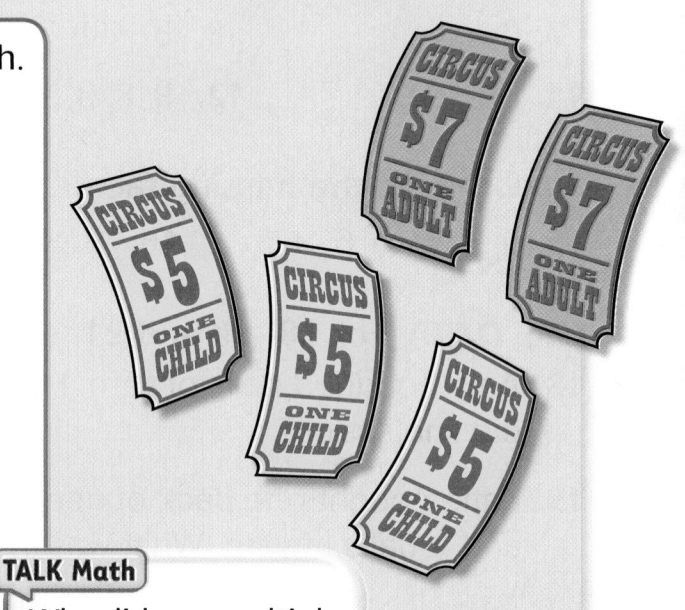

- Mr. Kimble buys 2 adult tickets that cost $7 each. Multiply to find the cost for the adult tickets.

$$2 \times \$7 = \$14$$

- He buys 3 child tickets that cost $5 each. Multiply to find the cost for the child tickets.

$$3 \times \$5 = \$15$$

- Add to find the total cost.

$14	+	$15	=	$29
↑		↑		↑
Cost of adult tickets		Cost of child tickets		Total cost

TALK Math
Why did you multiply in this problem?

So, the total cost is $29.

Think and Discuss

Reading Skill Visualize **Draw a picture to show the problem. Solve the problem. Explain the steps you used.**

a. There are 5 clowns with balloons. Four of the clowns have 8 balloons each. One clown has only 6 balloons. How many balloons in all do the clowns have?

b. Sam has a $20 bill. He buys 4 sheets of circus stickers. Each sheet costs $3. How much money does Sam have left?

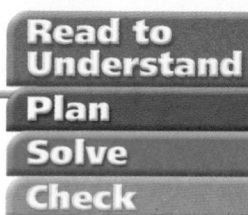
1. Maddie and Sasha buy 2 boxes of popcorn and 4 balloons. The popcorn costs $5 a box. Each balloon costs $2. How much do Maddie and Sasha spend in all?

   Visualize the problem.

   Which operation combines equal amounts?

   Which operation can you use to find the total cost?

   Solve the problem.

✓ 2. **What if** each balloon costs $3? How much do Maddie and Sasha spend in all for balloons and popcorn?

✓ 3. The animal trainers give 6 horses apples as rewards. The trainers reward each with 3 apples. If the trainers started with 30 apples, how many apples are left?

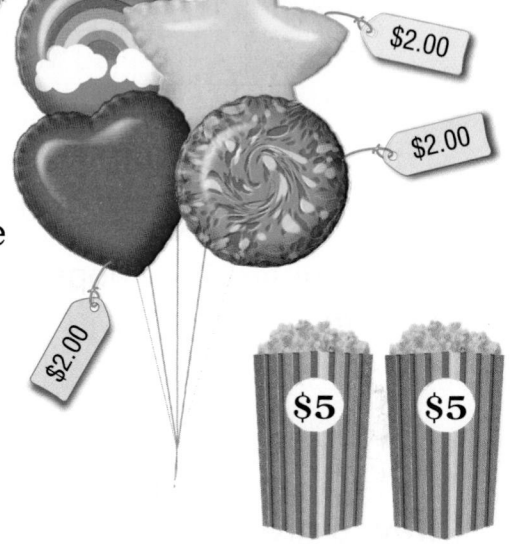

Mixed Applications

4. Mr. Brown's four children all have pets. Three of his children have 2 hamsters each. One child has 3 goldfish. How many pets in all do Mr. Brown's children have?

5. Jodi is saving money to buy a new bike. The bike costs $127. She has saved $75. How much more does Jodi need to buy the bike?

USE DATA For 6–8 use the menu.

6. Mr. Werner ordered turkey on rye, a salad, and juice. He paid with a $20 bill. How much change did he get back?

7. The baseball team went to David's Deli after the game. Each player ordered a hamburger and milk. There are 9 players on the team. What was the total cost of the team's order?

8. WRITE Math ▶ Mrs. Quigley bought twice as many apples as bananas. She bought 4 bananas. How much did Mrs. Quigley spend on fruit? **Explain** how you got your answer.

David's Deli

Hot Roast Beef Sandwich . .	$8
Turkey on Rye	$6
Hamburger	$4
Macaroni and Cheese	$5
Salad	$2
Fruit per piece	$1
banana, apple, orange	
Juice	$3
Milk	$2

Extra Practice

Set A Write a rule for each table. Then copy and complete the table. (pp. 256–257)

1.

Cars	1	2	3	4	5
Wheels	4	8	■	■	■

2.

Weeks	3	4	5	6	7
Days	21	28	■	■	■

Set B Find the missing factor. (pp. 258–259)

1. $3 \times \blacksquare = 21$ **2.** $b \times 5 = 35$ **3.** $a \times 3 = 30$ **4.** $5 \times \blacksquare = 25$

5. There are 18 scoops of ice cream. If there are 6 bowls, how many scoops will go in each bowl?

6. There are 32 children and 8 slides on the playground. If the students are divided evenly into groups, how many can play on each slide?

Set C Find the product. Write another way to group the factors. (pp. 260–261)

1. $(2 \times 2) \times 4 = \blacksquare$ **2.** $(1 \times 3) \times 3 = \blacksquare$ **3.** $(5 \times 2) \times 3 = \blacksquare$ **4.** $8 \times (1 \times 2) = \blacksquare$

Use parentheses. Find the product.

5. $3 \times 3 \times 1 = \blacksquare$ **6.** $2 \times 4 \times 5 = \blacksquare$ **7.** $1 \times 7 \times 4 = \blacksquare$ **8.** $2 \times 2 \times 2 = \blacksquare$

9. For Arbor Day, Nora wants to plant 3 groups of 3 trees in 4 different parks. How many trees in all will she plant?

10. Nora's friend Dion plants 2 groups of 4 trees in 7 different parks. How many trees will he plant?

Find the missing factor.

11. $(1 \times \blacksquare) \times 2 = 8$ **12.** $4 \times (2 \times \blacksquare) = 16$ **13.** $\blacksquare \times (5 \times 2) = 80$

Set D Find the product. Tell which property you used. (pp. 262–263)

1. $(2 \times 1) \times 5$ **2.** $(3 \times 3) \times 5$ **3.** 8×3 **4.** 6×1

Find the missing factor.

5. $2 \times \blacksquare = 10 \times 1$ **6.** $(2 \times 2) \times \blacksquare = 6 \times 2$ **7.** $0 \times 7 = 7 \times \blacksquare$

8. $7 \times \blacksquare = 5 \times 7$ **9.** $(4 \times \blacksquare) \times 3 = 4 \times 6$ **10.** $\blacksquare \times 9 = 9$

CD ROM **Technology**
Use Harcourt Mega Math, Ice Station Exploration, *Arctic Algebra,* Level C.

TECHNOLOGY ★ CONNECTION

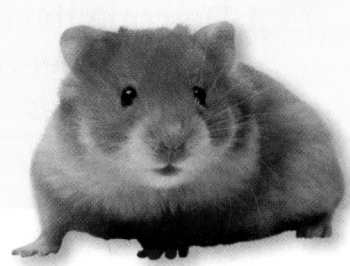

Calculator: Multiplication Facts

Use a Calculator for Multiplication

Eleanor is making a food mix for her hamsters. She wants equal numbers of sunflower seeds, corn kernels, peanuts, round pellets, and flat pellets. If she uses 12 of each item, how many items will be in the mix?

Write a number sentence for the word problem.
$5 \times 12 = $ ■

Use a calculator to solve.

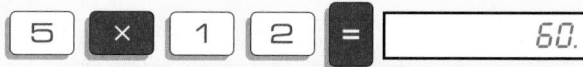

```
[5] [×] [1] [2] [=]     60.
```

So, Eleanor will use 60 items in the food mix.

Try It

Use a calculator to multiply.

1. $11 \times 7 = $ ■   **2.** $8 \times 4 = $ ■   **3.** $12 \times 6 = $ ■   **4.** $7 \times 4 = $ ■

5. $8 \times 5 = $ ■   **6.** $12 \times 8 = $ ■   **7.** $10 \times 11 = $ ■   **8.** $9 \times 4 = $ ■

9. $3 \times 12 = $ ■   **10.** $7 \times 3 = $ ■   **11.** $6 \times 9 = $ ■   **12.** $2 \times 11 = $ ■

13. Ferris went bird watching 7 times in May. On each trip, he wrote about 9 new bird sightings in his journal. How many new birds did he see in May?

14. Carter collects old coins. He has 6 dimes, 6 quarters, and 6 half dollars. How many coins does he have in all? Write a number sentence, and then use a calculator to multiply.

15. Maria has 12 pennies, 12 nickels, 12 dimes, and 12 silver dollars in her wallet. How many coins does she have in all? Write a number sentence, and then use a calculator to multiply.

16. **Explore More** Yvette has invited 8 friends to her party. She plans to give each friend 4 party favors. She has 35 favors in all. How many will she have left over? **Explain.**

Little Pieces

Jake's baby sister tore his multiplication table into little pieces. Where in the table does this piece belong?

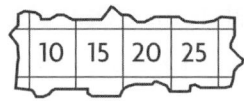

Example

Step 1 Find the pattern.
Five is added to each number.

Step 2 Describe the pattern using multiplication.
The numbers 10, 15, 20, and 25 are all multiples of 5.

Step 3 Look at the first and last numbers.

$10 = \mathbf{2} \times 5$

$25 = \mathbf{5} \times 5$

So, this piece is from row 5 between columns 2 and 5.

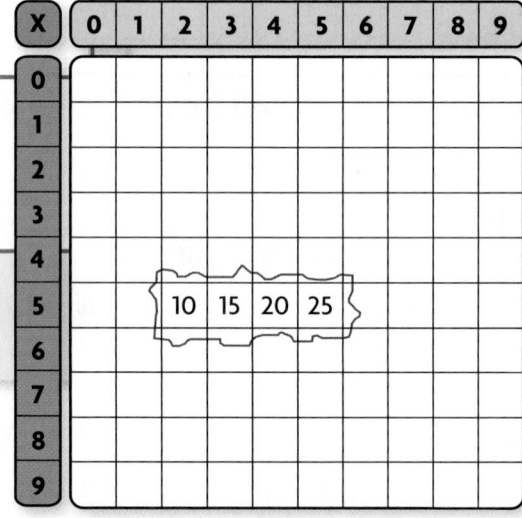

Try It

Below are parts of a multiplication table. In which row or column is each part found?

1.
6
12
18
24

2.
21
28
35
42

3.
18
27
36
45

4. 18 | 21 | 24 | 27

5. 2 | 4 | 6 | 8

6. ▐WRITE Math ▶ In what part of the table is this piece found? **Explain.**

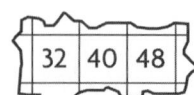

Chapter 10 Review/Test

Check Vocabulary and Concepts

Choose the best term from the box.

1. A __?__ is a letter or symbol that stands for an unknown number. (p. 258)

2. The __?__ states that the product of 1 and any number equals that number. (p. 262)

3. The __?__ states that when the grouping of factors is changed, the product remains the same. (p. 260)

Check Skills

Find the missing factor. (pp. 258–259)

4. $7 \times a = 28$ **5.** $\blacksquare \times 5 = 45$ **6.** $6 \times \blacksquare = 30$ **7.** $d \times 3 = 9$

8. $8 \times \blacksquare = 64$ **9.** $\blacksquare \times 4 = 20$ **10.** $g \times 10 = 40$ **11.** $9 \times b = 27$

Find the product. (pp. 260–261)

12. $3 \times (5 \times 2) = \blacksquare$ **13.** $(2 \times 4) \times 8 = \blacksquare$ **14.** $(1 \times 9) \times 5 = \blacksquare$

15. $6 \times (3 \times 3) = \blacksquare$ **16.** $7 \times (2 \times 2) = \blacksquare$ **17.** $(4 \times 2) \times 3 = \blacksquare$

Find the missing factor. (pp. 262–263)

18. $3 \times (3 \times \blacksquare) = 27$ **19.** $\blacksquare \times (4 \times 2) = 40$ **20.** $5 \times (\blacksquare \times 10) = 50$

21. $3 \times 4 = \blacksquare \times 2$ **22.** $\blacksquare \times 5 = 3 \times 10$ **23.** $6 \times \blacksquare = 9 \times 2$

Check Problem Solving

Solve. (pp. 264–265)

24. Michelle bought 2 necklaces for $3 each and 3 rings for $4 each. How much money did Michelle spend in all?

25. **WRITE Math** Rick put 5 baseball cards on each of 2 pages, and 8 cards on each of 4 pages. How many baseball cards did he put in the book altogether? **Explain** how you solved the problem.

Unit Review/Test
Chapters 8–10

Multiple Choice

1. ■ ■ ■ ■ ■ ■ ■
■ ■ ■ ■ ■ ■ ■

How many squares in all? (p. 206)

A 14

B 16

C 18

D 20

2. Clarence put 0 books on each of 3 shelves. How many books in all did he put on the shelves? (p. 214)

A 3

B 2

C 1

D 0

3. Which addition sentence represents 3×9? (p. 204)

A $9 + 9 = $ ■

B $9 + 9 + 9 = $ ■

C $9 + 9 + 9 + 9 = $ ■

D $9 + 9 + 9 + 9 + 9 = $ ■

4. Tina has $4. Use the table to find how many quarters this is. (p. 256)

Dollars	1	2	3	4
Quarters	4	8	12	■

A 14   **C** 18

B 16   **D** 20

5. Which number sentence is represented by the counters? (p. 240)

A $35 \div 6$

B 9×3

C 7×5

D $7 + 5$

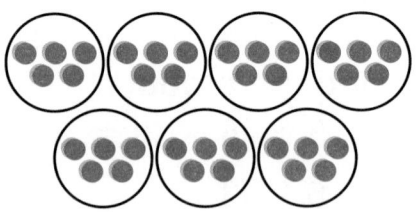

6. The graph shows the number of fish in each tank.

Fish Tanks	
Tank 1	⋐⋑ ⋐⋑ ⋐⋑ ⋐⋑ ⋐⋑ ⋐⋑
Tank 2	⋐⋑ ⋐⋑ ⋐⋑ ⋐⋑ ⋐⋑ ⋐⋑ ⋐⋑
Tank 3	⋐⋑ ⋐⋑ ⋐⋑ ⋐⋑ ⋐⋑
Key: Each ⋐⋑ = 8 fish.	

How many fish in all are there in Tank 2? (p. 236)

A 48

B 52

C 56

D 64

GO ONLINE Technology Use *Online Assessment.*

7. How many members belong to the Science Club? (p. 244)

Club Members	
Drama	○ ○ ○ ○
Chorus	○ ○ ○ ○ ○ ○
Science	○ ○ ○ ○ ○
Key: Each ○ = 12 members.	

A 48   **C** 60

B 56   **D** 64

8. Aunt Ester baked 3 dozen cookies. Which number sentence shows how many cookies Aunt Ester baked? (p. 244)

A $3 \times 12 = 36$ **C** $3 \times 4 = 12$

B $3 + 12 = 15$ **D** Not here

9. How many students voted for blue as their favorite color? (p. 218)

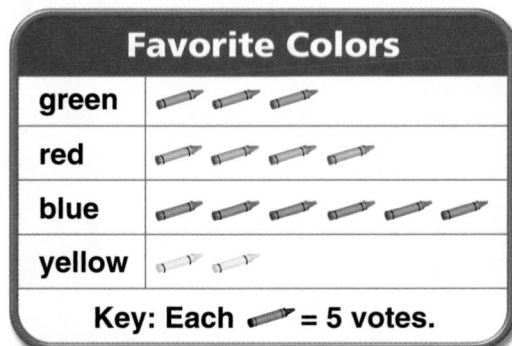

Favorite Colors

green	
red	
blue	
yellow	
Key: Each = 5 votes.	

A 10   **C** 20

B 15   **D** 30

Short Response

10. Multiply $9 \times (3 \times 4)$. (p. 260)

11. Mr. Ruiz bought 5 sandwiches for $5 each and 7 desserts for $3 each. How much did he spend in all? (p. 264)

Extended Response

12. **Explain** how you can find the number of days in 10 weeks. (p. 240)

June						
Sun	Mon	Tue	Wed	Thu	Fri	Sat
1	2	3	4	5	6	7
8	9	10	11	12	13	14
15	16	17	18	19	20	21
22	23	24	25	26	27	28
29	30	31				

13. **Explain** all of the different ways that you can show the product 16 using arrays of counters. (p. 236)

14. **Explain** how to find the total number of flowers you will need to fill 8 vases if each vase holds 7 flowers. (p. 240)

THE WORLD ALMANAC FOR KIDS

All About Animals

Strange Animal Parts

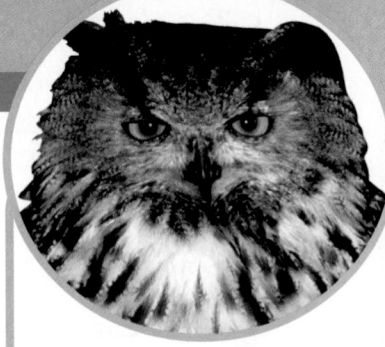

Many animals have 2 eyes, 2 ears, and 1 mouth—just as humans do. Some animals, however, have unusual numbers of eyes, ears, and even hearts.

A slug has 4 noses.

An earthworm has 5 hearts.

An owl has 3 eyelids on each eye.

An ostrich has 2 toes on each foot.

A bee has 5 eyes.

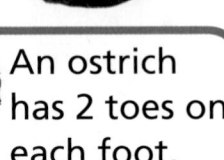

A praying mantis has 1 ear.

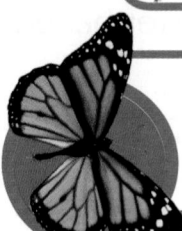

A butterfly has 4 wings.

A giraffe has 0 vocal cords.

FACT·ACTIVITY

Use facts above to answer these questions.
Write a number sentence for each problem.

❶ There are 9 slugs. How many noses are there?

❷ How many wings are there in a swarm of 7 butterflies?

❸ How many ears do 4 praying mantises have?

❹ There are 6 earthworms. How many hearts in all?

❺ How many vocal cords do 8 giraffes have?

❻ How many eyelids do 7 owls have?

❼ **Pose a Problem** Look at Problems 1 and 2. Write a similar problem about any of the animals shown on this page.

Strange Names

Have you ever seen a *gaggle* fly overhead or a *school* in the water? *Gaggle* and *school* are strange names for groups of animals: a *gaggle* of geese, a *school* of fish. You might shiver from fright if you saw some sharks in the water, but did you know that a group of sharks is called a *shiver*?

ALMANAC Fact

Names of Some Animal Groups

army of frogs
band of gorillas
pack of wolves
kindle of kittens
pod of whales
pride of lions
troop of monkeys

FACT·ACTIVITY

Write multiplication sentences to solve.

1. A kitten has 4 paws. How many paws are in a kindle of 8 kittens?

2. A goose has 2 wings. How many wings are in a gaggle of 9 geese?

3. Design an animal that has an unusual number of parts. Think about the number of legs, tails, wings, eyes, noses, ears, or other parts that your animal has.

   ► Draw your animal, and label its parts.

   ► Copy the chart. You may include more parts. Remember, you may choose 0 for some parts.

   ► Complete the table to show how many parts there are in 1, 2, and 3 animals.

   ► Suppose there are 10 of your animal in a group. Make up a name for the group.

Part	Number of parts		
	In 1 animal	In 2 animals	In 3 animals
eyes			
legs			
tails			
wings			
noses			
ears			

My Animal

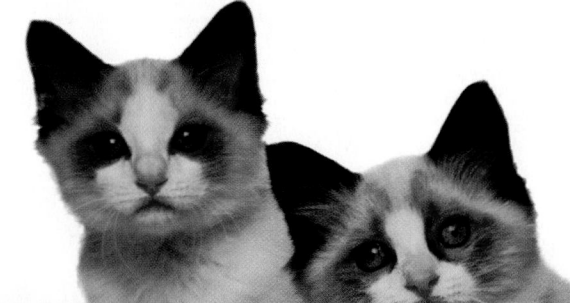

4 Division Concepts and Facts

Math on Location

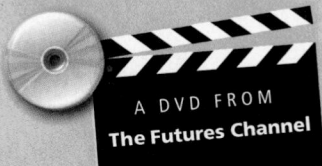

with
Chapter Projects

1

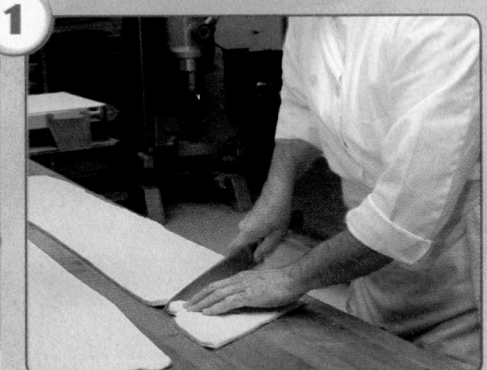

Each batch of dough is cut into the same number of triangular shapes.

2

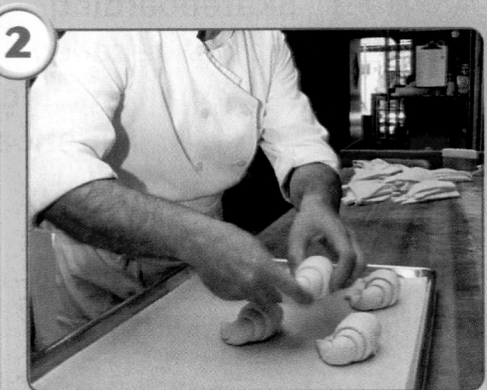

The croissants are rolled and placed in rows on baking trays to form an array.

3

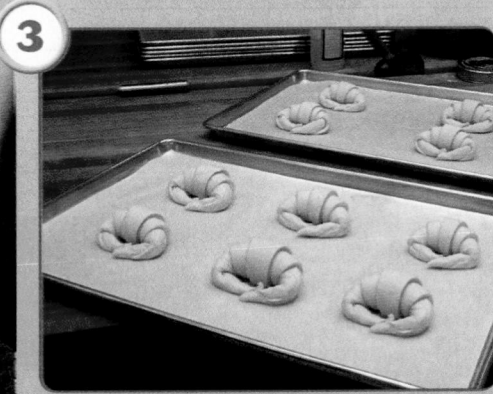

The baker divides 18 croissants onto 3 trays to put in the oven to bake.

VOCABULARY POWER

TALK Math

What math do you see in the **Math on Location** photographs? How can you use division to tell how many croissants are in each row?

READ Math

REVIEW VOCABULARY You learned the words below when you learned about division in grade 2. How do these words relate to **Math on Location**?

division the operation that separates objects into equal groups

equal shares equal groups of items

WRITE Math ▶

Copy and complete a Semantic Map like the one below. Use Math on Location and what you know about division to fill in the blanks.

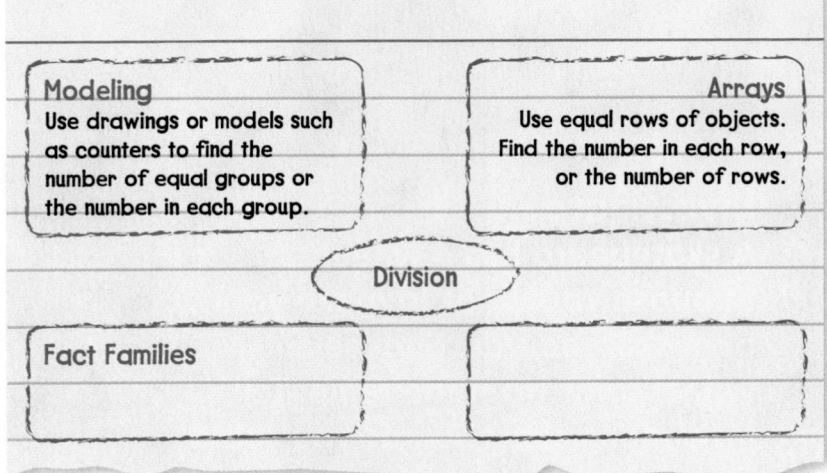

Modeling
Use drawings or models such as counters to find the number of equal groups or the number in each group.

Arrays
Use equal rows of objects. Find the number in each row, or the number of rows.

Division

Fact Families

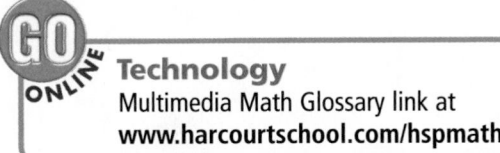

Technology
Multimedia Math Glossary link at
www.harcourtschool.com/hspmath

11 Understand Division

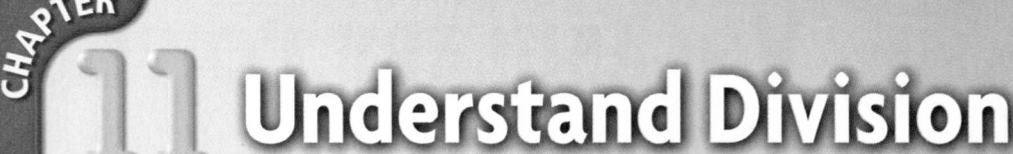

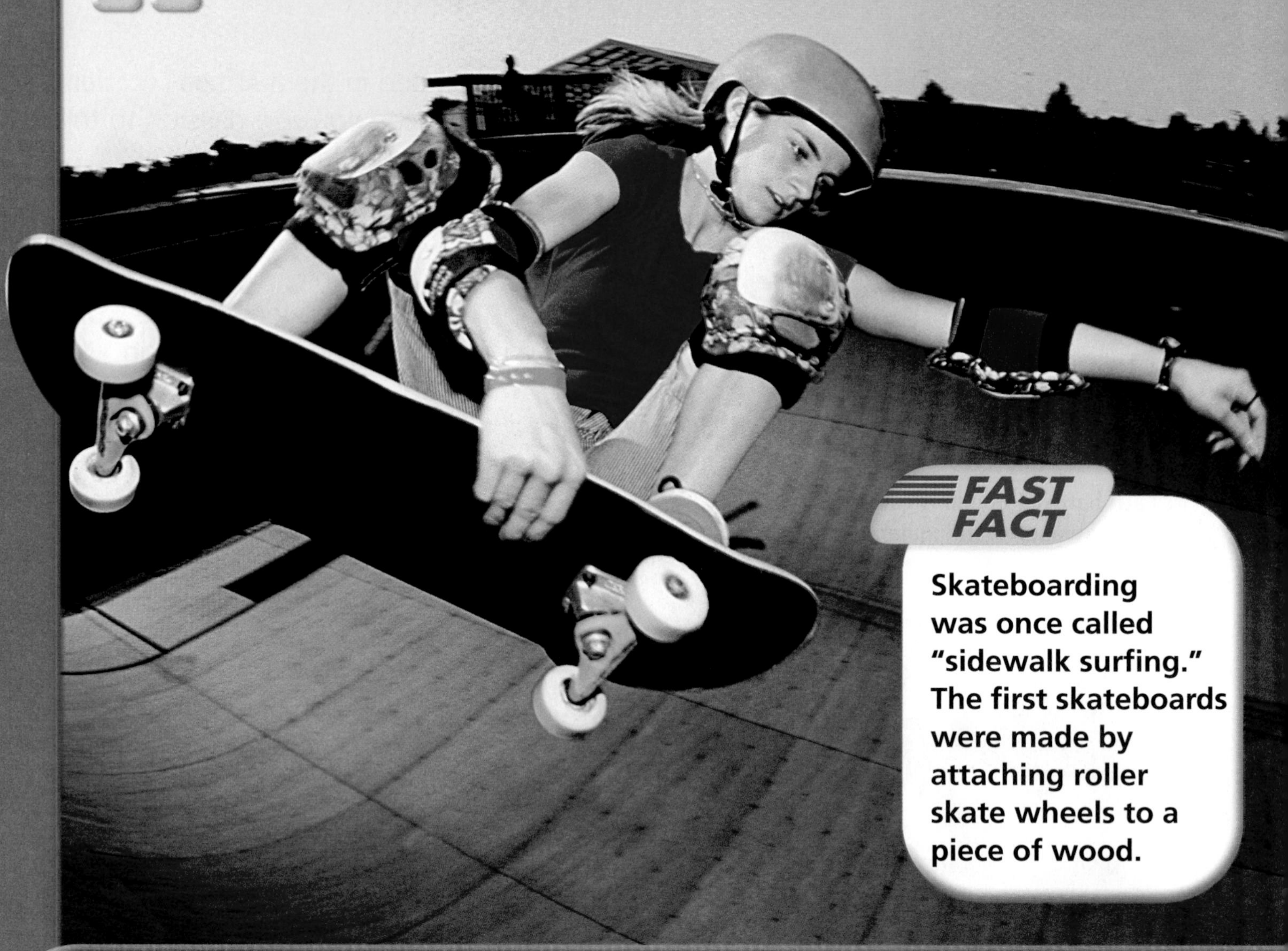

≡**FAST FACT**

Skateboarding was once called "sidewalk surfing." The first skateboards were made by attaching roller skate wheels to a piece of wood.

Investigate

A skateboard has 4 wheels. Suppose you want to make your own skateboards. Choose a wheel color from the table. Tell how many skateboards you could make using only that wheel color.

Wheels in Skate Shop	
Color	**Number of Wheels**
Red	24
White	40
Black	12
Green	36
Blue	28

GO ONLINE

Technology
Student pages are available in the Student eBook.

Check your understanding of important skills needed for success in Chapter 11.

▶ **Counting Equal Groups**

Complete.

1.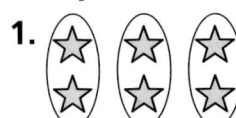

■ groups
■ in each group

2.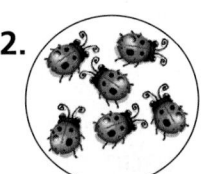

■ groups
■ in each group

3.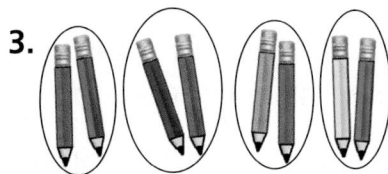

■ groups
■ in each group

4.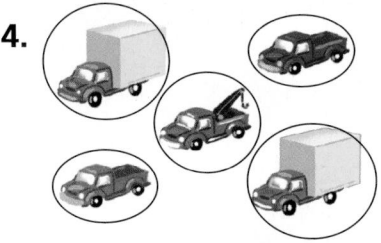

■ groups
■ in each group

5.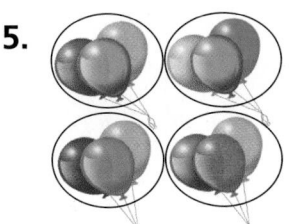

■ groups
■ in each group

6.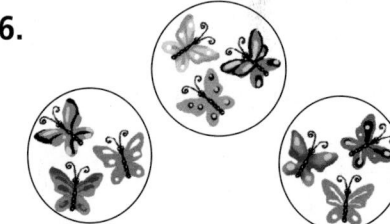

■ groups
■ in each group

▶ **Multiplication Facts Through 10**

Find the product.

7. $5 \times 3 = $ ■   **8.** ■ $= 6 \times 4$ **9.** $2 \times 8 = $ ■   **10.** $5 \times 6 = $ ■

11. $9 \times 3 = $ ■   **12.** $4 \times 2 = $ ■   **13.** ■ $= 7 \times 7$ **14.** $8 \times 5 = $ ■

VOCABULARY POWER

CHAPTER VOCABULARY

array
divide
dividend
divisor
fact family
quotient

WARM-UP WORDS

divide To separate into equal groups; the opposite operation of multiplication

fact family A set of related addition and subtraction, or multiplication and division, number sentences

LESSON 1

Model Division

OBJECTIVE: Use models to explore the meaning of division.

Quick Review

1. 2×3
2. 5×7
3. 4×5
4. 3×6
5. 7×4

Vocabulary

divide

Learn

PROBLEM William has 12 shells. He wants to put the same number of shells in each of 3 boxes. How many shells will be in each box?

When you multiply, you put equal groups together. When you **divide**, you separate into equal groups.

◀ A pink conch shell can be as long as 1 foot!

HANDS ON Activity

Materials ■ counters

Example 1 You can divide to find the number in each group.

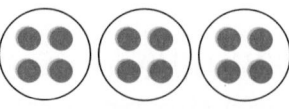

Step 1	Step 2	Step 3
Use 12 counters.	Show 3 groups. Place 1 counter in each group.	Continue until all 12 counters are used.

So, there will be 4 shells in each box.

William has decided that he wants to put his 12 shells in groups of 3. How many boxes will he need for his shells?

Example 2 You can divide to find the number of equal groups.

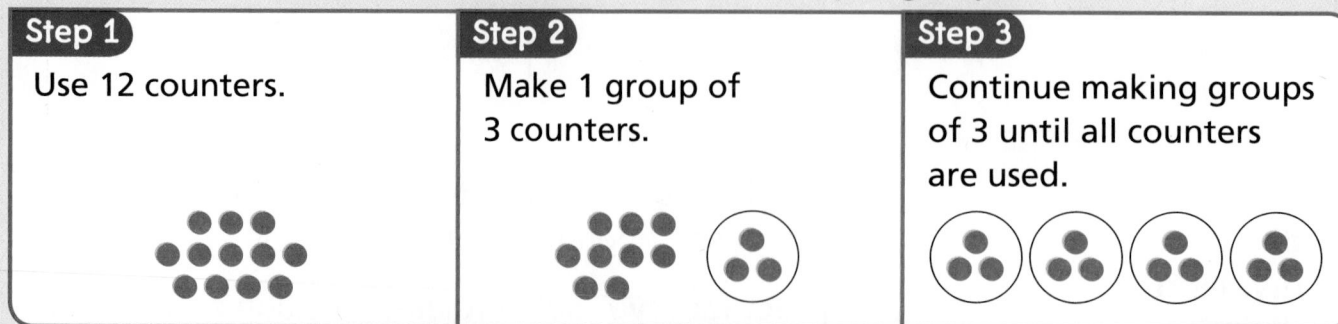

Step 1	Step 2	Step 3
Use 12 counters.	Make 1 group of 3 counters.	Continue making groups of 3 until all counters are used.

So, William will need 4 boxes for his shells.

1. Jon has 8 counters. He wants to put 2 in each group. Draw a picture to show the groups.

Copy and complete the table. Use counters to help.

	Counters	Number of Equal Groups	Number in Each Group
2.	10	2	■
3.	24	■	4

4. **TALK Math** **Explain** two ways you could divide 18 counters into equal groups. Draw a picture to show each way.

Independent Practice and Problem Solving

Copy and complete the table. Use counters to help.

	Counters	Number of Equal Groups	Number in Each Group
5.	14	7	■
6.	21	■	3
7.	20	5	■

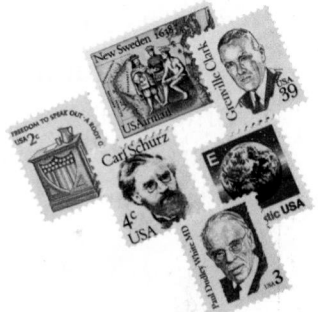

8. Jackie has 28 stamps. She put an equal number of her stamps on each of 4 pages. How many stamps are on each page?

9. Joe has 25 stamps and Martha has 15 stamps. They put their stamps in the same book. Each page has 5 stamps. How many pages did they fill?

10. **WRITE Math** Elijah has 16 stamps. He put 4 stamps each on 4 pages. **Explain** another way to arrange his stamps with an equal number of stamps on each page.

Mixed Review and Test Prep

11. What is the missing factor? (p. 258)

$$6 \times ■ = 48$$

12. Lee has 3,943 coins. What is the value of the 9 in 3,943? (p. 10)

13. **Test Prep** Zana has 9 rocks. She put 3 rocks in each bag. How many bags did she use in all?

A 27   **C** 6

B 12   **D** 3

Relate Division and Subtraction

OBJECTIVE: Relate division to repeated subtraction.

Learn

PROBLEM Sarah and Mandy take a total of 12 newspapers to school for the recycling program. Each girl takes the same number. How many newspapers does each girl take?

Divide. $12 \div 2 = \blacksquare$

ONE WAY Count back on a number line.

Start at 12.
Count back by 2s until you reach 0.
Count the number of times you subtract 2.

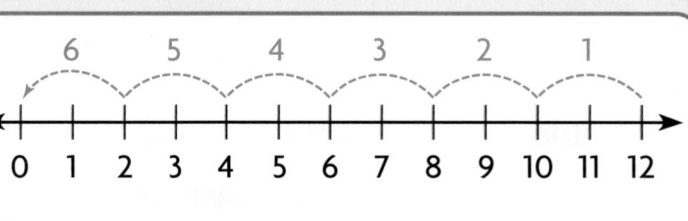

You subtract 2 six times, so each girl takes 6 newspapers.

ANOTHER WAY Use repeated subtraction.

Start with 12. Subtract 2 until you reach 0.
Count the number of times you subtract 2.

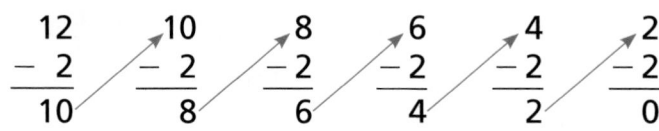

$\begin{array}{r}12\\-2\\\hline10\end{array}$	$\begin{array}{r}10\\-2\\\hline8\end{array}$	$\begin{array}{r}8\\-2\\\hline6\end{array}$	$\begin{array}{r}6\\-2\\\hline4\end{array}$	$\begin{array}{r}4\\-2\\\hline2\end{array}$	$\begin{array}{r}2\\-2\\\hline0\end{array}$

Number of times you subtract 2: 1 2 3 4 5 6

ERROR ALERT

Be sure to keep subtracting until you reach 0 as the answer.

Since you subtract 2 from 12 six times, there are 6 groups of 2 in 12.

Write: $12 \div 2 = 6$, or $2\overline{)12}^{\,6}$ **Read:** Twelve divided by two equals six.

Guided Practice

1. Use the number line to complete the number sentence. $12 \div 4 = \blacksquare$

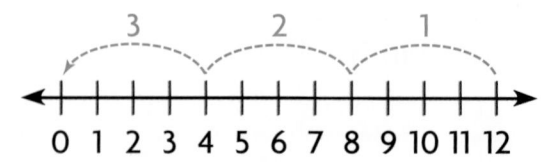

Use a number line or repeated subtraction to solve.

2. $16 \div 4 = $ ■　　**3.** $10 \div 5 = $ ■　　✓**4.** $3\overline{)21}$　　✓**5.** $8\overline{)32}$

6. [**TALK Math**] Explain how you can use subtraction to find $18 \div 3$.

Independent Practice and Problem Solving

Write a division sentence for each.

7.

```
      ⌒         ⌒         ⌒
  ←——+——+——+——+——+——+——+——+——+——→
     0  1  2  3  4  5  6  7  8  9
```

8.
$$
\begin{array}{ccc}
24 & 16 & 8 \\
-\ 8 & -\ 8 & -\ 8 \\
\hline
16 & 8 & 0
\end{array}
$$

Use a number line or repeated subtraction to solve.

9. $14 \div 7 = $ ■　　**10.** $35 \div 5 = $ ■　　**11.** $27 \div 9 = $ ■　　**12.** $20 \div 4 = $ ■

13. $4\overline{)28}$　　　**14.** $6\overline{)24}$　　　**15.** $2\overline{)16}$　　　**16.** $9\overline{)36}$

USE DATA For 17–19, use the graph.

17. Carl put his box tops in 6 equal piles. How many box tops were in each pile?

18. Reasoning Miguel brought an equal number of box tops to school each day for 5 days. Jane also brought an equal number of box tops each day for 5 days. How many box tops did they bring in altogether in 1 day? **Explain.**

19. [**WRITE Math**] **What's the Question?** Genna put an equal number of box tops in each of 3 bins. The answer is 5.

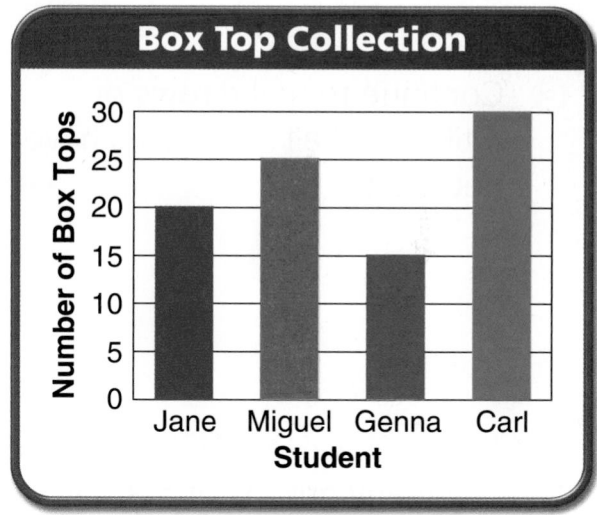

Box Top Collection

Mixed Review and Test Prep

20. Kara has 3 packs of paintbrushes. Each pack has 8 brushes. How many brushes does Kara have? (p. 236)

21. A figure has 4 vertices and 4 equal sides. What is the figure? (Grade 2)

22. Test Prep Mya collected 7 shells each day. She collected 21 shells in all. For how many days did Mya collect shells?

A 2 days　　　**C** 4 days

B 3 days　　　**D** 6 days

(**Extra Practice** on page 294, Set B)

3 Model with Arrays

OBJECTIVE: Model division by using arrays.

Investigate

Materials ■ square tiles

You can use arrays to model division and find equal groups.

A Count out 30 tiles. Make an array to find how many groups of 5 are in 30.

B Make a row of 5 tiles.

C Continue to make rows of 5 tiles until all of the tiles have been used.

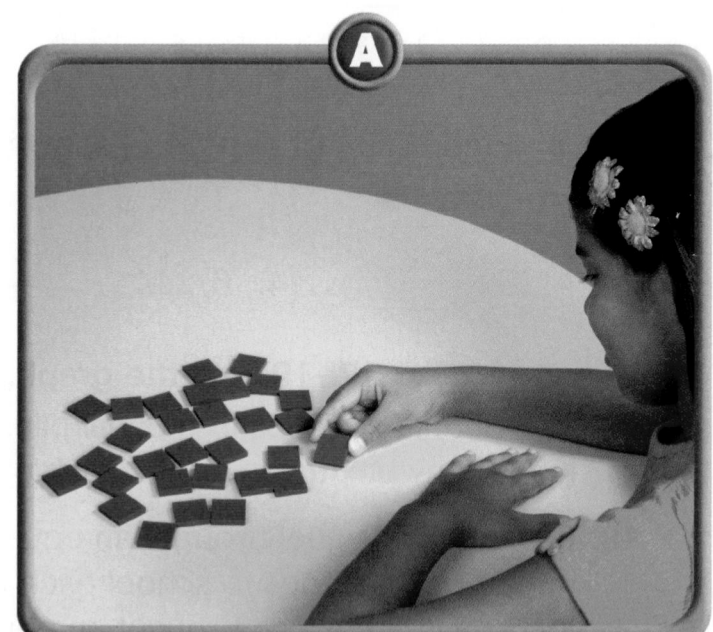

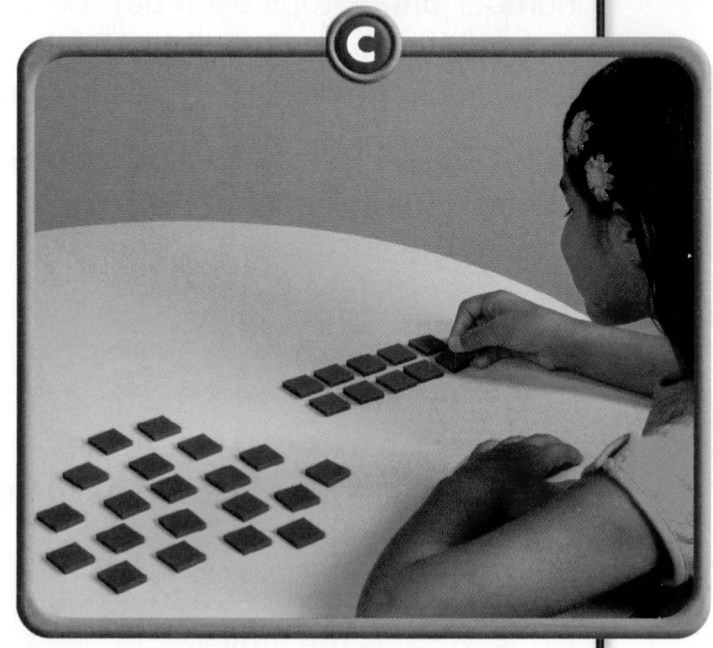

Draw Conclusions

1. How many groups of 5 are in 30?

2. Explain how you used the tiles to find the number of groups of 5 in 30.

3. **Application** Tell how to use an array to find how many groups of 6 are in 30.

Connect

You can write a division sentence to show what you did.

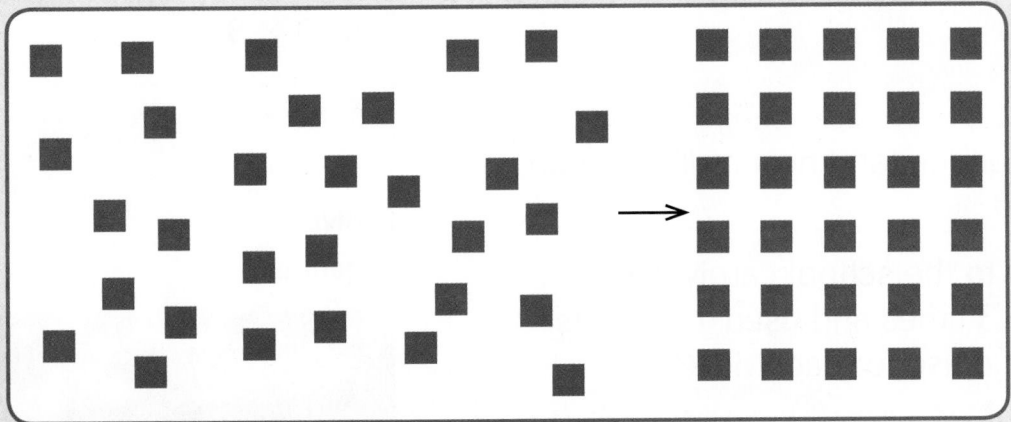

There are 6 rows of 5 tiles in 30.

So, 30 ÷ 5 = 6.

TALK Math

How does making an array help you divide?

- Use 24 tiles. Make an array by placing 6 tiles in each row. Use all of the tiles.

- How many groups of 6 are in 24?

- What division sentence can you write about your array?

Practice

Use square tiles to make an array. Solve.

1. How many groups of 3 are in 18?

2. How many groups of 7 are in 28?

3. How many groups of 9 are in 27?

4. How many groups of 8 are in 24?

5. How many groups of 5 are in 20?

6. How many groups of 6 are in 36?

Make an array. Write a division sentence for each one.

7. 16 tiles in 4 groups

8. 21 tiles in 3 groups

9. 24 tiles in 8 groups

10. 14 tiles in 2 groups

11. 25 tiles in 5 groups

12. 12 tiles in 4 groups

13. Reggie made an array with 32 tiles. He placed 8 tiles in each row. How many rows did he make?

14. **WRITE Math** Explain how to use an array to find 18 ÷ 6.

ALGEBRA
Multiplication and Division

OBJECTIVE: Relate multiplication and division.

Vocabulary

dividend

divisor

quotient

Learn

You can use arrays to understand how multiplication and division are related.

PROBLEM Mark went to the school carnival. He went on the same ride 3 times and used 12 tickets. How many tickets did he use for each ride?

Example Divide. $12 \div 3 = \blacksquare$

Show an array with 12 counters in 3 equal rows. Find how many are in each row.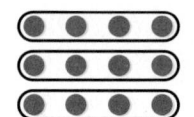

Since $3 \times 4 = 12$, then $12 \div 3 = 4$.

$$12 \div 3 = 4$$
$$\uparrow \qquad \uparrow \qquad \uparrow$$
dividend   divisor   quotient

$$\text{divisor} \longrightarrow 3\overline{)12} \longleftarrow \text{quotient (4)}$$
$$\uparrow$$
$$\text{dividend}$$

So, Mark used 4 tickets for each ride.

Math Idea
Multiplication and division are opposite, or inverse, operations.

More Examples

A 2 rows of $4 = 8$
   $8 \div 2 = 4$

B 3 rows of $6 = 18$
   $18 \div 3 = 6$

Guided Practice

1. What division sentence does the array represent?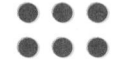

Copy and complete.

2.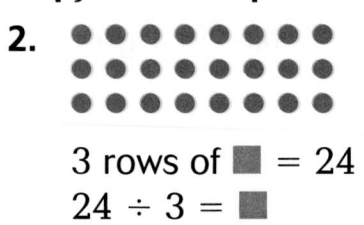

   3 rows of $\blacksquare = 24$
   $24 \div 3 = \blacksquare$

3.

   2 rows of $\blacksquare = 12$
   $12 \div 2 = \blacksquare$

4.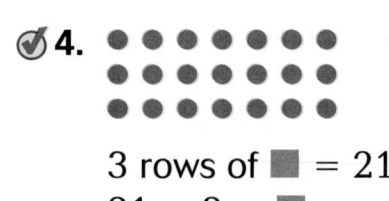

   3 rows of $\blacksquare = 21$
   $21 \div 3 = \blacksquare$

5. **TALK Math** Explain how you can use an array to find $25 \div 5$.

Copy and complete.

6. ● ● ● ●
   ● ● ● ●
   ● ● ● ●
   ● ● ● ●

   4 rows of ■ = 16
   16 ÷ 4 = ■

7. ● ● ● ● ●
   ● ● ● ● ●
   ● ● ● ● ●

   3 rows of ■ = 15
   15 ÷ 3 = ■

8. ● ● ● ● ● ● ●
   ● ● ● ● ● ● ●
   ● ● ● ● ● ● ●
   ● ● ● ● ● ● ●

   4 rows of ■ = 28
   28 ÷ 4 = ■

Complete each number sentence. Draw an array to help.

9. $6 \times$ ■ $= 24$ $24 \div 6 =$ ■
10. $5 \times$ ■ $= 35$ $35 \div 5 =$ ■
11. $8 \times$ ■ $= 32$ $32 \div 8 =$ ■
12. $9 \times$ ■ $= 18$ $18 \div 9 =$ ■

Complete.

13. $3 \times 3 = 27 \div$ ■
14. $16 \div 2 =$ ■ $\times 2$
15. ■ $\times 1 = 25 \div 5$

USE DATA For 16–19, use the signs.

16. Jill has 15 tickets. How many times can she ride the Scooter?

17. Philip bought 8 tickets for the Wildcat ride 3 different times. How many times did he ride the Wildcat?

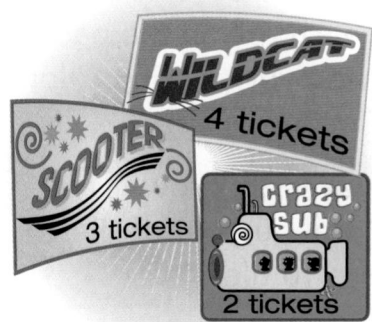

18. **Reasoning** Joe rode the Scooter 3 times, and Kate rode the Crazy Sub 4 times. Who used more tickets? **Explain.**

19. **WRITE Math** ► **Sense or Nonsense** Scott has 13 tickets. He says that to ride the Scooter 4 times, he needs more tickets. Is he correct? **Explain.**

Mixed Review and Test Prep

20. What is a possible outcome of using a spinner with 2 red and 2 blue sections? (p. 180)

21. A ticket to the zoo costs $4. How much do 9 tickets cost? (p. 238)

22. **Test Prep** At a game booth, there are 32 prizes in 4 equal rows. How many prizes are in each row?

   A 36   **C** 8

   B 28   **D** 6

Technology
Use Harcourt Mega Math, Ice Station Exploration, *Arctic Algebra*, Level E.

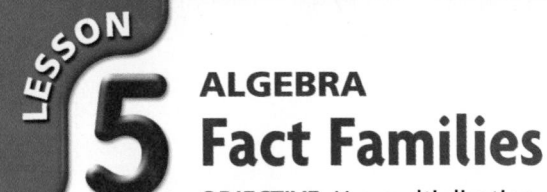

ALGEBRA
Fact Families

OBJECTIVE: Use multiplication and division fact families.

Learn

A **fact family** is a set of related multiplication and division number sentences.

PROBLEM Kim's pack of modeling clay has 2 rows of 5 colors. What is the fact family for 2, 5, and 10?

Activity

Materials ■ square tiles

Step 1

Count the number of rows and the number of colors in each row in the pack of clay.
There are 2 rows with 5 colors in each row.

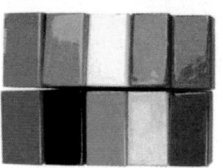

Step 2

Make an array with 2 rows of 5.
Count the total number of tiles.
There are 10 tiles.

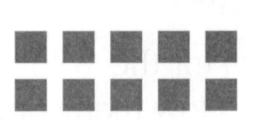

Step 3

Write two multiplication sentences and two division sentences that describe the array.

2 × 5 = 10	10 ÷ 5 = 2
5 × 2 = 10	10 ÷ 2 = 5

So, these related number sentences make the fact family for 2, 5, and 10.

Example

The array shows the fact family for 4, 4, and 16.
4 × 4 = 16   16 ÷ 4 = 4
Since both factors are the same, there are only two number sentences in this fact family.

• Write another set of numbers that has only two number sentences in the fact family for it.

Quick Review

Complete.

1. ■ × 5 = 15
2. 3 × ■ = 15
3. 15 ÷ 5 = ■
4. 5 × ■ = 25
5. 25 ÷ 5 = ■

Vocabulary

fact family

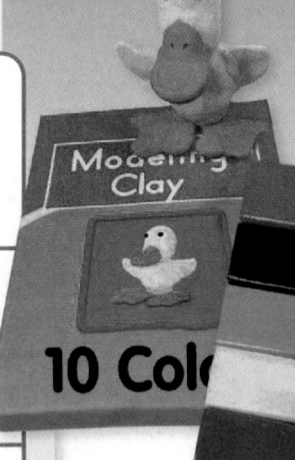

Modeling Clay

10 Col

Remember

$$4 \quad \times \quad 4 \quad = \quad 16$$
$$\uparrow \qquad \uparrow \qquad \uparrow$$
factor   factor   product

Use a Multiplication Table to Divide

Since division is the opposite of multiplication, you can use a multiplication table to find a quotient or a missing divisor.

Examples

Ⓐ Find the quotient.

$20 \div 4 = \blacksquare$

Think: $4 \times \blacksquare = 20$

Find the row for the factor 4. Look to the right to find the product 20. Look up to find the missing factor, 5.

$4 \times 5 = 20$

So, $20 \div 4 = 5$.

Ⓑ Find the missing divisor.

$18 \div \blacksquare = 3$

Think: $\blacksquare \times 3 = 18$

Find the factor 3 in the top row. Look down to find the product 18. Look left to find the missing factor, 6.

$6 \times 3 = 18$

So, $18 \div 6 = 3$.

×	0	1	2	3	4	5	6	7
0	0	0	0	0	0	0	0	0
1	0	1	2	3	4	5	6	7
2	0	2	4	6	8	10	12	14
3	0	3	6	9	12	15	18	21
4	0	4	8	12	16	20	24	28
5	0	5	10	15	20	25	30	35
6	0	6	12	18	24	30	36	42
7	0	7	14	21	28	35	42	49

Guided Practice

1. Complete the fact family for this array.

$3 \times 8 = 24$ $24 \div 3 = 8$

Write the fact family for each array.

2.

3.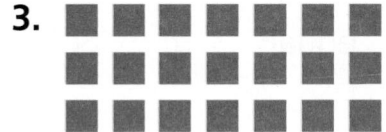

⊘4.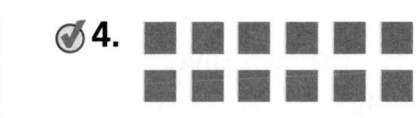

Write the fact family for each set of numbers.

5. 6, 7, 42

6. 2, 3, 6

7. 4, 8, 32

⊘8. 5, 5, 25

9. **TALK Math** Explain how you can use a multiplication table to find the missing divisor in $36 \div \blacksquare = 6$.

Write the fact family for each array.

10.

11.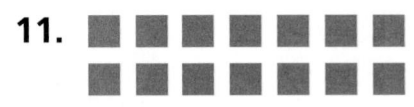

12.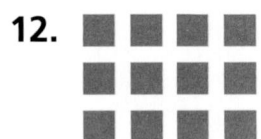

Write the fact family for each set of numbers.

13. 2, 4, 8   **14.** 4, 6, 24   **15.** 3, 3, 9   **16.** 5, 8, 40

Copy and complete each fact family.

17. $4 \times 7 = 28$
$7 \times \blacksquare = 28$
$28 \div \blacksquare = 4$
$28 \div 4 = \blacksquare$

18. $5 \times 6 = \blacksquare$
$6 \times \blacksquare = 30$
$30 \div 6 = \blacksquare$
$30 \div 5 = \blacksquare$

19. $4 \times \blacksquare = 36$
$9 \times \blacksquare = 36$
$36 \div 4 = \blacksquare$
$36 \div 9 = \blacksquare$

20. $\blacksquare \times 9 = 27$
$\blacksquare \times 3 = 27$
$\blacksquare \div 9 = 3$
$27 \div \blacksquare = 9$

Find the quotient or the missing divisor.

21. $20 \div \blacksquare = 5$ **22.** $45 \div 5 = \blacksquare$ **23.** $15 \div 3 = \blacksquare$ **24.** $36 \div \blacksquare = 6$

USE DATA For 25–26, use the table.

25. Mrs. Lee divides one package of clay and one package of glitter dough equally among 4 students. How many more glitter dough sections does each student have than clay sections?

26. ⬛WRITE Math ▸ **What's the Error?** Ty has a package of glitter dough. He says he can give 9 friends 5 equal sections. Describe his error.

Clay Supplies	
Item	**Number in Package**
Clay	12 sections
Clay tool set	11 tools
Glitter dough	36 sections

27. Pose a Problem Write a division word problem using $35 \div 5 = 7$. Solve your problem.

Mixed Review and Test Prep

28. What is the missing factor? (p. 258)

$$6 \times \blacksquare = 42$$

29. Jake has 57 pens and 49 pencils. How many more pens than pencils does Jake have? (p. 80)

30. Test Prep Which number sentence is not included in the same fact family as $9 \times 4 = 36$?

A $4 \times 9 = 36$ **C** $36 \div 4 = 9$

B $36 \div 6 = 6$ **D** $36 \div 9 = 4$

Justify an Answer

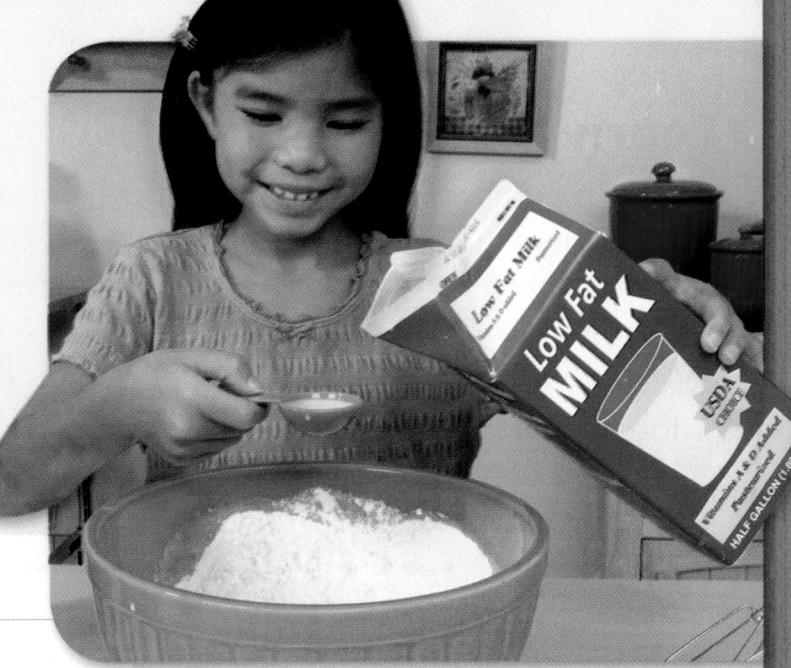

Tamara is making a recipe that calls for 15 teaspoons of milk. She doesn't have a teaspoon measure. She knows that 3 teaspoons equal 1 tablespoon. So, she uses 5 tablespoons of milk. How do you know whether she used the right amount of milk?

Jamal wrote this paragraph to justify Tamara's solution to her problem.

I know that a teaspoon is a smaller unit than a tablespoon. First, I use a teaspoon to fill a tablespoon of water. It takes 3 teaspoons of water to fill 1 tablespoon.

Then, I divide 15 by 3 to find out if 5 tablespoons is the correct amount of milk. I use the fact family for 5, 3, and 15 to check my answer.

$$5 \times 3 = 15 \qquad 3 \times 5 = 15$$
$$15 \div 5 = 3 \qquad 15 \div 3 = 5$$

I know that Tamara used the right amount of milk because $3 \times 5 = 15$.

Tips

To justify an answer:
- First, check that the information given in the problem is correct.
- Next, check whether the answer given is correct.
- Last, write a sentence to justify the answer, or explain why it is correct.

Problem Solving Write a paragraph to justify each answer.

1. Tara says, "I can share 12 crackers evenly with 3 friends."

2. Darin says, "I can share 6 sports cards evenly with 2 friends."

Problem Solving Workshop
Strategy: Write a Number Sentence

OBJECTIVE: Solve problems by using the strategy *write a number sentence.*

Learn the Strategy

Writing a number sentence can help you understand how the numbers in a problem are related.

You can write an addition number sentence.

Joe has 14 crayons. He gets 12 more crayons. Now he has 26 crayons.

$$14 + 12 = 26$$

↑	↑	↑
crayons Joe has	crayons Joe got	crayons Joe has now

You can write a subtraction number sentence.

Kat has 23 shells. She gives 10 shells to her brother. She has 13 shells left.

$$23 - 10 = 13$$

↑	↑	↑
shells Kat has	shells Kat gave away	shells Kat has left

You can write a multiplication number sentence.

April has 4 boxes of books. Each box has 8 books in it. There are 32 books in all.

$$4 \times 8 = 32$$

↑	↑	↑
boxes April has	books in each box	books in all

You can write a division number sentence.

Scott has 40 stickers. There are 8 stickers on each sheet. He has 5 sheets of stickers.

$$40 \div 8 = 5$$

↑	↑	↑
stickers Scott has	stickers on each sheet	sheets of stickers

TALK Math

What question could you ask about each number sentence above?

Use the Strategy

PROBLEM In Michelle's third grade class, the desks are in 4 equal rows. There are 24 desks in all. How many desks are in each row?

Read to Understand

 Reading Skill
- Identify the details in the problem.
- What information is given?

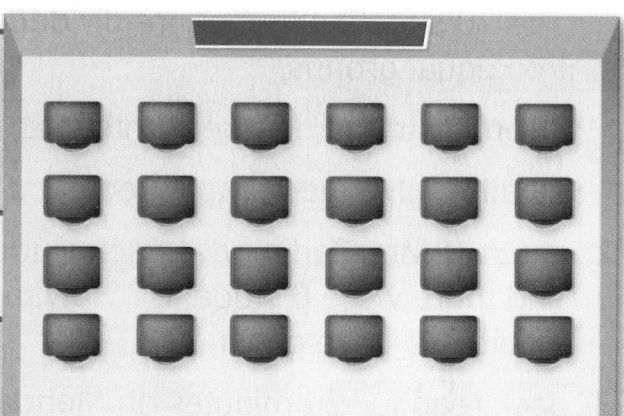

Plan

- **What strategy can you use to solve the problem?**

  You can *write a number sentence* to help you solve the problem.

Solve

- **How can you use the strategy to solve the problem?**

  The desks are divided into equal rows.
  This helps you know to use division.
  Write a division sentence. Find the quotient.

$$24 \div 4 = 6$$

number | number | number of desks
of desks | of rows | in each row

So, there are 6 desks in each row.

Check

- **How can you check your answer?**
- **What other strategy could you use to solve the problem?**

 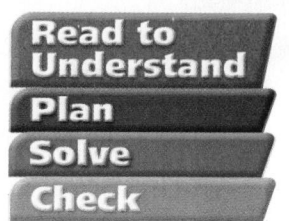

1. Mrs. Partin gave each student at Jenna's table 5 sheets of paper. She gave out 20 sheets of paper in all. How many students are at Jenna's table?

   First, decide what operation to use. The 20 sheets of paper are divided into equal groups.

   Then, write the number sentence.

   Finally, solve the number sentence.

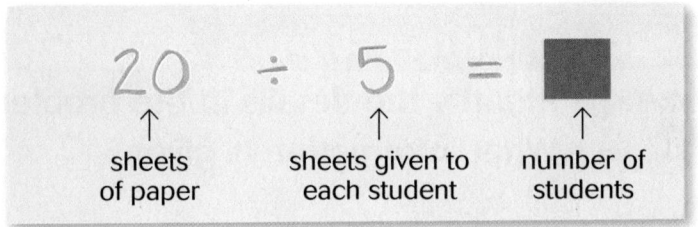

20	÷	5	=	■
↑		↑		↑
sheets of paper		sheets given to each student		number of students

2. **What if** Mrs. Partin gave each student 6 sheets of paper and there were 6 students? How many sheets of paper would she have given out?

3. Jack read for 20 minutes on Monday. He read 15 minutes more on Tuesday than on Monday. For how many minutes did Jack read on Tuesday?

Problem Solving Strategy Practice

For 4–5, choose the number sentence from the box. Solve.

> 4 × 10 = ■   10 + 4 = ■   27 − 3 = ■   27 ÷ 3 = ■

4. One eraser costs 3¢. Lizzie spends 27¢ on erasers. How many erasers does Lizzie have?

5. Jeremy has 10 pencils. His teacher gives him 4 more pencils. How many pencils does Jeremy have now?

Write a number sentence to solve.

6. Elizabeth reads for 360 minutes each week. She has read for 215 minutes so far this week. How many more minutes will Elizabeth read this week?

7. Mrs. Vargas has 30 students in her math class. There are 5 tables in her classroom. The same number of students sit at each table. How many students sit at each table?

8. **WRITE Math** At a store, there are 6 notebooks on each of 7 shelves. There are 5 notebooks on the 8th shelf. How many notebooks are on the shelves altogether? **Explain.**

Mixed Strategy Practice

USE DATA For 9–12, use the table.

9. Mr. Clark buys a pack of pencils for his students. He gives the same number of pencils to 8 students. How many pencils does each student get?

10. **Pose a Problem** Look back at Problem 9. Write a similar problem by changing the number of students.

11. Min bought 3 packs of erasers. She kept 8 erasers and divided the rest of them equally among 4 of her classmates. How many erasers did Min give to each of her 4 classmates? **Explain** your answer.

12. There are blue pencils and red pencils in a pencil pack. There are twice as many red pencils as blue pencils. How many red pencils are there?

13. **Open-Ended** ≡**FAST FACT** The first box of Crayola® crayons was sold in 1903 for 5¢. List two different groups of coins you could use to pay for 7 boxes of crayons.

CHALLENGE YOURSELF

The school store has these items for sale:

pencil	25¢	ruler	75¢
marker	45¢	sharpener	15¢
pen	65¢	notebook	95¢

14. Amy spends $1.25 on 3 different items. What items does she buy?

15. Frank buys 4 different items. He pays with three $1 bills, and receives two dimes in change. What items does Frank buy?

Choose a
STRATEGY

Draw a Diagram or Picture
Make a Model or Act It Out
Make an Organized List
Find a Pattern
Make a Table or Graph
Predict and Test
Work Backward
Solve a Simpler Problem
Write an Equation
Use Logical Reasoning

Items Sold

Items	Number
Crayons	8 per pack
Erasers	12 per pack
Pencils	24 per pack
Stickers	100 per roll

Extra Practice

Set A Copy and complete the table. Use counters to help. (pp. 278–279)

	Counters	Number of Equal Groups	Number in Each Group
1.	30	5	■
2.	28	■	7
3.	24	8	■
4.	12	4	■

Set B Write a division sentence for each. (pp. 280–281)

1.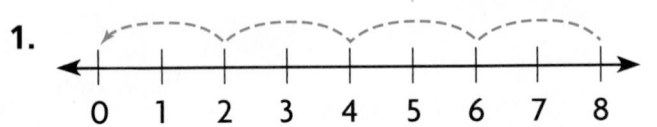

2.
$$\begin{array}{r} 12 \\ -\ 4 \\ \hline 8 \end{array} \qquad \begin{array}{r} 8 \\ -4 \\ \hline 4 \end{array} \qquad \begin{array}{r} 4 \\ -4 \\ \hline 0 \end{array}$$

Use a number line or repeated subtraction to solve.

3. $15 \div 3 = $ ■

4. $4\overline{)16}$

5. $12 \div 2 = $ ■

6. $5\overline{)20}$

7. If Desiree can make 6 necklaces in 36 minutes, how long does it take her to make each necklace?

8. Desiree can make 5 bracelets in 25 minutes. How long does it take to make each bracelet?

Set C Copy and complete. (pp. 284–285)

1. ● ● ● ●
● ● ● ●
● ● ● ●

3 rows of ■ = 12
$12 \div 3 = $ ■

2. ● ● ● ● ● ● ● ● ●
● ● ● ● ● ● ● ● ●

2 rows of ■ = 18
$18 \div 2 = $ ■

3. ● ● ● ● ● ●
● ● ● ● ● ●
● ● ● ● ● ●

3 rows of ■ = 18
$18 \div 3 = $ ■

Complete each number sentence. Draw an array to help.

4. $5 \times$ ■ $= 30$ $30 \div 5 = $ ■

5. $8 \times$ ■ $= 40$ $40 \div 8 = $ ■

Set D Write the fact family for each set of numbers. (pp. 286–289)

1. 3, 5, 15   **2.** 4, 7, 28   **3.** 2, 8, 16   **4.** 3, 7, 21

All in the Family

Draw Your Cards

2–4 players

Are They a Family?

- Gameboard
- Counter for each player
- Number cards
- Paper and pencils

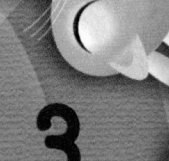

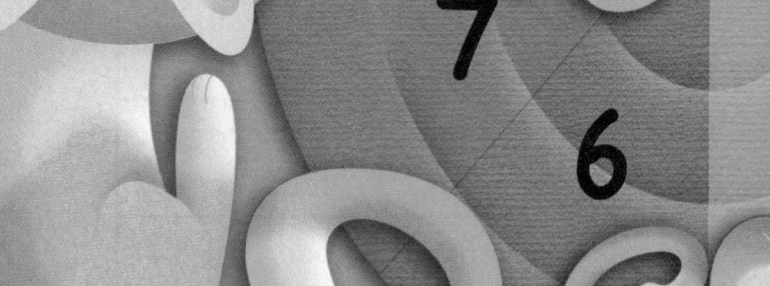

```
6
  2
12
```

```
2 × 6 = 12
6 × 2 = 12
12 ÷ 2 = 6
12 ÷ 6 = 2
```

9 2

8   3

7   4

6 5

Coming Home

- Players place their counter on any number on the gameboard.

- Each player is dealt 5 number cards. The remaining cards are placed facedown in a pile.

- Player 1 tries to make a fact family, either by using 3 of his or her cards or by using 2 cards and the number on which the counter lies. The player writes down the fact family, and the other players check it.

- Player 1 then discards the cards used, draws cards to replace them, and advances 1 space, clockwise, on the gameboard. It is then the next player's turn.

- If a player cannot make a fact family, he or she exchanges some or all of his or her cards with the cards from the pile, and his or her turn is over.

- The first player to return to his or her start space is the winner.

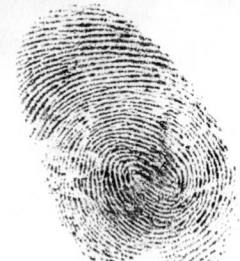

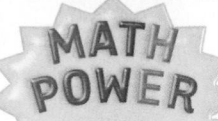

SPY GAMES

Use the Decoder to help Sam Sleuth solve the secret message. Match the symbol to the correct factor pair and letter in the Decoder.

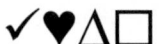 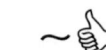 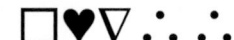  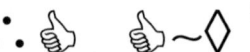

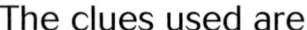

The clues used are:

	DECODER		
4, 5	**A**	4, 6	**G**
6, 7	**R**	2, 6	**W**
3, 8	**M**	2, 9	**N**
4, 9	**E**	3, 6	**I**
5, 7	**X**	3, 7	**S**
3, 9	**H**	2, 4	**T**

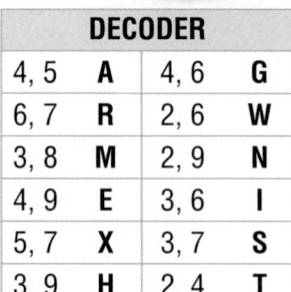

♥ Their product is odd. Their difference is 6.	△ Their product ends in zero and is less than 30.
▽ Their product equals 21 + 21.	□ Their product is a single digit.
∴ Their product is equal to 18 + 18.	∅ Their product is 18. The larger factor is odd.
✹ Their product is between 20 and 25. Their sum is 11.	👍 Their product is equal to 30 − 9.
~ Their product is 18. The smaller factor is odd.	✓ Their product is equal to 16 − 4.
≈ Their product is 24. Both factors are even.	◊ Their product is odd. Their difference is 2.

Example

A Read the clue for the first symbol. Their product is equal to 16 − 4.

B Find the factor pair that satisfies the clue.   2, 6

C Write the letter for the symbol.   W

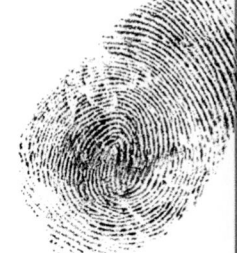

Try It

1. Solve the rest of the secret message.

2. **WRITE Math** ▸ Sam Sleuth sent this message: ∴ ~ ≈ ♥ □ ∴ ∴ ∅. What does it mean? **Explain** how you know.

Chapter 11 Review/Test

Check Vocabulary and Concepts

Choose the best term from the box.

VOCABULARY
divide
divisor
fact family
quotient

1. You _?_ when you separate into equal groups. (p. 278)

2. A _?_ is a set of related multiplication and division number sentences. (p. 286)

3. How many times a divisor goes into a dividend is the _?_. (p. 284)

Check Skills

Copy and complete the table. Use counters to help. (pp. 278–279)

	Counters	Number of Equal Groups	Number in Each Group
4.	21	3	■
5.	16	■	4
6.	36	9	■

Use a number line or repeated subtraction to solve. (pp. 280–281)

7. $28 \div 7 = $ ■   **8.** $2\overline{)10}$ **9.** $8 \div 4 = $ ■   **10.** $7\overline{)35}$

Complete each number sentence. Draw an array to help. (pp. 284–285)

11. $5 \times $ ■ $= 15$ $15 \div 5 = $ ■   **12.** $3 \times $ ■ $= 24$ $24 \div 3 = $ ■

13. $6 \times $ ■ $= 42$ $42 \div 6 = $ ■   **14.** $6 \times $ ■ $= 30$ $30 \div 6 = $ ■

Write the fact family for each set of numbers. (pp. 286–289)

15. 3, 9, 27   **16.** 3, 4, 12   **17.** 6, 6, 36   **18.** 3, 6, 18

Check Problem Solving

Solve. (pp. 290–293)

19. At a party, Dolly the Clown gave each child 4 balloons. She gave out 36 balloons in all. How many children were at the party?

20. **WRITE Math** ▶ There were 5 students at a table. Each student drew 5 pictures. How many pictures did the students draw in all? **Explain** how you know.

Standardized Test Prep
Chapters 1–11

Number and Operations

1. There were 1,457 people at a play. What is the value of the 4 in 1,457?
   (p. 10)

   A 4

   B 40

   C 400

   D 4,000

Test Tip Eliminate choices.

> See item 2. Since you need to subtract to find the answer, you can eliminate the answer choices that are greater than 312. Then subtract carefully, remembering to regroup.

2. Katie and Juan are reading books. Katie has read 312 pages in her book. Juan has read 259 pages in his book. How many more pages has Katie read than Juan? (p. 84)

   A 571

   B 153

   C 147

   D 53

3. **WRITE Math** ▶ **Explain** how to use the number line to find 12 ÷ 3.
   (p. 304)

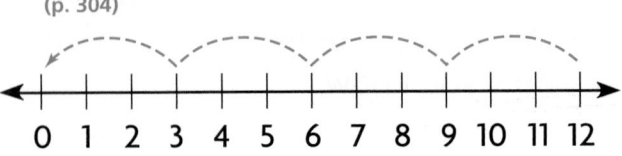

Algebraic Reasoning

4. Spiders have 8 legs. Marcy wants to find out how many legs are on 5 spiders. Use the table below to find the answer. (p. 256)

Spiders	1	2	3	4	5
Legs	8	16	24	32	■

   A 36

   B 38

   C 40

   D 42

5. Which number sentence is in the same fact family as $4 \times 8 = 32$?
   (p. 286)

   A $32 \div 8 = 4$

   B $8 \div 4 = 2$

   C $4 \times 4 = 16$

   D $4 \times 2 = 8$

6. **WRITE Math** ▶ Sammy wrote the pattern below. (Grade 2)

   $$4, 7, 10, 13, 16$$

   Write a rule for Sammy's pattern. **Explain** how to find the next number in his pattern.

Geometry

7. Which figure is a cone? (Grade 2)

A

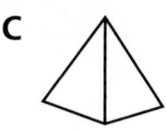

B

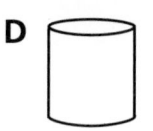

C

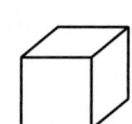

D

8. How many faces does a cube have?
(Grade 2)

A 3 **C** 6

B 4 **D** 8

9. **WRITE Math** Are the two figures
below congruent? **Explain** how you
know. (Grade 2)

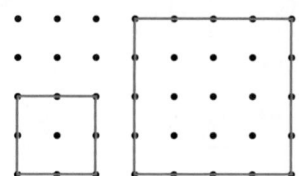

Data Analysis and Probability

10. How many more points does Drake
need to score to equal the number of
points Tio scored? (p. 154)

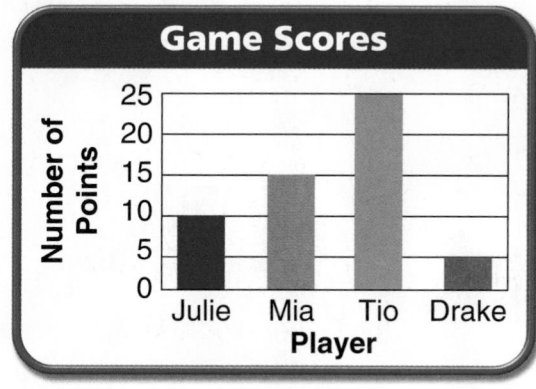

A 10 **C** 20

B 15 **D** 30

11. On which color is the spinner most
likely to stop? (p. 178)

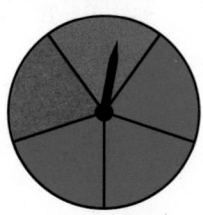

A Blue **C** Red

B Green **D** Yellow

12. **WRITE Math** Tina made a pictograph
to show how many books she owns.

Each 📕 = 10 books.

How many books does 📕📕📕📕📕
stand for? **Explain.** (p. 148)

12 Division Facts

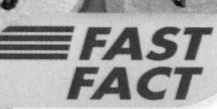

FAST FACT

A candy company in Bethlehem, Pennsylvania, makes Marshmallow Peeps®. It takes about 6 minutes to make one Marshmallow Peep®.

Investigate

Choose a candy from the table that you could share equally among the people who live at your house. Tell how you would find how many pieces to give to each person and if you would have any pieces left over.

Candy	Number of Pieces Per Package
Peeps®	10
Gobstoppers®	32
Mike and Ike®	36
M&M's®	54
Skittles®	63

GO ONLINE

Technology
Student pages are available in the Student eBook.

Check your understanding of important skills needed for success in Chapter 12.

▶ **Arrays**
Complete.

1. ▪▪▪▪▪▪
▪▪▪▪▪▪
▪▪▪▪▪▪

3 rows of ▪ = 18
18 ÷ 3 = ▪

2. ▪▪▪▪
▪▪▪▪

2 rows of ▪ = 8
8 ÷ 2 = ▪

3. ▪▪▪
▪▪▪
▪▪▪
▪▪▪

4 rows of ▪ = 12
12 ÷ 4 = ▪

4. ▪▪▪▪▪
▪▪▪▪▪
▪▪▪▪
▪▪▪▪

4 rows of ▪ = 20
20 ÷ 4 = ▪

5. ▪▪▪▪▪▪▪
▪▪▪▪▪▪▪

2 rows of ▪ = 14
14 ÷ 2 = ▪

6. ▪▪▪▪
▪▪▪▪
▪▪▪▪

3 rows of ▪ = 12
12 ÷ 3 = ▪

▶ **Multiplication and Division Fact Families**
Write the fact family.

7. 4, 6, 24   **8.** 3, 5, 15   **9.** 3, 8, 24   **10.** 5, 5, 25

11. 4, 9, 36   **12.** 8, 9, 72   **13.** 2, 4, 8   **14.** 6, 7, 42

VOCABULARY POWER

CHAPTER VOCABULARY

divide
dividend
divisor
fact family
quotient

WARM-UP WORDS

dividend The number that is to be divided in a division problem

divisor The number that divides the dividend

quotient The number, not including the remainder, that results from division

1 Divide by 2 and 5

OBJECTIVE: Divide by 2 and 5.

Quick Review

1. ■ × 2 = 10
2. 5 × ■ = 15
3. 3 × ■ = 6
4. ■ × 2 = 18
5. 5 × ■ = 25

Learn

PROBLEM Mrs. Benson needs feeders for 12 hummingbirds. If there will be 2 birds at each feeder, how many feeders does she need?

■ ← quotient

$$12 \div 2 = ■$$
↑   ↑   ↑
dividend   divisor   quotient

divisor → $2\overline{)12}$
↑
dividend

Example 1 Divide. 12 ÷ 2 = ■

ONE WAY Count back on a number line.

Start at 12. Count back by 2s until you reach 0. Count the number of times you subtract 2.

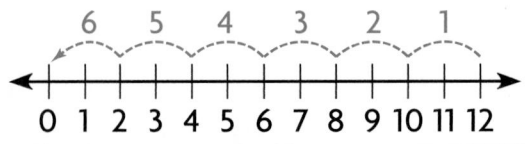

You subtract 2 six times. So, Mrs. Benson needs 6 feeders.

ANOTHER WAY Use a related multiplication fact.

12 ÷ 2 = ■   Think: ■ × 2 = 12

6 × 2 = 12   So, 12 ÷ 2 = 6, or $2\overline{)12}^{\,6}$.

Example 2 Divide. 20 ÷ 5 = ■

ONE WAY Count back on a number line.

Start at 20. Count back by 5s until you reach 0. Count the number of times you subtract 5.

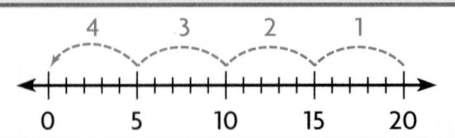

You subtract 5 four times. So, 20 ÷ 5 = 4.

ANOTHER WAY Use a related multiplication fact.

20 ÷ 5 = ■   Think: ■ × 5 = 20

4 × 5 = 20   So, 20 ÷ 5 = 4, or $5\overline{)20}^{\,4}$.

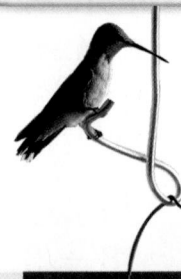

▲ A hummingbird can beat its wings as many as 80 times per second and can fly at a speed of 25 miles per hour!

Guided Practice

1. Use the number line to find $25 \div 5$.

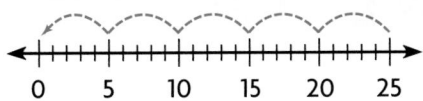

Find each quotient.

2. $16 \div 2 = \blacksquare$ **3.** $\blacksquare = 30 \div 5$ ✓**4.** $20 \div 2 = \blacksquare$ ✓**5.** $\blacksquare = 15 \div 5$

6. [TALK Math] Explain how $5 \times 8 = 40$ can help you find $40 \div 5$.

Independent Practice and Problem Solving

Find each quotient.

7. $6 \div 2 = \blacksquare$ **8.** $\blacksquare = 35 \div 5$ **9.** $10 \div 5 = \blacksquare$ **10.** $\blacksquare = 18 \div 2$

11. $\blacksquare = 45 \div 5$ **12.** $\blacksquare = 10 \div 2$ **13.** $8 \div 2 = \blacksquare$ **14.** $5 \div 5 = \blacksquare$

15. $5\overline{)15}$ **16.** $2\overline{)16}$ **17.** $5\overline{)35}$ **18.** $2\overline{)2}$

★**Algebra** Copy and complete each table.

19.

÷	25	30	35	40
5	$\blacksquare$	$\blacksquare$	$\blacksquare$	$\blacksquare$

20.

÷	12	14	16	18
2	$\blacksquare$	$\blacksquare$	$\blacksquare$	$\blacksquare$

USE DATA For 21–22, use the table.

21. The total mass of 2 hummingbirds of the same type is 8 grams. Which type of hummingbird are they? Write a division sentence to show the answer.

Hummingbirds

Type	Mass in Grams
Magnificent	7
Rubythroat	3
Anna's	4

22. [WRITE Math] Five hummingbirds of the same type have a total mass of 15 grams. What type are they? **Explain** how to find the answer.

Mixed Review and Test Prep

23. What is 5×7? (p. 240)

24. What is the missing number? (p. 262)
$$3 \times 8 = \blacksquare \times 3$$

25. Test Prep Jo sees the same number of birds each hour for 2 hours. She sees 16 birds in all. How many birds does Jo see each hour?

A 6   **B** 7   **C** 8   **D** 9

Extra Practice on page 314, Set A

Divide by 3 and 4

OBJECTIVE: Divide by 3 and 4.

Learn

PROBLEM For field day, 15 students have signed up for the relay race. Each relay team needs 3 students. How many teams can be made?

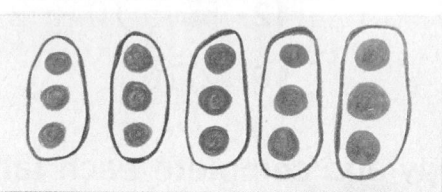

Example 1 Divide. 15 ÷ 3 = ▇

ONE WAY Draw a picture.

Draw 15 counters in groups of 3.
Count the number of equal groups.
There are 5 groups of 3.
So, 5 teams can be made.

ANOTHER WAY Use a related multiplication fact.

15 ÷ 3 = ▇   Think: ▇ × 3 = 15

5 × 3 = 15   So, $15 \div 3 = 5$, or $3\overline{)15}$ with quotient 5.

Math Idea
You can divide to find the number of equal groups or to find how many are in each group.

Example 2 Divide. 12 ÷ 4 = ▇

ONE WAY Draw a picture.

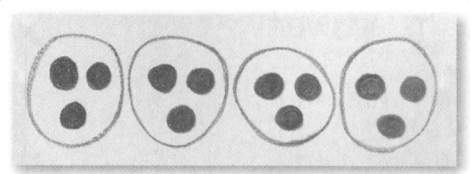

There are 3 counters in each group. So, $12 \div 4 = 3$.

ANOTHER WAY Use a related multiplication fact.

Think: 4 × ▇ = 12
        4 × 3 = 12

So, $12 \div 4 = 3$, or $4\overline{)12}$ with quotient 3.

Guided Practice

1. Use the picture to find 21 ÷ 3 = ▇.

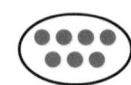 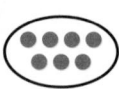 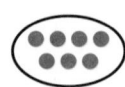

Find each quotient.

2. $9 \div 3 = \blacksquare$ **3.** $28 \div 4 = \blacksquare$ ✓**4.** $32 \div 4 = \blacksquare$ ✓**5.** $24 \div 3 = \blacksquare$

6. (TALK Math) **Explain** how you can use multiplication to find $20 \div 4$.

Independent Practice and Problem Solving

Find each quotient.

7. $30 \div 3 = \blacksquare$ **8.** $8 \div 4 = \blacksquare$ **9.** $\blacksquare = 27 \div 3$ **10.** $16 \div 4 = \blacksquare$

11. $24 \div 4 = \blacksquare$ **12.** $\blacksquare = 35 \div 5$ **13.** $6 \div 3 = \blacksquare$ **14.** $\blacksquare = 14 \div 2$

15. $3\overline{)12}$ **16.** $4\overline{)36}$ **17.** $5\overline{)20}$ **18.** $3\overline{)18}$

⭐**Algebra** Copy and complete each table.

19.

÷	6	9	12	15
3	■	■	■	■

20.

÷	20	24	28	32
4	■	■	■	■

USE DATA For 21–22, use the table.

21. Reasoning Students doing the beanbag toss and the jump-rope race competed in groups of 3. How many more groups participated in the jump-rope race than in the beanbag toss? **Explain** how you know.

22. What if students ran the relay race in groups of 4? Write a number sentence to show the number of groups that would have competed.

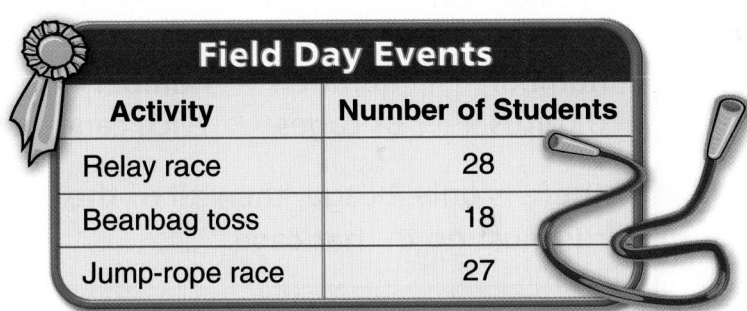

Field Day Events

Activity	Number of Students
Relay race	28
Beanbag toss	18
Jump-rope race	27

23. (WRITE Math) **What's the Question?** Cara put 36 sports cards into 4 equal piles. The answer is 9 sports cards.

Mixed Review and Test Prep

24. Lee used 35 beads to make 5 bracelets. How many beads did she use for each bracelet? (p. 302)

25. A bag has 5 red tiles and 2 blue tiles. Are you likely or unlikely to pull a blue tile? (p. 178)

26. Test Prep Carlos has 24 pretzels. He puts 4 pretzels in each bag. How many bags does Carlos fill?

A 4   **C** 6

B 5   **D** 7

(Extra Practice) on page 314, Set B

Division Rules for 1 and 0

OBJECTIVE: Divide using the rules for 1 and 0.

Quick Review

1. $6 \times \blacksquare = 6$
2. $\blacksquare \times 9 = 0$
3. $1 \times \blacksquare = 3$
4. $8 \times \blacksquare = 0$
5. $\blacksquare \times 1 = 5$

Learn

These division rules can help you divide with 1 and 0.

RULE A: Any number divided by 1 equals that number.

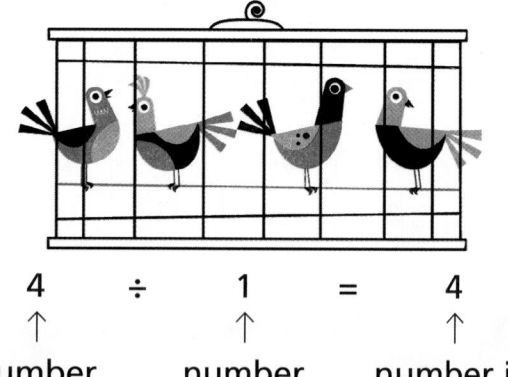

4	÷	1	=	4
↑		↑		↑
number of birds		number of cages		number in each cage

If there is only 1 cage, then all of the birds must go in that cage.

RULE B: Any number (except 0) divided by itself equals 1.

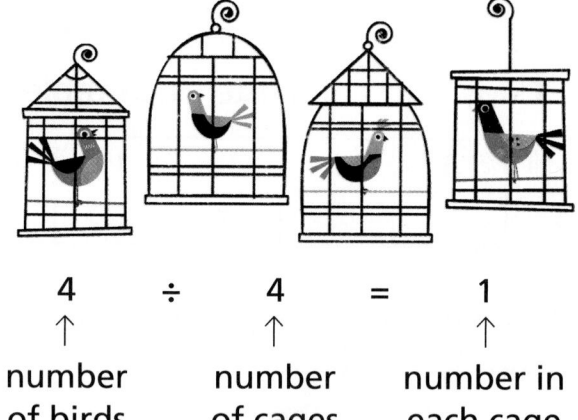

4	÷	4	=	1
↑		↑		↑
number of birds		number of cages		number in each cage

If there are the same number of birds and cages, then 1 bird goes in each cage.

RULE C: Zero divided by any number (except 0) equals 0.

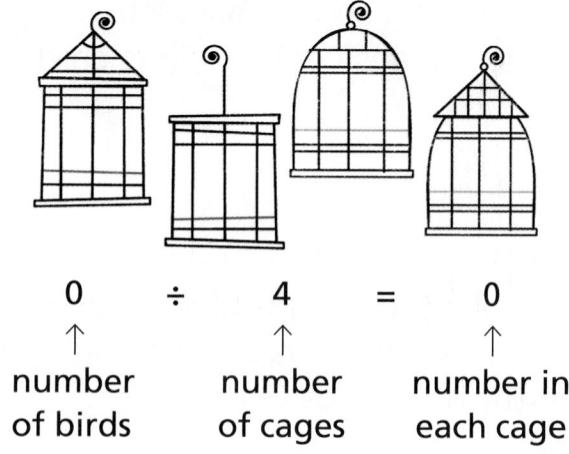

0	÷	4	=	0
↑		↑		↑
number of birds		number of cages		number in each cage

If there are 0 birds and 4 cages, there will not be any birds in the cages.

RULE D: You cannot divide by 0.

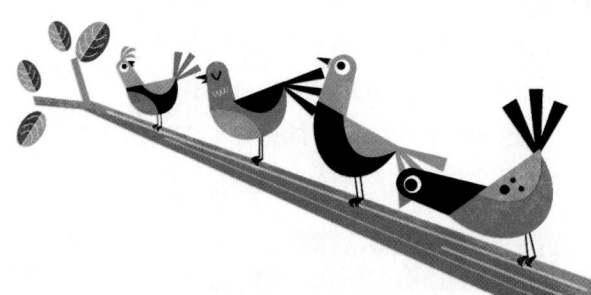

If there are 0 cages, then you cannot separate the birds into equal groups. Dividing by 0 is not possible.

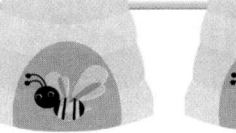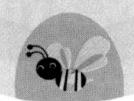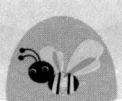

1. Use the picture to find $3 \div 3 = \blacksquare$.

Find each quotient.

2. $7 \div 1 = \blacksquare$ **3.** $2 \div 2 = \blacksquare$ ✅ **4.** $0 \div 5 = \blacksquare$ ✅ **5.** $6 \div 6 = \blacksquare$

6. [**TALK Math**] **Explain** why it is easy to find $9 \div 1$. Solve.

Independent Practice and Problem Solving

Find each quotient.

7. $0 \div 8 = \blacksquare$ **8.** $5 \div 5 = \blacksquare$ **9.** $\blacksquare = 2 \div 1$ **10.** $0 \div 7 = \blacksquare$

11. $6 \div 1 = \blacksquare$ **12.** $\blacksquare = 25 \div 5$ **13.** $\blacksquare = 0 \div 10$ **14.** $18 \div 3 = \blacksquare$

15. $14 \div 2 = \blacksquare$ **16.** $\blacksquare = 9 \div 9$ **17.** $32 \div 4 = \blacksquare$ **18.** $\blacksquare = 8 \div 1$

19. $4\overline{)24}$ **20.** $5\overline{)10}$ **21.** $3\overline{)0}$ **22.** $10\overline{)10}$

⭐ **Algebra** Compare. Write $<$, $>$, or $=$ for each ●.

23. $7 \div 7 \ ● \ 7 \div 1$ **24.** $9 \times 1 \ ● \ 9 \div 1$ **25.** $2 \div 2 \ ● \ 0 \div 2$

26. Angie has 7 parakeets. She put 4 of them in a cage. She let 3 friends hold the other parakeets. How many parakeets did each friend get to hold?

27. Pose a Problem Look back at Problem 26. Change the number of parakeets and friends so you can use the division sentence $6 \div 6 = 1$.

28. ≡**FAST FACT** There are more than 340 different types of parrots. Mary has 5 different parrots. She gives each parrot 1 grape. How many grapes does she give to her parrots?

29. [**WRITE Math**] ▸ Suppose a zoo has 59 birds in each of 59 cages. Use what you know to find the number of birds in each cage. **Explain** your answer.

Mixed Review and Test Prep

30. A flower shop sold 795 flowers last week. What is the value of the 9? (p. 8)

31. Use a related multiplication fact to find the quotient. $18 \div 3 = \blacksquare$ (p. 304)

32. Test Prep Farmer Joe has 4 stables. There is 1 horse in each stable. How many horses are there?

A 0   **B** 1   **C** 2   **D** 4

ALGEBRA
Practice the Facts

OBJECTIVE: Practice division facts through 5 using various strategies.

Quick Review

1. $4 \times \blacksquare = 32$
2. $\blacksquare \times 7 = 21$
3. $\blacksquare \times 5 = 10$
4. $2 \times \blacksquare = 12$
5. $1 \times \blacksquare = 9$

Learn

PROBLEM Tory made cottonball snowmen for her friends. She glued 3 cottonballs together to make each snowman. She used a total of 24 cottonballs. How many snowmen did Tory make?

Divide. $24 \div 3 = \blacksquare$

There are many ways to find the quotient.

A Draw a picture.

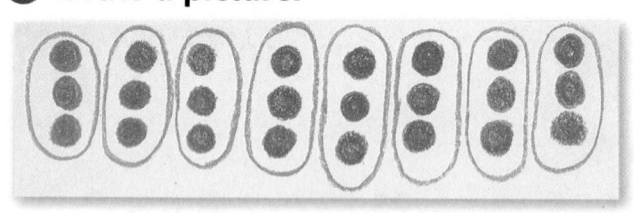

There are 8 groups of 3.
So, $24 \div 3 = 8$.

B Count back on a number line.

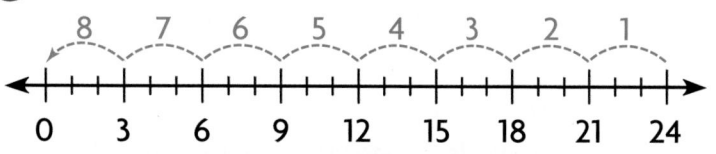

You subtract 3 eight times.
So, $24 \div 3 = 8$.

ERROR ALERT

Be sure to count back the same number of spaces each time you subtract on the number line.

C Use an array.

Make an array with 24 tiles.
Place 3 tiles in each row.
Count the number of rows.
There are 8 rows of 3 tiles.

Since $8 \times 3 = 24$, then $24 \div 3 = 8$.

D Use a fact family.

$3 \times 8 = 24$ $24 \div 8 = 3$

$8 \times 3 = 24$ $24 \div 3 = 8$

So, $24 \div 3 = 8$.

So, Tory made 8 snowmen.

E **Use a multiplication table.**

Think of a related multiplication fact.

Think: $3 \times \blacksquare = 24$

Find the row for the factor 3.
Look right to find the product 24.
Look up to find the missing factor, 8.

Since $3 \times 8 = 24$, then $24 \div 3 = 8$.

×	0	1	2	3	4	5	6	7	8	9
0	0	0	0	0	0	0	0	0	0	0
1	0	1	2	3	4	5	6	7	8	9
2	0	2	4	6	8	10	12	14	16	18
3	0	3	6	9	12	15	18	21	24	27
4	0	4	8	12	16	20	24	28	32	36
5	0	5	10	15	20	25	30	35	40	45
6	0	6	12	18	24	30	36	42	48	54
7	0	7	14	21	28	35	42	49	56	63
8	0	8	16	24	32	40	48	56	64	72
9	0	9	18	27	36	45	54	63	72	81

Guided Practice

1. Use the array to find $10 \div 5$.

Write a division sentence for each.

2.

3.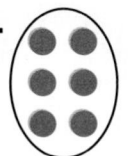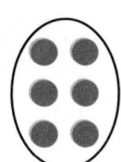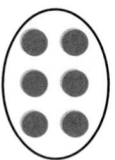

4.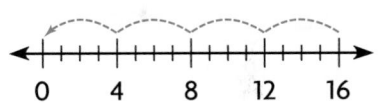

Find each missing factor and quotient.

5. $5 \times \blacksquare = 30$ $30 \div 5 = \blacksquare$

6. $1 \times \blacksquare = 7$ $7 \div 1 = \blacksquare$

7. $2 \times \blacksquare = 16$ $16 \div 2 = \blacksquare$

8. $4 \times \blacksquare = 32$ $32 \div 4 = \blacksquare$

9. **TALK Math** Explain two ways to find $15 \div 3$.

Independent Practice and Problem Solving

Write a division sentence for each.

10.

11.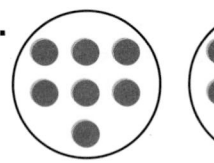

12.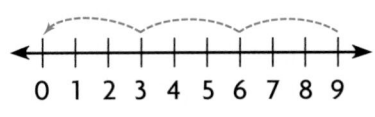

Extra Practice on page 314, Set D

Find each missing factor and quotient.

13. $4 \times \blacksquare = 24$ $24 \div 4 = \blacksquare$ **14.** $5 \times \blacksquare = 40$ $40 \div 5 = \blacksquare$

15. $5 \times \blacksquare = 0$ $0 \div 5 = \blacksquare$ **16.** $2 \times \blacksquare = 8$ $8 \div 2 = \blacksquare$

Find each quotient.

17. $4 \div 4 = \blacksquare$ **18.** $27 \div 3 = \blacksquare$ **19.** $\blacksquare = 12 \div 2$ **20.** $25 \div 5 = \blacksquare$

21. $\blacksquare = 6 \div 1$ **22.** $15 \div 5 = \blacksquare$ **23.** $0 \div 9 = \blacksquare$ **24.** $\blacksquare = 20 \div 4$

25. $\blacksquare = 36 \div 4$ **26.** $\blacksquare = 6 \div 2$ **27.** $18 \div 3 = \blacksquare$ **28.** $35 \div 5 = \blacksquare$

29. $8\overline{)0}$ **30.** $3\overline{)6}$ **31.** $4\overline{)32}$ **32.** $3\overline{)12}$

33. $2\overline{)18}$ **34.** $5\overline{)45}$ **35.** $5\overline{)5}$ **36.** $1\overline{)3}$

Compare. Write <, >, or = for each ●.

37. $30 \div 5 \;●\; 2 \times 3$ **38.** $12 \div 2 \;●\; 21 \div 3$ **39.** $9 \div 1 \;●\; 4 \times 2$

40. $27 \div 3 \;●\; 45 \div 5$ **41.** $24 \div 4 \;●\; 4 \times 2$ **42.** $16 \div 2 \;●\; 28 \div 4$

Write +, −, ×, or ÷ for each ●.

43. $14 \;●\; 2 = 6 \times 2$ **44.** $12 \div 4 = 27 \;●\; 9$ **45.** $21 \div 3 = 5 \;●\; 2$

USE DATA For 46–47, use the table.

46. Each snowman gets 2 bead eyes. How many bags of bead eyes do you need for 8 snowmen?

47. If you use 5 buttons for each snowman, how many snowmen can you decorate with one bag of buttons?

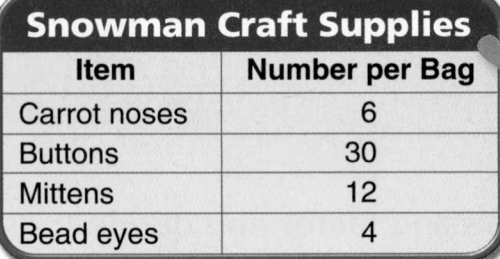

Snowman Craft Supplies	
Item	**Number per Bag**
Carrot noses	6
Buttons	30
Mittens	12
Bead eyes	4

48. Pose a Problem Write a word problem for the number sentence.

$$12 \div 2 = 6$$

49. Reasoning Martin has several boxes that hold 6 jars of paint each. Can 25 jars of paint fit in 4 of his boxes? **Explain** how you know.

50. **WRITE Math** **What's the Error?** Kim drew 3 equal groups of 9 to model $24 \div 3$. Describe her error. Draw a picture to model the division sentence.

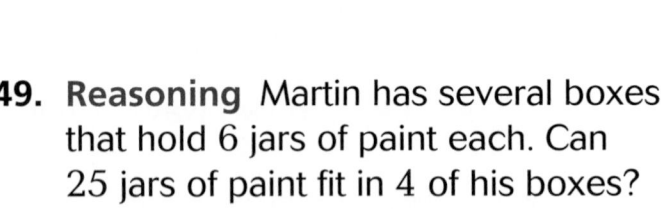

CD ROM Technology Use Harcourt Mega Math, The Number Games, *Up, Up, and Array,* Level E.

ALGEBRA
Finding the Cost

You can use multiplication to find the cost of multiple items.
You can use division to find the cost of one item.

Example 1 Mr. Lee buys 8 poster boards. Each poster board costs $2. How much does Mr. Lee spend?

8	×	$2	=	$16
↑		↑		↑
number of poster boards		cost of one		total spent

So, Mr. Lee spends $16.

Example 2 Courtney buys a pack of 5 paintbrushes. A pack costs $10. How much does each paintbrush cost?

$10	÷	5	=	$2
↑		↑		↑
total spent		number of paintbrushes		cost of one

So, each paintbrush costs $2.

Try It
Write a number sentence. Then solve.

51. Ms. Jenkins spends $28 on 4 picture frames. How much does each frame cost?

52. Glenn buys 4 rubber stamps. Each rubber stamp costs $5. How much does he spend?

53. The craft store sells baskets for $7 each. Karen buys 4 baskets. How much does she spend?

54. Books are on sale 3 for $12. What is the cost of one book?

Mixed Review and Test Prep

55. How many sides and vertices does this figure have? (Grade 2)

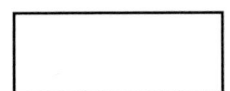

56. **Test Prep** Which division sentence is related to $6 \times 2 = 12$?

   A $12 \div 3 = 4$ **C** $6 \div 2 = 3$

   B $12 \div 6 = 2$ **D** $6 \div 3 = 2$

57. Mr. Lowry put 36 chairs in equal rows. He put 4 chairs in each row. How many rows did he make? (p. 304)

58. **Test Prep** Mrs. Kapp has 18 students in her class. She needs to divide them into groups of 3 for a project. **Explain** how you could use a number line to find how many groups there will be.

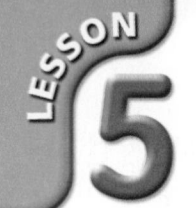

Problem Solving Workshop
Skill: Choose the Operation

OBJECTIVE: Solve problems by using the skill *choose the operation.*

Use the Skill

PROBLEM Miss Kent's class went to the science center to visit the new water and animal exhibits.

Sometimes, you need to decide which operation to use to solve a problem.

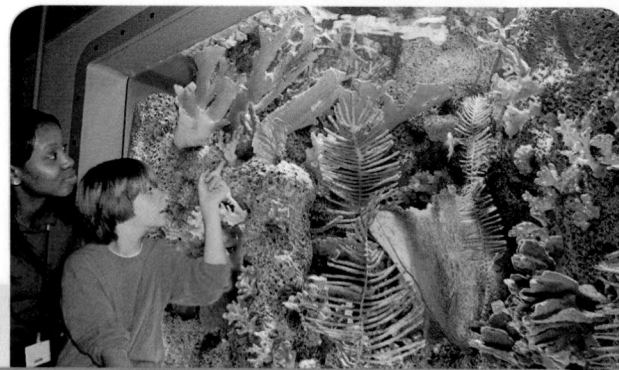

Examples

A Add to join groups of different sizes.
The water exhibit has 26 displays, and the animal exhibit has 18 displays. How many displays are in the exhibits in all?

$$
\begin{array}{ll}
26 & \leftarrow \text{ water displays} \\
+18 & \leftarrow \text{ animal displays} \\
\hline
44 & \leftarrow \text{ total number of displays}
\end{array}
$$

B Subtract to find the number left or to compare amounts.
Three of the 26 displays in the water exhibit were closed. How many were open?

$$
\begin{array}{ll}
26 & \leftarrow \text{ total water displays} \\
-3 & \leftarrow \text{ closed displays} \\
\hline
23 & \leftarrow \text{ open displays}
\end{array}
$$

C Multiply to join equal amounts.
The gift shop has world map puzzle books for $8 each. What is the cost of 5 puzzle books?

$$5 \quad \times \quad \$8 \quad = \quad \$40$$

| number of books | cost of one book | total cost |

D Divide to separate into equal groups or to find the number in each group.
The 24 students who went on the trip were separated into 4 equal groups. How many were in each group?

$$24 \quad \div \quad 4 \quad = \quad 6$$

| number of students | number of groups | students in each group |

Think and Discuss

Choose the operation. Write a number sentence. Then solve.

a. The Davis family spent $30 for 5 tickets to the ocean show. How much did each ticket cost?

b. There were 24 students and 13 adults on the bus for the science center trip. How many people rode on the bus?

Solve.

1. The show about the ocean was 17 minutes long, and the show about dolphins was 32 minutes long. How much longer was the dolphin show than the ocean show?

Which operation can you use to compare amounts? Write a number sentence and solve.

2. **What if** Problem 1 asked you to find the total time of the two shows? What operation would you use? Write a number sentence and solve.

3. T-shirts are sold for $9 each at the gift shop. What is the cost of 3 T-shirts?

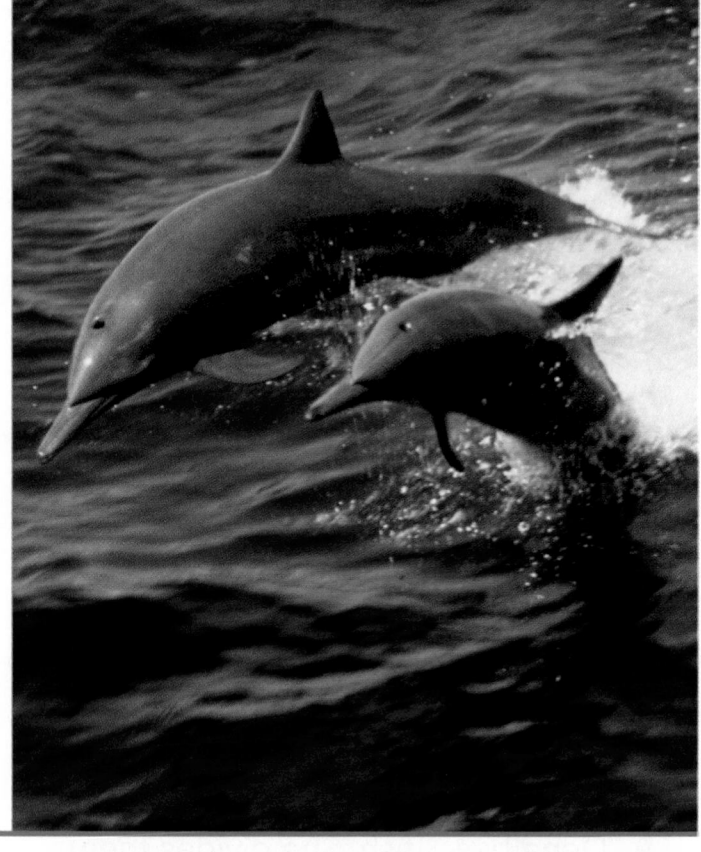

Mixed Applications

4. There are 45 books in the gift shop. There are an equal number of books on each of 5 shelves. How many books are on each shelf?

5. There are 54 fourth graders and 62 third graders who will enter projects in the science fair. Each project will be set up on its own table. How many tables are needed?

USE DATA For 6–8, use the table.

6. After visiting the science center, Miss Kent's class made this table about water use. In two days, how much water would a family of 4 use for brushing teeth in the morning and at bedtime?

7. Jonas took a bath, and his sister took a shower. How much more water did Jonas use than his sister?

8. **WRITE Math** ▸ Mr. Foster washed his clothes, washed his car, and ran the dishwasher. How much water did he use? **Explain** how you found your answer.

Water Use	
Activity	**Amount in Gallons**
Brush teeth	1
Wash clothes	30
Take a shower	30
Take a bath	40
Wash car	20
Run dishwasher	15

Extra Practice

Set A Find each quotient. (pp. 302–303)

1. $6 \div 2 = \blacksquare$ **2.** $\blacksquare = 25 \div 5$ **3.** $18 \div 2 = \blacksquare$ **4.** $\blacksquare = 40 \div 5$

5. $5\overline{)30}$ **6.** $2\overline{)12}$ **7.** $5\overline{)15}$ **8.** $2\overline{)4}$

9. Gina bought movie tickets for $20. Each ticket cost $5. How many tickets did she buy?

10. Carl placed a total of 14 chairs in 2 equal rows. How many chairs were in each row?

Set B Find each quotient. (pp. 304–305)

1. $\blacksquare = 21 \div 3$ **2.** $28 \div 4 = \blacksquare$ **3.** $\blacksquare = 18 \div 3$ **4.** $36 \div 4 = \blacksquare$

5. $4\overline{)12}$ **6.** $3\overline{)24}$ **7.** $4\overline{)32}$ **8.** $3\overline{)9}$

Set C Find each quotient. (pp. 306–307)

1. $3 \div 1 = \blacksquare$ **2.** $\blacksquare = 0 \div 9$ **3.** $\blacksquare = 5 \div 1$ **4.** $7 \div 7 = \blacksquare$

5. $4\overline{)0}$ **6.** $5\overline{)5}$ **7.** $2\overline{)0}$ **8.** $1\overline{)9}$

9. Dena has 3 fish. She divides them equally among 3 fishbowls. How many fish are in each bowl?

10. Steve has 4 flowers. He puts all of his flowers in 1 vase. How many flowers are in the vase?

Set D Write a division sentence for each. (pp. 308–311)

1. 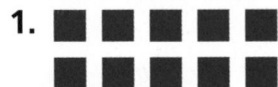 **2.** 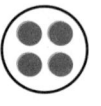 **3.**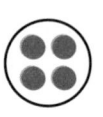

Find each missing factor and quotient.

4. $5 \times \blacksquare = 45$ $45 \div 5 = \blacksquare$

5. $1 \times \blacksquare = 6$ $6 \div 1 = \blacksquare$

Find each quotient.

6. $8 \div 2 = \blacksquare$ **7.** $35 \div 5 = \blacksquare$ **8.** $0 \div 7 = \blacksquare$ **9.** $16 \div 2 = \blacksquare$

10. $9\overline{)9}$ **11.** $3\overline{)15}$ **12.** $1\overline{)8}$ **13.** $4\overline{)24}$

CD ROM **Technology** — Use Harcourt Mega Math, The Number Games, *Up, Up, and Array,* Level E.

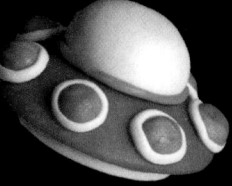

Division Cover-Up

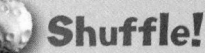 **Shuffle!**
2 players

 Draw!
- Division fact cards
- 10 counters for each player

1	27	14	6	15	5
21	8	7	32	12	2
16	0	18	30	10	24
9	3	45	35	4	36
40	4	28	50	8	3

⭐ Cover Them Up!

- Players shuffle the division fact cards and place them facedown in a pile.
- Player 1 draws the card from the top of the pile and says the number that is missing from the division number sentence on that card.
- Player 1 finds the missing number on the gameboard and places a counter on it.

- Players take turns. If a player cannot place a counter on the gameboard because the number is already covered, that player's turn ends.
- The first player to place all 10 of his or her counters on the gameboard wins the game.

MATH POWER · Odd and Even

Beat the Odds

Marco and his brother choose pairs of numbers and guess if their products are odd or even. What is the best guess for Marco—will most of the products be odd or even?

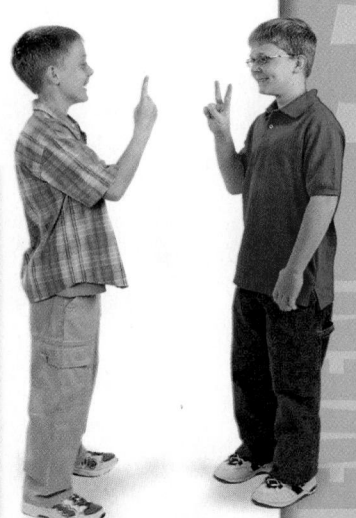

Example

Marco made a table to decide.

Step 1 Find the product of each example.

Step 2 Determine if each product is even or odd.

NUMBERS	EXAMPLE	PRODUCT	ODD OR EVEN?
odd × odd	3 × 9	■	odd
even × even	4 × 8	32	■
odd × even	5 × 8	■	even
even × odd	2 × 7	14	■

Step 3 Make a conclusion based on the table results. Three of the four possibilities result in an even product.

So, Marco should guess that the product will usually be even.

Try It
Complete the table.

	NUMBERS	EXAMPLE	QUOTIENT	ODD OR EVEN?
1.	odd ÷ odd	21 ÷ 3	■	■
2.	odd ÷ odd	35 ÷ 5	■	■
3.	even ÷ even	10 ÷ 2	■	■
4.	even ÷ even	24 ÷ 4	■	■
5.	even ÷ odd	20 ÷ 5	■	■
6.	even ÷ odd	18 ÷ 3	■	■

7. **WRITE Math** ▸ Make a conclusion based on the table results. **Explain** how you reached that conclusion.

Chapter 12 Review/Test

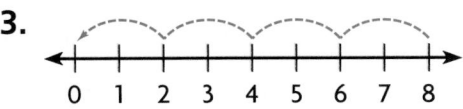

Check Concepts

Write a division sentence for each. (pp. 308–311)

1.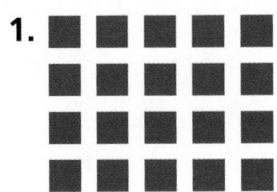

2. (circles with dots)

3.

0 1 2 3 4 5 6 7 8

Check Skills

Find each quotient. (pp. 302–303, 304–305, 306–307, 308–311)

4. $14 \div 2 = \blacksquare$ **5.** $8 \div 8 = \blacksquare$ **6.** $20 \div 5 = \blacksquare$ **7.** $\blacksquare = 0 \div 3$

8. $5 \div 1 = \blacksquare$ **9.** $\blacksquare = 20 \div 2$ **10.** $12 \div 3 = \blacksquare$ **11.** $16 \div 4 = \blacksquare$

12. $\blacksquare = 30 \div 5$ **13.** $24 \div 3 = \blacksquare$ **14.** $\blacksquare = 6 \div 6$ **15.** $12 \div 2 = \blacksquare$

16. $4\overline{)36}$ **17.** $6\overline{)0}$ **18.** $5\overline{)45}$ **19.** $3\overline{)6}$

20. $5\overline{)25}$ **21.** $4\overline{)28}$ **22.** $1\overline{)9}$ **23.** $2\overline{)18}$

Find each missing factor and quotient. (pp. 308–311)

24. $4 \times \blacksquare = 8$ $8 \div 4 = \blacksquare$ **25.** $3 \times \blacksquare = 27$ $27 \div 3 = \blacksquare$

26. $1 \times \blacksquare = 7$ $7 \div 1 = \blacksquare$ **27.** $2 \times \blacksquare = 10$ $10 \div 2 = \blacksquare$

Check Problem Solving

Solve. (pp. 312–313)

28. Mark put all of his shirts in 4 equal stacks. There are 6 shirts in each stack. How many shirts does Mark have altogether?

29. Beverly has 6 apples, 8 oranges, and 12 bananas. How many pieces of fruit does Beverly have in all?

30. **WRITE Math** ▶ Mike scored 18 points in the flag football game. He scored only touchdowns, and each touchdown he made scored 3 points. How many touchdowns did Mike make? **Explain** how you know which operation to use to solve the problem.

Standardized Test Prep
Chapters 1–12

Number and Operations

1. Sarah is setting tables for a party. She puts the same number of plates on each of 5 tables. There are 40 plates in all. How many plates are on each table? (p. 302)

   A 6

   B 7

   C 8

   D 9

Test Tip Look for important words.

See item 2. Key words can help you solve a problem. The word *altogether* indicates that you should find a total. Since there are two numbers that are different, find the total by adding.

2. There are 346 books on the first shelf in a library. There are 299 books on the second shelf. How many books are on both shelves altogether? (p. 58)

   A 535   **C** 635

   B 545   **D** 645

3. **WRITE Math** ▸ **Explain** how you can use the counters to find 20 ÷ 5. (p. 308)

Algebraic Reasoning

4. Which number completes the fact family? (p. 286)

   ■ × 9 = 63   63 ÷ ■ = 9
   9 × ■ = 63   63 ÷ 9 = ■

   A 6

   B 7

   C 8

   D 9

5. Which number is missing in the pattern below? (Grade 2)

   98, 85, 72, 59, 46, 33, ■

   A 22

   B 21

   C 20

   D 19

6. **WRITE Math** ▸ **Explain** how the arrays show the Commutative Property of Multiplication. (p. 262)

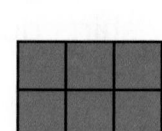 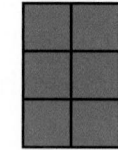

Measurement

7. Which figure has an area of 15 square units? (Grade 2)

A

B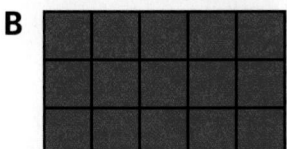

C

D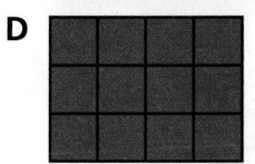

8. Which temperature does the thermometer show? (Grade 2)

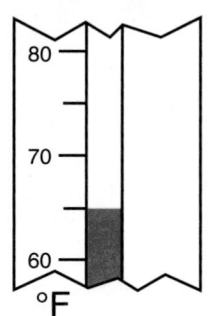

A 70°F

B 65°F

C 60°F

D 55°F

9. ⬛WRITE Math ▶ A paper clip is about 1 inch long. **Explain** how you could use a paper clip to measure the length of your pencil. (Grade 2)

Data Analysis and Probability

10. Jerry pulls a marble out of the bag without looking. Which color marble is he most likely to pull? (p. 178)

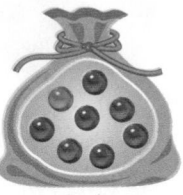

A Green

B Yellow

C Red

D Blue

11. How many letters did Thomas send? (p. 148)

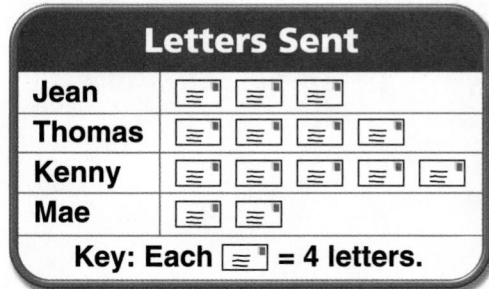

A 4　　　　**C** 16

B 12　　　**D** 20

12. ⬛WRITE Math ▶ A bar graph shows the number of students in each grade at Faber School. The bars for third grade and fourth grade are the same height. What does this mean? **Explain.** (p. 154)

13 Facts Through 12

Investigate

A hot-air balloon carries passengers in a basket. The size of the basket determines the number of passengers. Choose a balloon from the pictograph. How many balloon rides would be needed for all the students in your class to ride in that balloon?

Hot-Air Balloon Rides

Balloon A	🎈 🎈
Balloon B	🎈
Balloon C	🎈 🎈 🎈 🎈 🎈
Balloon D	🎈 🎈 🎈

Key: Each 🎈 = 2 passengers.

FAST FACT

Hot-air balloons fly because the hot air inside the balloon rises and lifts the balloon. Over 4,000 people in the United States are pilots of hot-air balloons.

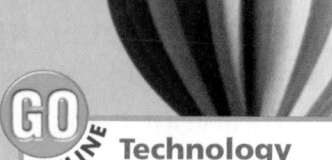

GO ONLINE

Technology
Student pages are available in the Student eBook.

Check your understanding of important skills needed for success in Chapter 13.

▶ **Multiplication Facts Through 12**

Find the product.

1. $7 \times 3 = \blacksquare$　　**2.** $4 \times 9 = \blacksquare$　　**3.** $\blacksquare = 5 \times 6$　　**4.** $\blacksquare = 10 \times 3$

5. $11 \times 8 = \blacksquare$　　**6.** $\blacksquare = 6 \times 4$　　**7.** $2 \times 12 = \blacksquare$　　**8.** $\blacksquare = 8 \times 7$

▶ **Missing Factors**

Find the missing factor.

9. $4 \times \blacksquare = 32$　　**10.** $18 = \blacksquare \times 3$　　**11.** $\blacksquare \times 9 = 54$　　**12.** $49 = 7 \times \blacksquare$

▶ **Multiplication Properties**

Use the properties of multiplication to help you find each product.

13. $6 \times 8 = \blacksquare$　　$8 \times 6 = \blacksquare$　　**14.** $(3 \times 2) \times 4 = \blacksquare$　　$3 \times (2 \times 4) = \blacksquare$

15. $7 \times 1 = \blacksquare$　　　　　　　　　**16.** $0 \times 12 = \blacksquare$

▶ **Division Facts Through 5**

Find the quotient.

17. $28 \div 4 = \blacksquare$　　**18.** $12 \div 3 = \blacksquare$　　**19.** $\blacksquare = 30 \div 5$　　**20.** $8 \div 1 = \blacksquare$

21. $\blacksquare = 18 \div 2$　　**22.** $20 \div 4 = \blacksquare$　　**23.** $27 \div 3 = \blacksquare$　　**24.** $40 \div 5 = \blacksquare$

VOCABULARY POWER

CHAPTER VOCABULARY	
array	equation
divide	expression
dividend	fact family
divisor	quotient

WARM-UP WORDS

equation A number sentence that uses the equal sign to show that two amounts are equal

expression The part of a number sentence that combines numbers and operation signs, but does not have an equal sign

1 Divide by 6

OBJECTIVE: Divide by 6.

Learn

PROBLEM Ms. Moore needs to buy 30 juice boxes for the class picnic. Juice boxes come in packs of 6. How many packs does she need to buy?

Divide. $30 \div 6 = \blacksquare$ $6\overline{)30}$

ONE WAY Use counters.

Use 30 counters.
Make groups of 6 until all counters are used.
Count the number of groups.

There are 5 groups of 6 counters.

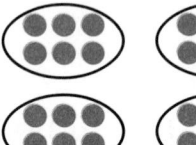
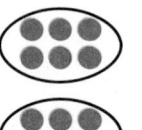

So, Ms. Moore needs to buy 5 packs of juice.

OTHER WAYS

A Use a related multiplication fact.

Think: ■ × 6 = 30
5 × 6 = 30

So, $30 \div 6 = 5$, or $6\overline{)30}^{5}$.

B Use factors.

$3 \times 2 = 6$
factors   product

Since 3 and 2 are factors of 6, you can divide by 6 using 3 and then 2.

$30 \div 3 = 10$ $10 \div 2 = 5$
So, $30 \div 6 = 5$.

• How can you solve $24 \div 6$ by using the factors 3 and 2?

Guided Practice

1. Use the model to find $18 \div 6$.

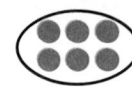
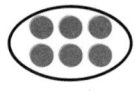
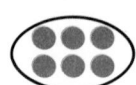

Find each missing factor and quotient.

2. $6 \times \blacksquare = 36$ $36 \div 6 = \blacksquare$ **3.** $6 \times \blacksquare = 12$ $12 \div 6 = \blacksquare$

✓**4.** $6 \times \blacksquare = 6$ $6 \div 6 = \blacksquare$ ✓**5.** $6 \times \blacksquare = 42$ $42 \div 6 = \blacksquare$

6. **TALK Math** **Explain** how $6 \times 9 = 54$ helps you find $54 \div 6$.

Independent Practice and Problem Solving

Find each missing factor and quotient.

7. $6 \times \blacksquare = 30$ $30 \div 6 = \blacksquare$ **8.** $6 \times \blacksquare = 48$ $48 \div 6 = \blacksquare$

9. $6 \times \blacksquare = 18$ $18 \div 6 = \blacksquare$ **10.** $6 \times \blacksquare = 24$ $24 \div 6 = \blacksquare$

Find each quotient.

11. $12 \div 6 = \blacksquare$ **12.** $\blacksquare = 6 \div 2$ **13.** $\blacksquare = 42 \div 6$ **14.** $15 \div 5 = \blacksquare$

15. $\blacksquare = 60 \div 6$ **16.** $20 \div 4 = \blacksquare$ **17.** $7 \div 1 = \blacksquare$ **18.** $\blacksquare = 54 \div 6$

19. $4\overline{)28}$ **20.** $6\overline{)36}$ **21.** $6\overline{)0}$ **22.** $3\overline{)21}$

Algebra Find the missing number.

23. $6 \div \blacksquare = 6$ **24.** $27 \div \blacksquare = 9$ **25.** $16 \div \blacksquare = 8$ **26.** $42 \div \blacksquare = 7$

27. Ms. Moore bought a bag of 12 apples for the class picnic. How many apples can each of 6 students have if they each get the same number?

28. There are 30 students in a relay race at the picnic. The students are divided into 6 equal teams. How many students are on each team?

29. **Reasoning** Cody baked 24 muffins. He ate 6 of them. How many muffins does he have left? How many can he give to each of 6 friends if they each get the same number? **Explain.**

30. **WRITE Math** **What's the Error?** Mary has 36 stickers to give to 6 friends. She says she can give each friend only 5 stickers. Use a division sentence to describe Mary's error.

Mixed Review and Test Prep

31. What is the missing number? (p. 262)

$$7 \times 8 = 8 \times \blacksquare$$

32. What is 8,024 written in expanded form? (p. 10)

33. **Test Prep** The same number of students are at each of 6 tables. There are 48 students in all. How many students are at each table?

A 9   **B** 8   **C** 7   **D** 6

Divide by 7 and 8

OBJECTIVE: Divide by 7 and 8.

Quick Review

1. ■ × 7 = 21
2. 3 × ■ = 24
3. 2 × ■ = 14
4. ■ × 7 = 42
5. 8 × ■ = 16

Learn

PROBLEM Firewood is sold in bundles of 7 logs. Steve has 28 logs. How many bundles of firewood can he make?

Example 1 Divide. 28 ÷ 7 = ■

ONE WAY Make an array.

Use 28 tiles. Make rows of 7 tiles until all tiles are used. Count the number of rows.

There are 4 rows of 7 tiles.

ANOTHER WAY Use a related multiplication fact.

Think: ■ × 7 = 28
      4 × 7 = 28

So, 28 ÷ 7 = 4, or 7)28̄ .

So, Steve can make 4 bundles of firewood.

Example 2 Divide. 32 ÷ 8 = ■

ONE WAY Make an array.

Use 32 tiles. Make rows of 8 tiles until all tiles are used. Count the number of rows.

There are 4 rows of 8 tiles.

ANOTHER WAY Use a related multiplication fact.

Think: ■ × 8 = 32
      4 × 8 = 32

So, 32 ÷ 8 = 4, or 8)32̄ .

Guided Practice

1. Use the array to find 14 ÷ 7 = ■.

Find each missing factor and quotient.

2. 7 × ■ = 35   35 ÷ 7 = ■   3. 8 × ■ = 48   48 ÷ 8 = ■

✓4. 8 × ■ = 56   56 ÷ 8 = ■   ✓5. 7 × ■ = 63   63 ÷ 7 = ■

6. **TALK Math** Explain how you can use an array to find 24 ÷ 8 = ■.

Find each missing factor and quotient.

7. $8 \times \blacksquare = 40$ $40 \div 8 = \blacksquare$ **8.** $7 \times \blacksquare = 49$ $49 \div 7 = \blacksquare$

9. $7 \times \blacksquare = 7$ $7 \div 7 = \blacksquare$ **10.** $8 \times \blacksquare = 64$ $64 \div 8 = \blacksquare$

Find each quotient.

11. $21 \div 7 = \blacksquare$ **12.** $\blacksquare = 8 \div 8$ **13.** $18 \div 2 = \blacksquare$ **14.** $\blacksquare = 25 \div 5$

15. $24 \div 6 = \blacksquare$ **16.** $\blacksquare = 15 \div 3$ **17.** $\blacksquare = 16 \div 8$ **18.** $56 \div 7 = \blacksquare$

19. $\blacksquare = 36 \div 4$ **20.** $70 \div 7 = \blacksquare$ **21.** $\blacksquare = 6 \div 1$ **22.** $72 \div 8 = \blacksquare$

23. $8\overline{)80}$ **24.** $5\overline{)40}$ **25.** $7\overline{)14}$ **26.** $6\overline{)54}$

★**Algebra** **Copy and complete each table.**

27.

÷	48	56	64	72
8	■	■	■	■

28.

÷	35	42	49	56
7	■	■	■	■

USE DATA **For 29–31, use the table.**

29. **Reasoning** There are 58 people camping at Zoe's family reunion. They have Columbia tents and Vista tents. How many of each type of tent do they need to sleep 58 people? **Explain.**

30. **Pose a Problem** Look back at Problem 29. Write a similar problem by changing the number of people and the types of tents used.

Tent Sizes

Type	Number of People
Columbia	10
Vista	8
Condor	7
Gamma 450	5

31. **⌇WRITE Math** ▸ There are 42 people going camping. How many Condor tents do they need? **Explain.**

Mixed Review and Test Prep

32. A Columbia tent costs $286. Mrs. Kent has $177. How much more money does she need to buy the tent? (p. 84)

33. There are 30 tents set up in groups with 5 tents in each group. How many groups are there? (p. 302)

34. **Test Prep** There are 24 benches in 8 equal rows at a picnic area. How many benches are in each row?

A 32   **C** 4

B 16   **D** 3

Problem Solving Workshop
Strategy: Work Backward

OBJECTIVE: Solve problems by using the strategy *work backward*.

Learn the Strategy

When you know the final amount, you can work backward
to solve a problem.

You can use subtraction and addition.

Zach paid $1.70 for lunch. Then his mom gave him $5.00. Now, Zach has $7.50. How much money did Zach have to start?

So, Zach had $4.20 to start.

Begin with the final amount of money.

Subtract the money Zach's mom gave him.

$7.50	−	$5.00	=	$2.50
↑		↑		↑
final amount		money from mom		money after lunch

Add the amount Zach spent on lunch.

$2.50	+	$1.70	=	$4.20
↑		↑		↑
money after lunch		money spent on lunch		money to start

You can use addition and multiplication.

Troy cuts a board in 2 equal pieces. Then he cuts 4 inches off one piece. The piece is now 6 inches long. What was the length of the original board?

So, the board was 20 inches long.

Begin with the final length of the board.

Add the number of inches Troy cut off.

6	+	4	=	10
↑		↑		↑
final length		inches cut off		length of one piece

Multiply to find the length of the original board.

10	×	2	=	20
↑		↑		↑
length of one piece		number of pieces		length of board

TALK Math

In the last problem, why did you use multiplication when you worked backward?

Use the Strategy

PROBLEM Chad bought 4 packs of T-shirts. He gave 5 T-shirts to his brother. Now Chad has 19 shirts. How many T-shirts were in each pack?

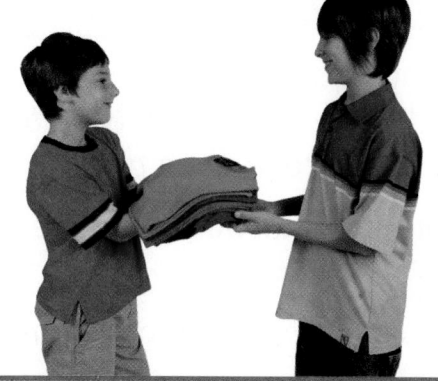

Read to Understand

- **What information is given?**
- **How can you sequence the information?**

Plan

- **What strategy can you use to solve the problem?**
  You can work backward to help you solve the problem.

Solve

- **How can you use the strategy to solve the problem?**
  Work backward from the number of T-shirts Chad has now.

  Begin with the final number of T-shirts. Add the number of T-shirts Chad gave away.

$$19 \quad + \quad 5 \quad = \quad 24$$

↑	↑	↑
final number of T-shirts	T-shirts given away	T-shirts in 4 packs

  Then divide to find the number of T-shirts in each pack.

$$24 \quad \div \quad 4 \quad = \quad 6$$

↑	↑	↑
T-shirts in 4 packs	number of packs	number in each pack

So, each pack had 6 T-shirts.

Check

- **How can you check your answer?**

Guided Problem Solving

Read to Understand

Plan

Solve

Check

1. Mac collects Matchbox® cars. He bought 4 packs of cars. Then his friend gave him 9 cars. Now Mac has 21 cars. How many cars are in each pack?

   Work backward from the total number of cars Mac has now.

   First, subtract the cars Mac's friend gave him.

   $$21 \quad - \quad 9 \quad = \quad 12$$
   ↑   ↑   ↑
   total cars   cars given to Mac   cars in 4 packs

   Then, divide to find the number of cars in each pack.

   $$12 \quad \div \quad 4 \quad = \quad \blacksquare$$
   ↑   ↑   ↑
   cars in 4 packs   number of packs   number in each pack

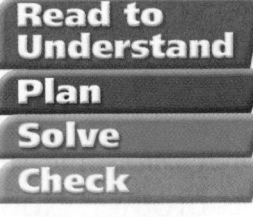

2. **What if** Mac bought 8 packs of cars and then his friend gave him 3 cars? If Mac has 19 cars now, how many cars are in each pack?

3. Ryan collects model cars. He gave half of his model car collection to a friend. Then he bought 6 more cars. Now Ryan has 14 cars. How many cars did Ryan have to start?

Problem Solving Strategy Practice

USE DATA For 4–6, use the table. Work backward to solve.

4. After lunch, 16 bracelets were sold. Then 2 bracelets were returned. How many bracelets were sold before lunch?

5. During the day, 9 customers each bought the same number of key chains. Then 9 more key chains were sold. How many key chains did each of the 9 customers buy?

6. **WRITE Math** ▶ First, Jan bought half of the total number of one item shown in the table. Then she bought 2 craft books. She bought 12 items in all. Which item did she buy first? Explain.

Items Sold in One Day	
Item	**Number**
bracelets	25
craft books	30
key chains	45
model car kits	20

Mixed Strategy Practice

USE DATA For 7–10, use the table.

7. Tim and Erica have eaten at all of the restaurants. Tim's restaurants are all different from Erica's. He has eaten at 10 more of the restaurants than Erica. How many restaurants has Tim eaten at?

8. ☰**FAST FACT** The Mall of America is the largest mall in the United States. Suppose there are 6 food stores on each level of the mall. How many levels would there be?

9. **Pose a Problem** Look back at Problem 8. Write a similar problem by using a different fact from the table and changing the number on each level.

10. **Open-Ended** Mark visited every food store. He visited the same number of food stores each day. List 3 different ways he could have done this.

11. Rose saw a movie, shopped in a store, and ate at a restaurant. She did not see the movie first. She shopped last. In what order did Rose do these activities?

12. Mr. Acosta went to the same number of stores each day for 4 days. On the fifth day, he went to 10 stores. He visited 34 stores in all. How many stores did he visit each of the 4 days?

Choose a STRATEGY

Draw a Diagram or Picture
Make a Model or Act It Out
Make an Organized List
Find a Pattern
Make a Table or Graph
Predict and Test
Work Backward
Solve a Simpler Problem
Write an Equation
Use Logical Reasoning

Mall of America Facts

Stores	520
Restaurants	50
Food stores	36
Movie screens	14

MALL OF AMERICA

CHALLENGE YOURSELF

A store sells pants for $12. The store also gives shoppers one free shirt for each $9 shirt they buy.

13. Dillon paid $30 for pants and shirts. How many pairs of pants did he buy? How many shirts did he get?

14. Pants usually sell for $16. Anna saved a total of $8 on her pants. She received 3 free shirts. How much did Anna spend?

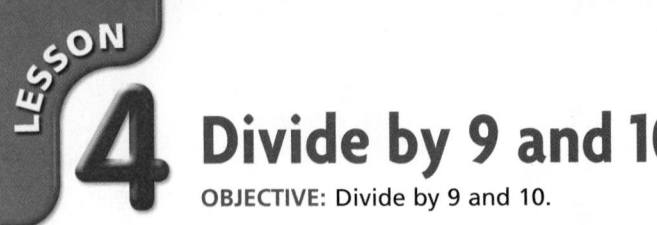

LESSON 4 Divide by 9 and 10

OBJECTIVE: Divide by 9 and 10.

Quick Review

1. $2 \times \blacksquare = 20$
2. $\blacksquare \times 10 = 50$
3. $9 \times \blacksquare = 36$
4. $\blacksquare \times 7 = 70$
5. $6 \times \blacksquare = 54$

Learn

PROBLEM Mateo's class goes to the aquarium. They have 45 minutes to visit 9 exhibits. How much time can they spend at each exhibit if they spend the same amount of time at each one?

Example 1 Divide. $45 \div 9 = \blacksquare$

$$\blacksquare$$
$$9\overline{)45}$$

▲ The Georgia Aquarium has more than 100,000 animals.

ONE WAY Use repeated subtraction.

Start with 45. Subtract 9 until you reach 0.

$$
\begin{array}{ccccc}
45 & 36 & 27 & 18 & 9 \\
-\ 9 & -\ 9 & -\ 9 & -\ 9 & -\ 9 \\
\hline
36 & 27 & 18 & 9 & 0
\end{array}
$$

Number of times you subtract 9: 1   2   3   4   5

You subtract 9 from 45 five times.

ANOTHER WAY Use a related multiplication fact.

$45 \div 9 = \blacksquare$ Think: $\blacksquare \times 9 = 45$ So, $45 \div 9 = 5$, or $9\overline{)45}^{\,5}$.

$5 \times 9 = 45$

So, Mateo's class can spend 5 minutes at each exhibit.

Example 2 Divide. $40 \div 10 = \blacksquare$

ONE WAY Use repeated subtraction.

Start with 40. Subtract 10 until you reach 0.

$$
\begin{array}{cccc}
40 & 30 & 20 & 10 \\
-\ 10 & -\ 10 & -\ 10 & -\ 10 \\
\hline
30 & 20 & 10 & 0
\end{array}
$$

  1   2   3   4

Count the number of times you subtract 10. You subtract 10 from 40 four times.

ANOTHER WAY Use a related multiplication fact.

$40 \div 10 = \blacksquare$

Think: $\blacksquare \times 10 = 40$

$4 \times 10 = 40$

So, $40 \div 10 = 4$, or $10\overline{)40}^{\,4}$.

1. Use the related multiplication fact to find $27 \div 9$.
$3 \times 9 = 27$

Find each quotient.

2. $80 \div 10 = $ ▪   **3.** $36 \div 9 = $ ▪   ✓**4.** $63 \div 9 = $ ▪   ✓**5.** $30 \div 10 = $ ▪

6. TALK Math **Explain** how to use repeated subtraction to find $60 \div 10$.

Independent Practice and Problem Solving

Find each quotient.

7. $18 \div 9 = $ ▪   **8.** ▪ $= 30 \div 5$ **9.** $50 \div 10 = $ ▪   **10.** ▪ $= 81 \div 9$

11. ▪ $= 20 \div 10$ **12.** $9 \div 9 = $ ▪   **13.** ▪ $= 12 \div 6$ **14.** $28 \div 7 = $ ▪

15. $4\overline{)32}$ **16.** $9\overline{)72}$ **17.** $10\overline{)10}$ **18.** $8\overline{)56}$

⯈**Algebra** Copy and complete each table.

19.

÷	36	45	54	63
9	▪	▪	▪	▪

20.

÷	70	80	90	100
10	▪	▪	▪	▪

USE DATA For 21–23, use the table.

21. Which jellyfish is four times the length of the sea wasp?

22. A marlin can be 87 inches long. This is 6 inches more than 9 times the length of which jellyfish?

23. WRITE Math ▸ **What's the Question?** A striped bass is 45 inches long. The answer is sea wasp. What is the question?

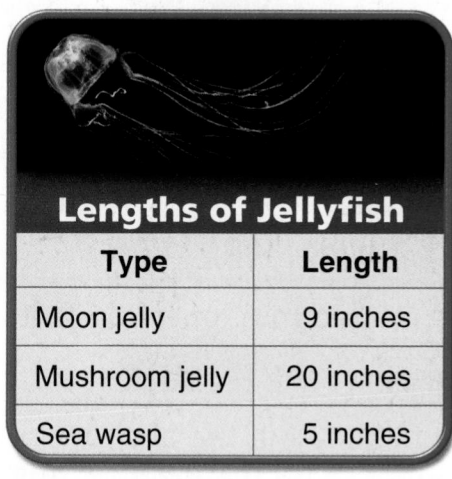

Lengths of Jellyfish

Type	Length
Moon jelly	9 inches
Mushroom jelly	20 inches
Sea wasp	5 inches

Mixed Review and Test Prep

24. What is the quotient? $45 \div 5 = $ ▪
(p. 302)

25. Compare the numbers. Write $<$, $>$, or $=$. $3{,}346$ ● $3{,}374$ (p. 28)

26. **Test Prep** Fifty people form 10 equal lines. How many people are in each line?

A 500   **B** 50   **C** 5   **D** 1

ALGEBRA
Division Facts Through 12

OBJECTIVE: Practice division facts through 12 using various strategies.

Quick Review

1. $12 \times \blacksquare = 24$
2. $\blacksquare \times 11 = 55$
3. $2 \times \blacksquare = 22$
4. $\blacksquare \times 12 = 72$
5. $10 \times \blacksquare = 120$

Learn

PROBLEM Kenny collects model cars. Each shelf in his room can hold 11 cars. Kenny has 44 cars. How many shelves will Kenny use to display his cars?

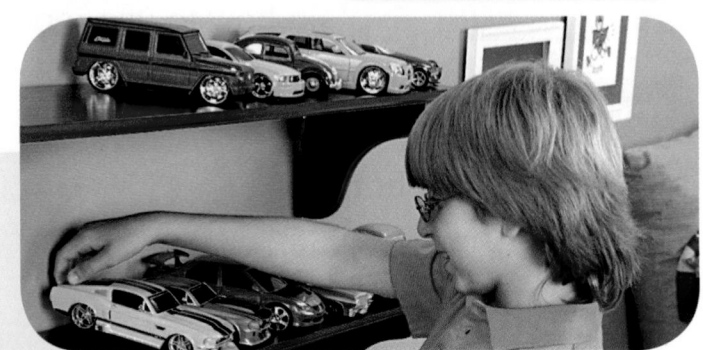

Example 1 Divide. $44 \div 11 = \blacksquare$

Think of a related multiplication fact.

Think: $\blacksquare \times 11 = 44$

- Find the factor 11 in the top row.
- Look down to find the product, 44.
- Look left to find the missing factor, 4.

Since $4 \times 11 = 44$, then $44 \div 11 = 4$.

So, Kenny will use 4 shelves.

Tara collects postcards. She has 108 postcards that she wants to divide equally among 12 boxes. How many postcards will Tara put in each box?

Example 2 Divide. $108 \div 12 = \blacksquare$

Think of a related multiplication fact.

Think: $\blacksquare \times 12 = 108$

- Find the factor 12 in the top row.
- Look down to find the product, 108.
- Look left to find the missing factor, 9.

Since $9 \times 12 = 108$, then $108 \div 12 = 9$.

So, Tara will put 9 postcards in each box.

- What if Tara had 72 postcards to divide equally among 12 boxes? How many postcards would she put in each box?

×	0	1	2	3	4	5	6	7	8	9	10	11	12
0	0	0	0	0	0	0	0	0	0	0	0	0	0
1	0	1	2	3	4	5	6	7	8	9	10	11	12
2	0	2	4	6	8	10	12	14	16	18	20	22	24
3	0	3	6	9	12	15	18	21	24	27	30	33	36
4	0	4	8	12	16	20	24	28	32	36	40	44	48
5	0	5	10	15	20	25	30	35	40	45	50	55	60
6	0	6	12	18	24	30	36	42	48	54	60	66	72
7	0	7	14	21	28	35	42	49	56	63	70	77	84
8	0	8	16	24	32	40	48	56	64	72	80	88	96
9	0	9	18	27	36	45	54	63	72	81	90	99	108
10	0	10	20	30	40	50	60	70	80	90	100	110	120
11	0	11	22	33	44	55	66	77	88	99	110	121	132
12	0	12	24	36	48	60	72	84	96	108	120	132	144

Practice the Facts

There are many ways to solve division problems.

Divide. 21 ÷ 7 = ■

> **Ⓐ Use counters.**
>
>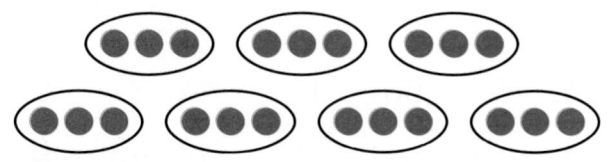
>
> There are 3 counters in each of 7 groups.

So, 21 ÷ 7 = 3.

> **Ⓑ Use a fact family.**
>
> **Fact Family for 3, 7, and 21**
>
> | factor | | factor | | product | | dividend | | divisor | | quotient |
> |---|---|---|---|---|---|---|---|---|---|---|
> | 3 | × | 7 | = | 21 | | 21 | ÷ | 7 | = | 3 |
> | 7 | × | 3 | = | 21 | | 21 | ÷ | 3 | = | 7 |

So, 21 ÷ 7 = 3.

> **Ⓒ Use repeated subtraction.**
>
> 21   14   7
> − 7 − 7 −7
> ―― ―― ――
> 14   7   0
> 1   2   3
>
> You subtract 7 from 21 three times.

> **Ⓓ Use an array.**
>
>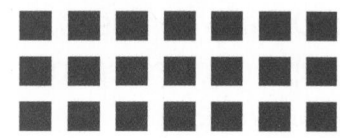
>
> There are 3 rows of 7 tiles.
> Since 3 × 7 = 21, then 21 ÷ 7 = 3.

• How would you find 27 ÷ 9 by using counters?

Guided Practice

1. Use the multiplication table on page 332 to find 88 ÷ 11.

Find each missing factor and quotient.

2. 11 × ■ = 55   55 ÷ 11 = ■   3. 12 × ■ = 24   24 ÷ 12 = ■

✓ 4. 12 × ■ = 48   48 ÷ 12 = ■   ✓ 5. 11 × ■ = 99   99 ÷ 11 = ■

6. **[TALK Math]** Explain how to use multiplication to find 84 ÷ 12 = ■.

Find each missing factor and quotient.

7. $11 \times \blacksquare = 66$ $66 \div 11 = \blacksquare$ **8.** $9 \times \blacksquare = 45$ $45 \div 9 = \blacksquare$

9. $12 \times \blacksquare = 132$ $132 \div 12 = \blacksquare$ **10.** $10 \times \blacksquare = 100$ $100 \div 10 = \blacksquare$

Find each quotient.

11. $45 \div 5 = \blacksquare$ **12.** $50 \div 10 = \blacksquare$ **13.** $\blacksquare = 88 \div 11$ **14.** $27 \div 9 = \blacksquare$

15. $\blacksquare = 96 \div 12$ **16.** $\blacksquare = 121 \div 11$ **17.** $10 \div 2 = \blacksquare$ **18.** $48 \div 6 = \blacksquare$

19. $7)\overline{42}$ **20.** $3)\overline{21}$ **21.** $8)\overline{56}$ **22.** $12)\overline{72}$

Compare. Write <, >, or = for each ●.

23. $49 \div 7$ ● $35 \div 5$ **24.** $100 - 16$ ● 9×9 **25.** $96 \div 8$ ● $4 + 9$

26. $49 + 12$ ● 11×6 **27.** $120 \div 12$ ● $23 - 13$ **28.** 6×7 ● 4×10

Write +, −, ×, or ÷ for each ●.

29. 3 ● $3 = 72 \div 8$ **30.** 9 ● $2 = 63 \div 9$ **31.** $10 \times 3 = 6$ ● 5

USE DATA For 32–34, use the table.

32. Hannah likes to visit the Davis Mountains in Texas. During her visits, she saw 4 equal groups of deer eating grass. How many deer were in each group?

33. The number of horned lizards Hannah saw is 9 times the number Manuel saw during his visits. How many horned lizards did Manuel see?

34. **WRITE Math** When Todd visited the Davis Mountains, he saw half as many elk and half as many deer as Hannah saw. How many elk and deer did Todd see in all? **Explain** your answer.

Animals Hannah Saw in the Davis Mountains	
Animal	**Number**
Rattlesnakes	14
Deer	12
Horned lizards	45
Quails	42
Elk	18

35. **Reasoning** Hannah took 60 photos of animals. She put 4 photos in a picture frame and put the rest in her photo album. Each page in the album holds 8 photos. How many pages did Hannah fill? **Explain.**

Technology
Use Harcourt Mega Math, The Number Games, *Up, Up, and Array*, Levels H, T.

Extra Practice on page 338, Set D

MENTAL MATH
Near Facts

You can use *near facts* to help you find quotients for division problems that do not come out evenly.

Example Rosa wants to share 25 cookies equally among 4 friends. How many cookies should each friend get?

Divide. $25 \div 4 = \blacksquare$

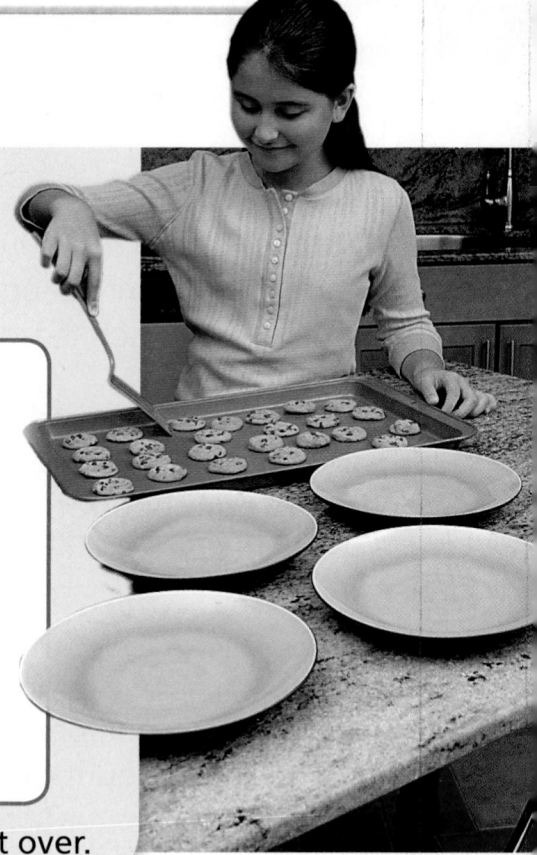

To find the quotient, look for a *near fact*. A near fact for this problem is a multiplication fact with 4 as a factor and a product as close to 25 as possible without going over.

Think: $4 \times 5 = 20$ (too low)
$4 \times 6 = 24$ (close)
$4 \times 7 = 28$ (too high)

Since $4 \times 6 = 24$ gives the closest product without going over, the quotient is 6. Since $25 - 24 = 1$, 1 is left over.
$25 \div 4 = 6$ with 1 left over

So, each friend should get 6 cookies. There will be 1 cookie left over.

Try It

Use near facts to solve. Write the near fact you used.

36. Mrs. Hart wants to put 33 desks in 4 equal rows. How many desks will be in each row? How many desks will be left over?

37. Keisha has 47 plates. She sets tables with 5 plates each. How many tables can she set? How many plates will she have left over?

Mixed Review and Test Prep

38. Gabe walked 3 miles each day for a total of 27 miles. What multiplication fact can you use to find the number of days Gabe walked? Solve. (p. 304)

39. **Test Prep** There are 80 miles of trails at a mountain. Each trail is 10 miles long. How many trails are there?

A 8   **B** 10   **C** 70   **D** 90

40. Sarah has a purple shirt, a blue shirt, and a pink shirt. She has brown pants, black pants, and tan pants. How many outfits can Sarah make with these shirts and pants? (p. 186)

41. **Test Prep** What is $77 \div 11$?

A 9   **B** 8   **C** 7   **D** 6

ALGEBRA

Expressions and Equations

OBJECTIVE: Write expressions and equations that represent situations and find missing operation signs.

Quick Review

1. $15 \div 5$
2. $28 \div 7$
3. $32 \div 4$
4. $40 \div 10$
5. $48 \div 8$

Vocabulary

expression   equation

Learn

PROBLEM There are 20 children at a bowling party. They are divided into 5 equal teams. How many children are on each team?

You can write an expression for this problem. An **expression** is part of a number sentence. It combines numbers and operation signs but does not have an equal sign.

20	÷	5
↑	↑	↑
20 children	divided into	5 teams

An **equation** is a number sentence. It uses an equal sign to show that two amounts are equal. You can use the expression above to write an equation to solve the problem.

20	÷	5	=	4
↑	↑	↑	↑	↑
20 children	divided into	5 teams	is equal to	4 children on each team.

So, there are 4 children on each team.

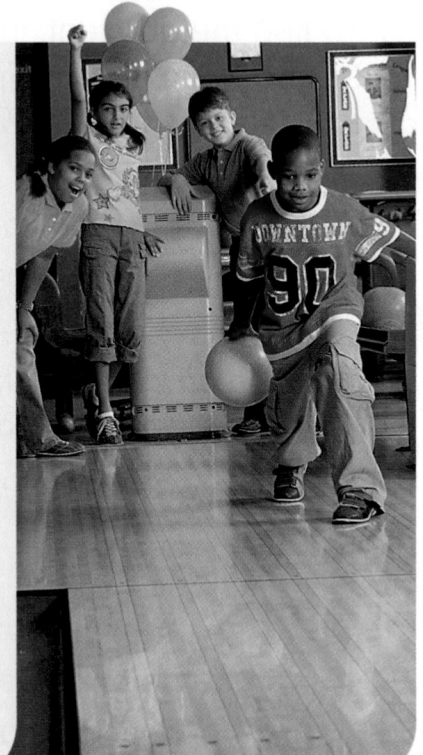

You need to know what operation symbol to use in an equation.

There are 3 children eating pizza at each of 5 tables. There are 15 children eating pizza.

$5 \bullet 3 = 15$

Which symbol correctly completes the equation?

Try +. $5 + 3 = 15$ is false.   Try −. $5 - 3 = 15$ is false.
Try ÷. $5 \div 3 = 15$ is false.   Try ×. $5 \times 3 = 15$ is true.

So, the correct symbol is ×.

Guided Practice

1. Write an expression to show 6 children bowling and 5 more children joining the game.

Write an expression. Then write an equation to solve.

✓ **2.** There were 7 children who each paid $4 to bowl. How much did the children pay in all?

✓ **3.** There were 28 slices of pizza. The children ate 19 slices. How many slices of pizza were left?

4. (TALK Math) **Explain** how you know which operation symbol will complete the equation 26 ● 13 = 39.

Independent Practice and Problem Solving

Write an expression. Then write an equation to solve.

5. There were 42 children and 23 adults at a roller-skating rink. How many people were at the rink in all?

6. There were 45 balloons tied in 9 equal bunches at a party. How many balloons were in each bunch?

Write +, −, ×, or ÷ to complete each equation.

7. 3 ● 2 = 48 ÷ 8

8. 16 ● 12 = 4 × 1

9. 11 ● 10 = 7 × 3

USE DATA For 10–12, use the graph and the equations in the box.

10. Troy scored 8 points each time it was his turn to bowl. Which equation shows how many turns Troy had?

11. John scored 10 more points than Max. Which equation shows how many points John scored?

12. (WRITE Math) Who scored more points during the bowling games—the boys or girls? **Explain** how you know.

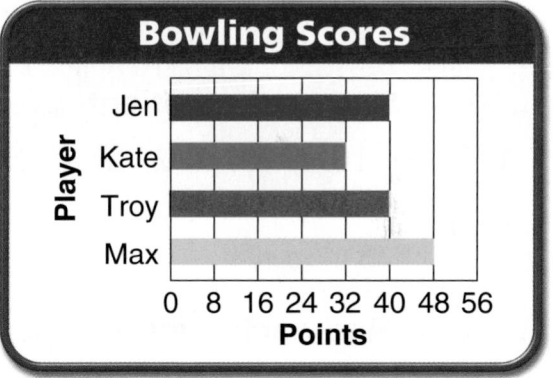

Bowling Scores

$8 \times 5 = 40$	$48 + 10 = 58$
$40 \div 8 = 5$	$48 - 10 = 38$

Mixed Review and Test Prep

13. There are 36 score sheets in 9 packages. How many score sheets are in each package? (p. 330)

14. How many sides does a triangle have? (Grade 2)

15. Test Prep There are 4 pizzas each with 8 slices. Which equation shows the number of slices in all?

A $4 + 8 = 12$ **C** $4 \times 8 = 32$

B $8 - 4 = 4$ **D** $8 \div 4 = 2$

(Extra Practice) on page 338, Set E

Extra Practice

Set A Find each missing factor and quotient. (pp. 322–323)

1. $6 \times \blacksquare = 36$ $36 \div 6 = \blacksquare$ 2. $6 \times \blacksquare = 54$ $54 \div 6 = \blacksquare$

Find each quotient.

3. $12 \div 6 = \blacksquare$ 4. $\blacksquare = 42 \div 6$ 5. $30 \div 6 = \blacksquare$ 6. $\blacksquare = 24 \div 6$

7. $6\overline{)48}$ 8. $6\overline{)6}$ 9. $6\overline{)60}$ 10. $6\overline{)18}$

Set B Find each missing factor and quotient. (pp. 324–325)

1. $7 \times \blacksquare = 28$ $28 \div 7 = \blacksquare$ 2. $8 \times \blacksquare = 40$ $40 \div 8 = \blacksquare$

Find each quotient.

3. $\blacksquare = 56 \div 7$ 4. $16 \div 8 = \blacksquare$ 5. $\blacksquare = 72 \div 8$ 6. $21 \div 7 = \blacksquare$

7. $8\overline{)48}$ 8. $7\overline{)35}$ 9. $8\overline{)32}$ 10. $7\overline{)63}$

Set C Find each quotient. (pp. 330–331)

1. $70 \div 10 = \blacksquare$ 2. $\blacksquare = 27 \div 9$ 3. $\blacksquare = 50 \div 10$ 4. $81 \div 9 = \blacksquare$

5. $9\overline{)54}$ 6. $10\overline{)20}$ 7. $10\overline{)100}$ 8. $9\overline{)36}$

Set D Find each quotient. (pp. 332–335)

1. $\blacksquare = 32 \div 4$ 2. $60 \div 12 = \blacksquare$ 3. $45 \div 9 = \blacksquare$ 4. $\blacksquare = 88 \div 11$

5. $12\overline{)108}$ 6. $8\overline{)56}$ 7. $11\overline{)110}$ 8. $12\overline{)84}$

9. Mr. Jones divided 33 students into 11 equal groups. How many students were in each group?

10. Marie has 72 CDs. She has them arranged in stacks of 12. How many stacks of CDs does she have?

Set E Write an expression. Then write an equation to solve. (pp. 336–337)

1. There are 35 seeds planted equally among 7 pots. How many seeds are in each pot?

2. Daniel earned $75 mowing lawns. Pat earned $90. How much more money did Pat earn than Daniel?

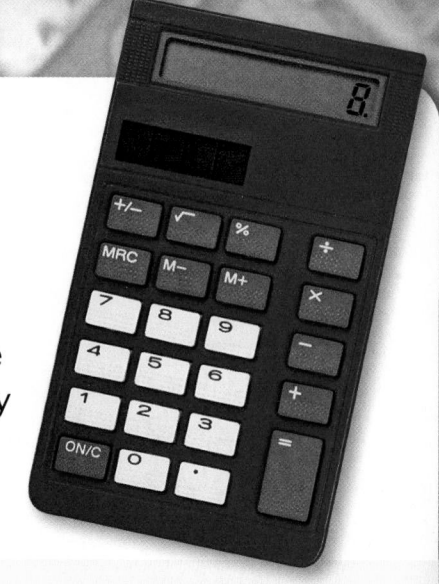

TECHNOLOGY ★ CONNECTION

Calculator: Division Facts

Use a Calculator for Division

Ms. Andrews bought 56 new books for her class library. There are 7 shelves on her bookshelf. If she divides the books evenly on the shelves, how many will go on each shelf?

Write a number sentence for the word problem. $56 \div 7 = $ ■

Use a calculator to solve.

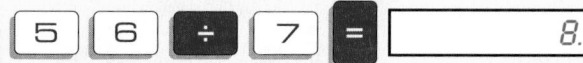
```
5  6  ÷  7  =  |          8. |
```

So, Ms. Andrews can put 8 books on each shelf.

What if Ms. Andrews bought 58 books? How many books would go on each shelf? How many would be left over?

A calculator gives the remainder as a decimal. A remainder is the amount left over when a number cannot be divided evenly.

```
5  8  ÷  7  =  | 8.2857142 |
```

To find out how many books are left over, use a *near fact*.

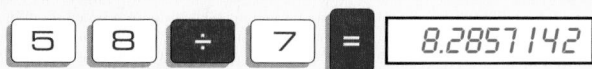
```
8  ×  7  =  |          56. |
```

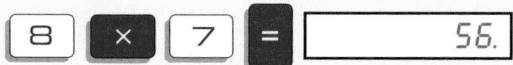
```
5  8  -  5  6  =  |          2. |
```

So, Ms. Andrews can put 8 books on each shelf and have 2 left over.

Try It

Use a calculator to divide.

1. $63 \div 7 = $ ■   **2.** $60 \div 12 = $ ■   **3.** $54 \div 9 = $ ■   **4.** $48 \div 6 = $ ■

Use a calculator to divide. Then use a near fact to find the remainder.

5. $32 \div 5 = $ ■   **6.** $65 \div 9 = $ ■   **7.** $76 \div 8 = $ ■   **8.** $68 \div 11 = $ ■

    remainder ■   remainder ■   remainder ■   remainder ■

Getting the SAME Answer

Find $6 - 2 \div 2$.

ONE WAY

Think: $6 - 2 = 4$

$6 - 2 \div 2 = 4 \div 2$

$4 \div 2 = 2$

ANOTHER WAY

Think: $2 \div 2 = 1$

$6 - 2 \div 2 = 6 - 1$

$6 - 1 = 5$

There seem to be two correct answers. Over the years, mathematicians have created rules so that everyone solves the problem the same way and gets the same answer.

Order of Operations

1. Solve operations inside parentheses first.

2. When there are no parentheses, multiply and divide from left to right.

3. Then, add and subtract from left to right.

So, the correct answer to $6 - 2 \div 2$ is 5.

Examples

A Find $12 \div (4 - 1)$

Think: Subtract inside the parentheses first. Then divide.

$12 \div (4 - 1) = 12 \div 3$

$12 \div 3 = 4$

B Find $6 + 4 \times 5$

Think: There are no parentheses. So, multiply first. Then add.

$6 + 4 \times 5 = 6 + 20$

$6 + 20 = 26$

Try It

Find the sum or difference.

1. $(8 - 2) \times 6 = \blacksquare$

2. $5 + 10 \div 5 = \blacksquare$

3. $3 \times (4 + 6) = \blacksquare$

4. $6 + 4 \div 2 = \blacksquare$

5. $(15 - 3) \times 2 = \blacksquare$

6. $14 - 7 \times 2 = \blacksquare$

7. **WRITE Math** ▶ **Explain** how to find $8 - 2 \times 3$.

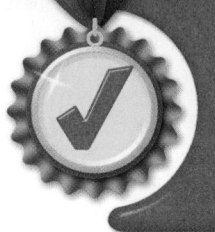

Chapter 13 Review/Test

Check Concepts

Write a division sentence for each. (pp. 332–335)

1.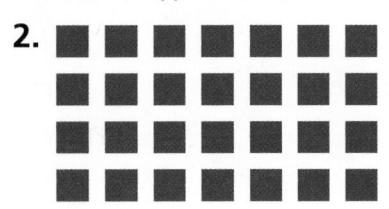

2. [grid of squares]

3.
$$
\begin{array}{ccccc}
27 & & 18 & & 9 \\
-\ 9 & & -\ 9 & & -\ 9 \\
\hline
18 & & 9 & & 0
\end{array}
$$

Check Skills

Find each quotient. (pp. 322–323, 324–325, 330–331, 332–335)

4. $32 \div 8 = \blacksquare$ 5. $70 \div 10 = \blacksquare$ 6. $21 \div 3 = \blacksquare$ 7. $\blacksquare = 45 \div 5$

8. $99 \div 11 = \blacksquare$ 9. $54 \div 9 = \blacksquare$ 10. $60 \div 12 = \blacksquare$ 11. $0 \div 2 = \blacksquare$

12. $16 \div 2 = \blacksquare$ 13. $\blacksquare = 48 \div 6$ 14. $20 \div 4 = \blacksquare$ 15. $\blacksquare = 63 \div 7$

16. $100 \div 10 = \blacksquare$ 17. $35 \div 5 = \blacksquare$ 18. $121 \div 11 = \blacksquare$ 19. $81 \div 9 = \blacksquare$

20. $9\overline{)36}$ 21. $1\overline{)7}$ 22. $3\overline{)9}$ 23. $8\overline{)24}$

24. $7\overline{)28}$ 25. $6\overline{)36}$ 26. $8\overline{)0}$ 27. $12\overline{)144}$

28. $1\overline{)4}$ 29. $11\overline{)55}$ 30. $4\overline{)24}$ 31. $2\overline{)10}$

Write an expression. Then write an equation to solve. (pp. 336–337)

32. There were 30 students in each of 6 groups. How many students were in each group?

33. There were 54 girls and 47 boys in line for a ride. How many students were in line?

Check Problem Solving

Solve. (pp. 326–329)

34. Mary gave half of her markers to a friend. Then she bought 8 more markers. Now Mary has 21 markers. How many markers did she have to start?

35. **WRITE Math** Tim bought 3 packs of baseball cards. He gave 4 cards to his friend. Now Tim has 14 cards. How many cards were in each pack? **Explain** how you know.

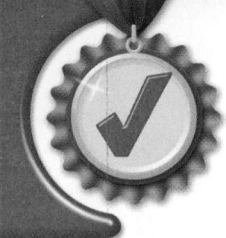

Unit Review/Test
Chapters 11–13

Multiple Choice

1. Which division sentence is represented by this array? (p. 282)

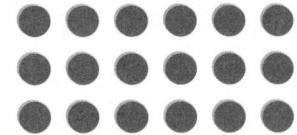

   A $18 \div 2 = 9$

   B $18 \div 3 = 6$

   C $24 \div 3 = 8$

   D $24 \div 6 = 4$

2. Which number makes this number sentence true? (p. 322)

$$54 \div \blacksquare = 9$$

   A 8

   B 7

   C 6

   D 5

3. Which number sentence is in the same fact family as $32 \div 8 = 4$?

   (p. 286)

   A $8 \times 5 = 40$

   B $4 \times 8 = 32$

   C $24 \div 8 = 3$

   D $8 \div 4 = 2$

4. Luis has 20 model cars. He puts 5 cars on each shelf. How many shelves does he use? (p. 302)

   A 2

   B 3

   C 4

   D 5

5. A pet shop has 108 goldfish. There are 12 goldfish in each fish tank. How many fish tanks have goldfish? (p. 332)

   A 6

   B 7

   C 8

   D 9

6. Which division sentence is represented by the following? (p. 332)

$$\begin{array}{ccc} 21 & 14 & 7 \\ -7 & -7 & -7 \\ \hline 14 & 7 & 0 \end{array}$$

   A $7 \div 1 = 7$

   B $14 \div 2 = 7$

   C $28 \div 7 = 4$

   D $21 \div 7 = 3$

7. Which number is missing from the table? (p. 304)

÷	16	■	24	28
4	4	5	6	7

A 21

B 20

C 19

D 18

8. Melissa spent $40 on tickets to the school play. She bought 8 tickets. Each ticket cost the same amount. What was the cost of each ticket?

(p. 324)

A $8

B $6

C $5

D $4

9. The school store has 80 pencils in boxes. Each box holds 10 pencils. How many boxes of pencils does the store have? (p. 330)

A 7

B 8

C 9

D 10

Short Response

10. What number makes this number sentence true? (p. 332)

$$77 \div \blacksquare = 7$$

11. Sammy picked 24 apples and divided them equally among 3 friends. How many apples did he give to each friend? (p. 304)

12. Write a division sentence for the array. (p. 282)

Extended Response

13. Darrin picked 63 strawberries. He wants to divide them equally among 9 friends. **Explain** how to use repeated subtraction to find how many strawberries Darrin will give to each of his friends. (p. 330)

14. Aimee baked 36 cookies. She wants to divide them equally among 6 bags. How many cookies will go in each bag? **Explain** how to use a related multiplication fact to find the answer.

(p. 322)

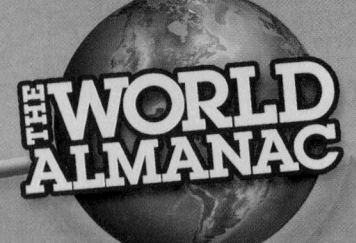
The Wheel Is a Big Deal

AROUND THE WHEEL

Think about the wheel. Without it, almost no one could travel anywhere. Buses, trains, cars, skateboards, and even planes and space shuttles use wheels.

FACT·ACTIVITY

Vehicles with Different Numbers of Wheels

	Vehicle	Number of Wheels
	unicycle	1
	bicycle	2
	tricycle	3
	car	4
	space shuttle	6
	tractor trailer	18

School teams are making models of vehicles with a given number of wheels. Use the table to answer the questions.

❶ Team A has 22 wheels. How many bicycles can they make?

❷ Team B has 48 wheels. How many space shuttles can they make?

❸ Team A wants to make cars instead of bicycles. How many cars can they make? What can they make with the extra wheels?

❹ Make your own vehicle.

► Invent a new vehicle that uses 7 wheels.

► Draw your vehicle and name it.

► How many of these new vehicles could you make if you had 21 wheels?

REUSING TIRED TIRES

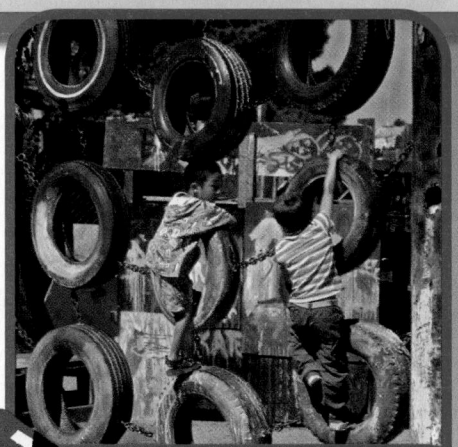

Trucks, motorcycles, and cars all use tires. These tires are strong, but they do wear out. What happens to old tires? Ground-up tires can be used to make roads, playground surfaces, and jogging tracks. Some tires are even made into park benches and waste containers. Whole tires can be used to make playground equipment.

FACT·ACTIVITY

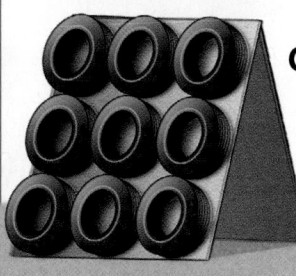

**Climbing Wall
9 tires**

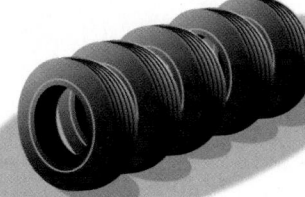

**Tunnel
5 tires**

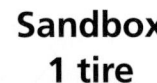

**Sandbox
1 tire**

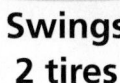

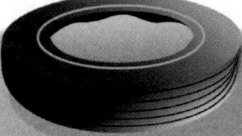

**Swings
2 tires**

Some playgrounds use tires for swings, tunnels, and climbing walls. Use the data from the playground pictures to answer the questions.

❶ How many tires are needed for this playground?

❷ How many climbing walls can be made from 63 tires?

❸ **WRITE Math** ▸ Are 19 tires enough to make 4 tire tunnels? **Explain.**

❹ It takes 6 tires to make the tunnel and sandbox combined. How many sets of these can be made from 30 tires?

5 Geometry and Patterns

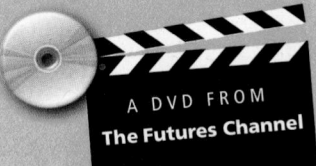

A DVD FROM
The Futures Channel

with
Chapter Projects

1

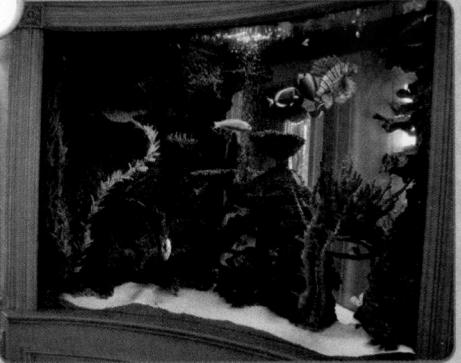

Fresh or saltwater aquariums of all shapes and sizes bring nature into a home or office.

2

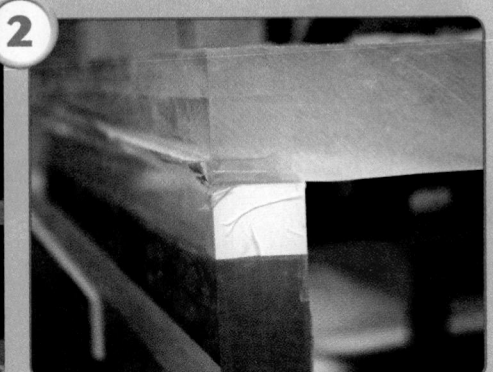

This large tank, a rectangular prism, will hold 32,000 pounds of water. It needs thick acrylic faces!

3

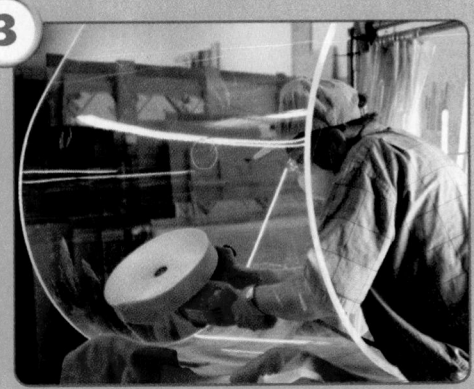

Some customers want curved-shaped aquariums like the half-cylinder surface that is being polished.

VOCABULARY POWER

TALK Math

What math ideas do you see in the **Math on Location** photographs? How many faces does the large rectangular tank have?

READ Math

REVIEW VOCABULARY You learned the words below when you learned about geometry last year. How do these words relate to **Math on Location**?

rectangle

square

solid figure a figure such as a sphere, a cube, a rectangular prism, a cylinder, a cone, or a pyramid

WRITE Math

Copy and complete a Degree of Meaning Grid like the one below. Use what you know about geometry.

General	Less General	Specific	More Specific
Plane figure	Lines	Line segment	Yarn
Polygon	Quadrilateral	Square	Napkin
Solid figure			

GO ONLINE
Technology
Multimedia Math Glossary link at
www.harcourtschool.com/hspmath

14 Plane Figures

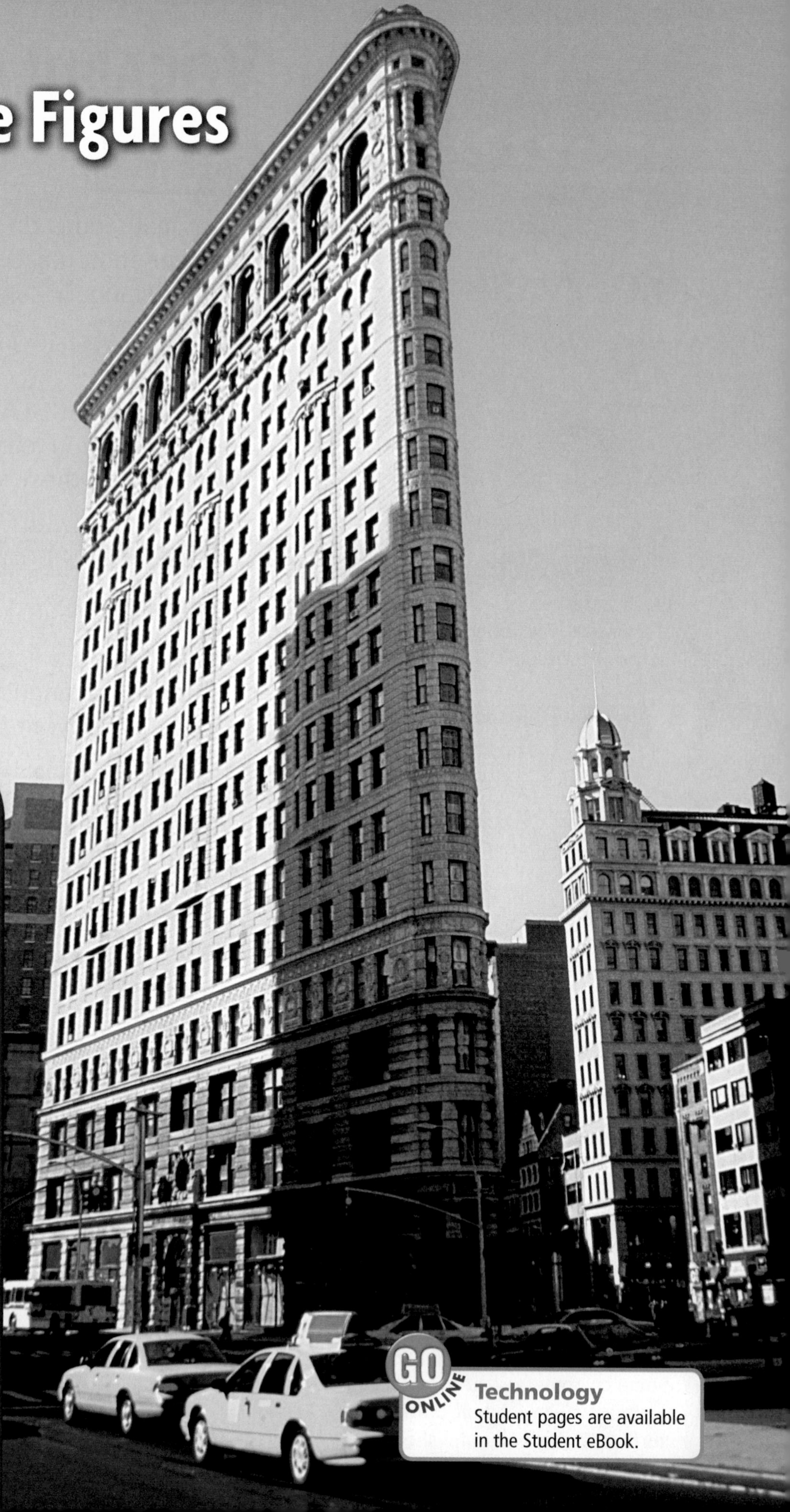

FAST FACT

The Flatiron Building is one of the oldest skyscrapers in New York City. The sides of the three-sided building connect to form a right triangle!

Investigate

Each side of the Flatiron Building is in the shape of a rectangle. Below are pictures of other skyscrapers. Make a list of the plane figures you see.

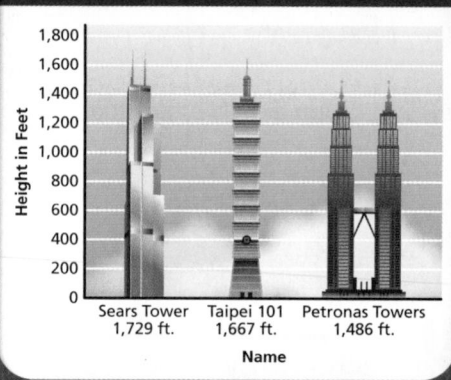

Skyscrapers

Height in Feet

Name	Height
Sears Tower	1,729 ft.
Taipei 101	1,667 ft.
Petronas Towers	1,486 ft.

GO ONLINE
Technology
Student pages are available in the Student eBook.

Check your understanding of important skills
needed for success in Chapter 14.

▶ Plane Figures

Name each figure.

1.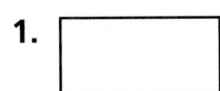

2.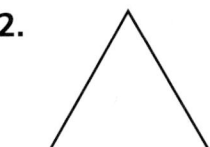

3. ◯

4.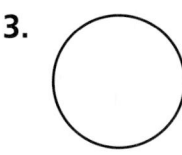

5.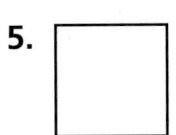

6.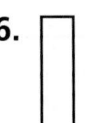

▶ Sides and Vertices

Tell the number of sides and vertices in each figure.

7.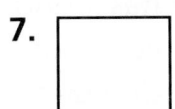

8.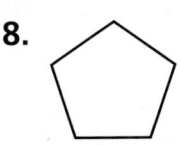

9.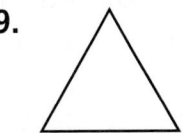

10. ▱

VOCABULARY POWER

CHAPTER VOCABULARY

acute angle
acute triangle
angle
center
circle
circumference
diameter
equilateral
  triangle
hexagon
intersecting
  lines
isosceles triangle

line
line segment
obtuse angle
obtuse triangle
octagon
parallel lines
parallelogram
pentagon
perpendicular
  lines
plane figure
point
polygon

quadrilateral
radius
ray
rhombus
right angle
right triangle
scalene triangle
straight angle
trapezoid
2-dimensional
  figures
vertex

WARM-UP WORDS

angle A figure formed by two rays that share an endpoint

line A straight path extending in both directions with no endpoints

quadrilateral A polygon with four sides

Line Segments and Angles

OBJECTIVE: Identify points, lines, line segments, rays, and angles.

Learn

PROBLEM Carmen drew this figure. What math words can you use to describe the figure?

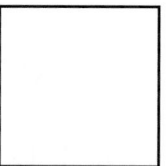

Vocabulary

point	line	line segment
ray	angle	vertex

right angle   acute angle

obtuse angle   straight angle

The words below can help you describe figures.

point
- is an exact position or location

point ↓

line
- is straight
- continues in both directions
- does not end

line segment
- is straight
- is part of a line
- has 2 endpoints

ray
- is straight
- is part of a line
- has 1 endpoint
- continues in one direction

An **angle** is formed by two rays that share an endpoint. The shared endpoint is called a **vertex**. The plural of *vertex* is *vertices*.

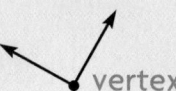

vertex

A **right angle** forms a square corner.

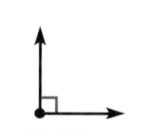

An **acute angle** is less than a right angle.

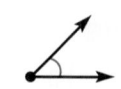

An **obtuse angle** is greater than a right angle.

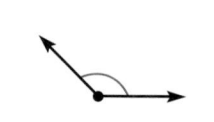

In a **straight angle**, two rays point in opposite directions and form a line.

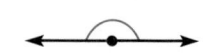

So, the 4 sides of Carmen's figure are line segments. There are 4 right angles and 4 vertices.

- How are lines and line segments alike? How are they different?

350

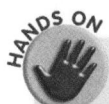

Activity   Draw Angles

Materials ■ dot paper, ruler

Step 1	Step 2	Step 3
Draw a point.	Use a ruler to draw 2 rays that meet at the point.	Label your angle.
		right angle

- Draw and label an acute angle, an obtuse angle, and a straight angle.

- Explain how you can use the corner of a sheet of paper to check the angles you drew.

Guided Practice

1. How many line segments are in this figure?

Tell whether each is a _point, line, line segment,_ or _ray_.

2. 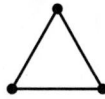   3. •   4.   ✓5.

Use the corner of a sheet of paper to tell whether each angle is _right, acute, obtuse,_ or _straight._

6.   7.   8.   ✓9.

10. **TALK Math** **Explain** the difference between a ray and a line segment.

Independent Practice and Problem Solving

Tell whether each is a *point*, *line*, *line segment*, or *ray*.

11. 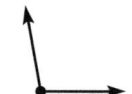 12. 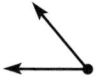 13.   14.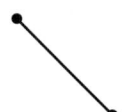

Use the corner of a sheet of paper to tell whether each angle is *right*, *acute*, *obtuse*, or *straight*.

15. 16. 17. 18.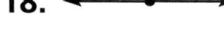

19. Katie made the figure on the right on grid paper. How many angles does Katie's figure have? Tell how many are right, acute, and obtuse.

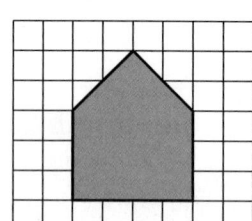

20. Use a ruler and dot paper to draw an acute angle.

21. **≡FAST FACT** The first pocket watch was invented in 1524. What time is shown? What type of angle do the hands form?

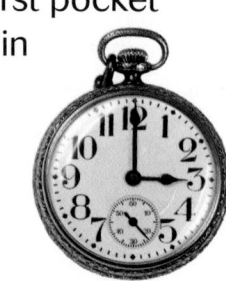

22. **WRITE Math** ▸ **What's the Error?** Zoey says this angle is an acute angle. Is she correct? **Explain.**

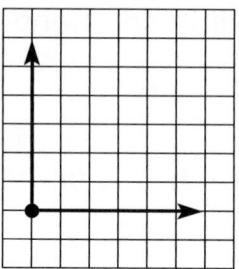

Mixed Review and Test Prep

23. Bruce has 8 bags of marbles. There are the same number of marbles in each bag. He has a total of 56 marbles. How many marbles are in each bag? (p. 324)

24. The drama club sold 3,500 tickets for three shows. They sold 987 tickets for the Thursday show and 1,215 tickets for the Friday show. How many tickets did they sell for the Saturday show? (p. 58, 88)

25. **Test Prep** Which shows a ray?

A ●⟶

B ╱●

C ↖

D ●

Extra Practice on page 370, Set A

Write to Explain

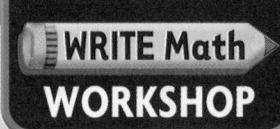

One way to explain two different things is to write about ways they are alike and ways they are different. In doing so, you compare the things.

Allen is learning about line segments, rays, and angles. He compares two angles by explaining how they are alike and how they are different.

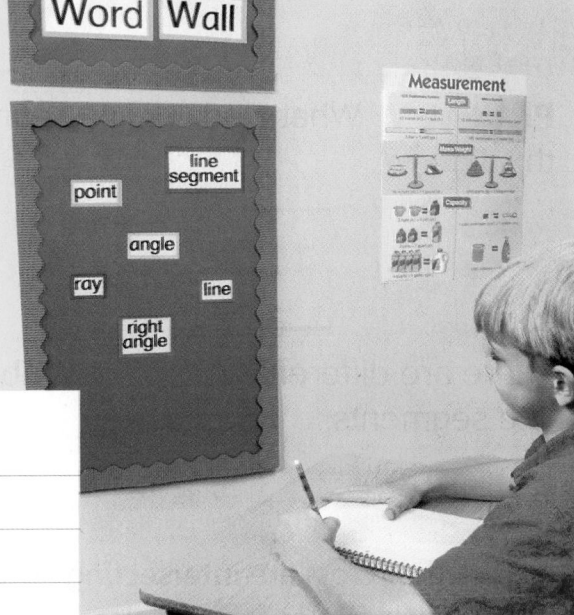

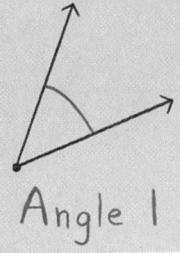

Angle 1

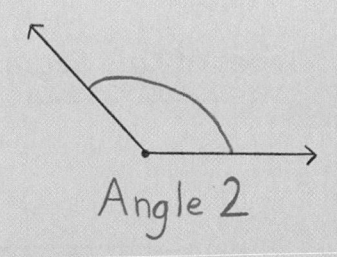

Angle 2

The two angles are alike. They are both made of two rays that share one endpoint.

The two angles are different. The angles are different sizes. Angle 1 is an acute angle. It is smaller than a right angle. Angle 2 is an obtuse angle. It is larger than a right angle.

Tips

To compare two drawings:

- First, describe the ways the drawings are alike.
- Then, describe the ways the drawings are different.
- Use correct definitions of math words.

Problem Solving Write a paragraph to explain how the drawings are alike and how they are different.

1.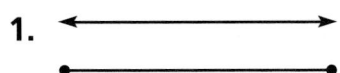

2.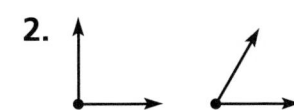

Types of Lines

OBJECTIVE: Identify and classify lines as intersecting, perpendicular, or parallel.

 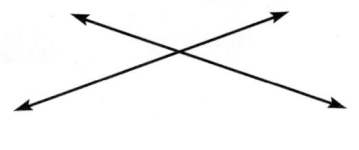
Learn

PROBLEM What kinds of line segments are in this figure?

There are different ways to describe lines and line segments.

Vocabulary

intersecting lines

perpendicular lines

parallel lines

Types of Lines

Lines that cross are **intersecting lines**. Intersecting lines form angles.

Intersecting lines that cross to form right angles are **perpendicular lines**.

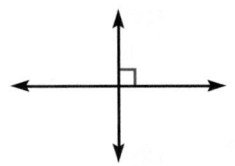

Lines that appear never to cross are **parallel lines**. They are always the same distance apart. They do not form any angles.

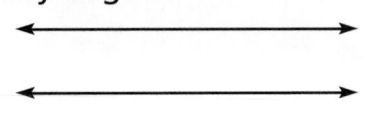

Types of Line Segments

The yellow and blue line segments meet. So, they form an angle.

The red and blue line segments meet at a right angle. So, they are perpendicular.

The green and blue line segments never cross. They are always the same distance apart. So, they appear to be parallel.

Guided Practice

1. The lines cross to form angles. Are they perpendicular lines or intersecting lines?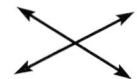

Describe the green line segments. Tell if the line segments appear to be *perpendicular* or *parallel*.

2.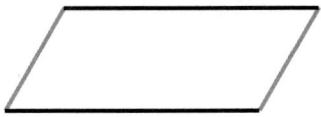

✓ 3.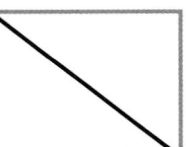

✓ 4.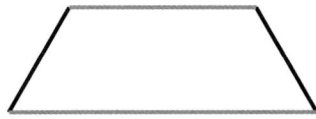

5. **TALK Math** **Explain** the difference between parallel lines and perpendicular lines.

Independent Practice and Problem Solving

Describe the lines. Tell if the lines appear to be *intersecting, perpendicular,* or *parallel*.

6.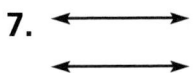

7.

8.

Describe the green line segments. Tell if the line segments appear to be *perpendicular* or *parallel*.

9.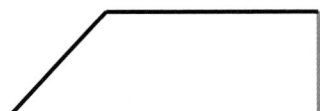

10.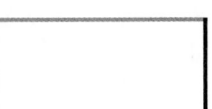

11.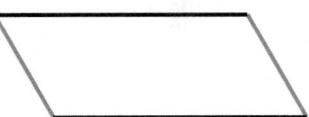

12. Use a ruler to draw pairs of intersecting, parallel, and perpendicular lines. Label each pair of lines.

13. **WRITE Math** **What's the Error?** Katie says the lines below appear to be parallel. **Explain** her error.

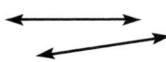

Mixed Review and Test Prep

14. Which operation sign goes in the box to make this number sentence true?

$$12 \bullet 4 = 3 \text{ (p. 304)}$$

15. Name this angle. (p. 350)

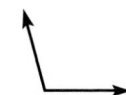

16. **Test Prep** Which of these pairs of lines appear to be perpendicular?

A 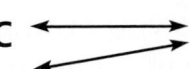   C

B   D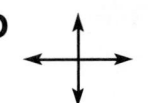

Extra Practice on page 370, Set B

Identify Plane Figures

OBJECTIVE: Identify, classify, and describe plane figures.

Learn

A **plane figure** is a figure on a flat surface. It is formed by lines that are curved, straight, or both.

A **polygon** is a closed plane figure with straight sides that are line segments.

Polygons have length and width, so they are called **two-dimensional figures**.

Polygons can be named by the number of sides or number of angles they have.

triangle
3 sides
3 angles

quadrilateral
4 sides
4 angles

pentagon
5 sides
5 angles

hexagon
6 sides
6 angles

octagon
8 sides
8 angles

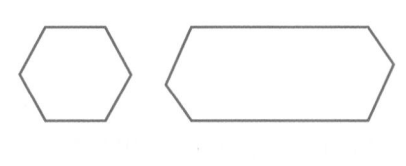

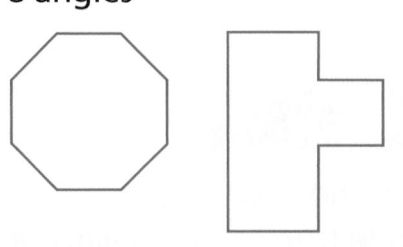

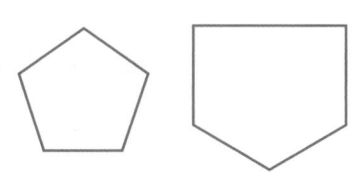

• What do you notice about the number of sides and the number of angles in each of the polygons shown above?

Guided Practice

1. Tell why the figure at the right is not a polygon.

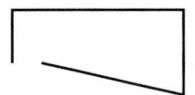

Name each polygon. Tell how many sides.

2.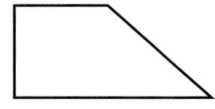

3.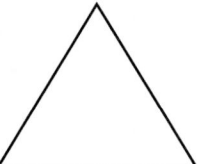

✓ 4.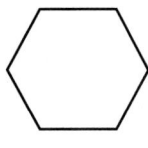

✓ 5.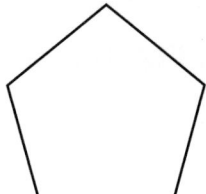

6. **TALK Math** **Explain** why a pentagon is a polygon.

Independent Practice and Problem Solving

Name each polygon. Tell how many sides.

7.

8.

9.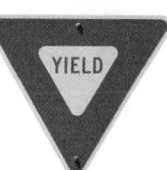

10.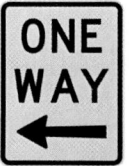

Tell whether each figure is a polygon. Write *yes* or *no*.

11.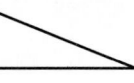

12.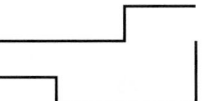

13.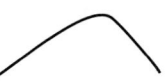

14.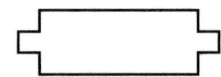

15. Draw a polygon with 4 sides and 4 angles. Then name the polygon.

16. Val has 25 craft sticks. She glues some sticks together to make 6 triangles. How many sticks does she have left?

17. **WRITE Math** Are figures *A–E* all polygons? **Explain** why or why not.

   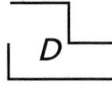

Mixed Review and Test Prep

18. Is this angle *right, acute, obtuse,* or *straight*? (p. 350)

19. How many endpoints does a ray have? (p. 350)

20. **Test Prep** How many sides does a pentagon have?

A 4   **B** 5   **C** 6   **D** 8

Extra Practice on page 370, Set C

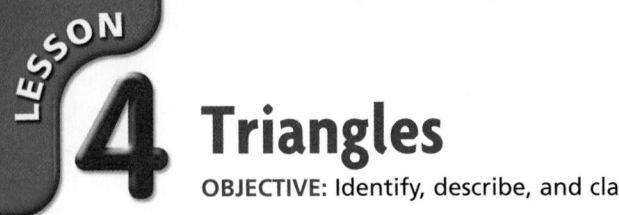

Triangles

OBJECTIVE: Identify, describe, and classify triangles.

Learn

PROBLEM The sculpture in the photo is called *Moondog*. The artist used triangles and other polygons. Name the types of triangles outlined in the sculpture.

Quick Review

Is the angle a right angle? Write *yes* or *no*.

1.   2.   3.

4.   5.

Vocabulary

equilateral triangle	**right triangle**
isosceles triangle	**obtuse triangle**
scalene triangle	**acute triangle**

ONE WAY You can name triangles by their equal sides.

equilateral triangle	isosceles triangle	scalene triangle
3 equal sides	2 equal sides	0 equal sides
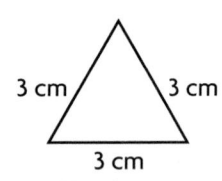	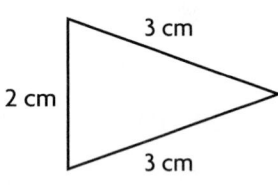	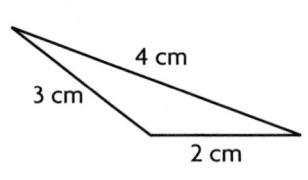

So, the red and white triangles are equilateral triangles, the yellow, purple, and green triangles are isosceles triangles, and the blue triangles are scalene triangles.

▲ The sculpture *Moondog*, by Tony Smith, is at the National Gallery of Art in Washington, D.C.

ANOTHER WAY You can name triangles by their angles.

right triangle	obtuse triangle	acute triangle
1 right angle	1 obtuse angle	3 acute angles
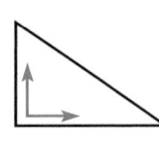	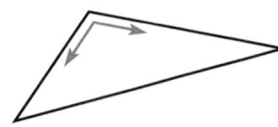	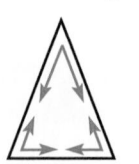

• Can a right triangle also be an isosceles triangle? **Explain.**

Remember

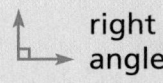 right angle

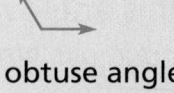 obtuse angle

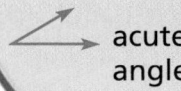 acute angle

1. Name each triangle.
Write *equilateral, isosceles,* or *scalene.*

Think: How many equal sides does each triangle have?

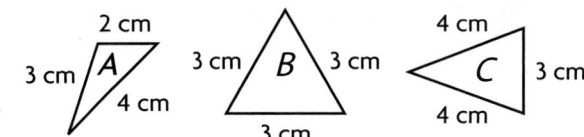

Name each triangle. Write *right, obtuse,* or *acute.*

2.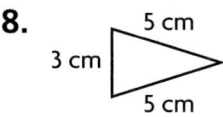

3.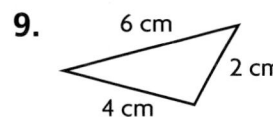

✓4.

✓5.

6. TALK Math Describe how a triangle can be both equilateral and acute.

Independent Practice and Problem Solving

Name each triangle. Write *equilateral, isosceles,* or *scalene.*

7. 5 cm, 5 cm, 5 cm

8. 5 cm, 3 cm, 5 cm

9. 6 cm, 2 cm, 4 cm

10. 4 cm, 4 cm, 2 cm

Name each triangle. Write *right, obtuse,* or *acute.*

11. 3 cm, 5 cm, 4 cm

12. 9 cm, 3 cm, 7 cm

13. 6 cm, 3 cm, 6 cm

14. 4 cm, 3 cm, 5 cm

15. Two of my sides are 5 inches long. My third side is shorter. All of my angles are less than a right angle. What kind of triangle am I?

16. WRITE Math How are an equilateral triangle and a scalene triangle alike? How are they different? **Explain.**

Mixed Review and Test Prep

17. Aaron drew a plane figure with 5 sides and 5 angles. Name the figure Aaron drew. (p. 356)

18. You toss a coin. What are the possible outcomes? (p. 180)

19. Test Prep Which correctly names this triangle?

A scalene and obtuse

B isosceles and acute

C scalene and acute

D isosceles and obtuse

5 cm, 9 cm, 6 cm

Extra Practice on page 371, Set D

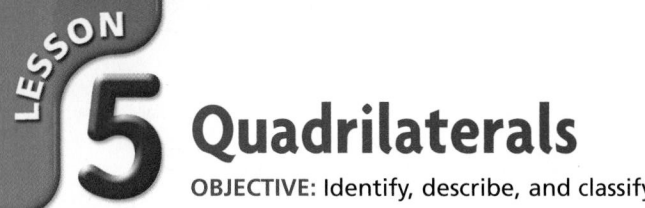

LESSON 5

Quadrilaterals

OBJECTIVE: Identify, describe, and classify quadrilaterals.

Quick Review

Write the number of sides.

1. 2. 3.

4. 5.

Learn

PROBLEM Lynn's aunt sent her this postcard of the Eiffel Tower, in Paris, France. What type of quadrilateral do you see in the tower?

Vocabulary

rhombus   parallelogram

trapezoid

Some quadrilaterals are named by their sides and their angles.

Examples

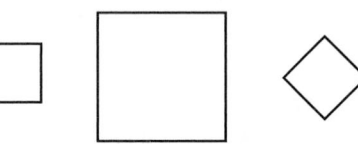

Square

- 2 pairs of parallel sides
- 4 equal sides
- 4 right angles

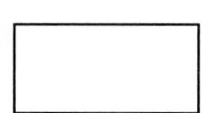

Rectangle

- 2 pairs of parallel sides
- 2 pairs of equal sides
- 4 right angles

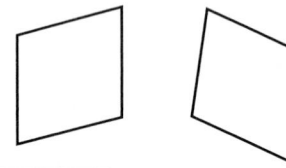

Rhombus

- 2 pairs of parallel sides
- 4 equal sides

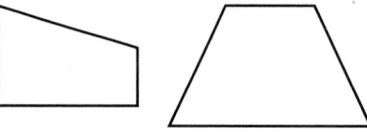

Trapezoid

- exactly 1 pair of parallel sides
- lengths of sides may not be the same
- sizes of angles may not be the same

The quadrilateral in the tower has 1 pair of parallel sides.

So, the quadrilateral in the Eiffel Tower is a trapezoid.

- What types of angles are in the trapezoid?

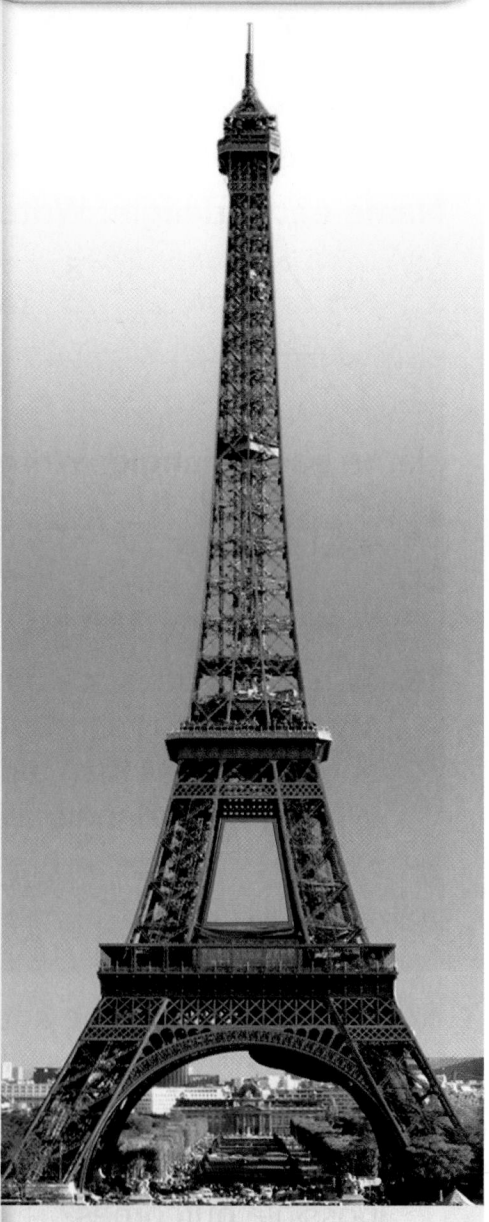

▲ The Eiffel Tower is 984 feet high. From the top you can see the city of Paris.

360

Another Example

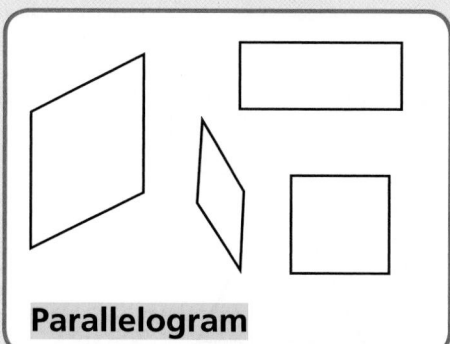

Parallelogram

- 2 pairs of parallel sides
- 2 pairs of equal sides

- Explain why a trapezoid is not a parallelogram.

- Explain why a square is a parallelogram, a rectangle, a quadrilateral, and a rhombus.

Guided Practice

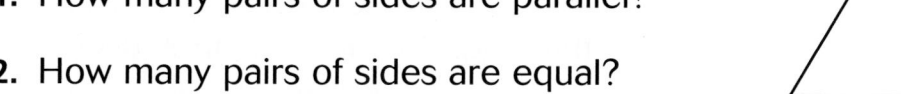

Look at the quadrilateral at the right.

1. How many pairs of sides are parallel?

2. How many pairs of sides are equal?

3. What types of angles are in the quadrilateral?

4. Name the quadrilateral.

Write as many names for each quadrilateral as you can.

5.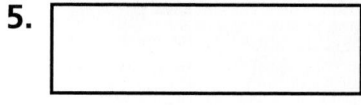

6.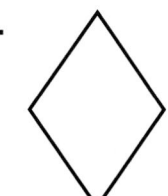

✓ 7.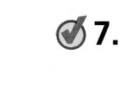

8.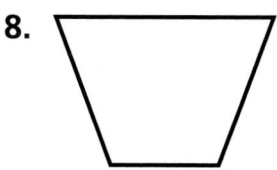

9.

✓ 10.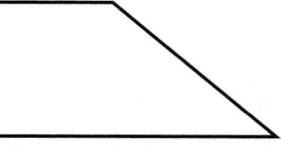

11. **TALK Math** Describe a square by its sides and by its angles.

Write as many names for each quadrilateral as you can.

12.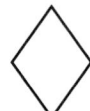

13.

14.

15.

16.

17.

For 18–21, use the quadrilaterals at the right.

18. Which quadrilaterals have 4 right angles?

19. Which quadrilaterals have 2 pairs of parallel sides?

20. Which quadrilaterals have no right angles?

21. How are quadrilateral B and quadrilateral C alike? How are they different?

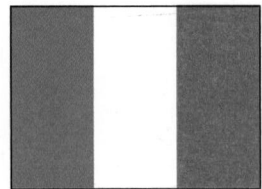

22. Describe the quadrilaterals you see in the flag of France below.

23. Below is a diagram of Jay's bedroom. His bedroom is a rectangle. What is the length of the side labeled s?

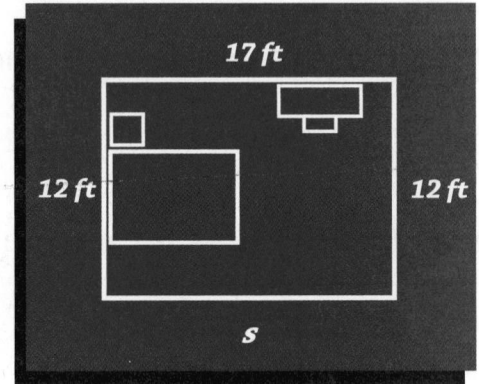

24. I am a quadrilateral with 1 pair of parallel sides. My sides may not be the same length. What figure am I?

25. I am a quadrilateral with 2 pairs of parallel sides and 2 pairs of equal sides. What figure am I?

26. **Reasoning** Describe how a rhombus is like a square and how it is different.

27. **WRITE Math** ▸ **Sense or Nonsense** Joe said all parallelograms have 4 equal sides. Does his statement make sense? **Explain.**

Technology
Use Harcourt Mega Math, Ice Station
ROM Exploration, *Polar Planes,* Level G.

Learn About) Venn Diagrams

A Venn diagram shows how sets of things are related. Look at the Venn diagram below. One circle shows figures that are rectangles. The other circle shows figures that are rhombuses. The figures inside the area where the circles overlap are both rectangles and rhombuses.

Rectangles   Rhombuses

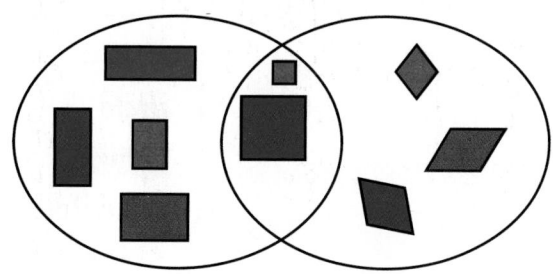

Try It

Use the Venn diagram.

28. How many rectangles are there?

29. How many rhombuses are there?

30. How many figures are both rectangles and rhombuses?

31. What type of quadrilateral is in both circles?

32. Where in the Venn diagram would you put this figure? ■

Mixed Review and Test Prep

33. Chris, Lee, and Jill played a video game. Chris scored 6,852 points. Lee scored 6,781 points and Jill scored 6,917 points. Write the scores in order from least to greatest. (p. 32)

34. Name this triangle by its sides. (p. 358)

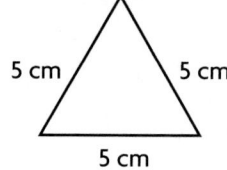

5 cm   5 cm

5 cm

35. Test Prep What figure has 2 pairs of parallel sides, no right angles, and 4 equal sides?

36. Test Prep Rita glued craft sticks together to make this shape. Which best describes the quadrilateral Rita made?

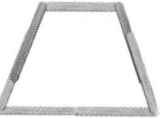

A parallelogram   **C** rhombus

B rectangle   **D** trapezoid

6 Circles

OBJECTIVE: Identify and draw the parts of a circle.

Quick Review

Name each figure.

1. ◺

2. ◯

3. ▭

4. ⬡

5. ▱

Learn

A **circle** is a closed plane figure made of points that are the same distance from the center. The **center** is the point in the middle of a circle.

Vocabulary

circle   center

radius   diameter

circumference

Parts of a Circle

A **radius** is a line segment. Its endpoints are the center of the circle and any point on the circle.	A **diameter** is a line segment. It passes through the center of the circle. It has endpoints on the circle.	The **circumference** is the distance around the circle.
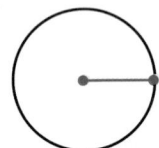	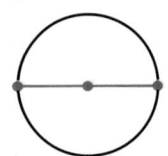	

Activity

Materials ■ large paper clip, 2 pencils, ruler

- Draw a point on a sheet of paper.

- Place a pencil in each end of a paper clip. Place one pencil on the point. Move the other pencil around to draw a circle.

- Use a ruler. Draw a radius and a diameter.

- Label the parts of your circle.

- When you moved the pencil around the point, what part of the circle were you drawing?

ERROR ALERT

The pencil on the point should not move when you draw your circle.

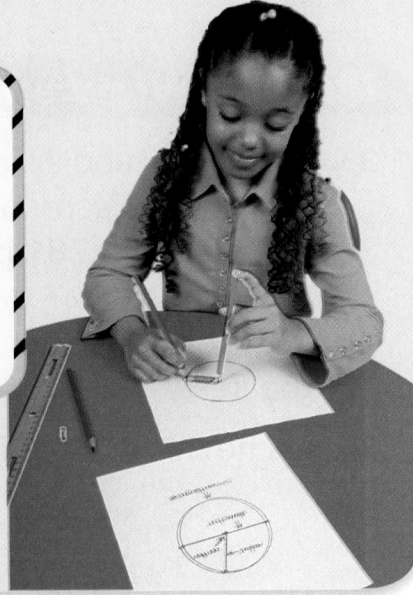

Guided Practice

1. Which figures are circles?

 A   B   C   D   E

Name the blue part in each circle.

2.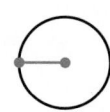

3.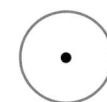

✓4.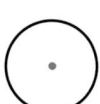

✓5.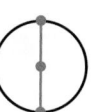

6. **TALK Math** How are the radius and diameter of a circle related? **Explain.**

Independent Practice and Problem Solving

Name the blue part in each circle.

7.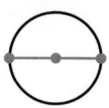

8.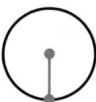

9.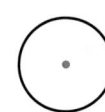

10.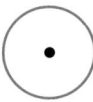

Is the blue part a diameter? Write *yes* or *no*.

11.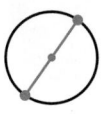

12.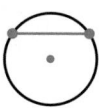

13.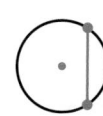

14.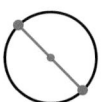

15. Darcy's swimming pool is in the shape of a circle. She swims the diameter of the pool. Draw Darcy's pool. Label the part Darcy swims.

16. **Reasoning** If the diameter of a circle is 4 inches, what is the radius? How do you know?

17. **WRITE Math** Cindy and Reggie drew the figures at the right. How are their figures alike? How are they different?

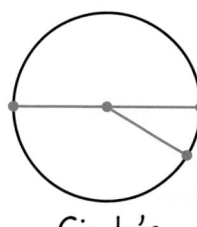

Cindy's circle

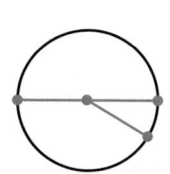

Reggie's circle

Mixed Review and Test Prep

18. What number makes this number sentence true?

$$\blacksquare \div 3 = 4 + 3?$$ (p. 304)

19. A quadrilateral has 2 pairs of parallel sides and no right angles. All sides measure 5 inches. Name the quadrilateral. (p. 360)

20. **Test Prep** Angie drew a circle and colored the diameter red. Which picture is Angie's circle?

A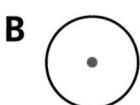

B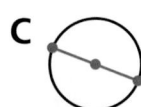

C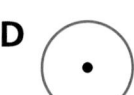

D

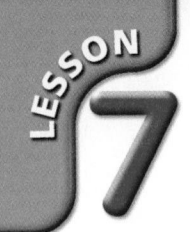

LESSON 7

Problem Solving Workshop
Strategy: Draw a Diagram

OBJECTIVE: Solve problems by using the strategy *draw a diagram*.

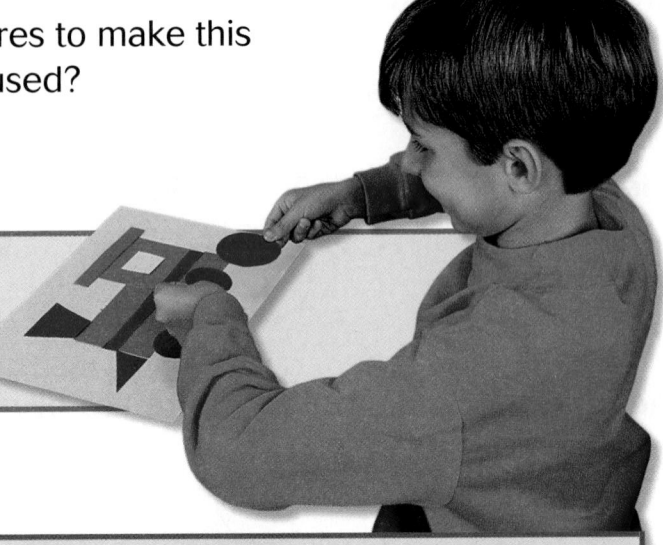

Use the Strategy

PROBLEM In art class, Harry used 11 figures to make this train. How can you sort the figures Harry used?

Read to Understand

Reading Skill

- Classify and categorize the figures Harry used.
- What information is given?

Plan

- **What strategy can you use to solve the problem?**

  You can draw a diagram to sort the figures Harry used.

Solve

- **How can you use the strategy to solve the problem?**

  Draw a Venn diagram. A Venn diagram shows how sets of things are related.

  Draw one circle, and label it *Quadrilaterals*.

  Draw another circle that overlaps the first circle. Label this circle *Blue*.

  Sort the figures into the two circles.

  The figures inside the area where the circles overlap are both blue and quadrilaterals.

Quadrilaterals   Blue

Check

- **What other strategy could you use?**

1. Georgia used these figures to make a picture.

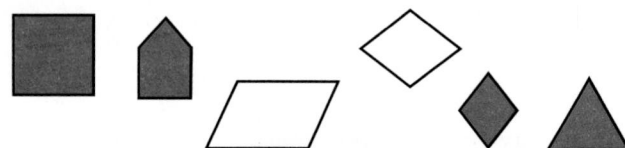

How are the figures alike, and how are they different?

First, draw a Venn diagram with two overlapping circles.

Then, label the circles.

Next, sort the figures.

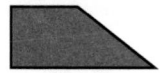

Last, tell how the figures are alike and how they are different.

2. **What if** Georgia added this figure to her picture?

Where should it be placed in the Venn diagram?

3. Copy the Venn diagram, showing multiples of 2 and 3. Complete the diagram, using the numbers through 24.

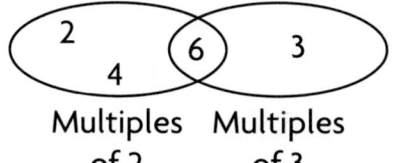

Multiples of 2   Multiples of 3

What do the numbers in the overlapping section represent?

Mixed Strategy Practice

USE DATA For 4–6, use the Venn diagram.

4. The Venn diagram shows the figures Cory used to make a picture. How many quadrilaterals with right angles did he use?

5. How many red figures have right angles but are not quadrilaterals?

6. **WRITE Math ▶ Explain** what the figures in the overlapping section represent.

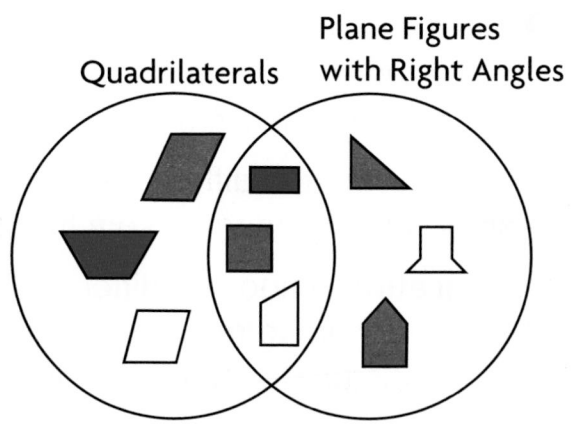

7. **Reasoning** Twenty pictures were entered in an art contest. The pictures were done with either paint or chalk. There were 8 more done with paint than with chalk. How many pictures were done with paint? How many with chalk?

8 Combine Plane Figures

OBJECTIVE: Combine and take apart plane figures.

Quick Review

Name each figure.

1. ⬡ 2. ▭

3. ◹ 4. ⬠

5. ▱

Investigate

Materials ■ pattern blocks

You can combine plane figures or take them apart to make new figures.

A Combine 2 triangles and record the name of the figure.

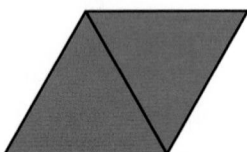

B Predict the new figure that can be made by adding a third triangle. Add it and make a new figure.

C Combine other pattern blocks to make several new figures.

D Trace your figures on paper and label them.

Draw Conclusions

1. What figure can you make by combining 4 triangles in a row?

2. Make a list of the different figures that can be combined to make a trapezoid.

3. **Application** Choose 4 different blocks. Combine them to make a new figure. Draw a picture to show your figure.

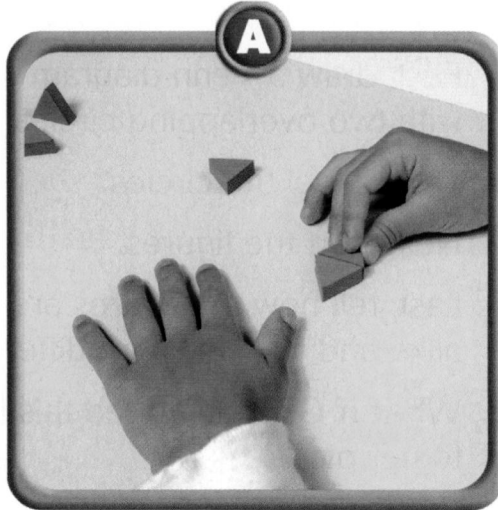

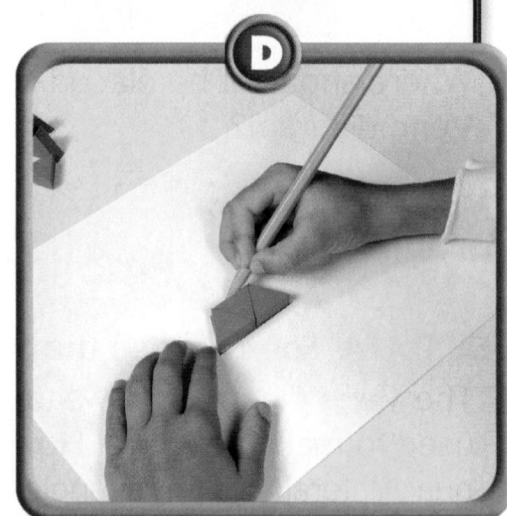

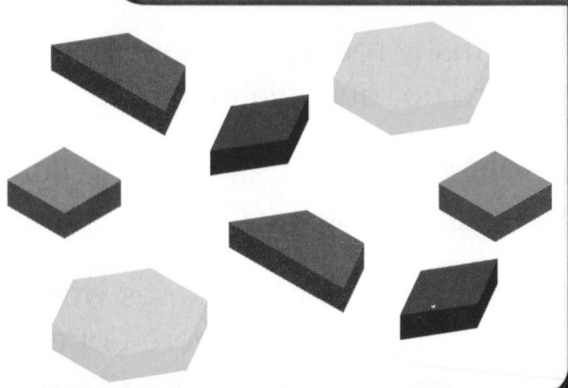

Some figures can be combined to make other figures.
Some figures can be taken apart to become other figures.

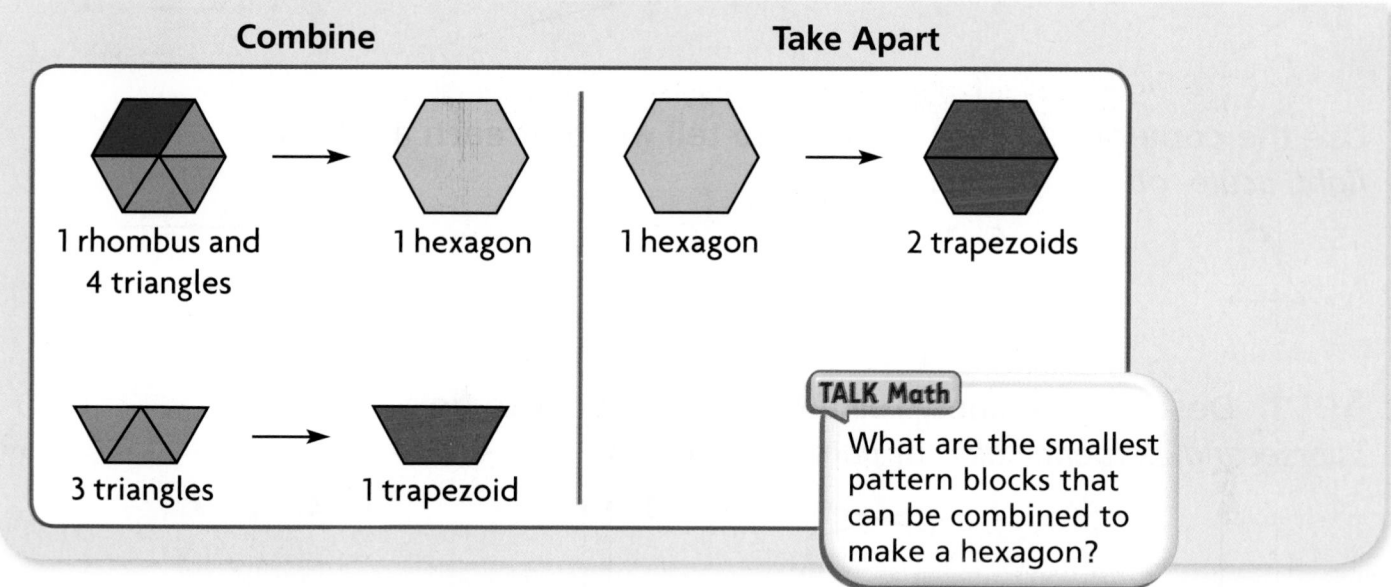

Combine

1 rhombus and 4 triangles → 1 hexagon

3 triangles → 1 trapezoid

Take Apart

1 hexagon → 2 trapezoids

TALK Math

What are the smallest pattern blocks that can be combined to make a hexagon?

Practice

What figures could have been combined to make each figure?

1.

2.

3.

✔ 4.

Draw and name a figure that could be made by using the figures shown.

5.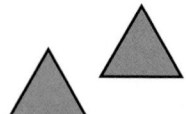

6.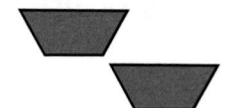

7.

✔ 8.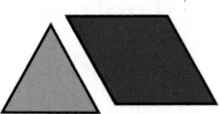

9. Jamie cut a rhombus into 2 equal parts. What plane figures does she have?

10. Violet used two figures to make a trapezoid. One of the figures was a triangle. What was the other figure?

11. **WRITE Math** ▶ Mary has 6 triangles. How many triangles will she have left if she makes 1 trapezoid and 1 rhombus? **Explain** your answer and draw a picture.

Extra Practice

Set A Tell whether each is a *point, line, line segment,* or *ray.* (pp. 350–353)

1. ↘

2. •

3. ↙

4. •——•

Use the corner of a sheet of paper to tell whether each angle is
right, acute, obtuse, or *straight.*

5. ∠

6. ⌐→

7. ∟

8. ←•→

Set B Describe the lines. Tell if the lines appear to be
intersecting, perpendicular, or *parallel.* (pp. 354–355)

1. +

2. ✕

3. ‖

4. ⤬

Set C Name each polygon. Tell how many sides. (pp. 356–357)

1.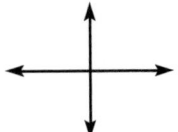

2.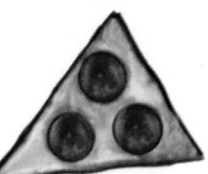

3.

4.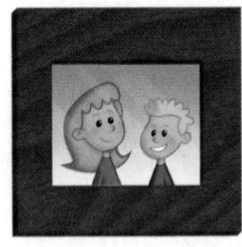

Tell whether each figure is a polygon. Write *yes* or *no.*

5.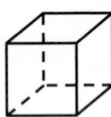

6.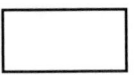

7.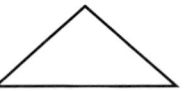

8.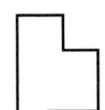

9. Which figures have vertices?

A B C D E

CD ROM Technology
Use Harcourt Mega Math, Ice Station
Exploration, *Polar Planes,* Levels A–G.

Set D Name each triangle. Write *equilateral, isosceles,* or *scalene.* (pp. 358–359)

1.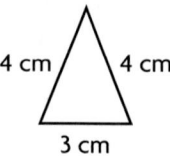
4 cm 4 cm
3 cm

2.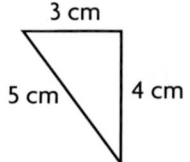
3 cm
5 cm 4 cm

3.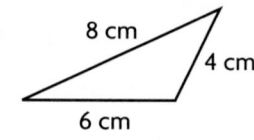
8 cm
4 cm
6 cm

4.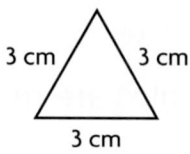
3 cm 3 cm
3 cm

Name each triangle. Write *right, obtuse,* or *acute.*

5.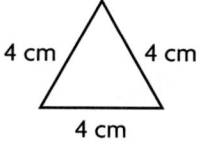
4 cm 4 cm
4 cm

6.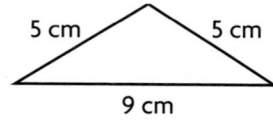
5 cm 5 cm
9 cm

7.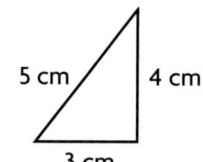
5 cm 4 cm
3 cm

8.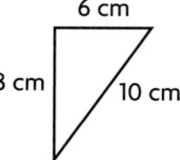
6 cm
8 cm 10 cm

Set E Write as many names for each quadrilateral as you can. (pp. 360–363)

1.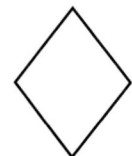

2.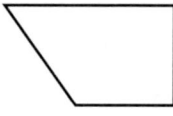

3.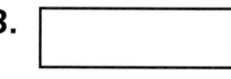

4.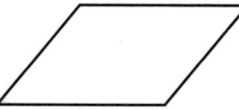

For 5–6, use the quadrilaterals below.

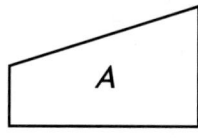 A

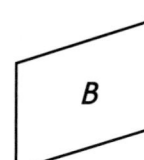 B

C

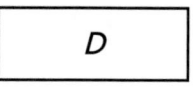 D

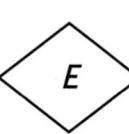 E

5. Which quadrilaterals have no right angles?

6. How are quadrilateral B and quadrilateral D alike? How are they different?

Set F Name the blue part in each circle. (pp. 364–365)

1.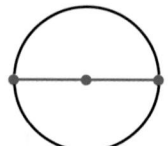

2.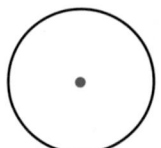

3.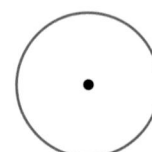

4.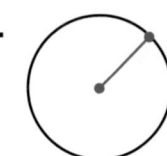

Angle Measures

How Do They Turn?

Angles are measured in units called degrees. The rotation, or turn, of an object is named by the angle the object turns. The symbol for degree is °. A circle can help you understand the measure of degrees.

Examples

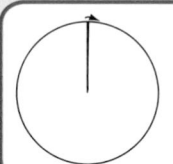 One degree is a very small turn or rotation around a circle. It is written 1°.

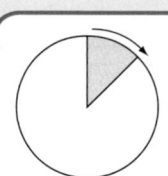 A rotation $\frac{1}{8}$ of the way around a circle measures 45°.

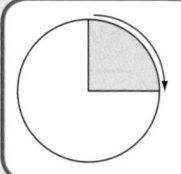 A rotation $\frac{1}{4}$ of the way around a circle measures 90°.

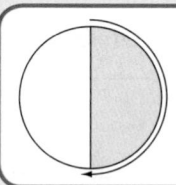 A rotation $\frac{1}{2}$ of the way around a circle measures 180°.

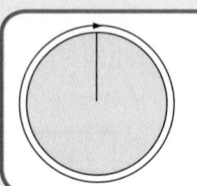 A rotation around the whole circle measures 360°.

Try It

Tell if the turn is about 45°, 90°, 180°, or 360°.

1.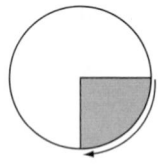

2.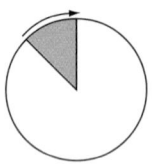

3.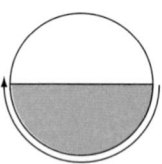

4.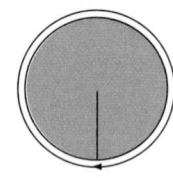

5.

6.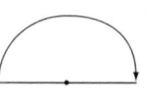

7.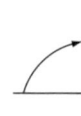

8. **WRITE Math** What is the measure of the angle formed on a clock when the minute hand points to 12 and the hour hand points to 3? **Explain.**

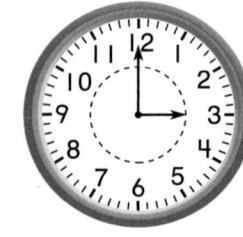

Chapter 14 Review/Test

Check Vocabulary and Concepts

Choose the best term from the box.

1. A __?__ forms a square corner. (p. 350)

2. An __?__ is a triangle with 3 equal sides. (p. 358)

3. A __?__ is a quadrilateral with 2 pairs of equal sides and 2 pairs of parallel sides. (p. 361)

4. A __?__ has 6 sides and 6 angles. (p. 356)

5. A __?__ is a line that passes through the center of a circle and has 2 endpoints on the circle. (p. 364)

VOCABULARY

diameter
equilateral triangle
hexagon
isosceles triangle
parallelogram
right angle

Check Skills

Name each polygon. Tell how many sides. (pp. 356–357)

6.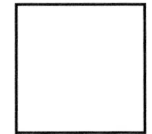

7.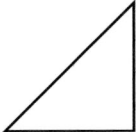

8.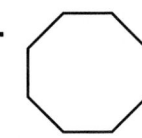

9.

Name each triangle. Write *equilateral*, *isosceles*, or *scalene*. (pp. 358–359)

10.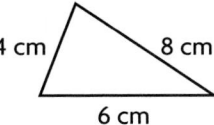

11.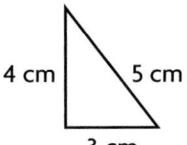

12.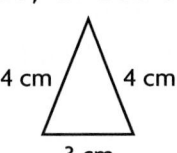

13.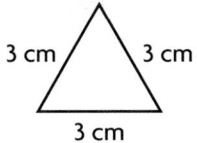

Check Problem Solving

Solve. (pp. 366–367)

14. The Venn diagram shows the figures Ethan used to make a picture. What does the overlapping section represent?

Quadrilaterals   Red

15. **WRITE Math** ▶ Ethan added this figure to his picture. **Explain** where it should be placed in the Venn diagram.

Standardized Test Prep
Chapters 1–14

Number and Operations

1. Joan flew 908 miles to visit her grandmother. What is 908 rounded to the nearest hundred? (p. 36)

   A 910

   B 908

   C 900

   D 800

Test Tip **Understand the problem.**

See item 2. Read the question again. What are you asked to find? Look in the problem for the information you need to answer the question.

2. Bill is putting his stamps in an album. There are 8 stamps on each page. Bill has filled 8 pages. How many stamps does Bill have? (p. 236)

   A 1

   B 16

   C 56

   D 64

3. **WRITE Math** ▸ **Explain** how this array models $6 \times 9 = 54$. (p. 206)

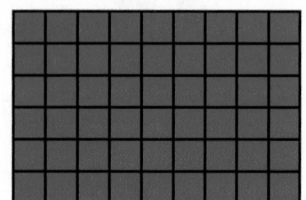

Algebraic Reasoning

4. Look at the table. How many wheels do 4 wagons have? (p. 256)

Number of Wagons	Number of Wheels
1	4
2	8
3	12
4	■

   A 8

   B 16

   C 20

   D 22

5. Which number completes the fact family? (p. 286)

   $$4 \times ■ = 32 \qquad ■ \times 4 = 32$$
   $$32 \div 4 = ■ \qquad 32 \div ■ = 4$$

   A 4

   B 8

   C 9

   D 32

6. **WRITE Math** ▸ **Explain** how knowing $(2 \times 4) \times 8 = 64$ helps you find $2 \times (4 \times 8)$. (p. 262)

Geometry

7. Look at the figure below. Which does NOT describe the shape? (p. 360)

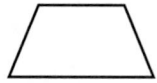

A It is a rhombus.

B It is a trapezoid.

C It is a polygon.

D It is a quadrilateral.

8. Which polygon has more sides than this figure? (p. 356)

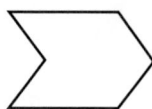

A Triangle

B Quadrilateral

C Hexagon

D Octagon

9. **WRITE Math** **Explain** how parallel lines are different than perpendicular lines. (p. 354)

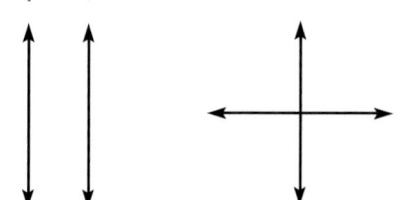

Data Analysis and Probability

10. A tally table shows ⱦⱦ ⱦⱦ ⱦⱦ || for the number of students who rode bikes to school. How many students rode bikes to school? (p. 146)

A 20   **C** 15

B 17   **D** 12

11. The graph shows some of the activities Jason did during the day. How many more hours did Jason spend sleeping than reading? (p. 154)

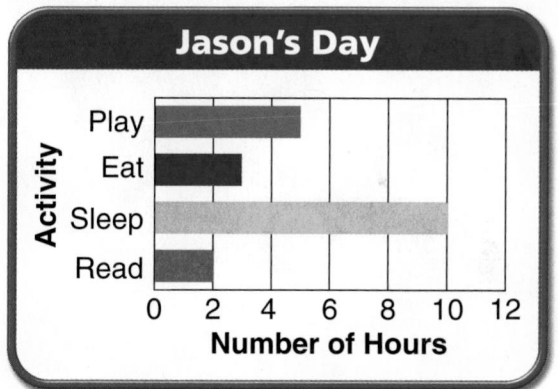

A 2 hours   **C** 10 hours

B 8 hours   **D** 12 hours

12. **WRITE Math** Rosanna chooses a card from the cards shown. Is she more likely or less likely to choose an *A* than a *B*? **Explain** how you know. (p. 182)

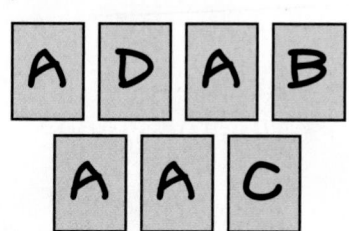

15 Congruence and Symmetry

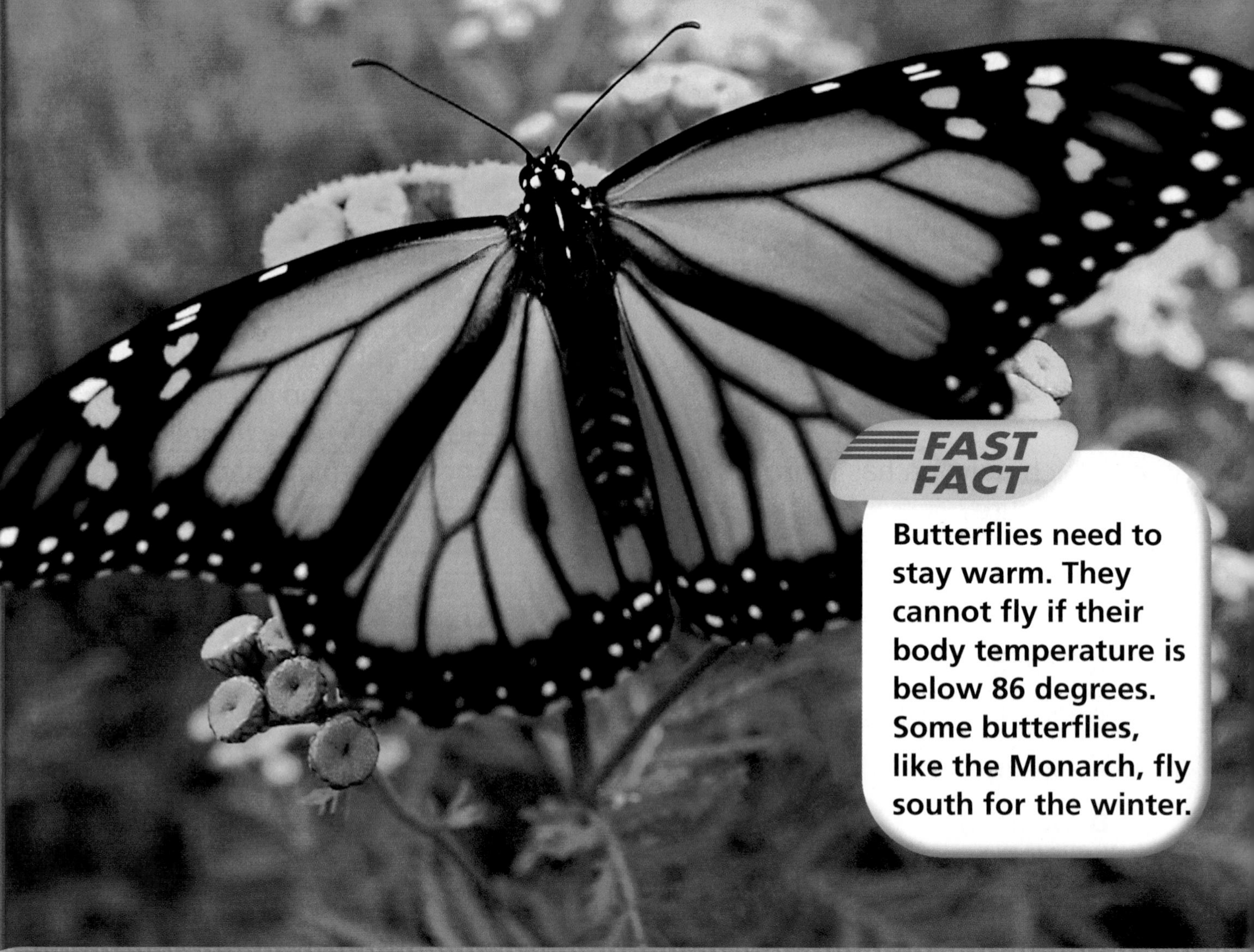

≡**FAST FACT**

Butterflies need to stay warm. They cannot fly if their body temperature is below 86 degrees. Some butterflies, like the Monarch, fly south for the winter.

Investigate
All butterflies are symmetrical. Their left and right wings have the same designs and colors. Look at the drawings. Which cannot be real butterflies? How do you know? Draw a butterfly that has a line of symmetry.

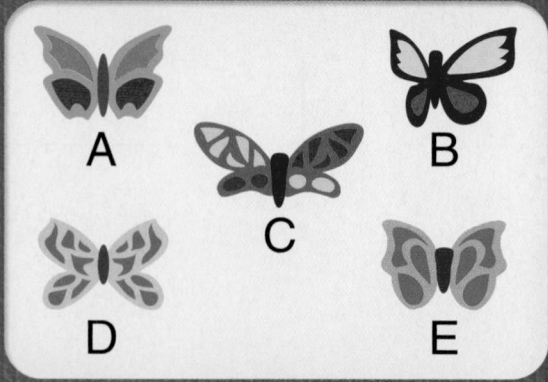

A   B   C   D   E

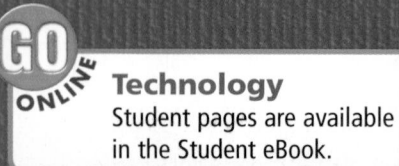

GO ONLINE

Technology
Student pages are available in the Student eBook.

Check your understanding of important skills needed for success in Chapter 15.

▶ **Same Size, Same Shape**

Tell whether the figures are the same size and shape.

Write *yes* or *no*.

1.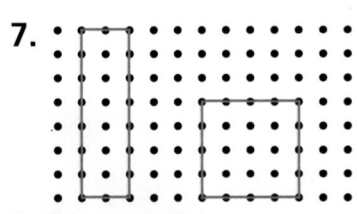

2.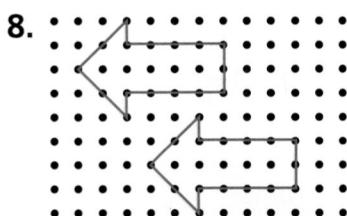

3.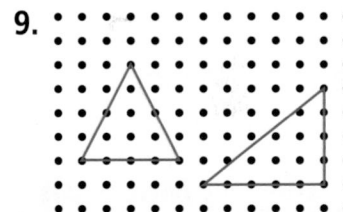

4.

5.

6.

7.

8.

9.

VOCABULARY POWER

CHAPTER VOCABULARY

congruent
flip (reflection)
line of symmetry
similar
slide (translation)
symmetry
turn (rotation)

WARM-UP WORDS

congruent Figures that have the same size and shape

similar Figures that have the same shape and the same or different size

symmetry A figure has symmetry if it can be folded along a line so that the two parts match exactly

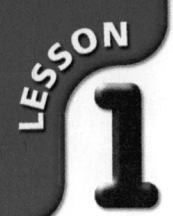

LESSON 1

Congruent Figures

OBJECTIVE: Identify 2-dimensional congruent figures.

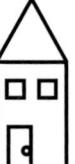
Learn

Figures with the same size and shape are **congruent**. Congruent figures can be in different positions.

The figures in each pair appear to be congruent.	The figures in each pair do not appear to be congruent.
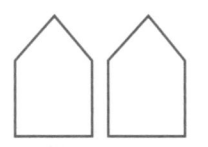 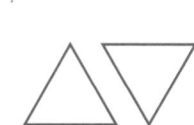	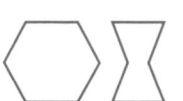 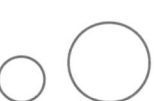
Same size, same shape	Same size, not the same shape Same shape, not the same size

PROBLEM Molly put a red hexagon on the front of her scrapbook. She wants to put a congruent figure on the back. Which figure should she use?

Activity   Materials ■ tracing paper

Use tracing paper to find the congruent figure.

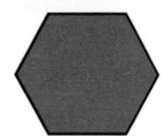  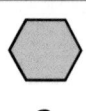 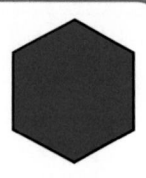

Molly's hexagon   **1**   **2**   **3**

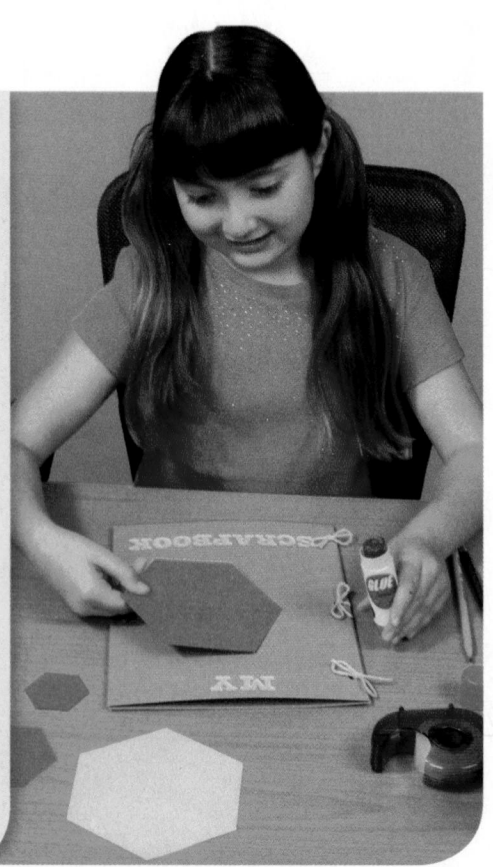

- Trace and cut out Molly's figure, the red hexagon.

- Place your tracing over Figure 1. Do the figures appear to be congruent?

- Place it over Figures 2 and 3. Do they appear to be congruent?

So, Molly should use Figure 3, the blue hexagon, because it appears to be congruent to her red hexagon.

1. Trace triangle A. Which triangle appears to be the same size and shape as A?

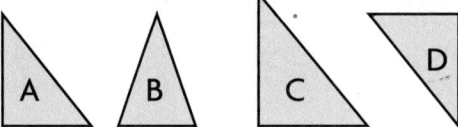

Trace and cut out each pair of figures. Tell if the figures appear to be congruent. Write *yes* or *no*.

2.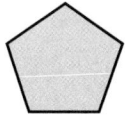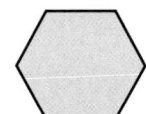

✓3.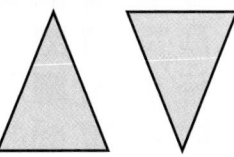

✓4.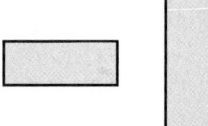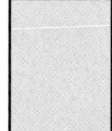

5. **TALK Math** **Explain** how to tell if two figures appear to be congruent.

Independent Practice and Problem Solving

Trace and cut out each pair of figures. Tell if the figures appear to be congruent. Write *yes* or *no*.

6.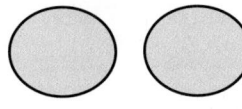

7.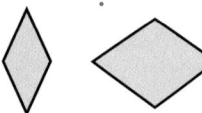

8.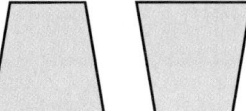

For 9–11, use the figures in the chart.

9. Johnny used two congruent star figures for his picture. Which figures did he use?

10. One of the figures in Mae's picture is triangle F. Which figure appears to be congruent to triangle F?

11. **WRITE Math** Look at stars A and C. Do they appear to be congruent? **Explain.**

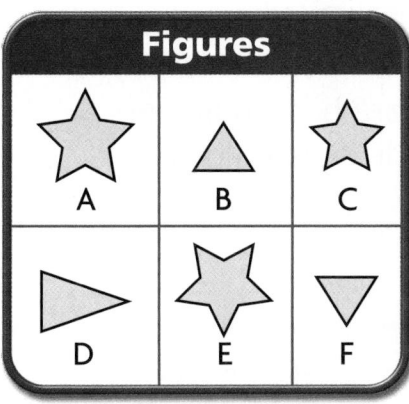

Mixed Review and Test Prep

12. A puzzle in Jill's classroom has 2,039 pieces in it. Write the number 2,039 in expanded form. (p. 10)

13. A figure has 4 equal sides and 4 right angles. What is the figure? (p. 360)

14. **Test Prep** Which figure appears to be congruent to this figure?

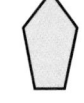

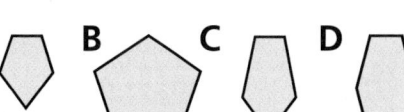

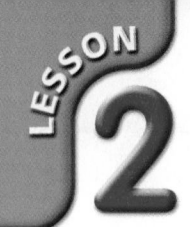
Problem Solving Workshop
Strategy: Make a Model

OBJECTIVE: Use the strategy *make a model* to solve problems.

Learn the Strategy

Making models can help you solve problems. You can use many different kinds of models.

You can use base-ten blocks.

There were 45 people at a play on Tuesday. There were 32 people at the play on Wednesday.

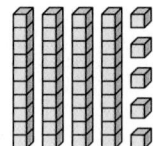 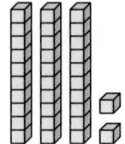

You can use square tiles.

There are 5 rows of desks with 6 desks in each row.

You can use counters.

Kara has 28 flowers. She puts 4 flowers in each vase.

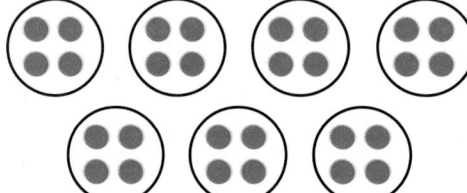

You can use pattern blocks.

Ben is tiling his floor. He uses triangles and squares to make a border.

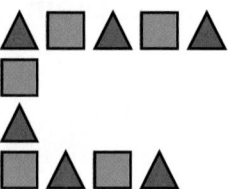

TALK Math

What problem can be solved by using each of the models shown?

Use the Strategy

PROBLEM Mr. Miller is making a path in his garden by
using stones that are shaped like hexagons. He needs one
more stone to complete the path. How can he use the
stone shapes below to make the last stepping stone?

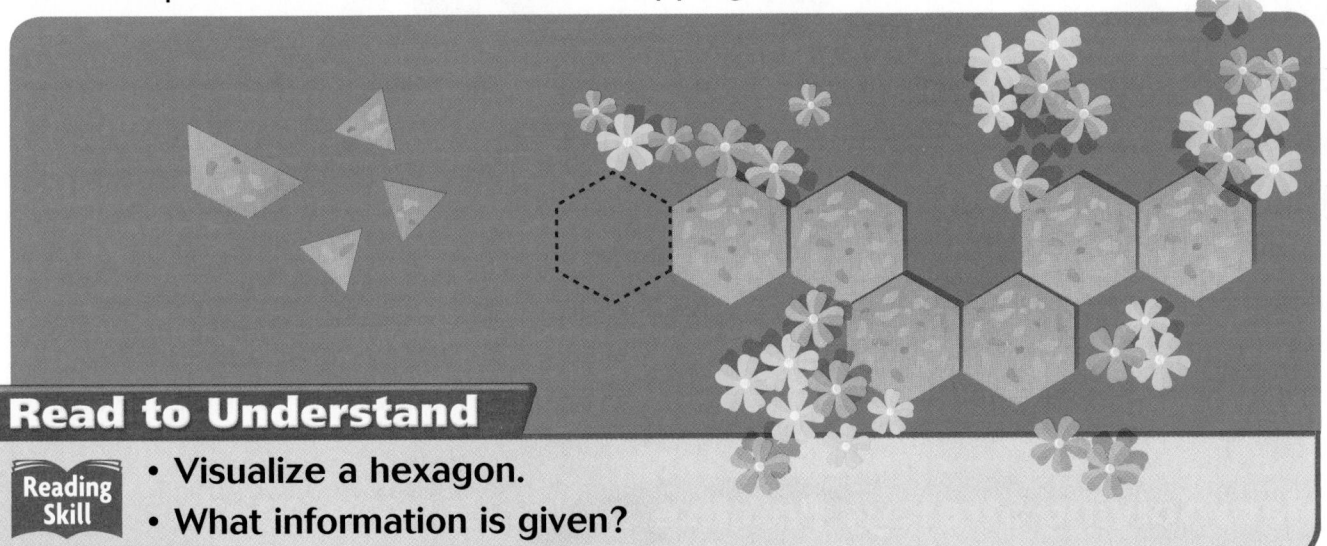

Read to Understand

Reading Skill
- Visualize a hexagon.
- What information is given?

Plan

- **What strategy can you use to solve the problem?**
  You can *make a model*.

Solve

- **How can you use the strategy to solve the problem?**
  Use pattern blocks to model the problem. Use the yellow
  hexagon, the green triangles, and the red trapezoid to model
  the stones.

  Arrange the pattern blocks to make a hexagon.

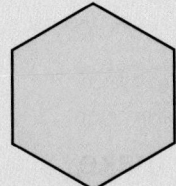

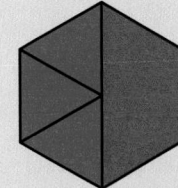

  hexagon stone   pieces of stone

  So, Mr. Miller can put the 3 triangles and 1 trapezoid together
  to make the last stepping stone.

Check

- **How do you know your answer is correct?**

1. Jillian is making a pattern. What pieces are missing from her pattern?

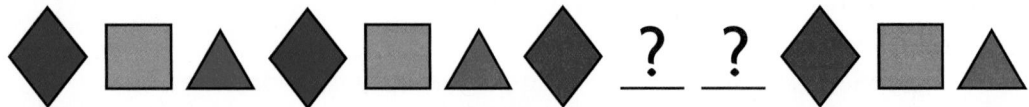

First, decide what model to use.
You can use pattern blocks to make the design.

Then, use the blocks to fill in the missing pieces.
Explain how you completed the pattern.

2. What if Jillian added 1 hexagon after each triangle? How many hexagons would be in her design?

3. Hunter uses square tiles to make an array with 4 rows and 3 columns. How many square tiles does he use?

Problem Solving Strategy Practice

Make a model to solve.

4. Two apples are the same size. Jenna ate $\frac{1}{2}$ of an apple. Caitlin ate $\frac{1}{3}$ of an apple. Who ate the larger part?

5. Mrs. Parker bought 48 muffins. There are 8 muffins in each box. How many boxes are there?

6. Ashley is making a photo album. Each page holds 6 photos. There are 12 pages. How many photos can her album hold?

7. Mary has 24 napkins. She puts the same number of napkins on each of 3 tables. How many napkins does Mary put on 2 of the tables?

8. Jessica is saving money to buy a bike. She saved $4 the first month, $8 the second month, $12 the third month, and $16 the fourth month. If the pattern continues, how much will she save the sixth month?

9. Patrick picked 3 baskets of apples. Each basket held 12 apples. How many apples in all did he pick?

10. **WRITE Math** John used 1 hexagon and 2 triangles to make this rhombus. What other pattern blocks can be used to make a rhombus congruent to this one?

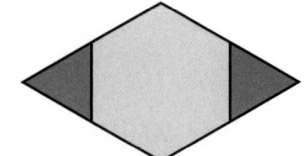

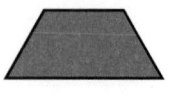   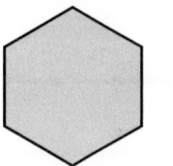 

Mixed Strategy Practice

USE DATA For 11–13, use the table.

11. Tina buys 9 pattern-block stamp kits. How many stamps does Tina have in all?

12. There are 4 fraction circles in each bag. How many bags of fraction circles are in 1 kit?

13. There are 4 different kinds of number cards in a kit. How many of each kind of card are there if there are the same number of each kind?

14. Sierra chose a square, a trapezoid, and a triangle from the pattern blocks. The block she chose first did not have 4 sides. She did not choose the square last. In what order did Sierra choose the blocks?

15. **Pose a Problem** Look back at problem 14. Write a similar problem using a rhombus, a hexagon, and a square. **Explain** the answer.

16. **Open-Ended** Choose 6 plane figures. Draw a Venn diagram with two overlapping circles. Label the circles. Sort the figures. Tell how the figures are alike and how they are different.

17. Marti used pattern blocks to make this pattern. What is the twelfth block in her pattern?

Choose a
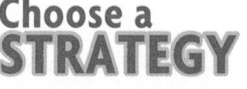
STRATEGY

Draw a Diagram or Picture

Make a Model or Act It Out

Make an Organized List

Find a Pattern

Make a Table or Graph

Predict and Test

Work Backward

Solve a Simpler Problem

Write an Equation

Use Logical Reasoning

Math Kit	
Item	Number in Each Kit
Pattern blocks	100
Number cards	36
Pattern-block stamps	6
Fraction circles	12

CHALLENGE YOURSELF

Glenn's town has 4 school supply stores.
Each store has 95 pattern-block stamp kits for sale.

18. Two schools each bought 28 pattern-block stamp kits from one store in September. Then one school returned 17 stamp kits. How many pattern-block stamp kits were in stock after the kits were returned?

19. Each pattern-block stamp kit costs $9. On Tuesday, two stores sold 5 kits, and three stores sold 2 kits. How much money was paid for the kits on Tuesday?

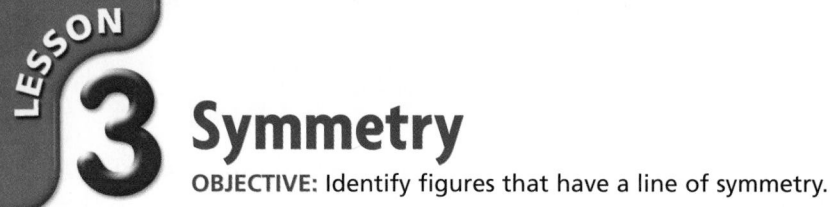

LESSON 3

Symmetry

OBJECTIVE: Identify figures that have a line of symmetry.

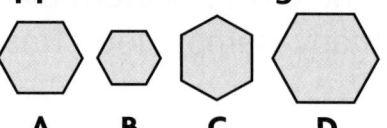

Quick Review

Which two figures appear to be congruent?

A B C D

Vocabulary

symmetry

line of symmetry

Learn

A figure has **symmetry** if it can be folded in half so that the halves match exactly.

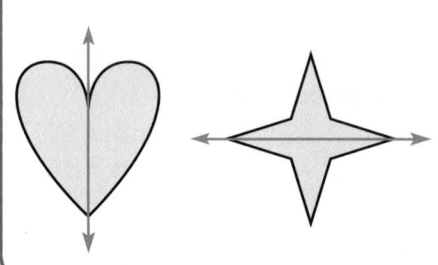

These figures appear to have a line of symmetry.

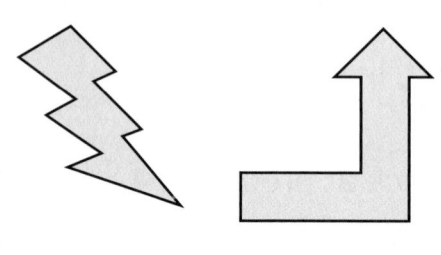

These figures do not appear to have a line of symmetry.

A line that divides a figure into two congruent parts is a **line of symmetry**.

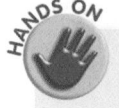

HANDS ON

Activity

Materials ■ paper, scissors, crayon or marker

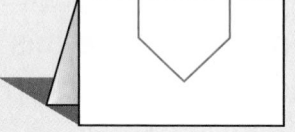

You can fold paper to explore symmetry.

• Fold a sheet of paper in half.

• Draw a figure that begins and ends on the fold. Cut out the figure with the paper still folded.

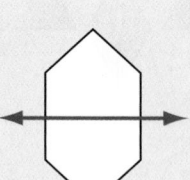

• Unfold the figure, and draw a line on the fold. The line on the fold is a line of symmetry.

• Do the halves match exactly? Explain.

Guided Practice

1. Does the blue line appear to be a line of symmetry? **Explain.**

Think: Do the halves match exactly?

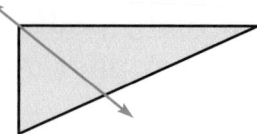

Tell if the blue line appears to be a line of symmetry.
Write *yes* or *no*.

2.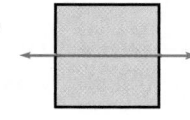

3.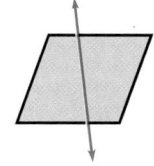

☑ **4.**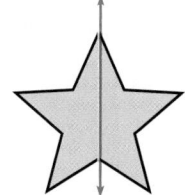

☑ **5.**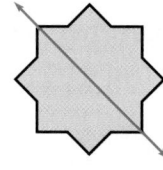

6. [**TALK Math**] **Explain** how you can fold paper to find a line of symmetry.

Independent Practice and Problem Solving

Tell if the blue line appears to be a line of symmetry.
Write *yes* or *no*.

7.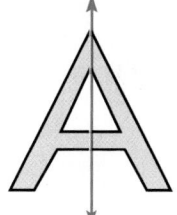

8.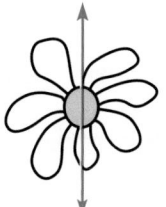

9.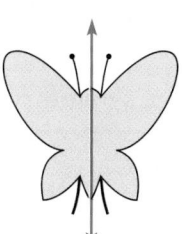

10.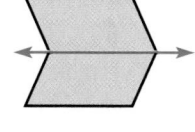

11. Reasoning Trace and cut out the figure at the right. Fold it to find a line of symmetry. **Explain** how you know your line shows symmetry.

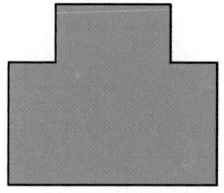

12. [**WRITE Math**] ▶ **What's the Error?** Julia says that the figure at the right shows a line of symmetry. Describe her error.

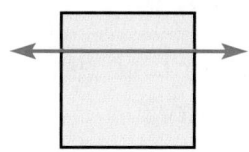

Mixed Review and Test Prep

13. A Favorite Drinks tally table shows 卌 卌 ||| next to juice. How many voted for juice? (p. 146)

14. Do the lines appear to be parallel or perpendicular? (p. 354)

15. Test Prep Which does not appear to be a line of symmetry?

A

C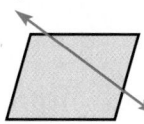

B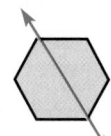

D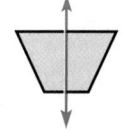

(**Extra Practice**) on page 392, Set B

CD ROM **Technology**
Use Harcourt Mega Math, Ice Station Exploration, *Polar Planes,* Level K.

4 Lines of Symmetry

OBJECTIVE: Identify and draw lines of symmetry in plane figures.

 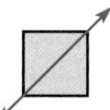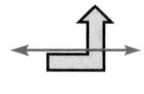
Learn

Some figures appear to have one or more lines of symmetry. Some figures have no lines of symmetry.

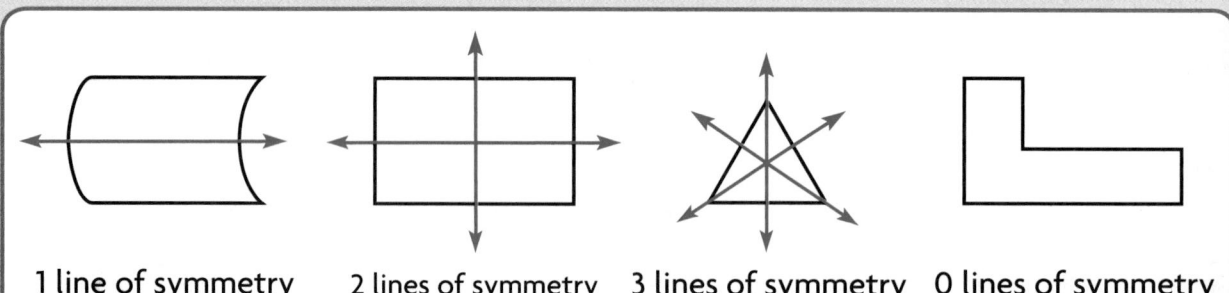

| 1 line of symmetry | 2 lines of symmetry | 3 lines of symmetry | 0 lines of symmetry |

Some letters and numbers appear to have lines of symmetry.

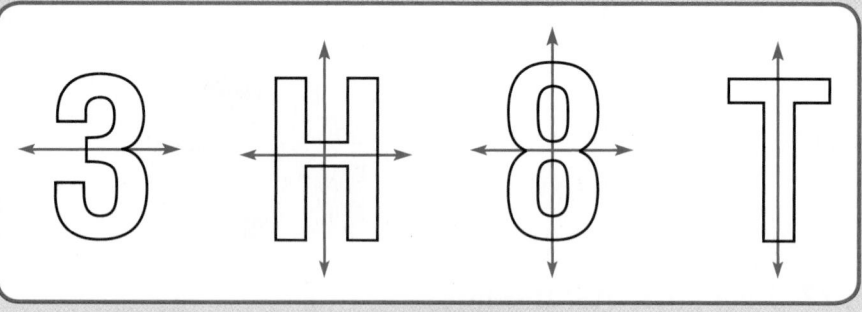

• Which other letters or numbers have more than 1 line of symmetry?

ERROR ALERT

Make sure that both halves of the figure match, or are congruent, when you draw lines of symmetry.

Guided Practice

1. Which of these letters appear to have more than 1 line of symmetry? Trace the letters, and draw the lines of symmetry.

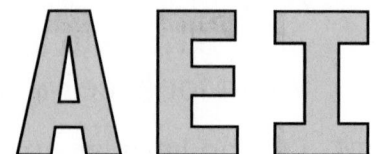

Trace each figure. Then draw the line or lines of symmetry.

2. 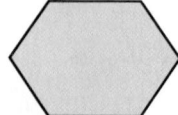   3. 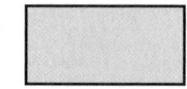   ✓ 4. 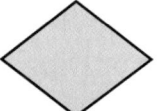   ✓ 5.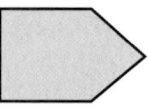

6. **TALK Math** Trace and cut out this figure. **Explain** how you can find all the lines of symmetry.

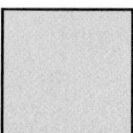

Trace each figure. Then draw the line or lines of symmetry.

7.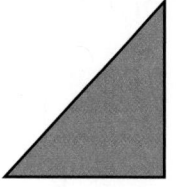

8.

9.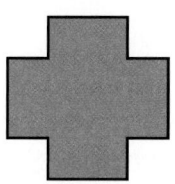

10.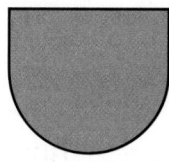

Decide if each figure appears to have 0 lines, 1 line, or more than 1 line of symmetry. Write *0, 1*, or *more than 1*.

11.

12.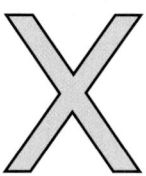

13.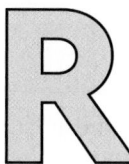

14.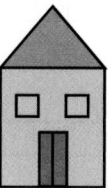

For 15–16, use shapes A–C.

15. Gillian is making a book cover. She drew a figure on it that has 2 lines of symmetry. Which figure did she draw?

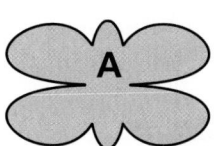 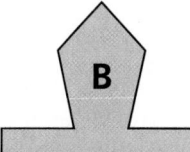 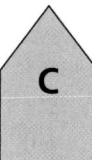

16. **≣FAST FACT** A nonagon is a polygon with 9 sides. Which of Gillian's book cover shapes is a nonagon? How many lines of symmetry does it have?

17. **WRITE Math** ▸ **Sense or Nonsense** Sienna says that this pattern block she traced has only 1 line of symmetry. Does her statement make sense? **Explain.**

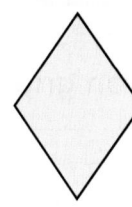

Mixed Review and Test Prep

18. Max drew a figure that is congruent to a hexagon. How many sides does his figure have? (p. 378)

19. What division number sentence is in the same fact family as $2 \times 8 = 16$? (p. 286)

20. **Test Prep** Which letters appear to have only 1 line of symmetry?

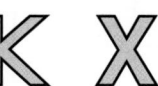

A K and X **C** B and O

B X and O **D** K and B

Extra Practice on page 392, Set C

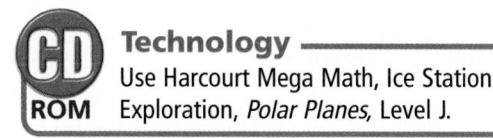 **Technology** ——— Use Harcourt Mega Math, Ice Station Exploration, *Polar Planes,* Level J.

Chapter 15 387

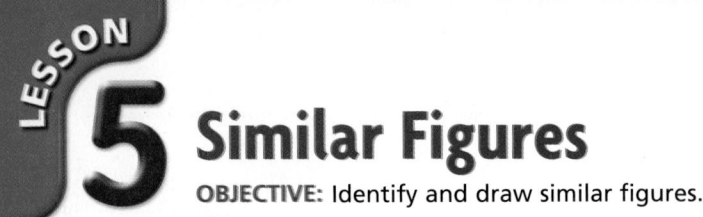

LESSON 5
Similar Figures

OBJECTIVE: Identify and draw similar figures.

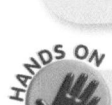

Learn

Similar figures have the same shape. Sometimes they are different sizes.

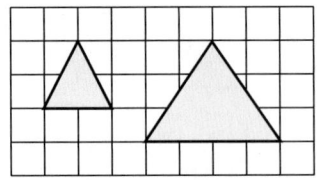

These figures are similar.

• same shape, different size

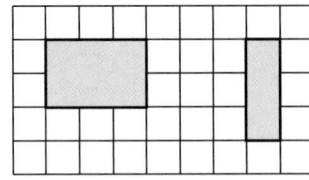

These figures are not similar.

• not the same shape

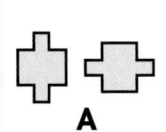 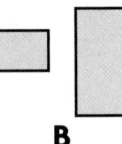

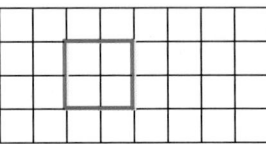

Activity   Materials ■ 1-centimeter grid paper

Explore similar figures on grid paper.

Step 1

Draw a 2 by 2 square on grid paper.

Step 2

On the same grid paper, draw a 3 by 3 square, a 4 by 4 square, and a 1 by 1 square.

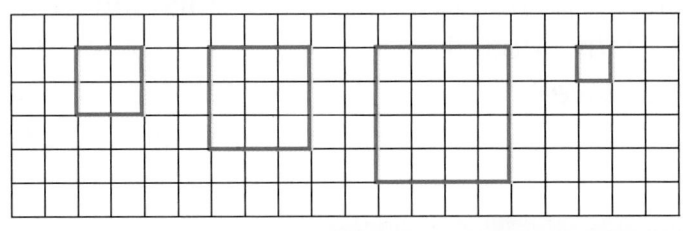

All figures that are the same shape are similar. If the figures are the same size, they are also congruent.

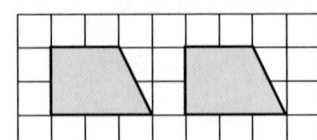

• same size
• same shape
• similar
• congruent

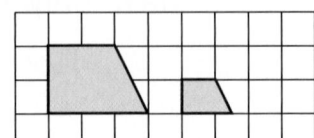

• same shape
• not the same size
• similar
• not congruent

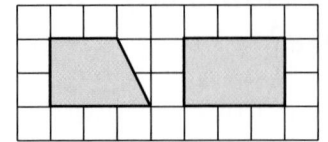

• not the same shape
• not similar
• not congruent

Quick Review

Tell if the figures appear to be congruent. Write *yes* or *no*.

A

B

Vocabulary

similar

Guided Practice

1. Look at the figures at the right. Do they appear to be the same shape? the same size?

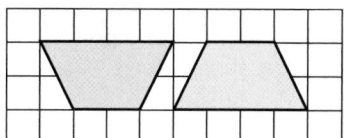

Tell if each pair of figures appears to be similar. Write *yes* or *no*.

2.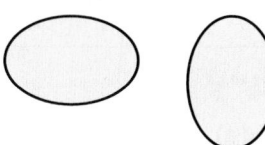

✓ 3.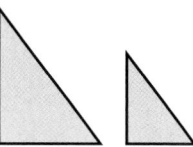

✓ 4.

5. **TALK Math** **Explain** why the figures at the right appear to be similar but not congruent.

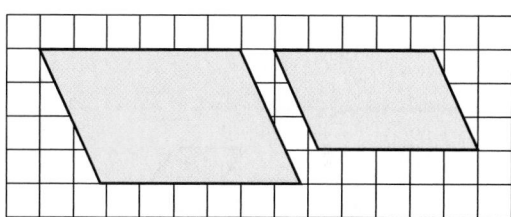

Independent Practice *and Problem Solving*

Tell if each pair of figures appears to be similar. Write *yes* or *no*.

6.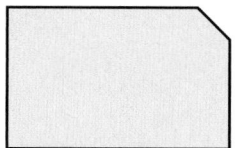

7.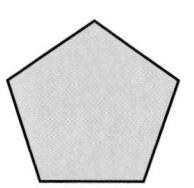

8.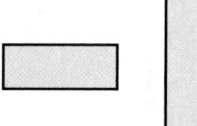

9. **WRITE Math** ▸ **What's the Error?** Joanna says that rectangles *A* and *B* appear to be similar. **Explain** her error.

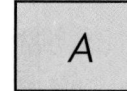

Mixed Review and Test Prep

10. Tonya has 15 crayons. She gives 3 crayons to each of her cousins. How many cousins does Tonya have? Multiply to check your answer. (p. 304)

11. Erin measured a rug. She measured the line segment shown. Did she measure the diameter or the radius? (p. 364)

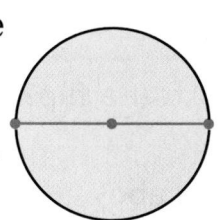

12. **Test Prep** Which pair of hexagons appears to be similar?

A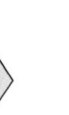

C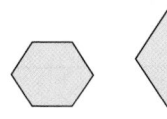

B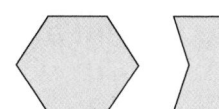

D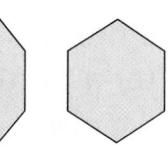

Extra Practice on page 392, Set D

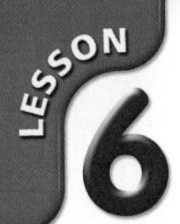

LESSON 6

Slides, Flips, and Turns

OBJECTIVE: Identify and predict the position of a figure after a slide, flip, or turn.

Quick Review

Tell if the figures appear to be congruent. Write *yes* or *no*.

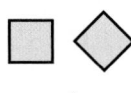 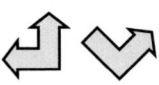

A   B

Learn

Figures can be moved in different ways without changing their shape or their size.

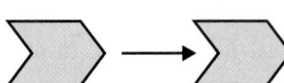

slide (translation)

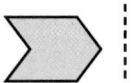

flip (reflection)

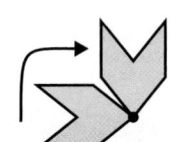

turn (rotation)

HANDS ON

Activity

Materials ■ paper, pattern blocks

Step 1

Trace a trapezoid pattern block on your paper.

Step 2

Slide the block and trace it. Label your drawing *slide*.

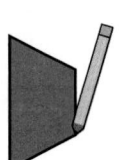

slide

Step 3

Flip the block and trace it. Label your drawing *flip*.

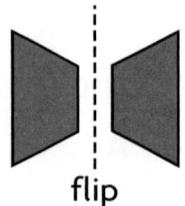

flip

Step 4

Turn the block around a point and trace it. Label your drawing *turn*.

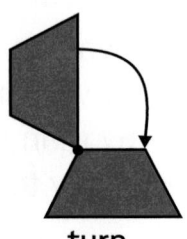

turn

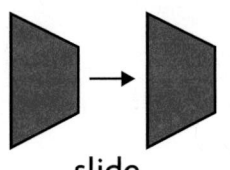

- Are the two figures congruent after a slide? After a flip? After a turn? Explain.

- Use a different pattern block. Repeat the steps above.

1. How was this figure moved?

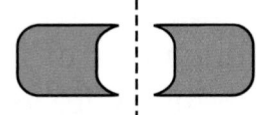

Tell how each figure was moved. Write *slide, flip,* or *turn.*

2.

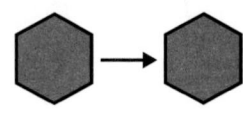

✅ **3.**

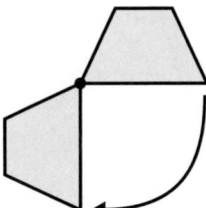

✅ **4.**

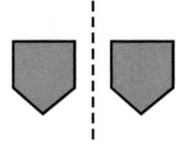

5. **TALK Math** Does the size or shape of a plane figure change after a slide, flip, or turn? **Explain.**

Independent Practice and Problem Solving

Tell how each figure was moved. Write *slide, flip,* or *turn.*

6.

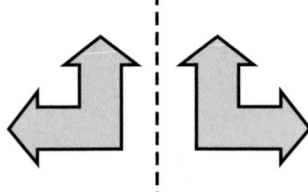

7.

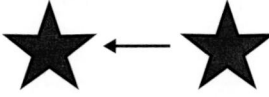

8.

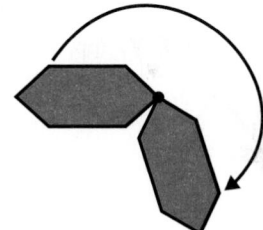

9. **WRITE Math** **What's the Error?** Mike traced Figure A. Then he moved it twice and traced it again. Figure B shows the new position. He said he slid the figure. What's his error?

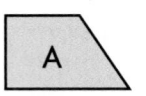 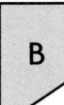

Mixed Review and Test Prep

10. What is the missing number in Jack's pattern? (Grade 2)

26, 37, ■, 59, 70

11. A quadrilateral has 2 pairs of parallel sides and no right angles. Name the quadrilateral. (p. 360)

12. Test Prep Which shows a turn?

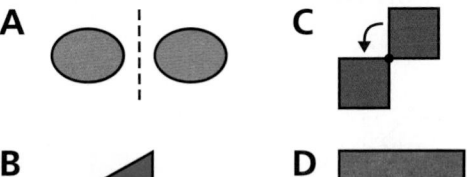

Extra Practice

Set A Trace and cut out each pair of figures. Tell if the figures appear to be congruent. Write *yes* or *no*. (pp. 378–379)

1.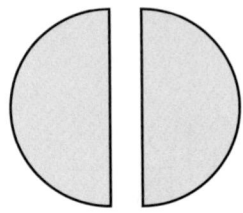
2.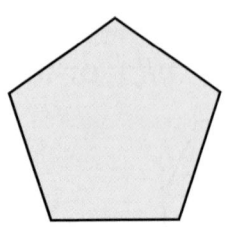
3.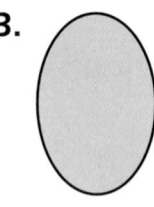

Set B Tell if the blue line appears to be a line of symmetry. Write *yes* or *no*. (pp. 384–385)

1.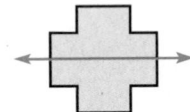
2.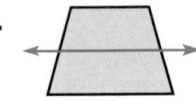
3.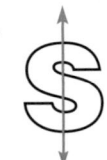
4.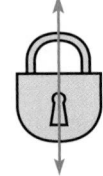

Set C Trace each figure. Then draw the line or lines of symmetry. (pp. 386–387)

1.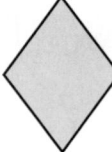
2.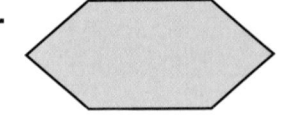
3.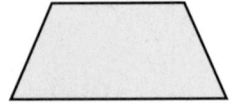
4.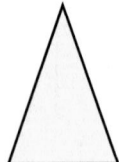

Set D Tell if each pair of figures appears to be similar. Write *yes* or *no*. (pp. 388–389)

1.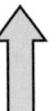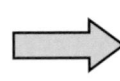
2.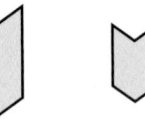
3.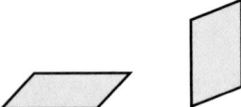

Set E Tell how each figure was moved. Write *slide, flip,* or *turn.* (pp. 390–391)

1.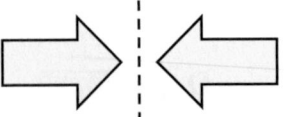
2.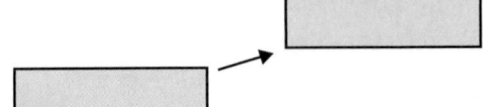
3.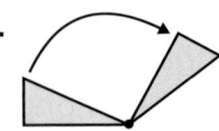

CD ROM **Technology**
Use Harcourt Mega Math, Ice Station
Exploration, *Polar Planes*, Levels H, I, J, K.

TECHNOLOGY ★ CONNECTION

*i*Tools: Geometry

Find out if a Plane Figure has Symmetry

Jane made invitations for her party. She used figures that had lines of symmetry and then folded them to make cards.

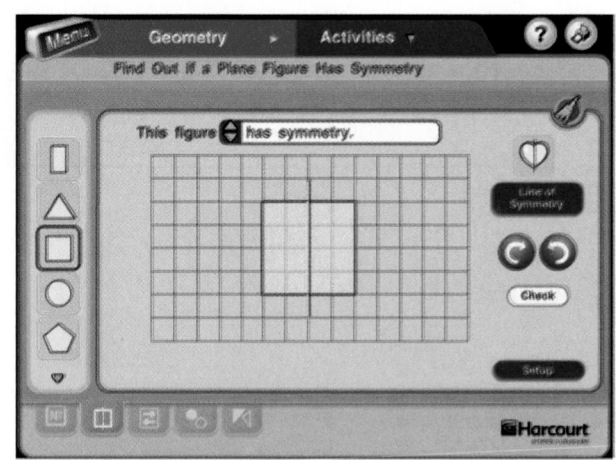

Step 1	Click on *Geometry*. Then click on *Plane Figures* in the *Activities* menu. Now click on the second tab at the bottom.
Step 2	Click on the square on the left to place it on the grid.
Step 3	Click on the arrows at the top of the screen to make the sentence true. Then click on *Check*.
Step 4	Click on *Line of Symmetry*.

Click on the broom to clear the workspace.

Try It

1. Look at the figures on the left of the screen. Find a figure that has 2 lines of symmetry. Then find a figure with more than 2 lines of symmetry.

2. Click on the arrow below the figures. Find a figure that has no lines of symmetry.

3. **Explore More** How many lines of symmetry does the hexagon have? Use the *i*Tool to show the lines of symmetry, and then draw what you see. **Explain** the lines of symmetry.

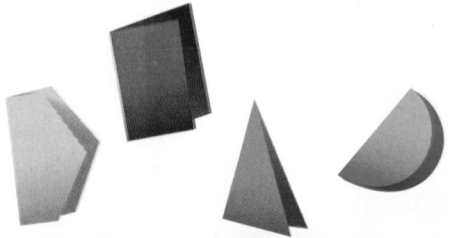

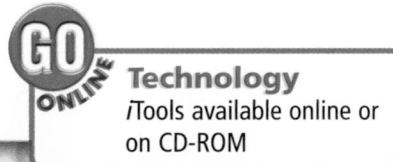

Technology
*i*Tools available online or on CD-ROM

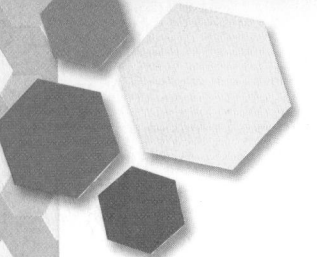

MATH POWER Tessellations

Make a Pattern

Some geometric figures can make a tessellation. A **tessellation** is a repeating pattern made of a closed plane figure that covers a surface with no overlapping or empty space.

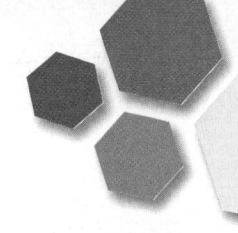

Examples
Will the figures below make a tessellation?

▲ *Sun and Moon* by M.C. Escher

Step 1

Repeat the figure in a row, as close together as possible without overlapping.

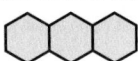   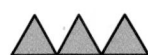   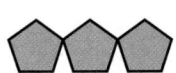

Step 2

Place a second row on top of the first.

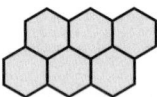   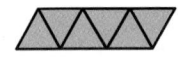   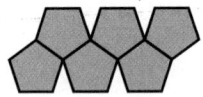

Step 3

Add more rows. If there is no empty space, the figure has made a tessellation.

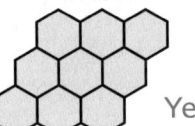 Yes   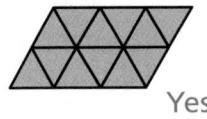 Yes   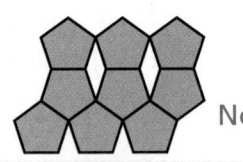 No

So, the hexagon and triangle will make a tessellation, but the pentagon will not.

Try It
Tell if each figure will make a tessellation. Write *yes* or *no*.

1.    2. 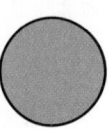   3. 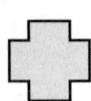   4.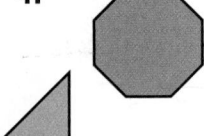

5. **WRITE Math** ▸ Will this figure make a tessellation? **Explain.**

Chapter 15 Review/Test

Check Vocabulary and Concepts

Choose the best term from the box.

> **VOCABULARY**
> symmetry
> line of symmetry
> similar
> congruent

1. Figures with the same size and shape are __?__. (p. 378)

2. Figures that have the same shape and may have the same size are __?__. (p. 388)

3. A __?__ divides a figure into two congruent parts. (p. 384)

Check Skills

For 4–7, tell if the blue line appears to be a line of symmetry. Write yes or no. (pp. 384–385)

4. 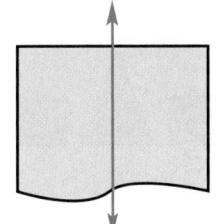   5. 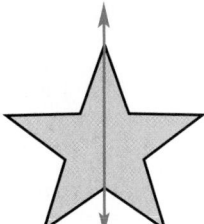   6. 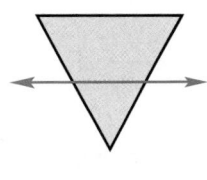   7.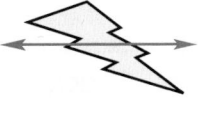

For 8–10, tell if each pair of figures appears to be similar. Write *yes* or *no*. (pp. 388–389)

8.    9. 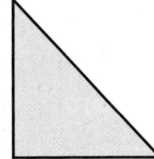   10.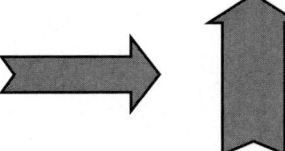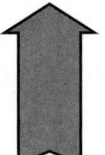

Check Problem Solving

Make a model to solve. (pp. 380–383)

11. Mrs. Thompson baked 4 apple pies. Each pie is cut into 8 slices. How many pieces of pie are there?

12. **WRITE Math** ▸ Bailey used 2 triangles and 2 trapezoids to make this rhombus. What other pattern blocks can be used to make a rhombus congruent to this one? **Explain.**

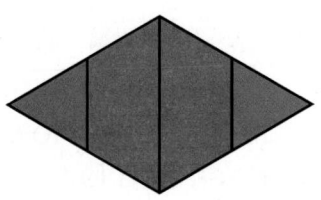

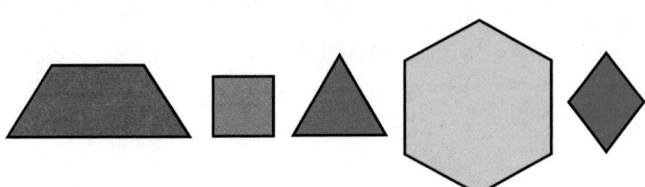

Standardized Test Prep
Chapters 1–15

Number and Operations

1. At the craft store, there are 447 wooden beads. There are 600 glass beads. How many more glass beads than wooden beads are there? (p. 88)

   A 47

   B 153

   C 247

   D 1,047

Test Tip **Check your work.**

See item 2. It is important to check your answer after you have solved a problem. You can use multiplication to check division. To check problem 2, multiply your answer by 10.

2. It takes Eli 10 minutes to read 5 pages in his book. Eli reads for 90 minutes. How many pages does he read? (p. 218)

   A 100

   B 80

   C 45

   D 9

3. **WRITE Math** Ben has 2 half dollars, 1 quarter, 5 dimes, and 6 pennies in his bank. How much money does Ben have? **Explain** how you know. (p. 110)

Algebraic Reasoning

4. What related multiplication fact can help you find $132 \div 11$? (p. 244)

   A $10 \times 11 = 110$

   B $11 \times 1 = 11$

   C $66 \times 2 = 132$

   D $12 \times 11 = 132$

5. Which shape comes next in the pattern? (Grade 2)

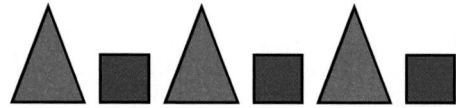

   A blue triangle

   B red triangle

   C blue square

   D red square

6. How many wheels do 4 wagons have? (p. 256)

Wagons	1	2	3	4
Wheels	4	8	12	■

   A 16

   B 15

   C 14

   D 13

7. **WRITE Math** How can you use a fact family to find $32 \div 8$? **Explain** your answer. (p. 286)

Geometry

8. Which figure appears to be congruent to this figure? (p. 378)

A

B

C

D

9. How many right angles are in a square? (p. 360)

A 1

B 2

C 3

D 4

10. ▐ WRITE Math ▶ How many lines of symmetry does this figure appear to have? Draw a picture to help you **explain.** (p. 386)

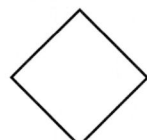

Data Analysis and Probability

11. The pictograph shows the number of trading cards Maria's friends have. Maria has 30 cards. How many symbols are needed to show this on the graph? (p. 150)

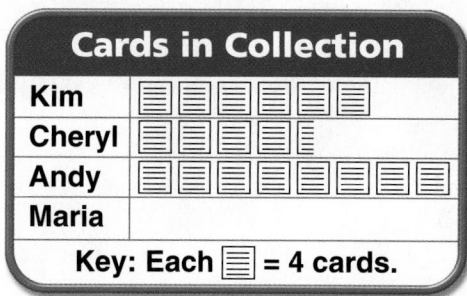

Cards in Collection		
Kim		
Cheryl		
Andy		
Maria		

Key: Each ▤ = 4 cards.

A 6

B 7 $\frac{1}{2}$

C 8

D 9

12. ▐ WRITE Math ▶ The graph shows the insects Stephen saw on a walk. How many insects did Stephen see in all? **Explain** how you found the answer. (p. 154)

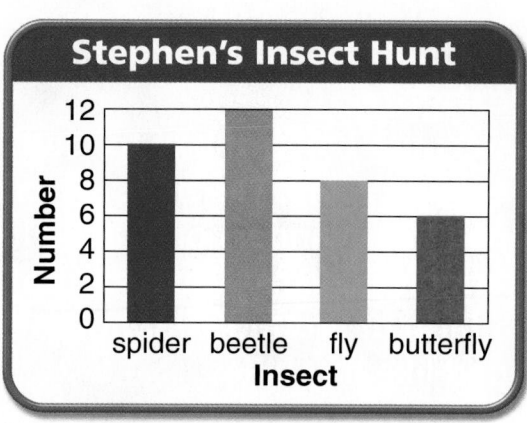

16 Solid Figures

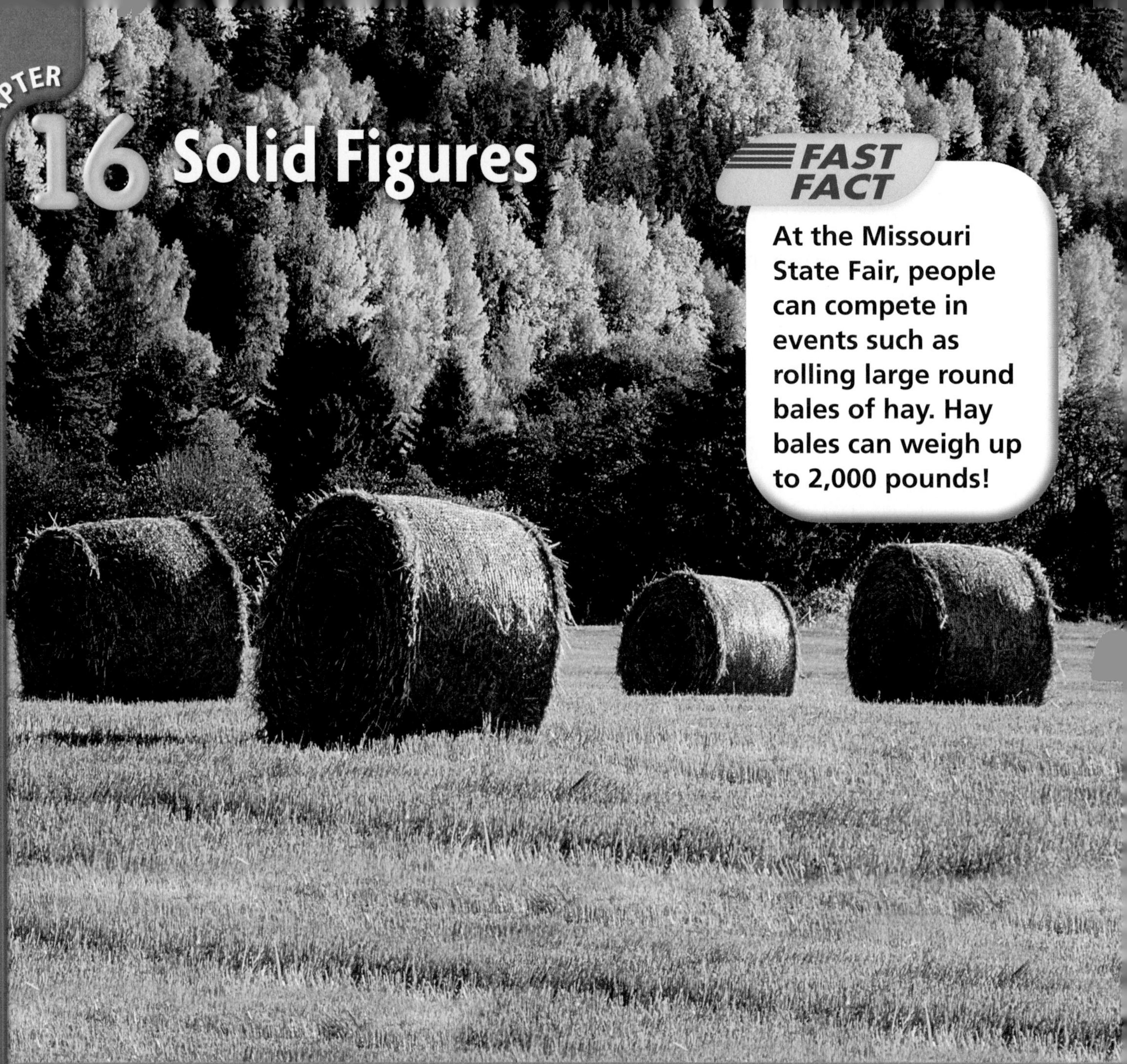

Investigate

Farmers use bales of hay to feed horses, sheep, and cows. The bales of hay can be shaped like cylinders or shaped like rectangular prisms. Make a list of other items on a farm or around your house that are shaped like hay bales.

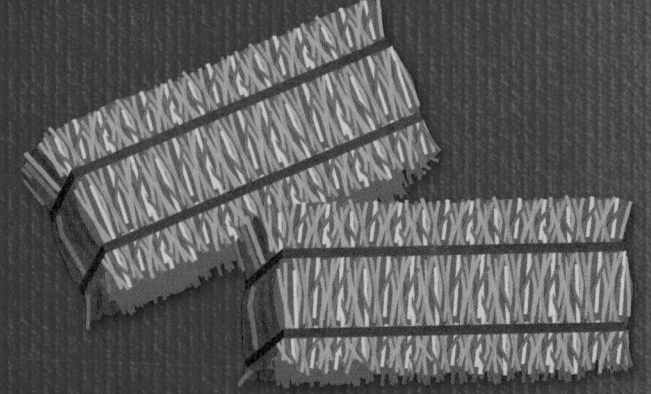

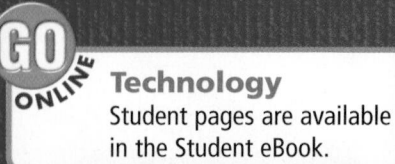

GO ONLINE

Technology
Student pages are available in the Student eBook.

Check your understanding of important skills needed for success in Chapter 16.

▶ **Solid Figures**

Choose the best term from the box.

| cone |
| cube |
| cylinder |
| rectangular prism |
| sphere |
| square pyramid |

1.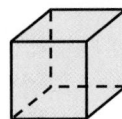

2.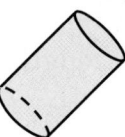

3.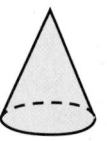

4.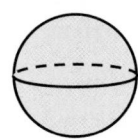

5.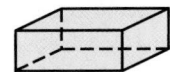

6.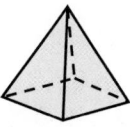

Name the solid figure that each object looks like.

7.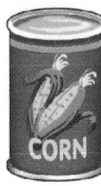

8.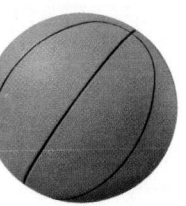

9.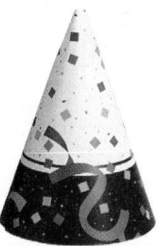

10.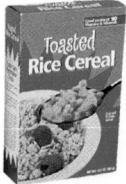

VOCABULARY POWER

CHAPTER VOCABULARY

cone
cube
cylinder
edge
face
net
rectangular prism

sphere
square pyramid
three-dimensional figure
vertex

WARM-UP WORDS

cube A solid figure with six faces that are all squares

face A flat surface of a solid figure

three-dimensional figure A figure having length, width, and height

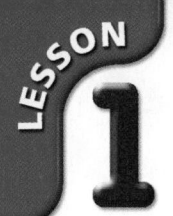

1 Identify Solid Figures

OBJECTIVE: Identify, describe, and classify solid figures.

Quick Review

Name each plane figure.

1. ☐ 2. △ 3. ▭

4. ○ 5. ◹

Learn

Solid figures have length, width, and height. They are also called **three-dimensional figures**.

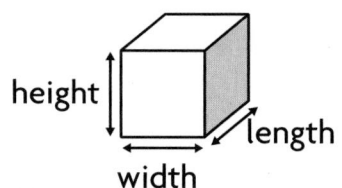

PROBLEM Jodie's grandmother gave her a charm bracelet. Which charm on her bracelet is shaped like a sphere?

Vocabulary

cone	edge
cube	face
cylinder	vertex
sphere	
rectangular prism	
square pyramid	
three-dimensional figure	

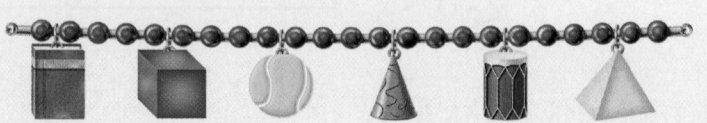

rectangular prism	cube
sphere	cone
cylinder	square pyramid

Math Idea
Some three-dimensional figures have curved surfaces.

curved surface

So, the tennis ball is shaped like a sphere.

• Which charm is shaped like a cylinder?

A **face** is a flat surface of a solid figure.

An **edge** is the line segment formed where two faces meet.

A **vertex** is a point where three or more edges meet. The plural of *vertex* is *vertices*.

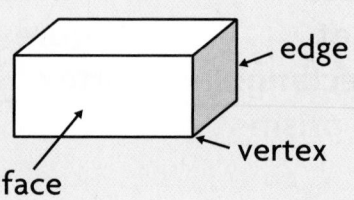

400

Naming Faces

Activity

Materials ■ solid figures (cube, square pyramid, rectangular prism), paper, crayons

- Copy the table below.
- Trace the faces of a cube. Name the plane figures.
- Count the numbers of faces, edges, and vertices. Record the numbers in the table.

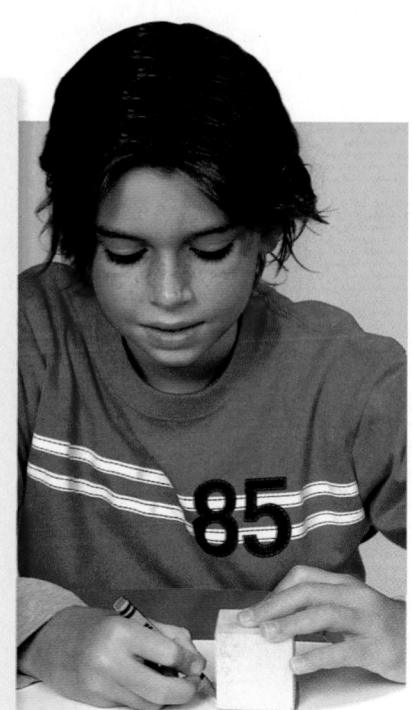

Name of Figure	Shapes of Faces	Names of Faces	Number of		
			Faces	Edges	Vertices
cube	□ □ □ □ □ □	6 squares	6	12	8

- Repeat the steps for a square pyramid and a rectangular prism.
- Describe the faces of a square pyramid.
- How many edges does a rectangular prism have?

Guided Practice

1. Which solid figure has the faces shown?

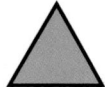

Name the solid figure that each object is shaped like.

2.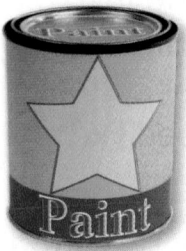

3.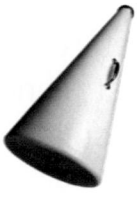

✓ 4.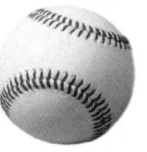

✓ 5.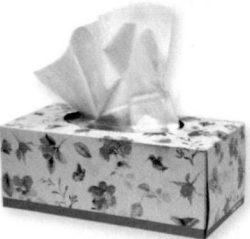

6. **TALK Math** **Explain** the difference between a cube and a square.

Name the solid figure that each object is shaped like.

7.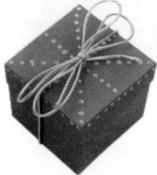

8.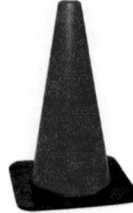

9.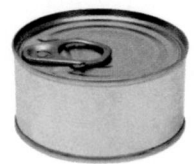

10.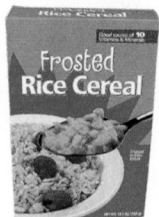

Name the solid figure. Then tell the number of faces, edges, and vertices.

11.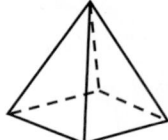

12.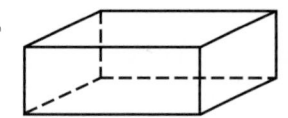

13.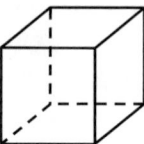

For 14–17, use the grocery items.

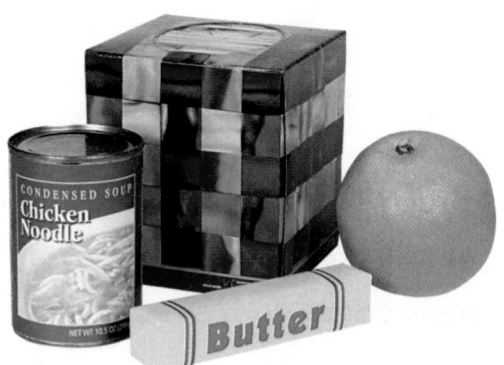

14. Which grocery item is shaped like a sphere?

15. Which grocery item has the faces shown below?

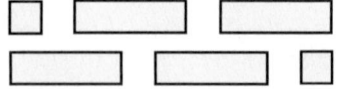

16. Describe the faces of the box of tissues.

17. Which solid figure is the can of soup shaped like?

18. I am a solid figure with 5 faces. One of my faces is a quadrilateral with 4 right angles and 4 sides the same length. What figure am I?

19. **Pose a Problem** Look at Problem 18. Write a similar problem about a different solid figure.

20. Rick built a tower using 7 rectangular prisms, 4 cylinders, 8 cubes, and 1 square pyramid. Half of the figures were blue and half were red. How many figures were blue?

21. **≡FAST FACT** Earth is the third planet from the sun and the fifth-largest planet in our solar system. What solid figure is shaped like Earth?

22. **Reasoning** Explain how a rectangular prism and a cube are alike and how they are different.

23. **WRITE Math** **What's the Question?** The answer is 6 square faces.

Extra Practice on page 414, Set A

Learn About) Parallel Faces

Some solid figures have parallel faces.
Parallel faces are always the same distance apart.

Megan made a jewelry box in
the shape of a rectangular prism.
She painted the parallel faces the
same colors.
How many colors did she use?

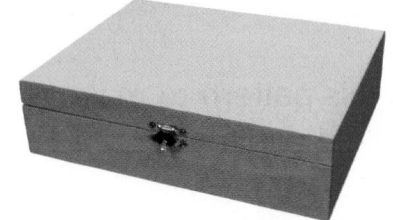

Remember
Parallel lines
are lines that
appear never to
cross. They are
always the same
distance apart.

Example Identify the parallel faces.

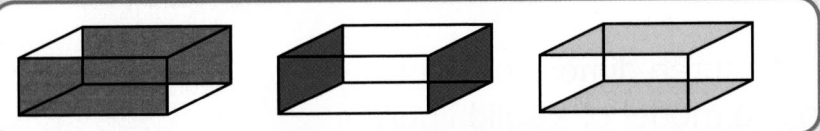

A rectangular prism has 3 pairs of parallel faces.
So, Megan used 3 different colors to paint her jewelry box.

Try It

24. Trace the solid figure below. Color
one pair of parallel faces. Write
the number of parallel faces.

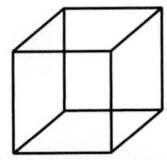

25. Megan said the figure below has
2 pairs of parallel faces. Do you
agree? **Explain.**

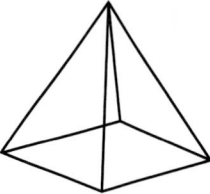

Mixed Review and Test Prep

26. A bag contains 8 balls numbered
1 through 8. You pull 1 ball from
the bag. List the possible outcomes.
(p. 182)

27. Test Prep Which solid figure is
shaped like a party hat?

  A cone   **C** cylinder

  B cube   **D** prism

28. What kind of motion was used to
move this figure? (p. 390)

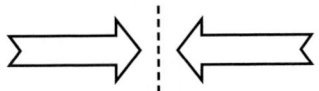

29. Test Prep How many faces does a
square pyramid have?

  A 12   **B** 8   **C** 6   **D** 5

**CD
ROM**

Technology
Use Harcourt Mega Math, Ice Station
Exploration, *Frozen Solids*, Level A.

Model Solid Figures

OBJECTIVE: Identify and make a model of a solid figure from a net.

Quick Review

Name the figure. Then tell how many faces, edges, and vertices.

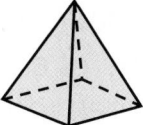

Learn

PROBLEM Lori folded this pattern to make a solid figure. What figure did she make?

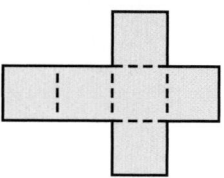

A **net** is a two-dimensional pattern of a three-dimensional, or solid, figure. When folded, it becomes a model of a solid figure.

Vocabulary

net

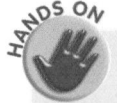

Activity 1

Materials ■ cube pattern, scissors, tape

• Cut out the net along the solid lines.

• Fold along the dashed lines. Tape the edges together.

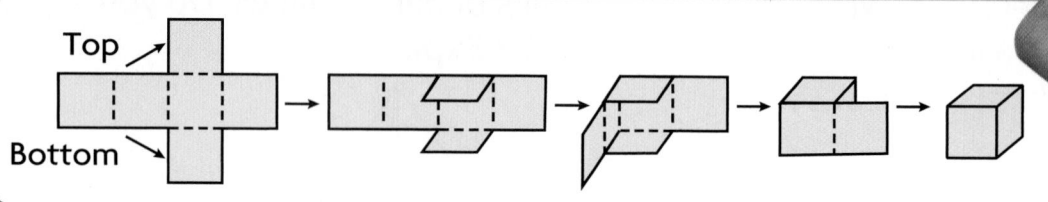

Top

Bottom

• Identify the solid figure you made.

The net can be folded to make a cube. So, Lori made a cube.

• What plane figures are the faces of a cube?

Examples of Nets

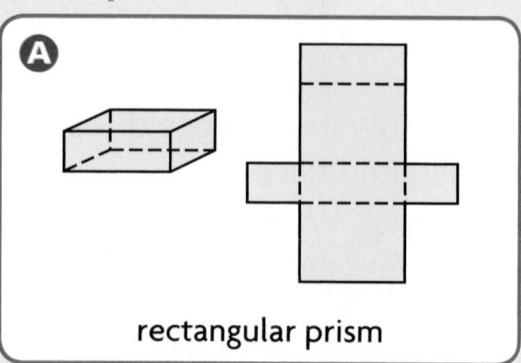

Ⓐ

rectangular prism

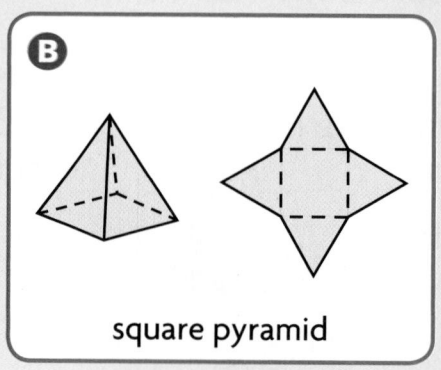

Ⓑ

square pyramid

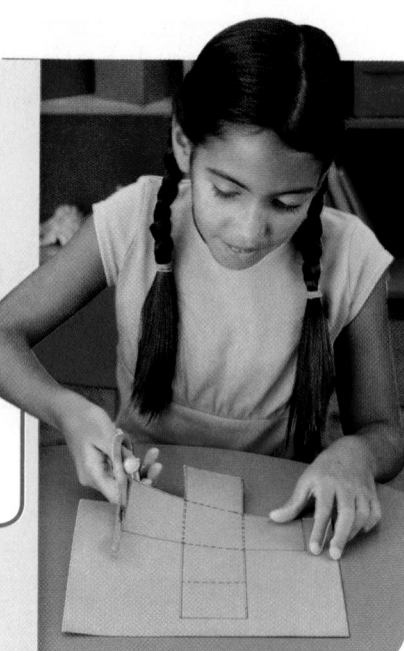

Making a Net

You can cut apart a three-dimensional figure to make a net.

Activity 2

Materials ■ box, paper, scissors, tape

• Cut along the edges of a box until it is flat.
  Lay it on a sheet of paper.

• Trace around the flattened box to make a net.

• Cut out the net. Fold it the same way the original box
  was folded. Tape the edges together.

• What are the plane figures on the net you made?

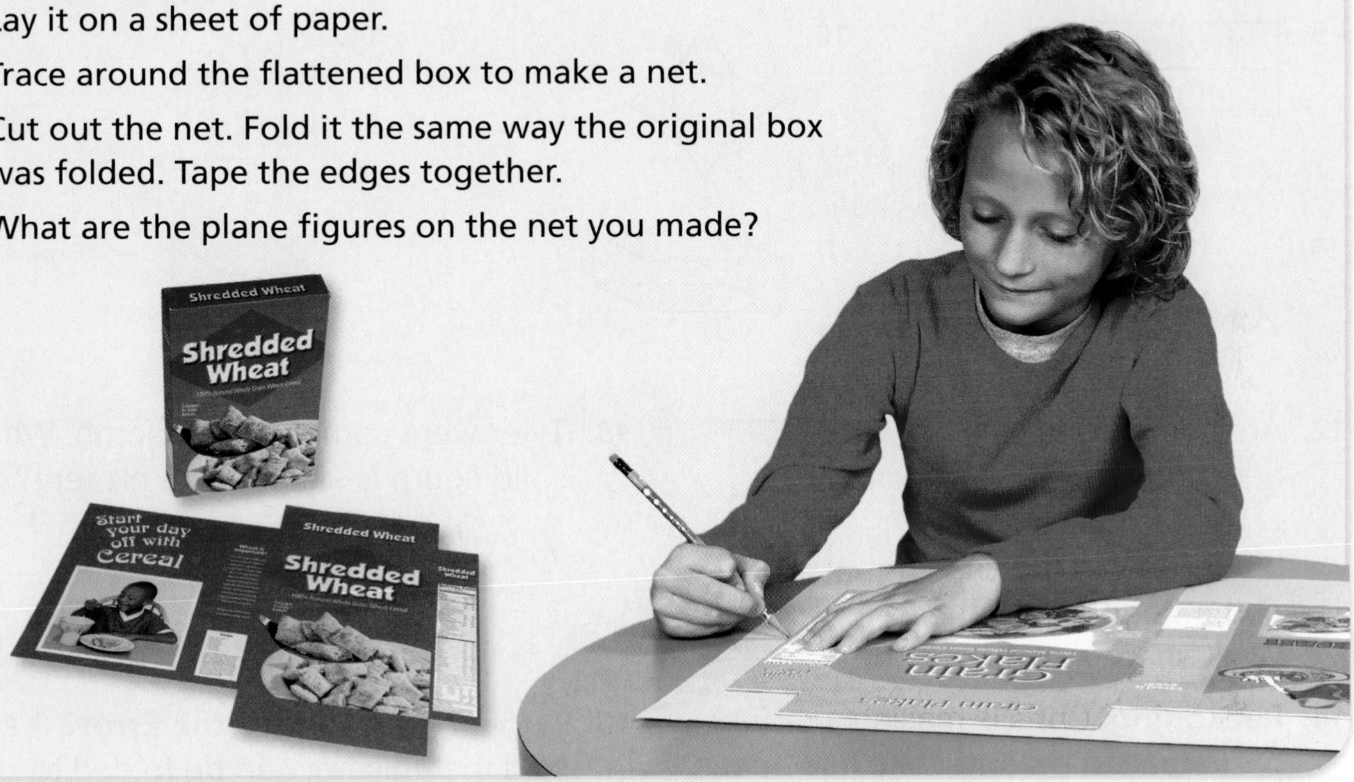

Guided Practice

1. What plane figures are the faces of this net?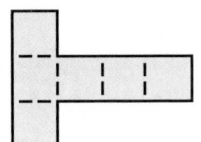

Identify the solid figure that can be made from each net.

2.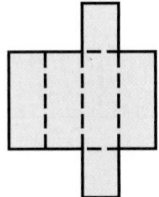

✓ **3.**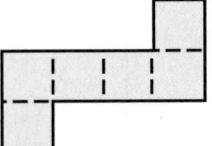

✓ **4.**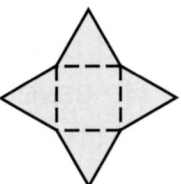

5. [TALK Math] **Explain** how a net for a cube is different
from a net for a rectangular prism.

Identify the solid figure that can be made from each net.

6.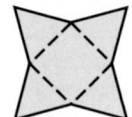

7.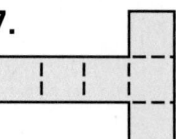

8.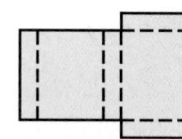

Write the letter of the solid figure that matches each net.

9.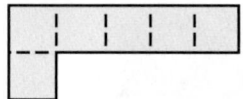

10.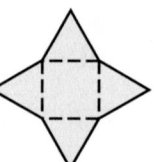

11.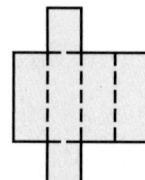

a.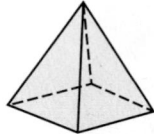

b.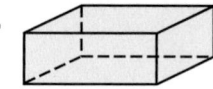

c.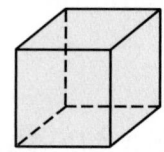

12. Arnie is moving to a new house. He has a cardboard packing box that is now in the shape of the net on the right. What shape will the box be?

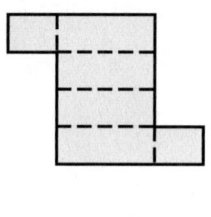

13. Tyler went camping last month. What solid figure is shaped like his tent?

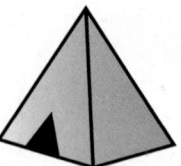

14. **Reasoning** Chris is mailing a basketball to his sister. He has boxes shaped like a cube, a rectangular prism, and a cylinder. Which box should he use? **Explain** your choice.

15. **WRITE Math** ▶ **What's the Error?** Kara said that this net can be folded to make a cube. **Explain** her error.

Mixed Review and Test Prep

16. Nick made a model of a rectangular prism. How many faces, edges, and vertices did Nick's model have? (p. 400)

17. Kit bought 3 puzzles. Each puzzle cost $7. He gave the cashier $30. How much change did he receive?

    (p. 264)

18. **Test Prep** Which solid figure could be made from this net?

    A cube

    B sphere

    C square pyramid

    D cylinder

    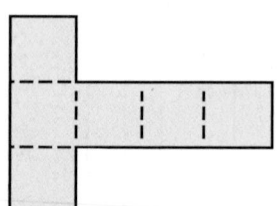

Extra Practice on page 414, Set B

The Art of Origami

 Reading Skill **Classify and Categorize**

Origami is the art of folding paper. The only material needed is paper. Some people can make models of animals and geometric shapes. Look at the origami models below.

When you classify three-dimensional figures, you organize them into groups by ways they are alike.

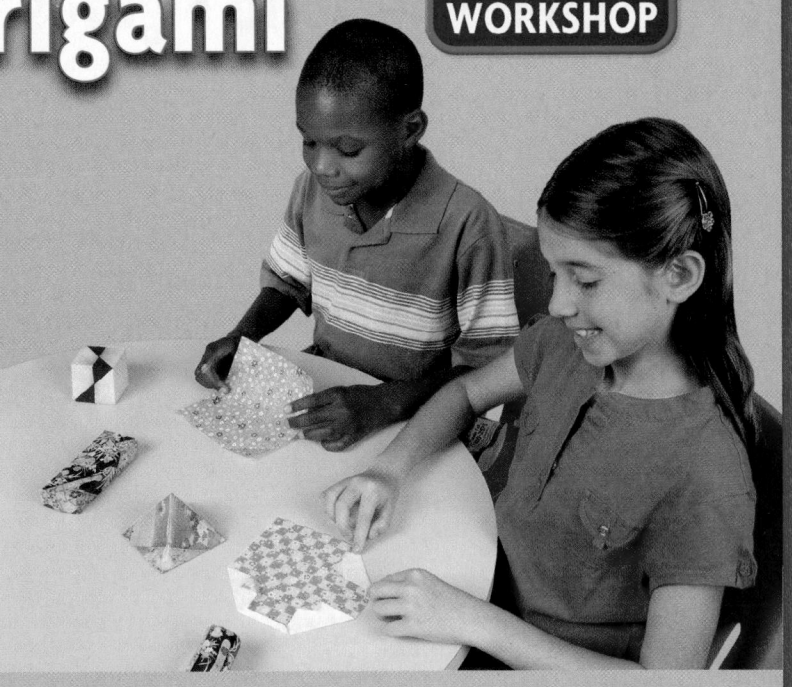

▲ The name *origami* comes from the Japanese word "oru," which means to fold, and "kami," which means paper.

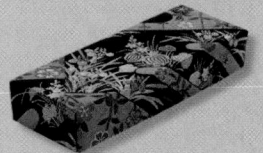 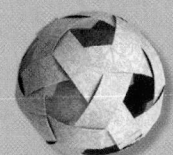 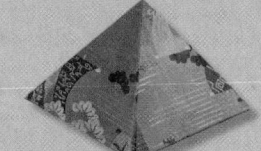 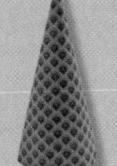 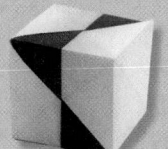 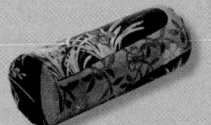

Figures that stack	Figures that roll	Figures with flat surfaces	Figures with curved surfaces	Figures with right angles	Figures with no right angles
cylinder rectangular prism cube	cylinder cone sphere	rectangular prism square pyramid cube	cylinder cone sphere	rectangular prism square pyramid cube	cylinder cone sphere

Problem Solving Use *classify and categorize* to solve.

1. How are the cube and the square pyramid alike?

2. Teresa sorted the solid figures shown below into two groups. Tell two ways Teresa could classify the models. Which models would you place in each category?

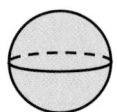 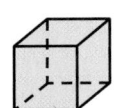 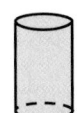 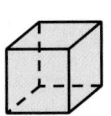 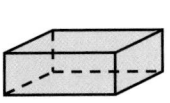 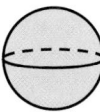 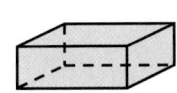

Combine Solid Figures

OBJECTIVE: Identify common solid figures in complex solid figures.

 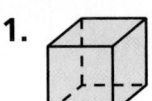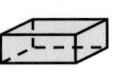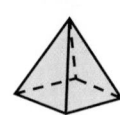
Learn

PROBLEM Randy and his sister built this sand castle at the beach. What solid figures make up the sand castle?

Example

Look at each part of the sand castle separately.

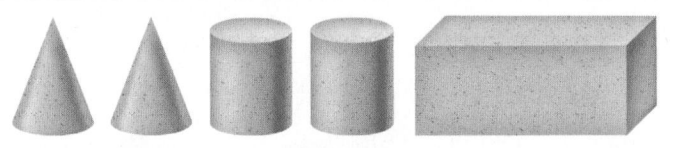

So, the sand castle is made up of 2 cones, 2 cylinders, and a rectangular prism.

More Examples

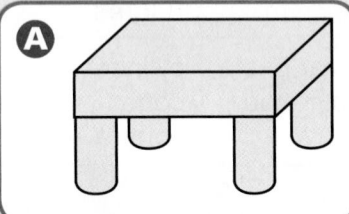   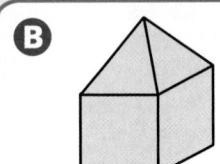   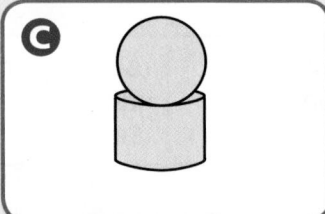

Ⓐ   Ⓑ   Ⓒ

• What solid figures were used to make Object A? Object B? Object C?

Guided Practice

1. How many solid figures were used to make this object?

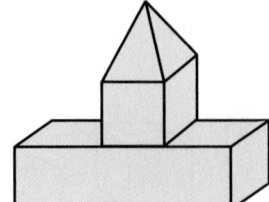

Name the solid figures used to make each object.

2.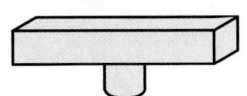

3.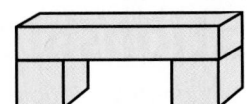

4.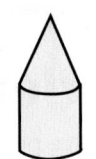

5. **[TALK Math]** **Explain** how to make Object B in More Examples look like this object.

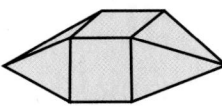

Independent Practice and Problem Solving

Name the solid figures used to make each object.

6.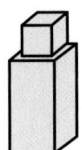

7.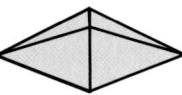

8.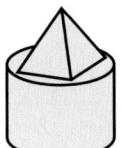

Each pair of objects should be the same.
Name the solid figure that is missing.

9.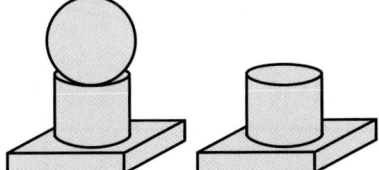

10.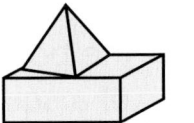

11.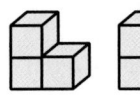

12. **Reasoning** What solid figures would you get if you cut a cube in half like this?

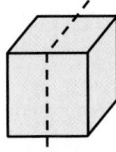

13. **[WRITE Math]** **What's the Error?** Wes says he used a cylinder and a cone to make this figure. Does this make sense? **Explain.**

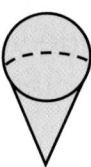

Mixed Review and Test Prep

14. What solid figure can be made from this net? (p. 404)

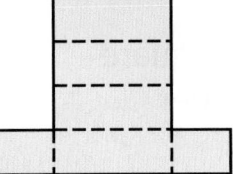

15. Write a rule for the pattern. Then write the next two numbers in the pattern. 3, 7, 11, 15, ___, ___. (p. 256)

16. **Test Prep** Which object is made by combining a cube and a cylinder?

A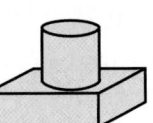

C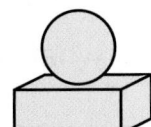

B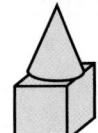

D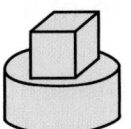

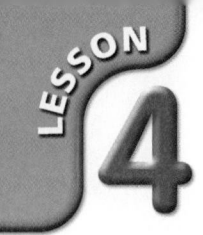

Problem Solving Workshop
Skill: Identify Relationships

OBJECTIVE: Solve problems by using the skill *identify relationships*.

Use the Skill

PROBLEM Trisha traced the face of a solid figure to make this plane figure. Which solid figure did she use?

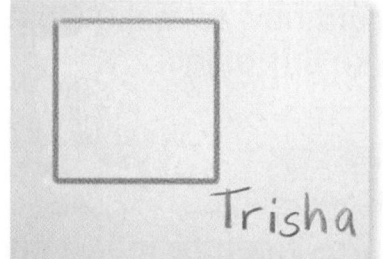

You can identify solid figures by looking at the different views.

A circle can be • the bottom view of a cone • the top or bottom view of a cylinder • any view of a sphere	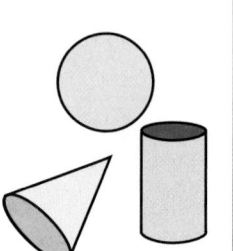	A square can be • any view of a cube • the top, bottom, or side view of a rectangular prism • the bottom view of a square pyramid	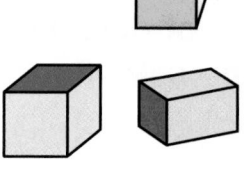
A rectangle can be • the top, bottom, or side view of a rectangular prism	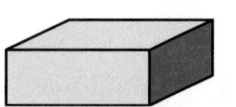	A triangle can be • the side view of a square pyramid	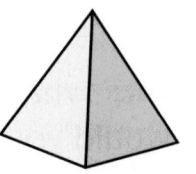

So, Trisha could have used a cube, a square pyramid, or a rectangular prism to make her drawing.

Think and Discuss
Use plane and solid figures to solve.

a. Natalie has a wooden block shaped like a square pyramid. If you look at the bottom view of her block, what plane figure would you see?

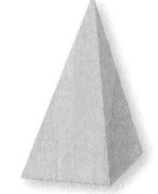

b. Eileen pressed a solid figure into clay. It left the outline of a circle. What solid figure did she use?

c. Karl made this pattern. Which solid figures could he have traced?

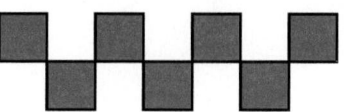

Solve.

1. Jannelle used a sponge to paint a border of circles around a picture frame. She has three different sponges in the shapes of a cylinder, a cube, and a rectangular prism. Which sponge did she use to make the border?

   Think about the three solid figures from different views.

   Which figure has a circle as the top, bottom, or side view?

   Now solve the problem.

2. **What if** Jannelle made a border of squares? Which sponge could she have used?

3. Casey made a sponge paint border of triangles around a poster. Was his sponge in the shape of a cylinder, a sphere, or a square pyramid?

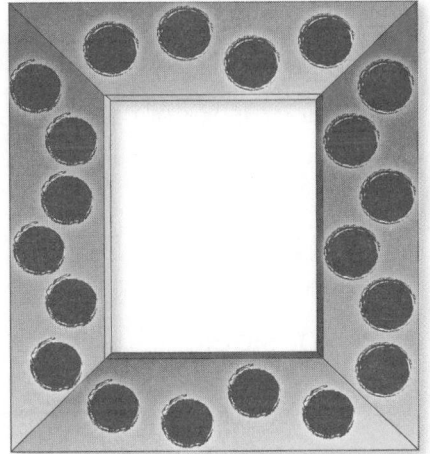

Mixed Applications

For 4–7, use the pictures.

4. Matt bought an item at the store. He said that if you look at the item from the side, it looks like a rectangle. Which item could Matt have bought?

5. Martin bought some items. He paid with a $20 bill. He got $3 in change. Which items could Martin have bought?

6. Mrs. Garrett bought 6 cans of peanuts and 2 boxes of crayons. Find the total amount she spent.

7. **Pose a Problem** Look at Problem 6. Write a similar problem by changing the items that Mrs. Garrett bought.

8. On Saturday, 482 people visited the aquarium. On Sunday, 621 people visited the aquarium. How many more people visited the aquarium on Sunday?

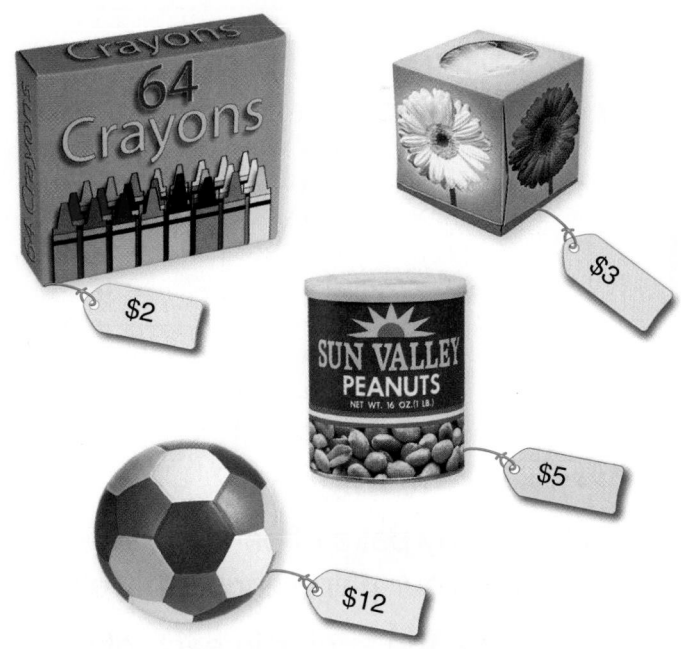

9. **WRITE Math** Nick painted a fence for 75 minutes in the morning and 90 minutes in the afternoon. How many minutes in all did Nick spend painting? How many hours and minutes? **Explain.**

5 Draw Figures

OBJECTIVE: Draw plane and solid figures.

 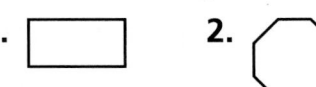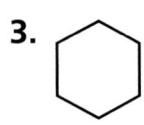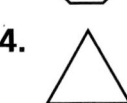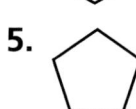
Investigate

Materials ■ dot paper, ruler

You can draw plane figures using line segments.

A Use a ruler. Draw a plane figure on dot paper. Name your figure based on the number of sides.

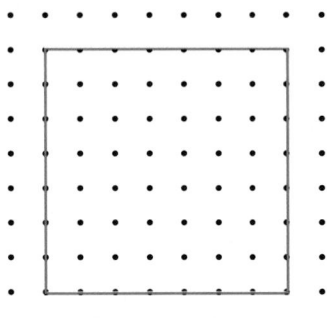

B Draw different plane figures.

Remember

A closed plane figure with straight sides that are line segments is a polygon.

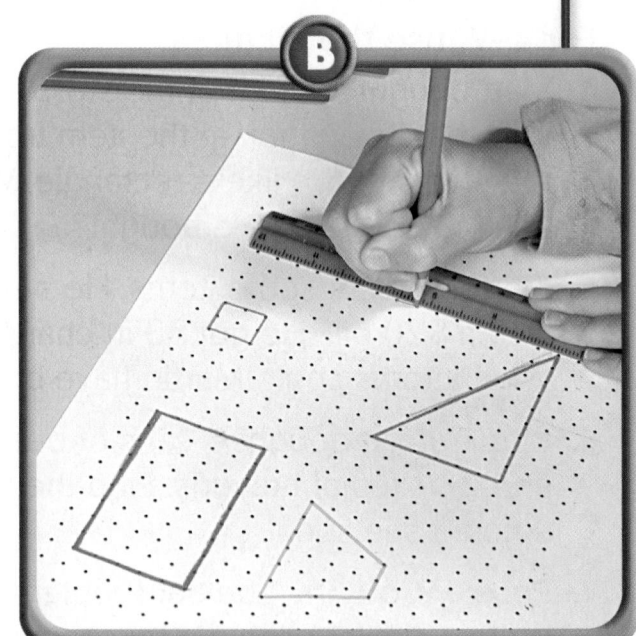

Draw Conclusions

1. How many pairs of parallel sides does each of your plane figures have?

2. Describe the angles in each of your plane figures.

3. **Analysis** Compare your plane figures with those of your classmates. Explain how they are alike and how they are different.

Connect

You can use what you know about faces, edges, and vertices to draw solid figures using line segments.

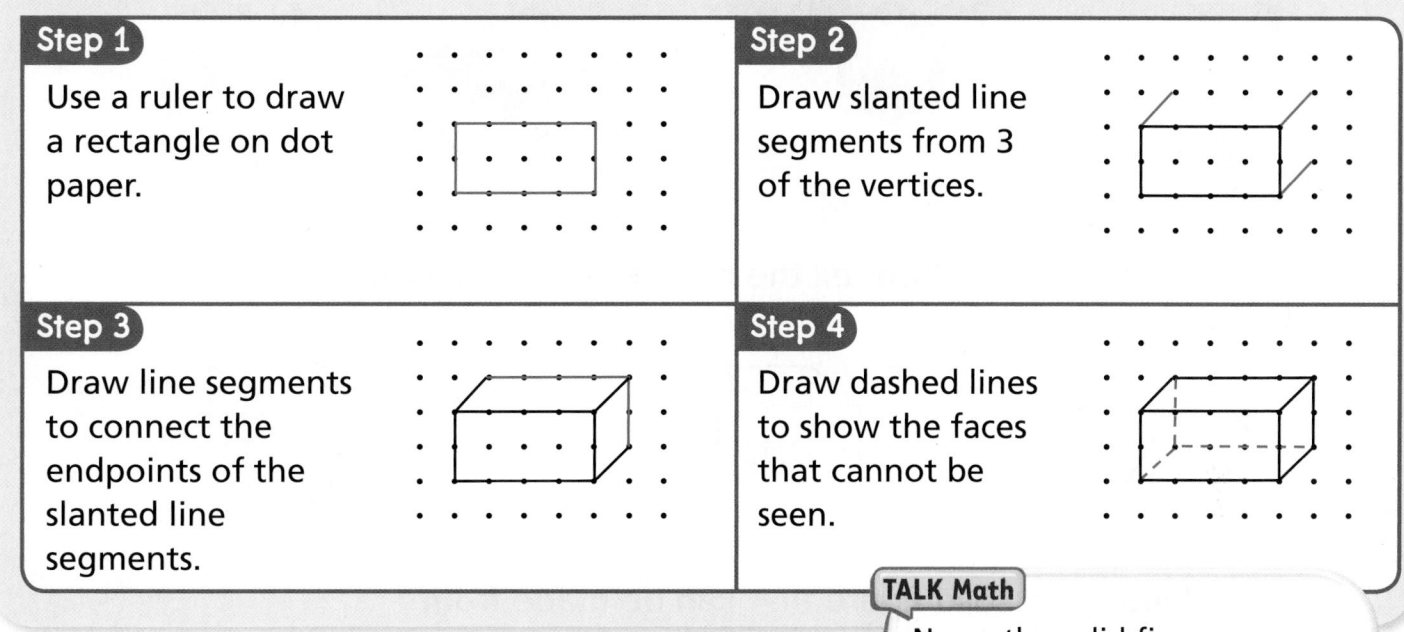

Step 1

Use a ruler to draw a rectangle on dot paper.

Step 2

Draw slanted line segments from 3 of the vertices.

Step 3

Draw line segments to connect the endpoints of the slanted line segments.

Step 4

Draw dashed lines to show the faces that cannot be seen.

TALK Math

Name the solid figure you drew. Then tell how many faces, edges and vertices the figure has.

Practice

For 1–6, copy each figure on dot paper. Then name the figure.

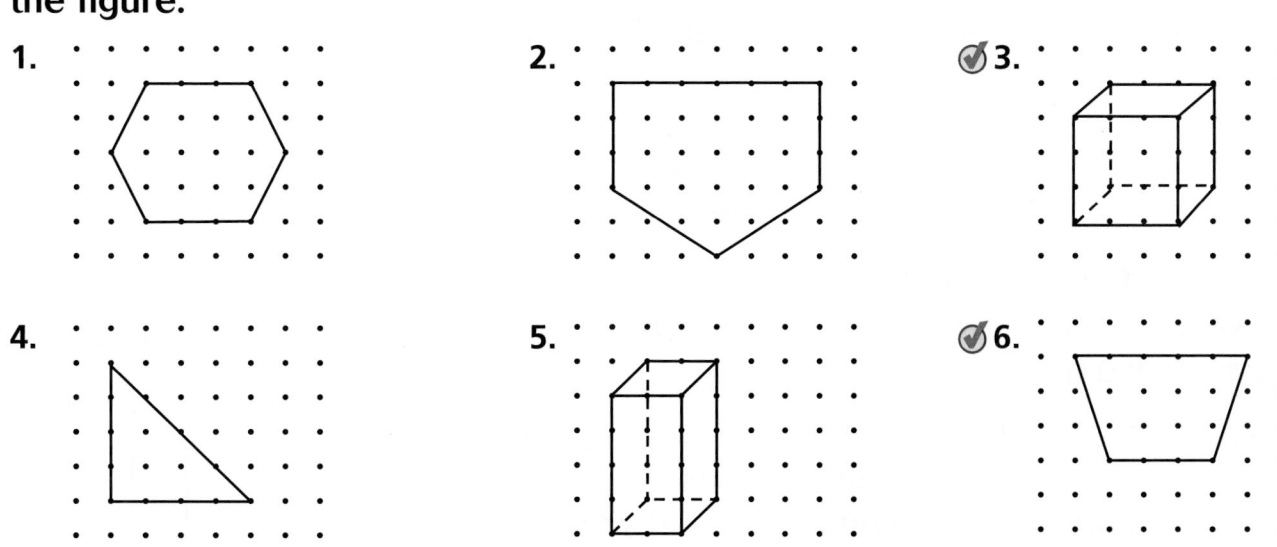

1.

2.

✓ 3.

4.

5.

✓ 6.

7. **WRITE Math** Explain how a square and a cube are alike. Use dot paper to draw each figure.

Extra Practice

Set A Name the solid figure that each object is shaped like. (pp. 400–403)

1.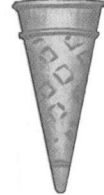
2.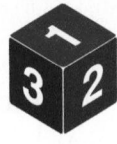
3.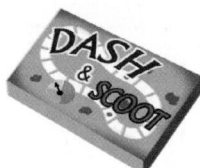
4.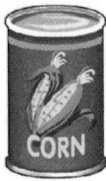

Name the solid figure. Then tell the number of faces, edges, and vertices.

5.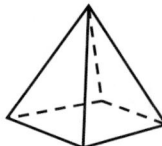
6.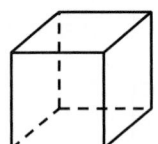
7.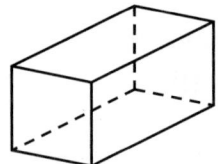

Set B Identify the solid figure that can be made from each net. (pp. 404–407)

1.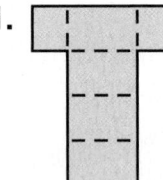
2.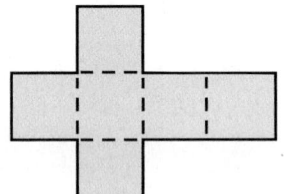
3.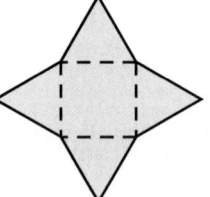

Set C Name the solid figures used to make each object. (pp. 408–409)

1.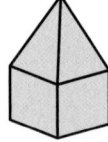
2.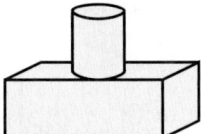
3.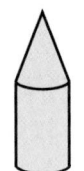

For 4–5, use the wooden shapes.

4. Everett made a tower of 2 yellow shapes. What solid figures did he use?

5. Madison used the remaining 3 shapes in her tower. Name the solid figures she used. What shape is probably on the top? Why?

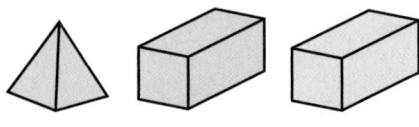
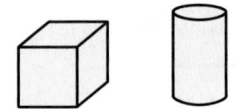

CD ROM **Technology**
Use Harcourt Mega Math, Ice Station
Exploration, *Frozen Solids*, Levels A, B, G.

PRACTICE GAME

Rolling Figures

Shake!

2–4 players

Rattle!

- Gameboard
- 2 solid figure game cubes
- Game card, crayon or pencil, and counter for each player

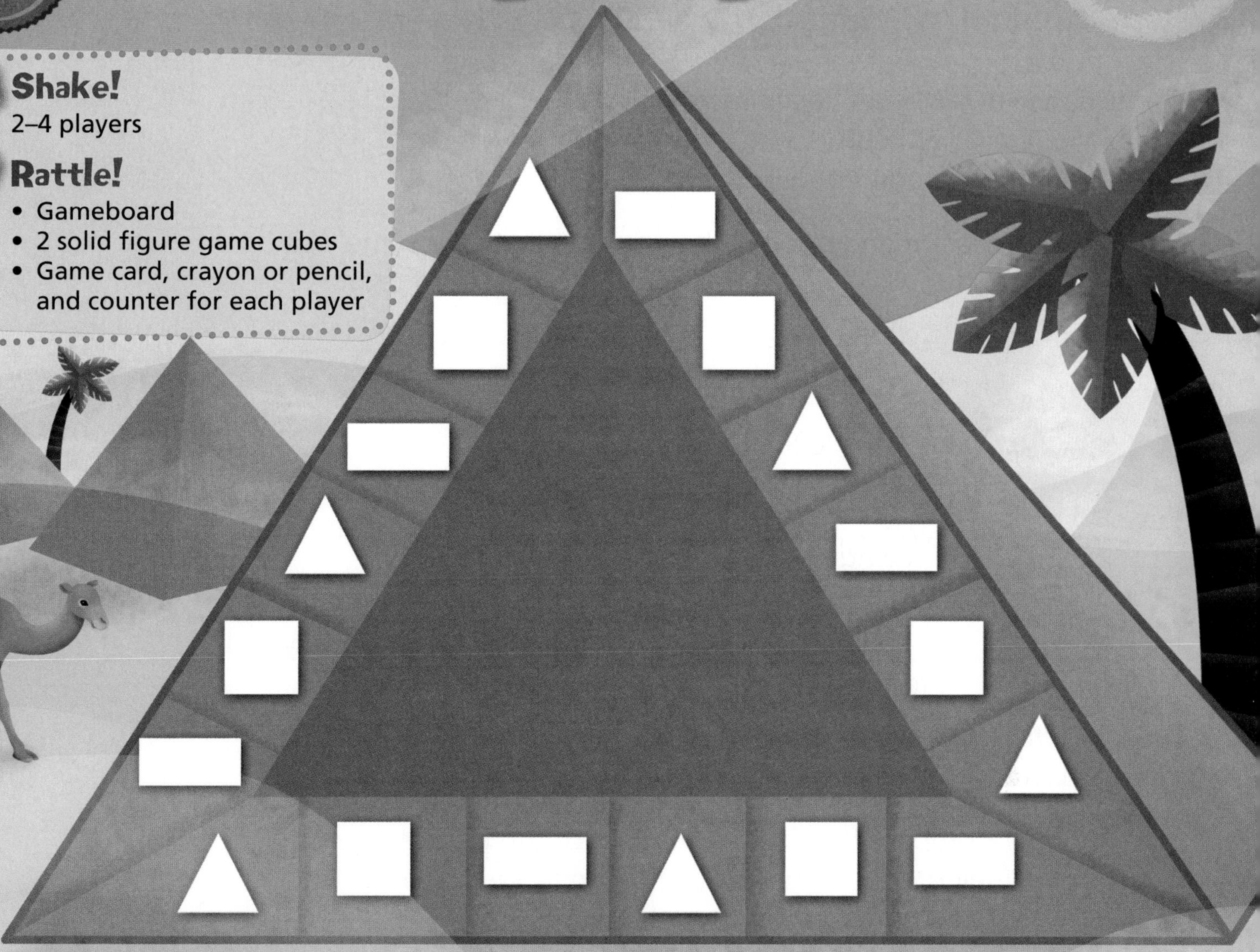

Roll!

- Each player places a counter on any space on the gameboard.

- The first player rolls both solid figure cubes and then tells whether the two figures that land face up can be combined.

- If the two figures can be combined, Player 1 shades a face on his or her game card that matches the face on which the counter lies. Player 1 then moves 1 space in any direction.

- Player 2 follows the same steps as Player 1. If the rolled figures cannot be combined, it is the next player's turn.

- The game continues as players roll the cubes, shade faces, and move around the gameboard.

- The first player to shade all the faces of any solid figure on his or her game card wins.

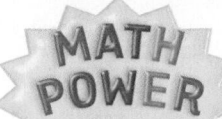

Congruent Solid Figures

Building Blocks

Chantal and Miguel each made a solid figure with cubes. Are the two solid figures congruent?

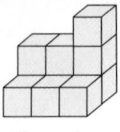 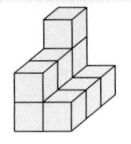

Chantal   Miguel

Two figures are congruent if they have exactly the same shape and size. Look at each layer of the figures to tell if they are congruent.

▲ The small plastic Lego® bricks were invented in Denmark. There is a LEGOLAND® Park in Carlsbad, California.

Example

Step 1 Make a table to compare the figures.

Step 2 Find the number of cubes in each row.

Step 3 Find the number of cubes in the layer.

	CHANTAL'S FIGURE	NUMBER OF CUBES	MIGUEL'S FIGURE	NUMBER OF CUBES
Layer 1	2 rows of 3 cubes	6	2 rows of 3 cubes	6
Layer 2	1 row of 3 cubes	3	1 row of 3 cubes	3
Layer 3	1 cube	1	1 cube	1

Step 4 Compare the sizes and shapes of the figures at each layer. If all of the sizes and shapes are the same, then the figures are congruent.

So, Chantal's figure is congruent to Miguel's figure.

Try It
Are the solid figures congruent?

1.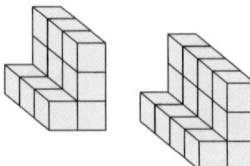

2.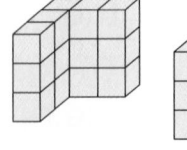

3.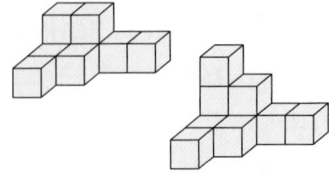

4. **WRITE Math** Use cubes to build a figure congruent to the one shown. **Explain** how you know they are congruent.

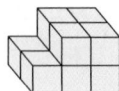

Chapter 16 Review/Test

Check Vocabulary and Concepts

Choose the best term from the box.

1. The line segment formed where two faces meet is an ___?___ . (p. 400)
2. The flat surface of a solid figure is called a ___?___ . (p. 400)
3. A ___?___ is a two-dimensional pattern used to make a three-dimensional figure. (p. 404)
4. A ___?___ is a solid figure with 6 square faces. (p. 400)

Check Skills

Name the solid figure. Then tell the number of faces, edges, and vertices. (pp. 400–403)

5.
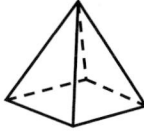

6.
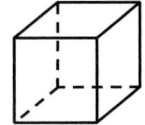

7.
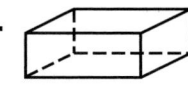

Identify the solid figure that can be made from each net. (pp. 404–407)

8.
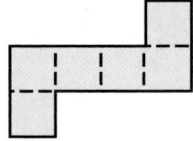

9.
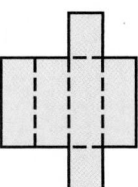

10.
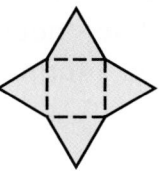

Name the solid figures used to make each object. (pp. 408–409)

11.
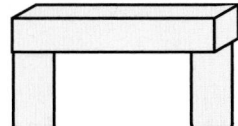

12.
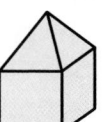

13.
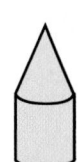

Check Problem Solving

Solve. (pp. 410–411)

14. Paul pressed a solid figure into clay. It left the outline of a square. Name 2 solid figures he could have used.

15. **WRITE Math** Jenita has 2 cubes, 2 rectangular prisms, and 1 square pyramid. She is painting them all blue. How many faces will she paint in all? **Explain** how you found the answer by writing number sentences.

Standardized Test Prep
Chapters 1–16

Number and Operations

1. At the science center, 299 people visited one exhibit. Another exhibit had 431 visitors. Which is the best estimate of the number of visitors at the exhibits altogether? (p. 52)

A 100

B 600

C 700

D 800

Test Tip **Get the information you need.**

See item 2. First, find the information given in the problem. Next, read the question again. Then, decide if there is information that is not needed. Finally, use the needed information to solve the problem.

2. Linda bought 7 packages of hot dog rolls. She bought 56 rolls in all. How many hot dog rolls were in each package? (p. 324)

A 63

B 49

C 9

D 8

3. **WRITE Math** What is 5×4. **Explain** two ways to find the product. (p. 212)

Algebraic Reasoning

4. The students in Charlie's class put tennis balls on the legs of their chairs. How many tennis balls were used for 9 chairs? (p. 256)

Chairs	Tennis Balls
1	4
2	8
3	12
4	16

A 4   **C** 20

B 13   **D** 36

5. Which number sentence belongs to the same fact family as $25 \div 5 = 5$? (p. 286)

A $5 + 5 = 10$

B $5 \times 5 = 25$

C $5 \div 5 = 1$

D $25 \div 1 = 25$

6. **WRITE Math** What is a rule for this pattern? What is the next number? **Explain** how you got your answer. (p. 256)

193, 183, 173, 163, ■

Geometry

7. Which shows a radius of the circle? (p. 364)

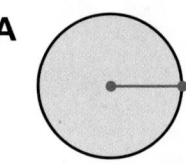
A

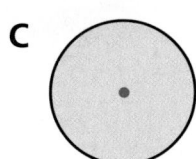
C

B

D

8. How many faces does this figure have? (p. 402)

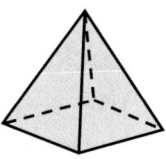

A 8   **C** 5

B 6   **D** 4

9. ⬛WRITE Math▶ Do these figures appear to be similar? **Explain** your answer. (p. 388)

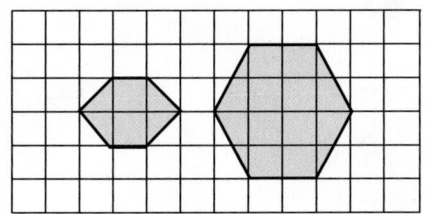

Data Analysis and Probability

10. Jay has the shirts and pants shown below. How many combinations of 1 shirt and 1 pair of pants does Jay have? (p. 186)

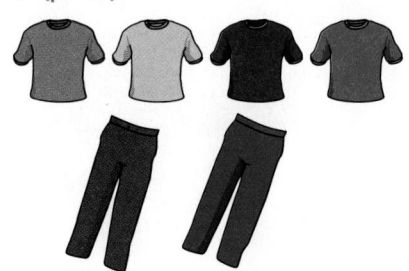

A 2

B 4

C 6

D 8

11. Jane made the line plot to show the height of the students in her class. How many students are exactly 53 inches tall? (p. 162)

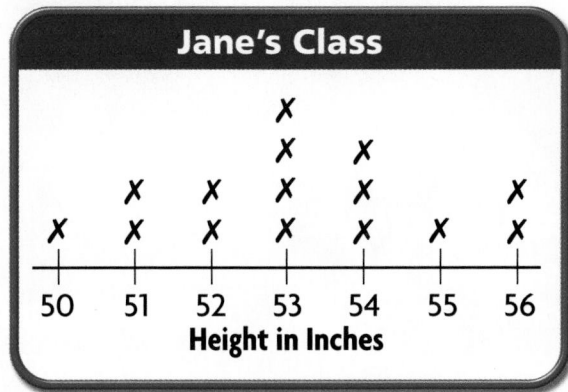

Jane's Class

Height in Inches

A 1   **C** 3

B 2   **D** 4

12. ⬛WRITE Math▶ **Explain** how to find the range of the data in the line plot in Problem 11. (p. 162)

17 Algebra: Patterns

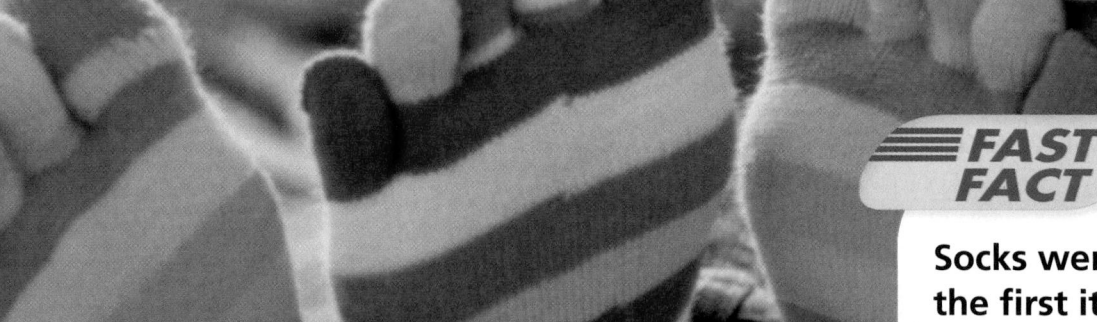

≡ FAST FACT

Socks were one of the first items that were hand-knitted. In 1589, William Lee invented the first knitting machine in England.

Investigate

Socks can be one color or many colors. Design your own socks. Create a color pattern using two or more colors of yarn. Draw what your socks might look like.

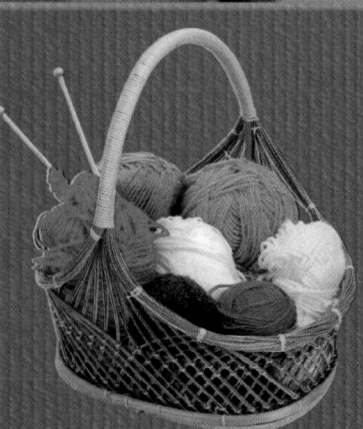

GO ONLINE

Technology
Student pages are available in the Student eBook.

Check your understanding of important skills
needed for success in Chapter 17.

▶ Find a Number Pattern

Write a rule. Then copy and complete the table.

1.

Boxes	1	2	3	4	5
Pencils	4	8	12	16	■

2.

Bicycles	1	2	3	4	5
Wheels	2	4	6	■	■

3.

T-shirt	1	2	3	4	5
Cost	$5	$10	■	$20	■

4.

Shelf	1	2	3	4	5
Books	10	■	30	40	■

▶ Plane Shape Patterns

Describe the pattern. Then draw the next two shapes.

5.

6. ☆★◆☆★◆☆★◆☆

7.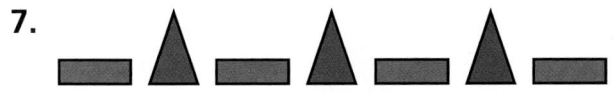

8.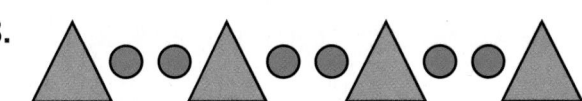

VOCABULARY POWER

CHAPTER VOCABULARY	WARM-UP WORDS
growing pattern **pattern unit** **repeating pattern**	**growing pattern** A pattern that increases by the same amount from one figure to the next **pattern unit** The part of a pattern that repeats **repeating pattern** A pattern that uses the same pattern unit over and over again

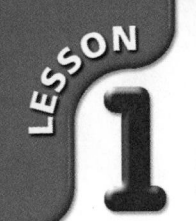

LESSON 1

Patterns

OBJECTIVE: Identify and extend number and geometric patterns to solve problems.

Quick Review

Name each shape.

1. 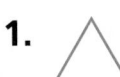 2.

3. 4.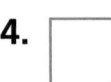

5.

Vocabulary

pattern unit

Learn

A pattern is an ordered set of numbers or objects. A **pattern unit** is the part of a pattern that repeats.

PROBLEM Karen enjoys sewing and making pillows. The chart shows the number of pillows she made each week. If the pattern continues, how many pillows will she make in Week 10?

Week	one	two	three	four	five	six	seven	eight	nine	ten
Number of pillows	3	2	4	3	2	4	3	2	4	▪

Example

> Look at the number pattern. Find the pattern unit.
>
> The number pattern is 3, 2, 4, 3, 2, 4, 3, 2, 4.
>
> The pattern unit is *3, 2, 4.*
>
> To continue the pattern, repeat the pattern unit.
> 3, 2, 4, 3, 2, 4, 3, 2, 4, 3, 2, 4

So, Karen will make 3 pillows in Week 10.

Math Idea
Both numbers and shapes can form patterns.

Another Example

> Karen sewed shapes across a pillow. Look at the pattern she used. What is the missing shape?
>
>   ?
>
> The pattern unit is *red circle, blue square.*

So, the missing shape is a red circle.

• Predict what the next two shapes in her pattern will be.

• What if the pattern unit was *red circle, blue square, green circle?* What would the pattern look like?

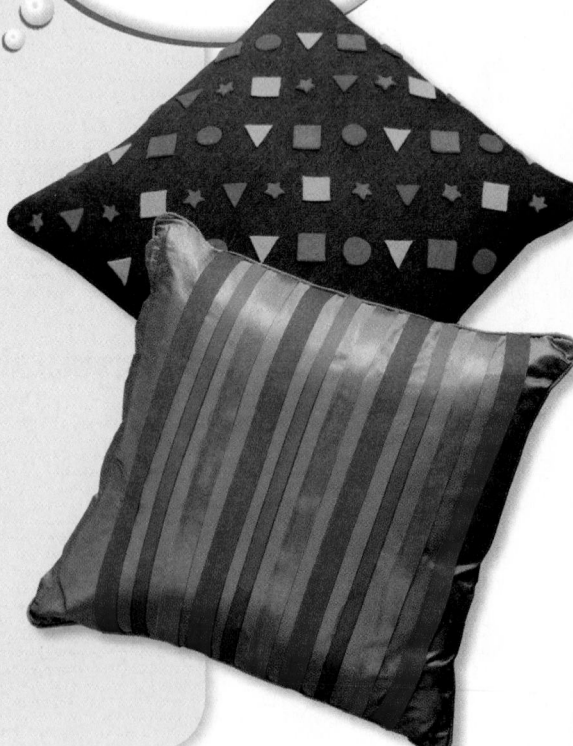

1. What are the next two shapes in this pattern?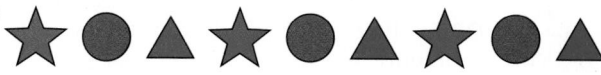

Name a pattern unit. Find the missing number or shape.

⊘2. 6, 6, 5, 6, 6, 5, 6, 6, 5, 6, ■, 5   **⊘3.** ▲▮▢▲▮▢▲▮▢ ? ▮

4. [TALK Math] **Explain** how to find a pattern unit.

Independent Practice (and Problem Solving

Name a pattern unit. Find the missing number or shape.

5. 8, 4, 2, 8, 4, 2, 8, 4, 2, 8, ■, 2   **6.** 2, 0, 0, 1, 2, 0, 0, 1, 2, 0, 0, 1, 2, 0, ■

7. ☆ ▭ ▭ ☆ ▭ ▭ ☆ ▭ ▭ ☆ ▭ ▭ ? ▭ ▭

Predict the next two numbers or shapes in each pattern.

8. 5, 1, 1, 5, 5, 1, 1, 5, 5, 1, 1, 5, ■, ■   **9.** ▽▽△▽▽△▽▽△ ? ?

USE DATA For 10–11, use the photo frames.

A.   B.

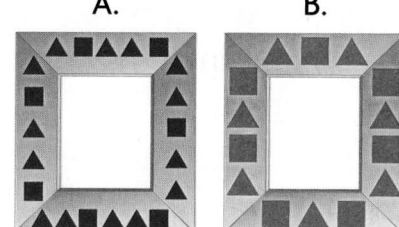

10. Greg put a photo of his dog in one of the frames. A pattern unit on the frame is *triangle, square, triangle.* Which frame did Greg use?

11. What is a pattern unit on Frame B?

12. [WRITE Math] ▸ **What's the Error?** Helena lost a bead from her pattern bracelet. She says the missing bead is a green square. What is Helena's error?

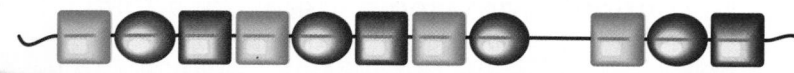

Mixed Review and Test Prep

13. The bottom view and top view of a solid figure is a circle. Name the solid figure. (p. 400)

14. I am a polygon with four sides the same length. I have no right angles. What am I? (p. 356)

15. Test Prep What are the next two numbers in this pattern?

1, 6, 1, 1, 6, 1, 1, 6, 1, 1, 6, ■, ■

A 6, 1   **C** 6, 6

B 1, 6   **D** 1, 1

Technology
Use Harcourt Mega Math, The Number Games, *Tiny's Think Tank,* Levels J and K.

Extra Practice on page 434, Set A

Geometric Patterns

OBJECTIVE: Identify and extend geometric patterns to solve problems.

Quick Review

Kylie drew this pattern.

What is the pattern unit?

Vocabulary

repeating pattern

growing pattern

Learn

PROBLEM Vicky and Will make rubber stamp patterns. What are the next two shapes in each pattern?

Vicky's pattern is a **repeating pattern** because it uses the same pattern unit over and over again.

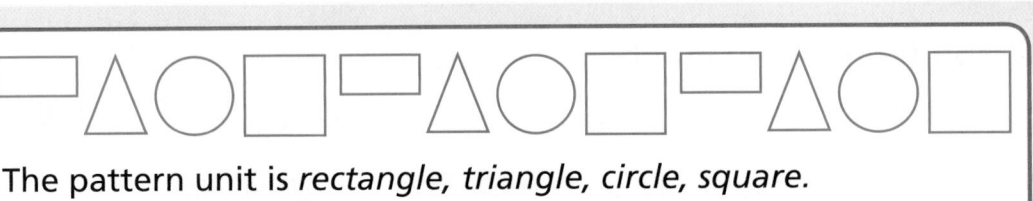

The pattern unit is *rectangle, triangle, circle, square*.

To continue a repeating pattern, use the pattern unit.

So, the next two shapes in Vicky's pattern are: *rectangle, triangle*.

Will's pattern is called a **growing pattern** because the number of rectangles increases by the same amount from one figure to the next.

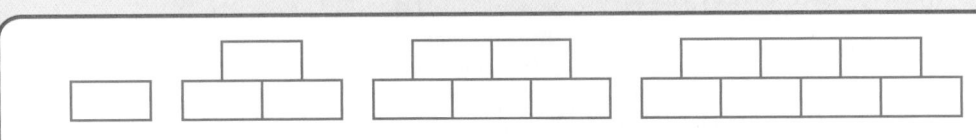

The rule is *add 2 rectangles*.

To continue a growing pattern, use a rule.

So, the next two figures in Will's pattern will have 9 rectangles and 11 rectangles.

• This is Lee's pattern. Is it a repeating or a growing pattern?

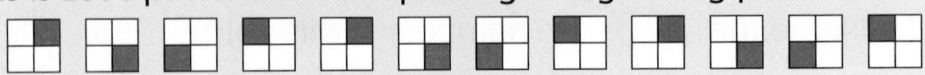

Guided Practice

1. Draw the pattern unit Lee used to make the pattern shown above.

Find the pattern unit or rule. Then name the next figure.

2. 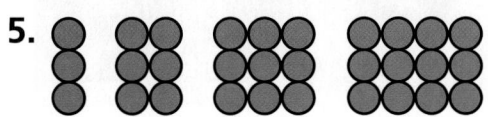   3. ▮▮ ▮▮▮ ▮▮▮▮ ▮▮▮▮▮

4. **[TALK Math]** **Explain** the difference between a repeating pattern and a growing pattern. Draw an example of each.

Independent Practice and Problem Solving

Find the pattern unit or rule. Then name the next figure.

5. ⦿⦿⦿⦿⦿⦿⦿⦿⦿⦿

6. ☆ △ ☆ △ ☆ △

Find the pattern unit or rule. Draw the missing figure.

7.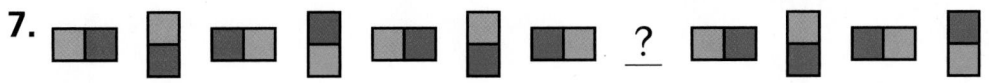

8. △ △   △△ △△   △△△
   △ △△ △△ △△△ △   ?   △△△△

9. ≡**FAST FACT** The non-venomous king snake looks much like the venomous coral snake. Look at the photos. Describe the color pattern unit for each.

king snake

coral snake

10. Draw a pattern. Tell whether your pattern is repeating or growing.

11. **[WRITE Math]** **What's the Question?** The answer is 9 tiles.

Mixed Review and Test Prep

12. The zoo sold 785 adult tickets and 418 child tickets. To the nearest hundred, how many tickets were sold? (p. 52)

13. What mailbox number is missing?

(p. 422)

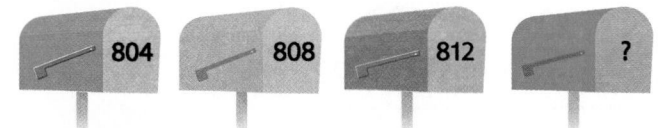

14. **Test Prep** Which is the missing figure?

▲▽ ▽ ▲▽ ▽ ▲▽ ? ▲

A △△

C ▷

B ◁

D ▽

Extra Practice on page 434, Set B

Number Patterns

OBJECTIVE: Identify and extend whole-number patterns to find rules and solve problems.

Learn

A rule can be used to describe a pattern.

PROBLEM Mr. Rome wrote a number pattern. What rule describes his pattern? What will the next number be?

2, 5, 8, 11, 14

Example

Look at the number pattern. Find the rule.

Think: What do I do to 2 to get 5? What do I do to 5 to get 8?

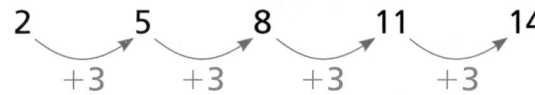

The numbers increase by 3. So, the rule *add 3* describes the pattern.

Use the rule to extend the pattern.

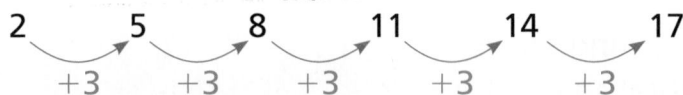

Math Idea

A rule must be true for all the numbers in the pattern.

So, the next number in the pattern is 17.

More Examples

A 27, 23, 19, 15, ___, 7

Think: What do I do to 27 to get 23?

What do I do to 23 to get 19?

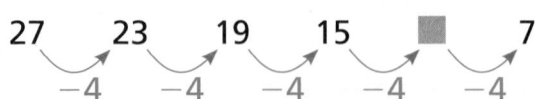

So, the rule is *subtract 4.*

To find the missing number, subtract 4.

$$15 - 4 = 11$$

So, the missing number is 11.

B 1, 2, 4, 7, 11, 16, ___

Think: What do I do to 1 to get 2?

to 2 to get 4? to 4 to get 7?

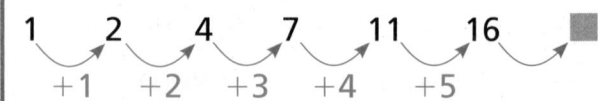

So, the rule is *add 1, then add 2, then add 3 and so on.*

To find the next number, add 6.

$$16 + 6 = 22$$

So, the next number is 22.

1. What is a rule for this number pattern?   1, 5, 9, 13, 17

Write a rule for each pattern. Then find the next number.

2. 28, 33, 38, 43, 48   ✓**3.** 52, 45, 38, 31, 24   ✓**4.** 4, 12, 20, 28, 36

5. [TALK Math] **Explain** how you can find a rule for a pattern.

Independent Practice (and Problem Solving)

Write a rule for each pattern. Then find the next number.

6. 7, 16, 25, 34, 43, 52   **7.** 81, 75, 69, 63, 57, 51   **8.** 211, 198, 185, 172, 159

9. 3, 5, 8, 10, 13, 15, 18, 20, 23   **10.** 12, 18, 17, 23, 22, 28, 27, ■

Find the missing numbers.

11. 109, 119, 129, ■, 149, 159, 169   **12.** 96, 93, 90, 87, ■, ■, 78, 75

13. 5, 15, 13, 23, ■, 31, 29, ■, 37, ■   **14.** 324, 316, 308, ■, 292, ■, ■, 268, ■

USE DATA For 15–17, use the table.

15. How much money does Erik save each week?

16. How much money is in Erik's account in Week 5?

17. **Reasoning** Erik wants a bike that costs $76. If he continues the savings pattern, will he have enough saved by Week 10? **Explain.**

18. [WRITE Math] **What's the Error?** Tim wrote this pattern: 5, 12, 15, 22, 25, 32, 35. Louie said the rule is *add* 7. Describe his error. Write a correct rule.

Erik's Savings	
Week	**Amount**
1	$25
2	$31
3	$37
4	$43
5	■
6	$55

Mixed Review and Test Prep

19. Morgan has 2 quarters, 3 dimes, and 6 nickels. How much money does she have in all? (p. 110)

20. Zoey ate breakfast at the time shown on the clock. At what time did she eat?

(p. 128)

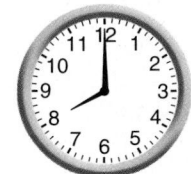

21. **Test Prep** Valerie wrote the following pattern:

262, 259, 256, 253, ■, 247, ■

What numbers are missing?

A 250, 245   **C** 250, 244

B 249, 243   **D** 256, 250

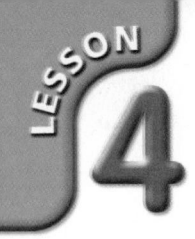

Problem Solving Workshop
Strategy: Find a Pattern

OBJECTIVE: Solve problems by using the strategy *find a pattern*.

Learn the Strategy

Finding patterns can help you solve problems. To find a pattern, see whether the numbers in the problem increase or decrease or if the colors or shapes repeat.

Number Patterns

Hannah is saving money to buy a new bike. She saved $3 the first week, $6 the second week, $9 the third week, and $12 the fourth week.

Week	1	2	3	4
Savings	$3	$6	$9	$12

Color Patterns

Josie made this bracelet in art class. She used red and blue beads to make a pattern.

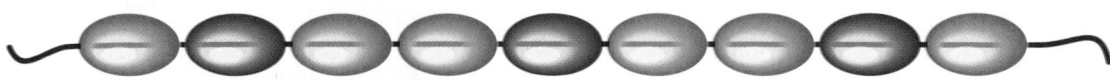

Geometric Patterns

Dan made this pattern with pattern blocks.

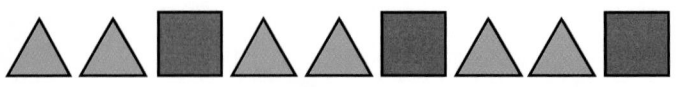

TALK Math

Look at each pattern above. Is the pattern repeating or growing? What number, color, or shape comes next in each pattern?

Use the Strategy

PROBLEM Sean is using square tiles to make patterns. He used 20 tiles to make the 4 rows in the pattern at the right.

How many tiles will he need for the fifth row?

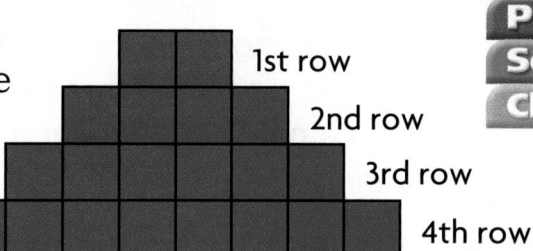

1st row
2nd row
3rd row
4th row

Read to Understand

Reading Skill

- **Summarize what you are asked to find.**
- **What information is given?**

Plan

- **What strategy can you use to solve the problem?**
  You can find a pattern.

Solve

- **How can you use the picture of tiles and the strategy to solve the problem?**

  Look at the tile pattern. Is the pattern repeating or growing? How are the rows related?

  The number of tiles increases by 2 from one row to the next. *Add 2 tiles* is a rule that describes the pattern.

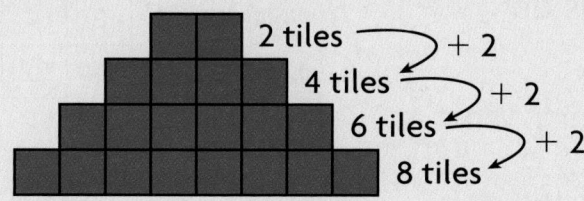

2 tiles ⟶ + 2
4 tiles ⟵ + 2
6 tiles ⟵ + 2
8 tiles ⟵

  To make the fifth row, add 2 tiles to the number of tiles in the fourth row.

$$8 + 2 = 10$$

  So, Sean will need 10 tiles for the fifth row.

Check

- **How can you check your answer?**
- **In what other ways could you solve the problem?**

Guided Problem Solving

1. Dylan and his dad are putting a Native American border on his bedroom wall. The pattern shows two bears facing each other with a paw print between them. How many figures are in the pattern unit?

   First, look at all of the figures in the border.

   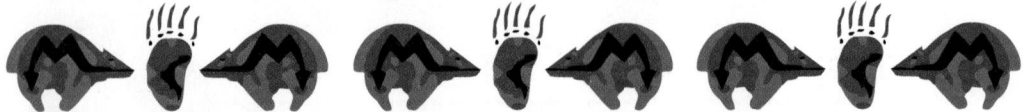

   Next, find the pattern unit where the pattern repeats.

   Then, count the number of figures in the pattern unit.

2. **What if** the border pattern included a right paw print between every other pair of facing bears? How many figures would be in this pattern unit?

   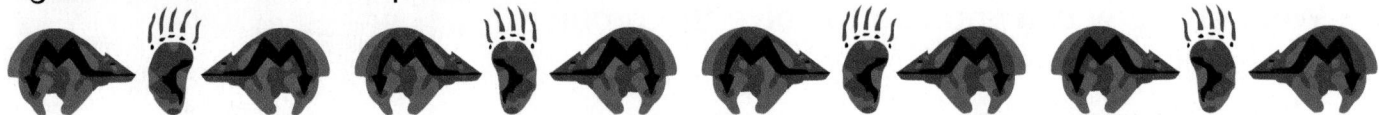

3. Steven painted a border around a picture frame. His pattern unit was *3 circles, 1 triangle*. He painted a total of 24 figures. What shape was the 12th figure?

   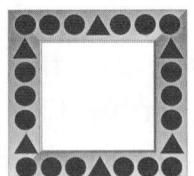

Problem Solving Strategy Practice

Find a pattern to solve.

4. A spider has 8 legs. How many legs do 7 spiders have?

   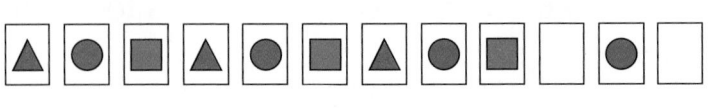

5. Mr. Tanner wrote this number pattern. What is the rule and the next two numbers?

   385, 381, 377, 373, 369, 365, ▨, ▨

6. Elise arranged shape cards to make a pattern. Then she turned 2 of the cards face down. What shapes are on those 2 cards?

   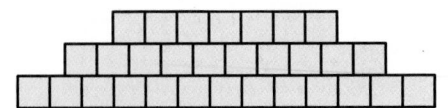

7. **WRITE Math** ▸ Curt is using 35 tiles to make a pattern. The bottom 3 rows are shown at the right. How many rows will Curt make? How many tiles will be in each row? **Explain** how you found the answer.

Mixed Strategy Practice

8. Some of the seat numbers in the stadium have worn off. Here is a row of seats. What seat numbers are missing?

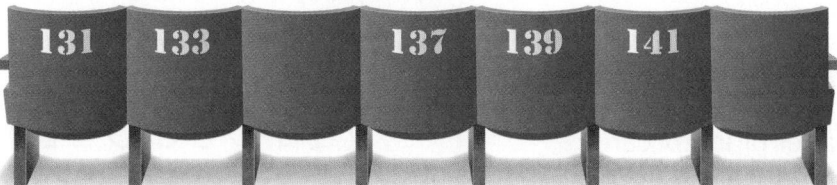

131 | 133 | | 137 | 139 | 141 |

9. Abe made a spinner that has 4 colors. The pointer is most likely to land on blue and equally likely to land on red, yellow, and green. What could Abe's spinner look like?

Choose a STRATEGY

Find a Pattern
Draw a Diagram or Picture
Make a Model or Act It Out
Make an Organized List
Make a Table or Graph
Predict and Test
Work Backward
Solve a Simpler Problem
Write an Equation
Use Logical Reasoning

USE DATA For 10–12, use the jersey information.

10. Some students in Mr. Jenson's class play soccer. They wore their soccer jerseys to school. Write the numbers in order from least to greatest.

11. Lisa's jersey number is a two-digit number. The ones digit is greater than the tens digit. The sum of the digits is less than 6. What is Lisa's jersey number?

12. **Open-Ended** Use all of the numbers on the soccer jerseys to write a pattern. Find a rule for your pattern. Then tell what the next two numbers would be if you continued your pattern.

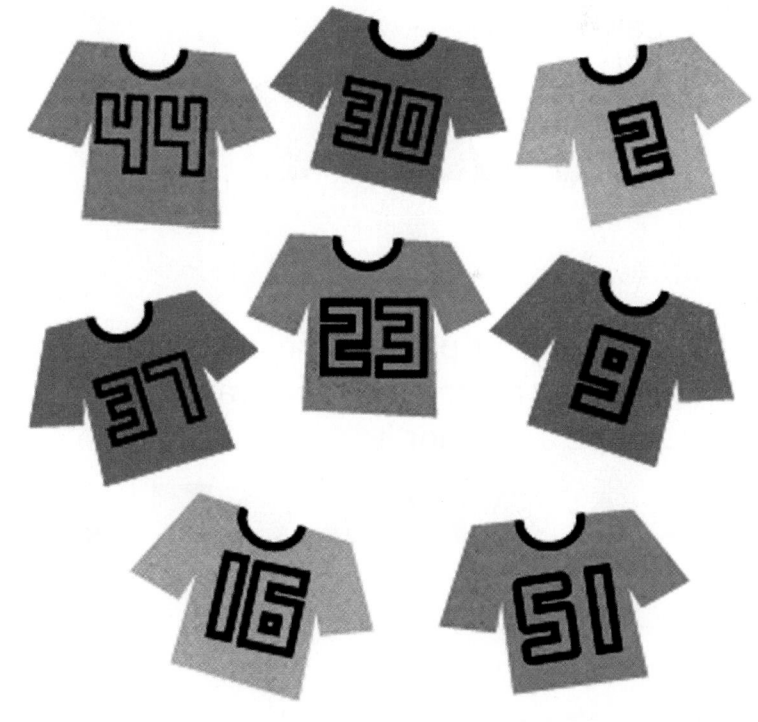

CHALLENGE YOURSELF

Five teams played in a soccer tournament.
Each team played each other only 1 time.

13. How many games in all were played in the tournament?

14. During the season, Team 1 won 2 fewer games than Team 5. Team 2 won 2 fewer games than Team 1. Team 1 won twice as many games as Team 3. Team 4 won 3 more games than Team 3. Team 5 won 10 games. How many games did Team 4 win?

5 Make a Pattern

OBJECTIVE: Use a rule or a pattern unit to make a pattern.

Investigate

Materials ■ plane shapes, crayons, paper or index cards

You can make patterns by using a repeating pattern unit.

Ⓐ Choose several shapes from a set of plane shapes. Use the shapes to make a pattern unit.

Ⓑ Repeat your pattern unit at least three times to make a pattern. Trace each shape and color it.

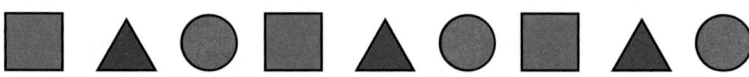

Draw Conclusions

1. Describe your pattern unit.

2. If you continued your pattern, what would be the next two shapes?

3. **Analysis** What will be the 20th figure in your pattern? **Explain** how you know.

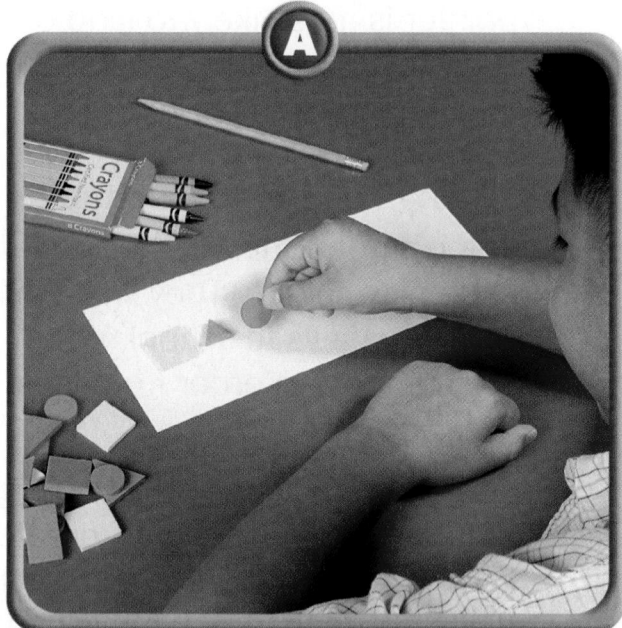

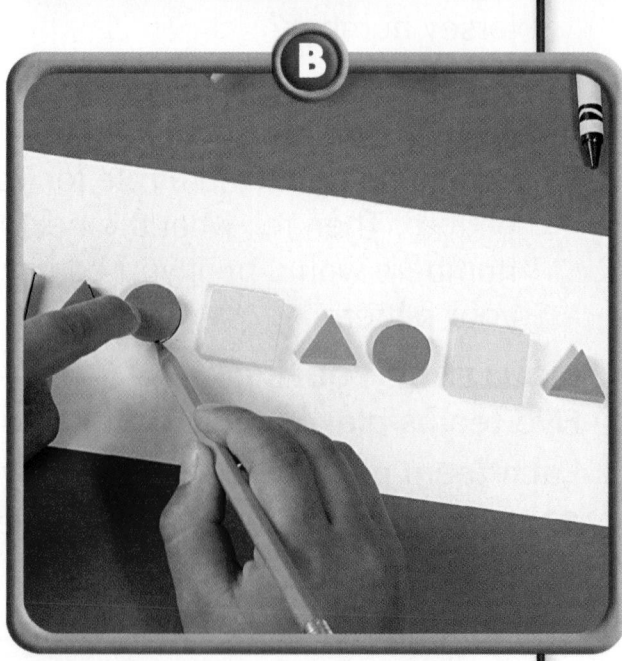

You can use a rule to make a growing number pattern.

A Think of a rule you would like to use for a number pattern.

B Choose a number to begin your pattern. Write this number on an index card or paper.

C Use your rule to write the next five numbers in your pattern. Make a card for each number.

| 7 | 11 | 15 | 19 | 23 | 27 |

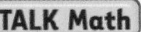

TALK Math

Describe your number pattern rule. Then write the next three numbers in your pattern.

Practice

Draw each geometric pattern.

1. Use four different shapes to make a pattern unit. Repeat the pattern unit three times. Draw your pattern.

2. Select two different shapes. Trace and color the shapes to make a pattern. Describe your pattern unit.

Make each number pattern.

3. Choose a two-digit number. Write a number pattern that begins with that number and uses addition as the rule.

4. Write the first five numbers of a number pattern. Describe the rule you used.

5. Thomas made a pattern with the pattern unit *red square, blue triangle, red square*. He drew 16 shapes. What figure was the 16th shape?

6. The band director put the band members in rows. The drawing shows the first five rows. Describe the pattern. How many band members will be in the 8th row?

7. Reasoning Trish wrote a number pattern. The third number in her pattern is 15. She used the rule *add 2*. What number did Trish choose as the starting number?

8. WRITE Math Explain how to find the missing number in this pattern: 12, 17, 22, 27, ■, 37, 42.

Extra Practice

Set A **Name a pattern unit. Find the missing number or shape.** (pp. 422–423)

1. 7, 6, 3, 7, 6, 3, ■, 6, 3, 7, 6, 3

2. 9, 1, 7, 9, 1, 7, 9, 1, 7, 9, 1, ■

3.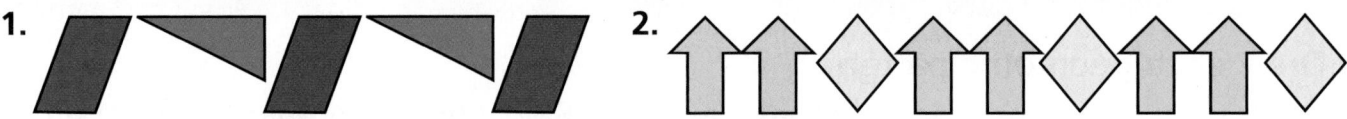

Predict the next two numbers in each pattern.

4. 3, 0, 8, 8, 3, 0, 8, 8, 3, 0, 8, ■,■

5. 4, 5, 6, 5, 4, 5, 6, 5, 4, 5, 6, 5, ■,■

6. Mark ran the following number of miles during training so far this month: 3, 3, 2, 3, 3, 2, 3, 3. If he continues the same pattern of miles, what are the next two distances he will run?

Set B **Find the pattern unit or rule. Then name the next figure.** (pp. 424–425)

1.

2.

Find the pattern unit or rule. Draw the missing figures.

3.

Set C **Write a rule for each pattern. Then find the next number.** (pp. 426–427)

1. 25, 37, 49, 61, 73, 85   **2.** 65, 58, 51, 44, 37, 30   **3.** 4, 8, 13, 17, 22, 26, 31, 35

Find the missing numbers.

4. 26, 34, 33, 41, 40, 48, 47, ■, 54

5. 5, 10, 8, 13, 11, ■, 14, 19, ■

6. The balances in Vivian's bank account for the last six months were $112, $127, $142, $157, $172, and $187. How much did Vivian save each month?

7. Matt read the first 20 pages of his book on Monday. He reads 3 pages more each day than the day before. How many pages will he read on Friday?

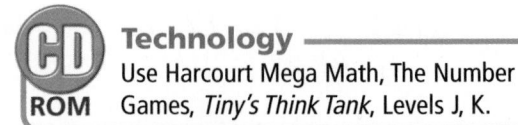

Technology
Use Harcourt Mega Math, The Number Games, *Tiny's Think Tank*, Levels J, K.

TECHNOLOGY CONNECTION

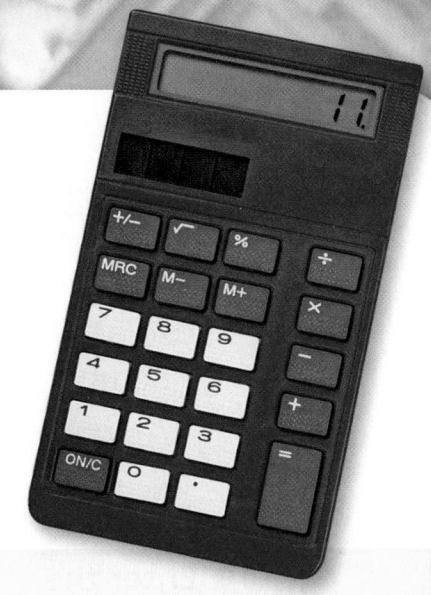

Calculator: Number Patterns

Use a calculator to find number patterns.

Elizabeth is taking a bead-making class. In her first lesson, she makes 8 beads. In each of the next lessons, she makes 3 more beads than in the lesson before. How many beads does she make in her fifth lesson?

Identify the first number and a rule for the pattern.

First lesson: 8 beads   **Pattern rule:** add 3

Add 3 to find out how many beads Elizabeth made in the second lesson.

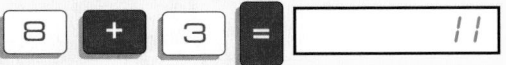

So, Elizabeth made 11 beads in the second lesson.

To continue the pattern, press the = key for the next three lessons. You do not have to press + 3 again.

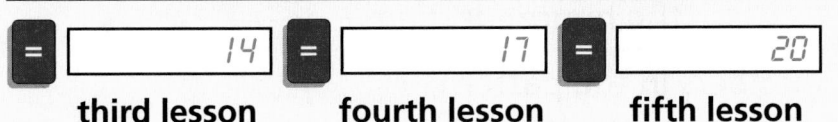

third lesson   fourth lesson   fifth lesson

So, Elizabeth made 20 beads in the fifth lesson.

Try It

Use a calculator to find the first five numbers in each number pattern.

1. First number: 5
   Pattern rule: add 9

2. First number: 74
   Pattern rule: subtract 8

3. First number: 15
   Pattern rule: add 12

Use a calculator to find a rule for each pattern. Fill in the missing numbers.

4. 56, 50, ■, 38, 32   5. 26, 39, 52, ■, 78   6. 140, 122, 104, 86, ■

7. **Explore More** Ethan made this table to show how long he read on each day of one week. How many minutes did he read on Friday? **Explain** your answer.

	Monday	Tuesday	Wednesday	Thursday	Friday
minutes	18	31	44	57	■

Nifty Numbers

You can use a calculator to find number patterns with large numbers.

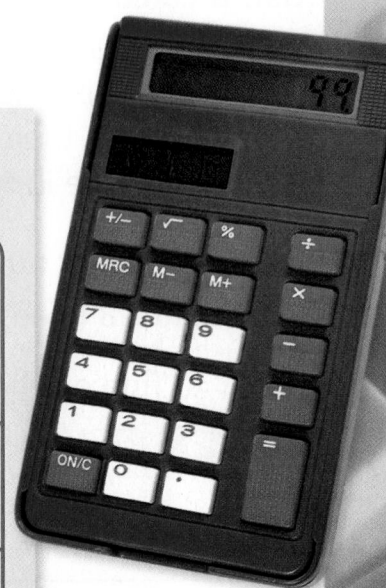

Example

Start with 0. Add 99 five times. What patterns do you see?

Step 1 Enter the starting number, 99.

 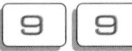

Press the plus key and then the equal key.

Step 2 Record each sum.

| 99 | 198 | 297 | 396 | 495 | 594 |

Step 3 Look for the patterns.

- What did you notice about the ones digits?
    the tens digits?
    the hundreds digits?

Step 4 Predict the next four numbers in the pattern. Check your predictions on your calculator.

So, you can predict the results of adding 99, using patterns.

Try It

Find a pattern. Write the next 3 numbers in each pattern.

1. Multiply 6 × 2. Record the product. Press the equal key 10 times. Record the products. What pattern do you notice in the ones digits?

2. Start with 7. Add 6 ten times. What patterns do you notice in the ones digits of the sums?

3. **WRITE Math** ▸ Choose a number from 1 through 9. Then choose a second number from 1 through 9 to add at least 10 times. Record each sum. Describe the patterns you find in the ones digits.

Chapter 17 Review/Test

Check Vocabulary and Concepts

Choose the best term from the box.

1. A __?__ is a pattern that uses a rule and increases by the same amount from one figure to the next. (p. 424)

2. The part of the pattern that repeats is the __?__. (p. 422)

3. A pattern that uses the same pattern unit over and over is a __?__. (p. 424)

Check Skills

Find the pattern unit or rule. Then draw the missing figure. (pp. 424–425)

4. △ ▽ △ ▽ △ ▽ △ __?__

5. ○ ○○ ○○○ ○○○○ __?__
   ○ ○○ ○○○ ○○○○

6. [grid figures with dots] __?__

Write a rule for each pattern. Then find the next number. (pp. 426–427)

7. 27, 34, 41, 48, 55, 62, ■

8. 8, 14, 19, 25, 30, 36, ■

9. 7, 9, 13, 19, 27, 37, ■

10. 93, 87, 85, 79, 77, 71, ■

11. 19, 28, 36, 43, 49, 54 ■

12. 1, 2, 4, 7, 11, 16, 22, 29, 37, ■

Check Problem Solving

Solve. (pp. 428–431)

13. Malik has a border on his bedroom wall that follows a pattern unit of two trees, a deer, and a leaf. What is the 14th figure in the pattern?

14. Melissa's rug has this pattern:

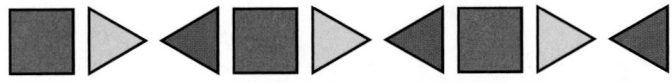

What is the pattern unit for the rug? What is the next shape?

15. **WRITE Math** ▶ Keisha is making a necklace with 9 red beads, 6 blue beads, and 3 yellow beads. What pattern can Keisha use so that she includes all the beads in the necklace? **Explain.**

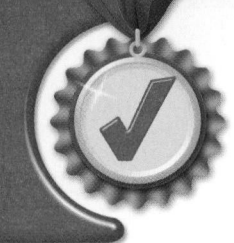

Unit Review/Test
Chapters 14–17

Multiple Choice

1. Which does NOT describe this figure? (p. 360)

   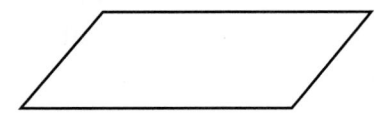

   A Parallelogram

   B Quadrilateral

   C Rectangle

   D Polygon

2. Which figure has the fewest number of sides? (p. 356)

   A Hexagon

   B Triangle

   C Quadrilateral

   D Pentagon

3. How many lines of symmetry does this figure appear to have? (p. 386)

   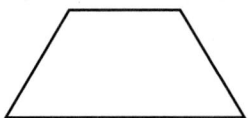

   A 1

   B 2

   C 3

   D 4

4. Which figure has 5 vertices? (p. 400)

   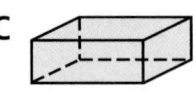
   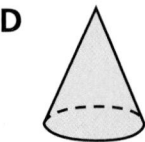

5. Which pair of lines is parallel? (p. 354)

   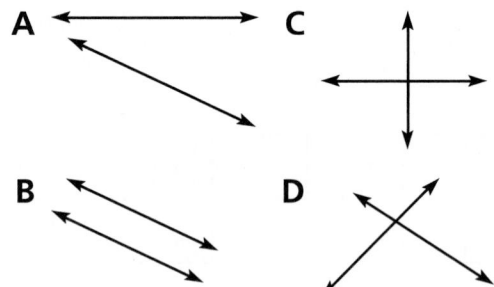

6. Which pair of figures appears to be congruent? (p. 378)

   A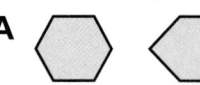

   B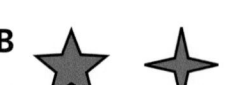

   C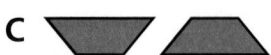

   D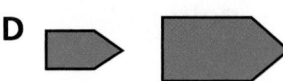

GO ONLINE Technology Use *Online Assessment.*

7. What is the pattern unit in this number pattern? (p. 426)

$$3, 2, 1, 3, 2, 1, 3, 2, 1$$

A 3, 2, 1

B 2, 3, 1

C 2, 3, 4

D 1, 2, 3

8. Which figure best describes the can of corn? (p. 400)

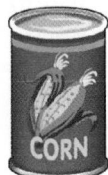

A Cylinder   **C** Sphere

B Cone   **D** Square pyramid

9. Rosanna made a number pattern. The rule for the pattern was *add 3, subtract 1*. Which could be her number pattern? (p. 426)

A 5, 8, 11, 14, 17, 21

B 5, 8, 7, 10, 9, 12

C 5, 4, 7, 6, 9, 8

D 5, 8, 9, 12, 13, 16

10. Which is the missing shape in this pattern? (p. 424)

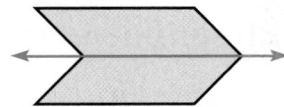

A ◯   **C** ☐

B △   **D** ▯

Short Response

11. Which figure has more faces, a cube or a square pyramid? (p. 400)

12. Annemarie drew the figure below. Does the blue line appear to be a line of symmetry? (p. 386)

Extended Response [WRITE Math]

13. Barry made towers with blocks. The towers form a pattern. How many blocks would be needed to make the 5th tower in the pattern? **Explain.**

(p. 424)

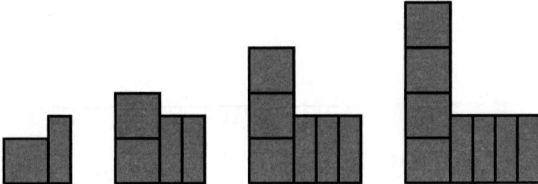

THE WORLD ALMANAC FOR KIDS

Native American Culture

FOOD SYMMETRY

The Caddo people lived in East Texas. They were farmers, hunters, and builders. They made pottery and carved wood. They grew many types of plants including corn, pumpkins, squash, beans, and sunflowers. Parts of the plants were used for food.

▲ The Caddo people cut pumpkins and squash into long strips and wove the strips together to make a mat. This would make the round vegetables flat and easier to store.

FACT·ACTIVITY

Look at the pictures to answer the questions.

1 Which sunflower pictures appear to have a line of symmetry?

A   B   C   D

2 How can you draw a bean that is congruent to the bean below?

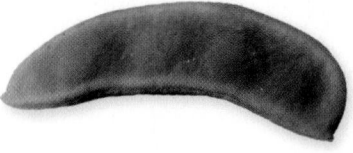

3 How many lines of symmetry does this squash appear to have?

USEFUL CADDO OBJECTS

Many objects made by the Caddo people are in museums. Some objects were for everyday use. Others were for decoration or for special occasions. Often these objects tell us a lot about the Caddo people.

ALMANAC Fact

Caddo houses were made of grass with domed roofs. Some were large enough to hold 30 people! It only took one day to build a house, because the whole village worked together.

FACT·ACTIVITY

Pictures of Caddo objects can be congruent, even if they are moved.

1. Object A shows a turn. Are the objects congruent?

2. Object B shows a flip. Are the objects congruent?

3. Object C shows a slide. Are the objects congruent?

4. Draw 2 congruent objects that are not in the same position.

A
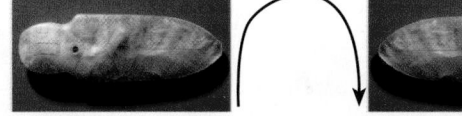

B
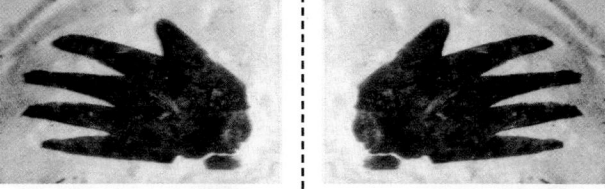

C
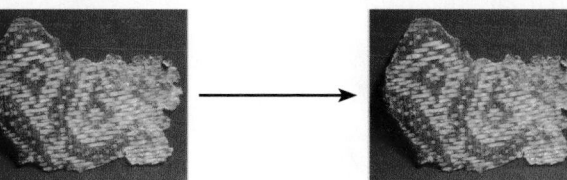

6 Fractions and Decimals

Math on Location

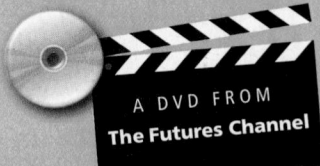

A DVD FROM
The Futures Channel

with
Chapter Projects

1

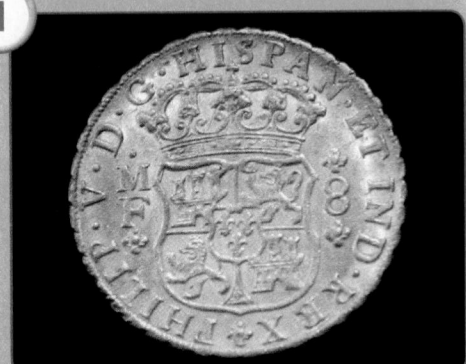

Some gold coins were cut into 4 or 8 equal pieces to make change in colonial times.

2

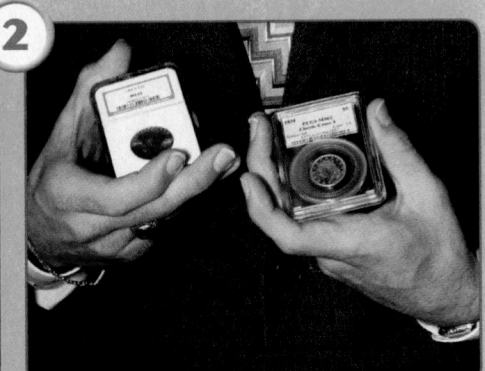

Today people buy and sell rare coins, which have values much greater than their face value.

3

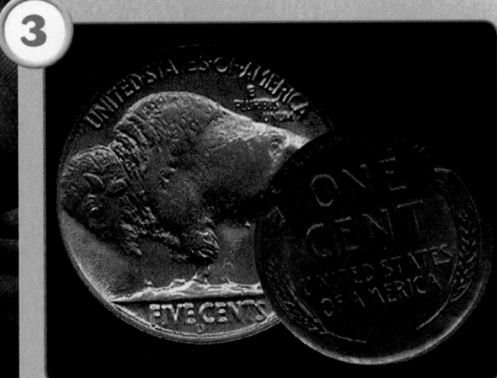

If you find an old wheat penny or buffalo nickel, you might be able to sell them for more than 1 cent or 5 cents!

VOCABULARY POWER

TALK Math

What math do you see in the **Math on Location** photographs? If a coin was cut into 4 equal pieces, what fraction of the whole coin would each piece represent?

READ Math

REVIEW VOCABULARY You learned about fractions and money in grade 2. How do these words relate to **Math on Location**?

numerator the part of a fraction above the line, which tells how many parts are being counted

denominator the part of a fraction below the line, which tells how many equal parts there are in the whole or in the group

cent 1 penny; 100 cents equal 1 dollar

WRITE Math

Copy and complete a Word Association Map like the one below. Use **Math on Location** and what you know about fractions to complete the map.

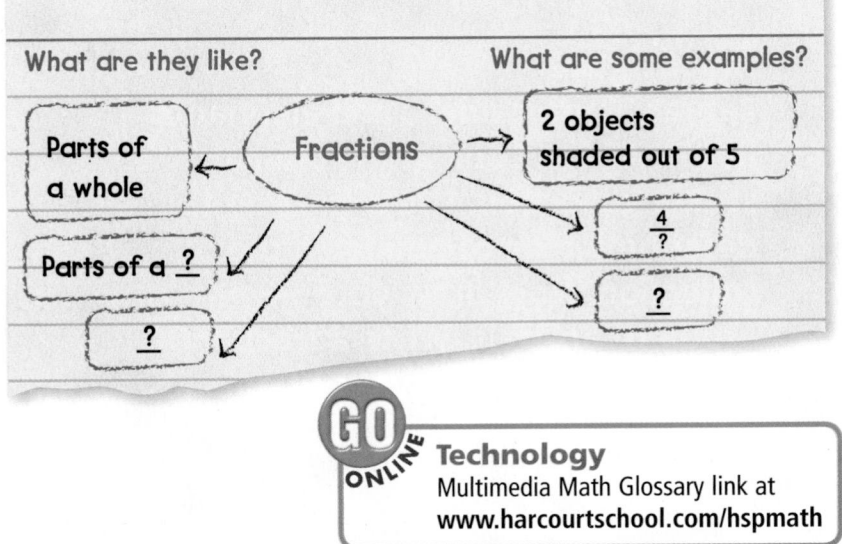

What are they like?   What are some examples?

Parts of a whole ← Fractions → 2 objects shaded out of 5

$\frac{4}{?}$

Parts of a ?

?

?

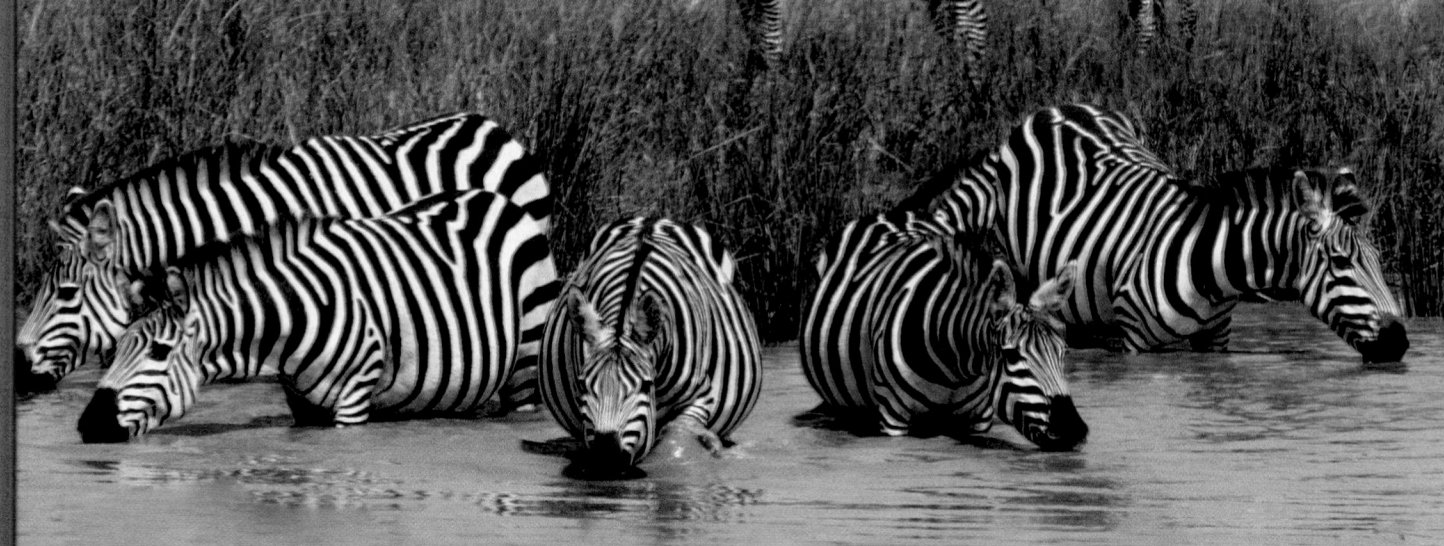

CHAPTER

18 Understand Fractions

≡ **FAST FACT**

The stripes on a
zebra are like a
fingerprint. Zebras
can be identified
by the color,
thickness, and
pattern of their
stripes.

Investigate

Zebras, lions, camels, and elephants
live in Africa. Look at the animal
sticker collection. Use a fraction to
describe a type of animal in the
collection. Now draw your own
group of animals. Write a fraction to
describe one of the types of animals.

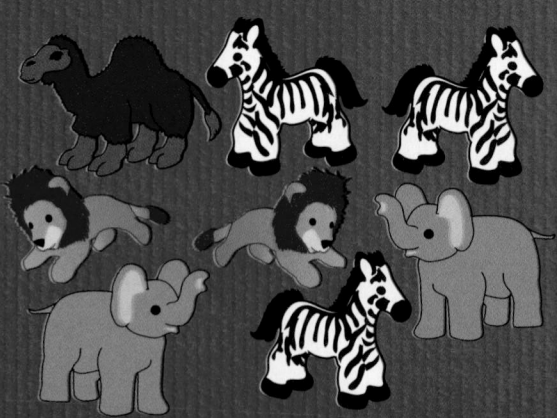

GO ONLINE

Technology
Student pages are available
in the Student eBook.

Check your understanding of important skills
needed for success in Chapter 18.

▶ **Parts of a Group**

Write the number in each set. Then write the number
in each set that are striped.

1.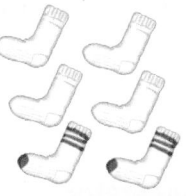

2.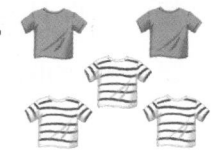

3.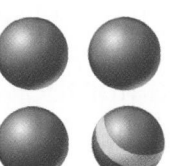

4.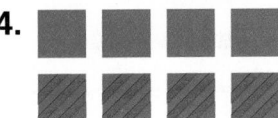

5.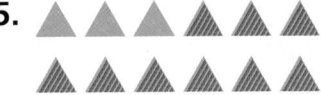

6.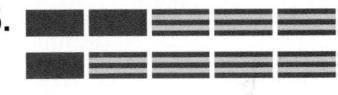

▶ **Parts of a Whole**

Write how many equal parts make up the whole figure.
Then write how many parts are shaded.

7.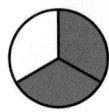

8.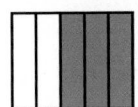

9.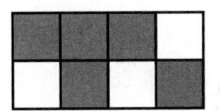

10.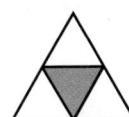

11.

12.

VOCABULARY POWER

CHAPTER VOCABULARY

denominator
equivalent fractions
fraction
like fractions
mixed number
numerator
simplest form

WARM-UP WORDS

fraction A number that names part of a whole
or part of a group

numerator The part of a fraction above the line,
which tells how many parts are being counted

denominator The part of a fraction below the
line, which tells how many equal parts there
are in the whole or in the group

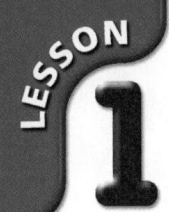

LESSON 1

Model Part of a Whole

OBJECTIVE: Read, write, and model fractional parts of a whole.

Quick Review

Tell how many equal parts are in each.

1.

2.

3.

4.

5.

Learn

PROBLEM The first pizzeria in America opened in New York in 1905. The pizza recipe came from Italy. Look at Italy's flag. What fraction of Italy's flag is red?

A **fraction** is a number that names part of a whole or part of a group.

The flag is divided into 3 equal parts, and 1 part is red.

| 1 red part | $\rightarrow \frac{1}{3} \leftarrow$ | numerator |
| 3 equal parts in all | | denominator |

Read: one third   **Write:** $\frac{1}{3}$

one part out of three equal parts   1 divided by 3

So, $\frac{1}{3}$ of Italy's flag is red.

The **numerator** tells how many parts are being counted.

The **denominator** tells how many equal parts are in the whole or in the group.

Vocabulary

fraction

numerator

denominator

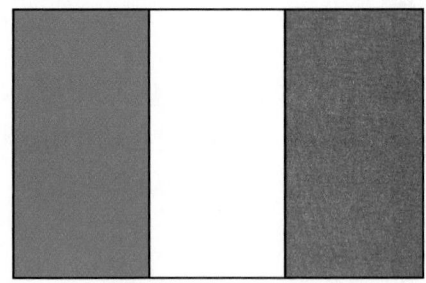

▲ The ingredients of some pizzas—basil, mozzarella, and tomato—show the colors of Italy's flag.

Activity   Materials ■ fraction circle pieces

Maria ate 2 out of 6 slices of pizza.
Find the fraction of the pizza that is left.

Step 1	Step 2	Step 3
Use fraction circle pieces to model a pizza with 6 equal slices.	Remove 2 of the pieces to show that 2 slices were eaten.	Count the number of slices left. $\frac{4}{6}$ 4 slices 6 equal slices in all
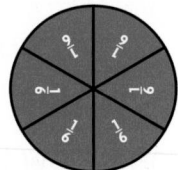	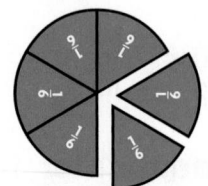	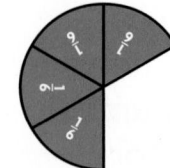

So, $\frac{4}{6}$ of the pizza is left.

A figure or a number line can show parts of a whole.

Examples

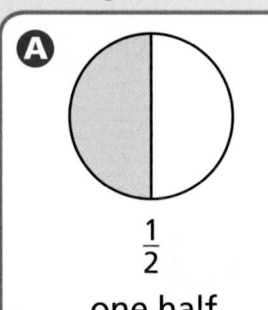

$\frac{1}{2}$

one half

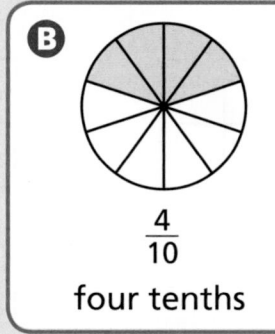

$\frac{4}{10}$

four tenths

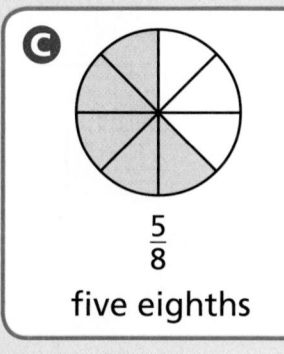

$\frac{5}{8}$

five eighths

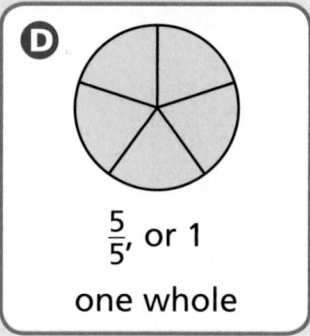

$\frac{5}{5}$, or 1

one whole

A number line can show parts of one whole. The space from one whole number to the next represents one whole. The line can be divided into any number of equal parts.

E This number line shows thirds.

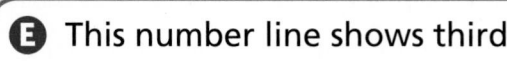

The point shows the location of $\frac{2}{3}$.

F This number line shows fourths.

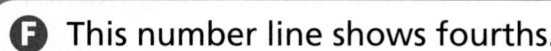

The point shows the location of $\frac{3}{4}$.

Guided Practice

1. **What fraction names the point?**

   Think: What number comes after 4?

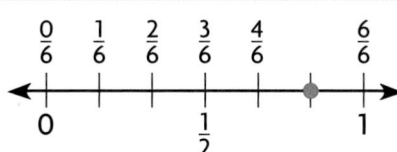

Write a fraction in numbers and in words to name the shaded part.

2.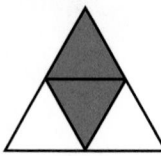

3.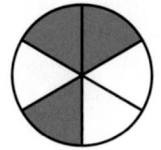

✓4.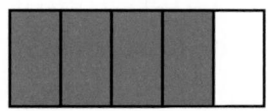

Use fraction circle pieces to make a model of each. Then write the fraction by using numbers.

5. nine twelfths

6. two divided by ten

✓7. seven out of nine

8. **TALK Math** Explain how to write a fraction for the part that is not shaded.

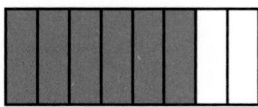

Write a fraction in numbers and in words to name the shaded part.

9.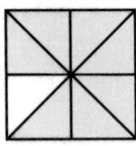

10.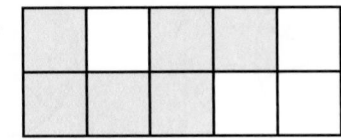

11.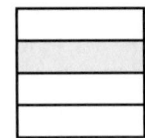

12.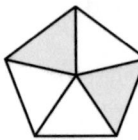

13.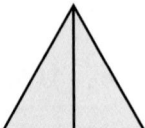

14.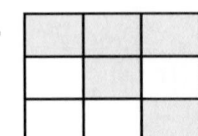

Use fraction circle pieces to make a model of each. Then write the fraction by using numbers.

15. five sixths

16. four out of twelve

17. one divided by three

18. six out of eight

19. two fourths

20. eight tenths

Write a fraction for the shaded part of each figure.

21.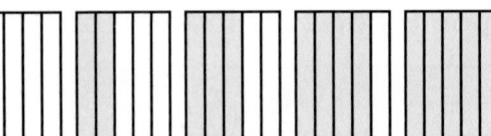

22.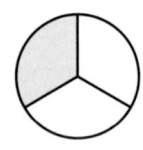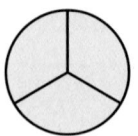

Write a fraction that names each point.

23.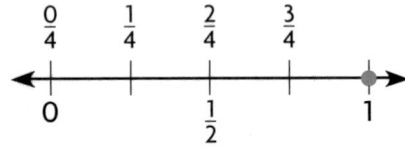

24.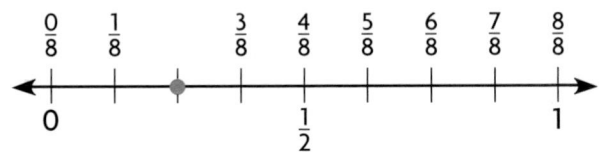

USE DATA For 25–27, use the pizzas.

25. Mrs. Ormond ordered pizza. Each pizza had 8 equal slices. What fraction of the pepperoni pizza is left?

26. What fraction of the cheese pizza is left?

27. **Pose a Problem** Use the picture of the veggie pizza to write a problem that can be answered by using fractions.

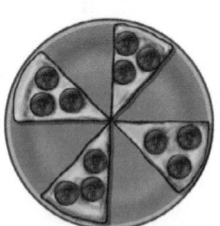 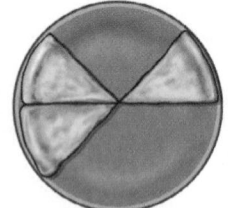 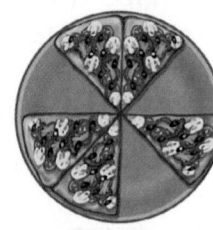

Pepperoni   Cheese   Veggie

28. Randy's family ate six eighths of a pizza. Draw a picture to show the amount that Randy's family ate.

Technology
Use Harcourt Mega Math, Fraction Action, *Fraction Flare Up*, Level B.

448 **Extra Practice** on page 476, Set A

29. Reasoning Two pizzas are the same size. The cheese pizza is cut into 6 equal slices. The meat pizza is cut into 8 equal slices. Which pizza has larger slices? **Explain.**

30. [WRITE Math] ▸ **What's the Error?** Kate says that $\frac{2}{3}$ names the shaded part. Describe her error. Write the correct fraction.

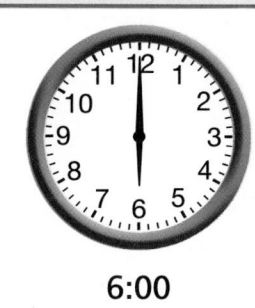

Learn About **Fractions on a Clock**

The minute hand can divide a clock into equal parts. So, you can use fractions when you tell time.

Example

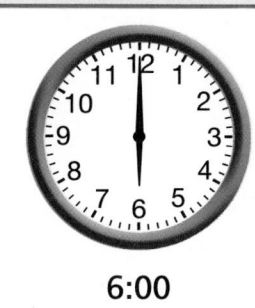

6:00

6:15
$\frac{1}{4}$, or quarter after 6

6:30
$\frac{1}{2}$, or half past 6

6:45
$\frac{1}{4}$, or quarter to 7

Try It

Complete each sentence. Write *one fourth*, *one half*, or *three fourths*.

31. At 6:30, the minute hand has moved __?__ of the way around the clock.

32. At 6:15, the minute hand has moved __?__ of the way around the clock.

33. At 6:45, the minute hand has moved __?__ of the way around the clock.

Mixed Review and Test Prep

34. John said these two figures are congruent. Do you agree? **Explain.**
(p. 378)

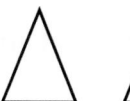

35. Test Prep Write in numbers and words the fraction that names the shaded part.

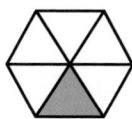

36. What is the area of the figure? (Grade 2)

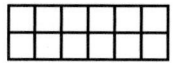

37. Test Prep What fraction of the figure is blue?

A $\frac{3}{5}$ **B** $\frac{8}{5}$ **C** $\frac{3}{8}$ **D** $\frac{5}{8}$

Model Part of a Group

OBJECTIVE: Read, write, and model fractional parts of a group.

 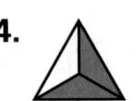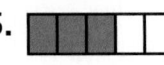
Learn

PROBLEM Jake and Emma each have a collection of marbles. What fraction of each collection is blue?

Math Idea
A fraction can name part of a group.

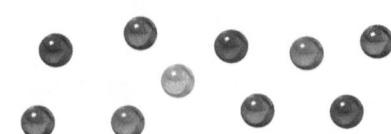

Jake's marbles

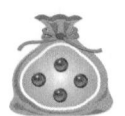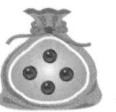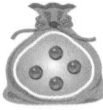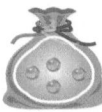

number of
blue marbles → $\frac{3}{10}$ ← numerator
total number → ← denominator
of marbles

Read: three tenths, or three out of ten

Write: $\frac{3}{10}$

So, $\frac{3}{10}$ of Jake's marbles are blue.

Emma's marbles

sets of
blue marbles → $\frac{1}{4}$ ← numerator
total number → ← denominator
of sets

Read: one fourth, or one out of four

Write: $\frac{1}{4}$

So, $\frac{1}{4}$ of Emma's marbles are blue.

Brian has 8 marbles. Two of them are red. What fraction of Brian's marbles are red? What fraction are not red?

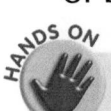 **Activity 1**   **Materials** ■ two-color counters

Step 1

Use 2 red counters and 6 yellow counters to show the marbles.

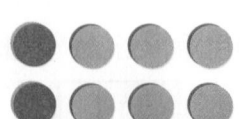

Step 2

Write the fraction of marbles that are red.

$\frac{2}{8}$ ← number of red counters
← total number of counters

Write the fraction of marbles that are not red.

$\frac{6}{8}$ ← number of yellow counters
← total number of counters

So, $\frac{2}{8}$ of Brian's marbles are red and $\frac{6}{8}$ are not red.

Twelve students signed up to play in a marble tournament. One third of the students who signed up are girls. How many girls will play in the marble tournament?

Find $\frac{1}{3}$ of 12.

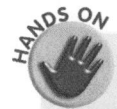

Activity 2

Materials ■ two-color counters

Step 1	**Step 2**	**Step 3**
Put 12 counters on your desk. 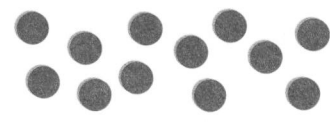	Place the counters in 3 equal groups. 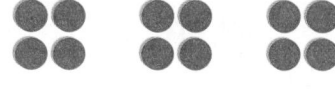	Count the number in one of the 3 groups. 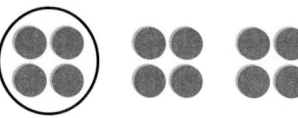

▲ The National Marble Tournament is held in Wildwood, New Jersey. It is for children ages 7 to 14.

There are 4 counters in one group. $\frac{1}{3}$ of 12 = 4

So, 4 girls will play in the marble tournament.

• What is $\frac{2}{3}$ of 12?

Guided Practice

1. Use the counters to find $\frac{1}{2}$ of 8.

Write a fraction that names the red part of each group.

2.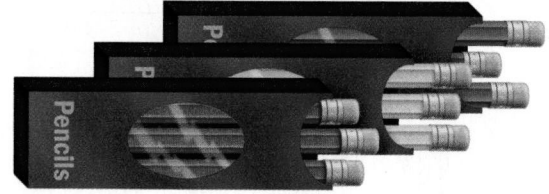

✓ 3.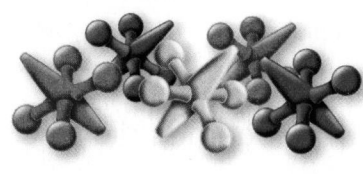

Draw each. Then write a fraction that names the shaded part.

4. Draw 10 squares.
   Shade 7 squares.

5. Draw 6 triangles.
   Make 2 equal groups.
   Shade 1 group.

✓ 6. Draw 8 circles.
   Shade 3 circles.

7. **TALK Math** Explain how to use counters to find $\frac{1}{5}$ of 10.

Write a fraction that names the blue part of each group.

8.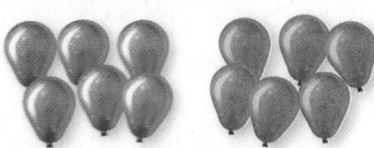

9.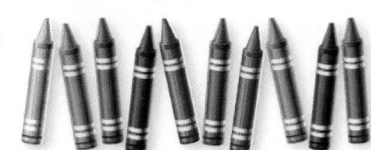

10.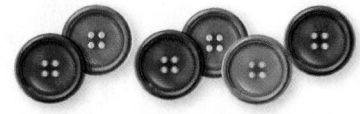

11.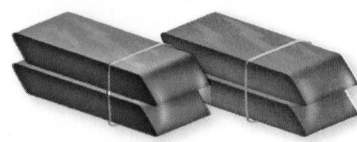

Draw each. Then write a fraction that names the shaded part.

12. Draw 3 circles.
    Shade 2 circles.

13. Draw 8 triangles.
    Make 4 equal groups.
    Shade 2 groups.

14. Draw 4 rectangles.
    Shade 1 rectangle.

Model each fraction with counters. Then write the fraction in words.

15. $\frac{4}{9}$

16. $\frac{1}{5}$

17. $\frac{6}{6}$

18. $\frac{2}{4}$

19. $\frac{5}{8}$

Use counters to solve.

20. $\frac{1}{2}$ of 4

21. $\frac{3}{4}$ of 8

22. $\frac{1}{3}$ of 9

23. $\frac{2}{6}$ of 12

24. $\frac{5}{5}$ of 10

USE DATA **For 25–27, use the bar graph.**

25. The bar graph shows the winners of the Smith Elementary School Marble Tournament. How many games were played? What fraction of the games did Scott win?

26. What fraction of the games did Robyn NOT win?

27. **Pose a Problem** Use the data from the bar graph. Write a problem that can be answered by using a fraction to name part of a group.

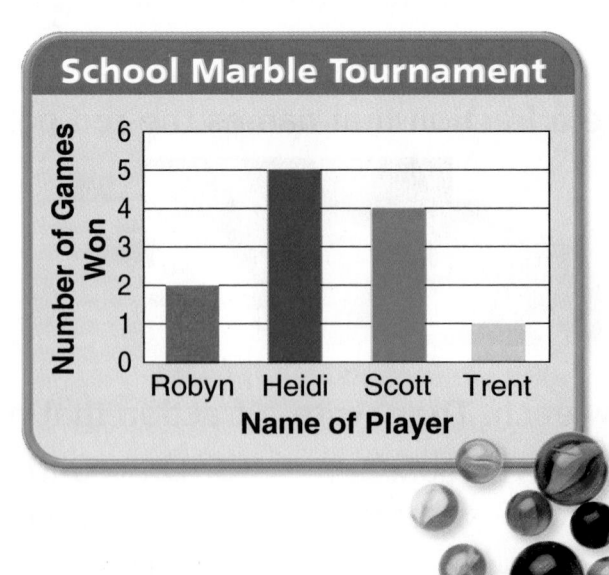

School Marble Tournament

Extra Practice on page 476, Set B

28. Kevin has 5 blue pens and 3 red pens. What fraction of Kevin's pens are red?

29. Lori has 10 flowers. Four of those flowers are pink. What fraction of the flowers are NOT pink?

30. Jess has a bag of 12 marbles. Of those marbles, $\frac{4}{12}$ are red, $\frac{3}{12}$ are white, and the rest are green. How many green marbles are in the bag?

31. **WRITE Math** ▸ **What's the Question?** A bag has 2 yellow cubes, 3 blue cubes, and 1 white cube. The answer is $\frac{5}{6}$.

Learn About) Fraction Patterns

You can use the models and patterns to complete the table.

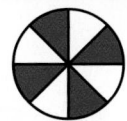

32.	Model	🟢🟢🟢🟢	⚫🟢🟢🟢	⬛	⚫⚫⚫🟢	⚫⚫⚫⚫
33.	Total number of parts	4	⬛	4	4	4
34.	Number of red parts	0	1	2	⬛	4
35.	Fraction of red parts	$\frac{0}{4}$	$\frac{1}{4}$	$\frac{2}{4}$	$\frac{3}{4}$	⬛

Mixed Review and Test Prep

36. What fraction of the circle is shaded? (p. 446)

37. **Test Prep** A basket is filled with 8 pieces of fruit. Of the pieces of fruit, $\frac{1}{4}$ are apples. How many apples are there?

   A 1   **C** 4

   B 2   **D** 6

38. Doug can choose ham, turkey, or beef for his sandwich. He can also choose white or wheat bread. How many different types of sandwiches can Doug make? (p. 186)

39. **Test Prep** What fraction of the coins are pennies?

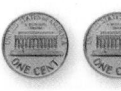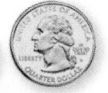

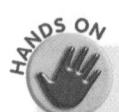

OBJECTIVE: Model and write equivalent fractions.

Learn

Two or more fractions that name the same amount are called **equivalent fractions**.

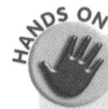

Activity 1

Materials ■ fraction bars

What is an equivalent fraction for $\frac{1}{4}$?

Step 1	Step 2	Step 3
Start with the bar for 1 whole. Line up a $\frac{1}{4}$ fraction bar. 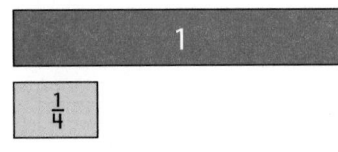	Use $\frac{1}{8}$ fraction bars to match the length of the bar for $\frac{1}{4}$. 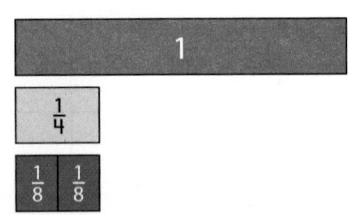	Count the number of $\frac{1}{8}$ bars that equal $\frac{1}{4}$. Write the equivalent fraction. **Count:** $\frac{1}{8},\ \frac{2}{8}$ **Write:** $\frac{1}{4} = \frac{2}{8}$

ERROR ALERT

Be sure that the fraction bars are lined up at the left.

Activity 2

Materials ■ fraction bars

What is an equivalent fraction for $\frac{2}{5}$?

Step 1	Step 2	Step 3
Start with the bar for 1 whole. Line up two $\frac{1}{5}$ bars for $\frac{2}{5}$. 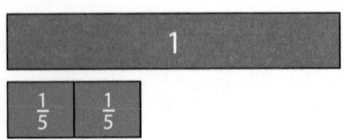	Use $\frac{1}{10}$ fraction bars to match the length of the bars for $\frac{2}{5}$. 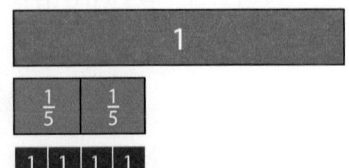	Count the number of $\frac{1}{10}$ bars that equal $\frac{2}{5}$. Write the equivalent fraction. **Count:** $\frac{1}{10},\ \frac{2}{10},\ \frac{3}{10},\ \frac{4}{10}$ **Write:** $\frac{2}{5} = \frac{4}{10}$

More Examples

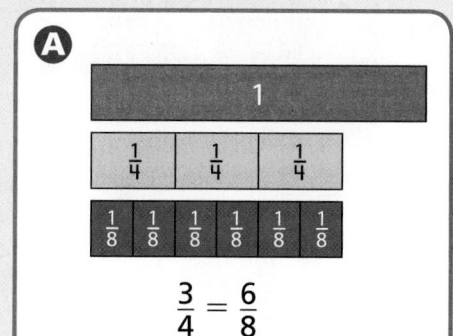

A

$$\frac{3}{4} = \frac{6}{8}$$

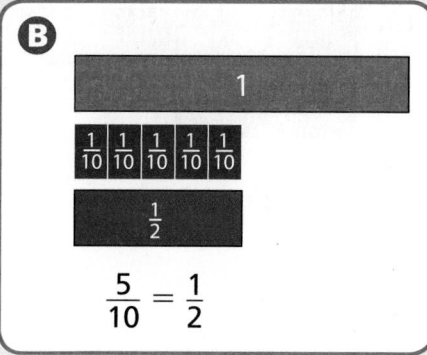

B

$$\frac{5}{10} = \frac{1}{2}$$

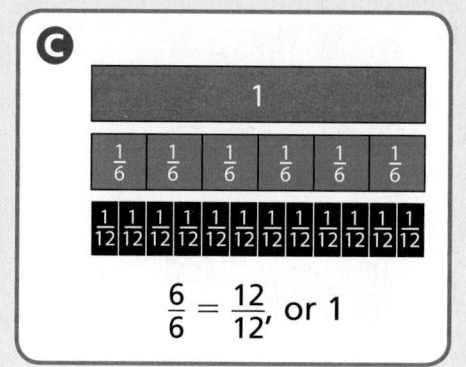

C

$$\frac{6}{6} = \frac{12}{12}, \text{ or } 1$$

Guided Practice

1. What fraction is equivalent to $\frac{2}{3}$?

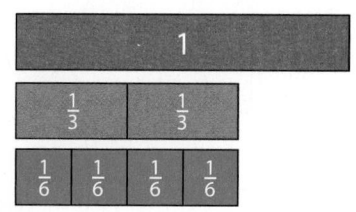

Find an equivalent fraction. Use fraction bars.

2.

3.

4.

5. [TALK Math] **Explain** how to use fraction bars to find a fraction that is equivalent to $\frac{3}{4}$.

Independent Practice and Problem Solving

Find an equivalent fraction. Use fraction bars.

6.

7.

8.

9.

10.

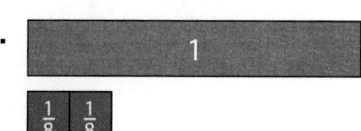

11.

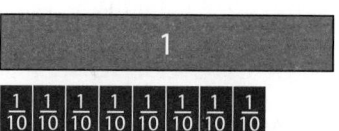

Extra Practice on page 476, Set C

Find the missing numerator. Use fraction bars.

12.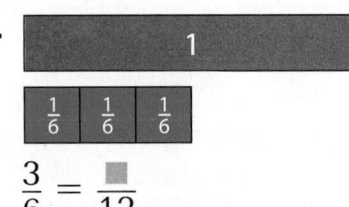

$$\frac{3}{6} = \frac{\blacksquare}{12}$$

13.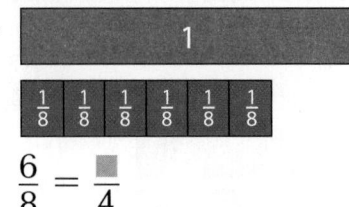

$$\frac{6}{8} = \frac{\blacksquare}{4}$$

14.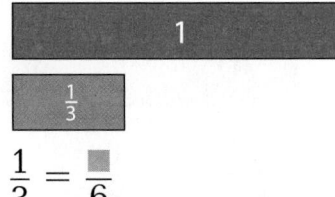

$$\frac{1}{3} = \frac{\blacksquare}{6}$$

15. $\frac{8}{10} = \frac{\blacksquare}{5}$

16. $\frac{1}{2} = \frac{\blacksquare}{8}$

17. $\frac{4}{12} = \frac{\blacksquare}{3}$

18. $\frac{2}{4} = \frac{\blacksquare}{12}$

19. $\frac{5}{5} = \frac{\blacksquare}{10}$

20. $\frac{4}{8} = \frac{\blacksquare}{2}$

21. Write the fraction that names the shaded part of each. Then tell which fractions are equivalent.

a. 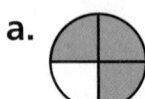　　**b.** 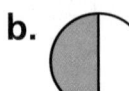　　**c.** 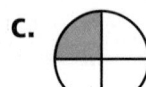　　**d.** 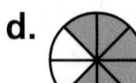　　**e.**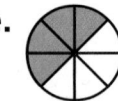

USE DATA For 22–24, use the table.

22. The table shows the lengths of three different types of ants. How many fire ants would it take to equal the length of one carpenter ant?

23. What fraction is equivalent to the length of a bulldog ant?

24. **Reasoning** Are any of the ants in the table the same length? **Explain.**

25. ▐▐ **WRITE Math** ▸ **Sense or Nonsense** Jay cut an orange into 8 equal pieces and ate 4 of the pieces. He says he ate one half of the orange. Does Jay's statement make sense? **Explain.**

Ants		
Type		**Length**
Fire ants		about $\frac{1}{4}$ inch
Bulldog ants		about $\frac{4}{5}$ inch
Carpenter ants		about $\frac{1}{2}$ inch

Mixed Review and Test Prep

26. Erin has 6 striped socks and 2 white socks in a drawer. What fraction of her socks are striped? (p. 450)

27. Each box of crayons costs $6. What is the cost of 4 boxes of crayons?

(p. 212)

28. **Test Prep** What is the missing numerator? $\frac{5}{6} = \frac{\blacksquare}{12}$

A 7　　　　　　**C** 9

B 8　　　　　　**D** 10

Draw to Explain

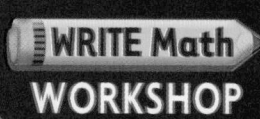

Sometimes you can best explain your thinking by drawing a picture or diagram.

Marta wants to find two fractions that are equivalent to $\frac{1}{3}$. She uses crayons and strips of paper to make diagrams of equivalent fractions.

She explains her thinking by describing what she did and showing her drawings.

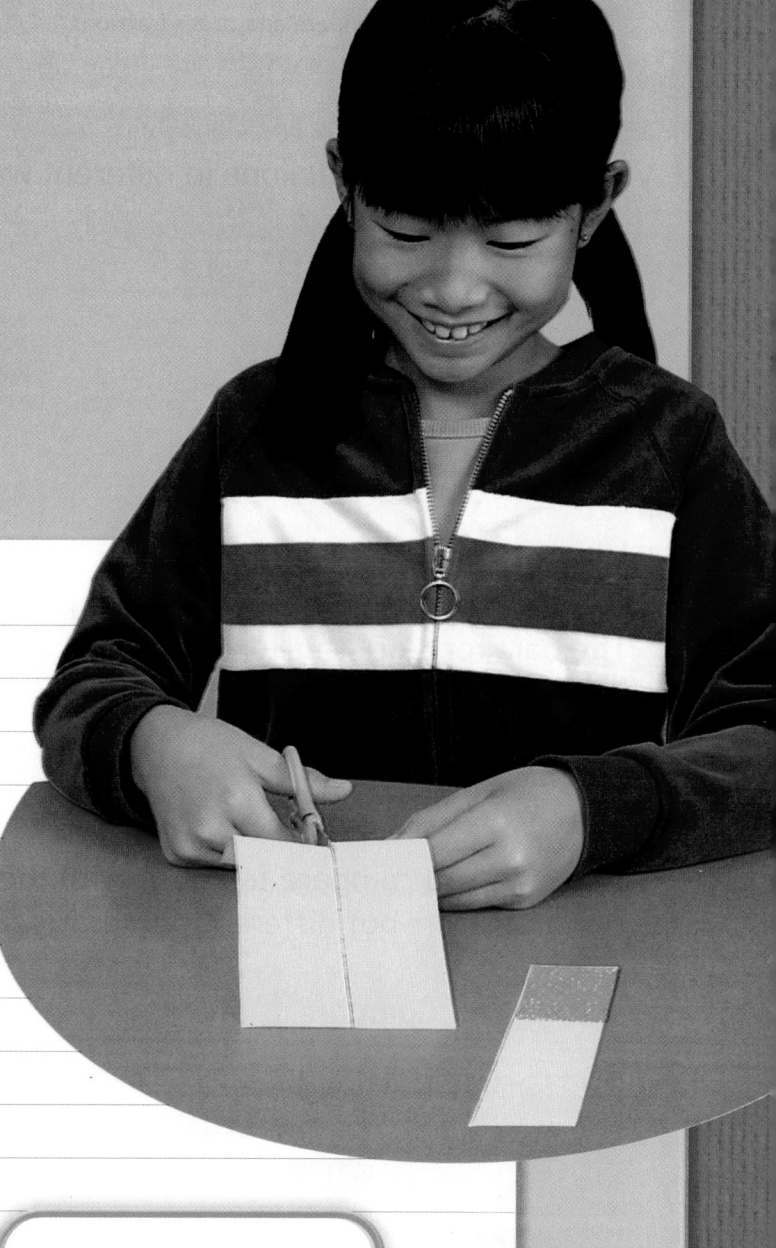

First, I cut three strips of paper that are the same size. Next, I folded the strips by using different numbers of folds to show $\frac{1}{3}$. I drew lines to show the folds and shaded $\frac{1}{3}$ of each strip.

| $\frac{1}{3}$ | $\frac{1}{3}$ | $\frac{1}{3}$ |

| $\frac{1}{6}$ | $\frac{1}{6}$ | $\frac{1}{6}$ | $\frac{1}{6}$ | $\frac{1}{6}$ | $\frac{1}{6}$ |

$$\frac{1}{3} = \frac{2}{6}$$

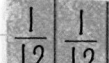   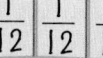 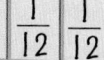

| $\frac{1}{12}$ | $\frac{1}{12}$ | $\frac{1}{12}$ | $\frac{1}{12}$ | $\frac{1}{12}$ | $\frac{1}{12}$ | $\frac{1}{12}$ | $\frac{1}{12}$ | $\frac{1}{12}$ | $\frac{1}{12}$ | $\frac{1}{12}$ | $\frac{1}{12}$ |

$$\frac{1}{3} = \frac{4}{12}$$

My drawings prove that $\frac{1}{3}$, $\frac{2}{6}$, and $\frac{4}{12}$ are equivalent fractions.

Problem Solving

Fold paper strips to show fractional parts. Draw lines to show the folds. Shade some parts to show the fractions. Then explain what you did. Use your drawings to show your solution.

1. Find an equivalent fraction for $\frac{2}{3}$.

2. Find an equivalent fraction for $\frac{3}{4}$.

Compare and Order Fractions

OBJECTIVE: Compare and order fractions.

Learn

You can compare fractions in different ways.

Example 1 Compare $\frac{2}{6}$ and $\frac{3}{6}$.

ONE WAY Use fraction bars.

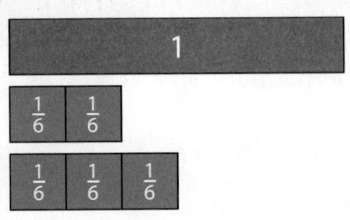

The bars for $\frac{2}{6}$ are shorter than the bars for $\frac{3}{6}$.

So, $\frac{2}{6} < \frac{3}{6}$,   or $\frac{3}{6} > \frac{2}{6}$.

ANOTHER WAY Use a number line.

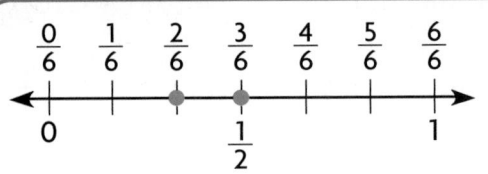

$\frac{3}{6}$ is to the right of $\frac{2}{6}$. It is closer to 1.

So, $\frac{3}{6} > \frac{2}{6}$,   or $\frac{2}{6} < \frac{3}{6}$.

• How can you compare fractions with the same denominators but different numerators?

Example 2 Compare $\frac{5}{10}$ and $\frac{1}{3}$.

ONE WAY Use fraction bars.

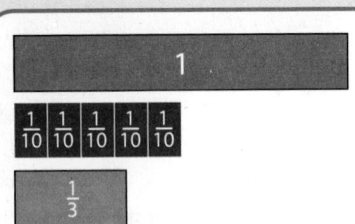

The bars for $\frac{5}{10}$ are longer than the bar for $\frac{1}{3}$.

So, $\frac{5}{10} > \frac{1}{3}$,   or $\frac{1}{3} < \frac{5}{10}$.

ANOTHER WAY Use number lines.

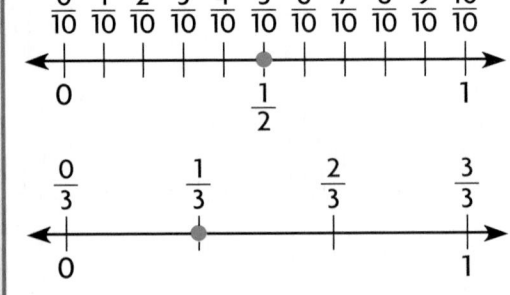

$\frac{1}{3}$ is to the left of $\frac{5}{10}$. It is closer to 0.

So, $\frac{1}{3} < \frac{5}{10}$,   or $\frac{5}{10} > \frac{1}{3}$.

You can use fraction bars or number lines to order fractions.

Example Compare and order $\frac{5}{8}$, $\frac{1}{4}$, and $\frac{4}{5}$.

ONE WAY Use fraction bars.

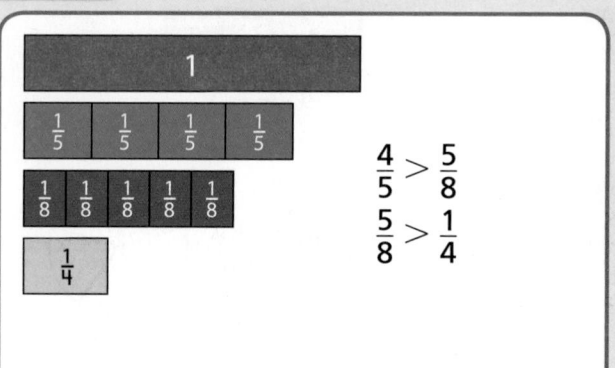

$\frac{4}{5} > \frac{5}{8}$

$\frac{5}{8} > \frac{1}{4}$

Think: $\frac{4}{5} > \frac{5}{8} > \frac{1}{4}$

So, the fractions in order from greatest to least are $\frac{4}{5}$, $\frac{5}{8}$, $\frac{1}{4}$.

ANOTHER WAY Use number lines.

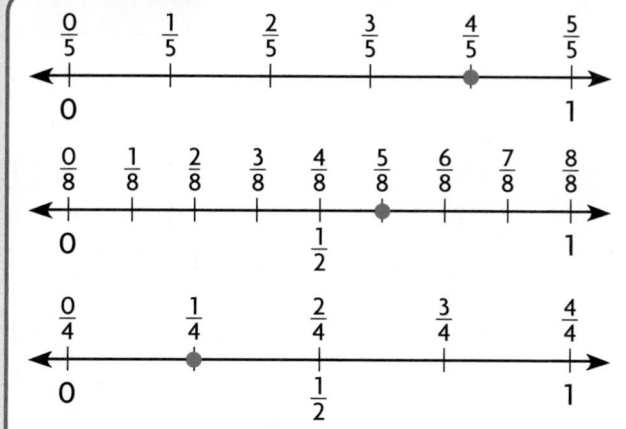

$\frac{4}{5}$ is closest to 1 and $\frac{1}{4}$ is closest to 0.

So, the fractions in order from greatest to least are $\frac{4}{5}$, $\frac{5}{8}$, $\frac{1}{4}$.

- What are the fractions in order from least to greatest?

- Compare and order $\frac{1}{8}$, $\frac{1}{4}$, and $\frac{1}{5}$. When the denominator is greater, are the fraction bars longer or shorter? Why?

Guided Practice

1. Which fraction is greater, $\frac{4}{6}$ or $\frac{2}{5}$?

   Think: The bars for $\frac{4}{6}$ are longer.

Compare. Write <, >, or = for each ●.

2.
   $\frac{6}{8}$ ● $\frac{4}{8}$

✓ 3.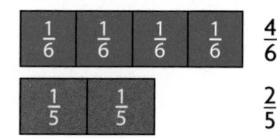

   $\frac{2}{4}$ ● $\frac{3}{4}$

✓ 4.
   $\frac{3}{12}$ ● $\frac{5}{10}$

5. **TALK Math** Explain how to use a number line to order $\frac{5}{6}$, $\frac{1}{6}$, and $\frac{3}{6}$ from least to greatest.

Compare. Write <, >, or = for each ⬤.

6.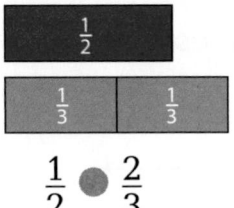

$$\frac{1}{2} \bullet \frac{2}{3}$$

7.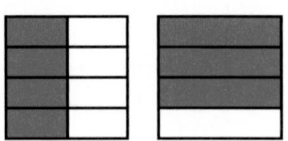

$$\frac{6}{8} \bullet \frac{9}{12}$$

8.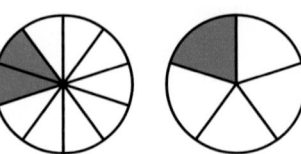

$$\frac{4}{5} \bullet \frac{6}{10}$$

9.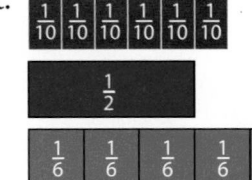

$$\frac{5}{6} \bullet \frac{1}{2}$$

10.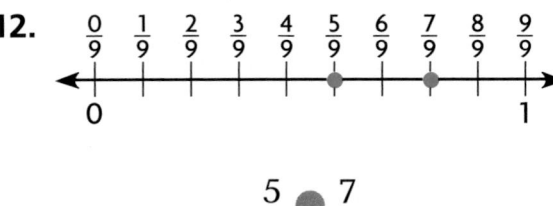

$$\frac{4}{8} \bullet \frac{3}{4}$$

11.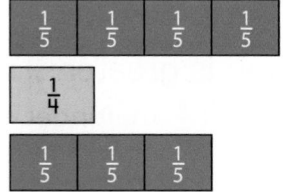

$$\frac{2}{10} \bullet \frac{1}{5}$$

12.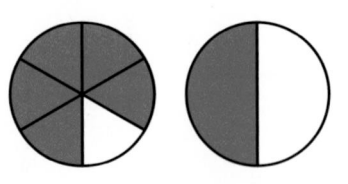

$$\frac{5}{9} \bullet \frac{7}{9}$$

13.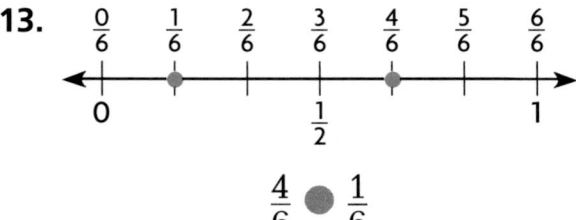

$$\frac{4}{6} \bullet \frac{1}{6}$$

Use fraction bars or number lines to compare.
Write <, >, or = for each ⬤.

14. $1 \bullet \frac{3}{3}$ **15.** $\frac{5}{9} \bullet \frac{10}{12}$ **16.** $\frac{1}{2} \bullet \frac{3}{6}$ **17.** $\frac{7}{8} \bullet \frac{3}{4}$

18. Order $\frac{6}{10}$, $\frac{1}{2}$, and $\frac{5}{6}$ from greatest to least.

19. Order $\frac{4}{5}$, $\frac{1}{4}$, and $\frac{3}{5}$ from least to greatest.

USE DATA For 20–21, use the map.

20. Which pet store is closer to Becky's house, Pet Mart or Super Pet?

21. Becky walked her dog from her house to Super Pet and then from Super Pet to the dog park. Which distance is greater?

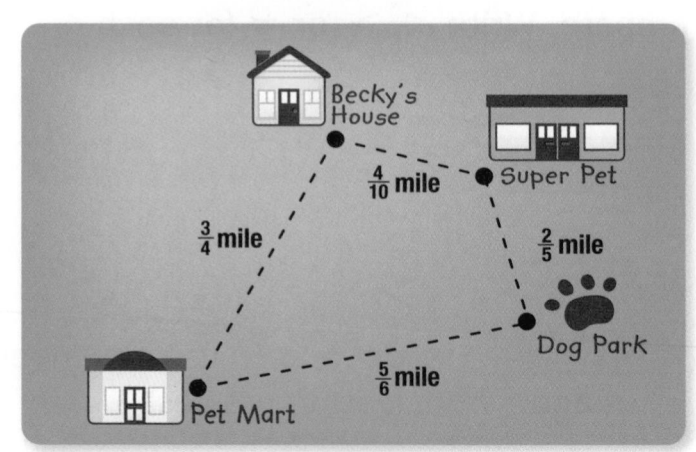

22. I am greater than $\frac{3}{6}$ and less than $\frac{4}{5}$. My denominator is 4. What fraction am I?

23. I am greater than $\frac{2}{8}$ and less than $\frac{1}{2}$. My denominator is 5. What fraction am I?

24. Jen found a recipe for dog biscuits. She needs $\frac{1}{3}$ cup butter, $\frac{3}{4}$ cup water, and $\frac{1}{2}$ cup powdered milk. Order these ingredients from the least to the greatest amount.

25. **WRITE Math** ▸ **Explain** how you can compare fractions that have different denominators.

Learn About Number Sense

Bobby and Jill went to a pizza restaurant and ordered the pizzas shown. Bobby and Jill each ate $\frac{1}{2}$ of his or her pizza.

Example

Did Bobby and Jill eat the same amount of pizza? Bobby and Jill did not eat the same amount. Since Bobby's pizza is larger, he ate more than Jill.

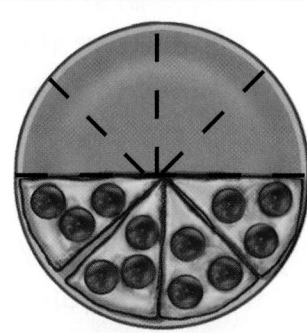

Bobby's pizza

Try It

Use the pictures of the pizzas to answer the questions below.

26. One slice of each pizza is $\frac{1}{8}$. Explain why Bobby's and Jill's slices aren't the same size.

27. Which pizza slices do you think cost less? Explain.

28. What if the pizzas were divided into thirds? Would Bobby's slices and Jill's slices be the same size?

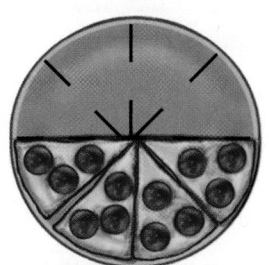

Jill's pizza

Mixed Review and Test Prep

29. One jar of jelly costs $3. Two jars cost $6, and three jars cost $9. What is the cost of 7 jars of jelly? (p. 256)

30. Test Prep Which fraction is greater than $\frac{5}{8}$?

A $\frac{1}{2}$　　**B** $\frac{4}{10}$　　**C** $\frac{3}{8}$　　**D** $\frac{3}{4}$

31. Write the fact family for 2, 7, and 9. (p. 76)

32. Test Prep Rick, Jerry, and Tabitha are all reading the same book. Rick has read $\frac{2}{3}$ of the book, Jerry has read $\frac{2}{5}$, and Tabitha has read $\frac{4}{12}$. Who has read most of the book?

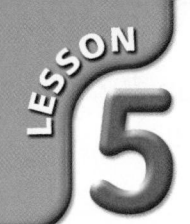

Problem Solving Workshop
Strategy: Compare Strategies

OBJECTIVE: Compare different strategies to solve problems.

Read to Understand
Plan
Solve
Check

Use the Strategy

PROBLEM Emma and her friends climbed a rock wall. Emma climbed $\frac{3}{4}$ of the wall, Elijah climbed $\frac{3}{6}$ of the wall, and Martin climbed $\frac{2}{3}$ of the wall. Who climbed the highest?

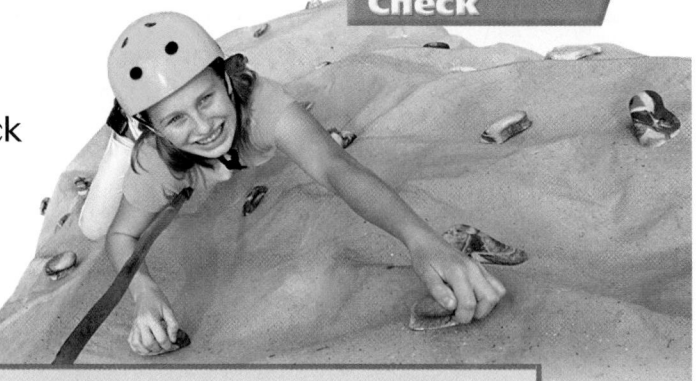

Read to Understand

- Visualize the problem.
- What information is given?

Plan

- **What strategy can you use to solve the problem?**

  Sometimes you can use more than one strategy to solve a problem. You can *make a model* or *draw a picture* to solve this problem.

Solve

- **How can you use each strategy to solve the problem?**

Make a Model Use fraction bars to model the problem.

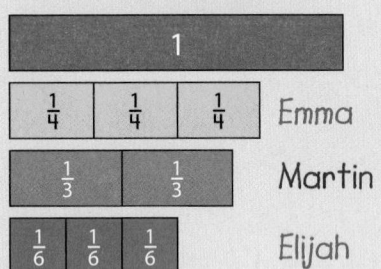

Compare the lengths.

$\frac{3}{4} > \frac{2}{3} > \frac{3}{6}$ So, Emma climbed the highest.

Draw a Picture Draw and label number lines to model the problem.

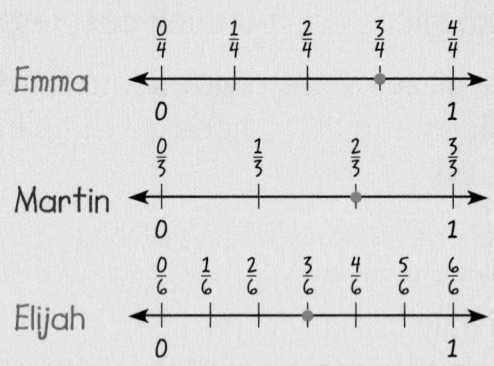

Compare the points.

Check

- **How do you know the answer is correct?**

462

Guided Problem Solving

1. Tracy and Kim ran on the track to see who could run farther without stopping. Tracy ran $\frac{4}{5}$ of a mile and Kim ran $\frac{8}{10}$ of a mile. Who ran farther?

   First, decide which strategy to use.

   Then, compare the fractions.

   Finally, find the greater fraction.

   $$\frac{4}{5} \bullet \frac{8}{10}$$

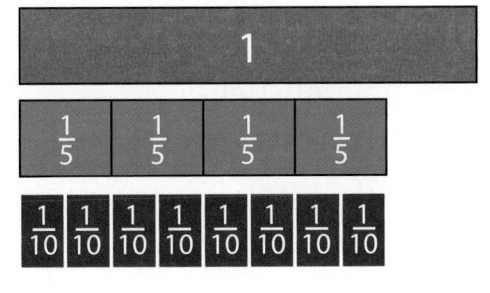

Choose a
STRATEGY

Draw a Diagram or Picture
Make a Model or Act It Out
Make an Organized List
Find a Pattern
Make a Table or Graph
Predict and Test
Work Backward
Solve a Simpler Problem
Write an Equation
Use Logical Reasoning

2. **What if** Cara decided to run on the track, too, and she ran $\frac{9}{10}$ of a mile? Who would have run the farthest?

3. Lewis made a wax candle at the carnival. He made $\frac{2}{8}$ of it blue, $\frac{1}{2}$ of it green, and $\frac{1}{4}$ of it yellow. Which color did he use the most?

Mixed Strategy Practice

USE DATA For 4–5, use the table.

4. For the Frisbee toss, players get 12 chances to toss Frisbees through a tire. Who threw the most Frisbees through the tire?

5. Who threw the fewest Frisbees through the tire? Write the fraction for that person in words.

6. Malia, Andy, and Jenna are in line for popcorn. Jenna is not first. Malia is last. In what position in line is Andy?

7. Joe and Mark did the balloon toss. Joe caught the balloon 3 more times than Mark. Together they caught the balloon 29 times. How many times did Mark catch the balloon?

8. **WRITE Math** Each team ran 1 lap in a relay race. Byron ran $\frac{1}{4}$ of a lap. Each person on his team ran the same distance. How many runners were on Byron's team? **Explain.**

Frisbee® Toss	
Name of Player	Fraction Thrown Through Tire
Lisa	$\frac{4}{12}$
Suri	$\frac{5}{6}$
Patrick	$\frac{3}{4}$

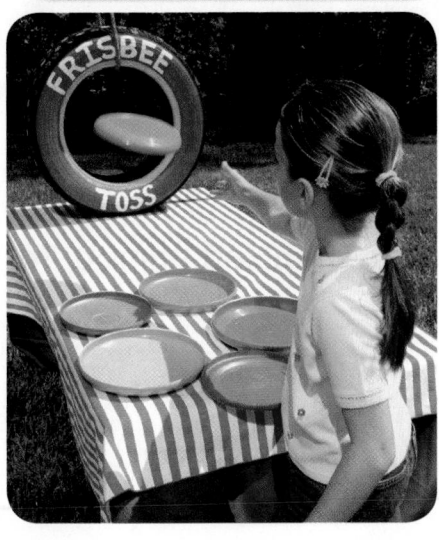

6 Mixed Numbers

OBJECTIVE: Identify, read, and write mixed numbers.

 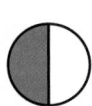
Learn

PROBLEM Sarah volunteers at an animal shelter. She feeds each kitten $\frac{1}{3}$ can of food. How many cans of food will she give to 5 kittens?

Here are two ways to find the total number of cans.

ONE WAY

Make a model.

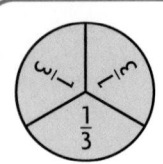 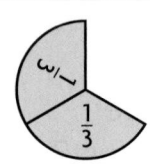

There are $\frac{5}{3}$ in all.

$\frac{3}{3} = 1$ whole

So, $\frac{5}{3} = 1 + \frac{2}{3}$, or $1\frac{2}{3}$.

ANOTHER WAY

Use a number line.

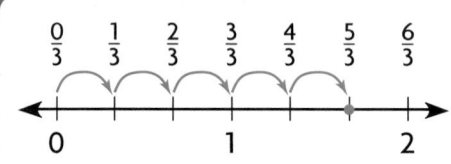

Show one jump for each $\frac{1}{3}$.

Five jumps on the number line is two thirds more than 1.

So, $\frac{5}{3} = 1 + \frac{2}{3}$, or $1\frac{2}{3}$.

So, Sarah will give 5 kittens $1\frac{2}{3}$ cans of food.

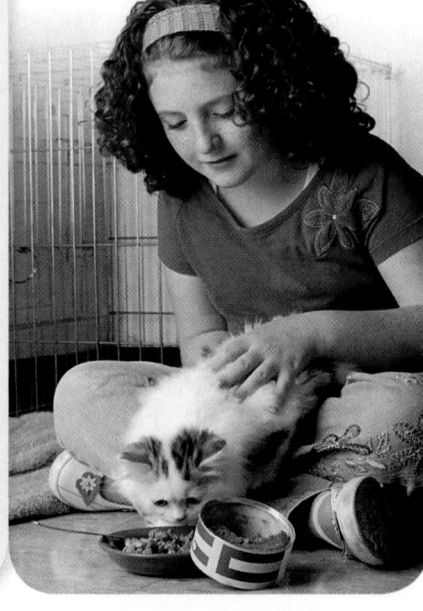

The number $1\frac{2}{3}$ is a mixed number. A **mixed number** is made up of a whole number and a fraction.

READ Math

Read $1\frac{2}{3}$ as *one and two thirds.*

Guided Practice

1. Write a mixed number for the model.

Think: There are $\frac{7}{4}$ in all.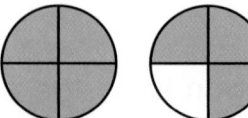

Write a mixed number for the parts that are shaded.

2.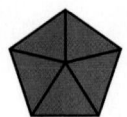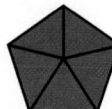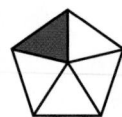

✓ **3.**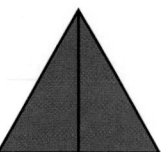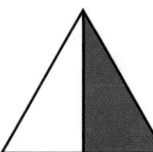

✓ **4.**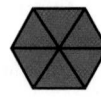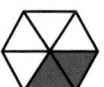

5. **TALK Math** Is $2\frac{1}{2}$ equal to $\frac{5}{2}$? **Explain** how you know.

Independent Practice and Problem Solving

Write a mixed number for the parts that are shaded.

6.   **7.** 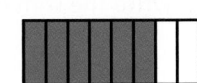   **8.**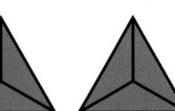

For 9–13, use the number line to write the mixed number.

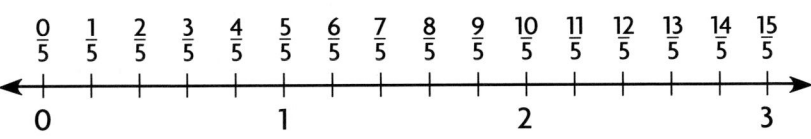

9. $\frac{6}{5}$ **10.** $\frac{8}{5}$ **11.** $\frac{12}{5}$ **12.** $\frac{9}{5}$ **13.** $\frac{13}{5}$

Make a model to show the mixed number.
Then write the mixed number using words.

14. $3\frac{2}{4}$ **15.** $1\frac{7}{10}$ **16.** $2\frac{5}{6}$ **17.** $3\frac{1}{2}$ **18.** $1\frac{3}{8}$

USE DATA For 19–21, use the table.

19. The table shows the weights of some kittens. What is Timber's weight written as a mixed number?

20. Which kitten weighs between 1 and $2\frac{1}{2}$ pounds?

21. Order the weights of the kittens from greatest to least. Write the weights as mixed numbers.

22. **WRITE Math** ▸ Buttercup is a cat at the animal shelter. She weighs $2\frac{5}{8}$ pounds. Is her weight closer to 2 pounds or 3 pounds? **Explain** how you know.

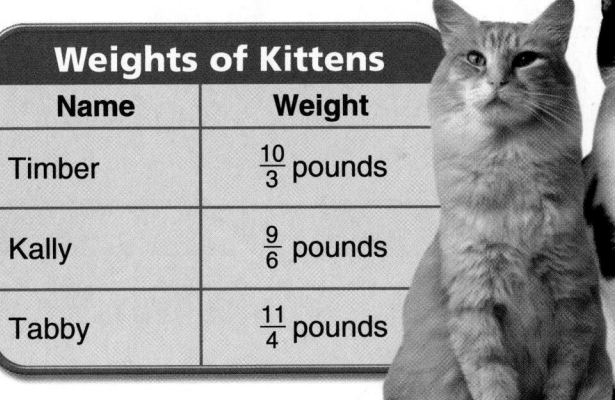

Weights of Kittens

Name	Weight
Timber	$\frac{10}{3}$ pounds
Kally	$\frac{9}{6}$ pounds
Tabby	$\frac{11}{4}$ pounds

Mixed Review and Test Prep

23. Jasmine drew a polygon that has five sides. Name the polygon she drew.
(p. 356)

24. What is the difference? (p. 88)
$3,006 - 1,165 = \blacksquare$

25. Test Prep Ms. Adams gave $\frac{1}{4}$ of an apple to each of 10 children. How many apples did she give to the children in all?

A $1\frac{4}{10}$ **B** $1\frac{2}{4}$ **C** $2\frac{1}{4}$ **D** $2\frac{2}{4}$

Extra Practice on page 477, Set E

Add Like Fractions

OBJECTIVE: Add like fractions and write the sum in simplest form.

Learn

Fractions that have the same denominator are called **like fractions**.

PROBLEM Jeb cut a pumpkin pie into 6 equal pieces. He ate 2 pieces. Claire ate 1 piece. How much of the pie did they eat altogether?

Add. $\frac{2}{6} + \frac{1}{6}$

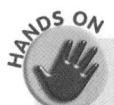

Activity   Materials ■ fraction bars

Step 1	Step 2	Step 3
Line up two $\frac{1}{6}$ fraction bars under the bar for 1.	Add one more $\frac{1}{6}$ fraction bar.	Count the number of $\frac{1}{6}$ fraction bars.

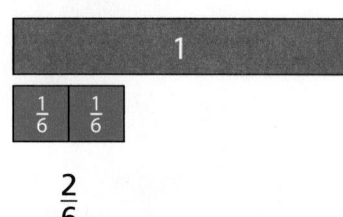
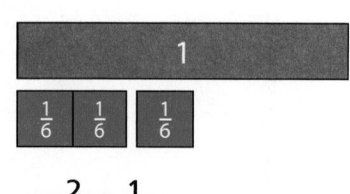
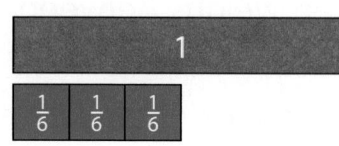

$\frac{2}{6}$ $\frac{2}{6} + \frac{1}{6}$ $\frac{1}{6}, \frac{2}{6}, \frac{3}{6},$ or $\frac{2}{6} + \frac{1}{6} = \frac{3}{6}$

So, Jeb and Claire ate $\frac{3}{6}$ of the pumpkin pie.

When you add fractions, you can show the sum in simplest form. A fraction is in **simplest form** when it uses the largest fraction bar or bars possible.

Find the largest fraction bar that is equivalent to $\frac{3}{6}$.
$\frac{3}{6}$ in simplest form is $\frac{1}{2}$.

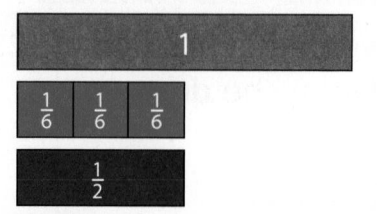

Remember
Equivalent fractions are two or more fractions that name the same amount.

So, Jeb and Claire ate $\frac{3}{6}$, or $\frac{1}{2}$ of the pumpkin pie.

Adding Numerators

You can add like fractions by adding the numerators.

Julie cut a loaf of pumpkin bread into 8 slices. She ate 2 slices, or $\frac{2}{8}$ of the loaf. Caleb ate 3 slices, or $\frac{3}{8}$ of the loaf. What fraction of the loaf did they eat in all?

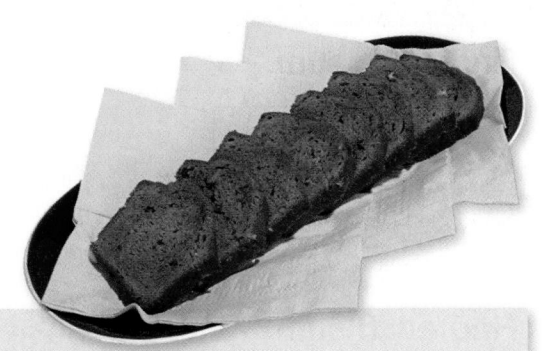

Example Add. $\frac{2}{8} + \frac{3}{8}$

MODEL	RECORD
Add the number of $\frac{1}{8}$ slices that Julie and Caleb ate.	2 slices $\quad + \quad$ 3 slices $\quad = \quad$ 5 slices
	$\downarrow \qquad\qquad \downarrow \qquad\qquad \downarrow$
$\frac{2}{8} \quad + \quad \frac{3}{8}$	$\frac{2}{8} \quad + \quad \frac{3}{8} \quad = \quad \frac{5}{8}$
	So, Julie and Caleb ate $\frac{5}{8}$ of the loaf.

Guided Practice

1. What is the sum of $\frac{2}{5}$ and $\frac{2}{5}$?

Think: $2 + 2 = 4$

$\frac{1}{5}$	$\frac{1}{5}$	$\frac{1}{5}$	$\frac{1}{5}$

Find each sum.

2.

$\frac{1}{6}$	$\frac{1}{6}$	$\frac{1}{6}$	$\frac{1}{6}$	$\frac{1}{6}$

$\frac{3}{6} + \frac{2}{6} = \blacksquare$

3.

$\frac{1}{4}$	$\frac{1}{4}$	$\frac{1}{4}$

$\frac{1}{4} + \frac{2}{4} = \blacksquare$

✓4.

$\frac{1}{12}$	$\frac{1}{12}$	$\frac{1}{12}$	$\frac{1}{12}$	$\frac{1}{12}$	$\frac{1}{12}$	$\frac{1}{12}$

$\frac{4}{12} + \frac{3}{12} = \blacksquare$

Find each sum. Write the answer in simplest form.

5.

$\frac{1}{8}$	$\frac{1}{8}$

$\frac{1}{4}$

$\frac{1}{8} + \frac{1}{8} = \blacksquare$, or $\blacksquare$

6.

$\frac{1}{10}$	$\frac{1}{10}$	$\frac{1}{10}$	$\frac{1}{10}$	$\frac{1}{10}$	$\frac{1}{10}$

$\frac{1}{5}$	$\frac{1}{5}$	$\frac{1}{5}$

$\frac{2}{10} + \frac{4}{10} = \blacksquare$, or $\blacksquare$

✓7.

$\frac{1}{5}$	$\frac{1}{5}$	$\frac{1}{5}$	$\frac{1}{5}$	$\frac{1}{5}$

1

$\frac{3}{5} + \frac{2}{5} = \blacksquare$, or $\blacksquare$

8. **TALK Math** Explain how to find $\frac{2}{12} + \frac{6}{12}$ in simplest form.

Independent Practice and Problem Solving

Find each sum.

9.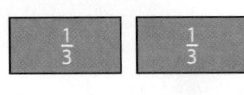

$$\frac{1}{3} + \frac{1}{3} = \blacksquare$$

10.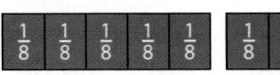

$$\frac{5}{8} + \frac{2}{8} = \blacksquare$$

11.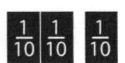

$$\frac{2}{10} + \frac{1}{10} = \blacksquare$$

Find each sum. Write the answer in simplest form.

12.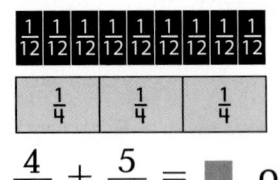

$$\frac{4}{12} + \frac{5}{12} = \blacksquare, \text{ or } \blacksquare$$

13.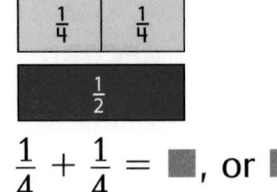

$$\frac{1}{4} + \frac{1}{4} = \blacksquare, \text{ or } \blacksquare$$

14.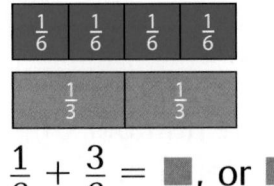

$$\frac{1}{6} + \frac{3}{6} = \blacksquare, \text{ or } \blacksquare$$

Find each sum.

15. $\frac{1}{5} + \frac{1}{5} = \blacksquare$

16. $\frac{2}{10} + \frac{3}{10} = \blacksquare$

17. $\frac{1}{3} + \frac{2}{3} = \blacksquare$

18. $\frac{6}{12} + \frac{4}{12} = \blacksquare$

19. $\frac{4}{6} + \frac{1}{6} = \blacksquare$

20. $\frac{1}{4} + \frac{3}{4} = \blacksquare$

21. $\frac{2}{8} + \frac{4}{8} = \blacksquare$

22. $\frac{5}{10} + \frac{2}{10} = \blacksquare$

23. $\frac{2}{10} + \frac{2}{10} = \blacksquare$

24. $\frac{1}{5} + \frac{2}{5} = \blacksquare$

25. $\frac{3}{12} + \frac{8}{12} = \blacksquare$

26. $\frac{2}{8} + \frac{1}{8} = \blacksquare$

USE DATA For 27–28, use the list of ingredients.

27. The ingredients list is for one batch of pumpkin bars. Amy made two batches of pumpkin bars. How much cinnamon did she use altogether?

28. Steve made pumpkin bars and pumpkin muffins. He used $\frac{1}{4}$ cup of cooking oil for the muffins. How much cooking oil did he use for both recipes?

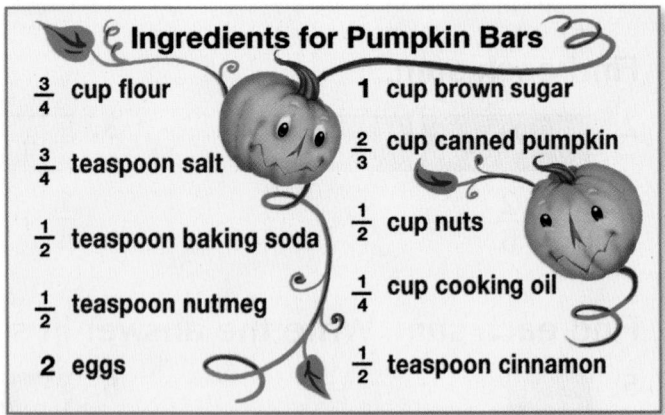

Ingredients for Pumpkin Bars

$\frac{3}{4}$ cup flour

$\frac{3}{4}$ teaspoon salt

$\frac{1}{2}$ teaspoon baking soda

$\frac{1}{2}$ teaspoon nutmeg

2 eggs

1 cup brown sugar

$\frac{2}{3}$ cup canned pumpkin

$\frac{1}{2}$ cup nuts

$\frac{1}{4}$ cup cooking oil

$\frac{1}{2}$ teaspoon cinnamon

29. The pumpkin bars were cut into 8 equal pieces. Jodi ate $\frac{3}{8}$, Maggie ate $\frac{1}{8}$, and Georgia ate $\frac{2}{8}$. What fraction of the pumpkin bars did they eat altogether?

30. **WRITE Math** **What's the Question?** Anna baked 12 muffins. Of the muffins, 6 were pumpkin, 4 were blueberry, and 2 were banana. The answer is $\frac{10}{12}$.

Find each sum. Write the answer in simplest form.

E	$\frac{1}{6} + \frac{3}{6}$	**H**	$\frac{1}{5} + \frac{1}{5}$	**L**	$\frac{1}{8} + \frac{3}{8}$	**A**	$\frac{2}{10} + \frac{1}{10}$
S	$\frac{2}{4} + \frac{1}{4}$	**T**	$\frac{3}{8} + \frac{2}{8}$	**P**	$\frac{3}{5} + \frac{1}{5}$	**E**	$\frac{5}{8} + \frac{2}{8}$
A	$\frac{4}{10} + \frac{5}{10}$	**N**	$\frac{6}{12} + \frac{4}{12}$	**O**	$\frac{1}{6} + \frac{1}{6}$	**F**	$\frac{4}{12} + \frac{4}{12}$

To answer the riddle, match the answers from above to the fractions below.

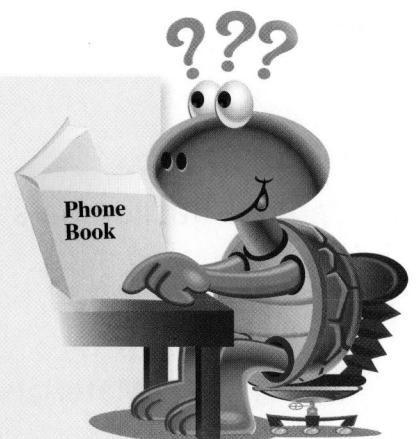

Phone Book

What kind of phone does a turtle use?

$$\frac{?}{\frac{9}{10}} \quad \frac{?}{\frac{3}{4}} \; \frac{?}{\frac{2}{5}} \; \frac{?}{\frac{7}{8}} \; \frac{?}{\frac{1}{2}} \; \frac{?}{\frac{1}{2}} \quad \frac{?}{\frac{4}{5}} \; \frac{?}{\frac{2}{5}} \; \frac{?}{\frac{1}{3}} \; \frac{?}{\frac{5}{6}} \; \frac{?}{\frac{7}{8}}!$$

Mixed Review and Test Prep

31. Ernie and Lupe rode along a bike trail. Ernie rode his bike $\frac{4}{5}$ of a mile. Lupe rode her bike $\frac{9}{10}$ of a mile. Who rode farther? (p. 458)

32. Test Prep Mandy is working on a crossword puzzle. Yesterday she filled in $\frac{3}{6}$ of the puzzle. Today she filled in $\frac{1}{6}$ of the puzzle. What fraction of the puzzle has Mandy filled in altogether?

A $\frac{2}{6}$ **C** $\frac{2}{12}$

B $\frac{4}{6}$ **D** $\frac{4}{12}$

33. Megan can choose to wear a blue shirt, a red shirt, or a yellow shirt. She can wear black pants, blue pants, or brown pants. How many different outfits can Megan choose to wear?

(p. 186)

34. Test Prep Reilly made a necklace and a bracelet. She used $\frac{6}{10}$ meter of string for the necklace and $\frac{2}{10}$ meter of string for the bracelet. How much string did she use in all? Write the fraction in simplest form.

Subtract Like Fractions

OBJECTIVE: Subtract like fractions and write the difference in simplest form.

Quick Review

Find each sum. Write the answer in simplest form.

1. $\frac{1}{4} + \frac{1}{4}$ **2.** $\frac{2}{6} + \frac{3}{6}$

3. $\frac{3}{10} + \frac{5}{10}$ **4.** $\frac{6}{12} + \frac{1}{12}$

5. $\frac{3}{8} + \frac{3}{8}$

Learn

You can use fraction bars to subtract like fractions.

Subtract. $\frac{8}{10} - \frac{5}{10}$

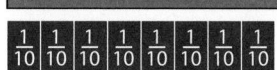

Activity 1   Materials ■ fraction bars

Step 1	Step 2	Step 3
Line up eight $\frac{1}{10}$ fraction bars under the bar for 1.	Take away five $\frac{1}{10}$ fraction bars.	Count the number of $\frac{1}{10}$ fraction bars left.

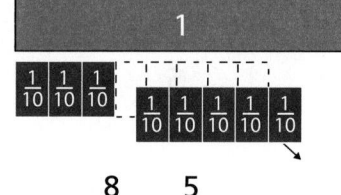
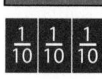

$$\frac{8}{10} \qquad \frac{8}{10} - \frac{5}{10} \qquad \text{So, } \frac{8}{10} - \frac{5}{10} = \frac{3}{10}.$$

Find $\frac{4}{8} - \frac{2}{8}$ in simplest form.

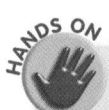

Activity 2   Materials ■ fraction bars

Step 1	Step 2	Step 3
Line up the fraction bars for $\frac{4}{8}$ and $\frac{2}{8}$ under the bar for 1.	Compare the bars to find the difference.	Find the largest fraction bar that is equivalent to $\frac{2}{8}$.

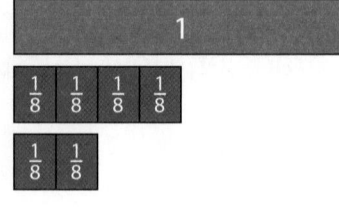
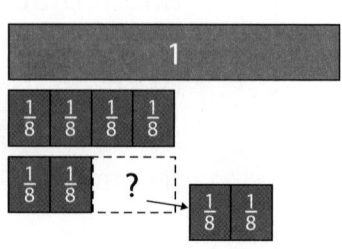
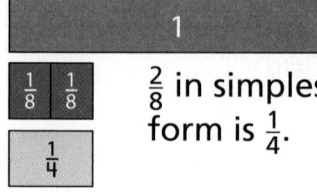

The difference is $\frac{2}{8}$.

$\frac{2}{8}$ in simplest form is $\frac{1}{4}$.

So, $\frac{4}{8} - \frac{2}{8} = \frac{2}{8}$, or $\frac{1}{4}$.

Subtracting Numerators

You can subtract like fractions by subtracting the numerators.

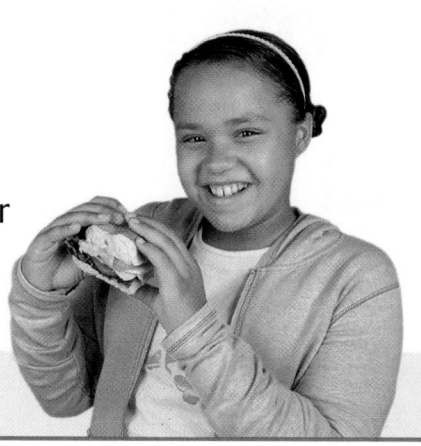

Molly had $\frac{7}{12}$ of a sub sandwich left to share with her friends. Her friends ate $\frac{6}{12}$ of the sandwich. What fraction of the sandwich is left?

Example Subtract. $\frac{7}{12} - \frac{6}{12}$

MODEL	RECORD
Subtract the number of $\frac{1}{12}$ pieces that Molly's friends ate. 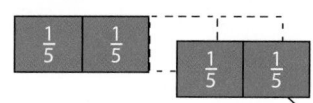 $\quad\frac{7}{12} \quad - \quad \frac{6}{12}$	7 pieces $\quad-\quad$ 6 pieces $\quad=\quad$ 1 piece $\qquad\downarrow\qquad\qquad\downarrow\qquad\qquad\downarrow$ $\quad\frac{7}{12}\qquad-\qquad\frac{6}{12}\qquad=\qquad\frac{1}{12}$ So, $\frac{1}{12}$ of the sandwich is left.

Guided Practice

1. What is the difference? $\frac{4}{5} - \frac{2}{5} = \blacksquare$

Think: $4 - 2 = 2$

Find each difference.

2. $\frac{7}{8} - \frac{4}{8} = \blacksquare$

3. $\frac{4}{4} - \frac{1}{4} = \blacksquare$

4. $\frac{9}{12} - \frac{2}{12} = \blacksquare$

Compare. Find each difference. Write the answer in simplest form.

5.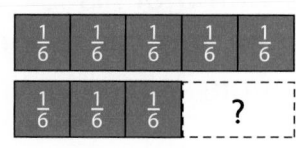

$\frac{5}{6} - \frac{3}{6} = \blacksquare$

6.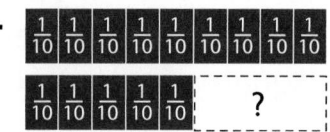

$\frac{9}{10} - \frac{5}{10} = \blacksquare$

7.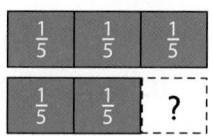

$\frac{3}{5} - \frac{2}{5} = \blacksquare$

8. **TALK Math** Explain how to use fraction bars to find $\frac{6}{8} - \frac{2}{8}$.

Find each difference.

9.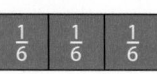

$$\frac{3}{6} - \frac{2}{6} = \blacksquare$$

10.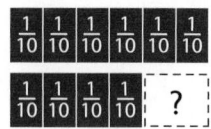

$$\frac{4}{5} - \frac{1}{5} = \blacksquare$$

11.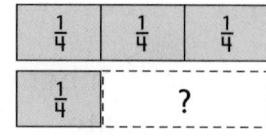

$$\frac{9}{10} - \frac{2}{10} = \blacksquare$$

Compare. Find each difference. Write the answer in simplest form.

12.

$$\frac{11}{12} - \frac{2}{12} = \blacksquare$$

13.

$$\frac{6}{10} - \frac{4}{10} = \blacksquare$$

14.

$$\frac{3}{4} - \frac{1}{4} = \blacksquare$$

Find each difference.

15. $\frac{5}{8} - \frac{3}{8} = \blacksquare$

16. $\frac{2}{3} - \frac{1}{3} = \blacksquare$

17. $\frac{10}{12} - \frac{7}{12} = \blacksquare$

18. $\frac{6}{6} - \frac{3}{6} = \blacksquare$

19. $\frac{5}{10} - \frac{2}{10} = \blacksquare$

20. $\frac{11}{12} - \frac{9}{12} = \blacksquare$

21. $\frac{7}{8} - \frac{1}{8} = \blacksquare$

22. $\frac{2}{4} - \frac{1}{4} = \blacksquare$

23. $\frac{3}{3} - \frac{2}{3} = \blacksquare$

24. $\frac{4}{6} - \frac{1}{6} = \blacksquare$

25. $\frac{7}{10} - \frac{3}{10} = \blacksquare$

26. $\frac{8}{12} - \frac{1}{12} = \blacksquare$

Algebra Compare. Write $<$, $>$, or $=$ for each ⬤.

27. $\frac{4}{5} - \frac{1}{5}$ ⬤ $\frac{3}{5} - \frac{2}{5}$

28. $\frac{3}{4} - \frac{2}{4}$ ⬤ $\frac{7}{8} - \frac{5}{8}$

29. $\frac{8}{10} - \frac{4}{10}$ ⬤ $\frac{9}{10} - \frac{3}{10}$

30. George used $\frac{5}{8}$ can of blue paint and $\frac{2}{8}$ can of white paint. How much more blue paint than white paint did he use?

31. A jar had $\frac{3}{4}$ cup of peanuts inside. Jill and Brad each ate $\frac{1}{4}$ cup of peanuts. How much of the peanuts are left?

32. Michelle made a pattern by using shapes. Of the shapes, $\frac{9}{12}$ were squares and $\frac{3}{12}$ were circles. What fraction tells how many more squares than circles she used?

33. Jacob cut a pie into 8 equal slices. He shared the pie with 5 of his friends. Jacob and each of his friends each ate 1 piece of pie. What fraction of the pie is left?

34. **WRITE Math** In a bag of 9 balloons, $\frac{5}{9}$ are blue and $\frac{1}{9}$ are red. The rest of the balloons are green. What fraction of the balloons are green? **Explain.**

Extra Practice on page 477, Set G

Learn About) Visual Thinking

You can use a number line to subtract like fractions.

Example

It is $\frac{9}{10}$ mile from the school to the library. It is $\frac{5}{10}$ mile from the museum to the library. How far is it from the school to the museum?

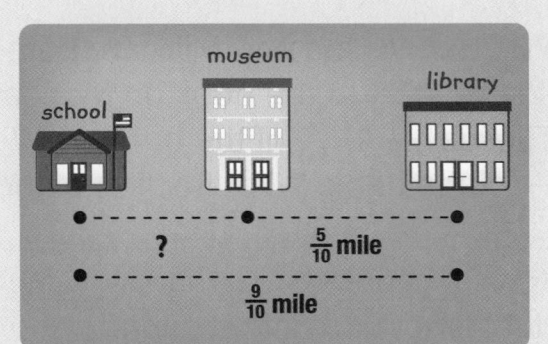

$$\frac{9}{10} - \frac{5}{10} = \blacksquare$$

school   museum   library

$\frac{0}{10}$ $\frac{1}{10}$ $\frac{2}{10}$ $\frac{3}{10}$ $\frac{4}{10}$ $\frac{5}{10}$ $\frac{6}{10}$ $\frac{7}{10}$ $\frac{8}{10}$ $\frac{9}{10}$ $\frac{10}{10}$

0                    $\frac{1}{2}$ 1

So, it is $\frac{4}{10}$ mile from the school to the museum.

Try It

Use a number line to find each difference.

35. $\frac{0}{6}$ $\frac{1}{6}$ $\frac{2}{6}$ $\frac{3}{6}$ $\frac{4}{6}$ $\frac{5}{6}$ $\frac{6}{6}$

0          $\frac{1}{2}$ 1

$$\frac{4}{6} - \frac{2}{6} = \blacksquare$$

36. $\frac{0}{8}$ $\frac{1}{8}$ $\frac{2}{8}$ $\frac{3}{8}$ $\frac{4}{8}$ $\frac{5}{8}$ $\frac{6}{8}$ $\frac{7}{8}$ $\frac{8}{8}$

0              $\frac{1}{2}$ 1

$$\frac{6}{8} - \frac{4}{8} = \blacksquare$$

Mixed Review and Test Prep

37. Write a rule for the pattern and find the next number. (p. 426)

5, 11, 17, 23, 29, 35, $\blacksquare$

38. Test Prep Kelly has $\frac{8}{8}$ yard of fabric. She uses $\frac{6}{8}$ yard to make a pillow. How much of the yard of fabric is left?

A $\frac{1}{4}$ **B** $\frac{3}{8}$ **C** $\frac{1}{2}$ **D** $\frac{3}{4}$

39. Tia collected 21 stamps. She divided the stamps into 3 groups. How many stamps were in each group? (p. 304)

40. Test Prep A log is $\frac{8}{10}$ meter long. Troy cuts off a piece that is $\frac{3}{10}$ meter long. What is the length of the log now? **Explain** how you know.

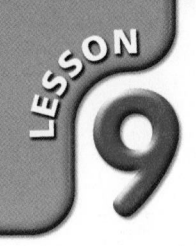

Problem Solving Workshop
Skill: Too Much/Too Little Information

Read to Understand
Plan
Solve
Check

OBJECTIVE: Solve problems by using the skill *too much/too little information.*

Use the Skill

PROBLEM Joe and Milly are both reading a 100-page book. Joe read $\frac{1}{10}$ of the book on Monday, $\frac{3}{10}$ of the book on Tuesday, and $\frac{2}{10}$ of the book on Wednesday. Milly has read $\frac{7}{10}$ of the book. What fraction of the book has Joe read?

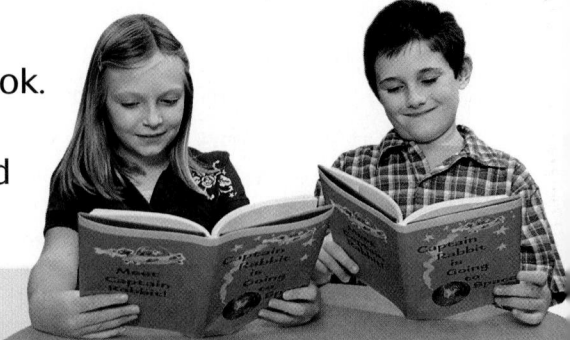

A word problem may have too much, too little, or the right amount of information.

Step 1	Step 2	Step 3
What do you need to find? the fraction of the book that Joe has read	**List the information you need.** Joe read $\frac{1}{10}$ of the book on Monday, $\frac{3}{10}$ on Tuesday, and $\frac{2}{10}$ on Wednesday.	**Is there information you do not need?** The book has 100 pages. Milly has read $\frac{7}{10}$ of the book.

Step 4

Solve the problem.
Add the amounts that Joe has read.

$\frac{1}{10} + \frac{3}{10} + \frac{2}{10} = \frac{6}{10}$ So, Joe has read $\frac{6}{10}$ of the book.

Think and Discuss
Tell whether there is too much or too little information. Solve if there is enough information.

a. Mrs. Charles cut a pie into equal-size pieces. She gave 6 pieces to Mike and his friends. What fraction of the pie is left?

b. In a relay race, Tom ran $\frac{1}{4}$ mile, Lori ran $\frac{3}{4}$ mile, and Raul ran $\frac{2}{4}$ mile. How far did Tom and Lori run altogether?

c. Isaiah bought 8 toy cars and 6 books. He gave 3 toy cars to his brother. What fraction of the toy cars did Isaiah keep?

474

Solve.

1. Mary used red, green, and blue ribbons to decorate a card. She used $\frac{5}{12}$ foot of red ribbon and $\frac{3}{12}$ foot of blue ribbon. How much ribbon did she use altogether?

    a. What do you need to find?

    b. What information do you need to solve the problem?

    c. Is there too much information? If so, what?

    d. Is there too little information? If so, what?

    e. Can you solve the problem? Explain.

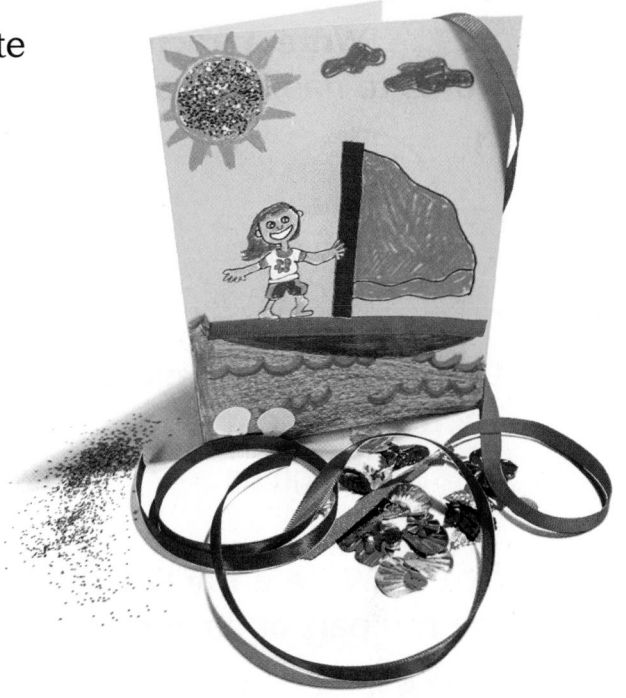

2. **What if** Mary used $\frac{2}{12}$ foot of green ribbon? How much ribbon did she use altogether?

3. There are 8 books on a shelf. Three of the books are short stories, some are coloring books, and the rest are sports books. What fraction of the books are NOT short stories?

Mixed Applications

4. Some children ate $\frac{4}{12}$ of a veggie pizza, $\frac{9}{12}$ of a pepperoni pizza, and $\frac{11}{12}$ of a cheese pizza. All 3 pizzas were the same size. What fraction tells how much more cheese pizza than veggie pizza the children ate?

5. **FAST FACT** The longest suspension bridge in the United States is in New York. Drivers pay $9 to cross in a car and $4 to cross on a motorcycle. What is the total cost for 5 cars and 2 motorcycles?

6. Betty has $25.00. She buys a book for $5.25 and a calendar for $6.50. How much money does she have now?

7. Matt has 129 books and Karly has 153 books. About how many books do they have altogether?

8. A box is filled with 5 books. Each book is 8 inches long and 6 inches wide. What is the perimeter of one book?

9. **WRITE Math** Lee read his book for 80 minutes on Saturday. How many hours and minutes is that? **Explain** how you know.

10. Mrs. Totten has 48 pencils. She keeps 12 pencils and divides the rest equally among 9 students. How many pencils does each student get?

Extra Practice

Set A Write a fraction in numbers and in words to name the shaded part. (pp. 446–449)

1.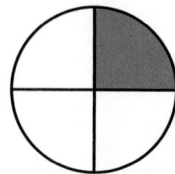

2.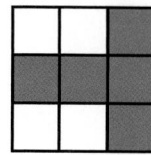

3.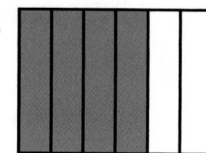

Use fraction circle pieces to make a model of each.
Then write the fraction by using numbers.

4. seven eighths   **5.** one divided by two   **6.** three out of five

Set B Write a fraction that names
the red part of each group. (pp. 450–453)

1.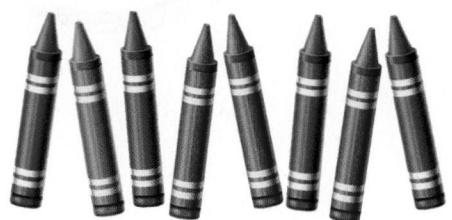

2.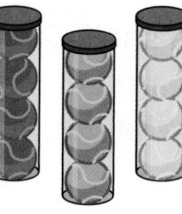

Set C Find an equivalent fraction. Use fraction bars. (pp. 454–457)

1.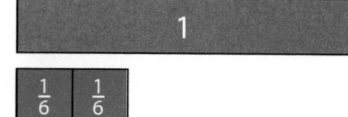

2.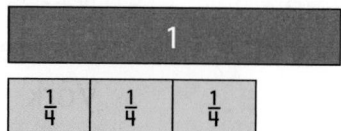

3.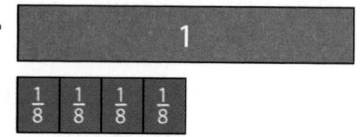

Set D Compare. Write <, >, or = for each ●. (pp. 458–461)

1.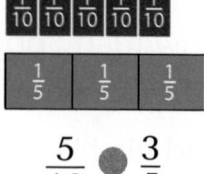

$\frac{5}{10}$ ● $\frac{3}{5}$

2.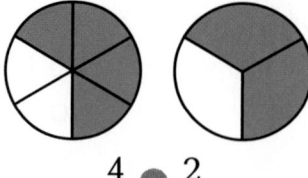

$\frac{4}{6}$ ● $\frac{2}{3}$

3.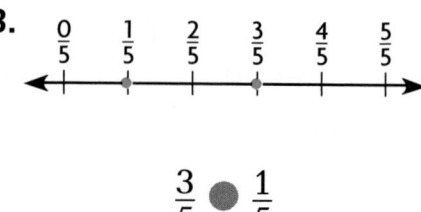

$\frac{3}{5}$ ● $\frac{1}{5}$

4. I am greater than $\frac{1}{2}$ and less than $\frac{3}{4}$. My denominator is 3. What fraction am I?

5. I am greater than $\frac{1}{3}$ and less than $\frac{3}{5}$. My denominator is 4. What fraction am I?

Technology
Use Harcourt Mega Math, Fraction Action,
Fraction Flare Up, Levels B, C, D, E, F, G, H.

Set E Write a mixed number for the parts that are shaded. (pp. 464–465)

1.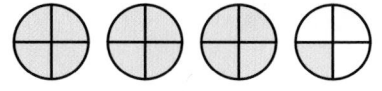

2.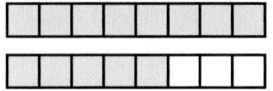

3.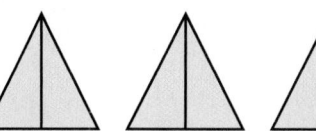

4.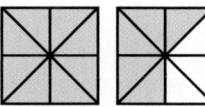

5.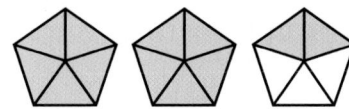

6.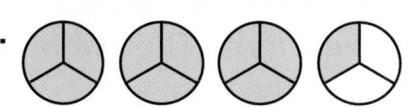

Set F Find each sum. Write the answer in simplest form. (pp. 466–469)

1.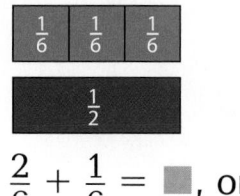

$$\frac{2}{6} + \frac{1}{6} = \blacksquare, \text{ or } \blacksquare$$

2.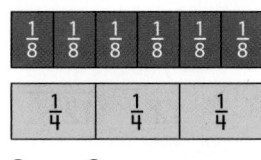

$$\frac{3}{8} + \frac{3}{8} = \blacksquare, \text{ or } \blacksquare$$

3.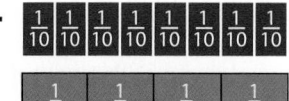

$$\frac{6}{10} + \frac{2}{10} = \blacksquare, \text{ or } \blacksquare$$

4. $\frac{1}{3} + \frac{1}{3} = \blacksquare$ **5.** $\frac{3}{12} + \frac{4}{12} = \blacksquare$ **6.** $\frac{2}{6} + \frac{2}{6} = \blacksquare$ **7.** $\frac{1}{4} + \frac{2}{4} = \blacksquare$

8. Bonnie ordered a pizza that was $\frac{1}{4}$ sausage, $\frac{1}{4}$ cheese, $\frac{1}{4}$ pepperoni, and $\frac{1}{4}$ mushroom. What fraction of the pizza had sausage or mushroom?

9. A submarine sandwich was cut into 12 equal pieces. Peter ate $\frac{3}{12}$, Taj ate $\frac{2}{12}$, and Marissa ate $\frac{5}{12}$. What fraction of the sandwich did they eat altogether?

Set G Compare. Find each difference.
Write the answer in simplest form. (pp. 470–473)

1.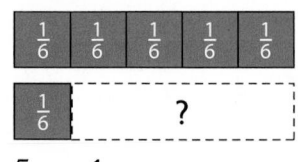

$$\frac{5}{6} - \frac{1}{6} = \blacksquare$$

2.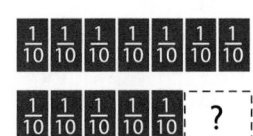

$$\frac{7}{10} - \frac{5}{10} = \blacksquare$$

3.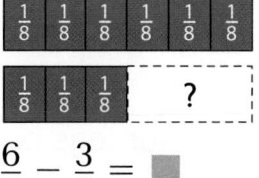

$$\frac{6}{8} - \frac{3}{8} = \blacksquare$$

4. $\frac{9}{12} - \frac{5}{12} = \blacksquare$ **5.** $\frac{3}{5} - \frac{2}{5} = \blacksquare$ **6.** $\frac{7}{9} - \frac{4}{9} = \blacksquare$ **7.** $\frac{6}{10} - \frac{1}{10} = \blacksquare$

8. $\frac{5}{6} - \frac{4}{6} = \blacksquare$ **9.** $\frac{4}{8} - \frac{2}{8} = \blacksquare$ **10.** $\frac{11}{12} - \frac{6}{12} = \blacksquare$ **11.** $\frac{2}{3} - \frac{1}{3} = \blacksquare$

THE RIDDLER

Copy the riddle below. Find the value of each letter in simplest form. Then write the letters in the correct spaces to solve the riddle.

Which weighs more, a pound of rocks or a pound of feathers? Neither, they both weigh one pound.

Example

$\frac{7}{12} - \frac{5}{12}$ **A**

Step 1
Add or subtract the numerators. $\frac{7}{12} - \frac{5}{12} = \frac{2}{12}$
The denominator stays the same.

Step 2
Simplify the answer. $\frac{2}{12} = \frac{1}{6}$

Step 3
Place the letter in the riddle.
Put the letter A on each line that is above $\frac{1}{6}$.

Try It

Add or subtract to answer the riddle.

1. $\frac{1}{5} + \frac{2}{5} = \blacksquare$ **R**

2. $\frac{7}{10} - \frac{3}{10} = \blacksquare$ **N**

3. $\frac{3}{6} - \frac{1}{6} = \blacksquare$ **O**

4. $\frac{4}{8} + \frac{2}{8} = \blacksquare$ **S**

5. $\frac{5}{9} + \frac{1}{9} = \blacksquare$ **T**

6. $\frac{3}{8} - \frac{1}{8} = \blacksquare$ **I**

7. $\frac{11}{12} - \frac{1}{12} = \blacksquare$ **F**

8. $\frac{4}{8} + \frac{1}{8} = \blacksquare$ **W**

9. $\frac{1}{4} + \frac{1}{4} = \blacksquare$ **P**

10. What has four legs but cannot walk?

$$\frac{?}{\frac{2}{3}} \quad \frac{?}{\frac{5}{8}} \quad \frac{?}{\frac{1}{3}} \qquad \frac{?}{\frac{1}{2}} \quad \frac{A}{\frac{1}{6}} \quad \frac{?}{\frac{1}{4}} \quad \frac{?}{\frac{3}{5}} \quad \frac{?}{\frac{3}{4}} \qquad \frac{?}{\frac{1}{3}} \quad \frac{?}{\frac{5}{6}} \qquad \frac{?}{\frac{1}{2}} \quad \frac{A}{\frac{1}{6}} \quad \frac{?}{\frac{2}{5}} \quad \frac{?}{\frac{2}{3}} \quad \frac{?}{\frac{3}{4}}$$

11. **WRITE Math** Write your own riddle using fractions.
Explain it to a classmate and have him or her solve it.

Chapter 18 Review/Test

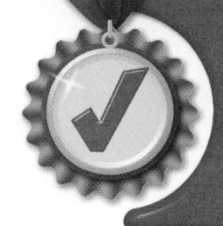

Check Vocabulary and Concepts

Choose the best term from the box.

1. The _?_ tells how many parts are being counted. (p. 446)

2. Two or more fractions that name the same amount are called _?_. (p. 454)

3. The _?_ tells how many equal parts are in the whole or in the group. (p. 446)

> **VOCABULARY**
> denominator
> equivalent fractions
> fraction
> numerator

Check Skills

Write a fraction in numbers and in words to name the blue part. (pp. 446–449, 450–453)

4.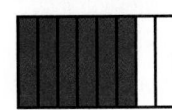

5.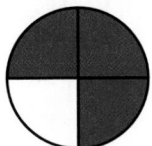

6.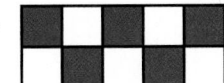

7.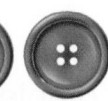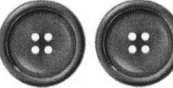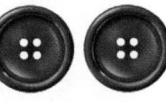

Find the missing numerator. Use fraction bars. (pp. 454–457)

8. $\frac{2}{8} = \frac{\blacksquare}{4}$

9. $\frac{4}{10} = \frac{\blacksquare}{5}$

10. $\frac{10}{12} = \frac{\blacksquare}{6}$

11. $\frac{1}{3} = \frac{\blacksquare}{9}$

Compare. Write $<$, $>$, or $=$ for each ●. (pp. 458–461)

12. $\frac{1}{2}$ ● $\frac{3}{4}$

13. $\frac{2}{3}$ ● $\frac{4}{5}$

14. $\frac{6}{10}$ ● $\frac{3}{5}$

15. $\frac{6}{8}$ ● $\frac{6}{12}$

Write a mixed number for the parts that are shaded. (pp. 464–465)

16.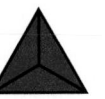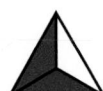

17.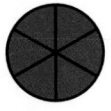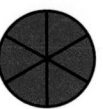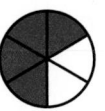

18.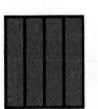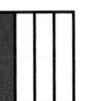

Check Problem Solving

Solve. (pp. 462–463, 474–475)

19. Colby, Fred, and Jim ran for six minutes. Colby ran $\frac{4}{6}$ mile, Fred ran $\frac{8}{10}$ mile, and Jim ran $\frac{8}{12}$ mile. Who ran the farthest?

20. ▌WRITE Math ▶ Amy ate $\frac{3}{8}$ of a pizza and Sue ate $\frac{2}{4}$ of it. Who ate more pizza? **Explain** how you know.

Standardized Test Prep
Chapters 1–18

Number and Operations

1. Which fraction names the shaded part? (p. 446)

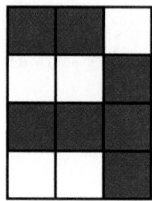

A $\frac{1}{7}$

B $\frac{5}{12}$

C $\frac{7}{12}$

D $\frac{7}{10}$

2. Charlie bought 6 packs of notepads. There were 10 notepads in each pack. How many notepads did Charlie buy? (p. 218)

A 4

B 16

C 54

D 60

3. ✏️ WRITE Math ▸ What is $\frac{5}{6} - \frac{2}{6}$ in simplest form? **Explain** your answer. (p. 470)

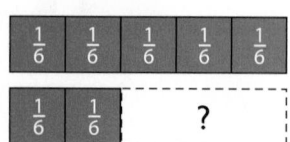

Algebraic Reasoning

4. Which number sentence is in the same fact family as $27 \div 9 = 3$? (p. 286)

A $9 \div 3 = 3$

B $3 \times 3 = 9$

C $3 \times 9 = 27$

D $6 \div 2 = 3$

 Test Tip **Check your work.**

See item 5. To check your work, place your answer in the table. Then make sure your number continues the pattern in the table.

5. Which number will complete the table below? (p. 256)

Cars	5	6	7	8	9
Wheels	20	24	28	32	▪

A 40

B 38

C 36

D 34

6. ✏️ WRITE Math ▸ **Explain** how you can use a related multiplication fact to find $49 \div 7$. (p. 324)

Geometry

7. How many lines of symmetry does the figure below appear to have? (p. 386)

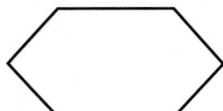

A 1

B 2

C 3

D 4

8. Which describes the triangle? (p. 358)

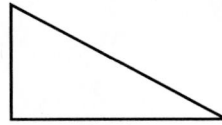

A right

B acute

C isosceles

D obtuse

9. **WRITE Math** ▶ What solid figure is shown? **Explain** how you know. (p. 400)

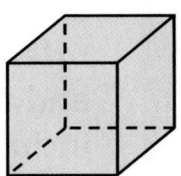

Data Analysis and Probability

10. How many more books did Julie read than Stephen? (p. 154)

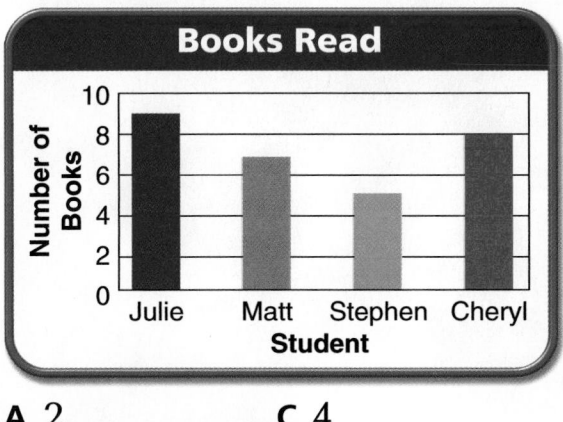

A 2   **C** 4

B 3   **D** 5

11. Kenny pulls a marble out of the bag without looking. Which color marble is he least likely to pull? (p. 178)

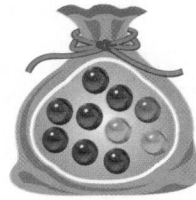

A Green

B Blue

C Red

D Yellow

12. **WRITE Math** ▶ Jennifer made a pictograph showing her classmates' favorite colors. The key for the graph is: Each 👤 = 6 students. How many symbols should she use to show that 15 students chose red as their favorite color? **Explain.** (p. 148)

19 Understand Decimals

Investigate

The table shows the top 5 runners who ran in the 100-meter race. The race times for runners are in decimals to show 100 parts of a second. Select two of the runners. Write each of their times in word form.

Special Olympics 100-Meter Run

Athlete	Time in Seconds
Rachel	17.24
Tim	17.37
Kayla	17.58
Caleb	18.84
Thomas	19.02

FAST FACT

Special Olympics offers 30 individual and team sports, including gymnastics, roller skating, and volleyball.

GO ONLINE
Technology
Student pages are available in the Student eBook.

Check your understanding of important skills
needed for success in Chapter 19.

▶ Name the Fraction
Write a fraction for the shaded part.

1.

2.

3.

4.

5.

6.

7.

8.

9.

▶ Name the Shaded Part
Write a fraction for the shaded part.

10.

11.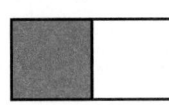

12.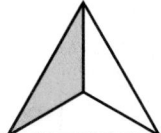

13.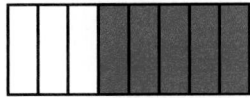

14.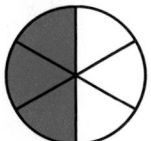

15.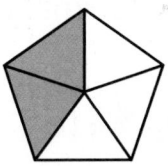

VOCABULARY POWER

CHAPTER VOCABULARY

decimal
hundredth
tenth

WARM-UP WORDS

decimal A number with one or more digits to the right of the decimal point

hundredth One of one hundred equal parts

tenth One of ten equal parts

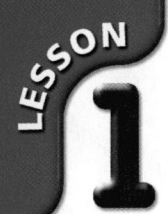
1 Model Tenths

OBJECTIVE: Model and write fractions and decimals in tenths.

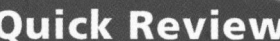
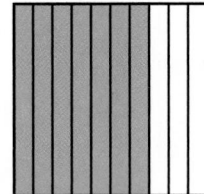 **Learn**

A **decimal** is a number with one or more digits to the right of the decimal point. A decimal shows values less than one, such as tenths.

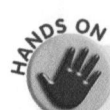 This model has 10 equal parts.
Each equal part is one **tenth**.
Seven parts are shaded.

Vocabulary

decimal

tenth

Fraction

Write: $\frac{7}{10}$

Read: seven tenths

Decimal

Write: 0.7

↳ decimal point

Read: seven tenths

Math Idea

A decimal is another way to write a fraction.

The fraction $\frac{7}{10}$ and the decimal 0.7 name the same amount.

You can use a decimal model to show part of a whole.

Activity

Materials ■ decimal model

Use a decimal model to show 0.3, or $\frac{3}{10}$.

Step 1	Step 2
Shade the decimal model to show three tenths. 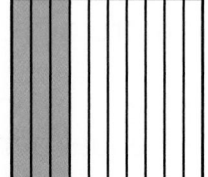	Write the fraction and the decimal for the amount of the model you shaded. **Fraction:** $\frac{3}{10}$ **Decimal:** 0.3

• How do you read 0.3?

• **What if** you shaded the model to show 0.6? How many parts would be shaded?

A decimal can name part of a whole or part of a group.

Example

There are 10 beanbags.
Five of the beanbags are red.

What part of the group of beanbags are red?

Fraction   **Decimal**

Write: $\frac{5}{10}$ Write: 0.5

                   ↑ decimal point

Read: five tenths   **Read:** five tenths

So, $\frac{5}{10}$, or 0.5, of the beanbags are red.

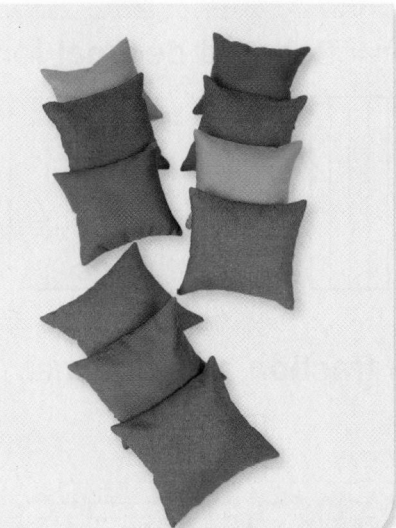

You can show tenths in different ways.

Use a decimal model.	Use a fraction.	Use a decimal place-value chart.
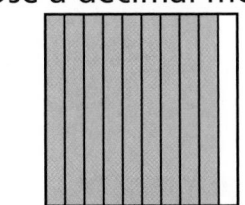	$\frac{9}{10}$	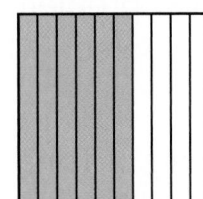

Use a decimal place-value chart.

ONES	.	TENTHS
0	.	9

Write: 0.9

Read: nine tenths

Guided Practice

1. What fraction of the square is shaded?

   Think: How many tenths are shaded?

Write the fraction and decimal for the shaded part.

2.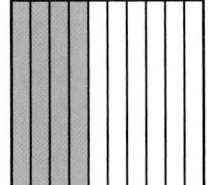

3.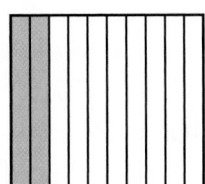

✔ 4.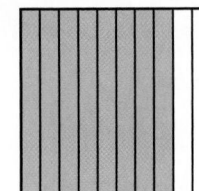

✔ 5.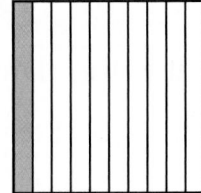

6. **TALK Math** Explain how fractions and decimals are related.

Write the fraction and decimal for the shaded part.

7.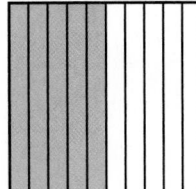

8.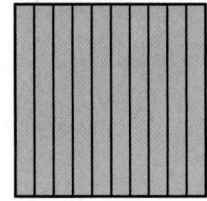

9.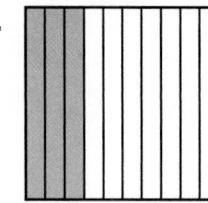

10.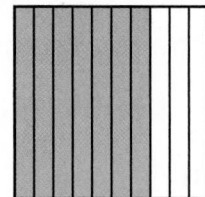

Write each fraction as a decimal.

11. $\frac{9}{10}$
12. $\frac{2}{10}$
13. $\frac{8}{10}$
14. $\frac{6}{10}$
15. $\frac{5}{10}$

Write each decimal as a fraction.

16.

ONES	.	TENTHS
0	.	4

17.

ONES	.	TENTHS
0	.	7

18.

ONES	.	TENTHS
0	.	1

19. 0.5
20. 0.2
21. 0.9
22. 0.3
23. 0.8

USE DATA For 24–26, use the pictograph.

24. Each player tossed 10 beanbags. The pictograph shows how many bags each person got in the goal. Write a decimal to show what part of the group of beanbags Travis tossed in the goal.

25. **Pose a Problem** Look back at Problem 24. Write a similar problem by changing the name of the person who tossed the beanbags.

26. Write a decimal for the part of Trina's tosses that did NOT land in the goal.

Beanbag Toss Results	
Name	**Tosses in Goal**
Travis	◇ ◇ ◇ ◇
Lee	◇ ◇ ◇
Carter	◇ ◇ ◇ ◇ ◇
Trina	◇ ◇ ◇ ◇ ◇ ◇

Key: Each ◇ = 1 beanbag.

27. **WRITE Math** **What's the Question?** Lisa tossed 10 beanbags and missed the goal 4 times. The answer is 0.6.

Mixed Review and Test Prep

28. What is the difference? (p. 84)

$$7,691 - 3,852 = \blacksquare$$

29. If $6 \times 9 = 54$, then what is 9×6?

(p. 262)

30. **Test Prep** Which shows the fraction for 0.2?

A $\frac{0}{2}$ B $\frac{1}{2}$ C $\frac{2}{10}$ D $\frac{8}{10}$

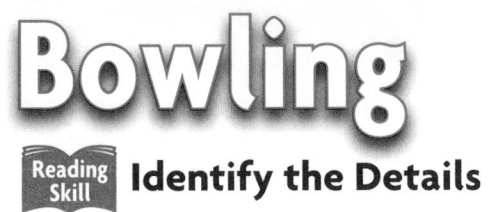

Bowling

Reading Skill **Identify the Details**

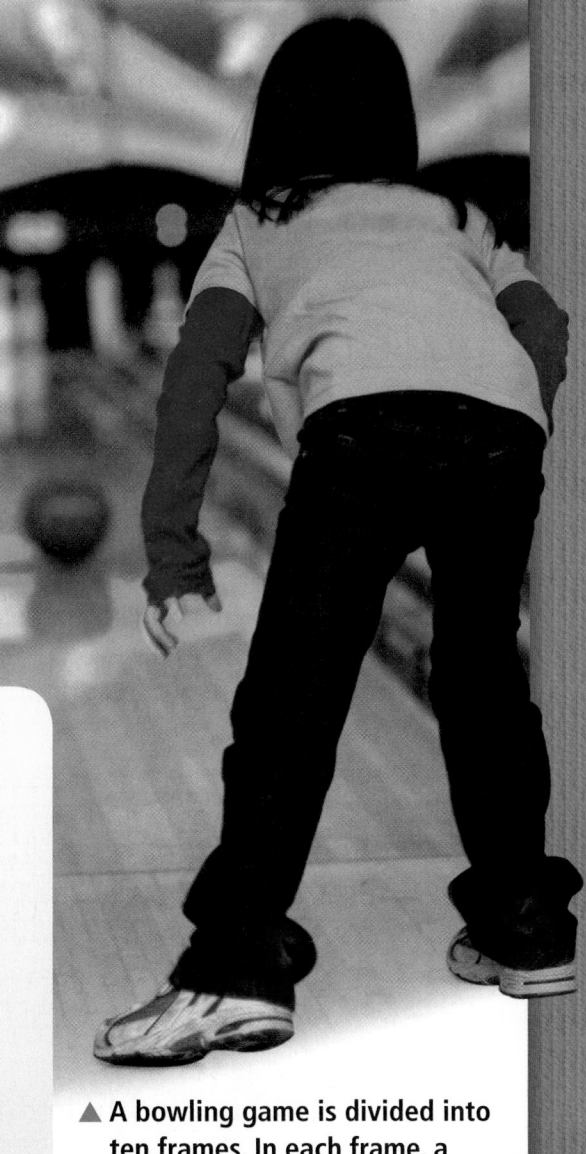

▲ A bowling game is divided into ten frames. In each frame, a player is given two chances to knock down all ten pins.

Bowling is a game in which players roll a ball to knock down ten pins. Each time you knock down a pin, you earn a point.

A player gets a *strike* when he or she knocks down all ten pins on the first roll. This is shown on the scorecard with an X. A player who knocks down all ten pins by the second roll gets a *spare*. A spare is shown on the scorecard with a /.

1	2	3	4	5	6	7	8	9	10
X	4 3	7 2	6 /	4 4	X	X	9 0	5 /	0 7

Look at the scorecard above. In what fraction of the ten frames did the bowler score a strike? Write your answer as a fraction and a decimal.

You can identify the details to help you answer the question.

Question: In what fraction of the frames did the bowler score a strike?

Details: A bowling game is divided into 10 frames. A strike is shown on the scorecard with an X.

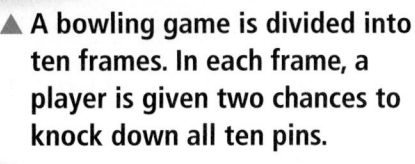

Problem Solving **Identify the details to solve the problems.**

1. Solve the problem above. **Explain** your answer.

2. Harvey went bowling. In his first game, he got two strikes and three spares. Write a decimal to show in what fraction of the ten frames Harvey knocked down all of the pins.

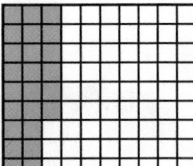

Model Hundredths

OBJECTIVE: Model and write fractions and decimals in hundredths.

Learn

This decimal model has 100 equal parts. Each equal part is one **hundredth**. In the model, 26 parts are shaded.

You can write the shaded parts as a decimal or as a fraction.

Write: 0.26, or $\frac{26}{100}$

Read: twenty-six hundredths

Vocabulary

hundredth

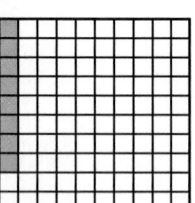

Activity   **Materials** ▪ decimal model

Use a decimal model to show 0.08, or $\frac{8}{100}$.

Step 1	Step 2
Shade the decimal model to show eight hundredths.	Write the fraction and the decimal for the amount you shaded. **Fraction:** $\frac{8}{100}$ **Decimal:** 0.08 **Read:** eight hundredths

You can show hundredths in different ways.

Use a model.	Use a fraction.	Use a place-value chart.
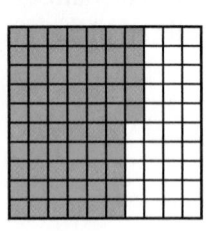	$\frac{65}{100}$	

ONES	.	TENTHS	HUNDREDTHS
0	.	6	5

Write: 0.65
Read: sixty-five hundredths
Expanded form: 0.6 + 0.05

Guided Practice

1. Write the fraction and the decimal for the model.

   Think: How many of the hundredths are shaded?

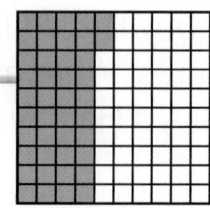

Write each fraction as a decimal. Use a decimal model to help.

2. $\frac{16}{100}$ **3.** $\frac{5}{100}$ **4.** $\frac{37}{100}$ ✓**5.** $\frac{60}{100}$ ✓**6.** $\frac{51}{100}$

7. [TALK Math] **Explain** how to write 0.32 as a fraction.

Independent Practice and Problem Solving

Write each fraction as a decimal. Use a decimal model to help.

8. $\frac{29}{100}$ **9.** $\frac{10}{100}$ **10.** $\frac{75}{100}$ **11.** $\frac{43}{100}$ **12.** $\frac{82}{100}$

Write each decimal as a fraction.

13.

ONES	.	TENTHS	HUNDREDTHS
0	.	1	2

14.

ONES	.	TENTHS	HUNDREDTHS
0	.	5	9

Write each decimal as a fraction and in expanded form.

15. 0.34   **16.** 0.18   **17.** 0.90   **18.** 0.03   **19.** 0.66

20. Reasoning There are 100 centimeters in 1 meter. Measure the paper clip in centimeters. Then write the length as a fraction and as a decimal of a meter.

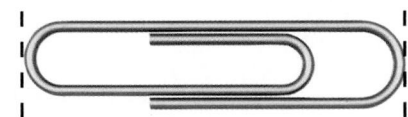

21. Lou surveyed 100 students. Of the 100 students, 0.38 of them have a dog for a pet. How many students have a dog?

22. [WRITE Math] ▸ **What's the Error?** Nikki says 0.20 is equal to $\frac{2}{100}$. Describe her error.

Mixed Review and Test Prep

23. Kim lives $\frac{9}{10}$ of a mile from Lydia. Write the distance as a decimal. (p. 484)

24. A rectangle is 5 units long and 3 units wide. What is the perimeter?

(Grade 2)

25. Test Prep Which decimal shows eight hundredths?

A 8.00   **C** 0.08

B 0.80   **D** 0.008

(Extra Practice) on page 500, Set B

CD ROM **Technology**
Use Harcourt Mega Math, Fraction
Action, *Fraction Flare Up,* Levels L, N.

Decimals Greater Than One

OBJECTIVE: Read and write decimals greater than one.

Learn

PROBLEM Mr. Branson is painting the fence around his yard. There are 10 sections. Each section has 10 boards. Mr. Branson has painted 16 boards so far. What decimal shows how many sections he has painted?

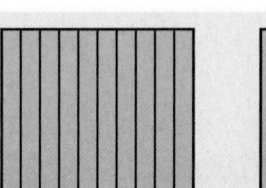 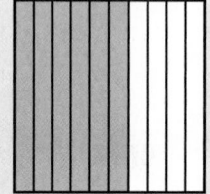

ONES	.	TENTHS
1	.	6

Write: 1.6
Read: one and six tenths
Expanded form: 1 + 0.6

So, Mr. Branson has painted 1.6 sections of fence.

Example

Show 2.84 in different ways.

ONES	.	TENTHS	HUNDREDTHS
2	.	8	4

Standard form: 2.84
Word form: two and eighty-four hundredths
Expanded form: 2 + 0.8 + 0.04
2.84 is the same as 2 ones 8 tenths 4 hundredths.

ERROR ALERT

When reading a decimal, use the place of the digit farthest to the right. 2.84 is read as two and eighty-four hundredths and not as two and eighty-four tenths.

Guided Practice

1. Write the decimal in expanded form.

ONES	.	TENTHS
3	.	2

■ + ■

Write the word form and the expanded form for each.

✓ **2.**

ONES	.	TENTHS
7	.	5

✓ **3.**

ONES	.	TENTHS	HUNDREDTHS
4	.	9	8

4. **TALK Math** **Explain** how to write five and thirty-one hundredths as a decimal.

Independent Practice and Problem Solving

Write the word form and the expanded form for each.

5.

ONES	.	TENTHS
6	.	4

6.

ONES	.	TENTHS	HUNDREDTHS
9	.	7	0

7. 1.53   **8.** 8.6   **9.** 3.26   **10.** 5.9   **11.** 2.48

Write the decimal for each.

12. four and three tenths   **13.** seven and two hundredths   **14.** nine and one tenth

15. Ms. Rich shares 2 boxes of markers and $\frac{7}{10}$ of another box of markers with her class. Write a decimal to show the total number of boxes of markers Ms. Rich shares.

16. **Reasoning** I am a decimal greater than 1 but less than 3. All my digits are even. My tenths digit is three times my ones digit. My hundredths digit is 8. What decimal am I?

17. Mr. Vo has 3 full boxes of crayons and $\frac{85}{100}$ of another box of crayons. Write a decimal to show the total number of boxes of crayons Mr. Vo has.

18. **WRITE Math** ▸ Does six and eighty hundredths name the same amount as six and eight tenths? **Explain.**

Mixed Review and Test Prep

19. What is the range of these numbers? (p. 162)

42, 36, 41, 35, 48, 44

20. Trace the figure and draw the line or lines of symmetry. (p. 386)

21. **Test Prep** Which shows 6.05 written in word form?

  A six hundred five

  B six and five hundredths

  C six and five tenths

  D six and fifty hundredths

Extra Practice on page 500, Set C

4 Compare and Order Decimals

OBJECTIVE: Compare and order decimals.

Quick Review

Write <, >, or = for each ●.

1. 9 ● 5
2. 63 ● 37
3. 449 ● 458
4. 2,698 ● 2,689
5. 1,346 ● 1,463

Learn

You can use models and place value charts to compare decimals. Compare 0.3 and 0.7.

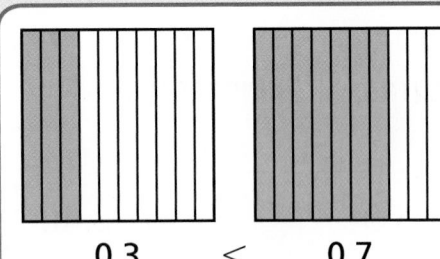

ONES	.	TENTHS
0	.	3
0	.	7

0.3 < 0.7

- **Compare ones.** 0 ones = 0 ones
- **Compare tenths.** 3 tenths < 7 tenths

So, 0.3 is less than 0.7.

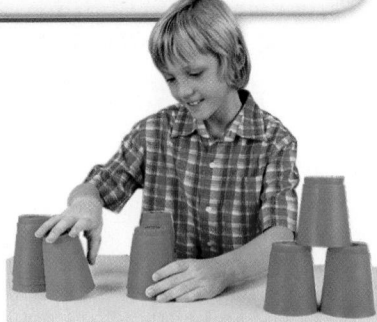

▲ Sport stacking is a sport where you race to stack and unstack cups in a special order.

In sport stacking, times are compared in hundredths of seconds. At a competition, Drew's time was 5.62 seconds. Mel's time was 5.47 seconds. Compare 5.62 and 5.47.

ONES	.	TENTHS	HUNDREDTHS
5	.	6	2
5	.	4	7

5.62 > 5.47

- Begin with the digit in the greatest place value.
- **Compare the ones.** 5 ones = 5 ones
- **Compare the tenths.** 6 tenths > 4 tenths

So, 5.62 is greater than 5.47.

Sam's time at the same competition was 5.49 seconds. Order 5.49, 5.62, and 5.47 from least to greatest.

ONES	.	TENTHS	HUNDREDTHS
5	.	4	9
5	.	6	2
5	.	4	7

- **Compare the ones.** 5 = 5 = 5
- **Compare the tenths.** 6 > 4, so 5.62 is the greatest.
- **Compare the hundredths.** 7 < 9, so 5.47 < 5.49.

So, the numbers from least to greatest are 5.47, 5.49, 5.62.

Guided Practice

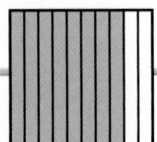
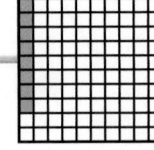

1. Which is greater, 0.8 or 0.08?

Compare. Write <, >, or = for each ●.

2.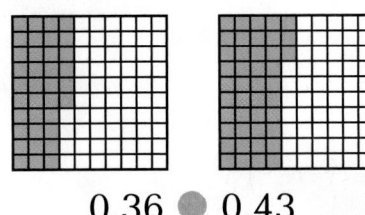

0.36 ● 0.43

3.

ONES	.	TENTHS
1	.	7
1	.	5

1.7 ● 1.5

4. [TALK Math] **Explain** how to order 0.4, 0.7, and 0.2 from least to greatest.

Independent Practice and Problem Solving

Compare. Write <, >, or = for each ●.

5.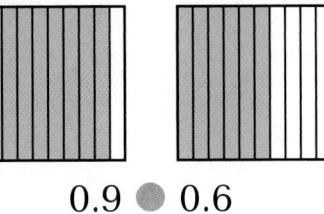

0.9 ● 0.6

6.

ONES	.	TENTHS	HUNDREDTHS
2	.	6	1
2	.	6	4

2.61 ● 2.64

7. 3.1 ● 2.8   **8.** 4.5 ● 4.3   **9.** 0.19 ● 0.24   **10.** 1.75 ● 1.57

Order the decimals from least to greatest.

11. 0.2, 0.5, 0.12   **12.** 0.6, 0.09, 0.1   **13.** 1.63, 1.89, 1.78

USE DATA For 14–16, use the table.

14. The stacker who holds the World Record for the 3-6-3 stack has the least time listed in the table. Who holds the World Record?

15. **Open-Ended** Jay said his time was greater than Timo's, but less than Robin's. What could his time be?

3-6-3 Stack Times	
Name	**Time in Seconds**
Robin Stangenberg	2.91
Emily Fox	2.72
Timo Reuhl	2.78

16. [WRITE Math] ▸ Brennan Fox did a 3-6-3 stack in 2.81 seconds. **Explain** how 2.81 compares to the times in the table.

Mixed Review and Test Prep

17. What is 428 + 373? (p. 58)

18. What is the value of the 5 in 5,861?

(p. 10)

19. **Test Prep** Which is greater than 1.64?

A 1.7   **B** 1.5   **C** 1.47   **D** 1.08

(Extra Practice) on page 500, Set D

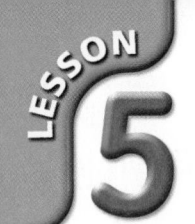

Problem Solving Workshop
Strategy: Compare Strategies

OBJECTIVE: Compare different strategies to solve problems.

Use the Strategy

PROBLEM Lynn was in a gymnastics competition. She scored 8.6 for her floor routine and 8.4 for her uneven bars routine. For which routine did she earn the greater score?

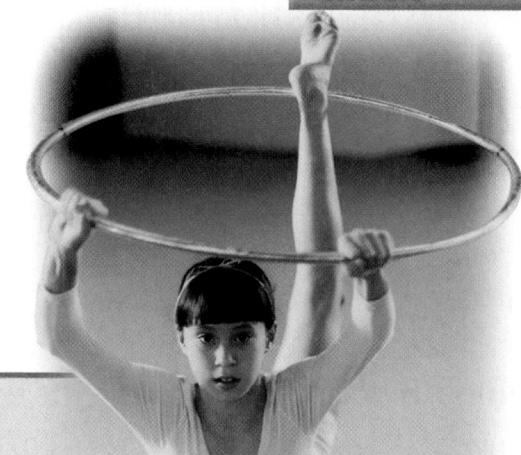

Read to Understand

Reading Skill

• **What information is given?**

• **Visualize the information.**

Plan

• **What strategy can you use to solve the problem?**

Sometimes you can use more than one strategy to solve a problem. You can *make a table* or *make a model* to solve this problem.

Solve

• **How can you use the strategies to solve the problem?**

Make a table to compare the decimals.

ONES	.	TENTHS
8	.	6
8	.	4

The ones are the same.
So, compare the tenths.
    0.6 > 0.4
    8.6 > 8.4

Make a Model to show and compare the decimals.

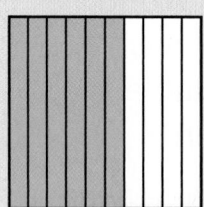 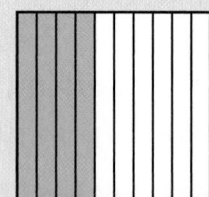

Since the ones are the same, compare the tenths.
    0.6 > 0.4
    8.6 > 8.4

So, Lynn earned a greater score for her floor routine.

Check

• **What other ways could you solve the problem?**

494

Guided Problem Solving

Choose a STRATEGY

Draw a Diagram or Picture
Make a Model or Act It Out
Make an Organized List
Find a Pattern
Make a Table or Graph
Predict and Test
Work Backward
Solve a Simpler Problem
Write an Equation
Use Logical Reasoning

1. Lynn and Shane take gymnastics classes together. Lynn lives 1.30 miles from the gym. Shane lives 1.15 miles from the gym. Who lives the least distance from the gym?

   First, choose a strategy. You can make a table or make a model.

   Then, use the strategy to solve the problem.

ONES	.	TENTHS	HUNDREDTHS
1	.	3	0
1	.	1	5

2. **What if** Nina lives 1.5 miles from the gym? How does this compare to the distances Lynn and Shane live from the gym?

3. In a gymnastics competition, Shane scored 8.39 on the rings, 8.75 on the parallel bars, and 8.7 on his floor routine. For which event did he earn the greatest score?

Mixed Strategy Practice

USE DATA For 4–8, use the table.

4. The table lists seven gymnasts and their scores in different events. Which gymnast had the greatest score on the vault?

5. Did more gymnasts score greater than 9 points or less than 9 points?

6. Which gymnast's score has a 7 in the hundredths place?

7. **Pose a Problem** Use the scores in the table to write a problem that can be solved by comparing two decimals.

8. **Open-Ended** Gretchen placed first and Beth placed third in the balance beam event. Give a possible score for the gymnast who placed second.

Gymnastics Competition		
Name	**Event**	**Points**
Tanya	Vault	8.65
Joel	Vault	8.48
Missy	Floor routine	9.20
Gretchen	Balance beam	9.54
Brad	Floor routine	8.95
Beth	Balance beam	9.37
Latesha	Vault	7.90

9. **WRITE Math** Vanessa's score on the uneven bars had the digits 5, 7, and 8. Her score was greater than 6.0 but less than 8.0. **Explain** how to find Vanessa's score.

Relate Fractions, Decimals, and Money

OBJECTIVE: Relate fractions, decimals, and money.

Learn

PROBLEM Julie and Sarah have $1.00 in quarters. They want to share the quarters equally. How many should each girl get? How much money is this?

Math Idea
Amounts less than $1.00 can be written as a fraction of a dollar.

$$\$0.75 = \frac{75}{100}$$

Example You can relate money and fractions.

4 quarters = 1 dollar = $1.00

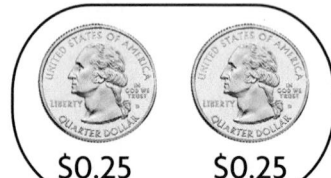 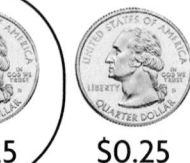 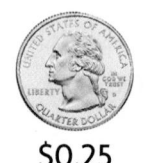

$0.25 $0.25 $0.25 $0.25

2 quarters are $\frac{2}{4}$, or $\frac{1}{2}$, of a dollar.

$\frac{1}{2}$ of a dollar = $0.50, or 50 cents

So, each girl should get 2 quarters, or $0.50.

More Examples

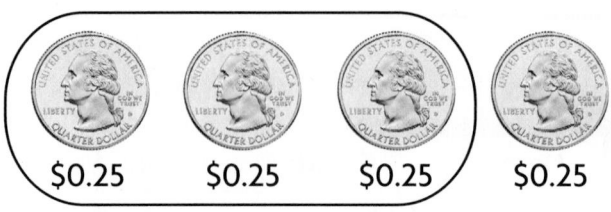

$0.25 $0.25 $0.25 $0.25

3 quarters are $\frac{3}{4}$ of a dollar.

$\frac{3}{4}$ of a dollar = $0.75, or 75 cents

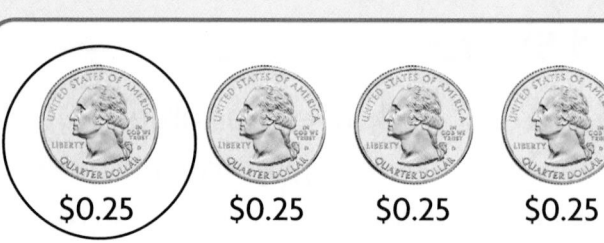

$0.25 $0.25 $0.25 $0.25

1 quarter is $\frac{1}{4}$ of a dollar.

$\frac{1}{4}$ of a dollar = $0.25, or 25 cents

10 dimes = 1 dollar = $1.00

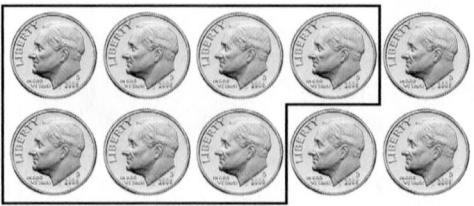

7 dimes are $\frac{7}{10}$ of a dollar.

$\frac{7}{10}$ of a dollar = $0.70, or 70 cents

100 pennies = 1 dollar = $1.00

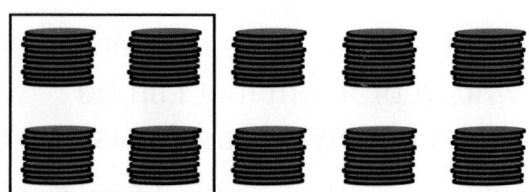

40 pennies are $\frac{40}{100}$ of a dollar.

$\frac{40}{100}$ of a dollar = $0.40, or 40 cents

Coin Combinations

You can write an amount of money as a decimal and
as a fraction of a dollar.

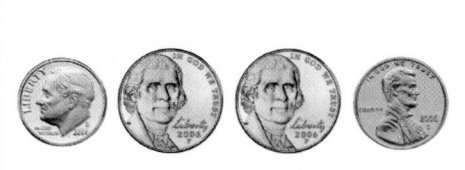

$0.21, or $\frac{21}{100}$ of a dollar

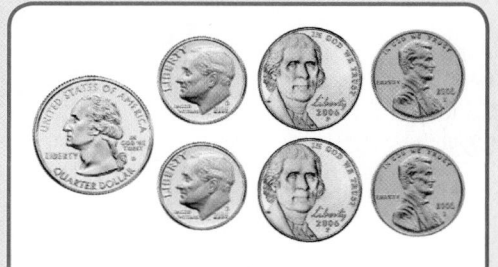

$0.57, or $\frac{57}{100}$ of a dollar

The table shows how to relate money, fractions, and decimals.

Coins	Money Amount	Fraction of a Dollar	Decimal
3 pennies	$0.03	$\frac{3}{100}$	0.03
9 dimes	$0.90	$\frac{90}{100}$ or $\frac{9}{10}$	0.90
1 quarter	$0.25	$\frac{25}{100}$ or $\frac{1}{4}$	0.25
6 nickels	$0.30	$\frac{30}{100}$ or $\frac{3}{10}$	0.30
2 quarters 1 dime	$0.60	$\frac{60}{100}$ or $\frac{6}{10}$	0.60

Guided Practice

1. Write the amount of money as a decimal.
   5 pennies $= \frac{5}{100} = $ ■

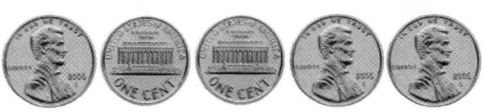

Write the amount of money shown. Then write the
amount as a fraction of a dollar.

2.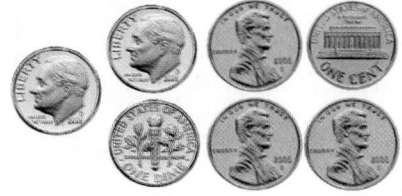

✓3.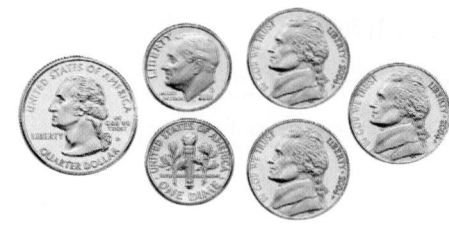

Write the money amount for each fraction of a dollar.

4. $\frac{92}{100}$ 5. $\frac{7}{100}$ 6. $\frac{16}{100}$ 7. $\frac{53}{100}$ ✓8. $\frac{71}{100}$

9. **TALK Math** Explain how $0.84 and $\frac{84}{100}$ are related.

Write the amount of money shown. Then write the amount as a fraction of a dollar.

10.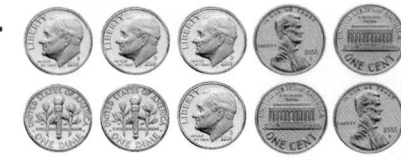

11.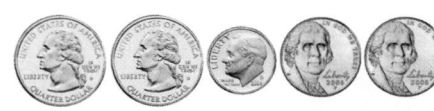

12.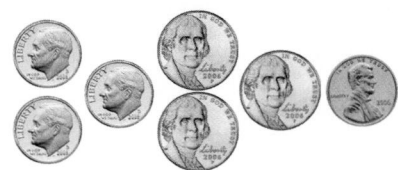

13.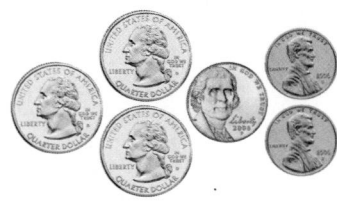

Write the money amount for each fraction of a dollar.

14. $\frac{27}{100}$ **15.** $\frac{4}{100}$ **16.** $\frac{75}{100}$ **17.** $\frac{98}{100}$ **18.** $\frac{61}{100}$

19. $\frac{83}{100}$ **20.** $\frac{11}{100}$ **21.** $\frac{32}{100}$ **22.** $\frac{9}{100}$ **23.** $\frac{52}{100}$

Write each money amount as a fraction of a dollar.

24. $0.68 **25.** $0.09 **26.** $0.20 **27.** $0.13 **28.** $0.47

29. $0.59 **30.** $0.70 **31.** $0.88 **32.** $0.35 **33.** $0.16

Write the money amount.

34. six hundredths of a dollar

35. fifty-two hundredths of a dollar

36. ninety hundredths of a dollar

USE DATA For 37–38, use the table.

37. The table shows the coins three students have. Write Nick's total amount as a fraction of a dollar.

38. Kim spent $\frac{40}{100}$ of a dollar on a snack. Write the amount she has left as a decimal.

39. **Reasoning** Travis has $\frac{1}{2}$ of a dollar. He has at least two different coins in his pocket. Draw two possible sets of coins that Travis could have.

Pocket Change				
Name	Quarters	Dimes	Nickels	Pennies
Kim	1	3	2	3
Tony	0	6	1	6
Nick	2	4	0	2

40. **WRITE Math** Would you rather have $0.25 or $\frac{3}{10}$ of a dollar? **Explain** why.

Showing Money with Decimal Models

You can use decimal models to show parts of a dollar.

Examples

Use a tenths model.
To show $0.70, shade 7 parts on the model.

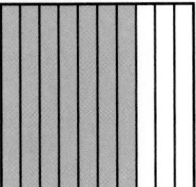

Use a hundredths model.
To show $0.38, shade 38 parts on the model.

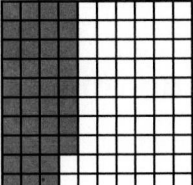

Try It

Write the amount of money shown by each model.

41.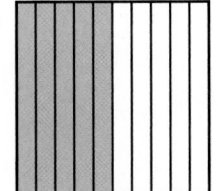

42.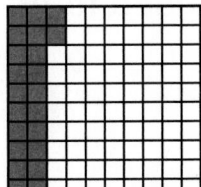

43.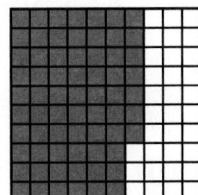

44.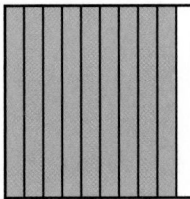

Mixed Review and Test Prep

45. Becky earns $7 an hour. Write a number sentence to find how many hours Becky needs to work to earn $56. (p. 290)

46. On Saturday, Greg rode his bike 4.25 miles and Nate rode his bike 4.40 miles. Who rode farther? (p. 492)

47. Test Prep Which amount equals $\frac{7}{10}$ of a dollar?

   A $0.07   **C** $0.70

   B $0.17   **D** $7.00

48. Test Prep Which amount of money shows the decimal $0.55?

A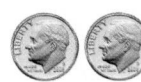

B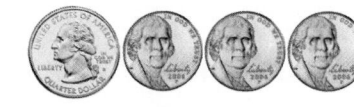

C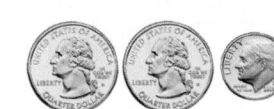

D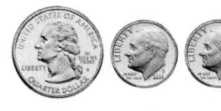

Extra Practice

Set A Write the fraction and decimal for the shaded part. (pp. 484–487)

1.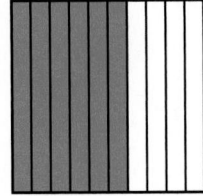
2.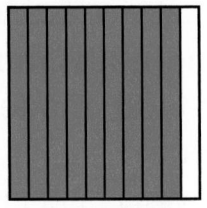
3.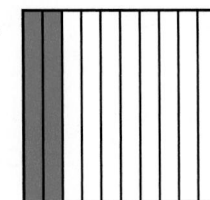
4.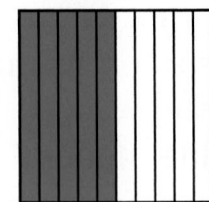

Write each fraction as a decimal.

5. $\frac{7}{10}$
6. $\frac{4}{10}$
7. $\frac{1}{10}$
8. $\frac{9}{10}$
9. $\frac{3}{10}$

Set B Write each fraction as a decimal. Use a decimal model to help. (pp. 488–489)

1. $\frac{35}{100}$
2. $\frac{17}{100}$
3. $\frac{80}{100}$
4. $\frac{62}{100}$
5. $\frac{94}{100}$

Write each decimal as a fraction and in expanded form.

6. 0.55
7. 0.72
8. 0.05
9. 0.40
10. 0.27

Set C Write the word form and the expanded form for each. (pp. 490–491)

1. 2.76
2. 3.15
3. 5.2
4. 9.61
5. 1.74

Set D Compare. Write <, >, or = for each ●. (pp. 492–493)

1. 1.2 ● 1.3
2. 5.8 ● 4.9
3. 0.27 ● 0.18
4. 2.79 ● 2.97

5. Order 0.5, 0.41, and 0.07 from least to greatest.

6. Order 1.89, 1.86, and 1.91 from greatest to least.

Set E Write the money amount for each fraction of a dollar. (pp. 496–499)

1. $\frac{52}{100}$
2. $\frac{82}{100}$
3. $\frac{14}{100}$
4. $\frac{61}{100}$
5. $\frac{49}{100}$

CD ROM Technology
Use Harcourt Mega Math, Fraction Action,
Fraction Flare Up, Levels L, N.

Decimal Trains

PRACTICE GAME

Draw It!
2 players

Connect It!
- Decimal Trains gameboard for each player
- Game cards

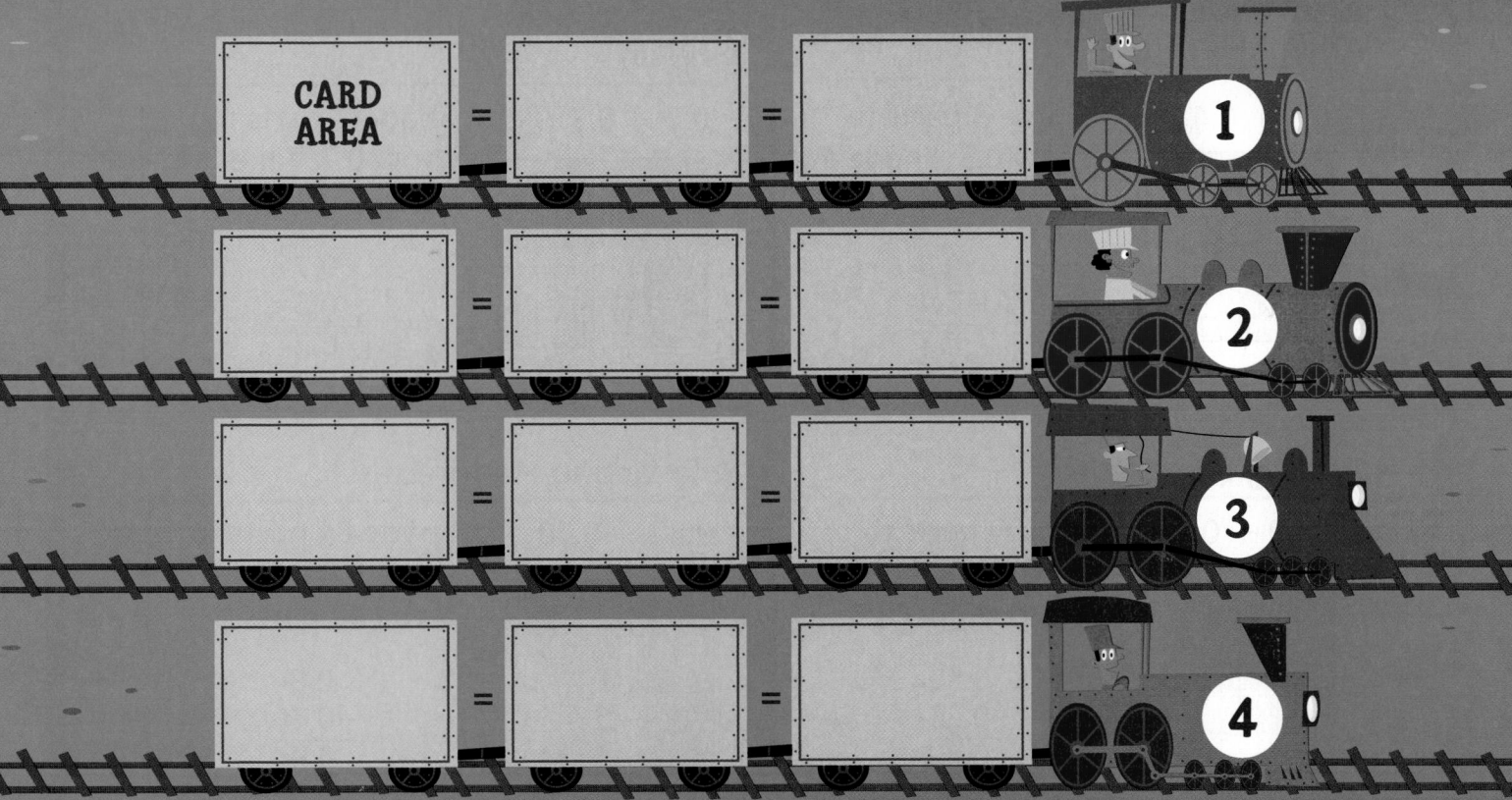

CARD AREA = =

Make a Train!

- Each player receives a gameboard.
- Shuffle the cards. Deal 5 cards to each player. Put remaining cards facedown in a pile.
- Players look at their cards and begin making trains by placing any equivalent fractions, decimals, and money on their gameboards.
- Player 1 draws a card from the pile and may begin a new train with it, add it to a train, or discard it.

- Player 2 may take the top card from the discard pile or draw the next card from the facedown pile. Players draw 1 card per turn.
- Play continues until a player has completed 4 trains. Cards in the same train must have a fraction, decimal, and money amount that are equal.
- The first player to complete all 4 trains wins the game.

MATH POWER

Add and Subtract Decimals

SHADING PARTS

Cody wants to add 0.3 and 0.4. You can use decimal models or paper and pencil to add and subtract decimals.

Examples

Adding Tenths

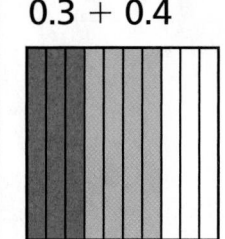

0.3 + 0.4

Shade 3 parts to show 0.3. Shade 4 parts to show 0.4.

$$\begin{array}{r} 0.3 \\ +0.4 \\ \hline 0.7 \end{array}$$

Subtracting Tenths

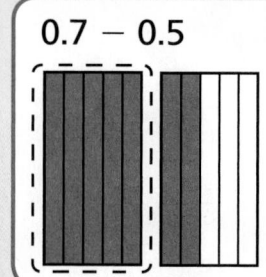

0.7 − 0.5

Shade 7 parts to show 0.7. Take away 5 parts.

$$\begin{array}{r} 0.7 \\ -0.5 \\ \hline 0.2 \end{array}$$

Adding Hundredths

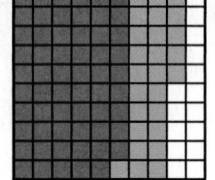

0.59 + 0.26

Shade 59 parts to show 0.59. Shade 26 parts to show 0.26.

$$\begin{array}{r} 0.59 \\ +0.26 \\ \hline 0.85 \end{array}$$

Subtracting Hundredths

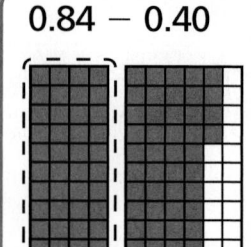

0.84 − 0.40

Shade 84 parts to show 0.84. Take away 40 parts.

$$\begin{array}{r} 0.84 \\ -0.40 \\ \hline 0.44 \end{array}$$

Try It

Add or subtract.

1. $\begin{array}{r} 0.54 \\ +0.39 \\ \hline \end{array}$

2. $\begin{array}{r} 0.9 \\ -0.3 \\ \hline \end{array}$

3. $\begin{array}{r} 3.46 \\ +1.44 \\ \hline \end{array}$

4. $\begin{array}{r} 1.75 \\ +0.52 \\ \hline \end{array}$

5. $\begin{array}{r} 5.67 \\ -2.80 \\ \hline \end{array}$

6. $\begin{array}{r} 0.4 \\ +0.6 \\ \hline \end{array}$

7. $\begin{array}{r} 0.87 \\ -0.53 \\ \hline \end{array}$

8. $\begin{array}{r} 6.5 \\ -3.8 \\ \hline \end{array}$

9. $\begin{array}{r} 1.6 \\ +0.8 \\ \hline \end{array}$

10. $\begin{array}{r} 1.57 \\ -1.14 \\ \hline \end{array}$

11. **WRITE Math** ▸ **Explain** how to find the sum of 1.15 and 2.64 by using decimal models or paper and pencil.

Chapter 19 Review/Test

Check Vocabulary and Concepts

Choose the best term from the box.

VOCABULARY

decimal
hundredth
tenth

1. A number with one or more digits to the right of the decimal point is called a ___?___. (p. 484)

2. A ___?___ is one of one hundred equal parts. (p. 488)

Check Skills

Write each fraction as a decimal. (pp. 484–487, 488–489)

3. $\dfrac{4}{10}$　　　**4.** $\dfrac{7}{10}$　　　**5.** $\dfrac{61}{100}$　　　**6.** $\dfrac{28}{100}$　　　**7.** $\dfrac{95}{100}$

Write each decimal as a fraction.

8.

ONES	.	TENTHS
0	.	9

9.

ONES	.	TENTHS	HUNDREDTHS
0	.	3	1

Write the word form and the expanded form for each. (pp. 490–491)

10. 3.16　　　**11.** 1.22　　　**12.** 6.5　　　**13.** 9.93　　　**14.** 2.7

Compare. Write <, >, or = for each ●. (pp. 492–493)

15. 3.2 ● 2.3　　　**16.** 4.49 ● 4.09　　　**17.** 0.01 ● 0.10　　　**18.** 1.20 ● 1.25

Write each money amount as a fraction of a dollar. (pp. 496–499)

19. $0.65　　　**20.** $0.20　　　**21.** $0.84　　　**22.** $0.05　　　**23.** $0.32

Check Problem Solving

Solve. (pp. 494–495)

24. Maria has 3 kittens. Molly weighs 1.9 pounds, Max weighs 2.18 pounds, and Toby weighs 2.05 pounds. What are the weights of the kittens in order from greatest to least?

25. **WRITE Math** ▸ At the long jump competition, Harvey's first jump was 2.97 meters. His second jump was 2.86 meters. **Explain** how to find which jump was longer.

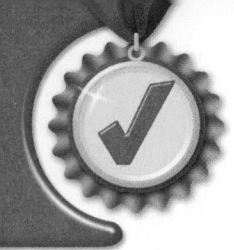

Unit Review/Test
Chapters 18–19

Multiple Choice

1. Which lists the fractions in order from least to greatest? (p. 458)

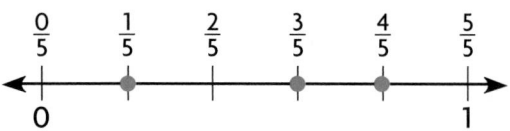

A $\frac{1}{5}, \frac{3}{5}, \frac{4}{5}$

B $\frac{1}{5}, \frac{4}{5}, \frac{3}{5}$

C $\frac{4}{5}, \frac{3}{5}, \frac{1}{5}$

D $\frac{3}{5}, \frac{4}{5}, \frac{1}{5}$

2. Gina shaded $\frac{3}{10}$ of the figure. (p. 484)

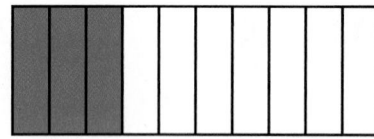

Which decimal equals $\frac{3}{10}$?

A 0.03   C 0.33

B 0.3   D 3.0

3. A pie was divided into sixths. Joey ate $\frac{1}{6}$ of the pie. Hannah ate $\frac{2}{6}$ of the pie. What fraction of the pie did Joey and Hannah eat altogether? (p. 466)

A $\frac{1}{6}$ C $\frac{3}{6}$

B $\frac{2}{6}$ D $\frac{4}{6}$

4. Which decimal is greater than 3.17? (p. 492)

A 3.2

B 3.09

C 2.18

D 2.17

5. Mandy made 12 cupcakes. She put sprinkles on $\frac{1}{3}$ of them. How many cupcakes had sprinkles? (p. 450)

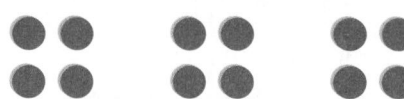

A 2

B 3

C 4

D 6

6. Which money amount is equal to $\frac{1}{2}$ of a dollar? (p. 496)

A $0.50

B $0.20

C $0.05

D $0.02

GO ONLINE Technology Use *Online Assessment.*

7. Which fraction is equivalent to $\frac{2}{5}$? (p. 454)

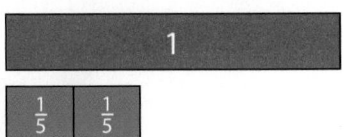

A $\frac{6}{10}$ **C** $\frac{4}{10}$

B $\frac{1}{2}$ **D** $\frac{2}{10}$

8. What fraction of the figure is shaded? (p. 446)

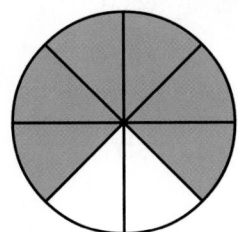

A $\frac{2}{10}$ **C** $\frac{6}{10}$

B $\frac{2}{8}$ **D** $\frac{6}{8}$

9. Len colored $\frac{7}{12}$ of his picture red and $\frac{3}{12}$ of his picture blue. How much more of the picture did Len color red than blue? (p. 470)

A $\frac{3}{12}$ **C** $\frac{5}{12}$

B $\frac{4}{12}$ **D** $\frac{10}{12}$

Short Response

10. Write the fraction and decimal for the shaded part of the model. (p. 488)

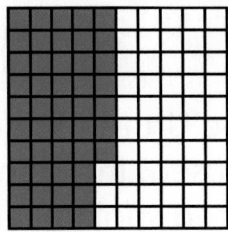

11. Write a mixed number for the parts that are shaded. (p. 464)

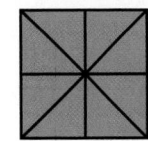 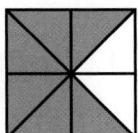

12. What is $\frac{4}{8} + \frac{3}{8}$? (p. 466)

Extended Response ▐WRITE Math▐▶

13. Lillianna gave $\frac{1}{8}$ of a batch of brownies to her sister. She took $\frac{6}{8}$ of the brownies to school. What fraction tells how much more of the brownies Lillianna took to school than she gave to her sister? **Explain** how you know. (p. 470)

14. Does one and two tenths name the same amount as one and twenty hundredths? **Explain.** (p. 490)

Hello, World

Ways to Say Hello

In the United States, about 380 different languages are used, including some signed languages. The most-used spoken languages are shown below. Tagalog is a language from the Philippines that is the sixth-most-used spoken language in the United States.

Saying Hello in Many Ways

Magandang araw!

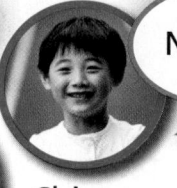

Tagalog

Ni hao!

Chinese

Hello!

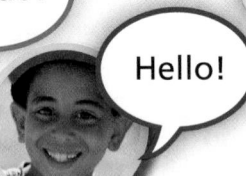

English

Guten Tag!

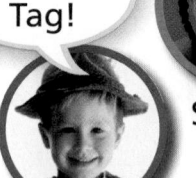

German

Hola!

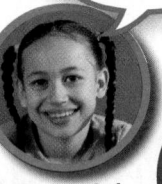

Spanish

Bonjour!

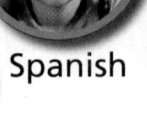

French

FACT·ACTIVITY

Hint: The vowels are A, E, I, O, and U.

For 1–3, use the greetings above.

1. How many of the greetings above begin with the letter *H*? How many greetings are shown in all? Write the fraction for the number of greetings that begin with *H*.

2. What fraction of the letters in the French greeting are vowels?

3. What fraction of the 6 greetings contain the letter *A*?

4. Say hello your way.
   - ► Work with a partner to make a new word for *hello*.
   - ► Look at your new word for *hello*. What fraction of the letters are vowels?
   - ► What other fraction can you write about the letters in your new word?

Sign Language

ALMANAC
Fact

The manual alphabet uses positions of the fingers on one hand to stand for each of the 26 letters in the alphabet.

Thomas Gallaudet and Laurent Clerc introduced sign language in the United States. They also founded the first school for the deaf in Hartford, Connecticut, in 1817.

Many people who cannot hear or speak use sign language to communicate. American Sign Language uses movements and positions of the hands and arms and expressions on the face. The American Manual Alphabet uses finger spelling.

American Manual Alphabet

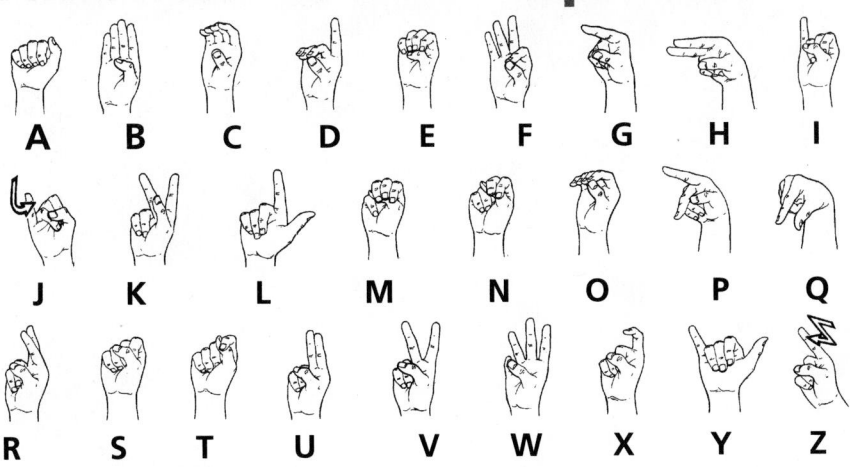

A B C D E F G H I

J K L M N O P Q

R S T U V W X Y Z

FACT·ACTIVITY

Use the alphabet chart above to help you answer the questions.

❶ To sign the letter *F*, what fraction of your fingers on one hand do you have to hold out?

❷ Look at the vowels, *A, E, I, O,* and *U.* For which vowel do you hold out $\frac{1}{5}$ of the fingers on your hand? For which vowel do you hold out $\frac{2}{5}$ of your fingers?

❸ For what fraction of the letters in *hello* do you need to hold out fingers?

❹ **WRITE Math** Explain how you found your answer to Problem 3.

UNIT 7

Measurement

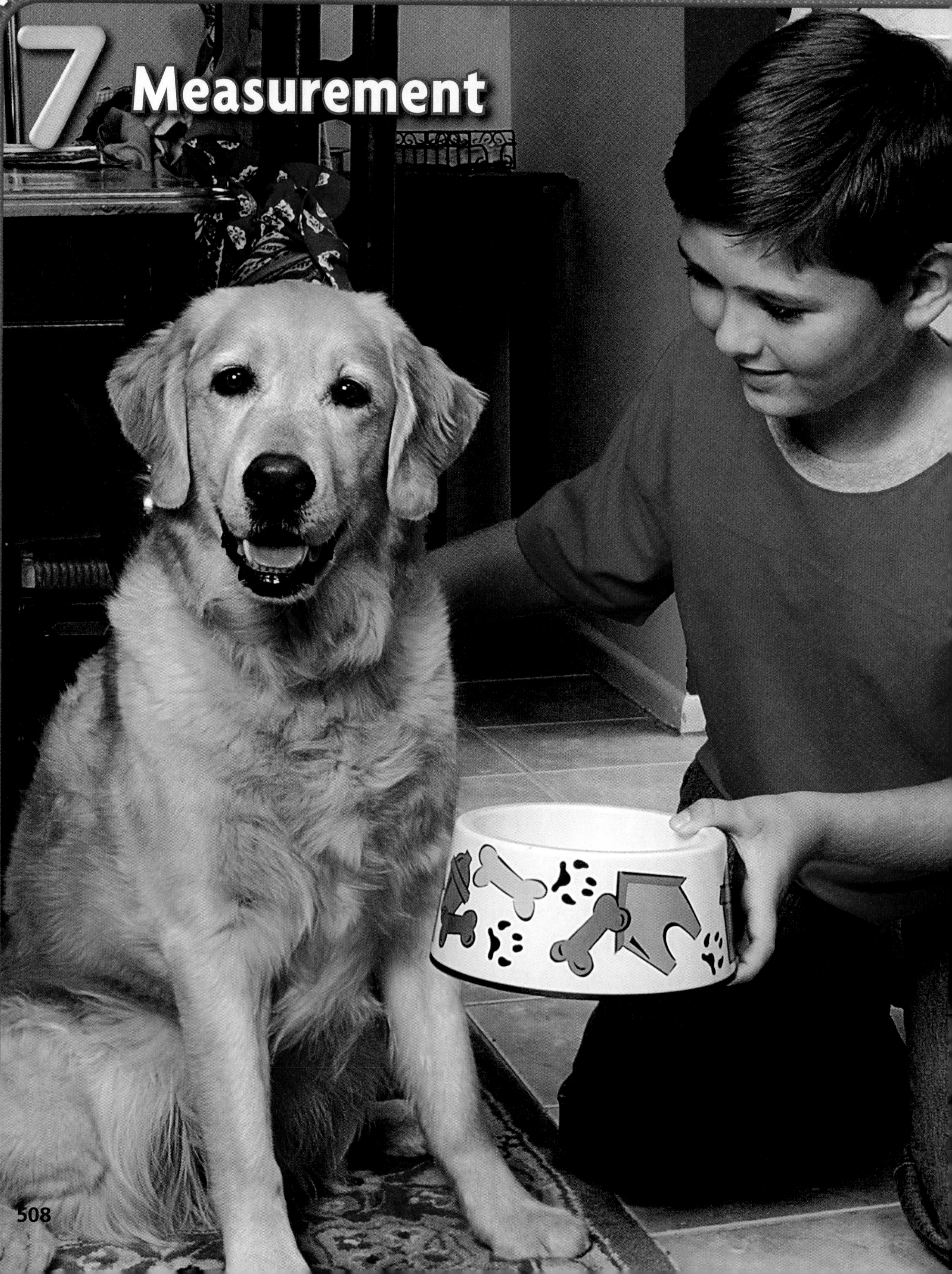

Math on Location

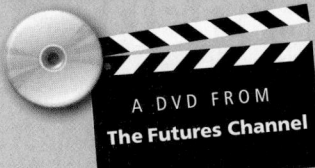

with
Chapter Projects

①

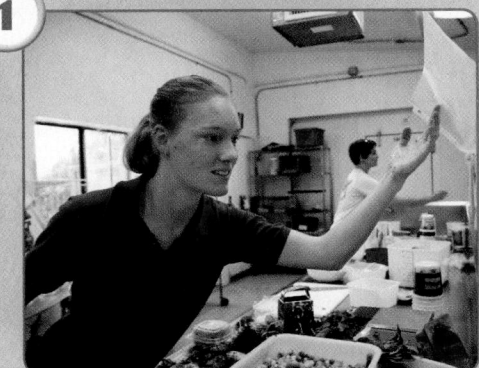

Daily chores at the zoo include cutting, measuring, and mixing food that keeps the animals healthy.

②

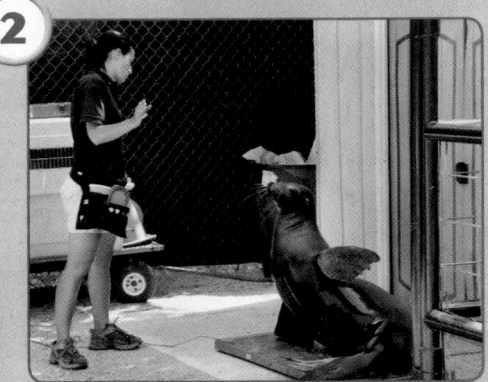

The sea lion on the scale weighs 180 pounds. The tank it swims in has more than 1,000 gallons of water.

③

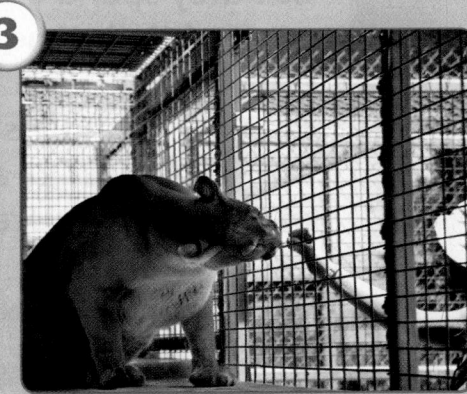

The cougar was measured to make sure its living space was large enough for it to move about easily.

VOCABULARY POWER

TALK Math

What math is being used in the **Math on Location** photographs? How can you find the weight of the sea lion in ounces?

READ Math

REVIEW VOCABULARY You learned the words below when you learned about measurement last year. How do these words relate to **Math on Location**?

gallon a customary unit for measuring capacity

kilogram a metric unit for measuring mass

ounce a customary unit for measuring weight

WRITE Math ▶

Copy and complete a Magic Square like the one below. Use what you know about measurement.

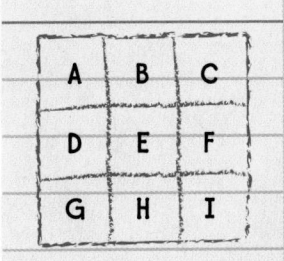

A	B	C
D	E	F
G	H	I

1. equals 12 inches
2. equals 1,000 milliliters
3. equals 4 quarts
4. equals 2 pints
5. equals 1,000 grams
6. equals 2 cups
7. equals 3 feet
8. equals 100 cm
9. equals 1,000 meters

A. liter   G. pint
B. kilometer   H. foot
C. quart   I. meter
D. yard
E. kilogram
F. gallon

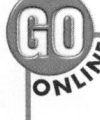

Technology
Multimedia Math Glossary link at
www.harcourtschool.com/hspmath

20 Customary Measurement

Investigate

There are 17 species of penguins. The bar graph shows the heights of some penguin species. Choose a penguin from the graph. Tell its height in inches. Then compare the penguin's height to your height.

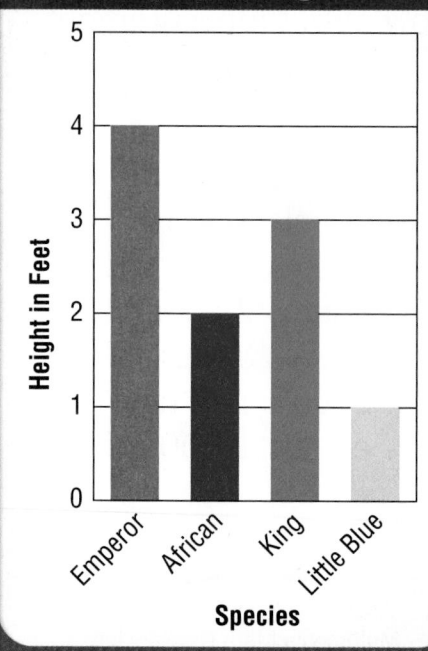

Penguin Heights

Height in Feet vs. *Species* (Emperor, African, King, Little Blue)

≡ **FAST FACT**

Penguins are birds, but they spend most of their time underwater. Emperor penguins are the largest of all penguins. They are about 4 feet tall.

GO ONLINE **Technology**
Student pages are available in the Student eBook.

Show What You Know

Check your understanding of important skills
needed for success in Chapter 20.

▶ **Use a Customary Ruler**

Use an inch ruler to measure.

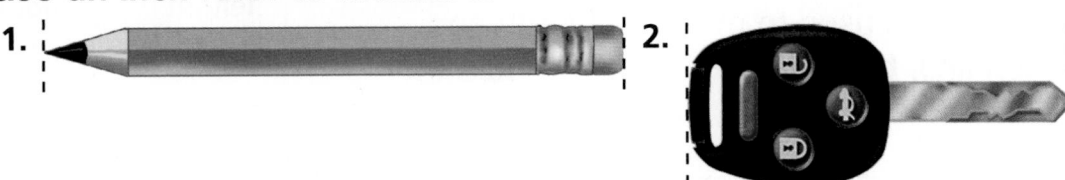

1.

2.

3.

4.

▶ **Measure to the Nearest Inch**

Use an inch ruler to measure to the nearest inch.

5.

6.

7.

8.

VOCABULARY POWER

CHAPTER VOCABULARY

capacity   mile (mi)
cup (c)   ounce (oz)
degrees   pint (pt)
  Fahrenheit (°F) pound (lb)
foot (ft)   quart (qt)
gallon (gal)   weight
length   yard (yd)

WARM-UP WORDS

capacity The amount a container will hold

length The measure of something from end to end

weight The measurement of how heavy an object is

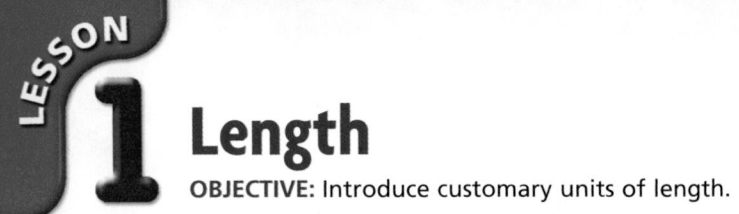

LESSON 1

Length

OBJECTIVE: Introduce customary units of length.

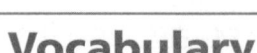
Learn

Length is the measurement of distance between two points. Customary units used to measure length and distance are inch (in.), **foot (ft)**, **yard (yd)**, and **mile (mi)**.

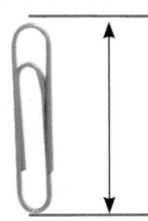

A small paper clip is about 1 inch long.

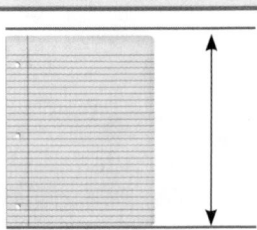

A sheet of notebook paper is about 1 foot long.

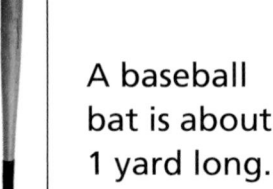

A baseball bat is about 1 yard long.

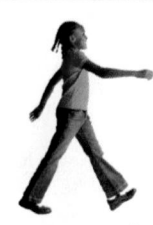

It takes about 20 minutes to walk 1 mile.

This chart shows how customary units of length are related.

Customary Units of Length

1 foot = 12 inches
1 yard = 3 feet = 36 inches
1 mile = 5,280 feet

Guided Practice

1. Would you measure the length of a pencil in inches or feet? **Think:** Is a pencil longer or shorter than a sheet of notebook paper?

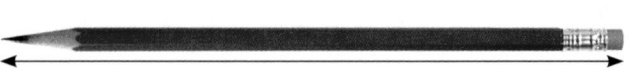

Choose the unit you would use to measure each. Write *inch*, *foot*, *yard*, or *mile*.

2.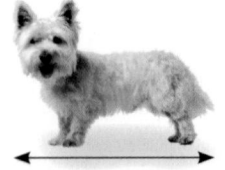

✓ 3.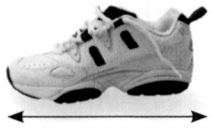

✓ 4.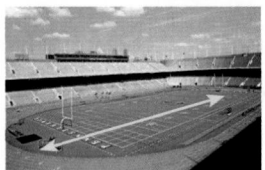

5. **TALK Math** **Explain** what unit you would use to measure the length of your classroom.

Choose the unit you would use to measure each.
Write *inch, foot, yard,* **or** *mile.*

6.

7.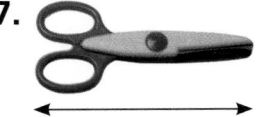

8.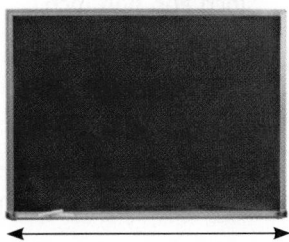

9. length of a one dollar bill

10. distance between two towns

11. length of a kitchen table

12. distance between two states

13. length of a car

14. length of a watch

15. Annie is going to walk to her friend's house. Her friend lives 3 houses away. What unit best measures how far Annie will have to walk?

16. Reasoning Jack is 2 weeks old. Andy is 12 years old. What unit would you use to measure how tall Jack is? Would you use the same unit to measure how tall Andy is? **Explain.**

17. Toni saw a giraffe at the zoo. What unit should Toni use to tell the height of the giraffe?

18. **WRITE Math** Madison visits her grandmother in another city. Does she travel 100 feet, 100 yards, or 100 miles? **Explain** your answer.

Mixed Review and Test Prep

19. There are 3 tennis balls in each of 5 cans. What expression shows the total number of tennis balls? (p. 336)

20. What shape comes next in this pattern? (p. 424)

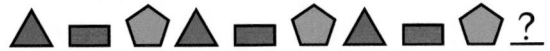

21. Test Prep Kenny uses a large piece of posterboard to draw a picture. About how long is the posterboard?

A 20 inches   **C** 20 yards

B 20 feet   **D** 20 miles

Estimate and Measure Inches

OBJECTIVE: Estimate and measure length to the nearest inch and half inch.

Learn

You can use an inch ruler to measure the length of an object to the nearest inch and nearest half inch.

Measure to the Nearest Inch

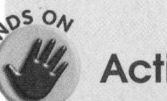

Activity   Materials ■ inch ruler

Step 1

Copy the table.

Length of Yarn		
Color	**Estimate**	**Measure**
red		
blue		
orange		
purple		
green		

Step 2

Estimate the length of the piece of red yarn. Record your estimate in your table.

Step 3

Use a ruler. Measure the length of the red yarn to the nearest inch. Record your measurement in your table.

Step 4

Repeat Steps 2 and 3 for the blue, orange, purple, and green yarn.

• Which color yarn is 2 inches longer than the shortest piece of yarn?

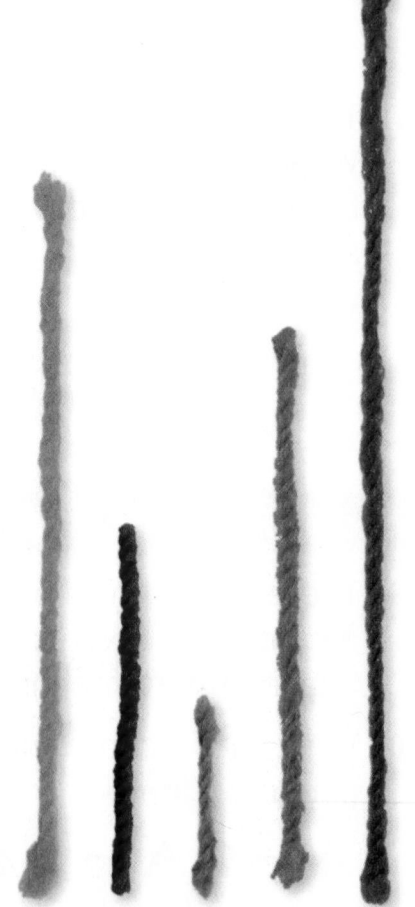

Measure to the Nearest Half Inch

You can also measure to the nearest half inch.

Examples

What is the length of each object to the nearest half inch?

A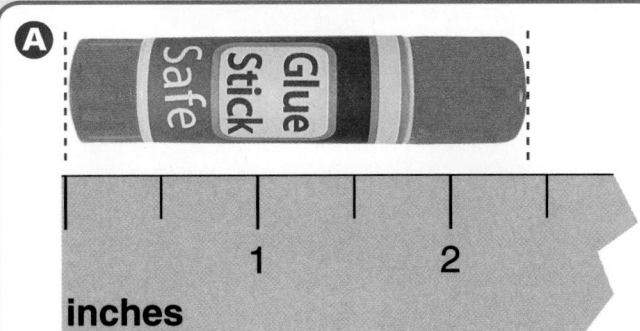

The left end of the glue stick is lined up with the 0 mark on the ruler.

The $\frac{1}{2}$ inch mark that is closest to the right end of the glue stick is $2\frac{1}{2}$.

So, the length of the glue stick to the nearest half inch is $2\frac{1}{2}$ inches.

B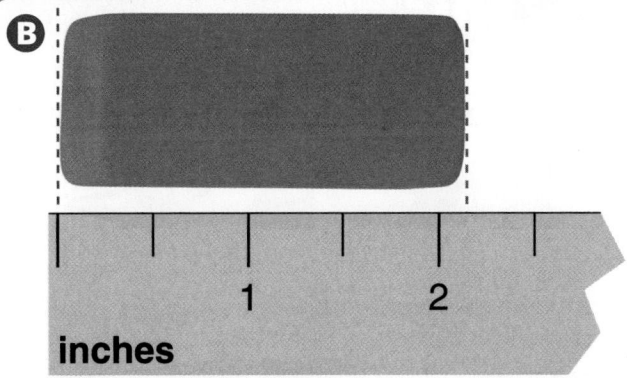

The left end of the eraser is lined up with the 0 mark on the ruler.

The $\frac{1}{2}$ inch mark that is closest to the right end of the eraser is 2.

So, the length of the eraser to the nearest half inch is 2 inches.

Guided Practice

1. Is the key $1\frac{1}{2}$ inches, 2 inches, or $2\frac{1}{2}$ inches long?

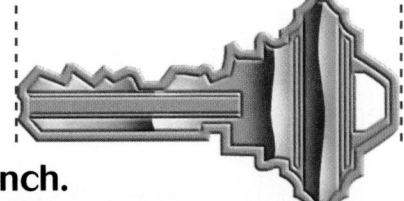

Measure the length to the nearest inch.

 2.

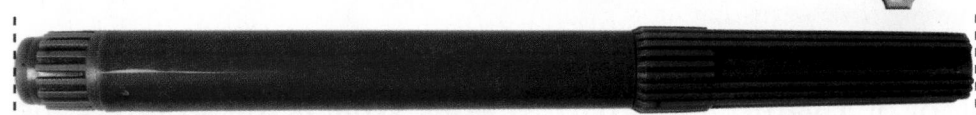

Measure the length to the nearest half inch.

3.

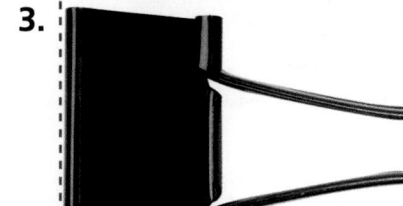

 4.

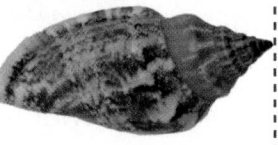

5. TALK Math Explain how you measured the shell to the nearest half inch.

Measure the length to the nearest inch.

6.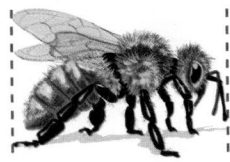

7.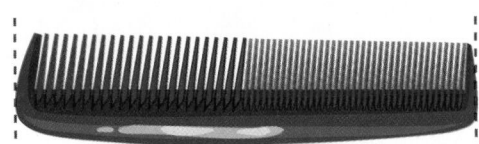

Measure the length to the nearest half inch.

8.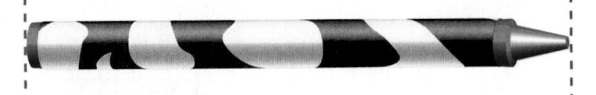

9.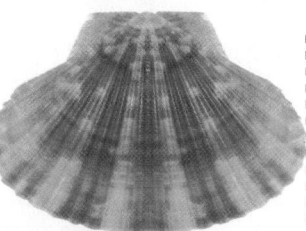

10.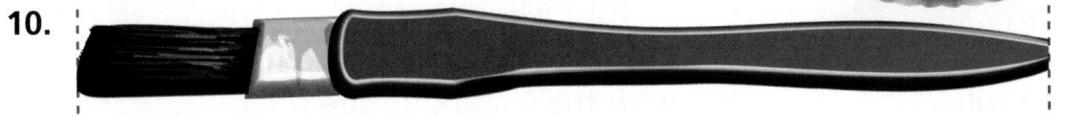

Use a ruler. Draw a line for each length.

11. 3 inches

12. $4\frac{1}{2}$ inches

13. 5 inches

14. $6\frac{1}{2}$ inches

15. Emily is measuring her hairbrush. It is $7\frac{1}{2}$ inches long. Between which two inch marks is the end of the hairbrush?

16. **WRITE Math** ▸ **What's the Error?** Joni said this piece of ribbon is 3 inches long. Describe her error.

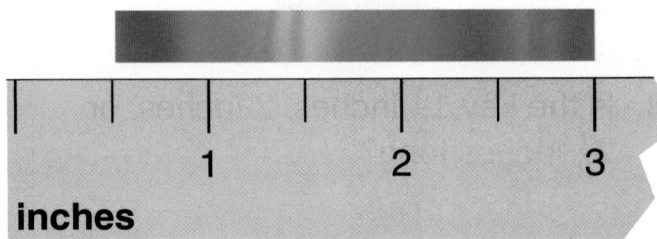

inches

17. Find two different-sized objects in your desk. Measure the length of each object to the nearest half inch. Use < or > to compare the measurements.

Mixed Review and Test Prep

18. Is a football about 1 foot or 1 yard long? (p. 512)

19. Mary spent $4.25 on a notebook and $5.15 on some trading cards. She paid with a $10 bill. How much change did she receive? (pp. 120, 122)

20. **Test Prep** What is the length of the bandage to the nearest half inch?

A $1\frac{1}{2}$ inches   **C** $2\frac{1}{2}$ inches

B 2 inches   **D** 3 inches

Extra Practice on page 530, Set B

CD ROM **Technology** Use Harcourt Mega Math, Ice Station Exploration, *Linear Lab,* Levels C and D.

Learn About) Measuring to the Nearest Quarter Inch

You learned to measure to the nearest inch and half inch. You can also measure to the nearest quarter inch. When you measure an object to the nearest quarter inch, your measurement is closer to the actual length of the object.

Examples

Measure the length to the nearest quarter inch.

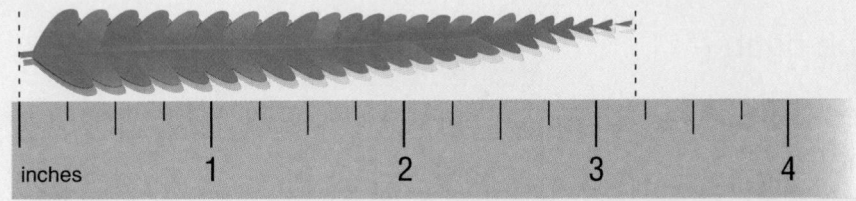 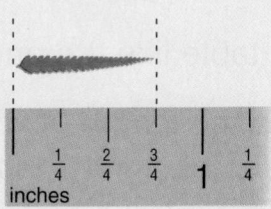

The left end of the leaf is lined up with the 0 mark on the ruler.

The $\frac{1}{4}$ inch mark that is closest to the right end of the leaf is $3\frac{1}{4}$ inches.

This leaf is $\frac{3}{4}$ inch long.

Try It

Measure the length to the nearest quarter inch.

21.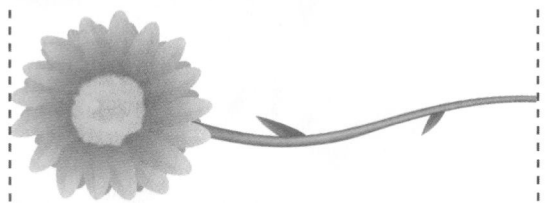

22.

23.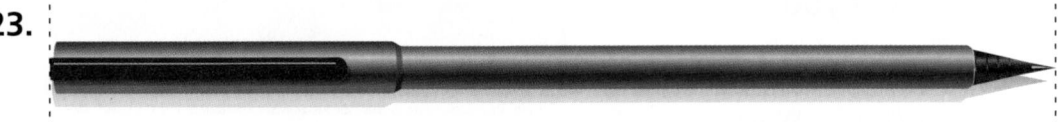

24. **WRITE Math** > **Explain** how you can measure the length of the crayon to the nearest quarter inch.

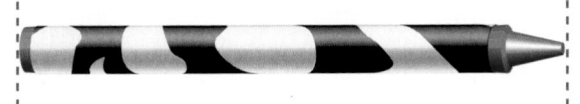

3 Estimate and Measure Feet and Yards

OBJECTIVE: Estimate and measure length to the nearest foot and yard.

You can use a ruler or yardstick to measure longer lengths.

Investigate

Materials ■ inch ruler and yardstick

A Make a table like the one at the right.

B Estimate the length of your desk, and record your estimate in the table.
Think: What unit should you use?

C Measure the length of your desk, and record the measurement in your table.

D Repeat Steps B and C for 2 other objects in your classroom. Some examples are the length of the teacher's desk, the height of the door, and the width of a window.

Length of Classroom Objects		
Object	Estimate	Measure
desk		

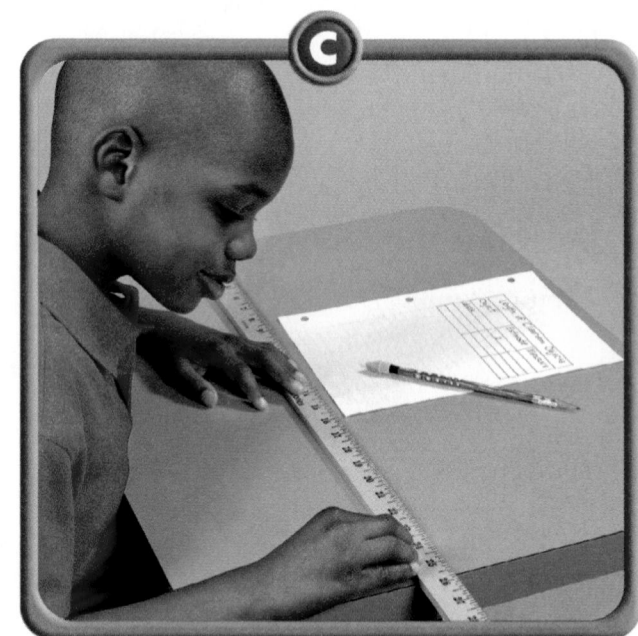

Draw Conclusions

1. When did you use a yardstick instead of a ruler to measure an object?

2. How does the length of your desk compare with another object you measured?

3. **Evaluation** You know about how long 1 foot is. How does that help you estimate the length of an object about 1 yard long? **Explain.**

Objects that are longer than 12 inches can be measured using a combination of units.

Suppose the length of your desk is 18 inches. You can write the length of the desk in inches or in feet and inches.

18 inches = ■ foot ■ inches

Think: 12 inches = 1 foot

18 inches = 12 inches + 6 inches

So, 18 inches = 1 foot 6 inches.

Table of Measures
1 foot = 12 inches
1 yard = 3 feet
1 yard = 36 inches

TALK Math

Explain how to write 40 inches as a combination of yards and inches.

Practice

Choose the better unit of measure.

1. the width of a small window

3 feet or 3 yards

2. the length of a car

9 feet or 9 yards

3. the height of a bookcase

4 feet or 4 yards

4. the length of a bathtub

2 feet or 2 yards

Use the Table of Measures above. Write the length in feet and inches or in yards and feet.

5. 28 inches = ■ feet ■ inches

6. 8 feet = ■ yards ■ feet

7. 11 feet = ■ yards ■ feet

8. 42 inches = ■ feet ■ inches

Algebra Compare. Write <, >, or = for each ●.

9. 4 feet ● 30 inches

10. 70 inches ● 2 yards

11. 24 inches ● 2 feet

12. Karl is building a pen for his rabbit. He needs 8 feet of wire. He has 2 yards of wire. Does he have enough wire to build the pen? **Explain.**

13. **WRITE Math** ▸ **What's the Error?** Mary said the length of the soccer field is 100 feet. Describe her error.

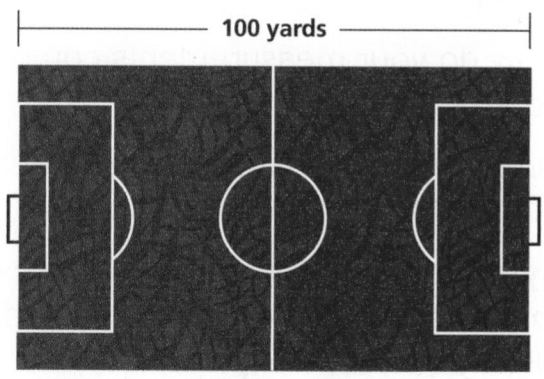

100 yards

4 Capacity

OBJECTIVE: Estimate and measure capacity.

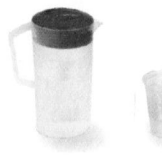
Capacity is the amount a container will hold. Customary units used to measure capacity are **cup (c)**, **pint (pt)**, **quart (qt)**, and **gallon (gal)**.

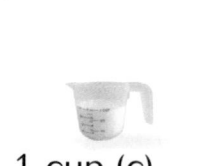 1 cup (c)	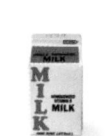 1 pint (pt)	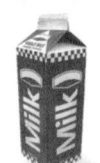 1 quart (qt)	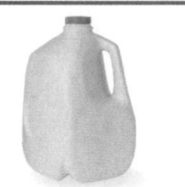 1 gallon (gal)

Investigate

Materials ■ cup, pint, quart, and gallon containers; water

A Make a table like the one at the right.

B Estimate the number of cups it will take to fill the pint container. Record your estimate.

C Fill a cup and pour it into the pint container. Repeat until the pint container is full.

D Record the number of cups it took to fill the pint container.

E Repeat Steps B–D for the quart and gallon containers.

Number of Cups		
	Estimate	Measure
Cups in a pint		
Cups in a quart		
Cups in a gallon		

Draw Conclusions

1. How do your measurements compare to your estimates?

2. How many cups are in a pint? a quart? a gallon?

3. **Synthesis** Which unit would you use to measure the amount of water needed to fill an aquarium? **Explain.**

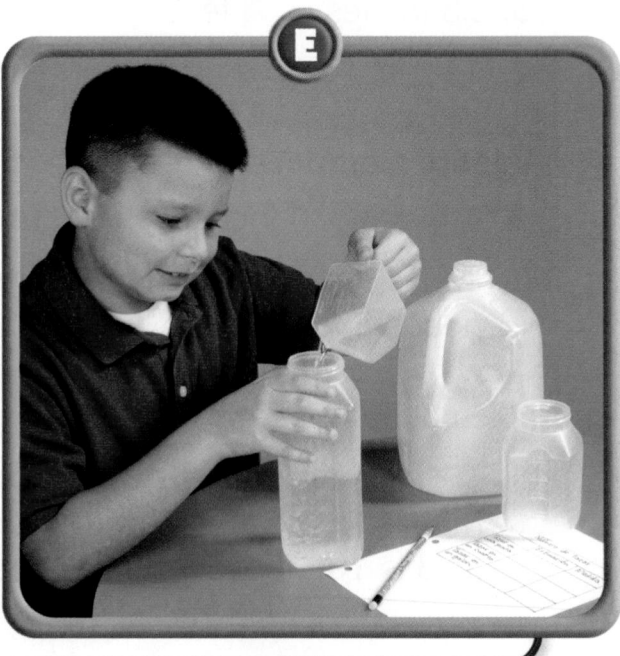

Connect

TALK Math

Explain how you can find the number of cups in 3 pints 1 cup.

How are cups, pints, quarts, and gallons related?

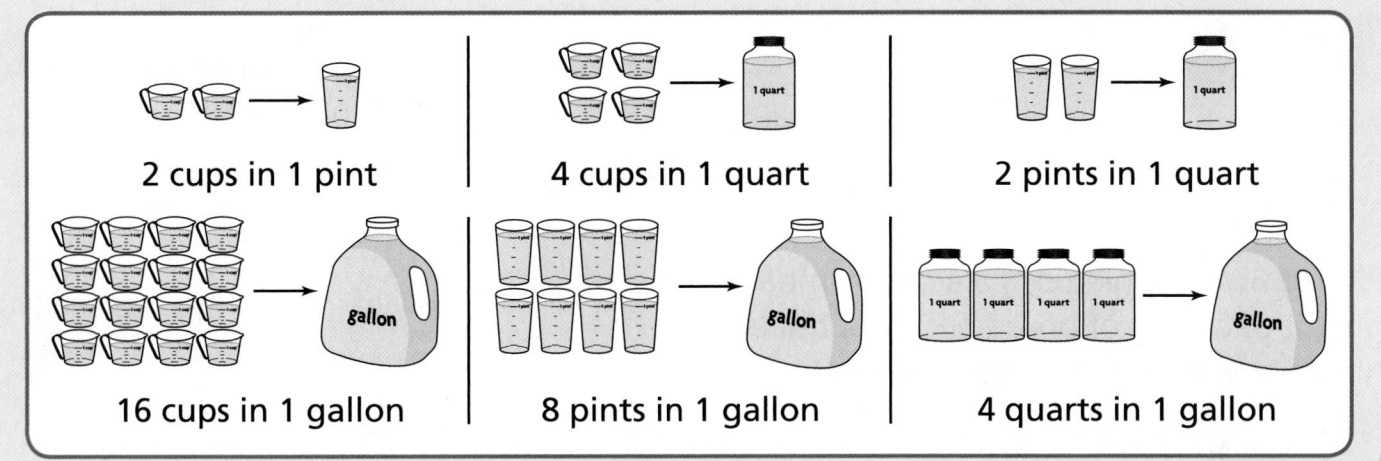

2 cups in 1 pint

4 cups in 1 quart

2 pints in 1 quart

16 cups in 1 gallon

8 pints in 1 gallon

4 quarts in 1 gallon

Practice

Choose the unit you would use to measure the capacity of each.
Write *cup, pint, quart,* or *gallon*.

1.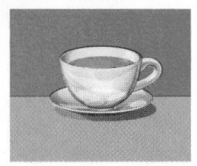

2.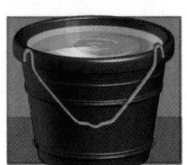

3.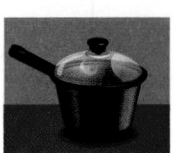

✓**4.**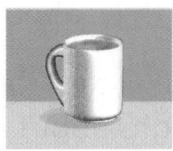

Tell how the units are related.

5. 8 cups = ■ pints

6. 6 pints = ■ quarts

✓**7.** 2 gallons = ■ quarts

⭐ **Algebra Compare. Write <, >, or = for each ●.**

8. 2 gallons ● 7 quarts

9. 3 cups ● 2 pints

10. 1 quart ● 5 cups

11. Find a container in the classroom that holds about 2 pints. Draw and label the container.

12. Write these amounts in order from greatest to least: 2 quarts, 6 pints, 10 cups.

13. [WRITE Math] **What's the Error?** Connor says it takes 8 cups to fill a 2-gallon container. Is he correct? **Explain.**

14. Lisa made 4 quarts of lemonade. How many cups can she pour?

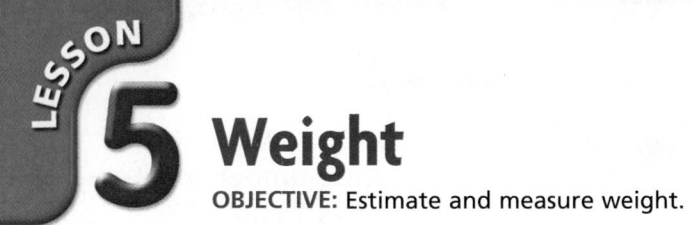

Weight

OBJECTIVE: Estimate and measure weight.

Learn

Weight is the measure of how heavy an object is. Customary units of weight include **ounce (oz)** and **pound (lb)**.

PROBLEM Sophie uses a scale to measure the weight of a slice of bread and a loaf of bread. About how much does each weigh?

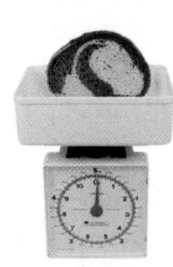
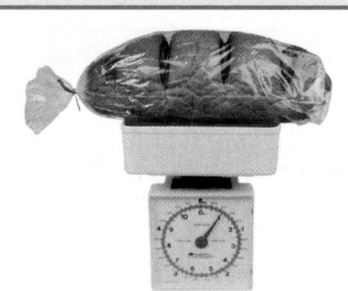

about 1 ounce   about 1 pound

So, a slice of bread weighs about 1 ounce, and a loaf of bread weighs about 16 ounces, or 1 pound.

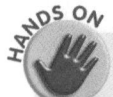

Activity

HANDS ON

Materials ■ scale, classroom objects

Estimate the weight of each object. Then use a scale to measure to the nearest ounce or pound.

- ■ tape dispenser   ■ book
- ■ apple   ■ pencil box

• How do your estimates compare to the actual measurements?

• Put the items you weighed in order from least to greatest weight.

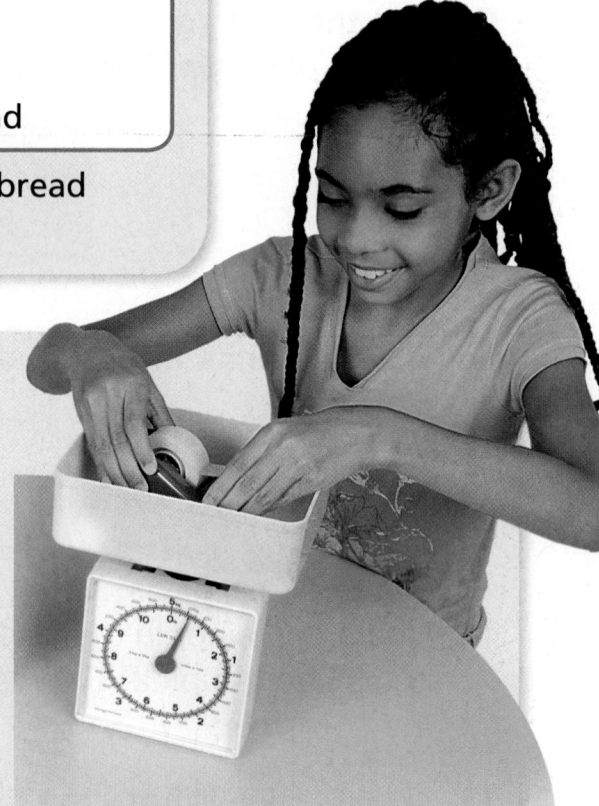

Customary Units of Weight
1 pound = 16 ounces

1. Does a strawberry weigh about 1 ounce or about 1 pound?

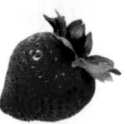

**Choose the unit you would use to weigh each.
Write *ounce* or *pound*.**

2.

3.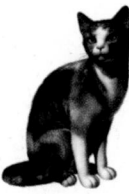

✓ 4.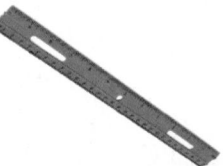

✓ 5.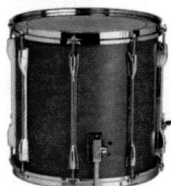

6. **TALK Math** Which weighs more—a key or a baseball bat? **Explain** how you know.

Independent Practice and Problem Solving

**Choose the unit you would use to weigh each.
Write *ounce* or *pound*.**

7.

8.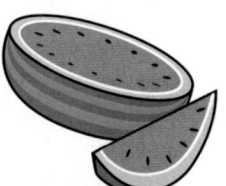

9.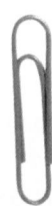

10.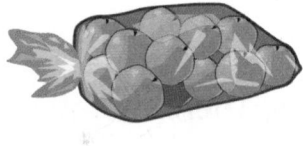

**Find an object in the classroom to match each weight.
Draw it, and label its weight.**

11. about 2 pounds

12. less than 1 pound

13. greater than 1 pound

14. **WRITE Math** **Sense or Nonsense** Hank says that 20 ounces is the same as 1 pound 4 ounces. Does his statement make sense? **Explain.**

Mixed Review and Test Prep

15. Two lines intersect and form right angles. Do the lines appear to be parallel or perpendicular? (p. 354)

16. $4 \times 3 = \blacksquare \times 6$ (p. 212)

17. **Test Prep** A store sells 4 ball caps. Each cap weighs 8 ounces. How much do the caps weigh in all?

A 8 ounces   **C** 2 pounds

B 12 ounces   **D** 4 pounds

Estimate or Measure

OBJECTIVE: Know when to estimate or when to measure.

Quick Review

1. 1 yard = ■ feet
2. 1 quart = ■ pints
3. 1 foot = ■ inches
4. 1 pint = ■ cups
5. 1 gallon = ■ quarts

Learn

Sometimes you need an exact measurement.
Sometimes an estimate is all you need.

Example 1 Theresa's father is making lemonade. The recipe
calls for 6 cups of water, $\frac{3}{4}$ cup sugar, and the juice from 4 lemons.
Should he estimate or measure the water and sugar?

When you use a recipe,
you should accurately
measure each ingredient.

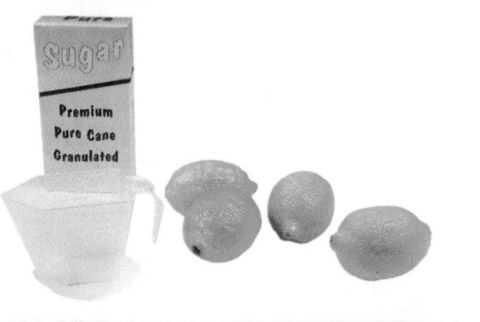

So, Theresa's father should measure the water and sugar.

Example 2 Theresa wants to pour 4 glasses of lemonade from
a pitcher that holds 2 quarts. Each glass holds 1 cup of lemonade.
Should Theresa measure the lemonade she pours into each glass,
or can she estimate whether there will be enough?

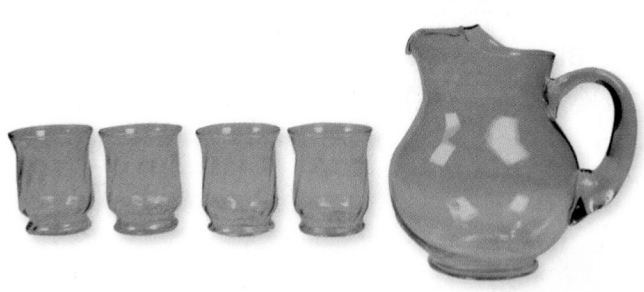

There are 4 cups in 1 quart, so Theresa can pour about
8 glasses from the 2-quart pitcher.

So, Theresa does not need to measure the lemonade she
pours into each glass.

• Why is it necessary to measure accurately when using a recipe?

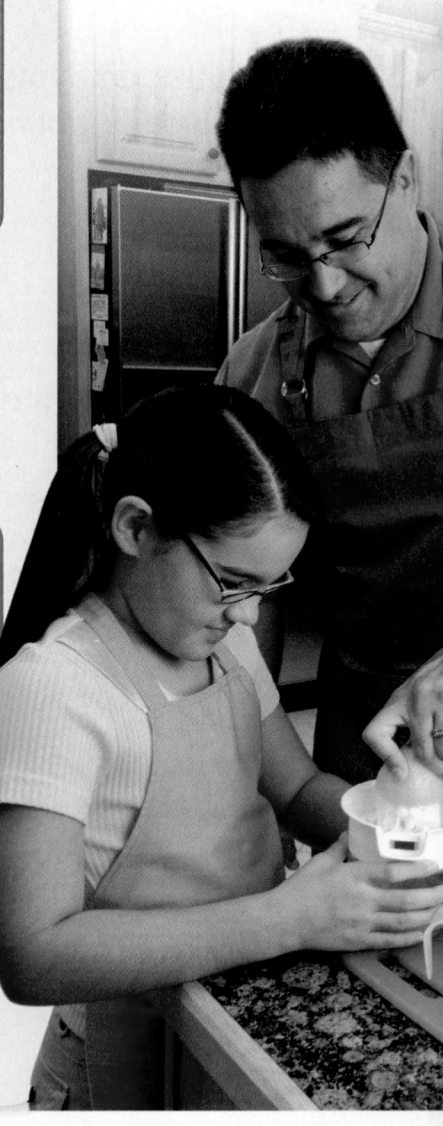

1. Ty filled a 1-quart container to water 3 plants. Each plant needs about 1 cup of water. Should he measure the water he gives each plant or can he estimate?

Choose *estimate* or *measure*.

2. Zach fills a water bowl for his kitten each day. Should Zach estimate or measure the water?

✓ 3. Morgan needs 36 inches of wire for each side of a rabbit pen. Should she estimate or measure the wire?

✓ 4. Jenna is cutting pieces of ribbon to glue on a picture frame. Should she estimate or measure the ribbon?

5. **TALK Math** Marta needs to mix 1 tablespoon of cocoa with 1 cup of milk to make hot chocolate. **Explain** why it is better for Marta to measure these amounts than to estimate them.

Independent Practice (and Problem Solving)

Choose *estimate* or *measure*.

6. Leigh is making cookies. The recipe calls for $\frac{3}{4}$ cup brown sugar. Should Leigh estimate or measure the brown sugar?

7. Jonas tore a poster when taking it off the wall. He needs 2 pieces of tape to fix the poster. Should Jonas estimate or measure the tape he needs?

8. Nathaniel has to be 48 inches tall to ride the Super Loop roller coaster. Should the theme park estimate or measure his height?

9. **WRITE Math** Sandra and Kailyn are making jump ropes. Should they estimate or measure the rope? **Explain.**

Mixed Review and Test Prep

10. Rory's room is 3 yards 2 feet long. How many feet long is the room?
    (p. 518)

11. Paula's volleyball practice lasts 90 minutes. It starts at 4:15. At what time does it end? (p. 130)

12. **Test Prep** Which amount should you measure?

    A the distance you can throw a ball

    B the amount of flour in a cake recipe

    C the amount of water in a teapot

    D the weight of a pair of skates

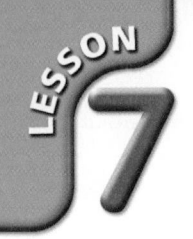

Problem Solving Workshop
Skill: Choose a Unit

OBJECTIVE: Solve problems by using the skill *choose a unit*.

Read to Understand

PROBLEM Ian's class is setting up a freshwater fish tank. What customary unit would Ian use to measure the capacity of the tank?

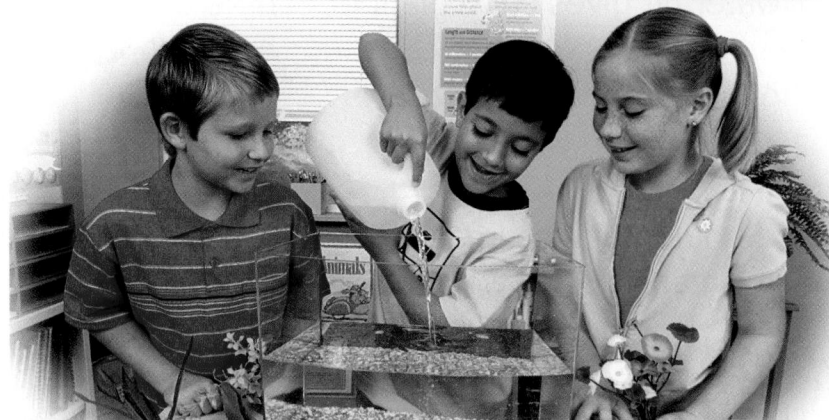

Remember how customary units of capacity are related.

> The smallest customary unit of capacity in Ian's class is a cup.
>
> A pint is larger than a cup.
> **Think:** there are 2 cups in 1 pint.
>
> A quart is larger than a pint.
> **Think:** there are 2 pints in 1 quart.
>
> A gallon is larger than a quart.
> **Think:** there are 4 quarts in 1 gallon.

Since the fish tank holds a lot of water, Ian would use gallons to measure the capacity.

Table of Measures
Length
12 inches = 1 foot
3 feet = 1 yard
Capacity
2 cups = 1 pint
4 cups = 1 quart
2 pints = 1 quart
8 pints = 1 gallon
4 quarts = 1 gallon
Weight
16 ounces = 1 pound

Think and Discuss

Choose the better unit of measure.

a. Marianna measures the length of a black swordtail fish in the classroom fish tank. Is the length closer to 2 inches or 2 feet?

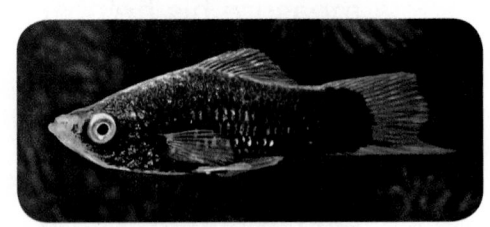

b. It takes Ned 12 minutes to drive from his house to the store. Is the distance he travels about 7 yards or 7 miles?

c. Ben likes to watch the pandas at the zoo. Is the weight of an adult panda measured in ounces or pounds?

TALK Math

How can you decide which unit is better to measure the weight of an object?

1. About 2 cars, end to end, will fit in Beth's driveway. What customary unit of length should Beth use to measure the length of her driveway?

   Think of the units of length.

   Which unit would be best to measure the length of a car?

   Which unit would be the best to measure a distance that is about 2 car lengths long?

   Solve the problem.

2. **What if** Beth helps her dad build a small birdhouse? What customary unit of length could they use to estimate the amount of wood they would need?

3. Mary enjoys drinking cocoa in the morning. Does her mug hold about 2 cups or 2 quarts?

Mixed Applications

4. Which unit would you use to measure the amount of water in a bathtub?

5. A bathtub is twice as long as Kia's dog. Kia's dog is 3 feet long. How many yards long is the bathtub?

For 6–8, use the items pictured.

6. Mike bought 2 bags of potting soil and 3 daylily plants. How much did he spend?

7. Which would cost more, 4 black-eyed Susan plants or 6 daisy plants? How much more?

8. Joe has $10. Name two combinations of items he could buy.

9. **WRITE Math** Judy bought 24 daisy plants. She wants to plant them in 4 equal rows. How many daisies will be in each row? **Explain** your answer by drawing an array.

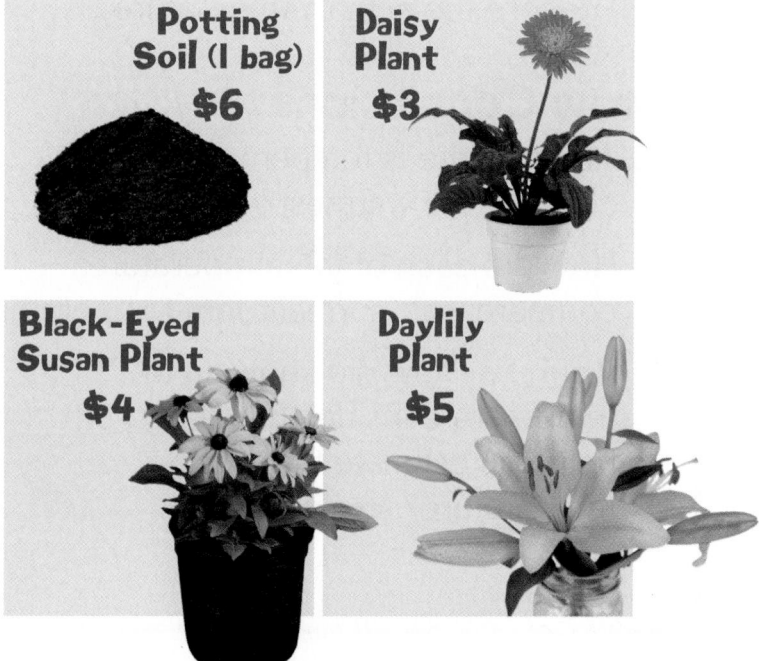

Potting Soil (1 bag) $6

Daisy Plant $3

Black-Eyed Susan Plant $4

Daylily Plant $5

8 Fahrenheit Temperature

OBJECTIVE: Estimate and measure temperature in degrees Fahrenheit.

Temperature is the measure of how hot or cold something is. **Degrees Fahrenheit (°F)** are customary units of temperature.

To read a thermometer, find the number closest to the top of the red bar. Use the scale along the side like a number line. On the thermometer at the right, each line on the scale stands for 1 degree. The top of the red bar is at 67°F. The temperature shown is 67°F.

Write: 67°F   Read: sixty-seven degrees Fahrenheit

Investigate

Materials ■ Fahrenheit thermometer

A Estimate what you think the outdoor temperature will be, in degrees Fahrenheit, 3 times during the day. Record your estimates.

B Use a Fahrenheit thermometer to measure the outdoor temperature at the listed times. Record the actual temperature.

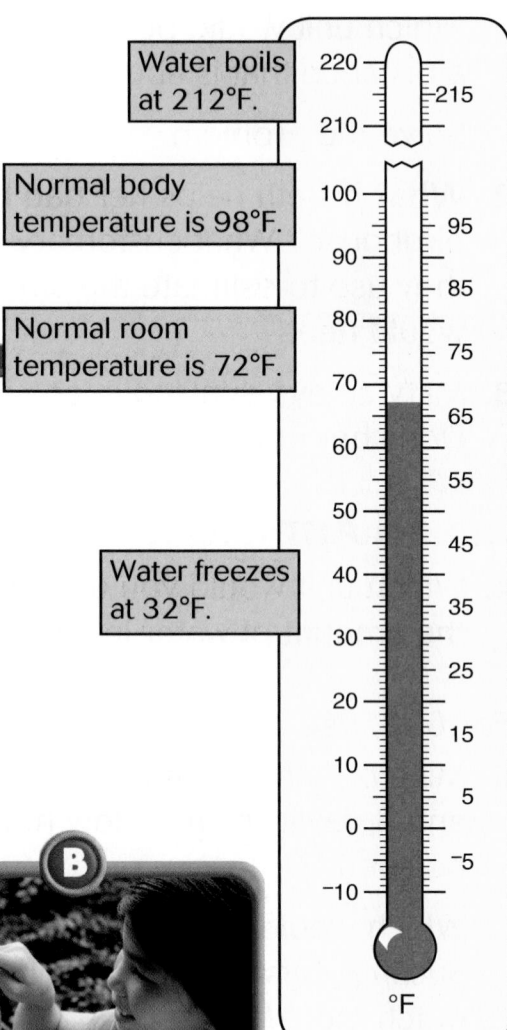

Water boils at 212°F.

Normal body temperature is 98°F.

Normal room temperature is 72°F.

Water freezes at 32°F.

Draw Conclusions

1. At what time is temperature the coolest? the warmest? **Explain.**

2. How did each of the temperatures compare with normal room temperature?

3. **Analysis** How did knowing the temperature inside your classroom help you estimate the outside temperature? **Explain.**

Below are outside activities you might do at 20°F, 75°F, and 90°F.

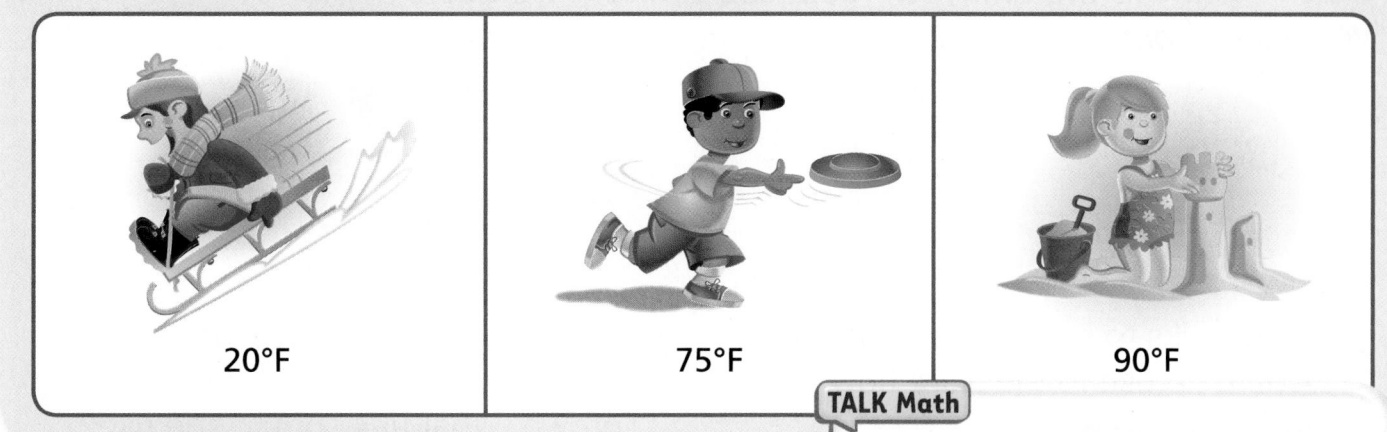

20°F   75°F   90°F

TALK Math

Explain how knowing the outside temperature can help you decide what clothes to wear.

Practice

Write each temperature in °F.

1. 2. 3. ✅ 4.

[thermometer reading between 40 and 50] °F   [thermometer reading near 10-20] °F   [thermometer reading near 70-80] °F   [thermometer reading near 90-100] °F

Choose the better temperature for each activity.

5.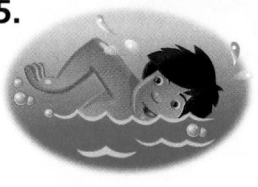

6.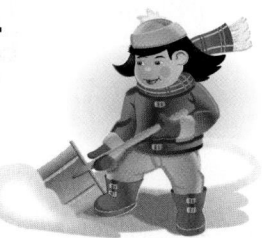

7.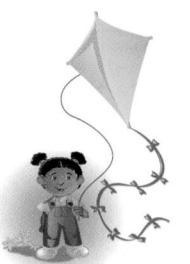

✅ 8.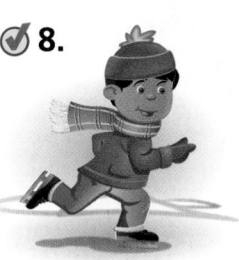

58°F or 88°F   23°F or 53°F   75°F or 105°F   90°F or 30°F

9. **WRITE Math** Kenny's father is building a fire in the fireplace. About what temperature might it be outside? **Explain.**

10. It is 85°F outside. What is an activity that Paige might do at this temperature? What clothes do you think she might wear?

Extra Practice

Set A Choose the unit you would use to measure each.
Write *inch, foot, yard,* or *mile.* (pp. 512–513)

1.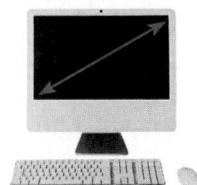

2.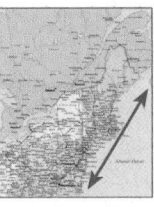

3.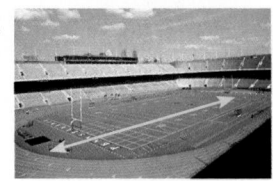

4. Sam walks to school. What unit would he use to measure how far he has to walk?

5. Helena is going to measure her kitten to see how much he has grown. What unit should she use?

Set B Measure the length to the nearest inch. (pp. 514–517)

1.

2.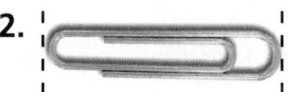

Measure the length to the nearest half inch.

3.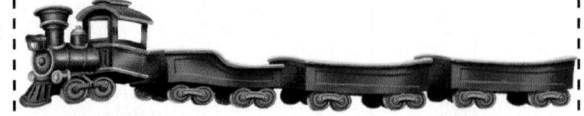

4.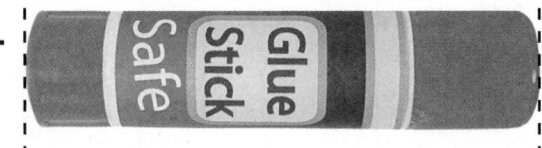

Set C Choose the unit you would use to measure each.
Write *ounce* or *pound.* (pp. 522–523)

1.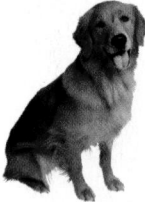

2.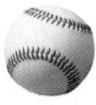

3.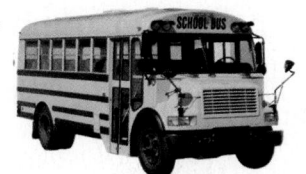

Set D Choose *estimate* or *measure.* (pp. 524–525)

1. Melanie wants to pour each of her 5 friends about 1 cup of orange juice. Her pitcher holds 2 quarts. Should Melanie estimate or measure the orange juice she pours?

2. Melanie is making cookies to serve with the orange juice. The recipe calls for 1 cup of sugar. Should Melanie estimate or measure the sugar?

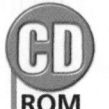 **Technology**
Use Harcourt Mega Math, The Number Games, *Tiny's Think Tank,* Levels N, O, P.

Measure Up!

LENGTH

How many inches are in 1 foot?

$100

| $200 |
| $300 |
| $400 |
| $500 |
| $600 |

CAPACITY

| $100 |
| $200 |
| $300 |
| $400 |
| $500 |
| $600 |

WEIGHT

| $100 |
| $200 |
| $300 |
| $400 |
| $500 |
| $600 |

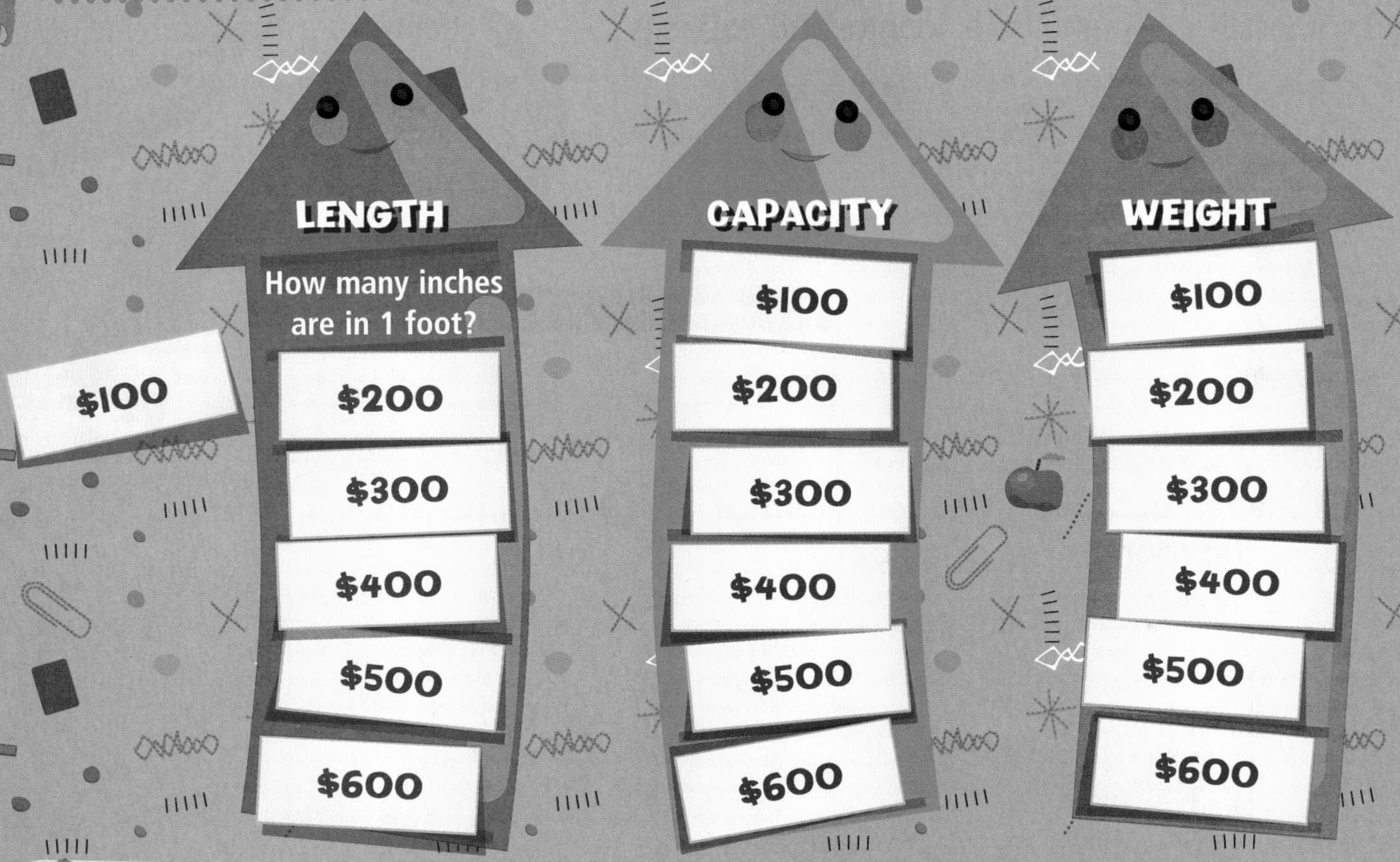

🐕 Your Answer, Please! ·············

■ Place the money cards over the gameboard sections as shown above.

■ The first player chooses Length, Capacity, or Weight, and begins with the $100 question. The reader uncovers the question and reads it aloud.

■ Player 1 answers the question. The reader uses the answer sheet to check Player 1's answer.

■ If the answer is correct, Player 1 keeps the money card and chooses the next question in the same category. If Player 1's answer is not correct, it is Player 2's turn.

■ Player 2 may continue in Player 1's category or begin a new category. Players may answer only 2 questions per turn.

■ Play continues until all questions are answered. The player with the greater amount of money wins.

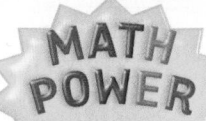 **MATH POWER** **Measurement**

CHOOSE A TOOL

Measurement tools such as thermometers, scales, clocks, rulers and measuring cups are used to measure temperature, weight, time, length, and capacity.

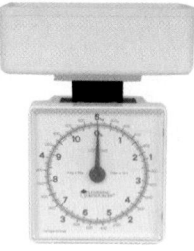 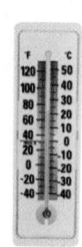 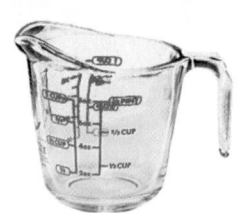 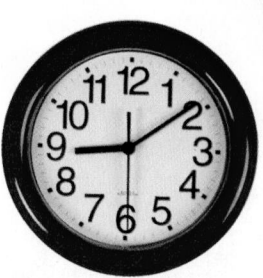

Examples
Which measurement tool would you use to measure each?

A the temperature of the room	**B** the weight of an object	**C** the time you get up
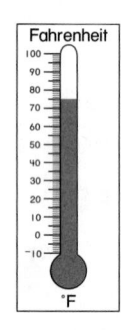	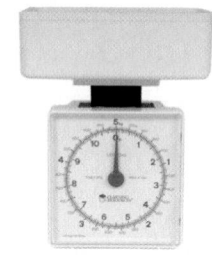	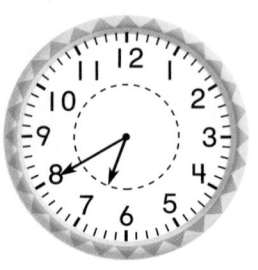

Try It
Which measurement tool would you use to measure each?

1. the time school starts

2. the height of a chair

3. the weight of a pencil

4. the capacity of a pitcher

5. |WRITE Math▶ What measurement tool would you use to find out which of two objects is heavier? **Explain.**

Chapter 20 Review/Test

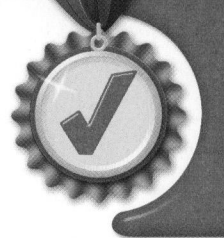

Check Concepts

Solve.

1. Would you use a cup, pint, quart, or gallon to measure the amount of juice in a glass? (pp. 520–521)

2. Would you use ounces or pounds to measure the weight of a tennis ball? (pp. 522–523)

Check Skills

Choose the unit you would use to measure each.
Write *inch*, *foot*, *yard*, **or** *mile*. (pp. 512–513)

3.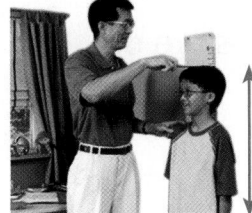

4.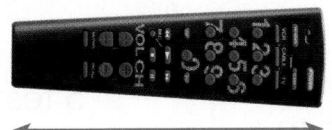

5.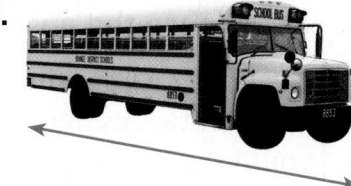

Measure to the nearest half inch. (pp. 514–517)

6.

7.

8.

Check Problem Solving

Solve. (pp. 526–527)

9. Christina's garden has 6 rows of corn, with 10 plants in each row. What unit of length should she use to measure the corn section of her garden?

10. **WRITE Math** ▸ Christina's mother is preparing 12 ears of corn. Should she put the corn in a pot that holds 3 cups or 3 gallons of water? **Explain.**

Standardized Test Prep
Chapters 1–20

Number and Operations

1. There are 204 people in the band. There are 289 people in the choir. Which shows the BEST estimate of how many more people are in the choir than in the band? (p. 78)

   A 400 C 50

   B 100 D 0

Test Tip Choose the answer.

See item 2. Order the numbers from greatest to least mentally. Then compare your list with the answers given. If your answer does not match any of the answers given, carefully solve the problem again.

2. One of Liz's books has 347 pages. Another book has 299 pages. A third book has 390 pages. Which lists the number of pages in order from greatest to least? (p. 32)

   A 299; 347; 390

   B 347; 390; 299

   C 390; 299; 347

   D 390; 347; 299

3. **WRITE Math** How can this picture help you find 5×8? **Explain.** (p. 236)

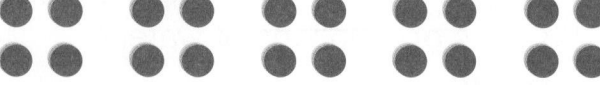

Algebraic Reasoning

4. What is the pattern unit in this number pattern? (p. 422)

   2, 0, 1, 4, 2, 0, 1, 4, 2, 0, 1, 4

   A 0, 1, 4, 2

   B 2, 0, 1, 4

   C 2, 0, 1

   D 1, 4, 2, 0

5. How many players are on 5 teams? (p. 218)

Teams	1	2	3	4	5
Players	5	10	15	20	■

   A 10

   B 15

   C 20

   D 25

6. **WRITE Math** What is a rule for the number pattern below? **Explain.**
   (p. 426)

   77, 66, 55, 44, 33

Measurement

7. Marisa used inches to measure an object. Which object did she measure? (p. 512)

A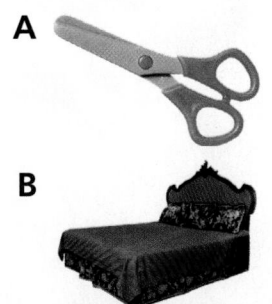

B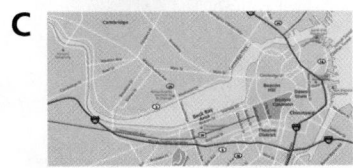

C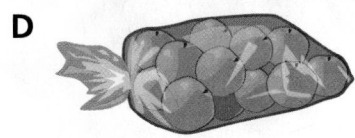

D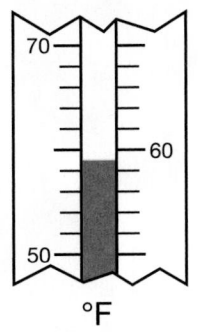

8. What temperature does the thermometer show? (p. 528)

A 51°F   **C** 59°F

B 54°F   **D** 61°F

9. ▌WRITE Math ▶ Would the height of a desk be 28 inches or 28 feet? **Explain.** (p. 512)

Data Analysis and Probability

10. Billy and Eric use this spinner to play a game. Which color are they more likely to spin? (p. 182)

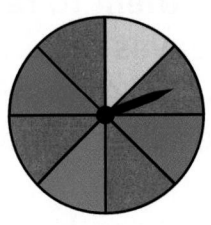

A Yellow

B Blue

C Green

D Red

11. John made a pictograph to show how many people played winter sports. He used the key: Each 🧍 = 8 people. The pictograph shows 🧍🧍🧍🧍🧍 next to ice-skating. How many people ice-skate? (p. 148)

A 36   **C** 44

B 40   **D** 48

12. ▌WRITE Math ▶ John wants to make a bar graph from the data in his pictograph. The bars for ice-skating and skiing are the same length. **Explain** what this means. (p. 154)

21 Metric Measurement

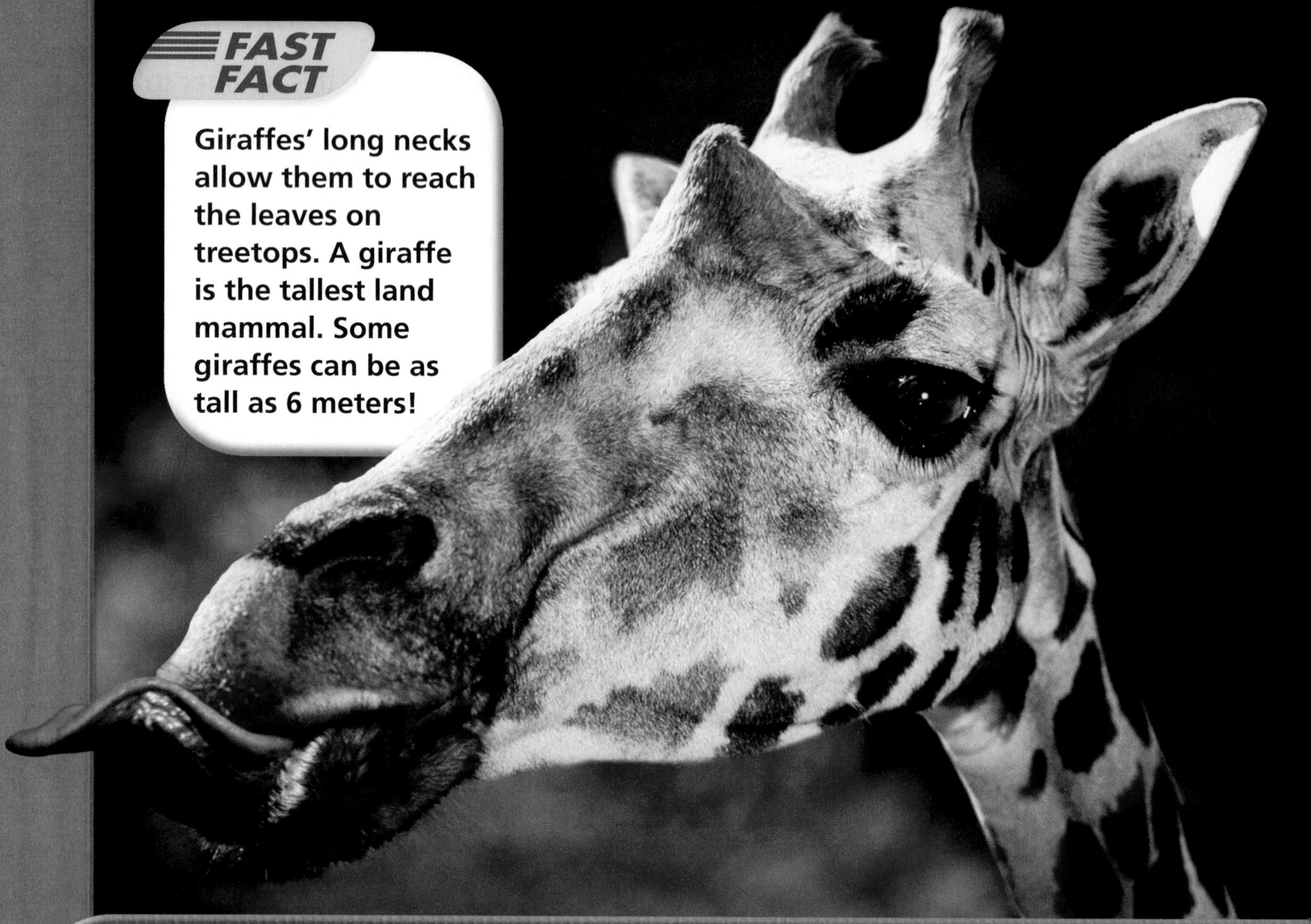

≡ FAST FACT

Giraffes' long necks allow them to reach the leaves on treetops. A giraffe is the tallest land mammal. Some giraffes can be as tall as 6 meters!

Investigate

The bar graph shows the heights of several items. Choose an item from the graph and compare it to the height of the giraffe. Find the difference between the two heights.

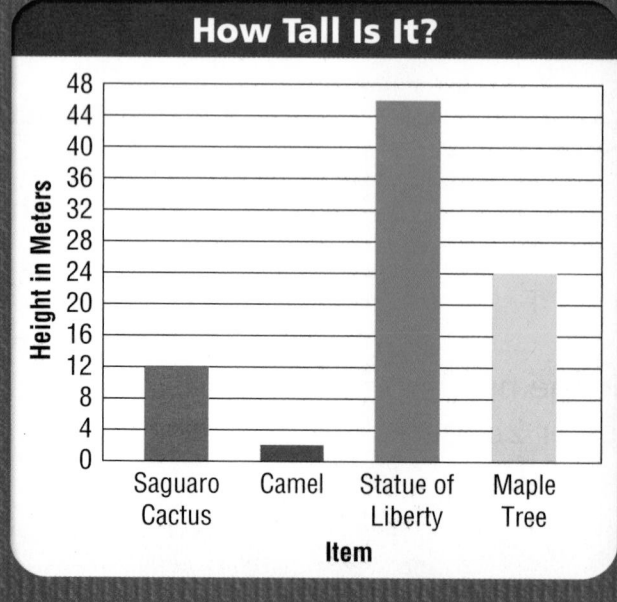

How Tall Is It?

Height in Meters (y-axis: 0, 4, 8, 12, 16, 20, 24, 28, 32, 36, 40, 44, 48)

Item (x-axis): Saguaro Cactus, Camel, Statue of Liberty, Maple Tree

GO ONLINE

Technology
Student pages are available in the Student eBook.

Check your understanding of important skills needed for success in Chapter 21.

▶ **Use a Metric Ruler**

Use a centimeter ruler to measure.

1.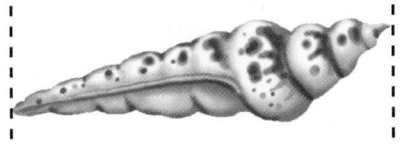

2.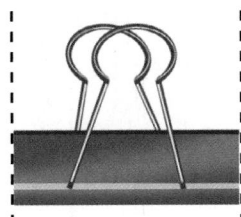

3.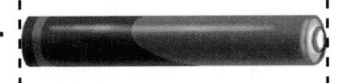

4.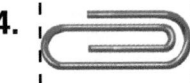

▶ **Measure to the Nearest Centimeter**

Use a ruler to measure to the nearest centimeter.

5.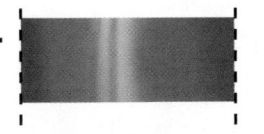

6.

7.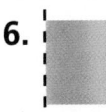

8.

VOCABULARY POWER

CHAPTER VOCABULARY

centimeter (cm) mass
decimeter (dm) meter (m)
gram (g) milliliter
kilogram (kg) (mL)
kilometer (km)
length
liter (L)

WARM-UP WORDS

centimeter (cm) A metric unit for measuring length or distance

gram A metric unit for measuring mass; 1 kilogram = 1,000 grams

liter A metric unit for measuring capacity; 1 liter = 1,000 milliliters

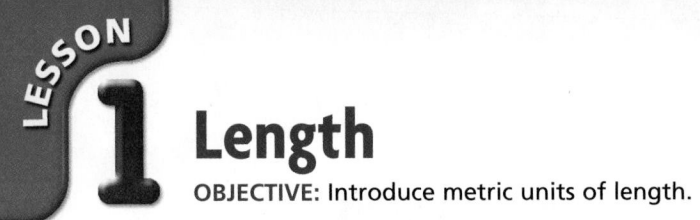

Length

OBJECTIVE: Introduce metric units of length.

Quick Review

Would you use an inch ruler or a yardstick to measure the length of a pencil?

Learn

Length and distance can be measured by using metric units such as **centimeter (cm)**, **decimeter (dm)**, **meter (m)**, and **kilometer (km)**.

PROBLEM Aaron plays basketball in college. Is Aaron about 2 centimeters, 2 decimeters, 2 meters, or 2 kilometers tall?

Vocabulary

centimeter (cm)
decimeter (dm)
meter (m)
kilometer (km)

Measure shorter lengths in centimeters and decimeters.

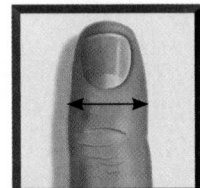

A child's finger is about 1 centimeter wide.

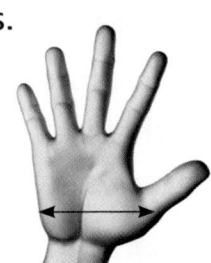

An adult's hand is about 1 decimeter wide.

Measure longer lengths in meters and kilometers.

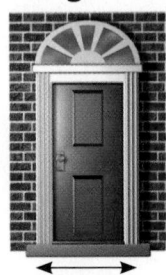

A doorway is about 1 meter wide.

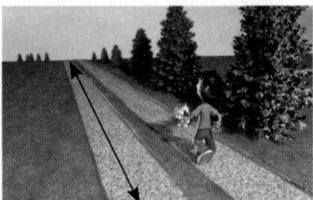

It takes about 10 minutes to walk 1 kilometer.

So, Aaron is about 2 meters tall.

Guided Practice

1. Would you measure the length of this crayon in centimeters or decimeters?

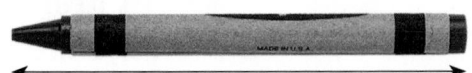

Choose the unit you would use to measure each.
Write cm, m, or km.

2.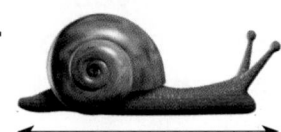

✓ 3.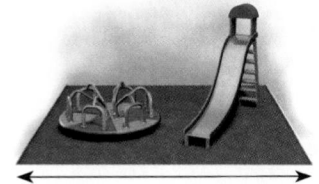

✓ 4.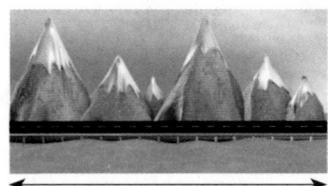

5. [TALK Math] Would you use centimeters or meters to measure the width of your school picture? **Explain.**

Independent Practice and Problem Solving

Choose the unit you would use to measure each.
Write cm, m, or km.

6.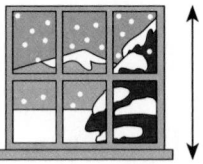

7.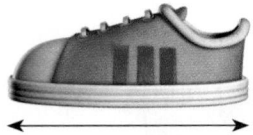

8.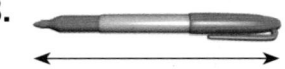

9. distance from your house to school

10. width of a bookshelf

11. height of a skyscraper

12. width of a butterfly

13. height of a flagpole

14. length of a dollar bill

15. Brad walks from his house to the park every afternoon to play basketball. It takes him 20 minutes to get to the park. Is the park 2 dm, 2 m, or 2 km from his house?

16. [WRITE Math] ▸ **What's the Error?**
Nancy's plant is about the same width as her front door. She says it is about 1 dm wide. Describe Nancy's error.

Mixed Review and Test Prep

17. Theresa has 5 quarters, 3 dimes, and 5 pennies. How much money does she have? (p. 110)

18. The temperature is 30°F. Is Eric planting flowers or shoveling snow?
(p. 528)

19. Test Prep About how long is this shell?

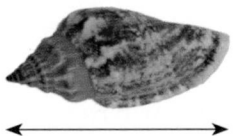

A 3 cm

B 3 dm

C 3 m

D 3 km

Estimate and Measure Centimeters, Decimeters, and Meters

OBJECTIVE: Estimate and measure length to the nearest centimeter, decimeter, and meter.

Learn

You can use a centimeter ruler to measure length to the nearest centimeter and decimeter.

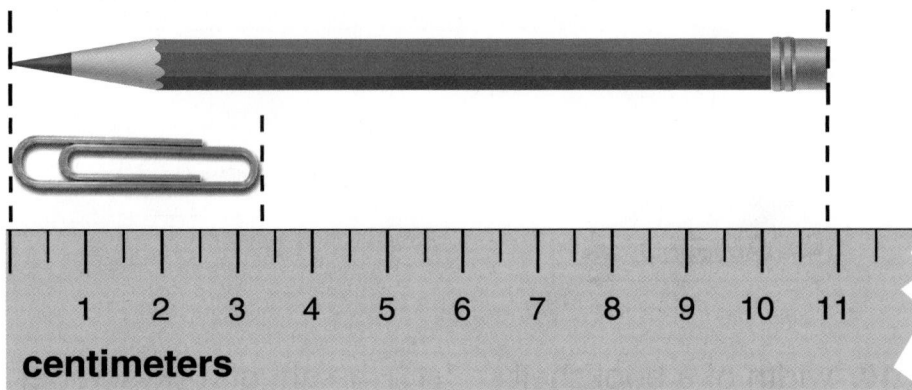

The right end of the paper clip is closest to the 3-centimeters mark. So, the paperclip is 3 centimeters long, to the nearest centimeter.

The right end of the pencil is closest to the 11-centimeters mark. So, the pencil is 11 centimeters long, to the nearest centimeter, and 1 decimeter long, to the nearest decimeter.

Remember
1 decimeter = 10 centimeters

Activity 1   **Materials** ■ centimeter ruler

Step 1

Make a table like the one at the right. Choose three objects to measure. Estimate the length of each object in cm or dm. Record your estimates.

Step 2

Use a centimeter ruler to measure each object. Record your measurements in the table.

Length of Objects		
Object	Estimate	Measure

• How did your estimates compare to the actual measurements?

• Write the lengths of the objects in order from least to greatest.

Relating Units

You can measure longer lengths in meters.

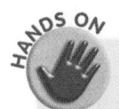

HANDS ON

Activity 2

Materials ■ centimeter grid paper, tape, crayons

Step 1 Use the Table of Measures to find the number of decimeters in one meter.	**Step 2** Cut enough decimeter strips out of grid paper to make a 1-meter strip. Color each decimeter strip a different color.
Step 3 Tape the decimeter strips together so that the edges do not overlap. 	**Step 4** Estimate the length of your classroom. Then use your meter strip to find the actual measure.

• How did you know how many decimeter strips were needed to make a meter strip?

Guided Practice

1. To the nearest centimeter, how long is this crayon?

Estimate the length in centimeters. Then use a ruler to measure to the nearest centimeter.

2. the length of your math book

☑ 3. the length of your shoe

4. the length of your pencil

☑ 5. the length of a marker

Choose the best estimate.

6. height of a fence
   2 cm   2 m   2 km

7. length of a roadrace
   5 dm   5 m   5 km

8. **TALK Math** Explain how you can measure the length of your notebook to the nearest centimeter.

Estimate the length in centimeters. Then use a ruler to measure to the nearest centimeter.

9. the length of a piece of chalk

10. the length of a ruler

11. the length of a pencil case

12. the length of an eraser

Use a ruler to measure to the nearest centimeter.

13.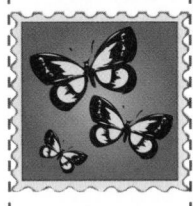

14.

Choose the best estimate.

15. length of a camera
   10 cm   10 dm   10 m

16. length of a banana
   2 cm   2 dm   2 m

17. length of a peanut
   4 cm   4 dm   40 dm

18. length of a marker
   12 cm   12 dm   12 m

19. length of a notebook
   3 cm   30 cm   300 cm

20. length of a paintbrush
   15 cm   15 dm   15 m

Use a centimeter ruler. Draw a line for each length.

21. 13 centimeters

22. 2 decimeters

23. 18 centimeters

24. **Reasoning** Peter is 8 dm tall. Mary is 86 cm tall. Susan is 9 dm tall and Jack is 84 cm tall. Who is tallest? **Explain.**

25. Suppose you measure your desk in centimeters and then in decimeters. Will there be more centimeters or more decimeters? **Explain.**

26. Choose 3 objects inside your classroom. Estimate and measure the lengths with a centimeter ruler. How do your estimates compare to the actual measurements?

27. **WRITE Math** ▸ **Sense or Nonsense** Justin said that 32 centimeters is the same as 3 decimeters plus 2 centimeters. Do you agree? **Explain.**

Mixed Review and Test Prep

28. Write <, >, or = to complete.
   8 ÷ 2 ● 2 + 2 (p. 308)

29. Write the fact family for 3, 9, and 27.
   (p. 286)

30. **Test Prep** June's book is 40 cm long. How many decimeters long is it?

   A 400 dm   **B** 40 dm   **C** 4 dm   **D** 4 cm

Technology
Use Harcout Mega Math, Ice Station Exploration, *Linear Lab,* Level H.

How Big is the Collection?

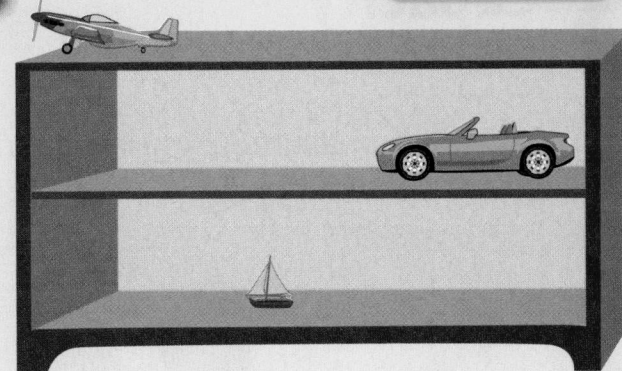

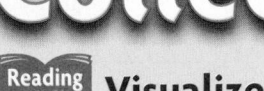 **Visualize**

Mike has a collection of model planes, cars, and boats. He wants to display each collection on one of the three shelves shown above. Each shelf is 12 dm long. The cars are about 4 dm long, the boats are about 1 dm long, and the planes are about 3 dm long. How many of each model will fit on one shelf?

You can visualize, or picture in your mind, how the models will fit on the shelves.

To solve the problem, use details from the problem and visualize the size of the models in Mike's collection. Then decide how many of each model will fit on one shelf.

Visualize
Each shelf is 12 dm long, or about 12 hand widths long.
The cars are about 4 dm long, or about 4 hand widths long.
The boats are about 1 dm long, or about 1 hand width long.
The planes are about 3 dm long, or about 3 hand widths long.

Remember
An adult's hand is about one decimeter wide.

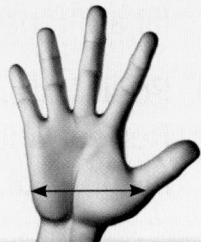

Problem Solving Visualize to understand the problem.

1. Solve the problem above. Which model will have the most on one shelf? Which model will have the fewest?

2. Mike also has 2 model trains. Each train is 6 dm long. Would both model trains fit on one shelf?

3. One motorcycle is about 5 dm long. If Mike has 3 motorcycles the same size, would they all fit on one shelf?

3 Capacity

OBJECTIVE: Estimate and measure capacity.

Capacity can be measured by using metric units such as **milliliter (mL)** and **liter (L)**.

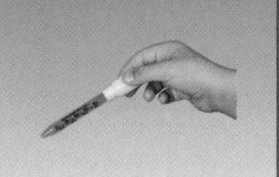

A dropper holds about 1 mL.

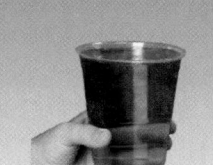

A full glass holds about 250 mL.

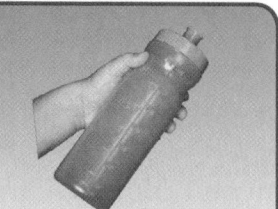

A water bottle holds about 1 L.

Quick Review

Which container holds more?

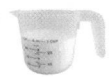 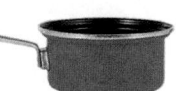

Vocabulary

milliliter (mL)   liter (L)

Investigate

Materials ■ 250-mL plastic water glass, liter container, pitcher

A Make a table like the one at the right to help find the capacity of different containers.

B Estimate the number of milliliters that are in 1 liter. Use the plastic glass. Pour 250 mL of water into the liter container.

C Repeat until the liter container is full. Record how many milliliters you poured.

D Estimate the number of liters it will take to fill a pitcher.

E Pour 1 liter of water into the pitcher. Repeat until the pitcher is full. Record the number of liters you poured.

Find the Capacity		
How many:	Estimate	Measure
milliliters in a liter?		
liters in a pitcher?		

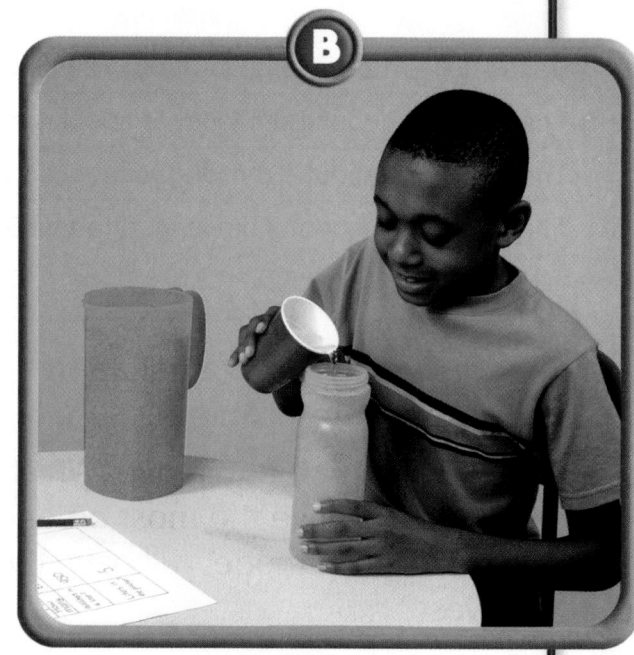

Draw Conclusions

1. How close were your estimates to the actual capacity of your containers?

2. **Evaluation** Suppose you drank a tall glass of orange juice. Did you drink about 4 mL or 400 mL of orange juice? **Explain.**

The table helps you see how liters and milliliters are related.

L	1	2	3	4	5
mL	1,000	2,000	3,000	4,000	5,000

1,000 mL = 1 L

TALK Math

Explain how to find the number of milliliters in 6 liters.

Practice

Choose the unit you would use to measure the capacity of each. Write *mL* or *L*.

1.
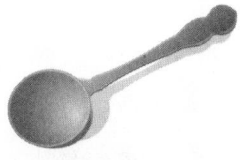

2.
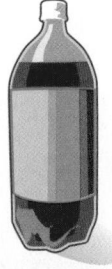

✓3.
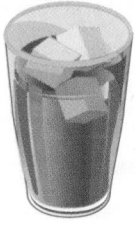

4.
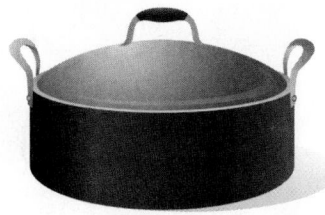

5.
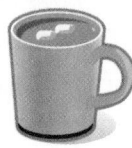

✓6.
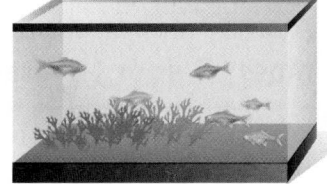

Find a container in the classroom that shows each capacity. Draw it and label its capacity.

7. less than 250 mL

8. greater than 1 L

9. greater than 2 L

⭐ **Algebra Find each missing number.**

10. ▪ mL = 4 L

11. 12,000 mL = ▪ L

12. 8 L = ▪ mL

13. **Reasoning** Jason made 1 liter of lemonade. He drank 450 milliliters of it. How much lemonade is left now? **Explain** how you got your answer.

14. **WRITE Math** ▸ Patrick's aquarium holds 10 L of water. He fills the aquarium using a 500-mL container. How many times will Patrick have to fill his container? **Explain.**

CD ROM Technology — Use Harcourt Mega Math, The Number Games, *Tiny's Think Tank*, Level N.

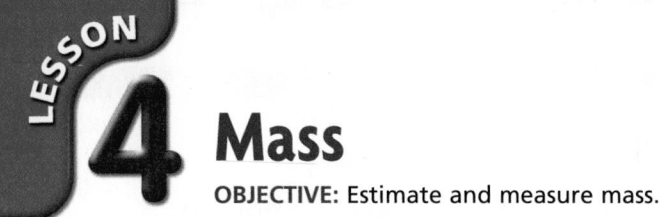

LESSON 4

Mass

OBJECTIVE: Estimate and measure mass.

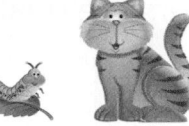

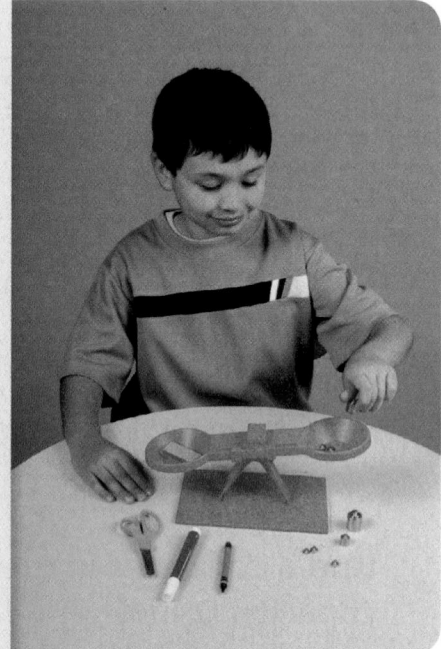

Learn

Mass is the amount of matter in an object. Mass can be measured by using metric units such as **gram (g)** and **kilogram (kg)**.

PROBLEM Ethan uses a balance to find the mass of a paper clip and a box of 1,000 paper clips. What is the mass of each object?

Vocabulary

mass   gram (g)   kilogram (kg)

Metric Units of Mass
1 kilogram = 1,000 grams

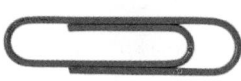

A small paper clip has a mass of about 1 gram.

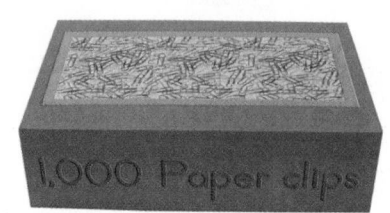

A box of 1,000 paper clips has a mass of about 1 kilogram.

HANDS ON Activity

Materials ■ balance, gram and kilogram weights, classroom objects

Estimate the mass of each object. Record your estimates in a table. Then find the mass of each object to the nearest gram or kilogram.

- marker
- scissors
- notebook
- dictionary
- eraser
- crayon

- How did your estimates compare with the actual measurements?
- Put the objects in order from greatest to least mass.

Mass		
Object	Estimate	Measure

Guided Practice

1. Does a nickel have a mass of about 5 grams or 5 kilograms?

**Choose the unit you would use to find the mass of each.
Write *gram* or *kilogram*.**

2.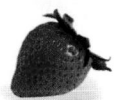

3.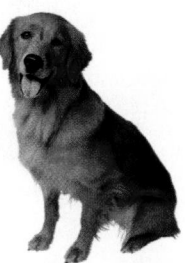

✓**4.**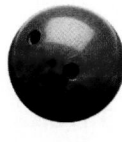

✓**5.**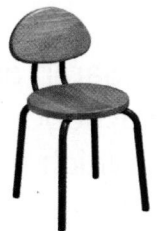

6. **[TALK Math]** Would you use grams or kilograms to find the mass of a toothbrush? **Explain.**

Independent Practice and Problem Solving

**Choose the unit you would use to find the mass of each.
Write *gram* or *kilogram*.**

7.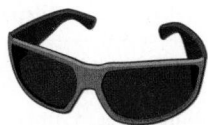

8.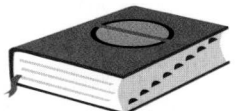

9.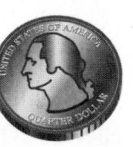

10.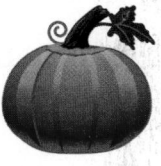

**Find an object in the classroom to match each mass.
Draw it and label its mass.**

11. less than
50 grams

12. greater than
100 grams

13. greater than
1 kilogram

14. **[WRITE Math]** Do objects of about the same size always have about the same mass? **Explain** your answer.

Mixed Review and Test Prep

15. Find the missing number.
108, 112, 116, 120, ■, 128 (p. 426)

16. Would you use centimeters or meters to measure the length of a carrot? (p. 538)

17. There are 2 fish in Javier's tank. One fish has a mass of 750 grams and one fish has a mass of 250 grams. What is the total mass of both fish?

A 500 grams

C 5 kilograms

B 1 kilogram

D 1,000 kilograms

Extra Practice on page 552, Set C

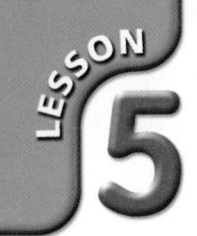

Problem Solving Workshop
Skill: Choose a Unit

OBJECTIVE: Solve problems by using the skill *choose a unit*.

Read to Understand

PROBLEM Sarah and her father are putting a wallpaper border around her bedroom. Which metric unit of length should Sarah use to measure the wallpaper border?

Think about how metric units of length are related.

Measure shorter lengths in centimeters and decimeters. Measure longer lengths in meters and kilometers.

Sarah's wallpaper border is too long to be measured in centimeters or decimeters, so think of the next largest unit.

Sarah's wallpaper border could be measured in meters.

Sarah's wallpaper border is too short to be measured in kilometers.

So, Sarah should use meters to measure the wallpaper border.

Metric Table of Measures	
Length	
10 centimeters	= 1 decimeter
100 centimeters	= 1 meter
1,000 meters	= 1 kilometer
Capacity	
1,000 milliliters	= 1 liter
Mass	
1,000 grams	= 1 kilogram

TALK Math

How can you decide which metric unit is best to measure the length of an object?

Think and Discuss
Choose the better unit of measure.

a. **≡FAST FACT** A newborn baby rabbit is about 4 cm long. Would you estimate the mass of the baby rabbit in grams or kilograms?

b. Jolene used chalk to draw a large rainbow on her driveway. The height of the rainbow is taller than she is. Is the rainbow about 3 meters or 3 decimeters tall?

c. Judy is making fruit punch for 6 of her friends. Which unit of capacity should she use to estimate the amount of fruit punch she needs: milliliters or liters?

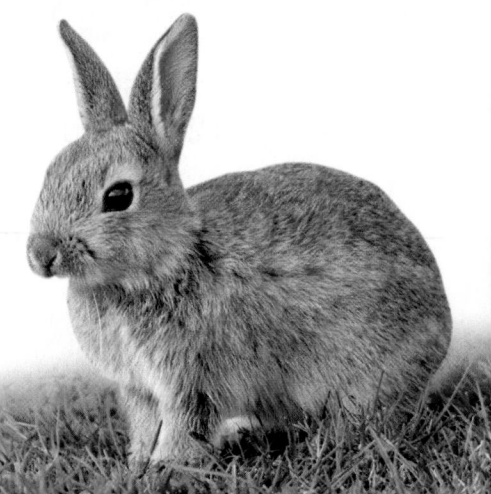

Guided Problem Solving

1. It takes about 30 minutes for Lizzie's family to drive from their house to her grandmother's house. Which unit of length should Lizzie use to measure the distance to her grandmother's house?

   Think of the units of length. How are the units related?

   Which unit would be best to measure a distance that takes about 30 minutes to drive? Solve the problem.

2. **What if** Lizzie's grandmother lived across the street? Which unit should Lizzie use to measure the distance to her grandmother's house?

3. George fills a bathtub with water. Does the bathtub hold about 100 L or 100 mL of water?

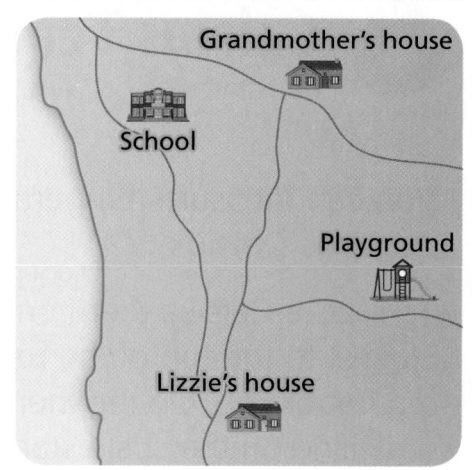

Mixed Applications

4. Gina collects miniature dolls. Her favorite doll is shorter than the width of her hand. Is the doll 6 cm or 6 dm tall?

5. Sam is making cookies. Should he use grams or kilograms to find the mass of one cookie?

USE DATA For 6–8, use the table.

6. Kendra bought 1 pack of felt and 5 meters of velvet fabric to make a costume. How much did she spend?

7. **Reasoning** Ben bought a leather belt and one other item with a $20 bill. How much change did he receive? **Explain.**

8. **WRITE Math** ▶ Maddie needs 3 meters of velvet and 2 leather belts. Will Maddie spend more money on the belts or the velvet? **Explain.**

9. Jim's costume comes with a walking stick, which is taller than he is. Is the walking stick 2 cm or 2 m tall?

Costume Items	
Felt for crown	$16.50 per pack
Leather belt	$9.50 each
Velvet for robe	$7.00 per meter

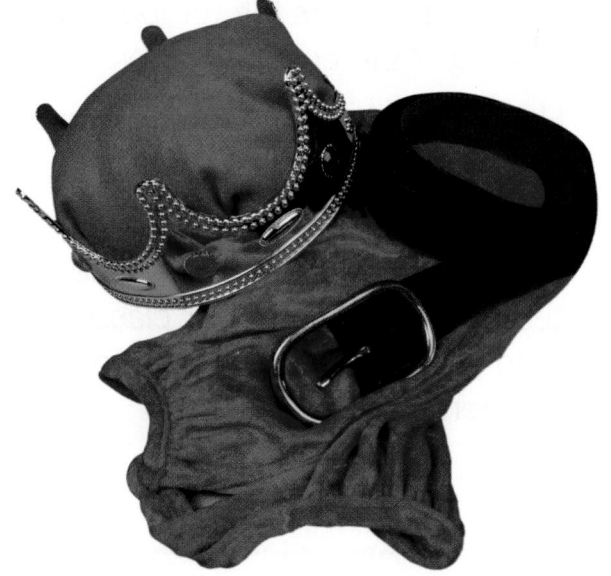

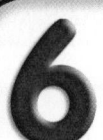

6 Celsius Temperature

OBJECTIVE: Estimate and measure temperature in degrees Celsius.

You can measure temperature in metric units as **degrees Celsius (°C)**.

To read a Celsius thermometer, find the number closest to the top of the red bar. Use the scale like a number line. On the thermometer at the right, each line on the scale stands for 5 degrees. The temperature shown is 20°C.

Write: 20°C   Read: twenty degrees Celsius

Investigate

Materials ■ Celsius thermometer

A Estimate what you think the outdoor temperature will be, in degrees Celsius, 3 times during the day. Record your estimates.

B Use a Celsius thermometer to measure the outdoor temperature at the listed times. Record the actual temperature.

Draw Conclusions

1. At what time was the temperature the warmest? the coolest?

2. How did each of the temperatures compare with normal room temperature?

3. **Analysis** How did knowing the temperature inside your classroom help you estimate the outside temperature?

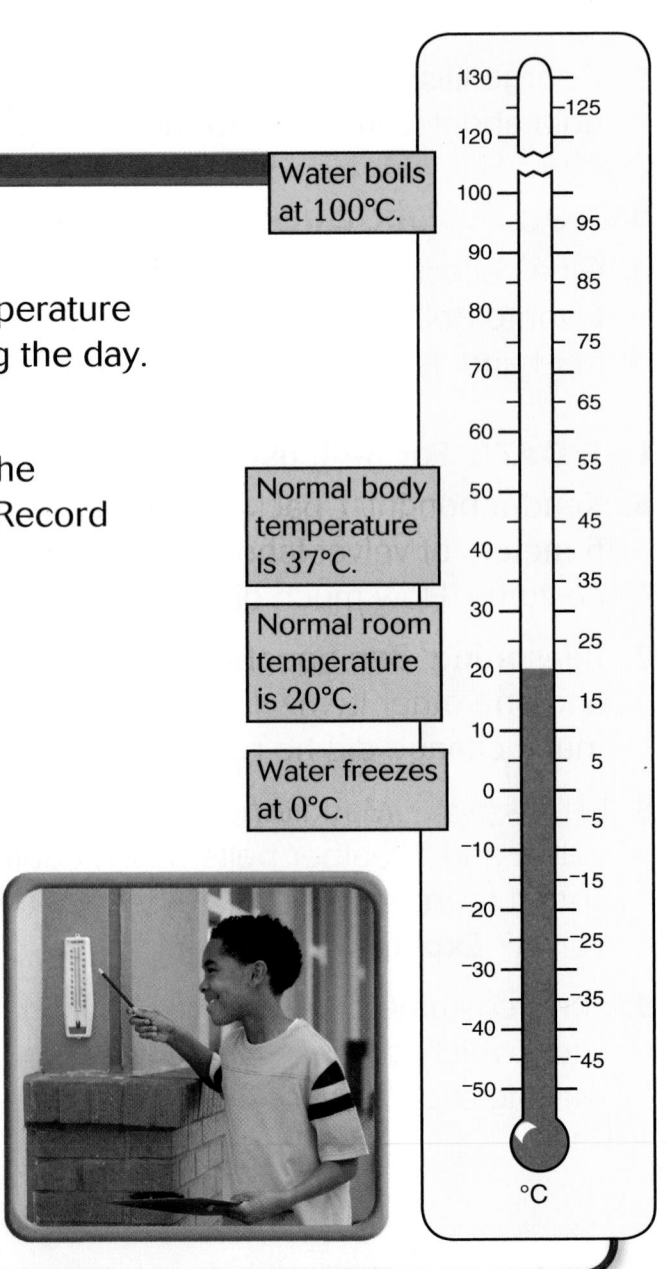

Water boils at 100°C.

Normal body temperature is 37°C.

Normal room temperature is 20°C.

Water freezes at 0°C.

Below are outside activities you might do at 0°C, 15°C, and 30°C.

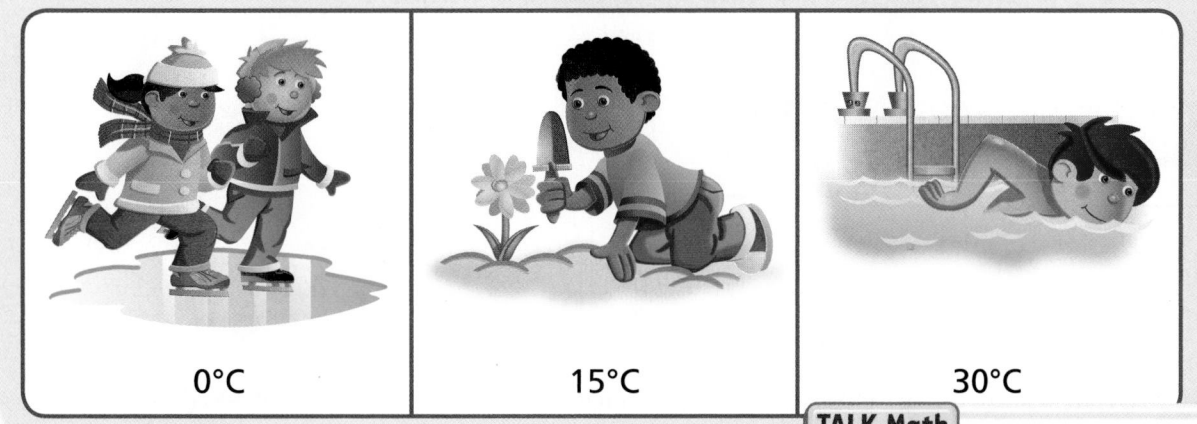

0°C   15°C   30°C

TALK Math

Explain how knowing the outside temperature can help you decide what clothes to wear to school.

Practice

Write each temperature in °C.

1. 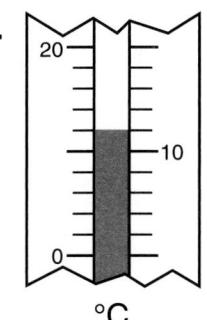 °C

2. °C

3. 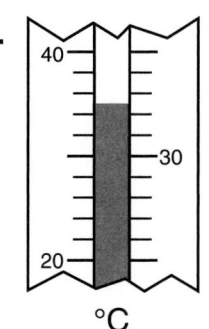 °C

✓4. 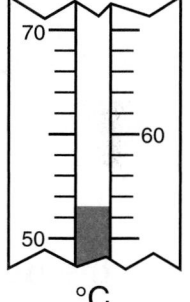 °C

Choose the better temperature for each activity.

5.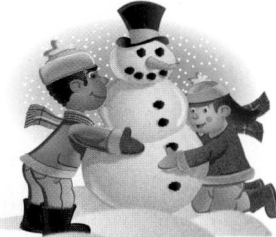

1°C or 33°C?

6.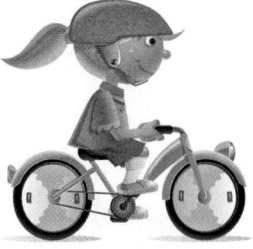

24°C or 6°C?

7.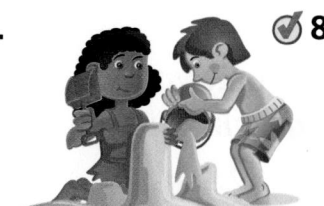

12°C or 31°C?

✓8.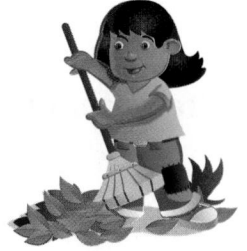

17°C or 35°C?

9. Lauren is wearing shorts and a pair of sandals. Is the outdoor temperature 5°C or 25°C?

10. **WRITE Math** It is 3°C outside. What is an activity that Jason might do at this temperature? What clothes do you think he might wear? **Explain.**

Extra Practice

Set A Choose the unit you would use to measure each.
Write *cm*, *m*, or *km*. (pp. 538–539)

1.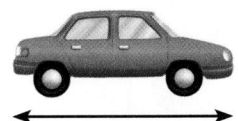

2.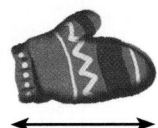

3.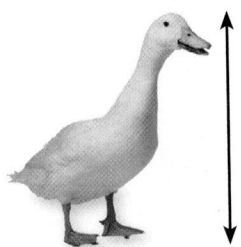

4. height of a drinking glass

5. distance from your home to school

6. length of a skating rink

7. distance from New Jersey to Illinois

8. length of a playground

9. height of a chair

Set B Estimate the length in centimeters. Then use a ruler to measure to the nearest centimeter. (pp. 540–543)

1.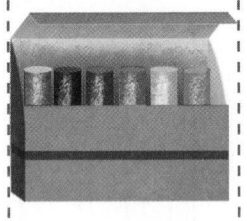

2.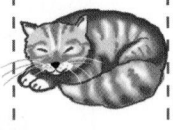

3.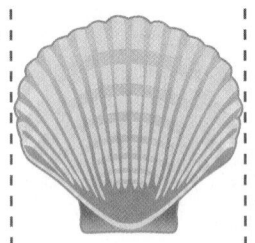

Choose the best estimate.

4. height of a window
   8 cm   8 dm   8 km

5. length of a safety pin
   3 cm   3 dm   3 m

6. length of a cell phone
   8 cm   8 dm   8 m

Set C Choose the unit you would use to find the mass of each.
Write *gram* or *kilogram*. (pp. 546–547)

1.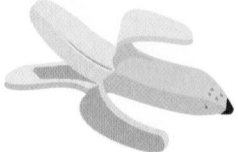

2.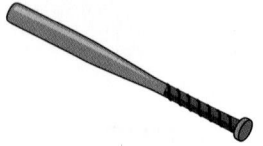

3.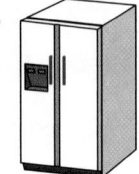

4.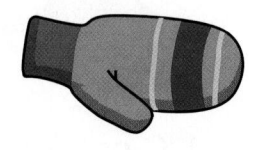

Collect-a-Meter

🍓 **Roll 'Em!** 🍃 **Measure 'Em!**

2–4 players
• Gameboard
• Centimeter rulers
• Number cube
• Counter, paper, and pencil for each player
• Action cards

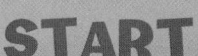
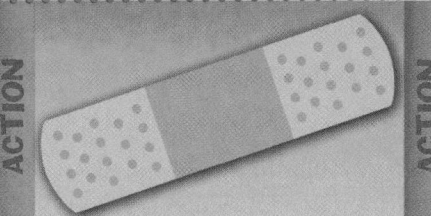
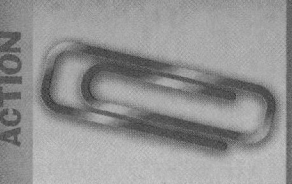
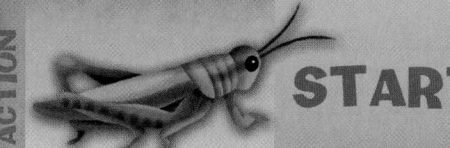

START

ACTION   ACTION   ACTION   **START**

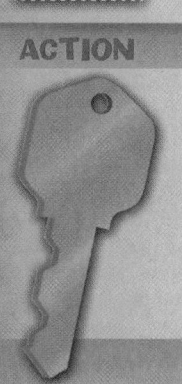

ACTION

ACTION CARDS

ACTION

START

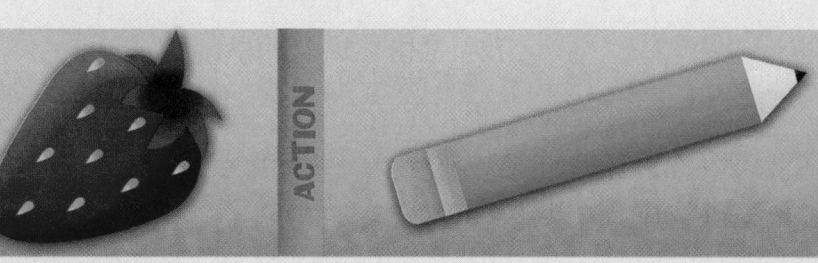

START

ACTION   ACTION

🧹 **Collect 'Em!**

■ Players shuffle the Action cards and place them facedown in the middle of the gameboard.

■ Each player places a counter in one of the START corners.

■ Player 1 rolls the number cube, moves the number of spaces rolled, measures the picture of the object on the space where he or she lands,

and writes the measurement on a score sheet. It is then Player 2's turn.

■ When players land on an Action space, they pick an Action card and follow its directions.

■ The first player to score a total of 100 centimeters wins.

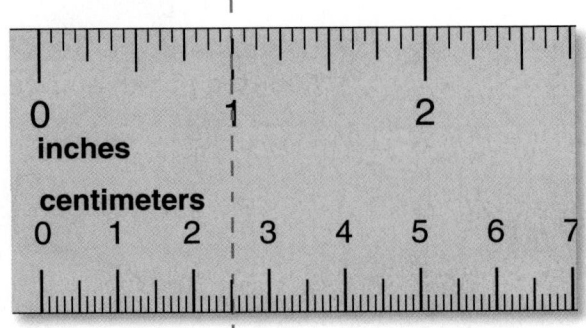

MATH POWER — Inches and Centimeters

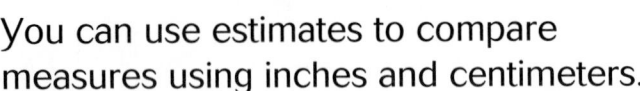

In the United States, we use the customary system of measurement, which includes inches as a unit of measure. Most other countries use the metric system of measurement, which includes centimeters as a unit of measure.

You can use estimates to compare measures using inches and centimeters.

Example

Look at the ruler.

One inch is about $2\frac{1}{2}$ centimeters.

Five inches is about how many centimeters?

Step 1 Make a table to compare inches and centimeters.
1 inch is about $2\frac{1}{2}$ centimeters.

inches	1	2	3	4	5	6
centimeters	$2\frac{1}{2}$	5	$7\frac{1}{2}$	10	$12\frac{1}{2}$	15

Step 2 Find 5 inches in the table and the estimated centimeter measure that matches it.

So, 5 inches is about $12\frac{1}{2}$ centimeters.

Try It

Copy and complete each comparison.

1. 4 inches is about _____ centimeters.

2. 5 centimeters is about _____ inches.

3. $17\frac{1}{2}$ centimeters is about _____ inches.

4. 10 inches is about _____ centimeters.

5. **WRITE Math** Explain how to compare centimeters to 1 foot.

Chapter 21 Review/Test

Check Concepts

Solve.

1. Which is a greater mass, a gram or a kilogram? (p. 546)

2. Which is a greater capacity, a liter or a milliliter? (p. 544)

3. Which is a greater distance, a kilometer or a meter? (p. 538)

Check Skills

**Choose the unit you would use to measure each.
Write *cm*, *m*, or *km*.** (pp. 538–539)

4. length of a driveway

5. distance from one city to another

6. length of a carrot

Choose the better estimate.

7.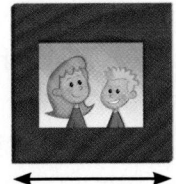

40 cm or 40 dm?

8.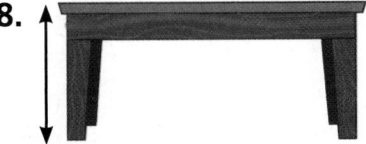

8 cm or 8 dm?

9.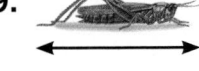

6 cm or 6 dm?

**Choose the unit you would use to find the mass of each.
Write *gram* or *kilogram*.** (pp. 546–547)

10.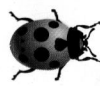

11.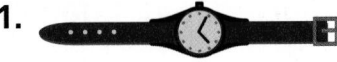

12.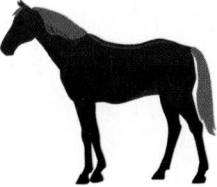

Check Problem Solving

Solve. (pp. 548–549)

13. Ed rides the bus 3,000 meters to school. How many kilometers does he ride?

14. Becky's bedroom is 5 meters long. How many decimeters long is her room?

15. **WRITE Math** ▶ Michael's puppy has a mass of 7,000 grams. Pauline's puppy has a mass of 8 kilograms. **Explain** how to find whose puppy has a greater mass.

Standardized Test Prep
Chapters 1–21

Number and Operations

1. Jackie baked cookies. She put 6 cookies in each of 9 bags. How many cookies in all did she bake? (p. 234)

   A 63   C 45

   B 54   D 15

2. The population of Alaska is about 663,700 people. What is the value of the digit 3 in 663,700? (p. 14)

   A 30

   B 300

   C 3,000

   D 30,000

3. Which number is between 3,165 and 3,217? (p. 32)

   A 3,098

   B 3,147

   C 3,185

   D 3,240

4. **WRITE Math** ▸ What division fact does this model show? **Explain** your answer. (p. 282)

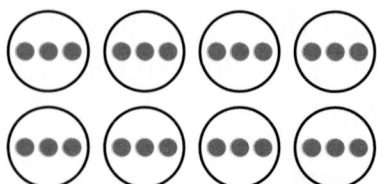

Algebraic Reasoning

5. Judy collects coins. If the pattern continues, how many coins will she collect in the fifth month? (p. 256)

Judy's Coins					
Month	1	2	3	4	5
Coins	6	12	18	24	■

   A 26   C 30

   B 28   D 32

   Test Tip **Decide on a plan.**

   See item 6. Make a plan to find the missing number. First, choose a number that completes one of the number sentences. Next, check if it completes the others. Then, find the number in the answer choices. Use the plan to find the answer.

6. Which number completes the fact family? (p. 286)

   $6 \times ■ = 42$ $■ \times 6 = 42$
   $42 \div ■ = 6$ $42 \div 6 = ■$

   A 6   C 8

   B 7   D 36

7. **WRITE Math** ▸ What is a rule in this pattern? **Explain** how you know. (p. 426)

   4, 5, 8, 9, 12, 13, 16

Geometry

8. Which pair of figures appears to be congruent? (p. 378)

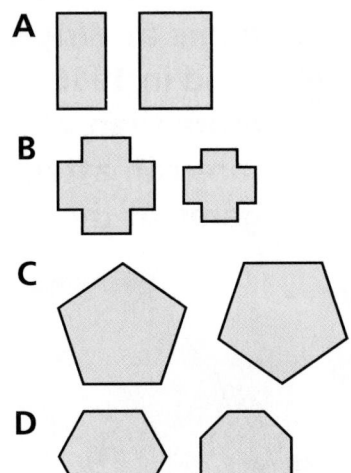

9. Cho drew these figures on the computer. Which figure appears to have a line of symmetry? (p. 384)

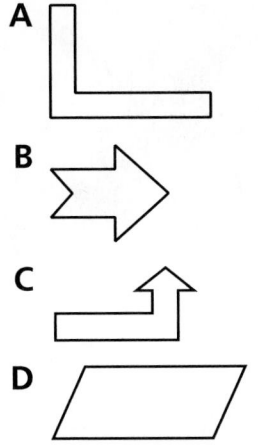

10. ⟨WRITE Math⟩ ▸ What kind of angle is shown? **Explain** how you know.

(p. 350)

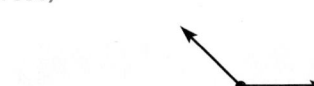

Data Analysis and Probability

11. How much money did the children earn altogether? (p. 148)

Money Earned	
Mia	$ $ $
Jeff	$ $
Carol	$ $ $ $ $
Key: Each $ = $3.	

A $10

B $12

C $30

D $40

12. Which color tile is most likely to be pulled? (p. 182)

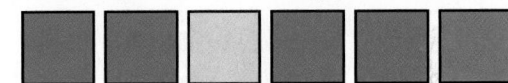

A Yellow

B Blue

C Green

D Red

13. ⟨WRITE Math⟩ ▸ Tory made a bar graph to show the number of pictures she took each day for a week. The bar for Wednesday ends at 12. What does this mean? **Explain.** (p. 156)

22 Perimeter, Area, and Volume

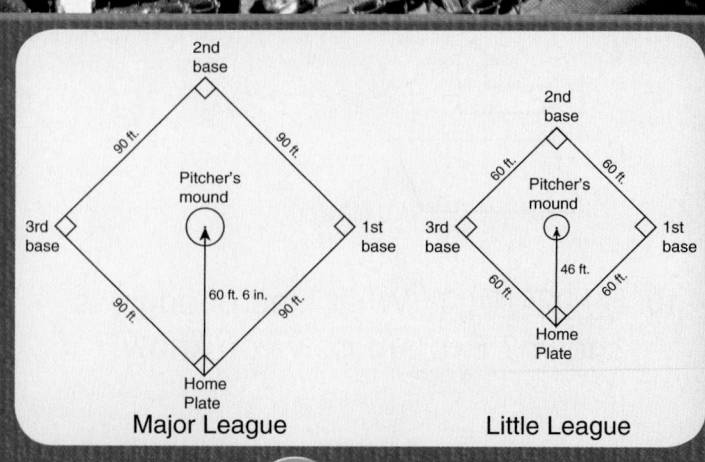

FAST FACT

The Chicago Cubs played their first game at Wrigley Field in 1916. Today, more than 41,000 fans can attend a game at the field.

Investigate

A Major League baseball infield is similar to a Little League baseball infield. Look at the two drawings. Describe how the infields are alike and how they are different.

Major League

2nd base
90 ft.
90 ft.
3rd base
Pitcher's mound
1st base
90 ft.
60 ft. 6 in.
90 ft.
Home Plate

Little League

2nd base
60 ft.
60 ft.
3rd base
Pitcher's mound
1st base
60 ft.
46 ft.
60 ft.
Home Plate

GO ONLINE

Technology
Student pages are available in the Student eBook.

**Check your understanding of important skills
needed for success in Chapter 22.**

▶ **Column Addition**

Find the sum.

	1.	2.	3.	4.
	1	2	5	4
	8	6	5	2
	9	7	8	2
	+4	+6	+3	+7

	5.	6.	7.	8.
	6	10	3	10
	7	9	5	10
	5	9	2	7
	+2	+4	+4	+ 2

▶ **Multiplication Facts Through 10**

Find the product.

9. $3 \times 4 = \blacksquare$ **10.** $7 \times 5 = \blacksquare$ **11.** $8 \times 2 = \blacksquare$ **12.** $6 \times 3 = \blacksquare$

13. $1 \times 5 = \blacksquare$ **14.** $4 \times 9 = \blacksquare$ **15.** $3 \times 2 = \blacksquare$ **16.** $5 \times 5 = \blacksquare$

17.	18.	19.	20.
3	10	6	7
$\times 8$	$\times 7$	$\times 4$	$\times 9$

VOCABULARY POWER

CHAPTER VOCABULARY

area
cubic unit
perimeter
square unit
volume

WARM-UP WORDS

area The number of square units needed to cover a flat surface

perimeter The distance around a figure

volume The amount of space a solid figure takes up

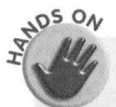

1 Estimate and Measure Perimeter

OBJECTIVE: Estimate and measure perimeter.

Quick Review

Find the sum.

1. $8 + 8 + 8 + 8$
2. $2 + 3 + 4$
3. $1 + 1 + 8 + 3$
4. $6 + 6 + 5 + 5$
5. $3 + 3 + 1 + 4 + 1$

Vocabulary

perimeter

Learn

Perimeter is the distance around a figure. You can estimate and measure perimeter in standard units, such as inches and centimeters.

Find the perimeter of a notebook.

HANDS ON

Activity   **Materials** ■ inch ruler

Step 1

Estimate the perimeter of a notebook in inches. Record your estimate.

Step 2

Use an inch ruler to measure the length of each side of the notebook.

Step 3

Add the lengths of the sides.
■ in. + ■ in. + ■ in. + ■ in. = ■ in.
Record the perimeter.

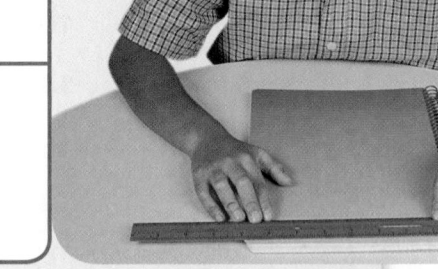

• How does your estimate compare with your measurement?

Examples

Estimate. Then use a ruler to find the length of each side in inches.	Estimate. Then use a ruler to find the length of each side in centimeters.

Add the lengths of the sides: 1 in. + 2 in. + 1 in. + 2 in. = 6 in. The perimeter is 6 inches.	Add the lengths of the sides: 3 cm + 3 cm + 3 cm + 3 cm = 12 cm The perimeter is 12 centimeters.

More Examples

Add the lengths of the sides to find the perimeter.

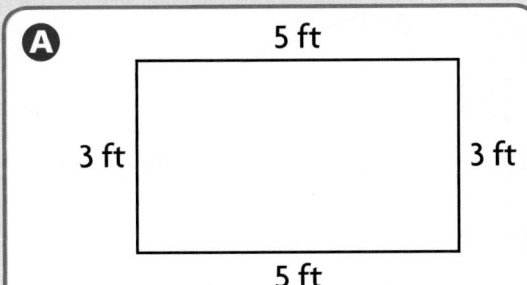

A

5 ft

3 ft   3 ft

5 ft

Add the lengths of the sides:
3 ft + 5 ft + 3 ft + 5 ft = 16 ft
The perimeter is 16 feet.

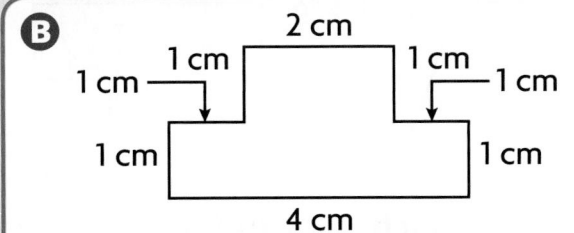

B

2 cm

1 cm

1 cm   1 cm   1 cm

1 cm   1 cm

4 cm

Add the lengths of the sides:
1 cm + 1 cm + 1 cm + 2 cm + 1 cm +
1 cm + 1 cm + 4 cm = 12 cm
The perimeter is 12 centimeters.

- What if you added 1 foot to each side of the rectangle in Example A? How would the perimeter change?

Guided Practice

1. Find the perimeter of the triangle in inches.
   Think: how long is each side?

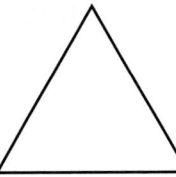

Estimate. Then use a centimeter ruler to find the perimeter.

2. 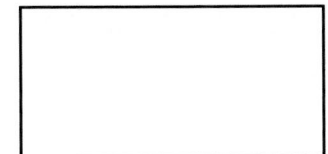   ✓ 3. 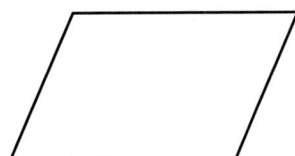   ✓ 4.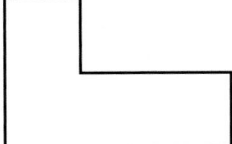

Estimate. Then use an inch ruler to find the perimeter.

5. 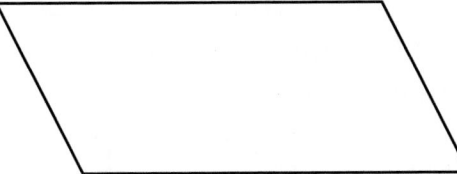   6.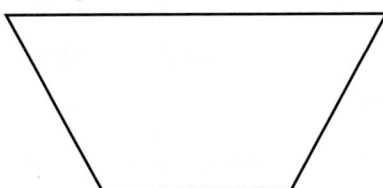

7. **TALK Math** **Explain** how to find the perimeter of this figure in centimeters.

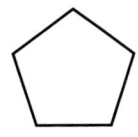

Estimate. Then use a centimeter ruler to find the perimeter.

8.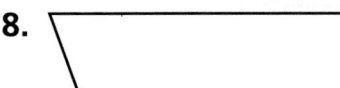

9.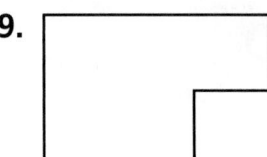

10.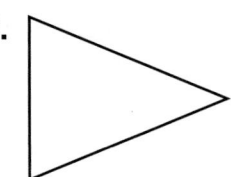

Estimate. Then use an inch ruler to find the perimeter.

11.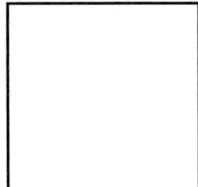

12.

13.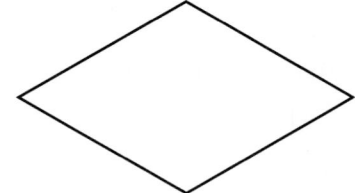

For 14–15, use the photos.

14. Which of the animal photos has a perimeter of 24 inches?

15. How much greater is the perimeter of the bird photo than the perimeter of the cat photo?

5 in.

7 in.

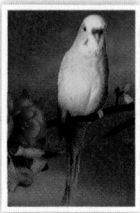

6 in.

4 in.

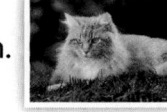

16. Open Ended Use grid paper or a ruler to draw a polygon with a perimeter of 20 cm. Label the length of each side.

17. Lacy is putting a fence around her square garden. Each side of her garden is 3 yards long. The fence costs $5 for each yard. How much will the fence cost?

18. **WRITE Math** One side of a rectangle is 4 feet long and one side is 10 feet long. What is the perimeter of the rectangle? **Explain.**

Mixed Review and Test Prep

19. A quadrilateral has two pairs of parallel sides and four right angles. Name this quadrilateral. (p. 360)

20. Which is the better estimate for the length of a room: 12 in. or 12 ft?

(p. 526)

21. Test Prep Use your centimeter ruler to find the perimeter of this rectangle.

A 8 cm **B** 10 cm **C** 12 cm **D** 16 cm

Technology
Use Harcourt Mega Math, Ice Station Exploration, *Polar Planes*, Level P.

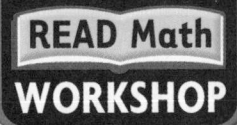

Take My Picture

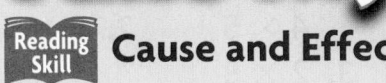 **Cause and Effect**

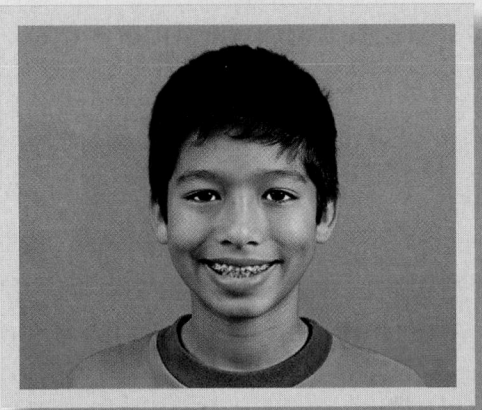

When you take a picture with a digital camera, the picture is stored in the camera's memory. Then you can print your picture later. Before you print the picture, you can choose the size. Look at the photo below. If each side of the photo is increased by 2 inches, how much will the perimeter increase? Cause and effect is a strategy that can help you understand a problem. A cause is the reason something happens. An effect is the result, or outcome.

Cause	Effect
Increase each side of the photo by 2 inches.	The perimeter increases.

So, if the length of each side changes, then the perimeter will also change.

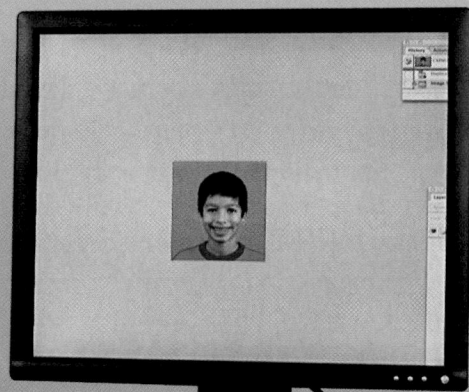

Problem Solving Use the information and the strategy to solve the problems.

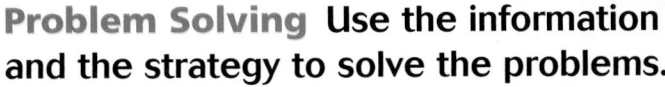

1. Solve the problem above. What operation did you use to solve the problem?

2. Courtney has a photo of her dog. The photo is 8 inches wide and 10 inches long. She wants to decrease the length of each side by 3 inches and reprint the photo. What will the new perimeter be? **Explain.**

2 Area of Plane Figures

OBJECTIVE: Estimate and measure the area of plane figures.

Quick Review

Multiply.

1. 4×5
2. 6×3
3. 2×8
4. 5×7
5. 9×9

Vocabulary

area   square unit

Learn

Area is the number of square units needed to cover a flat surface.

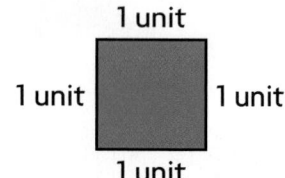

1 unit
1 unit   1 unit
1 unit

A **square unit** is a square with a side length of 1 unit.

 HANDS ON

Activity

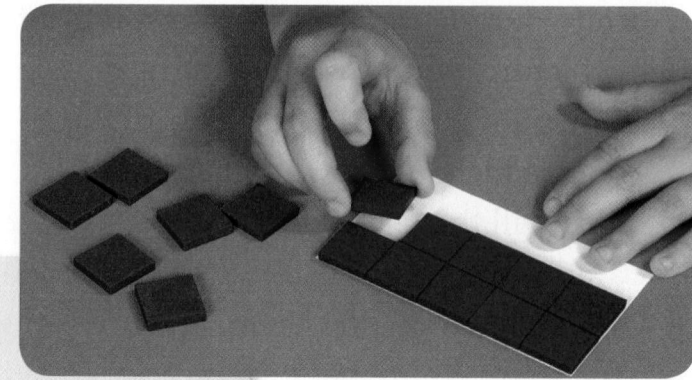

Materials ■ square tiles, index card, grid paper

Step 1

Estimate how many square tiles it will take to cover an index card. Record your estimate.

Step 2

Use square tiles to cover the surface of an index card.

Step 3

Use grid paper. Draw a picture to show how you covered the index card.

Step 4

Count and record the number of rows of tiles and the number of tiles in each row. The product of these numbers is the area of the index card in square units.

 ERROR ALERT

Do not leave any space between the square tiles when you use them to find area.

• What is the area of your index card?

• How does your estimate compare with your measurement?

• How is finding the area like making an array?

• **What if** you used larger paper squares to cover the surface of your index card? How would the number of paper squares compare to the number of tiles?

Examples

You can count or multiply square units to find area.

A Count units.

These are half square units.

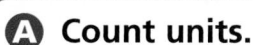

$\frac{1}{2}$ units

2 half square units = 1 square unit

1	2		
3	4		
5	6	7	8
9	10	11	12

12 square units

1	2		
3	4		
5	6	7	
8	9	10	11

$\frac{1}{2}$

$11\frac{1}{2}$ square units

B Multiply units.

To find area of a rectangle, multiply the number of rows by the number in each row.

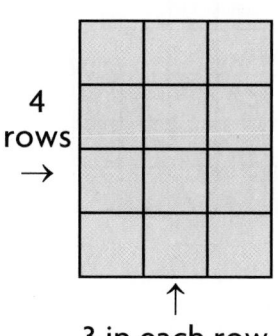

4 rows →

↑
3 in each row

number of rows	number in each row		area
↓	↓		↓
4	× 3	=	12 square units

Guided Practice

1. How many square tiles were used to make this figure? What is the area?

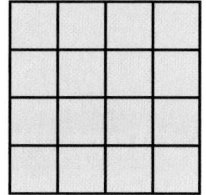

**Count or multiply to find the area of each figure.
Write the answer in square units.**

2.

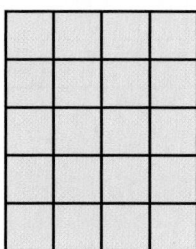

✓ 3.

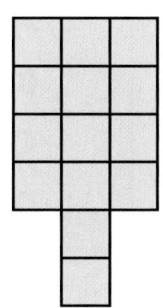

✓ 4.

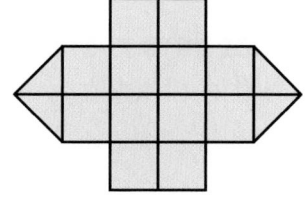

5. **TALK Math** On grid paper, draw a square that has a side length of 5 units. **Explain** two ways to find the area of the square.

Count or multiply to find the area of each figure.
Write the answer in square units.

6.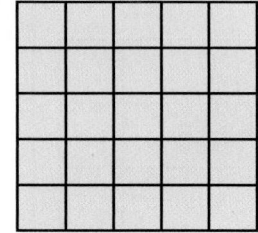

7.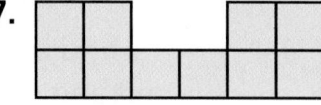

8.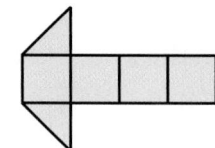

9.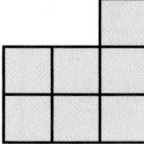

10.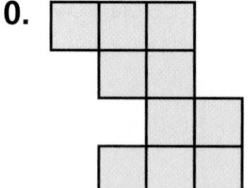

11.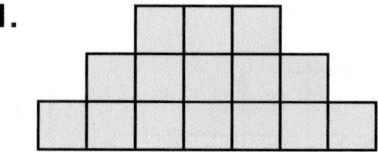

12. Use grid paper to draw a figure with an area of 16 square units.

13. Josh made a design with tiles. There are 6 rows with 6 square tiles in each row. What is the area?

14. Mr. Stephens put tile on a section of his floor. The section had 3 rows with 4 tiles in each row. Each tile cost $3. How much did Mr. Stephens spend?

15. **WRITE Math** ▸ **Sense or Nonsense** Mary says you can find the area of this rectangle by multiplying 2 times 3. Does this make sense? **Explain.**

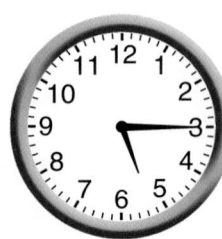

Mixed Review and Test Prep

16. Jade made a square pillow with 10 inch sides. She sewed a ribbon around the perimeter of the pillow. How much ribbon did she use? (p. 560)

17. What time is shown on the clock?

(p. 124)

18. **Test Prep** What is the area of this rectangle?

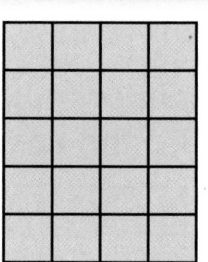

A 9 square units

B 10 square units

C 18 square units

D 20 square units

Extra Practice on page 574, Set B

CD ROM **Technology** Use Harcourt Mega Math, Ice Station Exploration, *Polar Planes,* Level Q.

Learn About Comparing Area

Lydia has plans for two different gardens. Each square unit represents 1 square yard. Which garden has the greater area?

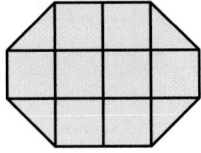

Garden A

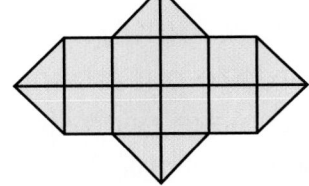

Garden B

Step 1 Count to find the number of whole square units in each garden.	Garden A has 8 whole square units. Garden B has 8 whole square units.
Step 2 Count the number of half square units in each garden.	Garden A has 4 half square units. Garden B has 8 half square units.
Step 3 Find the total area of each garden.	Garden A: 8 + 2 = 10 square units Garden B: 8 + 4 = 12 square units
Step 4 Compare the areas.	10 square units < 12 square units

So, Garden B has the greater area.

Try It

For each pair, find the area in square units. Which figure has the greater area?

19.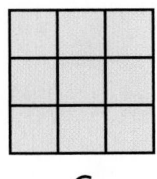

C   D

20.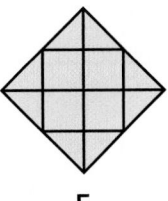

E   F

21. **WRITE Math** ▸ Can two rectangles with different shapes have the same area? **Explain.**

Relate Perimeter and Area

OBJECTIVE: Explore the relationship between the area and the perimeter of a figure.

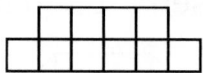
Learn

PROBLEM Cody has 20 feet of wood boards to put around a rectangular sandbox. How long should he make each side so that the area of the sandbox is as large as possible?

Example

Use square tiles. Make all the rectangles you can that have a perimeter of 20. Then find the area of each.

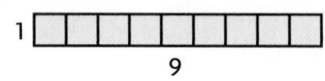
9

Perimeter: 9 + 1 + 9 + 1 = 20 units
Area: 1 × 9 = 9 square units

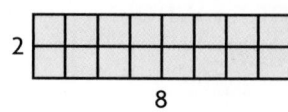
8

Perimeter: 8 + 2 + 8 + 2 = 20 units
Area: 2 × 8 = 16 square units

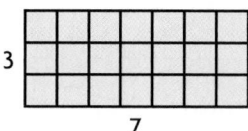
3
7

Perimeter:
7 + 3 + 7 + 3 = 20 units
Area: 3 × 7 = 21 square units

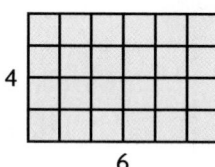
4
6

Perimeter:
6 + 4 + 6 + 4 = 20 units
Area: 4 × 6 = 24 square units

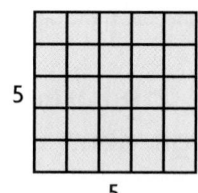
5
5

Perimeter:
5 + 5 + 5 + 5 = 20 units
Area: 5 × 5 = 25 square units

Order the areas: 9 < 16 < 21 < 24 < 25
25 square units is the greatest area.
So, to have a sandbox with the largest area possible,
Cody should make a square with sides 5 feet long.

More Examples

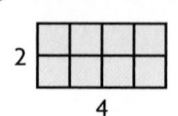
2
4

Perimeter:
4 + 2 + 4 + 2 = 12 units
Area:
2 × 4 = 8 square units

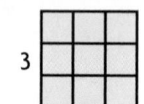
3
3

Perimeter:
3 + 3 + 3 + 3 = 12 units
Area:
3 × 3 = 9 square units

• What do you notice about the perimeters and areas of the two figures in More Examples?

Guided Practice

1. Use square tiles. Make a rectangle with the same perimeter but a different area as the one on the right. Which figure has the greater area?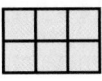

For each pair, find the perimeter and the area. Tell which figure has the greater area.

2.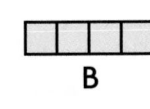

3.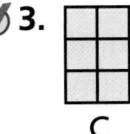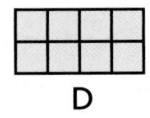

4. **TALK Math** Figures E and F have the same perimeter. **Explain** which figure has the greater area.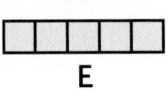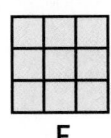

Independent Practice and Problem Solving

For each pair, find the perimeter and the area. Tell which figure has the greater area.

5.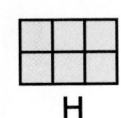

6.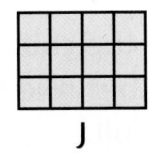

7. Julia made a rectangular flower garden with a perimeter of 16 feet and an area of 15 square feet. What are the lengths of the sides? Draw a picture to show your answer.

8. **WRITE Math** **What's the Question?** Todd's flower garden is 4 feet wide and 8 feet long. The answer is 32 square feet.

Mixed Review and Test Prep

9. A violin has 4 strings. How many strings are on 9 violins? (p. 212)

10. Ann glued strips of felt around the perimeter of a square picture frame. One side is 5 inches. How many inches of felt did she use? (p. 560)

11. **Test Prep** Which figure has an area of 16 square units and a perimeter of 16 units?

A 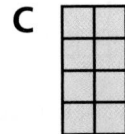   C

B 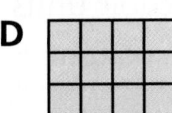   D

Extra Practice on page 574, Set C

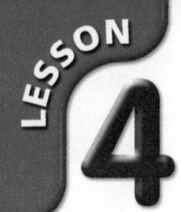

Estimate and Find Volume

OBJECTIVE: Estimate and find volume.

Learn

Volume is the amount of space a solid figure takes up.

A **cubic unit** is used to measure volume. A cubic unit is a cube with a side length of 1 unit.

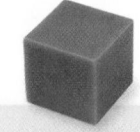

1 cubic unit

ONE WAY Count the cubes to find volume.

Activity **Materials** ■ small boxes, cubes

Step 1

Choose a box. Estimate the number of cubes it will take to fill the box. Record your estimate.

Step 2

Count the cubes you use. Place the cubes in rows along the bottom of the box. Continue to make layers of cubes until the box is full.

Step 3

Record how many cubes it took to fill the box. This is the volume of the box in cubic units.

• How does your estimate compare with the actual volume?

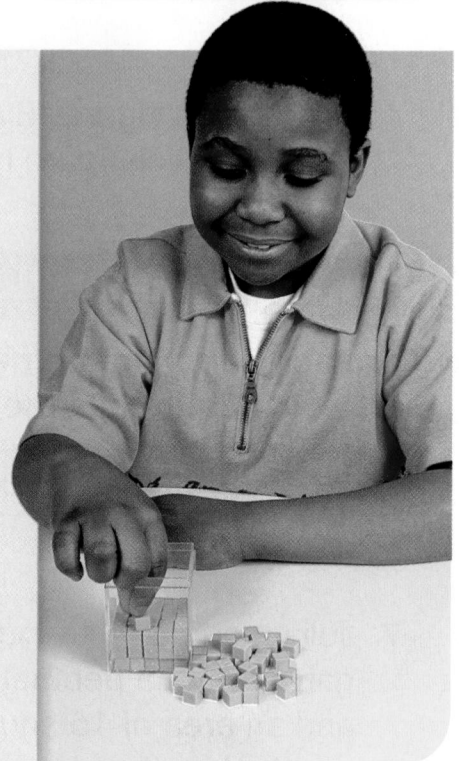

ANOTHER WAY Multiply to find volume.

When you cannot count each cube, count the number of cubes in the top layer. Then count the number of layers and multiply.

A

2 layers $\times$ 6 cubes per layer = 12 cubic units

The volume is 12 cubic units.

B

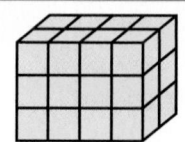

3 layers $\times$ 8 cubes per layer = 24 cubic units

The volume is 24 cubic units.

1. Find the volume of this solid figure.

Think: How many layers are there? How many cubes are in each layer?

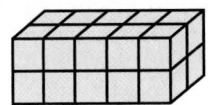

Use cubes to make each solid. Then write the volume in cubic units.

2.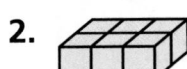

☑ 3.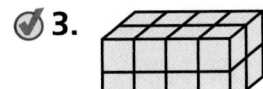

☑ 4.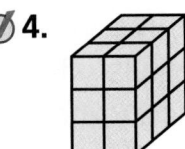

5. (TALK Math) **Explain** one way you can find the volume of a box that has 3 layers with 10 cubes in each layer.

Independent Practice and Problem Solving

Use cubes to make each solid. Then write the volume in cubic units.

6.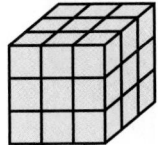

7.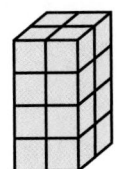

8.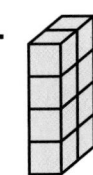

9. The volume of Chad's box is 36 cubic units. There are 4 layers. How many cubes are in each layer?

10. Look at the figure in Exercise 6. Write a multiplication sentence to find the volume of the figure.

11. Each layer of a prism is 6 cubic units. The volume is 24 cubic units. How many layers are in the prism?

12. (WRITE Math) **What's the Error?** Describe the error. Find the correct answer.

Volume = 6 cubic units

Mixed Review and Test Prep

13. If $(4 \times 2) \times 3 = 24$, what is $(2 \times 3) \times 4$? (p. 260)

14. Find the perimeter and area of this figure. (pp. 560, 564)

15. Test Prep What is the volume of this solid figure?

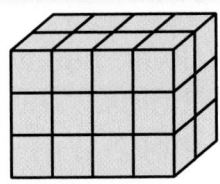

A 9 cubic units   **C** 24 cubic units

B 12 cubic units   **D** 36 cubic units

Problem Solving Workshop
Skill: Use a Model

OBJECTIVE: Solve problems by using the skill *use a model.*

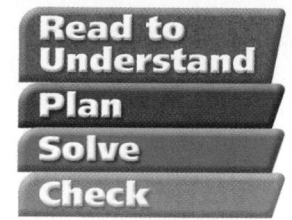

Use the Skill

PROBLEM Mr. Davis bought 12 baseballs. Each baseball comes in a cube-shaped box. He wants to put all the baseballs into one large box. Which box can Mr. Davis use to hold the 12 baseballs?

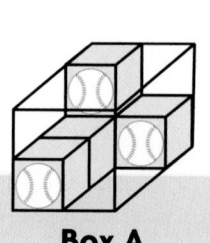 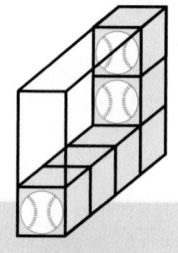

Box A   **Box B**

You can decide whether a box will hold 12 baseballs by using a model.

Make a model of Box A and Box B.
Use a cube to represent each baseball.

Box A

Place 3 rows of 2 cubes in the first layer.
Add a second layer.

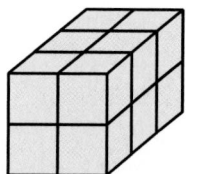

Find the volume:

2 layers × 6 cubes per layer = 12 cubic units

Box B

Place 1 row of 4 cubes in the first layer. Add two more layers.

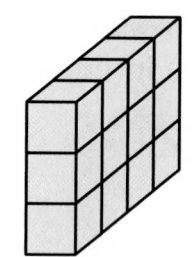

Find the volume:

3 layers × 4 cubes per layer = 12 cubic units

Both containers have a volume of 12 cubic units.

So, Mr. Davis can use Box A or Box B.
Both boxes will hold 12 baseballs.

Think and Discuss
Use a model to solve.

a. Lou filled a box with blocks. There are 2 layers. Each layer has 3 rows of 4 blocks. What is the volume of the box?

b. Ryan has two boxes. The red box has 4 layers. Each layer holds 3 rows of 3 cubes. The blue box has 5 layers. Each layer holds 2 rows of 4 cubes. Which box holds more cubes?

c. A box has a volume of 24 cubic units. There are 3 rows with 2 cubes in each row. How many layers does the box have?

Guided Problem Solving

Solve.

1. Mrs. Spencer collects teacups. She keeps each one in a cube-shaped box. She wants to pack her teacups in a larger box. There are two different-sized boxes she can use. Which box can hold 36 teacups?

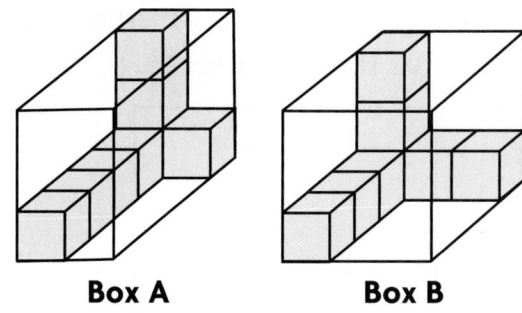

Box A   **Box B**

Make a model of each box.
Use a cube to represent each teacup box.
Count the cubes or multiply to find the volume of each box. Solve the problem.

2. **What if** Box A could hold 4 layers of teacups? What would be the volume of Box A in cubic units?

3. A carton is filled with 20 mugs in cube-shaped boxes. The carton has 2 layers. How many mugs are in each layer?

Mixed Applications

USE DATA For 5–6, use the table.

4. Ms. Wagner bought a box full of strawberry yogurt cups. The box has 2 layers. Each layer has 3 rows of 4 cups. How many yogurt cups are in the box?

Strawberry Snacks	
Snack	**Price**
Strawberry yogurt cup	$2.00
Strawberry pie slice	$3.50
Strawberry ice cream cone	$2.75

5. Brandon had $10. He bought 2 slices of strawberry pie and 1 strawberry ice cream cone. How much money does he have left?

6. Tom bought an ice cream cone and a yogurt cup. He did not use any quarters. What bills and coins could he have used?

7. **WRITE Math** Bob's box has 2 layers with 2 rows of 3 blocks. Tom's box has 3 layers with 2 rows of 2 blocks. Whose box has more blocks? **Explain.**

8. Steve traced around the bottom of a solid figure. He drew a circle. Which could he have traced: a square pyramid, a cone, or a cube?

9. Sandy can run 1 mile in 8 minutes. At that speed, about how long will it take Sandy to run a 3-mile race?

10. Bryanna is washing her dad's car. Is the temperature about 25°F or about 75°F?

Extra Practice

Set A Estimate. Then use a centimeter ruler
to find the perimeter. (pp. 560–563)

1.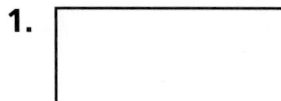

2.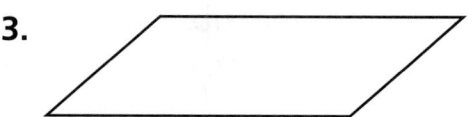

3.

Set B Count or multiply to find the area of each figure.
Write the answer in square units. (pp. 564–567)

1.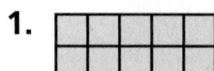

2.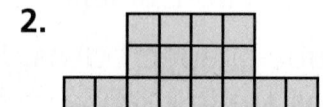

3.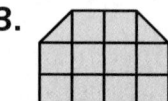

4. A checkerboard has 8 rows and
8 columns of red and black squares.
What is the area in square units?

5. Aidan put tiles on his bathroom
floor. There are four rows of five tiles
and two rows of two tiles. What is
the area?

Set C For each pair, find the perimeter and the area.
Tell which figure has the greater area. (pp. 568–569)

1.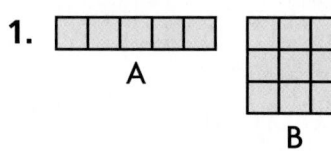

2.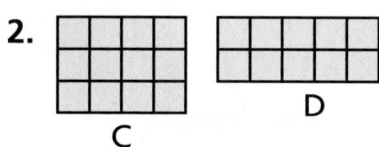

Set D Use cubes to make each solid. Then write the
volume in cubic units. (pp. 570–571)

1.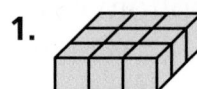

2.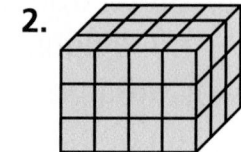

3.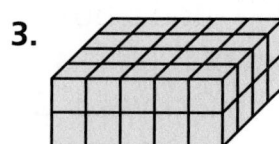

4. Each layer of a prism is 4 cubic units.
The volume is 24 cubic units. How
many layers are in the prism?

5. The volume of Sam's box is
25 cubic units. There are 5 layers.
How many cubes are in each layer?

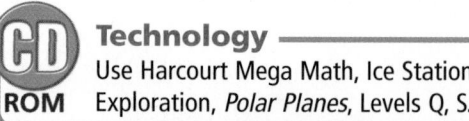

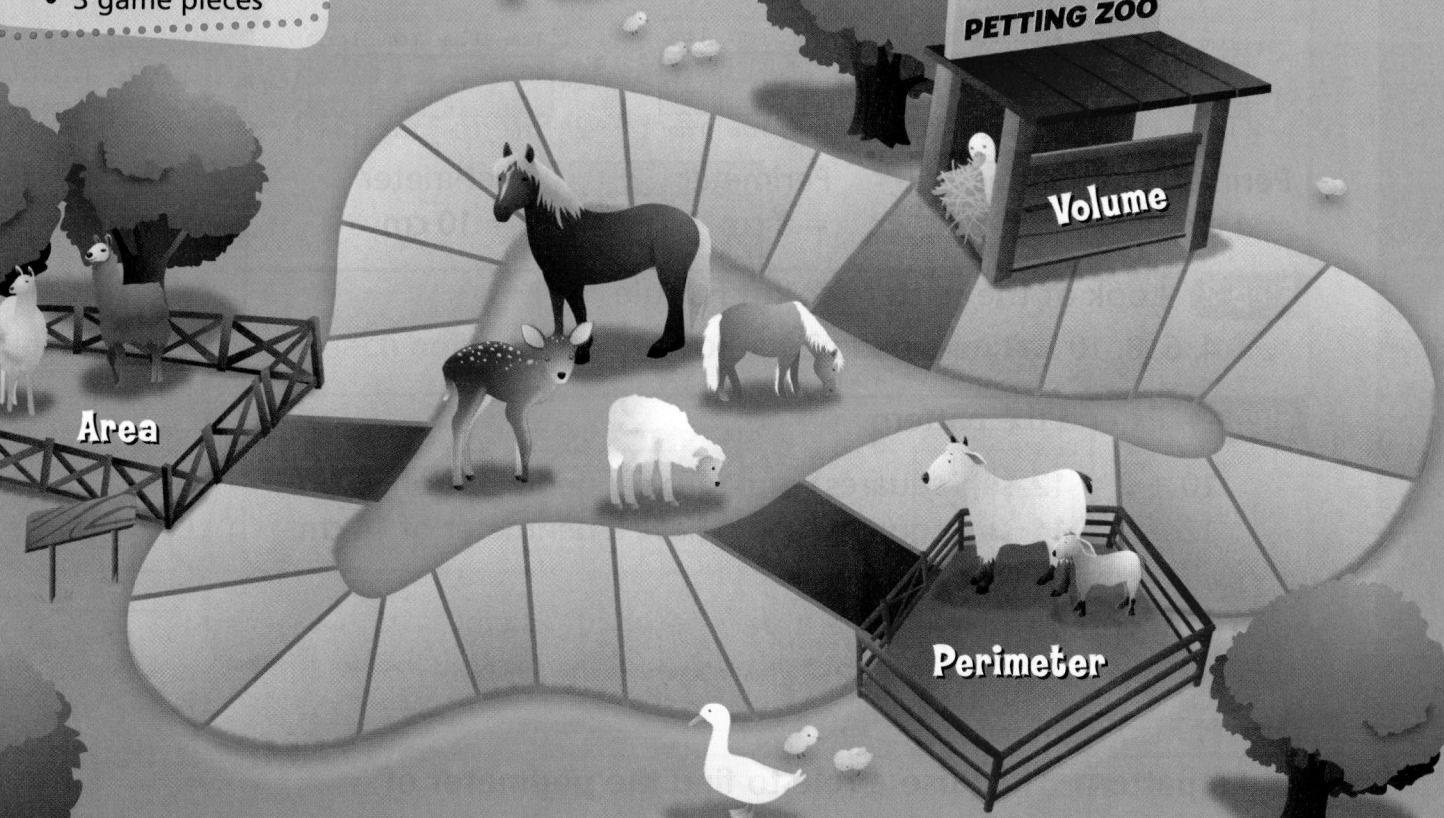

Find That Measure

Roll!
3 players

Move!
- Game cards
- 1 number cube
- 3 game pieces

PETTING ZOO

Volume

Area

Perimeter

Win!

- Each player places a game piece on either the Perimeter, Area, or Volume space on the gameboard.

- Players take turns tossing a number cube and moving clockwise that number of spaces.

- If a player lands on Perimeter, Area, or Volume, he or she draws a game card and finds the perimeter, area, or volume of the figure on the card.

- The other players check the answer. If it is correct, the player keeps the card and gets another turn.

- If the answer is incorrect, the player returns the card to the bottom of the deck, and play passes to the next player.

- The first player to collect one card each from Perimeter, Area, and Volume wins.

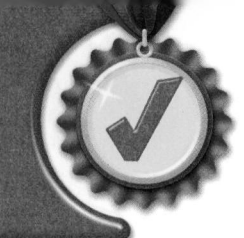

Unit Review/Test
Chapters 20–22

Multiple Choice

1. Which unit would be best to measure the weight of the dog? (p. 522)

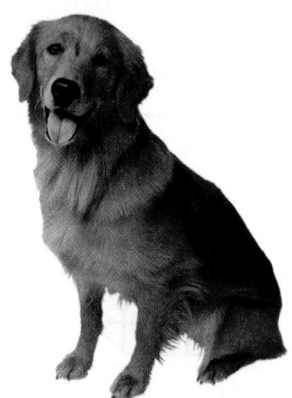

A Ounce   **C** Pound

B Foot   **D** Yard

2. Which measurement best describes the length of a student's desk? (p. 512)

A 2 inches

B 2 feet

C 20 feet

D 2 miles

3. Susan's pitcher contains 6 pints of lemonade. How many 1-cup glasses of lemonade can she fill from the pitcher? (p. 520)

A 3

B 6

C 10

D 12

4. Which distance is about 10 kilometers? (p. 538)

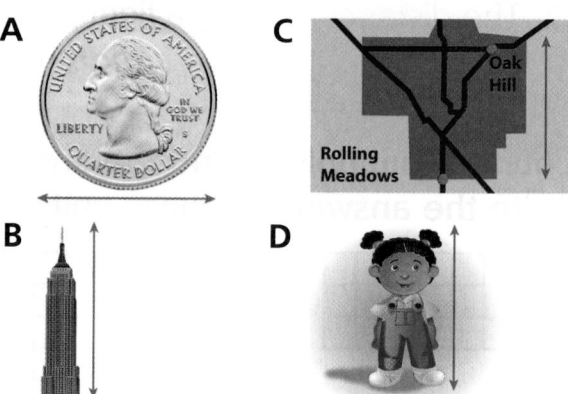

A   **C** Oak Hill / Rolling Meadows

B   **D**

5. Which statement is true? (p. 540)

A 700 cm = 7 m

B 700 cm = 70 m

C 700 cm = 700 m

D 700 cm = 7,000 m

6. What is the perimeter of this figure? (p. 560)

9 cm
7 cm   7 cm
7 cm   7 cm
9 cm

A 63 centimeters

B 49 centimeters

C 46 centimeters

D 42 centimeters

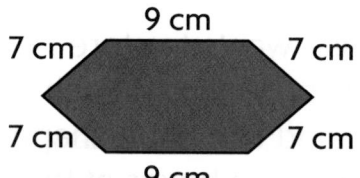 **Technology** Use *Online Assessment.*

Unit Review/Test
Chapters 20–22

Multiple Choice

1. Which unit would be best to measure the weight of the dog? (p. 522)

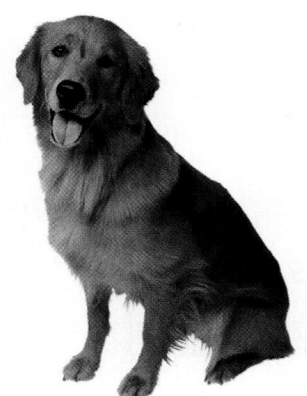

 A Ounce **C** Pound

 B Foot   **D** Yard

2. Which measurement best describes the length of a student's desk? (p. 512)

 A 2 inches

 B 2 feet

 C 20 feet

 D 2 miles

3. Susan's pitcher contains 6 pints of lemonade. How many 1-cup glasses of lemonade can she fill from the pitcher? (p. 520)

 A 3

 B 6

 C 10

 D 12

4. Which distance is about 10 kilometers? (p. 538)

 A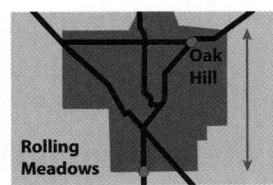

 B

 C

 D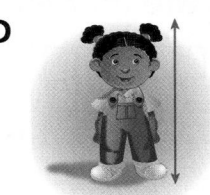

5. Which statement is true? (p. 540)

 A 700 cm = 7 m

 B 700 cm = 70 m

 C 700 cm = 700 m

 D 700 cm = 7,000 m

6. What is the perimeter of this figure? (p. 560)

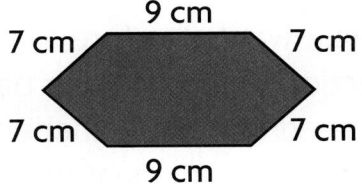

 A 63 centimeters

 B 49 centimeters

 C 46 centimeters

 D 42 centimeters

GO ONLINE Technology Use *Online Assessment.*

Chapter 22 Review/Test

Check Vocabulary and Concepts

Choose the best term from the box.

1. The __?__ is the amount of space a solid figure takes up. (p. 570)

2. The distance around a figure is the __?__ (p. 560)

Check Skills

Count or multiply to find the area of each figure.
Write the answer in square units. (pp. 564–567)

3.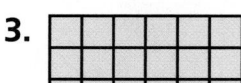

4.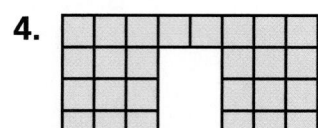

5.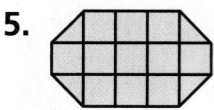

Find the volume of each solid. Write the volume in cubic units.

(pp. 570–571)

6.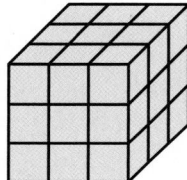

7.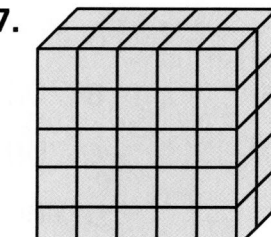

8.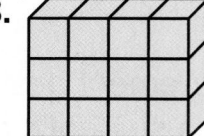

Check Problem Solving

Solve. (pp. 572–573)

9. Natasha wants to store her golf ball collection in a box. Each ball is packaged in a cube-shaped box. Which of the boxes at the right will hold Natasha's 20 golf balls?

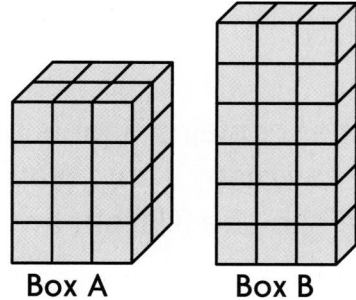

Box A   Box B

10. [WRITE Math] **Explain** why a box that has 6 layers of 6 cubes will not hold as much as a box that has 4 layers of 10 cubes.

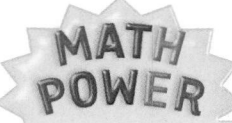

Perimeter Patterns

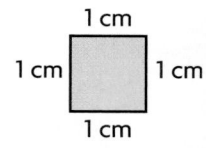

Look at the square. Its perimeter is 4 cm. You can use connected squares to form a perimeter pattern.

1 cm
1 cm ☐ 1 cm
1 cm

Example

Find the perimeter of 6 connected squares by using a pattern.

Step 1 Find the perimeters of the first few shapes.

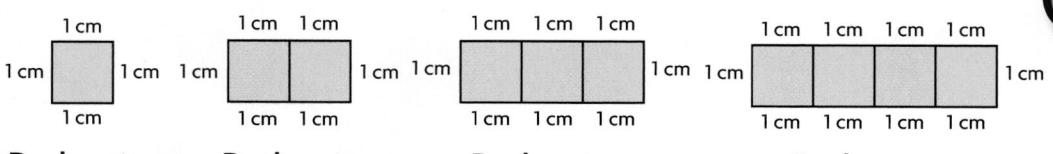

| Perimeter = 4 cm | Perimeter = 6 cm | Perimeter = 8 cm | Perimeter = 10 cm |

Step 2 Look at the pattern to find a rule.

4, 6, 8, 10   A rule is add 2.

Step 3 Extend the pattern.

10 + 2 = 12, so 5 squares would have a perimeter of 12 cm.
12 + 2 = 14, so 6 squares would have a perimeter of 14 cm.

So, 6 connected squares have a perimeter of 14 cm.

Try It

Find a pattern. Then use a rule to find the perimeter of 6 connected shapes.

1.
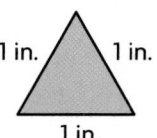
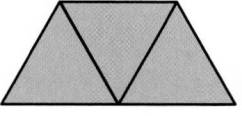
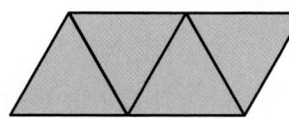

2.
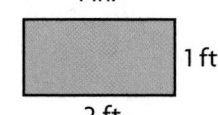
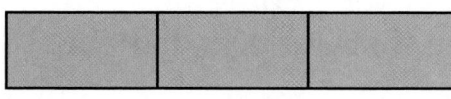

3. **WRITE Math ▶** Suppose the rectangles in exercise 2 were turned and the pattern at the right was made. Has the perimeter pattern changed? **Explain** how you know.

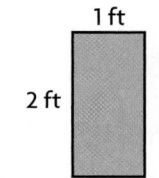
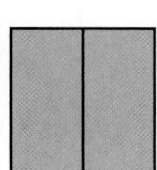
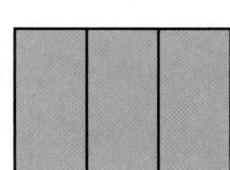

Find That Measure

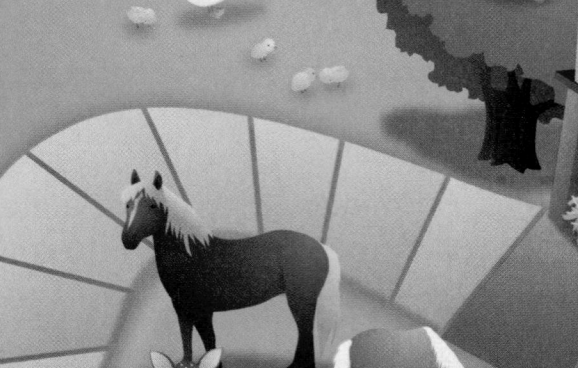

Roll!
3 players

Move!
- Game cards
- 1 number cube
- 3 game pieces

PETTING ZOO

Volume

Area

Perimeter

Win!

- Each player places a game piece on either the Perimeter, Area, or Volume space on the gameboard.

- Players take turns tossing a number cube and moving clockwise that number of spaces.

- If a player lands on Perimeter, Area, or Volume, he or she draws a game card and finds the perimeter, area, or volume of the figure on the card.

- The other players check the answer. If it is correct, the player keeps the card and gets another turn.

- If the answer is incorrect, the player returns the card to the bottom of the deck, and play passes to the next player.

- The first player to collect one card each from Perimeter, Area, and Volume wins.

7. A statue is 300 decimeters tall. How many meters tall is the statue?

(p. 540)

A 3,000 meters **C** 30 meters

B 300 meters **D** 3 meters

8. What activity could you do at the temperature shown? (p. 528)

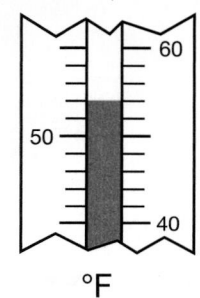

°F

A swimming **C** bike riding

B sledding **D** ice skating

9. What is the area of the figure?

(p. 564)

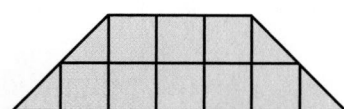

A 10 square units

B 12 square units

C 14 square units

D 20 square units

Short Response

10. Ginny has a ribbon that is 24 feet long. How many yards long is the ribbon? (p. 512)

11. What is the volume of this solid figure? (p. 570)

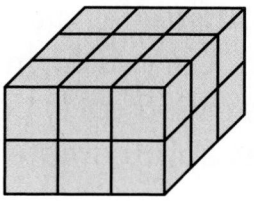

12. Annemarie has 20 cups of juice. Jerry has 6 quarts of juice. Who has more juice? (p. 520)

Extended Response ⟨ WRITE Math ⟩

13. Ted used milliliters to measure the amount of iced tea in a pitcher. Vanessa used liters to measure the same amount. Whose measurement was greater? **Explain.** (p. 544)

14. What is an activity you could do at the temperature shown? **Explain** your answer. (p. 550)

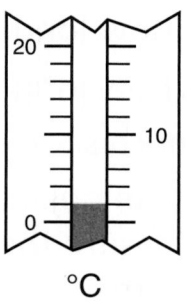

°C

The World Almanac FOR KIDS

Fish Stories

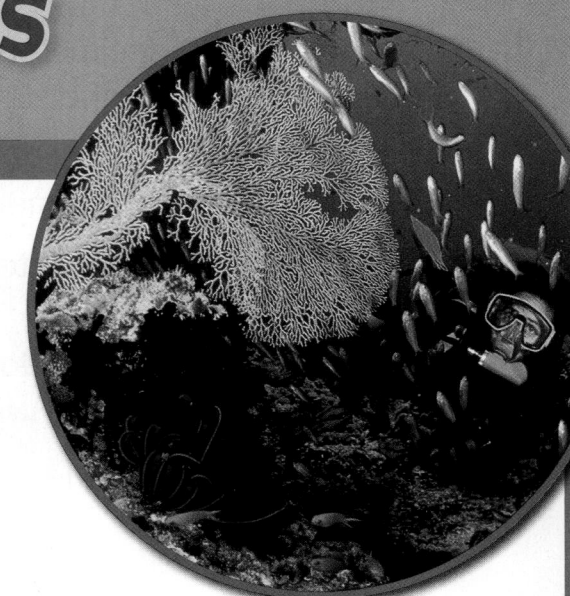

Great Barrier Reef

The Great Barrier Reef, located off the coast of Australia, is the home of colorful coral and fish. Coral is formed by colonies of tiny sea animals called coral polyps. The Great Barrier Reef has approximately 400 species of coral and 1,500 species of fish.

Some of the fish that live at the Great Barrier Reef are shown on these two pages.

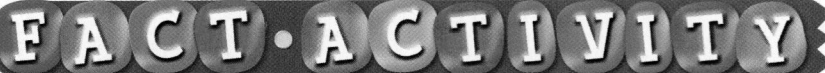

FACT·ACTIVITY

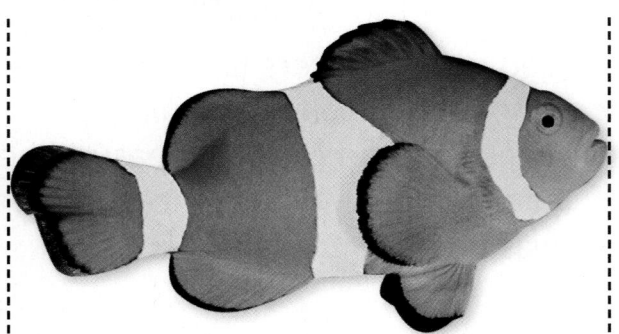

Clown fish

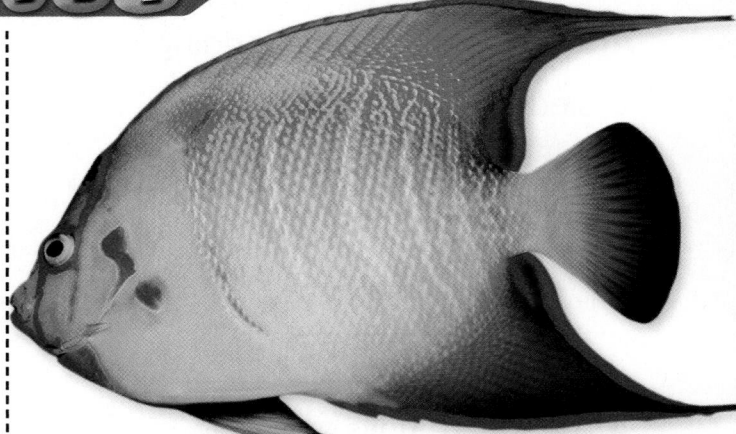

Angelfish

Use a ruler to measure to the nearest centimeter.

❶ About how long is the angelfish?

❷ About how long is the clown fish?

❸ How much shorter is the clown fish than the angelfish?

❹ Choose an object that is about the same length as each of these fish. Measure the objects. How do your measurements compare to the lengths of the fish?

You and the Fish

ALMANAC
Fact

The Great Barrier Reef is the world's largest coral reef.

Has anyone ever told you about "the fish that got away"? When people tell such "fish stories," they sometimes use their hands and arms to show the lengths of fish. It's easier to understand how long something is when you compare it to something familiar, such as the length of your arm span.

FACT·ACTIVITY

For 3–5, use the data on pages 580–581.

❶ Copy the chart. Estimate and record each length. Then, with a partner, use a centimeter ruler to measure to the nearest centimeter.

About How Many Centimeters?		
Body Unit	Estimate	Actual Measurement
Length of pointer finger		
Length of arm		
Length of foot		

❷ How close were your estimates to the actual measurements?

❸ Which fish is about as long as your pointer finger?

❹ Is the length of your foot greater than or less than the length of the clown fish?

❺ Is your height greater than or less than the length of the box jellyfish?

❻ **WRITE Math** ‣ Measure the width of your classroom with a meter stick. Then write a number sentence using <, >, or = to compare your measurement with the length of the hammerhead shark.

The hammerhead shark is about 6 meters long.

Including the tentacles, the box jellyfish is 3 meters long!

8 Multiply and Divide by 1 Digit

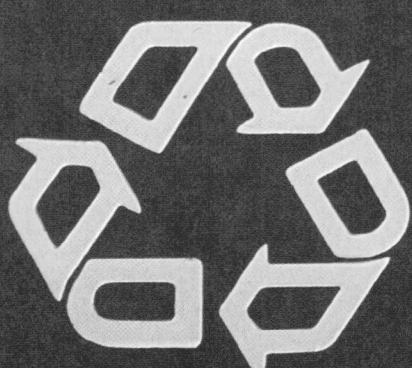

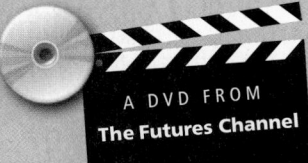

A DVD FROM
The Futures Channel

with
Chapter Projects

1

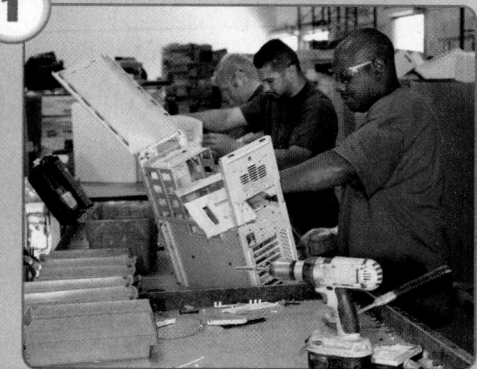

As old computers are taken apart, the number of cases, circuit boards, and keyboards multiply.

2

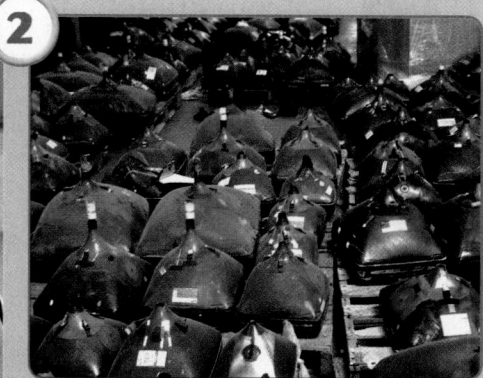

An equal number of CRT's (cathode ray tubes) are placed on wood pallets for safe handling.

3

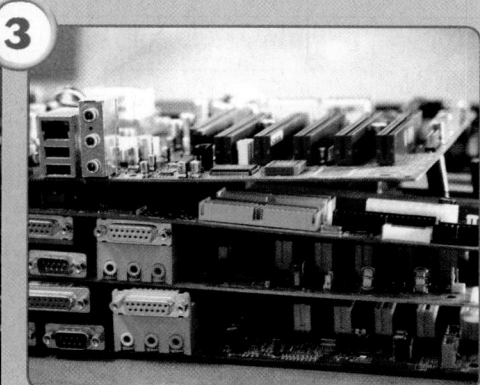

Three men can recycle 600 computers a day. That is 75 computers an hour in an 8-hour work day.

VOCABULARY POWER

TALK Math

What math do you see in the **Math on Location** photographs? How is multiplication or division used?

READ Math

REVIEW VOCABULARY You learned the words below when you learned about multiplication and division basic facts. How do these words relate to **Math on Location**?

Commutative Property of Multiplication the property that states that you can multiply two factors in any order and get the same product

quotient the answer in a division problem

dividend the number that is divided in a division problem

WRITE Math

Copy a Venn Diagram like the one below. Use what you know about multiplication and division to add more words.

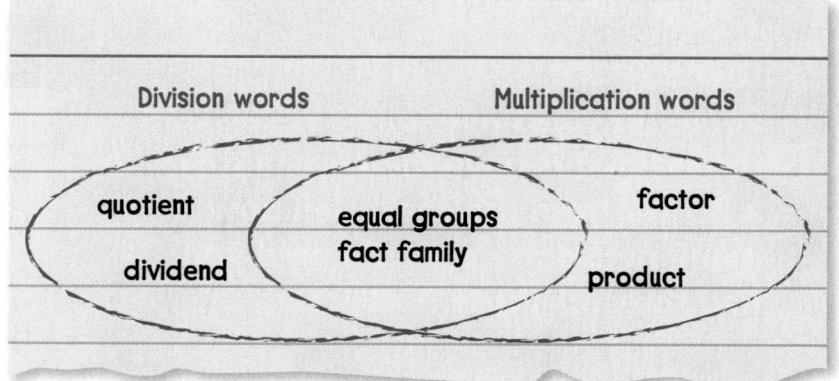

Division words   Multiplication words

quotient   equal groups   factor
                    fact family
dividend   product

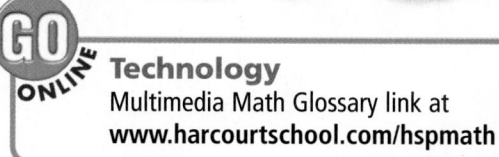

GO ONLINE
Technology
Multimedia Math Glossary link at
www.harcourtschool.com/hspmath

23 Multiply by 1 Digit

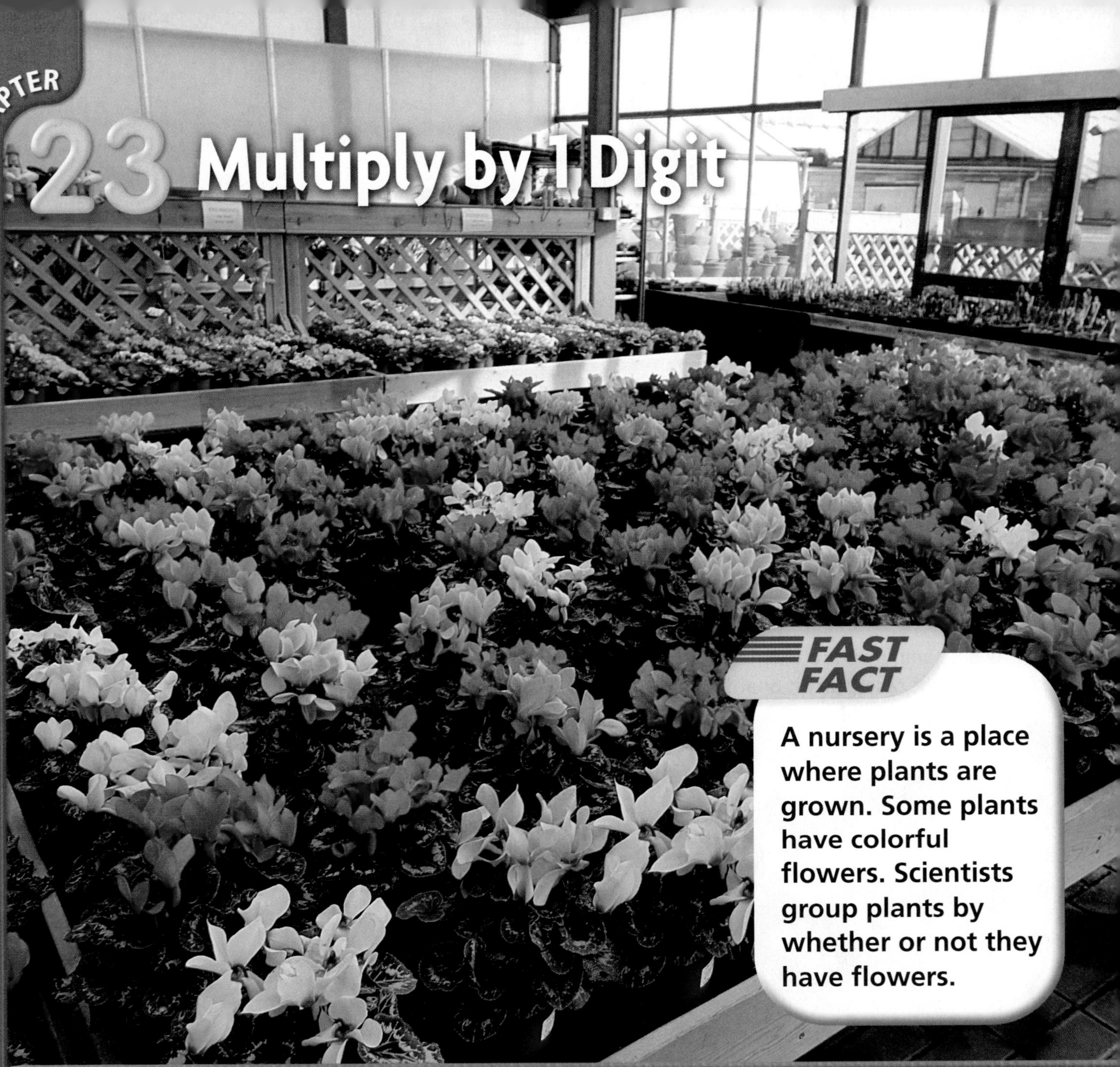

FAST FACT

A nursery is a place where plants are grown. Some plants have colorful flowers. Scientists group plants by whether or not they have flowers.

Investigate

Some flowers have only 3 petals and some flowers have many petals. Select a flower from the chart. Tell how many petals there would be if you had three of those flowers.

Flowers	
Type of Flower	**Number of Petals**
Sunflower	34
Marigold	12
Daisy	55
Black-eyed Susan	21

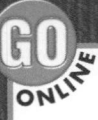

Technology
Student pages are available in the Student eBook.

Check your understanding of important skills needed for success in Chapter 23.

▶ Regroup Ones as Tens

Find the sum.

1. 7
   +9

2. 15
   + 8

3. 19
   +34

4. 36
   +27

5. 23
   +17

6. 29
   +11

7. 35
   +37

8. 32
   +48

9. $78 + 15 = $ ■   **10.** $47 + 39 = $ ■   **11.** $56 + 5 = $ ■   **12.** $33 + 8 = $ ■

▶ Multiplication Facts Through 10

Find the product.

13. $3 \times 5 = $ ■   **14.** $7 \times 7 = $ ■   **15.** $6 \times 4 = $ ■   **16.** $8 \times 9 = $ ■

17. 6
   ×6

18. 10
   × 8

19. 9
   ×3

20. 5
   ×8

21. 3
   ×2

22. 4
   ×9

23. 8
   ×3

24. 5
   ×4

VOCABULARY POWER

CHAPTER VOCABULARY	WARM-UP WORDS
array	**estimate** A number close to an exact amount
estimate	
factor	**factor** A number that is multiplied by another number to find a product
multiple	
pattern	**product** The answer in a multiplication problem
product	

ALGEBRA
Multiples of 10 and 100

OBJECTIVE: Use basic facts and patterns to multiply multiples of 10 and 100.

Learn

PROBLEM Kyle has 7 yo-yos in his collection. The world record holder for the largest yo-yo collection has about 600 times as many yo-yos as Kyle has. About how many yo-yos does the world record holder have?

You can use basic facts and patterns to multiply multiples of 10 and 100.

Example Multiply. 7×600

$7 \times 6 = 42$ ← basic fact
$7 \times 60 = 420$ The product has the same
$7 \times 600 = 4,200$ number of zeros as the factor.

So, the world record holder has about 4,200 yo-yos.

More Examples

A $5 \times 200 = \blacksquare$
$5 \times 2 = 10$
$5 \times 20 = 100$
$5 \times 200 = 1,000$

B $30 \times 3 = \blacksquare$
$3 \times 3 = 9$
$30 \times 3 = 90$
$300 \times 3 = 900$

Math Idea
The product has the same number of zeros as the factor unless the basic fact has a zero in the product.

- Look at Example B. What pattern do you notice with the zeros in the factors and the products? How is Example A different?

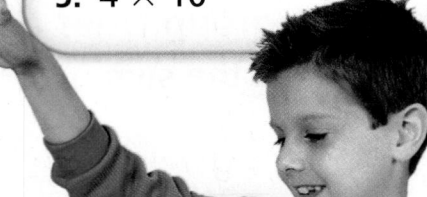

Guided Practice

1. What basic fact would you use to find 5×60?

Use a basic fact and patterns to find each product.

2. $3 \times 4 = \blacksquare$
$3 \times 40 = \blacksquare$
$3 \times 400 = \blacksquare$

✓**3.** $8 \times 5 = \blacksquare$
$80 \times 5 = \blacksquare$
$800 \times 5 = \blacksquare$

✓**4.** $6 \times 3 = \blacksquare$
$6 \times 30 = \blacksquare$
$6 \times 300 = \blacksquare$

5. **TALK Math** Explain how to find the product 9×500.

Use a basic fact and patterns to find each product.

6. $7 \times 3 = \blacksquare$
$70 \times 3 = \blacksquare$
$700 \times 3 = \blacksquare$

7. $2 \times 6 = \blacksquare$
$2 \times 60 = \blacksquare$
$2 \times 600 = \blacksquare$

8. $9 \times 9 = \blacksquare$
$9 \times 90 = \blacksquare$
$9 \times 900 = \blacksquare$

Find the product.

9. $60 \times 8 = \blacksquare$

10. $5 \times 400 = \blacksquare$

11. $\blacksquare = 4 \times 200$

12. $30 \times 8 = \blacksquare$

13. $\blacksquare = 7 \times 80$

14. $6 \times 400 = \blacksquare$

15. $\blacksquare = 1 \times 70$

16. $\blacksquare = 900 \times 3$

17. $300 \times 5 = \blacksquare$

USE DATA For 18–19, use the pictograph.

18. The pictograph shows how many yo-yo tricks each student did in 1 minute. How many tricks could Chuck do in 1 hour?

Think: 1 hour = 60 minutes

19. Max did yo-yo tricks for 20 minutes. Patty did yo-yo tricks for 30 minutes. Who did more yo-yo tricks? **Explain.**

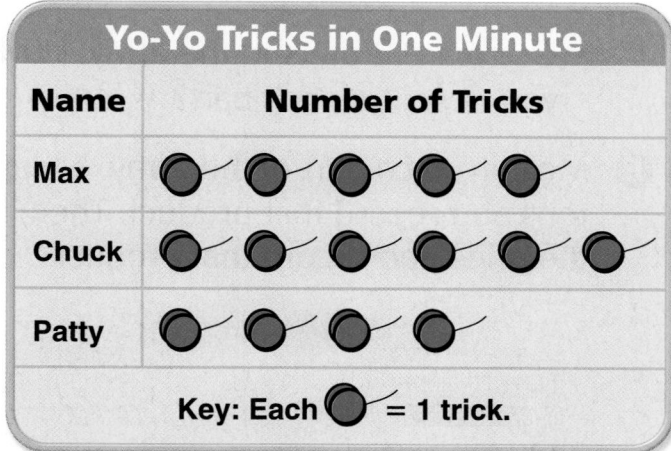

Yo-Yo Tricks in One Minute

Name	Number of Tricks
Max	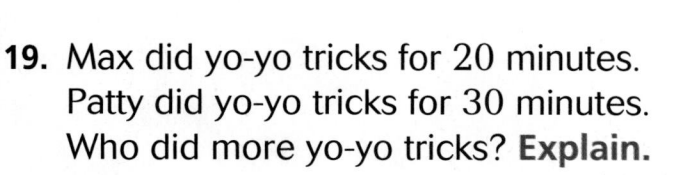
Chuck	
Patty	

Key: Each ⊘ = 1 trick.

20. A case contains 3 boxes of yo-yos. Each box holds 100 yo-yos. How many yo-yos are in 6 cases?

21. **⬛WRITE Math** ▸ **What's the Error?** Meg says that $5 \times 800 = 400$. Describe her error. Write the correct answer.

Mixed Review and Test Prep

22. Hugh bought 1.75 pounds of apples, 1.6 pounds of grapes, and 1.58 pounds of peaches. Of which fruit did he buy the greatest amount? (p. 492)

23. How many sides and angles does a hexagon have? (p. 356)

24. **Test Prep** The drama club is selling tickets for the school musical. There are 4 shows. They have 500 tickets for each show. How many tickets are there to sell?

A 200 tickets

C 1,000 tickets

B 900 tickets

D 2,000 tickets

2 Arrays with Tens and Ones

OBJECTIVE: Model multiplication using arrays with base-ten blocks.

Molly has a bookcase with 3 shelves. There are 14 books on each shelf. How many books are there in all?

Multiply. 3×14

Investigate

Materials ■ base-ten blocks

A Use base-ten blocks to model 3×14.

- There are 2 parts to the array. How can you describe each part?

B Multiply each part of the array. Multiply the tens and record that product. Then, multiply the ones and record that product.

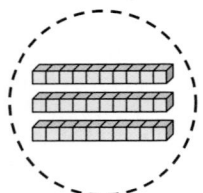   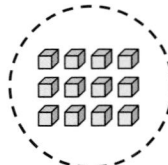

$3 \times 10 = 30$ $3 \times 4 = 12$

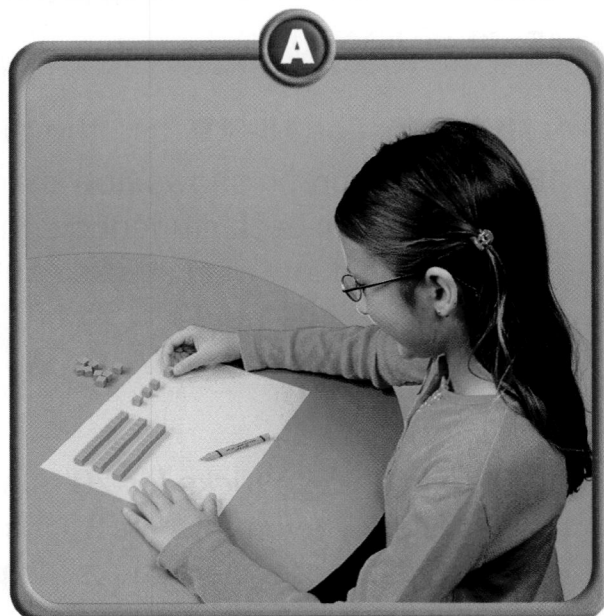

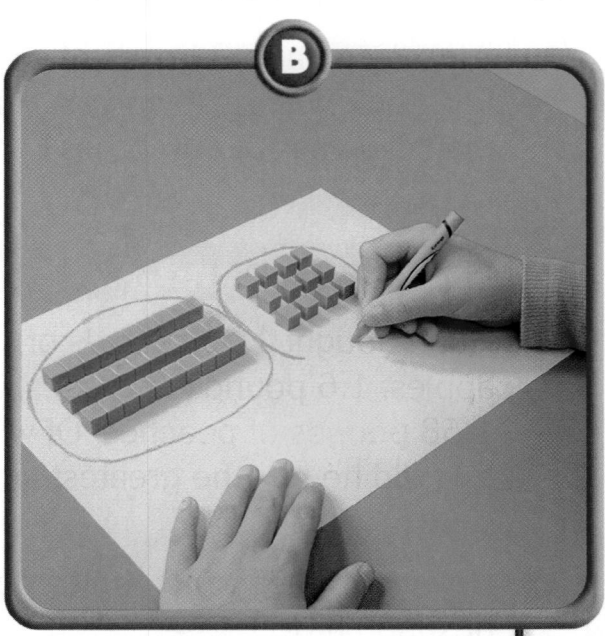

C Find the sum of the products. $30 + 12 = 42$

D Now use base-ten blocks to model 2×16. Multiply the tens and ones. Find the product.

Draw Conclusions

1. Describe the array you made to model 2×16.

2. How would you change the 2×16 array to model 2×26?

3. **Comprehension** One way to model 18 is 1 ten 8 ones. How can knowing this help you find 4×18?

Connect

You can draw arrays on grid paper to model multiplication.

Draw an array to model 3×14.

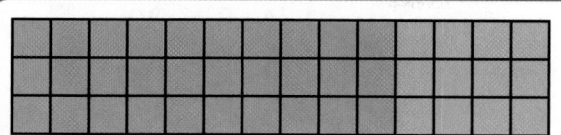

3 rows of 10
Multiply the tens.
$3 \times 10 = 30$

3 rows of 4
Multiply the ones.
$3 \times 4 = 12$

Add. $30 + 12 = 42$

So, $3 \times 14 = 42$.

TALK Math

Explain how to use an array to find 4×17.

Practice

Find the product. Show your multiplication and addition.

1.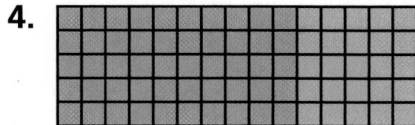

$3 \times 16 = \blacksquare$

2.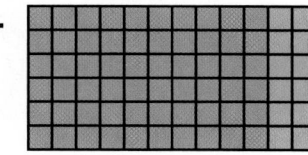

$5 \times 13 = \blacksquare$

✓ **3.**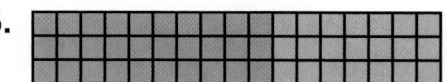

$4 \times 22 = \blacksquare$

4.

$5 \times 15 = \blacksquare$

5.

$6 \times 12 = \blacksquare$

✓ **6.**

$3 \times 17 = \blacksquare$

Use base-ten blocks or grid paper to find each product.

7. $4 \times 25 = \blacksquare$ **8.** $3 \times 18 = \blacksquare$ **9.** $5 \times 21 = \blacksquare$ **10.** $4 \times 34 = \blacksquare$

11. Reasoning The product of two numbers is 48. The sum of the two numbers is 16. What are the two numbers?

12. **WRITE Math** **Explain** how to use base-ten blocks to find the product 5×19.

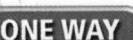

LESSON 3

Model 2-Digit Multiplication

OBJECTIVE: Model 2-digit multiplication with base-ten blocks using place value (partial products) and regrouping.

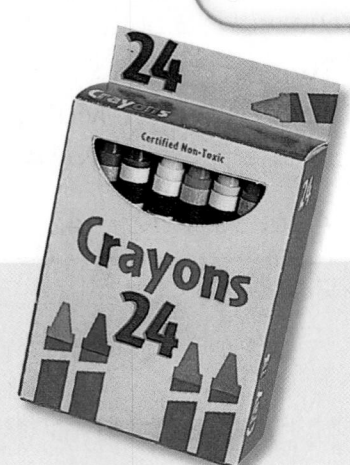

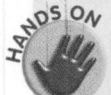

Quick Review

1. $5 \times 20 =$ ■
2. $7 \times 10 =$ ■
3. $9 \times 60 =$ ■
4. $8 \times 30 =$ ■
5. $3 \times 40 =$ ■

Learn

PROBLEM Sam has 3 boxes of crayons. Each box holds 24 crayons. How many crayons does Sam have in all?

You can model the problem using base-ten blocks.
Multiply. 3×24

ONE WAY Use place value.

HANDS ON Activity 1

Materials ■ base-ten blocks

Step 1	Step 2	Step 3
Model 3 groups of 24. Multiply the ones.	Multiply the tens.	Add to find the product.

Step 1

$$\begin{array}{c|c} T & O \\ \hline 2 & 4 \\ \times & 3 \\ \hline 1 & 2 \end{array}$$ (3×4 ones)

Step 2

$$\begin{array}{c|c} T & O \\ \hline 2 & 4 \\ \times & 3 \\ \hline 1 & 2 \\ 6 & 0 \end{array}$$ (3×4 ones)
(3×2 tens)

Step 3

$$\begin{array}{r} 12 \\ + 60 \\ \hline 72 \end{array}$$

So, Sam has 72 crayons in all.

More Examples

A
$$\begin{array}{r} 17 \\ \times \ 4 \\ \hline 28 \ (4 \times 7 \text{ ones}) \\ +40 \ (4 \times 1 \text{ ten}) \\ \hline 68 \end{array}$$

B
$$\begin{array}{r} 39 \\ \times \ 5 \\ \hline 45 \ (5 \times 9 \text{ ones}) \\ +150 \ (5 \times 3 \text{ tens}) \\ \hline 195 \end{array}$$

C
$$\begin{array}{r} 61 \\ \times \ 7 \\ \hline 7 \ (7 \times 1 \text{ one}) \\ +420 \ (7 \times 6 \text{ tens}) \\ \hline 427 \end{array}$$

• Why is 4×1 ten recorded as 40 and not 4?

ANOTHER WAY **Use regrouping.**

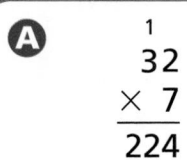

Activity 2

Materials ■ base-ten blocks

Step 1	**Step 2**
Use base-ten blocks to model 3 groups of 24.	Multiply the ones. $3 \times 4 = 12$ ones. Regroup 12 ones as 1 ten 2 ones.

Step 1 diagram of base-ten blocks.

Step 2:
$$\begin{array}{c|c} \overset{1}{T} & O \\ 2 & 4 \\ \times & 3 \\ \hline & 2 \end{array}$$

Step 3

Multiply the tens. 3×2 tens $= 6$ tens
Add the regrouped ten. 6 tens $+$ 1 ten $= 7$ tens

$$\begin{array}{c|c} \overset{1}{T} & O \\ 2 & 4 \\ \times & 3 \\ \hline 7 & 2 \end{array}$$

More Examples

A
$$\begin{array}{r} \overset{1}{32} \\ \times\ 7 \\ \hline 224 \end{array}$$

B
$$\begin{array}{r} \overset{3}{47} \\ \times\ 5 \\ \hline 235 \end{array}$$

C
$$\begin{array}{r} \overset{2}{58} \\ \times\ 3 \\ \hline 174 \end{array}$$

Guided Practice

1. What is 2×30?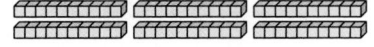

Find the product. Use place value or regrouping.

2.
$$\begin{array}{r} 16 \\ \times\ 4 \\ \hline \end{array}$$

✓3.
$$\begin{array}{r} 27 \\ \times\ 3 \\ \hline \end{array}$$

✓4.
$$\begin{array}{r} 39 \\ \times\ 2 \\ \hline \end{array}$$

5. **TALK Math** Find 3×45 using both place value and regrouping. Tell how the methods are alike and different.

Find the product. Use place value or regrouping.

6. $\begin{array}{r} 25 \\ \times\ 3 \\ \hline \end{array}$

7. $\begin{array}{r} 17 \\ \times\ 4 \\ \hline \end{array}$

8. $\begin{array}{r} 32 \\ \times\ 2 \\ \hline \end{array}$

Multiply. You may wish to use base-ten blocks to help you.

9. $\begin{array}{r} 23 \\ \times\ 6 \\ \hline \end{array}$

10. $\begin{array}{r} 39 \\ \times\ 2 \\ \hline \end{array}$

11. $\begin{array}{r} 45 \\ \times\ 3 \\ \hline \end{array}$

12. $\begin{array}{r} 26 \\ \times\ 4 \\ \hline \end{array}$

13. $\begin{array}{r} 52 \\ \times\ 5 \\ \hline \end{array}$

14. $\begin{array}{r} 31 \\ \times\ 4 \\ \hline \end{array}$

15. $\begin{array}{r} 16 \\ \times\ 5 \\ \hline \end{array}$

16. $\begin{array}{r} 41 \\ \times\ 3 \\ \hline \end{array}$

17. $\begin{array}{r} 18 \\ \times\ 3 \\ \hline \end{array}$

18. $\begin{array}{r} 14 \\ \times\ 8 \\ \hline \end{array}$

Algebra Use base-ten blocks to find the missing factor.

19. $3 \times \blacksquare = 93$
20. $\blacksquare \times 13 = 52$
21. $\blacksquare \times 24 = 72$
22. $5 \times \blacksquare = 80$

USE DATA For 23–24, use the bar graph.

23. There are 16 pencils in each box. How many pencils are in all of the boxes?

24. **Reasoning** There are 20 tubes of paint in each box. If each tube of paint costs $4, how much did the paint cost altogether?

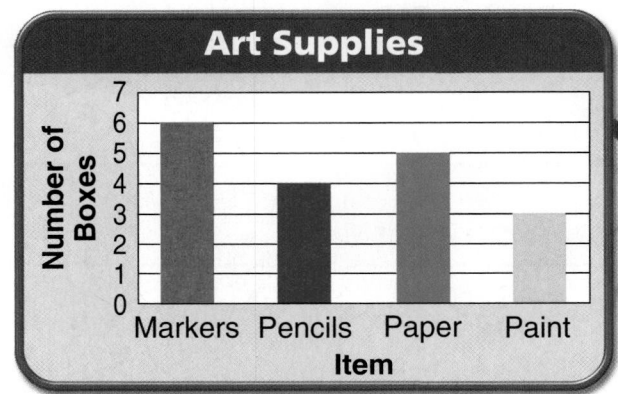

Art Supplies

25. ≡**FAST FACT** The first box of crayons was sold in 1903 and had the same 8 colors that are in an 8-crayon box today. If Holly has 13 of these boxes, how many crayons does she have?

26. ⌈WRITE Math⌉ **What's the Question?** Kate multiplied a 2-digit number by a 1-digit number. She says the product is a four-digit number. Does this make sense? **Explain.**

Mixed Review and Test Prep

27. One pack has 500 sheets of paper. How many sheets are in 4 packs? (p. 586)

28. Chris has a red, a blue, and a green shirt. He has blue and tan pants. How many combinations of 1 shirt and 1 pair of pants are there? (p. 186)

29. **Test Prep** A 3rd grade class went on a field trip. There were 26 students in each of 3 groups. How many students went on the field trip?

   A 29 students   **C** 78 students

   B 68 students   **D** 84 students

Making Crayons

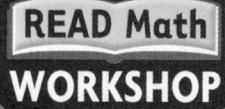

 Reading Skill **Identify the Details**

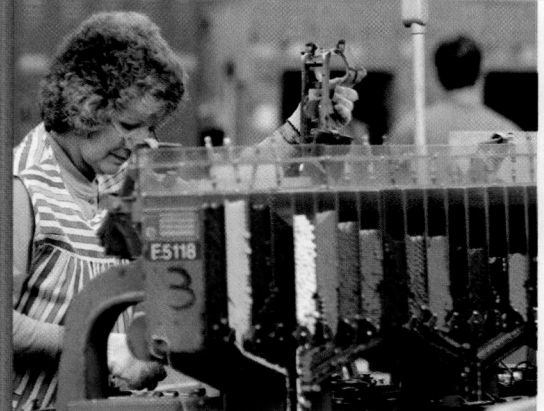 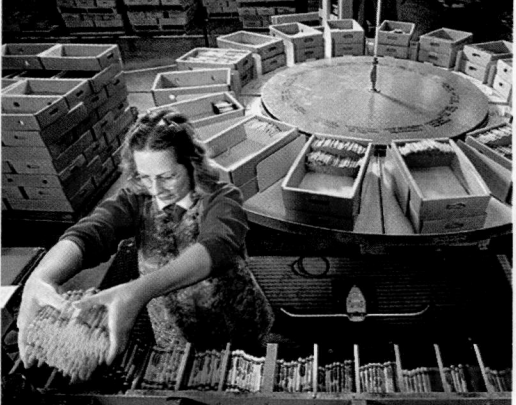

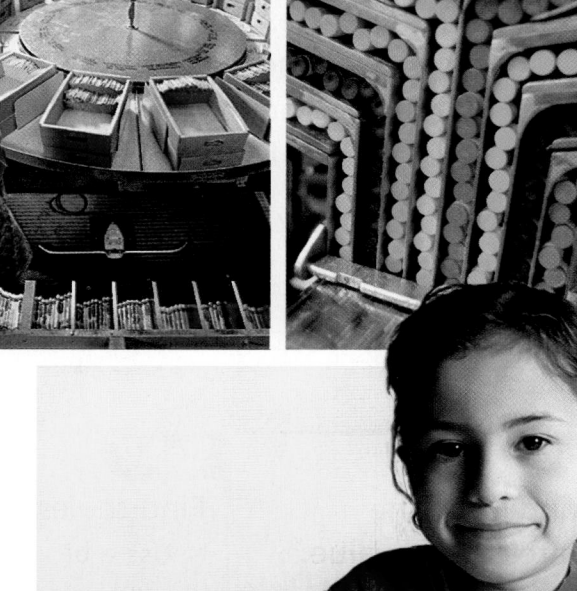

Have you ever wondered how your box of crayons was made?

Two main ingredients are pigment and wax. *Pigment* is another word for *color*. The wax is heated and mixed with pigment and hardening powder. The mixture is poured into a mold.

Cool water is used to cool the mold. After the mold cools, each crayon is wrapped with a paper label. Crayon labels are printed in different languages.

The crayons are separated by color and put into boxes. It can take 3 to 9 minutes to make one crayon.

Identify the details about making crayons:
- 2 main ingredients in crayons
- heated wax is mixed with color
- mixture is poured into mold
- mold is cooled
- crayons are wrapped with paper label
- 3 to 9 minutes to make one crayon

Problem Solving **Identify the details to solve the problems.**

1. How do crayons get their color?

2. If it takes 7 minutes to make 1 blue crayon, how long would it take to make 25 blue crayons?

Chapter 23 593

Estimate Products

OBJECTIVE: Use estimation to find a product.

Learn

PROBLEM The Bevilles drove 5 hours from their house to the beach. The family drove at an average speed of 62 miles an hour. About how many miles does the Beville family live from the beach?

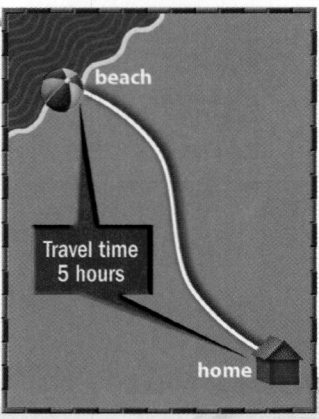

The question asks *about* how many. If you do not need an exact answer, you can find an estimate.
Estimate. 5×62

Example

Step 1	Step 2
Round 62 to the greatest place value. 5×62 $\downarrow$ 5×60	Find the estimated product. Use a basic fact and pattern of zeros. $5 \times 6 = 30$ $5 \times 60 = 300$

So, the Beville family lives about 300 miles from the beach.

Remember
To round a number:
• Decide on the place to be rounded.
• Look at the digit to its right.
• If the digit is less than 5, the digit being rounded stays the same.
• If the digit is 5 or more, the digit being rounded is increased by 1.

More Examples

Ⓐ Round to the nearest ten.

$$\begin{array}{cc} 78 \rightarrow & 80 \\ \times\ 7 & \times\ 7 \\ \hline & 560 \end{array}$$

Ⓑ Round to the nearest hundred.

$$\begin{array}{cc} 284 \rightarrow & 300 \\ \times\ \ 4 & \times\ \ 4 \\ \hline & 1{,}200 \end{array}$$

Guided Practice

1. Round 718 to the nearest hundred.

Estimate each product. Round to the greatest place value.

2. 3×93 ✓3. 7×826 ✓4. 6×39

5. **TALK Math** Explain how to estimate 5×59. Tell whether the exact answer is greater or less than the estimate and why.

Estimate each product. Round to the greatest place value.

6. 39×7 **7.** 52×9 **8.** 6×21 **9.** 3×76

10. 641×5 **11.** 8×925 **12.** 4×388 **13.** 872×3

14. $\begin{array}{r} 71 \\ \times\ 4 \\ \hline \end{array}$ **15.** $\begin{array}{r} 48 \\ \times\ 5 \\ \hline \end{array}$ **16.** $\begin{array}{r} 354 \\ \times\ 8 \\ \hline \end{array}$ **17.** $\begin{array}{r} 216 \\ \times\ 7 \\ \hline \end{array}$ **18.** $\begin{array}{r} 197 \\ \times\ 6 \\ \hline \end{array}$

19. $\begin{array}{r} 92 \\ \times\ 8 \\ \hline \end{array}$ **20.** $\begin{array}{r} 461 \\ \times\ 3 \\ \hline \end{array}$ **21.** $\begin{array}{r} 82 \\ \times\ 4 \\ \hline \end{array}$ **22.** $\begin{array}{r} 167 \\ \times\ 9 \\ \hline \end{array}$ **23.** $\begin{array}{r} 328 \\ \times\ 4 \\ \hline \end{array}$

USE DATA For 24–25, use the table.

24. If each room at the Beachfront Suites is filled, and there are 4 people per room, about how many people are staying at the hotel?

25. At the Flamingo, there are about 3 people per room. At the Sand and Surf, there are about 4 people per room. If all the rooms at both hotels are filled, which hotel has more people staying in it? About how many more?

26. Reasoning Marc owns a beach umbrella rental shop. Yesterday, he rented 6 umbrellas. Each umbrella costs $8 an hour and was rented for 8 hours. About how much did Marc earn yesterday?

Hotels at the Beach	
Name	**Number of Rooms**
Sand and Surf	52
Flamingo	132
Boardwalk Hotel	87
Beachfront Suites	48

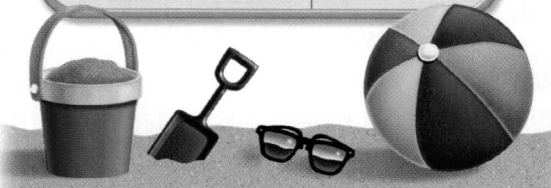

27. **WRITE Math** The Beville family stayed at a hotel that cost $77 a day. About how much did the hotel cost for 7 days? **Explain.**

Mixed Review and Test Prep

28. Ally brought 4 gallons of juice for the picnic. There are 16 servings in each gallon. How many servings of juice did Ally bring? (p. 590)

29. Oliver has 282 photos in an album and 72 photos that are not in the album. How many photos does Oliver have in all? (p. 58)

30. Test Prep Tom and his friends built 4 birdhouses. They used 177 craft sticks to build each birdhouse. About how many craft sticks did they use in all?

A 300   **C** 600

B 400   **D** 800

Extra Practice on page 604, Set C

Multiply 2-Digit Numbers

OBJECTIVE: Multiply 2-digit numbers using an algorithm.

Learn

PROBLEM The cafeteria has 68 tables. Each table has 4 chairs. How many chairs are in the cafeteria?

Multiply. 68×4 **Estimate.** $70 \times 4 = 280$

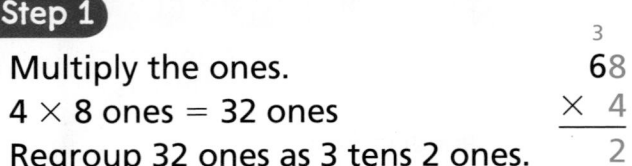

ONE WAY Use regrouping.

Step 1

Multiply the ones.

4×8 ones $= 32$ ones

Regroup 32 ones as 3 tens 2 ones.

$$\begin{array}{r} \overset{3}{68} \\ \times\ 4 \\ \hline 2 \end{array}$$

Step 2

Multiply the tens.

4×6 tens $= 24$ tens

24 tens $+$ 3 tens $= 27$ tens

Regroup 27 tens as 2 hundreds 7 tens.

$$\begin{array}{r} \overset{3}{68} \\ \times\ 4 \\ \hline 272 \end{array}$$

ANOTHER WAY Use place value.

Step 1

Multiply the ones. Record.

$$\begin{array}{r} 68 \\ \times\ 4 \\ \hline 32 \end{array} \quad (4 \times 8 = 32)$$

Step 2

Multiply the tens. Record.

$$\begin{array}{r} 68 \\ \times\ 4 \\ \hline 32 \\ 240 \end{array} \quad (4 \times 60 = 240)$$

Step 3

Add the products.

$$\begin{array}{r} 68 \\ \times\ 4 \\ \hline 32 \\ +\ 240 \\ \hline 272 \end{array}$$

So, the cafeteria has 272 chairs. Since 272 is close to the estimate, 280, the answer is reasonable.

Guided Practice

1. What is 5×4 tens?

Find each product.

2. $\begin{array}{r} 52 \\ \times\ 6 \\ \hline \end{array}$

3. $\begin{array}{r} 32 \\ \times\ 3 \\ \hline \end{array}$

✓4. $\begin{array}{r} 71 \\ \times\ 8 \\ \hline \end{array}$

✓5. $\begin{array}{r} 28 \\ \times\ 3 \\ \hline \end{array}$

6. **TALK Math** **Explain** how to find 7×54.

Find each product.

7. $\begin{array}{r} 24 \\ \times\ 3 \\ \hline \end{array}$	**8.** $\begin{array}{r} 76 \\ \times\ 8 \\ \hline \end{array}$	**9.** $\begin{array}{r} 45 \\ \times\ 6 \\ \hline \end{array}$	**10.** $\begin{array}{r} 19 \\ \times\ 5 \\ \hline \end{array}$	**11.** $\begin{array}{r} 37 \\ \times\ 4 \\ \hline \end{array}$
12. $\begin{array}{r} 37 \\ \times\ 9 \\ \hline \end{array}$	**13.** $\begin{array}{r} 93 \\ \times\ 3 \\ \hline \end{array}$	**14.** $\begin{array}{r} 31 \\ \times\ 7 \\ \hline \end{array}$	**15.** $\begin{array}{r} 82 \\ \times\ 4 \\ \hline \end{array}$	**16.** $\begin{array}{r} 63 \\ \times\ 7 \\ \hline \end{array}$

17. 98×5 **18.** 56×7 **19.** 9×44 **20.** 3×76

Algebra Find the missing factor.

21. $12 \times \blacksquare = 36$ **22.** $\blacksquare \times 4 = 44$ **23.** $16 \times \blacksquare = 64$ **24.** $\blacksquare \times 3 = 63$

USE DATA For 25–27, use the bar graph.

25. A box holds 48 cartons of milk. How many cartons of milk does the cafeteria have in all?

26. Reasoning If a box holds 32 bottles of juice and 64 bottles of water, does the cafeteria have more bottles of juice or water? **Explain.**

27. The cafeteria sold 58 bottles of lemonade. If one box holds 36 bottles, how many bottles of lemonade are left?

28. **WRITE Math** ▶ **What's the Question?** There are 24 bags of pretzels in each box. The answer is 72 bags.

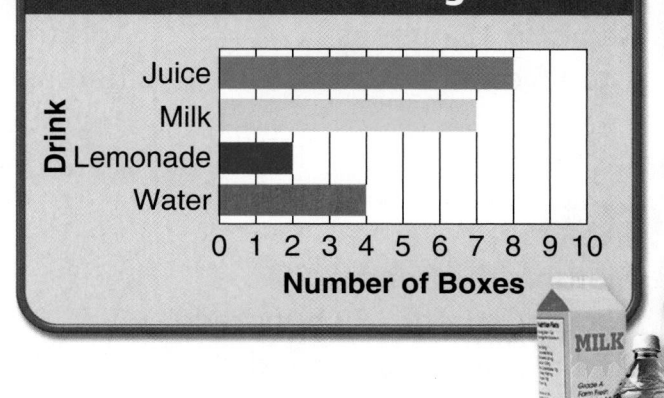

Cafeteria Beverages

Mixed Review and Test Prep

29. What is the missing addend? (p. 50)

$$12 - \blacksquare = 7$$

30. Nina uses 36 inches of ribbon to make a bow. About how much ribbon will she need to make 8 bows? (p. 594)

31. Test Prep Jamie rented three movies. Each movie is 97 minutes long. How long will it take Jamie to watch all three movies?

A 237 minutes   **C** 291 minutes

B 271 minutes   **D** 480 minutes

Extra Practice on page 604, Set D

CD ROM **Technology**
Use Harcourt Mega Math, The Number Games, *Up, Up, and Array,* Level J.

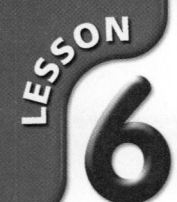

LESSON 6

Multiply 3-Digit Numbers

OBJECTIVE: Multiply 3-digit numbers using an algorithm.

Quick Review

1. 3×51
2. 6×37
3. 2×72
4. 8×50
5. 7×300

Learn

PROBLEM Mr. Brown walks his dog every day. If he walks 3 miles a day, how many miles will he walk in 1 year? (Hint: 1 year = 365 days)

Multiply. 365×3 **Estimate.** $400 \times 3 = 1,200$

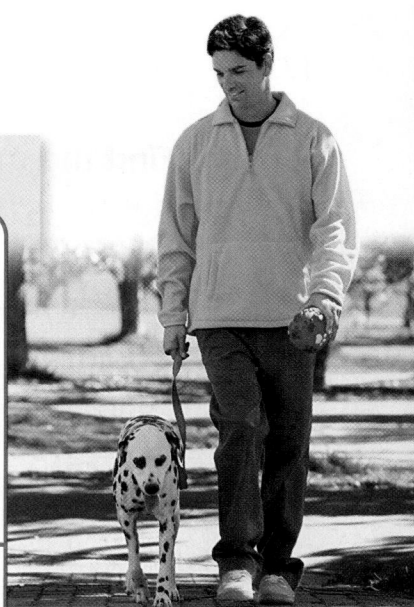

ONE WAY   Use regrouping.

Step 1

Multiply the ones.
3×5 ones = 15 ones
Regroup 15 ones as
1 ten 5 ones.

$$\begin{array}{r} \overset{1}{3}65 \\ \times\ \ 3 \\ \hline 95 \end{array}$$

Step 2

Multiply the tens.
3×6 tens = 18 tens
Add the regrouped ten.
18 tens + 1 ten = 19 tens
Regroup 19 tens as
1 hundred 9 tens.

$$\begin{array}{r} \overset{1\ 1}{3}65 \\ \times\ \ 3 \\ \hline 95 \end{array}$$

Step 3

Multiply the hundreds.
3×3 hundreds = 9 hundreds
Add the regrouped hundred. $9 + 1 = 10$
Regroup 10 hundreds as 1 thousand 0 hundreds.

$$\begin{array}{r} \overset{1\ 1}{3}65 \\ \times\ \ 3 \\ \hline 1,095 \end{array}$$

So, Mr. Brown will walk 1,095 miles in a year. Since 1,095 is close to the estimate, 1,200, the answer is reasonable.

ANOTHER WAY   Use place value.

Step 1

Multiply the ones.
Record.

$$\begin{array}{r} 305 \\ \times\ \ 3 \\ \hline 15\ (3 \times 5) \end{array}$$

Step 2

Multiply the tens.
Record.

$$\begin{array}{r} 305 \\ \times\ \ 3 \\ \hline 15\ (3 \times 5) \\ 0\ (3 \times 0) \end{array}$$

Step 3

Multiply the hundreds.
Record.

$$\begin{array}{r} 305 \\ \times\ \ 3 \\ \hline 15\ (3 \times 5) \\ 0\ (3 \times 0) \\ +900\ (3 \times 300) \end{array}$$

Step 4

Add the products.

$$\begin{array}{r} 305 \\ \times\ \ 3 \\ \hline 15 \\ 0 \\ +900 \\ \hline 915 \end{array}$$

1. What is 7×5 hundreds?

Find each product.

2. 218 $\times \ 4$	**3.** 451 $\times \ 6$	**4.** 132 $\times \ 3$	✓**5.** 333 $\times \ 4$	✓**6.** 537 $\times \ 5$

7. [TALK Math] **Explain** how to find 4×628.

Independent Practice and Problem Solving

Find each product.

8. 823 $\times \ 2$	**9.** 194 $\times \ 6$	**10.** 311 $\times \ 3$	**11.** 275 $\times \ 4$	**12.** 436 $\times \ 1$
13. 443 $\times \ 3$	**14.** 921 $\times \ 5$	**15.** 129 $\times \ 3$	**16.** 572 $\times \ 4$	**17.** 324 $\times \ 2$

18. 5×204 **19.** 3×152 **20.** 6×513 **21.** 2×789

USE DATA For 22–24, use the chart.

22. A calorie is a unit of energy that food gives you. The chart shows the number of calories used in one hour. Marcus swam for 4 hours. How many calories did he use?

23. Reasoning Matt practices the piano 5 times a week for 1 hour each time. How many calories does Matt use in 4 weeks?

Activity	Calories used per hour*
Playing Piano	76
Swimming	166
Jumping Rope	274

*For 60-pound student

24. [WRITE Math] ▸ Missy likes to jump rope. How many calories will Missy use by jumping rope for 3 hours? **Explain.**

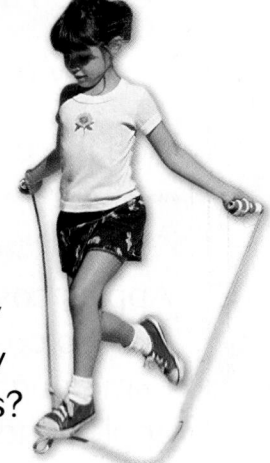

Mixed Review and Test Prep

25. Monique has 4 quarters, 3 dimes, and 2 nickels. How much money does she have? (p. 110)

26. $8,000 - 2,768 = $ ■ (p. 88)

27. Test Prep Mr. Jackson drives his company truck 417 miles each week. How far does he drive in 6 weeks?

A 2,402 miles **C** 2,502 miles

B 2,462 miles **D** 2,562 miles

Extra Practice on page 604, Set E

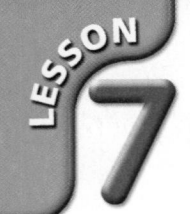

LESSON 7

Problem Solving Workshop
Strategy: Solve a Simpler Problem

OBJECTIVE: Solve problems by using the strategy *solve a simpler problem*.

Learn the Strategy

You can use a simpler problem to help you solve more complex problems. You can either break the problem into simpler parts or you can use estimation to help you solve the problem.

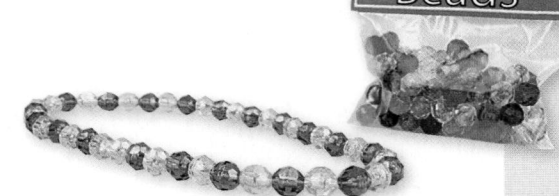

Break into Simpler Parts

Kendra uses beads to make necklaces. The beads come in packages of 75. If Kendra buys 6 packages, how many beads will she have?

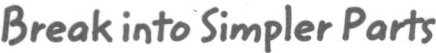

Break apart 75 into numbers that are easier to multiply.

Rewrite 75 as 70 + 5.

Multiply each addend by 6.

$$\begin{array}{r} 75 \\ \times\ 6 \end{array} = \begin{array}{r} 70 + 5 \\ \times\qquad 6 \\ \hline 30 \leftarrow 6 \times 5 \\ 420 \leftarrow 6 \times 70 \\ \hline 450 \end{array}$$

Add the products.   So, Kendra will have 450 beads.

Use Estimation

Apples cost $0.99 a pound. Grapes cost $0.89 a pound. Pam bought 4 pounds of apples and 3 pounds of grapes. Did she pay more or less than $5 in all?

$$\$0.99 \times 4 \rightarrow \$1 \times 4 = \$4$$
$$\$0.89 \times 3 \rightarrow \$1 \times 3 = \$3$$

$$\$4 + \$3 = \$7$$

Pam spent about $7.

So, Pam spent more than $5 in all.

TALK Math

Explain how rounding to the nearest dollar makes the second problem simpler to solve.

600

Use the Strategy

PROBLEM The students at Lincoln Elementary School are collecting food for the local food pantry. There are 87 third-grade students in the school. Each student brings in 4 cans of food. How many cans do the third-grade students collect altogether?

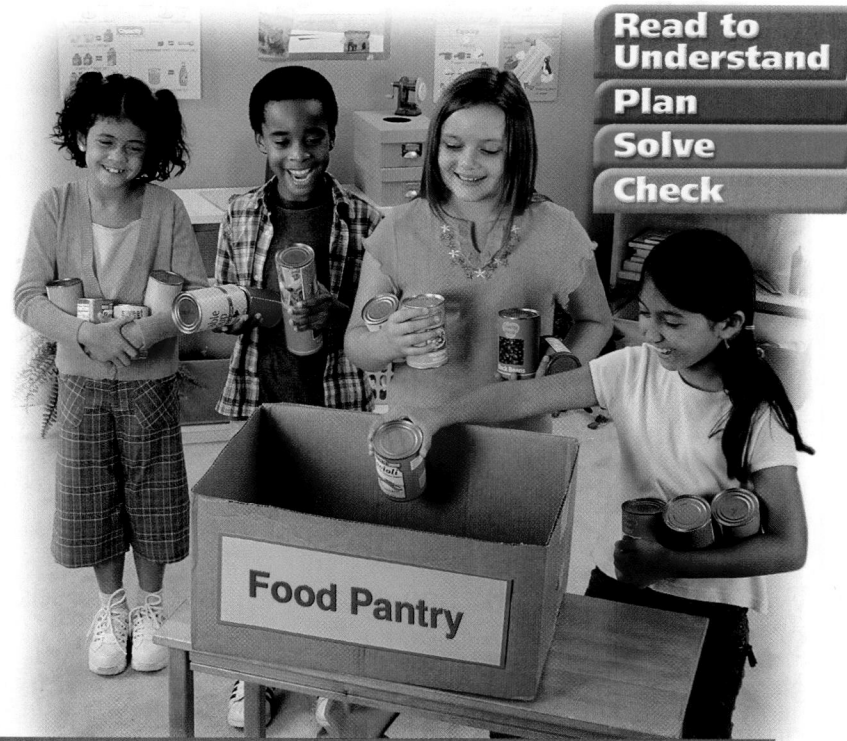

Read to Understand
Plan
Solve
Check

Food Pantry

Read to Understand

Reading Skill

- **Summarize the problem.**
- **What information is given?**

Plan

- **What strategy can you use to solve the problem?**
  You can solve a simpler problem.

Solve

- **How can you use the strategy to solve the problem?**
  You can find 87×4 by breaking apart 87 into numbers that are easier to multiply.

  Rewrite 87 as $80 + 7$.

  $$\frac{87}{\times\ 4} = \begin{array}{r} 80 + 7 \\ \times \qquad 4 \\ \hline \end{array}$$

  Multiply each addend by 4.

  $$\begin{array}{r} 28 \leftarrow 4 \times 7 \\ 320 \leftarrow 4 \times 80 \\ \hline 348 \end{array}$$

  Add the products.

  So, the third-grade students collect 348 cans altogether.

Check

- **Look back at the problem. Does the answer make sense for the problem? Explain.**

Guided Problem Solving

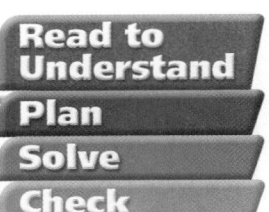

1. Ms. Reynolds volunteers at the food pantry. She organizes the donated food items. She puts the canned food on 5 shelves. Each shelf can hold 58 cans of food. How many cans can fit on the 5 shelves?

First, write a simpler problem.

Then, multiply each addend.

$$\begin{array}{r} 58 \\ \times\ 5 \\ \hline \end{array} = \begin{array}{r} 50 + 8 \\ \times\qquad 5 \\ \hline \end{array}$$

Finally, add the products to find the total number of cans.

2. **What if** there are 8 shelves and each shelf holds 96 cans of food? Describe how you would use a simpler problem to find the total number of cans on the shelves.

3. The recycling center collected 67 bags of aluminum cans in June and 92 bags of aluminum cans in July. If each bag weighed about 3 pounds, how many pounds of aluminum cans did the center collect in the two months?

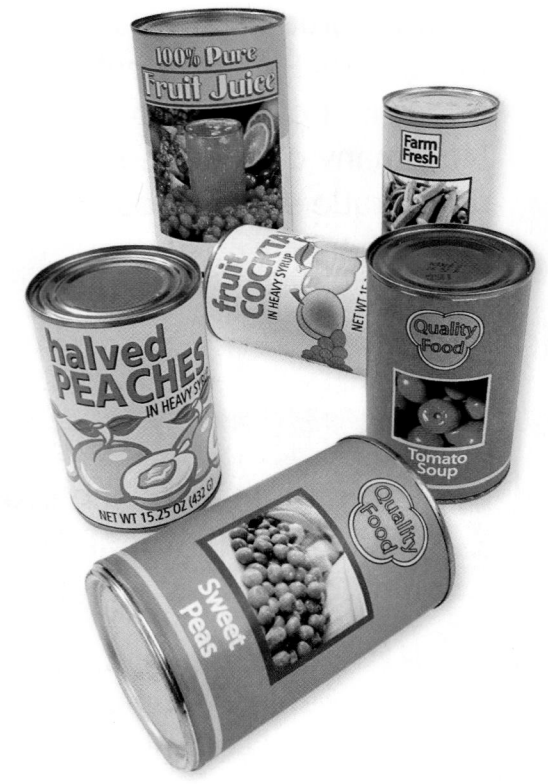

Problem Solving Strategy Practice

Use a simpler problem to solve.

4. The science club is collecting glass bottles to raise money for a trip to the planetarium. The students get 5 cents for each bottle they collect. So far the club has collected 96 bottles. How much money, in cents, did the club get for the bottles?

5. **Reasoning** The outdoor club hosted a hike-a-thon. Hikers earned 75 points for every $\frac{1}{2}$ mile they hiked. The course was 3 miles long. If Joe hiked the whole course, how many points did he earn?

6. **WRITE Math** ▸ The art club is making a paper chain to decorate the gym for a fund-raiser. Each student makes 8 links for the chain. There are 78 students in the art club. How many links will be on the chain? **Explain** how you found the answer.

Mixed Strategy Practice

USE DATA For 7–9, use the poster.

7. The school band held a car wash to raise money for the local animal shelter. If 36 cars, 8 vans, and 21 trucks came to the car wash, how much money did the band raise?

8. **Pose a Problem** Look back at Problem 7. Write a similar problem by changing the numbers of cars, vans, and trucks.

9. **Open-Ended** In the first two hours of the car wash, the band washed both cars and trucks and raised a total of $48. List a possible combination of cars and trucks that the band washed.

10. A green, a red, a white, and a blue car are in line at the car wash. The red car is not last. The white car is in front of the blue car. The blue car is second. Draw a picture to show the order of the cars.

Choose a
STRATEGY

Solve a Simpler Problem
Draw a Diagram or Picture
Make a Model or Act It Out
Make an Organized List
Make a Table or Graph
Predict and Test
Work Backward
Find a Pattern
Write an Equation
Use Logical Reasoning

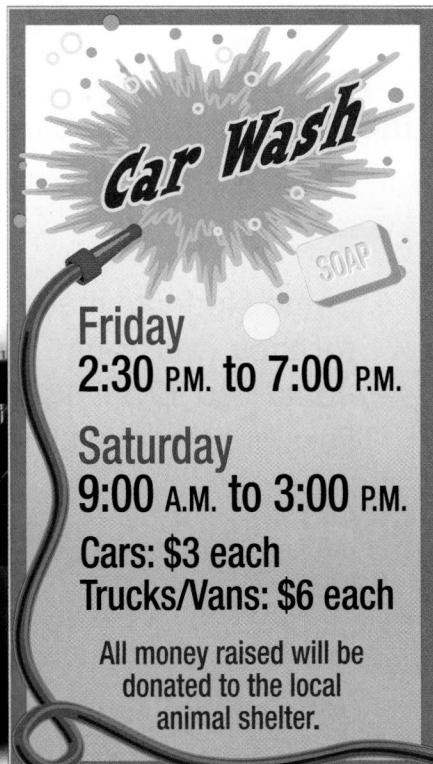

Car Wash

SOAP

Friday
2:30 P.M. to 7:00 P.M.

Saturday
9:00 A.M. to 3:00 P.M.

Cars: $3 each
Trucks/Vans: $6 each

All money raised will be donated to the local animal shelter.

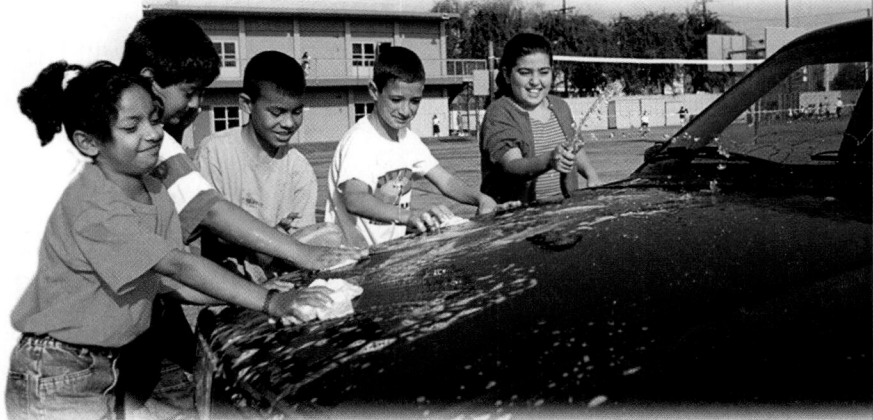

CHALLENGE YOURSELF

There are about 5,000 animal shelters nationwide. It costs about $10 a day to care for a cat or dog in a shelter.

11. Vanessa volunteers at her local animal shelter. There are 16 dogs and 24 cats at the shelter. What is the total cost per day to care for the animals?

12. Samuel also volunteers at an animal shelter. At the shelter, there are 12 dogs. Explain how to use a pattern to find the number of dogs nationwide that are in animal shelters if each shelter houses 12 dogs.

Extra Practice

Set A Use a basic fact and patterns to find each product. (pp. 586–587)

1. $2 \times 4 = \blacksquare$
$20 \times 4 = \blacksquare$
$200 \times 4 = \blacksquare$

2. $6 \times 3 = \blacksquare$
$60 \times 3 = \blacksquare$
$600 \times 3 = \blacksquare$

3. $8 \times 5 = \blacksquare$
$8 \times 50 = \blacksquare$
$8 \times 500 = \blacksquare$

Find the product.

4. $9 \times 30 = \blacksquare$

5. $4 \times 700 = \blacksquare$

6. $6 \times 900 = \blacksquare$

Set B Multiply. You may wish to use base-ten blocks to help you. (pp. 590–593)

1. $\begin{array}{r} 43 \\ \times\ 2 \\ \hline \end{array}$

2. $\begin{array}{r} 77 \\ \times\ 5 \\ \hline \end{array}$

3. $\begin{array}{r} 52 \\ \times\ 3 \\ \hline \end{array}$

4. $\begin{array}{r} 80 \\ \times\ 9 \\ \hline \end{array}$

5. $\begin{array}{r} 68 \\ \times\ 8 \\ \hline \end{array}$

Set C Estimate each product. Round to the greatest place value. (pp. 594–595)

1. 48×6

2. 73×8

3. $\begin{array}{r} 62 \\ \times\ 9 \\ \hline \end{array}$

4. $\begin{array}{r} 559 \\ \times\ 4 \\ \hline \end{array}$

5. $\begin{array}{r} 837 \\ \times\ 5 \\ \hline \end{array}$

6. Some students made 4 paper chains for their classroom. If each chain contained 175 links, about how many links are there in all of the chains?

7. Andy needs to reserve 22 tables for a party. If each table holds 8 people, about how many people will be attending the party?

Set D Find each product. (pp. 596–597)

1. $\begin{array}{r} 26 \\ \times\ 4 \\ \hline \end{array}$

2. $\begin{array}{r} 58 \\ \times\ 7 \\ \hline \end{array}$

3. $\begin{array}{r} 94 \\ \times\ 3 \\ \hline \end{array}$

4. $\begin{array}{r} 81 \\ \times\ 6 \\ \hline \end{array}$

5. $\begin{array}{r} 72 \\ \times\ 8 \\ \hline \end{array}$

6. John's team scored 48 touchdowns in a season. If a touchdown counts as 6 points, how many points in touchdowns did the team score?

7. A jar holds 35 pickles. Dana needs 244 pickles for a school lunch. Are 7 jars enough? Explain.

Set E Find each product. (pp. 598–599)

1. $\begin{array}{r} 101 \\ \times\ 4 \\ \hline \end{array}$

2. $\begin{array}{r} 247 \\ \times\ 3 \\ \hline \end{array}$

3. $\begin{array}{r} 658 \\ \times\ 5 \\ \hline \end{array}$

4. 7×431

5. 2×990

6. 3×145

7. 6×203

8. 4×318

9. 5×236

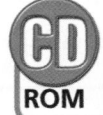

Technology
Use Harcourt Mega Math, The Number
Games, *Up, Up, and Array*, Levels I and J.

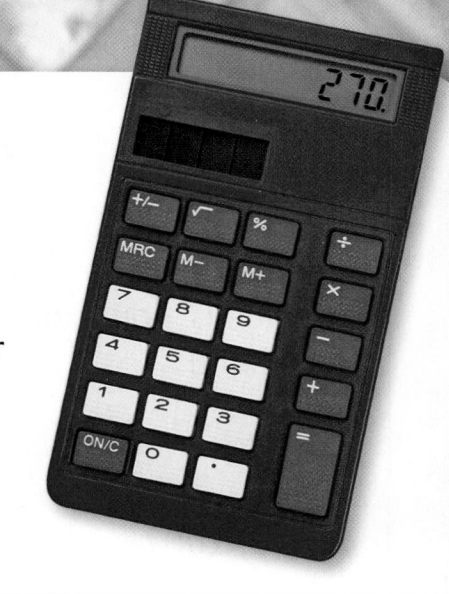

TECHNOLOGY ★ CONNECTION

Calculator: Multiplication

Use a Calculator for Multiplication

The Drama club sold sandwiches at lunch to raise money for a field trip. There were 6 kinds of sandwiches. They made 45 of each kind. How many sandwiches did they make?

Write a number sentence for the word problem.
$6 \times 45 = $ ■

Use a calculator to solve.

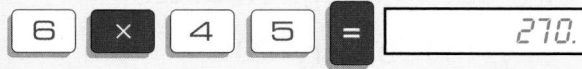
```
6  ×  4  5  =  [      270.]
```

So, the Drama club made 270 sandwiches.

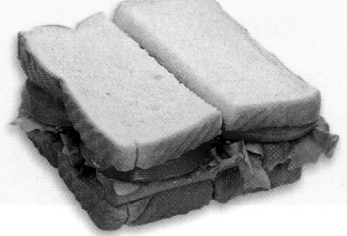

Try It

Use a calculator to multiply. Solve each problem twice to be sure that you have keyed in the correct information.

1. $64 \times 7 = $ ■   **2.** $32 \times 9 = $ ■   **3.** $83 \times 4 = $ ■   **4.** $89 \times 5 = $ ■

5. $55 \times 2 = $ ■   **6.** $49 \times 3 = $ ■   **7.** $53 \times 8 = $ ■   **8.** $77 \times 4 = $ ■

9. $5 \times 42 = $ ■   **10.** $3 \times 29 = $ ■   **11.** $7 \times 91 = $ ■   **12.** $4 \times 52 = $ ■

13. Janet read 9 magazines with 65 pages each during the month of June. How many pages did she read in June?

14. In December, Max read 8 books with 76 pages each. How many pages did he read in December?

15. Angie sold 8 toys for 50¢ each and 6 toys for 75¢ each. How much money, in cents, did she make?

16. What if Angie's mother doubled what Angie made? How much money does Angie have now?

17. Explore More Heather's piano teacher charges $30 for each half hour of lessons. Heather takes two hour-long lessons each month. How much does she pay each month? If her teacher charged $25 for a half-hour lesson and Heather took four half-hour lessons, would she pay more or less each month? **Explain.**

MATH POWER — How Old Are You?

Time Passes

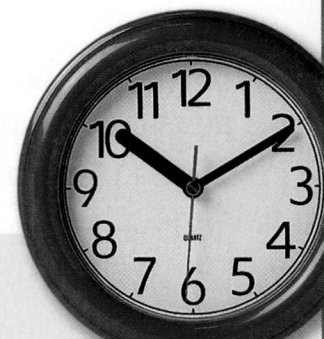

A person's age is usually given in years. Do you know how many days, hours, or minutes old you are? Use a calculator to find out!

Example

Abby was born on February 8, 1998. How old was she on April 3, 2007 in days, hours, and minutes?

Step 1 Multiply Abby's age in years by 365.	**Step 2** Add the number of days from the birthday to the given date.
$2007 - 1998 = 9$ $9 \times 365 = 3{,}285$	remaining days in February: 20 days in March: 31 days in April: 3 $20 + 31 + 3 = 54$ $3{,}285 + 54 = 3{,}339$
Step 3 Add one day for each leap year. Leap years are: . . . 1996, 2000, 2004, 2008, . . . $3{,}339 + 2 = 3{,}341$ So, Abby is 3,341 days old.	**Step 4** Multiply Abby's age in days by 24 hours. $3{,}341 \times 24 = 80{,}184$ So, Abby is 80,184 hours old.

Step 5 Multiply Abby's age in hours by 60 minutes. $80{,}184 \times 60 = 4{,}811{,}040$

So, Abby was 4,811,040 minutes old.

Try It

Find each age in years, days, hours, and minutes.

1. Jake's birthday is May 25, 1995. Find his age on January 16, 2006.

2. Elsie's birthday is August 3, 2001. Find her age on September 2, 2008.

3. **WRITE Math** ▶ Find your age in days, hours, and minutes. **Explain** how you know.

Chapter 23 Review/Test

Check Concepts

1. Explain how you could use base-ten blocks to help you solve 4×12. (p. 588)

2. What are the steps needed to multiply 23×4? (p. 590)

Check Skills

Find the product. (pp. 586–587)

3. $30 \times 6 =$ ■

4. $4 \times 300 =$ ■

5. $5 \times 200 =$ ■

6. ■ $= 7 \times 60$

7. $20 \times 8 =$ ■

8. ■ $= 3 \times 800$

Find each product. (pp. 596–597, 598–599)

9. $\begin{array}{r} 13 \\ \times\ 3 \\ \hline \end{array}$

10. $\begin{array}{r} 26 \\ \times\ 5 \\ \hline \end{array}$

11. $\begin{array}{r} 49 \\ \times\ 8 \\ \hline \end{array}$

12. $\begin{array}{r} 75 \\ \times\ 9 \\ \hline \end{array}$

13. $\begin{array}{r} 38 \\ \times\ 4 \\ \hline \end{array}$

14. $\begin{array}{r} 51 \\ \times\ 2 \\ \hline \end{array}$

15. $\begin{array}{r} 97 \\ \times\ 6 \\ \hline \end{array}$

16. $\begin{array}{r} 62 \\ \times\ 8 \\ \hline \end{array}$

17. $\begin{array}{r} 43 \\ \times\ 4 \\ \hline \end{array}$

18. $\begin{array}{r} 16 \\ \times\ 7 \\ \hline \end{array}$

19. $\begin{array}{r} 134 \\ \times\ \ \ 3 \\ \hline \end{array}$

20. $\begin{array}{r} 309 \\ \times\ \ \ 7 \\ \hline \end{array}$

21. $\begin{array}{r} 868 \\ \times\ \ \ 6 \\ \hline \end{array}$

22. $\begin{array}{r} 711 \\ \times\ \ \ 8 \\ \hline \end{array}$

23. $\begin{array}{r} 299 \\ \times\ \ \ 5 \\ \hline \end{array}$

Check Problem Solving

Solve. (pp. 600–603)

24. On a class trip to the zoo, 37 students and 5 teachers each paid $5 admission. How much did they pay in all for admission to the zoo?

25. **WRITE Math** ▸ Lindsay and Jeff live in towns that each have a population of 8 people per square mile. Lindsay's town is 64 square miles. Jeff's town is 120 square miles. How many people in all live in both towns? **Explain.**

Standardized Test Prep
Chapters 1–23

Number and Operations

1. Which is a true statement? (p. 458)

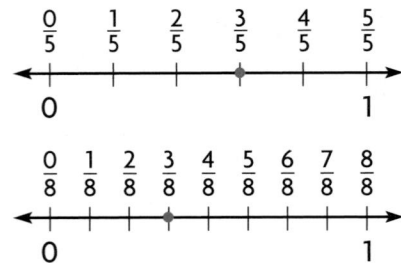

A $\frac{3}{8} > \frac{3}{5}$ **C** $\frac{3}{5} = \frac{3}{8}$

B $\frac{3}{5} < \frac{3}{8}$ **D** $\frac{3}{5} > \frac{3}{8}$

Test Tip **Choose the answer.**

See item 2. Multiply to find the answer. If the product does not match one of the answer choices, check your computation.

2. Caroline practiced 9 songs on the piano. She spent 12 minutes playing each song. For how many minutes did Caroline practice? (p. 244)

A 21   **C** 108

B 98   **D** 1,080

3. ⟦WRITE Math⟧ ▸ There are 65 treats in one bag of dog treats. How many treats are in 8 bags? **Explain** your answer. (p. 596)

Algebraic Reasoning

4. Which is the next figure in the pattern? (p. 424)

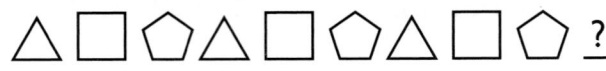

A △

B ⬡

C ⬠

D ▢

5. Which number sentence is in the same fact family as $72 \div 8 = 9$? (p. 286)

A $8 + 9 = 17$

B $72 - 8 = 64$

C $9 \times 8 = 72$

D $72 \div 12 = 6$

6. ⟦WRITE Math⟧ ▸ How many strings are on 6 guitars? **Explain** your answer. (p. 256)

Guitars	1	2	3	4	5	6
Strings	6	12	18	▪	▪	▪

Geometry

7. Jeremy drew a quadrilateral with all sides the same length. Which figure did Jeremy draw? (p. 360)

  A Trapezoid

  B Pentagon

  C Hexagon

  D Square

8. Which figure appears to have only 1 line of symmetry? (p. 386)

  A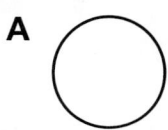

  B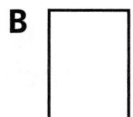

  C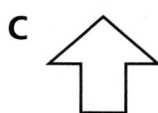

  D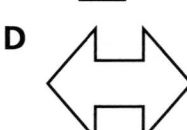

9. 〖WRITE Math〗▶ Which letter shows the location of $\frac{3}{5}$? **Explain** how you know. (p. 446)

Data Analysis and Probability

10. How many more books did Mark read than Deb? (p. 148)

Book Club Results

Pat	🖊 🖊 🖊 🖊
Mark	🖊 🖊 🖊 🖊 🖊
Deb	🖊 🖊 🖊

Key: Each 🖊 = 4 books.

  A 2   **C** 6

  B 4   **D** 8

11. On which day was the greatest number of books sold? (p. 154)

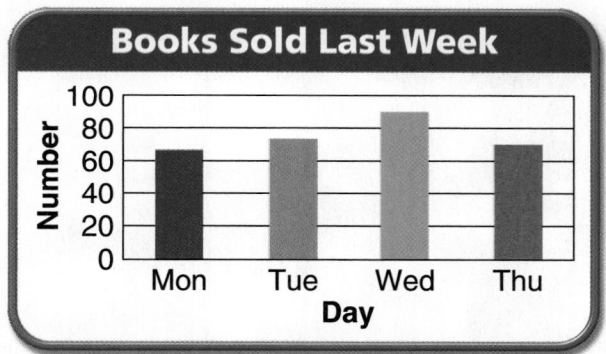

  A Monday   **C** Wednesday

  B Tuesday   **D** Thursday

12. 〖WRITE Math〗▶ Courtney has 8 blue pencils and 2 red pencils in a drawer. She reaches in the drawer and chooses a pencil without looking. Is she more likely to choose a blue pencil or a red pencil? **Explain.** (p. 178)

24 Divide by 1 Digit

≡FAST FACT

A pencil can draw a line 35 miles long. If all of the pencils made each year were laid end to end, they would circle the earth about 60 times!

Investigate

Suppose you have $80 to buy art supplies for your school. Use the graph to decide the greatest number and least number of items you could buy. Then choose two items and tell how many of each item you would buy.

Art Supplies	
Box of crayons	🗒️ 🗒️
Box of colored pencils	🗒️ 🗒️ 🗒️ 🗒️
Box of markers	🗒️ 🗒️ 🗒️
Pack of paper	🗒️ 🗒️ 🗒️

Key: Each 🗒️ = $2.

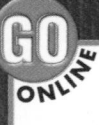

GO ONLINE

Technology
Student pages are available in the Student eBook.

Show What You Know

Check your understanding of important skills needed for success in Chapter 24.

▶ **Practice Subtraction Facts**

Find the difference.

1.	8	2.	36	3.	42	4.	61
	-2		-9		-5		-7

▶ **Practice Division Facts**

Find the quotient.

5. $5\overline{)20}$ 6. $7\overline{)42}$ 7. $3\overline{)21}$ 8. $4\overline{)36}$

▶ **Multiplication and Division Facts Through 10**

Find the product.

9. $8 \times 2 = \blacksquare$ 10. $9 \times 3 = \blacksquare$ 11. $5 \times 10 = \blacksquare$ 12. $3 \times 8 = \blacksquare$

13. $5 \times 7 = \blacksquare$ 14. $6 \times 2 = \blacksquare$ 15. $7 \times 7 = \blacksquare$ 16. $9 \times 4 = \blacksquare$

17. $3 \times 9 = \blacksquare$ 18. $5 \times 1 = \blacksquare$ 19. $10 \times 6 = \blacksquare$ 20. $0 \times 9 = \blacksquare$

Find the quotient.

21. $6 \div 3 = \blacksquare$ 22. $35 \div 5 = \blacksquare$ 23. $18 \div 2 = \blacksquare$ 24. $54 \div 6 = \blacksquare$

25. $4\overline{)36}$ 26. $7\overline{)70}$ 27. $5\overline{)25}$ 28. $8\overline{)72}$

VOCABULARY POWER

CHAPTER VOCABULARY

compatible numbers
dividend
divisor
quotient
remainder

WARM-UP WORDS

dividend The number that is to be divided in a division problem

divisor The number that divides the dividend

remainder The amount left over when a number cannot be divided evenly

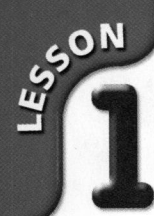

Model Division with Remainders

OBJECTIVE: Use counters to model division with remainders.

Learn

PROBLEM Zach has 13 shark teeth. He wants to make 4 necklaces, with the same number of teeth on each necklace. Can Zach divide the 13 teeth equally into 4 groups?

Activity 1   Materials ▪ counters

Use counters to find 13 ÷ 4.

Step 1	**Step 2**
Use 13 counters. Draw 4 circles for the 4 necklaces. 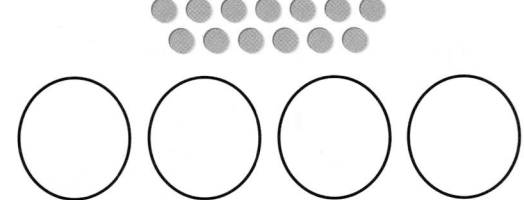	Divide the counters equally among the 4 circles. 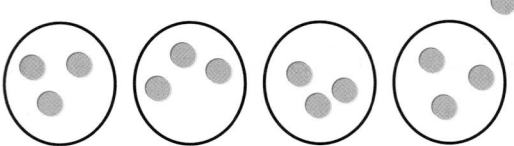 There is 1 counter left over.

So, Zach cannot divide the 13 teeth equally into 4 groups.

After dividing a number into equal groups as large as possible, the amount left over is called the **remainder**.

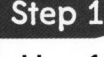

Activity 2   Materials ▪ counters

Use counters to find 20 ÷ 3.

Step 1	**Step 2**
Use 20 counters. Draw 3 circles. 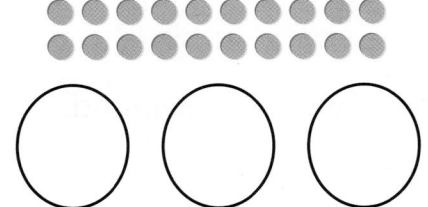	Divide the counters into 3 equal groups. 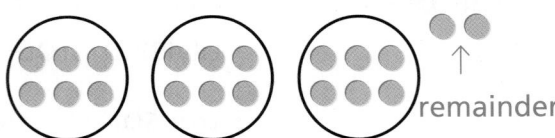 remainder 20 ÷ 3 = 6 r2 The quotient is 6. The remainder is 2.

READ Math

6 r2 is read
6 remainder 2.

1. Complete the number sentence. $11 \div 2 = \blacksquare \text{ r } \blacksquare$

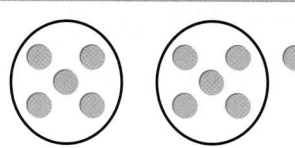

Use counters to find the quotient and remainder.

2. $14 \div 4$ 3. $17 \div 2$ 4. $13 \div 5$ ✅5. $15 \div 2$ ✅6. $18 \div 5$

7. **TALK Math** Explain why you can't have a remainder of 4 when you divide by 4.

Independent Practice and Problem Solving

Use counters to find the quotient and remainder.

8. $13 \div 2$ 9. $22 \div 3$ 10. $19 \div 2$ 11. $17 \div 7$ 12. $23 \div 8$

13. $14 \div 5$ 14. $15 \div 2$ 15. $16 \div 6$ 16. $21 \div 4$ 17. $18 \div 4$

★**Algebra** Find the missing number.

18. $19 \div n = 3 \text{ r}1$ 19. $12 \div 5 = n \text{ r}2$ 20. $11 \div 4 = 2 \text{ r}n$ 21. $n \div 2 = 5 \text{ r}1$

USE DATA For 22–23, use the graph.

22. **Reasoning** If Zach puts an equal number of tiger shark teeth into 3 boxes, what is the least number of shark teeth he will have left over?

23. **WRITE Math** If Zach divides the sand shark teeth evenly into 2 boxes, how many will be in each box? How many teeth will be left over? **Explain.**

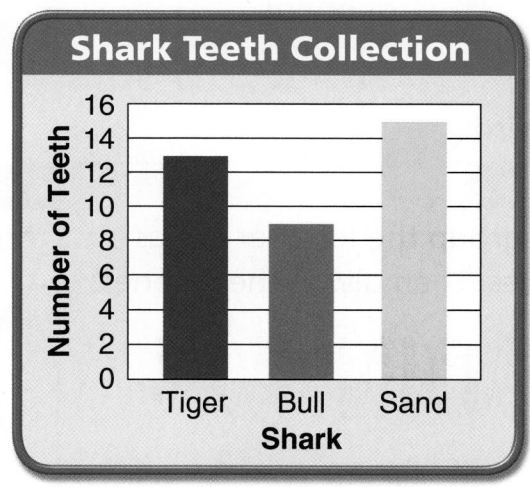

Mixed Review and Test Prep

24. Jake has 17 bull shark teeth and 26 sand shark teeth. How many shark teeth does he have in all? (p. 54)

25. Mary has 9 scarves. Of the scarves, 5 were given to her as presents. What fraction of Mary's scarves were not presents? (p. 450)

26. **Test Prep** Isabel wants to divide 16 lollipops evenly into 3 bags. How many lollipops will be left over?

   A 1   **C** 3

   B 2   **D** 4

Extra Practice on page 624, Set A

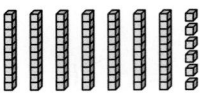

LESSON 2 Record Division

OBJECTIVE: Use base-ten blocks to show 2-digit division.

Quick Review

Find the quotient and remainder.

1. $19 \div 3$ 2. $14 \div 5$
3. $18 \div 7$ 4. $12 \div 5$
5. $19 \div 4$

Learn

PROBLEM Ray is making frozen lemonade popsicles. He has 76 ounces of lemonade. Each popsicle mold holds 6 ounces. How many molds can Ray fill? How many ounces of lemonade will be left over?

Example Divide. $76 \div 6$

Step 1

Use base-ten blocks to model the problem.

■ ← quotient

$6\overline{)76}$ ← dividend

↑
divisor

Step 2

$7 > 6$, so divide the 7 tens.

$\begin{array}{r} 1 \\ 6\overline{)76} \\ -6 \\ \hline 1 \end{array}$

Divide. $7 \div 6$
Multiply. 6×1
Subtract. $7 - 6$
Compare. $1 < 6$

Step 3

Regroup the leftover ten as 10 ones. Then divide the 16 ones.

$\begin{array}{r} 12 \text{ r4} \\ 6\overline{)76} \\ -6\downarrow \\ \hline 16 \\ -12 \\ \hline 4 \end{array}$ ←remainder

Divide: $16 \div 6$
Multiply: 6×2
Subtract: $16 - 12$
Compare: $4 < 6$

Step 4

Multiply to check your answer.

$\begin{array}{r} 12 \leftarrow \text{quotient} \\ \times\ 6 \leftarrow \text{divisor} \\ \hline 72 \end{array}$

$\begin{array}{r} 72 \\ +\ 4 \leftarrow \text{Add the remainder.} \\ \hline 76 \leftarrow \text{This should equal the} \\ \text{dividend.} \end{array}$

Math Idea
When checking your answer, use the inverse operation.

So, Ray can fill 12 popsicle molds. He will have 4 ounces of lemonade left over.

• Does a division problem have to have a remainder?

614

1. What division problem is modeled here?

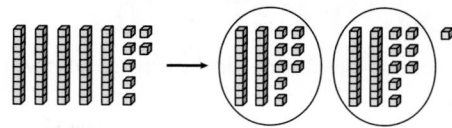

Use base-ten blocks. Write the quotient and remainder.

2. $32 \div 3$ 3. $62 \div 4$ ✓ 4. $4\overline{)58}$ ✓ 5. $6\overline{)78}$

6. **TALK Math** **Explain** how to use base-ten blocks to find $85 \div 6$.

Independent Practice and Problem Solving

Use base-ten blocks. Write the quotient and remainder.

7. $48 \div 7$ 8. $82 \div 3$ 9. $2\overline{)46}$ 10. $5\overline{)67}$

11. $6\overline{)85}$ 12. $2\overline{)54}$ 13. $85 \div 3$ 14. $58 \div 4$

Algebra Find the missing digit.

15. $3\overline{)8\blacksquare}$ $\quad$ 29 r2

16. $4\overline{)63}$ $\quad$ $\blacksquare$5 r3

17. $6\overline{)92}$ $\quad$ 1$\blacksquare$ r2

18. $5\overline{)88}$ $\quad$ 17 r$\blacksquare$

USE DATA For 19-21, use the recipe.

19. Kate poured 1 batch of lemonade equally into 6 tall glasses. How many ounces are in each glass? How many ounces are left over?

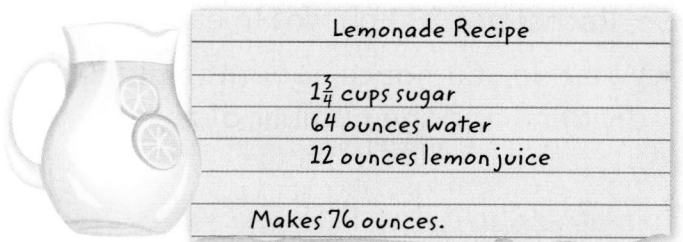

Lemonade Recipe

$1\frac{3}{4}$ cups sugar
64 ounces water
12 ounces lemon juice

Makes 76 ounces.

20. Erin uses an 8-ounce measuring cup to measure the water. How many times should she fill the cup? How much more water will she need?

21. **Reasoning** Mike made 6 batches of lemonade. He filled 4 pitchers with all of his lemonade. How many ounces of lemon juice are in each pitcher?

22. **WRITE Math** When you subtract in a division problem, why must the difference be less than the divisor? **Explain.**

Mixed Review and Test Prep

23. A bag contains 3 red marbles and 10 blue marbles. One marble is pulled. Name an impossible event.
(p. 178)

24. Estimate the product. 4×67 (p. 594)

25. **Test Prep** Paul divided 85 marbles into 4 bags with the same number in each bag. How many marbles were left over?

A 1 $\quad$ **B** 2 $\quad$ **C** 3 $\quad$ **D** 4

Extra Practice on page 624, Set B

ALGEBRA
Division Patterns

OBJECTIVE: Use basic facts and patterns to divide multiples of 10, 100, and 1,000.

Learn

PROBLEM Rachel took 600 photographs while visiting Chicago. She put the same number of photos in each of 3 albums. How many photos did she put in each one?

You can use basic division facts and patterns to divide multiples of 10, 100, and 1,000.

Example Divide. $600 \div 3$

> dividend   quotient
>   ↓   ↓
> $6 \div 3 = 2$ basic fact, no zeros
> $60 \div 3 = 20$ 1 zero in dividend, 1 zero in quotient
> $600 \div 3 = 200$ 2 zeros in dividend, 2 zeros in quotient

So, Rachel put 200 photos in each album.

• What do you notice about the number of zeros in the dividend and the number of zeros in the quotient?

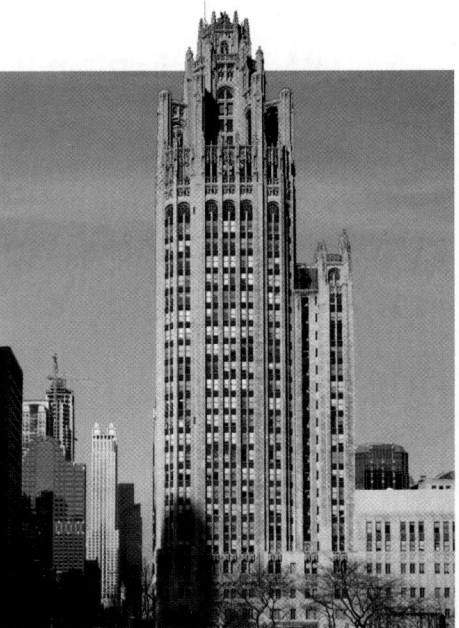

▲ Stones from sites in all 50 states and around the world are built into the walls of the Chicago Tribune Building.

More Examples

> **A** Basic fact without a zero
>
> $48 \div 6 = 8$ ← basic fact
>
> $480 \div 6 = 80$ ← 1 zero
>
> $4,800 \div 6 = 800$ ← 2 zeros

> **B** Basic fact with a zero
>
> $40 \div 8 = 5$ ← basic fact
>
> $400 \div 8 = 50$ ← 1 less zero
>
> $4,000 \div 8 = 500$ ← 1 less zero

• **What if** a basic fact already has a zero in the dividend? Explain what happens in the quotient.

Guided Practice

1. What basic fact can you use to help you find $810 \div 9$?

Use a basic fact and patterns to find each quotient.

2. $32 \div 8 = \blacksquare$ **3.** $56 \div 7 = \blacksquare$ ✓**4.** $30 \div 6 = \blacksquare$ ✓**5.** $18 \div 9 = \blacksquare$

     $320 \div 8 = \blacksquare$ $560 \div 7 = \blacksquare$ $300 \div 6 = \blacksquare$ $180 \div 9 = \blacksquare$

     $3{,}200 \div 8 = \blacksquare$ $5{,}600 \div 7 = \blacksquare$ $3{,}000 \div 6 = \blacksquare$ $1{,}800 \div 9 = \blacksquare$

6. **TALK Math** Explain how knowing $42 \div 6 = 7$ can help you find $4{,}200 \div 6$.

Independent Practice and Problem Solving

Use a basic fact and patterns to find each quotient.

7. $16 \div 2 = \blacksquare$ **8.** $72 \div 8 = \blacksquare$ **9.** $18 \div 3 = \blacksquare$ **10.** $50 \div 5 = \blacksquare$

     $160 \div 2 = \blacksquare$ $720 \div 8 = \blacksquare$ $180 \div 3 = \blacksquare$ $500 \div 5 = \blacksquare$

     $1{,}600 \div 2 = \blacksquare$ $7{,}200 \div 8 = \blacksquare$ $1{,}800 \div 3 = \blacksquare$ $5{,}000 \div 5 = \blacksquare$

Write the basic fact you can use. Then find the quotient.

11. $560 \div 7 = \blacksquare$ **12.** $\blacksquare = 4{,}500 \div 5$ **13.** $120 \div 6 = \blacksquare$ **14.** $\blacksquare = 3{,}600 \div 6$

15. $5{,}000 \div 5 = \blacksquare$ **16.** $4{,}000 \div 2 = \blacksquare$ **17.** $\blacksquare = 1{,}800 \div 2$ **18.** $\blacksquare = 900 \div 3$

★**Algebra** For 19–22, find each value of n.

19. $7{,}200 \div 9 = n$ **20.** $n \div 4 = 70$

21. $2{,}400 \div 8 = n$ **22.** $1{,}200 \div n = 300$

Solve.

23. **Reasoning** The area of a rectangle is 4,200 square feet. The length is 6 feet. What is the width? What is the perimeter?

24. **WRITE Math** **What's the Error?** Max says $400 \div 5 = 800$ because 400 has 2 zeros. Describe Max's error.

Mixed Review and Test Prep

25. Mrs. Walters cut a pizza into 8 equal slices. Jan ate 2 slices and Oscar ate 3 slices. What fraction of the pizza is left? (p. 470)

26. Kylie divided 32 cupcakes evenly into 5 boxes. How many cupcakes were left over? (p. 612)

27. **Test Prep** Which basic division fact can be used to find $400 \div 2$?

   A $40 \div 5 = 8$ **C** $4 \div 2 = 2$

   B $40 \div 8 = 5$ **D** $40 \div 10 = 4$

Extra Practice on page 624, Set C

Estimate Quotients

OBJECTIVE: Use compatible numbers to estimate quotients.

Quick Review

1. $300 \div 5$
2. $450 \div 9$
3. $320 \div 8$
4. $400 \div 4$
5. $7{,}200 \div 8$

Learn

PROBLEM A group of 50 girls have signed up for cheerleading. The girls will be divided into 6 squads. About how many girls will be on each squad?

Compatible numbers are numbers that are easy to compute mentally. When a problem does not need an exact answer, you can estimate by using compatible numbers.

Example 1 Estimate. $50 \div 6$

Step 1

Think of a number that is close to 50 and easy to divide by 6.

$50 \div 6$
$\downarrow$ Think:
$48 \div 6$ 48 is close to 50.

Step 2

Use the compatible numbers, 48 and 6, to find the estimated quotient.

$$48 \div 6 = 8$$

So, there will be about 8 girls on each squad.

• What other compatible numbers could you use to estimate $50 \div 6$? Explain.

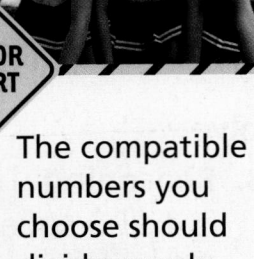

ERROR ALERT

The compatible numbers you choose should divide evenly.

Example 2 Estimate. $418 \div 6$

Step 1

Look at the first two digits. Think of a number that is close to 41 and easy to divide by 6.

$418 \div 6$ Think:
$\downarrow$ 42 is close to 41.
$420 \div 6$ $42 \div 6 = 7$

Step 2

Estimate using the compatible numbers, 420 and 6.

$$420 \div 6 = 70$$

So, $418 \div 6$ is about 70.

Guided Practice

1. What compatible numbers would you use to estimate $29 \div 3$?

Estimate. Tell the compatible numbers you used for each.

2. $60 \div 9$ **3.** $41 \div 5$ **4.** $293 \div 5$ ✓**5.** $472 \div 7$ ✓**6.** $358 \div 4$

7. [TALK Math] **Explain** how to estimate $251 \div 3$ using compatible numbers.

Independent Practice and Problem Solving

Estimate. Tell the compatible numbers you used for each.

8. $55 \div 8$ **9.** $37 \div 6$ **10.** $345 \div 7$ **11.** $234 \div 4$ **12.** $119 \div 2$

13. $75 \div 9$ **14.** $32 \div 6$ **15.** $128 \div 3$ **16.** $342 \div 5$ **17.** $226 \div 7$

18. $9\overline{)67}$ **19.** $7\overline{)51}$ **20.** $4\overline{)302}$ **21.** $8\overline{)152}$ **22.** $2\overline{)119}$

USE DATA For 23–26, use the table.

23. The baseball players will be divided into 5 teams. About how many players will be on each team?

24. The soccer players and hockey players are having a combined banquet. Eight players can sit at each table. About how many tables are needed?

25. **Reasoning** The basketball players are divided into 9 teams. The hockey players are divided into 7 teams. Which sport has more players per team? **Explain** how you estimated.

Springfield Recreation League	
Sport	**Number of Players**
Basketball	248
Baseball	216
Soccer	183
Hockey	134
Cheerleading	50

26. [WRITE Math] Look back at Problem 23. How did you decide which compatible numbers to use? **Explain.**

Mixed Review and Test Prep

27. Morgan has 2 quarters, 6 dimes, 3 nickels and 14 pennies. Caleb has 1 quarter, 9 dimes, 8 nickels and 27 pennies. Who has more money? How much more? (p. 114)

28. If $8 \div 4 = 2$, what is $800 \div 4$? (p. 616)

29. **Test Prep** Sal needs to estimate $57 \div 8$. Which expression shows the best choice of compatible numbers for Sal to use?

A $57 \div 10$ **C** $60 \div 8$

B $60 \div 10$ **D** $56 \div 8$

Extra Practice on page 624, Set D

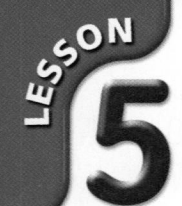

5 Divide 2- and 3-Digit Numbers

OBJECTIVE: Divide 2- and 3-digit numbers with and without remainders.

Learn

PROBLEM Miranda's elementary school is visiting the Children's Museum. There are 6 buses for the 288 students going to the museum. How many students will be on each bus?

Example 1 **Divide.** 288 ÷ 6 or 6)288   **Estimate.** 300 ÷ 6 = 50

Step 1

Decide where to place the first digit.

■
6)288

2 < 6, so divide the 28 tens.

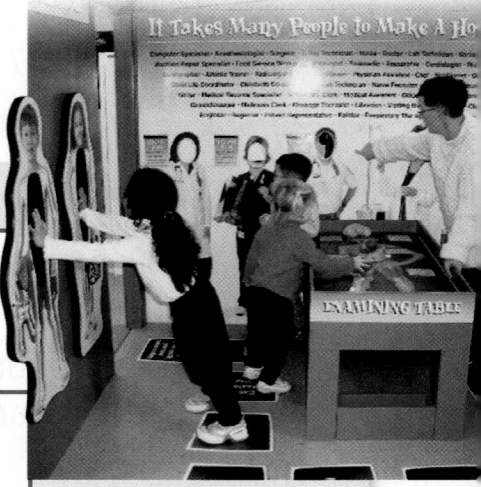

▲ the Children's Museum in Niantic, Connecticut

Step 2

Divide 28 tens by 6.

$$\begin{array}{r} 4 \\ 6\overline{)288} \\ -24 \\ \hline 4 \end{array}$$

Divide. 6)28
Multiply. 6 × 4
Subtract. 28 − 24
Compare. 4 < 6

Step 3

Bring down the 8 ones. Divide 48 ones by 6.

$$\begin{array}{r} 48 \\ 6\overline{)288} \\ -24\downarrow \\ \hline 48 \\ -48 \\ \hline 0 \end{array}$$

Divide. 6)48
Multiply. 6 × 8
Subtract. 48 − 48
Compare. 0 < 6

So, there will be 48 students on each bus. Since 48 is close to the estimate, 50, the answer is reasonable.

Example 2 **Divide.** 470 ÷ 3 or 3)470

$$\begin{array}{r} 156 \text{ r2} \\ 3\overline{)470} \\ -3 \\ \hline 17 \\ -15 \\ \hline 20 \\ -18 \\ \hline 2 \end{array}$$

Check your answer by multiplying the quotient by the divisor. Then add the remainder.

$$\begin{array}{r} 156 \\ \times\ \ 3 \\ \hline 468 \\ +\ \ 2 \\ \hline 470 \end{array}$$

◄——— Since the sum, 470, is equal to the dividend, 470, the quotient is correct.

1. Where should you place the first digit in the quotient $7\overline{)295}$ for the division problem at the right? **Explain.**

Divide. Use multiplication to check your answer.

2. $4\overline{)744}$ 3. $5\overline{)423}$ ✓4. $156 \div 6$ ✓5. $679 \div 3$ 6. $278 \div 3$

7. **TALK Math** Explain how you know how many digits are in the quotient $456 \div 2$ without dividing.

Independent Practice and Problem Solving

Divide. Use multiplication to check your answer.

8. $7\overline{)972}$ 9. $3\overline{)269}$ 10. $6\overline{)193}$ 11. $5\overline{)635}$ 12. $2\overline{)415}$

13. $8\overline{)973}$ 14. $2\overline{)374}$ 15. $7\overline{)113}$ 16. $9\overline{)189}$ 17. $6\overline{)286}$

18. $222 \div 6$ 19. $890 \div 7$ 20. $207 \div 5$ 21. $924 \div 9$ 22. $714 \div 8$

23. $261 \div 4$ 24. $632 \div 4$ 25. $644 \div 2$ 26. $742 \div 3$ 27. $398 \div 4$

USE DATA For 28–30, use the graph.

28. At the museum, 5 teachers volunteered the same number of hours. How many hours did each teacher volunteer?

29. Each of the gardening volunteers worked 6 hours. Each of the office staff volunteers worked 7 hours. Were there more gardening volunteers or office staff volunteers? **Explain.**

30. **WRITE Math** What's the Question? Each aide worked 5 hours. The answer is 50.

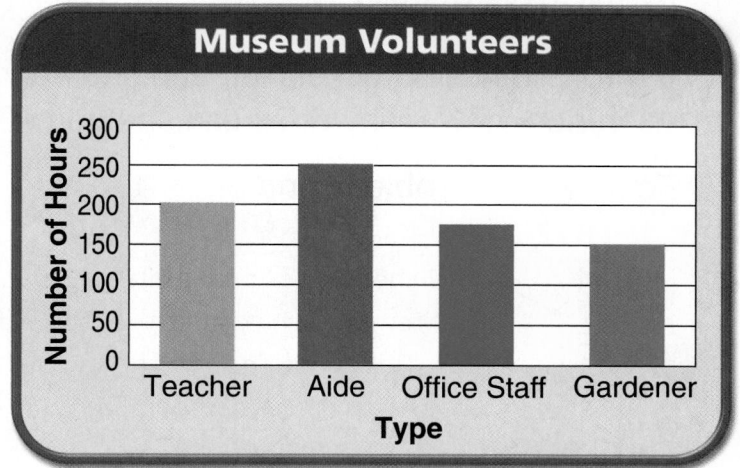

Museum Volunteers

Mixed Review and Test Prep

31. Gillian's dog weighs 8 pounds. How many ounces does the dog weigh? (pp. 522, 596)

32. Joe buys 4 tickets for $126. About how much does each cost? (p. 618)

33. **Test Prep** What is $431 \div 9$?

 A 52 r3   C 47 r8

 B 48 r1   D 31 r7

Technology
Use Harcourt Mega Math, The Number Games, *Up, Up, and Array,* Levels M, N.

Extra Practice on page 624, Set E

Problem Solving Workshop
Skill: Interpret the Remainder

OBJECTIVE: Solve problems by using the skill *interpret the remainder*.

Read to Understand

PROBLEM Michelle is at a carnival. She needs 49 tickets to go on her favorite rides. The tickets come in packs of 5. How many packs does she need to buy?

When you divide, sometimes you have to decide how to use the remainder to solve the problem.

To solve the problem, find $49 \div 5$.

```
    9 r4
5)49
 -45
    4
```

If Michelle buys 9 packs of tickets, she will only have 45 tickets. The remainder tells her she needs 4 more tickets, so she has to buy 1 more pack of tickets.

So, Michelle needs to buy 10 packs of tickets.

If Michelle has 34 tickets left and she needs 4 tickets for each ride, how many rides can she go on?

To solve the problem, find $34 \div 4$.

```
    8 r2
4)34
 -32
    2
```

If Michelle goes on 8 rides, she will use 32 tickets. The remainder tells her that she will have 2 tickets left. This is not enough for another ride, so drop, or ignore, the remainder.

So, Michelle can go on 8 rides.

TALK Math

Explain how you know when to drop, or ignore, the remainder.

Think and Discuss

Interpret the remainder to solve.

a. Eleven children want to ride a roller coaster at the carnival. Each car holds 3 children. How many cars will the children need?

b. Max uses 6 ounces of caramel to make 1 caramel apple. He has 94 ounces of caramel. How many caramel apples can he make?

1. Jamie and her family are at the school fair. It takes 5 minutes to make a spin-art picture. How many spin-art pictures can she make in 29 minutes?

   Divide 29 ÷ 5.

   What is the quotient? What is the remainder?

   Should you drop the remainder or increase the quotient?

   Solve the problem.

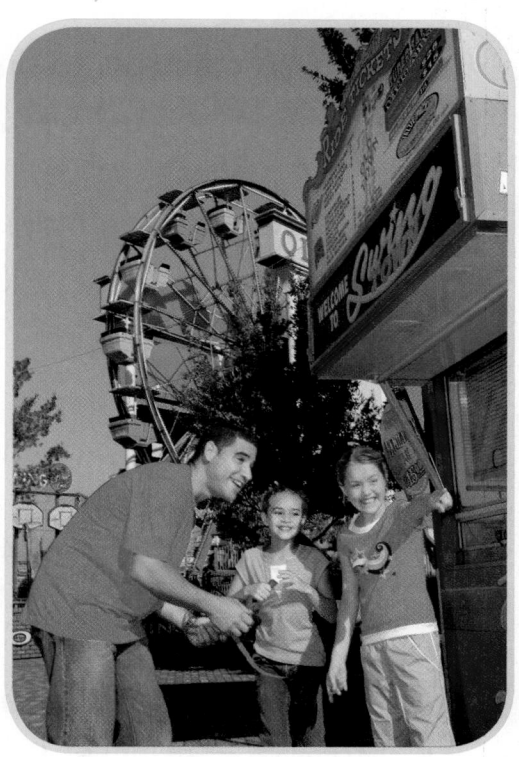

2. **What if** Jamie has 42 minutes to make spin-art pictures? How many pictures could Jamie make?

3. There are 60 children waiting in line at the bumper cars and 9 children can ride at a time. How many times does the ride need to run to give all the children a turn?

Mixed Applications

4. There are 30 picnic tables at the carnival that need to be placed under tents. Only 4 tables will fit under each tent. How many tents are needed?

5. It took Jimmy 35 minutes to get to the fair. Then he rode on 6 rides. Each ride took 8 minutes. How many minutes did Jimmy spend on the rides?

6. Nancy needs 4 tickets to go on the Safari Ride. She needs 3 tickets to go on the Ferris Wheel. Nancy wants to go on each ride 3 times. How many tickets does Nancy need in all?

7. Tommy has $25 to spend on food. He buys a cheese steak for $5.25, a fruit salad for $2.00, and 3 bottles of water for $1.25 each. How much money will Tommy have left?

8. Maggie, Pete, Ryan, and Olivia are waiting in line at the concession stand. Maggie is not last. Pete is behind Olivia. Ryan is first. In what order are the children standing?

9. **Reasoning** Jen rode on 14 rides that each used 5 tickets. Barry rode on 13 rides that each used 6 tickets. Who used more tickets? **Explain.**

10. **WRITE Math** A sheet of 20 tickets costs $23.75. Ned has $50. **Explain** how can he use estimation to decide if he has enough money to buy 2 sheets of tickets.

Extra Practice

Set A Use counters to find the quotient and remainder. (pp. 612–613)

1. $18 \div 5$ **2.** $15 \div 2$ **3.** $34 \div 6$ **4.** $22 \div 3$ **5.** $27 \div 8$

Set B Use base-ten blocks. Write the quotient and remainder. (pp. 614–615)

1. $38 \div 4$ **2.** $65 \div 3$ **3.** $7\overline{)94}$ **4.** $5\overline{)88}$ **5.** $6\overline{)95}$

6. $3\overline{)81}$ **7.** $4\overline{)97}$ **8.** $8\overline{)91}$ **9.** $2\overline{)59}$ **10.** $6\overline{)77}$

Set C Use a basic fact and patterns to find each quotient. (pp. 616–617)

1. $27 \div 3 = \blacksquare$ **2.** $42 \div 6 = \blacksquare$ **3.** $32 \div 4 = \blacksquare$ **4.** $35 \div 7 = \blacksquare$

    $270 \div 3 = \blacksquare$ $420 \div 6 = \blacksquare$ $320 \div 4 = \blacksquare$ $350 \div 7 = \blacksquare$

   $2{,}700 \div 3 = \blacksquare$ $4{,}200 \div 6 = \blacksquare$ $3{,}200 \div 4 = \blacksquare$ $3{,}500 \div 7 = \blacksquare$

Write the basic fact you can use. Then find the quotient.

5. $140 \div 2 = \blacksquare$ **6.** $6{,}400 \div 8 = \blacksquare$ **7.** $1{,}800 \div 9 = \blacksquare$ **8.** $200 \div 5 = \blacksquare$

Set D Estimate. Tell the compatible numbers you used for each. (pp. 618–619)

1. $70 \div 8$ **2.** $25 \div 6$ **3.** $111 \div 2$ **4.** $127 \div 5$ **5.** $218 \div 4$

6. $22 \div 3$ **7.** $61 \div 7$ **8.** $9\overline{)97}$ **9.** $6\overline{)176}$ **10.** $8\overline{)324}$

11. There are 129 players in a softball league. The league consists of 8 teams. About how many players will be on each team?

12. There are 453 coins in a jar. Gary will divide the coins into 9 equal groups. About how many coins will be in each group?

Set E Divide. Use multiplication to check your answer. (pp. 620–621)

1. $4\overline{)128}$ **2.** $5\overline{)229}$ **3.** $7\overline{)881}$ **4.** $365 \div 2$ **5.** $547 \div 3$

6. Larissa waters the plants in her garden once every 7 days for 175 days. How many times did Larissa water the plants?

7. Jonathan traveled by train for 3 hours. The train traveled 267 miles. How many miles did the train travel in each hour?

Technology
Use Harcourt Mega Math, The Number Games, *Up, Up, and Array*, Levels L, M, and N.

Division Toss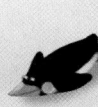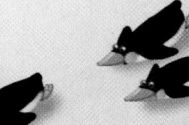

Start

Ready!
2–4 players

Set!
- Two prepared number cubes
- Counter for each player
- Gameboard
- Paper and pencils

Finish

Roll!

- Each player puts a counter on START.
- One player tosses both number cubes.
- The single number showing on one cube is the divisor. The greater number of the same color showing on the other cube is the dividend.
- All players find the quotient.

- The first player to find the quotient calls it out. Other players complete the division and check the first player's quotient. If correct, the player who called it out first moves 1 space.
- The next player tosses the cubes and players try to find the next quotient.
- The first player to reach FINISH wins.

Divide and Conquer

A number is divisible by another number if there is no remainder when the numbers are divided. Divisibility rules can be used to find out if one number is divisible by another.

Examples

A A number is divisible by 2 if the ones digit is 0, 2, 4, 6, or 8.

Divisible by 2:	Not divisible by 2:
64 98 412 6,940	65 97 413 6,949

B A number is divisible by 3 if the sum of the digits is divisible by 3.

Divisible by 3:	Not divisible by 3:
$516 \rightarrow 5 + 1 + 6 = 12$	$82 \rightarrow 8 + 2 = 10$
12 is divisible by 3. $12 \div 3 = 4$	10 is not divisible by 3.
So, 516 is divisible by 3.	So, 82 is not divisible by 3.

C A number is divisible by 5 if the ones digit is 0 or 5.

Divisible by 5:	Not divisible by 5:
40 65 230 6,495	41 63 237 6,498

D A number is divisible by 10 if the ones digit is 0.

Divisible by 10:	Not divisible by 10:
20 50 690 8,430	21 53 694 8,437

Try It

List if each number is divisible by 2, 3, 5, or 10.

1. 124 **2.** 875 **3.** 57 **4.** 377

5. 78 **6.** 207 **7.** 444 **8.** 214

9. 3,780 **10.** 6,208 **11.** 163,875 **12.** 119,000

13. ▌WRITE Math ▶ Write a 4-digit number. Tell whether your number is divisible by 2, 3, 5, or 10. **Explain** how you know.

Chapter 24 Review/Test

Check Vocabulary and Concepts

Choose the best term from the box.

1. The amount left over after dividing a number into equal groups is called the __?__. (p. 612)

2. The answer in a division problem, not including the remainder, is called a __?__. (p. 612)

Check Skills

Use a basic fact and patterns to find each quotient. (pp. 616–617)

3.
$30 \div 5 = $ ▪
$300 \div 5 = $ ▪
$3,000 \div 5 = $ ▪

4.
$42 \div 6 = $ ▪
$420 \div 6 = $ ▪
$4,200 \div 6 = $ ▪

5.
$81 \div 9 = $ ▪
$810 \div 9 = $ ▪
$8,100 \div 9 = $ ▪

6.
$24 \div 8 = $ ▪
$240 \div 8 = $ ▪
$2,400 \div 8 = $ ▪

Estimate. Tell the compatible numbers you used for each. (pp. 618–619)

7. $50 \div 3$

8. $23 \div 5$

9. $193 \div 6$

10. $276 \div 4$

Divide. Use multiplication to check your answer. (pp. 620–621)

11. $4\overline{)96}$

12. $7\overline{)266}$

13. $2\overline{)731}$

14. $8\overline{)304}$

15. $3\overline{)154}$

16. $5\overline{)297}$

17. $6\overline{)518}$

18. $7\overline{)677}$

19. $152 \div 8$

20. $203 \div 6$

21. $316 \div 2$

22. $872 \div 5$

Check Problem Solving

Solve. (pp. 622–623)

23. A movie theatre offers a free movie ticket for every 3 cans of pet food donated to the animal shelter. How many tickets can Dave receive if he donates 50 cans of pet food?

24. Kevin worked on a math puzzle for 32 minutes. If each part of the puzzle took 5 minutes to solve, how many parts did he solve?

25. **WRITE Math** A concert hall has 355 seats. Are there enough chairs to seat 40 groups of 9 students? If not, how many more seats are needed? **Explain.**

Multiple Choice

1. Debra sold 340 tickets for a play. She sold the same number of tickets each day for 5 days. How many tickets did she sell each day? (p. 620)

   A 68

   B 60

   C 56

   D 50

2. Which division problem does the model show? (p. 612)

   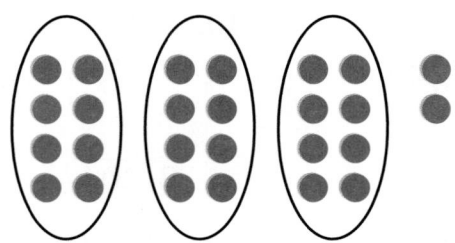

   A 24 ÷ 3 = 8

   B 23 ÷ 3 = 7 r2

   C 26 ÷ 3 = 8 r2

   D 21 ÷ 3 = 7

3. In Margaret's science class, 300 ants were placed in each of 6 ant houses. How many ants were there in all?

   (p. 586)

   A 180,000

   B 18,000

   C 1,800

   D 180

4. Which is the missing number? (p. 616)

   $$20 \div 5 = 4$$
   $$200 \div 5 = 40$$
   $$2{,}000 \div 5 = \blacksquare$$

   A 4

   B 40

   C 400

   D 4,000

5. Will drove 4 hours to visit his grandfather. He drove an average of 58 miles per hour. Which is the BEST estimate of the number of miles Will drove? (p. 594)

   A 160

   B 200

   C 240

   D 280

6. Tim is building with small building blocks. He uses 456 blocks to build 8 towers. He uses the same number of blocks in each tower. How many blocks does Tim use in each tower? (p. 620)

   A 68

   B 57

   C 46

   D 34

GO ONLINE **Technology** Use *Online Assessment.*

7. Which multiplication sentence is shown by the model? (p. 588)

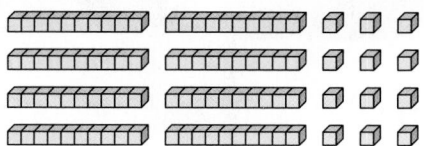

  A $4 \times 20 = 80$

  B $4 \times 13 = 52$

  C $1 \times 23 = 23$

  D $4 \times 23 = 92$

8. There are 465 students sitting in 9 rows in the auditorium of York School. There are about the same number of students in each row. Which is the BEST estimate of the number of students in each row?

(p. 618)

  A 40

  B 50

  C 60

  D 70

9. Bob placed 49 stamps on each of 8 pages in his stamp book. How many stamps did Bob place in all?

(p. 596)

  A 57

  B 322

  C 343

  D 392

Short Response

10. What is $2,400 \div 6$? (p. 616)

11. A kiln can fire 56 pieces of pottery at one time. How many pieces of pottery can be fired if the kiln is run 5 times? (p. 596)

12. What division sentence is shown by the model? (p. 612)

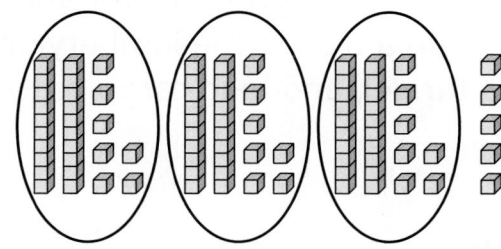

Extended Response ✏️ WRITE Math ▶

13. What is 5×200? **Explain** how you can use a basic fact and patterns to find the product? (p. 586)

14. How can you use compatible numbers to estimate $438 \div 6$? **Explain** your answer? (p. 618)

Model Trains

The Great Train Story

The 3,500 square foot Great Train Story at the Chicago Museum of Science and Industry shows a train's journey across the Western United States from Chicago to Seattle. The exhibit focuses on the materials that a train transports across the country. Some of the materials include fruit, logs, coal, and people.

This exhibit is not just for adults. Children can chop down a tree at the lumberyard, blow up rock to build a tunnel, and load cargo onto the train.

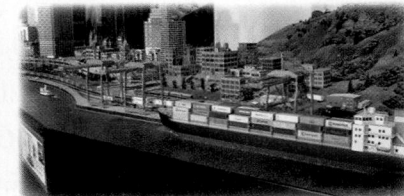

Children can load cargo onto the train.

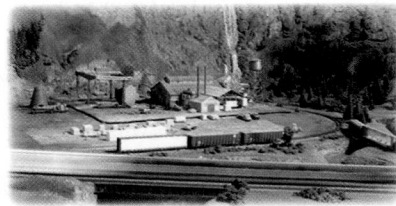

At the lumberyard, children can cut down a tree.

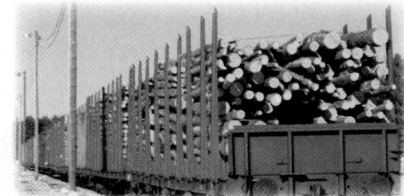

a real flatcar carrying lumber

FACT·ACTIVITY

Solve.

1. The exhibit designers took an 11-day train trip from Chicago to Seattle to look at the scenery. If it takes the same numbers of day to travel back to Chicago, for how many days were they traveling?

2. The designers tried 25 different layouts for the train exhibit before finding one that worked. If each layout took 1 week, how many days did it take before completing the final layout?

3. There are 192 hand-made buildings in the exhibit. If each team built 6 of them, how many teams would be needed to build all of the buildings?

4. **Pose a Problem** Look at Problem 1. Write a new problem by changing the train trip to last more than 2 weeks.

ALMANAC
Fact

At the Great Train Story, there are 34 operating trains traveling at one time.

Model Train Layouts

Model train layouts can be built by anyone. Whether young or old, model trains can provide hours of enjoyment. Model train layouts can be as simple as one train with a little scenery, or multiple trains and many different pieces of scenery.

To get started, you need a train, a track, and your imagination.

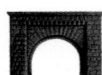

**stone tunnel:
2 per pack, $10**

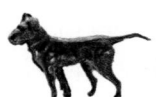 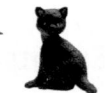 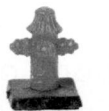

**dogs and cats, fire hydrant,
trash can: 9 pieces, $12**

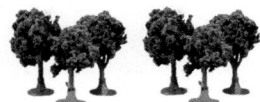

**ready-made trees:
38 per pack, $27**

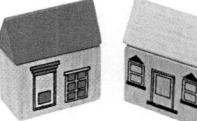 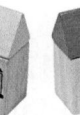 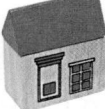

buildings: 3 per pack, $16

FACT·ACTIVITY

Suppose you want to build your own model railroad layout. The pictures show some possible items you can use in addition to the trains and tracks.

► Decide which items and how many packages of each you want in your layout. Find the total number of each item.

► Use the number of packages and the price per package to find the cost of each set of packages you buy. Find your total cost.

► Use grid paper to draw a picture of your model railroad layout.

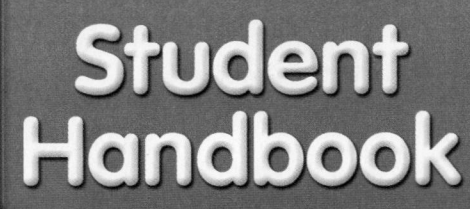

Student Handbook

Review the Key Concepts

These pages provide review of key concepts for your grade. They also help you avoid errors students often make.

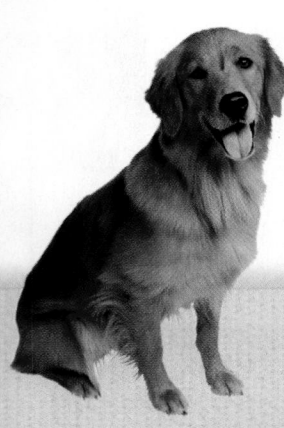

Review the Key Concepts

Place Value to 6 Digits

Key Concept Each digit in a number has a value.

A place-value chart can help you understand the value of each digit. In the number below, the digit 5 has a value of 50,000 because it is in the ten-thousands place.

HUNDRED THOUSANDS	TEN THOUSANDS	THOUSANDS	HUNDREDS	TENS	ONES
4	5	6,	7	1	8

You can write this number in different ways.

Standard form: 456,718

Expanded form: 400,000 + 50,000 + 6,000 + 700 + 10 + 8

Word form: four hundred fifty-six thousand, seven hundred eighteen

Examples

A Write the number 4,506 in expanded form.

When you write a number in expanded form, you show the value of each digit.

4,000 + 500 + 6

B What is the value of the digit 3 in the number 63,080?

The digit 3 in the thousands place.

The value of the digit 3 is 3,000.

ERROR ALERT

Be sure to look at the place the digit is in to find the value of the digit.

Try It

Write each number in expanded form.

1. 2,565

2. 74,406

3. 126,890

4. 650,111

Write the value of the underlined digit.

5. 23,1<u>4</u>8

6. 8<u>6</u>9,424

7. <u>8</u>45

8. <u>9</u>89,889

9. Read the problem below. **Explain** why C cannot be the correct answer choice. Then choose the correct answer. **COMMON ERROR**

There were 9,372 visitors to the Science Center in October. What is the value of the digit 3 in 9,372?

A 3,000   **C** 30

B 300   **D** 3

Review the Key Concepts

Compare and Order 3- and 4-Digit Numbers

Key Concept You can compare numbers to describe whether a
number is greater than, less than, or equal to another number.

THOUSANDS	HUNDREDS	TENS	ONES
6,	9	0	2
6,	7	4	3

Understanding place value can help you compare and order
numbers. To compare 6,902 and 6,743, start with the
greatest place value. The thousands are the same, so
compare the hundreds. 9 hundreds is greater than 7 hundreds.
So, 6,902 is greater than 6,743.

Examples

A Compare 567 and 435.

Compare digits in the same
place-value position from left
to right.

HUNDREDS	TENS	ONES
5	6	7
4	3	5

5 hundreds is greater than
4 hundreds.

So, 567 > 435.

B Spring School is voting
for class president. There
are 261 votes for Connie,
232 votes for Javon, and
248 votes for Gina. Put the
number of votes in order
from least to greatest.

Since the hundreds digits
are the same, you need to
compare the tens digits.

3 < 4 < 6

So, the order is 232, 248, 261.

ERROR ALERT

Remember to
compare digits
from left to
right.

Try It

Compare the numbers. Write <, >, or =
for each ●.

1. 681 ● 685

2. 526 ● 529

3. 3,659 ● 3,596

4. 7,894 ● 7,894

Write the numbers in order from least
to greatest.

5. 728; 721; 748

6. 1,176; 1,167; 1,178

7. Read the problem below.
Explain why B cannot be
the correct answer choice.
Then choose the correct answer.

COMMON ERROR

Which is a true statement?

A 1,025 < 978

B 5,672 = 5,762

C 1,428 > 1,432

D 6,319 < 6,340

Review the Key Concepts

Add 3- and 4-Digit Numbers

Key Concept When two numbers are added, the answer is called the sum.

To add 3- and 4-digit numbers, line up the digits by place value and add one column at a time from right to left. When the sum of one column is greater than 9, you must regroup.

$$\begin{array}{r} {}^{1\ 1} \\ 268 \\ +153 \\ \hline 421 \end{array}$$

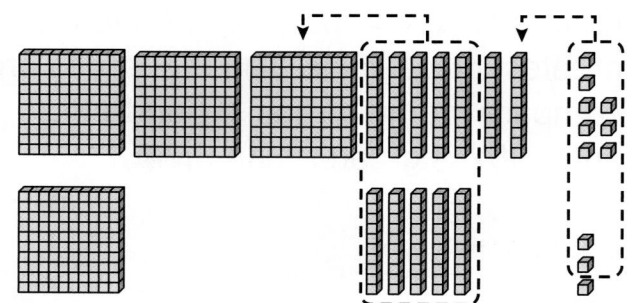

Examples

A Bobby has 1,290 baseball cards. Jack gives him 316 more cards. How many baseball cards does Bobby have now?

$$\begin{array}{r} {}^{1} \\ 1{,}290 \\ +\ \ 316 \\ \hline 1{,}606 \end{array}$$

B Find the sum.

$3{,}783 + 2{,}972 = \blacksquare$

$$\begin{array}{r} {}^{1\ \ 1} \\ 3{,}783 \\ +2{,}972 \\ \hline 6{,}755 \end{array}$$

ERROR ALERT

When regrouping, be sure to add the regrouped number to the next column.

Try It

Find each sum.

1. $\begin{array}{r} 352 \\ +378 \\ \hline \end{array}$

2. $\begin{array}{r} 545 \\ +297 \\ \hline \end{array}$

3. $\begin{array}{r} 1{,}016 \\ +4{,}592 \\ \hline \end{array}$

4. $\begin{array}{r} 8{,}876 \\ +\ \ 241 \\ \hline \end{array}$

5. $398 + 576 = \blacksquare$

6. $115 + 275 = \blacksquare$

7. $6{,}843 + 1{,}254 = \blacksquare$

8. $2{,}347 + 4{,}792 = \blacksquare$

9. Read the problem below. **Explain** why B cannot be the correct answer choice. Then choose the correct answer.

COMMON ERROR

Jane wants to count the number of tiles on the wall and on the floor. She counts 202 tiles on the wall and 189 tiles on the floor. How many tiles are there in all?

A 380	**C** 391
B 381	**D** 491

Review the Key Concepts

Subtract 3- and 4-Digit Numbers

Key Concept When two numbers are subtracted, the answer is called the difference.

To subtract 3- and 4-digit numbers, line up the digits vertically by place value. Then subtract one column at a time from right to left. If the number you are subtracting from is less than the number you are subtracting, then you need to regroup.

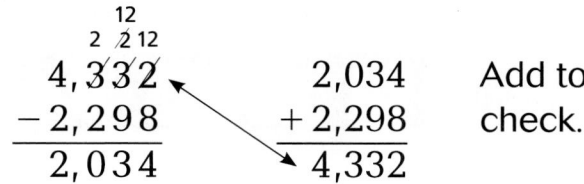

$$
\begin{array}{r}
\overset{\overset{12}{\overset{2\ \ \cancel{2}\ 12}{}}}{4,\cancel{3}\cancel{3}\cancel{2}} \\
-\ 2,298 \\
\hline
2,034
\end{array}
\qquad
\begin{array}{r}
2,034 \\
+\ 2,298 \\
\hline
4,332
\end{array}
\qquad
\begin{array}{l}
\text{Add to} \\
\text{check.}
\end{array}
$$

Examples

A Philip has 358 marbles. He gives 193 to his sister. How many marbles does Phillip have now?

$$
\begin{array}{r}
\overset{\overset{2\ 15}{}}{3\cancel{5}8} \\
-\ 193 \\
\hline
165
\end{array}
$$

B Subtract. 5,816 − 1,527

$$
\begin{array}{r}
\overset{\overset{10}{7\ \ 0\ \ 16}}{5,8\cancel{1}\cancel{6}} \\
-\ 1,527 \\
\hline
4,289
\end{array}
$$

ERROR ALERT

Be sure to start from the right and move to the left when subtracting vertically.

Try It

Find each difference.

1.
$$\begin{array}{r} 863 \\ -658 \\ \hline \end{array}$$

2.
$$\begin{array}{r} 413 \\ -262 \\ \hline \end{array}$$

3.
$$\begin{array}{r} 3,265 \\ -1,422 \\ \hline \end{array}$$

4.
$$\begin{array}{r} 6,721 \\ -4,632 \\ \hline \end{array}$$

5. $217 - 148 = \blacksquare$

6. $976 - 495 = \blacksquare$

7. $7,812 - 1,765 = \blacksquare$

8. $4,580 - 2,671 = \blacksquare$

9. Read the problem below. **Explain** why B cannot be the correct answer choice. Then choose the correct answer. **COMMON ERROR**

Juan's family is baking 225 cookies for a school picnic. If they have baked 155 cookies already, how many more do they need to bake?

A 180   **C** 130

B 170   **D** 70

Review the Key Concepts

Make Change from $5 and $10

Key Concept Count up from the cost of an item to make change.

When making change, start with the cost of the item, and count up with coins and bills until you get to the amount that was paid. Then count the value of the bills and coins you used.

A magazine costs $3.43 and Trish pays with a $10 bill. What change should Trish get?

Cost of item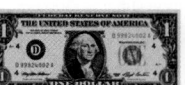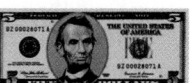
↓

$3.43   3.44 → 3.45 → $3.50 → $3.75 → $4.00 → $5.00 → $10.00 ← Amount paid

So, Trish should get $6.57 in change.

Examples

ERROR ALERT

Be sure to start with the cost of the item when finding the amount of change.

Ⓐ A dog toy costs $2.36. Sue pays with a $5 bill. How much change should she get?

$2.36 + 4 pennies + 1 dime + 2 quarters + 2 dollars = $5.00

Sue should get $2.64 in change.

Ⓑ A plant costs $7.82. Lee pays with a $10 bill. How much change should he get?

$7.82 + 3 pennies + 1 nickel + 1 dime + 2 dollars = $10.00

Lee should get $2.18 in change.

Try It

Find the amount of change from a $5 bill.

1. $4.20   **2.** $2.37

3. $1.89   **4.** $3.64

Find the amount of change from a $10 bill.

5. $6.14   **6.** $9.54

7. $4.78   **8.** $2.36

9. Read the problem below. **Explain** why D cannot be the correct answer choice. Then choose the correct answer.

COMMON ERROR

Maddie buys a pen for $1.79 and pays with a $5 bill. How much change should she receive?

A $1.79   **C** $3.21

B $2.79   **D** $5.21

Review the Key Concepts

Tell Time to the Nearest Minute

Key Concept To read the time on an analog clock, look at the hour hand and the minute hand.

When the hour hand is between two numbers, read the time as the number of minutes after the earlier hour or as the number of minutes before the later hour. To find the number of minutes past the hour, count forward by fives and ones. To find the number of minutes before the hour, count back by fives and ones. Digital clocks use numbers to show the time.

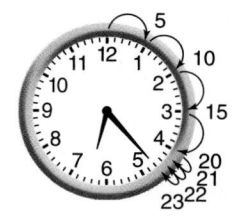

6:23 or 23 minutes after 6

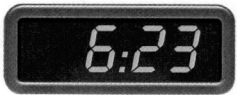

Examples

A What time is shown on this clock?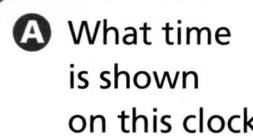

Write: 2:48

Read: • forty-eight minutes after two
• twelve minutes before three

B What time is shown on this clock?

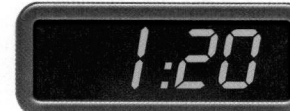

Write: 1:20

Read: • one twenty
• twenty minutes after one

ERROR ALERT

Remember that on an analog clock, the hour hand is shorter than the minute hand.

Try It

Write the time. Write two ways to read each time.

1.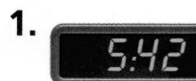

2.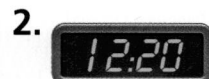

3.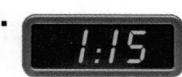

4.

5.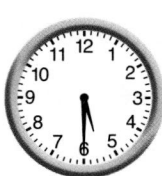

6.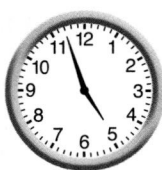

COMMON ERROR

7. Read the problem below. **Explain** why A cannot be the correct answer choice. Then choose the correct answer.

What time is shown on the clock below?

A 10:20

B 10:17

C 4:50

D 3:50

Review the Key Concepts

Read Bar Graphs

Key Concept A bar graph uses bars to show data.

A scale of numbers helps you read the number that each bar shows. In a horizontal bar graph, bars go across from left to right, and in a vertical bar graph, bars go up from the bottom.

Examples

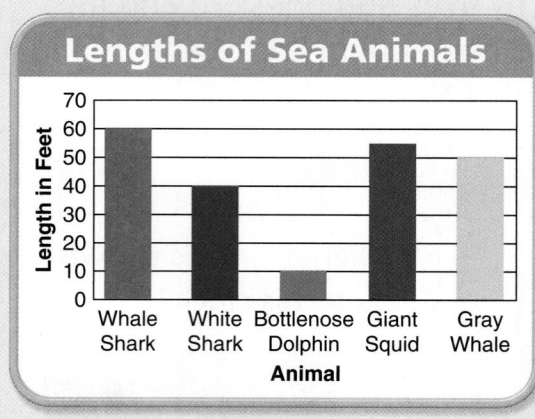

Lengths of Sea Animals

A How long is a giant squid?

The bar for the giant squid ends halfway between 50 and 60 feet.

A giant squid is 55 feet long.

B How much longer is a whale shark than a white shark?

A whale shark is 60 feet long.
A white shark is 40 feet long.
60 − 40 = 20

A whale shark is 20 feet longer than a white shark.

ERROR ALERT

Be sure to use the correct scale when reading a bar graph.

Try It

For 1–3, use the bar graph below.

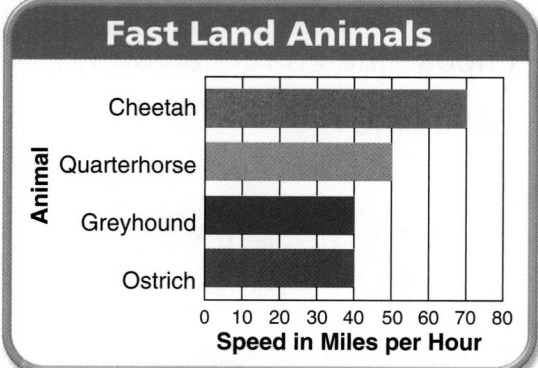

Fast Land Animals

1. How fast can a greyhound run?

2. Which animal is the fastest of the four?

3. Read the problem below. **Explain** why B cannot be the correct answer. Then choose the correct answer.

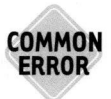
COMMON ERROR

How much faster is a cheetah than an ostrich?

A 70 miles per hour

B 40 miles per hour

C 30 miles per hour

D 10 miles per hour

Review the Key Concepts

Determine the Likelihood of Events

Key Concept You can use data to describe the probability, or likelihood, of events.

An event is something that might happen. Probability is the chance that an event will happen. Certain events will always happen, and impossible events will never happen. Likely events have a good chance of happening, and unlikely events do not have a good chance of happening.

> **ERROR ALERT**
>
> Be sure to identify the most likely outcome as the one that has the greatest chance of happening.

Examples

A Which color are you most likely to spin?

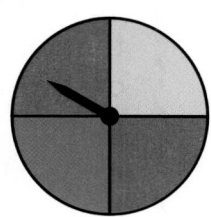

You have 2 out of 4 chances to land on red and only 1 out of 4 chances to land on any other color.

So, red is the most likely outcome.

B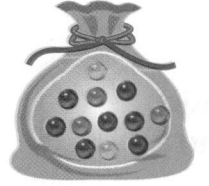

Is it likely or unlikely that a yellow marble will be pulled?

Yellow has the fewest marbles, so it is unlikely that a yellow marble will be pulled.

Is it certain or impossible that a purple marble will be pulled?

There are no purple marbles, so it is impossible.

Try It

If you spin the pointer one time, tell whether each event is *likely, unlikely, certain,* or *impossible.*

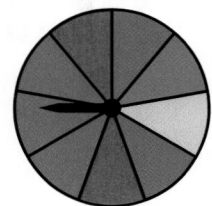

1. The pointer will land on brown.

2. The pointer will land on blue.

3. The pointer will land on green.

4. The pointer will land on a color.

5. Read the problem below. **Explain** why B cannot be the correct answer choice. Then choose the correct answer.

   COMMON ERROR

   Justin has a bag with 12 tiles. 7 tiles are green, 2 are red, 2 are blue, and 1 is yellow. If Justin pulls one tile out of the bag, which color will he most likely pull?

   A yellow   **C** green

   B blue   **D** red

Review the Key Concepts

Model Multiplication with Arrays

Key Concept An array is a group of objects in rows and columns.

Arrays can be used to help you understand and solve multiplication problems. The array at the right has 3 rows of 4 tiles. To find the total number of tiles, multiply the number of rows by the number in each row.

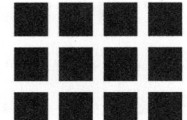

$$3 \times 4 = 12$$

Examples

A Write a multiplication sentence for the array.

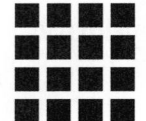

$4 \times 4 = 16$

B Multiply to find the product.

$5 \times 3 = 15$

ERROR ALERT

Be sure to multiply the number of rows by the number of objects in each row.

Try It

Solve.

1. How many tiles are there in all?

2. How many tiles are there in all?

3. Draw an array to show $5 \times 5 = 25$.

4. Draw an array and solve. $3 \times 6 = \blacksquare$

5. Read the problem below. **Explain** why A cannot be the correct answer choice. Then choose the correct answer.

COMMON ERROR

How many tiles are there in all?

A 8

B 12

C 15

D 24

Review the Key Concepts

Multiplication Facts

Key Concept When two numbers are multiplied together, the answer is called the product.

A multiplication table can be used to help you find products. The product is found where a row and column meet.

×	0	1	2	3	4	5	6	7	8	9	10
0	0	0	0	0	0	0	0	0	0	0	0
1	0	1	2	3	4	5	6	7	8	9	10
2	0	2	4	6	8	10	12	14	16	18	20
3	0	3	6	9	12	15	18	21	24	27	30
4	0	4	8	12	16	20	24	28	32	36	40
5	0	5	10	15	20	25	30	35	40	45	50
6	0	6	12	18	24	30	36	42	48	54	60
7	0	7	14	21	28	35	42	49	56	63	70
8	0	8	16	24	32	40	48	56	64	72	80
9	0	9	18	27	36	45	54	63	72	81	90
10	0	10	20	30	40	50	60	70	80	90	100

$5 \times 3 = \blacksquare$

$5 \times 3 = 15$

Examples

A Kim has 4 piles of photos. Each pile has 3 photos. How many photos does she have in all?

$$4 \times 3 = 12$$

So, Kim has 12 photos.

B Pierre saw 2 groups of 6 ducks in the pond. How many ducks did he see in all?

$$2 \times 6 = 12$$

So, he saw 12 ducks.

ERROR ALERT

Two factors can be multiplied in any order and the product is always the same.

Try It

Find each product.

1. $1 \times 4 = \blacksquare$ **2.** $5 \times 5 = \blacksquare$

3. $2 \times 5 = \blacksquare$ **4.** $6 \times 3 = \blacksquare$

5. $3 \times 3 = \blacksquare$ **6.** $2 \times 2 = \blacksquare$

7. $2 \times 4 = \blacksquare$ **8.** $4 \times 5 = \blacksquare$

9. $5 \times 3 = \blacksquare$ **10.** $6 \times 4 = \blacksquare$

11. $4 \times 4 = \blacksquare$ **12.** $1 \times 1 = \blacksquare$

13. Read the problem below. **Explain** why D cannot be the correct answer choice. Then choose the correct answer.

COMMON ERROR

Yasmin made 5 party favors with 7 paper flowers in each. How many flowers did she make in all?

A 28   **B** 32   **C** 35   **D** 45

Review the Key Concepts

Properties of Multiplication

Key Concept You can use multiplication properties to help find products.

Commutative Property You can multiply factors in any order, and the product is the same. $2 \times 5 = 5 \times 2$	Associative Property You can group factors in different ways and the product is the same. $(2 \times 4) \times 1 = 2 \times (4 \times 1)$
Identity Property The product of 1 and any number equals that number. $5 \times 1 = 5$	Zero Property The product of zero and any number equals 0. $6 \times 0 = 0$

Examples

A Use the Commutative Property of Multiplication to solve:

$$7 \times 4 = \blacksquare$$

$$4 \times 7 = \blacksquare$$

$7 \times 4 = 28$, so $4 \times 7 = 28$.

B Which property is shown below?

$$(2 \times 4) \times 3 = 2 \times (4 \times 3)$$

The Associative Property of Multiplication

ERROR ALERT

Be sure not to confuse one property with another.

Try It

Find the product. Tell which property you could use.

1. 17×1

2. $(3 \times 3) \times 2$

3. 32×0

4. 2×8

5. $(7 \times 3) \times 2$

6. 4×9

7. 1×9

8. 3×7

9. $(8 \times 2) \times 3$

10. 48×0

11. Read the problem below. **Explain** why D cannot be the correct answer choice. Then choose the correct answer.

COMMON ERROR

Which statement is true?

A $(8 \times 3) \times 2 = (3 \times 2) \times 7$

B $6 \times 1 = 6$

C $(13 - 3) \times 8 = (13 + 3) \times 8$

D $15 \times 0 = 15$

Review the Key Concepts

Relate Multiplication and Division

Key Concept Multiplication and division are inverse operations because they are opposites.

When you multiply, you combine equal groups, and when you divide, you separate into equal groups. Because multiplication and division are inverse operations, you can use multiplication to solve division problems and you can use division to solve multiplication problems.

$$2 \times 5 = 10 \text{ and } 10 \div 5 = 2$$

Examples

A Omar bought 12 apples. There were 4 apples in each bag. How many bags of apples did he buy?

Think: $4 \times \blacksquare = 12$

$4 \times 3 = 12$

So, $12 \div 4 = 3$. Omar bought 3 bags of apples.

B Find the quotient.

$18 \div 3 = \blacksquare$

Think: $3 \times \blacksquare = 18$

$3 \times 6 = 18$

So, $18 \div 3 = 6$.

ERROR ALERT

Be sure to use the correct numbers from the problem when multiplying or dividing to check your answer.

Try It

Use a related fact to solve.

1. $30 \div \blacksquare = 6$

2. $10 \times \blacksquare = 40$

3. $7 \times \blacksquare = 49$

4. $15 \div 3 = \blacksquare$

5. $\blacksquare \times 6 = 54$

6. $3 \times \blacksquare = 24$

7. $40 \div \blacksquare = 8$

8. $10 \times \blacksquare = 90$

9. $4 \times \blacksquare = 32$

10. $42 \div 7 = \blacksquare$

11. $\blacksquare \times 8 = 56$

12. $9 \times \blacksquare = 18$

13. $72 \div \blacksquare = 9$

14. $36 \div 6 = \blacksquare$

15. Read the problem below. **Explain** why C cannot be the correct answer choice. Then choose the correct answer.

COMMON ERROR

Which of these multiplication facts can be used to solve this division problem?

$$8 \div 2 = \blacksquare$$

A $2 \times 2 = 4$

B $2 \times 4 = 8$

C $4 \times 4 = 16$

D $8 \times 2 = 16$

Review the Key Concepts

Division Facts Through 5

Key Concept Learning division facts will help with solving larger problems.

There are several different ways to solve a division problem.

1. Use a multiplication table, like the one to the right.

2. Use a related multiplication fact to find the quotient.

3. Draw an array to represent the problem.

×	0	1	2	3	4	5	6	7	8	9	10
0	0	0	0	0	0	0	0	0	0	0	0
1	0	1	2	3	4	5	6	7	8	9	10
2	0	2	4	6	8	10	12	14	16	18	20
3	0	3	6	9	12	15	18	21	24	27	30
4	0	4	8	12	16	20	24	28	32	36	40
5	0	5	10	15	20	25	30	35	40	45	50
6	0	6	12	18	24	30	36	42	48	54	60
7	0	7	14	21	28	35	42	49	56	63	70
8	0	8	16	24	32	40	48	56	64	72	80
9	0	9	18	27	36	45	54	63	72	81	90
10	0	10	20	30	40	50	60	70	80	90	100

$$28 \div 4 = 7$$

dividend   divisor   quotient

Examples

A Jill has 20 marbles. She wants to separate her marbles into 4 equal groups. How many marbles will be in each group?

$20 \div 4 = 5$

So, there will be 5 marbles in each group.

B Use a related multiplication fact to find $40 \div 4$.

Think: $4 \times \blacksquare = 40$

$4 \times 10 = 40$

So, $40 \div 4 = 10$.

ERROR ALERT

Be sure not to mix up the dividend and the quotient.

Try It

Find each quotient.

1. $12 \div 2 = \blacksquare$ **2.** $20 \div 5 = \blacksquare$

3. $27 \div 3 = \blacksquare$ **4.** $24 \div 4 = \blacksquare$

5. $0 \div 5 = \blacksquare$ **6.** $9 \div 1 = \blacksquare$

7. $18 \div 2 = \blacksquare$ **8.** $30 \div 5 = \blacksquare$

9. $36 \div 4 = \blacksquare$ **10.** $7 \div 7 = \blacksquare$

11. $8 \div 2 = \blacksquare$ **12.** $15 \div 3 = \blacksquare$

13. Read the problem below. **Explain** why A cannot be the correct answer choice. Then choose the correct answer. **COMMON ERROR**

Sal wants to divide his collection of football cards evenly among his 4 brothers. If he has 32 cards, how many will each brother get?

A 32 cards   **C** 8 cards

B 9 cards   **D** 7 cards

Review the Key Concepts

Division Facts Through 12

Key Concept Using a strategy will help when solving difficult division problems.

You can use a multiplication table to solve division problems. First find the row that matches the divisor. Then look across to find the dividend. The number at the top of that column is the quotient.

$$5 \leftarrow \text{quotient}$$
$$6\overline{)30} \leftarrow \text{dividend}$$
$$\uparrow$$
$$\text{divisor}$$

×	0	1	2	3	4	5	6	7	8	9	10	11	12
0	0	0	0	0	0	0	0	0	0	0	0	0	0
1	0	1	2	3	4	5	6	7	8	9	10	11	12
2	0	2	4	6	8	10	12	14	16	18	20	22	24
3	0	3	6	9	12	15	18	21	24	27	30	33	36
4	0	4	8	12	16	20	24	28	32	36	40	44	48
5	0	5	10	15	20	25	30	35	40	45	50	55	60
6	0	6	12	18	24	30	36	42	48	54	60	66	72
7	0	7	14	21	28	35	42	49	56	63	70	77	84
8	0	8	16	24	32	40	48	56	64	72	80	88	96
9	0	9	18	27	36	45	54	63	72	81	90	99	108
10	0	10	20	30	40	50	60	70	80	90	100	110	120
11	0	11	22	33	44	55	66	77	88	99	110	121	132
12	0	12	24	36	48	60	72	84	96	108	120	132	144

Examples

A Billy collected 50 baseball cards. If he sorts them into 10 equal piles, how many cards will be in each pile?

$50 \div 10 = 5$
So, there will be 5 cards in each pile.

B Use the table to find $48 \div 8$.

Find the row for the divisor, 8. Look right to find the dividend, 48. Look up to find the quotient, 6.

So, $48 \div 8 = 6$.

ERROR ALERT

Remember that the steps for finding the quotient on a multiplication table are different than the steps for finding a product.

Try It

Find each quotient.

1. $18 \div 6 = \blacksquare$ **2.** $27 \div 9 = \blacksquare$

3. $14 \div 7 = \blacksquare$ **4.** $32 \div 8 = \blacksquare$

5. $70 \div 10 = \blacksquare$ **6.** $56 \div 7 = \blacksquare$

7. $36 \div 6 = \blacksquare$ **8.** $64 \div 8 = \blacksquare$

9. $48 \div 12 = \blacksquare$ **10.** $55 \div 11 = \blacksquare$

11. Read the problem below. **Explain** why A cannot be the correct answer choice. Then choose the correct answer.

COMMON ERROR

Which is the quotient?

$$42 \div 7 = \blacksquare$$

A 7   **C** 5

B 6   **D** 4

Review the Key Concepts

Identify and Compare Plane Figures

Key Concept A plane figure is a figure on a flat surface. It is made up of line segments that are straight, curved, or both.

A polygon is a closed plane figure with straight sides. Polygons are named by the number of sides and angles they have. Below are descriptions of some polygons.

Polygon	Number of Sides	Number of Angles
triangle	3	3
quadrilateral	4	4
pentagon	5	5
hexagon	6	6
octagon	8	8

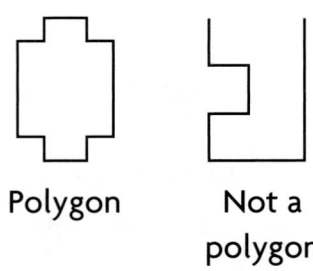

Polygon   Not a polygon

Examples

A Which figures are polygons?

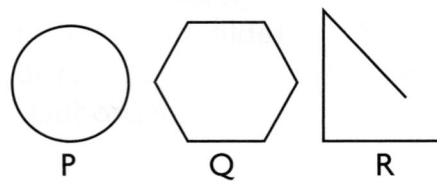

P   Q   R

Figures P, Q, and R are all plane figures. P does not have straight sides, and R is not closed. So, only Q is a polygon.

B Julio's yard has 4 sides. What is one name of the shape of Julio's yard?

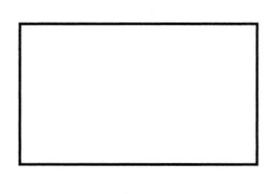

quadrilateral

ERROR ALERT

Be sure to count the number of sides and angles when naming plane figures.

Try It

For 1–2, use Figures A–E.

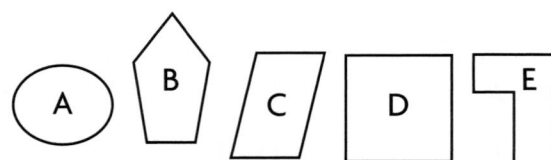

1. Which figure is a pentagon?

2. Which figures are polygons?

3. Read the problem below. **COMMON ERROR** **Explain** why D cannot be the correct answer choice. Then choose the correct answer.

   Which polygon has 8 sides?

   A octagon   **C** pentagon

   B square   **D** circle

Review the Key Concepts

Congruent Figures

Key Concept Congruent figures appear to have the same size and shape.

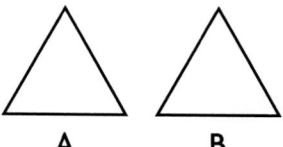

If you were to trace figure A, cut out the tracing, and place it on top of figure B, their sides and vertices would match.

Examples

Ⓐ Do these figures appear to be congruent?

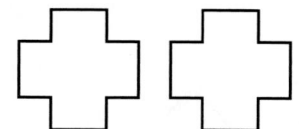

Yes, both figures appear to be the same shape and size.

Ⓑ Do these figures appear to be congruent?

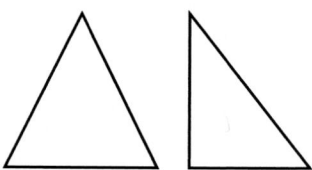

No, the figures are not congruent. They are both triangles, but they are different shapes and sizes.

ERROR ALERT

Remember that congruent figures can be in different positions.

Try It

Tell if each pair of figures appears to be congruent. Write *yes* or *no*.

1.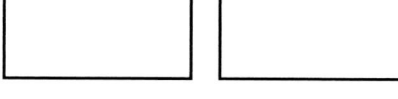

2.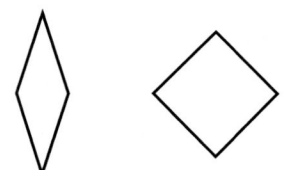

3.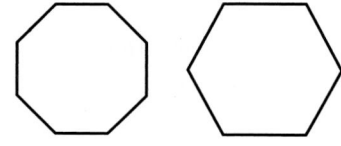

4.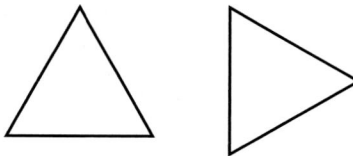

5. Read the problem below. **Explain** why C cannot be the correct answer. Then choose the correct answer. 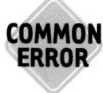 **COMMON ERROR**

   Which figure appears to be congruent to this figure?

   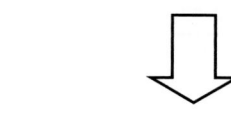

   A 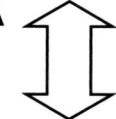   C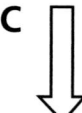

   B 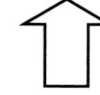   D

Review the Key Concepts

Identify Solid Figures

Key Concept Solid figures have length, width, and height. They are also called three-dimensional figures.

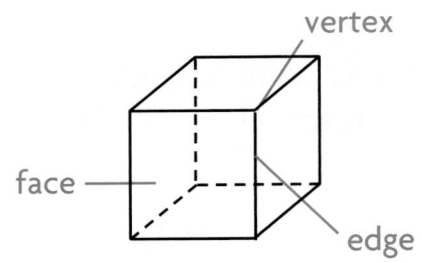

A **face** of a solid figure is a flat surface.

An **edge** is a line segment formed where two faces meet.

A **vertex** is a point where three or more edges meet.

Cubes, spheres, rectangular prisms, cones, square pyramids, and cylinders are some examples of solid figures.

Examples

A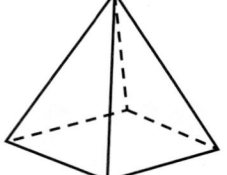

How many faces does the square pyramid have?

5 faces

How would you describe each of the faces?

Four faces are triangles, and one face is a square.

B Describe the figure by its faces, edges, and vertices. Then name this figure.

ERROR ALERT

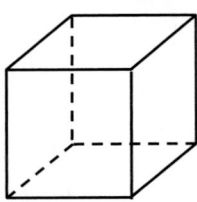

This solid figure has 6 faces that are squares, 12 edges, and 8 vertices. It is a cube.

Be sure to think about all the hidden faces of a solid figure.

Try It

Look at this rectangular prism.

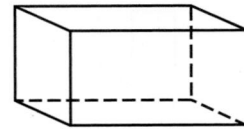

It has:

1. ▓ faces

2. ▓ vertices

3. ▓ edges

4. What two-dimensional figures make up the faces on the prism?

5. Read the problem below. **Explain** why D cannot be the correct answer choice. Then choose the correct answer.

COMMON ERROR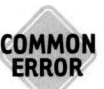

What two-dimensional figure forms the bottom of this figure?

A triangle

B square

C circle

D cube

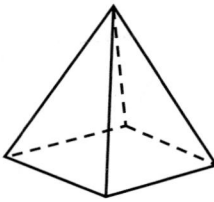

Review the Key Concepts

Number Patterns

Key Concept To understand relationships between numbers, you can find a pattern and then write a rule.

To find a pattern in a table, ask yourself how the numbers in the top row are related to the numbers in the bottom row. Once you understand the pattern, you can write the rule for the pattern. Knowing a rule helps you extend the table or find missing numbers.

6	9	12	15
2	3	■	5

Pattern: Each number in the top row is divided by 3 to get the number in the bottom row.

Rule: Divide by 3.

To find the missing number, divide 12 by 3.

$$12 \div 3 = 4$$

So, the missing number is 4.

Examples

A What is a rule for this table?

1	3	5	7	9
2	6	10	14	18

Each number in the top row is multiplied by 2 to get the number in the bottom row.
A rule is *multiply by 2*.

B Describe the pattern in this table.

10	20	30	40	50
2	4	6	8	10

Each number in the top row is divided by 5 to get the number in the bottom row.
A rule is *divide by 5*.

ERROR ALERT

Be sure the same rule works for all of the numbers in the table.

Try It

Write a rule. Then copy and complete the table.

1.

Pairs of shoes	3	4	■	6	7
Shoes	6	■	10	12	■

2.

Bottles of water	6	■	18	24	■
Runners	1	2	■	■	5

3. Read the problem below. **Explain** why A cannot be the correct answer choice. Then choose the correct answer.

COMMON ERROR

It takes Mr. Brown 8 minutes to run 1 mile. How many miles can he run in 40 minutes?

Miles	1	2	3	4	■
Minutes	8	16	24	32	40

A 320 miles   **C** 5 miles

B 40 miles   **D** 4 miles

Review the Key Concepts

Geometric Patterns

Key Concept A repeating pattern of geometric shapes uses the same pattern unit over and over again.

Different shapes and symbols can be used to make the same type of repeating pattern. The pattern unit is the part of the pattern that is repeated. If you give each shape a letter, you can see how the pattern repeats.

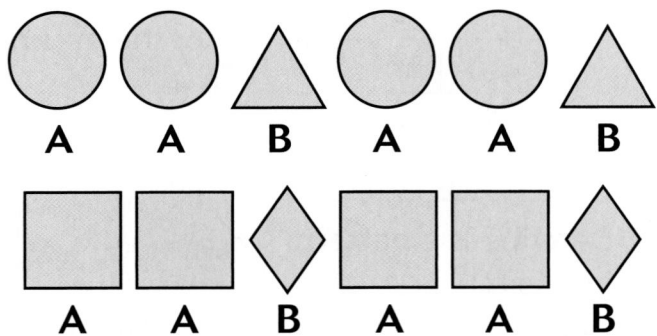

Examples

A Complete the pattern.

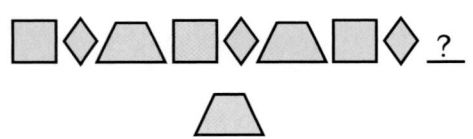

B Identify the pattern unit.

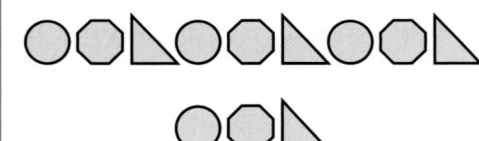

ERROR ALERT

When completing a pattern, be sure to add only the parts missing from the pattern unit.

Try It

Solve.

1. Use circles and squares to make the following pattern. AABBAABB

2. Name the pattern unit.

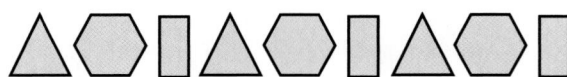

3. Read the problem below. **Explain** why A cannot be the correct answer choice. Then choose the correct answer. **COMMON ERROR**

   Which are the missing shapes?

   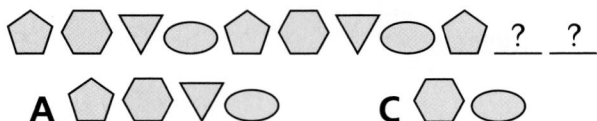

   A 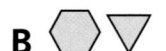   C

   B   D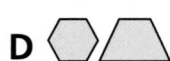

Review the Key Concepts

Customary Measurement: Estimate and Measure Length

Key Concept Estimating the length of an object can help you decide if your measurement is reasonable.

Customary units used to measure length and distance are inch, foot, yard, and mile.

1 foot (ft) = 12 inches (in.)
1 yard (yd) = 3 feet = 36 inches
1 mile (mi) = 5,280 feet

The length of a small paperclip is about one inch.

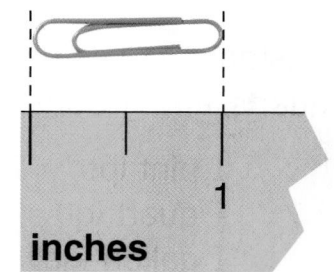

inches

Examples

A Estimate the length in inches. Then use a ruler to measure to the nearest half inch.

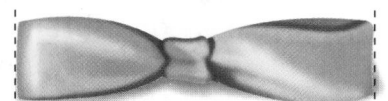

Estimate: about 2 inches
Measurement: The length to the nearest half inch is 2 inches.

B Would you use inches or feet to measure the height of a door?

feet

The height of a door is much more than a few inches.

ERROR ALERT

Be sure to consider the reasonableness of your estimates and measurements.

Try It

Choose the unit you would use to measure each. Write *inch, foot, yard,* or *mile*.

1. length of a pen
2. length of a classroom
3. distance between two schools

Estimate the length in inches. Then use a ruler to measure to the nearest half inch.

4.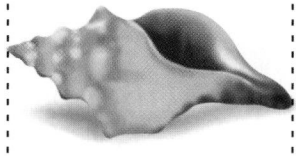

5. Read the problem below. **Explain** why D cannot be the correct answer choice. Then choose the correct answer.

COMMON ERROR

Mrs. Jones wants to know the length of her bracelet. Which unit could she use to measure its length?

A inch

B foot

C yard

D mile

Review the Key Concepts

Customary Measurement: Estimate and Measure Capacity and Weight

Key Concept Capacity is the amount a container can hold. Weight is the measurement of how heavy an object is.

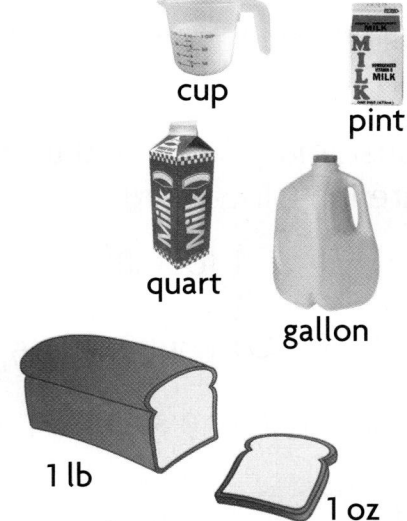

cup

pint

quart

gallon

1 lb

1 oz

Customary units used to measure capacity are cups, pints, quarts, and gallons.

> 1 pint (pt) = 2 cups (c)
> 1 quart (qt) = 2 pints or 4 cups
> 1 gallon (gal) = 4 quarts or 8 pints or 16 cups

Customary units used to measure weight are pounds and ounces.

> 1 pound (lb) = 16 ounces (oz)

Examples

A Janine is preparing punch for a party. Should she make 4 quarts or 4 cups of punch?

4 quarts; 4 cups would not be enough punch for the party.

B How many ounces are in 2 pounds?

1 lb = 16 oz

16 + 16 = 32

There are 32 ounces in 2 pounds.

ERROR ALERT

When comparing measurements of capacity, be sure to think about how the measurements are related.

Try It

Choose the better estimate.

1. bath tub

20 cups or
20 gallons

2. adult cat

10 ounces or
10 pounds

3. glass of milk

1 quart or
1 cup

4. desk chair

32 ounces or
32 pounds

Compare. Write <, >, or = for each ●.

5. 18 oz ● 1 lb

6. 2 pints ● 2 quarts

7. Read the problem below. **Explain** why A cannot be the correct answer choice. Then choose the correct answer.

COMMON ERROR

Michael is making a cake. The recipe calls for 2 pints of milk. Michael only has cups to measure in. How many cups of milk should Michael use?

A 2 cups   **C** 8 cups

B 4 cups   **D** 16 cups

Review the Key Concepts

Metric Measurement: Estimate and Measure Length

Key Concept Centimeter, decimeter, meter, and kilometer are used to measure length and distance in the metric system.

A useful way to estimate metric measurements is to think of lengths and objects that you know.

Centimeter (cm)   About the width of an index finger
Decimeter (dm)   About the width of a CD
Meter (m)   About your arm span
Kilometer (km)   A little more than half a mile

10 cm	=	1 dm
100 cm	=	1 m
1,000 m	=	1 km

Examples

A Kal and his family drove to visit his grandmother. She lives 5 km away. How many meters did Kal and his family travel?

1 km = 1,000 m

5 × 1,000 = 5,000 m

So, Kal and his family drove 5,000 meters.

B Estimate the length of the insect. Then use a ruler to measure it to the nearest centimeter.

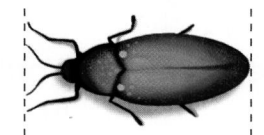

The insect measures 3 cm.

ERROR ALERT

Be sure to use the correct metric unit when you measure.

Try It

Estimate the length in centimeters. Then use a centimeter ruler to measure to the nearest centimeter.

1. 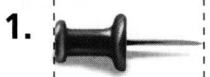   2.

3. 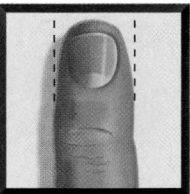   4.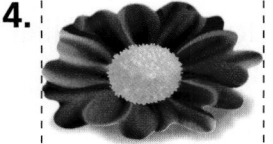

5. Read the problem below. **Explain** why B cannot be the correct answer choice. Then choose the correct answer.

COMMON ERROR

Which unit would you use to measure the distance between two cities?

A kilometer

B centimeter

C kilogram

D decimeter

Review the Key Concepts

Metric Measurements: Capacity and Mass

Key Concept Capacity is the amount a container can hold. Mass is the amount of matter in an object.

Milliliters (mL) and liters (L) are the metric units used to measure capacity. The capacity of smaller containers is measured in milliliters, and the capacity of larger containers is measured in liters.

$$1,000 \text{ mL} = 1 \text{ L}$$

Grams (g) and kilograms (kg) are the metric units used to measure mass. The mass of a strawberry would be measured in grams. The mass of a whale would be measured in kilograms.

$$1,000 \text{ g} = 1 \text{ kg}$$

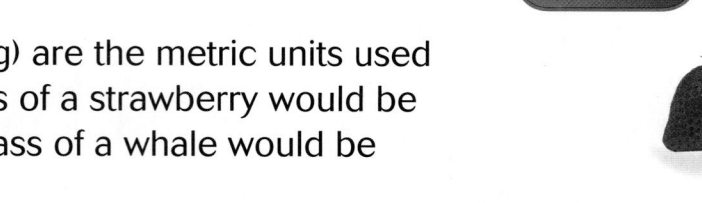

Examples

A Thomas wants to measure the capacity of his cereal bowl. Which metric unit should he use?

A cereal bowl holds less than 1 liter. So, Thomas should use milliliters.

B Would a mouse weigh 20 grams or 20 kilograms?

20 kilograms is very heavy. A mouse would weigh 20 grams.

ERROR ALERT Be sure to think about how the units are related.

Try It

For 1–2, choose the unit you would use to measure the capacity. Write *mL* or *L*.

1.

2.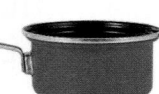

3. How many kilograms are there in 6,000 grams?

4. How many grams are there in 7 kilograms?

5. Read the problem below. **Explain** why B cannot be the correct answer choice. Then choose the correct answer.

COMMON ERROR

How many milliliters are in 8 liters?

A 8

B 80

C 800

D 8,000

Review the Key Concepts

Find Perimeter

Key Concept Perimeter is the distance around a figure.

You can find the perimeter by measuring each side
of a figure and adding the lengths of the sides.

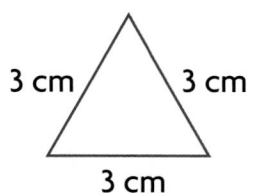

Perimeter =
3 cm + 3 cm + 3 cm = 9 cm

Examples

A Find the perimeter in
centimeters.

2 + 2 + 2 + 2 = 8
The perimeter is 8 cm.

B Find the perimeter in
centimeters.

ERROR ALERT

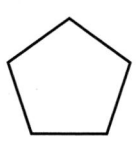

1 + 1 + 1 + 1 + 1 = 5
The perimeter is 5 cm.

Be sure to
measure and
add all of the
sides when
finding the
perimeter of a
figure.

Try It

Find the perimeter of each figure.

1.

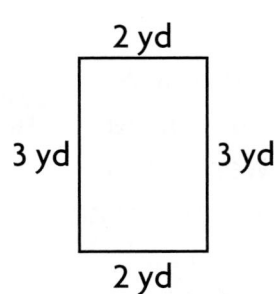

2.

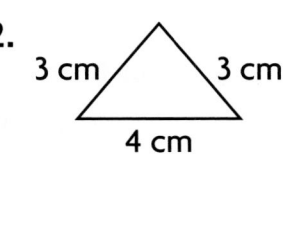

3.

4.

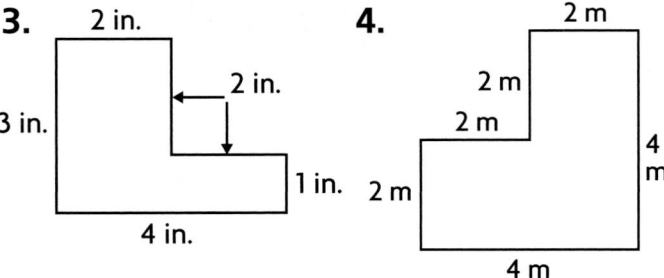

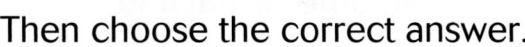

5. Read the problem below.
Explain why A cannot be
the correct answer choice.
Then choose the correct answer.

COMMON ERROR

Mrs. Brown builds a fence around
her square garden. Each side of her
garden measures 10 yards. Which
will help her decide how much
fence to buy?

A 10 + 10 = 20

B 10 + 10 + 10 = 30

C 10 + 10 + 10 + 10 = 40

D 10 + 10 + 10 + 10 + 10 = 50

Review the Key Concepts

Find Area and Volume

Key Concept Find the area of plane figures by covering them with squares. Find the volume of solid figures by counting the number of cubes that would fill them.

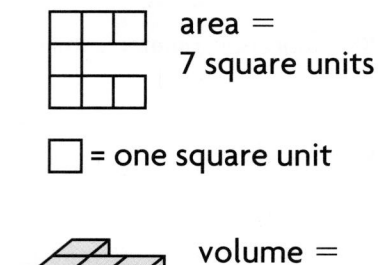

area = 7 square units

☐ = one square unit

Area is the number of square units needed to cover a flat surface. A square unit is a square with a side length of 1 unit.

Volume is the amount of space a solid figure takes up. It is measured in cubic units. A cubic unit is a cube with a side length of 1 unit.

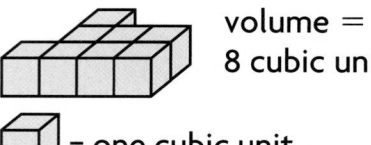

volume = 8 cubic units

= one cubic unit

Examples

A Find the area.

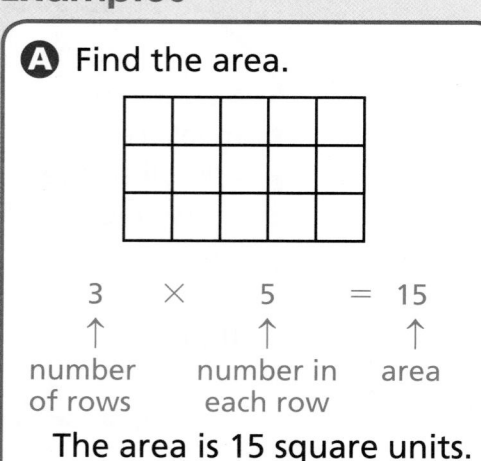

$$3 \quad \times \quad 5 \quad = \quad 15$$

number of rows   number in each row   area

The area is 15 square units.

B Find the volume.

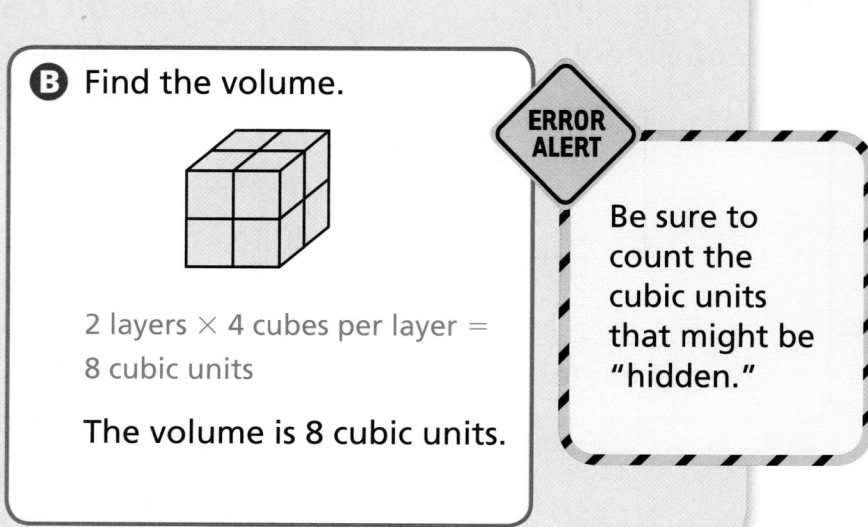

2 layers × 4 cubes per layer = 8 cubic units

The volume is 8 cubic units.

ERROR ALERT

Be sure to count the cubic units that might be "hidden."

Try It

Find the volume of each in cubic units.

1.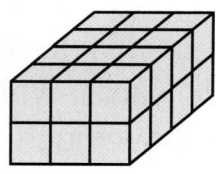

2.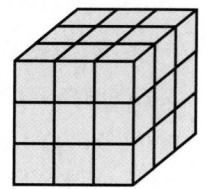

Find the area of each in square units.

3.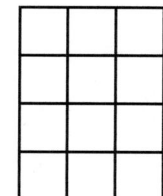

4.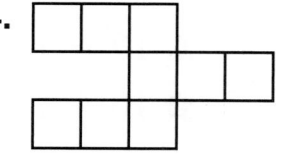

5. Read the problem below. **Explain** why A cannot be the correct answer choice. Then choose the correct answer.

COMMON ERROR

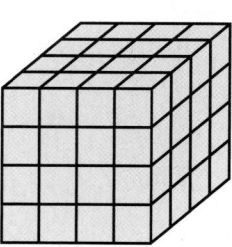

What is the volume of this figure?

A 16 cubic units   **C** 48 cubic units

B 32 cubic units   **D** 64 cubic units

Review the Key Concepts

Part of a Whole

Key Concept A number that names part of a whole is called a fraction.

The top number of a fraction, or numerator, tells how many parts are being counted. The bottom number, or denominator, tells how many equal parts are in the whole. The figure to the right shows a circle with four equal parts. Three parts are shaded. So, $\frac{3}{4}$ of the circle is shaded.

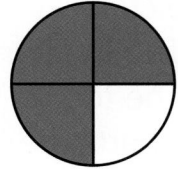

Examples

A What fraction of this pizza is left?

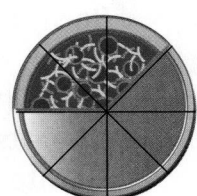

Count the number of slices left. That number is the numerator. Count the number of slices in all. That number is the denominator.

So, $\frac{3}{8}$ of the pizza is left.

B What fraction of the flag is blue?

Count the number of blue sections. That number is the numerator. The number of sections in all is the denominator.

So, $\frac{1}{2}$ of the flag is blue.

ERROR ALERT

Be sure to think of the denominator as the whole, and the numerator as the part that is being counted.

Try It

For 1–3, use the pizza.

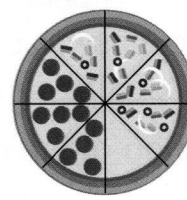

1. What fraction of the pizza has pepperoni?

2. What fraction of the pizza has vegetables?

3. What fraction of the pizza does not have pepperoni?

4. Read the problem below. **Explain** why C cannot be the correct answer choice. Then choose the correct answer.

COMMON ERROR

What fraction of the spinner is yellow?

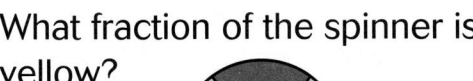
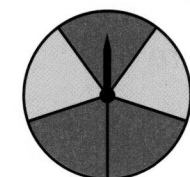

A $\frac{3}{5}$ **B** $\frac{2}{3}$ **C** $\frac{5}{2}$ **D** $\frac{2}{5}$

Review the Key Concepts

Part of a Group

Key Concept A number that names part of a group is called a fraction.

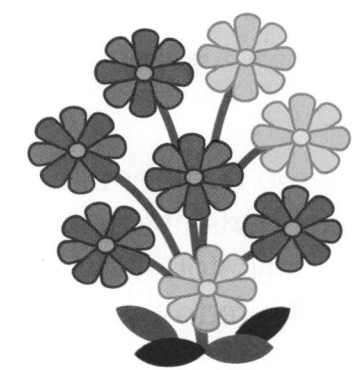

The picture at the right shows a group of flowers. Five are red. The fraction $\frac{5}{8}$ tells what part of the group of flowers is red. The top number of a fraction, or numerator, tells how many parts are being counted. The bottom number, or denominator, tells how many parts there are in the group.

Examples

A What fraction of the bikes are red?

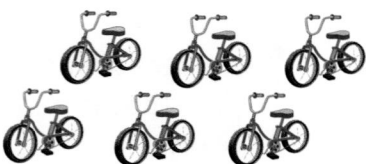

Count the number of red bikes. That number is the numerator. Count the number of bikes in all. That number is the denominator.

So, $\frac{2}{6}$ of the bikes are red.

B What fraction of the balls are striped?

ERROR ALERT

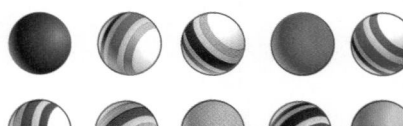

Count the number of striped balls. That number is the numerator. The number of balls in all is the denominator.

So, $\frac{6}{10}$ of the balls are striped.

Be sure to think of the numerator as the number of parts being counted and the denominator as the total number in the group.

Try It

For 1–4, use the socks.

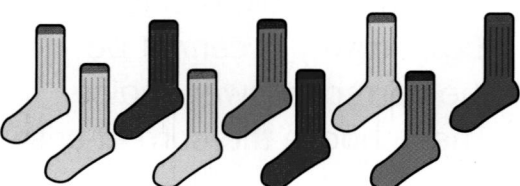

1. What fraction of the socks are red?

2. What fraction of the socks are blue?

3. What fraction of the socks are yellow?

4. What fraction of the socks are not green?

5. Read the problem below. **Explain** why A cannot be the correct answer choice. Then choose the correct answer.

COMMON ERROR

What fraction of the cars are blue?

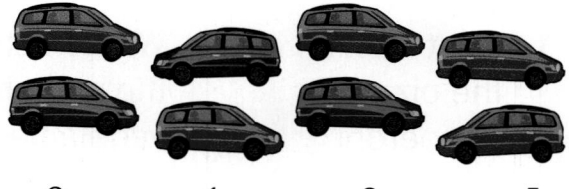

A $\frac{2}{6}$ **B** $\frac{1}{8}$ **C** $\frac{2}{8}$ **D** $\frac{5}{8}$

Review the Key Concepts

Tenths and Hundredths

Key Concept A tenth is one of ten equal parts. A hundredth is one of one hundred equal parts.

The decimal model on the right has 10 equal parts. Three parts out of the 10, or three tenths, are shaded. Three tenths can be shown as a fraction or as a decimal.

$$\frac{3}{10} = 0.3$$

A decimal is a number with one or more digits to the right of the decimal point. The first place to the right of the decimal point is the tenths place. The next place is the hundredths place.

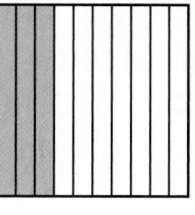

$$\frac{3}{10} = 0.3$$

Examples

A Write 0.5 as a fraction.

0.5 = 5 tenths

$$\frac{5}{10}$$

B Write $\frac{7}{100}$ as a decimal.

$$\frac{7}{100} = 7 \text{ hundredths}$$

0.07

ERROR ALERT

Be sure not to confuse the tenths and hundredths places.

Try It

Write each decimal as a fraction.

1. 0.05   **2.** 0.6

3. 0.9   **4.** 0.12

5. 0.78   **6.** 0.1

Write each fraction as a decimal.

7. $\frac{4}{10}$ **8.** $\frac{9}{100}$

9. $\frac{32}{100}$ **10.** $\frac{8}{10}$

11. $\frac{2}{10}$ **12.** $\frac{81}{100}$

13. $\frac{55}{100}$ **14.** $\frac{3}{10}$

15. Read the problem below. **Explain** why A cannot be the correct answer choice. Then choose the correct answer.

COMMON ERROR

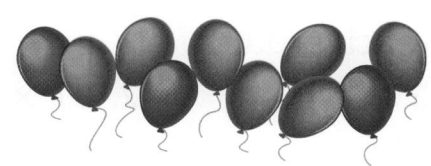

Which shows the decimal that represents the red balloons?

A 0.07

B 0.10

C 0.3

D 0.7

Review the Key Concepts

Multiply 2- and 3-Digit Numbers by 1-Digit Numbers

Key Concept To multiply 2- and 3-digit numbers by a 1-digit number, line up the numbers vertically by place value.

To correctly line up a multiplication problem, place the 1-digit number under the ones place of the multi-digit number. First, multiply the ones. Then, multiply the tens, and last, the hundreds.

$$\begin{array}{r} {\scriptstyle 1\ 1} \\ 243 \\ \times\quad 4 \\ \hline 972 \end{array}$$

If the product in any of the steps is greater than 9, then you must regroup to the next column.

Examples

ERROR ALERT

A Jan bought 2 packs of thank-you cards. If each pack contained 32 cards, how many cards did she buy in all?

$2 \times 32 = \blacksquare$

$$\begin{array}{r} 32 \\ \times\ 2 \\ \hline 64 \end{array}$$

So, Jan bought 64 cards.

B The ferry can transport 310 people in one trip. How many people can the ferry transport in 5 trips?

$5 \times 310 = \blacksquare$

$$\begin{array}{r} 310 \\ \times\ 5 \\ \hline 1{,}550 \end{array}$$

So, the ferry can transport 1,550 people in 5 trips.

Be sure to multiply vertically, starting with the ones column on the right.

Try It

Find each product.

1. $13 \times 2 = \blacksquare$

2. $21 \times 7 = \blacksquare$

3. $40 \times 8 = \blacksquare$

4. $103 \times 2 = \blacksquare$

5. $411 \times 6 = \blacksquare$

6. $513 \times 3 = \blacksquare$

7. $5 \times 216 = \blacksquare$

8. $2 \times 478 = \blacksquare$

9. $4 \times 341 = \blacksquare$

10. $7 \times 203 = \blacksquare$

11. Read the problem below. **Explain** why C cannot be the correct answer choice. Then choose the correct answer.

COMMON ERROR

Chris bought 3 packs of baseball cards. There were 127 cards in each pack. How many cards did he buy in all?

A 328

C 362

B 361

D 381

Review the Key Concepts

Divide 2- and 3-Digit Numbers by 1-Digit Numbers

Key Concept Recording division is helpful when dividing 2- and 3-digit numbers.

Divide, multiply, subtract, and compare are the steps you need to follow when solving division problems.

Sometimes, a number cannot be divided evenly. The amount left over when the dividend is not divided evenly by the divisor is called the remainder.

$$
\begin{array}{r}
9 \text{ r}3 \\
8\overline{)75} \\
-72 \\
\hline
3
\end{array}
$$

In the problem at the right, 8 is the divisor and 75 is the dividend. The quotient is 9 and the and the remainder is 3.

Examples

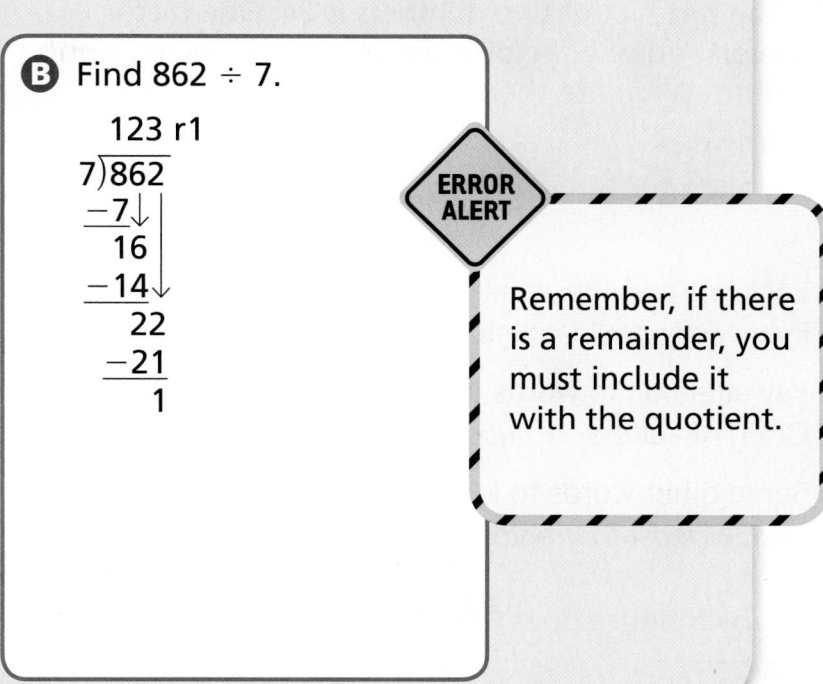

A Randy has 144 stamps. He puts the same number of stamps on each of 9 pages. How many stamps did Randy put on each page?

$$
\begin{array}{r}
16 \\
9\overline{)144} \\
-9\downarrow \\
\hline
54 \\
54 \\
\hline
0
\end{array}
$$

So, he put 16 stamps on each page.

B Find 862 ÷ 7.

$$
\begin{array}{r}
123 \text{ r}1 \\
7\overline{)862} \\
-7\downarrow \\
\hline
16 \\
-14\downarrow \\
\hline
22 \\
-21 \\
\hline
1
\end{array}
$$

ERROR ALERT

Remember, if there is a remainder, you must include it with the quotient.

Try It

Divide.

1. 79 ÷ 7

2. 44 ÷ 2

3. 6)79

4. 245 ÷ 7

5. 48 ÷ 5

6. 592 ÷ 8

7. 8)270

8. 6)834

9. Read the problem below. **Explain** why D cannot be the correct answer choice. Then choose the correct answer.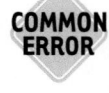

Find 95 ÷ 4.

| A | 25 r2 | C | 23 r3 |
| B | 25 | D | 23 |

Test-Taking Strategies

Tips for Taking Math Tests

Being a good test-taker is like being a good problem solver. When you answer test questions, you are solving problems. Remember to UNDERSTAND, PLAN, SOLVE, AND CHECK.

UNDERSTAND

Read the problem.

• Look for math terms and recall their meanings.

• Reread the problem and think about the question.

• Use the details in the problem and the question.

> 1. The product of two numbers is 24. One factor is even and one factor is odd. Both factors have one digit. What are the factors?
>
> A 1 × 24   C 3 × 8
>
> B 2 × 12   D 4 × 6

Test Tip **Understand the problem.**

Remember the meanings of *product, factor, even, odd,* and *digit*. Since all choices have a product of 24, look for the choices that have one odd and one even 1-digit number. The answer is **C**.

• Each word is important. Missing a word or reading it incorrectly could cause you to get the wrong answer.

• Pay attention to words that are in **bold** type, all CAPITAL letters, or *italics*.

• Some other words to look for are *round, about, only, best,* or *least to greatest*.

> 2. Which figure does NOT have $\frac{1}{2}$ shaded?
>
> A 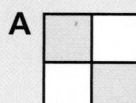   C
>
> B 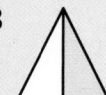   D

Test Tip **Look for important words.**

The word NOT is important. Without the word NOT, the answers would be A, B, and D. The answer is **C**.

PLAN

Think about how you can solve the problem.

- See if you can solve the problem with the information given.

- Pictures, charts, tables, and graphs may have the information you need.

- You may need to think about information you already know.

- The answer choices may have the information you need.

3. How many more girls than boys chose soccer as their favorite sport?

   Favorite Sport

	Boys	Girls
Soccer	4	6
Baseball	8	3

   A 2   C 4

   B 3   D 5

 Get the information you need.

Use the table to find how many girls and boys chose soccer. Find the difference by subtracting. The answer is **A**.

- You may need to write a number sentence and solve it.

- Some problems have two steps or more.

- In some problems you need to look at relationships instead of computing an answer.

- If the path to the solution isn't clear, choose a problem solving strategy and use it to solve the problem.

4. Jeremy bought 3 books that cost the same amount. He paid with a $20 bill and received $2 in change. How much did each book cost?

   A $3   C $5

   B $4   D $6

 Decide on a plan.

Begin with the amount of change. Subtract the change from $20. Then divide the difference by 3 to find how much each book cost. The answer is **D**.

SOLVE

Follow your plan, working logically and carefully.

- Estimate your answer. Look for unreasonable answer choices.

- Use reasoning to find the most likely choices.

- Solve all steps needed to answer the problem.

- If your answer does not match any answer choice, check your numbers and your computation.

5. Third-grade students went on a field trip on 6 buses. Each bus held 68 students. How many students went on the field trip?

   A 74   C 420

   B 408   D 3,400

Test Tip Eliminate choices.

Estimate the product (6×70). The only reasonable answers are B and C. Since 6 times the ones digit 8 is 48, the answer must end in 8. If you are still not certain, multiply and check your answer against B and C. The answer is **B**.

- If your answer still does not match, look for another form of the number, such as a decimal instead of a fraction.

- If answer choices are given as pictures, look at each one by itself while you cover the other three.

- Read answer choices that are statements and relate them to the problem one by one.

- If your strategy isn't working, try a different one.

6. Lauren is sewing a lace border around a tablecloth. The tablecloth is 60 inches wide and 80 inches long. How many inches of lace does she need?

   A 20 inches   C 220 inches

   B 140 inches   D 280 inches

Test Tip Choose the answer.

The lace goes around all 4 sides of the tablecloth. Add the lengths of the 4 sides ($60 + 80 + 60 + 80$). Find the answer choice that shows this sum. The answer is **D**.

CHECK

Take time to catch your mistakes.

- Be sure you answered the question asked.

- Check for important words you might have missed.

- Did you use all the information you needed?

- Check your computation by using a different method.

- Draw a picture when you are unsure of your answer.

7. Grant bought 2 shirts and a tie. Each shirt cost $24, and the tie cost $15. He gave the clerk $100. How much change did he receive?

A $63   C $47

B $61   D $37

 Test Tip Check your work.

Be sure to find the total cost of both shirts (2 × $24). Then add the cost of the tie ($48 + $15) before you subtract. The correct answer is **D**.

Tips for Short-Answer and Extended-Response Items

- Plan to spend from 3 to 5 minutes on each Short-Answer item and from 5 to 15 minutes on each Extended-Response item.

- Read the problem carefully and think about what you are asked to do. Plan how to organize your response.

- Short-Answer items will ask you to find a solution to a problem. Extended-Response items will ask you to use problem solving and reasoning skills to apply something you have learned.

- Think about how you solved the problem. You may be asked to use words, numbers, or pictures to explain how you found your answer.

- Leave time to look back at the problem, check your answer, and correct any mistakes .

Addition Facts

	K	L	M	N	O	P	Q	R
A	3 +2	0 +6	2 +4	5 +9	6 +1	2 +5	3 +10	4 +4
B	8 +9	0 +7	3 +5	9 +6	6 +7	2 +8	3 +3	7 +10
C	4 +6	9 +0	7 +8	4 +10	3 +7	7 +7	4 +2	7 +5
D	5 +7	3 +9	8 +1	9 +5	10 +5	9 +8	2 +6	8 +7
E	7 +4	0 +8	3 +6	6 +10	5 +3	2 +7	8 +2	9 +9
F	2 +3	1 +7	6 +8	5 +2	7 +3	4 +8	10 +10	6 +6
G	8 +3	7 +2	7 +0	8 +5	9 +1	4 +7	8 +4	10 +8
H	7 +9	5 +6	8 +10	6 +5	8 +6	9 +4	0 +9	7 +1
I	4 +3	5 +5	6 +4	10 +2	7 +6	8 +0	6 +9	9 +2
J	5 +8	1 +9	5 +4	8 +8	6 +2	6 +3	9 +7	9 +10

Subtraction Facts

	K	L	M	N	O	P	Q	R
A	9 −1	10 − 4	7 −2	6 −4	20 −10	7 −0	8 −3	13 − 9
B	9 −9	13 − 4	7 −1	11 − 5	9 −7	6 −3	15 −10	6 −2
C	10 − 2	8 −8	16 − 8	6 −5	18 −10	8 −7	13 − 3	15 − 6
D	11 − 7	9 −5	12 − 8	8 −1	15 − 8	18 − 9	14 −10	9 −4
E	9 −2	7 −7	10 − 3	8 −5	16 − 9	11 − 9	14 − 8	12 − 6
F	7 −3	12 −10	17 − 9	6 −0	9 −6	11 − 8	10 − 9	12 − 2
G	15 − 7	8 −4	13 − 6	7 −5	11 − 2	12 − 3	14 − 6	11 − 4
H	7 −6	13 − 5	12 − 9	10 − 5	13 − 8	11 − 3	16 −10	14 − 7
I	5 −0	10 − 8	11 − 6	9 −3	14 − 5	5 −4	7 −7	14 − 9
J	15 − 9	9 −8	13 − 7	8 −2	7 −4	13 −10	10 − 6	16 − 7

Multiplication Facts

	K	L	M	N	O	P	Q	R
A	2 ×7	0 ×6	6 ×6	9 ×2	8 ×3	3 ×4	2 ×8	6 ×1
B	7 ×7	5 ×9	2 ×2	7 ×5	2 ×3	10 ×8	4 ×10	8 ×4
C	4 ×5	5 ×1	7 ×0	6 ×3	3 ×5	6 ×8	7 ×3	9 ×9
D	0 ×9	6 ×4	6 ×10	1 ×6	9 ×8	4 ×4	3 ×2	9 ×3
E	0 ×7	9 ×4	1 ×7	9 ×7	2 ×5	7 ×9	5 ×6	5 ×8
F	4 ×3	6 ×9	1 ×9	7 ×6	7 ×10	6 ×0	2 ×9	10 ×3
G	5 ×3	1 ×5	7 ×1	3 ×8	3 ×6	8 ×10	3 ×9	6 ×7
H	7 ×4	7 ×2	3 ×7	2 ×4	7 ×8	4 ×7	5 ×10	8 ×6
I	4 ×6	5 ×5	5 ×7	3 ×3	9 ×6	8 ×0	4 ×9	8 ×8
J	8 ×9	6 ×2	4 ×8	9 ×5	5 ×4	0 ×5	10 ×6	9 ×10

Division Facts

	K	L	M	N	O	P	Q	R
A	1)‾1	3)‾9	2)‾6	2)‾4	1)‾6	3)‾12	5)‾15	7)‾21
B	6)‾24	8)‾56	5)‾40	6)‾18	6)‾30	7)‾42	9)‾81	5)‾45
C	5)‾30	2)‾16	3)‾21	7)‾35	3)‾15	9)‾9	8)‾16	9)‾63
D	4)‾32	9)‾90	4)‾8	8)‾48	9)‾54	3)‾18	10)‾50	6)‾48
E	7)‾28	3)‾0	5)‾20	4)‾24	7)‾14	3)‾6	5)‾50	10)‾60
F	9)‾18	4)‾36	5)‾25	7)‾63	1)‾5	8)‾32	9)‾45	6)‾54
G	2)‾14	8)‾24	4)‾4	5)‾40	3)‾9	4)‾12	7)‾56	8)‾72
H	5)‾35	1)‾4	8)‾64	5)‾10	8)‾40	2)‾12	6)‾42	10)‾70
I	7)‾49	9)‾27	10)‾90	3)‾27	9)‾36	4)‾20	9)‾72	8)‾80
J	8)‾0	4)‾28	2)‾10	7)‾70	1)‾3	10)‾80	6)‾60	10)‾100

Table of Measures

METRIC | CUSTOMARY

Length

1 decimeter (dm) = 10 centimeters (cm)	1 foot (ft) = 12 inches (in.)
1 meter (m) = 100 centimeters	1 yard (yd) = 3 feet, or 36 inches
1 meter (m) = 10 decimeters	1 mile (mi) = 1,760 yards, or 5,280 feet
1 kilometer (km) = 1,000 meters	

Mass/Weight

1 kilogram (kg) = 1,000 grams (g)	1 pound (lb) = 16 ounces (oz)

Capacity

1 liter (L) = 1,000 milliliters (mL)	1 pint (pt) = 2 cups (c)
	1 quart (qt) = 2 pints
	1 gallon (gal) = 4 quarts

TIME

1 minute (min) = 60 seconds (sec)	1 year (yr) = 12 months (mo), or about 52 weeks
1 hour (hr) = 60 minutes	
1 day = 24 hours	1 year = 365 days
1 week (wk) = 7 days	1 leap year = 366 days

MONEY

1 penny = 1 cent (¢)
1 nickel = 5 cents
1 dime = 10 cents
1 quarter = 25 cents
1 half-dollar = 50 cents
1 dollar ($) = 100 cents

SYMBOLS

< is less than
> is greater than
= is equal to
°F is degrees Fahrenheit
°C is degrees Celsius

Glossary

Pronunciation Key

a	add, map	f	fit, half	n	nice, tin	p	pit, stop	yōō	fuse, few
ā	ace, rate	g	go, log	ng	ring, song	r	run, poor	v	vain, eve
â(r)	care, air	h	hope, hate	o	odd, hot	s	see, pass	w	win, away
ä	palm, father	i	it, give	ō	open, so	sh	sure, rush	y	yet, yearn
b	bat, rub	ī	ice, write	ô	order, jaw	t	talk, sit	z	zest, muse
ch	check, catch	j	joy, ledge	oi	oil, boy	th	thin, both	zh	vision, pleasure
d	dog, rod	k	cool, take	ou	pout, now	t͟h	this, bathe		
e	end, pet	l	look, rule	ōō	took, full	u	up, done		
ē	equal, tree	m	move, seem	ōō	pool, food	û(r)	burn, term		

ə the schwa, an unstressed vowel representing the sound spelled *a* in **a**bove, *e* in sick**e**n, *i* in poss**i**ble, *o* in mel**o**n, *u* in circ**u**s

Other symbols:
- • separates words into syllables
- ′ indicates stress on a syllable

acute angle [ə•kyōōt′ ang′gəl] **ángulo agudo** An angle that has a measure less than a right angle (p. 350)
Example:

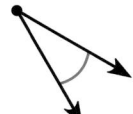

acute triangle [ə•kyōōt′ trī′ang•gəl] **triángulo acutángulo** A triangle that has three acute angles (p. 358)

addend [a′dend] **sumando** Any of the numbers that are added (p. 48)
Examples: 2 + 3 = 5
　　　　↑　↑
　　addend　addend

addition [ə•di′shən] **suma** The process of finding the total number of items when two or more groups of items are joined; the opposite operation of subtraction (p. 48)

A.M. [ā em] **a.m.** The hours between midnight and noon (p. 128)

analog clock [a′nəl•og kläk] **reloj analógico** A device for measuring time in which hands move around a circle to show hours, minutes, and sometimes seconds (p. 124)
Example:

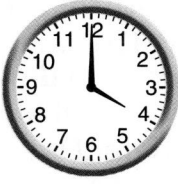

angle [ang′gəl] **ángulo** A figure formed by two rays that share an endpoint (p. 350)
Example:

Word History

When the letter *g* is replaced with the letter *k* in the word *angle*, the word becomes *ankle*. Both words come from the same Latin root, *angulus*, which means "a sharp bend."

area [âr′ē•ə] **área** The number of square units needed to cover a flat surface (p. 564)
Example:

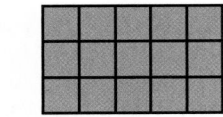

area = 15 square units

arrangement [ə•rānj′•mənt] **ordenación** A choice in which the order of items does matter (p. 194)

array [ə•rā′] **matriz** An arrangement of objects in rows and columns (p. 206)
Example:

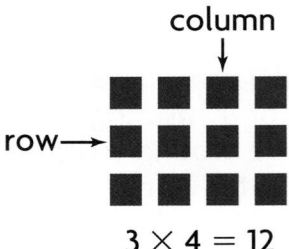

3 × 4 = 12

Associative Property of Addition [ə•sō′shē•ə•tiv prä′pər•tē əv ə•di′shən] **propiedad asociativa de la suma** The property that states that you can group addends in different ways and still get the same sum (p. 48)
Example:
4 + (2 + 5) = 11
(4 + 2) + 5 = 11

Associative Property of Multiplication [a•sō′shē•ə•tiv prä′pər•tē əv mul•tə•plə•kā′shən] **propiedad asociativa de la multiplicación** The property that states that when the grouping of factors is changed, the product remains the same (p. 260)
Example:
(3 × 2) × 4 = 24
3 × (2 × 4) = 24

bar graph [bär graf] **gráfica de barras** A graph that uses bars to show data (p. 154)
Example:

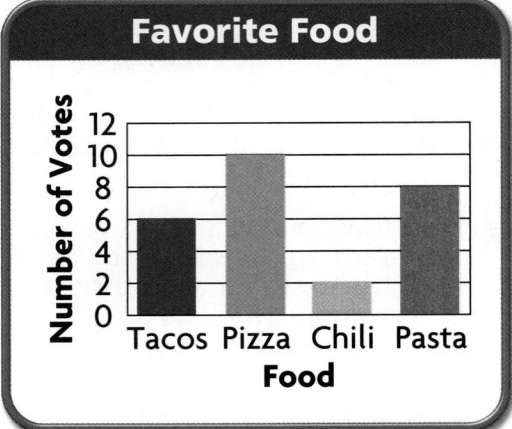

benchmark numbers [bench′märk num′bərz] **números de referencia** Numbers that help you estimate the number of objects without counting them, such as 25, 50, 100, or 1,000 (p. 42)

calendar [ka′lən•dər] **calendario** A chart that shows the days, weeks, and months of a year (p. 132)

capacity [kə•pa′sə•tē] **capacidad** The amount a container can hold (p. 520)
Example:
1 half gallon = 2 quarts

center [sen′tər] **centro** The point in the middle of a circle that is the same distance from anywhere on the circle (p. 364)
Example:

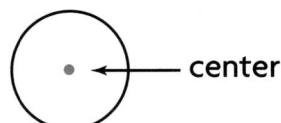

center

centimeter (cm) [sen′tə•mē•tər] **centímetro**
A metric unit that is used to measure
length or distance (p. 538)
Example:

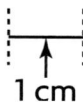

1 cm

certain [sûr′tən] **seguro** An event is certain
if it will always happen. (p. 178)

change [chānj] **cambio** The money you get
back if you have paid for an item with
coins or bills that have a value greater
than the cost of the item (p. 120)

circle [sûr′kəl] **círculo** A closed plane figure
made up of points that are the same
distance from the center (p. 364)

circle graph [sûr′kəl graf] **gráfica circular** A
graph in the shape of a circle that shows
data as a whole made up of different
parts (p. 172)

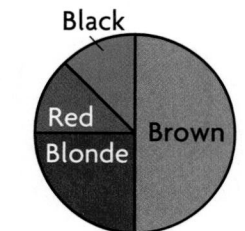

Classmates' Hair Color

circumference [sûr•kum′fər•əns]
circunferencia The distance around a
circle (p. 364)

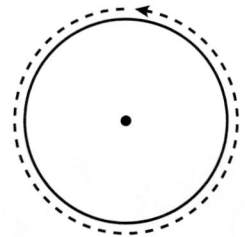

classify [kla′sə•fī] **clasificar** To group pieces
of data according to how they are the
same; for example, you can classify data
by size, color, or shape. (p. 160)

closed figure [klōzd fi′•gyər] **figura cerrada**
A shape that begins and ends at the
same point (p. 356)
Examples:

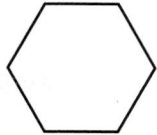 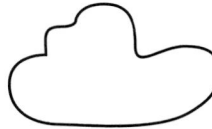

combination [kom•bə•nā′shən] **combinación**
A choice in which the order of the items
does not matter (p. 186)

Commutative Property of Addition
[kə•myōō′•tə•tiv prä′pər•tē əv ə•di′shən]
propiedad conmutativa de la suma The
property that states that you can add
two or more numbers in any order and
get the same sum (p. 48)
Example: 6 + 7 = 13
             7 + 6 = 13

Commutative Property of Multiplication
[kə•myōō•tə•tiv prä′pər•tē əv
mul•tə•plə•kā′shən] **propiedad
conmutativa de la multiplicación** The
property that states that you can
multiply two factors in any order and
get the same product (p. 206)
Example: 2 × 4 = 8
             4 × 2 = 8

compare [kəm•pâr′] **comparar** To describe
whether numbers are equal to, less than,
or greater than each other (p. 28)

compatible numbers [kəm•pat′ə•bəl
num′bərz] **números compatibles** Numbers
that are easy to compute mentally (pp. 52,
618)

cone [kōn] **cono** A solid, pointed figure
that has a flat, round base (p. 400)
Example:

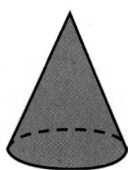

congruent [kən•grōō′ənt] **congruente**
Figures that have the same size and
shape (p. 378)
Example:

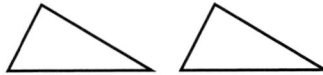

cube [kyōōb] **cubo** A solid figure with six
congruent square faces (p. 400)
Example:

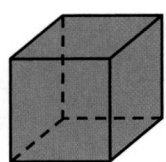

cubic unit [kyōō′bik yōō′nət] **unidad cúbica**
A cube with a side length of one unit,
used to measure volume (p. 570)

cup (c) [kup] **taza** A customary unit used to
measure capacity (p. 520)

cylinder [sil′in•dər] **cilindro** A solid or
hollow object that is shaped like a can
(p. 400)
Example:

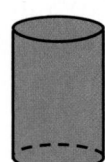

data [dā′tə] **datos** Information collected
about people or things (p. 146)

decimal [de′sə•məl] **decimal** A number with
one or more digits to the right of the
decimal point (p. 484)

decimal point [de′sə•məl point] **punto
decimal** A symbol used to separate
dollars from cents in money and to
separate the ones place from the tenths
place in decimals (pp. 110, 485)
Examples: $4.52   0.9
⌐ decimal point ⌐

decimeter (dm) [de′sə•mē•tər] **decímetro**
A metric unit that is used to measure
length or distance;
1 decimeter = 10 centimeters (p. 538)

degree Celsius (°C) [di•grē′ sel′sē•əs] **grado
Celsius** A metric unit for measuring
temperature (p. 550)

degree Fahrenheit (°F) [di•grē′ far′ən•hīt]
grado Fahrenheit A customary unit for
measuring temperature (p. 528)

denominator [di•nä′mə•nā•tər] **denominador**
The part of a fraction below the line,
which tells how many equal parts there
are in the whole or in the group (p. 446)
Example: $\frac{3}{4}$ ← denominator

diameter [dī•am′ə•tər] **diámetro** A line
segment that passes through the center
of a circle and has its endpoints on the
circle (p. 364)
Example:

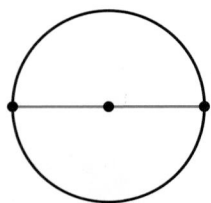

difference [di′frəns] **diferencia** The answer
in a subtraction problem (p. 78)
Example: 6 − 4 = 2
⌐ difference

digital clock [di′jə•təl kläk] **reloj digital**
A clock that shows time to the minute,
using digits (p. 124)
Example:

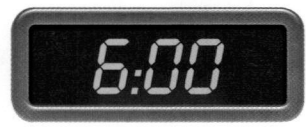

digits [di′jətz] **dígitos** The symbols 0, 1, 2, 3,
4, 5, 6, 7, 8, and 9 (p. 8)

dime [dīm] **moneda de 10¢** A coin worth
10 cents and equal to 10 pennies; 10¢
(p. 110)
Example:

H44   Glossary

divide [di•vīd'] **dividir** To separate into equal groups; the opposite operation of multiplication (p. 278)

dividend [di'və•dend] **dividendo** The number that is to be divided in a division problem (p. 284)
Example: 35 ÷ 5 = 7
    ↑ dividend

division [di•vi'zhen] **división** The process of sharing a number of items to find how many groups can be made or how many items will be in a group; the opposite operation of multiplication (p. 278)

divisor [di•vī'zər] **divisor** The number that divides the dividend (p. 284)
Example: 35 ÷ 5 = 7
    ↑ divisor

dollar [dol'ər] **dólar** Paper money worth 100 cents and equal to 100 pennies; $1.00 (p. 110)
Example:

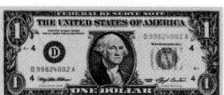 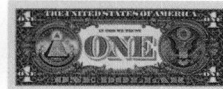

edge [ej] **arista** A line segment formed where two faces meet (p. 400)
Example:

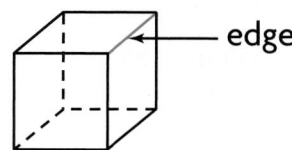

elapsed time [i•lapst'tīm] **tiempo transcurrido** The time that passes from the start of an activity to the end of that activity (p. 130)

equal sign (=) [ē'kwəl sīn] **signo de igualdad** A symbol used to show that two numbers have the same value (p. 28)
Example: 384 = 384

equal to (=) [ē'kwəl tōō] **igual a** Having the same value (p. 28)
Example: 4 + 4 is equal to 3 + 5

equally likely [ē'kwəl•lē lī'klē] **igualmente probable** Having the same chance of happening (p. 180)

equation [i•kwā'zhən] **ecuación** A number sentence that uses the equal sign to show that two amounts are equal (p. 336)
Examples:
    3 + 7 = 10
    4 − 1 = 3
    6 × 7 = 42

equilateral triangle [ē•kwə•la'tər•əl trī'ang•gəl] **triángulo equilátero** A triangle that has three equal sides and three equal angles (p. 358)
Examples:

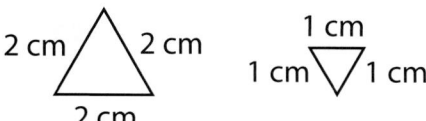

equivalent [ē•kwiv'ə•lənt] **equivalente** Two or more sets that name the same amount (p. 110)

equivalent fractions [ē•kwiv'ə•lənt frak'shənz] **fracciones equivalentes** Two or more fractions that name the same amount (p. 454)
Example:

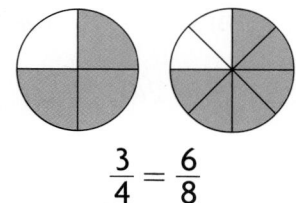

$$\frac{3}{4} = \frac{6}{8}$$

estimate [es'tə•māt] *verb* **estimar (v):** To find about how many or how much (p. 52)

estimate [es'tə•mət] *noun* **estimación (s):** A number close to an exact amount (p. 52)

even [ē'vən] **par** A whole number that has a 0, 2, 4, 6, or 8 in the ones place (p. 4)

event [i•vent'] **suceso** Something that might happen (p. 178)

expanded form [ik•spand'id fôrm] **forma desarrollada** A way to write numbers by showing the value of each digit (p. 8)
Example: 7,201 = 7,000 + 200 + 1

experiment [ik•sper′ə•mənt] **experimento**
A test that is done in order to find out
something (p. 182)

expression [ik•spre′shən] **expresión** The part
of a number sentence that combines
numbers and operation signs but doesn't
have an equal sign (p. 336)
Example: 5 × 6

face [fās] **cara** A flat surface of a solid
figure (p. 400)
Example:

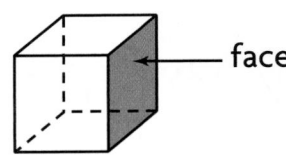
face

fact family [fakt fam′ə•lē] **familia de
operaciones** A set of related addition
and subtraction, or multiplication and
division, number sentences (pp. 76, 286)
Example:

4 × 7 = 28	28 ÷ 7 = 4
7 × 4 = 28	28 ÷ 4 = 7

factor [fak′tər] **factor** A number that is
multiplied by another number to find a
product (p. 206)
Examples: 3 × 8 = 24
          ↑   ↑
      factor factor

flip (reflection) [flip (ri•flek′shən)] **inversión
(reflexión)** A movement of a figure to a
new position by flipping the figure over
a line (p. 390)
Example:

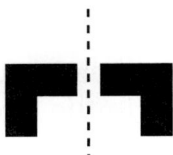

foot (ft) [foŏt] **pie** A customary unit used to
measure length or distance;
1 foot = 12 inches (p. 512)

fraction [frak′shən] **fracción** A number that
names part of a whole or part of a group
(p. 446)
Examples:

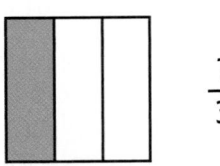 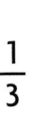 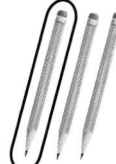
$\frac{1}{3}$

Word History

A *fraction* is part of a whole, or a whole
that is broken into pieces. *Fraction* comes
from the Latin word *frangere*, which
means "to break."

frequency table [frē′kwen•sē tā′bəl] **tabla de
frecuencia** A table that uses numbers to
record data (p. 146)
Example:

Favorite Color	
Color	**Number**
blue	10
red	7
green	8
yellow	4

gallon (gal) [ga′lən] **galón** A customary
unit for measuring capacity;
1 gallon = 4 quarts (p. 520)

gram (g) [gram] **gramo** A metric unit that is
used to measure mass (p. 546)

greater than (>) [grā′tər than] **mayor que**
A symbol used to compare two numbers,
with the greater number given first (p. 28)
Example: 6 > 4

grid [grid] **cuadrícula** Horizontal and
vertical lines on a map (p. 162)

Grouping Property of Addition [grōō′ping prä′pər•tē əv ə•dish′ən] **propiedad de agrupación de la suma** See Associative Property of Addition.

Grouping Property of Multiplication [grōō′ping prä′pər•tē əv mul•tə•plə•kā′shən] **propiedad de agrupación de la multiplicación** See Associative Property of Multiplication.

growing pattern [grō′ing pa′tərn] **patrón acumulativo** A pattern in which the number or number of figures increases by the same amount each time (p. 424)

half dollar [haf dol′ər] **moneda de 50¢** A coin worth 50 cents and equal to 50 pennies; 50¢ (p. 110)
Example:

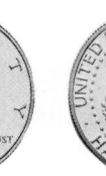 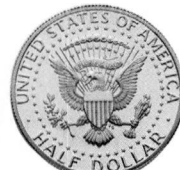

half hour [haf our] **media hora** 30 minutes (p. 124)
Example: Between 4:00 and 4:30 is one half hour.

hexagon [hek′sə•gän] **hexágono** A polygon with six sides and six angles (p. 356)
Examples:

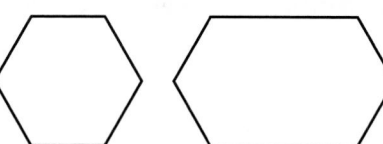

horizontal bar graph [hôr•ə•zän′təl bär graf] **gráfica de barras horizontales** A bar graph in which the bars go from left to right (p. 154)

hour (hr) [our] **hora** A unit used to measure time; in one hour, the hour hand on a clock moves from one number to the next;
1 hour = 60 minutes (p. 124)

hour hand [our hand] **horario** The short hand on an analog clock (p. 124)

hundredth [hun′drədth] **centésimo** One of one hundred equal parts (p. 488)
Example:

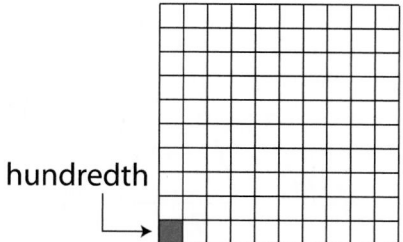

hundredth

Identity Property of Addition [ī•den′tə•tē prä′pər•tē əv ə•dish′ən] **propiedad de identidad de la suma** The property that states that when you add zero to a number, the result is that number (p. 48)
Example: 24 + 0 = 24

Identity Property of Multiplication [ī•den′tə•tē prä′pər•tē əv mul•tə•plə•kā′shən] **propiedad de identidad de la multiplicación** The property that states that the product of any number and 1 is that number (p. 214)
Examples: 5 × 1 = 5
1 × 8 = 8

impossible [im•pä′sə•bəl] **imposible** An event is impossible if it will never happen. (p. 178)

inch (in.) [inch] **pulgada** A customary unit used for measuring length or distance (p. 512)
Example:

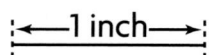

intersecting lines [in•tər•sek′ting līnz] **líneas secantes** Lines that cross (p. 354)
Example:

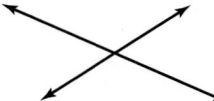

inverse operations [in′vûrs ä•pə•rā′shənz] **operaciones inversas** Opposite operations, or operations that undo one another, such as addition and subtraction or multiplication and division (pp. 76, 284)

isosceles triangle [ī•sä′sə•lēz trī′ang•gəl] **triángulo isósceles** A triangle that has two equal sides (p. 358)
Example:

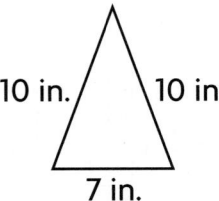

10 in.   10 in.

7 in.

key [kē] **clave** The part of a map or graph that explains the symbols (p. 148)

kilogram (kg) [kil′ə•gram] **kilogramo** A metric unit for measuring mass; 1 kilogram = 1,000 grams (p. 546)

kilometer (km) [kə•lä′mə•tər] **kilómetro** A metric unit for measuring length or distance; 1 kilometer = 1,000 meters (p. 538)

length [leng(k)th] **longitud** The measurement of the distance between two points (p. 512)

less than (<) [les ~~than~~] **menor que** A symbol used to compare two numbers, with the lesser number given first (p. 28)
Example: 3 < 7

like fractions [līk frak′shənz] **fracciones semejantes** Fractions that have the same denominator (p. 466)
Example: $\frac{3}{8}$ and $\frac{7}{8}$

likely [līk′lē] **probable** An event is likely if it has a good chance of happening. (p. 178)

line [līn] **línea** A straight path extending in both directions with no endpoints (p. 350)
Example:

⟵——————————⟶

line graph [līn graf] **gráfica lineal** A graph that uses line segments to show how data change over time (p. 168)
Example:

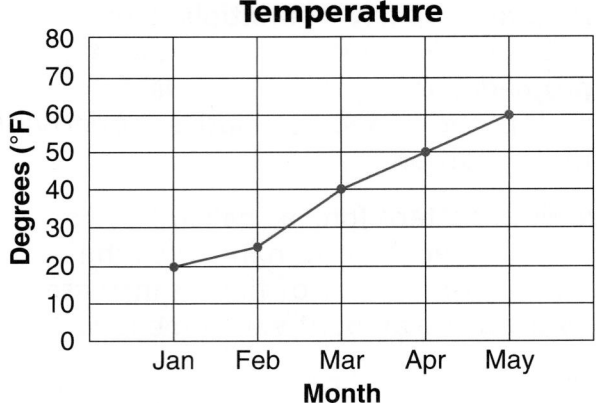

Temperature

line of symmetry [līn əv si′mə•trē] **eje de simetría** An imaginary line on a figure that when the figure is folded on this line, the two parts match exactly (p. 384)
Example:

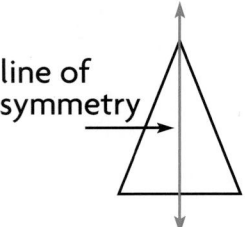

line of symmetry

line plot [līn plöt] **diagrama de puntos** A graph that records each piece of data on a number line (p. 162)
Example:

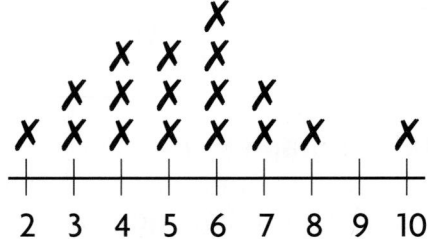

2 3 4 5 6 7 8 9 10

Word History

The word *line* comes from *linen*, a thread spun from the fibers of the flax plant. In early times, thread was held tight to mark a straight line between two points.

line segment [līn seg′mənt] **segmento** A part of a line that includes two points, called endpoints, and all of the points between them (p. 350)
Example:

liter (L) [lē′tər] **litro** A metric unit for measuring capacity;
1 liter = 1,000 milliliters (p. 544)

mass [mas] **masa** The amount of matter in an object (p. 546)

meter (m) [mē′tər] **metro** A metric unit for measuring length or distance;
1 meter = 100 centimeters (p. 538)

midnight [mid′nīt] **medianoche** 12:00 at night (p. 128)

mile (mi) [mīl] **milla** A customary unit for measuring length or distance;
1 mile = 5,280 feet (p. 512)

milliliter (mL) [mi′lə•lē•tər] **mililitro** A metric unit for measuring capacity (p. 544)

minute (min) [mi′nət] **minuto** A unit used to measure short amounts of time; in one minute, the minute hand moves from one mark to the next (p. 124)

minute hand [mi′nət hand] **minutero** The long hand on an analog clock (p. 124)

mixed number [mikst num′bər] **número mixto** A number represented by a whole number and a fraction (p. 464)
Example: $4\frac{1}{2}$

mode [mōd] **moda** The number or item found most often in a set of data (p. 162)

multiple [mul′tə•pəl] **múltiplo** A number that is the product of a given number and a counting number (p. 234)
Examples:

10	10	10	10	counting
× 1	× 2	× 3	× 4	← numbers
10	20	30	40	← multiples of 10

multiplication [mul•tə•plə•kā′shən] **multiplicación** The process of finding the total number of items in two or more equal groups; the opposite operation of division (p. 204)

multiply [mul′tə•plī] **multiplicar** When you combine equal groups, you can multiply to find how many in all; the opposite operation of division (p. 204)

multistep problem [mul′tē•step prä′bləm] **problema de varios pasos** A problem with more than one step (p. 264)

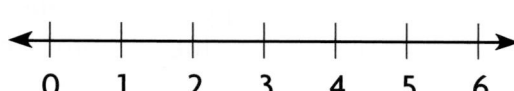

net [net] **plantilla** A two-dimensional pattern of a three-dimensional or solid figure (p. 404)
Example:

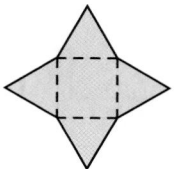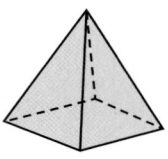

nickel [nik′əl] **moneda de 5¢** A coin worth 5 cents and equal to 5 pennies; 5¢ (p. 110)
Example:

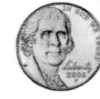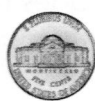

noon [nōōn] **mediodía** 12:00 in the day (p. 128)

number line [num′bər līn] **recta numérica** A line on which numbers can be located (p. 6)
Example:

```
←+——+——+——+——+——+——+→
  0   1   2   3   4   5   6
```

number sentence [num′bər sen′təns] **enunciado numérico** A sentence that includes numbers, operation symbols, and a greater than or less than symbol or an equal sign (p. 290)
Example: 5 + 3 = 8

numerator [nōō′mə•rā•tər] **numerador** The part of a fraction above the line, which tells how many parts are being counted (p. 446)

Example: $\frac{3}{4}$ ← numerator

obtuse angle [əb•t(y)ōōs′ ang′gəl] **ángulo obtuso** An angle that has a measure greater than a right angle (p. 350)
Example:

obtuse triangle [əb•t(y)ōōs′ trī′ang•gəl] **triángulo obtusángulo** A triangle that has 1 obtuse angle (p. 358)

octagon [ok′tə•gän] **octágono** A polygon with eight sides and eight angles (p. 356)
Examples:

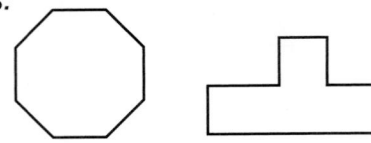

odd [od] **impar** A whole number that has a 1, 3, 5, 7, or 9 in the ones place (p. 4)

open figure [ō′pən fi′gyər] **figura abierta** A figure that does not begin and end at the same point (p. 356)
Examples:

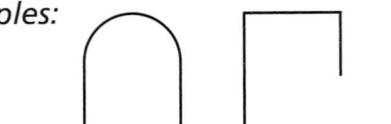

order [ôr′dər] **orden** A particular arrangement or placement of numbers or things, one after another (p. 32)

ordered pair [ôr′dərd pâr] **par ordenado** A pair of numbers that names a point on a grid (p. 166)
Example: (3,4)

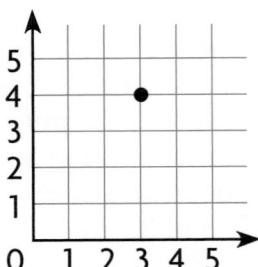

Order Property of Addition [ôr′dər prä′pər•tē əv ə•dish′ən] **propiedad de orden de la suma** *See* Commutative Property of Addition.

Order Property of Multiplication [ôr′dər prä′pər•tē əv mul•tə•plə•kā′shən] **propiedad de orden de la multiplicación** *See* Commutative Property of Multiplication.

ounce (oz) [ouns] **onza** A customary unit for measuring weight (p. 522)

outcome [out′kum] **resultado** A possible result of an experiment (p. 180)

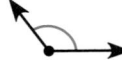

parallel lines [pâr′ə•lel līnz] **líneas paralelas** Lines that never cross; lines that are always the same distance apart (p. 354)
Example:

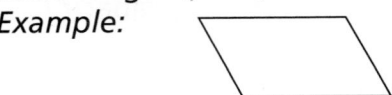

parallelogram [pâr•ə•le′lə•gram] **paralelogramo** A quadrilateral whose opposite sides are parallel and have the same length (p. 360)
Example:

pattern [pat′ərn] **patrón** An ordered set of numbers or objects; the order helps you predict what will come next. (p. 4)
Examples:
2, 4, 6, 8, 10

pattern unit [pat′ərn yōō′nət] **unidad de patrón** The part of a pattern that repeats (p. 422)
Example:

pattern unit

pentagon [pen′tə•gän] **pentágono**
A polygon with five sides and five angles
(p. 356)
Example:

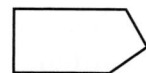

perimeter [pə•ri′mə•tər] **perímetro** The
distance around a figure (p. 560)
Example:

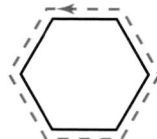

perpendicular [pûr•pən•di′kyə•lər]
perpendicular A line or plane that makes
a right angle with another line or plane
(p. 354)

perpendicular lines [pûr•pən•di′kyə•lər
līnz] **líneas perpendiculares** Lines that
intersect to form right angles (p. 354)
Example:

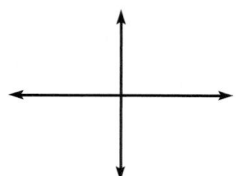

pictograph [pik′tə•graf] **pictografía** A graph
that uses pictures to show and compare
information (p. 148)
Example:

How We Got To School	
Walk	✹ ✹ ✹
Ride a Bike	✹ ✹ ✹ ✹
Ride a Bus	✹ ✹ ✹ ✹ ✹ ✹
Ride in a Car	✹ ✹
Key: Each ✹ = 10 students.	

pint (pt) [pīnt] **pinta** A customary unit for
measuring capacity;
1 pint = 2 cups (p. 520)

place value [plās val′yo͞o] **valor posicional**
The value of each digit in a number,
based on the location of the digit (p. 8)

plane figure [plān fi′•gyər] **figura plana**
A figure in a plane that is formed by
lines that are curved, straight, or both
(p. 356)
Example:

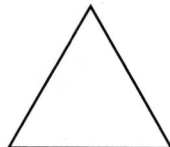

P.M. [pē em] **p.m.** The hours between noon
and midnight (p. 128)

point [point] **punto** An exact position or
location (p. 350)

polygon [po′lē•gän] **polígono** A closed
plane figure with straight sides that are
line segments (p. 356)
Examples:

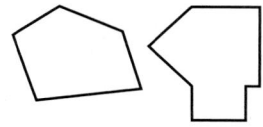 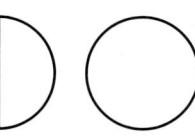

polygons   not polygons

Word History

Did you ever notice that a *polygon* looks
like a bunch of knees that are bent? This
is how the term got its name. *Poly-* is from
the Greek root *poli*, which means "many."
The ending *-gon* is from the Latin, *gonus*,
which means "to bend the knee."

possible [pos′ə•bəl] **posible** Having a chance
of happening (p. 180)

possible outcome [pos′ə•bəl out′kəm]
resultado posible Something that has a
chance of happening (p. 180)

pound (lb) [pound] **libra** A customary unit
for measuring weight;
1 pound = 16 ounces (p. 522)

predict [pri•dikt′] **predecir** To make a
reasonable guess about what will happen
(p. 180)

probability [prä•bə•bi′lə•tē] **probabilidad** The chance that a given event will occur (p. 178)
Example:

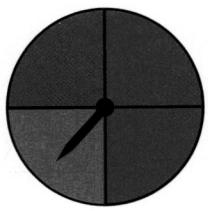

probability of red = 1 out of 4, or $\frac{1}{4}$

product [prä′dəkt] **producto** The answer in a multiplication problem (p. 206)
Example: 3 × 8 = 24
↳product

quadrilateral [kwä•drə•la′tə•rəl] **cuadrilátero** A polygon with four sides and four angles (p. 356)
Example:

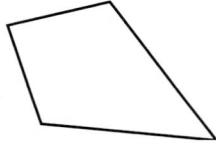

quart (qt) [kwôrt] **cuarto** A customary unit for measuring capacity;
1 quart = 2 pints (p. 520)

quarter [kwôr′•tər] **moneda de 25¢** A coin worth 25 cents and equal to 25 pennies;
25¢ (p. 110)
Example:

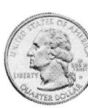 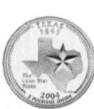

quarter hour [kwôr′tər our] **cuarto de hora** 15 minutes (p. 124)
Example: Between 4:00 and 4:15 is one quarter hour.

quotient [kwō′shənt] **cociente** The number, not including the remainder, that results from division (p. 284)
Example: 8 ÷ 4 = 2
↳quotient

radius [rā′dē•əs] **radio** A line segment with one endpoint at the center of a circle and the other endpoint on the circle (p. 364)
Example:

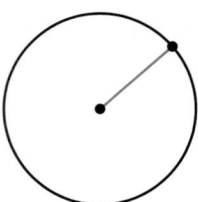

range [rānj] **rango** The difference between the greatest number and the least number in a set of data (p. 162)

ray [rā] **rayo** A part of a line, with one endpoint, that is straight and continues in one direction (p. 350)
Example:

rectangle [rek′tang•gəl] **rectángulo** A quadrilateral with 2 pairs of parallel sides, 2 pairs of equal sides, and 4 right angles (p. 360)
Example:

rectangular prism [rek•tang′gyə•lər pri′zəm] **prisma rectangular** A solid figure with six faces that are all rectangles (p. 400)
Example:

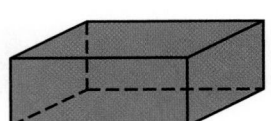

regroup [rē•grōōp′] **reagrupar** To exchange amounts of equal value to rename a number (p. 54)
Example: 5 + 8 = 13 ones or 1 ten 3 ones

remainder [ri•mān′dər] **residuo** The amount left over when a number cannot be divided evenly (p. 612)

repeating pattern [ri•pēt′ing pat′ərn] **patrón que se repite** A pattern which uses the same pattern unit over and over again (p. 424)

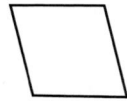
pattern unit

results [ri•zults′] **resultados** The answers from a survey (p. 158)

rhombus [räm′bəs] **rombo** A quadrilateral with 2 pairs of parallel sides and 4 equal sides and four angles (p. 360) ·
Example:

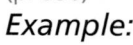

right angle [rīt ang′gəl] **ángulo recto** An angle that forms a square corner (p. 350)
Example:

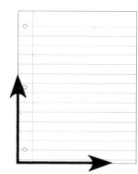

right triangle [rīt trī′ang•gəl] **triángulo rectángulo** A triangle with one right angle (p. 358)
Example:

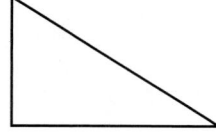

round [round] **redondear** Replace a number with another number that tells about how many or how much (p. 36)

rule [rool] **regla** An instruction that tells you the correct way to do something (pp. 256, 424)

scale [skāl] **escala** The numbers placed at fixed distances on a graph to help label the graph. (p. 154)

scalene triangle [skā′lēn trī′ang•gəl] **triángulo escaleno** A triangle in which no sides are equal (p. 358)
Example:

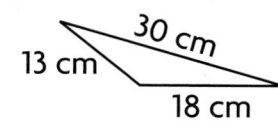

second [se′kənd] **segundo** A small unit of time;
60 seconds = 1 minute (p. 124)

sequence [sē′kwəns] **ordenar** To write events in order (p. 136)

similar [si′mə•lər] **semejante** Having the same shape and the same or different size (p. 388)
Example:

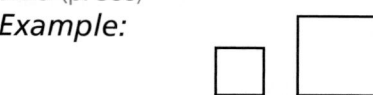

simplest form [sim′pləst fôrm] **mínima expresión** When a fraction is modeled with the largest fraction bar or bars possible (p. 466)

slide (translation) [slīd (trans•lā′shən)] **deslizar (traslación)** A movement of a figure to a new position without turning or flipping it (p. 390)
Example:

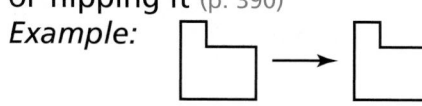

solid figure [so′lid fī′gyər] **cuerpo geométrico** A figure having length, width, and height (p. 400)
Example:

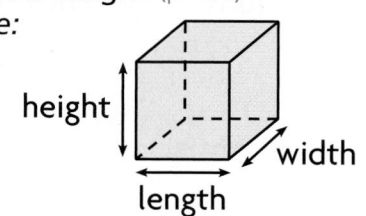
height   width   length

sphere [sfir] **esfera** A solid figure that has the shape of a round ball (p. 400)
Example:

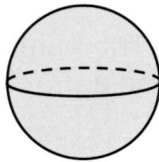

square [skwâr] **cuadrado** A quadrilateral with 2 pairs of parallel sides, 4 equal sides, and 4 right angles (p. 360)
Example:

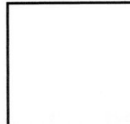

square number [skwâr num'bər] **número cuadrado** The product of two factors that are the same (p. 206)
Example: $2 \times 2 = 4$, so 4 is a square number

square pyramid [skwâr pir'ə•mid] **pirámide cuadrada** A solid, pointed figure with a flat base that is a square (p. 400)
Example:

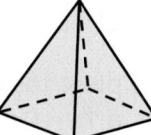

square unit [skwâr yōo'nət] **unidad cuadrada** A square with a side length of one unit; used to measure area (p. 564)

standard form [stan'dərd fôrm] **forma normal** A way to write numbers by using the digits 0–9, with each digit having a place value (p. 8)
Example: 345 ← standard form

straight angle [strāt ang'gəl] **ángulo llano** An angle in which two rays point in opposite directions so that they form a line (p. 350)
Example:

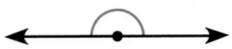

subtraction [sub•trak'shən] **resta** The process of finding how many are left when a number of items are taken away from a group of items; the process of finding the difference when two groups are compared; the opposite operation of addition (p. 78)

sum [sum] **suma o total** The answer to an addition problem (p. 48)

survey [sur'vā] **encuesta** A method of gathering information (p. 158)

symmetry [sim'ə•trē] **simetría** A figure has symmetry if it can be folded along a line so that the two parts match exactly; one half of the figure looks like the mirror image of the other half. (p. 384)

tally table [ta'lē tā'bəl] **tabla de conteo** A table that uses tally marks to record data (p. 146)
Example:

Favorite Sport	
Sport	Tally
Soccer	ЖH III
Baseball	III
Football	ЖH
Basketball	ЖH I

tenth [tenth] **décimo** One of ten equal parts (p. 484)
Example:

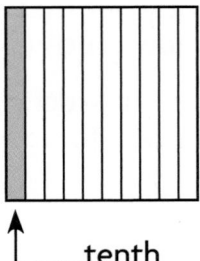

tenth

tessellation [te•sə•lā′shən] **teselación**
A repeating pattern made of a closed plane figure that covers a surface with no overlapping or empty space (p. 394)
Example:

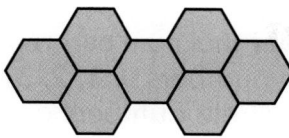

thermometer [thûr•mom′ə•tər] **termómetro**
An instrument for measuring temperature (p. 528)

three-dimensional figure
[thrē•di•men′shən•əl fig′yər] **figura tridimensional** A figure having length, width, and height (p. 400)
Example:

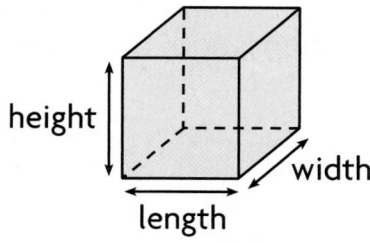

time line [tīm līn] **línea cronológica**
A drawing that shows when and in what order events took place (p. 136)

trapezoid [trap′ə•zoid] **trapecio**
A quadrilateral with exactly one pair of parallel sides and four angles (p. 360)
Example:

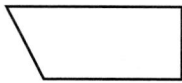

tree diagram [trē dí′ə•gram] **diagrama de árbol** An organized list that shows all possible outcomes of an event (p. 186)
Example:

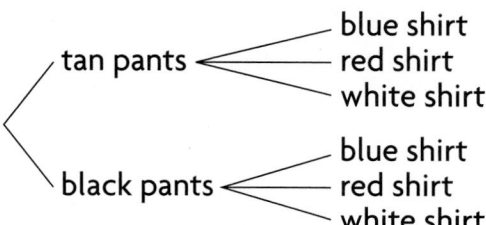

trends [trendz] **tendencias** On a graph, areas where the data increase, decrease, or stay the same over time (p. 168)

triangle [trī′ang′gəl] **triángulo** A polygon with three sides and three angles (p. 356)
Examples:

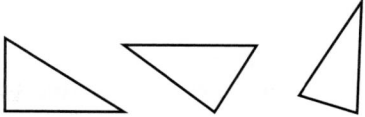

turn (rotation) [tûrn (rō•tā′shən)] **giro (rotación)** A movement of a figure to a new position by rotating the figure around a point (p. 390)
Example:

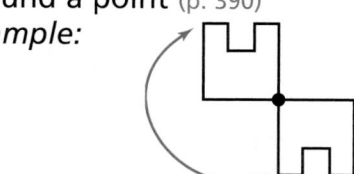

two-dimensional figure [tōō•di•men′shən•əl fig′yer] **figura bidimensional** A figure having length and width (p. 356)
Example:

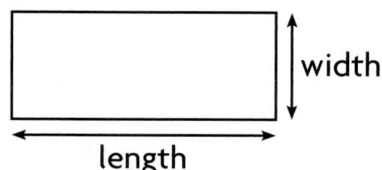

unlikely [un•lī′klē] **poco probable** An event is unlikely if it does not have a good chance of happening. (p. 178)

variable [vâr′ē•ə•bəl] **variable** A symbol or a letter that stands for an unknown number (p. 258)

> **Word History**
>
> *Variable* The word *vary* comes from the Latin word *variabilis*, meaning "changeable." At first, the word applied to changes of color, as in the speckled fur of animals. Eventually, the word was used for things that involve change of any kind.

Venn diagram [ven dī′ə•gram] **diagrama de Venn** A diagram that shows relationships among sets of things (p. 363)
Example:

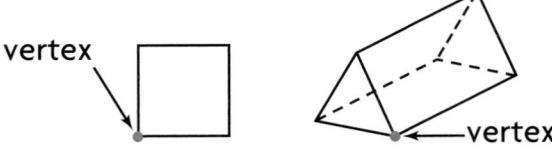

vertex [vûr′teks] **vértice** The point at which two rays of an angle or two (or more) line segments meet in a plane figure or where three or more edges meet in a solid figure (pp. 350, 400)
Examples:

vertex

vertex

vertical bar graph [vûr′ti•kəl bär graf] **gráfica de barras verticales** A bar graph in which the bars go up from bottom to top (p. 154)

volume [väl′yəm] **volumen** The amount of space a solid figure takes up (p. 570)

weight [wāt] **peso** How heavy an object is (p. 522)

whole number [hōl num′bər] **número entero** One of the numbers 0, 1, 2, 3, 4, ... The set of whole numbers goes on without end.

word form [wûrd fôrm] **en palabras** A way to write numbers by using words (p. 8)
Example: The word form of 212 is two hundred twelve.

yard (yd) [yärd] **yarda** A customary unit for measuring length or distance; 1 yard = 3 feet (p. 512)

Zero Property of Multiplication [zē′rō prä′pər•tē əv mul•tə•plə•kā′shən] **propiedad del cero de la multiplicación** The property that states that the product of zero and any number is zero (p. 214)
Example: $0 \times 6 = 0$

Index

B

C

G

Rounding
    to nearest hundred, 36–37, 52–53, 58–59, 78–79, 84–85, 88–91
    to nearest ten, 36–37, 52–53, 54–55, 78–79, 80–81
    to nearest thousand, 38–39, 58–59, 84–85, 88–91
    using number line, 36–37, 38–39
    rules for, 36–37, 38–39, 594
    See also Estimation
Rulers
    using customary, 514–517, 518–519, 560–563
    using metric, 540–543, 553, 560–563
Rules
    for changing units, 518–519
    divisibility, 626
    division, 306–307
    finding, 256–257, 424–425, 426–427
    for patterns, 256–257, 424–425, 426–427, 428–431, 432–433

S

Scale, 154–155, 156–157
Scalene triangles, 358–359
Seconds, 124–127
Sense or Nonsense, 12, 71, 155, 169, 181, 205, 261, 285, 362, 387, 409, 456, 523, 542, 566
Sequence of events, 136–137
Shapes. *See* Geometry
Show What You Know, 3, 27, 47, 75, 109, 145, 177, 203, 231, 255, 277, 301, 321, 349, 377, 399, 421, 445, 483, 511, 537, 559, 585, 611
Sides
    identify triangles by, 358–359
    in quadrilaterals, 356–357, 360–363
Similar figures, 388–389
Simplest form of fraction, 466–469, 470–473, 478
Skip–counting
    backward, 280–281, 302–303, 308–311
    on a hundred chart, 4–5
    on number line, 6–7, 280–281, 302–303, 308–311
Slides (translations), 390–391
Solid figures
    classifying, 400–403, 407
    combining, 408–409, 415
    cones, 400–403
    congruent, 416
    cubes, 400–403
    cylinders, 400–403
    drawing, 412–413
    edges of, 400–403
    faces of, 400–403, 410–411
    identifying, 400–403, 408–409, 410–411
    modeling, 404–407
    nets of, 404–407
    rectangular prisms, 400–403

    relationships to plane figures, 410–411
    spheres, 400–403
    square pyramids, 400–403
    surfaces of, 400–403
    vertices of, 400–403
    volume of, 570–571
Solve a Simpler Problem strategy, 600–603
Sorting, 363, 366–367, 383
Spheres, 400–403
Spreadsheets, 193
Square numbers, 209
Square pyramids, 400–403
Square units, 564–567
Squares, 360–363
Standard form, 8–9, 10–13, 14–15, 490–491
Standardized Test Prep, 24–25, 44–45, 72–73, 142–143, 174–175, 228–229, 252–253, 298–299, 318–319, 374–375, 396–397, 418–419, 480–481, 534–535, 556–557, 608–609
Statistics
    collecting data, 146–147
    graphs, 148–149, 150–153, 154–155, 156–157, 158–159, 165, 168–169, 172
    interpreting data, 148–149, 154–155, 162–165, 168–169, 172
    line plot, 162–164
    mode, 162–164
    range, 162–164
    survey, 158–159
    See also Data
Student Handbook, H1–H40
Subtraction
    across zeros, 88–91, 92
    basic facts, 76–77, 226, 250
    with a calculator, 92–93
    checking with addition, 80–81, 88–91
    choosing a method, 92–95
    of decimals, 502
    differences, 78–79, 80–81, 82–83, 84–85, 88–91, 92–95
    estimating differences, 78–79, 80–81, 84–85, 88–91
    fact families, 76–77
    four–digit numbers, 84–85, 88–91, 92–95
    of fractions, 470–473, 478
    as inverse of addition, 76–77
    mental math and, 80–81, 92–95
    modeling, 82–83, 88–91
    with money, 122–123
    number sentences, 290–293
    with regrouping, 80–81, 82–83, 84–85, 88–91, 92–95
    relating to division, 280–281
    repeated, 280–281, 330–331, 332–335
    three–digit numbers, 82–83, 84–85, 88–91, 92–95

T

Photo Credits

Prehistoric cave painters used charcoals that experts have dated to be nearly 17,000 years old.

Pastels come in more than 1,650 different colors.

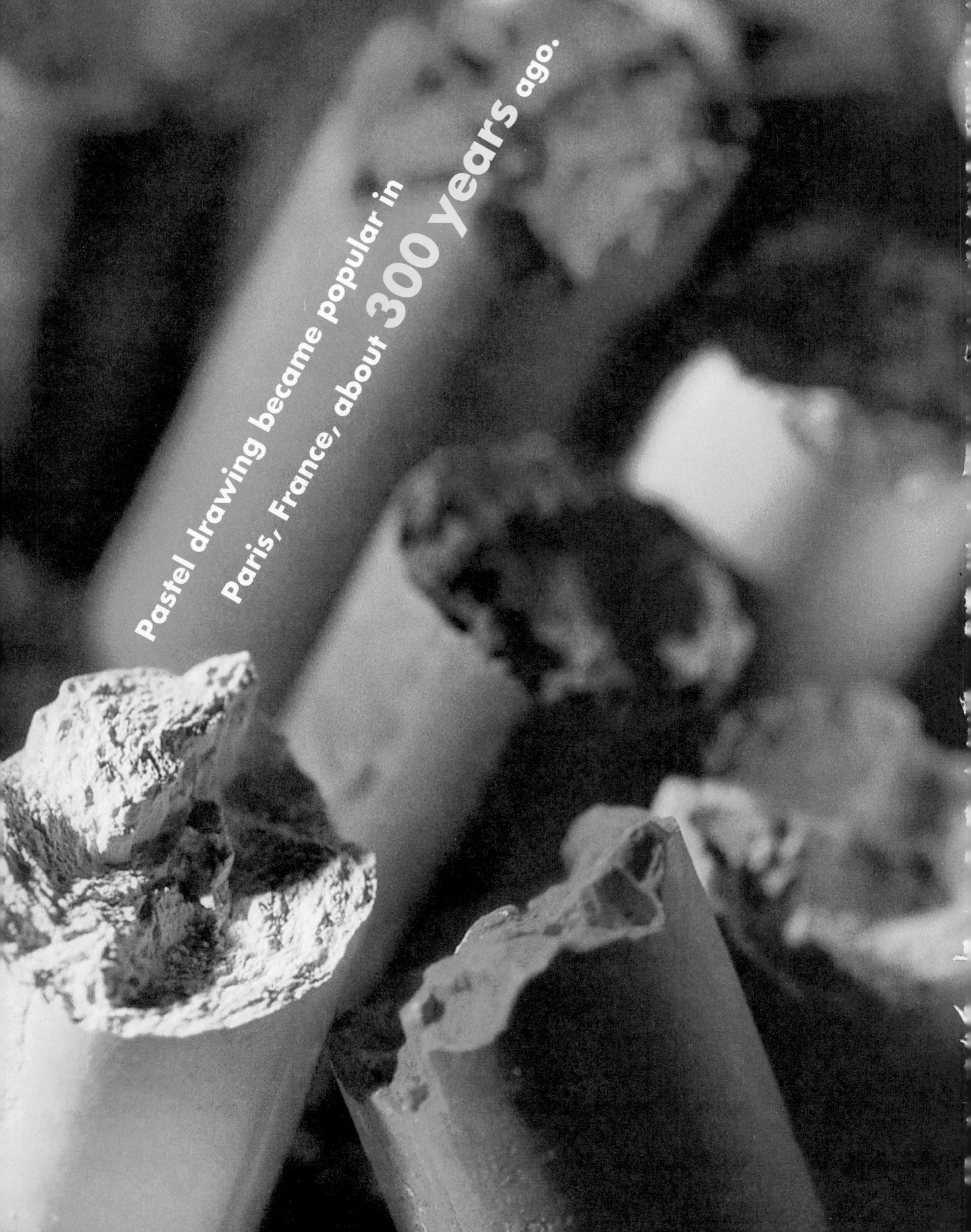

Pastel drawing became popular in Paris, France, about **300 years** ago.